Invitation to the Life Span

FOURTH EDITION

Kathleen Stassen Berger

Bronx Community College
of the City University of New York

worth publishers

Macmillan Learning

New York

Senior Vice President, Content Strategy: Charles Linsmeier

Program Director, Social Sciences: Shani Fisher

Executive Program Manager: Christine Cardone

Developmental Editor: Andrea Musick Page

Editorial Assistant: Dorothy Tomasini

Executive Marketing Manager: Katherine Nurre

Marketing Assistant: Chelsea Simens

Executive Media Editor: Laura Burden

Director, Content Management Enhancement: Tracey Kuehn

Senior Managing Editor: Lisa Kinne

Senior Content Project Manager: Peter Jacoby

Project Manager: Jana Lewis, Lumina Datamatics, Inc.

Media Project Manager: Joseph Tomasso

Senior Workflow Supervisor: Susan Wein

Senior Photo Editor: Sheena Goldstein

Photo Researcher: Donna Ranieri

Director of Design, Content Management: Diana Blume

Cover Designer: John Callahan

Interior Design: Lumina Datamatics, Inc.

Art Manager: Matthew McAdams

Illustrations: Lumina Datamatics, Charles Yuen, Matthew McAdams

Composition: Lumina Datamatics, Inc.

Printing and Binding: LSC Communications

Cover Photograph: Ariel Skelley/DigitalVision/Getty Images

Library of Congress Control Number: 2018955298

ISBN-13: 978-1-319-14064-9

ISBN-10: 1-319-14064-5

Printed in the United States of America

1 2 3 4 5 6   23 22 21 20 19 18

Worth Publishers

One New York Plaza

Suite 4500

New York, NY 10004-1562

www.macmillanlearning.com

ABOUT THE AUTHOR

Kathleen Stassen Berger received her undergraduate education at Stanford University and Radcliffe College, and then she earned an M.A.T. from Harvard University and an M.S. and a Ph.D. from Yeshiva University. Her broad experience as an educator includes directing a pre-school, serving as chair of philosophy at the United Nations International School, and teaching child and adolescent development to graduate students at Fordham University and to undergraduates at Montclair State University and Quinnipiac University. She also taught social psychology to inmates at Sing Sing Prison earning their paralegal degrees.

Currently, Berger is a professor at Bronx Community College of the City University of New York, as she has been for most of her professional career. She began as an adjunct in English, and for the past decades she has been a full professor in the Social Sciences Department, which includes sociology, economics, anthropology, political science, human services, and psychology. She has taught introduction to psychology, social psychology, abnormal psychology, human motivation, and all four developmental courses—child, adolescent, adulthood, and life span. Her students—who come from many ethnic, economic, and educational backgrounds, with varied ages, interests, and ambitions—consistently honor her with the highest teaching evaluations.

Berger is also the author of *The Developing Person Through the Life Span* and *The Developing Person Through Childhood and Adolescence.* Her developmental texts are currently being used at more than 700 colleges and universities worldwide and are available in Spanish, French, Italian, and Portuguese, as well as English. She is among the top 100 female authors assigned in colleges in the United States and the United Kingdom, an honor she shares with Jane Austen, Toni Morrison, and 97 other well-respected women. Her research interests include adolescent identity, immigration, bullying, and grandparents, and she has published articles on human development in the *Wiley Encyclopedia of Psychology* and in publications of the American Association for Higher Education and the National Education Association for Higher Education. She continues teaching and learning from her students, as well as from her four daughters and three grandsons.

Brief Contents

SHAPECHARGE/GETTY IMAGES

JOSE LUIS PELAEZ INC/GETTY IMAGES

CHRISTOPHER HOPE-FITCH/GETTY IMAGES

PHOTOALTO/JEROME GORIN/GETTY IMAGES

Contents

WOMEOWS/MOMENT/GETTY IMAGES

MARTINEDOUCET/E+/GETTY IMAGES

KARINA MIREYA SANCHEZ ANDINO / EYEEM/GETTY IMAGES

HERO IMAGES/GETTY IMAGES

AE PICTURES INC./DIGITALVISION/GETTY IMAGES

CAIAIMAGE/PAUL BRADBURY/GETTY IMAGES

MASKOT/GETTY IMAGES

PREFACE

If human development were simple, universal, and unchanging, there would be no need for a new edition of this textbook. Nor would anyone need to learn anything about human growth. But humans are complex, varied, and never the same.

This is evident to me in small ways as well as large ones. I made the mistake of taking two of my grandsons, then aged 6 and 7, to the grocery store, asking them what they wanted for dinner. I rejected immediately their first suggestions—doughnuts or store-made sandwiches. But, we lingered over the meat counter. Asa wanted hot dogs and Caleb wanted chicken. Neither would concede.

At least one universal is apparent in this anecdote: Grandmothers seek to nourish grandchildren. But, complexity and variability were evident in two stubborn cousins and one confused grandmother.

This small incident is not unlike today's news headlines. Indeed, another developmental question seems more urgent now—interweaving what is universally true about humans with what is new and immediate, using science to find a balance in order to move forward with our public and personal lives.

I found a compromise for dinner—chicken hot dogs, which both boys ate, with whole wheat buns and lots of ketchup. I wish I knew the solutions to public problems. Climate change, immigration, gun violence, and systemic racism all require a deep and accurate understanding of human development, but applying that knowledge is an ongoing dilemma.

That is why I wrote this new edition, which presents both enduring and current findings from the science of human development. Some of those findings have been recognized for decades, even centuries. Some are new, as thousands of scientists continue to study how humans grow and change.

I hope insight will advance the public and private aspects of our lives, moving us all forward from the moment of conception until the last breath. Often highlighted in the fourth edition, even more so than earlier, is the need for evidence, alternatives, and ethics as we seek to help everyone live happier, more fulfilling lives. If only it were as simple as cooking chicken hot dogs.

New Material

Every year, scientists discover and explain new concepts and research. The best of these are integrated into the text, including hundreds of new references on many topics such as epigenetics, prenatal nutrition, the microbiome, early-childhood education, autism spectrum disorder, vaping, high-stakes testing, opioid addiction, cohabitation, gender diversity, the grandmother hypothesis, living wills, continuing bonds, and variations of all kinds—ethnic, economic, genetic, and cultural.

Cognizant that the science of human development is interdisciplinary, I include recent research in biology, sociology, neuroscience, education, anthropology, political science, and more—as well as my home discipline, psychology. A list highlighting this material is available at macmillanlearning.com.

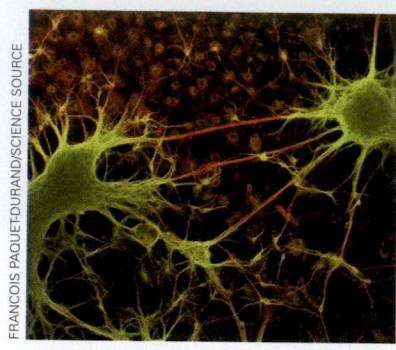

FRANCOIS PAQUET-DURAND/SCIENCE SOURCE

New *Inside the Brain* Feature

Since new discoveries in neuroscience abound, I have added *Inside the Brain* features to several chapters, exploring topics such as the intricacies of prenatal and infant neurological development, specialization, language advances, brain maturation, and emotional regulation.

New and Updated Coverage of Neuroscience

Of course, neuroscience is often discussed in the text as well. In addition to the new *Inside the Brain* features, cutting-edge research on the brain appears in virtually every chapter, often with charts, figures, and photos. A list highlighting this material is available at macmillanlearning.com.

Renewed Emphasis on Critical Thinking

STEVE RUSSELL/GETTY IMAGES

Critical thinking is essential for all of us lifelong. Virtually every page of this book presents not only facts but also questions with divergent interpretations, sometimes with references to my own cognitive reconsiderations. Often my family and students have made me realize the need to question my assumptions. Marginal *Think Critically* questions encourage students to examine the implications of what they read.

Every chapter is organized around learning objectives. Much of what I hope students will always remember from this course is a matter of attitude, approach, and perspective—all hard to quantify. The *What Will You Know?* questions at the beginning of each chapter indicate important ideas or provocative concepts—one for each major section of the chapter.

In addition, after every major section, *What Have You Learned?* questions help students review what they have just read. Some of these questions are straightforward, requiring only close attention to the chapter. Others are more complex, seeking comparisons, implications, or evaluations. Cognitive psychology and research on pedagogy show that vocabulary, specific knowledge, and critical thinking are all part of learning. These features are designed to foster all three; students and professors might add their own questions and answers, following this scaffolding.

Updated Features: *Opposing Perspectives, A View from Science*, and *A Case to Study*

In this edition of *Invitation to the Life Span*, I've included three unique features. *Opposing Perspectives* focuses on controversial topics—from prenatal sex selection to e-cigarettes. I have tried to present information and opinions on both sides so that students will weigh evidence, assess arguments, and recognize their biases, reaching their own conclusions. *A View from Science*, which explains research, and *A Case to Study*, which illustrates development via specific individuals, have been updated or replaced.

Visualizing Development

Data are often best understood visually and graphically. Every chapter of this edition includes a full-page illustration of a key topic that combines statistics, maps, charts, and photographs. These infographics focus on key issues ranging from changing U.S. demographics to the global prevalence of neurocognitive disorders. My editors and I worked closely with noted designer Charles Yuen to develop the *Visualizing Development* infographics.

Updated Online Data Connections Activities

Evidence is crucial for scientists. I hope students will understand this experientially via the interactive activities that require interpretation of data on important topics, from rates of vaccination to prevalence of risk-taking. These activities, some new, others with updated with more recent data, engage students in active learning, promoting a deeper understanding of the science of development. Instructors can assign the Data Connections in the online LaunchPad that accompanies this book.

New Integration with LaunchPad

Call-outs to accompanying online materials are in the margins throughout the book. These point to special videos, such as a video featuring Susan Beal, M.D., one of the Australian researchers who discovered a link between infant sleep position and sudden infant death syndrome. They also direct students to pertinent Data Connections and Video Activities from Worth's renowned collection.

Child Development and Nursing Career Correlation Guides

Many students taking this course seek to become licensed nurses or educators. This book and its accompanying Test Bank and practice quizzes are fully correlated to the NAEYC (National Association for the Education of Young Children) career preparation goals and the NCLEX (nursing) licensure exams. These two supplements are available in this book's accompanying online LaunchPad.

Ongoing Features

Many characteristics of this book have been acclaimed since the first edition.

Writing That Communicates the Excitement and Challenge of the Field

An overview of the science of human development should be lively, just as real people are. To that end, each sentence conveys tone as well as content. Chapter-opening vignettes describe real (not hypothetical) situations to illustrate the immediacy of

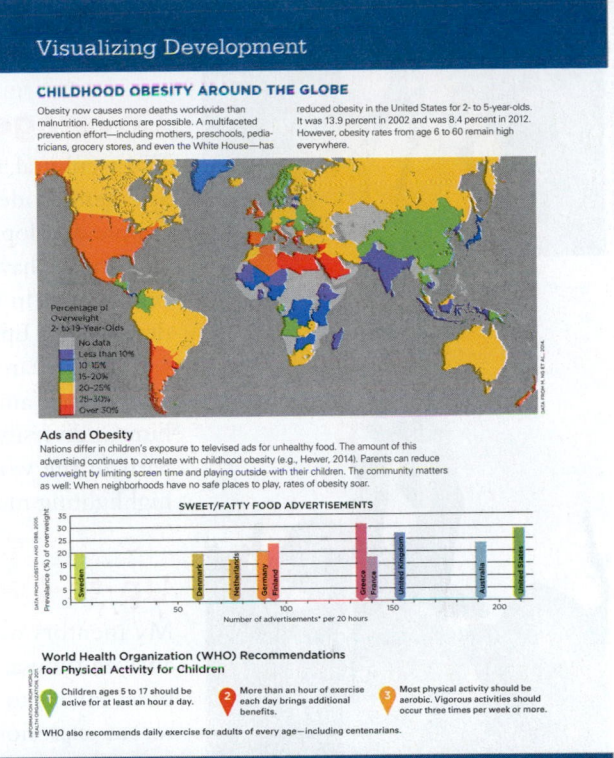

Visualizing Development

CHILDHOOD OBESITY AROUND THE GLOBE

Obesity now causes more deaths worldwide than malnutrition. Reductions are possible. A multifaceted prevention effort—including mothers, preschools, pediatricians, grocery stores, and even the White House—has reduced obesity in the United States for 2- to 5-year-olds. It was 13.9 percent in 2002 and was 8.4 percent in 2012. However, obesity rates from age 6 to 60 remain high everywhere.

Percentage of Overweight 2- to 19-Year-Olds
- No data
- Less than 10%
- 10–15%
- 15–20%
- 20–25%
- 25–30%
- Over 30%

Ads and Obesity
Nations differ in children's exposure to televised ads for unhealthy food. The amount of this advertising continues to correlate with childhood obesity (e.g., Hewer, 2014). Parents can reduce overweight by limiting screen time and playing outside with their children. The community matters as well: When neighborhoods have no safe places to play, rates of obesity soar.

SWEET/FATTY FOOD ADVERTISEMENTS

World Health Organization (WHO) Recommendations for Physical Activity for Children

1. Children ages 5 to 17 should be active for at least an hour a day.
2. More than an hour of exercise each day brings additional benefits.
3. Most physical activity should be aerobic. Vigorous activities should occur three times per week or more.

WHO also recommends daily exercise for adults of every age—including centenarians.

BRUESWU/MOMENTOPEN/GETTY IMAGES

development. Examples and explanations abound, helping students make the connections between theory, research, and their own experiences.

Coverage of Diversity

Cross-cultural, international, multiethnic, sexual orientation, socioeconomic status, age, gender identity—all of these words and ideas are vital to appreciating how people develop. Research uncovers surprising similarities and notable differences: All humans have much in common, yet each human is unique. From the emphasis on contexts in Chapter 1 to the coverage of historical and religious differences in death in the Epilogue, each chapter highlights variations.

New research on family structures, immigrants, bilingualism, and ethnic differences are among the many topics that illustrate human variations. Respect for human diversity is evident throughout. Examples and research findings from many parts of the world are included, not as add-ons but as integral to each age. A list highlighting multi-cultural material is available at www.macmillanlearning.com.

Up-to-Date Coverage

My mentors welcomed curiosity, creativity, and skepticism. As a result, I read and analyze thousands of articles and books on everything from how biology predisposes infants to autism spectrum disorder to the determination of brain death. The recent explosion of research in neuroscience and genetics has challenged me once again, first to understand and then to explain many complex findings and speculative leaps. My students ask nuanced questions and share current experiences, always adding perspective.

Topical Organization Within a Chronological Framework

I have devoted much thought to the organization of this text. Two chapters begin the book with definitions, theories, genetics, and prenatal development. These chapters provide a foundation for a life-span perspective on plasticity, nature and nurture, multi-cultural awareness, risk analysis, gains and losses, family bonding, and many other basic concepts.

The other six parts correspond to the major stages of development and proceed from biology, to cognition, to emotions, to social interaction, because human growth usually follows that path. Each stage begins when a new life event typically occurs: Puberty begins adolescence, for instance. The ages of such events vary among people, but 0–2, 2–6, 6–11, 11–18, 18–25, 25–65, and 65+ are the approximate and traditional ages of the various parts.

In some texts, emerging adulthood (Chapter 11) is subsumed in a stage called early adulthood (ages 20 to 40), which is followed by middle adulthood (ages 40 to 65). I decided against that for two reasons. First, there is no event that starts middle age, especially since the evidence for a "midlife crisis" has crumbled. Second, as Chapter 11 explains, current young adults merit their own chapter because they are distinct from both adolescents and adults.

I know, as you do, that life is not chunked—each passing day makes us older, each aspect of development affects every other aspect, and each social context affects us in a multitude of ways. However, we learn in sequence, with each thought building on the previous one. Thus, a topical organization within a chronological framework scaffolds comprehension of the interplay between age and domain.

Photographs, Tables, and Graphs That Are Integral to the Text

Students learn a great deal from this book's illustrations because Worth Publishers encourages their authors to choose the photographs, tables, and graphs and to write captions that extend the content. *Observation Quizzes* accompany some of them, directing readers to look closely at what they see. The online Data Connections further this process by presenting numerous charts and tables that contain detailed data for further study.

Teaching and Learning Aids

Supplements can make or break a class, as I and every other experienced instructor knows. Instructors use many electronic tools that did not exist a few decades ago. The publisher's representatives are trained every year to guide students and professors in using the most effective media for their classes. I have adopted texts from many publishers; the Worth representatives are a cut above the rest. Ask them for help with media, with testing, and with content.

LaunchPad with *Developing Lives*, LearningCurve Quizzing, and Data Connections Activities

Built to solve key challenges in the course, LaunchPad gives students what they need to prepare for class and exams, while offering instructors what they need to set up a course, shape the content to their syllabi, craft lectures, assign homework, and monitor the learning of each student and the class as a whole.

LaunchPad (preview at www.launchpadworks) includes:

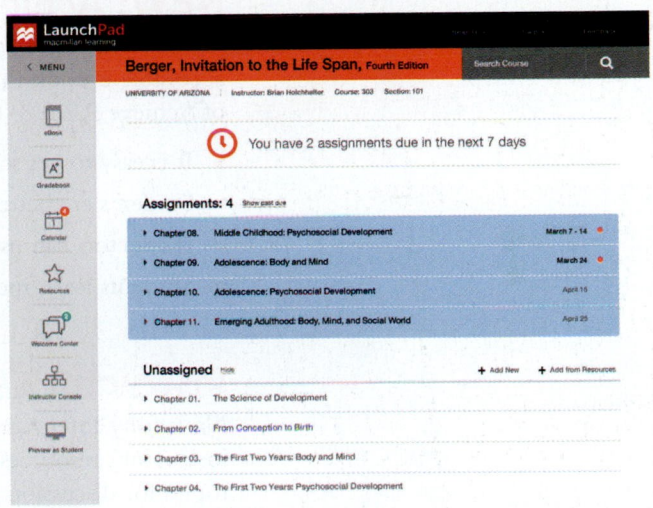

- An **interactive e-book,** which integrates the text and all student media, including videos, and much more.

- **Data Connections,** interactive activities that allow students to interpret data.

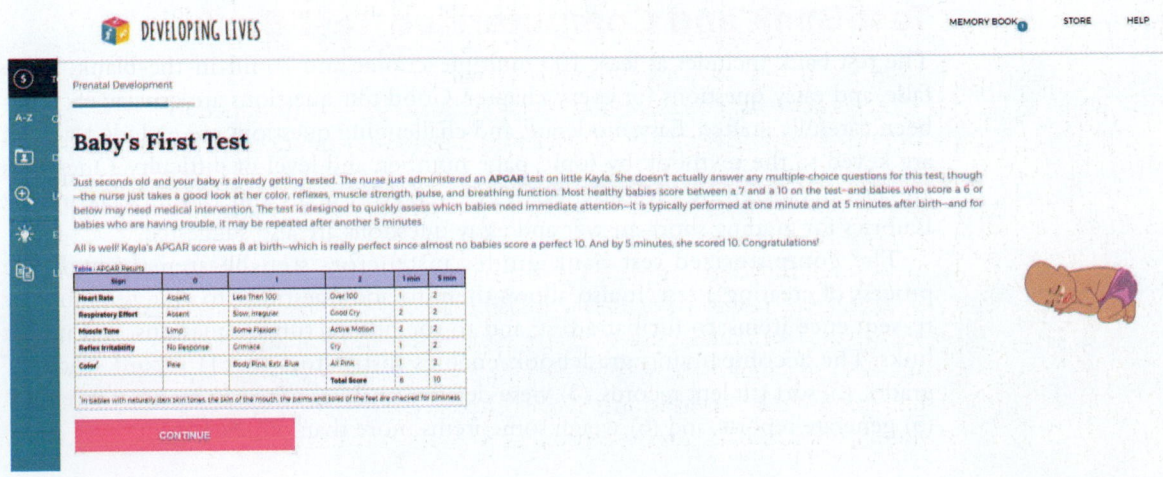

- **LearningCurve adaptive quizzing,** based on current research on learning and memory. It combines individualized question selection, immediate and valuable feedback, and a gamelike interface to engage students. Each LearningCurve quiz is integrated with other resources in LaunchPad through the Personalized Study Plan, so students can review using Worth's extensive library of videos and activities. Question analysis reports allow instructors to track the progress of individuals and the entire class.

- Worth's **Video Collection for Human Development** is an extensive archive of approximately 230 video clips and 60 video activities covering the full range of the course, from classic experiments (like Ainsworth's Strange Situation and Piaget's conservation task) to topics such as genetic disorders, nutrition, education, marriage, and grandparenting (to name a few). Instructors can assign these videos to students through LaunchPad or choose from 50 activities that combine videos with short-answer and multiple-choice questions. (For presentations, our videos are also available on flash drive.)

- **Developing Lives,** the robust interactive experience in which students "raise" their own virtual child. This simulation integrates more than 200 videos and animations, with quizzes and questions instructors can assign and assess.

NEW! Achieve Read & Practice

Achieve Read & Practice combines LearningCurve adaptive quizzing and our mobile, accessible e-book in one easy-to-use and affordable product. Among the advantages of Achieve Read & Practice:

- It is easy to get started.

- Students are better prepared: They can read and study in advance.

- Instructors can use analytics to help their students.

- Students learn more.

Instructor's Resources

Now fully integrated with LaunchPad, this collection is the richest collection of instructor's resources in developmental psychology. Included are learning objectives, topics for discussion and debate, handouts for student projects, course-planning suggestions, ideas for term projects, and a guide to videos and other online materials.

Test Bank and Computerized Test Bank

The test bank includes at least 100 multiple-choice and 70 fill-in-the-blank, true–false, and essay questions for every chapter. Good test questions are crucial; each has been carefully crafted. Easy, moderate, and challenging questions are included, and all are keyed to the textbook by topic, page number, and level of difficulty. Questions are also organized by NCLEX, NAEYC, and APA goals and Bloom's taxonomy. Rubrics for grading short-answer and essay questions are also suggested.

The computerized test bank guides instructors step-by-step through the process of creating a test. It also allows them to add questions; to edit, scramble, or re-sequence items; to format a test; and to include pictures, equations, and media links. The accompanying gradebook enables instructors to: (1) record students' grades, (2) sort student records, (3) view detailed analyses of test items, (4) curve tests, (5) generate reports, and (6) weigh some items more than others.

Thanks

Hundreds of academic reviewers and hundreds of thousands of students have read this book in every edition. Many have provided suggestions, criticisms, references, and encouragement. Because of them, each edition is better than the previous one. I especially thank those who have formally reviewed this edition:

Ty Abernathy, *Mississippi State University*

James Alverson, *Northern Kentucky University*

Karen Beck, *Rio Hondo College*

Malasri Chaudhery-Malgeri, *Schoolcraft College*

Debbie DeWitt, *Blue Ridge Community College*

Crystal Dunlevy, *The Ohio State University–Columbus*

Andrea Fillip, *College of the Mainland*

Nicole Hamilton, *St. Philip's College*

Sara Harris, *Illinois State University*

Kelly Munly, *Penn State Altoona*

Valerie Neeley, *University of Texas–Rio Grande Valley*

Alexis Nicholson, *St. Philip's College*

Laura Ochoa, *Bergen Community College*

Sujata Ponappa, *The Ohio State University–Columbus*

Lori Puterbaugh, *St. Petersburg College*

Lisa Rosen, *Texas Women's University*

Christine Ziemer, *Missouri Western State University*

The editorial, production, and marketing people at Worth Publishers are dedicated to high standards. They devote time, effort, and talent to every aspect of publishing, a model for the industry. I am particularly grateful to my executive program manager, Chris Cardone, to my developmental editor, Andrea Musick Page, and to Charles Linsmeier, Macmillan's Senior Vice President. I also thank other members of my Macmillan team: Diana Blume, Laura Burden, Matthew Christensen, Sheena Goldstein, Noel Hohnstine, Peter Jacoby, Lisa Kinne, Tracey Kuehn, Jana Lewis, Jennifer MacMillan, Matthew McAdams, Michael McCarty, Hilary Newman, Katherine Nurre, Donna Ranieri, Chelsea Simens, Dorothy Tomasini, Joseph Tomasso, Nik Toner, Susan Wein, and Charles Yuen. And, as always, I am grateful to my students, my colleagues, and my family. Without them, none of this would be possible.

Kathleen Stassen Berger

New York, June 2018

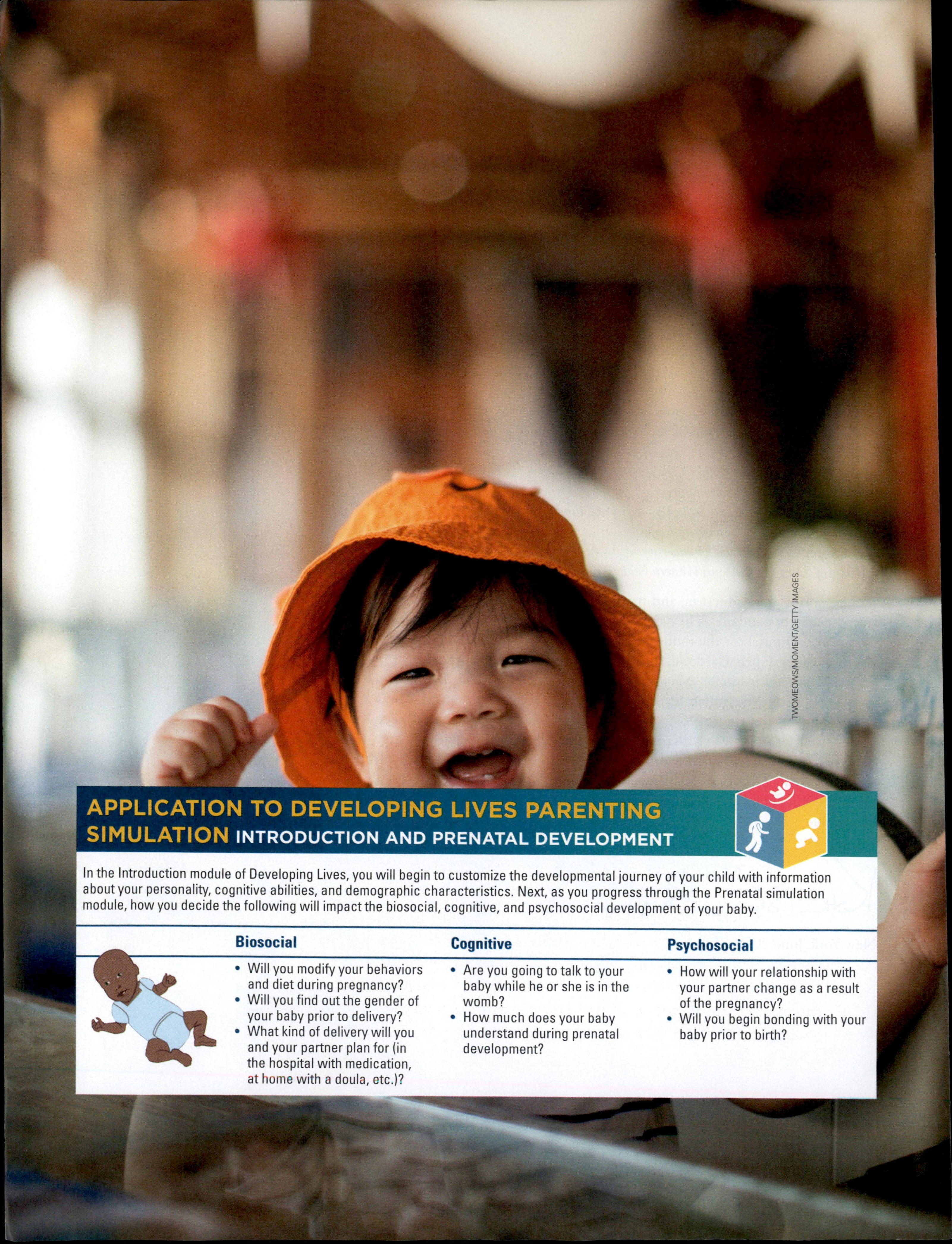

APPLICATION TO DEVELOPING LIVES PARENTING SIMULATION INTRODUCTION AND PRENATAL DEVELOPMENT

In the Introduction module of Developing Lives, you will begin to customize the developmental journey of your child with information about your personality, cognitive abilities, and demographic characteristics. Next, as you progress through the Prenatal simulation module, how you decide the following will impact the biosocial, cognitive, and psychosocial development of your baby.

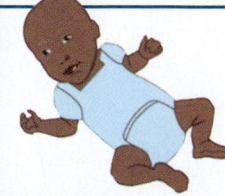

Biosocial	Cognitive	Psychosocial
• Will you modify your behaviors and diet during pregnancy? • Will you find out the gender of your baby prior to delivery? • What kind of delivery will you and your partner plan for (in the hospital with medication, at home with a doula, etc.)?	• Are you going to talk to your baby while he or she is in the womb? • How much does your baby understand during prenatal development?	• How will your relationship with your partner change as a result of the pregnancy? • Will you begin bonding with your baby prior to birth?

The Beginnings

The science of human development has many beginnings. Chapter 1 introduces the science and some theories, strategies, and methods that help us understand how people grow and change. Chapter 2 traces early development, from the genetic interactions that produce all inherited characteristics to the newborn's first movements, sounds, and reactions.

Throughout these two chapters, the interplay of nature (heredity) and nurture (the environment) is illustrated. For instance, whether or not a person will develop type 2 diabetes at age 60 depends on both nature (genetic vulnerability) and nurture (the mother's diet during pregnancy and the adult's health habits). Understanding the interplay of biology and culture is the foundation that allows us to reach **the goal of our study: a happy, productive, and meaningful life for the almost 8 billion people on Earth, of all ages, cultures, and aspirations**.

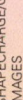

SHAPECHARGE/GETTY IMAGES

THE BEGINNINGS

The Science of Human Development

SHAPECHARGE/GETTY IMAGES

what will you know?*

- Why is the study of people a science?
- Are people the same, always and everywhere, or is each person unique, changing from day to day?
- Do all of the major theories of human development agree with each other?
- What cautions do developmental scientists need to remember?

I thought it was a small fix. I had a wayward toe, the one next to my big toe on my right foot. It stuck up; I had to push it down to wear dress shoes. I tried and failed to retrain it by taping it down.

I then followed what my culture suggests—see a doctor. I consulted a podiatrist, who sent me for X-rays and then recommended surgery. She said recovery would take a month. I told her I didn't have a month, that I walk for hours every day. She smiled: "That's what everyone says."

The toe had surgery; it then reminded me of the entire life span.

First, I regressed, clinging to the adolescent fable that I am an exception, that I could walk again in a day or two. Meanwhile, my four adult daughters arranged their schedules for the month so that at least one of them would be with me day and night. I wanted to be independent, as I have been all my life; they wanted to be caregivers, as adult women often do.

Sometimes we clashed. Two weeks after surgery I went to an evening meeting. When I arrived home at 10 P.M., my daughter Elissa was frantic, on the phone with another worried daughter, Sarah.

"You didn't tell us you had a meeting," she said angrily.

"I never tell you when I have a meeting. I am old enough to go out at night by myself."

One lesson from human development is that everyone should consider the perspective of everyone else; people at each age have needs and views that are typical of their age. I want to be independent; my daughters want to take care of me.

---

*"What Will You Know?" questions, one for each major heading, are a preview before each chapter. They are big ideas that you will still know a decade from now, unlike the "What Have You Learned?" questions after each major heading, which are more specific.

Another lesson regarded pain medication. I know the science: My 20 prescribed pills were addictive, and every day about 100 Americans die of opioid overdose. After I took two pills, I was afraid to take any more. But what to do with the rest? I remembered that flushing them down the toilet contaminates the water supply; I contemplated saving them for a future toothache. Then I thought about my curious, adventuresome grandsons. The solution—informed by science—was to destroy the pills by dissolving and incinerating them.

The final lesson occurred when the surgeon, pleased when I could walk again, sent me to physical therapy. Ridiculous, I thought, but I dutifully attended my first session. I expected the therapist to laugh, to say that the therapy was for legs, arms, and backs, not for toes.

She did not. Instead she massaged my toe and taught me six exercises to do every day.

"Your toe is connected to your entire body," she explained.

All this illustrates human development. As you will see in this chapter, our science is multi-directional, multi-contextual, multi-cultural, and plastic. Each small event, just like every toe and every family member, connects to the others. Understanding and appreciating these connections begins now.

Understanding How and Why

The **science of human development** *seeks to understand how and why people—all kinds of people, everywhere, of every age—change over time.* The goal is for everyone, of all ages, cultures, and aspirations, to have a happy, productive, and meaningful life.

Development over the life span is *multi-directional, multi-contextual, multi-cultural,* and *plastic*—four terms that will be explained soon. First we must emphasize that developmental study is a *science.* It depends on theories, data, analysis, critical thinking, and sound methodology, like every other science. Scientists ask questions and seek answers to ascertain "how and why."

Science is especially necessary when the topic is human development. People disagree about what pregnant women should eat; where babies should sleep; how children should be punished; whether adults should go to college, marry, divorce, and have children; and how older adults should approach aging, caregiving, and dying.

Some parents beat their children; other people put such parents in prison. Some people quit working as soon as they can; other people never retire. Some people welcome death; others take dangerous risks to defy it. Each person's choices affect everyone else. Scientists seek to progress from personal opinions to proven facts, from wishes to evidence.

The Scientific Method

As you surely realize, facts may be twisted, and applications sometimes spring from delusions. To rein in personal biases and avoid misinterpretations, researchers follow the **scientific method** (see Figure 1.1):

1. *Begin with curiosity.* Pose a question, guided by theory, research, or observation.

2. *Develop a hypothesis.* Shape the question into a testable **hypothesis.**

3. *Test the hypothesis.* Gather **empirical evidence** (data).

science of human development
The science that seeks to understand how and why people of all ages and circumstances change or remain the same over time.

scientific method
A way to answer questions using empirical research and data-based conclusions.

hypothesis
A specific prediction that can be tested, and proven or disproved.

empirical evidence
Evidence that is based on observation, experience, or experiment; not just theory or opinion. This makes it science-based.

1. Curiosity

2. Hypothesis

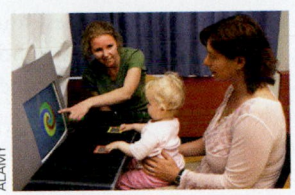
3. Test

4. Analyze data and draw conclusions

5. Report the results

FIGURE 1.1 Process, Not Proof Built into the scientific method—in questions, hypotheses, tests, and replication—is a passion for possibilities, especially unexpected ones.

4. *Draw conclusions.* Use evidence to support or refute the hypothesis.

5. *Report the results.* Share data, limitations, and conclusions.

Thus, developmental scientists begin with curiosity and then seek facts, drawing conclusions only after careful research.

Replication—repeating the procedures and methods of a study with different participants—is often a sixth and crucial step (Jasny et al., 2011). Scientists study the reports of other scientists and build on what has gone before. Sometimes they try to duplicate a study exactly; often they follow up with related research (Stroebe & Strack, 2014). Conclusions are revised, refined, rejected, or confirmed after replication.

Many scientists believe that psychology is now experiencing a replication crisis, since many important studies fail to replicate (Open Science Collaboration, 2015). But some scientists welcome the need for replication. One calls "the replication crisis as among psychological science's finest hours" (Lilienfeld, 2017, p. 660).

The scientific method is not foolproof. Scientists sometimes draw conclusions too hastily, misinterpret data, or ignore alternatives. The human mind is limited: That is why empirical research is crucial (Freese & Peterson, 2017).

replication
Repeating a study, usually using different participants, perhaps of another age, socioeconomic status (SES), or culture.

A VIEW FROM SCIENCE

Overweight Children and Adult Health*

Nutrition, health, and obesity are discussed in many chapters. Here we focus only on the implementation of the scientific method. Research on weight illustrates how scientists study and learn.

It has long been apparent that some children are plumper than others and that thin babies more often die. Even today, in some regions in Africa, about one of every ten newborns dies in the first days of life, with low birthweight (below 2,500 grams, 5½ pounds) a common cause (Grady et al., 2017). A century ago, death of underweight babies led to an untested assumption that is still held by some adults: that overweight children are healthier.

The results were predictable: Children were urged to finish their dinners, to eat more than they wanted. They were rewarded with sweets when they did as they were told. The notion that underweight children are more likely to die led to an unexamined assumption: Heavy children are healthy children (Laraway et al., 2010).

Sixty years ago, another untested assumption was that heart attacks could not be prevented. In 1948, scientists decided to study more than 5,000 adults in Framingham, Massachusetts, to see how their health in adulthood affected them later on (Levy & Brink, 2005; Mahmood et al., 2014). They collected data (step 3) and drew conclusions (step 4) that have revolutionized adult behavior.

Because of that study (since replicated hundreds of times), cigarette smoking is down, exercise is up, and doctors monitor blood pressure, weight, and cholesterol. Overweight is now recognized as a risk factor for heart disease and many other conditions.

Fatal heart attacks were only one-third as common in 2017 as in 1950, with reductions particularly apparent for

*Every chapter of this text features A View from Science, which explains surprising insights from recent scientific research.

men aged 40–60 (National Center for Health Statistics, 2017). Obesity is now considered "a chronic progressive relapsing disease" that often begins in childhood and continues lifelong (Bray et al., 2017, p. 717).

That research led to a new question: Is childhood obesity a health risk, too? This question (step 1) led to a hypothesis (step 2) that childhood overweight impairs adult health, which many believe is already proven. For instance, a poll found that most Californians consider childhood obesity "very serious," with one-third of them rating poor eating habits as riskier to child health than drug use or violence (Hennessy-Fiske, 2011). But science is needed to confirm or refute that hypothesis.

Research (step 3) needs to examine adult health in people who had been weighed and measured in childhood. Four teams of scientists did exactly that. They found that most people (83 percent) maintained their relative weight (see Figure 1.2a); thus, most overweight children became overweight adults and risked heart disease because of it.

A new question arose (step 1). What about overweight children who become normal-weight adults? That led to a new hypothesis (step 2): Childhood obesity predicts heart attacks, strokes, diabetes, and early death in adulthood, even if the person slims down.

The researchers measured health in normal-weight adults who had been overweight children (step 3). The data (step 4) (see Figure 1.2b) found that *the hypothesis was false:* Those who had slimmed down by adulthood were *not* at high risk of disease (Juonala et al., 2011).

Proving a hypothesis false is as useful for scientists as proving it true. In this case, childhood overweight is not a curse—welcome news leading to more studies. Other research finds that overweight children are at risk for some, but not all, measures of poor health (Ajala et al., 2017).

Many other issues, complications, and conclusions regarding obesity are discussed later in this book. For now, all you need to remember are the steps of the scientific method and that developmentalists are right: Significant "change over time" is possible.

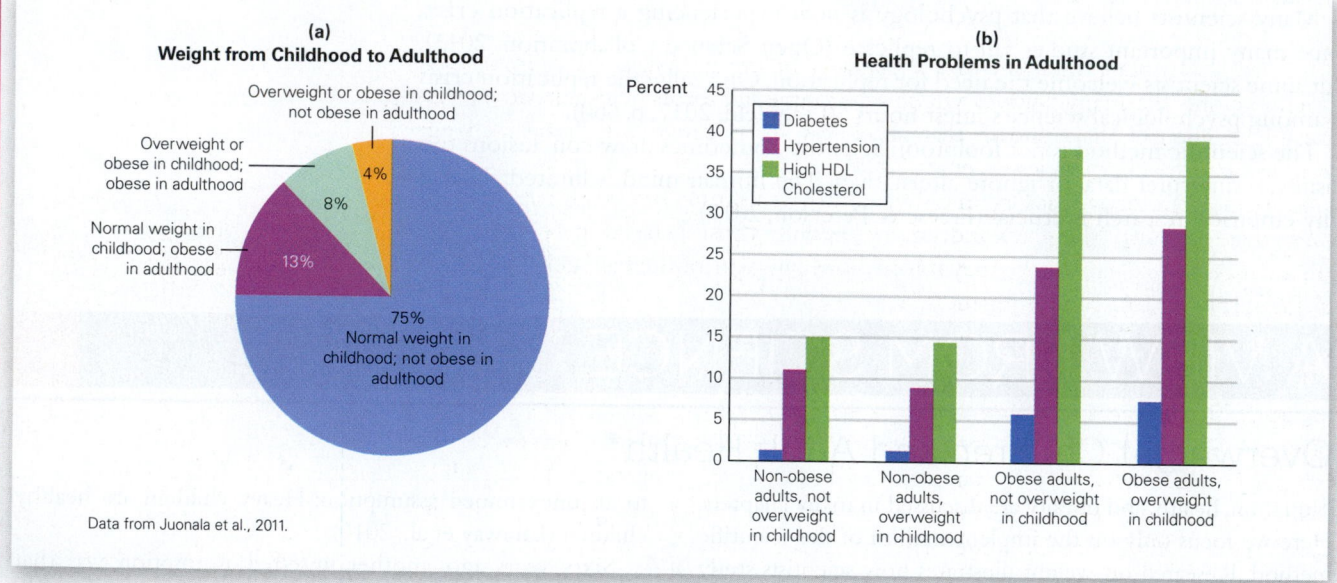

FIGURE 1.2 An Accurate Figure? As you probably know, more than half of all adults in the United States are overweight, so the pie graph—with only 21 percent of adults obese—may seem inaccurate. However, three facts explain why the data are accurate: (1) "Obese" is much heavier than overweight; (2) the average adult in this study was 34 years old (middle-aged and older adults are more often obese); and (3) one of the studies that provided much of the longitudinal data was in Finland, where rates of obesity are lower than in the United States.

Occasionally scientists discover, to their shock and dismay, that another scientist has not followed the procedures outlined above. This is one reason that reporting in detail (step 5) and replication are needed.

The most difficult part of the scientific method is to recognize that questions asked (step 1) and conclusions drawn (step 4) are limited by the people who designed the research. Ideally, with replication by scientists who were not part of the original study, conclusions become "robust," true not only for one group but for all humans everywhere (Freese & Peterson, 2017).

The Nature–Nurture Question

An easy example of the need for science concerns a great issue in development, the *nature–nurture question*. **Nature** refers to the influence of the genes that people inherit. **Nurture** refers to environmental influences, beginning with the health and diet of the embryo's mother and continuing lifelong, including family, school, community, culture, and society.

The nature–nurture issue has many other names, among them *heredity vs. environment* and *maturation vs. learning*. Under whatever name, the basic question is: *How much of any characteristic, behavior, or emotion is the result of genes and how much is the result of experience?*

Some people believe that most traits are inborn, that children are innately good (an "innocent child") or bad ("beat the devil out of them"). Other people stress nurture, blaming parents or neighborhoods or society or drugs when an adult is a criminal or disturbed or abhorrent in some other way.

Neither extreme is accurate. The question is "how much," not "which," because both genes *and* experience affect every characteristic: Nature always affects nurture, and then nurture affects nature.

Even "how much" may be misleading: It implies that nature and nurture each contribute a fixed amount when actually their explosive interaction is crucial (Eagly & Wood, 2013; Lock, 2013).

EPIGENETICS A new discipline that is related to nature and nurture is **epigenetics,** which explores the many ways in which environmental forces alter genetic expression. Neuroscientists have shown that loneliness, for example, can literally change structures in the brain (Cacioppo et al., 2014).

Sometimes protective factors, in either nature or nurture, outweigh liabilities. As one review explains, "there are, indeed, individuals whose genetics indicate exceptionally high risk of disease, yet they never show any signs of the disorder" (Friend & Schadt, 2014, p. 970). Why? Epigenetics.

DANDELIONS AND ORCHIDS There is increasing evidence of **differential susceptibility**—that is, the idea that the effect of any experience differs from one person to another because of the particular genes each person has inherited. For instance, if toddlers inherit the tendency to be disruptive, depressed, antisocial, or anxious, they benefit from a mother who provides structure and guidance. On the other hand, if a child is at low genetic risk for those problems, having such a mother might not matter, or might even be harmful (Harold et al., 2017).

Developmentalists use a metaphor for two kinds of children, those who seem to blossom no matter what kind of child rearing they experience, and those who need intense care—and wither without it. Some are like *dandelions*—hardy, growing and thriving in good soil or bad, with or without ample sun and rain. Others are like *orchids*—quite wonderful, but only when ideal growing conditions are met (Ellis & Boyce, 2008; Laurent, 2014).

For example, in one study, depression in pregnant women was assessed and then the emotional maturity of their children was measured. Those children who had a particular version of the serotonin transporter gene (5-HTTLPR) were orchids—likely to be emotionally immature if their mothers were depressed, but *more* mature than average if their mothers were not depressed (Babineau et al., 2015).

The interaction between nature and nurture is apparent for every topic in this book, as you will see, and in every moment of our lives, as I see in myself. My toe stuck up (nature) partly because I wore high heels with pointed toes for years (nurture); the pain and swelling from the surgery (nature) was reduced by the drugs

nature
In development, *nature* refers to genes. Thus, traits, capacities, and limitations inherited at conception are nature.

nurture
In development, *nurture* includes all environmental influences that occur after conception, from the mother's nutrition while pregnant to the culture of the nation.

epigenetics
The study of how environmental factors affect genes and genetic expression—enhancing, halting, shaping, or altering the expression of genes.

differential susceptibility
The idea that people vary in how sensitive (for better or worse) they are to particular experiences, either because of their genes or because of their past experiences. (Also called *differential sensitivity*.)

JANEK SKARZYNSKI/AFP/GETTY IMAGES

Chopin's First Concert
Frederick Chopin, at age 8, played his first public concert in 1818, before photographs. But this photo shows Piotr Pawlak, a contemporary prodigy playing Chopin's music in the same Polish palace where that famous composer played as a boy. How much of talent is genetic and how much is cultural is a nature–nurture question that applies to both boys, 200 years apart.

I took and by the ice packs my daughters brought me, but increased by my own insistence on walking more than the doctor advised (three aspects of nurture).

what have you learned?

1. What are the five steps of the scientific method?
2. Why is replication important?
3. What basic question is at the heart of the nature–nurture controversy?
4. How might differential susceptibility apply to adults?

The Life-Span Perspective

The **life-span perspective** (Baltes et al., 2006; Fingerman et al., 2011; Raz & Lindenberger, 2013) takes into account all phases of life (not just the first two decades, which were once the sole focus of developmental study), and all aspects of development (not just physical development, once the main focus). By including the entirety of life (see Table 1.1), this perspective has led to the realization that human development is multi-directional, multi-contextual, multi-cultural, and plastic.

Neuroscientists are among the most recent to apply a life-span perspective, recognizing that the connections in the brain are plastic and vary from one person to another (Zuo et al., 2017). Now we examine each of these four insights.

TABLE 1.1	Age Ranges for Different Periods of Development
Infancy	0 to 2 years
Early childhood	2 to 6 years
Middle childhood	6 to 11 years
Adolescence	11 to 18 years
Emerging adulthood	18 to 25 years
Adulthood	25 to 65 years
Late adulthood	65 years and older

As you will learn, developmentalists are reluctant to specify chronological ages for any period of development, since time is only one of many variables that affect each person. However, age is a crucial variable, and development can be segmented into periods of study. Approximate ages for each period are given here.

Development Is Multi-Directional

Multiple changes, in every direction, characterize the life span: Development is *multi-directional*. If human traits were all charted over time from birth to death, some traits would appear, others disappear, with increases, decreases, and zigzags (see Figure 1.3). The traditional idea—that all development advances until about age 18, steadies, and then declines—has been refuted by life-span research.

The pace of change varies as well. Sometimes *discontinuity* is evident: Change can occur rapidly and dramatically, as when caterpillars become butterflies. Sometimes *continuity* is found: Growth can be gradual, as when redwoods grow taller over hundreds of years.

Even stability is possible. Some characteristics seem not to change. For instance, chromosomal sex is lifelong: A zygote is XY or XX (male or female) for life. Of course, the power and meaning of that biological fact change, but the chromosomes themselves stay the same.

There is simple growth, radical transformation, improvement, and decline in almost every aspect of development. There is also stability and continuity—day to day, year to year, and generation to generation.

Life-span theorists see *gains and losses* throughout life, often at the same time (Lang et al., 2011; Villar, 2012). For example, when babies begin to talk, they are less able to distinguish sounds—especially the "l" and "r"—from other languages (a gain and a loss); when adults retire, they may become more creative (a loss and a gain).

life-span perspective
An approach to the study of human development that includes all phases, from conception to death.

---

*Think Critically questions occur several times in each chapter. They are intended to provoke thought, not simple responses, and hence have no obvious answers.

CRITICAL PERIODS The speed and timing of impairments or improvements vary as well. Some changes are sudden and profound because of a **critical period,** a time when something *must* occur for normal development, or the only time when an abnormality can occur. For instance, the critical period for humans to grow arms and legs, hands and feet, fingers and toes is between 28 and 54 days after conception.

After day 54, that critical period is over. Unlike some insects, humans never grow replacement limbs or digits. We know the critical period for limb formation because of a tragic occurrence. Between 1957 and 1961, thousands of newly pregnant women in 30 nations took *thalidomide,* an antinausea drug. This change in nurture (via the mother's bloodstream carried to the fetus via the umbilical cord) disrupted nature (the embryo's genetic program).

If an expectant woman took thalidomide between day 28 and day 54, her fetus's arms or legs were malformed or absent (Moore, et al., 2015, pp. 372–374). Whether all four limbs, or just arms, or just forearms were missing depended on dose and timing. If thalidomide was ingested only after day 54, the fetus had normal body structures.

SENSITIVE PERIODS As the life-span perspective recognizes, humans have few critical periods. Often, however, a particular development occurs more easily—not exclusively—at a certain time. Such a time is called a **sensitive period.**

An example is found in language. If children do not communicate in their first language between ages 1 and 3, they might do so later (hence, not critical), but their grammar is often impaired (hence, sensitive). Similarly, childhood is a sensitive period for learning to speak a second or third language. A new language can be learned later, but strangers might detect an accent and ask, "Where are you from?"

Often in development, individual exceptions to general patterns occur. Accent-free speech *usually* must be learned before puberty, but exceptional nature and nurture (an adult with excellent hearing and then immersion in a new language) can result in flawless second-language pronunciation (Birdsong, 2006; Muñoz & Singleton, 2011).

FIGURE 1.3 Patterns of Developmental Growth Many patterns of developmental growth have been discovered by careful research. Although linear progress seems most common, scientists now find that almost no aspect of human change follows the linear pattern exactly.

critical period
Time when a particular development must occur. If it does not, as when something toxic prevents that growth, then it cannot develop later.

sensitive period
A time when a particular developmental growth is most likely to occur, although it may still happen later.

JOHN MOORE/GETTY IMAGES

I Love You, Mommy We do not know what words, in what language, her son is using, but we do know that Sobia Akbar speaks English well, a requirement for naturalized U.S. citizens. Here she obtains citizenship for her two children born in Pakistan. Chances are they will speak unaccented American English, unlike Sobia, whose accent might indicate that she learned British English as a second language.

Because of sensitive periods for language development, such exceptions are rare. A study of native Dutch speakers who become fluent in English found only 5 percent had truly mastered native English (Schmid et al., 2014). Fluent English speakers who spoke another language first almost always stumbled with idioms, articles, or accents.

Added to the complexity are the varieties of each language. For example, many people in England, Hong Kong, Australia, and India speak English as their first language, but they do so unlike those in the United States, who differ among themselves depending on where they lived as a child (Sewell, 2016). Everyone, of course, "has an accent"—a fact which shows that childhood is a sensitive time for learning several languages, or several versions of one's native language.

Sensitive periods occur at many ages, not just early childhood. Consider the best time to learn about cultural differences, or infant care, or calculus: Not childhood!

Development Is Multi-Contextual

The second insight from the life-span perspective is that development is *multi-contextual*. It takes place within many contexts, including physical surroundings (climate, noise, population density, etc.) and family configurations (married couple, single parent, cohabiting couple, extended family, etc.). Each context influences development, sometimes for a moment, sometimes for years.

A college student might choose to go to a party instead of to the library. The social context of the party, such as the food and drinks, the music, and the other guests, influences that student's next several decisions. He or she might stay until 3 a.m., binge on alcohol, dance on a table—or leave as quickly as is socially acceptable, mumbling something about an exam tomorrow.

As you can imagine, the context of the party, and the decisions influenced by that context, affect later development: It may be hard for that student to attend class the next day, or, when in class, hard to remember math formulas or historical circumstances.

Of course, we are responsible for our actions, but social contexts are powerful, nudging us to do what we do (Thaler & Sunstein, 2008). This phenomenon has led many researchers to try to figure out the best techniques of "choice architecture"—how to design contexts so that people make good choices (Münscher et al., 2016).

ECOLOGICAL SYSTEMS Long before exploration of choice architecture, a leading developmentalist, Urie Bronfenbrenner (1917–2005), recognized that context is crucial. Just as a naturalist studying an organism examines the ecology (the multifaceted relationship between the organism and its environment), Bronfenbrenner recommended that developmentalists take an **ecological–systems approach** (Bronfenbrenner & Morris, 2006).

ecological-systems approach
A perspective on human development that considers all of the influences from the various contexts of development. (Later renamed *bioecological theory*.)

BARTCO/E+/GETTY IMAGES

Where in the World? Like every child, this boy is influenced by dozens of contexts from each of Bronfenbrenner's systems, some quite direct and some in the macro- and exosystems. His cap (called a kopiah), diligence, all-boys school, and slanted desk each affects his learning, but those could occur in many nations—in the Americas, Europe, or Africa. In fact, this is in Asia, in Kota Bharu, Malaysia.

The ecological-systems approach recognizes three nested levels that surround individuals and affect them (see Figure 1.4). Most obvious are *microsystems,* each person's immediate surroundings, such as family and peer group. Beyond the microsystems are the *exosystems* (local institutions such as school and church), and beyond that are *macrosystems* (the larger social setting, including cultural values, economic policies, and political processes).

Think of a high school graduate deciding whether or not to go to college. The decision is powerfully influenced by parents and friends. Would you be in college if your parents thought it was a waste of time and none of your friends chose to apply? However, the social context extends to the exosystem: Are there several

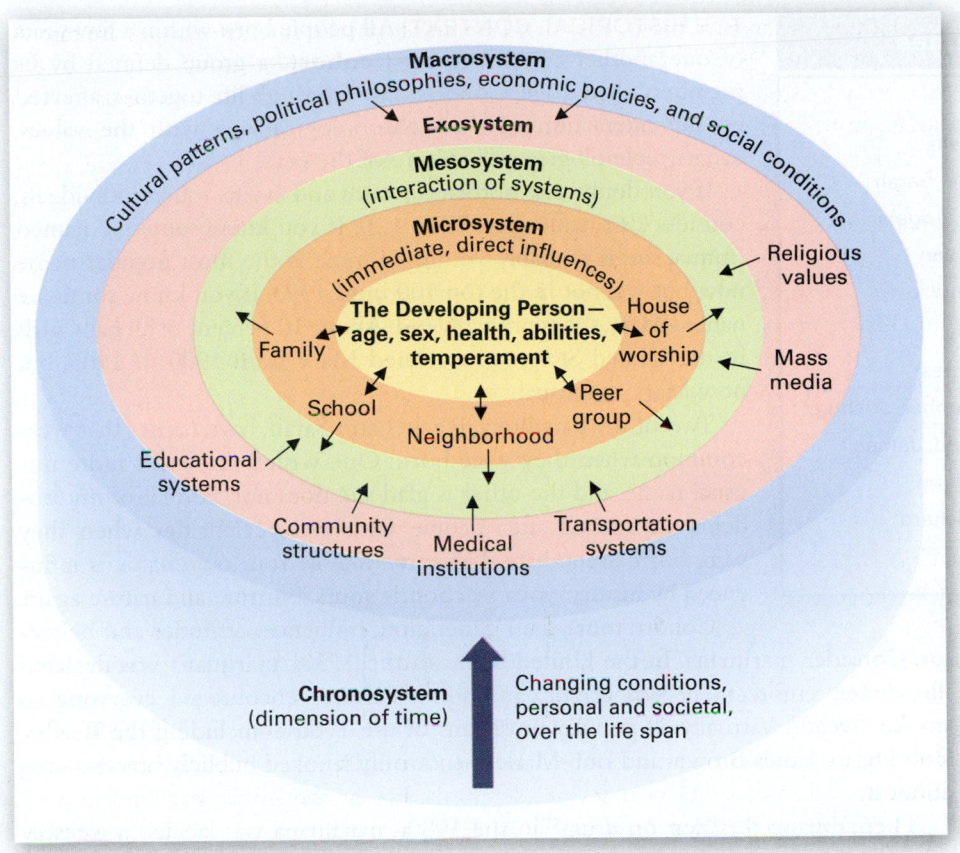

FIGURE 1.4 The Ecological Model According to developmental researcher Urie Bronfenbrenner, each person is significantly affected by interactions among a number of overlapping systems, which provide the context of development. *Microsystems*—family, peer group, classroom, neighborhood, house of worship—intimately and immediately shape human development. Surrounding and supporting the microsystems are the *exosystems*, which include all of the external networks, such as community structures and local educational, medical, employment, and communications systems, that affect the microsystems. Influencing both of these systems is the *macrosystem*, which includes cultural patterns, political philosophies, economic policies, and social conditions. *Mesosystems* refer to interactions among systems, as when parents and teachers coordinate to educate a child. Bronfenbrenner eventually added a fifth system, the *chronosystem*, to emphasize the importance of historical time.

nearby colleges? Did your high school prepare students for college and help with the admission process? Does the local government subsidize higher education? The macrosystem matters, too: Does the culture value education? Do the best jobs go to college grads?

No single system is decisive, but each nudges toward higher education or away from it. At some senior colleges, 94 percent of the freshmen earn a bachelor's degree; at other colleges, 8 percent do (Sneyers & De Witte, 2017). Family income, neighborhood, culture, gender, and field of study all matter, as does the college itself (Huang et al., 2017). Before a spaceship is launched, it must be "all systems go." This is true for individuals, too.

Bronfenbrenner also stressed the *chronosystem* (literally, "time system"), which encompasses historical conditions that affect each person. Further, to stress the dynamic interaction among all of the systems, he included a fifth system, the *mesosystem*, consisting of the connections between and among the other systems.

Throughout his life, Bronfenbrenner studied people in natural settings. He wanted to learn how people interact with each other at home, at school, or at work, and he did not want to study people in a scientist's laboratory or by having them answer questionnaires about their behavior. He watched them doing things in real life, not writing about what they did.

Bronfenbrenner renamed his approach *bioecological* to highlight the role of biology. He recognized that systems within the body (e.g., the sexual-reproductive system, the cardiovascular system) affect the external contexts (Bronfenbrenner & Morris, 2006).

As you can see, a contextual approach to development requires simultaneous consideration of many systems. Two contexts—historical and socioeconomic—are crucial in understanding all of the systems of life-span development, yet they are often ignored. They merit explanation now.

TABLE 1.2	Popular First Names

Girls:

2016: Emma, Olivia, Ava, Sophia, Isabella

1996: Jessica, Ashley, Emily, Samantha, Sarah

1976: Jennifer, Amy, Melissa, Heather, Angela

1956: Mary, Debra, Linda, Deborah, Susan

1936: Mary, Shirley, Barbara, Betty, Patricia

Boys:

2016: Noah, Liam, William, Mason, James

1996: Michael, Matthew, Jacob, Christopher, Joshua

1976: Michael, Jason, Christopher, David, James

1956: Michael, James, Robert, David, John

1936: Robert, James, John, William, Richard

Information from U.S. Social Security Administration.

cohort
People born within the same historical period who therefore move through life together, experiencing the same events, new technologies, and cultural shifts at the same ages.

↓ **OBSERVATION** QUIZ
Why is the line for the youngest cohort much shorter than the line for the older cohorts? (see answer, page 41)*

FIGURE 1.5 **Double Trends** Both cohort and generational trends are evident. Note that people of every age are becoming more accepting of marijuana, but the effect is most obvious for adults who never heard about "reefer madness."

THE HISTORICAL CONTEXT All people born within a few years of one another are said to be a **cohort,** a group defined by its members' shared age. Cohorts travel through life together, affected by the interaction of their chronological age with the values, events, technologies, and culture of the era.

If you doubt that historical trends and events touch individuals, consider first names (see Table 1.2). If you know someone named Emma, she is probably young—Emma is the most popular name now but was not in the top 100 until 1993. If you know someone named Mary, she is probably old: About 10 percent of all baby girls in the United States were named Mary from 1900 to 1965, but now Mary is unusual.

Two of my daughters, Rachel and Sarah, have names that were common when they were born: One wishes she had a more unusual name, and the other is glad she does not. Several of my students are named after people who were celebrities when they were born: Some hate that; some like it. Your own name is influenced by history; your reaction is yours. Nurture and nature again.

Cohort, more than generation, influences attitudes and behavior. Consider marijuana. In the United States in the 1930s, marijuana was declared illegal, but enforcement was erratic, and some cultures encouraged everyone to smoke "weed." Virtually all popular musicians of the 1960s—including the Beatles, Bob Dylan, James Brown, and Bob Marley—not only smoked publicly but also sang about it.

Then, during the "war on drugs" in the 1980s, marijuana was labeled a gateway drug, likely to open the floodgates to serious abuse and addiction (Kandel, 2002). People were arrested and jailed for possession of even a few grams.

From 1990 on, attitudes gradually shifted again (see Figure 1.5), such that by 2017 recreational marijuana use became legal in Uruguay and in 12 U.S. states, with medical use permitted in several others. A group of doctors advocates legalization of marijuana for reasons related to human development: They say it would be easier to keep drugs from children, to prevent teenagers from harming their brains, and to improve family life if marijuana potency were regulated and users never put in jail (Nathan et al., 2017).

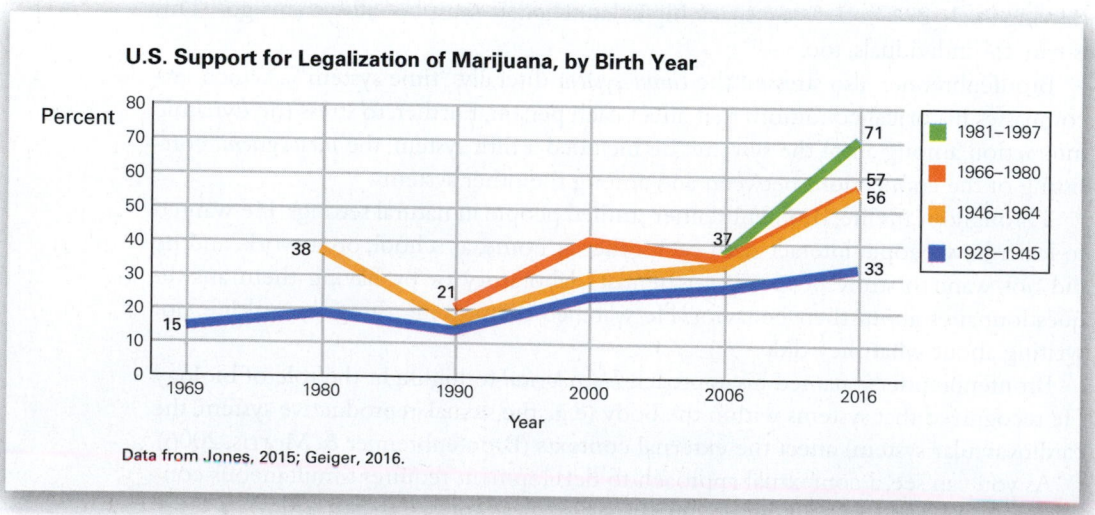

U.S. Support for Legalization of Marijuana, by Birth Year

Data from Jones, 2015; Geiger, 2016.

---

*Observation Quizzes are designed to help students practice a crucial skill, specifically to notice small details that indicate something about human development. Answers appear at the end of the chapter.

Adolescents are particularly affected by historical shifts, including those regarding marijuana use. In 1978, only 12 percent of high school students thought regular use of marijuana was a "great risk," and more than half had tried the drug. Thirteen years later, 80 percent thought there was "great risk" in regular use, and only 20 percent had tried it.

Every year since then, marijuana use has increased as attitudes changed again. In 2016, more than one-third of high school seniors had used it, and attitudes had flipped: Now more than 80 percent believe there is no great risk (Miech et al., 2017a and previous years). The developmental consequences of teenage drug use are discussed in Chapter 10; the point here is that cohort effects may be profound.

THE SOCIOECONOMIC CONTEXT Another influential context is economic, reflected in a person's **socioeconomic status,** abbreviated **SES.** (Sometimes SES is called *social class,* as in *middle class* or *working class.*) SES reflects income and much more, including occupation, education, and neighborhood.

Suppose a U.S. family is comprised of an infant, an unemployed mother, and a father who earns $18,000 a year. Their SES would be low if the wage earner is a high school dropout working 40 hours a week at minimum wage and living in an underserved neighborhood, but it would be much higher if the wage earner is a postdoctoral student living on campus and teaching part time.

Both are poor by official standards, because the poverty level is set by the relationship between income and the cost of food. A family of three is below the 2016 poverty threshold because its household income is less than $19,337, but they must be low in education as well to be considered low in SES.

SES brings opportunities or limitations—all affecting housing, health, nutrition, knowledge, and habits. Although low income obviously limits a person, other factors are pivotal, especially education and national policy. Voters choose leaders who decide taxes and policies that affect people of various ages and incomes.

socioeconomic status (SES)
A person's position in society as determined by income, occupation, education, and place of residence. (Sometimes called *social class.*)

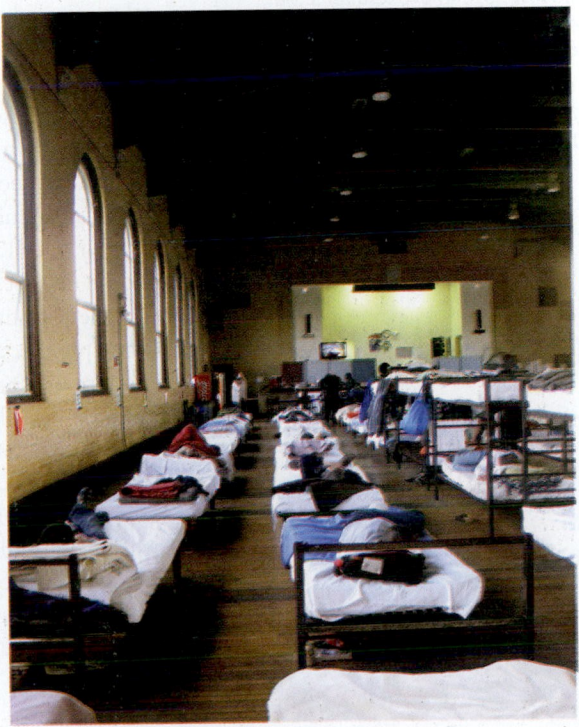

Same Situation, Far Apart: Shelter Rules The homeless shelter in Paris, France *(left)* allows dogs, Christmas trees, and flat-screen televisions for couples in private rooms. The one in Cranston, Rhode Island *(right)*, is only for men (no women, children, or dogs), who must leave each morning and wait in line each night for 1 of the 88 beds. Both places share one characteristic: Some of the homeless are turned away, as there is not room for everyone.

JOEL SAGET/AFP/GETTY IMAGES

AP PHOTO/DAVID KLEPPER

Poverty is a developmental issue as well as a personal one. Average income increases with age, which means that households headed by young adults are often poor. The result is that many children are in low-SES homes. Older adults, on average, are richer, but the greatest gap in income is among the very old; some of them are billionaires, and some have no money at all.

Education is particularly crucial here: Those with no income are often those without college degrees, because unemployment rises as education falls. In the United States, those 25- to 34-year-olds who did not graduate from high school but were employed earned an average of $25,000 annually, compared to twice that ($52,000) for those with at least a bachelor's degree (Snyder et al., 2016).

Some nations reduce the gap between rich and poor by providing paid day care or maternal leave for the youngest children and health care for everyone. In North America, that is more true for the old than the young, and more true in Canada than the United States. Among developed nations, the United States has "recently earned the distinction of being the most unequal" (Aizer & Currie, 2014, p. 856). Elsewhere in the world, however, the poorest nations have the largest SES disparities, where most people lack basic necessities but a few people are very rich (Ravallion, 2014).

The increasing gap between rich and poor may not be as troubling in the United States as it is in other advanced nations. A leading economist contends, "in America, people do not have a strong view against inequality per se, as long as inequality is fair" (Saez, 2017, p. 25).

That is *culture,* a topic discussed next. However, from a developmental perspective, if low SES makes it difficult for people to fulfill their potential, then it may be unfair.

Development Is Multi-Cultural

In order to study "all kinds of people, everywhere, at every age," as developmental science does, it is essential that people of many cultures be considered. For social scientists, **culture** is "the system of shared beliefs, conventions, norms, behaviors, expectations and symbolic representations that persist over time and prescribe social rules of conduct" (Bornstein et al., 2011, p. 30).

SOCIAL CONSTRUCTIONS Thus, culture is far more than food, clothes, or customs; it is a set of ideas that people share. This makes culture a powerful **social construction,** a concept constructed, or made, by a society. Social constructions affect how people think, what they do, and what they value.

Because culture is so basic to thinking and emotions, people are usually unaware of their social constructions. Fish do not realize that they are surrounded by water; people do not realize that their beliefs arise from their culture.

One assumption is evident if the word *culture* is used to refer to large groups of other people, as in "Asian culture" or "Hispanic culture." That invites stereotyping and prejudice, since such large groups include people of many backgrounds. For instance, people from Korea and Japan are aware of notable cultural differences between their nationalities, as are people from Mexico and Guatemala.

In today's United States, most people are influenced by several cultures, not just one. One observer contends that people with Jamaican heritage in the United States are tri-cultural (Jamaican, Black, American) (G. Ferguson et al., 2014). Given our awareness of contexts, each person is also influenced by more than their national culture. For example, middle-class culture, or California culture, or the culture of a particular college all affect what people think and do.

THINK CRITICALLY: When does money help and when does it hinder people from the goal of developmental psychology, for everyone to have a "happy, meaningful, and productive life"?

VIDEO: Interview with Barbara Rogoff to learn more about the role of culture in the development of Mayan children in Guatemala.

culture
A system of shared beliefs, norms, behaviors, and expectations that persist over time and prescribe social behavior and assumptions.

social construction
An idea that is built on shared perceptions, not on objective reality.

To appreciate that culture is a matter of beliefs and values, not superficial differences, consider language again. Of course, people speak distinct languages, but that itself is not a cultural difference. However, some people are offended by words that other people proudly say. That is cultural.

More generally, among some cultural groups, independent thinking is praised. In families in those groups, children are encouraged to talk freely, and when they do, the adults listen approvingly. Among other groups, a prime cultural value is that children respect their parents, and, by extension, every adult: Children should never interrupt an adult conversation.

One of my students remembered:

> My mom was outside on the porch talking to my aunt. I decided to go outside; I guess I was being nosey. While they were talking I jumped into their conversation which was very rude. When I realized what I did it was too late. My mother slapped me in my face so hard that it took a couple of seconds to feel my face again.
>
> *[C., personal communication]*

Notice how my student reflects her culture; she labels her own behavior "nosey" and "very rude." She later wrote that she expects children to be seen but not heard and that her own son makes her "very angry" when he interrupts. Do you agree? Your answer depends on your culture.

DEFICIT OR JUST DIFFERENCE? We humans tend to believe that we ourselves, our nation, our group, and our culture are better than others. That idea benefits us: Our self-esteem and our group loyalty are usually constructive. We strive for accomplishments because we believe we can do it; we care for our family members because we believe in them.

However, our personal pride becomes destructive if it reduces respect and appreciation. Developmentalists recognize this **difference-equals-deficit error,** the mistaken belief that people who are different from us are thereby deficient, which means lacking in some important way. Too quickly and without thought, differences are assumed to be problems (Akhtar & Jaswal, 2013).

difference-equals-deficit error
The mistaken belief that a deviation from some norm is necessarily inferior.

VIDEO: Research of Geoffrey Saxe further explores how difference does not equal deficit.

Difference, But Not Deficit This Syrian refugee living in a refugee camp in Greece is quite different from the aid workers who assist there, as evident in her head covering (hijab) and the cross on her tent. But the infant, with a pacifier in her mouth and a mother who tries to protect her, illustrates why developmentalists focus on similarities, rather than on differences.

MYRTO PAPADOPOULOS FOR THE WASHINGTON POST VIA GETTY IMAGES

Visualizing Development

DIVERSE COMPLEXITIES

It is often repeated that "the United States is becoming more diverse," a phrase that usually refers only to ethnic diversity and not to economic and religious diversity (which are also increasing and merit attention). From a developmental perspective, two other diversities are also important—age and region, as shown below. What are the implications for schools, colleges, employment, health care, and nursing homes in the notable differences in the ages of people of various groups? And are attitudes about immigration, or segregation, or multi-racial identity affected by the ethnicity of one's neighbors?

THE CHANGING ETHNIC MAKEUP OF THE UNITED STATES

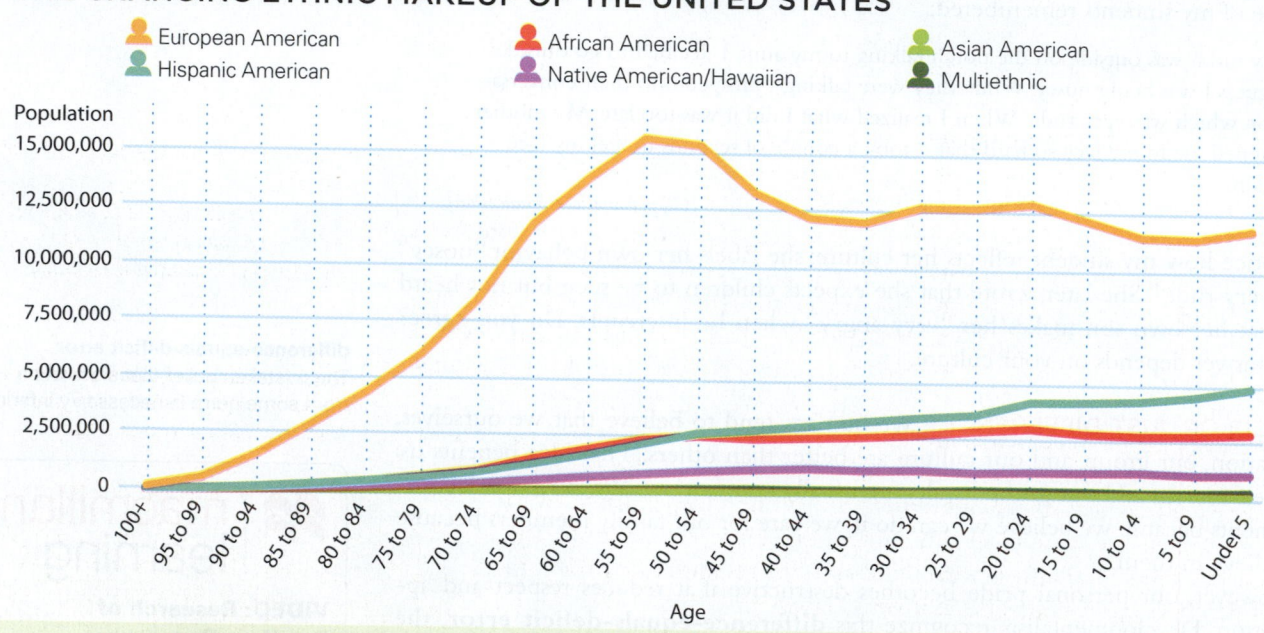

- European American
- Hispanic American
- African American
- Native American/Hawaiian
- Asian American
- Multiethnic

Regional Differences in Ethnicity Across the United States

In the United States, there are regional as well as age differences in ethnicity. This map shows which counties have an ethnic population greater than the national average. Counties where more than one ethnicity or race is greater than the national average are shown as multiethnic. Areas for which data are unavailable are left unshaded.

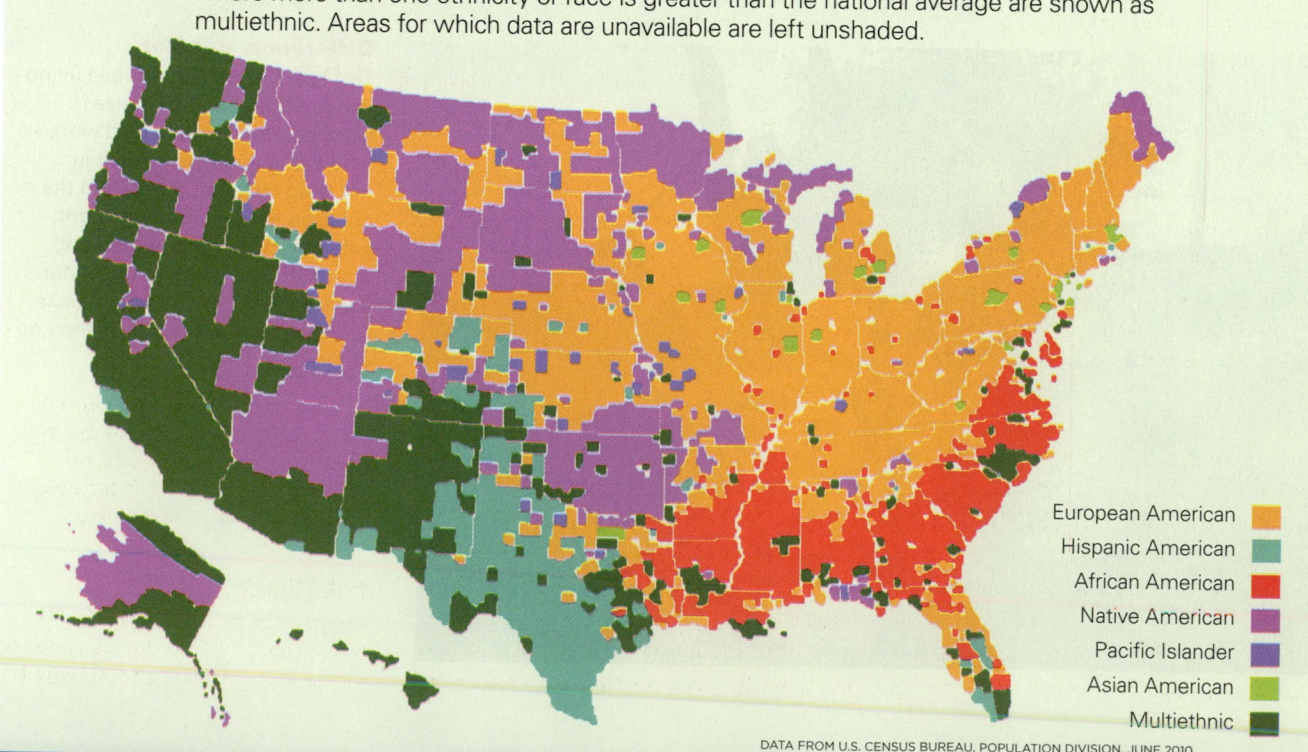

- European American
- Hispanic American
- African American
- Native American
- Pacific Islander
- Asian American
- Multiethnic

DATA FROM U.S. CENSUS BUREAU, POPULATION DIVISION, JUNE 2010.

Negative judgments are often made about how other people raise children, or worship God, or even eat. Age differences are also stereotyped. Have you heard adults complain about the attitudes, abilities, or actions of teenagers, or of senior citizens? Age stereotypes are evidence of differences judged as deficits. In the opening anecdote, did you judge either the caregiving daughters or their independent mother as wrong?

Gender differences are another easy example. We are amused when young girls say, "Boys stink," or their male classmates say, "Girls are stupid." However, even though the sexes have far more similarities than differences, humans of all ages notice differences and make sexist judgments. According to one scholar, even neuroscientists make that mistake. They are susceptible to "neurosexism," seeing and explaining gender differences "in the absence of data" (Fine, 2014, p. 915).

One of the very few proven gender differences is that women are more tenderhearted and men more sexually driven (Hyde, 2014). That is a difference, not a deficit. If you are male, do you think that women are weak because they are too emotional? If you are female, do you think men are too obsessed with sex? If you answer yes, how human of you. And how mistaken.

The difference-equals-deficit error is one reason a multi-cultural approach is crucial. Various ways of thinking or acting are not necessarily wrong or right, better or worse. The scientific method, which requires empirical data, is needed for accurate assessments.

Sometimes a difference is actually an asset (Marschark & Spencer, 2003). For example, cultures that discourage dissent also foster harmony. The opposite is also true—cultures that encourage dissent also value independence. Whatever your personal judgment on this cultural difference, the opposite opinion has some merit. A multi-cultural understanding requires recognition that some differences signify strengths, not weaknesses.

LEARNING WITHIN A CULTURE Russian developmentalist Lev Vygotsky (1896–1934) was a leader in describing the interaction between culture and education (Wertsch & Tulviste, 2005). He noticed that adults from the many cultures of the Soviet Union (Asians and Europeans of many religions) taught their children whatever beliefs and habits they might need as adults within their local community.

Vygotsky (discussed in more detail in Chapter 5) believed that *guided participation* is a universal process used by mentors to teach cultural knowledge, skills, and habits. Guided participation can occur via school instruction but more often happens informally, through "mutual involvement in several widespread cultural practices with great importance for learning: narratives, routines, and play" (Rogoff, 2003, p. 285). My grandson's third-grade teacher shakes each child's hand at the end of the day, smiles, and expects her students to look at her and say goodbye. In other cultures, this would not happen.

ETHNIC AND RACIAL GROUPS It is easy to confuse culture, ethnicity, and race because these terms sometimes overlap (see Figure 1.6). People of an **ethnic group** share certain attributes, almost always including ancestral heritage and usually national origin, religion, and language. This means that ethnic groups often—but not always—share a culture. Some people share ethnicity but not culture (consider people of Irish descent in Ireland, Australia, and North America), and some cultures include people of several ethnic groups (consider British culture).

Ethnic groups are primarily social constructions, dependent on context. For example, African-born people who live in North America typically consider themselves African,

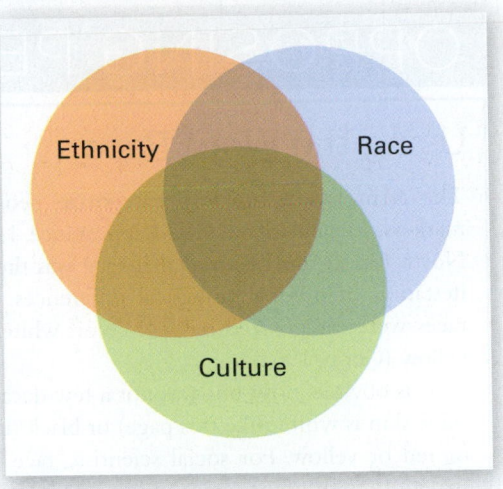

FIGURE 1.6 Overlap—But How Much? Ethnicity, culture, and race are three distinct concepts, but they often—though not always—overlap.

ethnic group
People whose ancestors were born in the same region. Usually they share a language, culture, and/or religion.

Affection for Children
Vygotsky lived in Russia from 1896 to 1934, when war, starvation, and revolution led to the deaths of millions. Throughout this turmoil, Vygotsky focused on learning.

↑ OBSERVATION QUIZ
Can you deduce anything about his attitude about children from this photo with his daughter? (see answer, page 41)

DR. JAMES WERTSCH

OPPOSING PERSPECTIVES*

Using the Word *Race*

The term **race** is used to categorize people via physical markers, particularly outward appearance. Historically, most North Americans believed that race was the outward manifestation of inborn biological differences. Fifty years ago, races were categorized by skin color: white, black, red, and yellow (Coon, 1962).

It is obvious now, but was not a few decades ago, that no one's skin is white (like this page) or black (like these letters) or red or yellow. For social scientists, race is a social construction, with color terms used to make it seem as if races are distinct.

Genetic analysis confirms that the biological concept of race is inaccurate, especially when based on skin color. A study of the genes for skin tones found marked diversity among people from Africa. The lead scientist explained, "There is so much diversity in Africans that there is no such thing as an African race" (Tishkoff, quoted in Gibbons, 2017, p. 158). Indeed, dark-skinned Australians or Maori in New Zealand share neither culture nor ethnicity with Africans. A study of East Asians found 20 genetic variants (most of them rare) that affect their skin color (Hider et al., 2013).

Race is more than a flawed concept; it is a destructive one. Slavery, lynching, and segregation in the United States were directly connected to the conviction that race was inborn; genocide in Nazi Germany and elsewhere in the world began with the notion that one group is biologically distinctive from another.

Since race is a social construction that leads to racism, most nations no longer refer to racial groups. Only 15 percent of nations use the word *race* on their census forms (Morning, 2008). The United States is the only nation whose census distinguishes race and ethnicity, stating that Hispanics "may be of any race." Such distinctions are not always clear or consistent: Between the 2000 U.S. Census and 2010 U.S. Census, 6 percent of individuals changed their racial or ethnic identification (Liebler et al., 2017).

Because of the way human cognition works, the terminology in the U.S. Census encourages stereotyping (Kelly et al., 2010). As one scholar explains:

> The United States' unique conceptual distinction between race and ethnicity may unwittingly support the longstanding belief that race reflects biological difference and ethnicity stems from cultural difference . . . [and]

preclude understanding of the ways in which racial categories are also socially constructed.

> *[Morning, 2008, p. 255]*

Perhaps to avoid racism, the word *race* should not be used.

But consider the opposite perspective. In a society with a history of racial discrimination, reversing that culture may *require* recognizing race. Although race is a social construction, not a biological distinction, it is powerful nonetheless. Many medical, educational, and economic conditions—from low birthweight to college graduation, from family income to health insurance—reflect racial disparities.

Indeed, many social scientists argue that pretending that race does not exist allows racism to thrive. Two political scientists studying criminal justice found that people who claim to be color-blind display "an extraordinary level of naiveté" (Peffley & Hurwitz, 2010, p. 113). A sociologist writes about people in the United States, "all are baptized in the waters of color-blind racism" (Bonilla-Silva, 2018, p. 241). This is true for those who see themselves as White, Black, or any other color, of every SES and ethnicity. He also contends that to call someone *racist* is a distraction from understanding the reality of racism (Bonilla-Silva, 2018).

A person's concept of race depends partly on their culture, cohort, and—particularly relevant to a life-span view—age. Adolescents of minority ethnicity who are proud of their racial identity are likely to achieve academically, resist drug addiction, and feel better about themselves (Crosnoe & Johnson, 2011; Zimmerman et al., 2013; Wittrup et al., 2016). To encourage racial pride, and to combat the distortions of seeing differences as deficits, we may need to keep the word *race*.

As you see, strong arguments support both sides. In this book, we refer to ethnicity more often than to race, but we use race or color when the original data are reported that way. Racial categories may crumble someday, but not here, not yet.

THINK CRITICALLY: To fight racism, must race be named and recognized?

race
The concept that some people are distinct from others because of physical appearance, typically skin color. Social scientists think race is a misleading idea, although race can be a powerful social construction, not based in biology.

---

*Every page of this text includes information that requires critical thinking and evaluation, and every chapter includes some brief Think Critically questions. In addition, once in each chapter you will find an Opposing Perspectives feature in which an issue that has compelling opposite perspectives is highlighted.

but African-born people living on that continent identify with a more specific ethnic group. A Nigerian might identify as Yoruba, or Ibo, or Hausa; a Kenyan might be Kikuyo, or Luhya, or Luo. Although many Americans consider warring participants within distant nations (e.g., Syria, Iraq, Russia) to be of the same ethnicity as their enemies, the rivals themselves do not.

Race is also a social construction—and a misleading one. There are good reasons to abandon the term and good reasons to keep it, as Opposing Perspectives (previous page) explains.

Development Is Plastic

The term *plasticity* denotes two complementary aspects of development: Human traits can be molded (as plastic can be), yet people maintain a certain durability (as plastic does). This provides both hope and realism—hope because change is possible and realism because development builds on what has come before.

Both brain and behavior are far more plastic than once was thought. Plasticity is basic to our life-span perspective because it simultaneously incorporates two facts:

1. People can change over time.
2. New behavior depends partly on what has already happened.

This is evident in the **dynamic-systems approach,** a framework that many contemporary developmentalists use. The idea behind this approach is that human development is an ongoing, ever-changing interaction between the individual and all the systems, domains, and cultures.

Note the word *dynamic:* Physical contexts, emotional influences, the passage of time, each person, and every aspect of the ecosystem are always interacting, always in flux, always in motion.

For instance, a useful strategy for developing motor skills in children with autism spectrum disorder (described in Chapter 7) is to think of the dynamic systems that undergird movement—the changing physical and social contexts (Lee & Porretta, 2013). Systematically considering contexts helps such children—not to make the autism disappear (past conditions are always influential) but to improve the child's ability to function. That's plasticity.

MIKE COPPOLA/GETTY IMAGES

Fitting In The best comedians are simultaneously outsider and insider, giving them a perspective that helps people laugh at the absurdities in their lives. Trevor Noah—son of a Xhosa South African mother and a German Swiss father—grew up within, yet outside, his native culture. For instance, he was seen as "Coloured" in his homeland, but as "White" on a video, which once let him escape arrest!

plasticity
The idea that abilities, personality, and other human characteristics are moldable, and thus can change.

dynamic-systems approach
A view of human development as an ongoing, ever-changing interaction between the physical, cognitive, and psychosocial influences.

MIKE COPPOLA/GETTY IMAGES

Comfortable Routine? This 37-year-old father in Stockholm, Sweden, uses his strong tattooed arm to buckle his daughter's sandals—caregiving as millions of contemporary men do. Plasticity means that many sex differences that were thought to be innate are actually the result of culture and experience. Is this an example?

A CASE TO STUDY*

My Nephew David

My sister-in-law contracted rubella (also called German measles) early in her third pregnancy, a fact not recognized until her son David was born, blind and dying. Heart surgery two days after birth saved his life, but surgery at 6 months to remove a cataract destroyed that eye. Malformations of his thumbs, ankles, teeth, feet, spine, and brain became evident. David did not walk or talk or even chew for years. Some people wondered why his parents did not place him in an institution.

Yet dire early predictions—from me as well as many others—have proven false. David is a productive adult, and happy. When I questioned him about his life he said, "I try to stay in a positive mood" (personal communication, 2011).

Remember that difference is not always deficit. When David's father died three years ago, most of us were sad. I am still affected by the loss of my brother. But David seemed upbeat: "I miss him, but I know that he is in a better place," he said. Does that indicate that part of David's brain was damaged or that David has internalized religious lessons that many of us forget?

Remember, plasticity cannot erase a person's genes, childhood experiences, or permanent damage. David's disabilities are always with him (he still lives with his mother). But his childhood experiences gave him lifelong strengths.

His family loved and nurtured him (consulting the Kentucky School for the Blind when he was a few months old). Educators taught him: He attended several preschools, each with a different schedule and specialty (for children with cerebral palsy, intellectual disability, and blindness), and then public kindergarten at age 6.

By age 10, David had skipped a year of school and was a fifth-grader, reading at the eleventh-grade level. He learned a second and a third language and joined the church choir.

My Brother's Children Michael, Bill, and David (*left to right*) are adults now, with quite different personalities, abilities, numbers of offspring (4, 2, and none), and contexts (in Massachusetts, Pennsylvania, and California). Yet despite genes, prenatal life, and contexts, I see the shared influence of Glen and Dot, my brother and sister-in-law—evident here in their similar, friendly smiles.

In young adulthood, after one failing semester (requiring family assistance again), he earned several As and graduated from college.

David now works as a translator of German texts, which he enjoys because "I like providing a service to scholars, giving them access to something they would otherwise not have" (personal communication, 2011). As his aunt, I have seen him repeatedly defy predictions. All four of the characteristics of the life-span perspective are evident in David's life, as summarized in Table 1.3.

TABLE 1.3 Four Characteristics of Development

Characteristic	Application in David's Story
Multi-directional. Change occurs in every direction, not always in a straight line. Gains and losses, predictable growth, and unexpected transformations are evident.	David's development seemed static (or even regressive, as when early surgery destroyed one eye), but then it accelerated each time he entered a new school or college.
Multi-contextual. Human lives are embedded in many contexts, including historical conditions, economic constraints, and family patterns.	The high SES of David's family made it possible for him to receive daily medical and educational care. His two older brothers protected him.
Multi-cultural. Many cultures—not just between nations but also within them—affect how people develop.	Appalachia, where David lived, is more accepting of people with disabilities.
Plasticity. Every individual, and every trait within each individual, can be altered at any point in the life span. Change is ongoing, although it is neither random nor easy.	David's measured IQ changed from about 40 (severely intellectually disabled) to about 130 (far above average), and his physical disabilities became less crippling as he matured.

*Most chapters of this text have A Case to Study. No single case can prove or disprove a hypothesis, but often one example illustrates a general finding or an important concept.

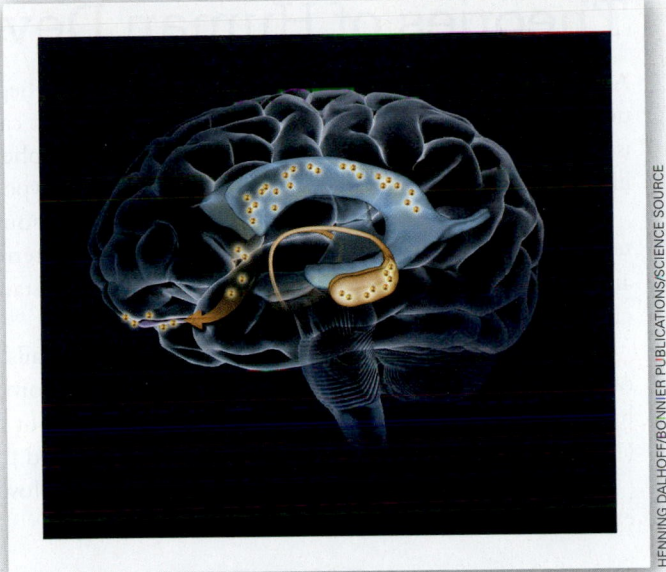

FIGURE 1.7 Birth of a Neuron A decade ago, neuroscientists thought that adult brains lost neurons, with age or alcohol, but never gained them. Now we know that precursors of neurons arise in the lateral ventricles (bright blue, center) to become functioning neurons in the olfactory bulb (for smell, far left) and the hippocampus (for memory, the brown structure just above the brain stem). Adult neurogenesis is much less prolific than earlier in life, but the fact that it occurs at all is astounding.

HENNING DALHOFF/BONNIER PUBLICATIONS/SCIENCE SOURCE

The most surprising example of plasticity in recent years involves the brain. Expansion of neurological structures, networks of communication between one cell and another, and even creation of neurons (brain cells) occurs in adulthood. This neurological plasticity is evident in hundreds of studies mentioned later in this text.

Plasticity is especially useful when anticipating growth of a particular person: Everyone is constrained by past circumstances, but no one is confined by them. Plasticity emphasizes that people can and do change, that predictions are not always accurate. Three insights already explained have improved predictions:

1. Nature and nurture always interact.

2. Certain ages are sensitive periods for particular kinds of development.

3. Genes predispose people to respond to certain circumstances, in differential susceptibility.

This was apparent for David, as A Case to Study shows: His inherited characteristics (from his intelligent parents) affected his ability to learn, his four preschools in early childhood (a sensitive period for language) helped him lifelong, and his inborn temperament (he is devastated by criticism but overjoyed by praise) helped him flourish. If I had known more about plasticity when he was born, I would have predicted a brighter—and more accurate—future for him.

what have you learned?

1. How can both continuity and discontinuity be true for human development?

2. What are some of the contexts of each person's life?

3. How does the exosystem affect children's schooling?

4. What are some cohort differences between young adults and their parents?

5. What factors comprise a person's SES (socioeconomic status)?

6. What are the differences between culture, race, and ethnicity?

7. In what two contrasting ways is human development plastic?

8. What is implied when human development is described as dynamic?

Theories of Human Development

As you read earlier in this chapter, the scientific method begins with observations, questions, and theories (step 1). That leads to hypotheses that can be tested (step 2). A *theory* is a comprehensive and organized explanation of many phenomena; a *hypothesis* is more limited and may be proven false. Theories are general; hypotheses are specific.

Theories sharpen perceptions and organize the thousands of behaviors we observe every day. Each **developmental theory** is a systematic statement of principles and generalizations, providing a framework for understanding how and why people change over the life span.

Imagine building a house from a heap of lumber, nails, and other materials. Without a plan and workers, the heap cannot become a home. Likewise, observations of human development are raw materials, but theories put them together. Kurt Lewin (1945) once quipped, "Nothing is as practical as a good theory."

Dozens of theories appear throughout this text. Now we explain four of them, each relevant lifelong.

developmental theory
A group of ideas, assumptions, and generalizations about human growth. A developmental theory provides a framework to interpret growth and change.

psychoanalytic theory
A theory of human development which contends that irrational, unconscious drives and motives underlie human behavior.

Psychoanalytic Theory

Inner drives and motives are the foundation of **psychoanalytic theory.** These basic underlying forces are thought to influence every aspect of thinking and behavior, from the smallest details of daily life to the crucial choices of a lifetime.

Freud at Work In addition to being the world's first psychoanalyst, Sigmund Freud was a prolific writer. His many papers and case histories, primarily descriptions of his patients' symptoms and sexual urges, helped make the psychoanalytic perspective a dominant force for much of the twentieth century.

AKG/PHOTO RESEARCHERS

FREUD'S STAGES Psychoanalytic theory originated with Sigmund Freud (1856–1939), an Austrian physician who treated patients suffering from mental illness. He listened to their dreams and fantasies and constructed an elaborate, multifaceted theory.

According to Freud, development in the first six years occurs in three stages, each characterized by sexual pleasure centered on a particular part of the body. Infants experience the *oral stage* because their erotic body part is the mouth, followed by the *anal stage* in early childhood, with the focus on the anus. In the preschool years (the *phallic stage*), the penis becomes a source of pride and fear for boys and a reason for sadness and envy for girls.

In middle childhood comes *latency,* a quiet period that ends with the *genital stage* at puberty. Freud thought that the genital stage continued throughout adulthood, which makes him the most famous theorist who thought that development stopped after puberty (see Table 1.4). As you remember, this assumption is no longer held by developmentalists.

Freud maintained that at each stage, sensual satisfaction (from the mouth, anus, or genitals) is linked to developmental needs, challenges, and conflicts. How people experience and resolve these conflicts—especially those related to weaning (oral), toilet training (anal), male roles (phallic), and sexual pleasure (genital)—determines personality then, because "the early stages provide the foundation for adult behavior" (Salkind, 2004, p. 125).

ERIKSON'S STAGES Many of Freud's followers became famous theorists themselves. The most notable for our study of human development was Erik Erikson (1902–1994), who described eight developmental stages, each characterized by a challenging crisis (summarized in Table 1.4).

TABLE 1.4 Comparison of Freud's Psychosexual and Erikson's Psychosocial Stages

Approximate Age	Freud (Psychosexual)	Erikson (Psychosocial)
Birth to 1 year	**Oral Stage** The lips, tongue, and gums are the focus of pleasurable sensations in the baby's body, and sucking and feeding are the most stimulating activities.	**Trust vs. Mistrust** Babies either trust that others will satisfy their basic needs, including nourishment, warmth, cleanliness, and physical contact, *or* develop mistrust about the care of others.
1–3 years	**Anal Stage** The anus is the focus of pleasurable sensations in the baby's body, and toilet training is the most important activity.	**Autonomy vs. Shame and Doubt** Children either become self-sufficient in many activities, including toileting, feeding, walking, exploring, and talking, *or* doubt their own abilities.
3–6 years	**Phallic Stage** The phallus, or penis, is the most important body part, and pleasure is derived from masturbation. Boys are proud of their penises; girls wonder why they don't have them.	**Initiative vs. Guilt** Children either try to undertake many adultlike activities *or* internalize the limits and prohibitions set by parents. They feel either adventurous *or* guilty.
6–11 years	**Latency** Not really a stage, latency is an interlude. Sexual needs are quiet; psychic energy flows into sports, schoolwork, and friendship.	**Industry vs. Inferiority** Children busily practice and then master new skills *or* feel inferior, unable to do anything well.
Adolescence	**Genital Stage** The genitals are the focus of pleasurable sensations, and the young person seeks sexual stimulation and satisfaction in heterosexual relationships.	**Identity vs. Role Confusion** Adolescents ask themselves "Who am I?" They establish sexual, political, religious, and vocational identities *or* are confused about their roles.
Adulthood	Freud believed that the genital stage lasts throughout adulthood. He also said that the goal of a healthy life is "to love and to work."	**Intimacy vs. Isolation** Young adults seek companionship and love *or* become isolated from others, fearing rejection. **Generativity vs. Stagnation** Middle-aged adults contribute to future generations through work, creative activities, and parenthood *or* they stagnate. **Integrity vs. Despair** Older adults try to make sense of their lives, either seeing life as a meaningful whole *or* despairing at goals never reached.

Although Erikson's first five stages build on Freud's theory, he added three adult stages, perhaps because of his own experience. He was a wandering artist in Italy, a teacher in Austria, and a Harvard professor in the United States.

Erikson named two polarities at each stage (which is why the word *versus* is used in each), but he recognized that many outcomes between these opposites are possible (Erikson, 1993a). For most people, development at each stage leads to neither extreme.

For instance, the generativity-versus-stagnation stage of adulthood rarely involves a person who is totally stagnant—no children, no work, no creativity. Instead, most adults are somewhat stagnant and somewhat generative. As the dynamic-systems theory would predict, the balance may shift year by year.

Erikson, like Freud, believed that adult problems echo childhood conflicts. For example, an adult who cannot form a secure, close relationship (intimacy versus isolation) may not have resolved the crisis of infancy (trust versus mistrust). However,

◆◆ **Especially for Teachers**
Your kindergartners are talkative and always moving. They almost never sit quietly and listen to you. What would Erik Erikson recommend? (see response, page 41)*

---

*Since many students reading this book are preparing to be teachers, healthcare professionals, police officers, or parents, every chapter contains Especially For questions, which encourage application of developmental concepts.

A Legendary Couple In his first 30 years, Erikson never fit into a particular local community, since he frequently changed nations, schools, and professions. Then he met Joan. In their first five decades of marriage, they raised a family and wrote several books. If Erikson had published his theory at age 73 (when this photograph was taken) instead of in his 40s, would he still have described life as a series of crises?

behaviorism
A theory of human development that studies observable actions. Behaviorism is also called *learning theory* because it describes how people learn to do what they do.

conditioning
According to behaviorism, the processes of learning. The word *conditioning* emphasizes the importance of repeated experiences, as when an athlete *conditions* his or her body by training day after day.

Erikson's stages differ significantly from Freud's in that they emphasize family and culture, not sexual urges. He called his theory *epigenetic,* partly to stress that genes and biological impulses are powerfully influenced by the social environment.

Behaviorism

Another influential theory, **behaviorism,** "began with a healthy skepticism about introspection" in direct opposition to the psychoanalytic emphasis on unconscious, hidden urges (differences are described in Table 1.5) (Staddon, 2014). Behaviorists emphasize nurture, including the social context and culture but especially the immediate responses from other people to whatever a person does.

Depending on the responses of other people, and the constraints of the culture, behaviorists believe that anything can be learned. For this reason, behaviorism is also called *learning theory.*

For every individual at every age, from newborn to centenarian, behaviorists have identified laws to describe how environmental responses shape what people do. All behavior—from reading a book to robbing a bank, from saying "Good morning" to a stranger to saying "I love you" to a spouse—follows these laws. Every action is learned, step by step.

CLASSICAL CONDITIONING The specific laws of learning apply to **conditioning,** the processes by which responses become linked to particular stimuli. Just as marathon runners try to condition themselves with daily runs for months, people are gradually conditioned to learn a particular behavior.

More than a century ago, Ivan Pavlov (1849–1936), a Russian medical doctor born in poverty who won a Nobel Prize for his work on digestion, noticed something in his experimental dogs that awakened his curiosity (step 1 of the scientific method) (Todes, 2014). The dogs drooled not only when they saw and smelled food but also when they heard the footsteps of the attendants who brought the food. This observation led Pavlov to hypotheses and experiments in which he conditioned dogs to salivate when they heard a specific noise (steps 2 and 3).

Pavlov began by sounding a tone just before presenting food. After a number of repetitions of the tone-then-food sequence, dogs began salivating at the sound, even when there was no food. This simple experiment demonstrated *classical conditioning,* when a person or animal learns to associate a neutral stimulus (the sound) with a meaningful stimulus (the food), gradually reacting to the neutral stimulus in the same way as to the meaningful one (step 4). The fact that Pavlov published (step 5) in Russian is one reason his research took decades to reach the United States (Todes, 2014).

TABLE 1.5 Three Types of Learning

Behaviorism is also called *learning theory* because it emphasizes the learning process, as shown here.

Type of Learning	Learning Process	Result
Classical conditioning	Learning occurs through association.	Neutral stimulus becomes conditioned response.
Operant conditioning	Learning occurs through reinforcement and punishment.	Weak or rare responses become strong and frequent—or, with punishment, unwanted responses become extinct.
Social learning	Learning occurs through modeling what others do.	Observed behaviors become copied behaviors.

OPERANT CONDITIONING The most influential North American behaviorist, B. F. Skinner (1904–1990), was inspired by Pavlov (Skinner, 1953). Skinner agreed that classical conditioning explains some behavior. Then he went further, experimenting to demonstrate another type of conditioning, **operant conditioning.**

In operant conditioning (also called *instrumental conditioning*), animals (including humans) perform some action and then a response occurs. If the response is useful or pleasurable, the animal is likely to repeat the action; if the response is painful, the animal is not likely to repeat the action. In both cases, the animal has been conditioned. Thus, responses are crucial; that is how learning occurs.

Pleasant consequences are sometimes called *rewards,* and unpleasant consequences are sometimes called *punishments.* Behaviorists hesitate to use those words, however, because what people think of as punishment can actually be a reward, and vice versa.

For example, how should a parent punish a child? Withholding dessert? Spanking? Not letting the child play? Speaking harshly? If a child hates that dessert, being deprived of it is actually a reward, not a punishment. Another child might not mind a spanking, especially if he or she craves parental attention. For that child, the intended punishment (spanking) is actually a reward (attention).

Any consequence that follows a behavior and makes the person (or animal) likely to repeat that behavior is called a **reinforcement,** *not* a reward. Once a behavior has been conditioned, humans and other creatures will repeat it even if reinforcement occurs only occasionally. Similarly, an unpleasant response makes a creature less likely to repeat a certain action.

Almost all daily behavior, from combing your hair to joking with friends, is a result of past operant conditioning, according to behaviorists. Likewise, things people fear, from giving a speech to eating raw fish, are avoided because of past punishment.

This insight has many practical applications for human development. Early responses are crucial because children learn habits that endure. For instance, if parents want their child to share, and their baby offers them a gummy, half-eaten cracker, they should take the gift with apparent delight and then return it, smiling.

HULTON-DEUTSCH/HULTON-DEUTSCH COLLECTION/ CORBIS VIA GETTY IMAGES

A Contemporary of Freud
Ivan Pavlov was a physiologist who received the Nobel Prize in 1904 for his research on digestive processes. It was this line of study that led to his discovery of classical conditioning, when his research on dog saliva led to insight about learning.

↑ **OBSERVATION** QUIZ How is Pavlov similar to Freud in appearance, and how do both look different from the other theorists pictured? (see answer, page 41)

operant conditioning
The learning process that reinforces or punishes behavior. (Also called *instrumental conditioning.*)

reinforcement
In behaviorism, the reward or relief that follows a behavior, making it likely that the behavior will occur again.

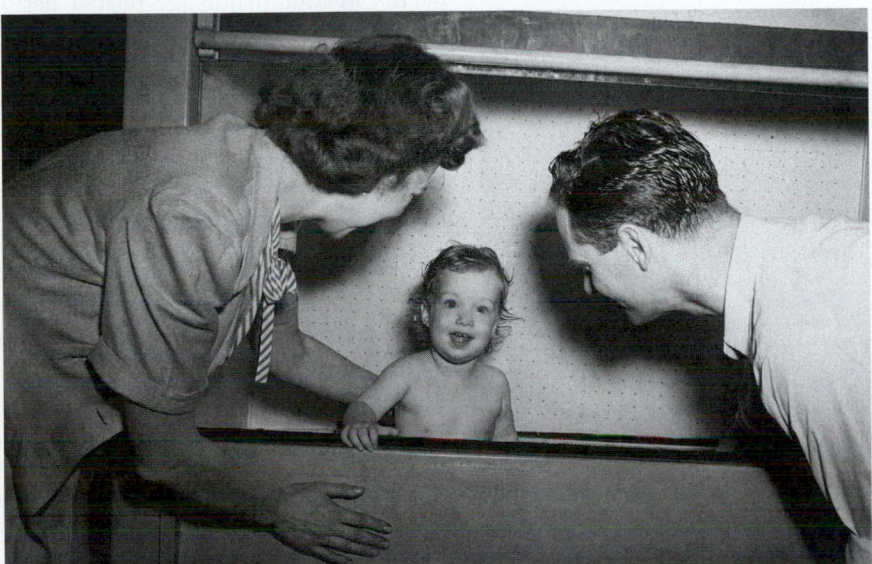

AP PHOTO

Rats, Pigeons, and People
B. F. Skinner is best known for his experiments with rats and pigeons, but he also applied his knowledge to human behavior. For his daughter, he designed a glass-enclosed crib in which temperature, humidity, and perceptual stimulation could be controlled to make her time in the crib enjoyable and educational. He encouraged her first attempts to talk by smiling and responding with words, affection, or other positive reinforcement.

According to behaviorism, people are never too old to learn. If an adult is afraid of speaking in public (a particular kind of social phobia, very common), then repeated reinforcement for talking (such as a professor praising a student's question) could eventually lead to speeches before an audience.

SOCIAL LEARNING THEORY A major extension of behaviorism is **social learning theory,** first described by Albert Bandura (b. 1925). This theory notes that, because humans are social beings, they learn from observing others, even without personally receiving any reinforcement (Bandura, 1977, 2006).

For example, children who witness domestic violence are influenced by it. As differential susceptibility and multi-contextualism would predict, the particular lesson learned depends on each individual's genes and experiences. If the father of three boys often hits their mother, one son might admire the abuser, another might try to protect the victim, and the third might disappear when fighting begins.

As adults, past social learning leads the first man to slap his wife and spank his children, the second to be especially kind, and the third to be more like a dandelion than an orchid, forgetting the past. If you know a family with many grown siblings, do they all agree on the kind of child rearing they experienced? Probably not: Each has a particular view of their parents.

Cognitive Theory

In **cognitive theory**, each person's ideas and beliefs are crucial. This theory has dominated psychology since about 1980 and has branched into many versions. The word *cognitive* refers not just to thinking but also to attitudes, beliefs, and assumptions.

The most famous cognitive theorist was Jean Piaget (1896–1980), who began by observing his own three infants and later studied thousands of older children (Inhelder & Piaget, 1958/2013b). Unlike other scientists of the early twentieth century, Piaget realized that babies are curious and thoughtful, creating their own interpretations about their world.

From this work, Piaget developed the central thesis of cognitive theory: How people think (not just what they know) changes with time and experience, and then human thinking influences actions. Piaget maintained that cognitive development occurs in four major age-related periods, or stages: *sensorimotor, preoperational, concrete operational,* and *formal operational* (see Table 1.6).

Intellectual advancement occurs because humans seek *cognitive equilibrium,* that is, a state of mental balance. An easy way to achieve this balance (called *assimilation*) is to interpret new experiences through the lens of preexisting ideas. For example, infants discover that new objects can be grasped in the same way as familiar ones; adolescents explain the day's headlines as evidence that supports their existing worldviews; older adults speak fondly of the good old days as embodying values that should endure.

Sometimes, however, a new experience is jarring and incomprehensible. That causes disequilibrium. As Figure 1.8 illustrates, disequilibrium leads to cognitive growth because

Would You Talk to This Man? Children loved talking to Jean Piaget, and he learned by listening carefully—especially to their incorrect explanations, which no one had paid much attention to before. All his life, Piaget was absorbed with studying the way children think. He called himself a "genetic epistemologist"—one who studies how children gain knowledge about the world as they grow.

© FARRELL GREHAN/CORBIS VIA GETTY IMAGES

TABLE 1.6 Piaget's Periods of Cognitive Development

	Name of Period	Characteristics of the Period	Major Gains During the Period
Birth to 2 years	Sensorimotor	Infants use senses and motor abilities to understand the world. Learning is active, without reflection.	Infants learn that objects still exist when out of sight *(object permanence)* and begin to think through mental actions. (The sensorimotor period is discussed further in Chapter 3.)
2–6 years	Preoperational	Children think symbolically, with language, yet they are *egocentric,* perceiving from their own perspective.	The imagination flourishes, and language becomes a significant means of self-expression and social influence. (The preoperational period is discussed further in Chapter 5.)
6–11 years	Concrete operational	Children understand and apply logic. Thinking is limited by direct experience.	By applying logic, children grasp concepts of conservation, number, classification, and many other scientific ideas. (The concrete operational period is discussed further in Chapter 7.)
12 years through adulthood	Formal operational	Adolescents and adults use abstract and hypothetical concepts. They can use analysis, not only emotion.	Ethics, politics, and social and moral issues become fascinating as adolescents and adults use abstract, theoretical reasoning. (The formal operational period is discussed further in Chapter 9.)

it forces people to reassess their old concepts (called *accommodation*) to include the new information. Learning occurs when new information requires more analysis (Brown et al., 2014).

Another influential cognitive theory, called *information processing,* is not a stage theory but rather provides a detailed description of the steps of cognition, focusing on what happens in the brain to cause intellectual growth. This theory is especially useful in understanding thinking in middle childhood and late adulthood, as you will see in Chapters 7 and 14.

Many researchers, not just those influenced by information-processing theory, now think that some of Piaget's conclusions were mistaken. However, every developmentalist appreciates his basic insight: Thoughts influence emotions and actions. This is sometimes called a *constructive* view of human cognition, because people of all ages build their understanding of themselves and their world, combining their experiences and their interpretations.

Evolutionary Theory

Charles Darwin's basic ideas were first published 150 years ago (Darwin, 1859), but serious research on human development inspired by **evolutionary theory** is quite recent. According to evolution, every species strives to survive and reproduce. That is true for humans, too. Consequently, many human impulses, needs, and behaviors evolved to help people survive and thrive over the past 100,000 years (Konner, 2010).

To understand contemporary human development, this theory contends, we must consider what humans needed thousands of years ago. For example, why do people fear snakes (which now cause less than one U.S. death in a million), and why does everyone ride in motor vehicles (which cause more than one death in a hundred)? Evolutionary theory suggests that the fear instinct evolved to protect life when snakes killed many people.

Fears have not caught up to modern life: The latest, fastest automobile is coveted by many, even though it may be a death trap. If everyone always drove slowly (under 30 miles an hour), thousands of lives would be saved. But I, and many other drivers, exceed speed limits and watch for police cars.

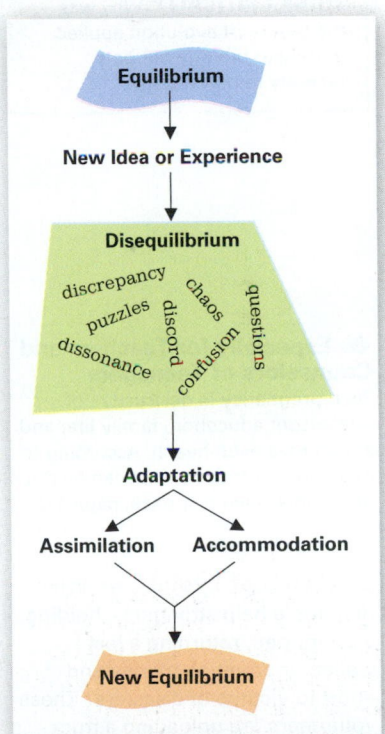

FIGURE 1.8 Challenge Me
Most of us, most of the time, prefer the comfort of our conventional conclusions. According to Piaget, however, when new ideas disturb our thinking, we have an opportunity to expand our cognition with a broader and deeper understanding.

evolutionary theory
When used in human development, the idea that many current human emotions and impulses are a legacy from thousands of years ago.

(a)

(b)

(c)

How to Think About Flowers A person's stage of cognitive growth influences how he or she thinks about everything, including flowers. *(a)* To an infant in Piaget's sensorimotor stage, flowers are "known" through pulling, smelling, and even biting. *(b)* At the concrete operational stage, children become more logical. This boy can understand that flowers need sunlight, water, and time to grow. *(c)* At the adult's formal operational stage, flowers can be part of a larger, logical scheme—for instance, to earn money while cultivating beauty. As illustrated by all three photos, thinking is an active process from the beginning of life until the end.

Evolutionary theory notes that, although fear of snakes, or blood, or thunder is irrational, some of our best human qualities, such as cooperation, spirituality, and self-sacrifice, also evolved thousands of years ago, when groups of people survived because they cared for one another. Childhood itself, particularly the long period when children depend on others while their brains grow, can be explained via evolution (Konner, 2010).

Notice that human mothers welcome child-rearing help from fathers, other relatives, and even strangers. Shared child rearing, called *allocare,* allows women to have children every two years or so, unlike chimpanzees, who space births four or five years apart (Hrdy, 2009). The reason, according to this theory, is that *Homo sapiens* (unlike all the other *Homo* species) found that allocare aided survival and reproduction. The result: almost 8 billion of our species alive today and only about 200,000 chimpanzees, a ratio of 35,000 to 1.

Evolutionary theory in developmental psychology has intriguing explanations for many phenomena: women's nausea in pregnancy, 1-year-olds' attachment to their parents, adolescent rebellion, emerging adults' sexual passions, parents' investment in their children, and the diseases of late adulthood.

THINK CRITICALLY: Why was the theory of evolution applied quickly to biology but only recently to psychology?

◆ **Especially for Teachers and Counselors of Teenagers**
Teen pregnancy is destructive of adolescent education, family life, and sometimes even health. According to evolutionary theory, what can be done about this? (see response, page 41)

Evidence of Evolution? Why do people help strangers—holding a door open, returning a lost wallet, or donating money and effort to victims of disasters? These volunteers are unloading a truck carrying relief supplies donated to the victims of Hurricane Harvey in Texas. In September 2017, millions of dollars were donated online to hurricane victims in Texas, Florida, Puerto Rico, and the U.S. Virgin Islands. The reason, according to evolutionary theory, is that cooperation aided homo sapiens, who survived and multiplied while other homo species became extinct. Helping strangers is part of the human genome.

All of these interpretations are controversial. Evolutionary explanations for male–female differences are particularly hotly disputed (Ellemers, 2018). Nonetheless, this theory provides many hypotheses to be explored.

what have you learned?

1. What is the role of the unconscious in psychoanalytic theory?
2. How do Erikson's stages differ from Freud's?
3. How is behaviorism a reaction to psychoanalytic theory?
4. How do classical and operant conditioning differ?
5. What is the basic idea of cognitive theory?
6. How does evolutionary theory apply to human development?

The Scientific Method

There are hundreds of ways to design scientific studies and analyze results as well as many ethical and practical issues related to science. Often statistical measures help scientists discover relationships between various aspects of the data. (Some statistical perspectives are presented in Table 1.7.) Statistics also force scientists to consider facts, not "fake news" or wishful thinking.

Every research design, method, and statistic has strengths as well as weaknesses. Now we describe three basic research designs—observation, the experiment, and the survey—and then three ways developmentalists study change over time.

TABLE 1.7	**Statistical Measures Often Used to Analyze Search Results**
Measure	**Use**
Effect size	There are many kinds of "effect sizes." The most useful in reporting studies of development is called Cohen's d, which can indicate the power of an intervention. An effect size of 0.2 is called small, 0.5 moderate, and 0.8 large.
Significance	Indicates whether the results might have occurred by chance. If chance would produce the results only 5 times in 100, that is significant at the 0.05 level; once in 100 times is 0.01; once in 1,000 is 0.001.
Cost-benefit analysis	Calculates how much a particular independent variable costs versus how much it saves. This is useful for analyzing public spending, e.g., finding that preschool education or preventative health measures save money over the long term.
Odds ratio	Indicates how a particular variable compares to a standard, set at 1. For example, one study found that, although less than 1 percent of all child homicides occurred at school, the odds were similar for public and private schools. The odds of it in high schools, however, were 18.47 times that of elementary or middle schools (set at 1.0) (MMWR, January 18, 2008).
Factor analysis	Hundreds of variables could affect any given behavior. In addition, many variables (such as family income and parental education) overlap. To take this into account, analysis reveals variables that can be clustered together to form a factor, which is a composite of many variables. For example, SES might become one factor, child personality another.
Meta-analysis	A "study of studies." Researchers use statistical tools to synthesize the results of previous, separate studies. Then they analyze the accumulated results, using criteria that weigh each study fairly. This approach improves data analysis by combining studies that were too small, or too narrow, to lead to solid conclusions.

Observation

Scientific observation requires researchers to record behavior systematically and objectively. Observations often occur in a naturalistic setting (such as a home, school, or public park), where people behave as they usually do and where the observer is ignored or even unnoticed. Observation can also occur in a laboratory, where scientists record human reactions in various situations, often with wall-mounted video cameras and the scientist in another room.

Observation is crucial for developing hypotheses. For example, you might wonder whether parents who are anxious about leaving their children at school make their children anxious. Worried children would be less likely to make friends and to learn whatever their teachers taught.

You might begin with observation, which is exactly what one team of scientists did. Several weeks after the beginning of a year of preschool, scientists observed how long parents stayed to hug and kiss their children before saying goodbye.

When parents lingered three minutes or more, their "children spent less time involved in the preschool peer social environment," measured by whether the child looked at or played with other children. The authors suggest that this "has implications for not only children's later peer interactions and peer status, but also for children's engagement in school and, ultimately, academic achievement" (Grady et al., 2012, p. 1690).

Perhaps, by staying, the parents made the children anxious about school. And *perhaps* that would affect the children later on, so they would be less engaged and therefore learn less.

But perhaps not. Observation found a correlation (to be defined later) but not proof. Might some children be naturally shy, causing their parents to stay and help them become more comfortable with school? Then those children would be less engaged with other children, not because their parents stayed but because they were shy. And, contrary to the researchers' speculation, those children might become academically strong later on because they would not be distracted by other children.

Thus, the data led to at least two alternative hypotheses: (1) Parental anxiety impairs child social engagement, or (2) shy children are given parental support. More research is needed.

Experiments

An **experiment** tests a hypothesis. In the social sciences, experimenters typically impose a particular treatment on a group of participants (formerly called *subjects*) or expose them to a specific condition and then note whether their behavior changes.

In technical terms, the experimenters manipulate an **independent variable,** the imposed treatment or special condition (also called the *experimental variable*). (A *variable* is anything that can vary.) They note whether this independent variable affects whatever they are studying, called the **dependent variable,** which *depends* on the independent variable.

Thus, the independent variable is the new, special treatment; any change in the dependent variable is the result. The purpose of an experiment is to find out whether an independent variable affects the dependent variable.

In a typical experiment (as diagrammed in Figure 1.9), two equal groups of participants are studied. One group, the *experimental group*, gets a particular treatment (the independent variable). The other group, the *control group* (also called the *comparison group*), does not.

scientific observation
Watching and recording participants' behavior in a systematic and objective manner—in a natural setting, in a laboratory, or in searches of archival data.

experiment
A research method in which the researcher adds one variable (called the *independent variable*) and then observes the effect on another variable (called the *dependent variable*) in order to learn if the independent variable causes change in the dependent variable.

independent variable
In an experiment, the variable that is added by the researcher to see if it affects the dependent variable.

dependent variable
In an experiment, the variable that may change as a result of the independent variable (whatever new condition the experimenter adds). In other words, the dependent variable *depends* on the independent variable.

The Experiment

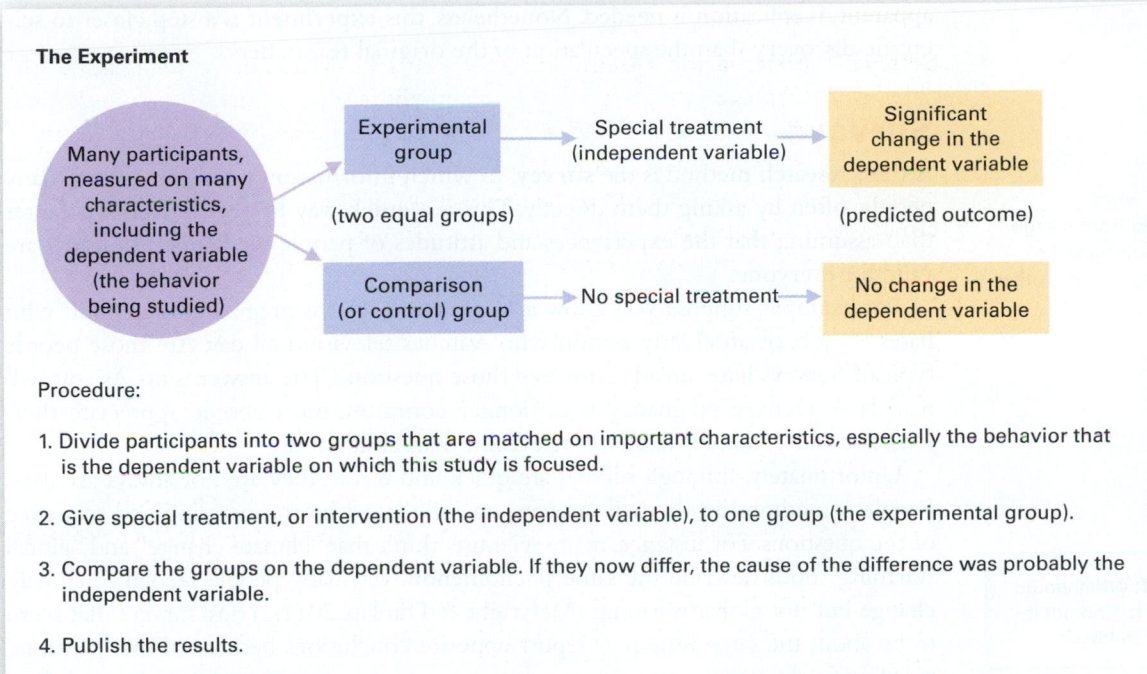

Procedure:

1. Divide participants into two groups that are matched on important characteristics, especially the behavior that is the dependent variable on which this study is focused.

2. Give special treatment, or intervention (the independent variable), to one group (the experimental group).

3. Compare the groups on the dependent variable. If they now differ, the cause of the difference was probably the independent variable.

4. Publish the results.

FIGURE 1.9 How to Conduct an Experiment The basic sequence diagrammed here applies to all experiments. Many additional features, especially the statistical measures listed in Table 1.7 and various ways of reducing experimenter bias, affect whether publication occurs. (Scientific journals reject reports of experiments that were not rigorous in method and analysis.)

To follow up on the observation study above, researchers could experiment. For example, they could assess the social skills (dependent variable) of hundreds of children in the first week of school and then require parents in half of the classes to linger at drop-off (independent variable, experimental group), and in the other classes, require parents to leave immediately.

It would be important to have the same rules for all parents in a class, so some children wouldn't feel unhappy that their parents left while they saw that other parents stayed. It would also be important to have several classes in each group, to balance out any effects of having a particular teacher.

Months later, the children's social skills (dependent variable) could be measured again. A few years later, their school achievement (another dependent variable) could be recorded.

Suppose the experimental group eventually had higher reading scores than the control group. Would this experiment prove that lingering at drop-off *caused* later academic success? Or suppose the leaving-quickly group did better academically. Did that *cause* learning?

Not exactly. Critical thinking is needed. Lingering might have caused other influences (more parental involvement, for instance). Or leaving right away may have encouraged the teachers to focus immediately on all of the children, and that may have led to higher achievement later on. Or, these particular classes might have differed in ways that were not

© RICK FRIEDMAN/CORBIS VIA GETTY IMAGES

What Can You Learn? Scientists first establish what is, and then try to change it. In one recent experiment, Deb Kelemen (shown here) established that few children under age 12 understand a central concept of evolution (natural selection). Then she showed an experimental group a picture book illustrating the idea. Success! The independent variable (the book) affected the dependent variable (the children's ideas), which confirmed Kelemen's hypothesis: Children can understand natural selection if instruction is tailored to their ability.

apparent. Replication is needed. Nonetheless, this experiment is a step closer to scientific discovery than the speculation of the original researchers.

Surveys

survey
A research method in which information is collected from a large number of people by interviews, written questionnaires, or some other means.

A third research method is the **survey,** in which information is collected from many people, often by asking them directly. This is a quick way to obtain data. It is better than assuming that the experiences and attitudes of people we happen to know are valid for everyone.

For example, suppose you know a 16-year-old who is pregnant, or an adult who hates his job, or an elderly person who watches television all day. Are those people typical? Surveys have already answered those questions. The answer is no. As you will read later, teenage pregnancy is no longer common, most people appreciate their jobs, and older people watch less television than children do.

Unfortunately, although surveys are quick and direct, they are not always accurate. People sometimes lie, or their answers are influenced by the wording and sequence of the questions. For instance, many scientists think that "climate change" and "global warming" both describe the same phenomenon, yet many people recognize climate change but not global warming (McCright & Dunlap, 2011). Thus, surveys that seem to be about the same issue may report opposite conclusions because of the questions' wording.

THINK CRITICALLY: What would be an accurate way to find out if parents abuse their children?

There is another problem with surveys: People do not want to admit whatever they are ashamed of, and many people want to say what they think the researcher wants to hear. This is a major problem in political polling: Most adults say they will vote, even if they will not.

Inaccuracy on surveys may harm development. For example, because hunger negatively affects children's health and education, developmentalists want to know how many families are "food insecure," which means they do not have sufficient food to meet their needs. Thus, the U.S. Department of Agriculture developed, tested, and revised the 18 questions of the Food Security Scale (Coleman-Jensen et al., 2017). The survey is accurate when answered honestly, but it is not quick to administer and score.

VIDEO ACTIVITY: What's Wrong with This Study? explores some of the major pitfalls of the process of designing a research study.

Instead, pediatricians use a briefer version (Council on Community Pediatrics, 2015). Parents answer yes or no to these two statements:

1. The food we bought just didn't last and we didn't have money to get more.
2. We worried whether the food we bought would run out before we got money to buy more.

People who say yes to one or both are almost always (97 percent) food insecure. So far, so good. But one-fourth of adults who say no are found to be food insecure when asked a longer set of questions (Cutts & Cook, 2017). For instance, they have sometimes gone hungry and skipped meals because there was not enough food.

It matters whether this survey asks "yes or no" or "often true, sometimes true, or never true" (Makelarski et al., 2017). In the minds of the professional, if parents sometimes run out of food, they should answer yes to that question, but many people who say "sometimes" are ashamed to say "yes." Food insecurity is "a highly stigmatized condition that is not commonly disclosed" (Makelarski et al., 2017, p. 1812). Therefore, to find everyone who is food insecure, more than two survey questions, and not just yes/no, may be needed.

Of course, each survey has specific liabilities, with some surveys being much better than others. However, this survey about food insecurity illustrates a general problem: Accuracy depends not only on the wording of the questions but also on the people who ask and answer.

Studying Development over the Life Span

In addition to conducting observations, experiments, and surveys, developmentalists must measure how people *change or remain the same over time,* as our definition stresses. Remember that systems are dynamic, ever-changing. To capture that dynamism, developmental researchers use one of three basic research designs: cross-sectional, longitudinal, or cross-sequential.

CROSS-SECTIONAL VERSUS LONGITUDINAL RESEARCH The quickest and least expensive way to study development over time is with **cross-sectional research,** in which groups of people of one age are compared with people of another age. Cross-sectional design seems simple. However, it is difficult to ensure that the various groups being compared are similar in every way except age.

For instance, comparing women in the United States in 1980 revealed that almost none of the 15-year-olds were married but that almost all (95 percent) of the 60-year-olds had married (Stevenson & Wolfers, 2007; Wang & Parker, 2014). Does that mean that current unmarried 20-year-olds will probably marry eventually? No. Those data came from women born between 1935 and 1955. Research on later cohorts found that the marriage rate steadily fell, such that 13 percent of the women who were born in 1970 never married.

Can we predict what happens next? If current trends continue, one-fourth (25 percent) of today's 20-year-olds will never marry (Wang & Parker, 2014). That projection is logical—but again it might be wrong. Marriage might increasingly seem like a poor choice, so maybe as many as half of all young women will never marry. Alternatively, marriage trends may reverse again—perhaps almost all current young women will marry eventually.

The point, of course, is that cross-sectional research is accurate about the difference between the average responses of people at one age compared to people of another age. In this study, if the research is carefully done, the results reveal exactly how many people are married at every age. However, it does not prove *why* marriage rates change with age, or what will happen in the future.

As in this example, new attitudes about marriage may have much more influence on whether or not a person decides to marry than the person's age does. To be an unmarried 30-year-old woman was a source of shame in 1900; it may be a source of pride today. Women of a particular age were once "old maids," but they now might be "swinging singles."

To help discover whether age itself, not cohort, causes a developmental change, scientists undertake **longitudinal research.** This requires collecting data repeatedly on the same individuals. Back to the feature on pages 5–6: Because parents are much

cross-sectional research
A research design that compares people who differ in age but not in other important characteristics.

longitudinal research
A research design that follows the same individuals over time.

All Smiling, All Multiethnic, All the Same? Cross-sectional research comparing these people would find age differences, but there might be cohort and context differences as well.

more aware of the lifelong problems of obesity, the current cohort of overweight children and adolescents may more often become normal-weight adults (Arigo et al., 2016). Cross-sectional research suggests that is happening, but only longitudinal research will prove it.

For insight about the life span, the best longitudinal research follows the same individuals from infancy to old age. Long-term research requires patience and dedication from a team of scientists, but it can pay off. For example, a longitudinal study of 790 low-SES children in Baltimore found that only 4 percent had graduated from college by age 28 (Alexander et al., 2014).

Without scientific data, a person might think that the problem was not enough counselors in high school. However, because this was a longitudinal study, the data pinpointed *when* those children were pushed toward, or away from, higher education.

Surprisingly, it was long before adolescence. The two most influential factors that increased the rate of college attendance for low-SES young adults were excellent education before high school and neighbors who were encouraging and friendly. High schools mattered, but they did not deserve most of the blame or credit.

Good as it is, longitudinal research has a problem, something already mentioned: the historical context. Science, popular culture, and politics change over time, and each alters the experiences of a child. Data collected on children born decades ago may not be relevant for today.

For example, many recent substances and processes that were once thought to be beneficial might be harmful, among them *phthalates* and *bisphenol A* (BPA) (chemicals used in manufacturing) in plastic baby bottles and other containers, *hydrofracking* (used to get gas for fuel from rocks), *e-waste* (from old computers and cell phones), and more. Some nations and states ban or regulate each of these; others do not.

Verified, longitudinal data are not yet possible.

Because of the outcry among parents, bisphenol A has been replaced with bisphenol S (BPS). But we do not know whether BPS is better, or worse, than BPA, because we do not have data on babies who drank from both kinds of bottles and are now adults (Zimmerman & Anastas, 2015).

Six Times of Life These photos show Sarah-Maria, born in 1980 in Switzerland, at six periods of her life: infancy (age 1), early childhood (age 3), middle childhood (age 8), adolescence (age 15), emerging adulthood (age 19), and adulthood (age 36).

↑ **OBSERVATION** QUIZ Longitudinal research best illustrates continuity and discontinuity. For Sarah-Maria, what changed over 30 years and what didn't? (see answer, page 41)

A newer example is *e-cigarettes*. They are less toxic (how much less?) to the heart and lungs than combustible cigarettes. Some (how many?) smokers reduce their risk of cancer and heart disease by switching to e-cigs (Bhatnagar et al., 2014). But some teenagers (how many?) are more likely to smoke cigarettes if they start by vaping.

The best research shows that nonsmoking teenagers who use e-cigarettes are almost four times as likely to say they "will try a cigarette soon," an ominous result (Parker et al., 2016). On the other hand, many teenagers think e-cigs are "cool," safer alternatives to cigarettes (Modesto-Lowe & Alvarado, 2017). But those are surveys, not longitudinal proof.

Until longitudinal data on addiction and death for e-cig smokers are known, 10 or 20 or 40 years from now, no one can be certain whether the harm outweighs the benefits (Ramo et al., 2015; Javed et al., 2017; Dutra & Glantz, 2014). [**Life-Span Link:** The major discussion of e-cigarette use is in Chapter 10.] Should we wait for longitudinal data?

CROSS-SEQUENTIAL RESEARCH Scientists now have a third strategy, a sequence of data collection that combines cross-sectional and longitudinal research. This combination is called **cross-sequential research** (also referred to as *cohort-sequential* or *time-sequential research*). In sequential designs, researchers study people of different ages (a cross-sectional approach), follow them for years (a longitudinal approach), and then combine the results.

A cross-sequential design lets researchers compare findings for, say, 6-year-olds with findings for the same individuals at birth as well as with data from people who were 6 long ago, who are now ages 12, 18, or even much older (see Figure 1.10). Cross-sequential research is complicated, in recruitment and analysis, but it lets scientists disentangle age from history.

The first well-known cross-sequential study (the *Seattle Longitudinal Study*) found that some intellectual abilities (vocabulary) increase even after age 60, whereas others (speed) start to decline at age 30 (Schaie, 2005/2013), confirming that development is multi-directional. This study also discovered that declines in adult math ability are more closely related to education than to age, something neither cross-sectional nor longitudinal research alone could reveal.

The advantages of cross-sequential research are evident. Accordingly, many researchers combine cross-sectional and longitudinal data collected by other scientists, thus using cross-sequential analysis without needing to do all the data collection themselves. For example, six scientists combined data from 14 longitudinal studies. They found that adolescent optimism about the future predicted health in middle age (Kern et al., 2016). Without a cross-sequential analysis, would people know that teenagers who say "life will be better when I grow up" are likely to be in good health decades later?

cross-sequential research
A hybrid research design that includes cross-sectional and longitudinal research. (Also called *cohort-sequential research* or *time-sequential research*.)

◆ **Especially for Future Researchers** What is the best method for collecting data? (see response, page 41)

Solutions and Challenges from Science

The scientific method illuminates and illustrates human development as nothing else does. Facts, consequences, and possibilities that would not be known without science have all emerged—and people of all ages are healthier, happier, and more capable than people of previous generations because of it.

For example, death of newborns, measles in children, girls not sent to school, boys sent to war, and older adults in nursing homes are all less prevalent today than a century ago. Science deserves credit. Even violent death—in war, homicide, or punishment for a crime—is less likely in recent centuries than in past ones: Inventions, discoveries, and education are reasons (Pinker, 2011).

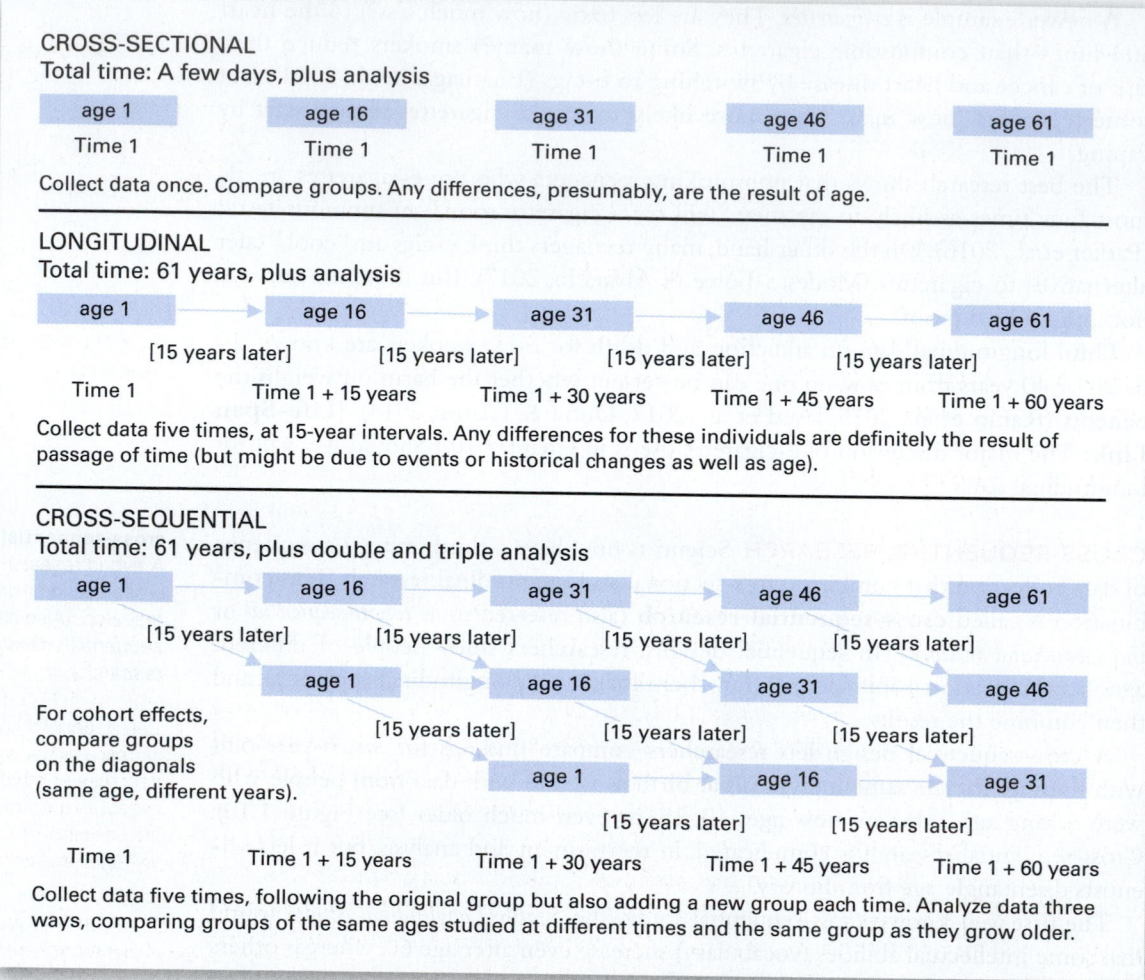

CROSS-SECTIONAL
Total time: A few days, plus analysis

age 1	age 16	age 31	age 46	age 61
Time 1	Time 1	Time 1	Time 1	Time 1

Collect data once. Compare groups. Any differences, presumably, are the result of age.

LONGITUDINAL
Total time: 61 years, plus analysis

| age 1 | → | age 16 | → | age 31 | → | age 46 | → | age 61 |

[15 years later]   [15 years later]   [15 years later]   [15 years later]

Time 1   Time 1 + 15 years   Time 1 + 30 years   Time 1 + 45 years   Time 1 + 60 years

Collect data five times, at 15-year intervals. Any differences for these individuals are definitely the result of passage of time (but might be due to events or historical changes as well as age).

CROSS-SEQUENTIAL
Total time: 61 years, plus double and triple analysis

| age 1 | → | age 16 | → | age 31 | → | age 46 | → | age 61 |

[15 years later]   [15 years later]   [15 years later]   [15 years later]

| age 1 | → | age 16 | → | age 31 | → | age 46 |

For cohort effects, compare groups on the diagonals (same age, different years).

[15 years later]   [15 years later]   [15 years later]

| age 1 | → | age 16 | → | age 31 |

[15 years later]   [15 years later]

Time 1   Time 1 + 15 years   Time 1 + 30 years   Time 1 + 45 years   Time 1 + 60 years

Collect data five times, following the original group but also adding a new group each time. Analyze data three ways, comparing groups of the same ages studied at different times and the same group as they grow older.

FIGURE 1.10 Which Approach Is Best? Cross-sequential research is the most time-consuming and complex, but it yields the best information. One reason that hundreds of scientists conduct research on the same topics, replicating one another's work, is to gain some advantages of cohort-sequential research without waiting for decades.

Developmental scientists have also discovered unexpected sources of harm. Video games, cigarettes, television, shift work, asbestos, and even artificial respiration are all less benign than people first thought.

These are challenging times for every American scientist. Most welcome the increased insistence on evidence and replication—even when it calls original results into question—but most also fear an anti-science mood that shuts down research.

Accordingly, the American Association for the Advancement of Science (AAAS, a national organization of 40,000 scientists from every discipline, including the many who study human development) adopted a statement on scientific freedom and responsibility. Both are crucial for good science:

Scientific freedom and scientific responsibility are essential to the advancement of human knowledge for the benefit of all. Scientific freedom is the freedom to engage in scientific inquiry, pursue and apply knowledge, and communicate openly. This freedom is inexorably linked and must be exercised in accordance with scientific responsibility. Scientific responsibility is the duty to conduct and apply science with integrity, in the interest of humanity, in a spirit of stewardship for the environment, and with respect for human rights.

[Jarvis, 2017, p. 462]

As the examples above attest, the benefits of science are many. However, there are also serious pitfalls. We now discuss three potential hazards: misinterpreting correlation, depending too heavily on numbers, and ignoring ethics.

A Pesky Third Variable
Correlation is often misleading. In this case, a third variable (the supply of fossil fuels) may be relevant.

CORRELATION AND CAUSATION Probably the most common mistake in interpreting research is confusing correlation with causation. A **correlation** exists between two variables if one variable is more (or less) likely to occur when the other does. A correlation is *positive* if both variables tend to increase together or decrease together, *negative* if one variable tends to increase while the other decreases, and *zero* if no connection is evident.

To illustrate: From birth to age 9, there is a positive correlation between age and height (children grow taller as they grow older), a negative correlation between age and amount of sleep (children sleep less as they grow older), and zero correlation between age and number of toes (children do not have more or fewer toes as they grow older).

Expressed in numerical terms, correlations vary from +1.0 (the most positive) to −1.0 (the most negative). Correlations are almost never that extreme; a correlation of +0.3 or −0.3 is noteworthy; a correlation of +0.8 or −0.8 is astonishing.

Many correlations are unexpected. For instance, first-born children are more likely to develop asthma than are later-born children, teenage girls have higher rates of mental health problems than do teenage boys, and counties in the United States with more dentists have fewer obese residents. That last study controlled for the number of medical doctors and the poverty of the community. The authors suggest that dentists provide information about nutrition that improves health (Holzer et al., 2014).

At this point, remember that *correlation is not causation*. Just because two variables are correlated does not mean that one causes the other—even if it seems logical that it does. It proves only that the variables are connected somehow. Can you think of other explanations for the correlation between the number of dentists and obesity?

correlation
Usually a number between +1.0 and −1.0 that indicates whether and how much two variables are related. Correlation indicates whether an increase in one variable will increase or decrease another variable. Correlation indicates only that two variables are somehow related, not that one variable *causes* the other to increase or decrease.

quantitative research
Research that provides data expressed with numbers, such as ranks or scales.

qualitative research
Research that considers individual qualities instead of quantities (numbers).

QUANTITY AND QUALITY A second caution concerns **quantitative research** (from the word *quantity*). Quantitative research data can be categorized, ranked, or numbered, and thus is easily translated across cultures and for diverse populations. One example of quantitative research is the use of children's school achievement scores to compare the effectiveness of education within a school or a nation.

Since quantities can be easily summarized, compared, charted, and replicated, many scientists prefer quantitative research. Statistics require numbers. Quantitative data are easier to replicate (Creswell, 2009). However, when data are presented in categories and numbers, some nuances and individual distinctions are lost.

Many developmental researchers thus turn to **qualitative research** (from the word *quality*)—asking open-ended questions, reporting answers in narrative (not numerical) form. Qualitative researchers are "interested in understanding how people interpret their experiences, how they construct their worlds . . ." (Merriam, 2009, p. 5).

Qualitative research reflects cultural and contextual diversity, but it is also more vulnerable to bias and harder to replicate. Both types of research, and research that combines the two, are needed (Mertens, 2014).

Ethics

The most important mandate for all scientists, especially for those studying humans, is to uphold ethical standards. Each academic discipline and professional society that

◆ **Especially for Future Researchers and Science Writers** Do any ethical guidelines apply when an author writes about the experiences of family members, friends, or research participants? (see response, page 41)

is involved in the study of human development has a *code of ethics* (a set of moral principles). The idea is that scientists need to adhere to high standards, and society needs to allow scientists the freedom to do so.

Ethical standards and codes are increasingly stringent. Most educational and medical institutions have an *Institutional Review Board* (IRB), a group that permits only research that follows certain guidelines. One crucial focus is on the well-being of the participants in a study: They must understand and consent to their involvement, and the researcher must keep results confidential and must ensure that no one is seriously or permanently harmed.

Although IRBs slow down science, some research conducted before IRBs was clearly unethical, especially when the participants were children, members of minority groups, prisoners, or animals.

As stressed early in this chapter, scientists, like all other humans, have strong opinions, which they expect research to confirm. They might try (sometimes without noticing it) to achieve the results they want. As one team explains:

> Our job as scientists is to discover truths about the world. We generate hypotheses, collect data, and examine whether or not the data are consistent with those hypotheses . . . [but we] often lose sight of this goal, yielding to pressure to do whatever is justifiable to compile a set of studies we can publish. This is not driven by a willingness to deceive but by the self-serving interpretation of ambiguity . . .
>
> *[Simmons et al., 2011, p. 1359, 1365]*

Obviously, collaboration, replication, and transparency are essential ethical safeguards. Hundreds of questions regarding human development need answers. Often, however, researchers uncover issues that have political implications or seek answers that people do not want to know.

Thus, every scientist, and every student of human development, needs to consider the implications of what is studied. This is apparent for almost every question, but we now look at two examples.

FAMILY PLANNING From 1980 to 2016, the government of China decided that the best way to decrease poverty for their 2 billion people was to allow—and sometimes force—each couple to have only one child. Some people credit that policy for an astonishing economic miracle: China was one of the poorest nations in the world and now it may be one of the richest. The Chinese government estimated that 400,000 births were averted, which helped the entire planet reduce starvation, pollution, and war. If true, that is a great gift to us all.

But note that 400,000 averted births is a government estimate. Other people consider that number a gross overestimate. In addition, some people refuse to credit the government for so many averted births, because even without coercion, people might have voluntarily had fewer children. Finally, those who praise the policy's success ignore the human costs, including tens of thousands of abortions. Many Western critics claim that the policy reduced far fewer births than the government claimed (Nie, 2016).

This dispute has smoldered for years, but recently it became a firestorm when the leading journal of demography, *The Science of Population,* published a paper suggesting that the Chinese government's estimates were not far off and that between 360,000 and 520,000 births were averted (Goodkind, 2017). Other scientists not only questioned the way Goodkind arrived at the estimates but also said that publishing that paper was "morally irresponsible" (Hvistendahl, 2017, p. 284).

GUN CONTROL The same is true regarding gun control. Some developmentalists believe that the availability of guns in the United States is the reason U.S. homicide

VIDEO ACTIVITY: Eugenics and the "Feebleminded": A Shameful History illustrates what can happen when scientists fail to follow a code of ethics.

rates are 25 times higher than those of other wealthy nations, and the gun–suicide rate 8 times as high (Cook and Donahue, 2017).

But others believe that guns are part of the American tradition of independence and that "guns don't kill people, people do." This is a contentious political issue, with the U.S. Congress forbidding federal research to "advocate or promote gun control."

Nevertheless, in 2014 the National Institutes of Health funded research on "objective, scientific inquiries into gun violence prevention." Whether or not to continue that research is hotly disputed, within the federal government and outside it (Wadman, 2017).

UNKNOWN UNKNOWNS An even greater question is about the "unknown unknowns," the topics that we assume we understand but do not, hypotheses that have not yet occurred to anyone because our thinking is limited by our cultures and contexts. Discovering a new idea is one of the pleasures of the study of human development, motivating thousands of scientists, professors and students, including me and, I hope, you.

Every topic in human development is controversial, with opposing perspectives and opinions. As a scientist and a textbook author, I often report statistics and try to stick to evidence, but I am aware of *confirmation bias*, that humans tend to seek evidence that confirms what they already think (Del Vicario et al., 2017).

To avoid that bias, scientists check facts and seek contrary evidence, keeping an open mind to see where the data lead. Critical thinking is my goal, and the goal of the scientific method, but my opinions may creep into my conclusions. I hope you will seek out the evidence yourself, especially when you disagree with my perspective.

The next cohort of developmental scientists will build on what is known, mindful of what needs to be explored, raising questions that no one has thought of before, seeking answers that surprise them. Remember that the goal is to help all 7 billion people on Earth fulfill their potential. Much more needs to be learned. The next 14 chapters are only a start; like every topic of life-span research, the challenge is lifelong.

what have you learned?

1. Why do careful observations not prove "what causes what"?
2. Why do experimenters use a control (or comparison) group as well as an experimental group?
3. What are the strengths and weaknesses of the survey method?
4. Why would a scientist conduct a cross-sectional study?
5. What are the advantages and disadvantages of longitudinal research?
6. Why do developmentalists prefer cross-sequential research?
7. Why does correlation not prove causation?
8. What are the pros and cons of quantitative and qualitative research?
9. Why are informed consent and confidentiality important?

SUMMARY

Understanding How and Why

1. The study of human development is a science that seeks to understand how people change or remain the same over time. As a science, it begins with questions and hypotheses and then gathers empirical data. Replication confirms, modifies, or refutes conclusions.

2. Nature (genes) and nurture (environment) always interact, and each human characteristic is affected by that interaction. In differential susceptibility, both genes and experiences can make some people change when others remain unaffected.

The Life-Span Perspective

3. The assumption that growth is linear and that progress is inevitable has been replaced by the idea that both continuity (sameness) and discontinuity (sudden shifts) are apparent at every age. A critical period is a time when something *must* occur or when an abnormality might occur.

4. Urie Bronfenbrenner's ecological-systems approach notes that each of us is situated within larger systems of family, school, community, and culture, as well as part of a historical cohort. Changes in the context affect all other aspects of the system.

5. Certain experiences or innovations shape people of each cohort because they were the same age when significant historical events and innovations occurred. Socioeconomic status (SES) affects each child's opportunities, health, and education.

6. Culture includes beliefs and patterns; ethnicity refers to ancestral heritage. Race is a social construction, not a biological one. Differences are not deficits; they are alternate ways to think or act.

7. Development is plastic, which means that change is ongoing, even as some things do not change.

Theories of Human Development

8. Psychoanalytic theory emphasizes that adult actions and thoughts originate from unconscious impulses and childhood conflicts. Freud theorized that sexual urges arise during three stages of childhood; Erikson described eight successive stages of development, each involving a crisis to be resolved, including three in adulthood.

9. Behaviorists, or learning theorists, emphasize conditioning—a lifelong learning process in which an association between one stimulus and another (classical conditioning) or the consequences of reinforcement and punishment (operant conditioning) guide behavior.

10. Social learning theory recognizes that people learn by observing others, even if they themselves have not been reinforced or punished. Children are particularly susceptible to social learning, but all humans are affected by what they notice in other people.

11. Cognitive theorists believe that thoughts and beliefs powerfully affect attitudes, actions, and perceptions, and those affect behavior. Piaget proposed four age-related periods of cognition. Information processing looks more closely at the relationship between brain activity and thought.

12. Evolutionary theory contends that contemporary humans inherit genetic tendencies that have fostered survival and reproduction of the human species for tens of thousands of years. Through selective adaptation, the fears, impulses, and reactions that were useful 100,000 years ago continue to this day.

The Scientific Method

13. Commonly used research methods are scientific observation, the experiment, and the survey. Each can provide insight and discoveries, yet each is limited.

14. Developmentalists study change over time, often with cross-sectional and longitudinal research. Ideally, results from both methods are combined in cross-sequential analysis.

15. A correlation shows that two variables are related, not that one *causes* the other: Both may be caused by a third variable.

16. Quantitative research provides numerical data. This makes it best for comparing contexts and cultures via verified statistics. By contrast, more nuanced data come from qualitative research, which reports on individual lives.

17. Ethical behavior is crucial in all of the sciences. Results must be fairly gathered, reported, and interpreted. Participants must understand and consent to their involvement. Scientists continue to study, report, discuss, and disagree—and eventually reach conclusions that aid all humankind.

KEY TERMS

science of human
  development (p. 4)
scientific method (p. 4)
hypothesis (p. 4)
empirical evidence (p. 4)
replication (p. 5)
nature (p. 7)
nurture (p. 7)
epigenetics (p. 7)
differential susceptibility (p. 7)
life-span perspective (p. 8)
critical period (p. 9)

sensitive period (p. 9)
ecological-systems approach
  (p. 10)
cohort (p. 12)
socioeconomic status (SES)
  (p. 13)
culture (p. 14)
social construction (p. 14)
difference-equals-deficit error
  (p. 15)
ethnic group (p. 17)
race (p. 18)

plasticity (p. 19)
dynamic-systems approach
  (p. 19)
developmental theory (p. 22)
psychoanalytic theory (p. 22)
behaviorism (p. 24)
conditioning (p. 24)
operant conditioning (p. 25)
reinforcement (p. 25)
social learning theory (p. 26)
cognitive theory (p. 26)
evolutionary theory (p. 27)

scientific observation (p. 30)
experiment (p. 30)
independent variable (p. 30)
dependent variable (p. 30)
survey (p. 32)
cross-sectional research (p. 33)
longitudinal research (p. 33)
cross-sequential research (p. 35)
correlation (p. 37)
quantitative research (p. 37)
qualitative research (p. 37)

APPLICATIONS

1. It is said that culture is pervasive but that people are unaware of it. List 30 things you did *today* that you might have done differently in another culture. Begin with how and where you woke up.

2. Developmentalists sometimes talk about "folk theories," which are theories developed by ordinary people, who may not know that they are theorizing. Choose three sayings that are commonly used in your culture, such as (from the dominant U.S. culture) "A penny saved is a penny earned" or "As the twig is bent, so grows the tree." Explain the underlying assumptions, or theory, that each saying reflects.

3. Design an experiment to answer a question that you have about human development. Specify the question and the hypothesis and then describe the experiment. How would you prevent your conclusions from being biased and subjective?

4. A longitudinal case study can be insightful but also limited in application to other people. Describe the life of one of your older relatives, explaining what aspects of their development are unique and what aspects might be relevant for everyone.

ESPECIALLY FOR ANSWERS

Response for Teachers (from page 23) Erikson would note that the behavior of 5-year-olds is affected by their developmental stage and by their culture. Therefore, you might design your curriculum to accommodate active, noisy children.

Response for Teachers and Counselors of Teenagers (from page 28) Evolutionary theory stresses the basic human drive for reproduction, which gives teenagers a powerful sex drive. Thus, merely informing teenagers of the difficulty of caring for a newborn (some high school sex-education programs simply give teenagers a chicken egg to nurture) is not likely to work. A better method would be to structure teenagers' lives so that pregnancy is impossible—for instance, with careful supervision or readily available contraception.

Response for Future Researchers (from page 35) There is no best method for collecting data. The method used depends on many factors, such as the age of participants (infants can't complete questionnaires), the question being researched, and the time frame.

Response for Future Researchers and Science Writers (from page 37) Yes. Anyone you write about must give consent and be fully informed about your intentions. They can be identified by name only if they give permission. For example, family members gave permission before anecdotes about them were included in this text. My nephew David read the first draft of his story (see page 38) and is proud to have his experiences used to teach others.

OBSERVATION QUIZ ANSWERS

Answer to Observation Quiz (from p. 12) Because surveys rarely ask children their opinions, and the youngest cohort on this graph did not reach adulthood until about 2005.

Answer to Observation Quiz (from page 17) A snapshot is only one moment, but her arm around him, and her happy, relaxed expression suggests a warm father–daughter relationship. At this point, he alrcady had symptoms of the tuberculosis that killed him.

Answer to Observation Quiz (from page 25) Both are balding, with white beards. Note also that none of the other theorists in this chapter has a beard—a cohort difference, not an ideological one.

Answer to Observation Quiz (from page 34) Of course, much changed and much did not change, but evident in the photos is continuity in Sarah-Maria's happy smile and discontinuity in her hairstyle (which shows dramatic age and cohort changes).

THE BEGINNINGS
From Conception to Birth

SHAPECHARGE/GETTY IMAGES

what will you know?

- How do genes affect each individual?
- How are each pair of twins alike and not alike?
- How can serious birth disorders be avoided?
- What causes postpartum depression?

W hen my daughter Elissa birthed her second child, her husband and midwife were with her in the labor room of the birthing center; I was in the family room with Asa, who was about to become a brother at age 5. His parents had packed a bag for him—snacks and a new Lego set—and my task was to keep him happy. Several times he ran down the hall to see his mother, who usually greeted him with a smile.

Five hours after we arrived, a nurse told us, "There's a new person who wants to meet you."

"Let me put this last Lego piece in," Asa replied. He then brought his Lego creation to show his parents. They introduced him to Isaac.

I saw a tiny baby, feeding on Elissa's breast, and I remembered the dangers of low birthweight.

"How much does he weigh?"

The midwife answered: "I can see that he is at least 7 pounds and healthy. I do not weigh them until after mother and baby get acquainted."

Five hours later, the entire family was home, and my daughter Sarah came to meet her new nephew. His two out-of-state aunts arrived in a few days.

The contrast between Isaac's birth and Elissa's own arrival is stark. Back then, midwives were banned from my hospital; fathers were relegated to waiting rooms. The nurses did not let me touch my daughter until she was 24 hours old. Her older sisters were not allowed on the maternity floor, where I stayed for four days and nights.

The science of human development is not only about how individuals change over time, it is about how contexts and cultures affect every moment of development, including family life and birth itself. Fathers, particularly, have become more active partners: In the United States they are now expected to attend the birth.

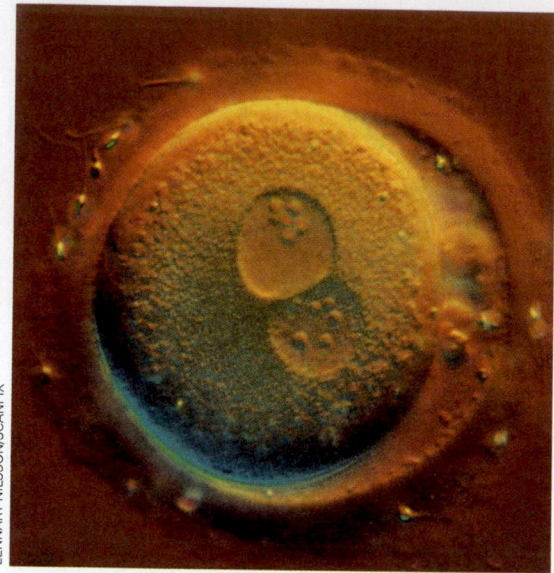

LENNART NILSSON/SCANPIX

The Moment of Conception
This ovum is about to become a
zygote. It has been penetrated by
a single sperm, whose nucleus
now lies next to the nucleus of the
ovum. Soon, the two nuclei will
fuse, bringing together about 21,000
genes to guide development.

deoxyribonucleic acid (DNA)
The chemical composition of the
molecules that contain the genes,
which are the chemical instructions for
cells to manufacture various proteins.

chromosome
One of the 46 molecules of DNA (in
23 pairs) that virtually every cell of
the human body contains and that,
together, contain all of the genes.
Other species have more or fewer
chromosomes.

Some things endure: Every pregnancy and birth is a miracle.
Genes endure, too. Babies get half their genes from each parent, so Isaac has one-fourth of mine, and mine came from my
ancestors, passed down over thousands of years. This chapter
describes genetics, prenatal development, and birth, as well as
some of the many differences from one era, one culture, even
one family to another. Possible harm is noted: causes and consequences of diseases, malnutrition, low birthweight, drugs,
pollution, stress, and so on.

The more we learn, the more we realize what we do not
know. All of us—governments, communities, professionals, and
parents—shape each life from the very beginning, which is one
reason this chapter is for everyone. Immediate social support
matters as well. Isaac arrived amidst many caring strangers
and relatives: Not every newborn is so fortunate, or so big.
Isaac was 9 pounds, 4 ounces.

Genes and Chromosomes

All living things are composed of cells that promote growth and sustain life according
to instructions in their molecules of **deoxyribonucleic acid (DNA)** (see Figure 2.1).
Each molecule of DNA is packaged into a **chromosome**. Almost all humans have
46 chromosomes; other creatures have more than or fewer than 46. Chromosomes contain *genes*, each located on a particular chromosome. Humans have about 21,000 genes.

With one exception, every cell has a copy of that person's chromosomes, arranged
in pairs. The exception is the reproductive cell, called a *gamete*. Each gamete—*sperm*

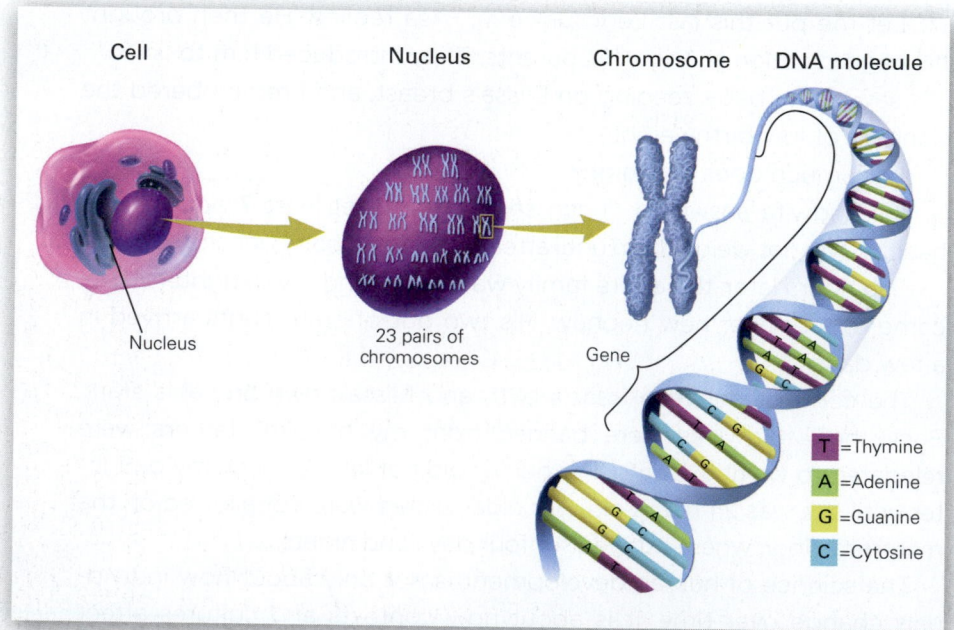

| Cell | Nucleus | Chromosome | DNA molecule |

Nucleus

23 pairs of
chromosomes

Gene

T = Thymine
A = Adenine
G = Guanine
C = Cytosine

FIGURE 2.1 How Proteins Are Made The genes on the chromosomes in the nucleus of
each cell instruct the cell to manufacture the proteins needed to sustain life and development. The
code for a protein is the particular combination of four bases, T-A-G-C (thymine, adenine, guanine,
and cytosine).

in a man and *ovum* in a woman—has only 23 chromosomes, one from each of that person's 23 pairs.

At conception, the genes on each of the 23 chromosomes from the sperm pair up with the genes on the same 23 chromosomes from the ovum, creating a new cell called a **zygote.** For instance, an eye-color gene from the father on chromosome 15 connects with an eye-color gene from the mother on the zygote's other chromosome 15. If the match between the two genes is exact (as it usually is since most genes are identical for every human), the person is said to be **homozygous** (literally, "same zygote") for that trait.

Variations Among People

Some genes come in slightly different versions, as in eye-color genes. Each version is called an **allele.** Genes that have various alleles are called *polymorphic* (many shapes). If the gene from one parent differs from the same gene from the other parent, the zygote is said to be **heterozygous** for that trait.

Since each gamete has only 23 chromosomes (one from each of the parent's 23 pairs), each man or woman can produce 2^{23} different gametes—more than 8 million versions of their chromosomes (actually 8,388,608). Thus, when a sperm and an ovum combine, the zygote they create is a new cell formed from one of 8 million possible sperm from the father interacting with 8 million possible ova from the mother. Your parents could have given you an astronomical number of siblings, each unique.

More variations occur. The DNA code on those chromosomes contains about *3 billion base pairs* of chemicals organized in *triplets* (sets of three pairs), each of which specifies production of one of 20 possible amino acids. Those amino acids combine to produce proteins, and those proteins combine to produce a person.

Small variations, mutations, or repetitions (called *copy number variations*) in the base pairs or triplets make a notable difference in the proteins and thus, eventually, in the person. Some genes have triplet transpositions, deletions, or repetitions not found in other versions of the same gene. Thus, genes "are themselves transmitted to individual cells with large apparent mistakes—somatically acquired deletions, duplications, and other mutations" (Macosko & McCarroll, 2013, p. 564).

Additional DNA and RNA (another molecule) surround each gene. In a process called *methylation,* this material enhances, transcribes, connects, empowers, silences, regulates, and alters genes. This material used to be called *junk*—but now "there is no such thing as junk DNA" (Larson, 2018, p. 1). As one team explains:

> One of the most important discoveries in genetics in the last 10 years is that the vast majority of trait-associated DNA variations occur in regions of the genome that were once labeled as 'junk DNA' because they do not code for proteins. We now know that these regions harbor genetic elements that control where, when, and to what extent specific genes are expressed.
>
> *[Furey & Sethupathy, 2013, p. 705]*

GENETIC EXPRESSION Pause for a moment to consider how significant this is. Obviously genes are crucial, but even more crucial is whether or not a gene is *expressed,* which means that it becomes active in forming the person. RNA turns some genes and alleles off. A person can have the gene for a particular trait, disease, or behavior, but that genetic possibility never appears in that person because it was never expressed.

zygote
The single cell formed from the union of two gametes, a sperm and an ovum.

homozygous
Referring to two genes of one pair that are exactly the same in every letter of their code. Most gene pairs are homozygous.

allele
A variation that makes a gene different in some way from other genes for the same characteristics. Many genes never vary; others have several possible alleles.

heterozygous
Referring to two genes of one pair that differ in some way. Typically one allele has only a few base pairs that differ from the other member of the pair.

Think of turning on a lamp. Many elements must be in place before the room is illuminated. The lamp needs an unspent bulb screwed into the socket, a cord correctly plugged in, an electric bill paid, and an electricity source. Yet the room will be dark until the switch is flipped. That's RNA.

Researchers who sought the gene for, say, schizophrenia, or homosexuality, or even for a tiny detail such as memory for chemistry formulas, have been disappointed. No such single genes exist. Instead, almost every trait arises from a combination of genes, each with a small potential impact, each dependent on epigenetic factors that determine if that gene is expressed or silenced (Ayyanathan, 2014).

THE MICROBIOME One epigenetic influence that profoundly affects each person is the **microbiome,** which refers to all of the microbes (bacteria, viruses, fungi, archaea, yeasts) that live within the body. The microbiome includes what people call "germs," which they try to kill with disinfectant and antibiotics. However, most microbes are helpful, not harmful. Microbes have their own DNA, reproducing throughout life.

There are thousands of varieties of these microbes. Together they have an estimated 3 million different genes—influencing immunity, weight, diseases, moods, and much else that affects us every day (Dugas et al., 2016; Koch, 2015). Particularly intriguing is the relationship between the microbiome and nutrition, since bacteria in the gut break down food for nourishment (Devaraj et al., 2013; Pennisi, 2016). A fetus gains weight because of the mother's microbiome. The mother's diet affects the fetal microbiome, and thus it affects the child (Prince et al., 2017).

Obese or thin mice change body size when the microbiome from another mouse with the opposite problem is implanted (Dugas et al., 2016). Thus, the microbiome affects genetic expression, another example of something that used to be considered junk becoming pivotal. The microbiome, like other epigenetic aspects, changes over each person's life, from birth to death.

In one telling study, researchers in Malawi studied young identical (*monozygotic*) and fraternal (*dizygotic*) twins, when one was severely malnourished and the other was not. Both lived in the same home and were fed the same food.

Did the greedier twin grab food from the other? No. When scientists analyzed each twin's microbiome, they found crucial differences that were the likely reason only one was starving (Smith et al., 2014).

SIBLINGS NOT ALIKE Siblings differ not only in their chromosomes and microbiome but also in the genes themselves. When the genes on the father's chromosome pair up with their counterparts from the mother, the interaction between the two determines the inherited traits of the future person. Since some alleles from the father differ from the alleles from the mother, their combination produces a zygote unlike either parent.

Even more than that, each zygote carries genes that are not exact duplicates of those inherited from the parents (Macosko & McCarroll, 2013). Small variations, mutations, or repetitions in the 3 billion base pairs could make a notable difference in the proteins and thus, eventually, in the person.

Attention has focused on **copy number variations,** which are repeats or deletions (from one to hundreds) of base pairs. Copy number variations are widespread—everyone has them—and they correlate with almost every disease and condition, including heart disease, intellectual disability, mental illness, and many cancers. Most, however, are insignificant. For example, about 30 percent of our skin cells include copy number variations (Macosko & McCarroll, 2013). No matter, our skin still protects us just fine.

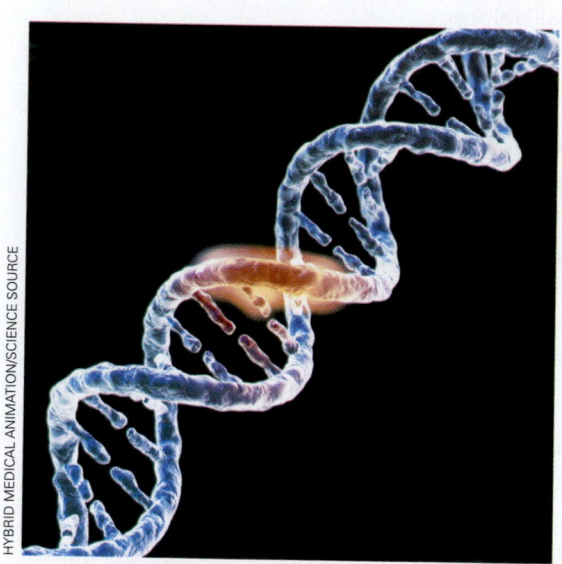

HYBRID MEDICAL ANIMATION/SCIENCE SOURCE

Twelve of 3 Billion Pairs This is a computer illustration of a small segment of one gene. Even a small difference in one gene can cause major changes in a person's phenotype.

microbiome
All of the microbes (bacteria, viruses, and so on) with all of their genes in a community; here, the millions of microbes of the human body.

copy number variations
The various repeats or deletions of base pairs that genes have.

Genetic diversity helps all humanity, because creativity, prosperity, and survival are enhanced when one person is unlike another. There is an optimal balance between diversity and similarity for each species: Human societies are close to that optimal level (Ashraf & Galor, 2013). Do you wish that everyone else were just like you? Of course not. That is one reason we should not see differences as deficits. We need those differences: males and females, extroverts and introverts, and so on (Cain, 2012).

Genotype and Phenotype

For each individual, the collection of his or her genes is called the **genotype.** It was once thought that the genotype led directly to facial characteristics, body formation, intelligence, personality, and so on, but this is much too simplistic. As you just read, not every gene is expressed.

The **phenotype,** which is a person's actual appearance and behavior, reflects much more than the genotype. The genotype is the beginning of diversity; the phenotype is the actual manifestation of it, the result of "multiple interactions among numerous genetic and environmental factors" (Nadeau & Dudley, 2011, p. 1015). If a gene is expressed, the influence of many environmental factors determines the particulars of that expression.

Humans are designed, by genes, to be profoundly shaped by their environment. Our many variations not only make us unique (you can spot a close friend in a crowd of thousands) but also let us adapt to our context. We are the only species that thrives on every continent, from the poles to the equator, eating blubber or locusts as the case may be.

One of the best parts of our adaptive genes is that we learn from each other. If you or I suddenly found ourselves thousands of miles from our native land, we would quickly learn how to dress, where to sleep, and what to eat. Humans like to teach each other: Strangers would show us what to do. If our descendants stayed in the new place, eventually our great-great-grandchildren would have genes slightly changed from ours, to help them thrive.

Thanks to our genetic diversity, even devastating diseases do not kill us all. For instance, a few people have alleles that defend them from HIV/AIDS; learning more about that helps us understand the immune system (Naranbhai & Carrington, 2017).

Similarly, genotype differences allowed some of our ancestors to survive tuberculosis, malaria, the Black Death, and other scourges, and some of our contemporaries to survive Ebola and to be resistant to Zika. The phenotype—such as whether we have been taught to wash our hands, hug our friends, or socialize with neighbors—matters, too, as we learned from Ebola survivors (Baers et al., 2018).

Shared and Divergent Genes

The entire packet of instructions that make a living organism is called the **genome.** There is a genome for every animal species, from *Homo sapiens* to the smallest insect, and for every kind of plant. Even yeast has a genome, detailed in 1996.

A worldwide effort to map all the human genes led to the *Human Genome Project,* which was virtually complete in 2003. Before then scientists thought humans had about 100,000 genes, but that turned out to be a gross overestimate to the surprise of every scientist. The Human Genome Project found only about 20,000 to 23,000 genes, almost all of which are present in every human being. (Mapping all the possible alleles takes much longer, and is ongoing.)

Genomes have since been sequenced for many other creatures, again with surprises. Dogs and mice have more genes than humans, and mice have several times more.

genotype
An organism's entire genetic inheritance, or genetic potential.

phenotype
The observable characteristics of a person, including appearance, personality, intelligence, and all other traits.

◆ **Especially for Medical Doctors**
Can you look at a person and then write a prescription that will personalize medicine to their particular genetic susceptibility? (see response, page 79)

genome
The full set of genes that are the instructions to make an individual member of a certain species.

Any two people, of whatever ethnicity, share 99.5 percent of their genetic codes, and humans are much more similar to other mammals than most people imagined. The genetic codes for humans and chimpanzees are 98 percent the same (although chimp genes are on 48, not 46, chromosomes), and the genomes for every other mammal are at least 90 percent the same as for people.

The genomes of brewer's yeast and a tiny worm (the nematode) are the only ones that have been completely sequenced, down to every letter of code. Virtually complete are the genomes of *Homo sapiens* and many other species, including the sweat bee, the olive fruit fly, the komodo dragon, the kakapo bird, and the monk seal (a list provided to help readers realize how many species and genomes there are) (Pennisi, 2017). Plant genomes are more complex, but several have been sequenced, including several kinds of rice.

Shared genes among mammals allow scientists to learn about human genetics from other creatures, especially mice, by transposing, deactivating, enhancing, and duplicating their genes. As more and more is learned from laboratory mice, some scientists now call for greater variety in which animals are studied and where they live. We need to learn from mammals that are not in laboratory cages (Yartsev, 2017). To understand humans, polymorphisms in diverse environments are key.

THE GENES OF DISEASES For humans, genetic differences that seem minor are significant. Some alleles are relatively common, detectable, and understood. For example, for the APOE gene, allele 4, unlike 2 or 3, renders a person susceptible to HIV/AIDS, heart disease, and Alzheimer's disease.

Most alleles have unknown effects, or perhaps no effects. And some are very rare: Each of us probably has one or two alleles that only one person in a million has. We have learned a lot about genes, but there is much more to be understood.

For example, about one woman in eight develops breast cancer. For women who have inherited a mutation in two alleles (named BRCA1 and BRCA2), the risk increases to one woman in two. About half of the women diagnosed with breast cancer have either of those alleles, or have one of ten other genes that increase the risk—although for those ten it is not known by how much (Kean, 2014).

◆ **Especially for Scientists**
A hundred years ago, it was believed that humans had 48 chromosomes, not 46; 20 years ago, it was thought that humans had 100,000 genes, not 20,000 or so. Why? (see response, page 79)

She Laughs Too Much No, not the smiling sister, but the 10-year-old on the right, who has Angelman syndrome. She inherited it from her mother's chromosome 15. Fortunately, her two siblings inherited the mother's other chromosome 15. If the 10-year-old had inherited the identical deletion on her father's chromosome 15, she would have Prader-Willi syndrome, which would cause her to be overweight, always hungry, and often angry. With Angelman syndrome, however, laughing, even at someone's pain, is a symptom.

MARIA PLATT-EVANS/SCIENCE SOURCE

That means that an unknown combination of genes, alleles, mutations, diet, and other epigenetic factors cause breast cancer in millions of other women. Uncertainty is difficult. About a fourth of those with cancer in one breast, who do not have BRCA1 or BRCA2, nonetheless choose to have *both* breasts removed, without any proven benefit (Hamilton et al., 2017).

Male and Female

One aspect of development that seems to be entirely determined by chromosomes is whether a person is male or female. Sex differences begin with chromosomes, but as you will see, the environment profoundly affects that difference.

Forty-five of a human's 46 chromosomes are equally likely to be inherited by a boy or a girl. That includes both halves of the first 22 pairs (called *autosomes*) and one half of the 23rd pair (the X). Thus, sex and gender are irrelevant for 97.8 percent of who we are, genetically.

THE 46TH CHROMOSOME However, one chromosome on the 23rd pair is crucial. In females, the 23rd pair is composed of two large X-shaped chromosomes. Accordingly, it is **XX.** In males, the 23rd pair has one large X-shaped chromosome and one quite small Y-shaped chromosome. That 23rd pair is **XY.**

Because a female's 23rd pair is XX, when that pair splits, every ovum contains one X or the other—but always an X. Because a male's 23rd pair is XY, when his 46 chromosomes divide to make gametes, half of his sperm carry an X chromosome and half carry a Y. (See Figure 2.2.)

The Y chromosome has fewer genes than the X, but it has one crucial gene (SRY) that directs the developing fetus to make male organs. Thus, the sex of the developing organism depends on which sperm penetrates the ovum—either an X sperm, which creates a girl (XX), or a Y sperm, which creates a boy (XY). The male organs of the fetus produce male hormones, which affect the developing brain.

Traditionally, male–female intellectual differences—males better at math, females better at verbal skills—were thought to be determined by that prenatal brain

XX
A 23rd chromosome pair that consists of two X-shaped chromosomes, one each from the mother and the father. XX zygotes become females.

XY
A 23rd chromosome pair that consists of an X-shaped chromosome from the mother and a Y-shaped chromosome from the father. XY zygotes become males.

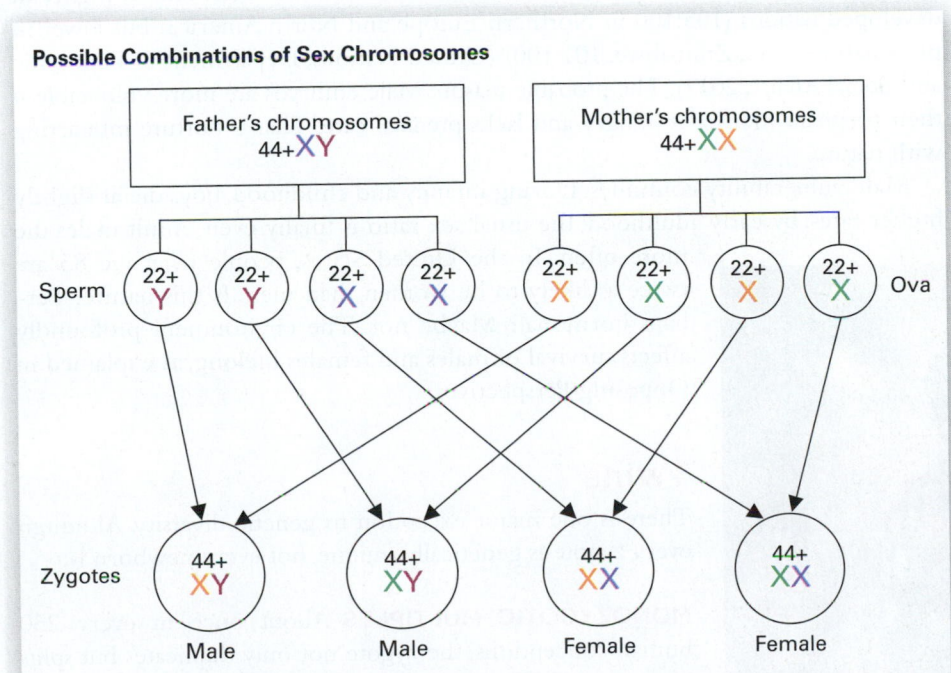

FIGURE 2.2 Determining a Zygote's Sex Any given couple can produce four possible combinations of sex chromosomes; two lead to female children and two lead to male children. In terms of the future person's sex, it does not matter which of the mother's Xs the zygote inherited. All that matters is whether the father's Y sperm or X sperm fertilized the ovum. However, for X-linked conditions it matters a great deal because typically one, but not both, of the mother's Xs carries the trait.

Uncertain Sex *Every now and then, a baby is born with "ambiguous genitals," meaning that the child's sex is not abundantly clear. When this happens, a quick analysis of the chromosomes is needed to make sure that there are exactly 46 and to see whether the 23rd pair is XY or XX. The karyotypes shown here indicate a typical baby boy (left) and girl (right).*

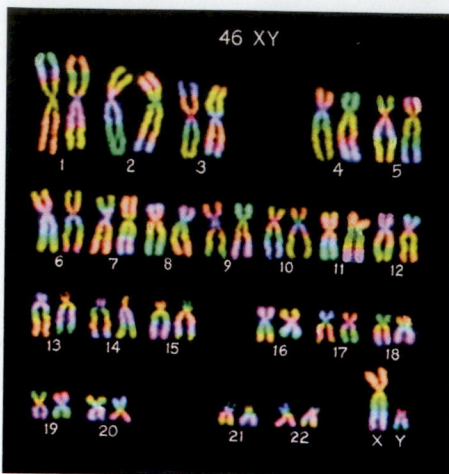
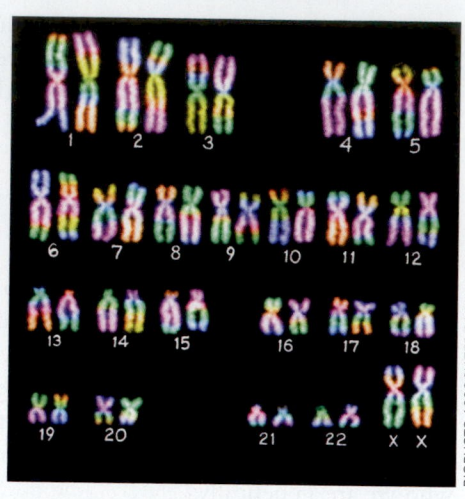

46 XY

differentiation. This was assumed until recently, when girls in some nations began to surpass boys in math. It is now thought that "gender differences . . . seem to be very sensitive to contextual influences (such as cultural values and schooling)" (Bonsang et al., 2017, p. 1210).

THE SEX RATIO This raises the issue of the natural and unnatural sex ratio. Since half the sperm carry an X and half a Y, one might think that half the newborns are male and half female. That is not what happens.

Even before birth, the environment affects male–female differences (called *gender* differences when caused by culture instead of biology, but remember that nature and nurture are intertwined). At conception, XY zygotes outnumber XX zygotes, with a ratio of about 120:100, perhaps because smaller Y sperm can swim faster than heavier X sperm and thus reach the ovum first. However, male embryos are more vulnerable than female ones (because of fewer genes, again?), so they are less likely to survive prenatally. At birth the natural boy:girl ratio is about 104:100.

Remember that nurture starts at conception. The newborn sex ratio is higher in developed nations (105:100 in Northern Europe and North America) but lower in poor nations (e.g., Zimbabwe, 101:100) (United Nations, Department of Economic and Social Affairs, 2017). The probable reason: Male embryos are more vulnerable if their pregnant mother is hungry and lacks prenatal care. That is nurture interacting with nature.

Male vulnerability continues. During infancy and childhood, boys die at slightly higher rates; by early adulthood, the usual sex ratio is finally even. Adult males die more often: In the United States, people over age 85 are twice as likely to be women than men. Is this nature? Perhaps hormonal? Maybe not. The environment profoundly affects survival of males and females lifelong, as explained in Opposing Perspectives.

Twins

There is one major exception to genetic diversity. Although every zygote is genetically unique, not every newborn is.

MONOZYGOTIC MULTIPLES About once in every 250 human conceptions, the zygote not only duplicates but splits apart completely, creating two, or four, or even eight separate

Not Exactly Alike *These two 4-year-old boys in South Carolina are identical twins, which means they originated from one zygote. But one was born first and heavier, and, as you see here, one appears to be more affectionate to his brother.*

OPPOSING PERSPECTIVES

Too Many Boys?

In past centuries, millions of newborns were killed because they were the wrong sex, a practice that is considered murder today. Now the same goal is achieved long before birth in three ways: (1) inactivating X or Y sperm before conception, (2) inserting only male or female zygotes after in vitro conception, or (3) aborting XX or XY fetuses.

Recently, millions of couples have used these methods. Should this be against the law? At least 36 nations say yes; the United States says no.

To some prospective parents, those 36 nations are unfair, since almost every nation allows similar measures to avoid severely disabled newborns. If a couple knows they might conceive a zygote with a lethal condition, they sometimes use in vitro fertilization, allowing implantation of only healthy zygotes. There are moral distinctions between prenatal selection of healthy embryos and prenatal selection of boys. But, should governments legislate morals? People disagree (Purewal & Eklund, 2017; Wilkinson, 2015).

One nation that since 1993 has forbidden prenatal sex selection is China. Fifteen years earlier, China began a one-child policy, urging and sometimes forcing couples to have only one child. That achieved the intended goal: fewer starving children. But in Chinese tradition it is sons, not daughters, who care for aging parents. Thinking ahead, many parents wanted their only child to be a boy. Among the unanticipated consequences:

- Since 1980, an estimated 10 million abortions of female fetuses
- Adoption of thousands of infant Chinese girls by Western families
- By 2010, millions of unmarried, childless men (called "bare branches")
- By 2017, far more deaths among young adult men than women

China rescinded the one-child policy in 2013. However, the 2017 male:female ratio at birth is 116:100. This suggests that, in defiance of their government, Chinese couples learn the sex of the embryo and then one in every seven female fetuses is aborted.

Many Americans believe that personal freedom means that couples can decide how many children to have and what sex they should be (Murray, 2014). They could abort in the early weeks, or, if they oppose abortion, they could select for a boy or a girl using the other two methods. Is that their private choice?

But maybe laws should forbid sex selection if it results in too many boys, because society suffers with too many men, especially if young women are scarce. If a man cannot find a partner, he is likely to take more risks and become depressed. In a nation with too few women, the rates of crime, heart attacks, and premature deaths (from accidents, suicide, and homicide) will be higher.

But wait: Chromosomes do not *determine* behavior. Every sex difference is influenced by culture. Even traits that originate with biology, such as vulnerability to heart attacks, are affected more by environment (in this case, diet and cigarettes) than by the Y chromosome. Nurture could change. For instance, societies could have better crime-prevention measures.

Indeed, every sex or gender difference is strongly influenced by culture and policy, not only for the fetus but also for the adult. For example, do you wonder why some nations allow polygamy? Perhaps when too many boys died, cultures encouraged men to have several wives so that every woman could be a wife and a mother, and every child could have a father at home. Couldn't customs adjust to the opposite problem, too many boys? Should they?

THINK CRITICALLY: Might laws against prenatal sex selection be unnecessary if culture shifted?

---

cells, each genetically identical to that original zygote. If each cell implants and grows, multiple births occur, as in the photo of the triplets on page 42.

One separation results in **monozygotic (MZ) twins,** from one *(mono)* zygote. Two or three separations create monozygotic quadruplets or octuplets. (An incomplete split creates *conjoined twins,* once called *Siamese twins.*)

Because monozygotic multiples originate from the same zygote, they have virtually identical genetic instructions for physical appearance, psychological traits, vulnerability to diseases, and everything else. However, because nurture always affects nature,

monozygotic (MZ) twins
Twins who originate from one zygote that splits apart very early in development. (Also called *identical twins.*) Other monozygotic multiple births (such as triplets and quadruplets) can occur as well.

dizygotic (DZ) twins
Twins who are formed when two separate ova are fertilized by two separate sperm at roughly the same time. (Also called *fraternal twins*.)

identical twins do not have exactly the same phenotype. Often the birthweight differs, especially if each twin was enveloped in its own placenta.

After birth, monozygotic twins usually develop distinct identities. They might inherit athletic ability, for instance, but one chooses basketball and the other, soccer. One MZ twin writes:

> Twins put into high relief *the* central challenge for all of us: self-definition. How do we each plant our stake in the ground, decide how sensitive, callous, ambitious, cautious, or conciliatory we want to be every day? . . . Twins come with a built-in constant comparison, but defining oneself against one's twin is just an amped-up version of every person's life-long challenge: to individuate—to create a distinctive persona in the world.

[Pogrebin, 2010, p. 9]

DIZYGOTIC MULTIPLES **Dizygotic (DZ) twins,** also called *fraternal twins,* are born three times as often as monozygotic twins. They began life as two zygotes created by two ova fertilized by two sperm. (Usually the ovaries release only one ovum per month, but sometimes two or more ova are released.)

Dizygotic multiples, like any offspring from the same parents, have half their genes in common. Their genotypes may differ (about half are male–female pairs) or they can look quite similar, again like other siblings, who also share half their genes.

A woman's tendency to ovulate more than one ovum is influenced by her genes, and thus it is more common in some families and groups than others. For example, about 1 in 11 Yorubas in Nigeria is a twin, as is about 1 in 45 European Americans, 1 in 75 Japanese and Koreans, and 1 in 150 Chinese. Age matters, too: Older women more often double-ovulate.

Because genes endure lifelong, if a woman has one set of DZ twins, she is more likely to have another set (Painter et al., 2010). Her daughters also have a 50/50 chance of inheriting her twin-producing X, and hence they often have twins themselves. Her sons are not likely to father twins because they do not ovulate. But her son's daughters may have twins because their X is from his mother, and half the time it is the multiple-ovulation X. That may explain why it is said that twinning skips a generation. In fact, the genotype doesn't skip, but the phenotype might.

Genetic Mix Dizygotic twins Olivia and Harrison have half their genes in common, as do all siblings from the same parents. If the parents are close relatives who themselves share most alleles, the nonshared half is likely to include many similar genes. That is not the case here, as their mother (Nicola) is from Wales and their father (Gleb) is from the nation of Georgia, which includes many people of Asian ancestry. Their phenotypes, and the family photos on the wall, show many additive genetic influences.

Genetic Interactions

No gene functions alone. Thus, almost every trait is *polygenic* (affected by many genes) and *multifactorial* (influenced by many factors). Almost daily, researchers discover new complexities in multifactorial interaction. Here we describe a few of them.

Most genes are **additive genes.** Their effects *add up* to make the phenotype. When genes interact additively, the phenotype may reflect all the genes that are involved. Height, hair curliness, and skin color, for instance, are influenced by additive genes. Indeed, height is probably influenced by 180 genes, each contributing a very small amount (Enserink, 2011).

Less common are *nonadditive* genes, which do not contribute equal shares. In one nonadditive form alleles interact in a **dominant–recessive pattern.** Then for a pair of genes (one from each parent), one gene, called *dominant,* is far more influential than the other, called *recessive.* When someone has a recessive gene that is not expressed that person is a **carrier** of that gene. The recessive gene is *carried* on the genotype.

CARRIERS Most recessive genes are harmless. For example, blue eyes are determined by a recessive allele and brown eyes by a dominant one, which means that a child conceived by a blue-eyed person and a brown-eyed person will usually have brown eyes.

"Usually" is accurate, because sometimes a brown-eyed person carries the blue-eye gene. In that case, in a blue-eye/brown-eye couple, every child inherits a blue-eye gene from the blue-eyed parent and has a 50/50 chance of having a second blue-eye gene from the carrier parent. Half of the children of this couple will have blue eyes and half will have brown eyes, on average.

Sometimes both parents are carriers. Then their children have one chance in four of inheriting the recessive gene from both parents. The phenotype of the child reflects the parents' genotype, even though it is not in either parent's phenotype. A blue-eyed baby can have brown-eyed parents (see Figure 2.3).

A special case of the dominant–recessive pattern occurs with genes that are **X-linked** (located on the X chromosome). If an X-linked gene is recessive—as are the genes for most forms of color blindness, many allergies, several diseases (including hemophilia and Duchenne muscular dystrophy), and some learning disabilities—the fact that it is on the X chromosome is critical (see Table 2.1).

COURTESY KATE NURRE

Sisters, But Not Twins, in Iowa From their phenotype, it is obvious that these two girls share many of the same genes, as their blond hair and facial features are strikingly similar. And you can see that they are not twins; in this photo, Lucy is 7 years old and Ellie is only 4. It may not be obvious that they have the same parents, but they do—and they are both very bright and happy because of it. This photo also shows that their genotypes differ in one crucial way: One of them has a dominant gene for a serious condition.

↑ **OBSERVATION** QUIZ Who has the genetic condition? (see answer, page 79)

additive genes Genes that each contribute to the characteristic—they "add up" rather than one being hidden (recessive). For example, skin color is additive: It shows the combined genes of both parents, rather than taking after one or the other.

dominant–recessive pattern The interaction of a heterozygous pair of alleles in such a way that the phenotype reflects one allele (the dominant gene) more than the other (the recessive gene).

carrier A person whose genotype includes a gene that is not expressed in the phenotype. The carried gene occurs in half of the carrier's gametes and thus is passed on to half of the carrier's children. If such a gene is inherited from both parents, the characteristic appears in the phenotype.

X-linked A gene carried on the X chromosome. If a male inherits an X-linked recessive trait from his mother, he expresses that trait because the Y from his father has no counteracting gene. Females are more likely to be carriers of X-linked traits but are less likely to express them.

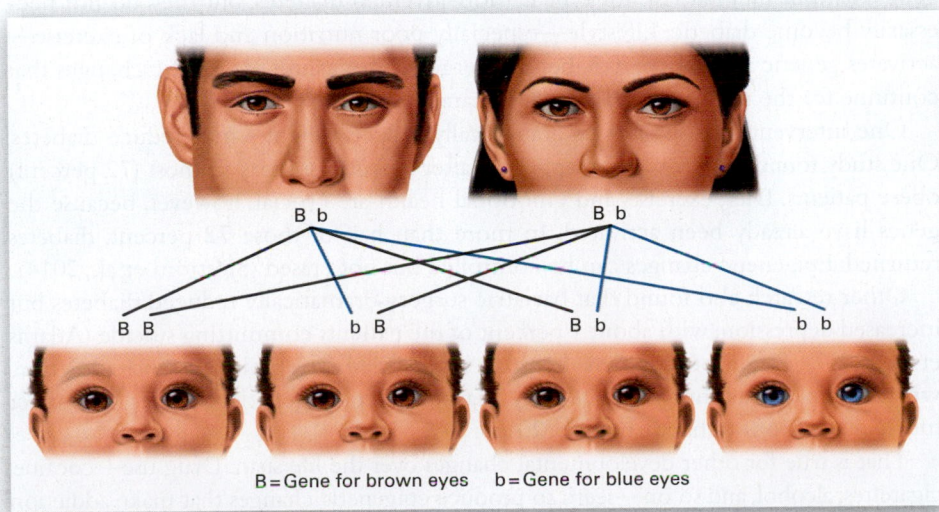

B = Gene for brown eyes   b = Gene for blue eyes

FIGURE 2.3 Changeling? No. If two brown-eyed parents both carry the blue-eye gene, they have one chance in four of having a blue-eyed child. Other recessive genes include the genes for red hair, Rh-negative blood, and many genetic diseases.

TABLE 2.1   The 23rd Pair and X-Linked Color Blindness

23rd Pair	Phenotype	Genotype	Next Generation
1. XX	Typical woman	Not a carrier	No color blindness.
2. XY	Typical man	Typical X from mother	No color blindness.
3. X**X**	Typical woman	Carrier from father	Half of her children will inherit her X. The girls with her X will be carriers; the boys with her X will have color blindness.
4. **X**X	Typical woman	Carrier from mother	Half of her children will inherit her X. The girls with her X will be carriers; the boys with her X will have color blindness.
5. **X**Y	Color-blind man	Inherited from mother	All of his daughters will have his X. None of his sons will have his X. All of his children will have normal vision unless their mother also had an X for color blindness.
6. **XX**	Color-blind woman (rare)	Inherited from both parents	Every child will have one X from her. Therefore, every son will have color blindness. Daughters will only be carriers unless they also inherit an X from the father, as their mother did.

X = **X** that carries recessive gene for color blindness

THINK CRITICALLY: If a woman has a color-blind brother, will her sons have color blindness?

This follows from what you already know. Since the Y chromosome is much smaller than the X, an X-linked recessive gene almost never has a dominant counterpart on the Y. Therefore, recessive traits carried on the X affect the phenotypes of sons more often than daughters. The girls are protected by their other X chromosome, which usually has the dominant gene. This explains why males with an X-linked disorder inherited it from their mothers, not their fathers. Because of their mothers, 20 times more boys than girls have color blindness (McIntyre, 2002).

EPIGENETIC The final complexity mentioned here is *epigenetic,* not solely genetic. As noted earlier, genes are affected from the moment of conception by other material. *Epi-* is a prefix that means "above, on, over, nearby, upon; outer; besides, in addition to; among; attached to; or toward." All important human characteristics are epigenetic including diseases known to be inherited, such as cancer, schizophrenia, and autism spectrum disorder (Kundu, 2013; Plomin et al., 2013). [**Life-Span Link**: Epigenetics is introduced in Chapter 1.]

Diabetes is a notable example. Many Americans, perhaps one in every four, inherit genes that put them at risk for type 2 (non-juvenile) diabetes, but they do not necessarily become diabetic. Lifestyle—especially poor nutrition and lack of exercise—activates genetic risk. Then, if diabetes emerges, it may cause epigenetic changes that continue for the rest of life (Reddy & Natarajan, 2013).

One intervention—surgery to dramatically reduce weight—may reduce diabetes. One study found that diabetes disappeared after bariatric surgery in most (72 percent) obese patients. Diet, exercise, and emotional health are crucial, however, because the genes have already been activated. In more than half of those 72 percent, diabetes returned: Epigenetic changes can be controlled but not erased (Sjöström et al., 2014).

Other research also found that bariatric surgery dramatically reduced diabetes but increased depression, with about 1 percent of the patients committing suicide (Adams et al., 2017). Some of that may because surgery led to opioid use and addiction, which again affects the genes. Obesity may produce epigenetic changes that affect future generations (Chapman et al., 2017).

That is true for other developmental changes over the life span. Drug use—cocaine, cigarettes, alcohol, and so on—seem to produce epigenetic changes that make addiction likely. That continues if a person has stopped using the drug for years (Bannon et al., 2014). Once addiction has occurred, addicts can never use the drug as they did before.

From Zygote to Newborn

Stunningly fast growth occurs before birth. You have already read that this growth is the result of rapidly multiplying cells, directed by genes, influenced by the prenatal environment. Now some details.

The First 14 Days

The first two weeks are called the **germinal period,** when the single cell, smaller than the period at the end of this sentence, germinates into an embryo with thousands of cells. Within hours after conception, the zygote begins *duplication* and *division.*

First, the 23 pairs of chromosomes duplicate, forming two complete sets of the genes contained within the developing organism (except for monozygotic twins, as already explained). These two new cells duplicate and divide, becoming four, which in turn duplicate and divide, becoming eight, each with the original genotype.

After about the eight-cell stage, a third process, *differentiation,* joins duplication and division. In differentiation, cells specialize, taking different forms and reproducing at various rates, depending on where they are located. They are no longer omnipotent stem cells that could develop into a new person. About a week after conception, the multiplying cells (now numbering more than 100) separate into two distinct masses.

The outer cells form a shell that will become the *placenta* (the organ that surrounds and protects the developing creature). It grows first because it must nourish the future embryo and then the fetus for the entire prenatal period.

germinal period
The first two weeks of prenatal development after conception, characterized by rapid cell division and the beginning of cell differentiation.

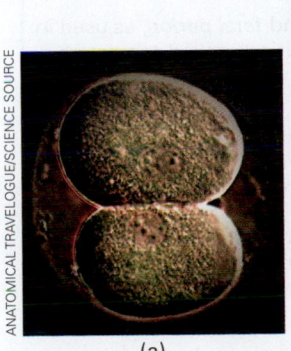

(a) (b) (c)

ANATOMICAL TRAVELOGUE/SCIENCE SOURCE

First Stages of the Germinal Period
The original zygote as it divides into *(a)* two cells, *(b)* four cells, and *(c)* eight cells. Occasionally at this early stage, the cells separate completely, forming the beginning of monozygotic twins, quadruplets, or octuplets.

implantation
The process, beginning about 10 days after conception, in which the developing organism burrows into the uterus, where it can be nourished and protected as it continues to develop.

embryo
The name for a developing human organism from about the third week through the eighth week after conception.

The first task of those outer cells is **implantation**—that is, to embed themselves in the lining of the uterus. This is far from automatic; half of all conceptions do not implant. Most new life ends before an embryo begins (Sadler, 2015). Successful implantation allows the cell mass to tap into nourishment from the mother's uterine wall, beginning the interdependence of mother and child.

Embryo: From the Third Through the Eighth Week

After implantation, the *embryonic period begins*. The formless mass of cells becomes a distinct being—not yet recognizably human but with a new name, **embryo.** (The word *embryo* is often used loosely, but each stage has a particular name. Here, embryo refers to the developing human from day 14 to day 56.) (See Table 2.2.)

DAY BY DAY Each day brings new growth in the embryo. At about day 14, a thin line called the *primitive streak* appears down the middle of the cell mass; it forms the neural tube 22 days after conception. The neural tube develops into the central nervous system (i.e., the brain and spinal column) (Sadler, 2015). Soon the head appears, as eyes, ears, nose, and mouth start to form and a minuscule blood vessel that will become the heart begins to pulsate.

By the fifth week, buds that will become arms and legs emerge. Upper arms and then forearms, palms, and webbed fingers grow. Legs, knees, feet, and webbed toes, in that order, appear a few days later, each with the beginning of a skeleton. Then, 52 and 54 days after conception, respectively, the fingers and toes separate (Sadler, 2015).

At the end of the eighth week after conception (56 days), the embryo weighs just one-thirtieth of an ounce (1 gram) and is about 1 inch (2½ centimeters) long. It moves frequently, about 150 times per hour, but the movement is imperceptible to

---

TABLE 2.2 Timing and Terminology

Popular and professional books use various phrases to segment the stages of pregnancy. The following comments may help to clarify the phrases used.

- *Beginning of pregnancy:* Pregnancy begins at conception, which is also the starting point of *gestational age*. However, the organism does not become an *embryo* until about two weeks later, and pregnancy does not affect the woman (and is not confirmed by blood or urine testing) until implantation. Perhaps because the exact date of conception is usually unknown, some obstetricians and publications count from the woman's last menstrual period (LMP), usually about 14 days *before* conception.

- *Length of pregnancy:* Full-term pregnancies last 266 days, or 38 weeks, or 9 months. If the LMP is used as the starting time, pregnancy lasts 40 weeks, sometimes expressed as 10 lunar months. (A lunar month is 28 days long.)

- *Trimesters:* Instead of *germinal period, embryonic period,* and *fetal period,* as used in this text, some writers divide pregnancy into three-month periods called *trimesters.* Months 1, 2, and 3 are called the *first trimester;* months 4, 5, and 6, the *second trimester;* and months 7, 8, and 9, the *third trimester.*

- *Due date:* Although a specific due date based on the LMP is calculated, only 5 percent of babies are born on that exact day. Babies born between two weeks before and one week after that date are considered *full term.* [This is recent; until 2012, three weeks before and two weeks after were considered full term.] Because of increased risks for postmature babies, labor is often induced if the baby has not arrived within seven days after the due date, although many midwives and doctors prefer to wait to see whether labor begins spontaneously.

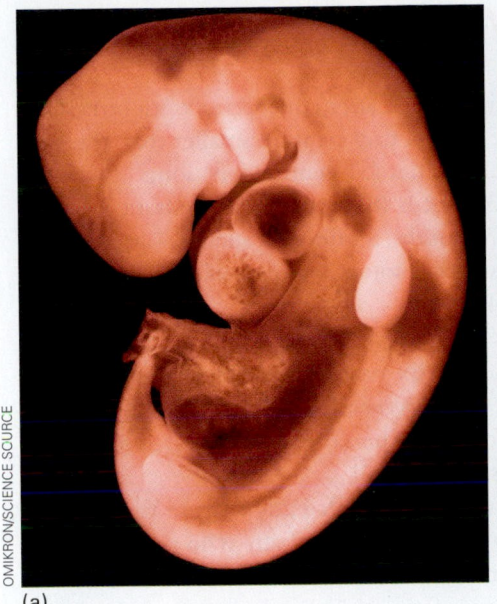

(a)

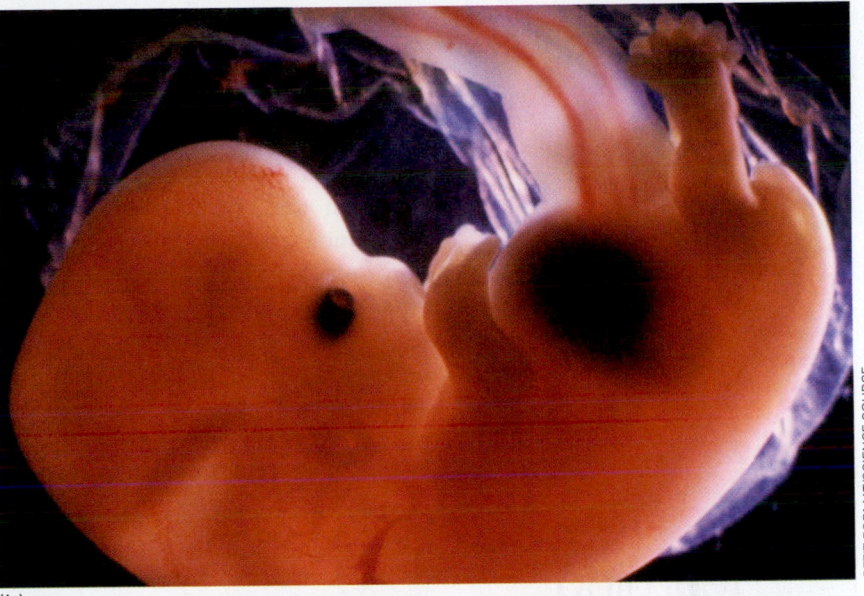

(b)

OMIKRON/SCIENCE SOURCE

PETIT FORMAT/SCIENCE SOURCE

the woman. Random arm and leg movements are more frequent early in pregnancy than later on (Rakic et al., 2016). By 8 weeks, the developing person has all of the organs and body parts of a human being, including elbows and knees.

The early embryo has both male (via *Wolffian ducts*) and female (via *Müllerian ducts*) potential, in a tiny intersex gonad. At the end of the embryonic period, hormonal and genetic influences typically cause one or the other to shrink, and then ovaries or testes, and a vagina or penis, grow from that omnipotent gonad (Zhao et al., 2017). As already mentioned, one gene—the SRY gene on the Y chromosome—is particularly influential, making the fetus become male. Rarely (less than 1 percent of the time), the process goes awry, and a fetus develops with traces of both male and female organs and brain organization.

PRENATAL TESTING Seeing a medical professional during the period of the embryo has many benefits: Women learn what to eat, what to do, and what to avoid. Some serious conditions, syphilis and HIV among them, can be diagnosed and treated, protecting the future fetus. A flu shot may increase immunity in the newborn. Prenatal tests (of blood, urine, and fetal heart rate) reassure parents, facilitating the crucial parent–child bond long before fetal movement is apparent.

In general, early care protects fetal growth, makes birth easier, and renders parents better able to cope. An **ultrasound** (sound waves that detect shape, also called *sonogram*) reveals growth and position. When complications appear (such as twins, gestational diabetes, and infections), early recognition increases the chance of a healthy birth.

Unfortunately, however, about 20 percent of early pregnancy tests *raise* anxiety instead of reducing it. It is now possible to use a simple blood test to indicate many chromosomal and genetic problems. The mother may learn information that she does not want to know (de Jong et al., 2015). Couples may argue about risks that they never discussed before.

One specific example comes from a test in place for decades: alpha–fetoprotein (AFP). If it is too high or too low, it may indicate multiple fetuses, abnormal growth, or Down syndrome. Many such warnings are **false positives;** that is, they falsely suggest a problem that does not exist. Any warning, whether false or true, requires further testing, worry, and soul-searching.

The Embryonic Period *(a)* At 4 weeks past conception, the embryo is only about 1/8 inch (3 millimeters) long, but already the head has taken shape. *(b)* By 7 weeks, the organism is somewhat less than an inch (2 centimeters) long. Eyes, nose, the digestive system, and even the first stage of toe formation can be seen.

COURTESY OF MANDY MCGUINNESS

Meet Your Baby The photo at the left is Elisa Clare McGuinness at 22 weeks postconception. She continued to develop well for the next four months, becoming a healthy, 3,572-gram newborn, finally able to meet her family—two parents and an older brother.

ultrasound
An image of a fetus (or an internal organ) produced by using high-frequency sound waves. (Also called *sonogram*.)

false positive
The result of a laboratory test that reports something as true when in fact it is not true. This can occur for pregnancy tests, when a woman might not be pregnant even though the test says she is, or during pregnancy, when a problem is reported that actually does not exist.

Fetus: From the Ninth Week Until Birth

The organism is called a **fetus** from the ninth week after conception until birth. The fetal period encompasses dramatic change, from a tiny creature smaller than the final joint of your thumb to a newborn about 20 inches (51 centimeters) long.

At 3 months, the fetus weighs about 3 ounces (87 grams) and is about 3 inches (7.5 centimeters) long. Those numbers—3 months, 3 ounces, 3 inches—are rounded off for easy recollection, but growth rates vary—some 3-month-old fetuses are not quite 3 ounces and others already weigh 4.

Mid-pregnancy (months 4, 5, and 6) is the period of the greatest brain growth of the entire life span. The brain increases about six times in size and develops many new neurons (*neurogenesis*) and synapses (*synaptogenesis*), and it divides into hemispheres (O'Rahilly & Müller, 2012). Before this, the cortex had been smooth, but now the brain folds and wrinkles to fit inside the head.

At about 22 weeks past conception, the brain is sufficiently mature to reach the **age of viability,** when a fetus born early might become a baby who survives. Note that brain maturation, not body size, is crucial: Twins born at 22 weeks sometimes survive, although they weigh less than a single fetus that young.

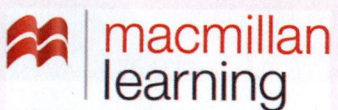

VIDEO: Brain Development Animation: Prenatal shows how the brain develops from just after conception until birth.

Thanks to intensive medical care, the age of viability decreased dramatically in the twentieth century, from 7 months to 5, but it seems stuck at 22 weeks because even the most advanced technology cannot maintain life without some brain response. Much better, of course, is for growth to continue in the uterus for another 16 weeks or so.

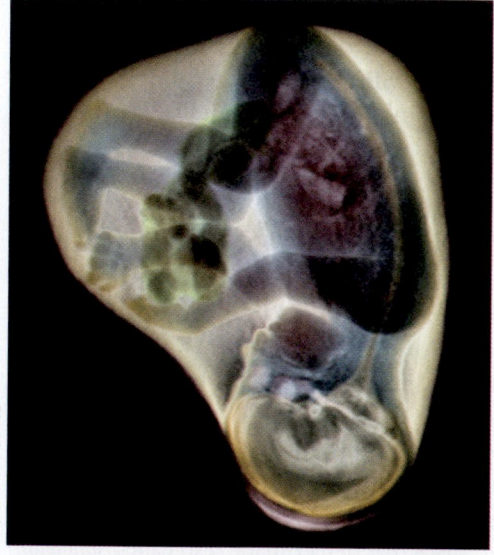

SPL/SCIENCE SOURCE

In the last trimester (months 7, 8, and 9) organs mature, weight is gained (an ounce a day!), and the fetus prepares for life outside the uterus with no medical help needed. The fetus practices breathing by swallowing fluid and then breathing it out, the eyes and ears prepare to see and hear, and, if the fetus is male, the testicles descend. The heart is one of the first organs to begin functioning (at about 5 weeks) and continues to mature throughout pregnancy, beating at a slower rate at birth (between 100 and 145 beats per minute) than at the beginning of the fetal period (about 200 beats per minute). Birth itself is described at the end of this chapter.

Ready for Birth? We hope not, but this fetus at 27 weeks postconception is viable, although very small. At full term (38 weeks), weight gain would mean that the limbs are folded close to the body, and the uterus is almost completely full.

what have you learned?

1. What must happen before the developing organism is called an embryo?
2. When and how do sex organs develop?
3. What brain growth occurs during prenatal development?
4. What are the arguments for and against prenatal testing?
5. What must happen before a fetus is viable?
6. Why is the age of viability unlikely to fall below 22 weeks?
7. What happens to the fetus in the final trimester?

Problems and Solutions

Those early months place the future person on the path toward health and success—or not. Sometimes inherited disorders, or unfavorable prenatal life, or a difficult birth, affect a person lifelong. Fortunately, healthy newborns are the norm, not the exception. However, if something is amiss, it may be part of a cascade of problems that begins at conception (Rossignol et al., 2014).

Chromosomal Anomalies

The sperm and ova do not always carry exactly 23 chromosomes; about half of all zygotes have more than or fewer than 46 chromosomes (Milunsky & Milunsky, 2016). Almost always they fail to duplicate, divide, differentiate, and implant, and they are spontaneously aborted before anyone knows that conception occurred.

If implantation does occur, many embryos with chromosomal miscounts are aborted, either by nature (miscarried) or by choice. Ninety-nine percent of fetuses that survive until birth have the usual 46 chromosomes. For the remaining 1 percent, birth is hazardous (Benn, 2016).

Survival is more common if only some cells have 47 chromosomes and the others have 46 (a condition called *mosaicism*), or if only a piece of a chromosome is missing or extra. Advanced analysis suggests that mosaicism of some sort "may represent the rule rather than the exception" (Lupski, 2013, p. 358). Usually mosaicism has no effect, although cancer in adulthood is more likely.

If an entire chromosome is missing or added, that leads to a recognizable *syndrome*, a cluster of distinct characteristics that tend to occur together. Usually the cause is three chromosomes at a particular location instead of the typical two (a condition called a *trisomy*).

DOWN SYNDROME The most common extra-chromosome condition that results in a surviving child is Down syndrome, with three chromosomes at the 21st site.

Universal Happiness All young children delight in painting brightly colored pictures on a big canvas, but this scene is unusual for two reasons: Daniel has trisomy-21, and this photograph was taken at the only school in Chile where typical children and those with special needs share classrooms.

↑OBSERVATION QUIZ
How many characteristics can you see that indicate Daniel has Down syndrome? (see answer, page 79)

REUTERS/CLAUDIA DAUT

In 1868, Dr. Langdon Down and his wife opened a home for such children (then called "Mongolian Idiots"), proving that they could be quite capable. The World Health Organization officially named trisomy-21 *Down syndrome* in 1965.

Some 300 distinct characteristics can result from trisomy-21. No individual with Down syndrome is identical to another, but this trisomy usually produces telltale physical characteristics—a thick tongue, round face, and slanted eyes, as well as distinctive hands, feet, and fingerprints. The brain is somewhat smaller; the *hippocampus* (important for memory) is especially affected.

Many people with Down syndrome also have hearing problems, heart abnormalities, muscle weakness, and short stature. They are slow to develop intellectually, especially in language, with a notable deficit in hearing sounds that rhyme (Næss, 2016).

However, remember plasticity. The impact of that third chromosome varies with every step of development, from conception on (Karmiloff-Smith et al., 2016). Always the brain and other organs are affected, but families, teachers, cultural conditions, and public policies are also influential (Kuehn, 2011).

Fifty years ago, most children with Down syndrome died before age 5. Now "people with Down syndrome are achieving success in school and employment and are very satisfied with their lives" (Skotko, quoted in Underwood, 2014, p. 965).

PROBLEMS AT THE 23RD PAIR Every human has at least 44 autosomes and one X chromosome; an embryo cannot develop without those 45. However, about 1 in every 300 infants is born with only one sex chromosome (no Y) or with three or more (not just two) (Benn, 2016). Each particular combination of sex chromosomes results in a particular syndrome (see Table 2.3).

Having an odd number of sex chromosomes impairs cognition and sexual maturation, with varied specifics (Hong & Reiss, 2014). It is not unusual for affected people to seem to be typical until adulthood, when they consult a doctor because they are infertile.

◆ Especially for Teachers

Suppose you know that one of your students has a sibling who has Down syndrome. What special actions should you take? (see response, page 79)

TABLE 2.3 Common Abnormalities Involving the Sex Chromosomes

Chromosomal Pattern	Physical Appearance	Psychological Characteristics	Incidence*
XXY (Klinefelter syndrome)	Males. Typical male characteristics at puberty do not develop—penis does not grow, voice does not deepen. Usually sterile. Breasts may develop.	Can have some learning disabilities, especially in language skills.	1 in 700 males
XYY (Jacob's syndrome)	Males. Typically tall.	Risk of intellectual impairment, especially in language skills.	1 in 1,000 males
XXX (Triple X syndrome)	Females. Typical appearance.	Impaired in most intellectual skills.	1 in 1,000 females
XO (only one sex chromosome) (Turner syndrome)	Females. Short, often "webbed" neck. Secondary sex characteristics (breasts, menstruation) do not develop.	Some learning disabilities, especially related to math and spatial understanding; difficulty recognizing facial expressions of emotion.	1 in 6,000 females

*Incidence is approximate at birth.

Information from Hamerton & Evans, 2005; Aksglaede et al., 2013; Powell, 2013; Benn, 2016.

Gene Disorders

If all anomalies and disorders are included, 92 percent of people do not develop a serious genetic condition by early adulthood—but that means 8 percent have a notable problem in their phenotype as well as their genotype (Chong et al., 2015). Everyone carries about 40 alleles that *could* cause serious disease. The phenotype is affected only when:

- the inherited gene is dominant, or
- a zygote received the same recessive gene from both parents, or
- multiple additive genes combine to cause a problem.

DOMINANT OR RECESSIVE? Most of the 7,000 *known* single-gene disorders are dominant (always expressed) (Milunsky & Milunsky, 2016). Most dominant disorders are relatively mild; severe ones are infrequent because children with a severe disorder usually die before puberty, and thus they never pass on that lethal gene.

However, a few dominant disorders are latent until adulthood. One is *Huntington's disease,* a fatal central nervous system disorder caused by a copy number variation—more than 35 repetitions of a particular set of three base pairs.

Although children with the dominant gene sometimes are affected (Milunsky & Milunsky, 2016), definite symptoms first appear in midlife. By then, a person could have had many children. Half of their children would inherit the dominant gene and thus develop Huntington's disease.

Recessive diseases are more numerous than dominant ones because they are passed down by carriers who are not affected. Most recessive disorders are on the autosomes and thus are not X-linked, which means that either parent could be a carrier (Milunsky & Milunsky, 2016). Only in the rare case when two carriers have a child who inherits the double recessive (true for one child in four when both parents are carriers) is the gene expressed. There are thousands of recessive diseases; advance carrier detection is currently possible for only several hundred.

A few recessive conditions are X-linked, which means they are carried on the X chromosome. One is *fragile X syndrome,* which is caused by more than 200 repetitions of one gene (Plomin et al., 2013). (Some repetitions are normal, but not this

Visit the **DATA CONNECTIONS ACTIVITY: Common Genetic Diseases and Conditions** to learn more about several different types of gene disorders.

Who Has the Fatal Dominant Disease? The mother, but not the children. Unless a cure is found, Amanda Kalinsky will grow weak and experience significant cognitive decline, dying before age 60. She and her husband, Bradley, wanted children without Amanda's dominant gene for a rare disorder, Gerstmann-Straussler-Scheinker disease. Accordingly, they used IVF and pre-implantation testing. Only zygotes without the dominant gene were implanted. This photo shows the happy result.

many.) The cognitive deficits caused by fragile X syndrome are the most common form of *inherited* intellectual disability. (Many forms are not usually inherited.) Boys are more often impaired by fragile X than are girls, because they have only one X.

THE MOST COMMON GENETIC DISORDERS About 1 in 12 North American men and women carries an allele for cystic fibrosis, thalassemia, or sickle-cell disease, all devastating in children who inherit the recessive gene from both parents. These conditions are common because carriers have benefited from the gene.

Consider the most studied example: sickle-cell disease. Carriers die less often from malaria. Indeed, four distinct alleles cause sickle-cell anemia, each originating in a malaria-prone region.

Selective adaptation allowed those alleles to become widespread because more people (the carriers) were protected than died (those who inherited the recessive gene from both parents). Odds were that if a couple were both carriers and had four children, one would die of sickle-cell disease, one would not be a carrier and thus might die of malaria, but two would be carriers, protected against a common, fatal disease. They would be more likely to survive to adulthood and become parents. In that way, the recessive trait became widespread.

Almost every disease and risk of death is more common in one group than in another (Weiss & Koepsell, 2014). Whenever a particular genetic condition is common, there are benefits for carriers. About 11 percent of Americans with African ancestors have the recessive gene for sickle-cell disease—they are protected against malaria. Cystic fibrosis is more common among Americans with ancestors from northern Europe; carriers may have been protected from cholera.

Benefits are apparent for additive genes as well. Dark skin is protective against skin cancer, and light skin allows more vitamin D to be absorbed from the sun—a benefit if a baby lives where sunlight is scarce or if cold weather causes everyone to cover up. Modern Europeans inherited between 1 and 4 percent of their genes from Neandertals, who became extinct about 30,000 years ago. Those genes protect contemporary humans against some skin conditions and other diseases but may also increase vulnerability to allergies and depression—depending on which Neandertal genes they inherit (Saey, 2016).

Double Trouble or Genetic Joy? Six-year-old Ethan Dean inherited two recessive genes for cystic fibrosis. That may prevent him from fulfilling his wish—to become a garbage man. But another genetic trait is evident: Humans want to care for children, especially those with deadly conditions. The Sacramento Department of Sanitation, and the Make-a-Wish Foundation, gave Ethan a day collecting trash, to his apparent delight.

SPONTANEOUS MUTATIONS Many genetic and chromosomal problems are spontaneous mutations (Arnheim & Calabrese, 2016; Reilly & Noonan, 2016). They are not present in the parents' genes, and thus they could not be predicted in advance. Nor are they likely to reappear in future embryos. Spontaneous mutations are more likely if the parents have been exposed to various pollutants or radiation, which then affects the sperm, ova, or zygote (Cassina et al., 2017).

Age matters, too: The frequency of chromosomal miscounts rises when the mother is over age 35; genetic mutations increase in the sperm when the father is over age 40. This does not mean that older parents should not have children: Serious problems are unusual no matter how old the parents are.

Nature aborts many such embryos early in pregnancy (one reason an early miscarriage is not necessarily a tragedy). Many other mutations are harmless. Some mutations are helpful and become more common in later generations, as with lactose tolerance.

However, some spontaneous mutations result in severe disabilities, indistinguishable from inherited disabilities except with genetic analysis. For parents of such children, genetic testing and counseling are especially helpful.

Genetic Counseling

Professionals who provide **genetic counseling** help prospective parents understand their genetic risk so that they can make informed decisions, not impulsive, irrational ones. They advise about special hazards, precautions, and treatments, before conception, during pregnancy, and after birth.

The genetic counselor's task is complicated. New genetic disorders—and treatments—are revealed almost weekly. For example, an inherited disorder that once meant lifelong neurological impairment (e.g., phenylketonuria, or PKU) might now mean a normal life.

Most parents need guidance in order to interpret the results of testing. For example, a particular gene may increase risk by only a tiny amount, perhaps 0.1 percent, and another genetic combination leads to a 50/50 chance of a severely disabled child. In both cases, the emotional impact of knowing that one's child might suffer leads some prospective parents to ignore the data and others to exaggerate the risks.

Consider the experience of one of my students. A month before she became pregnant, Jeannette's employer required her to have a rubella vaccination. Hearing that Jeannette had had the shot, her obstetrician gave her the following prognosis:

> My baby would be born with many defects, his ears would not be normal, he would be intellectually disabled. . . . I went home and cried for hours and hours. . . . I finally went to see a genetic counselor. Everything was fine, thank the Lord, thank you, my beautiful baby is okay.
>
> *[Jeannette, personal communication]*

Jeannette may have misunderstood what she was told, but that is exactly why a genetic counselor, trained to make information clear, is needed—especially for:

- women who fear that something they did or experienced affected a future or developing embryo;
- individuals who have a parent, sibling, or child with a serious genetic condition;
- couples who have had several spontaneous abortions or stillbirths;
- couples who are infertile;
- women over age 35 and men over age 40; and
- couples from the same ethnic group, particularly if they are relatives.

The latter is especially crucial among populations who often intermarry. This is true for Greeks in Cyprus, where about one-third of the population carries the recessive gene for thalassemia (either A or B). In the 1970s, one baby in 158 was born with serious thalassemia, which led to repeated hospitalization and premature death. Then Cyprus encouraged everyone to be tested, before conception or at least prenatally. Now virtually no newborns in Cyprus have the condition (Hvistendahl, 2013).

Prenatal Harm

Often an embryo with no genetic disorders implants and starts to grow, but then something in the prenatal environment affects growth. Every week, scientists discover another **teratogen,** which is anything—drugs, viruses, pollutants, malnutrition, stress, and more—that could harm an embryo or fetus.

VIDEO: Genetic Testing examines the pros and cons of knowing what diseases may eventually harm us or our offspring.

THINK CRITICALLY: Instead of genetic counseling, should we advocate health counseling?

genetic counseling
Consultation and testing by trained experts that enable individuals to learn about their genetic heritage, including harmful conditions that they might pass along to any children they may conceive.

teratogen
An agent or condition, including viruses, drugs, and chemicals, that can impair prenatal development and result in birth defects or even death.

A CASE TO STUDY

Blame the Mother?

About 20 percent of all children have difficulties that *could* be connected to teratogens. Almost every mother, noticing something amiss in her child, remembers something during pregnancy that was not optimal. Easy to remember is drug use, poor nutrition, or illness, but if that was not the case, the mother remembers being tired, or stressed, or exposed to some toxic chemical (from pesticides to cosmetics).

My adult daughter told me that her dentist said her gums were inflamed. My first thought was that I didn't drink enough milk when I was pregnant with her. She said, "Mom, if you are going to react that way, I will stop telling you about my health." She is right. As a culture we have zigzagged from thinking that the placenta protects against all harm to thinking that prenatal care determines everything, blaming mothers whenever something is amiss.

One of my students wrote:

I was nine years old when my mother announced she was pregnant. I was the one who was most excited. . . . My mother was a heavy smoker, Colt 45 beer drinker and a strong caffeine coffee drinker.

One day my mother was sitting at the dining room table smoking cigarettes one after the other. I asked, "Isn't smoking bad for the baby?" She made a face and said, "Yes, so what?"

I asked, "So why are you doing it?"

She said, "I don't know." . . .

During this time I was in the fifth grade and we saw a film about birth defects. My biggest fear was that my mother was going to give birth to a fetal alcohol syndrome (FAS) infant. . . . My baby brother was born right on schedule. The doctors claimed a healthy newborn. . . . Once I heard healthy, I thought everything was going to be fine. I was wrong, then again I was just a child. . . .

My baby brother never showed any interest in toys . . . he just cannot get the right words out of his mouth . . . he has no common sense . . .

Why hurt those who cannot defend themselves?

[J., personal communication]

J. blames her mother. Is that fair? Not only several teratogens but also genetic risks, inadequate prenatal care, and troubling postnatal experiences are part of her brother's sorry cascade. It is hard to separate out each risk. Should we blame the doctor who provided false reassurance? Could immediate intervention after birth have reduced the impact?

No One Knows Dozens of newborns in northern Brazil led doctors to discover that mosquitos carrying the Zika virus could cause microcephaly (small heads). More is now known: Zika brain damage is sometimes invisible, and newborns in North, Central, and South America are affected. However, certain diagnosis and long-term damage are still unknown. No wonder these pregnant women in a clinic in Colombia are worried, especially Sandra Ovallos (in the middle), who recently had a fever and a rash.

One complication is that newborns may appear to have escaped a teratogen (such as alcohol that causes facial deformities or rubella that causes blindness), but the brain is nonetheless damaged. Thousands of babies whose pregnant mothers drank alcohol only on weekends appear normal. They may nonetheless be affected by fetal alcohol spectrum disorders (Hoyme et al., 2016).

The long reach of a seemingly harmless teratogen (in this case, from a mosquito bite) is evident in the Zika virus, which caught the attention of obstetricians in 2015 in Brazil when several babies were born with abnormally small brains (*microcephaly*). Zika was then diagnosed in thousands of other Brazilian infants and then spread north, to many other South American and North American nations, including in the southeastern United States and in Puerto Rico.

We now know that Zika affects newborns who appear normal. Their senses and emotions are impaired (they are very irritable) (Rosen, 2016; Van den Pol et al., 2017).

Who is to blame? The mosquitos, the women who got bitten, the lack of family planning, the economy that results in homes without window screens, the public health officials who were slow to recognize the problem, the political leaders who did not instigate prevention, the scientists who have not found a vaccination? All of us?

Some teratogens cause no physical defects but affect the brain, making a child hyperactive, antisocial, or intellectually disabled. These are **behavioral teratogens.**

Behavioral teratogens can be subtle, yet their effects last a lifetime. That is one conclusion from longitudinal research on the babies born to women exposed to the influenza pandemic in 1918. By middle age, those born in flu-ravaged regions averaged less education, more unemployment, and lower income than those born a year earlier (Almond, 2006). They died a few years sooner than those born in 1917 or 1919. No fetus exposed to the flu lived to 100, although centenarians are the fastest growing age group.

OVERALL HEALTH Regarding prenatal health, women who maintain good nutrition and avoid drugs and teratogenic chemicals (often found in pesticides, cleaning fluids, and cosmetics) usually have healthy babies. Some medications are necessary (e.g., for women with epilepsy, diabetes, and severe depression), but advice regarding specific drugs should occur *before* conception.

Many women assume that herbal medicines or over-the-counter drugs are safe. Not so. As pediatrics professor Allen Mitchell explains, "Many over-the-counter drugs were grandfathered in with no studies of their possible effects during pregnancy" (quoted in Brody, 2013, p. D5). ("Grandfathered" means that if they were legal in days past, they remain legal—no modern testing needed.)

Sadly, a cascade of teratogens often begins with women who are already vulnerable and who have no preconception care. For example, smokers are more often drinkers (as was J.'s mother in A Case to Study), and migrant workers are more often exposed to chemicals and pesticides, and they rarely have early prenatal care.

EXPERT ADVICE Although prenatal care may protect the developing fetus, even doctors are not always careful. One concern is pain medication. Opioids (narcotics) may damage the fetus. Yet, one study found that 23 percent of pregnant women on Medicaid were given a prescription for a narcotic (Desai et al., 2014). Hopefully, the prescribing doctor didn't realize the patient was pregnant, and the women didn't take the drug.

Worse still is that some obstetricians do not ask about harmful life patterns. For example, one Maryland study found that almost one-third of pregnant women were not asked about alcohol (Cheng et al., 2011). Those who were over age 35 and who were college-educated were least likely to be queried. Did their doctors assume they

behavioral teratogens
Agents and conditions that can harm the prenatal brain, impairing the future child's intellectual and emotional functioning.

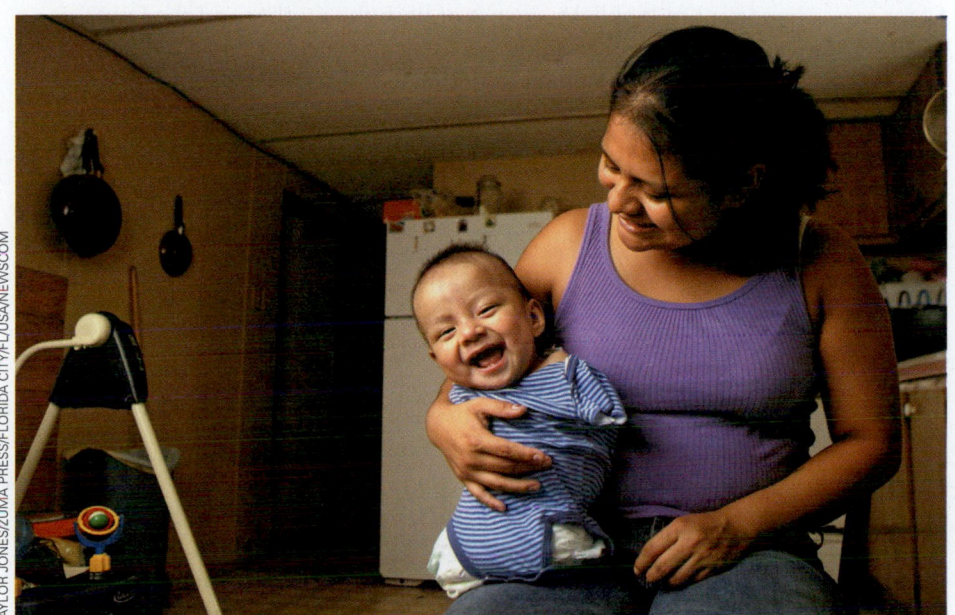

No More Pesticides Carlos Candelario, shown here at age 9 months, was born without limbs, a birth defect that occurred when his mother (Francisca, show here) and father (Abraham) worked in the Florida fields. Since his birth in 2004, laws prohibit spraying pesticides while people pick fruit and vegetables, but developmentalists worry about the effect of the residue on developing brains.

Welcome Home For many women in the United States, white wine is part of the celebration and joy of a house party, as shown here. Most people can drink alcohol harmlessly; there is no sign that these women are problem drinkers. However, danger lurks. Women get drunk on less alcohol than men, and females with alcohol use disorder tend to drink more privately and secretly, often at home, feeling more shame than bravado. All of that makes their addiction more difficult to recognize.

HERO IMAGES INC./ALAMY

◆ **Especially for Judges and Juries**
How much protection, if any, should the legal system provide for fetuses? Should women with alcohol use disorder who are pregnant be jailed to prevent them from drinking? What about people who enable them to drink, such as their partners, their parents, bar owners, and bartenders? (see response, page 79)

fetal alcohol syndrome (FAS)
A cluster of birth defects, including abnormal facial characteristics, slow physical growth, and reduced intellectual ability, that may occur in the fetus of a woman who drinks alcohol while pregnant.

DATA CONNECTIONS ACTIVITY: Teratogens examines both the effects of various teratogens and the preventive measures that mitigate their risk to a developing fetus.

already avoided that teratogen? If so, they were wrong. Older, educated women are the most likely to drink during pregnancy. The rate for pregnant woman overall is 10 percent, but the rate for older pregnant women is 19 percent and for college-educated women, 13 percent (Tan et al., 2015).

To learn what medications are safe, pregnant women often consult the Internet. However, a study of 25 Web sites that, together, approved 235 medications found that TERIS (expert teratologists who analyze drug safety) had declared only 60 (25 percent) safe. The rest were not *proven* harmful, but TERIS found insufficient evidence to confirm safety (Peters et al., 2013). Those 25 Internet sites sometimes used unreliable data: Some drugs on the safe list of one site were on the danger list of another.

GENES AND PRENATAL HEALTH Preventing harm to developing persons is multifaceted, certainly involving public health, pollution, and every family member. Specifics about the many teratogens could easily fill a book. In this chapter, one factor seems important to highlight—genes of both the mother and the fetus.

When a woman carrying dizygotic twins drinks alcohol, the umbilical cords deliver equal concentrations of alcohol to both fetuses, yet one may be more severely affected because of different alleles for the enzyme that metabolizes alcohol. Indeed, one twin may be born with all of the signs of **fetal alcohol syndrome (FAS),** including widely spaced eyes, a thin upper lip, feeding difficulties, and frequent crying. The other twin may appear normal but may have difficulty learning to read. Similar differential susceptibility occurs for many teratogens (McCarthy & Eberhart, 2014).

The mother's own genes interacting with her diet may also affect the fetus. One maternal allele results in low levels of folic acid in a woman's bloodstream and hence in the embryo, which can produce *neural-tube defects*—either *spina bifida,* in which the tail of the spine is not enclosed properly (enclosure normally occurs at about week 7), or *anencephaly,* when part of the brain is missing. Neural-tube defects are more common in certain ethnic groups (Irish, English, and Egyptian).

In the United States and 75 other nations (but none in Europe), folic acid is now added to flour, so women who eat cereal, pasta, or bread consume that vitamin—a measure that has reduced the incidence of spina bifida (MMWR, May 7, 2004).

Because of complicated interactions of genes, diet, pollution, drugs, and stress, results of teratogens cannot be predicted precisely for a particular fetus. However, low birthweight increases vulnerability to many hazards.

Low Birthweight: Causes and Consequences

With modern hospital care, babies born too early or too small usually survive, but ideally a newborn weighs at least 2,500 grams and is at least 35 weeks past conception. Ranking worse than most developed nations—and tied with Uruguay, Tanzania, Romania, and Spain—is the United States, whose low-birthweight rate is 46th in the world (World Bank, 2015).

The World Health Organization defines **low birthweight (LBW)** as under 2,500 grams. LBW babies are further grouped into **very low birthweight (VLBW),** under 1,500 grams (3 pounds, 5 ounces), and **extremely low birthweight (ELBW),** under 1,000 grams (2 pounds, 3 ounces). Some viable newborns weigh as little as 500 grams, but even with excellent care, about half of them die and most survivors suffer physical and intellectual disabilities (Lau et al., 2013) (see Figure 2.4).

MATERNAL BEHAVIOR AND LOW BIRTHWEIGHT The causes of LBW are many. Twins and other multiples gain weight more slowly than singletons. Babies born **preterm** (two or more weeks early; no longer called *premature*) are often LBW,

low birthweight (LBW)
A body weight at birth of less than 2,500 grams (5½ pounds).

very low birthweight (VLBW)
A body weight at birth of less than 1,500 grams (3 pounds, 5 ounces).

extremely low birthweight (ELBW)
A body weight at birth of less than 1,000 grams (2 pounds, 3 ounces).

preterm
A birth that occurs two or more weeks before the full 38 weeks of the typical pregnancy—that is, at 36 or fewer weeks after conception.

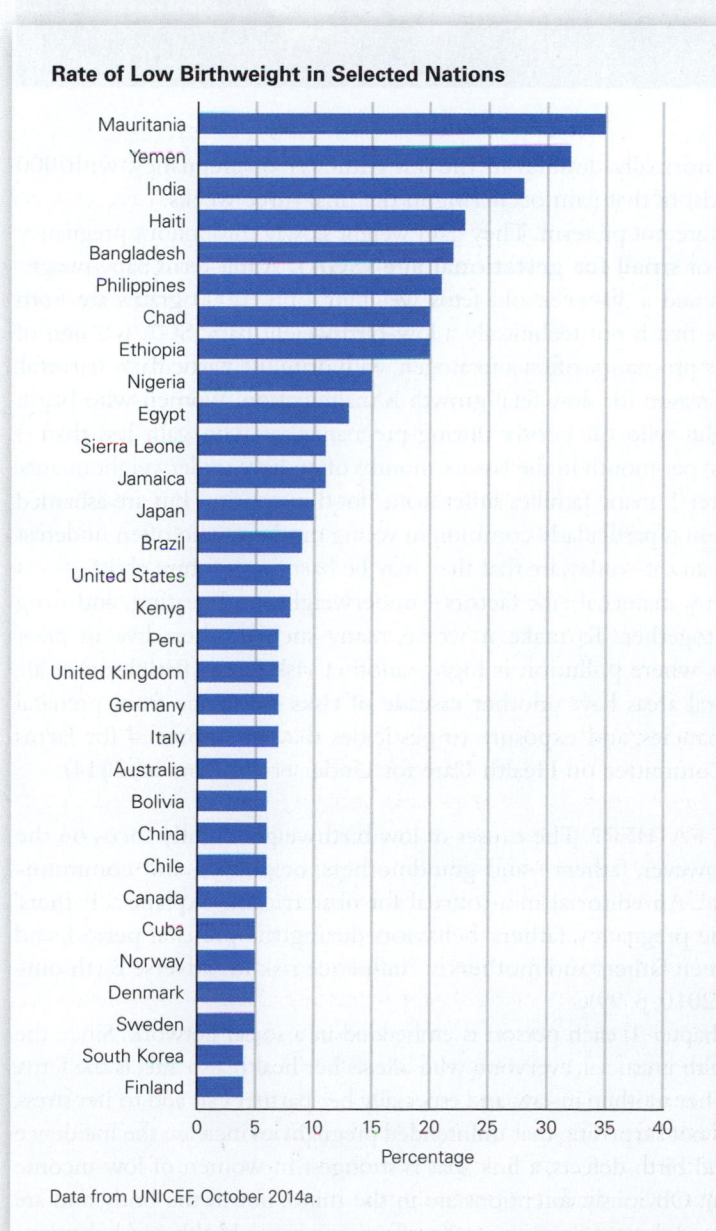

Rate of Low Birthweight in Selected Nations

Data from UNICEF, October 2014a.

FIGURE 2.4 **Getting Better** Some public health experts consider the rate of low birthweight to be indicative of national health, since both are affected by the same causes. If that is true, the world is getting healthier, since the LBW world average was 28 percent in 2009 but 16 percent in 2012. When all nations are included, 47 report LBW at 6 per 100 or lower. (The United States and the United Kingdom are not among them.)

Not the Fetus, the Mother!
Alicia Beltran, age 28, shown here pregnant with her first child, confided at her initial prenatal visit that she had been addicted to a painkiller but was now clean (later confirmed by a lab test). She refused a prescription to keep her away from illegal drugs. But that led to the police taking her to court in handcuffs and shackles when she was 14 weeks pregnant. She was neither represented nor allowed to defend herself, but a state-appointed lawyer for the fetus argued that she should be detained. After more than two months in involuntary confinement, a nonprofit lawyer got her released. More than a year later, a judge finally considered her petition that her constitutional rights had been violated, but the judge dismissed the case because the state had dropped the charges.

DARREN HAUCK/THE NEW YORK TIMES/REDUX

small for gestational age (SGA)
A term for a baby whose birthweight is significantly lower than expected, given the time since conception. For example, a 5-pound (2,265-gram) newborn is considered SGA if born on time but not SGA if born two months early. (Also called *small-for-dates*.)

because fetal weight normally doubles in the last trimester of pregnancy, with 900 grams (about 2 pounds) of that gain occurring in the final three weeks.

Some LBW babies are not preterm. They gain weight slowly throughout pregnancy and are *small-for-dates,* or **small for gestational age (SGA).** A full-term baby weighing only 2,600 grams and a 30-week-old fetus weighing only 1,000 grams are both SGA, even though the first is not technically a low-birthweight baby. SGA is a sign of something amiss in the pregnancy, often a teratogen, with drug use particularly harmful.

Another common reason for slow fetal growth is malnutrition. Women who begin pregnancy underweight, who eat poorly during pregnancy, or who gain less than 3 pounds (1.3 kilograms) per month in the last six months often have underweight infants. As described in Chapter 1, many families suffer from "food insecurity" but are ashamed to admit it. The problem is particularly common in young mothers, who often undereat so that their children can eat—unaware that they may be harming a future child.

Unfortunately, many maternal risk factors—underweight, undereating, and drug use—tend to occur together. To make it worse, many such mothers live in poor urban neighborhoods where pollution is high—another risk factor (Erickson et al., 2016). Women in rural areas have another cascade of risks—distance from prenatal care, unwanted pregnancies, and exposure to pesticides that are approved for farms but not for homes (Committee on Health Care for Underserved Women, 2014).

WHAT ABOUT THE FATHER? The causes of low birthweight rightly focus on the pregnant woman. However, fathers—and grandmothers, neighbors, and communities—are often crucial. An editorial in a journal for obstetricians explains: "Fathers' attitudes regarding the pregnancy, fathers' behaviors during the prenatal period, and the relationship between fathers and mothers . . . influence risk for adverse birth outcomes" (Misra et al., 2010, p. 99).

As explained in Chapter 1, each person is embedded in a social network. Since the pregnant woman's health is crucial, everyone who affects her health also affects the fetus. Her mother, her boss, her mother-in-law, and especially her partner can add to her stress, or reduce it. Thus, it is not surprising that unintended pregnancies increase the incidence of low birthweight and birth defects, a link that is strongest in women of low income (Finer & Zolna, 2016). Obviously, intentions are in the mind, not in the body, and are affected by the father and the community—who affect a woman's health and behavior.

Evidence for this is in the **immigrant paradox.** Many immigrants have difficulty getting education and well-paid jobs; their socioeconomic status is low. Low SES correlates with low birthweight, especially in the United States (Martinson & Reichman, 2016).

Thus, newborns born to immigrants are predicted to be underweight. But, paradoxically, they are not. They generally are heavier and healthier than newborns of U.S.-born women from the same income and gene pool (García Coll & Marks, 2012).

This paradox was first called the *Hispanic paradox,* because babies born to immigrants from Mexico or South America have fewer problems at birth than those born to Hispanics whose families have lived in the United States for generations. The same paradox is now apparent for immigrants from the Caribbean, Africa, eastern Europe, and Asia compared to U.S.-born women with ancestors from those places.

Why? One hypothesis is that fathers, other relatives, and cultural values are protective. Immigrant fathers tend to be very solicitous of their pregnant wives, keeping them drug-free, appreciated, and healthy, thus buffering the stress that poverty brings (Luecken et al., 2013).

CONSEQUENCES OF LOW BIRTHWEIGHT Life itself is uncertain for the smallest newborns. If they survive, every developmental milestone—smiling, holding a bottle, walking, talking—is delayed. On average, they experience cognitive difficulties as well as visual and hearing impairments. High-risk newborns become children who cry often, pay attention less, and disobey more (Aarnoudse-Moens et al., 2009; Stolt et al., 2014).

Problems continue. Children who were extremely SGA or preterm tend to have neurological impairments in middle childhood, including smaller brain volume, lower IQ, and behavioral difficulties (Clark et al., 2013; Hutchinson et al., 2013; Howe et al., 2016). Even in adulthood, risks persist: Adults who were VLBW are more likely to develop diabetes and heart disease. They also are more likely to become depressed (Lyall et al., 2016).

However, remember plasticity. By age 4, some ELBW infants exhibit typical brain development, especially if they had no medical complications and their mother was well educated. In adulthood, for the fortunate ones, early arrival may no longer be relevant.

immigrant paradox
The surprising, paradoxical fact that low-SES immigrant women tend to have fewer birth complications than native-born peers with higher incomes.

WATCH **VIDEO: Low Birthweight in India,** which discusses the causes of LBW among babies in India.

THINK CRITICALLY: Food scarcity, drug use, and single parenthood have all been suggested as reasons for the LBW rate in the United States. Which is it—or are there other factors?

A VIEW FROM SCIENCE

International Comparisons

As you remember from Chapter 1, scientists collect empirical data and then draw conclusions based on facts. Regarding low birthweight, the facts are clear; the conclusions are not. No less than six hypotheses might explain a puzzling fact: Low birthweight is less common in most nations than it was, but it is increasing in some nations—the United States among them. We begin with what is known.

In some northern European nations, only 4 percent of newborns weigh less than 2,500 grams; in several South Asian and African nations, including India, Pakistan, and Yemen, more than 20 percent do. Two conclusions are proven: First, less malnutrition means fewer hungry women and fewer underweight newborns in 2017 than a decade ago. For example, international records report only 19 deaths in the first month per thousand live births in 2015 compared to 36 such deaths in 1990 (World Bank, 2016).

Second, national goals matter. In China, Cuba, and Chile, low birthweight has plummeted in the twenty-first century because prenatal care has become a national priority. That is one

conclusion of a study, provocatively titled *Low birth weight outcomes: Why better in Cuba than Alabama?* (Neggers & Crowe, 2013).

In other nations, notably in sub-Saharan Africa, the LBW rate is rising because global warming, HIV, food shortages, wars, and other problems affect pregnancy. That distresses but does not puzzle doctors: We already know that pregnant women are particularly likely to suffer during times of war. For instance, low birthweight rates have been rising in the Ukraine, which has been mired in conflict since 2014.

Now the puzzle for scientists: In the United States, the rate fell throughout most of the twentieth century, reaching a low of 7.0 percent in 1990. But then it increased again, with the 2015 rate at 8.0 percent, ranging from less than 6 percent in Alaska to more than 11 percent in Mississippi. The U.S. rate is higher than most other developed nations.

More puzzling is that several changes in maternal ethnicity, age, and health since 1990 should have *decreased* LBW. For instance, although the rate of LBW among African Americans is higher than the national average (13 percent compared with

8 percent), and although teenagers have smaller babies than do women in their 20s, the LBW rate among both groups was much lower in 2015 than it was in 1990.

Similarly, unintended pregnancies are less common (Finer & Zolna, 2016), and two conditions that produce heavier babies (maternal obesity and diabetes) have increased since 1990. Yet, more underweight babies are born in the United States currently than decades ago. How is this explained?

Is prenatal care the crucial variable? Although 11 percent of pregnant Americans do not have adequate, early prenatal care (Partridge et al., 2012), the rates of women giving birth without prenatal care have decreased, so that may not be the reason. Although prenatal care benefits women in many ways, the hypothesis that it reduces LBW seems to have been disproven. Consequently, some scientists suggest that mere accessibility to prenatal care is not enough: Prenatal care needs to be redesigned (Krans & Davis, 2012). Aspects of that redesign are hypotheses that need testing.

Another logical hypothesis is that the United States has many more twin and triplet births because, unlike in most nations with high LBW rates, U.S. laws do not limit how many zygotes are implanted in assisted reproduction. Multiples tend to be of low birthweight. If laws changed, would LBW rates drop? Perhaps. The data confirm that multiple births are one reason that U.S. LBW rates are rising, but it is not the only reason, as rates are rising for naturally conceived singletons as well.

A more general suspect is nutrition. In the United States, the U.S. Department of Agriculture (Coleman-Jensen et al., 2015) reported an increase in the rate of *food insecurity* (measured by skipped meals, use of food stamps, and outright

hunger) between the first seven years of the twenty-first century and the next seven, from about 11 percent to about 15 percent (see Figure 2.5).

A related possibility is lack of health care among the poorest Americans, especially young adults. Since untreated infections and chronic illness correlate with LBW, health care may be an explanation. But again, rates of pregnancy among the ill are not high enough to be the only explanation.

A fifth possible culprit is drug use, which is more common among young women in the United States than in most other nations (Natarajan, 2017). There is good news here: Cigarette smoking is down, which may soon reduce the rate of low birthweight.

Many women quit cigarettes during pregnancy but take up e-cigarettes instead. We do not know how the rising rates of e-cigarette smoking will affect prenatal development. Scientists are watching the evidence. Pregnant smokers themselves are of mixed opinions. Most use cigarettes or other drugs to reduce stress (itself a correlate of low birthweight) (Oncken et al., 2017; Wigginton et al., 2017).

Sadly, cigarette-smoking trends outside of North America are ominous. In Asia, more young women are smoking and drinking than did two decades ago. Two nations where low birthweight is increasing are Korea and Japan; both now have more young women smokers (UNICEF, October 2014a). Correlation or causation?

This view from science illustrates why hundreds of scientists ask questions about the causes of low birthweight: Many hypotheses need testing, rejection, and/or confirmation, benefiting us all.

FIGURE 2.5 And Recovery? As you can see, all family types were affected by the Great Recession that began in 2007—especially single fathers, who were most likely to lose their jobs and not know how to get food stamps. But why are children of single mothers hungry more often than children of single fathers and three times as often as children of married parents? The data show correlation; researchers do not agree about causes.

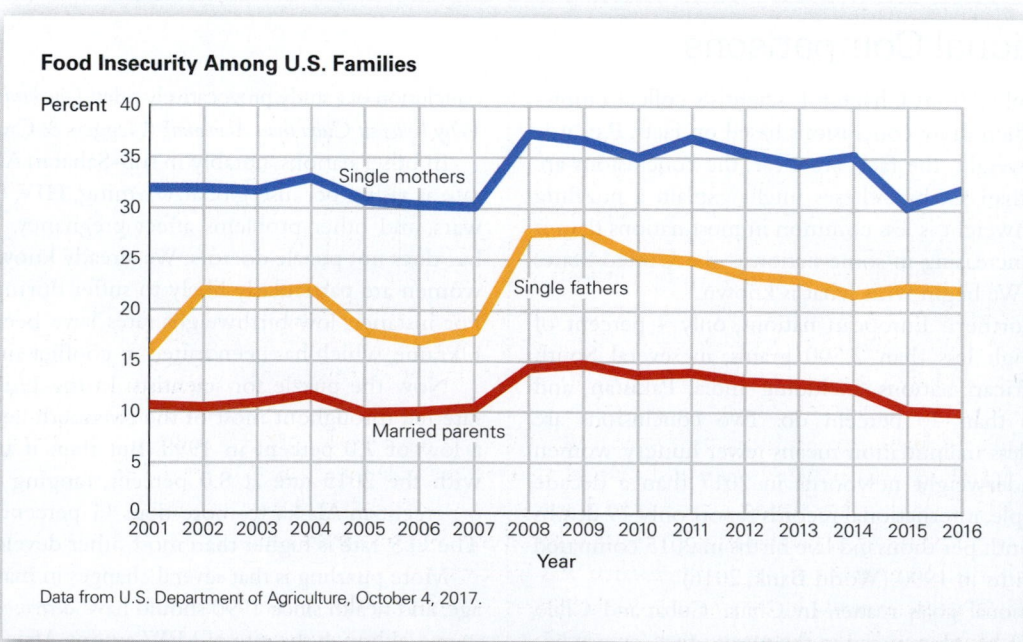

Data from U.S. Department of Agriculture, October 4, 2017.

Finally, a Baby

About 38 weeks (266 days) after conception, the fetal brain signals the release of hormones (especially oxytocin) to start labor. The average baby is born after about 12 hours of active labor for first births and 7 hours for subsequent births, with wide variations. The definition of "active" labor is usually decided by the woman herself, especially since women are encouraged to stay home until contractions are difficult to manage. Some women believe they are in active labor for days, and others say 10 minutes.

Women's birthing positions also vary—sitting, squatting, lying down. Some women give birth while immersed in warm water, which helps the woman relax (the fetus continues to get oxygen via the umbilical cord).

Preferences and opinions on birthing positions are partly cultural and partly personal. In general, physicians find it easier to see the head emerge if the woman lies on her back. However, it is easier for women to push the fetus out if they sit up. (Figure 2.6 shows the stages of birth.)

The Newborn's First Minutes

Newborns usually breathe and cry on their own. Between spontaneous cries, the first breaths of air bring oxygen to the lungs and blood, and the infant's color changes from bluish to pinkish. (Pinkish refers to blood color, visible beneath the skin, and applies to newborns of all hues.) Eyes open wide; tiny fingers grab; even tinier toes stretch and retract. The full-term baby is instantly, zestfully, ready for life.

Newborn health is often measured by the **Apgar scale,** first developed by Dr. Virginia Apgar. When she earned her M.D. in 1933, Apgar wanted to work in a hospital but was told that only men did surgery. She became an anesthesiologist, present at many births but never the doctor in charge.

Apgar saw that "delivery room doctors focused on mothers and paid little attention to babies. Those who were small and struggling were often left to die" (Beck, 2009, p. D1). To save those young lives, Apgar developed a simple rating scale of five vital signs—color, heart rate, cry, muscle tone, and breathing. Nurses could use the scale and raise the alarm immediately if a newborn was in crisis.

Since 1950, birth attendants worldwide have used the Apgar (often using the name as an acronym: Appearance, Pulse, Grimace, Activity, and Respiration) at one minute and again at five minutes after birth, assigning each vital sign a score of 0, 1, or 2.

Apgar scale
A quick assessment of a newborn's health, from 0 to 10. Below 6 is an emergency—a neonatal pediatrician is summoned immediately. Most babies are at 7, 8, or 9—almost never a perfect 10.

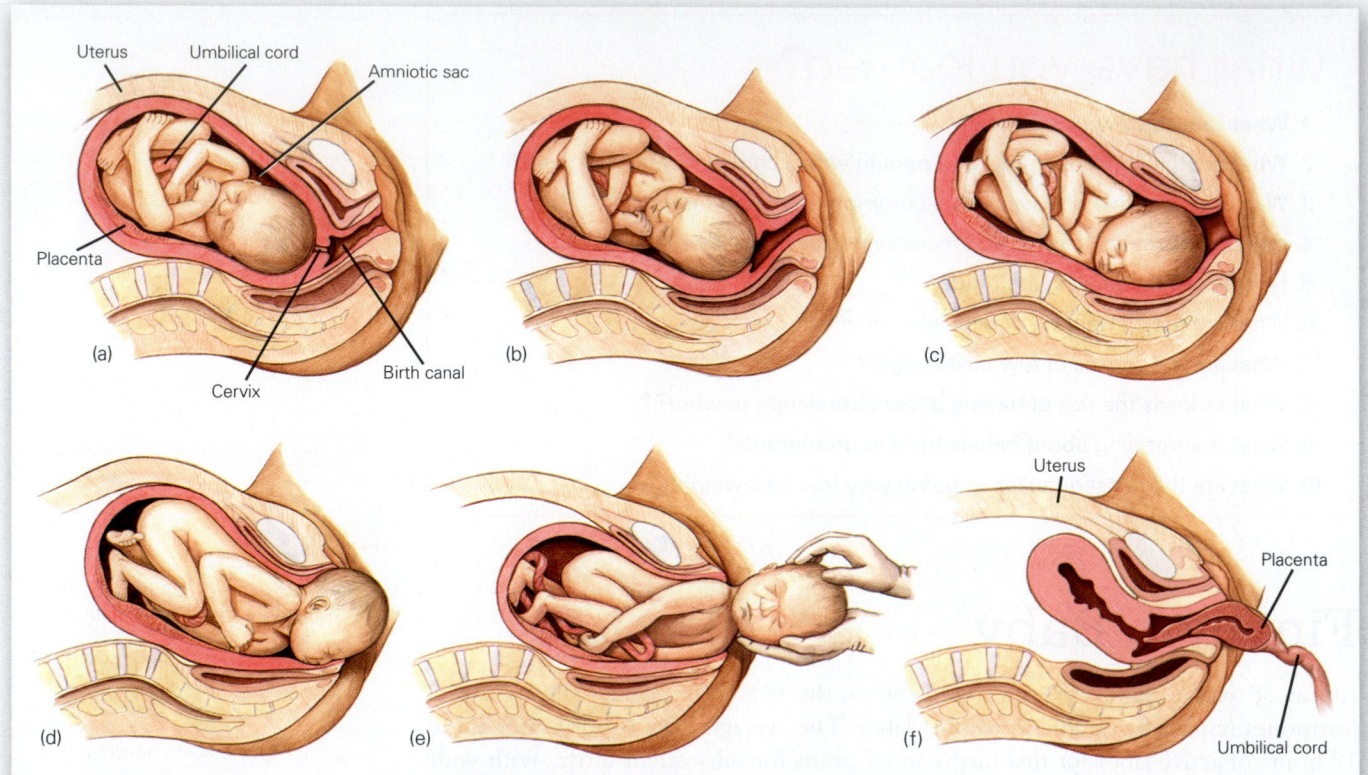

FIGURE 2.6 A Normal, Uncomplicated Birth *(a)* The baby's position as the birth process begins. *(b)* The first stage of labor: The cervix dilates to allow passage of the baby's head. *(c)* Transition: The baby's head moves into the "birth canal," the vagina. *(d)* The second stage of labor: The baby's head moves through the opening of the vagina (the baby's head "crowns") and *(e)* emerges completely. *(f)* The third stage of labor is the expulsion of the placenta. This usually occurs naturally, but the entire placenta must be expelled, so birth attendants check carefully. In some cultures, the placenta is ceremonially buried to commemorate its life-giving role.

Most babies are 8 or higher; below 6 requires immediate attention from a neonatal pediatrician. (See Visualizing Development on page 73.)

A study comparing Apgar rates in 23 nations found that birth attendants in some nations tended to score newborns as almost perfect (97 percent of newborns scored 9 or 10 in some nations, only 73 percent in others). Culture and custom, not objective data, seemed to be the reason, since high scores did not correlate with excellent obstetric practice. However, everywhere, babies with Apgars below 7 were at risk of early death (Siddiqui et al., 2017). Thus, worldwide, a low Apgar signals "baby emergency."

Medical Assistance at Birth

The specifics of birth depend on the fetus, the mother, the birth attendant, the birthplace, and the culture. In the United States, 98 percent of births occur in hospitals, with sterile procedures, electronic monitoring, and drugs to dull pain or speed contractions.

SURGERY Fifty years ago, in developed nations, hospital births required a medical doctor (M.D.), but now many hospitals allow midwives, who are trained specifically in pregnancy and birth but not in surgery. The data show that midwives are as skilled at delivering babies as physicians are, and the rates of various complications

Visualizing Development Infographic

A HEALTHY NEWBORN

Just moments after birth, babies are administered their very first test. The APGAR score is an assessment tool used by doctors and nurses to determine whether a newborn requires any medical intervention. It tests five specific criteria of health, and the medical professional assigns a score of 0, 1, or 2 for each category. A perfect score of 10 is rare—most babies will show some minor deficits at the 1-minute mark, and many will still lose points at the 5-minute mark.

GRIMACE RESPONSE/REFLEXES

2 A healthy baby will indicate his displeasure when his airways are suctioned—he or she will grimace, pull away, cough, or sneeze.

1 Baby will grimace during suctioning.

0 Baby shows no response to being suctioned and requires immediate medical attention.

RESPIRATION

2 A good strong cry indicates a normal breathing rate.

1 Baby has a weak cry or whimper, or slow/irregular breathing.

0 Baby is not breathing and requires immediate medical intervention.

PULSE

2 A pulse of 100 or more beats per minute is healthy for a newborn.

1 Baby's pulse is less than 100 beats per minute.

0 A baby with no heartbeat requires immediate medical attention.

APPEARANCE/COLOR

2 Body and extremities should show good color, with pink undertones indicating good circulation.

1 Baby has some blueness in the palms and soles of the feet. Many babies exhibit some blueness at both the 1- and 5-minute marks; most warm up soon after.

0 A baby whose entire body is blue, grey, or very pale requires immediate medical intervention.

Activity and muscle tone

2 Baby exhibits active motion of arms, legs, and body.

1 Baby shows some movement of arms and legs.

0 A baby who is limp and motionless requires immediate medical attention.

REFLEXES IN INFANTS

Never underestimate the power of a reflex. For developmentalists, newborn reflexes are mechanisms for survival, indicators of brain maturation, and vestiges of evolutionary history. For parents, they are mostly delightful and sometimes amazing.

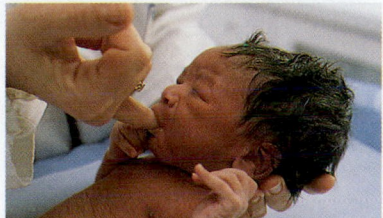

THE SUCKING REFLEX A newborn, just a few minutes old, demonstrates that he is ready to nurse by sucking on a doctor's finger.

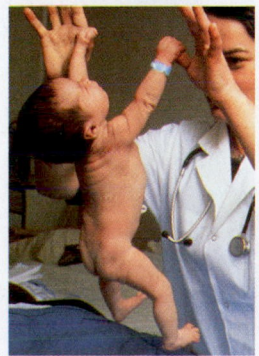

THE GRASPING REFLEX When the doctor places a finger on the palm of a healthy infant, he or she will grasp so tightly that the baby's legs can dangle in space.

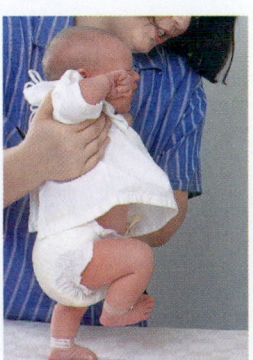

THE STEP REFLEX A 1-day-old girl steps eagerly forward on legs too tiny to support her body.

cesarean section (c-section)
A surgical birth, in which incisions through the mother's abdomen and uterus allow the fetus to be removed quickly, instead of being delivered through the vagina. (Also called simply *section*.)

and interventions are lower in midwife births (Bodner-Adler et al., 2017; Renfrew et al., 2014). If the birth needs surgical intervention, an M.D. is called.

Many midwives try to avoid such a call, believing that doctors are too quick to intervene. On the other hand, most U.S. births are attended by physicians, who deliver via **cesarean section** (**c-section,** or simply *section*) in about one birth in three. The fetus is removed through incisions in the mother's abdomen, avoiding a vaginal birth. C-sections were once very rare: a way to save the baby when it seemed that both mother and fetus were dying. Now c-sections save lives of both mother and child, and some women and doctors prefer them.

The World Health Organization suggests that cesareans are medically indicated in 10–15 percent of births, but many nations have too few or too many c-sections (World Health Organization, April, 2015). Fifty-four nations are below 10 percent; 69 are above 15 percent (Gibbons et al., 2012b). Nations with low cesarean rates have high rates of childbirth deaths, but nations with high cesarean rates are not necessarily healthier. The world region with the lowest rate is East Africa (4 percent) and with the highest, Latin America (40 percent) (Betrán et al., 2016). In the United States, the cesarean rate rose between 1996 and 2008 (from 21 percent to 34 percent) and since has stabilized or is slightly reduced.

Medical reasons for c-section include multiple births, breach (fetus is not positioned head down), prior c-section, long active labor (more than 24 hours), and advanced maternal age. None of those reasons *requires* a c-section. For instance, a large study of all births (78,880) in the state of Washington focused on the relationship between age and various complications. Of those new mothers aged 50 or older, 60 percent delivered by c-section and 40 percent vaginally (Richards et al., 2016).

Cesareans have immediate advantages for hospitals (easier to schedule, quicker, and more expensive than vaginal deliveries) and for women (they can plan ahead, and birth is quick). Convenience, rather than medical necessity, it the likely reason that c-sections are more than twice as common on weekdays than weekends (Martin et al., 2017).

Pick Up Your Baby! Probably she can't. In this maternity ward in Beijing, China, most patients are recovering from cesarean sections, making it difficult to cradle, breast-feed, or carry a newborn until the incision heals.

WANG ZHAO/AFP/GETTY IMAGES

Disadvantages appear later. Mothers giving birth by c-section are less likely to breast-feed and more likely to develop medical complications after birth. Children born by cesarean are more likely to develop asthma or become obese (Chu et al., 2017; Mueller et al., 2017). The reason may be that babies delivered vaginally have beneficial bacteria (the microbiome) in their gut, but those delivered surgically do not (Wallis, 2014).

OTHER INTERVENTIONS Less studied is the *epidural*, an injection in the spine that alleviates pain. Epidurals are often used in hospital births, but they may increase the rate of cesarean sections, decrease newborn sucking, and lead to other complications—at least according to a large study in Pennsylvania (Kjerulff, 2014).

Another medical intervention is *induced labor*, when labor is started, speeded, or strengthened with a drug. The rate of induced labor in developed nations has more than doubled since 1990, up to 20 or 25 percent. Sometimes induction is necessary for the health of the mother or the fetus. However, induced labor itself increases complications, including higher rates of cesareans (Grivell et al., 2012; Mikolajczyk et al., 2016).

Questions of costs and benefits abound, because c-section and epidural rates vary more by doctor, day of the week, and region than by medical conditions.

Complications vary by hospital. A study of 750,000 births in the United States divided hospitals into three categories—low, average, and high quality—based on obstetric complications for the woman. In low-quality hospitals, cesareans led to five times as many complications (20 percent) and vaginal births twice as many (23 percent) compared to high-quality hospitals (4 and 11 percent) (Glance et al., 2014).

HOME BIRTHS Only about 1 percent of U.S. births occur at home, about half of them planned and half unexpected because labor happened too quickly. The latter situation is hazardous if no one is nearby to rescue a newborn in distress. Higher rates of newborn death occur in poor nations, where most births occur at home without trained midwives or doctors.

Compared with the United States, *planned* home births are more common in many other developed nations (2 percent in England, 30 percent in the Netherlands) where professional birth attendants are supported by the government. In the Netherlands, special ambulances called *flying storks* speed mother and newborn to a hospital if needed. In nations where low-risk mothers can choose home births, and good medical care is available, mothers have fewer complications and newborn survival rates in home births are as good as or better than hospital births (de Jonge et al., 2015).

HELPERS AT BIRTH One reason women choose a home birth is that they want family members, friends, and nonmedical helpers nearby. Many U.S. hospitals now allow such people, although some still forbid anyone except nurses and doctors, and others limit the number of nonmedical people allowed at birth.

One helper often chosen is a **doula,** a person trained to support the laboring woman. Doulas time contractions, use massage, provide encouragement, and do whatever else is helpful. Often they come to the woman's home during early labor, and they provide breast-feeding advice for days after birth.

Every comparison study finds that the rate of medical intervention is lower when doulas are part of the birth team. Doulas have proven to be particularly helpful for immigrant, low-income, or unpartnered women who may be intimidated by doctors. Fathers also may be crucial supports, depending on their training and temperament (Kang, 2014; Saxbe, 2017). The midwife who delivered my grandson praised Elissa's husband, saying he was "as good as any doula."

◆◆ **Especially for Conservatives and Liberals**
Do people's attitudes about medical intervention at birth reflect their attitudes about medicine at other points in their life span, in such areas as assisted reproductive technology (ART), immunization, and life support? (see response, page 79)

doula
A woman who helps with the birth process. Traditionally in Latin America, a doula was the only professional who attended childbirth. Now doulas are likely to arrive at the woman's home during early labor and later work alongside a hospital's staff.

◆◆ **Especially for Nurses in Obstetrics**
Can the father be of any practical help in the birth process? (see response, page 79)

The New Family

Humans are social creatures, seeking interaction with their families and their societies. We have already seen how crucial social support is during pregnancy and birth; social interaction may become even more important in the first weeks after birth.

THE NEWEST MEMBER A newborn's appearance (big hairless head, tiny toes, and so on) stirs the heart, evident in adults' brain activity. Fathers are often enraptured by their scraggly newborn and protective of the exhausted mother, who may appreciate her husband more than before, for hormonal as well as practical reasons.

Newborns are responsive social creatures (Zeifman, 2013). They listen, stare, cry, stop crying, and cuddle. In the first day or two, a professional might administer the **Brazelton Neonatal Behavioral Assessment Scale (NBAS),** which records 46 behaviors, including 20 reflexes. A similar but simpler set of responsive behaviors can be assessed at birth (Nugent et al., 2017).

Parents who observe their newborn's responses are often amazed—and this fosters early parent–child connection. Months after birth, mothers who saw their baby respond at birth are more sensitive to their infants (Nugent et al., 2017).

Technically, a *reflex* is an involuntary response to a particular stimulus. Humans of every age reflexively protect themselves (the eye blink is an example). Reflexes seem automatic. Not quite. The strength and reliability of newborn reflexes varies depending on genes, drugs at birth, and overall health.

Newborns' senses are also on high alert—listening, looking, smelling, tasting. They are primed to suck, grasp, and cuddle. In many ways, newborns are ready to connect with their caregivers, who are predisposed to respond (Zeifman, 2013). If the baby performing these actions on the Brazelton NBAS were your own, you would be proud and amazed; that is part of being human.

NEW MOTHERS Many women experience significant physical problems soon after birth, such as healing from a c-section, painfully sore nipples, or problems with urination. However, worse than physical problems are psychological ones (O'Hara & McCabe, 2013). When the level of birth hormones drops, about one new mother in seven experiences **postpartum depression,** a sense of inadequacy and sadness (called *baby blues* in the mild version and *postpartum psychosis* in the most severe form).

With postpartum depression, baby care (feeding, diapering, bathing) feels very burdensome. The newborn's cry may not compel the mother to carry and nurse her infant. Instead, she may be terrified of harming her baby. The first sign that something is amiss may be euphoria after birth. A new mother may be unable to sleep or to stop talking. After the initial high, for between 8 and 15 percent of new mothers, severe depression sets in, typically peaking at 6 weeks after birth.

Postpartum depression is affected by anesthesia, hormones, pain, financial stress, marital problems, a birth that did not go as planned, surgery, and a baby with feeding or other problems. Successful breast-feeding reduces maternal depression (Figueiredo et al., 2014), but success is elusive for many new mothers. A lactation consultant may be an important part of the new mother's support team.

Some researchers believe that postpartum depression is a consequence of modern life, because contemporary women consume less omega-3 fatty acids (especially found in fish), exercise less (especially in the sun), and are far from their own mothers and other relatives (Hahn-Holbrook & Haselton, 2014). In any case, depressed mothers need help not only for their sake but for the sake of their babies, who begin learning how to respond to people based on how people respond to them.

Brazelton Neonatal Behavioral Assessment Scale (NBAS)
A test that is often administered to newborns which measures responsiveness and records 46 behaviors, including 20 reflexes.

reflex
An unlearned, involuntary action or movement in response to a stimulus. A reflex occurs without conscious thought.

postpartum depression
A new mother's feelings of inadequacy and sadness in the days and weeks after giving birth.

NEW FATHERS Whether or not he is present at the birth, the father's legal acceptance of the birth is important to mother and newborn. Currently, about half of all U.S. women are not married when their baby is born (Martin et al., 2017, p. 2), but fathers are usually listed on the birth certificate. When fathers acknowledge their role, birth is better for mother and child.

For example, a study of 151,869 babies and mothers (every single birth in Milwaukee from 1993 to 2006) found that complications correlated with several expected variables (e.g., maternal cigarette smoking) and one unexpected one—no father listed on the birth record. This connection was especially apparent for European Americans: When no father was listed, rates of long labor, cesarean section, and other complications increased (Ngui et al., 2009).

Fathers may experience pregnancy and birth biologically, not just psychologically. Many fathers experience symptoms, including weight gain and indigestion during pregnancy and pain during labor.

Paternal experiences of pregnancy and birth are called **couvade**—expected in some cultures such as India, normal in many, and considered pathological in others (M. Sloan, 2009; Ganapathy, 2014).

In the United States, couvade is unnoticed and unstudied, but many fathers are intensely involved with their future child (Brennan et al., 2007; Raeburn, 2014). Like new mothers, fathers are vulnerable to depression; other people need to help. Indeed, sometimes the father experiences more depression in the first few weeks than the mother (Bradley & Slade, 2011).

We close this chapter with the experience of one father, himself a nurse.

> Throughout most of this pregnancy I was able to form intelligent thoughts and remained relatively coherent, but as soon as we were admitted to the labor and delivery unit I felt my IQ plummet and all that I have learned as a nurse escaped me. . . .
>
> In my wife's own words, the whole ordeal was hot, sweaty, messy and a "crime scene of body fluids" . . . even when she felt "hot, sweaty and disgusting" I was in complete awe of her and couldn't have been prouder of her. She was as beautiful to me in those moments as she was on our wedding day and I will never forget it.

He continues, weeks after birth:

> . . . I am exhausted but I have been able to catch more naps than my poor wife who is up constantly to feed our little guy. . . . I joked with some of my new Dad friends (I'm already working on getting "Dad friends") that I would sell my soul or empty my life savings to buy my wife some much-deserved rest. . . .
>
> When I hear my boy cry I become a stupid and clueless mess. . . . I know logically that as long as he is clean/dry, warm, and fed that he is not suffering and just needs to be held and settled but that doesn't stop me from going into crisis mode. I know that in time this will get better.
>
> [cjcsoon2bnp, February 13, 2017]

Yes, in time people change—although not every parent thinks stubborn toddlers, or adventuresome adolescents, or any other age is "better." What does not change is the connection between people, who care for each other when someone is hot, messy, or exhausted. Knowledge helps—this man bragged about his skill in caring for others—but birth is a psychological experience, not just a physical one.

This chapter, rightly, explained genes and prenatal development. However, as you learn more about human development, remember that each life is an emotional journey as well as a biological sequence.

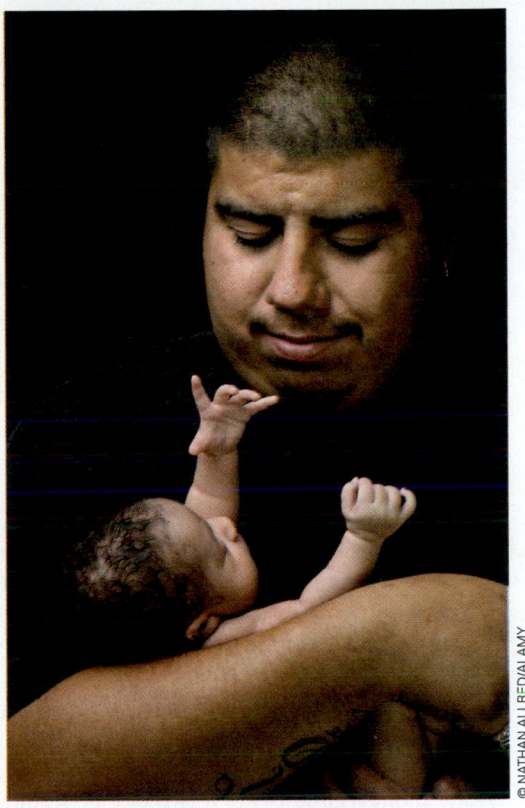

Mutual Joy Ignore this dad's tattoo and earring, and the newborn's head wet with amniotic fluid. Instead recognize that, for thousands of years, hormones and instincts propel fathers and babies to reach out to each other, developing lifelong connections.

couvade
Symptoms of pregnancy and birth experienced by fathers.

"Of course I know what he wants when he cries. He wants you."

what have you learned?

1. What five vital signs does the Apgar scale measure?

2. What are the advantages and disadvantages of cesarean sections?

3. What are the advantages and disadvantages of home birth?

4. In what ways do doulas support women before, during, and after labor?

5. What in the newborn's appearance and behavior helps with parental bonding?

6. How do fathers experience pregnancy and birth?

7. What are the consequences of postpartum depression?

SUMMARY

Genes and Chromosomes

1. Genes are the foundation for development. Human conception occurs when two gametes (an ovum and a sperm, each with 23 chromosomes) combine to form a zygote. Those 46 chromosomes contain the genes, about 20,000 in all.

2. Biological sex is determined by the 23rd pair of chromosomes, with a Y sperm creating an XY (male) zygote or an X sperm creating an XX (female) zygote. If one zygote splits, that creates monozygotic twins; if two ova are fertilized at the same time, that creates dizygotic twins.

3. Genes may interact additively, or they can follow a dominant–recessive pattern. The genotype may not be expressed in the phenotype, which is the actual characteristics of the person.

From Zygote to Newborn

4. In the germinal period (the first two weeks after conception), cells duplicate and differentiate, and the developing organism implants itself in the lining of the uterus. In the embryonic period (third through the eighth week), organs and body structures are formed, except the sex organs.

5. In the fetal period (ninth week until birth) the fetus grows and all the organs begin to function. Crucial for viability is brain development at 22 weeks, when a fetus born that early might survive. Every week after that increases weight and odds of survival.

Problems and Solutions

6. If a zygote has more or fewer than 46 chromosomes, it usually does not implant. However, if an extra chromosome is at the 21st site (Down syndrome) or at the 23rd site, that person has lifelong disabilities but may have a good life.

7. Everyone is a carrier for genetic abnormalities. Usually these conditions are recessive, and no fetus is affected unless both parents carry the same disorder. Genetic testing and counseling can help many couples avoid having a baby with serious chromosomal or genetic problems.

8. Thousands of teratogens, especially drugs and alcohol, have the potential to harm the embryo or fetus. Actual harm occurs because of a cascade: Genes, critical periods, dose, and frequency all have an impact.

9. Low birthweight (less than 5 ½ pounds, or 2,500 grams) may result from multiple fetuses, maternal illness, genes, malnutrition, smoking, drinking, or drug use. Underweight babies may experience physical and intellectual problems lifelong. Newborns that are small for gestational age (SGA) are especially vulnerable.

10. Maternal behavior increases the risk of every problem, including low birthweight. Fathers, other relatives, and the society also can affect the incidence of disabilities.

Finally, a Baby

11. Ideally, infants are born full term, weighing more than 5 ½ pounds, with an Apgar of at least 8. Medical assistance speeds contractions, dulls pain, and saves lives, but some interventions may be unnecessary, including about half of the cesareans performed in the United States.

12. Newborns are primed for social interaction, and fathers and mothers are often emotionally connected to their baby and to each other. Paternal support correlates with shorter labor and fewer complications.

13. About one women in seven experiences postpartum depression, feeling unhappy, incompetent, or unwell after giving birth. The most vulnerable time is when the baby is several weeks old, with social support crucial for mother, father, and infant.

KEY TERMS

deoxyribonucleic acid (DNA) (p. 44)

chromosome (p. 44)

zygote (p. 45)

homozygous (p. 45)

allele (p. 45)

heterozygous (p. 45)

microbiome (p. 46)

copy number variations (p. 46)

genotype (p. 47)

phenotype (p. 47)

genome (p. 47)

XX (p. 49)

XY (p. 49)

monozygotic (MZ) twins (p. 51)

dizygotic (DZ) twins (p. 52)
additive genes (p. 53)
dominant–recessive pattern (p. 53)
carrier (p. 53)
X-linked (p. 53)
germinal period (p. 55)
implantation (p. 56)
embryo (p. 56)

ultrasound (p. 57)
false positives (p. 57)
fetus (p. 58)
age of viability (p. 58)
genetic counseling (p. 63)
teratogen (p. 63)
behavioral teratogens (p. 65)
fetal alcohol syndrome (FAS) (p. 66)

low birthweight (LBW) (p. 67)
very low birthweight (VLBW) (p. 67)
extremely low birthweight (ELBW) (p. 67)
preterm (p. 67)
small for gestational age (SGA) (p. 68)
immigrant paradox (p. 69)

Apgar scale (p. 71)
cesarean section (c-section) (p. 74)
doula (p. 75)
Brazelton Neonatal Behavioral Assessment Scale (NBAS) (p. 76)
postpartum depression (p. 76)
couvade (p. 77)

APPLICATIONS

1. Many adults have a preference for having a son or a daughter. Interview adults of several ages and backgrounds about their preferences. If they give the socially preferable answer ("It does not matter"), ask how they think the two sexes differ. Listen and take notes—don't debate. Analyze the implications of the responses you get.

2. Draw a genetic chart of your biological relatives, going back as many generations as you can, listing all serious illnesses and causes of death. Include ancestors who died in infancy. Do you see any genetic susceptibility? If so, how can you overcome it?

3. People sometimes wonder how any pregnant woman could jeopardize the health of her fetus. Consider your own health-related behavior in the past month—exercise, sleep, nutrition, drug use, medical and dental care, disease avoidance, and so on. Would you change your behavior if you were pregnant? Would it make a difference if you, your family, and your partner did not want a baby?

4. Interview three mothers of varied backgrounds about their birth experiences. Make your interviews open-ended—let the mothers choose what to tell you, as long as they give at least a 10-minute description. Then compare and contrast the three accounts, noting especially any influences of culture, personality, circumstances, and cohort.

ESPECIALLY FOR ANSWERS

Response for Medical Doctors (from page 47): No. Personalized medicine is the hope of many physicians, but appearance (the phenotype) does not indicate alleles, recessive genes, copy number variations, and other genetic factors that affect drug reactions. Many medical researchers seek to personalize chemotherapy for cancer. This is urgently needed, but is still experimental, even when the genotype is known.

Response for Scientists (from page 48): There was some scientific evidence for the wrong numbers (e.g., chimpanzees have 48 chromosomes), but the reality is that humans tend to overestimate many things, from the number of genes to their grade on the next test. Scientists are very human: They tend to overestimate until the data prove them wrong.

Response for Teachers (from page 60): Your first step would be to make sure you know about Down syndrome by reading material about it. You would learn, among other things, that it is not usually inherited (your student need not worry about his or her progeny) and that some children with Down syndrome need extra medical and educational attention. This might mean that you need to pay special attention to your student, whose parents might focus on the sibling.

Response for Judges and Juries (from page 66): Some laws punish women who jeopardize the health of their fetuses, but a developmental view would consider the micro-, exo-, and macrosystems.

Response for Conservatives and Liberals (from page 75): Yes, some people are much more likely to want nature to take its course. However, personal experience often trumps political attitudes about birth and death; several of those who advocate hospital births are also in favor of spending one's final days at home.

Response for Nurses in Obstetrics (from page 75): Usually not, unless he is experienced, well taught, or has expert guidance. But his presence provides emotional support for the woman, which makes the birth process easier and healthier for mother and baby.

OBSERVATION QUIZ ANSWERS

Answer to Observation Quiz (from page 53): Ellie has a gene for achondroplasia, the most common form of dwarfism, which affects her limb growth, making her a little person. Because of her parents and her sister, she is likely to have a long and accomplished life: Problems are less likely to come from her genotype than from how other people perceive her phenotype.

Answer to Observation Quiz (from page 59): Individuals with Down syndrome vary in many traits, but visible here are five common ones. Compared to most children his age, including his classmate beside him, Daniel has a rounder face, narrower eyes, shorter stature, larger teeth and tongue, and—best of all—a happier temperament.

APPLICATION TO DEVELOPING LIVES PARENTING SIMULATION BABIES AND TODDLERS

As you progress through the Babies and Toddlers simulation module, how you decide the following will impact the biosocial, cognitive, and psychosocial development of your child.

	Biosocial	Cognitive	Psychosocial
	• Will you vaccinate your baby? • Will you breast-feed your baby? If so, for how long? • What kind of foods will you feed your baby during the first year? • How will you encourage motor skill development? • How do your baby's height and weight compare to national norms?	• What activities will you expose your baby to (music class, reading, educational videos)? • What activities will you do to promote language development? • Which of Piaget's stages of cognitive development is your child in?	• How will you soothe your baby when he or she is crying? • Can you identify your baby's temperament style? • Can you identify your baby's attachment style? • What kind of discipline will you use with your child?

The First Two Years

Adults don't change much in a year or two. They might have longer, grayer, or thinner hair; they might gain or lose a few pounds; they might learn something new. But if you saw friends you hadn't seen for two years, you'd recognize them immediately.

Imagine caring for a newborn day and night for a month and then leaving for two years. On your return, would you recognize him or her? The baby would have quadrupled in weight, grown a foot taller, and sprouted a new head of hair. Behavior and emotions change, too—less crying, but new joys and fears—including fear of you.

Two years are not much compared to the 80 or so years of the average life. However, in those 24 months humans reach half their adult height, learn to talk in sentences, and express almost every emotion—not just joy and fear but also love, jealousy, and shame. Now we describe these radical changes.

JOSE LUIS PELAEZ INC/GETTY IMAGES

THE FIRST TWO YEARS
Body and Mind

what will you know?

- What part of an infant grows most in the first two years?
- Does immunization protect or harm?
- What does it mean if a baby doesn't look for an object that disappears?
- Why do people talk to babies too young to talk back?

Our first child, Bethany, was born when I was in graduate school. I studiously memorized developmental norms, including sitting at 6 months, walking and talking at 12. But at 14 months, Bethany had not yet taken her first step.

I reassured my husband that genes were more influential than anything we did. I had read that babies in Paris are the latest walkers in the world, and my grandmother was French. My speculation was bolstered when our next two children, Rachel and Elissa, were also slow to walk, and Bethany was the fastest runner in kindergarten.

My genetic hypothesis was confirmed by my students, all devoted parents. Those with ancestors from Guatemala and Ghana had infants who walked before a year, unlike those of Asian or European heritage.

Fourteen years after Bethany, Sarah was born. I could afford a full-time caregiver, Mrs. Todd, from Jamaica. She thought Sarah was the most advanced baby she had ever known, except for her own daughter, Gillian. I told her that Berger children walk late.

"She'll be walking by a year," Mrs. Todd told me. "Gillian walked at 10 months."

"We'll see," I graciously replied, confident of my genetic explanation.

I underestimated Mrs. Todd. She bounced my delighted daughter on her lap, day after day, and spent hours giving her "walking practice." Sarah took her first step at 12 months, late for a Todd, early for a Berger, and a humbling lesson for me.

As a scientist, I know that a single case proves nothing. Sarah shares only half her genes with her sisters. Genetically, my daughters are only one-eighth French, a fraction I had conveniently ignored.

Nonetheless, evidence over the past decades from thousands of babies is overwhelming: Infants vary because of nurture, not only

VIDEO: Physical Development in Infancy and Toddlerhood offers a quick review of the physical changes that occur during a child's first two years.

because of nature. Caregiving enables growing, moving, and learning. Some caregivers massage babies every day, some talk in response to each burp, some keep them close every moment, others encourage them to run, climb, and explore. Babies respond.

Growth in Infancy

In infancy, growth is so rapid and the consequences of neglect are so severe that gains are closely monitored. Length, weight, and head circumference are measured monthly at first, and every organ is checked to make sure it functions well.

Body Size

Weight gain is dramatic. Newborns lose weight in the first three days and then gain an ounce a day for several months. Birthweight typically doubles by 4 months and triples by a year. An average 7-pound newborn will be 21 pounds at 12 months (9,525 grams, up from 3,175 grams at birth).

Physical growth in the second year is slower but still rapid. By 24 months, most children weigh almost 28 pounds (13 kilograms). They have added more than a foot in height—from about 20 inches at birth to about 34 inches at age 2 (from 51 to 86 centimeters). This makes them about half their adult height and about one-fifth their adult weight, four times heavier than they were at birth (see Figure 3.1).

Each of these numbers is a **norm,** which is a standard for a particular population. The "particular population" for the norms just cited is North American infants. Remember, however, genetic diversity: Some perfectly healthy, well-fed babies are smaller or larger than these norms. Each child follows his or her own trajectory.

At each checkup, growth is compared to that baby's previous numbers. Measurements are expressed as a **percentile,** from 0 to 100, comparing each infant to others the same age. For example, if a 1-month-old weighs at the 30th percentile, then 29 percent of 1-month-olds weigh less, and 69 percent weigh more.

If a baby's percentile changes markedly, either up or down, that is a signal that something might be amiss. If a baby moves down from, say, the 30th to the 10th percentile, that might be *failure to thrive.* Pediatricians consider it "outmoded" to blame

norm
An average, or standard, calculated from many individuals within a specific group or population.

percentile
A point on a ranking scale of 0 to 100. The 50th percentile is the midpoint; half of the people in the population being studied rank higher and half rank lower.

FIGURE 3.1 Averages and Individuals Norms and percentiles are useful—most 1-month-old girls who weigh 10 pounds should be at least 25 pounds by age 2. But although females weigh less than males on average lifelong, it is obvious that individuals do not always follow the norms. Do you know a 200-pound woman married to a 150-pound man?

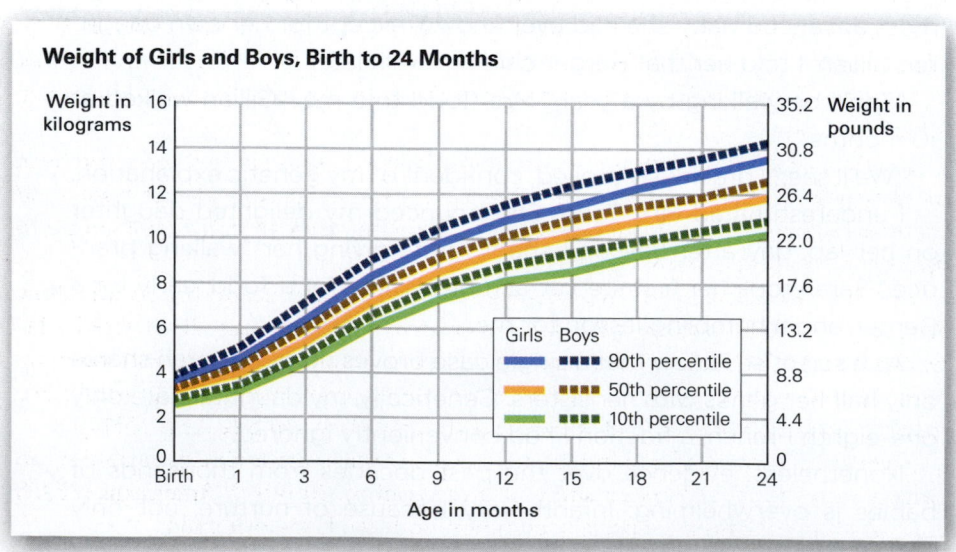

parents, but the biological or social cause of failure to thrive must be discovered and remedied (Jaffe, 2011, p. 100). Similarly, if weight moves up from the 30th to the 70th percentile, especially if height still is close to the 30th percentile, overfeeding might be a problem.

Sleep

Throughout life, health and growth correlate with regular and ample sleep (El-Sheikh & Kelly, 2017). As with many health habits, sleep patterns begin in the first year.

Newborns sleep about 15 to 17 hours a day. Every week brings a few more waking minutes. For the first two months the norm for total time asleep is 14¼ hours; for the next 3 months, 13¼ hours; for the next 12 months, 12¾ hours. Remember that norms are averages; individuals vary. Parents report that, among every 20 infants in the United States, one sleeps 9 hours or fewer per day and one sleeps 19 hours or more (Sadeh et al., 2009).

National averages vary as well. By age 2, the typical New Zealand toddler sleeps 15 percent more than the typical Japanese one (13⅓ hours compared to 11⅔) (Sadeh et al., 2010).

Infants also vary in how long they sleep at a stretch. Preterm and breast-fed infants wake up often, sometimes needing another meal soon after the previous one (called cluster feeding). "Sleeping through the night" is sought by every exhausted parent, but when this occurs depends not only on the baby but on the parent's interpretation. If a night is from midnight to 5 A.M., many babies occasionally sleep all night long at 3 months. But few 1-year-olds do so if night is from 8 P.M. to 6 A.M. (C. Russell et al., 2013).

Over the first few months, the time spent in each stage of sleep changes. Preterm babies may seem to be frequently dozing, never in deep sleep, but that may be caused partially by the constant bright lights and frequent feedings in the traditional NICU (neonatal intensive care unit). When they come home, they usually adjust to a day–night schedule (Bueno & Menna-Barreto, 2016).

About half the sleep of full-term newborns is **REM (rapid eye movement) sleep,** with flickering eyelids and rapid brain waves. That indicates dreaming, now thought to consolidate memories. REM sleep declines over the early weeks, as does "transitional sleep," the half-awake stage. At 3 or 4 months, quiet sleep (also called *slow-wave sleep*) increases markedly.

Sleep varies not only because of biology (maturation and genes) but also because of culture and caregivers. Infants who are fed formula and cereal sleep longer and more soundly—easier for parents but not better for the baby. The location of sleep depends primarily on the baby's age and culture, with **bed-sharing** (in the parents' bed) or **co-sleeping** (in the parents' room) the norm in some cultures but not in others (Esposito et al., 2015).

Bed-sharing is more common in breast-fed babies. A study in Sweden of preterm infants (who are fed every two or three hours) found that most slept with their mothers—especially if the mother had trouble getting back to sleep if she got up to feed her infant (Blomqvist et al., 2017).

Full-term newborns also have brain patterns and hunger needs that do not allow long stretches of deep sleep. If this lasts for months, the family may be affected: Maternal depression and family dysfunction are more common when infants wake up often (Piteo et al., 2013). This could be a cause or a consequence. Mothers' sleep patterns correlate with those of fathers and children (El-Sheikh & Kelly, 2017).

Overall, 25 percent of children under age 3 have sleeping problems, according to parents surveyed in an Internet study of more than 5,000 North Americans (Sadeh et al., 2009). Problems are especially common with the first-born child.

REM (rapid eye movement) sleep
A stage of sleep characterized by flickering eyes behind closed lids, dreaming, and rapid brain waves.

bed-sharing
When two or more people sleep in the same bed.

co-sleeping
A custom in which parents and their children (usually infants) sleep together in the same room.

◆ **Especially for New Parents**
You are aware of cultural differences in sleeping practices, which raises a very practical issue: Should your newborn sleep in bed with you? (see response, page 123)

Is Mom Awake? This 36-year-old mother in Hong Kong put her 7-month-old baby to sleep on her back, protecting her from SIDS as the Chinese have done for centuries. However, the soft pillow and comforter are hazards. Will she carry the baby to a safe place before she falls asleep?

IMAGES BY TANG MING TUNG/TAXI/GETTY IMAGES

Parents "are rarely well-prepared for the degree of sleep disruption a newborn infant engenders." As a result, many become "desperate" and institute patterns that they may later regret (C. Russell et al., 2013, p. 68). But what patterns are best? Experts, strangers, and relatives give conflicting advice, as Opposing Perspectives on page 87 suggests.

Brain Development

Findings from neuroscience are discussed in every chapter of this book. Some readers may already know the basics—neurons, axons, dendrites, neurotransmitters, synapses, the cortex, and the limbic system, and they could skip Inside the Brain on page 88. However, these terms appear often in later chapters, so this may be helpful to everyone.

Prenatal and postnatal brain growth is crucial for later cognition (Gilles & Nelson, 2012). From two weeks after conception to two years after birth, the brain grows more rapidly than any other organ, being about 25 percent of adult weight at birth and almost 75 percent at age 2. Over the same two years, brain circumference increases from about 14 inches to 19 inches. If teething or a stuffy nose temporarily slows weight gain, nature protects the brain, a phenomenon called **head-sparing.** (As discussed later, head-sparing cannot overcome prolonged malnutrition.)

One-year-olds can transfer learning from one object or experience to another, learn from strangers, and copy what they see in books and videos. The dendrites and neurons of several areas of the brain change to reflect remembered experiences.

Overall, infants remember not only specific events but also patterns (Keil, 2011). Babies know what to expect from a parent or a babysitter, which foods are delicious, or what details indicate bedtime. Every day of their young lives, infants are processing information and storing conclusions.

head-sparing
A biological mechanism that protects the brain when malnutrition disrupts body growth. The brain is the last part of the body to be damaged by malnutrition.

transient exuberance
The great but temporary increase in the number of dendrites that develop in an infant's brain during the first two years of life.

EXUBERANCE AND PRUNING Early dendrite growth is called **transient exuberance:** *exuberant* because it is rapid and *transient* because some is temporary. Expansive growth is followed by *pruning.* Just as a gardener might prune a rose bush by cutting away some growth to enable more, or more beautiful, roses to bloom, unused brain connections atrophy and disappear to enable children to connect the neurons needed in their culture.

OPPOSING PERSPECTIVES

Where Should Babies Sleep?

For many in Asia, Africa, and Latin America, the custom has been for infants to sleep beside their mothers. In those cultures, nighttime parent–child separation is often considered cruel. By contrast, most U.S. infants traditionally slept in cribs in their own rooms. Psychiatrists feared that babies would be traumatized if their parents had sex, and many nonprofessionals thought children would be spoiled if they depended too much on their mothers at night.

A 19-nation study found that Asian and African mothers worry about separation, whereas mothers with European roots worry more about privacy. In the extremes of that study, 82 percent of Vietnamese babies slept with their mothers, as did 6 percent in New Zealand (Mindell et al., 2010) (see Figure 3.2). Sleeping alone may encourage independence for both child and adult—a quality valued in some cultures but discouraged in others.

Sleeping patterns are changing in the United States. Since 2000, co-sleeping has been recommended by North Americans who advocate *attachment parenting* (Sears & Sears, 2001). Many companies sell "co-sleepers" that allow babies to sleep beside their mothers without a soft mattress or blankets.

Bed–sharing (not just co-sleeping) is becoming more popular in the United States: The rate doubled from 6.5 percent in 1993 to 13.5 percent in 2010 (Colson et al., 2013).

Many experts seek to safeguard infants who sleep with their parents (Ball & Volpe, 2013). Their advice includes *never* sleeping beside a baby if the parent has been drinking and *never* using a soft comforter, pillow, or mattress near a sleeping infant.

Some worry that co-sleeping will continue for months and years, disrupting the marital relationship and, perhaps, the entire family. One study found that U.S. families usually kept newborns in the parents' bedroom but moved them to a separate room by 6 months. In that study, mothers who were depressed, and who were unhappy with the father's involvement, were more likely to keep the baby in their room (Teti et al., 2015).

The authors suggest that depression and marital problems correlate with co-sleeping only if co-sleeping is not the norm. However, even in Japan, bed–sharing and marital strain often occur together. One Japanese mother wrote:

> I take care of my baby at night, since my husband would never wake up until morning whatever happens. Babies, who cannot turn over yet, are at risk of suffocation and SIDS because they would not be able to remove a blanket by themselves if it covers over their face. In my case, I sleep with my older child and baby. By the way, my husband sleeps in a separate room because of his bad snoring.
>
> *[Shimizu et al., 2014]*

Contrary to this woman's rationalization, sudden infant death syndrome (SIDS, discussed later) is twice as likely when babies sleep beside their parents. Researchers pinpoint the reason: Many parents occasionally sleep beside their baby after drinking or taking drugs. Then bed–sharing can be fatal (P. Fleming et al., 2015).

As one review explained, "There are clear reasons . . . [for bed–sharing] warmth, comfort, bonding, and cultural tradition, but there are also clear reasons against doing so, such as increased risk of sudden infant death syndrome" (Esposito et al., 2015). As with many aspects of child care, this decision is cultural and complex.

Over time, the sleep patterns of each family member affect the sleep of the others, and a good night's rest benefits everyone. So parents need to establish *sleep hygiene* (calming routines and regular schedules) (Bathory & Tomopoulos, 2017; El–Sheikh & Kelly, 2017). Exactly what that means is . . . opposing perspectives.

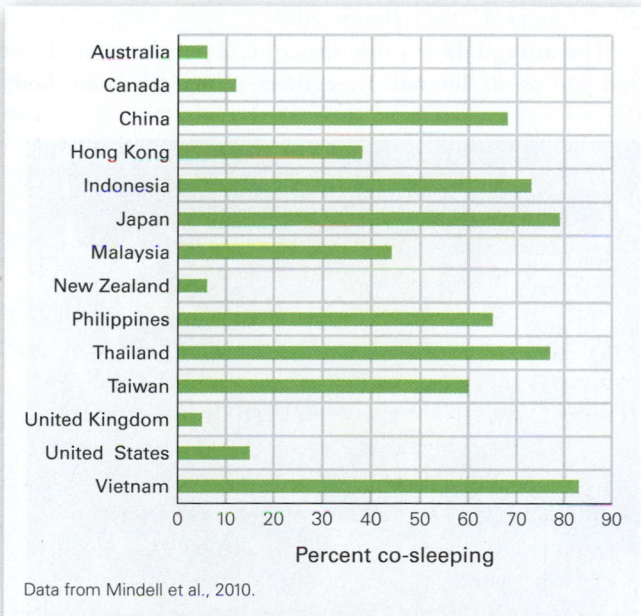

Data from Mindell et al., 2010.

FIGURE 3.2 Awake at Night Why the disparity between Asian and non-Asian rates of co-sleeping? It may be that Western parents use a variety of gadgets and objects—monitors, night-lights, pacifiers, cuddle cloths, sound machines—to accomplish some of what Asian parents do by having their infant next to them.

INSIDE THE BRAIN

Brain Basics

Communication within the central nervous system (CNS)—the brain and spinal cord—begins with nerve cells, called **neurons.** At birth, the human brain has an estimated 86 billion neurons, far more than any other primate. Especially in the **cortex** (the brain's six outer layers where most thinking, feeling, and sensing occur), humans have more neurons than other mammals (Herculano-Houzel et al., 2014b).

The cortex includes regions dedicated to particular aspects of brain function—the visual cortex, auditory cortex, and so on, all evident in newborns. The last part of the brain to mature is the **prefrontal cortex,** the area behind the forehead that is crucial for anticipation, planning, and impulse control. The prefrontal cortex is inactive in early infancy and gradually becomes more efficient in childhood, adolescence, and adulthood, with marked variation from one person to another (Walhovd et al., 2014).

Neurons connect to other neurons via intricate networks of nerve fibers called **axons** and **dendrites.** Each neuron typically has a single axon and numerous dendrites, which spread out like the branches of a tree. The axon of each neuron reaches toward

the dendrites of other neurons at intersections called **synapses,** which are critical communication links within the brain.

Axons and dendrites do not touch at synapses. Instead, electrical impulses in axons cause the release of chemicals called **neurotransmitters,** which carry information from the axon of the sending neuron to the dendrites of the receiving neuron. During the first months and years, rapid growth and refinement in axons, dendrites, and synapses occur, especially in the cortex. Dendrite growth is the main reason that brain weight triples from birth to age 2 (M. H. Johnson, 2011).

An estimated fivefold increase in dendrites in the cortex occurs in the 24 months after birth, with about 100 trillion synapses present at age 2. According to one expert, "40,000 new synapses are formed every second in the infant's brain" (Schore & McIntosh, 2011, p. 502).

Those synapses develop in every part of the brain, but during infancy this seems especially apparent in the **limbic system,** a cluster of brain areas deep in the forebrain that is heavily involved in emotions and motivation. Three crucial parts of the limbic system are the *amygdala,* the *hypothalamus,* and the *hippocampus.* These three develop early in life and are crucial for fear, depression, and anxiety lifelong (Ng et al., 2017; Qiu et al., 2015; Braun, 2011).

The **amygdala** is a tiny structure, about the same shape and size as an almond. It registers strong emotions, both

neuron
One of billions of nerve cells in the central nervous system, especially in the brain.

cortex
The outer layers of the brain in humans and other mammals. Most thinking, feeling, and sensing involves the cortex.

prefrontal cortex
The area of the cortex at the very front of the brain that specializes in anticipation, planning, and impulse control.

axon
A fiber that extends from a neuron and transmits electrochemical impulses from that neuron to the dendrites of other neurons.

dendrite
A fiber that extends from a neuron and receives electrochemical impulses transmitted from other neurons via their axons.

synapse
The intersection between the axon of one neuron and the dendrites of other neurons.

neurotransmitter
A brain chemical that carries information from the axon of a sending neuron to the dendrites of a receiving neuron.

limbic system
The parts of the brain that interact to produce emotions, including the amygdala, the hypothalamus, and the hippocampus. Many other parts of the brain also are involved with emotions.

amygdala
A tiny brain structure that registers emotions, particularly fear and anxiety.

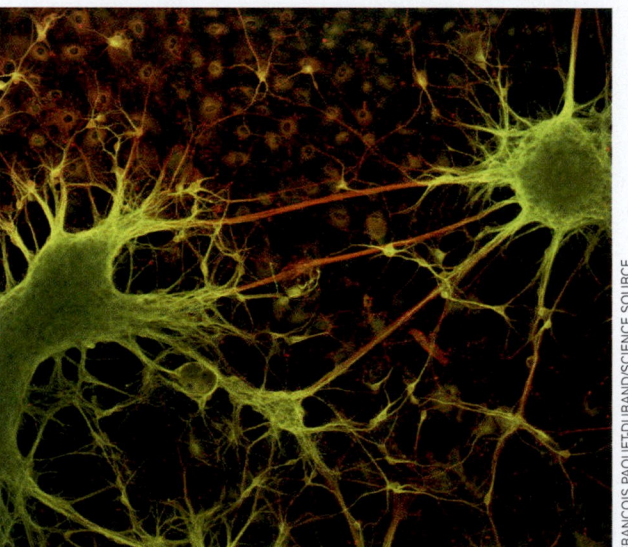

FRANCOIS PAQUET-DURAND/SCIENCE SOURCE

Connecting The color staining on this photo makes it obvious that the two cell bodies of neurons (stained chartreuse) grow axons and dendrites to each other's neurons. This tangle is repeated thousands of times in every human brain. Throughout life, those fragile dendrites will grow or disappear as the person continues thinking.

positive and negative—especially fear. The amygdala is present in infancy, growing with experience. Frightening a baby is likely to increase amygdala activity, causing terrifying nightmares or sudden terrors later on.

Another structure in the emotional network is the **hippocampus,** located next to the amygdala. A central processor of memory, especially memory for locations, the hippocampus responds to the amygdala by summoning memory.

Some places feel comforting (perhaps a childhood room) and others evoke fear (perhaps a doctor's office). Those emotions may continue even when the experiences that originated those emotions are long gone. The size of the hippocampus is markedly affected by maternal emotions during pregnancy and by **cortisol**—the hormone produced by stress.

Sometimes considered part of the limbic system is the **hypothalamus**, which responds to signals from the amygdala and to memories from the hippocampus by producing hormones, especially cortisol. [**Life-Span Link**: Many other hormones are discussed in Chapter 9, because

puberty is caused, enhanced, and bedeviled by rising hormones.]

For now, what you need to know is that social scientists—who once thought the crucial aspect of our species was walking on two legs and making tools—now believe the crucial difference between humans and other mammals is in the brain. All of the regions and functions mentioned above are especially active in humans: Our dendrites reach out to our neurons, making us unlike all other animals.

hippocampus
A brain structure that is a central processor of memory, especially memory for locations.

cortisol
The primary stress hormone; fluctuations in the body's cortisol level affect human emotions.

hypothalamus
A brain area that responds to the amygdala and the hippocampus to produce hormones that activate other parts of the brain and body.

As one expert explains it, there is an

> exuberant overproduction of cells and connections, followed by a several-year sculpting of pathways by massive elimination of much of the neural architecture.
>
> [Insel, 2014, p. 1727]

Notice the word *sculpting,* as if an artist created an intricate sculpture from raw marble or wood. Human infants are gifted sculptors, designing their brains for whatever family, culture, or society they happen to be born into, discarding the excess in order to think more clearly.

Thus, pruning is beneficial (Gao et al., 2016). Evidence comes from a sad symptom of fragile X syndrome (described in Chapter 2), "a persistent failure of normal synapse pruning" (Irwin et al., 2002, p. 194). Without pruning, the dendrites of children with fragile X are too dense and long, making thinking difficult.

Similar problems occur for children with autism spectrum disorder: Their brains are unusually large and full, impairing communication between neurons and making some sounds and sights overwhelming (Lewis et al., 2013).

EXPECTED OR DEPENDENT? Every child's experiences sculpt the brain (Kolb et al., 2017). Some sculpting is called **experience–expectant** and some is called **experience-dependent** (Greenough et al., 1987).

Brain development is experience-*expectant* when it is necessary for normal brain maturation. In deserts and in the Arctic, on isolated farms and in crowded cities, almost all babies have things to see, objects to manipulate, and people to love them. Without such expected experiences, dendrites and specific regions within the brain do not grow.

In contrast, certain facets of brain development are experience-*dependent*: They result from experiences that differ from one infant to another, resulting in brains that

experience-expectant
Brain functions that require certain basic common experiences (which an infant can be expected to have) in order to develop normally.

experience-dependent
Brain functions that depend on particular, variable experiences and therefore may or may not develop in a particular infant.

Face Lit Up, Brain Too Thanks to scientists at the University of Washington, this young boy enjoys the EEG of his brain activity. Such research has found that babies respond to language long before they speak. Experiences of all sorts connect neurons and grow dendrites.

AARON MCCOY/PHOTOLIBRARY/GETTY IMAGES

◆ **Especially for Parents of Grown Children**
Suppose you realize that you seldom talked to your children until they talked to you and that you often put them in cribs and playpens. Did you limit their brain growth and their sensory capacity? (see response, page 123)

also differ. What specific language is heard, whose faces are seen, or how emotions are expressed — from slight pursing of the lips to throwing oneself on the ground — vary from one family to another.

Depending on such variations, infant neurons connect in particular ways; some dendrites grow and others disappear (Stiles & Jernigan, 2010). In other words, every baby needs to develop language — that is expectant; brains are primed for it. But that language could be Tajik, Tamil, Thai, or Twi. That is experience-dependent; brains are shaped so that each baby will learn their native language. Infant brains are extraordinarily plastic, molded to their culture (Kolb et al., 2017).

STRESS AND THE BRAIN If the brain produces an overabundance of cortisol (the stress hormone) early in life (as when an infant is frequently terrified), that derails the connections between parts of the brain, causing atypical responses to stress lifelong. Years later that person may be hypervigilant (always on alert) or emotionally flat (never happy or sad).

Adults need to comfort crying babies, not tell them to stop crying. Indeed, because the prefrontal cortex has not yet developed, infants cannot *decide* to stop crying. If a frustrated adult shakes a crying baby, that may stop the crying because ruptured blood vessels in the brain break neural connections — a phenomenon called **shaken baby syndrome,** or *abusive head trauma* (Christian & Block, 2009). Death is the worst consequence; lifelong intellectual impairment is the more likely one.

Not every infant who has neurological symptoms of head trauma is the victim of abuse: Legal experts worry about false accusations (Byard, 2014). Nonetheless, infants are vulnerable, so the response to a screaming, frustrating baby should be to comfort or walk away, never to shake, yell, or hit.

shaken baby syndrome
A life-threatening injury that occurs when an infant is forcefully shaken back and forth, a motion that ruptures blood vessels in the brain and breaks neural connections.

sensation
The response of a sensory organ (eyes, ears, skin, tongue, nose) when it detects a stimulus.

perception
The mental processing of sensory information when the brain interprets a sensation.

The Senses

Every sense functions at birth. Newborns have open eyes, sensitive ears, and responsive noses, tongues, and skin. Very young babies use all of their senses to attend to everything, especially to people (Zeifman, 2013).

Meanwhile, adults also have an innate fondness of infant "cuteness," the sight, sounds, touch, and smell of the infant. Thus, from the very beginning, a mutual, multifaceted, sensory connection between infant and caregiver is apparent (Kringelbach et al., 2016). Infants are born with the ability to experience sensations, with a drive to perceive, and, as seen years later when they are adults, with an emotional impulse to care for the next generation.

FROM SENSING TO THINKING **Sensation** occurs when a sensory system detects a stimulus, as when the inner ear reverberates with sound or the eye's retina and pupil intercept light. Thus, sensations begin when an outer organ (eye, ear, nose, tongue, or skin) meets anything that can be seen, heard, smelled, tasted, or touched.

Perception occurs when the brain processes a sensation. This happens in the cortex, usually as the result of a message from one of the sensing organs, such as from the eye to the visual cortex.

The sight of a bottle, for instance, is conveyed from the retina to the optic nerve to the visual cortex, but it has no meaning unless the infant has been repeatedly bottle-fed. Similarly, a scrap of paper means nothing to adults unless they are searching for something written on just such a scrap or are trying to clean up

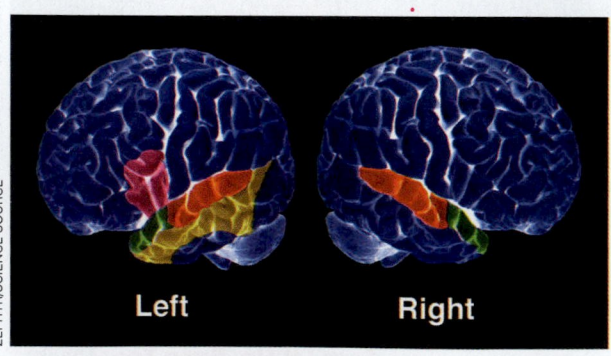

ZEPHYR/SCIENCE SOURCE

Left   **Right**

From Sound to Language Hearing occurs in the temporal lobe, in both hemispheres, the green and some of the orange parts of these brain images. Language comprehension, however, is mostly in the left hemisphere, shown here in the gold region that responds to known words, and in Broca's area, the orange bulb that produces speech. A person could hear but not understand (a baby) or understand but not speak (if Broca's area is damaged).

the floor, the room, the sidewalk. Perceptions require experience and motivation, not just sensation. Without them, the bottle or paper is unnoticed, not really seen.

Thus, perception follows sensation, when sensory stimuli are interpreted in the brain. Then cognition follows perception, when people think about what they have perceived. The baby might reach out for the bottle; the adult might pick up the paper, look at it, and discard it. The sequence from sensation to perception to cognition requires first that the sense organs function. No wonder the parts of the cortex dedicated to hearing, seeing, and so on develop rapidly: Thinking begins there.

HEARING The fetus hears during the last trimester of pregnancy; loud sounds trigger reflexes even without conscious perception. Familiar, rhythmic sounds such as a heartbeat are soothing: That's why newborns may stop crying if they are held with an ear on the mother's chest.

Because of early maturation of the language areas of the cortex, even 4-month-olds attend to voices, developing expectations of the rhythm, segmentation, and cadence of spoken words long before comprehension (Minagawa-Kawai et al., 2011). Soon, sensitive hearing combines with the maturing brain to distinguish patterns of sounds and syllables. That is why hearing is crucial: Ear infections, for instance, need to be treated promptly.

Thus, a newborn named Emily has no concept that *Emily* is her name, but she has the brain and auditory capacity to hear sounds in the usual speech range (not some sounds that other creatures can hear) and an inborn preference for repeated patterns and human speech.

By about 4 months, when her auditory cortex is rapidly creating dendrites, the repeated word *Emily* is perceived as well as sensed, especially because that sound emanates from interactions with the people she often sees, smells, and touches. By 6 months, Emily opens her eyes and smiles when her name is called, perhaps babbling in response.

This rapid development of hearing is the reason newborn hearing is tested. If necessary, remediation begins in infancy. By age 5, deaf children who got cochlear implants before age 2 are much better at understanding and expressing language than those with identical losses but whose implants came later (Tobey et al., 2013).

SEEING Compared to hearing, vision is immature at birth. Although in mid-pregnancy the eyes open and are sensitive to bright light (if a pregnant woman is sunbathing in a bikini, for instance), the fetus has nothing much to see. Newborns are legally blind; they focus only on things quite close to their eyes, such as the face of their breast-feeding mother.

Almost immediately, experience combines with maturation of the visual cortex to improve vision. By 2 months, infants not only stare at faces but also, with perception and the beginning of cognition, smile. (Smiling can occur earlier but not because of perception.)

Binocular vision (coordinating both eyes to see one image) cannot develop in the womb (nothing is far enough away), so many newborns use their two eyes independently, momentarily appearing wall-eyed or cross-eyed. Typically, between 2 and 4 months, experience allows both eyes to focus on a single thing (Wang & Candy, 2010). As with hearing, however, if cataracts or other problems affect infant vision, careful remediation is needed in the first weeks to enable the brain to correctly process what the eyes sense (Tailor et al., 2017).

◆ **Especially for Nurses and Pediatricians**
The parents of a 6-month-old have just been told that their child is deaf. They don't believe it because, as they tell you, the baby babbles as much as their other children did. What do you tell them? (see response, page 123)

binocular vision
The ability to focus the two eyes in a coordinated manner in order to see one image.

BLEND IMAGES · MIKE KEMP/BRAND X PICTURES/GETTY IMAGES

Who's This? Newborns don't know much, but they look intensely at faces. Repeated sensations become perceptions, so in about 6 weeks this baby will smile at Dad, Mom, a stranger, the dog, and every other face. If this father in Utah responds like typical fathers everywhere, by 6 months cognition will be apparent: The baby will chortle with joy at seeing him but become wary of unfamiliar faces.

As perception builds, visual scanning improves. Thus, 3-month-olds look closely at the eyes and mouth, smiling more at happy faces than at angry or expressionless ones. They pay attention to patterns, colors, and motion—the mobile above the crib, for instance.

Because of this rapid development, babies should be allowed to see many sights. A crying baby might be distracted by being taken outside to watch passing cars. Infant vision is attracted to movement and to eyes (more than to hair, for instance). By age 1, infants have learned to interpret facial expressions, to follow the eyes of someone else to see what they are looking at, and to use their own eyes to communicate (Grossman, 2017).

TASTING AND SMELLING As with vision and hearing, smell and taste function at birth and rapidly adapt to the social world. Infants learn to appreciate what their mothers eat, first through breast milk and then through smells and bits of the family dinner.

The foods of a culture may aid survival: For example, bitter foods provide some defense against malaria, hot spices help preserve food and may prevent food poisoning, and so on (Krebs, 2009). Thus, for 1-year-olds, enjoying the taste of their family cuisine not only joins them to their community, it may save their lives.

Notice once again how early experiences sculpt the brain. Taste preferences endure when a person migrates to another culture or when a particular food that was once protective is no longer so. Immigrants may pay high prices to buy the foods that were cheap in their native land because early on they developed an experience-dependent preference. Similarly, in communities threatened with starvation, people sought high-calorie foods. Now many of their descendants like French fries, whipped cream, and bacon, preferences that jeopardize their health.

Adaptation also occurs for the sense of smell. When breast-feeding mothers used a chamomile balm to ease cracked nipples, their babies preferred that smell almost two years later, unlike babies whose mothers used an odorless ointment (Delaunay-El Allam et al., 2010). The smell of bread baking, or garlic frying, or sour pickles brings happy memories to some people because of childhood moments.

As babies learn to recognize each person's scent, they prefer to sleep next to their caregivers, and they nuzzle into their caregivers' chests—especially when the adults are shirtless. One way to help infants who are frightened of the bath (some love bathing, some hate it) is for the parent to join the baby in the tub. The familiar smells of the adult's body and the soap, as well as the touch, sight, and voice of the caregiver, make the entire experience a pleasant one.

Learning About a Lime As with every other normal infant, Jacqueline's curiosity leads to taste and then to a slow reaction, from puzzlement to tongue-out disgust. Jacqueline's responses demonstrate that the sense of taste is acute in infancy and that quick brain perceptions are still to come.

TOUCH AND PAIN The sense of touch is acute in infants. Wrapping, rubbing, massaging, and cradling are comforting. Even when their eyes are closed, some infants stop crying and visibly relax when held securely by their caregivers. In the first year, the heartbeat slows and muscles relax when infants are stroked gently and rhythmically (Fairhurst et al., 2014).

That explains why, worldwide, parents cuddle their newborns—rocking, carrying, and so on. Some touch (gentle of course) seems experience-expectant, essential for normal growth. Beyond that, how much a baby is touched is experience-dependent, varying by culture. In some nations, daily massage begins soon after birth (Trivedi, 2015).

Indeed, in rural India, mothers need to be taught that the newborn's need for warmth is more important than immediate bathing and massage, since both of those common practices may inadvertently harm. Mothers are encouraged to wipe their newborns with a dry cloth and breast-feed immediately—practices that keep the baby warm, use the sense of touch, and reduce early death (Acharya et al., 2015).

Have you noticed that some adults are comforted by a reassuring touch and others cringe? Those opposite reactions reflect opposite childhood experiences.

Pain and temperature are not among the traditional five senses, but they are often connected to touch. Some babies cry when being changed, distressed at the sudden coldness on their skin. Some touches are painful—a poke, pinch, or pat—although at first babies look carefully at the person touching to discern intention, which tells the baby whether or not pain is involved.

Scientists are not certain about infant pain (Fitzgerald, 2015). Some believe that pain receptors are less sensitive at birth—otherwise, how could a baby endure being born? Some experiences that are painful to adults (circumcision, the setting of a broken bone) are much less so to newborns. However, this does not mean that newborns never feel pain (Reavey et al., 2014).

Physiological measures including hormones, heartbeat, and brain waves are studied to assess infant pain, but the conclusions are mixed. Infant brains are immature: They have some similar responses to pain and some dissimilar ones when compared to adults (Moultrie et al., 2016).

If surgery is required at birth, anesthesia is very sparingly used, since overuse might risk death due to slowed breathing. Fortunately, the other senses reduce pain: A drop of sugar water before a heel stick decreases crying, and listening to Mother's voice, or even to calming music, reduces distress (Filippa et al., 2017).

Many hospital NICUs have adopted practices that make the first days of life better for preterm babies, including allowing parents to touch their fragile infants,

THINK CRITICALLY: What political controversy makes objective research on newborn pain difficult?

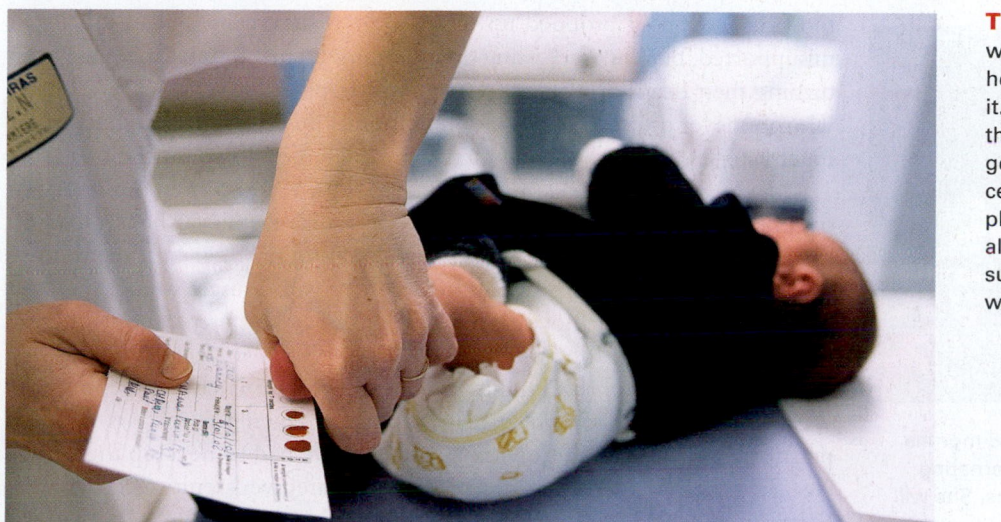

The First Blood Test This baby will cry, but most experts believe the heel prick shown here is well worth it. The drops of blood will reveal the presence of any of several genetic diseases, including sickle-cell disease, cystic fibrosis, and phenylketonuria. Early diagnosis allows early treatment, and the cries subside quickly with a drop of sugar water or a suck of breast milk.

BSIP/UIG VIA GETTY IMAGES

motor skill
The learned abilities to move some part of the body, in actions ranging from a large leap to a flicker of the eyelid. (The word *motor* here refers to movement of muscles.)

gross motor skills
Physical abilities involving large body movements, such as walking and jumping. (The word *gross* here means "big.")

↓ **OBSERVATION** QUIZ
Which of these skills has the greatest variation in age of acquisition? Why? (see answer, page 123)

At About This Time: Age Norms (in Months) for Gross Motor Skills

	When 50% of All Babies Master the Skill	When 90% of All Babies Master the Skill
Sits unsupported	6	7.5
Stands holding on	7.4	9.4
Crawls (creeps)	8	10
Stands not holding	10.8	13.4
Walks well	12.0	14.4
Walks backward	15	17
Runs	18	20
Jumps up	26	29

Note: As the text explains, age norms are affected by culture and cohort. The first five norms are based on babies from five continents [Brazil, Ghana, Norway, United States, Oman, and India] (World Health Organization, 2006). The next three are from a U.S.-only source [Coovadia & Wittenberg, 2004; based on Denver II (Frankenburg et al., 1992)]. Mastering skills a few weeks earlier or later does not indicate health or intelligence. Being very late, however, is a cause for concern.

Advancing and Advanced At 8 months, she is already an adept crawler, alternating hands and knees, intent on progress. She will probably be walking before a year.

eliminating bright lights and noisy monitors, reducing distress through careful swaddling and positioning, and so on. The result is improved social and cognitive development later on (Montirosso et al., 2017).

A few weeks after birth, infants seem to feel pain. Some cry inconsolably for more than three hours, more than three days a week. Digestive pain (colic) caused by the gut microbiome is the usual explanation (Pärtty & Kalliomäki, 2017). Pediatricians know that colic usually disappears by 3 months, so they are not troubled by it; but many parents are overwhelmed. Therefore, developmentalists take crying seriously; it may impair the relationship between infant and caregiver.

Motor Skills

Every **motor skill** (any movement ability), from the newborn's head-lifting to the toddler's stair-climbing, develops over the first two years.

Reflexes become skills if they are practiced and encouraged. As you saw in the chapter's beginning, Mrs. Todd set the foundation for my fourth child's walking when Sarah was only a few months old by encouraging her stepping reflex. Similarly, some 1-year-olds can swim—if adults have built on the swimming reflex by having the infants paddle in water in the early weeks.

GROSS MOTOR SKILLS Deliberate actions that use many parts of the body, producing large movements, are called **gross motor skills.** These skills emerge directly from reflexes and proceed in a *cephalocaudal* (head-down) and *proximodistal* (center-out) direction.

Infants first control their heads, lifting them up to look around, an early example of cephalocaudal maturation. Then control moves downward—upper bodies, arms, and finally legs and feet. (See At About This Time, which shows age norms for gross motor skills based on a large, representative, multiethnic sample of U.S. infants.)

Sitting requires muscles to steady the torso, no simple feat. By 3 months, most babies can sit propped up in a lap. By 6 months, they can usually sit unsupported, but "novice sitting and standing infants lose balance just from turning their heads or lifting their arms" (Adolph & Franchak, 2017). Babies who are never propped up (as in some institutions for orphaned children) sit much later, as do blind babies who cannot use vision to adjust their balance.

Crawling is another example of the head-down and center-out direction of skill mastery, as well as of the importance of practice. When placed on their stomachs, many newborns reflexively try to lift their heads and move their arms as if they were swimming. As they gain muscle strength, infants wiggle, attempting to move forward by pushing their arms, shoulders, and upper bodies against the floor.

Usually by 5 months, infants add their legs to this effort, inching forward (or backward) on their bellies. Exactly when this occurs depends partly on how much "tummy time" infants have had to develop their muscles, and that, of course, is affected by the caregiver's culture (Zachry & Kitzmann, 2011).

Most 8- to 10-month-olds can lift their midsections and crawl (or *creep,* as the British call it) on "all fours," coordinating the movements of their hands and knees. Crawling depends on experience, not just maturation. Some normal babies never do it, especially if the floor is cold, hot, or rough, or if they always lie on their backs. It is not true that babies must crawl to develop normally.

All babies find a way to move (inching, bear-walking, scooting, creeping, or crawling) before they walk, but many resist being placed on their stomachs. Heavier babies master gross motor skills later than leaner ones because practice and balance is harder when the body is heavy (Slining et al., 2010).

As soon as they are able, babies stand and then take some independent steps, falling frequently at first, about 32 times per hour. They persevere because walking is much quicker than crawling, and it has other advantages—better sight lines and free hands (Adolph & Tamis-LeMonda, 2014).

Once toddlers can walk by themselves, they practice obsessively, barefoot or not, at home or in stores, on sidewalks or streets, on lawns or in mud. Some caregivers offer many opportunities, holding infants to walk in the bath, after diapering, around the house, on the sidewalk. Indeed, "practice, not merely maturation, underlies improvements . . . in 1 hour of free play, the average toddler takes about 2400 steps, travels the length of about 8 U.S. football fields, and falls 17 times" (Adolph & Franchak, 2017).

FINE MOTOR SKILLS Small body movements are called **fine motor skills.** The most valued fine motor skills are finger movements, enabling writing, drawing, typing, tying, and so on. Movements of the tongue, jaw, lips, teeth, and toes are fine movements, too.

Actually, mouth skills precede hand skills by many months (newborns can suck; chewing precedes drawing by a year or more). Since every culture encourages finger dexterity, children practice finger movements, and adults give toddlers spoons, or chopsticks, or markers. By contrast, mouth skills such as spitting or biting are not praised. (Only other children admire blowing bubbles with gum.)

Regarding hand skills, newborns have a strong reflexive grasp but lack control. During their first 2 months, babies excitedly stare and wave their arms at objects dangling within reach. By 3 months they can usually touch such objects, but because of limited eye–hand coordination they cannot yet grab and hold on unless an object is placed in their hands.

By 4 months, infants sometimes grab, but their timing is off: They close their hands too early or too late. Finally, by 6 months, with a concentrated, deliberate stare, most babies

Bossa Nova Baby? This girl in Brazil demonstrates her joy at acquiring the gross motor skill of walking, which may quickly become dancing whenever music plays.

RADIUS IMAGES/ALAMY STOCK PHOTO

fine motor skills
Physical abilities involving small body movements, especially of the hands and fingers, such as drawing or picking up a coin. (The word *fine* here means "small.")

VIDEO: Fine Motor Skills in Infancy and Toddlerhood shows the sequence in which babies and toddlers acquire fine motor skills.

At About This Time: Age Norms (in Months) for Fine Motor Skills

	When 50% of All Babies Master the Skill	When 90% of All Babies Master the Skill
Grasps rattle when placed in hand	3	4
Reaches to hold an object	4.5	6
Thumb and finger grasp	8	10
Stacks two blocks	15	21
Imitates vertical line (drawing)	30	39

Data from World Health Organization, 2006.

can reach, grab, and grasp. Some can even transfer an object from one hand to the other.

Almost all can hold a bottle, shake a rattle, or yank a sister's braids. Toward the end of the first year and throughout the second, finger skills improve as babies master the pincer movement (using thumb and forefinger to pick up tiny objects) and self-feeding (first with hands, then fingers, then utensils) (Ho, 2010). (See At About This Time on page 95.)

As with gross motor skills, fine motor skills are shaped by practice, which is relentless from the third month of prenatal development throughout childhood. Practice is especially obvious in the first year, when "infants flap their arms, rotate their hands, and wiggle their fingers, and exhibit bouts of rhythmical waving, rubbing, and banging while holding objects" (Adolph & Franchak, 2017).

AGE AND CULTURE When U.S. infants are grouped by ethnicity, generally African American babies are ahead of Hispanic American babies when it comes to motor skills. In turn, Hispanic American babies are ahead of those of European descent. Internationally, the earliest walkers are in sub-Saharan Africa, where many well-nourished and healthy babies walk at 10 months.

As found in detailed studies in Senegal and Kenya, babies in many African communities are massaged and stretched from birth onward and are encouraged to walk. They may take their first independent step at 9 months. The latest walkers may be in rural China (15 months), where infants are bundled up against the cold (Adolph & Robinson, 2013).

Some cultures discourage walking if danger (poisonous snakes, open fires) abounds, so infants are safer if they cannot wander. By contrast, some cultures encourage running. Their offspring run marathons (Adolph & Franchak, 2017).

Remember that difference is not deficit. However, slow development *relative to local norms* may indicate a problem that needs attention; lags are much easier to remedy during infancy than later on.

The age at which walking occurs is a better predictor than simple chronological age of a child's verbal ability, perhaps because walking children elicit more language from caregivers than crawling ones do (Walle & Campos, 2014). The correlation could go in the opposite direction as well: Walkers see their caregivers more, so they talk more (Adolph & Tamis-LeMonda, 2014, p. 191).

what have you learned?

1. Why is it not worrisome if an infant is consistently at the 20th percentile in height and weight?

2. How do sleep patterns change over the first 18 months?

3. What are the reasons for and against bed-sharing?

4. How does the brain change from birth to age 2?

5. How can pruning increase brain potential?

6. How do experience-expectant and experience-dependent developments differ?

7. How does vision change over the first year?

8. How do the senses strengthen early social interactions?

9. What is the sequence for gross motor skills?

10. Which fine motor skills develop in infancy?

Infant Cognition

The rapid development of sensory and motor skills just described is impressive, but the intellectual growth that uses those sensorimotor skills is even more awesome. Recognition of this was one of Piaget's insights.

Sensorimotor Intelligence

Piaget called cognition in the first two years **sensorimotor intelligence.** He subdivided this period into six stages (see Table 3.1). [**Life-Span Link:** Piaget's theory of cognitive development is introduced in Chapter 1.]

STAGES ONE AND TWO Stage one, called the *stage of reflexes,* lasts only a month. It includes senses as well as motor reflexes, the foundations of infant thought. In this stage, infants adapt their sucking reflex to bottles or breasts, pacifiers or fingers, each requiring specific types of tongue pushing. This adaptation signifies that infants have begun to interpret sensations; they are using their minds—some would say "thinking."

Soon sensation leads to perception, which ushers in stage two, *first acquired adaptations* (also called the *stage of first habits*). During this stage, infant cognition leads babies to suck in some ways for hunger, in other ways for comfort—and not to suck fuzzy blankets.

STAGES THREE AND FOUR By 4 months (stage three), reactions are no longer confined to the infant's body; they are an *interaction* between the baby and

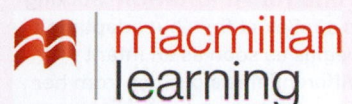

VIDEO: Sensorimotor Intelligence in Infancy and Toddlerhood shows how senses and motor skills fuel infant cognition.

sensorimotor intelligence
Piaget's term for the way infants think—by using their senses and motor skills—during the first period of cognitive development.

TABLE 3.1 The Six Stages of Sensorimotor Intelligence

For an overview of the stages of sensorimotor thought, it helps to group the six stages into pairs.

Primary Circular Reactions

The first two stages involve infants' responses to their own bodies.

Stage One (birth to 1 month)	*Reflexes:* sucking, grasping, staring, listening
	Example: sucking anything that touches the lips or cheek
Stage Two (1–4 months)	*The first acquired adaptations:* accommodation and coordination of reflexes
	Examples: sucking a pacifier differently from a nipple; attempting to hold a bottle to suck it

Secondary Circular Reactions

The next two stages involve infants' responses to objects and people.

Stage Three (4–8 months)	*Making interesting sights last:* responding to people and objects
	Example: clapping hands when mother says "patty-cake"
Stage Four (8–12 months)	*New adaptation and anticipation:* becoming more deliberate and purposeful in responding to people and objects
	Example: putting mother's hands together in order to make her start playing patty-cake

Tertiary Circular Reactions

The last two stages are the most creative, first with action and then with ideas.

Stage Five (12–18 months)	*New means through active experimentation:* experimentation and creativity in the actions of the "little scientist"
	Example: putting a teddy bear in the toilet and flushing it
Stage Six (18–24 months)	*New means through mental combinations:* thinking before doing, new ways of achieving a goal without resorting to trial and error
	Example: before flushing the teddy bear again, hesitating because of the memory of the toilet overflowing and mother's anger

Time for Adaptation Sucking is a reflex at first, but adaptation begins as soon as an infant differentiates a pacifier from her mother's breast or realizes that her hand is too big to fit into her mouth. This infant's expression of concentration suggests that she is about to make that adaptation and suck just her thumb from now on.

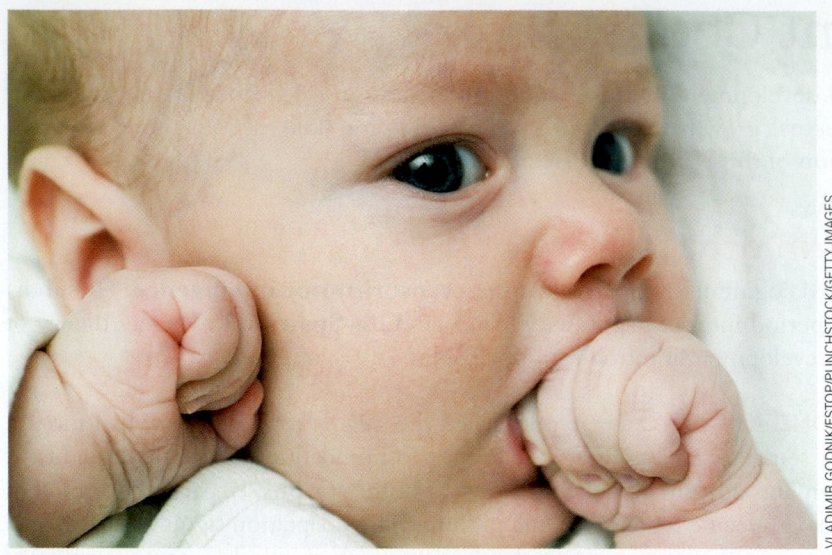

VLADIMIR GODNIK/FSTOP/PUNCHSTOCK/GETTY IMAGES

something—or someone—else. At first babies are merely responsive to what happens: Stage three is also called the stage of "making interesting sights last."

By stage four (between 8 and 12 months), babies initiate actions to get what they want. Seeing a parent putting on a coat, they might drag over their own jackets to signal that they want to go along. If the caregivers have been using sign language, among the first signs learned are "eat" and "more." Even without parental signing, babies this age begin displaying some universal signs—pointing, pushing, and reaching up to be held.

Piaget thought that, at about 8 months, babies first understand **object permanence**—the realization that objects or people continue to exist when they are no longer in sight. As Piaget discovered, not until about 8 months do infants search for toys that have fallen from the crib, rolled under a couch, or disappeared under a blanket. Babies with visual impairment also acquire object permanence toward the end of their first year, reaching for an object that they hear nearby (Fazzi et al., 2011).

As a recent statement of this phenomenon explains:

> Many parents in our typical American middle-class households have tried out Piaget's experiment in situ: Take an adorable, drooling 7-month-old baby, show her a toy she loves to play with, then cover it with a piece of cloth right in front of her eyes. What do you observe next? The baby does not know what to do to get the toy! She looks around, oblivious to the object's continuing existence under the cloth cover, and turns her attention to something else interesting in her environment. A few months later, the same baby will readily reach out and yank away the cloth cover to retrieve the highly desirable toy. This experiment has been done thousands of times and the phenomenon remains one of the most compelling in all of developmental psychology.

[Xu, 2013, p. 167]

object permanence
The realization that objects (including people) still exist when they can no longer be seen, touched, or heard.

THINK CRITICALLY: Why did Piaget call cognition in the first two years "sensorimotor intelligence"?

This excerpt describes Piaget's classic experiment to measure object permanence: An adult shows an infant an interesting toy, covers it with a lightweight cloth, and observes the response. The results:

- Infants younger than 8 months do not search for the object by removing the cloth.
- At about 8 months infants search, removing the cloth immediately after the object is covered but not if they have to wait a few seconds.

Family Fun Peek-a-boo makes all three happy, each for cognitive reasons. The 9-month-old is discovering object permanence, his sister (at the concrete operational stage) enjoys making Brother laugh, and their mother understands more abstract ideas—such as family bonding.

- At 18 months, they search quite well, even after a wait, but not if they have seen the object put first in one place and then moved to another. They search in the first place, not the second, a mistake called the *A-not-B error*. Thus, they search where they remember seeing it put (A), somehow not understanding that they saw it moved (to B).
- By 2 years, children fully understand object permanence, progressing through several stages of ever-advanced cognition (Piaget, 1954/2013a).

This sequence has intrigued scientists as well as parents for decades, as it clearly indicates cognition, maturation, and motivation together. However, as you will see later, Piaget misestimated the age of object permanence, because he did not take into account the brain activity of the infant.

STAGES FIVE AND SIX At about 12 months, Piaget found that infants begin to actively experiment. At first they do not think before acting, as when they squeeze all of the toothpaste out of the tube, draw on the wall, or uncover an anthill. Piaget called 1-year-olds "*little scientists*" who "experiment in order to see." Their devotion to discovery is familiar to every adult scientist—and to every parent.

Finally, toward the end of the second year, toddlers think about what they are doing before they do it, hesitating a moment before yanking the cat's tail or dropping a raw egg on the floor. Of course, the urge to explore may overtake caution: Things that are truly dangerous (cleaning fluids, swimming pools, open windows) need to be locked and gated.

The ability to combine thoughts and actions allows toddlers to pretend. For instance, they know that a doll is not a real baby, but they can strap it into a stroller and take it for a walk. At 22 months,

"IS THIS THE WAY YOU PLAN TO SPEND YOUR PEAK LEARNING YEARS?"

Still Wrong Parents used to ignore infant cognition. Now some make the opposite mistake, assuming that infants learn via active study.

Imitation Is Lifelong As this photo illustrates, at every age, people copy what others do—often to their mutual joy. The new ability at stage six is "deferred imitation"— this boy may have seen another child lie on a tire a few days earlier.

◆ **Especially for Parents**
One parent wants to put all breakable or dangerous objects away because the toddler is able to move around independently. The other parent says that the baby should learn not to touch certain things. Who is right? (see response, page 123)

information-processing theory
The idea that human cognition and comprehension occurs step by step, similar to the way that input, analysis, and output occur via computer.

VIDEO: Event-Related Potential (ERP) Research shows a procedure in which the electrical activity of an infant's brain is recorded to see whether the brain responds differently to familiar versus unfamiliar words.

my grandson gave me imaginary "shoe ice cream" and laughed when I pretended to eat it.

They also watch other people carefully and draw conclusions about what they see. *Deferred imitation* occurs when infants copy behavior that they noticed hours or even days earlier (Piaget, 1962/2013c). Piaget described his daughter, Jacqueline, who observed another child

> who got into a terrible temper. He screamed as he tried to get out of a playpen and pushed it backwards, stamping his feet. J. stood watching him in amazement, never having witnessed such a scene before. The next day, she herself screamed in her playpen and tried to move it, stamping her foot lightly several times in succession.
>
> *[Piaget, 1962/2013c, p. 63]*

These words illustrate Piaget's genius: He observed children carefully, noticing how they thought at each stage. Scientists were awed by Piaget's recognition that babies "learn so fast and so well" (Xu & Kushnir, 2013, p. 28). However, he underestimated the age at which various accomplishments occurred. You already saw this with object permanence; the same is true for deferred imitation.

Information Processing

Piaget's emphasis on senses and motor abilities limited his understanding of infant cognition. He missed many early cognitive accomplishments, now apparent from brain scans, heart rate, muscle tension, and gaze.

As explained in Chapter 1, Piaget's sweeping overview of cognition contrasts with **information-processing theory,** which breaks down cognition into hundreds of small steps between input and output. Computer analysis measures cognition long before the baby can demonstrate understanding.

Information-processing research has found that signs of attention may be a critical indication of cognition. Babies who focus intently on new stimuli and then turn away are more intelligent than babies who stare aimlessly (Bornstein & Colombo, 2012). Smart babies like novelty and try to understand it (Schulz, 2015).

MEMORY IN THE FIRST YEAR We focus now on one specific ability that Piaget underestimated and that information processing reveals: memory (Schneider, 2015).

BRUESWU/MOMENT OPEN/GETTY IMAGES

One crucial insight from information-processing theory is that the infant brain is a very active organ, ready from birth to take in experiences and remember repeated ones (Aslin, 2017). Within the first days after birth, infants recognize their caregivers by face, voice, and smell.

Innovative ways to measure cognition have been crucial to the research that finds that Piaget did not realize that the idea of object permanence can emerge before 8 months. The best-known example is a series of studies by Renee Baillargeon which proved that 3-month-old infants grasp object permanence, long before 8 months, when Piaget thought it began. They remember what they saw!

Baillargeon devised clever experiments that entailed showing infants an object, then covering it with a screen, and then removing the screen. If the object vanished behind the screen, the babies' brain waves, heart rate, or focused eyes showed surprise. That meant they expected the object to still be present—i.e., that an object's existence was permanent (Baillargeon & DeVos, 1991; Spelke, 1993).

SURPRISE AND THE BRAIN The conclusion that surprise indicates object permanence is accepted by most scientists. Other scientists are less convinced (Mareschal & Kaufman, 2012). They may interpret object permanence differently (Marcovitch et al., 2016), noticing the fragility of the concept in early infancy (Bremner et al., 2015) or suggesting other measures of surprise (Dunn & Bremner, 2017). But, everyone agrees that waiting until babies can physically uncover an object is waiting too long: Babies are thinking before bodies can demonstrate cognition.

Cognition can be measured via surprise, by gaze, by movement of arms and legs. Caregivers notice that babies look around and seem intently interested in what is happening. Adults also have better ways to interpret what they see. Instead of noticing children's many "faults or shortcomings relative to an adult standard," we need to appreciate that children remember what they need to remember (Bjorklund & Sellers, 2014, p. 142). Infants remember who their caregivers are, and soon remember what those caregivers do and say.

Repeated sensations and brain maturation are required in order to process and recall whatever happens. That is true later in life as well (Bauer et al., 2010). Everyone's memory fades with time, especially if that memory was never encoded into language, never compared with similar events, never discussed with a friend.

FORGET ABOUT INFANT AMNESIA! Piaget, Freud, and other early developmentalists described *infant amnesia*, the idea that people forget everything that happened to them before age 3. However, although adults do not remember what happened at age 1, they evidently do remember many simple things—especially when emotion is involved.

Selective Amnesia As we grow older, we forget about spitting up, nursing, crying, and almost everything else from our early years. However, strong emotions (love, fear, mistrust) may leave lifelong traces.

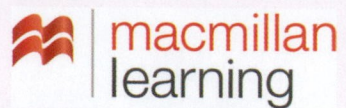

VIDEO: Contingency Learning in Young Infants shows Carolyn Rovee-Collier's procedure for studying instrumental learning during infancy.

An insight regarding infant amnesia begins with the distinction between *implicit* and *explicit* memory. Implicit memory is not verbal; it is memory for movement or thoughts that are not put into words. Implicit memory begins by 3 months, is stable by 9 months, continues to improve for the first two years, and varies from one infant to another (Vöhringer et al., 2017). Explicit memory takes longer to emerge, as it depends on language.

Thus, when people say "I don't remember," they mean "I cannot recall it," because it is not in explicit memory. Unconsciously and implicitly, a memory might be present. A person might have an irrational fear of doctors or hospitals, for instance, because of terrifying and painful experiences in the first year—experiences they do not consciously recall.

REMIND ME! The most dramatic proof of very early memory comes from a series of innovative experiments in which 3-month-olds learned to move a mobile by kicking their legs (Rovee-Collier, 1987, 1990). The infants lay on their backs connected to a mobile by means of a ribbon tied to one foot.

Virtually all of the babies realized that kicking made the mobile move. They then kicked more vigorously and frequently, sometimes laughing at their accomplishment. So far, this is no surprise—observing self-activated movement is highly reinforcing to infants.

When infants as young as 3 months had the mobile-and-ribbon apparatus reinstalled and reconnected *one week later,* most started to kick immediately, proof that they remembered their previous experience. But when other 3-month-old infants were retested *two weeks later,* they kicked randomly. Had they forgotten? It seemed so.

But then the lead researcher, Carolyn Rovee-Collier, *two weeks after* the initial training, allowed some infants to watch the mobile move when they were not connected to it. The next day, when a ribbon again tied their leg to the mobile, they kicked almost immediately.

Apparently, watching the mobile the previous day reminded them about what they had previously experienced. Other research similarly finds that reminders are powerful. If Daddy routinely plays with a 3-month-old, goes on a long trip, and the mother shows Daddy's picture and says his name on the day before his return, the baby might grin broadly when he reappears.

◆ **Especially for Teachers**
People of every age remember best when they are active learners. If you had to teach fractions to a class of 8-year-olds, how would you do it? (see response, page 123)

He Remembers! Infants are fascinated by moving objects within a few feet of their eyes—that's why parents buy mobiles for cribs and why Rovee-Collier tied a string to a mobile and a baby's leg to test memory. Babies not in her experiment, like this one, sometimes flail their limbs to make their cribs shake and thus make their mobiles move. Piaget's stage of "making interesting sights last" is evident to every careful observer.

IAN BODDY/SCIENCE SOURCE

OLDER INFANTS At 12 months, more improvement is evident. One-year-olds learn from parents and strangers, from other babies and older siblings, from picture books and family photographs, from their own walking and talking (Hayne & Simcock, 2009). Dendrites grow to reflect remembered experiences.

Every day of their young lives, infants are processing information and storing conclusions. Indeed, if you saw a photo of a grandmother who cared for you every day when you were an infant and who died when you were 2, your brain would still react, even though you thought she was forgotten. Information-processing research finds evidence of early memories, with visual memories particularly strong (Leung et al., 2016; Gao et al., 2016).

---

what have you learned?

1. How does stage one of sensorimotor intelligence lead to stage two?
2. In sensorimotor intelligence, what is the difference between stages three and four?
3. Why is the concept of object permanence important to an infant's development?
4. What does the active experimentation of the stage-five toddler suggest for parents?
5. Why did Piaget underestimate infant cognition?
6. What conditions help 3-month-olds remember something?

Language: What Develops in the First Two Years?

Human linguistic ability by age 2 far surpasses that of full-grown adults from every other species. Very young infants listen intensely, responding as best they can. One scholar explains, "infants are acquiring much of their native language before they utter their first word" (Aslin, 2012, p. 191). How do they do it?

The Universal Sequence

The sequence of language development is the same worldwide (see At About This Time on page 105). Some children learn several languages, some only one; some learn rapidly, others slowly. But all follow the same path.

LISTENING AND RESPONDING Newborns prefer to listen to the language their mother spoke when they were in the womb. They do not understand the words, of course, but they like the familiar rhythm, sounds, and cadence.

Surprisingly, newborns of bilingual mothers differentiate between the languages (Byers-Heinlein et al., 2010). Data were collected on 94 newborns (age 0 to 5 days) in a large hospital in Vancouver, Canada. Half were born to mothers who spoke both English and Tagalog (a language native to the Philippines), one-third to mothers who spoke only English, and one-sixth to mothers who spoke English and Chinese.

The infants in all three groups sucked on a pacifier connected to a recording of 10 minutes of English and 10 minutes of Tagalog. The two languages were matched for pitch, duration, and number of syllables.

Who Is Babbling? Probably both the 6-month-old and the 27-year-old. During every day of infancy, mothers and babies communicate with noises, movements, and expressions.

ARIEL SKELLEY/GETTY IMAGES

As evident in their sucking, most of the infants with bilingual mothers preferred Tagalog. For the Filipino babies, this was probably because their mothers spoke English in formal settings but not when with family and friends, so Tagalog was associated with more relaxed and animated talk. Those babies with English-only mothers preferred English (Byers-Heinlein et al., 2010).

Curiously, the Chinese bilingual babies, who had never heard Tagalog, nonetheless preferred it to English. The researchers believe that they liked Tagalog because the rhythm of that language is similar to Chinese (Byers-Heinlein et al., 2010).

Infants improve in their ability to distinguish sounds in whatever language they hear, whereas their ability to hear sounds never spoken in their native language (such as another way to pronounce "r" or "l") deteriorates (Narayan et al., 2010). If parents want a child to speak two languages, they should speak both of them to their baby from birth on.

By 12 months, analysis of brain waves finds that babies attend to sounds of their native language; unlike 6-month-olds, their brains seem indifferent to sounds of languages they never hear. The brains of bilingual 1-year-olds respond to both languages (Ramírez et al., 2017).

In every language, adults use higher pitch, simpler words, repetition, varied speed, and exaggerated emotional tone when talking to infants. Babies respond with attention and emotion. By 7 months, they begin to recognize words that are highly distinctive (Singh, 2008): *Bottle, doggie,* and *mama,* for instance, might be differentiated, but not *baby, Bobbie,* and *Barbie.*

Infants also like alliteration, rhymes, repetition, melody, rhythm, and varied pitch. Think of your favorite lullaby (itself an alliterative word); obviously, babies prefer sounds over content and singing over talking (Tsang et al., 2017). Early listening abilities and preferences are the result of brain function.

BABBLING AND GESTURING Between 6 and 9 months, babies repeat certain syllables (*ma-ma-ma, da-da-da, ba-ba-ba*), a vocalization called **babbling** because of the way it sounds. Babbling is experience-expectant; all babies babble and caregivers usually encourage those noises. Babbling predicts later vocabulary, even more than the other major influence—the education of the mother (McGillion et al., 2017).

babbling
An infant's repetition of certain syllables, such as *ba-ba-ba,* that begins when babies are between 6 and 9 months old.

At About This Time: The Development of Spoken Language in the First Two Years

Age*	Means of Communication
Newborn	Reflexive communication—cries, movements, facial expressions.
2 months	A range of meaningful noises—cooing, fussing, crying, laughing.
3–6 months	New sounds, including squeals, growls, croons, trills, vowel sounds.
6–10 months	Babbling, including both consonant and vowel sounds repeated in syllables.
10–12 months	Comprehension of simple words; speechlike intonations; specific vocalizations that have meaning to those who know the infant well. Deaf babies express their first signs; hearing babies also use specific gestures (e.g., pointing) to communicate.
12 months	First spoken words that are recognizably part of the native language.
13–18 months	Slow growth of vocabulary, up to about 50 words.
18 months	Naming explosion—three or more words learned per day. Much variation: Some toddlers do not yet speak.
21 months	First two-word sentence.
24 months	Multiword sentences. Half of the toddler's utterances are two or more words long.

*The ages in this table reflect norms. Many healthy, intelligent children attain each linguistic accomplishment earlier or later than indicated here.

Expectations appear early. Before uttering their first word, infants notice patterns of speech, such as which sounds are commonly spoken together. A baby who often hears that something is "pretty" expects the sound of *prit* to be followed by *tee* (MacWhinney, 2015) and is startled if someone says "prit-if."

Infants also learn the relationship between mouth movements and sound. In one study, 8-month-olds watched a film of someone speaking, with the audio a fraction of a second ahead of the video. Even when the actor spoke an unknown language, babies noticed the mistiming (Pons & Lewkowicz, 2014).

Some caregivers, recognizing the power of gestures, teach "baby signs" to their 6- to 12-month-olds. Then babies use hand signs months before they move their tongues, lips, and jaws to make words.

There is no evidence that baby signing accelerates talking (as had been claimed), but it may make parents more responsive, which itself is an advantage (Kirk et al., 2013). For deaf babies, sign language is crucial in the first year: It not only predicts later ability to communicate with signs but also advances crucial cognitive development (Hall et al., 2017).

Even without adult signing, gestures become a powerful means of communication (Goldin-Meadow, 2015). One early gesture is pointing and responding to pointing from someone else. The latter requires something quite sophisticated—understanding another person's perspective.

Most animals cannot interpret pointing; most 10-month-old humans can. They look at where someone else points and already point with their tiny index fingers. Pointing is well developed by 12 months, especially when the person who

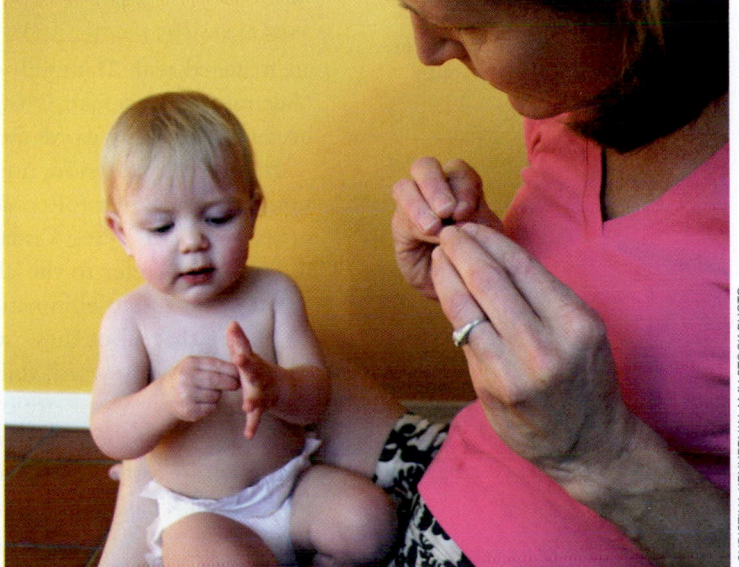

Are You Hungry? Pronunciation is far more difficult than hand skills, but parents want to know when their baby wants more to eat. One solution is evident here. This mother is teaching her 12-month-old daughter the sign for "more," a word most toddlers say months later.

© CHRISTINA KENNEDY/ALAMY STOCK PHOTO

Show Me Where Pointing is one of the earliest forms of communication, emerging at about 10 months. As you see here, pointing is useful lifelong for humans.

holophrase
A single word that is used to express a complete, meaningful thought.

naming explosion
A sudden increase in an infant's vocabulary, especially in the number of nouns, that begins at about 18 months of age.

is pointing also speaks (e.g., "look at that") (Daum et al., 2013).

FIRST WORDS Finally, at about a year, the average baby utters a few words, understood by caregivers if not by strangers. In the first months of the second year, spoken vocabulary increases gradually (perhaps one new word a week). Meanings are learned rapidly; babies understand much more than they say.

Initially, the first words are merely labels for familiar things (*mama* and *dada* are common). Each early word soon becomes a **holophrase,** a single word that expresses an entire thought. That is accompanied by gestures, facial expressions, and nuances of tone, loudness, and cadence (Saxton, 2010). Imagine meaningful communication in "Dada," "Dada?" and "Dada!" Each is a holophrase.

Of course, the thought in the baby's mind may not be what the adult understands. I know this personally. I was caring for my 16-month-old grandson when he said, "Mama, mama." He looked directly at me, and he didn't seem wistful.

"Mommy's not here," I told him. That didn't interest him; he repeated "mama, mama," more as a command than a complaint. I offered him milk in his sippy cup. He said, "No, no."

When his father appeared, Isaac repeated "mama." Then his dad lifted him up, and Isaac happily cuddled in his arms. I asked what "mama" means. The reply: "Pick me up." I now understand Isaac's logic: When he saw his mother, he said "mama" and she picked him up.

THE NAMING EXPLOSION Spoken vocabulary builds rapidly once the first 50 words are mastered, with 21-month-olds typically saying twice as many words as 18-month-olds (Adamson & Bakeman, 2006). This language spurt is called the **naming explosion** because many early words are nouns, that is, names of persons, places, or things.

Before the explosion, nouns are already favored. Infants learn the names of each significant caregiver (often *dada, mama, nana, papa, baba, tata*) and sibling (and sometimes each pet). (See Visualizing Development on page 107.) Other frequently uttered words refer to the child's favorite foods (*nana* can mean "banana" as well as "grandma") and to elimination (*pee-pee, wee-wee, poo-poo, ka-ka, doo-doo*).

Notice that all of these words have two identical syllables, a consonant followed by a vowel. Many words follow that pattern—not just *baba* but also *bobo, bebe, bubu, bibi*. Other early words are only slightly more complicated—*ma-me, ama,* and so on. The meaning of these words varies by language, but every baby says such words, and every culture assigns meaning to them. Such words are easier in the naming explosion as well: That's why rabbits are "bunnies" and stomachs are "tummies."

CULTURAL DIFFERENCES Early communication transcends culture. In one study, 102 adults listened to 40 recorded infant sounds and were asked which of five possibilities (pointing, giving, protesting, action request, food request) was the reason for each cry, grunt, or whatever. Half of the sounds, and about half of the adults, were from Scotland and the other half from Uganda. Adults in both cultures scored significantly better than chance (although no group or individual got everything right). It did not matter much whether the sounds came from Scottish or Ugandan infants, or whether the adults were parents or not (Kersken et al., 2017).

However, cultures and families vary in how much child-directed speech children hear. Some parents read to their infants, teach them signs, and respond to every burp

Visualizing Development

EARLY COMMUNICATION AND LANGUAGE DEVELOPMENT

Communication Milestones: The First Two Years

These are norms. Many intelligent and healthy babies vary in the age at which they reach these milestones.

Months	Communication Milestone
0	Reflexive communication—cries, movements, facial expressions
1	Recognizes some sounds Makes several different cries and sounds Turns toward familiar sounds
3	A range of meaningful noises—cooing, fussing, crying, laughing Social smile well established Laughter begins Imitates movements Enjoys interaction with others
6	New sounds, including squeals, growls, croons, trills, vowel sounds Meaningful gestures including showing excitement (waving arms and legs) Deaf babies express their first signs Expresses negative feelings (with face and arms) Capable of distinguishing emotion by tone of voice Responds to noises by making sounds Uses noise to express joy and unhappiness Babbles, including both consonant and vowel sounds repeated in syllables
10	Makes simple gestures, like raising arms for "pick me up" Recognizes pointing Makes a sound (not in recognizable language) to indicate a particular thing Responds to simple requests
12	More gestures, such as shaking head for "no" Babbles with inflection, intonation Names familiar people (like "mama," "dada," "nana") Uses exclamations, such as "uh-oh!" Tries to imitate words Points and responds to pointing First spoken words
18	Combines two words (like "Daddy bye-bye") Slow growth of vocabulary, up to about 50 words Language use focuses on 10–30 holophrases Uses nouns and verbs Uses movement, including running and throwing, to indicate emotion Naming explosion may begin, three or more words learned per day Much variation: Some toddlers do not yet speak
24	Combines three or four words together; half the toddler's utterances are two or more words long Uses adjectives and adverbs ("blue," "big," "gentle") Sings simple songs

Source: American Academy of Pediatrics

Universal First Words

Across cultures, babies' first words are remarkably similar. The words for mother and father are recognizable in almost any language. Most children will learn to name their immediate family and caregivers between the ages of 12 and 18 months.

Language	Mother	Father
English	mama, mommy	dada. daddy
Spanish	mama	papa
French	maman, mama	papa
Italian	mamma	bebbo, papa
Latvian	mama	te-te
Syrian Arabic	mama	babe
Bantu	be-mama	taata
Swahili	mama	baba
Sanskrit	nana	tata
Hebrew	ema	abba
Korean	oma	apa

AMPYANG/ISTOCK/GETTY IMAGES

Mastering Language

Children's use of language becomes more complex as they acquire more words and begin to master grammar and usage. A child's spoken words or sounds (utterances) are broken down into the smallest units of language to determine their length and complexity:

SAMPLES OF UTTERANCES

"Doggie!" = 1

"Doggie + Sleep" = 2

"Doggie + Sleep + ing" = 3

"Shh! + Doggie + Sleep + ing" = 4

"Shh! + Doggie + is + Sleep + ing" = 5

"Shh! + The + Doggie + is + Sleep + ing" = 6

Source: Courtesy of Monica Kalfur, SLP

or fart as if it were an attempt to talk. Other parents are much less verbal. They use gestures and touch; they say "hush" and "no" instead of expanding vocabulary.

Traditionally, in small agricultural communities, the goal was for everyone to be "strong and silent." If adults talked too much, they might be called a blabbermouth or gossip; a good worker did not waste time in conversation. In some rural areas of the world, that notion might continue, as in Senegal, where mothers traditionally feared talking to their babies lest that might encourage evil spirits to take over the child (Zeitlin, 2011).

However, communication is crucial in the twenty-first-century global economy, and verbal proficiency is needed in childhood. Government, teachers, and parents recognize this: A child's first words are celebrated as much as or more than a child's first steps. But many parents do not realize they should express joy and vocalize to infant noises.

In one study in Senegal, professionals from the local community (fluent in Wolof, the language spoken by the people) taught mothers in some villages about infant development. A year later those babies were compared to babies in similar towns where the educational intervention had not been offered.

The newly educated mothers talked more to their babies, and the babies, in turn, talked more, with more utterances in five minutes than the control group (A. Weber et al., 2017). Those who designed this study were careful not to challenge the traditional notions directly; instead they taught how early language development advanced infant cognition. The mothers did the rest.

PUTTING WORDS TOGETHER Grammar includes all of the methods that languages use to communicate meaning. Word order, prefixes, suffixes, intonation, verb forms, pronouns and negations, prepositions and articles—all of these are aspects of grammar.

Grammar is evident in holophrases: One word is spoken differently depending on meaning. Grammar becomes essential when babies combine words (Bremner & Wachs, 2010). That typically happens between 18 and 24 months.

For example, "Baby cry" and "More juice" follow grammatical word order. Children do not usually ask "Juice more," and even toddlers know that "cry baby" is not the same as "baby cry." By age 2, children combine three words. English grammar uses subject–verb–object order. Toddlers say, "Mommy read book" rather than any of the five other possible sequences of those three words.

Children's proficiency in grammar correlates with sentence length, which is why **mean length of utterance (MLU)** is used to measure a child's language progress (e.g., Miyata et al., 2013). The child who says "Baby is crying" is more advanced than the child who says "Baby crying" or simply "Baby!"

Theories of Language Learning

Worldwide, people who are not yet 2 years old express hopes, fears, and memories—sometimes in more than one language. By adolescence, people communicate with nuanced words and gestures, some writing poems and lyrics that move thousands of their co-linguists. How is language learned so easily and so well?

Answers come from at least three schools of thought. The first theory says that infants are directly taught, the second that social impulses propel infants to communicate, and the third that infants understand language because of brain advances that began several millennia ago.

THEORY ONE: INFANTS NEED TO BE TAUGHT One idea arises from behaviorism. The essential idea is that learning is acquired, step by step, through association and reinforcement.

◆ **Especially for Teachers**
An infant day-care center has a new child whose parents speak a language other than the one the teachers speak. Should the teachers learn basic words in the new language, or should they expect the baby to learn the teachers' language? (see response, page 123)

grammar
All of the methods—word order, verb forms, and so on—that languages use to communicate meaning, apart from the words themselves.

mean length of utterance (MLU)
The average number of words in a typical sentence (called utterance because children may not talk in complete sentences). MLU is often used to measure language development.

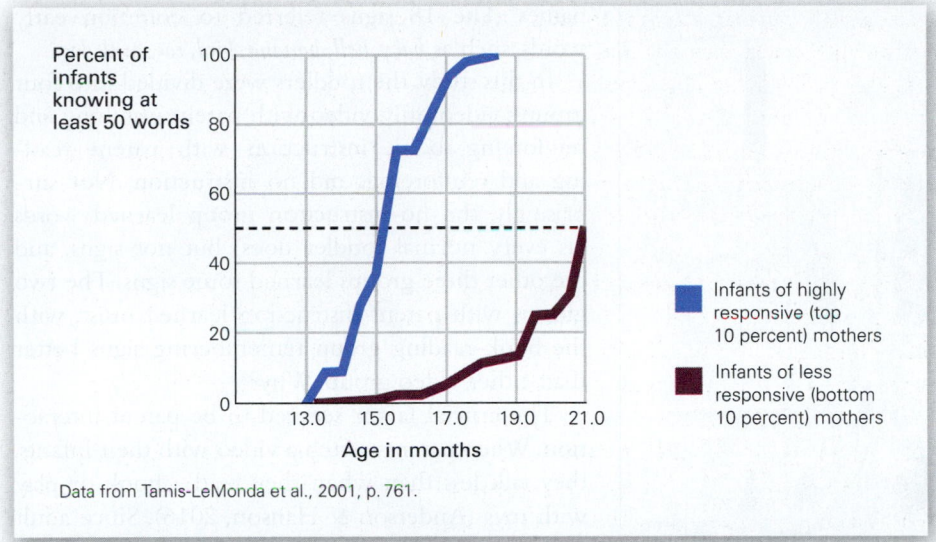

FIGURE 3.3 Maternal Responsiveness and Infants' Language Acquisition Learning the first 50 words is a milestone in early language acquisition, as it predicts the arrival of the naming explosion and the multiword sentence a few weeks later. Researchers found that half of the infants of highly responsive mothers (top 10 percent) reached this milestone at 15 months. The infants of less responsive mothers (bottom 10 percent) lagged significantly behind, with half of them at the 50-word level at 21 months.

B. F. Skinner (1957) noticed that spontaneous babbling is usually reinforced. Typically, when a baby says "ma-ma-ma-ma," a grinning mother appears, repeating the sound and showering the baby with attention, praise, and perhaps food.

Repetition strengthens associations, so infants learn language faster if parents speak to them often. Few parents know this theory, but many use behaviorist techniques. They may praise and respond to the toddler's simple, mispronounced speech, thus teaching language.

Behaviorists note that some 3-year-olds converse in elaborate sentences; others just barely put one simple word with another. Such variations correlate with the amount of language each child has heard. Parents of the most verbal children teach language throughout infancy—singing, explaining, listening, responding, and reading to their children every day, long before the first spoken word (Forget-Dubois et al., 2009) (see Figure 3.3).

THEORY TWO: SOCIAL IMPULSES FOSTER INFANT LANGUAGE The second theory arises from the sociocultural reason for language: communication. According to this perspective, infants communicate because humans are social beings, dependent on one another for survival and joy. All human infants (and no chimpanzees) seek to master words and grammar in order to join the social world (Tomasello & Herrmann, 2010).

According to this perspective, it is the social function of speech, not the words, that undergirds early language. This theory challenges child-directed videos, CDs, and MP3 downloads named to appeal to parents (*Baby Einstein, Brainy Baby,* and *Mozart for Mommies and Daddies—Jumpstart your Newborn's I.Q.*).

Since early language development is impressive, even explosive, some parents who allow infants to watch such programs believe that the rapid language learning is aided by video. Commercial apps for tablets and smartphones, such as *Shapes Game HD* and *VocabuLarry,* have joined the market.

However, developmental research finds that screen time during infancy may be harmful. One recent study found that toddlers could learn a word from either a book or a video but that only book-learning, not video-learning, enabled children to use the new word in another context (Strouse & Ganea, 2017).

Another study focused particularly on teaching "baby signs," 18 hand gestures that refer to particular objects (Dayanim & Namy, 2015). The babies in this study were 15 months old, an age at which all babies use gestures and are poised to learn object

"Keep in mind, this all counts as screen time."

Caught in the Middle Parents try to limit screen time, but children are beguiled and bombarded from many sides.

◆ **Especially for Nurses and Pediatricians**
Eric and Jennifer have been reading about language development in children. They are convinced that because language develops naturally, they need not talk to their 6-month-old son. How do you respond? (see response, page 123)

language acquisition device (LAD)
Chomsky's term for a hypothesized mental structure that enables humans to learn language, including the basic aspects of grammar, vocabulary, and intonation.

names. The 18 signs referred to common early words, such as *baby, ball, banana, bird, cat,* and *dog.*

In this study, the toddlers were divided into four groups: video only, video with parent watching and reinforcing, book instruction with parent reading and reinforcing, and no instruction. Not surprisingly, the no-instruction group learned words (as every normal toddler does) but not signs, and the other three groups learned some signs. The two groups with parent instruction learned most, with the book-reading group remembering signs better than either video group. Why?

The crucial factor seemed to be parent interaction. When parents watch a video with their infants, they talk less than when they read a book or play with toys (Anderson & Hanson, 2016). Since adult input is essential for language learning, cognitive development is reduced by video time.

Infants are most likely to understand and apply what they have learned when they learn directly from another person (R. Barr, 2103). Screen time cannot "substitute for responsive, loving face-to-face relationships" (Lemish & Kolucki, 2013, p. 335). Direct social interaction is pivotal for language, according to theory two.

THEORY THREE: INFANTS TEACH THEMSELVES

A third theory holds that language learning is genetically programmed. Adults need not teach it (theory one), nor is it a by-product of social interaction (theory two). Instead, it arises from a particular gene (FOXP2), brain maturation, and the overall human impulse to imitate.

For example, English articles (*the, an,* and *a*) signal that the next word will be the name of an object, and since babies have "an innate base" that primes them to learn, articles facilitate learning nouns (Shi, 2014, p. 9). Articles prove to be a useful clue for infants learning English but are frustrating for anyone who learns English as an adult. Adults may be highly intelligent and motivated, but their language-learning genes are past the sensitive learning time.

Our ancestors were genetically programmed to imitate for survival, but until a few millennia ago, no one needed to learn languages other than their own. Thus, human genes allow experience-dependent language learning, pruning the connections that our particular language does not need. If they are needed by another language that we want to learn in adulthood, our brains cannot resurrect them.

The prime spokesman for this perspective was Noam Chomsky (1968, 1980). Although behaviorists focus on variations among children in vocabulary size, Chomsky focused on similarities in language acquisition—the evolutionary universals, not the differences.

Noting that all young children master basic grammar according to a schedule, Chomsky hypothesized that children are born with a brain structure he called a **language acquisition device (LAD),** which allows children, as their brains develop, to derive the rules of grammar quickly and effectively from the speech they hear every day. For example, everywhere, a raised tone indicates a question, and infants prefer questions to declarative statements (Soderstrom et al., 2011).

This suggests that infants are wired to talk, and caregivers universally ask them questions long before they can answer back.

According to theory three, language is experience-expectant, as the developing brain quickly and efficiently connects neurons to support whichever language the infant hears. Because of this experience-expectancy, the various languages of the world are all logical, coherent, and systematic. Then some experience-dependent learning occurs as each brain adjusts to a particular language.

The LAD works for deaf infants as well. All 6-month-olds, hearing or not, prefer to look at sign language over nonlinguistic pantomime. For hearing infants, this preference disappears by 10 months, but deaf infants begin signing at that time, which is their particular expression of the universal LAD.

ALL TRUE? A master linguist explains that "the human mind is a hybrid system," perhaps using different parts of the brain for each kind of learning (Pinker, 1999, p. 279). Another expert agrees:

> our best hope for unraveling some of the mysteries of language acquisition rests with approaches that incorporate multiple factors, that is, with approaches that incorporate not only some explicit linguistic model, but also the full range of biological, cultural, and psycholinguistic processes involved.
>
> *[Tomasello, 2006, pp. 292–293]*

The idea that every theory is partially correct may seem idealistic. However, many scientists who are working on extending and interpreting research on language acquisition have arrived at this conclusion. They contend that language learning is neither the direct product of repeated input (behaviorism) nor the result of a specific human neurological capacity (LAD). From an evolutionary perspective, "different elements of the language apparatus may have evolved in different ways." Thus, a "piecemeal and empirical" approach is needed (Marcus & Rabagliati, 2009, p. 281).

Neuroscience is the most recent method to investigate the development of language. It was once thought that language was located in two specific regions of the brain (Wernicke's area and Broca's area). But now neuroscientists are convinced that

STEVEN J. KAZLOWSKI/ALAMY

Family Values Every family encourages the values and abilities that their children need to be successful adults. For this family in Ecuador, that means strong legs and lungs to climb the Andes, respect for parents, and keeping quiet unless spoken to. A "man of few words" is admired. By contrast, many North American parents babble in response to infant babble, celebrate the first spoken word, and stop their conversation to listen to an interrupting child. If a student never talks in class, or another student blurts out irrelevant questions, perhaps the professor should consider cultural influences.

language arises from other regions as well. Some genes and regions are crucial, but hundreds of genes and many brain regions contribute to linguistic fluency.

Neuroscientists describing language development write about "connections," "networks," "circuits," and "hubs" to capture the idea that language is interrelated and complex (Pulvermüller, 2018; Dehaene-Lambertz, 2017). Even when the focus is simply on talking, one neuroscientist notes that "speech is encoded at multiple levels in different parallel pathways" (Dehaene-Lambertz, 2017, p. 52).

That neuroscientist begins her detailed description of the infant brain and language with the same amazement that traditional linguists have expressed for decades:

> For thousands of years and across numerous cultures, human infants are able to perfectly master oral or signed language in only a few years. No other machine, be it silicon or carbon based, is able to reach the same level of expertise.
>
> *[Dehaene-Lambertz, 2017, p. 48]*

What conclusion can we draw from all of the research on infant cognition? It is clear that infants are amazing and active learners who advance their cognition in many ways—through understanding of objects, memory, and communication. Remember that before Piaget, many experts assumed that babies did not yet learn or think. How wrong they were!

what have you learned?

1. What aspects of language develop in the first year?
2. When does vocabulary develop slowly and when does it develop quickly?
3. What are the characteristics of the way adults talk to babies?
4. How would a caregiver who subscribes to the behaviorist theory of language learning respond when an infant babbles?
5. What is typical of the first words that infants speak?
6. What indicates that toddlers use some grammar?
7. According to behaviorism, how do adults teach infants to talk?
8. According to sociocultural theory, why do infants try to communicate?
9. Do people really have a language acquisition device?
10. Why do developmentalists accept several theories of language development?

Surviving and Thriving

None of this discussion of infant senses, motor skills, and cognition would be relevant if babies did not thrive and grow. In North America, most people probably now take that for granted, but throughout the world more than a billion infants died in the past half-century.

In 1950, one young child in seven died, but only about one child in 30 died in 2017 (United Nations, 2017). In earlier centuries, more than half of all children died at birth or in their first year. This progress is good news, not only for families but for developmentalists. It also presents a challenge: We are learning how to improve survival so that infant death in any nation becomes rare.

Better Days Ahead

The first month is the most hazardous. Now almost all newborns who survive the first month live to adulthood. Some nations have seen dramatic improvement. Chile's rate of infant mortality, for instance, was almost four times higher than the rate in the

© LOUISE GUBB/CORBIS

Well Protected Disease and early death are common in Ethiopia (where this photo was taken), but neither is likely for 2-year-old Salem. He is protected not only by the nutrition and antibodies in his mother's milk but also by the large blue net that surrounds them. Treated bed nets, like this one provided by the Carter Center and the Ethiopian Health Ministry, are often large enough for families to eat, read, as well as sleep in together, without fear of malaria-infected mosquitoes.

United States in 1970; now both nations have improved, and their rates are virtually identical (see Figure 3.4).

As more children survive, parents focus more effort and income on each child, having fewer children overall. Worldwide, the average woman had five (4.96) births in 1950; she now has two or three (2.52) (United Nations, 2017).

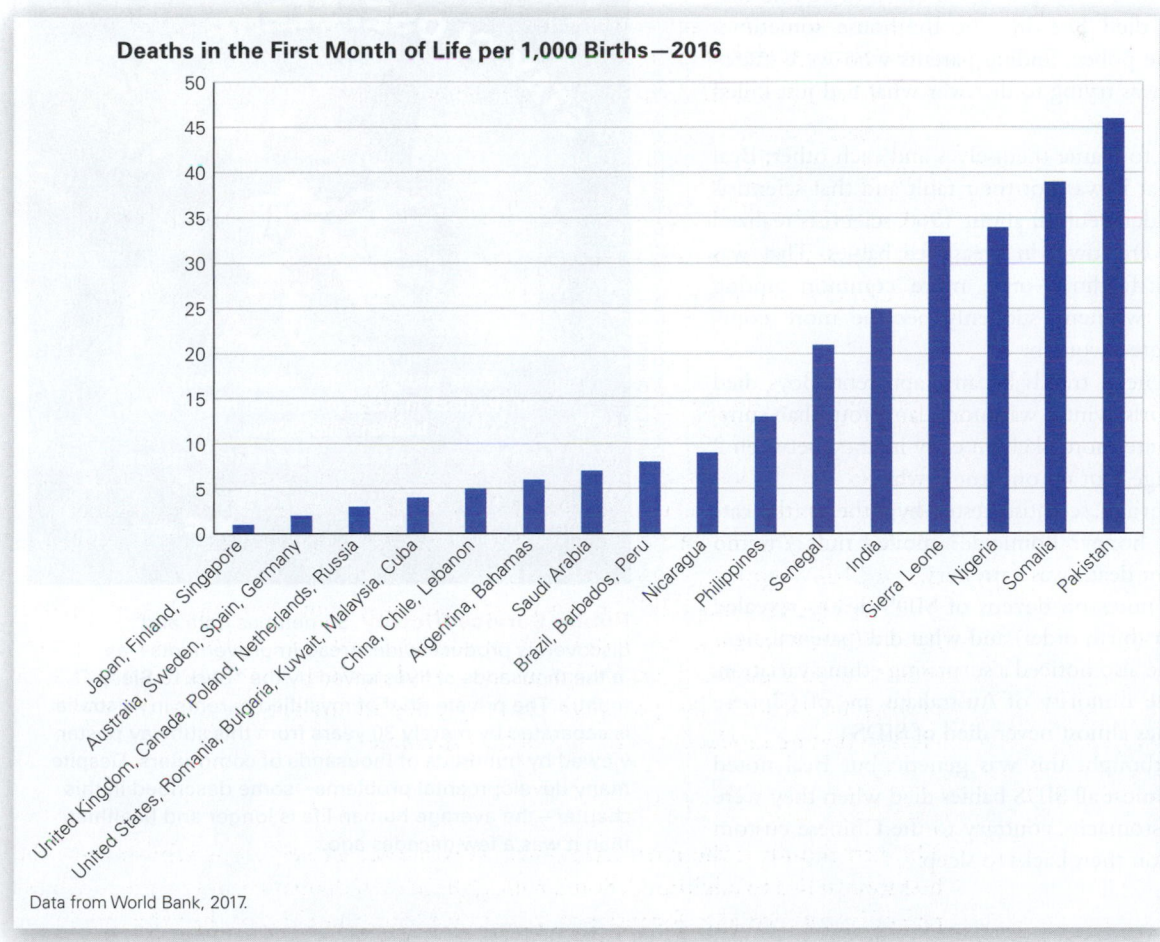

Deaths in the First Month of Life per 1,000 Births—2016

Data from World Bank, 2017.

FIGURE 3.4
A Better Life
It is easy to be critical of early deaths, such as to complain that more U.S. newborns die than Canadian ones, or that some nations have rates that reflect poor public health. However, a historical view makes these data worth celebrating. For example, fifty years ago, one in every two babies died in Pakistan; now it is one in every 22.

Infant survival and maternal education are the two main reasons the world's fertility rate is half the 1950 rate. This is found in data from numerous nations, especially developing ones, where educated women have far fewer children than those who are uneducated (de la Croix, 2013). That advances the national economy, allowing for better schools and health care—and fewer infant deaths.

Educated women have healthier children, in part because they are more aware of research that emphasizes breast-feeding, immunization, and other practices that protect health. Cultures vary in customs regarding newborn care, as you already read regarding bed-sharing. Usually variations are simply alternative ways to meet basic infant needs. However, not every cultural practice is equally good. Each practice needs to be considered carefully, especially when cultures differ: A mother's education helps her overcome harmful traditions.

For example, every year until the mid-1990s, tens of thousands of infants died of **sudden infant death syndrome (SIDS),** called *crib death* in North America and *cot death* in England. In every city and village, tiny infants smiled, waved their arms at rattles that small fingers could not yet grasp, went to sleep, and never woke up. That is much less common today, thanks to the work of one scientist who looked closely at cultural differences (see the feature below).

sudden infant death syndrome (SIDS)
A situation in which a seemingly healthy infant, usually between 2 and 6 months old, suddenly stops breathing and dies unexpectedly while asleep.

A VIEW FROM SCIENCE

Scientist at Work

Susan Beal, a young Australian scientist with four children, studied SIDS. Often she was phoned at dawn to be told that another baby had died. She drove to the house, sometimes arriving before the police, finding parents who were grateful that someone was trying to discover what had just killed their child.

Parents tended to blame themselves and each other; Beal reassured them that it was not their fault and that scientists shared their bewilderment. In about 1960, scientists realized that SIDS rates were lower in breast-fed babies. That was one reason breast-feeding—once more common among poor, uneducated women—suddenly became more common among educated women.

Some other general trends became apparent: Boys died more often than girls; winter was more dangerous than summer; and deaths were more likely in early infancy, between 2 and 6 months of age. But no one knew why.

As parents mourned, scientists tested hypotheses (the cat? the quilt? natural honey? homicide? spoiled milk?) to no avail. Sudden infant death was a mystery.

Beal's detailed notes on dozens of SIDS deaths revealed what didn't matter (birth order) and what did (parental cigarette smoking). She also noticed a surprising ethnic variation: Although a sizable minority of Australians are of Chinese descent, their babies almost never died of SIDS.

Most experts thought this was genetic, but Beal noted something else. Almost all SIDS babies died when they were sleeping on their stomachs, contrary to the Chinese custom of placing infants on their backs to sleep.

Public Service Victory Sometimes data and discoveries produce widespread improvements—as in the thousands of lives saved by the "Back to Sleep" mantra. The private grief of mystified parents in Australia is separated by merely 30 years from this subway poster viewed by hundreds of thousands of commuters. Despite many developmental problems—some described in this chapter—the average human life is longer and healthier than it was a few decades ago.

Beal convinced a large group of non-Chinese parents to put their babies to sleep on their backs, contrary to the advice of most pediatricians, including Dr. Benjamin Spock (author of *Baby and Child Care*, purchased more often than any other book except the Bible). Almost no back-sleeping Australian babies died. Beal concluded that back-sleeping protected against SIDS.

Beal's published report in the *Medical Journal of Australia* (Beal, 1988) caught the attention of doctors in the Netherlands. Two Dutch scientists (Engelberts & de Jonge, 1990) recommended back-sleeping. The Netherlands has one of the highest rates of educated women in the world; thousands of new mothers read the recommendation and followed it. SIDS was reduced in the Netherlands by 40 percent in one year—a stunning replication.

Worldwide, putting babies "Back to Sleep" has now cut the SIDS rate dramatically (Mitchell & Krous, 2015). According to the Centers for Disease Control and Prevention (the official body that tracks health throughout the United States), the SIDS death rate is now less than one-fourth of what it was (130 per 100,000 live births in 1990 versus 40 in 2015) (see Figure 3.5). In the United States alone, at least 100,000 children and young adults are alive who would be dead if they had been born before 1990.

Although SIDS is much less common than it was, culture still matters. Some parents still put newborns to sleep on their stomachs, partly because of past tradition. SIDS rates in the United States from 2011 to 2014 were five times higher among African American babies than among Asian American ones, with those of European descent midway between those two.

Stomach-sleeping is not the only risk. Beyond sleeping position, other risks include low birthweight, exposure to cigarette smoke, soft blankets or pillows, bed-sharing, and abnormalities in the brain stem, heart, mitochondria, or microbiome (Neary & Breckenridge, 2013; Hauck & Tanabe, 2017). Most SIDS victims experience several risks, a cascade of biological and social circumstances. But thanks to cross-cultural research, the major risk—stomach-sleeping—need not occur.

macmillan learning

VIDEO: Interview with Susan Beal http://www.youtube.com/watch?v=ZIPt5q2QJ9I

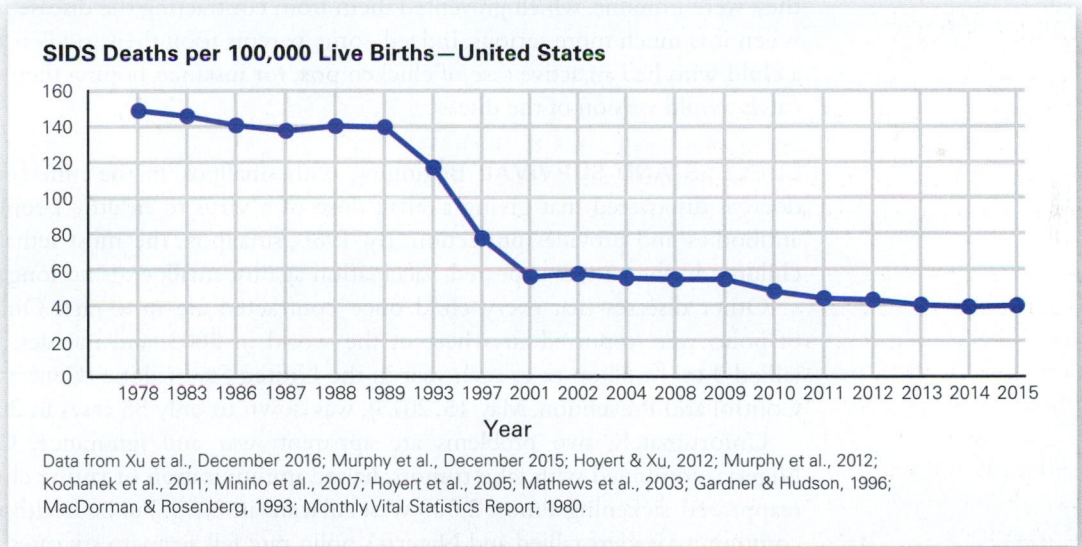

SIDS Deaths per 100,000 Live Births—United States

Data from Xu et al., December 2016; Murphy et al., December 2015; Hoyert & Xu, 2012; Murphy et al., 2012; Kochanek et al., 2011; Miniño et al., 2007; Hoyert et al., 2005; Mathews et al., 2003; Gardner & Hudson, 1996; MacDorman & Rosenberg, 1993; Monthly Vital Statistics Report, 1980.

FIGURE 3.5 Alive Today As more parents learn that a baby should be on his or her "back to sleep," the SIDS rate continues to decrease. Other factors are also responsible for the decline—fewer parents smoke cigarettes in the baby's room.

Immunization

Diseases that killed many infants (including measles, chicken pox, polio, mumps, rotavirus, and whooping cough) are now rare because of **immunization,** which primes the body's immune system to resist a particular disease. Immunization (often via *vaccination*) is said to have had "a greater impact on human mortality reduction and population growth than any other public health intervention besides clean water" (Baker, 2000, p. 199).

immunization
A process that stimulates the body's immune system by causing production of antibodies to defend against attack by a particular contagious disease. Creation of antibodies may be accomplished either naturally (by having the disease), by injection, by drops that are swallowed, or by a nasal spray.

True Dedication This young Buddhist monk lives in a remote region of Nepal, where until recently measles was a common, fatal disease. Fortunately, a UNICEF porter carried the vaccine over mountain trails for two days so that this boy—and his whole community—could be immunized.

In the first half of the twentieth century, almost every child had measles and chicken pox; many had other childhood diseases. Usually they recovered, and then they were immune, which prevented them from contracting the disease in adulthood when it is much more serious. Indeed, some parents took their toddlers to play with a child who had an active case of chicken pox, for instance, hoping their child would catch a mild version of the disease.

SUCCESS AND SURVIVAL Beginning with smallpox in the nineteenth century, doctors discovered that giving a small dose of a virus to healthy people stimulates antibodies and provides protection. By 1980, smallpox, the most lethal disease for children in the past, disappeared; vaccination against smallpox is no longer needed.

Other diseases that every child once contracted are now rare. Only 784 cases of polio were reported anywhere in the world in 2003, and measles, which once tallied 3 to 4 million cases each year in the United States alone (Centers for Disease Control and Prevention, May 15, 2015), was down to only 55 cases in 2012.

Unfortunately, two problems are apparent: war and ignorance. Civil war in Nigeria, combined with false rumors, halted immunization of young children. Polio reappeared, sickening almost 2,000 West Africans in 2005. Public health workers and community leaders rallied and Nigeria's polio rate fell again, to six cases in 2014.

However, due to globalization, when any group in any nation lets immunization rates fall, the infants in other nations become vulnerable. For polio, that happened in Pakistan and Afghanistan, where more than 300 children were diagnosed with polio in 2014. A rush to immunize led to fewer cases in 2015 (see Figure 3.6), but until no cases are reported worldwide for several years (as with smallpox), no nation can afford to relax for polio or any other disease (Martinez et al., August 18, 2017).

Measles is another example. In 2014, 667 people in the United States had measles—the highest rate since 1994 (MMWR, January 8, 2016). In the spring of 2017, an outbreak of measles in Minnesota put 20 people (mostly infants) in the hospital and led to emergency immunization of thousands (Hall et al., July 14, 2017).

Immunization protects not only from temporary sickness but also from complications, including deafness, blindness, sterility, and meningitis. Sometimes such damage is not apparent until decades later. Having mumps in childhood, for instance, can cause sterility and doubles the risk of schizophrenia in adulthood (Dalman et al., 2008).

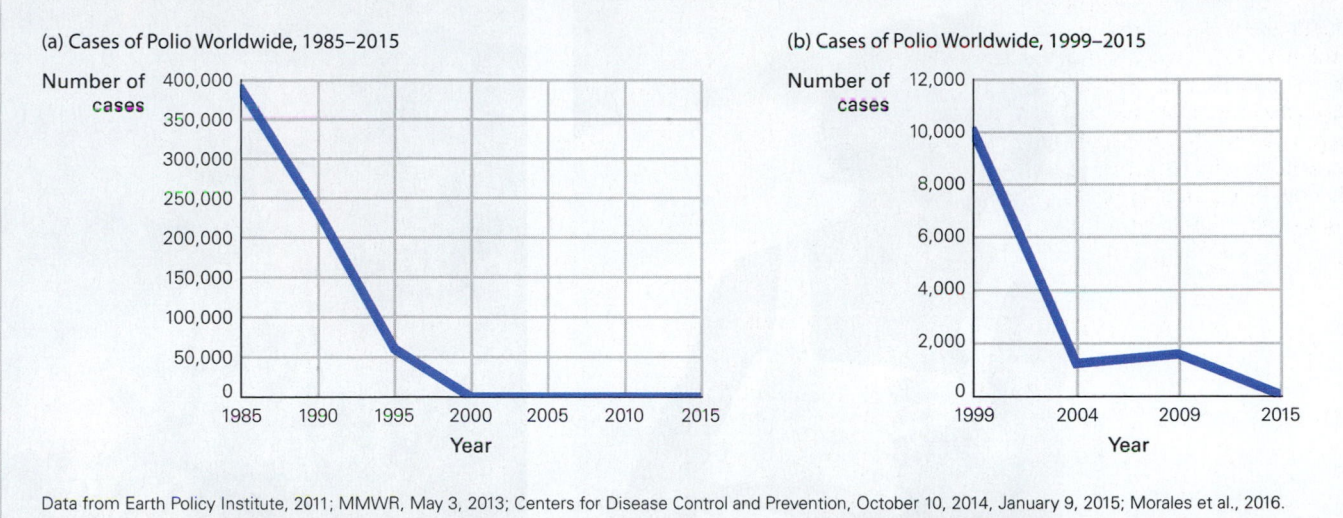

Data from Earth Policy Institute, 2011; MMWR, May 3, 2013; Centers for Disease Control and Prevention, October 10, 2014, January 9, 2015; Morales et al., 2016.

FIGURE 3.6 Not Yet Zero Many public health advocates hope polio will be the next infectious disease to be eliminated worldwide, as is the case in almost all of North America. The number of cases has fallen dramatically worldwide, to just 74 in 2015 *(a)*. However, there was a discouraging increase in polio rates from 2004 to 2009 *(b)*.

Immunization also protects those who cannot be safely vaccinated, such as infants under 3 months and people with impaired immune systems (HIV-positive, aged, or undergoing chemotherapy). Fortunately, each vaccinated child stops transmission of the disease, a phenomenon called *herd immunity*. Usually, if 90 percent of the people in a community (a herd) are immunized, no one dies of that disease.

Everywhere, some children are not vaccinated for valid medical reasons, but Minnesota is one of the 20 states that allow a child to be unvaccinated because a parent has a "personal belief" (Blad, 2014). Another such state is Colorado, where only 73 percent of 1- to 3-year-olds were fully immunized in 2014, a rate far below herd immunity. This terrifies public health workers, who know that the risks of the diseases—especially to babies—are far greater than the risks from immunization.

Many parents are concerned about the potential side effects of vaccines, in part because of the media attention that often results when a person is sickened by vaccination. A common source of irrational thinking is overestimating the frequency of a memorable case. However, no one notices when a child does *not* get polio, measles, or chicken pox, or when no one dies from those diseases.

Polio was an epidemic in the early 1950s, killing 2,000 people (mostly children) a year. Chicken pox was more common but less fatal. Before the varicella (chicken pox) vaccine, more than a hundred people in the United States died each year from that disease and a million were itchy and feverish for a week.

The fear that infant immunization leads to autism is unfounded, as detailed in Chapter 7. It is easy to understand why parents of children with serious developmental disorders seek to blame something other than genes or teratogens, but blaming immunization makes many parents fearful and some children sick.

◆◆ Especially for Nurses and Pediatricians
A mother refuses to have her baby immunized because she wants to prevent side effects. She wants your signature for a religious exemption, which in some jurisdictions allows the mother to refuse vaccination. What should you do? (see response, page 123)

Nutrition

As already explained, infant mortality worldwide has plummeted for several reasons: fewer sudden infant deaths, advances in prenatal and newborn care, clean water, and, as you just read, immunization. One more measure is making a huge difference: better nutrition.

Worldwide, about half of all childhood deaths occur because malnutrition makes a childhood disease lethal, not only the leading causes of childhood deaths—diarrhea and pneumonia—but also milder diseases such as measles (Walker et al., 2013; Roberts,

SELECTSTOCK/VETTA/GETTY IMAGES

HADYNYAH/VETTA/GETTY IMAGES

Same Situation, Far Apart: Breast-Feeding Breast-feeding is universal. None of us would exist if our fore-mothers had not successfully breast-fed their babies for millennia. Currently, breast-feeding is practiced worldwide, but it is no longer the only way to feed infants, and each culture has particular practices.

VIDEO: Nutritional Needs of Infants and Children: Breast-Feeding Promotion shows UNICEF's efforts to educate women on the benefits of breast-feeding.

2017). Some diseases result directly from malnutrition—including both *marasmus* during the first year, when body tissues waste away, and *kwashiorkor* after age 1, when growth slows down, hair becomes thin, skin becomes splotchy, and the face, legs, and abdomen swell with fluid (edema).

BREAST MILK The best defense against malnutrition is one that humans have relied on for 400,000 years, breast milk. The World Health Organization now recommends *exclusive* (no formula, juice, cereal, or water) breast-feeding for the first six months of life (see Table 3.2). That stunning endorsement of breast milk is based on extensive research from all nations of the world. The specific fats and sugars in breast milk make it more digestible and better for the brain than any substitute (Drover et al., 2009; Wambach & Riordan, 2014).

Ideally, nutrition starts with *colostrum,* a thick, high-calorie fluid secreted by the mother's breasts at birth. This benefit is not understood in some cultures, where mothers are forbidden to breast-feed until their milk "comes in" two or three days after birth. (Sometimes other women nurse the newborn; sometimes herbal tea is given.) This is one time when culture is harmful: Colostrum saves infant lives, especially if the infant is preterm (Moles et al., 2015; Andreas et al., 2015).

Breast-feeding mothers should be well nourished and hydrated; then their bodies will make the perfect food for their babies. Formula is preferable only in unusual cases, such as when the mother is HIV-positive, or uses toxic or addictive drugs. Even then, however, exclusive breast-feeding may be best. In some nations, the infants' risk of catching HIV from their HIV-positive mothers is lower than the risk of dying from infections, diarrhea, or malnutrition as a result of bottle-feeding (A. Williams et al., 2016).

In China, a study of more than a thousand babies in eight cities compared three groups of babies: those exclusively breast-fed (by their own mothers or wet nurses),

TABLE 3.2 The Benefits of Breast-Feeding

For the Baby

Balance of nutrition (fat, protein, etc.) adjusts to age of baby

Breast milk has micronutrients not found in formula

Less infant illness, including allergies, ear infections, stomach upsets

Less childhood asthma

Better childhood vision

Less adult illness, including diabetes, cancer, heart disease

Protection against many childhood diseases, since breast milk contains antibodies from the mother

Stronger jaws, fewer cavities, advanced breathing reflexes (less SIDS)

Higher IQ, less likely to drop out of school, more likely to attend college

Later puberty, fewer teenage pregnancies

Less likely to become obese or hypertensive by age 12

For the Mother

Easier bonding with baby

Reduced risk of breast cancer and osteoporosis

Natural contraception (with exclusive breast-feeding, for several months)

Pleasure of breast stimulation

Satisfaction of meeting infant's basic need

No formula to prepare; no sterilization

Easier travel with the baby

For the Family

Increased survival of other children (because of spacing of births)

Increased family income (because formula and medical care are expensive)

Less stress on father, especially at night

Information from Riordan & Wambach, 2014.

those fed no breast milk, and those fed a combination of foods, formula, and breast milk. Based on all of the data, the researchers suggest that the WHO recommendation for exclusive breast-feeding for the first six months "should be reinforced in China" (Ma et al., 2014, p. 290).

The more research is done, the better breast milk seems. For instance, the composition of breast milk adjusts to the age of the baby, with milk for premature babies distinct from that for older infants. Quantity increases to meet the demand: Twins and even triplets can be exclusively breast-fed for months. Each generation of scientists, and consequently each generation of mothers, knows more about breast milk (see A Case to Study on page 120).

Malnutrition

Protein–calorie malnutrition occurs when a person does not consume enough food to sustain normal growth. This form of malnutrition affects roughly one-third of children in developing nations (World Health Organization, 2014). Some experience **stunting** (being short for their age), because chronic malnutrition kept them from growing. Severe stunting is defined as 3 standard deviations from typical height. Less than 1 percent of children are genetically that short, but in many nations 35 percent are that short because they are chronically underfed (see Figure 3.7).

Even worse is **wasting,** when children are severely underweight for their age and height (3 or more standard deviations below average). Many nations, especially in East Asia, Latin America, and central Europe, have seen improvement in child nutrition in the past decades, with an accompanying decrease in wasting and stunting. India is one such nation (Dasgupta et al., 2016). However, much more is necessary. In India in 2014, 17 percent of young children were severely stunted and 5 percent were severely wasted (UNICEF, 2015).

protein-calorie malnutrition
A condition in which a person does not consume sufficient food of any kind. This deprivation can result in several illnesses, severe weight loss, and even death.

stunting
The failure of children to grow to a normal height for their age due to severe and chronic malnutrition.

wasting
The tendency for children to be severely underweight for their age and height as a result of malnutrition.

A CASE TO STUDY

Breast-Feeding in My Family

A hundred years ago, my grandmother, an immigrant who spoke accented English, breast-fed her 16 children. If women of her generation could not provide adequate breast milk (for instance, if they were very sick), the alternatives were milk from another woman (called a wet nurse), from a cow, or from a goat. Those alternatives increased the risk of infant malnutrition and death.

Grandma did not use any of these options. Four of her babies died in infancy.

By the middle of the twentieth century, scientists had analyzed breast milk and created *formula*, designed to be far better than cow's milk. Formula solved the problems of breast-feeding, such as insufficient milk and the exhaustion that breast-feeding mothers often experienced. Bottle-fed babies gained more weight than breast-fed ones; in many nations by 1950, only poor or immigrant women breast-fed.

That is why my mother formula-fed me. She explained that she wanted me to have the best that modern medicine could provide. She recounted an incident meant to convey that my father was less conscientious than she was. He had volunteered to give me my 2 A.M. feeding (babies were fed on a rigid four-hour schedule). But the next morning, she noticed the full bottle in the refrigerator. She queried him. He said I was sound asleep, so he decided I was "fat enough already." She told me this story to indicate that men are not good caregivers. I never told her that Dad was right.

When I had my children, I read that companies that sold formula promoted it in Africa and Latin America by paying local women to dress as nurses and to give new mothers free formula that lasted a week. When the free formula ran out, breast milk had dried up. So mothers used their little money to buy more formula—diluting it to make it last, not always sterilizing properly (fuel was expensive), and supplementing the formula with herbal tea.

Public health workers reported statistics: Formula-fed babies had more diarrhea (a leading killer of children in poor nations) and a higher death rate. The World Health Organization (WHO) recommended a return to breast-feeding and curbed promotion of formula.

In sympathy for those dying babies, I was among the thousands of North Americans who boycotted products from the offending corporations, and I breast-fed my children. But the recommended four-hour schedule had them hungry and me stressed: I gladly took my pediatrician's advice to feed my 2-month-olds occasional bottles of formula (carefully sterilized), juice, water, and spoons of baby cereal and bananas.

International research continues, producing another cohort change. Currently, most (about 80 percent) U.S. mothers breast-feed in the beginning (unlike my mother), and 19 percent breast-feed exclusively until 6 months (unlike me). My grandchildren consumed only breast milk for six months.

As of 2017, about 300 hospitals in the United States and hundreds more worldwide are "Baby-Friendly," a UNICEF designation that includes breast-feeding every newborn within half an hour of birth and giving them nothing but breast milk except in unusual circumstances. Some critics fear the other extreme—that the pressure to breast-feed punishes women who are unable to stay with their babies for six months (Jung, 2015).

The science of infant care advances with each generation. I wonder what the future will bring when my grandchildren become parents.

FIGURE 3.7 Evidence Matters Genes were thought to explain height differences among Asians and Scandinavians, until data on hunger and malnutrition proved otherwise. The result: starvation down and height up almost everywhere—especially in Asia. Despite increased world population, far fewer young children are stunted (255 million in 1970; 156 million in 2015). Evidence also identifies problems: Civil war, climate change, and limited access to contraception have increased stunting in East and Central Africa from 20 million to 28 million in the past 50 years.

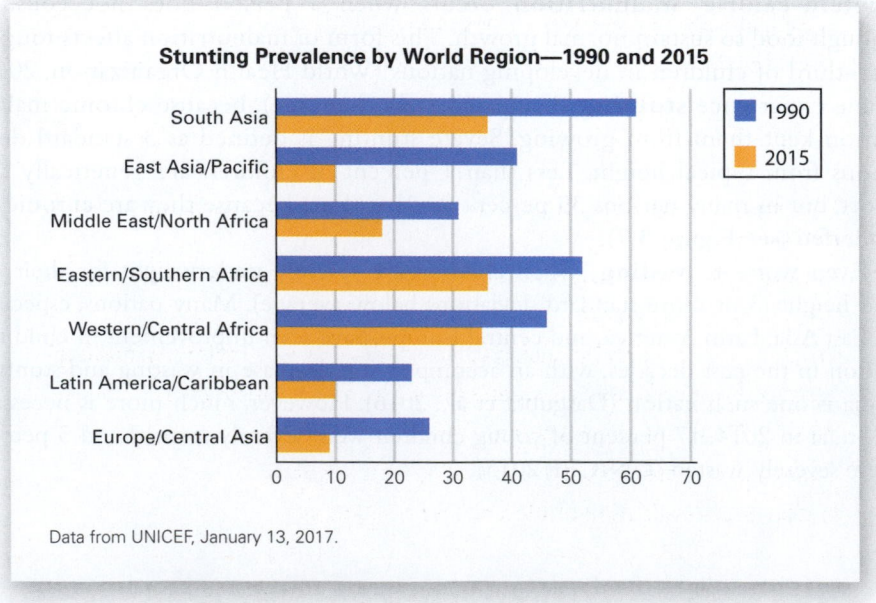

Stunting Prevalence by World Region—1990 and 2015

Data from UNICEF, January 13, 2017.

↑ **OBSERVATION** QUIZ
What regions have the most and least improvement since 1990? (see answer, page 123)

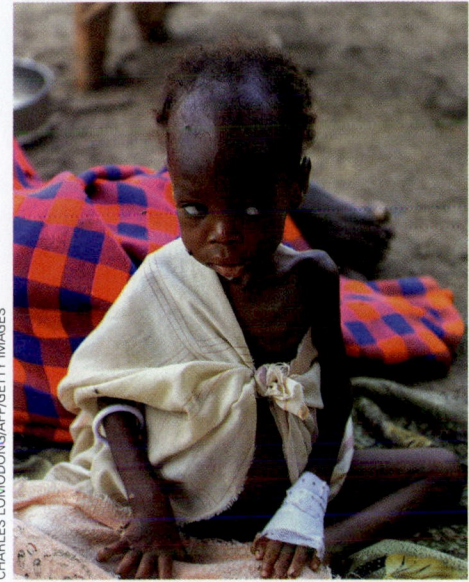
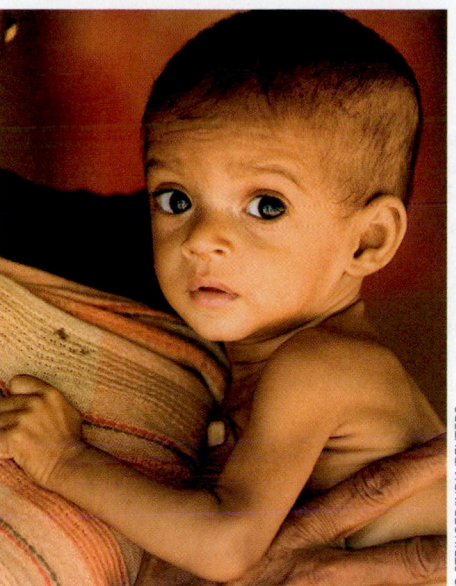

CHARLES LOMODONG/AFP/GETTY IMAGES

© STRINGER/INDIA/REUTERS

Same Situation, Far Apart: Children Still Malnourished Infant malnutrition is still common in some nations. The 16-month-old on the left is from South Sudan, a nation suffering from decades of civil war, and the 7-month-old boy in India on the right is a twin—a risk for malnutrition. Fortunately, they are getting medical help, and their brains are somewhat protected because of head-sparing.

In other nations, primarily in Africa, wasting is increasing. Most adults who were severely malnourished as infants have lower IQs throughout life, even if they eat enough later on (Waber et al., 2014).

Some of this is directly related to brain growth, but in addition, severely malnourished infants have less energy and reduced curiosity. Young children naturally want to do whatever they can: A child with no energy is a child who is not learning.

Prevention, more than treatment, is needed. Ideally, prenatal nutrition, then breast-feeding, and then supplemental iron and vitamin A stop malnutrition before it starts. Once malnutrition is apparent, highly nutritious formula (usually fortified peanut butter) often restores weight, and antibiotics can help. Sadly, some children hospitalized for marasmus or kwashiorkor die even with good medical care because their digestive systems are already failing (M. Smith et al., 2013; Gough et al., 2014).

That sad outcome is less common than it once was. Indeed, this entire chapter can be seen as good news: Infants are more likely to live and learn in the twenty-first century than at any previous time. Back to the opening anecdote: Babies have always been genetically primed to develop (see, hear, walk, talk, and so on), but we now have a better understanding of the impact of good caregiving. That is a reason to be thankful. My daughter Sarah makes me proud. Should I be grateful to Mrs. Todd for that?

what have you learned?

1. Why do public health doctors wish that all infants worldwide would get immunized?

2. Why would a parent blame immunization for autism spectrum disorder?

3. What is herd immunity?

4. What are the reasons for exclusive breast-feeding for the first six months?

5. What is the relationship between malnutrition and disease?

6. What diseases are caused directly by malnutrition?

7. What is the difference between stunting and wasting?

8. In what ways does malnutrition affect cognition?

SUMMARY

Growth in Infancy

1. In the first two years of life, infants grow taller, gain weight, and increase in head circumference—all indicative of development. On average, birthweight doubles by 4 months, triples by 1 year, and quadruples by 2 years, when toddlers weigh about 30 pounds.

2. Sleep gradually decreases over the first two years. As with all areas of development, variations are caused by both nature and nurture. Bed-sharing is the norm in many developing nations, and co-sleeping is increasingly common in developed ones.

3. Brain size increases dramatically, from about 25 percent to 75 percent of adult weight between birth and age 2. Complexity increases as well, with proliferating dendrites and synapses. Both growth and pruning aid cognition. Experience is vital.

4. At birth, the senses already respond to stimuli. Prenatal experience makes hearing the most mature sense. Vision is the least mature sense at birth, but it improves quickly. Infants use all of their senses to strengthen their early social interactions.

5. Infants gradually improve their motor skills as they grow and their brains develop. Gross motor skills are soon evident, from rolling over to sitting up (at about 6 months), from standing to walking (at about 1 year), from climbing to running (before age 2). Fine motor skills (to grab, aim, and manipulate almost anything within reach) develop over the first year.

Infant Cognition

6. Piaget realized that very young infants are active learners, seeking to understand their complex observations and experiences. Sensorimotor intelligence develops in six stages, beginning with reflexes and ending with mental combinations.

7. Infants gradually develop an understanding of objects. In Piaget's classic experiment, infants understand object permanence by about 8 months. Newer research finds that Piaget underestimated infant cognition, including when infants understand object permanence and when they defer imitation.

8. Another approach to understanding infant cognition involves information-processing theory, which looks at each step of the thinking process, from input to output. The data reveal very active infant minds months before motor skills can demonstrate understanding.

9. Infant memory is fragile but not completely absent. Reminder sessions help trigger memories, and by the second year infants remember sequences and object use, learning by observing other people.

Language: What Develops in the First Two Years?

10. Language distinguishes the human species from other animals and is an amazing accomplishment. Eager attempts to communicate are apparent in the first weeks and months. Infants babble at about 6 months, understand words and gestures by 10 months, and speak their first words at about 1 year.

11. Vocabulary builds slowly until the naming explosion begins. Grammar is evident in the first holophrases, and combining words together in proper sequence is further evidence that babies learn grammar as well as vocabulary.

12. Each major theory emphasizes different aspects of language learning: that infants must be taught, that their social impulses foster language learning, and that their brains are genetically attuned to language.

Surviving and Thriving

13. More than a billion infant deaths have been prevented in the past half-century because of improved health care. One major innovation is immunization, which has eradicated smallpox and virtually eliminated polio and measles. Too many parents avoid immunization, decreasing herd immunity.

14. Breast milk helps infants resist disease and promotes growth of every kind. Most babies are breast-fed at birth, but rates over the first year vary depending on family and culture. Pediatricians now recommend breast milk as the only nourishment for the first six months.

15. Severe malnutrition stunts growth and can cause death, both directly and indirectly. Stunting and wasting are signs of malnutrition, which has become less common worldwide except in some nations of sub-Saharan Africa.

KEY TERMS

norm (p. 84)
percentile (p. 84)
REM (rapid eye movement) sleep (p. 85)
bed-sharing (p. 85)
co-sleeping (p. 85)
head-sparing (p. 86)
transient exuberance (p. 86)
neuron (p. 88)
cortex (p. 88)
prefrontal cortex (p. 88)
axon (p. 88)

dendrite (p. 88)
synapse (p. 88)
neurotransmitter (p. 88)
limbic system (p. 88)
amygdala (p. 88)
hippocampus (p. 89)
cortisol (p. 89)
hypothalamus (p. 89)
experience-expectant (p. 89)
experience-dependent (p. 89)
shaken baby syndrome (p. 90)
sensation (p. 90)

perception (p. 90)
binocular vision (p. 91)
motor skill (p. 94)
gross motor skills (p. 94)
fine motor skills (p. 95)
sensorimotor intelligence (p. 97)
object permanence (p. 98)
information-processing theory (p. 100)
babbling (p. 104)
holophrase (p. 106)
naming explosion (p. 106)

grammar (p. 108)
mean length of utterance (MLU) (p. 108)
language acquisition device (LAD) (p. 110)
sudden infant death syndrome (SIDS) (p. 114)
immunization (p. 115)
protein–calorie malnutrition (p. 119)
stunting (p. 119)
wasting (p. 119)

APPLICATIONS

1. Observe three infants (whom you do not know) in a public place such as a store, playground, or bus. Look closely at body size and motor skills, especially how much control each baby has over his or her legs and hands. From that, estimate the baby's age in months, and then ask the caregiver how old the infant is.

2. Elicit vocalizations from an infant—babbling if the baby is under age 1, using words if the baby is older. Write down all of the baby's communication for 10 minutes. Then ask the primary caregiver to elicit vocalizations for 10 minutes, and write these down. What differences are apparent between the baby's two attempts at communication? Compare your findings with the norms described in the chapter.

3. Immunization regulations and practices vary, partly for social and political reasons. Ask at least two faculty or administrative staff members what immunizations the students at your college must have and why. If you hear "It's a law," ask why.

4. *This project can be done alone, but it is more informative if several students pool responses.* Ask three to 10 adults whether they were bottle-fed or breast-fed and, if breast-fed, for how long. If someone does not know, or expresses embarrassment, that itself is worth noting. Do you see any correlation between adult body size and infant feeding?

ESPECIALLY FOR ANSWERS

Response for New Parents (from page 85): From the psychological and cultural perspectives, babies can sleep anywhere as long as the parents can hear them if they cry. The main consideration is safety: Infants should not sleep on a mattress that is too soft, nor beside an adult who is drunk or on drugs. Otherwise, families should decide for themselves.

Response for Parents of Grown Children (from page 90): Probably not. Brain development is programmed to occur for all infants, requiring only the stimulation that virtually all families provide—warmth, reassuring touch, overheard conversation, facial expressions, movement. Extras such as baby talk, music, exercise, mobiles, and massage may be beneficial but are not essential.

Response for Nurses and Pediatricians (from page 91): Urge the parents to begin learning sign language and investigating the possibility of cochlear implants. Babbling has a biological basis and begins at a specified time in deaf as well as hearing babies. If their infant can hear, sign language does no harm. If the child is deaf, however, lack of communication may be destructive.

Response for Parents (from page 100): It is easier and safer to babyproof the house because toddlers, being "little scientists," want to explore. However, it is important for both parents to encourage and guide the baby. If having untouchable items prevents a major conflict between the adults, that might be the best choice.

Response for Teachers (from page 102): Remember the three principles of infant memory: real life, motivation, and repetition. Find something children already enjoy that involves fractions—even if they don't realize it. Perhaps get a pizza and ask them to divide it in half, quarters, eighths, sixteenths, and so on.

Response for Teachers (from page 108): Probably both. Infants love to communicate, and they seek every possible way to do so. Therefore, the teachers should try to understand the baby and the baby's parents, but they should also start teaching the baby the majority language of the school.

Response for Nurses and Pediatricians (from page 110): Although humans may be naturally inclined to communicate with words, exposure to language is necessary. You may not convince Eric and Jennifer about this, but at least convince them that their baby will be happier if they talk to him.

Response for Nurses and Pediatricians (from page 117): It is difficult to convince people that their method of child rearing is wrong, although you should try. In this case, listen respectfully and then describe specific instances of serious illness or death from a childhood disease. Suggest that the mother ask her grandparents whether they knew anyone who had polio, tuberculosis, or tetanus (they probably did). If you cannot convince this mother, do not despair: Vaccination of 95 percent of toddlers helps protect the other 5 percent. If the mother has genuine religious reasons, talk to her clergy adviser.

OBSERVATION QUIZ ANSWERS

Answer to Observation Quiz (from page 94): Jumping up, with a three-month age range for acquisition. The reason is that the older an infant is, the more impact both nature and nurture have.

Answer to Observation Quiz (from page 120) Most is East Asia, primarily because China has prioritized public health. Least is Western and Central Africa, primarily because of civil wars.

THE FIRST TWO YEARS
Psychosocial Development

JOSE LUIS PELAEZ INC/GETTY IMAGES

what will you know?

- Does a difficult newborn become a difficult child?
- What do infants do if they are securely attached to their caregivers?
- Is it best for infants to be cared for exclusively by their mothers?

My daughter Bethany came to visit her newest nephew, Isaac. She had visited him many times before, always expressing joy and excitement with her voice, face, and hands. At 3 months, he always responded in kind, with big smiles and waving arms. Mutual delight in interaction is typical for babies and aunts. But at this seven-month visit, when Bethany approached him, Isaac turned away, nuzzling into his mother. Later Bethany tried again, and this time he kept looking and smiling.

"You like me now," she said.

"He always liked you; he was just tired," said Elissa, his mother.

"I know," Bethany told her. "I didn't take it personally."

I appreciated both daughters. Elissa sought to reassure Bethany, and Bethany knew that Isaac's reaction was not really to her. But the person I appreciated most was Isaac, responsive to people as well-loved babies should be, but newly wary and seeking maternal comfort as he grew closer to a year. Emotions change month by month in the first two years; ideally caregivers change with them.

We open this chapter by tracing infants' emotions as their brains mature and their experiences accumulate. Next we explore caregiver–infant interaction, particularly *synchrony, attachment,* and *social referencing,* and some theories that explain those developments.

Finally, we explore a controversy: Who should care for infants? Only mothers? Or should fathers, grandmothers, nannies, and day-care teachers provide major care? Families and cultures answer this question in opposite ways. Fortunately, as this chapter explains, despite diversity of temperament and caregiving, most people develop well, as long as their basic physical and emotional needs are met. Isaac, Elissa, and Bethany continue to thrive.

At About This Time: Developing Emotions

Birth	Distress; contentment
6 weeks	Social smile
3 months	Laughter; curiosity
4 months	Full, responsive smiles
4–8 months	Anger
9–14 months	Fear of social events (strangers, separation from caregiver)
12 months	Fear of unexpected sights and sounds
18 months	Self-awareness; pride; shame; embarrassment

As always, culture and experience influence the norms of development. This is especially true for emotional development after the first 8 months.

Grandpa Knows Best Does her tongue sticking out signify something wrong with her mouth or mind? Some parents might worry, but one advantage of grandparents is that they have been through it before: All babies do something with their fingers, toes, or, as here, tongue (sometimes all three together!) that seems odd but is only a temporary exploration of how their body works.

social smile
A smile evoked by a human face, normally first evident in infants about 6 weeks after birth.

separation anxiety
An infant's distress when a familiar caregiver leaves; most obvious between 9 and 14 months.

stranger wariness
An infant's expression of concern—a quiet stare while clinging to a familiar person, or a look of fear—when a stranger appears.

Emotional Development

In their first two years, infants progress from reactive pain and pleasure to complex patterns of socioemotional awareness, a movement from basic instincts to learned responses.

Early Emotions

At first, comfort predominates: Newborns are happy and relaxed when fed and drifting off to sleep. Pain is also part of daily life: Newborns cry when they are hurt or hungry, tired or frightened (as by a loud noise or a sudden loss of support).

By the second week, some infants have bouts of uncontrollable crying, called *colic,* probably the result of immature digestion. Others have *reflux,* probably the result of immature swallowing. About 20 percent of babies cry "excessively," defined as more than three hours a day, more than three days a week, for more than three weeks (J. Kim, 2011).

SMILING AND LAUGHING Soon, crying decreases and additional emotions become recognizable. Curiosity is evident: Infants respond to objects and experiences that are new but not too novel. Happiness is expressed by the **social smile,** evoked by a human face at about 6 weeks. (Preterm babies smile later; the social smile is affected by age since conception, not age since birth.)

Laughter builds as curiosity does; a typical 6-month-old chortles upon discovering new things, particularly social experiences that balance familiarity and surprise, such as Daddy making a funny face. That is just what Piaget would expect, "making interesting experiences last." Very young infants prefer seeing happy faces over sad ones, even if the happy faces are not looking at them (Kim & Johnson, 2013).

ANGER AND SADNESS Crying in pain and smiling in pleasure are soon joined by more responsive emotions. Anger is notable at 6 months, usually triggered by frustration.

To study infant emotions, researchers "crouched behind the child and gently restrained his or her arms for 2 min[utes] or until 20 s[econds] of hard crying ensued" (Mills-Koonce et al., 2011, p. 390). "Hard crying" was not rare: Infants hate to be strapped in, caged in, closed in, or just held in place when they want to explore.

In infancy, anger is a healthy response to frustration, unlike sadness, which also appears in the first months (Thiam et al., 2017). Sadness indicates withdrawal instead of an active bid for help, and it is accompanied by a greater increase in the body's production of cortisol.

All social emotions, particularly sadness and fear, affect the hormones and hence the brain. Caregiving matters. Sad and angry infants whose mothers are depressed become fearful toddlers and depressed children (Dix & Yan, 2014).

Abuse and unpredictable responses from caregivers are likely among the "early adverse influences [that] have lasting effects on developing neurobiological systems in the brain" (van Goozen, 2015, p. 208). "Lasting effects" could be lifelong.

FEAR Note the transition from instinct to learning to expectation (Panksepp & Watt, 2011). Fear is not always focused on things and events; it also involves relationships. Two kinds of social fear are typical:

■ **Separation anxiety**—clinging and crying when a familiar caregiver is about to leave. Separation anxiety is normal at age 1, may intensify by age 2, and then usually subsides.

■ **Stranger wariness**—fear of unfamiliar people, especially when they move too close, too quickly. Wariness indicates memory: When Isaac hesitated at seeing Bethany, that meant his memory was maturing.

If separation anxiety remains intense after age 3, it may impair a child's ability to leave home, to go to school, or to play with other children. Then it is considered an emotional disorder.

Separation anxiety can be diagnosed as a disorder up to age 18 (American Psychiatric Association, 2013); some clinicians diagnose it in adults, as well (Bögels et al., 2013). Stranger wariness also may continue. It may become social phobia or a general anxiety (Rudaz et al., 2017). But both emotions are expected at age 1.

Curiosity is also normal, a sign of intelligence. Any unexpected or unfamiliar action attracts infant attention in the second half of the first year. In one study, infants first enjoyed watching a video of dancing to music as it normally occurs, on the beat. Then some watched a video in which the sound track was mismatched with dancing. Eight- to 12-month-old babies, compared to younger ones, were quite curious—but less delighted—about the offbeat dancing. That led the researchers to conclude that "babies know bad dancing when they see it" (Hannon et al., 2017).

Many 1-year-olds are wary of anything unexpected, from the flush of the toilet to the pop of a jack-in-the-box, from closing elevator doors to the tail-wagging approach of a dog. With repeated experience and reassurance, older infants might enjoy flushing the toilet (again and again) or calling the dog (crying if the dog does *not* come). Note the transition from instinct to learning to thought (Panksepp & Watt, 2011).

Developmentally Correct Both Santa's smile and Olivia's grimace are appropriate reactions for people of their age. Adults playing Santa must smile no matter what, and if Olivia smiled, that would be troubling to anyone who knows about 7-month-olds. Yet every Christmas, thousands of parents wait in line to put their infants on the laps of oddly dressed, bearded strangers.

◆ **Especially for Nurses and Pediatricians** Parents come to you concerned that their 1-year-old hides her face and holds onto them tightly whenever a stranger appears. What do you tell them? (see response, page 153)

Toddlers' Emotions

Emotions take on new strength during toddlerhood, as both memory and mobility advance. For example, throughout the second year and beyond, anger and fear become less frequent but more focused, targeted toward infuriating or terrifying experiences. Similarly, laughing and crying are louder and more discriminating.

TEMPER TANTRUMS The new strength of emotions is apparent in temper tantrums. Toddlers are famous for fury. When something angers them, they might yell, scream, cry, hit, and throw themselves on the floor. Logic is beyond them: If adults tease or get angry, that makes it worse. Parental insistence on obedience exacerbates the tantrum (Cierpka & Cierpka, 2016).

One child said, "I don't want my feet. Take my feet off. I don't want my feet." Her mother tried logic, which didn't work, and then offered to get scissors and cut off the offending feet. A new wail erupted, with a loud shriek "Nooooo!" (Katrina, quoted in Vedantam, 2011).

With temper tantrums, soon sadness comes to the fore. Then comfort—not punishment—is helpful (Green et al., 2011). Outbursts of anger are typical at age 2, but if they persist and lead to overt destruction, that signifies trouble, in parent or child (Cierpka & Cierpka, 2016).

Disgust is strongly influenced by culture as well as by maturation. Already by 10 months, infants looking at faces can distinguish disgust from anger (Ruba et al., 2017). In expressing disgust themselves, many 18-month-olds (but not younger infants) were disgusted at touching a dead animal (Stevenson et al., 2010). This is

Empathy Wins Crying babies whose caregivers sympathize often become confident, accomplished, and caring children. Sleep deprivation makes anyone unhappy, but this man's response is much better for both of them than anger or neglect.

self-awareness
A person's realization that he or she is a distinct individual whose body, mind, and actions are separate from those of other people.

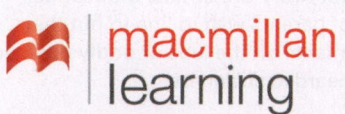

VIDEO ACTIVITY: Self-Awareness and the Rouge Test shows the famous assessment of how and when self-awareness appears in infancy.

My Finger, My Body, and Me
Mirror self-recognition is particularly important in her case, as this 2-year-old has a twin sister. Parents may enjoy dressing twins alike and giving them rhyming names, but each baby needs to know she is an individual, not just a twin.

considered innate: Humans have evolved to develop disgust at smells and objects that might make them sick, so toddlers naturally avoid rotting objects as soon as they are mature enough to notice (Herz, 2012).

However, toddlers are not disgusted when a teenager curses at an elderly person—something that parents and older children often find disgusting (Stevenson et al., 2010). Culture and upbringing make some disgusting items less so, while adding new items that once were accepted.

Toddlers who are unusually sensitive to disgust, raised by parents who frequently express disgust, may develop extreme reactions. By middle childhood, they may be diagnosed with obsessive-compulsive disorder (Ruba et al., 2017). Adults who are hypersensitive to disgust are also likely to suffer from phobia and anxiety (Olatunji et al., 2017).

As with this example, a toddler's innate reactions may evolve into moral values and psychic responses, with specifics depending on parents and experiences. For example, many children take off their clothes in public, unaware of the taboo of nakedness. Children are curious and unaware that some practices are taboo for some adults.

SELF AND OTHERS Temper can be seen as an expression of selfhood, as can other common toddler emotions: pride, shame, jealousy, embarrassment, disgust, and guilt. These emotions may begin with inborn sensitivities, but they involve social awareness.

Such awareness typically emerges from family interaction, which begins with the relationship between caregiver and baby. For instance, in a study of infant jealousy, when mothers were instructed to ignore their own baby and attend to another infant, the babies moved closer to their mothers, bidding for attention. Their brain activity also registered social emotions (Mize et al., 2014).

Positive emotions show social awareness and then learning as well. Most toddlers try to help a stranger who has dropped something or who is searching for a hidden object. Their response seems to be natural empathy, quite apart from any selfish motives (Warneken, 2015).

Over time, children learn when and whom to help; adults may teach them not to help. Some adults donate to beggars, others look away, and still others complain to the police that such people should not be seen in public. Attitudes about ethnicity, or immigration, or clothing, begin with the infant's preference for the familiar and interest in novelty, and then upbringing adds appreciation or rejection.

In addition to social awareness, another foundation for emotional growth is **self-awareness,** the realization that one's body, mind, and activities are distinct from those of other people (Kopp, 2011). Closely following the new mobility that results from walking is an emerging sense of "me" and "mine" that leads to a new awareness of others.

In a classic experiment (Lewis & Brooks, 1978), 9- to 24-month-olds looked into a mirror after a dot of rouge had been surreptitiously put on their noses. If they reacted by touching the red dot on their noses, that meant they knew the mirror showed their own faces. None of the babies younger than 12 months did that, although they sometimes smiled and touched the dot on the "other" baby in the mirror.

Between 15 and 24 months, babies become self-aware, touching their own red noses with curiosity and puzzlement. Self-recognition in the mirror/rouge test (and in photographs) usually emerges with two other advances: pretending and using first-person pronouns (*I, me, mine, myself, my*) (Lewis, 2010). Thus, "an explicit and hence reflective conception of the self is apparent at the early stage of language acquisition at around the same age that infants begin to recognize themselves in mirrors" (Rochat, 2013, p. 388).

This illustrates the interplay of infant abilities—walking, talking, social awareness, and emotional self-understanding all combine to make the 18-month-old quite unlike the 8-month-old. Again, timing and expression are affected by the social context (Ross et al., 2017). Does the parents' culture prize individuality (self-awareness) or cherish community (social understanding)?

Temperament

Temperament is defined as the "biologically based core of individual differences in style of approach and response to the environment that is stable across time and situations" (van den Akker et al., 2010, p. 485). "Biologically based" means that these traits originate with nature.

Confirmation that temperament arises from the inborn brain comes from an analysis of the tone, duration, and intensity of infant cries after the first inoculation, before much experience outside the womb. Cry variations at this very early stage correlate with later temperament: Those who scream loudest become quickest to protest later on (Jong et al., 2010).

Temperament is *not* the same as personality, although temperamental inclinations may lead to personality differences. Generally, personality traits (e.g., honesty and humility) are learned, whereas temperamental traits (e.g., shyness and aggression) are genetic. Of course, for every trait, nature and nurture interact, as the following makes clear.

temperament
Inborn differences between one person and another in emotions, activity, and self-regulation. It is measured by the person's typical responses to the environment.

VIDEO: Temperament in Infancy and Toddlerhood explores the unique ways infants respond to their environment.

INSIDE THE BRAIN

The Growth of Emotions

Brain maturation is crucial for emotional development, particularly for emotions that respond to other people. Experience connects the amygdala and the prefrontal cortex (van Goozen, 2015), teaching infants to align their own feelings with those of their caregivers (Missana et al., 2014). Joy, fear, and excitement become shared, mutual experiences—as anyone who successfully makes a baby laugh knows.

Maturation of the cortex and connections between parts of the brain are crucial for the social smile and then laughter—newborns can't do it (Konner, 2010). As the brain matures over the first two years, fear, self-awareness, jealousy, and anger become more pronounced, all evident in brain activity as well as in behavior.

Essentially, connections between innate emotional impulses from the amygdala and experience-based learning shows "dramatic age-dependent improvement," with genes, prenatal influences, and early caregiving all contributing to the development of the infant brain (Gao et al., 2017). Infant experience leads to adult reactions: If you know someone who cries, laughs, or angers quickly, ask about their childhood.

An example of the connection between the brain and caregiving came from a study of "highly reactive" infants (i.e., those whose brains naturally reacted with intense fear, anger, and other emotions). Highly reactive 15-month-olds

with responsive caregivers (not hostile or neglectful) became less fearful, less angry, and so on. By age 4, they were able to regulate their emotions, presumably because they had developed neurological links between brain excitement and emotional response. However, highly reactive toddlers with less responsive caregivers were often overwhelmed by later emotions (Ursache et al., 2013).

Differential susceptibility is apparent: Innate reactions and caregiver actions together sculpt the brain. Both are affected by culture: Some parents are especially sympathetic to distress, while others especially fear spoiling. Genes and prenatal influences also matter. Some newborns have been exposed to toxic drugs; some inherit genes that make them vulnerable to autism spectrum disorder. For them, particularly, postnatal experiences are crucial to promote healthy emotional development (Gao et al., 2017) (see Figure 4.1).

The social smile, for instance, is fleeting when 2-month-olds see a face—almost any face. As the brain develops, infants smile more quickly and openly at the sight of a familiar, loving caregiver but not at seeing a stranger. That occurs because caregivers appear frequently, and that causes neurons to repeatedly fire together, so the dendrites become closely connected.

In classic research, the brains of infant mice released more serotonin when their mothers licked them. That not

only increased the mouselings' pleasure but also started epigenetic responses, reducing cortisol from brain and body, including the adrenal glands. The effects were lifelong; those baby mice became smarter and more loving adults, with larger brains.

That research with mice has been replicated and extended, with neuroscientists in awe of the "remarkable capacity for plastic changes that influence behavioural outcomes throughout the lifetime" (Kolb et al., 2017, p. 1218).

For optimal brain development, some stimulation is needed (overprotection is harmful), but so is comfort. Too much fear and stress harms the hypothalamus, which then grows more slowly. If infants are maltreated, they develop abnormal responses to stress, anger, and other emotions, apparent in the many brain areas (hypothalamus, amygdala, hippocampus, prefrontal cortex) (Bernard et al., 2014; Cicchetti, 2013a). The immune system is impaired (Hostinar et al., 2018); abused children become sickly adults because of what has happened inside their brains decades earlier.

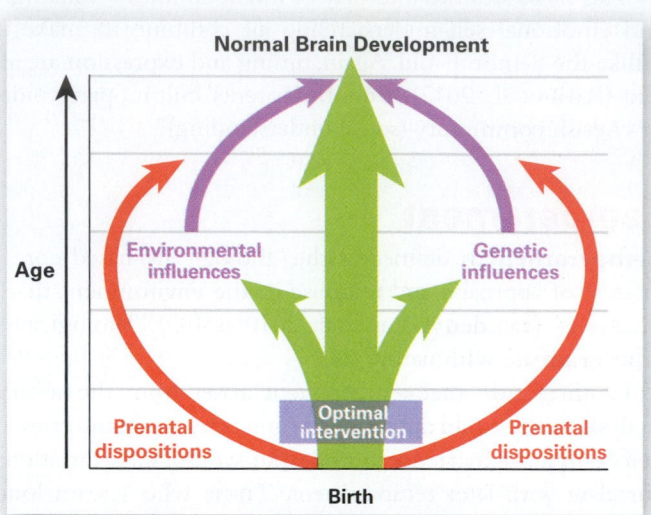

FIGURE 4.1 **Seven Arrows Pointing Up** This figure is intended to show the ongoing development of the brain. Prenatal, genetic, and experiential influences continue lifelong.

TEMPERAMENT OVER THE YEARS In laboratory studies of temperament, 4-month-old infants might see spinning mobiles or hear unusual sounds, and older babies might confront a clown who approaches quickly. During such experiences, some children laugh, some cry, and others are quiet. Infant reactions may be categorized as easy (40 percent), difficult (10 percent), slow-to-warm-up (15 percent), and hard-to-classify (35 percent).

These four categories originate from the *New York Longitudinal Study* (NYLS). Begun in the 1960s, the NYLS was the first large study to recognize that each newborn has a distinct temperament (Thomas & Chess, 1977). According to the NYLS, by 3 months, infants manifest nine traits that cluster into the four categories just listed.

Although the NYLS was the first major study to consider temperament longitudinally, its nine dimensions have not been replicated. Generally, only three (not nine) dimensions of temperament are found (Hirvonen et al., 2013; van den Akker et al., 2010; Degnan et al., 2011), each affecting later personality and achievement. The three are:

Effortful control (able to regulate attention and emotion, to self-soothe)

Negative mood (fearful, angry, unhappy)

Exuberance (active, social, not shy)

One longitudinal study analyzed temperament at least eight times, at 4, 9, 14, 24, and 48 months and then in middle childhood, adolescence, and adulthood. The scientists designed laboratory experiments to evoke emotions appropriate for the age of

Feliz Navidad Not only is every language and culture distinct, but each individual also has his or her own temperament. Here children watch the Cortylandia Christmas show in Madrid, Spain, where the Christmas holiday begins on the December 24 and lasts through January 6, which is Three Kings Day. As you see from the fathers and children, each person has his or her own reaction to the same event.

↑ **OBSERVATION** QUIZ
What indicates that each father has his own child on his shoulders? (see answer, page 153)

the participants, collected detailed reports from mothers and later from participants themselves, and gathered observational data and physiological evidence, including brain scans.

Past data on each person were reevaluated each time, and cross-sectional and international studies were considered (Fox et al., 2001, 2005, 2013; Hane et al., 2008; Williams et al., 2010; Jarcho et al., 2013). Half of the participants did not change much over time, reacting the same way and having similar brain-wave patterns in adulthood and in infancy.

Curiously, change was most likely for the inhibited, fearful infants and least likely for the exuberant ones (see Figure 4.2). Why was that? Are parents likely to coax frightened infants to be brave but willing to let exuberant babies stay happy?

The researchers found unexpected gender differences. As teenagers, relatively high rates of drug abuse occurred with the formerly inhibited boys, but low rates occurred in the girls (L. R. Williams et al., 2010). A likely explanation is cultural: Shy boys use drugs to mask their social anxiety, but shy girls may be more accepted as they are. Other research also finds that shyness is more stable in girls than boys over the years (Poole et al., 2017).

Continuity and change were seen in another study, which found that angry infants often provoked hostility from their mothers, and, if that happened, they became antisocial children. However, if the mothers were loving and patient despite the difficult temperament of the children, hostile traits were not evident later on (Pickles et al., 2013).

In general, infants with difficult temperaments are more likely than other babies to develop emotional problems, especially if their mothers had a difficult pregnancy and were depressed or anxious caregivers (Garthus-Niegel et al., 2017). This is a developmental cascade—no single factor determines later outcomes, but several can combine to cause a disorder.

Thus, childhood temperament endures, blossoming into adult personality, but innate tendencies are only part of the story. Context always shapes behavior.

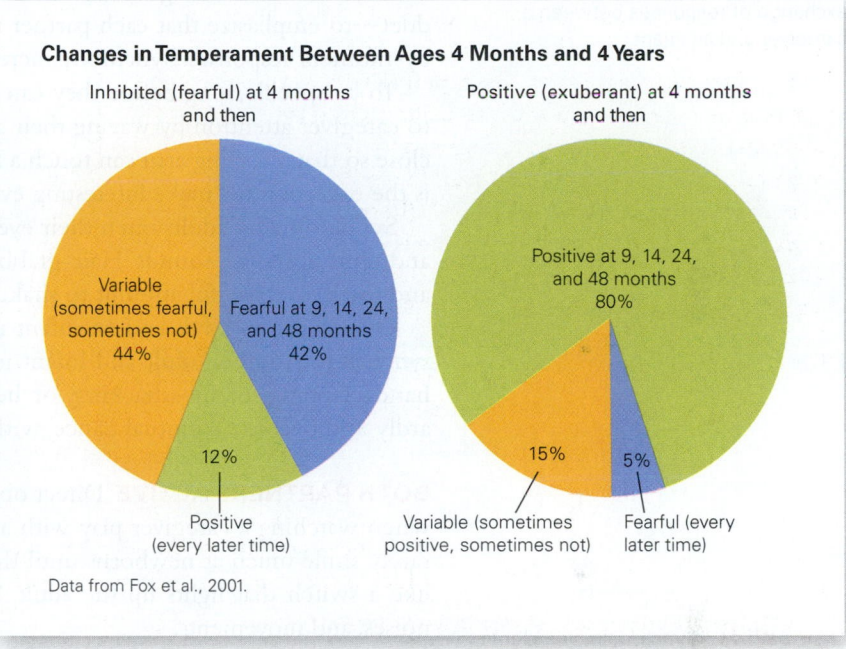

Changes in Temperament Between Ages 4 Months and 4 Years

Inhibited (fearful) at 4 months and then
- Variable (sometimes fearful, sometimes not) 44%
- Fearful at 9, 14, 24, and 48 months 42%
- Positive (every later time) 12%

Positive (exuberant) at 4 months and then
- Positive at 9, 14, 24, and 48 months 80%
- Variable (sometimes positive, sometimes not) 15%
- Fearful (every later time) 5%

Data from Fox et al., 2001.

FIGURE 4.2 Do Babies' Temperaments Change? Sometimes it is possible—especially if they were fearful babies. Adults can help children overcome fearfulness. If fearful children do not change, it is not known whether that's because their parents are not sufficiently reassuring (nurture) or because the babies themselves are temperamentally more fearful (nature).

what have you learned?

1. What experiences trigger happiness, anger, and fear?

2. How do emotions differ between the first and second year of life?

3. What is the significance of how toddlers react to seeing themselves in a mirror?

4. How do temperamental traits affect later personality?

The Development of Social Bonds

Humans are, by nature, social creatures. The specifics of social interaction during infancy depend on the age of the baby, with *synchrony, attachment,* and *social referencing* each evident in sequence during the first two years of life.

Synchrony

synchrony
A coordinated, rapid, and smooth exchange of responses between a caregiver and an infant.

Early parent–infant interactions are described as **synchrony,** a mutual exchange with split-second timing. Metaphors for synchrony are often musical—a waltz, a jazz duet—to emphasize that each partner must be attuned to the other, with moment-by-moment responses. Synchrony increases over the first year (Feldman, 2007).

To be specific, long before they can reach out and grab, infants respond excitedly to caregiver attention by waving their arms. Adults with animated expressions move close so that a waving arm can touch a face or, even better, a hand can grab hair. This is the eagerness to "make interesting events last" that was described in Chapter 3.

Synchronizing adults open their eyes wide, raise their eyebrows, smack their lips, and emit nonsense sounds. Hair-grabbing might make adults bob their heads back and forth, in a playful attempt to shake off the grab, to the infants' joy.

Over time, an adult and an infant might develop a routine of hair-grabbing in synchrony. Another adult and infant might develop another routine, perhaps with hand-clapping, or lip-smacking, or head-turning. Synchrony may begin haphazardly and become a mutual dance, with both knowing the steps.

BOTH PARTNERS ACTIVE Direct observation reveals synchrony; anyone can see it when watching a caregiver play with an infant who is far too young to talk. Adults rarely smile much at newborns until that first social smile, weeks after birth. That is like a switch that lights up the adult. Soon both partners synchronize smiles, eyes, noises, and movements.

Detailed research, typically with two cameras simultaneously recording infant and caregiver and later reviewed in slow motion to calibrate every millisecond of arched eyebrows, widening eyes, pursed lips, and so on, confirms the symbiosis of adult–infant partnership (Messinger et al., 2010). Recorded heart rate and brain waves also indicate synchrony, which explains why maternal depression leads to infant depression (Atzil et al., 2014).

Open Wide Synchrony is evident worldwide. Everywhere, babies watch their parents carefully, hoping for exactly what these two parents—each from quite different cultures—express, and responding with such delight that adults relish these moments.

In every interaction, infants read others' emotions and develop social skills, taking turns and watching expressions. Synchrony usually begins with adults imitating infants (not vice versa) in tone and rhythm. At first, adults respond to barely perceptible infant facial expressions and body motions (Beebe et al., 2016). This helps infants connect their internal state with behaviors that are understood within their family and culture.

NEGLECTED SYNCHRONY Experiments involving the **still-face technique** suggest that synchrony is experience-expectant (needed for normal brain growth) (Tronick, 1989; Tronick & Weinberg, 1997; Hari, 2017). [**Life-Span Link:** Experience-expectant and experience-dependent brain function are described in Chapter 3.]

In still-face studies, at first an infant is propped in front of an adult who responds normally. Then, on cue, the adult stops all expression, staring quietly with a "still face" for a minute or two. Sometimes by 2 months, and clearly by 6 months, infants are upset when their parents are unresponsive. Babies frown, fuss, drool, look away, kick, cry, or suck their fingers. By 5 months, they also vocalize, as if to say, "React to me!"

Many studies reach the same conclusion: Synchrony is experience-expectant, not simply experience-dependent. Responsiveness aids psychosocial and biological development, evident in heart rate, weight gain, and brain maturation.

For example, one study looked in detail at 4-month-old infants during and immediately after the still-face episode (Montirosso et al., 2015). The researchers found three clusters, which they called "socially engaged" (33 percent), "disengaged" (60 percent), and "negatively engaged" (7 percent).

When the mothers were still-faced, the socially engaged babies remained active, looking around at other things, apparently expecting that the caregivers would soon resume connection. When the still face was over, they quickly reengaged. The disengaged group became passive, taking longer to return to normal. The negatively engaged babies were upset and angry, crying even after the still face ended.

The mothers of each type differed in how they played with their infants before and after the still face. The socially engaged mothers matched the infants' actions (bobbing heads, opening mouth, and so on), but the negatively engaged mothers almost never matched and sometimes expressed anger—not sympathy—when the baby cried (Montirosso et al., 2015). That absent synchrony is a troubling sign for future emotional and brain development.

still-face technique
An experimental practice in which an adult keeps his or her face unmoving and expressionless in face-to-face interaction with an infant.

THINK CRITICALLY: What will happen if no one plays with an infant?

Hold Me Tight Synchrony is evident not only in facial expressions and noises but also in body positions. Note the mother's strong hands and extended arms, and her daughter's tucked in legs and arms. This is a caregiving dance that both have executed many times.

GUYLAIN DOYLE/LONELY PLANET/GETTY IMAGES

attachment
According to Ainsworth, "an affectional tie" that an infant forms with a caregiver—a tie that binds them together in space and endures over time.

Attachment

Responsive and mutual relationships are important throughout childhood and beyond. However, once infants can walk, the moment-by-moment, face-to-face synchrony is less common. Instead, **attachment**—the connection between one person and another, measured by how they respond to each other—comes to the fore. This connection helps infants learn to express as well as understand human emotions (Cooke et al., 2016).

Attachment can begin even before birth, but the scientific study of attachment has been most intense with infants who are about a year old. Research on mother–infant attachment began with John Bowlby (1983) in England and Mary Ainsworth (1967) in Uganda, and it has now been studied in virtually every nation, in both atypical populations (e.g., infants with Down syndrome or autism spectrum disorder) and typical ones. Attachment is lifelong. It begins before birth and influences relationships during early and late childhood, adolescence, and adulthood (e.g., Simpson & Rholes, 2015; Grossmann et al., 2014; Tan et al., 2016; Hunter & Maunder, 2016) (see At About This Time).

Developmentalists are convinced that attachment is basic to the survival of *Homo sapiens,* with the manifestation dependent on culture and the age of the person. For instance, Ugandan mothers never kiss their infants, but they often massage them, contrary to Westerners. American adults may phone their mothers every day—even when the mothers are a thousand miles away. Or attached family members may sit in the same room of a large house, each reading quietly, speaking only a few words every so often. All of these signify attachment.

SIGNS OF ATTACHMENT Infants show their attachment through *proximity-seeking* (such as approaching and following their caregivers) and through *contact-maintaining*

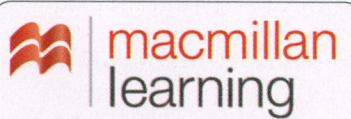

VIDEO ACTIVITY: Mother Love and the Work of Harry Harlow features classic footage of Harlow's research, showing the setup and results of his famous experiment.

At About This Time: Stages of Attachment

Birth to 6 weeks	*Preattachment.* Newborns signal, via crying and body movements, that they need others. When people respond positively, the newborn is comforted and learns to seek more interaction. Newborns are also primed by brain patterns to recognize familiar voices and faces.
6 weeks to 8 months	*Attachment in the making.* Infants respond preferentially to familiar people by smiling, laughing, babbling. Their caregivers' voices, touch, expressions, and gestures are comforting, often overriding the infant's impulse to cry. Trust (Erikson) develops.
8 months to 2 years	*Classic secure attachment.* Infants greet the primary caregiver, play happily when he or she is present, show separation anxiety when the caregiver leaves. Both infant and caregiver seek to be close to each other (proximity) and frequently look at each other (contact). In many caregiver–infant pairs, physical touch (patting, holding, caressing) is frequent.
2 to 6 years	*Attachment as launching pad.* Young children seek their caregiver's praise and reassurance as their social world expands. Interactive conversations and games (hide-and-seek, object play, reading, pretending) are common. Children expect caregivers to comfort and entertain.
6 to 12 years	*Mutual attachment.* Children seek to make their caregivers proud by learning whatever adults want them to learn, and adults reciprocate. In concrete operational thought (Piaget), specific accomplishments are valued by adults and children.
12 to 18 years	*New attachment figures.* Teenagers explore and make friendships independent from parents, using their working models of earlier attachments as a base. With formal operational thinking (Piaget), shared ideals and goals become influential.
18 years on	*Attachment revisited.* Adults develop relationships with others, especially relationships with romantic partners and their own children, influenced by earlier attachment patterns. Past insecure attachments from childhood can be repaired rather than repeated, although this does not always happen.

Information from Grobman, 2008.

(such as touching, snuggling, and holding). Attachment is evident when a baby cries if the caregiver closes the door when going to the bathroom, or fusses if a back-facing car seat prevents the baby from seeing the parent.

To maintain contact when driving in a car and to reassure the baby, some caregivers in the front seat reach back to give a hand, or they install a mirror angled so that driver and baby can see each other. Some caregivers take the baby into the bathroom: One mother complained that she hadn't been alone in the bathroom for two years (Senior, 2014). Contact need not be physical: Visual or verbal connections are often sufficient.

Attachment is mutual. Caregivers often keep a watchful eye on their baby, initiating contact with expressions, gestures, and sounds. Before going to sleep at midnight they might tiptoe to the crib to gaze at their sleeping infant, or, in daytime, absentmindedly smooth their toddler's hair.

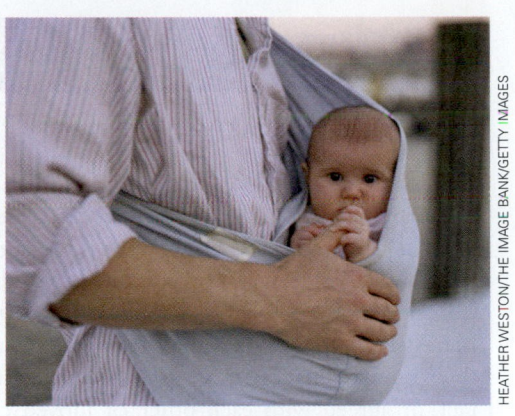

Stay in Touch In early infancy, physical contact is often part of secure attachment. No wonder many happy babies travel next to their caregivers in slings, wraps, and snugglies. Note that attachment is mutual—she holds on to the thumb that her father provides.

SECURE AND INSECURE ATTACHMENT Attachment is classified into four types: A, B, C, and D. Infants with **secure attachment** (type B) feel comfortable and confident. The caregiver is a *base for exploration,* providing assurance and enabling discovery. A toddler might, for example, scramble down from the caregiver's lap to play with an intriguing toy but periodically look back and vocalize (contact-maintaining) or bring the toy to the caregiver for inspection (proximity-seeking).

The caregiver's presence gives the child courage to explore; the caregiver's departure causes distress; the caregiver's return elicits positive social contact (such as smiling or hugging) and then more playing. This balanced reaction—being concerned but not overwhelmed by comings and goings—indicates security.

By contrast, insecure attachment (types A and C) is characterized by fear, anxiety, anger, or indifference. Some insecure children play independently without seeking contact; this is **insecure-avoidant attachment** (type A). The opposite reaction is **insecure-resistant/ambivalent attachment** (type C). Children with type C cling to their caregivers and are angry at being left.

Early research was on mothers and infants. Later, it was found that infants may be securely or insecurely attached to fathers or other caregivers. It was thought that temperament might affect attachment, but research shows that temperament does not determine attachment status (Groh et al., 2017).

Ainsworth's original schema differentiated only types A, B, and C. Later researchers discovered a fourth category (type D), **disorganized attachment.** Type D infants may suddenly switch from hitting to kissing their mothers, from staring blankly to crying hysterically, from pinching themselves to freezing in place.

Among the general population, almost two-thirds of infants are secure (type B). About one-third are insecure, either indifferent (type A) or unduly anxious (type C), and about 5 to 10 percent are disorganized (type D). The latter have no consistent strategy for social interaction, even avoidance or resistance. Instead, they may become hostile and aggressive, difficult for anyone to relate to. They are at high risk for later psychopathology, including severe aggression and major depression (Cicchetti, 2016; Groh et al., 2012).

ADOPTEES FROM ROMANIA No scholar doubts that close human relationships should develop in the first year of life and that the lack of such relationships risks dire consequences. Unfortunately, thousands of children born in Romania are proof.

When Romanian dictator Nicolae Ceauşescu forbade birth control and abortions in the 1980s, illegal abortions became the leading cause of death for Romanian women aged 15 to 45 (Verona, 2003), and 170,000 children were abandoned and sent to crowded, impersonal, state-run orphanages (Marshall, 2014). The children were severely deprived of social contact, experiencing virtually no synchrony, play, or conversation.

secure attachment (type B)
A relationship in which an infant obtains both comfort and confidence from the presence of his or her caregiver.

insecure-avoidant attachment (type A)
A pattern of attachment in which an infant avoids connection with the caregiver, as when the infant seems not to care about the caregiver's presence, departure, or return.

insecure-resistant/ambivalent attachment (type C)
A pattern of attachment in which an infant's anxiety and uncertainty are evident, as when the infant becomes very upset at separation from the caregiver and both resists and seeks contact on reunion.

disorganized attachment (type D)
A type of attachment that is marked by an infant's inconsistent reactions to the caregiver's departure and return.

A VIEW FROM SCIENCE

Measuring Attachment

Scientists take great care to develop valid measurements of various constructs because when studying people, it is crucial that other scientists know what is measured and how to replicate it. For instance, if you wanted to study love between romantic partners, what would your empirical measurement be? Ask the couple on a questionnaire? Record a video of their interaction, and count how often they made eye contact, or agreed with each other, or moved closer together? Or would you wait to see if they married, divorced, had sex, shared finances? As you might imagine, none of these is quite right, but all might be useful. Crucial is that to study an emotion such as love, some empirical measurement is defined.

The same is true for attachment.

Mary Ainsworth (1973) developed a now-classic laboratory procedure called the **Strange Situation** to measure attachment. In a well-equipped playroom, an infant is observed for eight episodes, each lasting no more than three minutes. First, the child and mother are together. Next, according to a set sequence, the mother and then a stranger come and go. Infants' responses to their mother indicate which type of attachment they have formed.

Researchers distinguish types A, B, C, and D. They focus on the following:

Exploration of the toys. A secure toddler plays happily.

Reaction to the caregiver's departure. A secure toddler notices when the caregiver leaves and shows some sign of missing him or her.

Strange Situation
A laboratory procedure for measuring attachment by evoking infants' reactions to the stress of various adults' comings and goings in an unfamiliar playroom.

Reaction to the caregiver's return. A secure toddler welcomes the caregiver's reappearance, seeking contact, and then plays again.

When scientists measure attachment, they are carefully trained to distinguish one type from another. That training involves watching videos, calibrating ratings, and studying manuals. Researchers are not certified to measure attachment until they reach a high standard of accuracy. Although such training is the standard, respected by scientists, in current studies many other measures are used—but always the published scientific report describes exactly how attachment was measured.

Research measuring attachment has revealed that some behaviors that might seem normal are, in fact, a sign of insecurity. For instance, an infant who clings to the caregiver and refuses to explore the toys might be type C. And young children who are immediately friendly to strangers might be type A (Tarullo et al., 2011).

In adulthood, signs of an insecure childhood are not only rejection of mother ("I never want to see her again") but also sanctification of her ("she was a saint"). It is especially troubling if an adult can provide few details about their awful or perfect childhood.

There are now many ways to measure attachment in older children, in adolescents, and in adults. At every age, the essential concept is that people who are securely attached are both independent and interdependent, neither anxious nor dismissive.

In recent decades, this research has spawned *attachment parenting,* which prioritizes the mother–infant relationship during the first three years of life far more than Ainsworth or Bowlby did (Sears & Sears, 2001; Komisar, 2017).

© 2016 MACMILLAN

Excited, Troubled, Comforted This sequence is repeated daily for 1-year-olds, which is why the same sequence is replicated to measure attachment. As you see, toys are no substitute for mother's comfort if the infant or toddler is secure, as this one seems to be. Some, however, cry inconsolably or throw toys angrily when left alone.

Attachment parenting mandates that mothers should always be near their infants (co-sleeping, "wearing" the baby in a wrap or sling, breast-feeding on demand). That may create two problems: (1) Mothers feel guilty if they are not available 24/7, and (2) other caregivers are less appreciated. Some experts suggest that attachment parenting is too distant from the research concept and evidence (Ennis, 2014).

The measurement of attachment via the Strange Situation has made longitudinal studies possible, with interesting results that could not have been established unless the measurement was understood and procedures carefully followed. Attachment affects brain development and the immune system (Pietromonaco & Powers, 2015). But insecure attachment in infancy does not always lead to later problems (Keller, 2014),

and the links from one generation to another are weaker than originally thought (Pasco Fearon & Roisman, 2017).

Nonetheless, thanks to a procedure developed by Mary Ainsworth half a century ago, we now know that securely attached infants are more likely to become secure toddlers, socially competent preschoolers, high-achieving schoolchildren, partners in loving couples, capable parents, and healthy adults (Shaver et al., 2019; Raby et al., 2017).

THINK CRITICALLY: Is the Strange Situation a valid way to measure attachment in every culture, or is it biased toward the Western idea of the ideal mother–child relationship?

In the two years after Ceauşescu was ousted and killed in 1989, thousands of those children were adopted by North American, western European, and Australian families. Infants under 6 months of age fared best; the adoptive parents established synchrony via play and caregiving. Many of those adopted between 6 and 18 months of age also fared well.

For those adopted later, early signs were encouraging: Skinny toddlers gained weight, started walking, and grew quickly, developing motor skills they had lacked (H. Park et al., 2011). However, if their social deprivation had lasted more than a year, their emotions and intellect suffered.

Many were overly friendly to strangers, a sign of past insecure attachment. By age 11, their average IQ was only 85, which is 15 points lower than the statistical norm. The older they had been at adoption, the worse they fared (Rutter et al., 2010). Some became impulsive, angry teenagers. Apparently, the stresses of adolescence and emerging adulthood exacerbated cognitive and social strains that they had encountered in infancy (Merz & McCall, 2011). (See Table 4.1 on page 139.)

These children are now adults, many with serious emotional or conduct problems (Sonuga-Barke et al., 2017). Other research on children adopted nationally and internationally finds that many develop quite well, but every stress—such as parental maltreatment, institutional life, and the uncertainty of the adoption process—makes it more difficult for a child to become a happy, well-functioning adult (Grotevant & McDermott, 2014).

Romania no longer permits international adoption, even though some infants are still institutionalized. Research confirms that early emotional deprivation, not genes or nutrition, is their greatest problem.

Romanian infants develop best in their own families, second best in foster families, and worst in institutions (Nelson et al., 2014). This is generally true for infants everywhere: Families usually nurture their babies better than strangers who provide good physical care but not emotional attachment. The longer children live in hospitals and orphanages, the higher the risk of social and intellectual harm (Julian, 2013).

Fortunately, most institutions have improved or closed, although many (estimated 8 million) children worldwide are still in institutions (Marshall, 2014). Recent adoptees are much less impaired than those Romanian orphans (Grotevant & McDermott, 2014), and many adoptive families are as strongly attached as any biological family, as A Case to Study demonstrates.

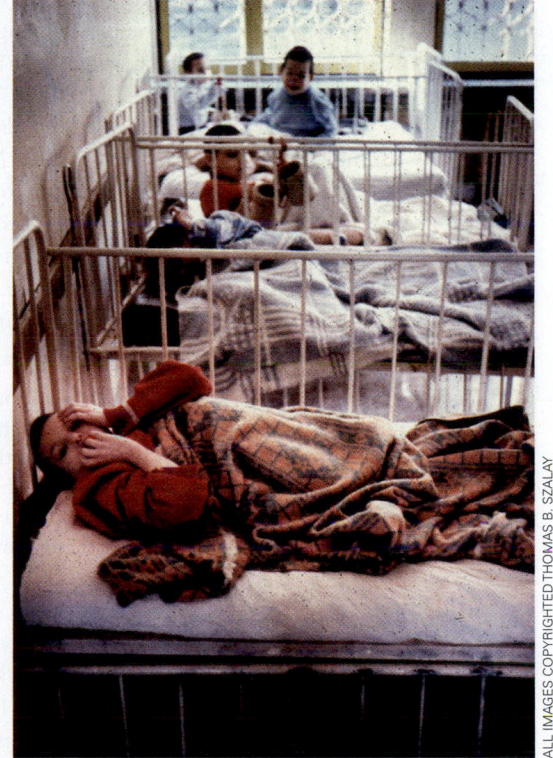

ALL IMAGES COPYRIGHTED THOMAS B. SZALAY

Hands on Head These children in Romania, here older than age 2, probably spent most of their infancy in their cribs, never with the varied stimulation that infant brains need. The sad results are evident here—that boy is fingering his own face, because the feel of his own touch is most likely one of the few sensations he knows. The girl sitting up in the back is a teenager. This photo was taken in 1982; Romania no longer destroys children so dramatically.

A CASE TO STUDY

Can We Bear This Commitment?

Parents and children capture my attention, wherever they are. Today I spotted one mother ignoring her stroller-bound toddler on a crowded subway (I wanted to tell her to talk to her child) and another mother breast-feeding a 7-month-old in a public park (I smiled approvingly, because that was illegal three decades ago). I look for signs of secure or insecure attachment—the contact-maintaining and proximity-seeking moves that parents do, seemingly unaware that they are responding to primordial depths of human love.

I particularly observe families I know. I am struck by the powerful bond between parent and child, as strong (or stronger) in adoptive families as in genetic ones.

One adoptive couple is Macky and Nick. I see them echoing my own experiences with my biological daughters. Two examples: When Alice was a few days old, I overheard Nick phone another parent, asking which detergent is best for washing baby clothes. That reminded me that I also switched detergents for my newborn. Years later, when Macky was engrossed in conversation, Nick interrupted to say they needed to stop talking because the girls needed to get home for their naps. Parents at social occasions everywhere do that, with one parent telling the other it's time to leave.

My appreciation of their attachment was cemented by a third incident. In Macky's words:

I'll never forget the Fourth of July at the spacious home of my mother-in-law's best friend. It was a perfect celebration on a perfect day. Kids frolicked in the pool. Parents socialized nearby, on the sun-drenched lawn or inside the cool house. Many guests had published books on parenting; we imagined they admired our happy, thriving family.

My husband and I have two daughters, Alice who was then 7 and Penelope who was 4. They learned to swim early and are always the first to jump in the pool and the last to leave. Great children, and doesn't that mean great parents?

After hours of swimming, the four of us scrambled up to dry land. I went inside to the library to talk with my father, while most people enjoyed hot dogs, relish, mustard, and juicy watermelon.

A Grateful Family This family photo shows (from *left* to *right*) Nick, Penelope (with their dog), Macky, and Alice Cooper. When they adopted Alice as a newborn, the parents said, "This is a miracle we feared would never happen."

Suddenly we heard a heart-chilling wail. Panicked, I raced to the pool's edge to see the motionless body of a small child who had gone unnoticed underwater for too long. His blue-face was still. Someone was giving CPR. His mother kept wailing, panicked, pleading, destroyed. I had a shameful thought—thank God that is not my child.

He lived. He regained his breath and was whisked away by ambulance. The party came to a quick close. We four, skin tingling from the summer sun, hearts beating from the near-death of a child who was my kids' playmate an hour before, drove away.

Turning to Nick, I asked, "Can we bear this commitment we have made? Can we raise our children in the face of all hazards—some we try to prevent, others beyond our control?"

That was five years ago. Our children are flourishing. Our confidence is strong and so are our emotions. But it takes only a moment to recognize just how entwined our well-being is with our children and how fragile life is. We are deeply grateful.

Many nations now restrict international adoptions, in part because some children were literally snatched from their biological parents to be sent abroad. According to government records, the number of international adoptees in the United States was 6,441 in 2014, down from 22,884 in 2004.

The decrease is influenced more by international politics than by infant needs. Ideally, no infant would be institutionalized, but if that ideal is not reached, scientists advocate quick adoption or change in institutions, because psychological health is crucial for well-being (McCall, 2013).

TABLE 4.1   Predictors of Attachment Type

Secure attachment (type B) is more likely if:

- The parent is usually sensitive and responsive to the infant's needs.
- The infant–parent relationship is high in synchrony.
- The infant's temperament is "easy."
- The parents are not stressed about income, other children, or their marriage.
- The parents have a working model of secure attachment to their own parents.

Insecure attachment is more likely if:

- The parent mistreats the child. (Neglect increases type A; abuse increases types C and D.)
- The mother is mentally ill. (Paranoia increases type D; depression increases type C.)
- The parents are highly stressed about income, other children, or their marriage. (Parental stress increases types A and D.)
- The parents are intrusive and controlling. (Parental domination increases type A.)
- The parents have alcohol use disorder. (Father with alcoholism increases type A; mother with alcoholism increases type D.)
- The child's temperament is "difficult." (Difficult children tend to be type C.)
- The child's temperament is "slow-to-warm-up." (This correlates with type A.)

Social Referencing

The third social connection that developmentalists look for during infancy, after synchrony and attachment, is **social referencing.** Much as a student might consult a dictionary or other reference work, social referencing means seeking emotional responses or information from other people. A reassuring glance, a string of cautionary words, a facial expression of alarm, pleasure, or dismay—those are social references.

Even at 8 months, infants notice where other people are looking and use that information to look in the same direction themselves (Tummeltshammer et al., 2014). After age 1, when infants can walk and are "little scientists," their need to consult others becomes urgent and more accurate—although they do not always respond to a shouted "No" or a worried look.

Toddlers search for clues in gazes, faces, and body position, paying close attention to emotions and intentions. They focus on their familiar caregivers, but they also use relatives, other children, and even strangers to help them assess objects and events. They are remarkably selective, noticing that some strangers are reliable references and others are not (Fusaro & Harris, 2013).

Social referencing has many practical applications for the infant. Consider mealtime. Caregivers the world over pretend to taste and say "yum-yum," encouraging toddlers to eat beets, liver, or spinach. Toddlers read expressions, insisting on the foods that the adults *really* like. If mother likes it, and presents it on the spoon, then they eat it—otherwise not (Shutts et al., 2013). Some tastes (spicy, bitter, sour, etc.) are rejected by very young infants, but if they repeatedly see that their caregivers eat it, they learn to like it (Forestel & Mennella, 2017).

Through this process, some children develop a taste for raw fish or curried goat or smelly cheese—foods that children in other cultures refuse. Similarly, toddlers use social cues to understand the difference between real and pretend eating, as well as to learn which objects, emotions, and activities are forbidden.

social referencing
Seeking information about how to react to an unfamiliar or ambiguous object or event by observing someone else's expressions and reactions. That other person becomes a social reference.

© BILL BACHMAN/ALAMY

Rotini Pasta? Look again. Every family teaches their children to relish delicacies that other people avoid. Examples are bacon (not in Arab nations), hamburgers (not in India), and, as shown here, a witchetty grub. This Australian aboriginal boy is about to swallow an insect larva.

DEVELOPING ATTACHMENT

Attachment begins at birth and continues lifelong. Much depends not only on the ways in which parents and babies bond, but also on the quality and consistency of caregiving, the safety and security of the home environment, and individual and family experience. While the patterns set in infancy may echo in later life, they are not determinative.

How Many Children are Securely Attached?

The specific percentages of children who are secure and insecure vary by culture, parent responsiveness, context, and specific temperament and needs of both the child and the caregiver. Generally, about a third of all 1-year-olds seem insecure.

50–70%	10–20%	10–20%	5–10%
Secure Attachment (Type B)	Avoidant Attachment (Type A)	Ambivalent Attachment (Type C)	Disorganized Attachment (Type D)

Attachment in the Strange Situation May Influence Relationships Through the Life Span

Attachment patterns formed in infancy affect adults lifelong, but later experiences of love and rejection may change early patterns. Researchers measure attachment by examining children's behaviors in the Strange Situation where they are separated from their parent and play in a room with an unfamiliar caregiver. These early patterns can influence later adult relationships. As life goes on, people become more or less secure, avoidant, or disorganized.

Securely Attached [Type B]
In the Strange Situation, children are able to separate from caregiver but prefer caregiver to strangers.
> Later in life, they tend to have supportive relationships and positive self-concept.

Insecure-Avoidant [Type A]
In the Strange Situation, children avoid caregiver.
> Later in life, they tend to be aloof in personal relationships, loners who are lonely.

Insecure-Resistant/Ambivalent [Type C]
In the Strange Situation, children appear upset and worried when separated from caregiver; they may hit or cling.
> Later in life, their relationships may be angry, stormy, unpredictable. They have few long-term friendships.

Disorganized [Type D]
In the Strange Situation, children appear angry, confused, erratic, or fearful.
> Later in life, they can demonstrate odd behavior—including sudden emotions. They are at risk for serious psychological disorders.

The Continuum of Attachment

Avoidance and anxiety occur along a continuum. Neither genes nor cultural variations were understood when the Strange Situation was first developed (in 1965). Some contemporary researchers believe the link between childhood attachment and adult personality is less straightforward than this table suggests.

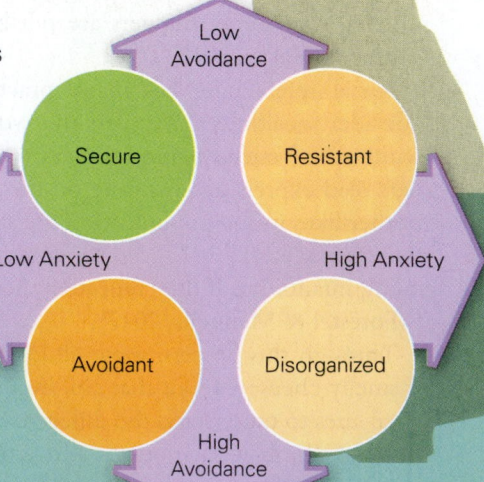

Fathers as Social Partners

Synchrony, attachment, and social referencing are evident with fathers as well as with mothers. Indeed, fathers tend to elicit more smiles and laughter from their infants than mothers do. They tend to play more exciting games, swinging and chasing, while mothers do more caregiving and comforting (Fletcher et al., 2013).

Although women do more child care than men in every nation, and men are more likely to play with their children, ideally both parents coordinate their efforts, with specifics attuned to their particular strengths (Shwalb et al., 2013). Too much can be made of gender roles. One researcher reports that "fathers and mothers showed patterns of striking similarity: they touched, looked, vocalized, rocked, and kissed their newborns equally" (Parke, 2013, p. 121).

Differences are more evident between couples than within couples, and variation is evident. One researcher reports only one enduring gender difference in child care: Women do more smiling (Parke, 2013).

Other researchers find that gender differences in child rearing vary by nation, by income, by cohort, and by ideology. For instance, a study in rural Indonesia found that fathers were almost never involved in direct care of infants but felt responsible for the household (Pardosi et al., 2017). A study of men in Italy found that younger generations were more often securely attached than older generations (Cassibba et al., 2017). A third study, this one of U.S. parents having a second child, found that mothers used slightly more techniques to soothe their crying infants than fathers did (7.7 versus 5.9). However, when fathers did active comforting, mothers were less stressed by infant crying (Dayton et al., 2015).

It is a stereotype that African American, Latin American, and Asian American fathers are less nurturing and stricter than other men (Parke, 2013). The opposite may be more accurate (Cabrera et al., 2011). Within the United States, contemporary fathers in all ethnic groups are, typically, more involved with their children than their own fathers were.

As with humans of all ages, social contexts are influential: Fathers are influenced by other fathers (Roopnarine & Hossain, 2013; Qin & Chang, 2013). Thus, fathers of every ethnic group know what other men are doing, and that affects their

> **THINK CRITICALLY:** Why are mothers less stressed by infant crying if fathers help? Do passive fathers blame mothers? Do mothers blame themselves?

Not Manly? Where did that idea come from? Fathers worldwide provide excellent care for their toddlers and enjoy it, evident in the United States *(left)* and India *(right)* and in every other nation.

own behavior. For both sexes, stress decreases parent involvement. That brings up another difference between mothers and fathers. When money is scarce and stress is high, some fathers opt out. That choice is less possible for mothers (Roopnarine & Hossain, 2013; Qin & Chang, 2013).

---

what have you learned?

1. Why does synchrony affect early emotional development?
2. How are proximity-seeking and contact-maintaining attachment expressed by infants and caregivers?
3. How does infant behavior differ in each of the four types of attachment?
4. How might each of the four types of attachment be expressed in adulthood?
5. What has been learned from the research on Romanian orphans?
6. How is social referencing important in toddlerhood?
7. What are the similarities and differences in mothers and fathers?

Theories of Infant Psychosocial Development

The fact that infants are emotional, social creatures is recognized by everyone who studies babies. However, each of the theories discussed in Chapter 1 has a distinct perspective on this universal reality, as you will now see.

Psychoanalytic Theory

Psychoanalytic theory connects biosocial and psychosocial development. Sigmund Freud and Erik Erikson each described two distinct stages of early development, one in the first year and one beginning in the second year.

◆ Especially for Nursing Mothers You have heard that if you wean your child too early, he or she will overeat or develop alcohol use disorder. Is it true? (see response, page 153)

All Together Now Toddlers in an employees' day-care program at a flower farm in Colombia learn to use the potty on a schedule. Will this experience lead to later personality problems? Probably not.

REUTERS/JOSE MIGUEL GOMEZ/NEWSCOM

FREUD: ORAL AND ANAL STAGES According to Freud (1935/1989, 2001), the first year of life is the *oral stage,* so named because the mouth is the young infant's primary source of gratification. In the second year, with the *anal stage,* pleasure comes from the anus—particularly from the sensual satisfaction of bowel movements and, eventually, the psychological pleasure of controlling them.

Freud believed that the oral and anal stages are fraught with potential conflicts. If a mother frustrates her infant's urge to suck—weaning too early or too late, for example, or preventing the baby from sucking a thumb or a pacifier—that may later lead to an *oral fixation.* Adults with an oral fixation are stuck (fixated) at the oral stage, and therefore they eat, drink, chew, bite, or talk excessively, still seeking the mouth-related pleasures of infancy.

Similarly, if toilet training is overly strict or if it begins before maturation allows sufficient control, that causes a clash between the toddler's refusal—or inability—to comply and the wishes of the adult, who denies the infant normal anal pleasures. That may lead to an *anal personality*—an adult who seeks self-control, with a strong need for regularity and cleanliness in all aspects of life.

ERIKSON: TRUST AND AUTONOMY According to Erikson, the first crisis of life is **trust versus mistrust,** when infants learn whether or not the world can be trusted to satisfy basic needs. Babies feel secure when food and comfort are provided with "consistency, continuity, and sameness of experience" (Erikson, 1993a, p. 247). If social interaction inspires trust, the child (later the adult) confidently explores the social world.

The second crisis is **autonomy versus shame and doubt,** beginning at about 18 months, when self-awareness emerges. Toddlers want autonomy (self-rule) over their own actions and bodies. Without it, they feel ashamed and doubtful. Like Freud, Erikson believed that problems in early infancy could last a lifetime, creating adults who are suspicious and pessimistic (mistrusting) or easily shamed (lacking autonomy).

Behaviorism

From the perspective of behaviorism, emotions and personality are molded as adults reinforce or punish children. Behaviorists believe that parents who respond joyously to every glimmer of a grin will have children with a sunny disposition. The opposite is also true:

> Failure to bring up a happy child, a well-adjusted child—assuming bodily health—falls squarely upon the parents' shoulders. [By the time the child is 3] parents have already determined . . . [whether the child] is to grow into a happy person, wholesome and good-natured, whether he is to be a whining, complaining neurotic, an anger-driven, vindictive, over-bearing slave driver, or one whose every move in life is definitely controlled by fear.
>
> *[Watson, 1928/1972, pp. 7, 45]*

Only in America Toddlers in every nation of the world sometimes cry when emotions overwhelm them, but in the United States young children are encouraged to express emotions—and Halloween is a national custom, unlike in other nations. Candy, dress-up, ghosts, witches, and ringing doorbells after sunset—no wonder many young children are overwhelmed.

Later behaviorists recognized that infants' behavior also reflects social learning, when infants learn from other people. You already saw an example, social referencing. Social learning occurs throughout life, not necessarily via direct teaching but often through observation (Shneidman & Woodward, 2016). Toddlers express emotions in various ways—from giggling to cursing—just as their parents or older siblings do.

For example, a boy might develop a hot temper if his father's outbursts seem to win his mother's respect; a girl might be coy, or passive-aggressive, if that is what she has seen at home. These examples are deliberately sexist: Gender roles, in particular, are learned, according to social learning.

Parents often unwittingly encourage certain traits in their children. Should babies have many toys, or will that make them too greedy? Should you pick up your crying baby or give her a pacifier? Should you breast-feed until age 2 or longer or switch to bottle-feeding before 6 months?

These questions highlight the distinction between **proximal parenting** (being physically close to a baby, often holding and touching) and **distal parenting** (keeping some distance—providing toys, encouraging self-feeding, and talking face-to-face instead of communicating by touch). Caregivers tend to behave in proximal or distal ways very early, when infants are only 2 months old (Kärtner et al., 2010). Each pattern reinforces some behavior.

For instance, toddlers who, as infants, were often held, patted, and hushed (proximal) became toddlers who are more obedient to their parents but less likely to recognize themselves in a mirror. This is one of those findings that has been replicated in many nations. In Greece, Cameroon, Italy, Israel, Zambia, Scotland, and Turkey, distal or proximal infant care correlates with whether adults value individual rather than collective action (Scharf, 2014; Keller et al., 2010; Ross et al., 2017; Carra et al., 2013; Borke et al., 2007; Kärtner et al., 2011).

trust versus mistrust
Erikson's first crisis of psychosocial development. Infants learn basic trust if the world is a secure place where their basic needs (for food, comfort, attention, and so on) are met.

autonomy versus shame and doubt
Erikson's second crisis of psychosocial development. Toddlers either succeed or fail in gaining a sense of self-rule over their actions and their bodies.

proximal parenting
Caregiving practices that involve being physically close to the baby, with frequent holding and touching.

distal parenting
Caregiving practices that involve remaining distant from the baby, providing toys, food, and face-to-face communication with minimal holding and touching.

Amusing or Neglectful?
Depends on the culture. In proximal cultures this father would be criticized for not interacting with his daughter, and the mother would be blamed for letting him do so. But in distal cultures Dad might be admired for multitasking: simultaneously reading the paper, waiting for the bus, and taking the baby to day care.

working model
In cognitive theory, a set of assumptions that the individual uses to organize perceptions and experiences. For example, a person might assume that other people are trustworthy and be surprised by an incident in which this working model of human behavior is erroneous.

Brainy Baby Fortunately, infant brains are designed to respond to stimulation of many kinds. As long as the baby has moving objects to see (an animated caregiver is better than any mobile), the synapses proliferate.

Cognitive Theory

Cognitive theory holds that thoughts determine a person's perspective. Early experiences are important because beliefs, perceptions, and memories make them so, not because they are buried in the unconscious (psychoanalytic theory) or burned into the brain's patterns (behaviorism).

According to many cognitive theorists, early experiences help infants develop a **working model,** which is a set of assumptions that becomes a frame of reference for later life (S. Johnson et al., 2010). It is a "model" because early relationships form a prototype, or blueprint; it is "working" because it is a work in progress, not fixed or final.

Ideally, infants develop "a working model of the self as lovable and competent" because the parents are "emotionally available, loving, and supportive of their mastery efforts" (Harter, 2012, p. 12). However, reality does not always conform to this ideal. A 1-year-old girl might develop a model, based on her parents' inconsistent responses to her, that people are unpredictable. She will continue to apply that model to everyone: Her childhood friendships will be insecure, and her adult relationships will be guarded.

The crucial idea, according to cognitive theory, is that an infant's early experiences themselves are not necessarily pivotal, but the interpretation of those experiences is (Olson & Dweck, 2009). Children may misinterpret their experiences, or parents may offer inaccurate explanations, and these form ideas that affect later thinking and behavior.

In this way, working models formed in childhood echo lifelong. A hopeful message from cognitive theory is that people can rethink and reorganize their thoughts, developing new models. Our mistrustful girl might marry someone who is faithful and loving, so she may gradually develop a new working model.

The form of psychotherapy that seems most successful at the moment is called *cognitive-behavioral,* in which new thoughts about how to behave are developed. In other words, a new working model is developed.

"Which one generates the most synapses?"

Evolutionary Theory

Remember that evolutionary theory stresses two needs: survival and reproduction. Human brains are extraordinarily adept at those tasks. However, not until after more than two decades of maturation is the human brain fully functioning. A human child must be nourished, protected, and taught much longer than offspring of any other species. Infant and parent emotions ensure this lengthy protection (Hrdy, 2009).

EMOTIONS FOR SURVIVAL Infant emotions are part of this evolutionary mandate. All of the reactions described in the first part of this chapter—from the hunger cry to the temper tantrum—can be seen from this perspective (Konner, 2010).

For example, newborns are extraordinarily dependent, unable to walk or talk or even sit up and feed themselves for months after birth. They must attract adult devotion—and they do. That first smile, the sound of infant laughter, and their role in synchrony are all powerfully attractive to adults—especially to parents.

Adults call their hairless, chinless, round-faced, big-stomached, small-limbed offspring "cute," "handsome," "beautiful," "adorable," yet all of these characteristics are often considered ugly in adults. Parents willingly devote hours to carrying, feeding, changing, and cleaning their infants, who never express their gratitude.

Adaptation is evident. Adults have the genetic potential to be caregivers, and grandparents have done it before, but, according to evolutionary psychology, whether or not that potential is expressed, turning busy adults into devoted caregivers and dependent infants into emotional magnets, is ruled by survival needs of the species.

If humans were motivated solely by money or power, no one would have children. Yet evolution has created adults who find parenting worth every sacrifice, and when they provide the care that evolution has ordained, children develop well (Narvaez et al., 2013). We can all be grateful for that.

THE COST OF CHILD REARING The financial costs of raising a child are substantial: Food, diapers, clothes, furniture, medical bills, toys, and child care (whether paid or unpaid) are just a start. Before a child becomes independent, many parents buy a bigger residence and pay for education—including such luxuries as piano lessons, karate class, or basketball camp. The emotional costs are greater—worry, self-doubt, fear, etc. A book about parenting is titled *All Joy and No Fun,* highlighting the paradox: People choose to sacrifice time, money, and fun because they find parenting deeply satisfying (Senior, 2014).

Evolutionary theory holds that the emotions of attachment—love, jealousy, even clinginess and anger—keep toddlers near caregivers who remain vigilant. Infants fuss at still faces, fear separation, and laugh when adults play with them—all to sustain caregiving. Emotions are our genetic legacy; we would die without them.

◆ **Especially for Pediatricians**
A mother complains that her toddler refuses to stay in the car seat, spits out disliked foods, and almost never does what she says. How should you respond? (see response, page 153)

Same Situation, Far Apart: Safekeeping Historically, grandmothers were sometimes crucial for child survival. Now, even though medical care has reduced child mortality, grandmothers still do their part to keep children safe, as shown by these two—in the eastern United States *(left)* and Vietnam *(right).*

allocare
Literally, "other-care"; the care of children by people other than the biological parents.

Evolutionary social scientists note that if mothers were the exclusive caregivers of each child until children were adults, a given woman could rear only one or two offspring—not enough for the species to survive. Instead, before the introduction of reliable birth control, the average interval between births for humans was two to four years. Humans bear children at relatively short intervals because of **allocare**—the care of children by *alloparents,* caregivers who are not the biological parents (Hrdy, 2009).

Allocare is essential for *Homo sapiens'* survival. Compared with many other species (mother chimpanzees space births by four or five years and never let another chimp hold their babies), human mothers have evolved to let other people help with child care (Kachel et al., 2011). That may be universal for our species—but each culture has distinct values and preferences for nonmaternal care, as the next topic explains.

> # what have you learned?
>
> 1. According to Freud, what might happen if a baby's oral needs are not met?
> 2. How might Erikson's crisis of "trust versus mistrust" affect later life?
> 3. How do behaviorists explain the development of emotions and personality?
> 4. What does the term *working model* mean within cognitive theory?
> 5. What is the difference between proximal and distal parenting?
> 6. How does evolution explain the parent–child bond?
> 7. Why is allocare necessary for survival of the human species?

Who Should Care for Babies?

Cultural variations and theoretical differences are vast in every aspect of infant care. You have read many examples: breast-feeding, co-sleeping, and language development among them. One way to illustrate these differences is to consider one issue. Who should care for babies?

Contrast This with That In stark contrast with the children on page 137, the infants in this day care center receive excellent care.

↑ OBSERVATION QUIZ
What three things do you see that suggest good care? (see answer, page 153)

TED RICHARDSON/RALEIGH NEWS & OBSERVER/MCT VIA GETTY IMAGES

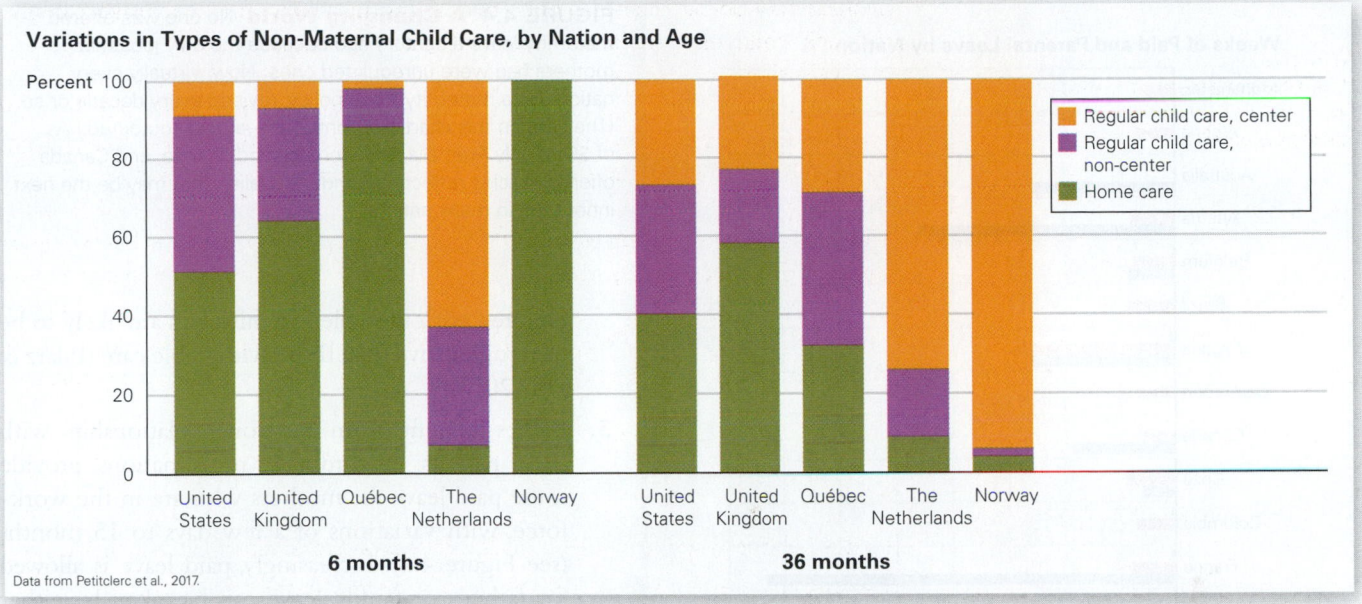

Variations in Types of Non-Maternal Child Care, by Nation and Age

Data from Petitclerc et al., 2017.

FIGURE 4.3 **Who Cares for the Baby?** Infants are the same everywhere, but cultures and governments differ dramatically. Does a 6-month-old need Mother more than a 3-year-old? Norway and Quebec say yes; the United States, United Kingdom, and the Netherlands say no.

Infant Day Care

About 150 million births occurred in 2017 (United Nations, Department of Economic and Social Affairs, Population Division, 2017). Most of these babies are cared for primarily by their mothers. Before age 2, marked differences in their allocare are evident.

Fathers and grandmothers frequently care for infants. The United States has more single mothers than other nations, but it also has higher rates of father care, unlike a few decades ago. Most married mothers are currently happy with how much infant care their husbands provide, although mothers are still primary caregivers (DeMaris & Mahoney, 2017). In some families in the United States and some other nations, grandmothers are primary caregivers from day 1. In other families, grandmothers are rarely, or never, alone with the infant.

In Western cultures, infant care provided by a nonrelative, either at the baby's home or at a day-care center, has increased since 1980. Since paid maternal leave is uncommon in the United States, 58 percent of the mothers of infants under 1 year of age were in the labor force in 2015 (U.S. Bureau of Labor Statistics, April 22, 2016). That requires allocare, either by a relative or a professional. As you can see from Figure 4.3, even among wealthy nations, care of infants varies markedly—the babies are all quite similar in their caregiving needs and responses, but nations and families vary dramatically in who cares for them at 6 months of age and again from ages 1 to 3.

By contrast, virtually no infant in some of the poorest nations receives regular nonmaternal care unless the mother is dead or severely ill. Not shown is the socioeconomic split: In most nations—except the United States—low-income children are most likely to be in exclusive maternal care (Petitclerc et al., 2017).

The United States has higher rates of infant day care for the working poor, whose infant care is subsidized, as well as higher rates for the wealthy, because they can afford it. Middle-class infants are usually in home care.

Almost every developmentalist agrees with three conclusions.

1. Attachment to one or several familiar caregivers is essential. That could be mothers, other close relatives, or regular day-care providers.

2. Frequent changes and instability are problematic. If an infant is cared for by a neighbor, a grandmother, a day-care center, and then another grandmother, each for only a month or two, or if an infant is with the biological mother, then a foster mother, then back with the biological mother, that is harmful. By age 3,

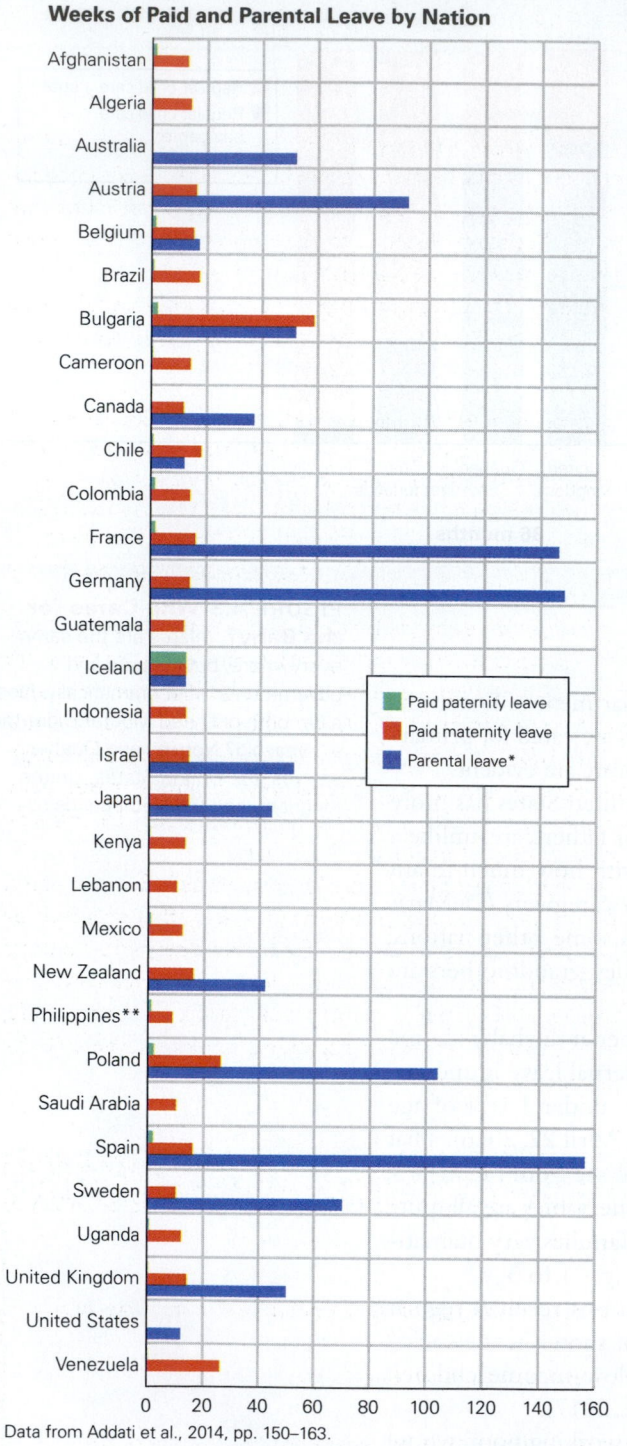

Weeks of Paid and Parental Leave by Nation

Legend:
- Paid paternity leave (green)
- Paid maternity leave (red)
- Parental leave* (blue)

Data from Addati et al., 2014, pp. 150–163.

Notes: *In some cases, leave can be shared between parents or other family members. Many nations have increased leave in the past four years.

**In the Philippines, parents must be married in order to receive paid leave.

FIGURE 4.4 A Changing World No one was offered maternity leave a century ago because the only jobs that mothers had were unregulated ones. Now, virtually every nation has a maternity leave policy, revised every decade or so. (The data on this chart are from 2011—already outdated.) As of 2014, only Australia, Sweden, Iceland, France, and Canada offered policies reflecting gender equality. That may be the next innovation in many nations.

children with unstable care histories are likely to be more aggressive than those with stable care (Pilarz & Hill, 2014).

3. Babies benefit from a strong relationship with their parents. Accordingly, most nations provide some paid leave for mothers who are in the workforce, with variations of a few days to 15 months (see Figure 4.4). Increasingly, paid leave is allowed for fathers, or family leave can be taken by either parent. In most nations, a mother's job is legally required to be available when her leave is over.

Beyond the need for attachment and stability, experts are split on whether infant day care is beneficial, harmful, or neutral. As one review explained: "This evidence now indicates that early nonparental care environments sometimes pose risks to young children and sometimes confer benefits" (Phillips et al., 2011, p. 44). The same is true for parental care: Some mothers and fathers are wonderful, some not.

People tend to believe that the practices of their own family or culture are best and that other patterns harm the infant. Because of the difference-equals-deficit error, false assumptions flourish.

Recent Past and Present

Research in the United States has found that center care benefits children of low-income families (Peng & Robins, 2010). For less impoverished children, questions arise.

An ongoing longitudinal study by the Early Child Care Network of the National Institute of Child Health and Human Development (NICHD) has followed the development of more than 1,300 children born in 1991. Early day care correlated with many cognitive advances, especially in language.

The social consequences were less clear, however. Most analyses find that secure attachment to the mother was as common among infants in center care as among infants cared for at home. Like other, smaller studies, the NICHD research confirms that the mother–child relationship is pivotal.

Indeed, although infants seem to benefit from nonmaternal care, the other half of the relationship—the mothers—have concerns of their own (Green, 2015). Some mothers feel guilty for allocare (remember attachment parenting), and others

◆ **Especially for Day-Care Providers**
A mother who brings her infant to you for day care says that she knows she is harming her baby, but economic necessity compels her to work. What do you say? (see response, page 153)

OPPOSING PERSPECTIVES

Infant Day Care

Adults disagree about the value and impact of nonparental care during the first two years of life. Such differences are affected by personal experience (those who, as infants, were in nonparental care are more likely to approve of it), by gender (males are more likely to think that mothers should provide exclusive care), and by education (higher education increases support for nonparental care) (Galasso et al., 2017; Rose et al., 2018; Shpancer & Schweitzer, 2016).

Beyond that, for cultural, ideological, and economic reasons, center-based infant care is common in France, Israel, China, Chile, the Netherlands, and Sweden, where it is heavily subsidized by the government. That much is the same in those nations, but specifics again reveal opposing perspectives.

For example, in France, such care can begin at 12 weeks, although there is a long waiting list for care. The infant–caregiver ratio is higher than would be accepted in other nations, as much as 7 to 1. In Norway, subsidized care does not begin until age 1, and spaces are available—and often taken—by everyone of every income level and ethnic background.

Many families in western Europe believe that subsidized infant care is a public right, just like fire, police, school, and medical care are available to everyone who needs them. By contrast, infant care paid by the government is rare in South Asia, Africa, and Latin America, where many parents believe it is harmful. (Table 4.2 lists five essential characteristics of high-quality infant day care, wherever it is located.)

Most nations are between those two. Germany recently began offering paid infant care as a successful strategy to increase the birth rate. One detailed example comes from Australia, where the government attempted to increase the birth rate by paying parents $5,000 for each newborn, providing paid parental leave, and offering low-cost child–care centers. Yet many Australians still believed that babies need exclusive maternal care (Harrison et al., 2014).

Parents are caught in the middle. For example, one Australian mother of a 12-month-old boy used center care, but said:

> I spend a lot of time talking with them about his day and what he's been doing and how he's feeling and they just seem to have time to do that, to make the effort to communicate. Yeah they've really bonded with him and he's got close to them. But I still don't like leaving him there.
>
> *[quoted in Boyd et al., 2013]*

Underlying every policy and practice are theories about what is best. In the United States, marked variations are apparent by state and by employer, with most states not contributing to center care until a child is 4 years old. It is not required for employers to pay for maternal leave, although some companies do so. Paternal leave is almost never paid, publicly or privately, with one exception: The U.S. military allows 10 days of paid leave for fathers.

In the United States, only 20 percent of infants are cared for *exclusively* by their mothers (i.e., no other relatives or babysitters) throughout their first year. This is in contrast to Canada, which has far more generous maternal leave and lower rates of maternal employment. In the first year of life, most Canadians are cared for only by their mothers (Babchishin et al., 2013).

TABLE 4.2 High-Quality Day Care

High-quality day care during infancy has five essential characteristics:

1 *Adequate attention to each infant*

   A small group of infants (no more than five) needs two reliable, familiar, loving caregivers. Continuity of care is crucial.

2 *Encouragement of language and sensorimotor development*

   Infants need language—songs, conversations, and positive talk—and easily manipulated toys.

3 *Attention to health and safety*

   Cleanliness routines (e.g., handwashing), accident prevention (e.g., no small objects), and safe areas to explore are essential.

4 *Professional caregivers*

   Caregivers should have experience and degrees/certificates in early-childhood education. Turnover should be low, morale high, and enthusiasm evident.

5 *Warm and responsive caregivers*

   Providers should engage the children in active play and guide them in problem solving. Quiet, obedient children may indicate unresponsive care.

Obviously, all of these differences are affected by culture, economics, and politics more than by universal needs of babies. What is your opinion? If you are, for instance, a well-educated North American woman whose mother was employed when you were young, you may think favorably of infant day care—but is your perspective the product of history and gender, or facts? Or if you are a man with roots in Latin America, you may look askance at any family who would entrust their infant to center care, but is your opinion based on evidence?

Double Winner For the father in this photo, baby and victory in the same year! He is one of many parents who are advocating for six weeks of paid maternity leave. The San Francisco Board of Supervisors voted yes, making this the first jurisdiction in the United States to mandate fully paid leave. The law went into effect in 2017—too late for both the mother and father shown here. Perhaps their next babies?

welcome the opportunity to continue their profession. The problems of multiple roles—parent, partner, professional etc.—are discussed in Chapter 13.

However, infant day care seemed detrimental if the mother was insensitive *and* the infant spent more than 20 hours a week in a poor-quality program with too many children per group (McCartney et al., 2010). Boys in such circumstances had more conflicts with their teachers than did the girls or other boys with a different mix of maternal traits and day-care experiences.

Many criticisms of early research—on children born more than 25 years ago, when caregivers knew less about infant development—seem valid. But day care itself has changed. For instance, it now seems that infants do best if they have regular, restful naps—and good day-care centers now structure the day accordingly. When they do, regular day care is likely to advance cognition (Plancoulaine, 2017).

Another criticism is that early research was almost exclusively on the United States (Dearing & Zachrisson, 2017). Other nations organize child care differently, and attitudes of mothers, fathers, and educators vary by culture.

More recent work finds that high-quality care in infancy benefits the cognitive skills of children of both sexes and all income groups, with no evidence of emotional harm, especially when it is followed by good preschool care (Li et al., 2013; Huston et al., 2015).

NORWAY The prior correlation between infant day care and childhood psychosocial problems, although not found in every study, raises concern. For that reason, the experience of Norway is instructive. In Norway, new mothers are paid at full salary to stay home with their babies for 47 weeks, and high-quality, free center day care is available from age 1 on. Most (62 percent) Norwegian 1-year-olds are in center care, as are 84 percent of the 2-year-olds and 93 percent of the 3-year-olds.

Longitudinal results in Norway find no detrimental results of center care, including when it begins at age 1. By kindergarten, Norwegian day-care children had slightly more conflicts with caregivers, but the authors suggest that this may be the result of shy children becoming bolder as a result of day care (Solheim et al., 2013). That raises another question: Was previous research biased to favor docile, passive children?

QUALITY CARE The issue of the quality of care has become crucial. A professional organization in the United States, the National Association for the Education of Young Children, updated its standards for care of babies from birth to 15 months, based on current research (NAEYC, 2014). Breast-feeding is encouraged (via bottles of breast milk that mothers have expressed earlier), babies are always put to sleep on

their backs, group size is small (no more than eight infants), and the ratio of adults to babies is 1:4 or fewer.

Many specific practices are recommended to keep infant minds growing and bodies healthy. For instance, "before walking on surfaces that infants use specifically for play, adults and children remove, replace, or cover with clean foot coverings any shoes they have worn outside that play area. If children or staff are barefoot in such areas, their feet are visibly clean" (NAEYC, 2014, p. 59). Another recommendation is to "engage infants in frequent face-to-face social interactions"—including talking, singing, smiling, and touching (NAEYC, 2014, p. 4).

All of the research on infant day care confirms that sociocultural and temperament differences matter. What seems best for one infant, in one culture, may not be best for another infant elsewhere. Good infant care—whether by mother, father, grandmother, or day-care center—depends on specifics, not generalities.

No matter what form of care is chosen or what theory is endorsed, individualized care with stable caregivers seems best (Morrissey, 2009). Frequent caregiver change is especially problematic for infants because each simple gesture or sound that a baby makes not only merits an encouraging response but also requires interpretation by someone who knows that particular baby well.

For example, "baba" could mean bottle, baby, blanket, banana, or some other word that does not even begin with *b*. This example is an easy one, but similar communication efforts—requiring individualized emotional responses, preferably from a familiar caregiver—are evident even in the first smiles and cries.

A related issue is the growing diversity of baby care providers. Especially when the home language is not the majority language, parents hesitate to let people of another background care for their infants. That is one reason that immigrant parents in the United States often prefer care by relatives instead of by professionals (P. Miller et al., 2014). Relationships are crucial, not only between caregiver and infant but also between caregiver and parent (Elicker et al., 2014).

However, especially for immigrants, young children need to learn the language and customs of the new nation in order to thrive. Many immigrant families understand this. They help the children adjust while maintaining cultural pride.

A study of West African immigrants in Italy, for instance, found that the mothers were more verbal than they would have been in their native country, thus encouraging language, but they retained some of their home culture (Carra et al., 2013). Obviously, the success of parents in raising successful, bicultural children depends on the attitudes within the host nation as well as on their own practices.

As is true of many topics in child development, controversies remain. But one fact is without question: Each infant needs personal responsiveness. Someone should serve as a partner in the synchrony duet, a base for secure attachment, and a social reference who encourages exploration. Then, infant emotions and experiences—cries and laughter, fears and joys—will ensure that development goes well.

what have you learned?

1. Why do cultures differ on the benefits of infant nonmaternal care?

2. How has father care changed in recent decades?

3. What lessons can be learned from the experiences of infant care in Norway?

4. Which infants are most likely to benefit from center care?

5. What aspects of infant care are agreed on by everyone?

SUMMARY

Emotional Development

1. Two emotions, contentment and distress, appear when an infant is born. Smiles and laughter are soon evident. Between 4 and 8 months of age, anger emerges in reaction to restriction and frustration, and it becomes stronger by age 1.

2. Reflexive fear is apparent in very young infants. Fear of something specific, including fear of strangers and of separation, typically arises in the second half of the first year, and it is strong by age 1.

3. In the second year, social awareness and self-awareness produce more selective and intense fear, anger, and joy. Emotions arise from the interaction of the self and others—specifically, pride, shame, and affection—and explosive temper. Self-recognition (measured by the mirror/rouge test) emerges at about 18 months, with culture a crucial influence.

4. Temperament is inborn, but the expression of temperament is influenced by the context, with evident plasticity.

The Development of Social Bonds

5. Often by 2 months, and clearly by 6 months, infants become more responsive and social, and synchrony is evident. Caregivers and infants engage in reciprocal interactions, with split-second timing.

6. Attachment is the relationship between two people who try to be close to each other (proximity-seeking and contact-maintaining). It is measured in infancy by a baby's reaction to the caregiver's presence, departure, and return in the Strange Situation.

7. Secure attachment provides encouragement for infant exploration. Adults are attached as well, evident not only as parents but also as romantic partners.

8. As they become more mobile and engage with their environment, infants use social referencing (looking to other people's facial expressions and body language) to detect what is safe, frightening, or fun.

9. Infants frequently use fathers as partners in synchrony, as attachment figures, and as social references, developing emotions

and exploring their world. Contemporary fathers often play with their infants.

Theories of Infant Psychosocial Development

10. According to all major theories, caregivers are especially influential in the first two years. Freud stressed the mother's impact on oral and anal pleasure; Erikson emphasized trust and autonomy. Both believed that the impact of these is lifelong.

11. Behaviorists focus on learning. They note that parents teach their babies many things, including when to be fearful or joyful, and how much physical and social distance (proximal or distal parenting) is best.

12. Cognitive theory holds that infants develop working models based on their experiences. Interpretation is crucial, and that can change with maturation.

13. Evolutionary theorists recognize that both infants and caregivers have impulses and emotions that have developed over millennia to foster the survival of each new member of the human species. Attachment is one example.

14. All theories agree with one conclusion from research in many nations: The relationship between the infant and caregivers is crucial. All aspects of early development are affected by policy and practice.

Who Should Care for Babies?

15. Research confirms that every infant needs responsive caregiving, secure attachment, and cognitive stimulation, and that these three can occur at home or in a good day-care center—but that quality matters.

16. Some people believe that infant day care benefits babies and that governments should subsidize high-quality infant care, just as governments pay professional firefighters to put out any fire. Other cultures believe the opposite—that infant care is best done by the mothers, who are solely responsible for providing it.

17. Still other nations take a middle ground. The Norwegian government pays for mothers to stay home with their infants until age 1, at which point excellent day-care centers are available for every child.

KEY TERMS

APPLICATIONS

1. One cultural factor that influences infant development is how infants are carried from place to place. Ask four mothers whose infants were born in each of the past four decades how they transported them—front or back carriers, facing out or in, strollers or carriages, in car seats or on mother's laps, and so on. Why did they choose the mode(s) they chose? What are their opinions and yours on how such cultural practices might affect infants' development?

2. Record video of synchrony for three minutes. Ideally, ask the parent of an infant under 8 months of age to play with the infant. If no infant is available, observe a pair of lovers as they converse. Note the sequence and timing of every facial expression, sound, and gesture of both partners.

3. Contact several day-care centers to try to assess the quality of care they provide. Ask about factors such as adult/child ratio, group size, and training for caregivers of children of various ages. Is there a minimum age? Why or why not? Analyze the answers, using Table 4.2 as a guide.

ESPECIALLY FOR ANSWERS

Response for Nurses and Pediatricians (from page 127): Stranger wariness is normal up to about 14 months. This baby's behavior actually might indicate secure attachment.

Response for Nursing Mothers (from page 142): Freud thought so, but there is no experimental evidence that weaning, even when ill-timed, has such dire long-term effects.

Response for Pediatricians (from page 145): Consider the origins of the misbehavior—probably a combination of the child's inborn temperament and the mother's distal parenting. Acceptance and consistent responses (e.g., avoiding disliked foods but always using the car seat) is more warranted than anger. Perhaps this mother is expressing hostility toward the child—a sign that intervention may be needed. Find out.

Response for Day-Care Providers (from page 148): Reassure the mother that you will keep her baby safe and will help to develop the baby's mind and social skills by fostering synchrony and attachment. Also tell her that the quality of mother–infant interaction at home is more important than anything else for psychosocial development; mothers who are employed full time usually have wonderful, secure relationships with their infants. If the mother wishes, you can discuss ways to be a responsive mother.

OBSERVATION QUIZ ANSWERS

Answer to Observation Quiz (from page 130): Watch the facial expressions.

Answer to Observation Quiz (from page 146): Remontia Green is holding the feeding baby in just the right position as she rocks back and forth—no propped-up bottle here. The two observing babies are at an angle and distance that makes them part of the social interaction, and they are strapped in. Finally, look at the cribs—no paint, close slats, and positioned so the babies can see each other.

APPLICATION TO DEVELOPING LIVES PARENTING SIMULATION EARLY CHILDHOOD

As you progress through the Early Childhood simulation module, how you decide the following will impact the biosocial, cognitive, and psychosocial development of your child.

Biosocial	Cognitive	Psychosocial
• How does your child's height and weight compare to national norms? • What foods will your child eat at this stage of development? • How much physical activity will you encourage?	• Which of Piaget's stages of cognitive development is your child in? • In what kind of school will you enroll your child? • Will your child be able to demonstrate impulse control? • How will your child compare to national averages in reading, math, and language?	• In what kind of social environment will you place your child? • How will your child react if you and your partner split up? • How will you discipline your child at this age? • How does your stress level impact your child's emotional health?

Early Childhood

From ages 2 to 6, young children spend most of their waking hours discovering, creating, laughing, and imagining, as they acquire the skills they need. They chase each other and attempt new challenges (developing their bodies); they play with sounds, words, and ideas (developing their minds); they invent games and dramatize fantasies (learning social skills and morals)—all under the guidance of their families, schools, and communities.

These years have been called the *preschool years,* but that is a misnomer. A *school* is a place of learning, and *pre-* means before. But most young children go somewhere every day to learn concepts, language, emotional regulation, and social skills while playing and growing. That means they are already in school. Consequently, ages 2 to 6 are best called *early childhood,* a joyful, playful, crucial time.

CHRISTOPHER HOPE-FITCH/GETTY IMAGES

EARLY CHILDHOOD
Body and Mind

what will you know?

- Why are some young children overweight?
- How should adults answer when children ask, "Why?"
- Does it confuse young children if they hear two or more languages?
- What do children learn in early education?

I often took 5-year-old Asa and his female friend, Ada, by subway from kindergarten in Manhattan to their homes in Brooklyn. Their bodies were quite similar to each other (no visible sex differences yet), but the two of them were unlike their fellow subway riders. Of course they had rounder heads, littler hands, and smaller bodies: Their feet did not touch the floor when they sat. But, appearance was not the most distinctive difference. Movement was.

I tried to keep their swinging feet from kicking other riders; I told them to stay beside me instead of careening up and down the subway car, oblivious to the strangers they bumped into or squeezed by. They were not disobedient; they sat for a moment. But then they quickly forgot my instructions. They left their seats again, unaware of the perspectives of other riders.

That is how nature makes young children: full of energy and action, with difficulty grasping viewpoints that are not theirs. Developmentalists call that *egocentrism*.

Adults must guide young children and keep them safe while enjoying their exuberance. Most tired subway riders did that; they smiled and seemed to sympathize with my attempt to teach proper behavior. This chapter describes growth during early childhood—in body and mind—and how to enjoy young children while helping them learn.

Body Changes

In early childhood, as in infancy, the body and mind develop according to powerful epigenetic forces. This means that nature and nurture continually interact: Growth is biologically driven and socially guided, experience-expectant and experience-dependent.

Growth Patterns

Compare the body of an unsteady 24-month-old with that of a cartwheeling 6-year-old. Physical differences are obvious. Height and weight increase. However, size is not the most radical change; shape is. Proportions shift: Children slim down as the lower body lengthens and fat gives way to muscle.

The average body mass index (BMI, a ratio of weight to height) is lower at ages 5 and 6 than at any other time of life. Gone are the infant's protruding belly, round face, short limbs, and large head. The center of gravity moves from the breast to the belly, enabling cartwheels, somersaults, rhythmic dancing, and pumping legs on a swing: Changing proportions enable new achievements.

During each year of early childhood, well-nourished children grow about 3 inches (about 7½ centimeters) and gain almost 4½ pounds (2 kilograms). By age 6, the average child in a developed nation:

■ is at least 3½ feet tall (more than 110 centimeters).

■ weighs between 40 and 50 pounds (between 18 and 23 kilograms).

■ looks lean, not chubby.

■ has adultlike body proportions (with legs constituting about half the total height).

Young children enjoy developing their motor skills as brain maturation allows advances. Adults need to provide space and guided practice; children do the rest.

Most North American 6-year-olds can climb a tree and jump over a puddle, as well as throw, catch, and kick a ball. Many can ride a bicycle, swim in a pool, and print their names. Some, on other continents, can embroider clothes, swim in oceans, and climb cliffs.

MARC ROMANELLI/GETTY IMAGES

Short and Chubby Limbs No Longer Siblings in New Mexico, ages 7 and almost 1, illustrate the transformation of body shape and skills during early childhood. Head size is almost the same, but arms are twice as long, evidence of proximodistal growth.

↑ **OBSERVATION** QUIZ
Can this toddler peddle the tricycle? (see answer, page 191)

Nutrition

Although they rarely starve, preschool children sometimes are malnourished, even in nations with abundant food. Small appetites are often satiated by unhealthy snacks, crowding out needed vitamins.

OBESITY AMONG YOUNG CHILDREN Older adults often encourage children to eat, protecting them against famine that was common a century ago. Unfortunately, that encouragement may be destructive. As family income decreases, obesity increases—a sign of poor nutrition, likely to reduce immunity and increase later disease (Rook et al., 2014).

There are many explanations for the connection between obesity and low SES. Families with little money or education are more likely to have family habits—less exercise, more television, fewer vegetables, more sweetened drinks, frequent fast food—that correlate with overweight (Cespedes et al., 2013). In addition, low-SES children more often live with grand-mothers who encourage eating patterns that, in other times and places, protected against starvation.

Problems endure lifelong. Children who grow up in food-insecure households learn to eat whenever food is available, becoming less attuned to hunger and satiety signals in their bodies. Consequently, as adults, they overeat when they are not hungry, risking obesity, diabetes, and strokes (Hill et al., 2016).

For all children, appetite decreases between ages 2 and 6. Parents need to know this, not enticing children to eat, nor feeding them candy or cake that will fill them up. If a young child develops poor eating habits, nutritional problems appear.

In 2012, 8 percent of 2- to 5-year-olds, 18 percent of 6- to 11-year-olds, and 21 percent of 12- to 19-year-olds in the United States were obese (Ogden et al., 2014). Some of those teenagers who were not obese had other eating problems, including anorexia and bulimia.

One reason parents urge children to eat is that they underestimate their children's weight. A review of 69 studies found that half the parents of overweight children believe their children are thinner than they actually are. This problem was particularly likely for children ages 2 to 5 (Lundahl et al., 2014), perhaps because parents do not know that 5-year-olds are naturally low in BMI.

Immigrant elders do not realize that traditional diets in low-income nations are healthier than foods advertised in developed nations (de Hoog et al., 2014). Sadly, many other nations are adopting Western diets. As a result, "childhood obesity is one of the most serious public health challenges of the 21st century. The problem is global and is steadily affecting many low- and middle-income countries, particularly in urban settings" (Sahoo et al., 2015, p. 187–188).

There is some good news in the United States, however. Young children (ages 2 to 5) are eating more fruit, and obesity rates fell accordingly, from 12.1 percent in 2010 to 8.4 percent in 2012 (Ogden et al., 2014).

Public education and parents both deserve credit. And many day-care centers have increased exercise and improved snacks: carrot sticks and apple slices, not cookies and chocolate milk (Sisson et al., 2016).

Catching Up, Slimming Down China has transformed its economy and family life since 1950, with far fewer poor families and malnourished children. Instead, problems and practices of the West are becoming evident, as in these two boys. They are attending a weight-loss camp in Zhengzhou, where the average 8- to 14-year-old child loses 14 pounds in one month.

© IMAGINECHINA/CORBIS

◆ **Especially for Early-Childhood Teachers**
You know that young children are upset if forced to eat a food they hate, but you have eight 3-year-olds with eight different preferences. What do you do? (see response, page 190)

"IT SAYS RIGHT HERE IN THE INGREDIENTS, 'THIS PRODUCT CONTAINS NO YUCKY STUFF'."

DAVE CARPENTER/CARTOONSTOCK

Who Is Fooling Whom? He doesn't believe her, but maybe she shouldn't believe what the label says, either. For example, "low fat" might also mean high salt.

This proves that weight gain is not inevitable. However, rates rose again in 2016, to 13.9 percent (Hales et al., 2017). That is bad news—with one hopeful twist: Since weight gain in early childhood is so fluid, parents and communities can make a difference if they choose to.

ORAL HEALTH Not surprisingly, tooth decay correlates with obesity; both result from too much sugar and too little fiber (Hayden et al., 2013). Sweetened beverages are usually the problem.

"Baby" teeth are replaced naturally from ages 6 to 10. The schedule is genetic, with girls a few months ahead of boys. However, tooth brushing and dentist visits should become habitual years before adult teeth erupt. Poor oral health in early childhood harms those permanent teeth (forming below the first teeth) and can cause jaw malformation, chewing difficulties, and speech problems.

Teeth are affected by diet and illness, so a young child's teeth can alert a professional to other health problems. The process works in reverse as well: Infected teeth can affect the rest of the child's body. In pregnant adults, tooth infections can cause preterm births (Puertas et al., 2018).

FOOD ALLERGIES An estimated 3 to 8 percent of children are allergic to a specific food, almost always a common, healthy one: Cow's milk, eggs, peanuts, tree nuts (such as almonds and walnuts), soy, wheat, fish, and shellfish are the usual culprits. Diagnostic standards for allergies vary (which explains the range of estimates), and treatment varies even more (Chafen et al., 2010).

For some foods the allergic reaction is a rash or an upset stomach when too much is consumed, but for others—especially peanuts or shellfish—the reaction is sudden shock and shortness of breath that could be fatal (Dyer et al., 2015). When a child has a severe allergic reaction, someone should immediately inject epinephrine to stop the reaction. In 2012, all Chicago schools had EpiPens, which were used in dozens of emergencies (DeSantiago-Cardenas et al., 2015).

Some experts advocate total avoidance of the offending food—there are peanut-free schools, where no one is allowed to bring a peanut-butter sandwich for lunch lest an allergic child take a bite. However, feeding children who are allergic to peanuts

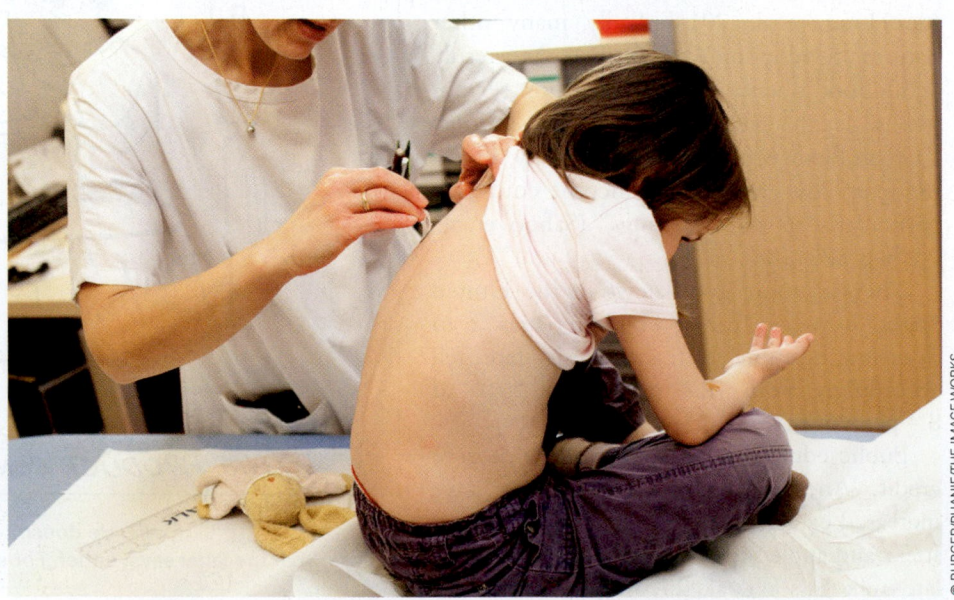

Not Allergic Anymore? Many food allergies are outgrown, so young children are more likely to have them than older ones. This skin prick will insert a tiny amount of a suspected allergen. If a red welt develops in the next half hour, the girl is still allergic. Hopefully, no reaction will occur, but if her breathing is affected, an EpiPen is within reach.

a tiny bit of peanut powder (under medical supervision) is usually a safe and effective way to decrease that allergic reaction (Vickery et al., 2017). Fortunately, many food allergies are outgrown.

Other food-related problems increase with age. During middle childhood, children who eat many snacks and fast foods (with high levels of saturated fatty acids, trans fatty acids, sodium, carbohydrates, and sugar) are likely to have asthma, stuffy noses, watery eyes, and itchy skin (Ellwood et al., 2013).

Brain Development

By age 2, most neurons have connected to other neurons and substantial pruning has occurred, as explained in Chapter 3. The 2-year-old's brain already weighs 75 percent of what it will weigh in adulthood; the 6-year-old's brain is 90 percent of adult weight.

Since most of the brain is already present and functioning by age 2, what remains to develop during early childhood? Connections!

MYELIN One crucial aspect of brain development is how well and rapidly the parts of the brain connect to each other. Essential for that is **myelin,** sometimes called the *white matter* of the brain. Myelin is a coating on the axons that protects and speeds signals between neurons. As you read, most neurons (the *gray matter* of the brain) are formed prenatally, and dendrites are pruned in late infancy. Despite those losses, the brain becomes heavier. One reason—more myelin.

Myelin helps every part of the brain, especially the connections between neurons that are far from each other. This provides more than insulation around the axons: "Myelin organizes the very structure of network connectivity . . . and regulates the timing of information flow through individual circuits" (Fields, 2014, p. 266). Myelin aids coordination of the left and the right halves of the brain, via the corpus callosum, as Inside the Brain explains.

myelin
The fatty substance coating axons that speeds the transmission of nerve impulses from neuron to neuron.

MATURATION OF THE PREFRONTAL CORTEX Connections between the prefrontal cortex and the rest of the brain are virtually absent at age 1, limited at age 2, and develop gradually at least until age 25. Gradual maturation is especially evident for actions that respond to other people (Eggebrecht et al., 2017) and for modulation of the limbic system. Nonetheless, some early brain maturation is evident by age 6:

- Sleep becomes more regular.
- Emotions become more nuanced and responsive.
- Temper tantrums subside.
- Uncontrollable laughter and tears are less common.

One specific example of the maturing brain is in the game Simon Says. Players are supposed to follow the leader *only* when orders are preceded by the words "Simon

◆ **Especially for Early-Childhood Teachers**
You know you should be patient, but frustration rises when your young charges dawdle on the walk to the playground a block away. What should you do? (see response, page 190)

Mental Coordination?
This brain scan of a 38-year-old depicts areas of myelination (the various colors) within the brain. As you see, the two hemispheres are quite similar, but not identical. For most important skills and concepts, both halves of the brain are activated.

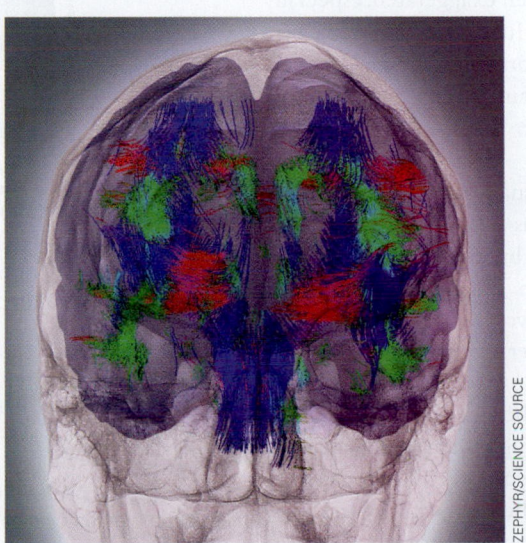

ZEPHYR/SCIENCE SOURCE

INSIDE THE BRAIN

Connected Hemispheres

The brain is divided into two halves, connected by the **corpus callosum,** a long, thick band of nerve fibers that grows and myelinates rapidly in early childhood (Ansado et al., 2015). For that reason, young children become much better at coordinating the two sides of their brains and, hence, both sides of their bodies. They can hop, skip, and gallop at age 6, unlike at age 2.

Serious disorders, almost always including intellectual disability, result when the corpus callosum fails to develop (Cavalari & Donovick, 2014). Abnormal growth of the corpus callosum is one symptom of autism spectrum disorder, as well as dozens of other disorders (Al-Hashim et al., 2016; Travers et al., 2015; J. Wolff et al., 2015).

To appreciate the corpus callosum, note that each side of the body and brain specializes and is therefore dominant for certain functions. This is **lateralization,** literally, "sidedness."

The entire human body is lateralized, apparent not only in right- or left-handedness but also in the feet, the eyes, the ears, and the brain itself. People prefer to kick a ball, wink an eye, or listen on the phone with their preferred foot, eye, or ear, respectively. Genes, prenatal hormones, and early experiences all affect which side does what.

Astonishing studies of humans whose corpus callosa were severed to relieve severe epilepsy, or who sustained major damage to their left or right brains, reveal how the brain's hemispheres specialize. Typically, the left half controls the body's right side as well as areas dedicated to logic, detailed analysis, and language. The brain's right half controls the body's left side and areas dedicated to emotional and creative impulses, including appreciation of music, art, and poetry. Thus, the left side notices details and the right side grasps the big picture.

This left–right distinction has been exaggerated, especially when broadly applied to people (Hugdahl & Westerhausen, 2010). No one is exclusively left-brained or right-brained, except individuals with severe brain injury in childhood, who may use half of their brain to do all of the necessary thinking.

For everyone else, every skill usually activates both sides of the brain. That makes the corpus callosum crucial. Logic (left brain) without emotion (right brain) is a severe impairment, as is the opposite (Damasio, 2012). As myelination progresses, signals between the two hemispheres become quicker and clearer, enabling better coordination of body parts, as well as part of the brain.

For example, no 2-year-old can hop but most 6-year-olds can—an example of brain balancing. Many songs, dances, and games that are beloved by young children (hokey-pokey, eensy-weensy spider, head/shoulders/knees and toes) involve moving their bodies in some coordinated way—challenging, but fun because of that.

The emotions of the young child (right brain) are gradually influenced by awareness of other people (left brain). Bursting into tears is less common at age 6 than at age 2.

Left-handed people tend to have thicker corpus callosa than right-handed people do, perhaps because they often need to use their nondominant hand. For example, most left-handed people brush their teeth with their left hand because using that hand is more natural, but they shake hands with their right hand because that is what social convention requires.

Left lateralization is an advantage in some professions, especially those involving creativity and split-second actions. A disproportionate number of artists, musicians, and sports stars were/are left-handed, including Pelé, Babe Ruth, Monica Seles, Bill Gates, Oprah Winfrey, Jimi Hendrix, Lady Gaga, and Justin Bieber. Five of the past eight presidents of the United States were lefties: Gerald Ford, Ronald Reagan, George H. W. Bush, Bill Clinton, and Barack Obama.

The corpus callosa of those celebrities may have been especially well-developed, enabling coordination of logic and emotion, body and mind. Scoring a goal, singing a song, or winning an election may seem to require only one skill, but to do them extraordinarily well requires the entire brain.

Dexterity in Evidence She already holds the pen at the proper angle with her thumb, index finger, and middle finger—an impressive example of dexterity for a 3-year-old. However, *dexter* is Latin for "right"—evidence of an old prejudice that is no longer apparent here.

corpus callosum
A long, thick band of nerve fibers that connects the left and right hemispheres of the brain and allows communication between them.

lateralization
Literally, "sidedness," referring to the specialization in certain functions by each side of the brain, with one side dominant for each activity. The left side of the brain controls the right side of the body, and vice versa.

says." Thus, if leaders touch their noses and say, "Simon says touch your nose," players are supposed to touch their noses, but when leaders touch their noses and say, "Touch your nose," no one should follow the example. Young children lose at this game because they cannot connect what they have been told with what they see and hear.

IMPULSIVENESS AND PERSE-VERATION Neurons have only two kinds of impulses: on–off or, in neuroscience terms, activate–inhibit. Each is signaled by a threshold of biochemical messages from dendrites to axons to neurons. Activation and inhibition keep adults from leaping too quickly or hesitating too long, neither lashing out in anger nor freezing in fear. If an elder becomes too impulsive or too cautious, that is a sign of cognitive loss.

STEPHANIE RAUSSER/GETTY IMAGES

However, it is normal for young children to be neurologically unbalanced, with poor **impulse control.** They might flit from one activity to another, unable to stay quietly on one task. That is apparent even in "circle time" in preschool, when teachers tell children to sit in place, not talking or touching anyone. Some instruct them, literally, to sit on their hands.

Ready to Learn? He is 5 years old, able to sit at a desk with impressive control of fine motor muscles in his upper lip, but probably not able to read the text on the board behind him. Should he be praised or punished? Perhaps neither; in another year or two, he will no longer be admired by his classmates for this trick.

impulse control
The ability to postpone or deny the immediate response to an idea or behavior.

Good Excuse It is true that emotional control of selfish instincts is difficult for young children because the prefrontal cortex is not yet mature enough to regulate some emotions. However, family practices can advance social understanding.

BARBARA SMALLER/THE NEW YORKER COLLECTION/CARTOONBANK.COM

"I would share, but I'm not there developmentally."

perseveration
The tendency to persevere in, or stick to, one thought or action for a long time.

At the other extreme, children may be captivated by one task, finding it hard to notice anything else or stop whatever they are doing. That is **perseveration:** They may play with one toy, hold one fantasy for hours, repeat a phrase or question again and again. Giggles or tears may be uncontrollable because the child is stuck in whatever triggered it.

No young child is perfect at regulating attention, because immaturity of the prefrontal cortex makes it impossible to moderate the limbic system. Impulsiveness and perseveration follow. Because the amygdala is not well connected to the more reflective parts of the brain, many children become suddenly terrified—even of something that exists only in imagination.

Gradually, preschoolers become less likely to perseverate, especially if they are taught how to stop one task to begin another (Zelazo, 2015). A study of children from ages 3 to 6 found increased ability to attend to what adults requested. Attention correlated with academic learning and behavioral control (fewer outbursts or tears) (Metcalfe et al., 2013).

◆ **Especially for Neurologists** Why do many experts think the limbic system is an oversimplified explanation of brain function? (see response, page 190)

Brain maturation (innate) and emotional regulation (learned) eventually allow most children to focus and switch as needed within their culture (Posner & Rothbart, 2017). By adolescence, most North American high school students can successfully change thoughts—from Chinese history to string theory, for instance—at the sound of the bell.

VIDEO ACTIVITY: The Childhood Stress-Cortisol Connection examines how high cortisol levels can negatively impact a child's overall health.

STRESS AND THE BRAIN The relationship between stress and brain activity depends partly on a person's age (childhood is most vulnerable) and partly on the degree of stress. Some stress may be good; too much is destructive.

In an experiment, brain scans and hormone measurements were taken of 4- to 6-year-olds immediately after a fire alarm (Teoh & Lamb, 2013). As measured by the hormone cortisol, some children were upset and some were not. Two weeks later, they were questioned, either by a friendly adult or by a stern one. Those with higher cortisol reactions to the alarm remembered more details. That conclusion is found in other research as well—some stress, but not too much, aids cognition (Keller et al., 2012).

However, this study and many others found that when adults ask questions in a stern, stressful manner, children's memories are less accurate. There are evolutionary reasons for both outcomes: People need to remember experiences that arouse their emotions so that they can avoid, or adjust to, similar experiences in the future. On the other hand, the brain protects itself from too much stress by shutting down.

Studies of maltreated children suggest that excessive stress-hormone levels in early childhood may permanently damage brain pathways, blunting or accelerating emotions lifelong (Evans & Kim, 2013; Wilson et al., 2011). Of course, every child experiences some stress, but especially then they need caregivers to help them manage. Sadly, this topic applies to the Romanian children mentioned in Chapter 4.

When adopted Romanian children saw pictures of happy, sad, frightened, or angry faces, their limbic systems were less reactive than were those of Romanian children who were never institutionalized. Their brains were also less lateralized, suggesting less efficient thinking (C. Nelson et al., 2014). Thus, institutional life, without the stress reduction of loving caretakers, impaired their brains.

Direct maltreatment may be worse, causing not only shrinkage of various regions of the brain but also decreases in white matter—and thus in the connections between parts of the brain (Puetz et al., 2017). A person who was abused as a child might get stuck—perhaps on fear, or on fantasy, or even on a happy or neutral thought, unable to coordinate and modulate the mixed emotions of most experiences.

what have you learned?

1. How are growth rates, body proportions, and motor skills related during early childhood?
2. What is changing in rates of early-childhood obesity and why?
3. What treatments are suggested for childhood allergies?
4. How does myelination advance skill development?
5. How is the corpus callosum crucial for learning?
6. What do impulse control and perseveration have in common?

Thinking During Early Childhood

You have just learned that every year of early childhood advances motor skills, brain development, and impulse control. That allows impressive learning, described by Piaget, Vygotsky, and others.

Piaget: Preoperational Thought

Early childhood is the time of **preoperational intelligence,** the second of Piaget's four periods of cognitive development (described in Table 1.6 on p. 27). Piaget called early-childhood thinking *pre*operational because children do not yet use *operations* (logical reasoning) (Inhelder & Piaget, 1964/2013a).

Preoperational children are beyond sensorimotor intelligence because they can think in symbols, not solely via senses and motor skills. In **symbolic thought,** an object or word can stand for something else, including something out of sight or imagined. Language is the most apparent example of symbolic thought. Words make it possible to think about things that are not immediately present.

Symbolic thought helps explain **animism,** the belief of many young children that natural objects (such as trees or clouds) are alive and that nonhuman animals have the same characteristics as human ones, especially the human each child knows

preoperational intelligence
Piaget's term for cognitive development between the ages of about 2 and 6; it includes language and imagination (which involve symbolic thought), but logical, operational thinking is not yet possible at this stage.

symbolic thought
A major accomplishment of preoperational intelligence that allows a child to think symbolically, including understanding that words can refer to things not seen and that an item, such as a flag, can symbolize something else (in this case, a country).

animism
The belief that natural objects and phenomena are alive, moving around, with sensations and abilities that are humanlike.

Not Happy Emotions are difficult for young children to understand, since they are not visible. The Disney-Pixar movie *Inside Out* uses symbolic thought to remedy that—here with green Disgust, red Anger, and purple Fear. What colors are Joy and Sadness?

↑ OBSERVATION QUIZ
What emotions are associated with green, red, and violet? (see answer, page 191)

WALT DISNEY STUDIOS MOTION PICTURES/PHOTOFEST

centration
A characteristic of preoperational thought in which a young child focuses (centers) on one idea, excluding all others.

egocentrism
Piaget's term for children's tendency to think about the world entirely from their own personal perspective.

focus on appearance
A characteristic of preoperational thought in which a young child ignores all attributes that are not apparent.

static reasoning
A characteristic of preoperational thought in which a young child thinks that nothing changes. Whatever is now has always been and always will be.

irreversibility
A characteristic of preoperational thought in which a young child thinks that nothing can be undone. A thing cannot be restored to the way it was before a change occurred.

conservation
The principle that the amount of a substance remains the same (i.e., is conserved) even when its appearance changes.

best, him or herself. Many children's stories include animals or objects that talk and listen (Aesop's fables; *Winnie-the-Pooh*; *Good Night, Gorilla*; *The Day the Crayons Quit*). Preoperational thought is symbolic and magical, not logical and realistic.

Among contemporary children, animism gradually disappears as the mind becomes more mature, by age 10 if not earlier (Kesselring & Müller, 2011). However, scholars contend that animism characterized preindustrial thought—people prayed to sky and trees, for instance—and that human history is best understood by considering Piaget's stages of cognition (e.g., Oesterdiekhoff, 2014).

OBSTACLES TO LOGIC Piaget noted four limitations that make logic difficult during preoperational thought: centration, focus on appearance, static reasoning, and irreversibility.

Centration is the tendency to focus on one aspect of a situation to the exclusion of all others. Young children may, for example, insist that Daddy is a father, not a brother, because they center on the role that he fills for them. This illustrates a type of centration that Piaget called **egocentrism**—literally, "self-centeredness." Egocentric children contemplate the world exclusively from their personal perspective.

A second characteristic of preoperational thought is a **focus on appearance** to the exclusion of other attributes. For instance, a girl given a short haircut might worry that she has turned into a boy. In preoperational thought, a thing is whatever it appears to be—evident in the joy young children have in wearing the hats or shoes of a grown-up, clomping noisily and unsteadily around the house.

Third, preoperational children use **static reasoning.** They believe that the world is stable, unchanging, always in the state in which they currently encounter it. Many children cannot imagine that their own parents were ever children. If they are told that Grandma is their mother's mother, they still do not understand how people change with maturation. One preschooler asked his grandmother to tell his mother not to spank him because "she has to do what her mother says."

The fourth characteristic of preoperational thought is **irreversibility.** Preoperational thinkers fail to recognize that reversing a process might restore whatever existed before. A young girl might cry because her mother put lettuce on her sandwich. She might reject the food even after the lettuce is removed because she believes that what is done cannot be undone.

CONSERVATION AND LOGIC Piaget discovered many examples of preoperational children disregarding logic. A famous set of experiments involved **conservation,** the notion that the amount of something remains the same (is conserved) despite changes in its appearance.

Suppose two identical glasses contain the same amount of pink lemonade, and the liquid from one of these glasses is poured into a taller, narrower glass. When young children are asked whether one glass contains more or, alternatively, if both glasses contain the same amount, those younger than 6 answer that the narrower glass (with the higher level) has more. (See Figure 5.1 for other examples.)

All four characteristics of preoperational thought are evident in this mistake. Young children fail to understand conservation because they focus (*center*) on what they see (*appearance*), noticing only the immediate (*static*) condition. It does not occur to them that they could pour the lemonade back into the wider glass and recreate the level of a moment earlier (*irreversibility*).

Piaget's original tests of conservation required children to respond verbally to an adult's questions. Contemporary researchers have made tests simple and playful, and then young children sometimes succeed. Moreover, before age 6, children indicate via eye movements or gestures that they understand some logic before they can put their understanding into words (Goldin-Meadow & Alibali, 2013).

VIDEO ACTIVITY: Achieving Conservation focuses on the cognitive changes that enable older children to pass Piaget's conservation-of-liquid task.

Tests of Various Types of Conservation

Type of Conservation	Initial Presentation	Transformation	Question	Preoperational Child's Answer
Volume	Two equal glasses of pink lemonade.	Pour one into a taller, narrower glass.	Which glass contains more?	The taller one.
Number	Two equal lines of candy.	Increase spacing of candy in one line.	Which line has more candy?	The longer one.
Matter	Two equal balls of cookie dough.	Squeeze one ball into a long, thin shape.	Which piece has more dough?	The long one.
Length	Two pencils of equal length.	Move one pencil.	Which pencil is longer?	The one that is farther to the right.

FIGURE 5.1 One Logical Concept (Conservation), Many Manifestations
According to Piaget, until children grasp the concept of conservation at (he believed) about age 6 or 7, they cannot understand that the transformations shown here do not change the total amount of liquid, candy, dough, and pencil.

Instead of sudden insight, many logical ideas are grasped bit by bit, via active, guided experience. Glimmers of understanding may be apparent at age 4 (Sophian, 2013).

Thus, as with sensorimotor intelligence in infancy, Piaget underestimated preoperational children. Piaget was right about his basic idea, however: Young children are not very logical (Lane & Harris, 2014). Their cognitive limits make smart 3-year-olds sometimes foolish, as Caleb was (see A Case to Study on page 168).

◆ **Especially for Nutritionists**
How can Piaget's theory help you encourage children to eat healthy foods? (see response, page 190)

Easy Question; Obvious Answer *(above left)* Sadie, age 5, carefully makes sure both glasses contain the same amount. *(above right)* When one glass of pink lemonade is poured into a wide jar, she triumphantly points to the tall glass as having more. Sadie is like all 5-year-olds; only a developmental psychologist or a 7-year-old child knows better.

A CASE TO STUDY

Stones in the Belly

As my grandson and I were reading a book about dinosaurs, 3-year-old Caleb told me that some dinosaurs (*sauropods*) have stones in their bellies. It helps them digest their food and then poop and pee.

I was amazed, never having known this before.

"I didn't know that dinosaurs ate stones," I said.

"They don't eat them."

"Then how do they get the stones in their bellies? They must swallow them."

"They don't swallow them."

"Then how do they get in their bellies?"

"They are just there."

"How did they get there?"

"They don't eat them," said Caleb. "Stones are dirty. We don't eat them."

I let it go, but my question apparently puzzled him. Later he asked his mother, "Do dinosaurs eat stones?"

"Yes, they eat stones so they can grind their food," she answered.

At that, Caleb was quiet.

In all of this, preoperational cognition is evident. Caleb is advanced in symbolic thought: He can name several kinds of dinosaurs. But logic eludes him. He is preoperational, not operational.

It seemed obvious to me that dinosaurs must have swallowed the stones. However, in his static thinking, Caleb said the stones "are just there."

He is egocentric, reasoning from his own experience, and animistic, in that he thinks animals would not eat stones because he does not. He trusts his mother more than me, and she told him never to eat stones, or sand from the sandbox, or food that fell on the floor. He would not trust anyone who, contrary to his mother's prohibition, told him to eat those things. Consequently, he did not accept my authority: The implications of my relationship to his mother are beyond his static thinking.

But, like many young children, he is curious, and my question raised his curiosity. He consulted his authority, my daughter.

Should he have acknowledged that I was right? He did not. That would have required far more understanding of reversibility and far less egocentrism than most young children can muster.

Vygotsky: Social Learning

For decades, the magical, illogical, and self-centered aspects of cognition dominated our conception of early-childhood thought. Scientists were understandably awed by Piaget, who demonstrated many aspects of egocentric thought in children.

Vygotsky emphasized another side of early cognition—that each person's thinking is shaped by other people. His focus on the *sociocultural* context contrasts with Piaget's emphasis on the individual (Vygotsky, 1987). As the term *sociocultural* suggests, Vygotsky was acutely aware of the social and cultural differences in his native Russia. In the early twentieth century, Russia was the only nation that spanned two continents (Europe and Asia), with citizens speaking a dozen languages, practicing many religions, and earning their living in hundreds of ways.

MENTORS It was obvious to Vygotsky that cognitive development is embedded in the social context—such as whether a child grew up in the affluent neighborhoods of Moscow or the frozen steppes of Siberia. Children in those disparate contexts are guided to learn different things. Everywhere, parents are the first to engage children in *guided participation*, although children are guided by many others, especially in an interactive pre-kindergarten (Broström, 2017).

Vygotsky stressed that children are curious and observant. They ask questions—about how machines work, why weather changes, where the sky ends—and seek answers from parents, teachers, older siblings, or strangers. The answers they get are affected by the mentors' perceptions and assumptions—that is, their culture—which shapes their thought.

Learning to Button Most shirts for 4-year-olds are wide-necked and without buttons, so preschoolers can put them on themselves. But the skill of buttoning is best learned from a mentor, who knows how to increase motivation.

According to Vygotsky, children learn because their mentors do the following:

- Present challenges.
- Offer assistance (without taking over).
- Add crucial information.
- Encourage motivation.

zone of proximal development (ZPD) Vygotsky's term for intellectual arena that is comprised of skills—cognitive as well as physical—that a person can learn with assistance.

scaffolding Temporary support that is tailored to a learner's needs and abilities and aimed at helping the learner master the next task in a given learning process.

SCAFFOLDING Vygotsky believed that all individuals learn within their **zone of proximal development (ZPD),** an intellectual arena in which new ideas and skills can be mastered. *Proximal* means "near," so the ZPD includes the ideas and skills children are close to mastering but cannot yet demonstrate independently. Learning depends, in part, on the wisdom and willingness of teachers to provide **scaffolding,** or temporary sensitive support, to help children within their developmental zone (Mermelshtine, 2017).

Good mentors offer extensive scaffolding, encouraging children to look both ways before crossing the street (pointing out speeding trucks, cars, and buses while holding the child's hand) or letting them stir the cake batter (perhaps covering the child's hand on the spoon handle, in guided participation). Crucial in every activity is joint engagement, when both learner and mentor are actively involved together in the ZPD (Adamson et al., 2014).

OVERIMITATION Sometimes scaffolding is inadvertent, as when children copy something that adults would rather the child not do. Young children curse, kick, and worse because someone else showed them how.

More benignly, children imitate meaningless habits and customs in *overimitation*. Children eagerly learn from mentors, allowing "rapid, high-fidelity intergenerational transmission of tool-use skills and for the perpetuation and generation of cultural forms" (Nielsen & Tomaselli, 2010, p. 735).

↓ **OBSERVATION** QUIZ Is the girl below right-handed or left-handed? (see answer, page 191)

Count by Tens A large, attractive abacus could be a scaffold. However, in this toy store the position of the balls suggests that no mentor is nearby. Children are unlikely to grasp the number system without a motivating guide.

Overimitation is universal: Young children follow what others do. Adults worldwide teach children, using words, gestures, eye contact, and facial expressions (Heyes, 2016). Young children are "socially motivated," which enables them to learn when someone structures and guides that learning. They also are eager to explore, deciding which actions to perform, whom to imitate, what to try (Gopnik, 2016).

LANGUAGE AS A TOOL Although all of the objects of a culture guide children, Vygotsky considered language pivotal.

First, talking to oneself, called **private speech,** is evident when young children talk aloud to review, decide, and explain events to themselves (and, incidentally, to anyone else within earshot) (Al-Namlah et al., 2012). Many adults use private speech as they talk to themselves when alone or as they write down ideas.

Second, language advances thinking by facilitating social interaction, which is vital to learning (Vygotsky, 2012). This **social mediation** function of speech occurs as mentors guide mentees in their zone of proximal development, learning numbers, recalling memories, and following routines.

STEM LEARNING A practical use of Vygotsky's theory concerns STEM (science, technology, engineering, math) education. Many adults wish that more college students would choose a STEM career. How to encourage that?

Developmentalists find that interest in STEM vocations begins when young children learn about numbers and science (counting, shapes, fractions, molecular structure, the laws of motion). Spatial understanding—how one object fits with another—is an accomplishment of early childhood that enhances later math skills (Verdine et al., 2017). During the preschool years, the understanding of math and physics develops month by month.

To be specific, by age 3 or 4, children's brains are mature enough to comprehend numbers, store memories, and recognize routines. Whether or not children actually demonstrate such understanding depends on what they hear and what they do within their families, schools, and cultures. "Scaffolding and elaboration from parents and teachers provide crucial input to spatial development," which itself leads to the math understanding that underpins STEM expertise (Verdine et al., 2017, p. 25).

Some 2-year-olds hear numbers such as "One, two, three, takeoff," "Here are two cookies," or "Dinner in five minutes" several times a day. They are encouraged to touch an interesting bit of moss, or to notice the phases of the moon outside their

private speech
The internal dialogue that occurs when people talk to themselves (either silently or out loud).

social mediation
Human interaction that expands and advances understanding, often through words that one person uses to explain something to another.

Same or Different? Which do you see? Most people focus on differences, such as ethnicity or sex. But a developmental perspective appreciates similarities: book-reading to a preliterate child cradled on a parent's lap.

Future Engineers in the Bronx Playing with Legos helps children learn about connecting shapes, which makes math and geometry easier to learn in school and STEM careers more likely. Once Legos were only marketed to boys, but no longer—there now are kits designed to appeal to girls.

window, or to play with toys that fit shapes, or to make the connection between their labored breathing and the steepness of a hill they are climbing.

Other children never have such experiences—and they have a harder time with math in first grade, with science in third grade, and with physics in high school. If Vygotsky is right that words mediate between brain potential and comprehension, STEM education begins long before first grade.

EXECUTIVE FUNCTION One manifestation of children's impressive learning ability is in the development of **executive function,** the ability to use the mind to plan, remember, inhibit some impulses, and execute others. Executive function (also called *executive control* and closely related to *emotional regulation*, explained in Chapter 6) develops throughout life, allowing students of all ages to learn from experience. It is first evident and measured during early childhood (Eisenberg & Zhou, 2016; Espy et al., 2016; Sasser et al., 2017).

Usually, three components comprise executive function: working memory, cognitive flexibility, and inhibitory control—which is the ability to focus on a task and ignore distractions. Executive function is a better predictor of later learning in kindergarten than a child's age or language ability (Pellicano et al., 2017).

Children's Theories

The contrast between Piaget and Vygotsky is apparent: Piaget highlighted the child's own curiosity and brain maturation, while Vygotsky stressed mentors, especially parents and teachers, in guiding children's learning. But do not let this difference obscure the more important truth: Both men recognized that young children are great learners, striving to understand their world. Children do more than master words and ideas; they develop theories to explain what they observe.

THEORY-THEORY Humans of all ages seek explanations. As a play on words, when naming their theory about how children think, psychologists explained that their theory is that children construct a theory. **Theory-theory** refers to the idea that children naturally construct theories to explain whatever they see and hear.

executive function
The cognitive ability to organize and prioritize the many thoughts that arise from the various parts of the brain, allowing the person to anticipate, strategize, and plan behavior.

theory-theory
The idea that children attempt to explain everything they see and hear by constructing theories.

According to theory-theory, humans both young and old seek reasons, causes, and underlying principles to make sense of their experience, connecting knowledge and observations. Especially in childhood, theories change as new evidence accumulates (Meltzoff & Gopnik, 2013; Bridgers et al., 2016; Gopnik, 2016).

Children follow the same processes that scientists do: asking questions, developing hypotheses, gathering data, and drawing conclusions. As a result, "preschoolers have intuitive theories of the physical, biological, psychological, and social world" (Gopnik, 2012, p. 1623).

Of course, the cognitive methods of children lack the rigor of scientific experiments, but children "not only detect statistical patterns, they use those patterns to test hypotheses about people and things" (Gopnik, 2012, p. 1625). Like all good scientists, they will revise theories based on new data, although, like all humans, children sometimes stick to their old theories despite conflicting evidence.

One common theory-theory is that everyone intends to do things correctly. For that reason, when asked to repeat something ungrammatical that an adult says, children often correct the grammar. They theorize that the adult intended to speak grammatically but failed to do so (Over & Gattis, 2010).

THEORY OF MIND Mental processes—thoughts, emotions, beliefs, motives, and intentions—are among the most complicated and puzzling phenomena that humans encounter every day. Adults wonder why people fall in love with the particular persons they do, why they vote for the odd political candidates they do, or why they make foolish choices—from signing for a huge mortgage to buying an overripe cucumber. Children are likewise puzzled about a playmate's unexpected anger, a sibling's generosity, or an aunt's too-wet kiss.

To know what goes on in another person's mind, people develop a *folk psychology,* which includes ideas about other people's thinking, called **theory of mind.** Theory of mind is "essential in communities that rely heavily on the exchange of information, ideas, and points of view" (Lillard & Kavanaugh, 2014, p. 1535). Longitudinal research finds that 2-year-olds do not know that other people think differently than they do, but 6-year-olds know this very well (Wellman et al., 2011).

Part of theory of mind is realizing that someone else might have a mistaken belief. In a classic experiment, children watch a puppet named Max put a toy dog into a red box. Then Max leaves and the child sees the dog taken out of the red box and put in a blue box.

When Max returns, the child is asked, "Where will Max look for the dog?" Without a theory of mind, most 3-year-olds confidently say, "In the blue box"; most 6-year-olds correctly say, "In the red box."

The development of theory of mind is evident when young children try to escape punishment by lying. Their faces often betray them: worried or shifting eyes, pursed lips, and so on. Parents might say, "I know when you are lying," and, to the consternation of most 3-year-olds, parents are usually right.

theory of mind
A person's theory of what other people might be thinking. In order to have a theory of mind, children must realize that other people are not necessarily thinking the same thoughts that they themselves are. That realization seldom occurs before age 4.

◆ **Especially for Social Scientists**
Can you think of any connection between Piaget's theory of preoperational thought and 3-year-olds' errors in this theory-of-mind task? (see response, page 190)

MACMILLAN PUBLISHERS

Candies in the Crayon Box Anyone would expect crayons in a crayon box, but once a child sees that candy is inside, he expects that everyone else will also know that candies are inside!

In one experiment, 247 children, ages 3 to 5, were left alone at a table that had an upside-down cup covering dozens of candies (Evans et al., 2011). The children were told *not* to peek, and the experimenter left the room. For 142 children (57 percent), curiosity overcame obedience. They peeked, spilling so many candies onto the table that they could not put them back under the cup.

The examiner returned, asking how the candies got on the table. Only one-fourth of the participants (more often the younger ones) told the truth. The rest lied, and their skill at lying increased with their age. The 3-year-olds typically told hopeless lies (e.g., "The candies got out by themselves"); the 4-year-olds told unlikely lies (e.g., "Other children came in and knocked over the cup"). Some of the 5-year-olds, however, told plausible lies (e.g., "My elbow knocked over the cup accidentally").

A study of prosocial lies (saying that a disappointing gift was appreciated) found that children who were advanced in theory of mind and in executive function were also better liars, able to stick to the lie that they liked the gift (S. Williams et al., 2016). This study was of 6- to 12-year-olds, not preschoolers, but the underlying abilities are first evident at about age 4.

Many studies have found that a child's ability to develop theories correlates with neurological maturation, which also correlates with advances in executive processing—the reflective, anticipatory capacity of the mind (Mar, 2011; Baron-Cohen et al., 2013). Detailed studies find that theory of mind activates several brain regions (Koster-Hale & Saxe, 2013). This makes sense: Theory of mind is a complex ability that humans develop in social contexts, so it is not likely to reside in just one neurological region.

Evidence for crucial brain maturation comes from the other research on the same 3- to 5-year-olds whose lying was studied. The children were asked to say "day" when they saw a picture of the moon and "night" when they saw a picture of the sun. They needed to inhibit their automatic reaction. Their success indicated advanced executive function, which correlated with maturation of the prefrontal cortex.

The crucial role of brain maturation was evident: Those who failed the day–night tests typically told impossible lies. Their age-mates who were higher in executive function (measured by the day–night tests) told better lies (Evans et al., 2011).

Does the prerequisite of neurological maturation make culture and context irrelevant for theory of mind? Not at all: Nurture is always important. Formal education traditionally began at about age 6 because by then the prefrontal cortex is naturally sufficiently mature to allow sustained attention. But, passive waiting for maturation may be foolish. Experiences before age 6 advance brain development and prepare children for first grade (Blair & Raver, 2015).

Many educators and parents focus on young children's intelligence and vocabulary. They are right to do so, because cognition and language development respond to encouragement. However, for brain development and later success in kindergarten and beyond, executive function seems even more crucial than scores on intelligence tests (Friedman & Miyake, 2017).

"Another milestone: the first step, first word, first excuse..."

The Dog Did It If only all parents were aware of cognitive development.

CHRIS WILDT/CARTOON STOCK

Some helpful experiences before age 6 occur for almost every child: Children develop theory of mind in talking with adults and in playing with other children. Games that require turn-taking encourage memory and inhibitory control, two crucial components of executive control.

As brothers and sisters argue, agree, compete, and cooperate, and as older siblings fool younger ones, it dawns on 3-year-olds that not everyone thinks as they do, a thought that advances theory of mind. Thus, siblings advance thinking.

By age 5, children have learned how to persuade their younger brothers and sisters to give them a toy. Meanwhile, younger siblings figure out how to gain sympathy by complaining that their older brothers and sisters have victimized them. Parents, beware: Asking, "Who started it?" may be irrelevant: Better is to help the siblings understand each other's perspective.

A VIEW FROM SCIENCE

Witness to a Crime

One application of early cognitive competency has received attention from lawyers and judges. Children may be the only witnesses to some crimes, especially of sexual abuse or of serious domestic violence. Can their accounts be trusted? Adults have gone to extremes in answering this question. As one legal discussion begins:

> Perhaps as a result of the collective guilt caused by disbelieving the true victims of abuse, there presently exists an unwavering conviction that a young child is incapable of fabricating a story of abuse, even when the tale of mistreatment is inherently incredible.
>
> *[Shanks, 2011, p. 517]*

As this quote implies, in past years children were never believed, and then they were always believed. Neither extreme was correct.

The answer to the question, "Can their accounts be trusted?" is: "Sometimes." People of all ages remember and misremember. Each age group misremembers in particular ways, depending partly on cognitive maturity and partly on social context. Memory itself is a social construction, not an infallible record of what occurred (Nash & Ost, 2017).

Younger children are sometimes more accurate than older witnesses who are influenced by prejudice and stereotypes. However, young children often confuse time, place, person, and action. They want to please adults, and they may lie to do so. With this in mind, developmental psychologists have developed many research-based suggestions to improve the accuracy of child witnesses (Lamb, 2014).

Words and expressions can plant false ideas in young children's minds, either deliberately (as an abuser might) or inadvertently (as a fearful parent might). Children's shaky grasp of reality makes them vulnerable to scaffolding memories that are imagined, not experienced (Bruck et al., 2006). This happened tragically 35 years ago. Some adults leapt to the conclusion that sexual abuse was rampant in preschools, and they set out to prove it.

For instance, biased questioning led 3-year-olds at Wee Care nursery school in New Jersey to convince a judge that a teacher had sexually abused them in bizarre ways (including making them lick peanut butter off her genitals) (Ceci & Bruck, 1995). In retrospect, it is amazing that any adult believed what they said. The accused were convicted, imprisoned, and finally exonerated. Partly because of that case, much has been learned about witnesses of all ages (Howe & Knott, 2015).

With sexual abuse in particular, a child might believe that some lewd act is OK if an adult says so. Only years later does the victim realize that it was abuse. Sometimes adults reinterpret what happened to them, with genuine memories of experiences that were criminal. However, people of all ages can be misled to believe that an event, including abuse, occurred when it did not (Howe & Knott, 2015).

As already explained, stress hormones may flood the brain and destroy part of the hippocampus, leading to permanent deficits in learning and health, causing major depressive disorder, post-traumatic stress disorder, attention-deficit/hyperactivity disorder, and distorted memories lifelong.

If children witness a crime, memory is more accurate when an interviewer is warm and attentive, listening carefully but not suggesting some answers instead of others (Teoh & Lamb, 2013; Johnson et al., 2016). Children should say what they remember, perhaps with eyes closed to limit the natural wish to please (Kyriakidou et al., 2014). No one, at any age, should be automatically believed or disbelieved.

Language Learning

Learning language is often considered the premier cognitive accomplishment of early childhood. Two-year-olds use short, telegraphic sentences ("Want cookie," "Where Daddy go?"), omitting adjectives, adverbs, and articles. By contrast, 5-year-olds seem to be able to say almost anything (see At About This Time) using every part of speech. Some kindergartners understand and speak two or three languages, an accomplishment that many adults struggle for years to achieve.

At About This Time: Language in Early Childhood

Approximate Age	Characteristic or Achievement in First Language
2 years	*Vocabulary:* 100–2,000 words *Sentence length:* 2–6 words *Grammar:* Plurals; pronouns; many nouns, verbs, adjectives *Questions:* Many "What's that?" questions
3 years	*Vocabulary:* 1,000–5,000 words *Sentence length:* 3–8 words *Grammar:* Conjunctions, adverbs, articles *Questions:* Many "Why?" questions
4 years	*Vocabulary:* 3,000–10,000 words *Sentence length:* 5–20 words *Grammar:* Dependent clauses, tags at sentence end ("... didn't I?" "... won't you?") *Questions:* Peak of "Why?" questions; many "How?" and "When?" questions
6 years and up	*Vocabulary:* 5,000–30,000 words *Sentence length:* Some seem unending ("... and ... who ... and ... that ... and ...") *Grammar:* Complex, depending on what the child has heard, with some children correctly using the passive voice ("Man bitten by dog") and subjunctive ("If I were ...") *Questions:* Some about social differences (male–female, old–young, rich–poor) and many other issues

A Sensitive Time

Brain maturation, myelination, scaffolding, and social interaction make early childhood ideal for learning language. As you remember from Chapter 1, scientists once thought that early childhood was a *critical period* for language learning—the *only* time when a first language could be mastered and the best time to learn a second or third one.

It is easy to understand why they thought so. Young children have powerful motivation and ability to sort words and sounds into meaning (theory-theory). That makes them impressive language learners. However, the critical-period hypothesis is false: A new language can be learned after age 6.

Still, while new language learning in adulthood is possible, it is not easy. Early childhood is a *sensitive period* for rapidly mastering vocabulary, grammar, and pronunciation. Young children are language sponges; they soak up every verbal drop they encounter.

One of the valuable (and sometimes frustrating) traits of young children is that they talk about many things to adults, to each other, to themselves, to their toys—unfazed by misuse, mispronunciation, ignorance, stuttering, and so on (Marazita & Merriman, 2010). Language comes easily partly because preoperational children are not self-critical about what they say. Egocentrism has advantages; this is one of them.

The Vocabulary Explosion

The average child knows about 500 words at age 2 and more than 10,000 at age 6 (Herschensohn, 2007). That's more than six new words a day. As with many averages in development, the range is vast: The number of root words (e.g., *run* is a root word, not *running* or *runner*) that 5-year-olds know ranges from 2,000 to 6,000 (Biemiller, 2009). In fact, it is very difficult to determine vocabulary size, although almost everyone agrees that building vocabulary is crucial (Milton & Treffers-Daller, 2013).

To understand why vocabulary is difficult to measure, consider the following: Children listened to a story about a raccoon that saw its reflection in the water, and then they were asked what *reflection* means. Five answers:

1. "It means that your reflection is yourself. It means that there is another person that looks just like you."

2. "Means if you see yourself in stuff and you see your reflection."

3. "Is like when you look in something, like water, you can see yourself."

4. "It mean your face go in the water."

5. "That means if you the same skin as him, you blend in." (Hoffman et al., 2014, pp. 471–472)

In another example, a story included "a chill ran down his spine." Children were asked what *chill* meant. One answer: "When you want to lay down and watch TV—and eat nachos" (Hoffman et al., 2014, p. 473).

Which of the five listed responses indicated that the child knew what *reflection* means? None? All? Some number in between? The last child was given no credit for *chill;* is that fair?

FAST-MAPPING Children develop interconnected categories for words, a kind of grid or mental map that makes speedy vocabulary acquisition possible. Learning a word after one exposure is called **fast-mapping** (Woodward & Markman, 1998) because, rather than figuring out the exact definition after hearing a word used in several contexts, children hear a word once and quickly stick it into a category in their mental language grid. For 2-year-olds, *mother* can mean any caregiving woman, for instance.

Picture books offer many opportunities to advance vocabulary through scaffolding and fast-mapping. A mentor might encourage the next steps in the child's zone

fast-mapping
The speedy and sometimes imprecise way in which children learn new words by tentatively placing them in mental categories according to their perceived meaning.

VIDEO ACTIVITY: Language Acquisition in Young Children features video clips of a new sign language created by deaf Nicaraguan children and provides insights into how language evolves.

What Is It? These two children at the Mississippi River Museum in Iowa might call this a crocodile, but really it is an alligator. Fast-mapping allows that mistake, and egocentrism might make them angry is someone tells them they chose the wrong name.

JASON LINDSEY / ALAMY

of proximal development, such as that tigers have stripes and leopards spots, or, for an older child, that calico cats are almost always female and that lions with manes are always male.

This process explains children's learning of colors. Generally, 2-year-olds fast-map color names (K. Wagner et al., 2013). For instance, *blue* is used for some greens or grays. The reason is *not* that children cannot see the hues. Instead, they apply words they know to broad categories and have not yet learned the boundaries that adults use, or specifics such as chartreuse, turquoise, olive, navy. As one team of scientists explains, adults' color words are the result of slow-mapping (K. Wagner et al., 2013), which is not what young children do.

WORDS AND THE LIMITS OF LOGIC Closely related to fast-mapping is a phenomenon called *logical extension:* After learning a word, children use it to describe other objects in the same category. One child told her father she had seen some "Dalmatian cows" on a school trip to a farm. Instead of criticizing her foolishness, he remembered that she petted a Dalmatian dog the previous weekend. He realized that she saw Holstein, not Jersey, cows.

Bilingual children who don't know a word in the language they are speaking often insert a word from the other language, code-switching in the middle of a sentence. That mid-sentence switch may be considered wrong, but actually it arises from the child's drive to communicate. By age 5, children realize who understands which language, and they avoid substitutions when speaking to a monolingual person. That illustrates theory of mind.

Some words are particularly difficult for every child, such as, in English, *who/ whom, have been/had been, here/there, yesterday/tomorrow*. More than one child has awakened on Christmas morning and asked, "Is it tomorrow yet?" A child told to "stay there" or "come here" may not follow instructions because the terms are confusing. It might be better to say, "Stay there on that bench" or "Come here to hold my hand." Every language has difficult concepts that are expressed in words; children everywhere learn them eventually.

Abstractions are particularly difficult; actions are easier to understand. A hole is to dig; love is hugging; hearts beat.

Camels Protected, People Confused Why the contrasting signs? Does everyone read English at the international airport in Chicago (O'Hare) but not on the main road in Tunisia?

Acquiring Grammar

Remember from Chapter 3 that *grammar* includes structures, techniques, and rules that communicate meaning. Knowledge of grammar is essential for learning to speak, read, and write. A large vocabulary is useless unless a person knows how to put words together. Each language has its own grammar rules; that's one reason children speak in one-word sentences first.

Children apply rules of grammar as soon as they figure them out, using their own theories about how language works and their experience regarding when and how various rules apply (Meltzoff & Gopnik, 2013). Careful research on language development during childhood reveals impressive mastery of grammar long before formal instruction.

For example, English-speaking children quickly learn to add an *s* to form the plural: Toddlers follow that rule when they ask for two cookies or more blocks. Soon they add an *s* to make the plural of words they have never heard before, even nonsense words. If preschoolers are shown a drawing of an abstract shape, told it is called a *wug,* and are then shown two of these shapes, they say there are two wugs (Berko, 1958). Young children learn the conventions of grammar almost as soon as they start talking (Pinker, 1999).

By age 3, children realize that verbs reflect singular or plural. This is difficult for people learning English, but it is grasped by most 3-year-old native speakers. They not only know that he *jumps* while they *jump* (difficult because the *s* is singular here) but also the difference between *are* and *is.* For example, careful monitoring of eye gaze reveals that as soon as they hear the word *are* when asked "Are there three cookies on the plate?" they look at the plate of cookies rather than a plate with one piece of cake (Deevy et al., 2017).

Sometimes children apply the rules of grammar when they should not. This error is called **overregularization.** By age 4, many children overregularize that final *s,* talking about *foots, tooths,* and *mouses.* This signifies knowledge, not lack of it.

Many children first say words correctly (*feet, teeth, mice*), repeating what they have heard. Later, they are smart enough to apply the rules of grammar, and they assume that all constructions follow the rules (Ramscar & Dye, 2011). The child who says, "I goed to the store" needs to hear, "Oh, you went to the store?" not criticism.

More difficult to learn is an aspect of language called **pragmatics**—knowing which words, tones, and grammatical forms to use with whom (Siegal & Surian, 2012). In some languages, it is essential to know which set of words to use when a

overregularization
The application of rules of grammar even when exceptions occur, making the language seem more "regular" than it actually is.

pragmatics
The practical use of language that includes the ability to adjust language communication according to audience and context.

person is older, or when someone is not a close friend, or when grandparents are on the mother's side or the father's.

English does not make those distinctions, but pragmatics is important for early-childhood learning nonetheless. Children learn variations in vocabulary and tone depending on the context, and once theory of mind is established, on the audience.

Knowledge of pragmatics is evident when a 4-year-old pretends to be a doctor, a teacher, or a parent. Each role requires different speech. On the other hand, children often blurt out questions or statements that embarrass their parents ("Why is that lady so fat?" or "I don't want to kiss Grandpa because his breath smells."): The pragmatics of polite speech requires more social understanding than many young children possess.

Learning Two Languages

Language-minority people (those who speak a language that is not their nation's dominant one) suffer if they do not also speak the majority language (Rosselli et al., 2016). In the United States, those who lack fluency in English often have lower school achievement, diminished self-esteem, and inadequate employment. Some of their problem comes from prejudice from native-English speakers, but some is directly connected to their English.

Early childhood is the best time to learn languages. Neuroscience finds that if adults mastered two languages before age 6, both languages are located in the same areas of the brain with no detriment to the cortex structure (Klein et al., 2014). Being bilingual seems to benefit the brain lifelong, further evidence for plasticity (Bialystok, 2017). Indeed, the bilingual brain may provide some resistance to neurocognitive disorder due to Alzheimer's disease in old age (Costa & Sebastián-Gallés, 2014).

When adults learn a new language, their pronunciation, idioms, and exceptions to the rules lag behind basic grammar and vocabulary. Thus, many immigrants speak the majority language with an accent and are confused by common metaphors, but they are proficient in comprehension (difference is not deficit).

From infancy on, listening is more acute than speaking. Almost all young children mispronounce whatever language they speak, blithely unaware of their mistakes.

Bilingual Learners These are Chinese children learning a second language. Could this be in the United States? No, this is a class in the first Chinese-Hungarian school in Budapest. There are three clues: the spacious classroom, the letters on the book, and the trees outside.

ATTILA KISBENEDEK/GETTY IMAGES

They comprehend more than they say, and they learn rapidly as long as many people use new words and phrases within their zone of proximal development. As the authors of a study of bilingual children summarized, "linguistic richness of a child's early learning experience is critical for language acquisition and cognitive growth, whether that child is learning one language or two" (Marchman et al., 2017).

For children to develop two languages, they must speak as well as hear two languages (Ribot et al., 2017). Thus, adults need to scaffold speaking (asking leading questions, listening attentively) instead of ignoring children or saying "Be quiet; listen to me."

LANGUAGE LOSS AND GAINS Language-minority parents have a legitimate fear: Their children might make a *language shift,* becoming fluent in the majority language and losing their home language. Language shift occurs whenever theory-theory leads children to conclude that their parents' language is inferior (Bhatia & Ritchie, 2013).

Some language-minority children in Mexico shift to Spanish; some children of Canada's First Nations shift to French; some U.S. children in non-English-speaking homes shift to English. In China, all speak some form of Chinese, but some shift from Wu, Hakka, or another dialect to Mandarin, a shift that troubles their parents.

Remember that young children are preoperational: They center on the immediate status of their language (not on future usefulness or past glory), on appearance more than substance. No wonder many shift.

Since language is integral to culture, if a child is to become fluently bilingual, everyone who speaks with the child should respect both cultures, in song, books, and conversation. Children learn from listening and talking, so a child needs to hear and speak twice as much to become fluent in two languages (Hoff et al., 2012).

If immigrant parents speak only their home language, they should talk often to the child in that language, because fluency in one language makes it easier to learn another (Hoff et al., 2014). Since early childhood is a sensitive time for language, such parents also need to find a social context (school, church, other relatives) where the child will learn the second language. The language shift is less likely if the child already speaks two languages before kindergarten.

The same practices make a child fluently trilingual, as some 5-year-olds are. Young children who are immersed in three languages may speak all three with no accent—except the accent of their mother, father, and friends.

LISTENING, TALKING, AND READING Because understanding the printed word is crucial, a meta-analysis of about 300 studies analyzed which activities in early childhood aided reading later on. Both vocabulary and phonics (precise awareness of spoken sounds) predicted literacy (Shanahan & Lonigan, 2010). Five specific strategies and experiences were particularly effective for children of all income levels, languages, and ethnicities.

1. *Code-focused teaching.* Before reading, children must "break the code" from spoken to written words. That means connecting letters and sounds (e.g., "*A*, alligators all around" or "*B* is for baby").

2. *Book-reading.* Vocabulary and print-awareness develop when adults read to children.

3. *Parent education.* Educated parents tend to be verbal parents who read books to their children and use a rich vocabulary that expands the child's vocabulary.

4. *Language enhancement.* Children who ask what a word means need someone to scaffold the explanation. That requires mentors who understand each child's zone of proximal development.

5. *Preschool programs.* Children learn from teachers, songs, excursions, and other children. (Early education advances language, as discussed next.)

◆ **Especially for Immigrant Parents**
You want your children to be fluent in the language of your family's new country, even though you do not speak that language well. Should you speak to your children in your native tongue or in the new language? (see response, page 190)

what have you learned?

1. What is the evidence that early childhood is a sensitive time for learning language?

2. How does fast-mapping aid the language explosion?

3. How can overregularization signify a cognitive advance?

4. When should children learn grammar?

5. What aspects of language seem difficult for young children?

6. Why is early childhood the best time to learn a second (or third) language?

7. What are three ways adults can foster language development?

Early-Childhood Education

Decades of research have led almost all developmentalists to agree that education of 3- to 6-year-olds aids learning in primary school. Benefits continue for decades.

Research on Costs and Benefits

Thousands of studies have examined the impact of early education on the development of children and on their families and nations. The first controlled studies 50 years ago echo in many homes and nations.

LONGITUDINAL STUDIES Evidence for the value of early education comes from three classic programs, each of which educated children for years—sometimes beginning with home visits in infancy, sometimes continuing in after-school programs through first grade. One program, called *Perry* (or *High/Scope*), was spearheaded in

"We teach them that the world can be an unpredictable, dangerous, and sometimes frightening place, while being careful not to spoil their lovely innocence. It's tricky."

Tricky Indeed Young children are omnivorous learners, picking up habits, curses, and attitudes that adults would rather not transmit. Deciding what to teach—by actions more than words—is essential.

FRANK PORTER GRAHAM CHILD DEVELOPMENT INSTITUTE

Lifetime Achievement The baby in the framed photograph escaped the grip of poverty. The woman holding it proved that early education can transform children. She is Frances Campbell, who spearheaded the Abecedarian Project. The baby's accomplishments may be the more impressive of the two.

Michigan (Schweinhart & Weikart, 1997); another, called *Abecedarian,* got its start in North Carolina (Campbell et al., 2001); a third, called *Child–Parent Centers,* began in Chicago (Reynolds, 2000). All of these programs focused on children from low-SES families; all provided intense education from well-trained teachers.

These three programs compared experimental groups of children with matched control groups and followed up on them for decades. The solid conclusion: Early education, when done well, results in benefits that become most apparent when children are in the third grade or later.

By age 10, children who had been enrolled in any one of these three programs scored higher on math and reading achievement tests than did other children from the same backgrounds, schools, and neighborhoods. They were less likely to be placed in classes for children with special needs or to repeat a year of school. Benefits were particularly likely if the early-childhood education was followed by learning within an effective elementary school (Reynolds et al., 2015).

As adolescents, the children who had undergone intensive preschool education had higher aspirations, possessed a greater sense of achievement, and were less likely to quit before graduation or become a teenage parent. As young adults, more of them attended college and fewer went to jail. As middle-aged adults, more were healthy, employed taxpayers (Reynolds & Ou, 2011; Schweinhart et al., 2005; Campbell et al., 2014; Reynolds et al., 2017).

INTERNATIONAL EARLY-CHILDHOOD EDUCATION Those three U.S. programs 50 years ago reached relatively few children, but they inspired thousands of educators who are teaching millions of 2- to 5-year-olds in virtually every nation. Currently, in most developed nations, over 90 percent of 3- to 5-year-olds attend school paid for by the government.

In nations where major government funding is scarce, preschools that are privately or religiously funded proliferate (Georgeson & Payler, 2013). In the United States, 54 percent of 3- to 4-year-olds are in some sort of educational program. That is the lowest rate among major developed nations, but it is five times as high as in 1965, according to the National Center for Education Statistics. About half of those young children are in programs funded by federal or local governments, and about half are in privately funded programs.

The highest rates are in Norway, where the government heavily subsidizes preschool education for every child from age 1 on (Ellingsaeter, 2014). More than 90 percent of young Norwegian children attend, with advances in language and social skills, and no apparent cognitive or emotional deficits (Zachrisson et al., 2013).

MOHD RASFAN/AFP/GETTY IMAGES

In Norway, because of paid parental leave, parents are more likely to stay home with their youngest babies and then most women return to their jobs when their children reach age 1. Most mothers—of all ethnic and economic backgrounds—are now convinced that the best care and ideal education for young children is in an educational program, not at home (Ellingsaeter et al., 2017).

HOME VERSUS PRESCHOOL The longitudinal evidence within the United States and the proliferation of early-education programs in many nations raise another question: Is *every* child better educated in a preschool of some sort than at home? No! Quality matters (Gambaro et al., 2014).

If the home learning environment is poor, a good preschool significantly advances health, cognition, and social skills. If, instead, a family provides excellent early education but the preschool is overcrowded, children may not benefit from attendance, at least according to studies in the United States (Karch, 2013).

The problem is that the easiest way for a preschool to reduce expenses is to hire fewer staff members. Many government subsidies are low. As one critic complained: "Parents can find cheap babysitting that's bad for their kids on their own. They don't need government help with that" (Barnett, quoted in Samuels & Klein, 2013, p. 21).

A U.S. program that gave mothers of young children a small subsidy for early child care if they had jobs found that many mothers entered the labor force, but their children learned no more than their peers whose mothers stayed home (A. Johnson et al., 2014). The exceptions were children of immigrants, who became better at English-reading skills. But, on most measures, the subsidized children did no better than the home-staying children, who actually learned more math than the children who attended low-quality preschools.

Quality is not indicated by name (preschool, nursery school, day-care center, pre-primary, or pre-K) or sponsorship (public or private, religious or secular, corporate or independent). What does matter is the training, warmth, and experience of the teachers.

Unfortunately, "because quality is hard for parents to observe, competition seems to be dominated by price" (Gambaro et al., 2014, p. 22), which means fewer, and less trained, adults. However, expensive preschools are not necessarily high in quality, because owners may spend money on attractive space, toys, and equipment, but not on teachers.

◆ **Especially for Unemployed Early-Childhood Teachers**
You are offered a job in a program that has ten 3-year-olds for every adult. You know that is too many, but you want a job. What should you do? (see response, page 191)

Quality of Early Education

Since price does not indicate quality, what does matter? Consider how many adults there are and what they do. Ideally caregivers talk, listen, laugh, guide, and play with the children; if they sit, watch, and command ("Stop hitting," "Sit here," "Share the toy"), that suggests low quality.

Another question is whether the goals of the program are to encourage each child's creative individuality (*child-centered*) or to prepare children for formal education (*teacher-directed*). Both approaches may succeed, but the teachers need to know the goals and work to accomplish them, not simply babysit. (See Visualizing Development, page 186.)

CHILD-CENTERED PROGRAMS Programs that are *child-centered,* or *developmental,* stress each child's development and growth. Teachers in such programs believe children need to follow their own interests. For example, they agree that "children should be allowed to select many of their own activities from a variety of learning areas that the teacher has prepared" (Lara-Cinisomo et al., 2011). The physical space and the materials (such as dress-up clothes, art supplies, puzzles, blocks, and other toys) are arranged to allow exploration.

Child-centered programs are often influenced by Piaget, who emphasized that each child will discover new ideas if given a chance, or by Vygotsky, who thought that children learn from playing, especially with other children, with adult guidance.

Most child-centered programs encourage artistic expression, including music and drama (Bassok et al., 2016). Some educators argue that young children are gifted in seeing the world more imaginatively than older people do. According to advocates of child-centered programs, creative vision should be encouraged; children need to tell stories, draw pictures, dance, and make music for their own delight.

One type of child-centered school began in the slums of Rome in 1907, when Maria Montessori opened a nursery school (Standing, 1998). She believed that children needed structured, individualized projects to give them a sense of accomplishment. Her students completed puzzles, used sponges and water to clean tables, traced shapes, and so on.

Contemporary **Montessori schools** still emphasize individual pride and achievement, presenting many literacy-related tasks (e.g., outlining letters and looking at books) to young children. Specific materials differ from those that Montessori

Montessori schools
Schools that offer early-childhood education based on the philosophy of Maria Montessori, which emphasizes careful work and tasks that each young child can do.

Tibet, China, India, and . . . Italy? Over the past half-century, as China increased its control of Tibet, thousands of refugees fled to northern India. Tibet traditionally had no preschools, but young children adapt quickly, as in this preschool program in Ladakh, India. This Tibetan boy is working a classic Montessori board.

MALIE RICH-GRIFFITH/INFOCUSPHOTOS.COM / ALAMY

developed, but the underlying philosophy is the same. Children seek out learning tasks; they do not sit quietly in groups while a teacher instructs them. That makes Montessori programs child-centered (Lillard, 2013).

Another child-centered form of early-childhood education is **Reggio Emilia,** named after the town in Italy where it began. In Reggio Emilia, children are encouraged to master skills that are not usually taught in North American schools until age 7 or so, such as writing and using tools. Although many educators worldwide admire the Reggio philosophy and practice, it is expensive to duplicate in other nations—there are few dedicated Reggio Emilia schools in the United States.

Reggio schools do not provide large-group instruction, with lessons in, say, forming letters or cutting paper. Instead, hands-on activities are chosen by each child, perhaps drawing, cooking, or gardening. Measurement of achievement, such as standardized testing to see whether children recognize the 26 letters of the alphabet, is antithetical to the conviction that every child should explore and learn in his or her own pace and manner. Each child's learning is documented via scrapbooks, photos, and daily notes—not to measure progress but to make the child and parent proud (Caruso, 2013).

Appreciation of the arts is evident. Originally, every Reggio Emilia school had a studio, an artist, and space to encourage creativity (Forbes, 2012). Children's art is displayed on white walls and hung from high ceilings, and floor-to-ceiling windows open to a spacious, plant-filled playground. Big mirrors are part of the schools' décor—again, with the idea of fostering individuality and self-expression. Cooperation is also valued. Group projects are encouraged, especially those that engage the young scientists to explore their natural world.

A third type of child-centered school is called **Waldorf,** first developed by Rudolf Steiner in Germany in 1919. The emphasis again is on creativity and individuality—with no homework, no tests, and no worksheets. As much as possible, children play outdoors—appreciation of nature is basic to Waldorf schools. Children of various ages learn together because older children serve as mentors for younger ones, and the curriculum follows the interests of the child, not the age of the child.

There is a set schedule—usually circle time in the beginning and certain activities on certain days (always baking on Tuesdays, for instance)—but children are not expected to master specific knowledge at certain ages. All child-centered schools emphasize creativity; in Waldorf schools, imagination is particularly prized (Kirkham & Kidd, 2017).

TEACHER-DIRECTED PROGRAMS Teacher-directed preschools stress academics, often taught by one adult to the entire group. The curriculum includes learning the names of letters, numbers, shapes, and colors.

Orderly, scheduled activities teach routines: Every child naps, snacks, and goes to the bathroom at certain times. Children learn to sit quietly and listen to the teacher. Praise and other reinforcements are given for good behavior, and time-outs (brief separation from activities) are imposed to punish misbehavior.

The goal of teacher-directed programs is to make all children "ready to learn" when they enter elementary school. For that reason, basic skills are stressed, including precursors to reading, writing, and arithmetic, perhaps via teachers asking questions that children answer together in unison. Behavior is also taught, as children learn to respect adults, to follow schedules, to hold hands when they go on outings, and so on.

Children practice forming letters, sounding out words, counting objects, and writing their names. If a 4-year-old learns to read, that is success. (In a child-centered program, that might arouse suspicion that there was too little time to play or socialize.)

Reggio Emilia
A program of early-childhood education that originated in the town of Reggio Emilia, Italy, and that encourages each child's creativity in a carefully designed setting.

Waldorf
An early-childhood education program than emphasizes creativity, social understanding, and emotional growth. It originated in Germany with Rudolf Steiner, and now is used in thousands of schools throughout the world.

ELIZABETH FLORES/TRIBUNE NEWS SERVICE/PLEASANT PRAIRIE/WI/USA/NEWSCOM

Child-Centered Pride How could Rachel Koepke, a 3-year-old from a Wisconsin town called Pleasant Prairie, seem so pleased that her hands (and cuffs) are blue? The answer arises from northern Italy—Rachel attended a Reggio Emilia preschool that encourages creative expression.

EARLY-CHILDHOOD SCHOOLING

Preschool can be an academic and social benefit to children. Around the world, increasing numbers of children are enrolled in early-childhood education.

Programs are described as "teacher-directed" or "child-centered," but in reality, most teachers' styles reflect a combination of both approaches. Some students benefit more from the order and structure of a teacher-directed classroom, while others work better in a more collaborative and creative environment.

TEACHER-DIRECTED APPROACH
Focused on Getting Preschoolers Ready to Learn
Direct instruction
Teacher as formal authority
Students learn by listening
Classroom is orderly and quiet
Teacher fully manages lesssons
Rewards individual achievement
Encourages academics
Students learn from teacher

CHILD-CENTERED APPROACH
Focused on Individual Development and Growth
Teacher as facilitator
Teacher as delegator
Students learn actively
Classroom is designed for collaborative work
Students influence content
Rewards collaboration among students
Encourages artistic expression
Students learn from each other

WORTH PUBLISHERS

DIFFERENT STUDENTS, DIFFERENT TEACHERS

There is clearly no "one right way" to teach children. Each approach has potential benefits and pitfalls. A classroom full of creative, self-motivated students can thrive when a gifted teacher acts as a competent facilitator. But students who are distracted or annoyed by noise, or who are shy or intimidated by other children, can blossom under an engaging and encouraging teacher in a more traditional environment.

Done Well

- engaging teacher
- clear, consistent assessment
- reading and math skills emphasized
- quiet, orderly classroom
- all students treated equally

- emphasizes social skills and emotion regulation
- encourages critical thinking
- builds communication skills
- fosters individual achievement
- encourages creativity and curiosity

Teacher-Directed ← → **Child-Centered**

- bored students
- passive learning
- less independent, critical thinking
- teacher may dominate

- chaotic/noisy classrooms
- students may miss important knowledge and skills
- inconclusive assessment of student progress
- some students may dominate others

Done Poorly

Many teacher-directed programs were inspired by behaviorism, which emphasizes step-by-step learning and repetition, with reinforcement (praise, gold stars, prizes) for accomplishment. Another inspiration for teacher-directed programs comes from information-processing research indicating that children who have not learned basic vocabulary and listening skills by kindergarten often fall behind in primary school. Many state legislatures mandate that preschoolers master specific concepts, an outcome best achieved by teacher-directed learning (Bracken & Crawford, 2010).

A program that now seems more teacher-directed than child-centered is **Head Start.** In the early 1960s, millions of young children in the United States were thought to need a "head start" on their formal education to foster better health and cognition before first grade. Consequently, since 1965, the federal government has funded preschool education for 4-year-olds from low-SES families or with disabilities.

The goals for Head Start have changed over the decades, from lifting families out of poverty to promoting literacy, from providing dental care and immunizations to teaching Standard English, from focusing on 4- and 5-year-olds to including younger children. In 2015, more than 8 billion dollars in federal funds were allocated to Head Start, which enrolled almost a million children.

In 2016, new requirements for Head Start included at least 6 hours a day and 180 days a year (initially, most programs were half-day), with priorities for children who are homeless, or have special needs, or are learning English. Those children were targeted partly because federal research found that Head Start benefits are strongest for them (U.S. Department of Health and Human Services, 2010). Moreover, they are least likely to be enrolled in private preschools (Crosnoe et al., 2016).

Historical data show that most Head Start children of every background advanced in language and social skills, but non–Head Start children often caught up in elementary school. However, there was one area in which the Head Start children maintained their superiority—vocabulary. This seems especially significant for Spanish-speaking children whose teachers instruct in English at least half of the time (Garcia, 2018).

Since there are about 8 million 3- and 4-year-olds in the United States, only about 12 percent of U.S. children that age are in Head Start. Many others are in private programs (about 83 percent of 4-year-olds from the wealthiest families are enrolled in private preschools) or state-sponsored programs, which range in quality from excellent to woefully inadequate (Barnett et al., 2016).

Head Start
A federally funded early-childhood intervention program for low-income children of preschool age.

© OCTAVIO JONES/ZUMA PRESS/CORBIS

If You're Happy and You Know It Gabby Osborne (pink shirt) has her own way of showing happiness, not the hand-clapping that Lizalia Garcia tries to teach. The curriculum of this Head Start class in Florida includes learning about emotions, contrary to the wishes of some legislators, who want proof of academics.

OPPOSING PERSPECTIVES

Comparing Child-Centered and Teacher-Directed Preschools

Most developmentalists advocate child-centered programs (Christakis, 2016; Golinkoff & Hirsh-Pasek, 2016). They believe that from ages 3 to 6 young children learn best when they can interact in their own way with materials and ideas (Sim & Zu, 2017). On the other hand, many parents and legislators want proof that early education will improve later school achievement.

The developmental critics of teacher-directed education fear "trad[ing] emotional grounding and strong language skills known to support learning for assembly-line schooling that teaches children isolated factoids" (Hirsh-Pasek & Golinkoff, 2016, p. 1158).

As Penelope Leach wrote, "Goals come from the outside.... It is important that people see early learning as coming from inside children because that's what makes clear its interconnectedness with play, and therefore the inappropriateness of many 'learning goals'" (Leach, 2011, p. 17). Another developmentalist asks, "Why should we settle for unimaginative goals . . . like being able to identify triangles and squares, or recalling the names of colors and seasons?" (Christakis, 2016).

However, children who enter kindergarten without knowing names and sounds of letters may become first-graders who cannot read (Ozernov-Palchik et al., 2017.) Understanding how written symbols relate to sounds is crucial, and children are unlikely to learn literacy skills in creative play (Gellert & Elbro, 2017). Early familiarity with numbers and shapes predicts school achievement later on.

As you read, Head Start programs have shifted over the past decades to be more teacher-directed, largely because national policy directives from the government have advocated that change—to the distress of many developmentalists (Walter & Lippard, 2017).

Finding the right balance between child-centered and teacher-directed learning is needed so that all young children learn in the manner that is best for them (Fuligni et al., 2012). The current trend is toward teacher-directed, according to a survey of kindergarten teachers (Bassok et al., 2016). (See Figure 5.2.)

Between 2010 and 2017, some states (e.g., Oklahoma, Georgia, Florida, New Jersey, and Illinois) and some cities (e.g., New York, Boston, Cleveland, San Antonio, and Los Angeles) have offered preschool to every 4-year-old. Overall, 29 percent of all 4-year-olds were in state-sponsored preschool, twice as many as a decade earlier (Barnett et al., 2015). Another 10 percent attended Head Start, and about 3 percent were in publicly funded programs for children with disabilities (U.S. Department of Education, 2015).

The increases in government-sponsored preschool—either child-centered or teacher-directed—for 4-year-olds is good news, although developmentalists note that in the United States, unlike in Europe, almost half of all 4-year-olds and most 3-year-olds are not in any educational program. The children *least* likely to be in such programs are

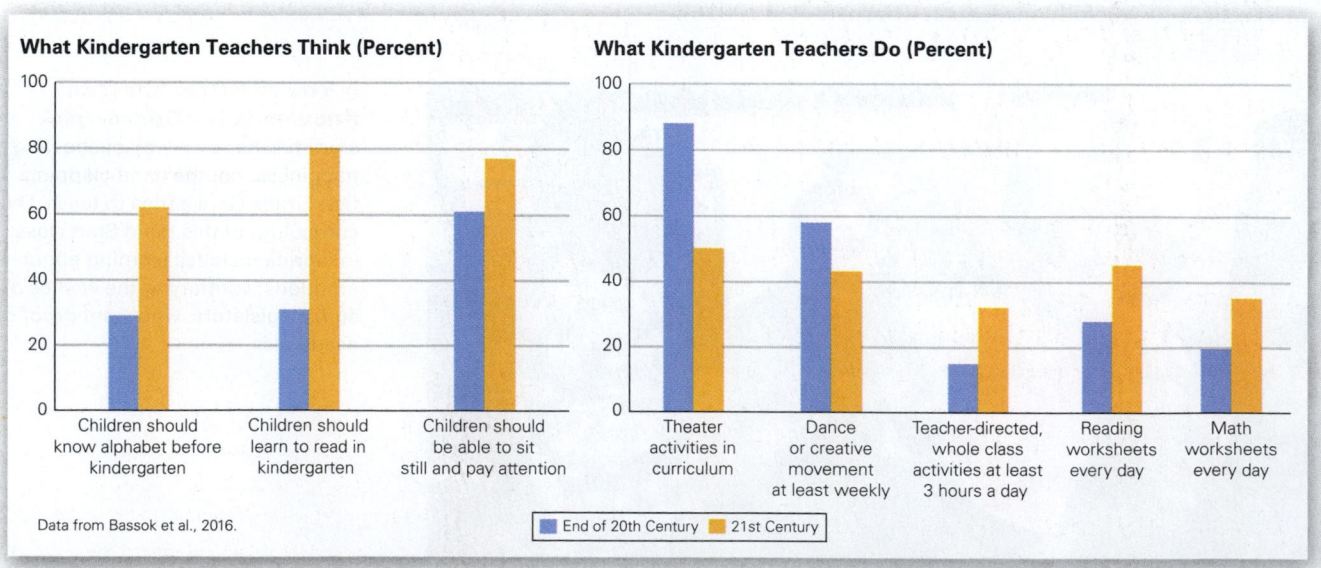

FIGURE 5.2 Less Play, More Work These data come from a large survey of more than 5,000 public school teachers throughout the United States. In 1998 and 2010, kindergarten teachers were asked identical questions but gave different answers. Smaller, more recent surveys suggest that these trends continue, and they now involve preschool teachers. Some use worksheets for 3-year-olds.

Spanish-speaking, or from families with income slightly above the poverty level, or whose mother is not employed.

Ironically, these are precisely the children for whom early education may be especially helpful, a conclusion found not only in Head Start but in other research as well (Weiland & Yoshikawa, 2013).

Many early-childhood educators of both opposing perspectives bewail the low U.S. rates of preschool attendance. Indeed, lack of early education in poor nations is considered a worldwide problem. An international review considered it a worldwide injustice that "less than 50% of children aged 3–6 years receive any form of pre-primary education" (Shawar & Shiffman, 2017, p. 119).

In the United States, economic and political pressures are reducing government funds for preschool education.

Adjusted for inflation, per-pupil spending by states was $5,129 per child in 2002 and $4,121 in 2014 (Barnett et al., 2015). Head Start funding is also down per pupil, and cuts of more than 10 percent are projected for 2018. This troubles educators on both sides of this opposing perspective.

Any cuts to preschool education not only mean less child-centered learning (which is more expensive) but also less high-quality teacher-directed learning.

In most states, kindergarten (always locally funded) is optional, and sometimes unavailable: Only 13 of the 50 states are required to offer all parents full-day kindergarten (E. Parker et al., 2016). Scientists who know the research on early-childhood cognition are dismayed when the wishes of adults supersede the education of children.

what have you learned?

1. What are the long-term benefits of early-childhood education?

2. In child-centered programs, what do the teachers do?

3. Why are Montessori schools still functioning 100 years after the first such schools opened?

4. What are the advantages and disadvantages of teacher-directed preschools?

5. Who benefits most from Head Start?

SUMMARY

Body Changes

1. Children continue to gain weight and add height during early childhood. Motor skills develop; clumsy 2-year-olds become agile 6-year-olds who move their bodies well.

2. Many adults overfeed children, not realizing that young children are naturally quite thin. Many children eat too much of the wrong foods: They may consume too much sugar and too little fiber, resulting in obesity and poor oral health.

3. The brain continues to grow in early childhood, reaching 75 percent of its adult weight at age 2 and 90 percent by age 6. Myelination accounts for much of that weight, beginning to connect the left and right brains as well as connecting the prefrontal cortex with the other regions. Impulsivity and perseveration decrease.

4. The two hemispheres of the brain work together, each controlling one side of the body. People are naturally left- or right-handed, as their brains dictate, with the corpus callosum connecting left and right.

Thinking During Early Childhood

5. Piaget called thinking at this stage "preoperational" because young children often cannot yet use logical operations. They may focus on only one thing (centration) and see things only from their own viewpoint (egocentrism), remaining stuck on appearances and current reality, unable to understand reversibility.

6. Vygotsky stressed the social aspects of childhood cognition, noting that children learn by guided participation, as mentors scaffold new information within the zone of proximal development to aid learning.

7. Children develop theories to explain human actions. One theory about children's thinking, called theory-theory, is that children develop theories because humans always seek explanations for everything they observe.

8. In early childhood, children develop a theory of mind—an understanding of what others may be thinking. Theory of mind results from brain maturation, with culture and experiences also influential.

Language Learning

9. Language develops rapidly during early childhood. Vocabulary increases dramatically, with thousands of words fast-mapped between ages 2 and 6. In addition, basic grammar is mastered, with impressive mastery as well as understandable exceptions.

10. Many children learn more than one language, gaining cognitive and social advantages. Ideally, that occurs before age 6, avoiding a language shift away from the home language.

11. Five specific strategies and experiences are known to be particularly effective for children's literacy: code-focused teaching,

book-reading, parent education, language enhancement, and pre-school programs.

Early-Childhood Education

12. Many types of early education advance language and social skills, with benefits lifelong. It is the quality of early education—whether at home or at school—that matters.

13. Many child-centered programs are inspired by Piaget and Vygotsky; they encourage children to follow their own interests. Teacher-directed early-childhood programs emphasize academics and good behavior. The goal is to prepare children for reading and writing in school.

KEY TERMS

myelin (p. 161)	animism (p. 165)	zone of proximal development (ZPD) (p. 169)	fast-mapping (p. 176)
corpus callosum (p. 162)	centration (p. 166)	scaffolding (p. 169)	overregularization (p. 178)
lateralization (p. 162)	egocentrism (p. 166)	private speech (p. 170)	pragmatics (p. 178)
impulse control (p. 163)	focus on appearance (p. 166)	social mediation (p. 170)	Montessori schools (p. 184)
perseveration (p. 164)	static reasoning (p. 166)	executive function (p. 171)	Reggio Emilia (p. 185)
preoperational intelligence (p. 165)	irreversibility (p. 166)	theory-theory (p. 171)	Waldorf (p. 185)
symbolic thought (p. 165)	conservation (p. 166)	theory of mind (p. 172)	Head Start (p. 187)

APPLICATIONS

1. Keep a food diary for 24 hours, writing down what you eat, how much, when, how, and why. Then think about nutrition and eating habits in early childhood. Did your food habits originate in early childhood, in adolescence, or at some other time? Explain.

2. Go to a playground or other place where many young children play. Note the motor skills that the children demonstrate, including abilities and inabilities, and keep track of age and sex. What differences do you see among the children?

3. Replicate one of Piaget's conservation experiments. The easiest one is conservation of liquids (illustrated in Figure 5.1). Work with a child under age 5 who tells you that two identically shaped glasses contain the same amount of liquid. Then ask the child to carefully pour one glass of liquid into a taller, narrower glass. Ask the child which glass now contains more or if the glasses contain the same amount.

ESPECIALLY FOR ANSWERS

Response for Early-Childhood Teachers (from page 159): Remember to keep food simple and familiar. Offer every child the same food, allowing refusal but no substitutes—unless for all eight. Children do not expect school and home routines to be identical; they eventually taste whatever other children enjoy.

Response for Early-Childhood Teachers (from page 161): One solution is to remind yourself that the children's brains are not yet myelinated enough to enable them to quickly walk, talk, or even button their jackets. Maturation has a major effect, as you will observe if you can schedule excursions in September and again in November. Progress, while still slow, will be a few seconds faster.

Response for Neurologists (from page 164): The more we discover about the brain, the more complex we realize it is. Each part has specific functions and is connected to every other part.

Response for Nutritionists (from page 167): Take each of the four characteristics of preoperational thought into account. Because of egocentrism, having a special place and plate might assure the child that this food is exclusively his or hers. Since

appearance is important, food should look tasty. Since static thinking dominates, if something healthy is added (e.g., grate carrots into the cake, add milk to the soup), do it before the food is given to the child. In the reversibility example in the text, the lettuce should be removed out of the child's sight and the "new" sandwich presented.

Response for Social Scientists (from page 172): According to Piaget, preschool children focus on appearance and on static conditions (so they cannot mentally reverse a process). Furthermore, they are egocentric, believing that everyone shares their point of view. No wonder they believe that they had always known the puppy was in the blue box and that Max would know that, too.

Response for Immigrant Parents (from page 180): Children learn by listening, so it is important to speak with them often. Depending on how comfortable you are with the new language, you might prefer to read to your children, sing to them, and converse with them primarily in your native language and find a good preschool where they will learn the new language. The worst thing you could do is to restrict speech in either tongue.

Response for Unemployed Early-Childhood Teachers (from page 183): It would be best for you to wait for a job in a program in which children learn well, organized along the lines explained in this chapter. You would be happier, as well as learn more, in a workplace that is good for children. Realistically, though, you might feel compelled to take the job. If you do, change the child/adult ratio—find a helper, perhaps a college intern or a volunteer grandmother. But choose carefully—some adults are not helpful at all. Before you take the job, remember that children need continuity: You can't leave simply because you find something better.

OBSERVATION QUIZ ANSWERS

Answer to Observation Quiz (from page 158): No. There are no pedals! Technically this is not a tricycle; it has four wheels. The ability to coordinate both legs follows corpus callosum development in the next few years, as explained on page 161.

Answer to Observation Quiz (from page 165): Green with jealousy, red-hot anger, and shrinking violet for fear.

Answer to Observation Quiz (from page 169): Right-handed. Her dominant hand is engaged in something more comforting than exploring the abacus.

EARLY CHILDHOOD
Psychosocial Development

CHRISTOPHER HOPE-FITCH/GETTY IMAGES

what will you know?

- Why do 2-year-olds have more sudden tempers, tears, and terrors than 6-year-olds?
- What happens if parents let their children do whatever they want?
- How does spanking affect children?
- Do maltreated children become abusive adults?

I t was a hot summer afternoon. My thirsty 3-year-old and 4-year-old were with me in the kitchen, which was in one corner of our living/ dining area. The younger one opened the refrigerator and grabbed a bottle of orange juice. The sticky bottle slipped, shattering on the floor. Both daughters stared at me, at the shards, at the spreading juice with extra pulp. I picked them up and plopped them on the couch.

"Stay there until I clean this up," I shouted.

They did, wide-eyed at my fury. As they watched me pick, sweep, and mop, I understood how parents could hit their kids. By the end of the chapter, I hope you also realize how a moment like this—in the heat, with two small children and unexpected work—can turn a loving, patient adult into something else. It is not easy, day after day, being the guide and model that parents should be.

Fortunately, many safeguards prevented serious maltreatment— the girls stayed on the couch; my values kept me from hitting them; I could afford more juice. Four aspects of psychosocial development—children learn to manage their emotions, parents learn to guide their children, the macrosystem (cultural values), and microsystem (personal income)—converged to allow understanding, not abuse. This chapter describes how all of these affect every young child.

Emotional Development

Controlling the expression of feelings, called **emotional regulation,** is the preeminent psychosocial task between ages 2 and 6. Emotional regulation is a lifelong endeavor, a crucial aspect of executive function, which develops most rapidly in early childhood (Gross, 2014; Lewis, 2013).

By age 6, most children can be angry, frightened, sad, anxious, or proud without the explosive outbursts of temper, terror, or tears of 2-year-olds. Depending on a child's training and temperament, some emotions are easier to control than others, but even temperamentally angry or fearful children learn to regulate their emotions (Moran et al., 2013; Tan et al., 2013; Suurland et al., 2016).

In the process of emotional regulation, children develop their **self-concept,** which is their idea of who they are. Remember that 1-year-olds begin to recognize themselves in the mirror, the start of self-awareness. By age 6, children can describe some of their characteristics, including what emotions they feel and how they express them. That is probably true for all children everywhere, although parental guidance and encouragement aid in self-awareness (LeCuyer & Swanson, 2016).

Indeed, for all aspects of self-concept and emotional regulation, culture and family matter. Children may be encouraged to laugh/cry/yell, or the opposite, to hide their emotions. Some adults guffaw, slap their knees, and stomp their feet for joy; others cover their mouths if a smile spontaneously appears. Anger is regulated in almost every culture, but the expression of it—when, how, and to whom—varies a great deal. No matter what the specifics, parents teach emotional regulation (Kim & Sasaki, 2014).

Emotional regulation is also called **effortful control** (Eisenberg et al., 2014), a term that emphasizes that controlling outbursts is not easy. Effortful control is more difficult when people—of any age—are in pain, or tired, or hungry.

Effortful control, executive function, and emotional regulation are similar constructs, with much overlap, at least in theory (Scherbaum et al., 2018; Slot et al., 2017). Executive function emphasizes cognition; effortful control emphasizes temperament; both undergird emotional regulation. Many neurological processes underlie these abilities; all advance during early childhood.

emotional regulation
The ability to control when and how emotions are expressed.

self-concept
A person's understanding of who they are, in relation to self-esteem, appearance, personality, and various traits.

effortful control
The ability to regulate one's emotions and actions through effort, not simply through natural inclination.

initiative versus guilt
Erikson's third psychosocial crisis, in which young children undertake new skills and activities and feel guilty when they do not succeed at them.

BLEND IMAGES-KIDSTOCK/GETTY IMAGES

Both Accomplished Note the joy and pride in this father and daughter in West New York, New Jersey. Who has achieved more?

Initiative Versus Guilt

Emotional regulation is part of Erikson's third developmental stage, **initiative versus guilt.** *Initiative* includes saying something new, beginning a project, or expressing an emotion. Depending on what happens next, children feel proud or guilty. Gradually, they learn to rein in boundless pride and avoid crushing guilt.

Pride is typical in early childhood. As one team expressed it:

> Compared to older children and adults, young children are the optimists of the world, believing they have greater physical abilities, better memories, are more skilled at imitating models, are smarter, know more about how things work, and rate themselves as stronger, tougher, and of higher social standing than is actually the case.
>
> [Bjorklund & Ellis, 2014, p. 244]

That *protective optimism* helps young children try new things, and thus, initiative advances learning. As Erikson predicted, their optimistic self-concept protects young children from guilt and shame, and encourages them to learn.

PRIDE AND PREJUDICE In many cultures, a young child's pride usually includes being proud of who they are. One example is pride in age, size, and maturation. They are very glad that they aren't babies. "Crybaby" is an insult; praise for being "a big kid" is welcomed. Bragging is common.

Indeed, many young children believe that whatever they are is good. They feel superior to children of another nationality or religion. This arises because of maturation: Cognition enables them to understand group categories, not only of ethnicity, gender, and nationality but even insignificant categories.

For instance, they remember more about cartoon characters whose names begin with the same letter as theirs (Ross et al., 2011). If their parents or other adults express prejudice against people of another group, they may mirror those prejudices (Tagar et al., 2017).

One amusing example occurred when preschoolers were asked to explain why one person would steal from another, as occurred in a story about two fictional tribes, the Zaz and the Flurps. As you would expect from theory-theory, the preschoolers readily found reasons. Their first explanation illustrated their belief that group loyalty was more important than any personal characteristic.

> "Why did a Zaz steal a toy from a Flurp?"
> "Because he's a Zaz, but he's a Flurp . . . They're not the same kind . . ."

Only when asked to explain a more difficult case, when group loyalty was insufficient, did they consider character, morality, and personality.

> "Why did a Zaz steal a toy from a Zaz?"
> "Because he's a very mean boy."

[Rhodes, 2013, p. 259]

Proud Peruvian In rural Peru, a program of early education (Pronoei) encourages community involvement and traditional culture. Preschoolers, like this girl in a holiday parade, are proud to be themselves, and that helps them become healthy and strong.

© MIKE THEISS/NATIONAL GEOGRAPHIC SOCIETY/CORBIS

THINK CRITICALLY: At what age, if ever, do people understand when pride becomes prejudice?

BRAIN MATURATION The new initiative that Erikson described results from myelination of the limbic system, growth of the prefrontal cortex, and a longer attention span—all results of neurological maturation. Emotional regulation and cognitive maturation develop together, each enabling the other to advance (Bell & Calkins, 2011; Lewis, 2013; Bridgett et al., 2015).

Normally, with the brain maturation that occurs at about age 4 or 5, and as family and preschool experiences guide them, the capacity for self-control, such as *not* opening a present immediately if asked to wait and *not* expressing disappointment at an undesirable gift, becomes more evident.

Consider the most recent time you gave someone a gift. If the receiver was a young child, you probably could tell whether the child liked the present. If the receiver was an adult, you may not be so sure (Galak et al., 2016).

You may be familiar with the famous marshmallow test, which now has longitudinal results (Mischel et al., 1972; Mischel, 2014). Children could eat one marshmallow immediately or eat two if they waited—sometimes as long as 15 minutes. Those who waited used various tactics—they looked away, closed their eyes, or sang to themselves. Young children who delayed gobbling up one marshmallow became

VIDEO ACTIVITY: Can Young Children Delay Gratification? illustrates how most young children are unable to overcome temptation even when promised an award.

Learning Emotional Regulation
Like this girl in Hong Kong, all 2-year-olds burst into tears when something upsets them—a toy breaks, a pet refuses to play, or it's time to go home. A mother who comforts them and helps them calm down is teaching them to regulate their emotions.

more successful as teenagers, young adults, and even middle-aged adults—doing well in college, for instance, and having happy marriages.

Of course, this is correlation, not causation: Some impatient preschoolers nonetheless became successful adults. However, emotional regulation predicts academic achievement and later success.

- **Maturation matters.** Three-year-olds are poor at impulse control. They improve by age 6.

- **Learning matters.** In the zone of proximal development, children learn from mentors, who offer tactics for delaying gratification.

- **Culture matters.** In the United States, many parents tell their children not to be afraid; in Japan, they tell them not to brag; in the Netherlands, not to be moody. Children regulate their emotions in accord with their culture.

Some of these cultural differences are apparent between nations. In the marshmallow test, children from the Nso people of Cameroon were far better able to wait than the California children in Mischel's original experiment (Lamm et al., 2017).

In the United States, when children experienced an unreliable examiner (who previously had reneged on a promise) they ate the marshmallow right away (Kidd et al., 2013). The studies suggest that the ability to delay gratification is not innate; it is a result of parents who do, or do not, keep their promises. That produces adults who expect their efforts to be rewarded.

Brain plasticity is evident. Children strengthen and develop their neuronal connections in response to the emotions of other people. The process is reciprocal and dynamic: Anger begets anger, which leads again to anger; joy begets joy, and so on.

This synergy of emotional regulation was found in brain scans when 3-year-olds did a puzzle with their mothers. When the mothers became frustrated, the children did too—and vice versa. As the scientists explain, "mothers and children regulate or deregulate each other" (Atzaba-Poria et al., 2017, p. 551).

The practical application benefits adults as well as children. If a happy young boy runs to you, try to laugh, pick him up, and swing him around; if a grinning young girl drums on the table, try to catch the rhythm and pound in return, smiling broadly. Your stress hormones will be reduced and your endorphins will increase. Of course, reciprocal joy is not always possible, but since emotions are infectious, catch the good ones and drop the bad ones.

Motivation

Motivation is the impulse that propels someone to act. It comes either from a person's own desires or from the social context.

Intrinsic motivation arises from within, when people do something for the joy of doing it: A musician might enjoy making music even if no one else hears it; the sound is intrinsically rewarding. Intrinsic motivation is thought to advance creativity, innovation, and emotional well-being (Weinstein & DeHaan, 2014).

All of Erikson's psychosocial needs—including the young child's initiatives— are intrinsic: A child feels inwardly compelled to act. This is very evident to adults, especially when they are in a hurry as they walk with a child: Their young companions may jump up to balance walking along a ledge, stop to throw a snowball, or pick up a piece of junk to explore, slowing down progress because of their internal motivation.

Extrinsic motivation comes from outside the person, when external praise or some other reinforcement is the goal, such as when a musician plays for applause or money. Social rewards are powerful lifelong: Four-year-olds brush their teeth because they are praised, sometimes even rewarded with musical toothbrushes and tasty toothpaste.

intrinsic motivation
A drive, or reason to pursue a goal, that comes from inside a person, such as the joy of reading a good book.

extrinsic motivation
A drive, or reason to pursue a goal, that arises from the wish to have external rewards, perhaps by earning money or praise.

If an extrinsic reward is removed, the behavior may stop unless it has become a habit. Young children might not brush their teeth if parents do not seem to care that they do so. For most of us, tooth brushing was extrinsically rewarded for long enough that it eventually became a habit, and then motivation is intrinsic. As an adult, because tooth brushing has become a comforting routine, if you skip it, your mouth feels mossy.

Intrinsic motivation is evident in childhood. Young children play, question, exercise, create, destroy, and explore for the sheer joy of it. That serves them well. For example, a longitudinal study found that 3-year-olds who were strong in intrinsic motivation were, two years later, advanced in early math and literacy (Mokrova et al., 2013). The probable reason: They enjoyed counting things and singing songs—when alone.

In contrast, exaggerated external praise ("your drawing is amazingly wonderful") undercuts motivation (Brummelman et al., 2017). If young children believe the praise, they might be afraid to try again, thinking they will not be able to do as well. If they suspect that the praise was inaccurate, they may discount the entire activity.

When playing a game, few young children keep score; intrinsic joy is the goal, more than winning. In fact, young children often claim to have won when objective scoring would say they lost; in this case, the children may really be winners.

Intrinsic motivation is also apparent when children invent dialogues for their toys, concentrate on creating a work of art or architecture, or converse with imaginary friends. Invisible companions are rarely encouraged by adults (thus, no extrinsic motivation), but many 2- to 7-year-olds have them.

An international study of 3- to 8-year-olds found that about one child in five said that they had one or more invisible companions, with notable variation by culture: 38 percent of children in the Dominican Republic, but only 5 percent in Nepal, said they had such a friend (Wigger, 2017). Is that because some cultures discourage imagination, so some children did not tell adults about their imaginary friends?

◆ Especially for College Students
Is extrinsic or intrinsic motivation more influential in your study efforts? (see response, page 229)

◆ Especially for Teachers of Young Children
Should you put gold stars on children's work? (see response, page 229)

what have you learned?

1. How might protective optimism lead to new skills and competencies?
2. What did Erikson think was crucial for young children?
3. Why might impulse control, as with marshmallows, predict adult success?
4. What is an example (not in the text) of intrinsic motivation?
5. What is an example (not in the text) of extrinsic motivation?

Play

Play is timeless and universal—apparent in every part of the world over thousands of years. Many developmentalists believe that play is children's most productive, enjoyable activity (Elkind, 2007; Bateson & Martin, 2013; P. Smith, 2010).

Not everyone agrees. Whether play is essential or merely fun is "a controversial topic of study" (Pellegrini, 2011, p. 3). Some educators want children to play less in order to learn reading and math; others predict emotional and academic problems if children rarely play (Golinkoff & Hirsh-Pasek, 2016).

This controversy underlies many of the disputes regarding early education. Some fear that "play in school has become an endangered species" (Trawick-Smith, 2012, p. 259). Among the theorists of human development, Vygotsky especially advocated play. He wrote that play makes children "a head taller" than their actual height (Vygotsky, 1980).

THINK CRITICALLY: Some experts believe that play should be encouraged at all ages. Do adults play too often or not often enough?

Real or Fake? This photo may be staged, but the children show the power of imagination—each responding to his or her cape in a unique way. Sociodramatic play is universal; children do it if given half a chance.

↑ **OBSERVATION** QUIZ
What suggests that this may be a staged photo? (see answer, page 229)

JGI/JAMIE GRILL/BLEND IMAGES/GETTY IMAGES

Playmates

Young children play best with *peers,* that is, people of about the same age and social status. Although infants are intrigued by other children, babies play only with toys or adults because peer play requires some social maturation (Bateson & Martin, 2013). Gradually, from age 2 to 6, most children learn how to join a peer group, manage conflict, take turns, find friends, and keep the action going (Şendil & Erden, 2014; Göncü & Gaskins, 2011).

Children need physical activity to develop muscle strength and control. Peers provide an audience, role models, and sometimes competition. For instance, running skills develop best when children chase or race each other, not when a child runs alone. Active social play—not solitary play—correlates with physical, emotional, and intellectual growth (Becker et al., 2014; Sutton-Smith, 2011).

THE HISTORICAL CONTEXT As you remember, one dispute in early education is finding the proper balance between child-centered creative play and teacher-directed learning. This was not an issue a century ago: Most families had many children, few mothers had jobs, and all of the children played outside with neighboring boys and girls, of several ages. The older children looked out for the younger ones, and games like tag, hide-and-seek, and stickball allowed each child to play at their own level.

In 1932, American sociologist Mildred Parten described five stages of play, each more advanced than the previous one:

1. *Solitary:* A child plays alone, unaware of other children playing nearby.
2. *Onlooker:* A child watches other children play.
3. *Parallel:* Children play in similar ways but not together.
4. *Associative:* Children interact, sharing toys, but not taking turns.
5. *Cooperative:* Children play together, creating dramas or taking turns.

Parten described play as intrinsic, with children gradually advancing, from age 1 to 6, from solitary to cooperative play.

Research on contemporary children finds much more age variation than Parten did, perhaps because family size is smaller and parents invest heavily in

LESS PLAY, LESS SAFE?

Play is universal—all young children do it when they are with each other, if they can. For children, play takes up more time than anything else, whether their family is rich or poor.

What 3-Year-Olds Do with Their Time

PERCENT OF KIDS WHOSE PARENTS PLAY OUTDOORS WITH THEM

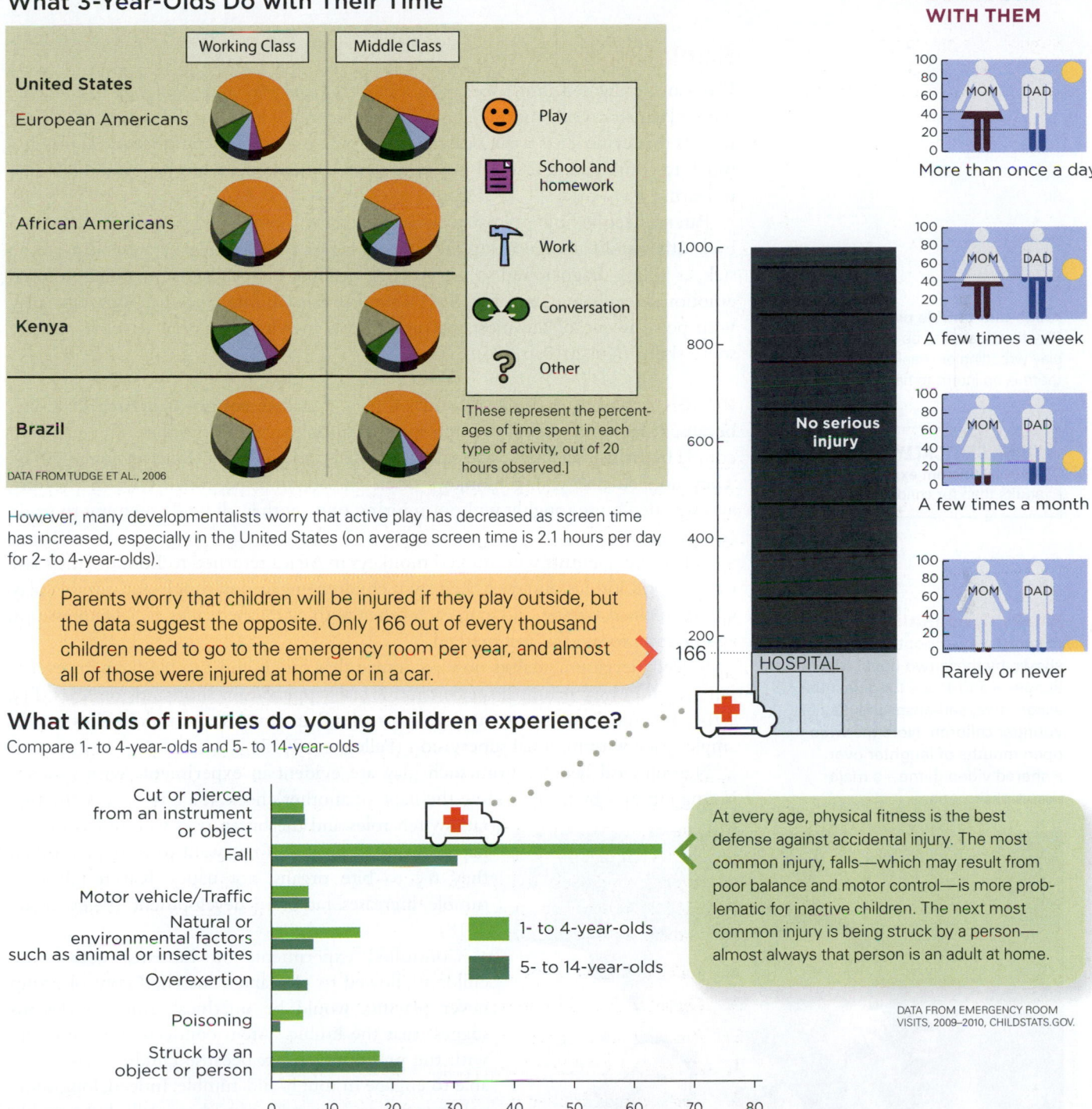

	Working Class	Middle Class
United States European Americans		
African Americans		
Kenya		
Brazil		

Legend:
- Play
- School and homework
- Work
- Conversation
- Other

[These represent the percentages of time spent in each type of activity, out of 20 hours observed.]

DATA FROM TUDGE ET AL., 2006

However, many developmentalists worry that active play has decreased as screen time has increased, especially in the United States (on average screen time is 2.1 hours per day for 2- to 4-year-olds).

Parents worry that children will be injured if they play outside, but the data suggest the opposite. Only 166 out of every thousand children need to go to the emergency room per year, and almost all of those were injured at home or in a car.

No serious injury

1,000 — 800 — 600 — 400 — 200 — 166

HOSPITAL

More than once a day — MOM DAD

A few times a week — MOM DAD

A few times a month — MOM DAD

Rarely or never — MOM DAD

What kinds of injuries do young children experience?

Compare 1- to 4-year-olds and 5- to 14-year-olds

- Cut or pierced from an instrument or object
- Fall
- Motor vehicle/Traffic
- Natural or environmental factors such as animal or insect bites
- Overexertion
- Poisoning
- Struck by an object or person

Legend:
- 1- to 4-year-olds
- 5- to 14-year-olds

0 10 20 30 40 50 60 70 80

Emergency room visits per 1,000 children

At every age, physical fitness is the best defense against accidental injury. The most common injury, falls—which may result from poor balance and motor control—is more problematic for inactive children. The next most common injury is being struck by a person—almost always that person is an adult at home.

DATA FROM EMERGENCY ROOM VISITS, 2009–2010, CHILDSTATS.GOV.

each child, rarely telling them to "go out and play and come back when it gets dark," as parents once did. Many Asian parents successfully teach 3-year-olds to take turns, share, and otherwise cooperate (stage 5). Many North American children, encouraged to be individuals, still engage in parallel play at age 6 (stage 3). Even in first grade, an only child who never attended school might stand at the edge of the recess yard, watching (stage 2).

Social Play

Play can be divided into two kinds: solitary *pretend play* and *social play* that occurs with playmates. One meta-analysis of the research on both (Lillard et al., 2013) reports that evidence is weak or mixed regarding pretend play but that social play has much to commend it. If social play is prevented, children are less happy and less able to learn.

Parents need to find playmates, because even the most playful parent is outmatched by another child at negotiating the rules of tag, at play-fighting, at pretending to be sick, at killing dragons, and so on. As they become better playmates, children learn emotional regulation, empathy, and cultural understanding. Specifics vary, but "play with peers is one of the most important areas in which children develop positive social skills" (Xu, 2010, p. 496).

ROUGH-AND-TUMBLE One form of play is called **rough-and-tumble play,** because it looks rough and children seem to tumble over one another. The term was coined by British scientists who studied animals in East Africa (Blurton-Jones, 1976). They noticed that young monkeys often chased, attacked, rolled over in the dirt, and wrestled quite roughly without injuring one another, all while seeming to smile (showing a *play face*).

When the scientists who studied monkeys in Africa returned to London, they saw that puppies, kittens, and even their own children engaged in rough-and-tumble play. Children chase, wrestle, and grab each other, with established rules, facial expressions, and gestures to signify "just pretend."

Indeed, developmentalists now recognize that rough-and-tumble happens everywhere, with every mammal species, and it has happened for thousands of years (Fry, 2014). It is much more common among males than females, and it flourishes best in ample space with minimal supervision (Pellegrini, 2013).

Neurological benefits from such play are evident in experiments with rodents. Young rats play by trying to bite the nape of another's neck. If a bite occurs, the two rats switch roles and the bitten tries to bite the other's nape. This is all playful: If rats want to hurt each other, they try to bite organs, not napes. Rat rough-and-tumble increases rat brain development (Pellis et al., 2018).

Controlled experiments on humans, with some children allowed to play and a matched control group never playing, would be unethical. But correlations suggest that the limbic system connects more strongly with the prefrontal cortex because children have been able to engage in rough-and-tumble. Indeed, longitudinal research on boys who played carefully but roughly with peers and parents (usually with fathers) suggests that they become caring, compassionate men (Fry, 2014; Raeburn, 2014).

---

rough-and-tumble play
Play that seems to be rough, as in play wrestling or chasing, but in which there is no intent to harm.

THINK CRITICALLY: Is "play" an entirely different experience for adults than for children?

Finally Cooperating The goal of social play—cooperation—is shown by these two boys, who at ages 8 and 11 are long past the associative, self-absorbed play of younger children. Note the wide-open mouths of laughter over a shared video game—a major accomplishment.

ISTOCKPHOTO/GIULIO FORNASAR/GETTY IMAGES

SOCIODRAMATIC PLAY Another major type of play is **sociodramatic play,** in which children act out various roles and plots. Through such acting, children:

- explore and rehearse social roles;

- learn to explain their ideas and persuade playmates;

- practice emotional regulation by pretending to be afraid, angry, brave, and so on; and

- develop self-concept in a nonthreatening context.

Sociodramatic play builds on pretending, which emerges in toddlerhood. But remember that solitary pretending does not advance social skills; dramatic play with peers does. As children combine their imagination with that of their friends, they advance in theory of mind (Kavanaugh, 2011).

Everywhere, as they age from 2 to 6, children increasingly prefer to play with children of their own sex. For example, a day-care center in Finland allowed extensive free play. The boys often enacted dramas of good guys versus bad guys. In one episode, four boys did so, with Joni as the bad guy. Tuomas directed the drama and acted in it.

> **Tuomas:** . . . and now he [Joni] would take me and would hang me . . . . this would be the end of all of me.
> **Joni:** Hands behind!
> **Tuomas:** I can't help it . . . I have to.
> *[The two other boys follow his example.]*
> **Joni:** I would put fire all around them.
> *[All three brave boys lie on the floor with hands tied behind their backs. Joni piles mattresses on them, and pretends to light a fire, which crackles closer and closer.]*
> **Tuomas:** Everything is lost!
> *[One boy starts to laugh.]*
> **Petterl:** Better not to laugh, soon we will all be dead. . . . I am saying my last words.
> **Tuomas:** Now you can say your last wish. . . . And now I say I wish we can be terribly strong.
> *[At that point, the three boys suddenly gain extraordinary strength, pushing off the mattresses and extinguishing the fire. Good triumphs over evil, but not until the last moment, because, as one boy explains, "Otherwise this playing is not exciting at all."]*
> *[adapted from Kalliala, 2006, p. 83]*

As with this example, boys' sociodramatic play often includes danger and then victory over evil. By contrast, girls typically act out domestic scenes, with themselves as the adults. In the same day-care center where Joni piled mattresses on his playmates, preparing to burn them, girls said their play is "more beautiful and peaceful . . . [but] boys play all kinds of violent games" (Kalliala, 2006, p. 110).

The prevalence of sociodramatic play varies by culture as well as gender, with parents often following cultural norms. Some cultures find make-believe frivolous and discourage it; in other cultures, parents teach toddlers to be lions, or robots, or ladies drinking tea. Then children elaborate on those themes (Kavanaugh, 2011). Many young children are avid television watchers, and they act out superhero themes from their favorite shows.

Joy Supreme Pretend play in early childhood is thrilling and powerful. For this dancing child in Brooklyn, New York, pretend play overwhelms mundane realities, such as an odd scarf or awkward arm.

sociodramatic play
Pretend play in which children act out various roles and themes in plots or roles that they create.

Good over Evil or Evil over Good? Boys everywhere enjoy "strong man" fantasy play, as the continued popularity of Spider-Man and Superman attests. These boys follow that script. Both are Afghan refugees now in Pakistan.

FIGURE 6.1 **Learning by Playing** Fifty years ago, the average child spent three hours a day in outdoor play. Video games and television have largely replaced that, especially in cities. Children seem safer if parents can keep an eye on them, but what are they learning? The long-term effects on brain and body may be dangerous.

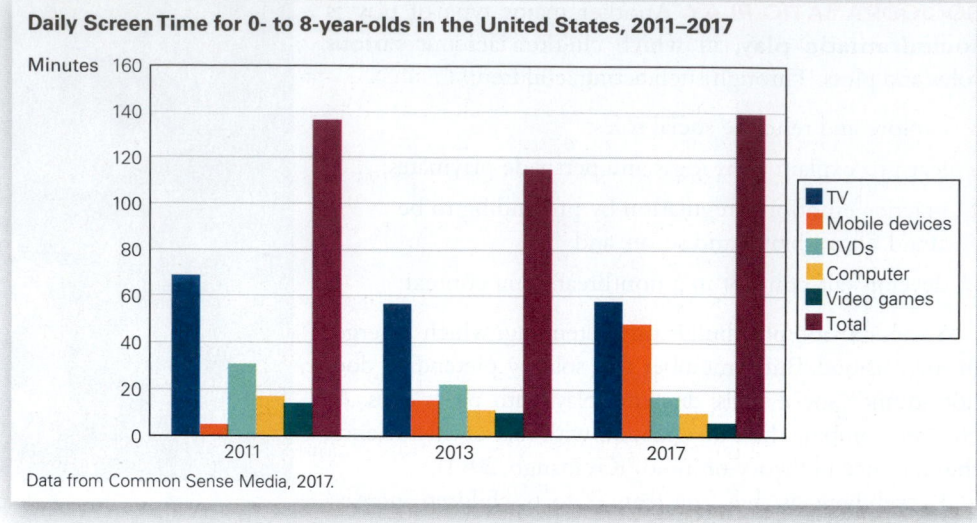

Data from Common Sense Media, 2017.

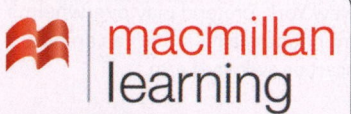

VIDEO: The Impact of Media on Early Childhood explores how screen time can affect young children's cognition.

In North America, most children watch screens at least two hours each day. That troubles developmentalists for many reasons. One is simply time—the more children are glued to screens, especially when they have their own hand-held device, the less time they have for active play (see Figure 6.1). Pediatricians, psychologists, and teachers all report extensive research that screen time reduces conversation, imagination, and outdoor activity (Downing et al., 2017).

Overall, the American Academy of Pediatrics (2016) recommends no more than an hour a day of any screen time for preschoolers and suggests that supervision should prevent exposure to violent or sexual media, and avoid racist and sexist stereotypes. However, many young children watch more than recommended, unsupervised, not only in the United States but also in other nations.

what have you learned?

1. What are children thought to gain from play?

2. Why does playing with peers increase physical development and emotional regulation?

3. What do children learn from rough-and-tumble play?

4. What do children learn from sociodramatic play?

5. Why do many experts want to limit children's screen time?

Challenges for Caregivers

Every developmentalist realizes that caring for a young child is difficult. Young children are energetic and curious, but not wise, and that tests the emotions and skills of every caregiver.

Styles of Caregiving

The more developmentalists study parents, the more styles of parenting they see. International variations are amazing—some are so strict that they seem abusive, and others are so lenient that they seem neglectful. Variations are apparent within nations, within ethnic groups, within neighborhoods, and sometimes within marriages.

◆ **Especially for Political Scientists** Many observers contend that children learn their political attitudes at home, from the way their parents teach them. Is this true? (see response, page 229)

BAUMRIND'S CATEGORIES Although thousands of researchers have traced the effects of parenting on child development, the work of one person, 60 years ago, remains influential. Diana Baumrind (1967, 1971) studied 100 preschool children, all from California, almost all middle-class European Americans.

She found that parents differed on four important dimensions:

1. *Expressions of warmth.* Some parents are warm and affectionate; others are cold and critical.

2. *Strategies for discipline.* Parents vary in how they explain, criticize, persuade, and punish.

3. *Expectations for maturity.* Parents vary in expectations for responsibility and self-control.

4. *Communication.* Some parents listen patiently; others demand silence.

Protect Me from the Water Buffalo These two are at the Carabao Kneeling Festival. In rural Philippines, hundreds of these large but docile animals kneel on the steps of the church, part of a day of gratitude for the harvest.

↑ OBSERVATION QUIZ

Is the father above authoritarian, authoritative, or permissive? (see answer, page 229)

On the basis of these dimensions, Baumrind identified three parenting styles (summarized in Table 6.1). A fourth style, not described by Baumrind, was suggested by other researchers.

Authoritarian parenting. The authoritarian parent's word is law, not to be questioned. Misconduct brings strict punishment, usually physical. Authoritarian parents set down clear rules and hold high standards. Discussion about emotions and expressions of affection are rare. One adult raised by authoritarian parents said that "How do you feel?" had only two possible answers: "Fine" and "Tired."

Permissive parenting. Permissive parents (also called *indulgent*) make few demands. Discipline is lax, partly because expectations are low. Permissive parents are nurturing and accepting, listening to whatever their offspring say, which may include "I hate you."

Authoritative parenting. Authoritative parents set limits, but they are flexible. They consider themselves guides, not authorities (unlike authoritarian parents) and not friends (unlike permissive parents). The goal of punishment is for the child to understand what was wrong and what should have been done differently.

Neglectful/uninvolved parenting. Neglectful parents are oblivious to their children's behavior; they seem not to care. Their children do whatever they want. This is quite different from permissive parents, who care very much.

Long-term effects of parenting styles have been reported in many nations. Cultural and regional differences are apparent, but everywhere authoritative parenting seems best (Pinquart & Kauser, 2018).

■ *Authoritarian* parents raise children who become conscientious, obedient, and quiet but not especially happy. Such children may feel guilty or depressed,

authoritarian parenting
An approach to child rearing that is characterized by high behavioral standards, strict punishment of misconduct, and little communication from child to parent.

permissive parenting
An approach to child rearing that is characterized by high nurturance and communication but little discipline, guidance, or control.

authoritative parenting
An approach to child rearing in which the parents set limits and enforce rules but are flexible and listen to their children.

neglectful/uninvolved parenting
An approach to child rearing in which the parents seem indifferent toward their children, not knowing or caring about their children's lives.

TABLE 6.1	Characteristics of Parenting Styles Identified by Baumrind				
				Communication	
Style	**Warmth**	**Discipline**	**Expectations of Maturity**	**Parent to Child**	**Child to Parent**
Authoritarian	Low	Strict, often physical	High	High	Low
Permissive	High	Rare	Low	Low	High
Authoritative	High	Moderate, with much discussion	Moderate	High	High

"He's just doing that to get attention."

Pay Attention Children develop best with lots of love and attention. They shouldn't have to ask for it!

internalizing their frustrations and blaming themselves when things don't go well. As adolescents, they sometimes rebel, leaving home before age 20. As adults, they are quick to blame and punish.

- *Permissive* parents raise children who lack self-control. Inadequate emotional regulation makes them immature and impedes friendships, so they are unhappy. They tend to continue to live at home, still dependent on their parents in adulthood.

- *Authoritative* parents raise children who are successful, articulate, happy with themselves, and generous with others. These children are usually liked by teachers and peers, especially in cultures that value individual initiative (e.g., the United States).

- *Neglectful/uninvolved* parents raise children who are immature, sad, lonely, and at risk of injury and abuse, not only in early childhood but also lifelong.

PROBLEMS WITH THE RESEARCH Baumrind's classification schema has been criticized, especially because she did not consider differences in cultural norms and child temperament. Developmentalists now believe that each child needs individualized care.

For example, fearful children require reassurance, while impulsive ones need strong guidelines. Parents of such children may, to outsiders, seem permissive or authoritarian. Every child needs protection and guidance; some more than others. The right balance depends on the particular child (differential susceptibility again).

A study of parenting at age 2 and children's competence in kindergarten (including emotional regulation and friendships) found "multiple developmental pathways," with the best outcomes dependent on both the child and the adult (Blandon et al., 2010). Simplistic advice—from a professional, a neighbor, or a textbook author (me) who does not know the child—may be misguided. Longitudinal, unbiased observation of parent–child interactions is needed before judging that a caregiver is too lax or too rigid.

Given a multi-cultural and multi-contextual perspective, developmentalists realize that many parenting practices are sometimes effective. But that does not mean that all families function equally well—far from it. Signs of emotional distress, including a child's anxiety, aggression, and inability to play with others, indicate that the family may not be the safe haven of support and guidance that it should be. Neglectful parenting is always harmful.

A detailed study of Mexican American mothers of 4-year-olds noted 1,477 instances when the mothers tried to change their children's behavior. Most of the time the mothers simply uttered a command and the children complied (Livas-Dlott et al., 2010).

This simple strategy, with the mother asserting authority and the children obeying without question, might be considered authoritarian. Almost never, however, did the mothers use physical punishment or even harsh threats when the children did not immediately do as they were told—which happened 14 percent of the time. For example:

> Hailey [the 4-year-old] decided to look for another doll and started digging through her toys, throwing them behind her as she dug. Maricruz [the mother] told Hailey she should not throw her toys. Hailey continued to throw toys, and Maricruz said her name to remind her to stop. Hailey continued her misbehavior,

and her mother repeated "Hailey" once more. When Hailey continued, Maricruz raised her voice but calmly directed, "Hailey, look at me." Hailey continued but then looked at Maricruz as she explained, "You don't throw toys; you could hurt someone." Finally, Hailey complied and stopped.

[Livas-Dlott et al., 2010, p. 572]

Note that the mother's first three efforts failed, and then a "look" accompanied by an explanation (albeit inaccurate in that setting, as no one could be hurt) succeeded. The Mexican American families did not fit any of Baumrind's categories; respect (*respeto*) for adult authority did not mean an authoritarian relationship. Instead, the relationship shows evident caring (*cariño*) (Livas-Dlott et al., 2010).

As in this example, parenting practices may arise from cultural values that need to be recognized and appreciated (Butler & Titus, 2015). This does not mean that every cultural practice is acceptable. Harsh or cold parenting is always harmful, increasing child anger and aggression no matter what the culture or the nature of the child (Dyer et al., 2014; Wang & Liu, 2018).

Discipline

Children misbehave. They do not always do what adults want them to do. Sometimes they do not know better, but sometimes they deliberately ignore a request, even doing exactly what they have been told not to do.

Since misbehavior is part of growing up, and since children need guidance to keep them safe and strong, parents must respond. Most do so—rates of punishment increase dramatically from infancy (when it is rare) to early childhood, when most parents use several methods (Thompson et al., 2017). Every form of discipline has critics as well as defenders (Larzelere et al., 2017).

PHYSICAL PUNISHMENT In the United States, young children are slapped, spanked, or beaten more often than are infants or older children, and more often than children in Canada or western Europe. Spanking is more frequent:

- in the southern United States than in New England,
- by mothers than by fathers,
- among conservative Christians than among nonreligious families,
- among African Americans than among European Americans,
- among European Americans than among Asian Americans,
- among U.S.-born Hispanics than among immigrant Hispanics, and
- in low-SES families than in high-SES families.

(MacKenzie et al., 2011; S. Lee et al., 2015; Lee & Altschul, 2015)

These are general trends, but do not stereotype. Contrary to these generalizations, some African American mothers living in the South never spank, and some secular, European American, high-SES fathers in New England routinely do. Local norms matter, but individual parents make their own decisions.

Controversy particularly swirls around physical punishment (called **corporal punishment** because it hurts the body). Such punishment usually succeeds momentarily because children become quiet, but longitudinal research finds that corporally punished children are more disobedient later on, and are more likely to become child bullies, adolescent delinquents, and then abusive adults (Gershoff et al., 2012).

That research is hard for some people to believe, because most North American adults were spanked as children and few consider themselves worse because of it. The effects of spanking vary from one person to another.

corporal punishment
Discipline techniques that hurt the body (*corpus*) of someone, from spanking to serious harm, including death.

Smack Will the doll learn never to disobey her mother again?

Longitudinal research finds that children who are *not* spanked are *more* likely to develop self-control. The correlation between spanking and later aggression is significant. Remember that correlation shows a connection between two variables; it does not prove that one variable always leads to another. Thus, many spanked children do not become unusually aggressive adults. Nonetheless, the correlation is found in all ethnic groups, in many nations (Lansford et al., 2014; Wang & Liu, 2018).

The influence of custom is notable. In 53 nations, including all of northern Europe, corporal punishment is illegal; in many other nations, it is the norm. A massive international study of low- and moderate-income nations found that 63 percent of 2- to 5-year-olds had been physically punished (slapped, spanked, hit with an object) in the past month (Deater-Deckard & Lansford, 2016).

In more than 100 nations, physical punishment is illegal in schools, but each U.S. state sets laws; teachers may legally paddle children in 22 of them. Overall, in the United States in one recent year, 218,466 children were corporally punished at school. Sixteen percent of those children had intellectual disabilities, and a disproportionate number were African American boys (Morones, 2013; Gershoff et al., 2015). Worldwide, boys are punished slightly more often than girls.

A study in one American state (Arkansas) that allows corporal punishment in school reports that whether or not a child is physically punished depends more on the school culture than on the state or district policy. Cohort is influential. In general, paddling decreased over the past decade. However, suspensions (the school equivalent of time-out) increased (McKenzie & Ritter, 2017).

The rate of discipline in Arkansas in the 2015–2016 school year was 59 per 100 students, with 5 per 100 including physical punishment. That ratio does not mean that more than half of the students were disciplined or that 5 percent of the students were paddled, because some students experienced more than 10 punishments (some were paddled several times) while most (especially the younger girls) were never punished. Rates were much higher in middle schools than elementary schools. The most common infractions were "minor, non-violent," when students did not obey their teacher or follow school guidelines.

Although some adults believe that physical punishment will "teach a lesson" to behave, others argue that the lesson learned is that "might makes right." Children who were physically disciplined tend to become more aggressive (Thompson et al., 2017). They also are more likely to use corporal punishment on others—first on their classmates, and later on their wives or husbands, and then their children.

THINK CRITICALLY: The varying rates of physical punishment in schools could be the result of prejudice, or they could be because some children misbehave more than others. Which is it?

◆ **Especially for Parents**
Suppose you agree that spanking is destructive, but you sometimes get so angry at your child's behavior that you hit him or her. Is your reaction appropriate? (see response, page 229)

ALTERNATIVES TO SPANKING If spanking is bad but discipline is good, what is a parent to do? Some employ **psychological control,** using children's shame, guilt, and gratitude to control their behavior (Barber, 2002). But this has its own problems (Alegre, 2011).

Consider Finland, where corporal punishment is forbidden. In one study, psychological control was measured by how much parents agreed with the following statements:

1. "My child should be aware of how much I have done for him/her."
2. "I let my child see how disappointed and shamed I am if he/she misbehaves."
3. "My child should be aware of how much I sacrifice for him/her."
4. "I expect my child to be grateful and appreciate all the advantages he/she has."

psychological control
A disciplinary technique that involves threatening to withdraw love and support, using a child's feelings of guilt and gratitude to the parents.

OPPOSING PERSPECTIVES

Is Spanking OK?

Opinions about spanking are influenced by past experience and cultural norms. That makes it hard for opposing perspectives to be understood by people on the other side (Ferguson, 2013). Try to suspend your own assumptions as you read this.

What might be right with spanking? Over the centuries, many parents have done it, so it has stood the test of time and has been a popular choice. Spanking is less common in the twenty-first century than in the twentieth (Taillieu et al., 2014), but 85 percent of U.S. adolescents who were children at the end of the twentieth century recall being slapped or spanked by their mothers (Bender et al., 2007). In low- and middle-income nations, more than a third of the mothers believe that physical punishment is essential to raise a child well (Deater-Deckard & Lansford, 2016).

Those who are pro-spanking need to explain the correlations reported by developmentalists (between spanking and later depression, low achievement, aggression, crime, and so on). They suggest that a third variable, not spanking itself, is the reason for that connection. One possible third variable is misbehavior: Perhaps disobedient children cause spanking, not vice versa. Such children may become delinquent, depressed, and so on not because they were spanked but in spite of being spanked.

Noting problems with correlational research, one team explains, "Quite simply, parents do not need to use corrective actions when there are no problems to correct" (Larzelere & Cox, 2013, p. 284). As these authors explain, although it is true that children who are spanked frequently are also children who misbehave frequently, the punishment may be the result of the child's actions, not the cause.

Further, since parents who spank their children often have less education and money than other parents, low SES may be another crucial variable. Perhaps spanking is a symptom of poverty and poor parenting. If that is true, the way to reduce the low achievement, aggression, and depression that correlates with spanking is to increase education and reduce poverty, not to ban spanking (Ferguson, 2013).

Another criticism is the way the scientists define spanking. If they do not distinguish between severe corporal punishment and milder, occasional spanking, then the data will show that spanking is harmful—but that conclusion may reflect the harmful effects of severe punishment (Larzelere et al., 2017).

What might be wrong with spanking? One problem is adults' emotions: Angry spankers may become abusive. Children have been seriously injured and even killed by parents who use corporal punishment.

Another problem is the child's immature cognition. Parents assume that the transgression is obvious, but children may think that the parents' anger, not the child's actions, caused spanking (Harkness et al., 2011). Most parents tell their children why they are being spanked, but when they are hit, children are less likely to listen or understand.

Almost all of the research finds that children who are physically punished suffer overall (Grogan-Kaylor et al., 2018). Compared to children punished in other ways, they are more depressed, antisocial, and lonely. Many hate school and have few close friends. Emotional and social problems in adulthood are more common in people who were spanked as children—true for relatively mild spanking as well as for more severe spanking.

One reason for these correlations is that spanked children more often have angry, depressed, unloving parents. However, even among children of warm and loving parents, spanked children tend to be more anxious, worried about doing something to lose their parents' affection (Lansford et al., 2014).

Of course, there are exceptions, spanked children who become happy and successful adults. For example, one U.S. study found that conservative Protestant parents spanked their children more often than other parents, but if that spanking occurred only in early (not middle) childhood, the children did not develop low self-esteem and increased aggression (Ellison et al., 2011).

The authors of the study suggest that, since spanking was the norm in that group, the children believed they were loved. Moreover, religious leaders tell parents never to spank in anger. As a result, their children may "view mild-to-moderate corporal punishment as legitimate, appropriate, and even an indicator of parental involvement, commitment, and concern" (Ellison et al., 2011, p. 957).

Another study of conservative Christians found that many thought their faith condoned spanking. Only when they learned biblical lessons opposing spanking (e.g., that "sparing the rod" refers to the guiding rod that shepherds use, not a punishing stick) and learned research on the long-term harm did they change their minds (Perrin et al., 2017). Many then conclude that physical punishment is contrary to the message of love and forgiveness that they believe.

As I write these words, I know which perspective is mine. I am one of many developmentalists who believe that alternatives to spanking are better for children and a safeguard against abuse. Indeed, the same study that found spanking common in developing nations also reported that 17 percent of the children experienced severe violence that no developmentalist would condone (Bornstein et al., 2016). That alone is reason to stop.

Nonetheless, a dynamic-systems, multi-cultural perspective reminds me that everyone is influenced by background and context. I know that I am; so is every scientist, and so are you.

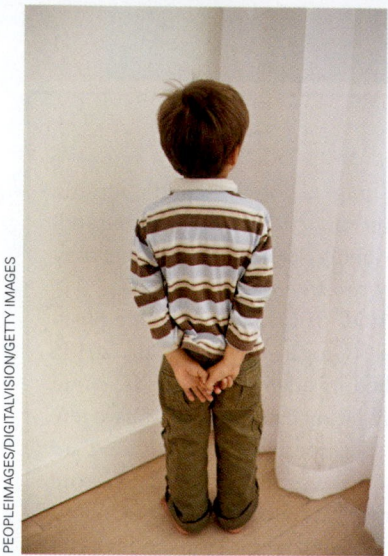

Bad Boy or Bad Parent? For some children and in some cultures, sitting alone is an effective form of punishment. Sometimes, however, it produces an angry child without changing the child's behavior.

↑ **OBSERVATION** QUIZ
We hope this is a staged photo, not a real one. Why? (see answer, page 229)

time-out
A disciplinary technique in which a person is separated from other people and activities for a specified time.

induction
A disciplinary technique in which the parent tries to get the child to understand why a certain behavior was wrong. Listening, not lecturing, is crucial.

sex differences
Biological differences between males and females, in organs, hormones, and body shape.

gender differences
Differences in male and female roles, behaviors, clothes, and so on that arise from society, not biology.

The higher the parents scored on these four measures of psychological control, the lower the children's math scores were—and this connection grew stronger over time. Moreover, the children tended to have negative emotions (depression, anger, and so on) (Aunola et al., 2013).

Another disciplinary technique often used in North America is the **time-out,** in which a misbehaving child is required to sit quietly, without toys or playmates, for a short time. Time-out is not to be done in anger, or for too long; it is recommended that parents use a calm voice and that the time-out last only one to five minutes (Morawska & Sanders, 2011). Time-out is punishment *if* the child enjoys "time-in," when the child is engaged with parents or with peers.

Time-out is favored by many experts. For example, in the large, longitudinal evaluation of the Head Start program highlighted in Chapter 5, an increase in time-outs and a decrease in spankings were considered signs of improved parental discipline (U.S. Department of Health and Human Services, 2010).

However, the same team who criticized the correlation between spanking and misbehavior also criticized the research favoring time-out. They added, "misbehavior is motivated by wanting to escape from the situation . . . time-out reinforces the misbehavior" (Larzelere & Cox, 2013, p. 289).

Often combined with the time-out is another alternative to physical punishment and psychological control—**induction,** in which the parents discuss the infraction with their child, hoping the children themselves will realize why their behavior was wrong. Ideally, a strong and affectionate parent–child relationship allows children to express their emotions and parents to listen.

Induction takes time and patience. Children confuse causes with consequences and tend to think they behaved properly, given the situation. Simple induction ("Why did he cry?") may be appropriate, but even that is hard before a child develops theory of mind. Nonetheless, induction may pay off over time. Children whose parents used induction when they were 3-year-olds became children with fewer externalizing problems in elementary school (Choe et al., 2013b).

What do parents actually do? A survey of discipline in early childhood found that most parents use more than one method (Thompson et al., 2017). In the United States, time-out is the most common punishment, and about half of the parents sometimes spank. The survey found that other methods—induction, counting, distraction, hand-smacking, removal of a toy or activity—were also used.

Specifics of parenting style and punishment seem less crucial than whether or not children know that they are loved, guided, and appreciated (Grusec et al., 2017). Many parents may seem to be authoritarian, but the crucial variable is how loving and warm they are: If that love is evident, their children may have higher achievement and pride than their peers (Pinquart & Kauser, 2018). Every parent needs to figure out the best way to love and guide their children.

Becoming Boys or Girls: Sex and Gender

Another challenge for caregivers is to promote a healthy understanding of sex and gender (Wilcox & Kline, 2013). This is difficult for every parent.

Biology determines whether an embryo is male or female (except in rare cases): Those XX or XY chromosomes shape organs and produce hormones, creating **sex differences,** which are biological. That is distinct from **gender differences,** which are cultural. In theory this distinction seems simple; in practice it is complex. Regarding sex and gender, scientists need to "treat culture and biology not as separate influences but as interacting components of nature and nurture" (Eagly & Wood, 2013, p. 349).

Many adults follow gender norms. A 2017 survey found that most adults thought parents should encourage their children to play with toys associated with the other sex,

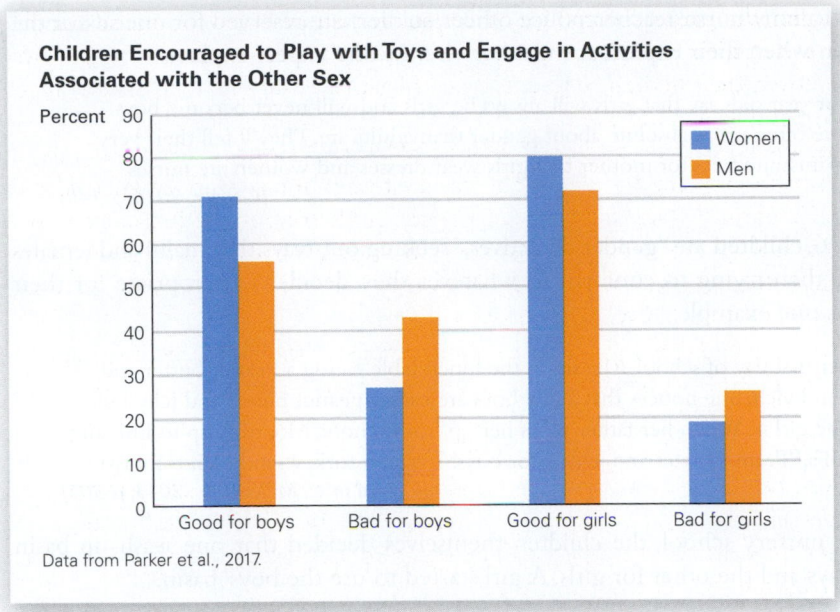

Children Encouraged to Play with Toys and Engage in Activities Associated with the Other Sex

Data from Parker et al., 2017.

FIGURE 6.2 Similarities? What is more remarkable—that most people think girls should be encouraged to play with trucks and boys encouraged to play with dolls, or that some people do not? Your answer probably depends on whether you thought gender equality was achieved, or is still far away.

↑ OBSERVATION QUIZ
Although this data can be read as evidence that we are moving toward gender equity, all four sets of percentages show strong gender influence. How? (See answer, page 229)

but a sizable minority disagreed (Parker et al., 2017). The highest disagreement was expressed by men regarding boys: 43 percent of the men thought boys should **not** be encouraged to do things usually stereotyped for girls, such as care for dolls, jump rope, or wear bracelets (see Figure 6.2).

Sex and gender issues are particularly challenging when children identify as *transgender*, wanting to be a gender that is not their biological sex. This presents their parents with a challenge that almost no parent anticipated a decade ago (Rahilly, 2015).

Gender distinctions are pervasive and lifelong, beginning with the blue or pink caps put on newborns' heads and ending with the clothes put on a corpse before burial. Already by age 2, children use gender labels (*Mrs., Mr., lady, man*) consistently. By age 4, children believe that certain toys (such as dolls or trucks) and roles

Same Situation, Far Apart: Culture Clash? He wears the orange robes of a Buddhist monk, and she wears the hijab of a Muslim girl. Although he is at a weeklong spiritual retreat led by the Dalai Lama and she is in an alley in Pakistan, both carry universal toys—a pop gun and a bride doll, identical to those found almost everywhere.

(Daddy, Mommy, nurse, teacher, police officer, soldier) are reserved for one sex or the other, even when their experience is otherwise. As one expert explains:

> ...four year olds say that girls will always be girls and will never become boys....
> they are often more absolute about gender than adults are. They'll tell their very
> own pantssuited doctor mother that girls wear dresses and women are nurses.
> [Gopnik, 2016, p. 140]

By age 6, children are "gender detectives," seeking out ways that males and females differ and then trying to conform to whatever they decide is appropriate for their sex. Mia is one example:

> On her first day of school, Mia sits at the lunch table eating a peanut butter and
> jelly sandwich. She notices that a few boys are eating peanut butter and jelly, but
> not one girl is. When her father picks her up from school, Mia runs up to him and
> exclaims, "Peanut butter and jelly is for boys! I want a turkey sandwich tomorrow."
> [Quoted in C. Miller et al., 2013, p. 307]

In one nursery school, the children themselves decided that one wash-up basin was for boys and the other for girls. A girl started to use the boys' basin.

> **Boy:** This is for the boys.
> **Girl:** Stop it. I'm not a girl and a boy, so I'm here.
> **Boy:** What?
> **Girl:** I'm a boy and also a girl.
> **Boy:** You, now, are you today a boy?
> **Girl:** Yes.
> **Boy:** And tomorrow what will you be?
> **Girl:** A girl. Tomorrow I'll be a girl. Today I'll be a boy.
> **Boy:** And after tomorrow?
> **Girl:** I'll be a girl.
> [Ehrlich & Blum-Kulka, 2014, p. 31]

Although they may not understand biological sex, many children accept rigid male–female roles. Thus, this girl did not dispute the rule against girls using the boys' sink. Instead, since she wanted to use the sink, she said she was a boy.

Despite their parents' and teachers' wishes, children say, "No girls [or boys] allowed." Most older children consider ethnic discrimination immoral, but they accept some sex discrimination (Møller & Tenenbaum, 2011). Transgender children, likewise, are insistent that they are not the sex that their parents thought (Rahilly, 2015), rather than suggesting that gender roles themselves are too narrow.

Why are male and female distinctions recognized by 2-year-olds, significant to 5-year-olds, and accepted as proper by 10-year-olds? All of the major theories "devote considerable attention to gender differences. . . . The primary difference among the theories resides in the causal mechanism responsible" (Bornstein et al., 2016, pp. 10, 11). Consider the four comprehensive theories in Chapter 1.

PSYCHOANALYTIC THEORY Freud (1938/1995) called the period from about ages 3 to 6 the **phallic stage,** named after the *phallus,* the Greek word for penis. At age 3 or 4, said Freud, boys become aware of their male sexual organ. They masturbate, fear castration, and develop sexual feelings toward their mother.

These feelings make every young boy jealous of his father—so jealous, according to Freud, that he wants to replace his dad. Freud called this the **Oedipus complex,** after Oedipus, son of a king in an ancient Greek drama. Abandoned as an infant and raised in a distant kingdom, Oedipus returned to his birthplace and, without realizing who they were, killed his father and married his mother. When he discovered the horror, he blinded himself.

phallic stage
Freud's third stage of development, when the penis becomes the focus of concern and pleasure.

Oedipus complex
The unconscious desire of young boys to replace their fathers and win their mothers' exclusive love.

Freud believed that this ancient story (immortalized in *Oedipus Rex,* a play written by Sophocles and first presented in Athens in 429 B.C.E., still presented every year somewhere in the world) dramatizes the overwhelming emotions that all 5-year-old boys feel about their parents—both love and hate. Every boy feels guilty about his incestuous and murderous impulses. In self-defense, he develops a powerful conscience called the *superego,* which is quick to judge and punish.

That marks the beginning of morality, according to psychoanalytic theory. This theory contends that a small boy's fascination with superheroes, guns, kung fu, and the like arises from his unconscious impulse to kill his father. Further, an adult man's homosexuality, homophobia, or obsession with guns, pornography, prostitutes, or hell arises from problems at the phallic stage.

Freud offered several descriptions of the moral development of girls. One, called the *Electra complex,* is again named after an ancient Greek drama. Freud thought that girls also want to eliminate their same-sex parent (mother) and become intimate with the opposite-sex parent (father). That explains why many 5-year-old girls dress in frills and lace, and are happy to be "daddy's girl."

Many psychologists criticize psychoanalytic theory as being unscientific. That was my opinion in graduate school, so I dismissed Freud's ideas and I deliberately dressed my baby girls in blue, not pink, so that they would not follow stereotypes. However, scientists seek to reconcile theory and experience. My daughters made me reconsider. (See A Case to Study on page 212.)

BEHAVIORISM Behaviorists believe that virtually all roles, values, and morals are learned. To behaviorists, gender distinctions result from reinforcement, punishment, and social learning, evident in early childhood.

Indeed, the push toward traditional gender behavior in play and chores (washing dishes versus fixing cars) is among the most robust findings of decades of research on this topic (Eagly & Wood, 2013). For example, a 2-year-old boy who asks for a train and a doll for his birthday is more likely to get the train. Sex differences are taught more to boys than girls.

Gender differentiation may be subtle, with adults unaware that they are reinforcing traditional masculine or feminine behavior. For example, parents talking to young children mention numbers and shapes more often with their sons (Chang et al., 2011; Pruden & Levine, 2017). This may be a precursor to the boys becoming more interested in math and science later on. Even with infants, fathers interact differently with their children, singing and talking more to their daughters but using words of achievement, such as *proud* and *win,* more with their sons (Mascaro et al., 2017).

Test Your Imagination
Preschool children have impressive imaginations and strong social impulses. When two friends are together, they launch into amazing fun, drinking tea, crossing swords, wearing special masks and bracelets, or whatever. Adults may be more limited—can you picture these two scenes with genders switched, the boys in the tea party and the girls in the sword fight?

A CASE TO STUDY

The Berger Daughters

It began when my eldest daughter, Bethany, was about 4 years old:

Bethany: When I grow up, I'm going to marry Daddy.
Me: But Daddy's married to me.
Bethany: That's OK. When I grow up, you'll probably be dead.
Me: *[Determined to stick up for myself]* Daddy's older than me, so when I'm dead, he'll probably be dead, too.
Bethany: That's OK. I'll marry him when he gets born again.

I was dumbfounded, without a good reply. Bethany saw my face fall, and she took pity on me:

Bethany: Don't worry, Mommy. After you get born again, you can be our baby.

The second episode was a conversation I had with Rachel when she was about 5:

Rachel: When I get married, I'm going to marry Daddy.
Me: Daddy's already married to me.
Rachel: *[With the joy of having discovered a wonderful plan]* Then we can have a double wedding!

The third episode was considerably more graphic. It took the form of a "Valentine" left on my husband's pillow on February 14 by my daughter Elissa (see Figure 6.3).

Finally, when Sarah turned 5, she also said she would marry her father. I tried one more time: I told her she

FIGURE 6.3 Pillow Talk Elissa placed this artwork on my husband's pillow. My pillow, beside it, had a less colorful, less elaborate note—an afterthought. It read, "Dear Mom, I love you too."

couldn't, because he was married to me. Her response revealed the hazard of screen time: "Oh, yes, a man can have two wives. I saw it on television."

As you remember from Chapter 1, a single example (or four daughters from one family) does not prove that Freud was correct. I still think he was wrong on many counts. But, his description of the phallic stage seems less bizarre than I once thought.

According to social learning theory, people model themselves after people they perceive to be nurturing, powerful, and yet similar to themselves. For young children, those people are usually their parents, who are the most gender-typed of their entire lives when they are raising young children.

Generally, if an employed woman is ever to leave her job to become a housewife, it is when she has a baby. Fathers tend to work longer hours—they are home less often—and mothers work fewer hours when children arrive. Since children learn gender roles from their parents, it is no surprise that they are quite sexist (Hallers-Haalboom et al., 2014). They follow the examples they see, unaware that their very existence is the reason for that behavior.

Reinforcement for distinct male and female actions is widespread. As the president of the Society for Research in Child Development observes, "parents, teachers, and peers . . . continue to encourage, model, and enforce traditional gender messages" (Liben, 2016, p. 24). The 3-year-old boy who brings his Barbie doll to preschool will be punished—not physically, but with words and social exclusion—by his male classmates. As social learning increases from age 2 to 22, so does gender divergence.

COGNITIVE THEORY Cognitive theory offers an alternative explanation for the strong gender identity of 5-year-olds (Kohlberg et al., 1983). Remember that cognitive theorists focus on how children understand various ideas. Regarding boys and girls, they construct a **gender schema,** an understanding of male–female differences (Bem, 1981; Martin et al., 2011).

As cognitive theorists point out, young children tend to perceive the world in simple, egocentric terms, as explained in Chapter 5. Therefore, they categorize male and female as opposites. Nuances, complexities, exceptions, and gradations about gender (and about everything else) are beyond them.

During the preoperational stage, appearance is stronger than logic. One group of researchers who endorse the cognitive interpretation note that "young children pass through a stage of gender appearance rigidity; girls insist on wearing dresses, often pink and frilly, whereas boys refuse to wear anything with a hint of femininity" (Halim et al., 2014, p. 1091).

In research reported by this group, the parents discouraged sexism, but that did not sway a girl who wanted a bright pink tutu and a sparkly tiara. The child's gender schema overcame the parents' fight against gender stereotypes. In effect, children develop a theory—theory to explain what they experience.

Not all parents think sexual distinctions are wrong. "Sometimes gender-traditional messages are conveyed deliberately. . . . Many fathers and mothers dream of raising their sons and daughters to join them in traditional masculine and feminine pastimes" (Liben, 2016, p. 24). Gender schemas are everywhere (Starr & Zurbriggen, 2016). Deliberate messages from the parents and the culture, added to children's simplistic thinking, explain gender stereotypes, according to cognitive theory.

EVOLUTIONARY THEORY Evolutionary theory holds that sexual passion is a basic human drive because all creatures have a powerful impulse to reproduce. Since conception requires an ovum and a sperm, males and females follow their evolutionary mandate by seeking to attract the other sex—walking, talking, and laughing in traditional feminine or masculine ways.

This evolutionary drive may explain why, already in early childhood, boys have a powerful urge to become like the men, and girls like the women. This will prepare them, later on, to mate and conceive a new generation.

Evolutionary theory emphasizes the urge to survive as well as the urge to reproduce. Over millennia of human history, genes, chromosomes, and hormones dictate that young boys are more active (rough-and-tumble play) and girls more domestic (playing house). That prepares them for adulthood, when fathers needed to defend against predators and mothers needed to care for the home and children.

MIKE BELLEME

Not Emma In a North Carolina kindergarten, each child had an "All About Me" day in which the teacher would draw a picture of the child for all the other children to copy. Emma was born with male sex organs but identifies as a girl. On her day, she proudly wore a light pink shirt with a heart, pink glittery shoes, and long hair—and came home bawling because the teacher drew this picture with her "boy name" (barely visible here). Her parents consoled her, had her edit her name and draw longer hair, with some other additions. Shouldn't children be allowed to be who they know themselves to be?

gender schema
A child's cognitive concept or general belief about male and female differences.

THINK CRITICALLY: Should children be encouraged to express both male and female characteristics, or is learning male and female roles crucial for becoming a happy man or woman?

What Is Best?

Each major developmental theory strives to explain the ideas that young children express and the roles they follow. No consensus has been reached. That challenges caregivers because they know they should not blindly follow the norms of their culture, yet they also know that they need to provide guidance regarding male–female differences and everything else.

Regarding sex or gender, those who contend that nature (sex) is more important than nurture (gender) tend to design, cite, and believe studies that endorse their perspective. That has been equally true for those who believe that nurture is more important than nature. Only recently has a true interactionist perspective, emphasizing how nature affects nurture and vice versa, been promoted (Eagly & Wood, 2013).

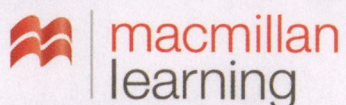

empathy
The ability to understand the emotions and concerns of another person, especially when they differ from one's own.

antipathy
Feelings of dislike or even hatred for another person.

prosocial behavior
Actions that are helpful and kind but that are of no obvious benefit to the person doing them.

antisocial behavior
Actions that are deliberately hurtful or destructive to another person.

Pinch, Poke, or Pat Antisocial and prosocial responses are actually a sign of maturation: Babies do not recognize the impact of their actions. These children have much more to learn, but they already are quite social.

Some recent research suggests a *gender similarities hypothesis,* the idea that our human emphasis on sex differences blinds us to the reality that the two sexes have far more in common than traditional theories recognize (Hyde, 2016). Perhaps instead of looking for sex differences, we should notice gender similarities. According to some researchers, similarities far outweigh differences in the brain, body, and behavior (Roseberry & Roos, 2016; Zhang, 2018).

Teaching Right and Wrong

Parents want their children to develop a morality that is in accord with the parents' understanding of right and wrong. Children have a sense of good and bad, an outgrowth of bonding, attachment, and cognitive maturation. Even infants may have a moral sense: An experiment found 6-month-olds preferring a puppet who helped another puppet, not an unhelpful one (Hamlin, 2014).

According to evolutionary theory, the survival of our species depended on protection, cooperation, and even sacrifice for one another. Humans needed group defense against harsh conditions and large predators. Morality evolved because humans need each other to survive (Dunning, 2011). Thus, our bodies produce hormones, especially oxytocin, that push people toward trust, love, and morality (Zak, 2012).

With the cognitive advances of early childhood, and increased interaction with peers, these innate moral impulses are strengthened. Children develop **empathy,** an understanding of other people's feelings and concerns, and **antipathy,** a feeling of dislike, disdain, or even hatred.

Empathy leads to compassion and **prosocial behavior**—helpfulness and kindness without any obvious personal benefit. Expressing concern, offering to share, and including a shy child in a game are examples of children's prosocial behavior. The opposite is **antisocial behavior,** hurting other people.

Prosocial behavior seems to result more from emotion than from intellect, more from empathy than from theory (Eggum et al., 2011). The origins of prosocial behavior can be traced to parents who help children understand their own emotions, not from parents who tell children what emotions others might have (Brownell et al., 2013).

The link between empathy and prosocial behavior was traced longitudinally in children from 18 months to 6 years. Empathetic 2-year-olds were more likely to share, help, and play with other children in the first grade (Z. Taylor et al., 2013).

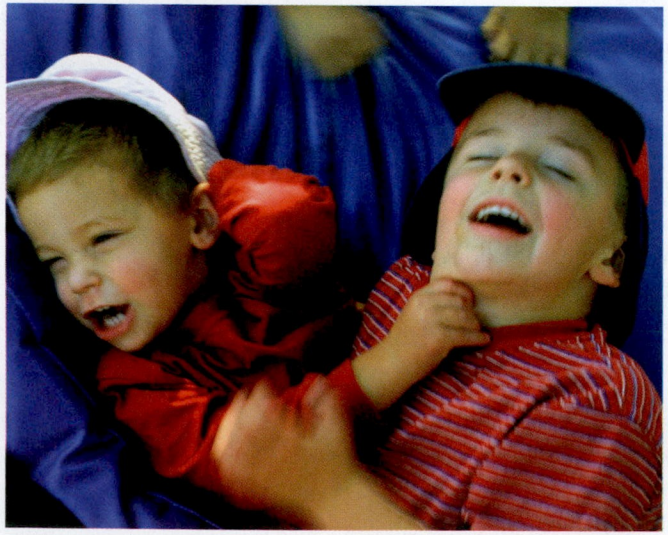

Prosocial reactions are inborn but not automatic. Some children limit empathy by "avoiding contact with the person in need [which illustrates] . . . the importance of emotion development and regulation in the development of prosocial behavior" and the influence of cultural norms (Trommsdorff & Cole, 2011, p. 136). Feeling distress may be a part of nature, but whether and how a child expresses it is nurture.

Antipathy leads to antisocial actions, which include verbal insults, social exclusion, and physical assaults (Calkins & Keane, 2009). That also may be inborn, as well as learned. A 2-year-old might look at another child, scowl, and then kick hard without provocation. Generally, parents and teachers teach better behavior, and children become more prosocial and less antisocial with age (Ramani et al., 2010).

An interesting example comes from attitudes about possessions. Two-year-olds find it hard to share, even to let another child use a crayon that they have already used. They have a sense of ownership: A teacher's crayon should be shared, but if a child brought it, the other children believe that child is allowed to be selfish (Neary & Friedman, 2014). This returns us to the nature–nurture controversy.

The rules of ownership are understood by children as young as 3, who apply them quite strictly. Consider how this develops over time. Some adolescents come to blows over sunglasses or shoes; some adults kill over what belongs to whom. Others are much more likely to lose, share, or give away. How much of those reactions are innate, and how much learned?

At every age, antisocial behavior indicates less empathy. That may originate in the brain. An allele or gene may have gone awry (Portnoy et al., 2013). But at least for children, lack of empathy correlates with parents who neither discuss nor respond to emotions (Z. Taylor et al., 2013; Richards et al., 2014).

AGGRESSION Not surprisingly, given their moral sensibilities, young children judge whether another child's aggression is justified or not. The focus is on effects, not motives: A child who accidentally spilled water on another's painting may be the target of that child's justified anger.

As with adults, impulsive self-defense is more readily forgiven than is a deliberate, unprovoked attack. As young children gain in social understanding, particularly theory of mind, they gradually become better at understanding intentions, and that makes them more likely to forgive an accident (Choe et al., 2013a).

The distinction between impulse and intention is critical in deciding when and how a child's aggression needs to be stopped. Researchers recognize four general types of aggression, each of which is evident in early childhood (see Table 6.2).

TABLE 6.2 The Four Forms of Aggression

Type of Aggression	Definition	Comments
Instrumental aggression	Hurtful behavior that is aimed at gaining something (such as a toy, a place in line, or a turn on the swing) that someone else has	Apparent from age 2 to 6; involves objects more than people; quite normal; more egocentric than antisocial.
Reactive aggression	An impulsive retaliation for a hurt (intentional or accidental) that can be verbal or physical	Indicates a lack of emotional regulation, characteristic of 2-year-olds. A 5-year-old can usually stop and think before reacting.
Relational aggression	Nonphysical acts, such as insults or social rejection, aimed at harming the social connections between the victim and others	Involves a personal attack and thus is directly antisocial; can be very hurtful; more common as children become socially aware.
Bullying aggression	Unprovoked, repeated physical or verbal attack, especially on victims who are unlikely to defend themselves	In both bullies and victims, a sign of poor emotional regulation; adults should intervene before the school years. (Bullying is discussed in Chapter 8.)

instrumental aggression
Hurtful behavior that is intended to get something that another person has.

reactive aggression
An impulsive retaliation for another person's intentional or accidental hurtful action.

relational aggression
Nonphysical acts, such as insults or social rejection, aimed at harming the social connection between the victim and other people.

bullying aggression
Unprovoked, repeated physical or verbal attack, especially on victims who are unlikely to defend themselves.

Instrumental aggression is common among 2-year-olds, who often want something and try to get it. This is called *instrumental* because it is a tool, or instrument, for getting something that is desired. The harm in grabbing a toy, and hitting if someone resists, is not understood by the child.

Because instrumental aggression occurs, **reactive aggression** also is common among young children. Almost every child reacts when hurt, whether or not the hurt was deliberate. The reaction may be aggressive—a child might punch in response to an unwelcome remark—but as the prefrontal cortex matures, the impulse to strike back becomes controlled. Both instrumental aggression and reactive aggression are less often physical when children develop emotional regulation and theory of mind (Olson et al., 2011).

Relational aggression (usually verbal) destroys self-esteem and disrupts social networks. A child might tell another, "You can't be my friend" or "You are fat," hurting another's feelings. Worse, a child might spread rumors, or tell others not to play with so-and-so. These are examples of relational aggression, which becomes more hurtful and sometimes more common as social understanding advances.

The fourth and most ominous type is **bullying aggression,** done to dominate. Bullying aggression occurs among young children but should be stopped before kindergarten, when it becomes more destructive. Not only does it destroy the self-esteem of victims, it impairs the later development of the bullies, who learn habits that harm them lifelong. A 10-year-old bully may be feared and admired; a 50-year-old bully may be hated and lonely. (An in-depth discussion of bullying appears in Chapter 8.)

Most types of aggression become less common from ages 2 to 6, as the brain matures and empathy increases. In addition, children learn to use aggression selectively, which decreases victimization (Ostrov et al., 2014). Parents, peers, and preschool teachers are pivotal mentors in this learning process.

It is a mistake to expect children to regulate their emotions on their own. If they are not guided, they may develop destructive patterns. It is also a mistake to punish aggressors too harshly because that may increase reactive aggression and make it hard for them to learn to regulate their anger.

In other words, although there is evidence that children spontaneously judge others who harm people, there also is evidence that prosocial and antisocial behavior are learned (Smetana, 2013). Who teaches them? Parents, peers, and teachers. Close teacher–student relationships in preschool decrease aggression and victimization in elementary school. The probable reason: Children want to please the teachers, who guide them toward prosocial, not antisocial, behavior (Runions & Shaw, 2013).

what have you learned?

1. What are the four main styles of parenting?

2. What are the consequences of each style of parenting?

3. Why is discipline part of being a parent?

4. What are the arguments for and against corporal punishment?

5. When is time-out effective and when is it not?

6. What are the differences between the psychoanalytic and behaviorist theories of gender development?

7. What are the differences between the cognitive and evolutionary theories of sex-role development?

8. How might children develop empathy and antipathy as they play with one another?

9. How much of moral development is innate and how much is learned?

10. What are the similarities and differences of the four kinds of aggression?

Harm to Children

We have saved the worst for last. The goal of the study of human development is to help all people to develop their full potential lifelong. Every culture particularly cherishes the young. Communities provide education, health care, and playgrounds; parents, grandparents, and strangers of every income, ethnicity, and nation seek to protect children while fostering their growth.

Nevertheless, far more children are harmed by acts of commission or omission (deliberate or accidental violence) than from any specific disease. In the United States, almost four times as many 1- to 4-year-olds die of accidents than of cancer, which is the leading cause of disease death during these years (National Center for Health Statistics, 2017).

Avoidable Injury

Worldwide, injuries cause millions of premature deaths among adults as well as children: Not until age 40 does any specific disease overtake accidents as a cause of mortality.

In some nations, malnutrition, malaria, and other infectious diseases *combined* cause more infant and child deaths than injuries do, but those nations also have high rates of child injury. Southern Asia and sub-Saharan Africa have the highest rates of motor-vehicle deaths, even though the number of cars is relatively low (World Health Organization, 2015). Most children who die in such accidents are pedestrians, or are riding—without a helmet—on motorcycles.

AGE-RELATED DANGERS In accidents overall, 2- to 6-year-olds are more often seriously hurt than 6- to 10-year-olds. Why are young children so vulnerable?

Immaturity of the prefrontal cortex makes young children impulsive; they plunge into danger. Unlike infants, their motor skills allow them to run, leap, scramble, and grab in a flash, before a caregiver can stop them. Their curiosity is boundless; their impulses are uninhibited. Then, if they do something dangerous, such as lighting a fire while playing with matches, fear and stress make them slow to get help.

Same Situation, Far Apart: Keeping Everyone Safe Preventing child accidents requires action by both adults and children. In the United States *(below left)*, adults passed laws and taught children—including this boy who buckles in his stuffed companion. In France *(below right)*, teachers stop cars while children hold hands to cross the street—each child keeping his or her partner moving ahead.

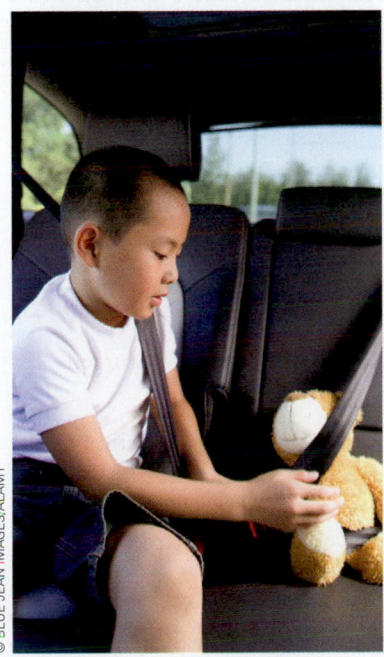

injury control/harm reduction
Reducing the potential negative consequences of behavior, such as safety surfaces replacing cement at a playground.

primary prevention
Actions that change overall background conditions to prevent some unwanted event or circumstance, such as injury, disease, or abuse.

secondary prevention
Actions that avert harm in a high-risk situation, such as using seat belts in cars.

tertiary prevention
Actions, such as immediate and effective medical treatment, after an adverse event (such as illness or injury).

◆ **Especially for Urban Planners**
Describe a neighborhood park that would benefit 2- to 5-year-olds. (see response, page 229)

Forget Baby Henry? Infants left in parked cars on hot days can die from the heat. Henry's father invented a disc to be placed under the baby that buzzes his cell phone if he is more than 20 feet away from the disc. He hopes all absent-minded parents will buy one.

Age-related trends are apparent in particulars. Falls are more often fatal for the youngest (under 24 months) and oldest (over 80 years) people; 1- to 4-year-olds have high rates of poisoning and drowning; motor-vehicle deaths peak from age 15 to 25.

Generally, as income falls, accident rates rise, but not for every cause. Not only are 1- to 4-year-olds more likely to die of drowning than any other age group, they drown in swimming pools six times more often than older children and adults (MMWR, May 16, 2014). Usually the deadly pool is in their own backyard, a luxury fewer low-income families enjoy.

INJURY CONTROL Instead of using the term *accident prevention,* public health experts prefer **injury control** (or **harm reduction**). Consider the implications. *Accident* implies that an injury is random, unpredictable; if anyone is at fault, it's a careless parent or an accident-prone child. Instead, *injury control* suggests that the impact of an injury can be limited, and *harm reduction* implies that harm can be minimized.

If young children are allowed to play to develop their skills, minor mishaps (scratches and bruises) are bound to occur. As explained in this chapter, children need to play. A child with no scrapes may be overprotected, but communities need to protect playing children. Serious injury is unlikely if a child falls on a safety surface instead of on concrete, if a car seat protects the body in a crash, if a bicycle helmet cracks instead of a skull, or if swallowed pills come from a tiny bottle.

Less than half as many 1- to 5-year-olds in the United States were fatally injured in 2015 as in 1980, thanks to laws that limit poisons, prevent fires, and regulate cars. Control has not yet caught up with newer hazards, however.

For instance, many new homes in California, Florida, Texas, and Arizona have swimming pools: In those states, drowning is a leading cause of child death. According to the American Association of Poison Control Centers' National Poison Data System, children under age 5 are now less often poisoned from pills and more often poisoned because of cosmetics or personal care products (deodorant, hair colorant, etc.) (Mowry et al., 2015, p. 968).

Prevention

Prevention begins long before any particular child, parent, or legislator does something foolish. Unfortunately, no one notices injuries and deaths that did not happen. However, developmentalists notice and advocate every level of prevention, especially primary prevention.

LEVELS OF PREVENTION Three levels of prevention apply to every health and safety issue.

- In **primary prevention,** the overall conditions are structured to make harm less likely. Laws and customs are crucial to reduce injury for people of every age.

- **Secondary prevention** is more targeted, averting harm in high-risk situations or for vulnerable individuals.

- **Tertiary prevention** begins after an injury has already occurred, limiting damage.

Tertiary prevention is the most visible, but primary prevention is the most effective. An example comes from data on pedestrian deaths. As compared with 20 years ago, although far more cars are on the road, far fewer children in the United States die in motor-vehicle crashes (see Figure 6.4). How does each level of prevention contribute?

Primary prevention includes sidewalks, pedestrian overpasses, streetlights, and traffic circles. Cars have been redesigned (e.g., better headlights, windows, and brakes), and drivers' competence has improved (e.g., stronger

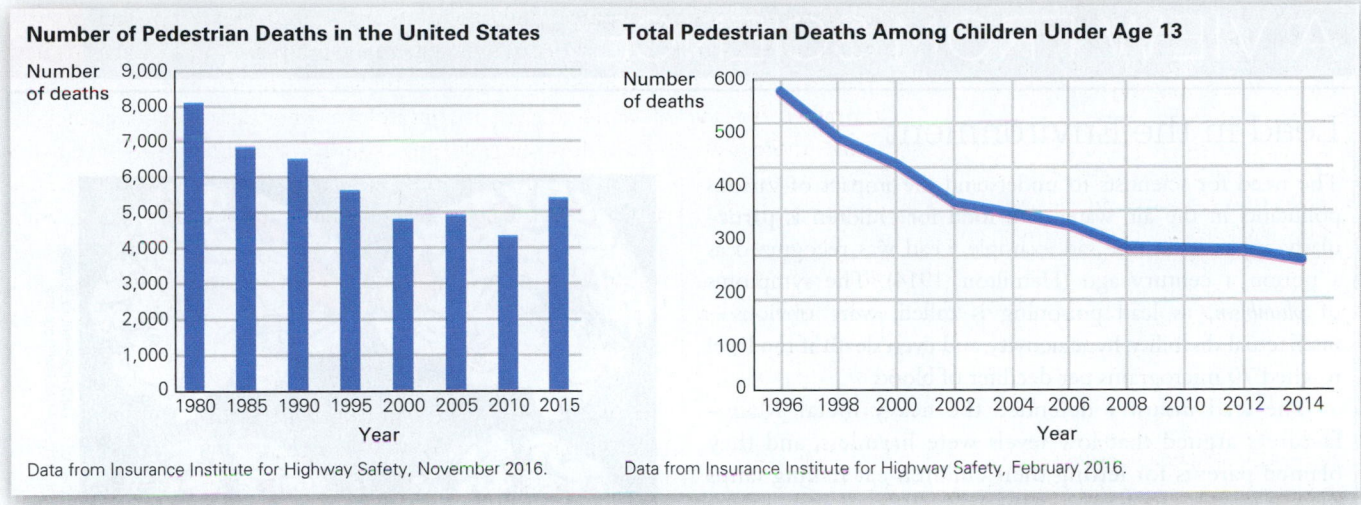

Number of Pedestrian Deaths in the United States

Data from Insurance Institute for Highway Safety, November 2016.

Total Pedestrian Deaths Among Children Under Age 13

Data from Insurance Institute for Highway Safety, February 2016.

FIGURE 6.4 **No Matter What Statistic** Motor-vehicle fatalities of pedestrians, passengers, and drivers, from cars, trucks, and motorcycles, for people of all ages, were all lower in 2015 than 1995, a dramatic difference since the population had increased by a third and the number of cars increased as well. Proof could be shown in a dozen charts, but here is one of the most telling: deaths of child pedestrians. All three levels of prevention, in roads, cars, drivers, police, caregivers, and the children themselves—contributed to this shift.

penalties for drunk driving). Reduction of traffic via improved mass transit can provide additional primary prevention.

Secondary prevention reduces danger in high-risk situations. Crossing guards and flashing lights on stopped schoolbuses are secondary prevention, as are salt on icy roads, warning signs before blind curves, speed bumps, and walk/don't walk signals at busy intersections.

Finally, *tertiary prevention* reduces damage after an accident. This includes speedy ambulances, efficient emergency room procedures, effective follow-up care, and laws against hit-and-run drivers, all of which have been improved from decades ago. Medical personnel speak of the *golden hour*, the hour following an accident, when a victim should be treated. Of course, there is nothing magical about 60 minutes in contrast to 61 minutes, but the faster an injury victim reaches a trauma center, the better the chance of recovery (Dinh et al., 2013).

The child death rate is lower for other reasons, as well. Air pollution has been reduced, so fewer children die of asthma. Poison control is more readily available, so fewer children die of swallowing toxins. And many pesticides are banned from home use, so fewer children swallow them.

In 1970, the rate of accident death was 10 per million children ages 1 to 14; in 2015, the rate was half of that (National Center for Health Statistics, 2017).

Evidence matters. It has led to community awareness and prevention. Children are no less curious than they were, cars are more common, and indeed, "the civilian gun stock has roughly doubled since 1968, from one gun per every two persons to one gun per person" according to a 2012 report to the U.S. Congress (Krouse, 2012, p. 9). Other sources also find more guns in homes. However, more parents hide and lock their guns, so only half as many children die of gun deaths.

Many pediatricians, newly aware of the research, advise safe firearm storage as well as locking up poisons. Sadly, school shootings (Sandy Hook, Parkland, Santa Fe) increase both gun purchases and accidental gun deaths of children (Levine & McKnight, 2017). Are newly purchased guns particularly lethal because purchasers are less careful?

For all these problems, the focus has been on physical injury, not on intellectual harm. That is the next challenge for developmentalists, as it is apparent that pollutants in air and water, and chemicals in household products and food, may harm the brain while having no impact on the body. This is particularly true in infancy and childhood, but it continues lifelong (Babadjouni et al., 2017).

It is difficult for any one person to prevent this harm, and government regulations are notoriously slow. Lead is a sobering example of this, as explained in A View from Science.

A VIEW FROM SCIENCE

Lead in the Environment

The need for scientists to understand the impact of various pollutants in the air, water, and food for children is particularly apparent in one sad example. Lead was recognized as a poison a century ago (Hamilton, 1914). The symptoms of *plumbism,* as lead poisoning is called, were obvious—intellectual disability, hyperactivity, and even death if the level reached 70 micrograms per deciliter of blood.

The lead industry defended the heavy metal. Manufacturers argued that low levels were harmless, and they blamed parents for letting their children eat flaking chips of lead paint (which tastes sweet).

Further, since children with high levels of lead in their blood were often from low-SES families, some argued that malnutrition, inadequate schools, family conditions, or a host of other causes were the reasons for their reduced IQ (Scarr, 1985). I am chagrined to confess that this argument made sense to me when I wrote the first edition of my textbook (Berger, 1980).

Lead remained a major ingredient in paint (it speeds drying) and in gasoline (it raises octane) for most of the twentieth century. Finally, chemical analyses of blood and teeth, with careful longitudinal and replicated research, proved that lead was indeed a poison for all children (Needleman et al., 1990; Needleman & Gatsonis, 1990).

The United States banned lead in paint (in 1978) and automobile fuel (in 1996). The blood level that caused plumbism was set at 40 micrograms per deciliter, then 20, and then 10. Danger is now thought to begin at 5 micrograms, but no level has been proven to be risk-free (MMWR, April 5, 2013). We now know that the fetus, infant, and young child absorb lead at a much higher rate than adults do, so lead's neurotoxicity is especially destructive of developing brains (Hanna-Attisha et al., 2016).

Regulation at the end of the twentieth century has made a difference (see Figure 6.5): The percentage of U.S. 1- to 5-year-olds with more than 5 micrograms of lead per deciliter of blood was 8.6 percent in 1999–2001, 4.1 percent in 2003–2006, 2.6 percent in 2007–2010, and less than 1 percent in 2010–2014 (Raymond & Brown, 2017). Children who are young, low-SES, and/or living in old housing tend to have higher levels (MMWR, April 5, 2013).

One preventive measure is to increase the consumption of dairy products, which help eliminate lead from the body (Kordas et al., 2018). Many parents now know to wipe window ledges clean, avoid child exposure to construction dust, test drinking water, discard lead-based medicines and crockery (available in some other nations), and prevent children from eating chips of lead-based paint. However, private

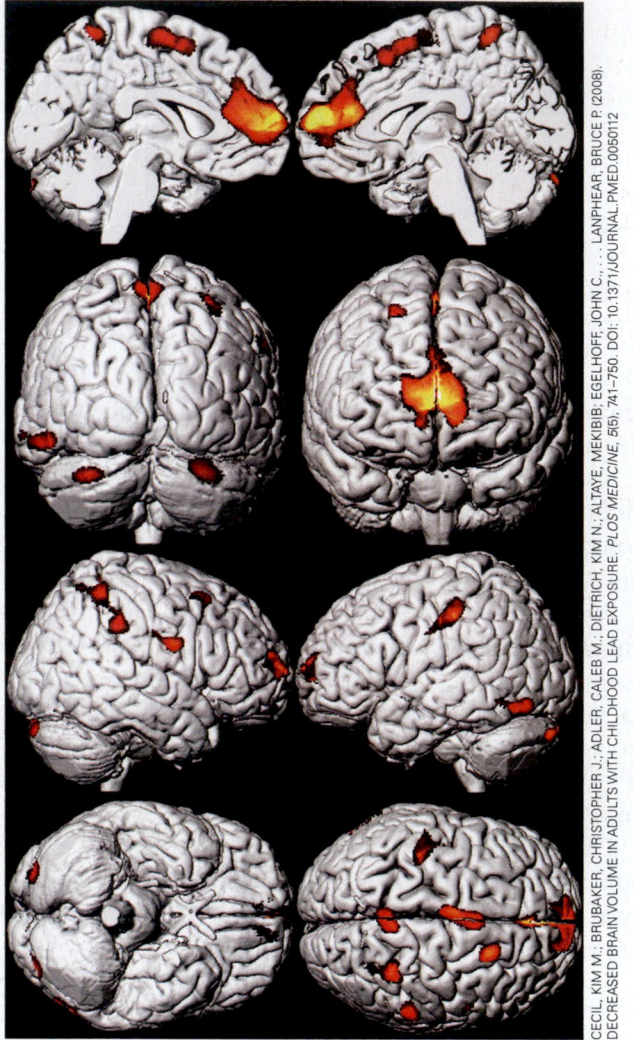

CECIL, KIM M.; BRUBAKER, CHRISTOPHER J.; ADLER, CALEB M.; DIETRICH, KIM N.; ALTAYE, MEKIBIB; EGELHOFF, JOHN C. . . . . LANPHEAR, BRUCE P. (2008). DECREASED BRAIN VOLUME IN ADULTS WITH CHILDHOOD LEAD EXPOSURE. *PLOS MEDICINE, 5*(5), 741–750. DOI: 10.1371/JOURNAL.PMED.0050112

Toxic Shrinkage A composite of 157 brains of adults—who, as children, had high lead levels in their blood—shows reduced volume. The red and yellow hot spots are all areas that are smaller than areas in a normal brain. No wonder lead-exposed children have multiple intellectual and behavioral problems.

actions alone are not sufficient to protect health. This is already proven with obesity, injury, abuse, and neglect. Parents are blamed, but often the larger community is also at fault.

A stark example occurred in Flint, Michigan, where in April 2014 cost-saving officials (appointed by the state to take over the city when the tax base shrunk as the auto industry left) changed the municipal drinking water from Lake Huron to the Flint River. That river contained chemicals that increased lead leaching from old pipes,

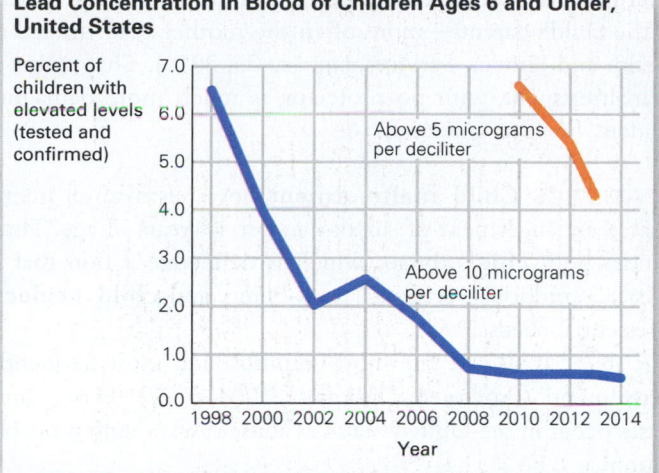

Lead Concentration in Blood of Children Ages 6 and Under, United States

Percent of children with elevated levels (tested and confirmed)

Above 5 micrograms per deciliter

Above 10 micrograms per deciliter

Data from Child Trends Data Bank, 2015; Centers for Disease Control and Prevention, 2016.

FIGURE 6.5 Dramatic Improvement in a Decade Once researchers established the perils of high lead levels in children's blood, the percentage of children suffering from plumbism fell by more than 300 percent. Levels are higher in states that once had heavy manufacturing and lower in mountain and Pacific states.

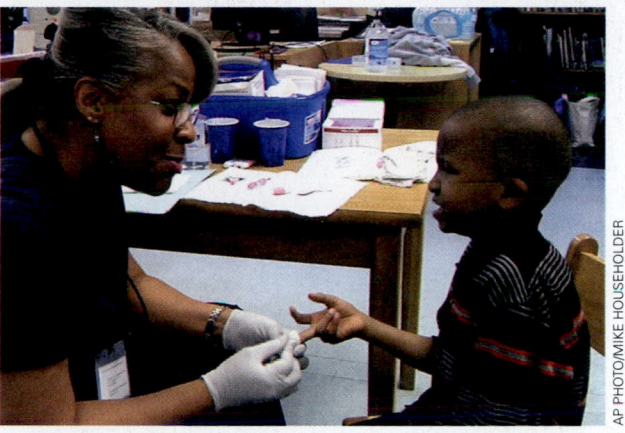

Too Late? Veronica Robinson is a University of Michigan nursing professor who volunteered to provide free lead testing for the children of Flint, Michigan. If 7-year-old Zyontae's level is high, brain damage in early life will trouble him lifelong.

contaminating the water supply—often used for drinking and mixing infant formula.

The percent of children in Flint with blood lead levels above 5 micrograms per deciliter doubled in two years, from 2.4 to 4.9 percent. It tripled in one neighborhood from 4.6 to 15.7 percent (Hanna-Attisha et al., 2016).

Apparently, the state-appointed emergency manager focused on saving money, ignoring possible brain damage to children who, unlike him, are mostly low-income and African American. This oversight is considered an "abject failure to protect public health" (Bellinger, 2016, p. 1101).

The consequences may harm these children lifelong, not only in their education but in their likelihood of going to jail. This prediction arises because scientists use data collected for other reasons to draw conclusions. About 15 years after the sharp decline in blood lead levels in young children, the rate of violent crime committed by teenagers and young adults fell sharply (Nevin, 2007).

Research in Canada, Germany, Italy, Australia, New Zealand, France, and Finland finds the same trends. Those nations that were earlier to legislate against lead had earlier crime reductions, about 20 years after the new laws. Research in many nations finds that blood lead levels predict attention deficits, school suspensions, and aggression (Amato et al., 2013; Goodlad et al., 2013; Nkomo et al., 2018).

There is no doubt that lead, even at low levels in a young child, harms the brain. That raises questions about the long-term effects of hundreds, perhaps thousands, of new chemicals in the air, water, or soil. It also makes the Flint tragedy more troubling. Developmentalists have known about the dangers of lead for decades. Why didn't the Michigan administrator know that?

Child Maltreatment

Accidental deaths are common worldwide, but the data reveal a worse problem. Some children are deliberately harmed. In recent years, as many 1- to 4-year-old U.S. children have been murdered as have died of cancer. (Rates for 2015: 369 homicides, 354 cancer deaths; in 2016: 339 homicides, 377 cancer deaths.)

Childhood disease deaths have decreased markedly with immunization and better nutrition; accidental deaths are down with better prevention, but maltreatment deaths are still high. We now consider child maltreatment in detail, because understanding precedes prevention.

Until about 1960, people thought child abuse was rare and consisted of a sudden attack by a disturbed stranger, usually a man. Today we know better, thanks to a pioneering study based on careful observation in one Boston hospital (Kempe & Kempe, 1978).

Maltreatment is neither rare nor sudden, and 92 percent of the time the perpetrators are one or both of the child's parents—more often the mother than the father (U.S. Department of Health and Human Services, January 25, 2016). That makes it worse: Ongoing home maltreatment, with no protector, is much more damaging than a single outside incident, however injurious.

DEFINITIONS AND STATISTICS **Child maltreatment** now refers to all intentional harm to, or avoidable endangerment of, anyone under 18 years of age. Thus, child maltreatment includes both **child abuse,** which is deliberate action that is harmful to a child's physical, emotional, or sexual well-being, and **child neglect,** which is failure to meet essential needs.

Neglect is worse than abuse. It also is "the most common and most frequently fatal form of child maltreatment" (Proctor & Dubowitz, 2014, p. 27). About three times as many neglect cases occur in the United States as abuse cases, a ratio probably found in many other nations.

Data on *substantiated* maltreatment in the United States in 2014 indicate that 77 percent were neglect, 17 percent physical abuse, 6 percent emotional abuse, and 8 percent sexual abuse. (A few were tallied in two categories [U.S. Department of Health and Human Services, January 25, 2016].) Ironically, neglect is often ignored by the public, who are "stuck in an overwhelming and debilitating" concept that maltreatment always causes bodily harm (Kendall-Taylor et al., 2014, p. 810). Neglect destroys emotional regulation, which is devastating for young children.

Substantiated maltreatment means that a case has been reported, investigated, and verified (see Figure 6.6). In 2015, about 800,000 children suffered substantiated abuse or neglect in the United States. Substantiated maltreatment harms about 1 in every 90 children aged 2 to 5 annually.

Reported maltreatment (technically a referral) means simply that the authorities have been informed. Since 1993, the number of children referred to authorities in the United States has ranged from about 2.7 million to 3.6 million per year, with 3.6 million in 2014 (U.S. Department of Health and Human Services, January 25, 2016).

child maltreatment
Intentional harm to or avoidable endangerment of anyone under 18 years of age.

child abuse
Deliberate action that is harmful to a child's physical, emotional, or sexual well-being.

child neglect
Failure to meet a child's basic physical, educational, or emotional needs.

substantiated maltreatment
Harm or endangerment that has been reported, investigated, and verified.

reported maltreatment
Harm or endangerment about which someone has notified the authorities.

FIGURE 6.6 Getting Better?
As you can see, the number of victims of child maltreatment in the United States has declined in the past decade. The legal and social-work response to serious maltreatment has improved over the years, which is a likely explanation for the decline. Other less sanguine explanations are possible, however.

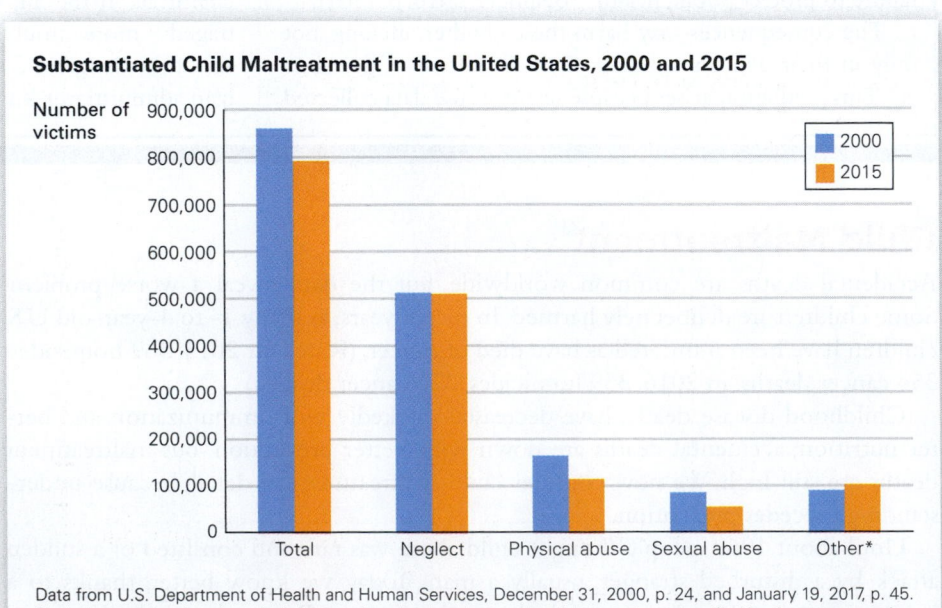

Substantiated Child Maltreatment in the United States, 2000 and 2015

Data from U.S. Department of Health and Human Services, December 31, 2000, p. 24, and January 19, 2017, p. 45.
*Includes emotional and medical abuse, educational neglect, and maltreatment not specified by the state records.

The 4.5-to-1 ratio of reported versus substantiated cases occurs because:

1. Each child is counted only once, so five verified reports about a single child result in one substantiated case.

2. Substantiation requires proof. Most investigations do not find unmistakable harm or a witness.

3. Many professionals are *mandated reporters,* required to report any signs of *possible* maltreatment. In 2014, two-thirds of all reports came from professionals. Usually an investigation finds no harm (Pietrantonio et al., 2013).

4. Some reports are "screened out" as belonging to another jurisdiction, such as the military or a Native American tribe, who have their own systems. In 2014, many (about 39 percent) referrals were screened out.

5. A report may be false or deliberately misleading (though few are) (Sedlak & Ellis, 2014).

FREQUENCY OF MALTREATMENT How often does maltreatment actually occur? No one knows. Not all instances are noticed, not all that are noticed are reported, and not all reports are substantiated. Part of the problem is in drawing the line between harsh discipline and abuse, and between momentary lapses and ongoing neglect. If the standard were perfect parenting all day and all night from birth to age 18, as judged by neighbors, professionals, as well as parents, then every child has been mistreated. Only severe cases are tallied.

If we rely on official U.S. statistics, positive trends are apparent. Substantiated child maltreatment increased from about 1960 to 1990 but decreased thereafter (see Figure 6.7). Other sources also report declines, particularly in sexual abuse.

Perhaps national awareness has led to better reporting and then more effective prevention. However, trends between 2010 and 2015 suggest that rates are increasing again (U.S. Department of Health and Human Services, January 19, 2017). There are many possible explanations. The growing gap between rich and poor families is the most plausible. But no matter what the reason, it is obvious that more work is needed.

Unfortunately, official reports raise doubt. For example, Pennsylvania reports about one-third fewer victims than a neighboring state (Ohio), but the child population of

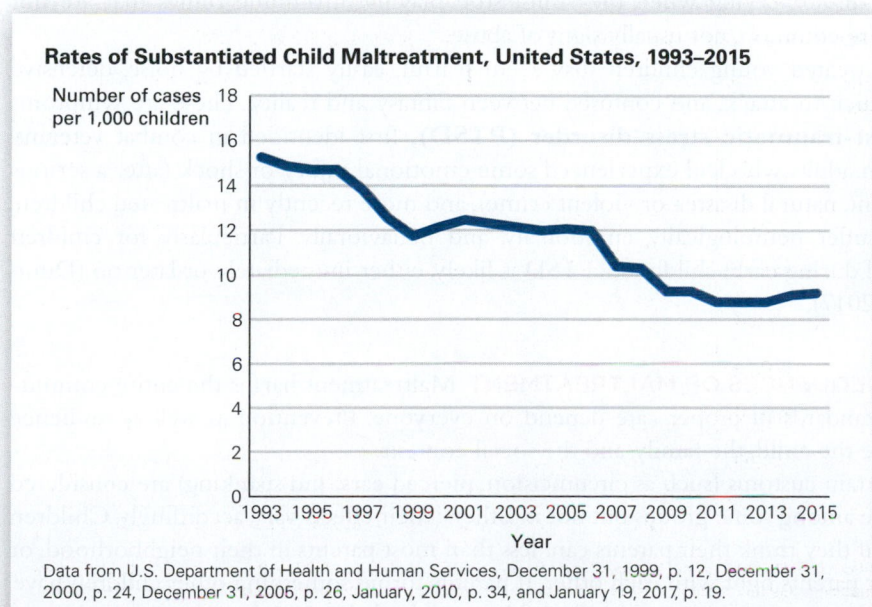

Rates of Substantiated Child Maltreatment, United States, 1993–2015

Number of cases per 1,000 children

Year

Data from U.S. Department of Health and Human Services, December 31, 1999, p. 12, December 31, 2000, p. 24, December 31, 2005, p. 26, January, 2010, p. 34, and January 19, 2017, p. 19.

FIGURE 6.7 Still Far Too Many The number of substantiated cases of maltreatment of children under age 18 in the United States is too high, but there is some good news: The rate has declined significantly from its peak (15.3) in 1993.

both states is about the same. The rate of child maltreatment is eight times higher in Vermont than Alabama—how can that be? When states are compared, states increase dramatically from year to year, not only overall but also in proportions of neglect, physical abuse, sexual abuse, and so on (U.S. Department of Health and Human Services, January 19, 2017).

Do some states ignore maltreatment that would have been spotted if the child lived across a state border? Or are people in some places quick to suspect harm?

How maltreatment is defined is powerfully influenced by culture (one of my students asked, "When is a child too old to be beaten?"). Willingness to report also varies. The United States has become more culturally diverse, and people have become more suspicious of government. Does that reduce reporting but not abuse?

From a developmental perspective, beyond the difficulty in getting accurate data, another problem is that most maltreatment occurs early in life. That is before children are required to attend school, where a teacher would notice a problem and be required to report. One infant in 45 is substantiated as maltreated, as is 1 preschooler in 90 (U.S. Department of Health and Human Services, January 25, 2016). Those are substantiated cases; some of the youngest victims never reach outsiders' attention.

An additional problem is that some children are abused in many ways by many people. Many studies have found that if a single episode of child abuse is followed by parental protection and love—never blaming the child—children recover. By contrast, repeated victimization causes lifelong harm, largely because such children are not protected by their parents. Indeed, often a family member is one of the abusers (Turner et al., 2016).

> **THINK CRITICALLY:** Why might Pennsylvania have so few cases of neglect?

WARNING SIGNS Instead of relying on official statistics and mandated reporters, every reader of this book can recognize developmental problems and prevent maltreatment. Often the first sign is delayed development, such as slow growth, immature communication, lack of curiosity, or unusual social interactions. These are all evident in infancy and early childhood.

Table 6.3 lists signs of child maltreatment, both neglect and abuse. None of these signs proves maltreatment, but whenever any of them occurs, investigation is needed. The opposite is also true: Some things that many young children do (not eating much dinner, crying when they must stop playing, imagining things that are not true) are common, not usually signs of abuse.

Maltreated young children may seem fearful, easily startled by noise, defensive and quick to attack, and confused between fantasy and reality. These are symptoms of **post-traumatic stress disorder (PTSD),** first identified in combat veterans, then in adults who had experienced some emotional injury or shock (after a serious accident, natural disaster, or violent crime), and more recently in maltreated children, who suffer neurologically, emotionally, and behaviorally. Particularly for children abused during early childhood, PTSD is likely, either immediately or later on (Dunn et al., 2017).

◆ **Especially for Nurses**
While weighing a 4-year-old, you notice several bruises on the child's legs. When you ask about them, the child says nothing and the parent says that the child bumps into things. What should you do? (see response, page 229)

post-traumatic stress disorder (PTSD)
An anxiety disorder that develops as a delayed reaction to having experienced or witnessed a shocking or frightening event. Its symptoms may include flashbacks, hypervigilance, anger, nightmares, and sudden terror.

CONSEQUENCES OF MALTREATMENT Maltreatment harms the entire community; standards of proper care depend on everyone. Prevention as well as resilience involve the child, the family, and the social context.

Certain customs (such as circumcision, pierced ears, and spanking) are considered abusive among some groups but not in others; their effects vary accordingly. Children suffer if they think their parents care less than most parents in their neighborhood, or if their parents fight with each other. If parents forbid something other children have, punish more severely, or not at all, children might feel unloved.

TABLE 6.3 Signs of Maltreatment in Children Aged 2 to 10
Injuries that do not fit an "accidental" explanation, such as bruises on both sides of the face or body; burns with a clear line between burned and unburned skin; "falls" that result in cuts, not scrapes
Repeated injuries, especially broken bones not properly tended (visible on X-ray)
Fantasy play, with dominant themes of violence or sexual knowledge
Slow physical growth, especially with unusual appetite or lack of appetite
Ongoing physical complaints, such as stomachaches, headaches, genital pain, sleepiness
Reluctance to talk, to play, or to move, especially if development is slow
No close friendships; hostility toward others; bullying of smaller children
Hypervigilance, with quick, impulsive reactions, such as cringing, startling, or hitting
Frequent absence from school
Frequent changes of address
Turnover in caregivers who pick up child, or caregiver who comes late, seems high
Expressions of fear rather than joy on seeing the caregiver

The long-term effects of maltreatment depend partly on the child's interpretation at the time and, in adulthood, on the current relationship between the adult and the punishing parent. If the grown child has a good relationship with the formerly abusive parent (more common if abuse was not chronic), then recovery is more likely (Schafer et al., 2014). It has been said that abused children become abusive parents, but this is not necessarily true (Widom et al., 2015a). Many people avoid the mistakes of their parents, especially if their friends or partners, or their reformed parents, show them a better way.

Nonetheless, the consequences of maltreatment may last for decades. Immediate impairment is obvious, as when a child is bruised, broken, afraid to talk, or failing in school. Later on, however, deficits in social skills and self-esteem are more crippling than physical or intellectual damage.

Maltreated children tend to hate themselves and then hate everyone else. Even if the child was mistreated in the early years and then not after age 5, emotional problems (externalizing for the boys and internalizing for the girls) linger (Godinet et al., 2014). Adult drug abuse, social isolation, and poor health may result from maltreatment decades earlier (Sperry & Widom, 2013; Mersky et al., 2013).

Hate is corrosive. A warm and enduring friendship can repair some damage, but maltreatment makes such friendships less likely. Many studies find that mistreated children typically regard other people as hostile; hence, they become less friendly, more aggressive, and more isolated than other children.

The earlier that abuse starts and the longer it continues, the worse the children's relationships are, with physically and sexually abused children likely to be irrationally angry and neglected children often withdrawn (Petrenko et al., 2012). That makes healthy romances and friendships difficult.

Further, finding and keeping a job is a critical aspect of adult well-being, yet adults who were maltreated suffer in this way as well. One study carefully matched 807 children who had experienced substantiated abuse with other children who were of the same sex, ethnicity, and family SES. About 35 years later, when maltreatment was a distant memory, those who had been mistreated were 14 percent less likely to be employed. The researchers concluded: "abused and neglected children experience large and enduring economic consequences" (Currie & Widom, 2010, p. 111).

In this study, women had more difficulty finding and keeping a job than men. It may be that self-esteem, emotional stability, and social skills are even more important

PHOTO JAPAN/ALAMY

DAVID JAKLE/IMAGE SOURCE/GETTY IMAGES

Family Protection Relatives are a safety net. Ideally, they feed and play with the young members of the family (as these grandfathers do). This is secondary prevention, allowing parents to provide good care. Rarely, tertiary prevention is needed. About 1 percent of all U.S. grandparents are foster or adoptive parents of their grandchildren. This does not benefit the adults, but it may be the best solution for mistreated children.

for female employees than for male ones. This study is just one of hundreds of lon-gitudinal studies, all of which find that maltreatment affects people decades after broken bones, or skinny bodies, or medical neglect.

Preventing Harm

For accidents, child abuse, and child neglect, the ultimate goal is *primary prevention,* a social network of customs and supports that help parents, neighbors, and profession-als protect every child. Neighborhood stability, parental education, income support, and fewer unwanted children all reduce injury.

All of these are primary prevention. Such measures are more effective in the long run, but governments and private foundations are more likely to fund projects that focus on high-risk families (Nelson & Caplan, 2014). The media's focus on shocking examples of parental abuse or social worker neglect ignores the many ways families, communities, and professionals stop harm before it begins.

Secondary prevention involves spotting warning signs and intervening to keep a risky situation from getting worse. For example, insecure attachment, especially of the disorganized type, is a sign of a disrupted parent–child relationship. Thus, inse-cure attachment should be repaired before it becomes harmful by leading to abuse, neglect, or lack of supervision. [**Life-Span Link:** Attachment types are explained in detail in Chapter 4.]

Tertiary prevention limits harm after injury has occurred. Reporting is the first step; investigating and substantiating is second. The final step, however, is helping the care-giver provide better care. That may include treating addiction, assigning a house-keeper, locating family helpers, securing better living quarters, and helping the child recover, with special medical, psychological, or education assistance, either with the same family or another one where better care is available.

The priority must be child protection. In every case, *permanency planning* is needed: planning how to nurture the child until adulthood (Scott et al., 2013). Uncertainty, moving, a string of temporary placements, and frequent changes in schools are all destructive.

When children are taken from their parents and entrusted to another adult, that is called **foster care.** The other adult might be a stranger or might be a relative, in which case it is called **kinship care.** Foster care sometimes is informal—a grandmother pro-vides custodial care because the parents do not—or may result from Child Protective Services provided by the government. Every year for the past decade in the United States, almost half a million children have been officially in foster care. At least another

foster care
When a person (usually a child) is cared for by someone other than the parents.

kinship care
A form of foster care in which a relative, usually a grandmother, becomes the approved caregiver.

million are unofficially in kinship care, because relatives realize that the parents are unable or unwilling to provide good care.

Most foster children are from low-income, ethnic-minority families—a statistic that reveals problems in the macrosystem as well as the microsystem. In the United States, most foster children have physical, intellectual, and emotional problems that arose in their original families—evidence of their abuse and neglect (Jones & Morris, 2012). Obviously, foster parents need much more than financial subsidies to provide good care for such children.

Sometimes a child's best permanency plan is adoption by another family, who will provide care lifelong. However, adoption is difficult, for many reasons:

Mother–Daughter Love, Finally After a difficult childhood, 7-year-old Alexia is now safe and happy in her mother's arms. Maria Luz Martinez was her foster parent and has now become her adoptive mother.

AURELIA VENTURA/LA OPINION/NEWSCOM

- Judges and biological parents are reluctant to release children for adoption.
- Most adoptive parents prefer infants, but few maltreating adults recognize how hard child care can be until they have tried, and failed, to provide for their children.
- Some agencies screen out families not headed by heterosexual couples.
- Some professionals insist that adoptive parents be of the same ethnicity and/or religion as the child.

As detailed many times in this chapter, caring for young children is not easy. Parents shoulder most of the burden, and their love and protection usually result in strong and happy children. However, when parents are inadequate and the community is not supportive, complications abound. We all benefit from well-nurtured people; how to achieve that goal is a question we all must answer.

what have you learned?

1. What can be concluded from the data on rates of childhood injury?
2. How do injury deaths compare in developed and developing nations?
3. What are some examples of primary prevention?
4. What are some examples of secondary prevention?
5. Why have the rates of child accidental death declined?
6. Why might poverty contribute to child maltreatment?
7. Why is reported abuse higher than substantiated abuse?
8. What is the difference between neglect and abuse in harm and frequency?
9. Why have rates of sexual abuse declined?
10. What are the short-term and long-term consequences of childhood maltreatment?
11. Why do developmentalists believe that tertiary prevention is too late?
12. What are the pros and cons of kinship care?
13. When is adoption part of permanency planning?

SUMMARY

Emotional Development

1. Emotional regulation is crucial during early childhood. It occurs in Erikson's third developmental stage, initiative versus guilt. Children normally feel pride when they demonstrate initiative, but sometimes they feel guilt or shame.

2. Intrinsic motivation is apparent when a child concentrates on a drawing or a conversation with an imaginary friend. It may endure when extrinsic motivation stops.

Play

3. All young children enjoy playing. They prefer play with other children of the same sex, who teach them lessons in social interaction that their parents do not.

4. Play with other children gradually changes as children mature. Peer experiences and television watching affect children's play as they progress from being onlookers to cooperators.

5. Active play takes many forms, with rough-and-tumble play fostering social skills and sociodramatic play developing emotional regulation.

Challenges for Caregivers

6. Three classic styles of parenting are authoritarian, permissive, and authoritative. Generally, children are more successful and happy when their parents express warmth and set guidelines.

7. A fourth style of parenting, neglectful/uninvolved, is always harmful. The particulars of parenting reflect the culture as well as the temperament of the child.

8. Parental punishment can have long-term consequences, with both corporal punishment and psychological control teaching lessons that few parents want their children to learn.

9. Even 2-year-olds correctly use sex-specific labels. Young children become aware of gender differences in clothes, toys, playmates, and future careers.

10. Every major theory interprets children's awareness of gender differences in a particular way, from Freud's emphasis on attraction to the opposite-sex parent, to behaviorist stress on reinforcement, cognitive gender-schema, and evolutionary need for procreation.

11. The sense of self and the social awareness of young children become the foundation for morality, influenced by both nature and nurture.

12. Prosocial emotions lead to caring for others; antisocial behavior includes instrumental, reactive, relational, and bullying aggression.

Harm to Children

13. Accidents cause more child deaths in the United States than all diseases combined. Close supervision and public safeguards can protect young children from their own eager, impulsive curiosity.

14. Harm reduction occurs on many levels, including long before and immediately after each harmful incident. Primary prevention protects everyone, secondary prevention focuses on high-risk conditions and people, and tertiary prevention occurs after harm has occurred.

15. A major problem is that pollution—in water, air, and food—harms the brains and lungs of children more intensely than those of older people.

16. The effects of child maltreatment may endure for decades in the life of an abused child. Many contextual factors influence the frequency of child abuse.

17. Substantiated maltreatment is less common than it was a few decades ago, but it still occurs for about 800,000 children in the United States each year. Victims are more often under age 6, and neglect is more common than abuse.

18. When maltreatment is substantiated, measures must ensure that it will stop. Sometimes foster care is needed, with kinship care—formal or not—a common practice.

KEY TERMS

emotional regulation (p. 194)
self-concept (p. 194)
effortful control (p. 194)
initiative versus guilt (p. 194)
intrinsic motivation (p. 196)
extrinsic motivation (p. 196)
rough-and-tumble play (p. 200)
sociodramatic play (p. 201)
authoritarian parenting (p. 203)
permissive parenting (p. 203)
authoritative parenting (p. 203)

neglectful/uninvolved parenting (p. 203)
corporal punishment (p. 205)
psychological control (p. 206)
time-out (p. 208)
induction (p. 208)
sex differences (p. 208)
gender differences (p. 208)
phallic stage (p. 210)
Oedipus complex (p. 210)
gender schema (p. 213)
empathy (p. 214)

antipathy (p. 214)
prosocial behavior (p. 214)
antisocial behavior (p. 214)
instrumental aggression (p. 216)
reactive aggression (p. 216)
relational aggression (p. 216)
bullying aggression (p. 216)
injury control/harm reduction (p. 218)
primary prevention (p. 218)
secondary prevention (p. 218)

tertiary prevention (p. 218)
child maltreatment (p. 222)
child abuse (p. 222)
child neglect (p. 222)
substantiated maltreatment (p. 222)
reported maltreatment (p. 222)
post-traumatic stress disorder (PTSD) (p. 224)
foster care (p. 226)
kinship care (p. 226)

APPLICATIONS

1. Children's television programming is rife with stereotypes about ethnicity, gender, and morality. Watch an hour of children's TV, especially on a Saturday morning, and describe the content of both the programs and the commercials. Draw conclusions about stereotyping, citing specific evidence, not generalities.

2. Gender indicators often go unnoticed. Go to a public place (park, restaurant, busy street) and spend at least 10 minutes recording examples of gender differentiation, such as articles of clothing, mannerisms, interaction patterns, and activities.

Quantify what you see, such as baseball hats on eight males and two females. Or (better, but more difficult) describe four male–female conversations, indicating gender differences in length and frequency of talking, interruptions, vocabulary, and so on.

3. Ask three parents about punishment, including their preferred type, at what age, for what misdeeds, and by whom. Ask your three informants how they were punished as children and how that affected them. If your sources all agree, find a parent (or a classmate) who has a different view.

ESPECIALLY FOR ANSWERS

Response for College Students (from page 197): Both are important. Extrinsic motivation includes parental pressure and the need to get a good job after graduation. Intrinsic motivation includes the joy of learning, especially if you can express that learning in ways others recognize. Have you ever taken a course that was not required and was said to be difficult? That was intrinsic motivation.

Response for Teachers of Young Children (from page 197): Perhaps, but only after the work is completed and if the child has put genuine effort into it. You do not want to undercut intrinsic motivation, as happens with older students who know a particular course will be an "easy A."

Response for Political Scientists (from page 202): There are many parenting styles, and it is difficult to determine each one's impact on children's personalities. At this point, attempts to connect early child rearing with later political outlook are speculative.

Response for Parents (from page 206): No. The worst time to spank a child is when you are angry. You might seriously hurt the child, and the child will associate anger with violence. You would do better to learn to control your anger and develop other strategies for discipline and for prevention of misbehavior.

Response for Urban Planners (from page 218): The adult idea of a park—a large, grassy open place—is not best for young children. For them, you would design an enclosed area, small enough and with adequate seating to allow caregivers to socialize while watching their children. The playground surface would have to be protective (since young children are clumsy), with equipment that encourages motor skills. Teenagers and dogs should have their own designated areas, far from the youngest children.

Response for Nurses (from page 224): Any suspicion of child maltreatment must be reported, and these bruises are suspicious. Someone in authority must find out what is happening so that the parent as well as the child can be helped.

OBSERVATION QUIZ ANSWERS

Answer to Observation Quiz (from page 198) The capes, probably furnished by the photographer. But, note that each child's individuality shines through.

Answer to Observation Quiz (from page 203): It is impossible to be certain based on one moment, but the best guess is authoritative. He seems patient and protective, providing comfort and guidance, neither forcing (authoritarian) nor letting the child do whatever he wants (permissive).

Answer to Observation Quiz (from page 208) His body proportions and his hands behind his back suggest that he is too young and too docile for effective time-out.

Answer to Observation Quiz (from page 209) Every number differs for boys and girls, and men and women.

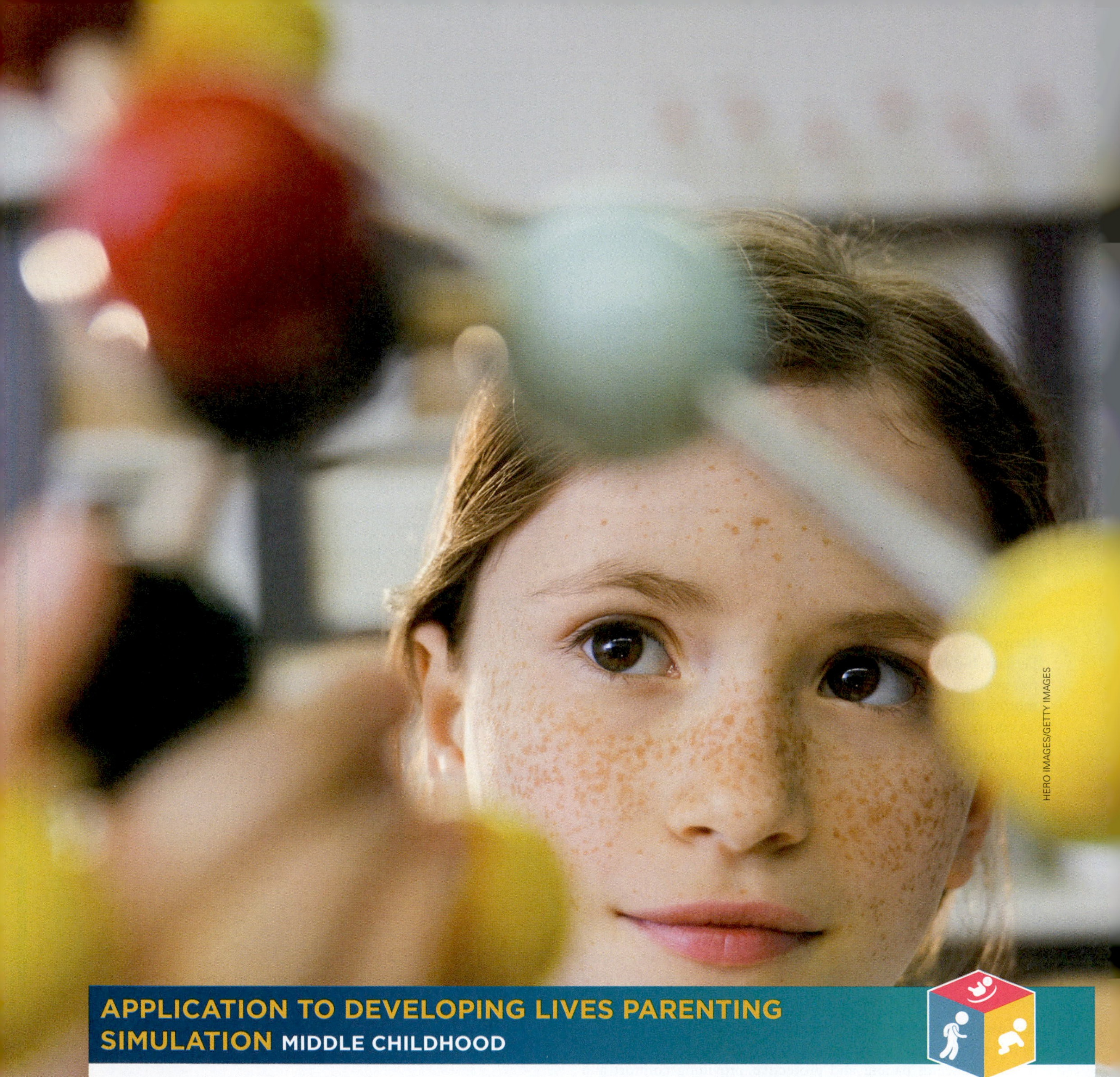

HERO IMAGES/GETTY IMAGES

APPLICATION TO DEVELOPING LIVES PARENTING SIMULATION MIDDLE CHILDHOOD

As you progress through the Middle Childhood simulation module, how you answer the following questions will impact the biosocial, cognitive, and psychosocial development of your child.

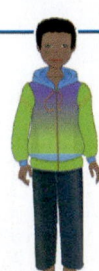

Biosocial	Cognitive	Psychosocial
• How will you adjust your child's diet and activity level in middle childhood? • Will you follow the recommended immunization schedule? • Will you regulate your child's screen time?	• Which of Piaget's stages of cognitive development is your child in? • How will your child score on an intelligence test? • Will you put your child in tutoring if needed? • Will you help with your child's homework?	• Will you eat meals as a family around the table or have a different routine? • What kind of elementary school will you choose for your child? • What stage of moral development is your child in? • Will your child be popular?

Middle Childhood

Every year has joys and sorrows, gains and losses. But if you were pushed to choose one best period, you might select middle childhood. The years from age 6 to 11 are usually a time of good health and steady growth. Children master new skills, learn thousands of words, and enter a wider social world. They are safe and happy; the dangers of adolescence (drugs, early sex, violence) are distant.

But not always. For some children, these years are the worst, not the best. They hate school or fear home; they suffer with asthma or disability; they are bullied or lonely.

Nor are these years straightforward for the adults who care for these children. Instead, controversies abound. Should children with special needs be medicated? How should learning be measured? Does single parenthood, divorce, cohabitation, or adult sexual orientation harm children? The next two chapters explore the many joys and problems of middle childhood.

PHOTOALTO/JEROME GORIN/GETTY IMAGES

MIDDLE CHILDHOOD
Body and Mind

what will you know?

- Whose fault is it if a child is obese?
- Why are some math concepts difficult at age 4 but easier at age 8?
- Are schools in the United States better than schools in other nations?
- What causes a child to have autism?

At age 9, I wanted a puppy. My parents said no; we already had Dusty, our big family dog. I wanted my own dog, and I said I would do all of the dog care. My promise was dismissed—my parents knew that more maturation was needed before I could be fully responsible for myself, much less for another creature. Then I dashed off a poem, promising "to brush his hair as smooth as silk" and "to feed him milk." Twice wrong. Poor cadence, and cow's milk makes puppies sick. But my father praised my poem; I got Taffy, a blonde cocker spaniel. I almost never brushed him, which did not surprise my parents.

At age 10, my daughter Sarah wanted her ears pierced, because her friends had pierced ears. I said no and explained that it would be unfair to her three older sisters, who had had to wait for ear-piercing until they were teenagers. Sarah wrote an affidavit and persuaded all three to sign "No objection." She got gold posts. She sometimes lost her earrings—no surprise.

Children's wishes differ by cohort and their strategies by context. My parents knew that I was too young to be responsible for a dog, but I expected my father to reward my poetry. Sarah understood that signed documents from her older sisters would persuade my husband (a lawyer) and me. We were both typical children, wanting something that we did not need and figuring out how to get it, despite adults who knew our limitations.

During these years, children still rely on adults, but they begin to join the wider world. Depending on their circumstances, children learn to divide fractions, text friends, memorize baseball stats, load rifles, or persuade parents.

Middle childhood is also the time when children want to fit in with their peers—they don't want to be odd, which is one reason Sarah wanted pierced ears and her sisters agreed. This chapter describes physical growth and cognitive advances before adolescence.

A Healthy Time

In marked contrast to infancy or adolescence, middle childhood is a time of slow and steady growth. Children gain about 2 inches and 5 pounds a year (more than 5 centimeters and 2 kilograms). Nature and nurture combine to make these the healthiest years of life.

To be specific, the death rate for 5- to 9-year-olds is by far the lowest of any age group, with the rates for 11- to 14-year-olds the second lowest (Murphy et al., 2017) (see Figure 7.1). Genetic diseases are most threatening in early infancy or old age; infectious diseases are kept away via immunization; and fatal accidents—although the most common cause of death—are lower than at every other period.

The naturally low death rate of children this age has continued to fall in recent years, thanks to better injury control and modern medicine. In the United States in 1950, the death rate per 100,000 5- to 14-year-olds was 60; in 2015, it was less than 13 (National Center for Health Statistics, 2017).

Oral health has improved, with more brushing and fluoride. A survey found that 75 percent of U.S. children saw a dentist for preventive care in the past year, and for 70 percent of them, the condition of their teeth was very good (Iida & Rozier, 2013) No wonder the boys on page 232 look proud of their new front teeth.

Health Habits

Children can maintain good health if adults teach them how and if regular doctor and dentist visits are part of their lives. Every child needs good medical care; without it, adult health is affected. Adults who now have good care still suffer if their childhood circumstances were poor (McEwen & McEwen, 2017; Juster et al., 2016).

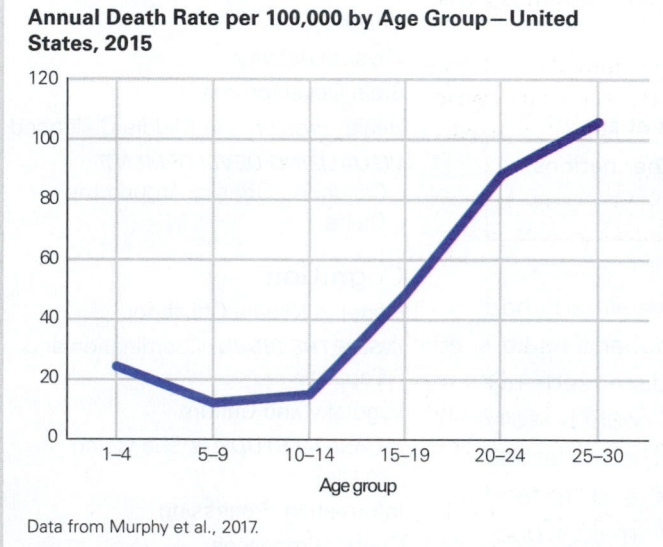

Annual Death Rate per 100,000 by Age Group—United States, 2015

Data from Murphy et al., 2017.

FIGURE 7.1 Rates continue to rise with age, up to 13,674 for those aged 85 and older, so this figure cannot portray the entire life span. Details are remarkable as well. Not only are fatal diseases rare, thanks to immunization, but accidents and homicide also dip during middle childhood—and rise rapidly thereafter.

Global Decay Thousands of children in Bangalore, India, gathered to brush their teeth together, part of an oral health campaign. Music, fast food, candy bars, and technology have been exported from the United States, and many developing nations have their own versions (Bollywood replaces Hollywood). Tooth decay has also reached many nations; preventive health now follows.

↑ **OBSERVATION** QUIZ
Beyond toothbrushes, what other health tools do most children here have that their parents did not? (see answer, page 273)

Peers and parents make a difference. If children see that others routinely care for their own health, social learning pushes them to do the same. Camps for children with asthma, cancer, diabetes, sickle-cell anemia, and so on are beneficial because other children and knowledgeable adults teach self-care. Health habits should be established before teenage rebellion erupts, often causing resistance to diets, pills, warning signs, and doctors (Dean et al., 2010; Naughton et al., 2014). Ideally self-care is already routine; rebellion focuses on curfews or hairstyles, not health habits.

Physical Activity

Beyond the sheer fun of playing, the benefits of physical activity—especially games with rules, which children now can follow—last a lifetime. Exercise advances physical, emotional, and mental health, as well as learning in school.

Harm from sports is also possible. Organizations have developed guidelines to prevent concussions among 7- and 8-year-olds in football and to halt full-body impact from ice hockey among children under age 12. The fact that regulations are needed to protect children from brain injury is sobering (Toporek, 2012).

Of course, many games that young children enjoy are unlikely to cause injury. However, adults tend to involve children in adult sports, providing child-size protective equipment (helmets, mitts, etc.) instead of child-friendly activities.

THE NEED FOR MOVEMENT Given the importance of physical activity for health and learning, many developmentalists are troubled when indoor activities (homework, television) crowd out active play. Parents used to tell their children "go out and play"; now they say, "don't leave the house." Such free play has many benefits, as does programmed activity that gets children to move.

Many parents now enroll their children in after-school sports that vary by culture—tennis, karate, cricket, yoga, rugby, baseball, or soccer (football). However, the children who most need to connect their bodies and their minds—those from low-SES families or who have physical disabilities—are least likely to join Little League and the like, even when enrollment is free. The reasons are many, the consequences sad (Dearing et al., 2009).

Ideally, all children learn various skills as well as exercise their bodies in school. However, a study of all elementary schools in Illinois found that schools with the least time scheduled for physical activity tend to be those with the most low-SES children, as well as the lowest reading scores (Kern et al., 2018).

In this example, understanding correlation provides a novel way to interpret the relationship between reading scores and recess. It is easy to assume that more

Are They Having Fun? Helmets, uniforms, and competition—more appropriate for adults? Children everywhere want to do what the adults do, so these ones are probably proud of their ice hockey team.

© HERO IMAGES/CORBIS

Idyllic Two 8-year-olds, each with a 6-year-old sister, all four daydreaming or exploring in a very old tree beside a lake in Denmark—what could be better? Ideally, all of the world's children would be so fortunate, but most are not.

VIDEO ACTIVITY: Brain Development: Middle Childhood depicts the changes that occur in a child's brain from age 6 to age 11.

reading instruction is needed in schools with low scores, so academic instruction crowds out time for physical education. But, the correlation might occur in the opposite direction: Less physical activity might cause less learning (Kern et al., 2018).

Even when policies mandate in-school physical education and recess, requirements may be ignored. For instance, although Alabama requires at least 30 minutes daily of physical education in primary schools, the average in one poor district was only 22 minutes. No school in that district had recess or after-school sports (Robinson et al., 2014).

PHYSICAL EXERCISE IN JAPAN In Japan, children score high on international tests, and yet many schools have more than an hour of recess (in several segments) a day, in addition to gym classes. The Japanese believe that physical activity promotes learning and character development (Webster & Suzuki, 2014).

Consequently, many Japanese public schools have swimming pools, indoor gyms, and outdoor yards with structures for climbing, swinging, and so on. The emphasis on exercise is lifelong; that is one explanation for the fact that the Japanese live longer, on average, than people in any other nation.

Even in Japan, however, teachers are hesitant to teach physical education to students with disabilities (Hodge et al., 2013). From what we know about the brain and the body during middle childhood, all children—*especially* those who are not athletically gifted—need daily physical activity.

Brain Development

How could body movement improve intellectual functioning? A review of the research suggests several possible mechanisms, including direct benefits on cerebral blood flow and neurotransmitters as well as indirect results from better moods (Singh et al., 2012). Many studies have found that children's brains benefit from physical exercise (Voelcker-Rehage et al., 2018).

While aerobic exercise directly affects brain structures, every movement can cause learning indirectly. Children learn by doing and then express what they know by moving, in *embodied cognition*, the idea that thinking is connected to body movement (Pexman, 2017). For example, the physical act of handwriting helps children learn to read (James, 2017).

PAYING ATTENTION Remember *executive control,* which includes the ability to inhibit some impulses to focus on others. Neurological advances allow children to pay special heed to the most important elements of their environment. *Selective attention,* concentrating on some stimuli while ignoring others, improves markedly at about age 7.

Selective attention is partly the result of maturation, but it is also greatly affected by experience, particularly social play. School-age children not only notice various stimuli (which is one form of attention) but also select appropriate responses when several possibilities conflict (Wendelken et al., 2011). In kickball, soccer, basketball, and baseball, it is crucial to attend to the ball, not to dozens of other stimuli.

For example, in baseball, young batters learn to ignore the other team's attempts to distract them; fielders start moving into position as soon as the bat connects; and

PRESSMASTER/SHUTTERSTOCK

Pay Attention Some adults think that computers make children lazy, because they can look up whatever they don't know. But imagine the facial expressions of these children if they were sitting at their desks with 30 classmates, listening to a lecture.

pitchers adjust to the height, handedness, and past performance of the person at bat. Another physical activity that seems to foster *executive function* is karate, which requires inhibition of some reactions in order to execute others (Alesi et al., 2014).

REACTION TIME Physical play as well as maturation during middle childhood also improves **reaction time,** which is how long it takes to respond to a stimulus. Preschoolers are sometimes frustratingly slow in putting on their pants, eating their cereal, throwing a ball. Reaction time is reduced every year of childhood, thanks to increasing myelination. Skill at games is an obvious example, from scoring on a video game, to swinging at a pitch, to kicking a soccer ball toward a teammate—timing on all of these improve every year from age 6 to 11, depending partly on practice.

Health Problems in Middle Childhood

Some chronic health conditions, including Tourette syndrome, stuttering, and allergies, may worsen during the school years, drawing unwanted attention to the affected child. Even minor problems—wearing glasses, repeatedly coughing or blowing one's nose, or having a visible birthmark—can affect children's self-esteem. We will now look at two other examples of physical conditions that affect learning.

CHILDHOOD OBESITY **Childhood overweight** is usually defined as a BMI above the 85th percentile, and **childhood obesity** is defined as a BMI above the 95th percentile for children of a particular age based on growth charts in 1980. In 2016, 18 percent of U.S. 6- to 11-year-olds were obese, a significant difference from 2- to 5-year-olds, whose obesity rate was 14 percent (Hales et al., 2017).

Childhood obesity is increasing worldwide, having more than doubled since 1980 in all three nations of North America (Mexico, the United States, and Canada) (Ogden et al., 2011). It also continues to creep higher in the United States, except for some reductions among 2- to 5-year-olds.

Recent increases are dramatic in developing nations as food becomes more plentiful and parents no longer need to worry that their children might starve. For instance, in China, in only two decades (from 1991 to 2011), overweight among 6- to

reaction time
The time it takes to respond to a stimulus, either physically (with a reflexive movement such as an eyeblink) or cognitively (with a thought).

childhood overweight
In a child, having a BMI above the 85th percentile, according to the U.S. Centers for Disease Control's 1980 standards for children of a given age.

childhood obesity
In a child, having a BMI above the 95th percentile, according to the U.S. Centers for Disease Control's 1980 standards for children of a given age.

◆ **Especially for Medical Professionals**
You notice that a child is overweight, but you are hesitant to say anything to the parents, who are also overweight, because you do not want to offend them. What should you do? (see response, page 272)

Same Situation, Far Apart Children have high energy but small stomachs, so they enjoy frequent snacks more than big meals. Yet snacks are typically poor sources of nutrition. Who is healthier: the American boy crunching buttered popcorn as he watches a 3-D movie, or the Japanese children eating *takoyaki* (an octopus dumpling) as part of a traditional celebration near Tokyo?

12-year-olds more than doubled (from 11 percent to 26 percent) (Jia et al., 2017) (see Visualizing Development, page 240). Many of the oldest generations remember when children died of malnutrition, but they do not know the dangers of obesity.

One Chinese father complained:

> I told my boy his diet needs some improvement . . . my mum said she is happy with his diet . . . [that he] eats enough meat and enough oil is used in cooking. . . . In their time, meat and oil were treasures so now they feel the more the better. . . . I decided to move out with my wife and son . . . his grandparents were a big problem . . . we couldn't change anything when we lived together.
>
> *[Li et al., 2015]*

This helps explain why, unlike for children whose families have lived in the United States for generations, children of recent immigrants are more likely to be overweight than their parents. A Canadian review of 49 studies on obesity among immigrants found that when they change their diet, from traditional to American, obesity increases (Sanou et al., 2014).

Childhood overweight correlates with asthma, high blood pressure, and elevated cholesterol (especially LDL, the "lousy" cholesterol), all of which increase death rates in adulthood. But during childhood, obesity is less a medical problem than a social one. As weight builds, school achievement decreases, self-esteem falls, and loneliness rises (Harrist et al., 2012).

Loneliness in middle childhood is especially painful, because friends become crucial. A vicious cycle may develop: Children with poor social skills and few friends are more likely to overeat and vice versa (Jackson & Cunningham, 2015; Vandewater et al., 2015).

Although obesity is somewhat affected by genes, culture is more influential. Look at the figure on obesity among 2- to 19-year-olds in the United States (see Figure 7.2). Are the large ethnic gaps (such as only 11 percent of Asian Americans but 26 percent of Hispanic Americans) genetic? But why the gender differences?

Boys and girls of the same ethnicity share 45 of their 46 chromosomes, yet African American *girls* are more often obese than boys, while Asian American and Hispanic American *boys* are more often obese than girls. Thus, the social context is crucial.

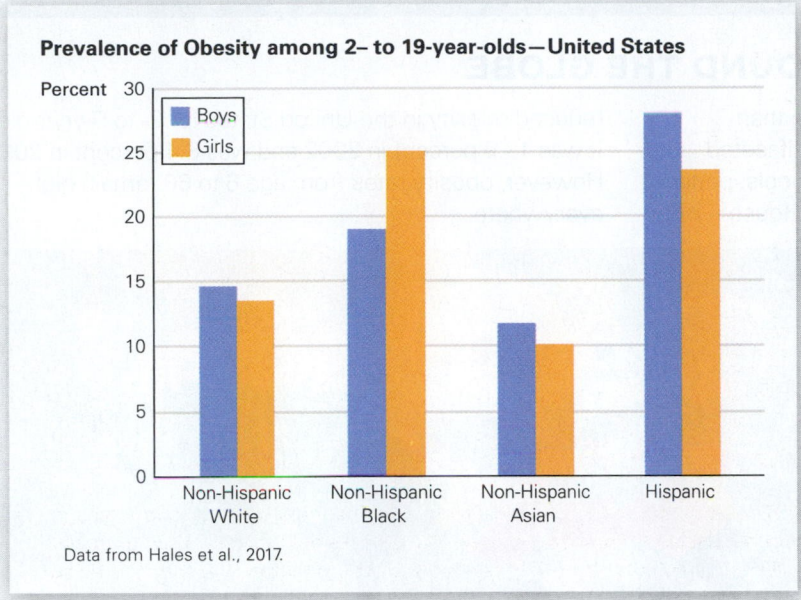

Prevalence of Obesity among 2– to 19-year-olds—United States

Data from Hales et al., 2017.

FIGURE 7.2 Ethnic or Economic? Obesity increases as income decreases. Is that obvious from this figure?

↑ **OBSERVATION** QUIZ
Since childhood obesity is defined as the top 5 percent, how can this be accurate? (see answer, page 273)

What parenting practices affect children's weight? Obesity rates rise if newborns are born too early, if infants are not breast-fed and begin eating solid foods before 4 months, if young children have televisions in their bedrooms and drink large quantities of soda, if older children sleep too little but have several hours of screen time (TV and so on) each day, if people of any age rarely play outside (Hart et al., 2011; Taveras et al., 2013).

During middle childhood, children themselves have *pester power*—the ability to get adults to do what they want (Powell et al., 2011). That often includes pestering their parents to buy calorie-dense snacks that are advertised on television or that other children eat.

However, there is hope for both parents and pestering children. Rather than targeting parents *or* children, educating parents *and* their children together improves weight and health, not just during the intervention but also over the long term (Yackobovitch-Gavan et al., 2018).

A dynamic-systems approach that considers individual differences, parenting practices, school lunches, fast-food restaurants, television ads, and community norms is needed. Prevention must be tailored to the particular child, family, and culture (Harrison et al., 2011; Baranowski & Taveras, 2018).

That makes progress slow—many treatments in isolation seem to have little impact—but given the long-term effects of childhood obesity, those who care about children must encourage every step.

ASTHMA Another childhood condition that can affect learning is **asthma,** a chronic inflammatory disorder of the airways that makes breathing difficult. Sufferers have periodic attacks, sometimes requiring a rush to the hospital emergency room, a frightening experience for children who know that asthma might kill them (although it almost never does in childhood).

If asthma continues in adulthood, which it does about half the time, it can be fatal (Banks & Andrews, 2015). But children's most serious problem related to asthma is frequent absence from school. This impedes not only learning but also friendships, which thrive between children who see each other every day.

asthma
A chronic disease of the respiratory system in which inflammation narrows the airways from the nose and mouth to the lungs, causing difficulty in breathing. Signs and symptoms include wheezing, shortness of breath, chest tightness, and coughing.

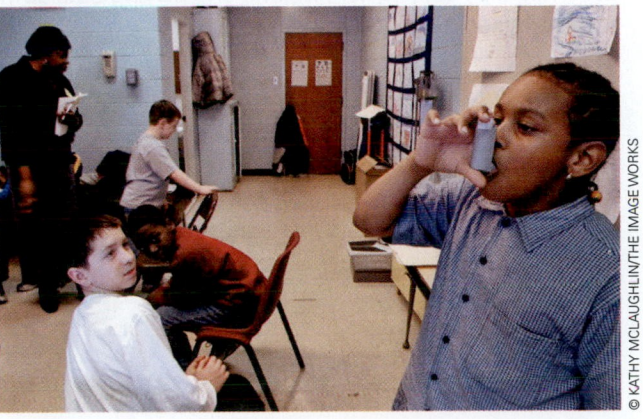

Pride and Prejudice In some city schools, asthma is so common that using an inhaler is a sign of pride, as suggested by the facial expressions of these two boys. The "prejudice" is beyond the walls of this school nurse's room, in a society that allows high rates of childhood asthma.

CHILDHOOD OBESITY AROUND THE GLOBE

Obesity now causes more deaths worldwide than malnutrition. Reductions are possible. A multifaceted prevention effort—including mothers, preschools, pediatricians, grocery stores, and even the White House—has reduced obesity in the United States for 2- to 5-year-olds. It was 13.9 percent in 2002 and was 8.4 percent in 2012. However, obesity rates from age 6 to 60 remain high everywhere.

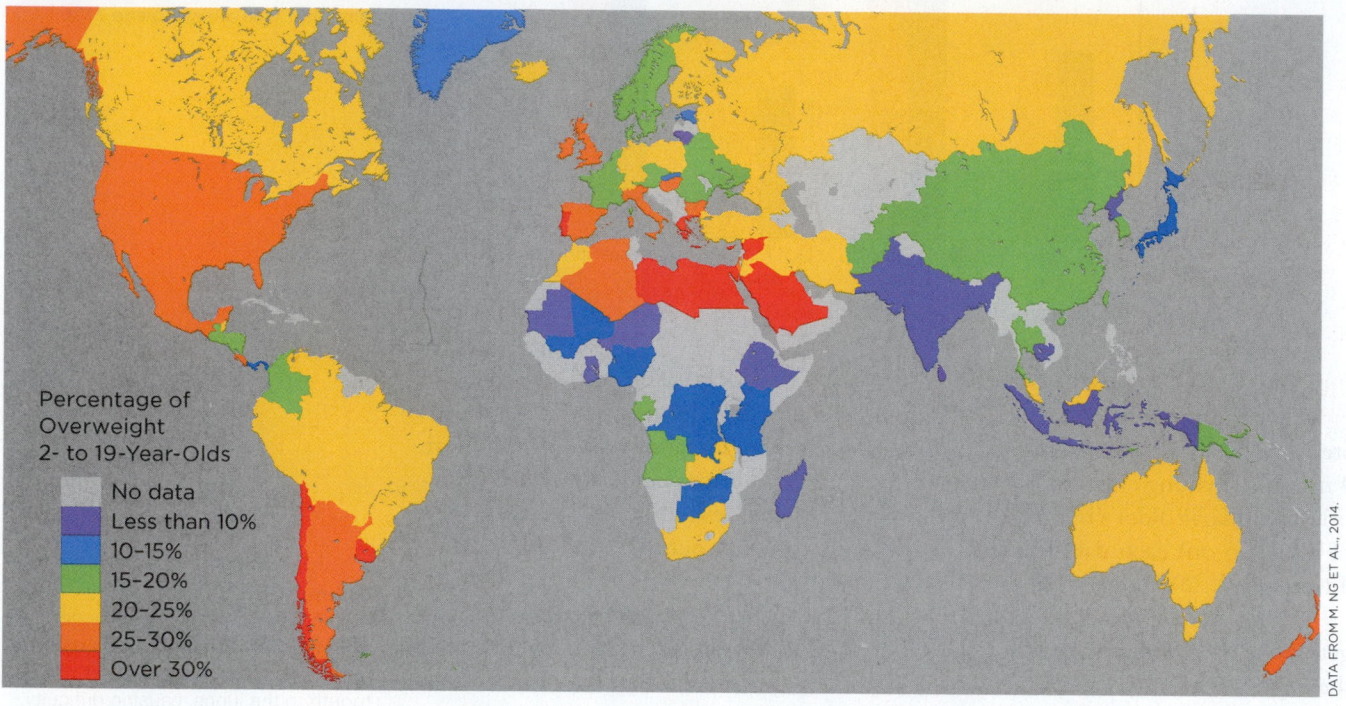

Percentage of Overweight 2- to 19-Year-Olds

- No data
- Less than 10%
- 10–15%
- 15–20%
- 20–25%
- 25–30%
- Over 30%

DATA FROM M. NG ET AL., 2014.

Ads and Obesity

Nations differ in children's exposure to televised ads for unhealthy food. The amount of this advertising continues to correlate with childhood obesity (e.g., Hewer, 2014). Parents can reduce overweight by limiting screen time and playing outside with their children. The community matters as well: When neighborhoods have no safe places to play, rates of obesity soar.

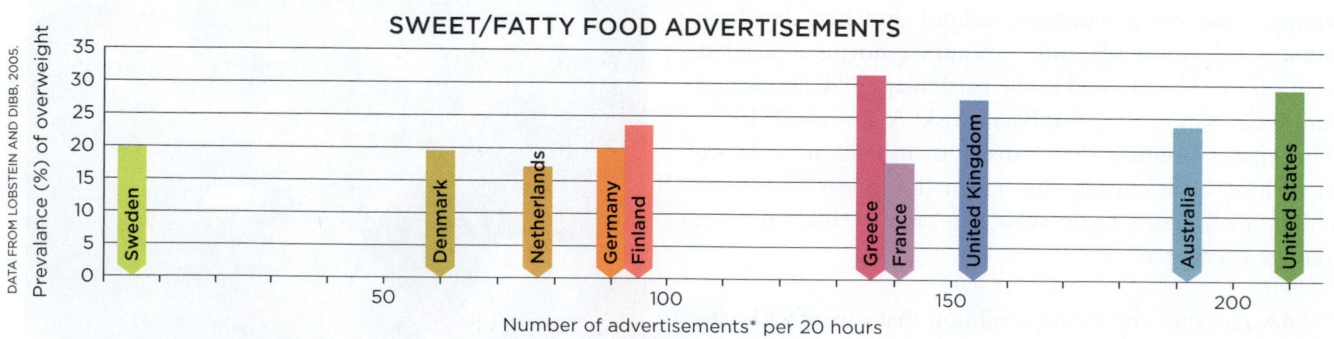

SWEET/FATTY FOOD ADVERTISEMENTS

Prevalance (%) of overweight — Number of advertisements* per 20 hours

DATA FROM LOBSTEIN AND DIBB, 2005.

Countries shown: Sweden, Denmark, Netherlands, Germany, Finland, Greece, France, United Kingdom, Australia, United States

World Health Organization (WHO) Recommendations for Physical Activity for Children

 1 Children ages 5 to 17 should be active for at least an hour a day.

 2 More than an hour of exercise each day brings additional benefits.

 3 Most physical activity should be aerobic. Vigorous activities should occur three times per week or more.

WHO also recommends daily exercise for adults of every age—including centenarians.

INFORMATION FROM WORLD HEALTH ORGANIZATION, 2011.

In the United States, childhood asthma rates tripled from 1980 to 2000, increased more gradually from 2000 to 2010, and then decreased somewhat (probably because smog has become less prevalent as clean air regulations have taken effect) (Zahran et al., 2018). Currently, 1 in every 10 U.S. 5- to 11-year-olds has been diagnosed with asthma and still suffers from the condition.

For more than half of them, asthma has meant missing school and having an attack in the past year. Rates are somewhat higher for boys, African Americans, and children of Puerto Rican descent (Zahran et al., 2018). Rates increase as income falls.

Researchers have found many causes. Some genetic alleles have been identified, as have many aspects of modern life—carpets, pollution, house pets, airtight windows, parental smoking, cockroaches, dust mites, less outdoor play. None acts in isolation. A combination of genetic sensitivity to allergies, early respiratory infections, and compromised lung functioning increases wheezing and shortness of breath (Mackenzie et al., 2014).

Some experts suggest a *hygiene hypothesis:* that "the immune system needs to tangle with microbes when we are young" (Leslie, 2012, p. 1428). Children may be over-protected from viruses and bacteria, especially in modern nations. In their concern about hygiene, parents mistakenly prevent exposure to minor infections, diseases, and family pets. All these would strengthen their child's immunity.

This hypothesis is supported by data showing that (1) first-born children develop asthma more often than later-born ones; (2) asthma and allergies are less common among farm-dwelling children; and (3) children born by cesarean delivery (very sterile) have a greater incidence of asthma. Overall, it may be "that despite what our mothers told us, cleanliness sometimes leads to sickness" (Leslie, 2012, p. 1428).

Remember the microbiome—those many bacteria within our bodies. Some in the lungs affect asthma (Singanayagam et al., 2017). Accordingly, changing the microbiome—via diet, drugs, or exposure to animals—may treat asthma. However, asthma has multiple, varied causes and types; no single treatment will help everyone.

what have you learned?

1. How does growth during middle childhood compare with growth earlier or later?

2. Why is middle childhood considered a healthy time?

3. How does physical activity affect a child's education?

4. What are several reasons why some children are less active than they should be?

5. What are the short-term and long-term effects of childhood obesity?

6. Why is asthma more common now than it was in 1980?

Cognition

Adults need to decide how and what to teach, because in middle childhood children can learn anything. Some, by age 11, beat their elders at chess, play music that adults pay to hear, publish poems, or solve complex math problems. Others survive on the streets or fight in civil wars.

Piaget in Middle Childhood

Piaget called middle childhood the time for **concrete operational thought,** characterized by new logical abilities. *Operational* comes from the Latin verb *operare,* meaning "to work; to produce." By calling this period operational, Piaget emphasized

concrete operational thought
Piaget's term for the ability to reason logically about direct experiences and perceptions.

How the Mind Works The official dictionary used for the Scripps National Spelling Bee has 472,000 words, which makes rote memorization impossible. Instead, winners recognize patterns, roots, and exceptions—all possible in middle childhood.

classification
The logical principle that things can be organized into groups (or categories or classes) according to some characteristic that they have in common.

Math and Money Third-grader Perry Akootchook understands basic math, so he might beat his mother at "spinning for money," shown here. Compare his concrete operational skills with those of a typical preoperational child, who would not be able to play this game and might give a dime for a nickel.

productive thinking. Piaget's theory is a classic stage theory: Concrete operational thinking is the stage after preoperational thought and before formal operational cognition.

In middle childhood, thinking is *concrete* operational, grounded in actual experience (like the solid concrete of a cement sidewalk). Concrete thinking arises from what is visible, tangible, and real, not abstract and theoretical (as at the next stage, formal operational thought). Children become more systematic, objective, scientific—and therefore educable.

A HIERARCHY OF CATEGORIES One logical operation is **classification,** the organization of things into groups (or *categories* or *classes*) according to some characteristic that they share. For example, *family* includes parents, siblings, and cousins. Other common classes are animals, toys, and food. Each class includes some elements and excludes others; each is part of a hierarchy.

Food, for instance, is an overarching category, with the next-lower level of the hierarchy being meat, grains, fruits, and so on. Most subclasses can be further divided: Meat includes poultry, beef, and pork, each of which can be divided again.

Adults grasp that items at the bottom of a classification hierarchy belong to every higher level: Bacon is always pork, meat, and food. They also know that each higher category includes many lower ones but not vice versa (most food, meat, and pork are not bacon). This mental operation of moving up and down the hierarchy is beyond preoperational children.

Piaget devised many classification experiments. In one, he showed a child a bunch of nine flowers—seven yellow daisies and two white roses. Then the child is asked, "Are there more daisies or more flowers?"

Until about age 7, most children answer, "More daisies." The youngest children offer no reason, but some 6-year-olds explain that "there are more yellow ones than white ones" or "because daisies are daisies, they aren't flowers" (Piaget et al., 2001).

INSIDE THE BRAIN

Coordination and Capacity

Brain scans were not available to Piaget, but his understanding of logic was prescient, reflecting what we now know as brain maturation. As children grow older, connections form between the various lobes and regions of the brain. Such connections are crucial for the complex tasks that children must master, which require "smooth coordination of large numbers of neurons" (P. Stern, 2013, p. 577).

Certain areas of the brain, called *hubs,* are locations where massive numbers of axons meet. Hubs tend to be near the corpus callosum, and damage to them correlates with brain dysfunction (as in major neurocognitive disorder and schizophrenia) (Crossley et al., 2014).

Particularly important are links between the hypothalamus and the amygdala, because emotions need to be regulated so that learning can occur. Stress impairs these connections: Slow academic mastery is one consequence of early maltreatment (Hanson et al., 2015).

On the other hand, the development of many logical concepts, including classification as Piaget described it, depends on neurological pathways from the general (food) to the particular (bacon) and back again. Those paths are not forged until brain maturation allows connective links in the hubs.

One example of the need for brain connections is learning to read, perhaps the most important intellectual accomplishment of middle childhood. Reading is not instinctual: Our ancestors never did it, and until recent centuries only a few scribes and scholars could make sense of marks on paper. Consequently, the brain has no areas dedicated to reading, the way it does for talking or gesturing (Sousa, 2014).

Instead, reading uses many parts of the brain—one for sounds, another for recognizing letters, another for sequencing, another for comprehension, and more. By working together, those parts foster listening, talking, and thinking, and then put it all together. That's reading (Lewandowski & Lovett, 2014).

Indeed, every skill, every logical idea, every thought from one circumstance that is applied to another requires connections between many neurons. As Piaget recognized, a cascade of new intellectual concepts results when connections allow a logical idea to extend to many specifics.

APPLICATION TO MATH Another example of concrete logic is **seriation,** the knowledge that things can be arranged in a logical *series*. Seriation is crucial for using (not merely memorizing) the alphabet or the number sequence. By age 5, most children can count up to 100. But because they do not yet grasp seriation, they cannot correctly estimate where any particular two-digit number would be placed on a line that starts at 0 and ends at 100 (Meadows, 2006).

Indeed, every logical concept helps with math. Concrete operational thinkers begin to understand that 15 is always 15 (conservation); that numbers from 20 to 29 are all in the 20s (classification); that 134 is less than 143 (seriation); and that because $5 \times 3 = 15$, it follows that $15 \div 5$ must equal 3 (reversibility). By age 11, children use mental categories and subcategories flexibly, inductively, and simultaneously, unlike at age 7.

seriation
The concept that things can be arranged in a logical series, such as the number sequence or the alphabet.

Vygotsky and Culture

Like Piaget, Vygotsky felt that educators should consider children's thought processes, not just the products. He also believed that middle childhood was a time for much learning, with the specifics dependent on the family, school, and culture.

Vygotsky appreciated children's curiosity and creativity. For that reason, he believed that an educational system based on rote memorization rendered the child "helpless in the face of any sensible attempt to apply any of this acquired knowledge" (Vygotsky, 1994a, pp. 356–357).

◆◆ **Especially for Teachers**
How might Piaget's and Vygotsky's ideas help in teaching geography to a class of third-graders? (see response, page 272)

Girls Can't Do It As Vygotsky recognized, children learn whatever their culture teaches. Fifty years ago, girls were in cooking and sewing classes. No longer. This 2012 photo shows 10-year-olds Kamrin and Caitlin in a Kentucky school, preparing for a future quite different from that of their grandmothers.

THE ROLE OF INSTRUCTION Unlike Piaget, who thought children would discover most concepts themselves, Vygotsky stressed direct instruction from teachers and other mentors. They provide the scaffold between potential and knowledge by engaging each child in his or her zone of proximal development.

Vygotsky would not be surprised at one finding of recent research: Internationally as well as nationally, children who begin school at age 4 or 5, not 6 or 7, tend to be ahead in academic achievement compared to those who enter later. The benefit of early schooling is still apparent at age 15, although not in every nation (Sprietsma, 2010). Vygotsky would explain the variation in impact by noting that in some nations early education is far more interactive, and hence better at guided participation, than in others.

Play with peers, screen time, dinner with families, neighborhood play—every experience, from birth on, teaches a child, according to Vygotsky. On their own, children gradually become more logical, but Vygotsky thought mentoring was helpful. Thus, when children are taught, they can master logical arguments (even counterfactual ones) by age 11.

For example, they know that *if* birds can fly, and *if* elephants are birds, *then* elephants can fly (Christoforides et al., 2016). Vygotsky emphasized that lessons vary by culture and school and are not simply the result of maturation. He recognized, however, that children are limited in grasping the philosophical issues of life and death. They tend to be quite matter-of-fact, absorbing whatever their parents and culture teach rather than seeking the deeper meaning—as was true for Philip in A Case to Study.

A CASE TO STUDY

Is She Going to Die?

Philip is a delightful 7-year-old, with many intellectual skills. He speaks French to his mother and English to everyone else; he can already read fluently and calculate Pokémon trades; he does his schoolwork conscientiously. He is well liked, because he knows how to cooperate when he plays soccer, to use "bathroom words" that make his peers laugh, and to use polite phrases that adults appreciate. Thus, his mind is developing just as it should.

Last year, his mother, Dora, needed open-heart surgery. She and her husband, Craig, told Philip who would take him to and from school and who would cook his dinner while she was recovering. Craig did the explaining, because Dora did not want to show her fear.

Philip responded to his parents' description by mirroring their attitude: quite factual, without emotions. He had few questions, mostly about exactly what the surgeon would cut. A day later he told his parents that when he told his classmates that his mother was having an operation, one of them asked, "Is she going to die?" Philip reported this to illustrate his friend's foolishness; he seemed unaware that the question was insensitive. His parents, wisely, exchanged wide-eyed glances but listened without comment. Later Craig asked Dora, "What is wrong with him? Does he have no heart?"

The fact that children are concrete operational thinkers (Piaget) and their perceptions arise from the immediate social context (Vygotsky) is illustrated not only by Philip but by every child in middle childhood. If they are told that their parents are divorcing, they might ask, "Where will I live?" instead of expressing sympathy, surprise, or anger. Aspects of cognition that adults take for granted—empathy, emotional sensitivity, hope and fears for the future—develop gradually.

Dora's surgery went well; no repeat surgery is expected. Someday Philip might blame his 7-year-old self for his nonchalance; Craig and Dora can reassure him that he reacted as a child. Adolescents have more than enough "heart"; they gain it during middle childhood.

Information Processing

Contemporary educators and psychologists find both Piaget and Vygotsky insightful. International research confirms the merits of their theories (Griffin, 2011; Mercer & Howe, 2012). Piaget described universal changes; Vygotsky noted cultural impact.

However, both grand theories of child cognition are limited, especially regarding school curriculum. Each domain of achievement may follow a particular path (Siegler, 2016). Developmentalists now recognize the need for a third approach to understanding cognition.

That third approach is *information-processing*, which benefits from technology that allows much more detailed data and analysis than were possible for Piaget or Vygotsky. Like computers that process information, people accumulate large amounts of facts. They then (1) seek relevant facts (as a search engine does) for each cognitive task, (2) analyze (as software programs do), and (3) express conclusions (as a printout might). By tracing the paths and links of each of these functions, scientists better understand the learning process.

The usefulness of the information-processing approach is evident in data on children's school achievement year by year and even month by month. Absences, vacations, new schools, and even new teachers may set back a child's learning because learning each day builds on the learning of the previous day. Brain connections and pathways are forged from repeated experiences, allowing advances in processing. Without careful building and repetition, fragile connections between neurons break.

One of the leaders of the information-processing perspective is Robert Siegler, who has studied the day-by-day details of children's cognition in math (Siegler & Braithwaite, 2017). Siegler compared the acquisition of knowledge to waves on an ocean beach when the tide is rising. After ebb and flow, eventually a new level is reached.

Similarly, math understanding accrues gradually, with new and better strategies for calculation tried, ignored, half-used, abandoned, and finally adopted (Siegler, 2016). The specifics are influenced by the culture, which may or may not emphasize math, and the teachers, who may or may not understand the need for patience as well as practice. Counting itself may be the product of culture: Some languages lack words for large numbers, fractions, and so on (Everett, 2017).

Overall, information processing guides teachers who want to know exactly which concepts and skills are crucial foundations for mastery of reading, writing, science, math, and human relations. Theory of mind, for example, turns out to be pivotal for understanding the scientific process and for estimating where a number might fall on a line (such as where the number 53 would be placed on a line from 0 to 100). That skill predicts later math achievement (Piekny & Maehler, 2013; Peng et al., 2017; Libertus et al., 2013).

KNOWLEDGE LEADS TO KNOWLEDGE The more people already know, the better they can learn. Having an extensive **knowledge base,** or a broad body of knowledge in a particular subject, makes it easier to remember and understand related new information. As children gain knowledge during the school years, they become better able to judge (1) accuracy, (2) what is worth remembering, and (3) what is not important (Woolley & Ghossainy, 2013).

© ARKO DATTA/X01337/REUTERS/CORBIS

Never Lost Unlike in the United States, in Varanasi, India, a sense of direction is essential in language and life, so all the children develop it. These children of Varanasi sleep beside the Ganges River in the daytime. At night they use their excellent sense of direction to guide devotees from elsewhere.

ARITHMETIC STRATEGIES: The Research of Robert Siegler demonstrates how children acquire math understanding.

knowledge base
A body of knowledge in a particular area that makes it easier to master new information in that area.

A Boy in Memphis Moziah Bridges (known as Mo Morris) created colorful bowties, which he first traded for rocks in elementary school. He then created his own company (Mo's Bows) at age 9, selling $300,000 worth of ties to major retailers by age 14. He is shown here with his mother, who encouraged his entrepreneurship.

GIOVANNI RUFINO/ABC VIA GETTY IMAGES

control processes
Mechanisms (including selective attention, metacognition, and emotional regulation) that combine memory, processing speed, and knowledge to regulate the analysis and flow of information within the information-processing system. (Also called *executive processes*.)

What Does She See? It depends on her knowledge base and personal experiences. Perhaps this trip to an aquarium in North Carolina is no more than a break from the school routine, with the teachers merely shepherding the children to keep them safe. Or, perhaps she has learned about sharks and dorsal fins, about scales and gills, about warm-blooded mammals and cold-blooded fish, so she is fascinated by the swimming creatures she watches. Or, if her personal emotions shape her perceptions, she feels sad about the fish in their watery cage or finds joy in their serenity and beauty.

MICHAEL PRINCE/CORBIS

Past experience, current opportunity, and personal motivation all facilitate increases in the knowledge base. Motivation explains why a child's knowledge base may not be what parents or teachers prefer. Some schoolchildren memorize words and rhythms of hit songs, know plots and characters of television programs, or recite names and statistics of basketball (or soccer, baseball, or cricket) stars. Yet they do not know whether World War I was in the nineteenth or twentieth century or whether Pakistan is in Asia or Africa.

Concepts are learned best when linked to personal and emotional experiences. For example, children from South Asia, or who have classmates from there, learn the boundaries of Pakistan when teachers appreciate and connect their students' heritage. On the other hand, children who are new to a nation, or even new to a particular school, may be confused by some kinds of learning that are easy for those who have always lived in that community.

Control Processes

The neurological mechanisms that put memory, processing speed, and the knowledge base together are **control processes;** they regulate the analysis and flow of information within the brain. Two terms are often used to refer to cognitive control—*metacognition* (sometimes called "thinking about thinking") and *metamemory* (knowing about memory).

Control processes require the brain to organize, prioritize, and direct mental operations, much as the CEO (chief executive officer) of a business organizes, prioritizes, and directs business operations. For that reason, control processes are also called *executive processes,* and the ability to use them is called *executive function* (already mentioned in Chapter 5). Control processes allow a person to step back from the specifics to consider more general goals and cognitive strategies.

Maturation and experience matter. For instance, in one study, children took a fill-in-the-blank test and indicated how confident

they were about each answer. Young children do not do well: They may be quite sure of a wrong answer. Then these children were allowed to delete some questions, with the remaining ones counting more. By age 9, children could estimate correctness; by age 11, they knew what to delete (Roebers et al., 2009).

Control processes develop spontaneously as the prefrontal cortex matures, but they can be taught. Examples include spelling rules ("*i* before *e* except after *c*") and ways to remember how to turn a lightbulb ("lefty-loosey, righty-tighty").

Preschoolers ignore such rules or use them only on command; 7-year-olds begin to use them; 9-year-olds can create and master more complicated rules. Efforts to teach executive control succeed if the particular neurological maturation of the child is taken into account, which is exactly what information-processing theorists would predict (Karbach & Unger, 2014).

Language

Language is crucial for cognition in middle childhood. It is the means by which children learn new concepts, and it also indicates how much children have learned. A school-age child who can explain ideas with complex sentences is a child who is thinking well. Every aspect of language—vocabulary, comprehension, communication skill, and code-switching—advances each year from age 6 to 11.

VOCABULARY Vocabulary builds during middle childhood. Concrete operational children are logical; they can understand prefixes, suffixes, compound words, phrases, and metaphors, even if they have not heard them before. For example, 2-year-olds know *egg*, but 10-year-olds also know *egg salad, egg-drop soup, egghead, a good egg,* and "*last one in is a rotten egg*"—a metaphor from my childhood that a 2017 Google search found still relevant today. By age 10, a child who has never smelled a rotten egg, nor heard that phrase, can figure out the meaning.

In middle childhood, some words become pivotal for understanding the curriculum, such as *negotiate, evolve, allegation, deficit, molecules.* Consequently, vocabulary is taught in every elementary school classroom.

ADJUSTING LANGUAGE TO THE CONTEXT Another aspect of language that advances markedly in middle childhood is pragmatics, defined in Chapter 5. This is evident when a child knows which words to use with teachers (never calling them a rotten egg) and informally with friends (who can be called rotten eggs or worse).

As children master pragmatics, they become more adept at making friends. Shy 6-year-olds cope far better with the social pressures of school if they use pragmatics well (Coplan & Weeks, 2009). By contrast, children with autism spectrum disorder are usually very poor at this aspect of language (Klinger et al., 2014).

Mastery of pragmatics allows children to change styles of speech, or *linguistic codes,* depending on their audience. Each code includes many aspects of language—not just vocabulary but also tone, pronunciation, grammar, sentence length, idioms, and gestures. Sometimes the switch is between *formal code* (used in academic contexts) and *informal code* (used with friends); sometimes it is between standard (or proper) speech and dialect or vernacular (used on the street).

All children need instruction because the logic of grammar and spelling (whether *who* or *whom* is correct or how to spell *you*) is almost impossible to deduce.

JONAS GRATZER/LIGHTROCKET VIA GETTY IMAGES

Go with the Flow This boat classroom in Bangladesh picks up students on shore and then uses solar energy to power computers linked to the Internet as part of instruction. The educational context will teach skills and metaphors that their parents will not understand.

FIGURE 7.3 Home and Country Do you see good news? A dramatic increase in the number of bilingual children is a benefit for the nation, but the increase in the number who have trouble with English suggests that more education is needed.

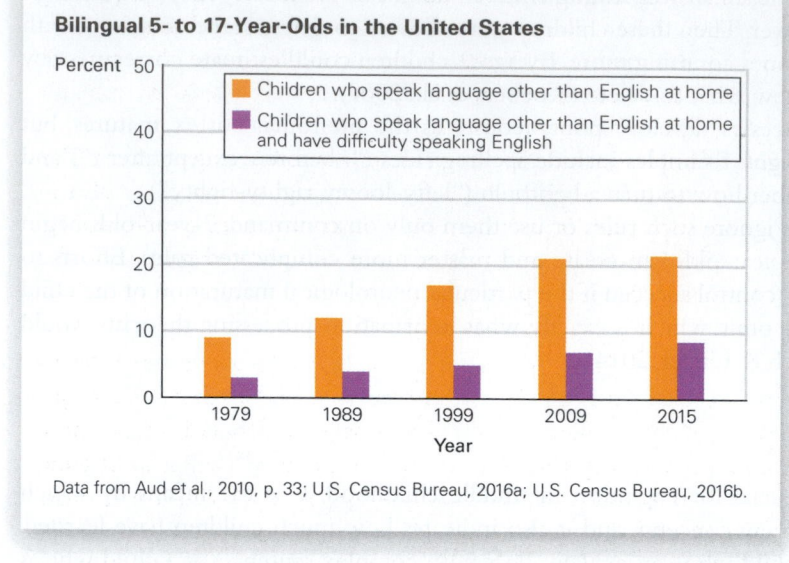

Data from Aud et al., 2010, p. 33; U.S. Census Bureau, 2016a; U.S. Census Bureau, 2016b.

English Language Learners (ELLs)
Children in the United States whose proficiency in English is low—usually below a cutoff score on an oral or written test. Many children who speak a non-English language at home are also capable in English; they are *not* ELLs.

immersion
A strategy in which instruction in all school subjects occurs in the second (usually the majority) language that a child is learning.

bilingual education
A strategy in which school subjects are taught in both the learner's original language and the second (majority) language.

ESL (English as a Second Language)
A U.S. approach to teaching English that gathers all of the non-English speakers together and provides intense instruction in English. Students' first languages are never used; the goal is to prepare them for regular classes in English.

Months or Years? ESL classes, like this one in Canada, often use pictures and gestures to foster word learning. How soon will these children be ready for regular classes?

Yet everyone will be judged by their ability to speak and write the formal code, so children need to learn it.

SPEAKING TWO LANGUAGES Code changes are obvious when children speak one language at home and another at school. Every nation includes many such children; most of the world's 6,000 languages are not school languages.

In the United States, about one school-age child in five speaks something other than English at home (see Figure 7.3). Many other U.S. children speak 1 of the 20 or so English dialects with regional or ethnic word use, pronunciation, and grammar. That creates a challenge for teachers, because code-switching correlates with school achievement yet pride in origins correlates with motivation (Terry et al., 2016). Fortunately, children can learn several codes—easily before age 5, with some help in middle childhood, and with effort after puberty—and they also need to be proud of their first language.

Educators and political leaders in the United States argue about how to teach English to **English Language Learners (ELLs),** whose first language is not Standard English. One strategy is **immersion,** with instruction entirely in the new code. The opposite strategy is to teach children in their first language initially and then to add instruction of the second as a "foreign" tongue (a strategy that is rare in the United States but common elsewhere).

Between these extremes lies **bilingual education,** with instruction in two languages, and **ESL (English as a Second Language),** with all non-English speakers taught English in one multilingual group, preparing them to join English-only classes.

Every method for teaching a second language sometimes succeeds and sometimes fails. Language-learning abilities change with age: The youngest children learn a new language fastest.

For cognitive advances during middle childhood, the information-processing perspective suggests that children should learn two languages. When bilingual individuals are asked to reason about something in their second language, they tend to be more rational and less emotional—which usually (but not always) leads to better thought (Costa et al., 2017).

Fluently bilingual children must inhibit one language while using another. This is a benefit because it increases cognitive control, not only in language but also in other aspects of executive function (Bialystok, 2018). Cognitive advances depend on linguistic proficiency: Children who are not fluent in at least one language are also impaired in cognitive skills.

POVERTY AND LANGUAGE Every study finds that SES affects cognitive development, with poor language mastery the prominent sign and perhaps the major cause. Children from low-SES families usually have smaller vocabularies than those from higher-SES families, and they also are impaired in grammar (fewer compound sentences, dependent clauses, and conditional verbs) (Hart & Risley, 1995; Hoff, 2013). That slows down school learning in every subject.

Brain scans confirm that development of the hippocampus is particularly affected by SES, and that may be critical for language learning (Jednoróg et al., 2012). How does poverty affect the brain? Possibilities include inadequate prenatal care, no breakfast, lead in the bloodstream, crowded households, few books at home, teenage parents, authoritarian child rearing, inexperienced teachers, air pollution, neighborhood violence, lack of role models . . . the list could go on and on (Van Agt et al., 2015; Kolb & Gibb, 2015; Rowe et al., 2016). All of these conditions correlate with low SES, slower language development, and less learning.

One factor seems to be a cause, not just a correlate: language heard early on. The mother's education is influential, especially if she continues her quest for learning by reading and asking questions. Children who grow up in homes with many books accumulate, on average, three more years of education than children who live in homes with no books (Evans et al., 2010). Remember the plasticity of the brain. In some families, neuronal connections are strengthened and dendrites grow to support language.

Low income per se is not as influential as maternal talk and listening. Educated parents are more likely to take their children to museums, zoos, and libraries, and to engage children in conversation about the interesting sights around them. Many sing to their children, not just a few simple songs but dozens of songs with varied vocabulary. Children benefit from conversations with relatives, strangers, friends, and teachers.

Some fortunate bilingual children speak one language at home and learn another language elsewhere, because they spend extensive time with speakers of that second language. It is amazing how much children can learn. One of my African students speaks five languages, all learned in childhood. His mother and his father each came from a different tribe, so he learned both local languages. He was schooled in Senegal (French-speaking) and Sierra Leone (English-speaking). Finally, he learned Arabic to study the Quran.

Some immigrant children then have another advantage. They are motivated to validate their parents'

◆ **Especially for Parents**
You've had an exhausting day but are setting out to buy groceries. Your 7-year-old son wants to go with you. Should you explain that you are so tired that you want to make a quick solo trip to the supermarket this time? (see response, page 272)

↓ **OBSERVATION** QUIZ
What in the daughter's behavior suggests that maternal grooming is a common event in her life? (see answer, page 273)

Priorities This family in London is low-income, evident in the stained walls, peeling paint, and old toilet, but that does not necessarily limit the girl's future. More important is what she learns about values and behavior. If this scene is typical, this mother is teaching her daughter about appearance and obedience. What would happen if the child had to care for her own grooming? Tangles? Short hair? Independence? Linguistic advances?

JW LTD/PHOTOGRAPHER'S CHOICE/GETTY IMAGES

decision to leave their native land (Ceballo et al., 2014; Fuller & García Coll, 2010). Their parents expect them to learn the school language and study hard. They do.

what have you learned?

1. What did Piaget mean when he called cognition in middle childhood *concrete operational thought*?

2. How do Vygotsky and Piaget differ in their explanation of cognitive advances in middle childhood?

3. How does information-processing theory differ from traditional theories of cognitive development?

4. According to Siegler, what is the pattern of learning math concepts?

5. How and why does the knowledge base increase in middle childhood?

6. How might control processes help a student learn?

7. What is the relationship between language and cognition?

8. Why would a child's linguistic code be criticized by teachers but admired by peers?

Teaching and Learning

As we have seen, middle childhood is a time of great learning. Children worldwide learn whatever adults in their culture teach, and their brains are ready. (See the accompanying At About This Time tables for some of the universally recognized sequences of learning reading and arithmetic.) Traditionally, they were educated at home, but now almost all of the world's 7-year-olds are in school.

The Hidden Curriculum

hidden curriculum
The unofficial, unstated, or implicit patterns within a school that influence what children learn. For instance, teacher background, organization of the play space, and tracking are all part of the hidden curriculum—not formally prescribed, but instructive to the children.

Differences between nations and between schools in the United States are stark in the **hidden curriculum**—all of the implicit values and assumptions of schools. Schedules, tracking, teacher characteristics, discipline, teaching methods, sports competitions, student government, and extracurricular activities are all part of the hidden curriculum. That teaches children far more than the formal, published curriculum that lists what is taught in each grade.

An obvious example is the physical surroundings. Some schools have spacious classrooms, wide hallways, and large, grassy playgrounds; others have cramped, poorly equipped classrooms and cement play yards. In some nations, school is held outdoors, with no chairs, desks, or books; classes are canceled when it rains. What does that tell the students?

TEACHER ETHNICITY Another aspect of the hidden curriculum is who the teachers are. If their gender, ethnicity, or economic background is unlike their students, children may conclude that education is irrelevant for them. School organization is also significant. If the school has gifted classes, the non-gifted may conclude that they are not capable of learning.

The United States is experiencing major demographic shifts. Since 2010, half of the babies born are from Hispanic, Black, Asian, or Native American families, whereas more than two-thirds of the adults are of European background. Given the

At About This Time

Math

Age	Norms and Expectations
4–5 years	• Count to 20. • Understand one-to-one correspondence of objects and numbers. • Understand *more* and *less.* • Recognize and name shapes.
6 years	• Count to 100. • Understand *bigger* and *smaller.* • Add and subtract one-digit numbers.
8 years	• Add and subtract two-digit numbers. • Understand simple multiplication and division. • Understand word problems with two variables.
10 years	• Add, subtract, multiply, and divide multi-digit numbers. • Understand simple fractions, percentages, area, and perimeter of shapes. • Understand word problems with three variables.
12 years	• Begin to use abstract concepts, such as formulas and algebra.

Math learning depends heavily on direct instruction and repeated practice, which means that some children advance more quickly than others. This list is only a rough guide, meant to illustrate the importance of sequence.

At About This Time

Reading

Age	Norms and Expectations
4–5 years	• Understand basic book concepts. For instance, children learning English and many other languages understand that books are written from front to back, with print from left to right, and that letters make words that describe pictures. • Recognize letters—name the letters on sight. • Recognize and spell own name.
6–7 years	• Know the sounds of the consonants and vowels, including those that have two sounds (e.g., *c, g, o*). • Use sounds to figure out words. • Read simple words, such as *cat, sit, ball, jump.*
8 years	• Read simple sentences out loud, 50 words per minute, including words of two syllables. • Understand basic punctuation, consonant–vowel blends. • Comprehend what is read.
9–10 years	• Read and understand paragraphs and chapters, including advanced punctuation (e.g., the colon). • Answer comprehension questions about concepts as well as facts. • Read polysyllabic words (e.g., *vegetarian, population, multiplication*).
11–12 years	• Demonstrate rapid and fluent oral reading (more than 100 words per minute). • Vocabulary includes words that have specialized meaning in various fields. For example, in civics, *liberties, federal, parliament,* and *environment* all have special meanings. • Comprehend paragraphs about unfamiliar topics. • Sound out new words, figuring out meaning using cognates and context. • Read for pleasure.
13+ years	• Continue to build vocabulary, with greater emphasis on comprehension than on speech. Understand textbooks.

Reading is a complex mix of skills, dependent on brain maturation, education, and culture. The sequence given here is approximate; it should not be taken as a standard to measure any particular child.

past history of sexual and racial discrimination, many experienced teachers are older white women. Thus, most children never have an elementary school teacher who is a man of minority background.

Of course, many older, European American women are excellent teachers, but schools also need more excellent male, minority teachers—not only for the minority boys. The hidden curriculum could teach that caring educators come in many colors. Does it?

TEACHER EXPECTATIONS Less visible but probably more influential is the hidden message that comes from teacher attitudes. If a teacher expects children to be disruptive, or unable to learn, children confirm those expectations. Fortunately, teacher expectations are malleable: Learning increases and absences decrease when teachers believe all of their students can learn and they teach accordingly, with encouragement (Sparks, 2016).

One teacher expectation is that students talk, or do not talk, in class. In the United States, adults are expected to voice their opinions. Accordingly, many teachers welcome student questions, call on children who do not speak up, ask children to work in pairs so that each child talks, and grant points for participation. North American students learn to speak, even when they do not know the answers. Elsewhere, children are expected to be quiet.

Room to Learn? In the elementary school classroom in Florida *(left),* the teacher is guiding two students who are working to discover concepts in physics—a stark contrast to the Filipino classroom *(right)* in a former storeroom. Sometimes the hidden curriculum determines the overt curriculum, as shown here.

This aspect of the hidden curriculum affects learning. In one study, middle-class children asked questions and requested help from their teachers more often than lower-SES students did (Calarco, 2014). The researchers suggested that the low-SES students sought to avoid teacher attention, fearing it would lead to criticism. Might that have given teachers the impression that they were disinterested? Thus, the hidden curriculum might prevent students who most need encouragement from getting it.

INTERNATIONAL TESTING Every nation now wants to improve education, because they believe that longitudinal data find that when achievement rises, the national economy advances (Hanushek & Woessmann, 2015). Better-educated children become more productive and healthier adults. That is one reason many developing nations are building more schools and colleges.

Nations also want to make education more effective for all students. To measure that, almost 100 nations have participated in at least one massive international test of children's learning.

Science and math achievement are tested in the **Trends in Math and Science Study (TIMSS).** The main test of reading is the **Progress in International Reading Literacy Study (PIRLS).** A third test is the **Programme for International Student Assessment (PISA),** which is designed to measure the ability to apply learning to everyday issues. East Asian nations always rank high, and scores of several nations (some in Europe, most in Asia) surpass the United States (see Tables 7.1 and 7.2).

One surprising example is that Finland's scores increased dramatically, especially in the PIRLS and the PISA, after a wholesale reform of its public education system. Reforms occurred in several waves (Sahlberg 2011, 2015). In 1985 ability grouping was abolished, and in 1994 the curriculum began to encourage collaboration and active learning rather than competitive passive education.

Currently, in Finland, all children learn together—no tracking—and teachers are mandated to help each child. If some children need special help to master the formal curriculum, teachers provide it *within* the regular class.

Over the past two decades, strict requirements for becoming a teacher have been put in place in Finland. Only the top 3 percent of Finland's high school graduates are

Trends in Math and Science Study (TIMSS)
An international assessment of the math and science skills of fourth- and eighth-graders. Although the TIMSS is very useful, different countries' scores are not always comparable because sample selection, test administration, and content validity are hard to keep uniform.

Progress in International Reading Literacy Study (PIRLS)
Inaugurated in 2001, a planned five-year cycle of international trend studies in the reading ability of fourth-graders.

Programme for International Student Assessment (PISA)
An international test taken by 15-year-olds in 50 nations that is designed to measure problem solving and cognition in daily life.

TABLE 7.1	TIMSS Ranking and Average Scores of Math Achievement for Fourth-Graders, 2011 and 2015	
	2011	**2015**
Singapore	606	618
Hong Kong	602	615
Korea	605	608
Chinese Taipei	591	597
Japan	585	593
N. Ireland	562	570
Russia	542	564
England	542	546
Belgium	549	546
United States	541	539
Canada (Quebec)	533	533
Finland	545	532
Netherlands	540	530
Germany	528	522
Sweden	504	519
Australia	516	517
Canada (Ontario)	518	512
Italy	508	507
New Zealand	486	491
Iran	431	431
Kuwait	342	353

TABLE 7.2	PIRLS Distribution of Reading Achievement for Fourth-Graders, 2011 and 2016	
	2011	**2016**
Hong Kong	571	569
Russian Federation	568	581
Finland	568	566
Singapore	567	576
N. Ireland	558	565
United States	556	549
Denmark	554	547
Chinese Taipei	553	559
Ireland	552	567
England	552	559
Canada	548	543
Italy	541	548
Germany	541	537
Israel	541	530
New Zealand	531	523
Australia	527	544
Poland	526	565
France	520	511
Spain	513	528
Iran	457	428

Information from Mullis et al., 2012b; 2017.

admitted to teachers' colleges. They study for five years at the university at no charge, earning a master's degree in the theory and practice of education.

Finnish teachers are granted more autonomy within their classrooms than is typical in other nations. Since the 1990s, they have had extra time and encouragement to work with colleagues (Sahlberg, 2011, 2015). They are taught to respond to each child's temperament as well as skills. This strategy has led to achievement, particularly in math (Viljaranta et al., 2015).

PROBLEMS WITH INTERNATIONAL COMPARISONS Elaborate and extensive measures are in place to make the PIRLS, TIMSS, and PISA valid. Test items are designed to be fair and culture-free, and participating children represent the diversity (economic, ethnic, etc.) of each nation's child population. Thousands of experts work to ensure validity and reliability. Consequently, most social scientists respect the data gathered from these tests.

The tests are far from perfect, however. Creating questions that are equally fair for everyone is impossible. For example, in math, should fourth-graders be expected to understand fractions, graphs, decimals, and simple geometry? Nations introduce these concepts at different ages, and some schools stress math more than others: Should every fourth-grader be expected to divide fractions?

THINK CRITICALLY: Finland's success has been attributed to many factors, some mentioned here and some regarding the geography and population of the nation. What do you think is the most influential reason?

"Big deal, an A in math. That would be a D in any other country."

After such general issues are decided, items are written. The following item tested math:

Three thousand tickets for a basketball game are numbered 1 to 3,000. People with ticket numbers ending with 112 receive a prize. Write down all the prize-winning numbers.

Only 26 percent of fourth-graders worldwide got this one right (112; 1,112; 2,112—with no additional numbers). About half of the children in East Asian nations and 36 percent of the U.S. children were correct. Those national scores are not surprising; children in Singapore, Japan, and China have been close to the top on every international test for 20 years, and the United States has been above average but not by much.

Children from North Africa did especially poorly; only 2 percent of Moroccan fourth-graders were correct. Is basketball, or 3,000 tickets for one game, or random prizes as common in North Africa as in the United States?

Another math item gives ingredients—4 eggs, 8 cups of flour, ½ cup of milk—and asks:

The above ingredients are used to make a recipe for 6 people. Sam wants to make this recipe for only 3 people. Complete the table below to show what Sam needs to make the recipe for 3 people. The number of eggs he needs is shown.

Eggs	2
Flour	
Milk	

The table lists 2 eggs, and the child needs to fill in amounts of flour and milk. Fourth-grade children in Ireland and England scored highest on this item (about half got it right), while those in Korea, China, and Japan scored lower (about 33 percent). The United States scored higher than East Asian nations but lower than England.

This is puzzling, since East Asians usually surpass others in math. Why not here? Are English and Irish children experienced with recipes for baked goods that include eggs, flour, and milk, unlike Japanese children? Or are Asian children distracted by the idea of a boy cooking?

GENDER DIFFERENCES IN SCHOOL PERFORMANCE In addition to marked national, ethnic, and economic differences, gender differences in achievement scores are reported. The PIRLS finds fourth-grade girls ahead of boys in reading in every nation, by an average of 19 points (Mullis et al., 2017).

The 2016 female verbal advantage on the PIRLS in the United States is 8 points, which is a difference of less than 2 percent. Several other nations are close to the U.S. norms, including France, Spain, and Hong Kong. Does that mean that those nations are more gender-equitable than the nation with the widest gender gap—Saudi Arabia with a 65-point gap (464/399)? Maybe, maybe not.

Historically, boys were ahead of girls in math and science. However, TIMSS reported that those gender differences among fourth-graders in math have narrowed, disappeared, or reversed. In many nations, boys are still slightly ahead, with the United States showing a male advantage (7 points—less than 2 percent). However, in other nations, girls are ahead, sometimes significantly, such as 10 points in Indonesia and 20 points in Jordan. Why? Is there an anti-male bias in their schools or culture?

In middle childhood, girls in every nation have higher report card grades, including in math and science. Is that biological (girls are better able to sit still, to

VIDEO ACTIVITY: Educating the Girls of the World examines the situation of girls' education around the world while stressing the importance of education for all children.

STEVE DEBENPORT/ASISEETT/GETTY IMAGES

Future Engineers After-school clubs now encourage boys to learn cooking and girls to play chess, and both sexes are active in every sport. The most recent push is for STEM (Science, Technology, Engineering, and Math) education—as in this after-school robotics club.

manipulate a pencil)? Or cultural (girls have been taught to do as they are told)? Or does the hidden curriculum favor girls (most of their elementary school teachers were women)?

The popularity of various explanations has shifted. Analysts once attributed girls' higher grades in school to their faster physical maturation. Now explanations are more often sociocultural—that parents and teachers expect girls to be good students and that schools are organized to favor female strengths. The same switch in explanations, from biology to culture, appears for male advantages in science. Is that change itself cultural?

Schooling in the United States

Many international tests indicate improvements in U.S. children's academic performance over the past decades. However, the United States has the largest disparities between income and ethnic groups. Some blame the disparity on immigration, but other nations (e.g., Canada) have more ethnic groups and immigrants than the United States, yet the Canadian achievement gap between groups is not as large.

NATIONAL STANDARDS For decades, the U.S. government has sponsored the **National Assessment of Educational Progress (NAEP),** which is a group of tests designed to measure achievement in reading, mathematics, and other subjects. The NAEP finds fewer children proficient than do state tests. For example, New York's tests reported 62 percent proficient in math, but the NAEP found only 32 percent; 51 percent were proficient in reading on New York's state tests but only 35 percent according to NAEP (Martin, 2014).

The NAEP also finds that Latino and African American fourth-graders are about 12 percent lower than their European American peers in reading and 9 percent lower in math (National Center for Health Statistics, 2016). Moreover, "Federal civil rights data show persistent and widespread disparities among disadvantaged students from prekindergarten to high school" with low-SES children, English Language Learners, and minority ethnic groups all suffering (McNeil & Blad, 2014, p. 8).

National Assessment of Educational Progress (NAEP)
An ongoing and nationally representative measure of U.S. children's achievement in reading, mathematics, and other subjects over time; nicknamed "the Nation's Report Card."

◆ **Especially for School Administrators**
Children who wear uniforms in school tend to score higher on reading tests. Why? (see response, page 273)

For some statistics—high school graduation, for instance—Asian American children achieve at higher rates than European Americans. However, the "model minority" stereotype obscures disadvantages for many children of Asian heritage. Further, Asian children may suffer from parental pressure and peer jealousy (Cherng & Liu, 2017).

The reason for disparities within the United States seems more economic than ethnic, because African Americans in some of the wealthier states (Massachusetts) score higher than European Americans in the poorer states (Mississippi).

Many suggest that the disparity in local funding for schools is at the root of the problem: High-SES children of all groups attend well-funded schools. That raises the first of several issues within U.S. education, ten of which are mentioned now.

TEN QUESTIONS

1. Should public schools be well-supported by public funds, or should smaller class sizes, special curricula, and expensive facilities (e.g., a stage, a pool, a garden) be available only in *private schools,* paid via tuition from wealthy parents? All told, about 11 percent of students in the United States attend private schools (see Figure 7.4). Other nations have higher and lower rates.

2. Should parents be given *vouchers* to pay for some tuition at a private school? Each state regulates vouchers differently, but a detailed look at vouchers in Wisconsin found that most parents who used vouchers were inclined to send their children to nonpublic schools in any case, partly for religious and safety reasons (D. Fleming et al., 2015). Thus, vouchers subsidize schools that differ from public schools, which may allow parents to choose a school that does not follow public school policy or curriculum.

3. Should more *charter schools* open or close? Charters are funded and licensed by states or local districts. Thus, they are public schools but are exempt from some regulations, especially those negotiated by teacher unions (hours, class size, etc.). Most have some control over admissions and expulsions, which makes them more ethnically segregated, with fewer children with special needs (Stern et al., 2015). Quality varies. Overall, more children (especially African American boys) and

FIGURE 7.4 Where'd You Go to School? Note that although home schooling is still the least-chosen option, the number of home-schooled children is increasing. Not shown is the percentage of children attending the nearest public school, which is decreasing slightly because of charter and magnet schools. More detailed data indicate that the average home-schooled child is a 7-year-old European American girl living in a rural area of the South with an employed father and a stay-at-home mother.

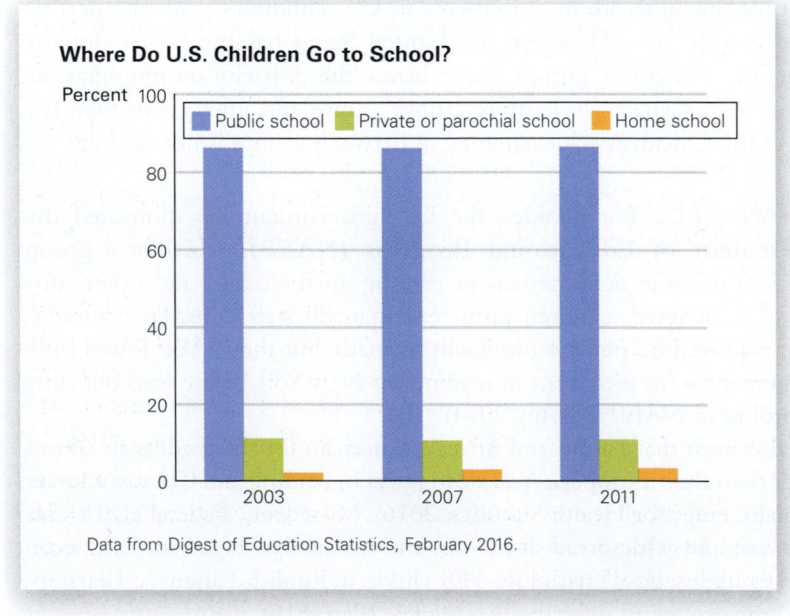

Where Do U.S. Children Go to School?

Data from Digest of Education Statistics, February 2016.

WILLIAM WIDMER/REDUX

Plagiarism, Piracy, and Public School Charter schools often have special support and unusual curricula, as shown here. These four children are learning about copyright law in a special summer school class at the ReNEW Cultural Arts Academy, a charter school in New Orleans.

teachers leave or are expelled from charter schools than from other public schools, a disturbing statistic. However, some charters report that children who stay learn more and are more likely to go to college than their peers in regular schools (Prothero, 2016).

4. In 35 of the 50 U.S. states, and in several other nations, parents can choose to *home school* their children, never sending them to school. In the United States, home-schooled children must learn certain subjects (reading, math, and so on), but each family decides schedules and discipline. About 2 percent of all U.S. children were home-schooled in 2003 and about 3 percent in 2007. Since then numbers have leveled off at between 3 and 4 percent (Snyder & Dillow, 2013; Ray, 2013; Redford et al., 2017). Home schooling requires intense family labor, typically provided by an educated, dedicated, patient mother in a two-parent family.

    The major problem with home schooling is not academic (some home-schooled children have high test scores) but social: no classmates. To compensate, many parents plan activities with other home-schooling families.

5. Should public education be free of *religion* to avoid bias toward one religion or another? In the United States, thousands of parochial schools were founded when Catholics perceived Protestant bias in public schools. In the past 20 years, many Catholic schools have closed, but schools teaching other religions—Judaism, Islam, conservative Christianity—have opened.

6. Should *the arts* be part of the curriculum? Music, drama, dance, and the visual arts are essential in some places, not in others. Half of all U.S. 18- to 24-year-olds say that they had no arts education in childhood, either in school or anywhere else (Rabkin & Hedberg, 2011). By contrast, schools in Finland consider arts education essential, with a positive impact on learning (Nevanen et al., 2014).

7. Should children learn a *second language* in primary school? In Canada and in most European nations, almost every child studies two languages by age 10. In the United States, less than 5 percent of children under age 11 study a language other than English in school (Robelen, 2011).

Ten Questions

1. Private schools?
2. Vouchers?
3. Charter schools?
4. Home-schooling?
5. Religion?
6. The Arts?
7. Second Language?
8. Computers?
9. Class size?
10. Soft skills?

"Copy and study this list of text messaging spelling words. We will have a test tomorrow."

LOL – LAUGHING OUT LOUD
BZ – BUSY
ADR– ADDRESS
BD – BIG DEAL
HB – HURRY BACK
KIT – KEEP IN TOUCH
BF – BEST FRIEND
OAO– OVER AND OUT
YW – YOU'RE WELCOME
IBRB– I'LL BE RIGHT BACK
JAS– JUST A SECOND
KIT – KEEP IN TOUCH

Basic Vocabulary? Should educators instruct children in texting? Maybe the adults are the ones who need instruction. One adult emailed a sympathy note to a friend whose mother died, and signed it "LOL." She thought that meant "Lots of Love."

Welcome Home Laura Stevens returns to her Maine elementary school after a whirlwind trip in Washington, D.C. She received the Presidential Award for Excellence in Math and Science Teaching, and $10,000. Which do you think makes her happier, the award, the hero's welcome from her students and colleagues, or the joy of teaching?

8. Can *computers* advance education? Some enthusiasts hope that connecting schools to the Internet or, even better, giving every child a laptop (as some schools do) will advance learning. The results are not dramatic, however. Sometimes computers improve achievement, but not always. Widespread, sustainable advances are elusive (Lim et al., 2013). Technology may be only a tool—a twenty-first-century equivalent of chalk—that depends on a creative, trained teacher to use well.

9. Are too many students in each class? Parents typically think that a smaller class size encourages more individualized education. That belief motivates many parents to choose private schools or home schooling. However, mixed evidence comes from nations where children score high on international tests. Sometimes they have large student–teacher ratios (Korea's average is 28-to-1) and sometimes small (Finland's is 14-to-1).

10. Should teachers nurture *soft skills* such as empathy, cooperation, and integrity as part of the school curriculum, even though these skills cannot be tested by multiple-choice questions? Many scholars argue that soft skills are crucial for academic success and later for employment (Reardon, 2013).

WHO DECIDES? An underlying issue for almost any national or international school is the proper role of parents. In most nations, matters regarding public education—curriculum, funding, teacher training, and so on—are set by the central government. Almost all children attend the local school, whose resources and standards are similar to those of the other schools in that nation. The parents' job is to support the child's learning by checking homework and so on.

In the United States, however, local districts provide most of the funds and guidelines, and parents, as voters and volunteers, are often active in their child's school. Although most U.S. parents send their children to the nearest public school, almost one-third send their children to private schools, charter schools, or magnet schools.

Parental choices may vary for each child, depending on the child's characteristics, the parents' current economic status, and the political rhetoric at the time. Every option has strengths and weaknesses, both for the child and for society.

It is difficult for parents to determine the best school for their child, partly because neither the test scores of students in any of these schools nor the moral values a particular school may espouse correlate with the cognitive skills that developmentalists seek to foster (Finn et al., 2014). Thus, parents may choose a school that advertises what the parents value, but the school may not actually be the best educational experience for their child.

Statistical analysis raises questions about home schooling, vouchers, and charter schools (Lubienski et al., 2013; Finn et al., 2014), but empirical data allow many interpretations. As one review notes, "the modern day, parent-led home-based education movement . . . stirs up many a curious query, negative critique, and firm praise" (Ray, 2013, p. 261).

Schoolchildren's ability to be logical and teachable, now that they are no longer preoperational and egocentric, makes this a good time to teach them—they will learn whatever adults deem important. Parents, politicians, and developmental experts all agree that

school is vital for development, but disagreements about teachers and curriculum—hidden or overt—abound.

what have you learned?

1. How does the hidden curriculum differ from the stated school curriculum?

2. What are the TIMSS, the PIRLS, and the PISA?

3. What nations score highest on international tests?

4. How do boys and girls differ in school achievement?

5. How do charter schools, private schools, and home schools differ?

6. How is it decided what curriculum children should receive?

Children with Special Brains and Bodies

Developmental psychopathology links usual with unusual development, especially when the unusual results in special needs (Cicchetti, 2013b; Hayden & Mash, 2014). This topic is relevant lifelong because "[e]ach period of life, from the prenatal period through senescence, ushers in new biological and psychological challenges, strengths, and vulnerabilities" (Cicchetti, 2013b, p. 458). Turning points, opportunities, and past influences are always apparent.

At the outset, four general principles should be emphasized.

1. *Abnormality is normal,* meaning that everyone has some aspects of behavior that are unusual. The opposite is also true: Everyone with a serious disorder is, in many respects, like everyone else. The cutoff between what is, and is not, a disorder is arbitrary (Clark et al., 2017).

2. *Disability changes year by year.* Most disorders are **comorbid,** which means that more than one problem is evident in the same person (Clark et al., 2017). A severe disorder in childhood may become milder, but another problem may become disabling.

3. *Life may get better or worse.* Prognosis is uncertain. Many children with severe disabilities (e.g., blindness) become productive adults. Conversely, some conditions (e.g., conduct disorder) become more disabling.

4. *Diagnosis, treatment, and prognosis reflect the social context.* Each individual interacts with the surrounding setting—including family, school, community, and culture—to modify, worsen, or even create psychopathology (Clark et al., 2017).

Measuring the Mind

Definitions of disorders change from decade to decade, criteria to criteria, and childhood to adolescence to adulthood. This is illustrated by the IQ test, a measure that was once used to indicate whether a child had special learning needs.

APTITUDE, ACHIEVEMENT, AND IQ The potential to master a specific skill or to learn a certain body of knowledge is called **aptitude.** A child might have the

developmental psychopathology
The field that uses insights into typical development to understand and remediate developmental disorders.

comorbid
Refers to the presence of two or more unrelated disease conditions at the same time in the same person.

aptitude
The potential to master a specific skill or to learn a certain body of knowledge.

© 2016 MACMILLAN

Typical 7-Year-Old? In many ways, this boy is typical. He likes video games and school, he usually appreciates his parents, and he gets himself dressed every morning. This photo shows him using blocks to construct a design to match a picture, one of the 10 kinds of challenges that comprise the WISC, a widely used IQ test. His attention to the task is not unusual for children his age, but his actual performance is more like that of an older child. That makes his IQ score significantly above 100.

Calculating IQ (answers on page 262)

1. Child is age 8. Mental age is 6. IQ is _____.
2. Child is age 8. Mental age is 10. IQ is _____.
3. Child is age 6. Mental age is 9. IQ is _____.

Flynn effect
The rise in average IQ scores that has occurred over the decades in many nations.

multiple intelligences
The idea that human intelligence is composed of a varied set of abilities rather than a single, all-encompassing one.

intellectual aptitude to be a proficient reader, for instance, even though that child has not learned to read or write. By middle childhood, most children have the aptitude to read and write; in adulthood, some people have the aptitude to be talented athletes, chefs, artists, or whatever.

Aptitude is distinct from *achievement,* which is what is actually mastered. We all have aptitudes that we never achieved, either because we chose not to develop those abilities or because our social context discouraged us. For children, academic achievement is measured by comparing a child with norms for each grade. Thus, a child who is at a third-grade reading level might, in fact, be in another grade—second or fifth, for instance. But nonetheless, the child reads at a third-grade level.

People assumed that, for intelligence, one general aptitude (often referred to as *g,* for *g*eneral intelligence) could be assessed by answers to a series of questions (vocabulary, memory, and so on). The number of correct answers was compared to the average for children of a particular age to compute an IQ. Such scores correlated with school achievement, because a child with a certain intellectual potential is able to learn if given the proper instruction. IQ scores could also indicate whether a child would have difficulty learning in class.

Originally, IQ tests produced a number that was literally a *quotient*: Mental age (the average chronological age of children who answer a certain number of questions correctly) was divided by the chronological age of a child taking the test. The answer from that division (the quotient) was multiplied by 100. An IQ of 100 was exactly average, because when mental age was the same as chronological age, the quotient was 1, and $1 \times 100 = 100$.

It was once assumed that aptitude was a fixed characteristic, present at birth. Longitudinal data show otherwise. Young children with a low IQ can become above average or even gifted adults, like my nephew David (discussed in Chapter 1).

Indeed, the average IQ scores of entire nations have risen substantially every decade for the past century—a phenomenon called the **Flynn effect.** This effect is more apparent for women than for men, and in southern Europe more than northern Europe, as educational opportunities for women and for southern Europeans improved in the twentieth century (D. Weber et al., 2017).

Most psychologists now agree that the brain is like a muscle, affected by mental exercise—which often is encouraged or discouraged by the social setting. This is proven in language and music (brains literally grow with childhood music training) and is probably true in other domains (Moreno et al., 2015; Zatorre, 2013). Both speed and memory are crucial for *g,* and they are affected by experience, evident in the Flynn effect.

MANY INTELLIGENCES Since scores change over time, IQ tests are much less definitive than they were once thought to be. Some scientists doubt whether any single test can measure the complexities of the human brain, especially if the test is designed to measure *g,* one general aptitude. People inherit and develop many abilities, some high and some low (e.g., Q. Zhu et al., 2010).

Two leading developmentalists (Robert Sternberg and Howard Gardner) are among those who believe that humans have **multiple intelligences,** not just one. Sternberg originally described three kinds of intelligence: *analytic, creative,* and *practical* (Sternberg, 2008, 2011). Children who are unusually creative, or very practical, may not be the best students in school, but they may flourish as adults, as explained more in Chapter 12.

Gardner originally described seven intelligences: *linguistic, logical-mathematical, musical, spatial, bodily-kinesthetic* (movement), *interpersonal* (social understanding), and *intrapersonal* (self-understanding), each associated with a particular brain region (Gardner, 1983). He subsequently added an eighth (*naturalistic:* understanding nature, as in biology, zoology, or farming) and a ninth (*spiritual/existential:* thinking about life and death) (Gardner, 1999, 2006; Gardner & Moran, 2006).

Although everyone has some of all nine intelligences, Gardner believes each individual excels in particular ones. For example, someone might be gifted spatially but not linguistically (a visual artist who cannot describe her work) or might have interpersonal but not naturalistic intelligence (an astute clinical psychologist whose houseplants die).

Schools, cultures, and families dampen or expand particular intelligences. If two children are born with creative, musical aptitude, the child whose parents are musicians is more likely to develop musical intelligence than the child whose parents are tone-deaf. Gardner (2011) believes that schools often are too narrow, teaching only some aspects of intelligence and thus stunting children's learning.

SCANNING THE BRAIN Another way to indicate aptitude is to measure the brain directly. In childhood, brain scans do not correlate with IQ scores (except for children with abnormally small brains), but they do later on (Brouwer et al., 2014). Brain scans can measure activity (reaction time, selective attention, emotional excitement) or the size of various brain areas, but they are not accurate in diagnosing cognitive disorders in childhood (Goddings & Giedd, 2014).

Neuroscientists and psychologists agree, however, on four generalities:

A Gifted Child Gardner believes every person is naturally better at some of his nine intelligences, and then the social context may or may not appreciate the talent. In the twenty-first century, verbal and mathematical intelligence is usually prized far more than artistic intelligence, but Georgie Pocheptsov was drawing before he learned to speak. The reason is tragic: His father suffered and died of brain cancer when Georgie was a toddler, and his mother bought paints and canvases to help her son cope with his loss. By middle childhood (shown here), Pocheptsov was a world-famous artist. Now as a young adult his works sell for hundreds of thousands of dollars — often donated to brain tumor research.

1. *Brain development depends on experiences.* Thus, a brain scan is accurate only at the moment, not for the future.

2. *Dendrites form and myelination changes throughout life.* Middle childhood is crucial, but developments before and after these years are also significant.

3. *Children with disorders often have unusual brain patterns, and training may change those patterns.* However, brain complexity and normal variation mean that diagnosis and remediation are far from perfect.

4. Each brain functions in a particular way, a concept called **neurodiversity.** Diverse neurological patterns are not necessarily better or worse; they are simply different, an example of the *difference is not deficit* idea explained first in Chapter 1 (Kapp et al., 2013).

Special Needs in Middle Childhood

Problems with testing are not the only reason diagnosis of psychopathology is complex (Hayden & Mash, 2014; Cicchetti, 2013b). One cause can have many (multiple) final manifestations, a phenomenon called **multifinality** (many final forms). The opposite is also apparent: Many causes can result in one symptom, a phenomenon called **equifinality** (equal in final form). Thus, a direct line from cause to consequence cannot be drawn with certainty.

◆ **Especially for Teachers**
What are the advantages and disadvantages of using Gardner's nine intelligences to guide your classroom curriculum? (see response, page 273)

neurodiversity
The idea that each person has neurological strengths and weaknesses that should be appreciated, in much the same way diverse cultures and ethnicities are welcomed. Neurodiversity seems particularly relevant for children with disorders on the autism spectrum.

multifinality
A basic principle of developmental psychopathology which holds that one cause can have many (multiple) final manifestations.

equifinality
A basic principle of developmental psychopathology which holds that one symptom can have many causes.

attention-deficit/hyperactivity disorder (ADHD)
A condition characterized by a persistent pattern of inattention and/or by hyperactive or impulsive behaviors; ADHD interferes with a person's functioning or development.

Calculating IQ: Answers (from page 260)

1. 1.75 (slow learner)
2. 2.125 (superior)
3. 3.150 (genius)

Almost Impossible The concentration needed to do homework is almost beyond Clint, age 11, who takes medication for ADHD. Note his furrowed brow, resting head, and sad face.

For example, an infant who has been flooded with stress hormones may become hypervigilant or irrationally placid, may be easily angered or quick to cry, or may not be affected (multifinality). Or a nonverbal child may have autism or hearing impairment, be electively mute or pathologically shy (equifinality).

To illustrate the many complexities, we discuss three disorders: attention-deficit/hyperactivity disorder (ADHD), specific learning disorder, and autism spectrum disorder (ASD). As a reference, we use DSM-5 (the fifth edition of the *Diagnostic and Statistical Manual of Mental Disorders,* published by the American Psychiatric Association in 2013). The DSM-5 is only one set of criteria—the World Health Organization has another (ICD-11), some experts are using a third (RDoC) for research. Psychiatrists are already discussing DSM-6 (Clark et al., 2017). There are hundreds of disorders: Some are added, combined, or deleted with each new edition of DSM. The following is only a beginning.

ATTENTION-DEFICIT/HYPERACTIVITY DISORDER Someone with **attention-deficit/hyperactivity disorder (ADHD)** is inattentive, active, and impulsive. DSM-5 says that symptoms must start before age 12 (in DSM-IV it was age 7) and must impact daily life. (DSM-IV said *impair,* DSM-III said *impact.*)

Partly because the definition now includes ADHD that first appears at puberty, the number of children diagnosed with ADHD has increased worldwide (Polanczyk et al., 2014). In 1980, about 5 percent of all U.S. 4- to 17-year-olds were diagnosed with ADHD; more recent rates are 7 percent of 4- to 9-year-olds, 13 percent of 10- to 13-year-olds, and 15 percent of 14- to 17-year-olds (Schwarz & Cohen, 2013).

All young children are sometimes inattentive, impulsive, and active, gradually settling down with maturation. However, those with ADHD "are so active and impulsive that they cannot sit still, are constantly fidgeting, talk when they should be listening, interrupt people all the time, can't stay on task, . . . accidentally injure themselves." All this makes them "difficult to parent or teach" (Nigg & Barkley, 2014, p. 75). Diagnosis can lead to helpful treatment, often involving medication.

Because many adults are upset by children's moods and actions, and because any physician can write a prescription to quiet a child, thousands of U.S. children may be overmedicated. *But,* because many parents do not recognize that their child needs help, or they are suspicious of drugs and psychologists (Moldavsky & Sayal, 2013; Rose, 2008), thousands of children may suffer needlessly. This dilemma is explored in Opposing Perspectives, on page 263.

In general, three problems are apparent.

■ *Misdiagnosis.* If ADHD is diagnosed when another disorder is the problem, treatment might make the problem worse (Miklowitz & Cicchetti, 2010). Many psychoactive drugs alter moods, so a child with disruptive mood dysregulation disorder (formerly called childhood bipolar disorder) might be harmed by ADHD medication.

■ *Drug abuse.* Although drugs sometimes are therapeutic for true ADHD cases, some older children want an ADHD diagnosis in order to obtain legal amphetamines (McCabe et al., 2014). In addition, parents or teachers may also overuse medication to quiet children.

■ *Typical behavior considered pathological.* If a child's activity, impulsiveness, and curiosity are diagnosed as ADHD, exuberance and self-confidence may suffer.

"Typical considered pathological" is one interpretation of data on 378,000 children in

OPPOSING PERSPECTIVES

Drug Treatment for ADHD and Other Disorders

Many child psychologists believe that the public discounts the devastation and lost learning that occur when a child's serious disorder is not recognized or treated. On the other hand, many parents are suspicious of drugs and psychotherapy and avoid recommended treatment (Gordon-Hollingsworth et al., 2015).

This controversy continues among experts. A leading book argues that ADHD is accurate for about a third of the children diagnosed with it and claims that drug companies and doctors are far too quick to push pills, making "ADHD by far, the most misdiagnosed condition in American medicine" (Schwarz, 2016, p. 2). A critical review of that book notes a failure to mention the millions of people who "have experienced life-changing, positive results" from treatment—including medication (Zametkin & Solanto, 2017, p. 9).

In the United States, more than 2 million people younger than 18 take prescription drugs to regulate their emotions and behavior. The rates are about 14 percent for teenagers (Merikangas et al., 2013), about 10 percent for 6- to 11-year-olds, and less than 1 percent for 2- to 5-year-olds (Olfson et al., 2010). Most children in the United States who are diagnosed with ADHD are medicated; in England and Europe, less than half are (Polanczyk et al., 2014).

In China, psychoactive medication is rarely prescribed for children: A Chinese child with ADHD symptoms is thought to need correction, not medication (Yang et al., 2013). An inattentive, overactive African child is more likely to be beaten than sent to the doctor. Wise or cruel?

The most common drug for ADHD is Ritalin (methylphenidate), but at least 20 other psychoactive drugs are prescribed for children to treat depression, anxiety, intellectual disability, autism spectrum disorder, disruptive mood dysregulation disorder, and many other conditions.

Some parents welcome the relief that drugs may provide; others refuse to medicate their children because they fear later drug abuse or shorter height. Neither of those consequences has been proven. Indeed, long-term benefits may include less drug abuse later on (Craig et al., 2015).

Some research finds a correlation between medicating children and the rate of mental illness in adulthood (Moran et al., 2015). On the other hand, one expert argues that teachers and doctors under-diagnose and under-treat African American children, and that increases another outcome—prison. If disruptive African American boys are punished, not treated, for ADHD symptoms, they may enter the "school-to-prison pipeline" (Moody, 2016).

All professionals agree that finding the best drug at the right strength is difficult, in part because each child's genes

CAITLIN TEAL PRICE/FOR THE WASHINGTON POST VIA GETTY IMAGES

A Family Learning When Anthony Suppers was diagnosed with ADHD, his mother, Michelle (shown here), realized she had it, too. That helps Anthony, because his mother knows how important it is to have him do his homework at his own desk as soon as he comes home from school. Does his brother have it, too?

and personality are unique, and in part because children's weight and metabolism change every year.

Given that, why are most children who are prescribed psychoactive drugs seen only by a general practitioner who does not follow up on dose and outcome (Patel et al., 2017)? Do pharmaceutical companies mislead parents about the benefits and liabilities of ADHD drugs?

Most professionals believe that contextual interventions (instructing caregivers and schools on child management, changing the diet, eliminating screens) should be tried before drugs (Daley et al., 2009; Leventhal, 2013). Many parents and teachers wonder whether those professionals understand how difficult managing an overactive child can be.

Genes, culture, health care, education, religion, and stereotypes all affect ethnic and economic differences. As two experts explain, "disentangling these will be extremely valuable to improving culturally competent assessment in an increasingly diverse society" (Nigg & Barkley, 2014, p. 98). Given the emotional and practical implications of that tangle, opposing perspectives are not surprising.

FIGURE 7.5 One Month Is One Year In the Taiwanese school system, the cutoff for kindergarten is September 1, so some boys enter school a year later because they were born a few days later. Those who are relatively young among their classmates are less able to sit still and listen. They are nearly twice as likely to be given drugs to quiet them down.

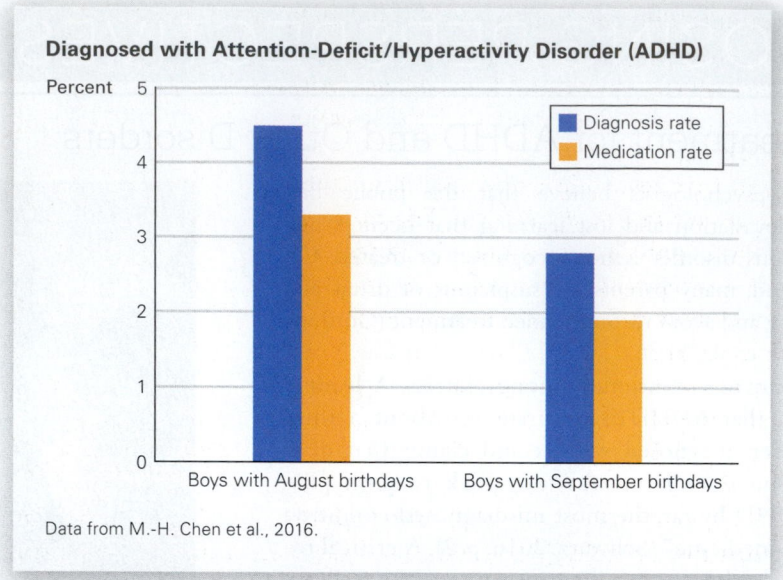

Taiwan, a Chinese nation whose rates of ADHD are increasing (M.-H. Chen et al., 2016). Boys who were born in August, and hence entered kindergarten when they had just turned 5, were diagnosed with ADHD at the rate of 4.5 percent, whereas boys born in September, starting kindergarten when they were almost 6, were diagnosed at the rate of 2.8 percent. Diagnosis typically occurred years after kindergarten, but August birthday boys were at risk throughout their school years. (See Figure 7.5.)

The example in Taiwan highlights another concern. For ADHD diagnosis, "boys outnumber girls 3-to-1 in community samples and 9-to-1 in clinical samples" (Hasson & Fine, 2012, p. 190). Could typical male activity, troubling to mothers and female teachers, be the reason?

Specific Learning Disorders

The DSM-5 diagnosis of **specific learning disorder** now includes problems in both perception and information processing that cause low achievement in reading, math, or writing (including spelling) (Lewandowski & Lovett, 2014). Disabilities in these areas undercut academic achievement, destroy self-esteem, and qualify a child for special education (according to U.S. law) or formal diagnosis (according to DSM-5).

The most commonly diagnosed learning disorder is **dyslexia**—unusual difficulty with reading. Historically, some children with dyslexia figured out themselves how to cope—as did Hans Christian Andersen and Winston Churchill.

Early theories hypothesized visual difficulties—for example, reversals of letters (reading *god* instead of *dog*) and mirror writing (*b* instead of *d*)—as causing dyslexia, but we now know that dyslexia more often originates with speech and hearing difficulties (Gabrieli, 2009; Swanson, 2013).

Another common learning disorder is **dyscalculia,** unusual difficulty with math. For example, when asked to estimate the height of a normal room, second-graders with dyscalculia might answer "200 feet." When shown both the 5 and 8 of hearts from a deck of playing cards and asked which is higher, they might use their fingers to count the hearts on each card (Butterworth et al., 2011).

macmillan learning

Learn more about how dyslexia affects children in **VIDEO: Dyslexia: Expert and Children.**

specific learning disorder
A marked deficit in a particular area of learning that is not caused by an apparent physical disability, by an intellectual disability, or by an unusually stressful home environment.

dyslexia
Unusual difficulty with reading; thought to be the result of some neurological underdevelopment.

dyscalculia
Unusual difficulty with math, probably originating from a distinct part of the brain.

Although learning disorders can appear in any skill, the DSM-5 recognizes only dyslexia, dyscalculia, and one more—*dysgraphia,* difficulty in writing. Few children write neatly at age 5, but practice allows most children to write easily and legibly by age 10.

Some children have several learning disabilities; they may be diagnosed as *intellectually disabled.* For them, as with children with only one learning disability, targeted help from teachers and guidance for parents make life easier for the child and family and may remediate learning problems (Crnic et al., 2017). Remember plasticity: Skills improve with precise practice (not general practice, such as doing homework, but specific practice, such as sounding out letters).

AUTISM SPECTRUM DISORDER Of all the children with special needs, those with **autism spectrum disorder (ASD)** are especially puzzling. Causes and treatments are hotly disputed.

A century ago, autism was a rare disorder affecting fewer than 1 in 1,000 children with "an extreme aloneness that, whenever possible, disregards, ignores, shuts out anything . . . from the outside" (Kanner, 1943). Children with autism were usually nonverbal and severely impaired.

Now, in the United States, among 8-year-olds, 1 child in every 59 (1 boy in 38; 1 girl in 151) is said to have ASD (MMWR, April 27, 2018). That's more than four times as many boys as girls. The other disparity is ethnic: The rate is higher for European American than Hispanic, Asian, or African American children.

- The increase could be real: Perhaps it is caused by the environment—chemicals in the food, pollution in the air and water.

- Or it could be that professionals are now aware of ASD and, since education for children with this diagnosis is now publicly funded, parents are more willing to seek a diagnosis (Klinger et al., 2014).

- Or it could be an expanded definition: The DSM-5 expanded the term autism to autism spectrum disorder, which now includes mild, moderate, and severe categories. Children who once were diagnosed as having an intellectual disability or Asperger syndrome are now "on the spectrum."

All children with ASD find it difficult to understand the emotions of others, which makes them feel alien, like "an anthropologist on Mars," as Temple Grandin, an educator and writer with ASD, expressed it (quoted in Sacks, 1995). Consequently, they are less likely to talk or play with other children, and they are delayed in developing theory of mind.

Verbal and social skills are impaired, but some children with ASD have special talents, such as in art or math. Many are above average in IQ tests (MMWR, March 28, 2014). This wide range of abilities illustrates *neurodiversity* (Graf et al., 2017). Because of their diverse abilities, adults should neither be dazzled by children's talents nor despairing at their deficiencies.

Many scientists are searching for biological ways to detect autism early in life, perhaps with blood tests or brain scans before age 1. At the moment, behavioral signs are the best we have. Most children with ASD show signs in early infancy (no social smile, for example, or less gazing at faces and eyes than most toddlers). Some improve by age 3; others deteriorate (Klinger et al., 2014).

BSIP/UIG VIA GETTY IMAGES

Happy Reading Those large prism glasses keep the letters from jumping around on the page, a boon for this 8-year-old French boy. Unfortunately, each child with dyslexia needs individualized treatment: These glasses help some, but not most, children who find reading difficult.

autism spectrum disorder (ASD) A developmental disorder marked by difficulty with social communication and interaction—including difficulty seeing things from another person's point of view—and restricted, repetitive patterns of behavior, interests, or activities.

VIDEO: Current Research into Autism Spectrum Disorder explores why the causes of ASD are still largely unknown.

Not a Cartoon At age 3, Owen Suskind was diagnosed with autism. He stopped talking and spent hour after hour watching Disney movies. His father said his little boy "vanished," as chronicled in the Oscar-nominated documentary *Life Animated*. Now, at age 23 (shown here), Owen still loves cartoons, and he still has many symptoms of autism spectrum disorder. However, he also has learned to speak and has written a movie that reveals his understanding of himself, *The Land of the Lost Sidekicks.*

> **THINK CRITICALLY:** Many adults are socially inept, insensitive to other people's emotions, and poor at communication—might they have been diagnosed as on the spectrum if they had been born more recently?

least restrictive environment (LRE)
A legal requirement that children with special needs be assigned to the most general educational context in which they can be expected to learn.

response to intervention (RTI)
An educational strategy intended to help children who demonstrate below-average achievement in early grades, using special intervention.

As more children are diagnosed, some people wonder whether ASD is a disorder needing a cure or whether, instead, our culture needs to adjust to a society in which not everyone is outgoing, flexible, and a fluent talker—the opposite of people with ASD. Instead of trying to make all children alike, we might welcome the neurological variation of human beings (Kapp et al., 2013; Silberman, 2015).

The neurodiversity perspective leads to new criticisms of the many treatments for ASD. When a child is diagnosed with ASD, parental responses vary from irrational hope to deep despair, from blaming doctors and chemical additives to feeling guilty for their genes, for their behavior during pregnancy, or for the circumstances they allowed at their child's birth.

A sympathetic observer describes one child who was medicated with

> Abilify, Topamax, Seroquel, Prozac, Ativan, Depakote, trazodone, Risperdal, Anafranil, Lamictal, Benadryl, melatonin, and the homeopathic remedy, Calms Forté. Every time I saw her, the meds were being adjusted again . . . [he also describes] physical interventions—putting children in hyperbaric oxygen chambers, putting them in tanks with dolphins, giving them blue–green algae, or megadosing them on vitamins . . . usually neither helpful nor harmful, though they can have dangers, are certainly disorienting, and cost a lot.
>
> *[Solomon, 2012, pp. 229, 270]*

Diagnosis and treatment are difficult; an intervention that seems to help one child proves worthless for another. It is known, however, that biology (genes, copy number abnormalities, birth complications, prenatal injury, perhaps chemicals during fetal or infant development) is crucial. Family nurture is not the cause.

Special Education

The overlap of the biosocial, cognitive, and psychosocial domains is evident to developmentalists, as is the need for parents, teachers, therapists, and researchers to work together to help each child. However, deciding whether a child should be educated differently than other children is not straightforward, nor is it closely related to individual needs. Parents, schools, and therapists often disagree.

The distinction between typical and atypical is not clear-cut (the first principle of developmental psychopathology) (Clark et al., 2017). In the United States, that realization led to a series of reforms in the education of children with special needs. According to the 1975 Education of All Handicapped Children Act, all children can learn, and all must be educated in the **least restrictive environment (LRE).**

This means that children with special needs are usually educated within a regular class (a practice once called *mainstreaming*) rather than restricted to a special class. Sometimes a class is an *inclusion class,* which means that children with special needs are "included" in the general classroom, with "appropriate aids and services" (ideally from a trained teacher who works with the regular teacher).

A more recent strategy is called **response to intervention (RTI)** (Al Otaiba et al., 2015; Jimerson et al., 2016; Ikeda, 2012). First, all children are taught specific skills—for instance, learning the sounds that various letters make. Then the children are tested, and those who did not master the skill receive special "intervention"—practice and individualized teaching, within the regular class.

Then they are tested again, and, if need be, intervention occurs again. If children do not respond adequately to repeated, focused intervention, they are referred for special education.

How It Should Be But Rarely Is
In this well-equipped classroom in Centennial, Colorado, two teachers are attentively working with three young children, indicating that each child regularly receives individualized instruction. At this school, students with developmental disabilities learn alongside typical kids, so the earlier a child's education begins the better. Sadly, few nations have classrooms like this, and in the United States, few parents can find or afford special help for their children. Indeed, most children with special needs are not diagnosed until middle childhood.

At that point, the school proposes an **individual education plan (IEP),** ideally designed for the particular child. Unfortunately, educators do not always know effective strategies, partly because research on remediation focuses on the less common problems. For example, in the United States "research funding in 2008–2009 for autistic spectrum disorder was 31 times greater than for dyslexia and 540 times greater than for dyscalculia" (Butterworth & Kovas, 2013, p. 304).

As Figure 7.6 shows, the proportion of children designated with special needs in the United States rose from 10 percent in 1980 to 13 percent in 2012. The greatest rise was in children called "learning disabled" (National Center for Education Statistics, 2016).

individual education plan (IEP)
A document that specifies educational goals and plans for a child with special needs.

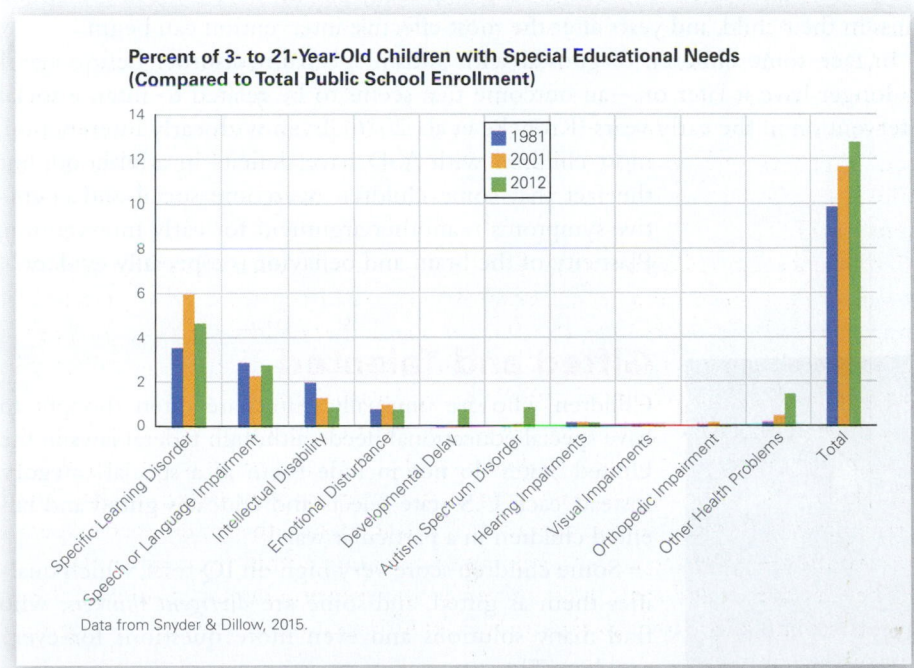

Percent of 3- to 21-Year-Old Children with Special Educational Needs (Compared to Total Public School Enrollment)

Legend: 1981, 2001, 2012

Categories (x-axis): Specific Learning Disorder, Speech or Language Impairment, Intellectual Disability, Emotional Disturbance, Developmental Delay, Autism Spectrum Disorder, Hearing Impairments, Visual Impairments, Orthopedic Impairment, Other Health Problems, Total

Data from Snyder & Dillow, 2015.

FIGURE 7.6 Nature or Nurture Some children have special needs, with physical, emotional, and neurological disorders of many kinds. In some eras, and even today in some nations, the education of such children was neglected. Indeed, many children were excluded from normal life. Now in the United States every child is entitled to school. As you see, the specific label for such children has changed over the past decades, because of nurture, not nature.

This increase could result from:

- more brain-damaging chemicals in the air, food, or water (as with the lead in Flint, Michigan).

- implicit prejudice, since a disproportional number of children in special education are from immigrant or African American families (Harry & Klingner, 2014).

- adults who are more likely to notice and test a child who isn't learning, and then quicker to decide that special education is the solution.

The U.S. school system designates more children as having special needs than does any other nation: Whether this is a reason for national pride or shame depends on which of the above reasons seems more accurate.

How many children really need special education? Some U.S. experts fear that neurodiversity, RTI, and inclusion may limit help for children with special needs. If everyone is special, will that prevent help for children who desperately need it (Kauffman et al., 2017)?

Early Intervention

One conclusion from all of the research on special education is that diagnosis and intervention often occur too late, or not at all. The numbers of children in public schools who are designated as needing special education increase as children grow older, which is the opposite of what would occur if early intervention were successful. This is apparent in each of the disorders we have discussed.

Sometimes the current approach is called "wait to fail," when ADHD and learning disorders are not diagnosed until a child has been struggling for years without help for sensory, familial, or cultural problems. As one expert says, "We need early identification, and . . . early intervention. If you wait until third grade, kids give up" (Shaywitz, cited in Stern, 2015, p. 1466).

A similar problem occurs with autism spectrum disorder. You read that autism appears in infancy, but children are not usually diagnosed until age 4, on average (MMWR, March 28, 2014). This is long after many parents have noticed something amiss in their child, and years after the most effective intervention can begin.

In fact, some children diagnosed with autism spectrum disorder before age 4 no longer have it later on—an outcome that seems to be related to intense social intervention in the early years (Kroncke et al., 2016). Even with early intervention, most children with ASD have deficits in adulthood, but the fact that some children overcome social and cognitive symptoms is another argument for early intervention. Plasticity of the brain and behavior is especially evident.

Gifted and Talented

Children who are unusually gifted are often thought to have special educational needs, although federal laws in the United States do not include them as a special category. Instead, each U.S. state selects and educates gifted and talented children in a particular way.

Some children score very high on IQ tests, which qualifies them as gifted, and some are *divergent thinkers,* who find many solutions and even more questions for every problem. These two characteristics sometimes coincide in the same child, but not always. Instead, a high-IQ child

And Tomorrow? The education of gifted children is controversial, as is the future of Sunny Pawar, "just a normal boy" from the slums of Mumbai (shown here at age 8) and also a talented star in *Lion,* a 2016 Oscar-nominated film made in Australia. After a worldwide tour to promote the film, he returned to his one-room home and attends school, where he gets none of the perks of being a movie star. What next?

STEVE GRANITZ/GETTY IMAGES

might be a *convergent thinker,* quickly finding one, and only one, correct answer for every problem. That child might be impatient not only with children who think more slowly but also with quick-thinking children who are highly creative.

Should children who are unusually intelligent, talented, or creative be home-schooled, skipped, segregated, or enriched? Each of these solutions has been tried and found lacking.

Historically, parents recognized their gifted or talented child, and then they taught the child themselves or hired a special coach or tutor. For example, Mozart composed music at age 3 and Picasso created works of art at age 4. Both boys had fathers who recognized their talent. Mozart's father transcribed his earliest pieces and toured Europe with his gifted son; Picasso's father removed him from school so that he could create all day.

Although intense early education nourished their talent, neither Mozart nor Picasso had a happy adult life. Mozart had a poor understanding of math and money. He had six children, only two of whom survived infancy. He died in debt at age 35. Picasso regretted never fully grasping how to read or write. He married at age 17 and had a total of four children by three women.

When school attendance became universal about a century ago, gifted children were allowed to skip early grades and join other children of the same mental age, not their chronological age. Many accelerated children never learned how to get along with others. As one woman remembers:

> Nine-year-old little girls are so cruel to younger girls. I was much smaller than them, of course, and would have done anything to have a friend. Although I could cope with the academic work very easily, emotionally I wasn't up to it. Maybe it was my fault and I was asking to be picked on. I was a weed at the edge of the playground.
>
> *[Rachel, quoted in Freeman, 2010, p. 27]*

Calling herself a weed suggests that she never overcame her conviction that she was less cherished than the other children. Her intellectual needs may have been met by skipping two grades, but her emotional and social needs were severely neglected.

My own father skipped three grades, graduating from high school at age 14. Because he attended a one-room school, and because he was the middle child of five, his emotional and social needs were met until he began college, where he almost failed because of his immaturity. He recovered, but some other children do not. A chilling example comes from:

> Sufiah Yusof [who] started her maths degree at Oxford [the leading University in England] in 2000, at the age of 13. She too had been dominated and taught by her father. But she ran away the day after her final exam. She was found by police but refused to go home, demanding of her father in an email: "Has it ever crossed your mind that the reason I left home was because I've finally had enough of 15 years of physical and emotional abuse?" Her father claimed she'd been abducted and brainwashed. She refuses to communicate with him. She is now a very happy, high-class, high-earning prostitute.
>
> *[Freeman, 2010, p. 286]*

The fate of creative children may be worse than that of intellectually gifted children. If not given an education that suits them, they joke in class, resist drudgery, ignore homework, and bedevil their teachers. They may become innovators, inventors, and creative forces in the future, but they also may become drug addicts or school dropouts. They may find it hard to earn a degree or get a steady job because they are eager to try new things and feel stifled by normal life. Among the well-known creative geniuses who were questionable students were Albert Einstein, Sigmund Freud, Isaac

Newton, Oliver Sacks, Steve Jobs, and hundreds of thousands of others, probably some of whom you know personally.

One such person was Charles Darwin, whose "school reports complained unendingly that he wasn't interested in studying, only shooting, riding, and beetle-collecting" (Freeman, 2010, p. 283). At the behest of his physician father, Darwin entered college to study medicine, but he dropped out. Without a degree, he began his famous five-year trip around South America at age 22, collecting specimens and developing the theory of evolution—which disputed conventional religious dogma as only a highly creative person could do.

Since both acceleration and intense home schooling have led to later social problems, a third education strategy has become popular, at least in the United States. Children who are bright, talented, and/or creative—all the same age but each with special abilities—are taught as a group in their own separate class. Ideally, such children are neither bored nor lonely; each is challenged and appreciated by classmates and teachers.

Some research supports the strategy of special education for children with exceptional music, math, or athletic gifts. Their brain structures develop in ways to support their talents (Moreno et al., 2015). Since plasticity means that children learn whatever their context teaches, perhaps some children need gifted-and-talented classes.

Such classes require unusual teachers—bright and creative, and able to individualize instruction. For example, a 7-year-old artist may need freedom, guidance, and inspiration for magnificent art but also need patient, step-by-step instruction in sounding out simple words.

Similarly, a 7-year-old classmate who already reads at the twelfth-grade level might have immature social skills, so the teacher must find another child to befriend him or her and then must help both of them share, compromise, and take turns. The teacher must also engage the child who is advanced in reading in conversation about books that most children cannot read until college.

The argument against gifted-and-talented classes is that *every* child needs such teachers, no matter what the child's abilities or disabilities. If each school district (and sometimes each school principal) hires and assigns teachers, as occurs in the United States, then the best teachers may have the most able students, and the school districts with the most money (the most expensive homes) have the highest paid teachers. Should it be the opposite?

High-achieving students are especially likely to have great teachers if the hidden curriculum includes *tracking,* putting children with special needs together, sorting regular classes by past achievement of the students, and allowing private or charter schools to select only certain students and expel difficult ones.

The problem is worse if the gifted students are in a separate class within the same school as the other students, or if two schools are in the same building, a regular school and a special school. Then all of the students suffer: Some feel inferior and others superior—with neither group motivated to try new challenges and no one learning how to work together (Herrmann et al., 2016; Van Houtte, 2016).

Mainstreaming, IEPs, and so on were developed when parents and educators saw that segregation of children with special needs led to less learning and impaired adult lives. The same may happen if gifted and talented children are separated from the rest. Some nations (China, Finland, Scotland, and many others) educate all children together, assuming that all children could become high achievers if they put in the effort and are guided by effective teachers. Since every child is special, should every child have special education?

what have you learned?

1. Should traditional IQ tests be discarded? Why or why not?
2. What are the four principles of psychopathology?
3. What is the difference between multifinality and equifinality?
4. What is the difference between ADHD and typical child behavior?
5. What are dyslexia, dyscalculia, and dysgraphia?
6. What are the symptoms of autism spectrum disorder?
7. How might the concept of neurodiversity affect treatment for special children?
8. What is the difference between mainstreaming and inclusion?
9. What are the problems when children with special needs are educated in regular classes?
10. What are the problems when children with special needs are educated together in separate classes?

SUMMARY

A Healthy Time

1. Physical activity aids health and joy in many ways. Benefits are apparent in bodies (strength and coordination) and brains (quicker reaction time, more selective attention). However, children who most need physical activity may be least likely to have it.

2. Worldwide obesity and asthma are increasing, with harm to children that is mostly social. Although genes make a child more vulnerable, parents and policies share the blame.

Cognition

3. According to Piaget, middle childhood is the time of concrete operational thought, when egocentrism diminishes and logical thinking begins. By contrast, Vygotsky stressed the social context of learning, including the specific lessons of school and learning from peers, adults, and culture.

4. An information-processing approach examines each step of the thinking process, from input to output, using the computer as a model. This highlights the role of the knowledge base and of control processes.

5. Language learning advances in many practical ways, including expanded vocabulary and pragmatics. Most children use one code, dialect, or language with their friends and another in school. Children who are adept at code-switching, or fluently bilingual, have a cognitive advantage.

6. Children of low SES are usually lower in linguistic skills, primarily because they hear less language at home. Parent and teacher expectations are crucial.

Teaching and Learning

7. The hidden curriculum may be more influential on children's learning than the formal curriculum. For example, some believe that elementary schools favor girls, although internationally gender similarities seem to outweigh gender differences.

8. International assessments are useful as comparisons. Reading is assessed with the PIRLS, math and science with the TIMSS, and practical intelligence with the PISA. Culture affects answers as well as learning: East Asian scores are high, Finland has improved, and the United States is middling.

9. In the United States, each state, each district, and sometimes each school retains significant control. This makes education a controversial topic in many communities. Most children attend their local public school, but some parents choose charter schools, others private schools, and still others home schooling.

Children with Special Brains and Bodies

10. Intellectual aptitude traditionally was measured with IQ tests, with scores that can change over time. Also changing is achievement—what a child has been learning. Aptitude and achievement are correlated and have risen in the past decades, as Flynn documented.

11. Critics of IQ testing contend that intelligence is manifested in multiple ways, which makes g (general intelligence) too narrow and limited. Gardner describes nine distinct intelligences.

12. Developmental psychopathology uses an understanding of typical development to inform the study of unusual development. Four general lessons have emerged: Abnormality is normal; disability changes over time; a condition may get better or worse later on; diagnosis depends on context.

13. Children with attention-deficit/hyperactivity disorder (ADHD) have potential problems in three areas: inattention, impulsiveness, and activity. DSM-5 recognizes learning disorders, specifically dyslexia (reading), dyscalculia (math), and dysgraphia (penmanship).

14. Children on the autism spectrum typically have problems with social interaction and language. ASD originates in the brain, with genetic and prenatal influences, but the course of development depends on parents, teachers, and an appreciation of neurodiversity.

15. About 13 percent of all school-age children in the United States receive special education services. These begin with an IEP (individual education plan) and assignment to the least restrictive environment (LRE), usually within the regular classroom.

16. Gifted and talented children receive special education in most U.S. states. There are sound cognitive reasons for and against this practice.

KEY TERMS

reaction time (p. 237)

childhood overweight (p. 237)

childhood obesity (p. 237)

asthma (p. 239)

concrete operational thought (p. 241)

classification (p. 242)

seriation (p. 243)

knowledge base (p. 245)

control processes (p. 246)

English Language Learners (ELLs) (p. 248)

immersion (p. 248)

bilingual education (p. 248)

ESL (English as a Second Language) (p. 248)

hidden curriculum (p. 250)

Trends in Math and Science Study (TIMSS) (p. 252)

Progress in International Reading Literacy Study (PIRLS) (p. 252)

Programme for International Student Assessment (PISA) (p. 252)

National Assessment of Educational Progress (NAEP) (p. 255)

developmental psychopathology (p. 259)

comorbid (p. 259)

aptitude (p. 259)

Flynn effect (p. 260)

multiple intelligences (p. 260)

neurodiversity (p. 261)

multifinality (p. 261)

equifinality (p. 261)

attention-deficit/hyperactivity disorder (ADHD) (p. 262)

specific learning disorder (p. 264)

dyslexia (p. 264)

dyscalculia (p. 264)

autism spectrum disorder (ASD) (p. 265)

least restrictive environment (LRE) (p. 266)

response to intervention (RTI) (p. 266)

individual education plan (IEP) (p. 267)

APPLICATIONS

1. Compare play spaces and school design for children in different neighborhoods—ideally, urban, suburban, and rural areas. Note size, safety, and use. How might this affect children's health and learning?

2. Visit a local elementary school and look for the hidden curriculum. For example, do the children line up? Why or why not, when, and how? Does gender, age, ability, or talent affect the grouping of children or the selection of staff? What is on the walls? For everything you observe, speculate about the underlying assumptions.

3. Interview a 6- to 11-year-old child to find out what he or she knows *and understands* about mathematics. Relate both correct and incorrect responses to the logic of concrete operational thought and to the information-processing perspective.

4. Parents of children with special needs often consult Internet sources. Pick one disorder and find 10 Web sites that describe causes and educational solutions. How valid, how accurate, and how objective is the information? What disagreements do you find? How might parents react to the information provided?

ESPECIALLY FOR ANSWERS

Response for Medical Professionals (from page 237): You need to speak to the parents, not accusingly (because you know that genes and culture have a major influence on body weight) but helpfully. Alert them to the potential social and health problems that their child's weight poses. Most parents are very concerned about their child's well-being and will work with you to improve the child's snacks and exercise levels.

Response for Teachers (from page 243): Here are two of the most obvious ways: (1) Use logic. Once children can grasp classification and class inclusion, they can understand cities within states, states within nations, and nations within continents. Organize your instruction to make logical categorization easier. (2) Make use of children's need for concrete and personal involvement. You might have the children learn first about their own location, then about the places where relatives and friends live, and finally about places beyond their personal experience (via books, photographs, videos, and guest speakers).

Response for Parents (from page 249): Your son would understand your explanation, but you should take him along if you can do so without losing patience. You wouldn't ignore his need for food or medicine, so don't ignore his need for learning. While shopping, you can teach vocabulary (does he know pimientos, pepperoni, polenta?), categories (root vegetables, freshwater fish), and math (which size box of cereal is cheaper?). Explain in advance that you need him to help you find items and carry them and that he can choose only one item that you wouldn't normally buy.

Seven-year-olds can understand rules, and they enjoy being helpful.

Response for School Administrators (from page 256): The relationship reflects correlation, not causation. Wearing uniforms is more common when the culture of the school emphasizes achievement and study, with strict discipline in class and a policy of expelling disruptive students.

Response for Teachers (from page 261): The advantages are that all of the children learn more aspects of human knowledge and that many children can develop their talents. Art, music, and sports should be an integral part of education, not just a break from academics. The disadvantage is that they take time and attention away from reading and math, which might lead to less proficiency in those subjects on standard tests and thus to criticism from parents and supervisors.

OBSERVATION QUIZ ANSWERS

Answer to Observation Quiz (from page 234): Water bottles, sun visors, and I.D. badges—although the latter might not be considered a healthy innovation.

Answer to Observation Quiz (from page 239): The definition harks back to early standards, when the obesity rate was only 5 percent.

Answer to Observation Quiz (from page 249): Her posture is straight; her hands are folded; she is quiet, standing while her mother sits. All of this suggests that this scene is a frequent occurrence.

MIDDLE CHILDHOOD
Psychosocial Development

PHOTOALTO/JEROME GORIN/GETTY IMAGES

what will you know?

- What helps children thrive in difficult family or neighborhood conditions?
- Should parents marry, risking divorce, or not marry, risking separation?
- What can be done to stop a bully?

"But Dad, that's not fair! Why does Keaton get to kill zombies and I can't?"

"Well, because you are too young to kill zombies. Your cousin Keaton is older than you, so that's why he can do it. You'll get nightmares."

"That's soooo not fair."

"Next year, after your birthday, I'll let you kill zombies."

[adapted from Asma, 2013]

This conversation between a professor and his 8-year-old son illustrates psychosocial development in middle childhood, explained in this chapter. All children want to do what the bigger children do, and all parents seek to protect their children, sometimes ineffectively.

Throughout middle childhood, issues of parents and peers, fairness and justice, inclusion and exclusion are pervasive. Age takes on new importance because concrete operational thinking makes chronology salient and because age-based cutoffs are used by schools, camps, and athletic leagues to decide whether a given child is "ready."

Children become well aware of age during these years. Birthdays are significant. I still remember who was the youngest, and the oldest, girl in my class—even though we all were less than a year apart.

In the excerpt above, the professor hoped that his son would no longer want to kill zombies when he was 9, but as you will see, a child's sense of fairness often differs from an adult's. Morality is the final topic of this chapter, but even the first topic, the nature of the child, raises ethical, not just psychosocial, issues.

The Nature of the Child

As explained in the previous chapter, steady growth, brain maturation, and intellectual advances make middle childhood a time for more independence (see At About This Time). One practical result is that between ages 6 and 11, children learn to care for themselves. They not only hold their own spoon but also make their own lunch, not only zip their own pants but also pack their own suitcases, not only walk to school but also organize games with friends. They venture outdoors alone.

industry versus inferiority The fourth of Erikson's eight psychosocial crises, during which children attempt to master many skills, developing a sense of themselves as either industrious or inferior, competent or incompetent.

Industry and Inferiority

Throughout the centuries and in every culture, school-age children have been industrious. They busily master whatever skills their culture values. Their mental and physical maturation, described in the previous chapter, makes such activity possible.

With regard to his fourth psychosocial crisis, **industry versus inferiority**, Erikson noted that the child "must forget past hopes and wishes, while his exuberant imagination is tamed and harnessed to the laws of impersonal things," becoming "ready to apply himself to given skills and tasks" (Erikson, 1993a, pp. 258, 259). Simply trying new things, as in the previous stage of initiative versus guilt, is no longer sufficient. Sustained activity that leads to accomplishments that make one proud is the goal.

Think of learning to read and to add, both of which are painstaking and tedious. For instance, slowly sounding out "Jane has a dog" or writing "3 + 4 = 7" for the hundredth time is not exciting. Yet school-age children busily practice reading and math: They are intrinsically motivated to read a page, finish a worksheet, memorize a spelling word, color a map, and so on. Similarly, they enjoy collecting, categorizing, and counting whatever they gather—perhaps stamps, stickers, stones, or seashells. That is industry.

Overall, children judge themselves as either *industrious* or *inferior*—deciding whether they are competent or incompetent, productive or useless, winners or losers. Self-pride depends not necessarily on actual accomplishments but on how others, especially peers, view one's accomplishments. Social rejection is both a cause and a consequence of feeling inferior (Rubin et al., 2013).

CHRISTINA KILGOUR/GETTY IMAGES

Learning from Each Other Middle childhood is prime time for social comparison. Swinging is done standing, or on the belly, or twisted, or head down (as shown here) if someone else does it.

At About This Time

Signs of Psychosocial Maturation over the Years of Middle Childhood.*

Children responsibly perform specific chores.

Children make decisions about a weekly allowance.

Children can tell time and have set times for various activities.

Children have homework, including some assignments over several days.

Children are punished less often than when they were younger.

Children try to conform to peers in clothes, language, and so on.

Children voice preferences about their after-school care, lessons, and activities.

Children are responsible for younger children, pets, and, in some places, work.

Children strive for independence from parents.

*Of course, culture is crucial. For example, giving a child an allowance is typical for middle-class children in developed nations since about 1960. It was rare, or completely absent, in earlier times and other places.

Same Situation, Far Apart: Helping at Home Sichuan, in China *(right)*, and Virginia, in the United States *(left)*, provide vastly different contexts for child development. Children everywhere help their families with household chores, as these two do, but gender expectations vary a great deal.

Parental Reactions

Did you pause a moment ago when you read that 6- to 11-year-olds can "venture outdoors alone"? Cohort and context changes can be dramatic. In the past few decades in the United States, many parents have not allowed their children outside without an adult, even to walk to a neighbor's house, much less to go to town with money in their pocket.

Universally, in middle childhood children become capable of doing things themselves that once they could not do, but parents react in diverse ways: Some children care for younger children and for the household while parents are away, some use power tools or drive tractors, and others are closely supervised for everything.

Although variation is apparent, in middle childhood parents shift from providing physical care (bathing, dressing, and so on) to engaging in dialogue, discussion, and shared activities, a trend particularly apparent with boys and their fathers (Keown & Palmer, 2014).

For all children, parents gradually grant more autonomy, which helps children feel happy and capable (Yan et al., 2017). Consequently, time spent with parents decreases while time alone, and with friends, increases. One study of U.S. families found that 8-year-olds, on average, spent 95 minutes a day with their mothers, 12-year-olds spent 70 minutes, and 18-year-olds, 35 minutes. This study found substantial variation by context and family structure (Lam et al., 2012).

Self-Concept

As children mature, they develop their *self-concept,* which is their idea about themselves, including their intelligence, personality, abilities, gender, and ethnic background. As you remember, in toddlerhood children discover that they are individuals, and in early childhood they develop a positive, global self-concept.

That general self-concept changes in middle childhood. The self-concept gradually becomes more specific and logical, the result of increases in cognitive development and social awareness (Orth & Robins, 2014).

COMPARED TO OTHERS Crucial during middle childhood is **social comparison**—comparing oneself to others (Lapan & Boseovski, 2017; Dweck, 2013). Ideally, social comparison helps school-age children value themselves for who they are, abandoning the imaginary, rosy self-evaluation of preschoolers.

The self-concept becomes more realistic: Children incorporate comparison to peers and become more specific when they judge their own competence. The usual result is still a positive self-concept, now grounded in reality (Thomaes et al., 2017).

social comparison
The tendency to assess one's abilities, achievements, social status, and other attributes by measuring them against those of other people, especially one's peers.

Black Panther Mythical superheroes, and the perpetual battle between good and evil, are especially attractive to boys in middle childhood but resonate with people of all ages, genders, and ethnic groups. *Black Panther* was first a comic-book hero in 1966 and then became a 2018 movie that broke records for attendance and impact. It features not only African American heroes but also an army of strong women—busting stereotypes and generating self-esteem for many children.

Some children—especially those from minority ethnic or religious groups—become newly aware of social prejudices that they need to overcome. Children also become aware of gender discrimination, with girls complaining that they are not allowed to play tougher sports and boys complaining that teachers favor the girls (Brown et al., 2011). Over the years of middle childhood, those children who affirm pride in their gender and ethnicity are likely to develop healthy self-esteem (Corenblum, 2014).

Especially when the outside world seems hostile, parents and schools who teach about ethnic heroes, gender stars, and immigration successes soon make a difference (Hernández et al., 2017). Much of the research focuses on adolescents and African Americans, but a recent review suggests that the same influences affect every group. Developing a sense of pride is more effective for self-confidence than directly preparing children for prejudice (Reynolds and Gonzales-Backen, 2017).

Affirming pride is an important counterbalance, because, during middle childhood, increasing self-understanding and social awareness come at a price. Self-criticism and self-consciousness rise from ages 6 to 11, and "by middle childhood . . . this [earlier] overestimate of their ability or judgments decreases" (Davis-Kean et al., 2009, p. 184). Children's self-concept becomes influenced by the opinions of others, even by other children whom they do not know (Thomaes et al., 2010).

CULTURE AND SELF-ESTEEM Both academic and social competence are aided by realistic self-perception. That is beneficial, because unrealistically high self-esteem reduces effortful control (deliberately modifying one's impulses and emotions). Reduced effortful control leads to lower achievement and increased aggression.

The same consequences occur if self-esteem is too low. Obviously, the goal then is to find a middle ground. This is not easy: Children may be too self-critical or not self-critical enough. Their self-control interacts with the reactions of their parents and culture. Cultures differ on what that middle ground is.

High self-esteem is neither universally valued nor universally criticized (Yamaguchi et al., 2007). Many cultures expect children to be modest, not prideful. For example, Australians say that "tall poppies are cut down"; the Chinese say, "the nail that sticks up is hammered"; and the Japanese discourage social comparison aimed at making oneself feel superior. This makes self-esteem a moral issue as well as a practical one: *Should* people believe that they are better than other people, as is typical in the United States but not in every nation? Answers vary.

> **THINK CRITICALLY:** When would a realistic, honest self-assessment be harmful?

Watch **VIDEO: Interview with Carol Dweck** to learn about how children's mindsets affect their intellectual development.

One crucial component of self-concept—process—has received considerable research attention (Dweck, 2013). As children become more self-aware, they benefit from praise for their process, not for their person: for *how* they learn, *how* they relate to others, and so on, not for static qualities such as intelligence and popularity.

For example, children who fail a test are devastated if failure means they are not smart. However, process-oriented children consider failure a "learning opportunity," a time to figure out how to study the next time. Self-conscious emotions (pride, shame, guilt) develop during middle childhood and serve to guide social interaction.

However, those emotions can overwhelm a healthy self-concept, leading to psychopathology (Muris & Meesters, 2014). Especially during middle childhood (less so in adolescence), school achievement is a crucial factor in developing self-esteem, and that affects later self-concept—as someone who is inferior or not.

Concrete thinking leads children to notice material possessions. Objects that adults find superficial (name-brand sunglasses, sock patterns) become important. Insecure 10-year-olds might desperately want the latest jackets, smartphones, and so on. Or they may want something else that makes them seem special, such as lessons in African dance, or a brilliant light for their bicycle, or—as one of my daughters did—a bread-maker (used often for several weeks, discarded after several years).

Same Situation, Far Apart: Play Ball In the recent war in Ukraine *(left),* volunteers guarded the House of Parliament against a Russian takeover, and in Liberia *(right),* thousands died in the Ebola epidemic. Nonetheless, in 2015, one boy practiced his soccer kick and four boys celebrated a soccer goal. Children can ignore national disasters as long as they have familiar caregivers nearby and a chance to play.

↑ OBSERVATION QUIZ
How can you tell that the Liberian boys are celebrating a soccer victory instead of the end of an epidemic? (see answer, page 307)

Resilience and Stress

In infancy and early childhood, children depend on their immediate families for food, learning, and life itself. Then, "experiences in middle childhood can sustain, magnify, or reverse the advantages or disadvantages that children acquire in the preschool years" (Huston & Ripke, 2006, p. 2). Some children continue to benefit from supportive families, and others escape destructive families by finding their own niche in the larger world.

Surprisingly, some children seem unscathed by early experiences. They have been called "resilient" or even "invincible." Current thinking about resilience (see Table 8.1), with insights from dynamic-systems theory, emphasizes that no one is truly untouched by past history or current context, but some weather early storms and a few not only survive but become stronger because of it (Masten, 2014).

DEFINING RESILIENCE **Resilience** has been defined as "a dynamic process encompassing positive adaptation within the context of significant adversity" (Luthar et al., 2000, p. 543) and "the capacity of a dynamic system to adapt successfully to disturbances

resilience
The capacity to adapt well to significant adversity and to overcome serious stress.

TABLE 8.1 Dominant Ideas About Resilience, 1965 to Present

1965	All children have the same needs for healthy development.
1970	Some conditions or circumstances—such as "absent father," "teenage mother," "working mom," and "day care"—are harmful for every child.
1975	All children are *not* the same. Some children are resilient, coping easily with stressors that cause harm in other children.
1980	Nothing inevitably causes harm. Both maternal employment and preschool education, once thought to be risks, are often helpful.
1985	Factors beyond the family, both in the child (low birthweight, prenatal alcohol exposure, aggressive temperament) and in the community (poverty, violence), can be very risky for children.
1990	Risk–benefit analysis finds that some children are "invulnerable" to, or even benefit from, circumstances that destroy others.
1995	No child is invincible. Risks are always harmful—if not in education, then in emotions; if not immediately, then long term.
2000	Risk–benefit analysis involves the interplay among many biological, cognitive, and social factors, some within the child (genes, disability, temperament), the family (function as well as structure), and the community (including neighborhood, school, church, and culture).
2008	Focus on strengths, not risks. Assets in child (intelligence, personality), family (secure attachment, warmth), community (schools, after-school programs), and nation (income support, health care) must be nurtured.
2010	Strengths vary by culture and national values. Both universal ideals and local variations must be recognized and respected.
2012	Genes as well as cultural practices can be either strengths or weaknesses; differential susceptibility means identical stressors can benefit one child and harm another.
2015	Communities are responsible for child resilience. Not every child needs help, but every community needs to encourage healthy child development.
2017	Resilience is seen more broadly as a characteristic of mothers and communities. Some are quite resilient, which fosters resilience in children.

that threaten system function, viability, or development" (Masten, 2014, p. 10). Note that both of these leading researchers emphasize three parts of this definition:

■ Resilience is *dynamic,* not a stable trait. That means a given person may be resilient at some periods but not others, and the effects from one period reverberate as time goes on.

■ Resilience is a *positive adaptation* to stress. For example, if parental rejection leads a child to a closer relationship with another adult, that is positive resilience, not passive endurance.

■ Adversity must be *significant*, a threat to development.

CUMULATIVE STRESS An important discovery is that stress accumulates over time, including minor disturbances (called "daily hassles"). A long string of hassles, day after day, takes a greater toll than an isolated major stress. Almost every child can withstand one trauma, but "the likelihood of problems increased as the number of risk factors increased" (Masten, 2014, p. 14).

One international example comes from Sri Lanka, where many children in the first decade of the twenty-first century were exposed to war, a tsunami, poverty, deaths of relatives, and relocation. A study of the Sri Lankan children found that accumulated stresses, more than any single problem, increased pathology and decreased

achievement. The authors point to "the importance of multiple contextual, past, and current factors in influencing children's adaptation" (Catani et al., 2010, p. 1188).

The social context, especially supportive adults who do not blame the child, is crucial. A chilling example comes from the "child soldiers" in the 1991–2002 civil war in Sierra Leone (Betancourt et al., 2013). Children witnessed and often participated in murder, rape, and other atrocities. When the war was over, 529 war-affected youth, then aged 10 to 17, were interviewed. Many were severely depressed, with crippling anxiety.

These war-damaged children were interviewed again two and six years later. Surprisingly, many had overcome their trauma and were functioning well. Recovery was more likely if they were in middle childhood, not adolescence, when the war occurred. If at least one caregiver survived, if their communities did not reject them, and if their daily routines were restored, the children usually regained emotional health.

FAMILY AS A BUFFER In England during World War II, many city children were sent to loving families in rural areas to escape the German bombs dropped every day. To the surprise of researchers, those children who stayed in London with their parents were more resilient, despite nights huddled in air-raid shelters, than those who were physically safe but without their parents (Freud & Burlingham, 1943).

Similar results were found in a longitudinal study of children exposed to a sudden, wide-ranging, terrifying wildfire in Australia. Almost all of the children suffered stress reactions at the time, but 20 years later the crucial factor was not how close they were to the fire but whether or not it separated them from their mothers (McFarlane & Van Hooff, 2009).

COGNITIVE COPING Obviously, these examples are extreme, but the general finding appears in many studies. Disasters take a toll, but resilience is possible. Factors in the child (especially problem-solving ability), in the family (consistency and care), and in the community (good schools and welcoming religious institutions) all help children recover (Masten, 2014).

The child's interpretation of events is crucial (Lagattuta, 2014). Cortisol increases in low-income children *if* they interpret events connected to their family's poverty as a personal threat and *if* the family lacks order and routines (thus increasing daily hassles) (E. Chen et al., 2010). If low-SES children do not feel personally to blame, and if their family is not chaotic, they may be resilient. Think of people you know: Some adults from low-SES families did not feel deprived. Thus, poverty may not have damaged them.

VIDEO ACTIVITY: Child Soldiers and Child Peacemakers examines the state of child soldiers in the world and then explores how adolescent cognition impacts the decisions of five teenage peace activists.

Same Situation, Far Apart: Praying Hands Differences are obvious between the Northern Indian girls entering their Hindu school *(left)* and the West African boy in a Christian church *(right)*, even in their clothes and hand positions. But underlying similarities are more important. In every culture, many 8-year-olds are more devout than their elders. That is especially true if their community is under stress. Faith aids resilience.

parentification
When a child acts more like a parent than a child. Parentification may occur if the actual parents do not act as caregivers, making a child feel responsible for the family.

THINK CRITICALLY: Is there any harm in having the oldest child take care of the younger ones? Why or why not?

In general, a child's interpretation of a family situation (poverty, divorce, and so on) determines how it affects him or her.

Some children consider the family they were born into a temporary hardship; they look forward to the day when they can leave childhood behind. If they also have personal strengths, such as problem-solving abilities and intellectual openness, they may shine in adulthood—evident in the United States in thousands of success stories, from Abraham Lincoln to Oprah Winfrey.

The opposite reaction is called **parentification,** when children feel responsible for the entire family. They become caregivers of everyone, including their parents.

Here again the child's interpretation is crucial. If children feel burdened and prevented from normal childhood experiences, they are likely to suffer; but if they think they are helpful (which occurs when their community respects their contribution), they may be resilient. This may explain why caregiving children who are European American suffer more from parentification than caregiving African American children (Khafi et al., 2014).

One final example. Many children of immigrants in the United States are translators for their parents, who speak little English. If those children feel burdened by their role as language brokers, that increases their depression; but if they feel they are making a positive contribution to their family well-being, they themselves benefit (Weisskirch, 2017b).

what have you learned?

1. How do Erikson's stages for preschool and school-age children differ?
2. Why is social comparison particularly powerful during middle childhood?
3. Why do cultures differ in how they value pride or modesty?
4. Why and when might minor stresses be more harmful than major stresses?
5. How might a child's interpretation of events help him or her cope with repeated stress?

Families During Middle Childhood

We have already mentioned the importance of parents during middle childhood; now we go deeper into family structure and function. This includes parents, of course, but also siblings, grandparents, and social forces.

Families are crucial lifelong. No one doubts that genes affect personality as well as ability, that peers are vital, and that schools and cultures influence what, and how much, children learn. Some have gone further, suggesting that genes, peers, and communities have so much influence that parents have little impact—unless they are grossly abusive (Harris, 1998, 2002; McLeod et al., 2007). This suggestion arose from studies about the impact of the environment on child development.

Shared and Nonshared Environments

Many studies have found that children are much less affected by *shared environment* (influences that arise from being in the same environment, such as for two siblings living in one home, raised by their parents) than by *nonshared environment* (e.g., the distinct experiences and surroundings of a person). Since nonshared environment is so much more influential than shared, might family influences be insignificant?

Shared Environment? All three children live in the same home in Brooklyn, New York, with loving, middle-class parents. But, it is not hard to imagine that family life is quite different for the 9-year-old girl than for her sister, born a year later, or their little brother, age 3.

It is true that most personality traits and intellectual characteristics can be traced to genes and nonshared environments, with little left over for shared influence. Even psychopathology, happiness, and sexual orientation (Burt, 2009; Långström et al., 2010; Bartels et al., 2013) can be attributed primarily to genes and nonshared environment. Some suggest that parents have little impact. This conclusion avoids "misplaced blame on parents for negative outcomes in their children . . . adding guilt to the grief parents are already feeling for their children's suffering" (Sherlock & Zietsch, 2018, p. 155). But might all the books, classes, and advisors who help parents become more effective be wasted efforts?

Could it be that parents are merely caretakers, necessary as providers of basic care (food, shelter), harmful when they are abusive, but inconsequential in daily restrictions, routines, and responses? If a child becomes a murderer or a hero, should parents be neither blamed nor credited?

Recent findings, however, reassert parent power. The analysis of shared and nonshared influences was correct, but the conclusion was based on a false assumption. Siblings raised together do *not* share the same environment.

For example, if relocation, divorce, unemployment, or a new job occurs in a family, the impact depends on each child's age, genes, resilience, and gender. Moving to another town upsets a school-age child more than an infant, divorce harms boys more than girls, poverty may hurt preschoolers the most, and so on.

Differential susceptibility adds to the variation: One child might be more affected by parents than another (Pluess & Belsky, 2010). When siblings are raised together, experiencing the same family conditions, the mix of genes, age, and gender may lead one child to become antisocial, another to be pathologically anxious, and a third to be resilient, capable, and strong (Beauchaine et al., 2009). Not only do children differ, but parents do not treat each child the same, as A View from Science makes clear.

Function and Structure

Family structure refers to the genetic and legal connections among related people living together. *Genetic* connections may be from parent to child, between cousins, between siblings, between grandparents and grandchildren, or more distantly. *Legal* connections may be through marriage or adoption.

family structure
The legal and genetic relationships among relatives living in the same home. Possible structures include nuclear family, extended family, stepfamily, single-parent family, and many others.

A VIEW FROM SCIENCE

"I Always Dressed One in Blue Stuff . . ."

To separate the effects of genes and environment, many researchers have studied twins (McAdams et al., 2014). As you remember from Chapter 2, some twins are dizygotic, with only half of their genes in common, and some are monozygotic, identical in all their genes. Many scientists assumed that children growing up with the same parents would have the same nurture (shared environment).

Therefore, if dizygotic twins are less alike than monozygotic twins are, genes must be the reason. Further, if one monozygotic twin differs from his or her genetically identical twin, raised by their parents in the same home, those differences must arise from the nonshared environment.

Logically, everyone is influenced by three forces: genes, shared environment (same home), and nonshared environment (different schools, friends, and so on). Many people were surprised when twin research discovered that almost everything could be attributed to genes and nonshared environment, with almost nothing left over for parents.

However, that conclusion is now tempered by another finding: Twins raised in the same home may have quite different family experiences for reasons that are not genetic. A seminal study in this regard occurred with twins in England.

An expert team of scientists compared 1,000 sets of monozygotic twins reared by their biological parents (Caspi et al., 2004). Obviously, the pairs were identical in genes, sex, and age. The researchers asked the mothers to describe each twin. Descriptions ranged from very positive ("my ray of sunshine") to very negative ("I wish I never had her. . . . She's a cow, I hate her") (quoted in Caspi et al., 2004, p. 153). Some mothers noted personality differences between their twins. For example, one mother said:

> Susan can be very sweet. She loves babies . . . she can be insecure . . . she flutters and dances around. . . .
> There's not much between her ears. . . . She's exceptionally vain, more so than Ann. Ann loves any game involving a ball, very sporty, climbs trees, very much a tomboy. One is a serious tomboy and one's a serious girlie girl. Even when they were babies I always dressed one in blue stuff and one in pink stuff.
> *[quoted in Caspi et al., 2004, p. 156]*

Some mothers rejected one twin but not the other:

> He was in the hospital and everyone was all "poor Jeff, poor Jeff" and I started thinking, "Well, what about me? I'm the one's just had twins. I'm the one's going through this, he's a seven-week-old baby and doesn't know a thing about it" . . . I sort of detached and plowed my emotions into Mike [Jeff's twin brother].
> *[quoted in Caspi et al., 2004, p. 156]*

This mother later blamed Jeff for favoring his father: "Jeff would do anything for Don but he wouldn't for me, and no matter what I did for either of them [Don or Jeff], it wouldn't be right" (p. 157). She said Mike was much more lovable.

The researchers measured personality at age 5 (assessing, among other things, antisocial behavior as reported by kindergarten teachers) and then measured each twin's personality two years later. They found that if a mother was more negative toward one of her twins, that twin *became* more antisocial, more likely to fight, steal, and hurt others at age 7 than at age 5, unlike the favored twin.

These researchers recognize that many other nonshared factors—peers, teachers, and so on—are significant. However, most developmental scientists now agree that genes, neighborhood, and parental influences are all important, and that—especially when genes or neighborhood push a child toward unhealthy development—parental intervention can be crucial (Liu & Neiderhiser, 2017).

Genes are still powerful, of course, because "a given DNA sequence operation in different environments can generate different products in different amounts at the cellular and phenotypic levels" (Waldinger & Schulz, 2018). That expresses an underlying theme of this book, that human development is multifactorial and complex. It begins with genes (DNA), but a simple calculation of genetic and family influence is impossible.

The fact that parents sometimes treat each of a pair of monozygotic twins differently confirms that parents matter. This will surprise no one who has a brother or a sister. Children from the same family do not always experience their family in the same way.

---

family function

The way a family works to meet the needs of its members. Children need families to provide basic material necessities, to encourage learning, to help them develop self-respect, to nurture friendships, and to foster harmony and stability.

Family function is distinct from structure. It refers to how the people in a family actually care for each other. Some families function well; others are dysfunctional.

Function is more important than structure. Ideally, every family provides love and encouragement. For most people, this comes from genetic relatives, so structure and function overlap. For foster children and adopted children who share few distinct genes with their caregivers, family function is crucial (Flannery et al., 2017).

Everyone enters the world with unique genes and a particular prenatal environment and that differential susceptibility influences how their family affects them. Beyond that, people's needs differ depending on their age: Infants need responsive caregiving, teenagers need guidance, young adults need freedom, the aged need respect. What do school-age children need?

THE NEEDS OF CHILDREN IN MIDDLE CHILDHOOD Ideally, families that function well for children aged 6 to 11 provide five things:

1. *Physical necessities.* In middle childhood, children can eat, dress, and wash themselves, but they need food, clothing, and shelter. Ideally, their families provide these things.

2. *Learning.* These are prime years for education. Families support, encourage, and guide schooling—connecting with teachers, checking homework, and so on.

3. *Self-respect.* Because children become self-critical and socially aware, families provide opportunities for success (in sports, the arts, or other arenas if academic success is difficult).

4. *Peer relationships.* Children need friends. Families choose schools and neighborhoods with friendly children and then arrange play dates, group activities, overnights, and so on.

5. *Harmony and stability.* Families provide protective, predictable routines in a home that is a safe, peaceful haven. Family conflict and chaos is avoided.

HARM FROM INSTABILITY The final item on the list above is especially significant in middle childhood: Children cherish safety and stability, not change (Turner et al., 2012). Ironically, many parents move from one neighborhood or school to another during these years. Children who move frequently are significantly affected academically and psychologically, but resilience is possible (Cutuli et al., 2013).

An example comes from children living in a shelter for homeless families. Compared to other children from the same kinds of families (often high-poverty, single-parent), homeless children were "significantly behind their low-income, but residentially more stable peers" in every measure (Obradović et al., 2009, p. 513). Learning and friendship suffered.

When added to other stresses, residential instability often becomes too much. Children who are homeless suffer physiologically as well as psychologically, evident in cortisol level, blood pressure, weight, and likelihood of hospitalization (Cutuli et al., 2017). Family function can buffer the impact: Children in shelters whose mothers provide stability, affection, routines, and hope sometimes are resilient. Their school achievement and friendship networks may seem unharmed.

A more benign example comes from children in military families. Enlisted parents tend to have higher incomes, better health care, and more education than do civilians from the same backgrounds. But they have one major disadvantage: instability.

◆ **Especially for Scientists**
How would you determine whether or not parents treat all of their children the same? (see response, page 307)

KIDSTOCK/BLEND IMAGES/GETTY IMAGES

Stay Home, Dad The rate of battle deaths for U.S. soldiers is lower for those deployed in Iraq and Afghanistan than for any previous conflict, thanks to modern medicine and armor. However, psychological harm from repeated returns and absences is increasing.

Military children (dubbed "military brats"—a pejorative that reflects how outsiders perceive them) have more emotional problems and lower school achievement than do their peers from civilian families. The reason is thought to be because their parents "are continually leaving, returning, leaving again. . . . School work suffers, more for boys than for girls, and . . . reports of depression and behavioral problems go up when a parent is deployed" (Hall, 2008, p. 52).

Most military children learn to cope (Russo & Fallon, 2014). To help them, the U.S. military has special programs for children whose parents are deployed. Caregivers of such children are encouraged to avoid changes in the child's life: no new homes, new rules, or new schools (Lester et al., 2011). Similar concerns arise when deployed parents come home: They are welcomed, of course, but the child's life might change again—and that causes more stress.

On a broader level, children who are displaced because of storms, fire, war, and so on may suffer psychologically. They may try to comfort their parents, not telling them about their distress, but the data on health and achievement show that moving from place to place is highly stressful (Masten, 2014). All children must cope with some disruption: Some children develop good coping skills and other children do not.

Various Family Structures

Two-parent families are composed only of children and their parents (married or not). Traditionally the parents are the biological parents of the children (*nuclear families*), but other two-parent families are headed by adoptive parents, foster parents, stepparents, or same-sex couples, most of whom provide good care.

About 31 percent of all U.S. 6- to 11-year-olds live in a **single-parent family.** Again, most have good caregivers. Some observers think that more than 31 percent of U.S. children are in single-parent families since more than half of all contemporary U.S. children will live in a single-parent family for at least a year before they reach age 18. However, as far as we can deduce, at any given moment most 6- to 11-year-olds are living in two-parent families. (See Visualizing Development, page 293.)

An **extended family** includes relatives in addition to parents and children. Usually the additional persons are grandparents or uncles, aunts, or cousins of the child. The crucial distinction for official tallies is who lives under the same roof. This measures family structure, not family function.

The distinction between one-parent, two-parent, and extended families is not as simple in practice as it is on the census. Many parents of young children live near, but not with, the grandparents, who provide meals, emotional support, money, and child care, functioning as an extended family. The opposite is true as well, especially in developing nations: Some extended families share a household but create separate living quarters for each set of parents and children, making these units somewhat like nuclear families.

In many nations, the **polygamous family** (one husband with two or more wives) is a legal family structure. Generally in polygamous families, income per child is reduced, and education, especially for the girls, is limited—in part because girls are expected to marry young. Polygamy is rare—and illegal—in the United States. Even in nations where it is allowed—many African and a few Southeast Asian nations— polygamy is less common than it was 30 years ago.

COHORT CHANGES There are more single-parent households, more divorces and remarriages, and fewer children per family than in the past. Specifics vary from decade to decade and nation to nation (see Figure 8.1). Nevertheless, although the proportions differ, problems within non-nuclear families are similar worldwide.

single-parent family
A family that consists of only one parent and his or her children.

extended family
A family of relatives in addition to the parents usually three or more generations living in one household.

polygamous family
A family consisting of one man, several wives, and their children.

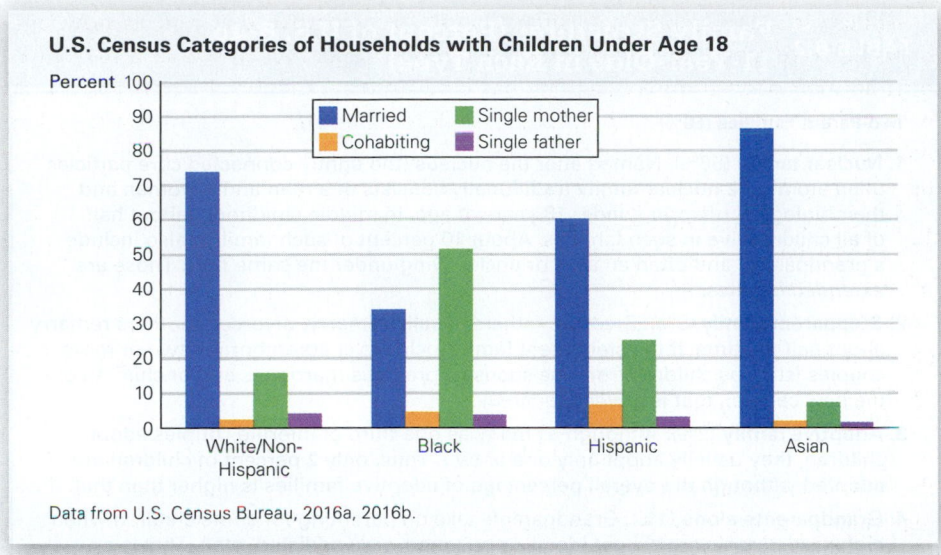

U.S. Census Categories of Households with Children Under Age 18

Percent

Legend: Married, Cohabiting, Single mother, Single father

Categories: White/Non-Hispanic, Black, Hispanic, Asian

Data from U.S. Census Bureau, 2016a, 2016b.

FIGURE 8.1 Possible Problems
As the text makes clear, structure does not determine function, but raising children is more difficult as a single parent, in part because income is lower. Single-parent African American families have at least one asset, however. They are more likely to live with grandmothers.

Such diversity should be acknowledged but neither exaggerated nor bemoaned. The United States has more single parents than other developed nations, yet more than two-thirds of all U.S. school-age children live with two parents (see Table 8.2), most often their biological parents.

Connecting Family Structure and Function

How a family functions is more important for children than their family structure. The two are related; structure influences (but does not determine) function. Some structures increase the possibility that the five family functions mentioned earlier (physical necessities, learning, self-respect, friendship, and harmony/stability) will be fulfilled.

TWO-PARENT FAMILIES On average, nuclear or other types of two-parent families function best; children living in such households tend to learn more in school and have fewer psychological problems. Why? Does this mean that all parents should marry and stay married? Not necessarily: Some benefits are correlates, not causes.

Education, earning potential, and emotional maturity increase the rate of marriage and parenthood and decrease the rate of divorce. For example, first-time mothers in the United States are usually (78 percent) married when they conceive their first child if they are highly educated, but they are usually unmarried (only 11 percent married at conception) if they are low in SES (Gibson-Davis & Rackin, 2014).

Thus, people tend to have personal assets *before* they marry and become parents, and those assets benefit their new family. The correlation between child success and married parents occurs partly because of who marries, not because of the wedding. These two factors—selection and income—explain some of the correlation between two-parent families and child well-being.

To the surprise of some outsiders, a large study comparing male–female and same-sex couples found that the major predictor of their children's well-being was not the parents' sexual orientation but their income and stability (Cenegy et al., 2018). Similar findings come from adoptive parents, grandparents raising children, and so on. A caregiver's emotional health and the family's economic security benefit the children.

In general, married parents (of whatever sexual orientation or gender identity) are more likely to stay together than unmarried parents, and they are more likely to become wealthier and healthier than either would alone. Further, seeing one's children day and night increases bonding, and that helps everyone. By contrast, single parenthood,

© 2016 MACMILLAN

Didn't Want to Marry This couple was happily cohabiting and strongly committed to each other but didn't wed until they learned that her health insurance would not cover him unless they were legally married. Twenty months after marriage, their son was born.

TABLE 8.2	Family Structures (Percent of U.S. 6- to 11-Year-Olds in Each Type)*

Two-Parent Families (69%)

1. **Nuclear family** (56%). Named after the nucleus (the tightly connected core particles of an atom), the nuclear family traditionally consists of a man and a woman and their biological offspring under 18 years of age. In middle childhood, about half of all children live in such families. About 10 percent of such families also include a grandparent, and often an aunt or uncle, living under the same roof. Those are *extended* families.

2. **Stepparent family** (9%). Divorced fathers usually remarry; divorced mothers remarry about half the time. If the stepparent family includes children born to two or more couples (such as children from the spouses' previous marriages and/or children of the new couple), that is a *blended family.*

3. **Adoptive family** (2%). Although as many as one-third of infertile couples adopt children, they usually adopt only one or two. Thus, only 2 percent of children are adopted, although the overall percentage of adoptive families is higher than that.

4. **Grandparents alone** (1%). Grandparents take on parenting for some children when biological parents are absent (dead, imprisoned, sick, addicted, etc.). That is a *skipped-generation* family.

5. **Same-sex parents** (1%). Some two-parent families are headed by a same-sex couple, whose legal status (married, step-, adoptive) varies.

Single-Parent Families (31%)

One-parent families are increasing, but they average fewer children than two-parent families. So in middle childhood, only 31 percent of children have a lone parent.

1. **Single mother—never married** (14%). In 2016, 40 percent of all U.S. births were to unmarried mothers; but when children are school age, many such mothers have married or have entrusted their children to their parents' care. Thus, only about 14 percent of 6- to 11-year-olds, at any given moment, are in single-mother, never-married homes.

2. **Single mother—divorced, separated, or widowed** (12%). Although many marriages end in divorce (almost half in the United States, fewer in other nations), many divorcing couples have no children. Others remarry. Thus, only 12 percent of school-age children currently live with single, formerly married mothers.

3. **Single father** (4%). About 1 father in 25 has physical custody of his children and raises them without their mother or a new wife. This category increased at the start of the twenty-first century but has decreased since 2005.

4. **Grandparent alone** (1%). Sometimes a single grandparent (usually the grandmother) becomes the sole caregiving adult for a child.

More Than Two Adults (15%) [Also listed as two-parent or single-parent family]

1. **Extended family** (15%). Some children live with a grandparent or other relatives, as well as with one (5 percent) or both (10 percent) of their parents. This pattern is most common with infants (20 percent) but occurs in middle childhood as well.

2. **Polygamous family** (0%). In some nations (not the United States), men can legally have several wives. This family structure is more favored by adults than children. Everywhere, polyandry (one woman, several husbands) is rare.

*Less than 1 percent of children under age 12 live without any caregiving adult; they are not included in this table.

The percentages in this table are estimates, based on data in U.S. Census Bureau (2011, 2015). The category "extended family" in this table is higher than most published statistics, since some families do not tell official authorities about relatives living with them.

especially after a bitter divorce, correlates with poor health and low income for everyone. Rarely seeing one parent increases children's internalizing and externalizing problems.

Contact tends to increase affection and care. Recent data come from Russia, where economic and social pressures have led many single men to drink and despair, dying years earlier than married men. The reason is thought to be that the husband/father role leads men to take better care of themselves and, wives to look out for their husband's health (Ashwin & Isupova, 2014).

AP PHOTO/CHARLES REX ARBOGAST

GREG ELMS/GETTY IMAGES

Shared parenting also decreases the risk of child maltreatment, because one parent is likely to protect their children if the other is abusive or neglectful. For all children, having two parents around every day makes it more likely that someone will read to them, check their homework, invite their friends over, buy them new clothes, and save for their education. Of course, living with both parents does not guarantee good care. One of my students wrote:

> My mother externalized her feelings with outbursts of rage, lashing out and break-ing things, while my father internalized his feelings by withdrawing, being silent and looking the other way. One could say I was being raised by bipolar parents. Growing up, I would describe my mom as the Tasmanian devil and my father as the ostrich, with his head in the sand. . . . My mother disciplined with corporal punishment as well as with psychological control, while my father was permissive. What a pair.
>
> [C., 2013]

This student is now a single parent, having twice married, given birth, and divorced. She is one example of a general finding: The effects of childhood family function echo in adulthood, financially as well as psychologically.

Remarried adults whose household income is comparable to that of nuclear parents contrib-ute less, on average, to children from their first marriage or to stepchildren (Turley & Desmond, 2011). Stepparents may be rejected by stepchil-dren, who are loyal to their absent parent. The new spouse has an additional challenge: It is diffi-cult to bond with the progeny of their new part-ner's former lover.

The primary advantage of the stepparent fam-ily structure is financial, especially when compared with most single-parent families. The primary disadvantage is in meeting the fifth family func-tion listed earlier—providing harmony and stability is (Martin-Uzzi & Duval-Tsioles, 2013). Often the child's loyalty to both biological parents is challenged by ongoing disputes between them. A solid parental alliance is elusive when it includes three adults—two of whom disliked each other enough to divorce, plus another adult who is a newcomer to the child.

Same Situation, Far Apart: Happy Families The boys in both photos are about 4 years old. Roberto lives with his single mother in Chicago *(left)*. She pays $360 a month for her two children to attend a day-care center. The youngest child in the Balmedina family *(right)* lives with his nuclear family—no day care needed—in the Philippines. Which boy has the better life? The answer is not known; family function is more crucial than family structure.

↓ **OBSERVATION** QUIZ
What is unusual about this family? (see answer, page 307)

DAVID MAXWELL/THE NEW YORK TIMES/REDUX

Middle American Family
This photo seems to show a typical breakfast in Brunswick, Ohio—Cheerios for 1-year-old Carson, pancakes that 7-year-old Carter does not finish eating, and family photos crowded on the far table.

◆ **Especially for Single Parents**
You have heard that children raised in one-parent families will have difficulty in establishing intimate relationships as adolescents and adults. What can you do about this possibility? (see response, page 307)

Don't Judge We know this is a mother and her child, but structure and function could be wonderful or terrible. These two could be half of a nuclear family, or a single mother with one adoptive child, or part of four other family structures. That does not matter as much as family function: If this scene is typical, with both enjoying physical closeness in the great outdoors, this family functions well.

© 2016 MACMILLAN

Further, compared with other two-parent families, stepfamilies more often change residence and community. In addition, the family constellation shifts: Older stepchildren are more likely to leave, new babies capture parental attention and affection, additional family members may join the household, and divorce is more common.

Children themselves impede the functioning of their new family structure. They often are angry or sad and act out, fighting with friends, failing in school, refusing to follow household rules, harming themselves (with cutting, accidents, eating disorders, and so on). Their parents often have opposite strategies for managing child misbehavior.

Added to that, disputes between half-siblings and stepsiblings are common. Remember, however, that structure affects function but does not determine it. Some stepparent families are troubled; others function well for everyone (van Eeden-Moorefield & Pasley, 2013).

SINGLE-PARENT FAMILIES On average, the single-parent structure functions less well for children because single parents have less income, time, and stability. That affects all five family functions needed by children in middle childhood. Most fill many roles—including wage earner, daughter or son (single parents often depend on their own parents), and lover (many seek a new partner). That reduces time for emotional and academic support for their children. If they are depressed (and many are), that makes it worse. Neesha, in A Case to Study, is an example.

STEPFAMILIES Generally, fathers who do not live with their children become less involved every year. When the children reach age 18, fathers are no longer legally responsible, and many divorced or unmarried fathers no longer pay for education or other expenses. This is a harsh reality in today's economy: Emerging adults usually need substantial funds before they become self-sufficient adults (Goldfarb, 2014). Laws and norms need updating.

When a father is the single parent, he suffers the same problems as single mothers—too much to do and not enough money to do it. Single parents of both sexes tend to seek a new spouse, in part to help with parenthood. This does not usually work out as planned (Booth & Dunn, 2014).

MANY EXCEPTIONS All of these are generalities. Structure encourages or undercuts healthy function, but many parents and communities overcome structural problems to support their children. Contrary to the averages, thousands of nuclear families are destructive, thousands of stepparents provide excellent care, and thousands of single-parent families are wonderful. In some European nations, single parents are given many public resources; in other nations, they are shamed as well as unsupported. Children benefit or suffer accordingly.

Culture is always influential. In contrast to data from the United States, a study in the slums of Mumbai, India, found rates of psychological disorders among school-age children *higher* in nuclear families than in extended families, presumably because grandparents, aunts, and uncles provided more care and stability in

A CASE TO STUDY

How Hard Is It to Be a Kid?

Neesha's fourth-grade teacher referred her to the school guidance team because Neesha often fell asleep in class, was late 51 days, and was absent 15 days. Testing found Neesha at the seventh-grade level in reading and writing and at the fifth-grade level in math. Since achievement was not Neesha's problem, something psychosocial must be amiss.

The counselor spoke to Neesha's mother, Tanya. She was a single parent who was depressed and worried about paying the rent on a tiny apartment where she had moved when Neesha's father left three years earlier. He lived with his girlfriend, now with a new baby as well. Tanya said she had no problems with Neesha, who was "more like a little mother than a kid," unlike her 15-year-old son, Tyrone, who suffered from fetal alcohol effects and whose behavior worsened when his father left.

Tyrone was recently beaten up badly as part of a gang initiation, a group he considered "like a family." He was currently in juvenile detention, after being arrested for stealing bicycle parts.

Note the nonshared environment: Although the siblings might be thought to have a shared environment, that was not the case, so Tyrone became rebellious whereas Neesha became parentified, "a little mother."

The school counselor spoke with Neesha.

> Neesha volunteered that she worried a lot about things and that sometimes when she worries she has a hard time falling asleep. . . . She got in trouble for being late so many times, but it was hard to wake up. Her mom was sleeping late because she was working more nights cleaning offices. . . . Neesha said she got so far behind that she just gave up. She was also having problems with the other girls in the class, who were starting to tease her about sleeping in class and not doing her work. She said they called her names

like "Sleepy" and "Dummy." She said that at first it made her very sad, and then it made her very mad. That's when she started to hit them to make them stop.

> [Wilmshurst, 2011, pp. 152–153]

Neesha is coping with poverty, a depressed mother, an absent father, a delinquent brother, and classmate bullying. She seemed resilient—her achievement scores are impressive—but shortly after Neesha was interviewed,

> The school principal received a call from Neesha's mother, who asked that her daughter not be sent home from school because she was going to kill herself. She was holding a loaded gun in her hand and she had to do it, because she was not going to make this month's rent. She could not take it any longer, but she did not want Neesha to come home and find her dead. . . . While the guidance counselor continued to keep the mother talking, the school contacted the police, who apprehended [the] mom while she was talking on her cell phone. . . . The loaded gun was on her lap. . . . The mother was taken to the local psychiatric facility.

> [Wilmshurst, 2011, pp. 154–155]

Whether Neesha's resilience will continue depends on her ability to find support beyond her family. Perhaps the school counselor will help:

> When asked if she would like to meet with the school psychologist once in a while, just to talk about her worries, Neesha said she would like that very much. After she left the office, she turned and thanked the psychologist for working with her, and added, "You know, sometimes it's hard being a kid."

> [Wilmshurst, 2011, p. 154]

that city than two parents alone (Patil et al., 2013). But see Opposing Perspectives on page 292.

Single parents are much less common in India and in most other nations than in the United States, but in this study as in every nation, on average, children in such families are more likely to have emotional or academic problems.

A close look at both structure and function finds that no structure always functions well, but some circumstances (such as genetic connections or adoptive choices) nudge adults to be more caring parents. Cultural norms also matter. In the United States, some immigrant households function well as extended families, especially when compared to single-parent families. That may not be true for those who are not immigrants (Areba et al., 2018).

Check out the **DATA CONNECTIONS ACTIVITY**: Family Structure in the United States and Around the World.

OPPOSING PERSPECTIVES

Extended Families

Why is this an "opposing perspective?" Aren't extended families always great? Some Americans think so. The question "What destroyed the extended family?" was posed in a newsletter called *Common Sense Home*. One answer:

> the idea that having Gram and Gramps living with the family was somehow low class and beneath the newly prosperous. … in searching for a better life, we destroyed what was good and true in the family unit to trade it for the affluent lifestyle.
>
> [Alice, quoted in Neverman, 2016]

But the data find that extended families are not always "good and true." In fact, extended families are often poor and conflicted, the two conditions known to harm children no matter what the family structure.

Then the question remains, but with the opposite answer: Extended families may *never* be great. Why is this an opposing perspective? Because every family structure is sometimes good and sometimes not. It depends not only on facts but also on attitudes.

Alice (above) got one thing right: Poverty makes extended families more likely. In the United States today, when three generations live together, usually the middle generation needs help with child care and living expenses, and the older generation pays the bills (Ho, 2015; Maroto, 2017). That makes the grandparents more stressed, less healthy, and more depressed than grandparents who live near but not with their grandchildren (Dunifon et al., 2014).

What about the children? Do they benefit from having several adults caring for them? Apparently not.

One study began with 194 young African American mothers of preschoolers, some of whom lived with their mothers and some who did not (Black et al., 2002). The researchers were not surprised that sharing a home took a toll on the older generation, because that finding has been replicated many times. But given "the enthusiasm of policymakers for three generation households" (Black et al., 2002, p. 573), they expected that co-residence would benefit the younger generations. Not so.

Compared to the mothers who lived apart from their parents, those in three-generation households were more often depressed. Their children were more often mistreated, disobedient, or withdrawn, and slow to develop language.

The researchers suggested a reason: Grandmother criticism accompanied grandmother care, and that reduced maternal pride and mother–child attachment. In addition, the mothers were less likely to have an independent source of income and less likely to have the children's father living with them. Resentment between mothers and grown daughters was common.

On reflection, that makes sense. When a mother and grandmother live together, conflicts are almost inevitable about how to feed, discipline, clean, and clothe the children.

I know this personally. My home had a major fire, so I lived with my adult daughter and her children for 8 months. We agreed on major issues and respected each other, but it was hard not to critique her choices of food, patterns of kitchen clean-up, placement of laundry.

I suspect she also tried to keep quiet about my habits. We avoided conflicts that would affect the children, but we both had to work at it.

This potential for conflict is evident worldwide. Sometimes Americans idealize extended families in African and Asian cultures. But research finds that many Asians and Africans no longer prefer extended families. Grandmother care—yes; living together—no (Johar & Maruyama, 2011; Goh et al., Tsai et al., 2014; Levetan & Wild, 2016).

But what about that study from India? (Patil et al., 2013). Another study in India found that college students who injured themselves (e.g., *cutting*) were more often from extended families than nuclear ones (Kharsati & Bhola, 2014). The likely explanation is that children in the first study were desperately poor: For them, extended families increased the odds that someone would feed and educate them. The children in the second study were from wealthier families. Abject poverty was not their problem, but conflict and stress were.

Are extended families wonderful or horrible? Probably neither. These opposing perspectives suggest that it depends on intergeneration attitudes and income. There is no simple answer.

THINK CRITICALLY: Can you describe a situation in which having a single parent would be better for a child than having two parents?

Family Trouble

All of the generalities just explained are averages; many families find their own way to function well, overcoming structural problems. However, no matter what ethnicity, culture, or structure, two factors inevitably undercut family function: low income and high conflict. If a family has one of these, they often have the other, because financial stress increases conflict and vice versa.

A WEDDING, OR NOT? FAMILY STRUCTURES AROUND THE WORLD

Children fare best when both parents actively care for them every day. This is most likely to occur if the parents are married, although there are many exceptions. Many developmentalists now focus on the rate of single parenthood, shown on this map. Some single parents raise children well, but the risk of neglect, poverty, and instability in single-parent households increases the chances of child problems.

RATES OF SINGLE PARENTHOOD

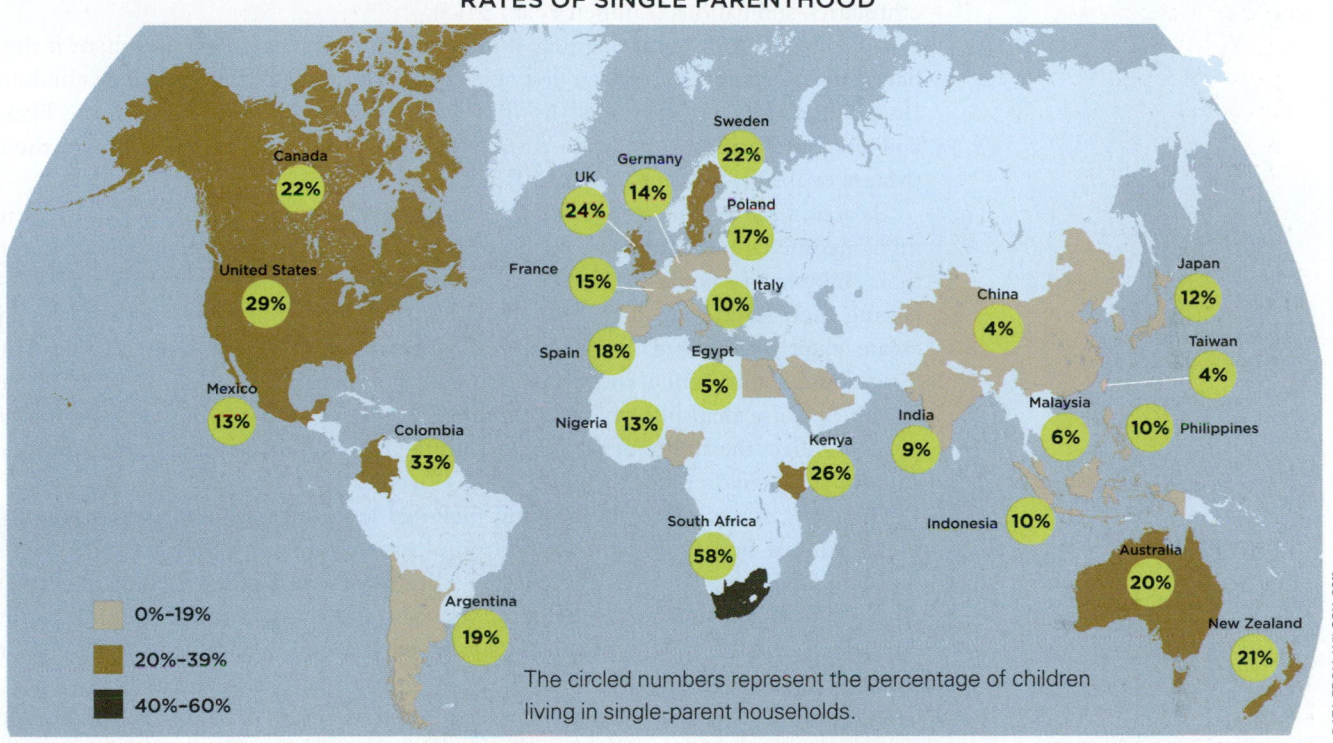

DATA FROM: WILCOX, 2011.

Legend:
- 0%–19%
- 20%–39%
- 40%–60%

The circled numbers represent the percentage of children living in single-parent households.

❤ A young couple in love and committed to each other—
WHAT NEXT?

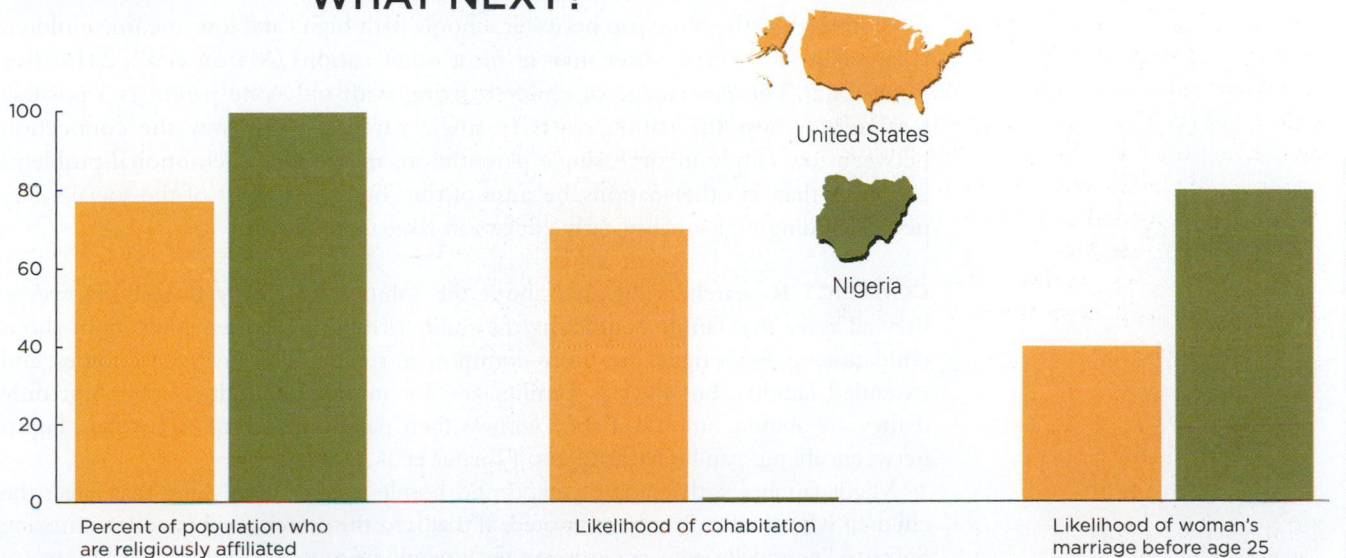

United States

Nigeria

DATA FROM COPEN ET AL., 2013, AND U.S. CENSUS BUREAU, 2012.

Chart axis labels:
- Percent of population who are religiously affiliated
- Likelihood of cohabitation
- Likelihood of woman's marriage before age 25

Cohabitation and marriage rates change from year to year and from culture to culture. These two examples are illustrative and approximate. Family-structure statistics like these often focus on marital status and may make it seem as if Nigerian children are more fortunate than American children. However, actual household functioning is more complex than that and involves many other factors.

WEALTH AND POVERTY Family income affects both function and structure. Marriage rates fall in times of recession, and divorce increases with unemployment. Low SES correlates with many other problems, and "risk factors pile up in the lives of some children, particularly among the most disadvantaged" (Masten, 2014, p. 95).

Several scholars have developed the *family-stress model,* which holds that any risk factor (such as poverty, divorce, single parenthood, unemployment) damages a family if, and only if, it increases stress on the parents, who become less patient and responsive to the children (Masarik & Conger, 2017). This is true for families of all types, ethnicities, and nations (Emmen et al., 2013).

If economic hardship is ongoing, if uncertainty about the future is high, or if they have little education, parents are less able to mentor and advocate for their children. Instead, they become tense and hostile. Low SES makes many stresses more likely, and then the parents' *reaction* to those stresses may exacerbate or minimize them (Mazza et al., 2017; Evans & Kim, 2013; Lee et al., 2013).

Reaction to wealth may also cause difficulty (Luthar et al., 2018). Children in high-income families are more likely to have developmental problems in adulthood than children of middle-SES parents. Wealthy parents may be anxious about maintaining their status, which makes them pressure their children to excel. That may create externalizing and internalizing problems in middle childhood that lead to drug abuse, delinquency, and poor academic performance. No one contends that wealth is worse than poverty for children. The crucial factor is how the economic pressures affect the ability of the parents and the community to provide the attention and guidance children need (Roubinov & Boyce, 2017).

Generally, adults whose upbringing included less education and impaired emotional control find it difficult to find employment, and then low income makes their children more likely to misbehave—a double whammy (Schofield et al., 2011). Their children are also more likely to have health problems that lead to "biologically embedded" stresses, which later impair adult well-being, affecting the next generation (Masten, 2013).

Nations that subsidize single parents (e.g., Austria and Iceland) tax wealthy adults at higher rates and have greater economic diversity within schools, which generally have smaller achievement gaps between low- and high-SES children. Reasons for the reduced gap are many, however, and those just mentioned may not be the crucial ones.

Nonetheless, the score gap between schools with high- and low-income children is larger in the United States than in most other nations (Martin et al., 2016) (see Figure 8.2). The percentage of children living with only one parent is a possible reason, as is how the nation reacts to single parents. In Norway the connection between low family income, single parenthood, and children's emotional problems is smaller than in other nations, because of the "buffering effect of the social safety net," including high-quality early education (Bøe et al., 2018).

CONFLICT Researchers disagree about the solution to family poverty. However, they all agree that family conflict harms children, especially when adults fight about child rearing. Such fights are more common in stepfamilies, divorced families, and extended families, but nuclear families are not immune. Children suffer not only if they are abused, but also if they witness their parents' abuse of each other. Fights between siblings can be harmful, too (Turner et al., 2012).

Might families with feuding parents and hostile siblings have genes that affect the children who are not directly mistreated? If that is so, the correlation between witnessing fights and personally suffering is deceptive: It would be caused by a third variable.

This hypothesis was tested in a longitudinal study of conflict in the families of 867 adult twins (388 monozygotic and 479 dizygotic), with both twins married and

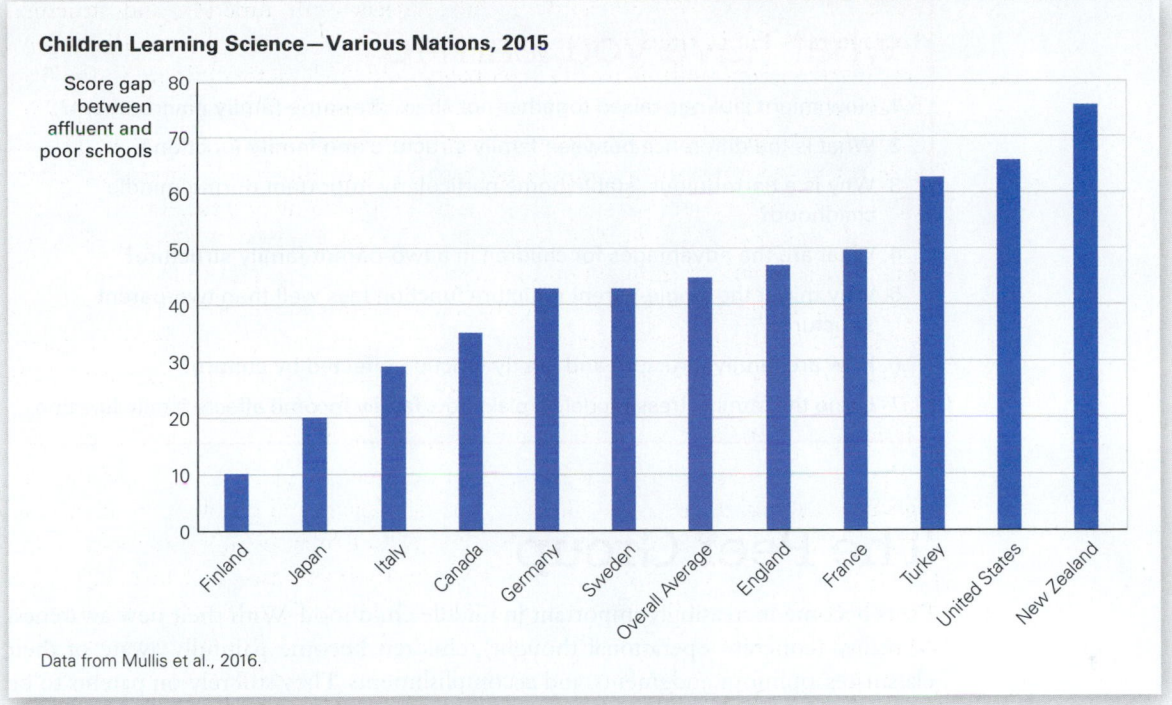

Children Learning Science—Various Nations, 2015

Score gap between affluent and poor schools

Data from Mullis et al., 2016.

FIGURE 8.2 Families and Schools This graph shows the score gap in fourth-grade science on the 2015 TIMSS between children in schools where more than 25 percent of the children are from affluent homes compared to children in schools where more than 25 percent are poor. Generally, the nations with the largest gaps are also the nations with the most schools at one or the other end of the spectrum and fewest in between. For example, only 23 percent of the children in the United States attended schools that were neither rich nor poor, but 37 percent of the Japanese children did.

having an adolescent child (Schermerhorn et al., 2011). Both parents were asked independently about marital conflict. Each teenager was compared to their cousin, who was the child of their parent's twin.

Thus, this study had data from 5,202 individuals—one-third of them adult twins, one-third of them spouses of twins, and one-third of them adolescents who were genetically linked to another adolescent. If their parent was a monozygotic twin, they had one-fourth of their genes in common with their cousin; if their parent was a dizygotic twin, one-eighth of the same genes.

Thus, the comparisons between cousins could distinguish genetic from family effects. The researchers found that witnessing conflict itself had a powerful effect, increasing externalizing problems in the boys and internalizing problems in the girls.

Quiet disagreements between the parents did little harm, but open conflict (e.g., yelling heard by the children) and divorce did (Schermerhorn et al., 2011). That leads to an obvious conclusion: Parents should not fight in front of their children.

You Idiot! Ideally, parents never argue in front of the children, as these two do here. However, *how* they argue is crucial. Every couple disagrees about specifics of family life; dysfunctional families call each other names. Hopefully, he said, "I know how to fit this bike into the car" and she answered, "I was just trying to help," rather than either one escalating the fight by saying, "It was your stupid idea to take this trip!"

what have you learned?

1. How might siblings raised together not share the same family environment?
2. What is the difference between family structure and family function?
3. Why is a harmonious, stable home particularly important during middle childhood?
4. What are the advantages for children in a two-parent family structure?
5. Why might the single-parent structure function less well than two-parent structures?
6. How are family structure and family function affected by culture?
7. Using the family-stress model, explain how family income affects family function.

The Peer Group

Peers become increasingly important in middle childhood. With their new awareness of reality (concrete operational thought), children become painfully aware of their classmates' opinions, judgments, and accomplishments. They still rely on parents to be supportive and available, but peer relationships become more important (Bosmans & Kerns, 2015).

The Culture of Children

child culture
The idea that each group of children has games, sayings, clothing styles, and superstitions that are not common among adults, just as every culture has distinct values, behaviors, and beliefs.

Peer relationships, unlike adult–child relationships, involve partners who negotiate, compromise, share, and defend themselves as equals. Consequently, children learn social lessons from one another (Rubin et al., 2013). Adults may follow a child's lead, but they are always much older and bigger, with their own values and experiences. They cannot substitute for a friend who is a peer.

Child culture includes the customs, rules, and rituals that are passed down to younger children from slightly older ones, with no thought about the origins or implications. The child's goal is to join a culture and thus be part of the peer group. Jump-rope rhymes, insults, and superstitions ensue.

For instance, "Ring around the rosy/Pocketful of posies/Ashes, ashes/We all fall down," may have originated as children coped with the Black Death, which killed half the population of Europe in the fourteenth century. (*Rosy* may be short for *rosary,* used by Roman Catholics for prayer.) Children have passed down that rhyme for centuries, laughing together with no thought of sudden death.

Throughout the world, child culture may be at odds with adult culture. Many children reject clothes that parents buy as too loose, too tight, too long, too short, or wrong in color, style, brand, decoration, or some other aspect that adults might not notice. If their schools are multiethnic, children may choose friends from other groups, even though their parents have no such friends.

Appearance is important for child culture, but more important is independence from adults. Classmates pity those (especially boys) whose parents kiss them ("mama's boy"), tease children who please the teachers ("teacher's pet," "suck-up"), and despise those who betray children to adults ("tattletale," "grasser," "snitch," "rat"). Keeping secrets from parents and teachers is a moral mandate.

The culture of children is not always benign. For example, because communication with peers is vital, children learn the necessary languages. Immigrant parents proudly note how well their children speak a second language, but all parents are

E. HANAZAKI PHOTOGRAPHY/MOMENT/GETTY IMAGES

No Toys Boys in middle childhood are happiest playing outside with equipment designed for work. This wheelbarrow is perfect, especially because at any moment the pusher might tip it.

distressed when their children spout their peers' curses, accents, and slang. Because they value independence, children may gravitate toward friends who defy authority, sometimes harmlessly (passing a note in class), sometimes not (shoplifting, smoking).

This is part of the nature of children, who often do what their parents do not want them to do, and it is in the nature of parents to be upset when that happens. This is easier to criticize in other cultures and centuries, as in the following example.

In 1922 the magazine *Good Housekeeping* published an article titled "Aren't You Glad You Are Not Your Grandmother?" In it, a daughter quotes letters from her dead grandmother that she found in the attic. One describes an incident that occurred when that daughter's father—also long dead—was a boy and snuck out of his house to play with other boys:

> When the door was left unlocked for a moment, out he ran in his little velvet suit. We did not miss him for a while because we thought he was doing his Latin Prose, and then some wealthy ladies . . . saw him literally in the gutter, groping in the mud for a marble. . . . Horace's father was white with emotion when he heard of it. He brought Horace in, gave him another whipping, and, saying that since he acted like a runaway dog he should be treated like one, he went out, bought a dog-collar and a chain, and chained Horace to the post of his little bed. He was there all the afternoon, crying so you could hear nothing else in all the house. . . . I went many times up to the hall before his door and knelt there stretching out my arms to my darling child, the tears flooding down my cheeks. But, of course, I could not open the door and go in to him, to interfere with his punishment.
>
> *[Fisher, 1922, p. 8]*

The author is grateful that mothers now (in 1922!) know more than did nineteenth-century parents with their "ignorance of child-life" (Fisher, 1922, p. 15). This raises the question: What ignorance of child-life do we have today? If I knew, that would not be ignorance, but this text makes me humble; each new generation develops a child culture that may teach their elders.

Friendships

Teachers sometimes separate friends, but that may be a mistake. Developmentalists find that children help each other learn both academic and social skills (Bagwell & Schmidt, 2011). The loyalty of children to their friends may work for their benefit or harm (Rubin et al., 2013).

Both aspects of friendship are expressed by these two Mexican American children.

Yolanda:

There's one friend . . . she's always been with me, in bad or good . . . She's always telling me, "Keep on going and your dreams are gonna come true."

Paul:

I think right now about going Christian, right? Just going Christian, trying to do good, you know? Stay away from drugs, everything. And every time it seems like I think about that, I think about the homeboys. And it's a trip because a lot of the homeboys are my family, too, you know?

[quoted in Nieto, 2000, pp. 220, 249]

Yolanda later went to college; Paul went to jail. This is echoed by other children. Many aspects of adult personality are influenced by the personality of childhood friends (Wrzus et al., 2016). Indeed, quite apart from a child's family, school, and IQ,

"Oh yeah? Well, my vocabulary is bigger than *your* vocabulary!"

Better Than Children of all genders, ethnic groups, religions, nations, and families think they are better than children of other groups. They can learn not to blurt out insults, but a deeper understanding of the diversity of human experience and abilities requires maturation.

JOHNNY HAWKINS/CARTOONSTOCK

THINK CRITICALLY: Do adults also choose friends who agree with them or whose background is similar to their own?

a study found that the intelligence of a best friend in sixth grade affected intelligence at age 15 (Meldrum et al., 2018).

Since children want to be liked, they learn faster and feel happier when they have friends. If they had to choose between being friendless but popular (looked up to by many peers) or having close friends but being unpopular (ignored by peers), most would choose the friends (Bagwell & Schmidt, 2011). A wise choice.

Friendships become more intense and intimate over the years of middle childhood, as social cognition and effortful control advance. Six-year-olds may befriend anyone of the same gender and age who will play with them. By age 10, children demand more. They choose carefully, share secrets, expect loyalty, change friends less often, are upset when they lose a friend, and find it harder to make new friends.

Older children tend to choose friends whose interests, values, and backgrounds are similar to their own. By the end of middle childhood, close friendships are almost always between children of the same gender, age, ethnicity, and socioeconomic status (Rubin et al., 2013). Both genders learn how to become good friends, with girls becoming better at sympathetic reassurance and boys becoming better at joint excitement. They all find friendship increasingly satisfying over the years of childhood (Rose & Asher, 2017).

Popular and Unpopular Children

In the United States, two types of popular children and three types of unpopular children have become apparent in middle childhood (Cillessen & Marks, 2011). At every age, children who are friendly and cooperative are well-liked and popular. By the end of middle childhood, as status becomes important, another avenue to popularity begins: Some popular children are also aggressive (Shi & Xie, 2012).

As for the three types of unpopular children, some are *neglected,* not rejected; they are ignored, but not shunned. The other two types are actively rejected, either **aggressive-rejected,** disliked because they are antagonistic and confrontational, or **withdrawn-rejected,** disliked because they are timid and anxious. Children as young as age 6 are aware if they are rejected and are able to decide whether they should try to be more accepted or should seek other friends (Nesdale et al., 2014).

aggressive-rejected
A type of childhood rejection, when other children do not want to be friends with a child because of his or her antagonistic, confrontational behavior.

withdrawn-rejected
A type of childhood rejection, when other children do not want to be friends with a child because of his or her timid, withdrawn, and anxious behavior.

Both aggressive-rejected and withdrawn-rejected children often misinterpret social situations, lack emotional regulation, and experience mistreatment at home. Each of these problems not only cause rejection but the rejection itself makes it worse for the child (Stenseng et al., 2015). If they do not learn when to assert themselves and when to be quiet, they may become bullies and victims.

Whether a particular child is popular or not depends on cultural norms, which may change over time. This is illustrated by research on shyness in China. A 1990 survey in Shanghai found that shy children were liked and respected (X. Chen et al., 1992), but 12 years later, when competition with the West became salient, shy children in the same schools were less popular (X. Chen et al., 2005).

Other research found that shyness was still valued in rural China (X. Chen et al., 2009), but in urban areas shyness predicted unhappiness—unless the shy child was also academically superior (X. Chen et al., 2013). Age mattered too: Shyness was less problematic in middle childhood than in adolescence (Liu et al., 2017). Obviously, cohort and context matter.

Now consider bullying, once quite acceptable ("boys will be boys!") and now seen as destructive, not only for victims but for bystanders and bullies as well.

VIDEO Bullying: Interview with Nikki Crick explores the causes and repercussions of the different types of bullying.

Bullying

Bullying is defined as repeated, systematic attacks intended to harm those who are unable or unlikely to defend themselves. It occurs in every nation, in every community, in every kind of school (religious/secular, public/private, progressive/traditional, large/medium/small), and perhaps in every child. As one girl said, "There's a little bit of bully in everyone" (Guerra et al., 2011, p. 303).

Bullying is of four types:

- *Physical* (hitting, pinching, shoving, or kicking)
- *Verbal* (teasing, taunting, or name-calling)
- *Relational* (destroying peer acceptance)
- *Cyberbullying* (using electronic means to harm another)

The first three types are common in primary school and begin in preschool. Cyberbullying is more common later on and is discussed in Chapter 10.

VICTIMS Almost every child experiences an isolated attack or is called a derogatory name at some point. Victims of bullying, however, endure shameful experiences again and again—pushed and kicked for no reason, called derogatory names, forced to do degrading sexual things, and so on—with no defense. Victims tend to be "cautious, sensitive, quiet . . . lonely and abandoned at school. As a rule, they do not have a single good friend in their class" (Olweus, 1999, p. 15).

Even having a friend who is also a victim helps. Such friends may not be able to provide physical protection, but they can and do provide psychological defense. They reassure victims that their condition is not their fault and that the bully is mean, stupid, racist, or whatever (Schacter & Juvonen, 2018). That is crucial, because the worst harm is loss of self-respect.

Although it is often thought that victims are particularly ugly or odd, this is not necessarily the case. Victims are chosen because of their emotional vulnerability and social isolation, not their appearance. Children who are new to a school, or whose background and therefore home culture are unlike that of their peers, or whose clothes indicate poverty are especially vulnerable. When bullying is pervasive, almost any trait can become an excuse to exclude and harass a vulnerable child.

As one boy said,

You can get bullied because you are weak or annoying or because you are different. Kids with big ears get bullied. Dorks get bullied. You can also get bullied because you think too much of yourself and try to show off. Teacher's pet gets bullied. If

bullying
Repeated, systematic efforts to inflict harm on other people through physical, verbal, or social attack on a weaker person.

THINK CRITICALLY: The text says that both former bullies and former victims suffer in adulthood. Which would you rather be, and why?

Who Suffers More? Physical bullying is typically the target of antibullying laws and policies, because it is easier to spot than relational bullying. But being rejected from the group, especially with gossip and lies, may be more devastating to the victim and harder to stop. It may be easier for the boy to overcome victimization than for the girl.

you say the right answer too many times in class you can get bullied. There are lots of popular groups who bully each other and other groups, but you can get bullied within your group too. If you do not want to get bullied, you have to stay under the radar, but then you might feel sad because no one pays attention to you.

[quoted in Guerra et al., 2011, p. 306]

Remember the three types of unpopular children? *Neglected* children are not victimized; they are ignored, "under the radar." *Rejected* children fit into the bully network. Withdrawn-rejected children are likely victims; they are isolated, depressed, and friendless. Aggressive-rejected children may be **bully-victims** (or *provocative victims*), with neither friends nor sympathizers (Kochel et al., 2015). They suffer the most, because they strike back ineffectively, which increases the bullying.

bully-victim
Someone who attacks others and who is attacked as well. (Also called *provocative victims* because they do things that elicit bullying.)

BULLIES Unlike bully-victims, most bullies are *not* rejected. Many are proud, pleased with themselves, with friends who admire them and classmates who fear them (Guerra et al., 2011). Some are quite popular, with bullying being a form of social dominance and authority (Pellegrini et al., 2011).

The link between bullying and popularity has long been apparent during early adolescence (Pouwels et al., 2016), but bullies are already "quite popular in middle childhood." What changes from ages 6 to 12 is that bullies become skilled at avoiding adult awareness, at picking rejected and defenseless victims, and at using nonphysical methods—which avoid adult punishment (Pouwels et al., 2017).

Boys are bullies more often than girls, typically attacking smaller, weaker boys. Girl bullies usually use words to demean shyer, more soft-spoken girls. Young boys sometimes bully girls, but by puberty (about age 11), boys who bully girls are not admired (Veenstra et al., 2010), although sexual teasing is. Especially in the final years of middle childhood, boys who are thought to be gay become targets, with suicide attempts one consequence (Hong & Garbarino, 2012).

◆ **Especially for Parents of an Accused Bully**
Another parent has told you that your child is a bully. Your child denies it and explains that the other child doesn't mind being teased. What should you do? (see response, page 307)

CAUSES AND CONSEQUENCES OF BULLYING Bullying may begin early in life. Most toddlers try to dominate other children (and perhaps their parents) at some point. When they hit, kick, and so on, usually their parents, teachers, and peers teach them to find other ways to interact. However, if home life is chaotic, if discipline is ineffectual, if siblings are hostile, or if attachment is insecure, children do not learn how to express their frustration. Instead, vulnerable young children develop externalizing and internalizing problems, becoming bullies or victims (Turner et al., 2012).

By middle childhood, bullying is not the outburst of a frustrated child but an attempt to gain status. That makes it a social action: Bullies rarely attack victims when the two of them are alone. Instead, a bully might engage in a schoolyard fight, with onlookers who are more likely to cheer the victor than stop the fight; or a bully might utter an insult that provokes laughter in all except the target. By the end of middle childhood, bullies choose victims whom other children reject.

Siblings matter. Some brothers and sisters defend each other; children are protected if bullies fear that an older sibling will retaliate. On the other hand, if children are bullied by peers in school *and* siblings at home, they are four times more likely to develop serious psychological disorders by age 18 (Dantchev et al., 2018).

Bullies and victims risk impaired social understanding, lower school achievement, and relationship difficulties, with higher rates of mental illness in adulthood (Copeland et al., 2013; Ttofi et al., 2014). Many victims become depressed; many bullies become increasingly cruel, with higher rates of prison and death (Willoughby et al., 2014).

"He followed me home—can I punch him?"

Much to Learn Children do not always know when something is hurtful, and adults do not always know when to intervene.

The damage spreads: In schools with high rates of bullying, all of the children are less likely to focus on academics and more likely to concentrate on the social dynamics of the classroom—hoping to avoid becoming the next victim.

CAN BULLYING BE STOPPED? Many victimized children find ways to halt ongoing bullying—by ignoring, retaliating, defusing, or avoiding. Friendships help.

We know what does *not* work: simply increasing students' awareness of bullying, instituting zero tolerance for fighting, or putting bullies together in a therapy group or a class of their own. This last measure tends to make daily life easier for teachers, but it increases aggression. Since one cause of bullying is poor parent–child interaction, talking to the bully's or victim's parents may "create even more problems for the child, for the parents, and for their relationship" (Rubin et al., 2013, p. 267).

To decrease bullying, the entire school must be involved (Juvonen & Graham, 2014). A Spanish concept, *convivencia*, describes a culture of cooperation and positive relationships within a community. Convivencia has been applied specifically to schools. When teachers are supportive and protective, and when friendships and cooperation among all students are encouraged, bullying decreases (Zych et al., 2017).

Programs that seem good might be harmful, especially if they call attention to bullying but do nothing about it. Longitudinal research on whole-school efforts finds variations depending on the age of the children (younger is easier), on the indicators (peer report, teacher report, absence rate, direct observation), as well as on the tactics (encouraging friendship and decreasing adult hostility is more effective than punishing overt bullying).

Bystanders are crucial: If they do not intervene—or worse, if they watch and laugh—bullying flourishes. Some children who are neither bullies nor victims feel troubled but also feel fearful and powerless (Thornberg & Jungert, 2013). However, if they empathize with victims, feel effective (high in effortful control), and refuse to admire bullies, aggression is reduced.

Appreciation of human differences is not innate (remember, children seek friends who are similar to them), so adults need to encourage multi-cultural sensitivity. Then peers are more effective than teachers at halting bullying (Palmer & Abbott, 2018).

As they mature, children become more socially conscious. That creates a conflict—they are more aware of how someone's actions might hurt a child but also more aware of the possible harm to themselves if they befriend a bullied child. This raises the final question related to peers in middle childhood—moral development.

Children's Morality

Middle childhood is prime time for moral development. These are:

> years of eager, lively searching on the part of children . . . as they try to understand things, to figure them out, but also to weigh the rights and wrongs. . . . This is the time for growth of the moral imagination, fueled constantly by the willingness, the eagerness of children to put themselves in the shoes of others.
>
> *[Coles, 1997, p. 99]*

Many lines of research have shown that children develop their own morality, guided by peers, parents, and culture (Killen & Smetana, 2014). Children's growing interest in moral issues is guided by three forces: (1) child culture, (2) empathy, and (3) education.

MORAL RULES OF CHILD CULTURE First, when child culture conflicts with adult morality, children often align themselves with peers. A child might lie to protect a friend, for instance. Friendship itself has a hostile side: Many close friends (especially girls) resist other children who want to join their play (Rubin et al., 2013). Boys are particularly likely to protect a bully if he is a friend.

Three moral imperatives of child culture in middle childhood are:

- Defend your friends.
- Don't tell adults about peers' misbehavior.
- Conform to peer standards of dress, talk, and behavior.

THINK CRITICALLY: If one of your moral values differs from that of your spouse, your parents, or your community, should you still try to teach it to your children? Why or why not?

STEVE RUSSELL/GETTY IMAGES

Universal Morality Remarkable? Not really. By the end of middle childhood, many children are eager to express their moral convictions, especially with a friend. Chaim Ifrah and Shai Reef believe that welcoming refugees is part of being a patriotic Canadian and a devout Jew, so they brought a welcoming sign to the Toronto airport where Syrian refugees (mostly Muslim) will soon deplane.

These three can explain both apparent boredom and overt defiance as well as standards of dress that mystify adults (such as jeans so loose that they fall off or so tight that they impede digestion—both styles worn by my children, who grew up in different cohorts). Given what is known about middle childhood, it is no surprise that children do not echo adult morality.

Part of child culture is that as children become more aware of their peers, they may reject other children who are outsiders as well as stay quiet about their own problems. When teachers ask, "Who threw that spitball?" or parents ask, "How did you get that bruise?" children may be mum. This does not mean that adults should back off from developing relationships with children. On the contrary, in middle childhood, children who consider two or more adults as friends are also likely to have better relationships with peers (Guhn et al., 2012). But adults should not expect children to tell them all the details of their lives.

EMPATHY The second factor, empathy, is key. As middle childhood advances, children become more socially perceptive and more able to learn about other people (Weissberg et al., 2016). This does not always lead to increased morality as adults might define it. One example was just described: Bullies become adept at picking victims, and bystanders become better at noticing victims. However, depending on the culture of their school and home, social awareness may make them either quicker to defend or more hesitant to act (Pozzoli & Gini, 2013).

The authors of a study of 7-year-olds "conclude that moral *competence* may be a universal human characteristic, but that it takes a situation with specific demand characteristics to translate this competence into actual prosocial performance" (van Ijzendoorn et al., 2010, p. 1). In other words, school-age children can think and act morally, but they do not always do so because the hidden curriculum, or adult values, lead them astray.

Here, diversity in schools and neighborhoods can be helpful. Empathy is not an abstract idea as much as an understanding of the basic humanity of other people. In order to achieve that, knowing children from other groups helps children understand them. Teachers and parents can help with this, not only through direct contact but, once children like to read on their own, by offering books about children in other lands, centuries, and cultures.

MORAL EDUCATION Finally, cognitive development might affect moral development, at least according to Piaget (1932/2013b) and then Kohlberg (1963), who described three levels of moral reasoning and two stages at each level (see Table 8.3), with parallels to Piaget's stages of cognition.

- **Preconventional moral reasoning** is similar to preoperational thought in that it is egocentric, with children most interested in their personal pleasure or avoiding punishment.
- **Conventional moral reasoning** parallels concrete operational thought in that it relates to current, observable practices: Children watch what their parents, teachers, and friends do and try to follow suit.
- **Postconventional moral reasoning** is similar to formal operational thought because it uses abstractions, going beyond what is concretely observed, willing to question "what is" in order to decide "what should be."

According to Kohlberg, intellectual maturation advances moral thinking. During middle childhood, children's answers shift from being primarily preconventional to

preconventional moral reasoning Kohlberg's first level of moral reasoning, emphasizing rewards and punishments.

conventional moral reasoning Kohlberg's second level of moral reasoning, emphasizing social rules.

postconventional moral reasoning Kohlberg's third level of moral reasoning, emphasizing moral principles.

TABLE 8.3	**Kohlberg's Three Levels and Six Stages of Moral Reasoning**

Level I: Preconventional Moral Reasoning

The goal is to get rewards and avoid punishments; this is a self-centered level.

- *Stage one: Might makes right* (a punishment-and-obedience orientation). The most important value is to maintain the appearance of obedience to authority, avoiding punishment while still advancing self-interest. Don't get caught!
- *Stage two: Look out for number one* (an instrumental and relativist orientation). Everyone prioritizes his or her own needs. The reason to be nice to other people is so that they will be nice to you.

Level II: Conventional Moral Reasoning

Emphasis is placed on social rules; this is a parent- and community-centered level.

- *Stage three: Good girl and nice boy.* The goal is to please other people. Social approval is more important than any specific reward.
- *Stage four: Law and order.* Everyone must be a dutiful and law-abiding citizen, even when no police are nearby.

Level III: Postconventional Moral Reasoning

Emphasis is placed on moral principles; this level is centered on ideals.

- *Stage five: Social contract.* Obey social rules because they benefit everyone and are established by mutual agreement. If the rules become destructive or if one party doesn't live up to the agreement, the contract is no longer binding. Under some circumstances, disobeying the law is moral.
- *Stage six: Universal ethical principles.* Universal principles, not individual situations (level I) or community practices (level II), determine right and wrong. Ethical values (such as "life is sacred") are established by individual reflection and religious ideas, which may contradict egocentric (level I) or social and community (level II) values.

being more conventional: Concrete thought and peer experiences help children move past the first two stages (level I) to the next two (level II). Postconventional reasoning is not usually present until adolescence or adulthood, if then.

Kohlberg posed moral dilemmas to school-age boys (and eventually girls, teenagers, and adults). The most famous example of these dilemmas involves a poor man named Heinz, whose wife was dying. He could not pay for the only drug that could cure his wife, a drug that a local druggist sold for 10 times what it cost to make.

> Heinz went to everyone he knew to borrow the money, but he could only get together about half of what it cost. He told the druggist that his wife was dying and asked him to sell it cheaper or let him pay later. But the druggist said "no." The husband got desperate and broke into the man's store to steal the drug for his wife. Should the husband have done that? Why?
>
> *[Kohlberg, 1963, p. 19]*

Kohlberg's assessment of morality depends *not* on what a person answers but *why* an answer is chosen. For instance, suppose a child says that Heinz should steal the drug. That itself does not indicate the level of morality. The reason could be that Heinz needs his wife to care for him (preconventional), or that people will blame him if he lets his wife die (conventional), or that the value of a human life is greater than the law (postconventional).

Or suppose another child says Heinz should not steal. Again, the reason is crucial. If it is that he will go to jail, that is preconventional; if it is that business owners will blame him, that is conventional; if it is that no one should deprive anyone else of their livelihood, that is postconventional.

Kohlberg has been criticized for not appreciating cultural or gender differences. For example, loyalty to family overrides other values in some cultures, so some people might avoid postconventional actions that hurt their family. Also, Kohlberg's

FIGURE 8.3 Sharing What Is Mine Children chose 10 stickers for themselves and then were asked to voluntarily and privately give some to an another child, whom they did not see or know. Some children—especially the younger ones, were quite stingy, giving only a few away, and some, especially the older ones, were quite generous, giving away more than half. Generosity was measured by how many of the ten stickers were donated. In every nation, as children grew older they became more generous. It also was apparent that national wealth had a greater impact than ideology: Children were more generous in the richer nations (Canada, United States, and China) than in the poorer ones (Turkey and South Africa).

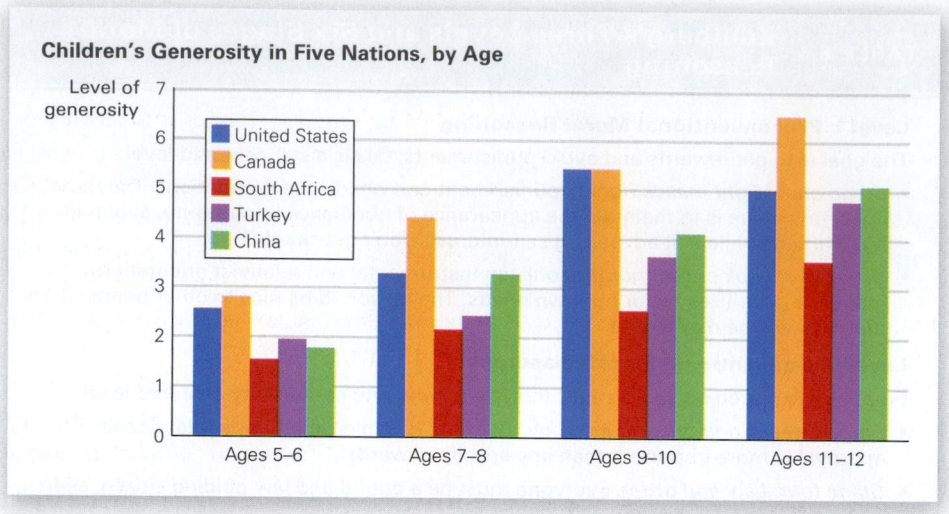

Children's Generosity in Five Nations, by Age

Level of generosity

- United States
- Canada
- South Africa
- Turkey
- China

Ages 5–6   Ages 7–8   Ages 9–10   Ages 11–12

↓ OBSERVATION QUIZ
What indicates that this sister often carries her younger sibling? (see answer, page 307)

KINZIE RIEHM/IMAGE SOURCE/GETTY IMAGES

Heavy Lift Carrying your barefoot little sister across a muddy puddle is not easy, but this 7-year-old has internalized family values. Note her expression: She and many other children her age are proud to do what they consider the right thing.

original participants were all boys, which may have led him to discount female values of nurturance and relationships (Gilligan, 1982).

Overall, Kohlberg seemed to value rational principles more than individual needs, unlike other scholars of moral development who consider emotions more influential than logic (Haidt, 2013). Regarding global warming, for instance, the facts about the world's temperature rising by a degree over a decade is less compelling for children in middle childhood than the stranded polar bear cub on a melting ice flow.

MATURATION AND MORALITY As discussed in Chapter 6, some prosocial values are evident in early childhood, such as caring for close family members, cooperating with other children, and not hurting anyone intentionally. Even very young children think stealing is wrong, and even infants seem to appreciate social support. They punish mean behavior in experiments with a good puppet and a mean puppet (Hamlin, 2014).

At the same time, young children have great difficulty with sharing. Many parents and teachers wisely tell children under age 6 not to bring a favorite toy to school unless they are willing to have other children play with it. The 3-year-old's moral rule about possessions seems to be "if I want it, it is mine, and you can't touch it," and some young children hurt others who grab their toy, or hat, or even their crayon.

Throughout childhood, maturation matters. One study measured generosity by counting how many chosen stickers 5- to 12-year-olds from five nations (United States, Canada, China, Turkey, South Africa) were willing to donate to another unknown child. Generosity increased with age: 5-year-olds gave away two and kept eight, while 12-year-olds gave away five and kept five (Cowell et al., 2017). (See Figure 8.3.)

Beyond that, culture had an impact. Children from Toronto, Canada, were most generous, and children from Cape Town, South Africa, were least generous, a difference thought to reflect national wealth (Cowell et al., 2017). Those national differences paled when individual behavior was considered: Some children from each of the five nations kept all or almost all stickers to themselves, and some from each nation gave more than half away.

TEACHING MORALITY Fortunately, children enjoy thinking about and discussing moral values, and then peers help one another advance in moral behavior. Children may be more ethical than adults (once they understand moral equity, they complain when adults are not fair), and they are better at stopping a bully than adults are, because a bully is more likely to listen to other children than to adults.

Since bullies tend to be low on empathy, they need peers to teach them when their actions are not admired. During middle childhood, morality can be scaffolded

just as cognitive skills are, with mentors—peers or adults—using moral dilemmas to advance moral understanding while they also advance the underlying moral skills of empathy and emotional regulation (Hinnant et al., 2013).

Usually, throughout middle childhood, moral judgment becomes more comprehensive, taking into account psychological as well as physical harm, intentions as well as consequences. For example, 5- to 11-year-olds were presented with anecdotes that involved a child hurting another child. In some anecdotes, the goal was to prevent further harm (stopping a child from a serious fall) and sometimes the behavior was simply mean. The younger children judged based on results, but the older children considered intention: They rated justifiable harm as less bad and unjustifiable harm as worse than the younger children did (Jambon & Smetana, 2014).

A detailed examination of the effect of peers on morality began with an update on one of Piaget's moral issues: whether punishment should seek *retribution* (hurting the transgressor) or *restitution* (restoring what was lost). Piaget found that children advance from retribution to restitution between ages 8 and 10 (Piaget, 1932/2013b). Many ethicists consider restitution more advanced (Claessen, 2017).

To learn how this occurs, researchers asked 133 9-year-olds:

> Late one afternoon there was a boy who was playing with a ball on his own in the garden. His dad saw him playing with it and asked him not to play with it so near the house because it might break a window. The boy didn't really listen to his dad, and carried on playing near the house. Then suddenly, the ball bounced up high and broke the window in the boy's room. His dad heard the noise and came to see what had happened. The father wonders what would be the fairest way to punish the boy. He thinks of two punishments. The first is to say: "Now, you didn't do as I asked. You will have to pay for the window to be mended, and I am going to take the money from your pocket money." The second is to say: "Now, you didn't do as I asked. As a punishment you have to go to your room and stay there for the rest of the evening." Which of these punishments do you think is the fairest?
>
> [Leman & Björnberg, 2010, p. 962]

The children were split almost equally in their answers. Then, 24 pairs were formed of children who had opposite views. Each pair was asked to discuss the issue, trying to reach agreement. (The other children did not discuss it.) Six pairs were boy–boy, six were boy–girl with the boy favoring restitution, six were boy–girl with the girl favoring restitution, and six were girl–girl.

FIGURE 8.4 Benefits of Time and Talking The graph on the left shows that most children, immediately after their initial punitive response, became even more likely to seek punishment rather than to repair damage. However, after some time and reflection, they affirmed the response that Piaget would consider more mature. The graph on the right indicates that children who had talked about the broken window example moved toward restorative justice even in examples that they had not heard before, which was not true for those who had not talked about the first story.

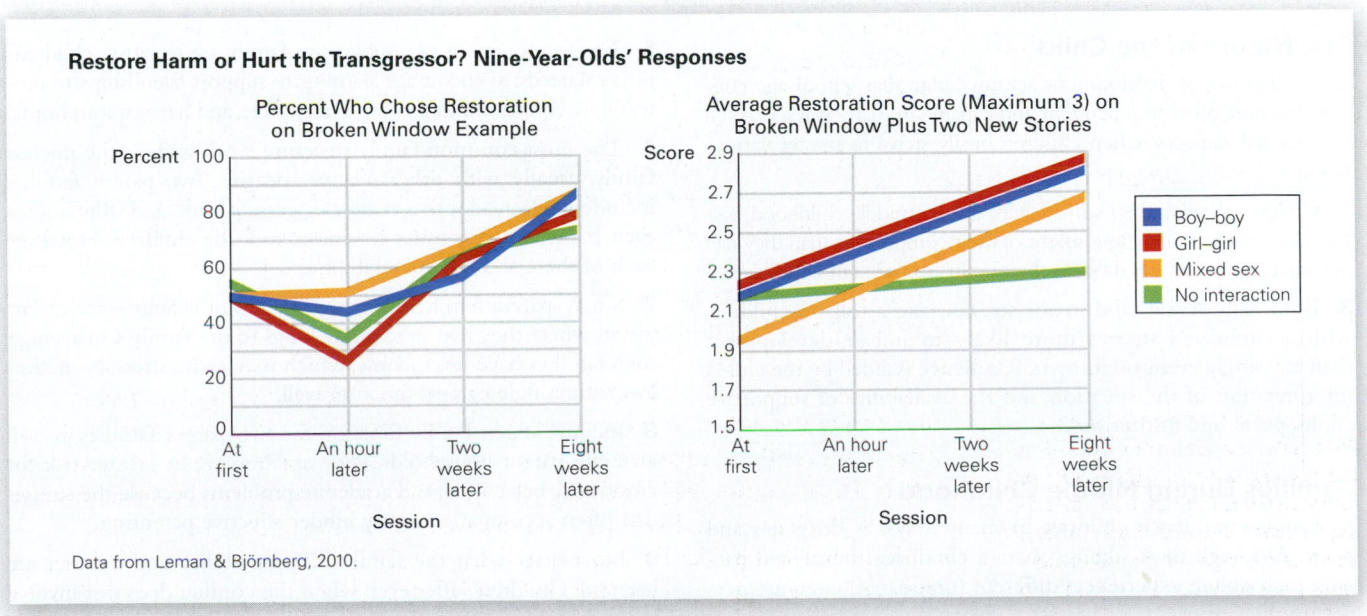

Data from Leman & Björnberg, 2010.

The conversations typically took only five minutes, and the retribution side was more often chosen—which Piaget would consider a moral backslide, since more restitution than retribution advocates switched. However, two weeks and eight weeks later all of the children were queried again. Their responses changed toward the more advanced, restitution thinking (see Figure 8.4). This advance occurred even for the children who merely thought about the dilemma again, but children who had discussed it with another child were particularly likely to decide that restitution was better.

The main conclusion from this study was that "conversation on a topic may stimulate a process of individual reflection that triggers developmental advances" (Leman & Björnberg, 2010, p. 969). Parents and teachers take note: Raising moral issues and letting children talk about them may advance morality—not immediately, but soon.

Think again about the opening anecdote for this chapter (killing zombies) or the previous chapter (piercing ears). In both cases, parents used age as a criterion and children rejected that argument. A better argument might raise a higher standard; in the first example, for instance, that killing is never justified, even for zombies. The child might disagree, but such conversations help children think more deeply about moral values.

That deeper thought might protect the child during adolescence, when life-changing moral issues arise.

what have you learned?

1. How does the culture of children differ from the culture of adults?

2. What are the different kinds of popular and unpopular children?

3. What do victims and bullies have in common?

4. How might bullying be reduced?

5. What three forces affect moral development during middle childhood?

6. What are the main criticisms of Kohlberg's theory of moral development?

7. What role do adults play in the development of morality in children?

SUMMARY

The Nature of the Child

1. All theories of development acknowledge that school-age children become more independent and capable in many ways. Erikson emphasized industry, when children busily strive to master various tasks.

2. Children develop their self-concept during middle childhood, basing it on a more realistic assessment of their competence than they had in earlier years. Cultures differ in their evaluation of high self-esteem.

3. Both daily hassles and major stresses take a toll on children, with accumulated stresses more likely to impair development than any single event on its own. Resilience is aided by the child's interpretation of the situation and the availability of supportive adults, peers, and institutions.

Families During Middle Childhood

4. Families influence children in many ways, as do genes and peers. Although most siblings share a childhood home and parents, each sibling experiences different (nonshared) circumstances within the family.

5. The five functions of a supportive family are to satisfy children's physical needs; to encourage learning; to support friendships; to protect self-respect; and to provide a safe, stable, and harmonious home.

6. The most common family structure worldwide is the nuclear family, usually with other relatives nearby. Two-parent families include nuclear, adoptive, same-sex, grandparent, and stepfamilies, each of which sometimes functions well for children. However, each of these also has vulnerabilities.

7. Single-parent families have higher rates of change—for example, in where they live and who belongs to the family. On average, such families have less income, which may cause stress. Nonetheless, some single parents function well.

8. Income affects family function for two-parent families as well as single-parent households. Poor children are at greater risk for emotional, behavioral, and academic problems because the stresses that often accompany poverty hinder effective parenting.

9. No matter what the family SES, instability and conflict are harmful. Children suffer even when the conflict does not involve them directly but their parents or siblings fight.

The Peer Group

10. Peers teach crucial social skills during middle childhood. Each cohort of children has a culture, passed down from slightly older children. Close friends are wanted and needed.

11. Popular children may be cooperative and easy to get along with or may be competitive and aggressive. Unpopular children may be neglected, aggressive, or withdrawn, sometimes becoming victims.

12. Bullying is common among school-age children. Both bullies and victims have difficulty with social cognition; their interpretation of the normal give-and-take of childhood is impaired.

13. Bullies themselves may be admired, which makes their behavior more difficult to stop. Overall, a multifaceted, long-term, whole-school approach—with parents, teachers, and bystanders working together—seems the best way to halt bullying.

14. School-age children seek to differentiate right from wrong as moral development increases over middle childhood. Peer values, cultural standards, empathy, and education all affect their personal morality.

15. Kohlberg described three levels of moral reasoning, each related to cognitive maturity. His description has been criticized for ignoring cultural and gender differences.

16. When values conflict, children often choose loyalty to peers over adult standards of behavior. When children discuss moral issues with other children, they develop more thoughtful answers to moral questions.

KEY TERMS

industry versus inferiority (p. 276)
social comparison (p. 277)
resilience (p. 279)
parentification (p. 282)
family structure (p. 283)

family function (p. 284)
single-parent family (p. 286)
extended family (p. 286)
polygamous family (p. 286)
child culture (p. 296)

aggressive-rejected (p. 298)
withdrawn-rejected (p. 298)
bullying (p. 299)
bully-victim (p. 300)
preconventional moral reasoning (p. 302)

conventional moral reasoning (p. 302)
postconventional moral reasoning (p. 302)

APPLICATIONS

1. Go someplace where many school-age children congregate (such as a schoolyard, a park, or a community center) and use naturalistic observation for at least half an hour. Describe what popular, average, withdrawn, and rejected children do. Note at least one potential conflict. Describe the sequence and the outcome.

2. Focusing on verbal bullying, describe at least two times when someone said something hurtful to you and two times when you said something that might have been hurtful to someone else. What are the differences between the two types of situations?

3. How would your childhood have been different if your family structure had been different, such as if you had (or had not) lived with your grandparents, if your parents had (or had not) gotten divorced, if you had (or had not) been adopted, if you had lived with one parent (or two), if your parents were both the same sex (or not)? Avoid blanket statements: Appreciate that every structure has advantages and disadvantages.

ESPECIALLY FOR ANSWERS

Response for Scientists (from page 285): Proof is very difficult when human interaction is the subject of investigation, since random assignment is impossible. Ideally, researchers would find identical twins being raised together and would then observe the parents' behavior over the years.

Response for Single Parents (from page 290): Do not get married mainly to provide a second parent for your child. If you were to do so, things would probably get worse rather than better. Do make an effort to have friends of both sexes with whom your child can interact.

Response for Parents of an Accused Bully (from page 300) The future is ominous if the charges are true. Your child's denial is a sign that there is a problem. (An innocent child would be worried about the misperception instead of categorically denying that any problem exists.) You might ask the teacher what the school is doing about bullying. Family counseling might help. Because bullies often have friends who egg them on, you may need to monitor your child's friendships and perhaps befriend the victim. Talk about the situation with your child. Ignoring the situation might lead to heartache later on.

OBSERVATION QUIZ ANSWERS

Answer to Observation Quiz (from page 279) They are hugging the ball.

Answer to Observation Quiz (from page 289) Both parents are women. The evidence shows that families with same-sex parents are similar in many ways to families with opposite-sex parents, and children in such families develop well.

Answer to Observation Quiz (from page 304) The legs and arms of the younger child suggest that she has learned how to hold her body to make carrying possible.

APPLICATION TO DEVELOPING LIVES PARENTING
SIMULATION ADOLESCENCE

As you progress through the Adolescence simulation module, how you answer the following questions will impact the biosocial, cognitive, and psychosocial development of your adolescent.

Biosocial	**Cognitive**	**Psychosocial**
• Will your child experiment with smoking, drinking, or drugs during adolescence? • How will you respond if you learn your child is experimenting with drugs? • How will you encourage your child to spend his or her free time after school (sports, part-time job)?	• Which of Piaget's stages of cognitive development is your child in? • What kind of path do you see your teenager pursuing after high school (college, military, work program)?	• How will you respond if your adolescent is struggling to fit in with peers? • How often do you think you and your teenager will have conflicts? • How social will your child be during his or her teen years? • How much privacy will you grant your teenager? • How will you respond when your teenager starts dating?

Adolescence

Acentury ago, adolescence did not begin until age 14 or so. Soon after that, most girls got married and most boys found work. It is said that *adolescence begins with biology and ends with culture.* If so, then a hundred years ago, adolescence lasted a few months.

Now adolescence lasts for years. Biological changes may begin at age 10 or even earlier, and adult responsibilities may be avoided for more than a decade. Not only are many teenagers far from "settling down" (which once meant marriage and full-time work or parenthood by age 18), but adolescence now is unsettled, attracting the high hopes and the worst fears of parents, teachers, police officers, social workers, and children themselves. Patterns and events can push a teenager toward a happy life or early death. Understanding the possibilities and pitfalls will help us make adolescence a fulfilling, not damaging, time.

HERO IMAGES/GETTY IMAGES

ADOLESCENCE
Body and Mind

what will you know?

- How can you predict when puberty will begin for a particular child?
- When is teenage sexuality a problem instead of a joy?
- Why do teenage emotions sometimes overwhelm reason?
- What kind of school is best for teenagers?

I overheard a conversation among three teenagers, including my daughter Rachel, all of them past their awkward years and now becoming beautiful young women. They were discussing the imperfections of their bodies. One spoke of her fat stomach (what stomach? I could not see it), another of her long neck (hidden by her silky, shoulder-length hair). Rachel complained about her fingers and her feet!

The reality that boys and girls become men and women is no shock to any adult. But for teenagers, heightened self-awareness may trigger surprise and sometimes horror, joy, and despair.

The details of growing bodies and the rational and irrational thinking of the adolescents who experience that growth are explained in this chapter. As you will see, bodies mature—physical development is usually complete by age 18—but the brain requires many more years to reach maturity.

Puberty Begins

Puberty is the time when a child's body is transformed into an adult body, capable of reproduction. Puberty begins at some point between ages 8 and 14, with rapid physical growth and sexual maturation continuing for several years. This is primarily a biological event, over by mid–adolescence.

Many hormones start this cascade, most notably growth and sex hormones. Those hormones include a major rush of estrogen for girls and testosterone for boys, although both sexes experience both.

puberty
The period of rapid growth and sexual development that begins adolescence.

Do They See Beauty? Both young women—the Mexican 15-year-old preparing for her Quinceañera and the Malaysian teen applying a rice facial mask—look wistful, even worried. They are typical of teenage girls everywhere, who do not realize how lovely they are.

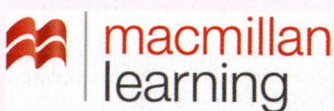

VIDEO: The Timing of Puberty depicts the usual sequence of physical development for adolescents.

THINK CRITICALLY: If a child seems to be unusually short or unusually slow in reaching puberty, would you give the child hormones? Why or why not?

menarche
A girl's first menstrual period, signaling that she has begun ovulation. Pregnancy is biologically possible, but ovulation and menstruation are often irregular for years after menarche.

spermarche
A boy's first ejaculation of sperm. Erections can occur as early as infancy, but ejaculation signals sperm production. Spermarche may occur during sleep (in a "wet dream") or via direct stimulation.

Sequence

First, the *hypothalamus* (a tiny brain part) signals the *pituitary* (a pea–sized gland behind the bridge of the nose) to send hormones to the *adrenals* (a pair of glands below the waist) to enlarge the *gonads* (the sex glands, testes or ovaries), which produce sex hormones. The entire body and brain are transformed (Goddings et al., 2012; Harden et al., 2017).

For girls, observable changes begin with nipple growth and a few pubic hairs. Soon the body increases in height while fat, especially on the breasts and hips, accumulates. Then the first menstrual period (**menarche**) is followed by more growth, with adolescent body growth complete by four years after it began and brain growth complete by the mid-20s.

For boys, the usual sequence is growth of the testes, initial pubic-hair growth, growth of the penis, first ejaculation of seminal fluid (**spermarche**), appearance of facial hair, a peak growth spurt, deepening of the voice, and final pubic-hair growth (Biro et al., 2001; Herman-Giddens et al., 2012; Susman et al., 2010). Final height is reached by age 20.

PSYCHOLOGICAL EFFECTS For all teenagers, hormones instigate attraction and thoughts about romance. Those thoughts bring horror, pleasure, or actual contact, depending more on the culture than on the body. Those hormones also precipitate emotions—rage, ecstasy, sadness—and sometimes psychopathology (Powers & Casey, 2015).

Most teenagers are simply moodier than they once were. However, at the extreme, adolescent males are almost twice as likely as adolescent females to develop schizophrenia, and girls are more than twice as likely as boys to become severely depressed.

Although emotional surges, irrational thoughts, and lustful urges arise with hormones, remember that body, brain, and behavior always interact, with genes and earlier experiences contributing to later events. Sexual thoughts themselves can *cause* physiological and neurological processes, not just result from them.

For example, other people's reactions to a young person's emerging breasts or beards (mocking, admiring, or merely commenting) may evoke adolescent emotions, which raise hormones and propel development. Emotions are typically expressed (with shouts and tears), which makes everyone—including the adolescent—escalate their reactions. A word of caution to adults: Do not comment!

PUBERTY AND THE BRAIN The effects of puberty on the adolescent body are visible, but more important are effects on the adolescent brain. All parts of the brain

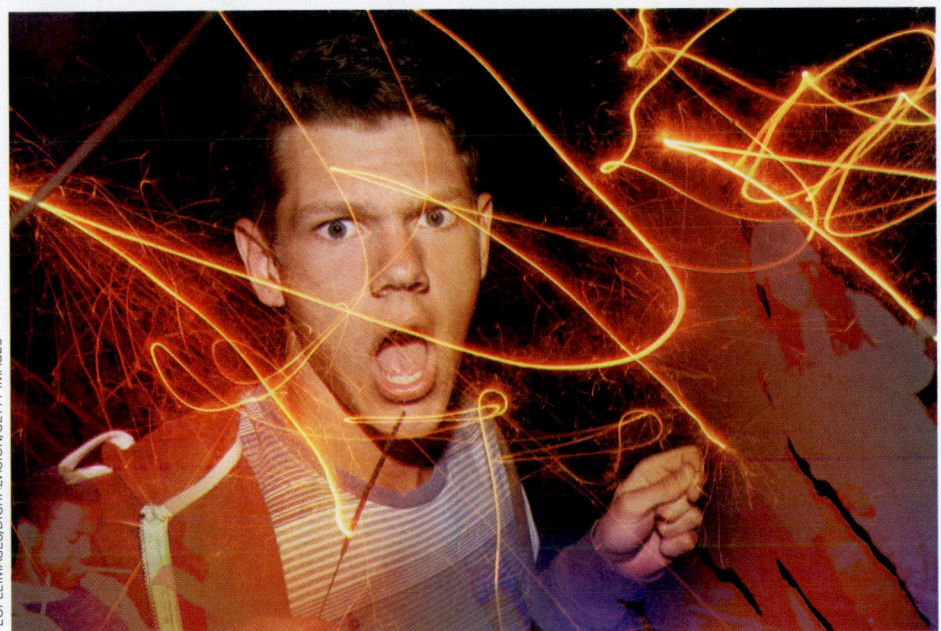

Fawkes, Not Fake Bonfires, fireworks, burning effigies, and—shown here—sparklers are waved in memory of Guy Fawkes, who tried to burn down the British Parliament and destroy the king in 1605. In theory, Guy Fawkes Night celebrates his capture; in fact, it is a time for rebellion.

as well as the body grow, but growth is uneven. The limbic system expands years ahead of the prefrontal cortex.

Pubertal hormones target the amygdala directly (Romeo, 2013). Powerful sensations—loud music, speeding cars, strong drugs—become compelling. Adolescents brag about being wasted, smashed, out of their minds—all conditions that adults try to avoid.

It is not that the prefrontal cortex shuts down. Actually, it continues to develop throughout adolescence and beyond. Maturation doesn't stop, but the emotional hot spots of the brain zoom ahead. Brain scans confirm that cognitive control, revealed by fMRI studies, is not fully developed until adulthood, because the prefrontal cortex is limited in connections and engagement (Luna et al., 2013; Hartley & Somerville, 2015) (see Figure 9.1).

A study compared 886 adolescents (ages 9 to 16) and their parents (average age 44) in Hong Kong and England. All of them were asked questions to assess their ability to reflect on what they thought. The adolescents were less accurate but notably quicker, confirming that the limbic system races ahead while the prefrontal cortex lags behind (Ellefson et al., 2017).

When stress, arousal, passion, sensory bombardment, intoxication, or deprivation is extreme, the adolescent brain is flooded with impulses that overwhelm the prefrontal cortex. Adults try to keep their thoughts coherent, but adolescents may enjoy such flooding. Many teenagers choose to spend a night without sleep, to eat nothing all day, to exercise in pain, to play music at deafening loudness, and to drink until they are drunk.

BODY RHYTHMS Hormones are affected by time—not only by the sudden rushes at puberty, pregnancy, birth, and so on but by the time of day and year. We all get sleepy or hungry at certain hours because of our hormones. Those rhythms, called *circadian,* interact with puberty.

About 15 genes influence whether someone is a natural night owl (evening alertness) or lark (morning alertness) (Hu et al., 2016). In addition to these genetic effects, daylight usually awakens the brain, especially for young children and adults. At

VIDEO ACTIVITY: Brain Development: Adolescence features animations and illustrations of the changes that occur in the teenage brain.

THINK CRITICALLY: Given the nature of adolescent brain development, how should society respond to adolescent thoughts and actions?

◆ **Especially for Health Practitioners**
How might you encourage adolescents to seek treatment for STIs? (see response, page 346)

FIGURE 9.1 **Same People, But Not the Same Brain** These brain scans are part of a longitudinal study that repeatedly compared the proportion of gray matter from childhood through adolescence. (Gray matter refers to the cell bodies of neurons, which are less prominent with age as some neurons are unused.) Gray matter is reduced as white matter increases, in part because pruning during the teen years (the last two pairs of images here) allows intellectual connections to build. As the authors of one study that included this chart explained, teenagers may look "like an adult, but cognitively they are not there yet" (Powell, 2006, p. 865).

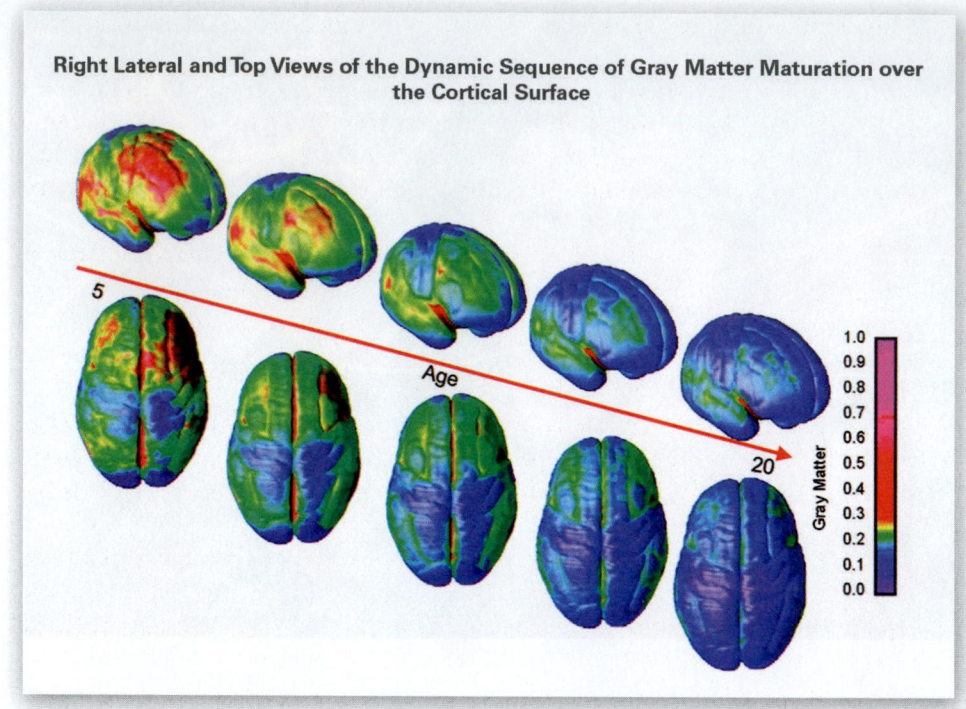

Right Lateral and Top Views of the Dynamic Sequence of Gray Matter Maturation over the Cortical Surface

GOGTAY, NITIN; GIEDD, JAY N.; LUSK, LESLIE; HAYASHI, KIRALEE M.; GREENSTEIN, DEANNA; VAITUZIS, A. CATHERINE,... UNGERLEIDER, LESLIE G. (2004) DYNAMIC MAPPING OF HUMAN CORTICAL DEVELOPMENT DURING CHILDHOOD THROUGH EARLY ADULTHOOD. *PROCEEDINGS OF THE NATIONAL ACADEMY OF SCIENCES OF THE UNITED STATES OF AMERICA.

puberty, however, night may be energizing. Many teens are wide awake and famished at midnight but half asleep, with no appetite or energy, all morning.

An added influence is "the blue spectrum light from TV, computer, and personal-device screens," which has "particularly strong effects on the human circadian system" (Peper & Dahl, 2013, p. 137). Many adolescents check e-mail or text friends late at night, which decreases sleep hormones and causes insomnia and sleep deprivation (see Figure 9.2). That increases nightmares, mood disorders (depression, conduct disorder, anxiety), and falling asleep while reading, driving, or just sitting in class.

Oblivious to adolescent circadian rhythms, some parents set early curfews for wide-awake adolescents and drag their sleepy teenager out of bed for school—the same children who a decade earlier were commanded to stay in bed until dawn.

FIGURE 9.2 **Sleepyheads** Three of every four high school seniors are sleep deprived. Even if they go to sleep by midnight, as many do, they must get up before 8 A.M., as almost all do. Then all day they are tired.

↑ OBSERVATION QUIZ
As you see, the problems are worse for the younger girls. Why is that? (see answer, page 347)

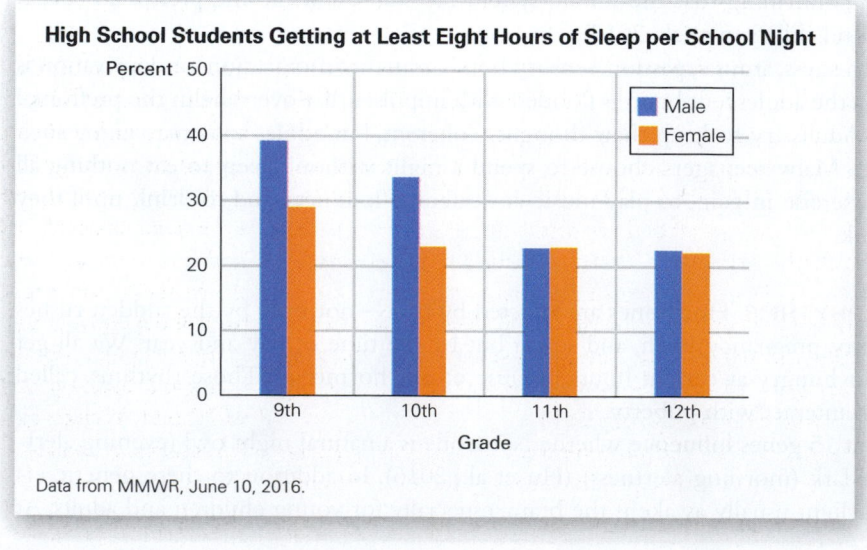

High School Students Getting at Least Eight Hours of Sleep per School Night

Data from MMWR, June 10, 2016.

Some schools expect high school students in class before 8:00 A.M. Some cities and towns pass laws that are contrary to adolescent biology.

For example, in 2014, Baltimore required everyone under age 14 to be home by 9:00 P.M. and 14- to 16-year-olds to be inside by 10:00 P.M. on school nights and 11:00 P.M. on weekends. This assumes that home is a safe, restful place and impedes adolescent friendships—not just hanging out but also studying with friends.

Some stores do not care that their rules discriminate. A major mall in Maryland (Towson) does not allow anyone under 18 to enter without an adult beginning at 5:00 P.M. on weekends. This policy is designed for the merchants and for adult shoppers who are intimidated by adolescents (Dresser & Dance, 2016).

About half of all U.S. high schools still start before 8:00 A.M., contrary to a recommendation of the American Academy of Pediatrics, who aim to prevent intellectual, behavioral, and health problems caused by sleep deprivation (Owens et al., 2014). The high schools set that start time for logical reasons (such as bus schedules), but is there unanticipated harm?

Twenty-nine high schools across seven states moved their start times to 8:30 A.M. or later. On average, graduation rates increased from 79 percent to 88 percent, and average daily attendance went from 90 percent to 94 percent (McKeever & Clark, 2017).

School schedules and town curfews are not the only examples of social norms clashing with what we know about teenage brains. A chilling example comes from teenage driving (legal at age 16 in most U.S. localities). Per mile driven, teenage drivers are three times more likely to die in a motor-vehicle crash than drivers over age 20 (Insurance Institute for Highway Safety, 2013b).

Apparently developing brains are not ready for the intellectual challenges of safe driving, even though legs are long enough to reach the pedals, arms are strong enough to turn the wheel, reaction time is quicker than at any other age, and memory is sharp enough to pass a multiple-choice test of rules of the road. (See Inside the Brain.) Again, unanticipated harm?

INSIDE THE BRAIN

Impulses, Rewards, and Reflection

Because the limbic system is activated by puberty while the prefrontal cortex is "developmentally constrained," maturing more gradually, adolescents are swayed by their emotions instead of by analysis (Hartley & Somerville, 2015, p. 109). Hormones, especially testosterone (rapidly increasing in boys but also increasing in girls), fuel new adolescent emotional impulses (Peper & Dahl, 2013).

Longitudinal research finds that heightened arousal occurs in the brain's reward centers, specifically the *nucleus accumbens,* a region of the *ventral striatum* that is connected to the limbic system (Braams et al., 2015). Many studies confirm that adolescents show "heightened activity in the striatum, both when anticipating rewards and when receiving rewards" (Crone et al., 2016, p. 360).

Consequently, in choosing between a small but guaranteed reward and a larger possible reward, adolescent brains show more activity for the larger reward than do the brains of children or adults. This means that when teenagers consider a risky action, they imagine the joy of success more than the fear of failure. Whether this makes them brave and bold or foolish and careless depends on specifics, but neurological circuits urge action.

Another crucial aspect of adolescent brains is that social acceptance is deeply sought, with activation throughout the limbic system as well as other subcortical areas. Humans always seek social support, but when social rejection is most painful depends on age (Nelson et al., 2016).

For example, maternal rejection is especially hurtful in infancy; a breakup with a romantic partner hurts most in adulthood. Rejection from other people of the same age (classmates, teammates, friends) is especially painful during adolescence.

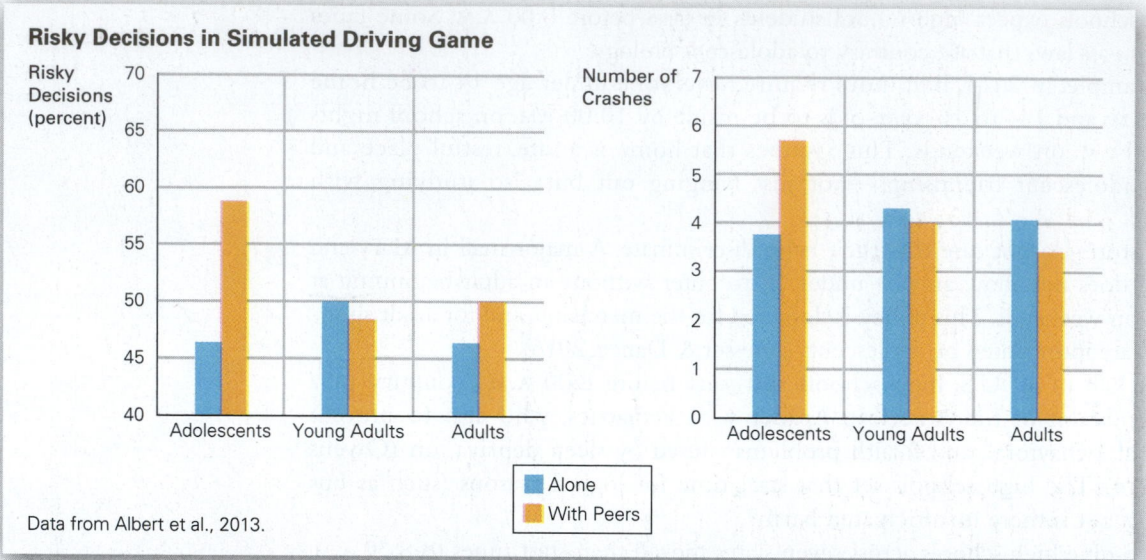

Risky Decisions in Simulated Driving Game

Data from Albert et al., 2013.

FIGURE 9.3 Losing Is Winning In this game, risk-taking led to more crashes and fewer points. As you see, adolescents were strongly influenced by the presence of peers, so much so that they lost points that they would have kept if they had played alone. In fact, sometimes they laughed when they crashed instead of bemoaning their loss. Note the contrast with emerging adults, who were more likely to take risks when alone.

That neurological sensitivity may push teens to follow impulses that promise social approval from friends. Many researchers have asked people of various ages to play video games in which taking risks might lead to crashes or additional points. Results are especially interesting when other people are watching the person playing the game.

Adolescents are more likely than adults to risk crashing, especially when they are with peers. By contrast, when the adolescent's mother is the observer, activity decreases in the same reward regions that increased with peer observers (Telzer et al., 2015).

These reactions are directly tied to activity in the ventral striatum. Brain scans reveal that the effect of peers on adult brains is to signal caution (inhibition), but the effect on adolescent brains is to signal activity (Albert et al., 2013) (see Figure 9.3).

An example from real life is texting while driving. This is illegal in most states and teenagers have heard that it is dangerous. But the "ping" of a text message from a friend evokes strong impulses to read and respond. In one survey of U.S. high school seniors who have driven a car in the past month, 61 percent had texted while driving (MMWR, June 10, 2016).

Teenage drivers like to fill (or overfill) their cars with teen passengers, who may admire them for speeding, for passing trucks, for beating trains at railroad crossings, and so on. Fatal accidents are more likely if the driver is a teenager; passengers aged 15 to 17 are more likely to be injured in a motor-vehicle crash than passengers of other ages (Bergen et al., 2014).

The power of peers is apparent in both sexes but is stronger in boys—particularly when they are with other boys (de Boer et al., 2017). This explains why boys die accidental deaths during adolescence twice as often as girls.

The accident rate among teenagers is affected by a third brain change in adolescence. Remember that myelin makes communication faster between neurons. As parts of the brain mature, myelination occurs in those regions.

Myelination occurs first in the basic sensory parts of the cortex—seeing, hearing, and so on: Toddlers coordinate their senses. Myelination is last in the prefrontal cortex, which is not fully myelinated until age 25 or later (Gibb & Kovalchuk, 2017).

During adolescence, myelination increases markedly in the areas that connect emotion and movement. Reaction time is probably faster in late adolescence than at any other time (Dykiert et al., 2012).

Thus, adolescent actions occur with lightning speed after an emotional signal, before their prefrontal cortex or slower-thinking adults can stop them. That is why "people who interact with adolescents often are frustrated by the mercurial quality of their decisions" (Hartley & Somerville, 2015, p. 112).

Don't blame teen crashes on inexperience; blame their brains. Some states now prohibit young drivers from transporting other teenagers. That reduces mortality. Teens advocate some laws (to protect the environment, to provide free access to the Internet), but they do not advocate this one. Now that you understand the teen brain, will you?

Early or Late?

Parents and children want to be ready for puberty yet not prepare years in advance, but healthy children can begin puberty anytime between ages 8 and 14. How can anyone know when to get ready? When it comes to individual children, more precise estimates are possible if genes, gender, weight, and stress are all considered.

BOYS AND GIRLS Girls mature before boys, so gender needs to be considered. In height, the average pubescent girl is about two years ahead of the average boy. The female peak height spurt occurs *before* menarche; the male peak *after* spermarche.

Therefore, for hormonal and sexual changes, girls are less than a year ahead of boys. This means that a short sixth-grade boy with sexual fantasies about the taller girls in his class is neither perverted nor precocious; his hormones are simply ahead of his height.

Genes also need to be taken into account. About two-thirds of the variation in age of puberty is genetic, not only due to the XX or XY chromosomes but also the genes common in families and ethnic groups (Dvornyk & Waqar-ul-Haq, 2012; Biro et al., 2013). If both of a child's parents were early or late to reach puberty, the child will likely be early or late as well.

A third influence on the onset of puberty is body fat. Heavy girls (over 100 pounds) reach menarche years earlier than thinner ones do. Although extreme underweight always delays puberty, body fat may be less necessary for boys. Indeed, one study found that male obesity may delay puberty (Tackett et al., 2014).

Malnutrition explains why youths reach puberty later in some parts of Africa, while their genetic relatives in North America mature much earlier. A more dramatic example arises from sixteenth-century Europe, where puberty may have started several years later than it does today (Gillis, 2013).

ADDED HORMONES Some scientists suspect that hormones in the food supply may cause precocious (before age 8) or delayed (after age 14) puberty. Cattle are

Ancient Rivals or New Friends? One of the best qualities of adolescents is that they identify more with their generation than their ethnic group, here Turk and German. Do the expressions of these 13-year-olds convey respect or hostility? Impossible to be sure, but given that they are both about mid-puberty (face shape, height, shoulder size), and both in the same school, they may become friends.

VICKY KASALA/GETTY IMAGES

Fully Grown These 14- to 17-year-old soccer players are in high school, probably already at their adult height, since girls typically mature before boys. We can be glad that U.S. law (Title IX) now mandates equal sports funding for both sexes, so all students can also experience the joys of teamwork, competition, and body strength. Adolescent and young-adult athletes are at their peak in power and reaction time—although they need to learn strategy and self-acceptance.

↑OBSERVATION QUIZ Do you see any sign that these girls are not yet comfortable with their new size and shape? (see answer, page 347)

◆◆ **Especially for Parents Worried About Early Puberty**
Suppose your cousin's 9-year-old daughter has just had her first period, and your cousin blames hormones in the food supply for this "precocious" puberty. Should you change your young daughter's diet? (see response, page 346)

leptin
A hormone that affects appetite and is believed to affect the onset of puberty. Leptin levels increase during childhood and peak at around age 12.

fed steroids to increase bulk and milk production, and hundreds of chemicals and hormones are used to produce most of the food that children consume. All of these substances *might* affect appetite, body fat, and sex hormones, with effects at puberty (Clayton et al., 2014; Wiley, 2011; Synovitz & Chopak-Foss, 2013).

Leptin, a hormone that is naturally produced by the human body, definitely affects puberty onset in girls. Low leptin is a problem, as this hormone is essential for appetite, energy, and puberty. However, too much leptin correlates with obesity, early puberty, and then early termination of growth.

Research to understand exactly how leptin and all the other hormones and chemicals affect puberty is ongoing and contradictory (M. Wolff et al., 2015; Bohlen, 2016). One puzzle is that early puberty does not predict later height. Indeed, the heaviest third-grade girl may become the tallest fifth-grader and then the shortest high school graduate.

Stress hastens puberty, especially if a child's parents are sick, drug-addicted, or divorced, or if the neighborhood is violent and impoverished. One study of sexually abused girls found that they began puberty as much as a year earlier than they otherwise would have, a result attributed not only to stress but also to the hormones activated by sexual abuse (Noll et al., 2017). Particularly for girls who are genetically sensitive, puberty comes early if their home is stressful (Ellis et al., 2011; James et al., 2012).

This may explain the fact that many internationally adopted children experience early puberty, especially if their first few years of life were in an institution or an abusive home. An alternative explanation is that their age at adoption was underestimated: Puberty then seems early but actually is not (Hayes, 2013).

what have you learned?

1. What are the first visible signs of puberty?
2. What body and brain parts are the last to reach full growth?
3. How do hormones affect the physical and psychological aspects of puberty?
4. How does the circadian rhythm affect adolescents?
5. What are the consequences of sleep deprivation?
6. What affects the age at which puberty begins?

Growth, Nutrition, and Sex

Puberty entails transformation of every body part, with each change affecting all of the others. For instance, growth of the heart muscle affects physical endurance, which affects the adolescent's ability to dance for hours, which affects sexual interaction, which affects sex hormones, which may affect what the adolescent chooses to eat. Of course, we must discuss these changes one by one. We first discuss biological growth and the nutrition that fuels that growth. Then we consider sexual maturation.

Growing Bigger and Stronger

Puberty causes a **growth spurt**—a sudden, uneven jump in size that turns children into adults. Growth proceeds from the extremities to the core (the opposite of the earlier proximodistal growth). Thus, fingers and toes lengthen before hands and feet, hands and feet before arms and legs, arms and legs before the torso. Because the torso is the last body part to grow, many pubescent children are temporarily big-footed, long-legged, and short-waisted.

As the growth spurt begins, children eat more and gain weight. Exactly when, where, and how much weight they gain depends on heredity, hormones, diet, exercise, and whether they are boys or girls. By age 17, the average girl's body has twice as much body fat as the average boy's. Obviously, gender and maturation are far from the only influences on body composition; genes and exercise affect shape lifelong.

A height spurt follows the weight spurt; a year or two later a muscle spurt occurs. Thus, the pudginess and clumsiness of early puberty are usually gone by late adolescence. Arm muscles grow, particularly in boys, who can lift twice as much at age 18 as at age 8. In both sexes the lungs triple in weight and the heart doubles in size, allowing the pulse to decrease and blood pressure to increase. Athletic ability and stamina improve every year.

Note that weight and height increase *before* muscles and internal organs grow: Athletic training and weight lifting should be tailored to an adolescent's size the previous year. Sports injuries are the most common school accidents, and they increase at puberty. One reason is that the height spurt precedes increases in bone mass, making young adolescents vulnerable to fractures (Mathison & Agrawal, 2010).

Meanwhile, the brain is impulsive, not cautious: The football player with a mild concussion is likely not to tell the coach, even though the player risks brain diseases in middle age. More than 1 million high school students play football each year, with about 400 concussions officially reported by coaches (Dompier et al., 2015).

Another organ system, the skin, becomes oilier, sweatier, and more prone to acne. Hair becomes coarser and darker, and the hairline might move. New hair grows under arms, on faces, and over sex organs (pubic hair, from the same Latin root as *puberty*).

growth spurt
The relatively sudden and rapid physical growth that occurs during puberty. Each body part increases in size on a schedule: Weight usually precedes height, and growth of the limbs precedes growth of the torso.

Both the Same? Yes, they are former U.S. Presidents. But what a difference 150 years makes! James Madison (*left*) was the fourth President of the United States, was popular and respected, and at 5 feet, 4 inches tall, weighed about 100 pounds. Barack Obama, the 44th President, was 6'1", and Trump (#45) is said to be 6'3". Lincoln (#16) was tallest of all—6'4"—which then was a reason to mock his appearance.

SCIENCE HISTORY IMAGES / ALAMY

JEWEL SAMAD/AFP/GETTY IMAGES

Diet Deficiencies

All of the changes of puberty depend on nourishment, yet many adolescents skip breakfast, binge at midnight, guzzle down unhealthy energy drinks, and munch on salty, processed snacks. In 2015, only 16 percent of U.S. high school seniors ate the recommended three or more servings of vegetables a day (MMWR, June 10, 2016).

Deficiencies of iron, calcium, zinc, and other minerals are especially common during adolescence. Because menstruation depletes iron, anemia is more common among adolescent girls than among any other age or sex group.

Boys may also be iron-deficient if they engage in physical labor or intensive sports: Muscles need iron for growth and strength. The teenager who is tired all the time may well be iron-deficient.

About half of adult bone mass is acquired from ages 10 to 20, with calcium required for bone growth. Although the recommended daily intake of calcium for adolescents is 1,300 milligrams, the average U.S. teen consumes less than 500 milligrams a day. One consequence: Many contemporary teenagers will develop *osteoporosis* (fragile bones), a major cause of disability, injury, and death in late adulthood, especially for women.

What Is in These Drinks? Milk and water are ideal for teens, but commercial coffee beverages often contain excessive sugar and fat.

body image
A person's idea of how his or her body looks.

CHOICES MADE Many social scientists advocate a "nudge" to encourage people to make better choices, in nutrition as well as other aspects of their lives (Thaler & Sunstein, 2008; Sunstein, 2014; Carroll et al., 2018). Teenagers may be nudged toward poor choices.

For example, fast-food establishments cluster around high schools, often with "extra seating" that encourages teenagers to eat and socialize. This is especially true for high schools with large Hispanic populations, who are most at risk for obesity. Forty-five percent of Hispanic American girls in U.S. high schools describe themselves as overweight, as do 28 percent of Hispanic American boys (MMWR, June 10, 2016). Before blaming their culture's diet, blame fast food.

Rates of obesity are falling in childhood but not in adolescence. In 2003, only three U.S. states (Kentucky, Mississippi, Tennessee) had high school obesity rates at 15 percent or higher; in 2015, 30 states did (MMWR, June 10, 2016).

BODY IMAGE One reason for poor nutrition is anxiety about **body image**—that is, a person's idea of how his or her body looks. Few teenagers welcome their sudden weight increase, so after eating because they are hungrier than before, they eat less to lose the body weight they naturally gain.

Teenagers try new diets, or go without food for 24 hours (as did 19 percent of U.S. high school girls in one typical month), or take diet drugs (6.6 percent) (MMWR, June 13, 2014). Some eat oddly (e.g., only rice or only carrots), begin unusual diets, or exercise intensely.

Two-thirds of U.S. high school girls are trying to lose weight, one-third think they are overweight, and only one-sixth are actually overweight (MMWR, June 10, 2016). This is one reason that depression increases rapidly at puberty, peaking at age 15 and then decreasing over the next several years, with many individual differences.

GRAHAM M. LAWRENCE/ALAMY

STEPHAN GLADIEU/GETTY IMAGES

Diet Worldwide, adolescent obesity is increasing. Parental responses differ, from indifference to major focus. For some U.S. parents, the response is to spend thousands of dollars trying to change their children, as is the case for the parents of these girls, eating breakfast at Wellspring, a California boarding school for overweight teenagers that costs $6,250 a month. Every day, these girls exercise more than 10,000 steps (tracked with a pedometer) and eat less than 20 grams of fat (normal is more than 60 grams).

The overall pattern is that, when height finally matches weight and the prefrontal cortex reins in the limbic system, fewer adolescents are seriously depressed. For some, however, dissatisfaction with body fat becomes dangerous.

EATING DISORDERS Many teenagers, mostly girls, eat erratically or ingest drugs (especially diet pills) to lose weight; others, mostly boys, take steroids to increase muscle mass. Eating disorders are rare in childhood but increase dramatically at puberty, accompanied by distorted body image, food obsession, and depression. (See Visualizing Development, page 323.)

Adolescents sometimes switch from obsessive dieting to overeating to overexercising and back again. Although girls are most vulnerable, boys are at risk too, especially those who aspire to be pop stars or who train to be wrestlers.

JON KOPALOFF/GETTY IMAGES

JAMES DEVANEY/GETTY IMAGES

Bingeing, Cutting, Starving Stardom Both Demi Lovato *(left)* and Zayn Malik *(right)* are world-famous stars, with best-selling albums and international tours. Demi starred in *Camp Rock* (a Disney film) and now has a highly successful musical career; Zayn was integral to One Direction (a leading "boy band" from England). Yet, both suffered serious eating disorders while millions of fans adored them, a sobering lesson for us all.

FRED DUFOUR/AFP/GETTY IMAGES

Not Just Dieting Elize, seen here sitting in a café in France, believes that she developed anorexia after she went on an extreme diet. Success with that diet led her to think that even less food would be better. She is recovering, but, as you can see, she is still too thin.

A body mass index (BMI) of 18 or lower, or a loss of more than 10 percent of body weight within a month or two, indicates **anorexia nervosa.** Fewer than 1 in 100 girls suffer from anorexia, but those who do starve themselves voluntarily and have a destructive and distorted attitude about their bodies. They become stick thin, risking death by organ failure.

About three times as common as anorexia is **bulimia nervosa.** Sufferers overeat compulsively, consuming thousands of calories within an hour or two, and then purge through vomiting or laxatives. Most are close to normal in weight and therefore unlikely to starve. However, they risk serious health problems, including damage to their gastrointestinal system and cardiac arrest from electrolyte imbalance (Mehler, 2018).

Bingeing and purging are common among adolescents. For instance, a 2013 survey found that *in the last 30 days,* 6.6 percent of U.S. high school girls and 2.2 percent of boys vomited or took laxatives to lose weight, with marked variation by state (from 3.6 percent in Nebraska to 9 percent in Arizona) (MMWR, June 13, 2014).

A disorder that is newly recognized in DSM-5 is **binge eating disorder.** Some adolescents periodically and compulsively overeat, quickly consuming large amounts of ice cream, cake, or snack food until their stomachs hurt. When bingeing becomes a disorder, overeating is typically done in private, at least weekly for several months. The sufferer does not purge (hence this is not bulimia) but feels out of control, distressed, and depressed.

anorexia nervosa
An eating disorder characterized by self-starvation. Affected individuals voluntarily undereat and often overexercise, depriving their vital organs of nutrition. Anorexia can be fatal.

bulimia nervosa
An eating disorder characterized by binge eating and subsequent purging, usually by induced vomiting and/or use of laxatives.

binge eating disorder
Eating much more in a short time period than is normal, to the point of feeling overfull and in pain. In this disorder, bingeing happens more than once a week for several months, and sufferers feel out of control—they can't stop. This disorder begins as bulimia does but does not involve purging.

primary sex characteristics
The parts of the body that are directly involved in reproduction, including the vagina, uterus, ovaries, testicles, and penis.

LIFE-SPAN CAUSES AND CONSEQUENCES From a life-span perspective, teenage eating disorders are not limited to adolescence, even though this is the age when first signs typically appear. The origins begin much earlier, in family eating patterns, if parents do not help their children eat sensibly—when they are hungry, without food being a punishment or a reward. Indeed, the origin could be at conception, since a genetic vulnerability is suspected.

For all eating disorders, family function (not structure) is crucial (Tetzlaff & Hilbert, 2014). During the teen years, many parents are oblivious to eating disorders. They might have given up trying to get their child to eat breakfast before school or to join the family for dinner. They delay getting the help that their children need (Thomson et al., 2014).

Some adolescents with eating disorders die during adulthood, especially of heart conditions, and others recover (Mehler, 2018). The chance of recovery is better if diagnosis and treatment occur during early adolescence (not adulthood) and if hospitalization is brief (Meczekalski et al., 2013; Errichiello et al., 2016).

Sexual Maturation

Sexuality is multidimensional, complicated, and variable—not unlike human development overall. For that reason, sexual interaction is discussed in several later chapters, including the next one on adolescent social life. Here we consider the impact of the biological aspects of sexual development.

The body characteristics that are directly involved in conception and pregnancy are called **primary sex characteristics.** During puberty, every primary sex organ

Visualizing Development

SATISFIED WITH YOUR BODY?

Probably not, if you are a teenager. At every age, accepting who you are—not just ethnicity and gender, but also body shape, size, and strength—correlates with emotional health. During the adolescent years, when everyone's body changes dramatically, body dissatisfaction rises. As you see, this is particularly true for girls—but if the measure were satisfaction with muscles, more boys would be noted as unhappy.

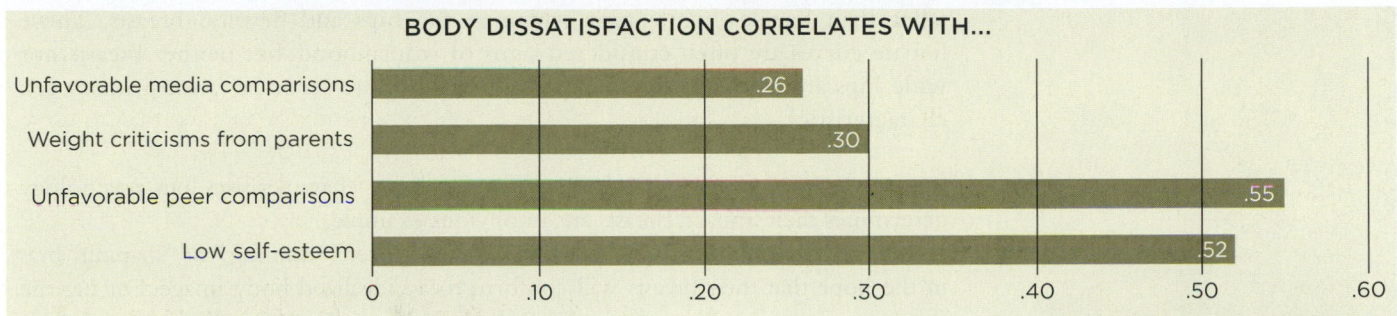

BODY DISSATISFACTION CORRELATES WITH...

Unfavorable media comparisons	.26
Weight criticisms from parents	.30
Unfavorable peer comparisons	.55
Low self-esteem	.52

0   .10   .20   .30   .40   .50   .60

DATA FROM VAN VONDEREN & KINNALLY, 2012.

Gender Differences in Body Dissatisfaction

Females of all ages tend to be dissatisfied with their bodies, but the biggest leap in dissatisfaction occurs when girls transition from early to mid-adolescence (Makinen et al., 2012).

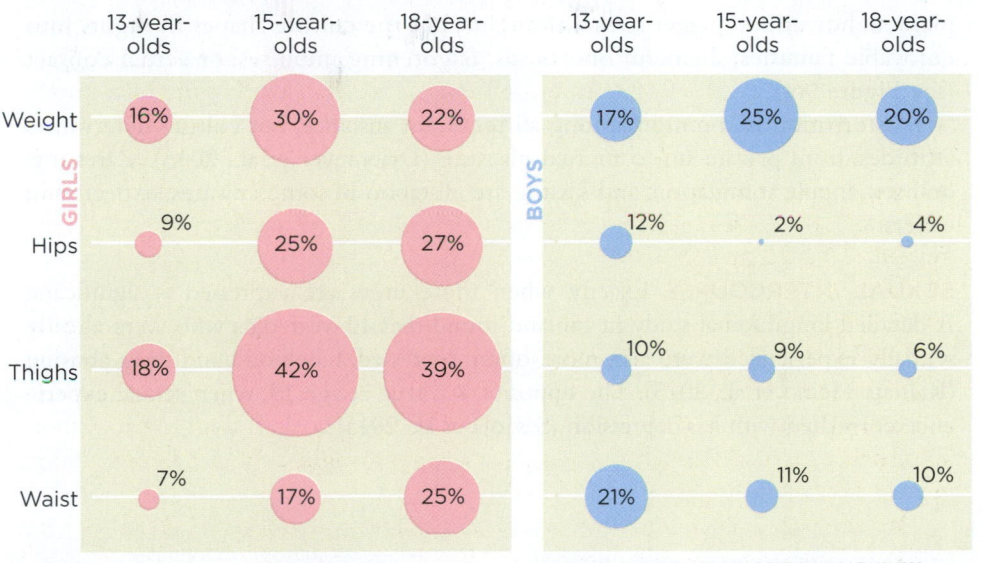

GIRLS

	13-year-olds	15-year-olds	18-year-olds
Weight	16%	30%	22%
Hips	9%	25%	27%
Thighs	18%	42%	39%
Waist	7%	17%	25%

BOYS

	13-year-olds	15-year-olds	18-year-olds
Weight	17%	25%	20%
Hips	12%	2%	4%
Thighs	10%	9%	6%
Waist	21%	11%	10%

DATA FROM WEINSHENKER, 2014; ROSENBLUM & LEWIS, 1999.

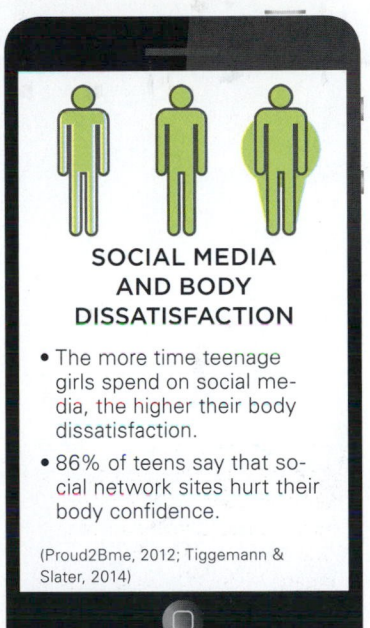

SOCIAL MEDIA AND BODY DISSATISFACTION

- The more time teenage girls spend on social media, the higher their body dissatisfaction.
- 86% of teens say that social network sites hurt their body confidence.

(Proud2Bme, 2012; Tiggemann & Slater, 2014)

Nutrition and Exercise

High school students are told, at home and at school, to eat their vegetables and not care about their looks. But they listen more to their peers and follow social norms. Fortunately, some eventually learn that, no matter what their body type, good nutrition and adequate exercise make a person feel more attractive, energetic, and happy.

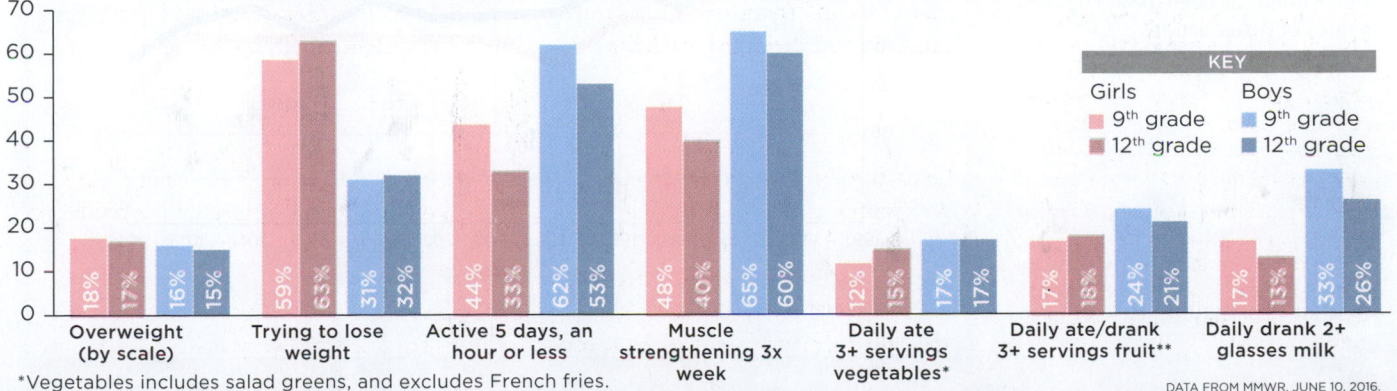

KEY

	Girls	Boys
9th grade	▮	▮
12th grade	▮	▮

	Girls 9th	Girls 12th	Boys 9th	Boys 12th
Overweight (by scale)	18%	17%	16%	15%
Trying to lose weight	59%	63%	31%	32%
Active 5 days, an hour or less	44%	33%	62%	53%
Muscle strengthening 3x week	48%	40%	65%	60%
Daily ate 3+ servings vegetables*	12%	15%	17%	17%
Daily ate/drank 3+ servings fruit**	17%	18%	24%	21%
Daily drank 2+ glasses milk	17%	13%	33%	26%

*Vegetables includes salad greens, and excludes French fries.
**Fruits include a glass of 100% fruit juice.

DATA FROM MMWR, JUNE 10, 2016.

(the ovaries, the uterus, the penis, and the testes) increases dramatically in size and matures in function. Reproduction becomes possible.

At the same time, **secondary sex characteristics** develop. They are body features that do not directly affect reproduction (hence they are secondary) but that signify masculinity or femininity.

One secondary characteristic is body shape. Young boys and girls have similar shapes, but at puberty males widen at the shoulders and grow about 5 inches taller than females, while girls widen at the hips and develop breasts. Those female curves are often considered signs of womanhood, but neither breasts nor wide hips are required for conception; thus, they are secondary, not primary, sex characteristics.

secondary sex characteristics
Physical traits that are not directly involved in reproduction but that indicate sexual maturity, such as a man's beard and a woman's breasts.

PSYCHOLOGICAL IMPACT Biology causes all sex characteristics, but psychology determines their impact. Breasts are an obvious example.

Many adolescent girls buy "minimizer," "maximizer," "training," or "shaping" bras in the hope that their breasts will conform to an idealized body image. During the same years, many overweight boys are horrified to notice a swelling around their nipples—a temporary result of the erratic hormones of early puberty.

The sex hormones that cause biological changes also affect the brain, so fantasizing, flirting, hand-holding, staring, standing, sitting, walking, displaying, and touching are all done in particular ways to reflect sexuality. As already explained, hormones trigger sexual thoughts, but the culture shapes thoughts into enjoyable fantasies, shameful obsessions, frightening impulses, or actual contact (see Figure 9.4).

Masturbation is common among all teens, for instance, but culture determines attitudes, from private sin to mutual pleasure (Driemeyer et al., 2016). Caressing, oral sex, nipple stimulation, and kissing are all taboo in some cultures, expected in others.

SEXUAL INTERCOURSE Exactly when those urges are expressed is significant. A detailed longitudinal study in Finland found that 13-year-olds who were already sexually experienced were also more often depressed, rebellious, and drug abusing (Kaltiala-Heino et al., 2015). The opposite was true at age 19, when sexual experience correlated with *less* depression (Savioja et al., 2015).

FIGURE 9.4 Boys and Girls Together Boys tend to be somewhat more sexually experienced than girls during the high school years. However, since the Youth Risk Behavior Survey began in 1991, the overall trend has been toward equality in rates of sexual activity.

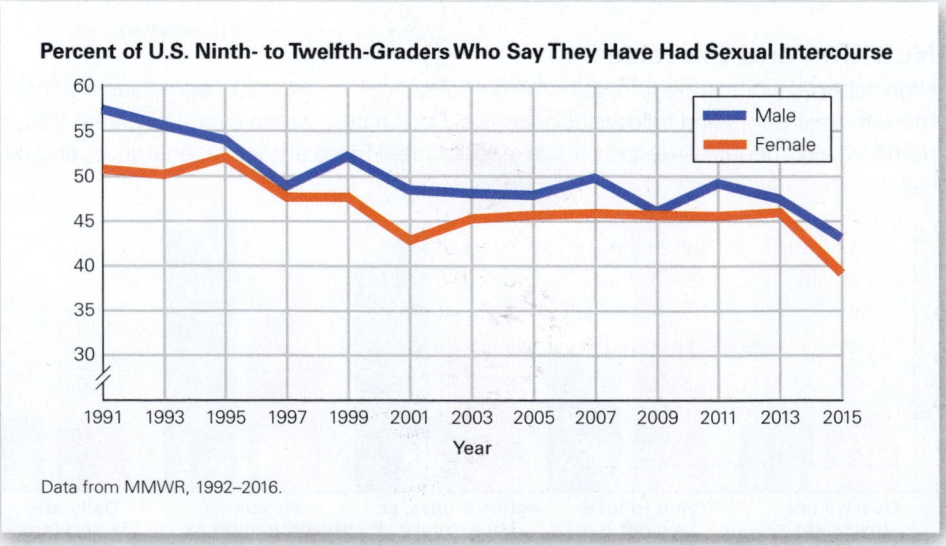

Data from MMWR, 1992–2016.

Overall, emotions regarding sexual experience, like the rest of puberty, are strongly influenced by cultural norms regarding what is expected at what age, with each teenager's own friends more influential than national culture. If you want to predict when a particular teen will be sexually active, instead of assessing age or body development, find out whether the teen's friends are active.

In many nations, including the United States, female rates of sexual activity are almost even with male rates. For example, among high school seniors, 57 percent of the girls and 59 percent of the boys have had sexual intercourse, with most of them sexually active in the past three months. The only notable difference is in the number of partners: Fewer girls than boys say they have had four or more (9 percent compared to 14 percent) (MMWR, June 10, 2016).

Over the past two decades in the United States, every gender, ethnic, and age group has become *less* sexually active than the previous cohort. Between 1991 and 2015, intercourse experience among African American high school students decreased 40 percent (to 49 percent); among European Americans, down 20 percent (to 40 percent); and among Latinos, down 19 percent (to 43 percent) (MMWR, June 10, 2016).

These were responses to an anonymous questionnaire. As you know from Chapter 1, people do not always answer honestly, but these trends (if not the specifics) are accurate because the same questions were asked over the decades. Many reasons for later sexual experience have been suggested: sex education, fear of HIV/AIDS, awareness of the hazards of pregnancy, more female education. To explore these hypotheses, more research is needed.

All of these examples demonstrate a universal experience (rising hormones) producing another universal experience (growth of primary and secondary sex characteristics) that is powerfully shaped by cohort, gender, and culture. The most important influence on adolescents' sexual activity is not their bodies but their close friends, who have more influence than do sex or ethnic group norms (van de Bongardt et al., 2015).

Sexual Problems in Adolescence

Sexual interest and interaction are part of adolescence, a biological imperative that ensures the survival of humankind. Guidance is needed, but teenagers are neither depraved nor degenerate in experiencing sexual urges: They are expressing an essential human trait.

Healthy adult relationships are more likely to develop when adolescent impulses are not haunted by shame and fear (Tolman & McClelland, 2011). Moreover, sex can be thrilling and affirming, providing a bonding experience. Before focusing on the hazards of adolescent sex, we should note that several "problems" are less common than they were 30 years ago:

- *Teen births have decreased.* In the United States, births to teenage mothers (ages 15 to 19) decreased 50 percent between 2007 and 2015

STEVE COLEMAN/OJO IMAGES RF/GETTY IMAGES

Everywhere Glancing, staring, and—when emotions are overwhelming—averting one's eyes are part of the universal language of love. Although the rate of intercourse among teenagers is lower than it was, passion is expressed in simple words, touches, and, as shown here, the eyes on a cold day.

The **DATA CONNECTIONS ACTIVITY Sexual Behaviors of U.S. High School Students** examines how sexually active teens really are.

Who Should Teens Talk to About Contraception?
This teenage girl is discussing contraception with her gynecologist.

PHOTOALTO/ERIC AUDRAS/GETTY IMAGES

across races and ethnicities, with the biggest drop among Hispanic teens (J. Martin et al., 2017). Similar declines are evident in other nations. The most dramatic results are from China, where the 2015 teen pregnancy rate was about one-tenth of the rate 50 years ago (reducing the 2015 projection of the world's population by about 1 billion).

■ *The use of "protection" has risen.* Contraception, particularly condom use among adolescent boys, has increased markedly in most nations since 1990. The U.S. Youth Risk Behavior Survey found that 63 percent of sexually active ninth-grade boys used a condom during their most recent intercourse (MMWR, June 10, 2016) (see Table 9.1).

■ *Teen abortions have decreased.* The teen abortion rate in the United States has steadily declined since abortion became safe and legal. From 2005 to 2015 the rate declined by half (Jatlaoui et al., 2017), even as the rate for women over age 35 (most of whom are married and already have children) has increased.

These are positive trends, but some other problems are still evident.

SEX TOO SOON Compared to a century ago, adolescent sexual activity—especially if it results in birth—has become more hazardous. Four circumstances have changed in recent decades:

1. Earlier puberty is one reason for some teens having sex before age 15. That correlates with depression, drug abuse, and lifelong problems (Kastbom et al., 2015).

2. Teen sex that led to pregnancy and birth was expected for young wives a century ago, whose husbands and parents welcomed the baby. Now only 9 percent of teen mothers are married, and often the father is not available to help (J. Martin et al., 2018).

3. Raising a child has become more time-consuming and expensive, and the traditional helper—the grandmother—is now often employed (Meyer, 2014).

4. **Sexually transmitted infections (STIs)** (also called sexually transmitted diseases [STDs]) are more likely than in former years. Sexually active teenagers have higher rates of STIs than do sexually active adults. Teens are slower to recognize symptoms, tell partners, and get medical treatment. That makes them more at risk of infertility and even death later on.

◆ Especially for Parents Worried About Their Teenager's Risk-Taking
You remember the risky things you did at the same age, and you are alarmed by the possibility that your child will follow in your footsteps. What should you do? (see response, page 346)

sexually transmitted infections (STIs)
Diseases that are spread by sexual contact, including syphilis, gonorrhea, genital herpes, chlamydia, and HIV/AIDS.

TABLE 9.1 Condom Use Among 15-Year-Olds (Tenth Grade)

Country	Sexually Active (% of total)	Used Condom at Last Intercourse (% of those sexually active)
France	20	84
England	29	83
Canada	23	78
Russia	33	75
Israel	14	72
United States	41	60

Data from MMWR, June 4, 2010, and June 10, 2016; Nic Gabhainn et al., 2009.

SEXUAL ABUSE **Child sexual abuse** is defined as any sexual activity (including fondling and photographing) between a juvenile and an adult. Age 18 is the usual demarcation between child and adult, although this varies by state. Pubescent girls—virginal, with newly developing breasts—are particularly vulnerable. Teenage boys are also at risk.

Although sexual abuse of younger children garners most headlines, adolescents are, by far, the most frequent victims. Virtually every problem, including pregnancy, drug abuse, eating disorders, and suicide, is more frequent in adolescents who are sexually abused.

This is true worldwide. Although solid numbers are unknown for obvious reasons, millions of girls in their early teens are forced into marriage or sold into prostitution each year. Adolescent girls are common victims of sex trafficking: Their youth makes them more alluring and their immaturity makes them more vulnerable (McClain & Garrity, 2011).

Estimates of the number of children annually trafficked for sex in the United States range from 1,000 to 336,000 (Miller-Perrin & Wurtele, 2017). Young people who are sexually exploited tend to fear sex and devalue themselves lifelong (Pérez-Fuentes et al., 2013).

Remember that perpetrators of child abuse are often people known to the child. After puberty, although sometimes abusers are adults (parents, coaches, or other authorities), often they are other teenagers. In the most recent U.S. Youth Risk Behavior Survey of high school students, 15 percent of the girls and 5 percent of the boys said that their dating partner had forced unwanted sexual activity (MMWR, June 10, 2016).

JEFF KOWALSKY/GETTY IMAGES

You, Too? Millions were shocked to learn that Larry Nassar, a physician for gymnasts training for the Olympics and at Michigan State University, sexually abused more than 150 young women. Among the victims was Kaylee Lorenz, shown here, addressing Nassar in court. Nassar was convicted of multiple counts of sexual assault and sentenced to 40 to 175 years in prison, but his victims wonder why no one stopped him. The president of Michigan State University resigned in disgrace; many others are still in office.

child sexual abuse
Any erotic activity that arouses an adult and excites, shames, or confuses a child, whether or not the victim protests and whether or not genital contact is involved.

what have you learned?

1. What is the pattern of growth in adolescent bodies?

2. What complications result from the sequence of growth (weight/height/muscles)?

3. What are examples of the difference between primary and secondary sex characteristics?

4. Why are fewer problems caused by adolescent sexuality now than a few decades ago?

5. Among sexually active people, why do adolescents have more STIs than adults?

6. What are the effects of child sexual abuse?

Cognitive Development

Brain maturation, additional years of schooling, moral challenges, increased independence, and intense conversations all occur between ages 11 and 18. The result is dramatic cognitive growth.

DIANNE AVERY PHOTOGRAPHY/MOMENT/GETTY IMAGES

Three California Girls Who takes selfies? Anyone with a smartphone can, but teenagers do so more than any other age group. Egocentrism is also evident in details of dress and grooming. All three of these girls, from Thousand Oaks, California, appear to spend many hours on their makeup and their hair, which they have likely grown for years.

adolescent egocentrism
A characteristic of adolescent thinking that leads young people (ages 10 to 13) to focus on themselves to the exclusion of others.

imaginary audience
The other people who, in an adolescent's egocentric belief, are watching and taking note of his or her appearance, ideas, and behavior. This belief makes many teenagers very self-conscious.

THINK CRITICALLY: How should you judge the validity of the idea of adolescent egocentrism?

Oblivious? When you see a teenager with purple hair, a nose ring, or riding a bicycle and reading, do you think they do not imagine what others think?

LEILA VALDUGA/MOMENT/GETTY IMAGES

Egocentrism

Adolescents thinking intensely about themselves and about what others think of them is a trait called **adolescent egocentrism** (Elkind, 1967). Especially in early adolescence, many adolescents regard themselves as much more special, admired, or despised than anyone else thinks they are.

Egocentric adolescents have trouble understanding other points of view because, egocentrically, they are overwhelmed by their own perspective. For example, few girls are attracted to boys with pimples and braces, but one boy's eagerness to be seen as growing up kept him from realizing this, according to his older sister:

> Now in the 8th grade, my brother has this idea that all the girls are looking at him in school. He got his first pimple about three months ago. I told him to wash it with my face soap but he refused, saying, "Not until I go to school to show it off." He called the dentist, begging him to approve his braces now instead of waiting for a year. The perfect gifts for him have changed from action figures to a bottle of cologne, a chain, and a fitted baseball hat like the rappers wear.
>
> [adapted from E., personal communication]

Acute self-consciousness about physical appearance may be more prevalent between ages 10 and 13 than at any other time, in part because adolescents notice changes in their body that do not exactly conform to social norms and ideals (Guzman & Nishina, 2014). Adolescents also instigate changes that they think other teenagers will admire.

For example, piercings, shaved heads, torn jeans—all contrary to adult conventions—signify connection to youth culture, and wearing suits and ties, or dresses and pearls, would attract unwelcome attention from other youth. Notice groups of adolescents waiting in line for a midnight show, or clustering near their high school, and you will see appearance that may seem rebellious to adults but that conforms to teen culture.

Egocentrism leads some adolescents to *ruminate* intensely and obsessively, going over problems via phone, text, conversation, social media, and private, quiet self-talk (as when they lie in bed, unable to sleep) about each nuance of everything they have done, are doing, might do, and should have done if only they had thought quickly enough. Rumination increases depression and anxiety (Topper et al., 2017; Burkhouse et al., 2017).

THE IMAGINARY AUDIENCE Egocentrism creates an **imaginary audience** in the minds of many adolescents. They believe they are at center stage, with all eyes on them, and they imagine how others might react to their appearance and behavior.

One woman remembers:

> When I was 14 and in the 8th grade, I received an award at the end-of-year school assembly. Walking across the stage, I lost my footing and stumbled in front of the entire student body. To be clear, this was

not falling flat on one's face, spraining an ankle, or knocking over the school principal—it was a small misstep noticeable only to those in the audience who were paying close attention. As I rushed off the stage, my heart pounded with embarrassment and self-consciousness, and weeks of speculation about the consequence of this missed step were set into motion. There were tears and loss of sleep. Did my friends notice? Would they stop wanting to hang out with me? Would a reputation for clumsiness follow me to high school?

[Somerville, 2013, p. 121]

This woman became an expert on the adolescent brain. She remembered from personal experience that "adolescents are hyperaware of others' evaluations and feel they are under constant scrutiny by an imaginary audience" (Somerville, 2013, p. 124).

FABLES Egocentricism leads naturally to a **personal fable,** the belief that one is unique, destined to have a heroic, fabled, even legendary life. Some 12-year-olds plan to star in the NBA, or to become billionaires, or to cure cancer. Some believe they are destined to die an early, tragic death. For that reason, evidence about smoking, junk food, vaping, or other destructive habits may be dismissed, as one of my young students did with "that's just a statistic."

Adolescents markedly overestimate the chance that they will die soon. One study found that teens estimate 1 chance in 5 that they will die before age 20 (Fischhoff et al., 2000). Another study found that 14 percent thought the odds were greater than 50/50 that they would die before age 21, including some who were quite certain they would be dead (Haynie et al., 2014).

In fact, the odds of death before age 21 for adolescents of all ethnic groups and genders are less than 1 in 1,000. Even those most at risk (urban African American males) survive 99 percent of the time. Ironically, if adolescents think that they will die young, they are likely to risk jail, HIV, drug addiction, and so on, increasing the odds of harm (Haynie et al., 2014).

If someone dies, the response is fatalistic ("his number was up"), unaware that a cognitive fable led to a dangerous risk. Fatalism may coexist with the **invincibility fable,** the idea that death will not occur unless it is destined. Believing that one is invincible—unless one is destined to die—removes any impulse to control one's behavior (Lin, 2016).

Similarly, egocentric teens post comments on Snapchat, Instagram, Facebook, and so on, and they expect others to understand, laugh, admire, or sympathize. Their imaginary audience is other teenagers, not parents, teachers, college admission officers, or future employers who might have another interpretation (boyd, 2014).

personal fable
An aspect of adolescent egocentrism characterized by an adolescent's belief that his or her thoughts, feelings, and experiences are unique, more wonderful, or more awful than anyone else's.

invincibility fable
An adolescent's egocentric conviction that he or she cannot be overcome or even harmed by anything that might defeat a normal mortal, such as unprotected sex, drug abuse, or high-speed driving.

formal operational thought
In Piaget's theory, the fourth and final stage of cognitive development, characterized by more systematic logical thinking and by the ability to understand and systematically manipulate abstract concepts.

Typical or Extraordinary? Francisca Vasconcelos, a San Diego high school senior, demonstrates formal operational thought. She used origami principles to create a 3-D printed robot. She calls herself an "aspiring researcher," and her project won second place in the INTEL 2016 Science Fair. Is she typical of older adolescents, or extraordinarily advanced?

Formal Operational Thought

Piaget described a shift toward **formal operational thought** as a child's concrete operational thinking becomes an adolescent's ability to consider abstractions, including "assumptions that have no necessary relation to reality" (Piaget, 1950/2001, p. 163). Is Piaget correct? Many educators think so. They adjust the curriculum between primary and secondary school, reflecting a shift from concrete thought to formal, logical thought. Here are three examples:

■ *Math.* Younger children multiply real numbers, such as $4 \times 3 \times 8$; adolescents multiply unreal numbers, such as $(2x)(3y)$ or even $(25xy^2)(-3zy^3)$.

- *Social studies.* Younger children study other cultures by considering daily life—drinking goat's milk or building an igloo, for instance. Adolescents consider the effects of GNP (gross national product) and TFR (total fertility rate) on global politics.

- *Science.* Younger students grow carrots and feed gerbils; adolescents study invisible particles and distant galaxies.

PIAGET'S EXPERIMENTS Piaget and his colleagues devised a number of tasks to assess formal operational thought (Inhelder & Piaget, 1958/2013b). In these tasks, "in contrast to concrete operational children, formal operational adolescents imagine all possible determinants . . . [and] systematically vary the factors one by one, observe the results correctly, keep track of the results, and draw the appropriate conclusions" (P. Miller, 2011, p. 57).

One of their experiments (diagrammed in Figure 9.5) required balancing a scale by hooking weights onto the scale's arms. To master this task, a person must realize the reciprocal interaction between distance from the center and heaviness of the weight.

Balancing was not understood by the 3- to 5-year-olds. By age 7, children balanced the scale by putting the same amount of weight on each arm, but they didn't realize that the distance from the center mattered. By age 10, children experimented with the weights, using trial and error, not logic.

Finally, by about age 13 or 14, some children hypothesized about reciprocity. They realize that a heavy weight close to the center can be counterbalanced with a light weight far from the center on the other side (Piaget & Inhelder, 1972).

HYPOTHETICAL-DEDUCTIVE REASONING One hallmark of formal operational thought is the capacity to think of possibility, not just reality. "Here and now" is only

VIDEO ACTIVITY: The Balance Scale Task shows children of various ages completing the task and gives you an opportunity to try it as well.

FIGURE 9.5 How to Balance a Scale Piaget's balance-scale test of formal reasoning, as it is attempted by a *(a)* 4-year-old, *(b)* 7-year-old, *(c)* 10-year-old, and *(d)* 14-year-old. The key to balancing the scale is to make weight times distance from the center equal on both sides of the center; the realization of that principle requires formal operational thought.

(a)

(b)

(c)

(d)

SUSAN WALSH/AP PHOTO

one of many possibilities, including "there and then," "long, long ago," "not yet," and "never." As Piaget said:

> The adolescent . . . thinks beyond the present and forms theories about everything, delighting especially in considerations of that which is not.
>
> *[Piaget, 1950/2001, p. 163]*

Adolescents are therefore primed to engage in **hypothetical thought,** reasoning about *if–then* propositions. Consider the following question, adapted from De Neys & Van Gelder (2009):

> If all mammals can walk,
> And whales are mammals,
> Can whales walk?

Children answer "No!" They know that whales swim, not walk; the logic escapes them. Some adolescents answer "Yes." They understand the conditional *if,* and therefore the counterfactual phrase "if all mammals."

> *Possibility* no longer appears merely as an extension of an empirical situation or of action actually performed. Instead, it is *reality* that is now secondary to *possibility.*
> *[Inhelder & Piaget, 1958/2013b, p. 251; emphasis in original]*

Hypothetical thought transforms perceptions, not necessarily for the better. Adolescents might criticize everything from their mother's spaghetti (it's not *al dente*) to the Gregorian calendar (it's not the Chinese or Jewish one). They criticize what *is* because of their hypothetical thinking about what might be and their growing awareness of other families and cultures (Moshman, 2011).

In developing the capacity to think hypothetically, by age 14 or so adolescents become more capable of **deductive reasoning,** or *top-down reasoning,* which begins with an abstract idea or premise and then uses logic to draw specific conclusions.

In the example above, "if all mammals can walk" is a premise. By contrast, **inductive reasoning,** or *bottom-up reasoning,* predominates during the school years, as children accumulate facts and experiences (the knowledge base) to aid their thinking. Since they know whales cannot walk, that knowledge trumps the logic.

hypothetical thought
Reasoning that includes propositions and possibilities that may not reflect reality.

inductive reasoning
Reasoning from one or more specific experiences or facts to reach (induce) a general conclusion. (Also called *bottom-up reasoning.*)

deductive reasoning
Reasoning from a general statement, premise, or principle, through logical steps, to figure out (deduce) specifics. (Also called *top-down reasoning.*)

◆**Especially for Natural Scientists**
Some ideas that were once universally accepted, such as the belief that the sun moved around Earth, have been disproved. Is it a failure of inductive reasoning or deductive reasoning that leads to false conclusions? (see response, page 346)

In essence, a child's reasoning goes like this: "This creature waddles and quacks. Ducks waddle and quack. Therefore, this must be a duck." This is inductive: It progresses from particulars ("waddles" and "quacks") to a general conclusion ("a duck"). By contrast, deduction progresses from the general to the specific: "If it's a duck, it will waddle and quack."

An example of the progress toward deductive reasoning comes from how children, adolescents, and adults change in their understanding of the causes of racism. Even before adolescence, almost every American is aware that racism exists—and almost everyone opposes it.

However, children tend to think the core problem is that some people are prejudiced. Using inductive reasoning, they think that the remedy is to argue against racism when they hear other people express it. By contrast, older adolescents think, deductively, that racism is a society-wide problem that requires policy solutions.

This example arises from a study of adolescent opinions regarding policies to remedy racial discrimination (Hughes & Bigler, 2011). Not surprisingly, most students of all ages recognized disparities between African Americans and European Americans and believed that racism was a major cause.

However, advanced cognition made a difference. Among those who recognized marked inequalities, older adolescents (ages 16 to 17) more often supported systemic solutions (e.g., affirmative action and desegregation) than did younger adolescents (ages 14 to 15). Similarly, in another study, when adolescents were asked how a person might overcome poverty, younger adolescents were more likely to emphasize personal hard work (an egocentric notion), while older adolescents used more complex analysis, noting systemic problems (formal operational thought), such as in national laws (Arsenio & Willems, 2017).

Two Modes of Thinking

As you see, Piagetians emphasize the sequence of thought, not only from egocentric to formal but throughout all four stages. Another group of scholars disagrees. They suggest that thinking does not develop in sequence but in parallel, with two processes that are not tightly coordinated within the brain (Baker et al., 2015).

To be specific, advanced logic in adolescence may be counterbalanced by the increasing power of intuition. Thus, thinking occurs in two ways, called **dual processing.** The terms and descriptions of these two processes vary, including intuitive/analytic, implicit/explicit, creative/factual, contextualized/decontextualized, unconscious/conscious, gist/quantitative, emotional/intellectual, experiential/rational, hot/cold, systems 1 and 2. Although they interact and can overlap, each mode is independent (Kuhn, 2013).

The thinking described by the first half of each pair is easier and quicker, preferred in everyday life. Sometimes, however, deeper thought is demanded. The discrepancy between the maturation of the limbic system and the prefrontal cortex reflects this duality.

INTUITIVE AND ANALYTIC PROCESSING In describing dual processing, we use the terms *intuitive* and *analytic,* defined as follows:

- **Intuitive thought** begins with a belief, assumption, or general rule (called a *heuristic*) rather than logic. Intuition is quick and powerful; it feels "right."
- **Analytic thought** is logical, hypothetical-deductive thinking described by Piaget.

dual processing
The notion that two networks exist within the human brain, one for emotional processing of stimuli and one for analytical reasoning.

intuitive thought
Thought that arises from an emotion or a hunch, beyond rational explanation, and is influenced by past experiences and cultural assumptions.

analytic thought
Thought that results from analysis, such as a systematic ranking of pros and cons, risks and consequences, possibilities and facts. Analytic thought depends on logic and rationality.

Impressive Connections This robot is about to compete in the Robotics Competition in Atlanta, Georgia, but much more impressive are the brains of the Oregon high school team (including Melissa, shown here) who designed the robot.

↑**OBSERVATION** QUIZ
Melissa seems to be working by herself, but what sign do you see that suggests she is part of a team who built this robot? (see answer, page 347)

When the two modes of thinking conflict, people of all ages sometimes use one and sometimes the other. Because of the uneven brain maturation described in the beginning of this chapter, adolescents are particularly likely to be intuitive thinkers, unlike their teachers and parents, who prefer slower, analytic thinking.

To test yourself on intuitive and analytic thinking, answer the following:

1. A bat and a ball cost $1.10 in total. The bat costs $1 more than the ball. How much does the ball cost?

2. If it takes 5 minutes for 5 machines to make 5 widgets, how long would it take 100 machines to make 100 widgets?

3. In a lake, there is a patch of lily pads. Every day the patch doubles in size. If it takes 48 days for the patch to cover the entire lake, how long would it take for the patch to cover half the lake?

[from Gervais & Norenzayan, 2012, p. 494]

Answers are on page 335. As you see, the quick, intuitive responses may be wrong.

Almost every adolescent is analytical and logical on some problems but not on others. As they grow older, adolescents sometimes gain in logic and sometimes regress, with the social context and training in statistics becoming major influences on cognition (Klaczynski & Felmban, 2014).

That finding has been confirmed by dozens of other studies (Kail, 2013). Being smarter as measured by an intelligence test does not advance cognition as much as having more experience, in school and in life, and studying statistics and linguistics that emphasize logic. However, even though the adolescent mind is capable of logic, sometimes "social variables are better predictors . . . than cognitive abilities" (Klaczynski & Felmban, 2014, pp. 103–104).

PREFERRING EMOTIONS Adolescents learn the scientific method in school, so they know the merits of empirical evidence and deductive reasoning. But, they do not always think like scientists. Why not?

A CASE TO STUDY

Biting the Policeman

The adolescent impulse to question traditional norms as development of the limbic system outpaces that of the prefrontal cortex can complicate simple conflicts. Added to that is suspicion of adult authority and idealism that is not tempered by experience.

One day, a student of mine, herself only 18, was with her 16-year-old cousin. A police officer stopped them, asked why the cousin was not in school, frisked him, and asked for identification. The cousin was visiting from another state; he did not carry ID.

My student cited a U.S. Supreme Court case that proved the officer did not have authority to "stop and frisk." The officer grabbed her cousin; my student bit the officer's hand—and was arrested. After weeks in jail (Rikers Island), she was brought before the judge. Her Legal Aid lawyer, and time in jail, led her to write an apology, which she read in a subdued, contrite voice. The officer did not press charges.

I appeared in court on her behalf; the judge praised me for caring and released her to me. Was it ironic that the judge listened to me but that the system did not address my student's needs? She was shivering; the first thing I did was put a warm coat around her.

This was dual processing. In her education, my student had gained a formal understanding of the U.S. Constitution. However, dispassionate analysis was missing. Her fast and furious intuition led her to defend her cousin in a way that an adult would not.

It is easy to conclude that more mature thought processes are wiser. I would not have bitten the officer. But this episode reveals that many adults do not understand the adolescent mind. However unwise at the moment, my student's adolescent mind-set combined with her childhood experience (she was taught to protect family members and be suspicious of the law) primed her to act as she did.

She is not the only one. Probably many readers of this book remember something they did in adolescence that arose from emotions but that with the wisdom of maturity they wish they had not done.

THINK CRITICALLY: When might an emotional response to a problem be better than an analytic one?

Dozens of experiments and extensive theorizing have found some answers (Albert & Steinberg, 2011). Essentially, logic is more difficult than intuition, and it requires questioning ideas that are comforting and familiar. Once people of any age reach an emotional conclusion (sometimes called a "gut feeling"), they resist changing their minds. Prejudice is not seen as prejudice; people develop reasons to support their feelings.

Moreover, it is comforting to stick to intuition. Fortunately, brains benefit from maturation and experience. As adolescents grow older, they are less likely to be illogical, overly optimistic, or too fatalistic. Compared to younger teens, they rely more on analysis than intuition (Klaczynski, 2017).

Ideally, they think things through before they act impulsively, and adults know when and how to allow them to reflect rather than to provoke immediate action—although that does not always happen, as when a police officer grabbed my student's cousin. (See A Case to Study.)

BETTER THINKING A developmental approach suggests that the adolescent way of thinking may have merit. For example, why do teenagers risk addiction by trying drugs, or risk HIV/AIDS by not using a condom? Of course, drug use is foolish and condom use is wise. But, perhaps we should not blame teenage irrationality and impulsiveness for those actions.

Perhaps adolescents are rational, but their priorities are not the same as those of their parents. Parents want healthy, long-lived children, so they blame faulty reasoning when adolescents risk their lives or break the law. Adolescents, however, value social warmth and friendship, and their hormones and brains are more attuned to those values than to long-term consequences (Crone & Dahl, 2012).

Thus, the reason may not be ignorance; it may be different values (Hartley & Somerville, 2015). For instance, is it important to postpone immediate pleasure in order to gain future rewards? That might mean rewriting an English paper, to hope for a better grade, to then be accepted in a better college, to then study for years to earn a degree, to then find a good job. That is what teachers and parents value.

Adolescents may value peer approval more than adult approval. If one's friends think they might die soon, those teenagers who believe that they themselves will survive are likely to take risks or break the law. Without faith in the future, "youth were willing to risk injury or death in pursuit of immediate rewards including, most notably, respect from friends" (Haynie et al., 2014, p. 177).

A 15-year-old who is offered a cigarette, for example, might rationally choose peer acceptance and the possibility of romance over the distant risk of cancer. Think of a teenager who wants to be "cool" or "bad," and then decide whether he or she might say, "No, thank you, my mother told me not to smoke."

Furthermore, weighing alternatives and thinking of future possibilities can be paralyzing. The systematic, analytic thought that Piaget described is slow and costly, not fast and frugal, wasting precious time when a young person wants to act. Some risks are taken impulsively, and that is not always bad.

Indeed, some experts suggest that the adolescent lust for excitement, responsiveness to peers, and willingness to explore new ideas may be adaptive in some contexts (Ernst, 2016). It may be that "the fundamental task of adolescence—to achieve adult levels of social competence—requires a great deal of learning about the social complexities of human social interactions" (Peper & Dahl, 2013, p. 135).

Societies need adolescents who question assumptions and reexamine traditions, lest old customs ossify and societies die. Of course, we also need people who follow norms and suspect innovation: Each age of the life span has a valuable perspective.

Answers	Intuitive	Analytic
1.	10 cents	5 cents
2.	100 minutes	5 minutes
3.	24 days	47 days

what have you learned?

1. How does adolescent egocentrism differ from early-childhood egocentrism?

2. What perceptions arise from belief in the imaginary audience?

3. Why are the personal fable and the invincibility fable called "fables"?

4. When might intuition and analysis lead to contrasting conclusions?

5. How might intuitive thinking increase risk-taking?

6. What are the benefits and liabilities of analytic thinking?

Secondary Education

What does our knowledge of adolescent cognition imply about school? There are dozens of schooling options: academic or practical skills, single-sex or co-ed, competitive or cooperative, large or small, public or private, and more.

To complicate matters, adolescents are far from a homogeneous group. As a result,

> some youth thrive at school—enjoying and benefiting from most of their experiences there; others muddle along and cope as best they can with the stress and demands of the moment; and still others find school an alienating and unpleasant place to be.
>
> *[Eccles & Roeser, 2011, p. 225]*

No school structure or pedagogy is best for everyone. A study of student emotional and academic engagement from fifth grade to eighth grade found that, as expected, the overall average was a slow and steady decline of engagement, but a distinctive group (about 18 percent) were highly engaged throughout while another distinctive group (about 5 percent) experienced precipitous disengagement year by year (Li & Lerner, 2011).

Those 18 percent are likely to do well in high school; those 5 percent are likely to drop out, but some of the latter are late bloomers who could succeed in college if given time and encouragement. Thus, schools and teachers need many strategies to reach every adolescent.

Various scientists, nations, schools, and teachers advocate reforms, based on opposite but logical hypotheses. To understand this complexity, we begin with facts.

Definitions and Facts

Each year of school advances human potential, a fact recognized by leaders and scholars in every nation and discipline. As you have read, adolescents are capable of deep and wide-ranging thought—no longer limited by concrete experience—yet they are often egocentric and impulsive.

Secondary education—traditionally grades 7 through 12—denotes the school years after elementary or grade school (known as *primary education*) and before college or university (known as *tertiary education*). Adults are healthier and wealthier if they complete primary education, learning to read and write, and then continue on through secondary and tertiary education. This is true within nations and between them.

Data on almost every condition, from all nations and ethnic groups, confirm that high school and college graduation correlate with better health, wealth, and family life. Some research focuses on people who grew up poor in toxic neighborhoods, because, particularly for them, education makes a marked difference.

Partly because political leaders recognize that educated adults advance national wealth and health, every nation is increasing the number of students in secondary schools. Education is compulsory until at least age 12 almost everywhere, and new high schools and colleges open daily in developing nations.

Traditionally, secondary education was divided into junior high (usually grades 7 and 8) and senior high (usually grades 9 through 12). As the average age of puberty declined, **middle schools** were created for grades 5 or 6 through 8. This makes sense, as you have learned: The pubescent 10- to 12-year-old is, cognitively, emotionally as well as biologically, unlike the 17-year-old or the 8-year-old.

Middle School

Adjusting to middle school is stressful: Teachers, classmates, and expectations all change. Developmentalists agree that "teaching is likely to be particularly complex for middle school teachers because it happens amidst a critical period of cognitive, socioemotional, and biological development of students who confront heightened social pressures from peers and gradual decline of parental oversight" (Ladd & Sorensen, 2017).

Regarding learning, "researchers and theorists commonly view early adolescence as an especially sensitive developmental period" (McGill et al., 2012, p. 1003). Middle schools have been called "developmentally regressive" (Eccles & Roeser, 2010, p. 13), which means that learning goes backward.

secondary education
Literally, the period after primary education (elementary or grade school) and before tertiary education (college). It usually occurs from about ages 12 to 18, although there is some variation by school and by nation.

middle school
A school for children in the grades between elementary school and high school. Middle school usually begins with grade 6 and ends with grade 8.

INCREASING BEHAVIORAL PROBLEMS For many middle school students, academic achievement slows down and behavioral problems increase. Puberty itself is part of the problem. At least for other animals, especially when they are under stress, learning takes longer at puberty (McCormick et al., 2010).

Students have good reason to dislike middle school. Bullying increases, particularly in the first year (Baly et al., 2014). Parents are less protective, partly because students want more independence.

Unlike primary school, in which each classroom had one teacher, middle school teachers have hundreds of students. They become impersonal and distant, opposite to the direct, personal engagement that young adolescents need (Meece & Eccles, 2010).

Academic achievement decreases particularly steeply for young adolescents of ethnic minorities, probably because they become more aware of the expectations of the larger society (Dotterer et al., 2009; McGill et al., 2012; Hayes et al., 2015).

One of the early signs of a future high school dropout is absenteeism in middle school, with experienced teachers and counselors able to stop this problem before it becomes chronic (Ladd & Sorensen, 2017). Most at risk are low-SES boys from African American or Latino families. Given the egocentric and intuitive thinking of many adolescents, role models who are similar to them are essential, yet few teachers are men from minority groups (Morris & Morris, 2013).

FINDING ACCLAIM No matter what a student's gender or ethnicity, middle school is challenging. Just when egocentrism leads young people to zigzag between feelings of shame and fantasies of stardom (the imaginary audience), schools may require them to change rooms, teachers, and classmates every 40 minutes or so. That limits both public acclaim and new friendships.

Middle school teachers grade more harshly than their primary school counterparts. Effort without accomplishment is not recognized, and achievement that was earlier "outstanding" is now only average. Many community after-school programs in the arts or sports lump adolescents of several ages together, so the younger ones feel inferior. Late developers, especially boys, are shorter, weaker, and less skilled than older youth.

Ironically, one factor that keeps students engaged in secondary school is participation on a sports team: Those who most need engagement may be least likely to get it.

School teams become competitive beginning in middle school, so those with fragile self-esteem protect themselves by not trying out. If sports require public showers, that is another reason for students with changing bodies to avoid them. Special camps for basketball, soccer, and so on may help develop skills, but they are expensive—beyond the reach of low-SES families.

As noted in the discussion of the brain, peer acceptance is more cherished at puberty than at any other time. Physical appearance—from eyebrows to foot size—suddenly becomes significant. Status symbols—from gang colors to trendy sunglasses—take on new meaning. Expensive clothes are coveted. Sexual conquests

© SPENCER GRANT/ALAMY STOCK PHOTO

Consequences Unknown
Few adolescents think about the consequences of their impulsive rage, responses, or retorts on social media or smartphones. This educator at a community center tries to explain that victims can be devastated—rarely suicidal, but often depressed.

◆ **Especially for Teachers**
You are stumped by a question your student asks. What do you do? (see response, page 346)

More Like Him Needed In 2014 in the United States, half of the public school students were non-White and non-Hispanic, and half are male. Meanwhile, only 17 percent of teachers are non-White and non-Hispanic, and only 24 percent are male. This Gardena, California, high school teacher is a welcome exception in two other ways—he rarely sits behind his desk, and he uses gestures as well as his voice to explain.

HILL STREET STUDIOS/BLEND IMAGES/NEWSCOM

Now Learn This Educators and parents disagree among themselves about how and what middle school children need to learn. Accordingly, some parents send their children to a school where biology is taught via dissecting a squid *(left),* others where obedience is taught via white shirts and lining up *(right).*

↑**OBSERVATION** QUIZ

Although the philosophy and strategy of these two schools are quite different, both share one aspect of the hidden curriculum. What is it? (see answer, page 347)

THINK CRITICALLY: The older people are, the more likely they are to be critical of social media. Is that wisdom or ignorance? Why?

are flaunted, which may be thoughtlessly destructive to other children. All of this adds stress to middle school students, who may have no psychic energy left for homework.

One solution is to educate boys and girls separately, which decreases the social anxiety of interacting with the other gender. A meta-analysis found some academic advantage to single-sex education in middle school but none in high school (Pahlke et al., 2014).

One review states, "both proponents and critics of single-sex schooling have studies that support their positions, stagnating the policy debate" (Pahlke & Hyde, 2016, p. 83). Perhaps the emphasis on academic achievement and self-esteem is too narrow: If the goal of secondary education is to prepare students for life, then coeducation may be better.

COPING WITH MIDDLE SCHOOL One way in which middle school students avoid feelings of failure in academics is to quit trying. Then they can blame a low grade on their choice ("I didn't study") rather than on their ability. Pivotal is how they think of their potential.

Some students have a "fixed mind-set," concluding that nothing they do can improve their academic skill. If they think they were born inept at math, or language, or whatever, they mask their self-assessment by claiming not to study, try, or care.

By contrast, if adolescents have a "growth mind-set," they will pay attention, participate in class, study, complete their homework, and learn. That is also called *mastery motivation,* an example of intrinsic motivation.

This is not hypothetical. In the first year of middle school, students with a fixed mind-set do not achieve much, whereas those with mastery motivation improve academically, true in many nations (e.g., Diseth et al., 2014; Zhao & Wang, 2014; Burnette et al., 2013). Beliefs lead to better coping—solving problems rather than blaming oneself—which is crucial for middle school achievement (Monti et al., 2017).

One possible set of problems arises with increased technology. Typically, adolescents get their first cell phone at about age 11, and in middle school teachers begin expecting them to research items on the Internet. During middle school, social media use and texting increase dramatically (Coyne et al., 2018). Research on this finds both harm and benefits, as described in the Opposing Perspectives and A View from Science features.

OPPOSING PERSPECTIVES

Digital Natives

Is technology a blessing or a curse? Some adults welcome the new information and connection that the Internet brings, while some think adolescents in particular should be protected from the harm of the omnipresent computer.

Teenagers may wonder why anyone would question the benefits of technology. Members of this generation are called *digital natives.* They have networked and texted all their lives with smartphones, tablets, and high-speed Internet. Their phones are with them day and night; some teens send hundreds of texts a day, with the "perpetual" texters more often male, mid-adolescent, and depressed (Coyne et al., 2018).

Even a decade ago, low-income and minority adolescents were less likely to have computers and smartphones. No longer. In the past few years, African American and Latino American teens are even more likely than European American teens to be online "almost constantly" (34, 32, and 19 percent, respectively) (Lenhart, 2015).

Most educators accept—even welcome—students' facility with technology. Teachers use laptops, smartphones, digital projectors, Smart Boards, and so on as tools for learning. In some districts, high school students are required to take at least one class completely online, and every student is given a tablet instead of a textbook.

Another benefit of technology arises from medical use. For example, using their smartphones, adolescents with type 1 diabetes can monitor their insulin level and send daily readings to their doctor—thus feeling more in control of their own health (Carroll et al., 2011).

Is technology a boon for every teenager? No. This is an Opposing Perspective because adults see many problems that digital natives do not (George & Odgers, 2015).

Many parents fear that sexual predators will lure innocent youth via the Internet. Fortunately, that is "extremely rare" (Mitchell et al., 2013, p. 1226), in part because teens are very suspicious of strangers online. When sexual harassment or harm occurs, the perpetrator is more likely to be someone the adolescent knows face-to-face.

Another worry is Internet addiction. Too much screen time may undercut schoolwork and friendship, a concern in every wired nation (Tang et al., 2014). Using criteria developed by psychiatrists for other addictions (gambling, drugs, and so on), one researcher believes that about 3 percent of U.S. adolescents suffer from Internet addiction, almost always with other disorders as well (Jorgenson et al., 2016) (see Table 9.2).

Those other disorders—often depression and conduct disorder—may be the underlying problem, with Internet use the symptom. Partly for that reason, the psychiatrists who wrote the DSM-5, after careful consideration of the evidence, did not include Internet use as an addiction.

TABLE 9.2 **Signs of Substance Use Disorder**	
In General	**How It Might Apply to Internet Addiction***
1. Impairs desired activity and accomplishment, notable in failed personal goals and broken promises to oneself.	1. Person denies, or lies about, how much time is spent online, which interferes with study, homework completion, household chores, or job-related concentration.
2. Normal cognitive processes—memory, motivation, logic—are impaired.	2. Person is less able to think deeply and analytically, or to remember things not online, such as phone numbers or appointments.
3. Social interactions disrupted, either disconnections when in a social group or isolation from other people.	3. Person spends less time in face-to-face communication with family and friends. Person ignores social interactions to check texts.
4. Basic body maintenance and health disturbed, such as loss of sleep, changed appetite, hygiene.	4. Person does not do usual health maintaining activities. Internet interferes with sleep, healthy eating, and so on.
5. Withdrawal symptoms: Person is agitated, physically or mentally, when unable to attain substance.	5. Person is angry or depressed when Internet unavailable, as when teachers or parents restrict cell phones, connections are broken, or recharging unavailable.
6. Increasing dependence: Need for substance or activity increases over time, as brain patterns change.	6. Person increases time spent; wants more devices (laptop, watch, tablet and more apps).

*This list is speculative. DSM-5 finds insufficient evidence of Internet addiction and does not use the word *addiction* because of "uncertain definition and potentially negative connotation" (American Psychiatric Association, 2013, p. 485).

Another major concern is **cyberbullying,** when electronic devices are used to harass someone, with rumors, lies, embarrassing truths, or threats. Some of those messages may involve what is called *sextortion*—for example, when sexual photos once shared consensually between two adolescents (called **sexting**) are then used maliciously. This can be especially damaging when a young adolescent is trying to establish sexual identity. [**Life-Span Link:** Sexting and sexual identity are discussed in Chapter 10.]

Since messages can be sent to many people—unlike face-to-face bullying—just one incident of cyberbullying can be devastating (Underwood & Ehrenreich, 2017). During the teen years, cyberbullying may be far worse than physical bullying (discussed in Chapter 8). Adolescent egocentrism and the imaginary audience magnify the sting.

No one condones cyberbullying, but some say the problem is in the bully, not the computer. Bullies need to be stopped and victims defended, no matter whether the mode is a face-to-face or electronic insult (Giumetti & Kowalski, 2015). Remember from the earlier discussion that the entire school needs to work together.

Especially in adolescence, adult lectures or zero-tolerance measures are ineffective. Measures that appeal to the better nature of the bully sometimes succeed: "I know that you don't want to hurt your classmates. How can you gain respect without trashing someone else?" (Yeager et al., 2018).

One final hazard: since emotional reactions overwhelm analytic thought, might adolescents believe fake news or biased accounts that they see on the Internet (Mihailidis & Viotty, 2017)? One careful observer claims that instead of being *native* users of technology, many teenagers are *naive* users—trusting sites that are markedly biased, believing news that is a lie (boyd, 2014). Adults can help—if they understand technology and teens. Time to get past both opposing views.

cyberbullying
Bullying that occurs when one person spreads insults or rumors about another by means of social media posts, e-mails, text messages, or cell phone videos.

sexting
Sending sexual content, particularly photos or videos, via cell phones or social media.

A VIEW FROM SCIENCE

Computer Use as a Symptom

Remember how easy is it to confuse correlation and causation. Might low school achievement, depression, and aggression (all correlates of excessive Internet use in some studies) precede video game playing and social media obsession rather than vice versa? Or might a third variable be the cause of the correlation?

If overuse is a symptom, then curtailing it is not a cure. In China, rehabilitation centers for Internet-addicted teens forbid any technology (Bax, 2014). Is that abusive?

A possible third variable is sleep deprivation. One study found that most teenagers use their cell phones to text after lights-out, which postpones going to sleep. The result was increased depression, which was correlated with cell phone use but not directly caused by it (Vernon et al., 2018). Those researchers suggest a "digital curfew" imposed by parents or initiated by the teenagers themselves.

Another study of the relationship between cell phone use and mental health problems (George et al., 2018) found that depression and anxiety actually decreased with cell phone use, probably because connecting with friends is an antidote to depression.

However, rates of attention deficit/hyperactivity disorder (ADHD) increased (George et al., 2018). Perhaps the quick responses required by texting and video games undercut the development of emotional regulation and concentration.

This view from science harks back to the conflicting theories explained in the first chapter. Psychoanalytic theory suggests that mental health problems arise from deep conflicts, and thus Internet use is a symptom, not the problem.

"What's the matter, sweetie? You haven't touched your food or your phone."

Why? For teenagers, it is more unusual to forgo texting than to forgo eating. Why is that?

By contrast, behaviorism contends that behavior itself may be the problem. In that case, directly stopping Internet overuse—charging smartphones overnight in the kitchen starting at 9 P.M., keeping the laptop in the living room—and substituting other behavior (maybe reading a book before lights-out) would not only stop Internet addiction but might also mitigate any related mental health problems.

Finally, evolutionary theory focuses on enduring needs, in this case the need for adolescents to connect with each other. Decades ago, adults worried about the automobile, and later the shopping mall, as places where teenagers would associate with each other without adult supervision and get into trouble. Now the Internet is seen as the culprit, when really the problem is adult misperception (boyd, 2014).

A question that attracts the most heated dispute is not whether adolescents overuse technology but whether the electromagnetic radiation from such devices is harmful to health. Some researchers suggest that even low levels of such radiation may harm the brain and body (Sage & Burgio, 2018).

Others not only disagree but add that it is harmful to suggest such an unproven possibility (Grimes & Bishop, 2018). Both sides agree that more scientific research in needed.

Researchers are far from consensus about adolescents and technology. We do know that times have changed and that research from only a decade ago is no longer valid. Determining exactly what are the best and worst features of technology for youth requires many researchers to consider the issue, and they are far from agreement.

High School

Many of the patterns and problems of middle school continue in high school, although once maturation reduces the sudden growth and unfamiliar sexual impulses of puberty, adolescents are better able to cope with school. They become increasingly able to think abstractly, analytically, hypothetically, and logically (all formal operational thought), as well as subjectively, emotionally, intuitively, and experientially.

THE COLLEGE-BOUND From a developmental perspective, the fact that high schools emphasize formal thinking makes sense, since many older adolescents are capable of abstract logic. In several nations, attempts are under way to raise standards so that all high school graduates will be ready for college, where analysis is required.

A mantra in the United States is "college for all," intended to encourage low achievers to aspire for tertiary education, although some authors believe the effect may be the opposite (Carlson, 2016). One result of the emphasis on college is that more students take classes that are assessed by externally scored exams, either the IB (*International Baccalaureate*) or the AP (*Advanced Placement*) tests. High scores allow students to bypass some college requirements.

◆ **Especially for High School Teachers**
You are much more interested in the nuances and controversies than in the basic facts of your subject, but you know that your students will take high-stakes tests on the basics and that their scores will have a major impact on their futures. What should you do? (see response, page 346)

Same Situation, Far Apart: How to Learn Although developmental psychologists find that adolescents learn best when they are actively engaged with ideas, most teenagers are easier to control when they are taking tests (*left,* Winston-Salem, North Carolina, United States) or reciting scripture (*right,* Kabul, Afghanistan).

WILL & DENI McINTYRE/CORBIS

MELANIE STETSON FREEMAN/THE CHRISTIAN SCIENCE MONITOR/GETTY IMAGES

In 2016, AP classes were taken by about one-third of all high school graduates, compared to less than one-fifth (19 percent) in 2003. The increase was particularly notable among low-income students, because the cost of taking the exam ($53) was subsidized by the federal government (students still paid part of the fee). The College Board reports that, in recent years, even though more students are taking the exam (1.1 million in 2016), the proportion who pass remains about 65 percent (Zubrzycki, 2017).

Other indicators of increasing standards are requirements for an academic diploma and restrictions on vocational or general diplomas. Most U.S. schools require two years of math beyond algebra, two years of laboratory science, three years of history, four years of English, and two years of a language other than English.

In addition to mandated courses, 74 percent of U.S. public high school students are required to pass a **high-stakes test** in order to graduate. (Any exam for which the consequences of failing are severe is called "high-stakes.") A decade ago, no state required exit exams. Increased testing is evident in every state, but it is controversial.

Overall, high school graduation rates in the United States have increased every year for the past decade, reaching 83.2 percent in 2016 after four years in high school (see Figure 9.6). A careful analysis finds that those increases represent real improvement (Gewertz, 2017).

It is possible that standards have risen and that challenge results in better performance. Others contend that the high-stakes tests discourage some students while making graduation too easy for others who are adept at test-taking (Hyslop, 2014).

Ironically, in the same decade during which U.S. schools are raising requirements, many East Asian nations, including China, Singapore, and Japan (all with high scores on international tests), have moved in the opposite direction. Particularly in Singapore, national high-stakes tests are being phased out, and local autonomy is increasing (Hargreaves, 2012).

International data support both sides of this controversy. One nation whose children generally score well is South Korea, where high-stakes tests have resulted in extensive studying. Many South Korean parents hire tutors to teach their children after school and on weekends to improve their test scores (Lee & Shouse, 2011).

Almost all Korean students graduate from high school and attend college—but that accomplishment is not valued by many Korean educators, including Seongho Lee, a professor of education in South Korea. He says that "oversupply in college

high-stakes test
An evaluation that is critical in determining success or failure. If a single test determines whether a student will graduate or be promoted, it is a high-stakes test.

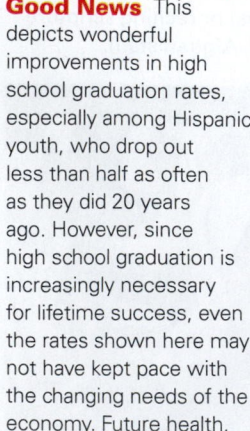

FIGURE 9.6 Mostly Good News This depicts wonderful improvements in high school graduation rates, especially among Hispanic youth, who drop out less than half as often as they did 20 years ago. However, since high school graduation is increasingly necessary for lifetime success, even the rates shown here may not have kept pace with the changing needs of the economy. Future health, income, and happiness may be in jeopardy for anyone who drops out.

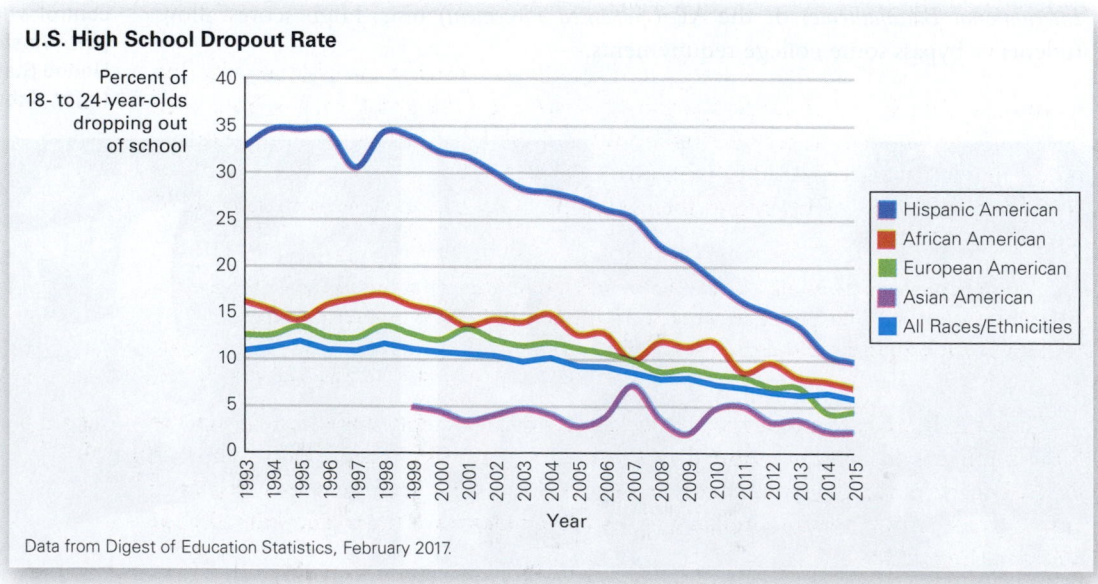

U.S. High School Dropout Rate

Percent of 18- to 24-year-olds dropping out of school

Hispanic American
African American
European American
Asian American
All Races/Ethnicities

Year

Data from Digest of Education Statistics, February 2017.

education is a very serious social problem" creating an "army of the unemployed" (quoted in Fischer, 2016, p. A25).

ALTERNATIVES TO COLLEGE In the United States, a sizable minority (about a third) of high school graduates do not enter college. Some have high test scores; they do not enroll even though they could succeed at a four-year college.

Variation is evident by state and city. When tallied by those who go directly from high school to college, the range is from 44 percent (Alaska) to 73 percent (Massachusetts) (Bransberger & Michelau, 2016). Data from two major cities in neighboring states (Albuquerque, New Mexico, and Fort Worth, Texas) had markedly different college enrollment rates (83 percent compared to 58 percent) (Center for Education Policy, 2012).

Most (about three-fourths) of those who enter public community colleges do not complete their associate's degree within three years, and almost half of those entering public or private four-year schools do not graduate. Some simply take longer or enter the job market first, but even 10 years after the usual age for high school graduation, only 37 percent of U.S. young adults have earned a bachelor's degree (Kena et al., 2016).

These sobering statistics suggest that many students should not go to college. If adolescents fail academic classes, will they feel bored, incapable, and disengaged? If students earn a high school diploma, go to college, and then drop out, wouldn't they be better off if they had entered the job market directly?

Business leaders have another concern—that high school graduates are unprepared for jobs because their education is abstract and irrelevant, with low standards for writing and analyzing. Some worry that the emphasis on test scores reduces learning through discussion, emotional maturation, and real-world experience.

Internationally, high school vocational education that explicitly prepares students for jobs via a combination of academic classes and practical experience seems to succeed better than a general curriculum (Eichhorst et al., 2012).

The data present a dilemma. Suggesting that a student should *not* go to college may be racist, classist, sexist, or worse. On the other hand, if students begin college but do not graduate, they lose time and gain debt when they could have advanced in a vocation. Everyone agrees that adolescents need to be educated for life as well as for employment, but it is difficult to decide what that means.

SAN DIEGO UNION-TRIBUNE/ZUMAPRESS/NEWSCOM

What Do They Need to Learn? Here, Jesse Olascoaga and José Perez assemble a desk as part of a class in Trade Tech High School in Vista, California. Are they mastering skills that will lead to a good job? Much depends on what else they are learning. It may be collaboration and pride in work done well, in which case this is useful education.

THINK CRITICALLY: Is it more important to prepare high school students for jobs or for college?

MEASURING PRACTICAL COGNITION Employers usually provide on-the-job training, which is much more specific and current than what high schools can provide. They hope their future employees will have learned how to think, explain, write, concentrate, and get along with other people.

As one executive of Boeing (which hired 33,000 new employees in two years) wrote:

> We believe that professional success today and in the future is more likely for those who have practical experience, work well with others, build strong relationships, and are able to think and do, not just look things up on the Internet.
>
> *[Stephens & Richey, 2013, p. 314]*

Those skills are hard to measure, especially on national high-stakes tests or on the three international tests mentioned in Chapter 7, the PIRLS, the TIMSS, and the PISA. Fourth-grade scores on the first two of these were presented in Chapter 7; eighth-grade assessments are similar, with East Asian nations at the top and the United States in the middle.

Programme for International Student Assessment (PISA) An international test taken by 15-year-olds in 50 nations that is designed to measure problem solving and cognition in daily life.

Now we look more closely at the third international test, the **Programme for International Student Assessment (PISA),** which was designed to measure students' ability to apply what they have learned. The PISA is taken at age 15, when students are close to the end of their secondary school career. The questions are supposed to be practical, measuring knowledge that might apply at home or on the job. As a PISA report described it:

> The tests are designed to generate measures of the extent to which students can make effective use of what they have learned in school to deal with various problems and challenges they are likely to experience in everyday life.
>
> *[PISA, 2009, p. 13]*

For example, among the 2012 math questions is this one:

> Chris has just received her car driving license and wants to buy her first car. The table below shows the details of four cars she finds at a local car dealer. What car's engine capacity is the smallest?

A. Alpha   B. Bolte   C. Castel   D. Dezal

Model	Alpha	Bolte	Castel	Dezal
Year	2003	2000	2001	1999
Advertised price (zeds)	4800	4450	4250	3990
Distance travelled (kilometers)	105 000	115 000	128 000	109 000
Engine capacity (liters)	1.79	1.796	1.82	1.783

For that and the other PISA questions, calculations are quite simple—most 10-year-olds can do them. However, almost half of the 15-year-olds worldwide got that question wrong. (The answer is D.) One problem is decimals: Some students do not remember how to interpret them when a practical question, not an academic one, is asked. Even in Singapore and Hong Kong, one out of five 15-year-olds got this question wrong.

Overall, the U.S. students score lower on the PISA compared to many other nations, including Canada, the nation most similar to the United States in ethnicity and location. Compared to peers in other nations, the 2012 results rank the U.S. 15-year-olds 36th in math, 28th in science, and 24th in reading—all lower than in 2009, when the U.S. scores were 31st, 23rd, and 17th, respectively.

Some 2012 results were not surprising (China, Japan, Korea, and Singapore were all high), but some were unexpected (high scores for Finland, Poland, and Estonia). The lowest results were for Peru, Indonesia, and Qatar. The results reflect the educational systems, not geography, since low-scoring Indonesia is close to Singapore.

International analysis finds that the following items correlate with high achievement of high school students on the PISA (OECD, 2010, p. 6):

- Leaders, parents, and citizens value education overall, with individualized approaches to learning so that all students learn what they need.

- Standards are high and clear, so every student knows what he or she must do, with a "focus on the acquisition of complex, higher-order thinking skills."

- Teachers and administrators are valued, and they are given "considerable discretion . . . in determining content" and sufficient salary as well as time for collaboration.

- Learning is prioritized "across the entire system," with high-quality teachers assigned to the most challenging schools.

The PISA and international comparisons of high school dropout rates suggest that U.S. secondary education can be improved, especially for those who do not go to college.

Now let us return to general conclusions for this chapter. Bodies grow according to insistent biological timetables, but the significance of puberty is strongly affected by the reactions of other people and the cultural context.

The cognitive skills that boost national economic development and personal happiness are creativity, flexibility, relationship building, and analytic ability. Whether or not an adolescent is college-bound, those skills are exactly what the adolescent mind can develop—with proper education and guidance. Every cognitive theorist and researcher believes that adolescents' logical, social, and creative potential is not always realized, but it can be. Does that belief end this chapter on a hopeful note?

what have you learned?

1. Why have most junior high schools disappeared?

2. What characteristics of middle schools make them more difficult for students than elementary schools?

3. What are the advantages and disadvantages of high-stakes testing?

4. Should high schools prepare everyone for college? Why or why not?

5. How does the PISA differ from other international tests?

SUMMARY

Puberty Begins

1. Puberty refers to the various changes that transform a child's body into an adult one. Biochemical signals are sent from the hypothalamus to the pituitary gland to the adrenal glands to the gonads, increasing hormones that cause rapid growth and sexual maturation. Some emotional reactions, such as quick mood shifts, both cause and result from the hormones of puberty.

2. The brain also grows rapidly but unevenly. The limbic system increases first, causing strong emotional reactions; the prefrontal cortex does not reach full maturation until the mid-20s.

3. Puberty normally starts between ages 8 and 14. Girls generally begin and end puberty before boys do, although the time gap in sexual maturity is less than the two-year gap in height. Body fat, genes, and stress all affect the onset of puberty.

Growth, Nutrition, and Sex

4. Peak weight usually precedes peak height, which is then followed by muscle growth. This sequence makes adolescents particularly vulnerable to sports injuries, as well as to poor body image.

5. Adolescents are vulnerable to nutritional deficiencies, particularly of calcium and iron, and to eating disorders—anorexia, bulimia, and binge eating. These are problems worldwide, with culture as well as biology influencing specifics.

6. Primary sex characteristics allow reproduction, which becomes increasingly possible in the years after puberty. Secondary sex characteristics are not directly involved in reproduction but signify that the child is becoming a man or a woman. Sexual activity is influenced more by culture than by physiology.

7. In the twenty-first century, hormones and nutrition cause earlier puberty, but teen pregnancy is far less common, condom use has increased, and the average age of first intercourse has risen. STIs are more common and dangerous among sexually active youth.

8. Sexual abuse is more likely to occur in early adolescence than at other ages. In the United States, the perpetrators are often known to the family. Worldwide, globalization has probably increased international sex trafficking.

9. Untreated STIs at any age can lead to infertility and even death. Rates among sexually active teenagers are rising for many reasons, with HIV/AIDS not yet halted.

Cognitive Development

10. Cognition in early adolescence may be egocentric, a kind of self-centered thinking. Adolescent egocentrism gives rise to the personal fable, the invincibility fable, and the imaginary audience.

11. In formal operational thought, Piaget explained that adolescents are no longer concrete in their thinking; they imagine the possible, the probable, and even the impossible. They develop hypotheses and explore, using deductive reasoning.

12. Many cognitive theories describe two types of thinking during adolescence. One set of names for these two types is intuitive and analytic. Both become more forceful during adolescence, but brain development means that intuitive, emotional thinking matures before analytic, logical thought.

Secondary Education

13. Achievement in secondary education—after primary education (grade school) and before tertiary education (college)—correlates with the health and wealth of individuals and nations.

14. In middle school, many students struggle both socially and academically. One reason may be that middle schools are not structured to accommodate egocentrism or intuitive thinking.

15. Education in high school emphasizes formal operational thought. In the United States, the demand for more accountability

has led to an increase in high-stakes testing and in requirements for graduation.

16. High school graduation rates have increased, but about one-third of high school students do not go on to college. About half of those who go to college leave without a degree.

17. Students who go directly to the job market are not as well served by U.S. education as are such students in some other nations. This is apparent in the PISA, a test taken by many 15-year-olds in 50 nations that measures how well students can apply their knowledge.

KEY TERMS

puberty (p. 311)
menarche (p. 312)
spermarche (p. 312)
leptin (p. 318)
growth spurt (p. 319)
body image (p. 320)
anorexia nervosa (p. 322)
bulimia nervosa (p. 322)
binge eating disorder (p. 322)

primary sex characteristics (p. 322)
secondary sex characteristics (p. 324)
sexually transmitted infections (STIs) (p. 326)
child sexual abuse (p. 327)
adolescent egocentrism (p. 328)
imaginary audience (p. 328)

personal fable (p. 329)
invincibility fable (p. 329)
formal operational thought (p. 329)
hypothetical thought (p. 331)
deductive reasoning (p. 331)
inductive reasoning (p. 331)
dual processing (p. 332)
intuitive thought (p. 332)

analytic thought (p. 332)
secondary education (p. 336)
middle school (p. 336)
cyberbullying (p. 340)
sexting (p. 340)
high-stakes test (p. 342)
Programme for International Student Assessment (PISA) (p. 344)

APPLICATIONS

1. Visit a fifth-, sixth-, or seventh-grade class. Note variations in the size and maturity of the students. Do you see any patterns related to gender, ethnicity, body fat, or self-confidence?

2. Interview several of your friends about their memories of menarche or spermarche, including how others reacted. Are cohort or cultural differences evident? Do their comments indicate that these events are emotionally troubling?

3. Talk to a teenager about politics, families, school, religion, or any other topic that might reveal the way he or she thinks. Do you hear any adolescent egocentrism? Intuitive thinking? Systematic thought? Flexibility? Cite examples.

4. Describe what happened and what you thought in the first year you attended a middle school or a high school. What made it better or worse than later years in that school?

ESPECIALLY FOR ANSWERS

Response for Health Practitioners (from page 313): Many adolescents are intensely concerned about privacy and fearful of adult interference. This means that your first task is to convince adolescents that you are nonjudgmental and that everything is confidential.

Response for Parents Worried About Early Puberty (from page 318): Probably not. If she is overweight, her diet should change, but the hormone hypothesis is speculative. Genes are the main factor; she shares only one-eighth of her genes with her cousin.

Response for Parents Worried About Their Teenager's Risk-Taking (from page 326): You are right to be concerned, but you cannot keep your child locked up for the next decade or so. Since you know that some rebellion and irrationality are likely, try to minimize them by not boasting about your own youthful exploits, by reacting sternly to minor infractions to nip worse behavior in the bud, and by making allies of your child's teachers and the parents of your child's friends.

Response for Natural Scientists (from page 331): Probably both. Our false assumptions are not logically tested because we do not realize that they might need testing.

Response for Teachers (from page 337): Praise the student by saying, "What a great question!" Egos are fragile, so it's best to always validate the question. Seek student engagement, perhaps by asking whether any classmates know the answer or telling the student to discover the answer online or saying you will find out. Whatever you do, don't fake it; if students lose faith in your credibility, you may lose them completely.

Response for High School Teachers (from page 341): It would be nice to follow your instincts, but the appropriate response depends partly on pressures within the school and on the expectations of the parents and administration. A comforting fact is that adolescents can think about and learn almost anything if they feel a personal connection to it. Look for ways to teach the facts your students need for the tests as the foundation for the exciting and innovative topics you want to teach. Everyone will learn more, and the tests will be less intimidating to your students.

OBSERVATION QUIZ ANSWERS

Answer to Observation Quiz (from page 314): Girls tend to spend more time studying, talking to friends, and getting ready in the morning. Other data show that many girls get less than seven hours of sleep per night.

Answer to Observation Quiz (from page 318): Look at their legs. The shortest is standing tall; the tallest is bending her knees.

Answer to Observation Quiz (from page 333): The flag on the robot matches her T-shirt. Often teenagers wear matching shirts to signify their joint identity.

Answer to Observation Quiz (from page 338): Both are single-sex. What does that teach these students?

ADOLESCENCE
Psychosocial Development

what will you know?

- Why might a teenager be into sports one year and into books the next?
- Should parents back off when their teenager disputes every rule, wish, or suggestion they make?
- Should we worry more about teen suicide or juvenile delinquency?
- Why are adolescents forbidden to drink and smoke, but adults can do so?

It's not easy being a teenager, as the previous chapter makes clear, but neither is it easy being the parent of one.

Sometimes I was too lenient. Once my daughter came home late. I was worried and angry but did not think about punishing her until she asked, "How long am I grounded?"

And sometimes I was too strict. For years, I insisted that my children wash the dinner dishes—until they told me, again and again, that none of their friends had such mean mothers.

At times, I reacted emotionally, not rationally. When our children were infants, my husband and I decided how we would deal with adolescent problems. We were ready to be firm, united, and consistent regarding illicit drugs, unsafe sex, and serious lawbreaking. More than a decade later, none of those issues appeared.

Instead, our children's clothes, neatness, and homework made us troubled, bewildered, inconsistent. My husband said, "I knew they would become adolescents. I didn't know we would become parents of adolescents."

This chapter is about adolescents' psychosocial development, including relationships with friends, parents, and the larger society. It begins with identity and ends with drugs, both of which may seem to be a personal choice but actually are strongly affected by social norms. I now understand that my children's actions and my reactions were influenced by my history (I washed family dishes) and by current norms (their friends did not).

Identity

Psychosocial development during adolescence is often understood as a search for a consistent understanding of oneself. Self-expression and self-concept become increasingly important at puberty. Each young person wants to know, "Who am I?"

According to Erik Erikson, life's fifth psychosocial crisis is **identity versus role confusion:** Working through the complexities of finding one's own identity is the primary task of adolescence (Erikson, 1968/1994). This crisis is resolved with **identity achievement,** when adolescents have reconsidered the goals and values of their parents and culture. They accept some and discard others, forging their own identity.

The result is neither wholesale rejection nor unquestioning acceptance of social norms. With their new autonomy, teenagers maintain continuity with the past so that they can move to the future, establishing their own identity. Simply following parental footsteps does not work, because the social context of each generation differs.

No Role Confusion These are high school students in Junior ROTC training camp. For many youths who cannot afford college, the military offers a temporary identity, complete with haircut, uniform, and comrades.

Not Yet Achieved

Over the past half-century, major psychosocial shifts have lengthened the duration of adolescence and made identity achievement more complex (Côté & Levine, 2015). How adolescents go about their search for identity also varies, depending on genes and the social context as well as whether their family encourages discussion (Markovitch et al., 2017).

Nonetheless, Erikson's insights have inspired thousands of developmentalists. Notable among those is James Marcia. He described and measured four ways in which young people cope with the identity crisis: (1) role confusion, (2) foreclosure, (3) moratorium, and finally (4) achievement (Marcia, 1966; Kroger & Marcia, 2011).

Role confusion is the opposite of achievement. It is characterized by lack of commitment to any goals or values. Erikson originally called this *identity diffusion* to emphasize that some adolescents seem diffuse, unfocused, and unconcerned about their future. Perhaps worse, adolescents in role confusion see no goals or purpose in their life, and thus they flounder, unable to move forward (Hill et al., 2013).

Identity **foreclosure** occurs when, in order to avoid the confusion of sorting through all the nuances of who they are and what they believe, young people lump traditional roles and values together, to be swallowed whole or rejected totally. They might follow every custom from their parents or their culture, never exploring alternatives.

Some do the opposite, foreclosing on an oppositional, *negative identity*—rejecting all of their elders' values and routines, again without thoughtful questioning. Foreclosure is comfortable but limiting. It is only a temporary shelter (Meeus, 2011).

A more mature shelter is **moratorium,** a time-out that includes exploration, either in breadth (trying many things) or in depth (following one path but with only tentative commitment). Moratoria usually occur after age 18, so they are discussed in the next chapter. Although the identity quest begins at puberty and is urgent throughout adolescence, it continues in adulthood (Fadjukoff & Kroger, 2016).

A recent study of almost 8,000 Belgian 14- to 30-year-olds confirms that most young adolescents are still uncertain and confused about their identity. With maturation, people are more likely to reach identity achievement (Verschueren et al., 2017).

identity versus role confusion
Erikson's term for the fifth stage of development, in which the person tries to figure out "Who am I?" but is confused as to which of many possible roles to adopt.

identity achievement
Erikson's term for the attainment of identity, or the point at which a person understands who he or she is as a unique individual, in accord with past experiences and future plans.

role confusion
A situation in which an adolescent does not seem to know or care what his or her identity is. (Sometimes called *identity diffusion* or *role diffusion*.)

foreclosure
Erikson's term for premature identity formation, which occurs when an adolescent adopts his or her parents' or society's roles and values wholesale, without questioning or analysis.

moratorium
An adolescent's choice of a socially acceptable way to postpone making identity-achievement decisions. Going to college is a common example.

SARA CALDWELL/STAFF/THE AUGUSTA CHRONICLE/ZUMAPRESS.COM/ALAMY

Four Arenas of Identity Formation

Erikson (1968/1994) highlighted four aspects of identity: religious, political, vocational, and sexual. Terminology and timing have changed, yet the crucial question remains: Does the person ponder the possibilities and actively seek to discover who he or she is?

RELIGIOUS IDENTITY Most adolescents question some aspects of their faith, but their *religious identity* is similar to that of their parents. Few reject their religion if they have been raised in it, especially if they have a good relationship with their parents (Kim-Spoon et al., 2012).

They may express their religious identity more devoutly. A Muslim girl might start to wear a headscarf, a Catholic boy might study for the priesthood, or a Baptist teenager might join a Pentecostal youth group, all surprising their parents. The more common pattern is in the opposite direction: Although adolescents identify with the religion of their childhood, often their attendance at places of worship gradually decreases (Lopez et al., 2011).

Although becoming more or less devout is common, major shifts in religious identity are rare. Almost no adolescent Muslims convert to Judaism, and almost no teenage Baptists become Hindu.

POLITICAL IDENTITY Parents also influence their children's *political identity*. In the twenty-first century in the United States, more adults identify as nonpartisan than as Republican, Democrat, or any other party. Their teenage children reflect their lack of party affiliation, perhaps boasting that they do not care about politics, echoing the parents without realizing it.

Others proudly vote for the first time at age 18—an event that is much more likely if they are living at home and their parents are voting than if they have already left home. Just like other aspects of political involvement, voting is a social activity, not an isolated, individual one (Hart & van Goethem, 2017).

In general, adolescents' interest in politics is predicted by their parents' involvement and by current events, as found in other aspects of identity formation (Stattin et al., 2017). Adolescents tend to be more liberal than their elders, especially on social issues (LGBTQ rights, reproduction, the environment, etc.), but major political shifts do not usually occur until later (P. Taylor, 2014). As adolescents, many current political leaders espoused views and were members of political parties that they abandoned by age 30.

ETHNIC IDENTITY Related to political identity is *ethnic identity*, a topic not discussed by Erikson. In the United States and Canada, about half of all current adolescents are of African, Asian, Latino, or Native American (Aboriginal in Canada) heritage. Many of them also have ancestors of another ethnic group. Those census categories are too broad; teenagers must forge a personal ethnic identity that is more specific.

Hispanic youth, for instance, must figure out how having grandparents from Mexico, Peru, or Cuba, and/or California, Texas, or New York, affects them. Many Latinos (some identifying as *Chicano*) also have ancestors from Spain, Africa, Germany, and/or indigenous groups such as the Maya or Inca.

Same Situation, Far Apart: Religious Identity Awesome devotion is characteristic of adolescents, whether devotion is to a sport, a person, a music group, or—as shown here—a religion. This boy *(left)* praying on a Kosovo street is part of a dangerous protest against the town's refusal to allow building another mosque. This girl *(right)* is at a stadium rally for young Christians in Michigan, declaring her faith for all to see. While adults see differences between the two religions, both teens share not only piety but also twenty-first-century clothing. Her T-shirt is a recent innovation, and on his jersey is Messi 10, for a soccer star born in Argentina.

THINK CRITICALLY: Since identity is formed lifelong, is your current identity different from what it was five years ago?

VIDEO ACTIVITY: Adolescence Around the World: Rites of Passage presents a comparison of adolescent initiation customs in industrialized and developing societies.

Similarly, those who are European American must decide the significance of having grandparents from, say, Italy, Ireland, or Sweden. No teenager adopts, wholesale, their ancestors' identity, but all reflect, somehow, their family's history.

Exactly how does a young person go about establishing an ethnic identity? Many influences affect the process, including knowledge of history (both family and group), and comments from friends (both from those of the same background and those of other backgrounds). If a high school student self-identifies as one ethnicity but others consider them another ethnicity, that correlates with depression and low self-esteem (Nishina et al., 2018). No wonder some wear certain colors, jewelry, and so on that broadcast ethnicity.

The process is often depicted in stages, from disagreeing with any ethnic identity ("I'm part of the human race; we are all the same") to insistence on specific connections ("your people enslaved my people") to final achievement ("I know my history, and I am proud to be who I am"). As with other aspects of identity, adolescents may fluctuate from one response to another.

A sign that overall identity as well as ethnic identity is more advanced is when adolescents report that ethnic identity has "relevance and consequence in their daily lives" (Yip, 2014, p. 218). In that case, ethnicity is an important source of pride.

On the other hand, when ethnic identity and self-concept are unclear to a person, that signifies psychological risk (Cicero & Cohn, 2018). In general, pride in ethnic identity correlates with academic achievement and overall well-being, but the relationship is "complex and nuanced" (Miller-Cotto & Byrnes, 2016).

VOCATIONAL IDENTITY *Vocational identity* originally meant envisioning oneself as a worker in a particular occupation. Choosing a vocation made sense a century ago, when most girls became housewives and most boys became farmers, small businessmen, or factory workers. Those few in professions were mostly generalists (doctors did family medicine, lawyers handled all kinds of cases, teachers taught all subjects).

No longer. No teenager can realistically choose among the tens of thousands of careers. The large Belgian study already referenced found that teenagers who choose employment rather than higher education are in foreclosure: Later they may be dissatisfied with their jobs. They may go back to school or seek a new vocation.

The typical young adult does not follow one vocational identity but instead changes jobs every year, a quest that may begin in adolescence but does not end there. They search for meaningful and satisfying work (Chao & Gardner, 2017).

It is a myth that having a job will keep teenagers out of trouble and establish vocational identity (Staff & Schulenberg, 2010). Sometimes work that is steady and not too time-consuming may be beneficial, but not usually. Adolescents who are employed more than 20 hours a week during the school year tend to quit school, fight with parents, smoke cigarettes, and hate their jobs—not only when they are teenagers but also later on (Osilla et al., 2015; Mortimer, 2010).

Typically, employed teenagers spend their wages on clothes, cars, drugs, fast food, and loud music, not on what some adults think they do (supporting their families or saving for college). Grades fall: Employment interferes with schoolwork and attendance, not only for U.S. high school students but in other nations, too (Lee et al., 2016; Mortimer, 2013).

Balancing work and home life is problematic throughout adulthood, and it is discussed in Chapter 13. Most adolescents are unbalanced: Those who work more than a few hours a week are less likely to graduate from high school and go to college.

There are exceptions. Especially for low-income adolescents from ethnic-minority families, employment during high school correlates with college enrollment (Hwang & Domina, 2017). That might be because they do not want to be stuck in a boring job.

THINK CRITICALLY: Why do African American teens more often benefit from employment than European Americans? Correlation? Cause? Or third variable?

GENDER IDENTITY The fourth type of identity described by Erikson is *sexual identity*. As you remember from Chapter 6, *sex* and *sexual* refer to biology, whereas *gender* refers to cultural and social attributes that differentiate males and females.

A half-century ago, Erikson and other theorists thought of the two sexes as opposites (Miller & Simon, 1980). They assumed that adolescents who were confused about sexual identity would soon adopt "proper" male or female roles (Erikson, 1968/1994; A. Freud, 1958/2000).

Thus, adolescence was once a time for "gender intensification," when people increasingly identified as male or female. No longer (Priess et al., 2009). Erikson's term *sexual identity* has been replaced by **gender identity,** which refers primarily to a person's self-definition as male, female, or other gender.

Sisters and Brothers Gender equality has become important to both sexes, as evidenced by the thousands of men who joined the Women's March on January 21, 2017—the day after President Trump's inauguration. This photo was taken in Washington, D.C., where more than half a million gathered.

Gender identity often (but not always) begins with the person's biological sex and leads to a gender role, but many adolescents use their analytic, hypothetical thinking to question traditional gender roles and expression. This may trouble their elders, who grew up with more traditional expectations. One mother thought she was helpful in suggesting that her daughter's skirt was too tight and short. Her angry daughter retorted, "Stop slut-shaming me."

Gender roles once meant that only men were employed; they were *breadwinners* (good providers) and women were *housewives* (married to their houses). As women entered the labor market, gender roles were evident (nurse/doctor, secretary/businessman, pink collar/blue collar).

Even today, women in every nation do far more child care and elder care than men. As one social scientist explains, there is a "slow but steady pace of change in gender divisions of domestic labor . . . combined with a persistence of gender differences and inequalities" (Doucet, 2015, p. 224). She considers gender disparities cultural; others disagree.

The speed and specifics of changing gender roles vary dramatically by culture and cohort. A new term, *cisgender,* refers to people whose gender identity is the same as their natal sex, but the fact that such a term exists is evidence of the complexity of gender identity. Fluidity and uncertainty regarding sex and gender are especially common during early adolescence, when hormones increase and fluctuate. That adds to the difficulty of self-acceptance. Complications multiply for those who identify as gay, lesbian, transgender, or other (Reisner et al., 2016).

Among Western psychiatrists in former decades, people who had "a strong and persistent cross-gender identification" were said to have *gender identity disorder,* a serious diagnosis according to DSM-IV. However, the DSM-5 instead describes *gender dysphoria,* when people are distressed at their biological gender.

This is more than a change in terminology. A "disorder" means something is amiss with the individual, no matter how he or she feels about it, whereas "dysphoria" means the problem is in the distress, which can be mitigated by social conditions, by cognitive framing, or by becoming the other gender (Zucker et al., 2013). As with all aspects of the identity crisis, self-definition and then acceptance is the psychosocial need.

gender identity
A person's self-perception as male, female, both, or neither.

KYODO NEWS/GETTY IMAGES

Although terms and society have changed, what has not changed is human biology: Hormones increase, independence is sought, and sexual drives are strong. As Erikson recognized, many adolescents are confused regarding when they need their parents' help and when they should be independent, and when, how, and with whom to express sexual drives.

Some foreclose by exaggerating male or female styles of dress and manner; others seek a moratorium, telling others via their clothes and mannerisms that they are not interested in sex or gender. Some deliberately disagree with whatever their parents advise.

Some who question their gender identity may aspire to a gender-stereotypic career (Sinclair & Carlsson, 2013). Choosing a career to establish gender identity, rather than to use skills, follow interests, and affirm values, is another reason why settling on a vocational identity during adolescence may be premature.

what have you learned?

1. What is Erikson's fifth psychosocial crisis, and how is it resolved?

2. How does identity foreclosure differ from identity moratorium?

3. What has changed over the past decades regarding political identity?

4. What role do parents play in adolescent religious and political identity?

5. Why is it premature for today's adolescents to achieve vocational identity?

6. What assumptions about gender identity did most adults hold 50 years ago?

7. What is the difference between gender identity disorder and gender dysphoria?

Close Relationships

The focus on adolescent identity may make it seem as if teenagers are intensely individualized, unaffected by the social situation in which they live. However, the opposite is more accurate. Parents, peers, teachers, and cultures shape adolescent lives.

Parents

Caregiver–adolescent relationships affect identity, expectations, and daily life. Parents may shift from providing direct guidance to being available, but close parent–child relationships continue (E. Chen et al., 2017). Peers do not replace parents.

FAMILY CONFLICT The fact that families are still important does not mean that family life is peaceful when an adolescent is in the house (Laursen & Collins, 2009). Disputes are common because biology, cognition, and culture all push for adolescent independence, which clashes with adults' desire for control and protection.

Normally, conflict peaks in early adolescence, especially between mothers and daughters. Usually this is not fighting but instead it is *bickering*—repeated, petty arguments (more nagging than fighting) about routine, day-to-day concerns such as cleanliness, clothes, chores, and schedules.

Each generation tends to misjudge the other, and that increases conflict. Adolescents want and need respect from adults, and they are quick to see disrespect, even if it is not really there. Adults need to stop lecturing (not "I'll ground you if I catch

A VIEW FROM SCIENCE

Teenagers, Genes, and Parents

A major challenge for developmentalists is to combine direct and practical programs that benefit adolescents with laboratory analysis of molecular genetics. Genes affect every behavior.

This is obvious in childhood. Some children are much more worried about the consequences of breaking rules than others. My kindergarten grandson refused to carry his backpack to school when he heard on the public-address system that the police have the right to check backpacks. [His parents finally convinced him that he would not be targeted.]

By contrast, his 3-year-old brother enjoys acting in ways that are contrary to adult rules. I told him it was cold outside, but he did not let me put his coat on him. He defiantly sat in his stroller—no hat, coat, or mittens.

It is not surprising that the two boys differ. As you read in Chapter 6, parents may need to modify authoritative, authoritarian, or permissive style in response to their child's temperament. This is as true in adolescence as in early childhood.

Thus, we need to understand the relationship between nature and nurture, avoiding the danger of blaming all teenage rebellion on the child, or on the parents, or on society. A leading researcher, Gene Brody, warns of overreliance on genetic analysis, even as he lauds the use of genetic research (Brody, 2017).

Brody's lifelong work is to help African American boys in rural Georgia, a "resource poor" social context that sometimes makes it difficult for Black children to succeed. He developed a program for parents and their sons.

In one of his studies, half of a group of 611 parents and 11-year-old sons had no special intervention: They were the control group. The other half were the experimental group, who participated in one of more than a dozen small groups, each of which was led by carefully chosen leaders who implemented a sequence of seven two-hour training sessions (Brody et al., 2009).

The leaders were energetic and creative as well as good role models: Most were African American men who had grown up in similar communities. Parents and sons were taught separately for an hour and then brought together. Teaching was active, with discussion and role-playing. (Brody had learned from earlier research by many other scientists that social interaction enhanced learning.)

The parents were taught the following:

- The importance of being nurturing and involved
- The importance of conveying pride in being African American
- How monitoring and control benefit adolescents
- Why clear norms and expectations reduce substance use
- Strategies for communication about sex

The 11-year-olds were taught the following:

- The importance of having household rules
- Adaptive behaviors when encountering racism
- The need for making plans for the future
- The differences between them and peers who use alcohol

After that first hour in each session, the parents and 11-year-olds were brought together. They engaged in games, structured interactions, and modeling designed to improve family communication and cohesion.

Three years after the intervention, both the experimental and comparison groups were reassessed regarding sex and alcohol/drug activity. The intervention decreased early sex, drinking, and smoking, but not by much. Apparently, any improvements in parent–son interaction were overwhelmed by social conditions.

Then, four years after the study began, research was published indicating that the short allele of the 5-HTTLPR gene heightened risks of depression, delinquency, and other problems. Might this apply to these African American boys?

Brody tracked down the sons from his original groups, who now were 16 years old. He convinced them to donate saliva to be analyzed for the 5-HTTLPR allele. As Figure 10.1

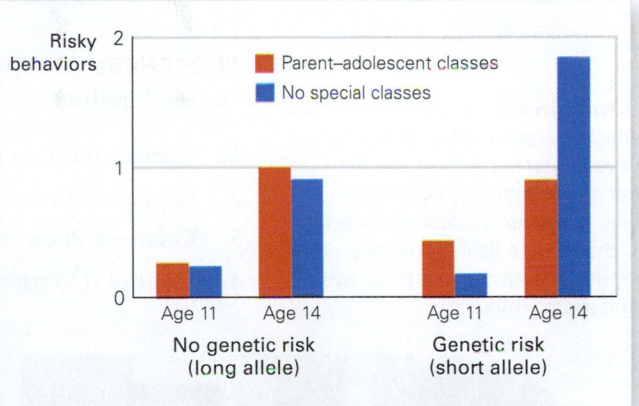

FIGURE 10.1 Not Yet The risk score was a simple one point for each of the following: had drunk alcohol, had smoked marijuana, had had sex. As shown, most of the 11-year-olds had done none of these. By age 14, most had done one (usually had drunk beer or wine)—except for those at genetic risk who did not have the seven-session training. Some of them had done all three, and many had done at least two. As you see, for those youths without genetic risk, the usual parenting was no better or worse than the parenting that benefited from the special classes: The average 14-year-old in either group had tried only one risky behavior. But for those at genetic risk, the special program made a decided difference.

shows, the training had a definitive effect on those who were genetically vulnerable. Four years later, blood analysis also showed that the intervention teens (now age 20) were less likely to smoke cigarettes (Y.-F. Chen et al., 2017).

How could parent–son training lasting 14 hours at most (some families skipped sessions) have an impact despite other influences of school and community? Apparently, since the parent–child relationship is crucial throughout adolescence,

those seven sessions provided insights and connections that affected each vulnerable pair from then on.

Differential susceptibility was apparent. In a follow-up study at age 19, the control group boys with the short 5-HTTLPR gene already had many indicators of poor health—physical and psychological (Brody et al., 2013). Nature and nurture work together, and parents make a difference.

---

you smoking," but "I am glad that you protect your lungs"). This is important advice not only for parents but also for every adult who seeks to influence teen behavior (Yeager et al., 2018).

Unspoken concerns need to be aired so that both generations better understand each other. Bickering begins with squabbling and nagging, but ideally it is replaced with understanding. This is not simple, especially for parents who think they know their child, because puberty awakens new thoughts, worries, and concerns (McLaren & Sillars, 2014).

Of course, close relationships often include conflict. The peace that results from neglect is as destructive in adolescence as it is earlier.

THINK CRITICALLY: When do parents forbid an activity they should approve of, or ignore a behavior that should alarm them?

Authors of research on mothers and their adolescents suggested that "although too much anger may be harmful . . . some expression of anger may be adaptive" (Hofer et al., 2013, p. 276). In this study, as well as generally, the parent–child relationship usually improved with time (Tighe et al., 2016; Tsai et al., 2013).

Crucial is that caregivers avoid extremes of strictness or leniency, instead maintaining support while adapting to increased autonomy. One review of dozens of studies found much variation but noted that "parent–adolescent conflict might signal the need for families to adapt and change . . . to accommodate adolescents' increasing needs for independence and egalitarianism" (Weymouth et al., 2016, p. 107).

CLOSENESS WITHIN THE FAMILY Several specific aspects of parent–child relationships have been studied, including:

1. Communication (Do family members talk openly and honestly?)
2. Support (Do they rely on each other?)
3. Connectedness (How emotionally close are family members?)
4. Control (Do parents undermine independence?)

A Study in Contrasts? These two teenagers appear to be opposites: one yelling at his mother and the other conscientiously helping his father. However, adolescent moods can change in a flash, especially with parents. Later in the day, these two might switch roles.

No social scientist doubts that the first two, communication and support, are crucial for healthy development. Patterns set in place during childhood continue, ideally buffering some of the turbulence of adolescence. Regarding the next two, connectedness and control, consequences vary and observers differ in what they see. How do you react to this example, written by one of my students?

> I got pregnant when I was sixteen years old, and if it weren't for the support of my parents, I would probably not have my son. And if they hadn't taken care of him, I wouldn't have been able to finish high school or attend college. My parents also helped me overcome the shame that I felt when . . . my aunts, uncles, and especially my grandparents found out that I was pregnant.
>
> *[I., personal communication]*

My student is grateful that she still lives with her parents, who provide most of the care for her son. However, did teenage motherhood give them too much control, preventing her from establishing her own identity? Had they unconsciously encouraged her dependence by neither chaperoning her time with her boyfriend nor explaining contraception?

I.'s parents are immigrants from South America, and culture may be a factor. Does this illustrate the best or the worst of **familism?** Should family members always protect each other, sometimes ignoring personal needs and outsiders to do so?

A related issue is **parental monitoring**—that is, parental knowledge about each child's whereabouts, activities, and companions. Many studies have shown that when parental knowledge is the result of a warm, supportive relationship, adolescents usually become confident, well-educated adults, avoiding drugs and risky sex. However, if the parents are cold, strict, and punitive, monitoring may lead to rebellion.

Thus, monitoring is not always a sign of good parenting. Much depends on the adolescent. A "dynamic interplay between parent and child behaviors" is evident: Teenagers choose what to reveal (Abar et al., 2014, p. 2177). They are more likely to drink alcohol and lie about it if their parents are controlling and cold (Lushin et al., 2017).

"So I blame you for everything—whose fault is that?"

BARBARA SMALLER/THE NEW YORKER COLLECTION/CARTOONBANK.COM

VIDEO: Parenting in Adolescence examines how family structure can help or hinder parent–teen relationships.

CULTURAL EXPECTATIONS FOR PARENTS OF TEENAGERS Several researchers have compared parent–child relationships in various cultures: Everywhere, parent–child communication and encouragement reduce teenage depression, suicide, and low self-esteem while increasing aspirations and achievements. However, expectations, interactions, and behavior vary by culture (Brown & Bakken, 2011).

Parent–child conflict is less evident in cultures that stress familism. Most refugee youth (Palestinian, Syrian, Iraqi, etc.) in Jordan agreed that parents have the right to decide their children's hairstyles, clothes, and music—contrary to what most U.S. teenagers believe (Smetana et al., 2016).

In many traditional cultures, teens do not let parents know about whatever they have done that might earn disapproval. By contrast, some U.S. adolescents might deliberately provoke an argument by advocating marijuana legalization, transgender inclusion, citizenship for immigrants, or abortion access, even if those policies would not affect them. The parents' challenge is to listen, not overreact.

Cultural variations in parent–child interaction are evident not only between nations but also within the United States and within ethnic groups. This is illustrated by a longitudinal study of Mexican American adolescents (Wheeler et al., 2017). Those who strongly endorse familism were less likely than those who were more

familism
The belief that family members should support one another, sacrificing individual freedom and success, if necessary, in order to preserve family unity and protect the family from outside forces.

parental monitoring
Parents' ongoing awareness of what their children are doing, where, and with whom.

Americanized to defy their parents. Instead, they behaved well—attending school, avoiding gangs, never carrying a weapon.

Within each family, as was evident in this study, adolescent development is dynamic. Over the years, devotion and respect between teens and their parents vary—as do adolescent risk-taking and whether the parents know what their children are doing. (A phone call from an arresting police officer may come as a shock to parents who thought their child was studying with a friend.)

Overall, when impulsive, fearful, or adventurous children are raised in a supportive family, they are *less* likely to do drugs or otherwise break the law than the average adolescent. If such a child is raised in a harsh family, all of those problems are *more* likely (Rioux et al., 2016).

The contrast is evident in academic achievement as well. A longitudinal study found that when parents are relatively harsh at puberty, fewer of their offspring complete high school and enroll in college. The particular adolescent actions that made college less likely varied by gender: Boys broke the law and girls became pregnant (Hentges et al., 2018).

EYESWIDEOPEN/GETTY IMAGES

More Familiar Than Foreign?
Even in cultures with strong and traditional family influence, teenagers choose to be with peers whenever they can. These boys play at Cherai Beach in India.

↑ **OBSERVATION** QUIZ
What evidence do you see that traditional norms remain in this culture? (see answer, page 379)

peer pressure
Encouragement to conform to one's friends or contemporaries in behavior, dress, and attitude; usually considered a negative force, as when adolescent peers encourage one another to defy adult authority.

Peer Power

Adolescents rely on peers to help them navigate the physical changes of puberty, the intellectual challenges of high school, and the social changes of leaving childhood. A longitudinal study found that friends help each other become better friends: Those who are more adept at sharing emotions become closer friends over time (von Salisch, 2018).

PEERS AND PARENTS Friendships are important at every stage. During early adolescence popularity (not just friendship) is also coveted. Especially when parents are harsh or neglectful, peer support can be crucial for healthy maturation (Birkeland et al., 2014; LaFontana & Cillessen, 2010).

Peers do not negate the need for parental support: Healthy relationships with parents during childhood enhance later peer friendships as well as more reciprocal romances (Flynn et al., 2017). However, parents alone are not enough.

For example, in one experiment, children and adolescents had to give a speech, with or without their parents present. For 9-year-olds, their parents' presence relieved stress, as indicated by lower levels of the stress hormone, cortisol, as well as visible signs. For 15-year-olds, however, the parents' presence was no help (Hostinar et al., 2015). Other research confirms that parent buffering of stress is less effective in adolescence.

The evidence for peers is complex. Some research finds that when friends help with speech preparation, stress increases (Doom et al., 2017).

PEER PRESSURE **Peer pressure** is usually depicted as peers pushing a teenager to do something that adults disapprove, such as using drugs or breaking laws. Peer pressure is especially strong in early adolescence, when adults seem clueless about biological and social stresses. However, peer pressure can be more helpful than harmful.

For example, many caregivers fear that social media corrupts innocent youth, but adolescents use social media to strengthen existing friendships. Of course, since most people post successes, not failures, social media may make teens feel less attractive, less social, or less competent than their peers, but that danger does not originate with the smartphone. If an adolescent has supportive friends offline, then online communication increases that support (Khan et al., 2016).

Almost all (92 percent) 13- to 17-year-olds in the United States go online every day, and 24 percent say they are online "almost constantly" (Lenhart, 2015, p. 16). Most connect with friends they see everyday, but some feel that none of their peers really understands them, because no one else is evangelical, atheist, Muslim, LGBTQ, disabled, or whatever. They can't find a close friend in their class or neighborhood. For them, the Internet provides a sympathetic, supportive peer.

Adults worry that an unseen friend might not be benign, but it is more likely that such a friend is helpful. Parents may advise caution, but they should recognize that everyone needs friends.

Peers may be particularly important for adolescents of minority and immigrant groups as they strive to achieve ethnic identity (not confused or foreclosed). The larger society provides stereotypes and prejudice, and parents may be stuck in past experiences, but peers bolster self-esteem as well as advise about romance, homework, and future education.

THE IMMEDIACY OF PEERS Given the areas of the brain that are quickest to myelinate and mature in adolescence, it is not surprising that the most influential peers are those nearby at the moment. This was found in a study in which all eleventh-graders in several public schools in Los Angeles were offered a free online SAT prep course (worth $200) that they could take if they signed up on a paper distributed by the organizers (Bursztyn & Jensen, 2015).

In this study, students were *not* allowed to talk before deciding whether or not to accept the offer. So, they did not know that, although all of the papers had identical, detailed descriptions of the SAT program, one word differed in who would learn of their decision—either no other students or only the students in that particular class. The two versions were:

> *Your decision to sign up for the course will be kept completely private from everyone, except the other students in the room.*

> *Your decision to sign up for the course will be kept completely private from everyone, including the other students in the room.*

A marked difference was found if students thought their classmates would learn of their decision: The honors students were *more* likely to sign up and the non-honors students *less* likely.

To verify the peer effect, not divergent motivation or ability between honors and non-honors students, the researchers compared students who took exactly two honors classes and several non-honors classes. There were 107 such students, some of whom happened to be in their honors class when they signed up for SAT prep; some not.

When the decisions of those two-honors students were kept totally private, acceptance rates were similar (72 and 79 percent) no matter which class students were in at the moment. But, if students thought their classmates might know their decision, imagined peer pressure affected them. When in an honors class, 97 percent signed up for the SAT program. Of those in a non-honors class, only 54 percent signed up (Bursztyn & Jensen, 2015).

Matthew Staver/Bloomberg via Getty Images

Everyday Danger
After cousins Alex and Arthur, ages 16 and 20, followed family wishes to shovel snow around their Denver home, they followed their inner risk impulses and jumped from the roof. Not every young man can afford the expense of motocross or hang gliding, but almost every one of them leaps into risks that few 40-year-olds would dare.

DRAGONIMAGES/GETTY IMAGES

Need an English Tutor Who Speaks Vietnamese?
Twenty years ago such tutors were hard to find, but now this Vietnamese girl can learn English from a multilingual computer program. This is one of many ways adolescents can utilize online technology to their benefit.

A CASE TO STUDY

The Naiveté of Your Author

Adults are sometimes unaware of adolescents' desire for respect from their peers who see them every day. I did not recognize this with my own children:

- Our oldest daughter wore the same pair of jeans in tenth grade, day after day. She washed them each night by hand, and I put them in the dryer early each morning. [Circadian rhythm—I was asleep hours before she was, and awake hours earlier.] My husband was bewildered. "Is this some weird female ritual?" he asked. Years later, our daughter explained that she was afraid that if she wore different pants each day, her classmates would think she cared about her clothes, which would prompt them to criticize her choices. To avoid criticism from that imaginary audience, she wore only one pair of jeans.

- Our second daughter, at 16, pierced her ears for the third time. I asked if this meant she would do drugs;

she laughed at my foolishness. Only later did I notice that many of her friends had multiple holes in their ear lobes.

- At age 15, our third daughter was diagnosed with cancer. My husband and I weighed opinions from four physicians, each explaining treatment that would minimize the risk of death. Our daughter had other priorities: "I don't care what you choose, as long as I keep my hair." (Now her health is good; her hair grew back.)

- Our youngest, in sixth grade, refused to wear her jacket (it was new; she had chosen it), even in midwinter. Years later she told me why—she wanted her classmates to think she was tough.

In retrospect, I am amazed that I was unaware of the power of the peers who my daughters saw every day—an influence stronger than the logic of having a long life, a warm body, or other goals that made sense to me.

◆ **Especially for Parents of a Teenager**
Your 13-year-old comes home after a sleepover at a friend's house with a new, weird hairstyle—perhaps cut or colored in a bizarre manner. What do you say and do? (see response, page 379)

deviancy training
Destructive peer support in which one person shows another how to rebel against authority or social norms.

THINK CRITICALLY: Why is peer pressure thought to be much more sinister than it actually is?

SELECTING FRIENDS Of course, peers *can* lead one another into trouble. A study of substance misuse and delinquency among twins found that—even controlling for genes and environment—when one twin became a delinquent, the other was more likely to do so (Laursen et al., 2017).

Collectively, peers provide **deviancy training,** whereby one person shows another how to resist social norms (Van Ryzin & Dishion, 2013; Dishion et al., 2001). However, innocent teens are not corrupted by deviants. Adolescents choose their friends and models—not always wisely, but never randomly.

A developmental progression can be traced: The combination of "problem behavior, school marginalization, and low academic performance" at age 11 leads to gang involvement two years later, deviancy training two years after that, and violent behavior at age 18 or 19 (Dishion et al., 2010, p. 603).

This cascade is not inevitable; adults need to engage marginalized 11-year-olds instead of blaming their friends years later. Teachers are crucial: If young adolescents are mildly disruptive (e.g., they don't follow directions), they are more likely to align with other troublemakers and their behavior worsens if their teachers are not supportive (e.g., sarcastic, demeaning, rigid, insensitive to student needs) (Shin & Ryan, 2017).

To further understand the impact of peers, examination of two concepts is helpful: *selection* and *facilitation*. Teenagers *select* friends whose values and interests they share, abandoning former friends who follow other paths. Then, friends *facilitate* destructive or constructive behaviors.

It is easier to do wrong ("Let's all skip school on Friday") or right ("Let's study together for the chem exam") with friends. Peer facilitation helps adolescents do things they are unlikely to do alone.

Thus, adolescents select and facilitate, choose and are chosen. Happy, energetic, and successful teens have close friends who themselves are high achievers, with no major emotional problems.

The opposite also holds: Those who are drug users, sexually active, and alienated from school choose compatible friends. In general, peers provide opportunity, companionship, and encouragement for what young adolescents already might do.

Research on teenage cigarette smoking finds that selection precedes peer pressure (Kiuru et al., 2010). Another study found that *after* young adolescents select peers who drink alcohol, they are then likely to start drinking themselves (Osgood et al., 2013). Finally, a third study, of teenage sexual activity, again found that selection was the crucial peer influence on behavior (van de Bongardt et al., 2015).

Selection and facilitation are evident lifelong, but the balance between the two shifts. Early adolescence is a time of selection; facilitation is more evident in later adolescence. In emerging adulthood, after age 18 or so, selection becomes important again, as young adults abandon some high school friends and establish new ones (Samek et al., 2016).

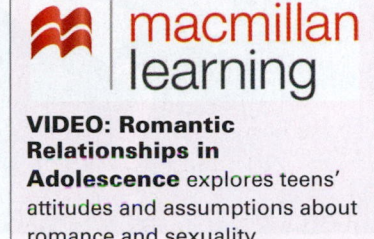

VIDEO: **Romantic Relationships in Adolescence** explores teens' attitudes and assumptions about romance and sexuality.

ROMANTIC PARTNERS Selection is obvious in romance. Adolescents choose and are chosen by romantic partners, and then they influence each other on almost everything—sex, music, work, play, education, food, and so on. Even small things matter: If one gets a new jacket, or tattoo, or sunglasses, the other might too.

Teens' first romances typically occur in high school, with girls having a steady partner more often than boys. Exclusive commitment is the ideal, but the fluidity and rapidity of the selection process mitigate against permanency.

Cheating, flirting, switching, and disloyalty are rife. Breakups are common, as are unreciprocated crushes. Emotions range from exhilaration to despair, leading to impulsive sex, cruel revenge, and deep depression.

Peer support is vital: Friends help adolescents cope with romantic ups and downs. They also make sexual intercourse more—or less—likely (see Figure 10.2). Their peers' actual sexual experience is not as influential as the perception of their peers' activity. Thus, friends influence each other by talking about what they are doing: The one who brags is more influential than the one who stays quiet.

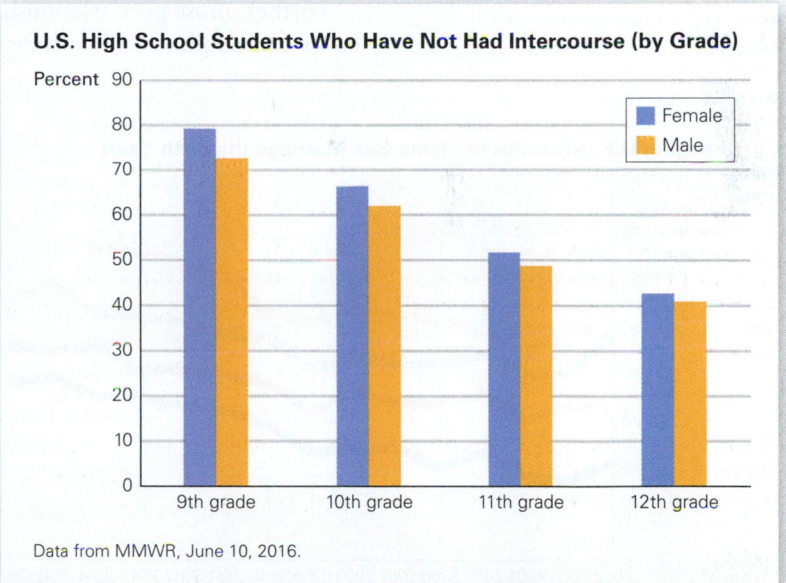

U.S. High School Students Who Have Not Had Intercourse (by Grade)

Data from MMWR, June 10, 2016.

FIGURE 10.2 Many Virgins
For 30 years, the Youth Risk Behavior Survey has asked high school students from all over the United States dozens of confidential questions about their behavior. As you can see, about one-fourth of all students have already had sex by the ninth grade, and more than one-third have not yet had sex by their senior year—a group whose ranks have been increasing in recent years. Other research finds that sexual behaviors are influenced by peers, with some groups all sexually experienced by age 14 and others not until age 18 or older.

SEXTING The importance of social learning from peers was apparent in a study of sexting, defined as sending an explicit sexual message or picture via cell phone. In a large Los Angeles high school, about half of the students knew someone who sexted.

Compared to the half who did not know any sexting peers, those who did know someone often sent and received sexts (twice as likely and 13 times more likely, respectively) themselves. Sexting increased sexual experiences, especially oral sex (seven times more likely) and sex without a condom (five times more likely) (Rice et al., 2018).

Sexting is a problem not only because it increases the rate of unsafe sex but because a jilted teen might resend a naked photo of a former lover. That is called *revenge porn,* and it is especially common among adolescents—who, as you remember

Girls Together These two girls from Sweden are comfortable lying close to one another. Many boys of this age wouldn't want their photograph taken if they were this close to each other. Around the world, there are cultural and gender norms about what are acceptable expressions of physical affection among friends during adolescence.

from the previous chapter, tend to act quickly and emotionally, not slowly and thoughtfully.

Sexting among adolescents is technically transmission of child pornography, illegal in many states, with girls more often feeling coerced than boys. However, sexting, including revenge porn, is almost never prosecuted (Salter et al., 2013). Adults may consider sexting dangerous and pornographic; teens usually do not (Erreygers et al., 2017).

Consequently, although young teens are especially vulnerable to sexual abuse of all kinds, we need to be careful not to condemn teen romances, including those that include texting and sexting. While Chapter 9 discusses many potential problems with early sexual experience, most cell phone use in romantic interaction is benign—bonding not harming, voluntary not coerced (Englander, 2015; Burén & Lunde, 2018).

Further, most peer relationships are asexual. As you remember from Chapter 9, fewer contemporary adolescents are sexually active than was true 20 years ago. Most teenagers have platonic friends of both sexes (Kreager et al., 2016). They also have romances that do not include intercourse. Most of them have dated someone but not had sex with that person.

Norms vary markedly from group to group, school to school, city to city, and nation to nation. For instance, twice as many high school students in Philadelphia as in San Francisco say they have had intercourse (52 percent versus 26 percent) (MMWR, June 10, 2016).

Obviously, within every city are many subgroups, each with specific norms. Girls from religious families with close relationships with their parents tend to date boys from similar families, and their shared values slow down sexual activity (Kim-Spoon et al., 2012).

sexual orientation
A term that refers to whether a person is sexually and romantically attracted to others of the same sex, the opposite sex, or both sexes.

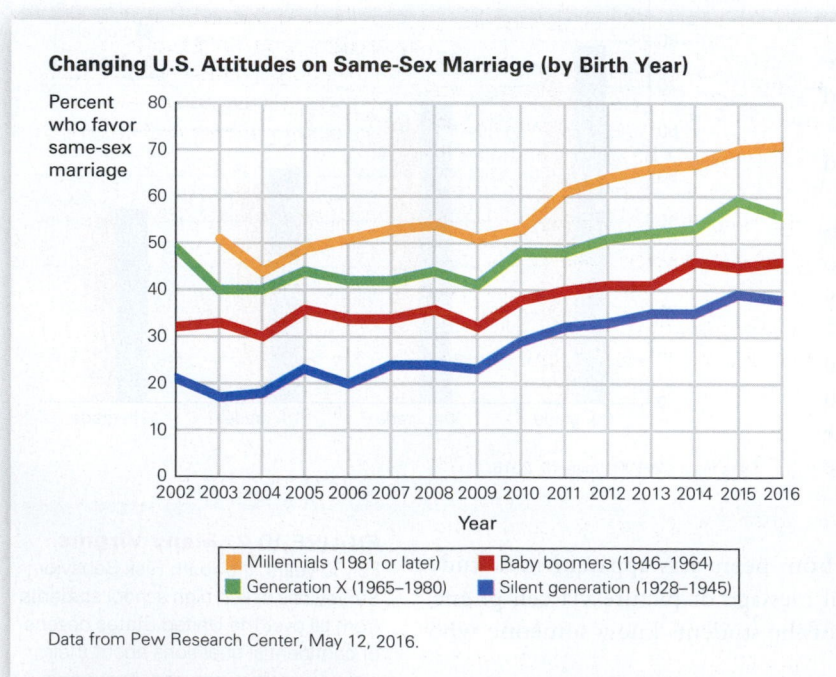

Data from Pew Research Center, May 12, 2016.

FIGURE 10.3 Young and Old Everyone knows that attitudes about same-sex relationships are changing. Less well known is that cohort differences are greater than the shift over the first decade of the twenty-first century.

SAME-SEX ROMANCES Some adolescents are attracted to peers of the same sex. **Sexual orientation** refers to the direction of a person's erotic desires. One meaning of *orient* is "to turn toward"; thus, sexual orientation refers to whether a person is romantically attracted to (turned on by) people of the other sex, the same sex, or both sexes. Sexual orientation can be strong, weak, overt, secret, or unconscious.

Obviously, culture and cohort are powerful (Bailey et al., 2016) (see Figure 10.3). Some cultures accept youth who identify as gay, lesbian, transgender, or other (the

census in India gives people three choices: male, female, or Hijra [transgender]). Other cultures criminalize LGBTQ youth (38 of the 53 African nations), even killing them (Uganda).

Worldwide, many gay and lesbian youths date the other sex to hide their orientation; deception puts them at risk for binge drinking, suicidal thoughts, and drug use. Those hazards are less common in cultures where same-sex partnerships are accepted, especially when parents affirm their offspring's sexuality.

At least in the United States, adolescents have similar difficulties and strengths whether they are gay or straight, and nonsexual friendships with peers of both sexes decrease loneliness and increase resilience (Van Harmelen et al., 2017). However, lesbian, gay, bisexual, and transgender youth have a higher risk of depression and anxiety, for reasons from every level of Bronfenbrenner's ecological-systems approach (Mustanski et al., 2014). [**Life–Span Link:** Ecological systems are described in Chapter 1.]

As with gender identity, sexual orientation is surprisingly fluid during adolescence. In one study, 10 percent of sexually active teenagers had had same-sex partners, but many of those 10 percent nonetheless identified as heterosexual (Pathela & Schillinger, 2010). In that study, those most at risk of sexual violence and sexually transmitted infections had partners of both sexes, a correlation also found in other studies (e.g., Russell et al., 2014). The reasons are unclear.

Learning About Sex

Many adolescents have strong sexual urges that push them toward romance with peers, but they have minimal logic about pregnancy and disease. They do not understand the relationship between lust and love. This mismatch is one consequence of the 10-year interval between maturation of the body and of the brain.

Millions of teenagers worry that they are oversexed, undersexed, or deviant, unaware that thousands, maybe millions, of others have the same sexual needs. Gay and lesbian teenagers may be especially troubled. In 2010, several LGBTQ youth, aged 13 to 15, killed themselves in despair. In response, 50,000 adults posted "it gets better" videos attesting that nontraditional sexual orientation and gender identity in adulthood is quite satisfying, a message that young people need to learn (Garrett, 2018).

Indeed, there is much that every young person needs to learn. As one observer wrote, adolescents "seem to waffle their way through sexually relevant encounters driven both by the allure of reward and the fear of negative consequences" (Wagner, 2011, p. 193). Where do they learn it?

FROM THE MEDIA Many adolescents learn about sex from the media. The Internet is a common source, particularly regarding sexually transmitted infections (Simon & Daneback, 2013). Unfortunately, Web sites are often frightening (featuring pictures of diseased organs), mesmerizing (pornography), or misleading (offering false information).

Media consumption peaks in early adolescence. Television programs that attract teen audiences include sexual content almost seven times per hour (Steinberg & Monahan, 2011). That content is deceptive: Almost never does a character develop an STI, deal with an unwanted pregnancy, or mention (much less use) a condom.

Adolescents with intense exposure to sex in music, print, social media, film, and television are more often sexually active, but the direction of this correlation is controversial (R. Collins et al., 2011; Steinberg & Monahan, 2011). The media may increase but not cause focus on external appearance, body objectification, and thus sexual activity (Vandenbosch & Eggermont, 2015).

Check out the **DATA CONNECTIONS ACTIVITY Sexual Behaviors of U.S. High School Students,** which examines how sexually active teens really are.

LAURA CAVANAUGH/GETTY IMAGES

To Be a Woman Here Miley Cyrus performs for thousands of fans in Brooklyn, New York. Does pop culture make it difficult for teenagers of all genders to reconcile their own sexual impulses with the images of their culture?

FROM PARENTS It may be that "the most important influences on adolescents' sexual behavior may be closer to home than to Hollywood" (Steinberg & Monahan, 2011, p. 575). As that quote implies, sex education begins at home.

Every study finds that parental communication influences adolescents' behavior. Effective programs of sex education explicitly require parental participation (Silk & Romero, 2014). However, embarrassment and ignorance are common on both sides.

Many parents underestimate their own child's sexual activity while fearing that the child's peers and media consumption are too sexual (Elliott, 2012). However, those fears do not lead to ongoing conversations about sex, love, and life. According to young women aged 15 to 24 chosen to represent the U.S. population, only 25 percent of adolescents remember receiving any sex education from either parent (Vanderberg et al., 2016).

Communication about the sexual aspects of romance is rare between parents and children. Mothers and daughters are more likely than fathers or sons to have detailed conversations, but the emphasis is on avoiding pregnancy and diseases, not on pleasure and intimacy.

Ironically, although mothers are worried about their daughters' sexual experiences and knowledge, and although daughters want to learn more about sex from someone they trust, both mothers and daughters consider such information private—and almost never share personal details (Coffelt, 2017).

"Smirking or non-smirking?"

Laugh and Learn Emotions are as crucial as facts in sex education.

FROM PEERS Especially when parents are silent, forbidding, or vague, adolescent sexual behavior is strongly influenced by peers. Boys learn about sex from other boys (Henry et al., 2012), girls from other girls, with the strongest influence being what peers say they have done, not something abstract (Choukas-Bradley et al., 2014).

Partners also teach each other. However, their lessons are more about pleasure than consequences: Few U.S. adolescent couples decide together *before* they have sex how they will prevent pregnancy and disease, and what they will do if their efforts fail.

When adolescents were asked with whom they discussed sexual issues, friends were the most common confidants, then parents, and last of all dating partners. Indeed, only half of them had *ever* discussed anything about sex with their sexual partner (Widman et al., 2014).

FROM EDUCATORS Sex education from teachers varies dramatically by school and nation. The curriculum for middle schools in most European nations includes information about masturbation, same-sex romance, oral and anal sex, and specific uses and failures of various methods of contraception. Those subjects are rarely covered in U.S. classes, even in high school.

Rates of teenage pregnancy in most European nations are less than half of those in the United States. Obviously, curriculum is part of the larger culture, and cultural differences regarding sex are vast, but sex education in schools is part of the reason.

Within the United States, the timing and content of sex education vary by state and community. Some high schools provide comprehensive education, free condoms, and medical treatment; others provide nothing. Some schools begin sex education in primary school; others wait until senior year of high school.

Because of HIV/AIDS, most U.S. adolescents (95 percent) receive sex education in school (Vanderberg et al., 2016), but content and timing limit effectiveness. Students are less likely to learn from sex education in school; they are more likely to listen to their peers who have already begun sexual activity and to consult the Internet.

One controversy has been whether schools should teach that sexual abstinence is the only acceptable strategy. It is true, of course, that abstaining from sex (including oral and anal sex) prevents STIs and that abstinence avoids pregnancy. But sexual drives overwhelm that logic.

Longitudinal data comparing students from the same communities, some who had abstinence-only education and others who had comprehensive sex education, find no difference in average age of beginning sexual activity. The only objective difference was that those with abstinence-only education had higher rates of sexually transmitted infections (Trenholm et al., 2007). Legislative support for abstinence-only education is an example of the problem described in Chapter 1: Opinions may ignore evidence (Hall et al., 2016).

Some social scientists complain that U.S. educators and parents present morals and facts about disease to adolescents, yet teen behavior is driven by peer norms and emotions. Sexual behavior does not spring from the prefrontal cortex: Knowing about STIs, or how to use a condom, does not guarantee a careful, wise behavior when passions run high. Consequently, effective sex education must engage emotions and peer support (Suleiman & Brindis, 2014).

Most educators and developmentalists want sex education to begin early and to convey medically accurate information (Hall et al., 2016; Lindberg et al., 2016). Most parents, including those who are evangelical Christians, want schools to teach children to make responsible as well as fulfilling choices about sex (Dent & Maloney, 2017).

However, a vocal minority sometimes blocks evidence-based sex education. One review reports that although sex education is part of the school curriculum in 49 of the 50 states, the emphasis is still on abstinence and male–female marriage (Hall et al., 2016). Only eight states mandate that sex education be medically accurate.

> ◆ **Especially for Sex Educators**
> Suppose adults in your community never talk to their children about sex or puberty. Is that a mistake? (see response, page 379)

> **THINK CRITICALLY:** Why has sex education become a political issue?

what have you learned?

1. Why do parents and adolescents often bicker?
2. How do parent–adolescent relationships change over time?
3. When is parental monitoring a sign of a healthy parent–adolescent relationship?
4. How does the influence of peers and parents differ for adolescents?
5. Why do many adults misunderstand the role of peer pressure?
6. How does culture affect sexual orientation?
7. From whom do adolescents usually learn about sex?
8. Why do some schools still teach abstinence-only sex education?

Sadness and Anger

Adolescence can be a wonderful time. Nonetheless, troubles plague about 20 percent of youths. For instance, one specific survey of more than 10,000 13- to 17-year-olds in the United States found that 23 percent had a psychological disorder in the past month (Kessler et al., 2012).

Most disorders are comorbid, with several problems occurring at once. Some are temporary—not too serious and soon outgrown. Parents and peers can help a sad or angry child so that emotions are regulated and expressed in healthy ways, or they can push a teenager toward deep despair or life in prison.

There is danger here. Sometimes sadness and anger can become intense, chronic, even deadly. To provide the social support that adolescents need, we must differentiate between pathology and normal moodiness, between behavior that is seriously troubled versus merely unsettling.

Depression

The general emotional trend from early childhood to early adolescence is toward less confidence and higher rates of depression. Then, gradually, self-esteem increases. A dip in self-esteem at puberty is found for children of every ethnicity and gender (Fredricks & Eccles, 2002; Greene & Way, 2005; Kutob et al., 2010; Zeiders et al., 2013a), with notable individual differences.

Universal trends, as well as gender and family effects, are apparent. For example, as in North America, a report from China also finds a dip in self-esteem at seventh grade (when many Chinese adolescents experience puberty) and then a gradual rise.

Contemporary Chinese teenagers have lower self-esteem than earlier cohorts, even though income has risen. This may be the consequence of reduced social connections: Most youth have no siblings or cousins, many parents work far from their children, and divorce is more common than it was (Liu & Xin, 2014).

In the United States, self-esteem tends to be higher in boys than in girls. Self-esteem is also, on average, higher in African Americans than in European Americans, who themselves have higher self-esteem than Latino and Asian Americans. All studies find notable variability, and these ethnic differences are not always found. The immediate social context—attitudes in the school, the family, and the community—is crucial.

For immigrant Latino youth with strong familism, self-esteem and ethnic pride are higher than for most other groups, and a rise over the years of adolescence is common. When compared to the high rates of depression among European American girls, the Latina rise in self-esteem from about age 16 is particularly notable (Zeiders et al., 2013a).

The likely reason is that family and cultural norms are protective. Latinas with high familism become increasingly helpful at home, which makes their parents appreciative and makes the girls themselves proud, unlike other U.S. teenage girls.

On the other hand, each subgroup is affected by current conditions. Latino Americans who are citizens of the United States but fear deportation of their parents often experience symptoms of depression, including sleep disturbance and lower school achievement (Gulbas et al., 2016).

Blot Out the World Teenagers sometimes despair at their future, as Anthony Ghost-Redfeather did in South Dakota. He tried to kill himself, and, like many boys involved in parasuicide, he is ashamed that he failed.

Adolescent immigrant youth are especially vulnerable to emotional stress, according to a statement by the Society for Research of Adolescence (Suárez-Orozco, 2017). The reason is that adolescents are newly aware of the wider culture and more concerned about their future identity. No wonder their emotions and motivation are affected.

Of course, immigrants are not the only ones affected by adolescent moodiness. Some families expect high achievement for every adolescent, and then teens are quick to criticize themselves and everyone else when any sign of failure appears (Bleys et al., 2016).

Perfectionism is dangerous at any age, but adolescents take rejection and failure particularly hard. When a teenager realizes that it is impossible to be perfect, depression may result (Damian et al., 2013). Perfectionism is considered one cause of teenage eating disorders (Wade et al., 2016).

MAJOR DEPRESSIVE DISORDER Some adolescents sink into **major depression,** a deep sadness and hopelessness that disrupts all normal, regular activities. The causes, including genes and early care, predate adolescence. Then puberty—with its myriad physical and emotional ups and downs—pushes vulnerable children, especially girls, into despair.

The rate of major depression more than doubles during this time, to an estimated 15 percent, affecting about one in five girls and one in ten boys. The gender difference occurs for many reasons, biological and cultural. One study found that the short allele of the serotonin transporter promoter gene (5-HTTLPR) increased the rate of depression among girls everywhere but increased depression among boys *only* if they lived in low-SES communities (Uddin et al., 2010). Is that surprising?

It is not surprising that vulnerability to depression is partly genetic, but why might neighborhood affect boys more than girls? Perhaps hormones depress females everywhere, but cultures protect boys unless jobs, successful adult men, and encouragement within their community are scarce?

And why girls more than boys? A cognitive explanation for such gender differences focuses on *rumination*—talking about, brooding, and mentally replaying past experiences, as already mentioned in Chapter 9. Girls ruminate much more than boys, and rumination often leads to depression (Michl et al., 2013).

But rumination is not always harmful. When it occurs with a close friend after a stressful event, the friend's support may be helpful (Rose et al., 2014). The fact that girls are more likely to express their emotions in conversation with their friends may be one reason girls are less likely to commit suicide. Differential susceptibility again.

SUICIDE Serious, distressing thoughts about killing oneself (called **suicidal ideation**) are most common at about age 15. More than one-third (40 percent) of U.S. high school girls felt so hopeless that they stopped doing some usual activities for two weeks or more in the previous year (an indication of depression), and nearly one-fourth (23 percent) seriously thought about suicide. The corresponding rates for boys were 20 percent and 12 percent (MMWR, June 10, 2016).

Suicidal ideation can lead to **parasuicide,** also called *attempted suicide* or *failed suicide*. Parasuicide includes any deliberate self-harm that could have been lethal.

Parasuicide is the preferred term because "failed" suicide implies that to die is to succeed(!). "Attempt" is likewise misleading because, especially in adolescence, the difference between attempt and completion may be luck and treatment, not intent.

As you see in Figure 10.4, parasuicide can be divided according to instances that require medical attention (surgery, pumped stomach, etc.) and those that do not, but any parasuicide is a warning. Among U.S. high school students in 2015, 11.6 percent of the girls and 5.5 percent of the boys attempted suicide in the previous year (MMWR, June 10, 2016). If there is a next time, the person may die.

Thus, parasuicide—even if it seems half-hearted—must be taken seriously. Thinking about suicide, even if not accompanied by any action, is also a warning that emotions may be overwhelming. An ominous sign, particularly for adolescent boys from low-SES families, is a Google search for "how to kill yourself" (Ma-Kellams et al., 2016).

Although suicidal ideation during adolescence is common, completed suicides are not. The U.S. annual rate of completed suicide for people aged 15 to 19 (in school or not) is less than 8 per 100,000, or 0.008 percent, which is only half the rate for adults aged 20 and older (Parks et al., 2014). Keep this statistic in mind if someone claims that adolescent suicide is "epidemic." They are wrong.

However, because they are more emotional and egocentric than logical and analytical, adolescents are particularly affected when they hear about someone else's

major depression
Feelings of hopelessness, lethargy, and worthlessness that last two weeks or more.

suicidal ideation
Thinking about suicide, usually with some serious emotional and intellectual or cognitive overtones.

parasuicide
Any potentially lethal action against the self that does not result in death. (Also called *attempted suicide* or *failed suicide*.)

THINK CRITICALLY: Suicide rates increase with income. Why?

FIGURE 10.4 Sad Thoughts
Completed suicide is rare in adolescence, but serious thoughts about killing oneself are frequent. Depression and parasuicide are more common in girls than in boys, but rates are high even in boys. There are three reasons to suspect that the rates for boys are underestimates: Boys tend to be less aware of their emotions than girls are; boys consider it unmanly to try to kill themselves and to fail; and completed suicide is also higher in males than in females.

↑ **OBSERVATION** QUIZ
Does thinking seriously about suicide increase or decrease during high school? (see answer, page 379)

◆ **Especially for Journalists**
You just heard that a teenage cheerleader jumped off a tall building and died. How should you report the story? (see response, page 379)

cluster suicides
Several suicides committed by members of a group within a brief period.

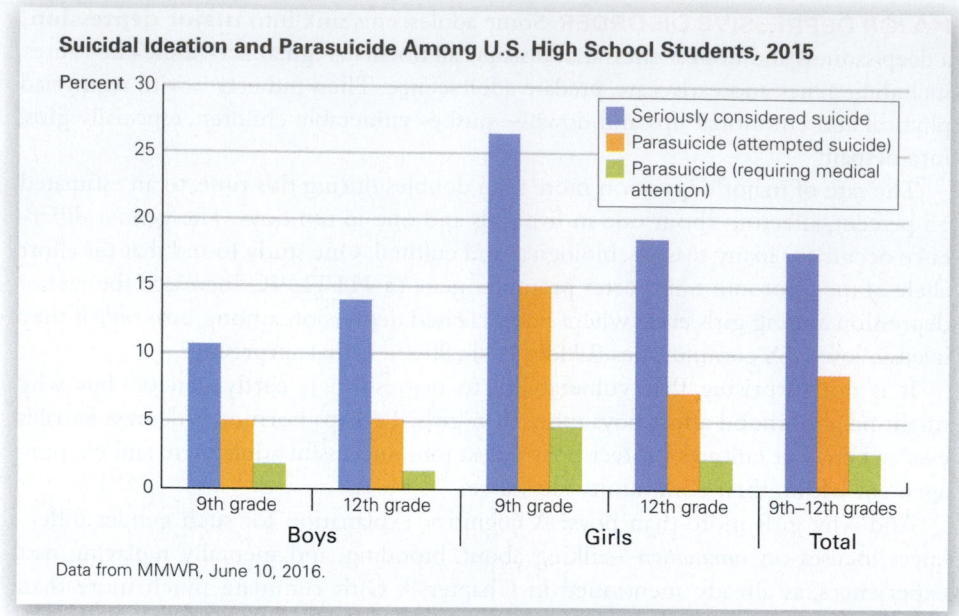

Suicidal Ideation and Parasuicide Among U.S. High School Students, 2015

Legend:
- Seriously considered suicide
- Parasuicide (attempted suicide)
- Parasuicide (requiring medical attention)

Data from MMWR, June 10, 2016.

suicide, either through the media or from peers (Niedzwiedz et al., 2014). They are susceptible to **cluster suicides,** which are several suicides within a group over a brief span of time. For that reason, media portrayals of a suicide may trigger more deaths.

Delinquency and Defiance

Like low self-esteem and suicidal ideation, bouts of anger are common in adolescence. In fact, a moody adolescent could be both depressed and delinquent because externalizing and internalizing behavior are closely connected during these years (Loeber & Burke, 2011). This may explain suicide in jail: Teenagers jailed for assault (externalizing) are higher suicide risks (internalizing) than adult prisoners.

Externalizing actions are obvious. Many adolescents slam doors, curse parents, and tell friends exactly how badly other teenagers (or siblings or teachers) have behaved. Some teenagers—particularly boys—"act out" by breaking laws. They steal, damage property, or injure others.

Is teenage anger necessary for normal development? That is what Anna Freud (Sigmund's daughter, herself a prominent psychoanalyst) thought. She wrote that adolescent resistance to parental authority was "welcome . . . beneficial . . . inevitable." She explained:

> We all know individual children who, as late as the ages of fourteen, fifteen or sixteen, show no such outer evidence of inner unrest. They remain, as they have been during the latency period, "good" children, wrapped up in their family relationships, considerate sons of their mothers, submissive to their fathers, in accord with the atmosphere, idea and ideal of their childhood background. Convenient as this may be, it signifies a delay of their normal development and is, as such, a sign to be taken seriously.
>
> [A. Freud, 1958/2000, p. 37]

However, most contemporary psychologists, teachers, and parents are quite happy with well-behaved, considerate teenagers, who often become happy adults. A 30-year longitudinal study found that adults who had never been arrested usually earned

In Every Nation Everywhere, older adolescents are most likely to protest against government authority. *(left)* Adolescents in Alabama celebrate the 50-year anniversary of the historic Selma-to-Montgomery march across the Pettus Bridge. In that historic movement, most of those beaten and killed were under age 25. *(right)* In the fall of 2014, thousands of students in Hong Kong led pro-democracy protests, which began peacefully but led, days later, to violent confrontations, shown here as they began.

degrees, "held high-status jobs, and expressed optimism about their own futures" (Moffitt, 2003, p. 61). Thus, teenage acting out, while not unusual, is not essential for healthy development.

BREAKING THE LAW Both the *prevalence* (how widespread) and the *incidence* (how frequent) of criminal actions are higher during adolescence than earlier or later. Arrest statistics in every nation reflect this fact, with 30 percent of African American males and 22 percent of European American males being arrested at least once before age 18 (Brame et al., 2014).

Many more adolescents have broken the law but have not been caught, or they have been caught but not arrested. Confidential self-reports suggest that most adolescents (male or female) break the law at least once before age 20. One reason for the high rate is that many behaviors that are legal for adults—buying cigarettes, having intercourse, skipping school, etc.—are illegal for adolescents.

Boys are three times as likely as girls to be caught, arrested, and convicted. In general, youth of minority ethnic groups, and low-SES families, are more likely to be arrested. Is this a reflection of ethnic and economic prejudice (Marotta & Voisin, 2017)?

The same question could be asked regarding boys. They are more overtly aggressive and rebellious at every age, but this may be nurture, not nature (Loeber et al., 2013). Some studies find that female aggression is typically limited to family and friends. Thus, it is less likely to lead to an arrest, because parents hesitate to call the police to arrest their daughters.

FALSE CONFESSIONS Determining accurate gender, ethnic, and income differences in actual lawbreaking, not just in arrests, is complex. Both self-reports and police responses may be biased. For instance, research in the Netherlands found that one-third of those interrogated by the police later denied any police contact (van Batenburg-Eddes et al., 2012).

On the other hand, adolescents sometimes tell the authorities that they committed a crime when they did

Change Their Uniforms
Juvenile offenders wear prison orange—easy to spot should they try to escape—as they listen to an ex-offender, Tony Allen, who grew up on the rough streets of Chicago. When this photo was taken, he earned 5 million dollars a year as a basketball player for the Memphis Grizzlies. If an adolescent-limited offender is imprisoned, talks like this have little effect unless at least two of the following four factors are also present: a supportive family, a dedicated teacher, a strong religious community, and a circle of friends and neighbors who encourage another path.

not. Overall, in the United States, about 20 percent of confessions are false, and that is more likely before age 20.

There are many reasons that a young person might confess falsely: Brain immaturity makes them less likely to consider long-term consequences, and sometimes they prioritize protecting family members, defending friends, and pleasing adults—including the police (Feld, 2013; Steinberg, 2009).

One dramatic case involved 13-year-old Tyler Edmonds, who said he murdered his brother-in-law. He was convicted and sentenced to life in prison. He then said that he confessed falsely to protect his 26-year-old sister, whom he admired. His conviction was overturned—after he spent four years behind bars.

The researchers who cited Tyler's case interviewed 194 boys, aged 14 to 17, all convicted of serious crimes. More than one-third (35 percent) said they had confessed falsely to a crime (not necessarily the one for which they were serving time).

False confessions were more likely after two hours of intense interrogation—the adolescents wanted it to stop; acting on impulse, they said they were guilty (Malloy et al., 2014). And the police believed them. Tyler's sister said that since he was only 13, he would have a light sentence. And he believed her.

A CRIMINAL CAREER? Many researchers distinguish between two kinds of teenage lawbreakers (Monahan et al., 2013; Jolliffe et al., 2017), as first proposed by Terrie Moffitt (2001, 2003). Both types are usually arrested for the first time in adolescence, for similar crimes, but their future diverges.

1. Most juvenile delinquents are **adolescence-limited offenders,** whose criminal activity stops by age 21. They break the law with their friends, facilitated by their chosen antisocial peers.

2. Some delinquents are **life-course-persistent offenders,** who become career criminals. Their lawbreaking is more often done alone than as part of a gang, and the cause is neurological impairment (either inborn or caused by early experiences). Symptoms include not only childhood defiance but also early disabilities with language and learning.

During adolescence, the criminal records of both types may be similar. However, if adolescence-limited delinquents can be protected from various snares (such as quitting school, entering prison, drug addiction), they will outgrow their criminal behavior. This is confirmed by other research: Few delinquent youths who are not jailed continue to be criminals in early adulthood (Monahan et al., 2009).

CAUSES OF DELINQUENCY The best way to reduce adolescent crime is to notice early behavior that predicts lawbreaking and to change patterns before puberty. Strong and protective social relationships, emotional regulation, and moral values from childhood keep many teenagers from jail. In early adolescence, three signs predict delinquency:

1. *Stubbornness* can lead to defiance, which can lead to running away. Runaways are often victims as well as criminals (e.g., falling in with human traffickers and petty thieves; being arrested for prostitution or robbery).

2. *Shoplifting* can lead to arson and burglary. Things become more important than people.

3. *Bullying* can lead to assault, rape, and murder.

Each of these pathways demands a different response. Stubbornness responds to social support—the rebel who feels understood, not punished, will gradually become less impulsive and more rational. The second pathway requires strengthening human relationships and moral education.

THINK CRITICALLY: If parents and society became more appreciative of this stage of life rather than fearful of it, might that lead to healthier and more peaceful teenagers?

---

adolescence-limited offender
A person whose criminal activity stops by age 21.

life-course-persistent offender
A person whose criminal activity typically begins in early adolescence and continues throughout life; a career criminal.

ADOLESCENT BULLYING

Bullying is defined as repeated attempts to hurt someone else, physically or socially. It can take many forms. For younger children, it was often physical—hitting, shoving, fighting. That is less common among adolescents, who can hurt each other with words or exclusion. Among teen-agers, not being invited to a party can be hurtful and is common—as teenagers develop dominance hierarchies and need peer support. The best protection is to have one or more close friends, and adults who encourage whatever talents the child has.

Types of Bullying

 **Physical**

hitting, pushing, tripping

 Verbal

name-calling, mean taunting, sexual comments, threatening

spreading rumors, posting embarrassing images, rejecting from group

Relational/Social

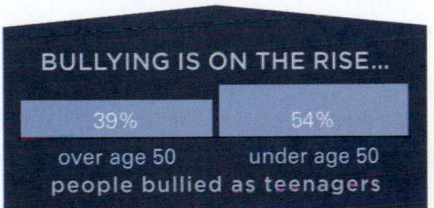

BULLYING IS ON THE RISE...

39%	54%
over age 50	under age 50

people bullied as teenagers

(DITCH THE LABEL, 2017; HARRIS INSIGHTS AND ANALYTICS, 2014; NATIONAL FOUNDATION FOR EDUCATIONAL RESEARCH, 2010)

The Nature of School Bullying

Much bullying takes place at school. Around two-thirds of all school bullying occurs in hallways, schoolyards, bathrooms, cafeterias, or buses. A full one-third occurs in classrooms, while teachers are present. It is estimated that 30% of school bullying goes unreported.

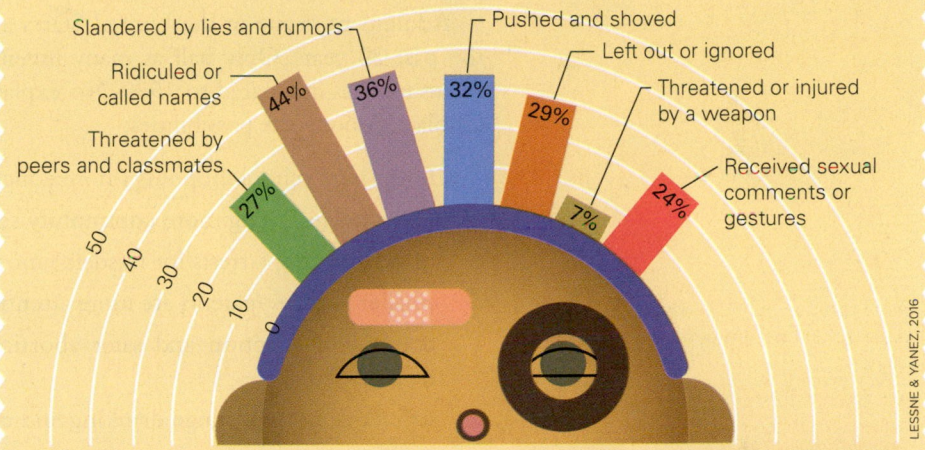

Slandered by lies and rumors — 44%
Ridiculed or called names — 44%
Pushed and shoved — 36%
32%
Left out or ignored — 29%
Threatened by peers and classmates — 27%
Threatened or injured by a weapon — 7%
Received sexual comments or gestures — 24%

LESSNE & YANEZ, 2016

Features of School Anti-Bullying Programs

- Increased supervision of students
- Delivery of consequences for bullying
- School-wide implementation of anti-bullying policies
- Cooperation among school staff, parents, and professionals across disciplines
- Identification of risk factors for bullying

Bullying prevention programs in schools reduce bullying between 25% and 50%.

(MCCALLION & FEDER, 2013)

Cyberbullying

Cyberbullying takes place through e-mail, text messaging, Web sites and apps, instant messaging, chat rooms, or posted videos or photos. Nearly half (47%) of all children and teens have been bullied online at least once. About 21% are bullied online frequently. Girls are more likely than boys to be cyberbullied on a regular basis (41% versus 29%). (DUGGAN, 2017)

 Like

Why Do Teens Cyberbully?

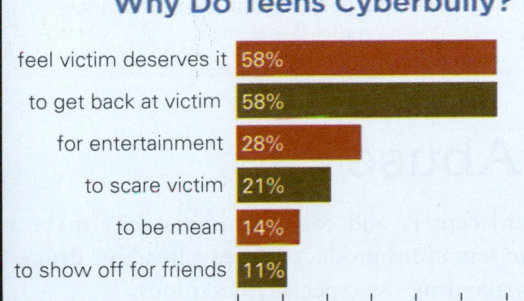

feel victim deserves it	58%
to get back at victim	58%
for entertainment	28%
to scare victim	21%
to be mean	14%
to show off for friends	11%

0 10 20 30 40 50 60

Social Media and Cyberbullying

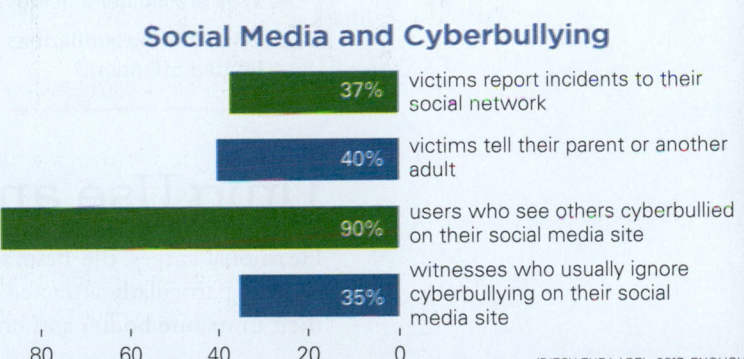

37%	victims report incidents to their social network
40%	victims tell their parent or another adult
90%	users who see others cyberbullied on their social media site
35%	witnesses who usually ignore cyberbullying on their social media site

80 60 40 20 0

(DITCH THE LABEL, 2017; ENOUGH IS ENOUGH, 2017; DUGGAN, 2017)

Those who exhibit the third behavior present the most serious problem. Bullying should have been stopped in childhood, as earlier chapters explained. If a bully still is granted respect and status in high school, something has gone wrong with the school climate and the family support.

Adolescents who still use force to get what they want need to develop other ways to connect with people, as well as other sources of status. Sometimes the problem is cognitive: Their earlier behavior prevented them from learning to achieve academically, so they need tutoring.

Meanwhile, they must be prevented from harming others. Many people believe that restriction on gun purchase and possession should begin with youth, especially those with a history of violence.

In all cases, early warning signs are present, and intervention is more effective earlier than later (Loeber & Burke, 2011). Childhood family relationships are crucial, particularly for girls (Rhoades et al., 2016).

Adolescent crime in the United States and many other nations has decreased in the past 20 years. Only half as many juveniles under age 18 are currently arrested for murder as compared to 1990. No explanation for this decline is accepted by all scholars. Among the possibilities:

- fewer high school dropouts (more education means less crime);
- wiser judges (using more community service than prison);
- better policing (arrests for misdemeanors are up, which may warn parents);
- smaller families (parents are more attentive to each of 2 children than each of 12);
- better contraception and safer abortion (wanted children less often become delinquents);
- stricter drug laws (binge drinking and crack cocaine increase crime);
- more immigrants (who are more law-abiding);
- less lead in the blood (early lead poisoning reduces brain functioning); and more.

Nonetheless, adolescents remain more likely to break the law than adults: The arrest rate for 15- to 17-year-olds is twice that for those over 18. The disproportion is true for almost every crime including rape, car theft, property destruction, and murder. The only exceptions are the "white collar" crimes of fraud, forgery, and embezzlement, which fewer adolescents commit (FBI, 2015).

what have you learned?

1. What is the difference between adolescent sadness and clinical depression?
2. Why do many adults think adolescent suicide is more common than it is?
3. Why are there gender differences in adolescent depression and arrest?
4. Why are cluster suicides more common in adolescence than in later life?
5. What are the similarities between life-course-persistent and adolescence-limited offenders?

Drug Use and Abuse

Hormonal surges, the brain's reward centers, and cognitive immaturity make adolescents particularly attracted to the sensations produced by psychoactive drugs. But their immature bodies and brains make drug use especially hazardous.

Variations in Drug Use

Most teenagers try *psychoactive drugs,* that is, drugs that activate the brain. Cigarettes, alcohol, and many prescription medicines are as addictive and damaging as illegal drugs such as cocaine and heroin.

AGE TRENDS For many developmental reasons, adolescence is a sensitive time for experimentation, daily use, and eventual addiction to psychoactive drugs (Schulenberg et al., 2014). Both prevalence and incidence increase from about ages 10 to 25 and then decrease when adult responsibilities and experiences make drugs less attractive.

Most worrisome is drinking alcohol and smoking cigarettes before age 15, because early use escalates. That makes depression, sexual abuse, bullying, and later addiction more likely (Merikangas & McClair, 2012; Mennis & Mason, 2012).

Although drug use increases every year from puberty until adulthood, one drug follows another pattern—*inhalants* (fumes from aerosol containers, glue, cleaning fluid, etc.). Sadly, the youngest adolescents are most likely to try inhalants, because inhalants are easy to get (hardware stores, drug stores, and supermarkets stock them) and cognitive immaturity means that few pubescent children have a realistic understanding of the risks—brain damage and even death (Nguyen et al., 2016).

A Man Now This boy in Tibet is proud to be a smoker—in many Asian nations, smoking is considered manly.

↓ **OBSERVATION** QUIZ
One line on this chart is troubling, not comforting. What is it? (see answer, page 379)

COHORT TRENDS Cohort differences are evident for every drug, even from one year to the next. Legalization of marijuana, stores selling electronic cigarettes in many flavors, thousands of deaths from opioids—these are three examples of changes in the psychoactive drug scene over the past few years.

Overall, drug use by adolescents has decreased in the United States since 1976 (see Figure 10.5), with use of synthetic narcotics and prescription drugs decreasing in the past two years (Miech et al., 2016). Cigarette smoking is down, but vaping is escalating—which may result in a later uptick in cigarette use (Park et al., 2016).

Longitudinal data are especially useful for drug use, because each new generation is pulled in new directions. This means that people who care about development (everyone reading this paragraph) need to know the current scene in order to guide adolescents.

Recent historical data shed light on the attempt to reduce drug availability. Apparently, it is easy for adolescents to obtain drugs, but that is not a major factor in drug use. Most high school students say that they could easily get alcohol, cigarettes, and marijuana: Perception of risk, not availability, reduces use (Miech et al., 2016).

As for e-cigarettes, although most states prohibit purchase by those under age 18, younger teens can buy them from 116 Internet vendors with no problem (Nikitin et al., 2016). Vaping is very common among teenagers, which worries some adults but is welcomed by others. See Opposing Perspectives on page 374.

U.S. High School Seniors Reporting Drug Use in the Past Year

Data from Miech et al., 2016.

Legend:
- Alcohol
- Marijuana
- Ritalin
- Illicit drugs other than marijuana
- Any prescription drug*
- Amphetamines
- Vicodin
- Cocaine
- OxyContin

FIGURE 10.5 Rise and Fall By asking the same questions year after year, the Monitoring the Future study shows notable historical effects. It is encouraging that something in society, not in the adolescent, makes drug use increase and decrease and that the most recent data show a continued decline in the drug most commonly abused—alcohol.

*Includes use of amphetamines, sedatives (barbiturates), narcotics other than heroin, or tranquilizers—without a doctor's prescription.

OPPOSING PERSPECTIVES

E-Cigarettes: Path to Addiction or Healthy Choice?

Electronic cigarettes (called e-cigs) are much less damaging to the lungs, because they deliver the drugs by vapor, called vaping. If e-cigs help adult smokers quit, then they save lives. Smokers with asthma, heart disease, or lung cancer find significant health benefits from vaping (Burstyn, 2014; Franck et al., 2014; Hajek et al., 2014).

However, many adults fear that adolescents who try e-cigarettes will become addicted to nicotine. Vaping smells better than tobacco, so might inhaling the vapor ease teenagers into smoking and then into using other drugs?

E-cigs are not harmless. They deliver fewer harmful chemicals than combustible cigarettes (Goniewicz et al., 2017), but one by-product is benzene, a known carcinogen (Pankow et al., 2017). If the choice is between combustible cigarettes and e-cigarettes, then e-cigs are better; but if the choice is between no smoking and e-cigs, e-cigs are worse.

A victory of North American public health has been in reducing use of regular cigarettes, resulting in fewer lives lost to lung cancer and many other diseases. There are only half as many adult smokers as there were in 1950, and smoking is now forbidden in most public places and in many homes.

The data on private residences are impressive: In the United States, no-smoking homes are now the majority (87 percent); there were virtually none in 1970 and 43 percent in 1992. Some smokers sleep in those homes: Cigarettes are banned in 46 percent of the homes where a smoker lives (MMWR, September 5, 2014). All of this indicates a massive cultural shift, far beyond a mere scientific discovery or legislative initiative.

The best news of all is that far fewer teens begin smoking. Adolescents once thought smoking was cool; now they know it is harmful. Ads remind them of immediate problems, such as yellow teeth and bad breath (see Figure 10.6). Smoking is no longer a sign of maturity; it is a sign of ignorance.

That is a reason to celebrate. But will e-cigarettes make smoking more acceptable? Will adolescent smoking increase again? Nicotine is addictive no matter how it is delivered, and many e-cigs contain nicotine.

E-cigs are illegal for people under age 18 (in some states, under 21), but they are marketed in flavors like bubble gum, can be placed for a fee in Hollywood films, and are permitted in many places where cigarettes are banned. Many teenagers use them; almost no one is arrested for that. Attitudes are powerful. If a "cancer stick" is now seen as a "glamour accessory," will public health progress stop?

The evidence confirms that teenagers who try e-cigs are likely to smoke tobacco later (Miech et al., 2017b). Is that because e-cigs open a door or because those adolescents would be smokers no matter what? Perhaps the correlation occurs because e-cigs are a sign of future drug use but not a cause of it? We do not know.

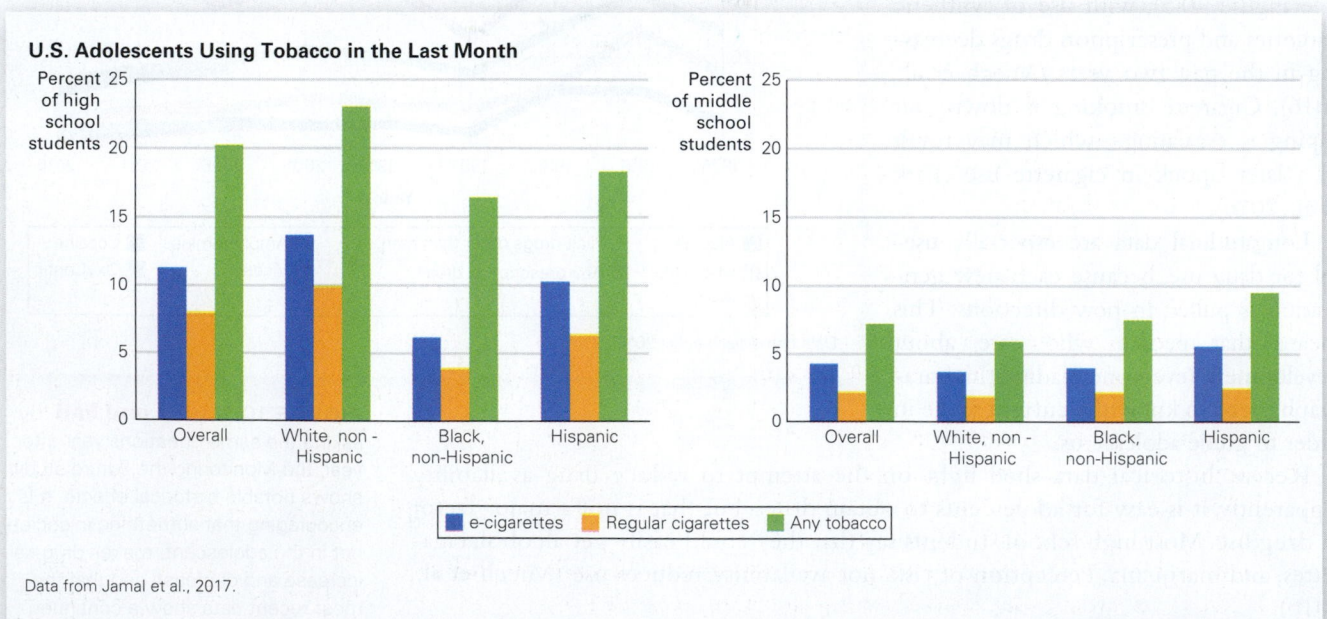

Data from Jamal et al., 2017.

FIGURE 10.6 Getting Better The fact that more than one in five high school students (that's 3 million people) used tobacco—even though purchase of any kind is illegal—in the past month is troubling. This means that more that 3 million students are at risk for addiction and poor health. The surprise (not shown) is that all of these rates are lower than a year earlier. Is that because laws are stricter or teenagers are getting wiser?

The argument from distributors of e-cigarettes is that their products are healthier than cigarettes, that people should make their own choices, and that the fear of adolescent vaping is exaggerated—part of the irrational fear that everything teenagers do is trouble.

Teenagers themselves, by the millions, use e-cigarettes, with use skyrocketing. Adults with chronic diseases, especially former smokers with chronic obstructive pulmonary disease (COPD), often use e-cigarettes (Kruse et al., 2017). Addiction counselors report that e-cigs reduce smoking, even for people who are not ready to quit (Rohsenow et al., 2018).

Yet most public health doctors advise against them, and pediatricians worry that fetal and infant lungs will suffer if the mother uses e-cigs (Carlsen et al., 2018). So far, no evidence of fetal harm has been reported. Perspectives depend on who is judging.

Harm from Drugs

Many researchers find that regular drug use before maturity harms body and brain growth. However, adolescents typically deny that they ever could become addicted, and many more deny drug use. Few adolescents notice when they or their friends move past *use* (experimenting) to *abuse* (experiencing harm) and then to *addiction* (needing the drug to avoid feeling nervous, anxious, sick, or in pain).

Are drugs really harmful? Yes, each one is in a particular way. An obvious negative effect of *tobacco* is that it impairs digestion and nutrition, slowing down growth. This is true not only for cigarettes but also for bidis, cigars, pipes, chewing tobacco, and probably e-cigarettes. Since internal organs continue to mature after the height spurt, drug-using teenagers who appear to be fully grown may damage their developing hearts, lungs, brains, and reproductive systems.

Alcohol is also harmful. Heavy drinking impairs memory and self-control by damaging the hippocampus and the prefrontal cortex, perhaps distorting the reward circuits of the brain lifelong (Guerri & Pascual, 2010).

Adolescence is a particularly sensitive period for alcohol use, because the regions of the brain that are connected to pleasure are more strongly affected by alcohol during adolescence than at later ages. That makes teenagers less conscious of the "intoxicating, aversive, and sedative effects" of alcohol (Spear, 2013, p. 155).

Ironically, alcohol is readily available in many homes, with some parents condoning adolescent drinking. A careful longitudinal study in Australia found that parents who provided alcohol to their teenagers thought they were teaching responsible drinking but were actually increasing binge drinking and substance use disorder six years later (Mattick et al., 2018).

Marijuana seems harmless to many people (especially teenagers), partly because users seem more relaxed than inebriated. Yet adolescents who regularly smoke marijuana are more likely to drop out of school, become teenage parents, be depressed, and later be unemployed—although the evidence comes from years when marijuana was illegal nationwide.

As Chapter 1 explains, some of this may be correlation, not causation. But a longitudinal study that used neurological evidence showed decreasing brain connections and lower intelligence among adolescents who used marijuana habitually, compared to another group who did not (Camchong et al., 2017).

Canada legalized marijuana for adults in the summer of 2018. Canadian health researchers hope that once the brain is mature, benefits will outweigh risks (Lake & Kerr, 2017). Marijuana will remain illegal in Canada for those under 18, although some doctors wish 21 were the cutoff (Rankin, 2017). Evidence needed!

◆◆ **Especially for Police Officers**
You see some 15-year-olds drinking beer in a local park when they belong in school. What do you do? (see response, page 379)

◆◆ **Especially for Parents Who Drink Socially**
You have heard that parents should allow their children to drink at home, to teach them to drink responsibly and not get drunk elsewhere. Is that wise? (see response, page 379)

Choose Your Weed No latte or beer offered here, although this looks like the place where previous generations bought drinks. Instead, at A Greener Today in Seattle, Washington, customers ask for 1 of 20 possibilities—all marijuana.

One problem with age restrictions is that most adolescents covet drugs used by slightly older youth. Many young adults in Canada and elsewhere buy drugs for younger siblings and classmates, supposedly being kind.

However, when New Zealand lowered the age for legal purchase of alcohol from 20 to 18, that nation experienced an uptick in hospital admissions for intoxication, car crashes, and injuries from assault, not only for 18- to 19-year-olds but also for 16- to 17-year-olds (Kypri et al., 2006, 2014).

As noted, some people suggest that the connection between drug use (including cigarettes, alcohol, marijuana, and illegal drugs) and later low achievement, depression, and poor health are correlations, not causes. Might the stress lead to drug use, and then might that reduce anxiety rather than make problems worse? Such self-medication is a plausible hypothesis, but it has been disproven.

Research suggests that drug use may make the user temporarily forget unpleasant emotions, but it *causes* more problems than it solves, often *preceding* anxiety disorders, depression, and rebellion (Maslowsky et al., 2014). Further, adolescents who use alcohol, cigarettes, and marijuana recreationally are likely to abuse these and other drugs after age 20 (Moss et al., 2014).

Longitudinal studies of twins (thus controlling for genes and early child care) confirm that many problems predate drug use: Genes and neighborhoods are, in part, the cause of addiction and rebellion. However, this research finds that although drugs do not cause all later problems, they do not help. Over the long term, the hypothesis that drugs relieve stress is false (Lynskey et al., 2012; Korhonen et al., 2012; Verweij et al., 2016).

Preventing Drug Abuse: What Works?

Evidence in the United States finds that adolescent drug use, legal and illegal, bought on the street and prescribed by doctors, has decreased in recent years. (E-cigs are an exception.) The most valid reporting refers to alcohol, because it is a legal substance that adolescents readily admit to consuming. When asked if they drank alcohol in the past month, half said yes in 1991 but only one-third said yes in 2015 (MMWR, June 10, 2016).

However, the same report found that binge drinking is still prevalent—and that binge drinkers usually found an older person to buy alcohol for them. That is dangerous. In the United States, an estimated 860 people under age 21 die every year by drinking too much (Esser et al., 2017). Peer pressure, and inexperience, probably leads them to keep drinking long after they should stop.

The Monitoring the Future study found that in 2016:

- 16 percent of high school seniors report having had five drinks in a row in the past two weeks.
- 2 percent smoked cigarettes every day for the past month.
- 6 percent smoked marijuana every day.

[Miech et al., 2017]

These figures suggest that addiction is the next step for these high school students. They are not the only ones in trouble. This survey did not include students who were absent or truant or had dropped out, yet they have higher rates of daily drug use and addiction.

Compared to three decades ago, drug use is reduced. Are teenagers wiser or have adults made drug use more difficult? Nonetheless, teenage drug use still is common. Is further reduction possible?

Relaxing on Marijuana?
Synthetic marijuana ("K-2," or "Spice") can be a deadly drug, evident in this unconscious young man on a Harlem sidewalk. Since secret chemicals are mixed and added in manufacturing, neither laws nor hospitals can keep up with new toxic substances.

SPENCER PLATT/GETTY IMAGES

Developmentalists are concerned not only about e-cigarettes but also about misuse of addictive prescription drugs—both stimulants (such as Ritalin and Adderall) and opioids (such as OxyContin and fentanyl). Should laws be more restrictive, or does that itself encourage drug use?

Remember that most adolescents think they are exceptions, sometimes feeling invincible, sometimes fearing social disapproval, but almost never realistic about their own potential addiction. Instead, some get a thrill from breaking the law, and some use stimulants to improve cognition or other drugs to relieve stress. They do not see that over time stress and depression increase, and achievement decreases (McCabe et al., 2017; Bagot, 2017).

Every psychoactive drug excites the limbic system and interferes with the prefrontal cortex. Because of these neurological reactions, drug users are more emotional (varying from euphoria to terror, from paranoia to rage) than they would otherwise be. They are also less reflective.

Moodiness and impulsivity are characteristic of adolescents, and drugs make them worse. Every hazard—including car crashes, unsafe sex, and suicide—is more common among teens who have taken a psychoactive drug.

With harmful drugs, as with many other aspects of life, people of each generation prefer to learn things for themselves. A common phenomenon is **generational forgetting,** that each new cohort forgets what the previous cohort learned (Chassin et al., 2014; Johnston et al., 2012).

This trait has evolutionary advantages, in that the young are adventurous and brave. Yet mistrust of the older generation, added to loyalty to one's peers, leads not only to generational forgetting but also to a backlash. Consequently, when adults forbid something, that is a reason to try it, especially if adults exaggerate the dangers. If a friend passes out from drug use, adolescents may be slow to get medical help—a dangerous hesitancy.

Some antidrug curricula and advertisements make drugs seem exciting. Antismoking announcements produced by cigarette companies (such as a clean-cut young person advising viewers to think before they smoke) actually increase use (Strasburger et al., 2009).

None of this means that trying to halt early drug use is hopeless. Massive ad campaigns by public health advocates in Florida and California cut adolescent smoking almost in half, in part because the publicity appealed to the young. Teenagers respond to graphic images. In one example:

> A young man walks up to a convenience store counter and asks for a pack of cigarettes. He throws some money on the counter, but the cashier says "that's not enough." So the young man pulls out a pair of pliers, wrenches out one of his teeth, and hands it over. . . . A voiceover asks: "What's a pack of smokes cost? Your teeth."
>
> [Krisberg, 2014]

Parental example and social changes also make a difference. Throughout the United States, higher prices, targeted warnings, and better law enforcement have led to a marked decline in smoking among younger adolescents. Looking internationally, laws have an effect.

In Canada, cigarette advertising is outlawed, and cigarette packs have lurid pictures of diseased lungs, rotting teeth, and so on; fewer Canadian 15- to 19-year-olds smoke than in the United States.

THINK CRITICALLY: Might the fear of adolescent drug use be foolish, if most adolescents use drugs whether or not they are forbidden?

generational forgetting The idea that each new generation forgets what the previous generation learned. As used here, the term refers to knowledge about the harm drugs can do.

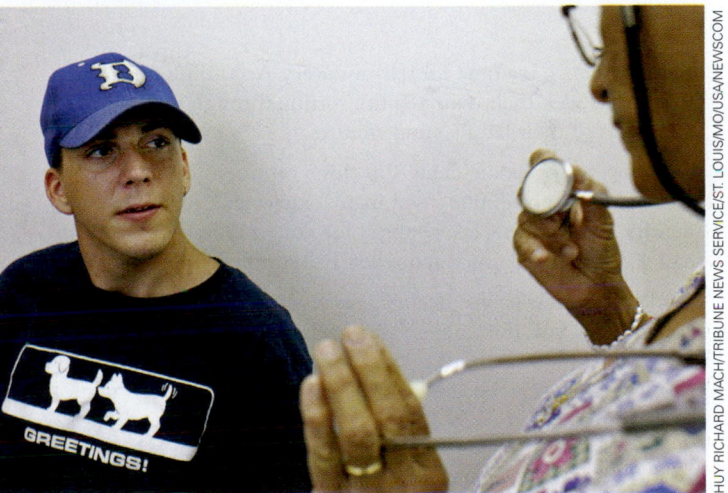

Serious Treatment A nurse checks Steve Duffer's blood pressure after a dose of Naltrexone, a drug with many side effects that combats severe addiction, in this case addiction to heroin. Steve is 24 in this photo; he was addicted the year before.

In the past chapters, we saw that the universal biological processes do not lead to universal psychosocial problems. This is particularly apparent in adolescence. Biology does not change, but context matters. Rates of teenage births and abortions are declining sharply, more students are graduating from high school, and fewer teens drink or smoke.

As explained at the beginning of these two chapters, adolescence starts with puberty; that much is universal. But what happens next depends on parents, peers, schools, communities, and cultures. In other words, the future of adolescents depends, in part, on you.

what have you learned?

1. Why are psychoactive drugs particularly attractive in adolescence?
2. Why are psychoactive drugs particularly destructive in adolescence?
3. What specific harm occurs with tobacco products?
4. How has adolescent drug use changed in the past decade?
5. What methods to reduce adolescent drug use are successful?

SUMMARY

Identity

1. Adolescence is a time for self-discovery. According to Erikson, adolescents seek their own identity, sorting through the traditions and values of their families and cultures.

2. Many young adolescents foreclose on their options without exploring possibilities, and many experience role confusion. Identity achievement takes longer for contemporary adolescents than it did a half-century ago when Erikson first described it.

3. Identity achievement occurs in many domains, including religion, politics, vocation, and gender. Each of these remains important over the life span, but timing, contexts, and often terminology have changed. Achieving vocational and gender identity is particularly difficult.

Close Relationships

4. Parents continue to influence their growing children, despite bickering over minor issues. Ideally, communication and warmth remain high, while parental control decreases and adolescents develop autonomy.

5. There are cultural differences in the timing of conflicts and in the benefits of parental monitoring. Too much parental control is harmful, as is neglect.

6. Peers and peer pressure can be beneficial or harmful. Adolescents select their friends, who then facilitate constructive and/or destructive behavior. Peer approval is particularly potent during adolescence.

7. Most adolescents in the United States use texting to connect with their peers. Sexting is also common, although adults see dangers in it, such as revenge porn, that peers do not.

8. Adolescents experience diverse sexual needs and may be involved in short-term or long-term romances, depending in part

on their peer group. Contemporary teenagers are less likely to have intercourse than was true a decade ago.

9. Some youths are sexually attracted to people of the same sex. Social acceptance of same-sex relationships is increasing, but in some communities and nations, gay, lesbian, bisexual, and transgender youth are bullied, rejected, or worse.

10. Many adolescents learn about sex from peers and the media—sources that are not comprehensive. Ideally, parents are the best teachers about sex, but many are silent or naive.

11. Some nations provide comprehensive sex education beginning in the early grades, and most U.S. parents want schools to teach adolescents about sex. Abstinence-only education is not effective at slowing down the age of sexual activity and may increase STIs.

Sadness and Anger

12. Almost all young adolescents become more self-conscious and self-critical than they were as children. A few become chronically sad and depressed.

13. Many adolescents (especially girls) think about suicide, and some attempt it. Few adolescents actually kill themselves; most who do so are boys.

14. At least in Western societies, almost all adolescents become more independent and angry as part of growing up, although most still respect their parents. Breaking the law and bursts of anger are common; boys are more likely to be arrested for violent offenses than are girls.

15. Adolescence-limited delinquents should be prevented from hurting themselves or others; life-course-persistent offenders may become career criminals. Early intervention—before the first arrest—is crucial to prevent serious delinquency.

Adulthood

We now begin the sixth part of this text. These three chapters cover 47 years (ages 18 to 65), when bodies mature, minds master new material, and people work productively.

No decade of adulthood is exclusively programmed for any one event: Adults at many ages get stronger and weaker, learn and produce, nurture friendships and marriages, care for children and aging relatives. Some experience hiring and firing, wealth and poverty, births and deaths, weddings and divorces, windfalls and disasters, illness and recovery. Adulthood is a long sweep, punctuated by momentous events, joyful and sorrowful.

There are some chronological norms, noted in these chapters. Early in adulthood, few people are married or settled in a career; later, most people have partners and offspring. Expertise is more likely at age 50 than 20.

Past development always matters: Adults are guided by nature and nurture, as they choose partners, activities, communities, and habits. For the most part, these are good years, when each person's goals become more attainable.

The experience of adulthood is not the same everywhere. In some nations and cultures, dominant influences are families, economics, and history; in others, genetic heritage and personal choice predominate. Economic forces are particularly strong when governments provide no safety nets, whereas genes and choices are more significant when governments and cultures help everyone. For example, virtually everyone marries in some nations, but genetic heritage and the ability to make a personal choice are stronger elsewhere. Many adults in such countries do not marry.

The following three chapters describe adulthood: the universals, the usual, and the diverse. As this introduction explains, be careful: Generalities are often wrong.

RAPIDEYE/ISTOCKIE+/GETTY IMAGES

Drug Use and Abuse

16. Most adolescents experiment with drugs, which may temporarily reduce stress and increase peer connections but may soon add to stress and social problems. Almost every adolescent tries alcohol, and many use e-cigarettes and marijuana. Both are technically illegal for those under 18 but are readily available to teenagers.

17. All psychoactive drugs are particularly harmful in adolescence, as they affect the developing brain and undermine impulse control. Prevention and moderation of adolescent drug use and abuse are possible. Price, perception, and parents have an effect.

KEY TERMS

identity versus role confusion (p. 350)

identity achievement (p. 350)

role confusion (p. 350)

foreclosure (p. 350)

moratorium (p. 350)

gender identity (p. 353)

familism (p. 357)

parental monitoring (p. 357)

peer pressure (p. 358)

deviancy training (p. 360)

sexual orientation (p. 362)

major depression (p. 367)

suicidal ideation (p. 367)

parasuicide (p. 367)

cluster suicides (p. 368)

adolescence-limited offender (p. 370)

life-course-persistent offender (p. 370)

generational forgetting (p. 377)

APPLICATIONS

1. Locate a news article about a teenager who committed suicide. Were there warning signs that were ignored? Does the report inadvertently encourage cluster suicides? Are parents, schools, or drugs unfairly blamed?

2. Research suggests that most adolescents have broken the law but that few have been arrested or incarcerated. Ask 10 of your fellow students whether they broke the law when they were under 18 and, if so, how often, in what ways, and with what consequences. (Assure them of confidentiality; remind them that drug use, breaking curfew, and skipping school were illegal.) Do you see any evidence of gender or ethnic differences? What additional research needs to be done?

3. Cultures vary in expectations for drug use. Interview three people from different backgrounds (not necessarily from different nations; each SES, generation, or religion has different standards) about their culture's drug use, including reasons for what is allowed and when. (Legal drugs should be included in your study.)

ESPECIALLY FOR ANSWERS

Response for Parents of a Teenager (from page 360): Remember: Communicate, do not control. Let your child talk about the meaning of the hairstyle. Remind yourself that a hairstyle in itself is harmless. Don't say, "What will people think?" or "Are you on drugs?" or anything that might give your child reason to stop communicating.

Response for Sex Educators (from page 365): Yes, but forgive them. Ideally, parents should talk to their children about sex, presenting honest information and listening to the child's concerns. However, many parents find it very difficult to do so because they feel embarrassed and ignorant. You might schedule separate sessions for adults over 30, for emerging adults, and for adolescents.

Response for Journalists (from page 368): Since teenagers seek admiration from their peers, be careful not to glorify the victim's life or death. Facts are needed, as is, perhaps, inclusion of warning signs that were missed or cautions about alcohol abuse. Avoid prominent headlines or anything that might encourage another teenager to do the same thing.

Response for Police Officers (from page 375): Avoid both extremes: Don't let them think this situation is either harmless or horrendous. You might take them to the police station and call their parents. These adolescents are probably not life-course-persistent offenders; jailing them or grouping them with other lawbreakers might encourage more crime.

Response for Parents Who Drink Socially (from page 375): No. Alcohol is particularly harmful for young brains. It is best to drink only when your children are not around. Children who are encouraged to drink with their parents are more likely to drink when no adults are present. It is true that adolescents are rebellious, and they may drink even if you forbid it. But if you allow alcohol, they might rebel with other drugs.

OBSERVATION QUIZ ANSWERS

Answer to Observation Quiz (from page 358): The girls are only observers, keeping a respectful distance.

Answer to Observation Quiz (from page 368): Both. It increases for boys but decreases for girls.

Answer to Observation Quiz (from page 373): Prescription drug use. The epidemic of opioid deaths among adults—which usually begin with misuse of a prescription drug—may soon emerge in adolescence, but there is no evidence yet.

RAPIDEYE/ISTOCK/E+/GETTY IMAGES

ADULTHOOD
Emerging Adulthood

what will you know?

- Why do young adults have so few children?
- Does college change the way people think?
- Do emerging adults still need and want their parents in their lives?

This chapter describes the pivot between childhood and adulthood, between growing up and being "a grown-up," as children call adults. The earlier and later periods discussed in this book are all explained in twin chapters—one for body and mind, and one for psychosocial development—but this period of life blurs the boundaries. One chapter is best.

Emerging adulthood is a time when people continue learning and exploring, postponing marriage, parenthood, and career while preparing for the rest of life. This once seemed to be a luxury stage for those with relatively high SES from developed nations, but now it is apparent worldwide (Padilla-Walker & Nelson, 2017).

In every nation, the average age of marriage and parenthood is later than it was 50 years ago. Millions of young adults are attending college and exploring vocations—unlike the generations preceding them, who were quick to settle down. Emerging adulthood is a dramatic example of a cohort change: Now we see it; then we did not.

Readers of this text have probably witnessed this stage in themselves or their friends. I witnessed it, too, in my children and me. For example, my husband and I worried that our youngest daughter was not taking life seriously, not doing what needed to be done, not sticking to any one goal, or friend, or hobby. When she was in high school we thought the problem was too much TV, so we hid the television. She was furious; she searched and found it. In desperation, my husband cut the wire (he reconnected it later).

That did not change our daughter's behavior; she still didn't study. Her English teacher said that he had seen dozens of students like her; she would eventually settle down. We waited.

She chose a small college in a semirural community; we hoped that context would stabilize her. Wrong. She still experimented and

Body Development
Strong and Active Bodies
OPPOSING PERSPECTIVES:
A Welcome Stage, or Just Weird?
Fertility, Then and Now
Taking Risks
A CASE TO STUDY: An Adrenaline
Junkie

Cognitive Development
A Fifth Stage
Countering Stereotypes
INSIDE THE BRAIN: Neurological
Advances in Emerging Adulthood
The Effects of College
A VIEW FROM SCIENCE: Stereotype
Threat
VISUALIZING DEVELOPMENT:
Why Study?
The Effects of Diversity

Psychosocial Development
Identity Achievement
Personality in Emerging Adulthood
Intimacy
Cohabitation

emerging adulthood
The period of life between the ages of 18 and 25. Emerging adulthood is now widely thought of as a distinct developmental stage.

TABLE 11.1	U.S. Deaths from the Top Three Causes*
Age Group	**Annual Rate per 100,000**
15–24	6
25–34	17
35–44	55
45–54	193
55–64	515
65–74	1,123
75–84	2,545
85+	6,224

Data from National Center for Health Statistics, 2014.
*Heart disease, cancer, and chronic lower respiratory diseases

organ reserve The capacity of organs to allow the body to cope with stress, via extra, unused functioning ability.

What a Body Can Do Here, at age 27, Tobin Heath leaps to celebrate her goal at the soccer World Cup final in Vancouver, after seven years of star performances. All young adults can have moments when their bodies and minds crescendo to new heights.

explored, as emerging adults do. She tutored refugees, got a part-time job at a chain restaurant, and transferred to another college. There she joined the crew team (which meant rising at dawn), majored in economics (as no one in our family ever had), spent a semester in a nation none of us had visited (Spain), and—to our happy surprise—graduated with honors.

But she was still restless. She lived in three places within a few years, was an intern at one company, a temporary worker at another, and unemployed for several months. Then, since age 25, she has had one employer, one apartment, one persona—and is warmly supportive of the family! In retrospect, I see emerging adulthood in her and in many other 18- to 25-year-olds.

Body Development

Biologically, the years from ages 18 to 25 have always been healthy, prime time for hard physical work and safe reproduction (see Table 11.1). However, the fact that young adults can carry rocks, plow fields, or produce babies is no longer admired.

If a contemporary young couple left high school to marry, build a home, and give birth year after year, neighbors would be appalled, not approving. Societies, families, and young adults expect more education, later marriage, and fewer babies than the norm a few decades ago.

By this point in your study, you may be skeptical of the previous paragraph; you know that cultural differences are vast. Might neighbors in some regions today approve of a young, fertile couple? Is this view of emerging adulthood too narrow, or distorted by personal experience? Scholars ask that question, too (see Opposing Perspectives).

Strong and Active Bodies

As has been true for thousands of years, every body system—including the digestive, respiratory, circulatory, and sexual-reproductive systems—functions optimally at the end of adolescence. The rapid and sometimes unsettling changes of adolescence are over: Emerging adults are at their peak of fertility and strength.

EXTRA CAPACITY, EXTRA BURDEN Neighborhoods, genes, and health habits from childhood have an impact in adulthood. Laboratory analysis of blood, urine, and body fat finds that some people age three times faster than others (Belsky et al., 2015).

About half of the difference between fast and slow aging is already evident by age 26. To appreciate this long reach of emerging adult health, it helps to understand three aspects of body functioning: *organ reserve, homeostasis,* and *allostatic load.*

Organ reserve refers to the extra power that each organ can employ when needed. Organ reserve shrinks each year of adulthood so that by old age a strain—shoveling snow, catching the flu, minor surgery—can overwhelm the body.

FRANCK FIFE/AFP/GETTY IMAGES

OPPOSING PERSPECTIVES

A Welcome Stage, or Just WEIRD?

This chapter is about emerging adulthood as a stage of human development, a time for questions, exploration, and experimentation. But is emerging adulthood universal? Might it be a cultural phenomenon for privileged youth who can afford to postpone work and family commitments?

The term *emerging adulthood* was coined by Jeffrey Arnett, a college professor in Missouri, who listened to his own students and realized they were neither adolescents nor adults. As a good researcher, he also queried young adults elsewhere in the United States, he read published research about "youth" or "late adolescence," and he thought about his own life. He decided that a new stage, requiring a new label, had appeared.

Arnett and others have now studied young adults in many Western European nations, and youth there meet the criteria for emerging adults. For example, when Danish 20- to 30-year-olds were asked what signified adulthood, they chose marriage, parenthood, financial self-sufficiency, and independence from parents. Relatively few of those under age 25 thought that they were adults (Arnett & Padilla-Walker, 2015).

But some scientists hold an opposing perspective. They are particularly critical of professors at U.S. universities who study their own students and then draw conclusions about all humankind.

Conclusions based on American college students may apply only to those who are **WEIRD**—from Western, Educated, Industrialized, Rich Democracies (Henrich et al., 2010). Most of the world's population are poor (even low-SES North Americans are rich by global measures), never reach college, and live in nations without regular elections. WEIRD people are unusual.

From that perspective, skewed perceptions are apparent. Indeed, referring to "the West" (North America and Western Europe) reveals a bias. Since Earth is round, people in "East Asia" (Japan, Korea, China) should call the United States the East, and call the "Middle East" (Israel, Jordan, Saudi Arabia, and so on) the Midwest.

The Canadian professor who developed the acronym WEIRD wrote "many psychologists . . . tend to think of cross-cultural research as a nuisance, necessary only to confirm the universality of their findings (which are usually based on WEIRD undergraduates)" (Henrich, 2015, p. 86). As one scientist says, "The WEIRD group represents maximally 5%

WEIRD
An acronym for Western, Educated, Industrialized, Rich Democracy. The criticism is that conclusions about human development based on people in such nations may not apply to most people in the world, who do not live in WEIRD nations.

of the world's population, but probably more than 90% of the researchers and scientists producing the knowledge that is represented in our textbooks work with participants from that particular context" (Keller, quoted in Armstrong, 2018).

Perhaps textbooks written for WEIRD people (most of you!) can be forgiven if they highlight the experience of WEIRD people. However, scientists seek evidence, and this text seeks to describe universals as well as variations. Is emerging adulthood a stage everywhere?

One group examined personality development among youth in 62 nations. They concluded that *when* emerging adulthood occurred varied (Bleidorn et al., 2013). The age when adulthood began was strongly affected by employment.

When people started work soon after adolescence ends (as in Pakistan, Malaysia, and Zimbabwe), personality maturation is rapid; when work began late (as in the Netherlands, Canada, and the United States), emerging adulthood lasts many years (Bleidorn et al., 2013). Other scientists have searched for this stage in many nations, and generally they have found it (Landberg et al., 2018).

Further confirmation comes from global statistics. A century ago, many women married in their teens. Now in sub-Saharan Africa, the average age when marriage occurs is 21 for women and 25 for men; in East Asia, 26 and 28; in Western Europe, 31 and 33.

The U.S. age of marriage has been rising every decade since 1960, and the median age at first marriage was 28 for women and 30 for men in 2016 (U.S. Census Bureau 2018). This does not include the millions who never marry. Data on childbearing, college attendance, and career commitment show similar trends worldwide.

By bestowing a label on this period, does that imply that it is acceptable or even laudable for young people to postpone adult responsibilities? Many postpone responsibility even after age 25. Deciding whether this stage is beneficial for communities or families is a matter of values—or opposing perspectives.

In emerging adulthood, however, organ reserve allows speedy recovery. A 20-year-old can stay awake all night, or take drugs that disrupt body function, and still get up the next day seemingly unharmed. Organ reserve has been activated, and the body has recovered.

Open Wide China has almost a billion adults who never saw dentists when they were young. They now have "Love Teeth Day," when, as shown here, professionals check their teeth and remedy any serious losses.

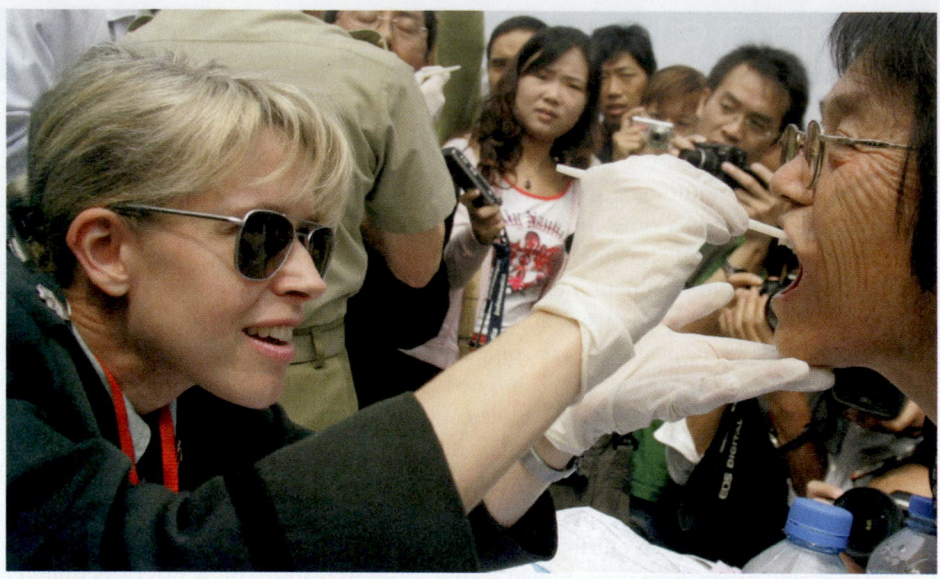

CHINA PHOTOS/GETTY IMAGES

homeostasis
The adjustment of all of the body's systems to keep physiological functions in a state of equilibrium. As the body ages, it takes longer for these homeostatic adjustments to occur, so it becomes harder for older bodies to adapt to stress.

allostasis
A dynamic body adjustment, related to homeostasis, that affects overall physiology over time. The main difference is that homeostasis requires an immediate response whereas allostasis requires longer-term adjustment.

allostatic load
The stresses of basic body systems that burden overall functioning, such as hypertension.

Closely related to organ reserve is **homeostasis**—a balance between various body reactions that keeps every physical function in sync with every other. For example, if the air temperature rises, people sweat, move slowly, and thirst for cold drinks—three aspects of body functioning that cool them. Homeostasis is quickest in early adulthood, partly because of organ reserve.

The next time you read about a rash of heat-wave deaths (e.g., Canada and Japan in 2018), note the age of the victims. As homeostasis slows down, the body dissipates heat less efficiently with age. Sometimes the demands temporarily overwhelm the heart, kidneys, or other organs. Even middle-aged adults are less protected from temperature changes—or any other stress on the body—than emerging adults (Larose et al., 2013).

Related to homeostasis is **allostasis,** a dynamic body adjustment that gradually changes overall physiology. The main difference between homeostasis and allostasis is time: Homeostasis requires an immediate response from body systems, whereas allostasis refers to long-term adjustment.

Allostasis depends on the biological circumstances of every earlier time of life, beginning at conception. The process continues with early adulthood conditions affecting later life, as evident in a measure called **allostatic load.** Although organ reserve usually protects emerging adults, the effects of lack of sleep, drug use, unhealthy eating, and so on accumulate. Some organ reserve is spent to maintain health, gradually adding to allostatic load.

EXAMPLES OF LOAD AND BALANCING Consider *sleep*. One night's poor sleep makes a person tired the next day—that is homeostasis, the body's way to maintain equilibrium. But if poor sleep quality is typical every day in youth, then appetite, mood, and activity adjust (more, down, less) to achieve homeostasis, while allostatic load rises (see Figure 11.1). By mid- and late adulthood, years of inadequate sleep load down overall health (McEwen & Karatsoreos, 2015; Carroll et al., 2014).

Another obvious example is *nutrition*. How much a person eats on a given day is affected by dozens of factors. An empty stomach triggers hormones, stomach pains, low blood sugar, and so on, all signaling that it is time to eat.

If an empty stomach is occasional, the cascade of homeostatic reactions makes people suddenly realize at 6 P.M. that they haven't eaten since breakfast. Dinner becomes a priority; the body signals that food is needed. Other factors, especially what food is available and whether other people are also eating, affect how much a person eats.

Over the years, allostasis is evident. If a person overeats or undereats day after day, the body adjusts: Appetite increases or decreases accordingly. But that ongoing homeostasis increases allostatic load, measured by body fat, factors in the blood, hypertension, and so on.

That high allostatic load makes a person vulnerable to diabetes, heart disease, stroke, and more—all the result of physiological adjustment (allostasis) to daily overeating (Sterling, 2012). At the opposite extreme, allostasis allows people with anorexia to feel energetic, not hungry, but the burden on their body eventually kills them.

Most young people learn to eat well, but some do not, making "emerging adulthood . . . a critical risk period in the development and prevention of disordered eating" (Goldschmidt et al., 2016, p. 480). The deadly consequences come later.

A third example comes from *exercise*. After a few minutes of exertion, the heart beats faster and breathing becomes heavier—these are homeostatic responses. Because of organ reserve, such temporary stresses on the body in early adulthood are no problem.

Over time, homeostasis adjusts and allows the person to exercise longer and harder. That decreases allostatic load by reducing the health risks evident in one's blood and weight.

The opposite is also true, as found in an impressive longitudinal study, CARDIA (Coronary Artery Risk Development in Adulthood), which began with thousands of healthy 18- to 30-year-olds. Many of them (3,154) were reexamined decades later. Those who were the least fit at the first assessment (more than 400 of them) were four times more likely to have diabetes and high blood pressure in middle age, because the adjustments of homeostasis affected organ reserve and allostatic load.

In CARDIA, problems for the least fit began but were unnoticed (except in blood work) when participants were in their 20s. Organ reserve allowed them to function quite well for the moment. Nonetheless, allostatic load increased (Camhi et al., 2013). By age 65, a disproportionate number had died.

Insufficient Sleep

Increases		Decreases
Appetite		Energy
Weight		Alertness
Depression		Health
Accidents		Life Expectancy

FIGURE 11.1 Don't Set the Alarm? Every emerging adult sometimes sleeps too little and is tired the next day—that is homeostasis. But years of poor sleep habits reduce years of life—a bad bargain. That is allostatic load.

Fastest Increase Obesity rates are rising faster in China than in any other nation as new American restaurants open every day. McDonald's and Starbucks each have about 5,000 outlets in China, catering especially to upwardly mobile young adults like these women in Beijing.

KEVIN FOY/ALAMY

See the Sweat This is "hot yoga," a 90-minute class in London with 26 positions and 2 breathing exercises, in 105°F (40.5°C) heat. Homeostasis allows young adults to stretch their muscles more easily in an overly heated room.

Attitudes about food are crucial. Young CARDIA adults were rarely obese, but if they sometimes felt their eating was out of control and had dieted, they were—25 years later—more often obese (Yoon et al., 2018).

These connections suggest an explanation for long-term effects of childhood poverty, racial discrimination, and maltreatment. Those problems affect all functions of the body, impairing health in middle age even if the childhood problems stopped decades ago (Destin, 2018; Widom et al., 2015b).

Fertility, Then and Now

As already mentioned, the sexual-reproductive system is quick and strong during emerging adulthood: Orgasms are frequent, the sex drive is powerful, erotic responses are thrilling, fertility is optimal, miscarriage is less common, and serious birth complications are unusual. Historically, most people married before age 20, had their first child within two years, and often a second and third before age 25; this is what their bodies did and what their culture expected.

That has changed dramatically. Bodies still crave sex, perhaps even earlier than they once did because puberty is earlier. Fertility peaks in late adolescence and early adulthood. But North American mores and emerging adult preferences are for births in the late 20s. Thus, biology and cognition conflict, which could cause a decade or more of sexual frustration or unwanted births.

Medical research has found a solution: sex without pregnancy. Young adults are as sexually active as ever, but the world's 2015 birth rate for women aged 20 to 24 was one-third lower than it was in 1960. In the United States, it was two-thirds lower (United Nations, 2017).

In earlier decades, premarital sex was forbidden, a taboo enforced in some cultures with diligent chaperoning, single-sex schools, and even the threat of death. Boys were less restricted, in the *double standard*, which seemed unfair to women.

A social construction developed that young women didn't want sex as much as young men did. Young adult men were supposed to make the first move, and brag about "scoring." The double standard has not disappeared completely, but particularly in the United States for premarital sex, it is changing rapidly (Bordini & Sperb, 2013) (see Figure 11.2). Of course, there was a good reason for the taboo on premarital intercourse.

Same Situation, Far Apart: The Bride and Groom Weddings everywhere involve special gowns and apparel—notice the gloves in Bali *(left)* and the headpiece in Malaysia *(right)*. They also involve families. In many places, the ceremony includes the new couple promising to care for their parents—a contrast to the U.S. custom of a father giving away his daughter to the groom.

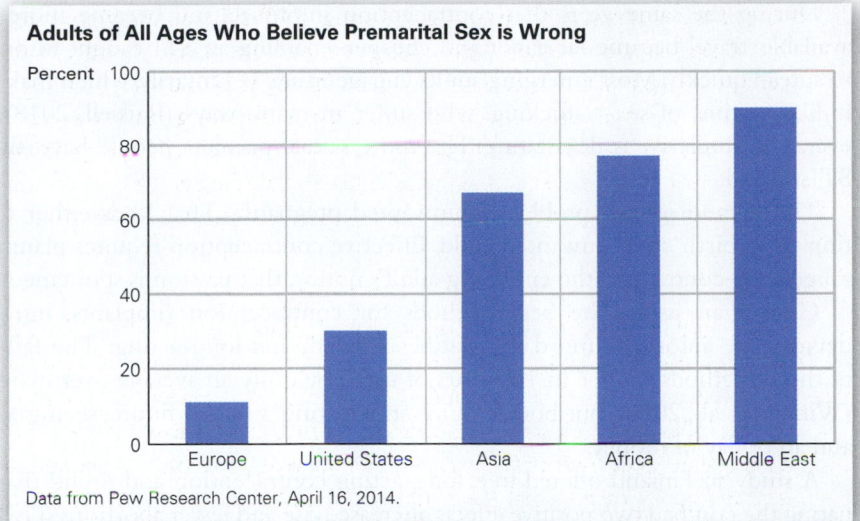

Adults of All Ages Who Believe Premarital Sex is Wrong

Data from Pew Research Center, April 16, 2014.

FIGURE 11.2 Everybody Is Doing It Cultural variation regarding sex before marriage, evident in this figure, illustrates a paradox: Sex is essential for community survival, yet attitudes about who, how, when, and why are diametrically opposite from one place, one era, and even one person to another.

Before effective contraception, premarital sex meant premarital pregnancy. Since children thrive best if their parents are committed to care for them, couples were pressured to wed. If an unmarried woman became pregnant, the man who got her pregnant was obligated to marry her (sometimes called a *shotgun wedding* because the girl's father threatened to kill the man if he did not marry her).

The shotgun wedding "is rapidly becoming a relic" of another era (Jayson, 2014), evidence of a cohort change. In the United States, if an unmarried woman becomes pregnant, she almost never is forced to marry the man. The opposite is sometimes true. Her parents may say that marriage would be a foolish choice.

In many ways, society has adjusted to the sexual revolution among young adults. For example, a century ago, thousands of private colleges were all male or all female (Miller-Bernal, 2000), a way to minimize sexual activity among students. By contrast, the United States in 2018 has only 4 all-male colleges and 27 all-female colleges.

The very fact that many women attend college is evidence that motherhood is no longer expected for sexually active young women. In the United States, almost twice as many men were in college than women 50 years ago. Now, for every 11 college men there are 15 women (National Center for Education Statistics, 2018). In almost every nation, more women than men attend college.

PROBLEMS WITH THE SEXUAL REVOLUTION The advent of effective contraception allowed a sexual revolution, welcomed by many young adults who, unlike earlier cohorts, no longer consider premarital sex a moral issue. For example, a survey of college students found that 85 percent agreed with this statement: "Any kind of consensual sex is okay as long as both persons freely agree to it" (England & Bearak, 2014, p. 1331).

However, the sexual revolution has led to two serious developmental problems in emerging adults. One is that the rate of sexually transmitted infections (STIs) is rising among unmarried people in their 20s.

Organ reserve and medical treatment almost always prevent death in emerging adulthood, but halting STIs requires medication. The age group with the lowest rate of doctor visits are 18- to 25-year-olds. In 2015, one out of every four emerging adults *never* saw a health professional (National Center for Health Statistics, 2017).

This lack of prevention, diagnosis, and early treatment for STIs is tragic. Sexual infections spread when their carriers are unaware of them. In this case, ignorance is dangerous. STIs increase infertility, disease, and death later in life, including from diseases that may seem unrelated, such as cancer and tuberculosis.

◆ **Especially for Nurses**
When should you suspect that a patient has an untreated STI? (see response, page 417)

During the same years that contraception improved and became more widely available, travel became far easier and cheaper, enabling an STI caught in one place to spread quickly. Most emerging adults engage in sex voluntarily, which makes them unlike victims of sex-trafficking, who suffer in many ways (Russell, 2018). However, one similarity is devastating: The more sexual partners people have, the more STIs spread.

The second serious problem is unwanted pregnancy. That leads either to abortion or to birth of an unwanted child. Effective contraception requires planning and diligence—contrary to the emerging adult's notion that passion is spontaneous.

Cost is an issue. The best methods for contraception (implants, intrauterine devices) are automatic (no daily routines needed) and long-acting. The failure rate of those methods is once in 100 years of use (obviously an average over many users) (Winner et al., 2012), but both require anticipating a sexual future, seeing a doctor, and an outlay of money.

A study in Finland offered free, long-acting contraception and found that eliminating the cost had two positive effects: increased use and fewer abortions (Gyllenberg et al., 2018). But, making contraception free for all emerging adults requires a massive cultural shift among older adults. Most people over age 50 who hope young adults do not engage in sexual activity remember when fear of unwanted pregnancy led to less sex and thus do not want to pay for their contraception.

Taking Risks

The spread of sexual diseases is one example of a generalization first expressed in Chapter 1: Every behavior and every age entails gains and losses. Some emerging adults bravely, or foolishly, take risks—a behavior that is gender- and age-related, as well as genetic and hormonal. Those who are genetically impulsive *and* male *and* in emerging adulthood are most likely to be brave and foolish.

BENEFITS OF RISK-TAKING In one study, 10- to 30-year-olds judged "how good or bad an idea is it to . . ." do various risky things (such as riding a bicycle down the stairs or taking pills at a party) (Shulman & Cauffman, 2014, p. 170). The participants

Who and Where? Knowing the attraction to danger of emerging-adult men makes it easy to guess *who*—a 19-year-old male. But *where* is harder—that dangerous leap into the ocean could be occurring in many nations. This one is taking place in the Indian Ocean in Sri Lanka.

STUART DUNN/ALAMY

had only two seconds to make a snap judgment on a sliding scale from 0 to 100. For instance, the bicycle-riding could be rated at 70 (a somewhat bad idea) and the pills at 99 (a very bad idea). There also were eight items that were not risky at all, such as eating a sandwich.

Risky items were rated increasingly more favorably (closer to a good idea) every year from age 10 to age 20 and then rated less favorably (closer to a bad idea) every year from age 20 to age 30. More of the older respondents had done the risky things (the average 15- to 17-year-old had done four of the items; the average 20- to 25-year-old had done seven), but that did not affect how good or bad each item was thought to be.

For example, whether or not a person had taken pills at a party was not related to whether or not they thought that was very risky. Instead, the crucial factor was maturation. The participants saw more risk in various items as they grew older, whether or not they personally had done them (Shulman & Cauffman, 2014).

Of course, risk-taking is not always bad. An emerging adult's bravery may lead to enrolling in college, moving to a new place, joining a sports team, finding a new job, enlisting in the military, or volunteering for work in a poor nation or troubled neighborhood. Emerging adults do these more often than older adults; societies benefit.

A historic example are the thousands of soldiers over the centuries who volunteered to fight against foes they never knew. Most national leaders and citizens are glad for this risk-taking.

A CASE TO STUDY

An Adrenaline Junkie

The fact that extreme sports are age-related is evident in Travis Pastrana, "an extreme sports renaissance man—a pro adrenaline junkie/daredevil/speed demon—whatever you want to call him" (Giblin, 2014). After several accidents that almost killed him, Pastrana won the 2006 X Games motocross competition at age 22 with a double backflip because, he explained,

> "The two main things are that I've been healthy and able to train at my fullest, and a lot of guys have had major crashes this year" (quoted in Higgins, 2006, p. D-7).

Four years later, Pastrana set a new record for leaping through big air in an automobile, as he drove over the ocean from a ramp on the California shoreline to a barge more than 250 feet out. He crashed into a barrier on the boat but emerged, seemingly ecstatic and unhurt, to the thunderous cheers of thousands of other young adults on the shore (Roberts, 2010).

In 2011, a broken foot and ankle made him temporarily halt extreme sports—but soon he returned to the acclaim of his cohort, winning races rife with flips and other hazards. In 2013, after some more serious injuries, he said that he was "still a couple of surgeries away" from racing on a motorcycle, so he turned to NASCAR.

In 2014 at age 30, after becoming a husband and a father (twice), he quit NASCAR. He said that his most hazardous race days were over, which is similar to many emerging adults who become less inclined to risk-taking with marriage and maturity. Now Pastrana is an icon for the next generation of daredevil young men.

Dangerous Pleasure Here, Travis Pastrana prepares to defy death once again as a NASCAR driver. Two days later, his first child was born, and two months later, he declared his race record disappointing. At age 30 he quit, declaring on Facebook that he would devote himself to his wife and family. Is that maturation, fatherhood, or failure?

JOHN HARRELSON/GETTY IMAGES

EXTREME SPORTS Is recreation that challenges the player a positive risk or a negative one? Many emerging adults climb mountains with perpendicular cliffs, surf in oceans with 20-foot waves, run in pain, play past exhaustion, and so on. An attraction to danger is characteristic of this age, the reason for what demographers call the *accident bump* in early adulthood.

New extreme sports—skydiving, bungee jumping, pond swooping, parkour, potholing (in caves), waterfall kayaking, shark-diving, jet skiing, and ziplining hundreds of feet above the ground—attract thousands of emerging adults. Is their fun foolish? A Case to Study explores this further.

Many doctors try to mitigate the risks of each sport, and equipment is designed to protect the skull or the spine in a fall (Denq & Delasobera, 2018). However, broken ankles, twisted muscles, and dislocated shoulders are common—and many young adults with a cast or crutches proudly explain how that injury occurred.

Popular college sports entail physical risks. Football not only injures the body (star players often are on the disabled list) but also can lead to concussions that increase the risk severe of brain damage and disease (Vos et al., 2018). A study compared college football players with matched college athletes who were stars of track and field. Brains of the former were significantly impaired (Adler et al., 2018).

Why, then, would any college promote that sport? Because the students want it! Large stadiums, tailgate parties, cheerleaders, mascots, homecoming weekends, and so on are integral to college life on many campuses.

THINK CRITICALLY: In 40 of the 50 U.S. states, the highest salary for a public employee is not paid to the governor or the college president but to the football coach. Is that how it should be?

DANGEROUS RISKS Risk-taking is often destructive. Although their bodies are strong and their reactions quick, emerging adults nonetheless have more serious accidents than do people of any other age (see Figure 11.3). The low rate of disease between ages 18 and 25 is counterbalanced by a high rate of violent death.

Risks that are more common in emerging adulthood than any other time include:

- unprotected sex with a new partner;
- driving without a seat belt;
- carrying a loaded gun;
- abusing drugs;
- addictive gambling.

All these are done partly for a rush of adrenaline (Cosgrave, 2010). In the United States, the peak age for serious crime is 19, for unintended pregnancy 18 to 19, for automobile driver death 21 (Shulman & Cauffman, 2014).

Fatal accidents, homicide, and suicide result in more deaths in emerging adulthood than all other causes *combined*. This is true even in nations with high rates of infectious diseases and malnutrition. The contrast between sudden, violent deaths and slower, disease deaths is most stark in nations with good medical care.

In 2015 in the United States, of the 15- to 24-year-olds who died, fewer than 5 percent were victims of cancer, although that was the leading cause of disease death. Compared to cancer, homicides were three times, suicide four times, and fatal accidents nine times as likely. Rates of all of these rise in late adolescence and peak in the early 20s (National Center for Health Statistics, 2017).

FIGURE 11.3 Send Them Home Accidents, homicides, and suicides occur more frequently during emerging adulthood than later. Note that the age range of more patients falls within the 7 years of emerging adulthood than within the 20 years of adulthood. If all data were reported by 7-year age groups, the chart would be much starker. Fewer young adults stay in the hospital, however. They are usually stitched, bandaged, injected, and sent home.

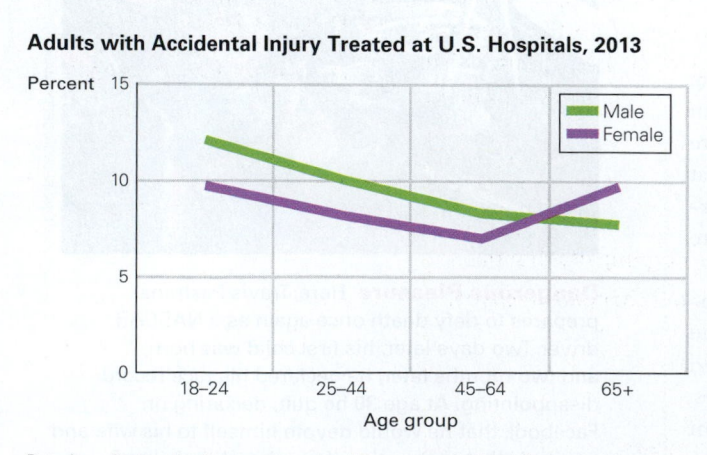

Adults with Accidental Injury Treated at U.S. Hospitals, 2013

Data from Centers for Disease Control and Prevention, National Center for Injury Prevention and Control, Division of Analysis, Research, and Practice Integration, 2013.

DRUG ABUSE By definition, **drug abuse** occurs whenever a drug (legal or illegal, prescribed or not) is used in a harmful way, damaging a person's physical, cognitive, or psychosocial well-being. The interaction between age and drug abuse illustrates the nature of emerging adults, who seem attracted rather than repulsed by the potential for jail in buying, carrying, and using an illegal drug.

Illegal drug use peaks at about age 20 and declines sharply with age (see Figure 11.4). Addiction to legal drugs (no arrest imminent) has a much slower quit rate, probably because be-

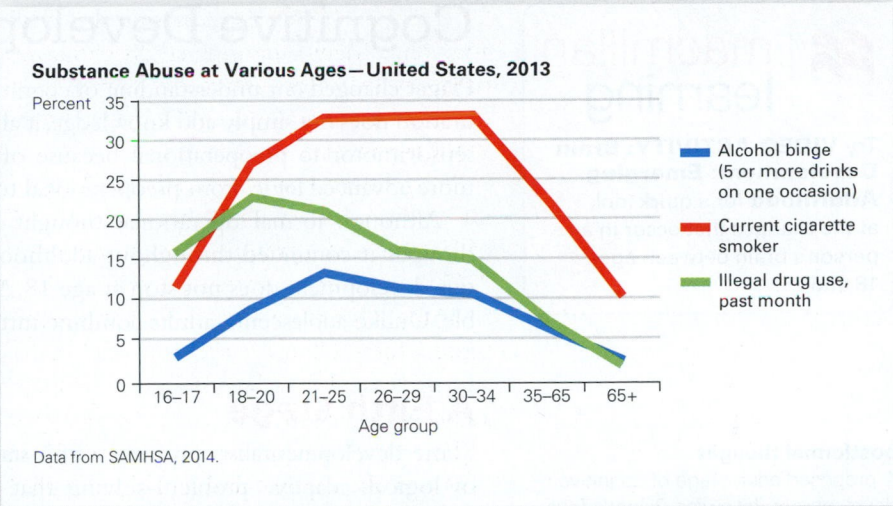

Substance Abuse at Various Ages—United States, 2013

Data from SAMHSA, 2014.

cause the excitement of avoiding the police is not part of the addiction. Death from opioids, including heroin, fentanyl, and legally prescribed opioids, peaks after age 25, probably because opioid drug use is less driven by thrill and rebellion (Seth et al., 2018).

Quitting addiction is difficult at any age, but when emerging adulthood is over, the thrill is gone and drugs are used to stop unpleasant emotions more than to promote exciting ones. For that reason, abstinence becomes more common after emerging adulthood, now a source of pride not embarrassment (Heyman, 2013).

Men tend to take more risks and use more drugs, but in the United States young women are also vulnerable. A nationwide study found that 24 percent of women aged 18 to 25 had binged on alcohol in the past month (for women a binge is defined as four or more drinks on one occasion). That emerging adult rate was higher than the rate for either younger or older women (MMWR, January 11, 2013). Moreover, those 24 percent *averaged* four binge episodes per month and six drinks per occasion, both more than older female bingers. Rates *rose* with income and education!

Many colleges restrict alcohol on campus, not only for legal reasons but to decrease property destruction and sexual assault (rates rise when both parties have been drinking or doing drugs [Zinzow & Thompson, 2015]). Colleges only have limited success, however, because local bars and national fraternities resist (McMurtrie, 2014).

A large part of the problem is the students themselves, many of whom use alcohol and drugs to overcome the awkwardness of social interaction with strangers. Students at residential colleges use alcohol and drugs far more than young adults the same age who live with their parents or who are married and living with their spouse. That leads us to the next topics of this chapter—cognitive and psychosocial development.

FIGURE 11.4 Too Old for That As you can see, emerging adults are the biggest substance abusers, but illegal drug use drops much faster than does cigarette use or binge drinking.

drug abuse
When drug use is harmful, either to the body or to society—as when alcohol makes a person risk their own health or hurt others.

> **THINK CRITICALLY:** Why are college students more likely to abuse drugs than emerging adults who are not in college?

what have you learned?

1. Why is maximum physical strength usually attained in emerging adulthood?

2. Over the past decades, what has changed, and what has not changed, in sexual activity?

3. Why are STIs more common currently than 50 years ago?

4. What are the social benefits of risk-taking?

5. Why are some sports more attractive at some ages than others?

6. Why are serious accidents more common in emerging adulthood than later?

Try **VIDEO ACTIVITY: Brain Development: Emerging Adulthood** for a quick look at the changes that occur in a person's brain between ages 18 and 25.

Cognitive Development

Piaget changed our understanding of cognitive development. He recognized that maturation does not simply add knowledge, it allows a leap forward at each stage: first from sensorimotor to preoperational because of language (symbolic thought), then with more advanced logic, from preoperational to concrete to formal (abstract) operations.

Although formal operational thought was the final one of Piaget's stages (he thought it continued throughout adulthood), psychologists now realize that cognitive development does not stop at age 18. Adult thinking is more practical and flexible. Unlike adolescents, adults combine intuitive and analytic thought.

A Fifth Stage

Some developmentalists propose a fifth stage, called **postformal thought**, a "type of logical, adaptive problem-solving that is a step more complex than scientific formal-level Piagetian tasks" (Sinnott, 2014, p. 3). In postformal cognition, "thinking needs to be integrated with emotional and pragmatic aspects, rather than only dealing with the purely abstract" (Labouvie-Vief, 2015, p. 89).

As you remember from Chapter 9, adolescents use two modes of thought (dual processing) but have difficulty combining them. The first mode is formal analysis to learn science, distill principles, develop arguments, and resolve the world's problems. In the second mode, teenagers think spontaneously and emotionally about personal issues, such as what to wear, whom to befriend, whether to skip class. For such issues, they prefer quick actions and reactions, only later realizing the consequences.

Postformal thinkers are better at using both modes together. They are less impulsive and reactive. They are flexible, noting difficulties and anticipating problems instead of denying, avoiding, or procrastinating. Postformal thinking is more practical.

Countering Stereotypes

Cognitive flexibility, particularly the ability to change childhood assumptions, helps counter stereotypes. Young adults show many signs of such flexibility. The very fact that emerging adults postpone marriage and parenthood shows that adult thinking

postformal thought
A proposed adult stage of cognitive development, following Piaget's four stages, that goes beyond adolescent thinking by being more practical, more flexible, and more dialectical (i.e., more capable of combining contradictory elements into a comprehensive whole).

Where Is This? Hundreds of health professionals offer free medical care at this Buddhist temple, likely employing postformal thought as they identify problems and risks and recommend strategies for promoting health. One of the professionals here is Daniel Garcia, who volunteers with APA Healthcare, an undergraduate organization from UCLA.

↑ **OBSERVATION** QUIZ
What city is this? (see answer, page 417)

MARCUS YAM / LOS ANGELES TIMES VIA GETTY IMAGES

INSIDE THE BRAIN

Neurological Advances in Emerging Adulthood

Piaget himself never used the term *postformal*. If the definition of a cognitive *stage* is to attain a new set of brain connections (such as the left brain dominance of language that distinguishes sensorimotor from preoperational thought), then adulthood has no stages. But if cognition is the product of neurological advances, then emerging adulthood may be a new intellectual stage.

This idea is suggested by research on the brain. As described in Chapter 9, the prefrontal cortex is not fully mature until the early 20s, and new dendrites connect throughout life. Thinking changes as the brain matures (Lemieux, 2012), with brain development affected by experiences more than by time alone (Sinnott, 2014). As is evident throughout childhood, adult brains benefit from better neurological connections and greater experience of the social world (Grayson & Fair, 2017).

A summary of the research on neurological advances in emerging adulthood finds that three factors are particularly important: socioeconomic status, peer involvement, and culture (Foulkes & Blakemore, 2018). Putting these three together is the task of the brain during late adolescence and early adulthood. That might explain why sensation-seeking peaks at about age 19 but emotional regulation peaks at about age 25, according to a study of 11 cultures (Steinberg et al., 2018).

Particularly interesting is the role of peers. When a person must assess and connect with new people—as occurs after high school graduation when the emerging adult enters college or joins a new workforce—the brain must engage in mentalizing, which is understanding the thoughts, attitudes, and emotions of other people.

Mentalizing is far more advanced than the precursor ability, theory of mind, which you remember from Chapter 5. It continues to develop in adolescence and emerging adulthood.

Several parts of the brain, called the *social brain network* (specifically the dorso lateral prefrontal cortex, the anterior temporal cortex, and the posterior superior temporal sulcus), continue to add gray matter in late adolescence and early adulthood (Foulkes & Blakemore, 2018). You do not need to know those names, but all of these parts of the brain are far more developed in adult humans than other animals. It may be that, as social interaction demands (later marriage, more education) on young adults have increased in recent years, the social brain continues to grow to accommodate new analysis.

That is not yet proven, but it is known that neurological maturation continues in emerging adulthood. The brains of young adults do much more than respond to simple rewards, such as food, shelter, and sex (as is true for lower animals). Instead, the social demands from new peers in the wider world are met with brain maturation (Reniers et al., 2017).

Thus, considerable neurological maturation during emerging adulthood, with pruning and more myelination of both the prefrontal and parietal lobes, is evident (Sherman et al., 2018). This brain maturation allows better cognitive control of impulses—a welcome development that eventually reduces impulsive risk-taking and allows a more mature understanding of society.

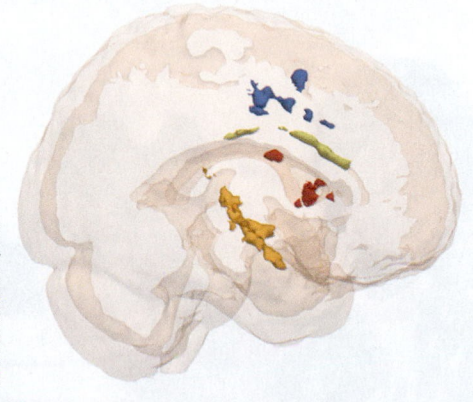

(a)

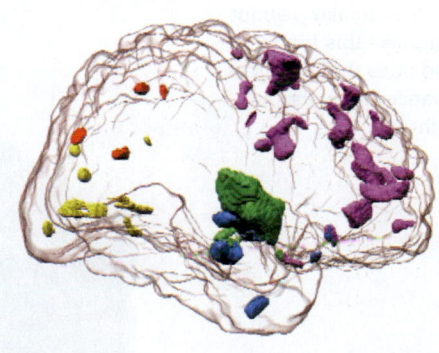

(b)

Thinking Away from Home *(a)* Entering a residential college means experiencing new foods, new friends, and new neurons. A longitudinal study of 18-year-old students at the beginning and end of their first year in college (Dartmouth) found increases in the brain areas that integrate emotion and cognition—namely, the cingulate (blue and yellow), caudate (red), and insula (orange). Researchers also studied one-year changes in the brains of students over age 25 at the same college and found no dramatic growth. *(b)* Shown here are the areas of one person's brain that changed from age 14 to age 25. The frontal cortex (purple) demonstrated many changes in particular parts, as did the areas for processing speech (green and blue)—a crucial aspect of young-adult learning. Areas for visual processing (yellow) showed minimal change.

Researchers now know that brains mature in many ways between adolescence and adulthood; scientists are not yet sure of the cognitive implications.

is not determined by childhood experience or tradition. Early life is influential, but postformal thinkers are not stuck there.

Research on racial prejudice is an example. Many people are less prejudiced than their parents, and they believe they are not biased. For example, few think that race is an important consideration in choosing a spouse, and 17 percent marry someone of another race (Bialik, 2017). But, research on implicit prejudice finds that many people of all races and ages have *both* unconscious prejudice and rational tolerance—a combination that illustrates dual processing.

Fortunately, postformal reasoning allows rational thinking to overcome emotional reactions, with responses dependent on reality, not stereotypes (Sinnott, 2014). A characteristic of adult thinking may be the flexibility that allows recognition and reconciliation of contradictions, thus reducing prejudice.

Unfortunately, many people do not recognize their own stereotypes, even when false beliefs harm them. One of the most pernicious results is **stereotype threat**, arising in people who worry that other people might judge them as stupid, lazy, oversexed, or worse because of their ethnicity, sex, age, or appearance.

The idea is that people have a stereotype that other people have a stereotype: Then, the imagined *possibility* of being stereotyped arouses anxiety, impairs the hippocampus, and hijacks memory, disrupting cognition. That is stereotype threat, as further explained in A View from Science on page 397.

The Effects of College

A major reason why emerging adulthood has become a new period of development, when people postpone the usual markers of adult life (marriage, a steady job), is that many older adolescents seek further education instead of taking on adult responsibilities. Of course, many do not attend college. However, here we focus on college, because, at least in theory, college promotes cognitive development.

There is no dispute that tertiary education improves health and wealth. The data on virtually every physical condition, and every indicator of material success, confirm that college graduates are ahead of high school graduates, who themselves are ahead of those without high school diplomas. This is apparent even when the comparisons are between students of equal ability: It is the education, not just the potential, that makes a difference.

stereotype threat
The thought in a person's mind that one's appearance or behavior will be misread to confirm another person's oversimplified, prejudiced attitudes.

◆ **Especially for Those Considering Studying Abroad**
Given the effects of college, would it be better for a student to study abroad in the first year or the last year of college education? (see response, page 417)

Anxiety? Does thinking about taking a test make this man anxious, and does that undercut his performance? If so, that is stereotype threat.

PEOPLEIMAGES/E+/GETTY IMAGES

A VIEW FROM SCIENCE

Stereotype Threat

One statistic has troubled social scientists for decades: African American men have lower grades in high school and earn only half as many college degrees as African American women (Chronicle of Higher Education, 2014a). This cannot be genetic, since the women have the same genes (except one chromosome) as the men.

Most scientists have blamed the historical context, parental practice, and current racism. One African American scholar, Claude Steele, thought of another possibility—that the problem originated in the mind, not in the family or society. He labeled it *stereotype threat,* a "threat in the air," not in reality (Steele, 1997). The mere *possibility* of being negatively stereotyped may disrupt cognition and emotional regulation.

Steele suspected that African American males who know the stereotype that they are poor scholars will become anxious in educational settings. Their anxiety may increase stress hormones that reduce their ability to respond to intellectual challenges.

Then, if they score low, they protect their pride by denigrating academics. They come to believe that school doesn't matter, that people who are "book smart" are not "street smart." That belief leads them to disengage from high school and college, which results in lower achievement. The greater the threat, the worse they do (Taylor & Walton, 2011).

Stereotype threat is more than a hypothesis. Hundreds of studies show that anxiety reduces achievement. The threat of a stereotype causes women to underperform in math, older people to be forgetful, bilingual students to stumble with English, and every member of a stigmatized minority in every nation to handicap themselves because of what they imagine others might think (Inzlicht & Schmader, 2012).

Not only academic performance but also athletic prowess and health habits may be impaired if stereotype threat makes people anxious (Aronson et al., 2013). Every sphere of life may be affected. One recent example is that blind people are underemployed if stereotype threat makes them hesitate to learn new skills (Silverman & Cohen, 2014).

The worst part of stereotype threat is that it is self-imposed. People alerted to the possibility of prejudice are not only hypersensitive when it occurs, but their minds are hijacked, undercutting potential. Their initial reaction may be to try harder to prove the stereotype wrong, and if that extra effort fails, they stop trying (Mangels et al., 2012; Aronson et al., 2013).

The harm from anxiety is familiar to those who study sports psychology. When star athletes unexpectedly underperform (called "choking"), stereotype threat arising from past team losses may be the cause (Jordet et al., 2012). Many female players imagine they are not expected to play as well as men (e.g., someone told them "you throw like a girl"), and that itself impairs performance (Hively & El-Alayli, 2014).

The next step for many developmentalists is figuring out how stereotype threat can be eliminated, or at least reduced (Inzlicht & Schmader, 2012; Sherman et al., 2013; Dennehy et al., 2014). Reminding people of their own potential, and the need to pursue their goals, is one step.

The question for each of us is what imagined criticisms from other people impair our own achievement. Then we can examine those criticisms and decide that they are not really held by the other people, or decide that they are the product of someone else's prejudice. Those decisions make us realize that the stereotypes have no power over us unless we let them. The creativity of adult cognition allows people to "challenge your stigma," reframing stereotypes to make them empowering, not debilitating (Wang et al., 2017).

THINK CRITICALLY: What imagined criticisms impair your own achievement, and how can you overcome them?

GOVERNMENT SUPPORT The United States was the first major nation to believe that everyone might benefit from college, and thus every state opened and funded state colleges and universities, often several per state (California has 36). Among the nations of the world, the United States has one of the highest rates of older citizens who are college graduates.

Recently, however, many other nations have increased public funding for college while the United States has decreased it. As a result, among the 35 developed nations in the OECD (Organization for Economic Cooperation and Development) nine other nations have a higher proportion of 25- to 34-year-olds who are college graduates (OECD, 2018) (see Figure 11.5).

FIGURE 11.5 How Things Have Changed This chart reveals two things. First, it shows whether young college graduates have grandparents and parents who did not attend college—dramatically true in Korea and Poland. Second, it reveals whether public support for college has increased in the past 20 years—not true in the United States, Israel, and Finland. In the United States, although more people begin college, fewer graduate, partly because the income gap is wider than it once was, while public funding is reduced. Finding four years of tuition money is increasingly difficult for North Americans, and college loans are seen as a boon to banks but not individuals—making young adults wary of signing on the dotted line.

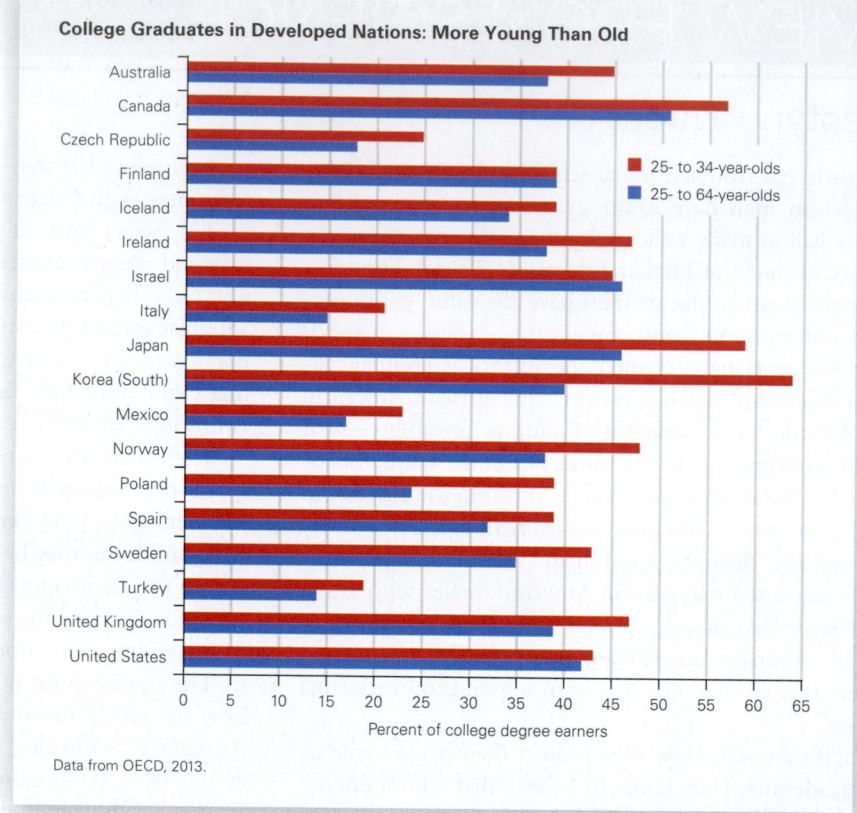

College Graduates in Developed Nations: More Young Than Old

Data from OECD, 2013.

◆ **Especially for High School Teachers**
One of your brightest students doesn't want to go to college. She would rather keep waiting tables in a restaurant, where she makes good money in tips. What do you say? (see response, page 417)

This is ironic because U.S. Census data and surveys find that college education benefits individuals and society *more* than it did 30 years ago. The average college man earns an additional $17,558 per year compared to a high school graduate. Women also benefit, but not as much, earning $10,393 more per year (Autor, 2014). That higher salary is averaged over the years of employment: Most new graduates do not see such a large wage difference; by middle age, the differences are dramatic.

DEBTS AND DROPOUTS The financial benefits of college seem particularly strong for ethnic minorities and low-income families. Ironically, they are least likely to enter college or earn a degree even though they are most likely to benefit when they do so.

The longitudinal data make it clear that a college degree is worth the expense, because investing in college education returns the initial expense more than five times. That means if a student spends a nickel now, they get a quarter back in a few years, or if a degree costs $200,000, over a lifetime the return is $1 million.

However, there is a major problem with that calculation. Although virtually all freshmen expect to graduate, about half leave college before graduating. They lose out, because most of the lifelong income benefits come from earning a degree. Since the expenses begin with enrollment but the benefits result from the degree, beginning college may not be as great an investment as the previous paragraph suggests.

Statistics on college graduation are discouraging. Only about one-third of students at private, for-profit colleges earn a degree; about half the students at public institutions do so, as do almost two-thirds of the students at private, nonprofit colleges. Sadly, schools with the lowest graduation rates are the most popular. The reasons may be the marketing efforts of the for-profit schools, which are designed to appeal to the emotional, intuitive thinking of the adolescent, not the logical reflection of the adult.

Since students pay when they enroll each semester, parental SES is the strongest predictor of whether or not someone will earn a college degree. Most (60 percent)

of those of high SES earning a bachelor's degree, but few (14 percent) of those with low family SES do so (Kena et al., 2015). Money is a major reason that many college students drop out before graduation (McKinney & Burridge, 2015). Both money and role models make college seem essential to some young adults and irrelevant to others. One young man said:

> People always ask me, why don't you go to college? My dad, he never went. You work, you pay your bills, you help with the rent. My priority right now is to be responsible, to know how adult life works. It might go bad for me, or it might go good. It's going to be hard. . . . I'm scared we'll wake up some day and say "We don't got nothing to eat."
>
> *[Maldonado, quoted in Healy, 2017]*

What this young man does not know is that when students of equal ability and family background are compared, education still makes a notable difference in later health and wealth.

COLLEGE AND COGNITION For developmentalists interested in cognition, the crucial question about college education is not about wealth, health, rates, expense, or even graduation. Instead, developmentalists wonder whether college advances critical thinking and postformal thought. The answer seems to be yes, but some studies dispute that.

Let us begin with the classic work of William Perry (1981, 1970/1998). After repeatedly questioning students at Harvard, Perry described students' thinking through nine levels of complexity over the four years that led to a bachelor's degree.

Perry found that freshmen arrived thinking in a simplistic dualism. Most 18-year-olds tended to think in absolutes, believing that things were either right or wrong. Answers to questions were yes or no, the future led to success or failure, and the job of the professor (the Authority) was to distinguish between the two and then tell the students.

By the end of college, Perry's subjects believed strongly in relativism, recognizing that many perspectives might be valid and that almost nothing was totally right or wrong. But they were able to move past that: They had become critical thinkers, realizing that they needed to move forward in their lives by adopting one point of view, yet expecting to change their thinking if new challenges and experiences produced greater insight. They no longer thought professors had the answers.

Perry found that the college experience itself caused this progression: Peers, professors, books, and class discussion all stimulated new questions and thoughts. Other research confirmed Perry's conclusions. In general, the more years of higher education a person had, the deeper and more postformal that person's reasoning became (Pascarella & Terenzini, 1991).

VIDEO: The Effects of Mentoring on Intellectual Development: The University-Community Links Project shows how an after-school study enhancement program has proven beneficial for both its mentors and the at-risk students who attend it.

CURRENT CONTEXTS But wait. You probably noticed that Perry's study was first published decades ago. His research was valid: Hundreds of other studies in the twentieth century also found that college deepens cognition. However, since you know that historical conditions have a major impact, you are right to wonder whether those conclusions still hold.

Many recent books criticize college education on exactly those grounds. Notably, a twenty-first-century longitudinal study of a cross section of U.S. college students found that students' growth in critical thinking, analysis, and communication over the four years of college was only half as much as among college students two decades ago. In the first two years of college, 45 percent of the students did not advance at all (Arum & Roksa, 2011).

The reasons were many. Compared to decades ago, students study less, professors expect less, and students avoid classes that require reading at least 40 pages a week or

Culture and Cohort Ideally, college brings together people of many backgrounds who learn from each other. This scene from a college library in the United Arab Emirates would not have happened a few decades ago. The dress of these three suggests that culture still matters, but education is recognized worldwide as benefiting every young person in every nation.

writing 20 pages a semester. Administrators and faculty still hope for intellectual growth, but rigorous classes are not required, and many are canceled for low enrollment.

A follow-up study of the same individuals after graduation found that those who did more socializing than studying were likely to be unemployed or have low-income jobs. College gave them a sense that things would get better, not the critical-thinking skills or the self-discipline that they needed for adult success (Arum & Roksa, 2014).

Some other observers blame the wider culture for forcing colleges to follow a corporate model, with students as customers who need to be satisfied rather than youth who need to be challenged (Deresiewicz, 2014). Customers, apparently, demand costly dormitories and sports facilities.

A related development is that U.S. young adults are less proficient in various skills, including reading comprehension, problem solving, and especially math, according to international tests (see Figure 11.6). A report on these data is particularly critical of the disparity between the cognitive skills of the rich and the poor, stating "to put it bluntly, we no longer share the growth and prosperity of the nation the way we did in the decades between 1940 and 1980" (Goodman et al., 2015, p. 2).

MOTIVATION TO ATTEND COLLEGE Motivation is crucial for every intellectual accomplishment. But motives are mixed for attending college, and that undercuts learning. Students, who are motivated to accomplish one thing, clash with professors, who are motivated to teach something else. Parents and governments, who subsidize college, may have a third goal in mind.

To be specific, developmentalists, most professors, and many college graduates believe that the purpose of higher education is "personal and intellectual growth." Professors hope to foster critical thinking and analysis. However, adults who have never attended college believe that "acquiring specific skills and knowledge" is more important. For them, success is a high-paying job.

FIGURE 11.6 Blue Is Higher Except... Since blue is for emerging adults and red is for adults of all ages (including emerging ones), it is no surprise that massification has produced higher scores among the young adults than the old ones. Trouble appears when young adults score about the same as older ones.

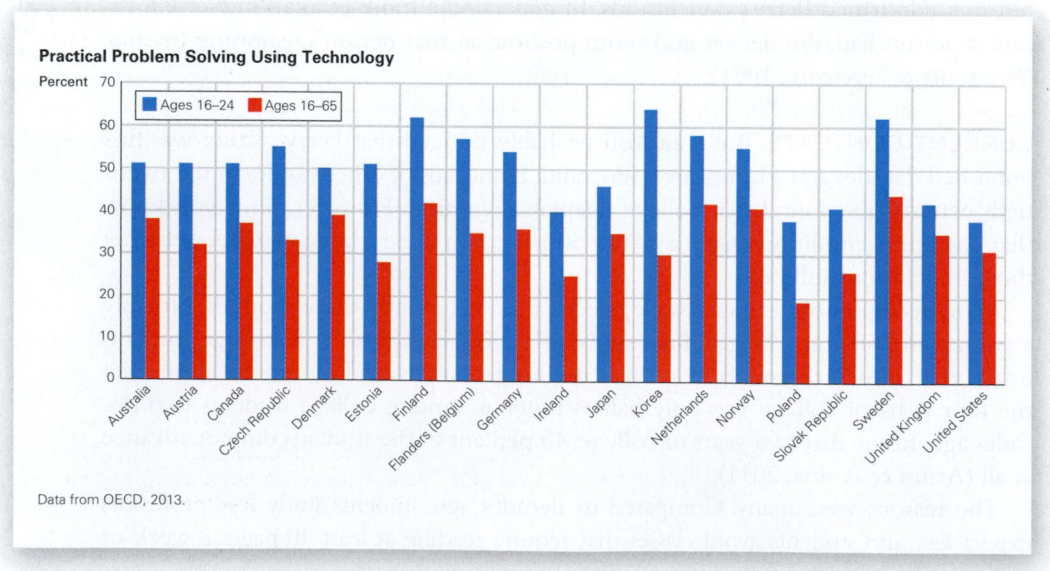

Practical Problem Solving Using Technology

Data from OECD, 2013.

Visualizing Development

WHY STUDY?

From a life-span perspective, college graduation is a good investment, for individuals (they become healthier and wealthier) and for nations (national income rises). That long-term perspective is the main reason why nations that control enrollment, such as China, have opened dozens of new colleges in the past two decades. However, when the effort and cost of higher education depend on immediate choices made by students and families, as in the United States, many decide it is not worth it, as illustrated by the number of people who earn bachelor's degrees.

EDUCATION IN THE UNITED STATES

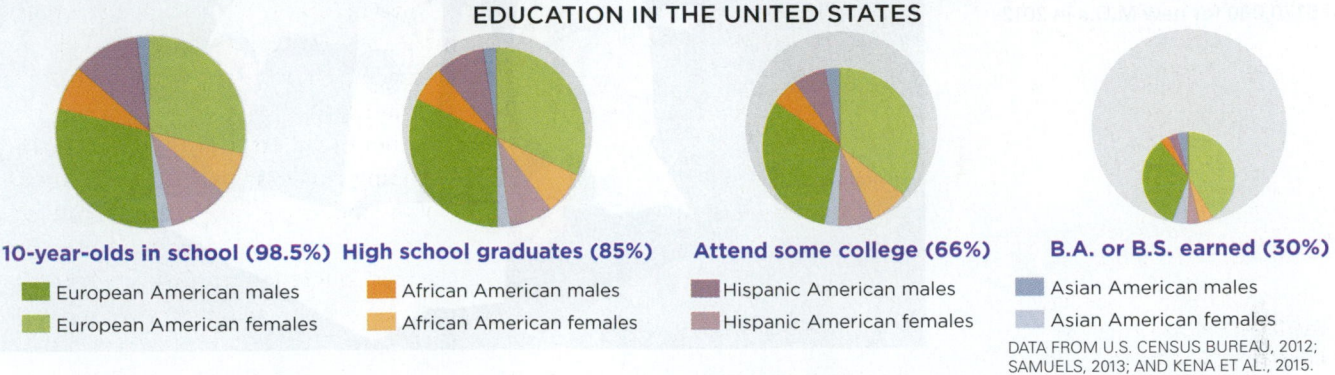

10-year-olds in school (98.5%)   **High school graduates (85%)**   **Attend some college (66%)**   **B.A. or B.S. earned (30%)**

- 🟩 European American males
- 🟩 European American females
- 🟧 African American males
- 🟧 African American females
- 🟪 Hispanic American males
- 🟪 Hispanic American females
- 🟦 Asian American males
- 🟦 Asian American females

DATA FROM U.S. CENSUS BUREAU, 2012; SAMUELS, 2013; AND KENA ET AL., 2015.

AMONG ALL ADULTS

The percentage of U.S. residents with high school and college diplomas is increasing as more of the oldest cohort (often without degrees) dies and the youngest cohorts aim for college. However, many people are insufficiently educated and less likely to find good jobs.

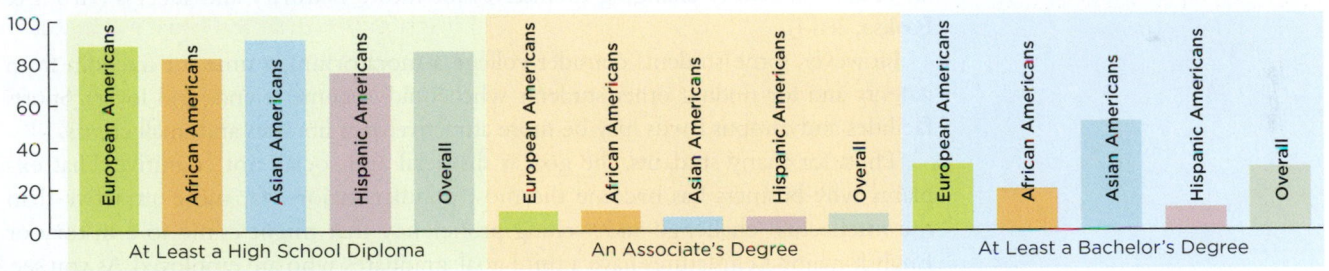

DATA FROM U.S. CENSUS BUREAU, 2013B.

INCOME IMPACT

Over an average of 40 years of employment, someone who completes a master's degree earns $500,000 more than someone who leaves school in eleventh grade. That translates into about $90,000 for each year of education from twelfth grade to a master's. The earnings gap is even wider than those numbers indicate because this chart includes only adults who have jobs, yet finding work is more difficult for those with less education.

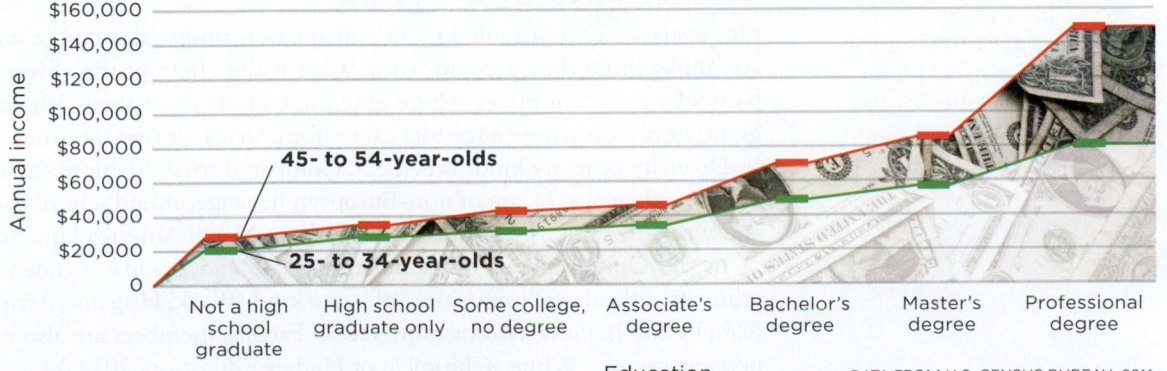

JUPITERIMAGES/THINKSTOCK/PHOTOS.COM/GETTY IMAGES PLUS

DATA FROM U.S. CENSUS BUREAU, 2011.

Educating Congress Justin Neisler is a medical student, about to testify before Congress. As an openly gay man, he hopes to serve LGBTQ youth, a group with many unmet medical needs. However, he and all of his classmates have a major problem: the clash between their idealism and the money they owe for their education—a median of $170,000 for new M.D.s in 2012.

ANDREW HARRER/BLOOMBERG VIA GETTY IMAGES

In the Arum and Roksa report (2011), students majoring in business and other career fields were less likely to gain in critical thinking compared to those in the liberal arts (courses that demand more reading and writing). These researchers suggest that colleges, professors, and students themselves who seek easier, more popular courses are short-changing themselves for future maturity and success (Arum & Roksa, 2014).

However, some students consider college a moratorium, a time for freedom from parents and for finding other students who could become friends and lovers. Sports facilities and campus lawns may be more attractive than libraries and small classes.

Thus, for many students, the goal is financial and social, not cognitive. That explains why business has become the most popular major—far more attractive than the intellectual challenge and writing proficiency that might come to a history or English major. Legislatures have a third goal: graduates who are employed. As you see, the stakeholders clash.

This clash is evident in the proliferation of community colleges. In 1955, most U.S. colleges were four-year institutions. There were only 275 "junior" colleges. Now there are about 2,000 such colleges, often called community colleges. For-profit colleges were scarce until about 1980; now there are hundreds of them.

THINK CRITICALLY: What is the purpose of college education?

The Effects of Diversity

Not every emerging adult attends college. But, almost all interact with people who are unlike those they grew up with. What is the effect of this diversity? Colleges in particular are often places where emerging adults meet their first atheist, or immigrant, or person whose ancestors came from Africa, or Asia, or South America.

Diversity of many kinds is evident. Compared to 1970, more students are parents, are older than age 24, are of non-European heritage, attend school part time, and live and work off campus. This is true not only in North America but also worldwide.

In the United States, when undergraduate and graduate students are tallied by ethnicity, a third are "minorities" of some kind (Black, Hispanic, Asian, American Indian, Pacific Islander, two or more races). Faculty members are also more diverse; 19 percent are non–White (Chronicle of Higher Education, 2014a).

CHARLES REX ARBOGAST/AP IMAGES

Love Thy Neighbor This is Larycia Hawkins, a tenured professor at a Christian college (Wheaton) who wore a hijab during Advent to show respect for Muslims, because "we worship the same God." The result was two-fold: demonstrations of support by many Wheaton students and several bouts of theological questioning by the president of the college, himself a Wheaton graduate ('88). She lost her job but became a symbol for emerging adults who welcome diversity.

This is much more likely in the twenty-first century than it was in the twentieth century. Many colleges have sizable populations of Americans of several ethnicities, as well as international students. Almost no college is exclusively for students of one ethnic or cultural background. Some have been, historically, Black or Catholic, but they now have students who are White, Protestant, or of other ethnic and religious backgrounds.

DIVERSITY AS THOUGHT-PROVOKING How does diversity affect cognition? It depends. Simply working or sitting in class beside someone of another background does not result in deeper thought. Instead, intellectual expansion comes from honest conversations among people of varied backgrounds and perspectives (Pascarella et al., 2014).

Colleges that make use of their diversity—via curriculum, assignments, discussions, cooperative education, learning communities, and so on—stretch student understanding. Employers who create teams of diverse workers to accomplish some goal reap the benefits of different perspectives.

Advances are not guaranteed. Emerging adults, like people of every age, tend to feel most comfortable with people who agree with them. Critical thinking develops outside the personal comfort zone, when cognitive dissonance requires reflection.

Regarding colleges, some people hypothesize that critical thinking is less likely to develop when students enroll in colleges near home or when they join fraternities or sororities. However, that hypothesis does not seem valid (Martin et al., 2015).

Meeting people from various backgrounds is a first step toward cognitive development. Every college has more diversity than once was the case. Of course, students must listen to others with opinions unlike their own. Openness and flexibility are characteristic of postformal thought.

The validity of this conclusion is illustrated by the remarkable acceptance of homosexuality over the past 50 years, not only in allowing marriage but in everything from bullying in middle school to adoption of children. Fourteen percent of Americans—including members of groups that once rejected gay, lesbian, and bisexual individuals—have changed their minds (Pew Research Center, March 30, 2013).

The main reason that individuals became more accepting of same-sex relationships and gender nonconformity is that people realized they knew someone personally who was LGBTQ. That occurred not only because people were more open about their orientation but also because young adults, in particular, spoke with peers of various identities and backgrounds. The research finds that those in the vanguard of this social revolution were emerging adults, for all the reasons just described about cognitive development.

what have you learned?

1. Why did scholars choose the term *postformal* to describe the fifth stage of cognition?

2. How does postformal thinking differ from typical adolescent thought?

3. Why might the threat of a stereotype affect cognition?

4. Why do people disagree about the goals of a college education?

5. In what way does diversity affect cognition?

Psychosocial Development

A theme of all human development is that continuity and change are evident throughout life. In emerging adulthood, the legacy of childhood is apparent amidst new achievements, as young adults establish new friends and partners. The task for scientists, as well as for emerging adults, is to understand what has changed and what endures.

In general, there are shifts but not entirely new developments. For example, emerging adults are less religious than older or younger people and are less likely to attend worship services, but they consider themselves no less spiritual (Alper, 2015).

Identity Achievement

Although the identity crisis begins in adolescence, "identity development in the areas of love, work, and worldviews is a central task of the third decade of life" (Padilla-Walker & Nelson, 2017, p. 5). This crisis sometimes causes confusion or foreclosure (see Table 11.2). A more mature response is to seek a moratorium, postponing identity achievement and avoiding marriage and parenthood while exploring possibilities.

TABLE 11.2 Erikson's Eight Stages of Development

Stage	Virtue / Pathology	Possible in Emerging Adulthood If Not Successfully Resolved
Trust vs. mistrust	Hope / withdrawal	Suspicious of others, making close relationships difficult
Autonomy vs. shame and doubt	Will / compulsion	Obsessively driven, single-minded, not socially responsive
Initiative vs. guilt	Purpose / inhibition	Fearful, regretful (e.g., very homesick in college)
Industry vs. inferiority	Competence / inertia	Self-critical of any endeavor, procrastinating, perfectionistic
Identity vs. role confusion	Fidelity / repudiation	Uncertain and negative about values, lifestyle, friendships
Intimacy vs. isolation	Love / exclusivity	Anxious about close relationships, jealous, lonely
Generativity vs. stagnation	Care / rejection	[In the future] Fear of failure
Integrity vs. despair	Wisdom / disdain	[In the future] No "mindfulness," no life plan

Information from Erikson, 1982/1998.

As you remember, the identity crisis was discussed in some detail in Chapter 10, but identity is reasserted, revised, and reestablished lifelong. This is especially apparent during emerging adulthood, which is said to have become "the period of life that offers the most opportunities for identity exploration" (Luyckx et al., 2013, p. 703). Emerging adults question who they really are in all four areas: gender (sex), vocation (career), politics (ethnicity), and religion (spiritual growth).

Evidence that identity is ongoing, not static, was found in a longitudinal study of Swedish 20- to 30-year-olds (Carlsson et al., 2015). Answers to questions designed to assess identity status indicated that by age 25, many (41 percent) had achieved identity, some (32 percent) had foreclosed, and 15 percent were in moratorium. In the next five years, about half switched, most often to achievement. Identity achievement became deeper and more meaningful as life experiences required reassessment and moving forward.

One example was Alice, who at 25 was considering several possible careers. Thus, she had not yet achieved vocational identity. By age 29, she was midway through an advanced degree in archeology, a firm choice. Thus, vocational identity had been achieved.

In contrast, Alice's gender identity seemed firm at age 25: She wanted to marry and have a child, and she said this was more important than her career. By age 29, she was still a committed heterosexual and had, in fact, become a wife and mother, but she had a new understanding of what that meant. She said, "To me, children should never hinder me from doing what I want, and a job should never ever hinder me from having children. It just can't be like that" (Carlsson et al., 2015, p. 340).

Research on almost 2,000 German emerging adults found that, for men as well as women, commitment to *both* work and family is most likely to lead to emotional satisfaction. However, in that study only 18 percent of emerging adults had reached firm identity achievement in both domains (Luyckx et al., 2013). Not only do many emerging adults need to figure out how to best combine their vocational and gender identity, researchers also struggle to understand this (see Chapter 13).

Grown Up Now? In Korean tradition, age 19 signifies adulthood, when people can drink alcohol and, in modern times, vote. In 2011, administrators invited 100 19-year-olds to a public Coming of Age ceremony, shown here, continuing a tradition that began centuries before. Emerging adults are torn between old and new. For example, in many nations, coming of age ceremonies are exclusive to one gender, but here young men and women participate.

ETHNIC IDENTITY One crucial aspect of identity formation is ethnic identity, which is "not a matter of one's idiosyncratic self-perception but, rather, is profoundly shaped by one's social context, including one's social role and place in society" (Seaton et al., 2017, p. 683). In other words, how people see themselves is deeply affected by family, friends, and the wider culture—which becomes increasingly influential when a person enters the adult world.

About half of all emerging adults in the United States have ancestors who were not European, but that simply describes who they are *not*—they need to figure out the specifics of having ancestors from China, or Colombia, or Cameroon, or wherever. Many non-European young people have forebears from more than one heritage and group—again posing challenges in establishing their own unique identity.

Young adults with European backgrounds also seek to figure out their ethnic identity—as Irish, or Italian, or whatever—and what it means to be from a particular part of the United States or Canada. As emerging adults enter colleges and workplaces in a global economy, interacting with people of many backgrounds, they need to know their own roots so that they can be proud of themselves while respecting everyone else (Rivas-Drake et al., 2014).

In the United States, for example, Hispanic American college students who resisted both assimilation ("I am just like everyone else") and alienation ("I have nothing in common with these people") fared best. Combining personal identity

Ordinary Workers Most children and adolescents want to be sports heroes, star entertainers, billionaires, or world leaders—yet fewer than one in 1 million succeed in doing so.

and social norms helped them maintain their self-esteem, deflect stereotype threat, and become good students (Rivas-Drake & Mooney, 2009). This is also true internationally as well as nationally. In Chile, youth of both Mapuche (indigenous) and mainstream Chilean descent benefited when they respected themselves and each other (González et al., 2017).

VOCATIONAL IDENTITY Moratoria include attending college; joining the military; taking on religious mission work; working as an intern in government, academia, or industry; and finding temporary work. All moratoria advance exploration and reduce the pressure to achieve identity.

As explained in Chapter 10, vocational identity is currently so complex that adolescents are wise to postpone selecting a particular career. Even in emerging adulthood, today's job market has made development of vocational identity harder.

Many young people take a series of temporary jobs. Between ages 18 and 25, the average U.S. worker has held seven jobs, with the college-educated changing jobs more often than those with less education. They want to try various kinds of work, and current economic conditions make this a wise course of action. Emerging adults may be "sagely avoiding foreclosure and premature commitment in a treacherous job market" (Konstam, 2015, p. 95).

Personality in Emerging Adulthood

Both continuity and change are evident in personality lifelong. Temperament, childhood trauma, and emotional habits endure: If self-doubt, anxiety, depression, and so on are present in childhood and adolescence, they are often still evident years later. Traits strongly present at age 5 or 15 do not disappear by age 25.

Yet personality is not static. Psychosocial continuity is apparent amidst new achievements, with emerging adulthood called the "crucible of personality development" (Roberts & Davis, 2016).

New Jobs, New Workers This barista in Germany *(left)* and these app developers in India *(right)* work at very different jobs. Yet they may have much in common: If they are like other emerging adults, their current employment is not what they imagined in high school, and not what they will be doing in 10 years.

After adolescence, new characteristics appear and negative traits diminish (Specht et al., 2011). Emerging adults make choices that break with the past. In modern times, emerging adulthood is characterized by years of freedom from a settled life-style, which allows shifts in attitude and personality.

A study of almost a million adolescents and adults from 62 nations found that "during early adulthood, individuals from different cultures across the world tend to become more agreeable, more conscientious, and less neurotic" (Bleidorn et al., 2013, p. 2530). They also feel more in control of their own lives (Vargas Lascano et al., 2015).

RISING SELF-ESTEEM Other research confirms both continuity and improvement in personality. A study of college students found a dip in self-confidence over their freshman year and then gradual improvement, with a significant—but not large—rise in self-esteem from the beginning to the end of college (Chung et al., 2014).

This is not surprising. Emerging adults are open to new experiences, reflecting their advanced cognition and spirit of adventure. Going to college, leaving home, paying one's way, stopping drug abuse, moving to a new city, finding satisfying work and performing it well, making new friends, committing to a partner—each of these might alter a person's life course and add to a person's self-esteem.

Total transformation does not occur, since genes, childhood experiences, and family circumstances always affect people. Nor do new experiences always lead to improvement. Cohort effects are always possible; target intervention can also occur (Mroczek, 2014). But, there is no doubt that personality *can* shift after adolescence.

Intimacy

In Erikson's theory, after achieving identity, people experience the sixth crisis of development, **intimacy versus isolation**. This crisis arises from the powerful desire to share one's life with someone else. Without intimacy, adults suffer from loneliness and isolation. Erikson explains:

> The young adult, emerging from the search for and the insistence on identity, is eager and willing to fuse his identity with others. He is ready for intimacy, that is, the capacity to commit himself to concrete affiliations and partnerships and to develop the ethical strength to abide by such commitments, even though they call for significant sacrifices and compromises.

[Erikson, 1993a, p. 263]

intimacy versus isolation
The sixth of Erikson's eight stages of development. Adults seek someone with whom to share their lives in an enduring and self-sacrificing commitment. Without such commitment, they risk profound aloneness and isolation.

The urge for social connection is a powerful human impulse, one reason our species has thrived. Other theorists use different words (*affiliation, affection, interdependence, communion, belonging, love*) for the same human need. Attachment experienced in infancy may well be a precursor to adult intimacy, especially if the person has developed a working model of attachment (Chow & Ruhl, 2014; Holt et al., 2018). Adults seek to become friends, lovers, companions, and partners.

All intimate relationships (friendship, family ties, and romance) have much in common—in both the psychic needs they satisfy and in the behaviors they require—with those sacrifices and compromises that Erikson mentioned (Padilla-Walker et al., 2017). Intimacy progresses from attraction to close connection to ongoing commitment. Each relationship demands some vulnerability, shattering the isolation caused by too much self-protection.

Social isolation is harmful at every age and in every culture (Holt-Lunstad et al., 2015). Humans have a powerful desire to share their personal lives with someone else. Without intimacy, adults suffer. As Erikson explains, to establish intimacy the emerging adult must

> face the fear of ego loss in situations which call for self-abandon:
> in the solidarity of close affiliations [and] sexual unions, in close
> friendship and in physical combat, in experiences of inspiration
> by teachers and of intuition from the recesses of the self. The
> avoidance of such experiences . . . may lead to a deep sense of
> isolation and consequent self-absorption.
>
> *[Erikson, 1993a, pp. 163–164]*

◆ Especially for Family Therapists
More emerging-adult children today live with their parents than ever before, yet you have learned that families often function better when young adults live on their own. What would you advise? (see response, page 417)

"This property comes complete with grown-up children left behind by the vendors."

No Thanks Even living with one's own adult children is problematic.

EMERGING ADULTS AND THEIR PARENTS Before turning to the romantic needs of emerging adults, we need to acknowledge the ongoing role of parents. It is hard to overestimate the importance of the family throughout the life span. Although a family is made up of individuals, in dynamic synergy, children grow, adults find support, and everyone is part of a collective that gives meaning to, and provides models for, daily life.

Parents today may be more important to emerging adults than they were in earlier times. Two experts in human development write, "With delays in marriage, more Americans choosing to remain single, and high divorce rates, a tie to a parent may be the most important bond in a young adult's life" (Fingerman & Furstenberg, 2012).

That bond may literally mean providing shelter. In the United States in 2016, 15 percent of adult children aged 25 to 35 lived with their parents. That was true of only 10 percent in 2000, which means the 2016 rate was one and a half times the rate before emerging adulthood was a recognized stage (Fry, 2017).

There is some debate as to whether this actually benefits the young adult. It saves money: Increasing housing costs and job scarcity are the main reasons the rate is increasing. Adults who live with their parents are less likely to marry and more likely to have experienced a divorce. For that reason (among others), a prolonged postponement of adult responsibilities may not be good for society.

On the other hand, it may protect against poverty and drug use. For example, in Thailand, researchers studied the data and concluded that young adults should be encouraged to stay home until they marry, avoiding the allure of Western independence that leads to increased risk-taking and drug use (Wongtongkam et al., 2015).

No matter where they live, family members have **linked lives;** that is, the experiences and needs of family members at one stage of life are affected by those at other stages (Elder, 1998; Macmillan & Copher, 2005; Settersten, 2015).

We have already described many examples. If parents fight, children suffer—even if no one lays a hand on them. Family financial stress and parental alliances shape children's lives, even if those children are parents themselves.

Those who are living with their parents, especially the "boomerang" group who once were on their own, are more likely to be depressed. However, if they are employed and are saving money to enable moving out soon, they may be quite happy (Copp et al., 2015). Family interaction continue to be more important than who lives where.

EMERGING ADULTS AND THEIR FRIENDS Because emerging adults are entering the worlds of work, college, and community, they have more friends at this time of life than at any other period. They need friends to navigate all of their new experiences.

An important aspect of close human connections is "self-expansion," the idea that each of us expands our experiences through our close friends and lovers (Aron et al., 2013). A crucial part of this is *mutuality*—the ability of both members of a dyad to care for the needs and emotions of someone else while attending to themselves.

Unlike relatives, friends are chosen (not inherited). They seek understanding, tolerance, loyalty, affection, and humor from one another—all qualities that make friends trustworthy, supportive, and enjoyable.

Friendships "reach their peak of functional significance during emerging adulthood" (Tanner & Arnett, 2011, p. 27). Since fewer emerging adults have the obligations that come with spouses, children, or frail parents, their friends provide companionship and critical support. Friends comfort each other when romance turns sour; they share experience and knowledge about everything, from what college to choose to what jeans to wear.

Who Needs It? Is Sophia grateful that her mother is making her bed as she moves into her freshman dorm at Saint Joseph's College in Maine? Your answer may be influenced by whether you identify with the mother or the daughter.

linked lives
Lives in which the success, health, and well-being of each family member are connected to those of other members, including those of another generation, as in the relationship between parents and children.

Same Situation, Far Apart: Good Friends Together These smiling emerging adults show that friendship matters everywhere. Culture matters, too. Would the eight Florida college students celebrating a 21st birthday at a Tex-Mex restaurant *(left)* be willing to switch places with the two Tibetan workers *(right)*?

A behavior called *self-silencing*—being quiet about one's own ideas and needs—undercuts true intimacy. Friends are particularly adept at helping each other find their voice. One crucial question for emerging adults is what and how to tell parents news that might upset them: Friends help with that, too.

Emerging adults often use social media to extend and deepen friendships that begin face-to-face, becoming more aware of the day-to-day tribulations of their friends (Burstein, 2013). Some find that writing down their worries, and responding to each other online, provides perspective.

Fears that increasing Internet use would diminish the number or quality of friendships have been proven to be false. Internet use is neither a boon nor a burden to emerging adults; the benefit or harm depends on the personality and lifestyle of the person (Castellacci & Tveito, 2018; Hood et al., 2017; Blank & Lutz, 2018).

Overall, friends are especially important during emerging adulthood, as confidants and buffers against stress and depression. Emerging adults typically gain new friends during this period, and that helps this period of life be one of flourishing, not floundering (Padilla-Walker et al., 2017).

GENDER DIFFERENCES A meta-analysis of 37 studies found some gender differences in friendship (Hall, 2011). Women's friendships are typically more intimate and emotional. Women expect to share secrets and engage in self-disclosing talk—including difficulties with their health, romances, and relatives—with their friends. Women reveal their weaknesses and problems and receive an attentive and sympathetic ear, a shoulder to cry on.

By contrast, men are less likely to touch each other except in aggressive activities, such as competitive athletics or military combat. The butt-slapping or body-slamming immediately after a sports victory, or the sobbing in a buddy's arms in the aftermath of a battlefield loss, are less likely in everyday life. By contrast, many women routinely hug friends in greeting or farewell.

Gender differences in friendship interactions have been found in many studies, but not all. It may be that this is a relic of past socialization, or it may be something deeper—brain wiring or hormones, for instance. Young LGBTQ adults also have many friends who are confidants, not romantic partners.

A study of 25,000 people found that, for emerging adults, the average number of friends who "you could call or text if you were in trouble late at night" was four (Gillespie et al., 2015). That was true regardless of the gender identity or sexual orientation of the individual (see Figure 11.7). The most significant variable was age: Adults under age 30 cited four friends, on average, whom they could call.

Most emerging adults of all orientations have close friends of all genders, which is particularly helpful when they seek romance. Problems arise if outsiders assume that every male–female relationship is sexual: Most of them are not.

Instead, intellectual expansion may be aided as emerging adults better understand the perspective of the other sex. Keeping a relationship "just friendly" may be difficult, and, if it becomes sexual, romance with a third person is almost impossible to sustain (Bleske-Rechek et al., 2012).

Friendship lines blur when sex is part of the relationship. The so-called "friends with benefits" are likely to become romantic partners, and, if not, are less likely to be sustained as friends (Furman & Shaffer, 2011).

ROMANTIC PARTNERS Falling in love is a common experience, as is sexual attraction, but exactly what that means is affected by many particulars—personality, age, and gender among them (Sanz Cruces et al., 2015).

Love, romance, and commitment are important for emerging adults, although specifics have changed. Most emerging adults are thought to be postponing, not

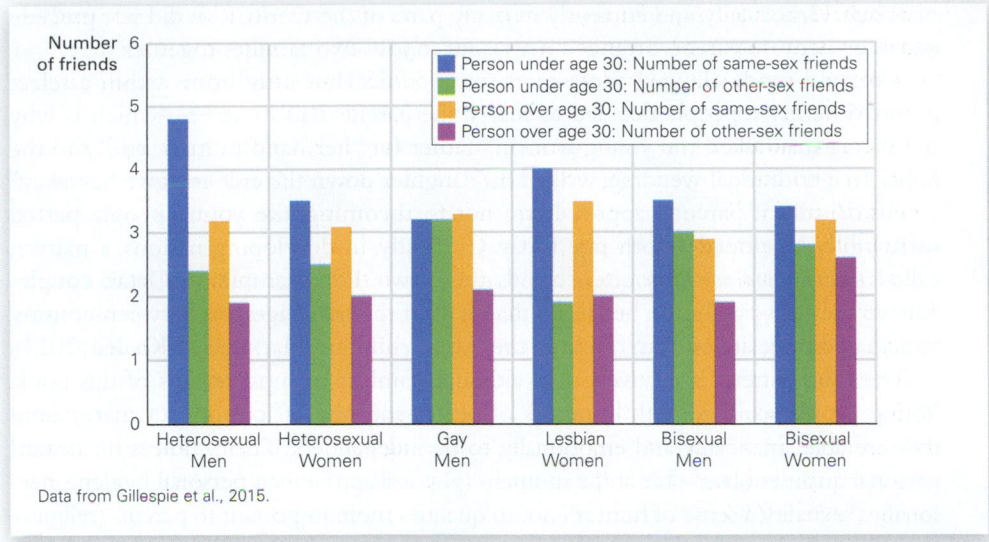

Data from Gillespie et al., 2015.

FIGURE 11.7 Same, Yet Different The authors of this study were struck by how similar the friendship patterns of sexual minority and majority people were. As you see, the one noticeable trend is age, not sexuality. People over 30 reported fewer friends overall, and fewer other-sex friends in particular, from an average of 2.6 to an average of 2.1.

abandoning, marriage, often because they want a college degree and a steady income first.

The fact that many emerging adults have had several romantic relationships may be helpful when they finally choose a life partner. With time and experience, young people become less sensitive to rejection, and that actually improves the quality of love relationships, because the young people learn to be less self-absorbed (Norona et al., 2018).

Romantic competence is multifaceted, with "mutual caring, trust, and emotional closeness; concern for, and sensitivity to, the needs . . . of others . . . and valuing faithfulness, loyalty, and honesty" (Raby et al., 2015, p. 117). Unlike in earlier times, currently it seems that the older couples are when they marry, the less likely they are to divorce.

From a developmental perspective, cohort and culture are pivotal in couple formation and bonding. Three distinct patterns are evident. The first is arranged

Postponing Parenthood? A challenge for many adults is how to combine work and family. Most postpone parenthood, but Shaun Creeden took another path. Here he holds his infant son, Dean, at his graduation from New York University.

marriage. Historically, and currently in many parts of the world, love did not precede marriage because parents arranged marriages to join two families together.

A second mode allowed adolescents some choice, but only from within a select group. When two people decided to marry, the parents had to agree—which is why the young man asked the young woman's father for "her hand in marriage," and the father, in a traditional wedding, walked his daughter down the aisle to "give her away."

Historically, if parental approval was not forthcoming, the young people parted sorrowfully or eloped—both rare today. Currently, in developing nations, a pattern called *modern traditionalism* often blends these two. For example, in Qatar, couples believe they have a choice, but more than half of the marriages are between cousins, anticipated by relatives from the time they were children (Harkness & Khaled, 2014).

The third pattern is relatively new, although familiar to most readers of this book. Young people socialize with hundreds of others and pair off but do not marry until they are able, financially and emotionally, to be independent. Their choices tilt toward personal qualities observable at the moment (physical appearance, personal hygiene, personality, sexuality, a sense of humor), not to qualities more important to parents (religion, ethnicity, politeness, long-term stability).

For most emerging adults, love is considered a prerequisite. Sexual exclusivity is expected, as found in a survey of 14,121 people of many ethnic groups and orientations (Meier et al., 2009). They were asked to rate from 1 to 10 (with 1 lowest and 10 highest) the importance of money, same racial background, long-term commitment, love, and faithfulness for a successful marriage or a serious, committed relationship.

Faithfulness to one's partner was considered most important of all (rated 10 by 89 percent), and love was almost as high (rated 10 by 86 percent). [Note that premarital sex is widely accepted; extramarital sex is not.] By contrast, most thought being of the same race did not matter much (57 percent rated it 1, 2, or 3). Money, while important to many, was not nearly as crucial as love and fidelity.

This survey was conducted in North America, but emerging adults worldwide share many of the same values. For example, 6,000 miles away, emerging adults in Kenya also reported that love was the primary reason for couples to connect and stay together; money was less important (S. Clark et al., 2010). A survey of 11,300 adults seeking partners in China found, as expected, that commitment was crucial but also found, unexpectedly, that love, "American style" was sought (Lange et al., 2015, p. 211).

Just Friends? This photo was taken in a public park in Isfala, Iran.

↑ OBSERVATION QUIZ
What indicates this is romance, not mere friendship?
(see answer, page 417)

GRIGVOVAN/SHUTTERSTOCK

FINDING A PARTNER From an evolutionary perspective, the emphasis on love and fidelity is not surprising. It may be that romantic love has been crucial for the survival of the human species for thousands of years. The different strategies for couple formation, including arranged marriages and polygamy, may be considered various ways to foster the love that bonds couples together (Fletcher et al., 2015).

Thus, the emphasis on love is worldwide, but other people remain influential, even when individuals say "all you need is love." Some romantic attachments are not those preferred by friends and family. Sometimes lovers resist parental advice, but that is more likely with cohabitation than marriage. Usually contrary choices are made reluctantly, not defiantly (Sinclair et al., 2015).

Traditionally, when parents did not arrange contact, friends did. Young people were invited to parties, set up for "blind" dates, introduced to people thought to be suitable. That is less true today.

One major innovation of the current cohort of emerging adults is the use of social media. Web sites such as Facebook and Instagram allow individuals to post their photos and personal information on the Internet, sharing the details of their daily lives with thousands of others. Almost all college students (93 percent) use social media sites, particularly to connect with each other (Chronicle of Higher Education, 2014a). Many also use Internet matching sites to find potential partners. In 2018, Match.com has 16 million users *per month;* 7.3 million messages are sent on OkCupid *per day.*

Having more choices may make decision-making harder (Sprecher & Metts, 2013). Contrary to the assumptions of most emerging adults, some research finds that love flourishes better when choice is limited—even severely limited—but supported by the family, as in an arranged marriage (Jaiswal, 2014).

At the other extreme, about a third of all marriages in the United States are the result of online matches between people unknown to friends or parents. Surprisingly, when online connections lead to face-to-face interactions and then to marriage, the likelihood of happy marriages is as high or higher than when the first contact was made in person (Cacioppo et al., 2013).

SEX WITHOUT COMMITMENT It seems that love occurs everywhere, and passion, intimacy, and commitment have been built into every culture. However, cultural differences and cohort effects are apparent.

This is particularly apparent in the **hookup**, a sexual interaction between partners who know little about each other, perhaps having met a few hours before. If that happened a few decades ago, it was prostitution, a fling, or a dirty secret. No longer.

It is estimated that about half of all emerging adults have hooked up. Hookups often involve intercourse, but that is not the defining characteristic. Lack of commitment is.

Hookups are more common among first-year college students than among those about to graduate, with the peak occurring in the spring of freshman year and the fall of sophomore year (Roberson et al., 2015). The reason may be that older students want partners, not pick-ups.

As one man put it, "If you hook up with somebody it probably is just a hookup and nothing is going to come of it" (quoted in Bogle, 2008, p. 38). Men as well as women hope to fall in love with a steady partner, although men are more accepting of men who have casual sex than of women who do the same (England & Bearak, 2014; Shulman et al., 2018).

Residential colleges and "Tinder culture" (referring to the app that is more often used for hookups than establishing long-term relationships) seem to encourage

JENA CUMBO PHOTOGRAPHY

How to Find Your Soul Mate Tiago and Mariela met on a dating site for people with tattoos, connected on Skype, moved in together, and soon were engaged to marry.

THINK CRITICALLY: Does the success of marriages between people who met online indicate that something is amiss with more traditional marriages?

hookup
A sexual encounter between two people who are not in a romantic relationship. Neither intimacy nor commitment are expected.

DATA CONNECTIONS ACTIVITY Technology and Romance: Trends for U.S. Adults examines how emerging adults find romantic partners.

uncommitted sex. Young adults who live at home are more likely to marry young—and then divorce. A survey of 2,195 emerging adults in the United States found a wide range of attitudes and suggested that parents should discuss love and commitment rather than directly bashing premarital sex and hookups (Weissbourd et al., 2017).

Cohabitation

cohabitation
An arrangement in which a couple lives together in a committed romantic relationship but are not formally married.

Many emerging adults combine their wish for commitment with their fear of marriage by choosing **cohabitation**, as living with an unmarried partner is called.

It is not that they don't want to marry; most young adults still value marriage but consider themselves not ready. The power of the institution is evident in the efforts that LGBTQ couples made to achieve marriage equality, the backlash in "defense of marriage," and the 400,000 same-sex couples who wed in the first two years it was possible to do so. Most of those newly married same-sex couples were over age 25.

Almost all young adults in some nations cohabit at some point—perhaps later marrying that person or someone else. In the United States, most (77 percent) emerging adults (same for men and women) disagree that "a young couple should not live together unless they are married" (Daugherty & Copen 2016, p. 10).

Another set of statistics that points to the popularity of cohabitation is that two-thirds of all newly married couples in the United States live together before marriage (Manning et al., 2014), as do most couples in Canada (especially Quebec), northern Europe, England, and Australia (see Figure 11.8). Many couples in Sweden, France, Jamaica, and Puerto Rico cohabit for decades, never marrying.

In the United States, the differences between couples who cohabit for years and those who cohabit for a shorter time and then either split up or marry seems more related to education than to parenthood. Although marriage rates are down and cohabitation up in every demographic group, education increases the chance of marriage and marital childbearing. Unmarried childbearing is more likely among people of low SES, perhaps partly because weddings have become expensive.

DEVELOPMENTAL CONSEQUENCES OF COHABITATION Many emerging adults consider cohabitation to be a wise choice as a prelude to marriage, a way for people to make sure they are compatible before tying the knot and thus reducing the chance of divorce. However, research suggests the opposite.

Contrary to widespread belief, living together before marriage does not prevent problems after a wedding. In a meta-analysis, a team of researchers examined the

↓ OBSERVATION QUIZ
Usually the rate of cohabitation increased at a steady rate, but there is one exception. When was that? (see answer, page 417)

FIGURE 11.8 More Together, Fewer Married As you see, the number of cohabiting male–female households in the United States has increased dramatically over the past decades. These numbers are an underestimate: Couples do not always tell the U.S. Census that they are living together, nor are cohabitants counted within their parents' households. Same-sex couples (not tallied until 2000) are also not included here.

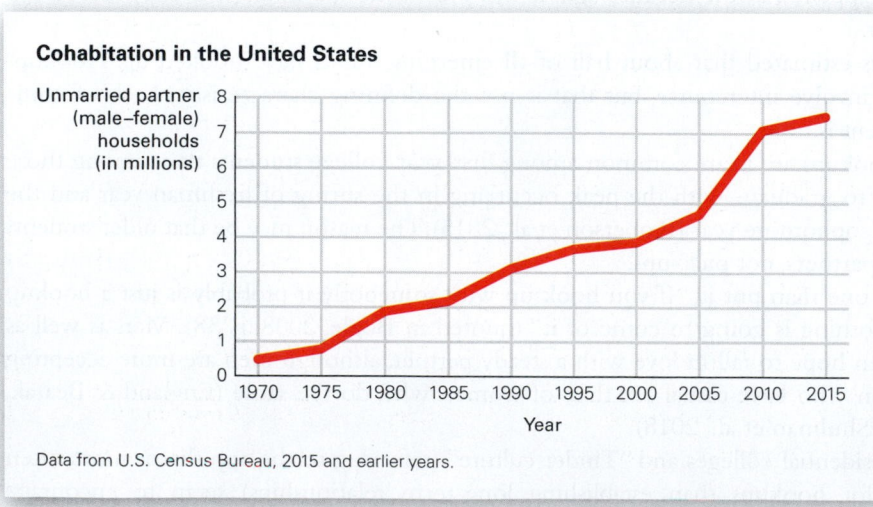

Cohabitation in the United States

Unmarried partner (male–female) households (in millions)

Year

Data from U.S. Census Bureau, 2015 and earlier years.

results of 26 scientific studies of the consequences of cohabitation for the subsequent stability and quality of marriages and found that those who had lived together were more likely to divorce (Jose et al., 2010). These results may be dated—each new cohort may have a different experience of cohabitation.

Some emerging adults want to avoid customs and old traditions. They believe that cohabitation allows a couple to have the advantages of marriage without the legal and institutional trappings.

But cohabitation is unlike marriage in many ways. Cohabiters are less likely to consolidate their finances, less likely to have close relationships with their parents or their partner's parents, less likely to take care of their partner's health, more likely to break the law, and more likely to break up (Forrest, 2014; Guzzo, 2014; Hamplova et al., 2014).

Particularly problematic is *churning,* when couples live together, then separate, and then get back together. Churning relationships have high rates of verbal and physical abuse (Halpern-Meekin et al., 2013) (see Figure 11.9). Cohabitation is fertile ground for churning because the partners are less committed to each other than if they were married, but they cannot slow down their relationship as easily as if they were not living together.

Although the research suggests many problems with cohabitation, most emerging adults do it, and most of their grandparents did not. Of course, humans tend to justify whatever they do. In this case, cohabiting adults typically think they have found intimacy without the restrictions of marriage, but they may be fooling themselves.

This raises an important caveat with research on the consequences of cohabitation. Much of it is based on people who cohabited 10 or 20 years ago. Those cohabitants were more rebellious and less religious than those who did not cohabit; that might explain why they were more likely to divorce if they did marry. Current research finds the implications of cohabitation less negative (Copen et al., 2013).

All of the research finds that cohabitation has one decided advantage and one decided disadvantage. The advantage is financial: People save money by living together. The disadvantage occurs if children are born: Cohabiting partners are less committed to the long decades of child rearing, and their children are less likely to excel in school, graduate, and go to college.

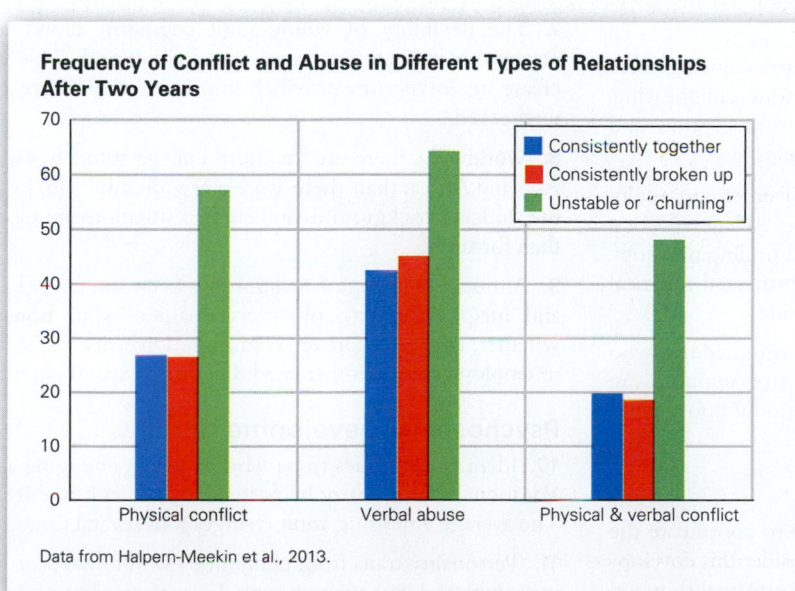

Frequency of Conflict and Abuse in Different Types of Relationships After Two Years

Data from Halpern-Meekin et al., 2013.

FIGURE 11.9 Love You, Love You Not In a longitudinal study of unmarried emerging adults (half men, half from two-parent homes, two-thirds European American, all from Toledo, Ohio) who had had a serious dating or cohabiting relationship in the past two years, some (15 percent) had broken up and not reunited, some (41 percent) had been together without breaking up, and some (44 percent) were churners, defined as having broken up and gotten together again with their partner. As you see, young-adult relationships are often problematic, but churning correlates with the stormiest relationships, with half of churners fighting both physically and verbally.

One other long-term effect should give everyone pause: Children tend to repeat the family structure of their youth. That means young adults whose parents divorced tend to marry children of divorce and then to divorce themselves, and children whose parents cohabited do likewise.

Looking at the broad picture of human development, it is clear that every human of every cohort and culture benefits from satisfying and enduring relationships. Emerging adults achieve romantic partnership in ways not chosen several generations ago, and they relate to parents and friends more intensely than ever. Some choices and partners are harmful, but overall, social isolation harms everyone of any age, so the impulse to connect should not be squashed (Holt-Lunstad et al., 2015).

This prepares us for the next period of development, adulthood. During the adult years, most people are immersed in a large social world, connecting to elders and children as well as partners and coworkers. On to Chapter 12.

what have you learned?

1. How is attending college a moratorium?

2. Why is vocational identity particularly elusive in current times?

3. How does personality change from adolescence to adulthood?

4. What is the general trend of self-esteem during emerging adulthood?

5. What kinds of support do parents provide their young-adult children?

6. What do emerging adults seek in a close relationship?

7. How has the process of mate selection changed over the past decades?

8. Why do many emerging adults cohabit instead of marrying?

SUMMARY

Body Development

1. Emerging adults usually have strong and healthy bodies. Homeostasis and organ reserve allow most emerging adults to withstand fatal disease. Over time, sleep, nourishment, and exercise are crucial for reducing allostatic load.

2. The sexual-reproductive system reaches a peak during these years, but most current emerging adults postpone childbearing. The results include both increased use of contraception and higher rates of sexually transmitted diseases.

3. Willingness to take risks is characteristic of emerging adults. This allows positive behaviors, such as entering college, meeting new people, volunteering for difficult tasks, and finding new jobs. It also leads to destructive actions, such as unprotected sex, fatal accidents, and an increase in suicide and homicide.

4. Extreme sports are attractive to some emerging adults, who find the risk of serious injury thrilling. The same impulses can lead to drug abuse, which peaks in emerging adulthood, especially among college students.

Cognitive Development

5. Adult thinking is more flexible, better able to coordinate the objective and the subjective. Some scholars consider this development a fifth stage of cognition, referred to as postformal thought.

6. Whether or not a fifth stage exists, there is no doubt that maturation of the prefrontal cortex allows more advanced thought. Emerging adults are more able to combine intuitive and analytic thought.

7. The flexibility of young-adult cognition allows people to reexamine stereotypes from their childhood. This may decrease stereotype threat, which impairs adult performance if left unchecked.

8. Worldwide, there are far more college students, especially in Asia and Africa, than there were a few decades ago. Everywhere, the students' backgrounds and current situations are more diverse than formerly.

9. Although a college education has been shown to have health and income benefits, observers disagree as to how, or even whether, college improves cognition. Diversity—in college and in employment—has increased. That may expand cognition.

Psychosocial Development

10. Identity continues to be worked out in emerging adulthood. Vocational identity may be particularly difficult in current times. The average emerging adult changes jobs several times.

11. Personality traits from childhood do not disappear in emerging adulthood, but many people learn to modify or compensate

for whatever negative traits they have. Personality is much more plastic than people once thought or experienced.

12. Family members continue to be important to emerging adults. Parental support—financial as well as emotional—may be more crucial than in earlier times.

13. The need for social connections and relationships is lifelong. Emerging adults tend to have more friends, of both sexes, than people of other ages do.

14. In earlier times, and in some cultures currently, emerging adults followed their parents' wishes in seeking marriage partners. Today's emerging adults are more likely to choose their own partners and postpone marriage.

15. Cohabitation is the current norm for emerging adults in many nations. Nonetheless, marriage still seems to be the goal, before or after parenthood.

KEY TERMS

emerging adulthood (p. 383)

organ reserve (p. 384)

WEIRD (p. 385)

homeostasis (p. 386)

allostasis (p. 386)

allostatic load (p. 386)

drug abuse (p. 393)

postformal thought (p. 394)

stereotype threat (p. 396)

intimacy versus isolation (p. 407)

linked lives (p. 409)

hookup (p. 413)

cohabitation (p. 414)

APPLICATIONS

1. Describe an incident during your emerging adulthood when taking a risk could have led to disaster. What were your feelings at the time? What would you do if you knew that a child of yours was about to do the same thing?

2. Read a biography or autobiography that includes information about the person's thinking from adolescence through adulthood. How did personal experiences, education, and maturation affect the person's thinking?

3. Statistics on cohort and culture in students and in colleges are fascinating, but only a few are reported here. Compare your nation, state, or province with another. Analyze the data and discuss causes and implications of differences.

4. Talk to three people you would expect to have contrasting views on love and marriage (differences in age, gender, upbringing, experience, and religion might affect attitudes). Ask each of them the same questions, and then compare their answers.

ESPECIALLY FOR ANSWERS

Response for Nurses (from page 389): Always. In this context, "suspect" refers to a healthy skepticism, not to prejudice or disapproval. Your attitude should be professional rather than judgmental, but be aware that education, gender, self-confidence, and income do not necessarily mean that a given patient is free of an STI.

Response for Those Considering Studying Abroad (from page 396): Since one result of college is that students become more open to other perspectives while developing their commitment to their own values, foreign study might be most beneficial after several years of college. If they study abroad too early, some students might be either too narrowly patriotic (they are not yet open) or too quick to reject everything about their national heritage (they have not yet developed their own commitments).

Response for High School Teachers (from page 398): Even more than ability, motivation is crucial for college success, so don't insist that she attend college immediately. Since your student has money and a steady job (prime goals for today's college-bound youth), she may not realize what she would be missing. Ask her what she hopes for, in work and in lifestyle, over the decades ahead.

Response for Family Therapists (from page 408): Remember that family function is more important than family structure. Sharing a home can work out well if contentious issues—like privacy, money, and household chores—are clarified before resentments arise. You might offer a three-session preparation package to explore assumptions and guidelines.

OBSERVATION QUIZ ANSWERS

Answer to Observation Quiz (from page 394): Los Angeles, California. Garcia is an undergraduate at UCLA. Clues—ethnic diversity and the temple's architecture.

Answer to Observation Quiz (from page 412): Note body position, hands, and her facial expression.

Answer to Observation Quiz (from page 414) Between 2005 and 2010. The probable reason: economic recession.

RAPIDEYE/E+/GETTY IMAGES

ADULTHOOD
Body and Mind

what will you know?

- Is there a difference between looking old and being old?
- Does drug addiction increase or decrease over the years of adulthood?
- Do adults get more intelligent or less intelligent as they grow older?
- Is everyone an expert in something?

Jenny was in her early 30s, a star in my human development class long ago, before my first textbook was published. She told the class that she was divorced, raising her 9-year-old daughter, her 7-year-old son, and two orphaned teenage nephews (sons of her former husband's sister) in public housing in the south Bronx. She spoke eloquently and enthusiastically about free activities for the four children—public parks, museums, the zoo, Fresh Air Fund camp. We were awed by her creativity and energy.

A year later, Jenny came to my office to speak privately. She had just discovered she was pregnant. The father, Billy, was a married man. He had told her he would not leave his wife but that he would pay for an abortion. She feared he would end their relationship if she had his child; she wanted my advice.

I asked questions. She did not think abortion was immoral; her 7-year-old son needed speech therapy; she thought she was too old to have another infant; she was a carrier for sickle-cell anemia, which had complicated her most recent pregnancy; her crowded apartment was not "babyproof"; her mother could not help because she needed caregiving herself.

Jenny would soon graduate with her associate's degree. She had found a job that would enable her to move her children to a better neighborhood, a job she could not take if she had a newborn. After a long conversation, she thanked me profusely.

Then she surprised me:

"I'll have the baby," she announced. "Men come and go, but children are always with you."

I had thought her narrative was leading to a different conclusion, but her values shaped *her* life, not mine. All adults decide about their own bodies and futures, ideally after discussing facts and implications with someone they trust.

Adulthood covers four decades, from ages 25 to 65. As with Jenny, questions about health, childbearing, and caretaking arise. This chapter explains facts about aging, sex, reproduction, disease, and more, and then it describes how adults think. Adults use their minds to combine analysis and emotions.

Expertise is the final topic in this chapter. Jenny came to me because she respected my knowledge of human development. I told her that she was *not* too old to have a baby and that Billy should be tested to see if he is a carrier of sickle-cell anemia. But my expertise is limited.

Jenny was the expert on her life, which you will appreciate at the end of this chapter. Adult cognition allowed us both to consider facts and values, using intuition and analysis. My most relevant expertise in this conversation came from life experience: I have learned to listen more than advise.

Growing Older

Most adults consider themselves strong, capable, and healthy. Economic analysis supports this perception: Adults aged 26 to 60 contribute more to the society than those who are older or younger, adding an economic and social surplus to support those not yet, or no longer, "in their prime" (Zagheni et al., 2015).

However, biological analysis suggests that **senescence,** as the aging process is called, begins when adulthood does. Every organ, every body system, and indeed every cell slows down with age. Senescence does not necessarily mean impairment. Consider breathing, the senses, and the brain.

Breathing

Because of homeostasis, the body naturally maintains a certain level of oxygen in the blood whether a person is old or young, awake or asleep, exercising or resting (Dominelli & Sheel, 2012). Aging may require more compensation. On average, oxygen

senescence
The process of aging, whereby the body becomes less strong and efficient.

↓ **OBSERVATION** QUIZ
Is Jared closer to 30, 40, or 50 in this photo? (see answer, page 459)

Just Keeping Rolling Along
After four years in Iraq and two in Afghanistan, Jared McCallum sought new challenges. He hiked the Appalachian Trail (2,180 miles) and, on September 1, 2014, began rowing the Mississippi River. Here, on October 1, 2014, he is at Rock Island, Iowa.

© QUADCITYTIMES/ZUMA WIRE/ALAMY LIVE NEWS

dispersal into the bloodstream from the lungs drops about 4 percent per decade after age 20. Thus, older adults may become "winded" after running, or they may pause after climbing a long flight of stairs to "catch their breath." That is homeostatic.

Some adults, especially if they are obese and heavy smokers, might seriously impair their lungs by middle age. They may develop chronic obstructive pulmonary disease (COPD, which includes emphysema), the fourth most common cause of death from age 45 to 65 (National Center for Health Statistics, 2017).

But impairment need not occur. Adults can maintain their breathing by exercising regularly and avoiding pollutants, especially cigarette smoke. Every year after age 25, far more people quit smoking than start it, and then lung functioning gradually improves. As a result, ex-smokers have stronger lungs at age 40 than they did at age 20. Indeed, an estimated 10 years of life are gained by quitting during adulthood (Jha et al., 2013).

This has practical applications. Suppose a 50-year-old who stops to catch his breath after climbing several flights of stairs decides he wants to run a marathon. That's possible—if he spends a year or more doing practice runs, eating and sleeping well, not smoking, and so on. Like the muscles of the legs, the lungs can be strengthened with judicious exercise.

The word *judicious* refers to judgment. People must judge how to protect their bodies. Improved functioning is not automatic—quite the opposite. Adults need to exercise without straining their muscles, to eat well by consuming many vegetables and not too much salt, sugar, or food overall, to avoid some drugs and use others.

Sleep is increasingly seen as crucial. Adults, like children, need to get ample, sound sleep in order to function well. This may mean deciding not to watch late-night television, or not to drink coffee after dinner, or even to take a midday nap.

Napping is sometimes beneficial to health and cognition and sometimes not. Adults need to figure out whether napping is best for them (Mantua & Spencer, 2017). By late adulthood, poor sleep is a direct impediment to health, as bad sleep habits in adulthood catch up to older adults (Spira, 2018).

For all health habits, decisions are crucial; without good decisions, that marathon is impossible. In other words, the effects of aging in adulthood depend as much on the mind as on the body.

Having Fun? Here are some of the 98,247 aspiring marathoners running on the Verrazano-Narrows Bridge from Staten Island to Brooklyn, New York, as part of a 26-mile race. Everyone should exercise and should figure out how to make that enjoyable to them. Some choose this.

VIDEO: Brain Development Animation: Middle Adulthood offers an animated look at how the brain changes and slows with age.

◆ **Especially for Drivers**
A number of states have passed laws requiring that hands-free technology be used by people who use cell phones while driving. Do those measures cut down on accidents? (see response, page 459)

The Brain with Age

The brain slows down with age. Neurons fire more slowly, and reaction time lengthens because messages from the axon of one neuron are not picked up as quickly by the dendrites of other neurons. Brain size decreases, with fewer neurons in adulthood than in adolescence. Myelination is reduced, and that means reaction time slows (Wang & Young, 2014).

But remember from Chapter 1 that gains and losses are evident at every point of the life span. This is true for the brain. As one expert describes it:

> The human brain is in a continuous state of flux defined by periods of relative development and periods of relative degeneration that together engender processes of growth, maturation, repair, and deterioration across the life span.
>
> [Sherin & Bartzokis, 2011, p. 333]

Gains? Brain growth? In adulthood? Yes! Myelination is reduced in some places, but new nodes develop in other parts of the brain (Wang & Young, 2014). Dendrites grow, reflecting experience. An adult who performs a particular action, time and time again, becomes better and quicker at it because of changes in the brain.

Of course, neurological advances are not automatic. For about 1 percent of all adults, significant brain loss occurs before age 65. There are five major causes of such adult brain reduction.

- *Traumatic brain injury (TBI).* Blows to the head—either at one time as in a car crash or repeated over time as in football, hockey, or boxing—reduce brain functioning. TBIs can occur at any age, but for adults they usually occur before age 40.

- *Viruses.* Various membranes, called the *blood–brain barrier,* protect the brain from most viruses, but a few—including HIV and the prion that causes mad cow disease—cross that barrier and destroy neurons. This can occur at any point in adulthood.

- *Genes.* About 1 in 1,000 people inherits a dominant gene for Alzheimer's disease, and even fewer people inherit genes for other severe neurocognitive disorders. Those can decrease brain function as early as age 30, although impairment usually appears after age 40.

- *Substance abuse.* All psychoactive drugs can harm the brain, especially chronic alcohol abuse, which stops absorption of vitamin B_1. That leads to Wernicke-Korsakoff syndrome ("wet brain"). Because long-term abuse is the cause, permanent brain damage is not usually apparent until age 40 or older.

- *Poor circulation.* Everything that impairs blood flow—such as hypertension and cigarette smoking—impairs circulation in the brain and thus harms thinking, evident by age 50.

For most adults, however, experience continues to advance brain development. Learning continues, links between one thought and another are strengthened, and adults are better able to understand how one event affects another. This may result not only from experience; the brain itself may grow, as Inside the Brain explains.

The Senses

All of the senses become less sharp over time. As with every aspect of adult development, experience is significant; the brain compensates for sensory loss in any one area by using the other senses (Collignon et al., 2011). For example, especially with age it is easier to hear what someone is saying if the listener can see them talking; it is easier to read a street sign if a person knows where to look and knows what street it might be.

INSIDE THE BRAIN

Neurons Forming in Adulthood

It has long been known that brains slow down with age and that parts of the brain often shrink. It also has long been known that neurons form rapidly during prenatal development and that most of them are eliminated by pruning, especially in infancy and in early adolescence. It was thought that brain growth and *neurogenesis* (the formation of neurons) stopped long before adulthood.

But in the past two decades, scientists have been surprised by discoveries that parts of the brain grow during adulthood (Ming & Song, 2011). Not only do dendrites form and pathways strengthen, but new neurons are born. One area that gains brain cells is the hippocampus, the brain structure that is most prominent in memory (Bergmann et al., 2015). That neurogenesis "appears to contribute significantly to hippocampal plasticity across the life span" (Kempermann et al., 2015).

The specific area of the hippocampus where new neurons settle is the *dentate gyrus,* a region activated in forming new memories and exploring new places. One conclusion is that the adult human brain is characterized by amazing plasticity (Kempermann et al., 2015).

Brain plasticity is evident lifelong, a finding now accepted by almost all scientists. But not everyone agrees that a significant number of new neurons are born in adulthood.

- One team of 19 scientists reported that the number of new neurons created after age 13 is so low as to be undetectable (Sorrells et al., 2018).

- Another team of 12 scientists found that new neurons form even at age 70 (Boldrini et al., 2018).

The number of scientists in each of these two contradictory studies highlights that this is not a controversy between an optimist and a pessimist; it is a dispute between two teams of careful scientists. For neuroscientists, this dispute is thrilling: They await new techniques to study the brain.

For our purposes, however, we sidestep the controversy to state what we know: cognitive reserve, homeostasis, and allostasis protect the brain. New learning occurs in adulthood. Dendrites sprout to reach hundreds of other neurons as new situations demand it.

Thus, although adult brains slow down a bit, that may allow more careful analysis. Is that why judges, bishops, and world leaders are almost always older adults?

Historically and to this day, people connect wisdom with age. Could this be evidence that brain functioning advances over time? That hope is not yet firmly established in laboratories by neuroscientists but seems recognized in daily life by millions of ordinary people.

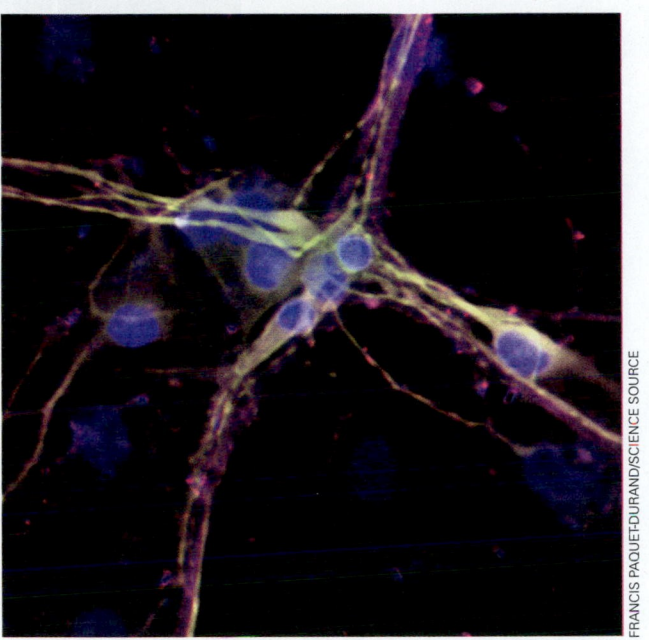

FRANCIS PAQUET-DURAND/SCIENCE SOURCE

Neurons Growing Even in adulthood, dendrites grow (pale yellow in this photo). Here the cells are in a laboratory and the growth is cancerous, but we now know that healthy neurons develop many new connections in adulthood.

In addition, current technology can compensate for most sensory losses. By middle age, most people wear corrective lenses; many have learned that conversations at crowded parties require a quiet corner.

Moreover, not just with technology and behavior, the brain itself compensates for all of the small losses that are inevitable with age, and for larger losses as well. For example, blind people who read Braille develop extraordinary sensitivity, not only in their fingers but also in their visual cortex, as axons from that area connect language and touch. For everyone, damage to parts of the cortex can be repaired, and functions redirected.

© FLANIGAN/FILMMAGIC/GETTY IMAGES

Compensation All of the senses decline with age. Some people accept these losses as inevitable, becoming socially isolated and depressed. Instead, compensation is possible in two ways. One is to increase use of the other senses and abilities. Stevie Wonder illustrates this well—he relies on hearing and touch, which have enabled him to sell over 100 million records and win 25 Grammys. The other way is more direct: Many technological and medical interventions are available for every sensory loss.

VISION Vision actually involves 30 distinct brain areas as well as at least a dozen aspects of the eye. Age affects each of them in specific ways long before the serious problems of late adulthood. For example, peripheral vision (at the sides) narrows faster than frontal vision; some colors fade more than others; adjusting to dark and glare takes longer with age, but the timetable varies; nearsightedness and farsightedness follow different paths.

The shape of the lens changes. If the eye is too curved, that causes nearsightedness (defined as seeing near better than far). If the eye is too flat, that causes farsightedness (far better than near). Nearsightedness increases gradually in childhood and then more rapidly in adolescence. Then it stabilizes and begins to reverse in midlife as the eye shape reverses.

When nearsightedness is reduced in midlife, farsightedness may increase. This explains why 40-year-olds hold the newspaper much farther away than 20-year-olds do: Their near focus is blurry (Aldwin & Gilmer, 2013). Adults who have never needed corrective lenses suddenly need reading glasses.

HEARING Hearing is most acute at about age 10, with variations from one person to another and from one sound to another. Those variations are both nature and nurture. For example, because of both genes and experience, professional musicians distinguish pitch much better than other people.

For everyone, however, high-frequency sounds (the voice of a young child) are lost earlier than low-frequency sounds (a man's voice). Although some middle-aged people hear better than others, everyone's hearing diminishes over time.

Actually, hearing is always limited: No one hears a conversation a hundred feet away. Because deafness is not absolute, gradual losses are unnoticed. *Presbycusis* (literally, "aging hearing") is rarely diagnosed until late adulthood.

Many nations mandate ear protection for construction workers, but no laws protect against extremely loud music, which some emerging adults enjoy. One sad consequence is that presbycusis may begin earlier, with whispers inaudible by age 30.

In one study, almost a third of a large group of high school students reported ringing in their ears, muffled sounds, or temporary deafness. They did not realize that music on their headphones or at concerts was damaging the hairs of the inner ear (Vogel et al., 2010).

Outward Appearance

It is reassuring to know that vital organs and the senses can function well throughout adulthood, if people take care of themselves. However, visible changes with age are inevitable, which troubles many in an age-conscious society.

Losing hair or getting wrinkles, moving stiffly or getting shorter, wearing glasses or not hearing a whisper—none of these is life-threatening, but all are signs of aging. These happen to almost everyone in adulthood. Few adults want to appear old. Eventually everyone does.

SKIN AND HAIR The first visible signs of age are in the skin, which becomes drier, rougher, and thinner with every decade after age 20. Wrinkles first become visible in areas exposed to weather, such as the face and hands.

Hormones and diet have an effect—fat slows down wrinkling—but aging is apparent in all four layers of the skin, with "looseness, withering, and wrinkling" particularly noticeable at about age 50 for women, caused by reduced estrogen after menopause (Piérard et al., 2015, p. 98).

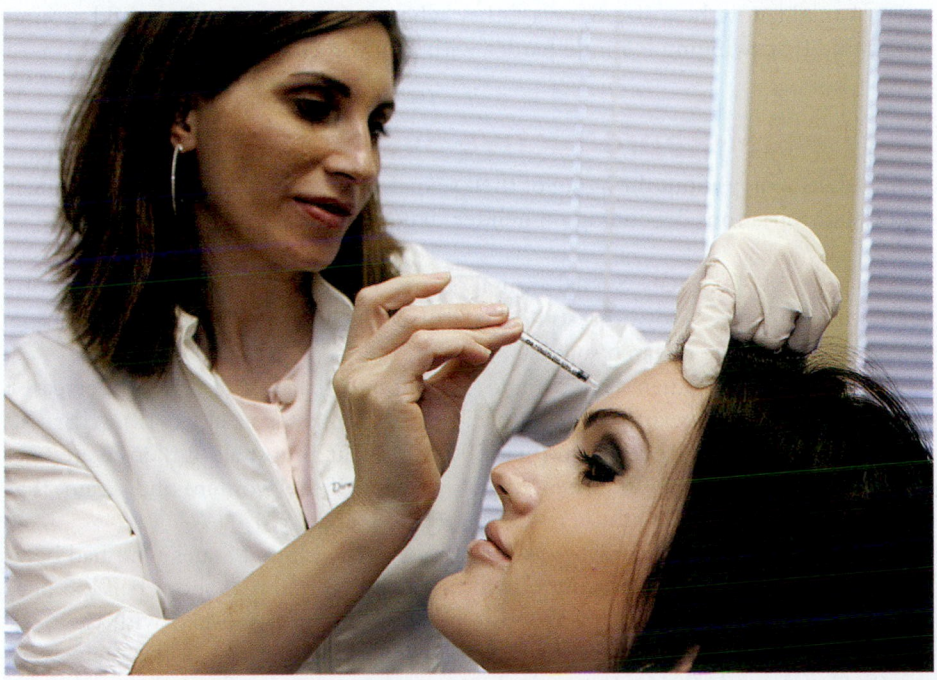

Look Your Age? Jennifer Roe is used to getting Botox injections—she has been doing this since she was 21. She is among an estimated 16 million people in the United States who, in 2017, turned to these injections, or more invasive cosmetic surgery, to mitigate the signs of aging.

↑ **OBSERVATION** QUIZ Guess her age (see answer, page 459)

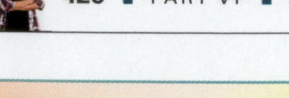

Hair usually becomes gray and thinner, first at the temples before age 40 and then over the rest of the scalp. This change does not affect health, but since hair is a visible sign of aging, many adults spend substantial money and time on coloring, thickening, styling, and more.

Both men and women lose hair, but the pattern differs. Women's hair becomes thinner overall, whereas some men lose hair on the top of their heads but not on the sides. That is *male pattern baldness.*

I saw a man wearing a T-shirt that read, "This is not a bald spot; it is a solar plate for a sex machine." Yes, male pattern baldness correlates with male hormones and sexual desire; it also correlates with increased risk of prostate cancer (Zhou et al., 2016).

Body hair (on the arms, legs, and pubic area) also becomes less dense as people age. An occasional thick, unwanted hair may appear on the chin, inside the nose, or in some other place. That has no known correlation with any disease, although many adults are distressed at every sign of aging.

SHAPE AND AGILITY The body changes shape between ages 25 and 65. Muscles weaken; pockets of fat settle on the abdomen, the upper arms, the buttocks, and the chin; people stoop slightly when they stand (Whitbourne & Whitbourne, 2014).

As joints lose flexibility, stiffness appears; bending is harder; agility is reduced. Rising from the floor, twisting in a dance, or even walking "with a spring in your step" is more difficult. A strained back, neck, or other muscle may occur.

By late middle age, even if they stretch to their tallest, adults are shorter than they were, because back muscles, connective tissue, and bones lose density, making the vertebrae in the spine shrink. People lose about an inch (2 to 3 centimeters) by age 65, a loss in the trunk because cushioning between spinal disks is reduced. As torsos shrink, waists widen, hence the dreaded middle-age spread.

This all begins before middle age. A 35-year-old woman who was proud of being a size 4 might now be a size 8, or a father who easily swung his first child around might find that swinging is a little harder with his third child.

The Sexual-Reproductive System

Many adults worry about the aging of their sexual and reproductive systems. Changes occur, with variations depending on gender, experience, and attitude.

SEXUAL SATISFACTION Sexual arousal occurs more slowly and orgasm takes longer with senescence. However, some say that sexual responses improve with age. Could that be? Some research suggests so.

A U.S. study of women aged 40 and older found that sexual activity decreased each decade but that sexual satisfaction did not (Trompeter et al., 2012). A British study of more than 2,000 adults in their 50s found that almost all of them were sexually active (94 percent of the men and 76 percent of the women) and, again, that most were quite satisfied with their sex lives (D. Lee et al., 2015).

Variability is evident. A study of 38,207 adults in the United States who had been in a committed relationship for more than three years found that about half (55 percent of the women and 43 percent of the men) were highly satisfied with their sex lives, but about a third (27 percent of the women and 41 percent of the men) were not (Frederick et al., 2016). Interestingly, age was not a major factor, but variety of sex acts (including oral sex) and quality of sexual communication was.

Overall, the research finds that some adults are satisfied, even thrilled, with their sex lives, and some are unhappy. Although sexual satisfaction tends to be highest

Long-Lasting Joy In every nation and culture, many couples who have been together for decades continue to delight in their relationship. Talk shows and headline stories tend to focus on bitter divorces, ignoring couples like these who are happy together.

in the early months of a relationship, some long-married couples report that their happiness with their sex lives is as strong as it was early on (Frederick et al., 2016).

Every large study finds a vast range of sexuality and sexual satisfaction. In most cultures, men are more interested in sex than women, but that may be nurture, not nature. Some adults have strong sexual drives and powerful sexual orientation, some to the same gender and most to other-gender adults. But some other people have weaker or bisexual drives. Some seem to be asexual—not interested or aroused.

All of these variations are affected by culture, experience, religion, and opportunity. Cognition may be more influential than biology (Brotto & Yule, 2011). As one humorist said, "For humans, the most important sexual organ is between the . . . ears."

SEEKING PREGNANCY Infertility (failure to conceive after years of trying) varies from nation to nation, primarily because the rate increases when medical care is scarce (Gurunath et al., 2011). Worldwide, primary infertility (never able to conceive) is estimated at 2 percent of all young couples, and secondary infertility (inability to have a second child after five years of trying) is about 10 percent (Mascarenhas et al., 2012).

infertility
The inability to conceive a child after trying for at least a year.

Those are rates for young couples, but age slows down fertility. In the United States, about 12 percent of all adult couples do not conceive after one year of trying, partly because they do not want a baby until they are "ready." Peak fertility is about age 17; the average U.S. woman has her first baby at age 27 (Martin et al., 2018). That suggests a decade of postponement.

If couples in their 40s try to conceive, about half fail and the other half risk various complications. Of course, risk is not reality: In 2016 in the United States, 122,183 babies were born to women age 40 or older, with about 20 percent of those a first birth for that woman (Martin et al., 2018). Most of those babies and mothers were quite healthy and happy.

A common reason for male infertility is low sperm count. Conception is most likely if a man ejaculates more than 20 million sperm per milliliter of semen, two-thirds of them mobile and viable. Each sperm's journey to the ovum is aided by millions of fellow travelers.

Depending on the man's age, each day about 100 million sperm reach maturity after a developmental process that lasts about 75 days. Anything that impairs

© XIXINXING/CORBIS

COMPASSIONATE EYE FOUNDATION/COLORBLIND IMAGES/GETTY IMAGES

Choosing Motherhood In 2018, U.S. Senator Tammy Duckworth, age 50, had her second baby via IVF and won the right to bring her infant daughter to the Senate floor. Next: Will the United States continue to be the only nation (except for New Guinea) without paid maternity leave?

CHIP SOMODEVILLA/GETTY IMAGES

body functioning over those 75 days (e.g., fever, radiation, drugs, time in a sauna, stress, environmental toxins, alcohol, cigarettes) reduces sperm number, shape, and motility (activity), making conception less likely. Sedentary behavior, perhaps watching too much television, also correlates with lower sperm count (Gaskins et al., 2013).

As with men, women's fertility is affected by anything that impairs physical functioning—including disease, smoking, extreme dieting, and obesity. Many infertile women have contracted *pelvic inflammatory disease (PID)* years earlier. PID creates scar tissue that may block the fallopian tubes, preventing sperm from reaching an ovum (Brunham et al., 2015).

ASSISTED CONCEPTION In the past 50 years, medical advances have solved about half of all fertility problems. Surgery can repair some problems directly, and *assisted reproductive technology (ART)* overcomes obstacles such as a low sperm count and blocked fallopian tubes. Some ART procedures, including in vitro fertilization (IVF), were explained in Chapter 2.

What was not discussed was the impact on the adults, who may be depressed if they are unable to have a baby. Infertility, and fertility measures, affect the psyche, not just the body. People may question their own morality ("Am I selfish for wanting a biological child?") and their partner's wishes.

This is a time when couples may benefit from seeing a marriage counselor. Remember that communication is crucial for a satisfying adult sex life; this is especially true when ART is involved.

Some ART is morally acceptable to virtually everyone, especially when couples anticipate disease-related infertility. For example, many cancer patients freeze their ova. When the treatment is over, if they want a baby, their IVF success rate (about one-third of attempts) is similar to those who freeze their ova for reasons not related to cancer (Cardozo et al., 2015).

ART has helped millions who thought they could never have a baby. One dramatic example is with HIV-positive adults. Three decades ago, their doctors recommended sterilization and predicted early death. Now, adults with HIV live happily for decades, with medical measures making birth of a healthy baby possible (Wu & Ho, 2015).

Remembering Younger Days When Chris McNulty was diagnosed with cancer, he and his wife decided to freeze his sperm so that they could later have children. He died, but his widow used his sperm five years after his death. Her twin sons, Kyle and Cole, are the result *(left)*. Bala Ram Devi Lohan and his wife Rajo *(right)* wanted a child but tried for 40 years without success. Finally, a donor egg and Bala Ram's sperm produced a zygote, implanted in Rajo's uterus. She gave birth to a 3-pound, 4-ounce girl, shown here with her happy parents, ages 70 and 72.

MENOPAUSE: MALE AND FEMALE During adulthood, the level of sex hormones circulating in the bloodstream declines—suddenly in women, gradually in men. Both sexes are affected by those changes, with some taking hormones to replace the hormones lost. That may be ill-advised—as you will see.

For women, sometime between ages 42 and 58 (the average age is 51), ovulation and menstruation stop because of a marked drop in production of several hormones. This is **menopause,** which is connected to many biological effects, including vaginal dryness and body temperature disturbances, causing hot flashes and cold sweats. Those bodily responses can be hardly noticeable, or they can be dramatic—interfering with sleep, which can make a woman tired and irritable.

The psychological effects of menopause also vary, with some women sad that they can no longer become pregnant and other women happy for the same reason. Some menopausal women are depressed, some are moody, and others are more energetic (Judd et al., 2012). Anthropologist Margaret Mead famously said, "There is no more creative force in the world than the menopausal woman with zest."

In the United States, about one in nine women has a *hysterectomy* (surgical removal of the uterus, and usually of the ovaries) (Wright et al., 2013). Most of them are pre-menopausal, and the sudden reduction of estrogen causes menopausal symptoms.

Early menopause, surgical or not, correlates with health problems later on (Hunter, 2012). This suggests that estrogen protects health, a major reason that the rate of hysterectomies has been dramatically reduced in recent decades.

Do men undergo anything like menopause? Some say yes. Even with erection-inducing drugs such as Viagra and Levitra, male sexual desire and speed of orgasm decline with age, as do many other physiological and cognitive functions. Perhaps age-related lower testosterone levels, which reduce sexual desire, erections, and muscle mass, should be called *andropause* (or *male menopause*) (Samaras et al., 2012).

But most experts think that the term *andropause* is misleading because it implies a sudden drop in reproductive ability or hormones. That does not occur in men, some of whom produce viable sperm at age 80 or older. Sexual inactivity and anxiety reduce testosterone—superficially similar to menopause but with a psychological,

menopause
The time in middle age, usually around age 50, when a woman's menstrual periods cease and the production of estrogen, progesterone, and testosterone drops. Strictly speaking, menopause is dated one year after a woman's last menstrual period, although many months before and after that date are menopausal.

Pausing, Not Stopping During the years of menopause, these two women experienced more than physiological changes: Jane Goodall *(left)* was widowed and Ellen Johnson-Sirleaf *(right)* was imprisoned. Both, however, are proof that post-menopausal women can be productive. After age 50, Goodall (shown visiting a German zoo at age 70) founded and led several organizations that educate children and protect animals, and Johnson-Sirleaf (shown speaking to the International Labor Organization at age 68) became the president of Liberia.

not physiological, cause. In addition, some medical conditions and treatments reduce testosterone.

hormone replacement therapy (HRT)

Taking hormones (in pills, patches, or injections) to compensate for hormone reduction. HRT is most common in women at menopause or after removal of the ovaries, but it is also used by men as their testosterone decreases. HRT has some medical uses but also carries health risks.

HORMONE REPLACEMENT Toward the end of the twentieth century, millions of post–menopausal women used **hormone replacement therapy (HRT)**. Some did so to alleviate symptoms of menopause, others to prevent osteoporosis (fragile bones), heart disease, strokes, or cognitive loss. Correlational studies found that these diseases occurred less often among women taking HRT.

However, that correlation was misleading. In a multiyear study of thousands of women, half (the experimental group) took HRT and half (the control group) did not. The results were a shock: Taking estrogen and progesterone *increased* the risk of heart disease, stroke, and some types of cancer (U.S. Preventive Services Task Force, 2002).

The most dramatic difference was an increase in breast cancer, at the rate of 6 per year for 1,000 women taking HRT compared to 4 per 1,000 for women who did not take the hormone (Chlebowski et al., 2013). International research has since confirmed the risk of breast cancer (Pizot et al., 2016). The original study was halted because the researchers concluded that the experimental group was at risk.

How could the prior conclusions have been mistaken? In retrospect, scientists realized that simply comparing women who chose HRT with women who did not resulted in women of higher SES being compared with women of lower SES (who could not afford HRT). Lower disease rates were the result of education, income, and health care, not of HRT.

Doctors now agree that HRT reduces hot flashes, decreases osteoporosis, and may improve hearing, but the costs need to be considered (Frisina & Frisina, 2016). Some experts still argue that for younger women the benefits may outweigh the risks (Langer et al., 2012). Now, "In most countries, HRT is only recommended for climacteric symptoms, at a dose as small as possible and for a limited period of time" (Kanis et al., 2013, p. 44).

To combat male hormonal decline, some men take HRT. Of course, their H is the hormone testosterone, not estrogen. The result seems to be less depression, more sexual desire, and leaner bodies. (Some women also take smaller amounts of testosterone to increase their sexual desire.)

Weighing costs and benefits is again needed (Hackett, 2016). One recent study found that men who took testosterone for years had lower rates of cardiovascular disease and fewer deaths, but in the short term more deaths occurred than usual (Wallis et al., 2016). These scientists rightly call for longitudinal randomized studies, a wise suggestion given the results of female HRT.

what have you learned?

1. How can people improve the function of their lungs?

2. How does brain aging suggest that senescence involves more than time and genes?

3. How does vision change with age?

4. How does experience affect hearing?

5. What aspects of appearance signify that a person is aging?

6. How does sexual arousal change with age?

7. What impairs fertility in men and in women?

8. What are the effects of menopause?

9. What are the consequences of HRT in women and in men?

Habits: Good and Bad

Surely you have noticed that much depends on habits. Allostatic load, described in Chapter 11, builds quickly or slowly, so some adults seem decrepit by age 50 while others seem youthful. In a longitudinal study of 26- to 38-year olds, measured with 18 indicators of health as well as by appearance, some aged three years per chronological year, and some aged hardly at all (Belsky et al., 2015).

Exercise, nutrition, and drugs influence how long, how strong, and how full each adult life is. We describe the impact of each of these in turn.

Exercise

Many people have sought the secret sauce, the fountain of youth, the magic bullet that will slow, or stop, or even reverse the effects of senescence. It has been found! Thousands of scientists, studying every disease of aging, have found something that helps every condition—exercise.

Regular physical activity protects against serious illness even if a person overeats, smokes, or drinks (all discussed soon). Exercise reduces blood pressure, strengthens the heart and lungs, promotes digestion, and makes depression, diabetes, osteoporosis, strokes, arthritis, and several cancers less likely. Health benefits from exercise are substantial for men and women, old and young, former sports stars and those who never joined a team (Aldwin & Gilmer, 2013).

Moving the body protects both mental health and physical health. Exercise strengthens the immune system (Davison et al., 2014). Active people feel happier and more energetic, and that increases other good habits.

"The fresh mountain air is starting to depress me."

Just Give Me the Usual Even bad habits feel comfortable—that's what makes them habits.

Taking Turns Workers such as Josh Baldonado at this insurance company must sign up to use one of the 30 treadmill workstations allowing exercise as they work. The company moves the worker's phone and computer to the workstation, and has fewer absences and lower health care costs.

© MICHAEL CONROY/CORBIS

Unfortunately, exercise takes time and effort. It cannot be put in a pill and sold. Perhaps this is one reason that no corporation subsidizes research to understand and promote it. Consequently, scientists do not know exactly which exercise—and for how long—is best, nor how to get every adult to do it.

As one cardiologist said, "It's almost like we have something more powerful than any drug that we have for cardiovascular disease—physical activity—but we don't know how to dose it" (Ashley, quoted in Servick, 2015, p. 1307). For example, is it better to exercise a little every day or a lot on weekends? Some research suggests that intensity is unnecessary: Regular movement is (Ross et al., 2015).

Drugs

Adults use many drugs, more in the United States than in most other nations. As you will see, there are diverse drug varieties, sources, reasons, and effects.

PRESCRIPTION DRUGS More than half of all 25- to 65-year-olds took at least one prescription drug in the past month, and one-fourth took three or more. About half of those prescriptions were for chronic conditions (such as high blood pressure) and about half were for pain. Many of the rest were for emotional problems: 14 percent of adults took a prescribed antidepressant (National Center for Health Statistics, 2017).

Over the past 50 years, prescription medication has cut the adult death rate in half and markedly reduced disability. Childhood diabetes (type 1), for instance, was once a death sentence; now diet and insulin allow diabetics to reach the highest levels of success, as Supreme Court Justice Sonia Sotomayor did. She began injecting herself at age 7; now she takes newer medication that is more precisely calibrated to her daily needs (Sotomayor, 2014).

CHIP SOMODEVILLA/GETTY IMAGES

Almost Died Twice As a younger woman, U.S. Supreme Court Justice Sonia Sotomayor twice survived loss of consciousness from her type 1 Diabetes. Fortunately her friends noticed her crisis. Now she has automatic monitoring and calibrated insulin, and is expected to interpret the Constitution for 30 more years or so.

COMMON NONPRESCRIPTION DRUGS There is no accurate tally of over-the-counter drugs, but almost every adult frequently takes vitamins, analgesics, laxatives, antihistamines, or some other medication. One benefit of growing older might be wisdom regarding drug use: Adults tell each other what works, pharmacists make suggestions, and each person notices his or her personal reactions to various drugs.

Look at the displays in every drugstore. There are hundreds of drugs that you have never taken, because you have a preferred pill for headaches, stomach upset, colds, or whatever. Chances are that you tried those because someone recommended them.

Furthermore, almost every adult eats specific foods for energy, comfort, or relaxation, and drinks soda, tea, or coffee, not for nutrition but to satisfy an emotional need. Evidence suggests that the use of ordinary substances may be another example of adults gaining from experience.

For example, the effect of coffee varies genetically, and adults learn how coffee affects them (Cornelis et al., 2015). For some, coffee does no harm but reduces various problems, including depression and type 2 diabetes (Palatini, 2015). For others, coffee disrupts nighttime sleep and undercuts daytime efficiency. Adults adjust accordingly.

NICOTINE Cigarette smoking in the United States illustrates marked cohort, culture, and gender effects. During World War II (1941–1945), American soldiers (always men) were given free cigarettes. Then in 1964, the U.S. surgeon general first reported on the health risks of smoking, with many follow-up reports in the next few decades. As a result, many former soldiers quit, and fewer young men began smoking.

Meanwhile, some women celebrated another historical happening, women's liberation, by smoking—encouraged by cigarette advertisements. (One brand launched in 1968, Virginia Slims, used the slogan "You've come a long way, baby.") Young women were particularly likely to begin smoking, and for a few years their rate of smoking was as high or higher than for young men.

For all adults, smoking rates dropped over recent decades. In 2015, only 19 percent of adult men and 15 percent of women were smokers. Rates peak at about age 30 and then decrease, indicating the advantages of maturation (National Center for Health Statistics, 2017). By age 60, most smokers have quit.

The changes over the past decades are reflected in lung cancer deaths. A half-century ago in the United States, five times as many men as women died of lung cancer. More recently, rates are closer to equal because "women who smoke like men die like men who smoke" (Schroeder, 2013, p. 389). In the past decades, lung cancer deaths have been reduced by 500 percent from the high of 1960—not primarily because of better medical care but because of wiser adults (see Figure 12.1).

ALCOHOL The harm from cigarettes is dose-related: Each puff, each day, each breath of secondhand smoke makes cancer, heart disease, strokes, and emphysema more likely. No such linear harm results from alcohol.

In fact, some alcohol may be beneficial: Adults who drink wine, beer, or spirits *in moderation*—never more than two drinks a day—live longer than abstainers.

IMAGE COURTESY OF THE ADVERTISING ARCHIVES

Wishful Thinking Would you like to be her, with a thin cigarette in your hand? If this was her usual appearance, she would now be at risk for cancer and heart disease.

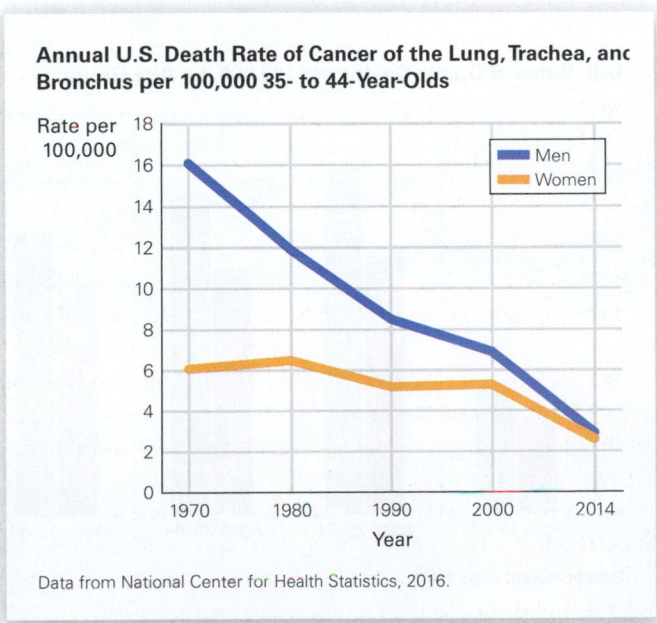

Annual U.S. Death Rate of Cancer of the Lung, Trachea, and Bronchus per 100,000 35- to 44-Year-Olds

Data from National Center for Health Statistics, 2016.

FIGURE 12.1 No More Cancer Sticks The rates of lung cancer deaths dropped dramatically about a decade after smoking rates decreased. Other age groups of adults show similar results, although improvements are not as dramatic for older adults because they learned too late about the damage done to their lungs. In another few decades we will know whether e-cigarettes reverse this trend.

◆ **Especially for Doctors and Nurses**
If you had to choose between recommending various screening tests and recommending various lifestyle changes to a 35-year-old, which would you do? (see response, page 459)

Some scientists consider this a misleading correlation because some of those abstainers were formerly heavy drinkers, so their death rate reflects damage done by earlier alcohol abuse (Chikritzhs et al., 2015; Knott et al., 2015). This is debatable, but everyone agrees that excessive drinking is harmful.

To be specific, alcohol use disorder destroys brain cells, causes liver damage and several cancers, contributes to osteoporosis, decreases fertility, and precipitates many suicides, homicides, and accidents—all while wreaking havoc in families. Even moderate consumption is unhealthy if it leads to smoking, overeating, casual sex, or other destructive habits.

Alcohol abuse also shows age, gender, cohort, and cultural differences. For example, the risk of accidental death while drunk is most common among young men: Law enforcement in the United States has cut their drunk-driving rate in half. However, middle-aged parents who abuse alcohol are more harmful to other people, because of their neglect and irrational rage (Blas & Kurup, 2010).

THE OPIOID EPIDEMIC Most of the data on adult use of drugs shows encouraging trends. Prescription drugs reduce blood pressure and heart disease; illegal drug use decreases markedly after age 25; cigarette smoking is less than half of what it was; a better understanding of alcohol abuse results in fewer abusers.

However, opioid deaths in the United States have increased every year of the past decade, particularly among adults ages 25–44, who are more often addicted than older or younger adults. Reliable data comparing 2015 to 2016 show an increase in 48 of the 50 U.S. states. Nationwide, in 2017, 200 people *per day* died of opioid overdose, according to the National Institute of Drug Abuse. (See Figure 12.2.)

Often the problem starts with a prescribed pain medication. If the doctor stops the prescription, some people switch to heroin, others obtain fentanyl (an illegal synthetic), and others try desperate means to get prescribed drugs.

One man (age 33) killed four people when he robbed a drugstore to get pills for himself and his addicted wife (age 30). The local attorney general said, "The genesis of the current prescription pill and heroin epidemic lies squarely at the feet of the medical establishment" (Spota, quoted in James, 2012).

Many doctors feel unjustly accused, and patients with severe surgical pain are sometimes refused drugs that they need. Is the problem in the addict, the dealer,

THINK CRITICALLY: How would you apportion blame for drug addiction?

FIGURE 12.2 **Bad News** Which is most troubling: that rates of opioid deaths have more than tripled in a decade, that rates continue to rise, or that rates in middle age are almost four times the rates for emerging adults? These data are for 2016; the epidemic continues to worsen.

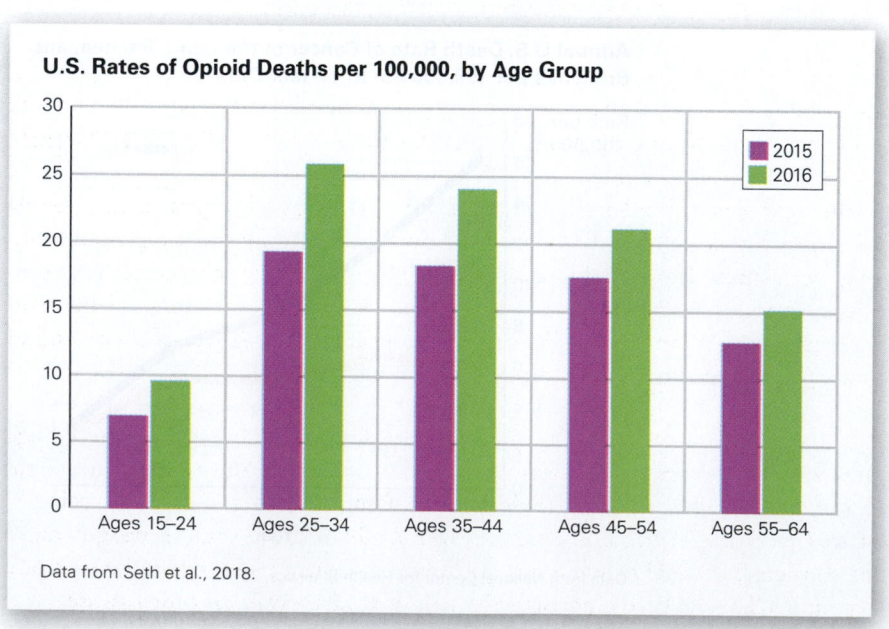

U.S. Rates of Opioid Deaths per 100,000, by Age Group

Data from Seth et al., 2018.

the doctor, the pharmaceutical companies, the community, the culture? From a developmental perspective, blame is unproductive: We need accurate understanding, effective prevention, and successful treatment.

Pain may be alleviated in other ways. For example, one study compared two groups of sufferers of severe back, hip, or knee pain. Half were prescribed opioids (usually morphine or oxycodone) and half nonsteroidal anti-inflammatory drugs (NSAIDS). Other opioids or non-opioid drugs were dispensed if needed. Pain relief was the same for both groups (Krebs et al., 2018).

Hope comes from data on other substances: Rates of alcohol abuse and cigarette smoking are much lower than a few decades ago because we better understand *how* to reduce alcohol abuse and cigarette smoking. Laws, taxes, awareness, and norms together reduce adolescent use. If a young person is prevented from smoking or drinking excessively, then addiction "ages out" in adulthood. The major battle is won, because few adults begin to abuse those substances.

However, that does not apply to opioids. What would stop drug abuse that *begins* in adulthood? At least we know how to reduce deaths. *Naloxone* (a medication that blocks the effects of opioids) is life-saving if given to someone who has stopped breathing from an opioid overdose. Campaigns to make naloxone more readily available are succeeding. The hope is that a near-death episode will motivate an addict toward treatment.

But, prevention should begin long before that. A clue may be in the geographic distribution of opioid addictions. Some states (New Hampshire, Ohio, West Virginia, Massachusetts) have death rates four times higher than in others (Iowa, Oregon, Texas, Hawaii). Some communities have much higher rates than others. Local policies and norms make a difference; scientists must understand what they are.

Nutrition

Diet is increasingly important as adults grow older, because metabolism decreases by one-third between ages 20 and 60, and digestion become less efficient. This means that, to stay healthy at the same weight, adults should eat less, add more vegetables, and move often as they grow older. That is not what happens.

PREVALENCE OF OBESITY Adults in the United States gain an average of 1 to 2 pounds each year, much more than prior generations did. Over the 40 years of adulthood, that adds 40 to 80 pounds. Thus, two-thirds of U.S. adults are overweight, defined as a body mass index (BMI) of 25 or more.

Healthy eating and good health care are important for all adults. Some people may be genetically destined to be outside the boundaries of normal weight, and thus they may be healthy despite being overweight. This may be connected to ethnicity: In the United States, adult obesity rates are higher in African Americans (48 percent) and lower in Asian Americans (11 percent). Should the cutoff (BMI of 30 or higher for obesity) be changed to take ethnicity into account?

CONSEQUENCES OF OBESITY A meta-analysis found that mortality rates by age for adults who were overweight but not obese were *lower* than the average rates. That conclusion comforted many large adults (Flegal et al., 2013).

Not so fast. Some of those people are overweight because muscle weighs more than fat, so their BMI is high while the fat content of their body is not. Excess body fat (no matter what the BMI) increases the risk of almost every chronic disease.

Pain Killer "Never meant to cause you any pain," sang Prince in his classic song, "Purple Rain." But his own pain led to an opioid addiction and then to an accidental overdose of fentanyl, a synthetic opioid 50 times more powerful than heroin. His death at age 57 hurt us all.

JOHN NORMILE/GETTY IMAGES

Winners or Losers? Erik Booker, Miki Sudo, Joey Chestnut, and Sonya Thomas (left to right) compete in the annual chicken-wing eating contest in Buffalo, New York. Chestnut won by eating 205 wings in 12 minutes; Sudo was second with 170. The festival was attended by 70,000 people; the contest was part of the International Federation of Competitive Eating.

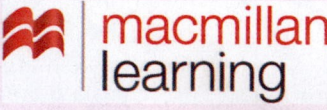

Try the **DATA CONNECTIONS** activity **Body Mass Index** for a demonstration of how BMI is determined.

For example, diabetes causes eye, heart, and foot problems as well as early death. Type 1 diabetes is primarily genetic, but type 2 diabetes is only partly genetic. It may be triggered by overweight. The United States is the world leader in both obesity and diabetes.

The consequences of obesity are psychological as well as physical, since adults who are obese are targets of scorn and prejudice. They are less likely to be chosen as marriage partners, as employees, and even as friends. The stigma leads them to avoid medical checkups, to eat more, and to exercise less—impairing their health far more than their weight alone (Puhl & Heuer, 2010).

For the morbidly obese, health risks increase with every kilogram or pound and surgery may be the best option. Each year, about 200,000 U.S. residents undergo bariatric surgery (via a band inserted laparoscopically in the gastric system) to restrict weight gain. The rate of serious complications is not insignificant: About 2 percent of the patients experience them, and about 1 percent of those with complications (.02 percent overall) die (Change et al., 2017).

Patients have fewer complications if they lose weight in preparation for the surgery (Anderin et al., 2015). That could be an aspect of homeostasis—the body is getting ready to adjust to a better diet.

Despite initial complications, such surgery saves lives because morbid obesity increases the likelihood of many diseases. The greatest benefits seem to occur for people with type 2 diabetes: 70 percent find that their diabetes disappears, usually not to return (Arterburn et al., 2013; Y. Chen et al., 2016). Currently, bariatric surgery is less often chosen by those who most need it—especially if they are of low SES—who are most likely to die of morbid obesity (Moussa et al., 2018).

Correlating Income and Health

The relationship between ethnicity and various health behaviors may reflect income more than national origin. Thus, the fact that Asian Americans are less often overweight could be a consequence of another fact: Asian Americans tend to have more education and income than other Americans.

Worldwide, high-SES adults live longer, avoiding morbidity and disability more than their fellow citizens. Even in nations with universal health care, the poorest people have shorter lives, on average.

THINK CRITICALLY: Should taxpayers subsidize kidney dialysis for young college students or intensive care for severely disabled 80-year-olds? Would it matter, though, if those damaged kidneys were the result of drug abuse, or if that older person was a former president?

Visualizing Development

ADULT OVERWEIGHT AROUND THE GLOBE

A century ago, being overweight was a sign of affluence, as the poor were less likely to enjoy a calorie-rich diet and more likely to be engaged in physical labor. Today, that link is less clear. Overweight—defined as having a body mass index (BMI) over 25—is common across socioeconomic groups and across borders, and obesity (a BMI over 30) is a growing health threat worldwide. In the United States, weight increases as income falls.

OVERWEIGHT AND GDP

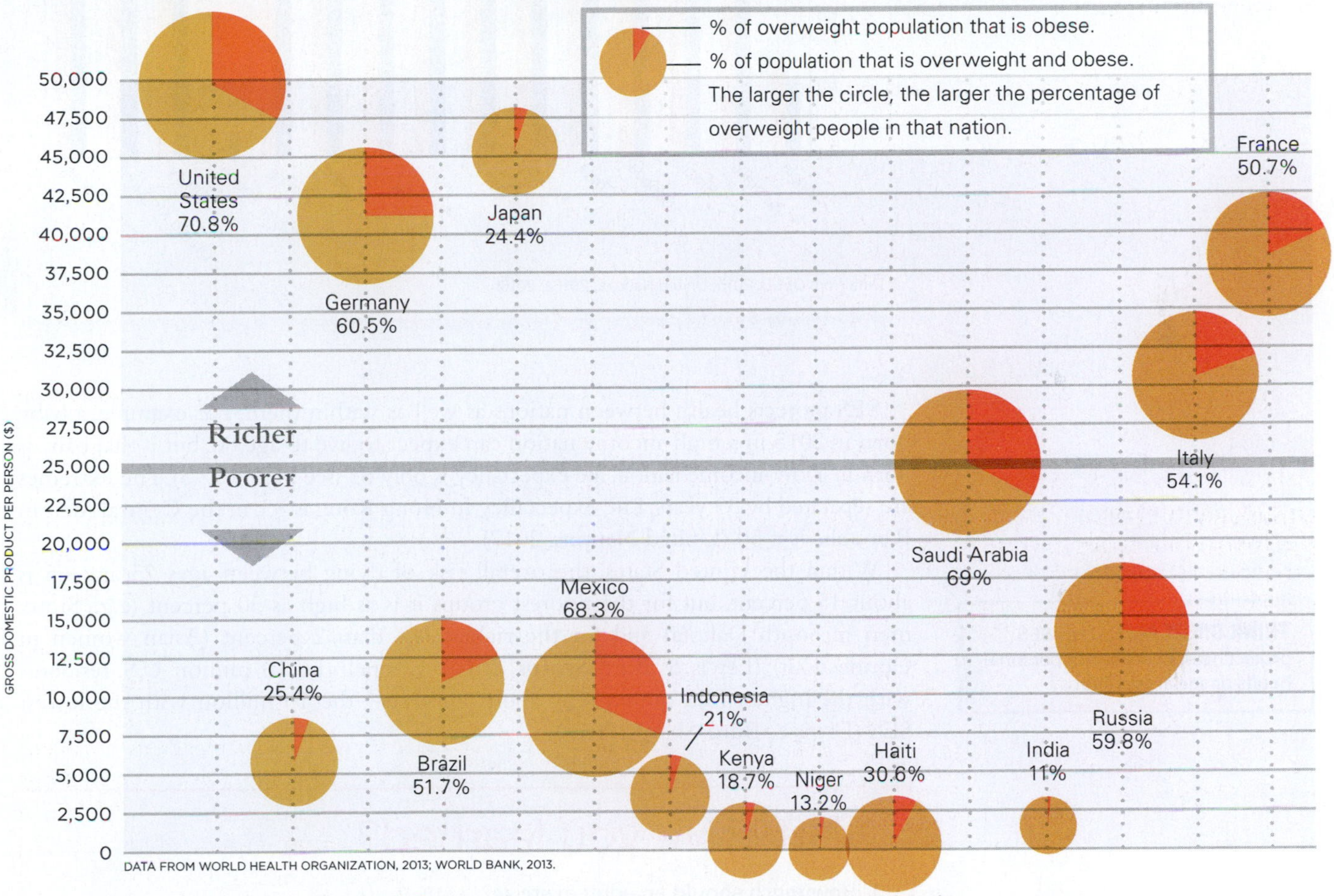

% of overweight population that is obese.
% of population that is overweight and obese.
The larger the circle, the larger the percentage of overweight people in that nation.
GROSS DOMESTIC PRODUCT PER PERSON ($)
50,000
47,500
45,000
42,500
40,000
37,500
35,000
32,500
30,000
27,500
25,000
22,500
20,000
17,500
15,000
12,500
10,000
7,500
5,000
2,500
0
Richer
Poorer
United States 70.8%
Germany 60.5%
Japan 24.4%
France 50.7%
Italy 54.1%
Saudi Arabia 69%
Russia 59.8%
Mexico 68.3%
China 25.4%
Brazil 51.7%
Indonesia 21%
Kenya 18.7%
Niger 13.2%
Haiti 30.6%
India 11%

DATA FROM WORLD HEALTH ORGANIZATION, 2013; WORLD BANK, 2013.

International cutoff weights for overweight and obesity are set at various levels. These numbers show proportions of adults whose BMI is over 25.

OBESITY IN THE UNITED STATES

While common wisdom holds that overweight and obesity correlate with income, recent data suggest that culture and gender may play a bigger role. Obesity tends to be less prevalent among wealthy American women; for men, the patterns are less consistent.

Male | Female

$$$ = Income 350%+ of poverty level
$$ = Income 130% to 349% of poverty level
$ = Income less than 130% of poverty level

OBESITY RATES (U.S.)

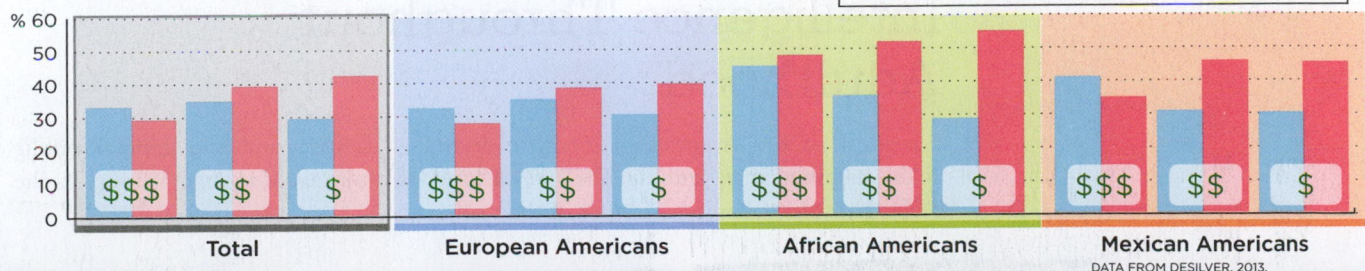

% 60
50
40
30
20
10
0
$$$
$$
$
Total
European Americans
African Americans
Mexican Americans

DATA FROM DESILVER, 2013.

FIGURE 12.3 More Widows Than Widowers Women live longer than men, but it matters where they live. The cause is probably both nature and nurture: Biology is that extra X chromosome, more estrogen, or less testosterone; Nurture is that men have fewer social supports, suppress their emotions, and use more harmful drugs.

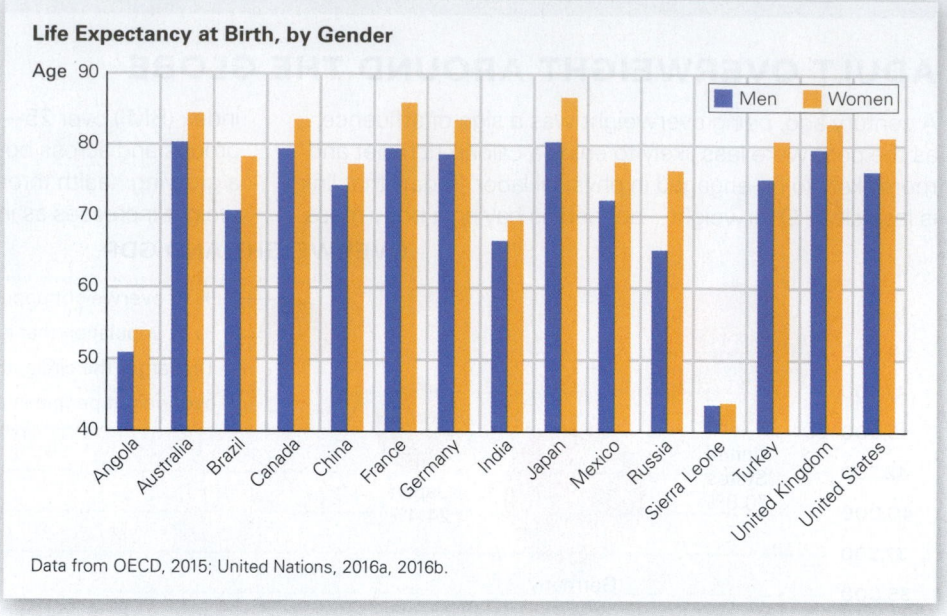

Life Expectancy at Birth, by Gender

Data from OECD, 2015; United Nations, 2016a, 2016b.

SES protects health between nations as well as within them. For example, a baby born in 2015 in a high-income nation can expect to live to age 80; but if that baby is born in a low-income nation, life expectancy is only 61 (see Figure 12.3). The extremes are separated by 33 years: Life expectancy in Hong Kong is 83; in the Central African Republic it is 50 (United Nations, 2017).

Within the United States, the overall risk of dying between ages 25 and 65 is about 15 percent, but for the poorest groups it is as high as 50 percent (e.g., Sioux men in South Dakota) and for the richest less than 2 percent (Asian women in Connecticut) (Lewis & Burd-Sharps, 2010). Overall, the 10 million U.S. residents with the highest SES outlive—by about 30 years—the 10 million with the lowest SES (Lewis & Burd-Sharps, 2010).

THINK CRITICALLY: Does SES protect health because of personal habits or social conditions?

what have you learned?

1. How much should an adult exercise?
2. Why do some experts think exercise is more important than weight?
3. What are the trends in adult weight in the United States?
4. How does lung cancer reflect trends in smoking cigarettes?
5. Which groups are smoking more, and which groups are smoking less?
6. Why would SES predict health, even in a nation with free, public health care?

Intelligence Throughout Adulthood

For most of the twentieth century, everyone—scientists and the general public alike—assumed that "intelligence" was a kind of physical thing, like a lump in the brain that some people had more of than others.

Talk and Think Stephen Hawking (1942–2018) wrote *A Brief History of Time*, which sold more than 10 million copies—an astounding number for a book about theoretical physics and cosmology. He also had ALS, diagnosed at age 21, which did not stop him from marriage (twice), and fatherhood (thrice), and becoming a leading international scholar. Toward the end of his life, he could not talk but communicated with a muscle in his cheek—striking evidence that intellect cannot always be assessed via speech.

As one scholar begins a book on intelligence:

> Homer and Shakespeare lived in very different times, more than two thousand years apart, but they both captured the same idea: we are not all equally intelligent. I suspect that anyone who has failed to notice this is somewhat out of touch with the species.
>
> *[Hunt, 2011a, p. 1]*

General Intelligence

One leading theoretician, Charles Spearman (1927), proposed that there was **general intelligence,** which he called **g**. Spearman contended that although *g* cannot be measured directly, it can be inferred from various abilities, such as vocabulary, memory, and reasoning.

The belief that there is a *g* continues to influence thinking on intelligence (Nisbett et al., 2012). Many scientists also seek one common factor that undergirds IQ—perhaps genes, prenatal brain development, experiences in infancy, or physical health. Other scientists suggest that this is a fool's quest, because *g* does not exist. As one scholar who studies intelligence states, "Intelligent researchers will likely continue to disagree about *g*" (Gignac, 2016, p. 84).

Neuroscientists have joined the debate. Areas of the prefrontal cortex or a part of the adult midbrain (the caudate nuclei) may indicate *g* (Barbey et al., 2013; Roca et al., 2010; Grazioplene et al., 2015). However, given brain plasticity, this could be a consequence rather than a cause of intelligence.

general intelligence (g)
The idea of *g* assumes that intelligence is one basic trait, underlying all cognitive abilities. According to this concept, people have varying levels of this general ability.

Putting It All Together

Many studies using sophisticated designs and statistics have supplanted early cross-sectional, longitudinal, and cross-sequential studies. No study is perfect, because "no design can fully sanitize a study so as to solve the age-cohort-period identification problem" (Hertzog, 2010, p. 5). Cultures, eras, and individuals vary substantially regarding which cognitive abilities are nurtured and tested.

OPPOSING PERSPECTIVES

How to Measure Dynamic Intelligence

As you might imagine, one question about measuring intelligence is whether it should be with written answers, spoken responses, or scans that record the activity of the prefrontal cortex or other areas of the brain. Thousands of scholars are trying to formulate accurate measures of intellectual prowess.

However, the major controversy about intelligence has not been about what measures to use but about how to capture changes over the life span. Consider in detail each of the three methods used for studying human development introduced in Chapter 1: cross-sectional, longitudinal, and cross-sequential.

For the first half of the twentieth century, psychologists thought that children gained intelligence each year, reaching a peak in late adolescence. They believed that intelligence gradually declined over the adult years so that a very old person has about as much intelligence as a child. Younger adults were considered smarter than older ones.

Hundreds of cross-sectional studies of IQ in many nations confirmed that younger adults outscored older ones. Age-related decline in IQ was considered proven. That is why, on both classic IQ tests (the Stanford-Binet and the WISC/WAIS), adult scores are not compared to chronological age (as occurs for children) but are compared to standards for 18-year-olds. [**Life-Span Link:** Intelligence and IQ tests are introduced in Chapter 7.]

An opposing perspective emerged when two young researchers analyzed the intelligence of the adults who had been identified as child geniuses by Lewis Terman decades earlier (Bayley & Oden, 1955). They knew that "invariable findings had indicated that most intellectual functions decrease after about 21 years of age" (Bayley, 1966, p. 117).

Instead, they found that IQ scores *increased* between ages 20 and 50. Follow-up research replicated that surprising finding. Why did these new data contradict previous conclusions?

As you remember from Chapter 1, cross-sectional research can be misleading because each cohort has unique life experiences. In this domain, the quality and extent of education, cultural opportunities (travel, movies), and sources of information (newspapers, radio, and later, television and the Internet) change every decade. No wonder adults, studied longitudinally, grow in intelligence.

It is now considered unfair—and scientifically invalid—to compare the IQ scores of adults of various ages to learn about age-related changes. Older adults score lower, but that does not mean that they have lost intellectual power. Longitudinal research finds that they gain, not lose, ability.

However, advocates of cross-sectional research point out problems with longitudinal research:

1. Repeated testing provides practice, which increases scores.
2. Participants who are not retested because they move without forwarding addresses, or die, tend to be the ones whose IQs are declining. That skews the results of longitudinal research.
3. Unusual events (e.g., a major war or a breakthrough in public health) affect each cohort. In addition, gradual changes—such as widespread use of the Internet or less pollution—make it hard to predict the future based on the history of the past.

A method for reconciling these opposing perspectives came from K. Warner Schaie, who tested a cross section of 500 adults, aged 20 to 50, on primary mental abilities. The cross-sectional results showed age-related decline, as expected.

Schaie then had a brilliant idea. Seven years later, he retested his initial participants (longitudinal) *and* tested a new group of people who were the same age as his earlier sample. Consequently, he could compare people not only to their own previous scores but also to people currently as old as his original group had been when first tested.

US SIGNAL CORPS/TIME LIFE PICTURES/GETTY IMAGES

Smart Enough for the Trenches? These young men were drafted to fight in World War I. Younger men (about age 17 or 18) did better on the military's intelligence tests than slightly older ones did.

↑ **OBSERVATION** QUIZ In addition to intellectual ability, what two aspects of this test situation might affect older men differently than younger men? (see answer, page 459)

He tested and retested, adding a new group every seven years. Known as the *Seattle Longitudinal Study*, this was the first *cross-sequential* study of adult intelligence.

Schaie found that each ability at each age has a distinct pattern. Men were initially better at number skills and women at verbal skills, but they grew closer over time. Vocabulary increased every decade, but speed notably declined beginning at age 30. Everyone declined by age 60 in at least one of their basic abilities, but everyone maintained or increased in other abilities.

But one conclusion has been verified. From about age 20 to age 70, national values, specific genes, and education are all more influential on IQ scores than is chronological age (W. Johnson et al., 2014).

The patterns cannot be predicted accurately for any particular person, even if genes and age are known. For instance, a study of Swedish twins aged 41 to 84 found differences in verbal ability even among the monozygotic twins with equal education. Age had an effect: Memory and spatial ability declined over time, but not at the same rate for everyone (Finkel et al., 2009).

Considering all of the research, adult intellectual abilities measured on IQ tests sometimes rise, fall, zigzag, or stay the same. Specific patterns are affected by each person's experiences, with "virtually every possible permutation of individual profiles" (Schaie, 2013, p. 497). This illustrates the life-span perspective: Intelligence is multi-directional, multi-cultural, multi-contextual, and plastic. Although scores on several subtests decline, overall ability is usually maintained until late adulthood.

Components of Intelligence: Many and Varied

Many developmentalists are now looking closely at patterns of cognitive gain and loss. They contend that, because virtually every pattern is possible, it is misleading to ask whether intelligence either increases or decreases; it does not move in lockstep with age. Each of dozens of distinct intellectual abilities independently rises or falls over time (Roberts & Lipnevich, 2012; Goldstein et al., 2015).

TWO CLUSTERS OF INTELLIGENCE In the 1960s, a leading personality researcher, Raymond Cattell, teamed up with a promising graduate student, John Horn, to study intelligence tests. They concluded that adult intelligence is best understood by grouping various measures into two categories, which they called *fluid* and *crystallized*.

As its name implies, **fluid intelligence** is like water, flowing to its own level no matter where it happens to be. Fluid intelligence is fast and flexible, enabling people to learn anything, even things that are unfamiliar and disconnected to what they already know. Curiosity, learning for the joy of it, solving abstract puzzles, and the thrill at discovering something new are marks of fluid intelligence (Silvia & Sanders, 2010).

People high in this intelligence can draw inferences, understand relationships between concepts, and readily process new ideas and facts in part because their working memory is large and flexible. Fluid intelligence makes a person quick and creative with words and numbers; intellectual puzzles are fun for them. The kinds of questions that test fluid intelligence among Western adults might be:

What comes next in each of these two series?* (Answers are at the bottom of page 442.)

4 9 1 6 2 5 3
V X Z B D

Puzzles are often used to measure fluid intelligence, with speedy solutions given bonus points (as on many IQ tests). Immediate recall—of nonsense words,

VIDEO ACTIVITY: Research Methods and Cognitive Aging explores how various research methods have been employed to study how intelligence changes with age.

THINK CRITICALLY: If an adult lived in another nation, would he or she be smarter? And, because of that, would that adult live longer and healthier?

fluid intelligence
Those types of basic intelligence that make learning of all sorts quick and thorough. Abilities such as short-term memory, abstract thought, and speed of thinking are all usually considered part of fluid intelligence.

of numbers, of a sentence just read—indicates working memory, an asset for fluid intelligence.

Since fluid intelligence appears to be disconnected from past learning, it may seem impractical. Not so. A study of adults aged 34 to 83 found that stressors varied not by age but by fluid intelligence. People high in fluid intelligence were more often exposed to stress but less likely to suffer from it: They used their intellect to turn stress into positive experiences (Stawski et al., 2010).

The ability to detoxify stress may be one reason that high fluid intelligence in emerging adulthood leads to longer life and higher IQ later on. Fluid intelligence is associated with openness to new experiences and overall brain health (Ziegler et al., 2012; Silvia & Sanders, 2010).

The accumulation of facts, information, and knowledge as a result of education and experience is called **crystallized intelligence.** The size of a person's vocabulary, the knowledge of chemical formulas, and the long-term memory for dates in history all indicate crystallized intelligence. Tests designed to measure this intelligence might include questions like these:

> What is the meaning of the word *eleemosynary*?
> Who was Nelson Mandela?
> Explain the difference between a tangent and a triangle.
> Why does the city of Peking no longer exist?

Although such questions seem to measure achievement more than aptitude, these two are connected, especially in adulthood. Intelligent adults read widely, think deeply, and remember what they learn, so their achievement reflects their aptitude. Thus, crystallized intelligence grows out of fluid intelligence (Nisbett et al., 2012).

Vocabulary, for example, improves with reading. Using the words *joy, ecstasy, bliss,* and *delight*—each appropriately, with distinct nuances (quite apart from the drugs, perfumes, or yogurts that use these names)—is a sign of intelligence. Remember the knowledge base (Chapter 7): As people know more, they learn more.

ALL KINDS OF INTELLIGENCE COMBINED To reflect the total picture of a person's intellectual aptitude, all aspects of intelligence need to be considered (Hunt, 2011a). Age complicates the IQ calculation because scores on items measuring fluid

---

crystallized intelligence
Those types of intellectual ability that reflect accumulated learning. Vocabulary and general information are examples. Some developmental psychologists think crystallized intelligence increases with age, while fluid intelligence declines.

Think Before Acting Both of these adults need to combine fluid intelligence and crystallized intelligence, insight and intuition, logic and experience. One *(left)* is a surgeon, studying X-rays before picking up her scalpel. The other *(right)* appears to be an architect, using working memory and abstract reasoning.

---

*The correct answers are 6 and F. The clue is to think of multiplication (squares) and the alphabet: Some series are much more difficult to complete.

intelligence decrease with age, whereas scores on items measuring crystallized intelligence increase. Further, there is some overlap between the two kinds of intelligence, such that someone high in fluid intelligence is likely to become high in crystalized intelligence (Ziegler et al., 2012).

The combination of these two types of intelligence makes IQ fairly steady throughout adulthood. Although brain slowdown begins at age 20 or so, it is rarely apparent until massive declines in fluid intelligence affect crystallized intelligence. Only then do overall IQ scores fall.

THREE FORMS OF INTELLIGENCE Robert Sternberg (1988, 2003, 2011, 2015) agrees that a single intelligence score is misleading. As first mentioned in Chapter 7, Sternberg proposed three fundamental forms of intelligence: analytic, creative, and practical, each of which can be tested. (See Table 12.1.)

Analytic intelligence includes all of the mental processes that foster academic proficiency by making efficient learning, remembering, and thinking possible. Thus, it draws on abstract planning, strategy selection, focused attention, and information processing, as well as on verbal and logical skills.

Strengths in those areas are valuable in emerging adulthood, particularly in college and in graduate school. Multiple-choice tests and brief essays that call forth remembered information, with only one right answer, indicate analytic intelligence.

Creative intelligence involves the capacity to be intellectually flexible and innovative. Creative thinking is divergent rather than convergent, valuing the unexpected, imaginative, and unusual rather than standard and conventional answers.

Sternberg developed tests of creative intelligence that include writing a short story titled "The Octopus's Sneakers" or planning an advertising campaign for a new doorknob. Those with many novel ideas earn high scores.

Practical intelligence involves the capacity to adapt one's behavior to the demands of a given situation. This capacity includes an accurate grasp of the expectations

analytic intelligence
A form of intelligence that involves abstract planning, strategy selection, focused attention, and information processing, as well as verbal and logical skills.

creative intelligence
A form of intelligence that involves the capacity to be intellectually flexible and innovative.

practical intelligence
The intellectual skills used in everyday problem solving. (Sometimes called *tacit intelligence*.)

TABLE 12.1	**Sternberg's Three Forms of Intelligence**		
	Analytic Intelligence	**Creative Intelligence**	**Practical Intelligence**
Mental processes	• Abstract planning • Strategizing • Focused attention • Verbal skills • Logic	• Imagination • Appreciation of the unexpected or unusual • Originality • Vision	• Adaptive actions • Understanding and assessing daily problems • Applied skills and knowledge
Valued for	• Analyzing • Learning and understanding • Remembering • Thinking	• Intellectual flexibility • Originality • Future hopes	• Adaptability • Concrete knowledge • Real-world experience
Indicated by	• Multiple-choice tests • Brief essays • Recall of information	• Inventiveness • Innovation • Resourcefulness • Ingenuity	• Performance in real situations • "Street smarts"

Information from Sternberg, 1988, 2003, 2011, 2015.

and needs of the people involved and an awareness of the particular skills that are called for, along with the ability to use these insights effectively.

Practical intelligence is sometimes called *tacit intelligence* because it is not obvious on tests. Instead, it comes from "the school of hard knocks" and is sometimes called "street smarts," not "book smarts."

THE THREE INTELLIGENCES IN ADULTHOOD

Think about what cognitive abilities are needed in adulthood. Analytic intelligence is useful in higher education, but practical intelligence aids daily life.

An idea resulting from analytic intelligence might fail because people resist academic brilliance as unrealistic and elite, as the term *ivory tower* implies. The history of science is filled with brilliant analysis that was rejected at first. For example, no one believed a young Australian doctor whose research convinced him that bacteria caused stomach ulcers until he drank infectious broth that made him sick. He then swallowed medication that would work on that bacteria. He got well; people believed him.

After college, few adults need to define obscure words or deduce the next element in a number sequence (analytic intelligence), and few need to compose new music, restructure local government, or invent a new gadget (creative intelligence). Ideally, those few find people with practical intelligence to implement their analytic or creative ideas.

Practical intelligence helps adults maintain a home, advance a career, manage money, distinguish real news from false news, respond to the emotional needs of lovers, relatives, neighbors, and coworkers. Schaie found that scores on tests of practical intelligence were steadier than scores on other kinds of tests from age 20 to age 70, with no notable decrement, in part because these skills are needed throughout life (Schaie, 2005/2013).

Smart Farmer; Smart Teacher This school field trip is not to a museum or a fire station but to a wheat field, where children study grains that will become bread. Like this creative teacher, modern farmers use every kind of intelligence. To succeed, they need to analyze soil, fertilizer, and pests (analytic intelligence); to anticipate market prices and food fads (creative intelligence); and to know what crops and seed varieties grow in each acre of their land as they manage their workers (practical intelligence).

Notice that a stunningly creative idea may be rejected as ridiculous and weird rather than serious and inspired. Stravinsky was 31 when his innovative *Rite of Spring* was first presented: The audience booed and almost rioted. It is now much admired.

Think about the political implication of these three intelligences in various nations. Creative individuals are critical of tradition and therefore are tolerated only in some regimes. Analytic individuals might be seen as absentminded, head-in-the-clouds dreamers; people who focus only on immediate results might ignore the results that scientists, using their analytic thought, might find.

As you see, practical intelligence is the most immediately useful. Of course, it could be used for evil as well as good. We all need to be suspicious of short-term benefits at the price of the long-term results from creative or analytic intelligence.

Currently in the United States, of Gardner's nine intelligences, linguistic and mathematical intelligence are the core of most tests of aptitude and achievement. But in some other cultures, the ability to dance (kinesthetic intelligence), or to grow herbs (naturalistic intelligence), or to pray (existential intelligence) might be more crucial. [**Life-Span Link:** Gardner's intelligences are discussed in Chapter 7.]

AMPLIFYING INTELLIGENCE Adults may learn to increase their intelligence by reading, talking to others, attending classes, and much more. Historically, written language, the number system, universities, and the scientific method were what are called **cognitive artifacts**—that is, ways to amplify and extend general cognitive ability. A psychologist who studies intelligence believes that the nations with the most advanced economies and greatest national wealth are those that make best use of cognitive artifacts (E. Hunt, 2012).

The germ theory of disease, for instance, was developed because doctors were able to research, write, publish, and then learn from each other (Hunt, 2011a). Those people who understood and benefited from that theory had longer and healthier lives, and that advanced entire nations.

In more recent times, preventive health care, clean water, electricity, global travel, and the Internet have resulted in advanced societies. According to this idea, smart people are better able to use the cognitive artifacts of their society to advance their own intelligence. Education at every level is often considered a cultural artifact that has benefited humankind. That produced what is called the Enlightenment, and that led to longer, happier lives for everyone (Pinker, 2018).

cognitive artifacts
Intellectual tools passed down from generation to generation that may assist in learning within societies.

What Kind of Intelligence?
Adult intelligence is difficult to assess because context is crucial. What kind of intelligence would you need to successfully herd camels in Saudi Arabia, or to drive a taxi using an app that connects you to customers in Beijing?

What Next? As an adolescent, Josh Groban wanted to be an actor, but fame came from singing. Now that he is 37 he is learning to combine singing and acting—another adult still pursuing a childhood dream.

A meta-analysis of 167 nations compared disaster deaths and the education of adult women (Lutz et al., 2014). Educated women were more likely to use cognitive artifacts: They built safer houses, stockpiled supplies, cared for physical and mental health, heard and understood warnings on various devices. All this required cognition, quite apart from other measures of adult success, such as income. The analysis found that "female education is indeed strongly associated with a reduction in disaster fatalities," but national wealth is not (Lutz et al., 2014, p. 1061).

One attractive concept is that cognition is enhanced when some adults develop artifacts and other intelligent adults use them. One summary explains:

> Because human cognition is a richly multidimensional phenomenon, there are many methods, technologies, and strategies to enhance it. Education, mental training, textbooks, healthy diets, shopping-lists, good-quality sleep, calculators, caffeine, notebooks, mnemonics, Modafinil, maps, methods of loci, and computing devices, in one way or another, enhance our cognitive abilities.
>
> *[Heersmink, 2017, p. 19]*

Most of these are methods that, over the years of adulthood, people learn to use, and then they think better because of it. Some are the result of discoveries by creative, analytic people (e.g., calculators) that are then picked up by intelligent adults. As stressed earlier in this chapter, exercise and diet improve health, moods, and thinking throughout adulthood.

But, as that author explains, some cognitive boosters are questioned by intelligent adults (Heersmink, 2017). For example, Modafinil is on that list; it is one of many drugs said to enhance memory and focus. Here again analytic thought is needed.

Every cognitive artifact, now including computers and mind-enhancing drugs, once including radios and cigarettes, needs to be considered for immediate and long-term effects. How, when, and why adults should advance thinking needs careful consideration—ideally the thought that postformal reflection allows.

what have you learned?

1. Have scientists found the source of *g*?
2. What does cross-sectional research on IQ throughout adulthood usually find?
3. What does longitudinal research on IQ throughout adulthood usually find?
4. How do historical changes affect the results of longitudinal research?
5. How does cross-sequential research control for cohort effects?
6. Why does IQ vary as much as it does?
7. Why would a person want more crystallized than fluid intelligence?
8. Why would a person want more fluid than crystallized intelligence?
9. When are each of Sternberg's three intelligences most useful?
10. How is a textbook a cognitive artifact?

Becoming an Expert

Aging neurons, cultural pressures, historical conditions, and past education all affect adult cognition. None of these can be controlled directly by an individual. Nonetheless, many researchers believe that adults can make crucial choices about intellectual development, deciding whether or not to develop their minds.

Optimization with Compensation

Paul and Margret Baltes (1990) developed a theory called **selective optimization with compensation** to describe the "general process of systematic functioning" (P. Baltes, 2003, p. 25), by which people maintain a balance in their lives as they grow older. They believe that people seek to *optimize* their development, *selecting* the best way to *compensate* for physical and cognitive losses, becoming more proficient at activities they want to perform well.

Selective optimization with compensation applies to every aspect of life, ranging from choosing friends to playing baseball. Each adult seeks to maximize gains and minimize losses, practicing some abilities and ignoring others. Choices are critical, because any ability can be enhanced or diminished, depending on how, when, and why a person uses it. It is possible to "teach an old dog new tricks," but learning requires that adults *want* to learn those new tricks.

When adults are motivated to do well, few age-related deficits are apparent. However, compared with younger adults, older adults are less motivated to put forth their best effort when the task at hand is not particularly engaging (Hess et al., 2009b). That works against them if they take an IQ test.

As Baltes and Baltes (1990) explain, selective optimization means that each adult selects certain aspects of intelligence to optimize and neglects the rest. If the ignored aspects happen to be the ones measured on intelligence tests, then IQ scores will fall, even if the adult's selection improves (optimizes) other aspects of intellect. The brain is plastic over the entire life span, developing new dendrites and activation sequences, adjusting to whatever the person chooses to learn (Karmiloff-Smith, 2010).

AN EXAMPLE: EAST TIMOR For example, suppose someone is highly motivated to learn about a particular area of the world, perhaps East Timor, a tiny nation that has been independent since 2002. That someone goes to the library, selecting key articles and the two dozen books about East Timor, ignoring other interesting topics (*selection*). Selection might also include getting someone else to do the tasks this person finds less interesting, such as balancing the checkbook, hanging the curtains, cleaning the garage.

Then suppose that person realizes that aging vision makes it hard to read the fine print of some news articles about East Timor. Time for *compensation*—new glasses, a magnifier, increased font size. The person might also notice that memory is sometimes shaky, so the person asks other scholars how they take notes. Then the person chooses note-taking strategies such as color coding, file folders, and underlining. The result: If a local lawmaker or newscaster wants to know about genocide, or Indonesia, or the United Nations, then our person shares knowledge about East Timor that few others have (*optimization*).

If the expert on East Timor takes an IQ test that includes *tamarind* as a vocabulary word, that person might score high. However, the same person might fail math questions. Thus, knowledge increases in depth but decreases in breadth.

MULTITASKING One example of selective optimization is multitasking—doing two or more things at once. Some time is saved if both tasks can be accomplished,

selective optimization with compensation
The theory, developed by Paul and Margaret Baltes, that people try to maintain a balance in their lives by looking for the best way to compensate for physical and cognitive losses and to become more proficient in activities they can already do well.

What's the Point? This time, you write the caption! (Use creative intelligence.)

but some slowdown always occurs (Koch et al., 2018). That is more evident with age: Older people who say "I can't do everything at once" and "Don't rush me" are making a wise choice.

The detriments of multitasking become obvious when people drive a car while texting or talking on a cell phone. Such behavior is dangerous for everyone but particularly for older drivers. As the brain focuses on the communication, the neurological shift needed to react to a darting pedestrian is slower (Asbridge et al., 2013).

Some jurisdictions require drivers to use hands-free phones, as if the distraction originates in the body. These misguided laws have not reduced traffic accidents resulting from cell phone use because the multitasking brain is the problem, not the fingers.

Some say that passenger conversation is as distracting as cell phone talk, but that is not true: Years of practice have taught adult passengers (though not young children) when to stop talking so that the driver can focus on the road (Charlton, 2009). If passengers do not quiet down on their own, experienced drivers stop listening and replying because they know they must concentrate.

One father tried to explain this concept to his son as follows:

I told my son: triage
Is the main art of aging.
At midlife, everything
Sings of it. In law
Or healing, learning or play,
Buying or selling—above all
In remembering—the rule is
Cut losses, let profits ring.
Specifics rise and fall
By selection.

[Hamill, 1991]

Expert Cognition

Another way to describe selective optimization is to say that everyone becomes a selective expert. No longer are adults subject to high school or college requirements that mandate that students learn some of everything (science, humanities, math, literature, etc.). Adults can specialize in anything from car repair to gourmet cooking, from illness diagnosis to fly fishing.

As people develop expertise in some areas, they pay less attention to others. For example, each adult chooses to watch only a few of the dozens of channels on television, with some adults never turning the TV on and others having it on all day.

Similarly, some people delete hundreds of unread e-mails every day, never responding to current events. Others cannot help but respond to everything. Some adults consider it a waste of time to go to certain concerts or rallies at which others spend hours standing as they wait for the event to begin.

Culture and context guide people in this process. Many adults who were school-children 60 years ago write letters with distinctive and legible handwriting because they practiced penmanship for hours, became experts in it, and maintained that expertise. Today's schools, and therefore today's young people, make other choices. Some adults never send handwritten letters, but virtually all can read, unlike a century ago when many adults were illiterate.

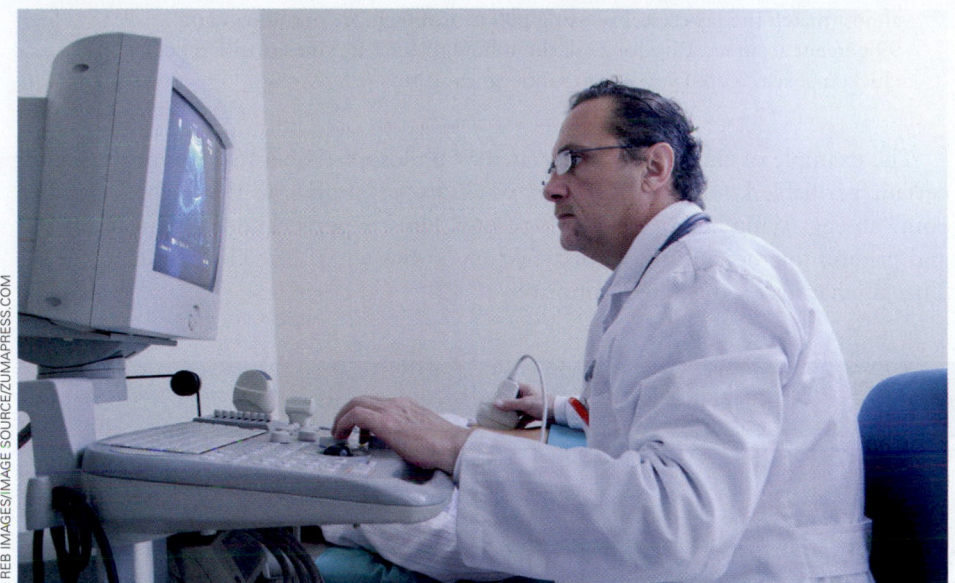

Cohort Changes This expert examining a sonogram illustrates the benefits of recent history. His lifetime experience has made him a better judge of healthy and diseased tissue. Another cohort change is evident here: This photo was taken in Valparaiso, Chile, where the 2015 death rate was only one-third of what it was in 1960.

An **expert,** as defined by cognitive scientists, is not necessarily someone with rare and outstanding knowledge or skills. Although most experts do, in fact, know more than the average person, to researchers expertise means more—and less—than that. Expertise is not innate, although it may begin with inherited abilities that are later developed (Hambrick et al., 2016).

After time and effort, some people have accumulated knowledge, practice, and experience that catapult them up—they enter a higher plane than most people. The quality as well as the quantity of their cognition is advanced. Expert thought is (1) intuitive, (2) automatic, (3) strategic, and (4) flexible, as we now describe.

EXPERTS ARE INTUITIVE Novices follow formal procedures and rules. Experts rely more on past experiences and immediate contexts; their actions are therefore more intuitive and less stereotypical than those of the novice.

The role of experience and intuition is evident, for example, in surgery (Norman et al., 2018). Data on physicians indicate that the single most important question to ask a surgeon is "How often have you performed this operation?" The novice, even with the best, most recent training, is less skilled than the expert.

Expertise is also evident in cooking. One study asked expert chefs to describe how they conceived of their extraordinarily sumptuous dishes. They spoke of sudden insight, not step-by-step analysis (Stierand & Dörfler, 2016).

In psychotherapy as well, experience matters. One study asked therapists to talk aloud as they analyzed a hypothetical case. Novices and experts all had the requisite academic knowledge. The experts did more "forward thinking," using inferences and developing a possible treatment plan. The novices were less likely to think about the person's social relationships, focusing more on the individual and a description of *what is* rather than wonder about what might be (Eells et al., 2011).

A classic example of expert intuition is *chicken-sexing*—the ability to tell whether a newborn chicken is male or female. As David Myers tells it:

> Poultry owners once had to wait five to six weeks before the appearance of adult feathers enabled them to separate cockerels (males) from pullets (hens). Egg producers wanted to buy and feed only pullets, so they were intrigued to hear that some Japanese had developed an uncanny ability to sex day-old chicks. . . . Hatcheries elsewhere then gave some of their workers apprenticeships under the Japanese. . . . After months of training and experience, the best Americans and Australians could

expert
Someone with specialized skills and knowledge developed around a particular activity or area of specific interest.

almost match the Japanese, by sexing 800 to 1,000 chicks per hour with 99 percent accuracy. But don't ask them how they do it. The sex difference, as any chicken-sexer can tell you, is too subtle to explain.

[Myers, 2002, p. 55]

The example of chicken-sexing is cited by philosophers because it is not based on certain, verifiable knowledge. Only six weeks later is it obvious that a chick will become an egg-laying hen or an eggless rooster. Thus, experts cannot articulate reasons and criteria for their intuition, or why they know what they know (Greco, 2014). That is what makes the expert intuitive.

A VIEW FROM SCIENCE

Who Wins in Soccer?

One experiment that studied the relationship between expertise and intuition involved 486 Dutch college students who were asked to predict the winners of soccer games not yet played. Those students who were avid fans (the experts) made better predictions when they had a few minutes of unconscious thought instead of when they had the same number of minutes to mull over their choice (see Figure 12.4). Those who didn't care much about soccer (the nonexperts) did worse overall, but they did especially poorly when they had time to use unconscious intuition (Dijksterhuis et al., 2009).

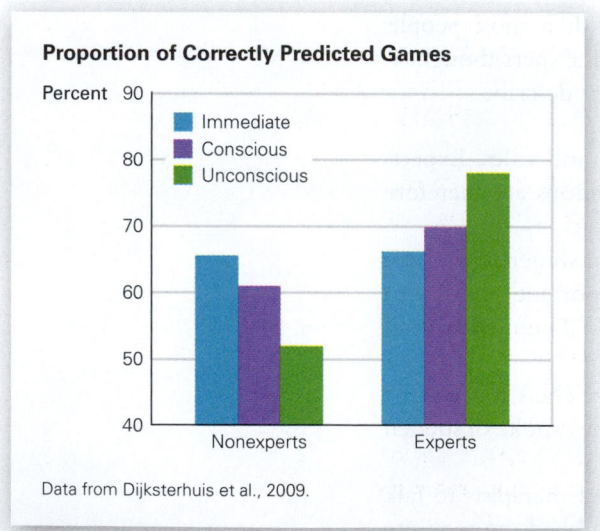

Data from Dijksterhuis et al., 2009.

FIGURE 12.4 If You Don't Know, Don't Think!
Undergraduates at the University of Amsterdam were asked to predict winners of four World Cup soccer matches in one of three conditions: (1) immediate—as soon as they saw the names of the nations that were competing in each of the contests, (2) conscious—after thinking for two minutes about their answers, and (3) unconscious—after two minutes of solving distracting math tasks. As you can see, the experts were better at predicting winners after unconscious processing, but the nonexperts became less accurate when they thought about their answers, either consciously or unconsciously.

The details of this experiment are intriguing. For 20 seconds, all participants were shown a computer screen with four soon-to-be-played soccer matches and were asked to predict the winners. One-third of the predictions were made immediately, one-third were made after two minutes of conscious thought, and one-third were made after two minutes when *only* unconscious thought could occur—because people randomly assigned to that group were required to calculate a series of mind-taxing math questions during those two minutes.

Nonexperts did no better than chance. They did worse after thinking about their answer, especially when the thought was unconscious. Did the stress of doing math interfere with their thinking?

By contrast, the predictions of the experts were not much better than those of the nonexperts when they guessed immediately, a little better when they had two minutes to think, and best of all after unconscious thought. Apparently, the experts' knowledge of soccer helped them most when they were consciously thinking of something else.

This experiment has led to many follow-up studies. One study examined people's impulsive food choices, which often are unhealthy. In this study, people were trained to prefer fruits and vegetables, and they chose those healthier foods later—if they had to choose quickly (Veling et al., 2017). When they had more time to think, their choices were the same as they always were.

Other studies concern medicine, where intuition sometimes finds a diagnosis that a textbook would not. One of the benefits of expert doctors is that they more quickly reach a diagnosis when the person has a common ailment, but they also note uncommon symptoms and diagnoses.

A meta-analysis cautioned against applying the benefits of quick thinking too broadly: Medical knowledge, and thoughtful analysis, may lead to better conclusions than intuition (Vadillo et al., 2015). Hopefully, your doctor is expert enough to realize that.

ADEK BERRY/GETTY IMAGES

Same Situation, Far Apart: Don't Be Afraid The police officer in Toronto collecting slugs and the violinist in Jakarta collecting donations have both spent years refining their skills. Many adults would fear being that close to a murder victim or that close to thousands of rushing commuters, but both men have learned to practice their vocation no matter where they are. They are now experts: The cop discovered that two guns were used, and the musician earns more than $5 a day (the average for street musicians in Indonesia).

EXPERTS ARE AUTOMATIC The experiment with soccer predictions confirms that many elements of expert performance are automatic; that is, the complex action and thought required by most people have become routine for experts, making it appear that most aspects of the task are performed instinctively.

Experts process incoming information quickly, analyze it efficiently, and then act in well-rehearsed ways that make their efforts appear unconscious. In fact, some automatic actions are no longer accessible to the conscious mind. Expert musicians, for instance, have changes in their brains that make hearing sounds more precise (with "perfect pitch") and allow movement of the hands with speed and sensitivity (Altenmuller & Furuya, 2018).

An everyday example of automaticity occurs in tying shoelaces. Adults can do that in the dark, without thinking about it. However, they cannot describe how they do it—unless they can remember what they were told as children. Children, however, can talk about it, but not always do it. For adults, talking about sequence may confuse rather than clarify their thinking (Dijksterhuis et al., 2009).

Automaticity is apparent if you are an experienced driver and try to teach someone else to drive. Excellent drivers who are inexperienced instructors find it hard to recognize or verbalize things that have become automatic—such as anticipating the future movements of cyclists on the far side of the road, or feeling the car shift gears as it heads up an incline, or hearing the tires lose traction on a bit of sand. Yet such factors differentiate the expert from the novice.

The same gap between knowledge and instruction occurs when a computer expert tries to teach a novice what to do, as I know myself when my daughters try to help me with the finer points of Microsoft Excel. They are unable to verbalize what they know, although they can do it very well with the computer. It is much easier to click the mouse or do the keystroke oneself than to teach what has become automatic.

Chess players have been studied intensely, in part because international rankings define levels of expertise. The general finding is that, although players show age-related decrements and slowdowns in general tests of cognition, age seems to have no effect on chess ability. This is particularly apparent for speedy recognition that the king is threatened: Older experts do that almost as quickly as younger

adults (in a fraction of a second) despite steep, age-related declines on standard tests (Gobet & Charness, 2018).

When something—such as an audience, a stressor, or too much conscious thought—interferes with automatic processing, the result may be clumsy performance. This is thought to be the problem when some experienced athletes "choke under pressure"—their automatic actions are hijacked (DeCaro et al., 2011).

In a final example, medical students and doctors were asked to diagnose a difficult case of cardiac failure and pulmonary embolus. They read details of the case while their eye movements were tracked (Vilppu et al., 2016). Less than half of the interns reached a correct diagnosis, but all of the experienced doctors did. The latter also read more quickly and focused on different paragraphs: They could automatically process some information and knew when unusual information was presented.

EXPERTS ARE STRATEGIC Experts have more and better strategies, especially when problems are unexpected. Indeed, strategy may be the pivotal difference between a skilled person and an unskilled person. Extensive study has occurred with pilots of aircraft, since one small lapse can become a disaster (Dismukes et al., 2007). Detailed checklists are followed before every takeoff, yet every now and then an error occurs.

The crucial factor that differentiates an expert pilot from a nonexpert one is not knowledge but strategic use of resources—that is, strategic use of all of the possible backup plans (Durso et al., 2018). For instance, if the plane must land somewhere other than the runway, an expert pilot can guide the aircraft to a safe stop on a field, or even on the water.

A strategy used by expert team leaders is ongoing communication, especially during slow times. Therefore, when stress builds, no team member misinterprets previously rehearsed plans, commands, and requirements. Expert teams include individuals from many backgrounds, but they all have learned to work together when need be (Sonesh et al., 2018).

The ability to plan ahead is evident in experts of many kinds. You have witnessed the same phenomenon in expert professors: At the beginning of the semester they institute routines and policies, strategies that avoid problems later in the

↓ **OBSERVATION** QUIZ
What expertise and skills does this nurse need? (see answer, page 459)

Many Skills Nurse Rolanda Florence checks the glucose level of a person with diabetes as part of three days of free health screenings in Los Angeles, California.

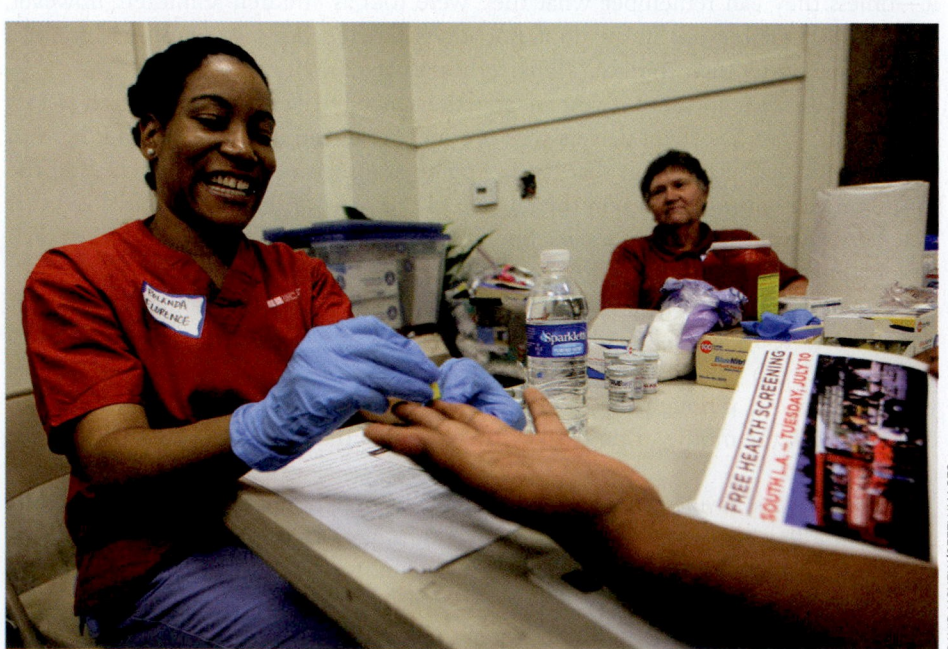

DAVID MCNEW/GETTY IMAGES

term. They also are able to change the plan on the fly if the class needs it, which leads to the final point.

Overall, strategies themselves need to be updated as situations change—and no chess game, or flight, or class is exactly like another. The monthly fire drill required by some schools, the standard lecture given by some professors, and the pat safety instructions read by airline attendants before takeoff become less effective over time. Strategy must change. I recently heard a flight attendant begin his standard talk with, "For those of you who have not ridden in an automobile since 1960, this is how you buckle a seat belt." During that preflight monologue, I actually listened.

EXPERTS ARE FLEXIBLE Finally, perhaps because they are intuitive, automatic, and strategic, experts are also flexible. The expert artist, musician, or scientist is creative and curious, deliberately experimenting and enjoying the challenge when unexpected things occur (Csikszentmihalyi, 2013).

Remember Pavlov (Chapter 1)? He already had won the Nobel Prize when he noticed his dogs' unexpected reaction to being fed. His expertise made him notice, then investigate, and eventually develop insights that opened a new perspective in psychology.

Consider the expert surgeon who takes the most complex cases and prefers unusual patients to typical ones, because operating on the unusual ones might reveal sudden, unexpected complications. Compared with the novice, the expert surgeon is not only more likely to notice telltale signs (an unexpected lesion, an oddly shaped organ, a rise or drop in a vital sign) that may signal a problem but is also more flexible and willing to deviate from standard textbook procedures if those procedures seem ineffective (Patel et al., 1999).

In the same way, experts in all walks of life adapt to individual cases and exceptions—much like an expert chef adjusts ingredients, temperature, technique, and timing as a dish develops, tasting to see whether a little more spice is needed, seldom following a recipe exactly. Standards are high: Some chefs throw food in the garbage rather than serve a dish that many people would happily eat. Expert chess players, auto mechanics, and violinists are similarly aware of nuances that might escape the novice.

In the field of education, best practices for the educator now emphasize flexibility and strategy, as each group of students has distinct and often erroneous assumptions, which change every year. It is not helpful to simply teach the right answers; flexibility requires matching the instruction to the individual students, discovering what learning is needed (Ford & Yore, 2012).

In order to be a flexible expert, many options need to be understood. It is estimated that expert chess players have memorized 100,000 possible opening sequences (Chassy & Gobet, 2011). Major airlines usually require pilots to have thousands of hours of flight experience before they can become a captain (Durso et al., 2018).

Expertise, Age, and Experience

The relationship between expertise and age is not straightforward. One of the essential requirements for expertise is time.

People who become experts need months—or even years—of practice (depending on the task) to develop that expertise. In some areas, practice must be extensive, several hours a day for at least 10 years. It also must be deliberate practice, done to improve skills. Circumstances, training, genes, ability, practice, and age all affect expertise, which means that experts in one specific field are often quite inexpert in other areas.

Many studies also show that people become more expert, and their brains adapt while they practice whatever skills are needed in their chosen field. This occurs not

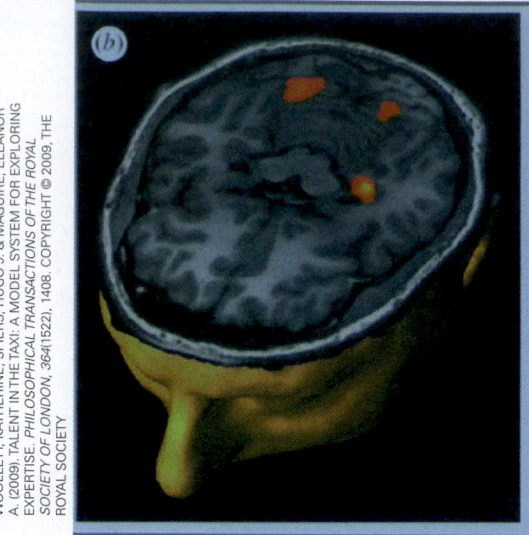

WOOLLETT, KATHERINE; SPIERS, HUGO J. & MAGUIRE, ELEANOR A. (2009). TALENT IN THE TAXI: A MODEL SYSTEM FOR EXPLORING EXPERTISE. PHILOSOPHICAL TRANSACTIONS OF THE ROYAL SOCIETY OF LONDON, 364(1522), 1408. COPYRIGHT © 2009, THE ROYAL SOCIETY

Red Means Go! The red shows the activated brain areas in London taxi drivers as they navigated the busy London streets. Not only were these areas more active than the same areas in the average person's brain, but they also had more dendrites. In addition, the longer a cabby had been driving, the more brain growth was evident. This research confirms plasticity, implying that we all could develop new skills, not only by remembering but also by engaging in activities that change the very structures of our brains.

only for motor skills—playing the violin, dancing, driving—but also for reasoning skills (Zatorre et al., 2012). An interesting example comes from perfumers: They need an acute sense of smell as they seek to develop new scents. Although the sense of smell typically declines with age, this is not so for perfumers. Experts outdid younger nonexperts: They had significantly developed those parts of the brain that were attuned to smell (Delon-Martin et al., 2013).

Indeed, as evident in typing, motor skills are almost always subsidiary to thought. The expert typist is very quick (automatic), but experience helps in that experts scan several letters beforehand—and that helps them with speed.

Young typists have an advantage when sheer speed is needed, but they are less adept at vocabulary and communication. This illustrates a general conclusion: Experienced adults often use selective optimization with compensation, becoming expert. In many workplaces, the best employees may be the older, more experienced ones—if they want to do their best.

One final example of the relationship between age and job effectiveness comes from an occupation familiar to all of us: driving a taxi. In major cities, taxi drivers must find the best route (factoring in traffic, construction, time of day, and many other details) while knowing where new passengers are likely to be found and how to relate to customers, some of whom want to talk, others not.

Research in England—where taxi drivers "have to learn the layout of 25,000 streets in London and the locations of thousands of places of interest, and pass stringent examinations" (Woollett et al., 2009, p. 1407)—found not only that the drivers became more expert with time but also that their brains adjusted to the need for particular knowledge. Some regions of their brains (areas dedicated to spatial representation) were more extensive and active than those of an average person (Woollett et al., 2009). On ordinary IQ tests, the taxi drivers' scores were average, but in navigating London, their expertise was apparent.

FAMILY SKILLS This discussion of expertise has focused so far on occupations—surgeons, pilots, taxi drivers—that once had far more male than female workers. In recent years, two important shifts have occurred that add to this topic.

First, more women are working in occupations traditionally reserved for men. Remember from Chapter 2 that Virginia Apgar, when she earned her M.D. in 1933, was told that she could not be a surgeon because only men were surgeons. Fortunately for the world, she became an anesthesiologist and her scale has saved millions of newborns.

Today that assumption has changed; almost half of the new M.D.s in the United States are women, and many of them have become surgeons (see Figure 12.5). More generally, most college women expect to have careers, husbands, and children, and many do so (Hoffnung & Williams, 2013).

The second major shift is that domestic work has gained new respect. In earlier generations, women sometimes said they were "just a housewife," even though

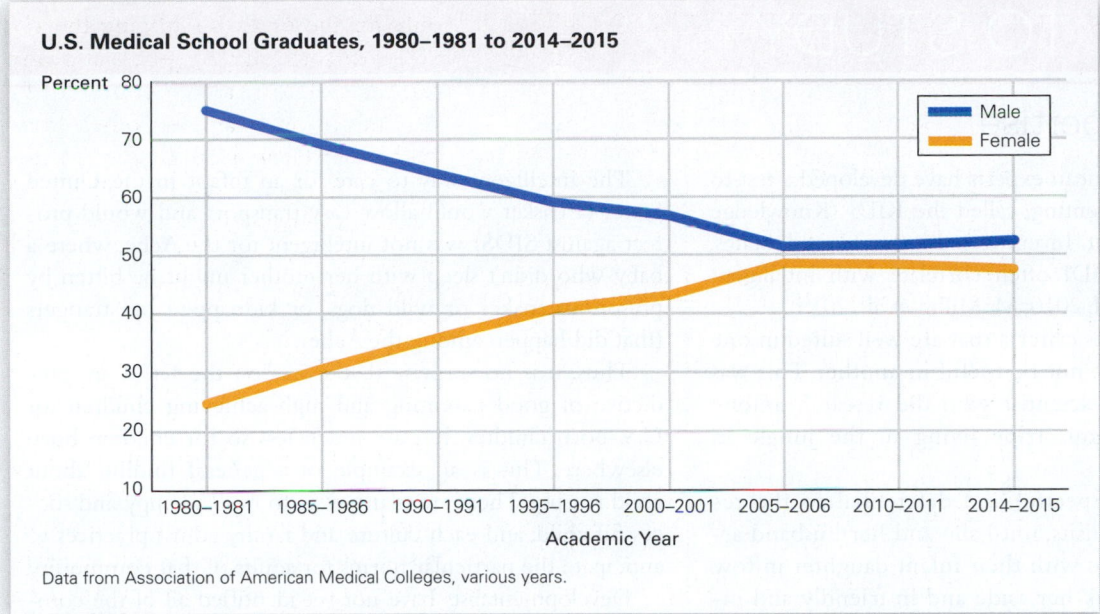

U.S. Medical School Graduates, 1980–1981 to 2014–2015

Data from Association of American Medical Colleges, various years.

FIGURE 12.5

Expect a Woman
Next time you hear "The doctor will see you now," the physician is as likely to be a woman as a man—unless the doctor is over age 40.

they not only cared for the house but also the biological, cognitive, and psychosocial needs of several children. Recently, however, the importance of work at home is increasingly recognized, and men as well as women do it.

We now know that women are not automatically good mothers and house-keepers, and that men can be experts in the domestic and emotional work that once only women were supposed to do. Couples who switch traditional roles are no longer rare. Most experts now believe that, especially when mothers work full time, children benefit when fathers have major responsibility for child rearing (Dunn et al., 2013).

It is no longer assumed that a "maternal instinct" is innate to every mother; many mothers experience postpartum depression, financial stress, or bursts of anger and do not provide responsive child care. Certainly in some families, fathers and grand-parents provide better care for children than mothers do. As with other adult tasks, motivation and experience are crucial for caregiving.

The skill, flexibility, and strategies needed to raise a family are a manifestation of expertise. Here again, age as well as gender is important. As noted in previous chapters, in their late teens and early 20s, humans are at their most fertile, and young women have the fewest complications of pregnancy. But conception is only a start: In general, older parents are more patient, with lower rates of child abuse as well as more successful offspring.

Of course, the mere passage of time does not make a person learn to be a better parent, but age correlates with better parenting. A review of the research by an expert on the science of parenting concludes that, in general, as people gain in maturity and experience, "the more appropriate and optimal their parenting cognitions and practices are likely to be" (Bornstein, 2015, p. 91).

This is especially true if the parents have learned from experience and can listen well, as mature parents more often do. Raising a child teaches adults how to become an expert parent—intuitive, strategic, and flexible. For this, the children themselves get some credit. As my first two daughters said to the next two, "You should be grateful to us. We broke them [my husband and me] in."

◆ Especially for Prospective Parents
In terms of the intellectual challenge, what type of intelligence is most needed for effective parenthood? (see response, page 459)

A CASE TO STUDY

Parenting Expertise

A team of North American experts have developed a test to measure intelligent parenting, called the KIDI (Knowledge of Infant Development Inventory). In the United States, high scores on the KIDI often correlate with intelligent baby care (e.g., Howard, 2010; McMillin et al., 2015).

However, sometimes criteria that are well suited in one cultural context might not be useful in another. This was illustrated by a social scientist who did research among the Ache, an indigenous tribe living in the jungle in Paraguay.

The Ache were respectful and deferential to the researcher on repeated visits, until she and her husband arrived at their study site with their infant daughter in tow. The Ache women took her aside and in friendly and intimate but no-nonsense terms told her all the things she was doing wrong as a mother. . . .

> This older woman sat with me and told me I *must* sleep with my daughter. They were horrified that I had a basket with me for her to sleep in. . . . Here was a group of forest hunter-gatherers, people living in what Westerners would call basic conditions, giving instructions to a highly educated woman from a technologically sophisticated culture.
>
> *[Hurtado, quoted in Small, 1998, pp. 213–214]*

The intelligent way to care for an infant in the United States (a basket would allow easy transport and would protect against SIDS) was not intelligent for the Ache, where a baby who didn't sleep with her mother might be bitten by poisonous snakes or wild dogs, or kidnapped by strangers (that did happen among the Ache).

Thus, it is no surprise that scores on the KIDI are predictive of good parenting and high-achieving children for U.S.-born children but are much less so for children born elsewhere. This is an example of a general finding about child rearing: There are many ways to raise a happy and successful child, and each culture and family adjust practices to anticipate the particular norms for adults of that community.

Developmentalists have not yet identified all of the components necessary to become an expert in child rearing, but at least we know that such expertise exists. Children raised by teenage parents are more likely to become high school dropouts and substance abusers; more experienced and mature parents are more likely to nip problems in the bud and recognize that some behaviors (that hairstyle, that music, that tattoo) are not worth fighting about.

As with all aspects of adult cognition, age does not guarantee intelligence. But experience, wisely understood, may help. Some parents are far more skilled than others.

As you have read, many types of expertise require flexibility. This is evident in parenting, which varies a great deal, depending on the particulars of the child and the culture. (See A Case to Study.)

JENNY AGAIN A dispassionate analysis of Jenny's situation when she consulted me would conclude that her decision to birth another baby—with no marriage, no job, a father who might disappear, and an apartment in the south Bronx—would doom her to poor health, poor prospects, and a depressing life. This is not a stereotype: The data show that lifelong poverty is the usual future for low-income single mothers who have several children.

But those statistics do not reflect Jenny's expertise. She already had a habit of gathering social support, evident by her seeking me out. She was not daunted by her poverty; remember, she found many free activities for her children to enjoy, including sending them on vacation in the country. She was exceptional, but not unique: Some low-SES people overcome the potential stressors of poverty (Chen & Miller, 2012).

Jenny used her knowledge well. She asked Billy to be tested for sickle-cell anemia (negative), and she knew that honest communication is crucial for human relationships. She told Billy she loved him but that she would have the baby, contrary to his advice. She continued to encourage her children in public school,

befriending their teachers, who in turn gave special attention to her speech-impaired son.

When she was 8 months pregnant, she interviewed for a city job tutoring children in her home. She hoped to earn money while caring for her newborn (a full-term, healthy girl). I brought baby clothes to her modest eighth-floor apartment in a public housing project.

I noticed that her framed Bronx Community College diploma was not displayed. She explained that she feared that the city investigator, who would come to her home to see if it was adequate for tutoring, might decide she was overqualified. That decision is evidence of Jenny's expertise: She got the job.

When her baby was a little older, Jenny headed back to college, earning a B.A. on a full scholarship. Her peers and professors recognized her intelligence: She was selected to give the student speech at graduation. By then the two nephews were over age 18 and moved out.

She then found work as a receptionist in a city hospital, a union job that provided day care and health benefits for her and her three children. That allowed her to move to a better neighborhood of the Bronx (Co-op City, once home to Justice Sotomayor).

Billy did not disappear. He sometimes visited Jenny and the daughter he had not wanted. His wife became suspicious and hired a detective to follow him—and then gave him an ultimatum: Stop seeing Jenny or file for divorce.

At that point, I realized that Jenny had insight into human relations that I did not anticipate in my office years earlier: Billy chose divorce and married Jenny. Within a few years, they moved to Florida, where Jenny earned a master's degree (she phoned to say she was assigned my textbook) and then worked as a supervisor in a school. Their young daughter graduated from high school in Florida.

The last time I saw her, I learned that she bikes, swims, and gardens every day. I met her son: He not only overcame his speech problem, he earned a Ph.D. in psychology. He was an adjunct at Bronx Community College for a year, and I observed him teach an excellent class. He was offered a tenure-track job, which he refused—he had a better offer elsewhere. Both of Jenny's daughters are now college graduates.

Not everyone becomes an expert mother, or wise in human relations; Jenny is exceptional in many ways. But one lesson from this chapter is that health, intelligence, and even wisdom may improve over the years of adulthood. As further explained in Chapter 13, choices and relationships affect how lives unfold—true for Jenny and for us all.

what have you learned?

1. How might a person compensate for fading memory skills?
2. What selective optimization can you see in your parents or grandparents?
3. In what domain are you an expert that most people are not?
4. How does automatic processing contribute to expertise?
5. Explain how intuition might help or diminish ability.
6. In what occupations would age be an asset, and why?
7. In what occupations would age be a liability, and why?
8. What do parents learn from experience?

SUMMARY

Growing Older

1. Senescence causes a universal slowdown during adulthood. The pace and significance depend on culture and on the decisions adults make.

2. For most people, brains continue to function well. However, for about 1 percent of adults, thinking is impaired, because serious brain damage occurs. The senses all lose acuity with age, but severe sensory problems are not typical in adulthood.

3. Appearance changes with age, especially evident in the skin. Ease of movement decreases as people become less agile. Shape and reaction time change as well.

4. Sexual satisfaction may improve with age, but infertility becomes more common. Sperm count gradually decreases in men, and every step of female reproduction—ovulation, implantation, fetal growth, labor, and birth—slows down.

5. A number of assisted reproductive technology (ART) procedures, including in vitro fertilization (IVF), offer potential answers to infertility.

6. At menopause, ovulation ceases and estrogen is markedly reduced, causing infertility and other symptoms. Hormone production declines more gradually in men. For everyone, hormone replacement therapy should be used cautiously, if at all.

Habits: Good and Bad

7. Good habits keep adults healthy. Most adults take prescription and over-the-counter drugs and eat or drink foods they hope will enhance health. What works depends on their own body chemistry.

8. Cigarette smoking has markedly declined, and abuse of alcohol and most illegal drugs also is markedly reduced in adulthood.

Rates of opioid addiction, however, are increasing, especially in adulthood.

9. Nutrition and exercise continue to be crucial for health. However, many adults overeat and under exercise, so more than half of all American adults are overweight, gaining weight every year of adulthood.

Intelligence Throughout Adulthood

10. It was traditionally assumed that there is one general intelligence (g), measurable by IQ tests. Cross-sectional research shows a decline in IQ with age; longitudinal research shows an increase in adulthood.

11. Crystallized intelligence, reflecting accumulated knowledge, increases, but fluid, flexible reasoning declines in adults. That makes IQ, overall, steady over the decades of adulthood until old age.

12. Sternberg proposed three fundamental forms of intelligence: analytic, creative, and practical. Analytic intelligence is needed in higher education, creative intelligence is valued only in some circumstances, and practical intelligence is particularly useful for adults in daily life.

Becoming an Expert

13. Selective optimization with compensation occurs in cognition, education, and many other aspects of adult life.

14. People become experts in some aspects of knowledge and intellect, allowing others to fade. Expertise is characterized by more intuitive, automatic, strategic, and flexible thinking.

15. Experienced adults may surpass younger adults if they specialize, compensating for any declines. Years of practice may be crucial for typists, taxi drivers, doctors, and parents.

KEY TERMS

senescence (p. 420)
infertility (p. 427)
menopause (p. 429)
hormone replacement therapy
  (HRT) (p. 430)

general intelligence (g)
  (p. 439)
fluid intelligence (p. 441)
crystallized intelligence
  (p. 442)

analytic intelligence
  (p. 443)
creative intelligence
  (p. 443)
practical intelligence (p. 443)

cognitive artifacts
  (p. 445)
selective optimization with
  compensation (p. 447)
expert (p. 449)

APPLICATIONS

1. Guess the age of five adults you know, ideally of different ages. Then ask them how old they are. Analyze the clues you used for your guesses and the reactions to your question.

2. Find a speaker willing to come to your class who is an expert on weight loss, adult health, smoking, or drinking. Write a one-page proposal explaining why you think this speaker would be good and what topics he or she should address. Give this proposal to your instructor, with contact information for your speaker. The instructor

will call the potential speakers, thank them for their willingness, and decide whether or not to actually invite them to speak.

3. Attend a gathering for people who want to stop a bad habit or start a good one, such as an open meeting of Alcoholics Anonymous or another 12-step program, an introductory session of Weight Watchers or Smoke Enders, or a meeting of prospective gym members. Report on who attended, what you learned, and what your reactions were.

ESPECIALLY FOR ANSWERS

Response for Drivers (from page 422): No. Car accidents occur when the mind is distracted, not the hands.

Response for Doctors and Nurses (from page 434): Obviously, much depends on the specific patient. Overall, however, far more people develop a disease or die because of years of poor health habits than because of various illnesses not spotted early. With some exceptions, age 35 is too early to detect incipient cancers or circulatory problems, but it's prime time for stopping cigarette smoking, curbing alcohol abuse, and improving exercise and diet.

Response for Prospective Parents (from page 455): Because parenthood demands flexibility and patience, Sternberg's practical intelligence is probably most needed. Anything that involves finding a single correct answer, such as analytic intelligence or math answers, would not be much help.

OBSERVATION QUIZ ANSWERS

Answer to Observation Quiz (from page 420) He is closer to 30—28 to be exact. Clues: He still has the strength, stamina, and risk-taking adventurousness of an emerging adult. Another clue is contextual and historical: His two years as a Marine in Afghanistan must have been recent when this photo was taken.

Answer to Observation Quiz (from page 425) She is only 24 in this photo. The clue is her smooth skin.

Answer to Observation Quiz (from page 440) Older adults might be more stressed by the proctors, and they might find it uncomfortable to sit on the floor while writing.

Answer to Observation Quiz (from page 452) Medical expertise and interpersonal skills. Puncturing the finger to draw blood must be automatic, but her response must be intuitive and flexible—that winning smile sometimes must become a look of serious competence.

RAPIDEYE+/GETTY IMAGES

ADULTHOOD
Psychosocial Development

what will you know?

- Does personality change from childhood to adulthood?
- Why doesn't everyone get married?
- Is being a parent work or joy?

"Your backpack is open."

I hear that several times a day from strangers at street corners, on subways, in stores. I say, "Thank you. I know," and continue whatever I am doing.

The backpack is large, with three deep pockets. It is easier for me to zip it up halfway, leaving the top open so that I can see which books and papers are in which section. Nothing visible has any value to anyone but me, and nothing ever falls out when the backpack is strapped to my back, half-open.

But one time, as I was waiting for the train, next to me sat a young boy with his father. The man seemed caring and friendly. He said, "Your backpack is open."

"Thank you. I know."

He was troubled.

"Do you want me to zip it for you?"

I smiled and shook my head.

"I know you must be tired and busy," he said. "My son could zip it for you."

He seemed upset. The boy seemed ready. I gave up.

"OK."

The son zipped it up; the father was happy.

I thanked them both, as if I were grateful.

The merits of open backpacks can be argued either way, but this incident begins this chapter because it reveals three characteristics of adult development, each soon described.

First, we describe adult personality: That man and I have quite different attitudes about things being closed. (I keep kitchen cabinets, closet doors, and jackets open, too.) One of the major traits on which people differ is called *openness*, with some people very open (me) and others troubled when they encounter such openness. My

daughter Rachel closes cabinets in my kitchen—she is unnerved when I leave them open.

We all know that people have personality differences, but our perceptions arise from our own minds and experiences, which makes misunderstandings common. That man assumed, incorrectly, that my backpack was open because I was too tired to zip it up. In this incident, that was not a problem. But, as you will learn, for many married adults, misunderstandings and personality differences lead to divorce.

The second major topic is relationships with other people. The focus is on family and friends. This man was a good role model for his son.

The final topic of this chapter is caregiving. Adults want to care for each other, yet each individual wants to be independent. Accepting care may be difficult. I did not need or want anyone to zip up my backpack, but I recognized the father's need to take care of me. When I rationalized that I would be caring for him by letting him care for me, I said OK.

Personality Development in Adulthood

Chapter 4 explains that every infant is born with a unique temperament, and Chapter 6 describes parenting styles. Those are two basic ingredients that contribute to adult personality. Continuity is evident: Few adults develop characteristics that are antithetical to their childhood temperament.

But, there is discontinuity sometimes. Adult personality arises from many influences, beginning with the particular alleles inherited at conception and always affected by the ongoing cultural and historical influences of the wider world.

Adults can change, not only in actions and attitudes but also in personality. Theories and descriptions about how that happens vary. However, everyone agrees that adult personality is influenced by each adult's motivation and context (Dweck, 2017).

Erikson's Theory

As you remember, Erikson described eight stages of development. His first stages (already explained) each begin in a particular chronological period. His adult stages are less age-based (see Table 13.1).

Identity, once thought to be confined to adolescence, continues into adulthood. In fact, echoes of the search for identity are still apparent in late adulthood (Erikson, 1993a). Similarly, the three adult stages—*intimacy versus isolation, generativity versus stagnation*, and *integrity versus despair*—do not always appear in chronological sequence; they overlap. People backtrack before moving forward.

Erikson emphasized the sociocultural influences on development. This is a key difference between his theory and that of his mentor, Freud. The ecological approach, now accepted by almost every developmentalist, builds on Erikson's recognition that many social and cultural factors influence each person.

Every adult seeks to connect with other people, experiencing the crisis Erikson called **intimacy versus isolation,** as explained in Chapter 11. The social nature of humans is particularly salient at this stage, because intimacy cannot be achieved alone. People need other people to avoid isolation, and those other people affect personality.

intimacy versus isolation
The sixth of Erikson's eight stages of development. Adults seek someone with whom to share their lives in an enduring and self-sacrificing commitment. Without such commitment, they risk profound aloneness and isolation.

TABLE 13.1	Erikson's Stages of Adulthood

Unlike Freud or other early theorists who thought adults simply worked through the legacy of their childhood, four of Erikson's eight psychosocial stages occur after puberty. His most famous book, *Childhood and Society* (1993a), devoted only two pages to each adult stage, but elaborations in later works have led to a much richer depiction.

Identity Versus Role Confusion

Although Erikson originally situated the identity crisis during adolescence, he realized that identity concerns could be lifelong. Identity combines values and traditions from childhood with the current social context. Since contexts keep evolving, many adults reassess all four types of identity (sexual/gender, vocational/work, religious/spiritual, and political/ethnic).

Intimacy Versus Isolation

Adults seek intimacy—a close, reciprocal connection with another human being. Intimacy is mutual, not self-absorbed, which means that adults need to devote time and energy to one another. This process begins in emerging adulthood and continues lifelong. Isolation is especially likely when divorce or death disrupts established intimate relationships.

Generativity Versus Stagnation

Adults need to care for the next generation, either by raising their own children or by mentoring, teaching, and helping others. Erikson's first description of this stage focused on parenthood, but later he included other ways to achieve generativity. Adults extend the legacy of their culture and their generation with ongoing care, creativity, and sacrifice.

Integrity Versus Despair

When Erikson himself reached his 70s, he decided that integrity, with the goal of combating prejudice and helping all humanity, was too important to be left to the elderly. He also thought that each person's entire life could be directed toward connecting a personal journey with the historical and cultural purpose of human society, the ultimate achievement of integrity.

According to Erikson, after intimacy comes **generativity versus stagnation,** when adults seek to be productive in a caring way. Erikson wrote that a mature adult "needs to be needed" (1993a, p. 266). Without generativity, adults experience "a pervading sense of stagnation and personal impoverishment" (Erikson, 1993a, p. 267).

Generativity is expressed by caring for the younger generation. If you notice adults who are devoted to children (not only parents but also grandparents, teachers, nurses, coaches, and many others), you see that adults are compelled to be generative. However, generativity occurs in ways other than child rearing. Meaningful employment, important creative production, and caregiving of other adults also avoid stagnation.

Generativity, like intimacy, is a social stage. Children affect their parents and grandparents, by their personalities, needs, and sheer existence. As Erikson said, "The fashionable insistence on dramatizing the dependence of children on adults often blinds us to the dependence of the older generation on the younger one" (1993a, p. 266). This continues. Middle-aged adults who care for their aging parents, and vice versa, are affected by their interaction.

The final adult stage, *integrity versus despair,* is described in Chapter 15.

Maslow's Theory of Personality

Some scientists are convinced that there is something hopeful, unifying, and noble in humans. People seek love, then respect, and finally, if all goes well, everyone will become quite wonderful in their own way. This is the central idea of **humanism,** a theory of personality developed by Abraham Maslow (1908–1970) and many others.

generativity versus stagnation
The seventh of Erikson's eight stages of development. Adults seek to be productive in a caring way, often as parents. Generativity also occurs through art, caregiving, and employment.

humanism
A theory that stresses the potential of all humans, who have the same basic needs, regardless of culture, gender, or background.

FIGURE 13.1 Moving Up, Not Looking Back Maslow's hierarchy is like a ladder: Once a person stands firmly on a higher rung, the lower rungs are no longer needed. Thus, someone who has arrived at step 4 might devalue safety (step 2) and be willing to risk personal safety to gain respect.

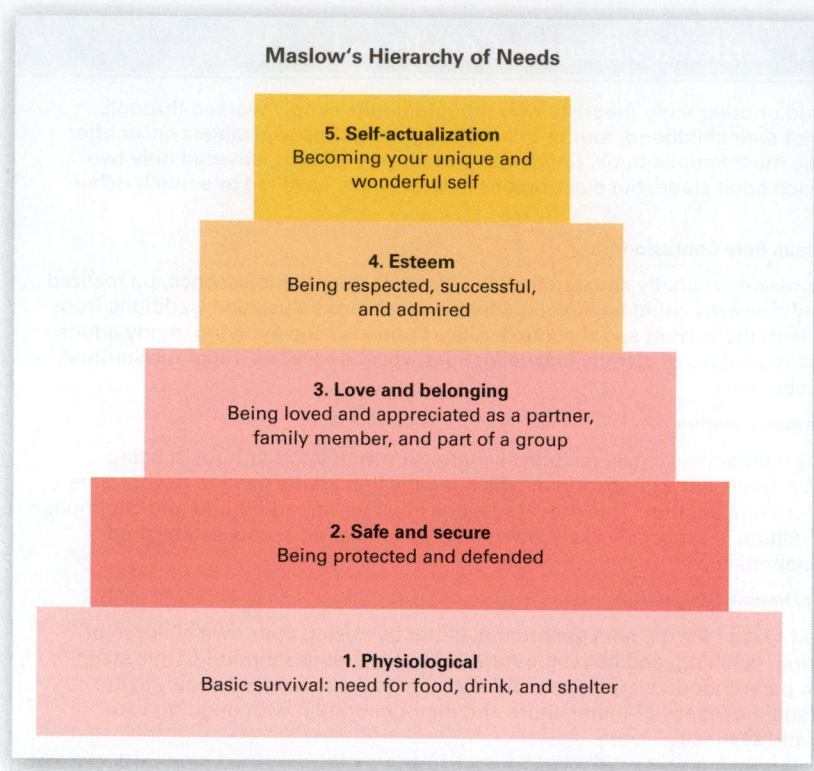

Maslow's Hierarchy of Needs

5. Self-actualization
Becoming your unique and wonderful self

4. Esteem
Being respected, successful, and admired

3. Love and belonging
Being loved and appreciated as a partner, family member, and part of a group

2. Safe and secure
Being protected and defended

1. Physiological
Basic survival: need for food, drink, and shelter

Maslow witnessed the Great Depression, the rise of the Nazis, the power of fascism, World War II, the atom bomb, and then the eventual decline and defeat of all of those horrors. He concluded that traditional psychological theories underrated humans by focusing on evil, not the potential for good. He wrote *Toward a Psychology of Being* (1962/1998), challenging psychoanalytic and behaviorist theories of personality.

Maslow believed that all people—no matter what their culture, gender, or background—have the same basic needs, eventually striving for appreciation of themselves and of everyone else. He arranged these needs in a hierarchy, often illustrated as a pyramid (see Figure 13.1):

1. Physiological: needing food, water, warmth, and air
2. Safety: feeling protected from injury and death
3. Love and belonging: having friends, family, and a community (often religious)
4. Esteem: being respected by the wider community as well as by oneself
5. Self-actualization: becoming truly oneself, fulfilling one's unique potential while appreciating all of life

This pyramid caught on almost immediately; it was one of the most "contagious ideas in behavioral science" because it seemed insightful about human psychology (Kenrick et al., 2010, p. 292). This theory is not a developmental theory in the traditional sense, in that Maslow did not believe that the five levels were connected to a particular stage or age. However, his hierarchy is sequential: Lower needs must be met before higher needs can be.

Thus, every person needs to have basic physiological needs satisfied, and to feel safe, before being able to seek love, respect, and finally self-actualization. At that

highest level, when all four earlier needs have been met, people can be fully themselves—creative, spiritual, curious, appreciative of nature, able to respect everyone else.

A UNIVERSAL THEORY? Humanists emphasize what all people have in common, not their national, ethnic, or cultural differences. Maslow contended that everyone, universally, has the same needs, which can lead to the unique self-fulfillment of each person.

A starving man, for instance, may not be concerned for his own safety when he seeks food (level 1 precedes level 2). Likewise, a woman who feels unloved might not care about self-respect because she needs love (level 3 precedes level 4).

Maslow proposed that people who seem mean-spirited, or selfish, or nationalistic feel insecure. Destructive and inhumane actions may be the consequence of unmet lower needs. When those needs are met, self-actualization becomes possible.

This theory is relevant for life-span development. Babies seek food and comfort, children seek approval, emerging adults seek love, older adults seek respect, and all people have an inner drive to self-actualize.

Early experiences can impede human growth: People may become thieves or even killers, unable to reach their potential, to self-actualize, if they were unsafe or unloved as children. Ideally, people get past those lower levels. Then each person can become their unique, best self, with all the diversity of humankind.

It does seem that adults tend to be more generous to others if they themselves feel secure. For instance, especially for single mothers (who may have many needs), having a steady, adequate income correlates with better parenting (Berger et al., 2017).

APPLICATIONS Humanism is prominent among medical professionals because they recognize that illness and pain are connected to the psychological needs of the patient (Felicilda-Reynaldo & Smith, 2018; J.C. Jackson et al., 2014). Even the very sick need love and belonging (never left alone) and esteem (the dying need respect). As a medical team from the famed Mayo Clinic states, "Solely addressing physiological recovery in the ICU, without also placing focus on psychological recovery, is limiting and not sufficient for recovery of the entire patient—both body and mind" (Karnatovskaia et al., 2015, p. 210).

Echoes of humanism are also evident in education and sports: The basic idea here is that people are motivated to achieve their "personal best"—that is, to reach the peak of their own potential—by challenging themselves to improve on their own past performance. If, instead, the competition is to be the only one to earn an A+ or to be the most valuable player, then most people will quit trying (Ravizza, 2007).

In their careers, too, self-actualization may be the reason people strive for success (Fernando & Chowdhury, 2015). Crude competition—which produces winners and losers—is antithetical to the core belief of humanism, that everyone is uniquely wonderful.

After Fame Why did Oprah *(left)* quit her popular TV show to pursue other projects? Why did Mark Ruffalo *(right)* donate his time to stop fracking? Perhaps Maslow was right. Self-actualization is the highest level in his famous hierarchy, when respect and esteem allow people to move past selfish concerns to care for the rest of humanity and nature. This applies to less famous adults as well.

If only I could accept that I can't accept being someone who finds it hard to accept acceptance from those who accept me for the person that I can't accept I really am.

Maybe Next Year Self-acceptance is a gradual process over the years of adulthood, aided by the appreciation of friends and family. At some point in adulthood, people shift from striving to fulfill their potential to accepting their limitations.

Big Five
The five basic clusters of personality traits that remain quite stable throughout adulthood: openness, conscientiousness, extroversion, agreeableness, and neuroticism.

Trait Theories

Many contemporary psychologists contend that adult personalities are too varied to be described by any grand theory, such as the ones proposed by Maslow and Erikson. Instead, they contend that each person has hundreds of traits, each comprising one pixel of the distinct picture of personality.

THE BIG FIVE One prominent theory is that all traits can be clustered on five dimensions, with each person relatively high or low on each. This has been called the **Big Five.** (To remember the Big Five, the acronym OCEAN is useful.)

- *Openness:* imaginative, curious, artistic, creative, open to new experiences
- *Conscientiousness:* organized, deliberate, conforming, self-disciplined
- *Extroversion:* outgoing, assertive, active
- *Agreeableness:* kind, helpful, easygoing, generous
- *Neuroticism:* anxious, moody, self-punishing, critical

Each personality is somewhere on a continuum on each of these five. The low end might be described, in the same order as above, with these five adjectives: *closed, careless, introverted, hard to please,* and *placid.*

According to trait theory, adults choose their contexts, selecting vocations, hobbies, health habits, mates, and neighborhoods to reflect their personality. Those high in extroversion might work in sales, those high in openness might be artists, and so on. International research confirms that human personality traits (there are hundreds of them) can be grouped on these five dimensions (Carlo et al., 2014; Ching et al., 2014).

Among the actions and attitudes linked to the Big Five are education (conscientious people are more likely to complete college), cheating on exams (low on agreeableness), marriage (more often extroverts), divorce (more likely for neurotics), IQ (higher in openness), verbal fluency (again, openness and extroversion), smoking cigarettes (low in conscientiousness), recovery from a stroke (low on neuroticism), and even political views (conservatives are less open) (Dwan & Ownsworth, 2017; Gerber et al., 2011; Silvia & Sanders, 2010; Giluk & Postlethwaite, 2015; Zvolensky et al., 2015).

Of course, all of this may reflect the values and prejudices of the community as well as the personalities of the individuals. Everyone agrees that personality is influenced by many factors beyond temperament. The paragraph above notes tendencies, not always reality.

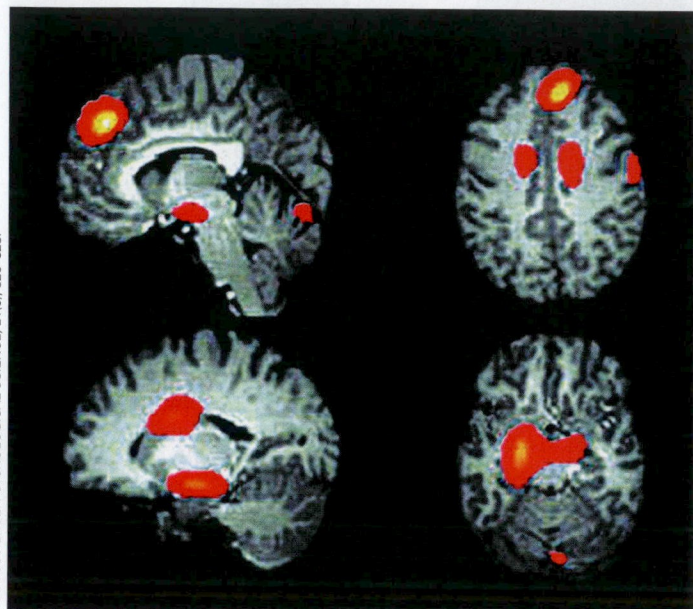

Active Brains, Active Personality The hypothesis that individual personality traits originate in the brain was tested by scientists who sought to find correlations between brain activity (shown in red) and personality traits. People who rated themselves high in four of the Big Five (conscientiousness, extroversion, agreeableness, neuroticism—but not openness) also had more activity in brain regions that are known to relate to those traits. Here are two side views *(left)* and a top and bottom view *(right)* of brains of people high in neuroticism. Their brain regions known to be especially sensitive to stress, depression, threat, and punishment (yellow bullseyes) were more active than the same brain regions in people low in neuroticism (DeYoung et al., 2010).

AGE CHANGES The strength of every trait is affected by adult maturation. Continuity over the life span is evident: When people are followed longitudinally, their Big Five traits are apparent *compared* to others their age. For example, extroversion decreases slightly overall with age, but 20-year-old extroverts will be extroverts at age 80, more outgoing than other 80-year-olds, although not necessarily more than most 20-year-olds.

The general age trend is positive: People are affected by the norms of their community. Adults gradually become less neurotic and more conscientious.

Personality shifts are more likely early or late in life, not in the middle (Specht et al., 2011). That may be one reason that self-esteem tends to rise from early

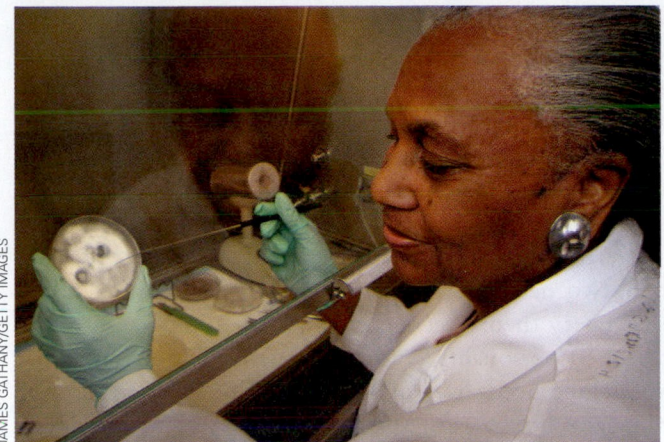

adulthood until about age 50, as people develop whatever personality is most appreciated within their community (Orth et al., 2012).

One indication of this is that adults become more accepting of themselves and their community. People under the age of 30 "actively try to change their environment," moving away from home and finding new friends, changing their nurture. Later in life, context shapes traits, because once adults have chosen their vocation, family, and neighborhoods, they "change the self to fit the environment" (Kandler, 2012, p. 294).

CULTURAL INFLUENCES That "change to fit the environment" is evident in how adults react to cultural mandates to have many, or few, children. Traits didn't affect childbearing much for men and women born in 1920 because the culture strongly valued fertility: Almost all adults, no matter what their personality, hoped to marry and have several children. Most did; infertility was a sad fact, not a choice. (My maternal grandparents had 16 babies; my paternal grandparents had 5.)

By 1960, however, culture was less enamored with frequent childbearing. For those born in that year, personality mattered. Women high in openness and conscientiousness had fewer children than average, sometimes choosing to have one or none (Jokela, 2012). (Some of my cousins had no children.) As in this example, cultural context matters, interacting with personality.

The ability to express temperament also changes. For example, in the 1960s women's work roles were constricted: Women got jobs out of necessity, and most became nurses, teachers, secretaries, and the like. Then more opportunities opened for women, and they were more likely to find careers that expressed their personality (George et al., 2011).

As in these examples, culture shapes personality. As one team wrote, "Personality may acculturate" (Güngör et al., 2013, p. 713). A study of well-being and self-esteem in 28 nations found that people are happiest if their personality traits match their social context. This has implications for immigrants, who might feel, and be, less appreciated when the personality values of their home culture clash with their new community (Fulmer et al., 2010).

For example, extroversion is relatively highly valued in Canada and less so in Japan; Canadians and Japanese have a stronger sense of well-being if their personal ratings on extroversion (high or low) are consistent with their culture's norms (Fulmer et al., 2010). Everywhere, some personality traits correlate with longer life, but the strength of this correlation varies by culture. Extroversion is particularly protective in North America, less so elsewhere (Graham et al., 2017).

Same Situation, Far Apart: Scientists at Work Most scientists are open-minded and conscientious (two of the Big Five personality traits), as both of these women are. Culture and social context are crucial, however. If the woman on the left were in Tanzania, would she be a doctor surrounded by patients in the open air, as the Tanzanian woman on the right is? Or is she so accustomed to her North American laboratory, protected by gloves and a screen, that she could not adjust? The answer depends on other aspects of the Big Five.

◆ **Especially for Immigrants and Children of Immigrants** Poverty and persecution are the main reasons some people leave their home for another country, but personality is also influential. Which of the Big Five personality traits do you think is most characteristic of immigrants? (see response, page 493)

THINK CRITICALLY: Would your personality fit better in another culture?

Common Themes

Cultural differences are evident, but do not exaggerate the power of culture. Every well-known theorist or scholar of adult personality sees the same themes.

Freud enunciated the basic two adult psychological needs first: He said that adults need *lieben und arbeiten* (to love and to work). As you just read, Maslow considered Love and Belonging, and then Success and Esteem, essential steps in his hierarchy. Trait theories recognize extroversion and conscientiousness, which are related to the same two and which correlate with long life (Graham et al., 2017).

Other theorists call these two needs *affiliation/achievement,* or *emotional/instrumental,* or *communion/agency.* Every theory recognizes both; all adults seek to love and to work in ways that fit their personality, culture, and gender. To organize our discussion of these two overarching needs, we will use Erikson's terms, *intimacy* and *generativity,* but other word pairs echo the same themes.

---

what have you learned?

1. How does personality differ from temperament?
2. What do all people strive for, according to Maslow?
3. What are the three needs of adults, according to Erikson?
4. What are the Big Five traits?
5. How are personality traits affected by age?
6. How does personality interact with culture?

Intimacy: Connecting with Others

Humans are not meant to be loners. Decades of research finds that physical health and psychological well-being more often flourish if both family members and friends are part of an adult's life (Li & Zhang, 2015).

Romantic Partners

We begin our discussion of intimacy with romance. Adults tend to be happiest and healthiest if they have a long-term partner, connected to them with bonds of affection and care.

MARRIAGE Traditionally, the romantic bond was codified via marriage. You already read that most emerging adults postpone marriage. That trend continues in adulthood: Although many say they would like a long and happy marriage, more and more adults never marry (see Figure 13.2).

Those trends are apparent worldwide. Despite marked variations between one region of the world and another, age of marriage is increasing everywhere, as is the number of adults who are unmarried (Cherlin, 2014b).

FIGURE 13.2 And Now? Not only are far fewer people marrying, but also they marry later, so it seemed misleading to include a bar for 1980–2000. If we did, the rates would be under 50 percent. Most emerging adults are unmarried.

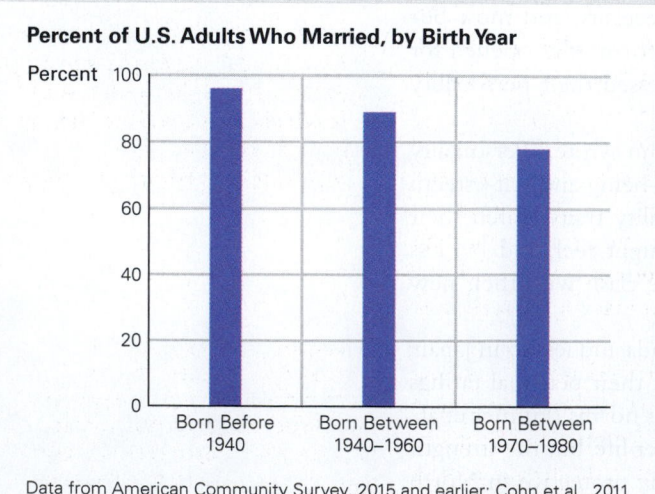

Percent of U.S. Adults Who Married, by Birth Year

Data from American Community Survey, 2015 and earlier; Cohn et al., 2011.

However, most adults continue to believe that marriage is desirable even as they postpone or avoid it. One example: Would you think that having a bad marriage would discourage people about the institution? That does not happen: Many people who divorce remarry. In the United States, 40 percent of new marriages have at least one partner who has been married before (Livingston, 2014).

What do these trends mean for societies and individuals? Societies benefit when most adults marry and stay married. Children are more likely to thrive if both parents are legally and emotionally dedicated to them, and adults are healthier, especially in old age, if they have a partner who cares for them—thus saving some social costs of child care and health care.

Partners may benefit, too: A satisfying marriage improves health, wealth, and happiness. However, not all marriages are satisfying, and divorce is always difficult (Fincham & Beach, 2010; R. Miller et al., 2013). The only sure way to avoid divorce is to never marry.

It was once thought that men were happier in marriage and women less happy (Bernard, 1982). Suggested reasons were that women had higher expectations for marriage and, thus, greater disillusionment, or that women did far more housework, child care, and emotional work. However, that is changing by cohort and varies by income, education, and culture (Stavrova et al., 2012).

A meta-analysis in the United States found no marked gender differences in marital happiness (J. B. Jackson et al., 2014). Early in a marriage, wives tended to be slightly more satisfied with the relationship than husbands, but this shifted by about the 15-year mark, with husbands slightly more satisfied. That study found one cultural exception to overall gender neutrality: In Chinese American and Japanese American marriages, wives were more often dissatisfied than husbands.

NONMARITAL ROMANTIC RELATIONSHIPS As explained in Chapter 11, romantic partnerships do not always mean marriage. Cohabitation is no longer the exclusive purview of young adults; cohabitation rates are increasing for adults of all ages. Many adults prefer cohabitation to marriage and, depending on the culture, many of the benefits of marriage are apparent for those who are in a long-term cohabiting relationship.

A sizable number of adults have found a third way (neither marriage nor cohabitation) to meet their intimacy needs with a steady romantic partner. They **live apart together (LAT).** They have separate residences, but especially when the partners are over age 30, they function as a couple for decades—sexually faithful, vacationing together, and so on (Duncan & Phillips, 2010).

Share My Life Marriage often requires one partner to support the other's aspirations. That is evident in the French couple *(right)*, as Nicole embraces her husband, Alain Maignan, who just completed a six-month solo sail around the world. For 20 years, he spent most of his money and time building his 10-meter boat. Less is known about the Nebraska couple *(left)*, but many farm wives forgo the pleasures of city life in order to support the men they love.

THINK CRITICALLY: Is marriage a failed institution?

VIDEO: Marriage in Adulthood features researcher Ronald Sabatelli and interviews of people discussing the joys and challenges of marriage.

Living Apart Together (LAT)
The term for couples who are committed to each other and spend time together but maintain separate homes. LAT couples are increasingly common in the United States and Europe.

One Love, Two Homes Their friends and family know that Jonathan and Diana are a couple, happy together day and night, year after year. But one detail distinguishes them from most couples: Each owns a house. They commute 10 miles and are living apart together—LAT.

Financial patterns are a particular issue for LAT couples. Most married couples pool their money; many cohabiting couples do not (Hamplová et al., 2014). LAT couples struggle with this aspect of their relationship, with the women particularly wanting to pay their own way (Lyssens-Danneboom & Mortelmans, 2014).

An adult's decision to marry, cohabit, or LAT is strongly influenced by children. Cohabiters who have had children together are more likely to marry than those who have not, especially when the children start school. Likewise, married couples sometimes stay together for the children and sometimes do the opposite, as when one parent leaves a violent mate to protect the children. As for LAT couples, many older parents maintain separate households because they do not want to upset their grown children (de Jong Gierveld & Merz, 2013).

PARTNERSHIPS OVER THE YEARS Love is complex. Steinberg described romantic love as having three aspects: passion, intimacy, and commitment. Passion typically is strong at the beginning of a relationship; intimacy occurs when a couple shares secrets, possessions, and a bed; and commitment is expressed in promises—typically a wedding with vows of faithfulness that are fulfilled. When all three occur together, that is *consummate love*—only sometimes attained. A wealth of research on adulthood over the years finds that, for most adults, mutual commitment is the most crucial of the three.

A long-term committed partnership correlates with health and happiness throughout life (R. Miller et al., 2013). The reasons for this correlation are both emotional and practical. People have a deep psychological need for someone who listens, understands, and shares heartfelt goals. Even when that does not happen, people benefit from a companion who monitors diet, exercise, and medical attention.

The passage of time makes a difference. In general, the honeymoon period tends to be happy, but frustration with a partner increases as conflicts—even those not directly between the couple—arise (see At About This Time). Partnerships (including heterosexual married couples, committed cohabiters, same-sex couples, and LAT couples) tend to be less happy when the first child is in infancy or toddlerhood and again when children reach puberty (Umberson et al., 2010). Divorce risk rises in the first years of marriage and then falls.

Remember, however, that averages obscure many differences of age, ethnicity, personality, and circumstances. In the United States, Asian Americans are least likely to divorce and African Americans are most likely to do so. These ethnic differences are partly cultural and partly economic, making any broad effort to promote marriage for everyone doomed to disappoint politicians, social workers, and individuals (Johnson, 2012).

Education and religion matter, too: College-educated couples are more likely to marry and less likely to divorce no matter what their ethnic background. Some unhappy couples stay married for religious reasons,

At About This Time: Marital Happiness Over the Years

Interval After Wedding	Characterization
First 6 months	Honeymoon period—happiest of all.
6 months to 5 years	Happiness dips; divorce is more common now than later in marriage.
5 to 10 years	Happiness holds steady.
10 to 20 years	Happiness dips as children reach puberty.
20 to 30 years	Happiness rises when children leave the nest.
30 to 50 years	Happiness is high and steady, barring serious health problems.

Not Always: These are trends, often masked by more pressing events. For example, some couples stay together because of the children, so unlike most couples, for them the empty-nest stage becomes a time of conflict or divorce.

A CASE TO STUDY

The Benefits of Marriage

Marriage can be a benefit or a problem, depending on whom you ask. A study of long-term cohabiting and married adults in England found a great variety of responses. Consider two quotations from that study (quoted in Soulsby & Bennett, 2017).

Dave, age 45, had been married for seven years when he said:

> Being married is molding the person that I am and who I'm becoming. It's helping me fulfil dreams and ambitions and goals, . . . it's giving me a deeper meaning of love, it's given me, a sense of achievement and a sense of encouragement.

Gina, age 50, had been married for 23 years, and said:

> As a single person you do what you want, you live your life as you like, you do what you want. . . . When

you get married, all of a sudden you've got washing to do, you've got to tidy up in case your mess is impinging on someone else, or theirs on you, you've got to think about eating at the same time. You've got someone else that you need to factor in, so your life changes completely.

Which of these two seems more valid to you? For this A Case to Study, the final case to be considered is your own. Consider the relationship between your own parents. If they were married or in a stable cohabiting relationship, was this a benefit for them? If they were not married, or if they married and divorced, would it have been better if they were together? Consider, as in the quotations above, both perspectives.

---

and the result may be a long-lasting, troubled relationship, or a marriage that seems stronger every year. Husbands and wives in happy marriages tend to agree that their marriage is a good one, but in unhappy marriages often one spouse is much less content than the other (Brown et al., 2012).

Contrary to outdated impressions, the **empty nest**—when parents are alone again after the children have left—is usually a time for improved relationships. Simply having time for each other, without crying babies, demanding children, or rebellious teenagers, improves intimacy. Partners can focus on their mates, doing together whatever they both enjoy. Remember *linked lives*. Partners are connected in many ways to their mate (Carr et al., 2014), as A Case to Study suggests.

JOHN MOORE/GETTY IMAGES

A Dream Come True When Melissa Adams and Meagan Martin first committed to each other, they thought they could never marry, at least in their South Carolina home. On July 11, 2015, they celebrated their union, complete with flower girl, bridesmaids, Reverend Sidden, and all the legal documents.

SAME-SEX COUPLES As you remember from Chapter 11, almost everything just described applies to gay and lesbian couples as well as to heterosexual ones. A review of 15 years of same-sex marriages in Denmark, Sweden, and Norway finds that neither the greatest fears nor hopes for such unions have been realized (Biblarz & Stacey, 2010).

Some same-sex couples are faithful and supportive of each other; their emotional well-being thrives on their intimacy and commitment, which increases over the decades. Others are conflicted: Problems of finances, communication, and domestic abuse resemble those in heterosexual marriages.

As the U.S. Supreme Court acknowledged in 2013, love between partners is the crucial bond. Same-sex couples fight about money and children just as heterosexual couples do. For every partnership, communication is crucial (Ogolsky & Gray, 2016).

The similarity of same-sex and other-sex couples surprised researchers who studied alcohol abuse in romantic couples. The scientists expected that the stress of minority

empty nest
The time in the lives of parents when their children have left the family home to pursue their own lives.

sexual orientation status would increase the rate of alcohol use disorder. That was *not* what the data revealed. Instead, the crucial variable was whether the couple was married or not. For both same-sex and other-sex couples, excessive drinking was more common among cohabiters than married couples (Reczek et al., 2014).

An increasing number of families headed by same-sex couples have children, some from a former marriage, some adopted, and some the biological child of one partner, conceived because the couple wanted a child. The well-being of such children depends on factors that affect other-sex couples as well. Family income is probably the crucial one: Same-sex couples more often have low income (Cenegy et al., 2018). As you remember from earlier chapters, low SES increases the risk of physical, academic, and emotional problems.

Another finding relates to all partnerships: family connections. In a study of married same-sex male couples in Iowa, one man decided to marry because of his mother: "I had a partner that I lived with. . . . And I think she, as much as she accepted him, it wasn't anything permanent in her eyes" (Ocobock, 2013, p. 196). In this study, most family members were supportive, but some were not—again eliciting deep emotional reactions.

In heterosexual marriages as well, in-laws usually welcome the new spouse, but when they do not, the partnership may be troubled. Family influences are hard to ignore.

DIVORCE AND REMARRIAGE Throughout this text, developmental events that seem isolated, personal, and transitory are shown to be interconnected and socially constructed, with enduring consequences. Family relationships are part of the microsystem, but the macrosystem, mesosytem, and exosystem all have an impact. Thus, a study of many nations found that a couple's happiness and separation are powerfully influenced by national norms (Wiik et al., 2012).

Separation occurs because at least one partner believes that he or she would be happier without the other, a conclusion reached fairly often. In 1980, in the United States, half as many divorces occurred as marriages. Then emerging adults, in large numbers, avoided marriage until they were older, and that itself reduced the divorce rate (Rotz, 2016). In the past decades, slightly more couples are marrying and slightly fewer divorcing, so the 2017 divorce rate is about 46 percent of the marriage rate.

Family problems from divorce arise not only with children (usually custodial parents become stricter and noncustodial parents become distant) but also with other relatives. The divorced adults' parents are often financially supportive but not emotionally supportive. Relationships with their in-laws that may once have been good are severed when the couple splits. No wonder divorce increases loneliness (van Tilburg et al., 2015).

Sometimes divorced adults confide in their children. That may help the adults but not the children. Even if adults avoid that trap, children need extra stability and understanding just when the parents are consumed by their own emotions (H. S. Kim, 2011).

Many divorced people seek another partner (remember, their marriage rate is higher than for never-married people the same age). Initially, remarriage restores intimacy, health, and financial security. For fathers, bonds with stepchildren or with a new baby may replace strained relationships with the children who live with the former wife (Noël-Miller, 2013a).

◆ **Especially for Young Couples**
Suppose you are one-half of a turbulent relationship in which moments of intimacy alternate with episodes of abuse. Should you break up? (see response, page 493)

"But you knew I was addicted to bad men when you married me."

Surprised? Many brides and grooms hope to rescue and reform their partners, but they should know better. Changing another person's habits, values, or addictions is very difficult.

Divorce is never easy, but the negative consequences just explained are not inevitable. If divorce ends an abusive, destructive relationship (as it does about one-third of the time), it usually benefits at least one spouse (Amato, 2010). Such divorces lead to stronger and warmer mother–child and/or father–child relationships after the marital fights are over. That helps children cope, not only immediately but also for years to come (Vélez et al., 2011).

Friends and Acquaintances

Each person is part of a **social convoy.** The term *convoy* originally referred to a group of travelers in hostile territory, such as the pioneers in ox-drawn wagons headed for California or soldiers marching across unfamiliar terrain. Individuals were strengthened by the convoy, sharing difficult conditions and defending one another.

Fellow Travelers Here that phrase is not a metaphor for life's journey but a literal description of a good friend, Tom, carrying 30-year-old Kevan Chandler, from Fort Wayne, Indiana, as they view the Paris Opera House. Kevan was born with spinal muscular atrophy because both his parents are carriers of the recessive gene. He cannot walk, but three of his friends agreed to take him on a three-week backpacking adventure through Europe. The trip was funded by hundreds of people who read about Kevan's plans online.

As people move through life, their social convoy functions as those earlier convoys did, a group of people who provide "a protective layer of social relations to guide, socialize, and encourage individuals as they move through life" (Antonucci et al., 2001, p. 572).

Sometimes a friend needs care and cannot reciprocate at the time, but it is understood that later the roles may be reversed. Friends provide practical help and useful advice when serious problems—death of a family member, personal illness, job loss—arise. They also add companionship, information, and laughter to daily life.

Friends are a crucial part of the social convoy; they are chosen for the traits that make them reliable fellow travelers. Mutual loyalty and aid characterize friendship: An unbalanced friendship (one giving and the other taking) often ends because both parties are uncomfortable.

Friendships tend to improve over the decades of adulthood. As adults grow older, they tend to have fewer friends overall, but they keep their close friends and nurture those relationships (English & Carstensen, 2014). One of the benefits of friendship is that a person has someone to talk with about problems and joys. That itself increases happiness, especially when a friend celebrates accomplishments (Demir et al., 2017).

Although most friendships last for decades, conflicting health habits may end a relationship (O'Malley & Christakis, 2011). For instance, a chain smoker and a friend who quit smoking are likely to part ways. On the other hand, shared health problems can bind a friendship together. For example, overweight people become friends with other overweight people, and together their food preferences and eating habits reinforce each other as both continue to gain weight (Powell et al., 2015).

If an adult has no close and positive friends, health suffers (Couzin, 2009; Fuller-Iglesias et al., 2013). This seems as true in poor nations as in rich ones: Universally, humans are healthier with social support and sicker when socially isolated (Kumar et al., 2012).

Family Bonds

Family links span generations and endure over time, even more than friendship networks or romantic partnerships. Childhood history influences people decades after they have left their childhood home. Parental death does not stop parental influence.

social convoy
Collectively, the family members, friends, acquaintances, and even strangers who move through the years of life with a person, all aging together.

Dinner Every Night Not only does the Shilts family eat together at 6 P.M. every night, but all six adults and five children also sleep under the same roof. The elderly couple is on the ground floor, and each adult daughter, with husband and children, has a wing on the second floor.

Framed by Birth In the twenty-first century, it is unusual for fathers and sons to work together, as these two do in a framing shop. It is even more unusual for both to enjoy working together.

For example, many studies have found that parental SES is a strong predictor of SES in adulthood. It is difficult to overcome the influence of poverty during youth. However, detailed studies found that low income alone is not as crucial as childhood family experiences.

For example, going to museums, reading books, discussing current events, and other practices influence adult habits and values and, thus, SES (Erola et al., 2016). Secure attachment and emotional support begin in early childhood; the benefits are evident lifelong.

This does not always mean that adults do what their own parents did: Sometimes the opposite occurs. One of my students complained about her life as one of 16 children; she had only one child, and she said that was enough. As she explained this to the class, it seemed apparent that her choice was in reaction to her childhood.

The power of family experiences was documented in data from all of the twins in Denmark. They married less often than single-born Danes, but if they wed, they were less likely to divorce. According to the researchers, twins may have their intimacy needs met by each other and therefore they are less likely to seek a spouse; but if they have a spouse, they know how to maintain a close relationship (Petersen et al., 2011).

PARENTS AND THEIR ADULT CHILDREN A crucial part of family life for many adults is raising children. That is discussed soon as part of generativity. Here we focus on family bonds that meet adult intimacy needs, providing companionship, support, and affection for parents and their grown children.

Do not confuse intimacy with residence. If income allows, most adults seek to establish their own households. A study of 7,578 adults in seven nations found that physical separation did not weaken family ties. Indeed, intergenerational relationships seem to be strengthened, not weakened, when adult children lived apart from their parents (Treas & Gubernskaya, 2012), because "the intergenerational support network is both durable and flexible" (Bucx et al., 2012, p. 101).

If a divorced son or daughter has custody of children, the grandparents (usually middle-aged adults) often provide child care and other help (Westphal et al., 2015).

Considerable research has recently focused on "boomerang children," adults who live with their parents for a while. In the United States, in 1980 only 11 percent of 25- to 34-year-olds lived with their parents for at least a few months, but between 2008 and 2011, 29 percent did (K. Parker, 2012).

Rates of adult children living with parents are continuing to rise, reaching a peak not seen in the past 135 years—except in 1940, when the Great Depression meant that few young people could afford to leave home (DeSilver, 2016). Sharing one's home with adults from different generations is not ideal for individual development, but the data illustrate that parents remain a resource for their children lifelong.

FICTIVE KIN Most adults maintain connections with brothers and sisters, sometimes traveling great distances to attend weddings, funerals, and holidays. The power of this link is apparent when we note that, unlike friends, family members may be on opposite sides of a political or social divide. Even radically different views do not usually keep them apart.

Sometimes, however, adults avoid their blood relatives because they find them toxic—not because they disagree on politics but because their personal interaction is hostile. Such adults may become **fictive kin** in another family. They are introduced by a family member who says this person is "like a sister" or "my brother" and so on. Over time, the new family accepts them. They are not technically related (hence *fictive*), but they are treated like a family member (hence *kin*).

Fictive kin can be a lifeline to those adults who are rejected by their original family (perhaps because of their sexual orientation), or are isolated far from home (perhaps because they are immigrants), or are changing their family habits (such as stopping addiction). A qualitative study of African American college students found that the influence of fictive kin, at college or at home, was pivotal in encouraging them to persist in their studies (Brooks & Allen, 2016).

The role of fictive kin reinforces a general theme: Adults benefit from kin, fictive or not.

Strangers or Twins? Both. Aysha Lord (left) is a "genetic twin" to Peter Milburn (right), a father of four who had a fatal blood cancer. He was saved by stem cells donated by a stranger—Aysha—whose cells were a perfect match.

fictive kin
People who become accepted as part of a family who have no genetic or legal relationship to that family.

what have you learned?

1. What needs do long-term partners meet?

2. How are marriage and cohabiting rates changing?

3. Why would people choose to live apart together?

4. How do same-sex marriages compare to heterosexual marriages?

5. What are the consequences of divorce?

6. How do remarriages differ from first marriages?

7. Why do people need a social convoy?

8. What roles do friends play in a person's life?

9. What is the usual relationship between adult children and their parents?

10. Why do people have fictive kin?

Generativity: The Work of Adulthood

Adults satisfy their need to be generative in many ways, especially through parenthood, caregiving, and employment.

Parenthood

Erikson thought that generativity often became manifest in "establishing and guiding the next generation" (Erikson, 1993a, p. 267). In his day, it was thought that everyone would become a parent if they could. As discussed many times in the previous chapters, children need parental warmth, discipline, and guidance—so that manifestation of generativity is to be commended. Now, however, we look at how having children affects adults.

Most nonparents underestimate how generative demands of parenthood affect adults. Indeed, "having a child is perhaps the most stressful experience in a family's life" (McClain, 2011, p. 889).

Parenthood is particularly difficult if intimacy, not generativity, is a person's most urgent psychosocial need. As already noted, marital happiness may dip in the first year or two after a birth, because intimacy needs must sometimes be postponed. Worse yet is having a baby as part of the search for identity—to prove manhood or womanhood to oneself.

Children reorder adult perspectives. One sign of a good parent is the parent's realization that the infant's cries are communicative, not selfish, and that adults need to care for children more than vice versa (Katz et al., 2011).

Values may change, too. Many emerging adults believe in gender equality, that men and women are equally suited for employment, housework, and child care. But with parenthood, both sexes tilt toward believing that women and men differ in their roles and abilities (Endendijk et al., 2018). This finding is directly connected to having children, not to cultural bias: The data came from a large study in the

↓ OBSERVATION QUIZ
In what ways might these fathers differ from mothers? (see answer, page 493)

More Dad . . . and Mom Worldwide, fathers are spending more time playing with their children—daughters as well as sons, as these two photos show. Does that mean that mothers spend less time with their children? No—the data show that mothers are spending more time as well.

Netherlands, where gender equity is a national value, and the tilt toward tradition was apparent in mothers as well as fathers.

Historical trends find that fathers have become more involved in child care than they were. For example, a 16-nation study concluded that fathers have become more involved parents and mothers are more likely to be employed. However, this does not mean that mothers do less child care—indeed, the data suggest that mothers are more intensely involved with their children than they were a few generations ago. A gender division of family labor remains (Kan et al., 2011). On average, mothers provide child care, schedule doctor appointments, plan birthday parties, arrange play dates, choose schools and after-school activities, and so on more than fathers.

What has changed is that there is more flexibility in roles. Each couple figures out what is best for them, and the number of couples in which the father provides primary child care while the mother is the chief wage earner has almost tripled, from 3 percent in 2004 to 8 percent in 2012 (Young & Schieman, 2018). Women in the workplace are earning more money, and have more responsibilities, than a few decades ago. However, old patterns persist, more in family life than in the workplace (Pepin & Cotter, 2018).

For example, one man became the prime caregiver for his infant and 2-year-old but wanted to earn a paycheck. He found a part-time job that allowed him to bring his children along (as a schoolbus driver). He said:

> In the last generation it's changed so much . . . it's almost like you're on ice that's breaking up. That's how I felt. Like I was on ice breaking up. You don't really know what or where the father role is. You kind of have to define it for yourself. . . . I think that's what I've learned most from staying home with the kids. . . . Does it emasculate me that my wife is making more money?
>
> *[Geoff, quoted in Doucet, 2015, p. 235]*

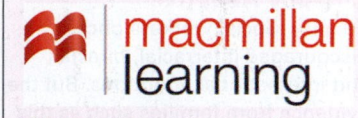

VIDEO: Interview with Jay Belsky explores how problematic parenting practices are transmitted (or not) from one generation to the next.

Another father in the same study opened a day-care business for his own children and several others. Neither of these men felt comfortable being solely caregivers; both felt they should contribute financially.

No matter who does what, adults find parenting an ongoing challenge. Just when they figure out how to care for their infants, or preschoolers, or schoolchildren, those children grow older, presenting new dilemmas. One exasperated mother told her criticizing teenager, "Give me a break. I'm learning on the job, I've never been a mother of an adolescent before."

Exactly how the parents collaborate may change as the children have new needs. Both parents tend to reduce outside work or choose more flexible hours when raising children, but specifics depend on the age of the children. Mothers are more likely to scale back (working part time instead of full time) during infancy; fathers reduce work hours or choose more flexible schedules when the children are in elementary school (Young & Schieman, 2018).

Throughout child rearing, privacy and income rarely seem adequate. Every child needs extra care and attention at some point. The more children a couple has, the more problems arise, as was found in a multinational study (Margolis & Myrskylä, 2011).

This makes sense, because almost every child encounters some difficulties—with reading or math, with talking too much or too little, with being clumsy at sports or having illegible handwriting, and so on. It is the nature of childhood that problems come and go, so a child with a problem in second grade might, with a different teacher or better friends, have a happy fourth-grade year.

Obviously, the more children a couple has, the more likely at least one child will need special attention—and each parent might have a different idea as to what is

A Happy Adoptive Family Social workers once discouraged interracial, biracial, and international adoptions. But the evidence from families such as this one finds a very positive result.

best. Such problems occur with all families, but stress is particularly likely for adults in two situations:

1. Parents of children with special needs. This puts additional strain on both parents and on the other children, and, sadly, it increases the rate of divorce (Shenaar-Golan, 2017; Emerson, 2015).

2. Adults who become nonbiological parents. Each form of such parenting provides opportunities for generativity, as well as distinct vulnerabilities.

ADOPTIVE PARENTS The easiest form of nonbiological parenting may be adoption, since those adults are legally connected to their children for life. Moreover, adoptive children are much wanted, so the parents are ready to sacrifice their own needs to be generative for the child.

Current adoptions are usually "open," which means that the birth parents decided that someone else would be a better parent, but they still want some connection to the child. The child knows about this arrangement; that makes it easier for everyone than the former "closed" adoption, when children and birth parents felt abandoned.

Strong parent–child attachments are often evident with adoption, especially when children are adopted as infants. Secure bonds can also develop if the adoptee is older, especially if the adopting mother was strongly attached to her own mother (Pace et al., 2011).

Sadly, some adopted children have spent their early years in an institution, never attached to anyone. Although some such children are resilient, many are afraid to love anyone (van IJzendoorn et al., 2011). That makes child rearing more difficult for the adoptive parent.

DSM-5 recognizes *reactive attachment disorder,* when a young child cannot seem to form any attachments. This can occur with children who live with their biological parents, but it is particularly likely with children who have spent infancy in institutions or who experienced a series of placements before adoption.

As you remember, adolescence—the time when teenagers seek their own identity—can stress any family. This stage is particularly problematic for adoptive families because all teenagers want to know their genetic and ethnic roots; normal conflicts with parents cut particularly deep (Klahr et al., 2011). One college student who feels well loved and cared for by her adoptive parents explains:

> In attempts to upset my parents sometimes I would (foolishly) say that I wish I was given to another family, but I never really meant it. Still when I did meet my birth family I could definitely tell we were related—I fit in with them so well. I guess I have a very similar attitude and make the same faces as my birth mother! It really makes me consider nature to be very strong in personality.
>
> *[A., personal communication]*

Attitudes in the larger culture often increase tensions between adoptive parents and children. For example, the mistaken notion that biological parents are the "real" parents is a common social construction. International and interethnic adoptions are especially controversial if outsiders think only someone from the same background can properly raise a child.

Adoptive parents who take on the complications of international or interethnic adoption are usually intensely dedicated to their children. They are very much "real" parents, seeking to protect their children from discrimination that they might not have noticed before it affected their child.

For example, one European American couple adopted a multiethnic baby and three years later requested a second baby. They said, "We made a commitment [to our daughter] that we would have a brown or Black baby. So we turned down a couple of situations because they were not right" (Sweeney, 2013, p. 51). These parents had noticed strangers' stares and didn't want their first child to be the only family member with dark skin.

Many such adoptive parents seek multiethnic family friends and educate their children about their heritage and the prejudice they may encounter. Such *racial socialization* often occurs within minority families for their biological children. When adoptive parents do so, their adolescents who encounter frequent prejudice experience less stress because they are ready to counter with pride in their background (Leslie et al., 2013).

The same is true if the child experiences discrimination because of same-sex parents, or single parents, or international origins, or even adoption itself. Each situation provides special insights and strengths. Adults realize that; children may need to be told.

As emphasized in earlier chapters, the child's first months and years are a sensitive period for language, attachment, and neurological maturation. The older a child is at adoption, the more difficult parenting might be (Schwarzwald et al., 2015). However, difficult parenting is what most parents do. Parents usually are devoted to their children, no matter what the child's special needs or biological heritage. Generativity is amazingly powerful.

STEPPARENTS The average new stepchild is 9 years old. This means that the stepparent becomes mother or father to a child who already has habits, morals, and a distinct personality.

Typically, stepchildren have lived with both biological parents and then with a single parent, a grandparent, other relatives, and/or a paid caregiver before becoming a stepchild. Each of those living situations affects the child, adding to adjustment complications for the adult.

Changes in living arrangements are always disruptive for children (Goodnight et al., 2013). The effects are cumulative; emotions erupt in adolescence if not before. Becoming a stepparent to such a child, especially if the child is coping with a new school, loss of friends, or puberty, is challenging. Stepchildren may intensify their attachment to their birth parents, a reaction that upsets a stepparent who wants to become a parent to the child.

Joy from Generativity Six smiling members of this family from New Port Richey, Florida are typical in one way and not in another. Unusual is that all four sisters are adopted. Typical is that the parents get great joy from their daughters, as is evident from their wide smiles.

TAMPA BAY TIMES/BRENDAN FITTERER/THE IMAGE WORKS

Stop to consider each person's perspective. The new stepparent may expect the child to welcome a loving new mother or father, especially because all humans tend to believe they are better than most other people. The stepparent has confirmation: Their new spouse rejected the former partner and chose the new one.

However, the children did not reject their biological parent. In loyalty they may be hostile or distant (Ganong et al., 2011). Added to that, their emotional turmoil may make them sick or injured, or, if they are teenagers, get them pregnant, drunk, or arrested. That childish reaction to disruption is understandable; so is the resentment that stepparents feel.

Few adults—biological parents or not—can live up to the generative ideal, day after day. Some stepparents quit trying. Hopefully, the new couple feels happy with each other, and the stepparent is sufficiently mature to react to hostility with patience.

Eventually, the adults may form a well-functioning, generative family (King et al., 2014). Be forewarned, however, that this is not easy: The divorce rate of second marriages is higher than for first marriages, and having stepchildren increases the risk of divorce.

FOSTER PARENTS An estimated 437,465 children were officially in foster care in the United States in 2016, about half of them cared for by adults who were strangers to them (Child Welfare Information Gateway, 2018). Many others are unofficially in foster care, because someone other than their biological parents has taken them in.

This is the most difficult form of parenting of all, partly because foster children typically have emotional and behavioral needs that require intense involvement. Foster parents need to spend far more time and effort on each child than biological parents do, yet the social context tends to devalue their efforts (J. Smith et al., 2013).

Contrary to popular prejudice, adults become foster parents more often for psychosocial than financial reasons, part of the adult generativity impulse (Geiger et al., 2013). Official foster parents are paid, but they typically earn far less than a babysitter would, or than they themselves would in a conventional job.

Most children are in foster care for less than a year, as the goal is usually reunion with the birth parent. Children may be moved back to the original family for reasons unrelated to the wishes, competence, or emotions of the foster parents or the children.

The average child entering the foster-care system is 6 years old (Child Welfare Information Gateway, 2013). Many spent their early years with their birth families and are attached to them. Such human bonding is normally beneficial, not only for the children but also for the adults.

However, if birth parents are so neglectful or abusive that their children are removed, the child's past insecure or disorganized attachment impedes acceptance of the foster parent. Most foster children have experienced long-standing maltreatment and have witnessed violence; they are understandably suspicious of any adult (Dorsey et al., 2012).

Given the realities of life for those half a million U.S. children in foster care, and the millions more in other nations, it is sad but unsurprising that a review of longitudinal research concludes that many foster children develop serious problems, including less education, more arrests, and earlier death (Gypen et al., 2017).

Your knowledge of human development leads you to understand something not recognized by usual

Here's Your Baby But only for a few weeks. More than 70 babies have spent days or weeks with Becky O'Connell until being united with their adoptive parents. As with baby Alex, shown here, the hardest part is giving them up—but, at age 64, Becky is unlikely to become a mother herself.

CHICAGO TRIBUNE/GETTY IMAGES

practices: It is difficult for foster parents to develop a generative attachment to their children. Nonetheless, sometimes such attachments develop, especially if the child is kept with one loving parent for years. When adolescents have been with a stable foster family, about half the time a healthy, mutual attachment develops, a marked contrast to the relationship with their biological parents (Joseph et al., 2014).

For all forms of parenting, generative caring does not occur in the abstract; it involves a particular caregiver and care receiver. It is never easy, but it is very satisfying for the adult as well as the child when it works well. That means everything needs to be done to encourage attachment between parent and child, no matter what their connection might be.

GRANDPARENTS As already mentioned, the empty-nest stage of a marriage, when children have finally grown up and started independent lives, is often a happy time for parents. Grown children are more often a source of pride than of stress.

A new opportunity for generativity, as well as a new source of stress, occurs if grandchildren appear. That event once occurred on average at age 40, but now, in developed nations, grandparenthood begins on average at about age 50 (Leopold & Skopek, 2015a).

Especially when the grandchildren's parents are troubled, grandparents worldwide believe that they must help raise their grandchildren (Herlofson & Hagestad, 2012). Specifics depend on policies, customs, gender, past parenting, and income of both adult generations, but for every adult, the generative impulse extends to caring for the youngest generation.

Grandparents try to be helpful, whether or not the grandchildren live with the grandparents, as about 5 percent do. Even when they share a home, the parents are often the major caregivers and grandparents are companions, not authorities. Three generations living together is not the usual pattern, but it is more common in families that are African American, Hispanic American, or recent immigrants. The reasons are partly economic necessity and partly past cultural tradition (Reyes, 2018).

This pattern may be idealized, with the reality much less benign. Conflicts may arise between the grandmother and mother about details of child rearing.

One study of young, low-income African American mothers—who are most likely to live with their own mothers—found that those who had their own residences were less often depressed than those who lived with their mothers. Their

JODI COBB/GETTY IMAGES

Everybody Contributes A large four-generation family such as this one helps meet the human need for love and belonging, the middle level of Maslow's hierarchy. When social scientists trace who contributes what to whom, the results show that everyone does their part, but the flow is more down than up: Grandparents give more money and advice to younger generations than vice versa.

children also fared better. The reason was thought to be that conflicts arose when two women both cared for the child. The grandmothers disrupted the normal mother–child attachment (Black et al., 2002).

Conflicts also arise when the two families have separate homes and the adult child needs more help than the grandparents want to provide.

If a grandmother is employed, she is likely to retire early if she has major responsibility for her grandchildren, because balancing the demands of job, marriage, and family reduces her own health and well-being (Meyer, 2014). Stress may strain her marriage. One working grandmother reports:

> When my daughter divorced, they nearly lost the house to foreclosure, so I went on the loan and signed for them. But then again they nearly foreclosed, so my husband and I bought it. . . . I have to make the payment on my own house and most of the payment on my daughter's house, and that is hard. . . . I am hoping to get that money back from our daughter, to quell my husband's sense that the kids are all just taking and no one is ever giving back. He sometimes feels used and abused.
>
> *[quoted in Meyer, 2014, pp. 5–6]*

This example is extreme. In every nation, grandparents usually enjoy helping their children and connecting with grandchildren. Some grandmothers are rhapsodic and spiritual about their experience. As one writes:

> Not until my grandson was born did I realize that babies are actually miniature angels assigned to break through our knee-jerk habits of resistance and to remind us that love is the real reason we're here.
>
> *[Golden, 2010, p. 125]*

Caregiving

Child care is the most common form of generativity for adults, but caregiving can and does occur in many other ways as well. Indeed, "life begins with care and ends with care" (Talley & Montgomery, 2013, p. 3). Some caregiving requires meeting

A VIEW FROM SCIENCE

The Skipped-Generation Family

Some U.S. households (about 1 percent) are two-generation families because the middle generation is missing. That is a *skipped-generation* family, with all parenting work done by the grandparents. Skipped-generation families require every ounce of generativity that grandparents can muster, often at the expense of their own health and happiness. This family type sometimes is designated officially to provide kinship care (true for one-third of the foster children), and it may include formal adoption by the grandparents.

In general, skipped-generation families have several strikes against them. Both the grandparents and the grandchildren are sad about the missing middle generation. In addition, difficult grandchildren (such as drug-affected infants and rebellious school-age boys) are more likely to live with grandparents (Hayslip & Smith, 2013). Many grandparents are resilient, but the challenges are real.

But, before concluding that grandparents suffer when they are responsible for grandchildren, consider China, where millions of grandparents outside the urban areas become full-time caregivers because members of the middle generation have jobs in the cities, unable to take children with them.

The Chinese parents who are employed far from their natal home typically send money and visit once a year, on a national holiday. Studies are contradictory regarding the welfare of the children, but those grandparents seem to have *better* physical and psychological health (Baker & Silverstein, 2012; Chen & Liu, 2012) than grandparents who are not caregivers.

This suggests that the social context is crucial: If grandparents are supported and appreciated by their children and the community, a skipped-generation family may benefit the grandparents.

Even in China, however, it seems best for children to be raised by parents, not grandparents.

physical needs—feeding, cleaning, and so on—but much of it involves fulfilling psychological needs. Caregiving is part of generative adulthood.

KINKEEPERS A prime example of caregiving in most multigenerational families is the **kinkeeper,** who gathers everyone for holidays; spreads the word about anyone's illness, relocation, or accomplishments; buys gifts for special occasions; and reminds family members of one another's birthdays and anniversaries. Kinkeepers keep the family history and connect family members (Hendry & Ledbetter, 2017). Guided by their kinkeeper, all of the relatives become more generative.

Fifty years ago, kinkeepers were almost always women, usually the mother or grandmother of a large family. Now families are smaller and gender equity is more apparent, so some men or young women are kinkeepers. This role may seem burdensome, but caregiving provides both satisfaction and power (Mitchell, 2010).

Middle-aged adults have been called the **sandwich generation,** a term that evokes an image of a layer of filling pressed between two slices of bread. This analogy suggests that the middle generation is squeezed because they are expected to support their parents and their growing children.

This sandwich metaphor is vivid but misleading (Gonyea, 2013). Longitudinal data found "relatively few cases where middle-aged adults were in a 'sandwich generation' of simultaneously providing care for aging parents and children younger than 15" (Fingerman et al., 2012d, p. 200).

Far from being squeezed, middle-aged adults who provide some financial and emotional help to their adult children are *less* likely to be depressed than those adults whose children no longer relate to them. The research finds that family members continue to care for each other, less as a matter of obligation but more as a result of past connections. For example, divorce weakens family bonds, especially for men, but ongoing relationships with emerging-adult children are typical, especially for women (Fingerman et al., 2012d).

Emerging adults, depicted as squeezing their parents, instead take care of their parents, not usually financially but culturally. They help their parents understand music, media, fashion, and technology—setting up their smartphones, sending digital photos, fixing computer glitches. They also are more cognizant of nutritional and medical discoveries and guidelines.

kinkeeper
Someone who becomes the gatherer and communication hub for their family.

sandwich generation
The generation of middle-aged people who are supposedly "squeezed" by the needs of the younger and older members of the families.

↓ **OBSERVATION** QUIZ
Both father and daughter are doing something that typifies their care for each other. What is it? (see answer, page 493)

A Peak Experience For many men, the best part of fatherhood is when their children become old enough to share interests in world events, sports, or, as shown here, climbing a mountain in Norway.

STANISLAW PYTEL/GETTY IMAGES

I have often experienced caregiving from my adult children. For years, one of my daughters insisted that *my* Christmas gift to *her* should be for *me* to have a mammogram. Another daughter said that her birthday present should be to go clothes shopping with her for *myself*. She told me what to try on and what to buy. All I did was pay for my own new clothes. She was thrilled.

As for caregiving on the other side of the supposed sandwich, from middle-aged adults to their elderly parents, this is typically much less demanding than the metaphor implies. Most members of the over-60 generation are capable of caring for themselves, and financial support is more likely to flow from them to their middle-aged children than vice versa.

If an older parent needs daily care, a spouse, another elderly person, or a paid caregiver is more likely to provide it than a daughter or son. Middle-aged adults do their part as members of a caregiving team for older relatives, but they are not often stuck in the middle of a sandwich. [Of course, caring for elders who are frail, intellectually challenged, and in poor health is a major burden. This topic is discussed in Chapter 15, in part because caregivers are often elders themselves.]

Every adult member of a family cares for every other one, each in their own way. The specifics depend on many factors, including childhood attachments, personality patterns, and the financial and practical resources of each generation. (See Visualizing Development on page 485.)

In general, middle-aged adults are well positioned "to connect generations rather than separate them." This is an asset for people at every point of the life span, from children to the very old, not as a burden but as a way for families and societies "to engage and value the assets found in every generation" (Butts, 2017, p. vi). Mutual caregiving and shared information strengthens family bonds; wise kinkeepers keep those intergenerational channels open; everyone is generative (Hendry & Ledbetter, 2017).

Lowered Expectations It was once realistic, a "secular trend," for adults to expect to be better off than their parents had been, but hard times have reduced the socioeconomic status of many adults.

Employment

Besides parenthood and caregiving, the other major avenue for generativity is employment. A well-established specialty within the field of psychology focuses on increasing the productivity of workers and companies. In general, wealthier nations provide better education and health for everyone, which means that increased production can benefit everyone—from newborns to centenarians.

There is extensive research regarding many aspects of economic development, such as when and where telecommuting is beneficial, how to organize work teams and times, and almost every aspect of job conditions—lighting, wall colors, coffee breaks, and more.

Here, however, we focus on human development, not productivity. So, we consider how employment affects people as they grow older.

GENERATIVITY AND WORK As is evident from many terms that describe healthy adult development—*generativity, success and esteem, instrumental,* and *achievement*—adults have many psychosocial needs that work can fill.

FAMILY CONNECTIONS, FAMILY CAREGIVING

Generally, family members remain connected to each other lifelong. However, burdensome caregiving from adults to their aged parents is not the norm. This is evident in nationwide data from the United States.

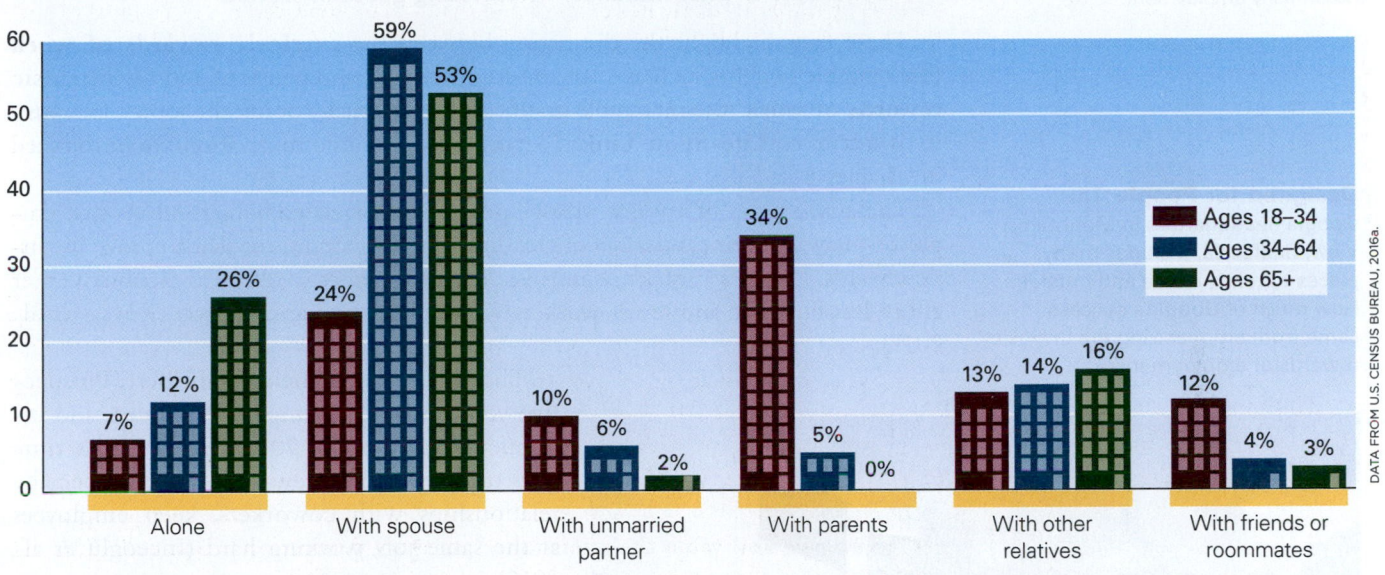

LIVING ARRANGEMENTS

Most families have only one generation of adults, but when two generations are present, parents are more often helping adult children than the reverse.

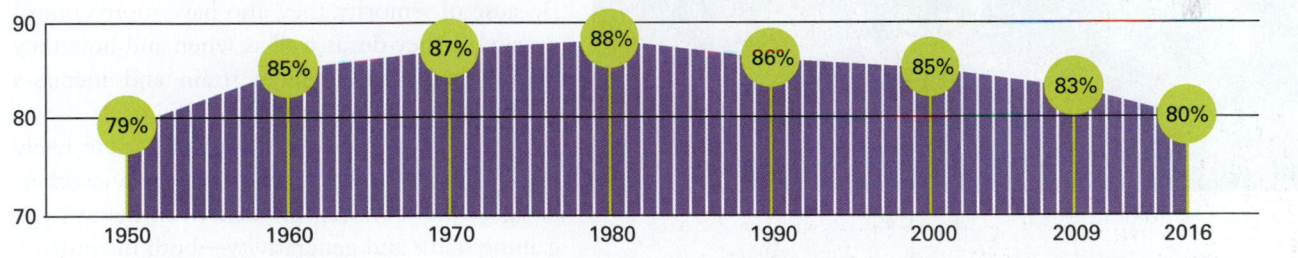

U.S. FAMILIES WITH ONLY ONE GENERATION OF ADULTS (OVER AGE 18)

As you see, there are only slightly more two-adult generation families in the United States today than 30 years ago. What *has* changed, however, is that those extra adults are usually adult children, not aged parents. So, what percentage of adults live with other generations of adults over age 18?

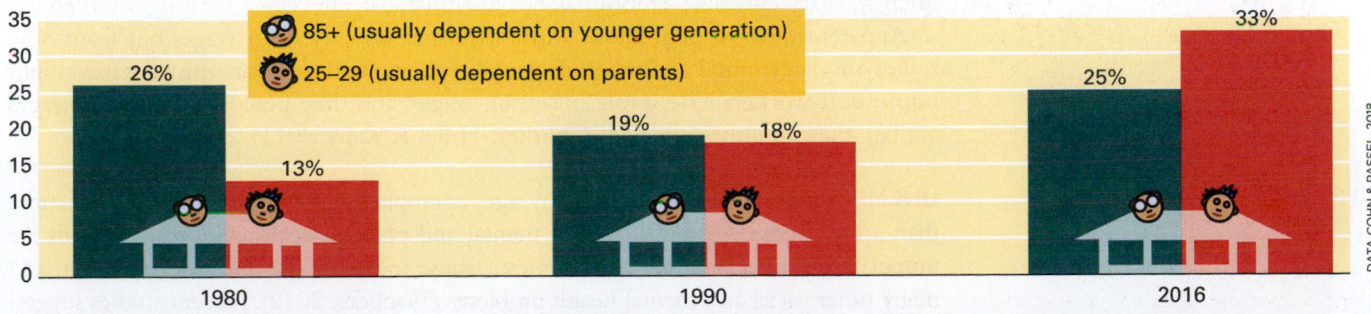

ADULTS LIVING WITH OTHER GENERATIONS

Currently about one-fourth of younger adults and about one-third of the oldest-old are living with the middle generation.

extrinsic rewards of work
The tangible benefits, usually in salary, insurance, pension, and status, that come with employment.

intrinsic rewards of work
The personal gratifications, such as pleasure in a job well done or friendship with coworkers that accompany employment.

Designed for People The Google headquarters in Mountain View, California, includes many places to relax, inside and outside. How much of Google's success came from emphasizing the intrinsic rewards of employment?

Work meets these needs by allowing people to do the following:

- Develop and use their personal skills
- Express their creative energy
- Aid and advise coworkers, as mentor or friend
- Support the education and health of their families
- Contribute to the community by providing goods or services

These facts highlight the distinction between the **extrinsic rewards of work** (the tangible benefits such as salary, health insurance, and pension) and the **intrinsic rewards of work** (the intangible gratifications of actually doing the job). Generativity is intrinsic. [**Life-Span Link:** Extrinsic and intrinsic motivation are introduced in Chapter 6.]

These two types of rewards may be negatively correlated, which means that employers may increase pay *instead* of creating working conditions that improve intrinsic rewards. That is a mistake, as intrinsic rewards predict worker satisfaction, worker effort, less burnout, and fewer workers who quit to find another job (Kuvaas et al., 2017).

There is a developmental shift here. Prospective young workers compare pay, hours, and insurance (Kooij et al., 2011). However, as time goes on, the intrinsic rewards of work, especially relationships with coworkers, keep employees at the same job, working hard (Inceoglu et al., 2012).

The power of intrinsic rewards explains why older employees are, on average, less often absent or late and more committed to doing a good job than younger workers are (Rau & Adams, 2014). Because of seniority, they also have more control over what they do, as well as when and how they do it. (Autonomy reduces strain and increases dedication.)

Further, experienced workers are more likely to be mentors—people who help new workers navigate the job. Mentors benefit in many ways, gaining status and generativity—both intrinsic.

Surprisingly, absolute income (whether a person earns $30,000 or $40,000 or even $100,000 a year, for instance) matters less for job satisfaction than how a person's income compares with others in their profession or neighborhood, or with their own salary a year or two ago.

It is a human trait to react more strongly to personal losses than to personal gains, ignoring systemic losses unless they become personal (Kahneman, 2011). Consequently, salary cuts have emotional, not just financial, effects.

Apparently, resentment about work arises not directly from wages but from how wages are determined and whether people believe that their income or status might improve. If workers have a role in setting wages, and they perceive that those wages are fair, they are more satisfied (Choshen-Hillel & Yaniv, 2011).

UNEMPLOYMENT For adults of any age, unemployment—especially if it lasts more than a few weeks—is destructive of mental and physical health. Generative needs are unmet, which increases the rate of domestic abuse, substance use disorder, depression, and many other social and mental health problems (Wanberg, 2012). Recent studies suggest

If You Had to Choose Which is more important, a high salary or comfortable working conditions? Intrinsic rewards of work are scarce for these workers in Mumbai, India *(left),* who talk to North Americans who call in confused about their computers, bills, or online orders, as well as for the man in eastern Colorado *(right).* His relationships with coworkers and supervisors may not be affirming comforting, and he has heard that fracking increases pollution, earthquakes, and cancer (hence the protective gear). Most workers who have few psychosocial benefits at work are much younger than the average employee.

that, in addition to the burden of unemployment, uncertainty about future income and work adds to family stress, and that, in turn, makes abuse more likely (Schneider et al., 2017).

A meta-analysis of research on eight stressful events found that losing a job was worst. A bout of unemployment reduced self-esteem more than even death of a parent or a divorce. The stress of unemployment lingered after finding a job (Luhmann et al., 2012).

Developmentalists are particularly concerned when the economy, or the automation of labor, results in fewer jobs for millions of adults. Current high rates of unemployment of emerging adults—people who are NEET (Not in Education, Employment, or Training)—may harm that generation lifelong, a "grave concern." One careful study of thousands of NEETs in Great Britain found that they seek work but are stymied by the job market and by their own traits (Goldman-Mellor et al., 2016, p. 201).

Unemployment is troubling at any age. Adults who are unemployed are 60 percent more likely to die than their age-mates, especially if they are younger than 40 (Roelfs et al., 2011). They are twice as likely to be clinically depressed (Wanberg, 2012) and almost twice as likely to be addicted to drugs (Compton et al., 2014).

These statistics need to be put in context. The death rate is low during these years, but the depression and drug-addiction rate is substantial. This means that unemployment is a significant drag on personal well-being. A crucial buffer is social support from family and friends—more evidence of the importance of linked lives (Crowe & Butterworth, 2016).

THINK CRITICALLY: Is the connection between employment and developmental health cause or correlation?

INCOME DISPARITY What about working conditions for those who have jobs? Most Americans are troubled about the large income gap between the rich and the poor. They wish that the salary distribution were less skewed. However, relatively few consider this a major problem (Norton & Ariely, 2011).

Given that a sense of fairness is innate, many psychologists wonder why people are not more troubled. One answer is that people believe that social mobility is possible—that they themselves will be able to earn more (Davidai & Gilovich, 2015).

THE CHANGING WORKPLACE Employment is changing in many ways that affect adult development. We focus here on only three—diversity among workers, job changes, and alternate schedules. Dramatic shifts have occurred in all three. We will

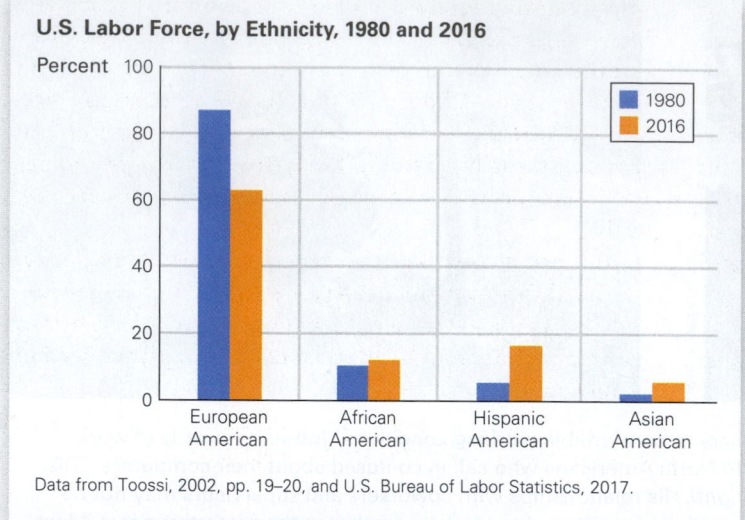

U.S. Labor Force, by Ethnicity, 1980 and 2016

Data from Toossi, 2002, pp. 19–20, and U.S. Bureau of Labor Statistics, 2017.

FIGURE 13.3 Better or Worse?
It depends on who you are. Ideally, everyone has a job.

use U.S. statistics to illustrate these shifts, but these phenomena are occurring worldwide.

As you can see from Figure 13.3, the workforce is becoming more diverse. Fifty years ago, the U.S. civilian labor force was 74 percent male and 89 percent non-Hispanic White. In 2012, 53 percent were male and 65 percent non-Hispanic White (16 percent were Hispanic, 12 percent African American, 5 percent Asian, and 2 percent multiracial).

This shift is also notable within occupations. For example, in 1960, male nurses and female police officers were rare, perhaps 1 percent. Now 11 percent of registered nurses are men and 14 percent of police officers are women—still an unbalanced ratio, but a dramatic shift nonetheless (Dey et al., 2016). Job discrimination relating to gender and ethnicity still exists—but it is much less prevalent than it once was.

These changes benefit millions of adults who would have been jobless in previous decades, but they also require workers and employers to be sensitive to differences that they did not previously notice. Younger adults may have an advantage: A 25-year-old employee is not surprised to have a female boss or a coworker of another ethnicity. Since a goal of human development is for everyone to fill their potential, reduced discrimination in employment is welcomed by developmentalists, as Opposing Perspectives suggests. The next two changes are not as welcome.

OPPOSING PERSPECTIVES

Accommodating Diversity

Accommodating the various sensitivities and needs of a diverse workforce requires far more than reconsidering the cafeteria menu and the holiday schedule. Private rooms for breast-feeding, revised uniform guidelines, new office design, and changing management practices may be necessary. Exactly what is needed depends on the particular culture of the workers: Some are satisfied with conditions that others would reject.

For example, many New Zealand supervisors of European descent criticize Maori workers (descendent from Polynesians who had arrived there several hundred years before the first Europeans) for "extending the leave they were given for attending a family or tribe *hui* (gathering or meeting) without notifying them. . . . If the reasons behind are not understood, such critical incidents may . . . easily lead to over-generalizations and stereotyping and finally to less employment of people who are labeled as 'unreliable'" (Podsiadlowski & Fox, 2011, p. 8).

What might those "reasons behind" be? For British New Zealanders, a funeral of a cousin might take a day. Employees from that culture resent that a Maori coworker might be gone much longer, appearing back at work a week or more later.

Yet, the Maori were expected by their families to stay for several days: It would be disrespectful to leave quickly. The cultural clash regarding work schedules and family obligations led to anger and rejection.

Less obvious examples occur daily, at every workplace. Certain words, policies, jokes, or mannerisms seem innocuous to one group but hostile to others.

- Women object to sexy calendars or photos hung in offices and to any gender-specific jokes or comments.

- Exchanging Christmas presents, as in the office "Secret Santa," may be troubling to those who are Jehovah's Witnesses or are not Christian.

- Resentment may stir if a man calls a woman "honey" or if a supervisor creates a nickname for an employee with a hard-to-pronounce name.

- Comments about a celebrity of another race, gender identity, or sexual orientation may be heard as insults.

Researchers have begun to explore *micro-aggressions*— small things unnoticed by one person that seem aggressive

to another (Sue, 2010). Mentioning "senior moments," or being "color-blind" or of the "fairer sex" can be perceived as aggressive, even though the speaker believes they are benign.

The question "Where are you from?" may seem innocent, or even friendly, but it implies that someone is from elsewhere. This question may be micro-aggressive to a Hispanic American born in Puerto Rico or Texas, whose family members have been U.S. citizens for decades (Nadal et al., 2014).

Micro-aggressions can affect anyone who feels different because of their ethnicity, age, gender identity, sexual orientation, religion, or anything else. For example, one research group found that older workers were particularly likely to notice ageist micro-aggression at their workplace but that some young men heard micro-aggressions about them as well (Chou & Choi, 2011). The implication that "Millennials" are less industrious than others, when they are actually suffering from (and often overcoming) economic decisions of much older people, is certainly ageist.

To create a workplace that respects diversity, mutual effort is needed. Not only must everyone learn about sensitivities and customs, but everyone also must communicate. When an innocent comment is heard as an insult, both parties need to be more aware.

CHANGING LOCATIONS Today's workers change employers more often than did workers decades ago. Hiring and firing are common. Employers constantly downsize, reorganize, relocate, outsource, or merge. Loyalty between employee and employer, once assumed, now seems quaint.

Whether they originate from the worker or the employer, changes may increase corporate profits, worker benefits, and consumer choice. However, churning employment may harm development. Losing work friendships means losing a source of social support. This problem may be worse for older adults for several reasons (Rix, 2011):

1. Seniority brings higher salaries, more respect, and greater expertise; workers who leave a job they have had for years lose these advantages.

2. Many skills required for employment were not taught decades ago, so older workers are less likely to find a new job.

3. Workers believe that age discrimination is widespread. Even if this is a misperception, stereotype threat undercuts successful job searching.

4. Especially if a new job requires relocation, long-standing intimacy and generativity are reduced.

From a developmental and family perspective, this last factor is crucial. Imagine that you are a 40-year-old who has always lived in West Virginia and your employer goes out of business. You try to find work, but no one hires you, partly because unemployment in West Virginia is among the highest in the nation. Would you move a thousand miles west to North Dakota, where the unemployment rate is less than half that of West Virginia? According to the Bureau of Labor Statistics (U.S. Bureau of Labor Statistics, June 15, 2018), the North Dakota unemployment rate was 2.6 compared to West Virginia, 5.4.

If you were unemployed and in debt, and a new job was guaranteed, you might. You would leave friends, community, and local culture, but at least you would have a paycheck.

But, would your family leave their homes, jobs, schools, places of worship, and friends to move with you? If not, you would be deprived of social support; but if they did, their food and housing would be expensive, their schools overcrowded, and their lives lonely (at least initially). For you and anyone who comes with you, moving means losing intimacy—harmful for psychosocial development.

◆ **Especially for Entrepreneurs**
Suppose you are starting a business. In what ways would middle-aged adults be helpful to you? (see response, page 493)

DAVE AND LES JACOBS/GETTY IMAGES

Insecurity More than 1 million people in the United States work as security guards, often spending long lonely nights watching video cameras, as this man does. How might his work hours, sleep schedule, and family life be different from the average office worker's?

Such difficulties are magnified for immigrants, who make up about 15 percent of the U.S. adult workforce and 22 percent of Canada's. Many depend on other immigrants for housing, work, religion, and social connections (García Coll & Marks, 2012). That may meet some of their intimacy and generativity needs, but their relationships with their original family and friends are strained by distance. The climate, the food, and the language are not comforting.

These developmental needs are ignored by most business owners and by many workers themselves. However, intimacy and generativity are best satisfied by a thriving social network, and each neighborhood and workplace fosters that. When that is disrupted, psychological and physical health suffers.

CHANGING SCHEDULES The standard workweek is 9 A.M. to 5 P.M., Monday through Friday—a schedule that is increasingly unusual. In the United States, about one-third of all workers have nonstandard schedules. Retail services (online and in-store) are increasingly available 24/7, which requires night and weekend employees. Many other parts of the economy (hospitals, police, hotels) need employees with nonstandard schedules. Employers, customers, and employees see many benefits.

It has long been recognized that varied schedules upset the body rhythms of adults, making them more vulnerable to physical illness as well as emotional problems. Recently, an entire issue of an academic journal was devoted to these problems (Chronobiology International, 2016).

Specific data find that, perhaps because of disrupted sleep, shift workers have higher rates of obesity, illness, and death—with women particularly more often developing breast cancer (McHill & Wright, 2017; Jehan et al., 2017; Wegrzyn et al., 2017). Specifics vary by study, with rotating schedules seeming worse than steady night work, and some research not finding harm. But, no study finds that shift work benefits the workers.

Beyond health, the impact on family life is a major concern for developmentalists. Those who are most likely to have mandatory, nonstandard schedules are parents of young children, who are most likely to suffer.

Weekend work, especially with mandatory overtime, is difficult for father–child relationships, because "normal rhythms of family life are impinged upon by irregular schedules" (Hook, 2012, p. 631). Mothers with nonstandard employment get less sleep and are more stressed (Kalil et al., 2014b). Couples who have less time together are more likely to divorce (Maume & Sebastian, 2012).

Choices about hours, overtime, and tasks increase job satisfaction. This is true no matter how experienced the workers are, what their occupation is, or where they live (Tuttle & Garr, 2012). For instance, a nationwide study of 53,851 nurses, ages 20 to 59, found that *required* overtime was one of the few factors that reduced job satisfaction in every cohort (Klaus et al., 2012). Apparently, although employment is often satisfying, working too long and not by choice may undercut the psychological and physical benefits.

In theory, part-time work or self-employment might allow adults to balance conflicting demands. But reality does not conform to the theory. In many nations, part-time work is underpaid and without benefits. Thus, workers avoid part-time employment if they can, again making a choice that inadvertently undercuts their emotional well-being and family life. Self-employment often means more work for less money.

The same problem occurs for temporary work. The use of temporary employees has increased in the past decade (Dey et al., 2016). This makes sense for the employers: It provides a buffer against another recession, and it is cheaper to hire workers without full

Happy Family Dad is a firefighter and has been on call for two weeks because of bushfires near his home in Victoria, Australia. The scene in this photo is idyllic, but often irregular schedules—typical of firefighters, nurses, police officers, and shift workers of all kinds—disrupt family life. Fortunately, this family may truly be as happy as they seem because of four factors: (1) wife and mother Helen's presence keeps the family running smoothly; (2) the children are old enough to understand why their father's schedule is necessary; (3) communities are usually quite proud of their firefighters; and (4), perhaps most importantly, he volunteered for this assignment.

FAIRFAX MEDIA/GETTY IMAGES

benefits. However, job uncertainty increases job dissatisfaction, which increases stress on families (Dawson et al., 2017). In this and many other ways, the needs of employers and employees conflict.

A major concern has arisen for all working adults, a conflict between the needs of employment and family life. Once thought to be a problem only for women, now men also experience this difficulty. It is apparent that, for adults of every gender and family situation, it is crucial to find a balance between all aspects of adult life, but this is not easy—especially for parents of young children. National policies make a difference, but no nation has yet made it possible for every adult to find a satisfying balance (Ollo-López & Goñi-Legaz, 2017).

Finding the Balance

As you see, adulthood is filled with opportunities and challenges. Adults choose their mates, their locations, their lifestyles to express their personality. Extroverts surround themselves with many social activities, and introverts choose a quieter, but no less rewarding, life.

Adults have many ways to meet their intimacy needs, with partners of the same or other sex, marriage or cohabitation, friends and family, parents or grown children. Ideally, they find some combination that results in solid social support. Similarly, generativity can focus on raising children, caring for others, or satisfying work, again with more choices and flexibility than in past decades.

In some ways, then, modern life allows adults to "have it all," to combine family and work in such a way that all needs are satisfied at once. However, some very articulate observers suggest that "having it all" is an illusion or, at best, a mistaken ideal achievable only by the very rich and very talented (Slaughter, 2012; Sotomayor, 2014).

Compromises, trade-offs, and selective optimization with compensation may be essential to find an appropriate work–family balance. Both halves of these two sources of generativity can bring joy, but both can bring stress—and often do.

In linked lives, spouses and partners usually adjust to each other's needs, allowing them to function better as a couple than they did as singles (Abele & Volmer, 2011). A large survey of heterosexual couples found that five years after their wedding, the man's salary is notably higher than it would have been if he were single, while their home was more comfortable, perhaps because the wife had worked to make it so (Kuperberg, 2012).

That result may reflect gender norms, but both spouses should be credited with improvements in each other's lives. In general, adults—mates, family, and friends—help each other, together balancing intimacy and generativity needs.

Because personality is enduring and variable, opinions about the impact of modern life reflect personality as well as objective research. Some people are optimists—high in extroversion and agreeableness—and they tend to believe that adulthood is better now than it used to be.

Others are pessimists—high in neuroticism and low in openness—and they are likely to conclude that adults were better off before the rise of cohabitation, LAT, divorce, and economic stress. They may laud the time when most people married and stayed married, raising their children on the man's steady salary from his nine-to-five job with one stable employer.

Data could be used to support both perspectives. For instance, in the United States, average education is higher than it used to be (life is better), but the gap between rich and poor is increasing (life is worse). Fewer people are marrying and fewer children are born: Is that evidence for improved adult lives or the opposite?

From a developmental perspective, personality, intimacy, and generativity continue to be important in every adult life. Many researchers study work–family balance; their conclusions differ.

Much depends on whether or not individual workers are able to feel in control of their lives, achieving the balance they want (Allen et al., 2012; Chan et al., 2016). As recognition of the macrosystem and exosystem makes clear, an adult's ability to balance work and family is affected by many aspects of the local and national economic culture.

Every adult benefits from friends and family, caregiving responsibilities, and satisfying work. Whether finding a satisfying combination of all these is easier or more difficult at this historical moment is debatable.

As you will read in the final two chapters, there are many possible perspectives on life in late adulthood as well. Some view the last years of life with dread, while others call them golden. Soon you will have your own view, informed by empirical data, not prejudice.

what have you learned?

1. How is generativity a distinct human need?
2. In what ways does parenthood satisfy the need to be generative?
3. Why might it be more difficult for parents to bond with nonbiological children?
4. What do kinkeepers do, and who becomes one?
5. What is the relationship between caregiving and generativity?
6. What is the relationship between the extrinsic and intrinsic rewards of work?
7. What are the advantages of greater ethnic diversity at work?
8. Why is changing jobs stressful?
9. How have innovations in work scheduling helped and harmed families?

SUMMARY

Personality Development in Adulthood

1. Erikson emphasized that people at every stage of life are influenced by their social context. The adulthood stages are much less age-based than the childhood stages because intimacy and generativity are needed throughout adulthood.

2. Maslow and other humanists believe that people of all ethnic and national origins have the same basic needs. They first must have their physical needs met and then feel safe. Beyond that, love and respect are crucial. Finally, people can be truly themselves, becoming self-actualized.

3. Personality traits over the years of adulthood are quite stable, although many adults become closer to their culture's ideal. The Big Five personality traits—openness, conscientiousness, extroversion, agreeableness, and neuroticism—characterize personality at every age. Culture and context affect everyone.

Intimacy: Connecting with Others

4. Intimacy is a universal human need, satisfied in diverse ways, with romantic partners, friends, and family. Variations are evident, by culture and cohort.

5. Marriage is no longer the only way to establish a romantic partnership. Although societies benefit if people marry and stay

married, many adults prefer cohabitation, or living apart together. Same-sex and other-sex relationships are similar in most ways.

6. Divorce sometimes may be the best end for a conflicted relationship, but divorce is difficult for both partners and their family members, not only immediately but for years before and after the decree.

7. Remarriage is common, especially for men. This solves some of the problems (particularly financial and social) of divorced adults, but the success of second marriages varies. Children add complications.

8. Friends are crucial for buffering stress and sharing secrets, for everyday companionship and guidance. This is true for both men and women, with younger adults having more friends but older adults preferring fewer, closer friends.

9. Family members have linked lives, continuing to affect one another as they all grow older. Parents and adult children are less likely to live together than in earlier times, but family members are often mutually supportive, emotionally and financially.

Generativity: The Work of Adulthood

10. Adults seek to be generative, successful, achieving, instrumental—all words used to describe a major psychosocial need that each adult meets in their own way.

11. Parenthood is a common expression of generativity. Wanted and planned-for biological children pose challenges. Adoptive children, stepchildren, and especially foster children bring additional stresses. Nonetheless, many adults become generative by raising children.

12. Caregiving is more likely to flow from the older generations to the younger ones, so the "sandwich generation" metaphor is misleading. Many families have a kinkeeper, who aids generativity within the family.

13. Employment brings many rewards to adults, including intrinsic benefits such as pride and friendship. Changes in employment patterns—job switches, shift work, and the diversity of fellow workers—affect other aspects of adult development. Unemployment is particularly difficult for self-esteem.

14. Balancing work and family life, personal needs, and social involvement is a major task for adults. This is true for men as well as women, since both now function in both spheres.

15. Combining work demands, caregiving requirements, intimacy, and generativity is not easy; consequences are mixed. Some adults benefit from new patterns within the labor market and in the overall culture; others cannot find a happy balance.

KEY TERMS

intimacy versus isolation (p. 462)
generativity versus stagnation (p. 463)
humanism (p. 463)

Big Five (p. 466)
living apart together (LAT) (p. 469)
empty nest (p. 471)

social convoy (p. 473)
fictive kin (p. 475)
kinkeeper (p. 483)
sandwich generation (p. 483)

extrinsic rewards of work (p. 486)
intrinsic rewards of work (p. 486)

APPLICATIONS

1. Describe a relationship that you know of in which a middle-aged person and a younger adult learned from each other.

2. Did your parents' marital and employment status affect you? How would you have fared if they had chosen other marriage or work patterns?

3. Imagine becoming a foster parent or adoptive parent. What do you see as the personal benefits and costs?

4. Ask several people how their personalities have changed in the past decade. The research suggests that changes are usually minor. Is that what people say?

ESPECIALLY FOR QUESTIONS

Response for Immigrants and Children of Immigrants (from page 467): Extroversion and neuroticism, according to one study (Silventoinen et al., 2008). Because these traits decrease over adulthood, fewer older adults migrate.

Response for Young Couples (from page 472): There is no simple answer, but you should bear in mind that, while abuse usually decreases with age, breakups become more difficult with every year, especially if children are involved.

Response for Entrepreneurs (from page 489): As employees and as customers. Middle-aged workers are steady, with few absences and good "people skills," and they like to work. In addition, household income is likely to be higher at about age 50 than at any other time, so middle-aged customers will probably be able to afford your products or services.

OBSERVATION QUIZ ANSWER

Answer to Observation Quiz (from page 476): Mothers could have those facial expressions or use their arms that way—but fathers do it more often.

Answer to Observation Quiz (from page 483): He carries the pack with supplies for both of them; she memorializes the hike with a selfie.

Late Adulthood

What emotions do you expect when you read about late adulthood? Sadness, fear, depression, resignation, sympathy, sorrow? Expect, instead, surprise and joy. You will learn that most older adults are active, alert, and self-sufficient; that dramatic loss of memory and logic ("senility") is unusual; and that many are independent and happy.

Earlier personality and the effects of SES continue lifelong, but time brings changes. Every older adult experiences disability—perhaps in the senses, in body movement, in the heart, or in digestion. However, most older adults, most of the time, overcome such difficulties and enjoy this time of life.

If you doubt this, you are not alone. Late adulthood, more than any other part of life, is a magnet for misinformation. Ageism may be worse than the other *-isms*, because everyone experiences it if they live long enough. Read on, and get ready.

JUPITERIMAGES/GETTY IMAGES

LATE ADULTHOOD
Body and Mind

JUPITERIMAGES/GETTY IMAGES

what will you know?

- What percentage of older people are in nursing homes?
- Are old men and women abnormal if they are interested in sex?
- Can most people live to 100?
- Will everyone become senile if they live long enough?
- Do decades of experience make a person wise?

I took my 1-year-old grandson to the playground. One mother, watching her son, warned that the sandbox would soon be crowded because the children from a nearby day-care center were coming. We chatted, and to my delight she explained details of the center's curriculum, staffing, scheduling, and tuition as if she assumed I was my grandson's mother, not his grandmother.

Soon I realized that she was merely being polite, because a girl glanced at me and asked:

"Is that your grandchild?"

I nodded.

"Where is the mother?" was her next question.

Later that afternoon came the final blow. As I opened the gate for a middle-aged man, he said, "Thank you, young lady." I don't think I look old, but no one would imagine I was young. That "young lady" was benevolent, but it made me realize that my pleasure at the first woman's words was a sign of my own self-deceptive prejudice.

Now we begin our study of the last phase of life, from age 65 or so until death. This chapter starts by exploring the prejudices that surround aging, evident in my reaction to all three people at the playground. We describe biosocial changes—and what can be done to mitigate them.

Then we provide a perspective on cognition after age 60—what changes, and what remains the same. For most people, analysis and self-reflection are at least as strong as ever until their last days of life.

New Understanding of Old Age

demographic shift
A shift in the proportions of the populations of various ages.

Major changes have occurred in social understanding of late adulthood because there are more older adults and because we have a better idea of what causes aging. This begins with science, and it ends with attitudes.

Demography

Demography is the science that describes populations, including by cohort, age, gender, or region. Demographers refer to "the greatest demographic upheaval in human history" (Bloom, 2011, p. 562), a **demographic shift** in the size of the age groups.

Two hundred years ago, there were 20 times more children under age 15 than people over age 64. Now there are only 3 times as many, with 8 percent of the world's population 65 or older in 2015. In some nations, the older population is even larger than that: 15 percent in the United States, 16 percent in Canada, 22 percent in Italy, and 26 percent in Japan (United Nations, Department of Economic and Social Affairs, Population Division, 2017) (see Figure 14.1).

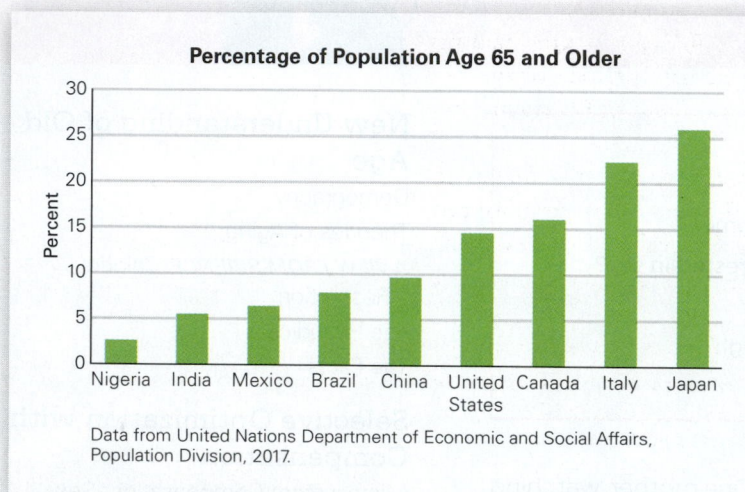

Data from United Nations Department of Economic and Social Affairs, Population Division, 2017.

FIGURE 14.1 Affluence and Age How does having more older adults affect national wealth and war? Some contend that civil war, poverty, and violence of all kinds are reduced when a nation has more wise elders and fewer rebellious young adults.

Demographers often depict the age structure of a population as a series of stacked bars, one bar for each age group, with the youngest at the bottom and the oldest at the top. Always, the shape was a *demographic pyramid*. Like a wedding cake, it was wide at the base, with each higher level narrower than the one beneath it (see Figure 14.2). There were three reasons, none true today:

1. More babies were born than the replacement rate of one per adult, so each new generation had more children than the previous one. (**NOW FALSE**)

FIGURE 14.2 Almost a Pyramid India's population still looks like a pyramid, but note that within the past few years the demographic shift has begun even here. There are fewer children under 5 than in the three higher age groups.

↑**OBSERVATION** QUIZ
Does India have more males or more females? (see answer, page 529)

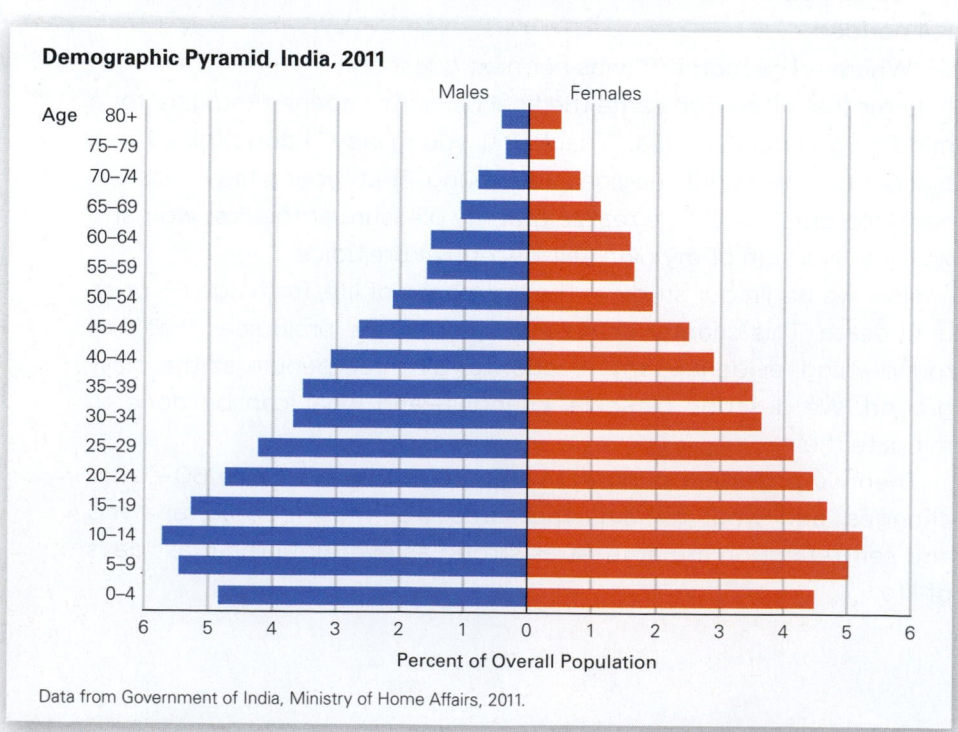

Data from Government of India, Ministry of Home Affairs, 2011.

2. Many young children died, which made the bottom bar much wider than upper ones. (**NOW FALSE**)

3. Serious illness was almost always fatal, reducing the size of each adult group. (**NOW FALSE**)

To appreciate that this is revolutionary, not a small change, consider the decades recently added to the life span. Demographers chart the *average life expectancy,* which is how long an average newborn in a particular place is likely to live.

Between 1950 and 2015, the average life expectancy in high-income nations became twenty years longer, from 60 to 80. In low-income nations, the average became 30 years longer, from 35 to 65 (United Nations, Department of Economic and Social Affairs, Population Division, 2017).

Most of these added averages resulted from fewer childhood deaths, thanks to clean water, immunization, nutrition, and newborn care. Recently, in more advanced nations, midlife deaths have also been reduced: about half because of lifestyle improvements (less smoking, more exercise) and half because of medical care (surgery, early detection).

Of course, improvements in average life expectancy are not inevitable. In the United States, opioid and gun deaths slightly reduced average life expectancy in 2017. However, once a U.S. resident reaches age 60, he or she is projected to live to 83, five years longer than was the case in 1950.

STATISTICS THAT FRIGHTEN Unfortunately, demographic data are sometimes reported in ways designed to alarm, suggesting that the increasing numbers of elderly comprise a time bomb about to explode. For instance, have you heard that people over age 80 are the fastest-growing age group? Or, that more and more people suffer from Alzheimer's disease? Both true; both misleading.

Yes, there are more old people alive. But the overall population has also grown. The *percentage* of U.S. residents age 80 and older has doubled, not quadrupled. In 2015 it was 3.8 percent. That does not overwhelm the other 96.2 percent.

Further, only about 3 percent of those over age 64 are in hospitals or nursing homes, because most elders are healthier than elders once were. Most people over age 65 are fiercely independent, more often care *givers* than care receivers. The leading British medical journal discusses "the time bomb that isn't" (Spijker & MacInnes, 2013).

Same Situation, Far Apart: Keep Smiling Good humor seems to be a cause of longevity, and vice versa. This is true for both sexes, including the British men on Founder's Day *(left)* and the two Indian women on an ordinary sunny day in Dwarka *(right).*

young-old
Healthy, vigorous, financially secure older adults (generally, those aged 65 to 75) who are well integrated into the lives of their families and communities.

old-old
Older adults (generally, those over age 75) who suffer from physical, mental, or social deficits.

oldest-old
Elderly adults (generally, those over age 85) who are dependent on others for almost everything, requiring supportive services such as nursing homes and hospital stays.

wear-and-tear theory
A view of aging as a process by which the human body wears out because of the passage of time and exposure to environmental stressors.

maximum life span
The oldest possible age that members of a species can live under ideal circumstances. For humans, that age is approximately 122 years.

WHAT KIND OF "OLD"? Gerontologists distinguish among the *young-old*, the *old-old*, and the *oldest-old*.

- The **young-old** are the largest group of older adults. They are healthy, active, financially secure, and independent. Few people notice them or realize their age.

- The **old-old** suffer losses in body, mind, or social support, but they care for themselves.

- Only the **oldest-old** are dependent, a small group, easy to notice. How many of your relatives (aunts, uncles, parents, grandparents, etc.) are over age 65? How many of them are now in nursing homes? As you see, the oldest-old are relatively few.

Theories of Aging

As it has become clear that not every older person is impaired, it has become important to understand why aging occurs. That can help slow the process, allowing more people to have a long and healthy life.

The biological consequences of age are sometimes divided into *primary aging* (the direct result of time) and *secondary aging* (the accumulated consequences of what people and societies do). We know how to reduce secondary aging (better health habits, as explained in Chapter 12). We need a better understanding of primary aging, because if we could reduce it, many diseases would disappear.

Many scientists say that "aging is modifiable" (Kennedy, 2016, p. 109) and "senescence is not inevitable" (Jones & Vaupel, 2017, p. 965). Theories of primary aging can be grouped in three major clusters: wear and tear, genetic adaptation, and cellular aging.

Is She Old Yet? Maggie Smith began her acting career in Shakespeare's *Twelfth Night* at age 17, and she has appeared every year since then in films, television, and on stage. Many people have watched her work as Professor Minerva McGonagall in eight *Harry Potter* movies and as Violet Crawley in the TV series *Downton Abbey*. She is still acting, making her a young-old person.

STOP MOVING? STOP EATING? The oldest, most general theory of aging is known as the **wear-and-tear theory.** The idea is that the body wears out after years of use. Organ reserve and repair processes are exhausted as the decades pass.

Evidence for this theory includes the following. Inclement weather, or harmful food, or toxic pollution, or unseen radiation take a toll on health. Too much sun causes skin cancer, too much animal fat clogs arteries, pollution causes cancer. Stress causes painful joints, smoke damages the lungs, blows to the head destroy the brain; allostatic load increases over time.

Thus, sometimes the body suffers from years of abuse. However, wear and tear does not explain all of aging, because some body parts benefit from activity. Exercise improves hearts and lungs; tai chi improves balance; weight-training increases muscle mass; and sexual activity stimulates the sexual-reproductive system. The slogan "use it or lose it" may apply to many body parts, including the brain.

A surprising study of 55- to 79-year-olds who bicycled over 100 miles per week (they enjoyed the exercise and the views!) found very little age-based deterioration of the muscles. Indeed, on most measures those older bikers had much stronger legs than the average 30-year-old (Pollock et al., 2018).

IT'S ALL GENETIC Another cluster of theories focuses on genes, both genes of the entire species and genes that vary from one person to another (Sutphin & Kaeberlein, 2011). This theory is widely accepted, in part because it contends that individuals are not responsible for the genetic effects of aging.

JOHN PHILLIPS/GETTY IMAGES

Every species has a **maximum life span,** defined as the oldest possible age that members of that species can attain. Genes determine the maximum: for rats, 4 years; rabbits, 13; tigers, 26; house cats, 30; brown bats, 34; brown bears, 37; chimpanzees, 55; Indian elephants, 70; finback whales, 80; humans, 122; lake sturgeon, 150; giant tortoises, 180.

Indeed, genes affect the entire aging process, from how long the fetus stays in the womb to the details of graying or loss of hair. Remember puberty: It begins when genes direct the pituitary to make growth and sexual hormones, and then every organ is affected. The same may occur for aging and, eventually, death.

This theory is supported by a fact: Some genes cause unusually fast or slow aging. Children born with Hutchinson-Gilford syndrome (a genetic disease also called *progeria*) stop growing at about age 5 and begin to look old, with wrinkled skin and balding heads in childhood. They die in their teens of diseases typically found in people five times their age.

Other genes program a long and healthy life. People who reach age 100 usually have alleles that other people do not (Govindaraju et al., 2015). Because of our genes, no one has proven to live longer than a French woman named Jeanne Calment, who died in 1997 at the age of 122. She had the DR1 allele, common in centenarians. Many other longevity alleles have been identified (Santos-Lozano et al., 2016). Most of us do not have them.

Don't believe that people are living past 122; our genes do not allow it. People in some regions are said to live to 150 or more, but when scientists look for proof of age, those elders are probably decades younger (Thorson, 1995). Jeanne Calment died more than two decades ago, yet no one with a verified birthday has surpassed her. Aging is in our DNA.

Two alleles of the ApoE gene prove the the importance of genes. ApoE2 is found in 12 percent of men in their 70s, but death is more common in the 88 percent without it. That explains why 17 percent of men over age 85 have ApoE2. Another allele of the same gene, ApoE4, increases the rate of death by heart disease, stroke, neurocognitive disorders, and—if a person is HIV-positive—by AIDS (Kuhlmann et al., 2010). Most people have neither; they have the neutral ApoE3.

Further evidence confirms that every disease of aging is partly genetic. That is one reason that disease rates vary among people with ancestors from particular parts of the world. For example, many scientists search for the genes that increase the risk for diabetes. Genetic-wide research (called GWAS), which looks at the entire genome, has found more than 100 genes that increase the risk a small amount (Visscher et al., 2017). Those genes can appear in someone of any ethnicity, but some groups have more of particular ones.

Thus, because of genes, people with Asian ancestors tend to develop diabetes at younger ages and lower weights than Europeans. In China, Han people have higher rates than other Chinese people (Wang et al., 2017; Hsu et al., 2015). In the United States, African Americans are particularly likely to develop diabetes (Layton et al., 2018).

As a theory of aging, looking at genes makes sense. However, the danger is that focusing on genes distracts people from other causes of

"If you give up alcohol, cigarettes, sex, red meat, cake and chocolate, and don't get too excited, you can enjoy life for a few more years yet."

World's Record for Centenarians Can you sprint 100 meters in less than 30 seconds? This man, Hidekichi Miyazaki, can. Maybe you need more practice. Hidekichi has been running for 103 years!

THINK CRITICALLY: For the benefit of the species as a whole, why would genes promote aging?

metabolic syndrome
Several conditions that tend to occur together and increase one's risk of diabetes, heart disease, and cancer.

cellular aging
The cumulative effect of stress and toxins, first causing cellular damage and eventually the death of cells.

Hayflick limit
The number of times a human cell is capable of dividing into two new cells. The limit for most human cells is approximately 50 divisions, an indication that the life span is limited by our genetic program.

telomeres
The area of the tips of each chromosome that is reduced a tiny amount as time passes. By the end of life, the telomeres are very short.

disease and death. As emphasized earlier, nature and nurture always interact, so genes alone do not cause the diseases and other signs of old age.

Diabetes, for instance, is strongly influenced by nongenetic factors. African Americans who live in areas with high residential segregation are more likely to develop diabetes—and the reasons are not genetic (Bancks et al., 2017).

More broadly, the complex relationship between aging, genes, and environment is shown by the **metabolic syndrome,** a cluster of factors that tend to occur together to increase risk of age-related diabetes, heart disease, and cancer (Gathirua-Mwangi et al., 2018; Kaur, 2014). Those factors are body fat around the waist (apple-shaped, not pear-shaped obesity), hypertension, insulin resistance, triglycerides, and LDL cholesterol. Every aspect of metabolic syndrome is affected by genes, but the total cluster is powerfully influenced by diet, exercise, and stress. .

AGING CELLS The third cluster of theories examines **cellular aging,** focusing on molecules and cells. Remember, cells duplicate many times over the life span. Minor errors—repetitions and deletions of base pairs—in copying accumulate. Early in life, the immune system repairs such errors, but eventually the immune system itself becomes less adept.

In general, when the organism can no longer repair cellular errors, senescence occurs. This process is first apparent in the skin, an organ that replaces itself often, particularly if damage occurs (such as peeling skin with sunburn). With age, cuts take a little longer to heal, scarring becomes more obvious. Cellular aging also occurs inside the body; the aging immune system is increasingly unable to control abnormal cells.

Cellular aging, with some cells out of normal control, is a major cause of all forms of cancer (Martincorena & Campbell, 2015). Before age 40, the biological mechanisms usually keep cancer cells from reproducing and metastasizing. However, once the childbearing years are over, cancer cells duplicate unchecked. In the United States in 2015, cancer rates were 2 percent of those aged 25 to 44 but 18 percent of those over age 64 (National Center for Health Statistics, 2017).

Cells eventually lose the ability to replicate. This point is referred to as the **Hayflick limit,** named after the scientist who discovered it. Hayflick believes that aging is caused primarily by a natural loss of molecular fidelity—that is, by inevitable errors in transcription as each cell reproduces itself. He believes that aging is natural, built into our cells (Hayflick, 2004).

There are dozens of cellular changes, from the seemingly insignificant mitochondria to the obviously crucial stem cells (López-Otín et al., 2013). One particular cell change that has been studied in connection with aging is the **telomere,** which is material at the end of each chromosome

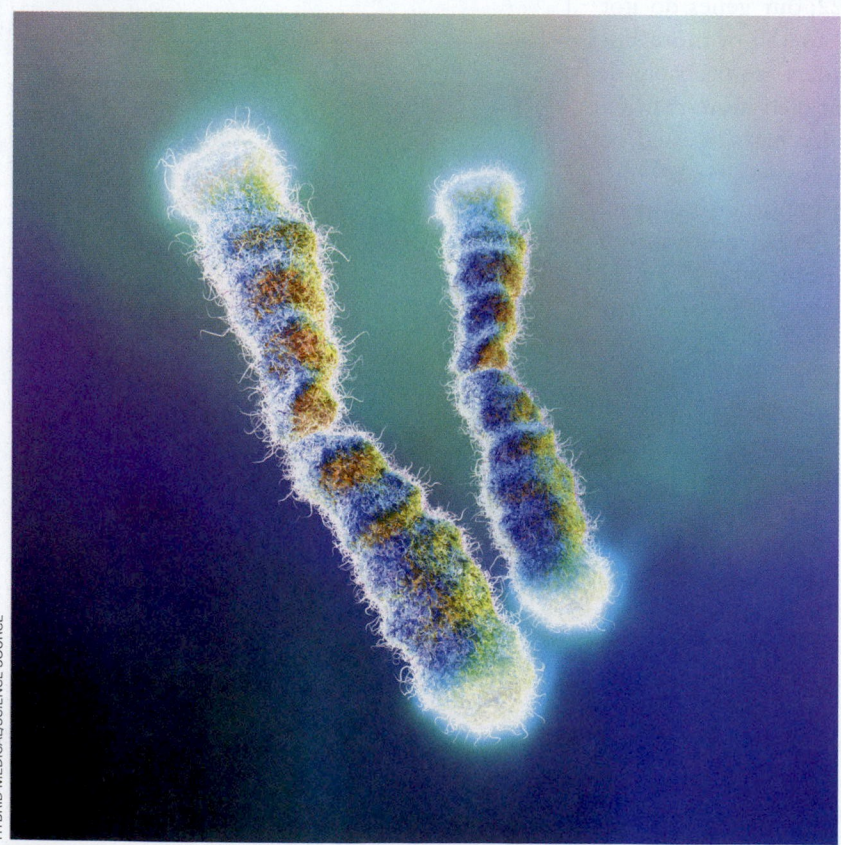

HYBRID MEDICAL/SCIENCE SOURCE

Old Caterpillars? No, these are young chromosomes, stained to show the glowing white telomeres at the ends.

that becomes shorter over time. Telomeres are longer in children (except those with progeria) and shorter in old adults. Eventually, at the Hayflick limit, the telomere is gone, duplication stops, and the creature dies.

The more stress a person experiences, from childhood on, the shorter his or her telomeres are and the sooner the person will die (J. Lin et al., 2012). Telomere length is about the same in newborns of all genders and ethnic groups, but by late adulthood telomeres are longer in women than in men and longer in European Americans than in African Americans (Aviv, 2011). There are many possible causes, but cellular-aging theorists focus on the consequences: Women outlive men, and European Americans outlive African Americans, at least until age 80.

Research on primary aging assumes that it would benefit society if more people lived to age 100 or more. But that is not accepted by everyone. As one scientist says:

> Interventions that merely extend the number of years during which humans suffer through diseased lives contribute no value to those lives, and perhaps have significant disutility for society.
>
> *[Crutchfield, 2018, p. 442]*

To understand this dilemma, we must first separate prejudice from fact.

◆ **Especially for Biologists**
What are some immediate practical uses for research on the causes of aging? (see response, page 529)

A VIEW FROM SCIENCE

Calorie Restriction

Calorie restriction—a drastic reduction in calories consumed—increases the life span in many creatures. The most dramatic evidence comes from fruit flies, which can live three times as long if they eat less. Many other species benefit from calorie restriction, including some primates such as rhesus monkeys (Mattison et al., 2017).

All three theories of aging help explain this. Eating half as many calories reduces wear on digestion and changes the cells—especially the cells that predispose to diseases. With animal research, not every species benefits, probably because of genetic differences between one species and another or because of details of the diet. Maybe a high-nutrient, low-protein diet is needed, or maybe periodic fasting (some days with very low consumption and other days with normal eating) is even better (Fontana & Partridge, 2015; Tinsley & Horne, 2018).

Does this apply to humans? Thousands of members of the Calorie Restriction Society voluntarily undereat (Roth & Polotsky, 2012). They give up some things that many people cherish, not just cake and cheeseburgers but also a strong sex drive. They have lower blood pressure, fewer strokes, less cancer, and almost no diabetes.

In several places (e.g., Okinawa, Denmark, and Norway), wartime occupation forced severe calorie reduction for almost everyone. People ate local vegetables, and not much else, and they were often hungry. But they were less likely to die of disease (Most et al., 2017).

calorie restriction
The practice of limiting dietary energy intake (while consuming sufficient quantities of vitamins, minerals, and other important nutrients) for the purpose of improving health and slowing down the aging process.

Similar results occurred in Cuba in the 1990s. Because of a U.S. embargo, meat and gas were scarce. People ate fewer calories and walked more. The average adult lost 14 pounds, putting less strain on their bodies. That reduced diabetes and heart disease (Franco et al., 2013).

However, in all these places where food scarcity was the consequence of international politics, when the crisis was over, people ate more and diseases increased. In Cuba, when the food supply improved, people regained weight, and the diabetes rate doubled (Franco et al., 2013).

Apparently, most people want the pleasures of a full stomach and tasty treats, just as some athletes choose sports that wear out their bodies. Perhaps seeking those pleasures is part of the genetics of being a person. Would you choose personal happiness over longevity?

THINK CRITICALLY: Do people want the comforts of daily life—driving and eating—more than longer lives?

Older and Wiser Contrary to ageist ideas, older mountain climbers are less likely to fall to their death than younger ones. Judgment is crucial; a strong safety rope like this one and climbing with a buddy are smart precautions.

ageism
A prejudice whereby people are categorized and judged solely on the basis of their chronological age.

THINK CRITICALLY: Why do many people contemplate aging with sorrow rather than joy?

The Prejudice

Ageism is the idea that age determines whom a person is and therefore that people should "act their age." Ageism leads to stereotypes and restrictions, especially harming those who are old. Such attitudes may seem benevolent, but that is still prejudice. People may not recognize their own ageism when they infantilize the elderly, as if they were children ("so cute!," "second childhood"), but their words do harm.

Surveys find that ageism is prevalent among people of all ages and nations (North & Fiske, 2015; Luo et al., 2013; Bratt et al., 2018). Do you think that Asians are more respectful of the old than Western cultures? That is another prejudice.

BELIEVING THE STEREOTYPE Ageism becomes a *self-fulfilling prophecy,* a prediction that comes true *because* people believe it. There are three harmful consequences:

- If younger adults treat older people as if they are frail and confused, that treatment itself makes the elderly become more dependent.

- If professionals believe that the norms for young adults should apply to everyone, they may try to make older people behave as younger adults do. If they fail, they give up.

- If older adults themselves focus on what they have lost instead of what they have gained, they lose the joy of old age.

One sign of ageism is believing that you, yourself, are in better health, with sharper memories and more happiness, than other people your age. Consider the logic: If *most* people say they are younger than average, then the average is not really average. That reflects ageism.

When 829 women, ages 40 to 75, were asked about how their health compared to the average person their age, most said their health was better and very few said their health was worse (Holahan et al., 2017).

Similar results came from a study comparing 1,877 adults, ages 30 to 95, in Germany, China, and the United States on eight aspects of aging. As expected, some cultural and contextual differences were found, but in every nation and every domain, the elders on average felt younger than their chronological age (O'Brien et al., 2017).

The results can be harmful. For instance, in the study above (Holahan et al., 2017), most of the older women were relatively inactive—despite evidence that activity would improve their health. Their belief that they were already healthier than their peers made them less healthy.

The Facts

Of course illness and disability with age are facts, not simply the result of ageism. Elders must find "a delicate balance . . . knowing when to persist and when to switch gears . . . some aspects of aging are out of one's control" (Lachman et al., 2011, p. 186).

As with those women above, recognition of the reality of primary and secondary aging is needed so that health can be protected. Let us look at three examples—sleep, exercise, and talk—trying to distinguish fact from prejudice.

HOW TO FIGHT INSOMNIA The day–night circadian rhythm diminishes with age: Many older people wake before dawn and are sleepy during the day. Older adults spend more time in bed, take longer to fall asleep, and wake frequently (about

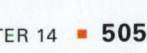

10 times per night) (Ayalon & Ancoli-Israel, 2009). They also are more likely to nap.

All of this is normal, but since ageism considers them problems, older people worry. If they avoid worrying and develop their own sleep schedules, elders feel less tired than young adults. Good sleep patterns are restorative at every age (Scullin, 2017).

In one study, older adults complaining of sleep problems were mailed six booklets (one each week) (K. Morgan et al., 2012). The booklets described normal sleep patterns for people their age and gave suggestions to relieve insomnia, such as not watching TV in bed and getting up when the body woke up.

Compared to similar older people who did not get the booklets, the informed elders used less sleep medication and reported better-quality sleep. Even six months after the last booklet, they were more satisfied with their sleep.

By contrast, uninformed elders in an ageist culture are distressed about sleep. Doctors might prescribe narcotics, or people might drink alcohol, to induce sleep. These remedies can overwhelm an aging body, causing heavy sleep, confusion, nausea, depression, and unsteadiness upon waking.

LESS EXERCISE OR MORE? The facts about exercise are clear. Movement aids health of the body and mind. Yet in the United States, only 28 percent of those age 75 and over meet the recommended guidelines for aerobic exercise, in contrast to 60 percent for adults aged 18 to 24 (National Center for Health Statistics, 2017) (see Figure 14.3). Meeting the guidelines for muscle strengthening was worse.

A sociocultural perspective finds that the context discourages exercise among the elderly in many ways:

- Most team sports are organized to accommodate the young.
- Ballroom dancing assumes that every woman has a male partner (although at the oldest ages, the ratio is 2:1).
- Most yoga, aerobics, and exercise classes are paced and designed for the young.
- Bikes are designed for speed, not stability.
- Laws requiring bike helmets often apply only to children.
- Younger players might reject an older man from a pickup basketball game.
- People might snicker if an elder dons spandex and jogs around the park.

All of this is ageism in the culture. Added to that, elders themselves choose comfort—reducing range of motion while impairing circulation and digestion. Shorter strides, shallower breathing, sitting not walking, elevators not stairs—all impair health.

Some people still hold the old ageist idea that exercise will cause heart problems. This means that some family members discourage exercise ("just sit and relax, Grandma") even though people of all ages are more likely to hike, bike, or join a team when other people do so as well (Franco et al., 2015).

Sadly, younger adults and the media discourage the elderly from leaving home. For example, whenever an older person is robbed, raped, or assaulted, ageist headlines add to fear. In fact, street crime targets young adults, not old ones.

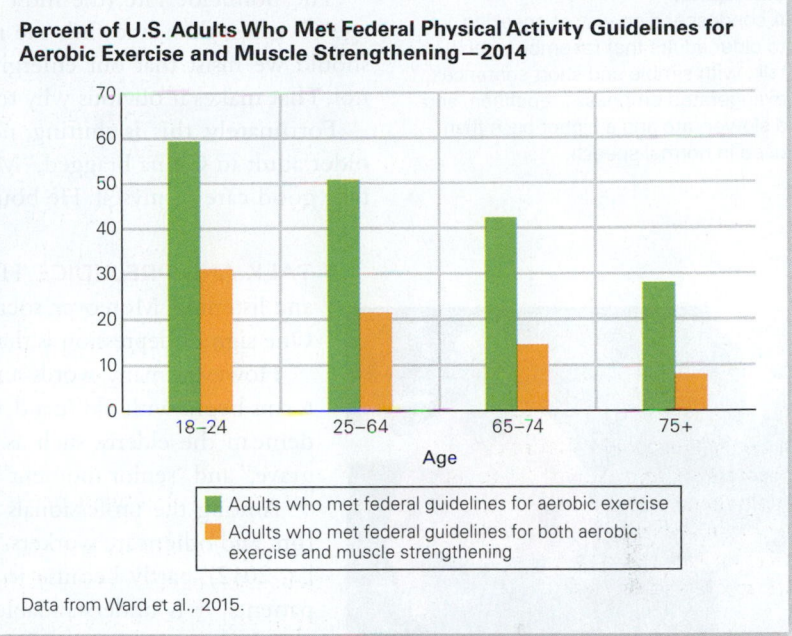

Percent of U.S. Adults Who Met Federal Physical Activity Guidelines for Aerobic Exercise and Muscle Strengthening—2014

■ Adults who met federal guidelines for aerobic exercise
■ Adults who met federal guidelines for both aerobic exercise and muscle strengthening

Data from Ward et al., 2015.

FIGURE 14.3 Hearts, Lungs, and Legs As you see, most of the elderly do not meet the minimum exercise standards recommended by the Centers for Disease Control—150 minutes of aerobic exercise a week and muscle-strengthening exercises twice a week. This is especially troubling since those activities have been proven many times to safeguard the health of all major organs, as well as to correlate with intelligence, memory, and joy.

elderspeak
A condescending way of speaking to older adults that resembles baby talk, with simple and short sentences, exaggerated emphasis, repetition, and a slower rate and a higher pitch than used in normal speech.

The homicide rate (the most reliable indicator of violent crime) for those over age 65 is less than one-fifth the rate for those in their 20s. To protect our relatives, should we insist that our emerging adults never leave the house alone? Of course not. That makes it obvious why telling older adults to stay home is shortsighted.

Fortunately, this is shifting, not only in the United States but worldwide. An older adult in China bragged, "My son told me that the most important thing is to take good care of myself. He bought a bike for me" (Li et al., 2013, p. 346).

© RONNIE KAUFMAN/CORBIS

TALK AND PREJUDICE Humans of every age develop their minds by talking and listening. Moreover, social interaction is needed for emotional equilibrium. One sign of depression is that a person does not talk much.

However, many words and phrases in standard vocabulary are ageist. Some terms begin with old (maid, fart, coot, geezer, battle ax, blue-hair); many phrases demean the elderly, such as "dirty old man," "over the hill," "one foot in the grave," and "senior moment" (Storlie, 2015).

Among the professionals most likely to harbor stereotypes are nurses, doctors, and other care workers. Their ageism is difficult to erase (Eymard & Douglas, 2012), partly because it is based on experience with a subgroup of older patients. It is understandable—and harmful—to generalize based on a biased sample (those who are sick and feeble).

Such professionals are likely to use **elderspeak.** Like baby talk, elderspeak uses simple and short sentences, slower talk, higher pitch, louder volume, and frequent repetition (Kemper, 2015; Nelson, 2011). Elderspeak is especially patronizing when people call an older person "honey" or "dear," or use a nickname instead of a surname ("Billy," not "Mr. White"). The consequences are harmful; older adults internalize the message (Storlie, 2015).

Ironically, many aspects of elderspeak *reduce* communication (Kemper, 2015). Higher frequencies are harder for the elderly to hear; stretching out words makes comprehension worse; shouting causes anxiety; and simplified vocabulary reduces clarity.

Safe Crossing Professionals least likely to use elderspeak are those like this one who interact with dozens of typical, community-dwelling elders every day.

what have you learned?

1. What are the facts from demography regarding late adulthood?
2. Regarding maximum and average life span, should both, neither, or only one be extended?
3. What is the connection between telomeres and the Hayflick limit?
4. What evidence supports and what evidence refutes the wear- and-tear theory of senescence?
5. How is benevolent ageism harmful?
6. What is elderspeak and how is it used?

Selective Optimization with Compensation

Now we highlight a strategy already described in Chapter 12, *selective optimization with compensation*. The elderly can compensate for the impairments of senescence and then can perform (optimize) whatever specific tasks they select.

Selective compensation occurs on each of Bronfenbrenner's levels—the microsystem, macrosystem, exosystem, and chronosystem. That means personal choice,

community practices, technological advances, and historical change are always relevant. To illustrate, we now explain four examples: sexual intercourse, driving, the senses, and the brain. Each involves every system, but here we emphasize one level for each.

Microsystem Compensation: Sex

Most people are sexually active in adulthood (see Figure 14.4), but frequency of intercourse slows down and sometimes stops during late adulthood. Nonetheless, sexual satisfaction often increases after middle age.

As one study explained, sex in late adulthood is "active, but with a different kind of desire" (McHugh & Interligi, 2015, p. 103). A five-nation study (United States, Germany, Japan, Brazil, Spain) found that kissing and hugging, not intercourse, predicted happiness in long-lasting romances (Heiman et al., 2011). The sex lives of most married people can be described as selective optimization.

A similar process occurs for individuals after divorce or death of a partner. Since the sex drive varies from person to person, some single elders are happy to forgo sexual interaction. Others date, cohabit, begin LAT (living apart together), or remarry. As A Case to Study (page 508) suggests, each older person decides how sexual to be—selecting, optimizing, and compensating in their own way.

This variability is crucial for professionals and relatives to understand. Because hospitals and nursing homes routinely separate elderly couples, the wish for the elderly to be privately affectionate is one reason why some fiercely resist attempts to hospitalize them.

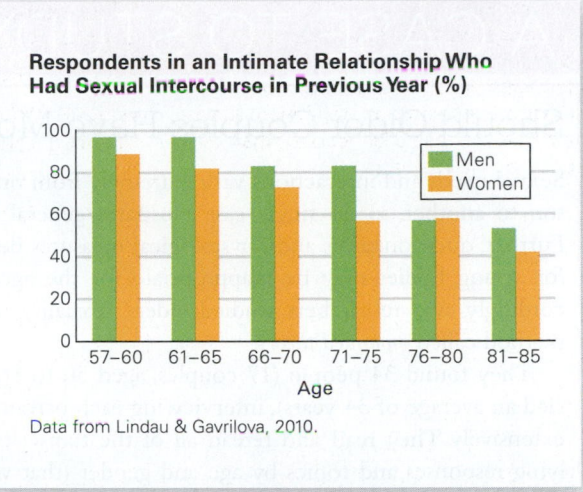

Respondents in an Intimate Relationship Who Had Sexual Intercourse in Previous Year (%)

Data from Lindau & Gavrilova, 2010.

FIGURE 14.4 Your Reaction Older adults who consider their health good (most of them) were asked if they had had sexual intercourse within the past year. If they answered yes, they were considered sexually active. What is your reaction to the data? Some young adults might be surprised that many adults aged 60 to 80 still experience sexual intercourse. Other people might be saddened that most healthy adults over age 80 do not. However, neither reaction may be appropriate. For many elders, sexual affection is expressed in many more ways than intercourse, and it continues lifelong.

↑OBSERVATION QUIZ
What are the male–female differences and how can they be explained, since all of these respondents had partners of another gender? (see answer, page 529)

Macrosystem Compensation: Driving

Older adults have more car accidents than younger adults. Since they drive slower, rarely drive drunk, and are less often on major highways, their accidents are more often fender benders than multiple-victim crashes. Nonetheless, accidents per mile increase with age, because reading road signs takes longer, hearing is muted, turning the neck is harder, grip weakens, reaction time lengthens, and night vision worsens.

Few older drivers notice the impact of their losses, so societies need to compensate. Often they do not. For instance, many jurisdictions renew licenses by mail, even at age 80. If an older adult causes a crash, the individual is blamed, not the community.

When retesting is required, it may entail answering multiple-choice questions about road rules, and reading letters on a well-lit chart straight ahead. Any elder who fails should have stopped driving long ago, but proficiency does not guarantee competence.

There is a solution that local jurisdictions could adopt, but few do. A national panel recommends simulated driving via a computer and video screen, with the prospective driver seated with a steering wheel, accelerator, and brakes (Staplin et al., 2012). The results of this test could allow some older adults to renew, some to have their licenses revoked, and many to recognize that they are less proficient than they thought.

BEN CAWTHRA/SIPA PRESS/WINDSOR/BERKSHIRE/UK

Should She Drive? Queen Elizabeth II was 91 years old when this photo taken. She is the only person in the United Kingdom who is not required to have a driver's license, but her driving is usually limited to her private estates.

A CASE TO STUDY

Should Older Couples Have More Sex?

Sexual needs and interactions vary extremely from one person to another, so no single case illustrates general trends. Further, questionnaires and physiological measures designed for young bodies may be inappropriate for the aged. Accordingly, two researchers studied elders' sexuality using a method called *grounded theory*.

They found 34 people (17 couples, aged 50 to 86, married an average of 34 years), interviewing each privately and extensively. They read and reread all of the transcripts, tallying responses and topics by age and gender (that was the grounded part). Then they analyzed common topics, interpreting trends (that was theory).

They concluded that sexual activity is more a social construction than a biological event (Lodge & Umberson, 2012). All of their cases said that intercourse was less frequent with age, including four couples for whom intercourse stopped completely because of the husband's health. Nonetheless, more respondents said that their sex life had improved than said it deteriorated (44 percent compared to 30 percent).

Surprisingly, those 30 percent were more likely to be middle-aged than older. Some midlife men were troubled by difficulty maintaining an erection, and many midlife women worried that they were not sexy.

One woman said:

All of a sudden, we didn't have sex after I got skinny. And I couldn't figure that out. I look really good now and we're not having sex. It turns out that he was going through a major physical thing at that point and just had lost his sex drive. . . . I went through years thinking it was my fault.

[*Irene, quoted in Lodge & Umberson, 2012, p. 435*]

The authors theorize that "images of masculine sexuality are premised on high, almost uncontrollable levels of penis-driven sexual desire" (p. 430), while the cultural ideals of feminine sexuality emphasize women's passivity and yet "implore women to be both desirable and receptive to men's sexual desires and impulses," deeming "older women and their bodies unattractive" (p. 430).

Thus, when middle-aged adults first realize that aging has changed them, they are distressed. By late adulthood they realize that the young idea of good sex (frequent intercourse) is irrelevant. Instead, they *compensate* for physical changes by *optimizing* their relationship in other ways. As one man over age 70 said:

I think the intimacy is a lot stronger . . . more often now we do things like holding hands and wanting to be close to each other or touch each other. It's probably more important now than sex is.

[*Jim, quoted in Lodge & Umberson, 2012, p. 438*]

An older woman said her marriage improved because:

We have more opportunities and more motivation. Sex was wonderful. It got thwarted, with . . . the medication he is on. And he hasn't been functional since. The doctors just said that it is going to be this way, so we have learned to accept that. But we have also learned long before that there are more ways than one to share your love.

[*Helen, quoted in Lodge & Umberson, 2012, p. 437*]

The next cohort of older adults may have other attitudes; the male/female and midlife/older differences evident with these 17 couples may not apply. These cases do suggest, however, that selective optimization with compensation is possible.

CULTURA RM EXCLUSIVE/KMM PRODUCTIONS/GETTY IMAGES

Hot or Cold The weather is chilly and the beach is lonely, but it is evident that this senior couple is enjoying the moment. Physical attraction and intimacy continue into later adulthood, despite what younger people might think.

Driving simulators are especially useful if an older adult has had a stroke, or if there are signs of neurological impairment. Some older adults are nonetheless competent drivers, and some are not: Age is a poor predictor, and medical doctors are not the best judges (Vardaki et al., 2016). Individuals are poor at self-assessment: An on-road analysis of older drivers found that some overestimated their competence and some underestimated it (Broberg & Willstrand, 2014).

Beyond retesting, the macrosystem could compensate in other ways. Larger-print signs before highway exits, mirrors that replace the need to turn one's neck, illuminated side streets and driveways, nonglare headlights and hazard flashers, and warnings of ice or fog ahead would reduce accidents.

Well-designed cars, roads, signs, lights, and guardrails, as well as appropriate laws and enforcement, are selective optimization. Competent elderly drivers can maintain independence. Some can drive safely at age 90, most cannot.

Exosystem Compensation: The Senses

Every sense becomes slower and less sharp with each passing decade. This is true for touch (particularly in fingers and toes), pain, taste (particularly for sour and bitter), smell, as well as for sight and hearing.

All of these losses begin as individual problems, unrelated to the exosystem. Specifics depend on genes, past practices, and current demands. However, the exosystem (including historical change and cultural assumptions) may be crucial. Hundreds of manufactured devices and "built" constructions can compensate for sensory loss; research and availability are supported, or impeded, by the exosystem.

VISION Only 10 percent of people over age 65 see well without glasses (see Table 14.1). But technology, from eyeglasses (first invented in the thirteenth century) to tiny video cameras worn on the forehead that connect directly to the brain (not yet commercially available), improves sight. Changing the environment—brighter lights, halogen streetlights, newspapers with large and darker print—makes a difference.

For those with severe vision loss, dogs, canes, and audio devices allow mobility and cognition. The availability of such implements depends on nationwide practices—they are free in some places, absent in others. That is the exosystem.

HEARING Everyone loses some hearing with age. Of those over age 65 in the United States, 39 percent acknowledge some trouble hearing, and 8 percent say that they are virtually deaf (National Center for Health Statistics, 2017). The rates among men are twice that of women. High frequencies—the voice of a small child—are lost more quickly than low frequencies.

THINK CRITICALLY: How does a driver decide whether his or her driving is impaired?

(a)

(b)

(c)

(d)

© ANNA STOWE/ALAMY

Through Different Eyes These photographs depict the same scene as it would be perceived by a person with (a) normal vision, (b) cataracts, (c) glaucoma, or (d) macular degeneration. Think about how difficult it would be to find your own car if you had one of these disorders. That may help you remember to have your vision checked regularly.

TABLE 14.1 Common Vision Impairments Among the Elderly

- *Cataracts.* As early as age 50, about 10 percent of adults have cataracts, a thickening of the lens, causing vision to become cloudy, opaque, and distorted. By age 70, 30 percent do. Cataracts can be removed in outpatient surgery and replaced with an artificial lens.

- *Glaucoma.* About 1 percent of those in their 70s and 10 percent in their 90s have glaucoma, a buildup of fluid pressure within the eye that damages the optic nerve. The early stages have no symptoms, but the later stages cause blindness, which can be prevented if an ophthalmologist or optometrist treats glaucoma before it becomes serious. African Americans and people with diabetes may develop glaucoma as early as age 40.

- *Macular degeneration.* About 4 percent of those in their 60s and about 12 percent over age 80 have a deterioration of the retina, called macular degeneration. An early warning occurs when vision is spotty (e.g., some letters missing when reading). Again, early treatment—in this case, medication—can restore some vision, but without treatment, macular degeneration is progressive, causing blindness about five years after it starts.

universal design
The creation of settings and equipment that can be used by everyone, whether or not they are able-bodied and sensory-acute.

As with vision, the exosystem is crucial. A psychiatrist argues that because of ageism in the culture, doctors, insurance policies, and public facilities all fail to compensate for fading hearing. He believes that, if compensation were readily available, the elderly would have far fewer mental disorders and cognitive problems (Blazer, 2018).

UNIVERSAL DESIGN Disability advocates hope more designers and engineers will think of **universal design,** which is the creation of settings and equipment that can be used by everyone, whether or not they are able-bodied and sensory-acute (Hussain et al., 2013; Holt, 2013). That would be a change in the exosystem. At the moment, just about everything, from houses to fashionable shoes, is designed for adults with no impairments. Many disabilities would disappear with better design.

Look around at the built environment (stores, streets, colleges, and homes); notice the print on medicine bottles; listen to the public-address systems in train stations; ask why most homes have entry stairs and narrow bathrooms, why most buses and cars require a big step up to enter, why smelling remains the usual way to detect a gas leak. Then, look for signs of compensation, and find out how accurate those signs are. Too often elevators are not in service, curb cuts are not smooth, ramps are steep or hidden, headphones are unavailable, and so on.

Sensory loss need not lead to morbidity or cognitive loss, but without compensation, any disability, especially deafness and blindness, correlates with isolation, inactivity, and reduced intellect. The blame is borne by aging individuals, but the exosystem is crucial.

Looped In? This sign indicates that a hearing loop is installed in this New York City subway booth, enabling most people with hearing aids and cochlear implants to receive important messages and communicate with transit personnel. Frequent riders of public transit, however, complain that the public address system malfunctions, the elevators are often broken, and the signs do not always reflect reality.

Chronosystem Compensation: The Brain

One more system described by Bronfenbrenner is the chronosystem, which includes both historical time and time over the life span. Effects on the brain from the chronosystem are numerous.

As Chapter 12 already explained, the brain shrinks with age. This is particularly notable in the hippocampus and the areas of the prefrontal cortex that are needed for planning, inhibiting unwanted responses, and coordinating thoughts (Rodrigue & Kennedy, 2011). Could this lead to selective optimization, with the brain developing the parts that are most needed?

Such compensation is suggested by research on elders who have experienced several falls. Their brains are enlarged in the hippocampus (memory for places) and somatosensory cortex (connecting senses and movement). The scientists write, "Falls may induce a compensatory increase in brain regions involved in multisensory integration and spatial navigation" (Allali et al., 2017).

As you remember, with age additional connections form and new neurons may be born. [**Life-Span Link:** Neurogenesis is introduced in Chapter 1.] Those new connections may compensate for less intense action in other areas of the brain. That is one explanation for an intriguing finding: When older people are presented with an intellectual task, they use more parts of their brain than younger people do. This often includes both hemispheres.

The chronosystem also considers the sweep of history. It may be that some intellectual capacities of the aged are advanced compared to people of similar ages a few centuries ago. Brains may have adapted to the social complexity of modern life. In the words of one researcher:

> Moving actively in a changing world and dealing with novelty and complexity regulate adult neurogenesis. New neurons might thus provide the cognitive adaptability to conquer ecological niches rich with challenging stimuli.
>
> *[Kempermann, 2012, p. 727]*

On a practical note, many of the elderly learn to deploy memory aids—the written reminder, the alarm clock, the routine, having "a place for everything and everything in its place." This need is recognized by many of the elderly themselves (Smarr et al., 2014).

DAVID MAXFIELD

Still Thinking New dendrites can lead to new ideas. Albert Bandura was a young scholar when he developed social learning theory to explain why preschoolers attacked a doll with a hammer. Here, at age 90, he signs copies of his most recent book that explains his theory of moral disengagement, in hopes that we can develop a more compassionate, humane society.

what have you learned?

1. How is it possible for older adults to have satisfying sex lives?
2. What can be done to maintain the independence of older drivers while reducing their risk of accidents?
3. How does selective optimization apply to decreases in the senses?
4. How would universal design affect an older person in your community?

Information Processing After Age 65

Particularly in late adulthood, cognition is variable, with some of the elderly quite sharp and others seemingly without any memory. A famous longitudinal study that began with 11-year-olds in Scotland who are now in their 80s and 90s reports that cognition over adulthood shows "a great divergence" with increasing variation with age (Underwood, October 31, 2014).

Some changes are universal. With each decade of adulthood, the volume of gray matter (crucial for processing new experiences) is reduced, as the cortex thins (Zhou et al., 2013). However, many people use their cognitive reserve to stave off serious impairment (Whalley et al., 2016). White matter generally is reduced as well. It also also increases in an odd way: Bright white spots appear on MRIs after age 50 or so.

What causes the diversity? Why do some adults grow increasingly wise with age while other adults have major losses? For all those in between, how much intellectual capacity is needed to function in everyday life?

INSIDE THE BRAIN

Thinking Slow

Senescence reduces the production of neurotransmitters, especially dopamine, that allow a nerve impulse to jump quickly across the synaptic gap from one neuron to another. Neural fluid decreases, myelination thins, cerebral blood circulates more slowly. The result is a slowdown, evident in reaction time, movement, speech, and thought.

This may be a serious problem, because speed is crucial for many aspects of cognition. In fact, some experts believe that processing speed is a basic element of *g* (see Chapter 12), underlying all other aspects of intelligence (Salthouse, 2004; Gow et al., 2011; Sandu et al., 2014).

Deterioration of cognition correlates with slower movement and almost every kind of physical disability. For example, gait speed correlates strongly with many measures of intellect (Hausdorff & Buchman, 2013). Walks slow? Talks slow? Oh no—thinks slow!

Indeed, researchers have studied the connection between walking speed and intellectual sharpness and found that the slower gait predicts cognitive impairment and brain disease (Montero-Odasso et al., 2017). Remember Jeanne Calment, the woman who lived to 122? Caregivers were astonished that she walked much faster after age 100 than most people in their 80s.

White-matter lesions increase the time it takes for a thought to be processed in the brain (Rodrigue & Kennedy,

◆ **Especially for People Who Are Proud of Their Intellect**
What can you do to keep your mind sharp all your life? (see response, page 533)

2011). Slowed transmission from one neuron to another is not the only problem. With age, transmission of impulses from entire regions of the brain, specifically from parts of the cortex and the cerebellum, is disrupted. Specifics correlate more with cognitive ability than with age (Bernard et al., 2013).

But wait—could there be ageism in this connection between speed and thought? Psychological tests are normed and validated based on younger adults. To avoid cultural bias, many questions are quite abstract and timed.

Some researchers suggest that the design of such tests may be unfair to the old, as abstractions are harder than more practical questions. One particular aspect is when the tests are given: Young brains are quicker in the afternoon, older brains in the morning (Maylor & Badham, 2018).

The crucial question is whether speed is essential for cognition. Our language connects the two. A smart person is said to be a *quick* thinker, the opposite of someone who is a *slow* learner. On the other hand, our culture questions those assumptions. A fable credited to Aesop, a Greek slave who lived 2,600 years ago, concerns a race between a tortoise and a hare. The rabbit lost: Slow and steady won the race.

Of course, older brains (as well as bodies) are slower than younger ones. But it is a mistake to expect cognition to be the same at every age and to focus only on losses over time. Slowness of thought may not be as crucial as people imagine, as Inside the Brain explains.

Given the complexity, variation, and diversity of late-life cognition, specific details are needed to combat general stereotypes. For this purpose, the information-processing approach is useful to examine input (sensing), memory (storage), control processes (programming), and output.

Input

The first step in information processing is input. Sensation precedes perception, which precedes comprehension. No sense is as sharp at age 65 as at age 15. In order to be perceived, information must cross the *sensory threshold*—the divide between what is sensed and what is not. Small sensory losses—not noticed by the person or family but inevitable with age—impair cognition.

Sensory losses may not be noticed because the brain automatically fills in missed sights and sounds, not always with complete accuracy. Elders miss some communication. For example, they are less accurate at knowing where someone is looking or

Atrophy Ranking

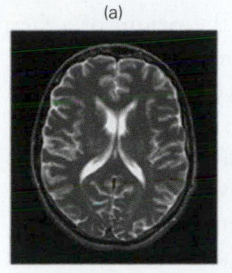
(a)
Lowest

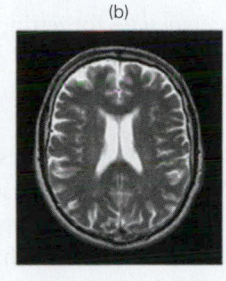
(b)
25th Percentile

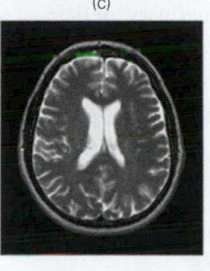
(c)
Median

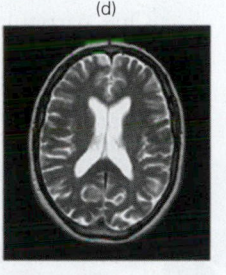
(d)
75th Percentile

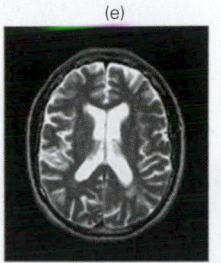
(e)
Highest

FROM FARRELL C, ET AL. DEVELOPMENT AND INITIAL TESTING OF NORMAL REFERENCE MR IMAGES FOR THE BRAIN AT AGES 65–70 AND 75–80 YEARS. EUROPEAN RADIOLOGY 2009;19: 177–183. COPYRIGHT J.M.WARDLAW.

Not All Average A team of neuroscientists in Scotland (Farrell et al., 2009) published these images of the brains of healthy 65- to 70-year-olds. The images show normal brain loss (the white areas) from the lowest (5th percentile) to the highest (95th percentile). Some atrophy is inevitable (even younger brains atrophy), but few elders are merely average.

what their facial expression means (Hughes & Devine, 2015). A study of point-light walkers (in the dark, the person sees only the lights on the joints) found that older adults were less accurate in judging movement and emotion, particularly of anger and sadness (J. Spencer et al., 2016).

Small hearing losses may make a difference. The cognition of almost 2,000 adults, average age 77, was repeatedly tested (Lin et al., 2013). An audiologist assessed their hearing. Between the start of the study and eleven years later, the average cognitive scores of the adults with hearing loss (who were often unaware of it) were down 7 percent; those with normal hearing lost 5 percent.

That 2-percent difference seems small, but statistically it was highly significant (.004). Furthermore, greater hearing losses correlated with greater cognitive declines (Lin et al., 2013). Many other researchers likewise find that small input losses have a notable effect on output.

There is an important qualifier here. Although every study of each sense in isolation finds significant input loss with age, one recent study found no loss in perception of emotion when the emotion was genuine (not produced by an actor, as in some standardized tests), and when participants could use three input sources (facial expressions, words, tone of voice) (Wieck & Kunzmann, 2017).

Memory

After input, information processing requires remembering what has been sensed. Stereotype threat impedes this. Simply knowing that they are taking a memory test makes older adults anxious, feeling years older (Hughes et al., 2013). More complex memory tasks (such as associative memory, connecting one idea with another) are particularly affected by stereotype threat (Brubaker & Naveh-Benjamin, 2018). [**Life-Span Link:** Stereotype threat is discussed in Chapter 11.]

Regarding memory, however, scientists now recognize that memory is not one function but many, each with a specific pattern of loss. Some age-related losses are quite typical and others are pathological (Markowitsch & Staniloiu, 2012).

Generally, explicit memory (recall of learned material) shows more loss than implicit memory (recognition and habits). This means that names are harder to

DOUG MCKINLAY/GETTY IMAGES

Keeping Alert These three men on a park bench in Malta are doing more than engaging in conversation; they are keeping their minds active through socialization and the discussion of current events and politics.

↑OBSERVATION QUIZ
Beyond conversation, what do you see that predicts cognition? (see answer, page 531)

remember than actions. Grandpa may still swim, bike, and drive, even if he cannot name both U.S. senators from his state.

One particular memory deficit is *source amnesia*—forgetting the origin of a fact, idea, or snippet of conversation. Source amnesia is particularly problematic currently, with uncensored Internet, many channels of television, and many printed sources bombarding the mind.

In practical terms, source amnesia means that elders might believe a rumor or political advertisement because they forget the biased source. Compensation requires deliberate attention to the reason behind a message before accepting a con artist's promises or the politics of a TV ad. However, elders are less likely than younger adults to analyze, or even notice, who said what and why (Boywitt et al., 2012).

A hot political debate in the United States is about "dark money," whereby financial contributions to political candidates are anonymous (Dawood, 2015). If dark money is banned, knowing the source will help, but older voters, with fragile source memory, may be less affected.

Another crucial type of memory is called *prospective memory*—remembering to do something in the future (to take a pill, to meet someone for lunch, to buy milk). Prospective memory also fades notably with age (Kliegel et al., 2008). This loss becomes dangerous if, for instance, a person cooking dinner forgets to turn off the stove, or if a driver is in the far lane of the highway when the exit appears.

Compensation or Crutch?
This phone is a speed dialer, able to quickly ring the people in the pictures. Other phones respond to voice commands. Is this type of technology helpful to the aging?

The crucial aspect of prospective memory seems to be the ability to shift the mind quickly from one task to another: Older adults get immersed in one thought and have trouble changing gears (Schnitzspahn et al., 2013). For that reason, many elders follow routine sequences (brush teeth, take medicine, get the paper) and set an alarm to remind them to leave for a doctor's appointment. That is compensation.

Thus far we have focused on what elders do not remember. But there are some things that are remembered well. Vocabulary is one example. Older people remember words, and languages, that they learned decades ago, and they continually learn new words and phrases.

For example, *Internet, smartphone, e-mail,* and *fax* appeared long after today's elders were young. With repeated hearing, most very old people understand and use these words, which demonstrates continued cognitive ability. The main problem with vocabulary is not in knowing what the words mean but in being able to recall a word on command. Control strategies are useful, such as allowing time, reducing stress, and using clues (remembering the first letter, remembering when that word was used, and many more).

◆◆ **Especially for Students**
If you want to remember something you learn in class for the rest of your life, what should you do? (see response, page 529)

Another crucial element is the person's experience. Thus, the current cohort of the elderly is more proficient in vocabulary than earlier generations were, probably because words—in the media and in social interaction—have become more important in the past decades (Hartshorne & Germine, 2015).

Control Processes

The next step in information processing involves control processes. Many scholars believe that the crucial impairment of cognition in late adulthood is in this step. Control processes include selective attention, strategic judgment, and then appropriate action—the so-called *executive function* of the brain.

ARNE DEDERT/AP IMAGES

Instead of using analysis and forethought, the elderly tend to rely on prior knowledge, general principles, familiarity, and rules of thumb as they make decisions (Peters et al., 2011), basing actions on past experiences and current emotions.

Inadequate control processes may explain why many older adults have extensive vocabularies (measured by written tests) but limited fluency (when they write or talk), why they are much better at recognition than recall, why tip-of-the-tongue forgetfulness is common, and why spelling is poorer than pronunciation. Efforts to improve their use of control strategies are successful, but only when the strategy is explicitly taught (B. Murray et al., 2015; Brom & Kliegel, 2014; McDaniel & Bugg, 2012).

BLOOMBERG/GETTY IMAGES

Output

The final step in information processing is output. Scientists usually measure output through use of standardized tests of mental ability. As already noted, if older adults think their memory is being tested, that alone awakens stereotype threat and impairs memory (Hughes et al., 2013). Even without stereotype threat, output on cognitive tests designed for the young may not reflect ability.

Since abstract thinking and processing speed are the aspects of cognition that fade most with age, is there a better way to measure output in late adulthood? Perhaps ability should be measured in everyday tasks and circumstances, not as laboratory tests assess it. To do measurements in everyday settings is to seek **ecological validity,** which may be particularly important when measuring cognition in the elderly.

For example, because of changes in their circadian rhythm, older adults are at their best in the early morning, when adolescents are half asleep. If a study were to compare 85-year-olds and 15-year-olds, both tested at 7 A.M., the teenagers would be at a disadvantage.

Or the opposite, if intellectual ability were assessed via a timed test, then faster thinkers (usually young) would score higher than slower thinkers (usually old), although the slower ones might be accurate with a few more seconds to think. Context matters, too: Who feels stressed if the tests occur on a college campus?

Indeed, age differences in prospective memory are readily apparent in laboratory tests but disappear in some naturalistic settings, a phenomenon called the *prospective memory paradox* (Schnitzspahn et al., 2011). Motivation seems crucial; elders are less likely to forget whatever they believe is important—phoning a child on his or her birthday, for instance.

Similarly, as already noted, older adults are not as accurate as younger adults when tested on the ability to read emotions by looking at someone's face or listening to someone's voice. Since seeing and hearing are less acute with age, that may not be the best way to measure empathy in older adults. Accordingly, a team decided to measure empathy when visual contact was impossible.

Their study included a hundred couples who had been together for years, and the participants were repeatedly asked to indicate their own emotions (how happy, enthusiastic, balanced, content, angry, downcast, disappointed, nervous they were) and to guess the emotions of their partner at that moment. Technology helped: The participants were beeped at various times and indicated their answers on a smartphone they kept with them. Sometimes they happened to be with their partner, sometimes not.

When the partner was present, accuracy was higher for the younger couples, presumably because they could see and hear their mate. But when the partner was absent, the older participants were as good as the younger ones (see Figure 14.5).

Active in the Community
One the best ways for the elderly to stay mentally active is to be active in their neighborhoods. Registering new voters, as this man is doing, benefits community while also helping seniors to maintain their control processes.

ecological validity
The idea that cognition should be measured in settings that are as realistic as possible and that the abilities measured should be those needed in real life.

macmillan learning

VIDEO: Old Age: Thinking and Moving at the Same Time features a research study demonstrating how older brains are quite adaptable.

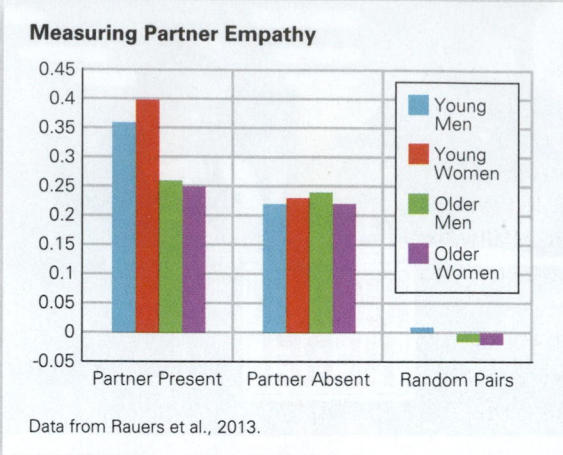

Measuring Partner Empathy

Legend:
- Young Men
- Young Women
- Older Men
- Older Women

Categories: Partner Present, Partner Absent, Random Pairs

Data from Rauers et al., 2013.

FIGURE 14.5 Always on My Mind When they were together, younger partners were more accurate than older ones at knowing their partner's emotions, but older partners were as good as younger ones when they were apart. This study used "smartphone experience sampling," buzzing both partners simultaneously to ask how they and their partner felt. Interestingly, differences were found with age but not length of relationship—5, 10, 20, or 30 years of togetherness did not necessarily increase empathy when apart, but men who were in their 70s were better at absent mood assessment than men in their 20s.

The authors asked if people could

> predict a social partner's feelings when that person is absent … although many abilities deteriorate with aging, this particular ability may remain reliable throughout your life.
>
> [Rauers et al., 2013, p. 2215]

The fundamental ecological issue for developmentalists is what should be assessed—pure, abstract thinking or practical, contextual thought; depersonalized abilities or everyday actions? Traditional tests of cognition emphasize fluid abilities, but problem solving and emotional sensitivity may be more crucial. Those practical abilities are not measured by traditional cognitive tests.

Awareness of the need for ecological validity has helped scientists restructure research on memory. Restructured studies find fewer deficits than originally thought. However, any test may overestimate or underestimate ability. For instance, what is an accurate test of long-term memory? Many older people recount, in vivid detail, events that occurred decades ago. That is impressive . . . if the memories are accurate.

Unfortunately, "there is no objective way to evaluate the degree of ecological validity . . . because ecological validity is a subjective concept" (Salthouse, 2010, p. 77). It is impossible to be totally objective in assessing memory; tests of memory always have a subjective component.

The final ecological question is "What is memory for?" Older adults usually think they remember well enough. Fear of memory loss is more typical at age 60 than at age 80, even though actual memory loss increases with age.

The old-old are correct in not fearing memory loss. Unless they develop a neurocognitive disorder such as Alzheimer's disease (soon described), they remember how to live their daily lives. Is that enough?

In daily life, output is usually verbal. If the timbre and speed of a person's speech sounds old, ageism might cause listeners to dismiss the content without realizing that the substance may be profound, or at least, no worse than it was decades ago.

If elders realize that what they say is ignored, they talk less. Output is diminished. This provides guidance for anyone who wants to respect and learn from someone else, perhaps a person from another culture, or ethnic group, or of another age. Listen carefully—the content may be more insightful than you think.

what have you learned?

1. How does sensory loss affect cognition?

2. Which kinds of things are harder to remember with age?

3. How might output be affected by the aging process?

4. What needs to be considered in ecologically valid measurement of adult intelligence?

5. What would be an ecologically valid test of cognition in late adulthood?

neurocognitive disorder (NCD) Any of a number of brain diseases that affect a person's ability to remember, analyze, plan, or interact with other people.

Neurocognitive Disorders

Most older people are less sharp than they once were, but they think and remember quite well. Others experience serious decline. They have a **neurocognitive disorder (NCD).**

The Ageism of Words

The rate of neurocognitive disorders increases with every decade after age 60, a fact that is distorted and exaggerated by ageism. To understand and prevent NCDs, we need to begin by using words carefully.

Senile simply means "old." If the word *senility* is used to mean "severe mental impairment," that would imply that old age always brings intellectual failure—an ageist myth. *Dementia* (used in DSM-IV) was a more precise term than *senility* for irreversible, pathological loss of brain functioning, but the Latin term *dementia* means "madness" or "insanity" and thus has inaccurate connotations.

The DSM-5 now describes neurocognitive disorders as either *major* (previously called *dementia*) or *mild* (previously called *mild cognitive impairment*). Mild cognitive impairment sometimes—but not certainly not always—precedes a neurocognitive disorder (Wakefield et al., 2018).

Memory problems occur in every cognitive disorder, although some people with NCDs have other notable symptoms, such as in judgment (they do foolish things) and moods (they are suddenly tearful or full of rage). The line between typical age-related changes, mild disorder, and major disorder is not clear, and symptoms vary depending on the specifics of both brain loss and context. Even when the disorder is major, the individual remains unique.

Many scientists seek biological indicators (called *biomarkers*, such as in the blood or cerebrospinal fluid) or brain indicators (as on brain scans) that predict major memory loss. None of these is completely accurate.

Prevalence of NCDs

How many people suffer from neurocognitive disorders in their older years? Young people might estimate 50 percent or more. A study of people already diagnosed with **major neurocognitive disorder (major NCD)** found much lower rates, about 8 percent of the aged population (Koller & Bynum, 2014).

The World Health Organization (March 2015) estimates that 47 million people are affected worldwide, 60 percent of them in low-income nations. In the poorest nations, as longevity increases, rates of major NCD rise. This has already occurred in China, where 9 million people had a serious NCD in 2010, compared to only 4 million in 1990 (K. Chan et al., 2013).

Worldwide, neurocognitive disorders are the most common cause of *morbidity* (the inability to function normally because of a disease or condition) and the second most common cause of death (Global Burden of Disease Neurological Disorders Collaborator Group, 2017).

Eventually, better education and public health will reduce the rate (if not the number) of neurocognitive disorders everywhere. In England and Wales, the rate of major NCD for people over age 65 was 8.3 percent in 1991 but only 6.5 percent in 2011 (Matthews et al., 2013). Sweden had a similar decline (Qiu et al., 2013). In China, rates are much higher in rural areas than in cities, perhaps because education and health care are more accessible in urban areas (Jia et al., 2014).

The Many Neurocognitive Disorders

As more is learned, it has become apparent that there are many types of brain disease, each beginning in a distinct part of the brain and having particular symptoms. Accordingly, we describe some of these disorders now.

ALZHEIMER'S DISEASE In the past century, millions of people in every large nation have been diagnosed with **Alzheimer's disease (AD)** (now formally referred

major neurocognitive disorder (major NCD)
Irreversible loss of intellectual functioning caused by organic brain damage or disease. Formerly called *dementia*, major NCD becomes more common with age, but it is abnormal and pathological even in the very old.

Alzheimer's disease (AD)
The most common cause of major NCD, characterized by gradual deterioration of memory and personality and marked by the formation of plaques of beta-amyloid protein and tangles of tau in the brain.

to as *major NCD due to Alzheimer's disease*). Severe and worsening memory loss is the main symptom, but the diagnosis is not definitive until an autopsy finds extensive plaques and tangles in the cerebral cortex (see Table 14.2).

Plaques are clumps of a protein called beta-amyloid in tissues surrounding the neurons; **tangles** are twisted masses of threads made of a protein called tau within the neurons. A normal brain contains some beta-amyloid and some tau, but in brains with AD these plaques and tangles proliferate, especially in the hippocampus. Forgetfulness is the dominant symptom, from momentary lapses to—after years of progressive disease—forgetting the names and faces of one's own children.

Alzheimer's disease is partly genetic. If it develops in middle age, the affected person either has trisomy-21 (Down syndrome) or has inherited one of three genes: amyloid precursor protein (APP), presenilin 1, or presenilin 2. The disease progresses quickly for these people, reaching the last phase within three to five years.

Most cases begin much later, at age 75 or so. Many genes have some impact, including SORL1 and ApoE4 (allele 4 of the ApoE gene). People who inherit one copy of ApoE4 (as about one-fifth of all U.S. residents do) have about a 50/50 chance of developing AD, with women more at risk than men (Altmann et al., 2014). Those who inherit two copies almost always develop the disorder if they live long enough.

VASCULAR DISEASE The second most common cause of neurocognitive disorder is a stroke (a temporary obstruction of a blood vessel in the brain) or a series of strokes, called *transient ischemic attacks* (*TIAs,* or *ministrokes*). The interruption in blood flow reduces oxygen, destroying part of the brain. Symptoms (blurred vision, weak or paralyzed limbs, slurred speech, and mental confusion) suddenly appear.

In a TIA, symptoms may vanish quickly, unnoticed. However, unless recognized and prevented, another TIA is likely, eventually causing **vascular disease,** formerly referred to as *vascular* or *multi-infarct dementia* (see Figure 14.6).

Vascular disease has many causes, none of which is the sole cause. It correlates with the ApoE4 allele (Cramer & Procaccio, 2012). For some of the elderly, vascular

The Alzheimer's Brain This computer graphic shows a vertical slice through a brain ravaged by Alzheimer's disease *(left)* compared with a similar slice of a normal brain *(right)*. The diseased brain is shrunken because neurons have degenerated. The red indicates plaques and tangles.

A. PAKIEKA / SCIENCE SOURCE

plaques
Clumps of a protein called beta-amyloid, found in brain tissue surrounding the neurons.

tangles
Twisted masses of threads made of a protein called tau within the neurons of the brain.

vascular disease
(formerly called *vascular* or *multi-infarct dementia*) Vascular disease is characterized by sporadic, and progressive, loss of intellectual functioning caused by repeated infarcts, or temporary obstructions of blood vessels, which prevent sufficient blood from reaching the brain.

In **VIDEO ACTIVITY: Alzheimer's Disease,** experts and family members discuss the progression of the disease.

TABLE 14.2 Stages of Alzheimer's Disease

Stage 1. People in the first stage forget recent events or new information, particularly names and places. For example, they might forget the name of a famous film star or how to get home from a familiar place. This first stage is similar to mild cognitive impairment—even experts cannot always tell the difference. In retrospect, it seems clear that President Ronald Reagan had early AD while in office, but no doctor diagnosed it.

Stage 2. Generalized confusion develops, with deficits in concentration and short-term memory. Speech becomes aimless and repetitious, vocabulary is limited, words get mixed up. Personality traits are not curbed by rational thought. For example, suspicious people may decide that others have stolen the things that they themselves have mislaid.

Stage 3. Memory loss becomes dangerous. Although people at stage 3 can care for themselves, they might leave a lit stove or hot iron on or might forget whether they took essential medicine and thus take it twice—or not at all.

Stage 4. At this stage, full-time care is needed. People cannot communicate well. They might not recognize their closest loved ones.

Stage 5. Finally, people with AD become unresponsive. Identity and personality have disappeared. When former president Ronald Reagan was at this stage, a longtime friend who visited him was asked, "Did he recognize you?" The friend answered, "Worse than that—I didn't recognize him." Death comes 10 to 15 years after the first signs appear.

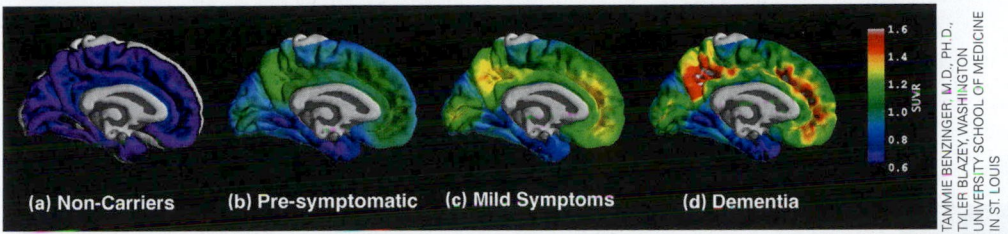

(a) Non-Carriers   (b) Pre-symptomatic   (c) Mild Symptoms   (d) Dementia

TAMMIE BENZINGER, M.D., PH.D., TYLER BLAZEY, WASHINGTON UNIVERSITY SCHOOL OF MEDICINE IN ST. LOUIS

Hopeful Brains Even the brain without symptoms *(a)* might eventually develop Alzheimer's disease, but people with a certain dominant gene definitely will. They have no symptoms in early adulthood *(b)*, some symptoms in middle adulthood *(c)*, and stage-five Alzheimer's disease *(d)* before old age. Research finds early brain markers (such as those shown here) that predict the disease. This is not always accurate, but it may soon lead to early treatment that halts AD, not only in those genetically vulnerable but also in everyone.

disease is caused by surgery that requires general anesthesia. They suffer a ministroke, which, added to reduced cognitive reserve, damages their brains (Y. Stern, 2013).

FRONTOTEMPORAL DISORDERS Several types of neurocognitive disorders affect the frontal lobes and thus are called **frontotemporal NCDs,** or *frontotemporal lobar degeneration.* (Pick disease is the most common form.) These disorders cause perhaps 15 percent of all cases of NCDs in the United States. Frontotemporal NCDs tend to begin before age 70, unlike Alzheimer's or vascular disease (Seelaar et al., 2011).

In frontotemporal NCDs, parts of the brain that regulate emotions and social behavior (especially the amygdala and prefrontal cortex) deteriorate. Emotional and personality changes are the main symptoms (Seelaar et al., 2011). A loving mother with a frontotemporal NCD might reject her children, or a formerly astute businessman might invest in a foolish scheme.

Frontal lobe problems may be worse than more obvious types of neurocognitive disorders in that compassion, self-awareness, and judgment fade in a person who otherwise seems normal. One wife, Ruth French, was furious because her husband

> threw away tax documents, got a ticket for trying to pass an ambulance and bought stock in companies that were obviously in trouble. Once a good cook, he burned every pot in the house. He became withdrawn and silent, and no longer spoke to his wife over dinner. That same failure to communicate got him fired from his job.
>
> [D. Grady, 2012, p. A1]

Finally, he was diagnosed with a frontotemporal NCD. Ruth asked him to forgive her fury. It is not clear that he understood either her anger or her apology.

Although there are many forms and causes of frontotemporal NCDs—including a dozen or so alleles—they usually progress rapidly, leading to death in about five years.

OTHER DISORDERS Many other brain diseases begin with impaired motor control (shaking when picking up a coffee cup, falling when trying to walk), not with impaired thinking. The most common of these is **Parkinson's disease,** the cause of about 3 percent of all cases of NCDs.

Parkinson's disease starts with rigidity or tremor of the muscles as dopamine-producing neurons degenerate, affecting movement long before cognition. Middle-aged adults with Parkinson's disease usually have sufficient cognitive reserve to avoid major intellectual loss, although about one-third have mild cognitive decline (S. Gao et al., 2014).

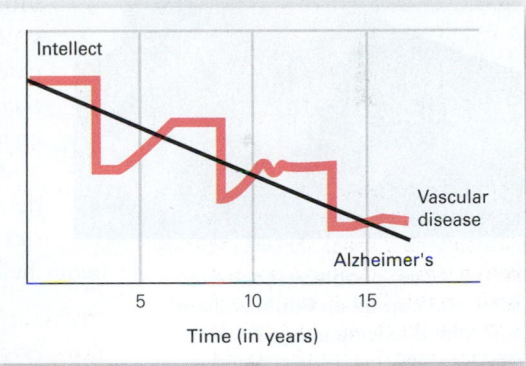

FIGURE 14.6 The Progression of Alzheimer's Disease and Vascular Disease Cognitive decline is apparent in both Alzheimer's disease (AD) and vascular disease (VaD). However, the pattern of decline for each disease is different. Individuals with AD show steady, gradual decline, while those with VaD get suddenly much worse, improve somewhat, and then experience another serious loss.

frontotemporal NCDs
Deterioration of the amygdala and frontal lobes that may be the cause of 15 percent of all major neurocognitive disorders. (Also called *frontotemporal lobar degeneration.*)

Parkinson's disease
A chronic, progressive disease that is characterized by muscle tremor and rigidity and sometimes major neurocognitive disorder; caused by reduced dopamine production in the brain.

Lewy body disease
A form of major neurocognitive disorder characterized by an increase in Lewy body cells in the brain. Symptoms include visual hallucinations, momentary loss of attention, falling, and fainting.

JASON KEMPIN/GETTY IMAGES

Why? Many people wonder why actor and comedian Robin Williams committed suicide at age 63. One explanation: He was in the early stages of a serious neurocognitive disorder. Williams was diagnosed with Parkinson's disease a few months before he died, but an autopsy revealed Lewy body disease, whose symptoms include loss of inhibition, severe anxiety, tremors, and difficulty reasoning.

Older people with Parkinson's develop cognitive problems sooner (Pfeiffer & Bodis-Wollner, 2012). If people with Parkinson's live ten years or more, almost always major neurocognitive impairment occurs (Pahwa & Lyons, 2013).

Another 3 percent of people with NCD in the United States suffer from **Lewy body disease:** excessive deposits of a particular kind of protein in their brains. Lewy bodies are also present in Parkinson's disease, but in Lewy body disease they are more numerous and dispersed throughout the brain, interfering with communication between neurons. The main symptom is loss of inhibition: A person might gamble or become hypersexual.

Comorbidity (several illnesses) is common with all of these disorders. For instance, most people with Alzheimer's disease also show signs of vascular impairment (Doraiswamy, 2012). Parkinson's, Alzheimer's, and Lewy body diseases can occur together: People who have all three experience more rapid and severe cognitive loss (Compta et al., 2011).

Some other types of NCDs begin in middle age or even earlier, caused by Huntington's disease, multiple sclerosis, a severe head injury, or the last stages of syphilis, AIDS, or bovine spongiform encephalopathy (BSE, or mad cow disease). Repeated blows to the head, even without concussions, can cause *chronic traumatic encephalopathy (CTE),* which first causes memory loss and emotional changes (Voosen, 2013).

Although the rate of systemic brain disease increases dramatically with every decade after age 60, brain disease can occur at any age, as revealed by the autopsies of a number of young professional athletes. For them, prevention includes better helmets and fewer body blows. Already, tackling is avoided in football practice.

Preventing Impairment

Severe brain damage cannot be reversed, although the rate of decline and some of the symptoms can be treated. However, education, exercise, and good health not only ameliorate mild losses but also may prevent worse ones.

Prevention seems to be happening: "A growing number of studies, at least nine over the past ten years, have shown a declining risk for dementia incidence or prevalence in high-income countries, including the US, England, The Netherlands, Sweden, and Denmark" (Langa, 2015, p. 34).

Because brain plasticity is lifelong, exercise that improves blood circulation not only prevents cognitive loss but also builds capacity and repairs damage. The benefits of exercise have been repeatedly cited in this text. Now we simply reiterate that physical exercise—even more than good nutrition and mental exercise—prevents, postpones, and slows cognitive loss of all kinds (Erickson et al., 2012; Gregory et al., 2012; Lövdén et al., 2013).

Medication to prevent strokes also protects against neurocognitive disorders. In a Finnish study, half of a large group of older Finns were given drugs to reduce lipids in their system (primarily cholesterol). Years later, fewer of them had developed NCDs than did a comparable group who were not given the drug (Solomon et al., 2010).

Avoiding specific pathogens is critical. For example, beef can be tested to ensure that it does not have BSE, condoms can protect against HIV/AIDS, and syphilis can be cured with antibiotics.

For most neurocognitive disorders, however, despite the efforts of thousands of scientists and millions of older people, no foolproof prevention or cure has been found. Avoiding toxins (lead, aluminum, copper, and pesticides) or adding supplements (hormones, aspirin, coffee, insulin, antioxidants, red wine, blueberries, and statins) have been tried as preventatives but have not proven effective in controlled, scientific research.

Thousands of scientists have sought to halt the production of beta-amyloid, and they have had some success in mice but not yet in humans. One current goal is to diagnose Alzheimer's disease ten or fifteen years before the first outward signs appear in order to prevent brain damage. That is one reason for the interest in mild NCDs: They often (though not always) progress to major problems. If it were known why some mild losses do not lead to major ones, prevention might be possible.

Among professionals, hope is replacing despair. Earlier diagnosis seems possible; many drug and lifestyle treatments are under review. "Measured optimism" (Moye, 2015, p. 331) comes from contemplating the success that has been achieved in combating other diseases. Heart attacks, for instance, were once the leading cause of death for middle-aged men. No longer.

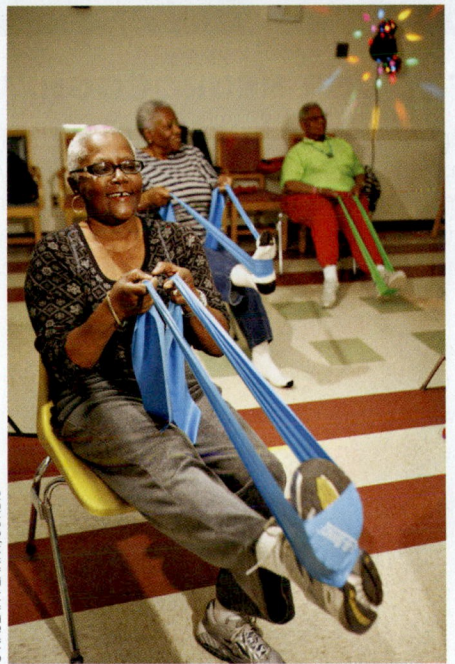

Same Situation, Far Apart: Strong Legs, Long Life As this woman in a Brooklyn seniors center *(left)* and this man on a Greek beach *(right)* seem to realize, exercise that strengthens the legs is particularly beneficial for body, mind, and spirit in late adulthood.

Reversible Neurocognitive Disorder?

Care improves when everyone knows what disease is undermining intellectual capacity. Accurate diagnosis is even more crucial when memory problems do not arise from a neurocognitive disorder. Brain diseases destroy parts of the brain, but some people are thought to be permanently "losing their minds" when a reversible condition is really at fault.

DEPRESSION The most common reversible condition that is mistaken for major NCD is depression. Normally, older people tend to be quite happy; frequent sadness or anxiety is not normal. Ongoing, untreated depression increases the risk of major NCD (Y. Gao et al., 2013).

Ironically, people with untreated anxiety or depression may exaggerate minor memory losses or refuse to talk. Quite the opposite reaction occurs with early Alzheimer's disease, when victims are often surprised that they cannot answer questions, or with Lewy body disease or frontotemporal NCDs, when people talk too much without thinking. Talk, or lack of it, provides an important clue.

Specifics provide other clues. People with neurocognitive loss might forget what they just said, heard, or did because current brain activity is impaired, but they might repeatedly describe details of something that happened long ago. The opposite may be true for emotional disorders, when memory of the past is impaired but short-term memory is not.

MALNUTRITION Malnutrition and dehydration can also cause symptoms that may seem like brain disease. The aging digestive system is less efficient but needs more nutrients and fewer calories. This requires new habits, less fast food, and more grocery money (which many do not have).

Visualizing Development

GLOBAL PREVALENCE OF MAJOR NEUROCOGNITIVE DISORDERS

Major neurocognitive disorder refers to several diseases, with Alzheimer's disease the most common. Estimates of the prevalence and number of people with major NCD vary depending on how studies are conducted, but numbers are increasing in most parts of the world, as more people live to their 80s and 90s. Rates are quite low in some places, such as sub-Saharan Africa, but that might be because most people die before they are very old. In developed nations, by contrast, a person could have major NCD and live a decade or longer.

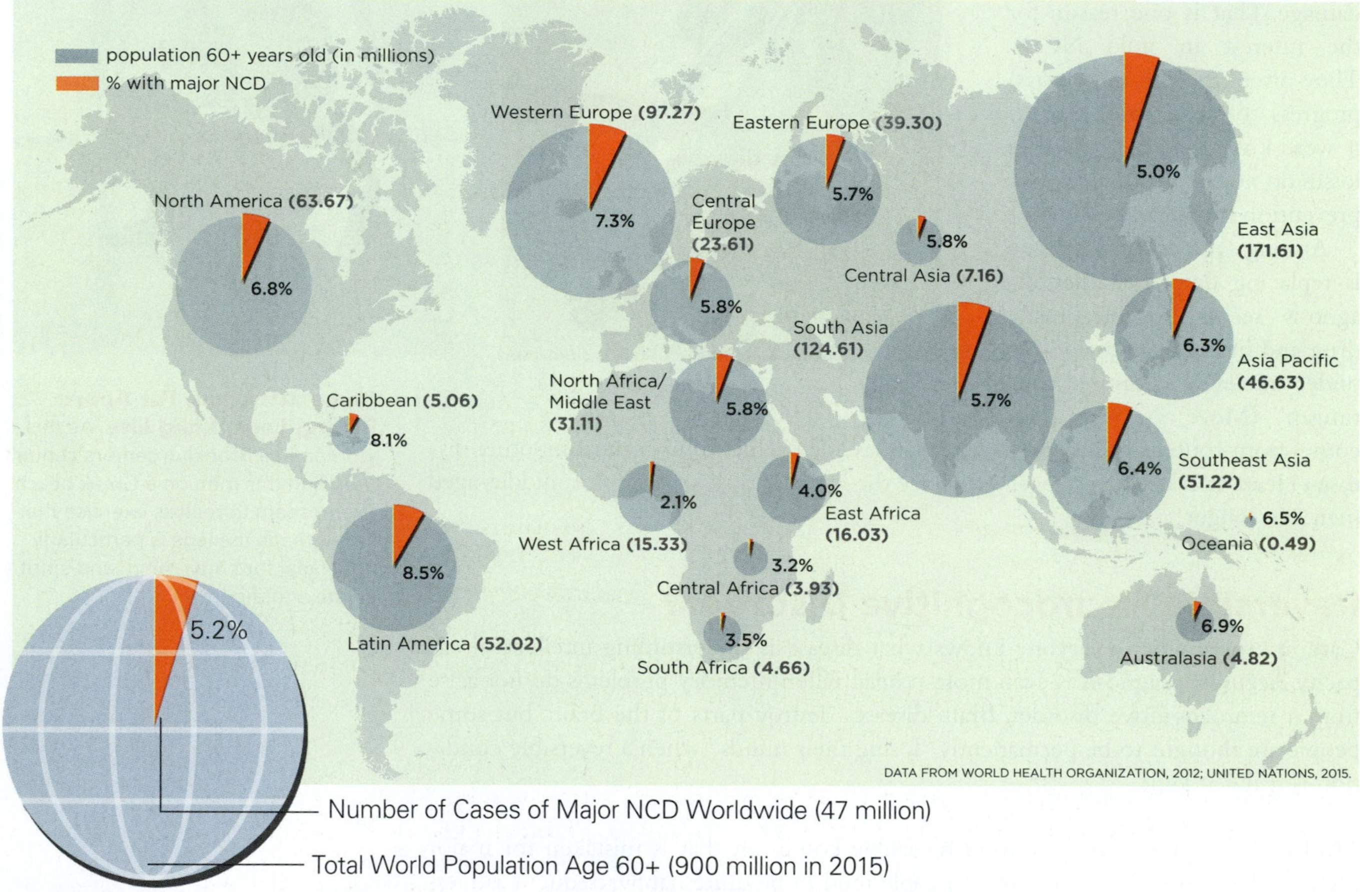

population 60+ years old (in millions)
% with major NCD

Western Europe (97.27) **7.3%**

Eastern Europe (39.30) **5.7%**

Central Europe (23.61) **5.8%**

Central Asia (7.16) **5.8%**

East Asia (171.61) **5.0%**

North America (63.67) **6.8%**

Asia Pacific (46.63) **6.3%**

Caribbean (5.06) **8.1%**

North Africa/Middle East (31.11) **5.8%**

South Asia (124.61) **5.7%**

Southeast Asia (51.22) **6.4%**

West Africa (15.33) **2.1%**

East Africa (16.03) **4.0%**

Oceania (0.49) **6.5%**

Latin America (52.02) **8.5%**

Central Africa (3.93) **3.2%**

South Africa (4.66) **3.5%**

Australasia (4.82) **6.9%**

5.2%

DATA FROM WORLD HEALTH ORGANIZATION, 2012; UNITED NATIONS, 2015.

Number of Cases of Major NCD Worldwide (47 million)

Total World Population Age 60+ (900 million in 2015)

How Will the Numbers Change in Decades to Come?

It is impossible to project future rates of neurocognitive disorders, since many scientists and doctors are trying to understand causes and cures, and many older people are trying to reduce their risk. However, one risk—old age—will increase. As more people reach age 80 and above, more people will experience major NCD of one kind or another.

Health Care Costs Associated with Major NCD

Alzheimer's disease and other major NCDs are among the costliest chronic diseases to society: Individuals with a major NCD have more hospital and skilled nursing facility stays and home health care visits than other older people. However, the human cost may be greater than these estimates: Many family members spend substantial time caring for people with major NCDs, but often that time is not calculated until the NCD is severe.

The Health Care Providers

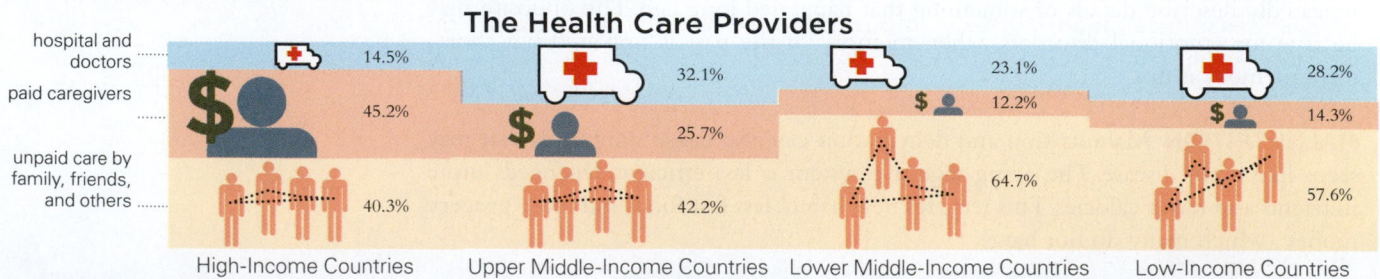

	High-Income Countries	Upper Middle-Income Countries	Lower Middle-Income Countries	Low-Income Countries
hospital and doctors	14.5%	32.1%	23.1%	28.2%
paid caregivers	45.2%	25.7%	12.2%	14.3%
unpaid care by family, friends, and others	40.3%	42.2%	64.7%	57.6%

DATA FROM WORLD HEALTH ORGANIZATION, 2012; UNITED NATIONS, 2015.

Some elderly people deliberately drink less because they want to avoid frequent urination, yet inadequate fluid in the body impedes cell health. Since homeostasis slows with age, older people are less likely to recognize and remedy their hunger and thirst, and thus they may inadvertently impair their cognition.

Beyond the need to drink water and eat vegetables, several specific vitamins may stave off cognitive impairment. Among the suggested foods to add are those containing antioxidants (vitamins C, A, E) and vitamin B_{12}. Homocysteine (from animal fat) may need to be avoided, since high levels correlate with major NCD (Perez et al., 2012; Whalley et al., 2014). Psychoactive drugs, especially alcohol, can cause confusion and hallucinations at much lower doses than in the young.

Obviously, any food that increases the risk of heart disease and stroke also increases the risk of vascular disease. In addition, some prescribed drugs destroy certain nutrients, although specifics require more research (Jyrkkä et al., 2012).

Indeed, well-controlled longitudinal research on the relationship between particular aspects of nutrition and NCD has not been done (Coley et al., 2015). It is known, however, that people who already suffer from NCD tend to forget to eat or tend to choose unhealthy foods, hastening their mental deterioration. It is also known that alcohol abuse interferes with nutrition, directly (reducing eating and hydration) and indirectly (blocking vitamin absorption).

POLYPHARMACY At home as well as in the hospital, most elderly people take numerous drugs—not only prescribed medications but also over-the-counter preparations and herbal remedies—a situation known as **polypharmacy.** Excessive reliance on drugs can occur on doctor's orders as well as via patient ignorance.

The rate of polypharmacy is increasing in the United States. For instance, in 1988 the number of people over age 65 who took five drugs or more was 13 percent; by 2015 that number had tripled to 38 percent (National Center for Health Statistics, 2017).

Unfortunately, recommended doses of many drugs are determined primarily by clinical trials with younger adults, for whom homeostasis usually eliminates excess medication (Herrera et al., 2010). When homeostasis slows down, excess lingers. In addition, most trials to test the safety of a new drug exclude people who have more than one disease. That means drugs are not tested on the people who will use them most.

The average elderly person in the United States sees a physician eight times a year (National Center for Health Statistics, 2017). Typically, each doctor follows "clinical practice guidelines," which are recommendations for one specific condition. A "prescribing cascade" (when many interacting drugs are prescribed) may occur.

In one disturbing case, a doctor prescribed medication to raise his patient's blood pressure, and another doctor, noting the raised blood pressure, prescribed a drug to lower it (McLendon & Shelton, 2011–2012). Usually, doctors ask patients what medications they are taking and why, which could prevent such an error. However, people who are sick and confused may not give accurate responses.

A related problem is that people of every age forget when to take which drugs (before, during, or after meals? after dinner or at bedtime?) (Bosworth & Ayotte, 2009). Short-term memory loss makes this worse, and poverty cuts down on pill purchases.

Even when medications are taken as prescribed and the right dose reaches the bloodstream, drug interactions can cause confusion and memory loss. Cognitive side effects can occur with almost any drug, but especially with drugs intended to reduce anxiety and depression.

The solution seems simple: Discontinue drugs. However, that may increase both disease and cognitive decline. One expert warns of polypharmacy but adds that "underuse of medications in older adults can have comparable adverse effects on quality of life" (Miller, 2011–2012, p. 21).

polypharmacy
A situation in which elderly people are prescribed several medications. The various side effects and interactions of those medications can result in symptoms typical of major neurocognitive disorder.

And That's Not All This 82-year-old man is shown with eight of his pill bottles. That polypharmacy alone causes side effects and drug interactions. Added to that are what he eats and drinks, including substances that might interfere with his medication.

For instance, untreated diabetes and hypertension cause cognitive loss. Lack of drug treatment for those conditions may be one reason why low-income elders experience more illness, more cognitive impairment, and earlier death than do high-income elders: They may not be able to afford good medical care or life-saving drugs.

Obviously, money complicates the issue: Prescription drugs are expensive, which increases profits for drug companies, but they can also reduce surgery and hospitalization, thus saving money. As one observer notes, the discussion about spending for prescription drugs is highly polarized, emotionally loaded, with little useful debate. A war is waged over the cost of prescriptions for older people, and it is a "gloves-off, stab-you-in-the-guts, struggle to the death" (Sloan, 2011–2012, p. 56).

what have you learned?

1. How does changing terminology reflect changing attitudes?
2. What changes in the prevalence of neurocognitive disorders have occurred in recent years?
3. What indicates that Alzheimer's disease is partly genetic?
4. How does the progression of Alzheimer's differ from that of vascular disease?
5. In what ways are frontotemporal NCDs worse than Alzheimer's disease?
6. Why is Lewy body disease sometimes mistaken for Parkinson's disease?
7. How successful are scientists at preventing major NCD?
8. What is the relationship between depression, anxiety, and neurocognitive disorders?
9. Why is polypharmacy particularly common among the elderly?

New Cognitive Development

You have learned that most older adults maintain adequate intellectual power. Some losses—in rapid reactions, for instance—are quite manageable, and most elders never experience a serious neurocognitive disorder.

Beyond that, the life-span perspective holds that gains as well as losses occur during every period. [**Life-Span Link:** The multi-directional characteristic of development is discussed in Chapter 1.] Are there cognitive gains in late adulthood? Yes, according to many developmentalists. New depth, enhanced creativity, and even wisdom are possible.

Erikson and Maslow

Both Erik Erikson and Abraham Maslow were particularly interested in the elderly, interviewing older people to understand their views. Erikson's final book, *Vital Involvement in Old Age* (Erikson et al., 1986/1994), written when he was in his 90s, was based on responses from other 90-year-olds—the cohort who had been studied since they were babies in Berkeley, California.

Erikson found that in old age many people gained interest in the arts, in children, and in human experience as a whole. He observed that elders are "social witnesses," aware of the interdependence of the generations as well as of all human experience. His eighth stage, *integrity versus despair,* marks the time when life comes together in a "resynthesis of all the resilience and toughness of the basic strengths already developed" (Erikson et al., 1986/1994, p. 40).

Maslow maintained that older adults are more likely than younger people to reach what he originally thought was the highest stage of development, **self-actualization.** Remember that Maslow rejected an age-based sequence of life, refusing to confine self-actualization to the old. However, Maslow also believed that life experience helps people move forward, so more of the old reach the final stage.

The stage of self-actualization is characterized by aesthetic, creative, philosophical, and spiritual understanding (Maslow, 1954/1997). A self-actualized person might have a deeper spirituality than ever; might be especially appreciative of nature; or might find life more amusing, laughing often.

This seems characteristic of many of the elderly. Studies of centenarians find that they often have a deep spiritual grounding and a surprising sense of humor—surprising, that is, if one assumes that people with limited sight, poor hearing, and frequent pain have nothing to laugh about.

Life Gets Better This couple has reached the time in their lives when having a beer in an outdoor cafe while checking the Internet is not only possible but also joyous. Not every older man is happy in late adulthood, but increasing self-actualization and laughter is common.

Learning Late in Life

Many people have tried to improve the intellectual abilities of older adults by teaching or training them in various tasks. Success has been reported in specific abilities, but not usually overall. In one part of the Seattle Longitudinal Study, 60-year-olds who had lost some spatial understanding had five sessions of personalized training and practice. As a result, they returned to the skill level of fourteen years earlier (Schaie, 2005/2013).

One intriguing strategy is using video games to develop perceptual skills and thus advance cognition. Although there are many variables that increase the effectiveness of this strategy, cognition benefits sometimes occur when people in their 60s and 70s are challenged to think quickly and pay attention (Bier et al., 2018).

Similar results have been found in many nations in which elders have been taught a specific skill. As a result, almost all researchers have accepted the conclusion that people younger than 80 can advance in cognition if the educational process is carefully targeted to their motivation and ability.

For instance, in one study in southern Europe, people who were cognitively typical but were living in senior residences were taught memory strategies and attended motivational discussions to help them understand why and how memory was important for daily functioning. Their memory improved compared to a control group, and the improvements were still evident six months later (Vranić et al., 2013).

What about the oldest-old? Learning is more difficult for them, but it is still possible. The older people are, the harder it is for them to master new skills and then apply what they know (Stine-Morrow & Basak, 2011). Older adults sometimes learn cognitive strategies and skills and maintain that learning if the strategies and skills are frequently used, but they may quickly forget new learning if it is not applied (Park & Bischof, 2013). They revert back to familiar, and often inferior, cognitive patterns.

Let's return to the question of cognitive gains in late adulthood. In many nations, education programs have been created for the old, called Universities for the Third Age in Europe and Australia, and Road Scholar (formerly Exploritas, or Elderhostel) in the United States.

There is a growing body of research on teaching older people. One aspect is that they have a wide range of needs and motivations: Some want intellectually challenging courses, and others want practical skills (Villar & Celdrán, 2012). All of the research finds that, when motivated, older adults can learn.

self-actualization
The final stage in Maslow's hierarchy of needs, characterized by aesthetic, creative, philosophical, and spiritual understanding.

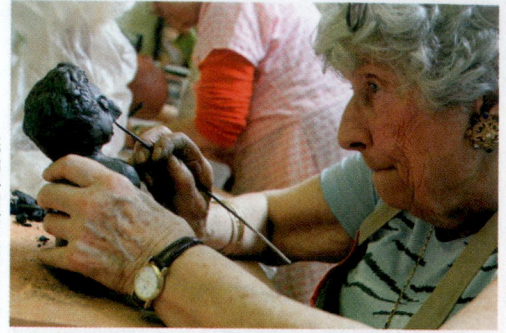

Exercise and the Mind

Creative activity may improve the intellect, especially when it involves social activity. Both the woman in a French ceramics class *(top)*, subsidized by the government for residents of Grenoble over age 60, and the man playing the tuba in a band in Cuba *(bottom)* are gaining much more than the obvious finger or lung exercise.

life review

An examination of one's own role in the history of human life, engaged in by many elderly people. This can be written or oral.

In **VIDEO: Portrait of Aging: Bill, Age 99,** one man shares his secret to longevity.

Aesthetic Sense and Creativity

Robert Butler was a geriatrician responsible for popularizing the study of aging in the United States. He coined the word "ageism" and wrote a book entitled *Why Survive: Being Old in America,* first published in 1975. Partly because his grandparents were crucial in his life, Butler understood that society needs to recognize the potential of the elderly.

Butler explained that "old age can be a time of emotional sensory awareness and enjoyment" (Butler et al., 1998, p. 65). For example, some of the elderly take up gardening, bird-watching, sculpting, painting, or making music, even if they have never done so before. Others have more time to pursue interests they have always had.

ELDERLY ARTISTS Many well-known artists continue to work in late adulthood, sometimes producing their best work. Michelangelo painted the awe-inspiring frescoes in the Sistine Chapel at age 75; Verdi composed the opera *Falstaff* when he was 80; Frank Lloyd Wright completed the design of New York City's Guggenheim Museum when he was 91.

In a study of extraordinarily creative people, very few felt that their ability, their goals, or the quality of their work had been much impaired by age. The leader of that study observed, "In their seventies, eighties, and nineties, they may lack the fiery ambition of earlier years, but they are just as focused, efficient, and committed as before . . . perhaps more so" (Csikszentmihalyi, 2013, p. 207).

But an older artist does not need to be extraordinarily talented. Some of the elderly learn to play an instrument, and many enjoy singing. In China, people gather spontaneously in public parks to sing together. The groups are intergenerational—but a disproportionate number are elderly (Wei, 2013).

Music and singing are often used to reduce anxiety in those who suffer from neurocognitive impairment, because the ability to appreciate music is preserved in the brain when other functions fail (Sacks, 2008; Ueda et al., 2013). Many experts believe that creative activities—poetry and pottery, jewelry making and quilting, music and sculpture—can benefit all of the elderly (Flood & Phillips, 2007; Malchiodi, 2012). Artistic expression may aid social skills, resilience, and even brain health (McFadden & Basting, 2010).

Research has focused particularly on those of the elderly who have some cognitive deficits (a focus itself that may be ageist). The evidence is clear: Music, visual arts, and creative work of all kinds help one's mind, mood, and overall well-being (Charise & Eginton, 2018).

One particular method often used is called the **life review.** In a life review, elders provide an account of their personal journey by writing or telling their story. They want others to know their history, not only their personal experiences but also those of their family, cohort, or ethnic group. According to Robert Butler:

> We have been taught that this nostalgia represents living in the past and a preoccupation with self and that it is generally boring, meaningless, and time-consuming. Yet as a natural healing process it represents one of the underlying human capacities on which all psychotherapy depends. The life review should be recognized as a necessary and healthy process in daily life as well as a useful tool in the mental health care of older people.
>
> *[Butler et al., 1998, p. 91]*

Hundreds of developmentalists, picking up on Butler's suggestions, have guided elderly people in self-review. Sometimes the elderly write down their thoughts, and sometimes they simply tell their story, responding to questions from the listener.

The result of the life review is almost always quite positive, especially for the person who tells the story. For instance, half of 202 elderly people in the Netherlands were randomly assigned to a life review process. For them, depression and anxiety were markedly reduced compared to the control group (Korte et al., 2012). A study of elders in the United States also found that telling their story helped them see a purpose in life—just what Erikson would hope (Robinson & Murphy-Nugen, 2018).

Wisdom

Is it possible that "older adults . . . understand who they are in a newly emerging stage of life, and discover the wisdom that they have to offer" (Bateson, 2011, p. 9)? A massive international survey of 26 nations from every corner of the world found that most people everywhere agree that wisdom is a characteristic of the elderly (Löckenhoff et al., 2009).

Contrary to these wishes and opinions, most objective research finds that wisdom does not necessarily increase with age. Starting at age 25 or so, some adults of every age are wise, but most, even at age 80, are not (Staudinger & Glück, 2011).

An underlying quandary is that a universal definition of wisdom is elusive: Each culture and each cohort has its own concept, with fools sometimes seeming wise (as happens in Shakespearean drama) and those who are supposed to be wise sometimes acting foolishly (provide your own examples). Older and younger adults differ in how they make decisions; one interpretation of these differences is that the older adults are wiser, but not every younger adult would agree (Worthy et al., 2011).

Several factors just mentioned, including self-reflective honesty (as in integrity), perspective on past living (the life review), and the ability to put aside one's personal needs (as in self-actualization), are considered part of wisdom.

If this is true, the elderly may have an advantage in developing wisdom, particularly if they have (1) dedicated their lives to the "understanding of life," (2) learned from their experiences, and (3) become more mature and integrated (Ardelt, 2011, p. 283). That may be why religious leaders and U.S. Supreme Court justices are usually quite old.

As two psychologists explain:

> Wisdom is one domain in which some older individuals excel. . . . [They have] a combination of psychosocial characteristics and life history factors, including openness to experience, generativity, cognitive style, contact with excellent mentors, and some exposure to structured and critical life experiences.
>
> [Baltes & Smith, 2008, p. 60]

These researchers posed life dilemmas to adults of various ages and asked others (who had no clue as to how old the participants were) to judge whether the responses were wise. They found that wisdom is rare at any age, but, unlike physical strength and cognitive quickness, wisdom does not fade with maturity.

Thus, some people of every age were judged as wise. A review of personality development over adulthood found that some people become wiser, but not everyone (Reitz & Staudinger, 2017). This returns us to a theme often seen in this chapter—late adulthood is a time of marked variation, a theme continued in Chapter 15. You need to define wisdom and decide who has it.

Wise or Foolish? Your opinion depends primarily on how you evaluate motorcycle transportation—as a more enjoyable and less expensive way to navigate the road, or dangerous and uncomfortable. Your evaluation could indicate wisdom—possible at any age but hard for anyone to define.

Long Past Warring Many of the oldest men in Mali, like this imam, are revered. Unfortunately, Mali has experienced violent civil wars and two national coups in recent years, perhaps because 75 percent of the male population are under age 30 and less than 2 percent are over age 70.

what have you learned?

1. What do Erikson and Maslow say about cognitive development in late adulthood?

2. What happens with creative ability as people grow older?

3. What is the special role of music in old age?

4. Why is the life review beneficial?

5. Why are scientists hesitant to say that wisdom comes from old age?

SUMMARY

New Understanding of Old Age

1. An increasing percentage of the population is older than 64, but the numbers are sometimes presented in misleading ways. Currently, about 15 percent of people in the U.S. population are elderly, and most of them are self-sufficient and productive.

2. Hundreds of theories address the causes of aging. The most common are theories of wear and tear, of genes, and of cellular change. All seem plausible, but none seems sufficient.

3. One attempt to stop the aging process is calorie restriction. That seems to benefit health and prolong life in many species, but experts are conflicted as to whether it would be useful for people.

4. Contrary to ageist stereotypes, most older adults are happy, quite healthy, and active. Benevolent as well as dismissive ageism reduces health and self-image, as elderspeak illustrates.

Selective Optimization with Compensation

5. Sexual intercourse occurs less often, driving a car becomes more difficult, and the senses all become less acute for older adults. However, selective optimization with compensation can mitigate almost any loss. A combination of personal determination, adjustment by society, and medical research is needed.

6. Speed of processing slows down, parts of the brain shrink, and more areas of the brain are activated in older people. New neurons may form, and new connections are established.

Information Processing After Age 65

7. Memory is affected by aging, but specifics vary. As the senses become dulled, some stimuli never reach the sensory memory. Working memory shows notable declines with age because slower processing means that some thoughts are lost.

8. Control processes are less effective with age, as retrieval strategies become less efficient. Anxiety may prevent older people

from using the best strategies for cognitive control. Ecologically valid, real-life measures of cognition are needed.

Neurocognitive Disorders

9. Major neurocognitive disorder, whether it occurs in late adulthood or earlier, is characterized by diseases that reduce brain functioning. Most people never suffer from a brain disease, but it is devastating when it occurs.

10. The most common cause of major NCD in the United States is Alzheimer's disease, an incurable ailment that becomes more prevalent with age and worsens over time. The main symptom is extreme memory loss.

11. Also common worldwide is vascular disease, which results from a series of ministrokes that occur when impairment of blood circulation destroys portions of brain tissue.

12. Other NCDs, including frontotemporal NCD and Lewy body disease, also become more common with age. Several other types of NCD can occur in early or middle adulthood. One is Parkinson's disease, which begins with loss of muscle control. Parkinson's disease can also cause significant cognitive decline, particularly in the old.

13. Major NCD is sometimes mistakenly diagnosed when individuals are suffering from a reversible problem, such as anxiety, depression, malnutrition, or polypharmacy. The elderly take many drugs, sometimes with uncertain side effects.

New Cognitive Development

14. Many people become more interested and adept in creative endeavors, as well as more philosophical, as they grow older. The life review helps many older people remember earlier experiences, allowing them to gain perspective and achieve integrity or self-actualization.

15. Wisdom does not necessarily increase as a result of age, but some elderly people are unusually wise or insightful.

KEY TERMS

demographic shift (p. 498)	cellular aging (p. 502)	neurocognitive disorder (NCD) (p. 516)	vascular disease (p. 518)
young-old (p. 500)	Hayflick limit (p. 502)	major neurocognitive disorder (major NCD) (p. 517)	frontotemporal NCDs (p. 519)
old-old (p. 500)	telomeres (p. 502)		Parkinson's disease (p. 519)
oldest-old (p. 500)	calorie restriction (p. 503)	Alzheimer's disease (AD) (p. 517)	Lewy body disease (p. 520)
wear-and-tear theory (p. 500)	ageism (p. 504)		polypharmacy (p. 523)
maximum life span (p. 500)	elderspeak (p. 506)	plaques (p. 518)	self-actualization (p. 525)
metabolic syndrome (p. 502)	universal design (p. 510)	tangles (p. 518)	life review (p. 526)
	ecological validity (p. 515)		

APPLICATIONS

1. Write down the degree of independence of all your relatives over age 65, such as grandparents and great-grandparents, great aunts and great uncles, and so on. What percent are in nursing homes? How and why is that percent higher or lower than the national average?

2. Compensating for sensory losses is difficult because it involves learning new habits. To better understand the experience, reduce your hearing or vision for a day by wearing earplugs or dark glasses that let in only bright lights. (Use caution and common sense: Don't drive a car while wearing earplugs or cross streets while wearing dark glasses.) Report on your emotions, the responses of others, and your conclusions.

3. Ask five people of various ages whether they want to live to age 100 and record their responses. Would they be willing to eat half as much, exercise much more, experience weekly dialysis, or undergo other procedures in order to extend life? Analyze the responses.

ESPECIALLY FOR ANSWERS

Response for Biologists (from page 503): Although ageism and ambivalence limit the funding of research on the causes of aging, the applications include prevention of AIDS, cancer, neurocognitive disorders, and physical damage from pollution—all urgent social priorities.

Response for People Who Are Proud of Their Intellect (from page 512): If you answered, "Use it or lose it" or "Do crossword puzzles," you need to read more carefully. No specific brain activity has proved to prevent brain slowdown. Overall health is good for the brain as well as for the body, so exercise, a balanced diet, and well-controlled blood pressure are some smart answers.

Response for Students (from page 514): Learn it very well now, and you will probably remember it in fifty years, with a little review.

OBSERVATION QUIZ ANSWERS

Answer to Observation Quiz (from page 498): More males, except for over age 55, when it is about even. Why is that?

Answer to Observation Quiz (from page 507): Overall, older men are about 15 percent more likely to be sexually active than older women. Why? One explanation is that, among this cohort, brides were about five years younger than grooms, so some of those older married women had partners who were no longer "sexually active." Another explanation is that men are still more likely to brag and women to demur—actual rates may be more gender-neutral than this figure depicts.

LATE ADULTHOOD
Psychosocial Development

what will you know?

- Do older people become more sad or more hopeful?
- Do the elderly want to move to a distant, warm place?
- Is home care better than nursing-home care?

Almost every week I walk through a park with my friend Doris, a widow who is now aged 90, to a meeting we both attend. Many people of all backgrounds greet her by name, including men playing cards on a park table and a woman who owns a nearby hotel. Doris is an icon for street performers, including Colin, who plays his piano (on wheels) on sunny days. The police watch the card players carefully because they suspect drug-dealing, and they ticketed Colin for not having a permit.

Doris organized a protest. She got Community Board 2 (she is the oldest member, reappointed by the City Council every two years since 1964) to pass a resolution supporting entertainment in the park. The city withdrew the ticket, and the Parks Department revised their policy.

We walk slowly because Doris greets babies and animals alike. Squirrels scamper up to grab peanuts from her hand, and sometimes pigeons perch on her arm. Tourists photograph her; the local press admires her (Google "Doris Diether").

Doris dresses well, appropriate for each season. One hot August day I was surprised that she wore a long-sleeved blouse. She proudly told me why: Her arm was scratched because two pigeons fought over the same spot. She tells me about her grandmother from Finland, her two marriages, her journalist days as a dance critic, her efforts to style her very white hair.

We often stop at a mailbox to drop in a timely greeting card: I have become one of hundreds on her list. Colorful envelopes arrive in my box—green for St. Patrick's Day, orange for Halloween, gray for Thanksgiving, red for July 4th, and multicolored for my birthday. She sends 426 Christmas cards and orders the stamps from a post office catalog.

Not a Puppet One park regular is a puppeteer, Ricky Syers, who entertains hundreds of tourists with an array of puppets. He recently made a puppet of Doris, one more bit of evidence that the real Doris is beloved by many—and not controlled by anyone.

Usually friends have much in common, but Doris and I have many differences. She has no children; I have four. I never send cards, feed squirrels, or protect pianists (although Doris did get me to help Colin). We belong to opposing political parties and often vote differently on Community Board resolutions.

How did we become friends? Ten years ago, Doris had knee surgery. Since she lives alone, she asked for volunteers to push her wheelchair to her many meetings, appointments, and social engagements. I offered to take her once a week.

Soon she could walk, but I grew to enjoy her anecdotes, her memories, her attitudes. I watch for cars when we cross the street; I lift her walker down the two stairs from her front door. But I get far more than I give.

Six years ago, Doris broke her hip. The hospital soon put her in a private room because her younger roommate complained that Doris had visitors at all times of the day. A year ago, another fracture occurred, and more evidence of Doris's personality appeared. Medicare paid for six weeks of therapy. When the six weeks were over, her therapist joked, "Don't break a bone again just to get me back." She laughed; he is yet another friend.

Doris defies stereotyping, which makes her an illustration of the theme of this chapter. Each older person is unique, not just one of the millions. Some are frail, lonely, and vulnerable. But even the very old, with several disabilities, are often like Doris—active, involved, and beloved. I hope to be like her someday.

Theories of Late Adulthood

Some elderly people run marathons and lead nations; others no longer walk or talk. Social scientists theorize about this diversity. In late adulthood, the "creation and maintenance of identity" is "a key aspect of healthy living" (Allen et al., 2011, p. 10).

Self Theories

self theories
Theories of late adulthood that emphasize the core self, or the search to maintain one's integrity and identity.

Certain theories of late adulthood can be called **self theories**; they focus on individuals, especially the self-concept and challenges to identity. Self-awareness begins, as you remember, before age 2, and it builds throughout childhood and adolescence. In those early decades, self-image is greatly affected by physical appearance and by other people's perceptions (Harter, 2012).

Appearance and external opinions become less crucial with age. One study found that as people grow older, they feel that they are closer to their "authentic self" (Seto & Schlegel, 2018). That particular study was limited in size and age span, but other studies point in the same direction.

Elders who feel more in control of their own lives also are happier and healthier. One impressive study began with over a thousand people ages 40 to 85 and followed them until ages 55 to 100. Those with a lower sense of control over their lives were more often lonely and dependent on family (Drewelies et al., 2017).

THE SELF AND AGING Ideally, people become more truly themselves with age. That is what Anna Quindlen found:

> It's odd when I think of the arc of my life from child to young woman to aging adult. First I was who I was, then I didn't know who I was, then I invented someone and became her, then I began to like what I'd invented, and finally I was what I was again. It turned out I wasn't alone in that particular progression.
>
> *[Quindlen, 2012, p. ix]*

Of course, one person's self-reflection on the "arc of life" should not be taken as a general truth. However, substantial research on both cognitive and personality traits find fluctuation earlier in life and then stability in late adulthood (Briley & Tucker-Drob, 2017). Thus, each person does seem to become more definitive and distinctive as time goes on.

For the oldest-old who have numerous disabilities, maintaining independence is crucial for the self, because it signifies resilience (Hayman et al., 2017). Even those with neurocognitive disorders seek to preserve the self when memory and health fade (Klein, 2012).

INTEGRITY The most comprehensive self theory came from Erik Erikson. His eighth and final stage of development, **integrity versus despair**, requires adults to integrate their unique experiences with their community concerns (Erikson et al., 1986/1994). The word *integrity* is often used to mean honesty, but it also means a feeling of being whole, not scattered, comfortable with oneself. The virtue of old age, said Erikson, is wisdom, which implies a broad perspective.

As an example of integrity, many older people are proud of their personal history. They glorify their past, even boasting about bad experiences such as skipping school, taking drugs, escaping arrest, or being physically abused. Feeling pride at having overcome past problems may explain an interesting finding: Several studies report that depression is more common in middle age than in late adulthood. A sense of mastery is protective of the self (Nicolaisen et al., 2017; Blanchflower & Oswald, 2017).

As Erikson explained it, self-glorifying memories and self-acceptance counteract despair, because "time is now short, too short for the attempt to start another life" (Erikson, 1993a, p. 269). For every stage, the tension between the two opposing aspects (here integrity versus despair) propels growth. In this final stage,

> life brings many, quite realistic reasons for experiencing despair: aspects of a past we fervently wish had been different; aspects of the present that cause unremitting pain; aspects of a future that are uncertain and frightening. And, of course, there remains inescapable death, that one aspect of the future which is both wholly certain and wholly unknowable. Thus, some despair must be acknowledged and integrated as a component of old age.
>
> *[Erikson et al., 1986/1994, p. 72]*

Integration of death and the self is the crucial accomplishment of Erikson's eighth stage. The life review (explained in Chapter 14) and one's acceptance of death (explained in the Epilogue) are crucial aspects of the integrity envisioned by Erikson (Zimmerman, 2012).

Self theory may explain why many of the elderly strive to maintain childhood cultural and religious practices. For instance, grandparents may painstakingly teach a grandchild a language that is rarely used, or they may encourage the child to repeat traditional rituals and prayers. In cultures such as the United States that emphasize newness, elders worry that their traditional values will be lost and thus that they themselves will disappear.

integrity versus despair
The final stage of Erik Erikson's developmental sequence, in which older adults seek to integrate their unique experiences with their vision of community.

Always Himself Leading nonviolent protest is a sign of lifelong integrity for John Lewis. In his early 20s, he was beaten and arrested dozens of times as he sought civil rights for African Americans. At age 23, he spoke at the 1963 March on Washington, when Martin Luther King, Jr. proclaimed his dream. In this photo, at age 73, he is at the unveiling of a stamp commemorating that march. Lewis was elected to represent Georgia in the U.S. Congress in 1986 and has been reelected 15 times. At age 76, he led a sit-in on the Congressional floor, asking the leadership for discussion and a vote on a bill requiring background checks for gun ownership. He has not succeeded . . . yet.

RICCARDO S. SAVI/U.S. POSTAL SERVICE/GETTY IMAGES

As Erikson wrote, the older person

> knows that an individual life is the accidental coincidence of but one life cycle with but one segment of history; and that for him all human integrity stands or falls with the one style of integrity of which he partakes. . . . In such a final consolation, death loses its sting.

> *[Erikson, 1993a, p. 268]*

HOLDING ON TO THE SELF Most older people consider their personalities and attitudes quite stable over their life span, even as they acknowledge physical changes of their bodies and lapses in their minds (Klein, 2012). One 103-year-old woman, wrinkled, shrunken, and severely crippled by arthritis, displayed a photo of herself as a beautiful young woman. She said, "My core has stayed the same. Everything else has changed" (quoted in Troll & Skaff, 1997, p. 166).

Many older people refuse to move from drafty and dangerous dwellings into safer apartments, because leaving old places means abandoning personal history. They keep objects and papers that a younger person would throw away, a habit now labeled **compulsive hoarding**.

That is irrational, but their intent is to maintain the self (see A Case to Study). Likewise, elders may refuse surgery, chemotherapy, or medicine because they fear anything that might distort their thinking or emotions: They want to be themselves, even if it shortens their life (Miller, 2011–2012).

SOCIO-EMOTIONAL SELECTIVITY THEORY Another self theory is **socio-emotional selectivity theory** (Carstensen, 1993), the idea that older people select familiar social contacts who reinforce their generativity, pride, and joy. As socio-emotional theory would predict, when people believe that their future time is limited, they think about the meaning of life and then decide that they should be more appreciative of family and old friends, thus furthering their happiness (Hicks et al., 2012).

Socio-emotional selectivity could be a specific version of *selective optimization with compensation,* which you read about in Chapters 12 and 14. As senescence changes appearance and status, older adults select the key aspects of their social world to optimize.

Selectivity is central to self theories. Individuals set personal goals, assess their abilities, and try to accomplish their goals despite limitations. When older people are resilient, they maintain their identity despite wrinkles, slowdowns, and losses (Resnick et al., 2011).

An outgrowth of both socio-emotional selectivity and selective optimization is known as the **positivity effect.** It seems that, in every nation, the elderly perceive, prefer, and remember positive images and experiences more than negative ones (Reed et al., 2014; Carstensen & DeLiema, 2018). Unpleasant experiences are ignored, forgotten, or reinterpreted.

For that reason, stressful events (economic loss, serious illness, and death of friends or relatives) become less central to identity with age. That perspective protects emotional health (Boals et al., 2012), because the positivity effect makes a person happier. A strong

---

compulsive hoarding
The urge to accumulate and hold on to familiar objects and possessions, sometimes to the point of their becoming health and/or safety hazards. This impulse tends to increase with age.

socio-emotional selectivity theory
The theory that older people prioritize regulation of their own emotions and seek familiar social contacts who reinforce generativity, pride, and joy.

positivity effect
The tendency for elderly people to perceive, prefer, and remember positive images and experiences more than negative ones.

Trash or Treasure? Tryphona Flood, threatened with eviction, admitted she's a hoarder and got help from Megan Tolen, shown here discussing what in this four-room apartment can be discarded. Flood sits on the only spot of her bed that is not covered with stuff. This photo was taken midway through a three-year effort to clean out the apartment—the clutter was worse a year earlier.

JIM WILKES/THE TORONTO STAR/ZUMAPRESS.COM/NEWSCOM

A CASE TO STUDY

Saving Old Newspapers

My friend Doris (in the opening anecdote) keeps old newspaper clippings, records (some of which she recently sold to a music collector), and many other things. She has accumulated these possessions over the 50 years she has lived in a small apartment, about 200 square feet in total, with almost every wall and surface covered.

To her, all of her saved items are meaningful; she sometimes offers them to libraries and other institutions. She lives alone, with two cats. Remember that she sends hundreds of cards; she also receives hundreds, displayed all around her small space, only taken down when each holiday is over. Is that a problem?

A social worker might label that *compulsive hoarding,* which until recently was not considered a disorder. Many elderly hoarders grew up in the Great Depression and World War II. Saving, rationing, and reusing meant survival and patriotism, and homes typically had attics or basements with space for old magazines, clothes, toys, and knickknacks. Sayings like "a penny saved is a penny earned" were passed down as wisdom from one generation to the next.

Saving is no longer admired; pennies on the street are rarely picked up. In the twenty-first century, expiration dates are stamped on food and drugs; electronics, from computers to televisions, are designed to become quickly obsolete. Unlike all previous editions, the fifth edition of the *DSM* classifies hoarding as a psychological disorder (American Psychiatric Association, 2013, pp. 247–251).

Is saving old objects a sign of mental illness? Perhaps the elderly are expressing values formed decades ago. As an expression of the self, hoarding may bring emotional satisfaction (Frost et al., 2015), the same joy a younger person might get from buying the latest smartphone.

Self theory suggests that keeping possessions is part of self-expression. The elderly seek to maintain childhood mores, lifelong habits, and past history. Faded photographs and chipped china may help them do that.

However, hoarding correlates with social isolation and many physical and psychological problems (Roane et al., 2017). In today's smaller dwellings, there is no space for extra possessions. Hoarders cannot have friends over for visits (no room) and may be embarrassed for anyone to see their homes (at least Doris lets me in; she asks me to change the cats' water).

Because stacks of old papers and junk can attract dirt, mold, and small insects, not to mention pose a fire hazard, I thought of offering to help Doris get rid of her stuff. But then I realized that would be too painful for both of us.

I understand the general conclusions from the research: Hoarding may signify pathology, including social isolation that worsens over time. But to me, Doris's stacks of papers are part of her maintenance of identity, not hoarding. My view may be distorted; everyone sometimes ignores evidence when it applies to people they love. Have I lost my scientific mind?

---

sense of self-efficacy (the idea that a person has the power to control and change a situation) correlates with health, happiness, and a long life (Gerstorf et al., 2014).

The positivity effect may explain why, in every nation and religion, older people tend to be more patriotic and devout than younger ones. They see their national history and religious beliefs in positive terms, and they are proud to be themselves—Canadian, Czech, Chinese, or whatever. Past difficulties are reinterpreted as problems that are overcome, forgetting their contemporaries who did not survive past wars, diseases, prejudices.

As one review of resilience in old age notes:

> People in advanced age have a unique history to draw from when adapting to challenges. An 85 year old in 2015, for example, would have been born in 1930 and would have lived through global, formative experiences such as the Great Depression, WWII and social movements after WWII.... Reflecting upon past life events is an active strategy employed by older people when facing adversity.
>
> *[Hayman et al., 2017, p. 581]*

And those reflections result in pride in oneself, a person who coped with past troubles.

THINK CRITICALLY: Does the positivity effect avoid reality?

stratification theories
Theories that emphasize that social forces, particularly those related to a person's social stratum or social category, limit individual choices and affect a person's ability to function in late adulthood because past stratification continues to limit life in various ways.

Twice Fortunate Ageism takes many forms. Some cultures are youth-oriented, devaluing the old, while others are the opposite. These twin sisters are lucky to be alive: They were born in rural China in 1905, a period when most female twins died. When this photo was taken, they were age 103, and fortunate again, venerated because they have lived so long.

Twice-Abandoned Widows Traditionally in India, widows walked into the funeral pyre that cremated their husband's body, a suicide called sati. If the widow hesitated, the husband's relatives would sometimes push. Currently, sati is outlawed, but many Indian widows experience a social death: They are forbidden to meet men and remarry, except sometimes to the dead man's brother. Hundreds go to the sacred city of Vrindavan, where they are paid a pittance to chant prayers all day, as this woman does.

Stratification Theories

Self theories focus on the individual, specifically how unique, personal perceptions help older people cope with age. That contrasts with the second set of theories, called **stratification theories,** which emphasize social forces that position each person in a social stratum or level. That positioning creates disadvantages for some and advantages for others.

Stratification begins in the womb, as "individuals are born into a society that is already stratified—that is, differentiated—along key dimensions, including sex, race, and SES" (Lynch & Brown, 2011, p. 107). Indeed, stratification affects the prenatal environment, so some newborns already suffer from being born to a disadvantaged mother.

Stratification can arise from gender, ethnicity and immigration history, income, or age. Each of these can occur with other types of stratification, creating double, triple, or quadruple jeopardy.

GENDER STRATIFICATION Older women are typically financially disadvantaged. Many of them spent years as unpaid caregivers. And when they had jobs, their earnings were low. They are also more often victims of benevolent ageism ("sweet old lady").

Why do adult children urge their widow mothers more than their widower fathers to live with them? Is that sexist? It is certainly not logical, as men are more likely to experience a sudden health crisis, and thus living alone is more dangerous for them.

Gender stratification may harm males, too. Boys are taught to be stoic, repressing emotions and, later in life, avoiding medical attention, thus shortening their lives (Hamm et al., 2017). Males die more often than females at every age, yet in 2015 in the United States, twice as many men as women never saw a doctor (19.5 percent versus 10.8 percent) (National Center for Health Statistics, 2017).

Thus, all older people are affected adversely by gender stratification. One final example: Young women typically marry men a few years older and then outlive them. Because many married women traditionally relied on their husbands to manage money, and many men relied on their wives for everything domestic, many old widows were poor and dependent for decades, and many old widowers could not ask for help in caring for themselves. Thus, gender stratification may make men die too soon and may make women lonely for too long.

ETHNIC STRATIFICATION Remember that ethnic differences are sometimes codified as racial differences, with racial attitudes and experiences over a lifetime harming many elders. That coding itself is stratification, because people react to a person's apparent race rather than to their background. Past racial discrimination reduced quality of education, health of neighborhoods, wages earned—and all of this affects the current life of the aged.

Consider one detailed example, home ownership, a source of financial security for many seniors. Fifty years ago, stratification prevented many young-adult African Americans from buying homes. Thirty years ago, new laws reduced housing discrimination, which meant that many middle-aged African Americans bought homes.

However, at that point, mortgages had high interest rates but were easy to obtain. Thus, the foreclosure crisis that began in 2007 fell particularly hard on African Americans, whose homes were "under water"—more money owed than the houses were worth. Is this a new example of an old story: past stratification causing poverty in old age (Saegert et al., 2011)?

IMAGINECHINA/AP IMAGES

STUART FREEDMAN/IN PICTURES/CORBIS

A particular form of ethnic stratification affects immigrant elders. Most immigrants to North America come from cultures in which younger generations are expected to care for the old. However, U.S. homes are designed for two-generation families, and pensions and Social Security come to employees who worked for decades "on the books," or to their non-employed spouses, not to older immigrants who helped younger family members.

For that reason, U.S. practices leave many older immigrants poor, lonely, and dependent on their children, who live in homes and apartments not designed for extended families. That may lead to either of two harmful family dynamics: unwelcome closeness in crowded, multigenerational homes, or distressing distance between elders and their descendants.

INCOME STRATIFICATION Many of the poorest elderly never held jobs that qualify for Social Security benefits. Thus, an important source of income for most older Americans is absent. Further, people who were poor in adulthood have no savings for late adulthood because future planning was not expedient (Haushofer & Fehr, 2014).

Income stratification weighs heavily on the very old of every gender and ethnicity. And recent political and economic events in many nations have resulted in less governmental support for the poor of any age (Phillipson, 2013).

AGE STRATIFICATION Ageism and age segregation affects people of every income stratum. Even those middle-SES men who had good jobs and benefits find that after seniority builds in the workplace, employment stops, perhaps with a pension but never with as much income as before.

For every older person, health costs increase. Some young people think Medicare pays for all medical expenses of citizens older than age 65, but that is far from true. Health expenses can bankrupt those who thought they had enough money. Those who were unskilled or temporary workers are especially hard hit (Phillipson, 2013).

The most controversial version of age stratification is **disengagement theory** (Cumming & Henry, 1961), which holds that as people age, four significant changes occur: (1) Traditional roles become unavailable; (2) the social circle shrinks; (3) coworkers stop relying on them; and (4) adult children turn away to focus on their own children. Meanwhile, older people become less mobile and less able to engage in social interaction.

According to this theory, disengagement is a mutual process, chosen by both adult generations. Thus, younger adult workers and parents disengage from the old, who themselves disengage, withdrawing from life's action.

Disengagement theory provoked a storm of protest. Many gerontologists insisted that older people need and want new involvements. They proposed an opposing theory, **activity theory,** which holds that the elderly seek to remain active with relatives, friends, and community groups. Activity theorists contended that if the elderly disengage, they do so unwillingly and suffer because of it (Kelly, 1993; Rosow, 1985).

Extensive research supports activity theory. Being active correlates with happiness, intelligence, and health. This is true at younger ages as well, but the correlation between activity and well-being is particularly strong at older ages (Potočnik & Sonnentag, 2013; Bielak et al., 2012).

Disengagement is more likely among those low in SES, which suggests that it is another harmful outcome of past economic stratification (Clarke, 2011). Literally being active—bustling around the house, climbing stairs, and walking to work—lengthens life and increases satisfaction.

disengagement theory
The view that aging makes a person's social sphere increasingly narrow, resulting in role relinquishment, withdrawal, and passivity.

activity theory
The view that elderly people want and need to remain active in a variety of social spheres—with relatives, friends, and community groups—and become withdrawn only unwillingly, as a result of ageism.

A Soldier for Democracy Poll workers like Margaret Borcherding in Ohio are often patriotic senior citizens who work on election days, checking lists and guiding voters. Democracy in the United States depends on hundreds of thousands of such people. It is not an easy job, as both competence and friendliness are needed. In 2016, New York City had four election days, which meant 62 hours of training and work for thousands of retirees.

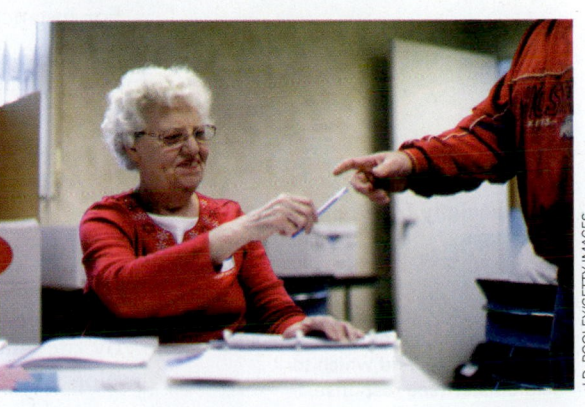

J.D. POOLEY/GETTY IMAGES

OPPOSING PERSPECTIVES

A Critique of Stratification Theories

Contrary to all of the preceding examples, might people develop habits and attitudes over their lifetime that protect them from the worst effects of stratification (Rosenfield, 2012)? Of course, poverty and ill health are harmful at every age, but perhaps gender, ethnicity, or low income are less damaging for the very old than they are earlier in life.

Both disengagement and activity theories need to be applied with caution. Remember the *positivity effect:* Older people may disengage from emotional events that cause anger, regret, and sadness, while actively enjoying other experiences.

Neither of the two age-related stratification theories—(1) that all elderly people want to disengage or (2) that all elderly people should be active—reflects the diversity of late adulthood (Johnson & Mutchler, 2014).

Similarly, people may break away from gender stratification. The traditional roles of married couples—with wives dedicated to home and family and husbands focused on work and politics—are less rigid in late adulthood. Each spouse incorporates the interests of the other (Carr et al., 2014). If a partner dies, past stratification may become a way to cope: Women become closer to friends and children while men remarry. In that way, both use the limitations of their young years to thrive in late adulthood.

Likewise, cautionary data come from comparing the aged of various ethnic groups. Although African Americans have poorer health and higher death rates than European Americans in childhood and adulthood, that inequality disappears at about age 80. Then, in a *race crossover,* the inequality

reverses, with the oldest-old African Americans living longer than the oldest-old European Americans. Elders from other minority ethnic groups also live longer than the national average. Deaths from suicide among older African Americans are half the rate of European Americans (National Center for Health Statistics, 2017).

One scholar suggests that older African American women in the United States have the best mental health of all. He does not think that "stratification systems such as gender, race and class" result in high risk for older adults. Instead, "multiple minority statuses affect mental health in paradoxical ways . . . that refute triple jeopardy approaches" (Rosenfield, 2012, p. 791).

Overall, past stratification might buffer the problems of old age. Might those who were stratified in adulthood develop coping strategies, such as being able to laugh at problems and developing strong social bonds, that improve late adulthood? That would reverse the effect of stratification. Indeed, immigrant elders generally are happier with their lives than nonimmigrants, a phenomenon called the *happiness paradox* (R. Calvo et al., 2017).

Data on longevity are not as reassuring, however. In the United States, the expected life span of low-SES adults is several years lower than that of high-SES adults, and it has been dropping since 2000, when income disparity in the United States began increasing. It may be that racism, sexism, and ageism are as strong now as ever, and suggesting that stratification is no longer a problem is wishful thinking.

That is why this is an opposing perspective.

DOUBLE AND TRIPLE JEOPARDY Every form of stereotyping makes it more difficult for people to break free from social institutions that assign them to a particular path. The results are cumulative, over the entire life span (Brandt et al., 2012). Often several forms of stratification co-occur. As one scholar contends, "[W]omen . . . are much more likely to live in households that fall below the federal poverty line. Black and Hispanic women are particularly vulnerable" (Jackson et al., 2011, p. 93).

For instance, newborns who are female *and* African American *and* poor are more likely to be underweight at birth. Their development is more likely to follow a downward path: They are less likely to attend a good preschool, read before age 5, graduate from high school, obtain a college degree, find a good job, or marry. Each of these outcomes is more likely because of the previous one.

Dozens of factors—including diet, exercise, stress, and neighborhood—place older people in one stratum or another. Those factors accumulate, and the consequences become apparent: The age-adjusted rate of cardiovascular death of African Americans is twice that for European Americans, for instance (National Center for Health Statistics, 2017).

By late adulthood, all of the past stratification makes some people more likely to develop cancer, diabetes, heart disease, or other serious problems. African American women older than 65 are the group most likely to say their health is poor.

◆ **Especially for Social Scientists**
The various social science disciplines tend to favor different theories of aging. Can you tell which theories would be more acceptable to psychologists and which to sociologists? (see response, page 563)

Resisting Jeopardy These men and women in Beijing, China, are gathering at dawn for a prayer meeting. Like many of the elderly who identify with a particular ethnic group, their community is a powerful antidote to the harm of stratification.

At each stage of life, some individuals break free from the usual path. For example, thousands of African American adults who were poor as children become successful and highly respected elders. Nonetheless, stratification theory contends that overcoming the liabilities of the past is increasingly difficult as life unfolds.

This explains why stratification theory seems particularly pertinent in late adulthood. People who have experienced poverty and prejudice all their lives almost never become healthy and wealthy. Stratification theory suggests that to help the aged, intervention needs to begin before birth. The fact that health problems result from a lifetime of stratification "suggests multiple intervention points at which disparities can be reduced" (Haas et al., 2012, p. 238).

what have you learned?

1. How does Erikson's use of the word *integrity* differ from its usual meaning?

2. How does hoarding relate to self theory?

3. Is there any harm in older people striving to become themselves?

4. Which type of stratification is most burdensome, economic, ethnic, or gender?

5. How can disengagement be mutual?

6. If activity theory is correct, what does that suggest older adults should do?

7. What is the evidence for, and against, stratification theory?

Activities in Late Adulthood

As you read, active, independent elders live longer and more happily than inactive, dependent ones. Elders themselves bear this out. Most of them wish they had more time to do all they want to do. They enjoy their active, busy lives.

Being active and finding joy in life correlates with health. To some extent, the direction of the correlation is from health to activity, in that healthy people can be more active. But the correlation is strong in the other direction: Elders who are active become healthier than those who are inactive.

Same Situation, Far Apart: Satisfying Work In Nice, France *(left),* two paleontologists examine a skull bone, and in Arizona *(right),* a woman said to be more than 100 years old prepares wool for weaving. Note their facial expressions: Elders are often happier when they continue working.

That many elders are active might surprise emerging adults. They see few gray hairs and wrinkles at sports events, political rallies, job sites, or midnight concerts. Ageism might lead them to imagine older people sitting quietly at home. Not so. Most of the elderly are far from inactive; it is just that their activities differ from those of the young. We now present specifics.

Working

A significant proportion of the elderly continue working, because work provides social support and status. Others retire from full-time, paid employment but remain productive in other ways.

PAID WORK Employment history affects current health and happiness of older adults (Wahrendorf et al., 2013). Those who lost their jobs involuntarily because of structural changes (a factory closing, a corporate division eliminated) are, decades later, less likely to be in good health (Schröder, 2013).

The employment rate for older workers has risen since 2005 (see Figure 15.1), largely because workers want or need to keep earning money. Pensions—federal as well as private—are less secure than they once were, and many investments have not worked out well. Health care expenses are costly as well, especially in the United States.

FIGURE 15.1 Along with Everyone Else Although younger adults might imagine that older people stop work as soon as they can, this is clearly not true for everyone.

↑ OBSERVATION QUIZ
What is the most significant change since 1970? (see answer, page 563)

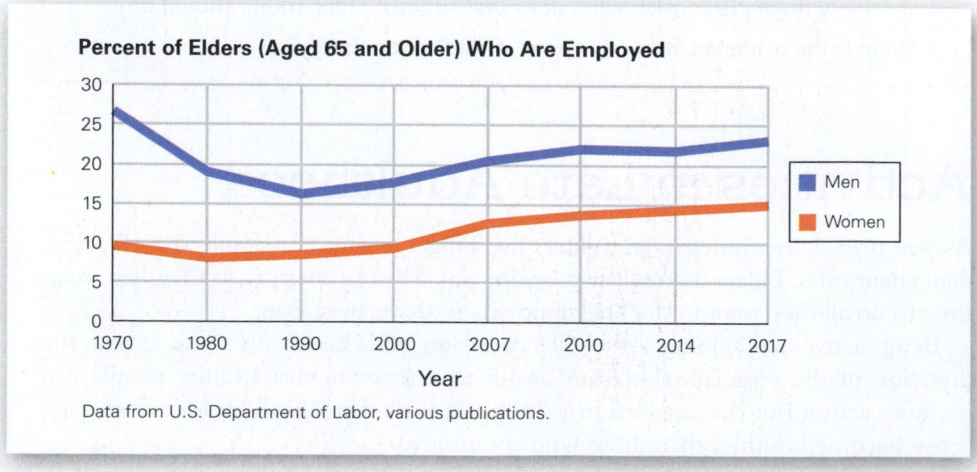

Percent of Elders (Aged 65 and Older) Who Are Employed

Data from U.S. Department of Labor, various publications.

Adequate income is a crucial predictor of health and happiness in late adulthood. Nonunionized low-wage workers (who need the income) and professionals (who welcome the status) are likely to stay employed in their 60s (Komp et al., 2010). Especially for low-wage workers, worries about retirement income are increasing: 41 percent of U.S. workers aged 45 to 65 fear post-retirement income will be inadequate (Morin & Fry, 2012).

RETIREMENT The United States is one of the few developed nations that does not mandate a particular age for retirement (except in some occupations, such as firefighters and airplane pilots). When employed adults can choose their retirement date, many continue working until they believe that their retirement income is adequate, or unless health concerns suggest that they must quit.

The Best New Hire Clayton Fackler, age 72, is shown here at his new job, a cashier at a Wal-Mart in Bowling Green, Ohio. He is among thousands of elderly people hired by that corporation, in part because retired seniors are reliable workers. They are also more willing than younger adults to work for minimum wage at part-time hours—a boon to employers but not for young adults.

Family interactions also matter. Generally, fathers tend to work a little longer than other men, perhaps because they want sufficient income to support their adult children. Mothers, on average, tend to retire a little earlier, perhaps because they want or need to become caregivers (Hank & Korbmacher, 2013). For many women, being a caregiving grandmother is a reason for earlier retirement (Hochman & Lewin-Epstein, 2013).

Many retirees hope to work part time or become self-employed, with small businesses or consulting work (Rix, 2011). Some employers provide *bridge* jobs, enabling older workers to transition from full employment.

Securing a bridge job depends on both the employer and the employee. Crafting an employment bridge, or consulting work, is an option more available to educated, long-term employees. SES also affects self-employment and second-career options. Thus, past stratification affects the feasibility of bridge jobs (E. Calvo et al., 2017).

Employment in late adulthood varies markedly, with many older workers convinced that age discrimination is common. In some occupations, physical ability is crucial and skill is minimal: In those occupations, older workers are rarely hired and often fired. In other jobs, the experience and reliability of older workers (who are less often absent, late, or hungover) make them particularly valuable (Dingemans et al., 2016; James et al., 2011).

A longitudinal study of older adults in the Netherlands before and after retirement found that self-esteem decreased in the five years *before* retirement (Bleidorn & Schwaba, 2018). Then for many, self-esteem rose again because of *role strain reduction*—apparently older workers found it hard to be a good worker, spouse, and grandparent simultaneously; they were happy to stop working.

Thus, retirement was a relief for many—but not everyone. Some followed the opposite trajectory, decreasing in self-esteem, presumably because the socialization and status of employment was lost. Is it significant that this study was of Dutch workers, where public support for retirees is relatively good? Many studies find that social context (particularly pensions and health care) makes a difference in how older adults feel about retirement.

VOLUNTEER WORK Volunteering provides some of the benefits of paid employment (generativity and social connections). Longitudinal as well as cross-sectional research finds a strong link between volunteering, health, and well-being, especially for older adults (Cutler et al., 2011; Kahana et al., 2013; Tabassum et al., 2016). A *regular* volunteer commitment to a social-service organization, religious institution, or community group is best.

As self theory would predict, volunteer work attracts older people who were always strongly committed to their community and had more social contacts

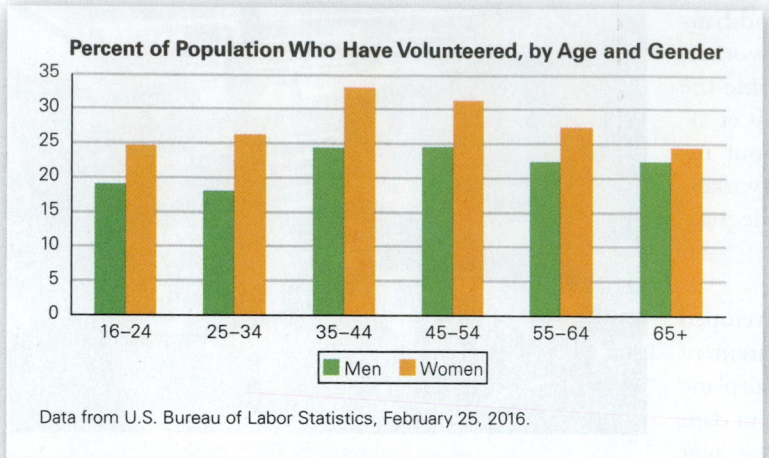

Percent of Population Who Have Volunteered, by Age and Gender

Data from U.S. Bureau of Labor Statistics, February 25, 2016.

FIGURE 15.2 Official Volunteers As you can see, older adults volunteer less often than do middle-aged adults, according to official statistics. However, this counts people who volunteer for organizations—schools, churches, social service groups, and so on. Not counted is help given to friends, family members, neighbors, and even strangers. If that were counted, would elders have higher rates than everyone else?

↑ **OBSERVATION** QUIZ
When is the gender gap least evident? (see answer, page 563)

age in place
To remain in the same home and community in later life, adjusting but not leaving when health fades.

(Pilkington et al., 2012). One meta-analysis found that volunteering cuts the death rate in half. Even when various confounds (such as marital status and health before volunteering) were taken into account, simply being a volunteer correlated with a longer and healthier life (Okun et al., 2013).

In one project, older people interested in "active retirement" attended a two-hour session that explained the benefits of volunteering, the importance of planning and initiative, and various ways to find an activity that suited one's values and preferences. They were given a list of nearby volunteer opportunities (Warner et al., 2014).

Six weeks later, the rate of volunteering among the attendees doubled. Some began volunteering for the first time, and many who already were volunteers increased their commitment.

Although the benefits of volunteering are many, in the United States the overall rate of volunteering is only 25 percent, with the rate for those over age 65 only 23.5 percent—lower than for middle-aged, employed adults (U.S. Bureau of Labor Statistics, February 25, 2016) (see Figure 15.2). Informal volunteering—helping a friend, visiting someone who is sick, or caring for a grandchild—is higher, although ideally older adults do both.

Home Sweet Home

One of the favorite activities of many retirees is caring for their own homes and taking care of their personal needs. Typically, all adults do more housework and meal preparation (less fast food, more fresh ingredients) after retirement (Luengo-Prado & Sevilla, 2012). They go to fewer restaurants, stores, and parties, because they like to stay put.

Older adults also do yard work, redecorate, build shelves, hang pictures, and rearrange furniture. One study found that husbands did much more housework and yard work when they retired, but that wives did not reduce their work when husbands became more helpful around the house. Apparently, couples find more things to do when they have more time to do them (Leopold & Skopek, 2015a).

Gardening is popular: More than half of the elderly in the United States do it. Growing flowers, herbs, and vegetables is productive because it involves creativity, exercise, and social interaction (Schupp & Sharp, 2012; Miller et al., 2018).

AGING IN PLACE In keeping up with household tasks and maintaining their property, almost all older people—about 90 percent, even when they are frail—prefer to **age in place** rather than move. That means they like to stay in their own homes.

The preference for aging in place is evident in state statistics. Of the 50 states, Florida has the largest percentage of people over age 65, many of whom moved there not only for the climate but also because they already knew people there. The next three states highest in proportion of population over age 65 are Maine, West Virginia, and Pennsylvania, all places where older people have aged in place.

Fortunately, aging in place has become easier. One successful project sent a team (a nurse, occupational therapist, and handyman) to vulnerable aged adults, most of whom became better able to take care of themselves at home, avoiding institutions

(Szanton et al., 2015). Elders themselves use selective optimization with compensation as they envision staying in their homes despite age-related problems (Fiske et al., 2015).

About 4,000 consultants are now certified by the National Association of Homebuilders to advise about universal design, which includes making a home livable for people who find it hard to reach the top shelves, to climb stairs, and to respond to the doorbell. Non-design aspects of housing also allow aging in place, such as bright lights without dangling cords, carpets affixed to the floor, and seats and grab bars in the shower.

Assistance to allow a person to age in place is particularly needed in rural areas, where isolation may become dangerous. Many public policies are designed for the elderly: Rents reduced; special transportation provided for those who cannot walk; aides, therapists, and meal services come to homes. Doris has made me well aware that all of these are flawed and inadequate. Nonetheless, she—and many others—could not age in place without them.

NORCs An ideal way to age in place is a neighborhood or apartment complex that has become a **naturally occurring retirement community (NORC)**. A NORC develops when young adults move into a new suburb or large building and then stay for decades as they age. People in NORCs may live alone, after children leave and partners die. They enjoy home repair, housework, and gardening, partly because their lifelong neighbors notice the new curtains, the polished door, and the blooming rosebush.

If low-income elders are in a NORC within a high-crime neighborhood, they and their neighbors sometimes form a protective social network. NORCs can be granted public money to replace after-school karate with senior centers, or piano teachers with visiting nurses, if that is what the community needs (Greenfield et al., 2012; Vladeck & Altman, 2015).

Religious Involvement

The old-old attend fewer religious services than do the young-old, but faith and praying increase over the life span. For example, two-thirds of Americans over age 65 pray every day, as do only about one-third of those in their 20s (Pew Research Center, November 3, 2015, p. 20). Many elders study religious texts.

The psychological construct of *attachment* has been applied to late-life religious activity. Remember that attachment was described Chapter 4: Some babies are securely attached to their caregivers and some are not. Attachment also appeared in Chapter 13, regarding romances and families. In late adulthood, attachment appears again, this time regarding a person's relationship with God (Granqvist & Kirkpatrick, 2013).

One study found that elders who feel securely attached to God (e.g., "When I talk to God, I know he listens to me") are more likely to be optimistic about the future and feel good about themselves—even as they are aware of their faults (Kent et al., 2018). Another study found that prayer itself does not seem to promote a sense of well-being. However, if prayer is part of a personal attachment to God, it benefits the old (Bradshaw & Kent, 2018).

Imagining the Future Couples like this one in Quebec, Canada, often build new homes with modifications in their current neighborhoods so they can age in place for 20 or more years. Note that the younger man in this photo (the architect) is pleased to show them a model of their new home—no stairs and fewer bedrooms.

naturally occurring retirement community (NORC)
A neighborhood or apartment complex whose population is mostly retired people who moved to the location as younger adults and never left.

Many of the older adults in **VIDEO: Active and Healthy Aging: The Importance of Community** frequent senior centers for continual social contact, and some benefit from volunteering.

◆ **Especially for Religious Leaders**
Why might the elderly have strong faith but poor church attendance? (see response, page 563)

Visualizing Development

LIFE AFTER 65: LIVING INDEPENDENTLY

Most people who reach age 65 not only survive a decade or more, but also live independently.

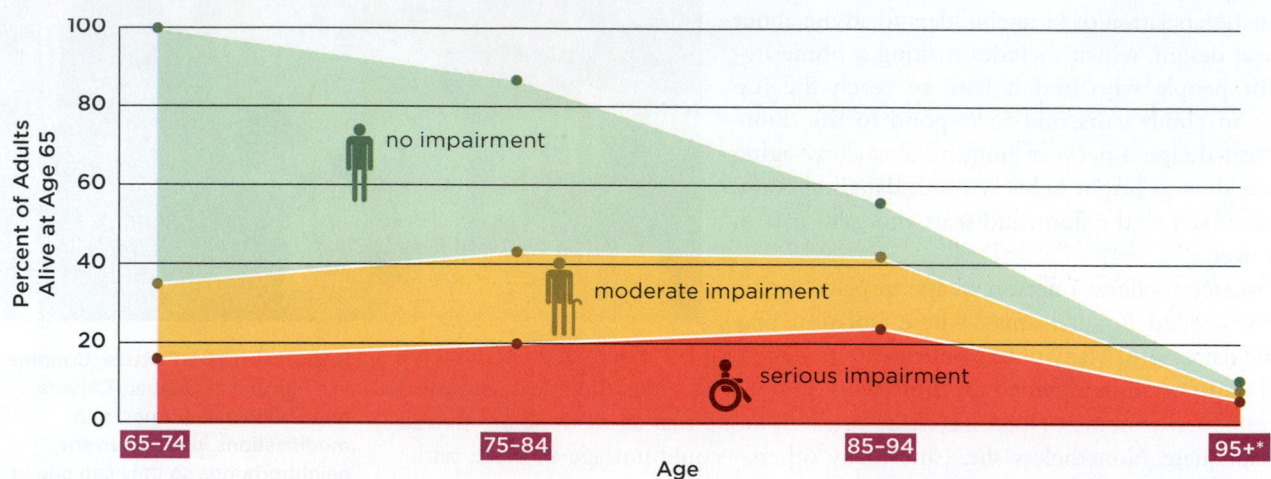

*With each year after 95, some survivors are still self-sufficient!

AGE 65

Of 100 people, in the next decade:

Most will care for all their basic needs. But, 35 will become unable to take care of at least one instrumental activity of daily living (IADL) like household chores, shopping, or taking care of finances, or one activity of daily living (ADL) like bathing, dressing, eating, or getting in and out of bed. And 16 are so impaired that they need extensive help, either at home or in a nursing home. 87 will survive another decade.

AGE 75

Of the 87 people who survived, in the next decade:

About half will not need help caring for their basic needs. But 43 will become unable to take care of at least one IADL or ADL. And half of these 43 become so impaired that they require extensive care. 56 will survive another decade.

AGE 85

Of the 56 people who survived, in the next decade:

Most need help. 42 will be unable to take care of at least one IADL or ADL. And 24 of them become so impaired that they require extensive care. Only 11 will survive another decade.

AGE 95

Of the 11 people who survived, in the next decade:

Those who reach 95 live for about four more years, on average. Almost three quarters will need some help caring for their basic needs and about half require extensive care.

DATA FROM NATIONAL VITAL STATISTICS REPORTS, MAY 8, 2013.

With Whom?

According to U.S. Census data from 2010, only about 10 percent of those over age 65 had moved in with an adult child, and less than 4% lived in a nursing home or hospital.

LIVING ARRANGEMENTS OF PERSONS 65+, 2010

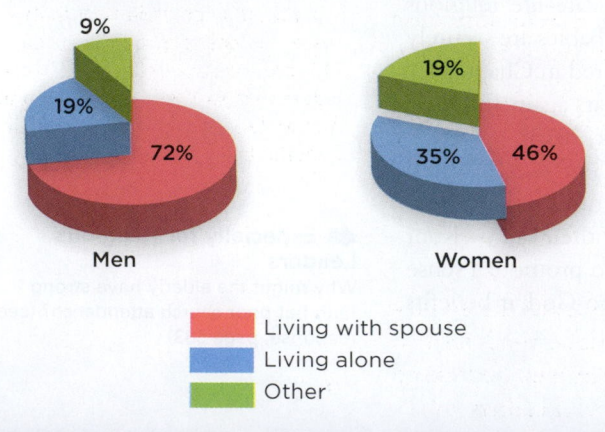

Men

Women

- Living with spouse
- Living alone
- Other

Where?

Not necessarily in a warm state.

PERSONS 65+ AS A PERCENTAGE OF TOTAL POPULATION, 2010

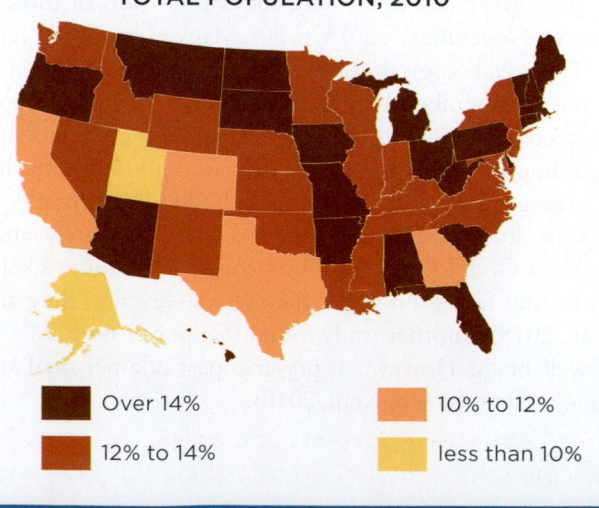

- Over 14%
- 12% to 14%
- 10% to 12%
- less than 10%

DATA FROM U.S. CENSUS BUREAU, 2011.

Religious activity correlates with physical and emotional health in late adulthood. Developmentalists have several explanations:

1. Religious prohibitions encourage good habits (e.g., less drug use).
2. Faith communities promote caring relationships.
3. Beliefs give meaning for life and death, thus reducing stress.

[Atchley, 2009; Lim & Putnam, 2010; Noronha, 2015]

Religious identity and institutions are especially important for older members of minority groups, who often identify more strongly with their religious heritage than with their national or ethnic background. A nearby house of worship, with familiar words, music, and rituals, is one reason that elders prefer to age in place.

Immigrants bring their religion with them. About a third of all U.S. Catholics are immigrants or children of immigrants, as are almost all of U.S. Hindus and Buddhists and many U.S. Muslims (Pew Research Center, May 12, 2015). Although the average congregant in these newer groups is younger than the average member of traditional U.S. Christian or Jewish groups, in every religious group the elderly members tend to be most devout.

Political Activity

It is easy to assume that elders are not political activists. Few turn out for rallies, and only about 2 percent are active in political campaigns. By other measures, however, the elderly are very political. More than any other age group, they write letters to their representatives, identify with a political party, and vote.

In addition, they keep up with the news. The Pew Research Center periodically asks a cross section of U.S. residents questions about current events and civic understanding. The elderly usually best the young.

For example, 73 percent of elders (65 and older) but only half as many (38 percent) of young adults (ages 18–29) knew that the vice president casts the deciding vote if the U.S. Senate is split 50/50 (as it was in 2017 for Secretary of Education Betsy DeVos's confirmation) (Pew Research Center, April 26, 2018).

Many government policies affect the elderly, especially those regarding housing, pensions, prescription drugs, and medical costs. However, members of this age group do not necessarily vote their own economic interests, or vote as a bloc. Instead they are divided on most national issues, including global warming, military conflicts, and public education.

Political scientists believe that the idea of "gray power" (that the elderly vote their own interests) is a myth, promulgated to reduce support for programs that benefit the old (Walker, 2012). Given that ageism zigzags from hostile to benign—and is often based on beliefs that are far from reality—it is not surprising that "older persons [are] attacked as too powerful and, at the same time, as a burdensome responsibility" (Schulz & Binstock, 2008, p. 8).

DOUGLAS GRAHAM/ASSOCIATED PRESS

Few for Many These seniors rally to keep the U.S. Congress from reducing Social Security, Medicare, and Medicaid benefits—part of a successful National Committee to Preserve Social Security (NCPSS) campaign that has been supported by politicians of both major political parties for 30 years. This organization relies mostly on letters sent to legislators and on the human tendency to resist reductions in benefits.

Friends and Relatives

Companions are particularly important during old age. As socio-emotional theory predicts, the size of the social circle shrinks, but close relationships are crucial. Bonds formed over the years allow people to share triumphs and tragedies with others who understand and appreciate them. Siblings, old friends, and spouses are ideal convoy members.

A Lover's Kiss Ralph Young awakens Ruth *(left)* with a kiss each day, as he has for most of the 78 years of their marriage. Here they are both 99, sharing a room in their Indiana residence, "more in love than ever." Half a world away, in Ukraine *(right)*, more kisses occur, with 70 newly married couples and one couple celebrating their golden anniversary. Developmental data suggest that now, several years after these photos, the two old couples are more likely to be happily married than the 70 young ones.

LONG-TERM PARTNERSHIPS For most of the current cohort of elders, their spouse is the central convoy member, a buffer against the problems of old age. Even more than other social contacts, a spouse is protective of health and well-being (Wong & Waite, 2015).

Mutual interaction is crucial: Each healthy and happy partner improves the other's well-being (Ruthig et al., 2012). A lifetime of shared experiences—living together, raising children, and dealing with financial and emotional crises—brings partners closer. Often couples develop "an exceedingly positive portrayal" (O'Rourke et al., 2010b) of their mate, seeing their partner's personality as better than their own.

Older couples have learned how to disagree, considering conflicts to be discussions, not fights. I know one example personally. Irma and Bill are both politically active, proud parents of two adults, devoted grandparents, and informed about current events. They seem happily married, and they cooperate admirably when caring for their grandsons.

However, they vote for opposing candidates. I was worried that their marriage might be an unhappy one until Irma explained: "We sit together on the fence, seeing both perspectives, and then, when it's time to vote, Bill and I fall on opposite sides." I know who will fall on which side, but for them, the discussion is productive. Their long-term affection keeps disagreements from becoming fights.

Outsiders might judge many long-term marriages as unequal, since one or the other spouse usually provides most of the money, needs most of the care, or does most of the housework. Yet such disparities may not bother older partners, who accept each other's dependencies, remembering times (perhaps decades ago) when the situation was reversed.

Older couples often find patterns of interaction that work for them. One study found that older husbands were generally satisfied with their marriages because their wives took good care of them, and wives were satisfied because they were able to take care of their husbands (Carr et al., 2014). This may seem sexist to younger people, but both partners may be quite content with their relationship.

A couple together can achieve selective optimization with compensation. For example, I know a couple in their early 90s. His memory is fading; her legs are so weak that she has difficulty getting out of bed. If either had been alone, he or she would need extensive care. However, the husband helps the wife move, and she keeps track of what needs to be done: Together they need minimal outside help.

INTERGENERATIONAL RELATIONSHIPS Since the average couple now has fewer children, the *beanpole family,* with multiple generations but with only a few members at each level, is becoming more common (Murphy, 2011) (see Figure 15.3). Some children have no cousins, brothers, or sisters but have a dozen elderly relatives.

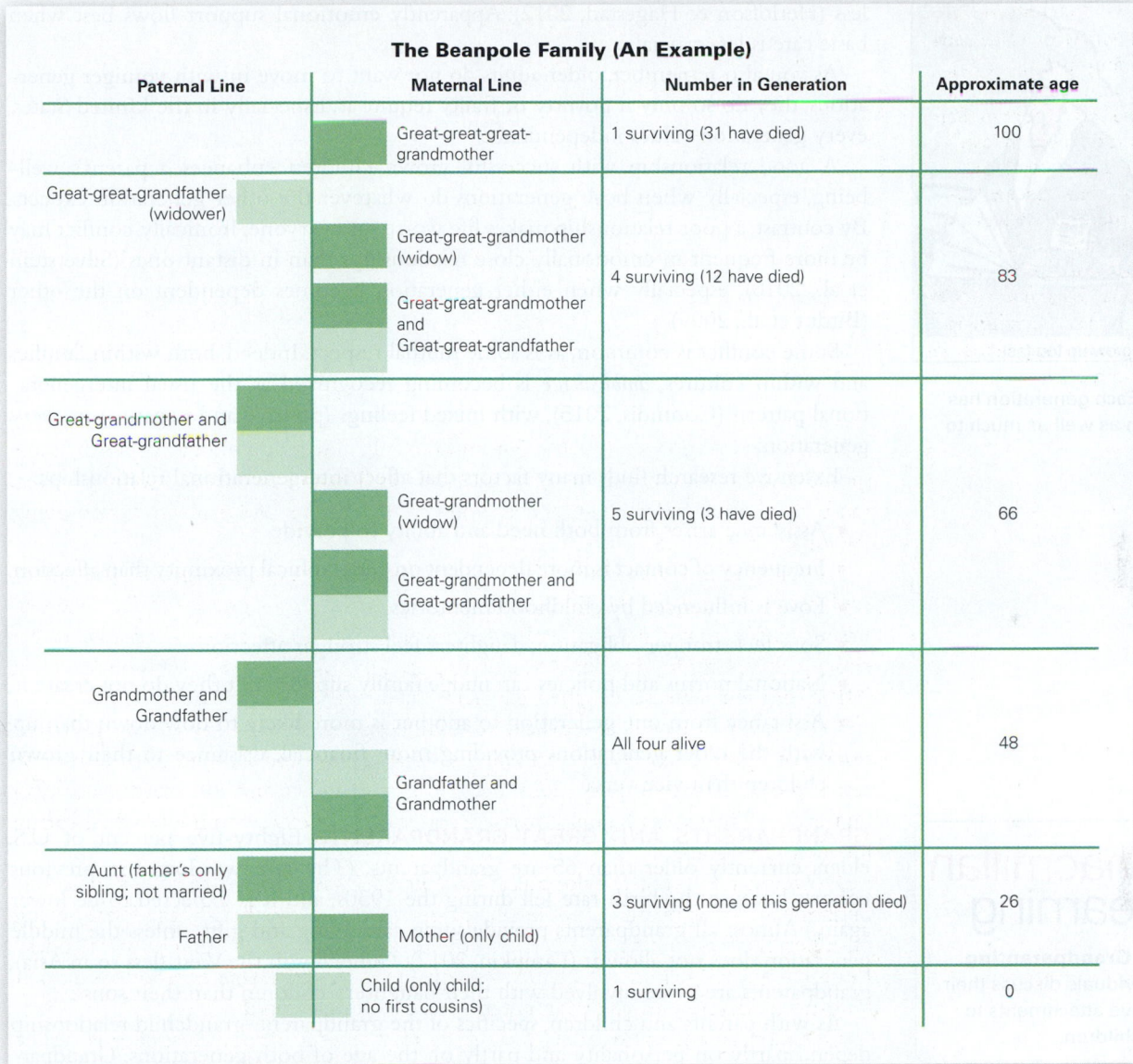

The Beanpole Family (An Example)			
Paternal Line	**Maternal Line**	**Number in Generation**	**Approximate age**
	Great-great-great-grandmother	1 surviving (31 have died)	100
Great-great-grandfather (widower)			
	Great-great-grandmother (widow)	4 surviving (12 have died)	83
	Great-great-grandmother and Great-great-grandfather		
Great-grandmother and Great-grandfather			
	Great-grandmother (widow)	5 surviving (3 have died)	66
	Great-grandmother and Great-grandfather		
Grandmother and Grandfather			
		All four alive	48
	Grandfather and Grandmother		
Aunt (father's only sibling; not married)		3 surviving (none of this generation died)	26
Father	Mother (only child)		
	Child (only child; no first cousins)	1 surviving	0

FIGURE 15.3 Fourteen Old Relatives This is a six-generation beanpole family as it might be for a baby born today. Currently parents have their first child, on average, at about age 26. A generation before that, it was about age 22, before that, age 18 and before that 17. As you see, most people die by age 80, but about 1 in every 30 reaches 100. This example does not take into account the possible remarriages. Many newborns also have step-grandparents or great-grandparents.

The result is fewer peers who are relatives but stronger connections across generational lines.

As you remember, *familism* prompts family caregiving among all relatives. One norm is **filial responsibility,** the obligation of adult children to care for their aging parents. This is a value in every nation, with some variation by culture (Saraceno, 2010).

As a cultural ideal, filial responsibility is strongest in Asia, but in practice, Asians are less likely to care for elderly parents than those in Western cultures. For example, a survey in China found that half of adult children saw their parents only once a year or less (Kim et al., 2015).

Many elders believe the older generation should help the younger ones, although specifics vary by culture. When the government provides assistance for the aged (housing, pensions, and so on), the generations are *more* involved with each other, not

filial responsibility
The obligation of adult children to care for their aging parents.

"They grow up too fast."

Ignorant? Each generation has much to teach as well as much to learn.

In **VIDEO: Grandparenting,** several individuals discuss their close, positive attachments to their grandchildren.

less (Herlofson & Hagestad, 2012). Apparently, emotional support flows best when basic care is less crucial.

As you also remember, older adults do not want to move in with younger generations; they do so only if poverty or frailty require it. Especially in the United States, every generation values independence.

A good relationship with successful grown children enhances a parent's well-being, especially when both generations do whatever the other generation expects. By contrast, a poor relationship makes life worse for everyone. Ironically, conflict may be more frequent in emotionally close relationships than in distant ones (Silverstein et al., 2010), especially when either generation becomes dependent on the other (Birditt et al., 2009).

Some conflict is common, as is some mutual respect. Indeed, both within families and within cultures, *ambivalence* is becoming recognized as the usual intergenerational pattern (Connidis, 2015), with mixed feelings (positive and negative) in every generation.

Extensive research finds many factors that affect intergenerational relationships:

- Assistance arises from both need and ability to provide.
- Frequency of contact is more dependent on geographical proximity than affection.
- Love is influenced by childhood memories.
- Sons feel stronger obligation; daughters feel stronger affection.
- National norms and policies can nudge family support, but they do not create it.
- Assistance from one generation to another is more likely to flow down than up, with the older generations providing more financial assistance to their grown children than vice versa.

GRANDPARENTS AND GREAT-GRANDPARENTS Eighty-five percent of U.S. elders currently older than 65 are grandparents. (The rate was lower in previous cohorts because the birth rate fell during the 1930s, and it is expected to be lower again.) Almost all grandparents provide some caregiving and gifts, unless the middle generation does not allow it (Lampkin, 2012). Generally in the West (less so in Asia), grandparents are more involved with their daughters' children than their sons'.

As with parents and children, specifics of the grandparent–grandchild relationship depend partly on personality and partly on the age of both generations. Grandparents typically are active caregivers of the youngest children, provide material support for the school-age children, and offer advice, encouragement, and a role model for the older grandchildren. One of my college students realized this when she wrote:

> Brian and Brianna are twins and are turning 13 years old this coming June. Over the spring break my family celebrated my grandmother's 80th birthday and I overheard the twins' talking about how important it was for them to still have grandma around because she was the only one who would give them money if they really wanted something their mom wasn't able to give them. . . . I lashed out . . . how lucky we were to have her around and that they were two selfish little brats. . . . Now that I am older, I learned to appreciate her for what she really is. She's the rock of the family and "the bank" is the least important of her attributes now.
>
> [Giovanna, personal communication]

Currently in developed nations, all three generations expect grandparents to be companions, not authorities. Contemporary elders usually enjoy their own independence. They provide babysitting and financial help but not advice or discipline (May et al., 2012).

As you remember from Chapter 13, in *skipped-generation* families, grandparent health and happiness are sometimes sacrificed when the grandparent takes on the

stresses and responsibilities of the parent role (Sampson & Hertlein, 2015). Usually such grandparents are relatively young, far more often age 50 than 70, and full parental responsibility ages them quickly.

Much depends on the culture and on the relationship between the grandparents and the parents. Generally in North America, skipped-generation families arise because the middle generation is abusive, neglectful, incarcerated, sick, or dead—obviously not the best situation for either the oldest or the youngest family members.

However, in China, skipped generations arise because the middle generation finds work in a distant city—and sends money, gives respect, and visits when possible. In China, grandparents with voluntary custody of the children tend to be healthier and happier than grandparents who live in three-generation families (Chen & Liu, 2012; Lou et al., 2013).

A middle ground is best. Just as too much responsibility impairs health and happiness, too little may be harmful as well. One Australian study focused on grandparents whose children prevented contact with the grandchildren.

For example, one reported this conversation with her daughter:

> She said: "You've never been a good mother, only when I was little". I said: "now that is ridiculous and you know that is ridiculous". She said: "you be quiet and listen to what I have to say, what I have to tell you now. . . I never want to see or hear from you the rest of your life". . . . I said: "I have fought hard. I have provided for both of your children. I've done all that I can to help you and [son-in-law]."
>
> [Marion, quoted in Sims & Rofail, 2014, p. 119]

Another grandmother in the same study first was thrilled with her grandchildren and then despondent.

> It was so enjoyable and now to think about it brings me to tears . . . this breaks our hearts . . . the consequence of this is that I have had issues of anxiety and depression, none of which I had previously and now I have been diagnosed with a severe heart problem, cardiomyopathy . . . this is more than I can bear – it breaks my heart to think of them.
>
> [Veronica, quoted in Sims & Rofail, 2014, pp. 120–121]

Sometimes past parent–child relationships provoke the middle generation to cut off grandparent–grandchild interaction. However, developmental research finds:

- Adults change over time, even in late adulthood. A grandparent can become less, or more, strict, following parental rules that differ from past practices. As with every human relationship, mutual compromise and explicit communication is essential.

Same Situation, Far Apart: Happy Grandfathers No matter where they are, grandparents and grandchildren often enjoy each other partly because conflict is less likely, as grandparents are usually not as strict as parents are. Indeed, Sam Levinson quipped, "The reason grandparents and grandchild get along so well is that they have a common enemy."

Grampa says it's what they used to use for social networking!

Universal Needs Hurray for grandparents who recognize that every generation needs to connect— even though the hayride, the soda fountain, and the balcony of the movie theater have all been replaced.

■ Relationships with the younger generation influence the emotional and physical well-being of the older generation. Not only heart problems, high blood pressure, and sleepless nights, but even life itself is affected by social interaction, sometimes reducing problems, sometimes increasing them (Paúl, 2014).

One of the realities of human development that appears in study after study is that family connections are pivotal for optimal growth, from pregnancy (when relatives help the expectant mother stay healthy and drug-free) to the end of life (when family members provide essential comfort). That is no less true in late adulthood, as the elderly benefit in many ways from connections to younger generations.

FRIENDSHIP Crucial for life satisfaction in later adulthood is friendship (Blieszner, 2014). Friendship networks are typically reduced with each decade. Emerging adults tend to average the most friends. By late adulthood, the number of people considered friends is notably smaller (Wrzus et al., 2013). Added to this normal shrinkage are two circumstances: Some older friends die, and retirees usually lose contact with work friends.

Family friends (friends who are also relatives, such as a favorite cousin) tend to be the most loyal. Elders are healthiest if some family friends are among their closest social circle, yet if the circle includes only relatives, and no nonfamily friends, that correlates with worse health (Shiovitz-Ezra & Litwin, 2015). Older adults are more likely to keep longtime friends than find new ones (Wrzus & Neyer, 2016), which is another reason they like to age in place.

Grown children who urge their distant parents to move closer to them may not appreciate the social networks—including those seen occasionally as well as those seen more often—that surround most older people. Gerontologists agree that "interrupting social connections . . . might be harmful, especially for women and the frailest" (Berkman et al., 2011, p. 347).

Same Situation, Far Apart: Partners Whether at the Vietnam Veterans Memorial in Washington, D.C. *(left)* or in the Philippines *(right),* elderly people support each other in joy and sorrow. These women are dancing together, and these men are tracing the name of one of their buddies who died 40 years earlier.

The Frail Elderly

Remember the diversity of development in late adulthood? As just described, most aging adults are active in many venues, enjoying supportive friends and family. But that is not true for everyone, for all their years.

Now we turn to the **frail elderly**—those who are infirm, inactive, seriously disabled. Frailty is not defined by any single disease, no matter how serious, but by an overall loss of energy and strength.

Most frail elders have several infirmities (taking many medications is a predictor), but some have no diagnosed illness (Theou et al., 2012; Jamsen et al., 2016). Frailty affects the entire body. One sign is weight loss (especially in men); another is extreme tiredness (especially in women); and a third is difficulty walking (everyone). Before death, about one-third of the elderly experience at least a year of frailty.

Activities of Daily Life

One way to measure frailty, according to insurance standards and medical professionals, is by assessing a person's ability to maintain self-care. Gerontologists often assess five physical **activities of daily life (ADLs):** eating, dressing, bathing, toileting, and moving (transferring) from a bed to a chair.

In part because mortality increases if a person cannot do the ADLs, a mnemonic sometimes used is DEATH [dressing, eating, ambulating (moving), toileting, hygiene (bathing)]. Sometimes additional ADLs are added to those five, including brushing teeth, walking 50 feet, and putting on shoes.

If a person cannot perform one or more of the ADLs, that may be a temporary problem, common after a major illness. The ADLs are dynamic: Most people who have difficulty with an ADL are able to recover (Ciol et al., 2014).

Recovery is especially likely if someone teaches them how to, for instance, put on shoes without needing to reach way down, or get out

frail elderly
People over age 65, and often over age 85, who are physically infirm, very ill, or cognitively disabled.

activities of daily life (ADLs)
Typically identified as five tasks of self-care that are important to independent living: eating, bathing, toileting, dressing, and transferring from a bed to a chair. The inability to perform any of these tasks is a sign of frailty.

Better or Worse? It depends. The advantage of having a motorized wheelchair is that a person can stay engaged in life, even, as shown here, on the streets of Beijing. The disadvantage is that riding may replace walking. This man might be on his way to strength-training at the gym, and if he gets there safely and regularly, his electric wheelchair can add years to his life.

WANG ZHAO/AFP/GETTY IMAGES

TABLE 15.1	Instrumental Activities of Daily Life
Domain	**Exemplar Task**
Managing medical care	Keeping current on checkups, including teeth, ears, and eyes
	Assessing supplements as good, worthless, or harmful
Food preparation	Evaluating nutritional information on food labels
	Preparing and storing food to prevent spoilage
Transportation	Comparing costs of car, taxi, bus, and train
	Determining quick and safe walking routes
Communication	Knowing when, whether, and how to use landline, cell, texting, mail, and e-mail
	Programming speed dial for friends, emergencies
Maintaining household	Following instructions for operating an appliance
	Keeping safety devices (fire extinguishers and CO_2 alarms) active
Managing one's finances	Budgeting future expenses (housing, utilities, etc.)
	Completing timely income tax returns
	Avoiding costly scams, unnecessary magazine subscriptions

Not Universal The IADLs vary from place to place, cohort to cohort. This list shows examples in developed nations in 2019.

instrumental activities of daily life (IADLs)
Actions (for example, paying bills and car maintenance) that are important to independent living and that require some intellectual competence and forethought. The ability to perform these tasks may be even more critical to self-sufficiency than ADL ability.

of bed without pain or risking a fall. Physical therapists show ways to accomplish self-care, recommend specialized equipment, and teach exercises that might increase the range of motion to make every task easier.

More important may be the **instrumental activities of daily life (IADLs)**, which require intellectual competence and forethought. Difficulty with IADLs often precede problems with ADLs since planning and problem-solving help elders maintain self-care.

IADLs vary from culture to culture. In developed nations, IADLs may include interpreting the labels on medicine bottles, preparing nutritious meals, filling out tax forms, keeping track of investments and expenses, scheduling doctor appointments, or using a computer, a cell phone, a kitchen gadget (see Table 15.1). In some nations, feeding one's animals, following religious rituals, and keeping the home clean, warm, and dry are IADLs.

Sometimes medical professionals are so focused on survival when someone has a health crisis that they ignore the need to recover ADLs and IADLs. True recovery includes self-care, and thus developmentalists are much more concerned about on-going life than on heart rate or oxygen saturation (Wahl et al., 2017).

Preventing Frailty

The ideal is to prevent frailty: Elders could be healthy and self-sufficient one day and dead the next. Instead, almost every older person eventually has difficulty with ADLs or IADLs. Such problems can be overcome, allowing capable self-care.

Prevention of frailty depends on everyone considering that disability is dynamic, not static, with self-sufficiency extended if individuals, families, and the larger community all do their part. We focus on two examples: first, mobility, and second, cognitive failure.

MUSCLE WEAKNESS The preeminent symptom of frailty is weakness. To some extent, that is everyone's problem: Muscles weaken with age, a condition called *sarcopenia*. In fact, muscle mass at age 90 is only half of what it was at age 30, with much of that loss occurring in late adulthood (McLean & Kiel, 2015).

Bones and balance are impaired as well. Thus, elderly people are more likely to fall than younger people, and they are more likely to break a bone when doing so. As already mentioned, osteoporosis (weak bones) is a common problem in old age, and broken bones—particularly the hip bone—cause immobility, morbidity, and eventual death.

Mobility is crucial for ADLs and IADLs. Yet there are many ways to prevent immobility. Some directly target bones: Drugs; diet; exercise; and replacement of hips, shoulders, knees, and so on are common. However, not every older person chooses such measures. Some fear falling and move less, increasing frailty, a choice sometimes encouraged by family and the community.

For example, if an elder wants to age in place, that saves money and is easier for the family and the society, even if it means staying in a home with steep stairs and a kitchen and bathroom far from the bedroom. Caregiving relatives might bring meals, buy a portable toilet, and get a remote control for a large bedroom TV. The community may not offer affordable and nearby housing alternatives and may not build smooth sidewalks. The TV news may highlight violent crime, further immobilizing the old. The result is an old, frail individual.

Instead, to prevent frailty, the individual, the family, and the community could change. The person could exercise daily, walking with family members on pathways built to be safe and pleasant. A physical therapist—paid by the individual, the family, or the government—could tailor the exercise and select appropriate equipment (a walker? a cane? special shoes?). The house could be redesigned, or the elder could move to a place where walking was safe and encouraged.

Extensive research has found again and again that lack of exercise leads to lower quality of life, increasing both ADLs and IADLs. On the other hand, more exercise improves life and health in the elderly who age in place or who live in senior residences or nursing homes. Indeed, a remarkable study in Australia found many positive results from an exercise program for the oldest-old with major neurocognitive disorder, living in long-term care facilities (Traynor et al., 2018).

Another study randomly assigned nursing-home residents to one of three groups: usual care, cognitive-behavioral intervention designed to increase exercise and reduce fear of falling, and the same cognitive-behavioral therapy plus a physical therapist to prescribe specific exercise. The latter group benefited most, not only in activity and muscle strength but in emotional outlook (T.-T. Huang et al., 2015).

In general, the research is clear that both attitude change and exercise carefully tailored to the individual are beneficial and that social support and companionship can dramatically increase movement. However, translating that research into action remains the problem, and loss of ADLs and IADLs is the result.

Don't Laugh One of the impediments to life and health is the notion that people who exercise must look young and attractive. This man is wise and brave, as well as admirably balanced.

Cognitive Failure

All three—the elder, the family, and the community—could prevent or at least postpone frailty, not only by improving mobility but also by helping with intellectual control.

Consider this example.

A 70-year-old Hispanic man came to his family doctor following a visit to his family in Colombia, where he had appeared to be disoriented (he said he believed he

Never Frail This man is playing the recorder at an Easter celebration in Arachova, a mountain town in Greece.

↑ OBSERVATION QUIZ

Impossible to be sure, but from what you see and know, there are seven clues that he will never be frail. How many can you name? (see answer, page 563)

was in the United States, and he did not recognize places that were known to be familiar to him) and he was very agitated, especially at night. An interview with the patient and a family member revealed a history that had progressed over the past six years, at least, of gradual worsening cognitive deficit, which that family had interpreted as part of normal aging. Recently his symptoms had included difficulty operating simple appliances, misplacement of items, and difficulty finding words, with the latter attributed to his having learned English in his late 20s. . . . [His] family had been very protective and increasingly had compensated for his cognitive problems.

. . . He had a lapse of more than five years without proper control of his medical problems [hypertension and diabetes] because of difficulty gaining access to medical care. . . .

Based on the medical history, a cognitive exam . . . and a magnetic resonance imaging of the brain . . . the diagnosis of moderate Alzheimer's disease was made. Treatment with ChEI [cholinesterase inhibitors] was started. . . . His family noted that his apathy improved and that he was feeling more connected with the environment.

[Griffith & Lopez, 2009, p. 39]

Both the community (those five years without treatment for hypertension and diabetes) and the family (making excuses, protecting him) contributed to major neurocognitive disorder that could have been delayed, if not prevented altogether.

Often with IADLs, the elderly themselves need to understand and prevent problems. In this case, the elderly man did not take care of his health, nor did any family member help him do so.

That trip to Colombia was the worst thing he could have done because disorientation worsens in an unfamiliar place. Nonetheless, family members helped him arrange the trip, a costly and foolish one. Why did no one realize how destructive such an excursion could be?

The social support networks that prevent physical decline also prevent cognitive decline (Boss et al., 2015). With many types of failing physical and mental health, delay, moderation, and sometimes prevention are possible. Often older individuals, and the people who love them, need to put in place all the safeguards and develop all the habits that will prevent frailty.

Caring for the Frail Elderly

Prevention is best, but it is not always sufficient. Some problems, such as major neurocognitive disorder or severe heart failure, can be postponed or slowed but not eliminated. Caregivers themselves are usually elderly, and they often have poor health, limited strength, and failing immune systems (Lovell & Wetherell, 2011). Thus, an aging parent who cares for the other parent is likely to need help.

Caregiving is especially difficult when people fail at their IADLs, because they do not realize what help they need. If people have trouble with an ADL, they know that they cannot walk, for instance. But if a person has trouble with an IADL, they might insist that they can submit taxes perfectly well and become angry if the Internal Revenue Service fines them.

FILIAL RESPONSIBILITY? There are marked cultural differences in norms and practices regarding care for the frail elderly, with some assuming that sons will do it, others that daughters should, others that the government should provide care. Recently, the governments of China and India have mandated that children care for their parents, a mandate that itself suggests that many older parents are not getting needed support.

The problem is that demographics have changed, which impacts filial responsibility. Some people still romanticize elder care, believing that frail older adults should

live with their caregiving children. That assumption worked when the demographic pyramid meant that each surviving elder had many descendants, but it may overburden beanpole families. [**Life-Span Link:** Demographic shift is discussed in Chapter 14.]

Some middle-aged couples have a dozen living ancestors. If those relatives had many children, care is shared by several siblings. A great-grandmother might have five children, 20 grandchildren, and 100 great-grandchildren.

However, with current longevity, some of those elders will need intensive care, and with current demographic changes, some stepparents will be added and fewer younger relatives will be available to provide care. Sometimes neither partner of a middle-aged couple has siblings, and then the filial responsibility for a dozen elderly relatives is theirs alone.

An added problem is that the designated caregiver of a frail elderly person is chosen less for logical reasons (e.g., the relative with the most patience, time, and skill) than for cultural ones. Grown children may assume that another relative has fewer responsibilities, or lives closest, and thus should be the caregiver. As you might imagine, resentment is common, particularly in daughters with more education (I.-F. Lin et al., 2012).

Sweet but Sad Family support is evident here, as an older sister (Lillian, age 75) escorts the younger sister (Julia, age 71) to the doctor. Unseen is how family support wrecked their lives: These sisters lost their life savings and their childhood home because their nephew had a substance use disorder.

Fortunately, most elderly relatives can care for themselves. Elders who believe that they are in control of their lives and are not dependent on their children are less likely to become frail (Elliot et al., 2018). But "not wanting to be a burden" can result in not accepting needed care.

Every solution is complicated, with costs and benefits, and adults of every gender and generation often disagree about what care is needed and who should provide it. Some older men, particularly, are fiercely independent, refusing help from family, doctors, and technology (such as walkers and hearing aids). That shortens their lives (Hamm et al., 2017). Some older women have held jobs and are unwilling to become dependent on their children.

Instead of the work–family conflicts that are common when children are young, a new conflict may arise, a family–family conflict. If a middle-aged couple have elders living with them, that can create tension for the marriage or their teenagers—who seek independence.

Adult siblings may also fight. In general, in North America, brothers expect their sisters to provide care for dependent elders. Although many midlife women do so, they resent that other family members do not do more.

SPOUSAL CAREGIVING This discussion thus far has focused on filial responsibility, but it should be noted that most of the elderly are cared for by their husbands and wives, who are elderly themselves. They become homebound, isolated from their friends and family—who visit less often and help even less. As one review explains:

> Spousal caregivers report more emotional, physical, and financial burden when compared with other caregivers, such as those who care for their elderly parents. They experience greater isolation and less help.
>
> [Glauber & Day, 2018, p. 537]

Remember variability, however. Some caregivers feel they are repaying past caregiving, and sometimes every other family member or friend, including the care receiver, expresses appreciation. That relieves resentment and makes caregiving easier (I.-F. Lin et al., 2012).

Caregiver burden varies but is often overwhelming, not only in the United States but wherever it occurs (Soto-Rubio et al., 2017). Currently in the United States, the

A Fortunate Man Henk Huisman gets care from his wife, Ria, who is happy to provide it. One reason is that this couple has three daughters, all of whom also help. Another reason may be that they live in the Netherlands, which provides extensive public assistance for everyone over age 65.

usual caregiver is the spouse (the wife twice as often as the husband), who often has no prior experience caring for a frail elder. Not only does the culture assume that it is her job, she herself assumes that she must provide care.

That may explain why many very frail husbands, with emotional and cognitive problems as well as physical ones, are cared for by their wives, who become depressed and exhausted. Indeed, while "spousal caregiving may be a labor of love, it is also a chronic stressor" (Glauber & Day, 2018, p. 538).

What if an elderly caregiver also has a part-time job? If she is the wife, that relieves some of the depression, because coworkers provide sympathy and comfort. But if he is the husband, part-time employment increases depression, presumably because men are socialized to work full time or to enjoy retirement—and these men can do neither (Glauber & Day, 2018).

THE ROLE OF THE GOVERNMENT Not only do individual assumptions about what is proper vary; nations, cultures, and ethnic groups vary as well. In northern European nations, most elder care is provided through a social safety net of senior day-care centers, senior homes, and skilled nurses; in African cultures, families are fully responsible for their older relatives.

In some cultures, an older person who is sick is taken to a hospital; in other cultures, such intervention is seen as interference with the natural order. In the United States, those who are elderly, sick, and destitute are cared for in understaffed nursing homes—unlike the luxury homes soon to be discussed.

In the United States, African Americans who enter nursing homes are more likely than European Americans to be poor and to suffer from major cognitive deficits, presumably because African American elderly people with merely physical frailties (ADLs not IADLs) are more often cared for by family. Only when care becomes emotionally crushing are alternatives considered.

Even in ideal circumstances, family members disagree about appropriate nutrition, medical help, and dependence. One family member may insist that an elderly person *never* enter a nursing home, and that insistence may create family conflict.

Public agencies rarely intervene unless a crisis arises. This troubles developmentalists, who study "change over time." From a life-span perspective, caregiver exhaustion and elder abuse are predictable and preventable.

ALL TOGETHER NOW Many elders are terrified of nursing homes and suspicious of strangers, and many informal caregivers do not ask for help. If one family member insists that a frail, disoriented relative be cared for at home, that may lead to family conflict, caregiver depression, poor health, and isolation—true in many cultures (Yıkılkan et al., 2014).

The ideal is **integrated care,** in which professionals and family members cooperate to provide comprehensive individualized care, whether at a long-term care facility, at the elder's home, or at someone else's home (Lopez-Hartmann et al., 2012). Just as a physical therapist knows which exercises and movements improve mobility, a professional can evaluate an impaired elder and figure out which tasks are best done by a relative, which by the frail person themselves, and which by a professional.

Multidisciplinary teams are needed, because frail elders need medical, social, and financial care (Pollina et al., 2017). Integrated care does not erase the burden of caregiving, but it helps. Much of the burden is emotional, and simply having someone else to explain what needs to be done, and what does not, is a comfort and relief.

In one study, a year after a professional helped plan and coordinate care, family caregivers improved in their overall attitude and quality of life. Although the total time spent on caregiving was not reduced by integrated care, the tasks performed changed, with more time on household tasks (e.g., meal preparation and cleanup) and less on direct care (Janse et al., 2014).

Often a professional will know what technology can help elders care for themselves. Dozens of devices are available (Rashidi & Mihailidis, 2013). For example, a pill container can be locked but then opened when an alarm rings and it is time to take the medicine. That avoids both over- and undermedication and allows the elder more independence.

Similarly, a large-screen video hookup can allow an older person to age in place while the caregiver lives elsewhere, visiting in person when necessary. This is much more advantageous than Skype or FaceTime—it provides a 24-hour connection that enables the elder and caregiver to talk face-to-face whenever either wants to say something.

Sometimes only standard equipment is needed (e.g., a chair in the shower, a raised seat on the toilet, a railing and nightlight in the hall).

The concept that a frail person is cared for *either* exclusively by one live-in family member *or* exclusively in a nursing home is not only wrong but is also destructive. Family members want and need to be involved, wherever care occurs. Isolation—either at home or in a nursing home—makes poor care more likely.

ELDER ABUSE When caregiving results in resentment and social isolation, the risk of depression, sickness, and abuse (of either the frail person or the caregiver) escalates (G. Smith et al., 2011; Dong, 2017; Johannesen & LoGiudice, 2013). Abuse is likely if:

- the *caregiver* suffers from emotional problems or substance abuse;
- the *care receiver* is frail, confused, and demanding; or
- the *care location* is isolated, where visitors are few.

Each of these factors increases the risk, and each of them is apparent before abuse begins (Chen & Dong, 2017). Ironically, although relatives are less able to cope with difficult patients than professionals are, they typically provide round-the-clock care, making abuse more likely. Those most likely to be abused live with their caregivers and suffer from neurocognitive problems as well as medical ones (Lachs & Pillemer, 2015).

Ideally, when one person becomes the caregiver, other family members should provide respite care. Instead they may avoid visiting. If they suspect abuse, they may accuse the abuser, but they often keep "family secrets," avoiding outsiders.

integrated care
Care of frail elders that combines the caregiving strengths of everyone—family, medical professionals, social workers, and the elders themselves.

Always There This elderly man can simply push one button to speak with his doctor.

Professionals typically begin care too late. Most doctors treat a patient in a medical crisis (a fall, heart attack, and so on) but not before, and most legal authorities intervene only after repeated and blatant abuse. Preventive care could have forestalled these problems.

As a result, some caregivers overmedicate, lock doors, and use physical restraints, all of which may be abusive. That may lead to inadequate feeding, medical neglect, or rough treatment. Obvious abuse is less likely in nursing homes and hospitals, not only because laws forbid it but also because workers are not alone, nor expected to work 24/7.

That statement may raise questions in your mind, because publicity is likely to occur when an instance of abuse occurs in a nursing home. However, most victims at home are never reported. A careful review laments inadequate definitions, comparisons, and reports, with actual prevalence in nursing homes "difficult to estimate" (Daly et al., 2011).

Of course, nursing homes are not exempt. The most common problem in nursing homes is that other residents can be abusive if supervision is inadequate. Typically, such abusers are men with a history of aggression who suffer from a major neurocognitive disorder; obviously such men need to be separated from vulnerable residents (Ferrah et al., 2015).

International research finds that elder abuse occurs everywhere, with a meta-analysis that estimated the prevalence at 16 percent (Yon et al., 2017). That number may be too high or too low because accurate incidence data and intervention are complicated by definitions: If an elder feels abused but a caregiver disagrees, who is right? Abused elders are often depressed, ill, and suffering from neurocognitive disorders. Does that prove abuse or absolve abusers (Dong et al., 2011)?

To prevent elder abuse, extensive public and personal safety nets are needed. Most social workers and medical professionals are suspicious if an elder is unexpectedly quiet, or losing weight, or injured. Professionals are "mandated reporters," which means that they must alert the authorities if they believe abuse is occurring.

However, most elder abuse is not physical, and some of the elderly are quiet, or lose weight, or accuse others for reasons other than abuse. Often elder abuse is financial, yet bankers, lawyers, and investment advisors are not trained to recognize it or obligated to respond and notify anyone (Jackson & Hafemeister, 2011).

Generally, abuse cases do not reach the courts unless the abuse is ongoing and extreme. Professionals and relatives alike hesitate to spot and then question a family caregiver who spends the Social Security check, disrespects the elder, or does not comply with the elder's demands. At what point is this abuse? Typically, abuse begins gradually and continues for years, unnoticed. Political and legal definitions and remedies are not clear-cut (Dong & Simon, 2011).

Consider this example.

> A sister made large withdrawals from her elderly brother's bank account. The victim, Mr Clark, was admitted to hospital after a serious fall. He had cognitive impairment and subsequently his mental capacity deteriorated. His sister began to look after his finances. Mrs Watson claimed that Mr Clark intended for her to have the money which she withdrew, describing it as her 'slush fund'. The Judge noted that Mr Clark was suffering from dementia and therefore was vulnerable, he trusted his sister but she had betrayed his trust, and she did not show remorse or appreciate that her actions were wrong, but acted out of greed rather than need. Mrs Watson was sentenced to ten months under house arrest followed by one year of probation. The Judge took into account that she had no prior criminal record, was unlikely to reoffend, and had provided personal care to her brother before he was admitted to hospital.
>
> [Matthews, 2018, p. 75]

As you see, the judge and the sister disagree as to whether this was greed, not need. Is a courtroom the best place to decide such a case?

Sometimes caregivers become victims, attacked by a confused elderly person. The victim is particularly likely to be a wife, who does not know how to handle an angry, confused husband. As with other forms of abuse, the dependency of the victim makes prosecution difficult, especially when secrecy, suspicion, and family pride keep outsiders away.

Long-Term Care

Same Situation, Far Apart: Diversity Continues No matter where they live, elders thrive with individualized care and social interaction, as is apparent here. Lenore Walker *(left)* celebrates her 100th birthday in a Florida nursing home with her younger sister nearby, and an elderly chess player in a senior residence in Kosovo *(right)* contemplates protecting his king. Both photos show, in details such as the women's earrings and the men's head coverings, that these elders maintain their individuality.

Although more than 90 percent of elders are independent and live in the community at any given moment, many of them will someday need institutional care. Nursing home and rehabilitation stays are often for less than a month, after a few days in a hospital. However, some elders need specialized institutional care for more than a year, and a very few—the oldest and least capable—stay for 10 years or more. Variations in such care are vast.

NURSING HOMES The trend in the United States and elsewhere is away from nursing homes and toward aging in place. Currently, residents of nursing homes tend to be very old—at least age 85—with significant cognitive decline and several medical problems (Moore et al., 2012). They also are disproportionately female (because men are usually married or remarried and die before their wives), with no capable descendants.

The skill of the staff, especially of the aides who provide frequent personal care, is crucial: Such simple tasks as helping a frail person out of bed can be done either clumsily and painfully or skillfully and patiently. Currently, however, many front-line workers have little training, low pay, and too many patients—and almost half leave each year (Golant, 2011).

Currently in the United States, many aides in nursing homes are immigrants, some with limited understanding of the language or background of the residents. Some of the more caring come from Africa, with a tradition of respect for the aged but frustration with the low pay and lack of mobility. They hope for better jobs soon, an understandable ambition but not ideal for their patients (Covington-Ward, 2017).

Even in the worst nursing homes, outright abuse is rare. Laws forbid the use of physical restraints except temporarily in specific, extraordinary circumstances. In the United States, nursing homes are frequently visited by government inspectors to "stop dreadful things from happening" (Baker, 2007).

In North America, excellent nursing-home care is available for those few who can afford it and know to seek individualized, humane care. Ideally, residents decide

what to eat, where to walk, whether to have a pet. Some excellent nonprofit homes are subsidized by religious organizations.

Good care encourages independence, individual choice, and privacy. This is called "person-centered care" and is now a goal of most nursing homes (Simmons & Rahman, 2014). As with day care for young children, continuity of care is crucial: A high rate of staff turnover is a bad sign.

◆ **Especially for Those Uncertain About Future Careers** Would you like to work in a nursing home? (see response, page 563)

At every age, relationships with other people are crucial: If the residents have the same caregivers, year after year, that improves well-being. A nationwide survey of nursing-home residents found that almost all thought it was very important that every effort be made to support relationships with family members—who should be able to visit at any time.

The best nursing homes now have special areas and accommodations for people with neurocognitive disorders. For example, some have "memory boxes," in addition to names on the doors of the rooms. A memory box displays photographs and other mementos so the residents know which room is theirs.

Many people with major neurocognitive disorders do not understand why they need care and often resist it. The easiest way to treat such resistance is with psycho-active drugs (Kleijer et al., 2014), but other tactics may be better at reducing anxiety (Konno et al., 2014). For instance, music, friendly dogs, and favorite foods can be appreciated by someone whose memory is so impaired that reading and conversing are impossible.

Quality care is much more labor-intensive and expensive than most people realize. Variations are dramatic, primarily because of the cost of personnel. According to John Hancock Life & Health Insurance Company in 2015, the cost of a year in a private room at a nursing home is $200,750 in Alaska and $56,575 in Louisiana. (Most people think that Medicare, Medicaid, or long-term care insurance covers the entire cost—a gross misconception.)

Some smaller nursing homes provide individualized care, where nurses and aides work closely together. Some homes are called Eden Alternative or Green, named after exemplars that stress individual autonomy. Such places increase the life and health of the residents, not only because of physical care but also because of attitude—residents are more hopeful about the future (Kubsch et al., 2018).

ALTERNATIVE CARE An ageist stereotype is that older people are either completely capable of self-care or completely dependent on others. In actuality, everyone is on a continuum, capable of some self-care and yet needing some help.

Once that is understood, a range of options can be envisioned. Recall the study cited in Chapter 14 that found that major NCD is less common in England than it used to be. That study also found that the percentage of people with neurocognitive disorders in nursing homes has risen, from 56 percent in 1991 to 65 percent in 2011, primarily because of a rise in the number of oldest-old women in such places (Matthews et al., 2013).

This means that more British elderly who need some care are now in the community. This is good news for the elderly, for developmentalists, and for the economy, because aging in place, assisted living, and other options cost less and have individualized care.

The number of assisted-living facilities has increased as nursing homes have decreased. Typically, assisted-living residences provide private apartments for each person and allow pets and furnishings, as in a traditional home.

The "assisted" aspects vary, often one daily communal meal, special transportation and activities, household cleaning, and medical assistance, such as supervision of pill-taking and blood pressure or diabetes monitoring, with a nurse, doctor, and ambulance if needed. In the United States, these assistances are additional expenses.

Many Possibilities This couple in Wyoming *(left)* sold their Georgia house and now live in this RV, and this Cuban woman *(right)* continues to live in her familiar home. Ideally, all of the elderly have a range of choices—and when that is true, almost no one needs nursing-home care.

As the number of assisted-living places increases, a concern arises about the lack of oversight (Han et al., 2017). As with nursing homes, quality varies a great deal.

Assisted-living facilities range from group homes for three or four elderly people to large apartments or townhouse developments for hundreds. Almost every state, province, or nation has its own standards for assisted-living facilities, but many such places are unlicensed. Some regions of the world (e.g., northern Europe) have many assisted-living options, while others (e.g., sub-Saharan Africa) have almost none.

Another form of elder care is sometimes called *village care*. Although not really a village, it is so named because of the African proverb, "It takes a whole village to raise a child." In village care, elderly people who live near each other pool their resources, staying in their homes but also getting special assistance when they need it. Such communities require that the elderly contribute financially and that they be relatively competent, so village care is not suited for everyone. However, for some it is ideal (Scharlach et al., 2012).

The first step in figuring out the best care—a step that should be taken long before a person needs to move to a nursing facility—is to invite a public health professional to the home to assess needs. As one advocate of personalized care wrote:

> In the home, nurses sit around all kinds of kitchen tables, on rickety wooden chairs and sleek bar stools, experiencing firsthand the diverse ways people live, care and connect. Interactions with family, friends and neighbours are generally frequent – and in some cases, noticeably absent.
>
> *[Sharkey & Lefebre, 2017, p. 11]*

Overall, as with many other aspects of aging, the emphasis in living arrangements is on selective optimization with compensation. Elders need settings that allow them to be safe, social, and respected, as independent as possible. Housing solutions vary depending not only on ADLs and IADLs but also on the elder's personality and social network of family and friends.

We close with a wonderful example of family care and nursing-home care at their best. A young adult named Rob related that his 98-year-old great-grandmother "began to fail. We . . . thought, well, maybe she is growing old" (quoted in Adler, 1995, p. 242). All three younger generations decided that she should move to a nearby nursing home, leaving the place she had lived for decades. She reluctantly agreed.

Fortunately, this nursing home did not assume that decline is always a sign of "final failing" (Rob's phrase). The doctors discovered that her pacemaker was not working properly. Rob tells what happened next:

> We were very concerned to have her undergo surgery at her age, but we finally agreed. . . . Soon she was back to being herself, a strong, spirited, energetic, independent woman. It was the pacemaker that was wearing out, not Great-grandmother.
>
> *[quoted in Adler, 1995, p. 242]*

This story contains a lesson repeated throughout this book. Whenever a toddler does not talk, a preschooler grabs a toy, a teenager gets drunk, an emerging adult takes risks, an adult seeks divorce, or an older person becomes frail, it is easy to conclude that such actions are normal. Indeed, each of these is common at the ages mentioned and may be appropriate and acceptable for some individuals. But none should simply be accepted without question. Each should also alert others to encourage talking, sharing, moderation, caution, communication, or self-care. The life-span perspective holds that, at every age, people can be "strong, spirited, and energetic."

what have you learned?

1. What factors make an older person frail?
2. What are the basic differences between ADLs and IADLs?
3. Why might IADLs be more important than ADLs in deciding whether a person needs care?
4. How is integrated care related to prevention of frailty?
5. What three factors increase the likelihood of elder abuse?
6. What are the advantages and disadvantages of assisted living for the elderly?
7. What factors distinguish a good nursing home from a bad one?

SUMMARY

Theories of Late Adulthood

1. Self theories hold that adults make personal choices in ways that allow them to become fully themselves. One such theory arises from Erikson's last stage, integrity versus despair, in which individuals seek integrity that connects them to the human community.

2. Compulsive hoarding can be understood as an effort to hold onto the self, keeping objects from the past that others might consider worthless.

3. Stratification theories maintain that social forces—such as ageism, racism, and sexism—limit personal choices throughout the life span, keeping people on a particular level or stratum of society.

4. Age stratification can be blamed for the disengagement of older adults. Activity theory counters disengagement theory, stressing that older people need to be active.

5. In late adulthood, some aspects of stratification theory seem apt, but others do not.

Activities in Late Adulthood

6. At every age, employment can provide social and personal satisfaction as well as needed income. Retirement may be welcomed because it enables other activities.

7. Some elderly people perform volunteer work and are active politically—writing letters, voting, staying informed. Many also value religious beliefs and practices.

8. Most of the elderly want to age in place. Many engage in home improvement.

9. Older adults in long-standing marriages tend to be satisfied with their relationships and to safeguard each other's health. As a result, married elders tend to live longer, happier, and healthier lives than unmarried ones.

10. Friends and other relatives are important for health and happiness. The social circle shrinks, but it may become more intense.

11. Relationships with adult children and grandchildren are usually mutually supportive, although conflicts arise as well. Financial support usually flows down the generational ladder.

The Frail Elderly

12. Most elderly people are self-sufficient, but some eventually become frail. They need help, either with physical tasks (ADLs such as eating and bathing) or with instrumental ones (IADLs such as completing income taxes).

13. Care of the frail elderly is usually undertaken by adult children or spouses, who are often elderly themselves. Most families have a strong sense of filial responsibility.

14. Elder abuse is a problem worldwide. It occurs because of a combination of caregiver and care receiver characteristics. Families are reluctant to get help when needed. Abuse can be financial, physical, or emotional.

15. Nursing homes, assisted living, and professional home care are of varying quality and availability. Good care for the frail elderly is personalized, combining professional and family support, recognizing diversity in needs and personality.

KEY TERMS

self theories (p. 532)
integrity versus despair (p. 533)
compulsive hoarding (p. 534)
socio-emotional selectivity theory (p. 534)

positivity effect (p. 534)
stratification theories (p. 536)
disengagement theory (p. 537)
activity theory (p. 537)

age in place (p. 542)
naturally occurring retirement community (NORC) (p. 543)
filial responsibility (p. 547)
frail elderly (p. 551)

activities of daily life (ADLs) (p. 551)
instrumental activities of daily life (IADLs) (p. 552)
integrated care (p. 557)

APPLICATIONS

1. Political attitudes vary by family and by generation. Interview several generations within the same family about issues of national and local importance. How do you explain the similarities and differences between the generations? What is more influential: experience, SES, heritage, or age?

2. People of different ages, cultures, and experiences vary in their values regarding family caregiving, including the need for safety, privacy, independence, and professional help. Find four people whose backgrounds (age, ethnicity, SES) differ. Ask their opinions and analyze the results.

3. A major expense for many older people is health care, both routine and catastrophic. Government payment for health care expenses (hospitals, drugs, and preventive care) varies widely from nation to nation. Compare two nations, your own and one other, on specifics of coverage and on data that indicate the health of the elderly (rates of longevity, diseases, etc.).

4. Visit a nursing home or assisted-living residence in your community. Record details about the physical setting, the social interactions of the residents, and the activities of the staff. Would you like to work or live in this place? Why or why not?

ESPECIALLY FOR ANSWERS

Response for Social Scientists (from page 538): In general, psychologists favor self theories, and sociologists favor stratification theories. Of course, each discipline respects the other, but each believes that its perspective is more honest and accurate.

Response for Religious Leaders (from page 543): There are many possible answers, including the specifics of getting to church (transportation, stairs), physical comfort in church (acoustics, temperature), and content (unfamiliar hymns and language).

Response for Those Uncertain About Future Careers (from page 560): Why not? The demand for good workers will obviously increase as the population ages, and the working conditions are likely to improve. An important problem is that the quality of nursing homes varies, so you need to make sure you work in one whose policies incorporate the view that the elderly can be quite capable, social, and independent.

OBSERVATION QUIZ ANSWERS

Answer to Observation Quiz (from page 540): Two good answers: 1) the drop in men's employment from 1970 to 1990, and 2) the steady rise in women's employment throughout. Does your choice between these two say anything about what you notice?

Answer to Observation Quiz (from page 542): Emerging adulthood. The hard question is why?

Answer to Observation Quiz (from page 554): He has an activity that he enjoys (recorder playing), he walks regularly (that walking stick), he breathes unpolluted air (mountain town), he is religious (it is Easter, so he is probably Greek Orthodox), his community values him (he was chosen to play), he is male (men are more likely to die quickly), and he has a healthy diet (the Mediterranean diet—with lots of fish, vegetables, and olive oil, the healthiest diet we know). Of course, we cannot be certain of any of these, but chances are this man has many more healthy years.

Death and Dying

what will you know?

- Why is death a topic of hope, not despair?
- What is the difference between a good death and a bad one?
- How does mourning help with grief?

"If someone must die, who should be saved, an unborn baby or a pregnant woman?"

That question was posed to me when I was a girl. My teacher wanted me to think about ethical choices that I might encounter, and neither that adult nor I considered that question inappropriate for an 8-year-old.

That reflected reality as my older teacher understood it: A century ago, death often took the lives of newborns and sometimes of birthing women. Death was once familiar, yet frightening. Everyone knew someone struck down "in their prime" by tuberculosis, heart attacks, cancer, or other diseases.

In my own life, by contrast, medical care and public health measures keep death at bay until old age. Only one of my high school classmates died in adulthood, and she ran into a burning building because she thought her children were inside. Only one person I know had a baby who died. The cause was sudden infant death syndrome (SIDS); that was 40 years ago.

Since death before old age was rare, I witnessed two new phases of thinking about death. When I was an adolescent, talking about death had become taboo. By the time I entered college, a third phase had begun, with crusaders who fought the "denial of death" (Becker, 1997), the "death industry" (Mitford, 2000), and the refusal of hospitals to acknowledge the emotions of the dying (Kübler-Ross, 1997). College courses, single-topic textbooks (e.g., Kastenbaum, 2012), and epilogues (like those in my texts) included death as part of life.

Are we entering a fourth phase? Children have video games in which creatures (and people) often die, drones are programmed to kill from thousands of miles away, smartphones "die" and then are recharged every day. Death is commonplace, but distant. Or are these superficial changes? Is death still an emotion-laden finality that we strive to understand?

This chapter notes the dilemmas of death and dying, such as determining when and why death occurs and how to help people who are grieving.

Death remains part of life. There is still *hope* in death, there are *choices* in dying, and there is *affirmation* in mourning, as each of the three main sections of this Epilogue describe. Ethical questions linger.

Death and Hope

A multi-cultural life-span perspective reveals that reactions to death are filtered through many cultural prisms, affected by historical changes and regional variations as well as by the age of both the dying and the bereaved.

One emotion is constant, however: hope. It appears in many ways: hope for life after death, hope that the world is better because someone lived, hope that death occurred for a reason, hope that survivors rededicate themselves to whatever they deem meaningful. Immortality of some kind seems evident as people think about death (Robben, 2018).

Cultures, Epochs, and Death

Few people in developed nations have witnessed someone die. This was not always the case (see Table EP.1). If someone reached age 50 in 1900 in the United States and had had 20 high school classmates, at least six of those fellow students would have already died. The survivors would have visited and reassured their dying friends at home, promising to see them in heaven.

Modern people are less sure about heaven but still have hope. We begin by describing traditional responses when familiarity with death was common.

ANCIENT TIMES Paleontologists have evidence from 120,000 years ago that the Neandertals buried their dead with tools, bowls, or jewelry, signifying belief in an afterlife (Stiner, 2017). The date is controversial: Burial with objects could have begun

---

TABLE EP.1 How Death Has Changed in the Past 100 Years

Death occurs later. A century ago, the average life span worldwide was less than 40 years (47 in the rapidly industrializing United States). Half of the world's babies died before age 5. Now newborns are expected to live to age 71 (79 in the United States); in many nations, centenarians are the fastest-growing age group.

Dying takes longer. In the early 1900s, death was usually fast and unstoppable; once the brain, the heart, or any other vital organ failed, the rest of the body quickly followed. Now death can often be postponed through medical technology: Hearts can beat for years after the brain stops functioning, respirators can supplement lungs, and dialysis does the work of failing kidneys.

Death often occurs in hospitals. For most of our ancestors, death occurred at home, with family nearby. Now most deaths occur in hospitals or other institutions, with the dying surrounded by medical personnel and machines.

The causes of death have changed. People of all ages once usually died of infectious diseases (tuberculosis, typhoid, and smallpox), or, for many women and most infants, in childbirth. Now disease deaths before age 50 are rare, and in developed nations most newborns (99 percent) and their mothers (99.99 percent) live.

And after death . . . People once knew about life after death. Some believed in heaven and hell; others, in reincarnation; and others, in the spirit world. Prayers were repeated—some on behalf of the souls of the deceased, some for remembrance, some to the dead asking for protection. Believers were certain that their prayers were heard. People now are aware of cultural and religious diversity; many raise doubts that never occurred to their ancestors.

earlier, but it is certain that long ago death was an occasion for hope, mourning, and remembrance.

Two Western civilizations with written records—Egypt and Greece—had elaborate death rituals millennia ago. The ancient Egyptians built magnificent pyramids, refined mummification, and scripted instructions (called the *Book of the Dead*) to help the soul (*ka*), personality (*ba*), and shadow (*akh*) reunite after death so that the dead could protect the living (Taylor, 2010).

Another set of beliefs came from the ancient Greeks. Again, continuity between life and death was evident, with hope for this world and the next. The fate of a dead person depended on his or her life. A few would have a blissful afterlife, a few were condemned to torture in Hades, and most would enter a shadow world until they were reincarnated.

Ancient Chinese, Mayan, Indian, and African cultures also had rituals about death, and they venerated ancestors as still connected to the living in some way (Hill & Hageman, 2016). That gave survivors hope for themselves. Everywhere:

- Actions during life were thought to affect destiny after death.
- The afterlife was more than a hope; it was assumed.
- Mourners said particular prayers and made specific offerings to prevent the spirit of the dead from haunting and hurting them and to gain blessing and strength from the ancestors.

CONTEMPORARY RELIGIONS Now consider contemporary religions. Each faith seems distinct in its practices surrounding death (Garces-Foley, 2015). One review states, "Rituals in the world's religions, especially those for the major tragic and significant events of bereavement and death, have a bewildering diversity" (Idler, 2006, p. 285).

Some details illustrate this diversity. The period of mourning could be a week, a month, or a year, or until a candle or a funeral pyre burns out. According to one expert, in Hinduism the dead body is always visible; in Islam, never (Gilbert, 2013). In many Muslim and Hindu cultures, the next of kin bathe the dead person; among some Native Americans (e.g., the Navajo), no family member touches the dead person.

Although religious traditions learned in childhood are carried by immigrants to distant lands, after several generations specific rituals vary as much by region as by religion. In North America, Christians of all sects are influenced by local traditions: The funeral of a Roman Catholic in Nebraska is more like a Nebraskan Methodist than an Indonesian Catholic.

According to many branches of Hinduism, a person should die on the floor, surrounded by family, who neither eat nor wash until the funeral pyre is extinguished. By contrast, among some (but not all) Christians today, the very sick should be taken to the hospital; if they die, then mourners gather to eat and drink, often with music and dancing.

HIP/ART RESOURCE, NY

Conversation Who is talking here? Unless you are an Egyptologist, you would not guess that this depicts a dead man conversing with the gods of the Underworld. Note that the deceased is relatively young and does not seem afraid—both typical for people in ancient Egypt.

COLIN MCCONNELL/GETTY IMAGES

Dance for the Dead This woman in Toronto, Ontario, dances on Dia de los Muertos, wearing a traditional skull headdress. People in many Latin American communities remember death and celebrate life on November 1 (All Saints Day) and November 2 (All Souls Day) each year.

Diversity is also evident in Buddhism. The First Noble Truth is that life is suffering. Some rituals help believers accept death and detach from the dying person. Other rituals help people connect to the dead as a way to mark the continuity between life and death (Cuevas & Stone, 2011).

That creates an ethical dilemma—not the one posed to me at age 8, but nonetheless a difficult one. Some Buddhists leave the dying alone; other Buddhists hover nearby. Evident is "a multiplicity of distinctive Buddhist philosophical and cultural traditions" (Tsomo, 2006, p. 22).

AUTOPSY AND CREMATION Acceptance of cremation, autopsy, and organ donation depends as much on local norms as on religious authority. Muslims in many nations are cremated, but those in the United States and Europe may be buried (Campo, 2015). Among the more than 500 Native American tribes in the United States, each has its own heritage and death customs.

Honor Your Father Worldwide, children mourn their deceased parents by performing rituals developed by their community, as these four young men do while they spread ashes in the sea. Some secular adults, born and raised in Western Europe or North America, fly thousands of miles back to India with their Hindu fathers' ashes, comforted by thus respecting their heritage.

Autopsies may be legally required and yet be considered a religious sacrilege. For instance, for the Hmong in Cambodia, any mutilation of the dead body has "horrifying meanings" and "dire consequences for . . . the spiritual well-being of surviving family and community" (Rosenblatt, 2013, p. 125).

In Minnesota, however, where many Hmong now live, autopsies are required—without the family's permission—if there is "any question about the cause of death." Such questions often arise when an older Cambodian person dies, because they choose to die at home.

As new generations with Cambodian heritage become more Americanized, death customs may change: Each generation responds to death with a combination of tradition and modernity. An example comes from Korea.

In the past, Koreans opposed autopsies because the body is a sacred gift. However, science and medicine are highly valued. This created a problem: Medical schools need autopsies. The Koreans developed a new custom: a special religious service honoring the dead who gave their body to teach aspiring doctors (J.-T. Park et al., 2011). The result: a dramatic increase in the number of bodies donated.

The conflict between religion and politics in organ donation is evident in many nations. In Egypt, people were suspicious of organ donation and chose to protect the dying and dead from any attempt to use their organs. However, again current needs affected beliefs. In the protests of 2011, many people were blinded by tear gas, which led many other Egyptians to donate the corneas of the dead so that protestors could see again (Hamdy, 2018).

In all religions, the hope for future generations combines with the respect for prior generations. Many people believe that spirits of ancestors can bless or curse the living. Those spirits may appear when needed, or they may come on special days, such as the Hungry Ghost Festival (in many East Asian nations), the Day of the Dead (in many Latin American nations), or All Souls Day (in many European nations).

Understanding Death Throughout the Life Span

Thoughts about death—as about everything else—are influenced by each person's age, cognitive maturation, and past experiences. Here are some of the specifics.

DBIMAGES/ALAMY STOCKPHOTO

DEATH IN CHILDHOOD Some adults think children are oblivious to death; others believe children should participate in funerals and other rituals, just as adults do (Talwar et al., 2011). You know from your study of childhood cognition that neither view is completely correct.

Very young children have some understanding of death, but their perspective differs from that of older people. They may believe that the dead can come alive again. For that reason, a child might not immediately be sad when someone dies. Later, moments of profound sorrow might occur when reality sinks in, or simply when the child realizes that a dead parent will never again tuck them into bed at night.

Children are affected by the attitudes of others. They may be upset if they see grown-ups moan and cry or if grown-ups keep them away from death rituals for someone they loved. Thus, adults should neither ignore the child's emotions nor expect adultlike reactions (Doering, 2010). Because the limbic system matures more rapidly than the prefrontal cortex, children may seem happy one day and morbidly depressed the next.

Young children who themselves are fatally ill typically fear that death means being abandoned (Wolchik et al., 2008). Consequently, parents should stay with a dying child—holding, reading, singing, and sleeping. A frequent and caring presence is more important than logic.

By school age, many children seek independence. Parents and professionals can be too solicitous; older children do not want to be babied. Often they want facts and a role in "management of illness and treatment decisions" (Varga & Paletti, 2013, p. 27).

Children who lose a friend, a relative, or a pet might, or might not, seem sad, lonely, or angry. For example, one 7-year-old boy seemed unfazed by the loss of three grandparents and an uncle within two years. However, he was extremely upset when his dog, Twick, died.

JOHAN ORDOÑEZ/GETTY IMAGES

Sorrow All Around When a 5-day-old baby died in Santa Rosa, Guatemala, the entire neighborhood mourned. Symbols and a procession help with grief: The coffin is white to indicate that the infant was without sin and will therefore be in heaven.

↑ OBSERVATION QUIZ
Beyond the coffin, do you see any other signs of ritual? (see answer, page 592)

That boy's parents, each grieving for a dead mother, were taken aback by the depth of his emotions. The boy was angry that they did not take him to the animal hospital before the dog was euthanized. He refused to go back to school, saying, "I had wanted to see him one more time. . . . You don't understand" (quoted in Kaufman & Kaufman, 2006, pp. 65–66).

Because the loss of a particular companion is a young child's concern, it is not helpful to say that a dog can be replaced. Even a 1-year-old knows that a new puppy is not the same dog. Nor should a child be told that Grandma is sleeping, that God wanted Sister in heaven, or that Grandpa went on a trip. The child may take such explanations literally, wanting to wake up Grandma, complain to God, or phone Grandpa to say, "Come home."

In any case, adults need to recognize that children have many emotions and thoughts about death. Adults need to listen to children, avoiding platitudes (Stevenson, 2017). If adults ignore the child, the child reaches the horrifying conclusion that death is so frightening that adults cannot talk about it. Even worse is the conclusion that adults lie to children.

Remember how cognition changes with development. Egocentric preschoolers might fear that they, personally, caused death with their unkind words. [**Life-Span Link:** Egocentrism is discussed in Chapter 5.] A child's cognition is also affected by the culture. Many developmentalists find that video games involving killing and rebirth make children less aware of the power of actual death and aggression (e.g., Greitemeyer, 2014).

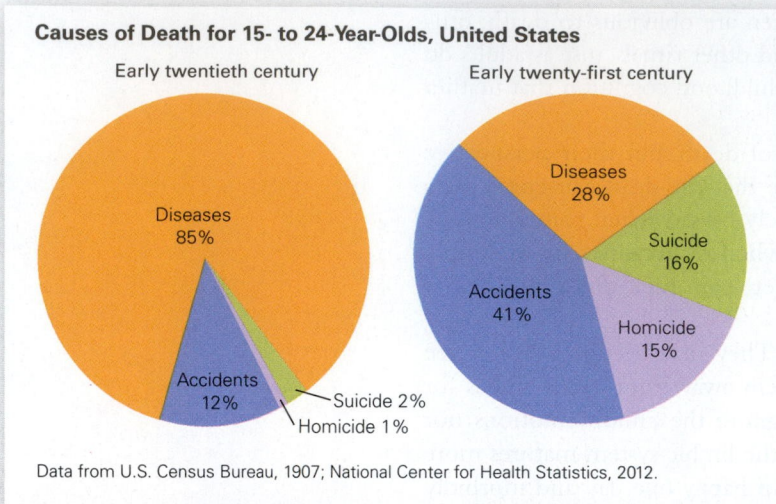

Causes of Death for 15- to 24-Year-Olds, United States

Early twentieth century

Diseases 85%
Accidents 12%
Suicide 2%
Homicide 1%

Early twenty-first century

Diseases 28%
Suicide 16%
Homicide 15%
Accidents 41%

Data from U.S. Census Bureau, 1907; National Center for Health Statistics, 2012.

FIGURE EP.1 Typhoid Versus Driving into a Tree In 1905, most young adults in the United States who died were victims of diseases, usually infectious ones like tuberculosis and typhoid. In 2012, almost three times more died violently (accidents, homicide, and suicide) than died of all diseases combined.

↑ **OBSERVATION** QUIZ
Which cause of death shows the greatest change over the past century? (see answer, page 592)

terror management theory
The idea that people adopt cultural values and moral principles in order to cope with their fear of death. This system of beliefs protects individuals from anxiety about their mortality and bolsters their self-esteem.

As children become concrete operational thinkers, they seek facts, such as exactly how a person died and where that person is now. They want something to do: bring flowers, repeat a prayer, write a letter. The boy who was so upset when his dog died went back to school after his parents framed and hung a poem that he wrote to Twick. Children accept both biological death and spiritual afterlife, as long as adults are honest with them (Talwar et al., 2011).

DEATH IN ADOLESCENCE AND EMERGING ADULTHOOD Adolescents may be self-absorbed, philosophical, analytic, or distraught—or all four at different moments. [**Life-Span Link:** Adolescent dual processing is discussed in Chapter 9.] Self-expression is part of the search for identity; death of a loved one does not put an end to that search. Some adolescents use social media to write to the dead person or to vent their grief—an effective way to express their personal identity concerns (DeGroot, 2012; Balk & Varga, 2017).

"Live fast, die young, and leave a good-looking corpse" is advice often attributed to actor James Dean, who died in a car crash at age 24. At what stage would a person be most likely to agree? Emerging adulthood, of course (see Figure EP.1).

Terror management theory explains some illogical responses to death. The idea is that people who fear death become more defensive of their own culture, more ageist, and sometimes more likely to take risks (Burke et al., 2010). By surviving a risk, they manage their terror by defying death. Terror management is particularly evident among college students and seems to disappear when people are middle-aged or older (Maxfield et al., 2017).

Terror management may explain an illogical action by adolescents in Florida who suffer from asthma. Compared to high school students without asthma, they are more likely to use tobacco products (28 percent versus 24 percent). That includes higher rates of smoking cigarettes and cigars, which they know are harmful for their lungs (Reid et al., 2018).

Research in many nations finds that when adolescents and emerging adults think about death, they may become more patriotic and religious but less tolerant of other worldviews (Ellis & Wahab, 2013; Jonas et al., 2013). Apparently, death fosters the hope that they and their group are worthy of living. If they are dying, they especially value friends and personal identity.

DEATH IN ADULTHOOD When adults become responsible for work and family, attitudes shift. Death is not romanticized. Many adults quit addictive drugs, start wearing seat belts, and adopt other death-avoiding behaviors when they become parents.

The death of a child is particularly hard on the parents, who may either distance themselves from one another or become closer. Indeed, several years after the loss of a child, the illness and death rate of parents rises (Brooten et al., 2018).

Adults who are dying may be less concerned about themselves than about the other people they will leave, especially children. It helps if they write a letter to the child to be opened at some age—such as 18—so they know that their love and care will continue after they die.

One dying middle-aged adult was Randy Pausch, a 47-year-old professor and father of three. Ten months before he died of cancer in 2008, he delivered a famous *last lecture,* detailing his childhood dreams and saluting those who would continue his work. After advising his students to follow their own dreams, he concluded, "This talk is not for you, it's for my kids" (Pausch & Zaslow, 2008).

Not surprisingly, that message was embraced by his wife, also in mid-adulthood. She wrote her own book, *Dream New Dreams*, in which she discusses overcoming death by focusing on life (J. Pausch, 2012).

To defend against the fear of death, adults do not readily accept the death of others. When Dylan Thomas was about age 30, he wrote to his dying father: "Do not go gentle into that good night/ Rage, rage against the dying of the light" (Thomas, 2003, p. 239). Nor do adults readily accept their own death. A woman diagnosed at age 42 with a rare and almost always fatal cancer (a sarcoma) wrote:

> I hate stories about people dying of cancer, no matter how graceful, noble, or beautiful. . . . I refuse to accept I am dying; I prefer denial, anger, even desperation.
>
> [Robson, 2010, pp. 19, 27]

When adults hear about another's death, their reaction depends on the dead person's age. Millions of people mourned James Dean, Prince, and Whitney Houston (ages 24, 57, and 48, respectively). Equally talented entertainers who die at age 80 or 90 are less mourned.

Logically, adults should work to change social factors that increase the risk of mortality—such as air pollution, junk foods, and unsafe transportation. Instead, many react more strongly to rare causes of death, such as anthrax and avalanches. They particularly fear deaths beyond their control.

For example, people fear travel by plane more than by car. In fact, flying is safer: In 2017 in the entire world, only 399 people were killed in airplane accidents; but in the United States alone, 40,100 were killed by motor vehicles, according to the National Safety Council.

Ironically, when four airplanes crashed on September 11, 2001, many North Americans drove long distances because they were afraid to fly. In the next few

PHOTOGRAPH © JAI PAUSCH. FROM THE BOOK *THE LAST LECTURE* BY RANDY PAUSCH WITH JEFFREY ZASLOW. COPYRIGHT © 2008 RANDY PAUSCH. PHOTO COURTESY OF DAVID BLACK AGENCY.

"For My Kids" Randy Pausch was a brilliant, innovative scientist at Carnegie Mellon University. When he was diagnosed with terminal pancreatic cancer, he gave a talk titled "The Last Lecture: Really Achieving Your Childhood Dreams" that became famous worldwide. He devoted the final 10 months of his life to his family—his wife, Jai, and their children, Chloë, Dylan, and Logan.

BRYAN WOOLSTON/REUTERS/NEWSCOM

MCT/GETTY IMAGES

Contrast or Commonality? Solemn faces and red eyes are evident in the brother, widow, children, and father of Beau Biden, former Vice President Joe Biden's son *(left)*—a contrast to the pop performances at Michael Jackson's funeral *(right)*. In both cases, however, survivors memorialized the dead. Vice President Biden, for instance, began a national campaign to fight brain cancer.

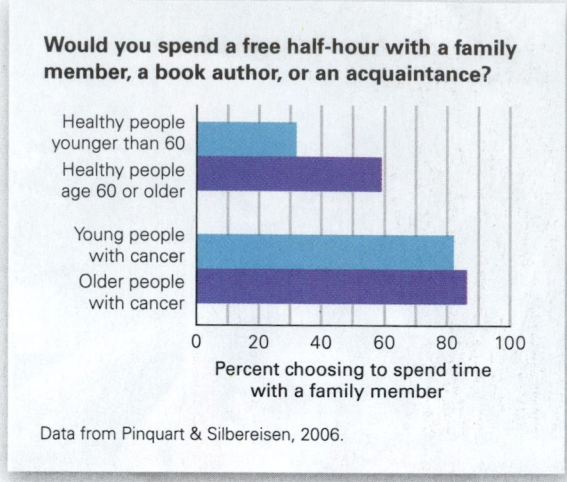

Would you spend a free half-hour with a family member, a book author, or an acquaintance?

Percent choosing to spend time with a family member

Data from Pinquart & Silbereisen, 2006.

FIGURE EP.2 Turning to Family as Death Approaches Both young and old people diagnosed with cancer (one-fourth of whom died within five years) more often preferred to spend a free half-hour with a family member rather than with an interesting person whom they did not know well.

months, 2,300 more U.S. residents died in car crashes than usual (Blalock et al., 2009). Not logical, but very human.

DEATH IN LATE ADULTHOOD In late adulthood, attitudes shift again. Anxiety decreases; hope rises (De Raedt et al., 2013).

Some older people remain happy when they are fatally ill. Many developmentalists believe that one sign of mental health among older adults is acceptance of mortality, which increases the concern for others. Some elders engage in *legacy work,* trying to leave something meaningful for later generations (Lattanzi-Licht, 2013).

As evidence of this attitude change, older people seek to reconcile with estranged family members and tie up loose ends (Kastenbaum, 2012). Do not be troubled when elders allocate heirlooms, discuss end-of-life wishes, or buy a burial plot: All of those actions are developmentally appropriate.

Acceptance of death does not mean that the elderly give up on living; rather, their priorities shift. In an intriguing series of studies (Carstensen, 2011), people were presented with the following scenario:

> Imagine that in carrying out the activities of everyday life, you find that you have half an hour of free time, with no pressing commitments. You have decided that you'd like to spend this time with another person. Assuming that the following three persons are available to you, whom would you want to spend that time with?
> - A member of your immediate family
> - The author of a book you have just read
> - An acquaintance with whom you seem to have much in common

Older adults, more than younger ones, choose the family member (see Figure EP.2). The researchers explain that family becomes more important when death seems near.

Near-Death Experiences

At every age, coming close to death may be an occasion for hope. This is most obvious in what is called a *near-death experience,* in which a person almost dies. Survivors sometimes report having left the body and moved toward a bright light while feeling peace and joy. The following classic report is typical:

> I was in a coma for approximately a week.... I felt as though I were lifted right up, just as though I didn't have a physical body at all. A brilliant white light appeared.... The most wonderful feelings came over me—feelings of peace, tranquility, a vanishing of all worries.
>
> [quoted in Moody, 1975, p. 56]

Near-death experiences often include religious elements (angels seen, celestial music heard). Survivors often become more spiritual, less materialistic.

A reviewer of near-death experiences is struck by their endorsement of religious beliefs. In every culture, "all varieties of the dying experience" move people toward the same realizations: (1) the limitations of social status, (2) the insignificance of material possessions, and (3) the narrowness of self-centeredness (Greyson, 2009).

In fact, people who have merely heard about near-death experiences from other people tend to have some of the same emotions, feeling more spiritual and less materialistic (Tassell-Matamua et al., 2017). That brings us back to a general theme. Thinking about death can make people more hopeful about the future—their own and that of others.

THINK CRITICALLY: When a person is almost dead, might thoughts occur that are not limited by the neuronal connections in the brain?

Choices in Dying

Do you recoil at the heading "Choices in Dying"? If so, you may be living in the wrong century. Every twenty-first–century death involves choices, beginning with risks taken or avoided, habits sustained, and specific measures to postpone or hasten death.

A Good Death

People everywhere hope for a good death, one that is:

- At the end of a long life
- Peaceful
- Quick
- In familiar surroundings
- With family and friends present
- Without pain, confusion, or discomfort

RICH PEDRONCELLI/AP IMAGES

Many would add that *control over circumstances* and *acceptance of the outcome* are also characteristic of a good death, but cultures and individuals differ. Some dying individuals willingly cede control to doctors or caregivers, and others fight every sign that death is near.

A review finds that family, medical personnel, and the dying person emphasize different aspects of "a good death" (Meier et al., 2016). For example, psychological and spiritual well-being are important for many patients but less so for physicians.

MEDICAL CARE In some ways, modern medicine makes a good death more likely. The first item on the list has become the norm: Death usually occurs at the end of a long life. Younger people still get sick, but surgery, drugs, radiation, and rehabilitation typically mean that the ill enter a hospital and then return home. If young people die, death is typically quick (a fatal accident or suicide) and without pain, although painful for their loved ones.

In other ways, however, medical advances make a bad death more likely. When a cure is impossible, physical and emotional comfort deteriorate (Kastenbaum, 2012). Instead of acceptance, people fight death with medical measures that increase pain. Hospitals may exclude visitors at the most critical point; patients may become delirious or unconscious, unable to die in peace.

Although most people want to die at home, most deaths in developed nations occur in hospitals. Even in England, where one goal of public medicine is a good

Too Late for Her When Brittany Maynard was diagnosed with progressive brain cancer that would render her unable to function before killing her, she moved from her native California to establish residence in Oregon so she could die with dignity. A year later, the California Senate Health Committee (shown here) debated a similar law, with Brittany's photo on a desk. They approved the law, 5–2.

VIDEO: End of Life: Interview with Laura Rothenberg features a young woman with a terminal illness discussing her feelings about death.

death, half of the deaths occur in hospitals, one-fourth in "care homes" (called nursing homes in the United States), and only one-fourth at home (Bone et al., 2018).

The underlying problem may be medical care itself, with "the dangers of well-intentioned over 'medicalization'" (Ashby, 2009, p. 94). From a developmental perspective, medication is not the answer. Dying involves emotions, values, and a community—not just a heart that might stop beating.

STAGES OF DYING Emotions were the focus of Elisabeth Kübler-Ross (1975, 1997). In about 1960, she asked the administrator of a large hospital for permission to speak with dying patients. He told her that no one was dying! Eventually, she found a few terminally ill patients who wanted very much to talk.

From ongoing interviews, Kübler-Ross identified reactions of dying people. She divided their emotions into five sequential stages.

1. Denial ("I am not really dying.")
2. Anger ("I blame my doctors, or my family, or my God for my death.")
3. Bargaining ("I will be good from now on if I can live.")
4. Depression ("I don't care; nothing matters anymore.")
5. Acceptance ("I accept my death as part of life.")

Another set of stages of dying is based on Maslow's hierarchy (Zalenski & Raspa, 2006):

1. Physiological needs (freedom from pain)
2. Safety (no abandonment)
3. Love and acceptance (from close family and friends)
4. Respect (from caregivers)
5. Self-actualization (appreciating one's unique past and present)

Maslow later suggested a possible sixth stage, *self-transcendence* (Koltko-Rivera, 2006), which emphasizes the acceptance of death.

Other researchers have *not* found either set of stages. Remember the woman dying of a sarcoma, cited earlier? She said that she would never *accept* death and that Kübler-Ross should have included desperation as a stage. Kübler-Ross said that her stages have been misunderstood, as "our grief is as individual as our lives. . . . Not everyone goes through all of them or goes in a prescribed order" (Kübler-Ross & Kessler, 2005, p. 7).

Nevertheless, both lists remind caregivers that each dying person has strong emotions and needs that may be unlike that same person's emotions and needs a few days or weeks earlier. They may differ from their doctors and loved ones, who themselves have varied emotions. A good death recognizes dynamic changes in everyone's thoughts.

◆ **Especially for Relatives of a Person Who Is Dying**
Why would a healthy person want the attention of hospice caregivers? (see response, page 592)

Same Situation, Far Apart: As It Should Be Dying individuals and their families benefit from physical touch and suffer from medical practices (gowns, tubes, and isolation) that restrict movement and prevent contact. A good death is likely for these two patients—a husband with his wife in their renovated hotel/hospital room in North Carolina *(left),* and a man with his family in a Catholic hospice in Andhra Pradesh, India *(right).*

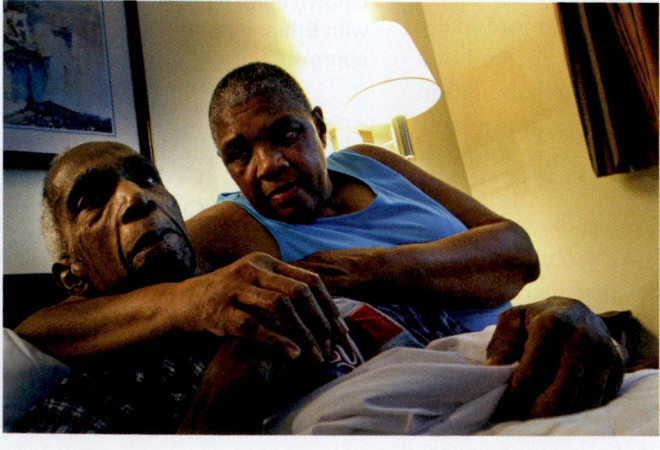
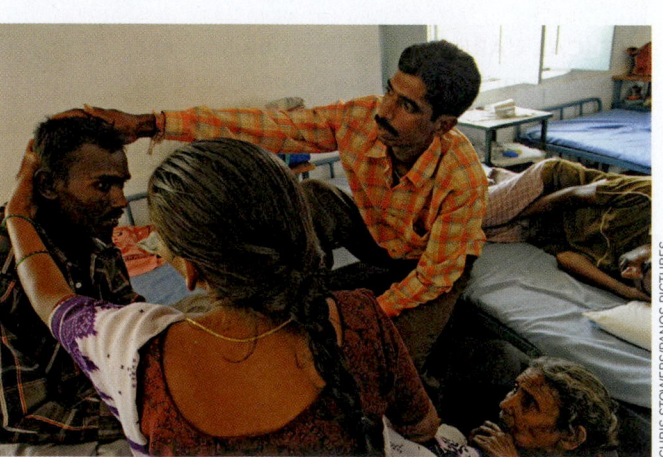

TELLING THE TRUTH Many wise contemporary physicians stress honest medical care in treatment of the dying (Gawande, 2014; Kalanithi 2016). Knowing the truth about prognosis allows appropriate care (including addictive painkillers, music, prayers, favorite foods, or distant relatives—whatever the dying person wants) (Lundquist et al., 2011).

This is difficult, because patients misunderstand, symptoms change, and priorities shift. Some dying people do *not* want the whole truth, some want every possible medical intervention, and some do *not* want visitors. Ideally, conversation among all concerned is interactive, occurring over weeks and months (Cripe & Frankel, 2017).

Better Ways to Die

Several practices have become more prevalent since the contrast between a good death and the usual hospital death has become clear. The hospice and palliative care are examples.

HOSPICE In London, in the 1950s, Cecily Saunders opened the first modern **hospice,** where terminally ill people could spend their last days in comfort. Since then thousands of hospices have opened in many nations, and hundreds of thousands of caregivers bring hospice care to dying people where they live. In the United States, hospice care is available in every state. Two-thirds of all hospice deaths occur at home.

Two principles characterize hospice care:

- Each patient's autonomy is respected. For example, pain medication is readily available, not on a schedule or set dosage, and decisions are made by the patient, not by administrators.

- Family members and friends are counseled before the death, taught to provide care, and guided in mourning afterward. Death is thought to happen to a family, not just to an individual.

Hospice allows measures that hospitals may forbid: acupuncture, special foods, flexible schedules, visitors at midnight, excursions outside, massage, aromatic oils, religious rituals, and so on (Doka, 2013). Comfort takes precedence over cure, but that itself may extend life. In fact, 16 percent of U.S. hospice patients are discharged alive.

Unfortunately, hospice does not reach everyone (see Table EP.2). It is more common in England than in mainland Europe, more common in the western part of the United

hospice
An institution or program in which terminally ill patients receive palliative care to reduce suffering; family and friends of the dying are helped as well.

THINK CRITICALLY: What are the possible reasons that fewer people in hospice are from non-European backgrounds?

TABLE EP.2 Barriers to Entering Hospice Care

- Hospice patients must be terminally ill, with death anticipated within six months, but predictions are difficult. For example, in one study of noncancer patients, physician predictions were 90 percent accurate for those who died within a week but only 13 percent accurate when death was predicted in three to six weeks (usually the patients died sooner) (Brandt et al., 2006). Other research confirms that "death is highly unpredictable" (Einav et al., 2018).

- Patients and caregivers must accept death. Traditionally, entering a hospice meant the end of curative treatment (chemotherapy, dialysis, and so on). This is no longer true. Now treatment can continue. Many hospice patients survive for months, and some are discharged alive (Salpeter et al., 2012).

- Hospice care is costly. Skilled workers—doctors, nurses, psychologists, social workers, clergy, music therapists, and so on—provide individualized care day and night.

- Availability varies. Hospice care is more common in England than in mainland Europe and is a luxury in poor nations. In the United States, western states have more hospices than midwestern states do. Even in one region (northern California) and among clients of one insurance company (Kaiser), the likelihood that people with terminal cancer will enter hospice depends on exactly where they live (Keating et al., 2006).

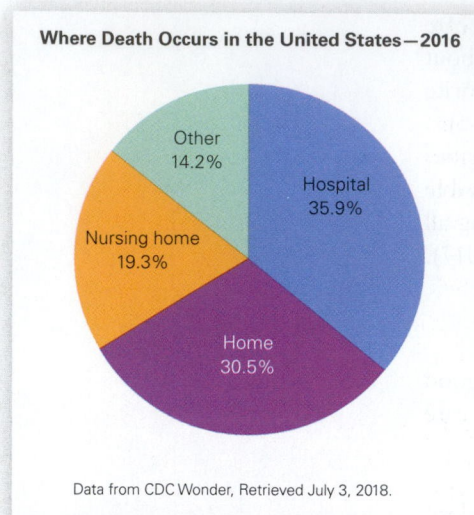

Where Death Occurs in the United States—2016

Other 14.2%

Hospital 35.9%

Nursing home 19.3%

Home 30.5%

Data from CDC Wonder, Retrieved July 3, 2018.

FIGURE EP.3 Not with Family Almost everyone prefers to die at home, yet most people die in an institution, surrounded by medical personnel and high-tech equipment, not by the soft voices and gentle touch of loved ones. The "other" category is even worse, as it includes most lethal accidents or homicides. But don't be too saddened by this chart—improvement is possible. Twenty years ago, the proportion of home deaths was notably lower.

palliative care
Medical treatment designed primarily to provide physical and emotional comfort to the dying patient and guidance to his or her loved ones.

double effect
When an action (such as administering opiates) has both a positive effect (relieving a terminally ill person's pain) and a negative effect (hastening death by suppressing respiration).

THINK CRITICALLY: At what point, if ever, should intervention stop to allow death?

States than the Southeast, and rare in poor nations. Everywhere, hospice care correlates with higher income, although now Medicare covers such care.

Ethnic differences are apparent. For example, African Americans choose hospice about half as often as European Americans do. They are more likely to seek aggressive, hospital care—which, ironically, means more pain and distress. One team suggests that African American churches should explain the spiritual benefits of hospice (Townsend et al., 2017).

Some insurance policies pay for hospice only if a doctor certifies that the patient has less than six months to live. Doctors may not want to admit defeat, so they wait until death is imminent. For that reason, hospice care usually begins within two weeks of death—too late for ideal personalized care (see Figure EP.3).

PALLIATIVE CARE In 2006, the American Medical Association approved a new specialty, **palliative care,** which focuses on relieving pain and suffering. That is essential in every hospice, but about half of all hospitals also include palliative care. That may help patients decades before death.

Some people refuse medical measures when they understand the risks and benefits (Mynatt & Mowery, 2013). Instead of painful procedures, palliative-care doctors prescribe powerful drugs and procedures that make patients comfortable, and treat nonlethal symptoms, such as rashes and nausea.

The need for palliative care is obvious when one considers the complications of pain relief. Doctors have become very cautious in prescribing addictive opioids. The first response to pain is to employ comfort care, but addictive drugs are also prescribed by palliative care doctors. Morphine and other opiates have a **double effect:** They relieve pain (a positive effect), but they also slow down respiration (a negative effect). A painkiller that reduces both pain and breathing is allowed by law, ethics, and medical practice.

In England, for instance, although it is illegal to cause death (even if dying patients request it), doctors can prescribe drugs that have a double effect. One-third of all English deaths include such drugs, which may hasten death as well as relieve pain (Billings, 2011).

Heavy sedation is another method sometimes used to alleviate pain. If recovery is unlikely, sedation may delay death more than extend life, since an unconscious patient cannot think or feel (Raus et al., 2011). Other measures—injections, salves, and meditation—may alleviate pain. Palliative-care doctors know them all, and ideally they advise patients as to what is best.

Ethical Issues

As you see, the success of medicine has created new dilemmas. Death is no longer the natural outcome of age and disease; when and how death occurs involves human choices.

DECIDING WHEN DEATH OCCURS No longer does death necessarily occur when a vital organ stops. Breathing continues with respirators, stopped hearts are restarted, stomach tubes provide calories, and drugs fight pneumonia. At what point, if ever, should intervention stop?

Almost every life-threatening condition results in treatments started, stopped, or avoided, with death postponed, prevented, or welcomed. This has fostered impassioned moral arguments, between nations (evidenced by radically different laws) and within them.

Religious advisers, doctors, and lawyers disagree with colleagues within their respective professions; family members have opposite opinions; and people within each group diverge. For example, outsiders might imagine that all Roman Catholic leaders share the same views, but that is far from the truth (Bedford et al., 2017).

EVIDENCE OF DEATH Historically, death was determined by listening to a person's chest: No heartbeat meant death. To make sure, a feather was put to the person's nose to indicate respiration—a person who had no heartbeat and did not exhale was pronounced dead. Very rarely, but widely publicized when it happened, death was declared when the person was still alive.

Modern medicine has changed that: Hearts and lungs need not function on their own. Many life-support measures and medical interventions circumvent the diseases and organ failures that once caused death. Checking breathing with feathers is a curiosity that, thankfully, is never used today.

But how is it determined that a person is dead? In the late 1970s, a group of Harvard physicians concluded that death occurred when brain waves ceased, a definition now used worldwide (Wijdicks et al., 2010). Current criteria involve several tests of brain functioning (see Table EP.3). However, the general public is still uneasy about the declaration of death (Lewis & Greer, 2017).

When are people in a permanent vegetative state (and thus will never be able to think) and when are they merely in a coma? Is a person with an unresponsive brain unable to ever breathe again without a respirator? Does "ever" mean 10 or 20 years hence?

Few laypeople understand all of the tests that determine brain death. Family members may cling to hope long after medical experts are convinced that recovery is impossible. Beyond the cost and psychic distress of this divide, people who want to donate their organs after death cannot do so if too much time elapses between brain death and donation.

EUTHANASIA Ethical dilemmas are particularly apparent with *euthanasia* (sometimes called *mercy-killing*). There are two kinds of euthanasia.

In **passive euthanasia,** a person near death is allowed to die. The person's medical chart may say **DNR (do not resuscitate),** instructing medical staff not to restore breathing or restart the heart if breathing or pulsating stops. A more detailed version is the **POLST (physician-ordered life-sustaining treatment),** which describes when antibiotics, feeding tubes, and so on should be used.

passive euthanasia
When a seriously ill person is allowed to die naturally, without active attempts to prolong life.

DNR (do not resuscitate) order
A written order from a physician (sometimes initiated by a patient's advance directive or by a health care proxy's request) that no attempt should be made to revive a patient who suffers cardiac or respiratory arrest.

POLST (physician-ordered life-sustaining treatment)
An order from a doctor regarding end-of-life care that advises nurses and other medical staff which treatments (e.g., feeding, antibiotics, and respirators) should be used or not used. It is similar to a living will, but it is written for medical professionals, and thus is more specific.

TABLE EP.3 Dead or Not? Yes, No, and Maybe
Brain death: Prolonged cessation of all brain activity with complete absence of voluntary movements; no spontaneous breathing; and no response to pain, noise, and other stimuli. Brain waves have ceased; the electroencephalogram is flat; and *the person is dead.*
Locked-in syndrome: The person cannot move, except for the eyes, but normal brain waves are still apparent; *the person is not dead.*
Coma: A state of deep unconsciousness from which the person cannot be aroused. Some people awaken spontaneously from a coma; others enter a vegetative state; and *the person is not yet dead.*
Vegetative state: A state of deep unconsciousness in which all cognitive functions are absent, although eyes may open, sounds may be emitted, and breathing may continue; *the person is not yet dead.* The vegetative state can be *transient, persistent,* or *permanent.* No one has ever recovered after two years; most who recover (about 15 percent) improve within three weeks (Preston & Kelly, 2006). After sufficient time has elapsed, the person may, effectively, be dead, although exactly how many days that requires has not yet been determined (Wijdicks et al., 2010).

active euthanasia
When someone does something that hastens another person's death, with the intention of ending that person's suffering.

physician-assisted suicide
A form of active euthanasia in which a doctor provides the means for someone to end his or her own life, usually by prescribing lethal drugs.

Passive euthanasia is legal everywhere, but many emergency personnel automatically start artificial respiration and stimulate hearts. POLSTs are not always followed as the original physician intended, and they raise additional ethical questions (Moore et al., 2016). Passive euthanasia may be contrary to patient wishes, but more often passive euthanasia was desired but medical intervention made it impossible.

Active euthanasia is deliberate action to cause death, such as turning off a respirator or giving a lethal drug. Some physicians condone active euthanasia when three conditions occur: (1) Suffering cannot be relieved, (2) the illness is incurable, and (3) the patient wants to die. Active euthanasia is legal in the Netherlands, Belgium, Luxembourg, Switzerland, Colombia, and Canada (each nation has different requirements) and illegal (but rarely prosecuted) elsewhere.

In every nation, some physicians would never perform active euthanasia, but others have done so. Opinions from the public vary as well (see Figure EP.4).

PHYSICIAN HELP WITH DEATH Between passive and active euthanasia is another option: A doctor may provide the means for patients to end their own lives in **physician-assisted suicide,** typically by prescribing lethal medication that a patient can choose to take when they are ready to die. Oregon was the first U.S. state to legalize this practice, asserting that such deaths are "death with dignity," not suicide. Physician-assisted suicide is now legal in Washington state, Montana, Vermont, and California.

The Oregon law requires the following:

- The dying person must be an Oregon resident, over age 17.
- The dying person must request the lethal drugs three times, twice spoken, and once in writing.
- Fifteen days must elapse between the first request and the prescription.
- Two physicians must confirm that the person is terminally ill, has less than six months to live, and is competent (i.e., not mentally impaired or depressed).

Even if all of this occurs, approval is not automatic. Only about one-third of the initial requests are granted.

Opposite opinions are deeply held. Some people believe that suicide can be noble. Buddhist monks publicly burned themselves to death to advocate Tibetan independence from China; one individual's suicide set off the Arab Spring; one woman's

FIGURE EP.4 Mercy or Sin?
Most Austrians of every age think euthanasia is sometimes merciful. But almost one-third disagree, and some of those think God agrees with them. If those opposite opinions are held by children of a dying parent, who should prevail?

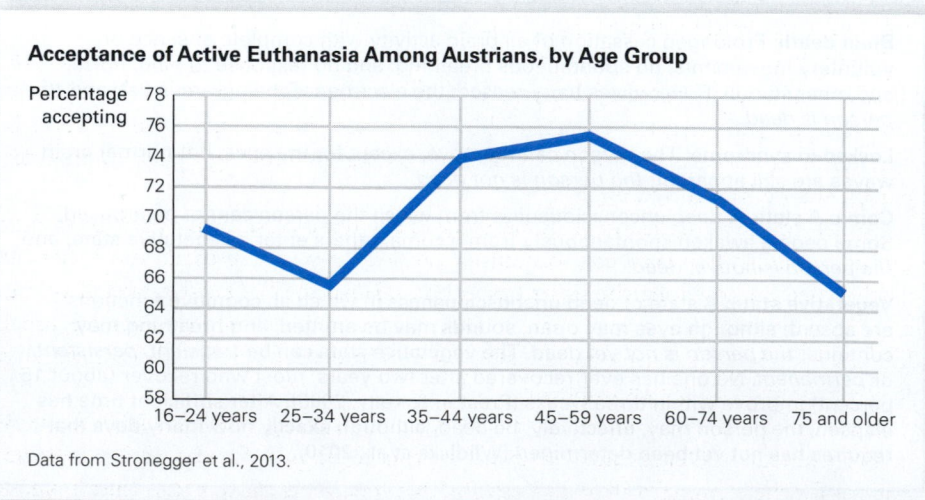

Data from Stronegger et al., 2013.

(Brittany Maynard) wish for help in suicide changed the laws of California. Everywhere, some people are praised because they choose to die for the honor of their nation, their family, or themselves.

On the other hand, personality and religion affect acceptance of physician-assisted suicide. The practice is anathema in Islamic nations; in North America, people who are devout Christians often are strongly opposed (Bulmer et al., 2017).

PAIN: PHYSICAL AND PSYCHOLOGICAL The Netherlands has permitted active euthanasia since 1980, a law extended in 2002. The patient must be clear and aware in making the request, and the goal is to halt "unbearable suffering" (Buiting et al., 2009). Dutch physicians first try to make the suffering bearable via medication.

The Netherlands' law was revised in 2002 to allow euthanasia not only when a person is terminally ill but also when a person is chronically ill and in pain. A qualitative analysis found that Dutch physicians considered "unbearable suffering" to include "fatigue, pain, decline, negative feelings, loss of self, fear of future suffering, dependency, loss of autonomy, being worn out, being a burden, loneliness, loss of all that makes life worth living, hopelessness, pointlessness and being tired of living" (Dees et al., 2011, p. 727).

Oregon residents also request lethal drugs primarily for psychological, not physiological, pain (see Table EP.4). That raises additional ethical questions, as Opposing Perspectives explains on page 580.

TABLE EP.4	Oregon Residents' Reasons for Requesting Physician Assistance in Dying, 2017
Percent of Patients Giving Reason (most had several reasons)	
Less able to enjoy life	88
Loss of autonomy	87
Loss of dignity	67
Burden on others	79
Loss of control over body	37
Pain	21
Financial implications of treatment	6

Data from Oregon Public Health Division, 2018, p. 10.

Advance Directives

Recognizing that people differ on all of these choices, many professionals hope everyone will express their wishes in **advance directives.** Such directives include medical treatment, where and how death occurs, what should happen to the body, and details of the funeral or memorial.

MEDICAL INTERVENTION The most complicated part of advance directives is on medical measures. Should artificial feeding, breathing, or heart stimulation be used? Are antibiotics that might merely prolong life or pain medication that causes coma or hallucinations desired? The legality of such directives varies by jurisdiction: Sometimes a lawyer is needed to ensure that documents are legal; sometimes a written request, signed and witnessed, is adequate.

Many people want personal choice about death and thus approve of advance directives in theory, but they are uncertain about specifics. For example, few know that restarting the heart may extend life for decades in a young, healthy adult but may result in major neurocognitive disorder, or merely prolong dying, in an elderly person whose health is failing.

Added to the complications are personal characteristics, such as other morbidities, timing, mobility. For example, sometimes cardiopulmonary resuscitation is harmful, partly based on how long the heart has stopped (Buss, 2013). Data on overall averages are contradictory (Elliot et al., 2011). One reason is that outcome data are usually for survivors, not for those who die after various interventions. So advance directives may be based on faulty assumptions.

Even talking about choices is controversial. Originally, the Affordable Care Act of 2013 (dubbed "Obamacare") allowed doctors to be paid for describing treatment options for the terminally ill (e.g., Kettl, 2010). Opponents called those "death panels,"

advance directives
Any description of what a person wants to happen as they die and after they die. This can include medical measures, visitors, funeral arrangements, cremation, and so on.

THINK CRITICALLY: Why would someone take all the steps to obtain a lethal prescription and then not use it?

OPPOSING PERSPECTIVES

The "Right to Die"?

Some legal scholars believe that people have a right to choose their death, but others believe that the right to life forbids the right to die (Wicks, 2012). Indeed, some people fear that legalizing euthanasia or physician-assisted suicide creates a *slippery slope,* leading toward ending life for people who are disabled, poor, or non-White.

The data refute that concern. In Oregon and elsewhere, the oldest-old, the poor, and those of non-European heritage are *less* likely to use fatal prescriptions. In Oregon, almost everyone who chose "death with dignity" was European American (96 percent), had health insurance, was educated (73 percent had some college), and had lived a long life (see Figure EP.5) but were not over age 85. Most died at home, with friends or family.

The number of Dutch people who choose euthanasia is increasing; is this a slippery slope? Some people think so; others think it shows that this option is one that people want.

Addressing the slippery-slope argument, a cancer specialist writes:

To be forced to continue living a life that one deems intolerable when there are doctors who are willing either to end one's life or to assist one in ending one's own life, is an unspeakable violation of an individual's freedom to live—and to die—as he or she sees fit. Those who would deny patients a legal right to euthanasia or assisted suicide typically appeal to two arguments: a "slippery slope" argument, and an argument about the dangers of abuse. Both are scare tactics, the rhetorical force of which exceeds their logical strength.

[Benatar, 2011, p. 206]

Not everyone agrees with that doctor. Might deciding to die be a sign of depression? Should physicians refer the patient to a psychiatrist rather than prescribe lethal drugs (Finlay & George, 2011)? Declining ability to enjoy life was cited by 88 percent of Oregonians who requested physician-assisted suicide in 2017 (see Table EP.4). Is that sanity or depression?

Might acceptance of death be mentally healthy in the old but not the young? If only those over age 64 were allowed

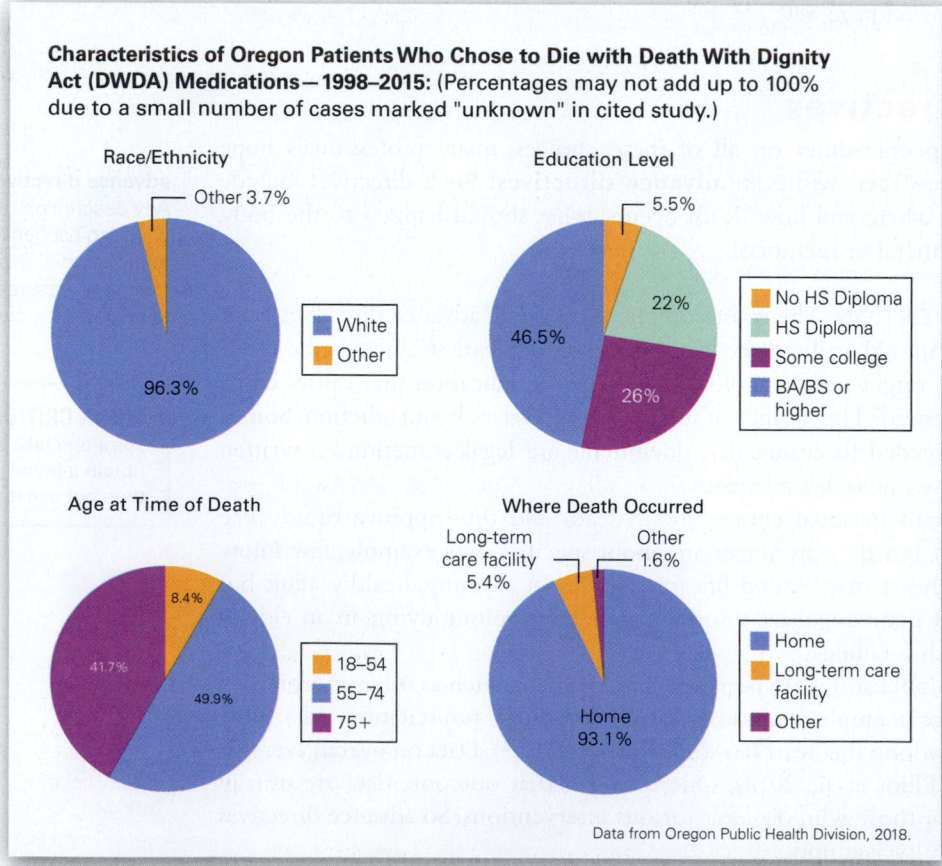

Characteristics of Oregon Patients Who Chose to Die with Death With Dignity Act (DWDA) Medications—1998–2015: (Percentages may not add up to 100% due to a small number of cases marked "unknown" in cited study.)

Race/Ethnicity
- Other 3.7%
- White 96.3%

Education Level
- No HS Diploma 5.5%
- HS Diploma 22%
- Some college 26%
- BA/BS or higher 46.5%

Age at Time of Death
- 18–54 8.4%
- 55–74 49.9%
- 75+ 41.7%

Where Death Occurred
- Long-term care facility 5.4%
- Other 1.6%
- Home 93.1%

Data from Oregon Public Health Division, 2018.

FIGURE EP.5 Death with Dignity? The data do not suggest that people of low SES are unfairly pushed to die. Quite the opposite—people who choose physician-assisted suicide tend to be among the better-educated, more affluent citizens.

the right to die, that would exclude 28 percent of Oregonians who opted to die with dignity. Is that idea ageist, in that it assumes that the young don't understand death, and that life is over for the old?

In 2017, of the 37,000 Oregonians who died naturally, 218 obtained lethal prescriptions, of whom 130 legally used those drugs to die. Most of the other 88 died naturally, but some were alive in January 2018 and are keeping the drugs for possible future use (in the past, about 10 percent use their prescriptions the year after obtaining them) (Oregon Public Health Division, 2018). Those numbers have increased every year: Only 16 died with physician assistance in 1998.

An increase is also evident in the Netherlands, where some form of euthanasia accounted for about 1 in 50 deaths when the law was first in place but 1 in 30 deaths in 2014. In Oregon, almost 1 in 200 used lethal prescriptions that year. Some might interpret these data as evidence of a slippery slope; others see it as proof that the law is useful but only in unusual circumstances.

There is another argument against physician-assisted suicide: that it distracts from care for the dying. In the words of one doctor:

> These interventions are for the 1% not the 99% of dying patients. We still need to deal with the problem that confronts most dying patients: how to get optimal symptom relief, and how to avoid the hospital and stay at home in the final weeks. Legalizing euthanasia and PAS is really a sideshow in end-of-life care — championed by the few for the few, extensively covered by the media, but not targeted to improve the care for most dying patients who still suffer.
>
> *[Emanuel, 2017]*

Could it be that a law designed to allow death with dignity actually undercuts dying with dignity?

A position statement from the International Association of Hospice and Palliative Care says:

> no country or state should consider the legalization of euthanasia or PAS until it ensures universal access to palliative care services and to appropriate medications, including opioids for pain and dyspnea.
>
> *[De Lima et al., 2017, p. 8]*

Since no state or nation has "universal access to palliative care," by that standard, no nation is ready to offer physician-assisted suicide. A contrary opinion is evident in Canada, where its Supreme Court unanimously approved physician-assisted suicide after the Canadian Medical Association withdrew their objection to it (Attaran, 2015).

Most jurisdictions recognize the dilemma: Doctors are almost never prosecuted for helping with death as long as it is done privately and quietly. Opposing perspectives, and opposite choices, are evident.

---

an accusation that almost torpedoed the entire bill. As a result, that measure was scrapped: Physicians are not reimbursed for time spent explaining palliative care, options for treatment, or dying.

Physicians are nonetheless encouraged to speak with their patients and write POLST instructions that specify treatment options. That is useful for other doctors and nurses, who, unlike the general public, know risks and benefits for every choice.

WILLS AND PROXIES Advance directives often include a living will and/or a health care proxy. Hospitals and hospices strongly recommend both of these. Nonetheless, most people resist: A study of cancer patients in a leading hospital found that only 16 percent had living wills and only 48 percent had designated a proxy (Halpern et al., 2011).

A **living will** indicates what medical intervention is desired if a person is unable to express preferences. (If the person is conscious, hospital personnel ask about each specific procedure, often requiring written consent. Patients who are lucid can override any instructions of their living will.)

Why would anyone want to override their own earlier wishes? Because living wills include phrases such as "incurable," "reasonable chance of recovery," and "extraordinary measures," and it is difficult to know what those phrases mean until a specific issue arises. Even then, doctors and family members disagree about what is "extraordinary" or "reasonable."

A **health care proxy** is another person delegated to make medical decisions if someone becomes unable to do so. That seems logical, but unfortunately neither a

◆ **Especially for People Without Advance Directives** Why do very few young adults have advance directives? (see response, page 592)

living will
A document that indicates what medical intervention an individual prefers if he or she is not conscious when a decision is to be expressed. For example, some do not want mechanical breathing.

health care proxy
A person chosen to make medical decisions if a patient is unable to do so, as when in a coma.

A CASE TO STUDY

Terri Schiavo

A heartbreaking example of the need for advance directives occurred with 26-year-old Theresa (Terri) Schiavo, whose eating disorder caused her heart to stop. Emergency personnel restarted her heart, but she fell into a deep coma. Like almost everyone her age, Terri had no advance directives. A court designated Michael, her husband of six years, as her proxy.

Michael attempted many measures to bring back his wife, but after 11 years he accepted her doctors' repeated diagnosis: Terri was in a persistent vegetative state. He petitioned to have her feeding tube removed. The court agreed, noting the testimony of witnesses who said that Terri had told them that she never wanted to be on life support. Terri's parents appealed the decision but lost. They then pleaded with the public.

The Florida legislature responded, passing a law that required that the tube be reinserted. After three more years of legal wrangling, the U.S. Supreme Court ruled that the lower courts were correct. By this point, every North American newspaper and TV station was following the case. Congress passed a law requiring that artificial feeding be continued, but that law, too, was overturned as unconstitutional.

The stomach tube was removed, and Terri died on March 31, 2005—although some maintained that she had really died 15 years earlier. An autopsy revealed that her brain had shrunk markedly; she had been unable to think for at least a decade.

Partly because of the conflicts among family members, and between appointed judges and elected politicians, Terri's case caught media attention, inspiring vigils and protests. Lost in that blitz are the thousands of other mothers and fathers, husbands and wives, sons and daughters, judges and legislators, and doctors and nurses who struggle less publicly with similar issues.

Advance directives may help make death "an event to be lived . . . [with] the same values that have given meaning to the story of our life" (Farber & Farber, 2014, p. 109) and provide caregivers some peace. But, as the Schiavo case makes clear, discussion with every family member is needed long before a crisis occurs (Rogne & McCune, 2014).

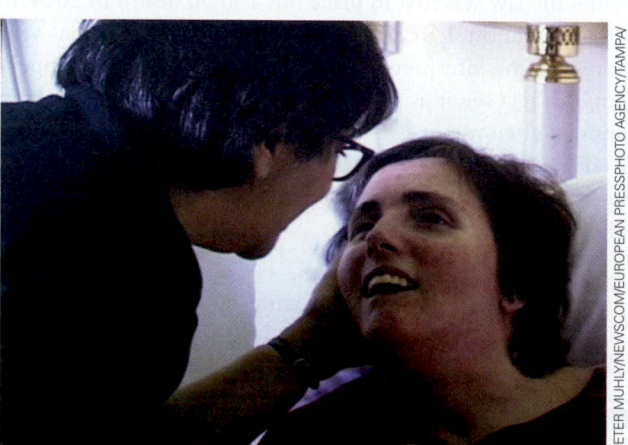

PETER MUHLY/NEWSCOM/EUROPEAN PRESSPHOTO AGENCY/TAMPA/ FLORIDA/UNITED STATES

Is She Thinking? This photo of Terri Schiavo with her mother was released by those who believed Terri could recover. Other photos (not released) and other signs told the opposite story. Although autopsy showed that Terri's brain had shrunk markedly, remember that hope is part of being human. That helps explain why some people were passionately opposed to removal of Terri's stomach tube.

living will nor a health care proxy guarantees that medical care will be exactly what a person would choose.

For one thing, proxies often find it difficult to allow a loved one to die, unless the living will is very explicit. A larger problem is that few people—experts included—understand the risks, benefits, and alternatives to every medical procedure. That makes it difficult to decide when the risks outweigh the benefits.

Medical professionals advocate advance directives, but they know there are problems with them. As one couple (both experts in end-of-life care) wrote:

> Working within the reality of mortality, coming to death is then an inevitable part of life, an event to be lived rather than a problem to be solved. Ideally, we would live the end of our life from the same values that have given meaning to the story of our life up to that time. But in a medical crisis, there is little time, language, or ritual to guide patients and families in conceptualizing or expressing their values and goals.

[Farber & Farber, 2014, p. 109]

what have you learned?

1. What is a good death?
2. What are Kübler-Ross's five stages of dying, and why doesn't everyone agree with them?
3. What determines whether or not a person will receive hospice care?
4. Why is the double effect legal, even though it speeds death?
5. How is it determined that death has occurred?
6. What is the difference between passive and active euthanasia?
7. What are the four prerequisites of "death with dignity" in Oregon?
8. Why would a person who has a living will also need a health care proxy?

Affirmation of Life

Human relationships are life sustaining, but all adults lose someone they love. Grief and mourning are part of living.

Grief

Grief is the powerful sorrow felt after a profound loss, especially when a loved one dies. Grief is deep and personal, an anguish that can overtake daily life.

NORMAL GRIEF Grief is normal, even when it includes odd actions and thoughts. The specifics vary from person to person, but uncontrollable sobbing, sleeplessness, and irrational and delusional thoughts are common (Doka, 2016).

Joan Didion remembers her reaction after her husband's sudden death. She refused the offers of her friends to come stay with her:

> Grief has no distance. Grief comes in waves, paroxysms, sudden apprehensions that weaken the knees and blind the eyes and obliterate the dailiness of life. . . I see now that my insistence on spending that first night alone was more complicated than it seemed, a primitive instinct. . .There was a level on which I believed that what had happened remained reversible. . . I needed to be alone so that he could come back.
> [Didion, 2005, pp. 27, 32, 33]

When a loved one dies, loneliness, denial, anger, and sorrow come in sudden torrents. Many people want some time alone; everyone also needs to be with other people.

Grief overtakes normal human needs—to sleep, to eat, to think—and other people are a comforting reminder that life continues. Grief typically hits hardest in the first week, but rushes can occur months or years later.

COMPLICATED GRIEF Sometimes grief may fester, becoming what is known as **complicated grief,** impeding life (Neimeyer & Jordan, 2013). The DSM-IV had a "bereavement exclusion," stating that major depression could not be diagnosed within two months of a death, but DSM-5 changed that. Major depression can occur whenever someone dies; treatment may be needed to avoid despair.

grief
The deep sorrow that people feel at the death of another. Grief is personal and unpredictable.

complicated grief
A type of grief that impedes a person's future life, usually because the person clings to sorrow or is buffeted by contradictory emotions.

JOHN MOORE/AP IMAGES

Empty Boots The body of a young army corporal killed near Baghdad has been shipped home to his family in Mississippi for a funeral and burial, but his fellow soldiers in Iraq also need to express their grief. The custom is to hold an informal memorial service, placing the dead soldier's boots, helmet, and rifle in the middle of a circle of mourners, who weep, pray, and reminisce.

Why Flags? This couple expresses their grief after a mass shooting at the Pulse nightclub by bringing flowers to a memorial at the Phillips Center for Performing Arts in Orlando, Florida. Some mourners bring candles and flags, and others join marches and protests. Grief is expressed in many ways—some simple, some complicated.

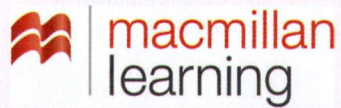

VIDEO: Bereavement: Grief in Early and Late Adulthood presents the views of a young-adult daughter and middle-aged mother on the death of the mother's brother, to whom they were both close.

absent grief
When mourners do not grieve, either because other people do not allow expressions of grief or because the mourners do not allow themselves to mourn.

disenfranchised grief
A situation in which certain people, although they are bereaved, are prevented from mourning publicly by cultural customs or social restrictions.

incomplete grief
When circumstances, such as a police investigation or an autopsy, interfere with the process of grieving.

One complication is called **absent grief,** when a bereaved person does not seem to grieve. This is a common first reaction, but ongoing unexpressed grief can trigger physical or psychological symptoms, such as trouble breathing, panic attacks, or depression.

Disenfranchised grief is "not merely unnoticed, forgotten, or hidden; it is socially disallowed and unsupported" (Corr & Corr, 2013b, p. 135). Some people experience deep grief but are forbidden by social norms to express it.

For instance, often only a current spouse or close blood relative is legally allowed to decide on funeral arrangements, disposal of the body, and other matters. This made sense when all family members were close, but it may now result in "gagged grief and beleaguered bereavement" (Green & Grant, 2008, p. 275).

Sometimes a long-time but unmarried partner is excluded, especially when the partner is of the same sex (Curtin & Garrison, 2018). Relatives, especially those who live far away, may not know the deceased person's friends at work or in the community. Thus, some mourners are disenfranchised—not invited to the funeral, unable to grieve with fellow mourners.

INCOMPLETE GRIEF Usually grief is a process, intense at first, diminishing over time, eventually reaching closure. Customs such as viewing the dead, or throwing dirt on the grave, or scattering ashes all bring closure. However, many circumstances can interfere, creating **incomplete grief.**

Traumatic death is always unexpected, and then denial, anger, and depression undercut the emotions of grief (Kauffman, 2013). Murders and suicides often trigger police, judges, and the press, so mourners who need time to grieve instead must answer questions. An autopsy may prevent closure if the griever believes that the body will rise or that the soul does not immediately leave the body.

Inability to recover a body, as with soldiers who are missing in action or victims of a major flood or fire, may prevent grief from being expressed and thereby hinder completion. That explains why, after the 9/11 terror attacks, when DNA identified a fragment of bone, the family often had a funeral and burial, a way to complete the grieving process.

In natural or human-caused disasters such as hurricanes and wars, incomplete grief is common, because survival—food, shelter, and medical care—takes precedence. In

the days and weeks after disasters, people die of causes not directly attributable to the trauma, becoming victims of the indifference of others and of their own diminished self-care.

The reality that grief is a process experienced by individuals who do not follow a script suggests that other people should not try to cut it short. No one should tell parents who lost a baby "You never knew that baby; you can have another," or pet owners "It was only a cat," or those with aged relatives "It was time for them to die." Grief has its own expressions and boundaries; others should not decide what is appropriate (Doka, 2016).

People who live and work where no one knows their personal lives have no community or recognized customs to help them grieve. The laws of some nations—China, Chile, and Spain, for example—allow paid bereavement leave, but this is not true in the United States (Meagher, 2013).

Indeed, for workers at large corporations or students in universities, grief becomes "an unwelcome intrusion (or violent intercession) into the normal efficient running of everyday life" (M. Anderson, 2001, p. 141). Many college professors (me included) wish students would not miss classes or delay assignments because of a death. This may be a mistake. My rationale is that people should move past intense grief, but incomplete grief impedes recovery.

Mourning

Grief splinters people into jumbled pieces, making them vulnerable. Mourning reassembles them, making them whole again and able to rejoin the larger community. To be more specific, **mourning** is the public and ritualistic expression of bereavement, the ceremonies and behaviors that a religion or culture prescribes to honor the dead and allow recovery in the living.

HOW MOURNING HELPS Mourning is needed because, as you just read, the grief-stricken are vulnerable not only to irrational thoughts but also to self-destructive acts. Some eat too little or drink too much; some forget caution as they drive or even as they walk across the street. Physical and mental health dips in the recently bereaved, and the rate of suicide increases.

mourning
The ceremonies and behaviors that a religion or culture prescribes for people to express their grief after a death.

Sometimes death continues to affect people years later. A large study in Sweden found that adults whose brother or sister died in childhood were more likely than other people their age to die prematurely. Risk of death increased somewhat no matter why the sibling died, but if the cause was suicide, surviving siblings were three times more likely to kill themselves than other Swedes of the same age and background (Rostila et al., 2013).

Similarly, after the suicide of a celebrity, rates rise for people who are not famous. This alerts us that shared mourning is especially important when suicide occurs. Survivors tend to blame themselves, feel angry at the deceased, or consider following their example. Outsiders may stay away because they do not know what to say. All of this adds difficulty to expressions of grief and rituals of mourning, yet both are especially crucial.

Many customs are designed to help people move from grief toward reaffirmation (Harlow, 2005; Corr & Corr, 2013b). For this reason, eulogies emphasize the dead person's good qualities; people who did not personally know the deceased attend wakes, funerals, or memorial services to comfort the survivors.

Prescribed expression of grief are ways to channel and contain private grief. Examples include the Jewish custom of sitting Shiva at home for a week and then walking around the block to signify return to life, or the three days of active sorrow among some Muslim groups, or the 10 days of ceremonies beginning at the next full moon following a Hindu death.

CULTURAL DIFFERENCES As you have read, beliefs about death vary a great deal. So do mourning rituals. Some religions believe in reincarnation—that a dead person is reborn and that the new life depends on the person's character in the past life. Other religions believe that souls are judged and then sent to heaven or hell. Still others contend that the spirits of the dead remain to help or haunt the living; others contend that the dead are gone forever, alive only in memory.

All of these beliefs affect how people mourn. If the dead are somehow still present, mourners may provide food and other comforts so that their spirits will be benevolent. If memory is crucial, a new baby is named after a dead person, and the dead are honored on a memorial day.

One example of cultural differences compares England and Japan. The British tend to see people as autonomous. Consequently, mourners take personal action to remember that particular person. The Japanese see people as interdependent. Therefore, mourning is more of a group event, reflecting continuity over the generations (Valentine, 2017).

The Western practice of building a memorial, dedicating a plaque, or naming a location for a dead person is antithetical to some Eastern cultures. Indeed, some

Same Situation, Far Apart: Gateway to Heaven or Final Rest? Many differences are obvious between a Roman Catholic burial in Mbongolwane, South Africa *(left),* and a Hindu cremation procession in Bali, Indonesia *(right).* The Africans believe the soul goes to heaven; the Indonesians believe the body returns to the elements. In both places, however, friends and neighbors gather to honor the dead and comfort their relatives.

Asian cultures believe that the spirit should be allowed to rest in peace, and thus all possessions, signs, and other evidence of the deceased are removed after proper prayers.

This created a cultural clash when terrorist bombs in Bali killed 38 Indonesians and 164 foreigners (mostly Australian and British). The Indonesians prayed intensely and then destroyed all reminders; the Australians raised money to build a memorial (de Jonge, 2011). The Indonesian officials posed many obstacles to prevent the construction; the Australians were frustrated; the memorial was never built. Neither group understood the deep emotions of the other.

GROWTH AFTER DEATH In recent decades, many people everywhere have become less religiously devout, and mourning practices are less ritualized. Has death then become a source of despair, not hope? Maybe not. People worldwide become more spiritual when confronted with death (Lattanzi-Licht, 2013).

If the dead person was a public figure, mourners may include thousands, even millions. They express their sorrow to one another, stare at photos, and listen to music that reminds them of the dead person, weeping as they watch funerals on television. Mourners often pledge to affirm the best of the deceased, forgetting any criticisms that they might have had in the past.

Some observers suggest that mourning can lead people to **post-traumatic growth** (the opposite of post-traumatic stress disorder, or PTSD) (Tedeschi et al., 2017). As you remember, Kübler-Ross found that reactions to death eventually lead to acceptance. Finding meaning may be crucial to the reaffirmation that follows grief. In some cases, this search starts with preserving memories: Displaying photographs and personal effects and telling anecdotes about the deceased person are central to many memorial services.

Organizations that are devoted to combating a particular problem (such as breast cancer or a harmful chemical) find their most dedicated donors, demonstrators, and advocates among people who have lost a loved one to that specific danger. That also explains why, when someone dies, survivors often designate a charity that is connected to the deceased. Then mourners contribute, hoping the death has led to good.

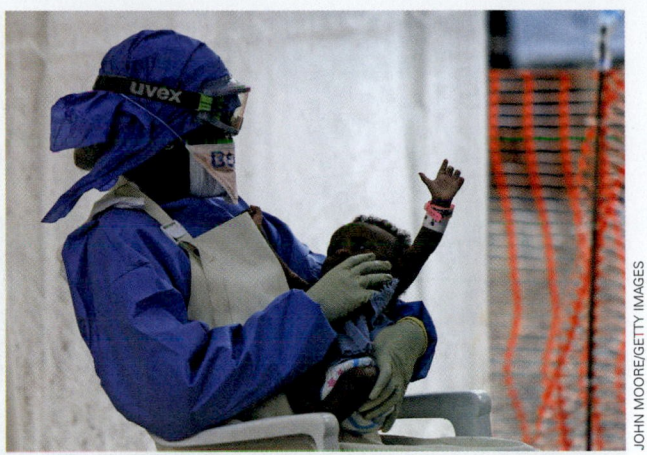

JOHN MOORE/GETTY IMAGES

The Human Touch Benetha Coleman fights Ebola in this treatment center by taking temperatures, washing bodies, and drawing blood, but she also comforts those with symptoms. Why would anyone risk working here? Benetha has recovered from Ebola, and, like many survivors of a disaster, she wants to help others who suffer.

post-traumatic growth The increased insight, compassion, and benevolence that some people feel after a trauma, such as surviving a disaster or sudden death of a loved one.

Placing Blame and Seeking Meaning

A common impulse after death is for the survivors to assess blame—for medical measures not taken, for laws not enforced, for unhealthy habits not changed. The bereaved sometimes blame the dead person, sometimes themselves, and sometimes others.

The medical establishment is often blamed. In November 2011, Michael Jackson's personal doctor, Conrad Murray, was found guilty and jailed for prescribing the drugs that led to the singer's death. Many fans and family members cheered at the verdict; Murray was one of the few who blamed Jackson, not himself.

In 2018, the doctor who prescribed painkillers to Prince was fined $30,000 but not prosecuted, because he was not the source of the illegal drugs that killed Prince. Many of Prince's friends knew about his addiction: They blamed themselves and each other.

For public tragedies, nations accuse one another. Blame is not rational or proportional to guilt. For instance, outrage at the assassination of Archduke Francis Ferdinand of Austria by a Serbian terrorist in 1914 provoked a conflict between Austria and Serbia—soon joined by a dozen other nations—that led to the four years and 16 million deaths of World War I.

THINK CRITICALLY: Do you think current wars are fueled by a misguided impulse to assign blame?

Childish Response? The survivors of the high school shooting in Parkland, Florida, sparked a nationwide protest against the National Rifle Association and the lawmakers and corporations who support it. Are these protestors in Washington, D.C., naive? People on both sides of the gun control debate believe so.

In **VIDEO: Bereavement and Grief: Late Adulthood,** people discuss their experiences with the loss of beloved family members and friends—and all agree that these losses have been very difficult experiences.

When death occurs from a major disaster, survivors often seek to honor the memory of the dead. Many people believe that Israel would not have been created without the Holocaust, or that same-sex marriage would not have been be legalized if the AIDS epidemic had not occurred.

Mourners often resolve to bring those responsible to justice. Blame can land on many people. In 2017, After 17 people died of a gun massacre in Parkland, Florida, surviving students accused adults of not curbing the National Rifle Association (NRA), and they persuaded major companies to discontinue discounts for NRA members. Florida enacted a law to raise the age for gun purchase to 21 and to require a wait period before a person can buy a gun (the NRA opposed that law); school districts nationwide considered arming teachers.

The search for blame in Parkland included the security guard who stayed outside the school, the adequacy of mental health workers, the design of the school classrooms, the specifics of gun manufacture (e.g., assault weapons and bump stocks), the local sheriff, and the national FBI. All of this illustrates that humans seek to blame someone—and the response may not be logical.

The impulse to assign blame and seek meaning is powerful but not always constructive. Revenge may arise, leading to long-standing and often fatal feuds between one family, one gang, or one cultural, ethnic, or religious group, and another. Nations go to war because some people in one nation killed someone from another. Ideally, counselors, politicians, and clergy can steer grief-stricken survivors toward beneficial ends.

In 2015, when a gunman killed nine people in a prayer group at Emanuel African Methodist Episcopal Church in Charleston, South Carolina, some people blamed those who still honor the Confederate soldiers who fought in the U.S. Civil War. Within a month, the state Senate voted to remove the Confederate flag from the center of Charleston, and major retailers stopped selling that flag. Instead of blame, the church members chose forgiveness.

Those church members may have had the right idea. When homicides occur, some family members want revenge, and others forgive. More generally, some people forgive the dead for past misdeeds rather than blaming them, a practice more likely to lead to psychological well-being (Gassin et al., 2017).

Diversity of Reactions

The specifics of bereavement vary. Blame cannot bring the dead back to life, and no single reaction is necessarily best. Culture matters. For example, mourners who keep the dead person's possessions, talk to the deceased, and frequently review memories are notably *less* well adjusted than other mourners 18 months after the death if they live in the United States, but they are *better* adjusted if they live in China (Lalande & Bonanno, 2006).

Past experiences affect bereavement. Children who lost their parents might be more distraught decades later when someone else dies. Past attachment also matters (Kosminsky, 2017). Older adults who were securely attached as children are more likely to experience normal grief; those whose attachment was insecure-avoidant are more likely to have absent grief; and those who were insecure-resistant may become stuck, focusing only on blame and unable to move forward with their own lives.

CONTINUING BONDS Reaffirmation does not mean forgetting; **continuing bonds** are evident years after death (Klass et al., 1996; Klass & Steffen, 2017; M. Stroebe et al., 2012). Such bonds are memories and connections that link the living and the dead. They may help or hinder reaffirmation, depending on the past relationship between the individuals and on the circumstances of the death. Often survivors write letters or talk to the deceased person, or consider events—a sunrise, a butterfly, a rainstorm—as messages of comfort.

Bereavement theory once held an "unquestioned assumption" that mourners should grieve and then move on, accepting that the dead person is gone forever (Neimeyer, 2017). It was thought that, if this progression did not take place, pathological grief could result, with the person either not grieving enough (absent grief) or grieving too long (incomplete grief).

But now a much wider variety of reactions (Rubin, 2012) are recognized. Continuing bonds are not only normal but the "centrality of relations between the living and the dead" is helpful to the mourner and to everyone else (Neimeyer, 2017, p. xii).

Crucial are the person's beliefs before the death (Mancini et al., 2011). If someone tends to have a positive perspective, believing that justice will prevail and that life has meaning, then the death of a close family member may deepen, not weaken, those beliefs. Depression is less likely if a person has already accepted the reality of death, and if the person does something—a public protest, a private contribution to charity, a written memorial—to give expression to emotions.

A bereaved person *might or might not* want to visit the grave, light a candle, cherish a memento, pray, or sob. Mourners may want time alone or may want company. Those who have been taught to bear grief stoically may be distressed if a friend advises them to cry but they cannot. Conversely, those whose cultures expect loud wailing may resent being told to hush.

She Didn't Forget Eleven years after planes crashed into the World Trade Center and the Pentagon, killing 2,977, several memorial ceremonies were held. Alice Watkins attended one of them, to remember a friend who died. Are continuing bonds an expression of our connection to heritage and history, or a sign that some people are stuck in the past?

continuing bonds
The ongoing memories and attachment that one person has for another even after that other person has died.

DON'T ASSUME Assumptions arising from one culture or religion might be inaccurate; people's reactions about death and hope vary for many reasons. One example came from a 13-year-old girl who refused to leave home after her 17-year-old brother was shot dead going to school. The therapist was supposed to get her to go to school again.

> It would have been easy to assume that she was afraid of dying on the street, and to arrange for a friend to accompany her on her way to school. But careful listening revealed the real reason she stayed home: She worried that her depressed mother might kill herself if she were left alone.
>
> *[Crenshaw, 2013]*

To help the daughter, the mother had to be helped.

No matter what fears arise, what rituals are followed, or what grief entails, mourning gives the living a deeper appreciation of themselves and others. In fact, a theme frequently sounded by those who work with the dying and the bereaved is that death leads to a greater appreciation of life, especially of the value of intimate, caring relationships.

A VIEW FROM SCIENCE

Resilience After a Death

Earlier studies overestimated the frequency of pathological grief. For obvious reasons, scientists usually began research on mourning with mourners—that is, with people who had recently experienced the death of a loved one. However, that made it impossible to backtrack and study a mourner's attitudes and personality before the death.

Furthermore, psychologists often treated people who had difficulty dealing with a death. Some patients experienced absent grief; others felt disenfranchised grief; some were overcome by unremitting sadness many months after the loss; still others could not find meaning in a violent, sudden, unexpected death. All of these people consulted therapists, who often helped them by allowing them to mourn and then move on. But they were not typical.

We now know that personality has a major effect on grief and mourning (Boyraz et al., 2012). Pathological mourners are *not* typical.

Everyone experiences several deaths over a lifetime—of parents and grandparents, of a spouse or close friend. Most grieve, mourn, and resume their life, functioning as well a few months later as they did before. Only a small subset, 10 to 15 percent, exhibit extreme or complicated grief.

The variety of reactions to death was evident in a longitudinal study that began by assessing married older adults in greater Detroit. Over several years, 319 became widows or widowers. Most were interviewed again six and 18 months after the death of their spouse. About one-third were seen again four years later (Boerner et al., 2004, 2005).

General trends were evident. Almost all of the widows and widowers idealized their past marriages, remembering them more positively after the death than they spoke about them years earlier, before the death. Other research finds that such idealization is connected to psychological health, not pathology (O'Rourke et al., 2010b).

The longitudinal study found notable variations in widows' and widowers' reactions. Four types of responses were evident (Galatzer-Levy & Bonanno, 2012):

1. Sixty-six percent were resilient. They were sad at first, but six months later they were about as happy and productive as they had been before the death.

2. Fifteen percent were depressed at every assessment, before as well as years after the death. If this research had begun only after the death, it might seem that the loss caused depression. However, the pre-loss assessment suggests that these people were chronically depressed, not stuck in grief.

3. Ten percent were *less* depressed after the death than before, often because they had been caregivers for their seriously ill partners.

4. Nine percent were slow to recover, functioning poorly at 18 months. By four years after the death, however, they functioned almost as well as they had before.

The slow recovery of this fourth group suggests that some of them experienced complicated grief. Note, however, that they were far from the majority of the participants.

Many other studies show that grief and then recovery form the usual pattern, with only about 10 percent needing professional help to deal with a death. A person's health, finances, and personality all contribute to postmortem reactions.

It is fitting to end this Epilogue, and this book, with a reminder of the creative work of living. As first described in Chapter 1, the study of human development is a science, with topics to be researched, understood, and explained. But the process of living is an art as well as a science, with strands of love and sorrow woven into each person's unique tapestry. Death, when it leads to hope; dying, when it is accepted; and grief, when it fosters affirmation—all add meaning to birth, growth, development, and love.

what have you learned?

1. What is grief, and what are some of its signs?
2. What are some complications of grief?
3. What are the differences among grief, mourning, and bereavement?
4. If a person still feels a loss six months after a death, is that pathological?
5. How can other people help someone who is grieving?

SUMMARY

Death and Hope

1. In ancient times, death connected the living, the dead, and the spirit world. People respected the dead and tried to live their lives so that their own death and afterlife would be good.

2. Every modern religion includes rituals and beliefs about death. These vary a great deal, but all bring hope to the living and strengthen the community.

3. Death has various meanings, depending partly on the age of the person involved. For example, young children want companionship; older children want to know specifics of death.

4. Terror management theory finds that some emerging adults cope with death anxiety by defiantly doing whatever is risky. In adulthood, people tend to worry about leaving something undone or abandoning family members. Older adults are more accepting of death.

Choices in Dying

5. Everyone wants a good death. A death that is painless and that comes at the end of a long life may be more possible currently than a century ago. However, other aspects of a good death—quick, at home, surrounded by loved ones—are less likely than it was.

6. The emotions of people who are dying change over time. Some may move from denial to acceptance, although stages of dying are much more variable than originally proposed. Honest conversation helps many, but not all, dying persons.

7. Hospice caregivers meet the biological and psychological needs of terminally ill people and their families.

8. Palliative care relieves pain and suffering. Much of the stress of dying is psychological, not physical, which is difficult for palliative-care physicians to remedy.

9. Drugs that reduce pain as well as hasten dying, producing a double effect, are allowed by most people and nations. However, euthanasia and physician-assisted suicide are controversial. Several nations and U.S. states condone some forms of these; most do not.

10. Since 1980, death has been defined as occurring when brain waves stop. However, many measures now prolong life when no conscious thinking occurs.

11. Advance directives, such as a living will and a health care proxy, are recommended for everyone. However, it is impossible to anticipate all possible interventions that may occur. Family members as well as professionals often disagree about specifics.

Affirmation of Life

12. Grief is overwhelming sorrow. It may be irrational and complicated, absent or incomplete.

13. Mourning rituals channel human grief, helping people move to affirm life. Specifics vary by culture and cohort. Ideally, post-traumatic growth occurs.

14. Continuing bonds with the deceased are no longer thought to be pathological. Past attachment history affects how a person responds to death.

KEY TERMS

terror management theory (p. 570)
hospice (p. 575)
palliative care (p. 576)
double effect (p. 576)
passive euthanasia (p. 577)

DNR (do not resuscitate) order (p. 577)
POLST (physician-ordered life-sustaining treatment) (p. 577)
active euthanasia (p. 578)

physician-assisted suicide (p. 578)
advance directives (p. 579)
living will (p. 581)
health care proxy (p. 581)
grief (p. 583)
complicated grief (p. 583)

absent grief (p. 584)
disenfranchised grief (p. 584)
incomplete grief (p. 584)
mourning (p. 585)
post-traumatic growth (p. 587)
continuing bonds (p. 589)

APPLICATIONS

1. Death is sometimes said to be hidden, even taboo. Ask 10 people whether they have ever been with someone who was dying. Note not only the yes and no answers but also the details and reactions. For instance, how many of the deaths occurred in hospitals?

2. Find quotes about death in *Bartlett's Familiar Quotations* or a similar collection. Do you see any historical or cultural patterns of acceptance, denial, or fear?

3. Every aspect of dying is controversial in modern society. Do an Internet search for a key term such as *euthanasia* or *grief*. Analyze the information and the underlying assumptions. What is your opinion, and why?

4. People of varying ages have different attitudes toward death. Ask people of different ages (ideally, at least one person younger than 20, one adult between 20 and 60, and one older person) what thoughts they have about their own death. What differences do you find?

ESPECIALLY FOR ANSWERS

Response for Relatives of a Person Who Is Dying (from page 574): Death affects the entire family, including children and grandchildren. I learned this myself when my mother was dying. A hospice nurse not only gave her pain medication (which made it easier for me to be with her) but also counseled me. At the nurse's suggestion, I asked for forgiveness. My mother indicated that there was nothing to forgive. We both felt a peace that would have eluded us without hospice care.

Response for People Without Advance Directives (from page 581): Young adults tend to avoid thinking realistically about their own deaths. This attitude is emotional, not rational. The actual task of preparing the documents is easy (the forms can be downloaded; no lawyer is needed). Young adults have less trouble doing other future-oriented things, such as getting a tetanus shot or enrolling in a pension plan.

OBSERVATION QUIZ ANSWER

Answer to Observation Quiz (from page 569): The chief mourners are wearing white (unlike the others) and the grandmother has red roses—a luxury often reserved for weddings and funerals.

Answer to Observation Quiz (from page 570): Homicide, which is 15 times more common. The question the chart does not answer—Why?

Appendix
More About Research Methods

This appendix explains how to learn about any topic. It is crucial that you distinguish valid conclusions from wishful thinking. Such learning begins with your personal experience.

Make It Personal

Think about your life, observe your behavior, and watch the people around you. Pay careful attention to details of expression, emotion, and behavior. The more you see, the more fascinated, curious, and reflective you will become. Ask questions and listen carefully and respectfully to what other people say regarding development.

Whenever you ask specific questions as part of an assignment, <u>remember that observing ethical standards (see Chapter 1) comes first.</u> *Before* you interview anyone, inform the person of your purpose and assure him or her of confidentiality. Promise not to identify the person in your report (use a pseudonym) and do not repeat any personal details that emerge in the interview to anyone (friends or strangers). Your instructor will provide further ethical guidance. If you might publish what you've learned, get in touch with your college's Institutional Review Board (IRB).

Read the Research

No matter how deeply you think about your own experiences, and no matter how intently you listen to others whose background is unlike yours, you also need to read scholarly published work in order to fully understand any topic that interests you. Be skeptical about magazine or newspaper reports; some are bound to be simplified, exaggerated, or biased.

Professional Journals and Books

Part of the process of science is that conclusions are not considered solid until they are corroborated in many studies, which means that you should consult several sources on any topic. Five journals in human development are:

- *Developmental Psychology* (published by the American Psychological Association)
- *Child Development* (Society for Research in Child Development)
- *Developmental Review* (Elsevier)
- *Human Development* (Karger)
- *Developmental Science* (Wiley)

These journals differ in the types of articles and studies they publish, but all are well respected and peer-reviewed, which means that other scholars review each article submitted and recommend that it be accepted, rejected, or revised. Every article includes references to other recent work.

Also look at journals that specialize in longer reviews from the perspective of a researcher.

- *Child Development Perspectives* (from Society for Research in Child Development)
- *Perspectives on Psychological Science* (This is published by the Association for Psychological Science. APS publishes several excellent journals, none specifically on development but every issue has at least one article that is directly relevant.)

Beyond these seven are literally thousands of other professional journals, each with a particular perspective or topic, including many in sociology, family studies, economics, and so on. To judge them, look for journals that are peer-reviewed. Also consider the following details: the background of the author (research funded by corporations tends to favor their products); the nature of the publisher (professional organizations, as in the first two journals above, protect their reputations); and how long the journal has been published (the volume number tells you that). Some interesting work does not meet these criteria, so you be careful before believing what you read.

Many *books* cover some aspect of development. Single-author books are likely to present only one viewpoint. That view may be insightful, but it is limited. You might consult a *handbook,* which is a book that includes many authors and many topics. One good handbook in development, now in its seventh edition (a sign that past scholars have found it useful) is:

- *Handbook of Child Psychology and Developmental Science* (7th ed.), edited by Richard M. Lerner, 2015, Hoboken, NJ: Wiley.
- Another set of handbooks—*Handbook of the Biology of Aging, Handbook of the Psychology of Aging,* and *Handbook of Aging and the Social Sciences*—is now in its eighth edition, published by Academic Press in 2016.

Dozens of other good handbooks are available, many of which focus on a particular age, perspective, or topic.

The Internet

The *Internet* is a mixed blessing, useful to every novice and experienced researcher but dangerous as well. Every library worldwide and most homes in North America, Western Europe, and East Asia have computers that provide access to journals and other information. If you're doing research in a library, ask for help from the librarians; many of them can guide you in the most effective ways to conduct online searches. In addition, other students, friends, and even strangers can be helpful.

Virtually everything is on the Internet, not only massive national and international statistics but also accounts of very personal experiences. Photos, charts, quizzes, ongoing experiments, newspapers from around the world, videos, and much more are available at a click. Every journal has a Web site, with tables of contents, abstracts, and sometimes full texts. (An abstract gives the key findings; for the full text, you may need to consult the library's copy of the print version.)

Unfortunately, you can spend many frustrating hours sifting through information that is useless, trash, or tangential. *Directories* (which list general topics or areas and then move you step by step in the direction you choose) and *search engines* (which give you all the sites that use a particular word or words) can help you select appropriate information. Each directory or search engine provides somewhat different lists; none provides only the most comprehensive and accurate sites. Sometimes organizations pay, or find other ways, to make their links appear first, even though they are biased. With experience and help, you will find quality on the Internet, but you will also encounter some junk no matter how experienced you are.

Anybody can put anything online, regardless of its truth or fairness, so you need a very critical eye. Make sure you have several divergent sources for every "fact" you find; consider who provided the information and why. Every controversial issue has sites that forcefully advocate opposite viewpoints, sometimes with biased statistics and narrow perspectives.

Here are four Internet sites that are quite reliable:

- *embryo.soad.umich.edu* The Multidimensional Human Embryo. Presents MRI images of a human embryo at various stages of development, accompanied by brief explanations.
- *childdevelopmentinfo.com* Child Development Institute. A useful site, with links and articles on child development and information on common childhood psychological disorders.
- *eric.ed.gov* Education Resources Information Center (ERIC). Provides links to many education-related sites and includes brief descriptions of each.
- *www.cdc.gov/nchs/hus.htm* The National Center for Health Statistics issues an annual report on health trends, called *Health, United States.*

Every source—you, your interviewees, journals, books, and the Internet—is helpful. Do not depend on any particular one. Avoid plagiarism and prejudice by citing every source and noting objectivity, validity, and credibility. Your own analysis, opinions, words, and conclusions are crucial, backed up by science.

Additional Terms and Concepts

As emphasized throughout the text, the study of development is a science. Social scientists spend years in graduate school, studying methods and statistics. Chapter 1 touches on some of these matters (observation and experiments; correlation and statistical significance; independent and dependent variables; experimental and control groups; cross-sectional, longitudinal, and cross-sequential research), but there is much more. A few additional aspects of research are presented here to help you evaluate research wherever you find it.

Who Participates?

The entire group of people about whom a scientist wants to learn is called a **population.** Generally, a research population is quite large—not usually the world's entire population of more than 7 billion, but perhaps all the 4 million babies born in the United States last year, or all the 31 million Japanese currently over age 65.

The particular individuals who are studied in a specific research project are called the **participants.** They are used as a **sample** of the larger group. Ideally, the participants are a **representative sample,** that is, a sample that reflects the population. Every peer-reviewed, published study reports details on the sample.

Selection of the sample is crucial. People who volunteer, or people who have telephones, or people who have some particular condition are not a *random sample;* in a random sample, everyone in a particular population is equally likely to be selected. To avoid *selection bias,* some studies are *prospective,* beginning with an entire cluster of people (for instance, every baby born on a particular day) and then tracing the development of some particular characteristic.

population
The entire group of individuals who are of particular concern in a scientific study, such as all the children of the world or all newborns who weigh less than 3 pounds.

participants
The people who are studied in a research project. Participants is the term now used in psychology; other disciplines still call these people "subjects."

sample
A group of individuals drawn from a specified population. A sample might be the low-birthweight babies born in four particular hospitals that are representative of all hospitals.

representative sample
A group of research participants who reflect the relevant characteristics of the larger population whose attributes are under study.

For example, prospective studies find the antecedents of heart disease, or child abuse, or high school dropout rates—all of which are much harder to find if the study is *retrospective*, beginning with those who had heart attacks, experienced abuse, or left school. Thus, although retrospective research finds that most high school dropouts say they disliked school, prospective research finds that some who like school still decide to drop out and then later say they hated school, while others dislike school but stay to graduate. Prospective research discovers how many students are in these last two categories; retrospective research on people who have already dropped out does not.

Research Design

Every researcher begins not only by formulating a hypothesis but also by learning what other scientists have discovered about the topic in question and what methods might be useful and ethical in designing research. Often they include measures to prevent inadvertently finding only the results they expect. For example, the people who actually gather the data may not know the purpose of the research. Scientists say that these data gatherers are **blind** to the hypothesized outcome. Participants are sometimes "blind" as well, because otherwise they might, for instance, respond the way they think they should.

Another crucial aspect of research design is to define exactly what is to be studied. Researchers establish an **operational definition** of whatever phenomenon they will be examining, defining each variable by describing specific, observable behavior. This is essential in quantitative research, but it is also useful in qualitative research.

For example, if a researcher wants to know when babies begin to walk, does walking include steps taken while holding on? Is one unsteady step enough? Some parents say yes, but the usual operational definition of *walking* is "takes at least three steps without holding on." This operational definition allows comparisons worldwide, making it possible to discover, for example, that well-fed African babies tend to walk earlier than well-fed European babies.

Operational definitions are difficult to formulate, but they are essential when personality traits are studied. How should *aggression* or *sharing* or *shyness* be defined? Lack of an operational definition leads to contradictory results. For instance, critics report that infant day care makes children more aggressive, but advocates report that it makes them less passive. In this case, both may be seeing the same behavior but defining it differently. For any scientist, operational definitions are crucial, and studies usually include descriptions of how they measured attitudes or behavior.

Reporting Results

You already know that results should be reported in sufficient detail so that another scientist can analyze the conclusions and replicate the research. Various methods, populations, and research designs may produce divergent conclusions. For that reason, handbooks, some journals, and some articles are called *reviews:* They summarize past research. Often, when studies are similar in operational definitions and methods, the review is a **meta-analysis,** which combines the findings of many studies to present an overall conclusion.

Table 1.7 (page 29) describes some statistical measures. One of them is *statistical significance,* which indicates whether or not a particular result could have occurred by chance.

A crucial statistic is **effect size,** a way of measuring how much impact one variable has on another. Effect size ranges from 0 (no effect) to 1 (total transformation, never found in actual studies). Effect size may be particularly important when the

blind
The condition of data gatherers (and sometimes participants, as well) who are deliberately kept ignorant of the purpose of the research so that they cannot unintentionally bias the results.

operational definition
A description of the specific, observable behavior that will constitute the variable that is to be studied, so that any reader will know whether that behavior occurred or not. Operational definitions may be arbitrary (e.g., an IQ score at or above 130 is operationally defined as "gifted"), but they must be precise.

meta-analysis
A technique of combining results of many studies to come to an overall conclusion. Meta-analysis is powerful, in that small samples can be added together to lead to significant conclusions, although variations from study to study sometimes make combining them impossible.

effect size
A way of indicating statistically how much of an impact the independent variable in an experiment had on the dependent variable.

sample size is large, because a large sample often leads to highly "significant" results (results that are unlikely to have occurred by chance) that have only a tiny effect on the variable of interest.

Hundreds of statistical measures are used by developmentalists. Often the same data can be presented in many ways: Some scientists examine statistical analysis intently before they accept conclusions as valid. A specific example involved methods to improve students' writing ability between grades 4 and 12. A meta-analysis found that many methods of writing instruction have a significant impact, but effect size is much larger for some methods (teaching strategies and summarizing) than for others (prewriting exercises and studying models). For teachers, this statistic is crucial, for they want to know what has a big effect, not merely what is better than chance (significant).

Numerous articles published in the past decade are meta-analyses that combine similar studies to search for general trends. Often effect sizes are also reported, which is especially helpful for meta-analyses since standard calculations almost always find some significance if the number of participants is in the thousands.

An added problem is the "file drawer" problem—that studies without significant results tend to be filed away rather than published. Thus, an accurate effect size may be much smaller than the published meta-analysis finds, or may be nonexistent. For this reason, replication is an important step.

Overall, then, designing and conducting valid research is complex yet crucial. Remember that with your own opinions: As this appendix advises, it is good to "make it personal," but do not stop there.

Glossary

A

absent grief When mourners do not grieve, either because other people do not allow expressions of grief or because the mourners do not allow themselves to feel sadness.

active euthanasia When someone does something that hastens another person's death, with the intention of ending that person's suffering.

activities of daily life (ADLs) Typically identified as five tasks of self-care that are important to independent living: eating, bathing, toileting, dressing, and transferring from a bed to a chair. The inability to perform any of these tasks is a sign of frailty.

activity theory The view that elderly people want and need to remain active in a variety of social spheres—with relatives, friends, and community groups—and become withdrawn only unwillingly, as a result of ageism.

additive genes Genes that each contribute to the characteristic—they "add up" rather than one being hidden (recessive). For example, skin color is additive: It shows the combined genes of both parents, rather than taking after one or the other.

adolescence-limited offender A person whose criminal activity stops by age 21.

adolescent egocentrism A characteristic of adolescent thinking that leads young people (ages 10 to 13) to focus on themselves to the exclusion of others.

advance directives Any description of what a person wants to happen as they die and after they die. This can include medical measures, visitors, funeral arrangements, cremation, and so on.

age in place To remain in the same home and community in later life, adjusting but not leaving when health fades.

age of viability The age (about 22 weeks after conception) at which a fetus might survive outside the mother's uterus if specialized medical care is available.

ageism A prejudice whereby people are categorized and judged solely on the basis of their chronological age.

aggressive-rejected A type of childhood rejection, when other children do not want to be friends with a child because of his or her antagonistic, confrontational behavior.

allele A variation that makes a gene different in some way from other genes for the same characteristics. Many genes never vary; others have several possible alleles.

allocare Literally, "other-care"; the care of children by people other than the biological parents.

allostasis A dynamic body adjustment, related to homeostasis, that affects overall physiology over time. The main difference is that homeostasis requires an immediate response, whereas allostasis requires longer-term adjustment.

allostatic load The stresses of basic body systems that burden overall functioning, such as hypertension.

Alzheimer's disease (AD) The most common cause of major NCD, characterized by gradual deterioration of memory and personality, and marked by the formation of plaques of beta-amyloid protein and tangles of tau in the brain.

amygdala A tiny brain structure that registers emotions, particularly fear and anxiety.

analytic intelligence A form of intelligence that involves abstract planning, strategy selection, focused attention, and information processing, as well as verbal and logical skills.

analytic thought Thought that results from analysis, such as a systematic ranking of pros and cons, risks and consequences, possibilities and facts. Analytic thought depends on logic and rationality.

animism The belief that natural objects and phenomena are alive, moving around, with sensations and abilities that are humanlike.

anorexia nervosa An eating disorder characterized by self-starvation. Affected individuals voluntarily undereat and often overexercise, depriving their vital organs of nutrition. Anorexia can be fatal.

antipathy Feelings of dislike or even hatred for another person.

antisocial behavior Actions that are deliberately hurtful or destructive to another person.

Apgar scale A quick assessment of a newborn's health, from 0 to 10. Below 6 is an emergency—a neonatal pediatrician is summoned immediately. Most babies are at 7, 8, or 9—almost never a perfect 10.

aptitude The potential to master a specific skill, or to learn a certain body of knowledge.

asthma A chronic disease of the respiratory system in which inflammation narrows the airways from the nose and mouth to the lungs, causing difficulty in breathing. Signs and symptoms include wheezing, shortness of breath, chest tightness, and coughing.

attachment According to Ainsworth, "an affectional tie" that an infant forms with a caregiver—a tie that binds them together in space and endures over time.

attention-deficit/hyperactivity disorder (ADHD) A condition characterized by a persistent pattern of inattention and/or by hyperactive or impulsive behaviors; ADHD interferes with a person's functioning or development.

authoritarian parenting An approach to child rearing that is characterized by high behavioral standards, strict punishment of misconduct, and little communication from child to parent.

authoritative parenting An approach to child rearing in which the parents set limits and enforce rules, but are flexible and listen to their children.

autism spectrum disorder (ASD) A developmental disorder marked by difficulty with social communication and interaction—including difficulty seeing things from another person's point of view—and restricted, repetitive patterns of behavior, interests, or activities.

autonomy versus shame and doubt Erikson's second crisis of psychosocial development. Toddlers either succeed or fail in gaining a sense of self-rule over their actions and their bodies.

axon A fiber that extends from a neuron and transmits electrochemical impulses from that neuron to the dendrites of other neurons.

B

babbling An infant's repetition of certain syllables, such as *ba-ba-ba,* that begins when babies are between 6 and 9 months old.

bed-sharing When two or more people sleep in the same bed.

behavioral teratogens Agents and conditions that can harm the prenatal brain, impairing the future child's intellectual and emotional functioning.

behaviorism A theory of human development that studies observable actions. Behaviorism is also called *learning theory,* because it describes how people learn to do what they do.

Big Five The five basic clusters of personality traits that remain quite stable throughout adulthood: openness, conscientiousness, extroversion, agreeableness, and neuroticism.

bilingual education A strategy in which school subjects are taught in both the learner's original language and the second (majority) language.

binge eating disorder Eating much more in a short time period than is typical, to the point of feeling overfull and in pain. In this disorder, bingeing happens more than once a week for several months, and sufferers feel out of control—they can't stop. This disorder begins as bulimia does, but does not involve purging.

binocular vision The ability to focus the two eyes in a coordinated manner in order to see one image.

blind The condition of data gatherers (and sometimes participants, as well) who are deliberately kept ignorant of the purpose of the research so that they cannot unintentionally bias the results.

body image A person's idea of how his or her body looks.

Brazelton Neonatal Behavioral Assessment Scale (NBAS) A test that is often administered to newborns which measures responsiveness and records 46 behaviors, including 20 reflexes.

bulimia nervosa An eating disorder characterized by binge eating and subsequent purging, usually by induced vomiting and/or use of laxatives.

bullying Repeated, systematic efforts to inflict harm on other people through physical, verbal, or social attack on a weaker person.

bullying aggression Unprovoked, repeated physical or verbal attack, especially on victims who are unlikely to defend themselves.

bully-victim Someone who attacks others and who is attacked as well. (Also called *provocative victim* because they do things that elicit bullying.)

C

calorie restriction The practice of limiting dietary energy intake (while consuming sufficient quantities of vitamins, minerals, and other important nutrients) for the purpose of improving health and slowing down the aging process.

carrier A person whose genotype includes a gene that is not expressed in the phenotype. The carried gene occurs in half of the carrier's gametes, and thus is passed on to half of the carrier's children. If such a gene is inherited from both parents, the characteristic appears in the phenotype.

cellular aging The cumulative effect of stress and toxins, first causing cellular damage and eventually the death of cells.

centration A characteristic of preoperational thought in which a young child focuses (centers) on one idea, excluding all others.

cesarean section (c-section) A surgical birth, in which incisions through the mother's abdomen and uterus allow the fetus to be removed quickly, instead of being delivered through the vagina. (Also called simply *section.*)

child abuse Deliberate action that is harmful to a child's physical, emotional, or sexual well-being.

child culture The idea that each group of children has games, sayings, clothing styles, and superstitions that are not common among adults, just as every culture has distinct values, behaviors, and beliefs.

child maltreatment Intentional harm to or avoidable endangerment of anyone under 18 years of age.

child neglect Failure to meet a child's basic physical, educational, or emotional needs.

child sexual abuse Any erotic activity that arouses an adult and excites, shames, or confuses a child, whether or not the victim protests and whether or not genital contact is involved.

childhood obesity In a child, having a BMI above the 95th percentile, according to the U.S. Centers for Disease Control's 1980 standards for children of a given age.

childhood overweight In a child, having a BMI above the 85th percentile, according to the U.S. Centers for Disease Control's 1980 standards for children of a given age.

chromosome One of the 46 molecules of DNA (in 23 pairs) that virtually every cell of the human body contains and that, together, contain all of the genes. Other species have more or fewer chromosomes.

classification The logical principle that things can be organized into groups (or categories or classes) according to some characteristic that they have in common.

cluster suicides Several suicides committed by members of a group within a brief period.

cognitive artifacts Intellectual tools passed down from generation to generation that may assist in learning within societies.

cognitive theory A theory of human development that focuses on how people think. According to this theory, our thoughts shape our attitudes, beliefs, and behaviors.

cohabitation An arrangement in which a couple lives together in a committed romantic relationship but are not formally married.

cohort People born within the same historical period who therefore move through life together, experiencing the same events, new technologies, and cultural shifts at the same ages.

comorbid Refers to the presence of two or more unrelated disease conditions at the same time in the same person.

complicated grief A type of grief that impedes a person's future life, usually because the person clings to sorrow or is buffeted by contradictory emotions.

compulsive hoarding The urge to accumulate and hold on to familiar objects and possessions, sometimes to the point of their becoming health and/or safety hazards. This impulse tends to increase with age.

concrete operational thought Piaget's term for the ability to reason logically about direct experiences and perceptions.

conditioning According to behaviorism, the processes of learning. The word *conditioning* emphasizes the importance of repeated experiences, as when an athlete *conditions* his or her body by training day after day.

conservation The principle that the amount of a substance remains the same (i.e., is conserved) even when its appearance changes.

Continuing bonds The ongoing memories and attachment that one person has for another even after that other person has died.

control processes Mechanisms (including selective attention, metacognition, and emotional regulation) that combine memory, processing speed, and knowledge to regulate the analysis and flow of information within the information-processing system. (Also called *executive processes*.)

conventional moral reasoning Kohlberg's second level of moral reasoning, emphasizing social rules.

copy number variations The various repeats or deletions of base pairs that genes have.

corporal punishment Discipline techniques that hurt the body (*corpus*) of someone, from spanking to serious harm, including death.

corpus callosum A long, thick band of nerve fibers that connects the left and right hemispheres of the brain and allows communication between them.

correlation Usually a number between +1.0 and −1.0 that indicates whether and how much two variables are related. Correlation indicates whether an increase in one variable will increase or decrease another variable. Correlation indicates only that two variables are somehow related, not that one variable *causes* the other to increase or decrease.

cortex The outer layers of the brain in humans and other mammals. Most thinking, feeling, and sensing involves the cortex.

cortisol The primary stress hormone; fluctuations in the body's cortisol level affect human emotions.

co-sleeping A custom in which parents and their children (usually infants) sleep together in the same room.

couvade Symptoms of pregnancy and birth experienced by fathers.

creative intelligence A form of intelligence that involves the capacity to be intellectually flexible and innovative.

critical period Time when a particular development must occur. If it does not, as when something toxic prevents that growth, then it cannot develop later.

cross-sectional research A research design that compares people who differ in age but not in other important characteristics.

cross-sequential research A hybrid research design that includes cross-sectional and longitudinal research. (Also called *cohort-sequential research* or *time-sequential research*.)

crystallized intelligence Those types of intellectual ability that reflect accumulated learning. Vocabulary and general information are examples. Some developmental psychologists think crystallized intelligence increases with age, while fluid intelligence declines.

culture A system of shared beliefs, norms, behaviors, and expectations that persist over time and prescribe social behavior and assumptions.

cyberbullying Bullying that occurs when one person spreads insults or rumors about another by means of social media posts, e-mails, text messages, or cell phone videos.

D

deductive reasoning Reasoning from a general statement, premise, or principle, through logical steps, to figure out (deduce) specifics. (Also called *top-down reasoning*.)

demographic shift A shift in the proportions of the populations of various ages.

dendrite A fiber that extends from a neuron and receives electrochemical impulses transmitted from other neurons via their axons.

deoxyribonucleic acid (DNA) The chemical composition of the molecules that contain the genes, which are the chemical instructions for cells to manufacture various proteins.

dependent variable In an experiment, the variable that may change as a result of the independent variable (whatever new condition the experimenter adds). In other words, the dependent variable *depends* on the independent variable.

developmental psychopathology The field that uses insights into typical development to understand and remediate developmental disorders.

developmental theory A group of ideas, assumptions, and generalizations about human growth. A developmental theory provides a framework to interpret growth and change.

deviancy training Destructive peer support in which one person shows another how to rebel against authority or social norms.

difference-equals-deficit error The mistaken belief that a deviation from some norm is necessarily inferior.

differential susceptibility The idea that people vary in how sensitive (for better or worse) they are to particular experiences, either because of their genes or because of their past experiences. (Also called *differential sensitivity*.)

disenfranchised grief A situation in which certain people, although they are bereaved, are prevented from mourning publicly by cultural customs or social restrictions.

disengagement theory The view that aging makes a person's social sphere increasingly narrow, resulting in role relinquishment, withdrawal, and passivity.

disorganized attachment (type D) A type of attachment that is marked by an infant's inconsistent reactions to the caregiver's departure and return.

distal parenting Caregiving practices that involve remaining distant from the baby, providing toys, food, and face-to-face communication with minimal holding and touching.

dizygotic (DZ) twins Twins who are formed when two separate ova are fertilized by two separate sperm at roughly the same time. (Also called *fraternal twins*.)

DNR (do not resuscitate) order A written order from a physician (sometimes initiated by a patient's advance directive or by a health care proxy's request) that no attempt should be made to revive a patient if they suffer cardiac or respiratory arrest.

dominant–recessive pattern The interaction of a heterozygous pair of alleles in such a way that the phenotype reflects one allele (the dominant gene) more than the other (the recessive gene).

double effect When an action (such as administering opiates) has both a positive effect (relieving a terminally ill person's pain) and a negative effect (hastening death by suppressing respiration).

doula A woman who helps with the birth process. Traditionally in Latin America, a doula was the only professional who attended childbirth. Now doulas are likely to arrive at the woman's home during early labor and later work alongside a hospital's staff.

drug abuse When drug use is harmful, either to the body or to society—as when alcohol makes a person risk their own health or hurt others.

dual processing The notion that two networks exist within the human brain, one for emotional processing of stimuli and one for analytical reasoning.

dynamic-systems approach A view of human development as an ongoing, ever-changing interaction between the physical, cognitive, and psychosocial influences.

dyscalculia Unusual difficulty with math, probably originating from a distinct part of the brain.

dyslexia Unusual difficulty with reading; thought to be the result of some neurological underdevelopment.

E

ecological validity The idea that cognition should be measured in settings that are as realistic as possible and that the abilities measured should be those needed in real life.

ecological-systems approach A perspective on human development that considers all of the influences from the various contexts of development. (Later renamed *bioecological theory*.)

effect size A way of indicating statistically how much of an impact the independent variable in an experiment had on the dependent variable.

effortful control The ability to regulate one's emotions and actions through effort, not simply through natural inclination.

egocentrism Piaget's term for children's tendency to think about the world entirely from their own personal perspective.

elderspeak A condescending way of speaking to older adults that resembles baby talk, with simple and short sentences, exaggerated emphasis, repetition, and a slower rate and a higher pitch than used in normal speech.

embryo The name for a developing human organism from about the third week through the eighth week after conception.

emerging adulthood The period of life between the ages of 18 and 25. Emerging adulthood is now widely thought of as a distinct developmental stage.

emotional regulation The ability to control when and how emotions are expressed.

empathy The ability to understand the emotions and concerns of another person, especially when they differ from one's own.

empirical evidence Evidence that is based on observation, experience, or experiment; not just theory or opinion. This makes it science-based.

empty nest The time in the lives of parents when their children have left the family home to pursue their own lives.

English Language Learners (ELLs) Children in the United States whose proficiency in English is low—usually below a cutoff score on an oral or written test. Many children who speak a non-English language at home are also capable in English; they are *not* ELLs.

epigenetics The study of how environmental factors affect genes and genetic expression—enhancing, halting, shaping, or altering the expression of genes.

equifinality A basic principle of developmental psychopathology, which holds that one symptom can have many causes.

ESL (English as a Second Language) A U.S. approach to teaching English that gathers all of the non-English speakers together and provides intense instruction in English. Students' first languages are never used; the goal is to prepare them for regular classes in English.

ethnic group People whose ancestors were born in the same region. Usually they share a language, culture, and/or religion.

evolutionary theory When used in human development, the idea that many current human emotions and impulses are a legacy from thousands of years ago.

executive function The cognitive ability to organize and prioritize the many thoughts that arise from the various parts of the brain, allowing the person to anticipate, strategize, and plan behavior.

experience-dependent Brain functions that depend on particular, variable experiences and therefore may or may not develop in a particular infant.

experience-expectant Brain functions that require certain basic common experiences (which an infant can be expected to have) in order to develop normally.

experiment A research method in which the researcher adds one variable (called the *independent variable*) and then observes the effect on another variable (called the *dependent variable*) in order to learn if the independent variable causes change in the dependent variable.

expert Someone with specialized skills and knowledge developed around a particular activity or area of specific interest.

extended family A family of relatives in addition to the parents usually three or more generations living in one household.

extremely low birthweight (ELBW) A body weight at birth of less than 1,000 grams (2 pounds, 3 ounces).

extrinsic motivation A drive, or reason to pursue a goal, that arises from the wish to have external rewards, perhaps by earning money or praise.

extrinsic rewards of work The tangible benefits, usually in salary, insurance, pension, and status, that come with employment.

F

false positive The result of a laboratory test that reports something as true when in fact it is not true. This can occur for pregnancy tests, when a woman might not be pregnant even though the test says she is, or during pregnancy, when a problem is reported that actually does not exist.

familism The belief that family members should support one another, sacrificing individual freedom and success, if necessary, in order to preserve family unity and protect the family from outside forces.

family function The way a family works to meet the needs of its members. Children need families to provide basic material necessities, to encourage learning, to help them develop self-respect, to nurture friendships, and to foster harmony and stability.

family structure The legal and genetic relationships among relatives living in the same home. Possible structures include nuclear family, extended family, stepfamily, single-parent family, and many others.

fast-mapping The speedy and sometimes imprecise way in which children learn new words by tentatively placing them in mental categories according to their perceived meaning.

fetal alcohol syndrome (FAS) A cluster of birth defects, including abnormal facial characteristics, slow physical growth, and reduced intellectual ability, that may occur in the fetus of a woman who drinks alcohol while pregnant.

fetus The name for a developing human organism from the start of the ninth week after conception until birth.

fictive kin People who become accepted as part of a family who have no genetic or legal relationship to that family.

filial responsibility The obligation of adult children to care for their aging parents.

fine motor skills Physical abilities involving small body movements, especially of the hands and fingers, such as drawing or picking up a coin. (The word *fine* here means "small.")

fluid intelligence Those types of basic intelligence that make learning of all sorts quick and thorough. Abilities such as short-term memory, abstract thought, and speed of thinking are all usually considered part of fluid intelligence.

Flynn effect The rise in average IQ scores that has occurred over the decades in many nations.

focus on appearance A characteristic of preoperational thought in which a young child ignores all attributes that are not apparent.

foreclosure Erikson's term for premature identity formation, which occurs when an adolescent adopts their parents' or society's roles and values wholesale, without questioning or analysis.

formal operational thought In Piaget's theory, the fourth and final stage of cognitive development, characterized by more systematic logical thinking and by the ability to understand and systematically manipulate abstract concepts.

foster care When a person (usually a child) is cared for by someone other than the parents.

frail elderly People over age 65, and often over age 85, who are physically infirm, very ill, or cognitively disabled.

frontotemporal NCDs Deterioration of the amygdala and frontal lobes that may be the cause of 15 percent of all major neurocognitive disorders. (Also called *frontotemporal lobar degeneration.*)

G

gender differences Differences in male and female roles, behaviors, clothes, and so on that arise from society, not biology.

gender identity A person's self-perception as male, female, both, or neither.

gender schema A child's cognitive concept or general belief about male and female differences.

general intelligence (g) The idea of *g* assumes that intelligence is one basic trait, underlying all cognitive abilities. According to this concept, people have varying levels of this general ability.

generational forgetting The idea that each new generation forgets what the previous generation learned. As used here, the term refers to knowledge about the harm drugs can do.

generativity versus stagnation The seventh of Erikson's eight stages of development in which adults seek to be productive in a caring way, often as parents. Generativity also occurs through art, caregiving, and employment.

genetic counseling Consultation and testing by trained experts that enable individuals to learn about their genetic heritage, including harmful conditions that they might pass along to any children they may conceive.

genome The full set of genes that are the instructions to make an individual member of a certain species.

genotype An organism's entire genetic inheritance, or genetic potential.

germinal period The first two weeks of prenatal development after conception, characterized by rapid cell division and the beginning of cell differentiation.

grammar All of the methods—word order, verb forms, and so on—that languages use to communicate meaning, apart from the words themselves.

grief The deep sorrow that people feel at the death of another. Grief is personal and unpredictable.

gross motor skills Physical abilities involving large body movements, such as walking and jumping. (The word *gross* here means "big.")

growth spurt The relatively sudden and rapid physical growth that occurs during puberty. Each body part increases in size on a schedule: Weight usually precedes height, and growth of the limbs precedes growth of the torso.

H

Hayflick limit The number of times a human cell is capable of dividing into two new cells. The limit for most human cells is approximately 50 divisions, an indication that the life span is limited by our genetic program.

Head Start A federally funded early-childhood intervention program for low-income children of preschool age.

head-sparing A biological mechanism that protects the brain when malnutrition disrupts body growth. The brain is the last part of the body to be damaged by malnutrition.

health care proxy A person chosen to make medical decisions if a patient is unable to do so, as when in a coma.

heterozygous Referring to two genes of one pair that differ in some way. Typically one allele has only a few base pairs that differ from the other member of the pair.

hidden curriculum The unofficial, unstated, or implicit patterns within a school that influence what children learn. For instance, teacher background, organization of the play space, and tracking are all part of the hidden curriculum—not formally prescribed, but instructive to the children.

high-stakes test An evaluation that is critical in determining success or failure. If a single test determines whether a student will graduate or be promoted, it is a high-stakes test.

hippocampus A brain structure that is a central processor of memory, especially memory for locations.

holophrase A single word that is used to express a complete, meaningful thought.

homeostasis The adjustment of all of the body's systems to keep physiological functions in a state of equilibrium. As the body ages, it takes longer for these homeostatic adjustments to occur, so it becomes harder for older bodies to adapt to stress.

homozygous Referring to two genes of one pair that are exactly the same in every letter of their code. Most gene pairs are homozygous.

hookup A sexual encounter between two people who are not in a romantic relationship. Neither intimacy nor commitment are expected.

hormone replacement therapy (HRT) Taking hormones (in pills, patches, or injections) to compensate for hormone reduction. HRT is most common in women at menopause or after removal of the ovaries, but it is also used by men as their testosterone decreases. HRT has some medical uses, but it also carries health risks.

hospice An institution or program in which terminally ill patients receive palliative care to reduce suffering; family and friends of the dying are helped as well.

humanism A theory that stresses the potential of all humans, who have the same basic needs, regardless of culture, gender, or background.

hypothalamus A brain area that responds to the amygdala and the hippocampus to produce hormones that activate other parts of the brain and body.

hypothesis A specific prediction that can be tested, and proved or disproved.

hypothetical thought Reasoning that includes propositions and possibilities that may not reflect reality.

I

identity achievement Erikson's term for the attainment of identity, or the point at which a person understands who they are as a unique individual, in accord with past experiences and future plans.

identity versus role confusion Erikson's term for the fifth stage of development, in which the person tries to figure out "Who am I?" but is confused as to which of many possible roles to adopt.

imaginary audience The other people who, in an adolescent's egocentric belief, are watching and taking note of his or her appearance, ideas, and behavior. This belief makes many teenagers very self-conscious.

immersion A strategy in which instruction in all school subjects occurs in the second (usually the majority) language that a child is learning.

immigrant paradox The surprising, paradoxical fact that low-SES immigrant women tend to have fewer birth complications than native-born peers with higher incomes.

immunization A process that stimulates the body's immune system by causing production of antibodies to defend against attack by a particular contagious disease. Creation of antibodies may be accomplished either naturally (by having the disease), by injection, by drops that are swallowed, or by a nasal spray.

implantation The process, beginning about 10 days after conception, in which the developing organism burrows into the uterus, where it can be nourished and protected as it continues to develop.

impulse control The ability to postpone or deny the immediate response to an idea or behavior.

incomplete grief When circumstances, such as a police investigation or an autopsy, interfere with the process of grieving.

independent variable In an experiment, the variable that is added by the researcher to see if it affects the dependent variable.

individual education plan (IEP) A document that specifies educational goals and plans for a child with special needs.

induction A disciplinary technique in which the parent tries to get the child to understand why a certain behavior was wrong. Listening, not lecturing, is crucial.

inductive reasoning Reasoning from one or more specific experiences or facts to reach (induce) a general conclusion. (Also called *bottom-up reasoning*.)

industry versus inferiority The fourth of Erikson's eight psychosocial crises, during which children attempt to master many skills, developing a sense of themselves as either industrious or inferior, competent or incompetent.

infertility The inability to conceive a child after trying for at least a year.

information-processing theory The idea that human cognition and comprehension occurs step by step, similar to the way that input, analysis, and output occur via computer.

initiative versus guilt Erikson's third psychosocial crisis, in which young children undertake new skills and activities and feel guilty when they do not succeed at them.

injury control/harm reduction Reducing the potential negative consequences of behavior, such as safety surfaces replacing cement at a playground.

insecure-avoidant attachment (type A) A pattern of attachment in which an infant avoids connection with the caregiver, as when the infant seems not to care about the caregiver's presence, departure, or return.

insecure-resistant/ambivalent attachment (type C) A pattern of attachment in which an infant's anxiety and uncertainty are evident, as when the infant becomes very upset at separation from the caregiver, and both resists and seeks contact on reunion.

instrumental activities of daily life (IADLs) Actions (for example, paying bills and car maintenance) that are important to independent living and that require some intellectual competence and forethought. The ability to perform these tasks may be even more critical to self-sufficiency than ADL ability.

instrumental aggression Hurtful behavior that is intended to get something that another person has.

integrated care Care of frail elders that combines the caregiving strengths of everyone—family, medical professionals, social workers, and the elders themselves.

integrity versus despair The final stage of Erik Erikson's developmental sequence, in which older adults seek to integrate their unique experiences with their vision of community.

intimacy versus isolation The sixth of Erikson's eight stages of development. Adults seek someone with whom to share their lives in an enduring and self-sacrificing commitment. Without such commitment, they risk profound aloneness and isolation.

intrinsic motivation A drive or reason to pursue a goal, which comes from inside a person, such as the joy of reading a good book.

intrinsic rewards of work The personal gratifications, such as pleasure in a job well done or friendship with coworkers that accompany employment.

intuitive thought Thought that arises from an emotion or a hunch beyond rational explanation, and is influenced by past experiences and cultural assumptions.

invincibility fable An adolescent's egocentric conviction that he or she cannot be overcome or even harmed by anything that might defeat a normal mortal, such as unprotected sex, drug abuse, or high-speed driving.

irreversibility A characteristic of preoperational thought in which a young child thinks that nothing can be undone. A thing cannot be restored to the way it was before a change occurred.

K

kinkeeper Someone who becomes the gatherer and communication hub for their family.

kinship care A form of foster care in which a relative, usually a grandmother, becomes the approved caregiver.

knowledge base A body of knowledge in a particular area that makes it easier to master new information in that area.

L

language acquisition device (LAD) Chomsky's term for a hypothesized mental structure that enables humans to learn language, including the basic aspects of grammar, vocabulary, and intonation.

lateralization Literally, "sidedness," referring to the specialization in certain functions by each side of the brain, with one side dominant for each activity. The left side of the brain controls the right side of the body, and vice versa.

least restrictive environment (LRE) A legal requirement that children with special needs be assigned to the most general educational context in which they can be expected to learn.

leptin A hormone that affects appetite and is believed to affect the onset of puberty. Leptin levels increase during childhood and peak at around age 12.

Lewy body disease A form of major neurocognitive disorder characterized by an increase in Lewy body cells in the brain. Symptoms include visual hallucinations, momentary loss of attention, falling, and fainting.

life review An examination of one's own role in the history of human life, engaged in by many elderly people. This can be written or oral.

life-course-persistent offender A person whose criminal activity typically begins in early adolescence and continues throughout life; a career criminal.

life-span perspective An approach to the study of human development that includes all phases, from conception to death.

limbic system The parts of the brain that interact to produce emotions, including the amygdala, the hypothalamus, and the hippocampus. Many other parts of the brain are also involved with emotions.

linked lives Lives in which the success, health, and well-being of each family member are connected to those of other members, including those of another generation, as in the relationship between parents and children.

Living Apart Together (LAT) The term for couples who are committed to each other and spend time together but maintain separate homes. LAT couples are increasingly common in the United states and Europe.

living will A document that indicates what medical intervention an individual prefers if he or she is not conscious when a decision is to be expressed. For example, some do not want mechanical breathing.

longitudinal research A research design that follows the same individuals over time.

low birthweight (LBW) A body weight at birth of less than 2,500 grams (5½ pounds).

M

major depression Feelings of hopelessness, lethargy, and worthlessness that last two weeks or more.

major neurocognitive disorder (major NCD) Irreversible loss of intellectual functioning caused by organic brain damage or disease. Formerly called *dementia,* major NCD becomes more common with age, but it is abnormal and pathological even in the very old.

maximum life span The oldest possible age that members of a species can live under ideal circumstances. For humans, that age is approximately 122 years.

mean length of utterance (MLU) The average number of words in a typical sentence (called utterance because children may not talk in complete sentences). MLU is often used to measure language development.

menarche A girl's first menstrual period, signaling that she has begun ovulation. Pregnancy is biologically possible, but ovulation and menstruation are often irregular for years after menarche.

menopause The time in middle age, usually around age 50, when a woman's menstrual periods cease and the production of estrogen, progesterone, and testosterone drops. Strictly speaking, menopause is dated one year after a woman's last menstrual period, although many months before and after that date are menopausal.

meta-analysis A technique of combining results of many studies to come to an overall conclusion. Meta-analysis is powerful, in that small samples can be added together to lead to significant conclusions, although variations from study to study sometimes make combining them impossible.

microbiome All of the microbes (bacteria, viruses, and so on) with all of their genes in a community; here, the millions of microbes of the human body.

middle school A school for children in the grades between elementary school and high school. Middle school usually begins with grade 6 and ends with grade 8.

monozygotic (MZ) twins Twins who originate from one zygote that splits apart very early in development. (Also called *identical twins.*) Other monozygotic multiple births (such as triplets and quadruplets) can occur as well.

Montessori schools Schools that offer early-childhood education based on the philosophy of Maria Montessori, which emphasizes careful work and tasks that each young child can do.

moratorium An adolescent's choice of a socially acceptable way to postpone making identity-achievement decisions. Going to college is a common example.

motor skill The learned abilities to move some part of the body, in actions ranging from a large leap to a flicker of the eyelid. (The word *motor* here refers to movement of muscles.)

mourning The ceremonies and behaviors that a religion or culture prescribes for people to express their grief after a death.

multifinality A basic principle of developmental psychopathology that holds that one cause can have many (multiple) final manifestations.

multiple intelligences The idea that human intelligence is composed of a varied set of abilities rather than a single, all-encompassing one.

myelin The fatty substance coating axons that speeds the transmission of nerve impulses from neuron to neuron.

N

naming explosion A sudden increase in an infant's vocabulary, especially in the number of nouns, that begins at about 18 months of age.

National Assessment of Educational Progress (NAEP) An ongoing and nationally representative measure of U.S. children's achievement in reading, mathematics, and other subjects over time; nicknamed "the Nation's Report Card."

naturally occurring retirement community (NORC) A neighborhood or apartment complex whose population is mostly retired people who moved to the location as younger adults and never left.

nature In development, *nature* refers to genes. Thus, traits, capacities, and limitations inherited at conception are nature.

neglectful/uninvolved parenting An approach to child rearing in which the parents seem indifferent toward their children, not knowing or caring about their children's lives.

neurocognitive disorder (NCD) Any of a number of brain diseases that affect a person's ability to remember, analyze, plan, or interact with other people.

neurodiversity The idea that each person has neurological strengths and weaknesses that should be appreciated, in much the same way diverse cultures and ethnicities are welcomed. Neurodiversity seems particularly relevant for children with disorders on the autism spectrum.

neuron One of billions of nerve cells in the central nervous system, especially in the brain.

neurotransmitter A brain chemical that carries information from the axon of a sending neuron to the dendrites of a receiving neuron.

norm An average, or standard, calculated from many individuals within a specific group or population.

nurture In development, *nurture* includes all environmental influences that occur after conception, from the mother's nutrition while pregnant to the culture of the nation.

O

object permanence The realization that objects (including people) still exist when they can no longer be seen, touched, or heard.

Oedipus complex The unconscious desire of young boys to replace their fathers and win their mothers' exclusive love.

oldest-old Elderly adults (generally, those over age 85) who are dependent on others for almost everything, requiring supportive services such as nursing homes and hospital stays.

old-old Older adults (generally, those over age 75) who suffer from physical, mental, or social deficits.

operant conditioning The learning process that reinforces or punishes behavior. (Also called *instrumental conditioning*.)

operational definition A description of the specific, observable behavior that will constitute the variable that is to be studied, so that any reader will know whether that behavior occurred or not. Operational definitions may be arbitrary (e.g., an IQ score at or above 130 is operationally defined as "gifted"), but they must be precise.

organ reserve The capacity of organs to allow the body to cope with stress, via extra, unused functioning ability.

overregularization The application of rules of grammar even when exceptions occur, making the language seem more "regular" than it actually is.

P

palliative care Medical treatment designed primarily to provide physical and emotional comfort to the dying patient and guidance to his or her loved ones.

parasuicide Any potentially lethal action against the self that does not result in death. (Also called *attempted suicide* or *failed suicide*.)

parental monitoring Parents' ongoing awareness of what their children are doing, where, and with whom.

parentification When a child acts more like a parent than a child. Parentification may occur if the actual parents do not act as caregivers, making a child feel responsible for the family.

Parkinson's disease A chronic, progressive disease that is characterized by muscle tremor and rigidity and sometimes major neurocognitive disorder; caused by reduced dopamine production in the brain.

participants The people who are studied in a research project. Participants is the term now used in psychology; other disciplines still call these people "subjects."

passive euthanasia When a seriously ill person is allowed to die naturally, without active attempts to prolong life.

peer pressure Encouragement to conform to one's friends or contemporaries in behavior, dress, and attitude; usually considered a negative force, as when adolescent peers encourage one another to defy adult authority.

percentile A point on a ranking scale of 0 to 100. The 50th percentile is the midpoint; half of the people in the population being studied rank higher and half rank lower.

perception The mental processing of sensory information when the brain interprets a sensation.

permissive parenting An approach to child rearing that is characterized by high nurturance and communication but little discipline, guidance, or control.

perseveration The tendency to persevere in, or stick to, one thought or action for a long time.

personal fable An aspect of adolescent egocentrism characterized by an adolescent's belief that their thoughts, feelings, and experiences are unique, more wonderful, or more awful than anyone else's.

phallic stage Freud's third stage of development, when the penis becomes the focus of concern and pleasure.

phenotype The observable characteristics of a person, including appearance, personality, intelligence, and all other traits.

physician-assisted suicide A form of active euthanasia in which a doctor provides the means for someone to end his or her own life, usually by prescribing lethal drugs.

plaques Clumps of a protein called beta-amyloid, found in brain tissue surrounding the neurons.

plasticity The idea that abilities, personality, and other human characteristics are moldable, and thus can change.

POLST (physician-ordered life-sustaining treatment) An order from a doctor regarding end-of-life care that advises nurses and other medical staff about which treatments (e.g., feeding, antibiotics, respirators) should be used or not used. It is similar to a living will, but it is written for medical professionals, and thus is more specific.

polygamous family A family consisting of one man, several wives, and their children.

polypharmacy A situation in which elderly people are prescribed several medications. The various side effects and interactions of those medications can result in symptoms typical of major neurocognitive disorder.

population The entire group of individuals who are of particular concern in a scientific study, such as all the children of the world or all newborns who weigh less than 3 pounds.

positivity effect The tendency for elderly people to perceive, prefer, and remember positive images and experiences more than negative ones.

postconventional moral reasoning Kohlberg's third level of moral reasoning, emphasizing moral principles.

postformal thought A proposed adult stage of cognitive development, following Piaget's four stages, that goes beyond adolescent thinking by being more practical, more flexible, and more dialectical (i.e., more capable of combining contradictory elements into a comprehensive whole).

postpartum depression A new mother's feelings of inadequacy and sadness in the days and weeks after giving birth.

post-traumatic growth The increased insight, compassion, and benevolence that some people feel after a trauma, such as surviving a disaster or sudden death of a loved one.

post-traumatic stress disorder (PTSD) An anxiety disorder that develops as a delayed reaction to having experienced or witnessed a shocking or frightening event. Its symptoms may include flashbacks, hypervigilance, anger, nightmares, and sudden terror.

practical intelligence The intellectual skills used in everyday problem solving. (Sometimes called *tacit intelligence*.)

pragmatics The practical use of language that includes the ability to adjust language communication according to audience and context.

preconventional moral reasoning Kohlberg's first level of moral reasoning, emphasizing rewards and punishments.

prefrontal cortex The area of the cortex at the very front of the brain that specializes in anticipation, planning, and impulse control.

preoperational intelligence Piaget's term for cognitive development between the ages of about 2 and 6; it includes language and imagination (which involve symbolic thought), but logical, operational thinking is not yet possible at this stage.

preterm A birth that occurs two or more weeks before the full 38 weeks of the typical pregnancy—that is, at 36 or fewer weeks after conception.)

primary prevention Actions that change overall background conditions to prevent some unwanted event or circumstance, such as injury, disease, or abuse.

primary sex characteristics The parts of the body that are directly involved in reproduction, including the vagina, uterus, ovaries, testicles, and penis.

private speech The internal dialogue that occurs when people talk to themselves (either silently or out loud).

Programme for International Student Assessment (PISA) An international test taken by 15-year-olds in 50 nations that is designed to measure problem solving and cognition in daily life.

Progress in International Reading Literacy Study (PIRLS) Inaugurated in 2001, a planned five-year cycle of international trend studies in the reading ability of fourth-graders.

prosocial behavior Actions that are helpful and kind but that are of no obvious benefit to the person doing them.

protein-calorie malnutrition A condition in which a person does not consume sufficient food of any kind. This deprivation can result in several illnesses, severe weight loss, and even death.

proximal parenting Caregiving practices that involve being physically close to the baby, with frequent holding and touching.

psychoanalytic theory A theory of human development that contends that irrational, unconscious drives and motives underlie human behavior.

psychological control A disciplinary technique that involves threatening to withdraw love and support, using a child's feelings of guilt and gratitude to the parents.

puberty The period of rapid growth and sexual development that begins adolescence.

Q

qualitative research Research that considers individual qualities instead of quantities (numbers).

quantitative research Research that provides data expressed with numbers, such as ranks or scales.

R

race The concept that some people are distinct from others because of physical appearance, typically skin color. Social scientists think race is a misleading idea, although race can be a powerful social construction, not based in biology.

reaction time The time it takes to respond to a stimulus, either physically (with a reflexive movement such as an eyeblink) or cognitively (with a thought).

reactive aggression An impulsive retaliation for another person's intentional or accidental hurtful action.

reflex An unlearned, involuntary action or movement in response to a stimulus. A reflex occurs without conscious thought.

Reggio Emilia A program of early-childhood education that originated in the town of Reggio Emilia, Italy, and that encourages each child's creativity in a carefully designed setting.

reinforcement In behaviorism, the reward or relief that follows a behavior, making it likely that the behavior will occur again.

relational aggression Nonphysical acts, such as insults or social rejection, aimed at harming the social connection between the victim and other people.

REM (rapid eye movement) sleep A stage of sleep characterized by flickering eyes behind closed lids, dreaming, and rapid brain waves.

replication Repeating a study, usually using different participants, perhaps of another age, socioeconomic status (SES), or culture.

reported maltreatment Harm or endangerment about which someone has notified the authorities.

representative sample A group of research participants who reflect the relevant characteristics of the larger population whose attributes are under study.

resilience The capacity to adapt well to significant adversity and to overcome serious stress.

response to intervention (RTI) An educational strategy intended to help children who demonstrate below-average achievement in early grades, using special intervention.

role confusion A situation in which an adolescent does not seem to know or care what his or her identity is. (Sometimes called *identity diffusion* or *role diffusion*.)

rough-and-tumble play Play that seems to be rough, as in play wrestling or chasing, but in which there is no intent to harm.

S

sample A group of individuals drawn from a specified population. A sample might be the low-birthweight babies born in four particular hospitals that are representative of all hospitals.

sandwich generation The generation of middle-aged people who are supposedly "squeezed" by the needs of the younger and older members of the families.

scaffolding Temporary support that is tailored to a learner's needs and abilities, and aimed at helping the learner master the next task in a given learning process.

science of human development The science that seeks to understand how and why people of all ages and circumstances change or remain the same over time.

scientific method A way to answer questions using empirical research and data-based conclusions.

scientific observation Watching and recording participants' behavior in a systematic and objective manner—in a natural setting, in a laboratory, or in searches of archival data.

secondary education Literally, the period after primary education (elementary or grade school) and before tertiary education (college). It usually occurs from about ages 12 to 18, although there is some variation by school and by nation.

secondary prevention Actions that avert harm in a high-risk situation, such as using seat belts in cars.

secondary sex characteristics Physical traits that are not directly involved in reproduction but that indicate sexual maturity, such as a man's beard and a woman's breasts.

secure attachment (type B) A relationship in which an infant obtains both comfort and confidence from the presence of his or her caregiver.

selective optimization with compensation The theory, developed by Paul and Margaret Baltes, that people try to maintain a balance in their lives by looking for the best way to compensate for physical and cognitive losses, and to become more proficient in activities they can already do well.

self theories Theories of late adulthood that emphasize the core self, or the search to maintain one's integrity and identity.

self-actualization The final stage in Maslow's hierarchy of needs, characterized by aesthetic, creative, philosophical, and spiritual understanding.

self-awareness A person's realization that he or she is a distinct individual whose body, mind, and actions are separate from those of other people.

self-concept A person's understanding of who they are, in relation to self-esteem, appearance, personality, and various traits.

senescence The process of aging, whereby the body becomes less strong and efficient.

sensation The response of a sensory organ (eyes, ears, skin, tongue, nose) when it detects a stimulus.

sensitive period A time when a particular developmental growth is most likely to occur, although it may still happen later.

sensorimotor intelligence Piaget's term for the way infants think—by using their senses and motor skills—during the first period of cognitive development.

separation anxiety An infant's distress when a familiar caregiver leaves; most obvious between 9 and 14 months.

seriation The concept that things can be arranged in a logical series, such as the number sequence or the alphabet.

sex differences Biological differences between males and females, in organs, hormones, and body shape.

sexting Sending sexual content, particularly photos or videos, via cell phones or social media.

sexual orientation A term that refers to whether a person is sexually and romantically attracted to others of the same sex, the opposite sex, or both sexes.

sexually transmitted infections (STIs) Diseases that are spread by sexual contact, including syphilis, gonorrhea, genital herpes, chlamydia, and HIV/AIDS.

shaken baby syndrome A life-threatening injury that occurs when an infant is forcefully shaken back and forth, a motion that ruptures blood vessels in the brain and breaks neural connections.

single-parent family A family that consists of only one parent and his or her children.

small for gestational age (SGA) A term for a baby whose birthweight is significantly lower than expected, given the time since conception. For example, a 5-pound (2,265-gram) newborn is considered SGA if born on time but not SGA if born two months early. (Also called *small-for-dates*.)

social comparison The tendency to assess one's abilities, achievements, social status, and other attributes by measuring them against those of other people, especially one's peers.

social construction An idea that is built on shared perceptions, not on objective reality.

social convoy Collectively, the family members, friends, acquaintances, and even strangers who move through the years of life with a person, all aging together.

social learning theory A theory that emphasizes the influence of other people. Even without reinforcement, people learn via role models. (Also called *observational learning*.)

social mediation Human interaction that expands and advances understanding, often through words that one person uses to explain something to another.

social referencing Seeking information about how to react to an unfamiliar or ambiguous object or event by observing someone else's expressions and reactions. That other person becomes a social reference.

social smile A smile evoked by a human face, normally first evident in infants about 6 weeks after birth.

sociodramatic play Pretend play in which children act out various roles and themes in plots or roles that they create.

socioeconomic status (SES) A person's position in society as determined by income, occupation, education, and place of residence. (Sometimes called *social class*.)

socio-emotional selectivity theory The theory that older people prioritize regulation of their own emotions and seek familiar social contacts who reinforce generativity, pride, and joy.

specific learning disorder A marked deficit in a particular area of learning that is not caused by an apparent physical disability, by an intellectual disability, or by an unusually stressful home environment.

spermarche A boy's first ejaculation of sperm. Erections can occur as early as infancy, but ejaculation signals sperm production. Spermarche may occur during sleep (in a "wet dream") or via direct stimulation.

static reasoning A characteristic of preoperational thought in which a young child thinks that nothing changes. Whatever is now has always been and always will be.

stereotype threat The thought in a person's mind that one's appearance or behavior will be misread to confirm another person's oversimplified, prejudiced attitudes.

still-face technique An experimental practice in which an adult keeps his or her face unmoving and expressionless in face-to-face interaction with an infant.

Strange Situation A laboratory procedure for measuring attachment by evoking infants' reactions to the stress of various adults' comings and goings in an unfamiliar playroom.

stranger wariness An infant's expression of concern—a quiet stare while clinging to a familiar person, or a look of fear—when a stranger appears.

stratification theories Theories that emphasize that social forces—particularly those related to a person's social stratum or social category—limit individual choices, and affect a person's ability to function in late adulthood because past stratification continues to limit life in various ways.

stunting The failure of children to grow to a normal height for their age due to severe and chronic malnutrition.

substantiated maltreatment Harm or endangerment that has been reported, investigated, and verified.

sudden infant death syndrome (SIDS) A situation in which a seemingly healthy infant, usually between 2 and 6 months old, suddenly stops breathing and dies unexpectedly while asleep.

suicidal ideation Thinking about suicide, usually with some serious emotional and intellectual or cognitive overtones.

survey A research method in which information is collected from a large number of people by interviews, written questionnaires, or some other means.

symbolic thought A major accomplishment of preoperational intelligence that allows a child to think symbolically, including understanding that words can refer to things not seen and that an item, such as a flag, can symbolize something else (in this case, a country).

synapse The intersection between the axon of one neuron and the dendrites of other neurons.

synchrony A coordinated, rapid, and smooth exchange of responses between a caregiver and an infant.

T

tangles Twisted masses of threads made of a protein called tau within the neurons of the brain.

telomeres The area of the tips of each chromosome that is reduced to a tiny amount as time passes. By the end of life, the telomeres are very short.

temperament Inborn differences between one person and another in emotions, activity, and self-regulation. It is measured by the person's typical responses to the environment.

teratogen An agent or condition, including viruses, drugs, and chemicals, that can impair prenatal development and result in birth defects or even death.

terror management theory The idea that people adopt cultural values and moral principles in order to cope with their fear of death. This system of beliefs protects individuals from anxiety about their mortality and bolsters their self-esteem.

tertiary prevention Actions, such as immediate and effective medical treatment, after an adverse event (such as illness or injury).

theory of mind A person's theory of what other people might be thinking. In order to have a theory of mind, children must realize that other people are not necessarily thinking the same thoughts that they themselves are. That realization seldom occurs before age 4.

theory-theory The idea that children attempt to explain everything they see and hear by constructing theories.

time-out A disciplinary technique in which a person is separated from other people and activities for a specified time.

transient exuberance The great but temporary increase in the number of dendrites that develop in an infant's brain during the first two years of life.

Trends in Math and Science Study (TIMSS) An international assessment of the math and science skills of fourth-and eighthgraders. Although the TIMSS is very useful, different countries' scores are not always comparable because sample selection, test administration, and content validity are hard to keep uniform.

trust versus mistrust Erikson's first crisis of psychosocial development. Infants learn basic trust if the world is a secure place where their basic needs (for food, comfort, attention, and so on) are met.

U

ultrasound An image of a fetus (or an internal organ) produced by using high-frequency sound waves. (Also called *sonogram*.)

universal design The creation of settings and equipment that can be used by everyone, whether or not they are able-bodied and sensory-acute.

V

vascular disease Vascular disease is characterized by sporadic, and progressive, loss of intellectual functioning caused by repeated infarcts, or temporary obstructions of blood vessels, which prevent sufficient blood from reaching the brain. (formerly called *vascular* or *multi-infarct dementia*.)

very low birthweight (VLBW) A body weight at birth of less than 1,500 grams (3 pounds, 5 ounces).

W

Waldorf An early-childhood education program than emphasizes creativity, social understanding, and emotional growth. It originated in Germany with Rudolf Steiner, and now is used in thousands of schools throughout the world.

wasting The tendency of children to be severely underweight for their age and height as a result of malnutrition.

wear-and-tear theory A view of aging as a process by which the human body wears out because of the passage of time and exposure to environmental stressors.

WEIRD An acronym for Western, Educated, Industrialized, Rich Democracy that refers to emerging adults. The criticism is that conclusions about human development based on people in such nations may not apply to most people in the world, who do not live in WEIRD nations.

withdrawn-rejected A type of childhood rejection, when other children do not want to be friends with a child because of his or her timid, withdrawn, and anxious behavior.

working model In cognitive theory, a set of assumptions that the individual uses to organize perceptions and experiences. For example, a person might assume that other people are trustworthy and be surprised by an incident in which this working model of human behavior is erroneous.

X

X-linked A gene carried on the X chromosome. If a male inherits an X-linked recessive trait from his mother, he expresses that trait because the Y from his father has no counteracting gene. Females are more likely to be carriers of X-linked traits but are less likely to express them.

XX A 23rd chromosome pair that consists of two X-shaped chromosomes, one each from the mother and the father. XX zygotes become females.

XY A 23rd chromosome pair that consists of an X-shaped chromosome from the mother and a Y-shaped chromosome from the father. XY zygotes become males.

Y

young-old Healthy, vigorous, financially secure older adults (generally, those aged 65 to 75) who are well integrated into the lives of their families and communities.

Z

zone of proximal development (ZPD) Vygotsky's term for intellectual arena that is comprised of skills—cognitive as well as physical—that a person can learn with assistance.

zygote The single cell formed from the union of two gametes, a sperm and an ovum.

References

Aarnoudse-Moens, Cornelieke S. H.; Smidts, Diana P.; Oosterlaan, Jaap; Duivenvoorden, Hugo J. & Weisglas-Kuperus, Nynke. (2009). Executive function in very preterm children at early school age. *Journal of Abnormal Child Psychology*, *37*(7), 981–993.

Abar, Caitlin C.; Jackson, Kristina M. & Wood, Mark. (2014). Reciprocal relations between perceived parental knowledge and adolescent substance use and delinquency: The moderating role of parent–teen relationship quality. *Developmental Psychology*, *50*(9), 2176–2187.

Abele, Andrea E. & Volmer, Judith. (2011). Dual-career couples: Specific challenges for work-life integration. In Stephan Kaiser, et al. (Eds.), *Creating balance? International perspectives on the work-life integration of professionals* (pp. 173–189). Heidelberg, Germany: Springer.

Acharya, Arnab; Lalwani, Tanya; Dutta, Rahul; Knoll Rajaratnam, Julie; Ruducha, Jenny; Varkey, Leila Caleb, . . . Bernson, Jeff. (2015). Evaluating a large-scale community-based intervention to improve pregnancy and newborn health among the rural poor in India. *American Journal of Public Health*, *105*(1), 144–152.

Adams, Ted D.; Davidson, Lance E.; Litwin, Sheldon E.; Kim, Jaewhan; Kolotkin, Ronette L.; Nanjee, Nazeem, . . . Hunt, Steven C. (2017). Weight and metabolic outcomes 12 years after gastric bypass. *New England Journal of Medicine*, *377*, 1143–1155.

Adamson, Lauren B. & Bakeman, Roger. (2006). Development of displaced speech in early mother-child conversations. *Child Development*, *77*(1), 186–200.

Adamson, Lauren B.; Bakeman, Roger; Deckner, Deborah F. & Nelson, P. Brooke. (2014). From interactions to conversations: The development of joint engagement during early childhood. *Child Development*, *85*(3), 941–955.

Addati, Laura; Cassirer, Naomi & Gilchrist, Katherine. (2014). *Maternity and paternity at work: Law and practice across the world*. Geneva: International Labour Office.

Adler, Caleb; DelBello, Melissa, P; Weber, Wade; Williams, Miranda; Duran, Luis Rodrigo Patino; Fleck, David, . . . Divine, Jon. (2018). MRI evidence of neuropathic changes in former college football players. *Clinical Journal of Sport Medicine*, *28*(2), 100–105.

Adler, Lynn Peters. (1995). *Centenarians: The bonus years*. Santa Fe, NM: Health Press.

Adolph, Karen E. & Franchak, John M. (2017). The development of motor behavior. *WIREs*, *8*(1–2), e1430.

Adolph, Karen E. & Robinson, Scott. (2013). The road to walking: What learning to walk tells us about development. In Philip D. Zelazo (Ed.), *The Oxford handbook of developmental psychology* (Vol. 1, pp. 402–447). New York, NY: Oxford University Press.

Adolph, Karen E. & Tamis-LeMonda, Catherine S. (2014). The costs and benefits of development: The transition from crawling to walking. *Child Development Perspectives*, *8*(4), 187–192.

Ainsworth, Mary D. Salter. (1967). *Infancy in Uganda: Infant care and the growth of love*. Baltimore, MD: Johns Hopkins Press.

Ainsworth, Mary D. Salter. (1973). The development of infant-mother attachment. In Bettye M. Caldwell & Henry N. Ricciuti (Eds.), *Child development and social policy* (pp. 1–94). Chicago, IL: University of Chicago Press.

Aizer, Anna & Currie, Janet. (2014). The intergenerational transmission of inequality: Maternal disadvantage and health at birth. *Science*, *344*(6186), 856–861.

Ajala, Olubukola; Mold, Freda; Boughton, Charlotte; Cooke, Debbie & Whyte, Martin. (2017). Childhood predictors of cardiovascular disease in adulthood: A systematic review and meta-analysis. *Obesity Reviews*, *16*(9), 1061–1070.

Akhtar, Nameera & Jaswal, Vikram K. (2013). Deficit or difference? Interpreting diverse developmental paths: An introduction to the special section. *Developmental Psychology*, *49*(1), 1–3.

Aksglaede, Lise; Link, Katarina; Giwercman, Aleksander; Jørgensen, Niels; Skakkebæk, Niels E. & Juul, Anders. (2013). 47,XXY Klinefelter syndrome: Clinical characteristics and age-specific recommendations for medical management. *American Journal of Medical Genetics Part C: Seminars in Medical Genetics*, *163*(1), 55–63.

Al Otaiba, Stephanie; Wanzek, Jeanne & Yovanoff, Paul. (2015). Response to intervention. *European Scientific Journal*, *1*, 260–264.

Albert, Dustin; Chein, Jason & Steinberg, Laurence. (2013). The teenage brain: Peer influences on adolescent decision making. *Current Directions in Psychological Science*, *22*(2), 114–120.

Albert, Dustin & Steinberg, Laurence. (2011). Judgment and decision making in adolescence. *Journal of Research on Adolescence*, *21*(1), 211–224.

Aldwin, Carolyn M. & Gilmer, Diane Fox. (2013). *Health, illness, and optimal aging: Biological and psychosocial perspectives* (2nd ed.). New York, NY: Springer.

Alegre, Alberto. (2011). Parenting styles and children's emotional intelligence: What do we know? *The Family Journal*, *19*(1), 56–62.

Alesi, Marianha; Bianco, Antonino; Padulo, Johnny; Vella, Francesco Paolo; Petrucci, Marco; Paoli, Antonio, . . .

Pepi, Annamaria. (2014). Motor and cognitive development: The role of karate. *Muscle, Ligaments and Tendons Journal, 4*(2), 114–120.

Alexander, Karl L.; Entwisle, Doris R. & Olson, Linda Steffel. (2014). *The long shadow: Family background, disadvantaged urban youth, and the transition to adulthood.* New York, NY: Russell Sage Foundation.

Al-Hashim, Aqeela H.; Blaser, Susan; Raybaud, Charles & MacGregor, Daune. (2016). Corpus callosum abnormalities: Neuroradiological and clinical correlations. *Developmental Medicine & Child Neurology, 58*(5), 475–484.

Allali, Gilles; Verghese, Joe & Beauchet, Olivier. (2017). Neural substrates of falls in aging: A compensatory mechanism. *Neurology, 88*(16, Suppl.).

Allen, Rebecca S.; Haley, Philip P.; Harris, Grant M.; Fowler, Stevie N. & Pruthi, Roopwinder. (2011). Resilience: Definitions, ambiguities, and applications. In Barbara Resnick, et al. (Eds.), *Resilience in aging: Concepts, research, and outcomes* (pp. 1–14). New York, NY: Springer.

Allen, Tammy D.; Johnson, Ryan C.; Saboe, Kristin N.; Cho, Eunae; Dumani, Soner & Evans, Sarah. (2012). Dispositional variables and work–family conflict: A meta-analysis. *Journal of Vocational Behavior, 80*(1), 17–26.

Almond, Douglas. (2006). Is the 1918 influenza pandemic over? Long-term effects of in utero influenza exposure in the post-1940 U.S. population. *Journal of Political Economy, 114*(4), 672–712.

Al-Namlah, Abdulrahman S.; Meins, Elizabeth & Fernyhough, Charles. (2012). Self-regulatory private speech relates to children's recall and organization of autobiographical memories. *Early Childhood Research Quarterly, 27*(3), 441–446.

Alper, Becka A. (2015, November 23). *Millennials are less religious than older Americans, but just as spiritual.* Fact Tank. Washington, DC: Pew Research Center.

Altenmüller, Eckart & Furuya, Shinichi. (2018). Brain changes associated with acquisition of musical expertise. In K. Anders Ericsson, et al. (Eds.), *The Cambridge handbook of expertise and expert performance* (2nd ed., pp. 550–575). New York, NY: Cambridge University Press.

Altmann, Andre; Tian, Lu; Henderson, Victor W. & Greicius, Michael D. (2014). Sex modifies the *APOE*-related risk of developing Alzheimer disease. *Annals of Neurology, 75*(4), 563–573.

Amato, Michael S.; Magzamen, Sheryl; Imm, Pamela; Havlena, Jeffrey A.; Anderson, Henry A.; Kanarek, Marty S. & Moore, Colleen F. (2013). Early lead exposure (<3 years old) prospectively predicts fourth grade school suspension in Milwaukee, Wisconsin (USA). *Environmental Research, 126,* 60–65.

Amato, Paul R. (2010). Research on divorce: Continuing trends and new developments. *Journal of Marriage and Family, 72*(3), 650–666.

American Academy of Pediatrics. (2016). Media and young minds. *Pediatrics, 138*(5).

American Community Survey. (2015). *American community survey.* Washington, DC: U.S. Census Bureau.

American Psychiatric Association. (2013). *Diagnostic and statistical manual of mental disorders: DSM-5* (5th ed.). Washington, DC: American Psychiatric Association.

Anderin, Claes; Gustafsson, Ulf O.; Heijbel, Niklas & Thorell, Anders. (2015). Weight loss before bariatric surgery and postoperative complications: Data from the Scandinavian Obesity Registry (SOReg). *Annals of Surgery, 261*(5), 909–913.

Anderson, Daniel R. & Hanson, Katherine G. (2016). Screen media and parent–child interactions. In Rachel Barr & Deborah Nichols Linebarger (Eds.), *Media exposure during infancy and early childhood: The effects of content and context on learning and development* (pp. 173–194). Cham, Switzerland: Springer.

Anderson, Michael. (2001). 'You have to get inside the person' or making grief private: Image and metaphor in the therapeutic reconstruction of bereavement. In Jenny Hockey, et al. (Eds.), *Grief, mourning, and death ritual* (pp. 135–143). Buckingham, UK: Open University Press.

Andreas, Nicholas J.; Kampmann, Beate & Le-Doare, Kirsty Mehring. (2015). Human breast milk: A review on its composition and bioactivity. *Early Human Development, 91*(11), 629–635.

Ansado, Jennyfer; Collins, Louis; Fonov, Vladimir; Garon, Mathieu; Alexandrov, Lubomir; Karama, Sherif, . . . Beauchamp, Miriam H. (2015). A new template to study callosal growth shows specific growth in anterior and posterior regions of the corpus callosum in early childhood. *European Journal of Neuroscience, 42*(1), 1675–1684.

Antonucci, Toni C.; Akiyama, Hiroko & Merline, Alicia. (2001). Dynamics of social relationships in midlife. In Margie E. Lachman (Ed.), *Handbook of midlife development* (pp. 571–598). New York, NY: Wiley.

Ardelt, Monika. (2011). Wisdom, age, and well-being. In K. Warner Schaie & Sherry L. Willis (Eds.), *Handbook of the psychology of aging* (7th ed., pp. 279–291). San Diego, CA: Academic Press.

Areba, Eunice M.; Eisenberg, Marla E. & McMorris, Barbara J. (2018). Relationships between family structure, adolescent health status and substance use: Does ethnicity matter? *Journal of Community Psychology, 46*(1), 44–57.

Arigo, Danielle; Butryn, Meghan L.; Raggio, Greer A.; Stice, Eric & Lowe, Michael R. (2016). Predicting change in physical activity: A longitudinal investigation among weight-concerned college women. *Annals of Behavioral Medicine, 50*(5), 629–641.

Armstrong, Kim. (2018). The WEIRD science of culture, values, and behavior [Web log post]. Association for Psychological Science.

Arnett, Jeffrey J. & Padilla-Walker, Laura M. (2015). Brief report: Danish emerging adults' conceptions of adulthood. *Journal of Adolescence, 38*(1), 39–44.

Arnheim, Norman & Calabrese, Peter. (2016). Germline stem cell competition, mutation hot spots, genetic disorders, and older fathers. *Annual Review of Genomics and Human Genetics, 17,* 219–243.

Aron, Arthur; Lewandowski, Gary W.; Mashek, Debra & Aron, Elaine N. (2013). The self-expansion model of motivation and cognition in close relationships. In Jeffry A. Simpson &

Lorne Campbell (Eds.), *The Oxford handbook of close relationships* (pp. 90–115). New York, NY: Oxford University Press.

Aronson, Joshua; Burgess, Diana; Phelan, Sean M. & Juarez, Lindsay. (2013). Unhealthy interactions: The role of stereotype threat in health disparities. *American Journal of Public Health, 103*(1), 50–56.

Arsenio, William F. & Willems, Chris. (2017). Adolescents' conceptions of national wealth distribution: Connections with perceived societal fairness and academic plans. *Developmental Psychology, 53*(3), 463–474.

Arterburn, David E.; Bogart, Andy; Sherwood, Nancy E.; Sidney, Stephen; Coleman, Karen J.; Haneuse, Sebastien, . . . Selby, Joe. (2013). A multisite study of long-term remission and relapse of type 2 diabetes mellitus following gastric bypass. *Obesity Surgery, 23*(1), 93–102.

Arum, Richard & Roksa, Josipa. (2011). *Academically adrift: Limited learning on college campuses.* Chicago, IL: University of Chicago Press.

Arum, Richard & Roksa, Josipa. (2014). *Aspiring adults adrift: Tentative transitions of college graduates.* Chicago, IL: University of Chicago Press.

Asbridge, Mark; Brubacher, Jeff R. & Chan, Herbert. (2013). Cell phone use and traffic crash risk: A culpability analysis. *International Journal of Epidemiology, 42*(1), 259–267.

Ashby, Michael. (2009). The dying human: A perspective from palliative medicine. In Allan Kellehear (Ed.), *The study of dying: From autonomy to transformation* (pp. 76–98). New York, NY: Cambridge University Press.

Ashraf, Quamrul & Galor, Oded. (2013). The 'Out of Africa' hypothesis, human genetic diversity, and comparative economic development. *American Economic Review, 103*(1), 1–46.

Ashwin, Sarah & Isupova, Olga. (2014). "Behind every great man . . .": The male marriage wage premium examined qualitatively. *Journal of Marriage and Family, 76*(1), 37–55.

Aslin, Richard N. (2012). Language development: Revisiting Eimas et al.'s /ba/ and /pa/ study. In Alan M. Slater & Paul C. Quinn (Eds.), *Developmental psychology: Revisiting the classic studies* (pp. 191–203). Thousand Oaks, CA: Sage.

Aslin, Richard N. (2017). Statistical learning: A powerful mechanism that operates by mere exposure. *WIREs Cognitive Science, 8*(1/2), e1373.

Asma, Stephen T. (2013). *Against fairness.* Chicago, IL: University of Chicago Press.

Atchley, Robert C. (2009). *Spirituality and aging.* Baltimore, MD: Johns Hopkins University Press.

Attaran, Amir. (2015). Unanimity on death with dignity—Legalizing physician-assisted dying in Canada. *New England Journal of Medicine, 372*, 2080–2082.

Atzaba-Poria, Naama; Deater-Deckard, Kirby & Bell, Martha Ann. (2017). Mother-child interaction: Links between mother and child frontal electroencephalograph asymmetry and negative behavior. *Child Development, 88*(2), 544–554.

Atzil, Shir; Hendler, Talma & Feldman, Ruth. (2014). The brain basis of social synchrony. *Social Cognitive and Affective Neuroscience, 9*(8), 1193–1202.

Aud, Susan; Hussar, William; Planty, Michael; Snyder, Thomas; Bianco, Kevin; Fox, Mary Ann, . . . Drake, Lauren. (2010). *The condition of education 2010.* Washington, DC: National Center for Education Statistics, Institute of Education Sciences, U.S. Department of Education.

Aunola, Kaisa; Tolvanen, Asko; Viljaranta, Jaana & Nurmi, Jari-Erik. (2013). Psychological control in daily parent–child interactions increases children's negative emotions. *Journal of Family Psychology, 27*(3), 453–462.

Autor, David H. (2014). Skills, education, and the rise of earnings inequality among the "other 99 percent." *Science, 344*(6186), 843–851.

Aviv, Abraham. (2011). Leukocyte telomere dynamics, human aging and life span. In Edward J. Masoro & Steven N. Austad (Eds.), *Handbook of the biology of aging* (7th ed., pp. 163–176). San Diego, CA: Academic Press.

Ayalon, Liat & Ancoli-Israel, Sonia. (2009). Normal sleep in aging. In Teofilo L. Lee-Chiong (Ed.), *Sleep medicine essentials* (pp. 173–176). Hoboken, NJ: Wiley-Blackwell.

Ayyanathan, Kasirajan (Ed.). (2014). *Specific gene expression and epigenetics: The interplay between the genome and its environment.* Oakville, Canada: Apple Academic Press.

Babadjouni, Robin M.; Hodis, Drew M.; Radwanski, Ryan; Durazo, Ramon; Patel, Arati; Liu, Qinghai & Mack, William J. (2017). Clinical effects of air pollution on the central nervous system; A review. *Journal of Clinical Neuroscience, 43*, 16–24.

Babchishin, Lyzon K.; Weegar, Kelly & Romano, Elisa. (2013). Early child care effects on later behavioral outcomes using a Canadian nation-wide sample. *Journal of Educational and Developmental Psychology, 3*(2), 15–29.

Babineau, Vanessa; Green, Cathryn Gordon; Jolicoeur-Martineau, Alexis; Minde, Klaus; Sassi, Roberto; St-André, Martin, . . . Wazana, Ashley. (2015). Prenatal depression and 5-HTTLPR interact to predict dysregulation from 3 to 36 months—A differential susceptibility model. *Journal of Child Psychology and Psychiatry, 56*(1), 21–29.

Baers, Justin H.; Wiley, Katelyn; Davies, J. M.; Caird, Jeff K.; Hallihan, Greg & Conly, John. (2018). A health system's preparedness for the "next Ebola." *Ergonomics in Design, 26*(1), 24–28.

Bagot, Kara. (2017). Making the grade: Adolescent prescription stimulant use. *Journal of the American Academy of Child & Adolescent Psychiatry, 56*(3), 189–190.

Bagwell, Catherine L. & Schmidt, Michelle E. (2011). *Friendships in childhood & adolescence.* New York, NY: Guilford Press.

Bailey, J. Michael; Vasey, Paul L.; Diamond, Lisa M.; Breedlove, S. Marc; Vilain, Eric & Epprecht, Marc. (2016). Sexual orientation, controversy, and science. *Psychological Science in the Public Interest, 17*(2), 45–101.

Baillargeon, Renée & DeVos, Julie. (1991). Object permanence in young infants: Further evidence. *Child Development, 62*(6), 1227–1246.

Baker, Beth. (2007). *Old age in a new age: The promise of transformative nursing homes.* Nashville, TN: Vanderbilt University Press.

Baker, Jeffrey P. (2000). Immunization and the American way: 4 childhood vaccines. *American Journal of Public Health, 90*(2), 199–207.

Baker, Lindsey A. & Silverstein, Merril. (2012). The well-being of grandparents caring for grandchildren in rural China and the United States. In Sara Arber & Virpi Timonen (Eds.), *Contemporary grandparenting: Changing family relationships in global contexts* (pp. 51–70). Chicago, IL: Policy Press.

Baker, Simon T. E.; Lubman, Dan I.; Yücel, Murat; Allen, Nicholas B.; Whittle, Sarah; Fulcher, Ben D., . . . Fornito, Alex. (2015). Developmental changes in brain network hub connectivity in late adolescence. *Journal of Neuroscience, 35*(24), 9078–9087.

Balk, David & Varga, Mary Alice. (2017). Continuing bonds and social media in the lives of bereaved college students. In Dennis Klass & Edith Maria Steffen (Eds.), *Continuing bonds in bereavement: New directions for research and practice.* New York, NY: Routledge.

Ball, Helen L. & Volpe, Lane E. (2013). Sudden infant death syndrome (SIDS) risk reduction and infant sleep location—Moving the discussion forward. *Social Science & Medicine, 79*(1), 84–91.

Baltes, Paul B. (2003). On the incomplete architecture of human ontogeny: Selection, optimization and compensation as foundation of developmental theory. In Ursula M. Staudinger & Ulman Lindenberger (Eds.), *Understanding human development: Dialogues with lifespan psychology* (pp. 17–43). Boston, MA: Kluwer Academic Publishers.

Baltes, Paul B. & Baltes, Margret M. (1990). Psychological perspectives on successful aging: The model of selective optimization with compensation. In Paul B. Baltes & Margret M. Baltes (Eds.), *Successful aging: Perspectives from the behavioral sciences* (pp. 1–34). New York, NY: Cambridge University Press.

Baltes, Paul B.; Lindenberger, Ulman & Staudinger, Ursula M. (2006). Life span theory in developmental psychology. In William Damon & Richard M. Lerner (Eds.), *Handbook of child psychology* (6th ed., Vol. 1, pp. 569–664). Hoboken, NJ: Wiley.

Baltes, Paul B. & Smith, Jacqui. (2008). The fascination of wisdom: Its nature, ontogeny, and function. *Perspectives on Psychological Science, 3*(1), 56–64.

Baly, Michael W.; Cornell, Dewey G. & Lovegrove, Peter. (2014). A longitudinal investigation of self- and peer reports of bullying victimization across middle school. *Psychology in the Schools, 51*(3), 217–240.

Bancks, Michael P.; Kershaw, Kiarri; Carson, April P.; Gordon-Larsen, Penny; Schreiner, Pamela J. & Carnethon, Mercedes R. (2017). Association of modifiable risk factors in young adulthood with racial disparity in incident type 2 diabetes during middle adulthood. *JAMA, 318*(24), 2457–2465.

Bandura, Albert. (1977). *Social learning theory.* Englewood Cliffs, NJ: Prentice Hall.

Bandura, Albert. (2006). Toward a psychology of human agency. *Perspectives on Psychological Science, 1*(2), 164–180.

Banks, James R. & Andrews, Timothy. (2015). Outcomes of childhood asthma to the age of 50 years. *Pediatrics, 136*(Suppl. 3).

Bannon, Michael J.; Johnson, Magen M.; Michelhaugh, Sharon K.; Hartley, Zachary J.; Halter, Steven D.; David, James A., . . . Schmidt, Carl J. (2014). A molecular profile of cocaine abuse includes the differential expression of genes that regulate transcription, chromatin, and dopamine cell phenotype. *Neuropsychopharmacology, 39*(9), 2191–2199.

Baranowski, Tom & Taveras, Elsie M. (2018). Childhood obesity prevention: Changing the focus. *Childhood Obesity, 14*(1), 1–3.

Barber, Brian K. (Ed.). (2002). *Intrusive parenting: How psychological control affects children and adolescents.* Washington, DC: American Psychological Association.

Barbey, Aron K.; Colom, Roberto; Paul, Erick J. & Grafman, Jordan. (2013). Architecture of fluid intelligence and working memory revealed by lesion mapping. *Brain Structure and Function, 219*(2), 485–494.

Barnett, W. Steven; Carolan, Megan E.; Squires, James H.; Brown, Kirsty Clarke & Horowitz, Michelle. (2015). *The state of preschool 2014: State preschool yearbook.* New Brunswick, NJ: National Institute for Early Education Research.

Barnett, W. Steven; Weisenfeld, G. G.; Brown, Kirsty; Squires, Jim & Horowitz, Michelle. (2016, July 29). *Implementing 15 essential elements for high quality: A state and local policy scan.* New Brunswick, NJ: National Institute for Early Education Research.

Baron-Cohen, Simon; Tager-Flusberg, Helen & Lombardo, Michael (Eds.). (2013). *Understanding other minds: Perspectives from developmental social neuroscience* (3rd ed.). New York, NY: Oxford University Press.

Barr, Rachel. (2013). Memory constraints on infant learning from picture books, television, and touchscreens. *Child Development Perspectives, 7*(4), 205–210.

Bartels, Meike; Cacioppo, John T.; van Beijsterveldt, Toos C. E. M. & Boomsma, Dorret I. (2013). Exploring the association between well-being and psychopathology in adolescents. *Behavior Genetics, 43*(3), 177–190.

Basak, Chandramallika; Boot, Walter R.; Voss, Michelle W. & Kramer, Arthur F. (2008). Can training in a real-time strategy video game attenuate cognitive decline in older adults? *Psychology and Aging, 23*(4), 765–777.

Bassok, Daphna; Latham, Scott & Rorem, Anna. (2016). Is kindergarten the new first grade? *AERA Open, 2*(1).

Bateson, Mary Catherine. (2011). *Composing a further life: The age of active wisdom.* New York, NY: Vintage Books.

Bateson, Patrick & Martin, Paul. (2013). *Play, playfulness, creativity and innovation.* New York, NY: Cambridge University Press.

Bathory, Eleanor & Tomopoulos, Suzy. (2017). Sleep regulation, physiology and development, sleep duration and patterns, and sleep hygiene in infants, toddlers, and preschool-age children. *Current Problems in Pediatric and Adolescent Health Care, 47*(2), 29–42.

Bauer, Patricia J.; San Souci, Priscilla & Pathman, Thanujeni. (2010). Infant memory. *Wiley Interdisciplinary Reviews: Cognitive Science, 1*(2), 267–277.

Baumrind, Diana. (1967). Child care practices anteceding three patterns of preschool behavior. *Genetic Psychology Monographs, 75*(1), 43–88.

Baumrind, Diana. (1971). Current patterns of parental authority. *Developmental Psychology, 4*(1, Pt. 2), 1–103.

Bax, Trent. (2014). *Youth and Internet addiction in China.* New York, NY: Routledge.

Bayley, Nancy. (1966). Learning in adulthood: The role of intelligence. In Herbert J. Klausmeier & Chester W. Harris (Eds.), *Analyses of concept learning* (pp. 117–138). New York, NY: Academic Press.

Bayley, Nancy & Oden, Melita H. (1955). The maintenance of intellectual ability in gifted adults. *The Journal of Gerontology Series B: Psychological Sciences and Social Sciences, 10*(1), 91–107.

Beal, Susan. (1988). Sleeping position and sudden infant death syndrome. *The Medical Journal of Australia, 149*(10), 562.

Beauchaine, Theodore P.; Klein, Daniel N.; Crowell, Sheila E.; Derbidge, Christina & Gatzke-Kopp, Lisa. (2009). Multifinality in the development of personality disorders: A Biology × Sex × Environment interaction model of antisocial and borderline traits. *Development and Psychopathology, 21*(3), 735–770.

Beck, Melinda. (2009, May 26). How's your baby? Recalling the Apgar score's namesake. *Wall Street Journal,* p. D1.

Becker, Derek R.; McClelland, Megan M.; Loprinzi, Paul & Trost, Stewart G. (2014). Physical activity, self-regulation, and early academic achievement in preschool children. *Early Education and Development, 25*(1), 56–70.

Becker, Ernest. (1997). *The denial of death.* New York, NY: Free Press.

Bedford, Elliott Louis; Blaire, Stephen; Carney, John G.; Hamel, Ron; Mindling, J. Daniel & Sullivan, M. C. (2017). Advance care planning, palliative care, and end-of-life care. *The National Catholic Bioethics Quarterly, 17*(3), 489–501.

Beebe, Beatrice; Messinger, Daniel; Bahrick, Lorraine E.; Margolis, Amy; Buck, Karen A. & Chen, Henian. (2016). A systems view of mother–infant face-to-face communication. *Developmental Psychology, 52*(4), 556–571.

Beilin, Lawrence & Huang, Rae-Chi. (2008). Childhood obesity, hypertension, the metabolic syndrome and adult cardiovascular disease. *Clinical and Experimental Pharmacology and Physiology, 35*(4), 409–411.

Bell, Martha Ann & Calkins, Susan D. (2011). Attentional control and emotion regulation in early development. In Michael I. Posner (Ed.), *Cognitive neuroscience of attention* (2nd ed., pp. 322–330). New York, NY: Guilford Press.

Bellinger, David C. (2016). Lead contamination in Flint—An abject failure to protect public health. *New England Journal of Medicine, 374*(12), 1101–1103.

Belsky, Daniel W.; Caspi, Avshalom; Houts, Renate; Cohen, Harvey J.; Corcoran, David L.; Danese, Andrea, ... Moffitt, Terrie E. (2015). Quantification of biological aging in young adults. *Proceedings of the National Academy of Sciences of the United States of America, 112*(30), E4104–E4110.

Bem, Sandra L. (1981). Gender schema theory: A cognitive account of sex typing. *Psychological Review, 88*(4), 354–364.

Benatar, David. (2011). A legal right to die: Responding to slippery slope and abuse arguments. *Current Oncology, 18*(5), 206–207.

Bender, Heather L.; Allen, Joseph P.; McElhaney, Kathleen Boykin; Antonishak, Jill; Moore, Cynthia M.; Kelly, Heather O'Beirne & Davis, Steven M. (2007). Use of harsh physical discipline and developmental outcomes in adolescence. *Development and Psychopathology, 19*(1), 227–242.

Benn, Peter. (2016). Prenatal diagnosis of chromosomal abnormalities through chorionic villus sampling and amniocentesis. In Aubrey Milunsky & Jeff M. Milunsky (Eds.), *Genetic disorders and the fetus: Diagnosis, prevention, and treatment* (7th ed., pp. 178–266). Hoboken, NJ: Wiley-Blackwell.

Bennett, Craig M. & Baird, Abigail A. (2006). Anatomical changes in the emerging adult brain: A voxel-based morphometry study. *Human Brain Mapping, 27*(9), 766–777.

Bergen, Gwen; Peterson, Cora; Ederer, David; Florence, Curtis; Haileyesus, Tadesse; Kresnow, Marcie-Jo & Xu, Likang. (2014). *Vital signs: Health burden and medical costs of non-fatal injuries to motor vehicle occupants — United States, 2012. Morbidity and Mortality Weekly Report, 63*(40), 894–900. Atlanta, GA: Centers for Disease Control and Prevention.

Berger, Kathleen S. (1980). *The developing person* (1st ed.). New York, NY: Worth.

Berger, Lawrence M.; Font, Sarah A.; Slack, Kristen S. & Waldfogel, Jane. (2017). Income and child maltreatment in unmarried families: Evidence from the earned income tax credit. *Review of Economics of the Household, 15*(4), 1345–1372.

Bergmann, Olaf; Spalding, Kirsty L. & Frisén, Jonas. (2015). Adult neurogenesis in humans. *Cold Spring Harbor Perspectives in Biology, 7,* a018994.

Berkman, Lisa F.; Ertel, Karen A. & Glymour, Maria M. (2011). Aging and social intervention: Life course perspectives. In Robert H. Binstock & Linda K. George (Eds.), *Handbook of aging and the social sciences* (7th ed., pp. 337–351). San Diego, CA: Academic Press.

Berko, Jean. (1958). The child's learning of English morphology. *Word, 14,* 150–177.

Bernard, Jessica A.; Peltier, Scott J.; Wiggins, Jillian Lee; Jaeggi, Susanne M.; Buschkuehl, Martin; Fling, Brett W., ... Seidler, Rachael D. (2013). Disrupted cortico-cerebellar connectivity in older adults. *NeuroImage, 83,* 103–119.

Bernard, Jessie S. (1982). *The future of marriage* (Revised ed.). New Haven, CT: Yale University Press.

Bernard, Kristin; Lind, Teresa & Dozier, Mary. (2014). Neurobiological consequences of neglect and abuse. In Jill E. Korbin & Richard D. Krugman (Eds.), *Handbook of child maltreatment* (pp. 205–223). New York, NY: Springer.

Best, Joel & Best, Eric. (2014). *The student loan mess: How good intentions created a trillion-dollar problem.* Berkeley, CA: University of California Press.

Betancourt, Theresa S.; McBain, Ryan; Newnham, Elizabeth A. & Brennan, Robert T. (2013). Trajectories of internalizing problems in war-affected Sierra Leonean youth: Examining conflict and postconflict factors. *Child Development, 84*(2), 455–470.

Betrán, Ana Pilar; Ye, Jianfeng; Moller, Anne-Beth; Zhang, Jun; Gülmezoglu, A. Metin & Torloni, Maria Regina. (2016). The increasing trend in caesarean section rates: Global, regional and national estimates: 1990–2014. *PLoS ONE*, *11*(2), e0148343.

Bhatia, Tej K. & Ritchie, William C. (Eds.). (2013). *The handbook of bilingualism and multilingualism* (2nd ed.). Malden, MA: Wiley-Blackwell.

Bhatnagar, Aruni; Whitsel, Laurie P.; Ribisl, Kurt M.; Bullen, Chris; Chaloupka, Frank; Piano, Mariann R., . . . Benowitz, Neal. (2014). Electronic cigarettes: A policy statement from the American Heart Association. *Circulation*, *130*(16), 1418–1436.

Bialik, Kristen. (2017, June 12). *Key facts about race and marriage, 50 years after Loving v. Virginia. Fact Tank*. Washington, DC: Pew Research Center.

Bialystok, Ellen. (2017). The bilingual adaptation: How minds accommodate experience. *Psychological Bulletin*, *143*(3), 233–262.

Bialystok, Ellen. (2018). Bilingualism and executive function: What's the connection? In David Miller, et al. (Eds.), *Bilingual cognition and language: The state of the science across its subfields* (pp. 283–306). Amsterdam, the Netherlands: John Benjamins.

Biblarz, Timothy J. & Stacey, Judith. (2010). How does the gender of parents matter? *Journal of Marriage and Family*, *72*(1), 3–22.

Bielak, Allison A. M.; Anstey, Kaarin J.; Christensen, Helen & Windsor, Tim D. (2012). Activity engagement is related to level, but not change in cognitive ability across adulthood. *Psychology and Aging*, *27*(1), 219–228.

Biemiller, Andrew. (2009). Parent/caregiver narrative: Vocabulary development (0 – 60 Months). In Linda M. Phillips (Ed.), *Handbook of language and literacy development: A roadmap from 0–60* (Online ed.). London, ON: Canadian Language and Literacy Research Network.

Bier, Bianca; Ouellet, Émilie & Belleville, Sylvie. (2018). Computerized attentional training and transfer with virtual reality: Effect of age and training type. *Neuropsychology*, *32*(5), 597–614.

Billings, J. Andrew. (2011). Double effect: A useful rule that alone cannot justify hastening death. *Journal of Medical Ethics*, *37*(7), 437–440.

Birditt, Kira S.; Miller, Laura M.; Fingerman, Karen L. & Lefkowitz, Eva S. (2009). Tensions in the parent and adult child relationship: Links to solidarity and ambivalence. *Psychology and Aging*, *24*(2), 287–295.

Birdsong, David. (2006). Age and second language acquisition and processing: A selective overview. *Language Learning*, *56*(Suppl. 1), 9–49.

Birkeland, Marianne S.; Breivik, Kyrre & Wold, Bente. (2014). Peer acceptance protects global self-esteem from negative effects of low closeness to parents during adolescence and early adulthood. *Journal of Youth and Adolescence*, *43*(1), 70–80.

Biro, Frank M.; Greenspan, Louise C.; Galvez, Maida P.; Pinney, Susan M.; Teitelbaum, Susan; Windham, Gayle C., . . . Wolff, Mary S. (2013). Onset of breast development in a longitudinal cohort. *Pediatrics*, *132*(6), 1019–1027.

Biro, Frank M.; McMahon, Robert P.; Striegel-Moore, Ruth; Crawford, Patricia B.; Obarzanek, Eva; Morrison, John A., . . . Falkner, Frank. (2001). Impact of timing of pubertal maturation on growth in Black and White female adolescents: The National Heart, Lung, and Blood Institute Growth and Health Study. *Journal of Pediatrics*, *138*(5), 636–643.

Bjorklund, David F. & Ellis, Bruce J. (2014). Children, childhood, and development in evolutionary perspective. *Developmental Review*, *34*(3), 225–264.

Bjorklund, David F. & Sellers, Patrick D. (2014). Memory development in evolutionary perspective. In Patricia Bauer & Robyn Fivush (Eds.), *The Wiley handbook on the development of children's memory* (Vol. 1, pp. 126–150). Malden, MA: Wiley.

Black, Maureen M.; Papas, Mia A.; Hussey, Jon M.; Hunter, Wanda; Dubowitz, Howard; Kotch, Jonathan B., . . . Schneider, Mary. (2002). Behavior and development of preschool children born to adolescent mothers: Risk and 3-generation households. *Pediatrics*, *109*(4), 573–580.

Blad, Evie. (2014). Some states overhauling vaccine laws. *Education Week*, *33*(31), 1, 23.

Blair, Clancy & Raver, C. Cybele. (2015). School readiness and self-regulation: A developmental psychobiological approach. *Annual Review of Psychology*, *66*, 711–731.

Blalock, Garrick; Kadiyali, Vrinda & Simon, Daniel H. (2009). Driving fatalities after 9/11: A hidden cost of terrorism. *Applied Economics*, *41*(14), 1717–1729.

Blanchflower, David G. & Oswald, Andrew. (2017). *Do humans suffer a psychological low in midlife? Two approaches (with and without controls) in seven data sets. NBER Working Paper*. Cambridge, MA: National Bureau of Economic Research. Working Paper No. 23724.

Blandon, Alysia Y.; Calkins, Susan D. & Keane, Susan P. (2010). Predicting emotional and social competence during early childhood from toddler risk and maternal behavior. *Development and Psychopathology*, *22*(1), 119–132.

Blank, Grant & Lutz, Christoph. (2018). Benefits and harms from Internet use: A differentiated analysis of Great Britain. *New Media & Society*, *20*(2), 618–640.

Blas, Erik & Kurup, Anand Sivasankara (Eds.). (2010). *Equity, social determinants, and public health programmes*. Geneva, Switzerland: World Health Organization.

Blazer, Dan G. (2018). Hearing loss: The silent risk for psychiatric disorders in late life. *Psychiatric Clinics of North America*, *41*(1), 19–27.

Bleidorn, Wiebke; Klimstra, Theo A.; Denissen, Jaap J. A.; Rentfrow, Peter J.; Potter, Jeff & Gosling, Samuel D. (2013). Personality maturation around the world: A cross-cultural examination of social-investment theory. *Psychological Science*, *24*(12), 2530–2540.

Bleidorn, Wiebke & Schwaba, Ted. (2018). Retirement is associated with change in self-esteem. *Psychology and Aging*, *33*(4), 586–594.

Bleske-Rechek, April; Somers, Erin; Micke, Cierra; Erickson, Leah; Matteson, Lindsay; Stocco, Corey, . . . Ritchie, Laura. (2012). Benefit or burden? Attraction in cross-sex friendship. *Journal of Social and Personal Relationships*, *29*(5), 569–596.

Bleys, Dries; Soenens, Bart; Boone, Liesbet; Claes, Stephan; Vliegen, Nicole & Luyten, Patrick. (2016). The role of intergenerational similarity and parenting in adolescent self-criticism: An actor–partner interdependence model. *Journal of Adolescence, 49*, 68–76.

Blieszner, Rosemary. (2014). The worth of friendship: Can friends keep us happy and healthy? *Generations, 38*(1), 24–30.

Bliss, Catherine. (2012). *Race decoded: The genomic fight for social justice.* Stanford, CA: Stanford University Press.

Blomqvist, Ylva Thernström; Nyqvist, Kerstin Hedberg; Rubertsson, Christine & Funkquist, Eva-Lotta. (2017). Parents need support to find ways to optimise their own sleep without seeing their preterm infant's sleeping patterns as a problem. *Acta Paediatrica, 106*(2), 223–228.

Bloom, David E. (2011). 7 billion and counting. *Science, 333*(6042), 562–569.

Blurton-Jones, Nicholas G. (1976). Rough-and-tumble play among nursery school children. In Jerome S. Bruner, et al. (Eds.), *Play: Its role in development and evolution* (pp. 352–363). New York, NY: Basic Books.

Boals, Adriel; Hayslip, Bert; Knowles, Laura R. & Banks, Jonathan B. (2012). Perceiving a negative event as central to one's identity partially mediates age differences in posttraumatic stress disorder symptoms. *Journal of Aging and Health, 24*(3), 459–474.

Bodner-Adler, Barbara; Kimberger, Oliver; Griebaum, Julia; Husslein, Peter & Bodner, Klaus. (2017). A ten-year study of midwife-led care at an Austrian tertiary care center: A retrospective analysis with special consideration of perineal trauma. *BMC Pregnancy and Childbirth, 17*, 357–371.

Bøe, Tormod; Serlachius, Anna; Sivertsen, Børge; Petrie, Keith & Hysing, Mari. (2018). Cumulative effects of negative life events and family stress on children's mental health: The Bergen Child Study. *Social Psychiatry and Psychiatric Epidemiology, 53*(1), 1–9.

Boerner, Kathrin; Schulz, Richard & Horowitz, Amy. (2004). Positive aspects of caregiving and adaptation to bereavement. *Psychology and Aging, 19*(4), 668–675.

Boerner, Kathrin; Wortman, Camille B. & Bonanno, George A. (2005). Resilient or at risk? A 4-year study of older adults who initially showed high or low distress following conjugal loss. *The Journals of Gerontology Series B: Psychological Sciences and Social Sciences, 60*(2), 67–73.

Bögels, Susan M.; Knappe, Susanne & Clark, Lee Anna. (2013). Adult separation anxiety disorder in *DSM-5. Clinical Psychology Review, 33*(5), 663–674.

Bogle, Kathleen A. (2008). *Hooking up: Sex, dating, and relationships on campus.* New York, NY: New York University Press.

Bohlen, Tabata M.; Silveira, Marina A.; Zampieri, Thais T.; Frazão, Renata & Donato, Jose. (2016). Fatness rather than leptin sensitivity determines the timing of puberty in female mice. *Molecular and Cellular Endocrinology, 423*, 11–21.

Boldrini, Maura; Fulmore, Camille A.; Tartt, Alexandra N.; Simeon, Laika R.; Pavlova, Ina; Poposka, Verica, . . . Mann, John. (2018). Human hippocampal neurogenesis persists throughout aging. *Cell Stem Cell, 22*(4), 589–599.e585.

Bone, Anna E.; Gomes, Barbara; Etkind, Simon N.; Verne, Julia; Murtagh, Fliss Em; Evans, Catherine J. & Higginson, Irene J. (2018). What is the impact of population ageing on the future provision of end-of-life care? Population-based projections of place of death. *Palliative Medicine, 32*(2), 329–336.

Bonilla-Silva, Eduardo. (2018). *Racism without racists: Color-blind racism and the persistence of racial inequality in America* (5th ed.). Lanham, MD: Rowman and Littlefield.

Bonsang, Eric; Skirbekk, Vegard & Staudinger, Ursula M. (2017). As you sow, so shall you reap: Gender-role attitudes and late-life cognition. *Psychological Science, 28*(9), 1201–1213.

Booth, Alan & Dunn, Judy (Eds.). (2014). *Stepfamilies: Who benefits? Who does not?* New York, NY: Routledge.

Bordini, Gabriela Sagebin & Sperb, Tania Mara. (2013). Sexual double standard: A review of the literature between 2001 and 2010. *Sexuality & Culture, 17*(4), 686–704.

Borke, Jörn; Lamm, Bettina; Eickhorst, Andreas & Keller, Heidi. (2007). Father-infant interaction, paternal ideas about early child care, and their consequences for the development of children's self-recognition. *Journal of Genetic Psychology, 168*(4), 365–379.

Bornstein, Marc H. (2015). Children's parents. In Richard M. Lerner (Ed.), *Handbook of child psychology and developmental science* (7th ed., Vol. 4, pp. 55–132). New York, NY: Wiley.

Bornstein, Marc H. & Colombo, John. (2012). Infant cognitive functioning and mental development. In Sabina Pauen (Ed.), *Early childhood development and later outcome.* New York, NY: Cambridge University Press.

Bornstein, Marc H.; Mortimer, Jeylan T.; Lutfey, Karen & Bradley, Robert. (2011). Theories and processes in life-span socialization. In Karen L. Fingerman, et al. (Eds.), *Handbook of life-span development* (pp. 27–56). New York, NY: Springer.

Bornstein, Marc H.; Putnick, Diane L.; Bradley, Robert H.; Deater-Deckard, Kirby & Lansford, Jennifer E. (2016). Gender in low- and middle-income countries: Introduction. *Monographs of the Society for Research in Child Development, 81*(1), 7–23.

Bosmans, Guy & Kerns, Kathryn A. (2015). Attachment in middle childhood: Progress and prospects. *New Directions for Child and Adolescent Development, 148*, 1–14.

Boss, Lisa; Kang, Duck-Hee & Branson, Sandy. (2015). Loneliness and cognitive function in the older adult: A systematic review. *International Psychogeriatrics, 27*(4), 541–553.

Bosworth, Hayden B. & Ayotte, Brian J. (2009). The role of cognitive and social function in an applied setting: Medication adherence as an example. In Hayden B. Bosworth & Christopher Hertzog (Eds.), *Aging and cognition: Research methodologies and empirical advances* (pp. 219–239). Washington, DC: American Psychological Association.

Bowlby, John. (1983). *Attachment* (2nd ed.). New York, NY: Basic Books.

boyd, danah. (2014). *It's complicated: The social lives of networked teens.* New Haven, CT: Yale University Press.

Boyd, Wendy; Walker, Susan & Thorpe, Karen. (2013). Choosing work and care: Four Australian women negotiating return to paid work in the first year of motherhood. *Contemporary Issues in Early Childhood, 14*(2), 168–178.

Boyle, Patricia A.; Wilson, Robert S.; Yu, Lei; Barr, Alasdair M.; Honer, William G.; Schneider, Julie A. & Bennett,

David A. (2013). Much of late life cognitive decline is not due to common neurodegenerative pathologies. *Annals of Neurology*, *74*(3), 478–489.

Boyraz, Guler; Horne, Sharon G. & Sayger, Thomas V. (2012). Finding meaning in loss: The mediating role of social support between personality and two construals of meaning. *Death Studies*, *36*(6), 519–540.

Boywitt, C. Dennis; Kuhlmann, Beatrice G. & Meiser, Thorsten. (2012). The role of source memory in older adults' recollective experience. *Psychology and Aging*, *27*(2), 484–497.

Braams, Barbara R.; van Duijvenvoorde, Anna C. K.; Peper, Jiska S. & Crone, Eveline A. (2015). Longitudinal changes in adolescent risk-taking: A comprehensive study of neural responses to rewards, pubertal development, and risk-taking behavior. *The Journal of Neuroscience*, *35*(18), 7226–7238.

Bracken, Bruce A. & Crawford, Elizabeth. (2010). Basic concepts in early childhood educational standards: A 50-state review. *Early Childhood Education Journal*, *37*(5), 421–430.

Bradley, Rachel & Slade, Pauline. (2011). A review of mental health problems in fathers following the birth of a child. *Journal of Reproductive and Infant Psychology*, *29*(1), 19–42.

Bradshaw, Matt & Kent, Blake Victor. (2018). Prayer, attachment to God, and changes in psychological well-being in later life. *Journal of Aging and Health*, *30*(5), 667–691.

Brame, Robert; Bushway, Shawn D.; Paternoster, Ray & Turner, Michael G. (2014). Demographic patterns of cumulative arrest prevalence by ages 18 and 23. *Crime & Delinquency*, *60*(3), 471–486.

Brandt, Hella E.; Ooms, Marcel E.; Ribbe, Miel W.; van der Wal, Gerrit & Deliens, Luc. (2006). Predicted survival vs. actual survival in terminally ill noncancer patients in Dutch nursing homes. *Journal of Pain and Symptom Management*, *32*(6), 560–566.

Brandt, Martina; Deindl, Christian & Hank, Karsten. (2012). Tracing the origins of successful aging: The role of childhood conditions and social inequality in explaining later life health. *Social Science & Medicine*, *74*(9), 1418–1425.

Bransberger, Peace & Michelau, Demarée K. (2016). *Knocking at the college door*. Boulder, CO: Western Interstate Commission for Higher Education.

Bratt, Christopher; Abrams, Dominic; Swift, Hannah J.; Vauclair, Christin-Melanie & Marques, Sibila. (2018). Perceived age discrimination across age in Europe: From an ageing society to a society for all ages. *Developmental Psychology*, *54*(1), 167–180.

Braun, Katharina. (2011). The prefrontal-limbic system: Development, neuroanatomy, function, and implications for socioemotional development. *Clinics in Perinatology*, *38*(4), 685–702.

Bray, George A.; Kim, K. K. & Wilding, John P. H. (2017). Obesity: A chronic relapsing progressive disease process. A position statement of the World Obesity Federation. *Obesity Reviews*, *18*(7), 715–723.

Bremner, J. Gavin; Slater, Alan M. & Johnson, Scott P. (2015). Perception of object persistence: The origins of object permanence in infancy. *Child Development Perspectives*, *9*(1), 7–13.

Bremner, J. Gavin & Wachs, Theodore D. (Eds.). (2010). *The Wiley-Blackwell handbook of infant development* (2nd ed.). Malden, MA: Wiley-Blackwell.

Brennan, Arthur; Ayers, Susan; Ahmed, Hafez & Marshall-Lucette, Sylvie. (2007). A critical review of the Couvade syndrome: The pregnant male. *Journal of Reproductive and Infant Psychology*, *25*(3), 173–189.

Bridgers, Sophie; Buchsbaum, Daphna; Seiver, Elizabeth; Griffiths, Thomas L. & Gopnik, Alison. (2016). Children's causal inferences from conflicting testimony and observations. *Developmental Psychology*, *52*(1), 9–18.

Bridgett, David J.; Burt, Nicole M.; Edwards, Erin S. & Deater-Deckard, Kirby. (2015). Intergenerational transmission of self-regulation: A multidisciplinary review and integrative conceptual framework. *Psychological Bulletin*, *141*(3), 602–654.

Briley, Daniel A. & Tucker-Drob, Elliot M. (2017). Comparing the developmental genetics of cognition and personality over the life span. *Journal of Personality*, *85*(1), 51–64.

Broberg, Thomas & Willstrand, Tania Dukic. (2014). Safe mobility for elderly drivers—Considerations based on expert and self-assessment. *Accident Analysis & Prevention*, *66*, 104–113.

Brody, Gene H. (2017). Using genetically informed prevention trials to test gene × environment hypotheses. In Patrick H. Tolan & Bennett L. Leventhal (Eds.), *Gene-environment transactions in developmental psychopathology: The role in intervention research* (pp. 211–233). Cham, Switzerland: Springer.

Brody, Gene H.; Beach, Steven R. H.; Philibert, Robert A.; Chen, Yi-fu & Murry, Velma McBride. (2009). Prevention effects moderate the association of 5-HTTLPR and youth risk behavior initiation: Gene × environment hypotheses tested via a randomized prevention design. *Child Development*, *80*(3), 645–661.

Brody, Gene H.; Yu, Tianyi; Chen, Yi-fu; Kogan, Steven M.; Evans, Gary W.; Windle, Michael, . . . Philibert, Robert A. (2013). Supportive family environments, genes that confer sensitivity, and allostatic load among rural African American emerging adults: A prospective analysis. *Journal of Family Psychology*, *27*(1), 22–29.

Brody, Jane E. (2013, February 26). Too many pills in pregnancy. *New York Times*.

Brom, Sarah S. & Kliegel, Matthias. (2014). Improving everyday prospective memory performance in older adults: Comparing cognitive process and strategy training. *Psychology and Aging*, *29*(3), 744–755.

Bronfenbrenner, Urie & Morris, Pamela A. (2006). The bioecological model of human development. In William Damon & Richard M. Lerner (Eds.), *Handbook of child psychology* (6th ed., Vol. 1, pp. 793–828). Hoboken, NJ: Wiley.

Brooks, Jada E. & Allen, Katherine R. (2016). The influence of fictive kin relationships and religiosity on the academic persistence of African American college students attending an HBCU. *Journal of Family Issues*, *37*(6), 814–832.

Brooten, Dorothy; Youngblut, Joanne M.; Caicedo, Carmen; Del Moral, Teresa; Cantwell, G. Patricia & Totapally, Balagangadhar. (2018). Parents' acute illnesses, hospitalizations, and medication changes during the difficult first year after infant or child NICU/PICU death. *American Journal of Hospice and Palliative Medicine*, *35*(1), 75–82.

Broström, Stig. (2017). A dynamic learning concept in early years' education: A possible way to prevent schoolification. *International Journal of Early Years Education, 25*(1), 3–15.

Brotto, Lori A. & Yule, Morag A. (2011). Physiological and subjective sexual arousal in self-identified asexual women. *Archives of Sexual Behavior, 40*(4), 699–712.

Brouwer, Rachel M.; van Soelen, Inge L. C.; Swagerman, Suzanne C.; Schnack, Hugo G.; Ehli, Erik A.; Kahn, René S., . . . Boomsma, Dorret I. (2014). Genetic associations between intelligence and cortical thickness emerge at the start of puberty. *Human Brain Mapping, 35*(8), 3760–3773.

Brown, B. Bradford & Bakken, Jeremy P. (2011). Parenting and peer relationships: Reinvigorating research on family–peer linkages in adolescence. *Journal of Research on Adolescence, 21*(1), 153–165.

Brown, Christia Spears; Alabi, Basirat O.; Huynh, Virginia W. & Masten, Carrie L. (2011). Ethnicity and gender in late childhood and early adolescence: Group identity and awareness of bias. *Developmental Psychology, 47*(2), 463–471.

Brown, Edna; Birditt, Kira S.; Huff, Scott C. & Edwards, Lindsay L. (2012). Marital dissolution and psychological well-being: Race and gender differences in the moderating role of marital relationship quality. *Research in Human Development, 9*(2), 145–164.

Brown, Peter C.; Roediger, Henry L. & McDaniel, Mark A. (2014). *Make it stick: The science of successful learning.* Cambridge, MA: Belknap Press of Harvard University Press.

Brownell, Celia A.; Svetlova, Margarita; Anderson, Ranita; Nichols, Sara R. & Drummond, Jesse. (2013). Socialization of early prosocial behavior: Parents' talk about emotions is associated with sharing and helping in toddlers. *Infancy, 18*(1), 91–119.

Brubaker, Matthew S. & Naveh-Benjamin, Moshe. (2018). The effects of stereotype threat on the associative memory deficit of older adults. *Psychology and Aging, 33*(1), 17–29.

Bruck, Maggie; Ceci, Stephen J. & Principe, Gabrielle F. (2006). The child and the law. In William Damon & Richard M. Lerner (Eds.), *Handbook of child psychology* (6th ed., Vol. 4, pp. 776–816). Hoboken, NJ: Wiley.

Brummelman, Eddie; Nelemans, Stefanie A.; Thomaes, Sander & Orobio De Castro, Bram. (2017). When parents' praise inflates, children's self-esteem deflates. *Child Development, 88*(6), 1799–1809.

Brunham, Robert C.; Gottlieb, Sami L. & Paavonen, Jorma. (2015). Pelvic inflammatory disease. *New England Journal of Medicine, 372,* 2039–2048.

Bucx, Freek; van Wel, Frits & Knijn, Trudie. (2012). Life course status and exchanges of support between young adults and parents. *Journal of Marriage and Family, 74*(1), 101–115.

Bueno, Clarissa & Menna-Barreto, Luiz. (2016). Environmental factors influencing biological rhythms in newborns: From neonatal intensive care units to home. *Sleep Science, 9*(4), 295–300.

Buiting, Hilde; van Delden, Johannes; Onwuteaka-Philpsen, Bregje; Rietjens, Judith; Rurup, Mette; van Tol, Donald, . . . van der Heide, Agnes. (2009). Reporting of euthanasia and physician-assisted suicide in the Netherlands: Descriptive study. *BMC Medical Ethics, 10*(18).

Bulmer, Maria; Böhnke, Jan R. & Lewis, Gary J. (2017). Predicting moral sentiment towards physician-assisted suicide: The role of religion, conservatism, authoritarianism, and Big Five personality. *Personality and Individual Differences, 105,* 244–251.

Burén, Jonas & Lunde, Carolina. (2018). Sexting among adolescents: A nuanced and gendered online challenge for young people. *Computers in Human Behavior, 85,* 210–217.

Burke, Brian L.; Martens, Andy & Faucher, Erik H. (2010). Two decades of terror management theory: A meta-analysis of mortality salience research. *Personality and Social Psychology Review, 14*(2), 155–195.

Burkhouse, Katie; Jacobs, Rachel; Peters, Amy; Ajilore, Olu; Watkins, Edward & Langenecker, Scott. (2017). Neural correlates of rumination in adolescents with remitted major depressive disorder and healthy controls. *Cognitive, Affective, & Behavioral Neuroscience, 17*(2), 394–405.

Burnette, Jeni L.; O'Boyle, Ernest H.; VanEpps, Eric M.; Pollack, Jeffrey M. & Finkel, Eli J. (2013). Mind-sets matter: A meta-analytic review of implicit theories and self-regulation. *Psychological Bulletin, 139*(3), 655–701.

Burstein, David D. (2013). *Fast future: How the millennial generation is shaping our world.* Boston, MA: Beacon Press.

Burstyn, Igor. (2014). Peering through the mist: Systematic review of what the chemistry of contaminants in electronic cigarettes tells us about health risks. *BMC Public Health, 14*(1), 18.

Bursztyn, Leonardo & Jensen, Robert. (2015). How does peer pressure affect educational investments? *Quarterly Journal of Economics, 130*(3), 1329–1367.

Burt, S. Alexandra. (2009). Rethinking environmental contributions to child and adolescent psychopathology: A meta-analysis of shared environmental influences. *Psychological Bulletin, 135*(4), 608–637.

Butler, Ashley M. & Titus, Courtney. (2015). Systematic review of engagement in culturally adapted parent training for disruptive behavior. *Journal of Early Intervention, 37*(4), 300–318.

Butler, Robert N.; Lewis, Myrna I. & Sunderland, Trey. (1998). *Aging and mental health: Positive psychosocial and biomedical approaches* (5th ed.). Boston, MA: Allyn & Bacon.

Butterworth, Brian & Kovas, Yulia. (2013). Understanding neurocognitive developmental disorders can improve education for all. *Science, 340*(6130), 300–305.

Butterworth, Brian; Varma, Sashank & Laurillard, Diana. (2011). Dyscalculia: From brain to education. *Science, 332*(6033), 1049–1053.

Butts, Donna. (2017). Foreword. In Matthew Kaplan, et al. (Eds.), *Intergenerational pathways to a sustainable society* (pp. v–vii). New York: NY: Springer.

Byard, Roger W. (2014). "Shaken baby syndrome" and forensic pathology: An uneasy interface. *Forensic Science, Medicine, and Pathology, 10*(2), 239–241.

Byers-Heinlein, Krista; Burns, Tracey C. & Werker, Janet F. (2010). The roots of bilingualism in newborns. *Psychological Science, 21*(3), 343–348.

Cabrera, Natasha J.; Hofferth, Sandra L. & Chae, Soo. (2011). Patterns and predictors of father–infant engagement across race/ethnic groups. *Early Childhood Research Quarterly, 26*(3), 365–375.

Cacioppo, John T.; Cacioppo, Stephanie; Gonzaga, Gian C.; Ogburn, Elizabeth L. & VanderWeele, Tyler J. (2013). Marital satisfaction and break-ups differ across on-line and off-line meeting venues. *PNAS, 110*(25), 10135–10140.

Cacioppo, Stephanie; Capitanio, John P. & Cacioppo, John T. (2014). Toward a neurology of loneliness. *Psychological Bulletin, 140*(6), 1464–1504.

Cain, Susan. (2012). *Quiet: The power of introverts in a world that can't stop talking.* New York, NY: Crown Publishers.

Calarco, Jessica McCrory. (2014). The inconsistent curriculum: Cultural tool kits and student interpretations of ambiguous expectations. *Social Psychology Quarterly, 77*(2), 185–209.

Calkins, Susan D. & Keane, Susan P. (2009). Developmental origins of early antisocial behavior. *Development and Psychopathology, 21*(4), 1095–1109.

Calvo, Esteban; Madero-Cabib, Ignacio & Staudinger, Ursula M. (2017). Retirement sequences of older Americans: Moderately destandardized and highly stratified across gender, class, and race. *The Gerontologist,* (In Press).

Calvo, Rocío; Carr, Dawn C. & Matz-Costa, Christina. (2017). Expanding the happiness paradox: Ethnoracial disparities in life satisfaction among older immigrants in the United States. *Journal of Aging and Health,* (In Press).

Camchong, Jazmin; Lim, Kelvin O. & Kumra, Sanjiv. (2017). Adverse effects of cannabis on adolescent brain development: A longitudinal study. *Cerebral Cortex, 27*(3), 1922–1930.

Camhi, Sarah M.; Katzmarzyk, Peter T.; Broyles, Stephanie; Church, Timothy S.; Hankinson, Arlene L.; Carnethon, Mercedes R., . . . Lewis, Cora E. (2013). Association of metabolic risk with longitudinal physical activity and fitness: Coronary artery risk development in young adults (CARDIA). *Metabolic Syndrome and Related Disorders, 11*(3), 195–204.

Campbell, Frances; Conti, Gabriella; Heckman, James J.; Moon, Seong H.; Pinto, Rodrigo; Pungello, Elizabeth & Pan, Yi. (2014). Early childhood investments substantially boost adult health. *Science, 343*(6178), 1478–1485.

Campbell, Frances A.; Pungello, Elizabeth P.; Miller-Johnson, Shari; Burchinal, Margaret & Ramey, Craig T. (2001). The development of cognitive and academic abilities: Growth curves from an early childhood educational experiment. *Developmental Psychology, 37*(2), 231–242.

Campo, Juan Eduardo. (2015). Muslim ways of death: Between the prescribed and the performed. In Kathleen Garces-Foley (Ed.), *Death and religion in a changing world.* New York, NY: Routledge.

Cardinal, Roger. (2001). The sense of time and place. In Jane Kallir & Roger Cardinal (Eds.), *Grandma Moses in the 21st century* (pp. 79–102). Alexandria, VA: Art Services International.

Cardozo, Eden R.; Thomson, Alexcis P.; Karmon, Anatte E.; Dickinson, Kristy A.; Wright, Diane L. & Sabatini, Mary E. (2015). Ovarian stimulation and in-vitro fertilization outcomes of cancer patients undergoing fertility preservation compared to age matched controls: A 17-year experience. *Journal of Assisted Reproduction and Genetics, 32*(4), 587–596.

Carlo, Gustavo; Knight, George P.; Roesch, Scott C.; Opal, Deanna & Davis, Alexandra. (2014). Personality across cultures: A critical analysis of Big Five research and current directions. In Frederick T. L. Leong, et al. (Eds.), *APA handbook of multicultural psychology* (Vol. 1, pp. 285–298). Washington, DC: American Psychological Association.

Carlsen, Karin C. Lødrup; Skjerven, Håvard O. & Carlsen, Kai-Håkon. (2018). The toxicity of e-cigarettes and children's respiratory health. *Paediatric Respiratory Reviews,* (In Press).

Carlson, Scott. (2016, May 1). Should everyone go to college?: For poor kids, 'College for all' isn't the mantra it was meant to be. *The Chronicle of Higher Education.*

Carlsson, Johanna; Wängqvist, Maria & Frisén, Ann. (2015). Identity development in the late twenties: A never ending story. *Developmental Psychology, 51*(3), 334–345.

Carr, Deborah; Freedman, Vicki A.; Cornman, Jennifer C. & Schwarz, Norbert. (2014). Happy marriage, happy life? Marital quality and subjective well-being in later life. *Journal of Marriage and Family, 76*(5), 930–948.

Carra, Cecilia; Lavelli, Manuela; Keller, Heidi & Kärtner, Joscha. (2013). Parenting infants: Socialization goals and behaviors of Italian mothers and immigrant mothers from West Africa. *Journal of Cross-Cultural Psychology, 44*(8), 1304–1320.

Carroll, Aaron E.; Dimeglio, Linda A.; Stein, Stephanie & Marrero, David G. (2011). Using a cell phone-based glucose monitoring system for adolescent diabetes management. *Diabetes Educator, 37*(1), 59–66.

Carroll, Kathryn A.; Samek, Anya & Zepeda, Lydia. (2018). Food bundling as a health nudge: Investigating consumer fruit and vegetable selection using behavioral economics. *Appetite, 121,* 237–248.

Carroll, Linda J.; Cassidy, David; Cancelliere, Carol; Côté, Pierre; Hincapié, Cesar A.; Kristman, Vicki L., . . . Hartvigsen, Jan. (2014). Systematic review of the prognosis after mild traumatic brain injury in adults: Cognitive, psychiatric, and mortality outcomes: Results of the international collaboration on mild traumatic brain injury prognosis. *Archives of Physical Medicine and Rehabilitation, 95*(3, Suppl.), S152–S173.

Carson, Valerie; Tremblay, Mark S.; Spence, John C.; Timmons, Brian W. & Janssen, Ian. (2013). The Canadian Sedentary Behaviour Guidelines for the Early Years (zero to four years of age) and screen time among children from Kingston, Ontario. *Paediatrics & Child Health, 18*(1), 25–28.

Carstensen, Laura L. (1993). Motivation for social contact across the life span. In Janis E. Jacobs (Ed.), *Developmental perspectives on motivation: Nebraska Symposium on Motivation (1992)* (pp. 209–254). Lincoln, NE: University of Nebraska.

Carstensen, Laura L. (2011). *A long bright future: Happiness, health, and financial security in an age of increased longevity.* New York, NY: PublicAffairs.

Carstensen, Laura L. & DeLiema, Marguerite. (2018). The positivity effect: A negativity bias in youth fades with age. *Current Opinion in Behavioral Sciences, 19,* 7–12.

Caruso, Federica. (2013). Embedding early childhood education and care in the socio-cultural context: The case of Italy. In Jan Georgeson & Jane Payler (Eds.), *International perspectives on early childhood education and care*. New York, NY: Open University Press.

Caspi, Avshalom; Moffitt, Terrie E.; Morgan, Julia; Rutter, Michael; Taylor, Alan; Arseneault, Louise, . . . Polo-Tomas, Monica. (2004). Maternal expressed emotion predicts children's antisocial behavior problems: Using monozygotic-twin differences to identify environmental effects on behavioral development. *Developmental Psychology, 40*(2), 149–161.

Cassibba, Rosalinda; Coppola, Gabrielle; Sette, Giovanna; Curci, Antonietta & Costantini, Alessandro. (2017). The transmission of attachment across three generations: A study in adulthood. *Developmental Psychology, 53*(2), 396–405.

Cassina, Matteo; Cagnoli, Giulia A.; Zuccarello, Daniela; Gianantonio, Elena Di & Clementi, Maurizio. (2017). Human teratogens and genetic phenocopies. Understanding pathogenesis through human genes mutation. *European Journal of Medical Genetics, 60*(1), 22–31.

Castellacci, Fulvio & Tveito, Vegard. (2018). Internet use and well-being: A survey and a theoretical framework. *Research Policy, 47*(1), 308–325.

Catani, Claudia; Gewirtz, Abigail H.; Wieling, Elizabeth; Schauer, Elizabeth; Elbert, Thomas & Neuner, Frank. (2010). Tsunami, war, and cumulative risk in the lives of Sri Lankan schoolchildren. *Child Development, 81*(4), 1176–1191.

Cavalari, Rachel N. S. & Donovick, Peter J. (2014). Agenesis of the corpus callosum: Symptoms consistent with developmental disability in two siblings. *Neurocase: The Neural Basis of Cognition, 21*(1), 95–102.

Ceballo, Rosario; Maurizi, Laura K.; Suarez, Gloria A. & Aretakis, Maria T. (2014). Gift and sacrifice: Parental involvement in Latino adolescents' education. *Cultural Diversity and Ethnic Minority Psychology, 20*(1), 116–127.

Ceci, Stephen J. & Bruck, Maggie. (1995). *Jeopardy in the courtroom: A scientific analysis of children's testimony*. Washington, DC: American Psychological Association.

Cecil, Kim M.; Brubaker, Christopher J.; Adler, Caleb M.; Dietrich, Kim N.; Altaye, Mekibib; Egelhoff, John C., . . . Lanphear, Bruce P. (2008). Decreased brain volume in adults with childhood lead exposure. *PLoS Medicine, 5*(5), 741–750.

Cenegy, Laura Freeman; Denney, Justin T. & Kimbro, Rachel Tolbert. (2018). Family diversity and child health: Where do same-sex couple families fit. *Journal of Marriage and Family, 80*(1), 198–218.

Center for Education Policy. (2012). *SDP strategic performance indicator: The high school effect on college-going. The SDP College-Going Diagnostic Strategic Performance Indicators*. Cambridge, MA: Harvard University, Center for Education Policy Research.

Centers for Disease Control and Prevention. (2014, October 10). *Updates on CDC's polio eradication efforts. Global Health — Polio*. Atlanta, GA: Centers for Disease Control and Prevention.

Centers for Disease Control and Prevention. (2015, January 9). *Updates on CDC's polio eradication efforts. Global Health – Polio*. Atlanta, GA: Centers for Disease Control and Prevention.

Centers for Disease Control and Prevention. (2015, May 15). *Epidemiology and prevention of vaccine-preventable diseases* (Jennifer Hamborsky, et al. Eds. 13th ed.). Washington DC: Public Health Foundation.

Centers for Disease Control and Prevention. (2016). *Number of children tested and confirmed bll's ≥10 μg/dl by state, year, and bll group, children < 72 months old. CDC's National Surveillance Data (1997–2014)*. Atlanta, GA: U.S. Department of Health & Human Services.

Centers for Disease Control and Prevention. (2017, November 3). Combined 4-vaccine series vaccination coverage among children 19-35 months by state, HHS region, and the United States, National Immunization Survey-Child (NIS-Child), 2016. ChildVaxView.

Centers for Disease Control and Prevention, National Center for Health Statistics. (2017). Underlying cause of death 1999–2016 on CDC WONDER Online Database, released December, 2017. Data are from the Multiple Cause of Death Files, 1999-2016, as compiled from data provided by the 57 vital statistics jurisdictions through the Vital Statistics Cooperative Program. CDC WONDER.

Centers for Disease Control and Prevention, National Center for Injury Prevention and Control, Division of Analysis, Research, and Practice Integration. (2013). *Fatal Injury Reports, 1999–2013, for National, Regional, and States*. Atlanta, GA: Centers for Disease Control and Prevention.

Centers for Medicare and Medicaid Services. (2014). *Beta amyloid positron tomography in dementia and neurodegenerative disease*. Baltimore, MD: Centers for Medicare and Medicaid Services.

Cespedes, Elizabeth M.; McDonald, Julia; Haines, Jess; Bottino, Clement J.; Schmidt, Marie Evans & Taveras, Elsie M. (2013). Obesity-related behaviors of US- and non-US-born parents and children in low-income households. *Journal of Developmental & Behavioral Pediatrics, 34*(8), 541–548.

Chafen, Jennifer J. S.; Newberry, Sydne J.; Riedl, Marc A.; Bravata, Dena M.; Maglione, Margaret; Suttorp, Marika J., . . . Shekelle, Paul G. (2010). Diagnosing and managing common food allergies. *JAMA, 303*(18), 1848–1856.

Chan, Kit Yee; Wang, Wei; Wu, Jing Jing; Liu, Li; Theodoratou, Evropi; Car, Josip, . . . Rudan, Igor. (2013). Epidemiology of Alzheimer's disease and other forms of dementia in China, 1990–2010: A systematic review and analysis. *The Lancet, 381*(9882), 2016–2023.

Chan, Xi Wen; Kalliath, Thomas; Brough, Paula; Siu, Oi-Ling; O'Driscoll, Michael P. & Timms, Carolyn. (2016). Work–family enrichment and satisfaction: The mediating role of self-efficacy and work–life balance. *The International Journal of Human Resource Management, 27*(15), 1755–1776.

Chang, Alicia; Sandhofer, Catherine M. & Brown, Christia S. (2011). Gender biases in early number exposure to preschool-aged children. *Journal of Language and Social Psychology, 30*(4), 440–450.

Chao, Georgia T. & Gardner, Philip D. (2017). Healthy transitions to work. In Laura M. Padilla-Walker & Larry J. Nelson (Eds.), *Flourishing in emerging adulthood: Positive development during the third decade of life*. New York, NY: Oxford University Press.

Chapman, Simon; Ford-Adams, Martha & Desai, Ashish. (2017). Bariatric surgery in adolescents. In Praveen Raj Palanivelu, et al. (Eds.), *Bariatric surgical practice guide* (pp. 9–17). Singapore: Springer.

Charise, Andrea & Eginton, Margaret L. (2018). Humanistic perspectives: Arts and the aging mind. In Matthew Rizzo, et al. (Eds.), *The Wiley handbook on the aging mind and brain*. Hoboken, NJ: Wiley.

Charlesworth, Christina J.; Smit, Ellen; Lee, David S. H.; Alramadhan, Fatimah & Odden, Michelle C. (2015). Polypharmacy among adults aged 65 years and older in the United States: 1988–2010. *The Journals of Gerontology Series A: Biological Sciences and Medical Sciences, 70*(8), 989–995.

Charlton, Samuel G. (2009). Driving while conversing: Cell phones that distract and passengers who react. *Accident Analysis and Prevention, 41*(1), 160–173.

Chassin, Laurie; Bountress, Kaitlin; Haller, Moira & Wang, Frances. (2014). Adolescent substance use disorders. In Eric J. Mash & Russell A. Barkley (Eds.), *Child psychopathology* (3rd ed., pp. 180–124). New York, NY: Guilford Press.

Chassy, Philippe & Gobet, Fernand. (2011). Measuring chess experts' single-use sequence knowledge: An archival study of departure from 'theoretical' openings. *PLoS ONE, 6*(11), e26692.

Chein, Jason; Albert, Dustin; O'Brien, Lia; Uckert, Kaitlyn & Steinberg, Laurence. (2011). Peers increase adolescent risk taking by enhancing activity in the brain's reward circuitry. *Developmental Science, 14*(2), F1–F10.

Chen, Edith; Brody, Gene H. & Miller, Gregory E. (2017). Childhood close family relationships and health. *American Psychologist, 72*(6), 555–566.

Chen, Edith; Cohen, Sheldon & Miller, Gregory E. (2010). How low socioeconomic status affects 2-year hormonal trajectories in children. *Psychological Science, 21*(1), 31–37.

Chen, Edith & Miller, Gregory E. (2012). "Shift-and-persist" strategies: Why low socioeconomic status isn't always bad for health. *Perspectives on Psychological Science, 7*(2), 135–158.

Chen, Feinian & Liu, Guangya. (2012). The health implications of grandparents caring for grandchildren in China. *The Journals of Gerontology Series B: Psychological Sciences and Social Sciences, 67B*(1), 99–112.

Chen, Gong & Gao, Yuan. (2013). Changes in social participation of older adults in Beijing. *Ageing International, 38*(1), 15–27.

Chen, Mu-Hong; Lan, Wen-Hsuan; Bai, Ya-Mei; Huang, Kai-Lin; Su, Tung-Ping; Tsai, Shih-Jen, . . . Hsu, Ju-Wei. (2016). Influence of relative age on diagnosis and treatment of Attention-deficit hyperactivity disorder in Taiwanese children. *The Journal of Pediatrics, 172*, 162–167.e161.

Chen, Ruijia & Dong, XinQi. (2017). Risk factors of elder abuse. In XinQi Dong (Ed.), *Elder abuse: Research, practice and policy* (pp. 93–107). New York, NY: Springer.

Chen, Xinyin; Cen, Guozhen; Li, Dan & He, Yunfeng. (2005). Social functioning and adjustment in Chinese children: The imprint of historical time. *Child Development, 76*(1), 182–195.

Chen, Xinyin; Rubin, Kenneth H. & Sun, Yuerong. (1992). Social reputation and peer relationships in Chinese and Canadian children: A cross-cultural study. *Child Development, 63*(6), 1336–1343.

Chen, Xinyin; Wang, Li & Wang, Zhengyan. (2009). Shyness-sensitivity and social, school, and psychological adjustment in rural migrant and urban children in China. *Child Development, 80*(5), 1499–1513.

Chen, Xinyin; Yang, Fan & Wang, Li. (2013). Relations between shyness-sensitivity and internalizing problems in Chinese children: Moderating effects of academic achievement. *Journal of Abnormal Child Psychology, 41*(5), 825–836.

Chen, Yi-Fu; Yu, Tianyi & Brody, Gene H. (2017). Parenting intervention at age 11 and cotinine levels at age 20 among African American youth. *Pediatrics, 140*(1).

Chen, Yijun; Corsino, Leonor; Shantavasinkul, Prapimporn Chattranukulchai; Grant, John; Portenier, Dana; Ding, Laura & Torquati, Alfonso. (2016). Gastric bypass surgery leads to long-term remission or improvement of type 2 diabetes and significant decrease of microvascular and macrovascular complications. *Annals of Surgery, 263*(6), 1138–1142.

Cheng, Diana; Kettinger, Laurie; Uduhiri, Kelechi & Hurt, Lee. (2011). Alcohol consumption during pregnancy: Prevalence and provider assessment. *Obstetrics & Gynecology, 117*(2), 212–217.

Cherlin, Andrew J. (2014a). *Labor's love lost: The rise and fall of the working-class family in America*. New York, NY: Russell Sage.

Cherlin, Andrew J. (2014b). First union patterns around the world: Introduction to the special issue. *Population Research and Policy Review, 33*(2), 153–159.

Cherng, Hua-Yu Sebastian & Liu, Jia-Lin. (2017). Academic social support and student expectations: The case of second-generation Asian Americans. *Asian American Journal of Psychology, 8*(1), 16–30.

Chikritzhs, Tanya; Stockwell, Tim; Naimi, Timothy; Andreasson, Sven; Dangardt, Frida & Liang, Wenbin. (2015). Has the leaning tower of presumed health benefits from 'moderate' alcohol use finally collapsed? *Addiction, 110*(5), 726–727.

Child Trends. (2015). *World family map 2015: Mapping family change and child well-being outcome*. Bethesda, MD: Child Trends.

Child Trends Data Bank. (2015, March). *Lead poisoning: Indicators on children and youth*. Bethesda, MD: Child Trends.

Child Welfare Information Gateway. (2013). *Foster care statistics, 2011*. Washington, DC: U.S. Department of Health and Human Services, Children's Bureau.

Child Welfare Information Gateway. (2018). *Foster care statistics, 2016*. Washington, DC: U.S. Department of Health and Human Services, Children's Bureau.

Ching, Charles M.; Church, A. Timothy; Katigbak, Marcia S.; Reyes, Jose Alberto S.; Tanaka-Matsumi, Junko; Takaoka, Shino, . . . Ortiz, Fernando A. (2014). The manifestation of traits in everyday behavior and affect: A five-culture study. *Journal of Research in Personality, 48*, 1–16.

Chlebowski, Rowan T.; Manson, JoAnn E.; Anderson, Garnet L.; Cauley, Jane A.; Aragaki, Aaron K.; Stefanick, Marcia L., . . . Prentice, Ross L. (2013). Estrogen plus progestin and breast cancer incidence and mortality in the Women's Health Initiative observational study. *Journal of the National Cancer Institute, 105*(8), 526–535.

Choe, Daniel E.; Lane, Jonathan D.; Grabell, Adam S. & Olson, Sheryl L. (2013a). Developmental precursors of young school-age children's hostile attribution bias. *Developmental Psychology, 49*(12), 2245–2256.

Choe, Daniel E.; Olson, Sheryl L. & Sameroff, Arnold J. (2013b). The interplay of externalizing problems and physical and inductive discipline during childhood. *Developmental Psychology, 49*(11), 2029–2039.

Chomsky, Noam. (1968). *Language and mind.* New York, NY: Harcourt Brace & World.

Chomsky, Noam. (1980). *Rules and representations.* New York, NY: Columbia University Press.

Chong, Jessica X.; Buckingham, Kati J.; Jhangiani, Shalini N.; Boehm, Corinne; Sobreira, Nara; Smith, Joshua D., . . . Bamshad, Michael J. (2015). The genetic basis of Mendelian phenotypes: Discoveries, challenges, and opportunities. *American Journal of Human Genetics, 97*(2), 199–215.

Choshen-Hillel, Shoham & Yaniv, Ilan. (2011). Agency and the construction of social preference: Between inequality aversion and prosocial behavior. *Journal of Personality and Social Psychology, 101*(6), 1253–1261.

Chou, Rita Jing-Ann & Choi, Namkee G. (2011). Prevalence and correlates of perceived workplace discrimination among older workers in the United States of America. *Ageing and Society, 31*(6), 1051–1070.

Choukas-Bradley, Sophia; Giletta, Matteo; Widman, Laura; Cohen, Geoffrey L. & Prinstein, Mitchell J. (2014). Experimentally measured susceptibility to peer influence and adolescent sexual behavior trajectories: A preliminary study. *Developmental Psychology, 50*(9), 2221–2227.

Chow, Chong Man & Ruhl, Holly. (2014). Friendship and romantic stressors and depression in emerging adulthood: Mediating and moderating roles of attachment representations. *Journal of Adult Development, 21*(2), 106–115.

Christakis, Erika. (2016). *The importance of being little: What preschoolers really need from grownups.* New York, NY: Viking.

Christian, Cindy W. & Block, Robert. (2009). Abusive head trauma in infants and children. *Pediatrics, 123*(5), 1409–1411.

Christoforides, Michael; Spanoudis, George & Demetriou, Andreas. (2016). Coping with logical fallacies: A developmental training program for learning to reason. *Child Development, 87*(6), 1856–1876.

Chronicle of Higher Education. (2014a). Almanac of higher education 2014–15. *The Chronicle of Higher Education, 60*(45).

Chronicle of Higher Education. (2014b). *Almanac of higher education 2014: Academe by the numbers.* Washington, DC: Chronicle of Higher Education.

Chronobiology International. (2016). 22nd International Symposium on Shiftwork and Working Time: Challenges and solutions for healthy working hours (Special Issue). *Chronobiology International, 33*(6).

Chu, Shuyuan; Chen, Qian; Chen, Yan; Bao, Yixiao; Wu, Min & Zhang, Jun. (2017). Cesarean section without medical indication and risk of childhood asthma, and attenuation by breastfeeding. *PLoS ONE, 12*(9), e0184920.

Chung, Joanne M.; Robins, Richard W.; Trzesniewski, Kali H.; Noftle, Erik E.; Roberts, Brent W. & Widaman, Keith F. (2014). Continuity and change in self-esteem during emerging adulthood. *Journal of Personality and Social Psychology, 106*(3), 469–483.

Cicchetti, Dante. (2013a). Annual research review: Resilient functioning in maltreated children – past, present, and future perspectives. *Journal of Child Psychology and Psychiatry, 54*(4), 402–422.

Cicchetti, Dante. (2013b). An overview of developmental psychopathology. In Philip D. Zelazo (Ed.), *The Oxford handbook of developmental psychology* (Vol. 2, pp. 455–480). New York, NY: Oxford University Press.

Cicchetti, Dante. (2016). Socioemotional, personality, and biological development: Illustrations from a multilevel developmental psychopathology perspective on child maltreatment. *Annual Review of Psychology, 67*, 187–211.

Cicero, David C. & Cohn, Jonathan R. (2018). The role of ethnic identity, self-concept, and aberrant salience in psychotic-like experiences. *Cultural Diversity and Ethnic Minority Psychology, 24*(1), 101–111.

Cierpka, Manfred & Cierpka, Astrid. (2016). Developmentally appropriate vs. persistent defiant and aggressive behavior. In Manfred Cierpka (Ed.), *Regulatory disorders in infants.* Cham, Switzerland: Springer.

Cillessen, Antonius H. N. & Marks, Peter E. L. (2011). Conceptualizing and measuring popularity. In Antonius H. N. Cillessen, et al. (Eds.), *Popularity in the peer system* (pp. 25–56). New York, NY: Guilford Press.

Ciol, Marcia A.; Rasch, Elizabeth K.; Hoffman, Jeanne M.; Huynh, Minh & Chan, Leighton. (2014). Transitions in mobility, ADLs, and IADLs among working-age Medicare beneficiaries. *Disability and Health Journal, 7*(2), 206–215.

cjcsoon2bnp. (2017, February 13). Becoming dad: A humbling birth experience of a new father and nurse [Web log post]. allnurses.

Claessen, Jacques. (2017). *Forgiveness in criminal law through incorporating restorative mediation.* Oisterwijk, the Netherlands: Wolf Legal Publishers.

Clark, Caron A. C.; Fang, Hua; Espy, Kimberly A.; Filipek, Pauline A.; Juranek, Jenifer; Bangert, Barbara, . . . Taylor, H. Gerry. (2013). Relation of neural structure to persistently low academic achievement: A longitudinal study of children with differing birth weights. *Neuropsychology, 27*(3), 364–377.

Clark, Lee Anna; Cuthbert, Bruce; Lewis-Fernández, Roberto; Narrow, William E. & Reed, Geoffrey M. (2017). Three approaches to understanding and classifying mental disorder: ICD-11, *DSM-5*, and the National Institute of Mental Health's Research Domain Criteria (RDoC). *Psychological Science in the Public Interest, 18*(2), 72–145.

Clark, Shelley; Kabiru, Caroline & Mathur, Rohini. (2010). Relationship transitions among youth in urban Kenya. *Journal of Marriage and Family, 72*(1), 73–88.

Clarke, Philippa; Marshall, Victor; House, James & Lantz, Paula. (2011). The social structuring of mental health over the adult life course: Advancing theory in the sociology of aging. *Social Forces, 89*(4), 1287–1313.

Clayton, P. E.; Gill, M. S.; Tillmann, V. & Westwood, M. (2014). Translational neuroendocrinology: Control of human growth. *Journal of Neuroendocrinology, 26*(6), 349–355.

Coffelt, Tina A. (2017). Deciding to reveal sexual information and sexuality education in mother-daughter relationships. *Sex Education, 17*(5), 571–587.

Cohen, Leslie B. & Cashon, Cara H. (2006). Infant cognition. In William Damon & Richard M. Lerner (Eds.), *Handbook of child psychology* (6th ed., Vol. 2, pp. 214–251). Hoboken, NJ: Wiley.

Cohn, D'Vera & Passel, Jeffrey S. (2018, April 5). *A record 64 million Americans live in multigenerational households. Fact Tank.* Washington, DC: Pew Research Center.

Cohn, D'Vera; Passel, Jeffrey S.; Wang, Wendy & Livingston, Gretchen. (2011, December 14). *Barely half of U.S. adults are married – A record low: New marriages down 5% from 2009 to 2010.* Washington, DC: Pew Research Center.

Coleman-Jensen, Alisha; Rabbitt, Matthew P.; Gregory, Christian & Singh, Anita. (2015). *Household food security in the United States in 2014.* Washington, DC: U.S. Department of Agriculture, Economic Research Service. ERR–194.

Coleman-Jensen, Alisha; Rabbitt, Matthew P.; Gregory, Christian A. & Singh, Anita. (2017). *Household food security in the United States in 2016.* Washington, DC: U.S. Department of Agriculture, Economic Research Service. ERR–237.

Coles, Robert. (1997). *The moral intelligence of children: How to raise a moral child.* New York, NY: Random House.

Coley, Nicola; Vaurs, Charlotte & Andrieu, Sandrine. (2015). Nutrition and cognition in aging adults. *Clinics in Geriatric Medicine, 31*(3), 453–464.

Collignon, Olivier; Champoux, François; Voss, Patrice & Lepore, Franco. (2011). Sensory rehabilitation in the plastic brain. *Progress in Brain Research, 191*, 211–231.

Collins, Rebecca L.; Martino, Steven C.; Elliott, Marc N. & Miu, Angela. (2011). Relationships between adolescent sexual outcomes and exposure to sex in media: Robustness to propensity-based analysis. *Developmental Psychology, 47*(2), 585–591.

Colson, Eve R.; Willinger, Marian; Rybin, Denis; Heeren, Timothy; Smith, Lauren A.; Lister, George & Corwin, Michael J. (2013). Trends and factors associated with infant bed sharing, 1993–2010: The National Infant Sleep Position study. *JAMA Pediatrics, 167*(11), 1032–1037.

Committee on Health Care for Underserved Women. (2014). Health disparities in rural women: Committee opinion no. 586. *Obstetrics & Gynecology, 123*(2), 384–388.

Common Sense Media. (2013). *Zero to eight: Children's media use in America 2013.* San Francisco, CA: Common Sense Media.

Common Sense Media. (2017). *The Common Sense Census: Media use by kids age zero to eight 2017.* San Francisco, CA: Common Sense Media.

Compta, Yaroslau; Parkkinen, Laura; O'Sullivan, Sean S.; Vandrovcova, Jana; Holton, Janice L.; Collins, Catherine, . . . Revesz, Tamas. (2011). Lewy- and Alzheimer-type pathologies in Parkinson's disease dementia: Which is more important? *Brain, 134*(5), 1493–1505.

Compton, Wilson M.; Gfroerer, Joe; Conway, Kevin P. & Finger, Matthew S. (2014). Unemployment and substance outcomes in the United States 2002–2010. *Drug & Alcohol Dependence, 142*, 350–353.

Connidis, Ingrid Arnet. (2015). Exploring ambivalence in family ties: Progress and prospects. *Journal of Marriage and Family, 77*(1), 77–95.

Cook, Philip J. & Donohue, John J. (2017, December 8). Saving lives by regulating guns: Evidence for policy. *Science, 358*(6368), 1259–1261.

Cooke, Jessica E.; Stuart-Parrigon, Kaela L.; Movahed-Abtahi, Mahsa; Koehn, Amanda J. & Kerns, Kathryn A. (2016). Children's emotion understanding and mother–child attachment: A meta-analysis. *Emotion, 16*(8), 1102–1106.

Coon, Carleton S. (1962). *The origin of races.* New York, NY: Knopf.

Coovadia, Hoosen M. & Wittenberg, Dankwart F. (Eds.). (2004). *Paediatrics and child health: A manual for health professionals in developing countries* (5th ed.). New York, NY: Oxford University Press.

Copeland, William E.; Wolke, Dieter; Angold, Adrian & Costell, E. Jane. (2013). Adult psychiatric outcomes of bullying and being bullied by peers in childhood and adolescence. *JAMA Psychiatry, 70*(4), 419–426.

Copen, Casey E.; Daniels, Kimberly & Mosher, William D. (2013). *First premarital cohabitation in the United States: 2006–2010 national survey of family growth. National Health Statistics Report.* Hyattsville, MD: U.S. Department of Health and Human Services, Centers for Disease Control and Prevention, National Center for Health Statistics.

Coplan, Robert J. & Weeks, Murray. (2009). Shy and soft-spoken: Shyness, pragmatic language, and socio-emotional adjustment in early childhood. *Infant and Child Development, 18*(3), 238–254.

Copp, Jennifer E.; Giordano, Peggy C.; Longmore, Monica A. & Manning, Wendy D. (2015). Living with parents and emerging adults' depressive symptoms. *Journal of Family Issues,* (In Press).

Corenblum, Barry. (2014). Relationships between racial–ethnic identity, self-esteem and in-group attitudes among First Nation children. *Journal of Youth and Adolescence, 43*(3), 387–404.

Cornelis, Marilyn C.; Byrne, E. M.; Esko, T.; Nalls, M. A.; Ganna, A.; Paynter, N., . . . Wojczynski, M. K. (2015). Genome-wide meta-analysis identifies six novel loci associated with habitual coffee consumption. *Molecular Psychiatry, 20*(5), 647–656.

Corr, Charles A. & Corr, Donna M. (2013a). Culture, socialization, and dying. In David K. Meagher & David E. Balk (Eds.), *Handbook of thanatology: The essential body of knowledge for the study of death, dying, and bereavement* (2nd ed., pp. 3–8). New York, NY: Routledge.

Corr, Charles A. & Corr, Donna M. (2013b). Historical and contemporary perspectives on loss, grief, and mourning. In David Meagher & David E. Balk (Eds.), *Handbook of thanatology: The essential body of knowledge for the study of death, dying, and bereavement* (2nd ed., pp. 135–148). New York, NY: Routledge.

Cosgrave, James F. (2010). Embedded addiction: The social production of gambling knowledge and the development of gambling markets. *Canadian Journal of Sociology, 35*(1), 113–134.

Costa, Albert & Sebastián-Gallés, Núria. (2014). How does the bilingual experience sculpt the brain? *Nature Reviews Neuroscience, 15*(5), 336–345.

Costa, Albert; Vives, Marc–Lluís & Corey, Joanna D. (2017). On language processing shaping decision making. *Current Directions in Psychological Science, 26*(2), 146–151.

Costa, Sara S. Fonseca & Ripperger, Jürgen A. (2015). Impact of the circadian clock on the aging process. *Frontiers in Neurology, 6*(43).

Côté, James E. & Levine, Charles. (2015). *Identity formation, youth, and development: A simplified approach*. New York, NY: Psychology Press.

Council on Community Pediatrics. (2015). Promoting food security for all children: Policy statement. *Pediatrics, 136*(5), e1431–e1438.

Couzin, Jennifer. (2009). Friendship as a health factor. *Science, 323*(5913), 454–457.

Couzin-Frankel, Jennifer. (2011a). A pitched battle over life span. *Science, 333*(6042), 549–550.

Couzin-Frankel, Jennifer. (2011b). Aging genes: The sirtuin story unravels. *Science, 334*(6060), 1194–1198.

Covington-Ward, Yolanda. (2017). African immigrants in low-wage direct health care: Motivations, job satisfaction, and occupational mobility. *Journal of Immigrant and Minority Health, 19*(3), 709–715.

Cowell, Jason M.; Lee, Kang; Malcolm-Smith, Susan; Selcuk, Bilge; Zhou, Xinyue & Decety, Jean. (2017). The development of generosity and moral cognition across five cultures. *Developmental Science, 20*(4), e12403.

Coyne, Sarah M.; Padilla-Walker, Laura M. & Holmgren, Hailey G. (2018). A six-year longitudinal study of texting trajectories during adolescence. *Child Development, 89*(1), 58–65.

Craig, Stephanie G.; Davies, Gregory; Schibuk, Larry; Weiss, Margaret D. & Hechtman, Lily. (2015). Long-term effects of stimulant treatment for ADHD: What can we tell our patients? *Current Developmental Disorders Reports, 2*(1), 1–9.

Cramer, Steven C. & Procaccio, Vincent. (2012). Correlation between genetic polymorphisms and stroke recovery: Analysis of the GAIN Americas and GAIN International Studies. *European Journal of Neurology, 19*(5), 718–724.

Crenshaw, David A. (2013). The family, larger systems, and traumatic death. In David K. Meagher & David E. Balk (Eds.), *Handbook of thanatology: The essential body of knowledge for the study of death, dying, and bereavement* (2nd ed., pp. 305–309). New York, NY: Routledge.

Creswell, John W. (2009). *Research design: Qualitative, quantitative, and mixed methods approaches* (3rd ed.). Thousand Oaks, CA: Sage.

Cripe, Larry D. & Frankel, Richard M. (2017). Dying from cancer: Communication, empathy, and the clinical imagination. *Journal of Patient Experience, 4*(2), 69–73.

Crnic, Keith A.; Neece, Cameron L.; McIntyre, Laura Lee; Blacher, Jan & Baker, Bruce L. (2017). Intellectual disability and developmental risk: Promoting intervention to improve child and family well-being. *Child Development, 88*(2), 436–445.

Crone, Eveline A. & Dahl, Ronald E. (2012). Understanding adolescence as a period of social–affective engagement and goal flexibility. *Nature Reviews Neuroscience, 13*(9), 636–650.

Crone, Eveline A.; van Duijvenvoorde, Anna C. K. & Peper, Jiska S. (2016). Annual research review: Neural contributions to risk-taking in adolescence–developmental changes and individual differences. *Journal of Child Psychology and Psychiatry, 57*(3), 353–368.

Crosnoe, Robert & Johnson, Monica Kirkpatrick. (2011). Research on adolescence in the twenty-first century. *Annual Review of Sociology, 37*(1), 439–460.

Crosnoe, Robert; Purtell, Kelly M.; Davis-Kean, Pamela; Ansari, Arya & Benner, Aprile D. (2016). The selection of children from low-income families into preschool. *Developmental Psychology, 52*(4), 599–612.

Crossley, Nicolas A.; Mechelli, Andrea; Scott, Jessica; Carletti, Francesco; Fox, Peter T.; McGuire, Philip & Bullmore, Edward T. (2014). The hubs of the human connectome are generally implicated in the anatomy of brain disorders. *Brain, 137*(8), 2382–2395.

Crowe, Laura & Butterworth, Peter. (2016). The role of financial hardship, mastery and social support in the association between employment status and depression: Results from an Australian longitudinal cohort study. *BMJ Open, 6*, e009834.

Crutchfield, Parker. (2018). The ethics of anti-aging clinical trials. *Science and Engineering Ethics, 24*(2), 441–453.

Csikszentmihalyi, Mihaly. (2013). *Creativity: Flow and the psychology of discovery and invention*. New York, NY: Harper Perennial.

Cuevas, Bryan J. & Stone, Jacqueline Ilyse (Eds.). (2011). *The Buddhist dead: Practices, discourses, representations*. Honolulu, HI: University of Hawaii Press.

Cumming, Elaine & Henry, William Earl. (1961). *Growing old: The process of disengagement*. New York, NY: Basic Books.

Currie, Janet & Widom, Cathy S. (2010). Long-term consequences of child abuse and neglect on adult economic well-being. *Child Maltreatment, 15*(2), 111–120.

Curtin, Nancy & Garrison, Mary. (2018). "She was more than a friend": Clinical intervention strategies for effectively addressing disenfranchised grief issues for same-sex couples. *Journal of Gay & Lesbian Social Services*, (In Press).

Cutler, Stephen J.; Hendricks, Jon & O'Neill, Greg. (2011). Civic engagement and aging. In Robert H. Binstock & Linda K. George (Eds.), *Handbook of aging and the social sciences* (7th ed., pp. 221–233). San Diego, CA: Academic Press.

Cutts, Diana & Cook, John. (2017). Screening for food insecurity: Short-term alleviation and long-term prevention. *American Journal of Public Health, 107*(11), 1699–1700.

Cutuli, J. J.; Ahumada, Sandra M.; Herbers, Janette E.; Lafavor, Theresa L.; Masten, Ann S. & Oberg, Charles N. (2017). Adversity and children experiencing family homelessness: Implications for health. *Journal of Children and Poverty, 23*(1), 41–55.

Cutuli, J. J.; Desjardins, Christopher David; Herbers, Janette E.; Long, Jeffrey D.; Heistad, David; Chan, Chi-Keung, . . . Masten, Ann S. (2013). Academic achievement trajectories of homeless and highly mobile students: Resilience in the context of chronic and acute risk. *Child Development, 84*(3), 841–857.

Daley, Dave; Jones, Karen; Hutchings, Judy & Thompson, Margaret. (2009). Attention deficit hyperactivity disorder in pre-school children: Current findings, recommended interventions and future directions. *Child, 35*(6), 754–766.

Dalman, Christina; Allebeck, Peter; Gunnell, David; Harrison, Glyn; Kristensson, Krister; Lewis, Glyn, . . . Karlsson, Håkan. (2008). Infections in the CNS during childhood and the risk of subsequent psychotic illness: A cohort study of more than one million Swedish subjects. *American Journal of Psychiatry, 165*(1), 59–65.

Daly, Jeanette M.; Gaskill, Kathryn J. & Jogerst, Gerald J. (2011). Essential data elements for reporters of elder abuse. *Journal of Elder Abuse & Neglect, 23*(3), 234–245.

Damasio, Antonio R. (2012). *Self comes to mind: Constructing the conscious brain.* New York, NY: Vintage.

Damian, Lavinia E.; Stoeber, Joachim; Negru, Oana & Băban, Adriana. (2013). On the development of perfectionism in adolescence: Perceived parental expectations predict longitudinal increases in socially prescribed perfectionism. *Personality and Individual Differences, 55*(6), 688–693.

Dantchev, Slava; Zammit, Stanley & Wolke, Dieter. (2018). Sibling bullying in middle childhood and psychotic disorder at 18 years: A prospective cohort study. *Psychological Medicine,* (In Press).

Darwin, Charles. (1859). *On the origin of species by means of natural selection.* London, UK: J. Murray.

Dasgupta, Rajib; Sinha, Dipa & Yumnam, Veda. (2016). Rapid survey of wasting and stunting in children: What's new, what's old and what's the buzz? *Indian Pediatrics, 53*(1), 47–49.

Daugherty, Jill & Copen, Casey. (2016). *Trends in attitudes about marriage, childbearing, and sexual behavior: United States, 2002, 2006–2010, and 2011–2013. National Health Statistics Reports, 92.* Hyattsville, MD: National Center for Health Statistics.

Daum, Moritz M.; Ulber, Julia & Gredebäck, Gustaf. (2013). The development of pointing perception in infancy: Effects of communicative signals on covert shifts of attention. *Developmental Psychology, 49*(10), 1898–1908.

Davidai, Shai & Gilovich, Thomas. (2015). Building a more mobile America: One income quintile at a time. *Perspectives on Psychological Science, 10*(1), 60–71.

Davis-Kean, Pamela E.; Jager, Justin & Collins, W. Andrew. (2009). The self in action: An emerging link between self-beliefs and behaviors in middle childhood. *Child Development Perspectives, 3*(3), 184–188.

Davison, Glen; Kehaya, Corinna & Jones, Arwel Wyn. (2014). Nutritional and physical activity interventions to improve immunity. *American Journal of Lifestyle Medicine.*

Dawood, Yasmin. (2015). Campaign finance and American democracy. *Annual Review of Political Science, 18,* 329–348.

Dawson, Chris; Veliziotis, Michail & Hopkins, Benjamin. (2017). Temporary employment, job satisfaction and subjective well-being. *Economic and Industrial Democracy, 38*(1), 69–98.

Dayanim, Shoshana & Namy, Laura L. (2015). Infants learn baby signs from video. *Child Development, 86*(3), 800–811.

Dayton, Carolyn Joy; Walsh, Tova B.; Oh, Wonjung & Volling, Brenda. (2015). Hush now baby: Mothers' and fathers' strategies for soothing their infants and associated parenting outcomes. *Journal of Pediatric Health Care, 29*(2), 145–155.

de Boer, Anouk; Peeters, Margot & Koning, Ina. (2017). An experimental study of risk taking behavior among adolescents: A closer look at peer and sex influences. *The Journal of Early Adolescence, 37*(8), 1125–1141.

de Hoog, Marieke L. A.; Kleinman, Ken P.; Gillman, Matthew W.; Vrijkotte, Tanja G. M.; van Eijsden, Manon & Taveras, Elsie M. (2014). Racial/ethnic and immigrant differences in early childhood diet quality. *Public Health Nutrition, 17*(6), 1308–1317.

de Jong, Antina; Maya, Idit & van Lith, Jan M. M. (2015). Prenatal screening: Current practice, new developments, ethical challenges. *Bioethics, 29*(1), 1–8.

de Jong Gierveld, Jenny & Merz, Eva-Maria. (2013). Parents' partnership decision making after divorce or widowhood: The role of (step)children. *Journal of Marriage and Family, 75*(5), 1098–1113.

de Jonge, Ank; Geerts, C. C.; van der Goes, Birgit Y.; Mol, Ben W.; Buitendijk, S. E. & Nijhuis, Jan. (2015). Perinatal mortality and morbidity up to 28 days after birth among 743,070 low-risk planned home and hospital births: A cohort study based on three merged national perinatal databases. *BJOG, 122*(5), 720–728.

de Jonge, Huub. (2011). Purification and remembrance: Eastern and Western ways to deal with the Bali bombing. In Peter Jan Margry & Cristina Sánchez-Carretero (Eds.), *Grassroots memorials: The politics of memorializing traumatic death* (pp. 262–284). New York, NY: Berghahn Books.

de la Croix, David. (2013). *Fertility, education, growth, and sustainability.* New York, NY: Cambridge University Press.

De Lima, Liliana; Woodruff, Roger; Pettus, Katherine; Downing, Julia; Buitrago, Rosa; Munyoro, Esther, . . . Radbruch, Lukas. (2017). International Association for Hospice and Palliative Care position statement: Euthanasia and physician-assisted suicide. *Journal of Palliative Medicine, 20*(1), 8–14.

De Neys, Wim & Van Gelder, Elke. (2009). Logic and belief across the lifespan: The rise and fall of belief inhibition during syllogistic reasoning. *Developmental Science, 12*(1), 123–130.

De Raedt, Rudi; Koster, Ernst H. W. & Ryckewaert, Ruben. (2013). Aging and attentional bias for death related and general threat-related information: Less avoidance in older as compared with middle-aged adults. *The Journals of Gerontology Series B: Psychological Sciences and Social Sciences, 68*(1), 41–48.

Dean, Angela J.; Walters, Julie & Hall, Anthony. (2010). A systematic review of interventions to enhance medication adherence in children and adolescents with chronic illness. *Archives of Disease in Childhood, 95*(9), 717–723.

Dearing, Eric; Wimer, Christopher; Simpkins, Sandra D.; Lund, Terese; Bouffard, Suzanne M.; Caronongan, Pia, . . . Weiss, Heather. (2009). Do neighborhood and home contexts help explain why low-income children miss opportunities to participate in activities outside of school? *Developmental Psychology, 45*(6), 1545–1562.

Dearing, Eric & Zachrisson, Henrik D. (2017). Concern over internal, external, and incidence validity in studies of child-care quantity and externalizing behavior problems. *Child Development Perspectives, 11*(2), 133–138.

Deater-Deckard, Kirby & Lansford, Jennifer E. (2016). Daughters' and sons' exposure to childrearing discipline and violence in low- and middle-income countries. *Monographs of the Society for Research in Child Development, 81*(1), 78–103.

DeCaro, Marci S.; Thomas, Robin D.; Albert, Neil B. & Beilock, Sian L. (2011). Choking under pressure: Multiple routes to skill failure. *Journal of Experimental Psychology, 140*(3), 390–406.

Dees, Marianne K.; Vernooij-Dassen, Myrra J.; Dekkers, Wim J.; Vissers, Kris C. & van Weel, Chris. (2011). 'Unbearable suffering': A qualitative study on the perspectives of patients who request assistance in dying. *Journal of Medical Ethics, 37*(12), 727–734.

Deevy, Patricia; Leonard, Laurence B. & Marchman, Virginia A. (2017). Sensitivity to morphosyntactic information in 3-year-old children with typical language development: A feasibility study. *Journal of Speech, Language & Hearing Research, 60*(2), 668–674.

Degnan, Kathryn A.; Hane, Amie Ashley; Henderson, Heather A.; Moas, Olga Lydia; Reeb-Sutherland, Bethany C. & Fox, Nathan A. (2011). Longitudinal stability of temperamental exuberance and social–emotional outcomes in early childhood. *Developmental Psychology, 47*(3), 765–780.

DeGroot, Jocelyn M. (2012). Maintaining relational continuity with the deceased on Facebook. *Omega, 65*(3), 195–212.

Dehaene-Lambertz, Ghislaine. (2017). The human infant brain: A neural architecture able to learn language. *Psychonomic Bulletin & Review, 24*(1), 48–55.

Del Vicario, Michela; Scala, Antonio; Caldarelli, Guido; Stanley, H. Eugene & Quattrociocchi, Walter. (2017). Modeling confirmation bias and polarization. *Scientific Reports, 7*(40391).

Delaunay-El Allam, Maryse; Soussignan, Robert; Patris, Bruno; Marlier, Luc & Schaal, Benoist. (2010). Long-lasting memory for an odor acquired at the mother's breast. *Developmental Science, 13*(6), 849–863.

Delon-Martin, Chantal; Plailly, Jane; Fonlupt, Pierre; Veyrac, Alexandra & Roye, Jean-Pierre. (2013). Perfumers' expertise induces structural reorganization in olfactory brain regions. *NeuroImage, 68*, 55–62.

DeMaris, Alfred & Mahoney, Annette. (2017). Equity dynamics in the perceived fairness of infant care. *Journal of Marriage and Family, 79*(1), 261–276.

Demir, Melikşah; Haynes, Andrew & Potts, Shannon K. (2017). My friends are my estate: Friendship experiences mediate the relationship between perceived responses to capitalization attempts and happiness. *Journal of Happiness Studies, 18*(4), 1161–1190.

Dennehy, Tara C.; Ben-Zeev, Avi & Tanigawa, Noriko. (2014). 'Be prepared': An implemental mindset for alleviating social–identity threat. *British Journal of Social Psychology, 53*(3), 585–594.

Denq, William & Delasobera, B. Elizabeth. (2018). Adaptive extreme sports: A clinical guide. In Arthur Jason De Luigi (Ed.), *Adaptive sports medicine* (pp. 343–357). Cham, Switzerland: Springer.

Dent, Lauren & Maloney, Patricia. (2017). Evangelical Christian parents' attitudes towards abstinence-based sex education: "I want my kids to have great sex!" *Sex Education, 17*(2), 149–164.

Deresiewicz, William. (2014). *Excellent sheep: The miseducation of the American elite and the way to a meaningful life.* New York, NY: Free Press.

Desai, Rishi J.; Hernandez-Diaz, Sonia; Bateman, Brian T. & Huybrechts, Krista F. (2014). Increase in prescription opioid use during pregnancy among Medicaid-enrolled women. *Obstetrics & Gynecology, 123*(5), 997–1002.

DeSantiago-Cardenas, Lilliana; Rivkina, Victoria; Whyte, Stephanie A.; Harvey-Gintoft, Blair C.; Bunning, Bryan J. & Gupta, Ruchi S. (2015). Emergency epinephrine use for food allergy reactions in Chicago public schools. *American Journal of Preventive Medicine, 48*(2), 170–173.

DeSilver, Drew. (2013, November 13). *Obesity and poverty don't always go together. Fact Tank.* Washington, DC: Pew Research Center.

DeSilver, Drew. (2016, June 8). *Increase in living with parents driven by those ages 25–34, non-college grads. Fact Tank: News in the Numbers.* Washington, DC: Pew Research Center.

Destin, Mesmin. (2018). Socioeconomic mobility, identity, and health: Experiences that influence immunology and implications for intervention. *American Psychologist,* (In Press).

Devaraj, Sridevi; Hemarajata, Peera & Versalovic, James. (2013). The human gut microbiome and body metabolism: Implications for obesity and diabetes. *Clinical Chemistry, 59*(4), 617–628.

Dey, Matthew; Houseman, Susan & Polivka, Anne. (2016). *Manufacturers' outsourcing to temporary help services: A research update.* Washington, DC: U.S. Department of Labor.

DeYoung, Colin G.; Hirsh, Jacob B.; Shane, Matthew S.; Papademetris, Xenophon; Rajeevan, Nallakkandi & Gray, Jeremy R. (2010). Testing predictions from personality neuroscience. *Psychological Science, 21*(6), 820–828.

Didion, Joan. (2005). *The year of magical thinking.* New York, NY: Knopf.

Digest of Education Statistics. (2016, February). *Table 205.10. Private elementary and secondary school enrollment and private enrollment as a percentage of total enrollment in public and private schools, by region and grade level: Selected years, fall 1995 through fall 2013.* Washington, DC: National Center for Education Statistics.

Digest of Education Statistics. (2017, February). *Table 219.80: Percentage of high school dropouts among persons 16 to 24 years old (status dropout rate) and number of status dropouts, by noninstitutionalized or institutionalized status, birth in or outside of the United States, and selected characteristics: Selected years, 2006 through 2015.* Washington, DC: National Center for Education Statistics.

Dijksterhuis, Ap; Bos, Maarten W.; van der Leij, Andries & van Baaren, Rick B. (2009). Predicting soccer matches after unconscious and conscious thought as a function of expertise. *Psychological Science, 20*(11), 1381–1387.

Dingemans, Ellen; Henkens, Kène & van Solinge, Hanna (2016). Access to bridge employment: Who finds and who does not find work after retirement? *The Gerontologist, 56*(4), 630–640.

Dinh, Michael M.; Bein, Kendall; Roncal, Susan; Byrne, Christopher M.; Petchell, Jeffrey & Brennan, Jeffrey. (2013). Redefining the golden hour for severe head injury in an urban setting: The effect of prehospital arrival times on patient outcomes. *Injury, 44*(5), 606–610.

Diseth, Åge; Meland, Eivind & Breidablik, Hans J. (2014). Self-beliefs among students: Grade level and gender differences in self-esteem, self-efficacy and implicit theories of intelligence. *Learning and Individual Differences, 35.*

Dishion, Thomas J.; Poulin, François & Burraston, Bert. (2001). Peer group dynamics associated with iatrogenic effects in group interventions with high-risk young adolescents. In Douglas W. Nangle & Cynthia A. Erdley (Eds.), *The role of friendship in psychological adjustment* (pp. 79–92). San Francisco, CA: Jossey-Bass.

Dishion, Thomas J.; Véronneau, Marie-Hélène & Myers, Michael W. (2010). Cascading peer dynamics underlying the progression from problem behavior to violence in early to late adolescence. *Development and Psychopathology, 22*(3), 603–619.

Dismukes, R. Key; Berman, Benjamin A. & Loukopoulos, Loukia. (2007). *The limits of expertise: Rethinking pilot error and the causes of airline accidents.* New York, NY: Routledge.

Ditch the Label. (2017). *The annual bullying survey 2017.* Los Angeles, CA: Ditch the Label.

Dix, Theodore & Yan, Ni. (2014). Mothers' depressive symptoms and infant negative emotionality in the prediction of child adjustment at age 3: Testing the maternal reactivity and child vulnerability hypotheses. *Development and Psychopathology, 26*(1), 111–124.

Doering, Katie. (2010). Death: The unwritten curriculum. *Encounter, 23*(4), 57–62.

Doka, Kenneth J. (2013). Historical and contemporary perspectives on dying. In David K. Meagher & David E. Balk (Eds.), *Handbook of thanatology: The essential body of knowledge for the study of death, dying, and bereavement* (2nd ed., pp. 17–23). New York, NY: Routledge.

Doka, Kenneth J. (2016). *Grief is a journey: Finding your path through loss.* New York, NY: Atria.

Dominelli, Paolo B. & Sheel, A. William. (2012). Experimental approaches to the study of the mechanics of breathing during exercise. *Respiratory Physiology & Neurobiology, 180*(2/3), 147–161.

Dompier, Thomas P.; Kerr, Zachary Y.; Marshall, Stephen W.; Hainline, Brian; Snook, Erin M.; Hayden, Ross & Simon, Janet E. (2015). Incidence of concussion during practice and games in youth, high school, and collegiate American football players. *JAMA Pediatrics, 169*(7), 659–665.

Dong, XinQi (Ed.). (2017). *Elder abuse: Research, practice and policy.* New York, NY: Springer.

Dong, XinQi & Simon, Melissa A. (2011). Enhancing national policy and programs to address elder abuse. *JAMA, 305*(23), 2460–2461.

Dong, XinQi; Simon, Melissa A.; Beck, T. T.; Farran, Carol; McCann, Judith J.; Mendes de Leon, Carlos F., . . . Evans, Denis A. (2011). Elder abuse and mortality: The role of psychological and social wellbeing. *Gerontology, 57*(6), 549–558.

Doom, Jenalee R.; Doyle, Colleen M. & Gunnar, Megan R. (2017). Social stress buffering by friends in childhood and adolescence: Effects on HPA and oxytocin activity. *Social Neuroscience, 12*(1), 8–21.

Doraiswamy, P. Murali. (2012). Silent cerebrovascular events and Alzheimer's disease: An overlooked opportunity for prevention? *American Journal of Psychiatry, 169*(3), 251–254.

Dorsey, Shannon; Burns, Barbara J.; Southerland, Dannia G.; Cox, Julia Revillion; Wagner, H. Ryan & Farmer, Elizabeth M. Z. (2012). Prior trauma exposure for youth in treatment foster care. *Journal of Child and Family Studies, 21*(5), 816–824.

Dotterer, Aryn M.; McHale, Susan M. & Crouter, Ann C. (2009). The development and correlates of academic interests from childhood through adolescence. *Journal of Educational Psychology, 101*(2), 509–519.

Doubleday, Justin. (2013). Earnings gap narrows, but college education still pays, report says. *The Chronicle of Higher Education,* A14.

Doucet, Andrea. (2015). Parental responsibilities: Dilemmas of measurement and gender equality. *Journal of Marriage and Family, 77*(1), 224–242.

Downing, Katherine L.; Hinkley, Trina; Salmon, Jo; Hnatiuk, Jill A. & Hesketh, Kylie D. (2017). Do the correlates of screen time and sedentary time differ in preschool children? *BMC Public Health, 17*(285).

Dresser, Michael & Dance, Scott. (2016, September 17). Towson mall bars hundreds of juveniles on first weekend of curfew without incidents. *Baltimore Sun.*

Drewelies, Johanna; Wagner, Jenny; Tesch-Römer, Clemens; Heckhausen, Jutta & Gerstorf, Denis. (2017). Perceived control across the second half of life: The role of physical health and social integration. *Psychology and Aging, 32*(1), 76–92.

Driemeyer, Wiebke; Janssen, Erick; Wiltfang, Jens & Elmerstig, Eva. (2016). Masturbation experiences of Swedish senior high school students: Gender differences and similarities. *The Journal of Sex Research,* (In Press).

Drover, James; Hoffman, Dennis R.; Castañeda, Yolanda S.; Morale, Sarah E. & Birch, Eileen E. (2009). Three randomized controlled trials of early long-chain polyunsaturated fatty acid supplementation on means-end problem solving in 9-month-olds. *Child Development, 80*(5), 1376–1384.

Duckworth, Angela L. & Kern, Margaret L. (2011). A meta-analysis of the convergent validity of self-control measures. *Journal of Research in Personality, 45*(3), 259–268.

Dugas, Lara R.; Fuller, Miles; Gilbert, Jack & Layden, Brian T. (2016). The obese gut microbiome across the epidemiologic transition. *Emerging Themes in Epidemiology, 13*(1).

Duggan, Maeve. (2017, July 11). *Online harassment 2017. Internet & Technology.* Washington, DC: Pew Research Center.

Duncan, Simon & Phillips, Miranda. (2010). People who live apart together (LATs)—How different are they? *The Sociological Review, 58*(1), 112–134.

Dunifon, Rachel E.; Ziol-Guest, Kathleen M. & Kopko, Kimberly. (2014). Grandparent coresidence and family well-being: Implications for research and policy. *The ANNALS of the American Academy of Political and Social Science, 654*(1), 110–126.

Dunn, Erin C.; Nishimi, Kristen; Powers, Abigail & Bradley, Bekh. (2017). Is developmental timing of trauma exposure associated with depressive and post-traumatic stress disorder symptoms in adulthood? *Journal of Psychiatric Research, 84*, 119–127.

Dunn, Kristy & Bremner, J. Gavin. (2017). Investigating looking and social looking measures as an index of infant violation of expectation. *Developmental Science, 20*(6), e12452.

Dunn, Marianne G.; Rochlen, Aaron B. & O'Brien, Karen M. (2013). Employee, mother, and partner: An exploratory investigation of working women with stay-at-home fathers. *Journal of Career Development, 40*(1), 3–22.

Dunning, David. (2011). *Social motivation.* New York, NY: Psychology Press.

Durso, Francis T.; Dattel, Andrew R. & Pop, Vlad L. (2018). Expertise and transportation. In K. Anders Ericsson, et al. (Eds.), *The Cambridge handbook of expertise and expert performance* (2nd ed., pp. 356–371). New York, NY: Cambridge University Press.

Dutra, Lauren M. & Glantz, Stanton A. (2014). Electronic cigarettes and conventional cigarette use among US adolescents: A cross-sectional study. *JAMA Pediatrics, 168*(7), 610–617.

Dvornyk, Volodymyr & Waqar-ul-Haq. (2012). Genetics of age at menarche: A systematic review. *Human Reproduction Update, 18*(2), 198–210.

Dwan, Toni & Ownsworth, Tamara. (2017). The Big Five personality factors and psychological well-being following stroke: A systematic review. *Disability and Rehabilitation,* (In Press).

Dweck, Carol S. (2013). Social development. In Philip D. Zelazo (Ed.), *The Oxford handbook of developmental psychology* (Vol. 2, pp. 167–190). New York, NY: Oxford University Press.

Dweck, Carol S. (2017). From needs to goals and representations: Foundations for a unified theory of motivation, personality, and development. *Psychological Review, 124*(6), 689–719.

Dyer, Ashley A.; Rivkina, Victoria; Perumal, Dhivya; Smeltzer, Brandon M.; Smith, Bridget M. & Gupta, Ruchi S. (2015). Epidemiology of childhood peanut allergy. *Allergy and Asthma Proceedings, 36*(1), 58–64.

Dyer, Nazly; Owen, Margaret T. & Caughy, Margaret O'Brien. (2014). Ethnic differences in profiles of mother–child interactions and relations to emerging school readiness in African American and Latin American children. *Parenting, 14*(3/4), 175–194.

Dykiert, Dominika; Der, Geoff; Starr, John M. & Deary, Ian J. (2012). Sex differences in reaction time mean and intra-individual variability across the life span. *Developmental Psychology, 48*(5), 1262–1276.

Eagly, Alice H. & Wood, Wendy. (2013). The nature–nurture debates: 25 years of challenges in understanding the psychology of gender. *Perspectives on Psychological Science, 8*(3), 340–357.

Earth Policy Institute. (2011). *Two stories of disease: Smallpox and polio.* Washington, DC: Earth Policy Institute.

Eccles, Jacquelynne S. & Roeser, Robert W. (2010). An ecological view of schools and development. In Judith L. Meece & Jacquelynne S. Eccles (Eds.), *Handbook of research on schools, schooling, and human development* (pp. 6–22). New York, NY: Routledge.

Eccles, Jacquelynne S. & Roeser, Robert W. (2011). Schools as developmental contexts during adolescence. *Journal of Research on Adolescence, 21*(1), 225–241.

Eells, Tracy D.; Lombart, Kenneth G.; Salsman, Nicholas; Kendjelic, Edward M.; Schneiderman, Carolyn T. & Lucas, Cynthia P. (2011). Expert reasoning in psychotherapy case formulation. *Psychotherapy Research, 21*(4), 385–399.

Eggebrecht, Adam T.; Elison, Jed T.; Feczko, Eric; Todorov, Alexandre; Wolff, Jason J.; Kandala, Sridhar, . . . Pruett, John R. (2017). Joint attention and brain functional connectivity in infants and toddlers. *Cerebral Cortex, 27*(3), 1709–1720.

Eggum, Natalie D.; Eisenberg, Nancy; Kao, Karen; Spinrad, Tracy L.; Bolnick, Rebecca; Hofer, Claire, . . . Fabricius, William V. (2011). Emotion understanding, theory of mind, and prosocial orientation: Relations over time in early childhood. *The Journal of Positive Psychology, 6*(1), 4–16.

Ehrlich, Paul R. (1968). *The population bomb.* New York, NY: Ballantine Books.

Ehrlich, Sara Z. & Blum-Kulka, Shoshana. (2014). 'Now I said that Danny becomes Danny again': A multifaceted view of kindergarten children's peer argumentative discourse. In Asta Cekaite, et al. (Eds.), *Children's peer talk: Learning from each other* (pp. 23–41). New York, NY: Cambridge University Press.

Eichhorst, Werner; Rodríguez-Planas, Núria; Schmidl, Ricarda & Zimmermann, Klaus F. (2012). *A roadmap to vocational education and training systems around the world.* Bonn, Germany: Institute for the Study of Labor.

Eisenberg, Nancy; Hofer, Claire; Sulik, Michael J. & Spinrad, Tracy L. (2014). Self-regulation, effortful control, and their socioemotional correlates. In James J. Gross (Ed.), *Handbook of emotion regulation* (2nd ed., pp. 157–172). New York, NY: Guilford Press.

Eisenberg, Nancy & Zhou, Qing. (2016). Conceptions of executive function and regulation: When and to what degree do they overlap? In James A. Griffin, et al. (Eds.), *Executive function in preschool-age children: Integrating measurement, neurodevelopment, and translational research* (pp. 115–136). Washington, DC: American Psychological Association.

Elder, Glen H. (1998). The life course as developmental theory. *Child Development, 69*(1), 1–12.

Elicker, James; Ruprecht, Karen M. & Anderson, Treshawn. (2014). Observing infants' and toddlers' relationships and interactions in group care. In Linda J. Harrison & Jennifer Sumsion (Eds.), *Lived spaces of infant-toddler education and care: Exploring diverse perspectives on theory, research and practice* (pp. 131–145). Dordrecht, the Netherlands: Springer.

Elkind, David. (1967). Egocentrism in adolescence. *Child Development, 38*(4), 1025–1034.

Elkind, David. (2007). *The power of play: How spontaneous, imaginative activities lead to happier, healthier children.* Cambridge, MA: Da Capo Press.

Ellefson, Michelle R.; Ng, Florrie Fei-Yin; Wang, Qian & Hughes, Claire. (2017). Efficiency of executive function: A two-generation cross-cultural comparison of samples from Hong Kong and the United Kingdom. *Psychological Science*, *28*(5), 555–566.

Ellemers, Naomi. (2018). Gender stereotypes. *Annual Review of Psychology*, *69*, 275–298.

Ellingsaeter, Anne L. (2014). Towards universal quality early childhood education and care: The Norwegian model. In Ludovica Gambaro et al. (Eds.), *An equal start?: Providing quality early education and care for disadvantaged children* (pp. 53–76). Chicago, IL: Policy Press.

Ellingsaeter, Anne Lise; Kitterød, Ragni Hege & Lyngstad, Jan. (2017). Universalising childcare, changing mothers' attitudes: Policy feedback in Norway. *Journal of Social Policy*, *46*(1), 149–173.

Elliot, Ari J.; Mooney, Christopher J.; Infurna, Frank J. & Chapman, Benjamin P. (2018). Perceived control and frailty: The role of affect and perceived health. *Psychology and Aging*, *33*(3), 473–481.

Elliott, Sinikka. (2012). *Not my kid: What parents believe about the sex lives of their teenagers.* New York, NY: New York University Press.

Elliott, Vanessa J.; Rodgers, David L. & Brett, Stephen J. (2011). Systematic review of quality of life and other patient-centred outcomes after cardiac arrest survival. *Resuscitation*, *82*(3), 247–256.

Ellis, Bruce J. & Boyce, W. Thomas. (2008). Biological sensitivity to context. *Current Directions in Psychological Science*, *17*(3), 183–187.

Ellis, Bruce J.; Shirtcliff, Elizabeth A.; Boyce, W. Thomas; Deardorff, Julianna & Essex, Marilyn J. (2011). Quality of early family relationships and the timing and tempo of puberty: Effects depend on biological sensitivity to context. *Development and Psychopathology*, *23*(1), 85–99.

Ellis, Lee & Wahab, Eshah A. (2013). Religiosity and fear of death: A theory-oriented review of the empirical literature. *Review of Religious Research*, *55*(1), 149–189.

Ellison, Christopher G.; Musick, Marc A. & Holden, George W. (2011). Does conservative Protestantism moderate the association between corporal punishment and child outcomes? *Journal of Marriage and Family*, *73*(5), 946–961.

Ellwood, Philippa; Asher, M. Innes; García-Marcos, Luis; Williams, Hywel; Keil, Ulrich; Robertson, Colin & Nagel, Gabriele. (2013). Do fast foods cause asthma, rhinoconjunctivitis and eczema? Global findings from the International Study of Asthma and Allergies in Childhood (ISAAC) Phase Three. *Thorax*, *68*(4), 351–360.

El-Sheikh, Mona & Kelly, Ryan J. (2017). Family functioning and children's sleep. *Child Development Perspectives*, *11*(4), 264–269.

Emanuel, Ezekiel J. (2017). Euthanasia and physician-assisted suicide: Focus on the data. *Medical Journal of Australia*, *206*(8), 1–2e1.

Emerson, Robert M. (2015). *Everyday troubles: The micro-politics of interpersonal conflict.* Chicago, IL: University of Chicago Press.

Emmen, Rosanneke A. G.; Malda, Maike; Mesman, Judi; van IJzendoorn, Marinus H.; Prevoo, Mariëlle J. L. & Yeniad, Nihal. (2013). Socioeconomic status and parenting in ethnic minority families: Testing a minority family stress model. *Journal of Family Psychology*, *27*(6), 896–904.

Endendijk, Joyce J.; Derks, Belle & Mesman, Judi. (2018). Does parenthood change implicit gender-role stereotypes and behaviors? *Journal of Marriage and Family*, *80*(1), 61–79.

Engelberts, Adèle C. & de Jonge, Guustaaf Adolf. (1990). Choice of sleeping position for infants: Possible association with cot death. *Archives of Disease in Childhood*, *65*(4), 462–467.

England, Paula & Bearak, Jonathan. (2014). The sexual double standard and gender differences in attitudes toward casual sex among U.S. university students. *Demographic Research*, *30*(46), 1327–1338.

Englander, Elizabeth. (2015). Coerced sexting and revenge porn among teens. *Bullying, Teen Aggression & Social Media*, *1*(2), 19–21.

English, Tammy & Carstensen, Laura L. (2014). Selective narrowing of social networks across adulthood is associated with improved emotional experience in daily life. *International Journal of Behavioral Development*, *38*(2), 195–202.

Ennis, Linda Rose (Ed.). (2014). *Intensive mothering: The cultural contradictions of modern motherhood.* Toronto: Demeter Press.

Enough Is Enough. (2017). *Cyberbullying statistics.* Great Falls, VA: Enough Is Enough.

Enserink, Martin. (2011). Can this DNA sleuth help catch criminals? *Science*, *331*(6019), 838–840.

Erickson, Anders C.; Ostry, Aleck; Chan, Hing Man & Arbour, Laura. (2016). Air pollution, neighbourhood and maternal-level factors modify the effect of smoking on birth weight: A multilevel analysis in British Columbia, Canada. *BMC Public Health*, *16*(1).

Erickson, Kirk I.; Miller, Destiny L.; Weinstein, Andrea M.; Akl, Stephanie L. & Banducci, Sarah. (2012). Physical activity and brain plasticity in late adulthood: A conceptual and comprehensive review. *Ageing Research*, *3*(1).

Erikson, Erik H. (1968). *Identity: Youth and crisis.* New York, NY: Norton.

Erikson, Erik H. (1982). *The life cycle completed: A review.* New York, NY: Norton.

Erikson, Erik H. (1993a). *Childhood and society* (2nd ed.). New York, NY: Norton.

Erikson, Erik H. (1993b). *Gandhi's truth: On the origins of militant nonviolence.* New York, NY: Norton.

Erikson, Erik H. (1994). *Identity: Youth and crisis.* New York, NY: Norton.

Erikson, Erik H. (1998). *The life cycle completed.* New York, NY: Norton.

Erikson, Erik H.; Erikson, Joan M. & Kivnick, Helen Q. (1986). *Vital involvement in old age.* New York, NY: Norton.

Erikson, Erik H.; Erikson, Joan M. & Kivnick, Helen Q. (1994). *Vital involvement in old age.* New York, NY: Norton.

Ernst, Monique. (2016). A tribute to the adolescent brain. *Neuroscience & Biobehavioral Reviews*, *70*, 334–338.

Erola, Jani; Jalonen, Sanni & Lehti, Hannu. (2016). Parental education, class and income over early life course and children's achievement. *Research in Social Stratification and Mobility, 44,* 33–43.

Erreygers, Sara; Vandebosch, Heidi; Vranjes, Ivana; Baillien, Elfi & De Witte, Hans. (2017). Nice or naughty? The role of emotions and digital media use in explaining adolescents' online prosocial and antisocial behavior. *Media Psychology, 20*(3), 374–400.

Errichiello, Luca; Iodice, Davide; Bruzzese, Dario; Gherghi, Marco & Senatore, Ignazio. (2016). Prognostic factors and outcome in anorexia nervosa: A follow-up study. *Eating and Weight Disorders, 21*(1), 73–82.

Esposito, Gianluca; Setoh, Peipei & Bornstein, Marc H. (2015). Beyond practices and values: Toward a physio-bioecological analysis of sleeping arrangements in early infancy. *Frontiers in Psychology, 6,* 264.

Espy, K. A.; Clark, C. A. C.; Garza, J. P.; Nelson, J. M.; James, T. D. & Choi, H.-J. (2016). Executive control in preschoolers: New models, new results, new implications. *Monographs of the Society for Research in Child Development, 81*(4), 111–128.

Esser, Marissa B.; Clayton, Heather; Demissie, Zewditu; Kanny, Dafna & Brewer, Robert D. (2017, May 12). *Current and binge drinking among high school students — United States, 1991–2015. Morbidity and Mortality Weekly Report, 66*(18), 474–478. Atlanta, GA: Centers for Disease Control and Prevention.

Evans, Angela D.; Xu, Fen & Lee, Kang. (2011). When all signs point to you: Lies told in the face of evidence. *Developmental Psychology, 47*(1), 39–49.

Evans, Gary W. & Kim, Pilyoung. (2013). Childhood poverty, chronic stress, self-regulation, and coping. *Child Development Perspectives, 7*(1), 43–48.

Evans, M. D. R.; Kelley, Jonathan; Sikora, Joanna & Treiman, Donald J. (2010). Family scholarly culture and educational success: Books and schooling in 27 nations. *Research in Social Stratification and Mobility, 28*(2), 171–197.

Everett, Caleb. (2017). *Numbers and the making of us: Counting and the course of human cultures.* Cambridge, MA: Harvard University Press.

Eymard, Amanda Singleton & Douglas, Dianna Hutto. (2012). Ageism among health care providers and interventions to improve their attitudes toward older adults: An integrative review. *Journal of Gerontological Nursing, 38*(5), 26–35.

Fadjukoff, Päivi & Kroger, Jane. (2016). Identity development in adulthood: Introduction. *Identity, 16*(1), 1–7.

Fairhurst, Merle T.; Löken, Line & Grossmann, Tobias. (2014). Physiological and behavioral responses reveal 9-month-old infants' sensitivity to pleasant touch. *Psychological Science, 25*(5), 1124–1131.

Fan, Hung; Conner, Ross F. & Villarreal, Luis P. (2014). *AIDS: Science and society* (7th ed.). Burlington, MA: Jones & Bartlett Learning.

Farber, Stu & Farber, Annalu. (2014). It ain't easy: Making life and death decisions before the crisis. In Leah Rogne & Susana Lauraine McCune (Eds.), *Advance care planning: Communicating about matters of life and death* (pp. 109–122). New York, NY: Springer.

Farrell, C.; Chappell, F.; Armitage, P. A.; Keston, P.; MacLullich, A.; Shenkin, S. & Wardlaw, J. M. (2009). Development and initial testing of normal reference MR images for the brain at ages 65–70 and 75–80 years. *European Radiology, 19*(1), 177–183.

Fazzi, Elisa; Signorini, Sabrina G.; Bomba, Monica; Luparia, Antonella; Lanners, Josée & Balottin, Umberto. (2011). Reach on sound: A key to object permanence in visually impaired children. *Early Human Development, 87*(4), 289–296.

FBI. (2015). *Crime in the United States, 2014.* Clarksburg, WV: U.S. Department of Justice, Federal Bureau of Investigation, Criminal Justice Information Services Division.

Feld, Barry C. (2013). *Kids, cops, and confessions: Inside the interrogation room.* New York, NY: New York University Press.

Feldman, Ruth. (2007). Parent-infant synchrony and the construction of shared timing; physiological precursors, developmental outcomes, and risk conditions. *Journal of Child Psychology and Psychiatry, 48*(3/4), 329–354.

Felicilda-Reynaldo, Rhea & Smith, Lucretia. (2018). Needs based frameworks. In Rose Utley, et al. (Eds.), *Frameworks for advanced nursing practice and research: Philosophies, theories, models, and taxonomies* (pp. 157–172). New York, NY: Springer.

Ferguson, Christopher J. (2013). Spanking, corporal punishment and negative long-term outcomes: A meta-analytic review of longitudinal studies. *Clinical Psychology Review, 33*(1), 196–208.

Ferguson, Gail M.; Iturbide, Maria I. & Gordon, Beverly P. (2014). Tridimensional (3D) acculturation: Ethnic identity and psychological functioning of tricultural Jamaican immigrants. *International Perspectives in Psychology: Research, Practice, Consultation, 3*(4), 238–251.

Fernando, Mario & Chowdhury, Rafi M. M. I. (2015). Cultivation of virtuousness and self-actualization in the workplace. In Alejo José G. Sison (Ed.), *Handbook of virtue ethics in business and management* (pp. 1–13). New York, NY: Springer.

Ferrah, Noha; Murphy, Briony J.; Ibrahim, Joseph E.; Bugeja, Lyndal C.; Winbolt, Margaret; LoGiudice, Dina, . . . Ranson, David L. (2015). Resident-to-resident physical aggression leading to injury in nursing homes: A systematic review. *Age and Ageing, 44*(3), 356–364.

Fields, R. Douglas. (2014). Myelin—More than insulation. *Science, 344*(6181), 264–266.

Figueiredo, B.; Canário, C. & Field, T. (2014). Breastfeeding is negatively affected by prenatal depression and reduces postpartum depression. *Psychological Medicine, 44*(5), 927–936.

Filippa, Manuela; Kuhn, Pierre & Westrup, Björn (Eds.). (2017). *Early vocal contact and preterm infant brain development: Bridging the gaps between research and practice.* Cham, Switzerland: Springer.

Fincham, Frank D. & Beach, Steven R. H. (2010). Of memes and marriage: Toward a positive relationship science. *Journal of Family Theory & Review, 2*(1), 4–24.

Fine, Cordelia. (2014). His brain, her brain? *Science, 346*(6212), 915–916.

Finer, Lawrence B. & Zolna, Mia R. (2016). Declines in unintended pregnancy in the United States, 2008–2011. *New England Journal of Medicine, 374,* 843–852.

Fingerman, Karen L.; Berg, Cynthia; Smith, Jacqui & Antonucci, Toni C. (2011). *Handbook of lifespan development.* New York, NY: Springer.

Fingerman, Karen L.; Cheng, Yen-Pi; Birditt, Kira & Zarit, Steven. (2012a). Only as happy as the least happy child: Multiple grown children's problems and successes and middle-aged parents' well-being. *The Journals of Gerontology Series B: Psychological Sciences and Social Sciences, 67B*(2), 184–193.

Fingerman, Karen L.; Cheng, Yen-Pi; Tighe, Lauren; Birditt, Kira S. & Zarit, Steve. (2012b). Relationships between young adults and their parents. In Alan Booth, et al. (Eds.), *Early adulthood in family context* (pp. 59–85). New York, NY: Springer.

Fingerman, Karen L.; Cheng, Yen-Pi; Wesselmann, Eric D.; Zarit, Steven; Furstenberg, Frank & Birditt, Kira S. (2012c). Helicopter parents and landing pad kids: Intense parental support of grown children. *Journal of Marriage and Family, 74*(4), 880–896.

Fingerman, Karen L. & Furstenberg, Frank F. (2012, May 30). You can go home again. *New York Times.*

Fingerman, Karen L.; Pillemer, Karl A.; Silverstein, Merril & Suitor, J. Jill. (2012d). The baby boomers' intergenerational relationships. *The Gerontologist, 52*(2), 199–209.

Finkel, Deborah; Andel, Ross; Gatz, Margaret & Pedersen, Nancy L. (2009). The role of occupational complexity in trajectories of cognitive aging before and after retirement. *Psychology and Aging, 24*(3), 563–573.

Finlay, Ilora G. & George, R. (2011). Legal physician-assisted suicide in Oregon and the Netherlands: Evidence concerning the impact on patients in vulnerable groups—Another perspective on Oregon's data. *Journal of Medical Ethics, 37*(3), 171–174.

Finn, Amy S.; Kraft, Matthew A.; West, Martin R.; Leonard, Julia A.; Bish, Crystal E.; Martin, Rebecca E., . . . Gabrieli, John D. E. (2014). Cognitive skills, student achievement tests, and schools. *Psychological Science, 25*(3), 736–744.

Fischer, Karin. (2016, May 1). When everyone goes to college: A lesson from South Korea. *The Chronicle of Higher Education.*

Fischhoff, Baruch; Parker, Andrew M.; Bruin, Wndi Bruine De; Downs, Julie; Palmgren, Claire; Dawes, Robyn & Manski, Charles F. (2000). Teen expectations for significant life events. *Public Opinion Quarterly, 64*(2), 189–205.

Fisher, Dorothy Canfield. (1922). *What grandmother did not know.* Boston: Pilgrim Press.

Fitzgerald, Maria. (2015). What do we really know about newborn infant pain? *Experimental Physiology, 100*(12), 1451–1457.

Flannery, Jessica E.; Beauchamp, Kathryn G. & Fisher, Philip A. (2017). The role of social buffering on chronic disruptions in quality of care: Evidence from caregiver-based interventions in foster children. *Social Neuroscience, 12*(1), 86–91.

Flegal, Katherine M.; Kit, Brian K.; Orpana, Heather & Graubard, Barry I. (2013). Association of all-cause mortality with overweight and obesity using standard body mass index categories: A systematic review and meta-analysis. *JAMA, 309*(1), 71–82.

Fleming, David J.; Cowen, Joshua M.; Witte, John F.; & Wolf, Patrick J. (2015). Similar students, different choices: Who uses a school voucher in an otherwise similar population of students? *Education and Urban Society, 47*(7), 785–812.

Fleming, Peter; Pease, Anna & Blair, Peter. (2015). Bed-sharing and unexpected infant deaths: What is the relationship? *Paediatric Respiratory Reviews, 16*(1), 62–67.

Fletcher, Erica N.; Whitaker, Robert C.; Marino, Alexis J. & Anderson, Sarah E. (2014). Screen time at home and school among low-income children attending Head Start. *Child Indicators Research, 7*(2), 421–436.

Fletcher, Garth J. O.; Simpson, Jeffry A.; Campbell, Lorne & Overall, Nickola C. (2015). Pair-bonding, romantic love, and evolution: The curious case of *Homo sapiens. Perspectives on Psychological Science, 10*(1), 20–36.

Fletcher, Richard; St. George, Jennifer & Freeman, Emily. (2013). Rough and tumble play quality: Theoretical foundations for a new measure of father–child interaction. *Early Child Development and Care, 183*(6), 746–759.

Flood, Meredith & Phillips, Kenneth D. (2007). Creativity in older adults: A plethora of possibilities. *Issues in Mental Health Nursing, 28*(4), 389–411.

Flynn, Heather Kohler; Felmlee, Diane H. & Conger, Rand D. (2017). The social context of adolescent friendships: Parents, peers, and romantic partners. *Youth & Society, 49*(5), 679–705.

Fontana, Luigi & Partridge, Linda. (2015). Promoting health and longevity through diet: From model organisms to humans. *Cell, 161*(1), 106–118.

Forbes, Deborah. (2012). The global influence of the Reggio Emilia Inspiration. In Robert Kelly (Ed.), *Educating for creativity: A global conversation* (pp. 161–172). Calgary, Canada: Brush Education.

Ford, Carole L. & Yore, Larry D. (2012). Toward convergence of critical thinking, metacognition, and reflection: Illustrations from natural and social sciences, teacher education, and classroom practice. In Anat Zohar & Yehudit Judy Dori (Eds.), *Metacognition in Science Education* (pp. 251–271). New York, NY: Springer.

Forestell, Catherine A. & Mennella, Julie A. (2017). The relationship between infant facial expressions and food acceptance. *Current Nutrition Reports, 6*(2), 141–147.

Forget-Dubois, Nadine; Dionne, Ginette; Lemelin, Jean-Pascal; Pérusse, Daniel; Tremblay, Richard E. & Boivin, Michel. (2009). Early child language mediates the relation between home environment and school readiness. *Child Development, 80*(3), 736–749.

Forrest, Walter. (2014). Cohabitation, relationship quality, and desistance from crime. *Journal of Marriage and Family, 76*(3), 539–556.

Foulkes, Lucy & Blakemore, Sarah-Jayne. (2018). Studying individual differences in human adolescent brain development. *Nature Neuroscience, 21*, 315–323.

Fox, Nathan A.; Henderson, Heather A.; Marshall, Peter J.; Nichols, Kate E. & Ghera, Melissa M. (2005). Behavioral inhibition: Linking biology and behavior within a developmental framework. *Annual Review of Psychology, 56*, 235–262.

Fox, Nathan A.; Henderson, Heather A.; Rubin, Kenneth H.; Calkins, Susan D. & Schmidt, Louis A. (2001). Continuity and discontinuity of behavioral inhibition and exuberance: Psychophysiological and behavioral influences across the first four years of life. *Child Development, 72*(1), 1–21.

Fox, Nathan A.; Reeb-Sutherland, Bethany C. & Degnan, Kathryn A. (2013). Personality and emotional development. In Philip D. Zelazo (Ed.), *The Oxford handbook of developmental psychology* (Vol. 2, pp. 15–44). New York, NY: Oxford University Press.

Franck, Caroline; Budlovsky, Talia; Windle, Sarah B.; Filion, Kristian B. & Eisenberg, Mark J. (2014). Electronic cigarettes in North America: History, use, and implications for smoking cessation. *Circulation, 129*(19), 1945–1952.

Franco, Manuel; Bilal, Usama; Orduñez, Pedro; Benet, Mikhail; Alain, Morejón; Benjamín, Caballero, . . . Cooper, Richard S. (2013). Population-wide weight loss and regain in relation to diabetes burden and cardiovascular mortality in Cuba 1980–2010: Repeated cross sectional surveys and ecological comparison of secular trends. *BMJ, 346*(7903), f1515.

Franco, Marcia R.; Tong, Allison; Howard, Kirsten; Sherrington, Catherine; Ferreira, Paulo H.; Pinto, Rafael Z. & Ferreira, Manuela L. (2015). Older people's perspectives on participation in physical activity: A systematic review and thematic synthesis of qualitative literature. *British Journal of Sports Medicine, 49*, 1268–1276.

Frankenburg, William K.; Dodds, Josiah; Archer, Philip; Shapiro, Howard & Bresnick, Beverly. (1992). The Denver II: A major revision and restandardization of the Denver Developmental Screening Test. *Pediatrics, 89*(1), 91–97.

Frederick, David A.; Lever, Janet; Gillespie, Brian Joseph & Garcia, Justin R. (2016). What keeps passion alive? Sexual satisfaction is associated with sexual communication, mood setting, sexual variety, oral sex, orgasm, and sex frequency in a national U.S. study. *The Journal of Sex Research*, (In Press).

Fredricks, Jennifer A. & Eccles, Jacquelynne S. (2002). Children's competence and value beliefs from childhood through adolescence: Growth trajectories in two male-sex-typed domains. *Developmental Psychology, 38*(4), 519–533.

Freeman, Joan. (2010). *Gifted lives: What happens when gifted children grow up?* New York, NY: Routledge.

Freese, Jeremy & Peterson, David. (2017). Replication in social science. *Annual Review of Sociology, 43*, 147–165.

Freud, Anna. (1958). Adolescence. *Psychoanalytic Study of the Child, 13*, 255–278.

Freud, Anna. (2000). Adolescence. In James B. McCarthy (Ed.), *Adolescent development and psychopathology* (pp. 29–52). Lanham, MD: University Press of America.

Freud, Anna & Burlingham, Dorothy T. (1943). *War and children*. New York, NY: Medical War Books.

Freud, Sigmund. (1935). *A general introduction to psychoanalysis.* New York, NY: Liveright.

Freud, Sigmund. (1938). *The basic writings of Sigmund Freud.* New York, NY: Modern Library.

Freud, Sigmund. (1989). *Introductory lectures on psycho-analysis.* New York, NY: Liveright.

Freud, Sigmund. (1995). *The basic writings of Sigmund Freud.* New York, NY: Modern Library.

Freud, Sigmund. (2001). An outline of psycho-analysis. In *The standard edition of the complete psychological works of Sigmund Freud* (Vol. 23). London, UK: Vintage.

Friedman, Naomi P. & Miyake, Akira. (2017). Unity and diversity of executive functions: Individual differences as a window on cognitive structure. *Cortex, 86*, 186–204.

Friend, Stephen H. & Schadt, Eric E. (2014). Clues from the resilient. *Science, 344*(6187), 970–972.

Frisina, Robert D. & Frisina, D. Robert. (2016). Hormone replacement therapy and its effects on human hearing. In Andrew H. Bass, et al. (Eds.), *Hearing and hormones* (pp. 191–209). New York, NY: Springer.

Frost, Randy O.; Steketee, Gail; Tolin, David F.; Sinopoli, Nicole & Ruby, Dylan. (2015). Motives for acquiring and saving in hoarding disorder, OCD, and community controls. *Journal of Obsessive-Compulsive and Related Disorders, 4*, 54–59.

Fry, Douglas P. (2014). Environment of evolutionary adaptedness, rough-and-tumble play, and the selection of restraint in human aggression. In Darcia Narvaez, et al. (Eds.), *Ancestral landscapes in human evolution: Culture, childrearing and social wellbeing* (pp. 169–188). New York, NY: Oxford University Press.

Fry, Richard. (2017, May 5). *It's becoming more common for young adults to live at home—and for longer stretches. Fact Tank.* Washington, DC: Pew Research Center.

Fuligni, Allison Sidle; Howes, Carollee; Huang, Yiching; Hong, Sandra Soliday & Lara-Cinisomo, Sandraluz. (2012). Activity settings and daily routines in preschool classrooms: Diverse experiences in early learning settings for low-income children. *Early Childhood Research Quarterly, 27*(2), 198–209.

Fuller, Bruce & García Coll, Cynthia. (2010). Learning from Latinos: Contexts, families, and child development in motion. *Developmental Psychology, 46*(3), 559–565.

Fuller-Iglesias, Heather R.; Webster, Noah J. & Antonucci, Toni C. (2013). Adult family relationships in the context of friendship. *Research in Human Development, 10*(2), 184–203.

Fulmer, C. Ashley; Gelfand, Micheke J.; Kruglanski, Arie W.; Kim-Prieto, Chu; Diener, Ed; Pierro, Antonio & Higgins, E. Tory. (2010). On "feeling right" in cultural contexts: How person-culture match affects self-esteem and subjective well-being. *Psychological Science, 21*(11), 1563–1569.

Furey, Terrence S. & Sethupathy, Praveen. (2013). Genetics driving epigenetics. *Science, 342*(6159), 705–706.

Furman, Wyndol & Shaffer, Laura. (2011). Romantic partners, friends, friends with benefits, and casual acquaintances as sexual partners. *Journal of Sex Research, 48*(6), 554–564.

Furukawa, Emi; Tangney, June & Higashibara, Fumiko. (2012). Cross-cultural continuities and discontinuities in shame, guilt, and pride: A study of children residing in Japan, Korea and the USA. *Self and Identity, 11*(1), 90–113.

Fusaro, Maria & Harris, Paul L. (2013). Dax gets the nod: Toddlers detect and use social cues to evaluate testimony. *Developmental Psychology, 49*(3), 514–522.

Gabrieli, John D. E. (2009). Dyslexia: A new synergy between education and cognitive neuroscience. *Science, 325*(5938), 280–283.

Galak, Jeff; Givi, Julian & Williams, Elanor F. (2016). Why certain gifts are great to give but not to get: A framework for understanding errors in gift giving. *Current Directions in Psychological Science, 25*(6), 380–385.

Galasso, Vincenzo; Profeta, Paola; Pronzato, Chiara & Billari, Francesco. (2017). Information and women's intentions: Experimental evidence about child care. *European Journal of Population, 33*(1), 109–128.

Galatzer-Levy, Isaac R. & Bonanno, George A. (2012). Beyond normality in the study of bereavement: Heterogeneity in depression outcomes following loss in older adults. *Social Science & Medicine, 74*(12), 1987–1994.

Gambaro, Ludovica; Stewart, Kitty & Waldfogel, Jane (Eds.). (2014). *An equal start?: Providing quality early education and care for disadvantaged children.* Chicago, IL: Policy Press.

Ganapathy, Thilagavathy. (2014). Couvade syndrome among 1st time expectant fathers. *Muller Journal of Medical Science Research, 5*(1), 43–47.

Ganong, Lawrence H.; Coleman, Marilyn & Jamison, Tyler. (2011). Patterns of stepchild–stepparent relationship development. *Journal of Marriage and Family, 73*(2), 396–413.

Gao, Sujuan; Unverzagt, Frederick W.; Hall, Kathleen S.; Lane, Kathleen A.; Murrell, Jill R.; Hake, Ann M., . . . Hendrie, Hugh C. (2014). Mild cognitive impairment, incidence, progression, and reversion: Findings from a community-based cohort of elderly African Americans. *The American Journal of Geriatric Psychiatry, 22*(7), 670–681.

Gao, Wei; Lin, Weili; Grewen, Karen & Gilmore, John H. (2017). Functional connectivity of the infant human brain: Plastic and modifiable. *The Neuroscientist, 23*(2), 169–184.

Gao, Yuan; Huang, Changquan; Zhao, Kexiang; Ma, Louyan; Qiu, Xuan; Zhang, Lei, . . . Xiao, Qian. (2013). Depression as a risk factor for dementia and mild cognitive impairment: A meta-analysis of longitudinal studies. *International Journal of Geriatric Psychiatry, 28*(5), 441–449.

Garces-Foley, Kathleen (Ed.). (2015). *Death and religion in a changing world.* New York, NY: Routledge.

Garcia, Elisa B. (2018). The classroom language context and English and Spanish vocabulary development among dual language learners attending Head Start. *Early Childhood Research Quarterly, 42*, 148–157.

García Coll, Cynthia T. & Marks, Amy K. (2012). *The immigrant paradox in children and adolescents: Is becoming American a developmental risk?* Washington, DC: American Psychological Association.

Gardner, Howard. (1983). *Frames of mind: The theory of multiple intelligences.* New York, NY: Basic Books.

Gardner, Howard. (1999). Are there additional intelligences? The case for naturalist, spiritual, and existential intelligences. In Jeffrey Kane (Ed.), *Education, information, and transformation: Essays on learning and thinking* (pp. 111–131). Upper Saddle River, NJ: Merrill.

Gardner, Howard. (2006). *Multiple intelligences: New horizons in theory and practice.* New York, NY: Basic Books.

Gardner, Howard. (2011). *Frames of mind: The theory of multiple intelligences.* New York, NY: Basic Books.

Gardner, Howard & Moran, Seana. (2006). The science of multiple intelligences theory: A response to Lynn Waterhouse. *Educational Psychologist, 41*(4), 227–232.

Gardner, Paula & Hudson, Bettie L. (1996). *Advance report of final mortality statistics, 1993. Monthly Vital Statistics Report, 44*(7, Suppl.). Hyattsville, MD: National Center for Health Statistics.

Garrett, Mallory. (2018). "It Gets Better" media campaign and gay youth suicide. In Chuck Stewart (Ed.), *Lesbian, gay, bisexual, and transgender Americans at risk: Problems and solutions* (pp. 119–128). New York, NY: Praeger.

Garthus-Niegel, Susan; Ayers, Susan; Martini, Julia; von Soest, Tilmann & Eberhard-Gran, Malin. (2017). The impact of postpartum post-traumatic stress disorder symptoms on child development: A population-based, 2-year follow-up study. *Psychological Medicine, 47*(1), 161–170.

Gaskins, Audrey Jane; Mendiola, Jaime; Afeiche, Myriam; Jørgensen, Niels; Swan, Shanna H. & Chavarro, Jorge E. (2013). Physical activity and television watching in relation to semen quality in young men. *British Journal of Sports Medicine, 49*(4), 265–270.

Gassin, Elizabeth A. (2017). Forgiveness and continuing bonds. In Dennis Klass & Edith Maria Steffen (Eds.), *Continuing bonds in bereavement: New directions for research and practice.* New York, NY: Routledge.

Gawande, Atul. (2014). *Being mortal: Medicine and what matters in the end.* New York, NY: Metropolitan Books.

Geiger, Abigail. (2016, October 12). *Support for marijuana legalization continues to rise. Fact Tank.* Washington, DC: Pew Research Center.

Geiger, Jennifer Mullins; Hayes, Megan J. & Lietz, Cynthia A. (2013). Should I stay or should I go? A mixed methods study examining the factors influencing foster parents' decisions to continue or discontinue providing foster care. *Children and Youth Services Review, 35*(9), 1356–1365.

Gellert, Anna S. & Elbro, Carsten. (2017). Does a dynamic test of phonological awareness predict early reading difficulties? A longitudinal study from kindergarten through grade 1. *Journal of Learning Disabilities, 50*(3), 227–237.

George, Linda G.; Helson, Ravenna & John, Oliver P. (2011). The "CEO" of women's work lives: How Big Five Conscientiousness, Extraversion, and Openness predict 50 years of work experiences in a changing sociocultural context. *Journal of Personality and Social Psychology, 101*(4), 812–830.

George, Madeleine J. & Odgers, Candice L. (2015). Seven fears and the science of how mobile technologies may be influencing adolescents in the digital age. *Perspectives on Psychological Science, 10*(6), 832–851.

George, Madeleine J.; Russell, Michael A.; Piontak, Joy R. & Odgers, Candice L. (2018). Concurrent and subsequent associations between daily digital technology use and high-risk adolescents' mental health symptoms. *Child Development, 89*(1), 78–88.

Georgeson, Jan & Payler, Jane (Eds.). (2013). *International perspectives on early childhood education and care.* New York, NY: Open University Press.

Gerber, Alan S.; Huber, Gregory A.; Doherty, David & Dowling, Conor M. (2011). The Big Five personality traits in the political arena. *Annual Review of Political Science, 14*, 265–287.

Gershoff, Elizabeth T.; Lansford, Jennifer E.; Sexton, Holly R.; Davis-Kean, Pamela & Sameroff, Arnold J.

(2012). Longitudinal links between spanking and children's externalizing behaviors in a national sample of White, Black, Hispanic, and Asian American families. *Child Development, 83*(3), 838–843.

Gershoff, Elizabeth T.; Purtell, Kelly M. & Holas, Igor. (2015). *Corporal punishment in U.S. public schools: Legal precedents, current practices, and future policy.* New York, NY: Springer.

Gerstorf, Denis; Heckhausen, Jutta; Ram, Nilam; Infurna, Frank J.; Schupp, Jürgen & Wagner, Gert G. (2014). Perceived personal control buffers terminal decline in well-being. *Psychology and Aging, 29*(3), 612–625.

Gervais, Will M. & Norenzayan, Ara. (2012). Analytic thinking promotes religious disbelief. *Science, 336*(6080), 493–496.

Gewertz, Catherine. (2017, May 3). Is the high school graduation rate inflated? No, study says [Web log post]. Education Week.

Gibb, Robbin & Kovalchuk, Anna. (2017). Brain development. In Robbin Gibb & Bryan Kolb (Eds.), *The neurobiology of brain and behavioral development.* San Diego, CA: Academic Press.

Gibbons, Ann. (2017). How Africans evolved a palette of skin tones. *Science, 358*(6360), 157–158.

Gibbons, Frederick X.; Kingsbury, John H. & Gerrard, Meg. (2012a). Social-psychological theories and adolescent health risk behavior. *Social and Personality Psychology Compass, 6*(2), 70–183.

Gibbons, Luz; Belizan, José M.; Lauer, Jeremy A.; Betran, Ana P.; Merialdi, Mario & Althabe, Fernando. (2012b). Inequities in the use of cesarean section deliveries in the world. *American Journal of Obstetrics and Gynecology, 206*(4), 331.e331–331.e319.

Giblin, Chris. (2014). Travis Pastrana makes comeback for Red Bull's inaugural straight rhythm competition. *Men's Fitness.*

Gibson-Davis, Christina & Rackin, Heather. (2014). Marriage or carriage? Trends in union context and birth type by education. *Journal of Marriage and Family, 76*(3), 506–519.

Gignac, Gilles E. (2016). On the evaluation of competing theories: A reply to van der Maas and Kan. *Intelligence, 57,* 84–86.

Gilbert, Richard B. (2013). Religion, spirituality, and end-of-life decision making. In David K. Meagher & David E. Balk (Eds.), *Handbook of thanatology: The essential body of knowledge for the study of death, dying, and bereavement* (2nd ed., pp. 63–71). New York, NY: Routledge.

Giles, Amy & Rovee-Collier, Carolyn. (2011). Infant long-term memory for associations formed during mere exposure. *Infant Behavior and Development, 34*(2), 327–338.

Gilles, Floyd H. & Nelson, Marvin D. (2012). *The developing human brain: Growth and adversities.* London, UK: Mac Keith Press.

Gillespie, Brian Joseph; Frederick, David; Harari, Lexi & Grov, Christian. (2015). Homophily, close friendship, and life satisfaction among gay, lesbian, heterosexual, and bisexual men and women. *PLoS ONE, 10*(6), e0128900.

Gilligan, Carol. (1982). *In a different voice: Psychological theory and women's development.* Cambridge, MA: Harvard University Press.

Gillis, John R. (2013). *Youth and history: Tradition and change in European age relations, 1770–present* (Expanded student ed.). San Diego, CA: Academic Press.

Giluk, Tamara L. & Postlethwaite, Bennett E. (2015). Big Five personality and academic dishonesty: A meta-analytic review. *Personality and Individual Differences, 72*(5), 59–67.

Giumetti, Gary W. & Kowalski, Robin M. (2015). Cyberbullying matters: Examining the incremental impact of cyberbullying on outcomes over and above traditional bullying in North America. In Raúl Navarro, et al. (Eds.), *Cyberbullying across the globe: Gender, family, and mental health* (pp. 117–130). New York, NY: Springer.

Glance, Laurent G.; Dick, Andrew W.; Glantz, Christopher; Wissler, Richard N.; Qian, Feng; Marroquin, Bridget M., . . . Kellermann, Arthur L. (2014). Rates of major obstetrical complications vary almost fivefold among US hospitals. *Health Affairs, 33*(8), 1330–1336.

Glauber, Rebecca & Day, Melissa D. (2018). Gender, spousal caregiving, and depression: Does paid work matter? *Journal of Marriage and Family, 80*(2), 537–554.

Global Burden of Disease Neurological Disorders Collaborator Group. (2017). Global, regional, and national burden of neurological disorders during 1990–2015: A systematic analysis for the Global Burden of Disease Study 2015. *The Lancet Neurology, 16*(11), 877–897.

Gobet, Fernand & Charness, Neil. (2018). Expertise in chess. In K. Anders Ericsson, et al. (Eds.), *The Cambridge handbook of expertise and expert performance* (2nd ed., pp. 597–615). New York, NY: Cambridge University Press.

Goddings, Anne-Lise & Giedd, Jay N. (2014). Structural brain development during childhood and adolescence. In Michael S. Gazzaniga & George R. Mangun (Eds.), *The cognitive neurosciences* (5th ed., pp. 15–22). Cambridge, MA: MIT Press.

Goddings, Anne-Lise; Heyes, Stephanie Burnett; Bird, Geoffrey; Viner, Russell M. & Blakemore, Sarah-Jayne. (2012). The relationship between puberty and social emotion processing. *Developmental Science, 15*(6), 801–811.

Godinet, Meripa T.; Li, Fenfang & Berg, Teresa. (2014). Early childhood maltreatment and trajectories of behavioral problems: Exploring gender and racial differences. *Child Abuse & Neglect, 38*(3), 544–556.

Gogtay, Nitin; Giedd, Jay N.; Lusk, Leslie; Hayashi, Kiralee M.; Greenstein, Deanna; Vaituzis, A. Catherine, . . . Ungerleider, Leslie G. (2004). Dynamic mapping of human cortical development during childhood through early adulthood. *Proceedings of the National Academy of Sciences of the United States of America, 101*(21), 8174–8179.

Goh, Esther C. L. (2011). *China's one-child policy and multiple caregiving: Raising little suns in Xiamen.* New York, NY: Routledge.

Golant, Stephen M. (2011). The changing residential environments of older people. In Robert H. Binstock & Linda K. George (Eds.), *Handbook of aging and the social sciences* (7th ed., pp. 207–220). San Diego, CA: Academic Press.

Golden, Marita. (2010). Angel baby. In Barbara Graham (Ed.), *Eye of my heart: 27 writers reveal the hidden pleasures and perils of being a grandmother* (pp. 125–133). New York, NY: HarperCollins.

Goldfarb, Sally F. (2014). Who pays for the 'boomerang generation'?: A legal perspective on financial support for young adults. *Harvard Journal of Law and Gender, 37*, 46–106.

Goldin-Meadow, Susan. (2015). From action to abstraction: Gesture as a mechanism of change. *Developmental Review, 38*, 167–184.

Goldin-Meadow, Susan & Alibali, Martha W. (2013). Gesture's role in speaking, learning, and creating language. *Annual Review of Psychology, 64*, 257–283.

Goldman, Dana P.; Cutler, David; Rowe, John W.; Michaud, Pierre-Carl; Sullivan, Jeffrey; Peneva, Desi & Olshansky, S. Jay. (2013). Substantial health and economic returns from delayed aging may warrant a new focus for medical research. *Health Affairs, 32*(10), 1698–1705.

Goldman-Mellor, Sidra; Caspi, Avshalom; Arseneault, Louise; Ajala, Nifemi; Ambler, Antony; Danese, Andrea, . . . Moffitt, Terrie E. (2016). Committed to work but vulnerable: Self-perceptions and mental health in NEET 18-year-olds from a contemporary British cohort. *Journal of Child Psychology and Psychiatry, 57*(2), 196–203.

Goldschmidt, Andrea B.; Wall, Melanie M.; Zhang, Jun; Loth, Katie A. & Neumark-Sztainer, Dianne. (2016). Over-eating and binge eating in emerging adulthood: 10-year stability and risk factors. *Developmental Psychology, 52*(3), 475–483.

Goldstein, Sam; Princiotta, Dana & Naglieri, Jack A. (Eds.). (2015). *Handbook of intelligence: Evolutionary theory, historical perspective, and current concepts.* New York, NY: Springer.

Golinkoff, Roberta M. & Hirsh-Pasek, Kathy. (2016). *Becoming brilliant: What science tells us about raising successful children.* Washington, DC: American Psychological Association.

Göncü, Artin & Gaskins, Suzanne. (2011). Comparing and extending Piaget's and Vygotsky's understandings of play: Symbolic play as individual, sociocultural, and educational interpretation. In Anthony D. Pellegrini (Ed.), *The Oxford handbook of the development of play* (pp. 48–57). New York, NY: Oxford University Press.

Goniewicz, Maciej L.; Gawron, Michal; Smith, Danielle M.; Peng, Margaret; Jacob, Peyton & Benowitz, Neal L. (2017). Exposure to nicotine and selected toxicants in cigarette smokers who switched to electronic cigarettes: A longitudinal within-subjects observational study. *Nicotine & Tobacco Research, 19*(2), 160–167.

Gonyea, Judith G. (2013). Midlife, multigenerational bonds, and caregiving. In Ronda C. Talley & Rhonda J. V. Montgomery (Eds.), *Caregiving across the lifespan: Research, practice, policy* (pp. 105–130). New York, NY: Springer.

González, Roberto; Lickel, Brian; Gupta, Manisha; Tropp, Linda R.; Luengo Kanacri, Bernadette P.; Mora, Eduardo, . . . Bernardino, Michelle. (2017). Ethnic identity development and acculturation preferences among minority and majority youth: Norms and contact. *Child Development, 88*(3), 743–760.

Goodkind, Daniel. (2017). The astonishing population averted by China's birth restrictions: Estimates, nightmares, and reprogrammed ambitions. *Demography, 54*(4), 1375–1400.

Goodlad, James K.; Marcus, David K. & Fulton, Jessica J. (2013). Lead and Attention-deficit/hyperactivity disorder (ADHD) symptoms: A meta-analysis. *Clinical Psychology Review, 33*(3), 417–425.

Goodman, Madeline J.; Sands, Anita M. & Coley, Richard J. (2015). *America's skills challenge: Millennials and the future.* Princeton, NJ: Educational Testing Service.

Goodnight, Jackson A.; D'Onofrio, Brian M.; Cherlin, Andrew J.; Emery, Robert E.; Van Hulle, Carol A. & Lahey, Benjamin B. (2013). Effects of multiple maternal relationship transitions on offspring antisocial behavior in childhood and adolescence: A cousin-comparison analysis. *Journal of Abnormal Child Psychology, 41*(2), 185–198.

Gopnik, Alison. (2012). Scientific thinking in young children: Theoretical advances, empirical research, and policy implications. *Science, 337*(6102), 1623–1627.

Gopnik, Alison. (2016). *The gardener and the carpenter: What the new science of child development tells us about the relationship between parents and children.* New York, NY: Farrar, Strauss and Giroux.

Gordon-Hollingsworth, Arlene T.; Becker, Emily M.; Ginsburg, Golda S.; Keeton, Courtney; Compton, Scott N.; Birmaher, Boris B., . . . March, John S. (2015). Anxiety disorders in Caucasian and African American children: A comparison of clinical characteristics, treatment process variables, and treatment outcomes. *Child Psychiatry & Human Development, 46*(5), 643–655.

Gough, Ethan K.; Moodie, Erica E. M.; Prendergast, Andrew J.; Johnson, Sarasa M. A.; Humphrey, Jean H.; Stoltzfus, Rebecca J., . . . Manges, Amee R. (2014). The impact of antibiotics on growth in children in low and middle income countries: Systematic review and meta-analysis of randomised controlled trials. *BMJ, 348*, g2267.

Government of India, Ministry of Home Affairs. (2011). Population in five year age-group by residence and sex.

Govindaraju, Diddahally; Atzmon, Gil & Barzilai, Nir. (2015). Genetics, lifestyle and longevity: Lessons from centenarians. *Applied & Translational Genomics, 4*(Suppl. 1), 23–32.

Gow, Alan J.; Johnson, Wendy; Pattie, Alison; Brett, Caroline E.; Roberts, Beverly; Starr, John M. & Deary, Ian J. (2011). Stability and change in intelligence from age 11 to ages 70, 79, and 87: The Lothian Birth Cohorts of 1921 and 1936. *Psychology and Aging, 26*(1), 232–240.

Grady, Denise. (2012, May 5). When illness makes a spouse a stranger. *New York Times.*

Grady, Jessica S.; Ale, Chelsea M. & Morris, Tracy L. (2012). A naturalistic observation of social behaviours during preschool drop-off. *Early Child Development and Care, 182*(12), 1683–1694.

Grady, Sue C.; Frake, April N.; Zhang, Qiong; Bene, Matlhogonolo; Jordan, Demetrice R.; Vertalka, Joshua, . . . Kutch, Libbey. (2017). Neonatal mortality in East Africa and West Africa: A geographic analysis of district-level demographic and health survey data. *Geospatial Health, 12*(1).

Graf, William D.; Miller, Geoffrey; Epstein, Leon G. & Rapin, Isabelle. (2017). The autism "epidemic": Ethical, legal, and social issues in a developmental spectrum disorder. *Neurology, 88*(14), 1371–1380.

**Graham, Eileen K.; Rutsohn, Joshua P.; Turiano, Nicholas A.; Bendayan, Rebecca; Batterham, Philip J.; Gerstorf,

Denis, . . . Piccinin, Andrea M. (2017). Personality predicts mortality risk: An integrative data analysis of 15 international longitudinal studies. *Journal of Research in Personality, 70*, 174–186.

Granqvist, Pehr & Kirkpatrick, Lee A. (2013). Religion, spirituality, and attachment. In Kenneth I. Pargament (Ed.), *APA handbook of psychology, religion, and spirituality* (Vol. 1). Washington, DC: American Psychological Association.

Grayson, David S. & Fair, Damien A. (2017). Development of large-scale functional networks from birth to adulthood: A guide to the neuroimaging literature. *NeuroImage, 160*, 15–31.

Grazioplene, Rachael G.; Ryman, Sephira G.; Gray, Jeremy R.; Rustichini, Aldo; Jung, Rex E. & DeYoung, Colin G. (2015). Subcortical intelligence: Caudate volume predicts IQ in healthy adults. *Human Brain Mapping, 36*(4), 1407–1416.

Greco, Daniel. (2014). Could KK be OK? *The Journal of Philosophy, 111*(4), 169–197.

Green, James A.; Whitney, Pamela G. & Potegal, Michael. (2011). Screaming, yelling, whining, and crying: Categorical and intensity differences in vocal expressions of anger and sadness in children's tantrums. *Emotion, 11*(5), 1124–1133.

Green, Lorraine & Grant, Victoria. (2008). "Gagged grief and beleaguered bereavements?" An analysis of multidisciplinary theory and research relating to same sex partnership bereavement. *Sexualities, 11*(3), 275–300.

Green, Ronald. (2015). Designer babies. In Henk ten Have (Ed.), *Encyclopedia of global bioethics*. Living Reference Work: Springer International Publishing.

Greene, Melissa L. & Way, Niobe. (2005). Self-esteem trajectories among ethnic minority adolescents: A growth curve analysis of the patterns and predictors of change. *Journal of Research on Adolescence, 15*(2), 151–178.

Greenfield, Emily A.; Scharlach, Andrew; Lehning, Amanda J. & Davitt, Joan K. (2012). A conceptual framework for examining the promise of the NORC program and Village models to promote aging in place. *Journal of Aging Studies, 26*(3), 273–284.

Greenough, William T.; Black, James E. & Wallace, Christopher S. (1987). Experience and brain development. *Child Development, 58*(3), 539–559.

Greenwood, Pamela M. & Parasuraman, R. (2012). *Nurturing the older brain and mind*. Cambridge, MA: MIT Press.

Gregory, Sara M.; Parker, Beth & Thompson, Paul D. (2012). Physical activity, cognitive function, and brain health: What is the role of exercise training in the prevention of dementia? *Brain Sciences, 2*(4), 684–708.

Greitemeyer, Tobias. (2014). Intense acts of violence during video game play make daily life aggression appear innocuous: A new mechanism why violent video games increase aggression. *Journal of Experimental Social Psychology, 50*, 52–56.

Greyson, Bruce. (2009). Near-death experiences and deathbed visions. In Allan Kellehear (Ed.), *The study of dying: From autonomy to transformation* (pp. 253–275). New York, NY: Cambridge University Press.

Griffin, Martyn. (2011). Developing deliberative minds: Piaget, Vygotsky and the deliberative democratic citizen. *Journal of Public Deliberation, 7*(1).

Griffith, Patrick & Lopez, Oscar. (2009). Disparities in the diagnosis and treatment of Alzheimer's disease in African American and Hispanic patients: A call to action. *Generations, 33*(1), 37–46.

Grimes, David Robert & Bishop, Dorothy V. M. (2018). Distinguishing polemic from commentary in science: Some guidelines illustrated with the case of Sage and Burgio (2017). *Child Development, 89*(1), 141–147.

Grivell, Rosalie M.; Reilly, Aimee J.; Oakey, Helena; Chan, Annabelle & Dodd, Jodie M. (2012). Maternal and neonatal outcomes following induction of labor: A cohort study. *Acta Obstetricia et Gynecologica Scandinavica, 91*(2), 198–203.

Grobman, Kevin H. (2008). Learning & teaching developmental psychology: Attachment theory, infancy, & infant memory development. DevPsy.

Grogan-Kaylor, Andrew; Ma, Julie & Graham-Bermann, Sandra A. (2018). The case against physical punishment. *Current Opinion in Psychology, 19*, 22–27.

Groh, Ashley M.; Narayan, Angela J.; Bakermans-Kranenburg, Marian J.; Roisman, Glenn I.; Vaughn, Brian E.; Fearon, R. M. Pasco & van IJzendoorn, Marinus H. (2017). Attachment and temperament in the early life course: A meta-analytic review. *Child Development, 88*(3), 770–795.

Groh, Ashley M.; Roisman, Glenn I.; van IJzendoorn, Marinus H.; Bakermans-Kranenburg, Marian J. & Fearon, R. Pasco. (2012). The significance of insecure and disorganized attachment for children's internalizing symptoms: A meta-analytic study. *Child Development, 83*(2), 591–610.

Gross, James J. (Ed.). (2014). *Handbook of emotion regulation* (2nd ed.). New York, NY: Guilford Press.

Grossmann, Klaus E.; Bretherton, Inge; Waters, Everett & Grossmann, Karin (Eds.). (2014). *Mary Ainsworth's enduring influence on attachment theory, research, and clinical applications*. New York, NY: Routledge.

Grossmann, Tobias. (2017). The eyes as windows into other minds: An integrative perspective. *Perspectives on Psychological Science, 12*(1), 107–121.

Grotevant, Harold D. & McDermott, Jennifer M. (2014). Adoption: Biological and social processes linked to adaptation. *Annual Review of Psychology, 65*, 235–265.

Grusec, Joan E.; Danyliuk, Tanya; Kil, Hali & O'Neill, David. (2017). Perspectives on parent discipline and child outcomes. *International Journal of Behavioral Development, 41*(4), 465–471.

Guerra, Nancy G.; Williams, Kirk R. & Sadek, Shelly. (2011). Understanding bullying and victimization during childhood and adolescence: A mixed methods study. *Child Development, 82*(1), 295–310.

Guerri, Consuelo & Pascual, María. (2010). Mechanisms involved in the neurotoxic, cognitive, and neurobehavioral effects of alcohol consumption during adolescence. *Alcohol, 44*(1), 15–26.

Guhn, Martin; Schonert-Reichl, Kim; Gadermann, Anne; Hymel, Shelley & Hertzman, Clyde. (2013). A population study of victimization, relationships, and well-being in middle childhood. *Journal of Happiness Studies, 14*(5), 1529–1541.

Gulbas, L. E.; Zayas, L. H.; Yoon, H.; Szlyk, H.; Aguilar-Gaxiola, S. & Natera, G. (2016). Deportation experiences and depression among U.S. citizen-children with undocumented Mexican parents. *Child, 42*(2), 220–230.

Güngör, Derya; Bornstein, Marc H.; De Leersnyder, Jozefien; Cote, Linda; Ceulemans, Eva & Mesquita, Batja. (2013). Acculturation of personality: A three-culture study of Japanese, Japanese Americans, and European Americans. *Journal of Cross-Cultural Psychology, 44*(5), 701–718.

Gurunath, Sumana; Pandian, Z.; Anderson, Richard A. & Bhattacharya, Siladitya. (2011). Defining infertility—A systematic review of prevalence studies. *Human Reproduction Update, 17*(5), 575–588.

Guzman, Natalie S. de & Nishina, Adrienne. (2014). A longitudinal study of body dissatisfaction and pubertal timing in an ethnically diverse adolescent sample. *Body Image, 11*(1), 68–71.

Guzzo, Karen Benjamin. (2014). Trends in cohabitation outcomes: Compositional changes and engagement among never-married young adults. *Journal of Marriage and Family, 76*(4), 826–842.

Gyllenberg, Frida; Juselius, Mikael; Gissler, Mika & Heikinheimo, Oskari. (2018). Long-acting reversible contraception free of charge, method initiation, and abortion rates in Finland. *American Journal of Public Health, 108*(4), 538–543.

Gypen, Laura; Vanderfaeillie, Johan; De Maeyer, Skrallan; Belenger, Laurence & Van Holen, Frank. (2017). Outcomes of children who grew up in foster care: Systematic-review. *Children and Youth Services Review, 76*, 74–83.

Haas, Steven A.; Krueger, Patrick M. & Rohlfsen, Leah. (2012). Race/ethnic and nativity disparities in later life physical performance: The role of health and socioeconomic status over the life course. *The Journals of Gerontology Series B: Psychological Sciences and Social Sciences, 67*(2), 238–248.

Hackett, Geoffrey Ian. (2016). Testosterone replacement therapy and mortality in older men. *Drug Safety, 39*(2), 117–130.

Hahn-Holbrook, Jennifer & Haselton, Martie. (2014). Is postpartum depression a disease of modern civilization? *Current Directions in Psychological Science, 23*(6), 395–400.

Haidt, Jonathan. (2013). *The righteous mind: Why good people are divided by politics and religion.* New York, NY: Vintage Books.

Hajek, Peter; Etter, Jean-François; Benowitz, Neal; Eissenberg, Thomas & McRobbie, Hayden. (2014). Electronic cigarettes: Review of use, content, safety, effects on smokers and potential for harm and benefit. *Addiction, 109*(11), 1801–1810.

Hales, Craig M.; Carroll, Margaret D.; Fryar, Cheryl D. & Ogden, Cynthia L. (2017, October). *Prevalence of obesity among adults and youth: United States, 2015–2016.* Atlanta, GA: Centers for Disease Control and Prevention: National Center for Health Statistics.

Halim, May Ling; Ruble, Diane N.; Tamis-LeMonda, Catherine S.; Zosuls, Kristina M.; Lurye, Leah E. & Greulich, Faith K. (2014). Pink frilly dresses and the avoidance of all things "girly": Children's appearance rigidity and cognitive theories of gender development. *Developmental Psychology, 50*(4), 1091–1101.

Hall, Jeffrey A. (2011). Sex differences in friendship expectations: A meta-analysis. *Journal of Social and Personal Relationships, 28*(6), 723–747.

Hall, Kelli Stidham; Sales, Jessica McDermott; Komro, Kelli A. & Santelli, John. (2016). The state of sex education in the United States. *Journal of Adolescent Health, 58*(6), 595–597.

Hall, Lynn K. (2008). *Counseling military families: What mental health professionals need to know.* New York, NY: Taylor & Francis.

Hall, Matthew L.; Eigsti, Inge-Marie; Bortfeld, Heather & Lillo-Martin, Diane. (2017). Auditory deprivation does not impair executive function, but language deprivation might: Evidence from a parent-report measure in deaf native signing children. *Journal of Deaf Studies and Deaf Education, 22*(1), 9–21.

Hall, Victoria; Banerjee, Emily; Kenyon, Cynthia; Strain, Anna; Griffith, Jayne; Como-Sabetti, Kathryn, . . . Ehresmann, Kristen. (2017, July 14). *Measles outbreak—Minnesota April–May 2017. Morbidity and Mortality Weekly Report, 66*(27), 713–717. Atlanta, GA: Centers for Disease Control and Prevention.

Hallers-Haalboom, Elizabeth T.; Mesman, Judi; Groeneveld, Marleen G.; Endendijk, Joyce J.; van Berkel, Sheila R.; van der Pol, Lotte D. & Bakermans-Kranenburg, Marian J. (2014). Mothers, fathers, sons and daughters: Parental sensitivity in families with two children. *Journal of Family Psychology, 28*(2), 138–147.

Halpern, Neil A.; Pastores, Stephen M.; Chou, Joanne F.; Chawla, Sanjay & Thaler, Howard T. (2011). Advance directives in an oncologic intensive care unit: A contemporary analysis of their frequency, type, and impact. *Journal of Palliative Medicine, 14*(4), 483–489.

Halpern-Meekin, Sarah; Manning, Wendy D.; Giordano, Peggy C. & Longmore, Monica A. (2013). Relationship churning, physical violence, and verbal abuse in young adult relationships. *Journal of Marriage and Family, 75*(1), 2–12.

Hambrick, David Z.; Macnamara, Brooke N.; Campitelli, Guillermo; Ullén, Fredrik & Mosing, Miriam A. (2016). Beyond born versus made: A new look at expertise. *Psychology of Learning and Motivation, 64*, 1–55.

Hamdy, Sherine. (2018). All eyes on Egypt: Islam and the medical use of dead bodies amidst Cairo's political unrest. In Antonius C. G. M. Robben (Ed.), *Death, mourning, and burial: A cross-cultural reader* (pp. 102–114). Hoboken, NJ: Wiley-Blackwell.

Hamerton, John L. & Evans, Jane A. (2005). Sex chromosome anomalies. In Merlin G. Butler & F. John Meaney (Eds.), *Genetics of developmental disabilities* (pp. 585–650). Boca Raton, FL: Taylor & Francis.

Hamill, Paul J. (1991). Triage: An essay. *The Georgia Review, 45*(3), 463–469.

Hamilton, Alice. (1914). Lead poisoning in the United States. *American Journal of Public Health, 4*(6), 477–480.

Hamilton, Jada G.; Genoff, Margaux C.; Salerno, Melissa; Amoroso, Kimberly; Boyar, Sherry R.; Sheehan, Margaret, . . . Robson, Mark E. (2017). Psychosocial factors associated with the uptake of contralateral prophylactic mastectomy among BRCA1/2 mutation noncarriers with newly diagnosed breast cancer. *Breast Cancer Research and Treatment, 162*(2), 297–306.

Hamlin, J. Kiley. (2014). The origins of human morality: Complex socio-moral evaluations by preverbal infants. In Jean Decety & Yves Christen (Eds.), *New frontiers in social neuroscience* (pp. 165–188). New York, NY: Springer.

Hamm, Jeremy M.; Chipperfield, Judith G.; Perry, Raymond P.; Parker, Patti C. & Heckhausen, Jutta. (2017). Tenacious self-reliance in health maintenance may jeopardize late life survival. *Psychology and Aging, 32*(7), 628–635.

Hamplová, Dana; Le Bourdais, Céline & Lapierre-Adamcyk, Évelyne. (2014). Is the cohabitation–marriage gap in money pooling universal? *Journal of Marriage and Family, 76*(5), 983–997.

Han, Kihye; Trinkoff, Alison M.; Storr, Carla L.; Lerner, Nancy & Yang, Bo Kyum. (2017). Variation across U.S. assisted living facilities: Admissions, resident care needs, and staffing. *Journal of Nursing Scholarship, 49*(1), 24–32.

Hane, Amie Ashley; Cheah, Charissa; Rubin, Kenneth H. & Fox, Nathan A. (2008). The role of maternal behavior in the relation between shyness and social reticence in early childhood and social withdrawal in middle childhood. *Social Development, 17*(4), 795–811.

Hank, Karsten & Korbmacher, Julie M. (2013). Parenthood and retirement: Gender, cohort, and welfare regime differences. *European Societies, 15*(3), 446–461.

Hanna-Attisha, Mona; LaChance, Jenny; Sadler, Richard Casey & Schnepp, Allison Champney. (2016). Elevated blood lead levels in children associated with the Flint drinking water crisis: A spatial analysis of risk and public health response. *American Journal of Public Health, 106*(2), 283–290.

Hannon, Erin E.; Schachner, Adena & Nave-Blodgett, Jessica E. (2017). Babies know bad dancing when they see it: Older but not younger infants discriminate between synchronous and asynchronous audiovisual musical displays. *Journal of Experimental Child Psychology, 159*, 159–174.

Hanson, Jamie L.; Nacewicz, Brendon M.; Sutterer, Matthew J.; Cayo, Amelia A.; Schaefer, Stacey M.; Rudolph, Karen D., . . . Davidson, Richard J. (2015). Behavioral problems after early life stress: Contributions of the hippocampus and amygdala. *Biological Psychiatry, 77*(4), 314–323.

Hanushek, Eric A. & Woessmann, Ludger. (2015). *The knowledge capital of nations: Education and the economics of growth.* Cambridge, MA: MIT Press.

Harden, K. Paige; Mann, Frank D.; Grotzinger, Andrew D.; Patterson, Megan W.; Steinberg, Laurence; Tackett, Jennifer L. & Tucker-Drob, Elliot M. (2017). Developmental differences in reward sensitivity and sensation seeking in adolescence: Testing sex-specific associations with gonadal hormones and pubertal development. *Journal of Personality and Social Psychology*, (In Press).

Hargreaves, Andy. (2012). Singapore: The Fourth Way in action? *Educational Research for Policy and Practice, 11*(1), 7–17.

Hari, Riitta. (2017). From brain–environment connections to temporal dynamics and social interaction: Principles of human brain function. *Neuron, 94*(5), 1033–1039.

Harkness, Geoff & Khaled, Rana. (2014). Modern traditionalism: Consanguineous marriage in Qatar. *Journal of Marriage and Family, 76*(3), 587–603.

Harkness, Sara; Super, Charles M. & Mavridis, Caroline J. (2011). Parental ethnotheories about children's socioemotional development. In Xinyin Chen & Kenneth H. Rubin (Eds.), *Socioemotional development in cultural context* (pp. 73–98). New York, NY: Guilford Press.

Harlow, Ilana. (2005). Shaping sorrow: Creative aspects of public and private mourning. In Samuel C. Heilman (Ed.), *Death, bereavement, and mourning* (pp. 33–52). New Brunswick, NJ: Transaction.

Harold, Gordon T.; Leve, Leslie D. & Sellers, Ruth. (2017). How can genetically informed research help inform the next generation of interparental and parenting interventions? *Child Development, 88*(2), 446–458.

Harris, Judith R. (1998). *The nurture assumption: Why children turn out the way they do.* New York, NY: Free Press.

Harris, Judith R. (2002). Beyond the nurture assumption: Testing hypotheses about the child's environment. In John G. Borkowski et al. (Eds.), *Parenting and the child's world: Influences on academic, intellectual, and social-emotional development* (pp. 3–20). Mahwah, NJ: Erlbaum.

Harris Insights and Analytics. (2014, February 19). *6 in 10 Americans say they or someone they know have been bullied.* New York, NY: Harris Interactive.

Harris-Kojetin, Lauren; Sengupta, Manisha; Park-Lee, Eunice; Valverde, Roberto; Caffrey, Christine; Rome, Vincent & Lendon, Jessica. (2016). *Long-term care providers and services users in the United States: Data from the National Study of Long-Term Care Providers, 2013–2014. Vital Health Statistics, 3*(38). Hyattsville, MD: National Center for Health Statistics.

Harrison, Kristen; Bost, Kelly K.; McBride, Brent A.; Donovan, Sharon M.; Grigsby-Toussaint, Diana S.; Kim, Juhee, . . . Jacobsohn, Gwen Costa. (2011). Toward a developmental conceptualization of contributors to overweight and obesity in childhood: The Six-Cs model. *Child Development Perspectives, 5*(1), 50–58.

Harrison, Linda J.; Elwick, Sheena; Vallotton, Claire D. & Kappler, Gregor. (2014). Spending time with others: A time-use diary for infant-toddler child care. In Linda J. Harrison & Jennifer Sumsion (Eds.), *Lived spaces of infant-toddler education and care: Exploring diverse perspectives on theory, research and practice* (pp. 59–74). Dordrecht, the Netherlands: Springer.

Harrist, Amanda W.; Topham, Glade L.; Hubbs-Tait, Laura; Page, Melanie C.; Kennedy, Tay S. & Shriver, Lenka H. (2012). What developmental science can contribute to a transdisciplinary understanding of childhood obesity: An interpersonal and intrapersonal risk model. *Child Development Perspectives, 6*(4), 445–455.

Harry, Beth & Klingner, Janette. (2014). *Why are so many minority students in special education?: Understanding race and disability in schools* (2nd ed.). New York, NY: Teachers College Press.

Hart, Betty & Risley, Todd R. (1995). *Meaningful differences in the everyday experience of young American children.* Baltimore, MD: P. H. Brookes.

Hart, Chantelle N.; Cairns, Alyssa & Jelalian, Elissa. (2011). Sleep and obesity in children and adolescents. *Pediatric Clinics of North America, 58*(3), 715–733.

Hart, Daniel & Van Goethem, Anne. (2017). The role of civic and political participation in successful early adulthood. In Laura M. Padilla-Walker & Larry J. Nelson (Eds.), *Flourishing in emerging adulthood: Positive development during the third decade of life* (pp. 139–166). New York, NY: Oxford University Press.

Harter, Susan. (2012). *The construction of the self: Developmental and sociocultural foundations* (2nd ed.). New York, NY: Guilford Press.

Hartley, Catherine A. & Somerville, Leah H. (2015). The neuroscience of adolescent decision-making. *Current Opinion in Behavioral Sciences, 5*, 108–115.

Hartshorne, Joshua K. & Germine, Laura T. (2015). When does cognitive functioning peak? The asynchronous rise and fall of different cognitive abilities across the life span. *Psychological Science, 26*(4), 433–443.

Hasson, Ramzi & Fine, Jodene Goldenring. (2012). Gender differences among children with ADHD on continuous performance tests: A meta-analytic review. *Journal of Attention Disorders, 16*(3), 190–198.

Hauck, Fern & Tanabe, Kawai O. (2017). Beyond "back to sleep": Ways to further reduce the risk of sudden infant death syndrome. *Pediatric Annals, 46*(8), e284–290.

Hausdorff, Jeffrey M. & Buchman, Aron S. (2013). What links gait speed and MCI with dementia? A fresh look at the association between motor and cognitive function. *The Journals of Gerontology Series A: Biological Sciences and Medical Sciences, 68*(4), 409–411.

Haushofer, Johannes & Fehr, Ernst. (2014). On the psychology of poverty. *Science, 344*(6186), 862–867.

Hayden, Ceara; Bowler, Jennifer O.; Chambers, Stephanie; Freeman, Ruth; Humphris, Gerald; Richards, Derek & Cecil, Joanne E. (2013). Obesity and dental caries in children: A systematic review and meta-analysis. *Community Dentistry and Oral Epidemiology, 41*(4), 289–308.

Hayden, Elizabeth P. & Mash, Eric J. (2014). Child psychopathology: A developmental-systems perspective. In Eric J. Mash & Russell A. Barkley (Eds.), *Child psychopathology* (3rd ed., pp. 3–72). New York, NY: Guilford Press.

Hayes, DeMarquis; Blake, Jamilia J.; Darensbourg, Alicia & Castillo, Linda G. (2015). Examining the academic achievement of Latino adolescents: The role of parent and peer beliefs and behaviors. *The Journal of Early Adolescence, 35*(2), 141–161.

Hayes, Peter. (2013). International adoption, "early" puberty, and underrecorded age. *Pediatrics, 131*(6), 1029–1031.

Hayflick, Leonard. (2004). "Anti-aging" is an oxymoron. *The Journals of Gerontology Series A: Biological Sciences and Medical Sciences, 59*(6), 573–578.

Hayman, Karen J.; Kerse, Ngaire & Consedine, Nathan S. (2017). Resilience in context: The special case of advanced age. *Aging & Mental Health, 21*(6), 577–585.

Hayne, Harlene & Simcock, Gabrielle. (2009). Memory development in toddlers. In Mary L. Courage & Nelson Cowan (Eds.), *The development of memory in infancy and childhood* (2nd ed., pp. 43–68). New York, NY: Psychology Press.

Haynes, Michelle C. & Heilman, Madeline E. (2013). It had to be you (not me)!: Women's attributional rationalization of their contribution to successful joint work outcomes. *Personality and Social Psychology Bulletin, 39*(7), 956–969.

Haynie, Dana L.; Soller, Brian & Williams, Kristi. (2014). Anticipating early fatality: Friends', schoolmates' and individual perceptions of fatality on adolescent risk behaviors. *Journal of Youth and Adolescence, 43*(2), 175–192.

Hayslip, Bert & Smith, Gregory C. (Eds.). (2013). *Resilient grandparent caregivers: A strengths-based perspective.* New York, NY: Routledge.

Healy, Jack. (2017, June 23). Out of high school, into real life. *New York Times.*

Heersmink, Richard. (2017). Extended mind and cognitive enhancement: Moral aspects of cognitive artifacts. *Phenomenology and the Cognitive Sciences, 16*(1), 17–32.

Heiman, Julia R.; Long, J. Scott; Smith, Shawna N.; Fisher, William A.; Sand, Michael S. & Rosen, Raymond C. (2011). Sexual satisfaction and relationship happiness in midlife and older couples in five countries. *Archives of Sexual Behavior, 40*(4), 741–753.

Hendry, Mandy P. & Ledbetter, Andrew M. (2017). Narrating the past, enhancing the present: The associations among genealogical communication, family communication patterns, and family satisfaction. *Journal of Family Communication, 17*(2), 117–136.

Hennessy-Fiske, Molly. (2011, February 8). California; Concern about child obesity grows, poll finds; Many Californians support restricting unhealthful food and drink in schools. *Los Angeles Times*, p. AA3.

Henrich, Joseph. (2015). Culture and social behavior. *Current Opinion in Behavioral Sciences, 3*, 84–89.

Henrich, Joseph; Heine, Steven J. & Norenzayan, Ara. (2010). The weirdest people in the world? *Behavioral and Brain Sciences, 33*(2/3), 61–83.

Henry, David B.; Deptula, Daneen P. & Schoeny, Michael E. (2012). Sexually transmitted infections and unintended pregnancy: A longitudinal analysis of risk transmission through friends and attitudes. *Social Development, 21*(1), 195–214.

Hentges, Rochelle F. & Wang, Ming-Te. (2018). Gender differences in the developmental cascade from harsh parenting to educational attainment: An evolutionary perspective. *Child Development, 89*(2), 397–413.

Herculano-Houzel, Suzana; Avelino-de-Souza, Kamilla; Neves, Kleber; Porfírio, Jairo; Messeder, Débora; Feijó, Larissa Mattos, . . . Manger, Paul R. (2014a). The elephant brain in numbers. *Frontiers in Neuroanatomy, 8*, 46.

Herculano-Houzel, Suzana; Manger, Paul R. & Kaas, Jon H. (2014b). Brain scaling in mammalian evolution as a consequence of concerted and mosaic changes in numbers of neurons and average neuronal cell size. *Frontiers in Neuroanatomy, 8*, 77.

Herlofson, Katharina & Hagestad, Gunhild. (2012). Transformations in the role of grandparents across welfare states. In Sara Arber & Virpi Timonen (Eds.), *Contemporary grandparenting: Changing family relationships in global contexts* (pp. 27–49). Chicago, IL: Policy Press.

Herman-Giddens, Marcia E.; Steffes, Jennifer; Harris, Donna; Slora, Eric; Hussey, Michael; Dowshen, Steven A., . . . Reiter, Edward O. (2012). Secondary sexual characteristics in boys: Data from the pediatric research in office settings network. *Pediatrics, 130*(5), e1058–e1068.

Hernández, Maciel M.; Robins, Richard W.; Widaman, Keith F. & Conger, Rand D. (2017). Ethnic pride, self-esteem, and school belonging: A reciprocal analysis over time. *Developmental Psychology, 53*(12), 2384–2396.

Herrera, Angelica P.; Snipes, Shedra A.; King, Denae W.; Torres-Vigil, Isabel; Goldberg, Daniel S. & Weinberg, Armin D. (2010). Disparate inclusion of older adults in clinical trials: Priorities and opportunities for policy and practice change. *American Journal of Public Health, 100*(51), S105–S112.

Herrmann, Julia; Schmidt, Isabelle; Kessels, Ursula & Preckel, Franzis. (2016). Big fish in big ponds: Contrast and assimilation effects on math and verbal self-concepts of students in within-school gifted tracks. *British Journal of Educational Psychology, 86*(2), 222–240.

Herschensohn, Julia R. (2007). *Language development and age.* New York, NY: Cambridge University Press.

Hertzog, Christopher. (2010). Regarding methods for studying behavioral development: The contributions and influence of K. Warner Schaie. *Research in Human Development, 7*(1), 1–8.

Herz, Rachel. (2012). *That's disgusting: Unraveling the mysteries of repulsion.* New York, NY: Norton.

Hess, Thomas M.; Hinson, Joey & Hodges, Elizabeth. (2009a). Moderators of and mechanisms underlying stereotype threat effects on older adults' memory performance. *Experimental Aging Research, 35*(2), 153–177.

Hess, Thomas M.; Leclerc, Christina M.; Swaim, Elizabeth & Weatherbee, Sarah R. (2009b). Aging and everyday judgments: The impact of motivational and processing resource factors. *Psychology and Aging, 24*(3), 735–740.

Hewer, Mariko. (2014). Selling sweet nothings: Science shows food marketing's effects on children's minds — and appetites. *Observer, 27*(10).

Heyes, Cecilia. (2016). Who knows? Metacognitive social learning strategies. *Trends in Cognitive Sciences, 20*(3), 204–213.

Heyman, Gene M. (2013). Quitting drugs: Quantitative and qualitative features. *Annual Review of Clinical Psychology, 9*, 29–59.

Hicks, Joshua A.; Trent, Jason; Davis, William E. & King, Laura A. (2012). Positive affect, meaning in life, and future time perspective: An application of socioemotional selectivity theory. *Psychology and Aging, 27*(1), 181–189.

Hider, Jessica L.; Gittelman, Rachel M.; Shah, Tapan; Edwards, Melissa; Rosenbloom, Arnold; Akey, Joshua M. & Parra, Esteban J. (2013). Exploring signatures of positive selection in pigmentation candidate genes in populations of East Asian ancestry. *BMC Evolutionary Biology, 13*, 150.

Higgins, Matt. (2006, August 7). A series of flips creates some serious buzz. *New York Times.*

Hill, Erica & Hageman, Jon B. (Eds.). (2016). *The archaeology of ancestors: Death, memory, and veneration.* Gainesville, FL: University Press of Florida.

Hill, Patrick L.; Burrow, Anthony L. & Sumner, Rachel. (2013). Addressing important questions in the field of adolescent purpose. *Child Development Perspectives, 7*(4), 232–236.

Hill, Sarah E.; Prokosch, Marjorie L.; DelPriore, Danielle J.; Griskevicius, Vladas & Kramer, Andrew. (2016). Low childhood socioeconomic status promotes eating in the absence of energy need. *Psychological Science, 27*(3), 354–364.

Hinnant, J. Benjamin; Nelson, Jackie A.; O'Brien, Marion; Keane, Susan P. & Calkins, Susan D. (2013). The interactive roles of parenting, emotion regulation and executive functioning in moral reasoning during middle childhood. *Cognition and Emotion, 27*(8), 1460–1468.

Hirsh-Pasek, Kathy & Golinkoff, Roberta M. (2016, March 11). The preschool paradox: It's time to rethink our approach to early education [Review of the book *The importance of being little: What preschoolers really need from grownups*, by Erika Christakis]. *Science, 351*(6278), 1158.

Hirvonen, Riikka; Aunola, Kaisa; Alatupa, Saija; Viljaranta, Jaana & Nurmi, Jari-Erik. (2013). The role of temperament in children's affective and behavioral responses in achievement situations. *Learning and Instruction, 27*, 21–30.

Hively, Kimberly & El-Alayli, Amani. (2014). "You throw like a girl:" The effect of stereotype threat on women's athletic performance and gender stereotypes. *Psychology of Sport and Exercise, 15*(1), 48–55.

Ho, Christine. (2015). Grandchild care, intergenerational transfers, and grandparents' labor supply. *Review of Economics of the Household, 13*(2), 359–384.

Ho, Emily S. (2010). Measuring hand function in the young child. *Journal of Hand Therapy, 23*(3), 323–328.

Hoare, Carol Hren. (2002). *Erikson on development in adulthood: New insights from the unpublished papers.* New York, NY: Oxford University Press.

Hochman, Oshrat & Lewin-Epstein, Noah. (2013). Determinants of early retirement preferences in Europe: The role of grandparenthood. *International Journal of Comparative Sociology, 54*(1), 29–47.

Hodge, Samuel R.; Sato, Takahiro; Mukoyama, Takahito & Kozub, Francis M. (2013). Development of the physical educators' judgments about inclusion instrument for Japanese physical education majors and an analysis of their judgments. *International Journal of Disability, Development and Education, 60*(4), 332–346.

Hofer, Claire; Eisenberg, Nancy; Spinrad, Tracy L.; Morris, Amanda S.; Gershoff, Elizabeth; Valiente, Carlos, . . . Eggum, Natalie D. (2013). Mother-adolescent conflict: Stability, change, and relations with externalizing and internalizing behavior problems. *Social Development, 22*(2), 259–279.

Hoff, Erika. (2013). Interpreting the early language trajectories of children from low-SES and language minority homes: Implications for closing achievement gaps. *Developmental Psychology, 49*(1), 4–14.

Hoff, Erika; Core, Cynthia; Place, Silvia; Rumiche, Rosario; Señor, Melissa & Parra, Marisol. (2012). Dual language exposure and early bilingual development. *Journal of Child Language, 39*(1), 1–27.

Hoff, Erika; Rumiche, Rosario; Burridge, Andrea; Ribota, Krystal M. & Welsh, Stephanie N. (2014). Expressive vocabulary development in children from bilingual and monolingual homes: A longitudinal study from two to four years. *Early Childhood Research Quarterly, 29*(4), 433–444.

Hoffman, Jessica L.; Teale, William H. & Paciga, Kathleen A. (2014). Assessing vocabulary learning in early childhood. *Journal of Early Childhood Literacy, 14*(4), 459–481.

Hoffnung, Michele & Williams, Michelle A. (2013). Balancing act: Career and family during college-educated women's 30s. *Sex Roles, 68*(5-6), 321–334.

Hogan, Michael J.; Staff, Roger T.; Bunting, Brendan P.; Deary, Ian J. & Whalley, Lawrence J. (2012). Openness to experience and activity engagement facilitate the maintenance of verbal ability in older adults. *Psychology and Aging, 27*(4), 849–854.

Holahan, Carole K.; Holahan, Charles J.; Li, Xiaoyin & Chen, Yen T. (2017). Association of health-related behaviors, attitudes, and appraisals to leisure-time physical activity in middle-aged and older women. *Women & Health, 57*(2), 121–136.

Holt, Laura J.; Mattanah, Jonathan F. & Long, Michelle W. (2018). Change in parental and peer relationship quality during emerging adulthood: Implications for academic, social, and emotional functioning. *Journal of Social and Personal Relationships, 35*(5), 743–769.

Holt, Raymond. (2013). Review of the book *Design for the ages: Universal design as a rehabilitation strategy*, by Erika Christakis. *Disability & Society, 28*(1), 142–144.

Holt-Lunstad, Julianne; Smith, Timothy B.; Baker, Mark; Harris, Tyler & Stephenson, David. (2015). Loneliness and social isolation as risk factors for mortality: A meta-analytic review. *Perspectives on Psychological Science, 10*(2), 227–237.

Holzer, Jessica; Canavan, Maureen & Bradley, Elizabeth. (2014). County-level correlation between adult obesity rates and prevalence of dentists. *JADA, 145*(9), 932–939.

Hong, David S. & Reiss, Allan L. (2014). Cognitive and neurological aspects of sex chromosome aneuploidies. *The Lancet Neurology, 13*(3), 306–318.

Hong, Jun Sung & Garbarino, James. (2012). Risk and protective factors for homophobic bullying in schools: An application of the social–ecological framework. *Educational Psychology Review, 24*(2), 271–285.

Hood, Michelle; Creed, Peter A. & Mills, Bianca J. (2017). Loneliness and online friendships in emerging adults. *Personality and Individual Differences*, (In Press).

Hook, Jennifer L. (2012). Working on the weekend: Fathers' time with family in the United Kingdom. *Journal of Marriage and Family, 74*(4), 631–642.

Hostinar, Camelia E.; Johnson, Anna E. & Gunnar, Megan R. (2015). Parent support is less effective in buffering cortisol stress reactivity for adolescents compared to children. *Developmental Science, 18*(2), 281–297.

Hostinar, Camelia E.; Nusslock, Robin & Miller, Gregory E. (2018). Future directions in the study of early-life stress and physical and emotional health: Implications of the neuroimmune network hypothesis. *Journal of Clinical Child & Adolescent Psychology, 47*(1), 142–156.

Howard, Kimberly S. (2010). Paternal attachment, parenting beliefs and children's attachment. *Early Child Development and Care, 180*(1/2), 157–171.

Howe, Mark L. & Knott, Lauren M. (2015). The fallibility of memory in judicial processes: Lessons from the past and their modern consequences. *Memory, 23*(5), 633–656.

Howe, Tsu-Hsin; Sheu, Ching-Fan; Hsu, Yung-Wen; Wang, Tien-Ni & Wang, Lan-Wan. (2016). Predicting neurodevelopmental outcomes at preschool age for children with very low birth weight. *Research in Developmental Disabilities, 48*, 231–241.

Hoyert, Donna L.; Kung, Hsiang-Ching & Smith, Betty L. (2005). *Deaths: Preliminary data for 2003. National Vital Statistics Reports, 53*(15). Hyattsville, MD: National Center for Health Statistics.

Hoyert, Donna L. & Xu, Jiaquan. (2012). *Deaths: Preliminary data for 2011. National Vital Statistics Reports, 61*(6). Hyattsville, MD: National Center for Health Statistics.

Hoyme, H. Eugene; Kalberg, Wendy O.; Elliott, Amy J.; Blankenship, Jason; Buckley, David; Marais, Anna-Susan, . . . May, Philip A. (2016). Updated clinical guidelines for diagnosing fetal alcohol spectrum disorders. *Pediatrics, 138*(2), e20154256.

Hrdy, Sarah B. (2009). *Mothers and others: The evolutionary origins of mutual understanding*. Cambridge, MA: Harvard University Press.

Hsu, William C.; Araneta, Maria Rosario G.; Kanaya, Alka M.; Chiang, Jane L. & Fujimoto, Wilfred. (2015). BMI cut points to identify at-risk Asian Americans for type 2 diabetes screening. *Diabetes Care, 38*(1), 150–158.

Hu, Youna; Shmygelska, Alena; Tran, David; Eriksson, Nicholas; Tung, Joyce Y. & Hinds, David A. (2016). GWAS of 89,283 individuals identifies genetic variants associated with self-reporting of being a morning person. *Nature Communications, 7*(10448).

Huang, Chiungjung. (2010). Mean-level change in self-esteem from childhood through adulthood: Meta-analysis of longitudinal studies. *Review of General Psychology, 14*(3), 251–260.

Huang, Liuli; Roche, Lahna R.; Kennedy, Eugene & Brocato, Melissa B. (2017). Using an integrated persistence model to predict college graduation. *International Journal of Higher Education, 6*(3), 40–56.

Huang, Tzu-Ting; Chung, Meng-Ling; Chen, Fan-Ru; Chin, Yen-Fan & Wang, Bi-Hwa. (2016). Evaluation of a combined cognitive-behavioural and exercise intervention to manage fear of falling among elderly residents in nursing homes. *Aging & Mental Health, 20*(1), 2–12.

Hugdahl, Kenneth & Westerhausen, René (Eds.). (2010). *The two halves of the brain: Information processing in the cerebral hemispheres*. Cambridge, MA: MIT Press.

Hughes, Claire & Devine, Rory T. (2015). Individual differences in theory of mind: A social perspective. In Richard M. Lerner (Ed.), *Handbook of child psychology and developmental science* (7th ed., Vol. 3). New York, NY: Wiley.

Hughes, Julie M. & Bigler, Rebecca S. (2011). Predictors of African American and European American adolescents' endorsement of race-conscious social policies. *Developmental Psychology, 47*(2), 479–492.

Hughes, Matthew L.; Geraci, Lisa & De Forrest, Ross L. (2013). Aging 5 years in 5 minutes: The effect of taking a memory test on older adults' subjective age. *Psychological Science, 24*(12), 2481–2488.

Hughey, Matthew W. & Parks, Gregory. (2014). *The wrongs of the Right: Language, race, and the Republican Party in the age of Obama*. New York, NY: New York University Press.

Hunt, Earl B. (2011a). *Human intelligence*. New York, NY: Cambridge University Press.

Hunt, Earl B. (2011b). Where are we? Where are we going? Reflections on the current and future state of research on intelligence. In Robert J. Sternberg & Scott Barry Kaufman (Eds.), *The Cambridge handbook of intelligence*. New York, NY: Cambridge University Press.

Hunt, Earl B. (2012). What makes nations intelligent? *Perspectives on Psychological Science, 7*(3), 284–306.

Hunter, Jonathan & Maunder, Robert (Eds.). (2016). *Improving patient treatment with attachment theory: A guide for primary care practitioners and specialists*. New York, NY: Springer.

Hunter, Myra Sally. (2012). Long-term impacts of early and surgical menopause. *Menopause, 19*(3), 253–254.

Hussain, Amjad; Case, Keith; Marshall, Russell & Summerskill, Steve J. (2013). An inclusive design method for addressing human variability and work performance issues. *International Journal of Engineering and Technology Innovation, 3*(3), 144–155.

Huston, Aletha C.; Bobbitt, Kaeley C. & Bentley, Alison. (2015). Time spent in child care: How and why does it affect social development? *Developmental Psychology, 51*(5), 621–634.

Huston, Aletha C. & Ripke, Marika N. (2006). Middle childhood: Contexts of development. In Aletha C. Huston & Marika N. Ripke (Eds.), *Developmental contexts in middle childhood: Bridges to adolescence and adulthood* (pp. 1–22). New York, NY: Cambridge University Press.

Hutchinson, Esther A.; De Luca, Cinzia R.; Doyle, Lex W.; Roberts, Gehan & Anderson, Peter J. (2013). School-age outcomes of extremely preterm or extremely low birth weight children. *Pediatrics, 131*(4), e1053–e1061.

Hvistendahl, Mara. (2013). China heads off deadly blood disorder. *Science, 340*(6133), 677–678.

Hvistendahl, Mara. (2017). Analysis of China's one-child policy sparks uproar. *Science, 358*(6361), 283–284.

Hwang, Na Young & Domina, Thurston. (2017). The links between youth employment and educational attainment across racial groups. *Journal of Research on Adolescence, 27*(2), 312–327.

Hyde, Janet S. (2014). Gender similarities and differences. *Annual Review of Psychology, 65*, 373–398.

Hyde, Janet S. (2016). Sex and cognition: Gender and cognitive functions. *Current Opinion in Neurobiology, 38*, 53–56.

Hyslop, Anne. (2014). *The case against exit exams. New American Education Policy Brief*. Washington DC: New America Education Policy Program.

Idler, Ellen. (2006). Religion and aging. In Robert H. Binstock & Linda K. George (Eds.), *Handbook of aging and the social sciences* (6th ed., pp. 277–300). Amsterdam, the Netherlands: Elsevier.

Iida, Hiroko & Rozier, R. Gary. (2013). Mother-perceived social capital and children's oral health and use of dental care in the United States. *American Journal of Public Health, 103*(3), 480–487.

Ikeda, Martin J. (2012). Policy and practice considerations for response to intervention: Reflections and commentary. *Journal of Learning Disabilities, 45*(3), 274–277.

Inceoglu, Ilke; Segers, Jesse & Bartram, Dave. (2012). Age-related differences in work motivation. *Journal of Occupational and Organizational Psychology, 75*(2), 300–329.

Inhelder, Bärbel & Piaget, Jean. (1958). *The growth of logical thinking from childhood to adolescence: An essay on the construction of formal operational structures*. New York, NY: Basic Books.

Inhelder, Bärbel & Piaget, Jean. (1964). *The early growth of logic in the child: Classification and seriation*. New York, NY: Harper & Row.

Inhelder, Bärbel & Piaget, Jean. (2013a). *The early growth of logic in the child: Classification and seriation*. New York, NY: Routledge.

Inhelder, Bärbel & Piaget, Jean. (2013b). *The growth of logical thinking from childhood to adolescence: An essay on the construction of formal operational structures*. New York, NY: Routledge.

Insel, Thomas R. (2014). Mental disorders in childhood: Shifting the focus from behavioral symptoms to neurodevelopmental trajectories. *JAMA, 311*(17), 1727–1728.

Insurance Institute for Highway Safety. (2013a). Older drivers.

Insurance Institute for Highway Safety. (2013b). Teenagers: Driving carries extra risks for them.

Insurance Institute for Highway Safety. (2016, February). Fatality facts: Pedestrians 2014.

Insurance Institute for Highway Safety. (2016, November). Fatality facts: Pedestrians and bicyclists 2015.

Inzlicht, Michael & Schmader, Toni. (2012). *Stereotype threat: Theory, process, and application*. New York, NY: Oxford University Press.

Irwin, Scott; Galvez, Roberto; Weiler, Ivan Jeanne; Beckel-Mitchener, Andrea & Greenough, William. (2002). Brain structure and the functions of FMR1 protein. In Randi Jenssen Hagerman & Paul J. Hagerman (Eds.), *Fragile X syndrome: Diagnosis, treatment, and research* (3rd ed., pp. 191–205). Baltimore, MD: Johns Hopkins University Press.

Ivcevic, Zorana & Brackett, Marc. (2014). Predicting school success: Comparing conscientiousness, grit, and emotion regulation ability. *Journal of Research in Personality, 52*, 29–36.

Jackson, James C.; Santoro, Michael J.; Ely, Taylor M.; Boehm, Leanne; Kiehl, Amy L.; Anderson, Lindsay S. & Ely, E. Wesley. (2014). Improving patient care through the prism of psychology: Application of Maslow's hierarchy to sedation, delirium, and early mobility in the intensive care unit. *Journal of Critical Care, 29*(3), 438–444.

Jackson, James S.; Govia, Ishtar O. & Sellers, Sherrill L. (2011). Racial and ethnic influences over the life course. In Robert H. Binstock & Linda K. George (Eds.), *Handbook of aging and the social sciences* (7th ed., pp. 91–103). San Diego, CA: Academic Press.

Jackson, Jeffrey B.; Miller, Richard B.; Oka, Megan & Henry, Ryan G. (2014). Gender differences in marital satisfaction: A meta-analysis. *Journal of Marriage and Family, 76*(1), 105–129.

Jackson, Sandra L. & Cunningham, Solveig A. (2015). Social competence and obesity in elementary school. *American Journal of Public Health, 105*(1), 153–158.

Jackson, Shelly L. & Hafemeister, Thomas L. (2011). Risk factors associated with elder abuse: The importance of differentiating by type of elder maltreatment. *Violence and Victims, 26*(6), 738–757.

Jaffe, Arthur C. (2011). Failure to thrive: Current clinical concepts. *Pediatrics in Review, 32*(3), 100–108.

Jaiswal, Tulika. (2014). *Indian arranged marriages: A social psychological perspective.* New York, NY: Routledge.

Jamal, Ahmed; Gentzke, Andrea; Hu, S. Sean; Cullen, Karen A.; Apelberg, Benjamin J.; Homa, David M. & King, Brian A. (2017, June 16). *Tobacco use among middle and high school students — United States, 2011–2016. Morbidity and Mortality Weekly Report, 66*(23), 597–603. Atlanta, GA: Centers for Disease Control and Prevention.

Jambon, Marc & Smetana, Judith G. (2014). Moral complexity in middle childhood: Children's evaluations of necessary harm. *Developmental Psychology, 50*(1), 22–33.

James, Jacquelyn B.; McKechnie, Sharon & Swanberg, Jennifer. (2011). Predicting employee engagement in an age-diverse retail workforce. *Journal of Organizational Behavior, 32*(2), 173–196.

James, Jenée; Ellis, Bruce J.; Schlomer, Gabriel L. & Garber, Judy. (2012). Sex-specific pathways to early puberty, sexual debut, and sexual risk taking: Tests of an integrated evolutionary–developmental model. *Developmental Psychology, 48*(3), 687–702.

James, Karin H. (2017). The importance of handwriting experience on the development of the literate brain. *Current Directions in Psychological Science, 26*(6), 502–508.

James, Will. (2012, May 25). Report faults doctors: Long Island grand jury blames physicians, pharmacists for epidemic of abuse. *Wall Street Journal.*

Jamsen, Kris M.; Bell, J. Simon; Hilmer, Sarah N.; Kirkpatrick, Carl M. J.; Ilomäki, Jenni; Couteur, David Le, . . . Gnjidic, Danijela. (2016). Effects of changes in number of medications and drug burden index exposure on transitions between frailty states and death: The Concord Health and Ageing in Men Project Cohort Study. *Journal of the American Geriatrics Society, 64*(1), 89–95.

Janse, Benjamin; Huijsman, Robbert; de Kuyper, Ruben Dennis Maurice & Fabbricotti, Isabelle Natalina. (2014). The effects of an integrated care intervention for the frail elderly on informal caregivers: A quasi-experimental study. *BMC Geriatrics, 14*(1).

Jarcho, Johanna M.; Fox, Nathan A.; Pine, Daniel S.; Etkin, Amit; Leibenluft, Ellen; Shechner, Tomer & Ernst, Monique. (2013). The neural correlates of emotion-based cognitive control in adults with early childhood behavioral inhibition. *Biological Psychology, 92*(2), 306–314.

Jarvis, Michaela. (2017, October 27). AAAS adopts scientific freedom and responsibility statement. *Science, 358*(6362), 462.

Jasny, Barbara R.; Chin, Gilbert; Chong, Lisa & Vignieri, Sacha. (2011). Again, and again, and again . . . *Science, 334*(6060), 1225.

Jatlaoui, Tara C.; Shah, Jill; Mandel, Michele G.; Krashin, Jamie W.; Suchdev, Danielle B.; Jamieson, Denise J. & Pazol, Karen. (2017). *Abortion surveillance — United States, 2014. Morbidity and Mortality Weekly Report, 66*(24), 1–48. Atlanta, GA: Centers for Disease Control and Prevention.

Javed, Fawad; Kellesarian, Sergio V.; Sundar, Isaac K.; Romanos, Georgios & Rahman, Irfan. (2017). Recent updates on electronic cigarette aerosol and inhaled nicotine effects on periodontal and pulmonary tissues. *Oral Diseases, 23*(8), 1052–1057.

Jayson, Sharon. (2014, April 26). Shotgun weddings becoming relics of another time. *USA Today.*

Jednoróg, Katarzyna; Altarelli, Irene; Monzalvo, Karla; Fluss, Joel; Dubois, Jessica; Billard, Catherine, . . . Ramus, Franck. (2012). The influence of socioeconomic status on children's brain structure. *PLoS ONE, 7*(8), e42486.

Jehan, Shazia; Zizi, Ferdinand; Pandi-Perumal, Seithikurippu R.; Myers, Alyson K.; Auguste, Evan; Jean-Louis, Girardin & Mcfarlane, Samy I. (2017). Shift work and sleep: Medical implications and management. *Sleep Medicine and Disorders, 1*(2).

Jha, Prabhat; Ramasundarahettige, Chinthanie; Landsman, Victoria; Rostron, Brian; Thun, Michael; Anderson, Robert N., . . . Peto, Richard. (2013). 21st-century hazards of smoking and benefits of cessation in the United States. *New England Journal of Medicine, 368*, 341–350.

Jia, Jianping; Wang, Fen; Wei, Cuibai; Zhou, Aihong; Jia, Xiangfei; Li, Fang, . . . Dong, Xiumin. (2014). The prevalence of dementia in urban and rural areas of China. *Alzheimer's & Dementia, 10*(1), 1–9.

Jia, Peng; Xue, Hong; Zhang, Ji & Wang, Youfa. (2017). Time trend and demographic and geographic disparities in childhood obesity prevalence in China—Evidence from twenty years of longitudinal data. *International Journal of Environmental Research and Public Health, 14*(4).

Jimerson, Shane R.; Burns, Matthew K. & VanDerHeyden, Amanda M. (Eds.). (2016). *Handbook of response to intervention: The science and practice of multi-tiered systems of support.* New York, NY: Springer.

Johannesen, Mark & LoGiudice, Dina. (2013). Elder abuse: A systematic review of risk factors in community-dwelling elders. *Age and Ageing, 42*(3), 292–298.

Johar, Meliyanni & Maruyama, Shiko. (2011). Intergenerational cohabitation in modern Indonesia: Filial support and dependence. *Health Economics, 20*(1), 87–104.

Johnson, Anna D.; Han, Wen-Jui; Ruhm, Christopher J. & Waldfogel, Jane. (2014). Child care subsidies and the school readiness of children of immigrants. *Child Development, 85*(6), 2140–2150.

Johnson, Jonni L.; McWilliams, Kelly; Goodman, Gail S.; Shelley, Alexandra E. & Piper, Brianna. (2016). Basic principles of interviewing the child eyewitness. In William T. O'Donohue & Matthew Fanetti (Eds.), *Forensic interviews regarding child sexual abuse* (pp. 179–195). New York, NY: Springer.

Johnson, Kimberly J. & Mutchler, Jan E. (2014). The emergence of a positive gerontology: From disengagement to social involvement. *The Gerontologist, 54*(1), 93–100.

Johnson, Mark H. (2011). *Developmental cognitive neuroscience: An introduction* (3rd ed.). Malden, MA: Wiley-Blackwell.

Johnson, Matthew D. (2012). Healthy marriage initiatives: On the need for empiricism in policy implementation. *American Psychologist, 67*(4), 296–308.

Johnson, Susan C.; Dweck, Carol S.; Chen, Frances S.; Stern, Hilarie L.; Ok, Su-Jeong & Barth, Maria. (2010). At the intersection of social and cognitive development: Internal working models of attachment in infancy. *Cognitive Science, 34*(5), 807–825.

Johnson, Wendy; McGue, Matt & Deary, Ian J. (2014). Normative cognitive aging. In Deborah Finkel & Chandra A. Reynolds (Eds.), *Behavior genetics of cognition across the lifespan: Advances in behavior genetics* (Vol. 1, pp. 135–167). New York, NY: Springer.

Johnston, Lloyd D.; O'Malley, Patrick M.; Bachman, Jerald G. & Schulenberg, John E. (2012). *Monitoring the future, national survey results on drug use, 1975–2011, Volume I: Secondary school students.* Ann Arbor, MI: Institute for Social Research, The University of Michigan.

Jokela, Markus. (2012). Birth-cohort effects in the association between personality and fertility. *Psychological Science, 23*(8), 835–841.

Jolliffe, Darrick; Farrington, David P.; Piquero, Alex R.; MacLeod, John F. & van de Weijer, Steve. (2017). Prevalence of life-course-persistent, adolescence-limited, and late-onset offenders: A systematic review of prospective longitudinal studies. *Aggression and Violent Behavior, 33,* 4–14.

Jonas, Eva; Sullivan, Daniel & Greenberg, Jeff. (2013). Generosity, greed, norms, and death – Differential effects of mortality salience on charitable behavior. *Journal of Economic Psychology, 35,* 47–57.

Jones, Andrea M. & Morris, Tracy L. (2012). Psychological adjustment of children in foster care: Review and implications for best practice. *Journal of Public Child Welfare, 6*(2), 129–148.

Jones, Jeffrey M. (2015, October 21). *In U.S., 58% back legal marijuana use.* Washington, DC: Gallup.

Jones, Owen R. & Vaupel, James W. (2017). Senescence is not inevitable. *Biogerontology, 18*(6), 965–971.

Jong, Jyh-Tsorng; Kao, Tsair; Lee, Liang-Yi; Huang, Hung-Hsuan; Lo, Po-Tsung & Wang, Hui-Chung. (2010). Can temperament be understood at birth? The relationship between neonatal pain cry and their temperament: A preliminary study. *Infant Behavior and Development, 33*(3), 266–272.

Jordet, Geir; Hartman, Esther & Vuijk, Pieter J. (2012). Team history and choking under pressure in major soccer penalty shootouts. *British Journal of Psychology, 103*(2), 268–283.

Jorgenson, Alicia Grattan; Hsiao, Ray Chih-Jui & Yen, Cheng-Fang. (2016). Internet addiction and other behavioral addictions. *Child & Adolescent Psychiatric Clinics, 25*(3), 509–520.

Jose, Anita; Daniel O'Leary, K. & Moyer, Anne. (2010). Does premarital cohabitation predict subsequent marital stability and marital quality? A meta-analysis. *Journal of Marriage and Family, 72*(1), 105–116.

Joseph, Michelle A.; O'Connor, Thomas G.; Briskman, Jacqueline A.; Maughan, Barbara & Scott, Stephen. (2014). The formation of secure new attachments by children who were maltreated: An observational study of adolescents in foster care. *Development and Psychopathology, 26*(1), 67–80.

Judd, Fiona K.; Hickey, Martha & Bryant, Christina. (2012). Depression and midlife: Are we overpathologising the menopause? *Journal of Affective Disorders, 136*(3), 199–211.

Julian, Megan M. (2013). Age at adoption from institutional care as a window into the lasting effects of early experiences. *Clinical Child and Family Psychology Review, 16*(2), 101–145.

Jung, Courtney. (2015). *Lactivism: How feminists and fundamentalists, hippies and yuppies, and physicians and politicians made breastfeeding big business and bad policy.* New York, NY: Basic Books.

Juonala, Markus; Magnussen, Costan G.; Berenson, Gerald S.; Venn, Alison; Burns, Trudy L.; Sabin, Matthew A., . . . Raitakari, Olli T. (2011). Childhood adiposity, adult adiposity, and cardiovascular risk factors. *New England Journal of Medicine, 365*(20), 1876–1885.

Juster, Robert-Paul; Russell, Jennifer J.; Almeida, Daniel & Picard, Martin. (2016). Allostatic load and comorbidities: A mitochondrial, epigenetic, and evolutionary perspective. *Development and Psychopathology, 28*(4), 1117–1146.

Juvonen, Jaana & Graham, Sandra. (2014). Bullying in schools: The power of bullies and the plight of victims. *Annual Review of Psychology, 65,* 159–185.

Jyrkkä, Johanna; Mursu, Jaakko; Enlund, Hannes & Lönnroos, Eija. (2012). Polypharmacy and nutritional status in elderly people. *Current Opinion in Clinical Nutrition & Metabolic Care, 15*(1), 1–6.

Kachel, A. Friederike; Premo, Luke S. & Hublin, Jean-Jacques. (2011). Modeling the effects of weaning age on length of female reproductive period: Implications for the evolution of human life history. *American Journal of Human Biology, 23*(4), 479–487.

Kahana, Eva; Bhatta, Tirth; Lovegreen, Loren D.; Kahana, Boaz & Midlarsky, Elizabeth. (2013). Altruism, helping, and volunteering: Pathways to well-being in late life. *Journal of Aging and Health, 25*(1), 159–187.

Kahneman, Daniel. (2011). *Thinking, fast and slow.* New York, NY: Farrar, Straus and Giroux.

Kail, Robert V. (2013). Influences of credibility of testimony and strength of statistical evidence on children's and adolescents' reasoning. *Journal of Experimental Child Psychology, 116*(3), 747–754.

Kalanithi, Paul. (2016). *When breath becomes air.* New York, NY: Random House.

Kalil, Ariel; Dunifon, Rachel; Crosby, Danielle & Su, Jessica Houston. (2014a). Work hours, schedules, and insufficient sleep among mothers and their young children. *Journal of Marriage and Family, 76*(5), 891–904.

Kalil, Ariel; Ryan, Rebecca & Chor, Elise. (2014b). Time investments in children across family structures. *The ANNALS of the American Academy of Political and Social Science, 654*(1), 50–168.

Kalliala, Marjatta. (2006). *Play culture in a changing world.* Maidenhead, UK: Open University Press.

Kaltiala-Heino, Riittakerttu; Fröjd, Sari & Marttunen, Mauri. (2015). Depression, conduct disorder, smoking and alcohol use as predictors of sexual activity in middle adolescence: A longitudinal study. *Health Psychology and Behavioral Medicine, 3*(1), 25–39.

Kan, Man Yee; Sullivan, Oriel & Gershuny, Jonathan. (2011). Gender convergence in domestic work: Discerning the effects of interactional and institutional barriers from large-scale data. *Sociology, 45*(2), 234–251.

Kandel, Denise B. (Ed.). (2002). *Stages and pathways of drug involvement: Examining the gateway hypothesis.* New York, NY: Cambridge University Press.

Kandler, Christian. (2012). Nature and nurture in personality development: The case of neuroticism and extraversion. *Current Directions in Psychological Science, 21*(5), 290–296.

Kang, Hye-Kyung. (2014). Influence of culture and community perceptions on birth and perinatal care of immigrant women: Doulas' perspective. *The Journal of Perinatal Education, 23*(1), 25–32.

Kanis, John A.; McCloskey, Eugene V.; Johansson, Helena; Cooper, Cyrus; Rizzoli, Rene & Reginster, Jean-Yves. (2013). European guidance for the diagnosis and management of osteoporosis in postmenopausal women. *Osteoporosis International, 24*(1), 23–57.

Kanner, Leo. (1943). Autistic disturbances of affective contact. *Nervous Child, 2*, 217–250.

Kapp, Steven K.; Gillespie-Lynch, Kristen; Sherman, Lauren E. & Hutman, Ted. (2013). Deficit, difference, or both? Autism and neurodiversity. *Developmental Psychology, 49*(1), 59–71.

Karbach, Julia & Unger, Kerstin. (2014). Executive control training from middle childhood to adolescence. *Frontiers in Psychology, 5*(390).

Karch, Andrew. (2013). *Early start: Preschool politics in the United States.* Ann Arbor, MI: University of Michigan Press.

Karmiloff-Smith, Annette. (2010). A developmental perspective on modularity. In Britt Glatzeder, et al. (Eds.), *Towards a theory of thinking* (pp. 179–187). Heidelberg, Germany: Springer.

Karmiloff-Smith, Annette; Al-Janabi, Tamara; D'Souza, Hana; Groet, Jurgen; Massand, Esha; Mok, Kin, . . . Strydom, Andre. (2016). The importance of understanding individual differences in Down syndrome. *F1000Research, 5*(389).

Karnatovskaia, Lioudmila V.; Gajic, Ognjen; Bienvenu, O. Joseph; Stevenson, Jennifer E. & Needham, Dale M. (2015). A holistic approach to the critically ill and Maslow's hierarchy. *Journal of Critical Care, 30*(1), 210–211.

Kärtner, Joscha; Borke, Jörn; Maasmeier, Kathrin; Keller, Heidi & Kleis, Astrid. (2011). Sociocultural influences on the development of self-recognition and self-regulation in Costa Rican and Mexican toddlers. *Journal of Cognitive Education and Psychology, 10*(1), 96–112.

Kärtner, Joscha; Keller, Heidi & Yovsi, Relindis D. (2010). Mother–infant interaction during the first 3 months: The emergence of culture-specific contingency patterns. *Child Development, 81*(2), 540–554.

Kastberg, David; Chan, Jessica Ying & Murray, Gordon. (2016). *Performance of U.S. 15-year-old students in science, reading, and mathematics literacy in an international context: First look at PISA 2015.* Washington, DC: National Center for Education Statistics. NCES 2017-048.

Kastbom, Åsa A.; Sydsjö, Gunilla; Bladh, Marie; Priebe, Gisela & Svedin, Carl-Göran. (2015). Sexual debut before the age of 14 leads to poorer psychosocial health and risky behaviour in later life. *Acta Paediatrica, 104*(1), 91–100.

Kastenbaum, Robert J. (2012). *Death, society, and human experience* (11th ed.). Boston, MA: Pearson.

Katz, Kathy S.; Jarrett, Marian H.; El-Mohandes, Ayman A. E.; Schneider, Susan; McNeely-Johnson, Doris & Kiely, Michele. (2011). Effectiveness of a combined home visiting and group intervention for low income African American mothers: The Pride in Parenting program. *Maternal and Child Health Journal, 15*(Suppl. 1), 75–84.

Kauffman, James M.; Anastasiou, Dimitris & Maag, John W. (2017). Special education at the crossroad: An identity crisis and the need for a scientific reconstruction. *Exceptionality, 25*(2), 139–155.

Kauffman, Jeffery. (2013). Culture, socialization, and traumatic death. In David K. Meagher & David E. Balk (Eds.), *Handbook of thanatology: The essential body of knowledge for the study of death, dying, and bereavement* (2nd ed.). New York, NY: Routledge.

Kaufman, Kenneth R. & Kaufman, Nathaniel D. (2006). And then the dog died. *Death Studies, 30*(1), 61–76.

Kavanaugh, Robert D. (2011). Origins and consequences of social pretend play. In Anthony D. Pellegrini (Ed.), *The Oxford handbook of the development of play* (pp. 296–307). New York, NY: Oxford University Press.

Kean, Sam. (2014). The 'other' breast cancer genes. *Science, 343*(6178), 1457–1459.

Keating, Nancy L.; Herrinton, Lisa J.; Zaslavsky, Alan M.; Liu, Liyan & Ayanian, John Z. (2006). Variations in hospice use among cancer patients. *Journal of the National Cancer Institute, 98*(15), 1053–1059.

Keil, Frank C. (2011). Science starts early. *Science, 331*(6020), 1022–1023.

Keller, Heidi. (2014). Introduction: Understanding relationships. In Hiltrud Otto & Heidi Keller (Eds.), *Different faces of attachment: Cultural variations on a universal human need* (pp. 3–25). New York, NY: Cambridge University Press.

Keller, Heidi; Borke, Jörn; Chaudhary, Nandita; Lamm, Bettina & Kleis, Astrid. (2010). Continuity in parenting strategies: A cross-cultural comparison. *Journal of Cross-Cultural Psychology, 41*(3), 391–409.

Keller, Peggy S.; El-Sheikh, Mona; Granger, Douglas A. & Buckhalt, Joseph A. (2012). Interactions between salivary cortisol and alpha-amylase as predictors of children's cognitive functioning and academic performance. *Physiology & Behavior, 105*(4), 987–995.

Kelly, Daniel; Faucher, Luc & Machery, Edouard. (2010). Getting rid of racism: Assessing three proposals in light of psychological evidence. *Journal of Social Philosophy, 41*(3), 293–322.

Kelly, John R. (1993). *Activity and aging: Staying involved in later life.* Newbury Park, CA: Sage.

Kempe, Ruth S. & Kempe, C. Henry. (1978). *Child abuse.* Cambridge, MA: Harvard University Press.

Kemper, Susan. (2015). Language production in late life. In Annette Gerstenberg & Anja Voeste (Eds.), *Language development: The lifespan perspective* (pp. 59–75). Philadelphia, PA: John Benjamins Publishing Company.

Kempermann, Gerd. (2012). New neurons for 'survival of the fittest.' *Nature Reviews Neuroscience, 13*(10), 727–736.

Kempermann, Gerd; Song, Hongjun & Gage, Fred H. (2015). Neurogenesis in the adult hippocampus. *Cold Spring Harbor Perspectives in Biology, 7*, a018812.

Kena, Grace; Hussar, William; McFarland, Joel; de Brey, Cristobal; Musu-Gillette, Lauren; Wang, Xiaolei, . . . Dunlop Velez, Erin. (2016). *The condition of education 2016.* Washington, DC: U.S. Department of Education, National Center for Education Statistics.

Kena, Grace; Musu-Gillette, Lauren; Robinson, Jennifer; Wang, Xiaolei; Rathbun, Amy; Zhang, Jijun, . . . Dunlop Velez, Erin. (2015). *The condition of education 2015.* Washington, DC: Department of Education, National Center for Education Statistics.

Kendall-Taylor, Nathaniel; Lindland, Eric; O'Neil, Moira & Stanley, Kate. (2014). Beyond prevalence: An explanatory approach to reframing child maltreatment in the United Kingdom. *Child Abuse & Neglect, 38*(5), 810–821.

Kennedy, Brian K. (2016). Advances in biological theories of aging. In Vern L. Bengtson & Richard Settersten (Eds.), *Handbook of theories of aging* (3rd ed., pp. 107–112). New York, NY: Springer Publishing Group.

Kenrick, Douglas T.; Griskevicius, Vladas; Neuberg, Steven L. & Schaller, Mark. (2010). Renovating the pyramid of needs: Contemporary extensions built upon ancient foundations. *Perspectives on Psychological Science, 5*(3), 292–314.

Kent, Blake Victor; Bradshaw, Matt & Uecker, Jeremy E. (2018). Forgiveness, attachment to God, and mental health outcomes in older U.S. adults: A longitudinal study. *Research on Aging, 40*(5), 456–479.

Keown, Louise J. & Palmer, Melanie. (2014). Comparisons between paternal and maternal involvement with sons: Early to middle childhood. *Early Child Development and Care, 184*(1), 99–117.

Kern, Ben D.; Graber, Kim C.; Shen, Sa; Hillman, Charles H. & McLoughlin, Gabriella. (2018). Association of school-based physical activity opportunities, socioeconomic status, and third-grade reading. *Journal of School Health, 88*(1), 34–43.

Kern, Margaret L.; Benson, Lizbeth; Larson, Emily; Forrest, Christopher B.; Bevans, Katherine B. & Steinberg, Laurence. (2016). The anatomy of developmental predictors of healthy lives study (TADPOHLS). *Applied Developmental Science, 20*(2), 135–145.

Kerr, Margaret; Stattin, Håkan & Burk, William J. (2010). A reinterpretation of parental monitoring in longitudinal perspective. *Journal of Research on Adolescence, 20*(1), 39–64.

Kersken, Verena; Zuberbühler, Klaus & Gomez, Juan-Carlos. (2017). Listeners can extract meaning from non-linguistic infant vocalisations cross-culturally. *Scientific Reports, 7.*

Kesselring, Thomas & Müller, Ulrich. (2011). The concept of egocentrism in the context of Piaget's theory. *New Ideas in Psychology, 29*(3), 327–345.

Kessler, Ronald C.; Avenevoli, Shelli; Costello, E. Jane; Georgiades, Katholiki; Green, Jennifer G.; Gruber, Michael J., . . . Merikangas, Kathleen R. (2012). Prevalence, persistence, and sociodemographic correlates of *DSM-IV* disorders in the National Comorbidity Survey Replication Adolescent Supplement. *Archives of General Psychiatry, 69*(4), 372–380.

Kettl, Paul. (2010). One vote for death panels. *JAMA, 303*(13), 1234–1235.

Khafi, Tamar Y.; Yates, Tuppett M. & Luthar, Suniya S. (2014). Ethnic differences in the developmental significance of parentification. *Family Process, 53*(2), 267–287.

Khan, Shereen; Gagné, Monique; Yang, Leigh & Shapk, Jennifer. (2016). Exploring the relationship between adolescents' self-concept and their offline and online social worlds. *Computers in Human Behavior, 55*(Part B), 940–945.

Kharsati, Naphisabet & Bhola, Poornima. (2014). Patterns of non-suicidal self-injurious behaviours among college students in India. *International Journal of Social Psychiatry, 61*(1), 39–49.

Kidd, Celeste; Palmeri, Holly & Aslin, Richard N. (2013). Rational snacking: Young children's decision-making on the marshmallow task is moderated by beliefs about environmental reliability. *Cognition, 126*(1), 109–114.

Killen, Melanie & Smetana, Judith G. (Eds.). (2014). *Handbook of moral development* (2nd ed.). New York, NY: Psychology Press.

Kim, Heejung S. & Sasaki, Joni Y. (2014). Cultural neuroscience: Biology of the mind in cultural contexts. *Annual Review of Psychology, 65*, 487–514.

Kim, Hojin I. & Johnson, Scott P. (2013). Do young infants prefer an infant-directed face or a happy face? *International Journal of Behavioral Development, 37*(2), 125–130.

Kim, Hyun Sik. (2011). Consequences of parental divorce for child development. *American Sociological Review, 76*(3), 487–511.

Kim, Joon Sik. (2011). Excessive crying: Behavioral and emotional regulation disorder in infancy. *Korean Journal of Pediatrics, 54*(6), 229–233.

Kim, Kyungmin; Cheng, Yen-Pi; Zarit, Steven H. & Fingerman, Karen L. (2015). Relationships between adults and parents in Asia. In Sheung-Tak Cheng, et al. (Eds.), *Successful aging* (pp. 101–122). Dordrecht, the Netherlands: Springer.

Kim-Spoon, Jungmeen; Longo, Gregory S. & McCullough, Michael E. (2012). Parent-adolescent relationship quality as a moderator for the influences of parents' religiousness on adolescents' religiousness and adjustment. *Journal of Youth and Adolescence, 41*(12), 1576–1587.

King, Valarie; Thorsen, Maggie L. & Amato, Paul R. (2014). Factors associated with positive relationships between stepfathers and adolescent stepchildren. *Social Science Research, 47*, 16–29.

Kirk, Elizabeth; Howlett, Neil; Pine, Karen J. & Fletcher, Ben. (2013). To sign or not to sign? The impact of encouraging infants to gesture on infant language and maternal mind-mindedness. *Child Development, 84*(2), 574–590.

Kirkham, Julie Ann & Kidd, Evan. (2017). The effect of Steiner, Montessori, and National Curriculum Education upon children's pretence and creativity. *Journal of Creative Behavior, 51*(1), 20–34.

Kiuru, Noona; Burk, William J.; Laursen, Brett; Salmela-Aro, Katariina & Nurmi, Jari-Erik. (2010). Pressure to drink but not to smoke: Disentangling selection and socialization in adolescent peer networks and peer groups. *Journal of Adolescence, 33*(6), 801–812.

Klaczynski, Paul A. (2017). Age differences in optimism bias are mediated by reliance on intuition and religiosity. *Journal of Experimental Child Psychology, 163*, 126–139.

Klaczynski, Paul A. & Felmban, Wejdan S. (2014). Heuristics and biases during adolescence: Developmental reversals and individual differences. In Henry Markovits (Ed.), *The developmental psychology of reasoning and decision-making* (pp. 84–111). New York, NY: Psychology Press.

Klahr, Ashlea M.; McGue, Matt; Iacono, William G. & Burt, S. Alexandra. (2011). The association between parent–child conflict and adolescent conduct problems over time: Results from a longitudinal adoption study. *Journal of Abnormal Psychology, 120*(1), 46–56.

Klass, Dennis; Silverman, Phyllis R. & Nickman, Steven L. (Eds.). (1996). *Continuing bonds: New understandings of grief.* Philadelphia, PA: Taylor & Francis.

Klass, Dennis & Steffen, Edith Maria (Eds.). (2017). *Continuing bonds in bereavement: New directions for research and practice.* New York, NY: Routledge.

Klaus, Susan F.; Ekerdt, David J. & Gajewski, Byron. (2012). Job satisfaction in birth cohorts of nurses. *Journal of Nursing Management, 20*(4), 461–471.

Kleijer, Bart C.; van Marum, Rob J.; Frijter, Dinnus H. M.; Jansen, Paul A. F.; Ribbe, Miel W.; Egberts, Antoine C. G. & Heerdink, Eibert R. (2014). Variability between nursing homes in prevalence of antipsychotic use in patients with dementia. *International Psychogeriatrics, 26*(3), 363–371.

Klein, Denise; Mok, Kelvin; Chen, Jen-Kai & Watkins, Kate E. (2014). Age of language learning shapes brain structure: A cortical thickness study of bilingual and monolingual individuals. *Brain and Language, 131*, 20–24.

Klein, Stanley B. (2012). The two selves: The self of conscious experience and its brain. In Mark R. Leary & June Price Tangney (Eds.), *Handbook of self and identity* (pp. 617–637). New York, NY: Guilford Press.

Kliegel, Matthias; Jäger, Theodor & Phillips, Louise H. (2008). Adult age differences in event-based prospective memory: A meta-analysis on the role of focal versus nonfocal cues. *Psychology and Aging, 23*(1), 203–208.

Klinger, Laura G.; Dawson, Geraldine; Burner, Karen & Crisler, Megan. (2014). Autism spectrum disorder. In Eric J. Mash & Russell A. Barkley (Eds.), *Child psychopathology* (3rd ed., pp. 531–572). New York, NY: Guilford Press.

Knott, Craig S.; Coombs, Ngaire; Stamatakis, Emmanuel & Biddulph, Jane P. (2015). All cause mortality and the case for age specific alcohol consumption guidelines: Pooled analyses of up to 10 population based cohorts. *BMJ, 350*, h384.

Koch, Iring; Poljac, Edita; Müller, Hermann & Kiesel, Andrea. (2018). Cognitive structure, flexibility, and plasticity in human multitasking—An integrative review of dual-task and task-switching research. *Psychological Bulletin, 144*(6), 557–583.

Koch, Linda. (2015). Shaping the gut microbiome. *Nature Reviews Genetics, 16*, 2–3.

Kochanek, Kenneth D.; Xu, Jiaquan; Murphy, Sherry L.; Miniño, Arialdi M. & Kung, Hsiang-Ching. (2011). *Deaths: Preliminary data for 2009. National Vital Statistics Reports, 59*(4). Hyattsville, MD: National Center for Health Statistics.

Kochel, Karen P.; Ladd, Gary W.; Bagwell, Catherine L. & Yabko, Brandon A. (2015). Bully/victim profiles' differential risk for worsening peer acceptance: The role of friendship. *Journal of Applied Developmental Psychology, 41*, 38–45.

Kohlberg, Lawrence. (1963). The development of children's orientations toward a moral order: I. Sequence in the development of moral thought. *Vita Humana, 6*(1/2), 11–33.

Kohlberg, Lawrence; Levine, Charles & Hewer, Alexandra. (1983). *Moral stages: A current formulation and a response to critics.* New York, NY: Karger.

Kolb, Bryan & Gibb, Robbin. (2015). Childhood poverty and brain development. *Human Development, 58*(4/5), 215–217.

Kolb, Bryan; Harker, Allonna & Gibb, Robbin. (2017). Principles of plasticity in the developing brain. *Developmental Medicine & Child Neurology, 59*(12), 1218–1223.

Koller, Daniela & Bynum, Julie P. W. (2014). Dementia in the USA: State variation in prevalence. *Journal of Public Health, 37*(4), 597–604.

Koltko-Rivera, Mark E. (2006). Rediscovering the later version of Maslow's hierarchy of needs: Self-transcendence and opportunities for theory, research, and unification. *Review of General Psychology, 10*(4), 302–317.

Komisar, Erica. (2017). *Being there: Why prioritizing motherhood in the first three years matters.* New York, NY: TarcherPerigee.

Komp, Kathrin; van Tilburg, Theo & van Groenou, Marjolein Broese. (2010). Paid work between age 60 and 70 years in Europe: A matter of socio-economic status? *International Journal of Ageing and Later Life, 5*(1), 45–75.

Konner, Melvin. (2010). *The evolution of childhood: Relationships, emotion, mind.* Cambridge, MA: Harvard University Press.

Konno, Rie; Kang, Hee Sun & Makimoto, Kiyoko. (2014). A best-evidence review of intervention studies for minimizing resistance-to-care behaviours for older adults with dementia in nursing homes. *Journal of Advanced Nursing, 70*(10), 2167–2180.

Konstam, Varda. (2015). *Emerging and young adulthood: Multiple perspectives, diverse narratives.* New York, NY: Springer.

Kooij, Dorien T. A. M.; Annet, H. D. E. Lange; Jansen, Paul G. W.; Kanfer, Ruth & Dikkers, Josje S. E. (2011). Age and work-related motives: Results of a meta-analysis. *Journal of Organizational Behavior, 32*(2), 197–225.

Kopp, Claire B. (2011). Development in the early years: Socialization, motor development, and consciousness. *Annual Review of Psychology, 62*, 165–187.

Kordas, Katarzyna; Burganowski, Rachael; Roy, Aditi; Peregalli, Fabiana; Baccino, Valentina; Barcia, Elizabeth, . . . Queirolo, Elena I. (2018). Nutritional status and diet as predictors of children's lead concentrations in blood and urine. *Environment International, 111*, 43–51.

Korhonen, Tellervo; Latvala, Antti; Dick, Danielle M.; Pulkkinen, Lea; Rose, Richard J.; Kaprio, Jaakko & Huizink, Anja C. (2012). Genetic and environmental influences underlying externalizing behaviors, cigarette smoking and illicit drug use across adolescence. *Behavior Genetics, 42*(4), 614–625.

Korte, J.; Bohlmeijer, E. T.; Cappeliez, P.; Smit, F. & Westerhof, G. J. (2012). Life review therapy for older adults with moderate depressive symptomatology: A pragmatic randomized controlled trial. *Psychological Medicine, 42*(6), 1163–1173.

Kosminsky, Phyllis. (2017). Working with continuing bonds from an attachment theoretical perspective. In Dennis Klass & Edith Maria Steffen (Eds.), *Continuing bonds in bereavement: New directions for research and practice.* New York, NY: Routledge.

Koster-Hale, Jorie & Saxe, Rebecca. (2013). Functional neuroimaging of theory of mind. In Simon Baron-Cohen, et al. (Eds.), *Understanding other minds: Perspectives from developmental social neuroscience* (3rd ed., pp. 132–163). New York, NY: Oxford University Press.

Krans, Elizabeth E. & Davis, Matthew M. (2012). *Preventing Low Birthweight*: 25 years, prenatal risk, and the failure to reinvent prenatal care. *American Journal of Obstetrics and Gynecology, 206*(5), 398–403.

Kreager, Derek A.; Molloy, Lauren E.; Moody, James & Feinberg, Mark E. (2016). Friends first? The peer network origins of adolescent dating. *Journal of Research on Adolescence, 26*(2), 257–269.

Krebs, Erin E.; Gravely, Amy; Nugent, Sean; Jensen, Agnes C.; DeRonne, Beth; Goldsmith, Elizabeth S., . . . Noorbaloochi, Siamak. (2018). Effect of opioid vs nonopioid medications on pain-related function in patients with chronic back pain or hip or knee osteoarthritis pain: The SPACE randomized clinical trial. *JAMA, 319*(9), 872–882.

Krebs, John R. (2009). The gourmet ape: Evolution and human food preferences. *American Journal of Clinical Nutrition, 90*(3), 707S–711S.

Kringelbach, Morten L.; Stark, Eloise A.; Alexander, Catherine; Bornstein, Marc H. & Stein, Alan. (2016). On cuteness: Unlocking the parental brain and beyond. *Trends in Cognitive Sciences, 20*(7), 545–558.

Krisberg, Kim. (2014). Public health messaging: How it is said can influence behaviors: Beyond the facts. *The Nation's Health, 44*(6), 1, 20.

Kroger, Jane & Marcia, James E. (2011). The identity statuses: Origins, meanings, and interpretations. In Seth J. Schwartz, et al. (Eds.), *Handbook of identity theory and research* (pp. 31–53). New York, NY: Springer.

Kroncke, Anna P.; Willard, Marcy & Huckabee, Helena. (2016). Optimal outcomes and recovery. In, *Assessment of autism spectrum disorder: Critical issues in clinical, forensic and school settings* (pp. 23–33). New York, NY: Springer.

Krouse, William J. (2012, November 14). *Gun control legislation. CRS Report for Congress.* Washington, DC: Congressional Research Service. RL32842

Kruse, Gina R.; Kalkhoran, Sara & Rigotti, Nancy A. (2017). Use of electronic cigarettes among U.S. adults with medical comorbidities. *AJPM, 52*(6), 798–804.

Kübler-Ross, Elisabeth. (1975). *Death: The final stage of growth.* Englewood Cliffs, NJ: Prentice-Hall.

Kübler-Ross, Elisabeth. (1997). *On death and dying.* New York, NY: Scribner.

Kübler-Ross, Elisabeth & Kessler, David. (2005). *On grief and grieving: Finding the meaning of grief through the five stages of loss.* New York, NY: Scribner.

Kubsch, Sylvia M.; Tyczkowski, Brenda L. & Passel, Cheryl. (2018). The impact of the Eden Alternative on hope. *Nursing and Residential Care, 20*(2), 91–94.

Kuehn, Bridget M. (2011). Scientists find promising therapies for fragile X and Down syndromes. *JAMA, 305*(4), 344–346.

Kuhlmann, Inga; Minihane, Anne; Huebbe, Patricia; Nebel, Almut & Rimbach, Gerald. (2010). Apolipoprotein E genotype and hepatitis C, HIV and herpes simplex disease risk: A literature review. *Lipids in Health and Disease, 9*(1), 8.

Kuhn, Deanna. (2013). Reasoning. In Philip D. Zelazo (Ed.), *The Oxford handbook of developmental psychology* (Vol. 1, pp. 744–764). New York, NY: Oxford University Press.

Kumar, Santosh; Calvo, Rocio; Avendano, Mauricio; Sivaramakrishnan, Kavita & Berkman, Lisa F. (2012). Social support, volunteering and health around the world: Cross-national evidence from 139 countries. *Social Science & Medicine, 74*(5), 696–706.

Kundu, Tapas K. (Ed.). (2013). *Epigenetics: Development and disease.* New York, NY: Springer.

Kuperberg, Arielle. (2012). Reassessing differences in work and income in cohabitation and marriage. *Journal of Marriage and Family, 74*(4), 688–707.

Kutob, Randa M.; Senf, Janet H.; Crago, Marjorie & Shisslak, Catherine M. (2010). Concurrent and longitudinal predictors of self-esteem in elementary and middle school girls. *Journal of School Health, 80*(5), 240–248.

Kuvaas, Bård; Buch, Robert; Weibel, Antoinette; Dysvik, Anders & Nerstad, Christina G. L. (2017). Do intrinsic and extrinsic motivation relate differently to employee outcomes? *Journal of Economic Psychology, 61*, 244–258.

Kypri, Kypros; Davie, Gabrielle; McElduff, Patrick; Connor, Jennie & Langley, John. (2014). Effects of lowering the minimum alcohol purchasing age on weekend assaults resulting in hospitalization in New Zealand. *American Journal of Public Health, 104*(8), 1396–1401.

Kypri, Kypros; Voas, Robert B.; Langley, John D.; Stephenson, Shaun C. R.; Begg, Dorothy J.; Tippetts, A. Scott & Davie, Gabrielle S. (2006). Minimum purchasing age for alcohol and traffic crash injuries among 15- to 19-year-olds in New Zealand. *American Journal of Public Health, 96*(1), 126–131.

Kyriakidou, Marilena; Blades, Mark & Carroll, Dan. (2014). Inconsistent findings for the eyes closed effect in children: The implications for interviewing child witnesses. *Frontiers in Psychology, 5*, 488.

Labouvie-Vief, Gisela. (2015). *Integrating emotions and cognition throughout the lifespan.* New York, NY: Springer.

Lachman, Margie E.; Neupert, Shevaun D. & Agrigoroaei, Stefan. (2011). The relevance of control beliefs for health and aging. In K. Warner Schaie & Sherry L. Willis (Eds.), *Handbook of the psychology of aging* (7th ed., pp. 175–190). San Diego, CA: Academic Press.

Lachs, Mark S. & Pillemer, Karl A. (2015, November 12). Elder abuse. *New England Journal of Medicine, 373*(20), 1947–1956.

Ladd, Helen F. & Sorensen, Lucy C. (2017). Returns to teacher experience: Student achievement and motivation in middle school. *Education Finance and Policy, 12*(2), 241–279.

LaFontana, Kathryn M. & Cillessen, Antonius H. N. (2010). Developmental changes in the priority of perceived status in childhood and adolescence. *Social Development, 19*(1), 130–147.

Lagattuta, Kristin H. (2014). Linking past, present, and future: Children's ability to connect mental states and emotions across time. *Child Development Perspectives, 8*(2), 90–95.

Laird, Robert D.; Marrero, Matthew D.; Melching, Jessica A. & Kuhn, Emily S. (2013). Information management strategies in early adolescence: Developmental change in use and transactional associations with psychological adjustment. *Developmental Psychology, 49*(5), 928–937.

Lake, Stephanie & Kerr, Thomas. (2017). The challenges of projecting the public health impacts of marijuana legalization in Canada. *International Journal of Health Policy Management, 6*(5), 285–287.

Lalande, Kathleen M. & Bonanno, George A. (2006). Culture and continuing bonds: A prospective comparison of bereavement in the United States and the People's Republic of China. *Death Studies, 30*(4), 303–324.

Lam, Chun Bun; McHale, Susan M. & Crouter, Ann C. (2012). Parent–child shared time from middle childhood to late adolescence: Developmental course and adjustment correlates. *Child Development, 83*(2), 2089–2103.

Lamb, Michael E. (2014). How I got started: Drawn into the life of crime: Learning from, by, and for child victims and witnesses. *Applied Cognitive Psychology, 28*(4), 607–611.

Lamm, Bettina; Keller, Heidi; Teiser, Johanna; Gudi, Helene; Yovsi, Relindis D.; Freitag, Claudia, . . . Lohaus, Arnold. (2017). Waiting for the second treat: Developing culture-specific modes of self-regulation. *Child Development,* (In Press).

Lampkin, Cheryl L. (2012, March). *Insights and spending habits of modern grandparents.* Washington, DC: AARP.

Landberg, Monique; Dimitrova, Radosveta & Syed, Moin. (2018). International perspectives on identity and acculturation in emerging adulthood: Introduction to the special issue. *Emerging Adulthood, 6*(1), 3–6.

Lane, Jonathan D. & Harris, Paul L. (2014). Confronting, representing, and believing counterintuitive concepts: Navigating the natural and the supernatural. *Perspectives on Psychological Science, 9*(2), 144–160.

Lang, Frieder R.; Rohr, Margund K. & Williger, Bettina. (2011). Modeling success in life-span psychology: The principles of selection, optimization, and compensation. In Karen L. Fingerman, et al. (Eds.), *Handbook of lifespan development* (pp. 57–86). New York, NY: Springer.

Langa, Kenneth M. (2015). Is the risk of Alzheimer's disease and dementia declining? *Alzheimer's Research & Therapy, 7*(1), 34.

Lange, Rense; Houran, James & Li, Song. (2015). Dyadic relationship values in Chinese online daters: Love American style? *Sexuality & Culture, 19*(1), 190–215.

Langer, Robert D.; Manson, JoAnn E. & Allison, Matthew A. (2012). Have we come full circle – or moved forward? The Women's Health Initiative 10 years on. *Climacteric, 15*(3), 206–212.

Långström, Niklas; Rahman, Qazi; Carlström, Eva & Lichtenstein, Paul. (2010). Genetic and environmental effects on same-sex sexual behavior: A population study of twins in Sweden. *Archives of Sexual Behavior, 39*(1), 75–80.

Lansford, Jennifer E.; Sharma, Chinmayi; Malone, Patrick S.; Woodlief, Darren; Dodge, Kenneth A.; Oburu, Paul, . . . Di Giunta, Laura. (2014). Corporal punishment, maternal warmth, and child adjustment: A longitudinal study in eight countries. *Journal of Clinical Child & Adolescent Psychology, 43*(4), 670–685.

Lapan, Candace & Boseovski, Janet J. (2017). When peer performance matters: Effects of expertise and traits on children's self-evaluations after social comparison. *Child Development, 88*(6), 1860–1872.

Lara-Cinisomo, Sandraluz; Fuligni, Allison Sidle & Karoly, Lynn A. (2011). Preparing preschoolers for kindergarten. In DeAnna M. Laverick & Mary Renck Jalongo (Eds.), *Transitions to early care and education* (Vol. 4, pp. 93–105). New York, NY: Springer.

Laraway, Kelly A.; Birch, Leann L.; Shaffer, Michele L. & Paul, Ian M. (2010). Parent perception of healthy infant and toddler growth. *Clinical Pediatrics, 49*(4), 343–349.

Larose, Joanie; Boulay, Pierre; Sigal, Ronald J.; Wright, Heather E. & Kenny, Glen P. (2013). Age-related decrements in heat dissipation during physical activity occur as early as the age of 40. *PLoS ONE, 8*(12), e83148.

Larsen, Peter A. (2018). Transposable elements and the multidimensional genome. *Chromosome Research, 26*(1–2), 1–3.

Larzelere, Robert E. & Cox, Ronald B. (2013). Making valid causal inferences about corrective actions by parents from longitudinal data. *Journal of Family Theory & Review, 5*(4), 282–299.

Larzelere, Robert E.; Gunnoe, Marjorie Lindner; Roberts, Mark W. & Ferguson, Christopher J. (2017). Children and parents deserve better parental discipline research: Critiquing the evidence for exclusively "positive" parenting. *Marriage & Family Review, 53*(1), 24–35.

Lattanzi-Licht, Marcia. (2013). Religion, spirituality, and dying. In David K. Meagher & David E. Balk (Eds.), *Handbook of thanatology: The essential body of knowledge for the study of death, dying, and bereavement* (2nd ed., pp. 9–16). New York, NY: Routledge.

Lau, Carissa; Ambalavanan, Namasivayam; Chakraborty, Hrishikesh; Wingate, Martha S. & Carlo, Waldemar A. (2013). Extremely low birth weight and infant mortality rates in the United States. *Pediatrics, 131*(5), 855–860.

Laurent, Heidemarie K. (2014). Clarifying the contours of emotion regulation: Insights from parent–child stress research. *Child Development Perspectives, 8*(1), 30–35.

Laursen, Brett & Collins, W. Andrew. (2009). Parent-child relationships during adolescence. In Richard M. Lerner & Laurence Steinberg (Eds.), *Handbook of adolescent psychology* (3rd ed., Vol. 2, pp. 3–42). Hoboken, NJ: Wiley.

Laursen, Brett; Hartl, Amy C.; Vitaro, Frank; Brendgen, Mara; Dionne, Ginette & Boivin, Michel. (2017). The spread of substance use and delinquency between adolescent twins. *Developmental Psychology, 53*(2), 329–339.

Layton, Jill; Li, Xiaochen; Shen, Changyu; de Groot, Mary; Lange, Leslie; Correa, Adolfo & Wessel, Jennifer.

(2018). Type 2 diabetes genetic risk scores are associated with increased type 2 diabetes risk among African Americans by cardiometabolic status. *Clinical Medicine Insights: Endocrinology and Diabetes, 11.*

Leach, Penelope. (2011). The EYFS and the real foundations of children's early years. In Richard House (Ed.), *Too much, too soon?: Early learning and the erosion of childhood.* Stroud, UK: Hawthorn.

LeCuyer, Elizabeth A. & Swanson, Dena Phillips. (2016). African American and European American mothers' limit setting and their 36-month-old children's responses to limits, self-concept, and social competence. *Journal of Family Issues, 37*(2), 270–296.

Lee, David M.; Nazroo, James; O'Connor, Daryl B.; Blake, Margaret & Pendleton, Neil. (2015). Sexual health and well-being among older men and women in England: Findings from the English longitudinal study of ageing. *Archives of Sexual Behavior,* (In Press).

Lee, Dohoon; Brooks-Gunn, Jeanne; McLanahan, Sara S.; Notterman, Daniel & Garfinkel, Irwin. (2013). The Great Recession, genetic sensitivity, and maternal harsh parenting. *Proceedings of the National Academy of Sciences, 110*(34), 13780–13784.

Lee, Jihyun & Porretta, David L. (2013). Enhancing the motor skills of children with autism spectrum disorders: A pool-based approach. *JOPERD, 84*(1), 41–45.

Lee, Moosung; Oi-yeung Lam, Beatrice; Ju, Eunsu & Dean, Jenny. (2016). Part-time employment and problem behaviors: Evidence from adolescents in South Korea. *Journal of Research on Adolescence,* (In Press).

Lee, Shawna J. & Altschul, Inna. (2015). Spanking of young children: Do immigrant and U.S.-born Hispanic parents differ? *Journal of Interpersonal Violence, 30*(3), 475–498.

Lee, Shawna J.; Altschul, Inna & Gershoff, Elizabeth T. (2015). Wait until your father gets home? Mother's and fathers' spanking and development of child aggression. *Children and Youth Services Review, 52,* 158–166.

Lee, Soojeong & Shouse, Roger C. (2011). The impact of prestige orientation on shadow education in South Korea. *Sociology of Education, 84*(3), 212–224.

Leman, Patrick J. & Björnberg, Marina. (2010). Conversation, development, and gender: A study of changes in children's concepts of punishment. *Child Development, 81*(3), 958–971.

Lemieux, André. (2012). Post-formal thought in gerontagogy or beyond Piaget. *Journal of Behavioral and Brain Science, 2*(3), 399–406.

Lemish, Daphna & Kolucki, Barbara. (2013). Media and early childhood development. In Pia Rebello Britto et al. (Eds.), *Handbook of early childhood development research and its impact on global policy.* New York, NY: Oxford University Press.

Lenhart, Amanda. (2015, April 9). *Teen, social media and technology overview 2015: Smartphone facilitate shifts in communication landscape for teens. Pew Research Center: Internet, Science & Tech.* Washington, DC: Pew Research Center.

Leopold, Thomas & Skopek, Jan. (2015a). The delay of grandparenthood: A cohort comparison in East and West Germany. *Journal of Marriage and Family, 77*(2), 441–460.

Leopold, Thomas & Skopek, Jan. (2015b). The demography of grandparenthood: An international profile. *Social Forces, 94*(2), 801–832.

Leslie, Leigh A.; Smith, Jocelyn R.; Hrapczynski, Katie M. & Riley, Debbie. (2013). Racial socialization in transracial adoptive families: Does it help adolescents deal with discriminative stress? *Family Relations, 62*(1), 72–81.

Leslie, Mitch. (2012). Gut microbes keep rare immune cells in line. *Science, 335*(6075), 1428.

Lessne, Deborah & Yanez, Christina. (2016, December 20). *Student reports of bullying: Results from the 2015 School Crime Supplement to the National Crime Victimization Survey.* Washington, DC: National Center for Education Statistics.

Lester, Patricia; Leskin, Gregory; Woodward, Kirsten; Saltzman, William; Nash, William; Mogil, Catherine, . . . Beardslee, William. (2011). Wartime deployment and military children: Applying prevention science to enhance family resilience. In Shelley MacDermid Wadsworth & David Riggs (Eds.), *Risk and resilience in U.S. military families* (pp. 149–173). New York, NY: Springer.

Leung, Sumie; Mareschal, Denis; Rowsell, Renee; Simpson, David; Laria, Leon; Grbic, Amanda & Kaufman, Jordy. (2016). Oscillatory activity in the infant brain and the representation of small numbers. *Frontiers in Systems Neuroscience, 10*(4).

Leventhal, Bennett L. (2013). Complementary and alternative medicine: Not many compliments but lots of alternatives. *Journal of Child and Adolescent Psychopharmacology, 23*(1), 54–56.

Levetan, Jessica L. & Wild, Lauren G. (2016). The implications of maternal grandmother coresidence and involvement for adolescent adjustment in South Africa. *International Journal of Psychology, 51*(5), 356–365.

Levine, Phillip B. & McKnight, Robin. (2017). Firearms and accidental deaths: Evidence from the aftermath of the Sandy Hook school shooting. *Science, 358*(6368), 1324–1328.

Levy, Daniel & Brink, Susan. (2005). *A change of heart: How the Framingham Heart Study helped unravel the mysteries of cardiovascular disease.* New York, NY: Knopf.

Lewandowski, Lawrence J. & Lovett, Benjamin J. (2014). Learning disabilities. In Eric J. Mash & Russell A. Barkley (Eds.), *Child psychopathology* (3rd ed., pp. 625–669). New York, NY: Guilford Press.

Lewin, Kurt. (1945). The Research Center for Group Dynamics at Massachusetts Institute of Technology. *Sociometry, 8*(2), 126–136.

Lewis, Ariane & Greer, David. (2017). Current controversies in brain death determination. *Nature Reviews Neurology, 13,* 505–509.

Lewis, John D.; Theilmann, Rebecca J.; Townsend, Jeanne & Evans, Alan C. (2013). Network efficiency in autism spectrum disorder and its relation to brain overgrowth. *Frontiers in Human Neuroscience, 7,* 845.

Lewis, Kristen & Burd-Sharps, Sarah. (2010). *The measure of America 2010–2011: Mapping risks and resilience.* New York, NY: New York University Press.

Lewis, Marc D. (2013). The development of emotional regulation: Integrating normative and individual differences through developmental neuroscience. In Philip D. Zelazo (Ed.), *The*

Oxford handbook of developmental psychology (Vol. 2, pp. 81–97). New York, NY: Oxford University Press.

Lewis, Michael. (2010). The emergence of human emotions. In Michael Lewis, et al. (Eds.), *Handbook of emotions* (3rd ed.). New York, NY: Guilford Press.

Lewis, Michael & Brooks, Jeanne. (1978). Self-knowledge and emotional development. In Michael Lewis & L. A. Rosenblum (Eds.), *Genesis of behavior* (Vol. 1, pp. 205–226). New York, NY: Plenum Press.

Li, Bai; Adab, Peymané & Cheng, Kar Keung. (2015). The role of grandparents in childhood obesity in China - evidence from a mixed methods study. *International Journal of Behavioral Nutrition and Physical Activity, 12,* 91.

Li, Ting & Zhang, Yanlong. (2015). Social network types and the health of older adults: Exploring reciprocal associations. *Social Science & Medicine, 130*(2), 59–68.

Li, Weilin; Farkas, George; Duncan, Greg J.; Burchinal, Margaret R. & Vandell, Deborah Lowe. (2013). Timing of high-quality child care and cognitive, language, and preacademic development. *Developmental Psychology, 49*(8), 1440–1451.

Li, Yanling; Du, Xiaojing; Zhang, Chunfang & Wang, Sibao. (2013). Physical activity among the elderly in China: A qualitative study. *British Journal of Community Nursing, 18*(7), 340–350.

Li, Yibing & Lerner, Richard M. (2011). Trajectories of school engagement during adolescence: Implications for grades, depression, delinquency, and substance use. *Developmental Psychology, 47*(1), 233–247.

Liben, Lynn S. (2016). We've come a long way, baby (but we're not there yet): Gender past, present, and future. *Child Development, 87*(1), 5–28.

Libertus, Melissa E.; Feigenson, Lisa & Halberda, Justin. (2013). Is approximate number precision a stable predictor of math ability? *Learning and Individual Differences, 25,* 126–133.

Liebler, Carolyn A.; Porter, Sonya R.; Fernandez, Leticia E.; Noon, James M. & Ennis, Sharon R. (2017). America's churning races: Race and ethnicity response changes between census 2000 and the 2010 census. *Demography, 54*(1), 259–284.

Lilienfeld, Scott O. (2017). Psychology's replication crisis and the grant culture: Righting the ship. *Perspectives on Psychological Science, 12*(4), 660–664.

Lillard, Angeline S. (2013). Playful learning and Montessori education. *American Journal of Play, 5*(2), 157–186.

Lillard, Angeline S. & Kavanaugh, Robert D. (2014). The contribution of symbolic skills to the development of an explicit theory of mind. *Child Development, 85*(4), 1535–1551.

Lillard, Angeline S.; Lerner, Matthew D.; Hopkins, Emily J.; Dore, Rebecca A.; Smith, Eric D. & Palmquist, Carolyn M. (2013). The impact of pretend play on children's development: A review of the evidence. *Psychological Bulletin, 139*(1), 1–34.

Lim, Chaeyoon & Putnam, Robert D. (2010). Religion, social networks, and life satisfaction. *American Sociological Review, 75*(6), 914–933.

Lim, Cher Ping; Zhao, Yong; Tondeur, Jo; Chai, Ching Sing & Tsai, Chin-Chung. (2013). Bridging the gap: Technology trends and use of technology in schools. *Educational Technology & Society, 16*(2), 59–68.

Lin, Frank R.; Yaffe, Kristine; Xia, Jin; Xue, Qian-Li; Harris, Tamara B.; Purchase-Helzner, Elizabeth, . . . Simonsick, Eleanor M. (2013). Hearing loss and cognitive decline in older adults. *JAMA Internal Medicine, 173*(4), 293–299.

Lin, I-Fen; Fee, Holly R. & Wu, Hsueh-Sheng. (2012). Negative and positive caregiving experiences: A closer look at the intersection of gender and relationship. *Family Relations, 61*(2), 343–358.

Lin, Jue; Epel, Elissa & Blackburn, Elizabeth. (2012). Telomeres and lifestyle factors: Roles in cellular aging. *Mutation Research/Fundamental and Molecular Mechanisms of Mutagenesis, 730*(1/2), 85–89.

Lin, Phoebe. (2016). Risky behaviors: Integrating adolescent egocentrism with the theory of planned behavior. *Review of General Psychology, 20*(4), 392–398.

Lindau, Stacy T. & Gavrilova, Natalia. (2010). Sex, health, and years of sexually active life gained due to good health: Evidence from two US population based cross sectional surveys of ageing. *BMJ, 340*(7746), c810.

Lindberg, Laura Duberstein; Maddow-Zimet, Isaac & Boonstra, Heather. (2016). Changes in adolescents' receipt of sex education, 2006–2013. *Journal of Adolescent Health, 58*(6), 621–627.

Liu, Chang & Neiderhiser, Jenae M. (2017). Using genetically informed designs to understand the environment: The importance of family-based approaches. In Patrick H. Tolan & Leventhal Bennett L. (Eds.), *Gene-environment transactions in developmental psychopathology: The role in intervention research* (pp. 95–110). New York: NY: Springer.

Liu, Dong & Xin, Ziqiang. (2014). Birth cohort and age changes in the self-esteem of Chinese adolescents: A cross-temporal meta-analysis, 1996–2009. *Journal of Research on Adolescence.*

Liu, Junsheng; Chen, Xinyin; Zhou, Ying; Li, Dan; Fu, Rui & Coplan, Robert J. (2017). Relations of shyness-sensitivity and unsociability with adjustment in middle childhood and early adolescence in suburban Chinese children. *International Journal of Behavioral Development, 41*(6), 681–687.

Livas-Dlott, Alejandra; Fuller, Bruce; Stein, Gabriela L.; Bridges, Margaret; Mangual Figueroa, Ariana & Mireles, Laurie. (2010). Commands, competence, and *cariño*: Maternal socialization practices in Mexican American families. *Developmental Psychology, 46*(3), 566–578.

Livingston, Gretchen. (2014). *Four-in-ten couples are saying 'I do,' again.* Washington, DC: Pew Research Center.

Lobstein, Tim & Dibb, Sue. (2005). Evidence of a possible link between obesogenic food advertising and child overweight. *Obesity Reviews, 6*(3), 203–208.

Lock, Margaret. (2013). The lure of the epigenome. *The Lancet, 381*(9881), 1896–1897.

Löckenhoff, Corinna E.; De Fruyt, Filip; Terracciano, Antonio; McCrae, Robert R.; De Bolle, Marleen; Costa, Paul T., . . . Yik, Michelle. (2009). Perceptions of aging across 26 cultures and their culture-level associates. *Psychology and Aging, 24*(4), 941–954.

Lococo, Kathy H.; Staplin, Loren; Martell, Carol A. & Sifrit, Kathy J. (2012). *Pedal application errors.* Washington, DC: National Highway Traffic Safety Administration. DOT HS 811 597.

Lodge, Amy C. & Umberson, Debra. (2012). All shook up: Sexuality of mid- to later life married couples. *Journal of Marriage and Family, 74*(3), 428–443.

Loeber, Rolf & Burke, Jeffrey D. (2011). Developmental pathways in juvenile externalizing and internalizing problems. *Journal of Research on Adolescence, 21*(1), 34–46.

Loeber, Rolf; Capaldi, Deborah M. & Costello, Elizabeth. (2013). Gender and the development of aggression, disruptive behavior, and delinquency from childhood to early adulthood. In Patrick H. Tolan & Bennett L. Leventh (Eds.), *Disruptive behavior disorders* (pp. 137–160). New York, NY: Springer.

Loftus, Patricia A. & Wise, Sarah K. (2016). Epidemiology of asthma. *Current Opinion in Otolaryngology & Head & Neck Surgery, 24*(3), 245–249.

Lopez, Anna B.; Huynh, Virginia W. & Fuligni, Andrew J. (2011). A longitudinal study of religious identity and participation during adolescence. *Child Development, 82*(4), 1297–1309.

Lopez-Hartmann, Maja; Wens, Johan; Verhoeven, Veronique & Remmen, Roy. (2012). The effect of caregiver support interventions for informal caregivers of community-dwelling frail elderly: A systematic review. *International Journal of Integrated Care, 12*, 1–16.

López-Otín, Carlos; Blasco, Maria A.; Partridge, Linda; Serrano, Manuel & Kroemer, Guido. (2013). The hallmarks of aging. *Cell, 153*(6), 1194–1217.

Lou, Vivian W. Q.; Lu, Nan; Xu, Ling & Chi, Iris. (2013). Grandparent–grandchild family capital and self-rated health of older rural Chinese adults: The role of the grandparent–parent relationship. *The Journals of Gerontology Series B: Psychological Sciences and Social Sciences, 68*(4), 599–608.

Lövdén, Martin; Xu, Weili & Wang, Hui-Xin. (2013). Lifestyle change and the prevention of cognitive decline and dementia: What is the evidence? *Current Opinion in Psychiatry, 26*(3), 239–243.

Lovell, Brian & Wetherell, Mark A. (2011). The cost of caregiving: Endocrine and immune implications in elderly and non elderly caregivers. *Neuroscience & Biobehavioral Reviews, 35*(6), 1342–1352.

Lubienski, Christopher; Puckett, Tiffany & Brewer, T. Jameson. (2013). Does homeschooling "work"? A critique of the empirical claims and agenda of advocacy organizations. *Peabody Journal of Education, 88*(3), 378–392.

Luecken, Linda J.; Lin, Betty; Coburn, Shayna S.; MacKinnon, David P.; Gonzales, Nancy A. & Crnic, Keith A. (2013). Prenatal stress, partner support, and infant cortisol reactivity in low-income Mexican American families. *Psychoneuroendocrinology, 38*(12), 3092–3101.

Luengo-Prado, María J. & Sevilla, Almudena. (2012). Time to cook: Expenditure at retirement in Spain. *The Economic Journal, 123*(569), 764–789.

Luhmann, Maike; Hofmann, Wilhelm; Eid, Michael & Lucas, Richard E. (2012). Subjective well-being and adaptation to life events: A meta-analysis. *Journal of Personality and Social Psychology, 102*(3), 592–615.

Luna, Beatriz; Paulsen, David J.; Padmanabhan, Aarthi & Geier, Charles. (2013). The teenage brain: Cognitive control and motivation. *Current Directions in Psychological Science, 22*(2), 94–100.

Lundahl, Alyssa; Kidwell, Katherine M. & Nelson, Timothy D. (2014). Parental underestimates of child weight: A meta-analysis. *Pediatrics, 133*(3), e689–e703.

Lundquist, Gunilla; Rasmussen, Birgit H. & Axelsson, Bertil. (2011). Information of imminent death or not: Does it make a difference? *Journal of Clinical Oncology, 29*(29), 3927–3931.

Luo, Baozhen; Zhou, Kui; Jin, Eun Jung; Newman, Alisha & Liang, Jiayin. (2013). Ageism among college students: A comparative study between U.S. and China. *Journal of Cross-Cultural Gerontology, 28*(1), 49–63.

Lupski, James R. (2013). Genome mosaicism: One human, multiple genomes. *Science, 341*(6144), 358–359.

Lushin, Viktor; Jaccard, James & Kaploun, Victor. (2017). Parental monitoring, adolescent dishonesty and underage drinking: A nationally representative study. *Journal of Adolescence, 57*, 99–107.

Lustig, Cindy; Shah, Priti; Seidler, Rachael & Reuter-Lorenz, Patricia A. (2009). Aging, training, and the brain: A review and future directions. *Neuropsychology Review, 19*(4), 504–522.

Luthar, Suniya S.; Cicchetti, Dante & Becker, Bronwyn. (2000). The construct of resilience: A critical evaluation and guidelines for future work. *Child Development, 71*(3), 543–562.

Luthar, Suniya S.; Small, Phillip J. & Ciciolla, Lucia. (2018). Adolescents from upper middle class communities: Substance misuse and addiction across early adulthood. *Development and Psychopathology, 30*(1), 315–335.

Lutz, Wolfgang; Muttarak, Raya & Striessnig, Erich. (2014). Universal education is key to enhanced climate adaptation. *Science, 346*(6213), 1061–1062.

Luyckx, Koen; Klimstra, Theo A.; Duriez, Bart; Van Petegem, Stijn & Beyers, Wim. (2013). Personal identity processes from adolescence through the late 20s: Age trends, functionality, and depressive symptoms. *Social Development, 22*(4), 701–721.

Lyall, Donald M.; Inskip, Hazel M.; Mackay, Daniel; Deary, Ian J.; McIntosh, Andrew M.; Hotopf, Matthew, . . . Smith, Daniel J. (2016). Low birth weight and features of neuroticism and mood disorder in 83,545 participants of the UK Biobank cohort. *British Journal of Psychiatry Open, 2*(1), 38–44.

Lynch, Scott M. & Brown, J. Scott. (2011). Stratification and inequality over the life course. In Robert H. Binstock & Linda K. George (Eds.), *Handbook of aging and the social sciences* (7th ed., pp. 105–117). San Diego, CA: Academic Press.

Lynskey, Michael T.; Agrawal, Arpana; Henders, Anjali; Nelson, Elliot C.; Madden, Pamela A. F. & Martin, Nicholas G. (2012). An Australian twin study of cannabis and other illicit drug use and misuse, and other psychopathology. *Twin Research and Human Genetics, 15*(5), 631–641.

Lyssens-Danneboom, Vicky & Mortelmans, Dimitri. (2014). Living apart together and money: New partnerships, traditional gender roles. *Journal of Marriage and Family, 76*(5), 949–966.

Ma, Defu; Ning, Yibing; Gao, Hongchong; Li, Wenjun; Wang, Junkuan; Zheng, Yingdong, . . . Wang, Peiyu.

(2014). Nutritional status of breast-fed and non-exclusively breast-fed infants from birth to age 5 months in 8 Chinese cities. *Asia Pacific Journal of Clinical Nutrition*, 23(2), 282–292.

MacDorman, Marian F. & Rosenberg, Harry M. (1993). *Trends in infant mortality by cause of death and other characteristics, 1960–88. Vital and Health Statistic*, 20(20). Hyattsville, MD: National Center for Health Statistics.

Mackenzie, Karen J.; Anderton, Stephen M. & Schwarze, Jürgen. (2014). Viral respiratory tract infections and asthma in early life: Cause and effect? *Clinical & Experimental Allergy*, 44(1), 9–19.

MacKenzie, Michael J.; Nicklas, Eric; Brooks-Gunn, Jeanne & Waldfogel, Jane. (2011). Who spanks infants and toddlers? Evidence from the fragile families and child well-being study. *Children and Youth Services Review*, 33(8), 1364–1373.

Macmillan, Ross & Copher, Ronda. (2005). Families in the life course: Interdependency of roles, role configurations, and pathways. *Journal of Marriage and Family*, 67(4), 858–879.

Macosko, Evan Z. & McCarroll, Steven A. (2013). Our fallen genomes. *Science*, 342(6158), 564–565.

MacWhinney, Brian. (2015). Language development. In Richard M. Lerner (Ed.), *Handbook of child psychology and developmental science* (7th ed., Vol. 2, pp. 296–338). New York, NY: Wiley.

Mahmood, Syed S.; Levy, Daniel; Vasan, Ramachandran S. & Wang, Thomas J. (2014). The Framingham Heart Study and the epidemiology of cardiovascular disease: A historical perspective. *The Lancet*, 383(9921), 999–1008.

Makelarski, Jennifer A.; Abramsohn, Emily; Benjamin, Jasmine H.; Du, Senxi & Lindau, Stacy T. (2017). Diagnostic accuracy of two food insecurity screeners recommended for use in health care settings. *American Journal of Public Health*, 107(11), 1812–1817.

Ma-Kellams, Christine; Or, Flora; Baek, Ji Hyun & Kawachi, Ichiro. (2016). Rethinking suicide surveillance Google search data and self-reported suicidality differentially estimate completed suicide risk. *Clinical Psychological Science*, 4(3), 480–484.

Makinen, Mauno; Puukko-Viertomies, Leena-Riitta; Lindberg, Nina; Siimes, Martti A. & Aalberg, Veikko. (2012). Body dissatisfaction and body mass in girls and boys transitioning from early to mid-adolescence: Additional role of self-esteem and eating habits. *BMC Psychiatry*, 12(35).

Malchiodi, Cathy A. (2012). Creativity and aging: An art therapy perspective. In Cathy A. Malchiodi (Ed.), *Handbook of art therapy* (2nd ed., pp. 275–287). New York, NY: Guilford Press.

Malloy, Lindsay C.; Shulman, Elizabeth P. & Cauffman, Elizabeth. (2014). Interrogations, confessions, and guilty pleas among serious adolescent offenders. *Law and Human Behavior*, 38(2), 181–193.

Mancini, Anthony D.; Prati, Gabriele & Bonanno, George A. (2011). Do shattered worldviews lead to complicated grief? Prospective and longitudinal analyses. *Journal of Social and Clinical Psychology*, 30(2), 184–215.

Mangels, Jennifer A.; Good, Catherine; Whiteman, Ronald C.; Maniscalco, Brian & Dweck, Carol S. (2012).

Emotion blocks the path to learning under stereotype threat. *Social Cognitive and Affective Neuroscience*, 7(2), 230–241.

Manning, Wendy D.; Brown, Susan L. & Payne, Krista K. (2014). Two decades of stability and change in age at first union formation. *Journal of Marriage and Family*, 76(2), 247–260.

Mantua, Janna & Spencer, Rebecca M. C. (2017). Exploring the nap paradox: Are mid-day sleep bouts a friend or foe? *Sleep Medicine*, 37, 88–97.

Mar, Raymond A. (2011). The neural bases of social cognition and story comprehension. *Annual Review of Psychology*, 62, 103–134.

Marazita, John M. & Merriman, William E. (2010). Verifying one's knowledge of a name without retrieving it: A U-shaped relation to vocabulary size in early childhood. *Language Learning and Development*, 7(1), 40–54.

Marchman, Virginia A.; Martínez, Lucía Z.; Hurtado, Nereyda; Grüter, Theres & Fernald, Anne. (2017). Caregiver talk to young Spanish-English bilinguals: Comparing direct observation and parent-report measures of dual-language exposure. *Developmental Science*, 20(1), e12425.

Marcia, James E. (1966). Development and validation of ego-identity status. *Journal of Personality and Social Psychology*, 3(5), 551–558.

Marcovitch, Stuart; Clearfield, Melissa W.; Swingler, Margaret; Calkins, Susan D. & Bell, Martha Ann. (2016). Attentional predictors of 5-month-olds' performance on a looking A-not-B task. *Infant and Child Development*, 25(4), 233–246.

Marcus, Gary F. & Rabagliati, Hugh. (2009). Language acquisition, domain specificity, and descent with modification. In John Colombo, et al. (Eds.), *Infant pathways to language: Methods, models, and research disorders* (pp. 267–285). New York, NY: Psychology Press.

Mareschal, Denis & Kaufman, Jordy. (2012). Object permanence in infancy: Revisiting Baillargeon's drawbridge study. In Alan M. Slater & Paul C. Quinn (Eds.), *Developmental psychology: Revisiting the classic studies*. Thousand Oaks, CA: Sage.

Margolis, Rachel & Myrskylä, Mikko. (2011). A global perspective on happiness and fertility. *Population and Development Review*, 37(1), 29–56.

Markovitch, Noam; Luyckx, Koen; Klimstra, Theo; Abramson, Lior & Knafo-Noam, Ariel. (2017). Identity exploration and commitment in early adolescence: Genetic and environmental contributions. *Developmental Psychology*, 53(11), 2092–2102.

Markowitsch, Hans J. & Staniloiu, Angelica. (2012). Amnesic disorders. *The Lancet*, 380(9851), 1429–1440.

Maroto, Michelle. (2017). When the kids live at home: Coresidence, parental assets, and economic insecurity. *Journal of Marriage and Family*, 79(4), 1041–1059.

Marotta, Phillip L. & Voisin, Dexter R. (2017). Testing three pathways to substance use and delinquency among low-income African American adolescents. *Children and Youth Services Review*, 75, 7–14.

Marschark, Marc & Spencer, Patricia E. (2003). What we know, what we don't know, and what we should know. In Marc Marschark & Patricia E. Spencer (Eds.), *Oxford handbook of deaf* *studies, language, and education* (pp. 491–494). New York, NY: Oxford University Press.

Marshall, Eliot. (2014). An experiment in zero parenting. *Science, 345*(6198), 752–754.

Marsiske, Michael & Margrett, Jennifer A. (2006). Everyday problem solving and decision making. In James E. Birren & K. Warren Schaie (Eds.), *Handbook of the psychology of aging* (6th ed., pp. 315–342). San Diego, CA: Academic Press.

Martin, Carmel. (2014). *Common Core implementation best practices. New York State Office of the Governor Common Core Implementation Panel.* Washington, DC: Center for American Progress.

Martin, Carol L.; Fabes, Richard; Hanish, Laura; Leonard, Stacie & Dinella, Lisa. (2011). Experienced and expected similarity to same-gender peers: Moving toward a comprehensive model of gender segregation. *Sex Roles, 65*(5/6), 421–434.

Martin, Georgianna L.; Parker, Gene; Pascarella, Ernest T. & Blechschmidt, Sally. (2015). Do fraternities and sororities inhibit intercultural competence? *Journal of College Student Development, 56*(1), 66–72.

Martin, Joyce A.; Hamilton, Brady E.; Osterman, Michelle J. K.; Driscoll, Anne K. & Drake, Patrick. (2018, January 31). *Births: Final data for 2016. National Vital Statistics Reports, 67*(1). Hyattsville, MD: National Center for Health Statistics.

Martin, Joyce A.; Hamilton, Brady E.; Osterman, Michelle J. K.; Driscoll, Anne K. & Mathews, T. J. (2017). *Births: Final data from 2015. National Vital Statistics Reports, 66*(1). Hyattsville, MD: National Center for Health Statistics.

Martin, Michael O.; Mullis, Ina V. S.; Foy, Pierre & Hooper, Martin. (2016). *TIMSS 2015 international results in science.* Chestnut Hill, MA: TIMSS & PIRLS International Study Center, Boston College.

Martincorena, Iñigo & Campbell, Peter J. (2015). Somatic mutation in cancer and normal cells. *Science, 349*(6255), 1483–1489.

Martinez, Maureen; Shukla, Hemant; Nikulin, Joanna; Wadood, Mufti Zubair; Hadler, Stephen; Mbaeyi, Chukwuma, . . . Ehrhardt, Derek. (2017, August 18). *Progress toward poliomyelitis eradication—Afghanistan, January 2016–June 2017. Morbidity and Mortality Weekly Report, 66*(32), 854–858. Atlanta, GA: Centers for Disease Control and Prevention.

Martinson, Melissa L. & Reichman, Nancy E. (2016). Socioeconomic inequalities in low birth weight in the United States, the United Kingdom, Canada, and Australia. *American Journal of Public Health, 106*(4), 748–754.

Martin-Uzzi, Michele & Duval-Tsioles, Denise. (2013). The experience of remarried couples in blended families. *Journal of Divorce & Remarriage, 54*(1), 43–57.

Marvasti, Amir B. & McKinney, Karyn D. (2011). Does diversity mean assimilation? *Critical Sociology, 37*(5), 631–650.

Masarik, April S. & Conger, Rand D. (2017). Stress and child development: A review of the Family Stress Model. *Current Opinion in Psychology, 13*, 85–90.

Mascarenhas, Maya N.; Flaxman, Seth R.; Boerma, Ties; Vanderpoel, Sheryl & Stevens, Gretchen A. (2012). National, regional, and global trends in infertility prevalence since 1990: A systematic analysis of 277 health surveys. *PloS Medicine, 9*(12), e1001356.

Mascaro, Jennifer S.; Rentscher, Kelly E.; Hackett, Patrick D.; Mehl, Matthias R. & Rilling, James K. (2017). Child gender influences paternal behavior, language, and brain function. *Behavioral Neuroscience, 131*(3), 262–273.

Maslow, Abraham H. (1954). *Motivation and personality* (1st ed.). New York, NY: Harper & Row.

Maslow, Abraham H. (1962). *Toward a psychology of being* (1st ed.). Princeton, NJ: D. Van Nostrand.

Maslow, Abraham H. (1997). *Motivation and personality* (3rd ed.). New York, NY: Pearson.

Maslow, Abraham H. (1998). *Toward a psychology of being* (3rd ed.). New York, NY: Wiley.

Maslowsky, Julie; Schulenberg, John E. & Zucker, Robert A. (2014). Influence of conduct problems and depressive symptomatology on adolescent substance use: Developmentally proximal versus distal effects. *Developmental Psychology, 50*(4), 1179–1189.

Masten, Ann S. (2013). Risk and resilience in development. In Philip D. Zelazo (Ed.), *The Oxford handbook of developmental psychology* (Vol. 2, pp. 579–607). New York, NY: Oxford University Press.

Masten, Ann S. (2014). *Ordinary magic: Resilience in development.* New York, NY: Guilford Press.

Mathews, T. J.; Menacker, Fay & MacDorman, Marian F. (2003). *Infant mortality statistics from the 2001 period linked birth/infant death data set. National Vital Statistics Reports, 52*(2). Hyattsville, MD: National Center for Health Statistics.

Mathison, David J. & Agrawal, Dewesh. (2010). An update on the epidemiology of pediatric fractures. *Pediatric Emergency Care, 26*(8), 594–603.

Matthews, Fiona E.; Arthur, Antony; Barnes, Linda E.; Bond, John; Jagger, Carol; Robinson, Louise & Brayne, Carol. (2013). A two-decade comparison of prevalence of dementia in individuals aged 65 years and older from three geographical areas of England: Results of the Cognitive Function and Ageing Study I and II. *The Lancet, 382*(9902), 1405–1412.

Matthews, Timothy C. (2018). Perspectives on financial abuse of elders in Canada. *Trusts & Trustees, 24*(1), 73–78.

Mattick, Richard P.; Clare, Philip J.; Aiken, Alexandra; Wadolowski, Monika; Hutchinson, Delyse; Najman, Jackob, . . . Degenhardt, Louisa. (2018). Association of parental supply of alcohol with adolescent drinking, alcohol-related harms, and alcohol use disorder symptoms: A prospective cohort study. *The Lancet Public Health, 3*(2), e64–e71.

Mattison, Julie A.; Colman, Ricki J.; Beasley, T. Mark; Allison, David B.; Kemnitz, Joseph W.; Roth, George S., . . . Anderson, Rozalyn M. (2017). Caloric restriction improves health and survival of rhesus monkeys. *Nature Communications, 8*(14063).

Maume, David J. & Sebastian, Rachel A. (2012). Gender, nonstandard work schedules, and marital quality. *Journal of Family and Economic Issues, 33*(4), 477–490.

Maxfield, Molly; Pyszczynski, Tom; Greenberg, Jeff & Bultmann, Michael N. (2017). Age differences in the effects of mortality salience on the correspondence bias. *The International Journal of Aging and Human Development, 84*(4), 329–342.

May, Vanessa; Mason, Jennifer & Clarke, Lynda. (2012). Being there, yet not interfering: The paradoxes of grandparenting. In Sara Arber & Virpi Timonen (Eds.), *Contemporary grandparenting: Changing family relationships in global contexts* (pp. 139–158). Chicago, IL: Policy Press.

Maylor, Elizabeth A. & Badham, Stephen P. (2018). Effects of time of day on age-related associative deficits. *Psychology and Aging, 33*(1), 7–16.

Mazza, Julia Rachel; Pingault, Jean-Baptiste; Booij, Linda; Boivin, Michel; Tremblay, Richard; Lambert, Jean, . . . Côté, Sylvana. (2017). Poverty and behavior problems during early childhood: The mediating role of maternal depression symptoms and parenting. *International Journal of Behavioral Development, 41*(6), 670–680.

McAdams, Tom A.; Neiderhiser, Jenae M.; Rijsdijk, Fruhling V.; Narusyte, Jurgita; Lichtenstein, Paul & Eley, Thalia C. (2014). Accounting for genetic and environmental confounds in associations between parent and child characteristics: A systematic review of children-of-twins studies. *Psychological Bulletin, 140*(4), 1138–1173.

McCabe, Janice. (2011). Doing multiculturalism: An interactionist analysis of the practices of a multicultural sorority. *Journal of Contemporary Ethnography, 40*(5), 521–549.

McCabe, Sean Esteban; Veliz, Philip; Wilens, Timothy E. & Schulenberg, John E. (2017). Adolescents' prescription stimulant use and adult functional outcomes: A national prospective study. *Journal of the American Academy of Child and Adolescent Psychiatry, 56*(3), 226–233.e224.

McCabe, Sean Esteban; West, Brady T.; Teter, Christian J. & Boyd, Carol J. (2014). Trends in medical use, diversion, and nonmedical use of prescription medications among college students from 2003 to 2013: Connecting the dots. *Addictive Behaviors, 39*(7), 1176–1182.

McCall, Robert B. (2013). The consequences of early institutionalization: Can institutions be improved? – Should they? *Child and Adolescent Mental Health, 18*(4), 193–201.

McCallion, Gail & Feder, Jody. (2013, October 18). *Student bullying: Overview of research, federal initiatives, and legal issues.* Washington, DC: Congressional Research Service. R43254.

McCarrey, Anna C.; Henry, Julie D.; von Hippel, William; Weidemann, Gabrielle; Sachdev, Perminder S.; Wohl, Michael J. A. & Williams, Mark. (2012). Age differences in neural activity during slot machine gambling: An fMRI study. *PLoS ONE, 7*(11), e49787.

McCarthy, Neil & Eberhart, Johann K. (2014). Gene–ethanol interactions underlying fetal alcohol spectrum disorders. *Cellular and Molecular Life Sciences, 71*(14), 2699–2706.

McCartney, Kathleen; Burchinal, Margaret; Clarke-Stewart, Alison; Bub, Kristen L.; Owen, Margaret T. & Belsky, Jay. (2010). Testing a series of causal propositions relating time in child care to children's externalizing behavior. *Developmental Psychology, 46*(1), 1–17.

McClain, Lauren Rinelli. (2011). Better parents, more stable partners: Union transitions among cohabiting parents. *Journal of Marriage and Family, 73*(5), 889–901.

McClain, Natalie M. & Garrity, Stacy E. (2011). Sex trafficking and the exploitation of adolescents. *Journal of Obstetric, Gynecologic, & Neonatal Nursing, 40*(2), 243–252.

McCormick, Cheryl M.; Mathews, Iva Z.; Thomas, Catherine & Waters, Patti. (2010). Investigations of HPA function and the enduring consequences of stressors in adolescence in animal models. *Brain and Cognition, 72*(1), 73–85.

McCright, Aaron M. & Dunlap, Riley E. (2011). The politicization of climate change and polarization in the American public's views of global warming, 2001–2010. *Sociological Quarterly, 52*(2), 155–194.

McDaniel, Mark A. & Bugg, Julie M. (2012). Memory training interventions: What has been forgotten? *Journal of Applied Research in Memory and Cognition, 1*(1), 45–50.

McEwen, Bruce S. & Karatsoreos, Ilia N. (2015). Sleep deprivation and circadian disruption: Stress, allostasis, and allostatic load. *Sleep Medicine Clinics, 10*(1), 1–10.

McEwen, Craig A. & McEwen, Bruce S. (2017). Social structure, adversity, toxic stress, and intergenerational poverty: An early childhood model. *Annual Review of Sociology, 43*, 445–472.

McFadden, Susan H. & Basting, Anne D. (2010). Healthy aging persons and their brains: Promoting resilience through creative engagement. *Clinics in Geriatric Medicine, 26*(1), 149–161.

McFarlane, Alexander C. & Van Hooff, Miranda. (2009). Impact of childhood exposure to a natural disaster on adult mental health: 20-year longitudinal follow-up study. *The British Journal of Psychiatry, 195*(2), 142–148.

McGill, Rebecca K.; Hughes, Diane; Alicea, Stacey & Way, Niobe. (2012). Academic adjustment across middle school: The role of public regard and parenting. *Developmental Psychology, 48*(4), 1003–1018.

McGillion, Michelle; Herbert, Jane S.; Pine, Julian; Vihman, Marilyn; dePaolis, Rory; Keren-Portnoy, Tamar & Matthews, Danielle. (2017). What paves the way to conventional language? The predictive value of babble, pointing, and socioeconomic status. *Child Development, 88*(1), 156–166.

McHill, A. W. & Wright, K. P. (2017). Role of sleep and circadian disruption on energy expenditure and in metabolic predisposition to human obesity and metabolic disease. *Obesity Reviews, 18*(S1), 15–24.

McHugh, Maureen C. & Interligi, Camille. (2015). Sexuality and older women: Desirability and desire. In Varda Muhlbauer, et al. (Eds.), *Women and aging: An international, intersectional power perspective* (pp. 89–116). New York, NY: Springer.

McIntyre, Donald A. (2002). *Colour blindness: Causes and effects.* Chester, UK: Dalton Publishing.

McKeever, Pamela M. & Clark, Linda. (2017). Delayed high school start times later than 8:30 a.m. and impact on graduation rates and attendance rates. *Sleep Health, 3*(2), 119–125.

McKenzie, Sarah C. & Ritter, Gary W. (2017). School discipline in Arkansas. *Policy Briefs, 14*(4).

McKinney, Lyle & Burridge, Andrea Backscheider. (2015). Helping or hindering? The effects of loans on community college student persistence. *Research in Higher Education, 56*(4), 299–324.

McLaren, Rachel M. & Sillars, Alan. (2014). Hurtful episodes in parent–adolescent relationships: How accounts and attributions contribute to the difficulty of talking about hurt. *Communication Monographs, 81*(3), 359–385.

McLean, Robert R. & Kiel, Douglas P. (2015). Developing consensus criteria for sarcopenia: An update. *Journal of Bone and Mineral Research, 30*(4), 588–592.

McLendon, Amber N. & Shelton, Penny S. (2011–2012). New symptoms in older adults: Disease or drug? *Generations, 35*(4), 25–30.

McLeod, Bryce D.; Wood, Jeffrey J. & Weisz, John R. (2007). Examining the association between parenting and childhood anxiety: A meta-analysis. *Clinical Psychology Review, 27*(2), 155–172.

McMillin, Stephen Edward; Hall, Lacey; Bultas, Margaret W.; Grafeman, Sarah E.; Wilmott, Jennifer; Maxim, Rolanda & Zand, Debra H. (2015). Knowledge of child development as a predictor of mother-child play interactions. *Clinical Pediatrics, 54*(11), 1117–1119.

McMurtrie, Beth. (2014). Why colleges haven't stopped students from binge drinking. *Chronicle of Higher Education, 61*(14), A23–A26.

McNeil, Michele & Blad, Evie. (2014). U.S. comes up short on education equity, federal data indicate. *Education Week, 33*(26), 8.

Meadows, Sara. (2006). *The child as thinker: The development and acquisition of cognition in childhood* (2nd ed.). New York, NY: Routledge.

Meagher, David K. (2013). Ethical and legal issues and loss, grief, and mourning. In David K. Meagher & David E. Balk (Eds.), *Handbook of thanatology: The essential body of knowledge for the study of death, dying, and bereavement* (2nd ed.). New York, NY: Routledge.

Meczekalski, Blazej; Podfigurna-Stopa, Agnieszka & Katulski, Krzysztof. (2013). Long-term consequences of anorexia nervosa. *Maturitas, 75*(3), 215–220.

Meece, Judith L. & Eccles, Jacquelynne S. (Eds.). (2010). *Handbook of research on schools, schooling, and human development.* New York, NY: Routledge.

Meeus, Wim. (2011). The study of adolescent identity formation 2000–2010: A review of longitudinal research. *Journal of Research on Adolescence, 21*(1), 75–94.

Mehler, Philip S. (2018). Medical complications of anorexia nervosa and bulimia nervosa. In W. Stewart Agras & Athena Robinson (Eds.), *The Oxford handbook of eating disorders* (2nd ed.). New York, NY: Oxford University Press.

Meier, Ann; Hull, Kathleen E. & Ortyl, Timothy A. (2009). Young adult relationship values at the intersection of gender and sexuality. *Journal of Marriage and Family, 71*(3), 510–525.

Meier, Emily A.; Gallegos, Jarred V.; Thomas, Lori P. Montross; Depp, Colin A.; Irwin, Scott A. & Jeste, Dilip V. (2016). Defining a good death (successful dying): Literature review and a call for research and public dialogue. *The American Journal of Geriatric Psychiatry, 24*(4), 261–271.

Meldrum, Ryan; Kavish, Nicholas & Boutwell, Brian. (2018). On the longitudinal association between peer and adolescent intelligence: Can our friends make us smarter? *PsyArXiv,* (In Press).

Meltzoff, Andrew N. & Gopnik, Alison. (2013). Learning about the mind from evidence: Children's development of intuitive theories of perception and personality. In Simon Baron-Cohen, et al. (Eds.), *Understanding other minds: Perspectives from developmental social neuroscience* (3rd ed., pp. 19–34). New York, NY: Oxford University Press.

Mennis, Jeremy & Mason, Michael J. (2012). Social and geographic contexts of adolescent substance use: The moderating effects of age and gender. *Social Networks, 34*(1), 150–157.

Mercer, Neil & Howe, Christine. (2012). Explaining the dialogic processes of teaching and learning: The value and potential of sociocultural theory. *Learning, Culture and Social Interaction, 1*(1), 12–21.

Merikangas, Kathleen R.; He, Jian-ping; Rapoport, Judith; Vitiello, Benedetto & Olfson, Mark. (2013). Medication use in US youth with mental disorders. *JAMA Pediatrics, 167*(2), 141–148.

Merikangas, Kathleen R. & McClair, Vetisha L. (2012). Epidemiology of substance use disorders. *Human Genetics, 131*(6), 779–789.

Mermelshtine, Roni. (2017). Parent–child learning interactions: A review of the literature on scaffolding. *British Journal of Educational Psychology, 87*(2), 241–254.

Merriam, Sharan B. (2009). *Qualitative research: A guide to design and implementation.* San Francisco, CA: Jossey-Bass.

Mersky, Joshua P.; Topitzes, James & Reynolds, Arthur J. (2013). Impacts of adverse childhood experiences on health, mental health, and substance use in early adulthood: A cohort study of an urban, minority sample in the U.S. *Child Abuse & Neglect, 37*(11), 917–925.

Mertens, Donna M. (2014). *Research and evaluation in education and psychology* (4th ed.). Thousand Oaks, CA: Sage.

Merz, Emily C. & McCall, Robert B. (2011). Parent ratings of executive functioning in children adopted from psychosocially depriving institutions. *Journal of Child Psychology and Psychiatry, 52*(5), 537–546.

Messinger, Daniel M.; Ruvolo, Paul; Ekas, Naomi V. & Fogel, Alan. (2010). Applying machine learning to infant interaction: The development is in the details. *Neural Networks, 23*(8/9), 1004–1016.

Metcalfe, Lindsay A.; Harvey, Elizabeth A. & Laws, Holly B. (2013). The longitudinal relation between academic/cognitive skills and externalizing behavior problems in preschool children. *Journal of Educational Psychology, 105*(3), 881–894.

Meyer, Madonna Harrington. (2014). *Grandmothers at work: Juggling families and jobs.* New York, NY: New York University Press.

Michl, Louisa C.; McLaughlin, Katie A.; Shepherd, Kathrine & Nolen-Hoeksema, Susan. (2013). Rumination as a mechanism linking stressful life events to symptoms of depression and anxiety: Longitudinal evidence in early adolescents and adults. *Journal of Abnormal Psychology, 122*(2), 339–352.

Miech, Richard A.; Johnston, Lloyd D.; O'Malley, Patrick M.; Bachman, Jerald G. & Schulenberg, John E. (2016). *Monitoring the future, national survey results on drug use, 1975–2015: Volume I, secondary school students.* Ann Arbor, Michigan: Institute for Social Research, The University of Michigan.

Miech, Richard A.; Johnston, Lloyd D.; O'Malley, Patrick M.; Bachman, Jerald G.; Schulenberg, John E. & Patrick, Megan E. (2017a). *Monitoring the future, national survey results on drug use, 1975–2016: Volume I, secondary school students.* Ann Arbor, Michigan: Institute for Social Research, The University of Michigan.

Miech, Richard A.; Patrick, Megan E.; O'Malley, Patrick M. & Johnston, Lloyd D. (2017b). E-cigarette use as a predictor of cigarette smoking: Results from a 1-year follow-up of a national sample of 12th grade students. *Tobacco Control, 26,* e106–e111.

Mihailidis, Paul & Viotty, Samantha. (2017). Spreadable spectacle in digital culture: Civic expression, fake news, and the role of media literacies in "post-fact" society. *American Behavioral Scientist, 61*(4), 441–454.

Miklowitz, David J. & Cicchetti, Dante (Eds.). (2010). *Understanding bipolar disorder: A developmental psychopathology perspective.* New York, NY: Guilford Press.

Mikolajczyk, Rafael T.; Zhang, Jun; Grewal, Jagteshwar; Chan, Linda C.; Petersen, Antje & Gross, Mechthild M. (2016). Early versus late admission to labor affects labor progression and risk of cesarean section in nulliparous women. *Frontiers in Medicine, 3*(26).

Miller, Cindy F.; Martin, Carol Lynn; Fabes, Richard A. & Hanish, Laura D. (2013). Bringing the cognitive and the social together: How gender detectives and gender enforcers shape children's gender development. In Mahzarin R. Banaji & Susan A. Gelman (Eds.), *Navigating the social world: What infants, children, and other species can teach us* (pp. 306–313). New York, NY: Oxford University Press.

Miller, Evonne; Donoghue, Geraldine; Sullivan, Debra & Buys, Laurie. (2018). Later life gardening in a retirement community: Sites of identity, resilience and creativity. In David Davenport, et al. (Eds.), *Resilience and ageing: Creativity, culture and community.* Bristol, UK: Policy Press.

Miller, Greg. (2012). Engineering a new line of attack on a signature war injury. *Science, 335*(6064), 33–35.

Miller, Patricia H. (2011). *Theories of developmental psychology* (5th ed.). New York, NY: Worth Publishers.

Miller, Patricia Y. & Simon, William. (1980). The development of sexuality in adolescence. In Joseph Adelson (Ed.), *Handbook of adolescent psychology* (pp. 383–407). New York, NY: Wiley.

Miller, Portia; Votruba-Drzal, Elizabeth; Coley, Rebekah Levine & Koury, Amanda S. (2014). Immigrant families' use of early childcare: Predictors of care type. *Early Childhood Research Quarterly, 29*(4), 484–498.

Miller, Richard B.; Hollist, Cody S.; Olsen, Joseph & Law, David. (2013). Marital quality and health over 20 years: A growth curve analysis. *Journal of Marriage and Family, 75*(3), 667–680.

Miller, Susan W. (2011–2012). Medications and elders: Quality of care or quality of life? *Generations, 35*(4), 19–24.

Miller-Bernal, Leslie. (2000). *Separate by degree: Women students' experiences in single-sex and coeducational colleges.* New York, NY: Peter Lang.

Miller-Cotto, Dana & Byrnes, James P. (2016). Ethnic/racial identity and academic achievement: A meta-analytic review. *Developmental Review, 41,* 51–70.

Miller-Perrin, Cindy & Wurtele, Sandy K. (2017). Sex trafficking and the commercial sexual exploitation of children. *Women & Therapy, 40*(1/2), 123–151.

Mills-Koonce, W. Roger; Garrett-Peters, Patricia; Barnett, Melissa; Granger, Douglas A.; Blair, Clancy & Cox, Martha J. (2011). Father contributions to cortisol responses in infancy and toddlerhood. *Developmental Psychology, 47*(2), 388–395.

Milton, James & Treffers-Daller, Jeanine. (2013). Vocabulary size revisited: The link between vocabulary size and academic achievement. *Applied Linguistics Review, 4*(1), 151–172.

Milunsky, Aubrey & Milunsky, Jeff M. (2016). *Genetic disorders and the fetus: Diagnosis, prevention, and treatment* (7th ed.). Hoboken, NJ: Wiley-Blackwell.

Minagawa-Kawai, Yasuyo; van der Lely, Heather; Ramus, Franck; Sato, Yutaka; Mazuka, Reiko & Dupoux, Emmanuel. (2011). Optical brain imaging reveals general auditory and language-specific processing in early infant development. *Cerebral Cortex, 21*(2), 254–261.

Mindell, Jodi A.; Sadeh, Avi; Wiegand, Benjamin; How, Ti Hwei & Goh, Daniel Y. T. (2010). Cross-cultural differences in infant and toddler sleep. *Sleep Medicine, 11*(3), 274–280.

Ming, Guo-li & Song, Hongjun. (2011). Adult neurogenesis in the mammalian brain: Significant answers and significant questions. *Neuron, 70*(4), 687–702.

Miniño, Arialdi M.; Heron, Melonie P.; Murphy, Sherry L. & Kochanek, Kenneth D. (2007). *Deaths: Final data for 2004. National Vital Statistics Reports, 55*(19). Hyattsville, MD: National Center for Health Statistics.

Mischel, Walter. (2014). *The marshmallow test: Mastering self-control.* New York, NY: Little, Brown.

Mischel, Walter; Ebbesen, Ebbe B. & Raskoff Zeiss, Antonette. (1972). Cognitive and attentional mechanisms in delay of gratification. *Journal of Personality and Social Psychology, 21*(2), 204–218.

Misra, Dawn P.; Caldwell, Cleopatra; Young, Alford A. & Abelson, Sara. (2010). Do fathers matter? Paternal contributions to birth outcomes and racial disparities. *American Journal of Obstetrics and Gynecology, 202*(2), 99–100.

Missana, Manuela; Rajhans, Purva; Atkinson, Anthony P. & Grossmann, Tobias. (2014). Discrimination of fearful and happy body postures in 8-month-old infants: An event-related potential study. *Frontiers in Human Neuroscience, 8,* 531.

Mitchell, Barbara A. (2010). Happiness in midlife parental roles: A contextual mixed methods analysis. *Family Relations, 59*(3), 326–339.

Mitchell, Edwin A. & Krous, Henry F. (2015). Sudden unexpected death in infancy: A historical perspective. *Journal of Paediatrics and Child Health, 51*(1), 108–112.

Mitchell, Kimberly J.; Jones, Lisa M.; Finkelhor, David & Wolak, Janis. (2013). Understanding the decline in unwanted online sexual solicitations for U.S. youth 2000–2010: Findings from three Youth Internet Safety Surveys. *Child Abuse & Neglect, 37*(12), 1225–1236.

Mitford, Jessica. (2000). *The American way of death* (Revisited ed.). New York, NY: Vintage.

Miyata, Susanne; MacWhinney, Brian; Otomo, Kiyoshi; Sirai, Hidetosi; Oshima-Takane, Yuriko; Hirakawa, Makiko, . . . Itoh, Keiko. (2013). Developmental sentence scoring for Japanese. *First Language, 33*(2), 200–216.

Mize, Krystal D.; Pineda, Melannie; Blau, Alexis K.; Marsh, Kathryn & Jones, Nancy A. (2014). Infant physiological and behavioral responses to a jealousy provoking condition. *Infancy, 19*(3), 338–348.

MMWR. (2004, May 7). *Spina bifida and anencephaly before and after folic acid mandate—United States, 1995–1996 and 1999–2000. Morbidity and Mortality Weekly Report, 53*(17), 362–365. Atlanta, GA: U.S. Department of Health and Human Services, Centers for Disease Control and Prevention.

MMWR. (2008, January 18). *School-associated student homicides—United States, 1992–2006. Morbidity and Mortality Weekly Report, 57*(2), 33–36. Atlanta, GA: U.S. Department of Health and Human Services, Centers for Disease Control and Prevention.

MMWR. (2010, June 4). *Youth risk behavior surveillance—United States, 2009. Morbidity and Mortality Weekly Report Surveillance Summaries, 59*(SS05). Atlanta, GA: U.S. Department of Health and Human Services, Centers for Disease Control and Prevention.

MMWR. (2013, January 11). *Vital signs: Binge drinking among women and high school girls—United States, 2011. Morbidity and Mortality Weekly Report, 62*, 9–13. Atlanta, GA: Department of Health and Human Services, Centers for Disease Control and Prevention.

MMWR. (2013, April 5). *Blood lead levels in children aged 1–5 Years—United States, 1999–2010. Morbidity and Mortality Weekly Report, 62*(13), 245–248. Atlanta, GA: U.S. Department of Health and Human Services, Centers for Disease Control and Prevention.

MMWR. (2013, May 3). *Progress toward eradication of polio—Worldwide, January 2011–March 2013. Morbidity and Mortality Weekly Report, 62*(17), 335–338. Atlanta, GA: Centers for Disease Control and Prevention.

MMWR. (2014, March 28). *Prevalence of autism spectrum disorder among children aged 8 years—Autism and Developmental Disabilities Monitoring Network, 11 sites, United States, 2010. Morbidity and Mortality Weekly Report, 63*(2). Atlanta, GA: U.S. Department of Health and Human Services, Centers for Disease Control and Prevention.

MMWR. (2014, May 16). *Racial/ethnic disparities in fatal unintentional drowning among persons aged ≤29 years—United States, 1999–2010. Morbidity and Mortality Weekly Report, 63*(19), 421–426. Atlanta, GA: U.S. Department of Health and Human Services, Centers for Disease Control and Prevention.

MMWR. (2014, June 13). *Youth risk behavior surveillance—United States, 2013. Morbidity and Mortality Weekly Report, 63*(4). Atlanta, GA: U.S. Department of Health and Human Services, Centers for Disease Control and Prevention.

MMWR. (2014, September 5). *Prevalence of smokefree home rules—United States, 1992–1993 and 2010–2011. Morbidity and Mortality Weekly Report, 63*(35), 765–769. Atlanta, GA: Department of Health and Human Services, Centers for Disease Control and Prevention.

MMWR. (2016, January 8). *Notifiable diseases and mortality tables. Morbidity and Mortality Weekly Report, 64*(52). Atlanta, GA: U.S. Department of Health and Human Services, Centers for Disease Control and Prevention.

MMWR. (2016, April 8). *QuickStats: Percentage distribution of deaths, by place of death—United States, 2000–2014. Morbidity and Mortality Weekly Report, 65*(13), 357. Atlanta, GA: Centers for Disease Control and Prevention.

MMWR. (2016, June 10). *Youth risk behavior surveillance—United States, 2015. Morbidity and Mortality Weekly Report, 65*(6). Atlanta, GA: U.S. Department of Health and Human Services, Centers for Disease Control and Prevention.

MMWR. (2018, June 15). *Youth risk behavior surveillance—United States, 2017. Morbidity and Mortality Weekly Report, 67*(8). Atlanta, GA: U.S. Department of Health and Human Services, Centers for Disease Control and Prevention.

Modesto-Lowe, Vania & Alvarado, Camille. (2017). E-cigs . . . Are they cool? Talking to teens about e-cigarettes. *Clinical Pediatrics, 56*(10), 947–952.

Moffitt, Terrie E. (2003). Life-course-persistent and adolescence-limited antisocial behavior: A 10-year research review and a research agenda. In Benjamin B. Lahey et al. (Eds.), *Causes of conduct disorder and juvenile delinquency* (pp. 49–75). New York, NY: Guilford Press.

Moffitt, Terrie E.; Caspi, Avshalom; Rutter, Michael & Silva, Phil A. (2001). *Sex differences in antisocial behaviour: Conduct disorder, delinquency, and violence in the Dunedin Longitudinal Study.* New York, NY: Cambridge University Press.

Mokrova, Irina L.; O'Brien, Marion; Calkins, Susan D.; Leerkes, Esther M. & Marcovitch, Stuart. (2013). The role of persistence at preschool age in academic skills at kindergarten. *European Journal of Psychology of Education, 28*(4), 1495–1503.

Moldavsky, Maria & Sayal, Kapil. (2013). Knowledge and attitudes about Attention-deficit/hyperactivity disorder (ADHD) and its treatment: The views of children, adolescents, parents, teachers and healthcare professionals. *Current Psychiatry Reports, 15*, 377.

Moles, Laura; Manzano, Susana; Fernández, Leonides; Montilla, Antonia; Corzo, Nieves; Ares, Susana, . . . Espinosa-Martos, Irene. (2015). Bacteriological, biochemical, and immunological properties of colostrum and mature milk from mothers of extremely preterm infants. *Journal of Pediatric Gastroenterology & Nutrition, 60*(1), 120–126.

Møller, Signe J. & Tenenbaum, Harriet R. (2011). Danish majority children's reasoning about exclusion based on gender and ethnicity. *Child Development, 82*(2), 520–532.

Monahan, Kathryn C.; Steinberg, Laurence & Cauffman, Elizabeth. (2009). Affiliation with antisocial peers, susceptibility to peer influence, and antisocial behavior during the transition to adulthood. *Developmental Psychology, 45*(6), 1520–1530.

Monahan, Kathryn C.; Steinberg, Laurence; Cauffman, Elizabeth & Mulvey, Edward P. (2013). Psychosocial (im)maturity from adolescence to early adulthood: Distinguishing between adolescence-limited and persisting antisocial behavior. *Development and Psychopathology, 25*(4), 1093–1105.

Montero-Odasso, Manuel M.; Sarquis-Adamson, Yanina; Speechley, Mark; Borrie, Michael J.; Hachinski, Vladimir C.; Wells, Jennie, . . . Muir-Hunter, Susan. (2017). Association of dual-task gait with incident dementia in mild cognitive impairment: Results from the gait and brain study. *JAMA Neurology, 74*(7), 857–865.

Monthly Vital Statistics Report. (1980). *Final mortality statistics, 1978: Advance report. Monthly Vital Statistics Report, 29*(6, Suppl. 2). Hyattsville, MD: National Center for Health Statistics.

Monti, Jennifer D.; Rudolph, Karen D. & Miernicki, Michelle E. (2017). Rumination about social stress mediates the association between peer victimization and depressive symptoms during middle childhood. *Journal of Applied Developmental Psychology, 48*, 25–32.

Montirosso, Rosario; Casini, Erica; Provenzi, Livio; Putnam, Samuel P.; Morandi, Francesco; Fedeli, Claudia & Borgatti, Renato. (2015). A categorical approach to infants' individual differences during the Still-Face paradigm. *Infant Behavior and Development, 38*, 67–76.

Montirosso, Rosario; Tronick, Ed & Borgatti, Renato. (2017). Promoting neuroprotective care in neonatal intensive care units and preterm infant development: Insights from the neonatal adequate care for quality of life study. *Child Development Perspectives, 11*(1), 9–15.

Moody, Myles. (2016). From under-diagnoses to over-representation: Black children, ADHD, and the school-to-prison pipeline. *Journal of African American Studies, 20*(2), 152–163.

Moody, Raymond A. (1975). *Life after life: The investigation of a phenomenon—Survival of bodily death.* Atlanta, GA: Mockingbird Books.

Moore, Keith L.; Persaud, T. V. N. & Torchia, Mark G. (2015). *The developing human: Clinically oriented embryology* (10th ed.). Philadelphia, PA: Saunders.

Moore, Kelly L.; Boscardin, W. John; Steinman, Michael A. & Schwartz, Janice B. (2012). Age and sex variation in prevalence of chronic medical conditions in older residents of U.S. nursing homes. *Journal of the American Geriatrics Society, 60*(4), 756–764.

Moore, Kendra A.; Rubin, Emily B. & Halpern, Scott D. (2016). The problems with physician orders for life-sustaining treatment. *JAMA, 315*(3), 259–260.

Morales, Michelle; Tangermann, Rudolf H. & Wassilak, Steven G. F. (2016). Progress toward polio eradication—Worldwide, 2015–2016. *Morbidity and Mortality Weekly Report, 65*(18), 470–473. Atlanta, GA: Centers for Disease Control and Prevention.

Moran, Lauren V.; Masters, Grace A.; Pingali, Samira; Cohen, Bruce M.; Liebson, Elizabeth; Rajarethinam, R. P. & Ongur, Dost. (2015). Prescription stimulant use is associated with earlier onset of psychosis. *Journal of Psychiatric Research, 71*, 41–47.

Moran, Lyndsey R.; Lengua, Liliana J. & Zalewski, Maureen. (2013). The interaction between negative emotionality and effortful control in early social-emotional development. *Social Development, 22*(2), 340–362.

Morawska, Alina & Sanders, Matthew. (2011). Parental use of time out revisited: A useful or harmful parenting strategy? *Journal of Child and Family Studies, 20*(1), 1–8.

Moreno, Sylvain; Lee, Yunjo; Janus, Monika & Bialystok, Ellen. (2015). Short-term second language and music training induces lasting functional brain changes in early childhood. *Child Development, 86*(2), 394–406.

Morgan, Kevin; Gregory, Pamela; Tomeny, Maureen; David, Beverley M. & Gascoigne, Claire. (2012). Self-help treatment for insomnia symptoms associated with chronic conditions in older adults: A randomized controlled trial. *Journal of the American Geriatrics Society, 60*(10), 1803–1810.

Morin, Rich & Fry, Richard. (2012, October 22). *More Americans worry about financing retirement: Adults in their late 30s most concerned.* Pew Research, Social and Demographic Trends. Washington, DC: Pew Research Center.

Morning, Ann. (2008). Ethnic classification in global perspective: A cross-national survey of the 2000 census round. *Population Research and Policy Review, 27*(2), 239–272.

Morones, Alyssa. (2013). Paddling persists in U.S. schools. *Education Week, 33*(9), 1, 10–11.

Morris, Vivian G. & Morris, Curtis L. (2013). A call for African American male teachers: The supermen expected to solve the problems of low-performing schools. In Chance W. Lewis & Ivory A. Toldson (Eds.), *Black male teachers: Diversifying the United States' teacher workforce* (pp. 151–165). Bingley, UK: Emerald Group.

Morrissey, Taryn. (2009). Multiple child-care arrangements and young children's behavioral outcomes. *Child Development, 80*(1), 59–76.

Mortimer, Jeylan T. (2010). The benefits and risks of adolescent employment. *Prevention Researcher, 17*(2), 8–11.

Mortimer, Jeylan T. (2013). Work and its positive and negative effects on youth's psychosocial development. In Carol W. Runyan et al. (Eds.), *Health and safety of young workers: Proceedings of a U.S. and Canadian series of symposia* (pp. 66–79). Washington, DC: U.S. Department of Health and Human Services, Centers for Disease Control and Prevention, National Institute for Occupational Safety and Health.

Moshman, David. (2011). *Adolescent rationality and development: Cognition, morality, and identity* (3rd ed.). New York, NY: Psychology Press.

Moss, Howard B.; Chen, Chiung M. & Yi, Hsiao-ye. (2014). Early adolescent patterns of alcohol, cigarettes, and marijuana polysubstance use and young adult substance use outcomes in a nationally representative sample. *Drug & Alcohol Dependence, 136*(Suppl. 1), 51–62.

Most, Jasper; Tosti, Valeria; Redman, Leanne M. & Fontana, Luigi. (2017). Calorie restriction in humans: An update. *Ageing Research Reviews, 39*, 36–45.

Moultrie, Fiona; Goksan, Sezgi; Poorun, Ravi & Slater, Rebeccah. (2016). Pain in neonates and infants. In Anna A. Battaglia (Ed.), *An introduction to pain and its relation to nervous system disorders* (pp. 283–293). New York, NY: Wiley.

Mowry, James B.; Spyker, Daniel A.; Brooks, Daniel E.; Mcmillan, Naya & Schauben, Jay L. (2015). 2014 annual report of the American Association of Poison Control Centers' National Poison Data System (NPDS): 32nd annual report. *Clinical Toxicology, 53*(10), 962–1146.

Moye, Jennifer. (2015). Evidence-based treatment of neurocognitive disorders: Measured optimism about select outcomes. *The American Journal of Geriatric Psychiatry, 23*(4), 331–334.

Mroczek, Daniel K. (2014). Personality plasticity, healthy aging, and interventions. *Developmental Psychology, 50*(5), 1470–1474.

Mueller, Noel T.; Mao, G.; Bennett, Wendy L.; Hourigan, Suchi K.; Dominguez-Bello, Maria G.; Appel, Lawrence J. & Wang, Xiaobin. (2017). Does vaginal delivery mitigate or strengthen the intergenerational association of overweight and obesity? Findings from the Boston Birth Cohort. *International Journal of Obesity, 41,* 497–501.

Mullally, Sinéad L. & Maguire, Eleanor A. (2014). Learning to remember: The early ontogeny of episodic memory. *Developmental Cognitive Neuroscience, 9*(13), 12–29.

Mullis, Ina V. S.; Martin, Michael O.; Foy, Pierre & Arora, A. (2012a). *TIMSS 2011 international results in mathematics.* Chestnut Hill, MA: TIMSS & PIRLS International Study Center, Boston College.

Mullis, Ina V. S.; Martin, Michael O.; Foy, Pierre & Drucker, Kathleen T. (2012b). *PIRLS 2011 international results in reading.* Chestnut Hill, MA: TIMSS & PIRLS International Study Center, Boston College.

Mullis, Ina V. S.; Martin, Michael O.; Foy, Pierre & Hooper, Martin. (2016). *TIMSS 2015 international results in mathematics.* Chestnut Hill, MA: TIMSS & PIRLS International Study Center, Boston College.

Mullis, Ina V. S.; Martin, Michael O.; Foy, Pierre & Hooper, Martin. (2017). *International results in reading PIRLS 2016.* Chestnut Hill, MA: TIMSS & PIRLS International Study Center, Boston College.

Mullis, Ina V. S.; Martin, Michael O.; Kennedy, Ann M. & Foy, Pierre. (2007). International student achievement in reading. In, *IEA's progress in international reading literacy study in primary school in 40 countries* (pp. 35–64). Chestnut Hill, MA: TIMSS & PIRLS International Study Center, Boston College.

Muñoz, Carmen & Singleton, David. (2011). A critical review of age-related research on L2 ultimate attainment. *Language Teaching, 44*(1), 1–35.

Münscher, Robert; Vetter, Max & Scheuerle, Thomas. (2016). A review and taxonomy of choice architecture techniques. *Journal of Behavioral Decision Making, 29*(5), 511–524.

Muris, Peter & Meesters, Cor. (2014). Small or big in the eyes of the other: On the developmental psychopathology of self-conscious emotions as shame, guilt, and pride. *Clinical Child and Family Psychology Review, 17*(1), 19–40.

Murphy, Michael. (2011). Long-term effects of the demographic transition on family and kinship networks in Britain. *Population and Development Review, 37*(Suppl. 1), 55–80.

Murphy, Sherry L.; Kochanek, Kenneth D.; Xu, Jiaquan & Arias, Elizabeth. (2015, December). *Mortality in the United States, 2014. NCHS Data Brief,* (229). Hyattsville, MD: National Center for Health Statistics.

Murphy, Sherry L.; Xu, Jiaquan & Kochanek, Kenneth D. (2012). *Deaths: Preliminary data for 2010. National Vital Statistics Reports, 60*(4). Hyattsville, MD: National Center for Health Statistics.

Murphy, Sherry L.; Xu, Jiaquan; Kochanek, Kenneth D.; Curtin, Sally C. & Arias, Elizabeth. (2017, November 27). *Deaths: Final data for 2015. National Vital Statistics Reports, 66*(6). Hyattsville, MD: National Center for Health Statistics.

Murray, Brendan D.; Anderson, Michael C. & Kensinger, Elizabeth A. (2015). Older adults can suppress unwanted memories when given an appropriate strategy. *Psychology and Aging, 30*(1), 9–25.

Murray, Thomas H. (2014). Stirring the simmering "designer baby" pot. *Science, 343*(6176), 1208–1210.

Murtin, Fabrice; Mackenbach, Johan; Jasilionis, Domantas & Mira d'Ercole, Marco. (2017). Inequalities in longevity by education in OECD countries: Insights from new OECD estimates. *OECD Statistics Working Papers, 2017*(2).

Mustanski, Brian; Birkett, Michelle; Greene, George J.; Hatzenbuehler, Mark L. & Newcomb, Michael E. (2014). Envisioning an America without sexual orientation inequities in adolescent health. *American Journal of Public Health, 104*(2), 218–225.

Musu-Gillette, Lauren; Zhang, Anlan; Wang, Ke; Zhang, Jizhi & Oudekerk, Barbara A. (2017). *Indicators of school crime and safety: 2016.* Washington, DC: National Center for Education Statistics, U.S. Department of Education, and Bureau of Justice Statistics, Office of Justice Programs, U.S. Department of Justice. NCES 2017-064/NCJ 250650.

Myers, David G. (2002). *Intuition: Its powers and perils.* New Haven, CT: Yale University Press.

Mynatt, Blair Sumner & Mowery, Robyn L. (2013). The family, larger systems, and end-of-life decision making. In David K. Meagher & David E. Balk (Eds.), *Handbook of thanatology: The essential body of knowledge for the study of death, dying, and bereavement* (2nd ed., pp. 91–99). New York, NY: Routledge.

Nadal, Kevin L.; Mazzula, Silvia L.; Rivera, David P. & Fujii-Doe, Whitney. (2014). Microaggressions and Latina/o Americans: An analysis of nativity, gender, and ethnicity. *Journal of Latina/o Psychology, 2*(2), 67–78.

Nadeau, Joseph H. & Dudley, Aimée M. (2011). Systems genetics. *Science, 331*(6020), 1015–1016.

Næss, Kari-Anne B. (2016). Development of phonological awareness in Down syndrome: A meta-analysis and empirical study. *Developmental Psychology, 52*(2), 177–190.

NAEYC. (2014). *NAEYC Early Childhood Program Standards and Accreditation Criteria & Guidance for Assessment.* Washington, DC: National Association for the Education of Young Children.

Naranbhai, Vivek & Carrington, Mary. (2017). Host genetic variation and HIV disease: From mapping to mechanism. *Immunogenetics, 69*(8/9), 489–498.

Narayan, Chandan R.; Werker, Janet F. & Beddor, Patrice Speeter. (2010). The interaction between acoustic salience and language experience in developmental speech perception: Evidence from nasal place discrimination. *Developmental Science, 13*(3), 407–420.

Narvaez, Darcia; Gleason, Tracy; Wang, Lijuan; Brooks, Jeff; Lefever, Jennifer Burke & Cheng, Ying. (2013). The evolved development niche: Longitudinal effects of caregiving practices on early childhood psychosocial development. *Early Childhood Research Quarterly, 28*(4), 759–773.

Nash, Robert A. & Ost, James (Eds.). (2017). *False and distorted memories.* New York, NY: Routledge.

Natarajan, Mangai (Ed.). (2017). *Drugs of abuse.* New York, NY: Routledge.

Nathan, David L.; Clark, H. Westley & Elders, Joycelyn. (2017). The physicians' case for marijuana legalization. *American Journal of Public Health, 107*(11), 1746–1747.

National Center for Education Statistics. (2016, October). *Table 202.10: Enrollment of 3-, 4-, and 5-year-old children in preprimary programs, by level of program, control of program, and attendance status: Selected years, 1970 through 2015.* Washington, DC: Institute of Education Sciences, U.S. Department of Education.

National Center for Education Statistics. (2017, August). *Table 202.10: Enrollment of 3-, 4-, and 5-year-old children in preprimary programs, by level of program, control of program, and attendance status: Selected years, 1970 through 2016.* Washington, DC: Institute of Education Sciences, U.S. Department of Education.

National Center for Education Statistics. (2018). *Digest of education statistics, 2017.* Washington, DC: Institute of Education Sciences, U.S. Department of Education.

National Center for Health Statistics. (2012). *Health, United States, 2011: With special feature on socioeconomic status and health.* Hyattsville, MD: U.S. Department of Health and Human Services, Centers for Disease Control and Prevention.

National Center for Health Statistics. (2014). *Health, United States, 2013: With special feature on prescription drugs.* Hyattsville, MD: U.S. Department of Health and Human Services, Centers for Disease Control and Prevention.

National Center for Health Statistics. (2015). *Health, United States, 2014: With a special feature on adults aged 55–64.* Hyattsville, MD: U.S. Department of Health and Human Services, Centers for Disease Control and Prevention.

National Center for Health Statistics. (2016). *Health, United States, 2015: With a special feature on racial and ethnic health disparities.* Hyattsville, MD: U.S. Department of Health and Human Services, Centers for Disease Control and Prevention.

National Center for Health Statistics. (2016, December). Data are from the Compressed Mortality File 1999-2015 Series 20 No. 2U, 2016, as compiled from data provided by the 57 vital statistics jurisdictions through the Vital Statistics Cooperative Program. CDC WONDER.

National Center for Health Statistics. (2017). *Health, United States, 2016: With chartbook on long-term trends in health.* Hyattsville, MD: U.S. Department of Health and Human Services.

National Foundation for Educational Research. (2010). *Tellus4 national report.* Berkshire, UK: National Foundation for Educational Research. DCSF Research Report 218.

National Gardening Association. (2014). *Garden to table: A 5-year look at food gardening in America.* Williston, VT: National Gardening Association.

National Vital Statistics Reports. (2013, May 8). *Deaths: Final data for 2010. National Vital Statistics Reports, 61*(4). Hyattsville, MD: National Center for Health Statistics.

Naughton, Michelle J.; Yi-Frazier, Joyce P.; Morgan, Timothy M.; Seid, Michael; Lawrence, Jean M.; Klingensmith, Georgeanna J., . . . Loots, Beth. (2014). Longitudinal associations between sex, diabetes self-care, and health-related quality of life among youth with type 1 or type 2 diabetes mellitus. *The Journal of Pediatrics, 164*(6), 1376–1383.e1371.

Neary, Karen R. & Friedman, Ori. (2014). Young children give priority to ownership when judging who should use an object. *Child Development, 85*(1), 326–337.

Neary, Marianne T. & Breckenridge, Ross A. (2013). Hypoxia at the heart of sudden infant death syndrome? *Pediatric Research, 74*(4), 375–379.

Needleman, Herbert L. & Gatsonis, Constantine A. (1990). Low-level lead exposure and the IQ of children: A meta-analysis of modern studies. *JAMA, 263*(5), 673–678.

Needleman, Herbert L.; Schell, Alan; Bellinger, David; Leviton, Alan & Allred, Elizabeth N. (1990). The long-term effects of exposure to low doses of lead in childhood. *New England Journal of Medicine, 322*(2), 83–88.

Neggers, Yasmin & Crowe, Kristi. (2013). Low birth weight outcomes: Why better in Cuba than Alabama? *Journal of the American Board of Family Medicine, 26*(2), 187–195.

Neimeyer, Robert A. (2017). Series foreword. In Dennis Klass & Edith Maria Steffen (Eds.), *Continuing bonds in bereavement: New directions for research and practice.* New York, NY: Routledge.

Neimeyer, Robert A. & Jordan, John R. (2013). Historical and contemporary perspectives on assessment and intervention. In David K. Meagher & David E. Balk (Eds.), *Handbook of thanatology: The essential body of knowledge for the study of death, dying, and bereavement* (2nd ed., pp. 219–237). New York, NY: Routledge.

Nelson, Charles A.; Fox, Nathan A. & Zeanah, Charles H. (2014). *Romania's abandoned children: Deprivation, brain development, and the struggle for recovery.* Cambridge, MA: Harvard University Press.

Nelson, Eric E.; Jarcho, Johanna M. & Guyer, Amanda E. (2016). Social re-orientation and brain development: An expanded and updated view. *Developmental Cognitive Neuroscience, 17,* 118–127.

Nelson, Geoffrey & Caplan, Rachel. (2014). The prevention of child physical abuse and neglect: An update. *Journal of Applied Research on Children, 5*(1).

Nelson, Todd D. (2011). Ageism: The strange case of prejudice against the older you. In Richard L. Wiener & Steven L. Willborn (Eds.), *Disability and aging discrimination: Perspectives in law and psychology* (pp. 37–47). New York, NY: Springer.

Nesdale, Drew; Zimmer-Gembeck, Melanie J. & Roxburgh, Natalie. (2014). Peer group rejection in childhood: Effects of rejection ambiguity, rejection sensitivity, and social acumen. *Journal of Social Issues, 70*(1), 12–28.

Nevanen, Saila; Juvonen, Antti & Ruismäki, Heikki. (2014). Does arts education develop school readiness? Teachers' and artists' points of view on an art education project. *Arts Education Policy Review, 115*(3), 72–81.

Neverman, Laurie. (2016, May 5). What destroyed the extended family? [Web log post]. Common Sense Home.

Nevin, Rick. (2007). Understanding international crime trends: The legacy of preschool lead exposure. *Environmental Research, 104*(3), 315–336.

Ng, Marie; Fleming, Tom; Robinson, Margaret; Thomson, Blake; Graetz, Nicholas; Margono, Christopher, . . . Gakidou, Emmanuela. (2014). Global, regional, and national prevalence of overweight and obesity in children and adults during 1980—2013: A systematic analysis for the Global Burden of Disease Study 2013. *The Lancet, 384*(9945), 766–781.

Ng, Rowena; Lai, Philip; Brown, Timothy T.; Järvinen, Anna; Halgren, Eric; Bellugi, Ursula & Trauner, Doris. (2017). Neuroanatomical correlates of emotion-processing in children with unilateral brain lesion: A preliminary study of limbic system organization. *Social Neuroscience,* (In Press).

Ngui, Emmanuel; Cortright, Alicia & Blair, Kathleen. (2009). An investigation of paternity status and other factors associated with racial and ethnic disparities in birth outcomes in Milwaukee, Wisconsin. *Maternal and Child Health Journal, 13*(4), 467–478.

Nguyen, Jacqueline; O'Brien, Casey & Schapp, Salena. (2016). Adolescent inhalant use prevention, assessment, and treatment: A literature synthesis. *Drug Policy, 31,* 15–24.

Nic Gabhainn, Saoirse; Baban, Adriana; Boyce, William & Godeau, Emmanuelle. (2009). How well protected are sexually active 15-year-olds? Cross-national patterns in condom and contraceptive pill use 2002–2006. *International Journal of Public Health, 54*(Suppl. 2), 209–215.

Nicolaisen, Magnhild; Moum, Torbjørn & Thorsen, Kirsten. (2017). Mastery and depressive symptoms: How does mastery influence the impact of stressors from midlife to old age? *Journal of Aging and Health,* (In Press).

Nie, Jing-Bao. (2016). Erosion of eldercare in China: A socio-ethical inquiry in aging, elderly suicide and the government's responsibilities in the context of the one-child policy. *Ageing International, 41*(4), 350–365.

Niedzwiedz, Claire; Haw, Camilla; Hawton, Keith & Platt, Stephen. (2014). The definition and epidemiology of clusters of suicidal behavior: A systematic review. *Suicide and Life-Threatening Behavior, 44*(5), 569–581.

Nielsen, Mark & Tomaselli, Keyan. (2010). Overimitation in Kalahari Bushman children and the origins of human cultural cognition. *Psychological Science, 21*(5), 729–736.

Nieto, Sonia. (2000). *Affirming diversity: The sociopolitical context of multicultural education* (3rd ed.). New York, NY: Longman.

Nigg, Joel T. & Barkley, Russell A. (2014). Attention-deficit/hyperactivity disorder. In Eric J. Mash & Russell A. Barkley (Eds.), *Child psychopathology* (3rd ed., pp. 75–144). New York, NY: Guilford Press.

Nikitin, Dmitriy; Timberlake, David S. & Williams, Rebecca S. (2016). Is the e-liquid industry regulating itself? A look at e-liquid Internet vendors in the United States. *Nicotine & Tobacco Research, 18*(10), 1967–1972.

Nisbett, Richard E.; Aronson, Joshua; Blair, Clancy; Dickens, William; Flynn, James; Halpern, Diane F. & Turkheimer, Eric. (2012). Intelligence: New findings and theoretical developments. *American Psychologist, 67*(2), 130–159.

Nishina, Adrienne; Bellmore, Amy; Witkow, Melissa R.; Nylund-Gibson, Karen & Graham, Sandra. (2018). Mismatches in self-reported and meta-perceived ethnic identification across the high school years. *Journal of Youth and Adolescence, 47*(1), 51–63.

Nkomo, Palesa; Naicker, Nisha; Mathee, Angela; Galpin, Jacky; Richter, Linda M. & Norris, Shane A. (2018). The association between environmental lead exposure with aggressive behavior, and dimensionality of direct and indirect aggression during mid-adolescence: Birth to Twenty Plus cohort. *Science of the Total Environment, 612,* 472–479.

Noël-Miller, Claire M. (2013a). Repartnering following divorce: Implications for older fathers' relations with their adult children. *Journal of Marriage and Family, 75*(3), 697–712.

Noël-Miller, Claire M. (2013b). Former stepparents' contact with their stepchildren after midlife. *The Journals of Gerontology Series B: Psychological Sciences and Social Sciences, 68*(3), 409–419.

Noll, Jennie G.; Trickett, Penelope K.; Long, Jeffrey D.; Negriff, Sonya; Susman, Elizabeth J.; Shalev, Idan, . . . Putnam, Frank W. (2017). Childhood sexual abuse and early timing of puberty. *Journal of Adolescent Health, 60*(1), 65–71.

Norman, Geoffrey R.; Grierson, Lawrence E. M.; Sherbino, Jonathan; Hamstra, Stanley J.; Schmidt, Henk G. & Mamede, Silvia. (2018). Expertise in medicine and surgery. In K. Anders Ericsson, et al. (Eds.), *The Cambridge handbook of expertise and expert performance* (2nd ed., pp. 331–355). New York, NY: Cambridge University Press.

Norona, Jerika C.; Tregubenko, Valerya; Boiangiu, Shira Bezalel; Levy, Gil; Scharf, Miri; Welsh, Deborah P. & Shulman, Shmuel. (2018). Changes in rejection sensitivity across adolescence and emerging adulthood: Associations with relationship involvement, quality, and coping. *Journal of Adolescence, 63,* 96–106.

Noronha, Konrad J. (2015). Impact of religion and spirituality on older adulthood. *Journal of Religion, Spirituality & Aging, 27*(1), 16–33.

North, Michael S. & Fiske, Susan T. (2012). An inconvenienced youth? Ageism and its potential intergenerational roots. *Psychological Bulletin, 138*(5), 982–997.

North, Michael S. & Fiske, Susan T. (2015). Modern attitudes toward older adults in the aging world: A cross-cultural meta-analysis. *Psychological Bulletin, 141*(5), 993–1021.

Norton, Michael I. & Ariely, Dan. (2011). Building a better America: One wealth quintile at a time. *Perspectives on Psychological Science, 6*(1), 9–12.

Nugent, J. Kevin; Bartlett, Jessica Dym; Von Ende, Adam & Valim, Clarissa. (2017). The effects of the Newborn Behavioral Observations (NBO) system on sensitivity in mother–infant interactions. *Infants & Young Children, 30*(4), 257–268.

O'Hara, Michael W. & McCabe, Jennifer E. (2013). Postpartum depression: Current status and future directions. *Annual Review of Clinical Psychology, 9,* 379–407.

O'Malley, A. James & Christakis, Nicholas A. (2011). Longitudinal analysis of large social networks: Estimating the effect of health traits on changes in friendship ties. *Statistics in Medicine, 30*(9), 950–964.

O'Rourke, Norm; Cappeliez, Philippe & Claxton, Amy. (2010a). Functions of reminiscence and the psychological well-being of young-old and older adults over time. *Aging & Mental Health, 15*(2), 272–281.

O'Rourke, Norm; Neufeld, Eva; Claxton, Amy & Smith, JuliAnna Z. (2010b). Knowing me-knowing you: Reported personality and trait discrepancies as predictors of marital idealization between long-wed spouses. *Psychology and Aging, 25*(2), 412–421.

O'Brien, Erica L.; Hess, Thomas M.; Kornadt, Anna E.; Rothermund, Klaus; Fung, Helene & Voss, Peggy. (2017). Context influences on the subjective experience of aging: The impact of culture and domains of functioning. *The Gerontologist, 57*(Suppl. 2), S127–S137.

O'Rahilly, Ronan & Müller, Fabiola. (2012). Prenatal development of the brain. In Ilan Timor-Tritsch, et al. (Eds.), *Ultrasonography of the prenatal brain* (3rd ed., pp. 1–14). New York, NY: McGraw-Hill.

Obradović, Jelena; Long, Jeffrey D.; Cutuli, J. J.; Chan, Chi-Keung; Hinz, Elizabeth; Heistad, David & Masten, Ann S. (2009). Academic achievement of homeless and highly mobile children in an urban school district: Longitudinal evidence on risk, growth, and resilience. *Development and Psychopathology, 21*(2), 493–518.

Ocobock, Abigail. (2013). The power and limits of marriage: Married gay men's family relationships. *Journal of Marriage and Family, 75*(1), 191–205.

OECD. (2010). *PISA 2009 results: Learning to learn: Student engagement, strategies and practices* (Vol. 3) Paris: PISA, OECD Publishing.

OECD. (2013). *Education at a glance 2013: OECD indicators.* Paris, France: Organisation for Economic Cooperation and Development.

OECD. (2015). Life expectancy at birth. In *Health at a glance 2015: OECD indicators* (pp. 46–47). Paris, France: Organisation for Economic Cooperation and Development.

OECD. (2018). Adult education level (indicator). OECDiLibrary.

Oesterdiekhoff, Georg W. (2014). The role of developmental psychology to understanding history, culture and social change. *Journal of Social Sciences, 10*(4), 185–195.

Ogden, Cynthia L.; Carroll, Margaret D.; Kit, Brian K. & Flegal, Katherine M. (2014). Prevalence of childhood and adult obesity in the United States, 2011–2012. *JAMA, 311*(8), 806–814.

Ogden, Cynthia L.; Gorber, Sarah C.; Dommarco, Juan A. Rivera; Carroll, Margaret; Shields, Margot & Flegal, Katherine. (2011). The epidemiology of childhood obesity in Canada, Mexico and the United States. In Luis A. Moreno, et al. (Eds.), *Epidemiology of obesity in children and adolescents* (Vol. 2, pp. 69–93). New York, NY: Springer.

Ogolsky, Brian G. & Gray, Christine R. (2016). Conflict, negative emotion, and reports of partners' relationship maintenance in same-sex couples. *Journal of Family Psychology, 30*(2), 171–180.

Okun, Morris A.; Yeung, Ellen WanHeung & Brown, Stephanie. (2013). Volunteering by older adults and risk of mortality: A meta-analysis. *Psychology and Aging, 28*(2), 564–577.

Olatunji, Bunmi O.; Armstrong, Thomas & Elwood, Lisa. (2017). Is disgust proneness associated with anxiety and related disorders? A qualitative review and meta-analysis of group comparison and correlational studies. *Perspectives on Psychological Science, 12*(4), 613–648.

Olfson, Mark; Crystal, Stephen; Huang, Cecilia & Gerhard, Tobias. (2010). Trends in antipsychotic drug use by very young, privately insured children. *Journal of the American Academy of Child and Adolescent Psychiatry, 49*(1), 13–23.

Ollo-López, Andrea & Goñi-Legaz, Salomé. (2017). Differences in work–family conflict: Which individual and national factors explain them? *The International Journal of Human Resource Management, 28*(3), 499–525.

Olson, Kristina R. & Dweck, Carol S. (2009). Social cognitive development: A new look. *Child Development Perspectives, 3*(1), 60–65.

Olson, Sheryl L.; Lopez-Duran, Nestor; Lunkenheimer, Erika S.; Chang, Hyein & Sameroff, Arnold J. (2011). Individual differences in the development of early peer aggression: Integrating contributions of self-regulation, theory of mind, and parenting. *Development and Psychopathology, 23*(1), 253–266.

Olweus, Dan. (1999). Sweden. In Peter K. Smith, et al. (Eds.), *The nature of school bullying: A cross-national perspective* (pp. 7–27). New York, NY: Routledge.

Oncken, Cheryl; Ricci, Karen A.; Kuo, Chia-Ling; Dornelas, Ellen; Kranzler, Henry R. & Sankey, Heather Z. (2017). Correlates of electronic cigarettes use before and during pregnancy. *Nicotine & Tobacco Research, 19*(5), 585–590.

Open Science Collaboration. (2015). Estimating the reproducibility of psychological science. *Science, 349*(6251), 943.

Oregon Public Health Division. (2018). *Oregon Death with Dignity Act: 2017 data summary.* Portland, OR: Oregon Health Authority, Public Health Division.

Orth, Ulrich & Robins, Richard W. (2014). The development of self-esteem. *Current Directions in Psychological Science, 23*(5), 381–387.

Orth, Ulrich; Robins, Richard W. & Widaman, Keith F. (2012). Life-span development of self-esteem and its effects on important life outcomes. *Journal of Personality and Social Psychology, 102*(6), 1271–1288.

Osgood, D. Wayne; Ragan, Daniel T.; Wallace, Lacey; Gest, Scott D.; Feinberg, Mark E. & Moody, James. (2013). Peers and the emergence of alcohol use: Influence and selection processes in adolescent friendship networks. *Journal of Research on Adolescence, 23*(3), 500–512.

Osilla, Karen Chan; Miles, Jeremy N. V.; Hunter, Sarah B. & Amico, Elizabeth J. D. (2015). The longitudinal relationship between employment and substance use among at-risk adolescents. *Journal of Child & Adolescent Behavior Genetics, 3*(3).

Ostrov, Jamie M.; Kamper, Kimberly E.; Hart, Emily J.; Godleski, Stephanie A. & Blakely-McClure, Sarah J. (2014). A gender-balanced approach to the study of peer victimization and aggression subtypes in early childhood. *Development and Psychopathology, 26*(3), 575–587.

Over, Harriet & Gattis, Merideth. (2010). Verbal imitation is based on intention understanding. *Cognitive Development, 25*(1), 46–55.

Owens, Judith A.; Adolescent Sleep Working Group & Committee on Adolescence. (2014). Insufficient sleep in adolescents and young adults: An update on causes and consequences. *Pediatrics, 134*(3), e921–e932.

Ozernov-Palchik, Ola; Norton, Elizabeth S.; Sideridis, Georgios; Beach, Sara D.; Wolf, Maryanne; Gabrieli,

John D. E. & Gaab, Nadine. (2017). Longitudinal stability of pre-reading skill profiles of kindergarten children: Implications for early screening and theories of reading. *Developmental Science*, *20*(5), e12471.

Pace, Cecilia Serena; Zavattini, Giulio Cesare & D'Alessio, Maria. (2011). Continuity and discontinuity of attachment patterns: A short-term longitudinal pilot study using a sample of late-adopted children and their adoptive mothers. *Attachment & Human Development*, *14*(1), 45–61.

Padilla-Walker, Laura; Memmott-Elison, Madison & Nelson, Larry. (2017). Positive relationships as an indicator of flourishing during emerging adulthood. In Laura M. Padilla-Walker & Larry J. Nelson (Eds.), *Flourishing in emerging adulthood: Positive development during the third decade of life* (pp. 212–235). New York, NY: Oxford University Press.

Padilla-Walker, Laura M. & Nelson, Larry J. (Eds.). (2017). *Flourishing in emerging adulthood: Positive development during the third decade of life.* New York, NY: Oxford University Press.

Pahlke, Erin & Hyde, Janet Shibley. (2016). The debate over single-sex schooling. *Child Development Perspectives*, *10*(2), 81–86.

Pahlke, Erin; Hyde, Janet Shibley & Allison, Carlie M. (2014). The effects of single-sex compared with coeducational schooling on students' performance and attitudes: A meta-analysis. *Psychological Bulletin*, *140*(4), 1042–1072.

Pahwa, Rajesh & Lyons, Kelly E. (Eds.). (2013). *Handbook of Parkinson's disease* (5th ed.). Boca Raton, FL: CRC Press.

Painter, Jodie N.; Willemsen, Gonneke; Nyholt, Dale; Hoekstra, Chantal; Duffy, David L.; Henders, Anjali K., . . . Montgomery, Grant W. (2010). A genome wide linkage scan for dizygotic twinning in 525 families of mothers of dizygotic twins. *Human Reproduction*, *25*(6), 1569–1580.

Palatini, Paolo. (2015). Coffee consumption and risk of type 2 diabetes. *Diabetologia*, *58*(1), 199–200.

Palmer, Sally B. & Abbott, Nicola. (2018). Bystander responses to bias-based bullying in schools: A developmental intergroup approach. *Child Development Perspectives*, *12*(1), 39–44.

Pankow, James F.; Kim, Kilsun; McWhirter, Kevin J.; Luo, Wentai; Escobedo, Jorge O.; Strongin, Robert M., . . . Peyton, David H. (2017). Benzene formation in electronic cigarettes. *PLoS ONE*, *12*(3), e0173055.

Panksepp, Jaak & Watt, Douglas. (2011). What is basic about basic emotions? Lasting lessons from affective neuroscience. *Emotion Review*, *3*(4), 387–396.

Pardosi, Jerico Franciscus; Parr, Nick & Muhidin, Salut. (2017). Fathers and infant health and survival in Ende, a rural district of Eastern Indonesia. *Journal of Population Research*, *34*(2), 185–207.

Park, Denise C. & Bischof, Gérard N. (2013). The aging mind: Neuroplasticity in response to cognitive training. *Dialogues in Clinical Neuroscience*, *15*(1), 109–119.

Park, Hyun; Bothe, Denise; Holsinger, Eva; Kirchner, H. Lester; Olness, Karen & Mandalakas, Anna. (2011). The impact of nutritional status and longitudinal recovery of motor and cognitive milestones in internationally adopted children. *International Journal of Environmental Research and Public Health*, *8*(1), 105–116.

Park, Ji-Yeun; Seo, Dong-Chul & Lin, Hsien-Chang. (2016). E-cigarette use and intention to initiate or quit smoking among US youths. *American Journal of Public Health*, *106*(4), 672–678.

Park, Jong-Tae; Jang, Yoonsun; Park, Min Sun; Pae, Calvin; Park, Jinyi; Hu, Kyung-Seok, . . . Kim, Hee-Jin. (2011). The trend of body donation for education based on Korean social and religious culture. *Anatomical Sciences Education*, *4*(1), 33–38.

Parke, Ross D. (2013). Gender differences and similarities in parental behavior. In Bradford Wilcox & Kathleen K. Kline (Eds.), *Gender and parenthood: Biological and social scientific perspectives* (pp. 120–163). New York, NY: Columbia University Press.

Parker, Emily; Atchison, Bruce & Workman, Emily. (2016). *State pre-K funding for 2015–16 fiscal year: National trends in state preschool funding. 50-state review.* Denver, CO: Education Commission of the States.

Parker, Kim. (2012). *The boomerang generation: Feeling OK about living with Mom and Dad. Pew social and demographic trends.* Washington, DC: Pew Research Center.

Parker, Kim; Horowitz, Juliana Menasce & Stepler, Renee. (2017, December 5). *On gender differences, no consensus on nature vs. nurture: Americans say society places a higher premium on masculinity than on femininity. Social & Demographic Trends.* Washington, DC: Pew Research Center.

Parker, Kim & Patten, Eileen. (2013, January 30). *The sandwich generation: Rising financial burdens for middle-aged Americans. Social & Demographic Trends.* Washington, DC: Pew Research Center.

Parker, Philip D.; Jerrim, John & Anders, Jake. (2016). What effect did the global financial crisis have upon youth well-being? Evidence from four Australian cohorts. *Developmental Psychology*, *52*(4), 640–651.

Parks, Sharyn E.; Johnson, Linda L.; McDaniel, Dawn D. & Gladden, Matthew. (2014, January 17). *Surveillance for violent deaths — National Violent Death Reporting System, 16 states, 2010. Morbidity and Mortality Weekly Report*, *63*(SS01), 1–33. Atlanta, GA: U.S. Department of Health and Human Services, Centers for Disease Control and Prevention.

Parten, Mildred B. (1932). Social participation among preschool children. *The Journal of Abnormal and Social Psychology*, *27*(3), 243–269.

Partridge, Sarah; Balayla, Jacques; Holcroft, Christina A. & Abenhaim, Haim A. (2012). Inadequate prenatal care utilization and risks of infant mortality and poor birth outcome: A retrospective analysis of 28,729,765 U.S. deliveries over 8 years. *American Journal of Perinatology*, *29*(10), 787–794.

Pärtty, Anna & Kalliomäki, Marko. (2017). Infant colic is still a mysterious disorder of the microbiota–gut–brain axis. *Acta Paediatrica*, *106*(4), 528–529.

Pascarella, Ernest T.; Martin, Georgianna L.; Hanson, Jana M.; Trolian, Teniell L.; Gillig, Benjamin & Blaich, Charles. (2014). Effects of diversity experiences on critical thinking skills over 4 years of college. *Journal of College Student Development*, *55*(1), 86–92.

Pascarella, Ernest T. & Terenzini, Patrick T. (1991). *How college affects students: Findings and insights from twenty years of research.* San Francisco, CA: Jossey-Bass.

Pasco Fearon, R. M. & Roisman, Glenn I. (2017). Attachment theory: Progress and future directions. *Current Opinion in Psychology, 15,* 131–136.

Patel, Ayush; Medhekar, Rohan; Ochoa-Perez, Melissa; Aparasu, Rajender R.; Chan, Wenyaw; Sherer, Jeffrey T., . . . Chen, Hua. (2017). Care provision and prescribing practices of physicians treating children and adolescents with ADHD. *Psychiatric Services, 68*(7), 681–688.

Patel, Vimla L.; Arocha, José F. & Kaufman, David R. (1999). Expertise and tacit knowledge in medicine. In Robert J. Sternberg & Joseph A. Horvath (Eds.), *Tacit knowledge in professional practice: Researcher and practitioner perspectives* (pp. 75–99). Mahwah, NJ: Erlbaum.

Pathela, Preeti & Schillinger, Julia A. (2010). Sexual behaviors and sexual violence: Adolescents with opposite-, same-, or both-sex partners. *Pediatrics, 126*(5), 879–886.

Patil, Rakesh N.; Nagaonkar, Shashikant N.; Shah, Nilesh B. & Bhat, Tushar S. (2013). A cross-sectional study of common psychiatric morbidity in children aged 5 to 14 years in an urban slum. *Journal of Family Medicine and Primary Care, 2*(2), 164–168.

Paúl, Constança. (2014). Loneliness and health in later life. In Nancy A. Pachana & Ken Laidlaw (Eds.), *The Oxford handbook of clinical geropsychology.* New York, NY: Oxford University Press.

Pausch, Jai. (2012). *Dream new dreams: Reimagining my life after loss.* New York, NY: Crown Archetype.

Pausch, Randy & Zaslow, Jeffrey. (2008). *The last lecture.* New York, NY: Hyperion.

Peffley, Mark & Hurwitz, Jon. (2010). *Justice in America: The separate realities of Blacks and Whites.* New York, NY: Cambridge University Press.

Pellegrini, Anthony D. (2011). Introduction. In Anthony D. Pellegrini (Ed.), *The Oxford handbook of the development of play* (pp. 3–6). New York, NY: Oxford University Press.

Pellegrini, Anthony D. (2013). Play. In Philip D. Zelazo (Ed.), *The Oxford handbook of developmental psychology* (Vol. 2, pp. 276–299). New York, NY: Oxford University Press.

Pellegrini, Anthony D.; Roseth, Cary J.; Van Ryzin, Mark J. & Solberg, David W. (2011). Popularity as a form of social dominance: An evolutionary perspective. In Antonius H. N. Cillessen, et al. (Eds.), *Popularity in the peer system* (pp. 123–139). New York, NY: Guilford Press.

Pellicano, Elizabeth; Kenny, Lorcan; Brede, Janina; Klaric, Elena; Lichwa, Hannah & McMillin, Rebecca. (2017). Executive function predicts school readiness in autistic and typical preschool children. *Cognitive Development, 43,* 1–13.

Pellis, Sergio M.; Himmler, Brett T.; Himmler, Stephanie M. & Pellis, Vivien C. (2018). Rough-and-tumble play and the development of the social brain: What do we know, how do we know it, and what do we need to know? In Robbin Gibb & Bryan Kolb (Eds.), *The neurobiology of brain and behavioral development* (pp. 315–337). San Diego, CA: Academic Press.

Peng, Duan & Robins, Philip K. (2010). Who should care for our kids? The effects of infant child care on early child development. *Journal of Children and Poverty, 16*(1), 1–45.

Peng, Peng; Yang, Xiujie & Meng, Xiangzhi. (2017). The relation between approximate number system and early arithmetic: The mediation role of numerical knowledge. *Journal of Experimental Child Psychology, 157,* 111–124.

Pennisi, Elizabeth. (2016). The right gut microbes help infants grow. *Science, 351*(6275), 802.

Pennisi, Elizabeth. (2017, February 24). Biologists propose to sequence the DNA of all life on Earth [Web log post]. Science.

Peper, Jiska S. & Dahl, Ronald E. (2013). The teenage brain: Surging hormones—brain-behavior interactions during puberty. *Current Directions in Psychological Science, 22*(2), 134–139.

Pepin, Joanna R. & Cotter, David A. (2018). Separating spheres? Diverging trends in youth's gender attitudes about work and family. *Journal of Marriage and Family, 80*(1), 7–24.

Perez, L.; Helm, L.; Sherzai, A. Dean; Jaceldo-Siegl, K. & Sherzai, A. (2012). Nutrition and vascular dementia. *The Journal of Nutrition, Health & Aging, 16*(4), 319–324.

Pérez-Fuentes, Gabriela; Olfson, Mark; Villegas, Laura; Morcillo, Carmen; Wang, Shuai & Blanco, Carlos. (2013). Prevalence and correlates of child sexual abuse: A national study. *Comprehensive Psychiatry, 54*(1), 16–27.

Perrin, Robin; Miller-Perrin, Cindy & Song, Jeongbin. (2017). Changing attitudes about spanking using alternative biblical interpretations. *International Journal of Behavioral Development, 41*(4), 514–522.

Perry, William G. (1970). *Forms of intellectual and ethical development in the college years: A scheme.* New York, NY: Holt, Rinehart and Winston.

Perry, William G. (1981). Cognitive and ethical growth: The making of meaning. In Arthur Chickering (Ed.), *The modern American college: Responding to the new realities of diverse students and a changing society* (pp. 76–116). San Francisco, CA: Jossey-Bass.

Perry, William G. (1998). *Forms of intellectual and ethical development in the college years: A scheme.* San Francisco, CA: Jossey-Bass.

Peters, Ellen; Dieckmann, Nathan F. & Weller, Joshua. (2011). Age differences in complex decision making. In K. Warner Schaie & Sherry L. Willis (Eds.), *Handbook of the psychology of aging* (7th ed., pp. 133–151). San Diego, CA: Academic Press.

Peters, Stacey L.; Lind, Jennifer N.; Humphrey, Jasmine R.; Friedman, Jan M.; Honein, Margaret A.; Tassinari, Melissa S., . . . Broussard, Cheryl S. (2013). Safe lists for medications in pregnancy: Inadequate evidence base and inconsistent guidance from Web-based information, 2011. *Pharmacoepidemiology and Drug Safety, 22*(3), 324–328.

Petersen, Inge; Martinussen, Torben; McGue, Matthew; Bingley, Paul & Christensen, Kaare. (2011). Lower marriage and divorce rates among twins than among singletons in Danish birth cohorts 1940–1964. *Twin Research and Human Genetics, 14*(2), 150–157.

Petitclerc, Amélie; Côté, Sylvana; Doyle, Orla; Burchinal, Margaret; Herba, Catherine; Zachrisson, Henrik Daae, . . . Raat, Hein. (2017). Who uses early childhood education and care services? Comparing socioeconomic selection across five western policy contexts. *International Journal of Child Care and Education Policy, 11*(3).

Petrenko, Christie L. M.; Friend, Angela; Garrido, Edward F.; Taussig, Heather N. & Culhane, Sara E. (2012). Does subtype matter? Assessing the effects of maltreatment on functioning in preadolescent youth in out-of-home care. *Child Abuse & Neglect, 36*(9), 633–644.

Pew Research Center. (2012, May 17). *College graduation: Weighing the cost . . . and the payoff.* Washington, DC: Pew Research Center.

Pew Research Center. (2013, March 20). *Growing support for gay marriage: Changed minds and changing demographics.* Washington, DC: Pew Research Center.

Pew Research Center. (2014, April 16). *Global views on morality: Compare values across 40 countries. Global Attitudes & Trends.* Washington, DC: Pew Research Center.

Pew Research Center. (2015, May 12). *America's changing religious landscape: Christians decline sharply as share of population; unaffiliated and other faiths continue to grow. Religion & Public Life.* Washington, DC: Pew Research Center.

Pew Research Center. (2015, November 3). *U.S. public becoming less religious: Modest drop in overall rates of belief and practice, but religiously affiliated Americans are as observant as before. Religion & Public Life.* Washington, DC: Pew Research Center.

Pew Research Center. (2016, May 12). *Changing attitudes on gay marriage. Religion & Public Life.* Washington, DC: Pew Research Center.

Pew Research Center. (2018, April 26). *The public, the political system and American democracy.* Washington, DC: Pew Research Center.

Pexman, Penny M. (2017). The role of embodiment in conceptual development. *Language, Cognition and Neuroscience,* (In Press).

Pfeiffer, Ronald E. & Bodis-Wollner, Ivan (Eds.). (2012). *Parkinson's disease and nonmotor dysfunction.* New York, NY: Springer.

Phillips, Deborah A.; Fox, Nathan A. & Gunnar, Megan R. (2011). Same place, different experiences: Bringing individual differences to research in child care. *Child Development Perspectives, 5*(1), 44–49.

Phillipson, Chris. (2013). *Ageing.* Malden, MA: Polity Press.

Piaget, Jean. (1932). *The moral judgment of the child.* London, UK: K. Paul, Trench, Trubner & Co.

Piaget, Jean. (1950). *The psychology of intelligence.* London, UK: Routledge & Paul.

Piaget, Jean. (1954). *The construction of reality in the child.* New York, NY: Basic Books.

Piaget, Jean. (1962). *Play, dreams and imitation in childhood.* New York, NY: Norton.

Piaget, Jean. (2001). *The psychology of intelligence.* New York, NY: Routledge.

Piaget, Jean. (2013a). *The construction of reality in the child.* New York, NY: Routledge.

Piaget, Jean. (2013b). *The moral judgment of the child.* New York, NY: Routledge.

Piaget, Jean. (2013c). *Play, dreams and imitation in childhood.* New York, NY: Routledge.

Piaget, Jean & Inhelder, Bärbel. (1972). *The psychology of the child.* New York, NY: Basic Books.

Piaget, Jean; Voelin-Liambey, Daphne & Berthoud-Papandropoulou, Ioanna. (2001). Problems of class inclusion and logical implication. In Robert L. Campell (Ed.), *Studies in reflecting abstraction* (pp. 105–137). Hove, UK: Psychology Press.

Pickles, Andrew; Hill, Jonathan; Breen, Gerome; Quinn, John; Abbott, Kate; Jones, Helen & Sharp, Helen. (2013). Evidence for interplay between genes and parenting on infant temperament in the first year of life: Monoamine oxidase A polymorphism moderates effects of maternal sensitivity on infant anger proneness. *Journal of Child Psychology and Psychiatry, 54*(12), 1308–1317.

Piekny, Jeanette & Maehler, Claudia. (2013). Scientific reasoning in early and middle childhood: The development of domain-general evidence evaluation, experimentation, and hypothesis generation skills. *British Journal of Developmental Psychology, 31*(2), 153–179.

Piérard, Gérald E.; Hermanns-Lê, Trinh; Piérard, Sébastien & Piérard-Franchimont, Claudine. (2015). Effects of hormone replacement therapy on skin viscoelasticity during climacteric aging. In Miranda A. Farage, et al. (Eds.), *Skin, mucosa and menopause: Management of clinical issues* (pp. 97–103). New York, NY: Springer.

Pietrantonio, Anna Marie; Wright, Elise; Gibson, Kathleen N.; Alldred, Tracy; Jacobson, Dustin & Niec, Anne. (2013). Mandatory reporting of child abuse and neglect: Crafting a positive process for health professionals and caregivers. *Child Abuse & Neglect, 37*(2/3), 102–109.

Pietromonaco, Paula R. & Powers, Sally I. (2015). Attachment and health-related physiological stress processes. *Current Opinion in Psychology, 1,* 34–39.

Pilarz, Alejandra Ros & Hill, Heather D. (2014). Unstable and multiple child care arrangements and young children's behavior. *Early Childhood Research Quarterly, 29*(4), 471–483.

Pilkington, Pamela D.; Windsor, Tim D. & Crisp, Dimity A. (2012). Volunteering and subjective well-being in midlife and older adults: The role of supportive social networks. *The Journals of Gerontology Series B: Psychological Sciences and Social Sciences, 67*(2), 249–260.

Pinker, Steven. (1999). *Words and rules: The ingredients of language.* New York, NY: Basic Books.

Pinker, Steven. (2011). *The better angels of our nature: Why violence has declined.* New York, NY: Viking.

Pinker, Steven. (2018). *Enlightenment now: The case for reason, science, humanism, and progress.* New York, NY: Viking.

Pinquart, Martin & Kauser, Rubina. (2018). Do the associations of parenting styles with behavior problems and academic achievement vary by culture? Results from a meta-analysis. *Cultural Diversity and Ethnic Minority Psychology, 24*(1), 75–100.

Pinquart, Martin & Silbereisen, Rainer K. (2006). Socioemotional selectivity in cancer patients. *Psychology and Aging, 21*(2), 419–423.

PISA. (2009). *Learning mathematics for life: A perspective from PISA.* Paris, France: OECD.

Piteo, A. M.; Roberts, R. M.; Nettelbeck, T.; Burns, N; Lushington, K.; Martin, A. J. & Kennedy, J. D. (2013). P[…] natal depression mediates the relationship between infa[…]

maternal sleep disruption and family dysfunction. *Early Human Development, 89*(2), 69–74.

Pizot, Cécile; Boniol, Mathieu; Mullie, Patrick; Koechlin, Alice; Boniol, Magali; Boyle, Peter & Autier, Philippe. (2016). Physical activity, hormone replacement therapy and breast cancer risk: A meta-analysis of prospective studies. *European Journal of Cancer, 52*, 138–154.

Plancoulaine, Sabine; Stagnara, Camille; Flori, Sophie; Bat-Pitault, Flora; Lin, Jian-Sheng; Patural, Hugues & Franco, Patricia. (2017). Early features associated with the neurocognitive development at 36 months of age: The AuBE study. *Sleep Medicine, 30*, 222–228.

Plomin, Robert; DeFries, John C.; Knopik, Valerie S. & Neiderhiser, Jenae M. (2013). *Behavioral genetics.* New York, NY: Worth Publishers.

Pluess, Michael & Belsky, Jay. (2010). Differential susceptibility to parenting and quality child care. *Developmental Psychology, 46*(2), 379–390.

Podsiadlowski, Astrid & Fox, Stephen. (2011). Collectivist value orientations among four ethnic groups: Collectivism in the New Zealand context. *New Zealand Journal of Psychology, 40*(1), 5–18.

Pogrebin, Abigail. (2010). *One and the same: My life as an identical twin and what I've learned about everyone's struggle to be singular.* New York, NY: Anchor.

Polanczyk, Guilherme V.; Willcutt, Erik G.; Salum, Giovanni A.; Kieling, Christian & Rohde, Luis A. (2014). ADHD prevalence estimates across three decades: An updated systematic review and meta-regression analysis. *International Journal of Epidemiology, 43*(2), 434–442.

Pollina, Laura Di; Guessous, Idris; Petoud, Véronique; Combescure, Christophe; Buchs, Bertrand; Schaller, Philippe, . . . Gaspoz, Jean-Michel. (2017). Integrated care at home reduces unnecessary hospitalizations of community-dwelling frail older adults: A prospective controlled trial. *BMC Geriatrics, 17*(53).

Pollock, Ross D.; O'Brien, Katie A.; Daniels, Lorna J.; Nielsen, Kathrine B.; Rowlerson, Anthea; Duggal, Niharika A., . . . Harridge, Stephen D. R. (2018). Properties of the vastus lateralis muscle in relation to age and physiological function in master cyclists aged 55–79 years. *Aging Cell, 17*(2), e12735.

Pons, Ferran & Lewkowicz, David J. (2014). Infant perception of audio-visual speech synchrony in familiar and unfamiliar fluent speech. *Acta Psychologica, 149*, 142–147.

Poole, Kristie L.; Jetha, Michelle K. & Schmidt, Louis A. (2017). Linking child temperament, physiology, and adult personality: Relations among retrospective behavioral inhibition, salivary cortisol, and shyness. *Personality and Individual Differences, 113*, 68–73.

Portnoy, Jill; Gao, Yu; Glenn, Andrea L.; Niv, Sharon; Peskin, Melissa; Rudo-Hutt, Anna, . . . Raine, Adrian. (2013). The biology of childhood crime and antisocial behavior. In Chris L. Gibson & Marvin D. Krohn (Eds.), *Handbook of life-*... *criminology: Emerging trends and directions for future research* ...1–42). New York, NY: Springer.

Posner, Michael I. & Rothbart, Mary K. (2017). Integrating brain, cognition and culture. *Journal of Cultural Cognitive Science, 1*(1), 3–15.

Potočnik, Kristina & Sonnentag, Sabine. (2013). A longitudinal study of well-being in older workers and retirees: The role of engaging in different types of activities. *Journal of Occupational and Organizational Psychology, 86*(4), 497–521.

Pouwels, J. Loes; Lansu, Tessa A. M. & Cillessen, Antonius H. N. (2016). Participant roles of bullying in adolescence: Status characteristics, social behavior, and assignment criteria. *Aggressive Behavior, 42*(3), 239–253.

Pouwels, J. Loes; Salmivalli, Christina; Saarento, Silja; Van Den Berg, Yvonne H. M.; Lansu, Tessa A. M. & Cillessen, Antonius H. N. (2017). Predicting adolescents' bullying participation from developmental trajectories of social status and behavior. *Child Development,* (In Press).

Powell, Cynthia M. (2013). Sex chromosomes, sex chromosome disorders, and disorders of sex development. In Steven L. Gersen & Martha B. Keagle (Eds.), *The principles of clinical cytogenetics* (pp. 175–211). New York, NY: Springer.

Powell, Katie; Wilcox, John; Clonan, Angie; Bissell, Paul; Preston, Louise; Peacock, Marian & Holdsworth, Michelle. (2015). The role of social networks in the development of overweight and obesity among adults: A scoping review. *BMC Public Health, 15*(996).

Powell, Kendall. (2006). Neurodevelopment: How does the teenage brain work? *Nature, 442*(7105), 865–867.

Powell, Shaun; Langlands, Stephanie & Dodd, Chris. (2011). Feeding children's desires? Child and parental perceptions of food promotion to the "under 8s." *Young Consumers: Insight and Ideas for Responsible Marketers, 12*(2), 96–109.

Powers, Alisa & Casey, B. J. (2015). The adolescent brain and the emergence and peak of psychopathology. *Journal of Infant, Child, and Adolescent Psychotherapy, 14*(1), 3–15.

Pozzoli, Tiziana & Gini, Gianluca. (2013). Why do bystanders of bullying help or not? A multidimensional model. *The Journal of Early Adolescence, 33*(3), 315–340.

Preston, Tom & Kelly, Michael. (2006). A medical ethics assessment of the case of Terri Schiavo. *Death Studies, 30*(2), 121–133.

Priess, Heather A.; Lindberg, Sara M. & Hyde, Janet Shibley. (2009). Adolescent gender-role identity and mental health: Gender intensification revisited. *Child Development, 80*(5), 1531–1544.

Prince, Amanda; Chu, Derrick; Meyer, Kristen; Ma, Jun; Baquero, Karalee; Blundell, Peter, . . . Aagaard, Kjersti. (2017). The fetal microbiome is altered in association with maternal diet during gestation. *American Journal of Obstetrics and Gynecology, 216*(1, Suppl.), S17.

Proctor, Laura J. & Dubowitz, Howard. (2014). Child neglect: Challenges and controversies. In Jill E. Korbin & Richard D. Krugman (Eds.), *Handbook of child maltreatment* (pp. 27–61). New York, NY: Springer.

Prothero, Arianna. (2016, April 20). Charters help alums stick with college. *Education Week, 35*(28), 1, 13.

Proud2Bme. (2012, March 26). Overall, do social networking sites like Facebook and Twitter help or hurt your body confidence.

Pruden, Shannon M. & Levine, Susan C. (2017). Parents' spatial language mediates a sex difference in preschoolers' spatial-language use. *Psychological Science, 28*(11), 1583–1596.

Puccioni, Olga & Vallesi, Antonino. (2012). Conflict resolution and adaptation in normal aging: The role of verbal intelligence and cognitive reserve. *Psychology and Aging, 27*(4), 1018–1026.

Puertas, Alberto; Magan-Fernandez, Antonio; Blanc, Vanessa; Revelles, Laura; O'Valle, Francisco; Pozo, Elena, . . . Mesa, Francisco. (2018). Association of periodontitis with preterm birth and low birth weight: A comprehensive review. *Journal of Maternal-Fetal and Neonatal Medicine, 31*(5), 597–602.

Puetz, Vanessa B.; Parker, Drew; Kohn, Nils; Dahmen, Brigitte; Verma, Ragini & Konrad, Kerstin. (2017). Altered brain network integrity after childhood maltreatment: A structural connectomic DTI-study. *Human Brain Mapping, 38*(2), 855–868.

Puhl, Rebecca M. & Heuer, Chelsea A. (2010). Obesity stigma: Important considerations for public health. *American Journal of Public Health, 100*(6), 1019–1028.

Pulvermüller, Friedemann. (2018). Neural reuse of action perception circuits for language, concepts and communication. *Progress in Neurobiology, 160*, 1–44.

Purewal, Navtej & Eklund, Lisa. (2017). 'Gendercide', abortion policy, and the disciplining of prenatal sex-selection in neoliberal Europe. *Global Public Health*, (In Press).

Qin, Desiree B. & Chang, Tzu-Fen. (2013). Asian fathers. In Natasha J. Cabrera & Catherine S. Tamis-LeMonda (Eds.), *Handbook of father involvement: Multidisciplinary perspectives* (2nd ed., pp. 261–281). New York, NY: Routledge.

Qiu, A.; Anh, T. T.; Li, Y.; Chen, H.; Rifkin-Graboi, A.; Broekman, B. F. P., . . . Meaney, M. J. (2015). Prenatal maternal depression alters amygdala functional connectivity in 6-month-old infants. *Translational Psychiatry, 5*, e508.

Qiu, Chengxuan; von Strauss, Eva; Bäckman, Lars; Winblad, Bengt & Fratiglioni, Laura. (2013). Twenty-year changes in dementia occurrence suggest decreasing incidence in central Stockholm, Sweden. *Neurology, 80*(20), 1888–1894.

Quindlen, Anna. (2012). *Lots of candles, plenty of cake.* New York, NY: Random House.

Rabkin, Nick & Hedberg, Eric C. (2011). *Arts education in America: What the declines mean for arts participation.* Washington, DC: National Endowment for the Arts.

Raby, K. Lee; Labella, Madelyn H.; Martin, Jodi; Carlson, Elizabeth A. & Roisman, Glenn I. (2017). Childhood abuse and neglect and insecure attachment states of mind in adulthood: Prospective, longitudinal evidence from a high-risk sample. *Development and Psychopathology, 29*(2), 347–363.

Raby, K. Lee; Lawler, Jamie M.; Shlafer, Rebecca J.; Hesemeyer, Paloma S. & Collins, W. Andrew. (2015). The interpersonal antecedents of supportive parenting: A prospective, longitudinal study from infancy to adulthood. *Developmental Psychology, 51*(1), 115–123.

Raeburn, Paul. (2014). *Do fathers matter?: What science is telling us about the parent we've overlooked.* New York, NY: Farrar, Straus and Giroux.

Rahilly, Elizabeth P. (2015). The gender binary meets the gender-variant child: Parents' negotiations with childhood gender variance. *Gender & Society, 29*(3), 338–361.

Rakic, Snezana; Jankovic Raznatovic, Svetlana; Jurisic, Aleksandar; Anicic, Radomir & Zecevic, Nebojsa. (2016). Fetal neurosonography and fetal behaviour: Genesis of fetal movements and motor reflexes. *Ultrasound in Obstetrics and Gynecology, 48*(Suppl. 1), 196.

Ramani, Geetha B.; Brownell, Celia A. & Campbell, Susan B. (2010). Positive and negative peer interaction in 3- and 4-year-olds in relation to regulation and dysregulation. *Journal of Genetic Psychology, 171*(3), 218–250.

Ramírez, Naja Ferjan; Ramírez, Rey R.; Clarke, Maggie; Taulu, Samu & Kuhl, Patricia K. (2017). Speech discrimination in 11-month-old bilingual and monolingual infants: A magnetoencephalography study. *Developmental Science, 20*(1), e12427.

Ramo, Danielle E.; Young-Wolff, Kelly C. & Prochaska, Judith J. (2015). Prevalence and correlates of electronic-cigarette use in young adults: Findings from three studies over five years. *Addictive Behaviors, 41*, 142–147.

Ramscar, Michael & Dye, Melody. (2011). Learning language from the input: Why innate constraints can't explain noun compounding. *Cognitive Psychology, 62*(1), 1–40.

Rankin, Jay. (2017). Physicians disagree on legal age for cannabis. *CMAJ, 189*(4), E174–E175.

Rashidi, Parisa & Mihailidis, Alex. (2013). A survey on ambient-assisted living tools for older adults. *IEEE Journal of Biomedical and Health Informatics, 17*(3), 579–590.

Rau, Barbara L. & Adams, Gary A. (2014). Recruiting older workers: Realities and needs of the future workforce. In Daniel M. Cable, et al. (Eds.), *The Oxford handbook of recruitment* (pp. 88–109). New York, NY: Oxford University Press.

Rauers, Antje; Blanke, Elisabeth & Riediger, Michaela. (2013). Everyday empathic accuracy in younger and older couples: Do you need to see your partner to know his or her feelings? *Psychological Science, 24*(11), 2210–2217.

Raus, Kasper; Sterckx, Sigrid & Mortier, Freddy. (2011). Is continuous sedation at the end of life an ethically preferable alternative to physician-assisted suicide? *The American Journal of Bioethics, 11*(6), 32–40.

Ravallion, Martin. (2014). Income inequality in the developing world. *Science, 344*(6186), 851–855.

Ravizza, Kenneth. (2007). Peak experiences in sport. In Daniel Smith & Michael Bar-Eli (Eds.), *Essential readings in sport and exercise psychology* (pp. 122–125). Champaign, IL: Human Kinetics.

Ray, Brian D. (2013). Homeschooling rising into the twenty-first century: Editor's introduction. *Peabody Journal of Education, 88*(3), 261–264.

Raymond, Jaime & Brown, Mary Jean. (2017, January 20). *Childhood blood lead levels in children aged <5 Years— United S...*

2009–2014. *Morbidity and Mortality Weekly Report, 66*(3), 1–10. Atlanta, GA: Centers for Disease Control and Prevention.

Raz, Naftali & Lindenberger, Ulman. (2013). Life-span plasticity of the brain and cognition: From questions to evidence and back. *Neuroscience & Biobehavioral Reviews, 37*(9), 2195–2200.

Reardon, Sean F. (2013). The widening income achievement gap. *Educational Leadership, 70*(8), 10–16.

Reavey, Daphne; Haney, Barbara M.; Atchison, Linda; Anderson, Betsi; Sandritter, Tracy & Pallotto, Eugenia K. (2014). Improving pain assessment in the NICU: A quality improvement project. *Advances in Neonatal Care, 14*(3), 144–153.

Reczek, Corinne; Liu, Hui & Spiker, Russell. (2014). A population-based study of alcohol use in same-sex and different-sex unions. *Journal of Marriage and Family, 76*(3), 557–572.

Reddy, Marpadga A. & Natarajan, Rama. (2013). Role of epigenetic mechanisms in the vascular complications of diabetes. In Tapas K. Kundu (Ed.), *Epigenetics: Development and disease* (pp. 435–454). New York, NY: Springer.

Redford, Jeremy; Battle, Danielle & Bielick, Stacey. (2017). *Homeschooling in the United States: 2012.* NCES 2016-096.REV.

Reed, Andrew E.; Chan, Larry & Mikels, Joseph A. (2014). Meta-analysis of the age-related positivity effect: Age differences in preferences for positive over negative information. *Psychology and Aging, 29*(1), 1–15.

Reid, Keshia M.; Forrest, Jamie R. & Porter, Lauren. (2018, June 1). *Tobacco product use among youths with and without lifetime asthma—Florida, 2016. Morbidity and Mortality Weekly Report, 67*(21), 599–601. Atlanta, GA: Centers for Disease Control and Prevention.

Reilly, Steven K. & Noonan, James P. (2016). Evolution of gene regulation in humans. *Annual Review of Genomics and Human Genetics, 17*, 45–67.

Reisner, Sari L.; Katz-Wise, Sabra L.; Gordon, Allegra R.; Corliss, Heather L. & Austin, S. Bryn. (2016). Social epidemiology of depression and anxiety by gender identity. *Journal of Adolescent Health, 59*(2), 203–208.

Reitz, Anne K. & Staudinger, Ursula M. (2017). Getting older, getting better? Toward understanding positive personality development across adulthood. In Jule Specht (Ed.), *Personality Development Across the Lifespan* (pp. 219–241). Cambridge, MA: Academic Press.

Renfrew, Mary J.; McFadden, Alison; Bastos, Maria Helena; Campbell, James; Channon, Andrew Amos; Cheung, Ngai Fen, . . . Declercq, Eugene. (2014). Midwifery and quality care: Findings from a new evidence-informed framework for maternal and newborn care. *The Lancet, 384*(9948), 1129–1145.

Reniers, Renate L. E. P.; Beavan, Amanda; Keogan, Louise; Furneaux, Andrea; Mayhew, Samantha & Wood, Stephen J. (2017). Is it all in the reward? Peers influence risk-taking behaviour in young adulthood. *British Journal of Psychology, 108*(2), 276–295.

Resnick, Barbara; Gwyther, Lisa P. & Roberto, Karen A. (Eds.). (2011). *Resilience in aging: Concepts, research, and outcomes.* New York, NY: Springer.

. . . . driana M. (2018). The economic organization . . . . family households by race or ethnicity and socioeconomic status. *Journal of Marriage and Family, 80*(1), 119–133.

Reynolds, Arthur J. (2000). *Success in early intervention: The Chicago Child-Parent Centers.* Lincoln, NE: University of Nebraska Press.

Reynolds, Arthur J. & Ou, Suh-Ruu. (2011). Paths of effects from preschool to adult well-being: A confirmatory analysis of the Child-Parent Center Program. *Child Development, 82*(2), 555–582.

Reynolds, Arthur J.; Ou, Suh-Ruu; Mondi, Christina F. & Hayakawa, Momoko. (2017). Processes of early childhood interventions to adult well-being. *Child Development, 88*(2), 378–387.

Reynolds, Arthur J.; Rolnick, Arthur J. & Temple, Judy A. (Eds.). (2015). *Health and education in early childhood: Predictors, interventions, and policies.* New York, NY: Cambridge University Press.

Reynolds, Jamila E. & Gonzales-Backen, Melinda A. (2017). Ethnic-racial socialization and the mental health of African Americans: A critical review. *Journal of Family Theory & Review, 9*(12), 182–200.

Rhoades, Kimberly A.; Leve, Leslie D.; Eddy, J. Mark & Chamberlain, Patricia. (2016). Predicting the transition from juvenile delinquency to adult criminality: Gender-specific influences in two high-risk samples. *Criminal Behaviour and Mental Health, 26*(5), 336–351.

Rhodes, Marjorie. (2013). The conceptual structure of social categories: The social allegiance hypothesis. In Mahzarin R. Banaji & Susan A. Gelman (Eds.), *Navigating the social world: What infants, children, and other species can teach us* (pp. 258–262). New York, NY: Oxford University Press.

Ribot, Krystal M.; Hoff, Erika & Burridge, Andrea. (2017). Language use contributes to expressive language growth: Evidence from bilingual children. *Child Development*, (In Press).

Rice, Eric; Craddock, Jaih; Hemler, Mary; Rusow, Joshua; Plant, Aaron; Montoya, Jorge & Kordic, Timothy. (2018). Associations between sexting behaviors and sexual behaviors among mobile phone-owning teens in Los Angeles. *Child Development, 89*(1), 110–117.

Richards, Jennifer S.; Hartman, Catharina A.; Franke, Barbara; Hoekstra, Pieter J.; Heslenfeld, Dirk J.; Oosterlaan, Jaap, . . . Buitelaar, Jan K. (2014). Differential susceptibility to maternal expressed emotion in children with ADHD and their siblings? Investigating plasticity genes, prosocial and antisocial behaviour. *European Child & Adolescent Psychiatry, 24*(2), 209–217.

Richards, Morgan K.; Flanagan, Meghan R.; Littman, Alyson J.; Burke, Alson K. & Callegari, Lisa S. (2016). Primary cesarean section and adverse delivery outcomes among women of very advanced maternal age. *Journal of Perinatology, 36*, 272–277.

Riediger, Michaela; Voelkle, Manuel C.; Schaefer, Sabine & Lindenberger, Ulman. (2014). Charting the life course: Age differences and validity of beliefs about lifespan development. *Psychology and Aging, 29*(3), 503–520.

Riordan, Jan & Wambach, Karen (Eds.). (2009). *Breastfeeding and human lactation* (4th ed.). Sudbury, MA: Jones and Bartlett Publishers.

Rioux, Charlie; Castellanos-Ryan, Natalie; Parent, Sophie & Séguin, Jean R. (2016). The interaction between temperament and the family environment in adolescent substance use and externalizing behaviors: Support for diathesis–stress or differential susceptibility? *Developmental Review, 40*(10), 117–150.

Rivas-Drake, Deborah & Mooney, Margarita. (2009). Neither colorblind nor oppositional: Perceived minority status and trajectories of academic adjustment among Latinos in elite higher education. *Developmental Psychology, 45*(3), 642–651.

Rivas-Drake, Deborah; Seaton, Eleanor K.; Markstrom, Carol; Quintana, Stephen; Syed, Moin; Lee, Richard M., . . . Yip, Tiffany. (2014). Ethnic and racial identity in adolescence: Implications for psychosocial, academic, and health outcomes. *Child Development, 85*(1), 40–57.

Rix, Sara E. (2011). Employment and aging. In Robert H. Binstock & Linda K. George (Eds.), *Handbook of aging and the social sciences* (7th ed., pp. 193–206). San Diego, CA: Academic Press.

Roane, David M.; Landers, Alyssa; Sherratt, Jackson & Wilson, Gillian S. (2017). Hoarding in the elderly: A critical review of the recent literature. *International Psychogeriatrics, 29*(7), 1077–1084.

Robben, Antonius C. G. M. (2018). Death and anthropology: An introduction. In Antonius C. G. M. Robben (Ed.), *Death, mourning, and burial: A cross-cultural reader* (2nd ed., pp. 1–16). Hoboken, NJ: Wiley-Blackwell.

Robelen, Erik W. (2011). More students enrolling in Mandarin Chinese. *Education Week, 30*(27), 5.

Roberson, Patricia N. E.; Olmstead, Spencer B. & Fincham, Frank D. (2015). Hooking up during the college years: Is there a pattern? *Culture, Health & Sexuality, 17*(5), 576–591.

Roberts, Brent W. & Davis, Jordan P. (2016). Young adulthood is the crucible of personality development. *Emerging Adulthood, 4*(5), 318–326.

Roberts, Leslie. (2017, April 7). Nigeria's invisible crisis. *Science, 356*(6333), 18–23.

Roberts, Richard D. & Lipnevich, Anastasiya A. (2012). From general intelligence to multiple intelligences: Meanings, models, and measures. In Karen R. Harris, et al. (Eds.), *APA educational psychology handbook* (Vol. 2, pp. 33–57). Washington, DC: American Psychological Association.

Roberts, Soraya. (2010, January 1). Travis Pastrana breaks world record for longest rally car jump on New Year's Eve. *New York Daily News.*

Robinson, Julia T. & Murphy-Nugen, Amy B. (2018). It makes you keep trying: Life review writing for older adults. *Journal of Gerontological Social Work, 61*(2), 171–192.

Robinson, Leah E.; Wadsworth, Danielle D.; Webster, E. Kipling & Bassett, David R. (2014). School reform: The role of physical education policy in physical activity of elementary school children in Alabama's Black Belt region. *American Journal of Health Promotion, 38*(Suppl. 3), S72–S76.

Robson, Ruthann. (2010). Notes on my dying. In Nan Bauer Maglin & Donna Marie Perry (Eds.), *Final acts: Death, dying, and the choices we make* (pp. 19–28). New Brunswick, NJ: Rutgers University Press.

Roca, María; Parr, Alice; Thompson, Russell; Woolgar, Alexandra; Torralva, Teresa; Antoun, Nagui, . . . Duncan, John. (2010). Executive function and fluid intelligence after frontal lobe lesions. *Brain, 133*(1), 234–247.

Rochat, Philippe. (2013). Self-conceptualizing in development. In Philip D. Zelazo (Ed.), *The Oxford handbook of developmental psychology* (Vol. 2, pp. 378–397). New York, NY: Oxford University Press.

Rodrigue, Karen M. & Kennedy, Kristen M. (2011). The cognitive consequences of structural changes to the aging brain. In K. Warner Schaie & Sherry L. Willis (Eds.), *Handbook of the psychology of aging* (7th ed., pp. 73–91). San Diego, CA: Academic Press.

Roebers, Claudia M.; Schmid, Corinne & Roderer, Thomas. (2009). Metacognitive monitoring and control processes involved in primary school children's test performance. *British Journal of Educational Psychology, 79*(4), 749–767.

Roelfs, David J.; Shor, Eran; Davidson, Karina W. & Schwartz, Joseph E. (2011). Losing life and livelihood: A systematic review and meta-analysis of unemployment and all-cause mortality. *Social Science Medicine, 72*(6), 840–854.

Rogne, Leah & McCune, Susana Lauraine (Eds.). (2014). *Advance care planning: Communicating about matters of life and death.* New York, NY: Springer.

Rogoff, Barbara. (2003). *The cultural nature of human development.* New York, NY: Oxford University Press.

Rohsenow, Damaris J.; Tidey, Jennifer W.; Martin, Rosemarie A.; Colby, Suzanne M. & Eissenberg, Thomas. (2018). Effects of six weeks of electronic cigarette use on smoking rate, CO, cigarette dependence, and motivation to quit smoking: A pilot study. *Addictive Behaviors, 80*, 65–70.

Romeo, Russell D. (2013). The teenage brain: The stress response and the adolescent brain. *Current Directions in Psychological Science, 22*(2), 140–145.

Rook, Graham A. W.; Lowry, Christopher A. & Raison, Charles L. (2014). Hygiene and other early childhood influences on the subsequent function of the immune system. *Brain Research,* (Corrected Proof).

Roopnarine, Jaipaul L. & Hossain, Ziarat. (2013). African American and African Caribbean fathers. In Natasha J. Cabrera & Catherine S. Tamis-LeMonda (Eds.), *Handbook of father involvement: Multidisciplinary perspectives* (2nd ed., pp. 223–243). New York, NY: Routledge.

Rose, Amanda J. & Asher, Steven R. (2017). The social tasks of friendship: Do boys and girls excel in different tasks? *Child Development Perspectives, 11*(1), 3–8.

Rose, Amanda J.; Schwartz-Mette, Rebecca A.; Glick, Gary C.; Smith, Rhiannon L. & Luebbe, Aaron M. (2014). An observational study of co-rumination in adolescent friendships. *Developmental Psychology, 50*(9), 2199–2209.

Rose, Katherine K.; Johnson, Amy; Muro, Joel & Buckley, Rhonda R. (2018). Decision making about nonparental child care by fathers: What is important to fathers in a nonparental child care program. *Journal of Family Issues, 39*(2), 299–327.

Rose, Steven. (2008). Drugging unruly children is a method of social control. *Nature, 451*(7178), 521.

Roseberry, Lynn & Roos, Johan. (2016). *Bridging the gender gap: Seven principles for achieving gender balance.* New York, NY: Oxford University Press.

Rosen, Meghan. (2016). Concern grows over Zika birth defects. *Science News, 190*(9), 14–15.

Rosenblatt, Paul C. (2013). Culture, socialization, and loss, grief, and mourning. In David K. Meagher & David E. Balk (Eds.), *Handbook of thanatology: The essential body of knowledge for the study of death, dying, and bereavement* (2nd ed., pp. 121–126). New York, NY: Routledge.

Rosenblum, Gianine D. & Lewis, Michael. (1999). The relations among body image, physical attractiveness, and body mass in adolescence. *Child Development, 70*(1), 50–64.

Rosenfield, Sarah. (2012). Triple jeopardy? Mental health at the intersection of gender, race, and class. *Social Science & Medicine, 74*(11), 1791–1801.

Rosow, Irving. (1985). Status and role change through the life cycle. In Robert H. Binstock & Ethel Shanas (Eds.), *Handbook of aging and the social sciences* (2nd ed., pp. 62–93). New York, NY: Van Nostrand Reinhold.

Ross, Josephine; Anderson, James R. & Campbell, Robin N. (2011). *I remember me: Mnemonic self-reference effects in preschool children.* Boston, MA: Wiley-Blackwell.

Ross, Josephine; Yilmaz, Mandy; Dale, Rachel; Cassidy, Rose; Yildirim, Iraz & Zeedyk, M. Suzanne. (2017). Cultural differences in self-recognition: The early development of autonomous and related selves? *Developmental Science, 20*(3), e12387.

Ross, Robert; Hudson, Robert; Stotz, Paula J. & Lam, Miu. (2015). Effects of exercise amount and intensity on abdominal obesity and glucose tolerance in obese adults: A randomized trial. *Annals of Internal Medicine, 162*(5), 325–334.

Rosselli, Mónica; Ardila, Alfredo; Lalwani, Laxmi N. & Vélez–Uribe, Idaly. (2016). The effect of language proficiency on executive functions in balanced and unbalanced Spanish–English bilinguals. *Bilingualism: Language and Cognition, 19*(3), 489–503.

Rossignol, Michel; Chaillet, Nils; Boughrassa, Faiza & Moutquin, Jean-Marie. (2014). Interrelations between four antepartum obstetric interventions and cesarean delivery in women at low risk: A systematic review and modeling of the cascade of interventions. *Birth, 41*(1), 70–78.

Rostila, Mikael; Saarela, Jan & Kawachi, Ichiro. (2012). Mortality in parents following the death of a child: A nationwide follow-up study from Sweden. *Journal of Epidemiol Community Health, 66*(10), 927–933.

Rostila, Mikael; Saarela, Jan & Kawachi, Ichiro. (2013). Suicide following the death of a sibling: A nationwide follow-up study from Sweden. *BMJ Open, 3*(4), e002618.

Roth, Lauren W. & Polotsky, Alex J. (2012). Can we live longer by eating less? A review of caloric restriction and longevity. *Maturitas, 71*(4), 315–319.

Rotz, Dana. (2016). Why have divorce rates fallen?: The role of women's age at marriage. *Journal of Human Resources, 51*(4), 961–1002.

Roubinov, Danielle S. & Boyce, William Thomas. (2017). Parenting and SES: Relative values or enduring principles? *Current Opinion in Psychology, 15*, 162–167.

Rovee-Collier, Carolyn. (1987). Learning and memory in infancy. In Joy Doniger Osofsky (Ed.), *Handbook of infant development* (2nd ed., pp. 98–148). New York, NY: Wiley.

Rovee-Collier, Carolyn. (1990). The "memory system" of prelinguistic infants. *Annals of the New York Academy of Sciences, 608*, 517–542.

Rowe, Meredith L.; Denmark, Nicole; Harden, Brenda Jones & Stapleton, Laura M. (2016). The role of parent education and parenting knowledge in children's language and literacy skills among White, Black, and Latino families. *Infant and Child Development, 25*(2), 198–220.

Ruba, Ashley L.; Johnson, Kristin M.; Harris, Lasana T. & Wilbourn, Makeba Parramore. (2017). Developmental changes in infants' categorization of anger and disgust facial expressions. *Developmental Psychology, 53*(10), 1826–1832.

Rubin, Kenneth H.; Bowker, Julie C.; McDonald, Kristina L. & Menzer, Melissa. (2013). Peer relationships in childhood. In Philip D. Zelazo (Ed.), *The Oxford handbook of developmental psychology* (Vol. 2, pp. 242–275). New York, NY: Oxford University Press.

Rubin, Simon Shimshon; Malkinson, Ruth & Witztum, Eliezer. (2012). *Working with the bereaved: Multiple lenses on loss and mourning.* New York, NY: Routledge.

Rudaz, Myriam; Ledermann, Thomas; Margraf, Jürgen; Becker, Eni S. & Craske, Michelle G. (2017). The moderating role of avoidance behavior on anxiety over time: Is there a difference between social anxiety disorder and specific phobia? *PLoS ONE, 12*(7), e0180298.

Runions, Kevin C. & Shaw, Thérèse. (2013). Teacher–child relationship, child withdrawal and aggression in the development of peer victimization. *Journal of Applied Developmental Psychology, 34*(6), 319–327.

Russell, Ashley. (2018). Human trafficking: A research synthesis on human-trafficking literature in academic journals from 2000–2014. *Journal of Human Trafficking, 4*(2), 114–136.

Russell, Charlotte K.; Robinson, Lyn & Ball, Helen L. (2013). Infant sleep development: Location, feeding and expectations in the postnatal period. *The Open Sleep Journal, 6*(Suppl. 1: M9), 68–76.

Russell, Stephen T.; Everett, Bethany G.; Rosario, Margaret & Birkett, Michelle. (2014). Indicators of victimization and sexual orientation among adolescents: Analyses from youth risk behavior surveys. *American Journal of Public Health, 104*(2), 255–261.

Russo, Theresa J. & Fallon, Moira A. (2014). Coping with stress: Supporting the needs of military families and their children. *Early Childhood Education Journal, 43*(5), 407–416.

Ruthig, Joelle C.; Trisko, Jenna & Stewart, Tara L. (2012). The impact of spouse's health and well-being on own well-being: A dyadic study of older married couples. *Journal of Social and Clinical Psychology, 31*(5), 508–529.

Rutter, Michael; Sonuga-Barke, Edmund J.; Beckett, Celia; Castle, Jennifer; Kreppner, Jana; Kumsta, Robert, . . . Gunnar, Megan R. (2010). Deprivation-specific psychological patterns: Effects of institutional deprivation. *Monographs of the Society for Research in Child Development, 75*(1).

Sacks, Oliver. (1995). *An anthropologist on Mars: Seven paradoxical tales.* New York, NY: Knopf.

Sacks, Oliver. (2008). *Musicophilia: Tales of music and the brain.* New York, NY: Vintage Books.

Sadeh, Avi; Mindell, Jodi A.; Luedtke, Kathryn & Wiegand, Benjamin. (2009). Sleep and sleep ecology in the first 3 years: A web-based study. *Journal of Sleep Research, 18*(1), 60–73.

Sadeh, Avi; Tikotzky, Liat & Scher, Anat. (2010). Parenting and infant sleep. *Sleep Medicine Reviews, 14*(2), 89–96.

Sadler, Thomas W. (2015). *Langman's medical embryology* (13th ed.). Philadelphia, PA: Lippincott Williams & Wilkins.

Saegert, Susan; Fields, Desiree & Libman, Kimberly. (2011). Mortgage foreclosure and health disparities: Serial displacement as asset extraction in African American populations. *Journal of Urban Health, 88*(3), 390–402.

Saey, Tina Hesman. (2016). Neandertal DNA poses health risks. *Science News, 189*(5), 18–19.

Saez, Emmanuel. (2017). Income and wealth inequality: Evidence and policy implications. *Contemporary Economic Policy, 35*(1), 7–25.

Sage, Cindy & Burgio, Ernesto. (2018). Electromagnetic fields, pulsed radiofrequency radiation, and epigenetics: How wireless technologies may affect childhood development. *Child Development, 89*(1), 129–136.

Sahlberg, Pasi. (2011). *Finnish lessons: What can the world learn from educational change in Finland?* New York, NY: Teachers College Press.

Sahlberg, Pasi. (2015). *Finnish lessons 2.0: What can the world learn from educational change in Finland?* (2nd. ed.). New York, NY: Teachers College.

Sahoo, Krushnapriya; Sahoo, Bishnupriya; Choudhury, Ashok Kumar; Sofi, Nighat Yasin; Kumar, Raman & Bhadoria, Ajeet Singh. (2015). Childhood obesity: Causes and consequences. *Journal of Family Medicine and Primary Care, 4*(2), 187–192.

Salkind, Neil J. (2004). *An introduction to theories of human development.* Thousand Oaks, CA: Sage.

Salpeter, Shelley R.; Luo, Esther J.; Malter, Dawn S. & Stuart, Brad. (2012). Systematic review of noncancer presentations with a median survival of 6 months or less. *The American Journal of Medicine, 125*(5), 512.e511–512.e516.

Salter, Michael; Crofts, Thomas & Lee, Murray. (2013). Beyond criminalisation and responsibilisation: Sexting, gender, and young people. *Current Issues in Criminal Justice, 24*(3), 301–316.

Salthouse, Timothy A. (2004). What and when of cognitive aging. *Current Directions in Psychological Science, 13*(4), 140–144.

Salthouse, Timothy A. (2010). *Major issues in cognitive aging.* New York, NY: Oxford University Press.

Samaras, Nikolass; Frangos, Emilia; Forster, Alexandre; Lang, P. O. & Samaras, Dimitrios. (2012). Andropause: A review of the definition and treatment. *European Geriatric Medicine, 3*(6), 368–373.

Samek, Diana R.; Goodman, Rebecca J.; Erath, Stephen A.; McGue, Matt & Iacono, William G. (2016). Antisocial peer affiliation and externalizing disorders in the transition from adolescence to young adulthood: Selection versus socialization effects. *Developmental Psychology, 52*(5), 813–823.

Sampson, Deborah & Hertlein, Katherine. (2015). The experience of grandparents raising grandchildren. *GrandFamilies, 2*(1), 75–96.

Samuels, Christina A. & Klein, Alyson. (2013). States faulted on preschool spending levels. *Education Week, 32*(30), 21, 24.

Sandu, Anca-Larisa; Staff, Roger T.; McNeil, Chris J.; Mustafa, Nazahah; Ahearn, Trevor; Whalley, Lawrence J. & Murray, Alison D. (2014). Structural brain complexity and cognitive decline in late life—A longitudinal study in the Aberdeen 1936 Birth Cohort. *NeuroImage, 100*, 558–563.

Sanou, Dia; O'Reilly, Erin; Ngnie-Teta, Ismael; Batal, Malek; Mondain, Nathalie; Andrew, Caroline, . . . Bourgeault, Ivy L. (2014). Acculturation and nutritional health of immigrants in Canada: A scoping review. *Journal of Immigrant and Minority Health, 16*(1), 24–34.

Santos-Lozano, Alejandro; Santamarina, Ana; Pareja-Galeano, Helios; Sanchis-Gomar, Fabian; Fiuza-Luces, Carmen; Cristi-Montero, Carlos, . . . Garatachea, Nuria. (2016). The genetics of exceptional longevity: Insights from centenarians. *Maturitas, 90*, 49–57.

Sanz Cruces, José Manuel; Hawrylak, María Fernández & Delegido, Ana Benito. (2015). Interpersonal variability of the experience of falling in love. *International Journal of Psychology and Psychological Therapy, 15*(1), 87–100.

Saraceno, Chiara. (2010). Social inequalities in facing old-age dependency: A bi-generational perspective. *Journal of European Social Policy, 20*(1), 32–44.

Sasser, Tyler R.; Bierman, Karen L.; Heinrichs, Brenda & Nix, Robert L. (2017). Preschool intervention can promote sustained growth in the executive-function skills of children exhibiting early deficits. *Psychological Science, 28*(12), 1719–1730.

Savioja, Hanna; Helminen, Mika; Fröjd, Sari; Marttunen, Mauri & Kaltiala-Heino, Riittakerttu. (2015). Sexual experience and self-reported depression across the adolescent years. *Health Psychology and Behavioral Medicine, 3*(1), 337–347.

Saxbe, Darby E. (2017). Birth of a new perspective? A call for biopsychosocial research on childbirth. *Current Directions in Psychological Science, 26*(1), 81–86.

Saxton, Matthew. (2010). *Child language: Acquisition and development.* Thousand Oaks, CA: Sage.

Scarr, Sandra. (1985). Constructing psychology: Making facts and fables for our times. *American Psychologist, 40*(5), 499–512.

Schacter, Hannah L. & Juvonen, Jaana. (2018). Dynamic changes in peer victimization and adjustment across middle school: Does friends' victimization alleviate distress? *Child Development*, (In Press).

Schafer, Markus H.; Morton, Patricia M. & Ferraro, Kenneth F. (2014). Child maltreatment and adult health in a national sample: Heterogeneous relational contexts, divergent effects? *Child Abuse & Neglect, 38*(3), 395–406.

Schaie, K. Warner. (2005). *Developmental influences on adult intelligence: The Seattle Longitudinal Study.* New York, NY: Oxford University Press.

Schaie, K. Warner. (2013). *Developmental influences on adult intelligence: The Seattle Longitudinal Study* (2nd ed.). New York, NY: Oxford University Press.

Schanler, Richard. J. (2011). Outcomes of human milk-fed premature infants. *Seminars in Perinatology, 35*(1), 29–33.

Scharf, Miri. (2014). Parenting in Israel: Together hand in hand, you are mine and I am yours. In Helaine Selin (Ed.), *Parenting across cultures: Childrearing, motherhood and fatherhood in non-Western cultures* (pp. 193–206). Dordrecht: Springer.

Scharlach, Andrew; Graham, Carrie & Lehning, Amanda. (2012). The "Village" model: A consumer-driven approach for aging in place. *The Gerontologist, 52*(3), 418–427.

Scherbaum, Stefan; Frisch, Simon; Holfert, Anna-Maria; O'Hora, Denis & Dshemuchadse, Maja. (2018). No evidence for common processes of cognitive control and self-control. *Acta Psychologica, 182*, 194–199.

Schermerhorn, Alice C.; D'Onofrio, Brian M.; Turkheimer, Eric; Ganiban, Jody M.; Spotts, Erica L.; Lichtenstein, Paul, . . . Neiderhiser, Jenae M. (2011). A genetically informed study of associations between family functioning and child psychosocial adjustment. *Developmental Psychology, 47*(3), 707–725.

Schmid, Monika S.; Gilbers, Steven & Nota, Amber. (2014). Ultimate attainment in late second language acquisition: Phonetic and grammatical challenges in advanced Dutch–English bilingualism. *Second Language Research, 30*(2), 129–157.

Schneider, William; Waldfogel, Jane & Brooks-Gunn, Jeanne. (2017). The Great Recession and risk for child abuse and neglect. *Children and Youth Services Review, 72*, 71–81.

Schneider, Wolfgang. (2015). *Memory development from early childhood through emerging adulthood.* Switzerland: Springer International.

Schnitzspahn, Katharina M.; Ihle, Andreas; Henry, Julie D.; Rendell, Peter G. & Kliegel, Matthias. (2011). The age-prospective memory-paradox: An exploration of possible mechanisms. *International Psychogeriatrics, 23*(4), 583–592.

Schnitzspahn, Katharina M.; Stahl, Christoph; Zeintl, Melanie; Kaller, Christoph P. & Kliegel, Matthias. (2013). The role of shifting, updating, and inhibition in prospective memory performance in young and older adults. *Developmental Psychology, 49*(8), 1544–1553.

Schofield, Thomas J.; Martin, Monica J.; Conger, Katherine J.; Neppl, Tricia M.; Donnellan, M. Brent & Conger, Rand D. (2011). Intergenerational transmission of adaptive functioning: A test of the interactionist model of SES and human development. *Child Development, 82*(1), 33–47.

Schore, Allan & McIntosh, Jennifer. (2011). Family law and the neuroscience of attachment: Part I. *Family Court Review, 49*(3), 501–512.

Schröder, Mathis. (2013). Jobless now, sick later? Investigating the long-term consequences of involuntary job loss on health. *Advances in Life Course Research, 18*(1), 5–15.

Schroeder, Steven A. (2013). New evidence that cigarette smoking remains the most important health hazard. *New England Journal of Medicine, 368*(4), 389–390.

Schulenberg, John; Patrick, Megan E.; Maslowsky, Julie & Maggs, Jennifer L. (2014). The epidemiology and etiology of adolescent substance use in developmental perspective. In Michael Lewis & Karen D. Rudolph (Eds.), *Handbook of Developmental Psychopathology* (pp. 601–620). New York, NY: Springer.

Schulz, James H. & Binstock, Robert H. (2008). *Aging nation: The economics and politics of growing older in America.* Baltimore, MD: Johns Hopkins University Press.

Schulz, Laura. (2015). Infants explore the unexpected. *Science, 348*(6230), 42–43.

Schupp, Justin & Sharp, Jeff. (2012). Exploring the social bases of home gardening. *Agriculture and Human Values, 29*(1), 93–105.

Schwarz, Alan. (2016). *ADHD nation: Children, doctors, big pharma, and the making of an American epidemic.* New York, NY: Scribner.

Schwarz, Alan & Cohen, Sarah. (2013, March 31). A.D.H.D. seen in 11% of U.S. children as diagnoses rise. *New York Times.*

Schwarzwald, Heidi; Collins, Elizabeth Montgomery; Gillespie, Susan & Spinks-Franklin, Adiaha I. A. (2015). *International adoption and clinical practice.* New York, NY: Springer.

Schweinhart, Lawrence J.; Montie, Jeanne; Xiang, Zongping; Barnett, W. Steven; Belfield, Clive R. & Nores, Milagros. (2005). *Lifetime effects: The High/Scope Perry Preschool Study through age 40.* Ypsilanti, MI: High/Scope Press.

Schweinhart, Lawrence J. & Weikart, David P. (1997). *Lasting differences: The High/Scope Preschool curriculum comparison study through age 23.* Ypsilanti, MI: High/Scope Educational Research Foundation.

Scott, Diane L.; Lee, Chang-Bae; Harrell, Susan W. & Smith-West, Mary B. (2013). Permanency for children in foster care: Issues and barriers for adoption. *Child & Youth Services, 34*(3), 290–307.

Scullin, Michael K. (2017). Do older adults need sleep? A review of neuroimaging, sleep, and aging studies. *Current Sleep Medicine Reports, 3*(3), 204–214.

Sears, William & Sears, Martha. (2001). *The attachment parenting book: A commonsense guide to understanding and nurturing your baby.* Boston, MA: Little Brown.

Seaton, Eleanor K.; Quintana, Stephen; Verkuyten, Maykel & Gee, Gilbert C. (2017). Peers, policies, and place: The relation between context and ethnic/racial identity. *Child Development, 88*(3), 683–692.

Sedlak, Andrea J. & Ellis, Raquel T. (2014). Trends in child abuse reporting. In Jill E. Korbin & Richard D. Krugman (Eds.), *Handbook of child maltreatment* (pp. 3–26). New York, NY: Springer.

Seelaar, Harro; Rohrer, Jonathan D.; Pijnenburg, Yolande A. L.; Fox, Nick C. & van Swieten, John C. (2011). Clinical, genetic and pathological heterogeneity of frontotemporal dementia: A review. *Journal of Neurology, Neurosurgery, & Psychiatry, 82*(5), 476–486.

Şendil, Çağla Öneren & Erden, Feyza Tantekin. (2014). Peer preference: A way of evaluating social competence and behavioural well-being in early childhood. *Early Child Development and Care, 184*(2), 230–246.

Senior, Jennifer. (2014). *All joy and no fun: The paradox of modern parenthood.* New York, NY: Ecco.

Servick, Kelly. (2015). Mind the phone. *Science, 350*(6266), 1306–1309.

Seth, Puja; Scholl, Lawrence; Rudd, Rose A. & Bacon, Sarah. (2018). *Overdose deaths involving opioids, cocaine, and psychostimulants — United States, 2015–2016. Morbidity and Mortality Weekly Report, 67*(12), 349–358. Atlanta, GA: Centers for Disease Control and Prevention.

Seto, Elizabeth & Schlegel, Rebecca J. (2018). Becoming your true self: Perceptions of authenticity across the lifespan. *Self and Identity, 17*(3), 310–326.

Settersten, Richard A. (2015). Relationships in time and the life course: The significance of linked lives. *Research in Human Development, 12*(3/4), 217–223.

Sewell, Andrew. (2016). *English pronunciation models in a globalized world: Accent, acceptability and Hong Kong English.* New York, NY: Rutledge.

Shanahan, Timothy & Lonigan, Christopher J. (2010). The National Early Literacy Panel: A summary of the process and the report. *Educational Researcher, 39*(4), 279–285.

Shanks, Laurie. (2011). Child sexual abuse: How to move to a balanced and rational approach to the cases everyone abhors. *American Journal of Trial Advocacy, 34*(3), 517–564.

Sharkey, Shirlee & Lefebre, Nancy. (2017). Leadership perspective: Bringing nursing back to the future through people-powered care. *Nursing Leadership, 30*(1), 11–22.

Shaver, Phillip R.; Mikulincer, Mario & Cassidy, Jude. (2019). Attachment, caregiving in couple relationships, and prosocial behavior in the wider world. *Current Opinion in Psychology, 25*, 16–20.

Shawar, Yusra Ribhi & Shiffman, Jeremy. (2017). Generation of global political priority for early childhood development: The challenges of framing and governance. *The Lancet, 389*(10064), 119–124.

Shenaar-Golan, Vered. (2017). Hope and subjective well-being among parents of children with special needs. *Child and Family Social Work, 22*(1), 306–316.

Sherin, Jonathan E. & Bartzokis, George. (2011). Human brain myelination trajectories across the life span: Implications for CNS function and dysfunction. In Edward J. Masoro & Steven N. Austad (Eds.), *Handbook of the biology of aging* (7th ed., pp. 333–346). San Diego, CA: Academic Press.

Sherlock, James M. & Zietsch, Brendan P. (2018). Longitudinal relationships between parents' and children's behavior need not implicate the influence of parental behavior and may reflect genetics: Comment on Waldinger and Schulz (2016). *Psychological Science, 29*(1), 154–157.

Sherman, David K.; Hartson, Kimberly A.; Binning, Kevin R.; Purdie-Vaughns, Valerie; Garcia, Julio; Taborsky-Barba, Suzanne, . . . Cohen, Geoffrey L. (2013). Deflecting the trajectory and changing the narrative: How self-affirmation affects academic performance and motivation under identity threat. *Journal of Personality and Social Psychology, 104*(4), 591–618.

Sherman, Lauren E.; Greenfield, Patricia M.; Hernandez, Leanna M. & Dapretto, Mirella. (2018). Peer influence via Instagram: Effects on brain and behavior in adolescence and young adulthood. *Child Development, 89*(1), 37–47.

Shi, Bing & Xie, Hongling. (2012). Popular and nonpopular subtypes of physically aggressive preadolescents: Continuity of aggression and peer mechanisms during the transition to middle school. *Merrill-Palmer Quarterly, 58*(4), 530–553.

Shi, Rushen. (2014). Functional morphemes and early language acquisition. *Child Development Perspectives, 8*(1), 6–11.

Shimizu, Mina; Park, Heejung & Greenfield, Patricia M. (2014). Infant sleeping arrangements and cultural values among contemporary Japanese mothers. *Frontiers in Psychology, 5*, 718.

Shin, Huiyoung & Ryan, Allison M. (2017). Friend influence on early adolescent disruptive behavior in the classroom: Teacher emotional support matters. *Developmental Psychology, 53*(1), 114–125.

Shiovitz-Ezra, Sharon & Litwin, Howard. (2015). Social network type and health among older Americans. In Fredrica Nyqvist & Anna K. Forsman (Eds.), *Social capital as a health resource in later life: The relevance of context* (pp. 15–31). Dordrecht, the Netherlands: Springer.

Shneidman, Laura & Woodward, Amanda L. (2016). Are child-directed interactions the cradle of social learning? *Psychological Bulletin, 142*(1), 1–17.

Shpancer, Noam & Schweitzer, Stefanie N. (2016). A history of non-parental care in childhood predicts more positive adult attitudes towards non-parental care and maternal employment. *Early Child Development and Care*, (In Press).

Shulman, Elizabeth P. & Cauffman, Elizabeth. (2014). Deciding in the dark: Age differences in intuitive risk judgment. *Developmental Psychology, 50*(1), 167–177.

Shulman, Shmuel; Seiffge-Krenke, Inge; Scharf, Miri; Boiangiu, Shira Bezalel & Tregubenko, Valerya. (2018). The diversity of romantic pathways during emerging adulthood and their developmental antecedents. *International Journal of Behavioral Development, 42*(2), 167–174.

Shutts, Kristin; Kinzler, Katherine D. & DeJesus, Jasmine M. (2013). Understanding infants' and children's social learning about foods: Previous research and new prospects. *Developmental Psychology, 49*(3), 419–425.

Shwalb, David W.; Shwalb, Barbara J. & Lamb, Michael E. (Eds.). (2013). *Fathers in cultural context.* New York, NY: Psychology Press.

Siddiqui, Ayesha; Cuttini, Marina; Wood, Rachel; Velebil, Petr; Delnord, Marie; Zile, Irisa, . . . Macfarlane, Alison. (2017). Can the Apgar score be used for international comparisons of newborn health? *Paediatric and Perinatal Epidemiology, 31*(4), 338–345.

Siegal, Michael & Surian, Luca (Eds.). (2012). *Access to language and cognitive development.* New York, NY: Oxford University Press.

Siegler, Robert S. (2016). Continuity and change in the field of cognitive development and in the perspectives of one cognitive developmentalist. *Child Development Perspectives, 10*(2), 128–133.

Siegler, Robert S. & Braithwaite, David W. (2017). Numerical development. *Annual Review of Psychology, 68*, 187–213.

Silberman, Steve. (2015). *Neurotribes: The legacy of autism and the future of neurodiversity.* New York, NY: Avery.

Silk, Jessica & Romero, Diana. (2014). The role of parents and families in teen pregnancy prevention: An analysis of programs and policies. *Journal of Family Issues, 35*(10), 1339–1362.

Silventoinen, Karri; Hammar, Niklas; Hedlund, Ebba; Koskenvuo, Markku; Ronnemaa, Tapani & Kaprio, Jaakko. (2008). Selective international migration by social position, health behaviour and personality. *European Journal of Public Health, 18*(2), 150–155.

Silverman, Arielle M. & Cohen, Geoffrey L. (2014). Stereotypes as stumbling-blocks: How coping with stereotype threat affects life outcomes for people with physical disabilities. *Personality and Social Psychology Bulletin, 40*(10), 1330–1340.

Silverstein, Merril; Gans, Daphna; Lowenstein, Ariela; Giarrusso, Roseann & Bengtson, Vern L. (2010). Older parent–child relationships in six developed nations: Comparisons at the intersection of affection and conflict. *Journal of Marriage and Family, 72*(4), 1006–1021.

Silvia, Paul J. & Sanders, Camilla E. (2010). Why are smart people curious? Fluid intelligence, openness to experience, and interest. *Learning and Individual Differences, 20*(3), 242–245.

Sim, Zi L. & Xu, Fei. (2017). Learning higher-order generalizations through free play: Evidence from 2- and 3-year-old children. *Developmental Psychology, 53*(4), 642–651.

Simmons, Joseph P.; Nelson, Leif D. & Simonsohn, Uri. (2011). False-positive psychology: Undisclosed flexibility in data collection and analysis allows presenting anything as significant. *Psychological Science, 22*(11), 1359–1366.

Simmons, Sandra F. & Rahman, Anna N. (2014). Next steps for achieving person-centered care in nursing homes. *JAMDA, 15*(9), 615–619.

Simon, Laura & Daneback, Kristian. (2013). Adolescents' use of the Internet for sex education: A thematic and critical review of the literature. *International Journal of Sexual Health, 25*(4), 305–319.

Simpson, Jeffry A. & Rholes, W. Steven (Eds.). (2015). *Attachment theory and research: New directions and emerging themes.* New York, NY: Guilford.

Sims, Margaret & Rofail, Maged. (2014). Grandparents with little or no contact with grandchildren-impact on grandparents. *Journal of Aging Science, 2*(1), 117–124.

Sinclair, H. Colleen; Felmlee, Diane; Sprecher, Susan & Wright, Brittany L. (2015). Don't tell me who I can't love: A multimethod investigation of social network and reactance effects on romantic relationships. *Social Psychology Quarterly, 78*(1), 77–99.

Sinclair, Samantha & Carlsson, Rickard. (2013). What will I be when I grow up? The impact of gender identity threat on adolescents' occupational preferences. *Journal of Adolescence, 36*(3), 465–474.

Singanayagam, Aran; Ritchie, Andrew I. & Johnston, Sebastian L. (2017). Role of microbiome in the pathophysiology and disease course of asthma. *Current Opinion in Pulmonary Medicine, 23*(1), 41–47.

Singh, Amika; Uijtdewilligen, Léonie; Twisk, Jos W. R.; van Mechelen, Willem & Chinapaw, Mai J. M. (2012). Physical activity and performance at school: A systematic review of the literature including a methodological quality assessment. *Archives of Pediatrics & Adolescent Medicine, 166*(1), 49–55.

Singh, Leher. (2008). Influences of high and low variability on infant word recognition. *Cognition, 106*(2), 833–870.

Sinnott, Jan D. (2014). *Adult development: Cognitive aspects of thriving close relationships.* New York, NY: Oxford University Press.

Sisson, Susan B.; Krampe, Megan; Anundson, Katherine & Castle, Sherri. (2016). Obesity prevention and obesogenic behavior interventions in child care: A systematic review. *Preventive Medicine, 87*, 57–69.

Sjöström, Lars; Peltonen, Markku; Jacobson, Peter; Ahlin, Sofie; Andersson-Assarsson, Johanna; Anveden, Åsa, . . . Carlsson, Lena M. S. (2014). Association of bariatric surgery with long-term remission of type 2 diabetes and with microvascular and macrovascular complications. *JAMA, 311*(22), 2297–2304.

Skinner, B. F. (1953). *Science and human behavior.* New York, NY: Macmillan.

Skinner, B. F. (1957). *Verbal behavior.* New York, NY: Appleton-Century-Crofts.

Slaughter, Anne-Marie. (2012). Why women still can't have it all. *The Atlantic, 310*(1), 84–102.

Slining, Meghan; Adair, Linda S.; Goldman, Barbara D.; Borja, Judith B. & Bentley, Margaret. (2010). Infant overweight is associated with delayed motor development. *The Journal of Pediatrics, 157*(1), 20–25.e21.

Sloan, John. (2011–2012). Medicating elders in the evidence-free zone. *Generations, 35*(4), 56–61.

Sloan, Mark. (2009). *Birth day: A pediatrician explores the science, the history, and the wonder of childbirth.* New York, NY: Ballantine Books.

Slot, Pauline Louise; Mulder, Hanna; Verhagen, Josje & Leseman, Paul. (2017). Preschoolers' cognitive and emotional self-regulation in pretend play: Relations with executive functions and quality of play. *Infant and Child Development, 26*(6), e2038.

Small, Meredith F. (1998). *Our babies, ourselves: How biology and culture shape the way we parent.* New York, NY: Anchor Books.

Smarr, Cory-Ann; Long, Shelby K.; Prakash, Akanksha; Mitzner, Tracy L. & Rogers, Wendy A. (2014). Understanding younger and older adults' needs for home organization support. *Proceedings of the Human Factors and Ergonomics Society Annual Meeting, 58*(1), 150–154.

Smetana, Judith G. (2013). Moral development: The Social Domain Theory view. In Philip D. Zelazo (Ed.), *The Oxford handbook of developmental psychology* (Vol. 1, pp. 832–866). New York, NY: Oxford University Press.

Smetana, Judith G.; Ahmad, Ikhlas & Wray-Lake, Laura. (2016). Beliefs about parental authority legitimacy among refugee youth in Jordan: Between- and within-person variations. *Developmental Psychology, 52*(3), 484–495.

Smith, G. Rush; Williamson, Gail M.; Miller, L. Stephen & Schulz, Richard. (2011). Depression and quality of informal care: A longitudinal investigation of caregiving stressors. *Psychology and Aging, 26*(3), 584–591.

Smith, Hannah E.; Ryan, Kelsey N.; Stephenson, Kevin B.; Westcott, Claire; Thakwalakwa, Chrissie; Maleta, Ken, . . . Manary, Mark J. (2014). Multiple micronutrient supplementation transiently ameliorates environmental enteropathy in Malawian children aged 12–35 months in a randomized controlled clinical trial. *Journal of Nutrition, 144*(12), 2059–2065.

Smith, Jacqueline; Boone, Anniglo; Gourdine, Ruby & Brown, Annie W. (2013). Fictions and facts about parents and parenting older first-time entrants to foster care. *Journal of Human Behavior in the Social Environment, 23*(2), 211–219.

Smith, Michelle I.; Yatsunenko, Tanya; Manary, Mark J.; Trehan, Indi; Mkakosya, Rajhab; Cheng, Jiye, . . . Gordon, Jeffrey I. (2013). Gut microbiomes of Malawian twin pairs discordant for kwashiorkor. *Science, 339*(6119), 548–554.

Smith, Peter K. (2010). *Children and play: Understanding children's worlds.* Malden, MA: Wiley-Blackwell.

Sneyers, Eline & De Witte, Kristof. (2017). The interaction between dropout, graduation rates and quality ratings in universities. *Journal of the Operational Research Society, 68*(4), 416–430.

Snyder, Thomas D.; Brey, Cristobal de & Dillow, Sally A. (2016). *Digest of education statistics, 2015.* Washington, DC: National Center for Education Statistics, Institute of Education Sciences, U.S. Department of Education.

Snyder, Thomas D. & Dillow, Sally A. (2013). *Digest of education statistics, 2012.* Washington, DC: National Center for Education Statistics, Institute of Education Sciences, U.S. Department of Education.

Snyder, Thomas D. & Dillow, Sally A. (2015, May). *Digest of education statistics, 2013.* Washington, DC: National Center for Education Statistics, Institute of Education Sciences, U.S. Department of Education.

Soderstrom, Melanie; Ko, Eon-Suk & Nevzorova, Uliana. (2011). It's a question? Infants attend differently to yes/no questions and declaratives. *Infant Behavior and Development, 34*(1), 107–110.

Solheim, Elisabet; Wichstrøm, Lars; Belsky, Jay & Berg-Nielsen, Turid Suzanne. (2013). Do time in child care and peer group exposure predict poor socioemotional adjustment in Norway? *Child Development, 84*(5), 1701–1715.

Solomon, Alina; Sippola, Risto; Soininen, Hilkka; Wolozin, Benjamin; Tuomilehto, Jaakko; Laatikainen, Tiina & Kivipelto, Miia. (2010). Lipid-lowering treatment is related to decreased risk of dementia: A population-based study (FINRISK). *Neuro-Degenerative Diseases, 7*(1/3), 180–182.

Solomon, Andrew. (2012). *Far from the tree: Parents, children and the search for identity.* New York, NY: Scribner.

Somerville, Leah H. (2013). The teenage brain: Sensitivity to social evaluation. *Current Directions in Psychological Science, 22*(2), 121–127.

Sonesh, Shirley C.; Lacerenza, Christina; Marlow, Shannon & Salas, Eduardo. (2018). What makes an expert team? A decade of research. In K. Anders Ericsson et al. (Eds.), *The Cambridge handbook of expertise and expert performance* (2nd ed., pp. 506–532). New York, NY: Cambridge University Press.

Sonuga-Barke, Edmund J. S.; Kennedy, Mark; Kumsta, Robert; Knights, Nicky; Golm, Dennis; Rutter, Michael, . . .

Kreppner, Jana. (2017). Child-to-adult neurodevelopmental and mental health trajectories after early life deprivation: The young adult follow-up of the longitudinal English and Romanian Adoptees study. *The Lancet, 389*(10078), 1539–1548.

Sophian, Catherine. (2013). Vicissitudes of children's mathematical knowledge: Implications of developmental research for early childhood mathematics education. *Early Education and Development, 24*(4), 436–442.

Sorrells, Shawn F.; Paredes, Mercedes F.; Cebrian-Silla, Arantxa; Sandoval, Kadellyn; Qi, Dashi; Kelley, Kevin W., . . . Alvarez-Buylla, Arturo. (2018). Human hippocampal neurogenesis drops sharply in children to undetectable levels in adults. *Nature, 555*, 377–381.

Sotomayor, Sonia. (2014). *My beloved world.* New York, NY: Vintage Books.

Soto-Rubio, Ana; Pérez-Marín, Marián & Barreto, Pilar. (2017). Frail elderly with and without cognitive impairment at the end of life: Their emotional state and the wellbeing of their family caregivers. *Archives of Gerontology and Geriatrics, 73*, 113–119.

Soulsby, Laura K. & Bennett, Kate M. (2017). When two become one: Exploring identity in marriage and cohabitation. *Journal of Family Issues, 38*(3), 358–380.

Sousa, David A. (2014). *How the brain learns to read* (2nd ed.). Thousand Oaks, CA: Sage.

Sowell, Elizabeth R.; Thompson, Paul M. & Toga, Arthur W. (2007). Mapping adolescent brain maturation using structural magnetic resonance imaging. In Daniel Romer & Elaine F. Walker (Eds.), *Adolescent psychopathology and the developing brain: Integrating brain and prevention science* (pp. 55–84). New York, NY: Oxford University Press.

Sparks, Sarah D. (2016, July 20). Dose of empathy found to cut suspension rates. *Education Week, 35*(36), 1, 20.

Spear, Linda. (2013). The teenage brain: Adolescents and alcohol. *Current Directions in Psychological Science, 22*(2), 152–157.

Spearman, Charles E. (1927). *The abilities of man, their nature and measurement.* New York, NY: Macmillan.

Specht, Jule; Egloff, Boris & Schmukle, Stefan C. (2011). Stability and change of personality across the life course: The impact of age and major life events on mean-level and rank-order stability of the Big Five. *Journal of Personality and Social Psychology, 101*(4), 862–882.

Spelke, Elizabeth S. (1993). Object perception. In Alvin I. Goldman (Ed.), *Readings in philosophy and cognitive science* (pp. 447–460). Cambridge, MA: MIT Press.

Spencer, Justine M. Y.; Sekuler, Allison B.; Bennett, Patrick J.; Giese, Martin A. & Pilz, Karin S. (2016). Effects of aging on identifying emotions conveyed by point-light walkers. *Psychology and Aging, 31*(1), 126–138.

Sperry, Debbie M. & Widom, Cathy S. (2013). Child abuse and neglect, social support, and psychopathology in adulthood: A prospective investigation. *Child Abuse & Neglect, 37*(6), 415–425.

Spijker, Jeroen & MacInnes, John. (2013). Population ageing: The timebomb that isn't? *BMJ, 347*, f6598.

Spira, Adam P. (2018). Sleep and health in older adulthood: Recent advances and the path forward. *Journal of Gerontology Series A, 73*(3), 357–359.

Sprecher, Susan & Metts, Sandra. (2013). Logging on, hooking up: The changing nature of romantic relationship initiation and romantic relating. In Cindy Hazan & Mary I. Campa (Eds.), *Human bonding: The science of affectional ties* (pp. 197–225). New York, NY: Guilford Press.

Sprietsma, Maresa. (2010). Effect of relative age in the first grade of primary school on long-term scholastic results: International comparative evidence using PISA 2003. *Education Economics, 18*(1), 1–32.

Staddon, John. (2014). *The new behaviorism* (2nd ed.). New York, NY: Psychology Press.

Staff, Jeremy & Schulenberg, John. (2010). Millennials and the world of work: Experiences in paid work during adolescence. *Journal of Business and Psychology, 25*(2), 247–255.

Standing, E. M. (1998). *Maria Montessori: Her life and work.* New York, NY: Plume.

Staplin, Loren; Lococo, Kathy H.; Martell, Carol & Stutts, Jane. (2012). *Taxonomy of older driver behaviors and crash risk.* Washington, DC: Office of Behavioral Safety Research, National Highway Traffic Safety Administration, U.S. Department of Transportation.

Starr, Christine R. & Zurbriggen, Eileen L. (2016). Sandra Bem's gender schema theory after 34 years: A review of its reach and impact. *Sex Roles,* (In Press).

Stattin, Håkan; Hussein, Oula; Özdemir, Metin & Russo, Silvia. (2017). Why do some adolescents encounter everyday events that increase their civic interest whereas others do not? *Developmental Psychology, 53*(2), 306–318.

Staudinger, Ursula M. & Glück, Judith. (2011). Psychological wisdom research: Commonalities and differences in a growing field. *Annual Review of Psychology, 62,* 215–241.

Stavrova, Olga; Fetchenhauer, Detlef & Schlösser, Thomas. (2012). Cohabitation, gender, and happiness: A cross-cultural study in thirty countries. *Journal of Cross-Cultural Psychology, 43*(7), 1063–1081.

Stawski, Robert S.; Almeida, David M.; Lachman, Margie E.; Tun, Patricia A. & Rosnick, Christopher B. (2010). Fluid cognitive ability is associated with greater exposure and smaller reactions to daily stressors. *Psychology and Aging, 25*(2), 330–342.

Steele, Claude M. (1997). A threat in the air: How stereotypes shape intellectual identity and performance. *American Psychologist, 52*(6), 613–629.

Steinberg, Laurence. (2009). Should the science of adolescent brain development inform public policy? *American Psychologist, 64*(8), 739–750.

Steinberg, Laurence & Monahan, Kathryn C. (2011). Adolescents' exposure to sexy media does not hasten the initiation of sexual intercourse. *Developmental Psychology, 47*(2), 562–576.

Stenseng, Frode; Belsky, Jay; Skalicka, Vera & Wichstrøm, Lars. (2015). Social exclusion predicts impaired self-regulation: 2-year longitudinal panel study including the transition from school to school. *Journal of Personality, 83*(2), 212–220.

Stephens, Rick & Richey, Mike. (2013). A business view on education. *Science, 340*(6130), 313–314.

Sterling, Peter. (2012). Allostasis: A model of predictive regulation. *Physiology & Behavior, 106*(1), 5–15.

Stern, Gavin. (2015). For kids with special learning needs, roadblocks remain. *Science, 349*(6255), 1465–1466.

Stern, Mark; Clonan, Sheila; Jaffee, Laura & Lee, Anna. (2015). The normative limits of choice: Charter schools, disability studies, and questions of inclusion. *Educational Policy, 29*(3), 448–477.

Stern, Peter. (2013). Connection, connection, connection . . . *Science, 342*(6158), 577.

Stern, Yaakov (Ed.). (2013). *Cognitive reserve: Theory and applications.* New York, NY: Psychology Press.

Sternberg, Robert J. (1988). Triangulating love. In Robert J. Sternberg & Michael L. Barnes (Eds.), *The psychology of love* (pp. 119–138). New Haven, CT: Yale University Press.

Sternberg, Robert J. (2003). *Wisdom, intelligence, and creativity synthesized.* New York, NY: Cambridge University Press.

Sternberg, Robert J. (2008). Schools should nurture wisdom. In Barbara Z. Presseisen (Ed.), *Teaching for intelligence* (2nd ed., pp. 61–88). Thousand Oaks, CA: Corwin Press.

Sternberg, Robert J. (2011). The theory of successful intelligence. In Robert J. Sternberg & Scott Barry Kaufman (Eds.), *The Cambridge handbook of intelligence* (pp. 504–526). New York, NY: Cambridge University Press.

Sternberg, Robert J. (2015). Multiple intelligences in the new age of thinking. In Sam Goldstein et al. (Eds.), *Handbook of intelligence* (pp. 229–241). New York, NY: Springer.

Stevenson, Betsey & Wolfers, Justin. (2007). Marriage and divorce: Changes and their driving forces. *Journal of Economic Perspectives, 21*(2), 27–52.

Stevenson, Richard J.; Oaten, Megan J.; Case, Trevor I.; Repacholi, Betty M. & Wagland, Paul. (2010). Children's response to adult disgust elicitors: Development and acquisition. *Developmental Psychology, 46*(1), 165–177.

Stevenson, Robert G. (2017). Children and death: What do they know and when do they learn it? In Robert G. Stevenson & Gerry R. Cox (Eds.), *Children, adolescents, and death: Questions and answers.* New York, NY: Routledge.

Stierand, Marc & Dörfler, Viktor. (2016). The role of intuition in the creative process of expert chefs. *Journal of Creative Behavior, 50*(3), 178–185.

Stiles, Joan & Jernigan, Terry. (2010). The basics of brain development. *Neuropsychology Review, 20*(4), 327–348.

Stine-Morrow, Elizabeth A. L. & Basak, Chandramallika. (2011). Cognitive interventions. In K. Warner Schaie & Sherry L. Willis (Eds.), *Handbook of the psychology of aging* (7th ed., pp. 153–171). San Diego, CA: Academic Press.

Stiner, Mary C. (2017). Love and death in the stone age: What constitutes first evidence of mortuary treatment of the human body? *Biological Theory, 12*(4), 248–261.

Stolt, Suvi; Matomäki, Jaakko; Lind, Annika; Lapinleimu, Helena; Haataja, Leena & Lehtonen, Liisa. (2014). The prevalence and predictive value of weak language skills in children with very low birth weight – A longitudinal study. *Acta Paediatrica, 103*(6), 651–658.

Storlie, Timothy A. (2015). *Person-centered communication with older adults: The professional provider's guide.* London, UK: Academic Press.

Strasburger, Victor C.; Wilson, Barbara J. & Jordan, Amy B. (2009). *Children, adolescents, and the media* (2nd ed.). Los Angeles, CA: Sage.

Stroebe, Margaret S.; Abakoumkin, Georgios; Stroebe, Wolfgang & Schut, Henk. (2012). Continuing bonds in adjustment to bereavement: Impact of abrupt versus gradual separation. *Personal Relationships, 19*(2), 255–266.

Stroebe, Wolfgang & Strack, Fritz. (2014). The alleged crisis and the illusion of exact replication. *Perspectives on Psychological Science, 9*(1), 59–71.

Stronegger, Willibald J.; Burkert, Nathalie T.; Grossschädl, Franziska & Freidl, Wolfgang. (2013). Factors associated with the rejection of active euthanasia: A survey among the general public in Austria. *BMC Medical Ethics, 14,* 26.

Strouse, Gabrielle A. & Ganea, Patricia A. (2017). Toddlers' word learning and transfer from electronic and print books. *Journal of Experimental Child Psychology, 156,* 129–142.

Suárez-Orozco, Carola. (2017). Conferring disadvantage: Behavioral and developmental implications for children growing up in the shadow of undocumented immigration status. *Journal of Developmental & Behavioral Pediatrics, 38*(6), 424–428.

Sue, Derald Wing (Ed.). (2010). *Microaggressions and marginality: Manifestation, dynamics, and impact.* Hoboken, NJ: Wiley.

Suleiman, Ahna B. & Brindis, Claire D. (2014). Adolescent school-based sex education: Using developmental neuroscience to guide new directions for policy and practice. *Sexuality Research and Social Policy, 11*(2), 137–152.

Sullivan, Shannon. (2014). *Good White people: The problem with middle-class White anti-racism.* Albany, NY: State University of New York Press.

Sunstein, Cass R. (2014). *Why nudge?: The politics of libertarian paternalism.* New Haven, CT: Yale University Press.

Susman, Elizabeth J.; Houts, Renate M.; Steinberg, Laurence; Belsky, Jay; Cauffman, Elizabeth; DeHart, Ganie, . . . Halpern-Felsher, Bonnie L. (2010). Longitudinal development of secondary sexual characteristics in girls and boys between ages 9-1/2 and 15-1/2 years. *Archives of Pediatrics & Adolescent Medicine, 164*(2), 166–173.

Sutphin, George L. & Kaeberlein, Matt. (2011). Comparative genetics of aging. In Edward J. Masoro & Steven N. Austad (Eds.), *Handbook of the biology of aging* (7th ed., pp. 215–242). San Diego, CA: Academic Press.

Sutton-Smith, Brian. (2011). The antipathies of play. In Anthony D. Pellegrini (Ed.), *The Oxford handbook of the development of play* (pp. 110–115). New York, NY: Oxford University Press.

Suurland, Jill; van der Heijden, Kristiaan B.; Huijbregts, Stephan C. J.; Smaling, Hanneke J. A.; de Sonneville, Leo M. J.; Van Goozen, Stephanie H. M. & Swaab, Hanna. (2016). Parental perceptions of aggressive behavior in preschoolers: Inhibitory control moderates the association with negative emotionality. *Child Development, 87*(1), 256–269.

Swanson, H. Lee. (2013). Meta-analysis of research on children with learning disabilities. In H. Lee Swanson et al. (Eds.), *Handbook of learning disabilities* (2nd ed., pp. 627–642). New York, NY: Guilford Press.

Sweeney, Kathryn A. (2013). Race-conscious adoption choices, multiraciality and color-blind racial ideology. *Family Relations, 62*(1), 42–57.

Synovitz, Linda & Chopak-Foss, Joanne. (2013). Precocious puberty: Pathology, related risks, and support strategies. *Open Journal of Preventive Medicine, 3*(9), 504–509.

Szanton, Sarah L.; Wolff, Jennifer L.; Leff, Bruce; Roberts, Laken; Thorpe, Roland J.; Tanner, Elizabeth K., . . . Gitlin, Laura N. (2015). Preliminary data from Community Aging in Place, advancing better living for elders, a patient-directed, team-based intervention to improve physical function and decrease nursing home utilization: The first 100 individuals to complete a Centers for Medicare and Medicaid Services innovation project. *Journal of the American Geriatrics Society, 63*(2), 371–374.

Tabassum, Faiza; Mohan, John & Smith, Peter. (2016). Association of volunteering with mental well-being: A life-course analysis of a national population-based longitudinal study in the UK. *BMJ Open, 6*(8), 6:e011327.

Tackett, Jennifer L.; Herzhoff, Kathrin; Harden, K. Paige; Page-Gould, Elizabeth & Josephs, Robert A. (2014). Personality × hormone interactions in adolescent externalizing psychopathology. *Personality Disorders: Theory, Research, and Treatment, 5*(3), 235–246.

Tagar, Michal Reifen; Hetherington, Chelsea; Shulman, Deborah & Koenig, Melissa. (2017). On the path to social dominance? Individual differences in sensitivity to intergroup fairness violations in early childhood. *Personality and Individual Differences, 113,* 246–250.

Taillieu, Tamara L.; Afifi, Tracie O.; Mota, Natalie; Keyes, Katherine M. & Sareen, Jitender. (2014). Age, sex, and racial differences in harsh physical punishment: Results from a nationally representative United States sample. *Child Abuse & Neglect, 38*(12), 1885–1894.

Tailor, Vijay K.; Schwarzkopf, D. Samuel & Dahlmann-Noor, Annegret H. (2017). Neuroplasticity and amblyopia: Vision at the balance point. *Current Opinion in Neurology, 30*(1), 74–83.

Talley, Ronda C. & Montgomery, Rhonda J. V. (2013). Caregiving: A developmental lifelong perspective. In Ronda C. Talley & Rhonda J. V. Montgomery (Eds.), *Caregiving across the lifespan: Research, practice, policy* (pp. 3–10). New York, NY: Springer.

Talwar, Victoria; Harris, Paul L. & Schleifer, Michael (Eds.). (2011). *Children's understanding of death: From biological to religious conceptions.* New York, NY: Cambridge University Press.

Tamis-LeMonda, Catherine S.; Bornstein, Marc H. & Baumwell, Lisa. (2001). Maternal responsiveness and children's achievement of language milestones. *Child Development, 72*(3), 748–767.

Tan, Cheryl H.; Denny, Clark H.; Cheal, Nancy E.; Sniezek, Joseph E. & Kanny, Dafna. (2015, September 25). *Alcohol use and binge drinking among women of childbearing age—United States, 2011–2013. Morbidity and Mortality Weekly Report, 64*(37), 1042–1046. Atlanta, GA: Centers for Disease Control and Prevention.

Tan, Joseph S.; Hessel, Elenda T.; Loeb, Emily L.; Schad, Megan M.; Allen, Joseph P. & Chango, Joanna M. (2016). Long-term predictions from early adolescent attachment state of mind to romantic relationship behaviors. *Journal of Research on Adolescence, 26*(4), 1022–1035.

Tan, Patricia Z.; Armstrong, Laura M. & Cole, Pamela M. (2013). Relations between temperament and anger regulation over early childhood. *Social Development, 22*(4), 755–772.

Tang, Jie; Yu, Yizhen; Du, Yukai; Ma, Ying; Zhang, Dongying & Wang, Jiaji. (2014). Prevalence of Internet addiction and its association with stressful life events and psychological symptoms among adolescent Internet users. *Addictive Behaviors, 39*(3), 744–747.

Tanner, Jennifer L. & Arnett, Jeffrey Jensen. (2011). Presenting emerging adulthood: What makes emerging adulthood developmentally distinctive. In Jeffrey Jensen Arnett et al. (Eds.), *Debating emerging adulthood: Stage or process?* (pp. 13–30). New York, NY: Oxford University Press.

Tarullo, Amanda R.; Garvin, Melissa C. & Gunnar, Megan R. (2011). Atypical EEG power correlates with indiscriminately friendly behavior in internationally adopted children. *Developmental Psychology, 47*(2), 417–431.

Tassell-Matamua, Natasha; Lindsay, Nicole; Bennett, Simon; Valentine, Hukarere & Pahina, John. (2017). Does learning about near-death experiences promote psycho-spiritual benefits in those who have not had a near-death experience? *Journal of Spirituality in Mental Health, 19*(2), 95–115.

Taveras, Elsie M.; Gillman, Matthew W.; Kleinman, Ken P.; Rich-Edwards, Janet W. & Rifas-Shiman, Sheryl L. (2013). Reducing racial/ethnic disparities in childhood obesity: The role of early life risk factors. *JAMA Pediatrics, 167*(8), 731–738.

Taylor, John H. (Ed.). (2010). *Journey through the afterlife: Ancient Egyptian Book of the Dead.* Cambridge, MA: Harvard University Press.

Taylor, Paul. (2014). *The next America: Boomers, millennials, and the looming generational showdown.* New York, NY: PublicAffairs.

Taylor, Valerie J. & Walton, Gregory M. (2011). Stereotype threat undermines academic learning. *Personality and Social Psychology Bulletin, 37*(8), 1055–1067.

Taylor, Zoe E.; Eisenberg, Nancy; Spinrad, Tracy L.; Eggum, Natalie D. & Sulik, Michael J. (2013). The relations of ego-resiliency and emotion socialization to the development of empathy and prosocial behavior across early childhood. *Emotion, 13*(5), 822–831.

Tedeschi, Richard; Orejuela-Davila, Ana & Lewis, Paisley. (2017). Posttraumatic growth and continuing bonds. In Dennis Klass & Edith Maria Steffen (Eds.), *Continuing bonds in bereavement: New directions for research and practice.* New York, NY: Routledge.

Telzer, Eva H.; Ichien, Nicholas T. & Qu, Yang. (2015). Mothers know best: Redirecting adolescent reward sensitivity toward safe behavior during risk taking. *Social Cognitive and Affective Neuroscience, 10*(10), 1383–1391.

Teoh, Yee San & Lamb, Michael E. (2013). Interviewer demeanor in forensic interviews of children. *Psychology, Crime & Law, 19*(2), 145–159.

Terry, Nicole Patton; Connor, Carol McDonald; Johnson, Lakeisha; Stuckey, Adrienne & Tani, Novell. (2016). Dialect variation, dialect-shifting, and reading comprehension in second grade. *Reading and Writing, 29*(2), 267–295.

Teti, Douglas M.; Crosby, Brian; McDaniel, Brandon T.; Shimizu, Mina & Whitesell, Corey J. (2015). Marital and emotional adjustment in mothers and infant sleep arrangements during the first six months. *Monographs of the Society for Research in Child Development, 80*(1), 160–176.

Tetzlaff, Anne & Hilbert, Anja. (2014). The role of the family in childhood and adolescent binge eating. A systematic review. *Appetite, 76*(1), 208.

Thaler, Richard H. & Sunstein, Cass R. (2008). *Nudge: Improving decisions about health, wealth, and happiness.* New Haven, CT: Yale University Press.

Theou, Olga; Rockwood, Michael R. H.; Mitnitski, Arnold & Rockwood, Kenneth. (2012). Disability and co-morbidity in relation to frailty: How much do they overlap? *Archives of Gerontology and Geriatrics, 55*(2), e1–e8.

Thiam, Melinda A.; Flake, Eric M. & Dickman, Michael M. (2017). Infant and child mental health and perinatal illness. In Melinda A. Thiam (Ed.), *Perinatal mental health and the military family: Identifying and treating mood and anxiety disorders.* New York, NY: Routledge.

Thomaes, Sander; Brummelman, Eddie & Sedikides, Constantine. (2017). Why most children think well of themselves. *Child Development, 88*(6), 1873–1884.

Thomaes, Sander; Reijntjes, Albert; Orobio de Castro, Bram; Bushman, Brad J.; Poorthuis, Astrid & Telch, Michael J. (2010). I like me if you like me: On the interpersonal modulation and regulation of preadolescents' state self-esteem. *Child Development, 81*(3), 811–825.

Thomas, Alexander & Chess, Stella. (1977). *Temperament and development.* New York, NY: Brunner/Mazel.

Thomas, Dylan. (2003). *The poems of Dylan Thomas* (Rev. ed.). New York, NY: New Directions.

Thompson, Richard; Kaczor, Kim; Lorenz, Douglas J.; Bennett, Berkeley L.; Meyers, Gabriel & Pierce, Mary Clyde. (2017). Is the use of physical discipline associated with aggressive behaviors in young children? *Academic Pediatrics, 17*(1), 34–44.

Thomson, Samuel; Marriott, Michael; Telford, Katherine; Law, Hou; McLaughlin, Jo & Sayal, Kapil. (2014). Adolescents with a diagnosis of anorexia nervosa: Parents' experience of recognition and deciding to seek help. *Clinical Child Psychology Psychiatry, 19*(1), 43–57.

Thornberg, Robert & Jungert, Tomas. (2013). Bystander behavior in bullying situations: Basic moral sensitivity, moral disengagement and defender self-efficacy. *Journal of Adolescence, 36*(3), 475–483.

Thorson, James A. (1995). *Aging in a changing society.* Belmont, CA: Wadsworth.

Tiggemann, Marika & Slater, Amy. (2014). NetTweens: The Internet and body image concerns in preteenage girls. *The Journal of Early Adolescence, 34*(5), 606–620.

Tighe, Lauren A.; Birditt, Kira S. & Antonucci, Toni C. (2016). Intergenerational ambivalence in adolescence and early adulthood: Implications for depressive symptoms over time. *Developmental Psychology, 52*(5), 824–834.

Tinsley, Grant M. & Horne, Benjamin D. (2018). Intermittent fasting and cardiovascular disease: Current evidence and unresolved questions. *Future Cardiology, 14*(1), 47–54.

Tishkoff, Sarah A.; Reed, Floyd A.; Friedlaender, Françoise R.; Ehret, Christopher; Ranciaro, Alessia; Froment, Alain, . . . Williams, Scott M. (2009). The genetic structure and history of Africans and African Americans. *Science, 324*(5930), 1035–1044.

Tobey, Emily A.; Thal, Donna; Niparko, John K.; Eisenberg, Laurie S.; Quittner, Alexandra L. & Wang, Nae-Yuh. (2013). Influence of implantation age on school-age language performance in pediatric cochlear implant users. *International Journal of Audiology, 52*(4), 219–229.

Todes, Daniel P. (2014). *Ivan Pavlov: A Russian life in science.* New York, NY: Oxford University Press.

Tolman, Deborah L. & McClelland, Sara I. (2011). Normative sexuality development in adolescence: A decade in review, 2000–2009. *Journal of Research on Adolescence, 21*(1), 242–255.

Tomasello, Michael. (2006). Acquiring linguistic constructions. In William Damon & Richard M. Lerner (Eds.), *Handbook of child psychology* (6th ed., Vol. 2, pp. 255–298). Hoboken, NJ: Wiley.

Tomasello, Michael & Herrmann, Esther. (2010). Ape and human cognition. *Current Directions in Psychological Science, 19*(1), 3–8.

Toossi, Mitra. (2002). *A century of change: The U.S. labor force, 1950–2050. Monthly Labor Review,* 15–28. Washington, DC: U.S. Bureau of Labor Statistics, United States Department of Labor.

Toporek, Bryan. (2012). Sports rules revised as research mounts on head injuries. *Education Week, 31*(22), 8.

Topper, Maurice; Emmelkamp, Paul M. G.; Watkins, Ed & Ehring, Thomas. (2017). Prevention of anxiety disorders and depression by targeting excessive worry and rumination in adolescents and young adults: A randomized controlled trial. *Behaviour Research and Therapy, 90,* 123–136.

Toril, Pilar; Reales, José M. & Ballesteros, Soledad. (2014). Video game training enhances cognition of older adults: A meta-analytic study. *Psychology and Aging, 29*(3), 706–716.

Tough, Paul. (2012). *How children succeed: Grit, curiosity, and the hidden power of character.* Boston, MA: Houghton Mifflin Harcourt.

Townsend, Apollo; March, Alice L. & Kimball, Jan. (2017). Can faith and hospice coexist: Is the African American church the key to increased hospice utilization for African Americans? *Journal of Transcultural Nursing, 28*(1), 32–39.

Travers, Brittany G.; Tromp, Do P. M.; Adluru, Nagesh; Lange, Nicholas; Destiche, Dan; Ennis, Chad, . . . Alexander, Andrew L. (2015). Atypical development of white matter microstructure of the corpus callosum in males with autism: A longitudinal investigation. *Molecular Autism, 6.*

Trawick-Smith, Jeffrey. (2012). Teacher–child play interactions to achieve learning outcomes: Risks and opportunities. In Robert C. Pianta (Ed.), *Handbook of early childhood education* (pp. 259–277). New York, NY: Guilford Press.

Traynor, Victoria; Veerhui, Nadine & Gopalan, Shiva. (2018). Evaluating the effects of a physical activity program on agitation and wandering experienced by individuals living with a dementia in care homes. *Australian Nursing & Midwifery Journal, 25*(7), 44.

Treas, Judith & Gubernskaya, Zoya. (2012). Farewell to moms? Maternal contact for seven countries in 1986 and 2001. *Journal of Marriage and Family, 74*(2), 297–311.

Trenholm, Christopher; Devaney, Barbara; Fortson, Ken; Quay, Lisa; Wheeler, Justin & Clark, Melissa. (2007). *Impacts of four Title V, Section 510 abstinence education programs final report.* Washington, DC: U.S. Department of Health and Human Services, Mathematica Policy Research, Inc.

Trivedi, Daksha. (2015). Cochrane Review Summary: Massage for promoting mental and physical health in typically developing infants under the age of six months. *Primary Health Care Research & Development, 16*(1), 3–4.

Troll, Lillian E. & Skaff, Marilyn McKean. (1997). Perceived continuity of self in very old age. *Psychology and Aging, 12*(1), 162–169.

Trommsdorff, Gisela & Cole, Pamela M. (2011). Emotion, self-regulation, and social behavior in cultural contexts. In Xinyin Chen & Kenneth H. Rubin (Eds.), *Socioemotional development in cultural context* (pp. 131–163). New York, NY: Guilford Press.

Trompeter, Susan E.; Bettencourt, Ricki & Barrett-Connor, Elizabeth. (2012). Sexual activity and satisfaction in healthy community-dwelling older women. *The American Journal of Medicine, 125*(1), 37–43.e31.

Tronick, Edward. (1989). Emotions and emotional communication in infants. *American Psychologist, 44*(2), 112–119.

Tronick, Edward & Weinberg, M. Katherine. (1997). Depressed mothers and infants: Failure to form dyadic states of consciousness. In Lynne Murray & Peter J. Cooper (Eds.), *Postpartum depression and child development* (pp. 54–81). New York, NY: Guilford Press.

Truman, Jennifer L. & Langton, Lynn. (2015). *Criminal victimization, 2014.* Washington, DC: U.S. Department of Justice, Office of Justice Programs, Bureau of Justice Statistics.

Tsai, Feng-Jen; Motamed, Sandrine & Rougemont, André. (2013). The protective effect of taking care of grandchildren on elders' mental health? Associations between changing patterns of intergenerational exchanges and the reduction of elders' loneliness and depression between 1993 and 2007 in Taiwan. *BMC Public Health, 13*(567).

Tsai, Kim M.; Telzer, Eva H. & Fuligni, Andrew J. (2013). Continuity and discontinuity in perceptions of family relationships from adolescence to young adulthood. *Child Development, 84*(2), 471–484.

Tsang, Christine; Falk, Simone & Hessel, Alexandria. (2017). Infants prefer infant-directed song over speech. *Child Development, 88*(4), 1207–1215.

Tsomo, Karma Lekshe. (2006). *Into the jaws of Yama, lord of death: Buddhism, bioethics, and death.* Albany, NY: State University of New York Press.

Ttofi, Maria M.; Bowes, Lucy; Farrington, David P. & Lösel, Friedrich. (2014). Protective factors interrupting the continuity from school bullying to later internalizing and externalizing problems: A systematic review of prospective longitudinal studies. *Journal of School Violence, 13*(1), 5–38.

Tudge, Jonathan R. H.; Doucet, Fabienne; Odero, Dolphine; Sperb, Tania M.; Piccinini, Cesar A. & Lopes, Rita S. (2006). A window into different cultural worlds: Young children's everyday activities in the United States, Brazil, and Kenya. *Child Development, 77*(5), 1446–1469.

Tummeltshammer, Kristen S.; Wu, Rachel; Sobel, David M. & Kirkham, Natasha Z. (2014). Infants track the reliability of potential informants. *Psychological Science, 25*(9), 1730–1738.

Turley, Ruth N. López & Desmond, Matthew. (2011). Contributions to college costs by married, divorced, and remarried parents. *Journal of Family Issues, 32*(6), 767–790.

Turner, Heather A.; Finkelhor, David; Ormrod, Richard; Hamby, Sherry; Leeb, Rebecca T.; Mercy, James A. & Holt, Melissa. (2012). Family context, victimization, and child trauma symptoms: Variations in safe, stable, and nurturing relationships during early and middle childhood. *American Journal of Orthopsychiatry, 82*(2), 209–219.

Turner, Heather A.; Shattuck, Anne; Finkelhor, David & Hamby, Sherry. (2016). Polyvictimization and youth violence exposure across contexts. *Journal of Adolescent Health, 58*(2), 208–214.

Tuttle, Robert & Garr, Michael. (2012). Shift work and work to family fit: Does schedule control matter? *Journal of Family and Economic Issues, 33*(3), 261–271.

U.S. Bureau of Labor Statistics. (2012, June 22). *American time use survey — 2011 results.* Washington, DC: U.S. Department of Labor.

U.S. Bureau of Labor Statistics. (2016, February 25). *Volunteering in the United States — 2015.* Washington, DC: U.S. Department of Labor.

U.S. Bureau of Labor Statistics. (2016, April 22). *Employment characteristics of families — 2015.* Washington, DC: U.S. Department of Labor.

U.S. Bureau of Labor Statistics. (2017, August 24). *Number of jobs held, labor market activity, and earnings growth among the youngest baby boomers: Results from a longitudinal survey summary.* Washington, DC: U.S. Department of Labor.

U.S. Bureau of Labor Statistics. (2018, June 15). *Local area unemployment statistics for May 2018.* Washington, DC: U.S. Bureau of Labor Statistics.

U.S. Census Bureau. (1907). *Statistical abstract of the United States 1906.* Washington, DC: U.S. Department of Commerce.

U.S. Census Bureau. (2011). *America's families and living arrangements: 2011.* U.S. Department of Commerce, Economics and Statistics Administration, U.S. Census Bureau.

U.S. Census Bureau. (2012). *Statistical abstract of the United States: 2012.* Washington, DC: U.S. Department of Commerce.

U.S. Census Bureau. (2015). *America's families and living arrangements: 2015: Households (H table series). Table H3: Households by race and Hispanic origin of household reference person and detailed type.* Washington, DC: U.S. Department of Commerce, Economics and Statistics Administration, U.S. Census Bureau.

U.S. Census Bureau. (2016a). *Selected population profile in the United States: 2014 American community survey 1-year estimates. American FactFinder.* Washington, DC: U.S. Department of Commerce.

U.S. Census Bureau. (2016b). *Selected population profile in the United States: 2009 American community survey 1-year estimates. American FactFinder.* Washington, DC: U.S. Department of Commerce.

U.S. Census Bureau. (2017, September 8). *Historical poverty tables: People and families — 1959 to 2016.* Washington, DC: U.S. Census Bureau.

U.S. Census Bureau. (2018). *American community survey.* Washington, DC: U.S. Census Bureau.

U.S. Census Bureau, Population Division. (2010, June). *Monthly resident population estimates by age, sex, race and Hispanic origin for the United States: April 1, 2000 to July 1, 2009.* Washington, DC: U.S. Census Bureau.

U.S. Department of Agriculture. (2016, October 11). *Key statistics & graphics: Food insecurity by household characteristics.* Washington, DC: U.S. Department of Agriculture.

U.S. Department of Agriculture. (2017, October 4). *Key statistics & graphics: Food insecurity by household characteristics.* Washington, DC: U.S. Department of Agriculture.

U.S. Department of Education. (2015, April). *A matter of equity: Preschool in America.* Washington, DC: U.S. Department of Education.

U.S. Department of Health and Human Services. (1999, December 31). *Child maltreatment 1999.* Washington, DC: Administration on Children, Youth and Families, Children's Bureau.

U.S. Department of Health and Human Services. (2000, December 31). *Child maltreatment 2000.* Washington, DC: Administration on Children, Youth and Families, Children's Bureau.

U.S. Department of Health and Human Services. (2003). *Child maltreatment 2001.* Washington, DC: Administration on Children, Youth and Families, Children's Bureau.

U.S. Department of Health and Human Services. (2005, December 31). *Child maltreatment 2005.* Washington, DC: Administration on Children, Youth and Families, Children's Bureau.

U.S. Department of Health and Human Services. (2008). *Child maltreatment 2006.* Washington, DC: Administration on Children, Youth and Families, Children's Bureau.

U.S. Department of Health and Human Services. (2010). *Head Start impact study: Final report.* Washington, DC: Administration for Children and Families.

U.S. Department of Health and Human Services. (2010, January). *Child maltreatment 2009.* Washington, DC: Administration for Children and Families, Administration on Children, Youth and Families, Children's Bureau.

U.S. Department of Health and Human Services. (2011). *The Surgeon General's call to action to support breastfeeding.* Washington, DC: U.S. Department of Health and Human Services, Office of the Surgeon General.

U.S. Department of Health and Human Services. (2011, December 31). *Child maltreatment 2010.* Washington, DC: Administration on Children, Youth and Families, Children's Bureau.

U.S. Department of Health and Human Services. (2012, December 12). *Child maltreatment 2011.* Washington, DC: Administration on Children, Youth and Families, Children's Bureau.

U.S. Department of Health and Human Services. (2016, January 25). *Child maltreatment 2014.* Washington, DC: Administration for Children and Families, Administration on Children, Youth and Families, Children's Bureau.

U.S. Department of Health and Human Services. (2017, January 19). *Child maltreatment 2015.* Washington, DC: Administration for Children and Families, Administration on Children, Youth and Families, Children's Bureau.

U.S. Preventive Services Task Force. (2002). Postmenopausal hormone replacement therapy for primary prevention of chronic conditions: Recommendations and rationale. *Annals of Internal Medicine, 137*(10), 834–839.

Uddin, Monica; Koenen, Karestan C.; de los Santos, Regina; Bakshis, Erin; Aiello, Allison E. & Galea, Sandro. (2010). Gender differences in the genetic and environmental determinants of adolescent depression. *Depression and Anxiety, 27*(7), 658–666.

Ueda, Tomomi; Suzukamo, Yoshimi; Sato, Mai & Izumi, Shin-Ichi. (2013). Effects of music therapy on behavioral and psychological symptoms of dementia: A systematic review and meta-analysis. *Ageing Research Reviews, 12*(2), 628–641.

Umberson, Debra; Pudrovska, Tetyana & Reczek, Corinne. (2010). Parenthood, childlessness, and well-being: A life course perspective. *Journal of Marriage and Family, 72*(3), 612–629.

Underwood, Emily. (2014, February 28). Can Down syndrome be treated? *Science, 343*(6174), 964–967.

Underwood, Emily. (2014, October 31). Starting young. *Science, 346*(6209), 568–571.

Underwood, Marion K. & Ehrenreich, Samuel E. (2017). The power and the pain of adolescents' digital communication: Cyber victimization and the perils of lurking. *American Psychologist, 72*(2), 144–158.

UNICEF. (2014a, October). Low birthweight: Percentage of infants weighing less than 2,500 grams at birth. UNICEF global databases, based on DHS, MICS, other national household surveys, data from routine reporting systems, UNICEF and WHO.

UNICEF. (2014b, October). Infant and young child feeding. UNICEF Global Databases.

UNICEF. (2015). *Rapid survey on children (RSOC) 2013–14: National report.* Ministry of Women and Child Development, Government of India.

UNICEF. (2017, January 13). *Global overview child malnutrition 1990–2015. UNICEF Data and Analytics: Joint Malnutrition Estimates 2016 Edition.* New York, NY: United Nations.

United Nations. (2016a). *Life expectancy at birth, females.* United Nations Statistics Division.

United Nations. (2016b). *Life expectancy at birth, males.* United Nations Statistics Division.

United Nations, Department of Economic and Social Affairs, Population Division. (2017). *World population prospects: The 2017 revision.* New York, NY.

Ursache, Alexandra; Blair, Clancy; Stifter, Cynthia & Voegtline, Kristin. (2013). Emotional reactivity and regulation in infancy interact to predict executive functioning in early childhood. *Developmental Psychology, 49*(1), 127–137.

Vaala, Sarah E.; Linebarger, Deborah L.; Fenstermacher, Susan K.; Tedone, Ashley; Brey, Elizabeth; Barr, Rachel, . . . Calvert, Sandra L. (2010). Content analysis of language-promoting teaching strategies used in infant-directed media. *Infant and Child Development, 19*(6), 628–648.

Vadillo, Miguel A.; Kostopoulou, Olga & Shanks, David R. (2015). A critical review and meta-analysis of the unconscious thought effect in medical decision making. *Frontiers in Psychology, 6*(636).

Valentine, Christine. (2017). Identity and continuing bonds in cross-cultural perspective: Britain and Japan. In Dennis Klass & Edith Maria Steffen (Eds.), *Continuing bonds in bereavement: New directions for research and practice.* New York, NY: Routledge.

Van Agt, H. M. E.; de Ridder-Sluiter, J. G.; Van den Brink, G. A.; de Koning, H. J. & Reep van den Bergh, C. (2015). The predictive value of early childhood factors for language outcome in pre-school children. *Journal of Child and Adolescent Behaviour, 3*(6).

van Batenburg-Eddes, Tamara; Butte, Dick & van de Looij-Jansen, Petra. (2012). Measuring juvenile delinquency: How do self-reports compare with official police statistics? *European Journal of Criminology, 9*(1), 23–37.

van de Bongardt, Daphne; Reitz, Ellen; Sandfort, Theo & Deković, Maja. (2015). A meta-analysis of the relations between three types of peer norms and adolescent sexual behavior. *Personality and Social Psychology Review, 19*(3), 203–234.

van den Akker, Alithe; Deković, Maja; Prinzie, Peter & Asscher, Jessica. (2010). Toddlers' temperament profiles: Stability and relations to negative and positive parenting. *Journal of Abnormal Child Psychology, 38*(4), 485–495.

van den Pol, Anthony N.; Mao, Guochao; Yang, Yang; Ornaghi, Sara & Davis, John N. (2017). Zika virus targeting in the developing brain. *Journal of Neuroscience, 37*(8), 2161–2175.

van Eeden-Moorefield, Brad & Pasley, Kay. (2013). Remarriage and stepfamily life. In Gary W. Peterson & Kevin R. Bush (Eds.), *Handbook of marriage and the family* (pp. 517–546). New York, NY: Springer.

van Goozen, Stephanie H. M. (2015). The role of early emotion impairments in the development of persistent antisocial behavior. *Child Development Perspectives, 9*(4), 206–210.

Van Harmelen, A.-L.; Kievit, R. A.; Ioannidis, K.; Neufeld, S.; Jones, P. B.; Bullmore, E., . . . Goodyer, I. (2017). Adolescent friendships predict later resilient functioning across psychosocial domains in a healthy community cohort. *Psychological Medicine, 47*(13), 2312–2322.

Van Houtte, Mieke. (2016). Lower-track students' sense of academic futility: Selection or effect? *Journal of Sociology, 52*(4), 874–889.

van IJzendoorn, Marinus H.; Bakermans-Kranenburg, Marian J.; Pannebakker, Fieke & Out, Dorothée. (2010). In defence of situational morality: Genetic, dispositional and situational determinants of children's donating to charity. *Journal of Moral Education, 39*(1), 1–20.

van IJzendoorn, Marinus H.; Palacios, Jesús; Sonuga-Barke, Edmund J. S.; Gunnar, Megan R.; Vorria, Panayiota; McCall, Robert B., . . . Juffer, Femmie. (2011). Children in institutional care: Delayed development and resilience. *Monographs of the Society for Research in Child Development, 76*(4), 8–30.

Van Rheenen, Derek. (2012). A century of historical change in the game preferences of American children. *Journal of American Folklore, 125*(498), 411–443.

Van Ryzin, Mark J. & Dishion, Thomas J. (2013). From antisocial behavior to violence: A model for the amplifying role of coercive joining in adolescent friendships. *Journal of Child Psychology and Psychiatry, 54*(6), 661–669.

van Tilburg, Theo G.; Aartsen, Marja J. & van der Pas, Suzan. (2015). Loneliness after divorce: A cohort comparison among Dutch young-old adults. *European Sociological Review, 31*(3), 243–252.

Van Vonderen, Kristen E. & Kinnally, William. (2012). Media effects on body image: Examining media exposure in the broader context of internal and other social factors. *American Communication Journal, 14*(2), 41–57.

Vandenbosch, Laura & Eggermont, Steven. (2015). The role of mass media in adolescents' sexual behaviors: Exploring the explanatory value of the three-step self-objectification process. *Archives of Sexual Behavior, 44*(3), 729–742.

Vanderberg, Rachel H.; Farkas, Amy H.; Miller, Elizabeth; Sucato, Gina S.; Akers, Aletha Y. & Borrero, Sonya B. (2016). Racial and/or ethnic differences in formal sex education and sex education by parents among young women in the United States. *Journal of Pediatric and Adolescent Gynecology, 29*(1), 69–73.

Vandewater, Elizabeth A.; Park, Seoung Eun; Hébert, Emily T. & Cummings, Hope M. (2015). Time with friends and physical activity as mechanisms linking obesity and television viewing among youth. *International Journal of Behavioral Nutrition and Physical Activity, 12*(Suppl. 1), S6.

Vardaki, Sophia; Dickerson, Anne E.; Beratis, Ion; Yannis, George & Papageorgiou, Sokratis G. (2016). Simulator measures and identification of older drivers with mild cognitive impairment. *American Journal of Occupational Therapy, 70*(2).

Varga, Mary Alice & Paletti, Robin. (2013). Life span issues and dying. In David K. Meagher & David E. Balk (Eds.), *Handbook of thanatology: The essential body of knowledge for the study of death, dying, and bereavement* (2nd ed., pp. 25–31). New York, NY: Routledge.

Vargas Lascano, Dayuma I.; Galambos, Nancy L.; Krahn, Harvey J. & Lachman, Margie E. (2015). Growth in perceived control across 25 years from the late teens to midlife: The role of personal and parents' education. *Developmental Psychology, 51*(1), 124–135.

Vedantam, Shankar. (2011, December 5). *What's behind a temper tantrum? Scientists deconstruct the screams. Hidden Brain.* Washington DC: NPR.

Veenstra, René; Lindenberg, Siegwart; Munniksma, Anke & Dijkstra, Jan Kornelis. (2010). The complex relation between bullying, victimization, acceptance, and rejection: Giving special attention to status, affection, and sex differences. *Child Development, 81*(2), 480–486.

Vélez, Clorinda E.; Wolchik, Sharlene A.; Tein, Jenn-Yun & Sandler, Irwin. (2011). Protecting children from the consequences of divorce: A longitudinal study of the effects of parenting on children's coping processes. *Child Development, 82*(1), 244–257.

Veling, Harm; Chen, Zhang; Tombrock, Merel C.; Verpaalen, Iris A. M.; Schmitz, Laura I.; Dijksterhuis, Ap & Holland, Rob W. (2017). Training impulsive choices for healthy and sustainable food. *Journal of Experimental Psychology, 23*(2), 204–215.

Verburgh, Kris. (2018). *The longevity code: The new science of aging.* New York, NY: Experiment.

Verdine, Brian N.; Golinkoff, Roberta Michnick; Hirsh-Pasek, Kathy & Newcombe, Nora S. (2017). Spatial skills, their development, and their links to mathematics. *Monographs of the Society for Research in Child Development: Links between spatial and mathematical skills across the preschool, 82*(1), 7–30.

Vernon, Lynette; Modecki, Kathryn L. & Barber, Bonnie L. (2018). Mobile phones in the bedroom: Trajectories of sleep habits and subsequent adolescent psychosocial development. *Child Development, 89*(1), 66–77.

Verona, Sergiu. (2003). Romanian policy regarding adoptions. In Victor Littel (Ed.), *Adoption update* (pp. 5–10). New York, NY: Nova Science.

Verschueren, Margaux; Rassart, Jessica; Claes, Laurence; Moons, Philip & Luyckx, Koen. (2017). Identity statuses throughout adolescence and emerging adulthood: A large-scale study into gender, age, and contextual differences. *Psychologica Belgica, 57*(1), 32–42.

Verweij, Karin J. H.; Creemers, Hanneke E.; Korhonen, Tellervo; Latvala, Antti; Dick, Danielle M.; Rose, Richard J., . . . Kaprio, Jaakko. (2016). Role of overlapping genetic and environmental factors in the relationship between early adolescent conduct problems and substance use in young adulthood. *Addiction, 111*(6), 1036–1045.

Vickery, Brian P.; Berglund, Jelena P.; Burk, Caitlin M.; Fine, Jason P.; Kim, Edwin H.; Kim, Jung In, . . . Burks, A. Wesley. (2017). Early oral immunotherapy in peanut-allergic preschool children is safe and highly effective. *Journal of Allergy and Clinical Immunology, 139*(1), 173–181.e178.

Viljaranta, Jaana; Aunola, Kaisa; Mullola, Sari; Virkkala, Johanna; Hirvonen, Riikka; Pakarinen, Eija & Nurmi, Jari-Erik. (2015). Children's temperament and academic skill development during first grade: Teachers' interaction styles as mediators. *Child Development, 86*(4), 1191–1209.

Villar, Feliciano. (2012). Successful ageing and development: The contribution of generativity in older age. *Ageing and Society, 32*(7), 1087–1105.

Villar, Feliciano & Celdrán, Montserrat. (2012). Generativity in older age: A challenge for Universities of the Third Age (U3A). *Educational Gerontology, 38*(10), 666–677.

Vilppu, Henna; Mikkilä-Erdmann, Mirjamaija; Södervik, Ilona & Österholm-Matikainen, Erika. (2016). Exploring eye movements of experienced and novice readers of medical texts concerning the cardiovascular system in making a diagnosis. *Anatomical Sciences Education,* (In Press).

Visscher, Peter M.; Wray, Naomi R.; Zhang, Qian; Sklar, Pamela; McCarthy, Mark I.; Brown, Matthew A. & Yang, Jian. (2017). 10 years of GWAs discovery: Biology, function, and translation. *AJHG*, 101(1), 5–22.

Vladeck, Fredda & Altman, Anita. (2015). The future of the NORC-supportive service program model. *Public Policy Aging Report*, 25(1), 20–22.

Voelcker-Rehage, Claudia; Niemann, Claudia & Hübner, Lena. (2018). Structural and functional brain changes related to acute and chronic exercise effects in children, adolescents and young adults. In Romain Meeusen, et al. (Eds.), *Physical activity and educational achievement: Insights from exercise neuroscience* (pp. 143–163). New York: Routledge.

Vogel, Ineke; Verschuure, Hans; van der Ploeg, Catharina P. B.; Brug, Johannes & Raat, Hein. (2010). Estimating adolescent risk for hearing loss based on data from a large school-based survey. *American Journal of Public Health*, 100(6), 1095–1100.

Vöhringer, Isabel A.; Kolling, Thorsten; Graf, Frauke; Poloczek, Sonja; Fassbender, Iina; Freitag, Claudia, . . . Knopf, Monika. (2017). The development of implicit memory from infancy to childhood: On average performance levels and interindividual differences. *Child Development*, (In Press).

von Salisch, Maria. (2018). Emotional competence and friendship involvement: Spiral effects in adolescence. *European Journal of Developmental Psychology*, (In Press).

Voosen, Paul. (2013, July 15). A brain gone bad: Researchers clear the fog of chronic head trauma. *The Chronicle Review*, B6–B10.

Vos, Bodil C.; Nieuwenhuijsen, Karen K. & Sluiter, Judith K. (2018). Consequences of traumatic brain injury in professional American football players: A systematic review of the literature. *Clinical Journal of Sport Medicine*, 28(2), 91–99.

Vranić, Andrea; Španić, Ana Marija; Carretti, Barbara & Borella, Erika. (2013). The efficacy of a multifactorial memory training in older adults living in residential care settings. *International Psychogeriatrics*, 25(11), 1885–1897.

Vygotsky, Lev S. (1980). *Mind in society: The development of higher psychological processes*. Cambridge, MA: Harvard University Press.

Vygotsky, Lev S. (1987). Thinking and speech. In Robert W. Rieber & Aaron S. Carton (Eds.), *The collected works of L. S. Vygotsky* (Vol. 1, pp. 39–285). New York, NY: Springer.

Vygotsky, Lev S. (1994a). The development of academic concepts in school aged children. In René van der Veer & Jaan Valsiner (Eds.), *The Vygotsky reader* (pp. 355–370). Cambridge, MA: Blackwell.

Vygotsky, Lev S. (1994b). Principles of social education for deaf and dumb children in Russia. In Rene van der Veer & Jaan Valsiner (Eds.), *The Vygotsky reader* (pp. 19–26). Cambridge, MA: Blackwell.

Vygotsky, Lev S. (2012). *Thought and language*. Cambridge, MA: MIT Press.

Waber, Deborah P.; Bryce, Cyralene P.; Fitzmaurice, Garrett M.; Zichlin, Miriam L.; McGaughy, Jill; Girard, Jonathan M. & Galler, Janina R. (2014). Neuropsychological outcomes at midlife following moderate to severe malnutrition in infancy. *Neuropsychology*, 28(4), 530–540.

Wade, Tracey D.; O'Shea, Anne & Shafran, Roz. (2016). Perfectionism and eating disorders. In Fuschia M. Sirois & Danielle S. Molnar (Eds.), *Perfectionism, health, and well-being* (pp. 205–222). New York, NY: Springer.

Wadman, Meredith. (2017). Emails reveal pressures on NIH gun research. *Science*, 358(6361), 286.

Wagner, Katie; Dobkins, Karen & Barner, David. (2013). Slow mapping: Color word learning as a gradual inductive process. *Cognition*, 127(3), 307–317.

Wagner, Paul A. (2011). Socio-sexual education: A practical study in formal thinking and teachable moments. *Sex Education: Sexuality, Society and Learning*, 11(2), 193–211.

Wahl, Hans-Werner; Tesch-Romer, Clemens; Hoff, Andreas & Hendricks, Jon (Eds.). (2017). *New dynamics in old age: Individual, environmental and societal perspectives*. New York, NY: Routledge.

Wahrendorf, Morten; Blane, David; Bartley, Mel; Dragano, Nico & Siegrist, Johannes. (2013). Working conditions in mid-life and mental health in older ages. *Advances in Life Course Research*, 18(1), 16–25.

Wakefield, Sarah J.; Blackburn, Daniel J.; Harkness, Kirsty; Khan, Aijaz; Reuber, Markus & Venneri, Annalena. (2018). Distinctive neuropsychological profiles differentiate patients with functional memory disorder from patients with amnestic-mild cognitive impairment. *Acta Neuropsychiatrica*, 30(2), 90–96.

Waldinger, Robert & Schulz, Marc. (2018). The blind psychological scientists and the elephant: Reply to Sherlock and Zietsch. *Psychological Science*, 29(1), 158–160.

Walhovd, Kristine B.; Tamnes, Christian K. & Fjell, Anders M. (2014). Brain structural maturation and the foundations of cognitive behavioral development. *Current Opinion in Neurology*, 27(2), 176–184.

Walker, Alan. (2012). The new ageism. *The Political Quarterly*, 83(4), 812–819.

Walker, Christa L. Fischer; Rudan, Igor; Liu, Li; Nair, Harish; Theodoratou, Evropi; Bhutta, Zulfiqar A., . . . Black, Robert E. (2013). Global burden of childhood pneumonia and diarrhoea. *The Lancet*, 381(9875), 1405–1416.

Walle, Eric A. & Campos, Joseph J. (2014). Infant language development is related to the acquisition of walking. *Developmental Psychology*, 50(2), 336–348.

Wallis, Christopher J. D.; Lo, Kirk; Lee, Yuna; Krakowsky, Yonah; Garbens, Alaina; Satkunasivam, Raj, . . . Nam, Robert K. (2016). Survival and cardiovascular events in men treated with testosterone replacement therapy: An intention-to-treat observational cohort study. *The Lancet Diabetes & Endocrinology*, 4(6), 498–506.

Wallis, Claudia. (2014). Gut reactions: Intestinal bacteria may help determine whether we are lean or obese. *Scientific American*, 310(6), 30–33.

Walter, Melissa Clucas & Lippard, Christine N. (2017). Head Start teachers across a decade: Beliefs, characteristics, and time spent on academics. *Early Childhood Education Journal, 45*(5), 693–702.

Wambach, Karen & Riordan, Jan. (2014). *Breastfeeding and human lactation* (5th ed.). Burlington, MA: Jones & Bartlett Publishers.

Wanberg, Connie R. (2012). The individual experience of unemployment. *Annual Review of Psychology, 63,* 369–396.

Wang, Cynthia S.; Whitson, Jennifer A.; Anicich, Eric M.; Kray, Laura J. & Galinsky, Adam D. (2017). Challenge your stigma: How to reframe and revalue negative stereotypes and slurs. *Current Directions in Psychological Science, 26*(1), 75–80.

Wang, Jingyun & Candy, T. Rowan. (2010). The sensitivity of the 2- to 4-month-old human infant accommodation system. *Investigative Ophthalmology and Visual Science, 51*(6), 3309–3317.

Wang, Limin; Gao, Pei; Zhang, Mei; Huang, Zhengjing; Zhang, Dudan; Deng, Qian, . . . Wang, Linhong. (2017). Prevalence and ethnic pattern of diabetes and prediabetes in China in 2013. *JAMA, 317*(24), 2515–2523.

Wang, Meifang & Liu, Li. (2018). Reciprocal relations between harsh discipline and children's externalizing behavior in China: A 5-year longitudinal study. *Child Development, 89*(1), 174–187.

Wang, S. & Young, K. M. (2014). White matter plasticity in adulthood. *Neuroscience, 276,* 148–160.

Wang, Wendy & Parker, Kim. (2014). *Record share of Americans have never married. Social & Demographic Trends.* Washington, DC: Pew Research Center.

Wang, Wendy & Taylor, Paul. (2011). *For millennials, parenthood trumps marriage.* Washington, DC: Pew Social & Demographic Trends.

Ward, Brian W.; Clarke, Tainya C.; Freeman, Gulnur & Schiller, Jeannine S. (2015, June). *Early release of selected estimates based on data from the 2014 National Health Interview Survey. National Health Interview Survey Early Release Program.* Washington, DC: U.S. Department of Health and Human Services, Centers for Disease Control and Prevention, National Center for Health Statistics.

Warneken, Felix. (2015). Precocious prosociality: Why do young children help? *Child Development Perspectives, 9*(1), 1–6.

Warner, Lisa M.; Wolff, Julia K.; Ziegelmann, Jochen P. & Wurm, Susanne. (2014). A randomized controlled trial to promote volunteering in older adults. *Psychology and Aging, 29*(4), 757–763.

Watson, John B. (1924). *Behaviorism.* New York, NY: The People's Institute Pub. Co.

Watson, John B. (1928). *Psychological care of infant and child.* New York, NY: Norton.

Watson, John B. (1972). *Psychological care of infant and child.* New York, NY: Arno Press.

Watson, John B. (1998). *Behaviorism.* New Brunswick, NJ: Transaction.

Webber, Douglas A. (2015). *Are college costs worth it?: How individual ability, major choice, and debt affect optimal schooling decisions.* Bonn, Germany: Institute for the Study of Labor.

Weber, Ann; Fernald, Anne & Diop, Yatma. (2017). When cultural norms discourage talking to babies: Effectiveness of a parenting program in rural Senegal. *Child Development, 88*(5), 1513–1526.

Weber, Daniela; Dekhtyar, Serhiy & Herlitz, Agneta. (2017). The Flynn effect in Europe—Effects of sex and region. *Intelligence, 60,* 39–45.

Webster, Collin A. & Suzuki, Naoki. (2014). Land of the rising pulse: A social ecological perspective of physical activity opportunities for schoolchildren in Japan. *Journal of Teaching in Physical Education, 33*(3), 304–325.

Wegrzyn, Lani R.; Tamimi, Rulla M.; Rosner, Bernard A.; Brown, Susan B.; Stevens, Richard G.; Eliassen, A. Heather, . . . Schernhammer, Eva S. (2017). Rotating night-shift work and the risk of breast cancer in the nurses' health studies. *American Journal of Epidemiology, 186*(5), 532–540.

Wei, Si. (2013). A multitude of people singing together. *International Journal of Community Music, 6*(2), 183–188.

Weiland, Christina & Yoshikawa, Hirokazu. (2013). Impacts of a prekindergarten program on children's mathematics, language, literacy, executive function, and emotional skills. *Child Development, 84*(6), 2112–2130.

Weinshenker, Naomi J. (2014). Teenagers and body image. Education.com. Education.

Weinstein, Netta & DeHaan, Cody. (2014). On the mutuality of human motivation and relationships. In Netta Weinstein (Ed.), *Human motivation and interpersonal relationships: Theory, research, and applications* (pp. 3–25). New York, NY: Springer.

Weiss, Noel S. & Koepsell, Thomas D. (2014). *Epidemiologic methods: Studying the occurrence of illness* (2nd ed.). New York, NY: Oxford University Press.

Weissberg, Roger P.; Durlak, Joseph A.; Domitrovich, Celene E. & Gullotta, Thomas P. (2016). Social and emotional learning: Past, present, and future. In Joseph A. Durlak, et al. (Eds.), *Handbook of social and emotional learning: Research and practice* (pp. 3–19). New York: Guilford Press.

Weissbourd, Richard; Ross Anderson, Trisha; Cashin, Alison & McIntyre, Joe. (2017). *The talk: How adults can promote young people's healthy relationships and prevent misogyny and sexual harassment. Making Caring Common Project.* Cambridge, MA: Harvard Graduate School of Education.

Weisskirch, Robert S. (2017a). A developmental perspective on language brokering. In Robert S. Weisskirch (Ed.), *Language brokering in immigrant families: Theories and contexts.* New York, NY: Routledge.

Weisskirch, Robert S. (2017b). *Language brokering in immigrant families: Theories and contexts.* New York, NY: Routledge.

Wellman, Henry M.; Fang, Fuxi & Peterson, Candida C. (2011). Sequential progressions in a theory-of-mind scale: Longitudinal perspectives. *Child Development, 82*(3), 780–792.

Wendelken, Carter; Baym, Carol L.; Gazzaley, Adam & Bunge, Silvia A. (2011). Neural indices of improved attentional modulation over middle childhood. *Developmental Cognitive Neuroscience, 1*(2), 175–186.

Wertsch, James V. & Tulviste, Peeter. (2005). L. S. Vygotsky and contemporary developmental psychology. In Harry Daniels (Ed.), *An introduction to Vygotsky*. New York, NY: Routledge.

Westphal, Sarah Katharina; Poortman, Anne-Rigt & Van der Lippe, Tanja. (2015). What about the grandparents? Children's postdivorce residence arrangements and contact with grandparents. *Journal of Marriage and Family*, 77(2), 424–440.

Weymouth, Bridget B.; Buehler, Cheryl; Zhou, Nan & Henson, Robert A. (2016). A meta-analysis of parent–adolescent conflict: Disagreement, hostility, and youth maladjustment. *Journal of Family Theory & Review*, 8(1), 95–112.

Whalley, Lawrence J.; Duthie, Susan J.; Collins, Andrew R.; Starr, John M.; Deary, Ian J.; Lemmon, Helen, . . . Staff, Roger T. (2014). Homocysteine, antioxidant micronutrients and late onset dementia. *European Journal of Nutrition*, 53(1), 277–285.

Whalley, Lawrence J.; Staff, Roger T.; Fox, Helen C. & Murray, Alison D. (2016). Cerebral correlates of cognitive reserve. *Psychiatry Research Neuroimaging*, 247, 65–70.

Wheeler, Lorey A.; Zeiders, Katharine H.; Updegraff, Kimberly A.; Umaña-Taylor, Adriana J.; Rodríguez de Jesús, Sue A. & Perez-Brena, Norma J. (2017). Mexican-origin youth's risk behavior from adolescence to young adulthood: The role of familism values. *Developmental Psychology*, 53(1), 126–137.

Whitbourne, Susan K. & Whitbourne, Stacey B. (2014). *Adult development and aging: Biopsychosocial perspectives* (5th ed.). Hoboken, NJ: Wiley.

Wicks, Elizabeth. (2012). The meaning of 'life': Dignity and the right to life in international human rights treaties. *Human Rights Law Review*, 12(2), 199–219.

Widman, Laura; Choukas-Bradley, Sophia; Helms, Sarah W.; Golin, Carol E. & Prinstein, Mitchell J. (2014). Sexual communication between early adolescents and their dating partners, parents, and best friends. *The Journal of Sex Research*, 51(7), 731–741.

Widom, Cathy Spatz; Czaja, Sally J. & DuMont, Kimberly A. (2015a). Intergenerational transmission of child abuse and neglect: Real or detection bias? *Science*, 347(6229), 1480–1485.

Widom, Cathy Spatz; Horan, Jacqueline & Brzustowicz, Linda. (2015b). Childhood maltreatment predicts allostatic load in adulthood. *Child Abuse & Neglect*, 47, 59–69.

Wieck, Cornelia & Kunzmann, Ute. (2017). Age differences in emotion recognition: A question of modality? *Psychology and Aging*, 32(5), 401–411.

Wigger, J. Bradley. (2017). Invisible friends across four countries: Kenya, Malawi, Nepal and the Dominican Republic. *International Journal of Pyschology*, (In Press).

Wigginton, Britta; Gartner, Coral & Rowlands, Ingrid J. (2017). Is it safe to vape? Analyzing online forums discussing e-cigarette use during pregnancy. *Women's Health Issues*, 27(1), 93–99.

Wiik, Kenneth Aarskaug; Keizer, Renske & Lappegård, Trude. (2012). Relationship quality in marital and cohabiting unions across Europe. *Journal of Marriage and Family*, 74(3), 389–398.

Wijdicks, Eelco F. M.; Varelas, Panayiotis N.; Gronseth, Gary S. & Greer, David M. (2010). Evidence-based guideline update: Determining brain death in adults; Report of the quality standards subcommittee of the American Academy of Neurology. *Neurology*, 74(23), 1911–1918.

Wilcox, W. Bradford (Ed.). (2011). *The sustainable demographic dividend: What do marriage and fertility have to do with the economy?* New York, NY: Social Trends Institute.

Wilcox, William B. & Kline, Kathleen K. (2013). *Gender and parenthood: Biological and social scientific perspectives*. New York, NY: Columbia University Press.

Wiley, Andrea S. (2011). Milk intake and total dairy consumption: Associations with early menarche in NHANES 1999-2004. *PLoS ONE*, 6(2), e14685.

Wilkinson, Stephen. (2015). Prenatal screening, reproductive choice, and public health. *Bioethics*, 29(1), 26–35.

Williams, Anne M.; Chantry, Caroline; Geubbels, Eveline L.; Ramaiya, Astha K.; Shemdoe, Aloisia I.; Tancredi, Daniel J. & Young, Sera L. (2016). Breastfeeding and complementary feeding practices among HIV-exposed infants in coastal Tanzania. *Journal of Human Lactation*, 32(1), 112–122.

Williams, Lela Rankin; Fox, Nathan A.; Lejuez, C. W.; Reynolds, Elizabeth K.; Henderson, Heather A.; Perez-Edgar, Koraly E., . . . Pine, Daniel S. (2010). Early temperament, propensity for risk-taking and adolescent substance-related problems: A prospective multi-method investigation. *Addictive Behaviors*, 35(2), 1148–1151.

Williams, Shanna; Moore, Kelsey; Crossman, Angela M. & Talwar, Victoria. (2016). The role of executive functions and theory of mind in children's prosocial lie-telling. *Journal of Experimental Child Psychology*, 141, 256–266.

Willoughby, Michael T.; Mills-Koonce, W. Roger; Gottfredson, Nisha C. & Wagner, Nicholas J. (2014). Measuring callous unemotional behaviors in early childhood: Factor structure and the prediction of stable aggression in middle childhood. *Journal of Psychopathology and Behavioral Assessment*, 36(1), 30–42.

Wilmshurst, Linda. (2011). *Child and adolescent psychopathology: A casebook* (2nd ed.). Thousand Oaks, CA: Sage.

Wilson, Kathryn R.; Hansen, David J. & Li, Ming. (2011). The traumatic stress response in child maltreatment and resultant neuropsychological effects. *Aggression and Violent Behavior*, 16(2), 87–97.

Winner, Brooke; Peipert, Jeffrey F.; Zhao, Qiuhong; Buckel, Christina; Madden, Tessa; Allsworth, Jenifer E. & Secura, Gina M. (2012). Effectiveness of long-acting reversible contraception. *New England Journal of Medicine*, 366, 1998–2007.

Wittrup, Audrey R.; Hussain, Saida B.; Albright, Jamie N.; Hurd, Noelle M.; Varner, Fatima A. & Mattis, Jacqueline S. (2016). Natural mentors, racial pride, and academic engagement among Black adolescents: Resilience in the context of perceived discrimination. *Youth & Society*, (In Press).

Wolchik, Sharlene A.; Ma, Yue; Tein, Jenn-Yun; Sandler, Irwin N. & Ayers, Tim S. (2008). Parentally bereaved children's grief: Self-system beliefs as mediators of the relations between grief and stressors and caregiver-child relationship quality. *Death Studies, 32*(7), 597–620.

Wolff, Jason J.; Gerig, Guido; Lewis, John D.; Soda, Takahiro; Styner, Martin A.; Vachet, Clement, . . . Piven, Joseph. (2015). Altered corpus callosum morphology associated with autism over the first 2 years of life. *Brain, 138*(7), 2046–2058.

Wolff, Mary S.; Teitelbaum, Susan L.; McGovern, Kathleen; Pinney, Susan M.; Windham, Gayle C.; Galvez, Maida, . . . Biro, Frank M. (2015). Environmental phenols and pubertal development in girls. *Environment International, 84,* 174–180.

Wong, Jaclyn S. & Waite, Linda J. (2015). Marriage, social networks, and health at older ages. *Journal of Population Ageing, 8*(1/2), 7–25.

Wongtongkam, Nualnong; Ward, Paul R.; Day, Andrew & Winefield, Anthony H. (2015). Exploring family and community involvement to protect Thai youths from alcohol and illegal drug abuse. *Journal of Addictive Diseases, 34*(1), 112–121.

Woodward, Amanda L. & Markman, Ellen M. (1998). Early word learning. In Deanna Kuhn & Robert S. Siegler (Eds.), *Handbook of child psychology* (5th ed., Vol. 2, pp. 371–420). Hoboken, NJ: Wiley.

Woollett, Katherine; Spiers, Hugo J. & Maguire, Eleanor A. (2009). Talent in the taxi: A model system for exploring expertise. *Philosophical Transactions of the Royal Society of London, 364*(1522), 1407–1416.

Woolley, Jacqueline D. & Ghossainy, Maliki E. (2013). Revisiting the fantasy–reality distinction: Children as naïve skeptics. *Child Development, 84*(5), 1496–1510.

World Bank. (2013). *World DataBank.* Washington, DC: World Bank.

World Bank. (2015). Population estimates and projections: Fertility and mortality by country.

World Bank. (2016). World development indicators: Mortality rate, infant (per 1,000 live births).

World Health Organization. (2006). WHO Motor Development Study: Windows of achievement for six gross motor development milestones. *Acta Paediatrica, 95*(Suppl. 450), 86–95.

World Health Organization. (2011). *Global recommendations on physical activity for health: Information sheet: global recommendations on physical activity for health 5–17 years old.* Geneva, Switzerland: World Health Organization.

World Health Organization. (2012). *Dementia: A public health priority.* Geneva, Switzerland: World Health Organization.

World Health Organization. (2013). *World health statistics 2013.* Geneva, Switzerland: World Health Organization.

World Health Organization. (2014). Malnutrition prevalence, height for age (% of children under 5).

World Health Organization. (2015). *Global status report on road safety 2015.* Geneva, Switzerland: World Health Organization.

World Health Organization. (2015, March 16–17). *First WHO ministerial conference on global action against dementia.* Geneva, Switzerland: World Health Organization.

World Health Organization. (2015, April). *WHO statement on caesarean section rates: Executive summary.* Geneva, Switzerland: World Health Organization. WHO/RHR/15.02.

Worthy, Darrell A.; Gorlick, Marissa A.; Pacheco, Jennifer L.; Schnyer, David M. & Maddox, W. Todd. (2011). With age comes wisdom: Decision making in younger and older adults. *Psychological Science, 22*(11), 1375–1380.

Wright, Jason D.; Herzog, Thomas J.; Tsui, Jennifer; Ananth, Cande V.; Lewin, Sharyn N.; Lu, Yu-Shiang, . . . Hershman, Dawn L. (2013). Nationwide trends in the performance of inpatient hysterectomy in the United States. *Obstetrics & Gynecology, 122*(2), 233–241.

Wrzus, Cornelia; Hänel, Martha; Wagner, Jenny & Neyer, Franz J. (2013). Social network changes and life events across the life span: A meta-analysis. *Psychological Bulletin, 139*(1), 53–80.

Wrzus, Cornelia & Neyer, Franz J. (2016). Co-development of personality and friendships across the lifespan: An empirical review on selection and socialization. *European Psychologist, 21*(4), 254–273.

Wu, Ming-Yih & Ho, Hong-Nerng. (2015). Cost and safety of assisted reproductive technologies for human immunodeficiency virus-1 discordant couples. *World Journal of Virology, 4*(2), 142–146.

Xu, Fei. (2013). The object concept in human infants: Commentary on Fields. *Human Development, 56*(3), 167–170.

Xu, Fei & Kushnir, Tamar. (2013). Infants are rational constructivist learners. *Current Directions in Psychological Science, 22*(1), 28–32.

Xu, Jiaquan; Murphy, Sherry L.; Kochanek, Kenneth D. & Arias, Elizabeth. (2016, December). *Mortality in the United States, 2015. NCHS Data Brief,* (267). Hyattsville, MD: National Center for Health Statistics.

Xu, Yaoying. (2010). Children's social play sequence: Parten's classic theory revisited. *Early Child Development and Care, 180*(4), 489–498.

Yackobovitch-Gavan, Michal; Wolf Linhard, D.; Nagelberg, Nessia; Poraz, Irit; Shalitin, Shlomit; Phillip, Moshe & Meyerovitch, Joseph. (2018). Intervention for childhood obesity based on parents only or parents and child compared with follow-up alone. *Pediatric Obesity,* (In Press).

Yamaguchi, Susumu; Greenwald, Anthony G.; Banaji, Mahzarin R.; Murakami, Fumio; Chen, Daniel; Shiomura, Kimihiro, . . . Krendl, Anne. (2007). Apparent universality of positive implicit self-esteem. *Psychological Science, 18*(6), 498–500.

Yan, J.; Han, Z. R.; Tang, Y. & Zhang, X. (2017). Parental support for autonomy and child depressive symptoms in middle childhood: The mediating role of parent–child attachment. *Journal of Child and Family Studies, 26*(7), 1970–1978.

Yang, Rongwang; Zhang, Suhan; Li, Rong & Zhao, Zhengyan. (2013). Parents' attitudes toward stimulants use in China. *Journal of Developmental & Behavioral Pediatrics, 34*(3), 225.

Yartsev, Michael M. (2017). The emperor's new wardrobe: Rebalancing diversity of animal models in neuroscience research. *Science, 358*(6362), 466–469.

Yeager, David S.; Dahl, Ronald E. & Dweck, Carol S. (2018). Why interventions to influence adolescent behavior often fail but could succeed. *Perspectives on Psychological Science*, *13*(1), 101–122.

Yıkılkan, Hülya; Aypak, Cenk & Görpelioğlu, Süleyman. (2014). Depression, anxiety and quality of life in caregivers of long-term home care patients. *Archives of Psychiatric Nursing*, *28*(3), 193–196.

Yip, Tiffany. (2014). Ethnic identity in everyday life: The influence of identity development status. *Child Development*, *85*(1), 205–219.

Yon, Yongjie; Mikton, Christopher R.; Gassoumis, Zachary D. & Wilber, Kathleen H. (2017). Elder abuse prevalence in community settings: A systematic review and meta-analysis. *The Lancet Global Health*, *5*(2), e147–e156.

Yoon, Cynthia; Jacobs, David R.; Duprez, Daniel A.; Dutton, Gareth; Lewis, Cora E.; Neumark-Sztainer, Dianne, . . . Mason, Susan M. (2018). Questionnaire-based problematic relationship to eating and food is associated with 25 year body mass index trajectories during midlife: The Coronary Artery Risk Development In Young Adults (CARDIA) Study. *International Journal of Eating Disorders*, *51*(1), 10–17.

Young, Marisa & Schieman, Scott. (2018). Scaling back and finding flexibility: Gender differences in parents' strategies to manage work–family conflict. *Journal of Marriage and Family*, *80*(1), 99–118.

Zachrisson, Henrik D.; Dearing, Eric; Lekhal, Ratib & Toppelberg, Claudio O. (2013). Little evidence that time in child care causes externalizing problems during early childhood in Norway. *Child Development*, *84*(4), 1152–1170.

Zachry, Anne H. & Kitzmann, Katherine M. (2011). Caregiver awareness of prone play recommendations. *American Journal of Occupational Therapy*, *65*(1), 101–105.

Zagheni, Emilio; Zannella, Marina; Movsesyan, Gabriel & Wagner, Brittney. (2015). Time is economically valuable: Production, consumption and transfers of time by age and sex. In Emilio Zagheni, et al. (Eds.), *A comparative analysis of European time transfers between generations and genders* (pp. 19–33). New York, NY: Springer.

Zahran, Hatice S.; Bailey, Cathy M.; Damon, Scott A.; Garbe, Paul L. & Breysse, Patrick N. (2018). *Vital signs: Asthma in children — United States, 2001–2016. Morbidity and Mortality Weekly Report*, *67*(5), 149–155. Atlanta, GA: Centers for Disease Control and Prevention.

Zak, Paul J. (2012). *The moral molecule: The source of love and prosperity.* New York, NY: Dutton.

Zalenski, Robert J. & Raspa, Richard. (2006). Maslow's hierarchy of needs: A framework for achieving human potential in hospice. *Journal of Palliative Medicine*, *9*(5), 1120–1127.

Zametkin, Alan J. & Solanto, Mary V. (2017). A review of *ADHD nation* [Review of the book *ADHD nation: Children, doctors, big pharma, and the making of an American epidemic*, by Alan Schwarz]. *The ADHD Report*, *25*(2), 6–10.

Zatorre, Robert J. (2013). Predispositions and plasticity in music and speech learning: Neural correlates and implications. *Science*, *342*(6158), 585–589.

Zatorre, Robert J.; Fields, R. Douglas & Johansen-Berg, Heidi. (2012). Plasticity in gray and white: Neuroimaging changes in brain structure during learning. *Nature Neuroscience*, *15*, 528–536.

Zeiders, Katharine H.; Umaña-Taylor, Adriana J. & Derlan, Chelsea L. (2013a). Trajectories of depressive symptoms and self-esteem in Latino youths: Examining the role of gender and perceived discrimination. *Developmental Psychology*, *49*(5), 951–963.

Zeiders, Katharine H.; Updegraff, Kimberly A.; Umaña-Taylor, Adriana J.; Wheeler, Lorey A.; Perez-Brena, Norma J. & Rodríguez, Sue A. (2013b). Mexican-origin youths trajectories of depressive symptoms: The role of familism values. *Journal of Adolescent Health*, *53*(5), 648–654.

Zeifman, Debra M. (2013). Built to bond: Coevolution, coregulation, and plasticity in parent-infant bonds. In Cindy Hazan & Mary I. Campa (Eds.), *Human bonding: The science of affectional ties* (pp. 41–73). New York, NY: Guilford Press.

Zeitlin, Marian. (2011). *New information on West African traditional education and approaches to its modernization.* Dakar, Senegal: Tostan.

Zelazo, Philip David. (2015). Executive function: Reflection, iterative reprocessing, complexity, and the developing brain. *Developmental Review*, *38*, 55–68.

Zhang, Limei. (2018). *Metacognitive and cognitive strategy use in reading comprehension: A structural equation modelling approach.* Singapore: Springer.

Zhao, Jinxia & Wang, Meifang. (2014). Mothers' academic involvement and children's achievement: Children's theory of intelligence as a mediator. *Learning and Individual Differences*, *35*, 130–136.

Zhou, Cindy Ke; Levine, Paul H.; Cleary, Sean D.; Hoffman, Heather J.; Graubard, Barry I. & Cook, Michael B. (2016). Male pattern baldness in relation to prostate cancer–specific mortality: A prospective analysis in the NHANES I Epidemiologic Follow-Up Study. *American Journal of Epidemiology*, *183*(3), 210–217.

Zhou, Dongming; Lebel, Catherine; Evans, Alan & Beaulieu, Christian. (2013). Cortical thickness asymmetry from childhood to older adulthood. *NeuroImage*, *83*, 66–74.

Zhu, Qi; Song, Yiying; Hu, Siyuan; Li, Xiaobai; Tian, Moqian; Zhen, Zonglei, . . . Liu, Jia. (2010). Heritability of the specific cognitive ability of face perception. *Current Biology*, *20*(2), 137–142.

Ziegler, Matthias; Danay, Erik; Heene, Moritz; Asendorp, Jens & Bühner, Markus. (2012). Openness, fluid intelligence, and crystallized intelligence: Toward an integrative model. *Journal of Research in Personality*, *46*(2), 173–183.

Zimmerman, Julie B. & Anastas, Paul T. (2015). Toward substitution with no regrets. *Science*, *347*(6227), 1198–1199.

Zimmerman, Marc A.; Stoddard, Sarah A.; Eisman, Andria B.; Caldwell, Cleopatra H.; Aiyer, Sophie M. & Miller, Alison. (2013). Adolescent resilience: Promotive factors that inform prevention. *Child Development Perspectives*, *7*(4), 215–220.

Zimmermann, Camilla. (2012). Acceptance of dying: A discourse analysis of palliative care literature. *Social Science & Medicine*, *75*(1), 217–224.

Zinzow, Heidi M. & Thompson, Martie. (2015). Factors associated with use of verbally coercive, incapacitated, and forcible sexual assault tactics in a longitudinal study of college men. *Aggressive Behavior, 41*(1), 34–43.

Zosel, Amy; Bartelson, Becki Bucher; Bailey, Elise; Lowenstein, Steven & Dart, Rick. (2013). Characterization of adolescent prescription drug abuse and misuse using the Researched Abuse Diversion and Addiction-Related Surveillance (RADARS®) System. *Journal of the American Academy of Child & Adolescent Psychiatry, 52*(2), 196–204.e192.

Zubrzycki, Jackie. (2017). 1 in 5 public school students in the class of 2016 passed an AP exam [Web log post]. Education Week: Curriculum Matters.

Zucker, Kenneth J.; Cohen-Kettenis, Peggy T.; Drescher, Jack; Meyer-Bahlburg, Heino F. L.; Pfäfflin, Friedemann &

Womack, William M. (2013). Memo outlining evidence for change for Gender Identity Disorder in the *DSM-5*. *Archives of Sexual Behavior, 42*(5), 901–914.

Zuo, Xi-Nian; He, Ye; Betzel, Richard F.; Colcombe, Stan; Sporns, Olaf & Milham, Michael P. (2017). Human connectomics across the life span. *Trends in Cognitive Sciences, 21*(1), 32–45.

Zvolensky, Michael J.; Taha, Farah; Bono, Amanda & Goodwin, Renee D. (2015). Big Five personality factors and cigarette smoking: A 10-year study among US adults. *Journal of Psychiatric Research, 63*, 91–96.

Zych, Izabela; Farrington, David P.; Llorent, Vicente J. & Ttofi, Maria M. (Eds.). (2017). *Protecting children against bullying and its consequences*. Cham, Switzerland: Springer.

Name Index

Note: In page references, "p" indicates a photo, "f" indicates a figure, and "t" indicates a table.

Subject Index

Note: Page numbers followed by f, p, or t indicate figures, pictures, or tables, respectively. Boldface page numbers indicate key terms.

Brief Contents

Contents

Boxed Features

Gender/Diversity and Biopsychology Coverage

Preface

From psychology's inception as a separate discipline, authors of introductory psychology textbooks have been confronted with the need to convey a broad discipline to students in a book of reasonable length. To accomplish all that Les Sdorow originally intended in the first edition of *Psychology*, the book could easily have been twice as long as it is now. More than a century ago, William James, disturbed at the length of his now-classic *Principles of Psychology*, gave his own stinging review of it. He called it, among other things, "a bloated tumescent mass." Though this comment might have been written during one of James's frequent bouts with depression, it indicates the challenge of synthesizing a vast quantity of information. Given that psychology has become an even broader discipline and has accumulated an enormous information base, Les quickly discovered that he would somehow have to produce a textbook that adequately covered the discipline of psychology without becoming what textbook reviewers refer to as, perhaps euphemistically, "encyclopedic."

If you have not adopted this book in the past, we believe that you will find that your students will be eager to read it and to learn from it. You will find that the book achieves interest and readability while also accomplishing the following goals:

- Portraying psychology as a science
- Demonstrating the superiority of science over common sense
- Showing that psychological research occurs in a sociocultural context
- Illustrating the relevance of psychology to everyday life
- Encouraging critical thinking in all aspects of life, particularly in regard to the media
- Placing psychology in its intellectual, historical, biographical, and sociocultural contexts

To ensure that students will find the book appealing, we have made every effort to write clearly and concisely and to include interesting content. To make our prose as clear as possible, we have taken care that every sentence, paragraph, and section in the book presents a crisp, logical flow of ideas. To make the content more interesting, we have included many engaging examples of concepts and issues throughout the book. Because more readable textbooks provide vivid examples of the concepts and issues they cover, we have included concrete examples from psychological research and from virtually every area of life.

A textbook should be readable, but for students to respect psychology as a science, the textbook they use also must be scholarly. Though popular examples are provided throughout this text, they do not substitute for evidence provided by scientific research. If you skim the References section at the end of the book, you will note that it is as up-to-date as possible in its coverage of research studies, yet does not slight classic studies.

Themes Guiding *Psychology*

The seventh edition of *Psychology* includes special features that advance the five main themes of this text.

Psychology Is a Science

Over the years, several of our colleagues have expressed frustration that many people—including students—do not realize that psychology is a science, instead believing that it is based on common sense and the opinions of experts called "psychologists." Because of this misconception, one of our primary goals in this book is to show the student reader that psychology is indeed a science. Psychologists do have opinions, but as scientists, they try their best to hold opinions that do not come out of thin air but, rather, are supported by empirical data.

Yet, a psychology textbook should provide students with more than research findings. It should discuss "how we know" as well as "what we know." To give students enough background to appreciate the research process, in Chapter 2 we introduce psychology as a science, the methods of psychological research, and the statistical analysis of research data. The chapter includes a concrete example of the scientific method that shows how it relates to an interesting classic research study on interpersonal attraction. The chapter also includes data from a hypothetical experiment on the effects of melatonin on sleep and explains how to calculate descriptive statistics using that data.

Beginning with Chapter 2, each chapter features an in-depth discussion of a research study. This feature, *The Research Process*, highlights the rationale, methods, results, and interpretation of research studies in a manner accessible to beginning psychology students. The studies have been chosen for both their appeal and their ability to illustrate the scientific method. These studies include the following:

- David Buss and colleagues' (1992) evolutionary psychology study of emotional and sexual jealousy (Chapter 3)
- Nicholas Spanos and Erin Hewitt's (1980) study of hypnosis as an altered state of consciousness (Chapter 6)
- Lewis Terman's longitudinal study, the Genetic Studies of Genius (Chapter 10)

Psychology Is Superior to Common Sense

Many psychology professors we have known have stressed the need to demonstrate that psychology is more than formalized common sense. Though common sense is often correct and functionally useful, unlike science it is not self-correcting. False commonsense beliefs might survive indefinitely—and might be held tenaciously by introductory psychology students—despite being wrong. The text provides numerous examples of the failure of commonsense beliefs to stand up to scientific challenge. For example, Chapter 2 provides research evidence contradicting the commonsense belief that students should not change their answers on multiple-choice tests.

To demonstrate the superiority of the scientific approach, most chapters include the feature *Psychology Versus Common Sense.* This feature challenges widely held commonsense beliefs by evaluating them scientifically.

- Chapter 2 presents a study that showed how scientific research has countered the commonsense belief (upheld even in high-court decisions) that we can reliably determine if someone is legally drunk by observing their behavior.
- Chapter 5 discusses a research study indicating that it might be impossible for baseball players to follow the commonsense directive to "keep your eye on the ball" when they are at bat.
- Chapter 6 presents evidence that supports the commonsense belief that we need to sleep in order to maintain our physical health.

Psychology Is Relevant to Everyday Life

This textbook contains concrete examples that illustrate concepts while providing relief from the typically sober material often presented in psychology textbooks. Our examples—showing the relevance of psychology to everyday life—clarify concepts and make the material more interesting. These examples come from many areas of life, including art, sport, history, politics, biography, literature, entertainment, and student life, and are interwoven into the body of the text. Among these many examples are the following:

- Research-based suggestions for overcoming insomnia (Chapter 6)
- How operant conditioning is used to train animals (Chapter 7)
- Ways to improve one's memory and study habits (Chapter 8)

Psychology Improves Critical Thinking

If students learn nothing else from the introductory psychology course, they should learn to think more critically—that is, to be skeptical rather than gullible or cynical. Chapter 2 describes formal steps in thinking critically,

and critical thinking is encouraged throughout the book. Students will find that the ability to think critically benefits them in their daily lives when confronted with claims made by friends, relatives, politicians, advertisers, or anyone else. Every chapter of the book gives the student repeated opportunities to critically assess popular claims portrayed in the media, provide alternative explanations for research findings, and think of possible implications of research findings.

In a senior seminar course that Les has taught over the years, entitled "Current Issues in Psychology," students read many journal articles and some popular articles on a host of controversial topics, which they then discuss or debate. Because of the success of this course—students enjoy sinking their teeth into controversial issues—we have adapted its rationale in the *Critical Thinking About Psychology* features throughout the book. The topics chosen for this feature promote critical thinking by showing that psychologists use reason and empirical data to tackle controversies. Some of the topics include the following:

- The furor over Einstein's preserved brain (Chapter 3)
- The validity of "recovered memories" of childhood abuse (Chapter 8)
- The controversy over *The Bell Curve* (Chapter 10)

Psychology Has a Variety of Contexts

Psychology does not exist in a vacuum. It must consider sociocultural factors; it has an intellectual heritage; it reflects its times; and it is the product of individual human lives. That is, psychology has a variety of contexts: sociocultural, intellectual, historical, and biographical. This contextual variety is stressed throughout the book.

Psychology's Sociocultural Context Throughout the text, cross-cultural, ethnic, and gender differences are discussed within the context of human universals. Critical thinking about group differences must include consideration of the magnitude of these differences as well as the variables on which groups do not differ appreciably. For example, Chapter 2 includes a discussion of a research study that found that responses to rating scales might depend in part on one's cultural background. Students from North America were more willing to use the extremes of the scales than were students from East Asia. The discussion considers the possible cultural basis for this difference in the students' response tendencies. And Chapter 6 reports gender and ethnic differences in some aspects of the sleep cycle, noting that these differences may be attributable to variables that are correlated with gender and ethnicity, such as stress levels and sleep environments. Chapter 12 describes studies that report cross-cultural differences in the experience and socialization of emotion along with studies that report remarkable cross-cultural similarity in self-reported happiness and well-being. Moreover, the power of gender roles is emphasized in many discussions of gender differences. For example, in Chapters 11 and 17 we discuss the influence of gender roles on body satisfaction, eating disorders, physical attractiveness, and mate selection among heterosexual women and men, lesbians, and gay men.

Psychology's Intellectual Context Students need to realize that psychology is not intellectually homogeneous. Psychologists favor a variety of perspectives, including the psychoanalytic, the behaviorist, the cognitive, the humanistic, the biopsychological, and the sociocultural. Our text's attention to each of these perspectives reflects our belief that an introductory psychology textbook should introduce students to a variety of perspectives rather than reflect the author's favored one. That is, the introductory psychology textbook should be fair in representing psychology's intellectual context—while being critical of the various perspectives when research findings merit it. Students are introduced to the major psychological perspectives in Chapter 1 and continue to encounter them throughout the book, most obviously in the chapters on personality, psychological disorders, and therapy.

The text explains the different approaches to particular topics that are taken by psychologists who represent different perspectives. For example, Chapter 14's discussion on the possible causes of depression presents the differing views of psychologists who favor the psychoanalytic, behavioral, cognitive, humanistic, biopsychological, and sociocultural perspectives.

Psychology is diverse not only in its intellectual perspectives but also in its intellectual fields. Our students often express amazement at the breadth of psychology. One psychologist might devote a career to using fMRI techniques in studying cerebral hemispheric functions; another might devote a career to studying the relationship of childhood attachment patterns to adult romantic relationships. And whereas one member of a psychology department studies the causes of human aggression, another studies the nature of so-called flashbulb memories. Because of this breadth, we were forced to be selective in the topics, studies, and concepts presented in the book. Nonetheless, we believe that this book includes a representative sampling of the discipline of psychology.

Psychology's Historical Context An article dealing with psychology and the liberal arts curriculum in the June 1991 issue of the *American Psychologist* stressed that an essential goal in undergraduate psychology education is to provide students with the historical context of psychology. Introductory psychology textbooks should not present psychology as though it developed in ivory towers divorced from a historical context. Throughout this book, you will find many ways in which topics are given a historical grounding. Chapter 1 includes a discussion

of the contributions made by female psychologists to the early growth of psychology—as well as the obstacles they faced. By drawing a connection between Galvani's work on electricity, Mary Shelley's *Frankenstein*, and views on the nature of neural conduction, Chapter 3 reveals how, over the centuries, activity in one area of scientific endeavor can influence theorizing in another. And Chapter 10 traces the nature-nurture debate regarding intelligence back to the work of Francis Galton in the late 19th century. And, though this book is grounded in the history of psychology, studies throughout have been updated to reflect the current status of research in the field. Most notably, Chapter 14 has been extensively revised to reflect changes with the publication of the *DSM-5*.

Psychology's Biographical Context Psychology is influenced not only by the intellect of the psychologist but also by his or her own life experiences. Throughout this text, we show evidence that psychology is a human endeavor, practiced by people with emotions as well as intellects, and that scientific progress depends on serendipity as well as on purposeful scientific pursuits. For example, Chapter 3 points out that the first demonstration of the chemical basis of communication between nerve cells came to Otto Loewi in a dream. And Chapter 7 explains why the name *Pavlov* rings a bell but the name *Twitmyer* does not. Students tend to find this biographical information engaging, making them more likely to read assigned material in the text.

Pedagogical Features
Chapter Openers

We have made a special effort to include chapter openers that engage the student and promote interest in reading the chapter. Among the chapter openers are the following:

- **Chapter 1** begins with a description of the shootings at Columbine High School, which then is addressed later in the chapter through the lenses of the different psychological perspectives.
- **Chapter 4** begins with the story of Hulda Crooks, a 91-year-old mountain climber, which illustrates that people do not necessarily deteriorate in old age.
- **Chapter 7** begins with a discussion of the use of conditioned taste aversion to prevent coyotes from killing sheep, which indicates how basic research findings can be applied to practical problems.
- **Chapter 11** begins with the story of the life of "Mother" Joseph Cavellucci, a gay transvestite, which anticipates later coverage of theory and research on gender identity and sexual orientation.
- **Chapter 12** begins with a report of the use—and misuse—of the polygraph test to protect nuclear weapons secrets, which shows psychology's relationship to important current events.

- **Chapter 14** begins with the story of Norton I, Emperor of the United States, a man with schizophrenia who was renowned in 19th-century San Francisco, which demonstrates that even people with serious mental illnesses may live full lives.
- **Chapter 17** begins with a description of the Heaven's Gate mass suicide, which anticipates later text coverage of conformity, compliance, and obedience.

Running Marginal Glossary

A running marginal glossary is integrated throughout the book. This feature eliminates the need for us to torture our prose into the formal tone of a dictionary definition when we introduce new concepts. Terms that are printed in bold-face are defined in the margins and listed as *Key Terms* at the end of the chapter. The marginal definitions are also collected in the *Glossary* at the end of the book, which provides a handy tool for students when they encounter those terms in other chapters and when they are studying for exams.

Section Review Self-Quizzes

Each of the major sections within the chapters ends with a self-quiz called *Section Review.* These quizzes encourage students to pause and assess whether they can recall and comprehend important information from the relevant section. The quizzes include factual, conceptual, and applied questions. Answers to all the questions are provided at the end of the book and in the Online Edition.

Illustrations

We selected or helped design all the illustrations in this book. In doing so, we tried to make each of them serve a sound pedagogical purpose. Though the illustrations make the book aesthetically more appealing, they were chosen chiefly because their visual presentations complement material discussed in the text. The illustrations include beautifully executed drawings, graphs of research data, and many interesting photographs of people and events that students will recognize.

Chapter Summary

Each chapter ends with a bulleted *Chapter Summary* that captures the essential points made in the major sections of the chapter. The summaries provide a quick overview that will help students master what they have read.

Key Terms

Each chapter includes a list of *Key Terms* that were discussed in the chapter. The list is arranged alphabetically and according to each chapter's first-level headings and indicates the pages on which the terms were discussed. The list will help students in reviewing and studying for exams.

Experiencing Psychology

We have designed *Experiencing Psychology* activities to engage students in critical thinking about topics discussed in the text. These projects may be adapted for use as in-class activities or as out-of-class assignments. Activities include:

- Assessing the effectiveness of a mnemonic technique (Chapter 8)
- Replicating a classic study of the effects of mental sets on problem solving (Chapter 9)
- Testing the hypothesis that humorous professors are more effective educators (Chapter 12)
- Assessing the media's portrayal of mental illness (Chapter 14)
- Applying behavior modification techniques to increase adherence to an exercise regimen (Chapter 16)

Chapter Quiz and Thought Questions

Each chapter concludes with a multiple-choice *Chapter Quiz* and open-ended *Thought Questions* about material covered in the chapter. Answers for the quiz questions are provided at the end of the book and in the Online Edition, and possible answers for the Thought Questions are provided in the Instructor's Manual.

Online and in Print
Student Options: Print and Online Versions

This seventh edition of *Psychology* is available in multiple versions: online and in print as either a paperback or loose-leaf text. The most affordable version is the online book, with upgrade options including the online version bundled with a print version. What's nice about the print version is that it offers you the freedom of being unplugged—away from your computer. The people at YOLO Learning Solutions recognize that it's difficult to read from a screen at length and that most of us read much faster from a piece of paper. The print options are particularly useful when you have extended print passages to read.

The online edition allows you to take full advantage of embedded digital features, including search and notes. Use the search feature to locate and jump to discussions anywhere in the book. Use the notes feature to add personal comments or annotations. You can move out of the book to follow Web links. You can navigate within and between chapters using a clickable table of contents. These features allow you to work at your own pace and in your own style, as you read and surf your way through the material. (See "Harnessing the Online Version" for more tips on working with the online version.)

Appendixes

Three appendixes are available online and can be downloaded in PDF format and printed:

Appendix A   Majoring in Psychology
Appendix B   Industrial/Organizational Psychology
Appendix C   Statistics

Harnessing the Online Version

The online version of *Psychology* 7e offers the following features to facilitate learning and to make using the book an easy, enjoyable experience:

- *Easy-to-navigate/clickable table of contents*—You can surf through the book quickly by clicking on chapter headings, or first- or second-level section headings. And the Table of Contents can be accessed from anywhere in the book.
- *Key terms search*—Type in a term, and a search engine will return every instance of that term in the book; then jump directly to the selection of your choice with one click.
- *Notes and highlighting*—The online version includes study apps such as notes and highlighting. Each of these apps can be found in the tools icon embedded in the YOLO/Textbook Media's online eBook reading platform (http://www.yololearningsolutions.com).
- *Upgrades*—The online version includes the ability to purchase additional study apps and functionality that enhance the learning experience.

Supplements

In addition to the student-friendly features and pedagogy, the variety of student formats available, and the uniquely affordable pricing options, *Psychology* 7e comes with the following teaching and learning aids:

- *Test Item File*—An extensive set of multiple-choice, short answer, and essay questions for every chapter for creating original quizzes and exams.
- *Instructor's Manual*—An enhanced version of the book offering assistance in preparing lectures, identifying learning objectives, developing essay exams and assignments, and constructing course syllabi.
- *PowerPoint Presentations*—Key points in each chapter are illustrated in a set of PowerPoint files designed to assist with instruction.

Student Supplements and Upgrades (Additional Purchase Required)

- **Lecture Guide**—This printable lecture guide is designed for student use and is available as an in-class

resource or study tool. *Note:* Instructors can request the PowerPoint version of these slides to use as developed or to customize.

- **StudyUpGrade (Interactive Online Study Guide)**—Students can turbo-charge their online version of *Psychology* 7e with a unique study tool designed to "up your grade." StudyUpGrade is a software package that layers self-scoring quizzes and flash cards into the online version.

This inexpensive upgrade helps you improve your grades through the use of interactive content that's built into each chapter. Features include self-scoring multiple-choice quizzes, key concept reviews with fill-in-the-blank prompts, and e-flash cards comprised of key term definitions. For more on this helpful study tool, check out the flash demo at the YOLO Learning Solutions or Textbook Media websites.

- **Study Guide**—A printable version of the online study guide is available via downloadable PDF chapters for easy self-printing and review.

Acknowledgments

Because of their professionalism, good humor, and extensive knowledge of academic publishing, our editors at YOLO Learning Solutions have made writing this edition of our text a smooth, pleasurable process. We also would like to thank our production team at Putman Productions, especially Victoria Putman and Mary Monner, for providing us with their superb expertise and personal support throughout the process—while always being fun to work with.

Cheryl thanks her colleagues at the University of Redlands, especially Susan Goldstein, who cheerfully shared her expertise in cross-cultural psychology, and Sandi Richey, who helped in researching the text. Cheryl also thanks her sister, Gail Rickabaugh; her sister outlaw, Barbara Bridges, and her friends Kym Bennett, Jill Borchert, Dan Conte, Emily Culpepper, Susanne Pastuschek, and Judy Tschann for their respect, love, and support. And a special thanks to Oscar, who will always be her best friend and help her keep things in perspective.

Adrienne would like to thank her amazingly supportive family and friends. Without them, she would not be able to balance it all. She would also like to thank her colleagues at Quinnipiac University across all departments but most especially the Department of Psychology. She would also like to thank John Salamone for his unwavering support.

We hope that you enjoy the process of learning from our text. If you have any comments or questions, please contact YOLO Learning Solutions at info@yololearningsolutions.com or contact us directly at cheryl_rickabaugh@redlands.edu or adrienne.betz@quinnipiac.edu.

Reviewers

Thanks to the many reviewers of the various editions of this text.

Rahan s. Ali, *Pennsylvania State University*

Ronald Baenninger, *Temple University*

Ute Johanna Bayen, *University of North Carolina, Chapel Hill*

Robert C. Beck, *Wake Forest University*

Bethany Neal-Beliveau, *Indiana University–Purdue University Indianapolis*

John Benjafield, *Brock University*

Robert D. Boroff, M.D., *Modesto Junior College*

Linda Brannon, *McNeese State University*

Robert Paul Brown, *Jefferson Community College*

Dennis Cogan, *Texas Technical University*

John B. Connors, *Canadian Union College*

Stanley Coren, *University of British Columbia*

Randolph Cornelius, *Vassar College*

Verne C. Cox, *University of Texas at Arlington*

Jeffrey Ratliff-Crain, *University of Minnesota, Morris*

Ken Cramer, *University of Windsor*

Richard Cribs, *Motlow State Community College*

Hank Davis, *University of Guelph*

Scott Dickman, *University of Massachusetts, Dartmouth*

Deanna L. Dodson, *Lebanon Valley College*

Donald K. Freedheim, *Case Western Reserve University*

Larry Fujinaka, *Leeward Community College*

Preston E. Garraghty, *Indiana University*

Janet Gebelt, *University of Portland*

Ajaipal S. Gill, *Anne Arundel Community College*

Sandy Grossman, *Clackamas Community College*

Morton G. Harmatz, *University of Massachusetts, Amherst*

Debra L. Hollister, *Valencia Community College*

Daniel Houlihan, *Mankato State University*

Lera Joyce Jonson, *Centenary College*

Deanna Julka, *University of Portland*

Stanley K. Kary, *St. Louis Community College at Florrissant Valley*

Karen Kopera-Frye, *University of Akron*

Janet L. Kottke, *California State University, San Bernardino*

Gary LaBine, *Edinboro University of Pennsylvania*

Joan B. Lauer, *Indiana University–Purdue University Indianapolis*

Ting Lei, *Borough of Manhattan Community College*

Richard Lippa, *California State University, Fullerton*

Dennis Lorenz, *University of Wisconsin*

Gerald McRoberts, *Stanford University*

Ralph Miller, *State University of New York, Binghamton*

Joel Morgovsky, *Brookdale Community College*

James Mottin, *University of Guelph*

Ian Neath, *Purdue University*

Christopher Pagano, *Clemson University*

Richard Pisacreta, *Ferris State University*

Karen Quigley, *Pennsylvania State University*

Robert W. Ridel, *Maryhurst University*

Linda Robertello, *Iona College*

Sonya M. Sheffert, *Central Michigan University*

NC Silver, *University of Nevada, Las Vegas*

Brent D. Slife, *Brigham Young University*

Michael D. Spiegler, *Providence College*

George T. Taylor, *University of Missouri, St. Louis*

Lisa Valentino, *Seminole Community College*

Frank Vattano, *Colorado State University*

Benjamin Wallace, *Cleveland State University*

Wilse Webb, *University of Florida, Gainsville*

Amy Wilkerson, *Stephen F. Austin State University*

Ian Wishaw, *University of Lethbridge*

Michael Zicker, *Bowling Green University*

About the Authors

Les Sdorow was chairperson of the Department of Psychology at Arcadia University (formerly Beaver College). He received his B.A. from Wilkes College and his M.A. and Ph.D. from Hofstra University. He was chairperson of the Department of Behavioral Science at St. Francis College (Pa.) and the Department of Psychology at Allentown College (now DeSales University). Les was named Outstanding Educator at St. Francis College and Teacher of the Year at Allentown College. He also cofounded (with the late Richmond Johnson of Moravian College) the Annual Lehigh Valley Undergraduate Psychology Research Conference (one of the oldest such conferences in North America) and served as president of the Pennsylvania Society of Behavioral Medicine and Biofeedback. Les's research interests were in psychophysiology, sport psychology, and health psychology. His main teaching interests included introductory psychology, research methods, sport psychology, health psychology, and history of psychology. Les made numerous presentations on the teaching of psychology at local, regional, and national conferences. He also was invited to contribute a chapter to the first book published by NITOP (2005), *Voices of Experience: Memorable Talks from the National Institute on the Teaching of Psychology,* copublished by the American Psychological Society.

Cheryl A. Rickabaugh is Professor of Psychology at the University of Redlands. She received her B.A. from California State University, Los Angeles, and her M.A. and Ph.D. in social-personality psychology at the University of California, Riverside. She has received two Outstanding Faculty Awards for teaching during her 26 years at the University of Redlands. Cheryl teaches introductory psychology, research methods, social psychology, and psychology of gender, in addition to a travel abroad course, Jews, Muslims & Basques: Their sociocultural contributions to Spain. She also teaches an interdisciplinary course—women, wellness, and sport—in the University of Redlands Women and Gender Studies program. She has published research in social psychology, health psychology, psychology of gender, and the teaching of undergraduate psychology, and is the author of *Sex and Gender: Student Projects and Exercises*, 2nd ed. (2005). Believing that one is never too old to learn, she is taking Spanish classes at the University of Redlands and El Instituto de Cervantes. She lives in Spain during her summer breaks.

Adrienne J. Betz is a member of the Department of Psychology at Quinnipiac University. She received her B.A. from University of Connecticut in psychology. Her M.A. and Ph.D., also from University of Connecticut, were in behavioral neuroscience in the Psychology Department under the supervision of John D. Salamone. After receiving her Ph.D., she was a post-doctoral and associate at Yale School of Medicine in molecular psychiatry under the supervision of Jane R. Taylor. She is currently the Director of Behavioral Neuroscience at Quinnipiac University and organizes a regional neuroscience conference, NEURON, which supports undergraduate and graduate research in neuroscience. Adrienne's main teaching interests include physiological psychology, senior thesis and research methods in behavioral neuroscience. Her research, published in journals such as *Psychopharmacology, Frontiers in Behavioral Neuroscience, Neuroscience, Pharmacology,* and *Biochemistry & Behavior,* focuses on changes that occur in the brain after experiencing stress.

The Nature of Psychology

On April 20, 1999, Americans were horrified when two students went on a shooting rampage at Columbine High School in Jefferson County, Colorado. The students were Eric Harris, age 18, and Dylan Klebold, age 17. Armed with pistols, rifles, shotguns, and homemade bombs they held their fellow students and teachers hostage. Over the course of several hours, they systematically killed one teacher and 12 students and wounded 23 other students. The two then committed suicide. It took days for the police to defuse about 30 bombs Harris and Klebold had planted in the school to maim or kill would-be rescuers. Harris and Klebold were members of a group known as the Trench Coat Mafia, an "anti-jock" group of students who always wore black clothing and ridiculed students who conformed to traditional social norms.

The issue of school violence has become a pervasive one in the United States. The Columbine High School incident was but one in a series of similar incidents at schools in towns such as Pearl, Mississippi; West Paducah, Kentucky; Jonesboro, Arkansas; and Springfield, Oregon. In 2007, the fatal shooting of 32 people by a student at Virginia Tech University became the largest school massacre in American history. School violence of all kinds is of concern to psychologists. What would lead two intelligent teenagers from apparently stable, affluent families to commit a heinous act like the one at Columbine High School? How can we prevent other incidents like it? How can we help survivors cope with such incidents? The Columbine massacre, for example, led school districts across the United States to ask school psychologists to develop violence-prevention programs and crisis counseling programs for those affected by school violence (Crepeau-Hobson, Filaccio, & Gottfried, 2005).

The science of *psychology* seeks answers to questions about violence and all other aspects of human and animal behavior. Can the effects of brain damage be overcome by the transplantation of brain tissue? Do attachment patterns in infancy predict attachment patterns in adolescent and adult dating relationships? Do eyewitnesses give accurate testimony? Can chimpanzees learn to use language? Do lie detectors really detect lies? Is there a heart-attack-prone personality? What factors promote interpersonal attraction? These are some of the many questions about human and animal behavior answered in this book.

But what is psychology? The word *psychology* was coined in the 16th century from the Greek terms *psyche,* meaning "soul" or "mind," and *logos,* meaning "the study of a subject." Thus, the initial meaning of *psychology* was "the study of the soul or mind"

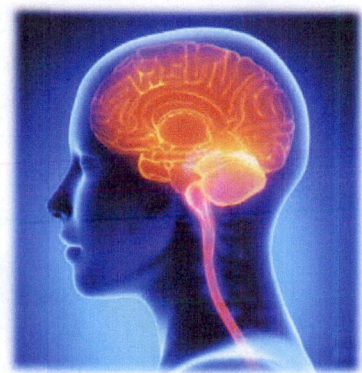

Source: CLIPAREA/Custom media/Shutterstock.com.

Chapter Outline

The Historical Context of Psychology

Contemporary Perspectives in Psychology

The Scope of Psychology

(Brozek, 1999). This definition reflected the early interest of theologians in topics that are now considered the province of psychologists. Psychology has continued to be defined by its subject matter, which has changed over time. By the late 19th century, when psychology emerged as a science, it had become "the Science of Mental Life" (James, 1890/1981, Vol. 1, p. 15).

Beginning in the 1910s, many psychologists—believing that a true science could study only directly observable, measurable events—abandoned the study of the mind in favor of the study of overt behavior. Psychologists moved from studying mental experiences, such as thirst or anger, to studying their observable manifestations, such as drinking or aggression. Consequently, by the 1920s, psychology was commonly defined as "the scientific study of behavior." This definition was dominant until the 1960s, when there was a revival of interest in studying the mind. As a result, **psychology** is now more broadly defined as "the science of behavior and cognitive processes."

psychology The science of behavior and cognitive processes.

What makes psychology a science? Psychology is a science because it relies on the *scientific method* (Holmes & Beins, 2009). Sciences are "scientific" because they share a common method, not because they share a common subject matter. Physics, chemistry, biology, and psychology differ in what they study, yet each uses the scientific method. Whereas a biochemist might use the scientific method to study the unhealthful effects of toxic pollutants on plants or animals, a psychologist might use it to study the behavior or cognitive experiences of a person suffering from severe depression. The role of the scientific method in psychology is discussed at length in Chapter 2.

The Historical Context of Psychology

Psychologists stress the importance of knowing the history of their discipline, with the vast majority of academic psychology departments offering a course devoted to the history of psychology (Fuchs & Viney, 2002). Like any other science, psychology has evolved over time. It has been influenced by developments in other disciplines and by its social, cultural, and historical contexts. To appreciate the state of psychology today, you should understand its origins (Danziger, 1994).

The Roots of Psychology

Psychology's historical roots are in philosophy and science. When psychologists of the late 19th century began to use the scientific method to study the mind, psychology became an independent scientific discipline (Hatfield, 2002). Though scientists and philosophers alike rely on systematic observation and reasoning as sources of knowledge, philosophers rely more on reasoning. For example, a philosopher might use reasoning to argue whether we are ever truly altruistic (that is, completely unselfish) in helping other people, whereas a psychologist might approach this issue by studying the cognitive, emotional and situational factors that determine the circumstances in which one person will help another (see Chapter 17).

The Philosophical Roots of Psychology

The philosophical roots of psychology reach back to the philosophers of ancient Greece, most notably Plato (c. 428–347 B.C.) and his pupil Aristotle (384–322 B.C.), who were especially interested in the origin of knowledge. Plato noted that our senses can deceive us, as in illusions such as the apparent bending of a straight stick partly immersed in a pool of water. Downplaying knowledge gained through the senses,

Plato (c. 428-347 B. C.)

Plato introduced the concepts of nativism and rationalism.
Source: Antonio Abrignani/ Shutterstock.com.

Plato believed that people enter the world with inborn knowledge—a philosophical position called **nativism.** Plato also believed that we can gain access to inborn knowledge through reasoning, a philosophical position called **rationalism.**

Though Aristotle accepted the importance of reasoning, he was more willing than Plato to accept sensory experience as a source of knowledge—a philosophical position called **empiricism.** Yet, he recognized the frailty of sensory data, as in "Aristotle's illusion." To experience this illusion for yourself, cross a middle finger over an index finger and run a pen between them. You will feel two pens instead of one. Aristotle was one of the first thinkers to speculate on psychological topics, as indicated by the titles of his works, including *On Dreams, On Sleep and Sleeplessness, On Memory and Reminiscence,* and *On the Senses and the Sensed.*

During the early Christian and medieval eras, answers to psychological questions were given more often by theologian philosophers than by secular philosophers like Plato or Aristotle. The dominant Western authority was Saint Augustine (354–430), who lived almost all of his life in what is now Algeria. Augustine wrote of his views on memory, emotion, and motivation in the self-analysis he presented in his classic autobiographical *Confessions.* He also speculated extensively on the nature of dreams (Sirridge, 2005) and anticipated Sigmund Freud by providing insight into the continual battle between our human reason and our animal passions, especially the powerful sex drive (Gay, 1986).

During the Middle Ages, when the Christian West was guided largely by religious dogma and those who dared to conduct empirical studies risked punishment, scientific research became almost the sole province of Islamic intellectuals. The most noteworthy of these was the Persian scientist, physician, and philosopher Abu Ibn Sina (980–1037)—better known in the West as Avicenna—who kept alive the teachings of Aristotle (Afnan, 1958/1980). Avicenna also contributed to our knowledge of medicine, even putting forth a theory of the cause of migraine headaches similar to one of the most influential theories today (Abokrysha, 2009). With the revival of Western intellectual activity in the late Middle Ages, scholars who had access to Arabic translations of the Greek philosophers rediscovered Aristotle. But most of these scholars limited their efforts to reconciling Aristotle's ideas with Christian teachings.

With the coming of the Renaissance, extending from the 14th to the 17th centuries, Western authorities once again relied less on theology and more on philosophy to provide answers to psychological questions. The spirit of the Renaissance inspired René Descartes (1596–1650), the great French philosopher-mathematician-scientist. Descartes, the first of the modern rationalists, insisted that we should doubt everything that is not proven to be self-evident by our own reasoning. In fact, in his famous statement, "I think, therefore I am," Descartes went to the extreme of using reasoning to prove to his own satisfaction that he existed. Descartes contributed to the modern intellectual outlook, which opposes blind acceptance of proclamations put forth by authorities— religious, political, scientific, or otherwise—unless they are supported by logical arguments (Kisner, 2005). Church leaders felt so threatened by Descartes's challenge to their authority that they put his works on their list of banned books.

Other intellectuals, though favoring empiricism instead of rationalism, joined Descartes in rejecting the authority of theologians to provide answers to scientific questions. Chief among these thinkers was the English politician-philosopher-scientist Francis Bacon (1561–1626). Bacon inspired the modern scientific attitude that favors skepticism, systematic observation, and verification of scientific claims by other observers (Hearnshaw, 1985). He also was a founder of applied science, which seeks practical applications of research findings. In support of applied science, Bacon asserted, "to be useless is to be worthless." Ironically, his interest in the application of scientific findings might have cost him his life. While studying the possible use of refrigeration to preserve food, he experimented by stuffing a chicken with snow in frigid weather—and came down with a fatal case of pneumonia.

Following in Francis Bacon's empiricist footsteps was the English philosopher John Locke (1632–1704). According to Locke (borrowing a concept from Aristotle), each of us is born with a blank slate—or *tabula rasa*—on which are written the life experiences

nativism The philosophical position that heredity provides individuals with inborn knowledge and abilities.

rationalism The philosophical position that true knowledge comes through correct reasoning.

empiricism The philosophical position that true knowledge comes through the senses.

René Descartes (1596–1650)

René Descartes was the first of the modern rationalists.
Source: Georgios Kollidas/Shutterstock.com.

Francis Bacon (1561–1626)

Francis Bacon inspired the modern scientific attitude that favors skepticism, systematic observation, and verification of scientific claims by other observers.
Source: Georgios Kollidas/Shutterstock.com.

John Locke (1632–1704)

According to John Locke, each of us is born with a blank slate, or *tabula rasa.*
Source: Georgios Kollidas/ Shutterstock.com.

Hermann von Helmholtz (1821–1894)

Through experimentation, Hermann von Helmholtz developed pioneering theories on vision and hearing.
Source: Nicku/Shutterstock.com.

psychophysics The study of the relationship between the physical characteristics of stimuli and the conscious psychological experiences that are associated with them.

we acquire through our senses. Whereas nativists such as Descartes believe that much of our knowledge is inborn, empiricists such as Locke believe that knowledge is acquired solely through life experiences (Gaukroger, 2009). Concern about the relative importance of heredity and life experiences is known as the *nature versus nurture* issue.

Because Locke's views were incompatible with the belief in the inborn right of certain people to be rulers over others, you can appreciate why Locke's writings helped inspire the American and French Revolutions. The nature versus nurture issue, a recurring theme in psychological theory and research, appears later in this book in discussions about a host of topics, including language, intelligence, personality, and psychological disorders.

The German philosopher Immanuel Kant (1724–1804) offered a compromise between Descartes's extreme rationalism and Locke's extreme empiricism. Kant was the ultimate "ivory tower" intellectual, never marrying and devoting his life to philosophical pursuits. Despite his international acclaim, he never left his home province—and probably never saw an ocean or a mountain (Paulsen, 1899/1963).

Kant taught that knowledge is the product of inborn cognitive faculties that organize and interpret sensory input from the physical environment (Slife, 2005). For example, though your ability to speak a language depends on inborn brain mechanisms, the specific language you speak (whether English or another) depends on experience with your native tongue (Newcombe, 2002).

The Physiological Roots of Psychology

By the 19th century, physiologists were making progress in answering questions about the nature of psychological processes that philosophers were having difficulty answering. As a consequence, intellectuals began to look more and more to physiology for guidance in the study of psychological topics. For example, in the mid 19th century, popular belief, based on reasoning, held that nerve impulses travel the length of a nerve as fast as electricity travels along a wire—that is, almost instantaneously—and were too fast to measure. This claim was contradicted by research conducted by the German physiologist Hermann von Helmholtz (1821–1894), one of the premier scientists of the 19th century (Cahan, 2006). In studying nerve impulses, Helmholtz found that they took a measurable fraction of a second to travel along a nerve. In one experiment, he had participants release a telegraph key as soon as they felt a touch on the foot or thigh. A device recorded their reaction time. Participants reacted more slowly to a touch on the foot than to a touch on the thigh. Helmholtz attributed this difference to the longer distance that nerve impulses must travel from the foot to the spinal cord and then on to the brain. This experiment indicated that nerve impulses are not instantaneous. In fact, Helmholtz found that human nerve impulses traveled at the relatively slow speed of 50 to 100 meters per second. Chapter 5 describes Helmholtz's pioneering theories on the psychology of vision and hearing.

Helmholtz's scientific contemporaries made important discoveries about brain functions that likewise could not have been discovered by philosophical speculation. The leading brain researcher was the French physiologist Pierre Flourens (1794–1867), the founder of scientific research on the localization of brain functions (Pearce, 2009). He found, for example, that damage to the cerebellum, a large structure at the back of the brain, caused motor incoordination. Animals with damage to the cerebellum would walk as though they were drunk. This study led him to conclude, correctly, that the cerebellum helps regulate the coordination of movements.

Other 19th-century scientists were more interested in the scientific study of cognitive processes apart from the brain structures that served them. The most notable of these researchers was the German mystic-physician-scientist Gustav Fechner (1801–1887). In his scientific research, Fechner used the methods of **psychophysics**, which was the intellectual offspring of the German physicist Ernst Weber (1795–1878), whose writings influenced Fechner (Marshall, 1990). Fechner, inspired to do so by a daydream, used psychophysical methods to quantify the relationship between physical stimulation and the mental experience of sensation (Heidelberger, 2004).

Psychophysics considers questions such as these: How much change in the intensity of a light is necessary for a person to experience a change in its brightness? And how much change in the intensity of a sound is necessary for a person to experience a change in its loudness? Psychophysics contributed to psychology's maturation from being a child of philosophy and physiology to being an independent discipline with its own subject matter, and it has had important applications. For example, the researchers who perfected television relied on psychophysics to determine the relationship between physical characteristics of the television picture and the viewer's mental experience of qualities such as color and brightness (Baldwin, 1954).

Psychologists of the late 19th century also were influenced by the theory of evolution put forth by the English naturalist Charles Darwin (1809–1882). Darwin announced his theory in *The Origin of Species* (Darwin, 1859/1975), which described the results of research he conducted while studying the plants and animals he encountered during a five-year voyage around the world on HMS *Beagle*. Though thinkers as far back as ancient Greece had proposed that existing animals had evolved from common ancestors, Darwin, along with fellow English naturalist Alfred Russell Wallace (Padian, 2008), was the first to propose a process that could account for it. According to Darwin, through *natural selection* physical characteristics that promote the survival of the individual are more likely to be passed on to offspring because individuals with these characteristics are more likely to live long enough to reproduce.

Darwin's theory had its most immediate impact on psychology through the work of his cousin, the English scientist Francis Galton (1822–1911). In applying Darwin's theory of evolution, Galton argued that natural selection could account for the development of human abilities. Moreover, he claimed that individuals with the most highly developed abilities, such as vision and hearing, would be the most likely to survive long enough to reproduce. This belief led him to found the field of **differential psychology** (Buss, 1976), which studies variations among people in physical, personality, and intellectual attributes. Galton's impact on the study of intelligence is discussed in Chapter 10.

differential psychology
The field of psychology that studies individual differences in physical, personality, and intellectual characteristics.

Differential psychology was introduced to North America by the psychologist James McKeen Cattell (1860–1944), who studied with Galton in England. In 1890 Cattell coined the term *mental test,* which he used to describe various tests of vision, hearing, and physical skills that he administered to his students. After being banished from academia for opposing America's entrance into World War I, Cattell started his own business, the Psychological Corporation, which to this day is a leader in the development of tests that assess abilities, intelligence, and personality. Thus, Cattell was a pioneer in the development of psychology as both a science and a profession (Landy, 1997).

The Founding Schools of Psychology

James McKeen Cattell became the first psychology professor in the world (that is, he was the first person to hold such a position independent of an academic biology or philosophy department) when he took a position at the University of Pennsylvania in 1889. Because he assumed his professorship more than a century ago, this supports a remark made by Hermann Ebbinghaus (1850–1909), a pioneer in psychology: "Psychology has a long past, but only a short history" (quoted in Boring, 1950, p. ix). By this, Ebbinghaus meant that though intellectuals have been interested in psychological topics since the era of ancient Greece, psychology did not become a separate discipline until the late 19th century.

Psychologists commonly attribute the founding of this new discipline to the German physiologist Wilhelm Wundt (1832–1920). In 1875 Wundt set up a psychology laboratory at the University of Leipzig in a small room that had served as a dining hall for impoverished students. Wundt's request for a more impressive laboratory had been rejected by the school's administrators, who did not want to promote a science they believed would drive students crazy by encouraging them to scrutinize the contents of their minds (Hilgard, 1987). Beginning in 1879 Wundt's laboratory became the site of formal research conducted by many students who later became some of the most renowned psychologists in the world. Wundt and his students conducted research on topics such as attention, sensation, and reaction time.

Wilhelm Wundt (1832–1920)

Wilhelm Wundt established the first psychology laboratory at the University of Leipzig in 1875.
Source: Nicku/Shutterstock.com.

More than 30 American psychologists, including Cattell, took their PhDs with Wundt (Benjamin, Durkin, Link, Vestal, & Acord, 1992). These students also included G. Stanley Hall (1846–1924), who founded the American Psychological Association in 1892. The growth of the new science was marked by the rise of competing intellectual schools of psychology championed by charismatic leaders, who often were trained in both philosophy and physiology. The earliest schools were *structuralism* and *functionalism.*

Structuralism

structuralism The early psychological viewpoint that sought to identify the components of the conscious mind.

The first approach—**structuralism**—arose in the late 19th century, championed by European psychologists inspired by the efforts of biologists, chemists, and physicists to analyze matter into cells, molecules, and atoms. Following the lead of these scientists, structuralists tried to analyze the mind into its component elements and discover how the elements interact. Structuralism was named and popularized by Wundt's student Edward Titchener (1867–1927). Titchener, an Englishman, introduced structuralism to the United States after receiving his PhD from Wundt in 1892 and then joining the faculty of Cornell University later that year.

analytic introspection A research method in which highly trained participants report the contents of their conscious mental experiences.

To study the mind, he had his participants use **analytic introspection,** a procedure aimed at analyzing complex mental experiences into what he believed were the three basic mental elements: images, feelings, and sensations. In a typical study using analytic introspection, Titchener would present a participant with a stimulus (for example, a repetitious sound produced by a metronome) and then ask the participant to report the images, feelings, and sensations evoked by it. Based on his research, Titchener concluded that there were more than 40,000 mental elements, with the great majority of them visual in nature (Lieberman, 1979).

Among Titchener's contributions was research on the sense of taste, which found that even complex tastes are mixtures of the four basic tastes of sour, sweet, salty, and bitter (Webb, 1981). Despite Titchener's renown, structuralism declined in its influence. This decline was, in part, because structuralism was limited to the laboratory. In fact, Titchener frowned on psychologists who tried to apply the new science of psychology to everyday life (White, 1994).

But the demise of structuralism owed more to its reliance on introspection, which limited it to the study of conscious mental experience in relatively intelligent adults with strong verbal skills. Psychologists also found introspection to be unreliable, because introspective reports in response to a particular stimulus by a given participant were inconsistent from one presentation of the stimulus to another. Similarly, introspective reports in response to the same stimulus were inconsistent from one participant to another. Though the shortcomings of analytic introspection made it fade into oblivion, some psychologists today rely on the related research procedure of having their participants give verbal reports of their mental experience—without necessarily trying to analyze them into their components.

Functionalism

functionalism The early psychological viewpoint that studied how the conscious mind helps the individual adapt to the environment.

Functionalism arose in America chiefly as a response to structuralism. Functionalists criticized the structuralists for limiting themselves to analyzing the contents of the mind. The functionalists preferred, instead, to study how the mind affects what people do. Whereas structuralists might study the mental components of tastes, functionalists might study how the ability to distinguish different tastes affects behavior. This approach reflected the influence of Darwin's theory of evolution, which stressed the role of inherited characteristics in helping the individual adapt to the environment. The functionalists assumed that the mind evolved because it promoted the survival of the individual. Your conscious mind permits you to evaluate your current circumstances and select the best course of action to adapt to them. Recall a time when you tasted food that had gone bad. You quickly spit it out, vividly demonstrating the functional value of the sense of taste.

The most prominent functionalist was the American psychologist and philosopher William James (1842–1910). In his approach to psychology, James viewed the mind as a stream, which, like a stream of water, cannot be meaningfully broken down into discrete elements. Thus, he believed that the mind—or *stream of consciousness*—is not suited to the kind of analytic study favored by structuralists. In 1875, the same year that Wundt established his laboratory at Leipzig, James established a psychology laboratory at Harvard University. But unlike Wundt, James used the laboratory for demonstrations, not for experiments. Instead, he urged psychologists to study how people function in the world outside the laboratory. James and Wundt were so influential that a survey of several major Canadian universities found that half of their psychology faculty members could trace their intellectual lineage through key faculty members back to one of the two (Lubek, Innis, Kroger, McGuire, Stam, & Herrmann, 1995).

Though he conducted few experiments, James made several contributions to psychology. His classic textbook, *The Principles of Psychology* (James, 1890/1981), highlighted the interrelationship of philosophy, physiology, and psychology. The book is so interesting, informative, and beautifully written that it is one of the few psychology books more than a century old still in print. An abridged version of the book, *Psychology: Briefer Course* (James, 1892/1985), became a leading introductory psychology textbook. William James also contributed a theory of emotion (discussed in Chapter 12) that is still influential today (Palencik, 2007). And his views influenced later theories and research in self psychology (Coon, 2000), which is discussed in Chapter 13.

As a group, the functionalists broadened the range of subjects used in psychological research by including animals, children, and people with psychological disorders. The functionalists also expanded the subject matter of psychology to include such topics as memory, thinking, and personality. And unlike the structuralists, who limited their research to the laboratory, the functionalists, in the tradition of Francis Bacon, applied their research to everyday life. The functionalist John Dewey (1859–1952) applied psychology to the improvement of educational practices and remains an influential intellectual figure in educational and developmental psychology (Fallace, 2010). The functionalist who founded the field of applied psychology itself was Hugo Münsterberg (1863–1916), who became a tragic figure in the history of psychology.

In 1892 William James, tiring of the demands of running the psychology laboratory at Harvard, hired Münsterberg, who had earned his PhD under Wilhelm Wundt in 1885 and had become a renowned German psychologist, to take over the laboratory. Münsterberg quickly gained stature in America. During the first decade of the 20th century, Münsterberg was second only to James in his fame as a psychologist. Ironically, though he was hired to run the Harvard psychology laboratory, Münsterberg's main contributions were in applied psychology (Van de Water, 1997). He conducted research, wrote books, and gave talks describing how psychology could be applied to law, industry, education, psychotherapy, and even the study of motion pictures (Bruno, 2009). But Münsterberg experienced extreme stress after being ostracized by his colleagues for trying to promote good relations between America and Germany during the years leading up to World War I (Spillmann & Spillmann, 1993). He died after suffering a stroke he experienced during a class lecture. Because Münsterberg and his functionalist colleagues dared to move psychology out of the laboratory and into the everyday world, they felt the wrath of structuralists, such as Titchener, who insisted that psychology could be a science only if it remained in the laboratory. Titchener established an organization called the Society of Experimentalists in part as a reaction against what he and his supporters saw as the American Psychological Association's movement away from the laboratory (Goodwin, 1985). Despite Titchener's criticisms, most psychologists today would applaud William James and the functionalists for increasing the kinds of research topics, methods, participants, and settings in psychological research (Yanchar, 1997).

James also helped open the door for the entry of women into the discipline of psychology. Most notably, he championed the career of Mary Whiton Calkins (1863–1930), the first prominent female psychologist. In 1903 Calkins, along with Margaret Floy Washburn, the leading animal psychologist of her time, and Christine Ladd-Franklin, who put forth an early theory of color vision, was included in James McKeen Cattell's influential list of the 50 most eminent American psychologists (O'Connell & Russo, 1990). But being one of James's students did not guarantee Calkins an easy path to a career as a psychologist (Furumoto, 1980).

Though Harvard did not permit women to enroll as matriculated students, Calkins's father, an influential Protestant minister, convinced its president to permit Calkins to audit courses. In her autobiography, Calkins describes being the only student in a course with William James (Calkins, 1930). Evidently, the male students dropped the course rather than attending it with a woman. Though Calkins completed all the coursework and the doctoral dissertation required for a doctoral degree, Harvard's administration refused the recommendation of her faculty sponsor, Hugo Münsterberg, that she be awarded the PhD in 1896. James had even called her oral defense of her doctoral dissertation "the most brilliant examination for the PhD that we have had at Harvard." Psychologists and student activists have continued to submit proposals to the Harvard administration for a posthumous PhD to be awarded to Calkins but to date have not been successful (Boatwright & Nolan, 2005).

Despite never receiving her doctorate, Calkins became a successful psychologist. She founded the psychology laboratory at Wellesley College, began the scientific study of dreams, invented the paired-associate technique of assessing memory, and wrote one of the first introductory psychology textbooks (Calkins, 1901). She spent most of her career developing her theory of self psychology, which viewed psychology as the empirical study of the person in conscious interaction with the environment (McDonald, 2007). In 1905 she became the first female president of the American Psychological Association. In 1918, Calkins, also a renowned philosopher, became the first female president of the American Philosophical Association. Calkins would be pleased that today many women earn doctoral degrees in psychology each year. In fact, more women than men now earn doctoral degrees in psychology (Denmark, 1998).

The Growth of Psychology

Structuralism and functionalism were soon joined by other intellectual schools of psychology, which included *Gestalt psychology, psychoanalysis,* and *behaviorism.* These schools broadened the subject matter, methodology, and applications of psychology. Though they were somewhat influenced by structuralism and functionalism, they became more influential than those two founding schools.

Gestalt Psychology

Gestalt psychology The early psychological viewpoint that claimed that we perceive and think about wholes rather than simply combinations of separate elements.

The structuralists' attempt to analyze the mind into its component parts was countered by the German psychologist Max Wertheimer (1880–1943), who founded **Gestalt psychology**. Wertheimer used the word *gestalt,* meaning "form" or "shape," to underscore his belief that we perceive wholes rather than combinations of individual elements. A famous tenet of Gestalt psychology asserts that "the whole is different from the sum of its parts" (Wertheimer & King, 1994). Because of this basic assumption, Wertheimer ridiculed structuralism as "brick-and-mortar psychology" for its attempt to analyze mental experience into discrete elements.

phi phenomenon Apparent motion caused by the presentation of different visual stimuli in rapid succession.

The founding of Gestalt psychology can be traced to a train trip taken by Wertheimer in 1912, when he daydreamed about the **phi phenomenon**, which involves seeing apparent motion in the absence of actual motion (as in a motion picture at a movie theater). At a stop, Wertheimer left the train and bought a toy stroboscope, which, like a motion picture, produces the illusion of movement by rapidly presenting a series of pictures that are slightly different from one another. On returning to his laboratory, he continued studying the phi phenomenon by using a more sophisticated device called a tachistoscope, which flashes visual stimuli for a fraction of a second. Wertheimer had the tachistoscope flash two lines in succession, first a vertical one and then a horizontal one. When the interval between flashes was just right, a single line appeared to move from a vertical to a horizontal orientation.

According to Wertheimer, the phi phenomenon shows that the mind does not respond passively to discrete stimuli, but instead organizes stimuli into coherent wholes. Thus, perception is more than a series of individual sensations. This conclusion is in keeping with Immanuel Kant's notion of the mind as an active manipulator of environmental input. If your mind only responded passively to discrete stimuli, when you observed Wertheimer's tachistoscope demonstration, you would first see the vertical line appear and disappear and then see the horizontal line appear and disappear. Gestalt psychology gave a new direction to psychology by stressing the active role of the mind in organizing sensations into meaningful wholes (Feest, 2007).

Though Wertheimer founded Gestalt psychology, it was popularized by his colleagues Kurt Koffka (1886–1941), the most prolific and influential writer among the Gestalt psychologists, and Wolfgang Köhler (1887–1967), who promoted Gestalt psychology as a natural science (Henle, 1993) and applied it to the study of problem solving. Koffka and Köhler introduced Gestalt psychology to the United States after fleeing Nazi Germany. Köhler, a Christian college professor, had provoked the Nazis by writing and speaking out against their persecution of his Jewish colleagues (Henle, 1978). He became a respected psychologist and in 1959 was elected president of the American Psychological Association.

Psychoanalysis

Unlike the other early approaches to psychology, which originated in universities, **psychoanalysis** originated in medical science. Sigmund Freud (1856–1939), the founder of psychoanalysis, was an Austrian neurologist who considered himself "a conquistador of the mind" (Gay, 1988). Freud noted that his theory, which views the human species as animals first and foremost, owed a debt to Darwin's theory of evolution. Psychoanalysis grew, in part, from Freud's attempts to treat patients suffering from physical symptoms, such as paralyzed legs, inability to speak, or loss of body sensations, that had no apparent physical causes. Based on his treatment of patients suffering from such symptoms of *conversion hysteria,* Freud concluded that the disorder was the result of unconscious psychological conflicts about sex caused by early sexual trauma or cultural prohibitions against sexual enjoyment (Guttman, 2006). These conflicts were "converted" into the physical symptoms seen in conversion hysteria, which might even provide the patient with an excuse to avoid engaging in the taboo behaviors.

Freud's case studies led him to infer that unconscious conflicts, usually related to repressed sexual or aggressive feelings that might elicit disapproval from one's self or others, were prime motivators of human behavior. Freud believed that all behavior—whether

psychoanalysis The early school of psychology that emphasized the importance of unconscious causes of behavior.

"It goes back to being pulled out of the hat."

Psychoanalysis

Sigmund Freud established psychoanalysis.

Source: Cartoonresource/Shutterstock.com.

psychic determinism
The Freudian assumption that all human behavior is influenced by unconscious motives.

normal or abnormal—was influenced by psychological motives, often unconscious ones. This belief is called **psychic determinism.** In his book *The Psychopathology of Everyday Life,* Freud (1901/2011) explained how even apparently unintentional behaviors could be explained by psychic determinism. Psychic determinism explains misstatements, popularly known as "Freudian slips," that arise when an unconscious wish overcomes the desire not to reveal it, as in the case of the radio announcer who began a bread commercial by saying, "For the breast in bed . . . I mean, for the best in bread . . . ." As a leading psychologist observed, the concept of psychic determinism meant that "the forgotten lunch engagement, the slip of the tongue, the barked shin could no longer be dismissed as accident" (Bruner, 1956, p. 465).

In addition to shocking the public of the Victorian era by claiming that people are motivated chiefly by unconscious—often sexual—motives, Freud made the controversial claim that early childhood experiences were the most important factors in personality development. Freud believed that memories of early childhood experiences stored in the unconscious mind continue to affect behavior throughout one's life. According to Freud, these unconscious influences explain the irrationality of much human behavior and the origins of psychological disorders.

Freudian psychoanalysis was so extraordinarily influential that a survey of chairs of graduate psychology departments found that they considered Freud to be the most important figure in psychology's first century (Davis, Thomas, & Weaver, 1982). Nonetheless, critics have pointed out that the unconscious mind can be too easily used to explain any behavior for which there is no obvious cause. William James had expressed this concern even before Freud's views had become known. James warned that the unconscious "is the sovereign means for believing whatever one likes in psychology and of turning what might become a science into a tumbling ground for whimsies" (James, 1890/1981,Vol.1, p.166).

Psychoanalysis also has been subjected to criticism for failing to provide adequate research evidence for its claims of the importance of sexual motives, unconscious processes, and early childhood experiences (Dufresne, 2007). Other critics claim that Freud's theory focuses on the male experience and thus has less relevance to women's lives (Masling, Bornstein, Fishman, & Davila, 2002). Moreover, Freud never tested his theory experimentally. Instead, he based his theory on notes written after seeing patients, which made his conclusions subject to his own memory lapses and personal biases. Moreover, Freud violated good scientific practice by generalizing to all people the results of his case studies of a relative handful of people with psychological disorders.

Despite these shortcomings, Freud's views have influenced the psychological study of topics as diverse as dreams, creativity, motivation, development, personality, psychopathology, and psychotherapy. Freud's views have also inspired the works of artists, writers, and filmmakers, including Eugene O'Neill's play *Mourning Becomes Electra* (1931) and the classic science fiction film *Forbidden Planet* (1956). Freud's contributions to a variety of psychological topics are discussed in several other chapters.

The decline of strictly Freudian psychoanalysis began when two of Freud's followers, Carl Jung (1875–1961) and Alfred Adler (1870–1937), developed psychoanalytic theories that contradicted important aspects of Freud's theory. Jung, Adler, and other so-called neo-Freudians placed less emphasis on the biological drives of sex and aggression and more emphasis on the importance of social relationships. Jung developed his own theory of personality, which included the concepts of the inner-directed *introvert* and the outer-directed *extravert.* Adler based his personality theory on his belief that each of us tends to compensate for natural childhood feelings of inferiority by striving for superiority, as in the case of students who study long hours to earn the necessary grades for admission to medical school, or athletes who train for Olympic competition. Other neo-Freudians also contributed to the psychoanalytic approach. Anna Freud (1895–1982), Sigmund Freud's daughter, was a leader in the field of child psychoanalysis, as was her intellectual rival Melanie Klein (1882–1960), who developed the technique of play therapy. The views of influential neo-Freudians are discussed in later chapters, particularly in Chapters 13.

Behaviorism

In 1913 a leading functionalist published an article entitled "Psychology as the Behaviorist Views It." It included the following proclamation:

> Psychology as the behaviorist views it is a purely objective experimental branch of natural science. Its theoretical goal is the prediction and the control of behavior. Introspection forms no essential part of its methods, nor is the scientific value of its data dependent on the readiness with which they lend themselves to interpretation in terms of consciousness. (Watson, 1913, p. 158)

This bold statement by the American psychologist John B. Watson (1878–1958) heralded the rise of **behaviorism**, an approach to psychology that dominated the discipline for half a century. He was influenced by Russian physiologist Ivan Pavlov (1849–1936), whose work he helped introduce to North American psychology (Buckley, 1989). Watson rejected the position shared by structuralists, functionalists, Gestalt psychologists, and psychoanalysts that the mind is the proper object of study for psychology. He and other behaviorists were emphatic in their opposition to the study of mental experience. Though Watson was fascinated by Freud's theory, like William James, he rejected the notion that unconscious cognitive processes could motivate human behavior.

behaviorism The psychological viewpoint that rejects the study of mental processes in favor of the study of overt behavior.

To Watson, the proper subject matter for psychological research was observable behavior. Unlike mental experiences, overt behavior can be recorded and subjected to verification by other scientists. For example, some psychologists might study the mental experience of hunger, but behaviorists would prefer to study the observable behavior of eating. Though Watson denied that cognitive processes could cause behaviors, he did not deny the existence of the mind. Thus, he would not have denied that people have the mental experience called "hunger," but he would have denied that the mental experience of hunger causes eating (Moore, 1990). Instead, he would have favored explanations of eating that placed its causes in the body (such as low blood sugar) or in the environment (such as a tantalizing aroma) instead of in the mind (such as feeling famished or craving a specific food).

Watson impressed his fellow psychologists enough to be elected president of the American Psychological Association in 1915. Watson was an attractive and charismatic person who popularized his brand of psychology by giving speeches and writing books and articles. Though he wrote about both heredity and environment, he placed great faith in the effect of environmental stimuli on the control of behavior, especially children's behavior (Horowitz, 1992). His "stimulus-response" psychology placed him firmly in the empiricist tradition of John Locke and is best expressed in his famous pronouncement on child development:

> Give me a dozen healthy infants, well-formed, and my own specified world to bring them up in and I'll guarantee to take any one at random and train him to become any type of specialist I might select—doctor, lawyer, artist, merchant-chief and, yes, even beggar man and thief, regardless of his talents, penchants, tendencies, abilities, vocations, and race of his ancestors. (Watson, 1930, p. 104)

Apparently, no parents rushed to offer their infants to be trained by Watson. Nonetheless, his views on child rearing became influential. Despite some of their excessive claims, behaviorists injected optimism into psychology by fostering the belief that people are minimally limited by heredity and easily changed by experience. In favoring nurture over nature, behaviorists assumed that people, regardless of their hereditary background, could improve themselves and their positions in life. Watson and his fellow behaviorists were more than willing to suggest ways to bring about such improvements. Watson even hoped to establish a utopian society based on behavioristic principles (Morawski, 1982).

Behaviorism dominated psychology through the 1960s (O'Neil, 1995). In fact, from 1930 to 1960 the term *mind* rarely appeared in psychological research articles (Mueller, 1979). But since then, the mind has returned as a legitimate object of study. The weakened influence of orthodox behaviorism is also shown by renewed respect for the constraints that heredity places on learning (a topic discussed in Chapter 7).

Watson's intellectual descendent was the American psychologist B. F. Skinner (1904–1990). As a young man, Skinner pursued a career as a writer and even spent six months living in Greenwich Village, New York, to soak up its creative Bohemian atmosphere. After discovering that he was not cut out to be a fiction writer and after being excited by the writings of John B. Watson, Skinner decided to become a psychologist (Keller, 1991). Though he eventually became a prominent figure in 20th-century psychology, second only to Sigmund Freud (Rutherford, 2000), it took many years for him to achieve that standing. His landmark book, *The Behavior of Organisms* (which had been published in 1938), sold only 80 copies by the end of World War II in 1945.

Like Watson, Skinner urged psychologists to ignore mental processes and to limit psychology to the study of observable behavior. He and other behaviorists insisted that psychology could not be on a scientific par with other natural sciences if psychologists tried to make it the study of mental experiences. Many behaviorists still refuse to treat verbal reports of mental experiences as appropriate subject matter for psychological research.

In contrast to Watson, Skinner stressed the role of the consequences of behavior, rather than environmental stimuli, in controlling behavior. He noted that animals and people tend to repeat behaviors that are followed by positive consequences. Consider your performance in school. If your studying (a behavior) pays off with an A on an exam (a positive consequence), you will be more likely to study in the future. In Skinner's terms, your behavior has been "positively reinforced."

Skinner, like Watson, was a utopian. In 1948 Skinner—showing that he did, in fact, have the ability to write fiction—published *Walden Two*, a novel that describes an ideal society based on behaviorist principles. In Skinner's utopia, benevolent behaviorists control the citizens by providing positive consequences for desirable behaviors. Several communities, most notably Twin Oaks in Louisa, Virginia, and Los Horcones near Hermosillo, Mexico, were founded on principles presented in *Walden Two* (Kuhlmann, 2005). Though there is still no behavioral utopia, the behavioral perspective has contributed to improvements in education, child rearing, industrial productivity, and therapy for psychological disorders. These topics are discussed in later chapters.

Despite Skinner's efforts, the influence of orthodox behaviorism has faded in recent years in the face of growing dissatisfaction with the lack of attention orthodox behaviorists give to cognitive processes. This dissatisfaction has prompted some behaviorists to study the relationship between cognitive processes such as thoughts or images, which cannot be directly observed, and overt behavior, which can. These psychologists are called cognitive behaviorists. One of their most influential leaders has been Albert Bandura (2001), who has noted that we can learn by observing as well as by doing. The views of Skinner and Bandura are discussed further in Chapter 7. Despite the rise of cognitivism, behaviorism remains a powerful force in psychology (Leigland, 2000).

Table 1-1 summarizes the major characteristics of the early perspectives of psychology.

TABLE 1-1 Major Psychological Perspectives

Perspective	Object of Study	Goal of Study	Method of Study
Structuralism	Conscious experience	Analyzing the structure of the mind	Analytic introspection
Functionalism	Conscious experience	Studying the functions of the mind	Introspection and testing
Gestalt psychology	Conscious experience	Demonstrating the active, holistic nature of the mind	Introspection and demonstrations
Psychoanalysis	Unconscious motivation	Studying unconscious motives of behavior	Clinical case studies
Behaviorism	Observable behavior	Controlling behavior	Observation and experiments

Section Review: The Historical Context of Psychology

1. How did the work of 19th-century scientists lead to the emergence of psychology as a science?

2. What were the contributions of functionalism to psychology?

3. What was Gestalt psychology's main criticism of structuralism?

4. What prompted the emergence of behaviorism?

Contemporary Perspectives in Psychology

According to Thomas Kuhn (1970), an influential philosopher of science, as a science matures, it develops a unifying **scientific paradigm**, or model, that determines its appropriate goals, methods, and subject matter. Though, as you have just read, psychology has been influenced by different approaches, the discipline still lacks a unifying scientific paradigm to which most psychologists would subscribe (Shapiro, 2005). Instead, diverse psychological perspectives exist, in addition to the psychoanalytic, behavioristic, and humanistic perspectives. The past half century has seen the emergence of three highly influential new perspectives—the *humanistic perspective,* the *cognitive perspective,* and the *biopsychological perspective*—as well as, more recently, the *sociocultural perspective.*

scientific paradigm A model that determines the appropriate goals, methods, and subject matter of a science.

The Humanistic Perspective

Because it provided the first important alternative to the highly influential psychoanalytic and behavioral perspectives, the **humanistic perspective** has been called the "third force" in psychology (Cosgrove, 2007). It was founded in the 1950s by the American psychologists Abraham Maslow (1908–1970) and Carl Rogers (1902–1987) to promote the idea that people have free will and are not merely pawns in the hands of unconscious motives or environmental stimuli. Maslow, who served as president of the American Psychological Association in 1967, had begun as a behaviorist but later rejected what he saw as behaviorism's narrow focus on observable behavior and the effects of the environment. He stressed people's natural tendency toward *self-actualization,* which was his term for the fulfillment of one's potentials.

 Rogers echoed Maslow, and both assumed that the subject matter of psychology should be the individual's unique subjective mental experience of the world. In favoring the study of mental experience, Maslow and Rogers showed their intellectual kinship to William James. Though Maslow and Rogers considered subjective mental experience to be one of several important aspects of humanistic psychology, the study of subjective mental experience is the overriding focus of the branch of humanistic psychology called **phenomenological psychology**. For example, phenomenological psychologists might study the mental experience of depression (Slavik & Croak, 2006) as opposed to behaviors exhibited by depressed people or the brain factors or unconscious motives that may underlie depression. And humanistic psychology's assumption that people have free will is central to **existential psychology**. This branch of humanistic psychology favors the study of how people respond to the basic givens of reality, including the responsibility of personal freedom, the isolation of one person from another, the need to find meaning in one's life, and the realization that we eventually will die.

 Humanistic psychology has been a prime mover in the field of psychotherapy, most notably through the efforts of Carl Rogers. His person-centered therapy, one of the chief kinds of psychotherapy, is discussed in Chapter 15. Though person-centered therapy has been the subject of extensive scientific research, other aspects of humanistic psychology, such as techniques that promote personal "growth experiences" and "consciousness raising," have been criticized for having little scientific support (Wertheimer, 1978). This lack of scientific rigor might be

humanistic perspective
The psychological viewpoint that holds that the proper subject matter of psychology is the individual's subjective mental experience of the world.

phenomenological psychology
A branch of humanistic psychology primarily concerned with the study of subjective mental experience.

existential psychology
A branch of humanistic psychology that studies how individuals respond to the basic philosophical issues of life, such as death, meaning, freedom, and isolation.

one reason why humanistic psychology has had only a relatively minor impact on academic psychology, a fact lamented by Rogers (1985) near the end of his life. Despite its scientific shortcomings, humanistic psychology has made a valuable contribution in promoting the study of positive aspects of human experience, including love, altruism, and healthy personality development. Moreover, many humanistic psychologists have become more willing to use experimentation to test their theories (Koole, Greenberg, & Pyszczynski, 2006)

The Cognitive Perspective

In his presidential address to the American Psychological Association, Wolfgang Köhler (1959) urged Gestalt psychologists and behaviorists to create a psychology that included the best aspects of both their schools. Psychologists who favor the *cognitive approach* have followed Köhler's advice, beginning with the "cognitive revolution" in psychology that began in the late 1950s. This revolution was largely provoked by the perceived shortcomings of behaviorism (Proctor & Kim-Phuong, 2006))—leading to the emergence of a **cognitive perspective**, which combines aspects of Gestalt psychology and the behavioral perspective (Simon, 1995). Like Gestalt psychologists, cognitive psychologists stress the active role of the mind in organizing perceptions, thinking, forming memories, and interpreting experiences. And like behavioral psychologists, cognitive psychologists stress the need for objective, well-controlled, laboratory studies. Thus, cognitive psychologists infer the presence of cognitive processes from observable responses without relying on verbal reports alone. But unlike strict behavioral psychologists, who claim that cognitive processes such as thoughts cannot affect behavior, many cognitive psychologists believe they can.

The cognitive perspective is illustrated in the work of the Swiss biologist-psychologist Jean Piaget (1896–1980), who put forth a cognitive theory of the child's mental development based on his interviews with children as they solved various problems. For example, he studied developmental changes in children's understanding of physical causality (Chandler, 2009). Piaget's research is discussed in Chapter 4. The cognitive perspective also has been influenced by the computer revolution that began in the 1950s, which stimulated research on the human brain as an information processor. A leader in this field was Herbert Simon (1916–2001), a psychologist who won the 1978 Nobel Prize in economics, the field in which he worked early in his career (Anderson, 2001). Some cognitive psychologists use computer programs to create models of human thought processes; others use their knowledge of human thought processes to improve computer programs, like those for computer chess games.

Beginning about 1980, the cognitive perspective surpassed the behavioral perspective and the psychoanalytic perspective in its influence on psychology (Robins, Gosling, & Craik, 1999). As you will realize while reading upcoming chapters, the cognitive perspective pervades almost every field of psychology. For example, the concept of cognitive schemas, or specialized knowledge structures, has been applied to the study of human development, memory, thought and language, social behavior, and personality.

The Biopsychological Perspective

Though several of the early approaches to psychology had their roots in 19th-century physiology, until relatively recently there was never a strictly biopsychological approach to psychology. But growing interest in the biological basis of behavior and cognitive processes, combined with the development of sophisticated research equipment, has led to the emergence of a **biopsychological perspective** Psychologists who favor this perspective are interested in studying the brain, the hormonal system, and the effects of heredity on psychological functions. Though most biopsychology researchers rely on animals as subjects, some of their most important studies have used human participants. For example, in the course of surgery on the brains of epilepsy victims to reduce their seizures, the Canadian neurosurgeon Wilder Penfield (1891–1976) mapped the brain by using weak electrical currents to stimulate points on its surface. He found that stimulation of particular points on one side of the brain caused movements of particular body parts on the opposite side.

cognitive perspective
The psychological viewpoint that favors the study of how the mind organizes perceptions, processes information, and interprets experiences.

biopsychological perspective
The psychological viewpoint that stresses the relationship of physiological factors to behavior and mental processes.

One branch of the biopsychological perspective is cognitive neuroscience, which studies topics such as the neurological bases of emotional memory (Labar & Cabeza, 2006), mental giftedness (Kalbfleisch, 2008), and attention deficit hyperactivity disorder (Vaidya & Stollstorff, 2008). Use of functional MRI (fMRI) to provide scans of ongoing brain activity has helped advance research in cognitive neuroscience (Poldrack & Wagner, 2008). In 1981 the American biopsychologist Roger Sperry (1913–1994) was awarded a Nobel Prize for his studies of the functions of the left and right brain hemispheres of epilepsy patients whose hemispheres had been surgically separated to reduce their seizures (Berlucchi, 2006). In conducting research on the brain, Sperry and his colleagues found that each hemisphere was somewhat superior to the other in performing particular psychological functions. Chapter 3 describes the research of Penfield, Sperry, and other contributors to biopsychology. Because of the increasing influence of this perspective, psychology might be moving toward an even broader definition as "the science of behavior and cognitive processes, and the physiological processes underlying them."

Some biopsychologists work in the field of **behavioral genetics**, which studies the relative influence of hereditary and environmental factors on human and animal behavior, such as the genetic bases of autism (Moy & Nadler, 2008) and psychological depression (Crowley & Lucki, 2006). Chapter 3 discusses the use of behavioral genetics in explaining differences in human intelligence and personality. Many of those who study the role of heredity rely on Charles Darwin's theory of evolution as the inspiration for their research. They champion the relatively new approach, based upon Darwinian principles and descended from functionalism, called **evolutionary psychology** (Barker, 2006). For example, evolutionary psychologists interpret some gender differences in social behavior to be the product of natural selection (Nicolson, 2002), in which traits and behaviors that have had survival value for men and women are passed from generation to generation. According to evolutionary psychology, men tend to be more physically aggressive than women in large part because physical aggression has had greater survival value for men than for women. Chapter 3 presents a study by evolutionary psychologist David Buss and his colleagues (1992) on the possible evolutionary basis of gender differences in sexual and emotional jealousy. And Chapter 17 considers evolutionary psychology's explanation of gender differences in the attributes that women and men find attractive in potential romantic partners.

The Sociocultural Perspective

Though Wilhelm Wundt is most famous for founding psychology as a laboratory science, he stressed the importance of considering sociocultural influences on human psychology (Cahan & White, 1992). In fact, his 10-volume *Folk Psychology,* which was published during the years 1900 to 1920, anticipated the **sociocultural perspective**. This perspective has developed as a reaction against what its proponents believe is the unfortunate tendency to presume that psychological research findings, obtained chiefly from research conducted in Europe and North America, are always generalizable to other cultures and other social groups. As two leading sociocultural psychologists have commented:

> The typical psychology text contains hundreds of concepts, terms, and theories . . . Most of these abstractions are used as if it has already been established that they are applicable everywhere. This is a premature if not dangerous assumption to make. (Lonner & Malpass, 1994, p. 2)

Throughout this text you will read about studies that have attempted to determine whether research findings obtained in one culture are, in fact, applicable to other cultures. Also, you will read about studies of the influence of sociocultural variables such as gender, ethnicity, and sexual orientation on the many aspects of human behavior and thought processes studied by psychologists. Harry Triandis (1990), one of the founders of the sociocultural perspective, takes a position that would be favored by functionalists. He suggests that we avoid ethnocentrism (viewing other cultures by using our own as the ideal standard of comparison) and, instead, view each culture as the outcome of attempts by its members to adapt to particular

behavioral genetics
The study of the relative effects of heredity and life experiences on behavior.

evolutionary psychology
The study of the evolution of behavior through natural selection.

sociocultural perspective
The psychological viewpoint that favors the scientific study of human behavior in its sociocultural context.

ecological niches. Then we would realize that, had we been born in another culture, our behavior and our views about what is normal and desirable might fit that culture's norms.

What has accounted for the relatively recent surge of interest in the sociocultural perspective? Perhaps the greatest influence has been the "shrinking" of our planet. Today people on opposite sides of the world can communicate instantly with one another using a variety of means, including telephone, radio, television, and the Internet. Other factors include tourism, immigration, international trade, and ethnic conflict. Thus, it behooves people from different cultures to be less ethnocentric so they can better understand one another.

But supporters of the sociocultural perspective take a variety of approaches to conducting their research. Some study **cross-cultural psychology**. Cross-cultural psychologists employ research methods designed to compare two or more cultures in an attempt to discover the degree to which psychological principles can be generalized across cultures. Cross-cultural psychologists study topics such as sociocultural factors involved in eating habits (Rozin, 2005), attitudes toward psychotherapy (Digiuni, Jones, & Camic, 2013), and psychological disorders such as depression in elderly women and men (Tiedt, 2013). Related to this topic is one of the central issues in cross-cultural psychology: *relativism* versus *universalism*. Whereas relativists stress the importance of identifying psychological differences across cultures and tend to support tolerance of differences, universalists stress the importance of identifying psychological commonalities across cultures and tend to stress universal phenomena.

The sociocultural perspective also has given rise to **multicultural psychology**, which studies psychological similarities and differences across the subcultures that commonly exist within individual countries. For example, the American Psychological Association and the American Counseling Association formally support the desirability of psychological counselors to have multicultural competencies to be able to deal effectively with clients from diverse cultural backgrounds (Cokley & Rosales, 2005).

Other psychologists believe that human behavior and cognitive processes are so molded by culture that we should be most concerned with studying how culture influences human behavior and cognitive processes. This approach is called **cultural psychology**, which includes, for example, research on how culture influences child development (Quintana et al., 2006). A related field, **ethnic psychology**, employs sociocultural methods to describe the experience of members of groups that have been historically underrepresented in psychology. For example, ethnic psychologists Mamie Phipps Clark, Kenneth B. Clark, and William E. Cross Jr. have studied the relationship between African Americans' self-concept and their mental health (Lal, 2002).

cross-cultural psychology An approach that tries to determine the extent to which research findings about human psychology hold true across cultures.

multicultural psychology The field that studies psychological similarities and differences across the subcultures that commonly exist within individual countries.

cultural psychology An approach that studies how cultural factors affect human behavior and mental experience.

ethnic psychology The field that employs culturally appropriate methods to describe the experience of members of groups that historically have been underrepresented in psychology.

Section Review: Contemporary Psychological Perspectives

1. In what way does the cognitive approach combine aspects of Gestalt psychology and behaviorism?

2. What are three areas of interest to psychologists who favor the biopsychological perspective?

3. Why has the sociocultural perspective become influential?

The Scope of Psychology

As psychology has evolved as a science, its fields of specialization have multiplied, and its educational and training requirements have become formalized. Today psychologists work in a wide variety of academic and professional settings (see Figure 1-1). Psychologists are so committed to the study of human behavior that some even study the factors associated with choosing to become an academic psychologist devoted mainly to teaching and research or a professional psychologist devoted mainly to applying psychology in practical settings (Leong, Zachar, Conant, & Tolliver, 2007).

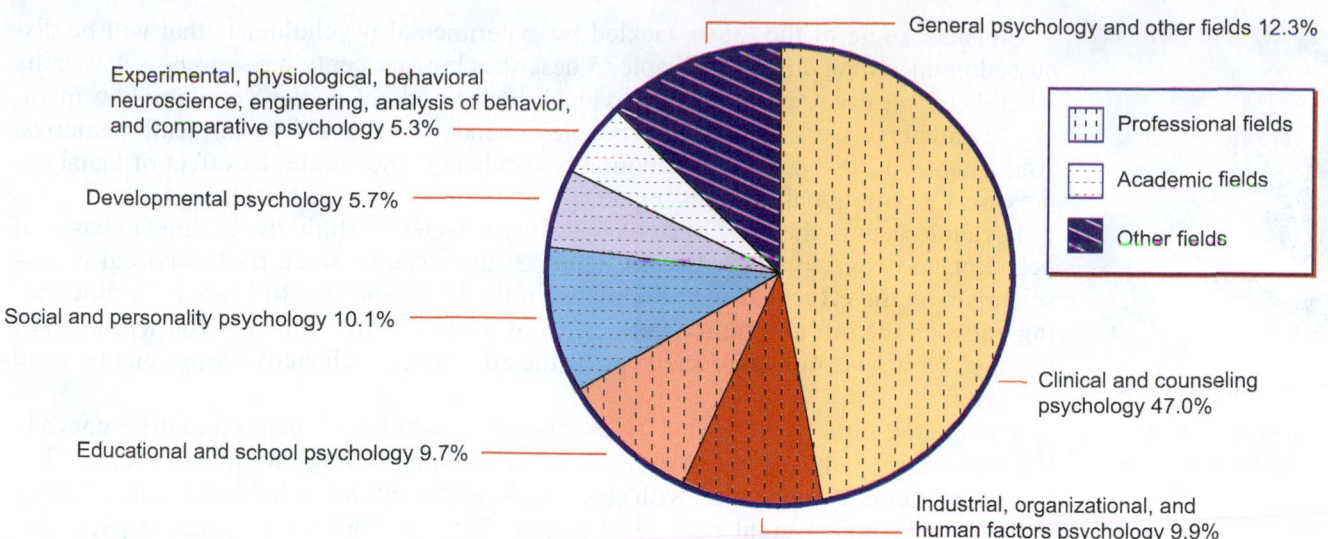

FIGURE 1-1 Fields of Specialization in Psychology

This graph presents the percentages of members of the American Psychological Association working in major fields of specialization.

Source: Data from the American Psychological Association (2014). Division Profiles by Division [Online] http://www.apa.org/about/division/officers/services/profiles.aspx

But how does one go about becoming a psychologist? Psychologists first earn a bachelor's degree, preferably, but not necessarily, in psychology. Earning a master's-level degree takes up to two years of additional schooling. Those who pursue a doctorate (PhD or PsyD) in psychology generally take 6 years or so beyond the bachelor's degree to do so. Those who pursue doctorates in clinical or counseling psychology complete internships and typically write a dissertation based on an original research study that they conduct. Some undergraduate psychology departments offer courses devoted to discussing career options in psychology and planning how to pursue a career in psychology (Macera & Cohen, 2006).

Academic Fields of Specialization

Most of the chapters in this book discuss academic fields of specialization in psychology, usually practiced by psychologists working at colleges or universities. In fact, colleges and universities are the main employment settings for psychologists. Because each field of psychology contains subfields, which in turn contain sub-subfields, a budding psychologist has hundreds of potential specialties from which to choose. For example, a psychologist specializing in the field of sensation and perception might be interested in the subfield of vision, with special interest in the sub-subfield of color vision.

Psychology researchers typically conduct either **basic research**, which is aimed at contributing to knowledge, or **applied research**, which is aimed at solving a practical problem. Note that basic research and applied research are not mutually exclusive, and many psychologists conduct both kinds of research. Findings from basic research can often be applied outside the laboratory. For example, psychologists have taken basic research findings on the interactive effects of alcohol and nicotine as the basis for treatment programs for individuals who are dependent on both alcohol and nicotine (Rohsenow, 2005).

The largest field of academic specialization in psychology is **experimental psychology**. Experimental psychologists restrict themselves chiefly to laboratory research on basic psychological processes, including perception, learning, memory, thinking, language, motivation, and emotion. Though this field is called experimental psychology, it is not the only field that uses experiments. Psychologists in almost all fields of psychology conduct experimental research.

basic research Research aimed at finding answers to questions out of theoretical interest or intellectual curiosity.

applied research Research aimed at improving the quality of life and solving practical problems.

experimental psychology The field primarily concerned with laboratory research on basic psychological processes, including perception, learning, memory, thinking, language, motivation, and emotion.

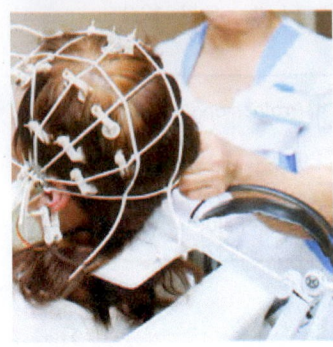

Behavioral Neuroscience

Psychologists in the field of behavioral neuroscience study the biological bases of behavior and cognitive processes.

Source: withGod/Shutterstock.com.

behavioral neuroscience
The field that studies the physiological bases of human and animal behavior and mental processes.

comparative psychology
The field that studies similarities and differences in the physiology, behaviors, and abilities of different species of animals, including human beings.

developmental psychology
The field that studies physical, perceptual, cognitive, and psychosocial changes across the life span.

personality psychology
The field that focuses on factors accounting for the differences in behavior and enduring personal characteristics among individuals.

social psychology The field that studies how the actual, imagined, or implied presence of other people affects one another's thoughts, feelings, and behaviors.

Consider some of the topics tackled by experimental psychologists that will be discussed in upcoming chapters. Chapter 5 describes how perception researchers determine whether people can identify other individuals by their odor. Chapter 8 explains how memory researchers assess the effect of people's moods on their ability to recall memories. And Chapter 12 discusses how emotion researchers demonstrate the effect of facial expressions on emotional experiences.

Psychologists in the field of **behavioral neuroscience** study the biological bases of behavior and cognitive processes. Chapter 3 discusses research by behavioral neuroscientists on the effects of natural opiates in the brain and the differences in functioning between the left and right hemispheres of the brain. In Chapter 6 you will learn of research by behavioral neuroscientists on the effects of psychoactive drugs on mind and behavior.

The related field of **comparative psychology** studies similarities and differences in the physiology, behaviors, and abilities of animals, including the human species. The field is particularly concerned with studying how evolution has led to animals adapting their behavior to different ecological niches (Tobach, 2006). Comparative psychologists study motives related to eating, drinking, aggression, courtship, sexual behavior, and parenting. Chapter 9 discusses how comparative psychologists study whether apes can learn to use language.

The field of **developmental psychology** is home to psychologists who study the factors responsible for physical, cognitive, and social changes across the life span. Research in developmental psychology has found, for example, that undergraduate students who report having had a lack of affectionate touching by parents in childhood are more prone to depression and problems in romantic relationships (Takeuchi et al., 2010). Chapter 4 presents research showing that infants are born with better perceptual skills than you might assume and that many gender differences might be smaller than is commonly believed.

Personality psychology is concerned with differences in behavior among individuals. As noted in Chapter 13, this field seeks answers to questions such as these: Are our personalities determined more by nature or by nurture? And to what extent do people behave consistently from one situation to another? Personality psychologists also devise tests for assessing personality, such as the famous Rorschach "inkblot test."

Psychologists in the field of **social psychology** study the effects people have on one another and the power of social situations. In Chapter 17 you will learn how social psychologists study the factors that influence interpersonal attraction, the problem of "groupthink" in making important decisions, and the reasons why people are often all too willing to follow orders to harm others.

Comparative Psychology

The field of comparative psychology is particularly concerned with studying how evolution has led to animals adapting their behavior to different ecological niches.

Source: Tratong/Shutterstock.com.

Professional Fields of Specialization

Professional psychologists commonly work in settings outside college or university classrooms and laboratories. Undergraduates are often surprised at the variety of professional fields of psychology (Stark-Wroblewski, Wiggins, & Ryan, 2006). Two of the largest are **clinical psychology** and **counseling psychology**, which deal with the causes, prevention, diagnosis, and treatment of psychological disorders. Counseling psychologists tend to deal with problems of everyday living related to career planning, academic performance, and personal relationships. In contrast, clinical psychologists typically treat more serious disorders, including phobias, alcoholism, drug abuse, and severe depression. Chapter 15 discusses the various techniques used by clinical and counseling psychologists as well as research concerning this important question: Is psychotherapy effective?

Clinical psychology and counseling psychology are distinctly different from the medical field of **psychiatry**. A psychiatrist is not a psychologist but a physician (with either an M.D. or a D.O.) who has served a residency in psychiatry, which takes a medical approach to the treatment of psychological disorders. Because psychiatrists are physicians, they may prescribe drugs or other biomedical treatments. Some clinical psychologists practicing in the state of New Mexico may undergo additional training and prescribe drugs. This controversial change has been made due to New Mexico's residents having comparatively less access to medical care than other Americans (Raw, 2003). Chapter 15 considers the various biopsychological treatments, including drugs to treat schizophrenia and electroconvulsive therapy to relieve depression. Some psychiatrists also offer psychotherapy to their clients.

Those who practice **health psychology** apply psychological principles to the maintenance of health and coping with illness. The major areas of health psychology include the relationship between stress and illness, the effects of behavior on health and illness, the individual's reaction to illness, and the role of psychology in serious and terminal illness. Health psychologists also develop interventions that reduce health-impairing habits, such as overeating and sedentary lifestyles (Baban & Cracian, 2007). Chapter 16 presents a comprehensive discussion of research findings and applications in health psychology.

Psychologists who practice **industrial/organizational psychology** work to increase productivity in businesses, industries, government agencies, and virtually any other kind of organization. They do so by improving working conditions, methods for hiring and training

clinical psychology The field that applies psychological principles to the prevention, diagnosis, and treatment of psychological disorders.

counseling psychology The field that applies psychological principles to help individuals deal with problems of daily living, generally less serious ones than those treated by clinical psychologists.

psychiatry The field of medicine that diagnoses and treats psychological disorders by using medical or psychological forms of therapy.

health psychology The field that applies psychological principles to the prevention and treatment of physical illness.

industrial/organizational psychology The field that applies psychological principles to improve productivity in businesses, industries, and government agencies.

Clinical and Counseling Psychology

Counseling psychologists tend to deal with problems of everyday living; clinical psychologists typically treat more serious disorders.

Source: wavebreakmedia/Shutterstock.com.

employees, and management techniques used by administrators. Some industrial/ organizational psychologists stress the importance of improving the quality of workers' lives, not just productivity (Zickar, 2003).

One of the oldest professional fields of specialization is **school psychology**. School psychologists work in elementary schools, middle schools, and high schools. They help improve students' academic performance and school behavior. For example, school psychologists take part in programs to improve students' reading acquisition (Bramlett, Murphy, Johnson, Wallingsford, & Hall, 2002). Today, school psychologists have been forced to also deal with serious issues, such as the prevention of suicide and the aftermath of suicides by schoolchildren (Debski, Spadafore, Jacob, Poole, & Hixson, 2007) and the plague of bullying, including cyber bullying via the Internet (Diamanduros, Downs, & Jenkins, 2008).

school psychology The field that applies psychological principles to improve the academic performance and social behavior of students in elementary, middle, and high schools.

The allied field of **educational psychology** tries to improve the educational process, including curriculum, teaching, and the administration of academic programs. For example, educational psychologists help school teachers understand the challenges faced by students with dyslexia (Regan & Woods, 2000). They also assess the effectiveness of inclusive programs versus traditional programs on the progress of students with intellectual or physical disabilities (Lindsay, 2007). There has been an influential movement in educational psychology to use only practices that have been supported by sound scientific research rather than simply relying on traditional practices or the opinions of educators (Stoiber & Waas, 2002). Educational psychologists usually are faculty members at colleges or universities.

educational psychology The field that applies psychological principles to help improve curriculum, teaching methods, and administrative procedures.

Sport psychology applies psychology to the acquisition of athletic skills, the improvement of athletic performance, and the maintenance of exercise programs. Sport psychologists typically work with elite collegiate, Olympic, or professional athletes to help them achieve excellence in performance. Some sport psychologists work with injured athletes to help them cope with the rehabilitation process (Hamson-Utley, Martin, & Walters, 2009) or wheelchair athletes to help them adjust to their physical disability while performing to their optimal level (Page, Martin, & Wayda, 2001). Chapter 11 discusses the relationship between motivation and sport performance.

sport psychology The field that applies psychological principles to help amateur and professional athletes improve their performance.

Psychologists who practice **forensic psychology** apply psychology to the legal system. The topics they study include the jury deliberation process and the best ways to select jurors. Forensic psychologists also help train police to handle domestic disputes, negotiate with hostage takers, and cope with job-related stress. And they seek to determine the fairest ways to present lineups of criminal suspects for identification by eyewitnesses (Kebbell, 2000), assess the competency of children to testify in court (Bala, Kang, Lindsay, & Talwar, 2010), develop training programs for law enforcement leaders (Miller, Watkins, & Webb, 2009), and conduct risk assessments of sex offenders being considered for parole (Freeman, Palk, & Davey, 2010). Chapter 8 describes another issue of interest to forensic psychologists: What is the best way to obtain accurate eyewitness testimony from children?

forensic psychology The field that applies psychological principles to improve the legal system, including the work of police and juries.

Environmental psychology studies the effect of the physical environment on human behavior, including how to design environments that improve the quality of life. Environmental psychologists work with a host of environmental settings and engage in activities as diverse as designing capsule habitats for exploring outer space, the deep sea, and the polar regions (Suedfeld & Steel, 2000) and designing exhibition centers, such as zoos and museums, to provide effective educational environments (Bitgood, 2002). Environmental psychologists also contribute to our knowledge of the role of changes in ambient light levels and other environmental factors implicated in seasonal affective disorder (discussed in Chapter 14), which is marked by the development of severe depression during a particular season of the year—typically the winter (Tonello, 2008).

environmental psychology The field that applies psychological principles to help improve the physical environment, including the design of buildings and the reduction of noise.

One of the newest fields of applied psychology is **peace psychology**, which aims at reducing conflicts and maintaining peace. Though the field is comparatively new, it became a formal subdiscipline during the Cold War, which began at the conclusion of World War II and ended in the early 1990s. During this time the world was threatened by nuclear annihilation as the then-Soviet Union and Western nations engaged in an escalating nuclear arms race (Christie, 2006). However, psychologists have long been interested in applying psychology to the promotion of peace. During the decade leading up to World War II, there was a symposium on the psychology of peace and war (Glover & Ginsberg, 1934). And near the

peace psychology The field that applies psychological principles to reducing conflict and maintaining peace.

Environmental Psychology

Environmental psychologists work with a host of environmental settings and design exhibition centers, such as zoos and museums, to provide effective educational environments.
Source: Andrev Burmakin/Shutterstock.com.

end of that war, psychologists discussed ways of applying psychology to the coming peace and reconstruction (Lerner, 1943). Today, peace psychologists are particularly interested in finding ways to reduce tensions that promote ethnic conflicts and terrorism (Wagner, 2006).

Section Review: Professional Fields of Specialization

1. What is the difference between basic and applied research?

2. How does psychiatry differ from psychology?

3. What is the nature of peace psychology?

Chapter Summary

The Historical Context of Psychology

- Psychology is the scientific study of behavior and cognitive processes.
- The roots of psychology are in philosophy and physiology.
- The commonly accepted founding date for psychology is 1879, when Wilhelm Wundt established the first formal psychology laboratory.
- Structuralism sought to analyze the mind into its component parts.

- Functionalism favored the study of how the conscious mind helps the individual adapt to the environment.
- Gestalt psychology favored the study of the mind as active and the study of perception as holistic.
- Psychoanalysis studies the influence of unconscious motives on behavior.
- Behaviorism rejects the study of the mind in favor of the study of observable behavior.

Contemporary Perspectives in Psychology

- To date, psychology has no unifying scientific paradigm, only competing psychological perspectives.
- The humanistic perspective, which favors the study of conscious mental experience and accepts the reality of free will, arose in opposition to psychoanalysis and behaviorism.
- The cognitive perspective views the individual as an active processor of information.
- The biopsychological perspective favors the study of the biological bases of behavior, mental experiences, and cognitive processes.
- The sociocultural perspective insists that psychologists must study people in their social and cultural contexts.

The Scope of Psychology

- Academic fields of specialization are chiefly concerned with conducting basic research.
- Professional fields of specialization in psychology are chiefly concerned with applying psychological research findings.

Key Terms

psychology (p. 2)

The Historical Context of Psychology

analytic introspection (p. 6)
behaviorism (p. 11)
differential psychology (p. 5)
empiricism (p. 3)
functionalism (p. 6)
Gestalt psychology (p. 8)
nativism (p. 3)
phi phenomenon (p. 8)
psychic determinism (p. 10)
psychoanalysis (p. 9)
psychophysics (p. 4)
rationalism (p. 3)
structuralism (p. 6)

Contemporary Perspectives in Psychology

behavioral genetics (p. 15)
biopsychological perspective (p. 14)
cognitive perspective (p. 14)
cross-cultural psychology (p. 16)
cultural psychology (p. 16)
ethnic psychology (p. 16)
evolutionary psychology (p. 15)
existential psychology (p. 13)
humanistic perspective (p. 13)
multicultural psychology (p. 16)
phenomenological psychology (p. 13)
scientific paradigm (p. 13)
sociocultural perspective (p. 15)

The Scope of Psychology

applied research (p. 17)
basic research (p. 17)

behavioral neuroscience (p. 18)
clinical psychology (p. 19)
comparative psychology (p. 18)
counseling psychology (p. 19)
developmental psychology (p. 18)
educational psychology (p. 20)
environmental psychology (p. 20)
experimental psychology (p. 17)
forensic psychology (p. 20)
health psychology (p. 19)
industrial/organizational psychology (p. 19)
peace psychology (p. 20)
personality psychology (p. 18)
psychiatry (p. 19)
school psychology (p. 20)
social psychology (p. 18)
sport psychology (p. 20)

Chapter Quiz

1. If you insisted that "seeing is believing," you would show your belief in
   a. nativism.
   b. empiricism.
   c. rationalism.
   d. psychic determinism.

2. The main difference between a psychiatrist and a clinical psychologist is that the psychiatrist
   a. is a physician.
   b. might analyze dreams.
   c. relies strictly on Freudian theory.
   d. deals with more serious kinds of disorders.

3. When you watch a cartoon in a movie theater, you are experiencing (the)
   a. phi phenomenon.
   b. Zeigarnik effect.
   c. psychic determinism.
   d. analytic introspection.

4. A psychologist would be most likely to
   a. prescribe drugs to treat anxiety.
   b. study the ability of apes to learn language.
   c. provide evidence for or against the existence of God.
   d. treat depression by administering electroshock therapy.

5. The philosopher who would most approve of Hugo Münsterberg's founding of applied psychology would be
   a. Plato.
   b. Saint Augustine.
   c. Immanuel Kant.
   d. Francis Bacon.

6. Darwin's theory of evolution had its greatest impact on
   a. structuralism.
   b. functionalism.
   c. Gestalt psychology.
   d. cognitive psychology.

7. Biology and psychology are both sciences because they
   a. study the brain.
   b. rely on statistics.
   c. share a common method.
   d. require specialized education.

8. Strict determinism would most likely be rejected by a
   a. psychoanalyst.
   b. biopsychologist.
   c. behavioral psychologist.
   d. humanistic psychologist.

9. The psychological perspective that is interested in studying the brain, the hormone system, and the effects of heredity on behavior is the
   a. differential perspective.
   b. neurochemical perspective.
   c. cerebrocortical perspective.
   d. biopsychological perspective.

10. The discussion of women in the early history of psychology noted that, since the early 20th century, psychology has been
    a. more hospitable to women than to men.
    b. more hospitable to women than other sciences have been.
    c. less hospitable to women than other sciences have been.
    d. about as hospitable to women as other sciences have been.

11. A research study on the effectiveness of psychological counseling techniques in helping Olympic athletes reach their potential would be an example of
    a. pure research.
    b. basic research.
    c. applied research.
    d. psychic determinism.

12. The discovery of possible universal psychological truths is central to
    a. parapsychology.
    b. cultural psychology.
    c. humanistic psychology.
    d. cross-cultural psychology.

13. If a psychologist insisted that a person's recent fall down a flight of stairs was more attributable to unconscious self-loathing than to clumsiness, she would be supporting the Freudian notion of
    a. stimulus control.
    b. psychic determinism.
    c. positive reinforcement.
    d. psychophysical parallelism.

14. Near the end of his life, Carl Rogers lamented that humanistic psychology had little impact on mainstream psychology, in part because it
    a. lacked scientific rigor.
    b. was too concerned with sex.
    c. likened the human mind to a computer.
    d. stressed unconscious motivation instead of conscious experience.

15. Neither behaviorism nor psychoanalysis
    a. studies the mind.
    b. uses case studies.
    c. considers the environment.
    d. focuses on the conscious mind.

16. Research in differential psychology, a field founded by Francis Galton, would be most likely to
    a. use placebo control groups.
    b. determine the effect of exercise on academic performance.
    c. study factors that make certain individuals more stress-resistant than others.
    d. assess changes in the personality of a single subject across various life stages.

17. A behaviorist would be most likely to agree with the belief that leaders
    a. are made, not born.
    b. are born, not made.
    c. use will power to dominate other people.
    d. are motivated by an unconscious desire for control.

18. An interest in the unconscious mind would be most characteristic of
    a. behaviorism.
    b. psychoanalysis.
    c. humanistic psychology.
    d. cognitive psychology.

19. B. F. Skinner would be most likely to attribute your desire to pursue a college education to
    a. your drive for self-actualization.
    b. an unconscious need to prove yourself.
    c. your past success in academic courses.
    d. intellectual interests inherited from your parents.

20. If a psychologist is interested in helping you to feel more self-actualized in your life, she is probably a(n)
    a. forensic psychologist.
    b. cognitive psychologist.
    c. humanistic psychologist.
    d. experimental psychologist.

21. The main employment settings of psychologists are
    a. private practices.
    b. businesses and industries.
    c. colleges and universities.
    d. governmental research laboratories.

22. Cognitive psychology can be viewed as the offspring of
    a. psychoanalysis and functionalism.
    b. behaviorism and Gestalt psychology.
    c. structuralism and humanistic psychology.
    d. biopsychology and differential psychology.

23. The idea that the proper subject matter of psychology should be a person's conscious mental experience was put forth by
    a. Ivan Pavlov.
    b. Roger Sperry.
    c. B. F. Skinner.
    d. Abraham Maslow.

24. According to philosopher Thomas Kuhn, as a science matures, it develops a paradigm shared by most scientists. Today, psychology
   a. lacks a unifying scientific paradigm.
   b. is dominated by the humanistic paradigm.
   c. is dominated by the behavioristic paradigm.
   d. is dominated by the psychoanalytic paradigm.

25. The first psychological laboratory was established in 1879 by
   a. Sigmund Freud.
   b. Wilhelm Wundt.
   c. John B. Watson.
   d. Edward Titchener.

Thought Questions

1. How would nativists and empiricists differ in their opinion of early childhood intervention projects, such as Head Start?

2. In the late 19th and early 20th centuries, many Americans believed that women's and men's lives should be lived in "separate spheres." How did this notion limit women's contributions to psychology?

3. Suppose you find that your professor is an unusually "happy" person—smiling, cracking jokes, and complimenting students on their brilliant insights. How would the different psychological perspectives explain this behavior?

Psychology as a Science

As discussed in Chapter 1, psychology is the science that studies human and animal behavior and cognitive processes. Psychology deals with topics of great interest to people, making them also of particular interest to the media. But the media at times are more interested in attracting readers, viewers, and listeners than in the objective reporting of scientific findings. This focus often leads the media to exaggerate or sensationalize research findings. Consider the media's coverage of the supposed effects of the hormone melatonin on the next page.

In discussing psychology as a science, this chapter will answer questions such as these: Why do psychologists use the scientific method? What are the goals of psychological research? How do psychologists employ the scientific method in their research? What techniques do psychologists rely on to analyze their data? And what ethical principles guide psychological research? The answers to these questions will help you appreciate the scientific basis of the issues, theories, research findings, and practical applications presented throughout this book.

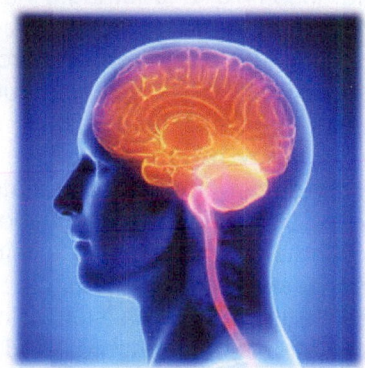

Source: CLIPAREA/Custom media/ Shutterstock.com.

Chapter Outline

Sources of Knowledge

Goals of Scientific Research

Methods of Psychological Research

Statistical Analysis of Research Data

Ethics of Psychological Research

Sources of Knowledge

Psychologists and other scientists favor the scientific method as their means of obtaining knowledge, such as knowledge about the effects of melatonin. To appreciate why they do, you need to understand the shortcomings of the everyday alternative to the scientific method: *common sense*.

Common Sense

When you rely on common sense, you assume that the beliefs you have obtained from everyday life are trustworthy. Commonsense knowledge has a variety of sources, including statements by recognized authorities, your own reasoning about things, and observations from your personal experience. Many college students view psychology as little more than common sense—until they are presented with examples of how scientific research has demonstrated that their commonsense beliefs are false (Osberg, 1993).

As an example of the frailty of common sense, consider sports fans' belief in the "hot hand," especially in professional basketball. According to this belief, a player's performance will temporarily improve following a string of successful shots. The accuracy of this commonsense belief was examined in a study of NBA Long Distance Shootout contests from 1994 through 1997. Analyses of videotaped free throws revealed that—contrary

Does Melatonin Have Beneficial Physical and Psychological Effects?

In November 1995, *Newsweek* magazine's cover story reported a craze inspired by the supposed beneficial physical and psychological effects of a "natural wonder drug": the hormone melatonin (Cowley, 1995). Melatonin, secreted by the pineal gland (located in the center of the brain), was touted in the article as a cure for aging, insomnia, and jet lag. And *Newsweek* was not alone. Reports by magazines, newspapers, radio stations, and television networks across the United States stimulated public excitement about melatonin.

The effects of the media reports were so powerful that many health-food stores could not keep up with consumer demand for melatonin. At the time the *Newsweek* article was published, a book praising the effects of melatonin was third on the *New York Times* best-seller list. Though the craze has subsided since 1995, the media still include periodic reports on the effects of melatonin—and the Internet is brimming with Web sites that praise the alleged benefits of melatonin, while they just so happen to offer it for sale online.

Should readers have accepted the claims about melatonin's alleged beneficial effects simply because they appeared in a popular news weekly that relied mainly on testimonials from people who used or marketed it? Psychologists, being scientists, do not accept such claims unless they are supported by sound scientific research findings—such as more recent research indicating that melatonin might indeed have beneficial psychological effects. Research studies have found that melatonin can be effective in treating insomnia (Wade et al., 2010) and cancer (Mills, Wu, Seely, & Guatt, 2005), countering jet lag (Paul et al., 2010), preventing heart disease (Veneroso, Tuñón, González-Gallego, & Collado, 2009), and slowing aging of the brain (Carretero et al., 2009). As you read this chapter, you will learn how a psychologist might use the scientific method to conduct an experiment to test the effects of melatonin. But you must first understand the nature of psychology as a science.

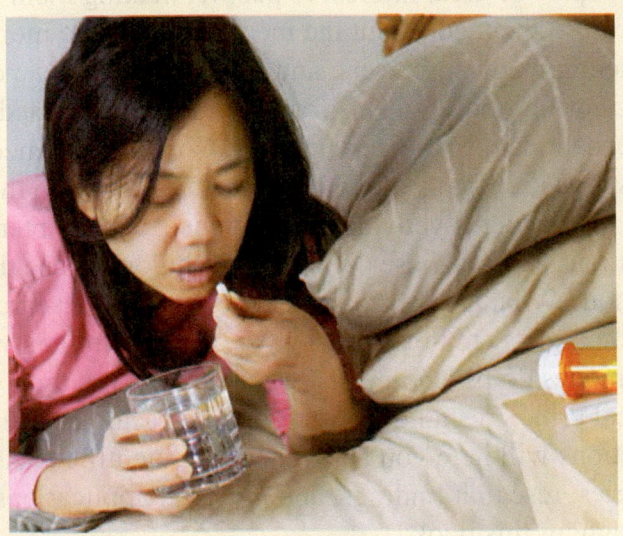

Science versus Pseudoscience

Should we accept media reports as strong evidence for popular claims, such as melatonin's alleged ability to promote sleep, overcome jet lag, and slow the aging process? Scientists require more rigorous standards of evidence than that.
Source: tab62/Shutterstock.com.

---

to common sense—players did *not* perform better following a "streak" of successes. In fact, players performed at about their base rate following a sequence of successful shots (Koehler & Conley, 2003). Thus, the best predictor of basketball players' next shots are their average performance, not the perception that they have "hot hands."

Even the judicial system, which strives for objectivity in courtroom deliberations, at times relies more on common sense than on scientific research to settle important issues, such as judges' and jurors' faith in the accuracy of eyewitness testimony (Benton, Ross, Bradshaw, Thomas, & Bradshaw, 2006). But we should not automatically discount the possibility that commonsense beliefs might be true. According to Harold Kelley (1921–2003), a leading researcher on commonsense thinking, "Discarding our commonsense psychology baggage would require us needlessly to separate ourselves from the vast sources of knowledge gained in the course of human history" (Kelley, 1992, p. 22). In other words, common sense may inspire scientific research, even though it cannot substitute for it—as in the research study inspired by a major social problem discussed in the "Psychology versus Common Sense" box on page 28.

Common Sense

Should you change your answers on multiple-choice tests? Student common sense would say no. You probably have heard the folk wisdom, "Don't change your answers on exams, because you'll be more likely to change a correct wrong answer to a wrong answer than a wrong answer to a correct answer." You might be surprised that scientific research has consistently found that students are slightly more likely to change a wrong answer to a correct answer than a correct answer to a wrong answer (N. F. Skinner, 1983).

Source: Tyler Olson/Shutterstock.com.

Science

Because of the weaknesses of common sense and the need for a more objective, self-correcting source of knowledge, scientists prefer the scientific method, which is based on certain assumptions and follows a formal series of steps. The fact that the scientific method is the dominant research method in psychology owes much to its origins in 19th-century natural science, particularly physiology.

Assumptions of Science

Scientists share some basic assumptions that guide their thinking about physical reality. Two of the most important of these assumptions are determinism and skepticism.

Determinism and Lawfulness Albert Einstein was fond of saying, "God does not play dice with the universe." In using the scientific method, psychologists and other scientists share his belief that there is order in the universe, meaning that the relationships among events are lawful rather than haphazard. In looking for these lawful relationships, scientists also share the assumption of **determinism**, which holds that every event has physical, possibly measurable, causes. Determinism rules out free will and supernatural influences as causes of behavior.

> **determinism** The assumption that every event has physical, potentially measurable, causes.

Yet, as pointed out more than a century ago by William James, scientists might be committed to determinism in conducting their research, while being tempted to assume the existence of free will in their everyday lives (Immergluck, 1964). They might succumb to this temptation because, if carried to its logical extreme, the assumption of strict determinism would lead them to unpalatable conclusions (Holton, 2009)—for example, that Mother Teresa did not deserve praise for her work with the poor and that Adolph Hitler did not deserve blame for his acts of genocide, because neither was free to choose otherwise. This logical extreme also means that strict determinism is incompatible with the legal system, which, because it assumes the existence of free will, holds criminals responsible for their actions.

Despite centuries of philosophical debate, neither side of the determinism versus free will debate has won. Even William James, after pondering this issue for many years,

Can We Reliably Detect When Someone is Drunk?

In the landmark 1961 *Zane* decision, a New Jersey court stated, "Whether the man is sober or intoxicated is a matter of common observation not requiring special knowledge or skill" (Langenbucher & Nathan, 1983, p. 1071). This assumption is an important one because state laws in the United States, based on the commonsense belief that drunkenness is easily detected, hold people such as party hosts and tavern owners legally responsible for the actions of people who become drunk at their homes or businesses. The ability to detect drunkenness was tested in a scientific study by researchers James Langenbucher and Peter Nathan (1983).

Langenbucher and Nathan had 12 bartenders, 49 social drinkers, and 30 police officers observe drinkers and judge whether they were legally drunk or sober. The drinkers in each case were two male and two female young adults. Each drinker consumed one of three drinks: tonic water, moderate doses of vodka (but not enough to become legally drunk), or high doses of vodka (enough to become legally drunk). A Breathalyzer ensured that the desired blood-alcohol concentrations were achieved for participants in the two vodka conditions.

The bartenders observed their participants being interviewed in a cocktail lounge. The social drinkers observed their participants being interviewed in the Alcohol Behavior Research Laboratory at Rutgers University. And the police officers observed their participants in a simulated nighttime roadside arrest in which they were given 3 minutes to determine whether the motorist they had pulled over was drunk or sober.

Langenbucher and Nathan found that the observers correctly judged the drinkers' level of intoxication only 25 percent of the time. Not a single legally drunk person was identified as such by a significant number of the observers. Of the 91 persons who served as judges, only five were consistently accurate—and all

of them were members of a New Jersey State Police special tactical unit for the apprehension of drunk drivers. Those five police officers had received more than 90 hours of training in the detection of drunkenness. The results implied that, without special training, even people with extensive experience in observing drinkers might be unable to determine whether a person is legally drunk or sober.

The social implication of these findings is that common sense is wrong in the assumption that people with experience in observing drinkers can detect whether someone is drunk. We are even more confident in the findings of this study because they were supported by the results of a different experiment conducted by a different researcher, using different participants, in a different research setting (Beatty, 1984). Perhaps bartenders, police officers, and habitual party givers should obtain special training similar to that given to the five police officers who performed well in the study.

The Detection of Drunkenness

Scientific research contradicts the commonsense belief that we can easily detect when someone is legally drunk.
Source: Andresr/Shutterstock.com.

---

failed to find enough evidence to favor either side of the determinism versus free will debate (Bricklin, 1999). This controversy is one that neither psychologists nor philosophers have been able to resolve, though some still try by resorting to soft determinism, which asserts that determinism generally governs events though at times we can impose free will on our actions (Clarke, 2010).

Skepticism and Critical Thinking Aside from assuming that the universe is an orderly place in which events—including behaviors—are governed by determinism, scientists today, like René Descartes and Francis Bacon before them (see Chapter 1), insist that open-minded **skepticism** is the best intellectual predisposition when judging the merits of any claim. Open-minded skepticism requires the maintenance of a delicate balance between cynicism and gullibility. As Mario Bunge, a leading philosopher of science, has noted, skeptics "do not believe anything in the absence of

skepticism An attitude that doubts all claims not supported by solid research evidence.

evidence, but they are willing to explore bold new ideas if they find reasons to suspect that they have a chance" (Bunge, 1992, p. 380). This skeptical attitude requires supportive evidence before accepting any claim. The failure to maintain a skeptical attitude leads to the acceptance of phenomena, such as ESP, that lack sufficient scientific support (Bartholomew & Radford, 2003), Nonetheless, researchers who accept the possible existence of ESP argue that critics tend to be more cynical than skeptical by not even considering sound scientific evidence supporting its existence (Radin, 2007).

Skepticism also is important in psychology because many psychological "truths" are tentative, in part because psychological research findings may depend on the times and places in which the research takes place. What generally is true of human behavior in one era or culture might be false in another era or culture. For example, gender differences in behavior in Western cultures have changed dramatically over the past few decades, and gender differences observed in Western cultures might be unlike those in non-Western cultures. More than two decades before the sociocultural perspective (see Chapter 1) achieved widespread acceptance in North American psychology, Anne Anastasi (1908–2001), in her presidential address to the American Psychological Association, showed foresight in urging psychologists not to confuse their ethnocentric personal beliefs and values with scientific "truths" (Anastasi, 1972).

Skepticism is valuable not only for scientists but for all of us in our everyday lives, as we evaluate information presented in academic courses, media reports, and Web sites. Skepticism also is the basis of *critical thinking*—the systematic evaluation of claims and assumptions. Students who major in psychology tend to become particularly adept at critical thinking by their senior year (Lawson, 1999). The following steps in critical thinking will serve you well as you evaluate claims encountered in your everyday life:

1. Identify the claim being made. Ask yourself whether it is based on empirical data (which would be subject to scientific evaluation) or on personal values, opinions, or religious beliefs (which would be less subject to scientific evaluation).

2. Examine the evidence in support of the claim. Try to assess whether the evidence has merit.

3. If the evidence does have merit, determine whether it logically supports the claim. The evidence might have merit in itself without necessarily being logically connected to the claim.

4. Consider possible alternative explanations of the claim. Perhaps there is a better explanation than the one that has been given.

Steps in Conducting Scientific Research

Because psychologists are skeptical about claims not supported by research findings, they employ the **scientific method** as their means of gaining knowledge. Though scientists vary in their approach to the scientific method, ideally they follow a formal series of steps:

Step 1: Provide a *rationale* for the study. The scientist identifies the problem, reviews the relevant research literature, decides on the research method to use, and states the research **hypothesis**. A hypothesis (from the Greek word for "supposition") is a testable prediction about the relationship between two or more events or characteristics.

Step 2: Conduct the study. The scientist carries out the research procedure and collects data.

Step 3: Analyze the data. The scientist usually uses mathematical techniques called *statistics* and discusses the implications of the research findings.

scientific method A source of knowledge based on the assumption that knowledge comes from the objective, systematic observation and measurement of particular variables and the events they affect.

hypothesis A testable prediction about the relationship between two or more events or characteristics.

replication The repetition of a research study, usually with some alterations in its methods or setting, to determine whether the principles derived from that study hold up under similar circumstances.

Step 4: Communicate the research findings. The scientist may present the research study at a professional meeting and publish an article describing the study in a professional journal. In doing so, the scientist includes the rationale for the research, the exact method that was used, the results of the research, and a discussion of the implications of the results.

Step 5: Replicate the study. **Replication** involves repeating the study, exactly or with some variation. Either the original researcher or other researchers may replicate the study. Successful replications of research studies strengthen confidence in their findings.

These steps were used by psychologist Donn Byrne and his colleagues (Byrne, Ervin, & Lamberth, 1970) in a classic research study of interpersonal attraction: Do opposites attract? Or do birds of a feather flock together? In this study, the problem concerned the relationship between interpersonal similarity and interpersonal attraction. After reviewing the research literature relevant to the problem, Byrne decided to conduct a *field experiment* that studied college students in a real-life setting instead of in a laboratory. In fact, his experiment was a replication conducted to determine whether the results of previous laboratory studies on the effects of attitude similarity on interpersonal attraction would generalize to a field setting.

Based on his review of the research literature, Byrne hypothesized that heterosexual men and women with similar attitudes would be more likely to be attracted to each other than would those with dissimilar attitudes. Byrne had his research participants complete a 50-item questionnaire that assessed their attitudes as part of a computer-dating service. He told them that their responses would be used to pair them with a student who shared their attitudes. But the students were actually paired so that some partners were similar in attitudes and others were dissimilar. Their similarity on the questionnaire provided a concrete definition of "similarity." The 44 heterosexual couples, selected from 420 volunteers, then were sent to the student union for a 30-minute get-acquainted date. Several weeks later, participants were asked to rate their partners, which provided Byrne with his research data.

Like almost all researchers, Byrne used statistics to summarize his data and to determine whether his hypothesis was supported. In this case, Byrne found that the data did support the hypothesis. Partners who were similar in attitudes were significantly more likely to recall each other's name, to have talked with each other since the date, and to desire to date each other again. Thus, in this study, the use of the scientific method found that birds of a feather tend to flock together.

Byrne communicated his findings by publishing them in a professional journal. He also might have shared his findings by presenting them at a research conference. Even undergraduate psychology researchers can present the results of their research studies at psychology research conferences—including undergraduate conferences—held each year.

Section Review: Sources of Knowledge

1. What are the basic assumptions of science?

2. What is critical thinking?

3. What are the formal steps in the scientific method?

Goals of Scientific Research

In conducting their research, psychologists and other scientists share common goals. They pursue the goals of description, prediction, control, and explanation of behavior and cognitive processes (Green & Powell, 1990).

Description

To a scientist, description involves noting the observable characteristics of an event, object, or individual. For example, we might note that participants who take daily doses of melatonin sleep longer. Psychologists, following in the intellectual tradition of Francis Bacon discussed in Chapter 1, are systematic in what they describe. Instead of arbitrarily describing everything that they observe, they describe only things that are relevant to their research topic. Thus, good observational skills are essential to psychologists. The need to be systematic in what you describe is expressed well in a statement about criminal investigations made by the fictional detective Sherlock Holmes to his friend Dr. Watson:

> A fool takes in all the lumber [facts] that he comes across, so that the knowledge which might be useful to him gets crowded out, or at best is jumbled up with a lot of other things . . . It is of the highest importance, therefore, not to have useless facts elbowing out the useful ones. (Doyle, 1930)

In science, descriptions must be more than systematic; they must be precise. Precise descriptions are concrete rather than abstract, and typically involve **measurement**, which is the use of numbers to represent events or characteristics. According to Francis Galton, one of the pioneers of psychology, "Until the phenomena of any branch of knowledge have been submitted to measurement . . . it cannot assume the status and dignity of a science" (quoted in Cowles, 1989, p. 2). Thus, describing a friend as "generous" would be acceptable in everyday conversation but would be too imprecise for scientific communication.

Scientists solve this problem by using **operational definitions**, which define behaviors or qualities in terms of the procedures used to measure or produce them (Feest, 2005). Donn Byrne did this when he defined *similarity* according to participants' responses to a questionnaire in his study of interpersonal attractiveness. More than a century ago, Galton, in studying audience behavior at plays and lectures, operationally defined *boredom* by recording the number of fidgets by audience members. You might operationally define *generous* as "donating more than 5 percent of one's salary to charity." And a common operational definition of being *legally drunk* is "a blood-alcohol concentration of at least 0.08 percent." Though operational definitions are desirable, psychologists sometimes find it difficult to agree on acceptable ones. For example, a series of journal articles argued about how best to operationally define "suicide attempt" (Kidd, 2003). Perhaps the main value of an operational definition is that it promotes more precise communication among scientists.

measurement The use of numbers to represent events or characteristics.

operational definition The definition of behaviors or qualities in terms of the procedures used to measure or produce them.

Prediction

Psychologists are not content just to describe things. They also make predictions in the form of hypotheses about changes in behavior, cognitive experiences, or physiological activity. A hypothesis is usually based on a **theory**, which is a set of statements that summarize and explain research findings and from which research hypotheses can be derived. For example, Sigmund Freud's theory of psychoanalysis integrates many observations he had made of the characteristics of people suffering from psychological disorders. Theories provide coherence to scientific research findings and suggest applications of research findings, making science more than the accumulation of isolated facts (Kukla, 1989).

Because we cannot know all the factors that affect a person or an animal at a given time, psychologists never are certain about the predictions made in their research hypotheses. In fact, it would be pointless to conduct a research study for which the outcome was certain. Moreover, scientific predictions about human participants or animal subjects usually are more accurate when applied to many people or animals than when applied to a specific case. For example, your automobile insurance company

theory An integrated set of statements that summarizes and explains research findings and from which research hypotheses can be derived.

can more accurately predict the percentage of people in your age group who will have an accident this year than it can predict whether you will have one. Likewise, though melatonin might prove effective in treating insomnia for most people, we would be unable to predict with certainty whether a particular person would benefit from it.

Psychology has nothing to apologize for in being limited to probabilistic prediction because this situation is no different in the other sciences, which likewise are limited to making predictions that scientists are not 100 percent certain are correct (Hedges, 1987). Your physician might prescribe an antibiotic that, based on medical research, is effective 98 percent of the time in treating pneumonia, but she or he cannot guarantee that it will cure your pneumonia. Similarly, flood forecasters know that regions along certain rivers are more likely to flood (Reggiani & Weerts, 2008) and earthquake forecasters know that regions along geological faults are more likely to experience earthquakes (Molchan & Keilis-Borok, 2008), but they cannot accurately predict well in advance the day, or even the year, that a flood or an earthquake will occur in a given region.

For example, the U.S. Geological Survey has estimated that there is a 76 percent chance that before 2030, a powerful earthquake measuring 6.7 or more on the seismic scale will occur in northern California (Perlman, 1999). But seismologists are far from being able to predict that "a magnitude 7.3 earthquake will strike 18 miles northeast of San Francisco in the spring of 2017." In the same vein, in regard to interpersonal attraction, people with similar attitudes will probably—but not always—be more attracted to each other than are people with dissimilar attitudes. We cannot predict with certainty whether two specific people with similar attitudes will be attracted to each other.

Control

Psychologists go beyond describing and predicting changes in behavior, cognitive processes, and physiological activity. They also try to influence those changes by controlling factors that affect them. The notion of control is used in two ways (Cowles, 1989). First, as you will read later in the chapter, control is an essential ingredient in the conduct of experiments. Second, psychologists try to apply their research findings to the control of behavior in everyday life (Smith, 2002). Thus, melatonin might be prescribed to control insomnia by promoting sleep, and young adults might be advised to find romance by seeking people who share their values and interests. Psychologists seek to help individuals gain control over phenomena as diverse as psychological disorders (Mansell & Carey, 2009) and Type 2 diabetes (Gonzales, Salas, & Umpierrez, 2011).

Explanation

The ultimate goal of psychology is explanation—the discovery of the causes of overt behaviors and cognitive processes. If it is demonstrated that people who ingest melatonin consistently overcome insomnia, the next step might be to explain how melatonin affects the brain to trigger sleep. Likewise, even though we know that attitude similarity promotes interpersonal attraction, we still would need to explain why we prefer people who have similar attitudes.

As discussed in Chapter 1, psychologists' favored perspectives determine where they look for explanations of psychological phenomena, such as psychological disorders (Lam, Salkovskis, & Warwick, 2005). Psychologists who favor the cognitive, humanistic, or psychoanalytic perspective will look for causes in the mind. Psychologists who favor the behavioral perspective will look for causes in the environment. Psychologists who favor the biopsychological perspective will look for causes in the brain or hormonal system. And psychologists who favor the sociocultural perspective will look for causes in the social or cultural context of the event.

Methods of Psychological Research

Given that psychologists favor the scientific method as their primary source of knowledge, how do they use it in their research? And once they have collected their data, how do they make sense of it? As shown in Table 2-1, psychologists use research methods that permit them to describe, predict, control, or explain relationships among variables. *Descriptive research* pursues the goal of description, *correlational research* pursues the goal of prediction, and *experimental research* pursues the goals of control and explanation.

Descriptive Research

Descriptive research is descriptive because researchers simply record what they have systematically observed. Descriptive research methods include *naturalistic observation, case studies, surveys, psychological testing,* and *archival research.*

descriptive research Research that involves the recording of behaviors that have been observed systematically.

Naturalistic Observation

In **naturalistic observation**, people or animals are observed behaving in their natural environment. Researchers who use naturalistic observation study topics as diverse as the ability to find where one has parked one's car (Lutz, Means, & Long, 1994), peer reactions to the bullying of children in school playgrounds (Hawkins, Pepler, & Craig, 2001), and factors related to smiling or laughing during group interactions (Mehu & Dunbar, 2008). To make sure that their observations represent natural behavior, observers refrain as much as possible from influencing the individuals they are observing. In other words, the observer remains unobtrusive. If you were studying the eating behavior of students in your school cafeteria, you would not announce your intention over a loudspeaker. Otherwise, your participants might behave unnaturally; a person who normally gorged on cake, ice cream, and chocolate pudding for dessert might eat fruit instead.

Naturalistic observation also is useful in studying animal behavior. Some of the best-known studies employing naturalistic observation were conducted by Jane Goodall, who spent decades observing chimpanzees in Gombe National Park in Tanzania (Crain, 2009). To prevent newly encountered chimpanzees from acting unnaturally because of her presence, Goodall spent her initial observation periods letting them get used to her.

naturalistic observation The recording of the behavior of people or animals in their natural environments, with little or no intervention by the researcher.

TABLE 2-1 The Goals and Methods of Psychology

Goal	Research Method	Relevant Question
Description	Descriptive	What are its characteristics?
Prediction	Correlational	How likely is it?
Control	Experimental	Can I make it happen?
Explanation	Experimental	What causes it?

ethology The study of animal behavior in the natural environment.

The study of animal behavior in the natural environment, as in Goodall's research, is called **ethology**. One of the advantages of an ethological approach is the potential discovery of behaviors not found in more artificial settings, such as zoos and laboratories. Goodall reported observations concerning mundane chimpanzee behavior, such as "fishing" for ants with sticks (O'Malley, Wallauer, Murray, & Goodall, 2012) and observations of chimpanzee behavior that have not been made in captivity, including cannibalism, infanticide, and unprovoked killing of other chimpanzees (Goodall, 1990). But researchers who use naturalistic observation, like those who use other research methods, must not be hasty in generalizing their findings. Even the generalizability of Jane Goodall's observations must be qualified. The behavior of the Gombe chimpanzees differs from the behavior of chimpanzees in the Mahali Mountains of western Tanzania. For example, female Mahali chimpanzees hunt more often than female Gombe chimpanzees do (Takahata, Hasegawa, & Nishida, 1984).

Naturalistic observation cannot determine the causes of the observed behavior because there are simply too many factors at work in a natural setting. So you could not determine *why* female chimpanzees hunt more in one part of Tanzania than in another. Is it due to differences in prey, in climate, in topography, or in another factor or some combination of factors? It would be impossible to tell just by using naturalistic observation.

Case Study

case study An in-depth study of an individual.

Another descriptive research method is the **case study**—an in-depth study of a person, typically conducted to gain knowledge about a particular psychological phenomenon that is relatively rare, such as psychosocial factors related to pathological hoarding of items (Koretz & Gutheil, 2009), or that would be unethical to study experimentally, such as psychosocial factors related to fibromyalgia (Griffies, 2010). The case-study researcher obtains as much relevant information as possible about a host of factors, perhaps including the person's thoughts, feelings, life experiences, and social relationships. The case study often is used in clinical studies of people suffering from psychological disorders. In fact, Sigmund Freud based his theory of psychoanalysis on data he obtained from clinical case studies, which are still a staple of psychoanalytic research (Midgley, 2006).

Most recently, the case study method has been used to gain insight into factors related to a rash of student shootings of their teachers and classmates. Researchers conducted case studies of 15 shooting incidents between 1995 and 2001 to examine the possible role of social rejection. Ostracism, bullying, or romantic rejection was present in all but two of the cases. The shooters also tended to have one or more of the following three risk factors: an interest in guns or explosives, a fascination with death or Satanism, or psychological problems involving depression, impulse control, or sadistic tendencies (Leary, Kowalski, Smith, & Phillips, 2003).

Because a person's behavior is affected by many variables, the case study method cannot determine the particular variables that caused the behavior being studied. Though it might seem reasonable to assume that the shooters' experiences of rejection caused them to lash out at their teachers and fellow students, that assumption might be wrong. Other factors, unrelated to social rejection, might have caused the violence. It even is conceivable that the shooters' peers rejected them only *after* discovering their fascination with death, Satanism, or guns.

Another shortcoming of the case study is that the results of a single case study, no matter how dramatic, cannot be generalized to all people. Even if the shooters lashed out at their teachers and students in response to social rejection, other people who commit violent acts might not have experienced social rejection. For example, as you will learn in Chapter 14, numerous studies have shown that both biopsychological and psychosocial factors play a role in violence.

Survey

When psychologists wish to collect information about behaviors, opinions, attitudes, life experiences, or personal characteristics of many people, they use a descriptive research method called the survey. A **survey** asks participants a series of questions about the topic of interest, such as product preferences or political opinions. Surveys deal with topics as varied as factors related to condom use (French & Holland, 2013), purchasing habits of students using school vending machines (Rose, 2011), occupational stress experienced by university professors (Slišković, Seršić, & Burić, 2011), and psychological symptoms related to video-game dependency (Rehbein, Kleimann, & Mödle, 2010). Surveys commonly are in the form of personal interviews or written questionnaires—sometimes presented over the Internet, as in product marketing surveys.

You probably have been asked to respond to several surveys in the past year, whether enclosed in the "You May Have Already Won!" offers that you receive in the mail or conducted by your student government association to get your views on campus policies. The prevalence of surveys, and the annoyance they may induce, is not new. More than a century ago, William James (1890/1981) was so irritated by the seeming omnipresence of surveys that he called them "one of the pests of life." Today, the most ambitious of these "pests" is the U.S. census, which is conducted every 10 years. Others you might be familiar with include the Gallup public opinion polls, the Pew Research Center surveys, Harris polls, and Nielsen television ratings surveys.

High-quality surveys use clearly worded questions that do not bias respondents to answer in a particular way. But surveys are limited by respondents' willingness to answer honestly and by social desirability—the tendency to give socially appropriate responses. You can imagine the potential effect of social desirability on responses to surveys on delicate topics such as child abuse, academic cheating, or sexual practices.

Still another issue to consider in surveys is the effect of sociocultural differences between test takers. You certainly are familiar with questionnaires that ask you to respond on a scale from, say, 1 to 7, with 1 meaning "strongly agree" and 7 meaning "strongly disagree." A cross-cultural study of high school students found that they differed in the degree to which they were willing to use the extreme points on scales like this. Students from Japan and Taiwan were more likely to use the midpoint than were students from Canada and the United States. This finding might be attributable to the greater tendency toward individualism in North American cultures and the greater tendency toward collectivism in East Asian cultures (Chen, Lee, & Stevenson, 1995). Consequently, survey researchers who use these kinds of scales should consider the cultural backgrounds of their participants when interpreting their findings.

Because of practical and financial constraints, surveys rarely include everyone of interest. Instead, researchers administer a survey to a **sample** of people who represent the target **population**. In conducting a survey at your school, you might interview a sample of 100 students. But for the results of your survey to be generalizable to the entire student population at your school, your sample must be representative of the student body in age, sex, and any other relevant characteristics. Generalizable results are best

survey A set of questions related to a particular topic of interest administered to a sample of people through an interview or questionnaire.

sample A group of participants selected from a population.

population A group of individuals who share certain characteristics.

achieved by **random sampling**, which makes each member of the population equally likely to be included in the sample. Surveys that have used random sampling have, for example, increased our knowledge of to the relationship between pornography and men's acceptance of violence against women (Malamuth, Hald, & Koss, 2012) and the relationship between religious orientation and health-relevant behaviors in residents of the greater Syracuse, New York, region (Masters & Knestel, 2011). Failure to achieve a random sample of respondents might produce bias because those selected to participate might be different from those not selected to participate in regard to the topic of the survey (Menachemi, 2011).

The need for a sample to be representative of its population was dramatically demonstrated in a notorious poll conducted by the *Literary Digest* during the 1936 U.S. presidential election. Until then, the *Literary Digest*'s presidential poll, based on millions of responses, had accurately predicted each presidential election from 1916 through 1932. In 1936, based on that poll, the editors predicted that Alf Landon, the Republican candidate, would easily defeat Franklin Roosevelt, the Democratic candidate. Yet, Roosevelt defeated Landon in a landslide.

What went wrong with the poll? Evidently, the participants included in the survey were a *biased sample,* not representative of those who voted. Many of the participants were selected from telephone directories or automobile registration lists in an era—the Great Depression—when telephones and automobiles were luxuries to many people, and those who had telephones or automobiles tended to be wealthier than those who did not. Because Republican candidates attracted wealthier voters than did Democratic candidates, people who had telephones or automobiles were more likely to favor the Republican (Landon) over the Democrat (Roosevelt). The previous polls did not suffer from this bias because economic differences among voters did not significantly affect their party allegiances until the 1936 election.

Psychological Testing

A widely used descriptive research method is the **psychological test**, which is a formal sample of a person's behavior, whether written or performed. The advantage of good tests is that they help us make less-biased decisions about individuals. There are many psychological tests, including tests of interests, attitudes, abilities, creativity, intelligence, and personality. Psychological testing has a variety of uses, including helping to decide child custody in divorce cases (Hagan & Hagan, 2008), determining law-enforcement leadership potential (Miller, Watkins, & Webb, 2009), and assessing the relationship of environmental lead exposure to cognitive, perceptual, and motor performance (Kmiecik-Małecka, Małecki, Pawlas, Woźniakova, & Pawlas, 2009) As noted by Anne Anastasi (1985), who was an influential authority on psychological testing for several decades (Hogan, 2003), a good test reflects important principles of test construction: *standardization, reliability,* and *validity.*

standardization

1. A procedure ensuring that a test is administered and scored in a consistent manner.
2. A procedure for establishing test norms by giving a test to large samples of people who are representative of those for whom the test is designed.

There are two major aspects of **standardization**. The first ensures that the test will be administered and scored in a consistent manner. In giving a test, all test administrators must use the same instructions, the same time limits, and the same scoring system. If they do not, test takers' scores might misrepresent their individual characteristics. The second establishes **norms**, which are the standards used to compare the scores of test takers. Without norms, a score on an intelligence test would be a meaningless number. Norms are established by giving the test to samples of hundreds or thousands of people who are representative of the people for whom the test is designed. If a test is to be used in North America, samples might include representative proportions of homosexual and heterosexual men and women; people from all ethnic groups; lower-, middle-, and upper-class individuals; and urban, rural, and suburban dwellers. Standardized norms have been established for tests that measure things such as factors involved in developmental changes in attention in children (Vakil, Blachstein, Sheinman, & Greenstein, 2009) and intelligence test scores of American and Canadian children (Reddon, Whipplet, & Reddon, 2007).

The use of testing norms became popular in North America in the early 20th century, in part because of the introduction of the Stanford-Binet Intelligence Scale in 1916 by Lewis Terman. In one case, Terman (1918) used the scale's norms to prevent the execution of a young man with intellectual disability who had committed a heinous murder. Should he have been tried as an adult and, therefore, be held responsible for his actions? Or was he so intellectually limited that he should not have been held responsible? The man's score on the Stanford-Binet indicated that his mental age was equivalent to that of a 7-year-old child. Terman testified as a defense witness in opposition to the prosecution's expert witness, who claimed that the young man could perform various activities that only an adult could perform. But the expert witness presented no evidence, only his personal opinion. Terman convinced the jury, using his intelligence scale's norms as objective evidence, that the activities noted by the prosecution witness could easily be performed by a child of 7 or 8 years of age. The jury, convinced by Terman, accepted that the man suffered from an intellectual disability and ruled out the death penalty in his case (Dahlstrom, 1993). The importance of standardized testing for grade school placement, college admissions, and other purposes increased throughout the 20th century. Today, standardized testing to ensure that children are progressing satisfactorily in school is mandatory in the United States under the widely publicized No Child Left Behind legislation (Mattai, 2002).

An adequate psychological test also must be *reliable*. The **reliability** of a test is the degree to which it gives consistent results over time and across administrators. Suppose you took an IQ test and scored 105 (average) one month, 62 (mentally retarded) the next month, and 138 (mentally gifted) the third month. Because your level of intelligence would not fluctuate that much in 3 months, you would argue that the test is unreliable. Likewise, you would doubt the reliability of a test that produced different results depending on who administered it.

One way to determine whether a test is reliable is to use the *test-retest method,* in which the same test is given to a group of people on two occasions. The greater the consistency of the scores on the tests from one occasion to the other, the higher the reliability of the test. Another way to determine a test's reliability is to determine its inter-rater reliability by assessing how strongly the results obtained by different administrators with the same test takers correlate with one another. The Preschool Behavioral and Emotional Rating Scale, for example, has both strong test-retest reliability and strong inter-rater reliability (Epstein & Synhorst, 2008).

A reliable test would be useless if it were not also valid. **Validity** is the extent to which a test measures what it is supposed to measure. An important kind of validity, *predictive validity,* indicates that the test accurately predicts behavior related to what the test is supposed to measure. A test of mechanical ability with predictive validity would accurately predict who would perform better as an automobile mechanic. The behavior or characteristic that is being predicted by a test, whether baking, automobile repair, or academic performance, is called a *criterion.*

One of the first studies of the predictive validity of a formal test was conducted by Francis Galton. He collected the civil service exam scores of hundreds of Englishmen who had taken the test in 1861 and compared them to their salaries 20 years later. He found that the exam had good predictive validity, in that those who had scored higher had higher salaries (the criterion) than did those who had scored lower. More recently, a large-scale review of the predictive validity of the Graduate Record Examination (GRE) found that it is a valid predictor of graduate school performance, as measured by first-year grade-point average (Kuncel, Hezlett, & Ones, 2001). That is, those who score high on the GRE tend to do better in graduate school than those who score low on it.

The sociocultural perspective has inspired greater interest in assessing the extent to which psychological tests, typically developed in North America, have cross-cultural reliability and validity. Tests that have shown cross-cultural reliability and validity include the Portuguese version of the Dental Anxiety Scale (Hu, Gorenstein, & Fuentes, 2007), the Japanese version of the Social Phobia Inventory (Nagata, Nakajima, Teo, Yamada, & Yoshimura, 2013), the Turkish version of the Beck Depression Inventory-II (Canel-Çınarbaş, Cui, & Lauridsen, 2011), and the Korean version of the Panic Disorder Severity Scale (Lee, Kim, & Yu, 2009). However, it is important to ensure that the research materials, samples, and participants' familiarity with the research task are culturally equivalent, or appropriate for the cultures under study (Allen & Walsh, 2000).

reliability The extent to which a test gives consistent results.

validity The extent to which a test measures what it is supposed to measure.

Archival Research

archival research
The systematic examination of collections of letters, manuscripts, tape recordings, video recordings, or other records.

The largest potential source of knowledge from descriptive research is **archival research**, which examines collections of letters, manuscripts, tape recordings, video recordings, or similar materials. The uses of archival research are virtually without limit. For example, archival research discussed in Chapter 3 attempts to answer the following controversial question: Do right-handed people live longer than left-handed people? An archival study of North American comic books found that their number of authoritarian themes increased during times of high perceived national social and economic threat and decreased during times of low perceived national social and economic threat (Peterson & Gerstein, 2005). And consider this question: Do women and men have different or similar physical fitness goals? In one archival study, researchers conducted Google Image searches for four consecutive years for the terms "burn fat" and "build muscle." They also recorded whether a woman, man, or no people appeared in the image. The researchers found that, regardless of the year, images of women were associated with the term "burn fat" and images of men were associated with the term "build muscle." This finding indicates that there are indeed gender differences in physical fitness goals (Salvatore & Maracek, 2010).

Archives also are valuable sources of historical information about psychology itself. Through the efforts of John Popplestone and Marion McPherson (Benjamin, 2002), the Archives of the History of American Psychology at The University of Akron has become the main repository of records related to the development of American psychology. The Archives provide insight into the major issues, pioneers, and landmark events in the history of American psychology (Popplestone & McPherson, 1976).

But note that, as is true of all descriptive research, archival research does not permit conclusive causal statements about its findings. For example, archival research cannot conclusively determine why women are more interested in burning fat than building muscle. Nor can archival research, by itself, explain why comic book themes become more authoritarian during times of perceived national social and threat.

Correlational Research

correlational research
Research that studies the degree of relationship between two or more variables.

correlation The degree of relationship between two or more variables.

variable An event, behavior, condition, or characteristic that has two or more values.

positive correlation
A correlation in which variables tend to change values in the same direction.

negative correlation
A correlation in which variables tend to change values in opposite directions.

causation An effect of one or more variables on another variable.

When psychologists want to predict changes in one variable based on changes in another, rather than simply describe something, they turn to **correlational research**. A **correlation** refers to the degree of relationship between two or more *variables*. A **variable** is an event, behavior, condition, or characteristic that has two or more values. Examples of possible variables include age, height, temperature, and intelligence.

Kinds of Correlation

A **positive correlation** between two variables indicates that they tend to change values in the same direction. That is, as the first increases, the second increases, and as the first decreases, the second decreases. For example, as hours of studying increase, grade-point average tends to increase. A **negative correlation** between two variables indicates that they tend to change values in opposite directions. For example, as age increases in adulthood, visual acuity tends to decrease. Correlations range in magnitude from zero, meaning that there is no systematic relationship between the variables, to 1.00, meaning that there is a perfect relationship between them. Thus, a perfect positive correlation would be +1.00, and a perfect negative correlation would be –1.00.

Consider the relationship between obesity and exercise. The more people exercise, the less they tend to weigh. This relationship indicates a negative correlation between exercise and body weight: As one increases, the other decreases. But it is essential to realize that when two variables are correlated, one can be used to *predict* the other, but the first does not necessarily have a causal relationship with the other (Brigham, 1989). That is, *correlation* does not necessarily imply **causation**. Even though it is plausible that exercise causes lower body weight, it is also possible that the opposite is true: Lower body weight might cause people to exercise. Lighter people might exercise more because they find it less strenuous, less painful, and less embarrassing than heavier people do.

Nonetheless, correlational research plays an important role when experimental research is either unethical or impractical to conduct, as is often true in certain settings, such as education (Thompson, Diamond, McWilliam, Snyder, & Snyder, 2005).

Causation versus Correlation

As another example of the need to distinguish between causation and correlation, consider the positive correlation between educational level and the likelihood of developing a deadly form of skin cancer called malignant melanoma ("Melanoma Risk and Socio-Economic Class," 1983). This positive correlation means that as educational level rises, the probability of getting the disease also rises. You would be correct in predicting that people who attend college will be more likely, later in life, to develop malignant melanoma than will people who never go beyond high school.

But does this finding mean that you should drop out of school today to avoid the disease? The answer is no, because the positive correlation between educational level and malignant melanoma does not necessarily mean that attending college causes the disease. Other factors common to people who attend college might cause them to develop the disease. Given that extensive exposure to the sun is a risk factor in malignant melanoma (Ivry, Ogle, & Shim, 2006), perhaps people who attend college increase their risk of malignant melanoma by exposing themselves to the sun more frequently than do those who have only a high school education. College students might be more likely to spend spring breaks in Florida, find summer jobs at beach resorts, or go on frequent Caribbean vacations after graduating and finding higher paying, full-time jobs. Instead of dropping out of college to avoid the disease, students might be wiser to spend less time in the sun.

Psychologists are careful not to confuse causation and correlation. They are aware that if two variables are positively correlated, the first might cause changes in the second, the second might cause changes in the first, or another variable might cause changes in both. Because of the difficulty in distinguishing causal relationships from mere correlational ones, correlational research has stimulated controversies in important areas of research. Does televised violence cause real-life aggression? A review of research on that question found a significant positive correlation between watching televised violence and exhibiting aggressive behavior. But this correlation does not indicate that televised violence *causes* aggressive behavior (Freedman, 1984). Perhaps people who are aggressive for other reasons simply prefer to watch violent television programs. Nonetheless, as discussed in Chapter 7, there have been a number of experimental studies that do support a causal link between media violence and viewer aggression (Bushman & Anderson, 2001).

Causation Versus Correlation

People who exercise regularly tend to be thinner than those who do not. But is exercise the cause of thin physiques? Perhaps not. Thin people might simply be more likely to exercise than people who are overweight. So, a negative correlation between exercise and body weight does not imply that exercise causes weight loss. Only experimental research can determine whether there is such a causal relationship.
Source: Flashon Studio/Shutterstock.com.

Experimental Research

The research methods discussed so far do not enable you to discover causal relationships between variables. Even when there is a strong correlation between variables, you cannot presume a causal relationship between them. To determine whether there is a causal relationship between variables, scientists use the **experimental method**. Psychologists have relied on the experimental method ever since the discipline finally completed its separation from philosophy in the late 19th century (Hatfield, 2002).

Experimental Method

Like the components of correlational research, the components of an experiment are called variables. Every experiment includes at least one *independent variable* and one *dependent variable*. The **independent variable** is manipulated by experimenters, which means that they determine its values before the experiment begins. The **dependent variable** shows any effects of the independent variable. In terms of cause-and-effect relationships, the independent variable would be the *cause* and changes in the dependent variable would be the *effect*. Thus, in a hypothetical experiment on the effects of drinking on driving, the independent variable of alcohol intake would be the cause of changes in the dependent variable of, say, steering accuracy.

experimental method
Research that manipulates one or more variables, while controlling other factors, to determine the effects on one or more other variables.

independent variable
A variable manipulated by the experimenter to determine its effect on another, dependent, variable.

dependent variable
A variable showing the effect of the independent variable

The simplest experiment uses one independent variable with two values (an experimental condition and a control condition) and one dependent variable. A group of participants, the **experimental group**, is exposed to the experimental condition, and a second group of participants, the **control group**, is exposed to the control condition. The control condition is often simply the absence of the experimental condition. For example, the experimental condition might be exposure to a particular advertisement, and the control condition might be nonexposure to the advertisement. The dependent variable might be the number of sales of the advertised product. The control group provides a standard of comparison for the experimental group. If you failed to include a control group in the suggested experiment on the effects of advertising, you would be unable to determine whether the advertising accounted for changes in the volume of sales.

This example illustrates the **field experiment**, which is conducted in real-life, as opposed to laboratory settings. Another example of a field experiment is one in which salesclerks had their moods altered by how alleged shoppers acted (that is, after interacting with a "shopper" trained by the experimenter—also called a *confederate*—which induced a positive or negative mood in the salesclerk). The salesclerks were then asked by another alleged shopper for help finding an item that the department store did not carry. The study found that the manipulation affected the extent to which inexperienced employees helped, but not the extent to which experienced employees helped. Positive mood induction led to more helping and negative mood induction led to less helping only among inexperienced salesclerks (Forgas, Dunn, & Granland, 2008).

To appreciate the nature of the experimental method, imagine you are a psychologist interested in conducting an experiment on the effect of melatonin on nightly sleep duration. A basic experiment on this topic is illustrated in Table 2-2. Assume that introductory psychology students volunteer to be participants in the study. Members of the experimental group receive the same dose of melatonin nightly for 10 weeks, while members of the control group receive a **placebo**, which has no demonstrated effect on sleep. As the experimenter, you would try to keep constant all other factors that might affect the two groups. By treating both groups the same except for the condition to which the experimental group is exposed, you would be able to conclude that any significant difference in average sleep duration between the experimental group and the control group was probably caused by the experimental group's receiving doses of melatonin. Without the use of a control group, you would have no standard of comparison and would be less secure in reaching that conclusion.

In the experiment on melatonin and nightly sleep duration, the independent variable (drug condition) has two values: melatonin and placebo. The experimenter is interested in the effect of the independent variable on the dependent variable. The dependent variable in this case is nightly sleep duration, with many possible values: 6 hours and 2 minutes, 7 hours and 48 minutes, and so on.

As an experimenter, you would try to hold constant all factors other than the independent variable, so that the effects of those factors are not confused with the effect of the independent variable. In the melatonin experiment, you would not want differences between the experimental group and the control group in diet, drugs, and other relevant factors to cause changes in the dependent variable that you would mistakenly attribute to the independent variable.

TABLE 2-2   A Basic Experimental Research Design

Group	Independent Variable	Dependent Variable
(Randomly assigned)	(Drug condition)	(Sleep)
Experimental group	Take melatonin	Hours of sleep
Control group	Take placebo	Hours of sleep

The effectiveness of melatonin in treating insomnia was, in fact, supported by a double-blind, placebo study of children with insomnia. Forty children, ages 6 to 12 years, with chronic difficulty falling asleep were randomly assigned to groups that received doses of melatonin or a placebo at 6 p.m. for four weeks. Thus, drug condition was the independent variable. The dependent variables included the time when the children turned the lights off in their bedrooms, the time when they fell asleep, and how long they slept. Those who received a placebo showed no significant change on these variables. In contrast, those who received doses of melatonin turned their lights off an average of 34 minutes earlier, fell asleep an average of 75 minutes earlier, and slept an average of 41 minutes longer (Smits, Nagtegaal, van der Heijden, & Coenen, 2001). Placebo control groups are essential in research on drug therapy, as in research on the effectiveness of drugs for treating depression (Hughes, Gabay, Funnel, & Dowrick, 2012) or anxiety (Bidzan, Mahableshwarkar, Jacobsen, Yan, & Sheehan, 2012).

Internal Validity

An experimenter must do more than simply manipulate an independent variable and record changes in a dependent variable. The experimenter must also ensure the **internal validity** of the experiment by *controlling* any extraneous factors whose effects on the dependent variable might be confused with those of the independent variable (Christ, 2007) in order to show a cause-and-effect relationship. Such extraneous factors are called **confounding variables**, because their effects are confused, or *confounded*, with those of the independent variable. A confounding variable might be associated with the experimental situation, participants, or experimenters involved in an experiment.

Situational Variables In carrying out the procedure in the melatonin experiment, you would not want any confounding variables to affect nightly sleep duration. You would want the participants to be treated the same, except that those in the experimental group would receive the same dose of melatonin nightly over a 10-week period. But suppose that some participants in the experimental group decided to take sleeping pills, to exercise more, or to practice meditation. If, at the end of the study, the experimental group had a longer nightly sleep duration than the control group, the results might be attributable not to the melatonin but to confounding variables—that is, differences between the groups in the extent to which they used sleeping pills, exercised, or practiced meditation.

As an example of the importance of controlling potential confounding procedural variables, consider what happened when the Pepsi-Cola company conducted a "Pepsi Challenge" taste test, an example of *consumer psychology* ("Coke-Pepsi Slugfest," 1976). Coca-Cola drinkers were asked to taste each of two unidentified cola drinks and state their preference. The drinks were Coca-Cola and Pepsi-Cola. The brand of cola was the independent variable, and the preference was the dependent variable. To keep the participants from knowing which cola they were tasting, they were given Pepsi-Cola in a cup labeled M and Coca-Cola in a cup labeled Q. To the delight of Pepsi-Cola stockholders, most of the participants preferred Pepsi-Cola.

The Pepsi-Cola company proudly—and loudly—advertised this finding as evidence that even Coca-Cola drinkers preferred Pepsi-Cola. But knowing the pitfalls of experimentation, the Coca-Cola company replicated the experiment, this time filling both cups with Coca-Cola. Most of the participants still preferred the cola in the cup labeled M. Evidently, the Pepsi Challenge had not demonstrated that Coca-Cola drinkers preferred Pepsi-Cola. It had demonstrated only that Coca-Cola drinkers preferred the letter M to the letter Q. The effect of the letters on the dependent variable (the taste preference) had been confounded with that of the independent variable (the kind of cola).

If you were asked to design a more scientifically sound Coke-Pepsi taste challenge, how would you control the effect of the letter on the cup? Pause to think about this question before reading on. One way to control it would be to use cups without letters. Of course, the experimenter would have to keep track of which cup contained Coke and which contained Pepsi. A second way to control the effect of the letter would be to label

internal validity The extent to which changes in a dependent variable can be attributed to one or more independent variables rather than to a confounding variable.

confounding variable A variable whose unwanted effect on the dependent variable might be confused with that of the independent variable.

Consumer Psychology: Example of a Blind Taste Test

How could you control for the effect of labeling each of the three products?
Source: John T Takai/ Shutterstock.com.

each of the colas M on half of the taste trials and Q on the other half. Thus, two ways to control potential confounding procedural variables are to eliminate them or to ensure that they affect all conditions equally.

Participant Variables Experimenters must likewise control potential confounding participant variables that might produce effects that would be confused with those of the independent variable. Suppose that in the melatonin experiment the participants in the experimental group initially differed from the participants in the control group on several variables, including their nightly sleep duration, psychoactive drug habits, and daily exercise practices. These differences might carry over into the experiment, affecting the participants' nightly sleep duration during the course of the study and giving the false impression that the independent variable (melatonin versus no melatonin) caused a significant difference on the dependent variable (nightly sleep duration) between the two groups.

Experimenters increase the chance that the experimental group and the control group will be initially equivalent on as many participant variables as possible by relying on *random assignment* of participants to groups (Enders, Laurenceau, & Stuetzle, 2006). In **random assignment**, participants are as likely to be assigned to one group as to another. Given a sufficiently large number of participants, random assignment will make the two groups initially equivalent on many, though not necessarily all, relevant participant variables.

After randomly assigning participants to the experimental group and the control group, you still would have to control other participant variables. One of the most important of these is **participant bias**, the tendency of people who know they are participants in a study to behave differently than they normally do. As in the case of naturalistic observation, you might choose to be unobtrusive, exposing people to the experimental condition without their being aware of it. If this were impossible, you might choose to misinform the participants about the true purpose of the study. (The ethical issues involved in using deception are discussed in the section entitled "Ethics of Psychological Research.") Placebos are used in conjunction with random assignment so that participants do not succumb to demand characteristics of the experimental situation, in which knowledge of the experimental hypothesis leads them to perform in a manner that supports it—even more so when they like the experimenter (Nichols & Maner, 2008).

Experimenter Variables Experimenters must control not only potential confounding variables associated with the research procedure or the research participants but also potential confounding variables associated with themselves. *Experimenter effects* on dependent variables can be caused by the experimenter's personal qualities, actions, and treatment of data. Experimenter effects have been studied most extensively by Robert Rosenthal and his colleagues, who have demonstrated them in many studies since the early 1960s. Rosenthal has found that the experimenter's personal qualities—including sex, attire, and attractiveness—can affect participants' behavior (Barnes & Rosenthal, 1985).

Also of concern is the effect of the experimenter's actions on the recording of data or on the participants' behavior, as in the **experimenter bias effect.** This occurs when the results are affected by the experimenter's expectancy about the outcome of a study, which is expressed through her or his unintentional actions. The tendency of participants to behave in accordance with experimenter expectancy is called *self-fulfilling prophecy.* Actions that might promote self-fulfilling prophecy include facial expressions (perhaps smiling at participants in one group and frowning at those in another), mannerisms (perhaps shaking hands with participants in one group but not with those in another), or tone of voice (perhaps speaking in an animated voice to participants in one group and speaking in a monotone to those in another). Self-fulfilling prophecy is especially important to control in studies of psychotherapy, because therapist expectancies, rather than therapy itself, might affect the outcome of therapy (Harris, 1994).

random assignment
The assignment of participants to experimental and control conditions so that each participant is as likely to be assigned to one condition as to another.

participant bias The tendency of people who know they are participants in a study to behave differently than they normally would.

experimenter bias effect
The tendency of experimenters to let their expectancies alter the way they treat their participants.

Can Experimenter Expectancies Affect the Behavior of Laboratory Rats?

Rationale

Robert Rosenthal noted that in the early 20th century, Ivan Pavlov had found that each succeeding generation of his animal subjects learned tasks faster than the preceding one. At first, Pavlov presumed that this improvement supported the (since-discredited) notion of the inheritance of acquired characteristics. But he eventually came to believe that the animals' improvement was caused by changes in the way in which his experimenters treated them. Rosenthal decided to determine whether experimenter expectancies could likewise affect the performance of laboratory animals.

Method

Rosenthal and his colleague Kermit Fode had 12 students act as experimenters in a study of maze learning in rats conducted at Harvard University (Rosenthal & Fode, 1963). Six of the students were told that their rats were specially bred to be "maze bright," and six were told that their rats were specially bred to be "maze dull." In reality, the rats did not differ in their inborn maze-learning potential. Each student was given five albino rats to run in a T-shaped maze, with one horizontal arm of the maze painted white and the other

Source: sextoacto/Shutterstock.com.

painted gray. The rats received a food reward whenever they entered into the gray arm. The arms were interchanged on various trials so that the rats had to learn to respond to the color gray rather than to the direction left or right. The students ran the rats 10 times a day for five days and recorded how long it took them to reach the food.

Results and Discussion

As shown in Figure 2-1, the results indicated the apparent influence of experimenter expectancy: On average, the "maze-bright" rats ran mazes faster than the "maze-dull" rats did. Because there was no evidence of cheating or misrecording of data by the students, the researchers attributed the results to experimenter expectancy. The students' expectancies apparently influenced the manner in which they trained or handled the rats, somehow leading the rats to perform in accordance with the expectancies. For example, those who trained "maze-bright" rats reported handling them more, and more gently, than did those who trained "maze-dull" rats. Confidence in the experimenter expectancy effect with animal subjects was supported in a replication study by a different researcher, using different rats, and involving a different learning task (Elkins, 1987). These findings indicate that those responsible for handling animals during an experiment should, if possible, be kept unaware of any presumed differences among the animals.

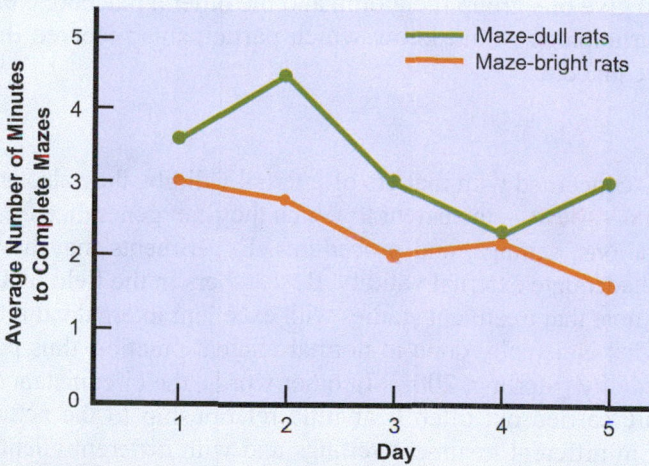

FIGURE 2-1   Experimenter Bias

The graph shows the results of the Rosenthal and Fode (1963) experiment, which found that allegedly maze-bright rats ran mazes faster than allegedly maze-dull rats did, depending on the experimenters' expectations.

Source: Data from Rosenthal and Fode (1963), "The Effect of Experimenter Bias on the Performance of the Albino Rat" in *Behavioral Science, 8,* 183–189.

Elementary School Teacher

Can teacher expectations affect student performance? *Source:* Andresr/Shutterstock. com.

double-blind technique

A procedure that controls experimenter bias and participant bias by preventing experimenters and participants from knowing which participants have been assigned to particular conditions.

external validity The extent to which the results of a research study can be generalized to other people, animals, or settings.

In a study of self-fulfilling prophecy that became widely publicized, Rosenthal found that elementary school teachers' expectancies for the performance of their students affected how well the children performed. Students whose teachers were led to believe they were fast learners performed better than did students whose teachers were led to believe they were slow learners. Yet, the students did not differ in their initial ability (Rosenthal & Jacobson, 1968). This finding became known as the *Pygmalion effect,* after the story in which an uneducated woman improves herself because of her mentor's faith in her. The Pygmalion effect also can occur between parents and children, therapists and patients, and employers and workers (McNatt, 2000). The classic research study discussed in "The Research Process" box demonstrated that experimenter expectancies can even affect the behavior of animal subjects.

How might experimenter bias affect the results of the hypothetical melatonin experiment? The experimenter might act more friendly and encourage the participants in the experimental group, perhaps motivating them to sleep better than they would have otherwise. Participants with a higher need for social approval would be especially susceptible to experimenter expectancy effects such as this special treatment (Hazelrigg, Cooper, & Strathman, 1991). One way to control experimenter bias would be to have those people who interact with the participants be unaware of the research hypothesis, eliminating the influence of the experimenter's expectancies on the participants' performance.

At times, both participant bias and experimenter bias might become confounding variables. This possibility might prompt experimenters to use the **double-blind technique**, in which neither the experimenter nor the participants know the conditions to which the participants have been assigned. This technique is common in studies of the effectiveness of drug treatments for psychological disorders. Consider a study on the effectiveness of nicotine-replacement therapy for smoking cessation. In a double-blind study, experimental groups received either nicotine gum or a nicotine inhaler, while the control group received a placebo. Participants in the nicotine replacement condition were significantly more likely to smoke fewer cigarettes or stop smoking altogether than the participants in the placebo condition (Kralikova, Kozak, Rasmussen, Gustavsson, & Le Houezec, 2009). In a double-blind melatonin experiment, instead of giving one group melatonin and the other nothing, it would be wise to give one group melatonin and the other a placebo. Neither the experimenter nor the participants would know which participants received the melatonin and which received the placebo.

External Validity

Though experimenters are chiefly concerned with matters of internal validity, they also are concerned with matters of **external validity**—the extent to which they can generalize their research findings to other populations, settings, and procedures. Experiments may have strong internal validity yet have inadequate external validity. Researchers in the field of alcoholism treatment, for example, note that treatment studies with excellent internal validity often bear little relationship to what is actually done in normal clinical practice, thus potentially limiting their external validity (Sterling, 2002). In other words, the circumstances under which treatment studies are carried out often bear little relationship to the actual treatment provided by clinicians in different treatment settings and with different clients. Similarly, laboratory experiments on consumer behavior often have strong internal validity but may lack external validity in regard to consumer behavior in everyday life, making those who run marketing campaigns unsure of whether consumer behavior that occurs in the laboratory will occur in everyday life too (Winer, 1999). Likewise, the external validity of experiments on automobile driving behavior using laboratory driving simulators depends on the simulation being relevant to real-life driving behavior (Araújo, 2007).

Because psychology relies heavily on college students as research participants, external validity is an important consideration (Blanton & Jaccard, 2008). One must ask if college students represent the sample population of what is being studied. In addition, those who volunteer to participate in experiments may differ in important characteristics from those who choose not participate, possibly weakening the external validity of experimental findings—as in experiments on smoking cessation programs aimed at finding techniques to use with smokers in general (Graham et al., 2008). Generalizability is enhanced when the characteristics of the sample used in the experiment are similar to those of the population it represents (Hughes & Callas, 2010).

Moreover, as stressed by Stanley Sue (1999) and other psychologists who favor the sociocultural perspective, the results of a research study done in one culture will not necessarily be generalizable to another culture or ethnic group. Researchers must identify the specific populations to which their research findings may be applied. An archival study of 14 psychology journals over a five-year period found that only 61 percent of 2,536 articles related to applied psychology reported participants' ethnicity. Of those that did, the ethnic breakdown of the samples was generally representative of the population estimates provided by the U.S. Census Bureau. However, Latinos—for whom English may be a second language—were underrepresented. The generalizability of research findings from those studies to non-English speakers is limited (Case & Smith, 2000).

But cross-cultural replications of research sometimes do demonstrate the possible universality of findings. Research has found cross-cultural similarities in coping strategies employed by Canadian and New Zealand women with a history of child sexual abuse (Barker-Collo, Read, & Cowie, 2012). Another study found that the same sociocultural factors that were associated with body self-image and eating disorders in American women also were found in Japanese women (Yamamiya, Shroff, & Thompson, 2008). And, researchers have found that marital discord also is associated with depression in both American and Brazilian women (Hollist, Miller, Falceto, & Fernandes, 2007).

Replication to assess external validity is not only important in experimental research but in other kinds of research as well. A national American survey found that about the same percentage of people had obsessions or compulsions as several previous national surveys had found (Ruscio, Stein, Chiu, & Kessler, 2010). A study that used psychological testing of self-esteem replicated prior research by showing that a major factor in overall self-esteem is one's perceived appraisal by significant others such as parents, teachers, and friends (Stephan & Maiano, 2007). And a study on the effectiveness of a high school suicide prevention program found results similar to that found by a previous study in regard to changing undesirable attitudes toward suicide and in decreasing reluctance to seek mental health treatment (Ciffone, 2007).

Another problem affecting external validity is the use of volunteer participants. People who volunteer to take part in a given experiment might differ from people who fail to, possibly limiting the generalizability of the research findings. In a study using volunteer participants, male and female undergraduates were given the choice of participating in either a study in which they would be given a sexual interview or a study in which they would watch an explicit sexual video. When compared with students who refused to volunteer, students who volunteered for either of the studies were more sexually experienced, held less traditional sexual attitudes, and scored higher on measures of sexual esteem and sexual sensation seeking. These findings indicate that people who participate in sexual research might not be representative of people in general, limiting the confidence with which sex researchers can generalize their findings (Wiederman, 1999).

Of course, differences between volunteers and nonvolunteers do not automatically mean that the results lack external validity. The best way to determine whether the results of research studies do in fact have external validity is to replicate them. Replication also enables researchers to determine whether the results of laboratory studies will generalize to the world outside the laboratory. Most replications are approximate; they rarely use the same setting, participants, or procedures. For example, confidence in the Pygmalion effect was strengthened when it was replicated by different researchers, using different teachers, with different students, in a different school (Meichenbaum, Bowers, & Ross, 1969). The ideal would be to replicate studies systematically several times, varying one aspect of the study each time (Hendrick, 1990). Thus, you would be more confident in your ability to generalize the findings of the melatonin experiment if people with insomnia, of a variety of ages, in several different cultures, succeeded in sleeping longer after habitually taking melatonin before bedtime.

Now that you have been introduced to the descriptive, correlational, and experimental methods of research, you should be able to recognize them as you read about research studies described in later chapters. As you read particular studies, try to determine which kind of method was used as well as its possible strengths and weaknesses—most notably, any potential confounding variables and any limitations on the generalizability of the research findings. You now are ready to learn how psychologists analyze the data generated by their research methods.

Section Review: Methods of Psychological Research

1. Why is it important to use unbiased samples in surveys?
2. What is validity in psychological testing?
3. What is an independent variable?
4. What is internal validity?

Statistical Analysis of Research Data

How would you make sense out of the data generated by the hypothetical melatonin experiment? In analyzing the data, you would have to do more than simply state that Ann Lee slept 9.1 hours, Steve White slept 7.8 hours, Sally Ramirez slept 8.2 hours, and so on. You would have to identify overall patterns in the data and whether the data support the research hypothesis that inspired the experiment.

As mentioned earlier, to make sense out of their data, psychologists rely on statistics. The term *statistics* was originally used to refer to the practice of recording quantitative political and economic information about European nation-states (Cowles, 1989). During the 20th century, the use of statistics to analyze research data became increasingly more prevalent in articles published in psychology journals (Parker, 1990). Psychologists use *descriptive statistics* to summarize data, *correlational statistics* to determine relationships between variables, and *inferential statistics* to test their experimental research hypotheses. Appendix C (available in the Online Edition) presents an expanded discussion of statistics and their calculation.

Descriptive Statistics

descriptive statistics
Statistics that summarize research data.

You would summarize your data by using **descriptive statistics**. An early champion of the use of descriptive statistics was Florence Nightingale (1820–1910), one of the founders of modern nursing. She urged that hospitals keep medical records on their patients. As a result, she demonstrated statistically that British soldiers during times of war were more likely to die from disease and unsanitary conditions than from combat. She also was a pioneer in the use of graphs to support her conclusions. Her work led to reforms in nursing and medicine and to her being made a fellow of the Royal Statistical Society and an honorary member of the American Statistical Association (Viney, 1993). Descriptive statistics include *measures of central tendency* and *measures of variability*.

Measures of Central Tendency

measure of central tendency
A statistic that represents the "typical" score in a set of scores.

mode The score that occurs most frequently in a set of scores.

A **measure of central tendency** is a single number used to represent a set of scores. The measures of central tendency include the *mode,* the *median,* and the *mean.* Psychological research uses the mode least often, the median somewhat more often, and the mean most often.

The **mode** is the most frequent score in a set of scores. As shown in Table 2-3, in the melatonin experiment the mode for the experimental group is 8.6 hours and the mode for

TABLE 2-3 Descriptive Statistics from a Hypothetical Experiment on the Effect of Melatonin on Average Nightly Sleep Duration

Experimental Group (Melatonin)				Control Group (No Melatonin)			
Participant	Duration	d	d^2	Participant	Duration	d	d^2
1	9.1	0.2	0.04	1	7.4	−0.5	0.25
2	8.6	−0.3	0.09	2	8.2	0.3	0.09
3	8.6	−0.3	0.09	3	9.5	1.6	2.56
4	8.8	−0.1	0.01	4	8.9	1.0	1.00
5	7.8	−1.1	1.21	5	6.7	−1.2	1.44
6	9.9	1.0	1.00	6	8.9	1.0	1.00
7	8.6	−0.3	0.09	7	7.5	−0.4	0.16
8	9.7	0.8	0.64	8	6.2	−1.7	2.89
9	9.0	0.1	0.01	9	7.8	−0.1	0.01
	Sum = 80.1		Sum = 3.18		Sum = 71.1		Sum = 9.40

Mode = 8.6 hours

Median = 8.8 hours

Mean = $\dfrac{80.1}{9}$ = 8.9 hours

Range = 9.9 − 7.8 = 2.1 hours

Variance = $\dfrac{\text{sum of } d^2}{\text{no. of participants}} = \dfrac{3.18}{9} = 0.35$

Standard deviation = $\sqrt{\text{Variance}}$

$= \sqrt{0.35}$

$= 0.59$ hours

Mode = 8.9 hours

Median = 7.8 hours

Mean = $\dfrac{71.1}{9}$ = 7.9 hours

Range = 9.5 − 6.2 = 3.3 hours

Variance = $\dfrac{\text{sum of } d^2}{\text{no. of participants}} = \dfrac{9.40}{9} = 01.04$

Standard deviation = $\sqrt{\text{Variance}}$

$= \sqrt{1.04}$

$= 1.02$ hours

Note: d = deviation from the mean.

the control group is 8.9 hours. The **median** is the middle score in a set of scores that have been arranged in numerical order. Thus, in the melatonin experiment the median score for each group is the fifth score after the scores are put in rank order. The median for the experimental group is 8.8 hours and the median for the control group is 7.8 hours. You are most familiar with the **mean**, which is the arithmetic average of a set of scores. You use the mean when you calculate your exam average, batting average, or average gas mileage. In the melatonin experiment, the mean for the experimental group is 8.9 hours and the mean for the control group is 7.9 hours.

One of the problems in the use of measures of central tendency is that they can be used selectively to create misleading impressions. Suppose you had the following psychology exam scores: 23, 23, 67, 68, 69, 70, 91. The mode (the most frequent score) would be 23, the median (the middle score) would be 68, and the mean (the average score) would be 58.7. In this case, you would prefer the median as representative of your performance. But what if you had the following scores: 23, 67, 68, 69, 70, 91, 91? The mode would be 91, the median would be 69, and the mean would be 68.43. In that case, you would prefer the mode as representative of your performance.

median The middle score in a set of scores that have been ordered from lowest to highest.

mean The arithmetic average of a set of scores.

Product advertisers, government agencies, and political parties also are prone to this selective use of measures of central tendency, as well as other statistics, to support their claims. But the use of statistics to mislead is not new. Its prevalence in the 19th century prompted British prime minister Benjamin Disraeli to declare, "There are three kinds of lies: lies, damned lies, and statistics." Even a basic understanding of statistics will make you less likely to be fooled by claims based on their misleading use.

Measures of Variability

measure of variability
A statistic describing the degree of dispersion in a set of scores.

range A statistic representing the difference between the highest and lowest scores in a set of scores.

To represent a distribution of scores, psychologists do more than report a measure of central tendency. They also report a **measure of variability**, which describes the degree of dispersion of the scores. That is, do the scores tend to bunch together, or are they scattered? Commonly used measures of variability include the range and the standard deviation. The **range** is the difference between the highest and the lowest score in a set of scores. In Table 2-3 the range of the experimental group is $9.9 - 7.8 = 2.1$ hours, and the range of the control group is $9.5 - 6.2 = 3.3$ hours. But the range can be misleading because one extreme score can create a false impression. Suppose that a friend conducts a similar experiment and reports that the range of sleep duration among the 15 participants in his experimental group is 4 hours, with the longest duration being 9.3 hours and the shortest duration being 5.3 hours. You might conclude that there was a great deal of variability in the distribution of scores. But what if he then reported that only one participant slept less than 9.1 hours? Obviously, the scores would bunch together at the high end, making the variability of scores much less than you had presumed.

standard deviation A statistic representing the degree of dispersion of a set of scores around their mean.

variance A measure based on the average deviation of a set of scores from their group mean.

Because of their need to employ more meaningful measures of variability than the range, psychologists prefer to use the standard deviation. The **standard deviation** represents the degree of dispersion of scores around their mean and is the square root of a measure of variability called the *variance*. The **variance** is a measure based on the average deviation of a set of scores from their group mean. Table 2-3 shows that the standard deviation of the experimental group is 0.59 hours, whereas the standard deviation of the control group is 1.02 hours. Thus, the distribution of scores in the experimental group has a larger mean, but the distribution of scores in the control group has a larger standard deviation.

Correlational Statistics

coefficient of correlation
A statistic that assesses the degree of association between two or more variables.

If you were interested in predicting one set of scores from another, you would use a measure of correlation. The concept of correlation was put forth in 1888 by Francis Galton, who wanted a way to represent the relationship between parents and offspring on factors, such as intelligence, presumed to be affected by heredity. Whereas the mean and standard deviation are useful in describing individual sets of scores, a statistic called the coefficient of correlation is useful in quantifying the degree of association between two or more sets of scores. The **coefficient of correlation** was devised by the English mathematician Karl Pearson (1851–1926) and is often called *Pearson's r* (with the *r* standing for "regression," another name for correlation).

As you learned earlier, a correlation can be positive or negative and can range from zero to +1.00 or –1.00. In a *positive correlation* between two sets of scores, relatively high scores on one set are associated with relatively high scores on the other, and relatively low scores on one set are associated with relatively low scores on the other (Branch, 1990). For example, there is a positive correlation between height and weight and between high school and college grade-point averages. In a *negative correlation* between two sets of scores, relatively high scores on one set are associated with relatively low scores on the other. For example, there is a negative correlation between driving speed and gas mileage. A *zero correlation* indicates that there is no relationship between one set of scores and another. You would find an approximately zero correlation between the intelligence levels of two groups of randomly selected strangers. The types of correlations are illustrated graphically in Figure 2-2.

The higher the correlation between two variables, the more accurately the scores on one variable will predict the scores on the other. For example, suppose you found a correlation of .83 between the number of milligrams of melatonin that people take each night

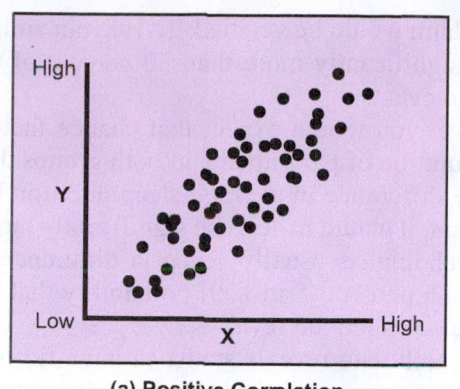

(a) Positive Correlation

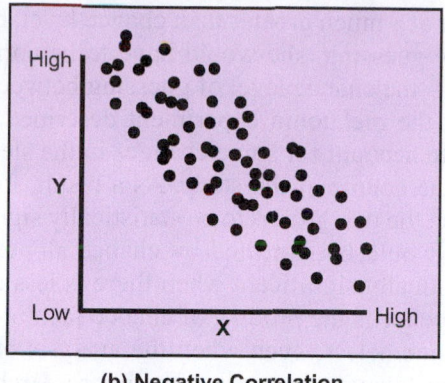

(b) Negative Correlation

(c) Zero Correlation

FIGURE 2-2 Correlations

(a) In a *positive correlation*, scores on the variables increase and decrease together. An example is the relationship between SAT verbal scores and college grade-point average. (b) In a *negative correlation*, scores on one variable increase as scores on another variable decrease. An example is the relationship between age and nightly sleep. (c) In a *zero correlation*, scores on one variable are unrelated to scores on another. A possible example is the relationship between the number of times people brush their teeth each day and the number of houseplants they have.

and their nightly sleep duration. This strong correlation would make you fairly confident in predicting that as the dose of melatonin increases, the average nightly duration of sleep would increase. If, instead, you found a weak correlation of .17, you would have less confidence in making that prediction.

Inferential Statistics

In the melatonin experiment, the experimental group had a longer average nightly sleep duration than the control group. But is the difference in average nightly sleep duration between the two groups large enough for you to conclude with confidence that melatonin was responsible for the difference? Perhaps the difference happened by chance—that is, because of a host of random factors unrelated to melatonin. To determine whether the independent variable, rather than chance factors, caused the changes in the dependent variable, psychologists use **inferential statistics**. By permitting psychologists to determine the causes of events, inferential statistics help them achieve the goal of explanation. Inferential statistics are "inferential" because they enable experimenters to make inferences from the samples used in their experiment to the populations of individuals they represent.

inferential statistics Statistics used to determine whether changes in a dependent variable are caused by an independent variable.

Statistical Significance

If there is a low probability that the difference between groups on the dependent variable is attributable to chance (that is, to random factors), the difference is statistically significant and is attributed to the independent variable. The concept of **statistical significance** was first put forth by the English mathematician Ronald Fisher (1890–1962) when he sought a way to test a noblewoman's claim that she could tell whether tea or milk had been added to her cup first (Tankard, 1984). Though he never carried out the demonstration, he proposed presenting her with a series of cups in which tea was sometimes added first and milk was sometimes added first. He assumed that if she could report the correct

statistical significance A low probability (usually less than 5 percent) that the results of a research study are due to chance factors rather than to the independent variable.

order at a much greater than chance level, her claim would be verified. To rule out simple lucky guessing, she would have to be correct significantly more than 50 percent of the time—the chance level of guessing between two events.

In the melatonin experiment described above, you would expect that chance factors would account for some changes in the sleep duration of participants in both groups during the course of the study. As a result, for the difference in average sleep duration between the two groups to be statistically significant, it would have to be significantly larger than would be expected by chance alone. Psychologists usually accept a difference as statistically significant when there is less than a 5 percent (5 in 100) probability that the difference is the product of chance factors—the so-called .05 level.

Nonetheless, even when the analysis of research data reveals statistical significance, the best way to determine whether research findings are generalizable is to replicate them (Falk, 1998). Two real experiments did, in fact, "replicate" the findings of the imaginary melatonin experiment described earlier. These experiments, which used the double-blind technique, found that participants who took melatonin slept longer than did participants who took the placebo—regardless of whether the participants were normal sleepers (Waldhauser, Saletu, & Trinchard, 1990) or insomnia sufferers (MacFarlane, Cleghorn, Brown, & Streiner, 1991). Thus, there is scientific support for the claims made in the *Newsweek* cover story that opened this chapter.

Another issue is the need to distinguish between statistical significance and clinical significance. Participants in an experimental group may differ on the target measure from participants in the control group, but the difference might not be large enough to produce meaningful clinical effects. Likewise, a small, but statistically significant difference between the experimental and control group might not be large enough to have practical significance outside the laboratory (Wijk, 2009).

Meta-analysis

meta-analysis A technique that combines the results of many similar studies to determine the effect size of a particular kind of independent variable.

Still another approach to assessing generalizability is to use the relatively new statistical technique called **meta-analysis**. Meta-analysis combines research findings from many, typically dozens, of related studies and goes beyond simply determining statistical significance. After gathering the studies under analysis, the researcher computes a statistic, d or *Cohen's d*, for each study in the analysis. This statistic compares the difference between the mean scores of each group and the distribution of scores (using the standard deviation) within each group. In other words, group differences are considered relative to individual differences. Then, the d statistic is averaged across all studies to compute the average size of the effect of the independent variable. As a general rule, effect sizes are described as small ($d = .20$), moderate ($d = .50$), or large ($d = .80$) (Cohen, 1969).

Because meta-analyses consider a large number of published, and sometimes unpublished studies, other factors influencing research findings may be evaluated in addition to effect sizes (Rosenthal & DiMatteo, 2002). For example, a meta-analysis of altruism found that men were more likely than women to help in risky situations, particularly when others were present (Eagly & Crowley, 1986). Thus, this gender difference might be attributable to the male gender role. Meta-analyses also enable psychologists to compare effect sizes across time, thus assessing the effect of sociocultural change. Two meta-analyses of gender differences in verbal and mathematical ability compared the effect sizes of studies published before and after 1973 (Hyde, Fennema, & Lamon, 1990; Hyde and Linn, 1988). In both analyses, the size of gender differences declined over the years.

Meta-analyses have been useful to psychologists interested in distilling the results of a large number of studies. However, the use of meta-analyses cannot overcome the methodological limitations of the studies on which they are based. Most important, studies that rely on selective recruitment of participants and poor assessment procedures are not improved by the use of meta-analysis (Halpern, 1995). Proponents such as Janet Shibley Hyde (1948–) (1994) assert that meta-analyses are helpful in understanding group differences, the effect of social roles and other situational factors on people's behavior, and how variables such as gender and ethnicity may influence each other. Psychologists have used the results of meta-analyses to shed light on a number of topics, including the psychological and physical health of elderly caregivers (Pinquart & Soerensen, 2003), gender differences and similarities in smiling (LaFrance, Hecht, & Paluck, 2003), gender differences and similarities in the quality of romantic attachment (Del Giudice, 2011).

Meta-analysis has been applied to many research topics, including some that even might be interesting to nonscientists. A meta-analysis of studies involving 3,401 participants found that the infamous commonsense "freshman 15"—a gain of 15 pounds—that supposedly marks the first year of college is off the mark. The meta-analysis found that there is an average weight gain of about 4 pounds during the first year—closer to a "freshman 5" (Vella-Zarb & Elgar, 2009). Chocolate lovers who are concerned about high blood pressure will appreciate that a meta-analysis of relevant studies found that eating dark chocolate significantly reduces high blood pressure (Ried, Sullivan, Fakler, Frank, & Stocks, 2010).

As you read the research studies discussed in later chapters, keep in mind that almost all were analyzed by one or more descriptive statistics, correlational statistics, or inferential statistics. You should also note that statistical significance does not necessarily imply practical or social significance (Favreau, 1997; Rachman, 1993). For example, a number of studies have reported small but consistent gender differences in social influence (Eagly, 1983). Though studies have found statistically significant differences in women's and men's behavior, these differences might not be of practical significance. In other words, they might not be large enough to account for the observed differences in men's and women's lives. Some journals that contain reports of research in counseling now require statements of not just statistical significance but also practical or clinical significance (Thompson, 2002).

Group Differences versus Individual Differences

When psychologists report gender, ethnic, or cross-cultural differences in research studies, they are describing group differences on the dependent variable. For example, one study might conclude that boys are more aggressive than girls. This conclusion is based on tests of inferential statistics—the mean for the sample of boys was greater than the mean for the sample of girls. And the difference between these two means was statistically significant. Thus, on average, boys were more aggressive than girls.

A statement about group differences—as in this case of gender differences in aggression—does not mean that the behavior of all the male participants differed from that of all the female participants. When frequency distributions of gender, ethnic, or cross-cultural group scores are plotted, there usually is overlap between the two curves. It is extremely unlikely that each participant in one group scored higher than each participant in the other group.

A statistically significant gender difference in aggression also might be smaller than individual differences in aggression. In this example, it is important to consider the magnitude of within-group variability. As you can see in Figure 2-3, many of the boys and girls in these

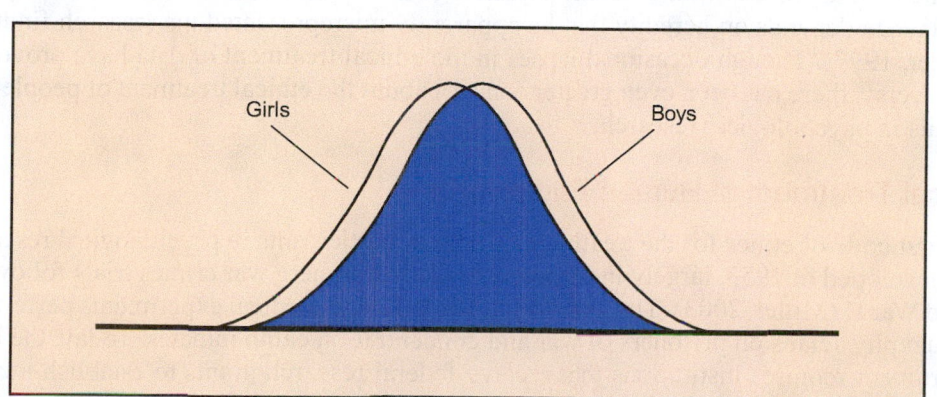

FIGURE 2-3 Statistically Significant Gender Differences

These overlapping curves represent frequency distributions of aggressiveness in a sample of girls and boys. Though these curves represent a statistically significant gender difference in aggressiveness, note that many of the boys and girls did not differ in their aggressiveness (the shaded area of the overlapping curves).

two samples did not differ in their aggressiveness. The areas shared by the overlapping curves represent this similarity. Moreover, some boys were not very aggressive at all whereas some girls were very aggressive. As you can see, the variability of the girls' and boys' scores—the spread of each curve—is greater than the distance between the two group means.

It is important, then, to understand that though there might be average group differences, it also is likely that there are considerable individual differences. And when individual differences are greater in magnitude than group differences, it is difficult to predict a particular person's behavior on the basis of group differences. Suppose a researcher reports significant cross-cultural differences between European American and Asian American participants in parenting behaviors. It would be a mistake to conclude from these findings that all European American parents treat their children differently than all Asian Americans. And the difference between two European American parents is likely to be greater in magnitude than the average cross-cultural difference.

Section Review: Statistical Analysis of Research Data

1. What are measures of central tendency?

2. What are measures of variability?

3. What is statistical significance?

4. How does meta-analysis summarize the results of many research studies?

Ethics of Psychological Research

Psychologists must be as concerned with the ethical treatment of their data and human participants and animal subjects as they are with the quality of their research methods and statistical analyses. Academic psychology departments place a premium on teaching their students the necessity of conducting ethically responsible research (Fisher, Fried, & Feldman, 2009).

Ethical Treatment of Research Data

A serious ethical violation in the treatment of data is falsification. Thus, in the hypothetical melatonin experiment, you would have to record your data accurately—even if it contradicted your hypothesis. During the past century, there have been several notorious cases in which researchers in physics, biology, medicine, or psychology have been accused of falsifying their data (Park, 2008). Chapter 10 discusses a prominent case in psychology in which Sir Cyril Burt, an eminent psychologist, was so intent on demonstrating that intelligence depends on heredity that he apparently misrepresented his research findings (Tucker, 1997). Though occasional lapses in the ethical treatment of data have provoked controversy, there has been even greater concern about the ethical treatment of people and animals in psychological research.

Ethical Treatment of Human Participants

The first code of ethics for the treatment of human participants in psychological research was developed in 1953, largely in response to the Nuremberg war crimes trials following World War II (Miller, 2003). The trials disclosed the cruel medical experiments performed by Nazi physicians on prisoners of war and concentration camp inmates. Today, the U.S. government requires institutions that receive federal research grants to establish a committee—known as an Institutional Review Board (IRB)—that reviews research proposals to ensure the ethical treatment of human participants and animal subjects (McGaha & Korn, 1995).

APA Code of Ethics

The code of ethics of the American Psychological Association (APA) contains specific requirements for the treatment of human participants and has published books detailing the ethical treatment of volunteers in experiments (Sales & Folkman, 2000).

1. The researcher must inform potential participants of all aspects of the research procedure that might influence their decision to participate. In the melatonin experiment, you would not be permitted to tell participants that they will be given melatonin and then give them a placebo instead unless they had been informed of the possibility. This requirement, informed consent, can be difficult to ensure because participants might be unable to give truly informed consent. Perhaps the participants are children (Vitiello, 2008), are prisoners (Regehr, Edward, & Bradford, 2000), or have schizophrenia (Beebe & Smith, 2010) or intellectual disabilities such as dementia (Cubit, 2010), and cannot comprehend the language used on informed consent documents.

2. Potential participants must not be forced to participate in a research study, which could become a problem with prisoners or hospitalized patients who fear the consequences of refusing to participate (Rosenthal, 1995). Though sometimes forcing the individual to undergo therapy, as in the case of adolescents with anorexia nervosa (a disorder marked by self-starvation), can be lifesaving (Manley, Smye, & Srikameswaran, 2001), it is not ethically permissible in research studies.

3. Participants must be permitted to withdraw from a study at any time. Of course, when participants withdraw, it can adversely affect the study because those who remain might differ from those who drop out. The loss of participants can therefore limit the ability to generalize research findings from those who complete the study to the desired target population (Trice & Ogden, 1987).

4. The researcher must protect the participants from physical harm and mental distress. Again, the use of deception might violate this provision by inducing mental distress. Certain research practices themselves might raise ethical concerns because of the distress they produce, such as contacting recently bereaved relatives to recruit them to participate in research on bereavement (Steeves, Kahn, Ropka, & Wise, 2001).

5. If a participant does experience harm or distress, the researcher must try to alleviate it. But some critics argue that it is impossible to routinely determine whether attempts to relieve distress produce long-lasting benefits (Norris, 1978).

6. Information gained from participants must be kept confidential. Confidentiality becomes a major issue when participants reveal information that indicates they might be in danger, such as children or adolescents being abused by parents (Wiles, Crow, Heath, & Charles, 2008).

Deception in Research

Despite their code of ethics, psychologists sometimes confront ethical dilemmas in their treatment of human participants, as in the use of deception to reduce participant bias. Psychologists might fail to inform people that they are participating in a study or might misinform participants about the true nature of a study. This deception is of concern, in part, because it violates the ethical norm of informed consent. Recall that the computer-dating study by Donn Byrne and colleagues (Byrne et al., 1970) used deception by falsely claiming that all participants would be matched with partners who shared their attitudes. Today, for this study to be considered ethical, the researcher would have to demonstrate to the IRB that the experiment could not be conducted without the use of deception and that its potential findings are important enough to justify the use of deception (Fisher & Fyrberg, 1994). Moreover, at the completion of the study, each participant would have to be debriefed. In **debriefing** participants, the researcher explains the reasons for the deception and tries to relieve any distress that

debriefing A procedure, after the completion of a research study, that informs participants of the purpose of the study and aims to remove any physical or psychological distress caused by participation.

Scientists Pro-Test in Support of Animal Research

In response to animal rights activists, scientists have begun to demonstrate their support for lifesaving medical research using animals.

Source: Professor David Jentsch. Used with permission.

might have been experienced (Benham, 2008). Some commentators insist that debriefing should be a component of nondeceptive research as well (Sharpe & Faye, 2009).

Some psychologists worry that deceptive research will make potential participants distrust psychological research (Hertwig & Ortmann, 2008). And Diana Baumrind (1985), a critic of deceptive research, argues that not even the positive findings of studies that use deception outweigh the distress of participants who learn that they have been fooled. Arguments against deceptive research have been countered by psychologists who argue that it would be unethical not to conduct deceptive studies that might produce important findings (Christensen, 1988). Still others urge psychologists not only to weigh the costs and benefits of using deception but also to inform participants that deception might be used as part of the study (Pittenger, 2002).

Whereas some psychologists argue about the use of deception, others try to settle the debate over deceptive research by using the results of empirical research. In one study, undergraduates who had participated in deceptive experiments rated their experience as more positive than did those who had participated in nondeceptive ones. Moreover, those in deceptive experiments did not rate psychologists as less trustworthy. Any negative emotional effects reported by participants seemed to be relieved by debriefing. The researchers concluded that debriefing eliminates any negative effects of deception, perhaps because the participants learn the importance of the research study (Smith & Richardson, 1983).

But this interpretation of the findings has been criticized. You might wish to pause to see if you can think of an alternative explanation for why participants in deceptive experiments responded more positively. One possibility is that the procedures used in deceptive experiments are more interesting and enjoyable than those used in nondeceptive ones (Rubin, 1985). Remembering that psychology, as a science, resolves issues through empirical research instead of through argument alone, how might you conduct a study to determine whether this assumption is correct? One way would be to conduct experiments whose procedures have been rated as equally interesting, and use deception in only half of them. If the participants still rate the deceptive experiments more positively, then the results would support Smith and Richardson (1983). If the participants rate the deceptive experiments less positively, then the results would support Rubin (1985).

Ethical Treatment of Animal Subjects

At the 1986 annual meeting of the American Psychological Association in Washington, D.C., animal rights advocates picketed in the streets and disrupted talks, including one by the prominent psychologist Neal Miller (1909–2002), a defender of the use of animals in psychological research (Miller, 1985). The present conflict between animal rights advocates and psychologists who study animals is not new. In the early 20th century, animal rights activists attacked the work of leading psychologists, including John B. Watson and G. Stanley Hall. In 1925, in part to blunt these attacks, the American Psychological Association's Committee on Precautions in Animal Experimentation established a code of regulations for the use of animals in research (Dewsbury, 1990).

Animal Rights versus Animal Welfare

Many *animal rights* advocates oppose all laboratory research using animals, regardless of its scientific merit or practical benefits. Thus, they would oppose testing the effects of melatonin on animal subjects. A survey of demonstrators at an animal rights march in Washington, D.C., in 1990 found that almost 80 percent of animal rights advocates valued animal life at least as much as human life, and 85 percent wanted to eliminate all animal research (Plous, 1991). Some animal rights advocates even have vandalized laboratories that conduct animal research to intimidate researchers and interfere with their research (Hadley, 2009).

Animal rights advocates go beyond *animal welfare* advocates, who would permit laboratory research on animals as long as the animals are given humane care and the potential benefits of the research outweigh any pain and distress caused to the animals (Wolfensohn

& Maguire, 2010). Thus, they would be more likely to approve the use of animals in testing the effects of melatonin on sleep. Bernard Rollin, an ethicist who has tried to resolve the ethical conflict between animal researchers and animal rights advocates, would permit animal research but urges that when in ethical doubt, experimenters should err in favor of the animal (Bekoff, Gruen, Townsend, & Rollin, 1992).

The current ethical standards of the American Psychological Association and other professional organizations, such as the Society for Neuroscience, for the treatment of animals are closer to those of animal welfare advocates than to those of animal rights advocates. The standards require that animals be treated with respect, housed in clean cages, and given adequate food and water. Researchers also must ensure that their animal subjects experience as little pain and distress as possible; when it is necessary to kill the animals, researchers must do so in a humane, painless way. Moreover, all institutions that receive research grants from the U.S. government must have approval from review boards (similar to IRBs) that judge whether research proposals for experiments using animal subjects meet ethical standards (Holden, 1987). The Canadian government likewise regulates the treatment of research animals in universities, government laboratories, and commercial institutions (Rowsell, 1988).

Research on Animals Is Beneficial

Source: Yurchyks/Shutterstock.com.

Reasons for Using Animals in Research

But with so many people available, why would psychologists be interested in studying animals? Advocates point to a number of benefits derived from animal research (Carroll & Overmier, 2001).

1. Some psychologists are simply intrigued by animal behavior and wish to learn more about it. To learn about the process of echolocation of prey, you would have to study animals such as bats rather than college students.

2. It is easier to control potential confounding variables that might affect the behavior of an animal. You would be less likely to worry about participant bias effects, for instance, when studying pigeons.

3. Developmental changes across the life span can be studied more efficiently in animals. If you were interested in the effects of the complexity of the early childhood environment on memory in old age, you might take 75 years to complete an experiment using human participants but only 3 years to complete one using rats.

4. Research on animals can generate hypotheses that are then tested using human participants. B. F. Skinner's research on learning in rats and pigeons stimulated research on learning in people.

5. Research on animals can benefit animals themselves. For example, as described in Chapter 7, psychologists have developed techniques to make coyotes feel nauseated by the taste of sheep; perhaps these techniques can someday be used to protect sheep from coyotes and coyotes from angry sheep ranchers.

6. Based on the assumption that animals do not have the same moral rights as people (Baldwin, 1993), certain procedures that are not ethically permissible with human participants are ethically permissible under current standards using animal subjects. Thus, if you wanted to conduct an experiment in which you studied the effects of surgically damaging a particular brain structure, you would be limited to the use of animals (Caminiti, 2009). But some critics of animal research note that the use of primates in invasive brain research because they most closely resemble people provides an argument against such research (Crum, 2009). Recent media attention has been drawn to the National Institute of Health's (NIH) decision to phase out much of its research on chimpanzees. As is common with any ethical dilemma, sound arguments can be raised for both sides regarding the use of animals in research. Often there is no resolution that is fully satisfactory to advocates of both sides.

1. Why has the use of deception in research provoked controversy?

2. What is debriefing in psychological research?

3. How do animal rights and animal welfare advocates differ from one other?

Chapter Summary

Sources of Knowledge

- Psychologists prefer the scientific method to common sense as a source of knowledge.
- The scientific method is based on the assumptions of determinism and skepticism.
- In using the scientific method to conduct research, a psychologist first provides a rationale for the research, then conducts the research study, analyzes the resulting data, and finally, communicates the results to other researchers.
- Replication of research studies is an important component of the scientific research process.

Goals of Psychological Research

- In conducting research, psychologists pursue the goals of description, prediction, control, and explanation.
- Scientific descriptions are systematic and rely on operational definitions.
- Scientific predictions are probabilistic, not certain.
- Scientists exert control over events by manipulating the factors that cause them.
- Scientific explanations state the probable causes of events.

Methods of Psychological Research

- Psychologists use descriptive, correlational, and experimental research methods.
- Descriptive research methods pursue the goal of description through naturalistic observation, case studies, surveys, psychological testing, and archival research.
- Correlational research pursues the goal of prediction by uncovering relationships between variables.
- When using correlational research, psychologists avoid confusing correlation with causation.
- Experimental research pursues the goals of control and explanation by manipulating an independent variable and measuring its effect on a dependent variable.
- Experimenters promote internal validity by controlling confounding variables whose effects might be confused with those of the independent variable.
- Confounding variables might be associated with the experimental situation, the participants in the experiment, or the experimenter.
- Random assignment is used to make the experimental group and control group equivalent before exposing them to the independent variable.

- Experimenters also must control for participant bias and experimenter bias.
- Another concern of experimenters is external validity—whether their results are generalizable from their participants and settings to other participants and settings.
- Experimenters rely on replication to determine whether their research has external validity.

Statistical Analysis of Research Data

- Psychologists typically make sense of their data by using mathematical techniques called statistics.
- Psychologists use descriptive statistics to summarize data, correlational statistics to determine relationships between variables, and inferential statistics to test their experimental hypotheses.
- Descriptive statistics include measures of central tendency (including the mode, median, and mean) and measures of variability (including the range, variance, and standard deviation).
- Correlational statistics let researchers use the values of one variable to predict the values of another.
- Inferential statistics examine whether numerical differences between experimental and control groups are statistically significant.
- Meta-analysis involves computation of the average effect size across a number of related studies.
- Statistical significance does not necessarily indicate social or practical significance. The magnitude of individual differences must be considered when examining group differences.

Ethics of Psychological Research

- American and Canadian psychologists have ethical codes for the treatment of human participants and animal subjects.
- In research using human participants, researchers must obtain informed consent, not force anyone to participate, let participants withdraw at any time, protect participants from physical harm and mental distress, alleviate any inadvertent harm or distress, and keep information obtained from the participants confidential.

- The use of deception in research has been an especially controversial issue.
- The use of animals in research also has been controversial.
- Many animal rights supporters oppose all research on animals.

- Animal welfare supporters approve of research on animals as long as the animals are treated humanely and the potential benefits of the research outweigh any pain and distress caused to the animals.
- Most psychologists support the use of animals in research because of the benefits of such research to both people and animals.

Key Terms

Sources of Knowledge

determinism (p. 28)
hypothesis (p. 30)
replication (p. 31)
scientific method (p. 30)
skepticism (p. 29)

Goals of Scientific Research

measurement (p. 32)
operational definition (p. 32)
theory (p. 32)

Methods of Psychological Research

archival research (p. 39)
case study (p. 35)
causation (p. 40)
confounding variable (p. 43)
control group (p. 41)
correlation (p. 39)
correlational research (p. 39)
dependent variable (p. 41)
descriptive research (p. 34)

double-blind technique (p. 46)
ethology (p. 35)
experimental group. (p. 41)
experimental method (p. 41)
experimenter bias effect (p. 44)
external validity (p. 46)
field experiment (p. 42)
independent variable (p. 41)
internal validity (p. 43)
naturalistic observation (p. 34)
negative correlation (p. 40)
norm (p. 37)
participant bias (p. 44)
placebo (p. 42)
population (p. 37)
positive correlation (p. 39)
psychological test (p. 37)
random assignment (p. 44)
random sampling (p. 37)
reliability (p. 38)
sample (p. 37)
standardization (p. 37)
survey (p. 36)

validity (p. 38)
variable (p. 39)

Statistical Analysis of Research Data

coefficient of correlation (p. 49)
descriptive statistics (p. 48)
inferential statistics (p. 51)
mean (p. 48)
measure of central tendency (p. 48)
measure of variability (p. 49)
median (p. 48)
meta-analysis (p. 52)
mode (p. 48)
range (p. 49)
standard deviation (p. 49)
statistical significance (p. 51)
variance (p. 49)

Ethics of Psychological Research

debriefing (p. 56)

Chapter Quiz

Note: Answers for the Chapter Quiz questions are provided at the end of the book.

1. The scientist is governed by an attitude of
   a. dualism.
   b. cynicism.
   c. dogmatism.
   d. skepticism.

2. Typically, for a statistical difference between the performances of experimental and control groups to be significant, its probability of occurring by chance must be less than
   a. 3 percent.
   b. 5 percent.
   c. 10 percent.
   d. 50 percent.

3. The prediction that "People high in psychological hardiness will be less likely to become ill than will people low in psychological hardiness" is an example of
   a. a fact.
   b. a hypothesis.
   c. inductive reasoning.
   d. an operational definition.

4. Deception is usually used in social psychological research to
   a. reduce participant bias.
   b. reduce experimenter bias.
   c. assess the reactions of people to being fooled.
   d. prevent potential participants from finding out about the experimental procedure in advance.

5. The more you smoke, the more likely you are to develop lung cancer. This demonstrates that smoking
   a. causes cancer.
   b. is caused by cancer.
   c. is positively correlated with cancer.
   d. is negatively correlated with cancer.

6. If people who score high on a test of mechanical ability perform better on tasks such as fixing a typewriter, building a bookcase, and replacing shock absorbers, this indicates that the test might have
   a. reliability.
   b. predictive validity.
   c. satisfactory norms.
   d. no relationship to mechanical ability.

7. You conduct an experiment to investigate the effect of meditation on the level of stress in men and women who vary in their religiosity. The dependent variable in your study is
   a. meditation.
   b. religiosity.
   c. sex of participants.
   d. level of stress.

8. Scientific predictions are
   a. invariably correct.
   b. probabilistic statements.
   c. based on the researcher's intuition.
   d. always made in the form of syllogisms.

9. Determinism is
   a. a procedure for ensuring that experimental and control groups are equivalent.
   b. a scientific assumption that every event has physical, potentially measurable causes.
   c. a means of finding out whether a confounding variable affected the dependent variable.
   d. a statistical technique for deciding whether research findings are statistically significant.

10. The most likely author of the statement "Never accept anything as true unless your own reasoning tells you it is true" is
    a. John Locke.
    b. B. F. Skinner.
    c. John B. Watson.
    d. René Descartes.

11. If the standard deviation of a set of scores is 4, the variance is
    a. 2.
    b. 4.
    c. 16.
    d. impossible to determine.

12. The best example of an operational definition would be defining
    a. *happy* as "being content with one's life."
    b. *beautiful* as "being physically attractive."
    c. *expert* as "being knowledgeable in one's own field."
    d. *strong* as "being able to bench-press one's body weight."

13. A child psychologist spends three hours a week watching and recording the play patterns of 3-year-old children in a nursery school. This is an example of (a)
    a. case study.
    b. archival research.
    c. experimental research.
    d. naturalistic observation.

14. The study discussed in the textbook that found that only 5 of 91 persons could identify a drunken person demonstrated the shortcomings of
    a. science.
    b. common sense.
    c. deductive reasoning.
    d. systematic observation.

15. A psychologist's favored perspective will determine where he or she looks for explanations of psychological events. For example, a humanistic psychologist will look for the causes of depression in the
    a. brain.
    b. environment.
    c. conscious mind.
    d. unconscious mind.

16. A psychologist who has designed a personality test administers it to a group of people on two occasions and determines how consistent the performances are. This is a procedure used to assess a test's
    a. reliability.
    b. validity.
    c. norms.
    d. criterion.

17. Both participant bias and experimenter bias can be controlled by
    a. using the double-blind technique.
    b. using more than one independent variable.
    c. replicating research studies several times.
    d. random assignment of participants to the experimental and control groups.

18. If you study the childhood diaries of adults you are seeing as psychotherapy clients to determine factors that are associated with adult emotional problems, then you are engaging in
    a. survey research.
    b. archival research.
    c. experimental research.
    d. naturalistic observation.

19. The "Pepsi Challenge" controversy discussed in the textbook revealed that
    a. Pepsi tastes better than Coke.
    b. Coke tastes better than Pepsi.
    c. taste preferences depended on a confounding variable.
    d. taste preferences cannot be determined by experiments.

20. The largest of the following correlations is
  a. .37
  b. .00
  c. −.01
  d. −.93

21. Cause is to effect as
  a. dependent variable is to independent variable.
  b. independent variable is to dependent variable.
  c. dependent variable is to confounding variable.
  d. confounding variable is to independent variable.

22. The generalizability of research findings is best determined by
  a. replication.
  b. common sense.
  c. archival research.
  d. deductive reasoning.

23. Given the numbers 2, 3, 22, 10, 3, 7, 9, the median is
  a. 3.
  b. 7.
  c. 8.
  d. 10.

24. Jane Goodall's research on chimpanzees in the wild is an example of
  a. ethology.
  b. evolutionary psychology.
  c. experimentation.
  d. archival research.

25. Every member of the population of interest has an equal chance of being selected in a
  a. quota sample.
  b. random sample.
  c. stratified sample.
  d. systematic sample.

Thought Questions

1. How would a skeptical attitude toward ESP, UFOs, and similar topics differ from either a cynical or a gullible attitude?

2. How would the four goals of scientific research influence research on violence?

3. In what way are medical treatments, weather forecasting, horse-race handicapping, college admissions decisions, and psychological child-rearing advice "probabilistic"?

4. Why is the experimental method considered a better means of determining causality than nonexperimental methods?

Biopsychological Bases of Behavior

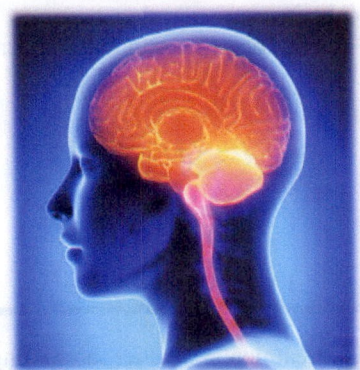

Source: CLIPAREA/Custom media/ Shutterstock.com.

Chapter Outline

Nature versus Nurture

Biological Communication Systems

Neuronal Activity

Brain Functions

unilateral neglect A disorder, caused by damage to a parietal lobe, in which the individual acts as though the side of her or his world opposite to the damaged lobe does not exist.

A 64-year-old, right-handed man was awakened by the sense that there was something strange in his bed. Opening his eyes, he observed to his horror that there was a strange arm reaching toward his neck. The arm approached nearer, as if to strangle him, and the man let out a cry of terror. Suddenly, he realized that the arm had on its wrist a silver-banded watch, which the man recognized to be his own. It occurred to him that the arm's possessor must have stolen his watch sometime during the night. A struggle ensued, as the man attempted to wrestle the watch off of the arm. During the struggle, the man became aware that his own left arm was feeling contorted and uncomfortable. It was then that he discovered that the strange arm in fact was his own. The watch was his, and it was on his left wrist. He was wrestling with his own arm! (Tranel, 1995, p. 885).

What could account for such bizarre behavior? It was caused by a stroke that damaged the right side of the man's brain. This made him exhibit **unilateral neglect**, in this case making it difficult for the man to attend to the left side of his body and immediate environment (Osawa & Maeshima, 2010). A person with unilateral neglect related to right-brain damage often acts as though the left side of his or her world, including his or her body, does not exist. A man with unilateral neglect might shave the right side of his face, but not the left, and might eat the pork chop on the right side of his plate but not the potatoes on the left. If the plate is turned for him, he might be surprised to see the food from the left side and deny it was ever there. About 25–30 percent of stroke victims develop unilateral neglect, with much functional recovery occurring during the first 2–3 months post-stroke. But large brain lesions usually lead to long-term impairment (Kerkhoff & Rossetti, 2006). Though more than 90% of cases of unilateral neglect are found after damage to the right side of the brain, it sometimes is found in people with damage to the left side of the brain; they show neglect for objects in the right half of their spatial world (Corbetta, Kincades, Lewis, Snyder, & Sapir, 2005).

Such profound effects of brain damage on physical and psychological functioning indicate that abilities we often take for granted require a properly functioning brain. If you have an intact brain, as you read this page your eyes inform your brain about what you are reading. At the same time, your brain interprets the meaning of that information and stores some of it in your memory. When you reach the end of a right-hand page, your brain will direct your hand to turn the page.

But how do your eyes inform your brain about what you are reading? How does your brain interpret and store the information it receives? And how does your brain direct the movements of your hand? The answers to these questions are provided by the field of **behavioral neuroscience,** which studies the relationship between neurological processes (typically, brain activity) and psychological functions (such as memory, emotion, and perception). More than a century ago William James (1890/1981), in his classic textbook, *The Principles of Psychology,* stressed the close association between physiology and psychology. James declared, "I have felt most acutely the difficulties of understanding either the brain without the mind or the mind without the brain" (quoted in Bjork, 1988, p. 107).

behavioral neuroscience
The field that studies the physiological bases of human and animal behavior and mental processes.

Nature versus Nurture

William James was influenced by Charles Darwin's (1859/1975) theory of evolution, which holds that individuals who are biologically well adapted to their environment are more likely to survive, reproduce, and pass on their physical traits to succeeding generations through their genes. Thus, the human brain has evolved into its present form because it helped people throughout history adapt successfully to their surroundings and survive long enough to reproduce. Our brain is remarkably flexible in helping us adapt to different circumstances and environments. For example our brain helped ancient people survive without automobiles, grocery stores, or electric lights. It helps people today survive in the arctic, outer space, and adapt to our current environments.

To what extent are you the product of your heredity, and to what extent are you the product of your environment? This issue of "nature versus nurture" (Sameroff, 2010) has been with us since the era of ancient Greece, when Plato championed nature and Aristotle championed nurture. Plato believed we are born with some knowledge; Aristotle believed that at birth our mind is a blank slate (or *tabula rasa*) and that life experiences provide us with knowledge.

Evolutionary Psychology

In modern times, the nature-nurture issue became even more heated after Charles Darwin (1859/1975) put forth his theory of evolution in the mid-19th century. Darwin noted that animals and people vary in their physical traits. Given the competition for resources (including food and water) and the need to foil predators (by avoiding them, defeating them, or escaping from them), animals and people with physical traits best adapted to these purposes would be the most likely to survive long enough to produce offspring, who would likely also have those traits. As long as particular physical traits provide a survival advantage, those traits will have a greater likelihood of showing up in succeeding generations. Darwin called this process *natural selection.*

Psychologists who champion **evolutionary psychology** employ Darwinian concepts in their research and theorizing (Ploeger, van der Maas, & Raijmakers, 2008). For example, research findings indicate that it is easier to condition fear responses to aversive stimuli than to neutral stimuli (Phelps and LeDoux, 2005). For example, natural threats such as snakes were more likely to elicit a fear response such as freezing (at the sight of one) as opposed to viewing a neutral stimuli, such as a house (Öhman, 2009). The possible role of evolution in human social relationships inspired the following study by evolutionary psychologist David Buss and his colleagues Randy Larsen, Drew Westen, and Jennifer Semmelroth (1992) at the University of Michigan.

evolutionary psychology
The study of the evolution of behavior through natural selection.

Has Evolution Influenced Gender Differences in Romantic Jealousy?

Rationale

Buss and his colleagues believe that evolution has left its mark on human behavior, even in the area of romance. Because women can be sure that their newborns are truly theirs, whereas men cannot, Buss hypothesized that men would exhibit more sexual jealousy than emotional jealousy. Because prehistoric women were, on the average, physically weaker and more responsible for caring for their children and depended on men to support them while pregnant and after giving birth, the researchers hypothesized that women would exhibit more emotional jealousy than sexual jealousy. The researchers believed that these differences were the product of thousands of generations of natural selection.

Method

Participants were 202 male and female undergraduate students. They were asked which of the following two dilemmas would distress them more: their romantic partner forming a deep emotional attachment to someone else or that partner enjoying passionate sexual intercourse with someone else. The participants also were asked to respond to a similar dilemma in which their romantic partner either fell in love with another person or tried a variety of sexual positions with that person.

Results and Discussion

The results showed that for the first dilemma 60 percent of the male participants reported greater jealousy over their partner's potential sexual infidelity. In contrast, 83 percent of the female participants reported greater jealousy over their partner's potential emotional infidelity. This pattern of responses was repeated in response to the second dilemma. Buss and other colleagues provided additional support for these findings in later research studies. For example, in an archival study, they examined 345 cases in which women were murdered by their husbands as part of lovers' triangles. They found that younger women, as compared with older women, were more likely to be killed by jealous husbands. The researchers noted that evolutionary psychology would have predicted this. Given that younger women have more reproductive potential than older women, evolutionary psychologists would predict more intense jealousy regarding the sexual infidelity of younger women than that of older women (Shackelford, Buss, & Weekes-Shackelford, 2003).

Of course, other interpretations of these findings—not dependent on evolutionary psychology—are possible. One alternative explanation has been put forward by Christine Harris (2003), who reviewed the relevant research. The most consistent evidence for gender differences in jealousy is found when researchers ask respondents to consider a hypothetical relationship. When participants are surveyed about their responses to personal experiences of sexual infidelity, gender differences disappear. And when the base rates for murders are taken into account, men are not proportionately more likely to murder their wives in a jealous rage. But evolutionary psychologists had pointed to research supporting the commonness of gender differences in sexual and emotional jealousy as evidence of its possible hereditary basis. And Buss and his colleagues' findings regarding gender differences in jealousy have been replicated in some research studies across different cultures (Wiederman & Kendall, 1999).

But the degree of the difference in female and male responses to sexual and emotional infidelity varies across cultures and ideologies. In one study, for example, gender differences in the two kinds of jealousy were stronger in the United States than in Germany or the Netherlands (Buunk, Angleitner, Oubaid, & Buss, 1996). Another study found that gender differences in sexual and emotional jealousy were greater among undergraduates who believed in gender inequality (Pratto & Hegarty, 2000). As you can see, research findings on gender differences in jealousy might be compatible with an evolutionary interpretation or a sociocultural interpretation (Wood & Eagly, 2000).

Behavioral Genetics

behavioral genetics

The study of the relative effects of heredity and life experiences on behavior.

Beginning in the 1970s, psychology has seen the growth of **behavioral genetics**, which studies how heredity affects behavior. In humans, this information is gathered through family, twin, and adoption studies. Research in behavioral genetics has found evidence of a hereditary basis for characteristics as diverse as delinquency (Taylor, Iacono, & McGue, 2000), intelligence (Loehlin, Horn, & Willerman, 1994), prosocial behavior (Gregory, Light-Häusermann, Rijsdijk, & Eley, 2009), marital satisfaction (Spotts et al., 2005), and antisocial personality disorder (Gunter, Vaughn, & Philibert, 2010). Antisocial personality disorder is discussed in Chapter 16.

Nonetheless, it is crucial to note that behavioral genetics does not presume that heredity is the most important factor in the development of these characteristics. All behavior is determined by interactions between people's genes and their environment. For most psychological traits, the proportion of individual variability attributable to heredity is less than 50 percent, so personal characteristics are almost always influenced more by environmental factors than by hereditary (Plomin & Asbury, 2001). Moreover, children reared in the same family tend to be less influenced by shared environmental factors than by nonshared environmental factors. This may help account for why children reared in the same family can turn out to be so different from one another. Perhaps they are treated somewhat differently by their parents and are subject to different outside environmental influences from their peers and other people they encounter in everyday life (Plomin, Asbury, & Dunn, 2001).

To appreciate behavioral genetics, you should have a basic understanding of genetics itself. The cells of the human body contain 23 pairs of *chromosomes,* which are long strands of *deoxyribonucleic acid (DNA)* molecules. (Unlike the other body cells, the egg cell and sperm cell each contain 23 single chromosomes.) DNA molecules are ribbon-like structures composed of segments called *genes.* Genes direct the synthesis of *ribonucleic acid (RNA).* RNA, in turn, directs the synthesis of proteins, which are responsible for the structure and function of our tissues and organs.

Though our genes direct our physical development, their effects on our behavior are primarily indirect. There are, for example, no "motorcycle daredevil genes." Instead, genes influence physiological factors, such as hormones, neurotransmitters, and brain structures. These factors, in turn, make people somewhat more likely to engage in particular behaviors. Perhaps people destined to become motorcycle daredevils inherit a less physiologically reactive nervous system for arousal, making them experience less anxiety in dangerous situations. Likewise, perhaps people destined to become motorcycle daredevils inherit a more physiologically reactive nervous system for arousal, making them experience thrill seeking in dangerous situations. Moreover, given current trends in molecular genetics, behavioral geneticists are on the threshold of identifying genes that affect specific behaviors. For example, the ambitious Human Genome Project has identified more than 20,000 human genes (van Ommen, 2005). Most researchers in behavioral genetics prefer to search for the effects of interactions among these genes, rather than single-gene effects, as influences on behavior (Wahlsten, 1999). This research also holds promise for the prevention and treatment of physical and psychological disorders that have possible genetic bases, such as obesity (see Chapter 11) and schizophrenia (see Chapter 16).

Our outward appearance and behavior might not indicate our exact genetic inheritance. In recognition of this, scientists distinguish between our genotype and our phenotype. Your **genotype** is your genetic inheritance. Your **phenotype** is the overt expression of your inheritance in your appearance or behavior. For example, your eye color is determined by the interaction of a gene inherited from your mother and a gene inherited from your father. The brown-eye gene is *dominant,* and the blue-eye gene is *recessive.* Dominant genes take precedence over recessive genes. Traits carried by recessive genes show up in phenotypes only when recessive genes occur together. If you are blue-eyed, your genotype includes two blue-eye genes (both recessive). If you have brown eyes, your genotype may include two brown-eye genes (both dominant) or one brown-eye gene (dominant) and one blue-eye gene (recessive).

In contrast to simple traits like eye color, most characteristics are governed by more than one pair of genes—that is, they are *polygenic.* With rare exceptions, this is especially true of genetic influences on human behaviors and abilities. Your athletic, academic, and social skills depend on the interaction of many genes as well as your life experiences. For example, your muscularity (your phenotype) depends on both your genetic endowment (your genotype) and your dietary, health, and exercise habits (your life experiences).

To appreciate research studies that try to determine the relative contributions of heredity and environment to human development, you should understand the concept of heritability. **Heritability** refers to the proportion of variability in a trait across a

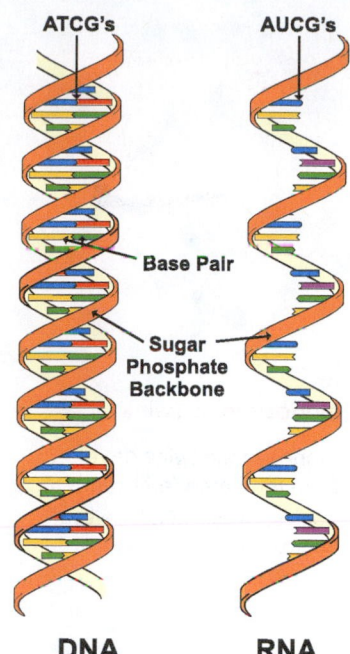

DNA and RNA

Chromosomes consist of long, ribbon-like strands of DNA. The chromosomes are recipes for making proteins. RNA directs the synthesis of proteins.
Source: udaix/Shutterstock.com.

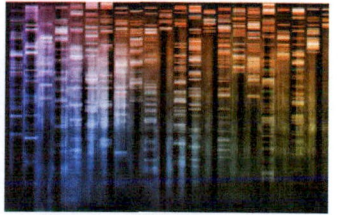

Human Genome Image

A digital representation of a human genome.
Source: kentoh/Shutterstock.com.

genotype An individual's genetic inheritance.

phenotype The overt expression of an individual's genotype (genetic inheritance) in his or her appearance or behavior.

heritability The proportion of variability in a trait across a population attributable to genetic differences among members of the population.

Monozygotic Twins

Monozygotic twins develop from the same fertilized egg.

Source: SvetlanaFedoseyeva/ Shutterstock.com.

population attributable to genetic differences among members of the population (Turkheimer, 1998). For example, people differ in their intelligence (as measured by IQ tests). To what extent is this variability caused by heredity, and to what extent is it caused by experience? Heritability values range from 0.0 to 1.0. If heritability accounted for none of the variability in intelligence, it would have a value of 0.0. If heritability accounted for all of the variability in intelligence, it would have a value of 1.0. In reality, the heritability of intelligence, as measured by IQ tests, is estimated to be between .50 (Chipuer, Rovine, & Plomin, 1990) and .70 (Bouchard, Lykken, McGue, Segal, & Tellegen, 1990). This indicates that the variability in intelligence is strongly, but not solely, influenced by heredity. Environmental factors also account for much of the variability. Moreover, note that heritability applies to groups, not to individuals. Heritability cannot be used, for example, to determine the relative contributions of heredity and environment to your own intelligence. Research procedures that assess the relative contributions of nature and nurture involve the study of relatives. These include studies of families, adoptees, and identical twins reared apart.

Family Studies

Family studies investigate similarities between relatives with varying degrees of genetic similarity. These studies find that the closer the genetic relationship (that is, the more genes that are shared) between relatives, the more alike they tend to be on a variety of traits. For example, the siblings of a person who has schizophrenia are significantly more likely to have schizophrenia than are the person's cousins. Though it is tempting to attribute this to their degree of genetic similarity, one cannot rule out that it is actually due to their degree of environmental similarity (Althoff, Faraone, Rettew, Morley, & Hudziak, 2005).

The best kind of family study is the *twin study,* which compares identical (or *monozygotic*) twins to fraternal (or *dizygotic*) twins. This kind of study was introduced by Francis Galton (1822–1911), who found more similarity between identical twins than between fraternal twins—and attributed this to heredity. Identical twins, because they come from the same fertilized egg, have identical genes. For this reason, they have the same genetic inheritance. Moreover, they are of the same sex. Fraternal twins, because they come from different fertilized eggs, do not have identical genes. Therefore, fraternal twins can be the same or other sex. They have merely the same degree of genetic similarity as ordinary siblings do.

Moreover, twins, whether identical or fraternal, are born at the same time and share more similar environments than other siblings do. Because research has found that identical twins reared in similar environments are more psychologically similar than fraternal twins reared in similar environments, it is reasonable to attribute the greater similarity of identical twins to heredity. Twin studies have been consistent across cultures in supporting the heritability of psychological characteristics, as in studies of the personality of twins in Russia (Saudino et al., 1999), sexual orientation and conformity to gender roles in Australian twins (Bailey, Dunne, & Martin, 2000), and schizophrenia in twins in Finland (Cannon et al., 1999). Nonetheless, there is an alternative, environmental explanation. Perhaps identical twins become more psychologically similar because they are treated more alike than fraternal twins are.

Adoption Studies

Another way to examine heritability is to study adopted children. *Adoption studies* measure the correlation in particular traits between adopted children and their biological parents and between those same children and their adoptive parents. Adoption studies have found that adoptees tend to be more similar to their biological parents than to their adoptive parents in characteristics such as drug abuse (Cadoret et al., 1995), vocational interests (Lykken, Bouchard, McGue, & Tellegen, 1993), and religious values (Waller, Kojetin, Bouchard, & Lykken, 1990). These findings indicate that with regard to such characteristics, the genes that adoptees inherit from their biological parents affect their development more than does the environment they are provided with by their adoptive parents.

Yet, the environment cannot be ruled out as an explanation for the greater similarity between adoptees and their biological parents. As you will see in Chapter 4, prenatal experiences can affect children's development. Perhaps adoptees are more like their biological parents not because they share the same genes but because during prenatal development the adoptees were subject to their mother's drug habits, health habits, nutritional intake, or other environmental influences. Moreover, their experiences with their biological parents in early infancy, before they were adopted, might likewise affect their development, possibly making them more similar to their biological parents.

Biological versus Adoptive Relatives: A Real-Life Experiment

Adoption creates two groups: genetic relatives and environmental relatives.
Source: DNF Style/Shutterstock.com.

Studies of Identical Twins Reared Apart

Perhaps the best procedure is to study identical twins reared apart. Research on a variety of traits has consistently found higher positive correlations between identical twins reared apart than between fraternal twins reared together. Because identical twins share identical genes, virtually identical prenatal environments, and highly similar neonatal environments, this research provides strong evidence in favor of the nature side of the debate. In keeping with this, a widely publicized ongoing study conducted at the University of Minnesota under the leadership of Thomas Bouchard has examined similarities between identical twins who were separated in infancy and reunited later in life. As part of the University of Minnesota study of twins reared apart, researchers administered a personality test to 71 pairs of adult identical and 53 pairs of adult fraternal twins reared apart and 99 pairs of adult identical and 99 pairs of adult fraternal twins reared together. The results found that the heritability estimate for personality was 0.46, indicating that heredity plays an important, but not dominant, role in personality (Bouchard, McGue, Hur, & Horn, 1998). Other studies of identical twins reared apart have found that the heritability of personality is approximately .40 (Bouchard & Loehlin, 2001).

The University of Minnesota twin studies have found some uncanny similarities in the habits, abilities, and physiological responses of the reunited twins. For example, one pair of twins at their first reunion discovered that they "both used Vademecum toothpaste, Canoe shaving lotion, Vitalis hair tonic, and Lucky Strike cigarettes. After that meeting, they exchanged birthday presents that crossed in the mail and proved to be identical choices, made independently in separate cities" (Lykken, McGue, Tellegen, & Bouchard, 1992).

But some of these similarities might be due to coincidence or being reared in similar environments or having some contact with each other before being studied. In fact, research on even unrelated people sometimes shows surprising similarities in their personality traits (Wyatt, 1993). Moreover, identical twins look the same and might elicit responses from others that indirectly lead to their developing similar interests and personalities. Consider how people might treat identical twins who are obese, muscular, attractive, or acne prone. Thus, identical twins who share certain physical traits might become more similar than ordinary siblings who do not share such traits—even when reared in different cultures (Ford, 1993). As you can see, no kind of study is flawless in demonstrating the superiority of heredity over environment in guiding development.

Regardless of the influence of heredity on development, behavioral genetics researcher Robert Plomin reminds us that life experiences also are important. In one study, personality test scores of identical and fraternal twins were compared at an average of 20 years of age and then at an average of 30 years of age. Plomin concluded that the stable core of personality is strongly influenced by heredity but that personality change is overwhelmingly influenced by environment (McGue, Bacon, & Lykken, 1993). Thus, heredity might have provided you with the personality traits needed to become a Nobel Prize winner, but without adequate academic experience in childhood, you might not perform well enough even to graduate from college. In fact, heredity and environment interact in influencing characteristics such as social smiling (Jones, 2008), childhood obesity (Levin, 2009), drug addiction (Agrawal & Lynskey, 2008), gender differences in religiosity (Bradshaw & Ellison, 2009), and psychological disorders (Wermter et al., 2010).

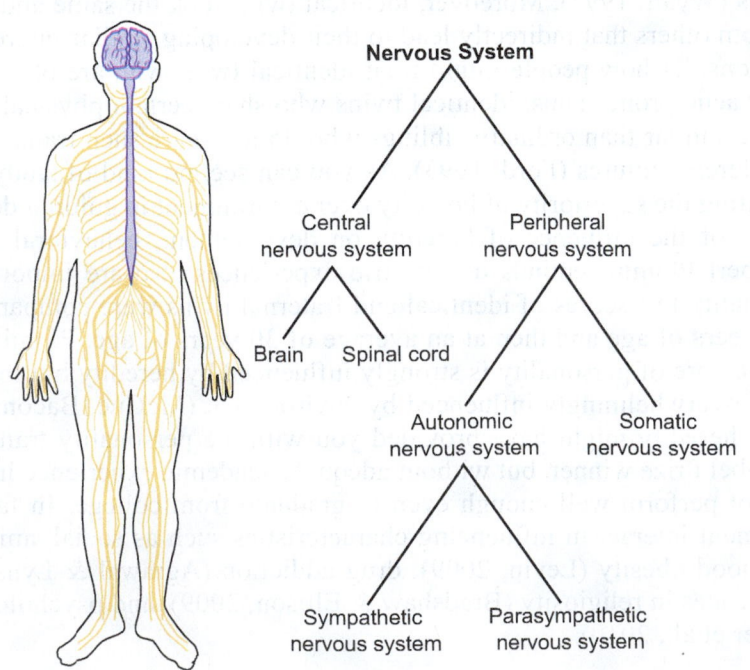

1. What is evolutionary psychology?

2. Why are the greater physical, cognitive, and personality similarities among relatives than among nonrelatives not enough evidence to demonstrate conclusively that they are the product of heredity?

nervous system The chief means of communication in the body.

neuron A cell specialized for the transmission of information in the nervous system.

central nervous system The division of the nervous system consisting of the brain and the spinal cord.

brain The structure of the central nervous system that is located in the skull and plays important roles in sensation, movement, and information processing.

spinal cord The structure of the central nervous system that is located in the spine and plays a role in bodily reflexes and in communicating information between the brain and the peripheral nervous system.

Biological Communication Systems

Biopsychological activity is regulated by two major bodily communication systems: the *nervous system* and the *endocrine system*. These systems regulate biopsychological functions as varied as hunger, memory, sexuality, and emotionality.

The Nervous System

The brain is part of the **nervous system**, the chief means of communication within the body. The basic unit of the nervous system is the **neuron**, a cell that is specialized for the transmission and reception of information. As illustrated in Figure 3-1, the two divisions of the nervous system are the *central nervous system* and the *peripheral nervous system*.

The Central Nervous System

The **central nervous system** comprises the *brain* and the *spinal cord*. The **brain**, protectively housed in the skull, is so important in psychological functioning that most of this chapter and many other sections of this book are devoted to it. As you will learn, the brain is intimately involved in learning, thinking, language, memory, emotion, motivation, body movements, social relationships, psychological disorders, perception of the world, and even immune-system activity.

The **spinal cord**, which runs through the bony, protective spinal column, provides a means of communication between the brain and the body. Motor output from the brain

FIGURE 3-1
The Nervous System

The nervous system comprises the central nervous system (brain and spinal cord) and the peripheral nervous system (nerves).

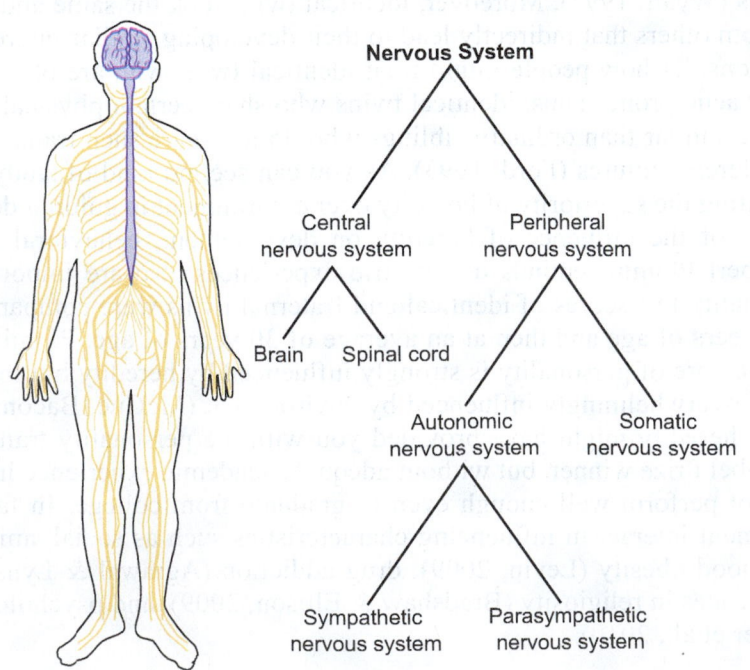

Nervous System

Central nervous system — Peripheral nervous system

Brain — Spinal cord

Autonomic nervous system — Somatic nervous system

Sympathetic nervous system — Parasympathetic nervous system

travels down the spinal cord to direct activity in muscles and certain glands. Sensory input from pain, touch, pressure, and temperature receptors in the body travels up the spinal cord to the brain, informing it of the state of the body. As discussed in the chapter section "Neuronal Activity," the spinal cord also plays a role in limb reflexes. A **reflex** is an automatic, involuntary, motor response to sensory stimulation. Thus, when you step on a sharp, broken shell at the beach, you immediately pull your foot away. This response occurs at the level of the spinal cord; it does not require input from the brain.

Damage to the spinal cord can have catastrophic effects. You might know people who have suffered a spinal-cord injury in a diving, vehicular, or contact-sport accident, causing them to lose the ability to move their limbs or feel bodily sensations below the point of the injury. Successful adjustment to spinal-cord injury is promoted by participating in physical activities to the extent possible (Ginis, Jetha, Dack, & Hetz, 2010) and by finding a purpose in life despite one's disability (Thompson, Coker, Krause, & Henry, 2003). Emotional reactions to spinal-cord injuries show the influence of gender and culture. Two studies of people with spinal-cord injuries in southern California found that men reported more distress over interpersonal problems than women did (Krause, 1998). Moreover, severe depression was more common among Latinos than among European Americans or African Americans (Kemp, Krause, & Adkins, 1999). As discussed in greater depth later in the chapter, research on the transplantation of healthy nerve tissue into damaged spinal cords of animals indicates that scientists may be on the threshold of discovering effective means of restoring motor and sensory functions to people who have suffered spinal-cord injuries (Kim et al., 1999).

The Peripheral Nervous System

The **peripheral nervous system** contains the **nerves**, which provide a means of communication between the central nervous system and the sensory organs, skeletal muscles, and internal bodily organs. The peripheral nervous system comprises the *somatic nervous system* and the *autonomic nervous system*. The **somatic nervous system** includes *sensory nerves,* which send messages from the sensory organs to the central nervous system, and *motor nerves,* which send messages from the central nervous system to the skeletal muscles. The **autonomic nervous system** controls automatic, involuntary processes (such as sweating, heart contractions, and intestinal activity) through the action of its two subdivisions: the *sympathetic nervous system* and the *parasympathetic nervous system.* The **sympathetic nervous system** arouses the body to prepare it for action, and the **parasympathetic nervous system** calms the body to conserve energy.

Imagine that you are playing a tennis match. Your sympathetic nervous system would speed up your heart rate to pump more blood to your muscles, make your liver release sugar into your bloodstream for quick energy, and induce sweating to keep you from overheating. As you cool down after the match, your parasympathetic nervous system would slow your heart rate and constrict the blood vessels in your muscles to divert blood for use by your internal organs. Chapter 12 describes the role of the autonomic nervous system in emotional responses and includes a diagram (Figure 12-1) illustrating its effects on various bodily organs. Chapter 13 explains how chronic activation of the sympathetic nervous system can contribute to the development of stress-related diseases. The peripheral nervous system is particularly subject to sport- and exercise-related injuries that produce temporary or chronic physical disability (Toth, McNeil, & Feasby, 2005).

The Endocrine System

The glands of the **endocrine system**, the other major means of communication within the body, exert their functions through hormones (Bauer, 2005). **Hormones** are chemicals that affect physical or psychological processes or both. The endocrine glands secrete hormones into the bloodstream, which transports them to their site of action. The actions of the endocrine system are slower, longer lasting, and more diffuse than those of the nervous system. Endocrine glands differ from *exocrine glands,* such as the sweat glands and salivary glands, which secrete their chemicals onto the body surface

---

reflex An automatic, involuntary motor response to sensory stimulation.

peripheral nervous system The division of the nervous system that conveys sensory information to the central nervous system and motor commands from the central nervous system to the skeletal muscles and internal organs.

nerve A bundle of axons that conveys information to or from the central nervous system.

somatic nervous system The division of the peripheral nervous system that sends messages from the sensory organs to the central nervous system and messages from the central nervous system to the skeletal muscles.

autonomic nervous system The division of the peripheral nervous system that controls automatic, involuntary, physiological processes.

sympathetic nervous system The division of the autonomic nervous system that arouses the body to prepare it for action.

parasympathetic nervous system The division of the autonomic nervous system that calms the body and performs maintenance functions.

endocrine system The physiological system whose glands secrete hormones into the bloodstream.

hormones Chemicals, secreted by endocrine glands, that play a role in a variety of functions, including synaptic transmission.

or into body cavities. Endocrine secretions have many behavioral effects, but exocrine secretions have few. Figure 3-2 illustrates the locations of major endocrine glands. Hormones can act directly on body tissues, serve as neurotransmitters, or modulate the effects of neurotransmitters.

The Pituitary Gland

pituitary gland An endocrine gland that regulates many of the other endocrine glands by secreting hormones that affect the secretion of their hormones.

The **pituitary gland**, an endocrine gland protruding from underneath the brain, regulates many of the other endocrine glands by secreting hormones that affect their activity. This is why the pituitary is known as the "master gland." The pituitary gland, in turn, is regulated by the brain structure called the *hypothalamus.* Feedback from circulating hormones stimulates the hypothalamus to signal the pituitary gland to increase or decrease their secretion (Charlton, 2008)

Pituitary hormones also exert a wide variety of direct effects. For example, *prolactin* levels increase in pregnant women—as well as in expectant fathers—shortly before childbirth (Storey, Walsh, Quintin, & Wynne-Edwards, 2000). Because an elevated prolactin level is also associated with both infertility (Grattan et al., 2001) and psychological stress (Sonino et al., 2004), prolactin might be involved in stress-related infertility. Women who are highly anxious about their inability to become pregnant might enter a vicious cycle in which their anxiety increases the level of prolactin, which in turn makes them less likely to conceive.

Growth hormone, another pituitary hormone, aids the growth and repair of bones and muscles. A child who secretes too much growth hormone might develop *giantism,* marked by excessive growth of the bones. A child who secretes insufficient growth hormone might develop *dwarfism,* marked by stunted growth. Giantism and dwarfism do not impair intellectual development. Children with growth-hormone deficiency may respond to growth hormone treatment (Rosenwald, 2009). Though it might seem logical to administer growth hormone to increase the height of extremely short children who are not diagnosed with dwarfism, this is unwise because the long-term side effects exposing children to hormone treatment for years are unknown (Tauer, 1994).

FIGURE 3-2
The Endocrine System

(a) Midsagittal section of the brain showing major structures of the endocrine system.
(b) Hormones secreted by the endocrine glands affect behavior, mood, cognitive activity, and a host of other physical and psychological processes.

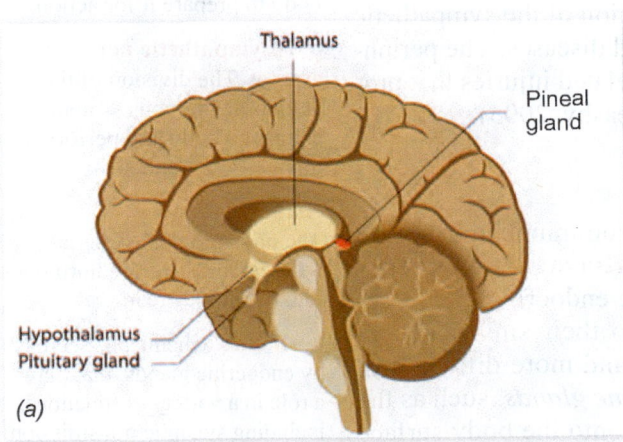

(a)

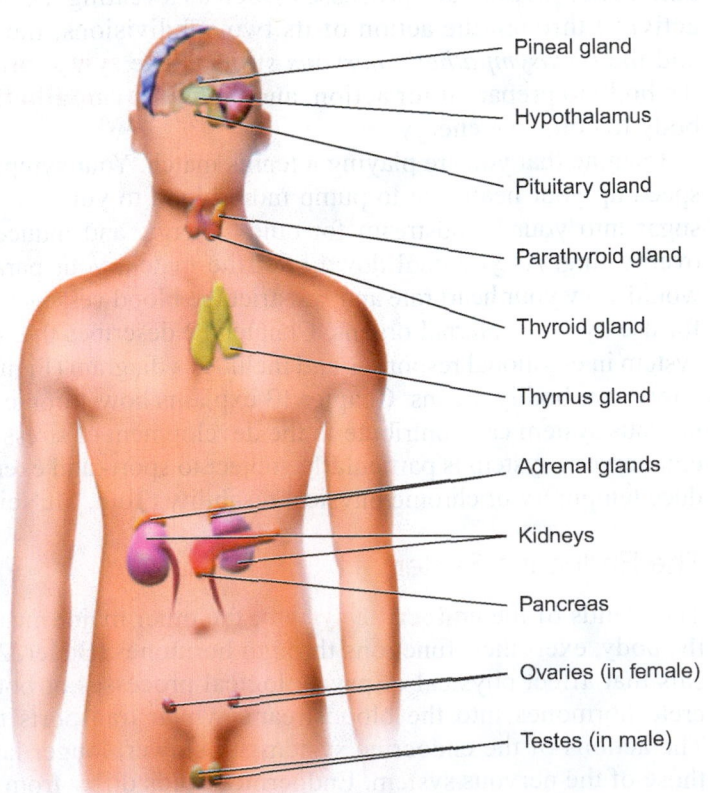

(b)

Adults who secrete high levels of growth hormone, often caused by a pituitary gland tumor, may develop *acromegaly*. This produces unusual enlargement of the hands, feet, jaw, and brow ridge. Because acromegaly increases the risk of mortality due to cardiovascular, cerebrovascular, or pulmonary dysfunction, it is treated by surgery, radiation, and medications (Melmed, 2009). Some competitive athletes take growth hormone alone or in combination with anabolic steroids to improve strength and stamina. Of course, they risk the effects of growth hormone overdose, much akin to acromegaly (Guhu, Sönksen, & Holt, 2010). Moreover, there is inconsistent evidence to support the effectiveness of growth hormone administration in improving athletic performance (Liu et al., 2008).

Other Endocrine Glands

Among the other psychologically important endocrine glands are the *adrenal glands* and the *gonads*. The **adrenal glands**, which lie on the kidneys, secrete important hormones. The *adrenal cortex*, the outer layer of the adrenal gland, secretes hormones, such as *aldosterone*, that regulate the excretion of sodium and potassium, which contribute to proper neural functioning. The adrenal hormone *cortisol* helps the body respond to stress by stimulating the liver to release sugar. Firefighters participating in simulated firefighting exercises show marked increases in cortisol secretion (Perroni et al., 2009). Cortisol levels decrease about 30% after massage therapy, providing evidence that massage therapy reduces stress (Field, Hernandez-Reif, Diego, Schanberg, & Kahn, 2005). Cortisol levels in premature infants are reduced by maternal touch, indicating that maternal touch might help relieve infants' stress (Gitau et al., 2002).

Moreover, cortisol levels have been found to be related to the levels of stress experienced by heterosexual couples who discuss the transition to marriage. In one study, cortisol levels were assessed in the laboratory after couples discussed the possibility of marriage. Cortisol levels were lower among couples who had previously discussed marriage during the course of their relationship. In contrast, higher levels of cortisol were found among couples who had not previously discussed marriage during the course of their relationships, and for whom the idea of being married was more novel, and presumably, more stressful (Loving, Gleason, & Pope, 2009).

In response to stimulation by the sympathetic nervous system, the *adrenal medulla*, the inner core of the adrenal gland, secretes *epinephrine* and *norepinephrine*, which function as both hormones and neurotransmitters. Epinephrine and norepinephrine play a role in stress-related responses. For example, spouses (especially wives) show increases in epinephrine and norepinephrine during marital conflict (Kiecolt-Glaser et al., 1996). Positive moods are associated with lower levels of cortisol and norepinephrine (Brummett, Boyle, Kuhn, Siegler, & Williams, 2009).

The **gonads**, the sex glands, affect sexual development and regulate the structure and organization of brain areas that control reproductive behavior. The **testes**, the male gonads, secrete *testosterone*, which regulates the development of the male reproductive system and secondary sex characteristics. Testosterone also stimulates sexual arousal in both males and females (Apperloo, Van Der Stege, Hoek, Schultz, & Willibrord, 2003). The **ovaries**, the female gonads, secrete *estrogen*, which regulates the development of the female reproductive system and secondary sex characteristics. The ovarian hormone *progesterone* regulates changes in the uterus that help maintain pregnancy. Physicians may administer progesterone to prevent premature delivery (Majhi, Bagga, Kalra, & Sharma, 2009). During prenatal development, sex hormones also affect certain structures and functions of the brain. The effects of sex hormones on human development and sexual behavior are discussed in Chapters 4 and 11.

Anabolic steroids, synthetic forms of testosterone, have provoked controversy during the past two decades. They have been used by athletes, bodybuilders, and weight lifters to promote muscle development, increase endurance, and boost athletic self-confidence (Wright, Grogan, & Hunter, 2000). Yet, studies have shown inconsistent effects of steroids on physical strength. It is unclear whether anabolic steroids directly increase strength or do so through a placebo effect in which users work out more regularly and more vigorously simply because they have faith in the effectiveness of steroids (Maganaris, Collins, & Sharp, 2000). Moreover, a dangerous side effect of anabolic steroid use is increased aggressiveness in some users (Trenton & Currier, 2005), which might be of particular concern to romantic partners.

adrenal gland An endocrine gland that secretes hormones that regulate the excretion of minerals and the body's response to stress.

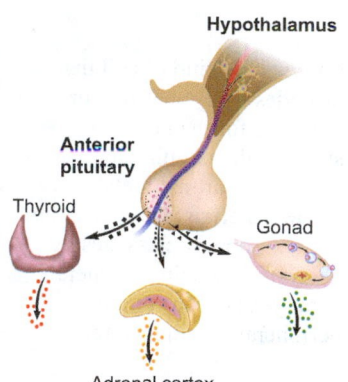

The Hypothalamic Pituitary Axes

Source: Alila Medical Media/ Shutterstock.com.

gonads The male and female sex glands.

testes The male gonads, which secrete hormones that regulate the development of the male reproductive system and secondary sex characteristics.

ovaries The female gonads, which secrete hormones that regulate the development of the female reproductive system and secondary sex characteristics.

Neuronal Activity

sensory neuron A neuron that sends messages from sensory receptors to the central nervous system.

You are able to read this page because *sensory neurons* are relaying input from your eyes to your brain. You will be able to write down information from this page because *motor neurons* from your spinal cord are sending commands from your brain to the muscles of your hand. A **sensory neuron** sends messages to the brain or spinal cord. A **motor neuron** sends messages to a gland, the cardiac muscle, or a skeletal muscle, as well as to a smooth muscle of an artery, small intestine, or other internal organ.

motor neuron A neuron that sends messages from the central nervous system to smooth muscles, cardiac muscle, or skeletal muscles.

Many motor neurons in the brain not only respond when a person initiates a movement but also when the person observes that movement being performed by another person. These are known as *mirror neurons* (Dushanova & Donoghue, 2010), and they play an important role in observational learning (see Chapter 7). Illnesses that destroy motor neurons, such as *amyotrophic lateral sclerosis* (also known as Lou Gehrig's disease, after the great baseball player struck down by it), cause muscle paralysis and eventual death from respiratory muscle paralysis (Beleza-Meireles & Al-Chalabi, 2009).

glial cell A kind of cell that provides a physical support structure for the neurons, supplies them with nutrition, removes neuronal metabolic waste materials, facilitates the transmission of messages by neurons, and helps regenerate damaged neurons in the peripheral nervous system.

Within the nervous system, about 10% of the cells are neurons and 90% are *glial cells* (Colon-Ramos & Shen, 2008). A **glial cell** may serve one of a number of functions, such as providing a physical support structure for the neurons (*glial* comes from the Greek word for "glue"), supplying neurons with nutrients, removing neuronal metabolic waste materials, guiding interneuronal connections, and helping regenerate damaged neurons in the peripheral nervous system . The 3 main types of glial cells are *astrocytes*, *microglia*, and *oligodendrocytes*. Glial cells even facilitate the transmission of messages by neurons (Cras, 2007). One of the most serious kinds of cancer is *glioblastoma,* a malignant glial cell tumor of the brain. It is treated by surgery, radiation, and chemotherapy. A recent addition to the treatment arsenal is monoclonal antibody therapy aimed at preventing angiogenesis—the development of blood vessels that nourish the tumor (Moen, 2010).

To appreciate the role of neurons in communication within the nervous system, consider the functions of the spinal cord. Neurons in the spinal cord convey sensory messages from the body to the brain and motor messages from the brain to the body. In 1730 the English scientist Stephen Hales demonstrated that the spinal cord also plays a role in limb reflexes. He decapitated a frog (to eliminate any input from the brain) and then pinched one of its legs. The leg reflexively pulled away. Hales concluded that the pinch had sent a signal to the spinal cord, which in turn sent a signal to the leg, eliciting its withdrawal. We now know that this limb-withdrawal reflex involves sensory neurons that convey signals from the site of stimulation to the spinal cord, where they transmit their signals to *interneurons* in the spinal cord (McCrea, 1992). An **interneuron** conveys messages between neurons in the brain or spinal cord. The interneurons then send signals to motor neurons, which stimulate flexor muscles to contract and pull the limb away from the source of stimulation—making you less susceptible to pain and injury.

interneuron A neuron that conveys messages between neurons in the brain or spinal cord.

The Structure of the Neuron

soma The cell body, which is the neuron's control center.

To understand how neurons communicate information, you should first become familiar with the structure of the neuron (see Figure 3-3). The **soma** (or cell body) contains the nucleus, which directs the neuron to act as a nerve cell rather than as a fat cell, a muscle cell, or any other kind of cell. The **dendrites** (from the Greek word for "tree") are short, branching fibers that receive neural impulses. The dendrites are covered by bumps called

dendrites The branchlike structures of the neuron that receive neural impulses.

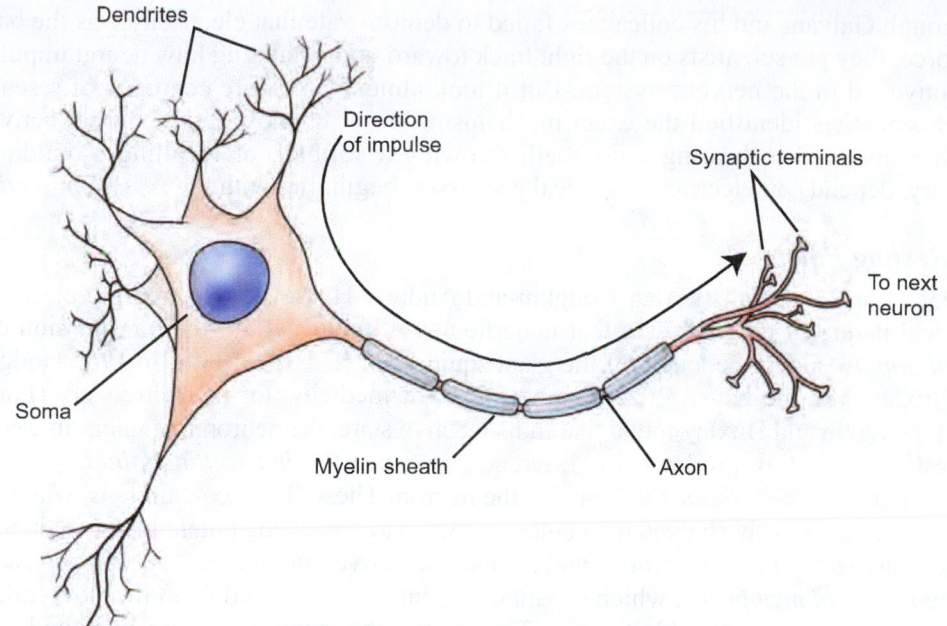

FIGURE 3-3
The Neuron

The main structures of the neuron are the dendrites, the soma, and the axon. The dendrites receive neural impulses from other neurons, the soma regulates neuronal functions, and the axon conveys signals to other neurons, skeletal muscles, or internal organs. When a neuron receives sufficient stimulation from other neurons, it transmits an electrical-chemical neural impulse along its entire axon.

dendritic spines, which provide more surface area for the reception of neural impulses from other neurons (Grutzendler, Kasthuri, & Gan, 2002) and play a critical role in learning and memory. The **axon** is a single fiber that sends neural impulses. Axons range from a tiny fraction of an inch (as in the brain) to more than 3 feet in length (as in the legs of a 7-foot-tall basketball player). Just as bundles of wires form telephone cables, bundles of axons form the nerves of the peripheral nervous system and tracks in the central nervous system. A nerve can contain motor neurons or sensory neurons, or both.

axon The part of the neuron that conducts neural impulses to glands, muscles, or other neurons.

The Neural Impulse

How does the neuron convey information? It took centuries of investigation by brilliant minds to find the answer. In the 17th century, René Descartes (1596–1650) was intrigued by moving statues in the royal gardens of King Louis XIII that were controlled hydraulically by fluid-filled tubes activated when visitors stepped on hidden levers. Descartes speculated that the body is controlled in a similar way by fluids, which he called vital spirits, flowing through the nerves. He assumed that our limbs move when vital spirits expand the muscles that control them.

Descartes was wrong about how muscles function. Though they shorten and thicken when contracted, their overall size remains the same. By the mid-18th century, an alternative explanation, put forth by the great scientist Isaac Newton, replaced Descartes's explanation (Wallace, 2003). Newton, who studied the nature of vibrating strings, believed that nerves communicated by vibrating. Thus, for example, a motor nerve would vibrate faster when we lift a heavy object than a light object. Newton's explanation was discredited by anatomical research, which found that nerves do not vibrate.

The first significant discovery regarding nerve conduction came in 1786, when demonstrations by the Italian physicist Luigi Galvani (1737–1798) hinted that the nerve impulse is electrical in nature. Galvani found that by touching the leg of a freshly killed frog with two different metals, such as iron and brass, he could create an electrical current that made the leg twitch. He believed he had discovered the basic life force—electricity. Some of Galvani's followers, who hoped to use electricity to raise the dead, obtained the fresh corpses of hanged criminals and stimulated them with electricity. To the disappointment of these would-be resurrectionists, they failed to induce more than the flailing of limbs (Hassett, 1978). Not much later, another of Galvani's contemporaries, Mary Shelley, applied what she called "galvanism" (apparently, the use of electricity) to revive the dead in her classic novel *Frankenstein.*

Though Galvani and his colleagues failed to demonstrate that electricity was the basic life force, they put scientists on the right track toward understanding how neural impulses are conveyed in the nervous system. But it took almost two more centuries of research before scientists identified the exact mechanism. We now know that neuronal activity, whether involved in hearing a doorbell, throwing a softball, or recalling a childhood memory, depends on electrical-chemical processes, beginning with the *resting potential.*

The Resting Potential

In 1952, English scientists Alan Hodgkin and Andrew Huxley discovered the electrical-chemical nature of the processes that underlie **axonal conduction**, the transmission of a *neural impulse* along the length of the giant squid axon (Huxley, 1959). In 1963 Hodgkin and Huxley won the Nobel Prize for physiology or medicine for their discovery (Lamb, 1999). Hodgkin and Huxley found that in its inactive state, the neuron maintains an electrical **resting potential**, produced by differences between the *intracellular fluid* inside the neuron and the *extracellular fluid* outside the neuron. These fluids contain *ions,* which are positively or negatively charged molecules. In regard to the resting potential, the main positive ions are *sodium* and *potassium,* and the main negative ions are *proteins* and *chloride.*

The *neuronal membrane,* which separates the intracellular fluid from the extracellular fluid, is selectively permeable to ions. This means that some ions pass back and forth through tiny *ion channels* in the membrane more easily than do others. Because ions with like charges repel each other and ions with opposite charges attract each other, you might assume the extracellular fluid and intracellular fluid would end up with the same relative concentrations of positive ions and negative ions. But, because of several complex processes, the intracellular fluid ends up with an excess of negative ions, and the extracellular fluid ends up with an excess of positive ions. This makes the inside of the resting neuron negative relative to the outside, so the membrane is said to be *polarized,* just like a battery. For example, at rest, the inside of a motor neuron has a charge of −70 millivolts relative to its outside. (A millivolt is one thousandth of a volt). In other words, when a neuron is at rest (not firing), it has an electrical charge.

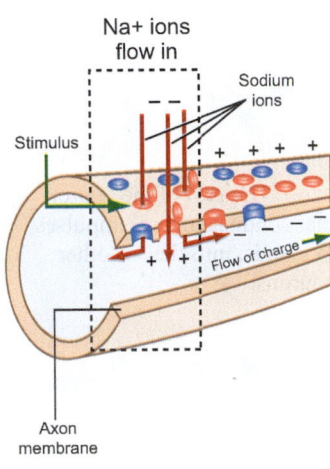

Na+ ions flow in

Sodium ions

Stimulus

Flow of charge

Axon membrane

(a)

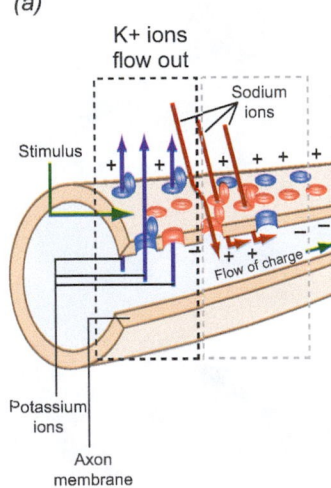

K+ ions flow out

Sodium ions

Stimulus

Flow of charge

Potassium ions

Axon membrane

(b)

The Action Potential

(a) Na+ ions flow into the axon causing a *depolarization* (i.e., a more positive charge inside the cell).
(b) Shortly after Na+ flows into the axon, K+ ions flow out of the axon.

The Action Potential

When a neuron is sufficiently stimulated by other neurons or by a sensory organ, it stops "resting." The neuronal membrane becomes more permeable to positively charged sodium ions, which, attracted by the negative ions inside, rush into the neuron. This movement makes the inside of the neuron less electrically negative relative to the outside, a process called *depolarization.* As sodium continues to rush into the neuron, and the inside becomes less and less negative, the neuron reaches its *firing threshold* (about −60 millivolts in the case of a motor neuron), and an *action potential* occurs at the point where the axon leaves the cell body.

An **action potential** is a change in the electrical charge across the axonal membrane, with the inside of the membrane becoming more electrically positive than the outside and, in the case of a motor neuron, reaching a charge of +40 millivolts. Once an action potential has occurred, that point on the axonal membrane immediately restores its resting potential through a process called *repolarization.* This occurs, in part, because the sudden excess of positively charged sodium ions inside the axon repels the positive potassium ions, driving many of them out of the axon. This loss of positively charged ions helps return the inside of the axon to its negatively charged state relative to the outside. The restored resting potential also is maintained by chemical "pumps" that transport sodium and potassium ions across the axonal membrane, helping return them to their original concentrations.

If an axon fails to depolarize enough to reach its firing threshold, no action potential occurs—not even a weak one. If you have ever been under general anesthesia, you became unconscious because you were given a drug that prevented the axons in your brain that are responsible for the maintenance of consciousness from depolarizing enough to fire off action potentials (Nicoll & Madison, 1982). When an axon reaches its firing threshold and an action potential occurs, a neural impulse travels the entire length of the axon at full strength, as sodium ions rush in at each successive point along the axon. This result is known as the **all-or-none law**. It is analogous to firing a gun: If you do not pull the trigger hard enough, nothing happens; but if you do pull the trigger hard enough, the gun fires and a bullet travels down the entire length of its barrel.

Thus, when a neuron reaches its firing threshold, a neural impulse travels along its axon, as each point on the axonal membrane depolarizes (producing an action potential) and then repolarizes (restoring its resting potential). This process of depolarization/repolarization is so rapid that an axon might conduct up to 1,000 neural impulses a second. The loudness of sounds you hear, the strength of your muscle contractions, and the level of arousal of your brain all depend on the number of neurons involved in those processes and the rate at which they conduct neural impulses.

The speed at which the action potential travels along the axon varies from less than 1 meter per second in certain neurons to more than 100 meters per second in others. The speed depends on several factors, most notably whether sheaths of a fatty white substance called **myelin** (which is produced by glial cells) are wrapped around the axon (Miller, 1994). At frequent intervals along myelinated axons, tiny areas are nonmyelinated. These areas are called *nodes of Ranvier*, after Louis-Antoine Ranvier, the French physiologist who identified them in the 19th century (Barbara, 2007). In myelinated axons, such as those forming much of the brain and spinal cord as well as the motor nerves that control our muscles, the action potential jumps from node to node instead of traveling from point to point along the entire axon. We call this phenomenon saltatory conduction (from the Latin word, *saltare*, which means "to dance"). This explains why myelinated axons conduct neural impulses faster than nonmyelinated axons. This increased speed allows humans and animals to think and react faster.

If you were to look at a freshly dissected brain, you would find that the inside appears mostly white and the outside appears mostly gray because the inside contains many more myelinated axons. You would be safe in concluding that the brain's white matter conveys information faster than its gray matter. Some neurological disorders are associated with abnormal myelin conditions. In the autoimmune demyelinating disease *multiple sclerosis (MS)*, portions of the myelin sheaths surrounding axons in the brain and spinal cord are destroyed, causing muscle weakness, sensory disturbances, memory loss, impaired reasoning, and other cognitive deterioration as a result of the disruption of normal axonal conduction (DeSousa, Albert, & Kalman, 2002).

To summarize, a neuron maintains a *resting potential* during which the inside is electrically negative relative to the outside. Stimulation of the neuron makes positive sodium ions rush in and *depolarize* the neuron (that is, make the inside less negative relative to the outside). If the neuron depolarizes enough, it reaches its *firing threshold*, and an *action potential* occurs. During the action potential, the inside of the neuron becomes electrically positive relative to the outside. Because of the *all-or-none law*, a *neural impulse* is conducted along the entire length of the axon at full strength. Axons covered by a *myelin sheath* conduct impulses faster than other axons. After an action potential has occurred, the axon *repolarizes* and restores its resting potential.

Synaptic Transmission

If all the neuron did was conduct a series of neural impulses along its axon, we would have an interesting but useless phenomenon. The reason we can enjoy a movie, feel a mosquito bite, think about yesterday, or ride a bicycle is because neurons can communicate with one another by the process of **synaptic transmission**—communication across gaps between neurons. Many psychological processes, such as detecting the direction of a sound by determining the slight difference in the arrival time of sound waves at the two ears, require rapid and precisely timed synaptic transmission (Sabatini & Regehr, 1999).

The question of how neurons communicate with one another provoked a heated debate in the late 19th century. The Spanish anatomist Santiago Ramón y Cajal (1852–1934) argued that neurons were separate from one another (Koppe, 1983), whereas

all-or-none law The principle that once a neuron reaches its firing threshold, a neural impulse travels at full strength along the entire length of its axon.

myelin A fatty white substance that forms sheaths around certain axons and increases the speed of neural impulses.

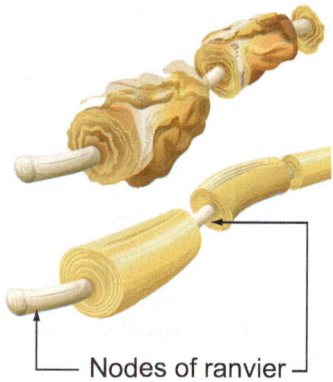

Nodes of ranvier

Damaged and Healthy Myelin Sheaths

The top image shows damage to the myelin of a section of a neuron associated with multiple sclerosis. The bottom image is of a healthy neuron. Arrows point to the nodes of Ranvier.

Source: BlueRingMedia/Shutterstock.com.

synaptic transmission The conveying of a neural impulse between a neuron and a gland, muscle, sensory organ, or another neuron.

synapse The junction between a neuron and a gland, muscle, sensory organ, or another neuron.

the Italian scientist Camillo Golgi (1843–1926) thought nervous tissue was a single system, not made up of separate cells. Ramón y Cajal won the debate by showing that neurons are units that form a network (Ramón y Cajal, 1937/1966). His finding led to the modern *neuron doctrine,* which views the neuron as the basic unit of nerve function, with the neurons physically separated by gaps (Albright et al., 2001). In 1897, the English physiologist Charles Sherrington (1857–1952) coined the term **synapse** (from the Greek word for "junction") to refer to the gaps that exist between neurons. You should note that synapses also exist between neurons and glands, between neurons and muscles, and between neurons and sensory organs.

Mechanisms of Synaptic Transmission

As is usually the case with scientific discoveries, the observation that neurons were separated by synapses led to still another question: How could neurons communicate with one another across these gaps? At first, some scientists assumed that the neural impulse simply jumped across the synapse, just as sparks jump across the gap in a spark plug. But the correct answer came in 1921—in a dream (Loewi, 1960).

The dreamer was Otto Loewi (1873–1961), an Austrian physiologist who had been searching without success for the mechanism of synaptic transmission. Loewi awoke from his dream and carried out the experiment it suggested. He removed the beating heart of a freshly killed frog, along with the portion of the *vagus nerve* attached to it, and placed it in a solution of salt water. By electrically stimulating the vagus nerve, he made the heart beat slower. He then put another beating heart in the same solution. Though he had not stimulated its vagus nerve, the second heart also began to beat slower. If you had made this discovery, what would you have concluded? Loewi concluded, correctly, that the vagus nerve of the hearts had released a chemical into the solution. He named the chemical "vagus stuff." It was this chemical, which other researchers identified as *acetylcholine* (Brown, 2006), that slowed the beating of both hearts (Sourkes, 2009). In 1936 Loewi and British physiologist Henry Dale were co-recipients of the Nobel Prize in physiology or medicine for their research identifying the chemical basis of synaptic transmission (Todman, 2008).

neurotransmitter Chemicals secreted by neurons that provide the means of synaptic transmission.

Acetylcholine is a **neurotransmitter**, a chemical that transmits neural impulses across synapses. Neurotransmitters are stored in round packets called *synaptic vesicles* in the intracellular fluid of *synaptic terminals* (bumps at the end of the axon; sometimes called *synaptic buttons*) that project from the end branches of axons. The discovery of the chemical nature of synaptic transmission led to a logical question: How do neurotransmitters facilitate this transmission? Subsequent research revealed the processes involved (see Figure 3-4):

1. When a neural impulse reaches the end of an axon, it induces a chemical reaction that makes some synaptic vesicles release neurotransmitter molecules into the synapse.

2. The molecules diffuse across the synapse and reach the dendrites of another neuron.

3. The molecules attach to tiny areas on the dendrites called *receptor sites*.

4. The molecules interact with the receptor sites to excite the neuron; this slightly depolarizes the neuron by permitting sodium ions to enter it. But for a neuron to depolarize enough to reach its firing threshold, it must be excited by neurotransmitters released by many neurons. To further complicate the process, a neuron also can be affected by neurotransmitters that inhibit it from depolarizing. Thus, a neuron will fire an action potential only when the combined effects of *excitatory neurotransmitters* sufficiently exceed the combined effects of *inhibitory neurotransmitters*.

5. Neurotransmitters do not remain attached to the receptor sites, continuing to affect them indefinitely. Instead, after the neurotransmitters have done their job, they either are broken down by chemicals called *enzymes* or taken back into the neurons that released them—in a process called *reuptake.*

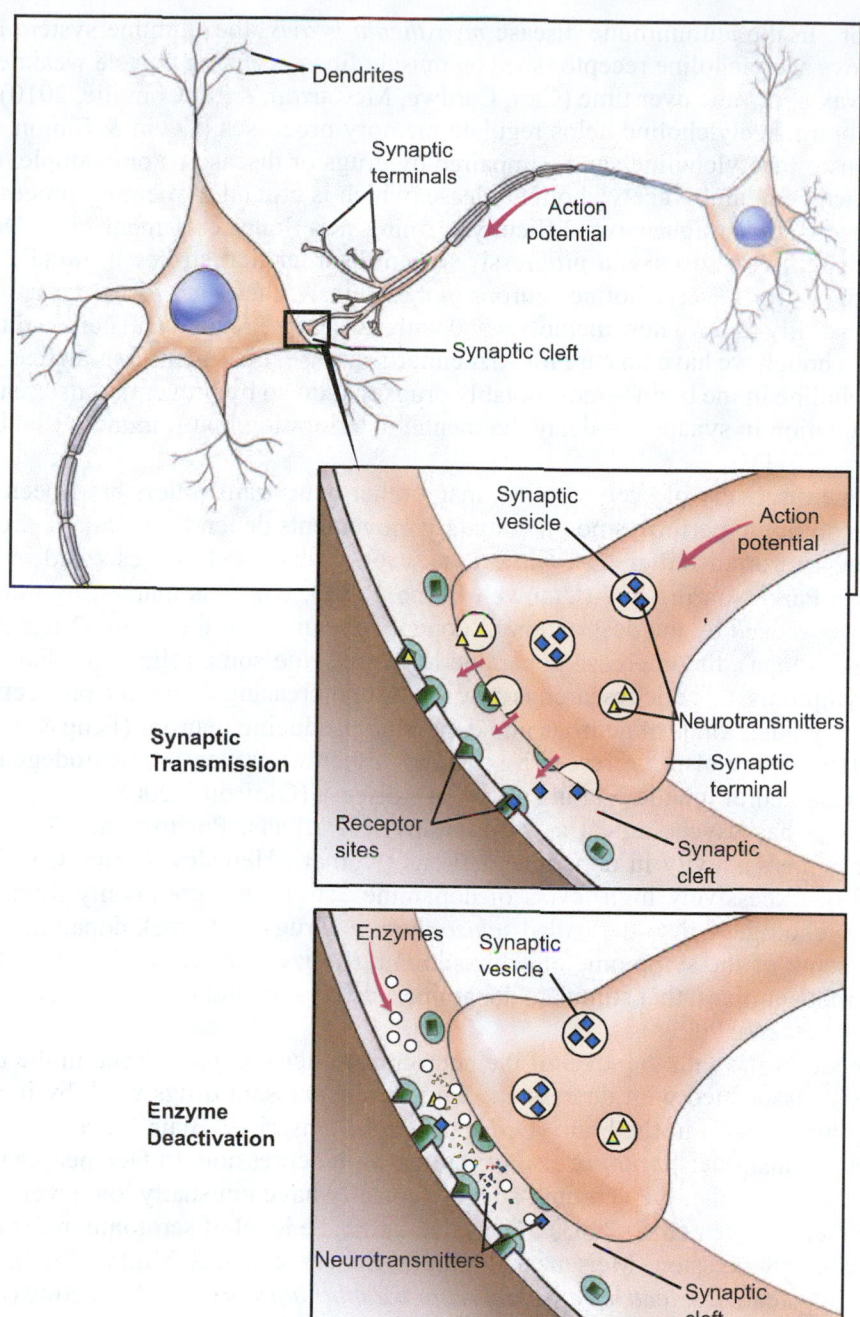

FIGURE 3-4
Mechanisms of Synaptic
Transmission

When a neural impulse
reaches the end of an axon,
it stimulates synaptic vesicles
to release neurotransmitter
molecules into the synaptic
cleft. The molecules diffuse
across the fluid in the synaptic
cleft and interact with receptor
sites on another neuron. The
molecules then disengage
from the receptor sites and
are either broken down by
enzymes or taken back into
the axon in a process called
reuptake.

Neurotransmitters and Drug Effects

Neurotransmitters affect our moods and are responsible for the mental and behavioral effects of psychoactive drugs. In fact, four of the main neurotransmitters out of the perhaps 100 that have been identified account for the effects of just about all psychoactive drugs (Snyder, 2002). Of the neurotransmitters, acetylcholine is the best understood and the first discovered. In the peripheral nervous system, it is the neurotransmitter at synapses between the neurons of the parasympathetic nervous system and the organs they control, such as the heart. Acetylcholine also is the neurotransmitter at synapses between motor neurons and muscle fibers, where it stimulates muscle contractions. *Curare,* a poison that Amazon Indians put on the darts they shoot from their blowguns into prey, paralyzes muscles by preventing acetylcholine from attaching to receptor sites on muscle fibers. The resulting paralysis of muscles, including the breathing muscles, causes death by suffocation. In the autoimmune disease *myasthenia gravis,* the immune system attacks and destroys acetylcholine receptor sites on muscle fibers, causing muscle weakness that tends to wax and wane over time (Carr, Cardwe, McCarron, & McConville, 2010).

In the brain, acetylcholine helps regulate memory processes (Levin & Simon, 1998). The actions of acetylcholine can be impaired by drugs or diseases. For example, chemicals in marijuana inhibit acetylcholine release, which is crucial in memory processes, so marijuana smokers might have difficulty forming new long-term memories (Domino, 1999). **Alzheimer's disease**, a progressive brain disorder that strikes in middle or late adulthood, destroys acetylcholine neurons in the brain. Alzheimer's disease is associated with the inability to form new memories and with severe intellectual and personality deterioration. Though we have no cure for Alzheimer's disease, treatments that increase levels of acetylcholine in the brain—most notably drugs that do so by preventing its breakdown and deactivation in synapses—delay the mental deterioration that it induces (Sabbagh & Cummings, 2011).

Since the discovery of acetylcholine, many other neurotransmitters have been identified. Your ability to perform smooth voluntary movements depends on brain neurons that secrete the neurotransmitter *dopamine.* **Parkinson's disease**, first described by physician James Parkinson in 1817 (Cranwell-Bruce, 2010), which is marked by movement disorders, is caused by the destruction of dopamine neurons in the brain. Drugs, such as levodopa (L-dopa), that increase dopamine levels provide some relief from Parkinson's disease symptoms. Genetic research is now aimed at increasing dopamine production and at converting other kinds of neurons into dopamine-producing neurons (Feng & Maguire-Zeiss, 2010). There also are research programs aimed at preventing neurodegeneration and restoring neural functioning in Parkinson's disease (Giovanni, 2008).

Dopamine has psychological as well as physical effects. Positive moods are maintained in part by activity in dopamine neurons (Kumari, Hemsley, Cotter, Checkley, & Gray,1998). Excessively high levels of dopamine activity are commonly found in the serious psychological disorder called *schizophrenia.* Drugs that block dopamine activity alleviate some of the symptoms of schizophrenia (Meizenzahl et al., 2007), and drugs, such as amphetamines, that stimulate dopamine activity may induce symptoms of schizophrenia (Adeyemo, 2002a).

Our moods vary with the level of the neurotransmitter *norepinephrine* in the brain. A low level is associated with depression. Some antidepressant drugs work by increasing norepinephrine levels in the brain (Dremencov, el Mensari, & Blair, 2009). A low level of the neurotransmitter *serotonin* also is implicated in depression. In fact, people who become so depressed that they commit suicide typically have unusually low levels of serotonin (Purselle & Nemeroff, 2003). Drugs that boost the level of serotonin in the nervous system relieve depression (Meisenzahl, Schmitt, Scheuerecker, & Möller, 2010). Antidepressant drugs called *selective serotonin reuptake inhibitors,* such as fluoxetine (Prozac), relieve depression by preventing the reuptake of serotonin into the axons that release it, thereby increasing serotonin levels in serotonin synapses (Racagni & Brunello, 1999).

Some neurotransmitters are amino acids. The main inhibitory amino acid neurotransmitter is *gamma aminobutyric acid* (or GABA). GABA promotes muscle relaxation and reduces anxiety. So-called tranquilizers, such as lorazepam (Ativan), relieve anxiety (Kalueff & Nutt, 2007) and insomnia (Winsky-Sommerer, 2009) by promoting the action of GABA. As discussed in Chapter 8, the main excitatory amino acid neurotransmitter, *glutamate,* helps in the formation of memories (Gravius, Pietraszek, Dekundy, & Danysz, 2010).

Endorphins

Another class of neurotransmitters comprises small proteins called *neuropeptides.* *Neuropeptide Y* promotes the deposit of abdominal fat, particularly in response to stressors (Kuo et al., 2007). The neuropeptide *substance P* has sparked interest because of its apparent role in the transmission of pain impulses (Ruiz, 2009), as in migraine headaches (Nakano, Shimomura, Takahashi, & Ikawa, 1993), sciatic nerve pain (Malmberg &

Alzheimer's disease A brain disorder characterized by difficulty in forming new memories and by general mental deterioration.

Parkinson's disease A degenerative disease of the dopamine pathway, which causes marked disturbances in motor behavior.

Basbaum, 1998), and following the accidental loosening of a hip replacement (Qian, Zeng, Zhang, & Jiang, 2008). During the past few decades, neuropeptides called **endorphins** have generated much research and publicity because of their possible roles in relieving pain and inducing feelings of euphoria.

The endorphin story began in 1973, when Candace Pert and Solomon Snyder of Johns Hopkins University discovered opiate receptors in the brains of animals (Pert & Snyder, 1973). Opiates are pain-relieving drugs (or *narcotics*)—including morphine, codeine, and heroin—derived from the opium poppy. Snyder and Pert became interested in conducting their research after finding hints in previous research studies by other scientists that animals might have opiate receptors. They took samples of brain tissue from mice, rats, and guinea pigs and treated them with radioactive morphine and naloxone, a chemical similar in structure to morphine that blocks morphine's effects. A special device detected whether the morphine and naloxone had attached to receptors in the brain tissue.

Pert and Snyder found that the chemicals had bound to specific receptors (opiate receptors). If you had been a member of Pert and Snyder's research team, what would you have inferred from this observation? Pert and Snyder inferred that the brain must manufacture its own opiate-like chemicals. This would explain why it had evolved opiate receptors, and it seemed a more likely explanation than that the receptors had evolved to take advantage of the availability of opiates such as morphine and codeine in the environment. Pert and Snyder's findings inspired the search for opiate-like chemicals in the brain.

The search bore fruit in Scotland when Hans Kosterlitz and his colleagues found an opiate-like chemical in brain tissue taken from animals (Hughes et al., 1975). They called this chemical *enkephalin* (from Greek terms meaning "in the head"). Enkephalin and similar chemicals discovered in the brain were later dubbed "endogenous morphine" (meaning "morphine from within"). This term was abbreviated into the now-popular term *endorphin*. Endorphins function as both neurotransmitters and *neuromodulators*—neurochemicals that affect the activity of other neurotransmitters. For example, endorphins serve as neuromodulators by inhibiting the release of substance P, thereby blocking pain impulses.

Once researchers had located the receptor sites for the endorphins and had isolated endorphins themselves, they then wondered, *Why has the brain evolved its own opiate-like neurochemicals?* Perhaps the first animals blessed with endorphins were better able to function in the face of pain caused by diseases or injuries, making them more likely to survive long enough to reproduce and pass this physical trait on to successive generations (Levinthal, 1988). Evidence supporting this speculation has come from both human and animal experiments.

In one experiment, researchers first recorded how long mice would allow their tails to be exposed to radiant heat from a light bulb before the pain made them flick their tails away from it. Those mice then were paired with more aggressive mice, which attacked and defeated them. The losers' tolerance for the radiant heat was then tested again. The results showed that the length of time the defeated mice would permit their tails to be heated had increased, which suggests that the aggressive attacks had raised their endorphin levels. But when the defeated mice were given naloxone, which blocks the effects of morphine, they flicked away their tails as quickly as they had done before being defeated. The researchers concluded that the naloxone had blocked the pain-relieving effects of the endorphins (Miczek, Thompson, & Shuster, 1982). Other studies have found that the endorphins likewise are associated with pain relief in people (Spinella, Znamensky, Moroz, Ragnauth, & Bodnar, 1999). And increases in pain may be associated with reductions in endorphin levels. Premenstrual pain, for example, is associated with low endorphin levels (Straneva et al., 2002).

Endorphin levels may rise in response to vigorous exercise (Harbach et al., 2000), perhaps accounting for the "exercise high" reported by many athletes, including runners, swimmers, and cyclists. This hypothesis was supported by a study that found increased endorphin levels after aerobic dancing (Pierce, Eastman, Tripathi, & Olson, 1993). Further support came from a study of bungee jumpers. After jumping, their feelings of euphoria showed a positive correlation with increases in their endorphin levels (Hennig, Laschefski, & Opper, 1994).

Defeated Mice

Social defeat stress is a test that is useful to study mood disorders. Test mice are repeatedly subjected to bouts of social defeat by larger and aggressive mice and this results in the test mouse having a depressive-like syndrome due to these social interactions.

Source: VectorShots/ Shutterstock.com.

The Runner's High

The euphoric "exercise high" experienced by long-distance runners might be caused by the release of endorphins.

Source: Jan Kranendonk/Shutterstock.com.

Section Review: Neuronal Activity

1. What are the major structures of the neuron?
2. What is the basic process underlying neural impulses?

Brain Functions

"Tell me, where is fancy bred, in the heart or in the head?" (*The Merchant of Venice,* act 3, scene 2). The answer to this question from Shakespeare's play might be obvious to you. You know that your brain, and not your heart, is your feeling organ—the site of your mind. But you have the advantage of centuries of research, which has made the role of the brain in all psychological processes obvious even to nonscientists. Of course, the cultural influence of early beliefs may linger. Just imagine the response of a person who received a gift of Valentine's Day candy in a box that was brain-shaped instead of heart-shaped.

The ancient Egyptians associated the mind with the heart and discounted the importance of the apparently inactive brain. In fact, when the pharaoh Tutankhamen ("King Tut") was mummified to prepare him for the afterlife, his heart and other bodily organs were carefully preserved, but his brain was discarded. The Greek philosopher Aristotle (384–322 B.C.) also believed that the heart was the site of the mind, because when the heart stops, mental activity stops (Laver, 1972). But the Greek physician-philosopher Hippocrates (460–377 B.C.), based on his observations of the effects of brain damage, did locate the mind in the brain:

> Some people say that the heart is the organ with which we think and that it feels pain and anxiety. But it is not so. Men ought to know that from the brain and from the brain alone arise our pleasures, joys, laughter, and tears. (quoted in Penfield, 1975, p. 7)

Techniques for Studying Brain Functions

Later in this chapter, you will learn about the function of the different substructures of the brain. But how did scientists discover them? They have relied on *clinical case studies, experimental manipulation, recording of electrical activity,* and *brain imaging.* But pause first to consider an alternative, commonsense approach to studying brain functions that dominated the 19th century and in various forms continued into the 20th century (see "Critical Thinking About Psychology" box).

Clinical Case Studies

For thousands of years, people have noticed that when individuals suffer brain damage from injuries, they may experience physical and psychological changes. Physicians and scientists sometimes conduct *clinical case studies* of such people to assess the acute and chronic effects of brain damage, as well as patterns of recovery following it (Muccio et al., 2009). For example, in the section "Functional Organization of the Brain," you will read about a clinical case study of Phineas Gage, a man who survived the tragic experience of having a 3-foot-long metal rod pierce his brain. Neurologist Oliver Sacks has written several books based on clinical case studies of patients who suffered brain damage that produced unusual—even bizarre—symptoms, including a man who lost the ability to recognize familiar faces. This disorder, *prosopagnosia,* is discussed in Chapter 5.

Experimental Manipulation

Clinical case studies involve individuals who have suffered brain damage from illness or injury. In contrast, techniques that involve *experimental manipulation* involve purposely damaging the brain, electrically or chemically stimulating the brain, or observing the effects of drugs on the brain.

When scientists use brain lesioning, they destroy specific parts of animal brains and, after the animal has recovered from the surgery, look for changes in behavior. Since the early 19th century, when the French anatomist Pierre Flourens formalized this practice, researchers who employ this technique have learned much about the brain. As described in Chapter 11, for example, researchers in the late 1940s demonstrated that destroying a specific part of the brain structure called the *hypothalamus* would make a rat starve itself even in the presence of food, whereas destroying another part of the hypothalamus would make a rat's appetite insatiable, and the rat would overeat until it became obese.

Some researchers, instead of destroying parts of the brain to see its effects on behavior, use electrical stimulation of the brain (ESB). They use weak electrical currents to stimulate highly localized sites in the brain and observe any resulting changes in behavior. Perhaps the most well-known research using ESB was conducted by neurosurgeon Wilder Penfield, who, in the course of operating on the brains of people with severe epilepsy, meticulously stimulated the surface of the brain. As a result, as discussed in the section "Brain Functions," Penfield discovered that specific sites on the brain control specific body movements and that specific sites are related to sensations from specific body sites.

The relatively new technique (first developed in the mid-1980s) of **transcranial magnetic stimulation (TMS)** involves electrically stimulating the cerebral cortex of the brain by using pulsed magnetic fields administered near the scalp. TMS has been used in cognitive studies of memory, language, and learning (Bailey, Karhu, & Ilmoniemi, 2001). Moreover, TMS has shown promise for reducing migraine headaches (McComas & Upton, 2009), clinical depression (Fitzgerald, Hoy, Daskalakis, & Kulkarni, 2009), and auditory hallucinations (Bagati, Nizamie, & Prakash, 2009).

Whereas some experimental researchers assess the effects of ESB or TMS, others observe the behavioral effects of drugs on the brain. In the section "Synaptic Transmission," you learned how animal subjects, when given the drug naloxone, do not show the same reduction in pain that they do when given a placebo. Because naloxone blocks the effects of opiates, this finding supported research implicating endorphins as the body's own natural opiates. Later in this chapter, you will learn of a technique that involves injecting a barbiturate into an artery serving either the left or right side of the brain and then observing any resulting effects. When the drug affects the left side of the brain, but rarely when it affects the right side, the person will lose the ability to speak. This result supports research indicating that the left half of the brain regulates speech in most people.

Lesioning the Brain

Feeding behavior is governed by inputs from neuronal signals (which were cut off by the lesion). Lesioning the lateral hypothalamus, a hunger center, in rats, results in underweight rats, whereas lesioning the ventromedial hypothalamus, a satiety center, results in obese rats.
Source: Cathy Keifer/ Shutterstock.com.

transcranial magnetic stimulation (TMS)

An experimental manipulation of the brain that involves electrically stimulating the cerebral cortex of the brain by using pulsed magnetic fields administered near the scalp.

What Can We Infer from the Size and Shape of the Brain?

"Research on Einstein's Brain Finds Size Does Matter" (*CBC Newsworld,* 6/19/99)

"Peek Into Einstein's Brain" (*Discovery* Online, 6/18/99)

"Einstein Was Bigger Where It Counts, Analysis Shows" (*Sydney Morning Herald,* 6/18/99)

"The Roots of Genius" (*Newsweek,* 6/24/99).

"Part of Einstein's Brain 15 Percent Bigger Than Normal" (NPR, 6/18/99)

"How Smart Can We Get?" (PBS, 10/24/2012)

"New Photos of Einstein's Brain" (NOVA Science now, 11/15/2012)

As you can gather from the preceding headlines, the international media responded with excitement when researchers at McMaster University in Ontario, Canada, announced that the brain of scientific genius Albert Einstein was anatomically distinct. That is, a particular region of it, the parietal lobe, was larger than that same region tended to be in other people. The media reports were based on a study of Einstein's preserved brain published in *The Lancet,* a respected British medical journal. Einstein, who conceived the theory of relativity, is considered one of the outstanding scientists in history. The reports attributed his scientific genius to that unusually large region of his brain—a region associated with spatial and mathematical ability. It seemed to be a matter of common sense; if you know the function of a brain structure, and that structure is unusually large in a particular person, then that person must have excelled in that function. But attempts to assess intellectual and personality functions by studying the size or shape of specific areas of the brain are not new—and typically have been fruitless, as in the case of the pseu-

doscience practice known as **phrenology** (Greek for "science of the mind").

"You need to have your head examined!" is a refrain heard by many people whose ideas and behavior upset other people. Today, this comment is simply a figure of speech, but for most of the 19th century and well into the early 20th century, it was common practice for people to—literally—have their heads examined for career counseling, contributing to the founding of that human service field (Hershenson, 2008). The pseudoscience of phrenology was perhaps the most dramatic example of the commonsense practice of inferring personal characteristics from the size and shape of the brain.

Phrenology began when the respected Viennese physician-anatomist Franz Joseph Gall (1758–1828) proclaimed that particular regions of the brain controlled specific psychological functions (Simpson, 2005). Gall not only believed that specific brain sites controlled specific mental faculties, he assumed that the shape of specific sites on the skull indicated the degree of development of the brain region beneath it. To Gall it was simply a matter of common sense to assume that a bumpy site would indicate a highly developed brain region; a flat site would indicate a less developed brain region.

But what did Gall use as evidence to support his practice? Much of his evidence came from his own casual observations. For example, as a child he noted, with some envy, that classmates with good memories had bulging eyes. He concluded that their eyes bulged because excess brain matter behind them pushed them out of their sockets, which led him to the commonsense conclusion that memory is controlled by the region of the brain just behind the eyes. Thus, phrenology was supported by commonsense reasoning about isolated cases, which is frowned on by scientists because of its unreliability.

---

phrenology A discredited technique for determining intellectual abilities and personality traits by examining the bumps and depressions of the skull.

electroencephalograph (EEG) A device used to record patterns of electrical activity produced by neuronal activity in the brain.

magnetoencephalography (MEG) A functional neuroimaging technique to measure brain activity using magnetic fields. MEG is useful to map brain changes across time and is often used together with fMRI.

Recording Electrical Activity

Consider the **electroencephalograph (EEG)**, which records the patterns of electrical activity produced by neuronal activity in the brain. The EEG has a peculiar history, going back to a day near the turn of the 20th century when an Austrian scientist named Hans Berger fell off a horse and narrowly escaped serious injury. That evening he received a telegram informing him that his sister felt he was in danger. The telegram inspired Berger to investigate the possible association between *mental telepathy* (the alleged, though scientifically unverified, ability of one mind to communicate with another by extrasensory means) and electrical activity from the brain (La Vaque, 1999). In 1924, after years of experimenting on animals and his son Klaus, Berger succeeded in perfecting a procedure for recording electrical activity in the brain. He attached small metal disks called *electrodes* to Klaus's scalp and connected them with wires to a device that recorded changes in the patterns of electrical activity in his brain.

Though Berger failed to find physiological evidence in support of mental telepathy, he found that specific patterns of brain activity are associated with specific mental states, such as coma, sleep, and wakefulness (Gloor, 1994). He also identified two distinct rhythms

What Can We Infer from the Size and Shape of the Brain? *continued*

Though phrenology had its scientific shortcomings and disappeared in the early 20th century, it sparked interest in the localization of brain functions (Miller, 1996). But what of Einstein's brain? If it did not make scientific sense to infer the size of brain areas and the degree of development of their associated functions from the shape of the skull, are inferences about brain functions from the size of particular structures any more scientifically credible?

When Einstein died in 1955 at the age of 76 in Princeton, New Jersey, his body was cremated and his ashes spread across the nearby Delaware River, but his brain was removed and kept by the pathologist, Thomas Harvey, who did the autopsy. Harvey took the brain with him when he moved to Wichita, Kansas, where he kept it in two mason jars. Most of it had been cut into sections that looked like cubes of tofu.

Over the years, Harvey had mailed small sections of the brain to scientists who wished to study its microscopic structure. But the 1999 study was the first to examine the structure of the brain as a whole. The researchers compared Einstein's brain with the preserved brains of 35 men and 56 women who were of presumably normal intelligence when they died. Einstein's brain was the same weight and overall size as those of the other men, including eight who were similar in age at the time of death. Though Sandra Witelson, the neuroscientist who led the research team, found that Einstein's brain was normal in size, she found specific differences between Einstein's brain and those of the other men. The lower portion of the parietal lobe was 15 percent wider than normal. This led Witelson to conclude there might have been more neural connections in that region of Einstein's brain.

"That kind of shape was not observed in any of our brains and is not depicted in any atlas of the human brain," noted Witelson (Ross, 1999, p. A-1). Because research has indicated that the parietal region is involved in spatial and mathematical functions, Witelson inferred that the larger size might account for Einstein's superiority as a physicist and mathematician—especially since Einstein always insisted that he did his scientific thinking spatially, not verbally.

But what can we make of this research report? Though some researchers have found that brain size on average is positively correlated with intellectual ability (Rushton & Ankney, 2009), Witelson warned that overall brain size is not a valid indicator of differences in intelligence between particular individuals. But she noted that the more specific anatomical differences between Einstein's brain and the others might indicate that mathematical genius is, at least to some extent, inborn. "What this is telling us is that environment isn't the only factor" (Ross, 1999, p. A-1). Nonetheless, Witelson added that she would not discount the importance of the environment in governing brain development. Perhaps Einstein was born with a brain similar to those of the people his was compared to, but a lifetime of thinking scientifically and mathematically (not to mention other experiences, such as diet and personal health habits) altered his brain and created distinctive anatomical differences between it and the others.

The media tend to seek the most interesting, controversial research studies to report. Scientific consumers are well advised to go beyond popular reports and articles and think critically about what they claim, perhaps even reading some of the scientific literature itself when it relates to topics of personal importance. One of the goals of this book is to make you that kind of critical consumer of information—whether presented by a scientist or a journalist.

---

of electrical activity. He called the relatively slow rhythm associated with a relaxed mental state the *alpha rhythm* and the relatively fast rhythm associated with an alert, active mental state the *beta rhythm*. Berger also used the EEG to provide the first demonstration of the stimulating effect of cocaine on brain activity. He found that cocaine increased the relative proportion of the beta rhythm in EEG recordings (Herning, 1985).

Berger's method of associating EEG activity with psychological processes is still used today. In one study, for example, researchers determined the EEG patterns that accompanied mental fatigue in white-collar workers (Okogbaa, Shell, & Filipusic, 1994). The EEG also has been used to record changes in infants' brain-wave patterns during their first year in response to music (Schmidt, Trainor, & Santesso, 2003) and in adults in response to aerobic exercise (Bailey et al., 2008) and the aroma of incense (Iijima, Osawa, Nishitan, & Iwata, 2009). Moreover, the EEG has been used clinically to assess patterns of brain activity associated with autism spectrum disorder (Bosl, Tierney, Tager-Rusberg, & Nelson, 2011), epilepsy (Vulliemoz, Lemieux, Daunizeau, Michel, & Duncan, 2010), and stages of sleep (Bersagliere & Achermann, 2010). **Magnetoencephalography (MEG)**, a

EEG

An EEG records momentary changes in electrical activity. The subject must wear electrodes placed close to the scalp.
Source: Oleg Senkov/Shutterstock.com.

Chapter 3 Biopsychological Bases of Behavior

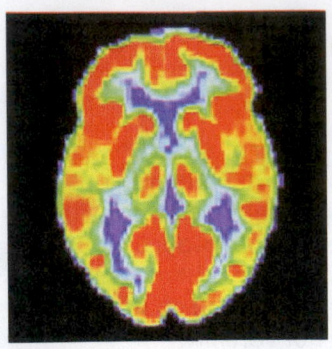

Pet Scan

Positron-emission tomography (PET) scans are a technique to record brain activity by injecting a radioactive substance called a tracer into human or animals. This PET scan shows the brain activity of a healthy person. Red indicates the highest activity during some task, followed by yellow, green, and blue.

Source: Courtesy Alzheimer's Disease Education and Referral Center, a service of the National Institute on Aging.

positron-emission tomography (PET) A brain-scanning technique that produces color-coded pictures showing the relative activity of different brain areas.

computed tomography (CT) A brain-scanning technique that relies on X-rays to construct computer-generated images of the brain or body.

magnetic resonance imaging (MRI) A brain-scanning technique that relies on strong magnetic fields to construct computer-generated images of the brain or body based on blood flow.

functional magnetic resonance imaging (fMRI) A brain-scanning technique that relies on strong magnetic fields to construct computer-generated images of physiological activity in the brain or body.

single photon emission computed tomography (SPECT) A brain-imaging technique that creates images of cerebral blood flow.

newer way of measuring brain activity, detects changes in the patterns of magnetic fields produced by neural activity. MEG has been used to map brain areas involved in speech disorders (Breier, Randle, Maher, & Papanicolaou, 2010), music perception (Brattico et al., 2009), clinical depression (Takei et al., 2009), and Alzheimer's disease (Abatzoglou, Anninos, Tsalafoutas, & Koukourakis,2009).

Brain-Imaging

The computer revolution has given rise to a major breakthrough in the study of the brain: brain-imaging techniques. Brain imaging involves scanning the brain to provide pictures of brain structures or "maps" of ongoing activity in the brain (Cacioppo, Berntson, & Nussbaum, 2008). One of the most important kinds of brain scan to psychologists is **positron-emission tomography (PET)**, which lets them measure ongoing activity in particular regions of the brain. In using the PET scan, researchers inject radioactive glucose (a type of sugar) into a participant. Because neurons use glucose as a source of energy, the most active region of the brain takes up the most radioactive glucose. The amount of radiation emitted by each region is measured by a donut-shaped device that encircles the head. This information is analyzed by a computer, which generates color-coded pictures showing the relative degree of activity in different brain regions. PET scans are useful in revealing the precise patterns of brain activity during the performance of motor, sensory, and cognitive tasks. For example, PET scans have been used to study brain activity of individuals while they smoked marijuana (Mathew et al., 2002) or played music in an ensemble (Satoh, Takeda, Nagata, Hatazawa, & Kuzuhara, 2001).

Two other brain-scanning techniques, which are more useful for displaying brain structures than for displaying ongoing brain activity, are **computed tomography (CT)** and **magnetic resonance imaging (MRI)**. The CT scan takes many X-rays of the brain from a variety of orientations around it. Detectors then record how much radiation has passed through the different regions of the brain. A computer uses this information to compose a picture of the brain. The MRI scan exposes the brain to a powerful magnetic field, and the hydrogen atoms in the brain align themselves along the magnetic field. A radio signal then disrupts the alignment. When the radio signal is turned off, the atoms align themselves again. A computer analyzes these changes, which differ from one region of the brain to another, to compose an even more detailed picture of the brain. Traditional CT and MRI scans have been useful in detecting structural abnormalities. For example, localized brain degeneration in adults with Alzheimer's disease has been verified by MRI scans (Appel et al., 2010).

A technique called **functional magnetic resonance imaging (fMRI)** has joined the PET scan as a tool for measuring ongoing activity in the brain. This ultrafast version of the traditional MRI detects increases in blood flow to active brain regions. Functional MRI has been used to study brain activity involved in pain (Yuan et al., 2010), orgasm (Komisaruk & Whipple, 2005), meditation (Engstrom & Söderfeldt, 2010), smelling odors (Katata et al., 2009) and mild cognitive impairment (Ries et al., 2008). Figure 3-5 illustrates images produced by functional MRI. A more recent version of computed tomography, **single photon emission computed tomography (SPECT)**, does more than provide images of brain structures. It creates images of regional cerebral blood flow. SPECT has been used in assessing brain activity in substance abuse (Amen, 2010), Alzheimer's disease (Habert et al., 2000), and epileptic seizures (Huberfeld et al., 2006).

Functional Organization of the Brain

The human brain's appearance does not hint at its complexity. Holding it in your hands, you might not be impressed by either its 3-pound weight or its walnut-like surface. You might be more impressed to learn that it contains billions of neurons. And you might be astounded to learn that any given brain neuron might communicate with thousands of others, leading to an enormous number of pathways and networks for messages to follow in the brain. Moreover, the brain is not homogeneous. It has many separate structures that interact to help you perform the myriad of activities that let you function

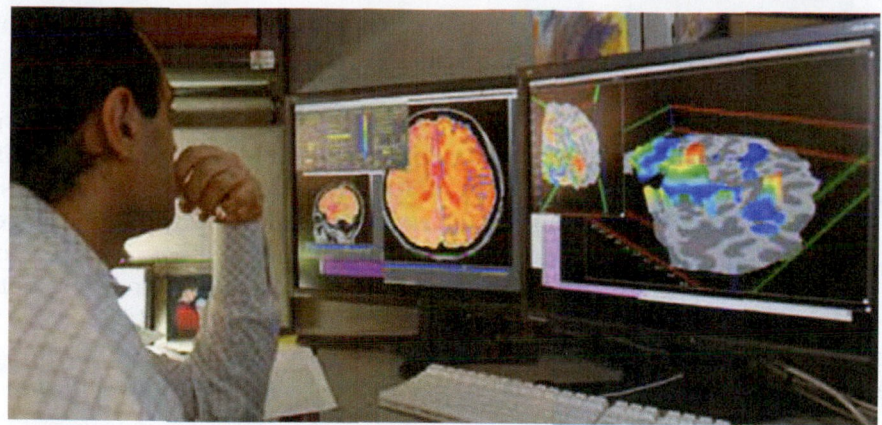

FIGURE 3-5
Functional MRI

Functional magnetic resonance imaging (fMRI) is a technique that uses magnetic detectors outside the head to measure metabolism in different parts of the brain. Researchers can thereby infer activity levels in various brain areas. Participants can perform cognitive tasks while in a fMRI scanner, and the areas that are most activated are generally represented in red and areas least activated are represented in blue.
Source: U.S. Department of Health and Human Services: National Institute of Mental Health.

in everyday life. When discussing the functions of the brain, it is customary to divide it into three major regions: the *brain stem,* the *limbic system,* and the *cerebral cortex* (see Figure 3-6).

The Brain Stem

Your ability to survive from moment to moment depends on your **brain stem**, located at the base of the brain. The brain stem includes the *medulla,* the *pons,* the *cerebellum,* the *reticular formation,* and the *thalamus.* The brain stem plays the primary role in maintaining breathing and consciousness. Cessation of breathing and loss of consciousness are components of what physicians define as "brain death" (Connie, Kelvin, Chung, Diana, & Gilberto, 2008).

brain stem A group of brain structures that provide life-support functions.

The Medulla Of all the brain stem structures, the most crucial to your survival is the **medulla**, which connects the brain and spinal cord. At this moment, your medulla is regulating your breathing, heart rate, and blood pressure. When called upon, your medulla also stimulates sneezing, coughing, vomiting, swallowing, and even hiccupping. By inducing vomiting, for example, the medulla prevents people who drink too much alcohol too fast from poisoning themselves. Damage to the medulla may cause difficulty in swallowing (Oku &

medulla A brain stem structure that regulates breathing, heart rate, blood pressure, and other life functions.

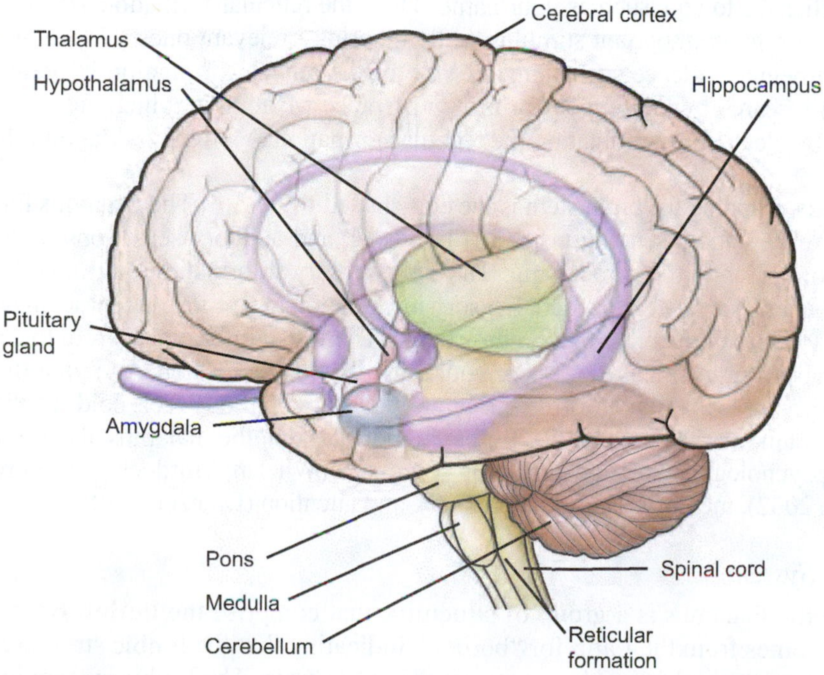

FIGURE 3-6
The Structure of the Human Brain

The structures of the brain serve a variety of life-support, sensory, motor, and cognitive functions.

Thalamus
Hypothalamus
Cerebral cortex
Hippocampus
Pituitary gland
Amygdala
Pons
Medulla
Cerebellum
Reticular formation
Spinal cord

Okada, 2008). The medulla also is important in regulating the transmission of pain impulses from the body to appropriate regions of the brain (Porreca & Gebhart, 2002).

pons A brain stem structure that regulates the sleep-wake cycle.

The Pons Just above the medulla lies the bulbous structure called the **pons** (which means "bridge" in Latin), which likewise plays a role in regulating breathing. As explained in Chapter 6, the pons helps regulate the sleep-wake cycle through its effect on consciousness (Datta, 2002). Surgical anesthesia induces unconsciousness by acting on the pons (Ishizawa, Ma, Dohi, & Shimonaka, 2000) and other brain regions. And if you have ever been the unfortunate recipient of a blow to the head that knocked you out, your loss of consciousness was caused by the blow's effect on your pons (Hayes et al., 1984). In more extreme cases, such as damage to the pons produced by a stroke, individuals might enter a comatose state in which they are unconscious and unresponsive to the environment (Claassen & Rao, 2008).

cerebellum A brain stem structure that controls the timing of well-learned movements.

The Cerebellum The pons connects the **cerebellum** (meaning "little brain" in Latin) to the rest of the brain. The cerebellum controls the timing and coordination of well-learned sequences of movements that are too rapid to be controlled consciously (Schmitt, Bitoun, & Manto, 2009), as in running a sprint, singing a song, playing the piano, or even throwing a ball (Timmann, Lee, Watts, & Hore, 2008). As you know from your own experience, conscious efforts to control normally automatic sequences of movements such as these can disrupt them. Pianists who think of each key they are striking while playing a well-practiced piece would be unable to maintain proper timing. Research indicates that the cerebellum may even affect the smooth timing and sequencing of mental activities, such as the use of language (Fabbro, 2000). Damage to the cerebellum can disrupt the ability to perform skills that we take for granted, such as using one's fingers to retrieve tiny objects (Glickstein, Waller, Baizer, Brown, & Timmann, 2005) and the tongue and oral muscles in speaking (Schweizer, Alexander, Gillingham, Cusimano, & Stuss, 2010). Moreover, cerebellar damage may lead to difficulty maintaining balance while walking and an increased risk of falls (Marsden, 2011).

reticular formation A diffuse network of neurons, extending through the brain stem, that helps maintain vigilance and an optimal level of brain arousal.

The Reticular Formation The brain stem also includes the **reticular formation**, a diffuse network of neurons that helps regulate vigilance and brain arousal. It also affects sleep, particularly dreaming (Blanco-Centurian & Salin-Pascual, 2001). The role of the reticular formation in maintaining vigilance is shown by the "cocktail party phenomenon," in which you can be engrossed in a conversation but still notice when someone elsewhere in the room says something of significance to you, such as your name. Thus, the reticular formation acts as a filter, letting you attend to an important stimulus while ignoring irrelevant ones (Haykin & Chen, 2005). Experimental evidence supporting the role of the reticular formation in brain arousal came from research by Giuseppe Moruzzi and Horace Magoun in which they awakened sleeping cats by electrically stimulating the reticular formation (Moruzzi & Magoun, 1949).

thalamus The brain stem structure that acts as a sensory relay station for taste, body, visual, and auditory sensations.

The Thalamus Capping the brain stem is the egg-shaped **thalamus**. The thalamus functions as a sensory relay station, sending taste, bodily, visual, and auditory sensations on to other areas of the brain for further processing. The only sensory information that is *not* relayed through the thalamus is related to smell. Sensory information from smell receptors in the nose goes directly to areas of the brain that process odors. The visual information from this page is being relayed by your thalamus to areas of your brain that process vision. And your thalamus is processing impulses that will inform your brain if part of your body feels cold (Davis et al., 1999) or is in pain (Narita et al., 2008). Research indicates that the thalamus also might take part in other psychological functions, including language (Whelan, Murdoch, Theodoros, Silburn, & Hall, 2002), memory (Hampstead, 2009), and attention (Dantzer, 2006).

limbic system A group of brain structures that, through their influence on emotion, motivation, and memory, promote the survival of the individual and, as a result, the continuation of the species.

The Limbic System

Surrounding the thalamus is a group of structures that comprise the **limbic system**. The word *limbic* comes from the Latin for "border," indicating that the limbic structures form a border between the higher and lower structures of the brain. The limbic system interacts with other brain structures to promote the survival of the individual and, as a result, the continuation of the species by engaging in functionally adaptive behaviors (Feinstein et al., 2010). Major components of the limbic system include the *hypothalamus,* the *amygdala,* and the *hippocampus.*

The Hypothalamus Just below the thalamus, on the underside of the brain, lies the **hypothalamus**. (In Greek the prefix *hypo-* means "below"). The hypothalamus helps regulate numerous functions, including eating, drinking, emotion, sexual behavior, blood pressure, and body temperature (Caqueret, Yang, Duplin, & Boucher, 2005). It exerts its influence by regulating the secretion of hormones by the pituitary gland and by signals sent along neurons to bodily organs controlled by the autonomic nervous system. The hypothalamus is especially important in stress because it regulates hormones secreted by both the pituitary gland and the adrenal glands (Armario, 2006). The hypothalamus also plays a role in sexual arousal, as demonstrated by a recent fMRI study of women's and men's responses to erotic stimuli. Whereas all participants were aroused by the erotica, as assessed by self-report and physiological measures, the researchers found significantly greater activation of the hypothalamus among male participants (Karama et al., 2002). As you will read in this book, gender differences and similarities are attributable to complex interactions of physiological and social-cultural factors.

The importance of the hypothalamus in emotionality was discovered by accident. Psychologists James Olds and Peter Milner (1954) of McGill University in Montreal inserted fine wire electrodes into the brains of rats to study the effects of electrical stimulation of the reticular formation. They had already trained the rats to press a lever to obtain food rewards. When a wired rat now pressed the lever, it obtained mild electrical stimulation of its brain. To the experimenters' surprise, the rats, even when hungry or thirsty, ignored food and water in favor of pressing the lever—sometimes thousands of times an hour—until they dropped from exhaustion up to 24 hours later (Olds, 1956). Olds and Milner examined brain tissue from the rats and discovered that they had mistakenly inserted the electrodes near the hypothalamus and not into the reticular formation. They concluded they had discovered a "pleasure center." But we now know that the hypothalamus is but one structure in an interconnected group of brain structures that induce feelings of pleasure when stimulated.

The Amygdala The **amygdala** of the limbic system, located in the temporal lobe, continuously evaluates information from the immediate environment and contributes to the formation of memories of emotionally significant events, particularly of stressful situations (Roozendaal, McEwen, & Chattarji, 2009; Phelps and LeDoux 2005). The amygdala is most notably important in regulating our responses to the social environment—such as facial expressions, tone of voice, and even laughing and crying—and helps elicit appropriate emotional and behavioral responses (Sander, Brechmann, & Scheich, 2003). If you saw a pit bull running toward you, your amygdala would help you quickly decide whether the dog was friendly, vicious, or simply roaming around. Depending on your evaluation of the situation, you might feel happy and pet the dog, feel afraid and jump on top of your desk, or feel relief and go back to studying. Research shows that the amygdala stimulates the profuse emotional sweating that some people exhibit when under extreme stress (Asahina, Suzuki, Mori, Kanesaka, & Hattori, 2003).

A functional MRI study of people with social anxiety disorder found that they experienced exaggerated amygdala responses to angry faces compared to people without that disorder (Evans et al., 2008). Amygdala responses to facial expressions also are influenced by culture. A functional MRI study of Japanese and American participants found greater activation of the amygdala in response to facial fear expressed by members of their own ethnic group. This makes sense from an evolutionary perspective; given that one would presume that fear expressed by a member of one's own ethnic group would indicate a greater threat to other members of the same group (Chiao et al., 2008).

hypothalamus A limbic system structure that, through its effects on the pituitary gland and the autonomic nervous system, helps regulate aspects of motivation and emotion, including eating, drinking, sexual behavior, body temperature, and stress responses.

amygdala A limbic system structure that evaluates information from the immediate environment, contributing to feelings of fear, anger, or relief.

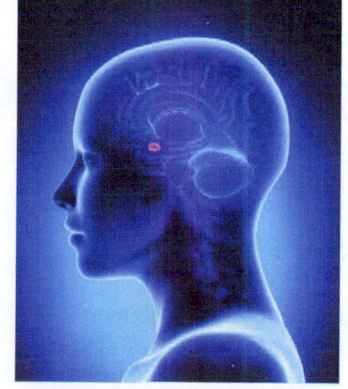

The Amygdala

A lateral view of the brain showing the location and shape of the amygdala (Greek for *almond*) within the brain. The amygdala is deep within the temporal lobe and responds to strong emotional situations and feelings.
Source: CLIPAREA/Custom media/Shutterstock.com.

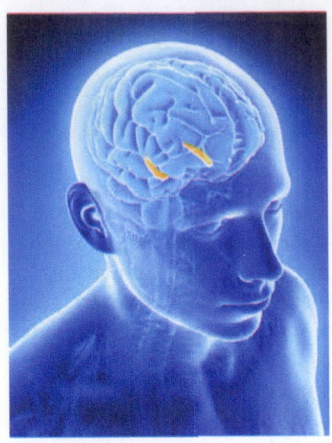

The Hippocampus

A frontal view of the brain showing the location and shape of the hippocampus (Greek for *seahorse*) within the brain. The hippocampus is deep within the temporal lobe and involved in the formation of new memories.

Source: Sebastian Kaulitzki/Shutterstock.com.

hippocampus A limbic system structure that contributes to the formation of memories.

cerebral cortex The outer covering of the brain.

cerebral hemisphere The left and right halves of the cerebrum.

primary cortical area Regions of the cerebral cortex that serve motor or sensory functions.

association area Region of the cerebral cortex that integrates information from the primary cortical areas and other brain areas.

frontal lobe A lobe of the cerebral cortex responsible for motor control and higher mental processes.

motor cortex The area of the frontal lobes that controls specific voluntary body movements.

In the late 1930s, Heinrich Klüver and Paul Bucy (1937) found that lesions of the amygdala in monkeys led to "psychic blindness," an inability to evaluate environmental stimuli properly. The monkeys indiscriminately examined objects by mouth, tried to mate with members of other species, and acted fearless when confronted by a snake. People who suffer amygdala damage also may exhibit symptoms of Klüver-Bucy syndrome (Unal et al., 2007).

The Hippocampus Whereas your amygdala helps you evaluate emotional information from your environment, the limbic system structure that is particularly important in helping you form memories of that information (including what you are now reading) is the **hippocampus** (Axmacher, Lenz, Haupt, Elger, & Fell, 2010). Much of what we know about the hippocampus comes from case studies of people who have suffered damage to it. The most famous study is of Henry Gustav Molaison(1926–2008) widely known as "H. M." (Scoville & Milner, 1957), whose hippocampus was surgically removed in 1953—when he was 27—to relieve his uncontrollable epileptic seizures. Following the surgery, H. M. formed few new memories, though he could easily recall events and information from before his surgery. It wasn't until his death in 2008, that H. M.'s identity was revealed. He was a Connecticut resident and played a critical role in the development of cognitive neuropsychology theories that explain the link between brain function and *memory*. You can read more about the implications of his case in regard to memory in Chapter 8. Damage to the hippocampus has been implicated in the memory loss associated with Alzheimer's disease. Victims of this disease suffer from degeneration of the neurons that serve as pathways between the hippocampus and other brain areas (Perl, 2010).

The Cerebral Cortex

Covering the brain is the crowning achievement of brain evolution—the **cerebral cortex**. Cortex means "bark" in Latin. And just as the bark is the outer layer of the tree, the cerebral cortex is the thin, 3-millimeter-thick outer layer of the uppermost portion of the brain called the *cerebrum*. The human cerebral cortex and that of other mammals has evolved folds called *convolutions,* which give it the appearance of kneaded dough. The convolutions permit more cerebral cortex to fit inside the skull. This is necessary because evolution has assigned so many complex brain functions to the mammalian cerebral cortex that the brain has, in a sense, outgrown the skull in which it resides. If the cerebral cortex were smooth (like other species) instead of convoluted, the human brain would have to be enormous to permit the same amount of surface area. The brain would be encased in a skull so large that it would give us the appearance of extraterrestrial creatures from science fiction movies.

The cerebrum is divided into left and right halves called the **cerebral hemispheres**. Figure 3-7 shows that the cerebral cortex covering each hemisphere is divided into four regions, or *lobes:* the *frontal lobe,* the *temporal lobe,* the *parietal lobe,* and the *occipital lobe.* The lobes have *primary cortical areas.* A **primary cortical area** serves motor or sensory functions. The lobes also have *association areas.* An **association area** integrates information from the primary cortical areas and other brain areas in activities such as speaking, problem solving, and recognizing objects.

Motor Cortex Your tour of the cerebral cortex begins in 1870, when the German physicians Gustav Fritsch and Eduard Hitzig (1870/1960) published their findings that electrical stimulation of a strip of cerebral cortex along the rear border of the right or left **frontal lobe** of a dog induces limb movements on the opposite side of the body. This phenomenon is known as *contralateral control.* The area they stimulated is called the **motor cortex.** They were probably the first to demonstrate conclusively that specific sites on the cerebral cortex control specific body movements (Gross, 2007).

Figure 3-8 presents a "map" of the motor cortex of the frontal lobe, represented by a *motor homunculus.* (*Homunculus* is a Latin term meaning "small human.") Each area of the motor cortex controls a particular contralateral body movement. Certain neurons on the motor cortex

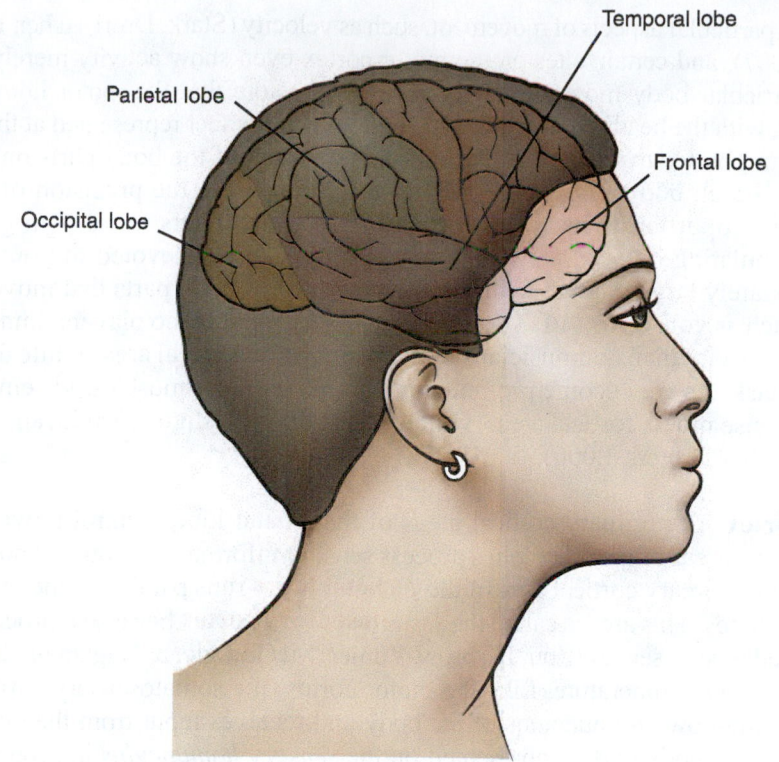

Temporal lobe

Parietal lobe

Occipital lobe

Frontal lobe

FIGURE 3-7

The Lobes of the Brain

The cerebral cortex covering each cerebral hemisphere is divided into four lobes: the frontal lobe, the temporal lobe, the parietal lobe, and the occipital lobe.

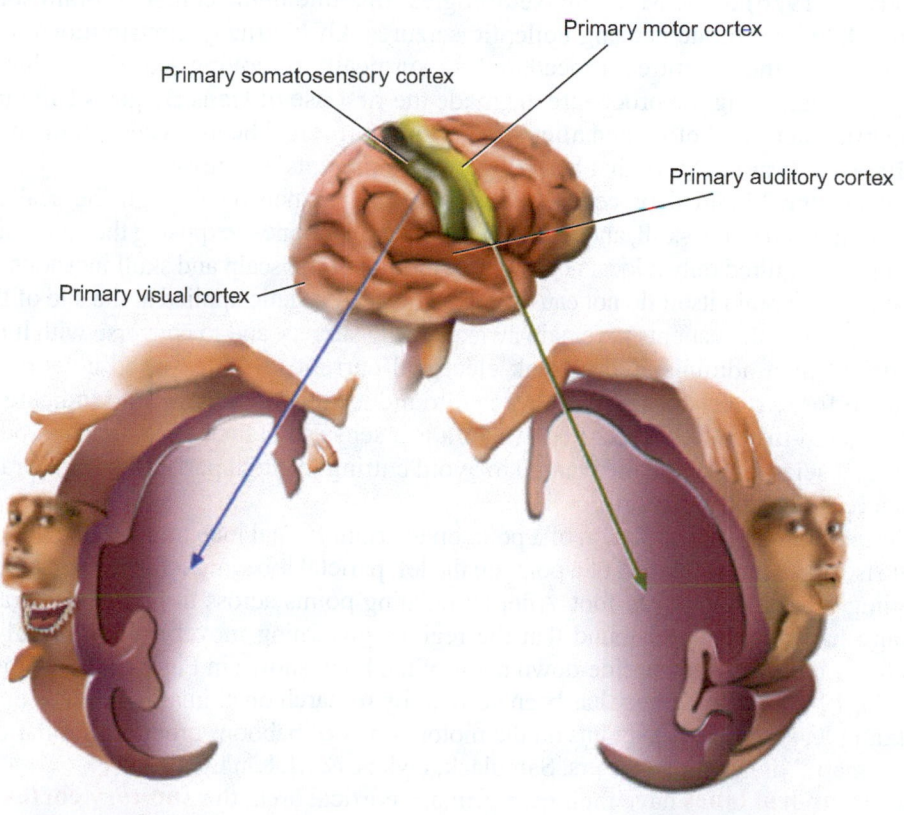

Primary motor cortex

Primary somatosensory cortex

Primary auditory cortex

Primary visual cortex

Primary Somatosensory Cortex

Primary Motor Cortex

FIGURE 3-8

The Motor Cortex and the Somatosensory Cortex

Both the motor cortex and the somatosensory cortex form distorted, upside-down maps of the contralateral side of the body. Activity in the motor cortex of a cerebral hemisphere produces contralateral movement. Touching a spot on one side of the body produces activity in the contralateral somatosensory cortex.

are related to particular aspects of movement, such as velocity (Stark, Drori, Asher, Ben-Shaul, & Abeles, 2007), and certain sites on the motor cortex even show activity merely in anticipation of particular body movements (Hyland, 1998). Note that the motor homunculus is upside down, with the head represented at the bottom and the feet represented at the top.

You also might be struck by the disproportionate sizes of the body parts on the motor homunculus—each body part is represented in proportion to the precision of its movements, not in proportion to its actual size. Because your fingers move with great precision in manipulating objects, the region of the motor cortex devoted to your fingers is disproportionately large relative to the regions devoted to body parts that move with less precision, such as your arms. An fMRI study of professional piano players found that they showed less activity than nonmusicians did in their motor cortical areas while doing a finger tapping task. As we become proficient at using our finger muscles, we employ more and more precise motor cortical areas, which eliminate even slightly irrelevant movement (Jaencke, Shah, & Peters, 2000).

parietal lobe A lobe of the cerebral cortex responsible for processing bodily sensations and perceiving spatial relations.

somatosensory cortex The area of the parietal lobes that processes information from sensory receptors in the skin.

Sensory Cortex The primary cortical areas of the frontal lobes control movements; the primary cortical areas of the other lobes process sensory information. You will notice in Figure 3-8 that the primary cortical area of the **parietal lobes** runs parallel to the motor cortex of the frontal lobes. This area is called the **somatosensory cortex** because it processes information related to skin senses (Zhu, Disbrow, Zumer, McGonigle, & Nagarajan, 2007), such as pain, touch, and temperature. Like the motor cortex, the somatosensory cortex forms a distorted, upside-down homunculus of the body and receives input from the opposite side of the body. Each body part is represented on the *sensory homunculus* in proportion to its sensory precision rather than its size. This is why the region devoted to your highly sensitive lips is disproportionately large relative to the region devoted to your less sensitive back.

How do we know that a motor homunculus and a sensory homunculus exist on the cerebral cortex? We know because of research conducted by neurosurgeon Wilder Penfield (1891–1976) of the Montreal Neurological Institute in the course of brain surgery to remove defective tissue causing epileptic seizures. Of his many contributions, his most important was the "Montreal procedure" for surgically removing scar tissue that caused epilepsy. In applying the procedure, he made the first use of Hans Berger's EEG by comparing brain activity before and after surgery to see if it had been successful in abolishing the abnormal brain activity that had triggered his patients' seizures.

In using the Montreal procedure, Penfield made an incision through the scalp, sawed through a portion of the skull, and removed a large flap of bone—exposing the cerebral cortex. His patients required only a local anesthetic at the site of the scalp and skull incisions because incisions in the brain itself do not cause pain. A local anesthetic applied at the site of the skull incision allowed the patients to remain awake during surgery and to converse with him.

Penfield then administered a weak electrical current to the exposed cerebral cortex. He did so for two reasons. First, he wanted to induce an *aura* that would indicate the site that triggered the patient's seizures. An aura is a sensation (such as an unusual odor) that precedes a seizure. Second, he wanted to avoid cutting through parts of the cerebral cortex that serve important functions.

Penfield found that stimulation of a point on the right frontal lobe might make the left forefinger rise and that stimulation of a point on the left parietal lobe might make the patient report a tingling feeling in the right foot. After stimulating points across the entire cerebral cortex of many patients, Penfield found that the regions governing movement and bodily sensations formed the distorted upside-down maps of the body shown in Figure 3-8 (Rasmussen & Penfield, 1947). His discovery has been verified by research on animals as well as on people. For example, stimulation of points on the motor cortex of baboons produces similar distorted motor "maps" of the body (Waters, Samulack, Dykes, & McKinley, 1990).

temporal lobe A lobe of the cerebral cortex responsible for processing hearing.

auditory cortex The area of the temporal lobes that processes sounds.

The **temporal lobes** have their own primary cortical area, the **auditory cortex**. Particular regions of the auditory cortex are responsible for processing sounds of particular frequencies (Menéndez-Colino et al., 2007), which enables the temporal lobes to analyze all kinds of sounds, including speech (Binder, JRao, Hammeke, & Yetkin, 1994) and music (Zatorre, Belin, & Penhune, 2002). There also is evidence from magnetoencephalography that an area of the temporal cortex involved in music perception is larger and responds faster in professional musicians than in amateur musicians (Schneider et al., 2002).

At the back of the brain are the **occipital lobes**, which contain the **visual cortex**. This region integrates input from your eyes into a visual "map" of what you are viewing (Swindale, 2000). Because of the nature of the pathways from your eyes to your visual cortex, visual input from objects in your *right visual field* is processed in your left occipital lobe, and visual input from objects in your *left visual field* is processed in your right occipital lobe. Certain neurons in the visual cortex process facial recognition (Pourtois, Schwartz, Seghier, Lazeyras, & Vuilleumier, 2009), and others process object movements (Mercier, Schwartz, Michel, & Blanke, 2009). Damage to a portion of an occipital lobe can produce a blind spot in the contralateral visual field (Trevethan & Sahraie, 2003). In some cases, damage can produce visual hallucinations, such as the perception of parts of objects that are not actually present (Anderson & Rizzo, 1994).

occipital lobe A lobe of the cerebral cortex responsible for processing vision.

visual cortex The area of the occipital lobes that processes visual input.

Association Cortex In reading about the brain, you might have gotten the impression that each area functions independently of the others. That is far from the truth. Consider the association cortex that composes most of the cerebral cortex. These areas combine information from other areas of the brain. For example, the association cortex of the frontal lobes integrates information involved in thinking, planning, and problem solving. The unusually large association cortex of the human cerebral cortex provides more area for processing information, which contributes to the human species' greater flexibility than other animals in adapting to diverse circumstances (Semendeferi, Lu, Schenker, & Damasio, 2002). The frontal lobes also play a role in motivated behavior. Research has found that college students who crave playing videogames on the Internet, as opposed to players who do not crave playing, show frontal lobe activity similar to people who are substance abusers in response to stimuli associated with the substances (Han, Kim, Lee, Min, & Renshaw, 2010).

Some of the evidence supporting the importance of the association areas of the frontal lobes in emotion and personality has come from case studies of people with damage to it, most notably the case of Phineas Gage (Harlow, 1993). On a fall day in 1848, Gage, the 25-year-old foreman of a Vermont railroad crew laying track, was clearing away rocks. While he was using an iron tamping rod to pack a gunpowder charge into a boulder, a spark ignited the gunpowder. The resulting explosion hurled the rod into Gage's left cheek, through his frontal lobes, and out the top of his skull. Miraculously, Gage survived, recuperated, and lived 12 more years, with little impairment of his intellectual abilities. But there were dramatic changes in his personality and emotionality. Instead of remaining the friendly, popular, hardworking man he had been before the accident, he became an ornery, disliked, irresponsible bully. Gage's friends believed he had changed so radically that "he was no longer Gage."

The case study of Phineas Gage implies that the frontal lobe structures damaged by the tamping rod might be important in emotion and personality. But, as explained in Chapter 2, it is impossible to determine causality from a case study. Perhaps Gage's emotional and personality changes were caused not by the brain damage itself, but instead by Gage's psychological response to his traumatic accident or by changes in how other people responded to him. Nonetheless, the frontal lobe's importance in emotion and personality has been supported by subsequent scientific research (Stuss, Gow, & Hetherington, 1992). As in the case of Phineas Gage, damage to the frontal lobes typically causes the person to become uninhibited, emotionally unstable, unable to plan ahead, and prone to socially inappropriate behavior (Macmillan, 2000). The association areas of the frontal lobes are especially important in helping us adapt our emotions and behavior to diverse situations. A case study of a 50-year-old man with frontal lobe damage similar to Gage's showed that he had intact cognitive abilities but had difficulty inhibiting his behavior and trouble behaving responsibly (Dimitrov, Phipps, Zahn, & Grafman, 1999).

Language Cortex The integration of different brain areas underlies many psychological functions. Consider the process of speech, one of the most distinctly human abilities. Speech depends on the interaction of the association cortex of the frontal and temporal lobes. In most left-handed people and almost all right-handed people, the left cerebral hemisphere is superior to the right in processing speech. The speech center of the frontal lobe, **Broca's area**, is

Broca's area The region of the frontal lobe responsible for the production of speech.

Phineas Gage's Skull and the Tamping Rod that Pierced His Frontal Lobe

Phineas Gage's horrible accident contributed to our knowledge of the possible roles of the frontal lobes in emotion and personality.

Source: AP Photo/Courtesy of Harvard Medical School.

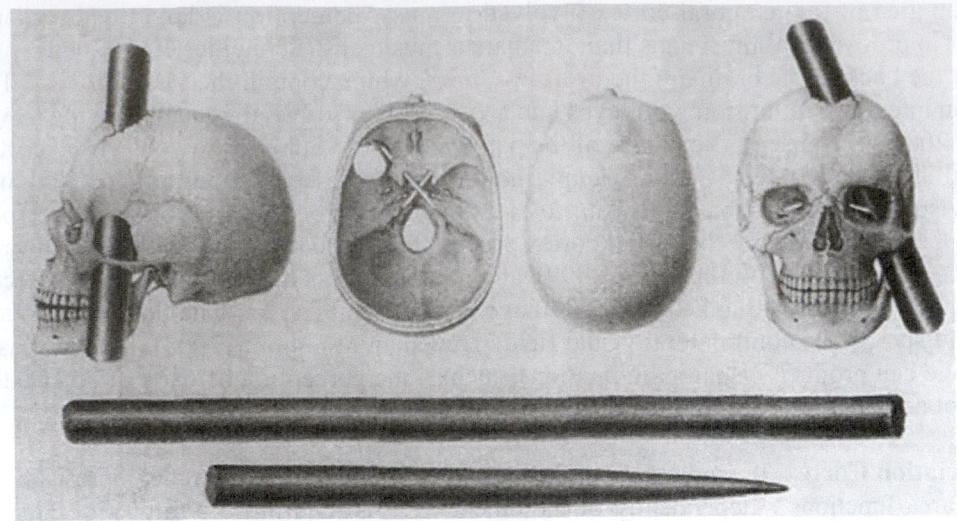

named for its discoverer, the French surgeon and anthropologist Paul Broca (1824–1880). In 1861 Broca treated a 51-year-old man named Leborgne, who was given the nickname "Tan" because he had a severe speech disorder that made *tan* the only syllable he could pronounce clearly. After Tan died of an infection, Broca performed an autopsy and found damage to a defined area of the left frontal lobe of his brain. Broca concluded that this area controls speech. Tan's speech disorder is now called *Broca's aphasia*. (*Aphasia* is the Greek word for "speechless.") Broca's observation was confirmed in later autopsies of the brains of people who had speech disorders similar to Tan's. CT scans have also verified that damage to Broca's area is, indeed, associated with Broca's aphasia (Breathnach, 1989).

What is the nature of Broca's aphasia? Though its victims retain the ability to comprehend speech, they speak in a telegraphic style that can be comprehended only by listeners who pay careful attention. For example, when one victim of Broca's aphasia was asked about a family dental appointment, he said, "Monday . . . Dad and Dick . . . Wednesday nine o'clock . . . doctors and teeth" (Geschwind, 1979, p. 186). The speaker expressed the important thoughts but failed to express the connections between them. Nonetheless, you probably got the gist of the statement.

Wernicke's area The region of the temporal lobe that controls the meaningfulness of speech.

Speech also depends on a region of the temporal lobe cortex called **Wernicke's area**, named for the German physician Karl Wernicke. In contrast to Broca's area, which controls the production of speech, Wernicke's area controls the meaningfulness of speech. In 1874, Wernicke reported that patients with damage to the rear margin of the left temporal lobe spoke fluently but had difficulty comprehending speech and made little or no sense to even the most attentive listener. This disorder became known as *Wernicke's aphasia*.

Consider the following statement by a victim of Wernicke's aphasia that describes a picture of two boys stealing cookies behind a woman's back: "Mother is away here working her work to get her better, but when she's looking the two boys looking in the other part. She's working another time" (Geschwind, 1979, p. 186). The statement seems more grammatical than the telegraphic speech of the victim of Broca's aphasia, but it is impossible to comprehend—it is almost meaningless.

The consensus among researchers is that, as presented in Figure 3-9, speech production requires the interaction of Wernicke's area, Broca's area, and the motor cortex (Geschwind, 1979). Wernicke's area selects the words that will convey your meaning and communicates them to Broca's area. Broca's area then selects the muscle movements to express those words and communicates them to the region of the motor cortex that controls the speech muscles. Finally, the motor cortex communicates these directions through motor nerves to the appropriate muscles, and you speak the intended words. As you can see, speaking phrases as simple as "let's go out for pizza" involves the interaction of several areas of your brain.

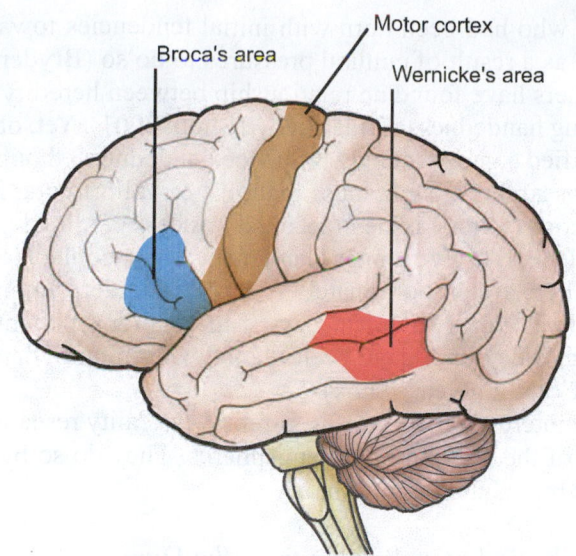

Broca's area
Motor cortex
Wernicke's area

FIGURE 3-9
Speech and the Brain

Wernicke's area, Broca's area, and the motor cortex interact in producing speech.

Cerebral Hemispheric Lateralization

You may have noted reports in the popular media alleging that the cerebral hemispheres control different psychological functions, leading to the notion of "left-brained" and "right-brained" people. Though most researchers would not assign complete responsibility for any psychological function to just one hemisphere, they have reached agreement on some of the psychological functions at which each hemisphere excels. The left hemisphere is somewhat superior at performing verbal, mathematical, analytical, and rational functions, and the right hemisphere is somewhat superior at performing nonverbal, spatial, holistic, and emotional functions (Springer & Deutsch, 1998). Some researchers believe we have evolved hemispheric lateralization because it makes us more efficient in carrying out multiple activities at the same time, such as speaking while remaining vigilant to potential threats (Rogers, 2000). Though each hemisphere has its own strengths, the hemispheres do not work in isolation. For example, the left hemisphere generally controls the production of speech, but the right hemisphere gives speech its appropriate emotional intonation (Snow, 2000).

Brain imaging has revealed that the area of the primary motor cortex that serves the dominant hand is larger on that side of the brain than on the other, providing people with the opportunity to learn to perform more precise movements (Hammond, 2002). Because about 90 percent of people are right-handed and, as a consequence, the manufactured environment favors right-handers, left-handers have more trouble functioning in the everyday world. For example, left-handers have difficulty operating control panels designed for right-handers, especially under stressful conditions that can cause confusion, as in airplane cockpits. Because of this difficulty, human-factors engineers must consider left-handed people when designing control consoles (Garonzik, 1989). Nonetheless, left-handedness has some advantages. For example, a disproportionate number of competitive athletes are left-handed, apparently because it provides a tactical and positional advantage (a left-handed baseball hitter is closer to first base) in sport competitions (Grouios, Tsorbatzoudis, Alexandris, & Barkoukis, 2000).

Because right-handedness is prevalent in almost all cultures, heredity evidently is more important than life experiences in determining handedness and cerebral lateralization of functions. Additional evidence of this comes from research findings that even newborns show evidence of cerebral lateralization of psychological functions (Fein, 1990), and most fetuses show a preference for sucking their right thumb while in the womb (Hepper, Shahidullah, & White, 1991). Yet, cultural factors can override hereditary tendencies, as revealed in a survey of natives of the Amazon region of Colombia. All of the persons in the survey reported that they were right-handed. The researchers who did the survey concluded that those who had been born with initial tendencies toward left-handedness became right-handed as a result of cultural pressures to do so (Bryden, Ardila, & Ardila, 1993). Some researchers have found no relationship between heredity and handedness in twin studies comparing handedness similarities (Bishop, 2001). Yet, other researchers believe they have identified a gene that may influence handedness, though this has not been confirmed by other researchers (McManus, Nicholls, & Vallortigara, 2009).

Perhaps the most controversial issue in recent decades regarding handedness is whether right-handed people tend to live longer than left-handed people. No controversy exists about this one fact: There are proportionately fewer left-handers among older adults than among younger adults in North America. Two of the main proponents of the belief that left-handers do in fact die sooner have been Stanley Coren and Diane Halpern (see the "Psychology versus Common Sense" box).

In addition to their interest in handedness, cerebral-laterality researchers study the psychological functions of the left and right hemispheres. They do so by studying the damaged brain, the intact brain, and the split brain.

Evidence of Hemispheric Lateralization from the Damaged Brain

As you read earlier in the chapter, the earliest source of knowledge about cerebral hemispheric lateralization was the study of unilateral brain damage—that is, damage to one cerebral hemisphere. If damage to one hemisphere of the brain produces symptoms that differ from symptoms produced by damage to the other hemisphere, researchers conclude that the damaged hemisphere plays more of a role in that function than does the other hemisphere.

Paul Broca, after finding that a specific kind of language disorder consistently followed damage to the left hemisphere, concluded that language depended more on the left hemisphere than on the right hemisphere (Harris, 1999). More recent research on brain damage has found that both hemispheres are involved in language but that their particular roles differ. For example, though the left hemisphere is more important for the production and comprehension of speech, the right hemisphere is more important for processing aspects of speech unrelated to the spoken words themselves. Damage to the right hemisphere produces greater deterioration in the ability to interpret the speaker's emotional tone of voice than does damage to the left hemisphere (Ross, Thompson, & Yenkosky, 1997).

Evidence of Hemispheric Lateralization from the Intact Brain

Psychologists interested in hemispheric lateralization have devised several methods for studying the intact brain. One of the chief methods has participants perform tasks while an EEG or brain scan measures the relative activity of their cerebral hemispheres. A study using fMRI found that people produce greater activity in certain areas of the left hemisphere while performing a verbal task and greater activity in certain areas of the right hemisphere while performing visual-spatial tasks (Stephan et al., 2003). Research using fMRI has demonstrated activity in the language areas of the left hemisphere even in people using American Sign Language. But American Sign Language also involves greater involvement of the right hemisphere than does English (Bavelier et al., 1998).

Another approach, the **Wada test**, studies human participants in whom a hemisphere has been anesthetized in the course of brain surgery to correct a neurological defect, often one that induces epileptic seizures . The Wada test is named for Juhn Wada, who introduced it in 1949 (Emde Boas, 1999). This procedure is done by injecting sodium amytal into either the right or the left carotid artery, which provides oxygenated blood to the associated cerebral hemisphere. The injection anesthetizes that hemisphere. As you might expect, anesthetization of the left hemisphere, but only rarely of the right hemisphere, induces temporary aphasia—the patient has difficulty speaking. Recent research and meta-analysis indicates that the use of fMRI may be preferable to the invasive Wada test in assessing lateralization of language (Abou-Khalill, 2007; Dym, Burns, Freeman, & Lipton, 2011).

Considerable controversy surrounds gender differences in cerebral lateralization. Whereas some studies have demonstrated gender differences in the structure of the two hemispheres, such as the number of convolutions in the cortex of each hemisphere (e.g.,

Wada test A technique in which a cerebral hemisphere is anesthetized to assess hemispheric lateralization.

Is Being Left-Handed a Pathological Condition?

Stanley Coren, a psychologist at the University of British Columbia, and Diane Halpern, a psychologist at Claremont McKenna College in California, pointed to earlier studies indicating that the percentage of right-handers was greater in older age groups (Coren & Halpern, 1991). Note that by age 80 there are virtually no left-handers in the population! To assess this handedness effect, Halpern and Coren (1988) conducted an archival study of longevity in professional baseball players, using the *Baseball Encyclopedia* as their source of data on more than 2,000 players. They found that, on the average, right-handers lived eight months longer than left-handers. This finding inspired them to replicate that study to determine if their findings would generalize to people other than baseball players.

Coren and Halpern sent brief questionnaires to the next of kin of 2,875 persons who recently had died in two southern California counties. The questionnaires asked questions about the deceased's handedness regarding writing, drawing, and throwing. Each person's age at death was obtained from death certificates. Despite the apparent intrusion of the questionnaires into the lives of grieving relatives, 1,033 questionnaires were returned. Of these, 987 were usable. Coren and Halpern determined whether the deceased had been right-handed or left-handed.

The results were startling: Right-handers lived an average of 9 years longer than left-handers. Thus, this study found a much larger longevity gap than the study of baseball players had found. Coren and Halpern attributed the gap to the earlier deaths of left-handers (the *elimination hypothesis*) rather than to cultural pressures to become right-handed (the *modification hypothesis*) that affected older generations more than younger ones. Coren and Halpern found that the most important factors accounting for this longevity gap were a greater tendency for left-handers to have accidents, immune disorders, and evidence of neurological defects. In an archival study of 975 women and 741 men, Coren found that non-right-handers are more susceptible to broken bones (Coren & Previc, 1996). Moreover, there is a somewhat greater risk of the sometimes fatal disease multiple sclerosis in left-handers than in right-handers (Gardener, Munrer, Chitnis, Spiegelman, & Ascherio, 2009). Left-handers are also more prone to clinical depression (Denny, 2009), which is associated with higher risk of mortality from suicide and illnesses exacerbated by depression. And in a study of more than 1,200 college students, Co-

ren found that left-handed people find it more difficult to fall asleep and stay asleep (Coren & Searleman, 1987). This finding is important because (as explained in Chapter 6) sleep is necessary for proper functioning of the immune system and optimal daytime alertness.

But research findings from other studies have not consistently supported Coren and Halpern's findings. Even the allegedly longer life spans of right-handed baseball players have been called into question. In fact, a study of more than 5,000 professional baseball players found that left-handers actually lived an average of 8 months longer than right-handers (Hicks, Johnson, Cuevas, & Debaro, 1994). Coren and Halpern's explanations for the apparent longevity difference favoring right-handers also have been disputed. For example, a study in the Netherlands found no relationship between accident proneness and handedness among undergraduate students (Merckelbach, Muris, & Kop, 1994). Moreover, research has been inconsistent on the relationship between handedness and immune disorders, with some studies even showing that right-handers are more susceptible to them (Bryden, 1993). And there is conflicting evidence about the greater likelihood of neurological disorders in left-handers, to which some researchers attribute the slightly higher rate of left-handedness in men (Bishop, 1990; Corballis, 2001).

One of the main reasons for the inconsistent findings regarding the susceptibility of left-handers to disease and injury may be inconsistency in how research studies have defined handedness. In one study of more than 5,000 deaths, instead of dividing handedness into either right-handed or left-handed, the researchers divided the deceased into extremely right-handed, generally right-handed, ambidextrous, generally left-handed, and extremely left-handed. The researchers found that only generally left-handed people died significantly younger than other people (Ellis & Engh, 2000).

The strongest response to Coren and Halpern has come from Lauren Harris (1993) of Michigan State University, who believes that the modification hypothesis is a better explanation for the decline in left-handers across the life span. According to Harris, today's older adults grew up at a time when left-handers were forced to use their right hands or simply chose to conform to a right-handed world. In contrast, over the past few decades left-handedness has lost its stigma, resulting in more left-handers remaining left-handed.

continued

Is Being Left-Handed a Pathological Condition? *continued*

Harris's hypothesis was supported by a study in Norway. In keeping with Coren and Halpern's findings, the researchers found that 15.2 percent of 21- to 30-year-olds were left-handed and that only 1.7 percent of those more than 80 years old were left-handed. But the researchers found that the apparent decline in left-handedness across the life span was, in reality, due to the fact that many left-handers in earlier generations had switched to being right-handed (Hugdahl, Satz, Mitrushina, & Miller, 1993). Despite these findings, which contradict their position, Halpern and Coren (1993) insist that most scientifically sound studies support their belief that left-handers tend to die younger.

Halpern and Coren's research findings prompted widespread interest and animosity. Halpern and Coren responded to critics of their research by noting that scientific research findings should not be affected by whether they please or displease particular groups of people. Instead, those who oppose research studies should criticize their methodology and, if possible, present research findings that contradict them (Halpern, Gilbert, & Coren, 1996).

In regard to the issue at hand, several questions remain to be answered, but the main one is this: If we follow groups of young people as they grow older, will the left-handers tend to die sooner than the right-handers? If they do, it would support Coren and Halpern's explanation. If they do not, it would support Harris's explanation. Of course, this determination would take many decades. In any case, as you can now appreciate, the commonsense belief that there are significantly fewer left-handers than right-handers in late adulthood because left-handers die younger may be wrong.

FIGURE 3-10 Left-handedness Has Lost Its Stigma

Over the past few decades, left-handedness has lost it's stigma. This has resulted in more left-handers remaining left-handed.

Source: DmitriMaruta/Shutterstock.com.

Luders, Narr, Bilder, Szaszko, Gurbani, & Hamilton, 2008), other researchers have investigated gender differences in the extent to which males and females exhibit cerebral lateralization and the extent to which gender differences in cerebral lateralization are correlated with cognitive abilities and performance. For example, two meta-analyses of research studies of the lateralization of spatial and verbal abilities found that male participants were slightly more lateralized than female participants (Medland, Geffen, & McFarland, 2002; Vogel, Bowers, & Vogel, 2003). Moreover, the size of the gender difference varies as a function of the laboratory task (Kansaku & Kitazawa, 2001) and test-taking strategy (Voyer & Flight, 2001). These inconsistent results are not surprising, as you will learn when you read about research described in Chapter 4. Whereas prenatal hormones do have an effect on brain structure and function, the observed gender differences in verbal and spatial skills generally are small and variable—especially for visual-spatial skills. So what accounts for the elusive "now you see it; now you don't" gender differences in hemispheric lateralization? One hypothesis is based on brain size. Larger brains are more lateralized. Because male brains are on average larger than female brains, gender differences in lateralization may be attributable to differences in brain size (Jancke & Steinmetz, 2003).

An alternative hypothesis emphasizes the interaction of sociocultural factors with biological factors such as hemispheric lateralization (Eviatar, 2000). Neuroscientists studying cross-cultural differences in the relation between thought and language provide support for this hypothesis (see Chapter 9). For example, one cross-cultural study tested the relationship between hemispheric laterality and the direction of written language (left to right in Italian and right to left in Arabic). The results indicated that performance on visual imaging tasks was influenced both by hemispheric lateralization and visual scanning (Maass & Russo, 2003).

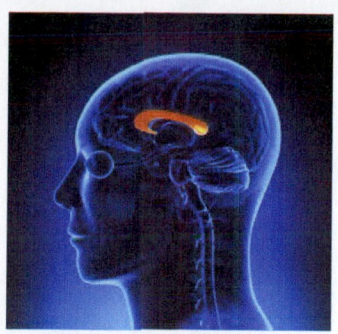

The Corpus Callosum

A lateral view of the brain showing the location and shape of the corpus callosum (Latin for *tough body*) within the brain. The corpus callosum is a wide band of axons that connects the right and left hemispheres.
Source: decade3d/Shutterstock.com.

Evidence of Hemispheric Lateralization from the Split Brain

Studies of damaged brains and intact brains have provided most of the evidence regarding cerebral hemispheric lateralization, but the most fascinating approach has been **split-brain research**. This research involves people whose hemispheres have been surgically separated from each other. Though split-brain research is only a few decades old, the idea was entertained in 1860 by Gustav Fechner, who was introduced in Chapter 1 as a founder of psychology. Fechner claimed that people who survived the surgical separation of their cerebral hemispheres would have two separate minds in one head (Springer & Deutsch, 1998). Decades later English psychologist William McDougall argued that such an operation would not divide the mind, which he considered indivisible. McDougall even volunteered to test Fechner's claim by having his own cerebral hemispheres surgically separated if he ever became incurably ill.

Though McDougall never had split-brain surgery, it was performed on patients in the early 1960s, when neurosurgeons Joseph Bogen and Phillip Vogel severed the **corpus callosum** of epileptic patients to reduce seizure activity that had not responded to drug treatments. The corpus callosum is a thick bundle of axons that provides the means of communication of information between the cerebral hemispheres (Pearce, 2007). Split-brain surgery works by preventing seizure activity in one hemisphere from spreading to the other. Split-brain patients function normally in their everyday lives, but special testing procedures have revealed an astonishing state of affairs: Their left and right hemispheres can no longer communicate with each other (Gazzaniga, 2005). Each acts independently of the other, as though each has its own independently functioning mind (Sperry, 1984). In *callosal agenesis*—the so-called natural split brain—the corpus callosum fails to develop prenatally, causing some of the same effects seen following split-brain surgery (Lassonde & Sauerwine, 2003).

Roger Sperry (1982) and his colleagues, most notably Jerre Levy and Michael Gazzaniga, have been pioneers in split-brain research. In a typical study, information is presented to one hemisphere and the participant is asked to give a response that depends more on one hemisphere than on the other. In a classic study (Gazzaniga, 1967), a split-brain patient performed a block-design task in which he had to arrange multicolored blocks so that their upper sides formed a pattern that matched the pattern printed on a card in front of him. Our left hands are controlled by the right hemisphere, and our right hands are controlled by the

split-brain research
A research technique for the study of cerebral hemispheric lateralization that involves people whose hemispheres have been surgically separated from each other.

corpus callosum A thick bundle of axons that provides a means of communication between the cerebral hemispheres and that is severed in so-called split-brain surgery.

left hemisphere. The experimental task is illustrated in Figure 3-11. When the participant performed with his left hand, he did well, but when he performed with his right hand, he did poorly. Can you explain why that happened?

Because the left hand is controlled by the right hemisphere, which is superior in perceiving spatial relationships, such as those in designs, he performed well with his left hand. And because the right hand is controlled by the left hemisphere, which is inferior in perceiving spatial relationships, he performed poorly with his right hand—even though he was right-handed. At times, when his right hand was having a hard time completing the design, his left hand would sneak up on it and try to help. This led to a bizarre battle for control of the blocks—as if each hand belonged to a different person. A similar conflict between competing behaviors has been observed in subsequent research on patients with damage to the corpus callosum (Nishikawa et al., 2001).

Despite the dramatic findings of split-brain studies, Jerre Levy (1983) has claimed that researchers, including Gazzaniga (1983), have exaggerated the extent to which each hemisphere regulates particular psychological processes, especially the supposed superiority of the left hemisphere. As always, only continued scientific research will resolve the Levy-Gazzaniga debate, which, you might note, is an example of the continual controversy over the degree to which psychological functions are localized in particular areas of the brain. The extent to which split-brain surgery produces two separate consciousnesses is controversial. Some commentators believe split-brain surgery leaves the patient with two complete, separate minds (Schechter, 2012). Others believe split-brain surgery leaves the patient with a complete stream of consciousness in the left hemisphere but only a primitive one in the right hemisphere, in part because the right hemisphere generally lacks language ability, which plays a crucial role in self-awareness (Morin, 2001).

Neural Plasticity

neural plasticity The brain's ability to learn from experience and to promote adaptive behavior.

The human brain is remarkable in its ability to learn from experience and to promote adaptive behavior. In doing so, the brain shows **neural plasticity**—that is, it is not completely "hardwired" at birth. Plasticity is shown by the elimination of excess synaptic connections (Huttenlocher, 1990) in childhood and the formation of new synaptic connections throughout life (Rosenzweig & Bennett, 1996). The biggest challenge to the plasticity of the brain is brain damage, whether caused by a stroke, a blow to the head, or

FIGURE 3-11
A Split-Brain Study

Gazzaniga (1967) had a split-brain patient arrange multicolored blocks to match a design printed on a card in front of him. The patient's left hand performed better than his right because the left hand is controlled by the right hemisphere, which is superior at perceiving spatial relationships. You would be able to perform a block-design task equally well with either your right or your left hand because your intact corpus callosum would let information from your spatially superior right hemisphere help your left hemisphere control your right hand.

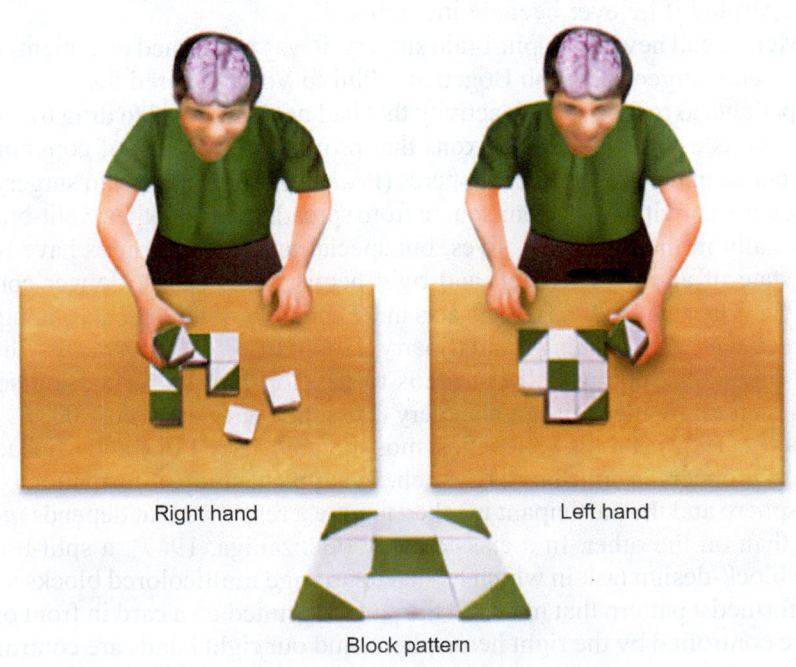

Right hand   Left hand

Block pattern

a disease such as Alzheimer's or Parkinson's. Natural processes in response to brain damage promote a limited degree of recovery. More recently, a technique formerly relegated to science fiction—the transplantation of neural tissue—has shown promise as a means of encouraging greater recovery from brain damage and spinal-cord damage.

Recovery from Neural Damage

Brain and spinal-cord damage can produce devastating effects, including paralysis, sensory loss, memory disruption, and personality deterioration. But what are the chances of recovering from such damage? It depends on the location of the damage and the kind of animal that has been damaged. Certain species of fish and amphibians, such as frogs (Krishnan, Sankar, & Muthusamy, 2001), can recover from spinal-cord damage by regenerating functional connections, but mammals—including people—do not.

People can regenerate damaged axons to regain lost functions only in the peripheral nervous system. Have you ever gotten a severe paper cut on your finger? The tingling sensation as it heals is the regeneration of peripheral nervous system axons. The regeneration is instigated, in part, by chemical signals that promote regrowth of the damaged axons (Vrbova et al., 2009). The possible effectiveness of a chemical called nerve growth factor in restoring neural functioning in the brain or spinal cord has been demonstrated in animal studies. For example, the administration of nerve growth factor has been effective in restoring functions after damage to the brain stem of rats (Alto et al., 2009). Glial cells in the peripheral nervous system form tunnels that guide the regrowth of damaged axons. In contrast, molecules released by glial cells in the brain and spinal cord block regeneration of axons (Bolsover, Fabes, & Anderson, 2008). This is why damage to your axons in your central nervous system can lead to paralysis. Christopher Reeve (1952–2004), the actor who played Superman in a series of motion pictures, was thrown from his horse in 1995 during an equestrian competition. Tragically, he landed on his head. The resulting injury to his spinal cord rendered him a quadriplegic, and he required a wheelchair and breathing assistance for the rest of his life.

In mammals, perhaps the most important factor in the recovery of functions that have been lost because of brain damage is the ability of intact brain areas to take over the functions of damaged ones (Johnston, 2009). In one experiment, researchers surgically destroyed portions of the motor cortex and somatosensory cortex that served one of the hind limbs of rats. The researchers found that the motor and somatosensory cortical "maps" representing those portions gradually shifted to intact adjacent areas of the cortex and to contralateral cortical areas, restoring the ability of the limb to function (Abo, Chen, Lai, Reese, & Bjelke, 2001). This likewise occurred in a case study of a boy who had suffered frontal lobe damage at age 7 due to an arterial rupture but showed remarkable recovery of functions over the years. The researchers found that fMRIs at age 24 indicated that undamaged cortical areas had taken over the processing of cognitive activities normally controlled by the damaged areas (Thompson et al., 2009).

Possible mechanisms by which spinal-cord injuries can be treated to regain some function include regeneration of axons and *collateral sprouting*, among others (Bradbury & McMahon, 2006). Through **collateral sprouting** (illustrated in Figure 3-12), branches from the axons of nearby healthy neurons grow into the pathways normally occupied by the axons of the damaged neurons. Ideally, the healthy neurons will take over the functions of the damaged ones. The younger the individual, the more likely collateral sprouting is to occur.

Neural plasticity following central nervous system damage, as in the spinal cord, is also promoted by exercise rehabilitation programs (Martinez, Brezun, Zennou-Azogui, Baril, & Xerri, 2009), particularly if there is incomplete severing of the spinal cord (Gregory et al., 2007). Apparently this occurs in part because it stimulates activity of neural stem cells that produce neuronal generation (Foret et al., 2010). Current cutting-edge research aims to activate endogenous neural stem cells to create new, fully functioning brain or spinal-cord neurons. Nonetheless, technical issues need to be worked out to make sure that newly generated neurons are functionally effective, given that haphazard regeneration can produce failure or even negative neurological effects (Okano, Sakaguchi, Ohki, & Suzuki, 2007).

collateral sprouting
The process in which branches from the axons of nearby healthy neurons grow into the pathways normally occupied by the axons of damaged neurons.

FIGURE 3-12
Collateral Sprouting

When an axon dies and its connections to the dendrites of other neurons degenerate, adjacent axons may sprout branches that form synapses with the vacated sites.

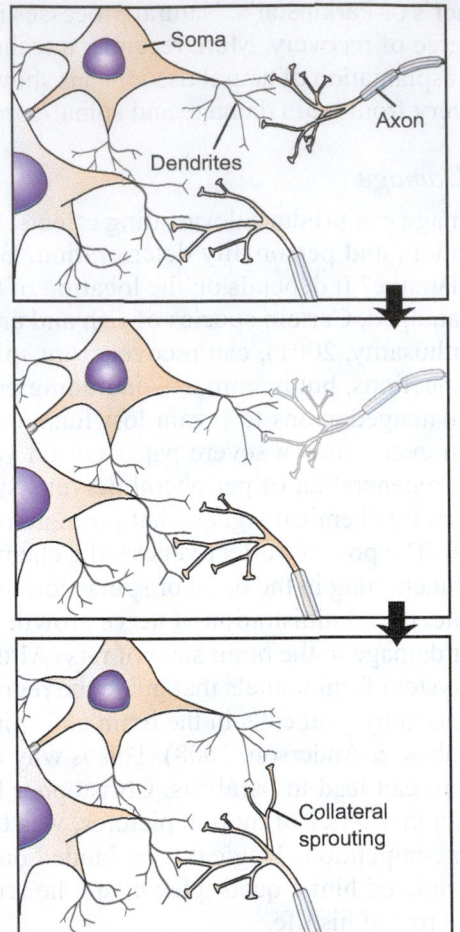

It should be noted that people's responses to brain or spinal-cord injury are not simply the product of the extent of injury and degree of recovery. Psychosocial factors also play a role. For example, recovery depends in part on cognitive interpretations and emotional reactions to injury. In fact, research indicates that variability in physical recovery after mild traumatic brain injury is more related to factors such as pain and depression than to the brain injury itself (Mooney, Speed, & Sheppard, 2005).

Another psychosocial factor in rehabilitation from spinal-cord injury is the culture's approach to medical care for people with neurological disabilities. A comparative study found that American spinal care medical professionals stress the desirability of getting patients into wheelchairs as soon as possible, whereas their colleagues in Italy and Canada are more concerned with attempting to restore as much self-ambulation as possible. The differences appear to be related to medical insurance policies. In the United States, to save on financial reimbursement, insurance providers direct physicians to move patients with brain or spinal-cord damage out of intensive rehabilitation as soon as they show even a minimal amount of mobility, whether while in a wheelchair or becoming self-ambulatory. Given that wheelchair functioning tends to come easier and faster, this may explain why American medical personnel favor wheelchair use as a primary goal. In contrast, in Italy and Canada, insurance providers permit patients to receive lengthy treatment aimed at maximizing their self-functioning before being released from intensive rehabilitation (Ditunno et al., 2006).

Neural Transplantation

Though plasticity might restore some lost functions, most people who have suffered brain or spinal-cord damage do not recover completely. This has led to research on possible ways to repair damaged brains and spinal cords, including attempts to administer chemicals that promote regeneration of neural connections (Santucci, Gluck, Kanof, & Haroutunian, 1993) or to stimulate the same processes that permit axons of the peripheral nerves to regenerate (Bertelli, Orsal, & Mira, 1994). The most widely publicized, and controversial, way has been to use **neural grafting**——the transplantation of healthy tissue into damaged nerves, brains, or spinal cords. For example, transplantation of retinal ganglion cells (which compose the optic nerves) to treat damaged ganglion cells in rats restored the rats' ability to respond to light, though their visual acuity remained impaired (Kittlerova & Valouskova, 2000).

Transplantation of human embryonic stem cells that are neuronal precursors has been successful in restoring some motor and sensory functioning in rats with brain damage, leading to greater interest in the possible use of this technique in people with similar damage (Hicks et al., 2009). Animal research also shows that transplantation of peripheral nerve grafts can help restore some motor function in rats with complete spinal-cord damage (Nordblom, Persson, Svensson, & Mattsson, 2009). A particularly promising preliminary study of people with ALS involved transplanted stem cells from the individual's blood into the motor cortex. Those who received the transplants showed improved functioning and longer survival than comparable ALS patients who received only typical medical treatment (Martinez et al., 2009).

Studies have reported a variety of successful applications of neural grafting in treating central nervous system disorders. Epileptic seizures that have been experimentally induced by surgically created brain damage in rats have been reduced by the transplantation of inhibitory GABA neurons from fetal rat brains (Fine, Meldrum, & Patel, 1990). And researchers have successfully used embryonic brain-tissue grafts to reduce epileptic seizures in people (Akimova et al., 2000). Neuroscientist Jacqueline Sagen works with the Miami Project to Cure Paralysis to help victims of spinal-cord injuries recover lost functions, potentially by using neural grafts to promote functional recovery.

Given the success of some experiments on fetal transplants in animals, it is natural to consider the possibility of using such transplants in people. Some studies in which fetal brain tissue has been transplanted to human patients with brain damage have produced significant, long-lasting restoration of lost functions. For example, more than twenty years ago, researchers in Sweden reported success in reducing symptoms of Parkinson's disease by using fetal cell transplants (Lindvall et al., 1990). Today, we know that such treatments are variable but can be as effective as levodopa (L-dopa). If these treatments are used early in the disease, they could substantially reduce the amount of medication a patient would need. What has yet to be determined is if early intervention with fetal transplants will significantly alter the course of the disease (Barker, Barrett, Mason, & Björklund, 2013). If such neural grafts are perfected, brain damage caused by strokes, tumors, diseases, or accidents might be treated by brain-tissue transplants. One application, which appears to be promising in the future but has yet to be tested in humans, is neural transplants for the treatment of Alzheimer's disease. Researchers who study animal models of Alzheimer's disease have used neural transplants containing acetylcholinergic neurons and transplanted them into the hippocampus of rodents. Once there, the acetylcholinergic neurons became anatomically and functionally incorporated into the hippocampus and delivered acetylcholine (Tarricone et al., 1996). Neural transplants appear to achieve their beneficial effects by secreting neurotransmitters that the damaged structure normally secretes (Becker, Curran, & Freed, 1990), by forming new neural circuits to replace damaged ones (Nunn & Hodges, 1994), or by secreting substances that promote neural regeneration (Lescaudron & Stein, 1990).

Pioneering research has produced promising findings, which indicate that the 21st century might see the cure of brain and spinal-cord damage. Adrenal-gland transplants in rats and mice have reduced symptoms akin to those found in Parkinson's disease (Espejo et al., 2001) and Huntington's disease (Jousselin-Hosaja et al., 2001) and have reduced memory loss caused by hippocampus damage (Tarricone, Simon, Li, & Low, 1996) and movement disturbances caused by cerebellum damage (Triarhou, 1995). Moreover, gene therapy designed to increase dopamine production in people with Parkinson's disease shows initial promise (Wakeman, Dodiya, & Kordower, 2011) and will likely replace invasive procedures such as fetal transplants.

Before becoming too optimistic about neural transplants, you should realize that many attempts at them have failed (Swenson, Danielsen, Klausen, & Erlich, 1989). And even "successful" transplants might not have the intended effects. The enhanced secretion of a neurotransmitter or the formation of new neural circuits might disrupt existing activity

neural grafting
The transplantation of healthy tissue into damaged nerves, brains, or spinal cords.

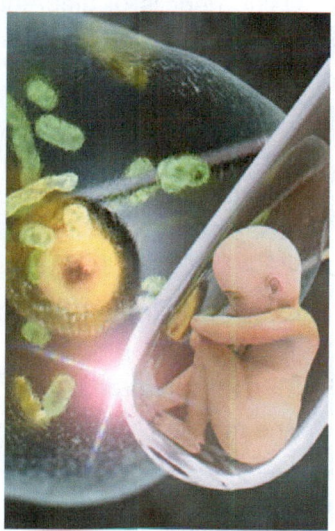

Fetal Stem Cells

Fetal stem cells, once harvested, cannot become embryos but can be coaxed into developing into any type of cell in the body; thus, they are helpful to scientists. Although controversial when obtained from a terminated pregnancy or collected from fertilization clinics, stem cells have helped advance treatment options for Parkinson's disease patients.
Source: Giovani Cancemi/ Shutterstock.com.

or neural pathways, creating even more functional deterioration, though recent research indicates that this might potentially be overcome by technical improvements in methodology (Politis, 2010). Though neural grafts have yet to demonstrate their everyday practical worth, research still might pay off with breakthroughs that will restore functions that have been lost as the result of brain or spinal-cord damage (Baisden, 1995). Recent research on transplantation of bone marrow stem cells from rats into regions of brain damage in those rats has produced neural generation and functional recovery. It remains for this to be applied in clinical trials with human participants (Bonilla et al., 2009).

Section Review: Brain Functions

1. What are the major functions of the brain stem, the limbic system, and the cerebral cortex?

2. What roles do Broca's area and Wernicke's area play in speech production?

3. What evidence is there for hemispheric lateralization based on split-brain research?

Experiencing Psychology

What Are the Locations and Functions of Brain Structures?

Using pencils of different colors, modeling clay of different colors, and any reference material you require, draw or sculpt the following brain structures. Use different colors for the different structures. Write a description of the functions of each of the structures. This exercise will reinforce what you have learned from class lectures and the chapter by providing you with two-dimensional or three-dimensional, as well as verbal understanding of the major brain structures and their functions.

Cerebral Cortex Structures

The language areas

The sensory areas

The motor areas

Limbic System Structures

The hippocampus

The amygdala

The hypothalamus

Brain Stem Structures

The thalamus

The cerebellum

The pons

The medulla

Chapter Summary

Nature versus Nurture

- Psychologists who champion evolutionary psychology employ Darwinian concepts in their research and theorizing.
- Scientists who study behavioral genetics are interested in how heredity affects behavior.
- Heritability refers to the proportion of variability in a trait across a population attributable to genetic differences among members of the population.

- Research procedures that assess the relative contributions of nature and nurture involve studies of families, adoptees, and identical twins reared apart.

Biological Communication Systems

- The field of behavioral neuroscience studies the relationships between physiological processes and psychological functions.

- The nervous system is composed of cells called neurons and serves as the main means of communication within the body.
- The nervous system is divided into the central nervous system, which comprises the brain and the spinal cord, and the peripheral nervous system, which comprises the nerves of the somatic nervous system and the autonomic nervous system.
- The autonomic nervous system is subdivided into the sympathetic nervous system, which arouses the body, and the parasympathetic nervous system, which conserves energy.
- Hormones, secreted into the bloodstream by endocrine glands, also serve as a means of communication within the body.
- Hormones participate in functions as diverse as sexual development and responses to stress. Most endocrine glands are regulated by hormones secreted by the pituitary gland, which in turn is regulated by the hypothalamus.

Neuronal Activity

- The nervous system carries information along sensory neurons, motor neurons, and interneurons, as in the limb-withdrawal reflex mediated by the spinal cord.
- The neuron generally receives signals through its dendrites and sends signals along its axon.
- The axon maintains a resting potential during which it is electrically negative on the inside relative to its outside, as a result of a higher concentration of negative ions inside.
- Sufficient stimulation of the neuron causes the axon to depolarize (become less electrically negative) and reach its firing threshold.
- Depolarization produces an action potential, which causes a neural impulse to travel along the entire length of the axon.
- The neural impulses stimulate the release of neurotransmitter molecules into the synapse.
- The molecules cross the synapse and attach to receptor sites on glands, muscles, or other neurons.
- These molecules exert either an excitatory or an inhibitory influence.
- In recent years, the neurotransmitters known as endorphins have inspired research because of their role in pain relief and euphoria.

Brain Functions

- The functions of the brain have been revealed by clinical case studies, experimental manipulation, recording of electrical activity, and brain-imaging techniques.
- The medulla regulates vital functions, such as breathing; the pons regulates arousal and attention; and the cerebellum controls the timing of well-learned sequences of movements.
- The reticular formation regulates brain arousal and helps maintain vigilance.
- The thalamus relays sensory information (except smell) to various regions of the brain for further processing.
- Within the limbic system, the hypothalamus regulates the pituitary gland as well as emotion and motives, such as eating, drinking, and sex.
- The amygdala continuously evaluates the immediate environment for potential threats, and the hippocampus processes information into memories.
- The cerebral cortex covers the brain and is divided into the frontal, temporal, parietal, and occipital lobes.
- Well-defined areas of the lobes regulate movements and process sensory information.
- Most areas of the cerebral cortex are association areas devoted to integrating information from different brain areas, such as those devoted to speech.
- Brain imaging techniques, including positron-emission tomography (PET), functional magnetic resonance imaging (fMRI), and single photon emission computed tomography (SPECT), have contributed to our understanding of the functions of different areas of the brain.
- Researchers historically have disagreed about the extent to which particular psychological functions are localized in particular areas of the brain.
- Each cerebral hemisphere has psychological functions at which it excels, though both hemispheres influence virtually all functions.
- Studies of the degree of activity in each hemisphere, of the effects of damage to one hemisphere, and of people whose hemispheres have been surgically disconnected show that the left hemisphere is typically superior at verbal tasks and the right hemisphere is typically superior at spatial tasks.
- Scientists have been making progress in treating brain and spinal-cord damage.
- One of the most promising, though controversial, treatments for brain and spinal-cord damage is neural grafting.

Key Terms

Biopsychological Bases of Behavior

behavioral neuroscience (p. 61)
unilateral neglect (p. 60)

Nature versus Nurture

behavioral genetics (p. 62)

evolutionary psychology (p. 61)
genotype (p. 63)
heritability (p. 63)
phenotype (p. 63)

Biological Communication Systems

adrenal gland (p. 69)

autonomic nervous system (p. 67)
brain (p. 66)
central nervous system (p. 66)
endocrine system (p. 67)
gonads (p. 69)
hormones (p. 67)
nerve (p. 67)

nervous system (p. 66)
neuron (p. 66)
ovaries (p. 69)
parasympathetic nervous system (p. 67)
peripheral nervous system (p. 67)
pituitary gland (p. 68)
reflex (p. 67)
somatic nervous system (p. 67)
spinal cord (p. 66)
sympathetic nervous system (p. 67)
testes (p. 69)

Neuronal Activity

action potential (p. 72)
all-or-none law (p. 73)
Alzheimer's disease (p. 76)
axon (p. 71)
axonal conduction (p. 72)
dendrites (p. 70)
endorphins (p. 77)
glial cell (p. 70)
interneuron (p. 70)
motor neuron (p. 70)
myelin (p. 73)
neurotransmitter (p. 74)
Parkinson's disease (p. 76)

resting potential (p. 72)
sensory neuron (p. 70)
soma (p. 70)
synapse (p. 74)
synaptic transmission (p. 73)

Brain Functions

amygdala (p. 85)
association areas (p. 86)
auditory cortex (p. 88)
brain stem (p. 83)
Broca's area (p. 89)
cerebellum (p. 84)
cerebral cortex (p. 86)
cerebral hemisphere (p. 86)
collateral sprouting (p. 97)
computed tomography (CT) (p. 82)
corpus callosum (p. 95)
electroencephalograph (EEG) (p. 80)
frontal lobe (p. 86)
functional magnetic resonance imaging
(fMRI) (p. 82)
hippocampus (p. 86)
hypothalamus (p. 85)
limbic system (p. 84)

magnetic resonance imaging (MRI)
(p. 82)
magnetoencephalography (MEG) (p. 81)
medulla (p. 83)
motor cortex (p. 86)
neural grafting (p. 99)
neural plasticity (p. 96)
occipital lobe (p. 89)
parietal lobe (p. 88)
phrenology (p. 80)
pons (p. 84)
positron-emission tomography (PET)
(p. 82)
primary cortical area (p. 86)
reticular formation (p. 84)
single photon emission computed tomography (SPECT) (p. 82)
somatosensory cortex (p. 88)
split-brain research (p. 95)
temporal lobe (p. 88)
thalamus (p. 84)
transcranial magnetic stimulation (TMS)
(p. 79)
visual cortex (p. 89)
Wada test (p. 92)
Wernicke's area (p. 90)

Chapter Quiz

1. The central nervous system comprises the
   a. brain and spinal cord.
   b. nerves and spinal cord.
   c. somatic and autonomic nervous systems.
   d. sympathetic and parasympathetic nervous systems.

2. Mary Shelley wrote the novel *Frankenstein* at about the same time that the possible electrical nature of nerve impulses was demonstrated by
   a. Isaac Newton.
   b. Luigi Galvani.
   c. Rene' Descartes.
   d. Charles Sherrington.

3. A football player is tackled and knocked unconscious. The blow probably affected his
   a. pons.
   b. thalamus.
   c. hippocampus.
   d. hypothalamus.

4. The convolutions of the cerebral cortex
   a. integrate sensory and motor information.
   b. act as biological radiators to cool the brain.
   c. permit more cerebral cortex to fit inside the skull.
   d. provide a means of communication between the hemispheres.

5. Myelinated axons conduct neural impulses faster because they
   a. contain nodes of Ranvier.
   b. tend to have smaller synaptic clefts.
   c. make impulses leap from one neuron to another.
   d. tend to be smaller in diameter than other neurons.

6. The nerves compose the
   a. brain.
   b. spinal cord.
   c. peripheral nervous system.
   d. reticular activating system.

7. An arrow from a careless archer pierces the brain of a bystander. The victim survives, recalls events from before the accident, but cannot form new memories. The arrow probably destroyed the
   a. pons.
   b. hippocampus.
   c. hypothalamus.
   d. parietal lobes.

8. If a split-brain patient were to draw a map, she would probably perform
   a. better with her left hand.
   b. better with her right hand.
   c. equally well with both hands.
   d. better using a foot rather than a hand.

9. Phrenology was based on the mistaken assumption that
   a. heredity affected brain development.
   b. brain neurons could regenerate after injury.
   c. brain structure could be determined by bumps on the skull.
   d. all psychological functions are processed bilaterally in the brain.

10. A classical pianist suffers a stroke and can no longer play the piano with proper timing, though she can use all of her fingers to strike the correct keys. The stroke probably affected her
   a. cerebellum.
   b. motor cortex.
   c. corpus callosum.
   d. somatosensory cortex.

11. The Wada test is used to
   a. measure the speed of neural conduction.
   b. identify the site of injury in stroke victims.
   c. determine the lateralization of particular psychological functions.
   d. assess the relative concentrations of extracellular and intracellular fluid.

12. Damage to the temporal cortex would most likely cause
   a. inability to move a body part.
   b. loss of sensation from a body part.
   c. a blind spot in the contralateral visual field.
   d. impaired ability to perceive sounds of certain pitches.

13. The sensory relay station of the brain is the
   a. thalamus.
   b. hypothalamus.
   c. corpus callosum.
   d. reticular activating system.

14. In Otto Loewi's demonstration of the chemical basis of neurotransmission in his study of frog hearts, he found that the chemical involved was
   a. dopamine.
   b. endorphins.
   c. acetylcholine.
   d. norepinephrine.

15. Electrical stimulation of the rear portion of the frontal lobe would most likely
   a. evoke an old memory.
   b. make a body part move.
   c. create images of lights or colors.
   d. cause a touch sensation from a body part.

16. The case study of railroad foreman Phineas Gage provided evidence that factors related to emotionality and personality are regulated by the
   a. limbic system.
   b. brain stem.
   c. frontal lobes.
   d. corpus callosum.

17. The probable existence of gaps between neurons was first demonstrated by
   a. Otto Loewi.
   b. Camillo Golgi.
   c. Luigi Galvani.
   d. Santiago Ramon y Cajal.

18. A stroke victim uses grammatically correct, but meaningless, speech. She most likely suffered damage to
   a. Broca's area.
   b. Wernicke's area.
   c. parietal association areas.
   d. occipital association areas.

19. In the 18th century, Stephen Hales's research on decapitated frogs demonstrated that they could still
   a. make croaking sounds.
   b. negotiate a water maze.
   c. form memories of visual events.
   d. respond reflexively to leg pinches.

20. A victim of a gunshot wound to the head dies immediately. The bullet most likely damaged the
   a. cerebellum.
   b. frontal lobes.
   c. corpus callosum.
   d. medulla.

21. A detective investigates a murder by poisoning in which the victim's skeletal muscles are completely relaxed. The detective suspects that the poison was
   a. curare.
   b. strychnine.
   c. tetanus toxin.
   d. acetylcholine.

22. The cell that is specialized for the transmission and reception of information is the
   a. soma.
   b. neuron.
   c. synapse.
   d. neuroglia.

23. Because of his views on the site of psychological functions, the philosopher who would most appreciate hearing the song "I Left My Heart in San Francisco" and receiving Valentine's Day candy in a heart-shaped box would be
   a. Plato.
   b. Socrates.
   c. Aristotle.
   d. Hippocrates.

24. A diving accident completely severs the spinal cord of a diver at mid-chest level. He would most likely experience
  a. initial leg paralysis, which would gradually disappear over time.
  b. permanent leg paralysis and permanent loss of feeling in the legs.
  c. almost immediate death due to destruction of control centers for breathing and heart rate.
  d. permanent loss of feeling in the body at the level of the injury, but retention of feeling above and below it.

25. The endocrine system would be most likely to be affected by a tumor of the
  a. tectum.
  b. amygdala.
  c. hypothalamus.
  d. corpus callosum.

Thought Questions

1. How do psychologists interested in behavioral genetics use studies of identical twins reared apart to assess the role of heredity in human development?

2. How would you determine whether the joy of a student who earns a 4.0 grade-point average is associated with an increase in endorphin levels?

3. Why do some psychologists believe that phrenology was an important but misguided approach to the localization of brain functions?

4. How does split-brain research provide evidence that the left cerebral hemisphere is somewhat superior in processing speech and the right cerebral hemisphere is somewhat superior in perceiving spatial relations?

Human Development

In 1987 Hulda Crooks climbed Mount Whitney in the Sierra Nevada Mountains of California for the 23rd time. This would be a noteworthy feat for any person, given that at 14,495 feet, Mount Whitney is the tallest mountain in the contiguous 48 states. What made it more impressive was that Hulda was 91 years old at the time, making her the oldest person ever to reach the summit. That year she also became the oldest woman to climb Mount Fuji, the tallest mountain in Japan. The Japanese sponsors of her ascent honored her with a banner reading "Grandma Fuji."

The following year Hulda decided to add the U.S. Capitol to her long list of conquests. She barely worked up a sweat as she ascended the 350-step staircase in the building's dome in just 30 minutes. Hulda, a physical fitness proponent who also held eight Senior Olympics world records in track and field at the time, made the climb to celebrate National Women in Sports Day (Connors, 1988).

In 1991 a peak near Mount Whitney was named Crooks Peak in Hulda's honor. "You have not only highlighted the importance of physical fitness for all Americans, but also served as a role model for senior citizens everywhere," wrote President George H. W. Bush in a letter recognizing her accomplishments. At the ceremony naming the peak, Hulda observed, "It's never too late to change your lifestyle if you realize it's not appropriate. I want to impress to young people that they're building their old age now" (Kuebelbeck, 1991).

Hulda, who died in 1997 at the age of 101, was a vegetarian who took up hiking in her 40s following a bout with pneumonia. She did not scale her first peak until she was 66, when many people are content to lead a more sedentary life. Hulda advocated a sparse diet, vigorous exercise, and avoiding caffeine and alcohol. She also credited her healthy life to her spirituality as a devout member of the Seventh Day Adventist Church. Hulda published her memoirs, *Conquering Life's Mountains,* as a testament to the importance of mental, physical, and spiritual well-being. At a book signing, she was treated as a celebrity. Mountaineers lined up to have her sign their copies. One of them laughed when he realized that he had retired from mountain climbing at 55, when he was more than 10 years younger than Hulda was when she began her climbing career (Fieckenstein, 1996).

Hulda Crooks' accomplishments in old age contradict the stereotype of the elderly as frail and lacking in vitality. Psychologists who study the aging process find that severe mental and physical decline is not necessarily a characteristic of old age. As Hulda noted, by keeping mentally and physically active in adulthood we can have rich, rewarding

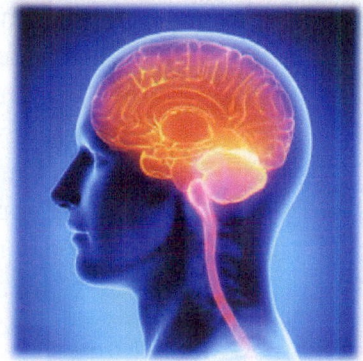

Source: CLIPAREA/Custom media/ Shutterstock.com.

Chapter Outline

Research Methods in Developmental Psychology

Prenatal Development

Infant and Child Development

Adolescent Development

Adult Development

Vigorous in Old Age

Hulda Crooks, who climbed her first mountain in her mid-60s and continued climbing into her 90s, illustrates the importance of maintaining physical fitness and a healthful lifestyle across the life span. Research indicates that physically and mentally active adults might age at a slower rate.
Source: Bettman/Corbis.

developmental psychology
The field that studies physical, perceptual, cognitive, and psychosocial changes across the life span.

maturation The sequential unfolding of inherited predispositions in physical and motor development.

lives throughout our later years. **Developmental psychology** is the study of the physical, perceptual, cognitive, and psychosocial changes that take place across the life span. Though opinions about the nature of human development can be found in the writings of ancient Greek philosophers, the scientific study of human development did not begin until the 1870s. That decade saw the appearance of the "baby biography," usually written by a parent, which described the development of an infant. Though much of infant development depends on learning, it also is guided by physical **maturation**—the sequential unfolding of inherited predispositions (as in the progression from crawling to standing to walking). Developmental psychologists recognize that most aspects of human development depend on the interaction of genetic and environmental factors (Belsky & Pluess, 2009).The 1890s saw the beginning of research on child development after infancy (White, 1990), most notably at Clark University by G. Stanley Hall (1844–1924). Hall based his views on Darwin's theory of evolution, earning him the title of "the Darwin of the mind." He applied research findings to the improvement of education and child rearing, and today he is recognized as the founder of *child psychology*. Until the 1950s the study of human development was virtually synonymous with child psychology. During that decade, psychologists began to study human development across the life span. More recently, psychologists have come to realize the importance of considering social-cultural factors in human development.

Research Methods in Developmental Psychology

Though developmental psychologists often use the same research methods as other psychologists, they also rely on methods that are unique to developmental psychology. These include *longitudinal research, cross-sectional research,* and *cohort-sequential research*, which enable researchers to study age-related differences and changes in their participants.

Longitudinal Research

longitudinal research
A research design in which the same group of participants is tested or observed repeatedly over a period of time.

Longitudinal research follows the same participants over a period of time, typically ranging from months to years. The researcher looks for changes in particular characteristics, such as language, personality, intelligence, or perceptual ability. Suppose you wanted to study changes in the social maturity of college students. If you chose to use a longitudinal design, you might assess the social maturity of an incoming class of first-year students and then note changes in their social maturity across their 4 years in college. Longitudinal research has been used to study numerous topics, such as factors associated with the development of creativity in children and adolescents (Weller, 2012), the relationship between identity, intimacy, and well-being in midlife (Sneed, Whitbourne, Schwartz, & Huang, 2012), and older adults' evaluations of their physical health as they age (Sargent-Cox, Anstey, & Luszcz, 2010).

Though longitudinal research has the advantage of permitting us to study individuals as they change across their life spans, it has major weaknesses. First, the typical longitudinal study takes months, years, or even decades to complete. This often requires ongoing financial support and continued commitment by researchers—neither of which can be guaranteed. Second, the longer the study lasts, the more likely it is that participants will drop out. They might refuse to continue or move away or even die. If those who drop out differ in important ways from those who remain, the results of the research might be less generalizable to the population of interest (Feng, Silverstein, Giarrusso, McArdle, & Bengtson, 2006). For example, a 14-year longitudinal study of changes in adult intelligence found that those who dropped out had scored lower on intelligence tests than did those who remained. This made it unwise to generalize the study's findings to all adults. Including only those who remained in the study would have led to the erroneous conclusion that as adults age they show a marked increase in intelligence (Schaie, Labouvie, & Barrett, 1973).

Cross-Sectional Research

The weaknesses of longitudinal research are overcome by **cross-sectional research**, which compares groups of participants of different ages at the same time. Each of the age groups is called a **cohort**. If you chose to use a cross-sectional design to study age-related differences in social maturity of college students, you might compare the current social maturity of four cohorts: first-year students, sophomores, juniors, and seniors. A cross-sectional research design was used in a study of differences in male sexuality across adulthood. The researchers compared samples of men in their 30s through 90s. The stereotypical view of old age as a time of asexuality was countered by the finding that all of the participants in the oldest groups reported feelings of sexual desire (Mulligan & Moss, 1991). Cross-sectional research designs have been used to study topics as varied as differences in attitudes about love, sex, and "hooking up" among students during their first year of college (Katz & Schneider, 2013) and the relationship between medical education and differences in moral reasoning across four years of medical school (Self & Baldwin, 1998).

Like longitudinal research, cross-sectional research has its own weaknesses. The main one is that cross-sectional research can produce misleading findings if a cohort in the study is affected by circumstances unique to that cohort (Fullerton & Dixon, 2010). Thus, cross-sectional studies can identify differences between cohorts of different ages, but those differences might not hold true if cohorts of those ages were observed during another era. Suppose that you conduct a cross-sectional study and find that older adults are more prejudiced against minorities than are younger adults. Does this mean that we become more prejudiced with age? Not necessarily. Perhaps, instead, the cohort of older adults was reared at a time when prejudice was more acceptable than it is today. Members of the cohort might simply have retained attitudes that they developed in their youth.

Cohort-Sequential Research

One way to deal with the shortcomings of longitudinal and cross-sectional research is to use **cohort-sequential research**, which begins as a cross-sectional study by comparing different cohorts and then follows the cohorts longitudinally. As an example, consider how a cohort-sequential research design was employed in a study of alcohol use in old age. Healthy cohorts ranging in age from 60 to 86 years were first compared cross-sectionally. The results showed a decline in the percentage of drinkers with age. The cohorts then were followed longitudinally for 7 years. The results remained the same: as the drinkers aged, they drank less. This made it more likely that the decline in drinking with age was related to age rather than to life experiences peculiar to particular cohorts (Adams, Garry, Rhyne, & Hunt, 1990). Another cohort-sequential study found that participation in sports, athletics, or exercising was related to lower levels of substance abuse by teenagers and young adults rather than merely being associated with different patterns of substance abuse for different age cohorts (Terry-McElrath & O'Malley, 2011).

Cohort-sequential research designs also may reveal age differences that are cohort effects rather than being age-related effects. This was the case in the Seattle Longitudinal Study. Cognitive abilities of participants in the longitudinal aspect of the study were measured in 1956, 1963, 1970, and 1977. At each of those times, the cognitive abilities of participants of different ages were compared cross-sectionally. The findings showed that there was a larger cognitive decline in the cross-sectional comparisons than in the longitudinal comparisons. This indicates that observed differences in cognitive ability at different ages is more related to factors affecting particular cohorts than to changes that naturally accompany aging (Williams & Klug, 1996).

cross-sectional research A research design in which groups of participants of different ages are compared at the same point in time.

cohort A group of people of the same age group.

cohort-sequential research A research design that begins as a cross-sectional study by comparing different cohorts and then follows the cohorts longitudinally.

Longitudinal research, cross-sectional research, and cohort-sequential research have long been staples of research on development from birth to death. Today, technology permits developmental psychologists to study ongoing developmental processes even before birth, during the prenatal period.

Section Review: Research Methods in Developmental Psychology

1. What is maturation?

2. What are the strengths and weaknesses of cross-sectional and longitudinal research designs?

Prenatal Development

All of us began life as a single cell. The formation of that cell begins the prenatal period, which lasts about 9 months and is divided into the germinal stage, the embryonic stage, and the fetal stage.

The Germinal Stage

germinal stage The prenatal period that lasts from conception through the second week.

The **germinal stage** begins with conception, which occurs when a *sperm* from the man unites with an egg (or *ovum*) from the woman, usually in one of her two *fallopian tubes*, forming a one-celled *zygote*. The zygote contains 23 pairs of chromosomes, one member of each pair coming from the ovum and the other coming from the sperm. The chromosomes, in turn, contain genes that govern the development of the individual. The zygote begins a trip down the fallopian tube, during which it is transformed into a larger, multicelled ball, called a *blastocyst*, by repeated cell divisions. By the end of the second week, the blastocyst attaches to the wall of the uterus. This marks the beginning of the embryonic stage.

The Embryonic Stage

embryonic stage The prenatal period that lasts from the end of the second week through the eighth week.

The **embryonic stage** lasts from the end of the second week through the eighth week of prenatal development. The embryo, nourished by nutrients that cross the placenta, increases in size and begins to develop specialized organs, including the eyes, heart, and brain. What accounts for this rapid, complex process? The development and location of bodily organs is regulated by genes, which determine the kinds of cells that will develop and also control the actions of *cell-adhesion molecules*. These molecules direct the movement of cells and determine which cells will adhere to one another, thereby determining the size, shape, and location of organs in the embryo (Rungger-Brändle, Ripperger, Steiger, Soltanieh, & Rungger, 2010). By the end of the embryonic stage, development has progressed to the point at which the heart is beating and the approximately one-inch-long embryo has facial features, limbs, fingers, and toes.

But what determines whether an embryo becomes a female or a male? The answer lies in the 23rd pair of chromosomes, the sex chromosomes, which are designated X or Y. Embryos that inherit two X chromosomes are genetic females, and embryos that inherit one X and one Y chromosome are genetic males. The presence of a Y chromosome directs the development of the testes; in the *absence* of a Y chromosome, the ovaries differentiate. Near the end of the embryonic period, the primitive gonads of male embryos secrete the hormone *testosterone*, which stimulates the development of male sexual organs. And the primitive gonads of female embryos secrete the hormones *estrogen* and *progesterone*, which stimulate the development of female sexual organs. Thus, the hormonal environments of female and male fetuses differ at the embryonic stage of development.

Prenatal hormones direct the differentiation of sexual organs and the brain, especially the hypothalamus (see Chapter 3). The secretion of testosterone by the male fetus directs the differentiation of the male sexual organs. In cases where testosterone is absent, female sexual organs differentiate. There is evidence, though, that estrogen plays a greater role in sexual differentiation of the female fetus than has been estimated in the past (Collaer, Geffner, Kaufman, Buckingham, & Hines 2002).

The Fetal Stage

The presence of a distinctly human appearance marks the beginning of the **fetal stage**, which lasts from the beginning of the third prenatal month until birth. By the fourth month, pregnant women report movement by the fetus. And by the seventh month, all of the major organs are functional, which means that an infant born even 2 or 3 months prematurely has a chance of surviving. The final 3 months of prenatal development are associated with most of the increase in the size of the fetus.

fetal stage The prenatal period that lasts from the end of the eighth week through birth.

The fetus also develops rudimentary sensory and cognitive abilities, including the ability to hear sounds and form long-term memories. In one study, 143 fetuses were exposed to a series of conditions. First, there was 2 minutes of silence. Second, there was a tape recording of their mother reading a story. The recording was played for 2 minutes through a speaker held about 4 inches from the mother's abdomen. Then, they were exposed to another 2 minutes of silence. Fetal heart rate increased in response to the mother's voice and decreased when they were exposed to silence. This indicates that the fetus can perceive and form a memory of its mother's voice (Kisilevsky & Haines, 2011).

Premature infants tend to be smaller and less physically and cognitively mature than full-term infants. For example, when an object approaches the eyes of a premature infant, the infant might not exhibit normal defensive blinking (Pettersen, Yonas, & Fisch, 1980). Moreover, though prenatal development usually produces a healthy infant, in some cases genetic defects produce distinctive physical and psychological syndromes. The chromosomal disorder called Down syndrome (discussed in Chapter 10), for example, is associated with intellectual disabilities and abnormal physical development. Other sources of prenatal defects are **teratogens**, which are noxious substances or other factors that can disrupt prenatal development and prevent the individual from reaching her or his inherited potential. (The word *teratogen* was coined from Greek terms meaning "that which produces a monster.")

teratogen A noxious substance, such as a virus or drug, that can cause prenatal defects.

Most teratogens affect prenatal development by first crossing the placenta. A potent teratogen is the German measles (rubella) virus, which can cause defects of the eyes, ears, and heart—particularly during the first 3 months of prenatal development. Many drugs, both legal and illegal, can cross the placenta and cause abnormal physical and psychological development. These drugs include nicotine (Piper, Gray, & Birkett, 2012) and marijuana (Keegan, Parva, Finnegan, Gersen, & Belden, 2010). And alcohol consumption during pregnancy is associated with **fetal alcohol syndrome**. Fetal alcohol syndrome is associated with facial deformities, hearing disorders, intellectual disabilities, attentional deficits, and poor impulse control.

fetal alcohol syndrome A disorder, marked by physical defects and intellectual disability, that can afflict the offspring of women who drink alcohol during pregnancy.

Factors that are correlated with parental substance abuse also may have harmful long-term effects. Recreational drug use has adverse effects on the father's health, including damaged DNA that results in abnormal sperm (Pollard, 2000). Parents with a history of substance abuse also are more likely to have turbulent relationships. One study found that women who were heavy cocaine users were more likely to report that the father of the child abused alcohol or other drugs. And fathers with a history of a drug or alcohol problems were more likely to subject their partner to physical or mental abuse during her pregnancy (Frank, Brown, Johnson, & Cabral 2002). Sadly, children with a history of prenatal drug exposure also are at risk of receiving poor-quality parental care after birth (Eiden, Schuetze, & Coles, 2011). Thus, teratogens not only have a direct effect upon prenatal development, they also may harm the child indirectly by contributing to an environment that fails to ensure the child's well-being.

Section Review: Prenatal Development

1. What are cell-adhesion molecules?

2. What are the symptoms of fetal alcohol syndrome?

Infant and Child Development

childhood The period that extends from birth until the onset of puberty.

infancy The period that extends from birth through 2 years of age.

Childhood extends from birth until puberty and begins with **infancy**, a period of rapid physical, cognitive, and psychosocial development, extending from birth to age 2 years. Many developmental psychologists devote themselves to studying the changes in physical, perceptual, cognitive, and psychosocial development that occur during childhood.

Physical Development

Newborn infants exhibit reflexes that promote their survival, such as blinking to protect their eyes from an approaching object and rooting (searching) for a nipple when their cheeks are touched. Through maturation and learning, the infant quickly develops motor skills that go beyond mere reflexes. The typical infant is crawling by 6 months and walking by 13 months. Though infant motor development follows a consistent sequence, the timing of motor milestones varies somewhat from one infant to another. Figure 4-1 depicts the major motor milestones.

Infancy also is a period of rapid brain development, when many connections between brain cells are formed and many others are eliminated. Though some of these changes are governed by maturation, research studies by Marian Diamond and her colleagues over the

FIGURE 4-1

Motor Milestones

Infancy is a period of rapid motor development. The infant begins with a set of motor reflexes and, over the course of little more than a year, develops the ability to manipulate objects and move independently through the environment. The ages at which healthy children reach motor milestones vary somewhat from child to child, but the sequence of motor milestones does not.

Holds up chin, then chest

Rolls over

Sits with support

Sits without support

Stands holding on

Pulls self to stand

Stands well alone

Walks well alone

Age (months)
0 1 2 3 4 5 6 7 8 9 10 11 12 13 14 15

past few decades have demonstrated that life experiences can affect brain development (Diamond, 1988). One of these studies determined the effect of enriched and impoverished environments on the brain development of rats (Camel, Withers, & Greenough, 1986). A group of infant rats spent 30 days in an enriched environment and another group spent 30 days in an impoverished environment. In the enriched environment, the rats were housed together in two large, toy-filled cages, one containing water and one containing food, which were attached to the opposite ends of a maze. The pattern of pathways and dead ends through the maze was changed daily. In the impoverished environment, the rats were housed individually in small, empty cages.

Microscopic examination of the brains of the rats found that those exposed to enriched environments had longer and more numerous dendrites (see Chapter 3) on their brain neurons than did those exposed to the impoverished environment. The increased size and number of dendrites would provide the rats exposed to the enriched environment with more synaptic connections among their brain neurons. The benefits of enriched environments on neural development also have been replicated in studies of children (Bryck & Fisher, 2012).

After infancy, the child's growth rate slows, and most children grow two or three inches a year until puberty. The child's motor coordination also improves. Children gradually learn to perform more sophisticated motor tasks, such as using scissors, tying their shoes, and riding bicycles. The development of motor skills even affects the development of cognitive skills. For example, children's ability to express themselves through language depends on the development of motor abilities that permit them to speak and to write.

Perceptual Development

Over a century ago, in describing what he believed was the chaotic mental world of the newborn infant, William James (1890/1981, Vol. 1, p. 462) claimed, "The baby, assailed by eyes, ears, nose, skin, and entrails at once, feels it all as one great blooming, buzzing confusion." But subsequent research has shown that newborn infants have more highly developed sensory, perceptual, and cognitive abilities than James believed. For example, though newborns cannot focus on distant objects, they can focus on objects less than a foot away—as though nature has programmed them to focus at the distance of the face of a person who might be holding them (Aslin & Smith, 1988). Newborn infants can use their sense of touch to discriminate between objects with different surface textures (Molina & Jouen, 1998). Newborns also have a more sophisticated sense of smell than James would have presumed. In one study, infants were exposed to either the odor of amniotic fluid (which they experienced while in the womb) or another odor they had not been exposed to before. The results showed that the infants were more likely to turn their heads toward the odor of amniotic fluid than toward the other odor (Schaal, Marlier, & Soussignan, 1998).

Ingenious studies have permitted researchers to infer what infants perceive by recording changes in their eye movements, head movements, body movements, sucking behavior, or physiological responses (such as changes in heart rate or brain-wave patterns). For example, a study of newborn American infants found that they could discriminate between Japanese words with different pitch patterns as indicated by their sucking harder on a rubber nipple in response to particular patterns (Nazzi, Floccia, & Bertoncini, 1998). Infant preferences can be determined by recording which targets they look at longer or by presenting them with a stimulus, waiting for them to *habituate* to it (that is, stop noticing it—as indicated by, for example, a stable heart rate), and then changing the stimulus. If they notice the change, they will show alterations in physiological activity, such as a *decrease* in heart rate.

Studies using these techniques have found that infants have remarkably well developed sensory-perceptual abilities. Tiffany Field has demonstrated that, as shown in Figure 4-2, infants less than 2 days old can imitate sad, happy, and surprised facial expressions (Field, Woodson, Greenberg, & Cohen, 1982.). Nonetheless, other studies have been inconsistent in their findings regarding neonatal imitation of facial expressions. The most consistent finding has been that neonates will respond to models who stick out their tongues by sticking out their own (Anisfeld, 1996).

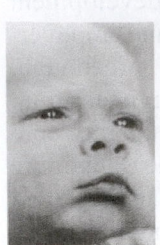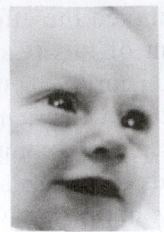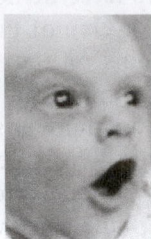

FIGURE 4-2 Abilities of Newborn Infants

Newborn infants not only see better than has been traditionally assumed, but also imitate facial expressions of surprise, sadness, and happiness.

Source: From Field, T. M., Woodson, R., Greenberg, R., and Cohen, D (1982). Discrimination and imitation of facial expressions by neonates. *Science*, 218, pp. 179–181. Reprinted with permission from AAAS.

The Research Process box illustrates one of the ways in which psychologists study infant perceptual development. The study made use of a "visual cliff" to test infant depth perception.

Infants also have good auditory abilities, including the ability to localize sounds. Between the ages of 8 and 28 weeks, infants can localize sounds that shift in location by only a few degrees, as indicated by head turns or eye movements in response to the shifts (Morrongiello, Fenwick, & Chance, 1990). Infants can even match the emotional tone of sounds to the emotional tone of facial expressions. In one study, 7-month-old infants were shown a sad face and a happy face. At the same time, they were presented with tones that either increased or decreased in pitch. When presented with a descending tone, they looked longer at a sad face than a happy face, as if they were equating the lower tones with a sad mood and the higher tones with a happy mood (Phillips, Wagner, Fells, & Lynch, 1990). As the preceding studies attest, infants are perceptually more sophisticated than William James presumed.

Cognitive Development

Infancy also is a time of rapid cognitive development, during which infants show the unfolding of inborn abilities and their talent for learning. In regard to inborn abilities, for example, newborn infants can distinguish groups of objects that differ in number (Wynn, 1995). In regard to learning, by 4 or 5 months of age, an infant's response to the sound of its own name differs from its response to hearing other names (Mandel, Jusczyk, & Pisoni, 1995).

Jean Piaget (1896–1980), a Swiss biologist and psychologist, put forth the most influential theory of cognitive development. Piaget (1952) proposed that children pass through four increasingly sophisticated cognitive stages of development (see Table 4-1).

TABLE 4-1 Piaget's States of Cognitive Development

Stage	Age	Description	Developmental Outcome
Sensorimotor	Birth–2 Years	Infants learn to integrate sensory input and motor output and begin to use symbolic thought.	Object permanence
Preoperational	2–7 Years	Children become more sophisticated in their use of language and symbolic thought, but they have difficulty in reasoning logically.	Loss of egocentrism
Concrete operational	7–11 Years	Children become proficient in reasoning logically about concrete situations, such as the ability to make transitive inferences.	Conservation
Formal operational	11–15 Years	Many adolescents learn to use abstract reasoning and to form hypotheses about future events based on relevant current knowledge.	Abstract reasoning and hypothesis testing

When Do Infants Develop Depth Perception?

Rationale

One of the most important perceptual abilities is depth perception. It lets us tell how far away objects are from us, preventing us from bumping into them and providing us with time to escape from potentially dangerous ones. But how early can infants perceive depth? This was the subject of a classic study by Eleanor Gibson (1910–2002) and Richard Walk (Gibson & Walk, 1960).

Method

Gibson and Walk used a "visual cliff" made from a piece of thick, transparent glass set about four feet off the ground (see Figure 4-3). Just under the "shallow" side was a red and white checkerboard pattern. The same pattern was placed at floor level under the "deep" side. The sides were separated by a one-foot-wide wooden board. The participants were 36 infants, aged 6 to 14 months. The infants were placed, one at a time, on the wooden board. The infants' mothers called to them, first from one side and then from the other.

Results and Discussion

When placed on the board, 9 of the infants refused to budge. The other 27 crawled onto the shallow side toward their mothers. But only 3 of the 27 crawled onto the deep side. The remaining ones instead cried or crawled away from it. This indicated that the infants could perceive the depth of the two sides—and feared the deep side. It also demonstrated that depth perception is present by 6 months of age. Replications of the study using a variety of animals found that depth perception develops by the time the animal begins moving about on its own—as early as the first day after birth for chicks and goats. This is adaptive, because it reduces their likelihood of being injured.

More recent research on human infants, using decreases in heart rate as a sign that they notice changes in depth, indicates that rudimentary depth perception is present in infants as young as 4 months (Aslin & Smith, 1988). But research findings indicate that human infants will not fear heights until they have had several weeks of crawling experience. Infants will not avoid the deep side of the visual cliff until they have been crawling for at 12 weeks (Kretch & Adolph, 2013).

FIGURE 4-3 The Visual Cliff

Eleanor Gibson and Richard Walk (1960) developed the *visual cliff* to test infant depth perception. The visual cliff consists of a thick sheet of glass placed on a table. The shallow end of the visual cliff has a checkerboard surface just below the glass. The deep end of the visual cliff has a checkerboard surface a few feet below the glass. Infants who have reached the crawling stage will crawl from the center of the table across the shallow end, but not across the deep end, to reach their mothers. This finding indicates that by 6 months infants can perceive depth. Of course, this study does not preclude the possibility that infants can perceive depth even before they can crawl.

According to Piaget, a child is more than an ignorant adult; the child's way of thinking is qualitatively different from the adult's. Moreover, infants are not passive in developing their cognitive views of the physical world. Instead, their views depend on their active interpretation of objects and events in the physical world.

Though Piaget assumed that complete passage through one stage is a prerequisite for success in the next one, research suggests that children can achieve characteristics of later stages without completely passing through earlier ones (Berninger, 1988). The issue of whether human cognitive development is continuous (gradual and quantitative) or discontinuous (in stages and qualitative) remains unresolved (Fischer & Silvern, 1985). The stages put forth by Piaget are the *sensorimotor stage*, *preoperational stage, concrete operational stage,* and *formal operational stage*. Some psychologists have criticized Piaget's theory for its assumption that cognitive development follows a universal pattern (Elkind, 1996). Cross-cultural research indicates that children throughout the world do tend to pass through these stages in the same order, though the timing varies (Segall, Dasen, Berry, & Poortings, 1990).

Sensorimotor Stage

Piaget called infancy the **sensorimotor stage**, during which the child learns to coordinate sensory experiences and motor behaviors. Infants learn to interact with the world by sucking, grasping, crawling, and walking. In little more than a year, they change from being reflexive and physically immature to being purposeful, locomoting, and language-using. By the age of 9 months, for example, sensorimotor coordination becomes sophisticated enough for the infant to grasp a moving object by aiming her or his reach somewhat ahead of the object—using its speed and direction—instead of where the object appears to be at that moment (Keen, Carrico, Sylvia, & Berthier, 2003).

Piaget claimed that experiences with the environment help the infant form **schemas**, which are cognitive structures incorporating the characteristics of persons, objects, events, procedures, or situations. This means that infants do more than simply gather information about the world. Their experiences actively change the way in which they think about the world. Schemas permit infants to adapt their behaviors to changes in the environment. But what makes schemas persist or change? They do so as the result of the interplay between **assimilation** and **accommodation**. We *assimilate* when we fit information into our existing schemas and *accommodate* when we revise our schemas to fit new information.

Young infants, prior to 6 months old, share an important schema in which they assume that the removal of an object from sight means that the object no longer exists. If an object is hidden by a piece of cloth, for example, the young infant will not look for it, even after watching the object being hidden. To the young infant, out of sight truly means out of mind. As infants gain experience with the coming and going of objects in the environment, they accommodate and develop the schema of **object permanence**—the realization that objects not in view may still exist. Infants generally fail to search for objects that are suddenly hidden from view until they are about 8 months old (Munakata, McClelland, Johnson, & Siegler, 1997). But researchers have questioned Piaget's explanation that young infants fail to search for hidden objects because they lack a schema for object permanence. Perhaps, instead, they simply forget the location of an object that has been hidden from view (Bjork & Cummings, 1984).

After the age of 8 months, most infants demonstrate their appreciation of object permanence by searching at other places for an object they have seen being hidden from view. At this point in their development, they can retain a mental image of a physical object even after it has been removed from their sight, and they realize that the object might be elsewhere. This also signifies the beginning of representational thought—the use of symbols to stand for physical objects. But Piaget might have placed the development of object permanence too late, because infants as young as 6 months have been found to show an appreciation of it (Shinskey, 2012).

sensorimotor stage
The Piagetian stage, from birth through the second year, during which the infant learns to coordinate sensory experiences and motor behaviors.

schema A cognitive structure that guides people's perception and information processing that incorporates the characteristics of particular persons, objects, events, procedures, or situations.

assimilation The cognitive process that interprets new information in light of existing schemas.

accommodation
1. The cognitive process that revises existing schemas to incorporate new information.
2. The process by which the lens of the eye increases its curvature to focus light from close objects or decreases its curvature to focus light from more distant objects.

object permanence
The realization that objects exist even when they are no longer visible.

Preoperational Stage

According to Piaget, when the child reaches the age of 2 years and leaves infancy, the sensorimotor stage gives way to the **preoperational stage**, which lasts until about age 7. The stage is called preoperational because the child cannot perform what Piaget called *operations*—mental manipulations of reality. For example, before about the age of 5 the early preoperational child cannot perform mental addition or subtraction of objects. During the preoperational stage, however, the child improves in the use of language, including a rapid growth in vocabulary and a more sophisticated use of grammar. Thus mental development sets the stage for language development. Unlike the sensorimotor-stage child, the preoperational-stage child is not limited to thinking about objects that are physically present.

During the preoperational stage, the child also exhibits what Piaget called **egocentrism**, the inability to perceive reality from the perspective of another person. Egocentrism declines between 4 and 6 years of age (Ruffman & Olson, 1989). Children display egocentrism when they draw a picture of their family but fail to include themselves in the drawing. In some capital criminal cases, lawyers might gain a reduced sentence for a child defendant if they can convince the jury that the child had not progressed beyond egocentrism and therefore was unaware of the effect of the criminal act on the victim (Ellison, 1987).

preoperational stage The Piagetian stage, extending from 2 to 7 years of age, during which the child's use of language becomes more sophisticated but the child has difficulty with the logical mental manipulation of information.

egocentrism The inability to perceive reality from the perspective of another person.

Concrete Operational Stage

At about the age of 7, the child enters what Piaget calls the **concrete operational stage**, which lasts until about the age of 11. The child learns to reason logically but is at first limited to reasoning about physical things. For example, when you first learned to do arithmetic problems, you were unable to perform mental calculations. Instead, until perhaps the age of 8, you counted by using your fingers or other objects. An important kind of reasoning ability that develops during this stage is the ability to make **transitive inferences**—the application of previously learned relationships to infer new ones. For example, suppose that a child is told that Pat is taller than Lee, and that Lee is taller than Terry. A child who can make transitive inferences will correctly conclude that Pat is taller than Terry. Though Piaget claimed that the ability to make transitive inferences develops by age 8, research has shown that children as young as 4 can make them—provided they are given age-appropriate tasks (Andrews & Halford, 1998).

By the age of 8, the child in the concrete operational stage also develops what Piaget called **conservation**—the realization that changing the form of a substance or the arrangement of a set of objects does not change the amount. Suppose that a child is shown two balls of clay of equal size. One ball is then rolled out into a snake, and the child is asked if either piece of clay has more clay. The child who has not achieved conservation will probably reply that the snake has more clay because it is longer. Figure 4-4 shows a classic means of testing whether a child has developed the schema of conservation. Conservation has implications for children as eyewitnesses. Children who have achieved conservation are less susceptible to leading questions than are children who have not achieved it (Muir-Broddus, King, Downey, & Petersen, 1998).

The effect of sociocultural experiences on the timing of conservation was demonstrated in a study of children in a Mexican village whose parents were pottery makers. The children who normally helped their parents in making pottery acquired conservation (at least of mass) earlier than other children did (Price-Williams, Gordon, & Ramirez, 1969). Moreover, certain nonverbal variations of the conservation of liquid volume problem show that children might develop conservation earlier than indicated by studies that have used the traditional verbal demonstration procedure (Wheldall & Benner, 1993).

In early adolescence, the concrete operational stage might give way to the formal operational stage, which is discussed in the section of this chapter devoted to adolescent development.

concrete operational stage The Piagetian stage, extending from 7 to 11 years of age, during which the child learns to reason logically about objects that are physically present.

transitive inference The application of previously learned relationships to infer new relationships.

conservation The realization that changing the form of a substance does not change its amount.

FIGURE 4-4
Conservation

During the concrete operational stage, children develop an appreciation of conservation. They come to realize that changing the form of something does not change its amount. For example, they realize that pouring water from a tall, narrow container into a short, wide container does not change the amount of water.

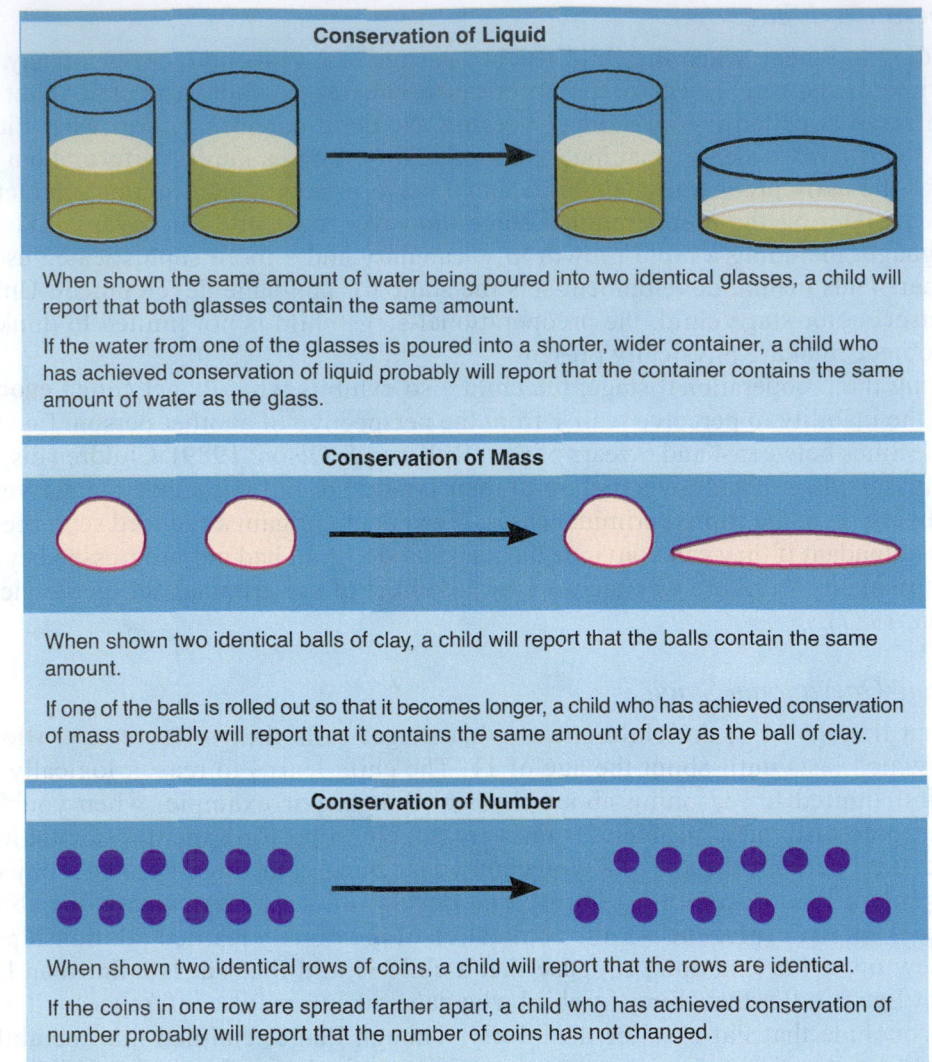

Conservation of Liquid

When shown the same amount of water being poured into two identical glasses, a child will report that both glasses contain the same amount.

If the water from one of the glasses is poured into a shorter, wider container, a child who has achieved conservation of liquid probably will report that the container contains the same amount of water as the glass.

Conservation of Mass

When shown two identical balls of clay, a child will report that the balls contain the same amount.

If one of the balls is rolled out so that it becomes longer, a child who has achieved conservation of mass probably will report that it contains the same amount of clay as the ball of clay.

Conservation of Number

When shown two identical rows of coins, a child will report that the rows are identical.

If the coins in one row are spread farther apart, a child who has achieved conservation of number probably will report that the number of coins has not changed.

Psychosocial Development

Just as Piaget believed that the child passes through stages of cognitive development, psychoanalyst Erik Erikson (1902–1994) believed that the child passes through stages of psychosocial development. Erikson observed that we go through eight distinct stages across the life span. Each stage is marked by a conflict that must be overcome, as described in Table 4-2. Research has supported Erikson's belief that we pass through the stages sequentially—though people differ in the ages at which they pass through them (Vaillant & Milofsky, 1980). Erikson also was one of the first researchers to consider sociocultural differences in psychosocial development, noting that the society, not just the family, affects the child's development (Eagle, 1997). This view was influenced by Erikson's studies of children in Sioux, Yurok, and other Native American cultures.

You also should be aware that there might be sociocultural differences among peoples we normally might consider to be members of a homogenous cultural group. In Central Africa, for example, infants have markedly different experiences among Ngandu farmers and neighboring Aka hunter-gatherers. Aka infants are more likely to be held, and Nkandu infants are more likely to be left alone, possibly contributing to early behavioral differences that are observed between them (Hewlett, Lamb, Shannon, Leyendecker, & Schoelmerich, 1998).

TABLE 4-2 Erikson's Stages of Psychosocial Development

Age	Social Conflict	Successful Resolution of Conflict
Birth–1 year	Trust vs. mistrust	A sense of security and attachment with caregivers.
2 years	Autonomy vs. shame and doubt	A sense of independence from caregivers.
3–5 years	Initiative vs. guilt	The ability to control impulses while still being spontaneous
6 years–puberty	Industry vs. inferiority	A sense of competence in regard to a variety of everyday activities
Adolescence	Identity vs. role confusion	A mature sense of self characterized by living according to one's own values, interests, and goals
Young adulthood	Intimacy vs. isolation	The establishment of mature relationships characterized by personal commitment and emotional attachment
Middle adulthood	Generativity vs. stagnation	An investment in others and concern about their well-being.
Late adulthood	Integrity vs. despair	A sense of acceptance from reflecting on a meaningful life.

Social Attachment and Interpersonal Relationships

Erikson found that the major social conflict of the first year of infancy is **trust versus mistrust**. One of the most important factors in helping the infant develop trust is **social attachment**, a strong emotional relationship between an infant and a caregiver that develops during the first year. Beginning in the 1930s, British psychiatrist John Bowlby (1907–1990) became interested in the effects of early maternal loss or deprivation on later personality development. Much of his theorizing was based on his study of orphans whose parents were killed in World War II. Bowlby favored an evolutionary viewpoint, suggesting that infants have evolved an inborn need for attachment because their survival depends on adult caregivers (Bowlby, 1988). Thus, infants seek to maintain physical proximity and evoke responses from adults through crying, cooing, smiling, and clinging. Similarly, Sigmund Freud assumed that an infant becomes attached to his or her mother for a functional reason—she provides nourishment through nursing.

Freud's assumption was contradicted by research conducted by Harry Harlow and his colleagues on social attachment in rhesus monkeys. Harlow separated infant monkeys from their parents and peers and raised them for 6 months with two "surrogate mothers." The surrogates were wire monkeys with wooden heads. One surrogate was covered with terry cloth and the other was left bare. Harlow found that the monkeys preferred to cling to the cloth-covered surrogate, even though milk was available only from a bottle attached to the bare-wire surrogate (see Figure 4-5). Harlow concluded that physical contact is a more important factor than nourishment in promoting infant attachment (Harlow & Zimmerman, 1959).

Harlow's research findings inspired interest in the possible role of attachment in human psychosocial development. Of course, today's ethical standards would prevent the replication of Harlow's experiment with human infants (and perhaps even with infant monkeys). Much of what we know about attachment in human infants comes from research by Mary Ainsworth (1913–1999) on the mother-infant relationship. She was inspired by her long-time collaboration with Bowlby. Ainsworth conducted her first studies of infant-mother attachment patterns after visiting Uganda. Though cross-cultural studies have found differences in infant behaviors and maternal behaviors and beliefs, the importance of infant-mother attachment patterns has been found to generalize across many cultures (Pierrehumbert et al., 2009).

trust versus mistrust
Erikson's developmental stage in which success is achieved by having a secure social attachment with a caregiver.

social attachment A strong emotional relationship between an infant and a caregiver.

FIGURE 4-5 Social Attachment

Harry Harlow found that infant monkeys became more attached to a terry-cloth-covered wire surrogate mother. Even when fed only from a nipple protruding from the bare-wire surrogate mother, the infant monkeys preferred to cling to the terry-cloth-covered surrogate mother. Harlow concluded that social attachment depended more on physical contact than on the provision of nourishment (Harlow & Zimmerman, 1959).

Source: Harlow Primate Laboratory.

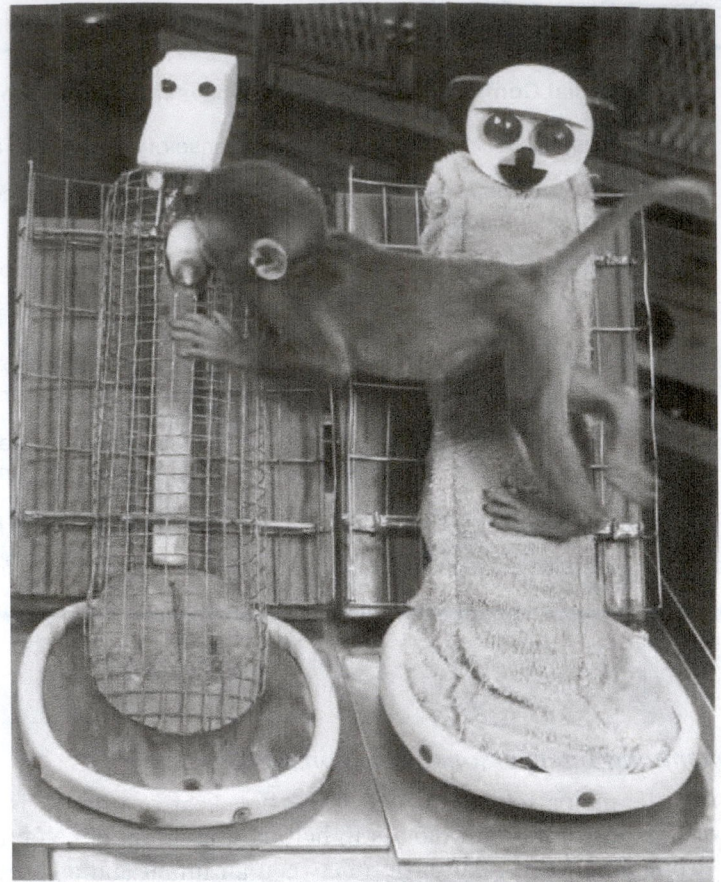

In assessing attachment, Ainsworth made a distinction between *securely attached* and *insecurely attached* infants. This becomes an especially important issue at about 8 months of age, when infants show a strong preference for their mothers over strangers and show separation anxiety. To test this, Ainsworth developed the Strange Situation: The mother and infant are in a room together; the mother leaves the room, a stranger enters the room, the stranger then leaves, and the infant's response to the mother is assessed when she then returns to the room. The securely attached infant seeks physical contact with the mother, yet, despite mildly protesting, freely leaves her to play and explore, using the mother as a secure base. In contrast, the insecurely attached infant clings to the mother, acts either apathetic or highly anxious when separated from her, and is either unresponsive or angry when reunited with her.

A meta-analysis of 21 studies using the Strange Situation with more than 1,000 infants found a moderately strong relationship between the mother's sensitivity and the infant's attachment security (De Wolff & van IJzendoorn, 1997). An infant whose mother is more sensitive, accepting, and affectionate will become more securely attached. Infants who are securely attached, in turn, have better relationships with their peers in childhood and adolescence than infants who are insecurely attached (Gorrese & Ruggieri, 2012). And research indicates that the relationship between maternal responsiveness and the quality of infant attachment generalizes across cultures. Cultural differences have been observed, though, in the maternal and infant behaviors observed in the Strange Situation, especially in measures of visual referencing—infants' willingness to play at a distance while keeping mothers within eyesight—and physical proximity seeking, such as clinging and cuddling (Leyendecker, Lamb, Fracasso, Schölmerich, & Larson, 1997; Zach & Keller, 1999).

Until recently, research on attachment has been limited to use of the Strange Situation in assessing the quality of attachment with the infant's primary caregiver—typically the mother (Field, 1996). Researchers investigating the role of the father in social development have found that paternal interaction also promotes secure attachment in infants. Moreover, families may be described as reflecting a system of attachments between infants, young children, and family members who provide care and engage them in social interaction (van IJzendoorn & DeWolff, 1997).

One study assessed the quality of attachment between mothers, fathers, and two of their children. The Strange Situation was used to measure attachment in the younger children (aged 18 to 24 months), and a questionnaire was used to measure attachment in older children (4 to 5 years of age). Parental caregiving was assessed through naturalistic observation and questionnaires. Results indicated that the majority of the children had developed secure attachments with both parents. Moreover, the quality of parental caregiving predicted secure attachment in only one case: between mothers and their younger children. Maternal caregiving was unrelated to the quality of attachment in older children. And paternal caregiving was unrelated to the quality of attachment of younger and older children (Schneider-Rosen & Burke, 1999). These findings suggest that caregiving is only one avenue by which parents, usually mothers, contribute to the development of a secure attachment in infancy. Moreover, the quality of attachment in older children appears to be related to other aspects of family interaction, such as the quality of parent-child play (Grossmann, Grossmann, Kremmer-Bombik, Scheuerer-Englisch, & Zimmerman, 2002). And, though neglected by early research in attachment, fathers do contribute to the development of attachment in infancy and early childhood.

Researchers also have investigated the stability of attachment security across the life span. Two longitudinal studies found that attachment security is remarkably stable from infancy through adolescence (Beijersbergen, Juffer, Bakermans-Kranenburg, & van IJzendoorn, 2012) and early adulthood (Fraley, Roisman, Booth-LaForce, Owen, & Holland, 2013). In these studies, attachment category had been assessed in infancy. Later, participants completed questionnaires assessing the quality of their attachment or were interviewed by raters blind to their original classification. In both studies, the majority of the securely attached participants' classification was unchanged. But what predicts changes in attachment security? Attachment security can be adversely affected by negative life events that disrupt a family's functioning and the psychological well-being of adults in the household—and in turn their responsiveness and sensitivity to their offspring (Waters, Weinfield, & Hamilton, 2000).

According to Erikson, during the second year the child experiences a conflict involving **autonomy versus shame and doubt**. The child explores the physical environment, begins to learn self-care skills, such as feeding, and tries out budding motor and language abilities. In doing so, the child develops a greater sense of independence from her or his parents. This might account for the popular notion of the "terrible twos," when the child enjoys behaving in a contrary manner and saying no to any request. Parents who stifle efforts at reasonable independence or criticize the child's awkward efforts will promote feelings of shame and doubt. Elementary and high school teachers who support autonomy in their students have a more positively motivating style of teaching (Reeve, Bolt, & Cai, 1999).

At 3 years of age, the child enters the stage that involves the conflict Erikson calls **initiative versus guilt**. The child shows initiative in play, social relations, and exploration of the environment. The child also learns to control his or her impulses, feeling guilt for actions that go beyond limits set by parents. So, at this stage, parents might permit their child to rummage through drawers but not to throw clothing around the bedroom. Thus, the stage of initiative versus guilt deals with the development of a sense of right and wrong.

At about the age of 6, and continuing until about the age of 12, Erikson observed, the child faces the conflict of **industry versus inferiority**. The industrious child who achieves successes during this stage is more likely to feel competent. This is important, because children who feel academically and socially competent are happier than other children and have more positive relationships with their peers (Mouratidis & Michou, 2011). A child who develops a sense of inferiority may lose interest in academics, avoid social interactions, or fail to participate in sports. Successful resolution of the conflict over industry versus inferiority also leads to more positive feelings of vocational competence in high-school students (Gribble, 2000). The importance of this stage in psychosocial development has been demonstrated in both Western and non-Western countries, including the People's Republic of China (Zhang & Nurmi, 2012).

autonomy versus shame and doubt Erikson's developmental stage in which success is achieved by gaining a degree of independence from one's parents.

initiative versus guilt Erikson's developmental stage in which success is achieved by behaving in a spontaneous but socially appropriate way.

industry versus inferiority Erikson's developmental stage in which success is achieved by developing a sense of competency.

Parent-Child Relationships

One of the most important factors in psychosocial development is the approach that parents take to child rearing. This is especially important, given the increasingly diverse family configurations within the United States. Stepparents, for example, who try to develop a friendship with their stepchildren before marrying and who continue their friendship after marrying have relationships with their stepchildren that are more likely to be marked by liking and affection. Stepparents who, instead, try to control their stepchildren are less likely to develop a positive relationship (Ganong, Coleman, Fine, & Martin, 1999). And a frequently expressed concern is whether the children of gay or lesbian parents will suffer from personal or social adjustment problems. An extensive review of research studies found no differences between the children of gay and lesbian parents and those of heterosexual parents on a number of measures of psychosocial adjustment (Wainright, Russell, & Patterson, 2004).

Parenting Style Psychologist Diana Baumrind (1966) distinguished three parenting styles: *permissive*, *authoritarian*, and *authoritative*. Permissive parents set few rules and rarely punish misbehavior. Permissiveness is undesirable because children will be less likely to adopt positive standards of behavior. At the other extreme, authoritarian parents set strict rules and rely on punishment. They respond to questioning of their rules by saying, "Because I say so!"

Authoritarian parenting, likewise, is undesirable. Authoritarian parents exert coercive power over their children, which is arbitrary and domineering (Baumrind, 2010), and which may lead to emotional abuse (Hamarman, Pope, & Czaja, 2002). Authoritarian parents also are more likely to resort to physical discipline—perhaps escalating to physical abuse. Aside from the potential for injury to the child, physical child abuse is associated with lasting emotional effects on the target of the abuse. Abused children have lower self-esteem and are more depressed (Leeson & Nixon, 2011), they tend to be more aggressive (Barry, Lochman, Fite, Wells, & Colder, 2012), and they are more likely to develop behavior problems in adolescence (Thompson, Hollis, & Richards, 2003).

Another form of physical and emotional child abuse is sexual abuse—in many cases by a parent or close family member. A review of research studies published between 1989 and 1999 found that about 10 percent of child abuse cases involve sexual abuse and about 17 percent of women and 8 percent of men had histories of sexual abuse as children (Putnam, 2003). The scourge of child sexual abuse makes it imperative that children be taught to avoid situations that might make them potential targets of sex abusers. Of great concern is the vicious cycle in which abused children become abusive parents. However, though most child abusers were abused as children, only one-third of abused children become abusers—a far cry from claims that being an abused child automatically makes one a future child abuser (Putnam, 2003). So, if you were unfortunate enough to have a history of child abuse, you may very well be able to break the vicious cycle when rearing your own children.

Baumrind has found that the best approach to child rearing is **authoritative parenting** (Baumrind, 1983). Authoritative parents tend to be warm and loving, yet insist that their children behave appropriately. They encourage independence within well-defined limits, show a willingness to explain the reasons for their rules, and permit their children to express verbal disagreement with them. By maintaining a delicate balance between freedom and control, authoritative parents help their children internalize standards of behavior.

Children of authoritative parents report better physical and psychological well-being than children of authoritarian or permissive parents Children who have authoritative parents are more likely to be socially competent, independent, and responsible. They are less likely to drink alcohol or smoke (Piko & Balázs, 2012) , more likely to perform well in school (Mattanah, Pratt, Cowan, & Cowan, 2005), and more likely to be autonomous and display a mastery orientation, which is essential for motivation (Kudo, Longhofer, & Floersch, 2012). But, as cautioned in Chapter 2, be wary of concluding that parenting style causes these effects. Remember that only experimental, not correlational, research permits statements about causality. Perhaps the direction of causality is the opposite of what one would assume. For example, children who behave properly might evoke authoritative parenting.

authoritative parenting
An effective style of parenting in which the parent is warm and loving yet sets well-defined limits that he or she enforces in an appropriate manner.

Research tends to support a positive relationship between authoritative parenting and children's competence. But we still do not know how or why it does so (Darling & Steinberg, 1993). Though the relationship between authoritative parenting and healthy child development appears to be a universal phenomenon (Zhou et al., 2008), we must be aware of cultural differences in child rearing—both between and within societies. Cultural differences in beliefs about parental and child roles and the nature of child rearing influence parents' interactions with their children (Rudy & Grusec, 2001). For example, Chinese parenting may be seen as authoritarian and controlling. Chinese cultural beliefs about parenting stress the concept of *chiao shun*, or training the child to meet social expectations. Thus, parental control may have different meanings in cross-cultural contexts (Chao, 1994; 2001).

Day Care Another important, and sometimes controversial, factor in child rearing is day care. The number of American children placed in day care increased during the 1990s, with more than half of infants and toddlers spending at least 20 hours per week in the care of adults other than their parents (Singer, Fuller, Keiley, & Wolf, 1998). Though day care, overall, seems to have neither strong benefits nor strong detrimental effects (Lamb, 1996), research findings are contradictory in regard to the effects of day care on infants. On the negative side are studies finding that infant day care of more than 20 hours a week in the first year of life is associated with insecure attachment during infancy and greater noncompliance and aggressiveness in early childhood (Hill, Wadlfogel, Brooks-Gunn, & Han, 2005) and that children who enter day care before age 2 later perform more poorly in high school than do children who enter day care after age 2 (Ispa, Thornburg, & Gray, 1990). Of course, we can never be sure about the cause and effect from studies such as these. On the positive side are studies finding that infants in day care do not become insecurely attached (Burchinal, Bryant, Lee, & Ramey, 1992) and that they later do well in school and act less aggressively than other children do (Field, 1991). And a longitudinal study that examined preschoolers' behavior before and after their mothers returned to work showed no negative outcomes (Chase-Lansdale et al., 2003). These contradictory findings reflect the complex nature of the issue, which involves numerous variables, including the characteristics of the infants, their parents, their caretakers, and their day-care settings.

Because many working parents have no choice but to place their infants in day care, it is reassuring to know that research indicates that high-quality infant day care is probably not harmful (Maccoby & Lewis, 2003). According to findings of the National Institute of Child Health and Human Development Study of Early Child Care, "high-quality" means that the number of children and the adult-child ratio are small, the adults practice nonauthoritarian caregiving, and the environment is safe, clean, and stimulating (NICHD Early Child Care Research Network, 1997). High-quality day care has been found to be especially influential in the prevention of behavior problems in low-income boys and African American children (Votruba-Drzal et al., 2010). Though, overall, day care has neither positive nor negative effects on infants or children, poor day care and lack of a stable care provider tend to have a negative effect (Lamb, 1996). But the cost of high-quality day care—if it is, in fact, available—makes it unaffordable to many families. Nonetheless, even day care that is not optimal tends not to have damaging effects on most children. Heredity and home environment tend to outweigh the effects of day care, even when it is not of high quality (Scarr, 1998).

Parental Conflict Children are affected not only by parenting styles and day-care practices but also by the quality of their parents' relationship. A meta-analysis of relevant studies found that parental discord spills over into negative parent-child relationships (Erel & Burman, 1995). Moreover, marital discord can undermine the child's feeling of emotional security and lead to adjustment problems in childhood and adolescence (Klahr, Rueter, McGue, Iacono, & Alexander, 2011) and marital discord in adulthood (Davies & Cummings, 1994).

In some cases marital discord leads to divorce. Because about half of all marriages in the United States end in divorce, many children spend at least part of their childhood primarily with one parent. Though it is easier for two adults to meet the stressful demands of providing the consistent, responsive caregiving that promotes children's well-being, research on single parents indicates that one responsible, emotionally available adult can provide the social and emotional bond that is essential to optimal childhood development (Silverstein & Auerbach, 1999). More than one-third of American children born in the past three decades will experience parental divorce. And they will be more likely to suffer emotional problems, particularly depression (Aseltine, 1996). The long-term effects of divorce on children include greater personal distress and more problems in intimate relationships in adulthood (Christensen & Brooks, 2001).

Because divorce involves so many variables, including the age and economic status of the parents, the age of the children, and the custody arrangements, different combinations of these variables can have different effects on the children (Lamb, 2012). The effects of each combination remain to be determined. It should be noted, however, that children from divorced families have a greater sense of well-being than children from intact families with intense parental conflict (Amato & Keith, 1991). Moreover, divorce itself might induce less distress in children than parental conflict prior to the divorce. A meta-analysis of research studies published during the 1990s on the well-being of children of divorce versus children from intact families found that children of divorce were worse off on variables such as self-esteem, personal conduct, psychological adjustment, interpersonal relationships, and academic performance. These differences were slightly greater in later studies than those reported in studies conducted during the 1980s (Reifman, Villa, Amans, Rethinam, & Telesca, 2001).

Interaction with Peers

Children are affected by their relationships with friends and siblings as well as those with their parents. Friendships provide the context for social and emotional growth (Newcomb & Bagwell, 1995). Secure attachment to both mothers and fathers provides a solid basis for friendships (Verissimo et al., 2011). And childhood friendships may have a bearing on adult emotional well-being. Consider a study that compared young adults who had a best friend in fifth grade and young adults who had no friends in fifth grade. Those who had a best friend had higher self-esteem than those who had no friends. And those who had no best friend were more likely to have symptoms of psychological disorders (Bagwell, Newcomb, & Bukowski, 1998). Of course, you must be careful not to assume that there is a causal relationship in which friendships promote healthy personalities. Perhaps, instead, children with certain personalities are simply more likely to make friends and to have higher self-esteem.

Few children develop friendships before the age of 3, and 95 percent of childhood friendships are between children of the same sex (Hartup, 1989). Girls tend to have fewer, but more intimate, friendships than boys do (Berndt & Hoyle, 1985). A meta-analysis of children's peer relations found that socially and academically competent children are popular with their peers. In contrast, children who are withdrawn, aggressive, or academically deficient tend to be rejected by their peers (Newcomb, Bukowski, & Pattee, 1993).

Peer relationships in childhood involve play. A classic study (Parten, 1932) found that the interactive play of children gradually increased between 2 and 4 years of age, but that throughout this period, children engaged mainly in parallel play, as when two children in a sandbox play separately from each other with pails and shovels. Parallel play provides a transition into social play, in which children play interactively, with children as old as 4 years alternating between the two (Anderson, 2001). There also are cultural differences in play. For example, whereas gender-segregated play appears to be a universal phenomenon, there are cultural differences in the extent to which children engage in cross-sex play (Aydt & Corsaro, 2003).

Gender-Role Development

gender roles Behaviors that are considered appropriate for women or men in a given culture.

One of the most frequently studied aspects of psychosocial development in childhood is the development of **gender roles**, which are behavior patterns that are considered appropriate for men or women in a given culture. The first formal theory of gender-role development was put forth by Sigmund Freud. He assumed that the resolution of what he called the Oedipus (in the case of boys) and Electra (in the case of girls) complexes (discussed in Chapter 13) at age 5 or 6 led the child to internalize the gender role of the same-sex parent. The Oedipus and Electra complexes begin with the child's sexual attraction to the other-sex parent. According to Freud, because the child fears punishment for desiring the other-sex parent, the child comes to identify with the same-sex parent. But studies of children show that children develop gender roles even when they live in single-parent households. Because of the lack of research support for Freud's theory, most researchers favor more recent theories of gender-role development.

Social learning theory stresses the importance of observational learning, rewards, and punishment. Thus, social learning theorists assume that the child learns gender-relevant behaviors by observing gender-role models and by being rewarded for appropriate, and corrected or punished for inappropriate, gender-role behavior. This process of gender typing begins on the very day of birth and continues through the life span. In one study, new parents were interviewed within 24 hours of the birth of their first child. Though there are no observable differences in the physical appearance of male and female newborns whose genitals are covered, newborn daughters were more likely to be described by their parents as cute, weak, and uncoordinated than newborn sons were (Rubin, Provenzano, & Luria, 1974). But an influential review of research by Eleanor Maccoby found that parents reported that they did not treat their sons and daughters differently (Maccoby & Jacklin, 1974). Of course, parents might believe that they treat their daughters and sons the same, while actually treating them differently. A meta-analysis, however, supported Maccoby by finding that gender-role development seems, at best, weakly related to differences in how parents rear their sons and daughters (Lytton & Romney, 1991).

Parents are not the only social influences contributing to gender-role development. As noted earlier in this chapter, children tend to socialize with same-sex peers and engage in sex-segregated play. Children reward each other for engaging in gender-appropriate activities and punish or exclude children who engage in cross-gender behavior. Moreover, this peer pressure is stronger for boys than for girls. Considering the inconsistent evidence for the role of differential parental reinforcement of children's behaviors, it is very likely that peers may wield a stronger influence on gender-role development than do parents (Bussey & Bandura, 1999). One such factor is the sex of one's siblings. A large-scale study of 3-year-olds found that both boys and girls with an older brother were more masculine and less feminine. Boys with an older sister were more feminine but not less masculine. And girls with an older sister were less masculine but not more feminine (Rust, Golombok, Hines, Johnston, & Golding, 2000).

An alternative to the social learning theory of gender-role development is Sandra Bem's (1981) **gender schema theory**, which combines elements of social learning theory and the cognitive perspective. Bem's theory holds that people differ in the schemas they use to organize their social world. People may have schemas relevant to age, ethnicity, gender, occupations, or any number of social categories. *Gender schemas* are specialized cognitive structures that assimilate and organize information about women and men. Children are *gender schematic* if they categorize people, behavior, activities, and interests as masculine or feminine. In contrast, *gender aschematic* children do not categorize these types of information into masculine and feminine categories. Gender schematic individuals are likely to notice, attend to, and remember people's behavior and attributes that are relevant to gender. For example, one study found that gender schematic adults recalled more gender-stereotypic information than did gender aschematic adults (Renn & Calvert, 1993).

Gender schemas develop early. One study found that toddlers were able to label same-sex toys—operationally defined as touching a masculine or feminine toy—as early as 2 years of age (Levy, 1999). Social experiences can modify the development of gender schema, though, as shown in studies of traditional and egalitarian families. A meta-analysis of 48 studies found that parents' gender schemas were correlated with their children's gender schemas. Though the effect size was small, traditional parents were more likely than nontraditional parents to have children who thought about themselves and others in gender-typed ways (Tenenbaum & Leaper, 2002). Gender schema theory provides a glimpse into the development of gender stereotypes and how gender stereotypes influence social behavior (Deaux & Major, 1987).

social learning theory
A theory of learning that assumes that people learn behaviors mainly through observation and mental processing of information.

gender schema theory
A theory of gender-role development that combines aspects of social learning theory and the cognitive perspective.

Moral Development

American psychologists have researched and tested the development of morality in children and adults for more than a century (Wendorf, 2001). Today, the most influential theory of moral development is Lawrence Kohlberg's (1981) cognitive-developmental theory.

Kohlberg's Theory of Moral Development Kohlberg's theory, formulated in the 1960s, is based on Piaget's (1932) proposal that a person's level of moral development depends on his or her level of cognitive development. Piaget found that children, in making moral judgments, are at first more concerned with the consequences of actions. Thus, a young child might insist that accidentally breaking ten dishes is morally worse than purposely breaking one dish. As children become more cognitively sophisticated, they base their moral judgments more on a person's intentions than on the consequences of the person's behavior. Kohlberg assumed that as individuals become more cognitively sophisticated, they reach more complex levels of moral reasoning. Research findings indicate that adequate cognitive development is, indeed, a prerequisite for each level of moral reasoning (Walker, 1986).

Kohlberg, agreeing with Piaget, developed a stage theory of moral development based on the individual's level of moral reasoning. Kohlberg determined the individual's level of moral reasoning by presenting a series of stories, each of which includes a moral dilemma. The person must suggest a resolution of the dilemma and give reasons for choosing that resolution. The person's stage of moral development depends not on the resolution, but instead on the reasons given for that resolution. What is your response to the following dilemma proposed by Kohlberg? Your reasoning in resolving it would reveal your level of moral development:

In Europe, a woman was near death from a very bad disease, a rare kind of cancer. There was one drug that the doctors thought might save her. It was a special form of radium that a druggist in the same town had recently discovered. The drug was expensive to make, but the druggist was charging 10 times what the drug cost him to make. He paid 200 dollars for the radium and charged two thousand dollars for a small dose of the drug. The sick woman's husband, Heinz, went to everyone he knew to borrow the money, but he could get together only about one thousand dollars, which was half of what it cost. He told the druggist that his wife was dying and asked him to sell it cheaper or let him pay later. But the druggist said, "No, I discovered the drug, and I am going to make money from it." So Heinz got desperate and broke into the man's store to steal the drug for his wife. (Kohlberg, 1981, p. 12)

The levels of moral development represented by particular responses to this dilemma are presented in Table 4-3. Kohlberg has identified three levels: the *preconventional*, the *conventional*, and the *postconventional*. Each level contains two stages, making a total of six stages of moral development. As Piaget noted, as we progress to higher levels of moral reasoning, we become more concerned with the actor's motives than with the consequences of the actor's actions. This was supported by a study of moral judgments about aggressive behavior, which found that high school and college students at higher stages of moral reasoning were more concerned with the aggressor's motivation than were students at lower stages (Berkowitz, Mueller, Schnell, & Padberg, 1986).

People at the **preconventional level** of moral reasoning, which typically characterizes children up to 9 years old, are mainly concerned with the consequences of moral behavior to themselves. In stage 1, the child has a punishment and obedience orientation, in which moral behavior serves to avoid punishment. In stage 2, the child has an instrumental-relativist orientation, in which moral behavior serves to get rewards or favors in return, as in "you scratch my back and I'll scratch yours."

People at the **conventional level** of moral reasoning, usually reached in late childhood or early adolescence, uphold conventional laws and values by favoring obedience to parents and authority figures. Kohlberg calls stage 3 the good boy/nice girl orientation because the child assumes that moral behavior is desirable because it gains social approval, especially from parents. Kohlberg calls stage 4 the society-maintaining orientation, in which the adolescent views moral behavior as a way to do one's duty, show respect for authority, and maintain the social order. These four stages have even been used to show differences in moral reasoning among members of the United States Congress about political issues (Shapiro, 1995).

At the end of adolescence, some of those who reach Piaget's formal operational stage of cognitive development also reach the **postconventional level** of morality. At this level of moral reasoning, people make moral judgments based on ethical principles that might conflict with their self-interest or with the maintenance of social order. In stage 5, the social-contract orientation, the person assumes that adherence to laws is in the long-term best interest of society but that unjust laws might have to be violated. The U.S. Constitution is based on this view. Stage 6, the highest stage of moral reasoning, is called the universal ethical principle orientation. The few people at this stage assume that moral reasoning must uphold human dignity and their conscience—even if that brings them into conflict with their society's laws or values. Thus, an abolitionist who helped runaway American slaves flee to Canada in the 19th century would be acting at this highest level of moral reasoning.

preconventional level
In Kohlberg's theory, the level of moral reasoning characterized by concern with the consequences that behavior has for oneself.

conventional level
In Kohlberg's theory, the level of moral reasoning characterized by concern with upholding laws and conventional values and by favoring obedience to authority.

postconventional level
In Kohlberg's theory, the level of moral reasoning characterized by concern with obeying mutually agreed-upon laws and by the need to uphold human dignity.

TABLE 4-3 Kohlberg's Theory of Moral Development

Level of Moral Development	Stage of Moral Development
Preconventional level: Concern with consequences of behavior for oneself	**Stage 1:** Moral choices made to avoid punishment
	Stage 2: Moral choices made to gain rewards
Conventional level: Concern with social laws and values	**Stage 3:** Moral choices made to gain social approval
	Stage 4: Moral choices made to fulfill duty, respect authority, and maintain social order
Postconventional level: Concern with moral principles, agreed-upon laws, and human dignity	**Stage 5:** Moral choices made to follow mutually agreed-upon principles and ensure mutual respect of others
	Stage 6: Moral choices made to uphold human dignity and one's own ethical principles

Criticisms of Kohlberg's Theory Kohlberg's theory has received mixed support from research studies. Children do appear to proceed through the stages he described in the order he described (Walker, 1989). And a study of adolescents on an Israeli kibbutz found that, as predicted by Kohlberg's theory, their stages of moral development were related to their stages of cognitive development (Snarey, Reimer, & Kohlberg, 1985). But Kohlberg's theory has been criticized on several grounds. First, the theory explains moral reasoning, not moral action. A person's moral actions might not reflect her or his moral reasoning. Yet some research supports a positive relationship between moral reasoning and moral actions. For example, one study found that college students who believed that the use of illegal drugs was morally wrong based on principle were, in fact, less likely to use drugs than peers who believed that illegal drug use was a matter of simple personal choice (Abide, Richards, & Ramsay, 2001).

A second criticism is that the situation, not just the person's level of moral reasoning, plays a role in moral decision making and moral actions. This was demonstrated in a study of male college students who performed a task in which their goal was to keep a stylus above a light moving in a triangular pattern—a tedious, difficult task. When provided with a strong enough temptation, even those at higher stages of moral reasoning succumbed to cheating (Malinowski & Smith, 1985).

Other critics insist that Kohlberg's theory might not be generalizable beyond Western cultures, with their greater emphasis on individualism (Sachdeva, Singh, & Medin, 2011). This criticism has been countered by Kohlberg and his colleagues. They found that when people in other cultures are interviewed in their own languages, using moral dilemmas based on situations that are familiar to them, Kohlberg's theory holds up well. Moreover, in other cultures, the stages of moral reasoning unfold in the order claimed by Kohlberg. For example, a study of Taiwanese children and young adults found that they progressed through the moral stages in the order and at the rate found in Americans (Lei, 1994). Nonetheless, postconventional moral reasoning is not found in all cultures (Snarey, Reimer, & Kohlberg, 1985).

Still another criticism of Kohlberg's theory is that it is biased in favor of a male view of morality. The main proponent of this criticism has been Carol Gilligan (1982). She points out that Kohlberg's theory was based on research on male participants, and she claims that Kohlberg's theory favors the view that morality is concerned with detached, legalistic justice (an allegedly masculine orientation) rather than with involved, interpersonal caring (an allegedly feminine orientation).

Thus, Gilligan believes that women's moral reasoning is colored by their desire to relieve distress, whereas men's moral reasoning is based on their desire to uphold rules and laws. Because Kohlberg's theory favors a male view, women are unfairly considered lower in moral development. Despite some research support for Gilligan's position (Garmon, Basinger, Gregg, & Gibbs, 1996), there does not appear to be a moral chasm between men and women—there are no significant differences between men and women in their use of justice and care orientations. For example, a recent study lent only mixed support to Gilligan's position. More than 200 men and women rated hypothetical mixed (containing elements of both care and justice orientations) and real-life (conflicts they had personally experienced) moral dilemmas. As Gilligan would predict, women scored higher on care reasoning and men scored higher on justice reasoning on the hypothetical mixed dilemmas. However, there were no gender differences in the ratings of the real-life moral dilemmas. Regardless of participant sex, real-life moral dilemmas involving ongoing personal relationships elicited care reasoning. And real-life moral dilemmas concerning the self or casual acquaintances elicited justice reasoning (Skoe, Cumberland, Eisenberg, Hansen, & Perry, 2002). Moreover, a meta-analysis found that females exhibit a care orientation only slightly more than males, and males exhibit a justice orientation only slightly more than females (Jaffee & Hyde, 2000).

Other critics claim that both Kohlberg's and Gilligan's theories are simplistic and do not consider enough of the factors that influence moral development. These critics believe that an adequate theory of moral development must consider the interaction of cultural, religious, and biological factors (Woods, 1996).

Adolescent Development

Change marks the entire life span, though it is more dramatic at certain stages than at others. Biological factors have a more obvious influence during adolescence and late adulthood than during early and middle adulthood. Social factors exert their greatest influence through the **social clock**, which includes major events that occur at certain times in the typical life cycle in a given culture. In Western cultures, for example, major milestones of the social clock include graduation from high school, leaving home, finding a job, getting married, having a child, and retiring from work. Being late in reaching these milestones can cause emotional distress (Rook, Catalano, & Dooley, 1989).

There also is some evidence for cross-cultural and cohort differences in young adults' beliefs about the timing of life events. For example, one study of Australian undergraduates found that the "best" ages associated with adult milestones differed from American age norms of the 1960s. Moreover, participants suggested later ages for marriage and grandparenthood and a wider age range for retirement (Peterson, 1996).

Cultural and historical factors can have different effects on different cohorts. Depending on your cohort, your adolescent and adult experiences might differ from those of other cohorts. A Swiss study compared young adult participants born between World Wars I and II (the "Between the Wars" cohort) participants born in the years immediately after World War II (the "Early Baby Boomers" cohort) and participants born in the early 1970s (the "Generation X" cohort) regarding their views concerning the main tasks of young adulthood. The largest difference was between the "Between the Wars" cohort and the "Generation X" cohort. Whereas the "Between the Wars" cohort placed relatively more value on work and family, the "Generation X" cohort placed relatively more value on higher education and leisure-time activities (Bangerter, Grob, & Krings, 2001). Thus, as you read, keep in mind that although common biological factors and social clocks might make generations somewhat similar in their development, cultural and historical factors that are unique to particular cohorts can make them somewhat different from cohorts that precede or succeed them.

Adolescence is unknown in many developing countries. Instead, adulthood begins with the onset of puberty and is commonly celebrated with traditional rites of passage. With the advent of universal free education and child labor laws in Western countries, children, who otherwise would have entered the adult work world by the time they reached puberty, entered a period of life during which they developed an adult body yet maintained a childlike dependence on parents. Formal study of **adolescence**, the transitional period between childhood and adulthood, began with the work of G. Stanley Hall (1904).

Physical Development

Recall your own adolescence. What you might recall most vividly are the rapid physical changes associated with **puberty** (from the Latin word for "adulthood"). As illustrated in Figure 4-6, puberty is marked by a rapid increase in height; girls show a growth spurt between the ages of 10 and 12, and boys show a growth spurt between the ages

social clock The typical or expected timing of major life events in a given culture.

adolescence The transitional period lasting from the onset of puberty to the beginning of adulthood.

puberty The period of rapid physical change that occurs during adolescence, including the development of the ability to reproduce sexually.

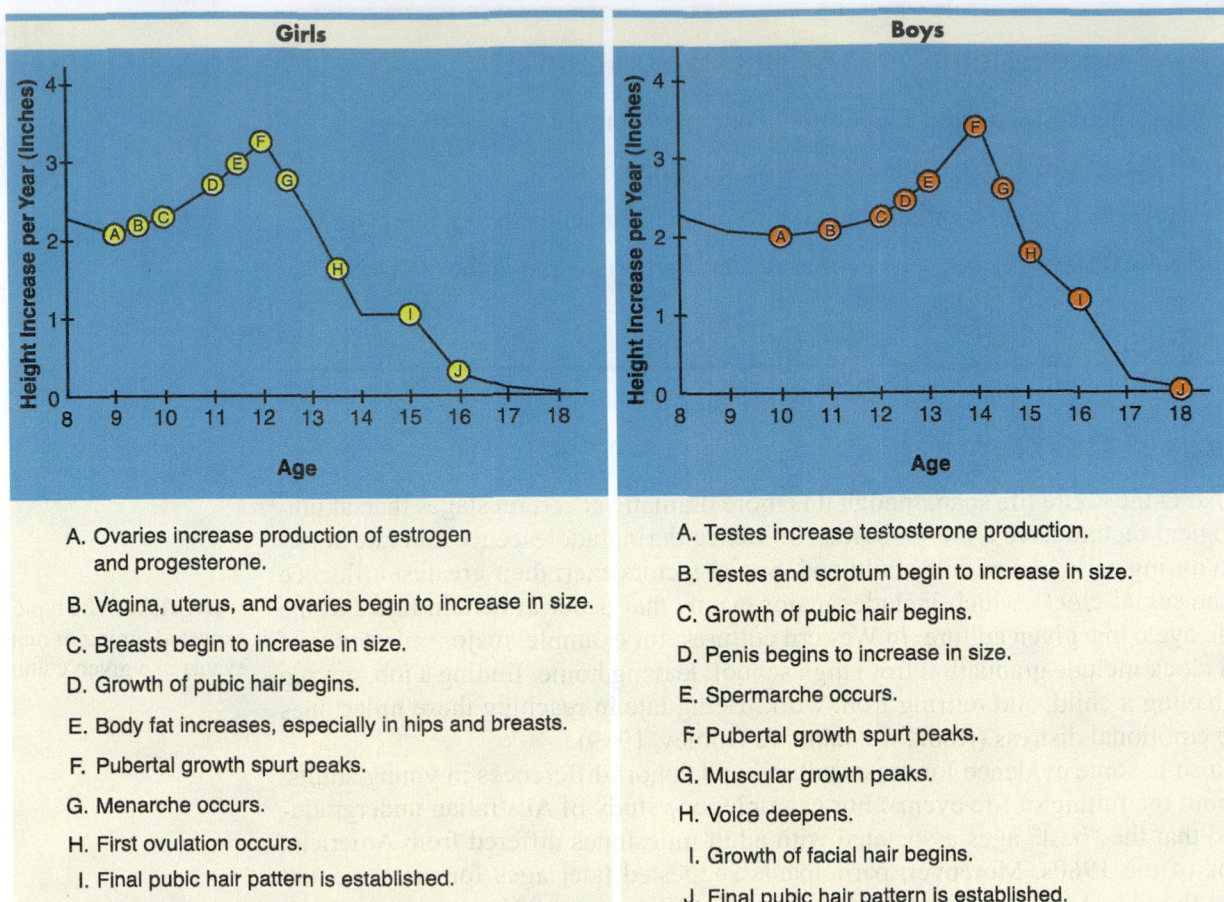

FIGURE 4-6 The Adolescent Growth Spurt and Pubertal Change

The onset of puberty is associated with a rapid increase in height. The growth spurt of girls occurs earlier than that of boys. Note that the ages given for the timing of particular physical changes during puberty are based on averages. Individual pubertal changes may vary from these averages without falling outside the range of normal development.

Girls

A. Ovaries increase production of estrogen and progesterone.

B. Vagina, uterus, and ovaries begin to increase in size.

C. Breasts begin to increase in size.

D. Growth of pubic hair begins.

E. Body fat increases, especially in hips and breasts.

F. Pubertal growth spurt peaks.

G. Menarche occurs.

H. First ovulation occurs.

I. Final pubic hair pattern is established.

J. Full breast growth is established.

Boys

A. Testes increase testosterone production.

B. Testes and scrotum begin to increase in size.

C. Growth of pubic hair begins.

D. Penis begins to increase in size.

E. Spermarche occurs.

F. Pubertal growth spurt peaks.

G. Muscular growth peaks.

H. Voice deepens.

I. Growth of facial hair begins.

J. Final pubic hair pattern is established.

of 12 and 14. The physical changes of puberty also include the maturation of primary and secondary sex characteristics. Primary sex characteristics are hormone-induced physical changes that enable us to engage in sexual reproduction. These changes include growth of the penis and testes in males and the vagina, uterus, and ovaries in females. Secondary sex characteristics are stimulated by sex hormones but are unrelated to sexual reproduction. Pubertal males develop facial hair, deeper voices, and larger muscles. Pubertal females develop wider hips, larger breasts, and more rounded physiques, caused in part by increased deposits of fat.

These physical changes are triggered in girls by a spurt in the secretion of the sex hormone estrogen between ages 10 and 11 and in boys by increased levels of the sex hormone testosterone between ages 12 and 13. Boys generally experience **spermarche**, their first ejaculation, between the ages of 13 and 15, typically while asleep (so-called nocturnal emissions). Girls exhibit earlier physical maturation than boys and generally experience **menarche**, their first menstrual period, between the ages of 11 and 13 (Paikoff & Brooks-Gunn, 1991). The average age at menarche is lower than in the past; this decline in the age of menarche has been attributed to improved health and nutrition. For example, the average age of menarche declined from 16.5 to 13.7 years over a span of 40 years in two rural counties of China. During this period of modernization, the health and living conditions of the rural Chinese population improved dramatically

spermarche The first ejaculation, usually occurring between the ages of 13 and 15.

menarche The beginning of menstruation, usually occurring between the ages of 11 and 13.

(Graham, Larsen, & Xu, 1999). And increasing rates of obesity across the globe are associated with a decline in the average age of menarche. The Health Behavior in School-Aged Children study assessed the relationship between obesity and the average age of menarche among girls in 34 countries. The researchers concluded that most cross-cultural differences in the average age of menarche were attributable to childhood obesity (Currie et al., 2012).

Though the dramatic physical changes of puberty are caused by hormonal changes, adolescent mood swings are not necessarily the byproducts of hormones run wild. Hormone fluctuations affect the adolescent's moods, but life events have a greater effect (Brooks-Gunn & Warren, 1989). Of course, the physical changes of puberty, including acne, rapid growth, and physical maturation, can themselves produce emotional distress. This is especially true if the adolescent is unprepared for them or is made to feel self-conscious by peers or parents. Boys find it difficult enough to deal with scruffy facial hair, unwanted penile erections, and voices that crack, without being made more anxious about those changes. Girls, likewise, find it difficult enough to discover suddenly that they have enlarged breasts, a monthly menstrual cycle, and possibly tower several inches above many of their male peers.

The timing of puberty may influence how adolescents respond to these physical changes. Research findings on the relative effects of early versus late puberty have been inconsistent, in part because of the different methodologies that have been used. Cross-sectional research findings indicate that late maturation is, overall, more negative for both males and females in regard to behavior and personal adjustment, but longitudinal research findings indicate that the timing of puberty, overall, has neither positive nor negative effects on adolescents (Dorn, Susman, & Ponirakis, 2003). Nonetheless, at times early maturation may bring with it certain problems. For example, boys and girls who enter puberty early drink more alcohol and become intoxicated more often than their peers who do not mature early. This correlation is stronger for boys than for girls (Kaltiala-Heino, Koivisto, Marttunen, & Fröjd, 2011).

Cognitive Development

Adolescent cognitive development is less dramatic, with no obvious surge in mental abilities to match the surge in physical development. According to Piaget's theory, at about 11 years of age, some adolescents pass from the concrete operational stage to

Puberty

Because adolescents enter puberty at different ages, groups of young adolescents include individuals who vary greatly in height and physical maturity. As a consequence, a typical middle-school class might appear to include a wider age range than it actually does.

Source: Tracy Whiteside/Shutterstock.com.

formal operational stage
The Piagetian stage, beginning at about age 11, marked by the ability to use abstract reasoning and to solve problems by testing hypotheses.

the **formal operational stage**. A person who reaches this stage is able to reason about abstract, not just concrete, situations. The adolescent who has reached the formal operational stage can apply abstract principles and make predictions about hypothetical situations. In contrast, an adolescent still in the concrete operational stage would rely more on blind trial and error than on a formal approach to problem solving.

To appreciate this, imagine that you are given four chemicals and are asked to produce a purple liquid by mixing them—but it is left up to you to discover the proper mixture. People at the concrete operational level would approach this task in an unsystematic manner, hoping that through trial and error they would hit upon the correct combination of chemicals. In contrast, people at the formal operational level would approach it systematically, perhaps by mixing each possible combination of two of the chemicals, then each possible combination of three, and finally all four. Thus, people who reach the formal operational stage perform better on more complex intellectual pursuits. A study of seventh and eighth graders found that those in transition between the concrete operational stage and the formal operational stage showed better understanding of abstract concepts presented in a physics textbook than did those still in the concrete operational stage (Renner, Abraham, Grzybowski, & Marek, 1990).

Piaget found that so few people reach the formal operational stage that he gave up his earlier belief that it was universal. Those who reach that stage are more likely to have been exposed to scientific thinking in their academic courses (Rogoff & Chavajay, 1995). Though educational interventions have been effective in fostering the development of formal operational thought in developing countries such as Pakistan (Iqbal & Shayer, 2000), people from cultures that do not stress science in their school curricula are less likely to achieve the formal operational stage.

Psychosocial Development

Erik Erikson noted that psychosocial development continues through adolescence into adulthood and old age. Perhaps the most important psychosocial tasks of adolescence are the formation of a personal identity and the development of healthy relationships with peers and parents.

Identity Achievement

identity versus role confusion
Erikson's developmental stage in which success is achieved by establishing a sense of personal identity.

According to Erikson (1963), the most important feat of adolescence is the resolution of the conflict of **identity versus role confusion**. The adolescent develops a sense of identity by adopting her or his own set of values and social behaviors. Erikson believed this is a normal part of finding answers to questions related to one's identity, such as these: What do I believe is important? What are my goals in life?

Erikson's emphasis on the importance of the identity crisis might reflect, in large part, his own life history. He was born in Germany, the child of a Danish Christian mother and father. Erik's father abandoned his mother while she was pregnant with him. She then married a Jewish physician, Theodore Homburger. Erik was given his new father's surname, making him Erik Homburger. But it was not until Erik reached adolescence that he was told that Homburger was not his biological father (Hopkins, 1995).

Erikson, uncomfortable among Jews and Christians alike, sought to find himself by traveling in European artistic and intellectual circles, as many young adults did in the 1920s. Eventually he met Anna Freud, Sigmund's daughter and an eminent psychoanalyst herself. Erikson underwent psychoanalysis with her almost daily for 3 years. In 1933 Erikson changed his name to Erik Homburger Erikson and left to pursue a career in the United States. His long, rich life was a testament to his success in finding his identity as a husband, writer, teacher, and psychoanalyst.

To appreciate the task that confronts the adolescent in developing an identity, consider the challenge of having to adjust simultaneously to a new body, a new mind, and a new social world. The adolescent body is larger and sexually mature. The adolescent mind can question the nature of reality and consider abstract concepts regarding ethical, political, and religious beliefs. The social world of the adolescent requires achieving a balance between childlike dependence and adultlike independence. This also manifests itself in the conflict between parental and peer influences. Children's values mirror their parents', but adolescents' values oscillate between those of their parents and those of their peers. Adolescents move from a world guided by parental wishes to a world in which they are confronted by a host of choices regarding sex, drugs, friends, schoolwork, and other things. Erikson's theory of adolescence has received support from longitudinal studies showing that, in fact, adolescents typically move from a state of role confusion to a state of identity achievement (Streitmatter, 1993). Among the factors that are related to successful identity achievement are positive parental involvement with the adolescent and active interest in the adolescent's school performance and social relationships (Brittain & Lerner, 2013).

There also is some evidence that Erikson's theory may generalize to adolescents' experiences across cultures. One study found that Hong Kong adolescents who achieved a sense of identity were more prosocial and exhibited fewer antisocial behaviors than adolescents who had not (Ma, Shek, Cheung, & Oi, 2000). And African adolescents who achieved a sense of identity reported more extensive exploration of career options and held broader vocational interests than adolescents who had not (Schmitt-Rodermund & Vondracek, 1999). Successful identity achievement is positively related to personal adjustment (Hunsberger, Pratt, & Pancer, 2001). Failure to achieve a sense of identity is associated with emotional distress, including feelings of emptiness and depression (Taylor & Goritsas, 1994).

But Carol Gilligan (1982) believes that Erikson's theory applies more to male than to female adolescents. She points out that Erikson based his theory on studies of men, who tend to place a greater premium on the development of self-sufficiency than do women, who tend to place a greater premium on intimate relationships in which there is mutual caring. Thus, female adolescents who fail to develop an independent identity at the same time as their male age peers might unfairly be considered abnormal. One recent study compared self-descriptions and personality attributes of male and female undergraduates. Self-descriptions of men and women who had achieved identity were more similar than the self-descriptions of men and women who had not. However, gender differences were found in the relationship of personality variables that have been thought to contribute to identity development (Cramer, 2000). Though intimate relationships are important to both men's and women's well-being, psychologists studying gender differences in identity development believe that women's identity development emphasizes the self in relation to others.

Psychologists also have investigated the nature of ethnic identity, particularly among immigrants and members of ethnic minority groups (Phinney, 1990). Studies of ethnic and American identity in multi-ethnic samples have found that ethnic identity is positively correlated with self-esteem—regardless of participants' ethnicities. Thus, positive attitudes toward one's ethnic group contribute to high self-esteem. Ethnic and

Identity Formation

During adolescence our peers play a large role in the development of our sense of identity. Generation after generation, this has distressed North American parents—though, as adolescents, their stylistic choices may have upset their own parents.

Sources: Left: Gina Smith/ Shutterstock.com. *Right:* marcogarrincha/Shutterstock. com.

American identity, however, tend to be strongly correlated only for European American participants (Phinney, Cantu, & Kurtz, 1997). Ethnic identity was found to be positively correlated with many measures of psychological adjustment, including optimism, mastery, and coping, in a multi-ethnic sample of over 5,400 American adolescents (Roberts et al., 1999). This research has important implications for members of ethnic minority groups, many of whom consider themselves to be bicultural. One study assessed ethnic identity and measures of acculturation among 1,367 American undergraduates, most of whom were of Mexican origin. Ethnic identity was strongest for first-generation and less acculturated participants. And higher levels of acculturation were associated with a diminished sense of ethnic identity and belongingness. More positive outcomes were associated with participants who were high in biculturalism—that is, feeling a part of both majority American and traditional Mexican cultures. Participants who scored high on a measure of biculturalism had higher ethnic identity scores and were more socially oriented than participants who scored low on biculturalism (Cuellar, Roberts, Nyberg, & Maldonado, 1997).

Once again, this demonstrates the importance of considering the cultural context of theoretical positions. For example, the Inuit people of Canada see personal identity as inseparable from the physical, animal, and human environments. The Inuits would find it maladaptive if members of their culture formed more individualistic identities (Stairs, 1992).

Social Relationships

Because the adolescent is dependent on parents while seeking an independent identity, adolescence has traditionally been considered a period of conflict between parents and children, or what G. Stanley Hall called a period of "storm and stress." Parents might be shocked by their adolescent's preferences in dress, music, and slang. In trying out various styles and values, adolescents are influenced by the cohort to which they belong. Thus, male adolescents shocked their parents by wearing pompadours in the 1950s, shoulder-length hair in the 1970s, spiked haircuts in the 1990s, and piercings and tattoos at the turn of the 21st century. Though parental conflict, moodiness, and a tendency for engaging in risky behavior are more common in adolescence, there are considerable cross-cultural differences. Adolescents in traditional cultures tend to maintain traditional values and practices—even those experiencing the rapid pace of modernization and globalization. Moreover, there are considerable individual differences in behavioral and mood disruptions among adolescents (Arnett, 1999).

Despite the normal conflicts between parental values and adolescent behaviors, most adolescents have positive relations with their parents. In general, adolescence is a time of only slightly increased parent-child conflict. Though the emotional intensity of parent-child conflicts is somewhat higher at puberty, the rate of parent-child conflict declines over the adolescent years (Laursen, Coy, & Collins, 1998) as both adolescents and their parents adopt more positive conflict resolution styles (Van Doom, Branje, & Meeus, 2011).

Adolescents' increasing autonomy and involvement with their peers often leads to disagreements with their parents about family obligations. For example, Jean Phinney and Anthony Ong assessed beliefs about family obligations in a large sample of Vietnamese-American and European-American adolescents and their parents. Regardless of socioeconomic status or cultural background, disagreement over family obligations was negatively correlated with the adolescent participants' life satisfaction (Phinney & Ong, 2003). Conflicts also may be more frequent among first-generation immigrants and their children due to differential rates of acculturation within the family. Compared to non-immigrant families, immigrant Armenian, Vietnamese, and Mexican parents were more likely to stress family obligations than their children. Moreover, among immigrant families, intergenerational discrepancies in familial values increased as a function of time spent living in the United States (Phinney, Ong, & Madden, 2000).

In regard to their friendships, adolescents have more intimate friendships than do younger children, possibly because they are more capable of sharing their thoughts and feelings and understanding those of others. Adolescents who fail to develop intimate friendships are especially prone to loneliness. In fact, adolescent friendships are more important than relationships with family members in preventing loneliness (Ciftci Uruk & Demir, 2003). Though the level of intimate feelings expressed by boys and girls when interacting with their same-sex friends does not differ, there are gender differences in the ways adolescents establish and experience intimate friendships. Adolescent girls tend to establish intimacy through self-disclosure and discussion, whereas adolescent boys tend to establish intimacy through shared activities (McNelles & Connolly, 1999).

Adolescence is associated with an important biologically based psychosocial conflict between the powerful urge to engage in sexual relations and societal values against premarital sex. The proportion of sexually active American adolescents increased steadily from the 1930s, when less than 10 percent had premarital sex, to today, when most older adolescents engage in it. But the sexes differ in their sexual attitudes. Male adolescents are more willing to engage in casual sex, whereas female adolescents are more likely to prefer sex as part of a committed relationship, though this gender difference is not large and gender similarities in sexual attitudes have increased over time (Petersen & Hyde, 2010; also see Chapter 11).

Psychologists recently have begun correcting the one-dimensional view of adolescent erotic relationships as consisting solely of sexual behavior. More researchers are focusing on the nature of adolescent romance, not just sexual behavior, including parental influences and changes in the nature of adolescent romance (Furman, 2002). A study of over 200 college students found that the quality of their romantic relationships was related to the nature of their relationships with their parents. Students who felt a low degree of trust, communication, and closeness in their relationships with their parents tended to feel devalued, disrespected, and emotionally controlled by their current romantic partner. Moreover, students who were unhappy in their current romantic relationship reported that their past relationships with their parents were marked by frequent, intense, and poorly resolved conflicts. A key factor moderating the relationship between their past negative relationships with their parents and their current romantic relationships was the expectation that their romantic partner would ultimately reject them. Such a pessimistic expectation may lead individuals to engage in behaviors that harm their romantic relationships (Gray, 2001).

Adolescence also is a period often involving experimentation with, or chronic use of, psychoactive drugs, including alcohol, nicotine, cocaine, and marijuana. Adolescent drug use, such as smoking, is influenced more by peers than by parents (Bauman, Carver, & Gleiter, 2001). But parental involvement, including monitoring their children's behavior, can help counter the possibility of the adolescent's being initiated into smoking by peers (Simons-Morton, 2002). The importance of avoiding unwise use of psychoactive drugs is highlighted by the association of adolescent smoking and drug use with risky sexual behavior, particularly engaging in sexual intercourse without using a condom (Wu, Witkiewitz, McMahon, & Dodge, 2010).

Drug use also has a negative effect on academic performance. A survey of more than 18,000 American adolescents assessed the relationship between using cigarettes, marijuana, alcohol, and cocaine and academic achievement. The main factors related to poor academic achievement were smoking cigarettes, getting drunk, and being under the influence of alcohol while at school. Cocaine use had a negligible relationship to academic achievement, perhaps because few adolescents reported being under the influence of cocaine while at school (Jeynes, 2002). Today alcohol is the main drug of choice among adolescents in many countries. A survey of more than 2,600 Canadian adolescents found that alcohol use was associated with more problem behaviors than was the use of other drugs (Gfellner & Hundleby, 1994). Fortunately, despite the risks associated with sexual irresponsibility and drug and alcohol abuse, almost all adolescents enter adulthood relatively unscathed.

Adult Development

adulthood The period beginning when the individual assumes responsibility for her or his own life.

In Western cultures, **adulthood** begins when adolescents become independent of their parents and assume responsibility for themselves. Interest in adult development accelerated in the 1950s after being inspired by Erikson's theory of life-span development (Levinson, 1986) and brought an increased realization that physical, cognitive, and psychosocial changes take place across the entire life span.

Physical Development

Adults reach their physical peak in their late twenties and then begin a slow physical decline that does not accelerate appreciably until old age. Most athletes peak in their twenties, as is shown by the ages at which world-class athletes achieve their best performances (Schulz & Curnow, 1988). Beginning in our twenties, our basal metabolic rate (the rate at which the body burns calories when at rest) also decreases, accounting in part for the tendency to gain weight in adulthood. This makes it especially important for adults to pay attention to diet and exercise, which are associated with healthier cardiovascular functioning in middle age and old age (Sawatzky & Naimark, 2002). Physical exercise also is associated with better cognitive functioning in old age (Colcombe & Kramer, 2003). Of course, one must be careful not to presume that exercise *causes* improved cardiovascular or cognitive functioning. Perhaps, for example, having a healthier cardiovascular system or good cognitive functioning makes individuals more likely to exercise.

menopause The cessation of menstruation, usually occurring between the ages of 40 and 55.

andropause The gradual decline of testosterone experienced by men after the age of 40.

The aging process is marked by hormonal changes in women and men. Typically, women experience **menopause**—the cessation of their menstrual cycle between the ages of 40 and 55. This is associated with a reduction in estrogen secretion, cessation of ovulation, and consequently the inability to become pregnant. The reduction in estrogen can cause sweating, hot flashes, and brittle bones, as well as atrophy of the vaginal tissue, uterus, and mammary glands (Freedman, 2002). Typically, men experience **andropause**—a gradual decline of testosterone after the age of 40. As testosterone levels decline, men produce fewer and fewer sperm and experience changes in their sexual response, such as slower erections and delayed or less frequent orgasms. However, they still can father children into old age (Morley, 2001).

Midlife hormonal changes do not signal an end to sexuality. Postmenopausal women still have fulfilling sex lives and social lives. A survey of 16,000 American women from five ethnic groups (European American, African American, Japanese American, Chinese American, and Latino) found that women's attitudes toward menopause were neutral to positive and that health status, not menopausal status, predicted the happiness of women in midlife (Sommer et al., 1999). Attitudes toward menopause, however, can vary by culture and social class. For example, one cross-cultural study found that French women generally reported positive attitudes toward menopause. However, Tunisian women, especially poor Tunisian women, reported more negative attitudes and physical symptoms than the French (Delanoë et al., 2012). Moreover, though the prevalence of erectile dysfunction does increase with age, many older men have satisfying sex lives. One large survey of more than 1,000 men aged 58 to 94 years found that positive sexual attitudes, good health, and a responsive sexual partner were associated with continued sexual activity (Bortz, Wallace, & Wiley, 1999).

Middle-aged adults tend to become farsighted and require reading glasses, as evidenced by an increasing tendency to hold books and newspapers at arm's length. But marked changes in physical abilities usually do not occur until late adulthood. The older adult exhibits deterioration in heart output, lung capacity, reaction time, muscular strength, and motor coordination (Maranto, 1984). Old age also brings a decline in hearing, particularly of high-pitched sounds.

Eventually, no matter how well we take care of our bodies, all of us reach the ultimate physical change—death. Though the upper limit of the human life span seems to be about 120 years, few people live to even 100 years of age. But why is death inevitable? Death seems to be genetically programmed into our cells by limiting their ability to repair or reproduce themselves (Hayflick, 1980). Animal research indicates that aging can be slowed by the reduction of daily caloric intake, which prevents the buildup of certain metabolic by-products that promote aging. For example, a study of rats found that those who ate a low-calorie diet lived longer (Masoro, Shimokawa, Higami, & McMahan, 1995). The effects of low-calorie diets on human aging and longevity remain unclear, but ongoing research with human participants suggests that there are positive benefits in reducing caloric intake (Roth & Polotsky, 2012). Longevity also is influenced by physical activity. One longitudinal study of 70-year-old residents of western Jerusalem found that mortality rates were significantly lower for participants who reported engaging in regular exercise. Moreover, walking as little as four hours per week was linked to increased survival in this sample (Stessman, Maaravi, Hammerman-Rozenberg, & Cohen, 2000).

We do know, however, that the mere act of continuing to work is associated with slower aging. In a study supporting this, elderly people who continued to work or who retired but participated in regular physical activities showed a constant level of cerebral blood flow over a 4-year period. In contrast, elderly retirees who did not participate in regular physical activities showed a significant decline in cerebral blood flow. Those who continued to work also scored better on cognitive tests than did the inactive retirees (Rogers, Meyer, & Mortel, 1990). One 30-year longitudinal study found that adults who were employed in occupations that required complex work—requiring thought and independent decision-making—demonstrated higher levels of intellectual functioning compared to adults who were employed in less demanding occupations. Moreover, the beneficial effect of complex work was more pronounced in late adulthood compared to young adulthood (Schooler, Mulatu, & Oates, 1999). There is even evidence that individuals who engage in complex activities can generate new synapses in the brain, partly countering some of the negative effects of aging (Black, Isaacs, & Greenough, 1991). Thus, whereas physical aging is inevitable, people who maintain an active lifestyle might age at a slower rate. Note that these results do not conclusively demonstrate that activity causes a slowing of the effects of aging. Perhaps, instead, people who age more slowly are more likely to stay active.

Aging and Physical Health

These adults show that diet and exercise can contribute to a healthy old age.
Source: Lisa F. Young/ Shutterstock.com.

Cognitive Development

One of the most controversial issues in developmental psychology is the pattern of adult cognitive development, particularly intellectual development. Early studies showed that we experience a steady decline in intelligence across adulthood. But this apparent decline is found more often in cross-sectional studies than in longitudinal studies. Longitudinal studies have found that a marked decline in intelligence does not begin until about age 60. This indicates that the decline in intelligence across adulthood found in cross-sectional studies might be a cohort effect (perhaps due to differences in early educational experiences) rather than an aging effect (Schaie & Hertzog, 1983). Moreover, the intellectual decline in old age does not encompass all facets of intelligence. Instead, it holds for fluid intelligence but not for crystallized intelligence (Ryan, Sattler, & Lopez, 2000). **Fluid intelligence** reflects the ability to reason and to process information; **crystallized intelligence** reflects the ability to gain and retain knowledge.

But what accounts for the decline in fluid intelligence in old age? The Seattle Longitudinal Study of 1,620 adults between 22 and 91 years of age conducted by K. Warner Schaie (1989) found that the speed of information processing slows in old age. This has been

fluid intelligence The form of intelligence that reflects reasoning ability, memory capacity, and speed of information processing.

crystallized intelligence The form of intelligence that reflects knowledge acquired through schooling and in everyday life.

Are There Significant Psychological Gender Differences?

In the 19th century, scientific interest in gender differences was stimulated by Darwin's theory of evolution and promoted by Francis Galton, whose views were influenced by sexist attitudes of the Victorian era (Buss, 1976). Galton assumed that women and men had evolved physical and psychological differences that help them function in particular roles, and he insisted that they should remain in those roles (Shields, 1975). As discussed in Chapter 10, views like his were countered by some psychologists, such as Leta Stetter Hollingworth (1886–1939), who insisted that gender differences were due to social factors and did not denote the inferiority of women.

The first major review of gender differences was published by Eleanor Maccoby and Carol Jacklin (1974). They reported that women were superior in verbal abilities and men were superior in spatial and mathematical abilities. They also found that men were more aggressive than women. Nonetheless, they found fewer differences, and generally smaller differences, than were commonly believed to exist. Today, researchers who study gender differences are particularly concerned with cognitive abilities and psychosocial variables. Many of these researchers have used the statistical technique meta-analysis, which enables them to assess the size of gender differences and situational or sociocultural factors that influence these effect sizes (see Chapter 2).

Cognitive Abilities

In studying cognitive differences between women and men, researchers have studied differences primarily in three kinds of abilities. They ask, Are there gender differences in verbal abilities? spatial abilities? mathematical abilities?

Verbal Abilities

Research on children supports the popular belief in the verbal superiority of girls and women. Girls tend to be superior to boys in speaking, spelling, vocabulary, and reading comprehension. Yet the size of these differences decreases by adolescence. Overall, gender differences in verbal abilities have declined in size in recent decades until they are virtually negligible (Hyde & Plant, 1995). But what about talkativeness, which the popular stereotype holds to be the province of women? Research indicates that, contrary to the stereotype, men are consistently more talkative than women (Hyde & Linn, 1988).

Spatial Abilities

Research has tended to consistently find a large gender difference in one test of spatial abilities. Men are superior in the rotation of mental images (Hyde, Fennema, & Lamon, 1990). Gender differences in other spatial abilities, though, tend to be smaller and inconsistent.

Moreover, a meta-analysis of research studies of gender differences in spatial abilities found that the sizes of the differences have decreased in recent years (Voyer, Voyer, & Bryden, 1995). However, gender differences in spatial abilities are observed in early childhood (Levine, Huttenlocher, Taylor, & Langrock 1999) and in many nonlaboratory settings. For example, when providing directions, women are more likely to rely upon landmarks, whereas men are more likely to refer to north-south-east-west strategies (Halpern & LeMay, 2000). A recent study revealed, though, that gender differences also may be influenced by regional differences. In the Midwest and Western United States and in regions characterized by a grid-like pattern of roads, *both* men and women were more likely to refer to compass or left-right directions (Lawton, 2001). Thus, social experiences can influence spatial abilities.

Mathematical Abilities

Perhaps the most strongly established cognitive gender difference is that adolescent and adult men have higher average scores than adolescent and adult women on standardized mathematics tests. A national talent search by Camilla Benbow and Julian Stanley (1983) found that among seventh- and eighth-graders who took the mathematics subtest of the Scholastic Aptitude Test (SAT), the average score for boys was higher than the average score for girls. In fact, among those scoring higher than 700 (out of 800), boys outnumbered girls by a ratio of 13 to 1. Could this be attributable to boys' having more experience in mathematics? Benbow and Stanley say no, having found little difference in the number of mathematics courses taken by females and males. And because they found no other life experiences that could explain their findings, Benbow and Stanley concluded that heredity probably accounts for the difference. This explanation has received some support from other researchers (Thomas, 1993).

But it has also provoked controversy. Critics argue that the gender differences in mathematical abilities reported by Benbow and Stanley might be attributable to as yet unidentified differences in girls' and boys' experiences with mathematics. Also, boys do not have a higher average score than girls on all measures of mathematical ability. Though boys have higher average scores on mathematics achievement tests, which stress problem solving, girls receive higher grades in mathematics courses (Halpern, 2000). A recent meta-analysis of 242 studies published between 1997 and 2007 based upon more than 1,200,000 participants found, overall, no gender differences in mathematical performance (Lindberg, Hyde, Peterson, & Linn, 2010).

Are There Significant Psychological Gender Differences? *continued*

It also is important to consider that gender differences in mathematics achievement are smaller than cross-cultural or ethnic differences in achievement (Kimball, 1995). In fact, the greatest gender difference in mathematics ability is found among European American samples (Hyde, Fennema, & Lamon, 1990). In cultures with comparatively smaller gender differences, parents are more likely to encourage academic achievement and advanced study in mathematics—for both sons and daughters (Hanna, Kundiger, & Larouche, 1990). Moreover, gender differences in mathematics are larger in countries where women do not share economic, social, and political power with men (Else-Quest, Hyde, & Linn, 2010).

As discussed in Chapter 17, people's beliefs about group differences may lead to a self-fulfilling prophecy, which ultimately influences their behavior. And research has shown that women's and men's beliefs about gender and ethnic differences can affect their performance on mathematics tests (Smith & White, 2002). (Thus, stereotypes about women's and men's cognitive abilities may contribute to gender differences in mathematics achievement.

Psychosocial Variables

Researchers also study gender differences in psychosocial behavior. They have been especially concerned with differences in personality and aggression.

Personality

Meta-analyses of research studies on personality differences have found that men are more assertive whereas women are slightly more extraverted ($d = -.14$) and more anxious, trusting, and, especially, tender-minded (that is, more caring and nurturing). These differences tended to be consistent across all ages and educational levels of participants, as well as across a variety of different cultures (Feingold, 1994). A recent meta-analysis found that male participants score slightly higher on standardized measures of self-esteem than do female participants. The size of this small gender difference does increase—at least temporarily—in adolescence (Kling, Hyde, Showers, & Buswell, 1999). And a recent meta-analysis (Else-Quest, Hyde, Goldsmith, & Van Hulle, 2006) found that girls score much higher on measures of self-control than do boys ($d = -1.01$) whereas there is a moderate gender difference favoring boys on factors related to rough-and-tumble play, such as activity level ($d = .30$) and the intensity of their emotional experiences ($d = .33$).

Researchers also have studied a variety of other personality variables with the use of meta-analysis. For example, do women reveal more of their private thoughts, feelings, and experiences than men do? Contrary to popular belief, women are only marginally more likely to self-disclose than men are (Dindia & Allen, 1992). But consistent with popular views,

Gender Differences and Similarities

Physiological and sociocultural factors play an important role in girls' and boys' cognitive abilities.
Source: Zurijeta/Shutterstock.com.

continued

Are There Significant Psychological Gender Differences? *continued*

males are slightly more likely than females to take risks across a variety of situations (Byrnes, Miller, & Shafer, 1999) and women and girls are slightly more able than men and boys to delay gratification (Silverman, 2003). But what of the popular belief that women are more empathetic than men? This apparent gender difference depends on how empathy is measured. When asked to report on their level of empathy, women score higher than men. But when empathy is measured by physiological arousal or overt behavior, gender differences disappear. Evidently, social expectations that women will be more emotionally sensitive than men create differences in their subjective views of themselves but not necessarily in their actual behavior or physiological responses (Eisenberg & Lennon, 1983). This hypothesis was tested in a recent meta-analysis that found women's empathy scores were higher than men's only when participants were aware that their empathy was being assessed. This gender difference disappeared in experimental situations that lacked this demand characteristic (Ickes, Gesn, & Graham, 2000).

One recent study provided more evidence of gender similarities in basic values. Over 11,000 participants were surveyed in eight cultures (Chinese East Asia, Eastern Europe, Finland, France, Israel, Japan, Latin America, and the United States). Whereas some cross-cultural differences were found, results indicated that there were no consistent gender differences in the meaning of personal values across cultures (Struch, Schwartz, & van der Kloot, 2002).

Aggression

Just as women are reputed to be more empathetic than men, men are reputed to be more aggressive than women. Research has found that men are somewhat more physically aggressive than are women (Eagly & Steffen, 1986). Moreover, gender differences in aggression might be the product of gender roles. This was the conclusion of a study in which male and female participants were tested in the laboratory. When they were singled out as individuals, men were more aggressive than women. When they were deindividuated (that is, made to feel anonymous), men and women did not differ in aggression. The researchers attributed this difference to the power of gender roles: When we feel that we are being noticed, we behave according to gender expectations (Lightdale & Prentice, 1994). Moreover, as discussed in Chapter 17, when operational definitions of aggression are broadened to include behaviors that are more stereotypically female—such as indirect aggression—gender differences in aggression are minimized.

Explanations for Possible Gender Differences

If psychological gender differences exist, what might account for them? Researchers point to physiological factors and sociocultural factors.

Physiological Factors

Because of the obvious physical differences between men and women, researchers have looked to physiological factors to explain psychological gender differences. David Buss believes that men and women inherit certain behavioral tendencies as a product of their long evolutionary history. According to Buss, "Men and women differ . . . in domains in which they have faced different adaptive problems over human evolutionary history. In all other domains, the sexes are predicted to be psychologically similar" (Buss, 1995, p. 164). Thus, men are more aggressive and women more nurturing because prehistoric males were more likely to be hunters and prehistoric females were more likely to be caregivers. They do not differ in traits unrelated to their prehistoric roles as males and females.

But how might heredity affect psychological gender differences? Evidence supporting the biological basis of gender differences in social behavior implicates hormonal factors. Girls whose adrenal glands secrete high prenatal levels of testosterone are more likely to become "tomboys" who prefer rough play and masculine activities (though most tomboys do not have this adrenal disorder). These girls' genitals look more similar to those of boys at birth (though they are usually modified by surgery), and this might make parents treat them as though they were boys, yet parents usually report that they treat these girls the same as parents treat girls without the disorder (Berenbaum & Hines, 1992). There is some evidence, though, for a hormonal basis for cognitive gender differences (Kimura & Hampson, 1994). There also is evidence of a hormonal basis for gender differences in play behavior in childhood and fairly strong evidence for its influence on gender differences in physical aggression (Collaer & Hines, 1995).

A second way that heredity might affect gender differences is through brain development. But efforts to associate specific cognitive differences with differences in brain structures have produced mixed results. As discussed in Chapter 3, some studies have found that men's brains may be more lateralized than women's brains. Studies of people with brain damage have found that damage to men's left cerebral hemisphere is associated with impaired verbal skills, and damage to men's right cerebral hemisphere is associated with impaired nonverbal skills. In contrast, women's verbal and nonverbal skills do not seem to be influenced by the side of the brain damaged (Springer and Deutsch, 1998). Other studies, though,

Are There Significant Psychological Gender Differences? *continued*

have failed to find gender differences in hemispheric lateralization (e.g., Snow & Sheese, 1985). And there are large individual differences in brain organization; biological sex is only one of many variables influencing brain organization (Kimura, 1987).

Sociocultural Factors

The possibility that gender differences in cognitive abilities are influenced more by sociocultural factors than by physiological factors is supported by studies that have found a narrowing of gender differences in cognitive abilities between North American male and female participants during the past 40 years (Hyde & Plant, 1995; Lindberg, Hyde, Peterson, & Linn, 2010). This might be explained in part by the cultural trend to provide girls and boys with somewhat more similar treatment and opportunities (Jacklin, 1989). Even Camilla Benbow (1988) agrees that environmental, as well as hereditary, factors play an important role in cognitive abilities such as mathematics. For example, minimal gender differences have been found among participants from the study of Mathematically Precocious Youth who had gone on to graduate study in math and sciences. The profiles of female and male participants included attributes that are critical to achieving excellence in these fields—exceptional quantitative abilities, scientific interests and values, and persistence in seeking out educational opportunities (Lubinski, Benbow, Shea, Eftekhari-Sanjani, & Halvorson, 2001).

After decades of extensive research, no gender differences have emerged that are large enough to predict with confidence how individual men and women will behave (Deaux, 1985). This has provoked a controversy about whether we should continue to study gender differences. Some psychologists, such as Roy Baumeister (1988), argue that we should no longer study them. Why study differences that are too few or too small to have practical significance? And why study gender differences when reports of even small differences might support sex discrimination? But Baumeister's view was countered by gender difference researchers Alice Eagly (1995) and Diane Halpern (1994), who believe that objective scientific research on gender differences should continue, even if it might find differences that some people would prefer did not exist.

A compromise position has been put forth by Janet Shibley Hyde, who favors studying gender differences but warns against relying on the results of studies that have not been replicated, interpreting gender differences as signs of female deficiencies, and automatically attributing such differences to inherited biological factors. She favors acknowledging the fact that gender similarities are the rule and that the few gender differences that have been found can be attributed primarily to sociocultural factors (Hyde, 2007).

---

replicated in other research studies (Zimprich & Martin, 2002). This slowing is especially detrimental to short-term memory (Salthouse, 1991), which is the stage of memory that involves the conscious, purposeful mental manipulation of information. But the decline in fluid intelligence can be slowed. The Seattle Longitudinal Study found that a group of older adults who were given cognitive training did not show the same decline in fluid intelligence shown by older adults who were not given such training (Saczynski, 2002).

Older adults tend to do more poorly than adolescents and young adults on cognitive tasks. One factor that explains why is that they have been out of school for many years. This was the finding of a study that compared the recall ability of college students of traditional age, their peers not attending college, and older people not attending college. The average age of the younger groups was 22, and the average age of the older group was 69. The three groups were equal in their level of intelligence.

The results showed that the recall ability of the college group was better than that of the other two groups. But there was no difference in the performance of the groups of older persons and younger persons who were not attending college. This indicates that it might be the failure to use one's memory, rather than simply brain deterioration accompanying aging, that accounts for the inferior performance of the elderly on tests of recall. When it comes to the maintenance of cognitive abilities, such as memory, the adage "Use it or lose it" might have some validity (Hultsch, Hertzog, Small, & Dixon 1999). One of the more intriguing longitudinal studies of cognitive aging and Alzheimer's disease is the Nun Study, which has involved following a large sample of Catholic religious sisters for more than 60 years—through the deaths of many of them (Santa Cruz et al., 2011).

Psychosocial Development

Social development continues through early, middle, and late adulthood. Keeping in mind that these divisions are somewhat arbitrary, assume that early adulthood extends from age 20 to age 40, middle adulthood from age 40 to age 65, and late adulthood from age 65 on. The similarities exhibited by people within these periods are related to the common social experiences of the "social clock." In recent decades, the typical ages at which some of these experiences occur have varied more than in the past. A graduate student might live at home with his parents until his late twenties, a woman working toward her medical degree might postpone marriage until her early thirties, and a two-career couple might not have their first child until they are in their late thirties. Of course, events that are unique to each person's life can also play a role in psychosocial development. Chance encounters in our lives, for example, contribute to our unique development (Bandura, 1982). You might reflect on chance encounters that influenced your choice of an academic major or that helped you meet your current boyfriend, girlfriend, husband, or wife.

Early Adulthood

Though Sigmund Freud paid little attention to adult development, he did note that normal adulthood is marked by the ability to love and to work. Erik Erikson agreed that the capacity for love is an important aspect of early adulthood, and he claimed that the first major task of adulthood is facing the conflict of **intimacy versus isolation.** Intimate relationships involve a strong sense of emotional attachment and personal commitment. The Rochester Adult Longitudinal study of a community sample supported Erikson's belief that the development of the capacity for intimacy depends on the successful formation of a psychosocial identity in adolescence. The achievement of identity during adolescence contributed to the development of intimacy in young adulthood. Participants who were capable of developing both identity in adolescence and a high degree of intimacy in young adulthood reported more successful romantic relationships and greater life satisfaction in midlife (Sneed, Whitbourne, Schwartz, & Huang, 2012).

Establishing Intimate Relationships About 95 percent of young adults eventually experience the intimate relationship of marriage. Of course there is a variety of family arrangements. And at any given time many adults are unmarried—they are either widowed, divorced, not ready, or committed to remaining single. However, the results of a longitudinal study of six countries (Austria, Germany, the Netherlands, Great Britain, Ireland, and the United States) found that men's and women's attitudes are shifting away from the norms of traditional marriage. Participants reported a remarkable diversity of lifestyles and individual differences in the timing of marriage and parenthood (Gubernskay, 2010).

A strong and consistent positive correlation has been found between marriage and psychological well-being. The World Values Survey, a survey of 159,169 adults in 42 countries, found that married women and men reported higher levels of life satisfaction than cohabiting couples, single adults, and divorced or separated adults. Though there were significant cross-cultural differences, these differences were negligible. And men and women derive similar benefits from marriage (Diener, Gohm, Suh, & Oishi, 2000). These results recently have been replicated in nationally representative samples from Australia, Germany, and Great Britain (Luhmann, Lucas, Eid, & Diener, 2013). Unmarried status is correlated with greater physical and psychological risks, especially for men. A survey of more than 18,000 men conducted in England found that unmarried middle-aged men of all kinds—single, widowed, divorced, or separated—had higher mortality rates than did married men (Ben-Shlomo, Smith, Shipley, & Marmot, 1993). One reason for this is a lower risk of illness in the married, especially if their partner is responsive to their needs (Selcuk & Ong, 2013).

What characteristics do adults look for in potential mates? As you might expect, both women and men tend to seek partners who are kind, loyal, honest, considerate, intelligent, interesting, and affectionate. But men tend to be more concerned than women with the potential spouse's physical attractiveness, and women tend to be more concerned than men with the potential spouse's earning capacity (Buss et al., 1990). As discussed in Chapter 17, psychologists argue whether these preferences reflect the influence of evolution or of cultural norms that differentially affect men's and women's marital expectations.

What determines whether a relationship will succeed? An important factor is similarity—in age, religion, attitudes, ethnicity, personality, intelligence, and educational level (O'Leary & Smith, 1991). Willingness to talk about problems is another important factor, as found in a 2-year longitudinal study of newlyweds. Those couples who believed that conflicts should be discussed openly reported greater marital happiness than those who believed they should be ignored (Crohan, 1992). A 4-year longitudinal study found that high-quality, positive communication between couples was associated with higher levels of marital satisfaction. Moreover, marital dissolution was associated with marital conflict and aggression—especially if present early in the marriage (Rogge & Bradbury, 1999).

Communication is essential to marital satisfaction. One study examined videotapes of 78 married or cohabiting couples discussing a conflict they were having. Positive interruptions (agreement with what the partner was saying) were positively correlated with the couples' feelings about the conversation and their relationship satisfaction. Negative interruptions (disagreement with what the partner was saying) were negatively correlated with the couples' feelings about the conversation and their relationship satisfaction (Daigen & Holmes, 2000). Research indicates that marital satisfaction is greater when partners take a collaborative approach to resolving conflicts than when one or both take a competitive approach (Greeff & de Bruyne, 2000).

Dissolving Intimate Relationships Unfortunately, for many couples, happiness is elusive, and they may eventually seek to end their relationship. In the United States, about half of first marriages are so unhappy that they end in divorce. In fact, the United States has the highest divorce rate of any industrialized country (O'Leary & Smith, 1991). A study that interviewed over 1,300 persons found that divorce has increased not because marriages were happier in the "good old days," but instead because barriers to divorce (such as conservative values or shared social networks) have fallen and alternatives to divorce (such as a wife's independent income or remarriage prospects) have increased. Thus, the threshold of marital happiness that will trigger divorce is lower than it was several decades ago.

The barriers to relationship dissolution associated with marriage are important in understanding the higher rate of relationship dissolution among gay and lesbian couples. One study compared relationship satisfaction and dissolution rates among heterosexual, gay, and lesbian couples. Heterosexual married couples' satisfaction with their relationship was similar to that reported by cohabiting gay and lesbian couples. Whereas relationship satisfaction declined among all three groups, gay and lesbian couples were more likely to have ended their relationships over the 5 years of the study. These results are attributed to the fact that gay and lesbian couples perceived fewer barriers to ending their relationship—for example, the cost of divorce or the loss of insurance or health benefits (Kurdek, 1998)

There are a variety of specific factors that contribute to divorce. One of the hallmarks of an unhappy marriage is the tendency of spouses to consistently offer negative explanations for their spouse's behavior (Karney & Bradbury, 2000). In dual-wage-earner marriages, perceived inequality in doing housework—particularly by wives—appears to contribute to divorces (Frisco & Williams, 2003). And even the nature of commitment may predict relationship dissolution. Couples who display avoidant commitment (that is, those who want to avoid the negative consequences of breaking up) are more likely than committed couples who display approach commitment (that is, those who want to retain the positive consequences of staying together) to break up (Frank & Brandstaetter, 2002).

Yet there is evidence that people might remain committed to spouses or partners who treat them poorly. You probably have known someone who sticks with a romantic partner who treats that person in a manner that you would not tolerate. Consider a study of 86 pairs of married couples from central Texas, with an average age of 32 years and an average length of marriage of 6 years (Swann, Hixon, & De La Ronde, 1992). The spouses took personality tests measuring their self-concepts. They also measured how the spouses appraised each other and how committed they were to each other. The results revealed that the degree of commitment to one's spouse depended on the degree of congruence between one's self-concept and how one was viewed by one's spouse. That is, those with positive self-concepts felt more committed when their spouses viewed them positively. Likewise, those with negative self-concepts felt more committed when their spouses viewed them negatively.

What could account for this finding, which runs counter to the commonsense notion that we all wish to be admired and treated well? The researchers found that though we might insist on being treated well in casual relationships, we insist on being treated in accordance with our self-concept within the intimacy of marriage. That is, we want our spouses to verify our self-concept so we are not confused about ourselves or about how other people will treat us. In addition, we will trust spouses more who do not try to "snow" us by telling us we're attractive when we feel ugly, intelligent when we feel stupid, and personally appealing when we feel socially inept. Moreover, whereas people with positive self-concepts might welcome high expectations of them, people with negative self-concepts might fear unrealistically high expectations that they could not meet.

Parenthood For most couples, parenthood is a major component of marriage. Raising children can be one of the greatest rewards in life, but it can also be one of life's greatest stresses. Because women still tend to be the primary caregiver, their parental responsibilities tend to be especially stressful. But couples who share childcare responsibilities are more likely to successfully weather the stress of becoming new parents (Belsky & Hsieh, 1998). Overall, parents who live with their biological children show greater declines in marital happiness over time than do married, childless couples or married couples living with stepchildren (Kurdek, 1999). Of course, some couples remain childless. They are not necessarily unhappy. In fact, especially if they are voluntarily childless, they might be as happy as couples with children. This is attributable, in part, to the fact that they do not have the stress that parents experience from money woes, children's illnesses, loss of sleep, and lack of recreational outlets. Women who are childless by choice show higher levels of psychological well-being than women who are involuntarily childless (Jeffries & Konnert, 2002).

But what of single parents? In the 1960s and 1970s, divorce was the chief cause of single parenting. This has been joined by planned or unplanned childbearing outside of marriage. Though single parents are usually women, one in five is male. Many single parents, given social and financial support, are successful in rearing children. For example, one study of single parents serving in the U.S. military found that mothers and fathers readily used social, financial, and organizational resources to balance their family and work obligations (Heath & Orthner, 1999). But according to the U.S. Bureau of the Census, single-parent families, on the average, suffer disadvantages in regard to income, health, and housing conditions. The most disadvantaged are families consisting of children and a never-married mother (Bianchi, 1995).

Middle Adulthood

In 1850 few Americans lived beyond what we now call early adulthood; the average life span was only 40 years (Shneidman, 1987). But improved nutrition, sanitation, and health care have almost doubled that life span. What was the end of the life span more than a century ago is today simply the beginning of middle adulthood. Daniel Levinson (1978) found that during the transition to middle adulthood, men commonly experience a midlife crisis, in which they realize that the "dream" they had pursued in regard to their life goals will not be achieved or, even if achieved, will seem transient in the face of the inevitability of death. Other studies indicate, however, that the midlife crisis is less intense than Levinson found in his research (Fagan & Ayers, 1982). Moreover, the life dreams of women tend to be more complex than the life dreams of men. Whereas men typically focus on their careers, women focus on marriage and children, as well as their careers (Kittrell, 1998).

According to Erik Erikson, the main task of middle adulthood is the resolution of the conflict of **generativity versus stagnation**. Those who achieve generativity become less self-absorbed and more concerned about being a productive worker, spouse, and parent (Slater, 2003). They are more competent, continue to strive for achievement, and are more altruistic and trusting (Cox, Wilt, Olson, & McAdams, 2010). They also are more satisfied with their lives (McAdams, de St. Aubin, & Logan, 1993). One way of achieving generativity is to serve as a mentor for a younger person. This lets mentors realize their life dreams vicariously and know that their dreams will continue even after their own deaths (Westermeyer, 2004).

Middle adulthood also brings transitions affected by one's parental status. You might be surprised to learn that parents become more distressed and experience more marital unhappiness after their first child leaves home than after their last child leaves home. In fact, after the last child has left home, parents tend to be relieved and experience improved marital relations (Harris, Ellicott, & Holmes, 1986). Perhaps the notion of an "empty nest syndrome" (after the last child has left home) should be replaced by the notion of a "partly empty nest syndrome" (after the first child has left home). Moreover, a growing trend in North America is the "revolving-door nest," caused by the return home of young adults who find it personally or financially difficult to live on their own (Dennerstein, Dudley, & Guthrie, 2002).

Late Adulthood

Now that more people in developed countries are living into their 70s and beyond, developmental psychologists have become more interested in studying late adulthood. In 1900 only one person in thirty was over 65. By 2020 one person in five will be over 65 (Eisdorfer, 1983). Though this increase in the elderly population, including many more retired people, will create more concern about physical well-being in old age, it also will create more concern about psychosocial development in old age. Research has provided inconsistent findings regarding whether retirement generally has positive, negative, or no effects on psychological well-being (Kim & Moen, 2001).

Erikson claimed that the main psychosocial task of late adulthood is to resolve the crisis of **integrity versus despair**. A sense of integrity results from reflecting back on a meaningful life through a "life review." In fact, Erikson claimed that pleasurable reminiscing is essential to satisfactory adjustment in old age. This was supported by a study of nursing home residents aged 70 to 88 years. Participants in the experimental group received a visitor who encouraged them to reminisce and engage in a life review.

Generativity
According to Erik Erikson, people who successfully resolve the midlife conflict of generativity versus stagnation become less self-absorbed and more concerned with the well-being of the next generation.
Source: Pressmaster/Shutterstock.com.

generativity versus stagnation
Erikson's developmental stage in which success is achieved by becoming less self-absorbed and more concerned with the well-being of others.

integrity versus despair
Erikson's developmental stage in which success is achieved by reflecting back on one's life and finding that it has been meaningful.

Participants in the control group received a friendly visit. Participants who engaged in a life review scored higher on a questionnaire that measured their level of ego integrity, as long as 3 years after the intervention (Haight, Michel, & Hendrix, 2000). Older adults who are able to review and accept their past are more likely to develop a sense of coherence and experience more positive psychological development (Wiesmann & Hannich, 2011).

And old age is not necessarily a time of physical decay, cognitive deterioration, and social isolation. For many, it is a time of physical activity, continued education, and rewarding social relations (Whitbourne & Hulicka, 1990). Many elderly adults optimize their cognitive and physical functioning by capitalizing on their strengths and compensating for their weaknesses. For example, they may allot more time to perform tasks, practice old skills, or learn new skills. The use of these strategies by elderly adults has been found to be associated with successful aging, characterized by more positive emotions, enhanced feelings of well-being, and less loneliness (Freund & Baltes, 1998).

Eventually, many adults must confront one of the greatest psychosocial challenges of old age—the death of a mate. During the period immediately following the death of their spouse, bereaved spouses are more likely to suffer depression, illness, or death than are their peers with living spouses. An increase in morbidity, mortality, and psychological well-being tends to be found among surviving spouses. This might stem from the loss of the emotional and practical support previously provided by the now-deceased spouse. One study tested this hypothesis with a sample of recently bereaved spouses. Widowers were more likely to experience greater deterioration in physical and mental health and receive less social support than were widows. However, there was no evidence that the loss of social support reported by widowers mediated this gender difference (Stroebe, Stroebe, & Abakoumkin, 1999). Thus, it is likely that other factors contribute to the poorer health and negative psychological outcomes experienced by bereaved widowers. For example, a study of older German adults found that widowers tend to be lonelier than widows (Pinquart, 2003). A variety of techniques have been used to aid the bereavement process, with varying success (Durland, 2000). In one study, 44 college students who had lost a loved one were randomly assigned to write about either their bereavement experience or about a trivial, unrelated topic. The results indicated that writing about one's bereavement experience helped reduce feelings of distress (Range, Kovac, & Marion, 2000). Similar findings were reported in a study in which college students wrote about their bereavement experience regarding a loved one who had committed suicide in the prior two years (Kovac & Range, 2000).

Though, as Benjamin Franklin observed in 1789, "in this world nothing's certain but death and taxes," we can at least improve the way in which we confront our own mortality. In old age, successful resolution of the crisis of ego integrity versus despair is associated with less fear of death (Goebel & Boeck, 1987). And a survey of 200 adults found that those with strong religious convictions and a greater belief in an afterlife have lower death anxiety (Alvarado, Templer, Bresler, & Thomas-Dobson, 1995).

Prior to the 20th century, death was accepted as a public part of life. People died at home, surrounded and comforted by loved ones. Today, people commonly die alone, in pain, in hospital rooms, attached to life-support systems. One of the most important developments to counter this approach to death and dying is the **hospice movement,** founded in 1958 by the British physician Cicely Saunders. She was motivated to do so by her colleagues' failure to respond sensitively to dying patients and their families. Hospices provide humane, comprehensive care for the dying patient in a hospital, residential, or home setting, with attention to alleviating the patient's physical, emotional, and spiritual suffering (Saunders, 1996). A study comparing hospices to traditional nursing homes found that elderly dying cancer patients received more effective pain relief and better quality of life during their time spent in hospice (Black et al., 2011).

What are the psychological experiences of the dying? The person who sparked interest in studying the experiences of dying persons was the Swiss psychiatrist

hospice movement
The providing of care for the dying patient with attention to alleviating the patient's physical, emotional, and spiritual suffering.

Elisabeth Kübler-Ross (1969). She saw death and suffering as a young adult as she traveled through France and Poland to help victims of World War II and later when she worked as a physician in the United States (Gill, 1980). Based on her observations of dying patients, she identified five stages commonly experienced by terminally ill patients: denial, anger, bargaining, depression, and acceptance. At first, the patients deny their medical diagnoses, then become angry at their plight, bargain with God to let them live, suffer depression at the thought of dying, and finally come to accept their impending death. Kübler-Ross and others, however, have found that not all terminally ill patients go through all the stages or go through them in the same order (Kübler-Ross, 1974). Though flawed by subjective interpretations and unsystematic recording of patients' reactions to terminal illness, her research has inspired others to study the psychology of dying (Corr, 1993).

Some researchers, including Kübler-Ross, also have studied so-called **near-death experiences**, which are sometimes reported by people as they die or of people who have come close to dying before being revived. In Western cultures there tends to be a core experience, which includes a peaceful state of mind; an out-of-body experience; and traveling into darkness or through a tunnel with a bright light at the end (Parker, 2001). Most, though not all, report that the experience was so pleasant that they would have preferred to stay. Though near-death experiences occur in both Eastern and Western cultures, they tend to contain culture-dependent content. Experiences of people in Thailand contain beliefs and customs more common to people from Southeast Asian cultures (Murphy, 2001).

near-death experience
A phenomenon reported by dying people that in Western cultures often includes a peaceful state of mind and an out-of-body experience.

Supposed out-of-body experiences are particularly intriguing, given that patients sometimes accurately report events that have taken place while they are under general anesthesia. These include describing the actions and remarks of relatives waiting elsewhere and reporting distinctive arm movements by the surgeon (Kelly, Greyson, & Stevenson, 1999–2000). A study of hospitalized cardiac patients found that those who related near-death experiences reported that they were difficult to put into words, provided a sense of profound peacefulness, involved the absence of pain, did not provoke fear, involved a feeling of detachment from one's body, and produced a loss of the sense of time and space (Schwaninger, Eisenberg, Schechtman, & Weiss, 2002).

But scientists and other skeptics tend to attribute near-death experiences to more mundane factors, such as unusual patterns of brain activity associated with different medically related factors that can alter one's consciousness (Mobbs & Watt, 2011). Though reports of near-death experiences convince few scientists of the reality of life after death, the experiences tend to convince many of those who experience them that their mind or soul will survive death (Potts, 2002). Given the difficulty of studying such an issue scientifically, it is likely that for each of us the ultimate mystery will be answered by our own experience, not by scientific research.

Section Review: Adult Development

1. What is the apparent relationship between caloric intake and aging?

2. What does research indicate about changes in intelligence in old age?

3. How do adults successfully resolve Erikson's conflict involving generativity versus stagnation?

An Analysis of Children's Toys

Rationale

As discussed in this chapter, children as young as toddlers learn to classify toys as masculine or feminine. In fact, toys are examples of how social and cultural factors influence gender-role development. In this exercise you will examine a selection of toys, observe any gender-specific messages or gender typing, and discuss your work in the context of what you learned from reading this chapter.

Procedure

Find a local toy store that has a well-stocked selection of toys for boys and girls of different ages. Before you make your trip, consider the ways that gender typing may be reflected in a toy's attributes. For example, you might consider colors of the toys or pictures of children playing with the toys on packaging materials. Other factors to consider might be indicators that toys are for girls or boys. Some packages might indicate that the toy is appropriate for boys of a certain age range. Or, the store might group toys that girls would be interested in together.

Spend about an hour in the store, examining the toys, their packaging, and their placement in the store and make notes of any evidence of gender typing. Summarize your findings by answering the following questions:

1. Could you find toys that were easily identifiable as boys' toys? What types of toys? What type of play or activities do they encourage?

2. Could you find toys that were easily identifiable as girls' toys? What types of toys? What type of play or activities do they encourage?

3. Could you find any gender-neutral toys—that is toys that were neither boys' nor girls' toys? What types of toys? What type of play or activities do they encourage?

Results and Discussion

Describe your findings. Did you find evidence of gender typing during your observation? As discussed in the chapter, cultural trends have indicated more similar treatment of boys and girls. Do your results support what you read in the chapter? Were there any other conclusions you reached after summarizing your observations?

Chapter Summary

Research Methods in Developmental Psychology

- Developmental psychology is the field that studies the physical, perceptual, cognitive, and psychosocial changes that take place across the life span.
- Research designs typical of developmental psychology include longitudinal research, cross-sectional research, and cohort-sequential research.

Prenatal Development

- The prenatal period is divided into the germinal, embryonic, and fetal stages.
- Cell-adhesion molecules direct the size, shape, and location of organs in the embryo.
- Teratogens can impair prenatal development.
- Women who drink alcohol, a teratogen, during pregnancy might have offspring who suffer from fetal alcohol syndrome.

Infant and Child Development

- Childhood extends from birth until puberty.
- The first 2 years of childhood are called infancy.
- Motor development follows a consistent sequence, though the timing of motor milestones varies somewhat among infants.
- Jean Piaget found that children pass through distinct cognitive stages of development.

- During the sensorimotor stage, the infant learns to coordinate sensory experiences and motor behavior, and forms schemas that represent aspects of the world.
- The preoperational stage is marked by egocentrism. In the concrete operational stage, the child learns to make transitive inferences and to appreciate conservation.
- Erik Erikson put forth an influential theory of psychosocial development. He believed that the life span consists of eight distinct stages, each associated with a crisis that must be overcome.
- An important factor in infant development is social attachment, a strong emotional relationship between an infant and a caregiver.
- Permissive and authoritarian child-rearing practices are less effective than authoritative ones.
- Children who receive high-quality day care do not appear to suffer ill effects from being separated from their parents, though this might not be true of infants.
- Research on the effects of divorce on children has produced inconsistent results, with some studies finding no effects, others finding negative effects, and still others finding positive effects.
- Though the causes of gender-role development are still unclear, social learning theory and gender-schema theory try to explain it.

- The most influential theory of moral development has been Lawrence Kohlberg's cognitive-developmental theory, which is based on Piaget's belief that a person's level of moral development depends on his or her level of cognitive development.
- Kohlberg proposes that we pass through preconventional, conventional, and postconventional levels of moral development.
- Carol Gilligan argues that Kohlberg's theory is biased toward a masculine view of morality. Research has provided mixed support for Kohlberg's theory.

Adolescent Development

- Adolescence is a transitional period between childhood and adulthood that begins with puberty.
- In regard to physical development, the adolescent experiences the maturation of primary and secondary sex characteristics.
- In regard to cognitive development, some adolescents enter Piaget's formal operational stage, meaning that they can engage in abstract, hypothetical reasoning.
- And, in regard to psychosocial development, adolescence is a time of identity formation, an important stage in Erik Erikson's theory of development.
- The adolescent also is increasingly influenced by peer values, especially in regard to fashion, sexuality, and drug use.
- Research on sex differences has found no consistent differences in male and female brains.
- Girls and boys differ little in their gross motor abilities until puberty, when boys begin to outperform girls.
- Women tend to have better verbal abilities, while men tend to have better spatial and mathematical problem-solving abilities.
- Men also tend to be more physically aggressive than women.
- Research on gender differences is controversial because of fears that its findings might be used to promote and legitimate discrimination.
- Gender differences are based on group averages, and most are so small that they should not be used to make decisions about individuals.

Adult Development

- Adulthood begins when adolescents become independent from their parents.
- In regard to physical development, adults reach their physical peak in their late twenties, at which point they begin a gradual decline that does not accelerate appreciably until old age.
- Middle-aged women experience menopause, which, contrary to popular belief, is rarely a traumatic event, and middle-aged men experience andropause.
- In regard to cognitive development, though aging brings some slowing of cognitive processes, people who continue to be mentally active show less cognitive decline than do their peers who do not stay active.
- In regard to social development, Erik Erikson saw the main task of early adulthood as the establishment of intimacy, typically between a husband and wife. About 95 percent of adults marry, but half of North American marriages will end in divorce.
- The most successful marriages are those in which the spouses discuss, rather than avoid, marital issues.
- Erikson saw the main task of middle adulthood as the establishment of a sense of generativity, which is promoted by parenting.
- After the last child leaves home, parents typically improve their emotional and marital well-being.
- Erikson saw the final stage of life as ideally promoting a sense of integrity in reflecting on a life well lived.
- Eventually, all people must face their own mortality.
- The hospice movement, founded by Cicely Saunders, has promoted more humane, personal, and homelike care for the dying patient.
- Elisabeth Kübler-Ross stimulated interest in the study of death and dying. She found that dying people typically go through the stages of denial, anger, bargaining, depression, and acceptance.
- Near-death experiences are controversial in that some researchers believe they indicate that the mind survives death and others believe that they are merely the byproduct of factors that induce an altered state of consciousness.

Key Terms

developmental psychology (p. 106)
maturation (p. 106)

Research Methods in Developmental Psychology

cohort (p. 107)
cohort-sequential research (p. 107)
cross-sectional research (p. 107)
longitudinal research (p. 106)

Prenatal Development

embryonic stage (p. 108)

fetal alcohol syndrome (p. 109)
fetal stage (p. 109)
germinal stage (p. 108)
teratogen (p. 109)

Infant and Child Development

accommodation (p. 114)
assimilation (p. 114)
authoritative parenting (p. 120)
autonomy versus shame and doubt (p. 119)
childhood (p. 110)
concrete operational stage (p. 115)

conservation (p. 115)
conventional level (p. 125)
egocentrism (p. 115)
gender roles (p. 122)
gender schema theory (p. 123)
industry versus inferiority (p. 119)
infancy (p. 110)
initiative versus guilt (p. 119)
object permanence (p. 114)
postconventional level (p. 125)
preoperational stage (p. 115)
preconventional level (p. 125)

Chapter Quiz

Note: Answers for the Chapter Quiz questions are provided at the end of the book.

1. A child who first believes that changing the form of something changes its amount, but eventually realizes that changing the form of something does not change its amount, would be exhibiting
   a. assimilation.
   b. accommodation.
   c. transitive inference.
   d. transductive reasoning.

2. In regard to the pubertal growth spurt,
   a. boys and girls typically show a spurt at about the same age.
   b. boys typically show a spurt about two years earlier than girls.
   c. girls typically show a spurt about two years earlier than boys.
   d. boys and girls a century ago typically showed a spurt several years earlier than boys and girls today.

3. A junior high school student shows excellent ability in designing and conducting experiments to test basic principles regarding the movement of objects. The student has probably reached what Piaget called the
   a. sensorimotor stage.
   b. preoperational stage.
   c. formal operational stage.
   d. concrete operational stage.

4. An important reason that adults tend to put on weight is that
   a. their appetite tends to increase.
   b. their basal metabolic rate slows.
   c. they reduce their secretion of insulin.
   d. they increase their secretion of insulin.

5. According to Erikson, the main psychosocial conflict of adolescence involves
   a. intimacy versus isolation.
   b. industry versus inferiority.
   c. identity versus role confusion.
   d. generativity versus stagnation.

6. A child who realizes that pouring all of the soda from a short, wide glass into a tall, narrow glass does not change the amount of soda is exhibiting an appreciation of
   a. object permanence.
   b. conservation.
   c. transitive inference.
   d. transductive reasoning.

7. Mary Ainsworth has contributed to our knowledge of infant
   a. social attachment.
   b. cognitive abilities.
   c. physical maturation.
   d. perceptual development.

8. Elderly persons would be most likely to show a decline in fluid intelligence if, for example, they
   a. lost the ability to swim.
   b. forgot the names of old friends.
   c. could no longer solve algebra problems.
   d. could no longer form new memories of daily events.

9. The "visual cliff" is used to test infant
   a. visual acuity.
   b. depth perception.
   c. movement detection.
   d. balance and coordination.

10. The sperm normally fertilizes the egg in the
    a. ovary.
    b. vagina.
    c. uterus.
    d. fallopian tube.

11. According to Diana Baumrind, authoritative parents
    a. prohibit "back talk."
    b. often rely on physical punishment.
    c. explain the reasons for their rules.
    d. often have children who become juvenile delinquents.

12. According to Sigmund Freud, resolution of the Oedipus and Electra complexes influences the development of
    a. weaning.
    b. gender roles.
    c. aggressiveness.
    d. social attachment.

13. In regard to moral development, Gilligan believes that girls and women
    a. favor justice more than caring.
    b. favor caring more than justice.
    c. favor caring and justice equally.
    d. are superior to males as children but not as adults.

14. According to Jean Piaget, assimilation and accommodation determine the infant's
    a. schemas.
    b. sensory acuity.
    c. motor maturation.
    d. social attachment.

15. A psychologist compares the language ability of a group of 12-month-olds, a group of 15-month-olds, and a group of 18-month-olds. This is an example of
    a. longitudinal research.
    b. cross-sectional research.
    c. cohort-sequential research.
    d. quasi-experimental research.

16. Research indicates that divorce has increased in the United States because
    a. barriers to divorce have fallen.
    b. marriages were happier in the past.
    c. children have become more burdensome.
    d. the age of first marriages continues to decline.

17. Jim is older than Phil. Susan is younger than Phil. A child who correctly concludes that Jim is older than Susan would be exhibiting
    a. conservation.
    b. transitive inference.
    c. preoperational thought.
    d. transductive reasoning.

18. According to Kohlberg, students who do not cheat on exams because they fear the teacher will punish them are at the
    a. concrete level of moral development.
    b. conventional level of moral development.
    c. preconventional level of moral development.
    d. postconventional level of moral development.

19. Teratogens
    a. may cause prenatal defects.
    b. guide embryonic development.
    c. depend on the individual's genotype.
    d. do not have effects until the last three months before birth.

20. According to Erikson the main conflict of old age is
    a. integrity versus despair.
    b. intimacy versus isolation.
    c. industry versus inferiority.
    d. generativity versus stagnation.

21. The average infant walks at age
    a. 5 months.
    b. 9 months.
    c. 13 months.
    d. 18 months.

22. The sequential unfolding of inherited predispositions is called
    a. eugenics.
    b. phylogeny.
    c. maturation.
    d. predeterminism.

23. In regard to gender differences in empathy, on the average,
    a. women report they are more empathetic than do men.
    b. women behave more empathetically than men.
    c. women show physiological changes indicating that they are more empathetic than men.
    d. men and women are equally empathetic on all measures of empathy.

24. The fact that college students who experienced the "Reagan revolution" of the 1980s might differ from those who experienced the "Woodstock era" of the 1960s may limit a psychologist to making only tentative conclusions about the psychological development of college students. This limitation would be most likely to affect the conclusions drawn from
    a. longitudinal research.
    b. cross-sectional research.
    c. naturalistic observation.
    d. quasi-experimental research.

Thought Questions

1. How would you use a longitudinal research design, a cross-sectional research design, and a cohort-sequential research design to study whether college students become more tolerant of ethnic groups that are not their own between their admission to college and their senior year?

2. A child insists on going out to play without first doing his homework. How might parents respond differently in using authoritarian parenting, permissive parenting, and authoritative parenting?

3. What are some of the major biological and sociocultural factors that contribute to the development of gender differences?

4. How might an adult successfully meet each of the last three crises in Erikson's theory of psychosocial development?

5

Sensation and Perception

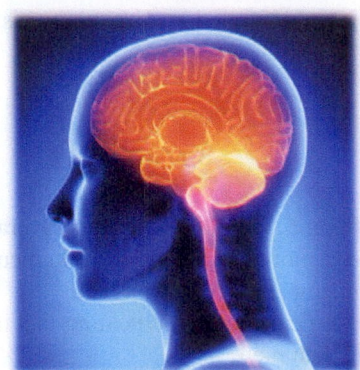

Source: CLIPAREA/Custom media/
Shutterstock.com.

Chapter Outline

Sensory Processes

Visual Sensation

Visual Perception

Hearing

Chemical Senses

Skin Senses

Body Senses

Extrasensory Perception

visual agnosia A condition in which an individual can see objects and identify their features but cannot recognize the objects.

prosopagnosia A condition in which an individual can recognize details in faces but cannot recognize faces as a whole.

> He reached out his hand and took hold of his wife's head, tried to lift it off, to put it on. He had apparently mistaken his wife for a hat! (Sacks, 1985, p. 10)

This bizarre scene was described in a case study presented in a best-selling book, *The Man Who Mistook His Wife for a Hat,* by neurologist Oliver Sacks. In the book, Sacks used case studies to illustrate the sometimes extraordinary effects of brain damage on human behavior. The man who mistook his wife for a hat, whom Sacks called "Dr. P.," was a talented singer and musician who taught at a music school. But his students began to notice that he could not recognize their faces. Yet, when they spoke, he identified them immediately. Dr. P. also saw people where they did not exist. As he strolled down a street, for example, he would kindly pat the tops of water hydrants and parking meters, mistaking them for the heads of children. At first people laughed and thought he was just joking—after all, he was known for his quirky sense of humor.

Did Dr. P. have a problem with his eyes? An eye examination found that he had good vision. Puzzled, the ophthalmologist sent him for a neurological examination by Dr. Sacks. After examining him, Sacks said, "His visual acuity was good: he had no difficulty seeing a pin on the floor" (Sacks, 1985, p. 9). But given that Dr. P. had normal vision, what accounted for his inability to recognize faces? Over time Sacks put the clues together to solve the mystery of Dr. P.'s peculiar problem. On one occasion, when Dr. P. perused an issue of *National Geographic,* he could identify individual details in scenes but not the scenes as a whole. When Sacks asked him to identify photographs of his family members, he could not—though he could identify their facial features. He identified his brother Paul based on his unusually large teeth. But Dr. P. did not recognize Paul's face. He simply inferred that it was Paul based on the size of the teeth.

Eventually, Sacks realized that Dr. P. suffered from brain damage (perhaps from an undetected stroke) that produced visual agnosia and prosopagnosia. In **visual agnosia,** the individual can see objects and identify their features, but cannot recognize them (Behrmann & Kimchi, 2003). When, for example, Dr. P. was shown a glove, he described it as being continuously curved, but he could not recognize it as a glove—until he put it on and used it. A person with **prosopagnosia** (a form of visual agnosia) can identify details of faces but cannot recognize them as a whole (de Gelder & Rouw, 2000). Imagine a man with prosopagnosia. He might fail to recognize his wife's face, yet still recognize her voice. Every time they met, she would have to speak so he could identify her.

Functional MRI reveals that when individuals with prosopagnosia look at familiar faces, they exhibit lower activity in a strip of association cortex (see Chapter 3) running along the underside of the occipital and temporal lobes of the brain (Hadjikhani & de Gelder, 2002). Visual agnosia and prosopagnosia illustrate the difference between **sensation**, the process that detects stimuli from the environment, and **perception**, the process that organizes sensations into meaningful wholes.

FIGURE 5-1
Sensation and Perception

Do you see anything in this picture? Though *sensation* lets you see the pattern of light and dark in the picture, *perception* lets you organize what you sense into a meaningful pattern—a person riding a horse.
Source: Dallenbach, K. M. (1951). A puzzle picture with a new principle of concealment. *American Journal of Psychology, 54,* 431–433.

Sensory Processes

The starting point for both sensation and perception is a stimulus (plural, stimuli), a form of energy (such as light waves or sound waves) that can affect sensory organs (such as the eyes or the ears). Visual sensation lets you detect the black marks on this page; visual perception lets you organize the black marks into letters and words. To appreciate the difference between sensation and perception, try to identify the picture in Figure 5-1. Most people cannot identify it because they sense the light and dark marks on the page but fail to perceive a meaningful pattern.

Sensation depends on specialized cells called **sensory receptors,** which detect stimuli and convert their energy into neural impulses. This process is called **sensory transduction.** Receptors serve our visual, auditory, smell, taste, skin, and body senses. But some animals have receptors that serve unusual senses. The blind cave salamander has electroreceptors that detect electrical fields produced by prey (Schlegel & Roth, 1997). Because whales and dolphins navigate by using receptors sensitive to the earth's magnetic field (Walker, Dennis, & Kirschvink, 2002), disruption of this sense might account for some of the periodic strandings of whales and dolphins on beaches.

Sensory Thresholds

How intense must a sound be for you to detect it? How much change in light intensity must occur for you to notice it? Questions like these are the subject matter of **psychophysics**, the study of the relationship between the physical characteristics of stimuli and the corresponding psychological responses to them. Psychophysics was developed by the German scientists Ernst Weber (1795–1878) and Gustav Fechner (1801–1887). Fechner, after the publication of his classic *Elements of Psychophysics* in 1860, devoted the rest of his life to studying the relationship between physical stimulation and cognitive experiences. Psychophysics has been used to assess, among other things, differences in digital video quality (Moore, 2002), infants' ability to detect differences between colors (Adams & Courage, 2002), and the ability of monkeys and baboons to detect changes in the sweetness of sugar solutions (Laska, Scheuber, Sanchez, & Luna, 1999).

Absolute Threshold

The minimum amount of stimulation that a person can detect is called the **absolute threshold**, or *limen.* For example, a cup of coffee would require a certain amount of sugar before you could detect a sweet taste. Weber used fine bristles to measure touch sensitivity by bending them against the skin. Because the absolute threshold for a particular sensory experience varies, psychologists operationally define the absolute threshold as the minimum level of stimulation that can be detected 50 percent of the time when a stimulus is presented. Thus, if you were presented with a low-intensity sound 30 times and you detected it 15 times, that level of intensity would be your absolute threshold for that stimulus. The absolute thresholds for certain senses are remarkable. For example, you can detect the sweetness from a teaspoon of sugar dissolved in two gallons of water, the odor of one drop of perfume diffused throughout a three-room apartment, the wing of a bee falling on your cheek from a height of one centimeter, the ticking of a watch under quiet conditions at a distance of 20 feet, and the flame of a candle seen from a distance of 30 miles on a clear, dark night

sensation The process that detects stimuli from the body or surroundings.

perception The process that organizes sensations into meaningful patterns.

sensory receptors Specialized cells that detect stimuli and convert their energy into neural impulses.

sensory transduction The process by which sensory receptors convert stimuli into neural impulses.

psychophysics The study of the relationship between the physical characteristics of stimuli and the conscious psychological experiences that are associated with them.

absolute threshold The minimum amount of stimulation that an individual can detect through a given sense.

(Galanter, 1962). The absolute threshold is used, for example, in testing the ability of people with hearing impairments to detect speech (Nejime & Moore, 1998).

Signal-Detection Theory The absolute threshold also is affected by factors other than the intensity of the stimulus. Because of this, researchers, inspired by Fechner's work, have devised **signal-detection theory,** which assumes that the detection of a stimulus depends on both its intensity and the physical and psychological state of the individual. One of the most important psychological factors is *response bias*—how ready the person is to report the presence of a particular stimulus. Imagine you are walking down a street at night. Your predisposition to detect a sound would partly depend on your estimate of the probability of being mugged, so you would be more likely to perceive the sound of footsteps in a neighborhood that you believe to be dangerous than in a neighborhood you believe to be safe.

Signal-detection researchers study four kinds of reports that a person might make in response to a stimulus. A *hit* is a correct report of the presence of a target stimulus. A *miss* is a failure to report the presence of a target stimulus that is, in fact, present. A *false alarm* is a report of the presence of a target stimulus that is not, in fact, present. And a *correct rejection* is a correct report of the absence of a target stimulus. Consider these four kinds of reports in regard to walking down a dark street at night. A hit would be perceiving footsteps when they actually occur. A miss would be failing to perceive footsteps when they actually occur. A false alarm would be perceiving footsteps when they do not occur. And a correct rejection would be failing to perceive footsteps when they do not occur.

Signal-detection theory has important applications to crucial tasks, such as identifying bombs put through airport X-ray machines. It has been used to assess differences in drivers' reactions to potentially dangerous situations, including merging into traffic and approaching a yellow traffic light (Rosenbloom & Wolf, 2002). Even caregivers' responses to infants' cries may depend on their response biases. In one study, 38 mothers were presented with taped cries of infants that they had been told were "easy" or "difficult." In reality, one of the labels was randomly assigned to each infant. Cries of supposedly "difficult" infants elicited greater detection sensitivity, such as response time and heart rate changes from the mothers (Donovan, Leavitt, & Walsh, 1997).

Subliminal Perception Research on **subliminal perception** investigates whether participants can unconsciously perceive stimuli that do not exceed the absolute threshold. In other words, such stimuli are below threshold detection. Nonetheless, some research studies have failed to support the existence of subliminal perception (Fox & Burns, 1993). Assuming that we might be able to perceive subliminal stimuli, could manufacturers make us buy their products by bombarding us with subliminal advertisements? This question is the heart of a controversy that arose in the late 1950s after a marketing firm subliminally flashed the words "Eat Popcorn" and "Drink Coca-Cola" during movies shown at a theater in Fort Lee, New Jersey. After several weeks of this subliminal advertising, popcorn sales had increased 50 percent and Coke sales had increased 18 percent (McConnell, Cutler, & McNeil, 1958). Marketing executives expressed glee at this potential boon to advertising, but the public feared that subliminal perception might be used as a means of totalitarian mind control.

Psychologists, however, pointed out that the uncontrolled conditions of the study made it impossible to determine the actual reason for the increase in sales. Perhaps sales increased because better movies, hotter weather, or more appealing counter displays attracted more customers during the period when subliminal advertising was used. Another problem is that the limen varies from trial to trial for each participant. This variation makes it difficult to assess when stimulation has truly been subliminal (Miller, 1991). Thus, perhaps moviegoers were, at times, consciously aware of the supposedly subliminal messages about Coke and popcorn. Moreover, there even is evidence that the original study just might have been a fabrication created by an overeager advertising executive (Pratkanis, 1992).

But some more recent controlled studies have provided support for the possible effectiveness of subliminal advertising. In one study, participants watched an episode of *The Simpsons* during which stimuli related to thirst were presented subliminally. A control group watched the episode without being exposed to the subliminal material.

signal-detection theory
The theory holding that the detection of a stimulus depends on both the intensity of the stimulus and the physical and psychological state of the individual.

subliminal perception
The unconscious perception of stimuli that are too weak to exceed the absolute threshold for detection.

The results showed that those who had been exposed to the subliminal thirst stimuli became thirstier than the control group and thirstier than they had been before watching the episode (Cooper & Cooper, 2002). Despite studies like this one, a meta-analysis of subliminal advertising studies found that it is generally ineffective in influencing consumers' product choices (Trappey, 1996).

But what of the popular subliminal self-help audiotapes that supposedly help you to improve yourself? Producers of subliminal self-help audiotapes claim that they can help listeners do everything from smoke less to improve their study habits. People who listen to these audiotapes typically hear soothing music or nature sounds. Messages (such as "Study harder") presented on audiotapes below the auditory threshold supposedly motivate the listener to improve in the desired area. Consider an experiment that examined the effectiveness of subliminal audiotapes (Froufe & Schwartz, 2001). Young adults were randomly assigned to one of four conditions. One group listened to audiotaped music with both supraliminal (above threshold detection) and subliminal self-esteem messages. A second group listened to music with only subliminal self-esteem messages. A third group listened to music, though they were told that the audiotape contained subliminal messages. And a fourth group did not listen to an audiotape. Each participant was given a self-esteem scale before and after each of the conditions had been administered. Whereas each of the first three groups showed an increase in self-esteem, the fourth group did not. This indicated that any improvements in self-esteem were no more than placebo effects.

Difference Threshold

In addition to detecting the presence of a stimulus, we must be able to detect changes in its intensity. The minimum amount of change in stimulation that can be detected is called the **difference threshold**. For example, you would have to increase or decrease the intensity of the sound from your CD player a certain amount before you could detect a change in its volume. Like the absolute threshold, the difference threshold for a particular sensory experience varies from person to person and from occasion to occasion. Therefore, psychologists formally define the difference threshold as the minimum change in stimulation that can be detected 50 percent of the time by a given person. The difference threshold has practical applications, as in a study of passengers' perception of differences in the comfort level of automobile rides based on changes in the intensity of vehicle vibrations (Mansfield & Griffin, 2000).

Weber and Fechner referred to the difference threshold as the **just noticeable difference (jnd).** They found that the amount of change in intensity of stimulation needed to produce a jnd is a constant fraction of the original stimulus. This fraction became known as **Weber's law** (Droesler, 2000). For example, because the jnd for weight is about 2 percent, if you held a 50-ounce weight, you would notice a change only if there was at least a 1-ounce change in it. But a person holding a 100-ounce weight would require the addition or subtraction of at least 2 ounces to notice a change. Research indicates that Weber's law holds better for mid-range stimuli than for stimuli at either the low or high extreme. Other factors also may play a role. For example, the jnd for two-dimensional bar graphs is smaller than for three-dimensional bar graphs. This means that three-dimensional bar graphs require larger differences between the heights of bars for those differences to be noticed (Hughes, 2001).

Sensory Adaptation

Given that each of your senses is constantly bombarded by stimulation, why do you notice only certain stimuli? One reason is that if a stimulus remains constant in intensity, you will gradually stop noticing it. For example, on entering a friend's dormitory room, you might be struck by the repugnant stench of month-old garbage. A few minutes later, though, you might not notice it at all. This tendency of sensory receptors to respond less and less to an unchanging stimulus is called **sensory adaptation.**

Sensory adaptation lets us detect potentially important changes in our environment while ignoring unchanging aspects of it. For example, when vibrations repeatedly

difference threshold
The minimum amount of change in stimulation that can be detected.

just noticeable difference (jnd)
Weber and Fechner's term for the difference threshold.

Weber's law The principle that the amount of change in stimulation needed to produce a just noticeable difference is a constant proportion of the original stimulus.

sensory adaptation
The tendency of the sensory receptors to respond less and less to a constant stimulus.

Can We Be Controlled by Subliminal Messages?

Since the 1950s, the media periodically have created alarm by sensationalizing claims that we can be influenced by stimulation that does not exceed the absolute threshold—subliminal stimulation. This attention has provoked fears among citizens and government officials that subliminal stimulation could be used to control people's behavior. Over the years, concern has been raised in the media about subliminal messages presented in movies, on television, on audiotapes, in advertisements, and in rock music recordings. Subliminal stimulation even became part of the 2000 U.S. presidential election when Democrats complained that Republicans had superimposed the subliminal message "RATS" over a televised campaign advertisement attacking candidate Al Gore's Medicare plan. Given an unusually close election like that one, might subliminal messages sway enough voters to determine who wins?

As another example, after the John Travolta movie *Phenomenon* was released in 1996, the *Globe* tabloid (Richard Baker, September 3, 1996) quoted two disc jockeys from Flint, Michigan, as saying that the movie was filled with subliminal messages about Travolta's belief in the religion of Scientology. These messages were supposedly conveyed through *backmasking*—the superimposing of a soundtrack backwards over

a forward one. This controversy even merited attention on the television tabloid show *Extra*. The show claimed, for example, that the movie's theme song, "I Have the Touch," sung by Peter Gabriel, included the words, "Don't you miss Ron?" when played backward. Some people took this phrase as a reference to L. Ron Hubbard, the founder of Scientology and author of *Dianetics*, the book that popularized it. Might a message like this be effective in encouraging readers to want to learn more about Scientology?

Parents likewise have expressed concerns about the alleged subliminal messages in rock music recordings, such as Led Zeppelin's "Stairway to Heaven," that supposedly can be heard clearly when the recording is played backward. Despite the lack of evidence that such messages exist, fear that they might cause crime, suicide, Satanism, and sexual promiscuity led California and other states to pass laws requiring warnings on recordings that allegedly contain subliminal messages. Yet, even if recordings (or movies) contain subliminal messages, there is no evidence that listeners will obey them like zombies any more than they will obey messages they are aware of (Vokey & Read, 1985). That is, subliminal *stimulation* should not be confused with subliminal *persuasion*.

stimulate your skin, you stop noticing them (Hollins, Delemos, & Goble, 1991). And once you have determined that the swimming pool water is cold, it would serve little purpose to continue noticing it—especially when more important changes might be taking place elsewhere in your surroundings. Of course, you will not adapt completely to extremely intense sensations, such as severe pain or freezing cold. This continuation of response also is adaptive, because to ignore such stimuli might be harmful or even fatal.

Section Review: Sensory Processes

1. What is the difference between sensation and perception?
2. What is psychophysics?
3. What is sensory adaptation?

Visual Sensation

vision The sense that detects objects by the light reflected from them into the eyes.

Because of our reliance on vision, psychologists have conducted more research on it than on all the other senses combined. **Vision** lets us sense objects by the light reflected from them into our eyes.

Light Waves

Light is the common name for the **visible spectrum,** a narrow band of energy within the *electromagnetic spectrum* (depicted in Figure 5-2). The wavelength of light corresponds to its *hue,* the perceptual quality that we call color. The wavelength is the distance between two wave peaks, measured in nanometers (billionths of a meter). Visible light varies in wavelength from about 350 nanometers to about 750 nanometers. A light composed of short wavelengths of light appears violet; a light composed of long wavelengths appears red. We see these wavelengths because we have receptors in our central nervous system that respond to them.

Though people have visual receptors that sense only the visible spectrum, certain animals have visual receptors that detect other forms of electromagnetic energy. Bats, for example, though they rely primarily on echolocation for detecting objects, also have visual receptors that are sensitive to the relatively short wavelengths of ultraviolet light, which affects people chiefly by causing sunburn (Winter, Lopez, & von Helversen, 2003). Pythons have receptors located in pits below their eyes that are sensitive to the relatively long wavelengths of infrared light, which conveys heat. This capability lets them hunt at night by detecting the heat emitted by nearby prey (Grace, Woodward, Church, & Calisch, 2001). Police and soldiers may use special infrared scopes and goggles to provide vision in the dark (Rabin & Wiley, 1994).

Returning to the visible spectrum, the height, or *amplitude,* of light waves determines the perceived intensity, or *brightness,* of a light. When you use a dimmer switch to adjust the brightness of a light bulb, you change the amplitude of the light waves emitted by it. The purity of a light's wavelengths determines its *saturation,* or vividness. The narrower the range of wavelengths, the more saturated the light. A highly saturated red light, for example, would seem "redder" than a less saturated one.

Vision and the Eye

Vision depends on the interaction of the eyes and the brain. The eyes sense light reflected from objects and convey this information to the brain, where visual perception takes place. The eye (see Figure 5-3) is a fluid-filled sphere. The "white" of your eye is a tough membrane called the **sclera,** which protects the eye from injury. At the front of the sclera is the round, transparent **cornea,** which focuses light into the eye. Are you blue-eyed? brown-eyed? green-eyed? Your eye color is determined by the color of your iris, a donut-shaped band of muscles behind the cornea. At the center of the iris is an opening called the pupil. The iris controls the amount of light that enters the eye by regulating the size of the pupil, dilating it to let in more light and constricting it to let in less. Your pupils dilate when you enter a dimly lit room and constrict when you go outside into sunlight.

You can demonstrate the pupillary response to light by first noting the size of your pupils in your bathroom mirror. Next, turn out the light for 30 seconds. Then turn on the

visible spectrum The portion of the electromagnetic spectrum that we commonly call light.

sclera The tough, white, outer membrane of the eye.

cornea The round, transparent area in the front of the sclera that allows light to enter the eye.

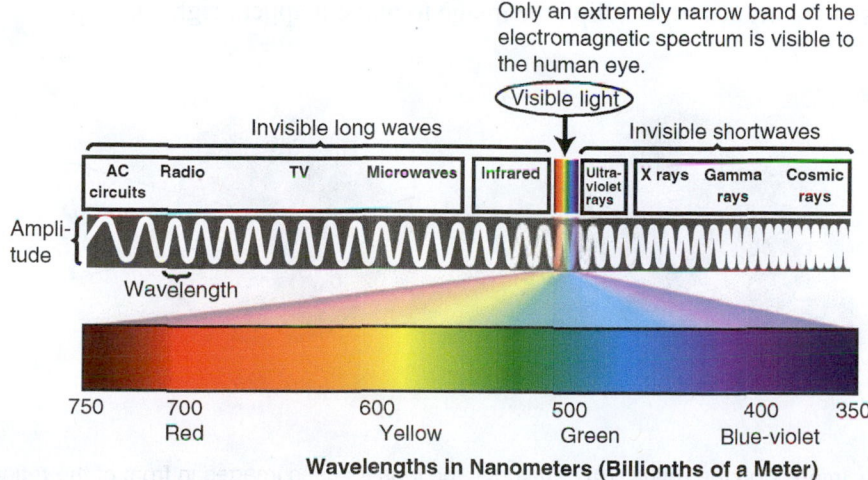

Only an extremely narrow band of the electromagnetic spectrum is visible to the human eye.

FIGURE 5-2

The Visible Spectrum

The human eye is sensitive to only a narrow slice (from about 400 to 700 nanometers) of the electromagnetic spectrum. This visible spectrum appears in rainbows, when sunlight is broken into its component wavelengths as it passes through raindrops in the atmosphere.

FIGURE 5-3
The Human Eye

The lens (from the Latin word *lentil*) is behind the pupil and focuses light onto the retina in this cross section of the eye. The letter R is in the visual field and is projected upside down onto the retina. Our brain interacts with the visual system and corrects the flip, and we perceive a letter R in front of us.

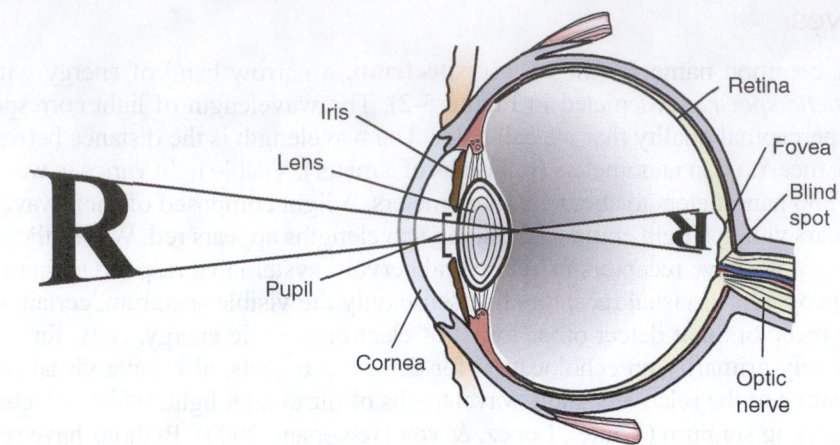

lens The transparent structure behind the pupil that focuses light onto the retina.

retina The light-sensitive inner membrane of the eye that contains the receptor cells for vision.

accommodation
1. The cognitive process that revises existing schemas to incorporate new information.
2. The process by which the lens of the eye increases its curvature to focus light from close objects or decreases its curvature to focus light from more distant objects.

light and look in the mirror. Notice how much larger your pupils have become and how quickly they constrict in response to the light.

The size of the pupil also is affected by a variety of psychological factors. When we are psychologically aroused, the sympathetic nervous system makes our pupils dilate. For example, the pupils dilate in response to emotional stimuli. In one study, young adults listened to negative sounds (such as a baby crying), positive sounds (such as a baby laughing), and neutral sounds (such as common office sounds). The participants' pupils became significantly larger in response to the negative and positive sounds than to the neutral sounds (Partala & Surakka, 2003). Because pupil dilation is a sign of emotional arousal, psychotherapists have used it to monitor the effectiveness of therapy, as in the treatment of snake phobia (that is, an intense fear of snakes that interferes with everyday functioning). As the participants' anxiety decreases, their pupils dilate less when they look at a snake (Sturgeon, Cooper, & Howell, 1989).

Regardless of the psychological phenomena associated with the pupil, its primary function is to regulate the amount of light that enters the eye. After passing through the pupil, light is focused by the **lens** onto the **retina**, the light-sensitive inner membrane of the eye. Tiny muscles connected to the lens control **accommodation**, the process by which the lens increases its curvature to focus light from close objects or decreases its curvature to focus light from more distant objects. Sustained accommodation, as when working at a computer monitor for a prolonged period, produces accommodation fatigue, which may reduce visual acuity (Hasebe, Graf, & Schor, 2001).

Today we know that the image cast on the retina is upside down. This phenomenon is illustrated in Figure 5-4. In the 15th century, Leonardo da Vinci (1452–1519) had rejected this possibility because he could not explain how the brain saw a right-side-up world from an upside-down image. Why, then, do we not see the world upside down? The neural pathways in the brain simply "flip" the image to make it appear right side up.

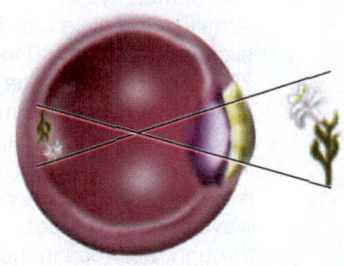

(a) Normal Vision

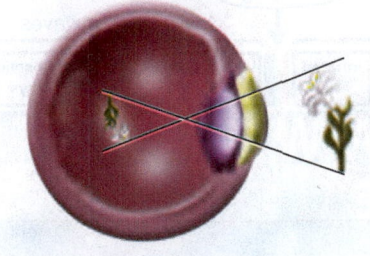

(b) Myopia

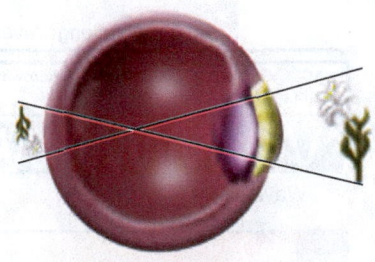

(c) Hyperopia

FIGURE 5-4 Visual Acuity

(a) In normal vision, the lens clearly focuses images on the retina. *(b)* In myopia, the lens focuses images in front of the retina. *(c)* In hyperopia, the lens focuses images at a point that would fall behind the retina.

Disruption of normal accommodation has important effects. As we age, the lens loses its elasticity, making it less able to accommodate when focusing on near objects. Adults typically discover this in their early 40s, when they find themselves holding books and newspapers at arm's length to focus the print more clearly on their retinas. Many people, whether young or old, have conditions that make them unable to focus clear images on the retina. The two most common conditions are illustrated in Figure 5-4. In **myopia,** or *nearsightedness,* the lens focuses images of near objects on the retina, but focuses images of far objects at a point in front of the retina. In **hyperopia,** or *farsightedness,* the lens focuses images of far objects on the retina, but focuses images of near objects at a point that would fall behind the retina. Both of these conditions often are corrected with prescription eyeglasses or contact lenses.

The Retina

As shown in Figure 5-5, the retina contains specialized neurons called *photoreceptors,* which respond when stimulated by light. There are two kinds of photoreceptors, **rods** and **cones,** whose names reflect their shapes. Each eye has about 120 million rods and about 6 million cones. The rods and cones stimulate *bipolar cells,* which in turn stimulate *ganglion cells.* The axons of the ganglion cells form the **optic nerve** of each eye, which conveys visual information to the brain.

The rods are especially important in night vision and peripheral vision; the cones are especially important in color vision and detailed vision. Rod vision and cone vision depend on different pathways in the brain (Hadjikhani & Tootell, 2000). The rods are more prevalent in the periphery of the retina, and the cones are more prevalent in the

myopia Visual nearsightedness, which is caused by an elongated eyeball.

hyperopia Visual farsightedness, which is caused by a shortened eyeball.

rods Receptor cells of the retina that play an important role in night vision and peripheral vision.

cones Receptor cells of the retina that play an important role in day vision and color vision.

optic nerve The nerve, formed from the axons of ganglion cells, that carries visual impulses from the retina to the brain.

FIGURE 5-5
The Cells of the Retina

Light must first pass through layers of ganglion cells and bipolar cells before striking the rods and cones. The rods and cones transmit neural impulses to the bipolar cells, which in turn transmit neural impulses to the ganglion cells. The axons of the ganglion cells form the optic nerves, which transmit neural impulses to the visual processing areas of the brain.

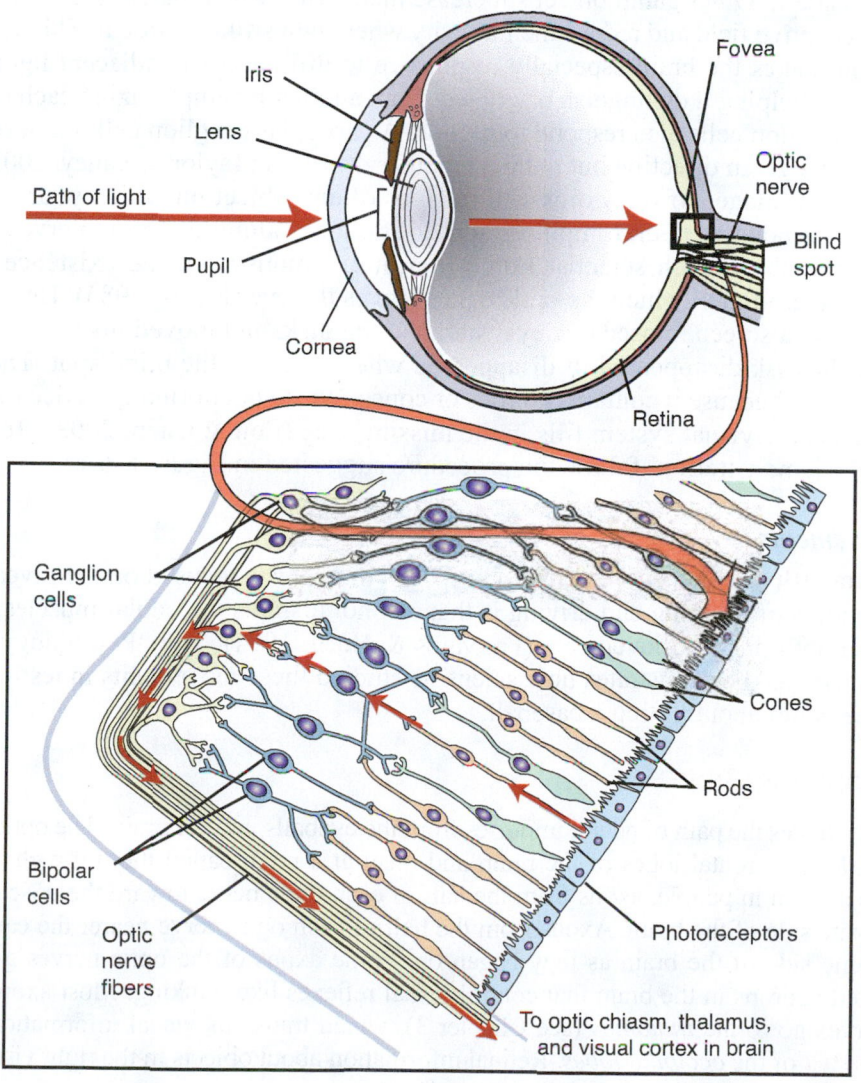

Iris
Lens
Path of light
Pupil
Cornea
Fovea
Optic nerve
Blind spot
Retina

Ganglion cells
Cones
Rods
Bipolar cells
Photoreceptors
Optic nerve fibers
To optic chiasm, thalamus, and visual cortex in brain

center. You can demonstrate this arrangement for yourself by taking small pieces of colored paper and selecting one without looking at it. Hold it beside your head, and slowly move it forward while staring straight ahead. Because your peripheral vision depends on your rods and your color vision depends on your cones, you will notice the paper before you can identify its color. Peripheral vision has survival value. For example, we rely on it to help avoid traffic hazards when crossing a street (David, Foot, & Chapman, 1990). Also, since rods are more sensitive to faint light, it is easier to see a faint star in the sky if you look slightly to the side of it instead of directly at it.

fovea A small area at the center of the retina that contains only cones and provides the most acute vision.

A small area in the center of the retina, the **fovea**, contains only cones. One reason why people differ in their visual acuity is that they vary in the number of foveal cones (Curcio, Sloan, Packer, Hendrickson, & Kalina 1987). Because the fovea provides our most acute vision, we try to focus images on it when we want to see fine details. As you read this sentence, words focused on your cone-rich fovea look clear. Meanwhile, words focused on the cone-poor area around your fovea look blurred. One reason foveal vision is more acute is that each cone transmits neural impulses to one bipolar cell. In other words, the exact retinal site of input from a given cone is communicated along the visual pathway. In contrast, neural impulses from an average of 50–100 rods are sent to a single bipolar cell (Cicerone & Hayhoe, 1990). Thus, the exact retinal site of stimulation of a given rod is lost. But in dim light the many rods sending their output to a given bipolar cell help make rod vision more sensitive than cone vision. A ganglion cell may receive input from many rods and cones in a given area of the retina. The area of the retina that feeds input to a ganglion cell is called its *receptive field*. Some ganglion cells increase their activity when light strikes inside the relevant receptive field and reduce their activity when light strikes outside it. Other ganglion cells increase their firing when light strikes outside the relevant receptive field and reduce their activity when light strikes inside it. This variation in reaction makes the brain especially responsive to differences in adjacent lighter and darker areas, helping it distinguish one object from another by emphasizing each object's borders. Ganglion cells also respond to motion. A particular ganglion cell might respond to motion in a given direction but not in any other direction (Taylor & Vaney, 2003).

The retinal images of the words you read, or of any object on which your eyes are focused, are coded as neural impulses sent to the brain along the optic nerves. In the 17th century, the French scientist Edmé Mariotte demonstrated the existence of the *blind spot,* the point at which the optic nerve leaves the eye (Riggs, 1985). He placed a small disk on a screen, closed one eye, stared at the disk, and moved his head until the image of the disk disappeared. It disappeared when it fell on the blind spot. The blind spot is "blind" because it contains no rods or cones. We do not normally notice the blind spot because the visual system fills in the missing area (Lou & Chen, 2003). To repeat Mariotte's demonstration, follow the procedure suggested in Figure 5-6.

Eye Movements

smooth pursuit movements Eye movements controlled by the ocular muscles that keep objects focused on the fovea.

We use **smooth pursuit movements** to keep moving objects focused on the foveae. One of the dangers of drinking and driving is that alcohol disrupts the ocular muscles, which control smooth pursuit movements (Freivalds & Horii, 1994). The "Psychology versus Common Sense" box illustrates how scientists studied these movements in testing commonsense belief about hitting a baseball.

Vision and the Brain

optic chiasm The point under the frontal lobes at which some axons from each of the optic nerves cross over to the opposite side of the brain.

visual cortex The area of the occipital lobes that processes visual input.

Figure 5-7 traces the path of neural impulses from the eyeballs into the brain. The optic nerves travel under the frontal lobes of the brain and meet at a point called the **optic chiasm**. At the optic chiasm in people, axons from the half of each optic nerve toward the nose cross to the opposite side of the brain. Axons from the half of each optic nerve nearer the ears travel to the same side of the brain as they began on. Some axons of the optic nerves go to the specialized neurons in the brain that control visual reflexes like blinking. Most axons of the optic nerves go to the *thalamus* (see Chapter 3), which transmits visual information to the **visual cortex** of the *occipital lobes*. Retinal information about objects in the right visual field

FIGURE 5-6
Finding Your Blind Spot

Because your retina has no rods or cones at the point where the optic nerve leaves the eye, the retina is "blind" at that spot. To find your blind spot, keep your eyes about an arm's length away from the figure, close your right eye, and focus your left eye on the black dot. Move your head slowly toward the figure. When your head is about a foot away, the image of the mouse should disappear. It disappears when it becomes focused on your blind spot. You do not normally notice your blind spot because your eyes see different views of the same scene, because your eyes constantly focus on different parts of the scene, and because your brain fills in the missing portion of the scene.

is processed in the left occipital lobe, and retinal information about objects in the left visual field is processed in the right occipital lobe. The visual cortex integrates visual information about objects, including their shape (Buechel, Price, Frackowiak, & Friston, 1998) and distance (Dobbins, Jeo, Fiser, & Allman, 1998) as well as their color (Engel, 1999), brightness (Rossi, Rittenhouse, & Paradiso, 1996), and movement (Moore & Engel, 1999). Functional MRI has shown that particular regions of the visual cortex also display distinctive patterns of activity in response to particular categories of objects, such as faces, houses, and chairs (Ishai, Ungerleider, Martin, & Haxby, 2000).

Because the visual cortex is covered by a "map" with a point-by-point representation of the retinas, people who have gone blind because of damage to their eyes or optic nerves might someday have their vision restored by devices that directly stimulate the visual cortex. Researchers have invented an electronic system that consists of a video camera connected to a microprocessor, which in turn is connected to a matrix of electrodes attached to the visual cortex. Stimulation of these electrodes produces a pattern of spots of light called *phosphenes*, from the Greek words *phos* (light) and *phainein* (to show), that can be used to represent the outlines of objects seen by the camera. In one experiment,

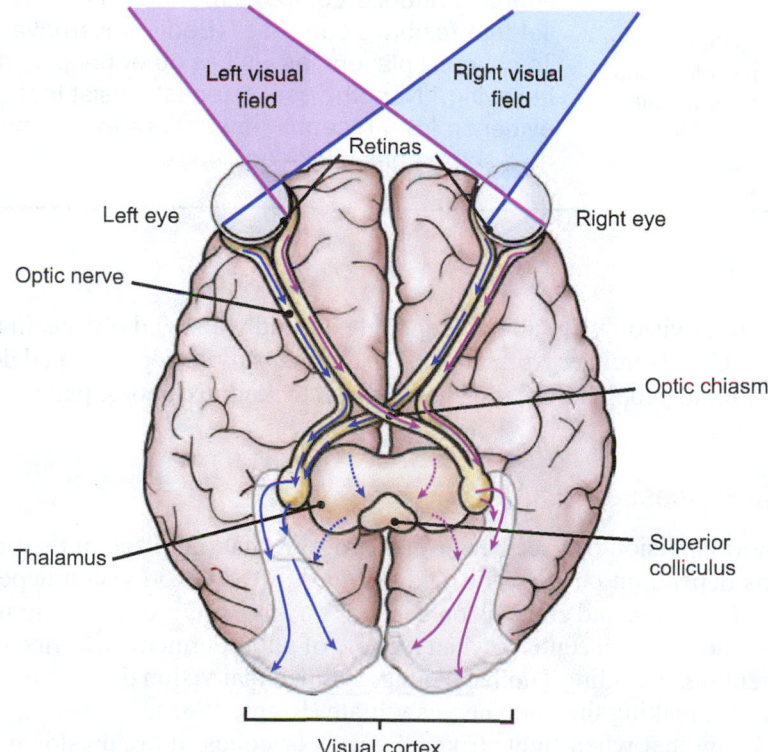

Visual cortex

FIGURE 5-7
The Visual Pathway

This illustration of a horizontal section of the brain shows that images of objects in the right visual field are focused on the left side of each retina, and images of objects in the left visual field are focused on the right side of each retina. This information is conveyed along the optic nerves to the optic chiasm and then on to the thalamus. The thalamus then relays the information to the visual cortex of the occipital lobes. Because of the nature of the visual pathway, images of objects in the right visual field are processed by the left occipital lobe, and images of the objects in the left visual field are processed by the right occipital lobe. Also note that a secondary visual pathway goes to the superior colliculus, a structure that contributes to visual reflexes, such as blinking when an object rapidly approaches your eyes.

Chapter 5 Sensation and Perception · 159

Can Baseball Batters Really Keep Their Eyes on the Ball?

Professional athletes make faster smooth pursuit eye movements than amateurs do (Harbin, Durst, & Harbin, 1989). This characteristic is important because, for example, a professional baseball batter might have to track a baseball thrown by a pitcher at more than 90 miles an hour from a distance of only 60 feet. Ted Williams, arguably the greatest hitter in the history of baseball, called hitting a baseball the most difficult single task in any sport. Given this difficulty, is there any scientific support for the commonsense suggestion to batters, "Keep your eye on the ball"? Take a look at a study by Terry Bahill and Tom LaRitz (1984), of the University of Arizona, in which they sought the answer to this question. Bahill and LaRitz rigged a device that propelled a ball toward home plate along a string at up to 100 miles an hour on a consistent path. A photoelectric device recorded the batter's eye movements as he tracked the ball. Several professional baseball players took part in the study.

Eye-movement recordings indicated that the batters were able to track the ball until it was about 5 feet from home plate. Over the last few feet they could not keep the ball focused on their foveae—it simply traveled too fast over those last few degrees of visual arc. Thus, the commonsense advice to keep your eye on the ball is well intentioned, but it is impossible to follow the ball's movement all the way from the pitcher's hand to home plate. The reason some hitters, including Ted Williams, claim they can see the ball strike the bat is that, based on their extensive experience in batting, their brains automatically calculate both the speed and the trajectory of the ball. This calculation allows them to anticipate the point in space at which the bat will meet the ball and make a final eye movement to that exact point. Years later Bahill likewise presented research evidence contradicting the commonsense belief that fastballs can "rise" (Bahill & Karnavas, 1993). To baseball players, as well as other people, "seeing is believing." Nonetheless, scientists insist that objective evidence from research is superior to common sense as a source of knowledge.

Keeping Your Eye on the Ball

The commonsense idea that batters can "keep their eye on the ball" is contradicted by scientific research. Professional hitters anticipate the point in space where the bat will meet the ball and make a final eye movement to that point.
Source: Peter Kim/Shutterstock.com.

people with normal vision were able to negotiate around walls and objects in a maze using this system (Cha, Horch, & Normann, 1992). Perhaps more sophisticated devices will one day permit blind people to use prosthetic vision to read textbooks, paint pictures, and drive automobiles.

Basic Visual Processes

photopigments Chemicals, including rhodopsin and iodopsin, that enable the rods and cones to generate neural impulses.

People with normal vision can see because of processes taking place in their retinas. Visual sensations depend on chemicals called **photopigments**. Rod vision depends on the photopigment *rhodopsin,* and cone vision depends on three kinds of photopigments called *iodopsin.* Until the late 19th century, when the role of photopigments was first discovered, prominent scientists, including Thomas Young, claimed that vision depended on light rays striking the retina, making the optic nerves vibrate (Riggs, 1985).

Today we know that when light strikes the rods or cones, it breaks down their photopigments. This breakdown begins the process by which neural impulses are eventually sent along the optic nerves to the brain. After being broken down by light, the photopigments are resynthesized—more rapidly in dim light than in bright light. The cones function better than the rods in normal light, but the rods function better than the cones in dim light. Because of this difference, in normal light we try to focus fine details on the fovea. But if you were to look directly at a star in the night sky, you would be unable to see it because it would be focused on the fovea. To see the star, you would have to turn your head slightly, thereby focusing the star on the rod-rich periphery of the retina. The photoreceptors are also important in the processes of *dark adaptation* and *color vision*.

Dark Adaptation

When you enter a darkened movie theater, you have difficulty finding a seat because your photoreceptors have been bleached of their photopigments by the light in the lobby. But your eyes adapt by increasing their rate of synthesis of iodopsin and rhodopsin, gradually increasing your ability to see the seats and people in the theater. The cones reach their maximum sensitivity after about 10 minutes of dim light. But your rods continue to adapt to the dim light, reaching their maximum sensitivity in about 30 minutes. So, you owe your ability to see in dim light to your rods. **Dark adaptation** is the process by which the eyes become more sensitive to light. Impaired dark adaptation, which accompanies aging (Jackson, Owsley, & McGwin, 1999), has been implicated in the disproportionate number of nighttime driving accidents that involve older adults. Dark adaptation also explains why motorists should dim their high beams when approaching oncoming traffic and why passengers should not turn on the dome light to read maps. High beams shining into the eyes or dome lights illuminating the inside of the vehicle bleach the rods, impairing the driver's ability to see objects that might be ahead. You also should note that the cones are most sensitive to the longer wavelengths of the visible spectrum (which produce the experience of red) and the rods are most sensitive to the medium wavelengths (which produce the experience of green). This fact explains why at dusk (when we shift from cone vision to rod vision) a red jacket looks dull while a patch of green grass looks vibrant.

dark adaptation The process by which the eyes become more sensitive to light when under low illumination.

Color Vision

Color enhances the quality of our lives, as manifested by our concern with the colors of our clothing, furnishings, and automobiles. Color also contributes to our survival, as exemplified by the orange or yellow life rafts used at sea that make search and rescue easier (Donderi, 1994). Primates such as apes, monkeys, and people have good color vision because they have three types of cones. Most other mammals, including dogs, cats, and cows, have poor color vision. They lack a sufficient number or variety of cones. Most birds and fish have good color vision. But fish that live in the dark depths of the ocean lack color vision, which would be useless to them because cones function well only in bright light (Levine & MacNichol, 1982).

A *Green* Fire Truck?

Because the rods are more sensitive to the green region of the visible spectrum than to the red region, green objects look brighter than red objects in dim light. As a result, though red fire trucks look bright in the daylight, they look grayish in dim light. This finding has prompted some fire departments to increase the evening visibility of their vehicles by painting them a yellowish green color.
Source: Gary Paul Lewis/ Shutterstock.com.

trichromatic theory
The theory that color vision depends on the relative degree of stimulation of red, green, and blue receptors.

Theories of Color Vision What processes account for color vision? One answer was offered in 1802 when British physicist Thomas Young presented the **trichromatic theory** of color vision, which was championed in the 1850s by German scientist Hermann von Helmholtz (1821–1894). Helmholtz's theories continue to influence research on the senses. Young and Helmholtz found that red, green, and blue lights could be mixed into any color, leading them to conclude that the brain pools the input of three receptors. Today the trichromatic theory is also called the *Young-Helmholtz theory.* It assumes that the retina has three kinds of receptors (which we now know are cones), each of which is maximally sensitive to red, green, or blue light (Chichilnisky & Wandell, 1999).

A century after Helmholtz put forth his theory, George Wald (1964) provided evidence for it in research that earned him a Nobel Prize. Wald found that some cones respond maximally to red light, others to green light, and still others to blue light. The colors we experience depend on the relative degree of stimulation of the cones. Figure 5-8 illustrates the principles of mixing colored lights and mixing colored pigments, which differ from each other. Mixing colored lights is an additive process: Wavelengths added together stimulate more cones. For example, mixing red light and green light produces yellow. Mixing pigments is a subtractive process: Pigments mixed together absorb more wavelengths than does a single pigment. For example, mixing blue paint and yellow paint subtracts those colors and leaves green to be reflected into the eyes. More recent research has lent support to the trichromatic theory (Jacobs, Neitz, Deegan, & Neitz, 1996).

In the 1870s, the German physiologist Ewald Hering (1834–1918) proposed an alternative explanation of color vision (Hurvich, 1969), the **opponent-process theory.** He did so in part to explain the phenomenon of color **afterimages**—images that persist after the removal of a visual stimulus. If you stare at a red or blue surface for a minute and then stare at a white surface, you will see an afterimage that is the complementary color. For example, staring at red will produce a green afterimage, and staring at blue will produce a yellow afterimage. See Figure 5-9 for a demonstration of an afterimage.

opponent-process theory
1. The theory that color vision depends on red-green, blue-yellow, and black-white opponent processes in the brain.
2. The theory that the brain counteracts a strong positive or negative emotion by evoking an opposite emotional response.

afterimage An image that persists after the removal of a visual stimulus.

The opponent-process theory assumes that there are *red-green, blue-yellow,* and *black-white* opponent processes (with the black-white opponent process determining the lightness or darkness of what we see). Stimulation of one process inhibits its opponent. When stimulation stops, the inhibition is removed and the complementary color is seen as a brief afterimage. This theory explains why staring at red leads to a green afterimage and staring at blue leads to a yellow afterimage. It also explains why we cannot perceive reddish greens or bluish yellows: Complementary colors cannot be experienced simultaneously because each inhibits the other.

Psychologist Russell de Valois and his colleagues (de Valois, Abramov, & Jacobs, 1966) provided evidence that supports the opponent-process theory. For example, certain ganglion cells in the retina and certain cells in the thalamus send impulses when the cones that send them input are stimulated by red and stop sending impulses when the cones that send them input are stimulated by the complementary color, green. Other ganglion cells and cells in the thalamus send impulses when the cones that send them input are stimulated by green and stop sending impulses when the cones that send them input are stimulated by red.

FIGURE 5-8

The Three Primary Colors of Light

By mixing the three primary colors of light—red, green, and blue—you can create any color. For example, mixing red and green produces yellow, and mixing all three together produces white.

Color Deficiency The opponent-process theory also explains another phenomenon that the trichromatic theory cannot explain by itself: **color blindness.** People with full color vision are *trichromats*—they have three kinds of iodopsin (red, blue, and green). Most people with color blindness are *dichromats*—they have a normal number of cones but lack one kind of iodopsin (Shevell & He, 1997). The most common form of color blindness is the inability to distinguish between red and green. People with red-green color blindness have cones with blue iodopsin, but their red and green cones have the same iodopsin, usually green. Because many people suffer from red-green color blindness, traffic lights always have the red light on top so that people with red-green color blindness will know when to stop and when to go. Figure 5-10 presents an example of one of the ways of testing for color blindness, the Ishihara color test (Birch, 1997). Interestingly, special lenses developed for medical professionals to view the blood vessels of the eye have demonstrated a potential use for treating color blindness. These lenses amplify the weak red-green sensitivity, allowing individuals with certain color blindness to distinguish colors for the first time.

Color blindness is a *sex-linked trait*. Genes on the sex chromosomes control the expression of sex-linked traits. Because color blindness is a recessive trait carried on the X chromosome, men are more likely than women to be color-blind. Approximately 1 in 15 men are color-blind (Bowmaker 1998). For traits carried on the X chromosome, a woman would inherit two genes (one on each X chromosome) controlling the trait. Men, because they have only one X chromosome, inherit a single gene controlling the trait. The Y chromosome is small relative to the X chromosome and lacks the gene controlling this trait. A woman must inherit two recessive genes to be color-blind. If a man inherits only one recessive gene on his single X chromosome, he will be color-blind. Few dichromats have blue-yellow color blindness. And even fewer people are *monochromats*—completely color-blind.

But how does color blindness support the opponent-process theory? It does so because, though dichromats cannot distinguish between the complementary colors of red and green or blue and yellow, they never fail to distinguish between red and blue, red and yellow, green and blue, or green and yellow. Today the trichromatic theory and the opponent-process theory are combined in explaining color vision this way (Boynton, 1988): Impulses from the red, green, and blue cones of the retina are sent to the opponent-process ganglion cells and then further integrated in the thalamus and visual cortex.

> **color blindness** The inability to distinguish between certain colors, most often red and green.

FIGURE 5-9
Color Afterimages

If you stare at this image for a minute and then stare at a white surface (such as a sheet of printer paper), you will see an afterimage in which the flag appears in familiar colors—red, white, and blue. This color afterimage comprises colors that are complementary to the ones in the original image.

Section Review: Visual Sensation

1. What structures do light waves pass through on their way from the cornea to the retina?

2. What is the trichromatic theory of color vision?

Visual Perception

Visual sensations provide the raw materials that are organized into meaningful patterns by *visual perception.* Do we have to learn through experience to convert sensations into accurate perceptions? This is the basic assumption of the *constructionist theory* of Hermann von Helmholtz. Or, instead, does visual perception depend mainly on inborn mechanisms that automatically convert sensations into perceptions of stimuli? This is the basic assumption of the *direct perception theory* of James J. Gibson (1904–1979). According to Gibson (1979), evolution has endowed us with brain mechanisms that create perceptions directly from information provided by the sense organs. Thus, we do not need to rely on experience to help us perceive this information properly (Nakayama, 1994). Research, discussed in Chapter 4, on the

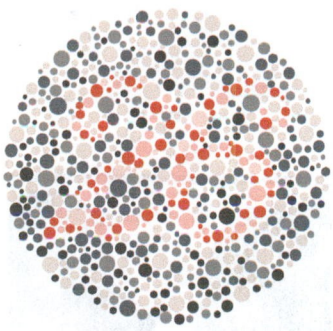

FIGURE 5-10
Color Deficiency

This figure provides an informal test for red-green color blindness. A person with red-green color blindness would not be able to read the number (26) contained in this design. Instead, he or she would see only scattered dots of different sizes. These reproduced figures are not appropriate for clinical use and only original plates with a qualified medical professional should be used for testing red-green color blindness.

sophisticated inborn perceptual abilities of newborn infants supports Gibson's theory. But most perception researchers believe that we "construct" our perceptions based on what Helmholtz called *unconscious inferences* that we make from our sensations (Wagemans et al., 2012a). These inferences are based on our experience with objects in the physical environment.

Form Perception

To perceive *forms* (meaningful shapes or patterns), we typically must distinguish a figure (an object) from its *ground* (its surroundings), though there is some evidence that form perception can precede the segmentation into figure and ground (Peterson & Gibson, 1994).

Figure-Ground Perception

Research on the monkey visual cortex has found cells that respond more to a stimulus when it is perceived as a figure than to a stimulus when it is perceived as a ground (Lamme, 1995). Gestalt psychologist Edgar Rubin (1886–1951) called this process **figure-ground perception.** The words on this page are figures against the ground of the white paper. Gestalt psychologists stress that form perception is an active rather than a passive process. Your expectancies might affect what you see in an ambiguous figure, for example (Davis, Schiffman, & Greis-Bousquet, 1990). If you first were shown pictures of pottery and then were shown Figure 5-11, you would be more likely to perceive a vase; if you first were shown pictures of faces, you would be more likely to perceive two profiles. The idea that our expectations impose themselves on sensations to form perceptions (so-called *top-down processing*) runs counter to the idea that we construct our perceptions strictly by mechanically combining sensations (so-called *bottom-up processing*). In fact, participants do not spontaneously reverse ambiguous figures. They must have experience with reversible figures or be informed that the figures are reversible before they will reverse them (Rock, Gopnik, & Hall, 1994). There is evidence that top-down and bottom-up processes interact in producing figure-ground perception (Wagemans et al., 2012b).

figure-ground perception
The distinguishing of an object (the figure) from its surroundings (the ground).

Gestalt Principles

Gestalt psychologists, including Max Wertheimer, Kurt Koffka, and Wolfgang Köhler, were the first to study the principles that govern form perception. Research has shown that these principles are more relevant to perceiving complex figures (Gillam, 1992). The principle of *proximity* states that stimuli that are close together tend to be perceived as parts of the same form. The principle of *closure* states that we tend to fill in gaps in forms. The principle of *similarity* states that stimuli similar to one another tend to be perceived as parts of the same form. And the principle of *continuity* states that we tend to group stimuli into forms that follow continuous lines or patterns. These principles are illustrated in Figure 5-12. The principles only recently have been subjected to experimental research, with initial support for the role of similarity, continuity, and proximity in grouping stimuli into coherent patterns (Pomerantz & Portillo, 2011).

According to Gestalt psychologists, forms are perceived as wholes rather than as combinations of features (Westheimer, 1999). This might prompt you to recall the famous Gestalt saying, mentioned in Chapter 1, that "the whole is different from the sum of its parts." Thus, in Figure 5-13 you see an image of a giraffe rather than a bunch of black marks.

To a Gestalt psychologist, you see a picture of a giraffe instead of a random grouping of black marks (bottom-up processing) because your brain, based on your experience seeing real giraffes and pictures of giraffes, imposes organization on what it perceives (top-down processing). A person who has never seen a picture of a giraffe might fail to perceive the marks as a meaningful form. How does your perception of the giraffe depend on each of the Gestalt principles of similarity, proximity, closure, and continuity?

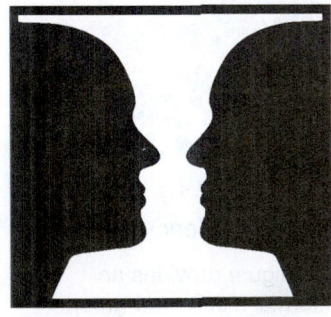

FIGURE 5-11
Figure-Ground Perception

As you view this picture, you will see that it seems to reverse. At one moment you see a vase, and at the next moment you see the profiles of two faces. What you see depends on what you perceive as figure and what you perceive as ground.

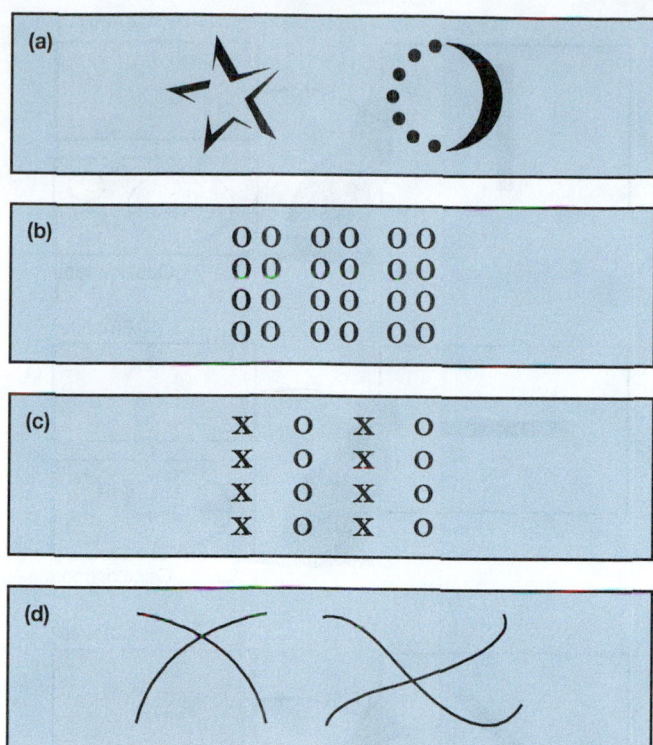

FIGURE 5-12
Gestalt Principles of Form
Perception

These patterns illustrate
the roles of *(a)* closure, *(b)*
proximity, *(c)* similarity, and *(d)*
continuity in form perception.

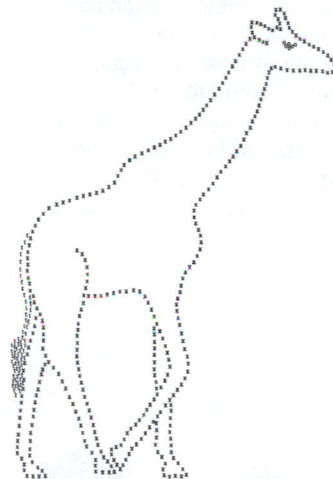

FIGURE 5-13
The Whole Is Different
From the Sum of Its Parts

According to Gestalt
psychologists, you see a
picture of a giraffe instead
of a random grouping of
marks because your brain
imposes organization on what
it perceives. Your perception
of the giraffe depends on the
Gestalt principles of similarity,
proximity, closure, and
continuity. As discussed later
in this chapter, your perception
of the giraffe also depends on
your prior experience. A person
from a culture unfamiliar with
giraffes might fail to perceive
the dots as a meaningful form.

Feature Analysis

Though some research findings support the Gestalt position that forms are perceived holistically(Wagemans et al., 2012b), other research findings suggest that forms can be perceived through the analysis of their features (Oden, 1984). Consider the letter A. Do we perceive it holistically as a single form or analytically as a combination of lines of various lengths and angles? Gestalt psychologists would assume that we perceive it holistically. But the **feature-detector theory** of David Hubel and Torsten Wiesel (1979) assumes that we construct it from its components. Hubel and Wiesel base their theory on studies in which they implanted microelectrodes into single cells of the visual cortex of cats and then presented the cats with lines of various sizes, orientations, and locations. Certain cells responded to specific features of images on the retina, such as a line of a certain length, a line at a certain angle, or a line in a particular location. Hubel and Wiesel concluded that we construct our visual perceptions from activity in such feature-detector cells. For their efforts, Hubel and Wiesel won a Nobel Prize in 1981. More recent studies indicate that whereas some *feature-detector cells* respond to component features of forms, others respond to whole forms (Wenderoth, 1994). Other neurons combine input from feature detectors into more complex patterns, such as letters, faces, or objects. Figure 5-14 illustrates Hubel and Wiesel's procedure for identifying feature-detector cells in the visual cortex.

Some feature-detector cells in the visual cortex respond to remarkably specific combinations of features. Feature-detector cells in the visual cortex even provide an anatomical basis for the **illusory contours** shown in Figure 5-15 because the cells respond to nonexistent contours as if they were the edges of real objects (Pan et al., 2012).

Depth Perception

If we lived in a two-dimensional world, form perception would be sufficient. Because we live in a three-dimensional world, we have evolved **depth perception**—the ability to judge the distance of objects.

Given that images on the retina (such as the image of a helicopter landing pad) are two-dimensional, how can we perceive depth? That is, how can we determine the

feature-detector theory
The theory that we construct perceptions of stimuli from activity in neurons of the brain that are sensitive to specific features of those stimuli.

illusory contours
The perception of nonexistent contours as if they were the edges of real objects.

depth perception
The perception of the relative distance of objects.

FIGURE 5-14
Feature Detectors

David Hubel and Torsten Wiesel implanted microelectrodes in the visual cortex of cats. The scientists found that specific cells responded to lines with certain features, such as lines that were tilted at a particular angle. An oscilloscope, a device used to display varying levels of electric potentials measured in voltages, was used to display increases in the activity of these feature-detector cells.

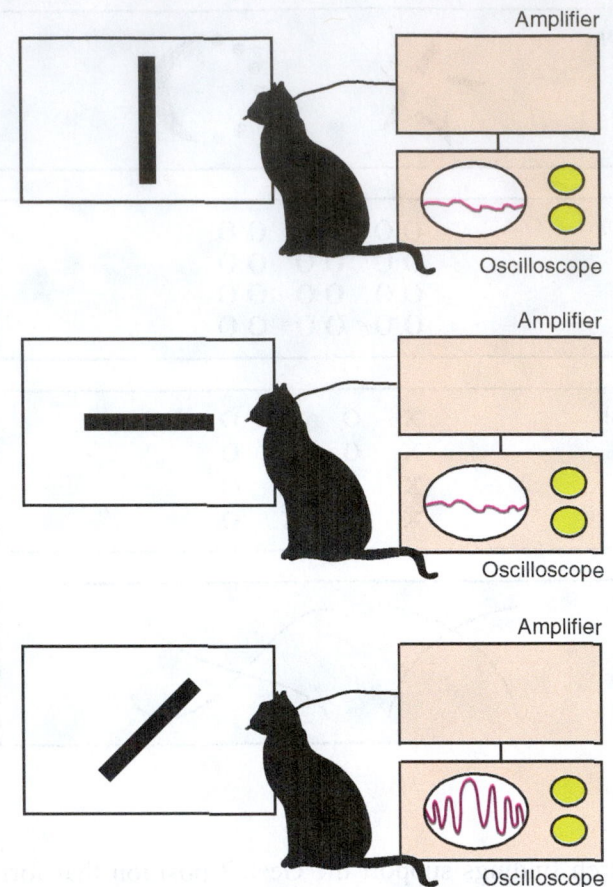

FIGURE 5-15
Illusory Contours

Seeing a complete triangle when only its corners are displayed is an example of the Gestalt principle of closure. Feature-detector cells in the visual cortex respond to such illusory contours as if they were real. This finding supports the Gestalt position that the brain imposes organization on stimuli.

Source: Based on an image from the Wikimedia Commons: Kanizsa, G. (1955).

binocular cues Depth perception cues that require input from the two eyes.

distance of an object (the *distal stimulus*) from the pattern of stimulation on our retinas (the *proximal stimulus*)? Researchers in the tradition of Helmholtz's constructionist theory maintain that depth perception depends on the use of *binocular cues* (which require two eyes) and *monocular cues* (which require one eye).

Binocular Depth Cues

The two kinds of **binocular cues** involve the interaction of both eyes. A study of accidents involving Canadian taxi drivers found that those with binocular depth perception problems tended to be involved in more crashes than those without such problems (Maag, Vanasse, Dionne, & Laberge-Nadeau, 1997).

One binocular cue is *binocular disparity,* the degree of difference between the images of an object that are focused on the two retinas. The closer the object, the greater the binocular disparity. To demonstrate binocular disparity for yourself, point a forefinger vertically between your eyes. Look at the finger with one eye closed. Then look at it with the other closed. You will notice that the background shifts as you view the scene with different eyes. This demonstration shows that the two eyes provide different views of the same stimulus. The "Viewmaster" device, a stereoscopic toy common in the 1960s and 1970s, creates the impression of visual depth by presenting slightly different images to the eyes at the same time—mimicking binocular disparity. Binocular disparity is greater when an object is near you than when it is farther away from you. Certain cells in the visual cortex detect the degree of binocular disparity, which the brain uses to estimate the distance of an object focused on the retinas (Minnini, Parker, & Bridge, 2010).

The second binocular cue to depth is *convergence,* the degree to which the eyes turn inward to focus on an object. As you can confirm for yourself, the closer the object, the greater the convergence of the eyes. Hold a forefinger vertically in front of your face and move it toward your nose. You should notice an increase in ocular muscle tension as your finger approaches your nose. Neurons in the cerebral cortex translate the amount of muscle tension into an estimate of the distance of your finger (Takagi, Yoshizawa, & Hara, 1992). Using a computer monitor for hours can induce eye fatigue caused by continuous convergence (Watten, Lie, & Birketvedt, 1994).

Monocular Depth Cues

There are many more monocular cues than binocular cues. **Monocular cues** require only one eye, so even people who have lost the sight in one eye still can have good depth perception. One monocular cue is *accommodation* (Meehan & Day, 1995), which, as explained earlier, is the change in the shape of the lens to help focus the image of an object on the retina. Specialized brain neurons respond so that the greater the accommodation of the lens, the closer the object appears (Judge & Cumming, 1986).

A second monocular cue is *motion parallax,* the tendency to perceive ourselves as passing objects faster when they are closer to us than when they are farther away. This phenomenon occurs because when you fix your eyes on the horizon, images of objects that are close to you move across your retinas faster than do images of objects that are far away from you (McDougal, Crowe, & Holland, 2003). Animal research indicates that particular brain cells might respond to motion parallax. For example, the pigeon's brain has specialized cells that code motion parallax (Xiao & Frost, 2013).

The remaining monocular cues are often called *pictorial cues* (see Figure 5-16) because artists use them to create depth in their drawings and paintings. They include occlusion, relative size, linear perspective, elevation, shading patterns, aerial perspective, and texture gradient. The ability of infants to make use of pictorial cues, such as linear perspective and texture gradient, appears at 22 to 28 weeks of age (Kavšek, Yonas, & Granrud, 2012).

Leonardo da Vinci formalized pictorial cues in the 15th century in teaching his students how to use them to make their paintings look more realistic (Haber, 1980). He noted that an object that overlaps another object will appear closer, a cue called occlusion (Anderson, 2003). Because your psychology professor overlaps the blackboard or whiteboard, you know she or he is closer to you than the board is. Comparing the relative size of familiar objects also provides a cue to their distance (Higashiyama & Kitano, 1991). If you know that two people are about the same height and one casts a smaller image on your retina, you will perceive that person as farther away.

You probably have noticed that parallel objects, such as railroad tracks, seem to get closer together as they get farther away (and farther apart as they get closer). This pictorial cue is called *linear perspective.* During World War II, naval aviation cadets flying at night sometimes crashed into airplanes ahead of them, apparently because of a failure to judge the distance of those planes. Taking advantage of linear perspective solved the problem. Two taillights set a standard distance apart replaced the traditional single taillight. As a result, when pilots noticed that the taillights of an airplane appeared to move farther apart, they realized that they were getting closer to it (Fiske, Conley, & Goldberg, 1987). Figure 5-17 shows another example of linear perspective.

An object's *elevation* provides another cue to its distance. Objects that are higher in your visual field seem to be farther away. If you paint a picture, you can create depth by placing more distant objects higher on the canvas. *Shading patterns* provide cues to distance because we tend to assume that light is striking objects from above (Lovell, Bloj, & Harris, 2012) and areas in shadow tend to recede, whereas areas in light tend to stand out. Painters use shading to make balls, balloons, and oranges appear round. *Aerial perspective* refers to the fact that objects that are closer to us seem clearer than more distant ones. A distant mountain will look hazier than a near one (O'Shea, Govan, & Sekuler, 1997).

The final monocular cue, the *texture gradient,* affects depth perception because the nearer an object, the more details we can make out, and the farther an object, the fewer

monocular cues Depth perception cues that require input from only one eye.

FIGURE 5-16 Pictorial Cues to Depth

Artists make use of pictorial cues to portray depth in their drawings and paintings. These cues include *(a)* occlusion, *(b)* aerial perspective, *(c)* linear perspective, *(d)* texture gradient, *(e)* elevation, and *(f)* shading patterns.

Source: *(a)* Dmitrydesign/Shutterstock.com. *(b)* behindlens/Shutterstock.com. *(c)* Viktor Gladkov/Shutterstock.com. *(d)* Haryadi CH/Shutterstock.com. *(e)* littlewormy/Shutterstock.com. *(f)* salajean/Shutterstock.com.

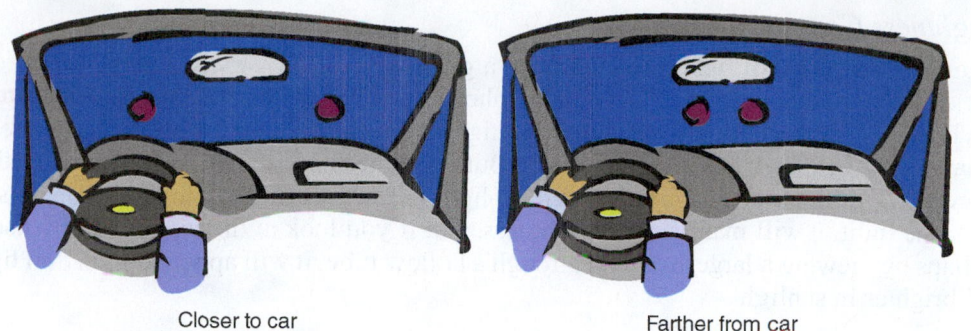

Closer to car   Farther from car

FIGURE 5-17
Linear Perspective from the Driver's Seat

Linear perspective is an important factor in everyday depth perception, as when you are determining the distance of a vehicle that you are following at night. As the two taillights of the vehicle you are following appear to move farther apart, you perceive yourself as getting closer to the vehicle. In contrast, as the two taillights appear to move closer together, you perceive yourself as getting farther from the vehicle.

details we can make out. When you look across a field, you can see every blade of grass near you, but only an expanse of green far away from you. Recent research has identified particular cortical neurons that respond to the texture gradient (Tsutsui, Sakata, Naganuma, & Taira, 2002).

Perceptual Constancies

The image of a given object focused on your retina may vary in size, shape, and brightness. Yet, because of *perceptual constancy,* you will continue to perceive the object as stable in size, shape, and brightness. There is evidence that size and shape constancy are present at birth (Slater, 1992). Perceptual constancy is adaptive because it provides you with a more visually stable world, making it easier for you to function in it.

Size Constancy

Size constancy is the perceptual process that makes an object appear to remain the same size despite changes in the size of the image it casts on the retina. The size of the object on your retina does not, by itself, tell you how far away it is. As an object gets farther away from you, it produces a smaller image on your retina. If you know the actual size of an object, size constancy makes you interpret a change in its retinal size as a change in its distance rather than as a change in its size. When you see a car a block away, it does not seem smaller than one that is half a block away, even though the more distant car produces a smaller image on your retina. Size constancy can be disrupted by alcohol. In one study, young adults drank alcohol and then were asked to estimate the size of an object. They consistently underestimated its size. Disruption of size constancy might be one way in which alcohol intoxication promotes automobile accidents (Farrimond, 1990). This should be a reminder that driving under the influence is dangerous.

size constancy The perceptual process that makes an object appear to remain the same size despite changes in the size of the image it casts on the retina.

Shape Constancy

Shape constancy ensures that an object of known shape will appear to maintain its normal shape regardless of the angle from which you view it. Pick up a book and hold it at various orientations relative to your line of sight. Unless you look directly at the cover when it is on a plane perpendicular to your line of vision, it will never cast a rectangular image on your retinas, yet you will continue to perceive it as rectangular. Shape constancy occurs because your brain compensates for the slant of an object relative to your line of sight (Wallach & Marshall, 1986).

Shape constancy is subject to top-down processes in that viewers' expectations can affect it. This effect is especially true for young children, as in a study in which 4- to 7-year-old children viewed a luminous circular disc oriented at a slant and presented in a darkened chamber. The children tended to overestimate the circularity of the disc when they knew the object was really a circle. This effect was greater in the younger children. In contrast, children who viewed an identical shape that they knew was an actual ellipse did not overestimate its circularity. Thus, the children's expectations affected their perception of the figure (Mitchell & Taylor, 1999).

shape constancy The perceptual process that makes an object appear to maintain its normal shape regardless of the angle from which it is viewed.

Chapter 5 Sensation and Perception

Brightness Constancy

Though the amount of light reflected from a given object can vary, we perceive the object as having a constant brightness. This phenomenon is called **brightness constancy**. A white shirt appears equally bright in dim light or bright light, and a black shirt appears equally dull in dim light or bright light. But brightness constancy is relative to other objects. If you look at a white shirt in dim light in the presence of nonwhite objects in the same light, it will maintain its brightness. But if you look at the white shirt by itself, perhaps by viewing a large area of it through a hollow tube, it will appear dull in dim light and brighter in sunlight.

Visual Illusions

You may have heard of so-called antigravity hills, which have been the subject of sensationalized media coverage. An antigravity hill is a short stretch of road, away from buildings, and surrounded by low-lying hills. When a car is put into neutral at one of these locations, it seems to roll uphill—an apparent violation of the law of gravity. This example shows how the misperception of visual cues can produce a **visual illusion**, in this case a false perception regarding the slope and horizon of the road. Visual illusions provide clues to the processes involved in normal visual perception (Gordon & Earle, 1992).

As with most illusions, the Ponzo illusion (see Figure 5-18) is caused by the misapplication of perceptual cues. As you read earlier, linear perspective is a cue to depth. Because the train tracks appear to come together in the distance, the horizontal bar higher in the figure appears to be farther away than the one lower in the figure. If you measure the bars, you will find that they are equal in length. Because the bars produce images of equal length on your retinas, the bar that appears to be farther away seems to be longer. And Figure 5-19 describes an example of a remarkable visual illusion, the Ames room.

As another example, from ancient times to modern times, people have been mystified by the **moon illusion,** in which the moon appears larger when it is at the horizon

brightness constancy
The perceptual process that makes an object maintain a particular level of brightness despite changes in the amount of light reflected from it.

visual illusion A misperception of physical reality usually caused by the misapplication of visual cues.

moon illusion
The misperception that the moon is larger when it is at the horizon than when it is overhead.

FIGURE 5-18
The Ponzo Illusion

Though the two horizontal lines are the same length in both *(a)* and *(b)*, the line that appears more distant appears longer. These illusions are the product of our perceptual assumption that if a more distant object produces the same size image on our retinas as a closer object, then the more distant object must be larger.
Source: (b) kenkistler/ Shutterstock.com.

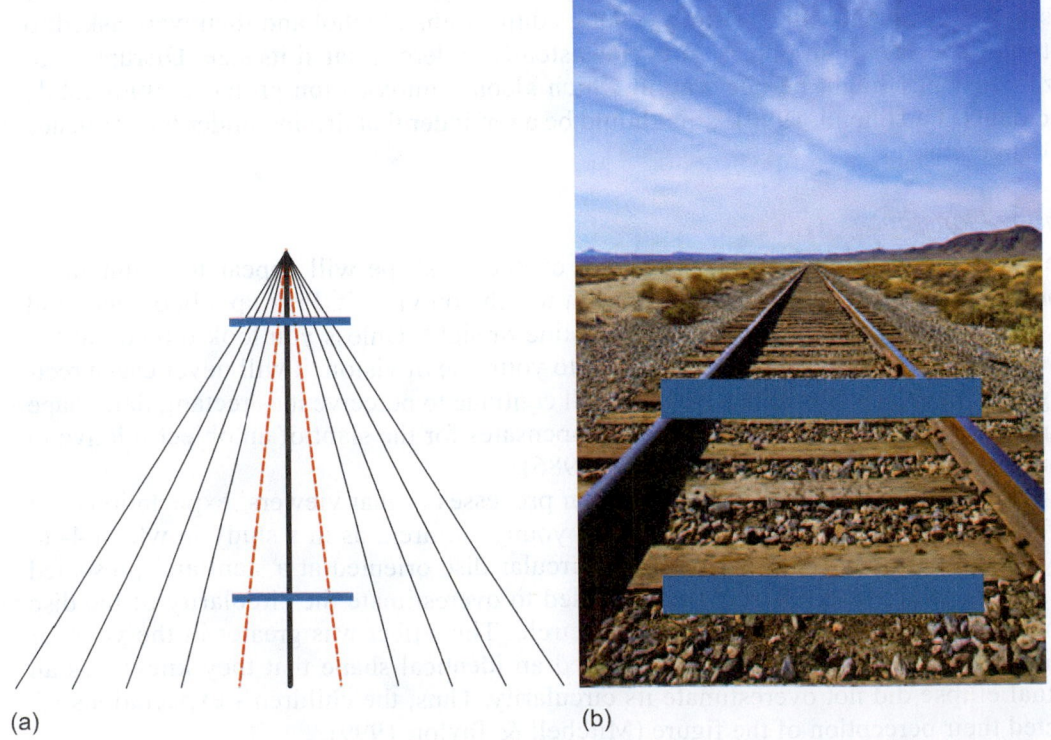

(a)   (b)

than when it is overhead. This is an illusion because the moon is the same distance from us at the horizon as when it is overhead. Thus, the retinal image it produces is the same size when it is at the horizon as when it is overhead. In the 2nd century the Greek astronomer Ptolemy put forth the earliest explanation of the moon illusion. His explanation, based on the principle of size constancy, is called the *apparent-distance hypothesis* (Kaufman & Rock, 1962). Ptolemy assumed that we perceive the sky as a flattened dome, with the sky at the horizon appearing *farther* away than it does overhead. Because the image of the moon on the retina is the same size whether the moon is overhead or at the horizon, the brain assumes the moon must be *larger* at the apparently more distant location—the horizon. But modern research has found that under certain conditions the sky can look farther away overhead than at the horizon. So if the apparent-distance hypothesis were correct, the moon under those conditions would appear larger overhead than it does at the horizon (Baird & Wagner, 1982).

(a)

(b)

FIGURE 5-19
The Ames Room

(a) The apparently giant man on the right, in reality, is of normal stature, and the boy on the left is actually taller than he appears to be. *(b)* The floor plan of the Ames room puts the individuals on the left farther away than the ones on the right, and the floor-to-ceiling height is greater on the left than on the right. Also, the window on the left is larger than the one on the right. These features create the illusion that all the individuals are in a rectangular room and are standing the same distance away from the viewer. The illusion occurs because the individuals on the right fill more of the space between the floor and the ceiling and because we assume that when two objects are the same distance away, the object that produces a smaller image on our retinas is, in fact, smaller.
Source: (a) © David Wells/The Image Works.

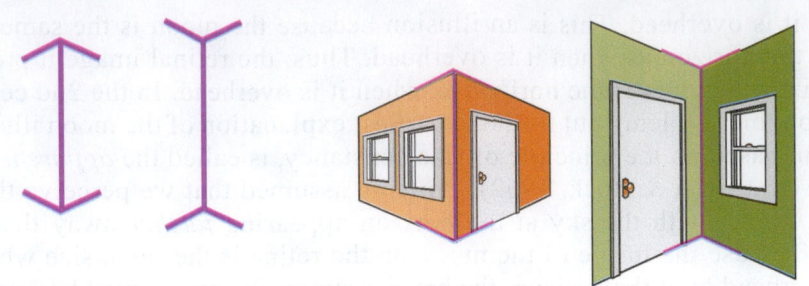

FIGURE 5-20
The Müller-Lyer Illusion

Perhaps the most widely studied illusion was developed more than a century ago by Franz Müller-Lyer. Note that the vertical line on the right appears longer than the one on the left. If you take a ruler and measure the lines, you will find that they actually are equal in length. Though no explanation has achieved universal acceptance(Mack, Heuer, Villardi, & Chambers, 1985), a favored one relies on size constancy and the resemblance of the figure on the right to the inside corner of a room and the resemblance of the figure on the left to the outside corner of a building. Given that the lines project images of equal length onto the retina, the line that appears farther away will be perceived as longer. Because an inside corner of a room appears farther away than an outside corner of a building, the line on the right appears farther away and therefore longer than the line on the left (Gillam, 1980).

Moreover, researchers have found that a variety of factors interact to create the moon illusion, so it remains to be seen whether researchers will find a single satisfactory explanation for it (Schmid, 2003).

Figure 5-20 depicts the Müller-Lyer illusion, another illusion that has stimulated many research studies. This illusion, developed more than a century ago by Franz Müller-Lyer, is perhaps the most widely studied of all illusions. Look at the two vertical lines with normal arrowheads and inverted arrowheads on the left in the figure. The line on the right should appear longer than the one on the left. If you take a ruler and measure the lines, you will find they are actually equal in length. The Müller-Lyer illusion may even impair our accuracy in estimating driving distances while reading maps when roads form patterns similar to those found in the illusion (Binsted & Elliott, 1999).

Experience, Culture, and Perception

As you have just read, visual perception depends on the interaction of the eyes and the brain. But it also depends on experience. Even the visual pathways themselves can be altered by life experiences, as demonstrated by the following study.

The Effect of Experience on Perception

As discussed in the section "Form Perception," David Hubel and Torsten Wiesel found that feature detectors in the visual cortex respond to lines of particular orientations. Other researchers (Hirsch & Spinelli, 1970) reared kittens with one eye exposed to vertical stripes and the other eye exposed to horizontal stripes. When the kittens later were exposed to lines of either orientation with one eye, certain feature-detector neurons in their visual cortexes responded only to lines of the orientation to which that eye had been exposed. But what would occur if kittens were reared in an environment that exposed both eyes to either only vertical or only horizontal stripes? This question was addressed in a study by Colin Blakemore and Graham Cooper (1970) of Cambridge University in England. Blakemore and Cooper reared kittens from the age of 2 weeks to the age of 5 months in darkness, except for 5 hours a day in a lighted, large cylinder with walls covered by either vertical or horizontal black and white stripes. Because the kittens also wore large saucer-shaped collars, they could not even see their own legs or bodies. This restriction prevented their being exposed to lines other than the vertical or horizontal stripes.

After 5 months, the kittens' vision was tested under normal lighting by waving a rod in front of them, sometimes vertically and sometimes horizontally. Kittens that had been exposed to vertical lines swatted at the vertical rod but not at the horizontal rod. And kittens that had been exposed to horizontal lines swatted at the horizontal rod but not at the vertical rod. Recordings of the activity in certain neurons in the visual cortex showed that particular neurons acted as feature detectors by responding to either vertical or horizontal lines, depending on the stripes to which the kittens had been exposed during the previous 5 months (Blakemore & Cooper, 1970). Later studies indicated that neurons in the visual cortex that are responsive to lines of different orientations are present at birth. But in an individual who is not exposed to lines of a particular orientation, the neurons responsive to that orientation will degenerate (Swindale, 1982).

Another source of evidence for the effect of experience on perception comes from studies of people blind from birth who have gained their sense of vision years later. The German physiologist Marius von Senden (1932–1960) reviewed all the studies of people who had been born blind because of lens cataracts and who gained their vision after surgical removal of the cataracts. He found that the newly sighted were immediately able to distinguish colors and to separate figure from ground, but had difficulty visually recognizing objects they had learned to identify by touch. They did, however, show gradual improvement in visual object recognition (von Senden, 1960).

Cultural Influences on Perception

Visual perception also can be influenced by cultural factors. This influence was demonstrated by the anthropologist Colin Turnbull (1961), who studied the Bambuti Pygmies of central Africa. Turnbull drove one of the Pygmies, Kenge, who lived in a dense forest, to an open plain. Looking across the plain at a herd of grazing buffalo, Kenge asked Turnbull to tell him what kind of insect they were. Turnbull responded by driving Kenge toward the herd. As the image of the "insects" got bigger and bigger on his retinas, Kenge accused Turnbull of witchcraft for turning the insects into buffaloes. Because he had never experienced large objects at a distance, Kenge had a limited appreciation of size constancy. To him the tiny images on his retinas could only be insects. Because of his understandable failure to apply size constancy appropriately, Kenge mistook the distant buffalo for a nearby insect.

Experiences with monocular cues to depth, such as linear perspective, even affect responses to the Ponzo illusion (Fujita, 1996). Rural Ugandan villagers, who have little experience with monocular cues in two-dimensional stimuli, are less susceptible to the Ponzo illusion than are Ugandan college students, who have more experience with such cues in art, photographs, and motion pictures (Leibowitz & Pick, 1972). Cross-cultural researchers have found substantial variability among populations in the susceptibility to visual illusions (Henrich, Heine, & Norenzayan, 2010). But research finding that infant monkeys respond to pictorial depth cues indicates that learning from exposure to these Western forms of depth representation is not necessary to produce such illusions (Gunderson, Yonas, Sargent, & Grant-Webster, 1993). Moreover, even pigeons and horses (Timney & Keil, 1996) are affected by the Ponzo illusion, making it less likely that it is simply the product of being exposed to Western art (Fujita, Blough, & Blough, 1993).

Section Review: Visual Perception

1. What are the Gestalt principles of form perception?

2. What are two binocular cues to depth perception?

Hearing

Like the sense of vision, the sense of hearing (or **audition**) helps us function by informing us about objects at a distance from us. Unlike vision, audition informs us about objects we cannot see because they are behind us, hidden by darkness, or blocked by another object. On average, women have better hearing sensitivity and experience greater deterioration from exposure to high-frequency noise. Men are better at sound localization and detecting specific sounds from among other sounds. Because these gender differences are not found in women who have a male twin, they have been attributed to prenatal exposure to male sex hormones, which may androgenize the auditory system of the female twin (McFadden, 1998; McFadden, 2002).

audition The sense of hearing.

Sound Waves

Sound is produced by vibrations carried by air, water, or other mediums. Because sound requires a medium through which to travel, it cannot travel in a vacuum. Sound vibrations create a successive bunching and spreading of molecules in the sound medium. A sound wave is composed of a series of these bunching-spreading cycles. The height of a sound wave is its *amplitude,* and the number of sound-wave cycles that pass a given point in a second is its *frequency.* Sound-wave frequency is measured in *hertz (Hz),* named for the 19th-century German physicist Heinrich Hertz. A 60-Hz sound would have a frequency of 60 cycles a second. Figure 5-21 illustrates the main properties of sound waves that affect perceived pitch and loudness.

The Auditory System

Sound waves are sensed and perceived by the auditory system, which begins at the ear. The structure of the ear is illustrated in Figure 5-22. The ear is divided into an outer ear, a middle ear, and an inner ear.

The Outer Ear

tympanic membrane
The eardrum; a membrane separating the outer ear from the middle ear that vibrates in response to sound waves that strike it.

The *outer ear* includes the *pinna,* the oddly shaped flap of skin and cartilage that we commonly call the "ear." Though the pinna plays a small role in human hearing, some animals, such as cats and deer, have large, movable pinnae that help them detect and locate faint sounds (Populin & Yin, 1998). Sound waves gathered by the pinna pass through the *external auditory canal* and reach the **tympanic membrane,** better known as the *eardrum.* Sound waves make the eardrum vibrate, and our hearing is responsive to even the slightest movement of the eardrum. If our hearing were any more acute, we would hear the air molecules that are constantly bouncing against the eardrum (Békésy, 1957).

A recent study found that temperature differences between the right and left tympanic membranes are associated with emotionality. That is, a warmer left tympanic membrane was associated with a more positive emotional state, and a warmer right tympanic membrane was associated with a more negative emotional state. As discussed in Chapter 12, positive emotions are associated with relatively greater activity in the left cerebral hemisphere, and negative emotions are associated with relatively greater activity in the right cerebral hemisphere. Thus, measurement of tympanic membrane temperature might help in assessing children who are at risk for emotional problems (Boyce et al., 2002).

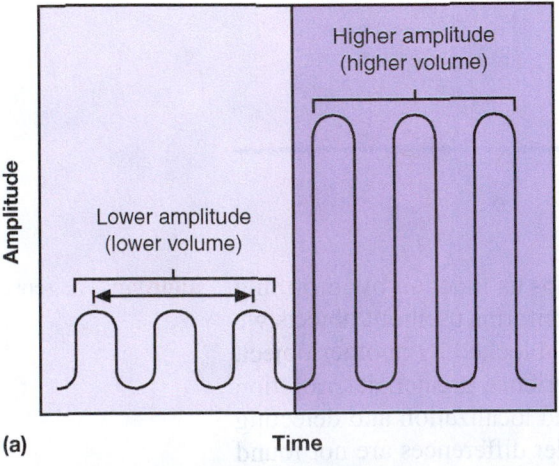
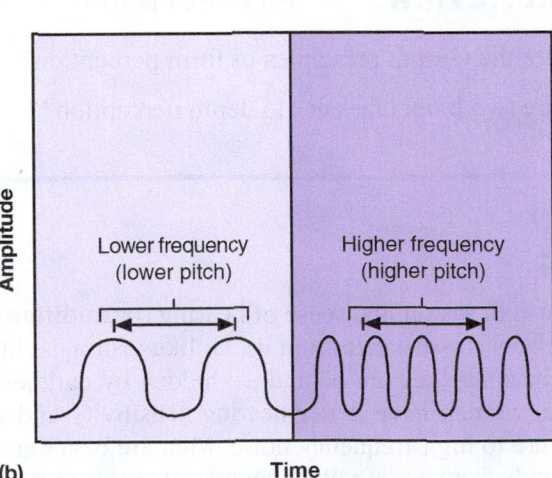

(a)   Time   (b)   Time

FIGURE 5-21 Sound Waves and Hearing

(a) The amplitude of a sound wave primarily affects loudness (volume), and *(b)* its frequency primarily affects pitch.
Source: From Seely, Stephens, and Tate, *Anatomy and Physiology,* 4th ed., McGraw-Hill, 1998.

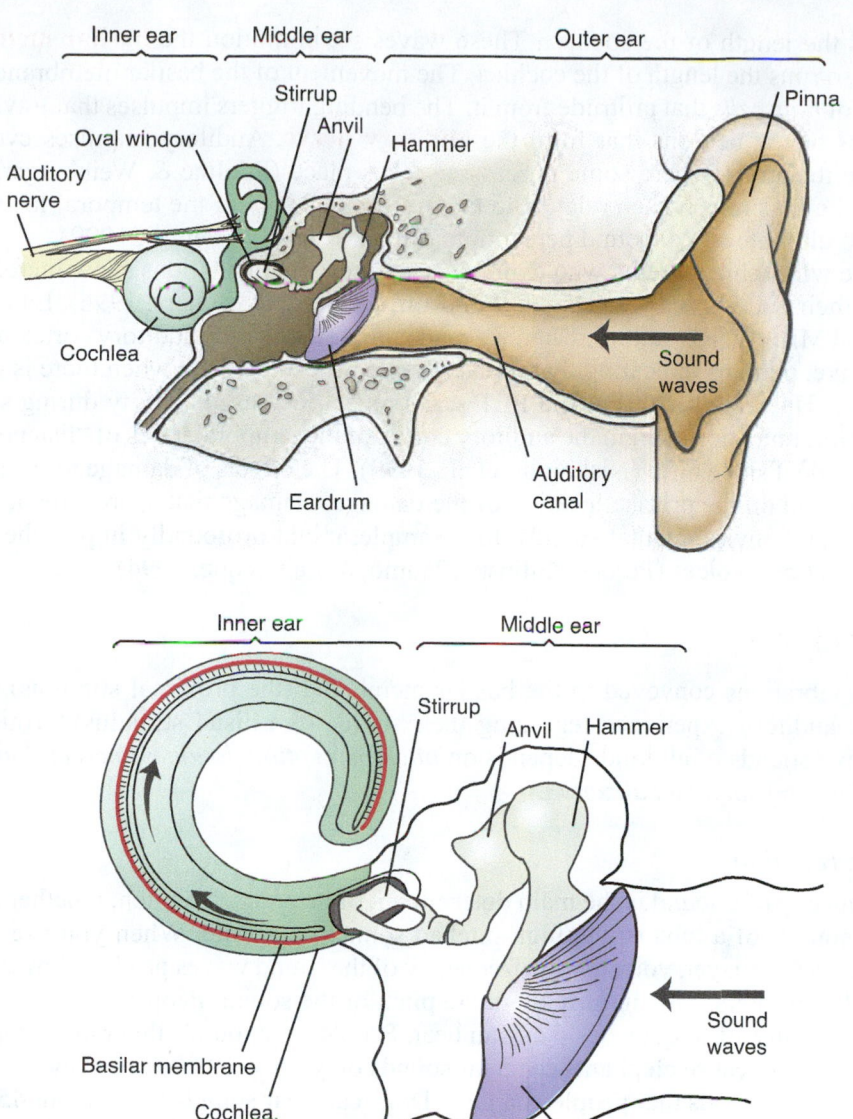

FIGURE 5-22
The Human Ear

The human ear is divided into an outer ear, middle ear, and inner ear. Sound waves pass through the outer ear and strike the eardrum, making it vibrate. This action produces vibrations in the bones (ossicles) of the middle ear (the hammer, the anvil, and the stirrup), which in turn convey the vibrations to the oval window of the inner ear. Vibrations of the oval window produce waves that travel through the fluid of the cochlea. The waves cause bending of hair cells that protrude from the basilar membrane, which stimulates the transmission of neural impulses along the neurons that form the auditory nerve. These impulses travel to the auditory cortex of the temporal lobes as well as to other regions of the brain involved in hearing.

The Middle Ear

The eardrum separates the outer ear from the *middle ear*. Vibrations of the eardrum are conveyed to the bones, or ossicles, of the middle ear. The ossicles are three tiny bones connected to one another by ligaments. The Latin names of the ossicles reflect their shapes: the *malleus* (hammer), the *incus* (anvil), and the *stapes* (stirrup). Infections of the middle ear must be taken seriously; in children they can produce hearing losses that adversely affect cognitive development, though most children recover within a few years (Johnson et al., 2000).

Connecting the middle ear to the back of the throat are the *eustachian tubes,* which permit air to enter the middle ear to equalize air pressure on both sides of the eardrum. You might become painfully aware of this function during airplane descents, when the pressure increases on the outside of the eardrum relative to the inside. Chewing gum can help open the eustachian tubes and equalize the pressure.

The Inner Ear

Vibrations of the stapes are conveyed to the *oval window* of the *inner ear.* The oval window is a membrane in the wall of a spiral structure called the **cochlea** (from a Greek word meaning "snail"). Vibrations of the oval window send waves through a fluid-filled chamber

cochlea The spiral, fluid-filled structure of the inner ear that contains the receptor cells for hearing.

basilar membrane
A membrane running the length of the cochlea that contains the auditory receptor (hair) cells.

auditory nerve The nerve that conducts impulses from the cochlea to the brain.

auditory cortex The area of the temporal lobes that processes sounds.

that runs the length of the cochlea. These waves set in motion the **basilar membrane**, which also runs the length of the cochlea. The movement of the basilar membrane causes bending of *hair cells* that protrude from it. The bending triggers impulses that travel along the axons of the neurons that form the **auditory nerve**. Auditory impulses eventually reach the thalamus, where some processing takes place (Edeline & Weinberger, 1991). Input to the thalamus is then relayed to the **auditory cortex** of the temporal lobes of the brain, the ultimate site of sound perception (Hirata, Kuriki, & Pantev, 1999).

People with schizophrenia who experience auditory hallucinations show increased activity in their auditory cortex (David, Woodruff, Howard, & Mellers, 1996). Likewise, in functional MRI (fMRI) studies, when we read words silently, the auditory cortex becomes more active, perhaps indicating that it plays a role in reading even when there is no auditory input (Haist et al., 2001). And PET scans reveal increased activity during sign language communication even in the auditory cortex of the temporal lobes of "listeners" who have been deaf since birth (Nishimura et al., 1999). The effects of damage to the auditory cortex depend on the precise location of the damage. Damage that spares the perception of speech and environmental sounds, for example, might profoundly impair the perception of tunes and voices (Peretz, Kolinsky, Tramo, & Labrecque, 1994).

Auditory Perception

How do vibrations conveyed to the basilar membrane (the proximal stimulus) create a complex auditory experience regarding their source (the distal stimulus)? Your ability to perceive sounds of all kinds depends on *pitch perception, loudness perception, timbre perception,* and *sound localization.*

Pitch Perception

The frequency of a sound is the main determinant of its perceived pitch, whether the low-pitched sounds of a tuba or the high-pitched sounds of a flute. When you use the tone control on a CD player, you alter the frequency of the sound waves produced by the vibration of the speakers. This in turn alters the pitch of the sound. People and other animals vary in the range of frequencies they can hear. People hear sounds that range from 20 Hz to 20,000 Hz. Because elephants can hear sounds only up to 10,000 Hz, they cannot hear higher-pitched sounds that people can hear. Dogs can hear sounds up to about 45,000 Hz (Heffner, 1983). Because dog whistles produce sounds between 20,000 and 45,000 Hz, they are audible to dogs but not to people. People with *absolute pitch* can identify and produce tones of a specific pitch. This ability appears to be learned best before the age of 6 and becomes difficult or impossible to develop afterward (Crozier, 1997). The potential to develop absolute pitch appears to be present from birth, provided that infants are presented with verbal labels for specific pitches (Deutsch, 2002).

pitch perception
The subjective experience of the highness or lowness of a sound, which corresponds most closely to the frequency of the sound waves that compose it.

place theory The theory of pitch perception that assumes that hair cells at particular points on the basilar membrane are maximally responsive to sound waves of particular frequencies.

Place Theory What accounts for **pitch perception**? In 1863 Hermann von Helmholtz put forth **place theory,** which assumes that particular points on the basilar membrane vibrate maximally in response to sound waves of particular frequencies. Georg von Békésy (1899–1972), a Hungarian scientist, won a Nobel Prize in 1961 for his research on place theory. He took the cochleas from the ears of guinea pigs and human cadavers, stimulated the oval window, and using a microscope, noted the response of the basilar membrane through a hole cut in the cochlea. He found that as the frequency of the stimulus increased, the point of maximal vibration produced by the traveling wave on the basilar membrane moved closer to the oval window. And as the frequency of the stimulus decreased, the point of maximal vibration moved farther from the oval window (Békésy, 1957).

Frequency Theory But place theory fails to explain pitch perception much below 1,000 Hz because such low-frequency sound waves do not make the basilar membrane vibrate maximally at any particular point. Instead, the entire basilar membrane vibrates equally. Because of this limitation, perception of sounds below 1,000 Hz is explained best by a theory first put forth by the English physicist Ernest Rutherford (1861–1937) in 1886.

His **frequency theory** assumes that the basilar membrane vibrates as a whole in direct proportion to the frequency of the sound waves striking the eardrum. The neurons of the auditory nerve will in turn fire at the same frequency as the vibrations of the basilar membrane. But because neurons can fire only up to 1,000 Hz, the frequency theory holds only for sounds up to 1,000 Hz.

Volley Theory Still another theory, the **volley theory** of psychologist Ernest Wever (Wever & Bray, 1937), explains pitch perception between 1,000 Hz and 5,000 Hz. Volley theory assumes that sound waves in this range induce certain groups of auditory neurons to fire in volleys. Though no single neuron can fire at more than 1,000 Hz, the brain might interpret the firing of volleys of particular auditory neurons as representing sound waves of particular frequencies up to 5,000 Hz (Zwislocki, 1981). For example, the pitch of a sound wave of 4,000 Hz might be coded by a particular group of five neurons, each firing at 800 Hz. Though there is some overlap among the theories, frequency theory best explains the perception of low-pitched sounds, place theory best explains the perception of high-pitched sounds, and volley theory best explains the perception of medium-pitched sounds.

Loudness Perception

Sounds vary in intensity, or loudness, as well as in pitch. The loudness of a sound depends mainly on the amplitude of its sound waves. When you use the volume control on a CD player, you alter the amplitude of the sound waves leaving the speakers. **Loudness perception** depends on both the number and the firing thresholds of hair cells on the basilar membrane that are stimulated. Because hair cells with higher firing thresholds require more intense stimulation, the firing of hair cells with higher thresholds increases the perceived loudness of a sound. A region of the auditory cortex processes differences in the intensity of sounds (Röhl, Kollmeier, & Uppenkamp, 2011).

The unit of sound intensity is the *decibel (dB)*. The decibel is one-tenth of a Bel, a unit named for Alexander Graham Bell, who invented the telephone. The faintest detectable sound has an absolute threshold of 0 dB. For each change of 10 decibels, the perceived loudness doubles. Thus, a 70-dB sound is twice as loud as a 60-dB sound. Table 5-1 presents the decibel levels of some everyday sounds. Exposure to high-decibel sounds promotes hearing loss. Chronic exposure to loud sounds first destroys hair cells nearest the oval window, which respond to high-frequency sound waves. A study of the effects of loud music found significant hearing loss among participants who listened to personal stereos for more than 7 hours a week. In addition, two-thirds of the participants who attended rock concerts at least twice monthly exhibited symptoms of hearing loss (Meyer-Bisch, 1996). Older Americans, after a lifetime of exposure to loud sounds, tend to have poor high-frequency hearing. In contrast, the typical 90-year-old in rural African tribes, whose surroundings only occasionally produce loud sounds, has better hearing than the typical 30-year-old North American (Raloff, 1982).

In extreme cases, individuals can lose more than their high-frequency hearing. They can become deaf. In **conduction deafness,** a mechanical problem in the outer or middle ear interferes with hearing. The auditory canal might be filled with wax, the eardrum might be punctured, or the ossicles might be fused and inflexible. Conduction deafness caused by deterioration of the ossicles can be treated by surgical replacement with plastic ossicles. Conduction deafness is more often overcome by hearing aids, which amplify sound waves that enter the ear.

In **nerve deafness,** there is damage to the basilar membrane, the auditory nerve, or the auditory cortex. Victims typically lose the ability to perceive sounds of certain frequencies. Nerve deafness responds poorly to surgery or hearing aids. But cochlear implants, which provide electronic stimulation of the neurons leaving the basilar membrane, promise to restore at least rudimentary hearing in people with nerve deafness caused by the destruction of basilar membrane hair cells. More than 20,000 children worldwide have had successful cochlear implants, which have improved their hearing, language ability, and social relationships (Balkany et al., 2002). Nonetheless, cochlear implants have provoked controversy

frequency theory
The theory of pitch perception that assumes that the basilar membrane vibrates as a whole in direct proportion to the frequency of the sound waves striking the eardrum.

volley theory The theory of pitch perception that assumes that sound waves of particular frequencies induce auditory neurons to fire in volleys, with one volley following another.

loudness perception
The subjective experience of the intensity of a sound, which corresponds most closely to the amplitude of the sound waves composing it.

conduction deafness Hearing loss usually caused by blockage of the auditory canal, damage to the eardrum, or deterioration of the ossicles of the middle ear.

nerve deafness Hearing loss caused by damage to the hair cells of the basilar membrane, the axons of the auditory nerve, or the neurons of the auditory cortex.

TABLE 5-1 Decibel Levels of Some Everyday Sounds

General Effect	Decibel Level	Example
Possible Hearing Loss	140	Jet airplane on runway
	130	Pain threshold
	120	Propeller airplane on runway
	110	Rock concert
	100	Jackhammer
Annoyingly Noisy	90	City street with traffic
	80	Downtown city apartment
	70	Active business office
Relatively Quiet	60	Normal conversation
	50	Suburban street
	40	Rural farm
	30	Soft whisper
	20	Quiet residence
	10	Fluttering leaf
	0	Hearing threshold

between those who believe they are an important means of correcting a disability and those who believe that routine practice of cochlear implants reflects a judgment that people who are deaf are inferior to those who can hear (Levy, 2002).

Timbre Perception

timbre The subjective experience that identifies a particular sound and corresponds most closely to the mixture of sound waves composing it.

Sounds vary in timbre as well as in pitch and loudness. **Timbre** is the quality of a sound, which reflects a particular mixture of sound waves. Timbre is especially apparent, for example, in the complex sounds produced in orchestral music (Tardieu & McAdams, 2012). Middle C on the piano has a frequency of 256 Hz, but it has a distinctive timbre because of overtones of varying frequencies. Timbre lets us identify the source of a sound, whether a voice, a musical instrument, or even—to the chagrin of students—a fingernail scratching across a chalkboard. The timbre of that spine-chilling sound is similar to that of the warning cry of macaque monkeys. Perhaps our squeamish response to it reflects a vestigial response inherited from our common distant ancestors who used it to signal the presence of predators (Halpern, Blake, & Hillerbrand, 1986).

The cortical areas that process differences in timbre, as between a violin and a trumpet, are more responsive in trained musicians than in non-musicians. Moreover, those cortical areas are even more responsive to the sound of the instrument on which professional musicians have been trained. Thus, the relevant cortical areas of violinists respond more strongly to the sound of a violin, and the relevant cortical areas of a trumpeter respond more strongly to the sound of a trumpet (Pantev, Roberts, Schulz, Engelien, & Ross, 2001).

Sound Localization

sound localization The process by which the individual determines the location of a sound.

We need to localize sounds as well as identify them. **Sound localization** involves discerning where sounds are coming from. People have an acute ability to localize sounds, whether of voices at a crowded party or of instruments in a symphony orchestra. Some animals have especially impressive sound localization ability. A barn owl can capture a mouse in the dark simply by following the faint sounds produced by its movements (Knudsen, 1981). The ability to localize sound is important for our survival, as in judging the distance of approaching vehicles. This aspect is especially important for young children, who are not proficient at detecting approaching vehicles from their sounds (Pfeffer & Barnecutt, 1996).

We are aided in localizing sounds by having two ears. Sounds that come from points other than those equidistant between our two ears, for example from behind you, reach one ear slightly before they reach the other. Our auditory system then determines the direction and source of the sound by comparing the messages from each ear. Such sounds also are slightly more intense at the ear closer to the sound source because it receives the sound waves first. The auditory cortex has cells that respond to these differences in intensity and arrival time, permitting the brain to determine the location of a sound (McAlpine & Grothe, 2003). Even sounds that come from points equidistant between our ears can be located because the irregular shape of the pinna alters sounds differently, depending on the direction from which they enter the ear (Middlebrooks & Green, 1991). The pinna is angled forward to help catch sounds coming toward you best. And the parietal cortex aids the auditory cortex in localizing sounds, in keeping with its role in spatial perception (Zatorre, Bouffard, Ahad, & Belin, 2002).

Section Review: Hearing

1. What are the major structures of the outer, middle, and inner ear?
2. What is the place theory of pitch perception?
3. What are the basic processes in sound localization?

Chemical Senses

The chemical senses of smell and taste let us identify things on the basis of their chemical content. These senses also provide us with both pleasure and protection.

Smell

Helen Keller (1880–1968), though deaf and blind from infancy, could identify her friends by their smell and could even tell whether a person had recently been in a kitchen, garden, or hospital room by his or her odor (Ecenbarger, 1987). Though most of us do not rely on smell to that extent, the sense of smell (or **olfaction**) is important to all of us. It warns us of dangers, such as fire, deadly gases, or spoiled food, and lets us enjoy the pleasant odors of food, nature, and other people.

North Americans find odors so important that they spend millions of dollars on perfumes, colognes, and deodorants to make themselves more socially appealing. Workers also might feel more motivated when in the presence of a pleasant fragrance. This reaction was demonstrated in a study in which men wore cologne for 10 days and reported their moods twice daily on those days as well as on 2 baseline days. The results showed that their moods while wearing cologne were improved over their moods during the 2 baseline days (Schiffman, Suggs, & Sattely-Miller, 1995). This finding was replicated in a study in which women exposed to pleasant odors had enhanced moods in response to them (Schiffman, Sattely-Miller, & Suggs, 1995). The possible influence of fragrances on moods has led some business owners to diffuse scents into their stores to gain a competitive advantage. Nonetheless, few research studies have supported the effectiveness of this technique (Spangenberg, Crowley, & Henderson, 1996).

Our responses to odors are influenced by culture, gender, and even disease states. Cultural differences in the perceived intensity and pleasantness of particular odors

olfaction The sense of smell, which detects molecules carried in the air.

appear to be attributable to cultural differences in people's experience with different odors (Ayabe-Kanamura et al., 1998). For example, a study of Mexican, German, and Japanese women found that participants rated familiar odors to be more intense and more pleasant than unfamiliar odors (Distal et al., 1999). Women tend to outperform men when detecting and identifying odors. This finding may be attributable to gender differences in experience and thus familiarity with various odors (Brand & Millot, 2001). In another experiment, patients with early-stage Alzheimer's disease were tested, with their eyes closed, for their ability to detect an odor, one nostril at a time. There were measurable distance differences in detection between Alzheimer's patients and a control group matched by age and gender (Stamps, Bartoshuck, & Heilman, 2013). This study reveals a non-invasive and inexpensive test that appears to be sensitive to identifying patients with early-stage Alzheimer's.

The ability of odors to affect our moods has led to the advent of so-called *aromatherapy,* which attempts to use different fragrances to enhance cognitive abilities or psychological well-being. In one experiment, groups of adults were exposed to either an alerting aroma (rosemary) or a relaxing odor (lavender) and were asked to perform mathematical calculations. The rosemary group showed heightened alertness as measured by self-reports and brain waves. Both groups increased their speed of calculations, but only the lavender group showed improved accuracy of calculations (Diego et al., 1998). In another experiment, agitated patients with Alzheimer's disease were randomly assigned to have either lemon-scented oil or a placebo oil rubbed on their arms and face twice a day for 4 weeks. The results showed that those who received lemon-scented oil became significantly calmer than those who received the placebo oil (Ballard, O'Brien, Reichelt, & Elaine, 2002). Despite some positive research findings regarding aromatherapy, some studies have failed to support its effectiveness (Lee, Choi, Posadzki, & Ernst, 2012). Consumers should remain skeptical of some of the extreme claims made for its effectiveness by those who stand to profit from aromatherapy products and services.

What accounts for our ability to smell odors? In part because of the practical difficulty of gaining access to the olfactory pathways, we have relatively limited knowledge of how olfactory anatomy affects the detection and recognition of odors. We do know that molecules carried in inhaled air stimulate smell receptor cells on the olfactory epithelium high up in the nasal passages. Figure 5-23 illustrates the major structures of the olfactory system.

Today, research findings indicate that molecules that reach the olfactory epithelium alter the resting potential and firing frequency of receptor cells, stimulating some and inhibiting others. Distinctive patterns in the firing of receptor cells evoke particular odors. Leading olfaction researcher Linda Bartoshuk has found that regardless of the exact mechanisms by which this occurs, olfaction depends on stimulation of different receptors, composed of proteins, on the olfactory epithelium by specific airborne chemicals (Bartoshuk & Beauchamp, 1994).

Neural impulses from the receptor cells travel along the short *olfactory nerves* to the frontal lobes of the brain. Smell is the only sense that is not processed first in the thalamus before being processed in other olfactory centers in the brain. The *limbic system,* a structure of the brain that is important in the experience of emotion, discussed in Chapter 3, receives many neural connections from the olfactory nerves. These connections might account for the powerful emotional effects of certain odors that evoke vivid memories of important events, places, or persons (Vermetten & Bremner, 2003). In one study, participants were exposed to 20 different odors and were asked to rate the odors and report whether they evoked a personal memory. In keeping with popular belief, memories evoked by the odors tended to be rare, vivid, emotional, and relatively old (Herz & Cupchik, 1992). And happiness, disgust, and to a lesser extent, anxiety, are reliably elicited by odors (Croy, Olgun, & Joraschky, 2011).

Our sense of smell has a remarkably low absolute threshold; we can detect minute amounts of chemicals diffused in the air. For example, *National Geographic* needed only 1 ounce of an odorous chemical to include a sample of it with 11 million copies of a smell survey (Gibbons, 1986). Our ability to identify familiar odors was highlighted

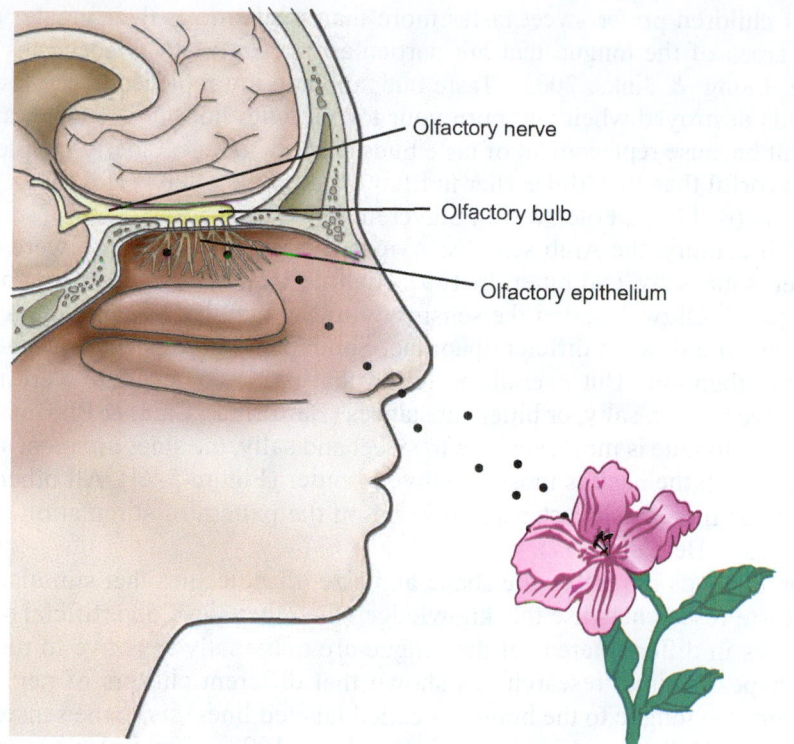

Olfactory nerve

Olfactory bulb

Olfactory epithelium

FIGURE 5-23
The Olfactory Pathway

Inhaled molecules attach to receptor cells high up in the nasal passages. This action stimulates neural activity in the olfactory bulbs, which generates olfactory-nerve impulses that are sent to brain regions that process smell sensations.

in a study of college students who showered themselves, put on fresh T-shirts, and used no soap, deodorant, or perfume for 24 hours. Participants then sniffed the shirts, one at a time, through an opening in a bag. Of the 29 participants, 22 correctly identified their own shirts (Russell, 1976). A more recent study assessed the reactions of participants to the odors of their relatives. The only odor aversions were between fathers and daughters and between brothers and sisters. The researchers concluded that odor aversion might contribute to the maintenance of the incest taboo (Weisfeld, Czilli, Phillips, Gall, & Lichtman, 2003).

Though smell is important to people, it is more important to many other animals. For example, salmon have an amazing ability to travel hundreds of miles to their home streams to spawn, following the familiar odors of the soil and plants on the banks of the waterways that mark the correct route home (Gibbons, 1986). Researchers have been especially interested in the effects of secretions called **pheromones**, intraspecies chemical signals, on the sexual behavior of animals. For example, *aphrodisin,* a vaginal pheromone released by female hamsters, stimulates copulation when inhaled by male hamsters (Singer & Macrides, 1990). Recent research indicates there may be human pheromones that affect emotions and behavior. For example, in one study, exposure to the pheromone *androstadienone,* which is primarily secreted by men, improved women's moods (Lundstrom, Goncalves, Esteves, & Olsson, 2003). But research results regarding the ability of any supposed human pheromone to consistently produce a particular effect are inconclusive (Hays, 2003). You should be wary of companies offering to sell you pheromones that they "guarantee" will help your romantic life.

pheromone An odorous chemical secreted by an animal that affects the behavior of other animals.

Taste

Our other chemical sense, taste (or **gustation**), protects us from harm by preventing us from ingesting poisons and enhances our enjoyment of life by letting us savor food and beverages. Taste depends on thousands of **taste buds**, which line the grooves between bumps called *papillae* on the surface of the tongue. The taste buds contain receptor cells that send neural impulses when stimulated by molecules dissolved in saliva (Smith & Margolis, 1999). Taste sensitivity also varies with the density of taste buds. One of the

gustation The sense of taste, which detects molecules of substances dissolved in the saliva.

taste buds Structures lining the grooves of the tongue that contain the taste receptor cells.

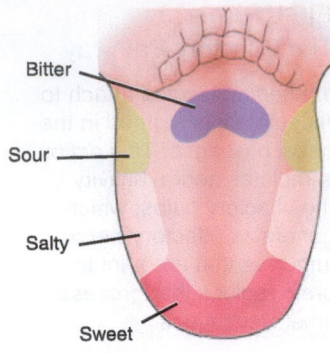

FIGURE 5-24

The Four Basic Tastes

All regions of the tongue are sensitive to each of the four basic tastes, but certain regions are more sensitive to particular ones. Sweet receptors line the tip of the tongue, sour and salty receptors line the sides, and bitter receptors line the back.

Labels on figure: Bitter, Sour, Salty, Sweet

reasons that children prefer sweet tastes more than adults do is their greater density of papillae in areas of the tongue that are particularly sensitive to sweet tastes (Segovia, Hutchinson, Laing, & Jinks, 2002). Taste buds die and are replaced every few days, so the taste buds destroyed when you burn your tongue with hot food or drink are quickly replaced. But because replacement of taste buds slows with age, elderly people may find food less flavorful than they did earlier in life. Older adults often prefer foods with more intense flavors (de Graaf, Polet, & van Staveren, 1994).

In the 11th century, the Arab scientist Avicenna proposed that there were four basic tastes: sweet, sour, salty, and bitter. In 1891 Hjalmar Ohrwall provided support for Avicenna's proposal. Ohrwall tested the sensitivity of the papillae by applying a variety of chemicals, one at a time, to different papillae. Some papillae responded to one taste and some to more than one. But overall, he found that particular papillae were maximally sensitive to sweet, sour, salty, or bitter substances (Bartoshuk, Cain, & Pfaffmann, 1985). The front of the tongue is most sensitive to sweet and salty, the sides are most sensitive to sour and salty, and the back is most sensitive to bitter (Figure 5-24). All other tastes are combinations of these basic tastes and depend on the pattern of stimulation of the taste receptors (Sato & Beidler, 1997).

Gustation depends in part on the shape and size of molecules that stimulate the taste receptors. Taste researchers use this knowledge when they develop artificial sweeteners. Taste receptors in different areas of the tongue are maximally sensitive to molecules of particular shapes. Animal research has shown that different clusters of nerve fibers in pathways from the tongue to the brain (so-called labeled lines) serve the senses of sweet, salty, and bitter (Hellekant, Ninomiya, & Danilova, 1998). There also are taste receptors that are sensitive to the presence of particular nutrients, such as fats and umami, the pleasurable taste elicited by monosodium glutamate, a common ingredient in Asian foods (Bellisle, 1999). Different regions of the somatosensory cortex respond more to certain tastes than to others (Kobayakawa et al., 1999).

Do not confuse taste with flavor, which is more complex. Whereas taste depends on sensations from the mouth, flavor relies on both taste and smell as well as on texture, temperature, and even pain—as in chili peppers (Bartoshuk, 1991). If you closed your eyes and held your nose, you would have trouble telling the difference between a piece of apple and a piece of potato placed in your mouth. Because smell is especially important for flavor, you might find that when you have a head cold that interferes with your ability to smell, food lacks flavor. In fact, people who lose their sense of smell because of disease or brain damage (a condition known as anosmia) find food less appealing (Ferris & Duffy, 1989).

Section Review: Chemical Senses

1. What are pheromones?
2. Why might a head cold affect your ability to enjoy the flavor of food?

Skin Senses

skin senses The senses of touch, temperature, and pain.

We rely on our **skin senses** of touch, temperature, and pain to identify objects, communicate feelings, and protect us from injury. Though there are a variety of receptors that produce skin sensations, there is no simple one-to-one relationship between specific kinds of receptors and specific skin senses. For example, there is only one kind of receptor in the cornea, but it is sensitive to touch, temperature, and pain. The pattern of stimulation of receptors, not the specific kind of receptor, determines skin sensations. Neural impulses from the skin receptors reach the thalamus, which relays them to the **somatosensory cortex** of the brain (see Chapter 3). Now consider what research has discovered about the senses of touch and pain.

somatosensory cortex The area of the parietal lobes that processes information from sensory receptors in the skin.

Touch

Your sense of *touch* lets you identify objects rapidly and accurately even when you cannot see them, as when you find your house key while fumbling with a key chain in the dark. Touch also helps us maintain our balance and equilibrium. Touch receptors on the soles of our feet, for example, help us maintain an upright posture while moving about (Roll, Kavounoudias, & Roll, 2002). Touch also is important in our social attachments, whether between lovers or between parent and child (Hertenstein, 2002), and in our well-being, as in helping physicians conduct medical examinations (Thompson & Lambert, 1995). Touch sensitivity depends on the concentration of receptors. The more sensitive the area of skin (such as the lips or fingertips), the larger is its representation on the somatosensory cortex. Touch sensitivity declines with age, perhaps because of the loss of touch receptors (Gescheider, Beiles, Checkosky, & Bolanowski, 1994) or alterations in the somatosensory cortex (Spengler, Godde, & Dinse, 1995).

The sense of touch is so precise that it can be used as a substitute for vision. In 1824 a blind Frenchman named Louis Braille invented the Braille system for reading and writing, which uses patterns of raised dots to represent letters. Blind adults who have used Braille for reading are superior to sighted adults in using their fingers to recognize fine details on objects. This sensitivity may be the result of a lifetime of using their fingers for reading (Van Boven, Hamilton, Kauffman, Keenan, & Pascual-Leone, 2000). The Braille concept has been extended to provide a substitute for vision. The blind person wears a camera on special eyeglasses and a special computer-controlled electronic vest covered with a grid of tiny Teflon cones. Outlines of images provided by the camera are impressed onto the skin by vibrations of the cones. People who have used the device have been able to identify familiar objects (Hechinger, 1981).

Pain

The sense of *pain* (or *nociception*) protects us from injury or even death. People born without a sense of pain, or who lose it through nerve injuries, may harm themselves without realizing it. Pain also interferes with functioning, as in back pain or headaches. Back pain is especially debilitating to certain professionals, such as truck drivers who commonly develop chronic lower back pain (Lyons, 2002). About 5 percent of the population experiences chronic daily headache (Lake & Saper, 2002). In the United States, headaches account for 18 million visits to physicians and the loss of more than 150 million workdays each year (Smith, 2000). Migraine headaches are generally more painful and debilitating than are tension headaches (Martins & Parriera, 2001). Migraine headaches are caused by dilation of arteries of the scalp, inflammation of nerves of the scalp, and decreased inhibition of pain transmission in the brain (Spierings, 2003). Based on the answers of almost 30,000 individuals who responded to a large-scale U.S. survey, 18.2 percent of female and 6.5 percent of male respondents reported having migraine headaches. European Americans are more likely to have migraines than African Americans, and migraines are more common among people of lower socioeconomic status. The frequency of migraines tends to increase through early adulthood and decline beginning in middle adulthood (Lipton, Stewart, Diamond, Diamond, & Reed, 2001).

Because acute pain can be extremely distressing and chronic pain is severely depressing (Banks & Kerns, 1996), researchers are studying the factors that cause pain and possible ways of relieving it.

Pain Factors

An injury or intense stimulation of sensory receptors induces pain. So, bright lights, loud noises, hot spices, and excessive pressure, as well as cuts, burns, and bruises are painful. Heredity plays a role in the pain response (Lariviere et al., 2002). The main pain receptors (or *nociceptors*) are free nerve endings in the skin. Two kinds of neuronal fibers transmit pain impulses: *A-delta fibers* carry sharp or pricking pain, and *C fibers* carry dull or burning pain (Mengel, Stiefenhofer, Jyvasjarvi, & Kniffki, 1993). Many pain receptor neurons transmit pain impulses by releasing the neuropeptide substance P from their axons (Meert, Vissers, Geenen, & Kontinen, 2003). For example, the intensity of arthritis pain varies with the amount of *substance P* released by neurons that convey pain impulses, and analgesics that reduce levels of substance P reduce arthritis pain intensity (Torri, Cecchettin, Bellometti, & Galzigna, 1995). Two substances implicated in pain are *bradykinin,* a chemical that accumulates at the site of an injury or inflammation (Banik, Kozaki, Sato, Gera, & Mizumura, 2001) and the neurotransmitter glutamate, which affects pain receptors in the brain, the spinal cord, and the body (Fundytus, 2001).

A brain region called the *periaqueductal gray* is an important pain-inhibiting center (Zanoto de Luca, Brandao, Motta, & Landeira-Fernandez, 2003). And pathways to the limbic system appear to affect emotional responses to pain (Giesler, Katter, & Dado, 1994). Painful stimulation of the skin triggers neural impulses that travel to the thalamus (Treede, 2002) and then are relayed to sites on the somatosensory cortex (Kanda et al., 2000).

The most influential theory of pain is the **gate-control theory,** formulated by psychologist Ronald Melzack and biologist Patrick Wall (1965). The theory assumes that pain impulses from the limbs or body pass through a part of the spinal cord that provides a "gate" for pain impulses, perhaps involving substance P neurons (Holland, Goldstein, & Aronstam, 1993). Stimulation of neurons that convey touch sensations "closes" the gate, preventing input from neurons that convey pain sensations. This theory might explain why rubbing a shin that you have banged against a table will relieve the pain. The closing of the pain gate is stimulated by the secretion of *endorphins* (Anderson, Sheth, Bencherif, Frost, & Campbell, 2002), which (as described in Chapter 3) are the brain's natural opiates. Endorphins might close the gate by inhibiting the secretion of substance P (Ruda, 1982). And exercise increases endorphin levels and reduces pain sensitivity (Sadigh-Lindell et al., 2001). The gate-control theory remains the most comprehensive, widely accepted theory of pain (Sufka & Price, 2002).

The pain gate also is affected by neural impulses that originate in the brain (Gilbert, 2003). In fact, merely anticipating pain increases activity in brain regions that process pain. In one study, participants were told that they would be given either painful or nonpainful stimulation of the foot. Cortical responses, as measured by fMRI, indicated that both kinds of stimulation increased activity in the area devoted to the foot, but the activity was more intense in response to anticipation of pain (Porro et al., 2002). This finding might explain why anxiety, relaxation, and other psychological factors can affect pain perception (Melzack, 1993). Cognitive factors are particularly important in moderating pain. Catastrophizing about pain, for example, by magnifying it and ruminating about it tends to intensify it (France, France, al'Absi, Ring, & McIntyre, 2002). And a feeling of control over pain's effects on one's life and over one's pain helps reduce people's distress (Tan et al., 2003). Thus, cognitive processes can affect physiological processes related to pain (Pincus & Morley, 2001).

Sociocultural factors, likewise, have been found to influence the perception of pain. A meta-analysis of experimental studies found that women report higher levels of pain sensitivity than do men. Moreover, effect sizes ranged from large to moderate depending on the type of painful stimulus (Riley, Robinson, Wise, Myers, & Fillingim, 1998). Women and men do appear to respond to some painful stimuli and analgesia differently, a difference that is attributable to biological, cognitive, and social factors (Miaskowski, 1999; Racine et al., 2012). African Americans and European Americans also respond to painful stimuli differently. This difference may be attributable to sociocultural factors, such as beliefs and attitudes, and psychological factors, such as coping strategies (Rahim-Williams, Riley, Williams, & Fillingim, 2012). Cross-cultural research has found that women find it more socially appropriate to admit to experiencing pain than do men (Nayak, Shiflett, Eshun, & Levine, 2000). And cultural factors can influence pain perception and responses to pain treatments (Goldberg & Remy-St. Louis, 1998), as in cross-cultural differences in the interpretation and expression of pain (Rollman, 1998) and research on reactions to childbirth of women from different cultures (see "The Research Process: Are There Cultural Differences in the Painfulness of Childbirth?" on the following page).

Pain Control

Chronic pain afflicts millions of Americans. The pain of cancer, surgery, injuries, headaches, and backaches makes pain control an important topic of research in both medicine and psychology. The most popular approach to the relief of severe pain relies on drugs

gate-control theory
The theory that pain impulses can be blocked by the closing of a neuronal gate in the spinal cord.

Are There Cultural Differences in the Painfulness of Childbirth?

Childbirth is both a physiological and cultural event of major importance in many women's lives. Italian researchers Alda Scopesi, Mirella Zanobini, and Paolo Carossino (1997), of the University of Genoa, wondered to what extent cultural factors would affect women's reactions to childbirth, including the degree of pain they experienced during labor and delivery. They decided to study the reactions of women in comparable cities in four different cultures.

Method

The research study was carried out in 18 hospitals in four industrialized cities: Boston in the United States, Genoa in Italy, Cologne in Germany, and Reims in France. Of the 414 women in the study, 93 were from Boston, 109 from Genoa, 107 from Cologne, and 105 from Reims. The women were asked to respond to a questionnaire with 29 questions about the course of their pregnancy and their subjective reactions to childbirth.

Results and Discussion

The results indicated that there was no statistically significant difference between the groups regarding pain during labor. But there was a statistically significant difference in their degree of pain during delivery. Most of the women in each city reported that delivery was bearable, but significantly fewer women in Genoa (only 6 percent) reported that delivery was unbearably painful. Boston and Reims had the highest percentage of women (22 percent in each city) reporting that delivery was unbearably painful.

The authors concluded that women in Genoa were less likely to experience delivery as unbearable because childbirth there is more likely to be considered a medical event in which pain is expected. This interpretation agrees with research findings that our expectations can affect our responses to pain. If we can predict that we will experience pain, we will experience it as less intense than if severe pain is not considered a part of delivery.

Another potentially important finding was that women who reported that pain during delivery was unbearable also tended to report that they experienced a greater degree of joy afterward. This phenomenon, in which a positive emotional experience follows a powerful negative one, is discussed in Chapter 12. This study provided evidence that women in different cultures will respond differently to the pain of childbirth. But it will take more cross-cultural studies like this one to determine the factors that account for this difference, including the reasons why women in four different cultures would differ in their subjective level of pain during delivery but not during labor. One possible explanation for these differences is the influence of the medical staff's expectations and treatment of their patients. Cross-cultural studies indicate that women's responses during labor might indeed be affected by the attitudes of their hospital caregivers (Sheiner, Sheiner, Shoham-Vardi, Mazor, & Katz, 1999).

such as morphine, a highly effective pain reliever, which affects endorphin receptors in the brain. Even **placebo** "sugar pills," which are supposedly inactive substances that are substituted for pain-relieving drugs, can relieve pain. One study found that patients with chronic pain who respond to placebos produce higher levels of endorphins than do those who fail to respond (Lipman et al., 1990). But other studies have failed to find a role for endorphins in the placebo effect (Montgomery & Kirsch, 1996).

Other techniques that do not rely on drugs or placebos also relieve pain by stimulating the release of endorphins. For example, the technique of **acupuncture**, popular in China for thousands of years, relies on the insertion of fine needles into various sites on the body. *Naloxone,* a drug that blocks the effects of opiates, inhibits the analgesic effects of acupuncture. This finding provides evidence for the role of endorphins in acupuncture (Murray, 1995), perhaps by blocking impulses at the pain gate in the spinal cord (Lee & Beitz, 1992). Research using functional MRI of the brain found that acupuncture might exert its pain-relieving effects in part by affecting the limbic system (Hui et al., 2000).

Acupuncture has been effective in reducing a variety of kinds of pain, including chronic neck pain (Irnich et al., 2002) and pain during labor (Nesheim et al., 2003). It has been particularly effective in treating chronic lower back pain. In one study, participants debilitated by lower back pain were randomly assigned to receive either acupuncture or a placebo treatment. After three months, the acupuncture group reported a significantly greater decrease in pain. Moreover, they used less pain medication, had better quality sleep, and were more likely to have returned to

placebo An inactive substance that might induce some of the effects of the drug for which it has been substituted.

acupuncture A pain-relieving technique that relies on the insertion of fine needles into various sites on the body.

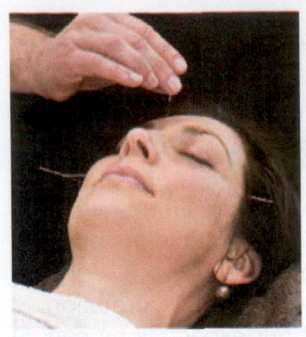

Acupuncture

Acupuncture appears to achieve its pain-relieving effects by stimulating the release of endorphins.

Source: VannPhotography/Shutterstock.com.

transcutaneous electrical nerve stimulation (TENS)
The use of electrical stimulation of sites on the body to provide pain relief, apparently by stimulating the release of endorphins.

work (Carlsson & Sjoelund, 2001). Though most studies on the use of acupuncture in treating pain have produced positive findings, the quality of acupuncture research needs to be improved in order to provide stronger evidence of its effectiveness (Ezzo et al., 2000).

A similar, more modern technique for pain relief relies on **transcutaneous electrical nerve stimulation (TENS),** which involves electrical stimulation of sites on the body. TENS has proved effective in relieving many kinds of pain, including back pain (Marchand, Charest, & Chenard, 1993) and headache pain (Solomon & Guglielmo, 1985). A survey of chronic-pain patients who used TENS found that the patients had a significant reduction in their use of pain-killing drugs (Chabal, Fishbain, Weaver, & Heine, 1998). As in the case of placebos and acupuncture, TENS might relieve pain by stimulating the release of endorphins because its effects are blocked by naloxone (Wang, Mao, & Han, 1992). TENS also might inhibit activity in the pain gate in the spinal cord (Garrison & Foreman, 1994).

Still another technique, hypnosis, is effective in relieving pain (Hawkins, 2001). For example, it has helped relieve pain experienced by burn victims (Patterson, Adcock, & Bombardier, 1997) and cancer patients (Liossi & Hatira, 2003). But unlike other pain-relieving techniques, hypnosis does not appear to work by stimulating the release of endorphins. Studies have found that hypnosis might exert its effects by sending neural impulses that block pain impulses at the spinal-cord pain gate (Kiernan, Dane, Phillips, & Price, 1995), by reducing attention to pain sensations (Crawford, Knebel, & Vendemia, 1998), or by inducing a state of consciousness in which the individual feels disconnected from the pain (Freeman, Barabasz, Barabasz, & Warner, 2000).

Pain victims also can control their pain by using distracting thoughts or distracting stimuli (Tsao, Fanurik, & Zeltzer, 2003). In a study of dental patients, participants distracted by music during procedures experienced less pain and distress than did participants in a control group who were not exposed to music (Anderson, Baron, & Logan, 1991). And a meta-analysis found that distraction is effective in reducing children's pain and distress during medical procedures (Kleiber & Harper, 1999). One mechanism by which distraction reduces pain is by stimulating activity in the periaqueductal gray, which receives sensory input from the cortex, limbic system, and brain stem as measured by fMRI (Tracey et al., 2002).

Section Review: Skin Senses

1. How has the sense of touch been used to provide an electronic substitute for vision?

2. What is the gate-control theory of pain?

3. How is naloxone used to determine whether a pain-relieving technique works by stimulating endorphin activity?

Body Senses

Just as your skin senses let you judge the state of your skin, your body senses tell you the position of your limbs and help you maintain your equilibrium. The body senses—the *kinesthetic sense* and the *vestibular sense*—often are taken for granted and have inspired less research than the other senses. But they are crucial to everyday functioning.

The Kinesthetic Sense

kinesthetic sense The sense that provides information about the position of the joints, the degree of tension in the muscles, and the movement of the arms and legs.

The **kinesthetic sense** informs you of the position of your joints, the tension in your muscles, and the movement of your arms and legs. This information is provided by special receptors in your joints, muscles, and tendons. Kinesthetic receptors in your muscles let you judge the force as well as the path of your limb movements. Limb movements produce activity in specific regions of the somatosensory cortex (Prud'homme, Cohen, & Kalaska, 1994).

If your leg has ever "fallen asleep" (depriving you of kinesthetic sensations) and collapsed when you stood up, you realize that the kinesthetic sense helps you maintain enough tension in your legs to stand erect. Your kinesthetic sense also protects you from injury. If you are holding an object that is too heavy, kinesthetic receptors signal you to put it down to prevent injury to your muscles and tendons. Alcohol intoxication interferes with kinesthetic feedback, impairing movement by disrupting the sense of limb position (Wang, Nicholson, Mahoney, & Li, 1993). Athletes may benefit from using mental imagery of kinesthetic sensations to improve their performance on tasks that demand precise timing and coordination of movements (Fery, 2003).

Imagine losing your kinesthetic sense permanently, as happened to a woman described in a case study by the neurologist Oliver Sacks (1985). This robust, athletic young woman developed a rare inflammatory condition that affected only her kinesthetic neurons. She lost all feedback from her body, making it impossible for her to sit, stand, or walk. Her body became as floppy as a rag doll, and she reported feeling like a disembodied mind. She was able to compensate only slightly by using her sense of vision to regulate her body posture and movements. Thus, our kinesthetic sense, which we usually take for granted, plays an important role in our everyday motor functioning, such as writing (Teasdale, Forget, Bard, & Paillard, 1995).

As in the case of other senses, kinesthetic perception is subject to top-down processes, as in its ability to judge the weight of objects. This finding was demonstrated in a study that compared the ability of golfers and non-golfers to judge the weights of practice golf balls and real golf balls. Though practice balls are normally heavier than real balls, the balls used in this study were equal in weight. The golfers, whose experience told them that practice balls are heavier than real balls, judged the practice balls to be heavier. The non-golfers, who had no experience with golf balls, correctly judged the balls to be equal in weight. Thus, the golfers' experience with golf balls affected their kinesthetic perception of the balls' comparative weights (Ellis & Lederman, 1998).

The Vestibular Sense

Whereas the kinesthetic sense informs you of the state of your body parts, your **vestibular sense**, which depends on organs in the inner ear, informs you of your head's position in space, helping you maintain your balance and orientation.

The Vestibular Organs

The **otolith organs** (the saccule and the utricle) detect horizontal or vertical linear movement of the head and help you orient yourself in regard to gravity. The other vestibular organs are the **semicircular canals**, which are three fluid-filled tubes oriented in different planes. Their location is indicated in Figure 5-25. When your head moves in a given direction, the jellylike fluid in the semicircular canal oriented in that direction at first lags behind the movement of the walls of the canal. This makes hair cells protruding into the fluid bend in the direction opposite to the direction of head movement. The bending of hair cells triggers neural impulses that are relayed to your cerebellum, to help you maintain your balance.

Motion Sickness

Though the vestibular sense helps you maintain your equilibrium, it also can induce motion sickness, particularly in the case of slow, rolling motions (Howarth & Griffin, 2003). Fortunately, repeated exposure to situations that induce motion sickness tends to produce tolerance (Hu & Stern, 1999), and a study of paratroopers found that two-thirds had motion sickness on their first jump but only one-quarter had it on their fifth jump (Antunano & Hernandez, 1989). Moreover, motion sickness is reduced by a sense of personal control—which might explain why you are less likely to develop motion sickness when you are driving an automobile than when you are a passenger in one (Golding, Bles, Bos, Haynes, & Gresty, 2003).

The mechanisms that underlie motion sickness are still debated, but an influential view holds that motion sickness is induced by conflict between visual and vestibular sensations. Suppose you are in a windowless cabin aboard a ship in a rough sea. Your eyes tell you

The Body Senses

The kinesthetic sense and the vestibular sense provide gymnasts, dancers, athletes, and other performers, with exquisite control over their body movements.
Source: Tutti Frutti/Shutterstock.com.

vestibular sense The sense that provides information about the head's position in space and helps in the maintenance of balance.

otolith organs The vestibular organs that detect horizontal or vertical linear movement of the head.

semicircular canals The curved vestibular organs of the inner ear that detect rotary movements of the head in any direction.

FIGURE 5-25
The Vestibular Organs

When your head moves, fluid movement in the vestibular organs of the inner ear causes hair cells to bend, generating neural impulses that travel along the vestibular nerve to the brain. The semicircular canals detect tilting or rotation of your head. The otolith organs (the saccule and the utricle) detect linear movements of the head.

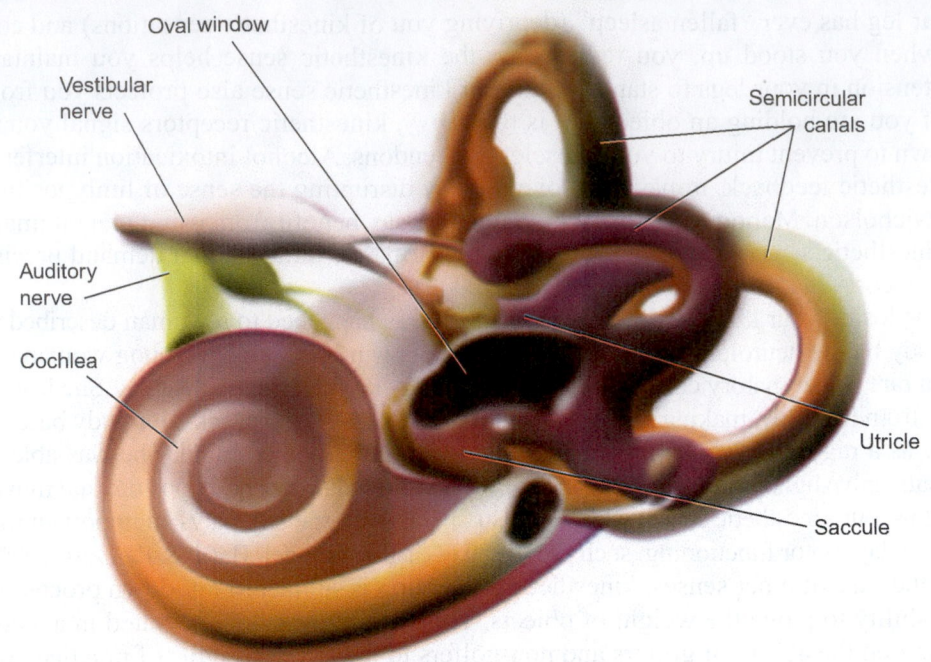

Oval window

Vestibular nerve

Semicircular canals

Auditory nerve

Cochlea

Utricle

Saccule

that you are stationary in relationship to one aspect of your environment—your cabin. Yet your vestibular sense tells you that you are moving in relationship to another aspect of your environment—the ocean. But this view does not explain why conflict between visual and vestibular sensations induces nausea. One hypothesis is that the motion-induced disruption of the normal association between visual and vestibular sensations is similar to the disruption produced by toxins, such as those in spoiled food, that induce nausea. As a result, motion induces nausea (Warwick-Evans, Symons, Fitch, & Burrows, 1998). As mentioned earlier, motion sickness is reduced by a sense of personal control—which might explain why if you look at the horizon while aboard a ship, you are less likely to develop motion sickness.

Section Review: Body Senses

1. What is the kinesthetic sense?
2. What is the role of the vestibular sense in motion sickness?

Extrasensory Perception

extrasensory perception (ESP) The alleged ability to perceive events without the use of sensory receptors.

parapsychology The study of extrasensory perception, psychokinesis, and related phenomena.

As you have just read, perception depends on the stimulation of sensory receptors by various kinds of energy. But you have certainly heard claims that support the possibility of perception independent of sensory receptors, so-called **extrasensory perception (ESP)**. The field that studies ESP and related phenomena is called **parapsychology** (*para-* means "besides"). The name indicates its failure to gain widespread acceptance within mainstream psychology. Parapsychological abilities are typically called *paranormal*. During the past decade, scientific interest in paranormal research has spread beyond Europe and North America, particularly into Latin American countries such as Brazil (Zangariand & Machado, 2001), Mexico (Ledezma & Monroig, 1997), and Argentina (Parra, 1997).

Despite scientific skepticism about paranormal abilities, a survey found that more than 99 percent of American college students believed in at least one paranormal ability and that more than 65 percent claimed a personal experience with at least one (Messer & Griggs, 1989). Moreover, mainstream journals in psychology, philosophy, and medicine periodically publish articles on paranormal abilities. Popular belief in paranormal abilities was exemplified in a

1986 lawsuit in which a Philadelphia woman who made a living as a psychic sued a hospital, insisting that a CT scan of her head made her lose her ESP abilities. A jury, impressed by the testimony of police officers who claimed she had helped them solve crimes by using ESP, awarded her $988,000 for the loss of her livelihood (Tulsky, 1986). (The jury's decision was later overturned on appeal.) Despite such widespread public acceptance of paranormal abilities, most psychologists are skeptical (Bem & Honorton, 1994). Before learning why they are, consider several of the paranormal abilities studied by parapsychologists.

Alleged Paranormal Abilities

More than three decades ago, members of the Grateful Dead rock band had their audiences at a series of six concerts in Port Chester, New York, try to transmit mental images of slides of art prints to a person asleep in a dream laboratory miles away at Maimonides Hospital in Brooklyn. When the sleeper awoke, he described the content of his dreams. Independent judges rated his dream reports as more similar to the content of the slides than were the dream reports of another person who had not been designated to receive the images (Ullman, Krippner, & Vaughan, 1973). It was reported as a successful demonstration of **mental telepathy**, the alleged ability to perceive the thoughts of others. This experiment was part of a series of ESP-dream studies carried out at Maimonides Hospital by Stanley Krippner and his colleagues (Krippner, 1993). Krippner is recognized as one of the contemporary leaders in the scientific approach to paranormal phenomena ("Stanley C. Krippner," 2003).

Dream-ESP studies conducted since the Maimonides studies have been less successful (Sherwood & Roe, 2003). One study of dream telepathy had a "sender" advertise in a national newspaper that he would send a dream telepathy image between midnight and 10 a.m. on a specified night. Different images were "sent" every 2 hours. More than 500 readers submitted dream reports and the times they "received" the images. Judges blind to the target sequence decided whether the reports matched the pictures. Unlike the results of the Grateful Dead demonstration, these judges' assessments provided no support for dream telepathy—the reports did not match the images that were sent (Hearne, 1989).

Related to mental telepathy is **clairvoyance,** the alleged ability to perceive objects or events without any sensory contact (Steinkamp, Milton, & Morris, 1998). You might be considered clairvoyant if you could identify all the objects in your psychology professor's desk drawer without looking in it. Many colleges host psychic entertainers, such as "the Amazing Kreskin," who impress their audiences by giving demonstrations such as "reading" the serial number of a dollar bill in an audience member's wallet. Reports that clairvoyant psychics have solved crimes by leading police to bodies or stolen items are exaggerated. A survey of police departments in the 50 largest American cities found not a single report of a clairvoyant who had solved a crime for them (Sweat & Durm, 1993).

Whereas mental telepathy and clairvoyance deal with the present, **precognition** is the alleged ability to perceive events in the future. An example would be predicting the next spin of a roulette wheel, one of the common ways of measuring precognitive ability (Kugel, 1990–1991). In regard to precognition about future events that come true, researchers must be aware that people who believe that they have had a precognitive experience might by their own behavior bring about the event that they predict (Steinkamp, 2000). Parapsychologists who are open to the possibility that precognition does exist are left with the daunting scientific problem of explaining how minds that exist in the present can perceive events that take place in the future (Randall, 1998).

Do not confuse precognition with **déjà vu,** an uncanny feeling that you have experienced a present situation in the past and that you can anticipate what will happen in the next few moments. There are four major viewpoints regarding the nature of déjà vu experiences. First, the *dual-processing* view holds that two cognitive processes are momentarily out of synchronization. Second, the *neurological* view holds that there is a momentary disruption in neurological transmission. Third, the *memory* view holds that we may be unconsciously aware of unfamiliar stimuli. Fourth, the *attention* view holds that we first perceive something without attending to it and then shortly thereafter perceive it while attending to it. There is not enough scientific evidence to strongly support or refute any of these views (Brown, 2003).

mental telepathy The alleged ability to perceive the thoughts of others.

clairvoyance The alleged ability to perceive objects or events without any sensory contact with them.

precognition The alleged ability to perceive events in the future.

déjà vu A feeling that you have experienced a present situation in the past and that you can anticipate what will happen next.

psychokinesis (PK)
The alleged ability to control objects with the mind alone.

Closely allied with ESP is **psychokinesis (PK),** the alleged ability to control objects with the mind alone. In an early experiment on PK, a person who supposedly had PK ability used a cup to throw six dice 2,376 times while trying to make a particular face come up. Each of the six possible faces was used as the designated face an equal number of times. The individual produced significantly more "hits" than would be expected by chance. The researchers concluded that this experiment provided evidence for the existence of PK (Herter & Rhine, 1945). More recent research has assessed people's ability to influence computer games (Broughton & Perlstrom, 1992) or a laser beam (Stevens, 1998–99). But a report by the National Academy of Sciences found no basis for any kind of paranormal ability (Palmer, Honorton, & Utts, 1989).

Problems with Paranormal Research

Parapsychology has attracted many prominent supporters. Mark Twain, William James, and G. Stanley Hall were members of the Society for Psychical Research, with James serving a term as president and Hall a term as vice president. James even established standards for research design in parapsychology, insisting that the scientific method was the only adequate means to determine whether paranormal phenomena were real (Schmeidler, 1993). Credit for making parapsychology a legitimate area of scientific research to some scientists goes to J. B. Rhine (1895–1980) of Duke University, who began a program of experimentation on paranormal phenomena in the 1930s (Matlock, 1991). His wife, Louisa Rhine, likewise became a leading parapsychologist (Feather, 1983). Several prestigious British universities also have lent credibility to parapsychology by sponsoring paranormal research. Edinburgh University in Scotland even set up the first faculty chair in parapsychology with a $750,000 grant from the estate of author Arthur Koestler (Dickson, 1984).

Despite the popular acceptance of parapsychology, most psychologists remain skeptical (Wesp & Montgomery, 1998). One reason is that many supposed instances of paranormal phenomena turn out to be the result of poorly controlled demonstrations (Schmidt & Walach, 2000). In a case reported by the magician James "The Amazing" Randi, a woman claimed she could influence fish by PK. Every time she put her hand against one side of an aquarium, the fish swam to the opposite side. Randi responded, "She calls it psychic; I call it frightened fish." He suggested she put dark paper over a side of the aquarium and test her ability on that side. After trying Randi's suggestion and finding that the fish no longer swam to the opposite side, she exclaimed, "It's marvelous! The power doesn't penetrate brown paper!" (Morris, 1980, p. 106). You might recognize her comment as an example of Piaget's concept of assimilation (see Chapter 4).

Supporters of parapsychology might also too readily accept chance events as evidence of paranormal phenomena (Brugger & Taylor, 2003). For example, at some time you probably have decided to call a friend, picked up the phone, and found your friend already on the other end of the line. Did mental telepathy make you call each other at the same time? Not necessarily. Perhaps the occurrence is simply due to coincidence, or perhaps you and your friend call each other often and at about the same time of day, so on occasion you might coincidentally call each other at exactly the same moment.

Another blow against the credibility of parapsychology is that some impressive demonstrations later have been found to involve fraud (Rhine, 1974). In a widely publicized case, the noted psychic Tamara Rand claimed to have predicted the 1981 assassination attempt on U.S. president Ronald Reagan in a videotape made before the attempt and later shown on the *Today* show. This case was considered evidence of precognition—until James Randi discovered that she had made the videotape after the assassination attempt ("Psychic Watergate," 1981).

Magic tricks also are often passed off as paranormal phenomena. In 1979 James McDonnell, chairman of the board of the McDonnell-Douglas corporation, gave $500,000 to Washington University in St. Louis to establish a parapsychology research laboratory. A respected physics professor took charge of the project and invited alleged psychics to be tested there. Randi sent two magicians, aged 17 and 18, to be tested as psychics. After demonstrating their PK "abilities" during 120 hours of testing over a 3-year period, the two were proclaimed the only participants with PK ability.

But both had relied on magic—in some instances, beginner's-level magic. For example, they demonstrated PK by moving a clock across a table through the use of an ultrathin thread held between their thumbs. Because of demonstrations like this one, Randi has urged parapsychologists to permit magicians to observe their research so that magic tricks are not mistaken for paranormal phenomena (Cox, 1984). Since 1965 Randi has offered a reward—now amounting to $1 million—to anyone who can demonstrate a true paranormal ability under well-controlled conditions. No one has done so.

Parapsychologists defend their research and insist that critics often reject positive findings by assuming they are impossible and therefore must be caused by some other factor, such as poor controls, magic tricks, or outright fraud (Child, 1985). Thus, opposition to paranormal research might reflect the current scientific paradigm as much as it does any methodological weaknesses in paranormal research (Krippner, 1995). Moreover, parapsychologists argue, paranormal abilities might be so subtle that they cannot be demonstrated at will or require highly motivated individuals to demonstrate them. For example, believers in paranormal abilities perform better on paranormal tests than do nonbelievers (Schmeidler, 1985). Likewise, experimenters who believe in paranormal abilities are more likely than nonbelievers to conduct research studies that produce positive findings. Gertrude Schmeidler (1997), a leading parapsychologist, notes that experimenter bias might account for the poor performance of some participants in ESP or PK studies. She insists that experimenters who are cynical about ESP or PK might inhibit talented people from performing well in research studies.

But even many parapsychologists agree that, from a scientific standpoint, the main weakness of research studies on paranormal abilities is the difficulty in replicating them (Galak, LeBoeuf, Nelson, & Simmons, 2012). As discussed in Chapter 2, scientists discredit events that cannot be replicated under similar conditions. Yet some parapsychologists insist that positive research findings related to paranormal phenomena have been replicated more often than critics of parapsychology will acknowledge (Roig, 1993), that meta-analyses show effects that are greater than those expected by chance alone (Storm, Tressoldi, & DiRisio, 2010), and that paranormal phenomena are so subtle that they are more likely to occur spontaneously in everyday life than on demand in a laboratory setting (Alvarado, 1996).

A final criticism of parapsychology is that there is no satisfactory explanation of paranormal phenomena (Fassbender, 1997). Their acceptance might require the discovery of new forms of energy. Evidence for the role of some sort of energy force comes from the finding that research studies conducted during periods of low geomagnetic activity have been associated with the most positive ESP research findings (Krippner, Vaughan, & Spottiswoode, 2000). But attempts to detect any unusual form of energy radiating from people with supposed paranormal abilities have failed (Balanovski & Taylor, 1978).

The Status of Parapsychology

Parapsychologists point out, however, that failure to know the cause of something does not mean that the phenomenon does not exist (Rockwell, 1979). They remind psychologists to be skeptical rather than cynical because many phenomena that are now scientifically acceptable were once considered impossible and unworthy of study. For example, scientists used to ridicule reports of stones falling from the sky and refused to investigate them. In 1807, after hearing of a report by two Yale University professors of a stone shower in Connecticut, President Thomas Jefferson, a scientist himself, said, "Gentlemen, I would rather believe that those two Yankee professors would lie than to believe that stones fell from heaven" (quoted in Diaconis, 1978). Today, even young children know that such stones are meteorites and that they indeed fall from the sky. Even William James, perhaps reflecting his being one of the most open-minded of scientists, believed at the end of his life that there was something to psychic phenomena but that he had still not found any convincing evidence of it. Nonetheless, because alleged paranormal abilities are so unusual, seemingly inexplicable, and difficult to demonstrate reliably, even open-minded psychologists will continue to discount them unless they receive more compelling evidence. The extraordinary claims made by parapsychologists will require extraordinary evidence for mainstream psychologists to accept their validity (Grey, 1994).

Section Review: Extrasensory Perception

1. What are the four alleged paranormal abilities?
2. What are the major shortcomings of paranormal research?

Experiencing Psychology

Do College Students Exhibit ESP Ability?

Rationale

As discussed in the section "Extrasensory Perception," psychologists for a variety of reasons tend to discount research findings that support ESP. Those who support the existence of ESP do so because of research in which performances on ESP tasks are significantly better than would be predicted from chance alone. In this exercise, you will be asked to participate in a study of telepathy in which participants try to identify the suits of common playing cards viewed by another student.

Method

Participants

The participants will be an equal number of male and female introductory psychology students, perhaps 10 to 20.

Materials

You will need a deck of playing cards and data sheets to record the participants' responses on each trial.

Procedure

The "sender" and the "receiver" should have their backs toward each other. The sender should turn the top card in the deck face up, write down its suit, and then try to send the image of the suit to the receiver for 5 seconds. The receiver should write down the suit that he or she believes the sender has seen. Do this for 20 trials for each participant, shuffling the deck after each trial.

Results and Discussion

Record the total number of correct responses for each participant and find the average number of correct responses for the group. Did the group's percentage of correct responses seem markedly different from chance expectancy (25 percent)? Did anyone's percentage of correct responses seem to indicate that the person had telepathic ability? If so, does that result necessarily indicate the presence of ESP ability? Why would it have been preferable to have used an inferential statistic instead of making a subjective judgment about the meaning of the percentage of correct responses? (See Chapter 2 and Appendix C—available in the Online Edition.) Discuss any important (not trivial) extraneous participant, experimenter, procedural, or environmental variables that might have affected the results and state how you would improve the study. How comfortable are you in generalizing the results of the study? Suggest another study that you would like to see conducted to test for the presence of ESP or PK.

Chapter Summary

Sensory Processes

- Sensation is the process that detects stimuli from one's body or environment.
- Perception is the process that organizes sensations into meaningful patterns.
- Psychophysics is the study of the relationships between the physical characteristics of stimuli and the conscious psychological experiences they produce.
- The minimum amount of stimulation that can be detected is called the absolute threshold.
- According to signal-detection theory, the detection of a stimulus depends on both its intensity and the physiological and psychological state of the receiver.

- Research on subliminal perception investigates whether participants can unconsciously perceive stimuli that do not exceed the absolute threshold.
- The minimum amount of change in stimulation that can be detected is called the difference threshold.
- Weber's law states that the amount of change in stimulation needed to produce a just noticeable difference is a constant proportion of the original stimulus.
- The tendency of our sensory receptors to be increasingly less responsive to an unchanging stimulus is called sensory adaptation.

Visual Sensation

- Vision lets us sense objects by the light reflected from them into our eyes.
- The lens focuses light onto the rods and cones of the retina.
- Visual input is transmitted by the optic nerves to the brain, ultimately reaching the visual cortex.
- During dark adaptation the rods and cones become more sensitive to light, with the rods becoming significantly more sensitive than the cones.
- The trichromatic theory of color vision considers the interaction of red, green, and blue cones.
- The opponent-process theory assumes that color vision depends on activity in red-green, blue-yellow, and black-white ganglion cells and cells in the thalamus.
- Color blindness is usually caused by an inherited lack of a cone pigment.

Visual Perception

- Form perception depends on distinguishing figure from ground.
- In studying form perception, Gestalt psychologists identified the principles of proximity, similarity, closure, and continuity.
- Whereas Gestalt psychologists claim that we perceive objects as wholes, other theories claim that we construct objects from their component parts.
- Depth perception lets us determine how far away objects are from us.
- Binocular cues to depth require the interaction of both eyes.
- Monocular cues to depth require only one eye.
- Experience in viewing objects contributes to size constancy, shape constancy, and brightness constancy.
- The misapplication of depth perception cues and perceptual constancies can contribute to visual illusions.
- Sensory experience and cultural background both affect visual perception.

Hearing

- The sense of hearing (audition) detects sound waves produced by the vibration of objects.
- Sound waves cause the tympanic membrane to vibrate.
- The ossicles of the middle ear convey the vibrations to the oval window of the cochlea, which causes waves to travel through fluid within the cochlea.
- The waves bend hair cells on the basilar membrane, sending neural impulses along the auditory nerve.
- Sounds are ultimately processed by the auditory cortex of the temporal lobes.
- The frequency of a sound determines its pitch.
- Pitch perception is explained by place theory, frequency theory, and volley theory.
- The intensity of a sound determines its loudness.
- People may suffer from conduction deafness or nerve deafness.
- The mixture of sound waves determines a sound's quality, or timbre.

- Sound localization depends on differences in a sound's arrival time and intensity at the two ears.

Chemical Senses

- The chemical senses of smell and taste detect chemicals in the air we breathe or the substances we ingest.
- The sense of smell (olfaction) depends on receptor cells on the nasal membrane that respond to particular chemicals.
- Odorous secretions called pheromones affect the sexual behavior of animals.
- The sense of taste (gustation) depends on receptor cells on the taste buds of the tongue that respond to particular chemicals.
- The basic tastes are sweet, salty, sour, and bitter.

Skin Senses

- Skin senses depend on receptors that send neural impulses to the somatosensory cortex.
- Touch sensitivity depends on the concentration of receptors in the skin.
- Pain depends on both physical and psychological factors.
- According to the gate-control theory of pain, stimulation of touch neurons closes a spinal gate, which inhibits neural impulses underlying pain from traveling up the spinal cord.
- Pain-relieving techniques such as placebos, acupuncture, and transcutaneous nerve stimulation relieve pain by stimulating the release of endorphins.
- Hypnosis appears to relieve pain by distracting the hypnotized person.

Body Senses

- Your body senses make you aware of the position of your limbs and help you maintain your equilibrium.
- The kinesthetic sense informs you of the position of your joints, the tension in your muscles, and the movement of your arms and legs.
- The vestibular sense informs you of your position in space, helping you maintain your equilibrium.
- The vestibular organs comprise the otolith organs (the saccule and the utricle) and the semicircular canals.
- An influential theory of motion sickness attributes it to conflict between the visual and vestibular senses.

Extrasensory Perception

- Most members of the lay public accept the existence of paranormal phenomena such as extrasensory perception and psychokinesis; most psychologists do not.
- Psychologists are skeptical because research in parapsychology has been marked by sloppy procedures, acceptance of coincidences as positive evidence, fraudulent reports, use of magic tricks, failure to replicate studies, and inability to explain paranormal phenomena.
- Supporters of parapsychology claim that their research has been subjected to unfair criticism.

Key Terms

perception (p. 151)
prosopagnosia (p. 150)
sensation (p. 151)
visual agnosia (p. 150)

Sensory Processes

absolute threshold (p. 151)
difference threshold (p. 153)
just noticeable difference (jnd) (p. 153)
psychophysics (p. 151)
sensory adaptation (p. 153)
sensory receptors (p. 151)
sensory transduction (p. 151)
signal-detection theory (p. 152)
subliminal perception (p. 152)
Weber's law (p. 153)

Visual Sensation

accommodation (p. 156)
afterimage (p. 162)
color blindness (p. 163)
cones (p. 157)
cornea (p. 155)
dark adaptation (p. 161)
fovea (p. 158)
hyperopia (p. 157)
lens (p. 156)
myopia (p. 157)
opponent-process theory (p. 162)
optic chiasm (p. 158)
optic nerve (p. 157)
photopigments (p. 160)
retina (p. 156)

rods (p. 157)
sclera (p. 155)
smooth pursuit movements (p. 158)
trichromatic theory (p. 162)
visible spectrum (p. 155)
vision (p. 154)
visual cortex (p. 158)

Visual Perception

binocular cues (p. 166)
brightness constancy (p. 170)
depth perception (p. 165)
feature-detector theory (p. 165)
figure-ground perception (p. 164)
illusory contours (p. 165)
monocular cues (p. 167)
moon illusion (p. 170)
shape constancy (p. 169)
size constancy (p. 169)
visual illusion (p. 170)

Hearing

audition (p. 173)
auditory cortex (p. 176)
auditory nerve (p. 176)
basilar membrane (p. 176)
cochlea (p. 175)
conduction deafness (p. 177)
frequency theory (p. 177)
loudness perception (p. 177)
nerve deafness (p. 177)
pitch perception (p. 176)
place theory (p. 176)

sound localization (p. 178)
timbre (p. 178)
tympanic membrane (p. 174)
volley theory (p. 177)

Chemical Senses

gustation (p. 181)
olfaction (p. 179)
pheromone (p. 181)
taste buds (p. 181)

Skin Senses

acupuncture (p. 185)
gate-control theory (p. 184)
placebo (p. 185)
skin senses (p. 182)
somatosensory cortex (p. 182)
transcutaneous electrical nerve
    stimulation (TENS) (p. 186)

Extrasensory Perception

kinesthetic sense (p. 186)
otolith organs (p. 187)
semicircular canals (p. 187)
vestibular sense (p. 187)
Extrasensory Perception
clairvoyance (p. 189)
dèjá vu (p. 189)
extrasensory perception (ESP) (p. 188)
mental telepathy (p. 189)
parapsychology (p. 188)
precognition (p. 189)
psychokinesis (PK) (p. 190)

Chapter Quiz

Note: Answers for the Chapter Quiz questions are provided at the end of the book.

1. Conflict between visual and vestibular sensations may induce
   a. psychokinesis.
   b. motion sickness.
   c. auditory dominance.
   d. mental dissociation.

2. The study of visual restriction in kittens (Blakemore & Cooper, 1970) found that kittens not exposed to lines of a particular orientation will
   a. fail to grow neurons responsive to that orientation.
   b. show degeneration of neurons responsive to that orientation.
   c. overcompensate by growing more neurons responsive to that orientation.
   d. show degeneration of neurons responsive to that orientation and perpendicular orientations.

3. A Viewmaster (a stereoscopic) toy creates a 3-D image by taking advantage of
   a. convergence.
   b. motion parallax.
   c. binocular disparity.
   d. linear perspective.

4. Smells may evoke powerful emotional responses because of pathways from the olfactory nerves to the
   a. brain stem.
   b. limbic system.
   c. corpus callosum.
   d. medulla.

5. Accommodation in the eye
   a. helps focus images on the retina.
   b. provides binocular depth perception.
   c. regulates the amount of light striking the retina.
   d. lets it rebound to its normal curvature after being poked by a finger or other object.

6. The kinesthetic sense enables one to
   a. perceive the movement of objects.
   b. detect the position of one's limbs.
   c. allegedly move objects with one's mind.
   d. sense changes in the temperature of objects.

7. While studying in the library you are, at first, distracted by the constant hum of the heating system. But you eventually stop noticing it. This is an example of
   a. synesthesia.
   b. sublimation.
   c. habituation.
   d. sensory adaptation.

8. Pheromones
   a. account for color vision.
   b. may explain motion sickness.
   c. affect the behavior of other animals.
   d. enable bats to locate prey by their echoes.

9. A hearing aid would be LEAST useful in treating deafness caused by damage to the
   a. pinna.
   b. eardrum.
   c. ossicles.
   d. auditory nerve.

10. A person suffers a wound that damages the temporal lobe. He would most likely experience difficulty in
    a. moving.
    b. seeing.
    c. hearing.
    d. smelling.

11. The study that used professional baseball players found that batters can keep their eyes on the ball
    a. only when it is about to hit their bat.
    b. only after it is about halfway to home plate.
    c. from the pitcher's hand until it reaches a few feet from home plate.
    d. from the pitcher's hand all the way to the point it makes contact with the bat.

12. The fact that the inner corner of a room looks farther away than the outer corner of a building provides one explanation of the
    a. Ponzo illusion.
    b. Ames room illusion.
    c. Poggendorf illusion.
    d. Müller-Lyer illusion.

13. If you could get the answers to this quiz by reading your professor's mind, you would demonstrate
    a. precognition.
    b. clairvoyance.
    c. psychokinesis.
    d. mental telepathy.

14. If a person's left optic nerve is completely severed, she would be
    a. blind in her left eye.
    b. blind in her left visual field.
    c. blind in her right visual field.
    d. able to detect objects, but not identify them, with her left eye.

15. The gate-control theory explains
    a. pain perception.
    b. taste perception.
    c. touch perception.
    d. pitch perception.

16. Papillae are found on the
    a. skin.
    b. tongue.
    c. basilar membrane.
    d. olfactory epithelium.

17. After observing that naval aviators sometimes crashed into airplanes ahead of them, researchers decided to set their taillights a standard distance apart. This improved depth perception by taking advantage of
    a. convergence.
    b. motion parallax.
    c. linear perspective.
    d. aerial perspective.

18. Advocates of top-down processing assume that the
    a. ability to perceive forms is based on heredity.
    b. mind is active, rather than passive, in perceiving forms.
    c. visual system composes perceptions mechanically from raw sensations.
    d. visual system processes the upper portions of objects and then proceeds to lower portions.

19. The frequency theory of hearing is best for sounds
    a. above 5,000 Hz.
    b. up to 1,000 Hz.
    c. between 1,000 and 5,000 Hz.
    d. within the range of human hearing.

20. Credit for trying to make ESP a legitimate topic of scientific interest is generally given to
    a. Uri Geller.
    b. J. B. Rhine.
    c. James Randi.
    d. Tamara Rand.

21. You should dim your high beams to oncoming traffic at night and not turn on the dome light to read a map because those actions would interfere with
    a. synesthesia.
    b. afterimages.
    c. color vision.
    d. dark adaptation.

22. The technical name for the "eardrum" is the
    a. pinna.
    b. oval window.
    c. basilar membrane.
    d. tympanic membrane.

23. The saying "the whole is different from the sum of its parts" would be most closely associated with
    a. John Locke.
    b. Ernst Weber.
    c. Max Wertheimer.
    d. Hermann von Helmholtz.

24. Touch sensations would most likely be disrupted by damage to the
    a. frontal lobes.
    b. temporal lobes.
    c. parietal lobes.
    d. occipital lobes.

25. An engineer designing a new television finds that for the middle ranges of light intensity a perceived change in brightness is a constant fraction of the original intensity. This is an example of
    a. Wundt's law.
    b. Weber's law.
    c. Young's law.
    d. Helmholtz's law.

Thought Questions

1. Why is it conceivable that creatures elsewhere in the universe have evolved sensory receptors that detect radio and television waves?

2. How does the opponent-process theory of color vision explain afterimages?

3. Why are both frequency theory and place theory needed to explain pitch perception?

4. Why do psychologists tend to discount the existence of paranormal abilities?

Consciousness

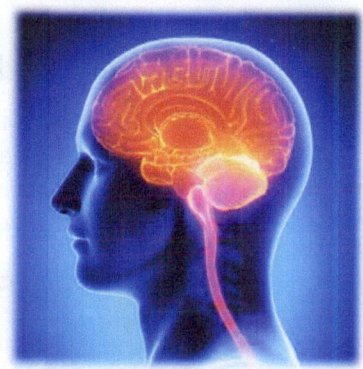

Source: CLIPAREA/Custom media/ Shutterstock.com.

Chapter Outline

The Nature of Consciousness

Sleep

Dreams

Hypnosis

Psychoactive Drugs

If you are like many students, you have experienced the dreaded "all-nighter"—staying awake through the night to write a paper or study for an exam. You probably felt exhausted the next night, collapsed into bed, slept a bit longer than usual, and awoke refreshed—none the worse for your experience. But what would happen to you if you stayed awake for several days? Would you suffer cognitive and physical deterioration? Would any negative effects be long-lasting?

Though research on prolonged sleep deprivation began in the 1890s, the first study to gain widespread attention took place in 1959. On January 21, Peter Tripp, a popular disc jockey in New York City, began a radiothon to raise money for the March of Dimes fight against polio. He decided to proceed despite anecdotal reports about animals and people who had died after prolonged sleep deprivation. He chose to believe, instead, other anecdotal reports about explorers and military troops who had survived bouts of extended sleep deprivation (Coren, 1996).

During his radiothon, Tripp stayed awake for 200 hours (more than 8 days), each evening broadcasting his 5 to 8 p.m. radio show from an Army recruiting booth in Times Square. He did this for the publicity and to permit passersby to look through the windows of the booth and verify that he was awake. Tripp periodically left the booth to go to the Astor Hotel across the street to wash up, use the toilet, change his clothes, and undergo medical examinations. Physicians and researchers monitored several of his physiological responses during the radiothon for his safety and to obtain scientific data about the effects of sleep deprivation.

As the days passed, Tripp showed signs of psychological deterioration. After 4 days he could not focus his attention well enough to do simple tasks, and he began experiencing hallucinations, such as seeing a rabbit run across the booth and flames shooting out of a drawer in his hotel room. Some accounts of Tripp's radiothon note that after 5 days he began taking a stimulant to stay awake (Luce & Segal, 1966). On the 8th and final day, he displayed delusional thinking, insisting that his physician was an undertaker coming to prepare him for burial. Tripp became so paranoid that he refused to undergo requested tests and insisted that unknown enemies were trying to force him to fall asleep by putting drugs in his food and drink. After his ordeal Tripp slept 13 hours and quickly returned to his customary level of psychological well-being.

Did Tripp's experience demonstrate that we need to sleep to maintain healthy psychological functioning and that a single night's sleep can overcome any ill effects of sleep deprivation? Possibly—but possibly not. First, Tripp's experiences were those of a single participant. His reactions to sleep deprivation might have been unique and not necessarily true of other people. Second, as you will learn later in the chapter, the delusions Tripp displayed near the end of his ordeal might have been caused by the stimulants he took to stay awake and not by his lack of sleep. Our knowledge of the effects of sleep deprivation and the effects of stimulants comes from research by psychologists and other scientists interested in the study of *consciousness*.

The Nature of Consciousness

What is consciousness? In 1690 John Locke wrote that "consciousness is the perception of what passes in a man's own mind" (Locke, 1690/1959, p. 138). Today psychologists share a similar view of **consciousness**, defining it as the subjective awareness of one's own cognitive activity, including thoughts, feelings, sensations, and surroundings.

The Stream of Consciousness

Two hundred years after Locke offered his definition of consciousness, William James (1890/1981) noted that consciousness is personal, selective, continuous, and changing. Consider your own consciousness. It is *personal* because you feel that it belongs to you—you do not share it with anyone else. Consciousness is *selective* because you can attend to certain things while ignoring other things. Right now you can shift your attention to a nearby voice, the first word in the next sentence, or the feel of clothing touching your body. Consciousness is *continuous* because its contents blend into one another—the mind cannot be broken down into meaningful segments. And consciousness is *changing* because its contents are in a constant state of flux, with one cognitive state following another in rapid succession. Because of this, you cannot focus on one thing more than momentarily without other thoughts, feelings, or sensations drifting through your mind.

Because consciousness is both continuous and changing, James likened it to a stream (Natsoulas, 1997–98). Your favorite stream remains the same stream even though the water at a particular site is continuously being replaced by new water. Even as you read this paragraph, you might notice irrelevant thoughts, feelings, and sensations passing through your own mind. Some might grab your attention; others might quickly fade away. If you were to write them down as they occurred, a person reading what you had written might think you were confused or even that you were mentally ill. The disjointed nature of stream-of-consciousness writing makes it hard to follow without knowing the context of the story. You can appreciate this by trying to make sense of the opening passage from James Joyce's *A Portrait of the Artist as a Young Man*:

> Once upon a time and a very good time it was there was a moocow coming down along the road and this moocow that was coming down along the road met a nicens little boy named baby tuckoo. . . . .
>
> His father told him that story: his father looked at him through a glass: he had a hairy face.
>
> He was baby tuckoo. The moocow came down the road where Betty Byrne lived: she sold lemon platt.
>
> *O, the wild rose blossoms*
>
> *On the little green place.*
>
> He sang that song. That was his song.
>
> *O, the green wothe botheth.*

When you wet the bed first it is warm then it gets cold. His mother put on the oilsheet. That had the queer smell.

His mother a nicer smell than his father. She played on the piano the sailor's hornpipe for him to dance. (Joyce, 1916/1967, p. 171)

As a functionalist, William James believed that consciousness is an evolutionary development that enhances our ability to adapt to the environment. James declared, "It seems reasonable to suppose that, unless consciousness served some useful purpose, it would not have been superadded to life" (quoted in Rieber, 1980, p. 205). That is, consciousness helps us function. Consciousness provides us with a cognitive representation of the world that permits us to try out courses of action in our mind before acting on them. This makes us more reflective and more flexible in adapting to the world, thereby reducing our tendency to engage in aimless, reckless, or impulsive behavior.

Attention

Today researchers are especially interested in an aspect of consciousness identified by James: its *selectivity*. We refer to the selectivity of consciousness as **attention**, which functions like a tuner to make us aware of certain stimuli while blocking out others. This selectivity is adaptive because it prevents our consciousness from becoming a chaotic jumble of thoughts, feelings, and sensations. For example, while you are reading this paragraph, it would be maladaptive for you to also be aware of irrelevant stimuli, such as the shoes on your feet or people talking. Of course, it would be adaptive to shift your attention if your shoes are too tight or someone yelled "Fire!" outside your room. The functional advantage of selective attention is demonstrated by the greater tendency of children with a history of physical abuse to notice angry facial expressions (Pollak & Tolley-Schell, 2003), and by people with schizophrenia who display deficits in selective attention (Ferchiou, Schühoff, Bulzacka, Leboyer, & Szöke, 2010).

Experimental research, as well as everyday experience, illustrates the selectivity of attention. Consider a study in which participants watched two videotapes superimposed on each other (Neisser & Becklen, 1975). One videotape portrayed two people playing a hand-slapping game, and the other portrayed three people bouncing and throwing a basketball. Participants were told to watch one of the games and to press a response key whenever a particular action occurred. Those watching the hand game had to respond whenever the participants slapped hands with each other. Those watching the ball game had to respond whenever the ball was thrown. The results showed that participants made few errors. But when they were asked to watch both games simultaneously, using their right hand to respond to one game and their left hand to respond to the other, their performances deteriorated, and they made significantly more errors than when they attended to just one of the games.

What determines whether we will attend to a given stimulus? Functional MRI indicates that the frontal lobe governs the ability to divide one's attention during divided-attention tasks (Loose, Kaufmann, Auer, & Lange, 2003). Among the many stimulus factors that affect attention are whether the stimulus is important, changing, shifting, or novel. We tend to notice stimuli that are personally important. You have certainly experienced the "cocktail party phenomenon," in which you might be engrossed in one conversation at a party yet notice that your name has been mentioned in another conversation. A change in stimulation is likely to attract our attention. When watching television, you are more likely to pay attention to a commercial that is much louder or quieter than the program it interrupts. The importance of attention in everyday life—and survival—is illustrated in the controversy regarding the use of cellular telephones in motor vehicles. Research indicates that using a cellular telephone while driving distracts drivers from possibly dangerous situations that they should respond to (Garcia-Larrea, Perchet, Perrin, & Amenedo, 2001). This recent rise in cellular phone use while driving has prompted researchers to investigate divided attention and simulated driving in the laboratory setting. Researchers have found that text messaging does indeed decrease reaction time and impair driving performance (Drews, Yazdani, Godfrey, Cooper & Strayer, 2009).

Though William James and other psychology pioneers stressed the importance of attention and other aspects of consciousness, interest in these topics declined after John B. Watson

attention The process by which the individual focuses awareness on certain contents of consciousness while ignoring others.

Multitasking

Driving while multitasking is dangerous.
Source: wavebreakmedia/ Shutterstock.com

stated that "the time seems to have come when psychology must discard all references to consciousness" (Watson, 1913, p. 163). The renewed interest in studying altered states of consciousness during the past few decades (Nelson, 1996) reflects James's observation that "normal waking consciousness, rational consciousness as we call it, is but one special type of consciousness, whilst all about it, parted from it by the filmiest of screens, there lie potential forms of consciousness entirely different" (James, 1902/1992, p. 388).

The Unconscious

In the late 19th century, William James (1890/1981), in his classic psychology textbook, included a section entitled "Can States of Mind Be Unconscious?" which presented 10 arguments answering yes and 10 answering no. Today the extent to which we are affected by unconscious influences still provokes animated debate. But the notion of the unconscious involves any of three different concepts: (1) *perception without awareness,* the unconscious perception of stimuli that normally exceed our absolute threshold (see Chapter 5) but that fall outside our focus of attention; (2) the *Freudian unconscious,* a region of the mind containing thoughts and feelings that motivate us without our awareness; and (3) *subliminal perception,* the unconscious perception of stimuli that are too weak to exceed the absolute threshold for detection. For a lengthier discussion of subliminal perception, see Chapter 5.

Perception Without Awareness

There is substantial evidence that we can be affected by stimuli that are above the normal absolute threshold but to which we are not attending at the time. At the turn of the 20th century, the existence of such **perception without awareness** (Merikle, Smilek, & Eastwood, 2001) led some psychologists to assume that suggestions given to people while they sleep might help children study harder or adults quit smoking (Jones, 1900). But subsequent research has failed to support such sleep learning. Any learning that does take place apparently occurs during brief awakenings (Wood, Bootzin, Kihlstrom, & Schacter, 1992). So, if you decide to study for your next psychology exam by playing an audiotape of class lectures while you are asleep, you will be more likely to disrupt your sleep than to learn significant amounts of material. Though there is no evidence that we can form memories while asleep, there is evidence that when we are awake, we can form memories of events and information that we are unaware of (Czyzewska, 2001). The formation of such *implicit memories* is discussed in Chapter 8.

Dichotic Listening Research on attention also has demonstrated the existence of perception without awareness. Consider studies of *dichotic listening,* in which the participant, wearing headphones, repeats—or "shadows"—a message being presented to one ear while another message is being presented to the other ear (Cherry, 1953). Dichotic listening is illustrated in Figure 6-1. By shadowing one message, the participant is prevented from consciously attending to the other one. Though participants cannot recall the unattended message, they might recall certain qualities of it, such as whether it was spoken in a sad, angry, happy, or neutral tone (Voyer & Rodgers, 2002). These studies demonstrate that our brain can process incoming stimuli that exceed the normal absolute threshold even when we do not consciously attend to them.

Blindsight Perception without awareness also is supported in studies of brain damage. Consider *prosopagnosia,* the inability to recognize faces. The disorder typically is caused by damage to a particular region of the cerebral cortex (see Chapter 5). In one study, two women with prosopagnosia were shown photographs of strangers, friends, and relatives while their galvanic skin response (a measure of arousal based on changes in the electrical activity of the skin due to moisture levels from sweat glands) was recorded. Though the women were unable to recognize their friends and relatives from the photographs, their galvanic skin responses to those photographs were larger than to the photographs of strangers. Intact visual pathways in the brain had distinguished between the familiar and the unfamiliar faces without the women's conscious awareness (Tranel & Damasio, 1985). This phenomenon of blindsight also may occur for visual stimuli other than faces.

FIGURE 6-1
Dichotic Listening

In studies of dichotic listening, participants repeat a message presented to one ear while a different message is presented to the other ear.

People who are blind in a portion of their visual field because of brain damage may still identify a particular target object in that field at greater than a chance level—even though they are not consciously aware of seeing it (Brogaard, 2011).

Controlled Versus Automatic Processing Of course, "awareness" is usually not an all-or-none phenomenon. For example, there is a continuum between controlled processing and automatic processing of information (Strayer & Kramer, 1990). At one extreme, when we focus our attention on one target, we use **controlled processing**, which involves more conscious awareness (attention) and cognitive effort and interferes with the performance of other activities. At the other extreme, when we do one thing while focusing our attention on another, we use **automatic processing**, which requires less conscious awareness and cognitive effort and does not interfere with the performance of other activities. Reading, for example, requires an interplay of controlled and automatic processing. We use controlled processing to read unfamiliar words or difficult passages and automatic processing to read familiar words or easy passages (Walczyk, 2000). Figure 6-2 illustrates the difference between controlled and automatic processing.

As we practice a task, we devote less and less attention to it because we move from controlled processing to automatic processing (Bargh, 1992). Think back to when you first learned to write in script or cursive in elementary school. You depended on controlled processing, which required you to focus your complete attention on forming each letter. Today, after years of practice, you make use of automatic processing. You can write notes in class while focusing your attention on the professor's lecture rather than on the movements of your pen. Automatic processing also is involved in *implicit attitudes*—attitudes that we are not consciously aware of (Cunningham, Preacher, & Banaji, 2001). The importance of implicit attitudes in prejudice is discussed in Chapter 17.

Automatic processing can, at times, interfere with controlled processing. Consider the Stroop effect, named for its discoverer, John Ridley Stroop (1897–1979), illustrated in Figure 6-3. Record the time it takes you to read the words. Then record the time for how long it takes you to name the colors of the words. You probably performed the first task faster, presumably because of your extensive experience in reading. But the automaticity of reading words interfered with your ability to name the colors, a task that you are rarely called on to do (Davidson, Zacks, & Williams, 2003). Thus, even when you try to name the colors and ignore the words, automatic, unconscious processes make it difficult for you not to read the words. Thus, the Stroop effect refers to your tendency to read the words rather than naming the color of the words.

(a)

(b)

FIGURE 6-2
Controlled Processing Versus Automatic Processing

(a) When we learn a new task, we depend on controlled processing, which makes us focus our attention on each aspect of the task. With experience, we depend less on automatic processing. *(b)* Eventually, we may be able to perform the task while focusing our attention on other activities.
Source: (a) szefei/Shutterstock.com. *(b)* Warren Goldswain/Shutterstock.com.

conscious mind The level of consciousness that includes the cognitive experiences that we are aware of at a given moment.

preconscious mind The level of consciousness that contains feelings and memories that we are unaware of at the moment but can become aware of at will.

unconscious mind The level of consciousness that contains thoughts, feelings, and memories that influence us without our awareness and that we cannot become aware of at will.

The Freudian Unconscious

During the 1988 National League baseball playoffs between the New York Mets and the Los Angeles Dodgers, relief pitcher Brian Holton of the Dodgers became so nervous that he could not grip the baseball. Suddenly he found himself singing the lyrics to a folk song, "You take the high road and I'll take the low road." This surprised him because he believed he had never heard the song. Yet, for some reason, singing it relaxed him enough to enable him to grip the baseball. When he told his mother about this mysterious behavior, she informed him that his father had comforted him by singing the song to him when he was a young child.

Levels of Consciousness Psychoanalytic theorists use anecdotal reports such as Holton's to support the existence of the Freudian unconscious. Sigmund Freud divided consciousness into three levels: the conscious, the preconscious, and the unconscious (see Figure 6-4). As had William James, Freud viewed the **conscious mind** as the awareness of fleeting images, feelings, and sensations. The **preconscious mind** contains memories of which we are unaware at the moment but of which we can become aware at will. And the **unconscious mind** contains repressed feelings, memories, and response tendencies of which we are unaware. Through what Freud called *psychic determinism,* these unconscious factors affect our behavior. Perhaps psychic determinism explains why we instantly like or dislike someone for no apparent reason or why we commit a "Freudian slip," in which we replace intended words with sexual or aggressive ones. Whereas psychologists who favor the reality of the Freudian unconscious point to evidence that our behavior can be influenced by unconscious emotional and motivational states, psychologists who accept the reality of a cognitive unconscious but not a Freudian unconscious point to a lack of evidence supporting the influence of unconscious emotional and motivational states (Ruys & Aarts, 2012).

Subliminal Psychodynamic Activation Until recently, the Freudian unconscious was considered impossible to study scientifically because evidence of its existence came solely from anecdotal or clinical reports and because it could not be observed directly. But more sophisticated techniques, though they have not necessarily convinced all psychologists of the existence of the Freudian unconscious, at least make it subject to scientific research (Epstein, 1994). One technique, developed by Lloyd Silverman and

FIGURE 6-4
Levels of Consciousness

According to Sigmund Freud, there are three levels of consciousness. The conscious level contains thoughts, images, and feelings that we are aware of. The preconscious level contains memories that we can retrieve at will. And the unconscious level contains repressed motives and memories that would evoke intense feelings of anxiety if we became aware of them.

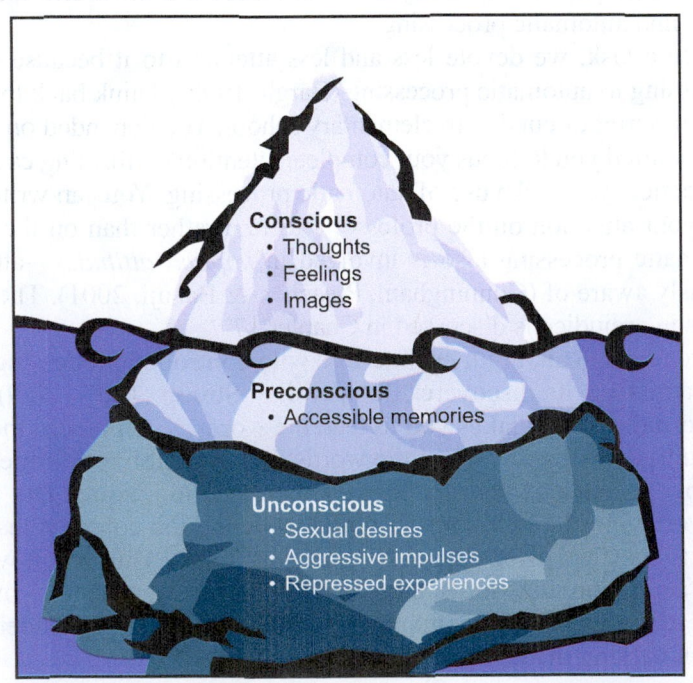

Conscious
• Thoughts
• Feelings
• Images

Preconscious
• Accessible memories

Unconscious
• Sexual desires
• Aggressive impulses
• Repressed experiences

called **subliminal psychodynamic activation,** is based on the assumption that emotionally charged subliminal messages will alter the recipient's moods and behaviors by stimulating unconscious fantasies (Weinberger & Silverman, 1990).

Silverman claimed that unconscious "oneness fantasies" (which express emotional union with one's mother, an important concept from Freud's theory that emphasizes the importance of maternal love and care in early childhood) relieve anxiety and enhance performance. For example, participants typically are presented with a oneness phrase, such as "Mommy and I are one," or a neutral phrase, such as "People are walking." The messages are presented by a device called a *tachistoscope,* which flashes visual stimuli too briefly (for only a fraction of a second) to exceed the absolute threshold. A study of subliminal psychodynamic activation used students who had failed a university mathematics assessment test who then took part in a summer mathematics enrichment program. One group viewed a subliminal oneness message and the other a neutral message. After 20 weeks of the program, the group exposed to the oneness message performed better on a mathematics test than did the group not exposed to it (Hudesman, Page, & Rautiainen, 1992).

But other studies have failed to find any effects of subliminal psychodynamic activation. For example, a study of subliminal psychodynamic activation examined the effect of subliminal messages on anxiety by using heart rate changes to measure the level of anxiety. The participants were 100 college students. They were divided into five groups, depending on which message they were shown: "Mommy and I are one," "Daddy and I are one," "Mommy has left me," "I'm happy and calm," and a neutral stimulus presumably without any emotional effect. The results showed that heart rate was unrelated to the kind of message presented, providing evidence against any special effect of oneness messages (Malik, Paraherakis, Joseph, & Ladd, 1996). Overall, studies of subliminal psychodynamic activation indicate that it produces small though statistically significant effects on moods and behaviors (Weinberger & Smith, 2011). Nonetheless, supporters of the effectiveness of subliminal psychodynamic activation have yet to explain how meaning can be extracted from phrases that are presented too briefly to be perceived consciously (Fudin, 2001).

Based on the foregoing discussion of unconscious influences, you should now realize that solid scientific evidence indicates that we can be affected by stimuli of which we are unaware. Some of the more extreme claims for unconscious influences on our moods and behaviors, however, have tainted an otherwise legitimate topic for psychological research.

subliminal psychodynamic activation The use of subliminal messages to stimulate unconscious fantasies.

Section Review: The Nature of Consciousness

1. What is the difference between automatic and controlled processing?

2. What is the cocktail party phenomenon?

3. How has subliminal psychodynamic activation been used to test Freud's notion of unconscious motivation?

Sleep

Perhaps the most obvious alternative to waking consciousness is *sleep*. The daily sleep-wake cycle is one of our **biological rhythms,** which are cyclical changes in physiological processes. Other examples of biological rhythms are the menstrual cycle in women and the annual cycle of waking and hibernation in bears. Be sure not to confuse biological rhythms, a legitimate topic of scientific research, with "biorhythms," a topic better left to pop psychology. Those who believe in biorhythms claim that each of us is born with physical, emotional, and intellectual cycles that stay constant in length and govern us for the rest of our lives. No scientifically worthy research supports these claims (Hines, 1998).

biological rhythms Repeating cycles of physiological changes.

Biological Rhythms and the Sleep-Wake Cycle

circadian rhythms Twenty-four-hour cycles of physiological changes, most notably the sleep-wake cycle.

The daily sleep-wake cycle is the most obvious of our **circadian rhythms**, which are 24-hour cycles of changes in physiological processes. Our circadian rhythm of body temperature parallels our circadian rhythm of brain arousal, with most people beginning the day at low points on both and rising on them through the day. College roommates who are out of phase with each other in their circadian rhythms are more likely to express dissatisfaction with their relationship (Watts, 1982). A student who is a "morning person"—already warmed up and chipper at 7 a.m.—might find it difficult to socialize with a roommate who can barely crawl out of bed at that time. Moreover, there is some evidence that these individual differences in circadian rhythm are established early in childhood (Cofer et al., 1999).

Factors in Biological Rhythms

pineal gland An endocrine gland that secretes a hormone that has a general tranquilizing effect on the body and that helps regulate biological rhythms.

What governs our circadian rhythms? A chief factor is a part of the hypothalamus called the *suprachiasmatic nucleus* (Schaap & Meijer, 2001), which regulates the secretion of the hormone *melatonin* by the **pineal gland,** an endocrine gland in the center of the brain. The suprachiasmatic nucleus, which is our body's main "clock," receives neural input from the eyes, making it sensitive to changes in light levels. As a result, melatonin secretion varies with light levels, decreasing in daylight and increasing in darkness (Caldwell, 2000).

When people are cut off from cues related to the day-night cycle, perhaps by living in a cave or a windowless room for several weeks, a curious thing happens. For unknown reasons, their sleep-wake cycle changes from 24 hours to 25 hours in length. They go to bed slightly later and get up just a few minutes later each successive day (Lavie, 2000). You may have experienced this phenomenon during vacations from work and school. Perhaps you find yourself going to bed later and later and, as a result, awakening later and later.

Jet Lag and Shift Work

phase advance Shortening the sleep-wake cycle, as occurs when traveling from west to east.

phase delay Lengthening the sleep-wake cycle, as occurs when traveling from east to west.

The natural tendency for the sleep-wake cycle to lengthen might explain why jet lag is more severe when we fly west to east than when we fly east to west. The symptoms of jet lag, caused by a disruption of the normal sleep-wake cycle, include fatigue, insomnia, irritability, and difficulty concentrating (Waterhouse, Reilly, Atkinson, & Edwards, 2007). Eastbound travel shortens the sleep-wake cycle (**phase advance**), countering its natural tendency to lengthen. In contrast, westbound travel lengthens the sleep-wake cycle (**phase delay**), which agrees with its natural tendency to lengthen. So, phase advance requires more adjustment by travelers. Thus, people traveling eastbound suffer from jet lag more than people traveling westbound. So, if you have just flown a few time zones east and are not sleepy, studies have shown that both melatonin and exposure to bright sunlight in the morning can help reduce the feeling of jet lag (Crowley & Eastman 2013).

Shift Work

Workers on rotating shifts might become less alert on the job. This could be especially dangerous in occupations such as law enforcement that require vigilance.

Source: John Roman Images/Shutterstock.com.

Workers on rotating shifts, including airline personnel, factory workers, and police officers, often find their sleep-wake cycles disrupted. A meta-analysis of research studies on the effects of rotating shifts found that workers with slowly rotating shifts slept longer than workers with rapidly rotating shifts. Adjustment to rotating shifts depended on an interaction between the nature of the job, the direction of rotation, the rapidity of rotation, and other factors (Pilcher, Lambert, & Huffcutt, 2000). Given the natural tendency of the sleep-wake cycle to increase in length, workers on rotating shifts might respond better to phase delay than to phase advance. This hypothesis was demonstrated in a study of industrial workers. Those on a phase-delay schedule moved from the night shift (12 midnight to 8 a.m.) to the day shift (8 a.m. to 4 p.m.) to the evening shift (4 p.m. to 12 midnight). Those on a phase-advance schedule moved in the opposite direction, from the night shift to the evening shift to the day shift. The results showed that workers on a phase-delay schedule had better health, greater satisfaction, higher productivity, and lower turnover (Czeisler, Moore-Ede, & Coleman, 1982). Nonetheless, some research studies—particularly ones involving air-traffic controllers—have failed to find that phase delay is superior to phase advance in improving adjustment to rotating shifts (Cruz, Boquet, Detwiler, & Nesthus, 2003).

Patterns of Sleep

In 1960, four leading introductory psychology textbooks made no mention of sleep, and the most extensive coverage in any introductory textbook was two pages (Webb, 1985). Today, in contrast, all introductory psychology textbooks include (usually extensive) coverage of sleep. This increased coverage indicates the explosion of scientific interest in the study of sleep since the 1960s. Two of the main topics of interest regarding sleep patterns are the sleep cycle and the duration of sleep.

A Typical Night's Sleep

Imagine that you are participating in a sleep study. You would first sleep a night or two in a sleep laboratory to get accustomed to the novel surroundings. You would then sleep several nights in the laboratory while special devices recorded changes in your brain waves, eye movements, heart rate, blood pressure, body temperature, breathing rate, muscle tension, and respiration rate. Your behavior, including any utterances you made, would be recorded on videotape and audiotape.

The physiological recordings would reveal that you do not simply drift into deep sleep, stay there all night, and suddenly awaken in the morning. Instead, they would show that you pass through repeated sleep cycles, which are biological rhythms marked by variations in the depth of sleep as defined by particular brain-wave patterns. Figure 6-5 illustrates these

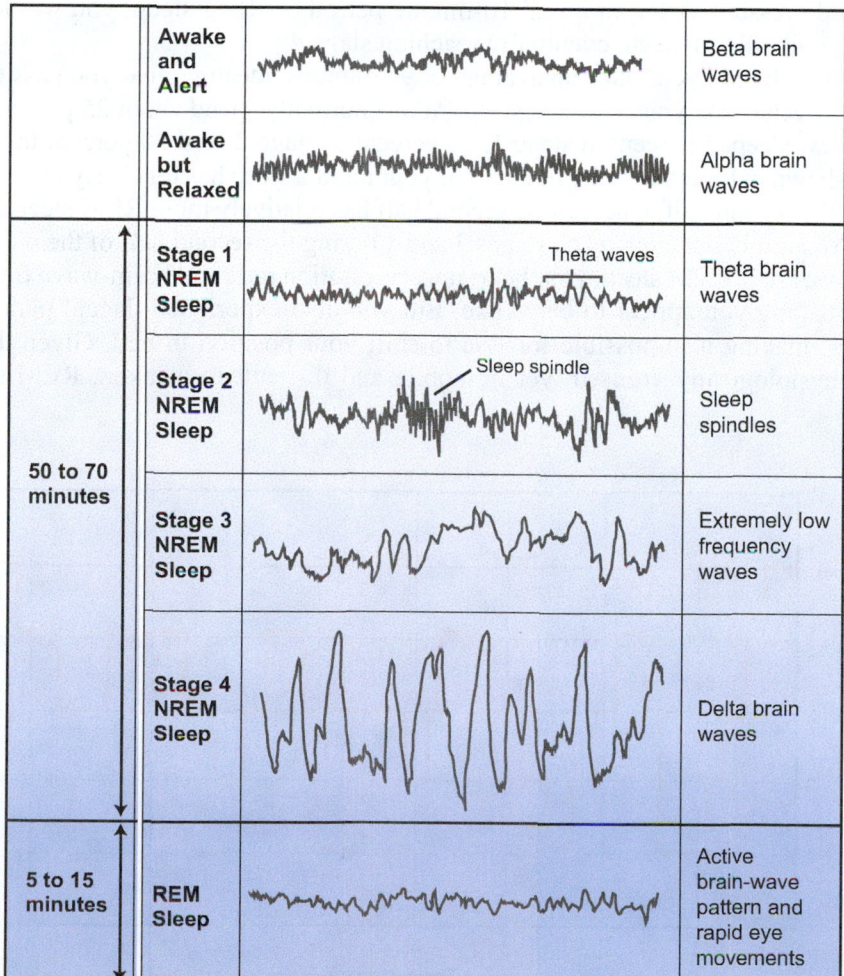

FIGURE 6-5
The Stages of Sleep

Studies of participants in sleep laboratories have found that the stages of sleep are associated with distinctive patterns of brain-wave activity. As we drift into deeper stages of sleep, our brain waves decrease in frequency and increase in amplitude. When we are in rapid eye movement (REM) sleep, our brain-wave patterns resemble the patterns of our waking state. Sometimes this is called paradoxical sleep.

patterns, which were first identified in the 1930s through the use of the electroencephalo-graph (EEG) (Loomis, Harvey, & Hobart, 1937).

Falling Asleep As you lie in bed with your eyes closed, an EEG recording would show that your brain-wave pattern changes from primarily high-frequency *beta waves* (14 to 30 cycles a second), which mark an alert cognitive state, to a higher proportion of lower-frequency *alpha waves* (8 to 13 cycles a second), which mark a relaxed, introspective cognitive state. As you drift off to sleep, you would exhibit slow, rolling eye movements, and your brain-wave pattern would show a higher proportion of *theta waves* (4 to 7 cycles a second), which have a lower frequency than alpha waves. You also would exhibit a decrease in other signs of arousal, including heart rate, breathing rate, muscle tension, and respiration rate.

The cessation of the rolling eye movements would signify the onset of sleep (Ogilvie, Mc-Donagh, Stone, & Wilkinson, 1988). This initial light stage of sleep is called *stage 1.* After 5 to 10 minutes in stage 1, you would enter the slightly deeper *stage 2,* associated with periodic bursts of higher-frequency (12 to 16 cycles a second) brain waves known as sleep spindles. After 10 to 20 minutes in stage 2, you would enter *stage 3,* marked by the appearance of extremely low-frequency (1/2 to 3 cycles a second) *delta waves.* When at least 50 percent of your brain waves are delta waves, you would be in *stage 4,* the deepest stage of sleep. After remaining in stages 3 and 4 for 30 to 40 minutes, you would drift up through stages 3, 2, and 1 until, about 90 minutes after falling asleep, you would reach the REM stage of sleep.

REM sleep The stage of sleep associated with rapid eye movements, an active brain-wave pattern, and vivid dreams.

NREM sleep The stages of sleep not associated with rapid eye movements and marked by relatively little dreaming.

The NREM-REM Cycle **REM sleep** gets its name from the darting eye movements that characterize it. You probably have seen these movements under the eyelids of sleeping people—or even a sleeping pet dog, or cat. Because stages 1, 2, 3, and 4 are not charac-terized by these eye movements, they are collectively called *non-REM,* or **NREM sleep.** NREM sleep is characterized by slow brain waves, deep breathing, regular heart rate, and lower blood pressure. After an initial 10-minute period of REM sleep, you would again drift down into NREM sleep, eventually reaching stage 4.

The NREM-REM cycles take an average of 90 minutes, meaning that you pass through four or five cycles in a typical night's sleep. Adults normally spend about 25 percent of the night in REM sleep, 5 percent in stage 1, 50 percent in stage 2, and 20 percent in stages 3 and 4. As shown in Figure 6-6, the first half of your night's sleep has relatively more NREM sleep than the second half, whereas the second half has relatively more REM sleep than the first half. You might not even reach stages 3 and 4 during the second half of the night.

While you are in REM sleep, your heart rate, respiration rate, and brain-wave frequency increase, making you appear to be awake. But you also experience flaccid paralysis of your limbs, making it impossible for you to shift your position in bed. Given that you become physiologically aroused, yet immobile and difficult to awaken, REM sleep is

FIGURE 6-6
A Typical Night's Sleep

During a typical night's sleep, we pass through cycles that involve stages of NREM sleep and the stage of REM sleep. Note that we obtain our deepest sleep during the first half of the night and that the periods of REM sleep become longer with each successive cycle (Cartwright, 1978).

Source: From *A Primer on Sleep and Dreaming* by Rosalind Cartwright. Copyright © 1978 Addison-Wesley. Reprinted by permission of the author.

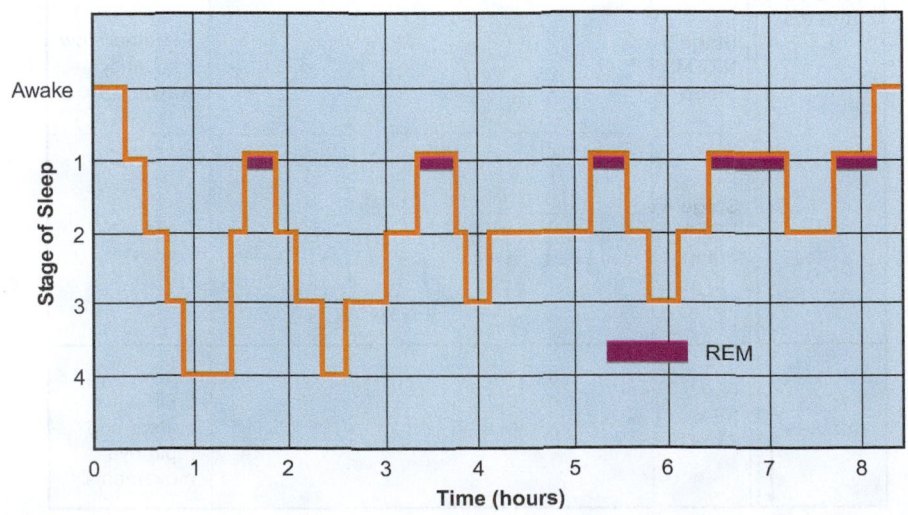

also called *paradoxical sleep*. Because we are paralyzed during REM sleep, sleepwalking (or *somnambulism*) occurs only during NREM sleep, specifically stages 3 and 4. In fact, sleepwalkers spend a greater proportion of their sleep in stages 3 and 4 than nonsleepwalkers do (Blatt, Peled, Gadoth, & Lavie, 1991). Sleepwalking is also more common in children than in adults. A survey of 5,000 people aged 18 years or older found that 2 percent engaged in sleepwalking (Bjorvatn, Grønli, & Pallesen, 2010).

Despite warnings to the contrary, sleepwalkers may be awakened without fear of doing physical or psychological harm to them. Of course, the habitual sleepwalker should be protected from injury by keeping doors and windows locked. Sleepwalking has been used successfully as a legal defense in criminal cases, as in the case of a man who was caught walking outside naked during the night (Thomas, 1997).

Another characteristic of REM sleep is erection of the penis and clitoris. Erection occurs spontaneously and is not necessarily indicative of a sexual dream. Clinicians use REM erections to determine whether men with erectile dysfunction are suffering from a physical or a psychological disorder. If a man has erections while in REM sleep, his problem is psychological, not physical (Mann, Pankok, Connemann, & Roeschke, 2003).

REM sleep is associated with dreaming. We know this because of research conducted in the early 1950s by Eugene Aserinsky and Nathaniel Kleitman (1953) of the University of Chicago. When they awakened sleepers displaying rapid eye movements, the sleepers usually reported that they had been dreaming. In contrast, sleepers awakened during NREM sleep rarely reported that they had been dreaming. Because the longest REM period occurs during the last sleep cycle of the night, you often find yourself in the middle of a dream when your alarm clock wakes you in the morning. You might be tempted to infer that rapid eye movements reflect the scanning of dream scenes, but Aserinsky and his colleagues (1985) have found that they do not—so if you were dreaming about, say, a tennis match, your rapid eye movements would not have been following the ball's flight.

Researchers are learning more and more about the physiological bases of the sleep cycle. Brain structures that help regulate sleep include the pons, thalamus, hypothalamus, and reticular formation. Neurotransmitters that help regulate sleep include serotonin, norepinephrine, and acetylcholine, with sleep onset related to a reduction in their secretion (Sharpley, 2002). More recently, the peptide neurotransmitter *orexin* (also called *hypocretin*), which is secreted by the hypothalamus, has been implicated in the sleep-wake cycle. Higher levels of orexin are associated with wakefulness, and lower levels of it are associated with sleep (Scammell, 2001; Lee, Hassani & Jones, 2005). Hence, orexin helps people stay awake.

Though sleep patterns are similar across cultures, there is some evidence for ethnic and gender differences in some aspects of the sleep cycle. A recent meta-analysis of 14 studies found small-to-moderate differences in the sleep cycles of African Americans compared to European Americans. African Americans experienced poorer quality sleep, including sleeping less, spending more time in stage 2 sleep and less time in stage 3 and 4 sleep. African Americans also awoke more frequently during the night (Ruiter, DeCoster, Jacobs, & Lichstein, 2011). Sleep continuity and duration were found to be influenced by biopsychosocial factors, whereas the differences in stages of sleep were not. And a study of elementary school students found that girls slept longer than boys and exhibited more "motionless sleep." However, there were no gender differences in the perceived quality of sleep (Sadeh, Raviv, & Gruber, 2000). Additionally, this study highlights different sleep patterns across childhood and indicates that older children (6th grade versus 2nd grade) go to bed later yet report increased daytime sleepiness. Sociologists have found that women self-report sleeping slightly longer than men, a difference that may be attributed to women's greater likelihood of being engaged in unpaid work and enjoying less high-quality leisure time than men (Burgard, & Ailshire, 2013). On the other hand, these findings could be attributed to different family responsibilities, such as caregiving for children, differences in napping, or other unknown factors. As you will read later in this chapter, there are many situational factors that affect sleep patterns, sleep continuity, and sleep disorders. These differences in the sleep-wake cycle may be attributable to factors such as stress levels, sleep environments, work and family responsibilities and other variables that are correlated with ethnicity and gender.

Sleep Deprivation

Many people, particularly college students burdened by academic responsibilities, suffer from sleep deprivation and snatch moments of sleep whenever they can. Sleep deprivation can impair the ability to perform academically, vocationally, and socially. *Source:* Arieliona/Shutterstock.com..

The Duration of Sleep

Sleep not only is cyclical but also varies in duration. People are moderately long sleepers, with young adults averaging 8 hours of sleep a day. In contrast, some animals, such as elephants, sleep as little as 2 hours a day, whereas other animals, such as bats, sleep as much as 20 hours a day. Efforts to wean people from sleep indicate that it cannot be reduced much below 4 hours without inducing extreme drowsiness and severe mood alterations (Webb, 1985). Figure 6-7 indicates that our daily need for sleep varies across the life span. At one extreme, infants typically sleep 16 hours a day and spend a significant portion of their sleep time in REM. At the other extreme, elderly people typically sleep 6 hours a day. Of course, you might need to sleep more or less than your age peers. This variability in normal sleep duration and sleep characteristics is different in children and adults and appears to have a hereditary basis (Barclay & Gregory, 2013). Researchers often have wondered about the contribution of genetic factors to sleep duration and quality. A recent longitudinal study using an adult twin cohort over the course of 15 years found that although genetic factors do play a stable and modest role in sleep stability and length, health issues and other environmental factors play stronger or more important roles (Hublin, Partinen, Koskenvuo, & Kaprio, 2013). This study implies that individuals experiencing short bouts of sleep or problematic sleep—for example, individuals suffering from insomnia—might gain relief from interventions such as sleep medications.

Regardless of how much sleep they need, North Americans habitually get less than their ideal quota. They might stay awake to watch television, do schoolwork, work on a computer, check social media, or perform other activities. You might go to bed when you want to (perhaps after watching the late movie) and awaken when you have to (perhaps in time for an 8 a.m. class), making you chronically sleep deprived. According to sleep researcher William Dement, "Most Americans no longer know what it feels like to be fully alert" (Toufexis, 1990, p. 79). His conclusion is supported by the results of a survey of over 4,000 Long Island, New York, mass-transit commuters. More than 50 percent of the respondents reported experiencing problems with sleep and wakefulness (Walsleben, Norman, Novak, O'Malley, Rapoport, & Strohl, 1999). Cross-cultural research, too, suggests that the proportion of Japanese adults who suffer from inadequate sleep is comparable to that reported in surveys of American samples (Liu et al., 2000).

FIGURE 6-7
Sleep Across the Life Span

Our amount of daily sleep declines across the life span, decreasing rapidly in infancy and childhood and more gradually in adulthood. The proportion of time spent in REM sleep also declines across the life span.

Source: Reprinted with permission from "Ontogenetic Development of the Human Sleep-Dream Cycle," by H. P. Roffwarg et al., *Science,* 152: 608, April 1996. Copyright © 1996 AAAS.

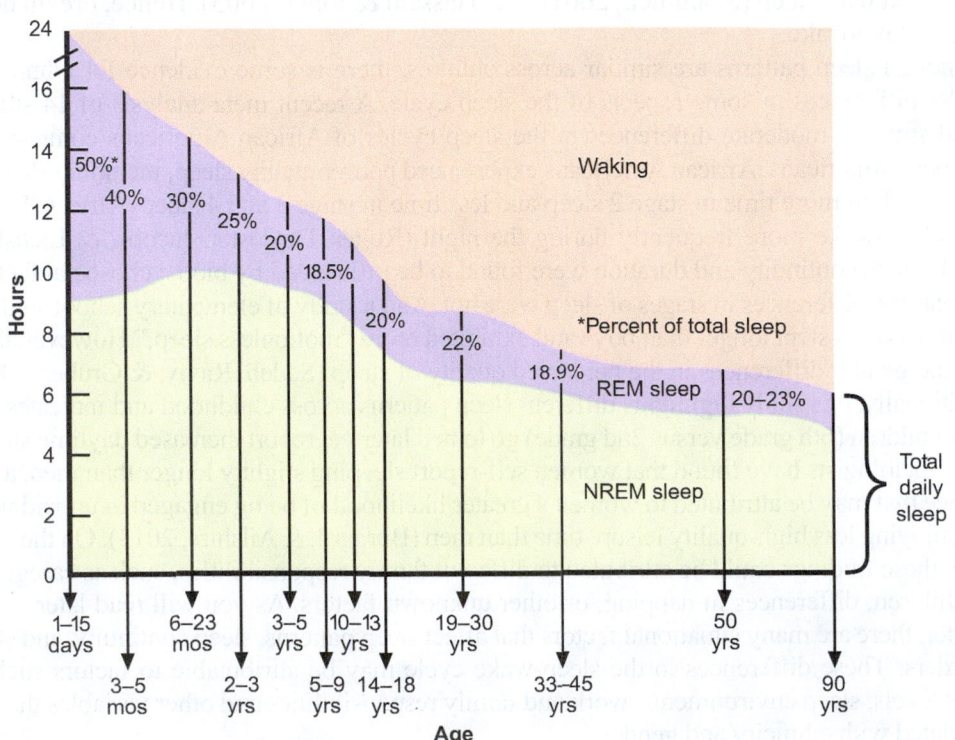

Moreover, in another study the prevalence of excessive daytime sleepiness among Japanese female workers was almost double that of Japanese male workers. The researchers attributed this difference to the additional family responsibilities that women face at the beginning and end of the workday (Doi & Minowa, 2003).

Difficulty in getting a good night's sleep has been increasing among college students. In a replication of an earlier study, a survey of college students published in 1992 found that they reported sleeping less and being less satisfied with their sleep than college students had reported in a survey conducted in 1978 (Hicks, Johnson, & Pellegrini, 1992). A common problem in regard to young adults' sleep patterns is the tendency to get too little sleep during the week because of staying up late and rising early, followed by sleeping late on Saturday and Sunday mornings. This tendency leads to "Sunday night insomnia" followed by "Monday morning blues." That is, young adults tend to report poorer moods and exhibit poorer cognitive performance on Monday mornings (Yang & Spielman, 2001).

Many people try to overcome the effects of inadequate nighttime sleep by taking daytime naps. Some cultures, typically in hot climates, even incorporate siestas as part of everyday life. Stores and businesses shut down for part of the afternoon so that individuals can rest or nap for an hour or two instead of being worn out by working during the hottest time of the day. With the growth of the European Union, though, many corporations in Mediterranean countries are adopting the workday schedules of their European neighbors. One recent survey conducted in Spain found that only 24 percent of the population were regular siesta takers. Moreover, anecdotal reports of chronic fatigue were on the rise (Boudreaux, 2000). However, many students and executives in non-siesta cultures have come to value their "power naps." They are being wise because an afternoon nap can increase alertness and improve task performance (Horne & Reyner, 1996). One study found that a 1-hour nap while on the night shift markedly improved workers' alertness and motivation for the rest of the shift (Bonneond et al., 2001). And research findings indicate that an afternoon nap improves alertness and driving performance in long-haul truck drivers (Macchi, Boulos, Ranney, Simmons, & Campbell, 2002).

The Functions of Sleep

Assuming that you live to be 90, you will have spent about 30 years asleep. Are you wasting one third of your life, or does sleep serve important functions for you? Among the many hypothesized functions of sleep, scientists have identified two that are the most prominent: *sleep as physical restoration* and *sleep as adaptive inactivity.*

Sleep as Physical Restoration

The most commonsense view of sleep holds that it restores the body and the mind after the wear and tear imposed by waking activities. Why else would we have a mechanism that forces us to spend at least one-third of our lives sleeping? Perhaps sleep repairs body tissues, removes metabolic waste products, and replenishes brain neurotransmitters (Inouye, Honda, & Komoda, 1995). One recent hypothesis suggests that sleep may help the brain sweep itself clean of toxins. Dr. Nedergaard and colleagues (Xie et al., 2013) discovered this while studying sleeping mice. The researchers noticed that the sleeping brain allowed for its cells to shrink and the fluid surrounding the brain to increase. This brain-cleaning process has yet to be observed in humans but could help us understand disorders such as Alzheimer's disease that are linked to sleep disorders. Alzheimer's disease is associated with an increase in a protein waste product called beta amyloid, and proper sleep can help clear the brain of it. Formal as well as anecdotal research has provided evidence of the detrimental effects of sleep loss and the restorative effects of sleep. Sleep deprivation is associated with a decline in the ability to perform physical and cognitive tasks (Quigley, Green, Morgan, Idzikowski, & King, 2000). For example, a survey of college students found a negative correlation between length of sleep and grade point average. That is, the fewer hours students slept each night, the lower their grade point averages tended to be (Kelly, Kelly, & Clanton, 2001).

The longer we stay awake, the more we crave sleep. In the case of Peter Tripp, sleep deprivation apparently produced hallucinations and delusional thinking, which disappeared after a single night's sleep. In a similar case in 1965, Randy Gardner, a 17-year-old San Diego high school student, stayed awake 264 hours (11 days) as his contribution to a science fair. He hoped to get his name in the Guinness Book of World Records. Two of his friends alternated shifts to keep him from falling asleep. Gardner stayed awake by remaining physically active—talking, walking, and playing games. He found it easier to stay awake during the daytime than at night—a finding in keeping with his natural circadian rhythm. At various times during the 11 days, Gardner had trouble focusing his eyes, suffered incoordination, became moody, showed memory deterioration, had difficulty concentrating, thought a street sign was a person, and experienced the delusion that he (though a person of European background) was a famous African American football player who was being oppressed by racism.

During the last 4 days, William Dement monitored Gardner's behavioral and physiological reactions to his prolonged sleep deprivation. When the media began covering Gardner near the end of his feat, he seemed to become more motivated. On the last night, he even defeated Dement in 100 consecutive games of pinball. Gardner also performed well at a press conference at the end of the eleventh day. When a reporter asked him how he managed to stay awake so long, he simply replied, "It's just mind over matter" (Dement, 1976, p. 12). Gardner then slept 14 hours, 40 minutes, and awoke practically recovered—recovering completely after a second night's sleep (Gulevich, Dement, & Johnson, 1966). Gardner's remarkable physical performance was attributed to his excellent physical condition, strong motivation, and support from those around him. But some scientists noted that he might have gained a boost from so-called microsleeps, which are repeated periods of sleep lasting only but a few seconds (which you might have experienced when exhausted and fighting to stay awake during a boring lecture). Microsleeps can be especially dangerous when performing tasks that require constant attention such as driving. The cumulative effect of these ultra-short "naps" might have helped Gardner combat the effects of sleep deprivation.

Another source of evidence for the restorative function of sleep is research on the effects of vigorous physical activity on subsequent sleep patterns. Sleep, especially deep sleep, increases on the nights after vigorous exercise (Vein, Sidorov, Martazaev, & Karlov, 1991). This finding was supported by a study of runners who participated in a 57-mile ultramarathon race. They experienced an increase in the duration of sleep, particularly stage 3 and stage 4, on the first two nights after the race (Shapiro, Bortz, Mitchell, Bartel, & Jooste, 1981). Though we still do not know exactly what, if anything, sleep restores, one explanation for the increase in deep sleep after vigorous exercise concerns the secretion of growth hormone, which increases during deep sleep. Growth hormone promotes the synthesis of proteins needed for the repair of muscles and other body tissues.

Sleep as Adaptive Inactivity

An alternative view, championed by Wilse Webb (1992), is that sleep evolved because it protected the sleeper from harm and prevented the useless expenditure of energy.

Sleep as Protection from Harm Our prehistoric ancestors who slept at night were less likely to gain the attention of hungry nocturnal predators. The limb paralysis accompanying REM sleep may have evolved because it prevented cave dwellers from acting out their dreams, when they might have bumped into trees, fallen off cliffs, or provided dinner for saber-toothed tigers. Evidence for this protective function of REM sleep comes from studies of cats. Destruction of a portion of the pons that normally induces REM paralysis in cats produces stalking and attacking movements during sleep, as though the cats are acting out their dreams (Morrison, 1983).

Further support for the protective function of sleep comes from studies showing that animals with little to fear while asleep (either because they are predators or because they sleep in safe places) sleep for much of the 24-hour day. In contrast, animals that have much to fear while asleep (either because they are prey or because they sleep in exposed places) sleep for relatively little of the 24-hour day. Thus, cats, which are predators, sleep much longer (15 hours) than rabbits (8 hours), which are prey. Likewise, bats, which sleep in caves, sleep much longer (20 hours) than horses (3 hours), which sleep in the open.

Sleep as a Conserver of Energy Another reason to believe that sleep might be a period of adaptive inactivity is that it conserves energy (Berger & Phillips, 1995). Evidence supportive of this view comes from studies of the food-finding habits of different species. Because the length of sleep for a given species is negatively correlated with how long it takes members of that species to find their daily food, perhaps animals stay awake only long enough to eat sufficient food to meet their energy needs. Animals might have evolved sleep in part to conserve energy the remainder of the time. Thus, the typical young adult's need for about 8 hours of nightly sleep might mean that our prehistoric ancestors needed about 16 hours to find their daily food (Cohen, 1979).

According to Wilse Webb (1992), both the restorative theory and the adaptive-inactivity theory must be included in an adequate theory of sleep. The restorative theory explains why sleepiness increases as sleep loss increases. The adaptive inactivity theory explains why sleep follows a circadian rhythm. You may have experienced this phenomenon if you have ever pulled an all-nighter while studying for exams. If you fight your sleepiness and force yourself to stay awake all night, you might be surprised to find yourself less sleepy in the morning (when your circadian rhythm would make you more alert). Later, you would find yourself becoming sleepy when your normal bedtime approaches again.

Sleep Disorders

You might take sleep for granted, but many people do not. They suffer from sleep disorders such as *insomnia, sleep apnea,* and *narcolepsy.*

Insomnia

Twenty to 30 million Americans suffer from **insomnia** (Roth, 1995), chronic difficulty in sleeping. There are two major forms of insomnia. People who suffer from *sleep-onset insomnia* have trouble falling asleep. You have experienced sleep-onset insomnia if you have ever lain in bed, perhaps for hours, fruitlessly waiting to drift off to sleep. Those who experience *sleep-maintenance insomnia* fall asleep normally but find themselves awakening repeatedly—typically during the second half of the night (Narita, Echizenya, Tekeshima, Inomata, & Shimizu, 2011).

If you suffer from insomnia, what should you do? Many people with insomnia resort to sedative drugs, including alcohol and barbiturates, to fall asleep. Though sedatives will, at least initially, help you fall asleep, they do so at a cost. First, they interfere with the normal sleep cycle, most notably by reducing REM sleep. Second, they eventually lose their effectiveness, leaving you with the same problem you began with. And third, they have harmful side effects, including drug dependence. Instead of turning to sedatives, insomnia victims can use psychological techniques to obtain a good night's sleep. If you suffer from insomnia, you should reduce your presleep arousal by avoiding exercise, stimulation from television, computer or cellular phone screens and caffeine too close to bedtime. A relatively new area of research addresses the effects of sleep and technology use. For example, researchers have found that LED-backlit device use or bright environmental light can contribute to sleep problems by inducing delayed bedtimes and shorter sleep time (NSF, 2011; Adams & Kisler, 2013). Another example that can help aid in sleep is practicing progressive muscle relaxation, which involves tensing and then relaxing major muscle groups in sequence (Taylor & Roane, 2010). It also is advisable to avoid napping. If you nap during the day, you might not feel sleepy enough to fall asleep at your desired bedtime. Because trying to suppress thoughts that might be racing through your mind as you lie in bed tends to promote insomnia (Harvey, 2003), you might even benefit from *paradoxical intention,* in which you try to stay awake while lying in bed. This method can, paradoxically, induce sleep by preventing fruitless, anxiety-inducing efforts to fall asleep. Another technique, *stimulus control,* requires arranging your bedtime situation to promote sleep. First, go to bed only when you feel sleepy. Second, to ensure that you associate lying in bed with sleep and not with being awake, do not eat, read, watch television, use your computer or phone, or listen to music while lying in bed. Third, if you toss and turn, get out of bed and return only when you are sleepy (Arnold, Miller, & Mehta, 2012).

insomnia Chronic difficulty in either falling asleep or staying asleep.

One Cause of Insomnia

Stimulation from computer monitors can delay sleep onset.

Source: Romanchuck Dimitry/ Shutterstock.com.

Is Sleep Necessary for Good Health?

Your parents may have repeatedly urged you to go to bed at a reasonable hour to maintain your health. Is this just another example of a well-intentioned but erroneous commonsense belief, or is it a commonsense belief with scientific backing? As mentioned in Chapter 2, commonsense beliefs are sometimes true, but scientists insist that they be supported by research findings before accepting them. But what of the effects of sleep deprivation on health? It seems that in this case, common sense might be right—sleep is necessary for proper functioning of the immune system. Many students anecdotally report that after obtaining only a few hours' sleep night after night during final exams, they often become ill a few days after their exams are over. And when we become ill, we tend to sleep more—perhaps because sleep promotes the immunological response to invading microorganisms (Majde & Krueger, 2005). One study that investigated the health effects of chronic sleep loss in people aged 18–34 found that participants suffered from increased daytime sleepiness and inflammatory cytokines (Pejovic et al., 2013). Inflammatory cytokines are a family of molecules produced by your immune system that help your body fight threats such as inflammation, stress, or infections. Thus people who fail to get an optimal night's sleep for extended periods may become less healthy and secrete higher levels of stress hormones and inflammatory markers, which can lead to illness. Thankfully, studies also show that these effects can be reversed with extended sleep.

Consider natural killer cell (NKC) activity. NKCs are lymphocytes—white blood cells—that help defend the body against cancer cells. Many studies have found that sleep loss is associated with a reduction in NKC activity. In one study, 29 persons, aged 40 to 78 years, spent three nights in a sleep laboratory. NKC activity was positively correlated with how long they slept (Hall et al., 1998). But additional research is needed to determine whether this reduction in NKC activity makes sleep-deprived people more susceptible to cancer by impairing the ability of NKCs to destroy cancer cells before they can reproduce and form invasive tumors.

Moreover, as noted in Chapter 2, scientists caution against confusing causation and correlation. The positive correlation between hours of sleep and NKC activity does not necessarily mean that sleep deprivation causes a reduction in NKC activity. Other factors might account for the relationship between sleep and NKC activity. In fact, it is conceivable that the presumed direction of causality is just the opposite: immunological activity might promote sleep, thereby accounting for the positive correlation between the two (Karnovsky, 1986).

Because of the possibility of misinterpretation, scientists rely on experimental rather than correlational research to determine causal relationships between variables. Experiments that have used hours of sleep as the independent variable and immunological activity as the dependent variable consistently have shown that depriving people and animals of sleep does in fact reduce immunological activity. In one experiment, laboratory rats were deprived of sleep for 8 hours. They showed a significant reduction in their immunological responses to foreign cells (Brown, Price, King, & Husband, 1989). Moreover, when animals are purposely subjected to infections, those who obtain more deep sleep are more likely to survive (Toth & Krueger, 1990).

In an experiment with human participants, 23 healthy men, aged 22 to 61 years, were prevented from obtaining a full night's sleep. Eighteen of the men showed a decrease in NKC activity, with a statistically significant reduction to 72 percent of their average baseline levels of NKC activity. After just a single full night's sleep, their NKC activity returned to baseline levels (Irwin et al., 1994).

These findings supporting the role of sleep in immune responses have practical implications. To prevent illness, make sure you get enough sleep. When you are ill, make sure to get more sleep than usual. Perhaps hospital patients, who need their immune systems to function optimally, should not be awakened to receive medication or have blood drawn. Table 6-1 offers you an opportunity to determine whether you are getting enough sleep.

Sleep Apnea

sleep apnea A condition in which a person awakens repeatedly in order to breathe.

Imagine that you stopped breathing hundreds of times every night and awakened each time in order to breathe. You would be suffering from **sleep apnea** (*apnea* means the absence of breathing). Victims of sleep apnea have repeated episodes throughout the night in which they fall asleep and then stop breathing for up to a minute or more. This cessation of breathing produces a decrease in blood oxygen that stimulates the brain to awaken them, permitting them to start breathing again. People with sleep apnea typically feel chronically sleepy during the day, yet do not recall their repeated nighttime awakenings. They also may lie in bed for 8–10 hours per night but get less than half of that time as quality sleep.

Psychology versus Common Sense

Is Sleep Necessary for Good Health? *continued*

TABLE 6-1 Are You Getting Enough Sleep?

Psychologist James Maas has developed the following questionnaire to measure people's sleep needs. To determine whether you might be suffering from sleep deprivation, answer "true" or "false" to the following items regarding your current life experiences.

True	False	
☐	☐	1. It's a struggle for me to get out of bed in the morning.
☐	☐	2. I need an alarm clock to wake up at the appropriate time.
☐	☐	3. Weekday mornings I hit the snooze bar several times to get more sleep.
☐	☐	4. I often sleep extra hours on weekend mornings.
☐	☐	5. I often need a nap to get through the day.
☐	☐	6. I have dark circles around my eyes.
☐	☐	7. I feel tired, irritable, and stressed out during the week.
☐	☐	8. I have trouble concentrating and remembering.
☐	☐	9. I feel slow with critical thinking, problem solving, and being creative.
☐	☐	10. I often fall asleep in boring meetings or lectures or in warm rooms.
☐	☐	11. I often feel drowsy while driving.
☐	☐	12. I often fall asleep watching TV.
☐	☐	13. I often fall asleep after heavy meals or after a low dose of alcohol.
☐	☐	14. I often fall asleep while relaxing after dinner.
☐	☐	15. I often fall asleep within five minutes of getting into bed.

If you answered "true" to three or more items, you probably are not getting enough sleep. Keep in mind that we differ in our individual sleep needs. If this questionnaire suggests that you may be sleep deprived, Maas recommends that you go to bed 15 minutes earlier every night for a week. Continue adding 15 more minutes each week until you are waking without the aid of an alarm clock and without feeling tired during the day. Encourage your family and friends to also try this exercise, and compare your experiences over the next few weeks to see if your daily alertness and energy level improves.

Source: "Are You Getting Enough Sleep? Questionnaire" from *Power Sleep: The Revolutionary Program That Prepared Your Mind for Peak Performance* by Dr. James B. Maas with Megan L. Wherry, David J. Axelrod, Barbara R. Hogan, and Jennifer A. Blumin, copyright © 1998 by James B. Maas, Ph.D. Used by permission of Villard Books, an imprint of Random House, a division of Random House LLC. All rights reserved.

There are two major causes of sleep apnea. One is a neurological dysfunction of brain stem structures that regulate breathing (Gilman et al., 2003). Cases with this cause sometimes respond to drug therapy (Mendelson, Maczaj, & Holt, 1991). The second major cause is the collapse of the breathing passage, which is more common in people who are obese (Fogel et al., 2003). The treatment of choice in 80 percent of these cases is *continuous positive airway pressure*—the use of a device that pumps a steady flow of air through a breathing mask worn by the sleeper. This apparatus helps prevent the breathing passage from collapsing, yet compliance with its use is challenging (Olsen, Smith, Simon, Oei, & Douglas, 2012).

Narcolepsy

Whereas victims of sleep apnea find it impossible to stay asleep at night, victims of **narcolepsy** find it impossible to stay awake all day. If you suffered from narcolepsy, you would experience repeated, irresistible sleep attacks. During these attacks, you would immediately fall into REM sleep for periods lasting from a few minutes to a half hour. Because of its association with REM sleep, narcolepsy is typically

narcolepsy A condition in which an awake person suffers from repeated, sudden, and irresistible REM sleep attacks.

accompanied by a sudden loss of muscle tone (*cataplexy*) that causes the victim to collapse. You can imagine how dangerous narcolepsy is for people performing hazardous activities. For example, many people with narcolepsy fall asleep while driving (Aldrich, 1992).

Because narcoleptic attacks such as cataplexy can be instigated by strong emotions, victims try to maintain a bland emotional life, avoiding both laughing and crying, which interferes with victims' sex lives, work performance, and social relationships (Goswami, 1998). The cause of narcolepsy is unknown, but given that it runs in families, we know that there is a strong genetic basis, and researchers have identified specific genes involved in the development of narcolepsy (Singh, Mahlios, and Mignot, 2013). The sleep disturbances of narcolepsy are caused by degeneration of neurons that secrete orexin (also known as hypocretin), which promotes wakefulness (Scammell, 2003). People with narcolepsy have fewer normal neurons that produce orexin. Though there is no cure for narcolepsy, stimulants and antidepressants drugs help reduce daytime sleep attacks (Littner et al., 2001). And one study found that the combination of taking daytime naps and maintaining a regular nightly bedtime is effective in reducing daytime sleep attacks in people with narcolepsy (Rogers, Aldrich, & Lin, 2001). Currently there are no available medications that target orexin specifically. In the future, it is very likely that research will discover such treatments.

Section Review: Sleep

1. What cycles take place during a typical night's sleep?

2. What evidence supports the view that sleep is a form of adaptive inactivity?

3. What helpful tips would you give to a person suffering from sleep-onset insomnia?

Dreams

dream A storylike sequence of visual images, usually occurring during REM sleep.

The most dramatic aspect of sleep is the **dream**, a storylike sequence of visual images that commonly evoke strong emotions. Though dreaming can occur during any sleep stage, intense dreaming is thought to occur during REM sleep (Hobson, Pace-Schott, & Stickgold, 2000). Actions that would be impossible in real life may seem perfectly normal in dreams. In a dream, you might find it reasonable to hold a conversation with a dinosaur or to leap across the Grand Canyon. But what are the major characteristics of dreams? This question was addressed in a classic study conducted more than a century ago by Mary Whiton Calkins (1893).

Though Sigmund Freud is famous for making the analysis of dreams an important part of psychoanalysis, beginning with the publication of *The Interpretation of Dreams* in 1900, he was not the first person to study them formally. An article published by Mary Whiton Calkins (1893) described a dream study she conducted with her colleague Edmund Clark Sanford. The study is noteworthy because Freud referred to it in his book and its findings have held up well. It also shows the transition in late 19th century psychology from philosophical speculation about psychological topics, such as dreams, to empirical research on them. This is a landmark study because Sanford presented a paper on it in 1892 at the first meeting of the American Psychological Association.

Calkins recorded her own dreams for 55 nights, and Sanford recorded his for 46 nights. They used alarm clocks to awaken themselves at various times during the night in order to jot down any dreams they were having. Calkins observed dream characteristics that later research has confirmed. One researcher, J. Allan Hobson (1988), credits Calkins with anticipating modern approaches to dream research and pioneering the intensive study of dreams over many nights with the use of dream diaries and reports. Her findings included the following:

- *We dream every night.* On several nights, Calkins believed she had not dreamed—only to find that she had written down several dreams during the night. Calkins hypothesized that we forget our dreams because of a lack of congruity between dreaming and the waking states of consciousness. This finding anticipated interest in *state-dependent memory,* which has inspired research studies only in the past few decades and is discussed in Chapter 8.

- *We have about four dreams a night.* Calkins recorded 205 dreams on 55 nights, and Sanford 170 on 46 nights. This finding agrees with modern research indicating that we have four or five REM periods on a typical night.

- *As the night progresses, we are more likely to be dreaming.* Calkins found that most dreams occurred during the second half of the night. Her conclusion agrees with later research findings, obtained with physiological recording equipment, that successive REM periods increase in length across the night. In other words, we have more dreams closer to when we wake in the morning.

- *Most dreams are mundane and refer to recent life events.* We might not realize that dreams are usually mundane because we tend to recall only the most dramatic ones.

- *Dreams can incorporate external stimuli.* In one of her dreams, Calkins found herself struggling to crawl from an elevator through a tiny opening into an eighth-floor apartment. She awoke to find herself in a cramped position with a heavy blanket over her face.

- *What Calkins called "real thinking" occurs during sleep.* This finding anticipated research findings that NREM sleep is marked by ordinary thinking, as opposed to the fantastic images and events common to REM dreaming.

- *We can reason while dreaming and even, to an extent, control our dreams.* This finding anticipated research on lucid dreaming, a serious topic of research only in the past decade that is discussed in the following section, "The Content of Dreams."

- *Dreams can disguise their true meaning.* This finding anticipated Freud's belief that dreams can use symbols to represent their true—often sexual—meaning.

The Content of Dreams

People have long been intrigued by dreams; references to the content of dreams are found on Babylonian clay tablets dating from 5000 B.C. As just described, Mary Whiton Calkins (1893) found that we tend to dream about mundane personal matters. This finding was supported by the research of Calvin Hall (1966), who analyzed the content of thousands of dreams reported by his participants, and by more recent studies that indicate that our dreams reflect recent events that affect us emotionally. For example, a study of individuals who regularly recorded their dreams compared their last 10 dreams before the suicide airliner attacks on the United States on September 11, 2001, and their first 10 dreams after the attacks found that the intensity of the dreams was markedly greater after the attacks (Hartmann & Basile, 2003). But what of people who have recurrent dreams? A study of 52 college students who recorded their dreams over a 14-day period found that recurrent dreamers tended to report more stress in their lives, lower levels of psychological well-being, and more negative content in their dreams (Zadra, O'Brien, & Donderi, 1998).

Dream content also is associated with sociocultural factors. Though Hall noted several gender-related differences in dreams, these differences have been decreasing. In fact, a recent study of the dreams of 40 male and 40 female college students found greater similarity in their dream content than would have been true several decades ago (Bursik, 1998), though there is some evidence that the content of males' dreams is somewhat more aggressive than that of females' dreams (Blume-Marcovici, 2010). A study of the relationship between culture and dream content examined the dreams of 205 children aged 7 to 12 years from peaceful Finland, from violence-prone regions of Gaza, and from relatively violence-free regions

Dreaming

As discussed earlier in this chapter compared to adults, infants spend more time in REM sleep—and dreaming.
Source: KieferPix/Shutterstock.com

of Gaza. The children recorded their dreams each morning for 7 days. The results showed that the children exposed to violence had more vivid dreams, incorporating more themes of persecution and aggression (Punamaecki & Joustie, 1998).

When you have a frightening dream, you are experiencing a **nightmare**. Children as young as two to three years of age report having nightmares (Byars, Yolton, Rausch, Lanphear, & Beebe, 2012), which are more common in children with high levels of anxiety (Mindell & Barrett, 2002). Nightmares tend to occur when we feel emotionally distressed. Frequent nightmares have been reported in studies of military personnel who have experienced intense combat (Long et al., 2011), people who have been exposed to terrorism (Soffar-Dudek & Shahar, 2010), and women who have been sexually assaulted (Karkow et al., 2002).

Do not confuse a nightmare, which is a frightening dream that occurs during REM sleep, with a **night terror**, which occurs during NREM sleep stages 3 and 4. The person experiencing a night terror will suddenly sit upright in bed, feel intense fear, let out a bloodcurdling scream, exhibit a rapid pulse and breathing rate, and speak incoherently. After a night terror, the person typically falls right back to sleep and does not recall the experience the next morning. As a result, a night terror can be more disturbing to the family members who are rudely awakened by it than to the person who has experienced it. Though night terrors are more common in children, especially those experiencing stress (Talarczyk, 2011), they can afflict adults as well (Llorente, Currier, Norman, & Mellman, 1992). A survey of almost 5,000 people aged 15 to 100 years found that 2 percent experienced night terrors (Ohayon, Guilleminault, & Priest, 1999).

As noted by Mary Whiton Calkins (1893), the content of dreams can be affected by immediate environmental stimuli. Even before Calkins made this observation, it was portrayed by Herman Melville in his novel *Moby Dick* in describing the effect of Captain Ahab's peg leg on the dreams of his ship's sailors. Melville wrote, "To his weary mates, seeking repose within six inches of his ivory heel, such would have been the reverberating crack and din of that bony step that their dreams would have been of the crunching teeth of sharks." Similarly, you might find yourself dreaming of an ice cream truck ringing its bell, only to awaken suddenly and discover that your dream had been stimulated by the ringing of your telephone.

Such anecdotal reports of the incorporation of stimuli into dreams have inspired laboratory experiments. In one of the first of these, researchers sprayed sleepers with a water mist when they were in REM sleep; on being awakened, many of the participants reported dreams with watery themes, such as a leaky roof or being caught in the rain (Dement & Wolpert, 1958). Experiments also have found that sleeping participants who are touched on their bodies (Nielsen, 1993) or rocked in a hammock (Leslie & Ogilvie, 1996) might incorporate that stimulation into their dreams. Despite these positive findings, stimuli that we experience when we are asleep are not always incorporated into our dreams. For example, a study of sleep apnea patients found no increase in dream content related to breathing problems (Gross & Lavie, 1994).

Mary Whiton Calkins (1893) also noted that we might be able to control our ongoing dreams. In **lucid dreaming**, an approach devised by Stephen LaBerge (Kahan & LaBerge, 1994), sleeping individuals learn how to be aware while dreaming and how to direct their dreams. Lucid dreamers report an enhanced sense of well-being (Wolpin, Marston, Randolph, & Clothier, 1992), though the reasons for this feeling are unclear. Lucid dreaming has been used to alleviate depression (Taitz, 2011) and help people with recurrent nightmares alter aspects of their dreams to make them less frightening (Zadra & Pihl, 1997).

The Purpose of Dreaming

REM sleep—dream sleep—is important. Participants who have been deprived of sleep, and then are allowed to sleep as long as they like, show an increase in REM sleep (Dement, 1960). This phenomenon is known as the *REM rebound effect* and indicates that dream sleep serves important functions. But what are the functions of dreams? People have pondered this question for thousands of years, and cultures vary in the significance and value they place on dreams (Wax, 1999). Native American cultures tend to make less of a demarcation between waking and dreaming realities and view dreams as messages from another realm that can enlighten the dreamer (Krippner & Thompson, 1996). The ancient Hebrews, Egyptians, and Greeks

nightmare A frightening dream occurring during REM sleep.

night terror A frightening NREM experience, common in childhood, in which the individual may suddenly sit up, let out a bloodcurdling scream, speak incoherently, and quickly fall back to sleep, yet usually fails to recall it on awakening.

lucid dreaming The ability to be aware that one is dreaming and to direct one's dreams.

believed that dreams brought prophecies from God or the gods, as in the Pharaoh's dream that was interpreted by Joseph in the Old Testament of the Bible and in dreams described in Homer's *Iliad* and *Odyssey*. But Aristotle, who at first accepted the divine origin of dreams, later rejected this belief, claiming that it is merely coincidental when prophetic dreams come true.

Dreaming as Wish Fulfillment

Sigmund Freud (1900/1990) provided the first formal view of dreaming as wish fulfillment. Freud claimed that dreams function as the "royal road to the unconscious" by serving as safe outlets for unconscious sexual or aggressive impulses that we cannot act on while we are awake because of cultural prohibitions against them. Freud distinguished between a dream's **manifest content**, which is the dream as recalled by the dreamer, and its **latent content**, which is the dream's hidden, underlying meaning. Thus, the manifest content of a dream hides its latent content. But why do we not dream about the latent content directly? If we dreamed directly about emotionally charged sexual or aggressive material, we might repeatedly awaken ourselves from our sleep.

But how can we uncover a dream's latent content from its manifest content? According to Freud, a dream's manifest content consists of symbols that disguise its latent sexual or aggressive content. Thus, in our dreams, trees, rifles, or skyscrapers might act as phallic symbols representing unconscious sexual impulses. The manifest content of a dream reported by a person is translated into its latent content during the process of psychoanalysis, which is discussed in Chapter 15. Nonetheless, even Freud said that "sometimes a cigar is just a cigar"—meaning that sometimes the manifest content is not symbolic but instead is the true content of the dream. Additionally, this approach to dream interpretations is difficult to study empirically; thus, Freud's approach to dream analysis in treatment settings is on the decline.

manifest content Sigmund Freud's term for the verbally reported dream.

latent content Sigmund Freud's term for the true, though disguised, meaning of a dream.

Dreaming as Problem Solving

The failure of psychoanalysts to provide convincing research support for dreaming as a form of disguised wish fulfillment (Fisher & Greenberg, 1985) led researchers to study other possible functions of dreams, such as problem solving. Anecdotal reports have long supported the view that dreaming serves the function of problem solving. For example, Elias Howe completed his invention of the sewing machine only after gaining insight from a dream. And there is research evidence that events we are concerned about from the previous day are more likely to be included in our dreams (Cipolli, Bolzani, Tuozzi, & Fagioli, 2001). Rosalind Cartwright (1978), a leading dream researcher, has conducted formal studies of the possible role of dreaming in solving practical and emotional problems.

According to Cartwright, dreaming provides a more creative approach to problem solving because it is freer and less constrained by the more logical thinking of waking life. In a study of people in the process of divorcing their spouse, Cartwright (1991) found that those who dreamed about their relationship with their spouse while they were going through the divorce were less depressed and better adjusted to single life a year later. This finding was particularly true of those who had highly emotional dreams. Note, however, that this study revealed a positive correlation between dreaming and emotional adjustment. It did not provide evidence that dreaming *caused* better emotional adjustment. Another experimental study found that participants who were directed to dream about particular problems later reported less distress and a reduction in the problems compared to participants who had not been directed to do so (White & Taytroe, 2003). Likewise, lucid dreamers who were directed to dream about a "guru" who knew the answers to particular problems later reported more creative solutions than did participants who were not lucid dreamers (Stumbrys and Daniels, 2010). Because these studies were experimental rather than correlational, it provides more convincing evidence that dreaming might play a role in helping us deal with personal problems.

Dreaming as an Aid to Memory

Do you ever stay up all night to study for exams? If so, you might be impairing your ability to memorize the material you have studied. Decades of research indicate that sleep can help you form long-term memories (Fenn, Nusbaum, & Margoliash, 2003), particularly emotional memories (Wagner, Gais, & Born, 2001). REM sleep appears to be even more beneficial to memory than NREM sleep. Researchers studying mice have found that the signaling molecules that are activated during memory processing in the hippocampus are also active during REM but not NREM sleep (Luo, Phan, Yang, Garelick, & Storm, 2013). Consider a study in which undergraduates learned a story during the day and then were awakened periodically to deprive them of equal periods of either REM sleep or stage 4 sleep. The next day they were asked to recall the story they had learned the day before. Participants who had been deprived of REM sleep showed poorer recall than participants who had been deprived of stage 4 sleep (Tilley & Empson, 1978).

Additional evidence for the importance of REM sleep comes from research findings that the more REM sleep we have during a night's sleep, the better our memory will be for material learned during the day before. In one study, undergraduates learned Morse code just before bedtime on three consecutive nights. After awakening, they were given a Morse code test. The results revealed a positive correlation between the length of REM sleep and their performance on the test (Mandai, Guerrien, Sockeel, & Dujardin, 1989). However, some researchers have pointed out that the evidence for the role of sleep in the formation of long-term memories is inconsistent (Vertes & Eastman, 2000). Thus, sleep may play a role in memory consolidation, and some researchers hypothesize that dreaming may enhance memory by facilitating a storehouse of memories that are unique to each individual (Oudiette & Paller, 2013).

Dreaming as the By-Product of Random Brain Activity

activation-synthesis theory
The theory that dreams are the by-products of the cortex's attempt to make sense of the spontaneous changes in physiological activity generated by the brain stem during REM sleep.

The **activation-synthesis theory** of J. Allan Hobson and Robert McCarley (1977) holds that dreams are the by-products of the cortex's attempt to make sense of activity generated by the brain stem during REM sleep. That is, the cortex interprets brain activation and *synthesizes* it into a dream. As an example, consider a dream in which you are being chased but feel that you cannot run away. According to the activation-synthesis theory, this dream might reflect the cortex's attempt to explain the failure of signals from the motor areas of the brain to stimulate limb movements during the paralysis that accompanies REM sleep—paralysis produced by activity in the brain stem. The inability of the cortex to make logical sense of patterns of random brain stem activity might explain why our REM dreams tend to be more bizarre than our daydreams (Williams, Merritt, Rittenhouse, & Hobson, 1992).

The activation-synthesis theory does not discount the influence of psychological factors on one's dreams. That is, the theory accepts that the cortex's interpretation of random brain stem activity presumably reveals something about the personality and experiences of the dreamer. The theory simply assumes that dreams are generated by random brain stem activity, not by unconscious wishes or emotional conflicts. Indeed, recent research indicates that dreams are not merely the meaningless by-products of brain activity (Colace, 2003). Psychological factors come into play only *after* the onset of brain stem activity (Rittenhouse, Stickgold, & Hobson, 1994). One problem with this theory is that there is no way to make clear testable hypotheses if a researcher were to design an experiment to test it. For example, there may be plenty of extraneous sounds or stimuli present while a person is sleeping, but a dream might only occasionally incorporate them. Also, consider if you have ever had a dream about a salient joyful or worrisome event that occurred long ago. Both examples would be difficult to explain using the activation-synthesis theory alone. Despite more than a century of research, no single dream theory has been clearly shown to be superior at explaining the functions of dreams. One of the difficulties in dream research is that the same dream can be explained equally well by different theories. This possibility is illustrated in Figure 6-8.

Section Review: Dreams

1. In what ways did Mary Whiton Calkins's 1893 study of dreams anticipate later research findings?

2. What is Freud's theory of dreaming?

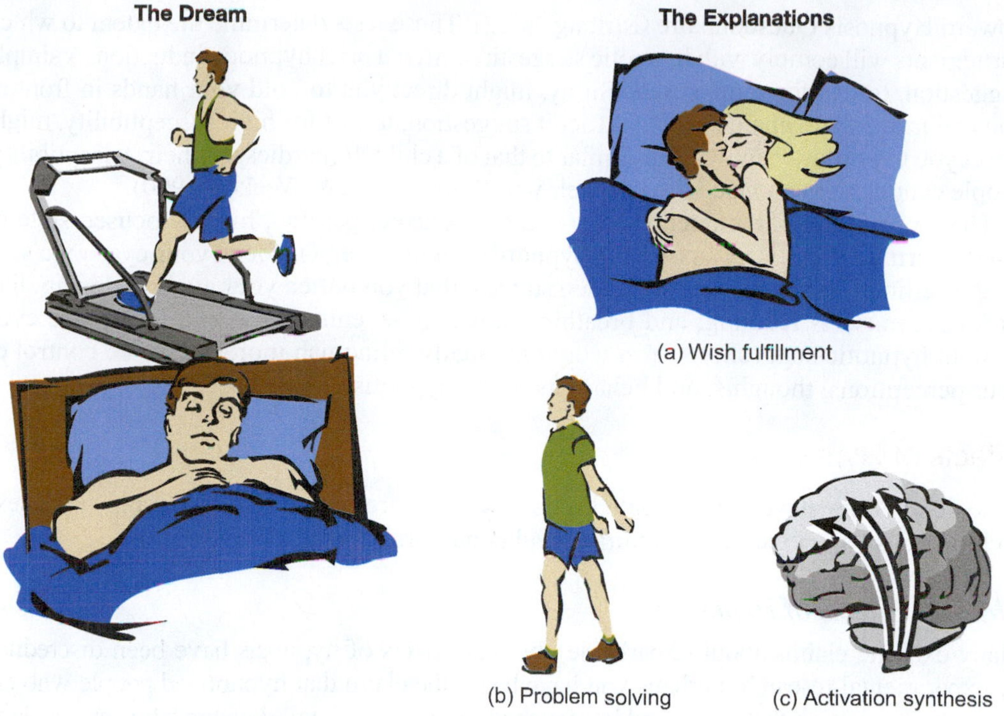

The Dream

The Explanations

(a) Wish fulfillment

(b) Problem solving

(c) Activation synthesis

FIGURE 6-8
One Dream, Three Explanations

The Dream: The person dreams that he is running in place and can neither move from the spot nor stop running. *Theoretical Explanations:* (a) Freud's wish fulfillment theory requires that the manifest content (the dream as reported) be interpreted to find its latent content (its true meaning). The dream might be interpreted as meaning that the dreamer has a conflict about his wish for sex (symbolized by his desire to move from the spot) and his guilt feelings about that wish (symbolized by his wish to stop running). (b) Cartwright's problem-solving theory assumes that dreaming helps us solve real-life problems. Perhaps the dreamer has been concerned with recent excessive weight gain but has been unable to decide on the best course of action for losing weight. The dream might be directing him to take up aerobic exercise. (c) Hobson and McCarley's activation-synthesis theory attributes dreaming to brain activity while we are asleep. During REM sleep, the pons generates neural impulses that activate random regions of the cerebral cortex. Perhaps it has activated the region of the motor cortex that controls leg movements. Because the sleeper's legs are paralyzed during REM sleep, he might synthesize the cortical arousal and leg paralysis into a dream about running in place without being able to move or stop.

Hypnosis

Whereas sleep is a naturally occurring state of consciousness, **hypnosis** is an induced state of consciousness in which one person responds to suggestions by another person to alter perception, thinking, feelings, and behavior. Hypnosis originated in the work of the Viennese physician Franz Anton Mesmer (1734–1815), who claimed that he could cure illnesses by transmitting to his patients a form of energy he called *animal magnetism,* a process that became known as *mesmerism.* In the late 18th century, Mesmer—a charismatic man—became the rage of Paris, impressing audiences with his demonstrations of mesmerism (Musikantow, 2011). Today we still use the word *mesmerized* to describe a person in a trancelike state and *animal magnetism* to describe people with charismatic personalities.

Mesmer's flamboyance and extravagant claims, as well as the professional jealousy of other physicians, provoked King Louis XVI to appoint a commission to investigate mesmerism. The commission was headed by Benjamin Franklin and included Antoine Lavoisier (the founder of modern chemistry) and J. I. Guillotin (the inventor of the infamous decapitation device, the guillotine). The commission completed its investigation in 1784, concluding that there was no evidence of animal magnetism and that the effects of mesmerism were attributable to the power of suggestion and people's active imagination (Franklin et al., 1784/2002). In 1842 the English surgeon James Braid (1795–1860) used mesmerism in his practice as an anesthetic and concluded that it induced a sleeplike state. He renamed mesmerism *hypnotism,* from Hypnos, the Greek god of sleep.

Hypnotic Induction and Susceptibility

How do hypnotists induce a hypnotic state? The process depends less on the skill of the hypnotist than on the suggestibility of the individual. Highly hypnotizable people have a superior ability to vividly and uncritically imagine things suggested to them and to become completely absorbed in what they are doing (Enea & Dafinoiu, 2013). Thus, these characteristics could be considered a cognitive trait associated with the responsiveness to suggestions. And perhaps of greatest importance, highly hypnotizable people tend to have strong empathy, or the ability to recognize other people's feelings (Wickramasekera & Szlyk, 2003).

Psychologists have developed tests of hypnotizability, such as the Stanford Hypnotic Susceptibility Scale (Weitzenhoffer & Hilgard, 1962) and more recently the Spanos Attitudes

hypnosis An induced state of consciousness in which one person responds to suggestions by another person for alterations in perception, thinking, and behavior.

Toward Hypnosis Questionnaire (Milling, 2012). These tests determine the extent to which participants will comply with hypnotic suggestions after a brief hypnotic induction. A simple suggestion, to test for some susceptibility, might direct you to hold your hands in front of you and move them apart. A more difficult suggestion, to test for high susceptibility, might direct you to produce handwriting similar to that of a child. Regardless of their susceptibility, people cannot be hypnotized against their will (Lynn, Rhue, & Weekes, 1990).

The aim of hypnotic induction is to create a relaxed, passive, highly focused state of mind. During hypnotic induction the hypnotist might have you focus your eyes on a spot on the ceiling. The hypnotist might then suggest that you notice your eyelids closing, feet warming, muscles relaxing, and breathing slowing—events that would take place even without hypnotic suggestions. You would gradually relinquish more and more control of your perceptions, thoughts, and behaviors to the hypnotist.

Effects of Hypnosis

Research studies have demonstrated a variety of impressive effects of hypnosis. These include physical, perceptual, cognitive, and behavioral effects.

Physical Effects of Hypnosis

Many extreme claims about remarkable physical effects of hypnosis have been discredited by experimental research. Perhaps you have heard the claim that hypnotized people who are given the suggestion that their hand has touched red-hot metal will develop a blister—a claim first made over two centuries ago (Gauld, 1990). Experiments have shown that such hypnotic suggestions can, at best, merely promote warming of the skin by increasing the flow of blood to it (Spanos, McNeil, & Stam, 1982). Nonetheless, there is evidence that hypnosis can have highly specific physical effects. One study found that postsurgical patients who received hypnotic suggestions for wound healing showed wound healing superior to that of patients who received supportive attention or usual medical care (Ginandes, Brooks, Sando, Jones, & Aker, 2003). Another study assessed the effect of hypnosis on the immune response. Dental and medical students were randomly assigned to receive either hypnosis or no hypnosis prior to a major exam. The results showed that those who received hypnosis did not show the normal stress-related decline in the immunological response (Kiecolt-Glaser, Marucha, Atkinson, & Glaser, 2001). At best, hypnosis might subtly inhibit pain pathways. Remember from Chapter 5 that pain is comprised of both sensory and emotional components.

Perceptual Effects of Hypnosis

Stage hypnotists commonly use hypnosis to induce alterations in perception, such as convincing participants that a vial of water is actually ammonia. Participants will jerk their heads away after smelling it. But the most important perceptual effect of hypnosis is in pain relief. In the mid-19th century, the Scottish surgeon James Esdaile (1808–1859) used hypnosis to induce anesthesia in more than three hundred patients undergoing surgery for the removal of limbs, tumors, or cataracts (Ellenberger, 1970).

A recent meta-analysis of laboratory and biomedical research studies (Montgomery, DuHamel, & Redd, 2000) found that hypnosis has a moderate to large effect in relieving pain, as in cancer pain (Shea, 2003), pain during labor and childbirth (Landolt & Milling, 2011), or postoperative pain (Lew, Kravits, Garberoglio, & Williams, 2011). But how does hypnosis produce its analgesic effects? As discussed in Chapter 5, one way is by using suggestions that help distract sufferers from their pain (Farthing, Venturino, & Brown, 1984). A second way is by sending neural impulses from the brain down the spinal cord that block the transmission of pain impulses from the body to the spinal cord (Holroyd, 1996). This method is in keeping with the gate-control theory of pain (see Chapter 5).

Cognitive Effects of Hypnosis

In 1976, 26 elementary schoolchildren and their bus driver were kidnapped in Chowchilla, California, and imprisoned in a buried tractor trailer. The bus driver and two of the children dug their way out and got help. The driver, Frank Ray, had seen the license plate number of the kidnappers' van but was unable to recall it. After being hypnotized and told to imagine himself watching the kidnapping unfold on television, he was able to recall all but one of the digits of the number. His recollection enabled the police to track down the kidnappers (Smith, 1983).

The Chowchilla case was a widely publicized example of one of the chief cognitive applications of hypnosis—**hypermnesia,** the enhancement of memory. Though many memories retrieved by hypnosis are accurate (Ewin, 1994), hypnosis also can create inaccurate memories, or pseudomemories (Spanos, Burgess, Burgess, Samuels, & Blois, 1999). In fact, one of the most common misconceptions that the American public holds about hypnosis is its role in restoring accurate memories (Johnson & Hauck, 1999). Because of the possibility of inaccuracy, the use of hypnosis in legal cases to enhance eyewitness memories is controversial, and its use is limited.

One problem is that hypnotized eyewitnesses feel more confident about the memories they recall under hypnosis—regardless of their accuracy (Weekes, Lynn, Green, & Brentar, 1992). In one study, 27 participants were hypnotized and then given the suggestion that they had been awakened by a loud noise one night during the preceding week. Later, after leaving the hypnotized state, 13 of the participants claimed that the suggested event had actually occurred. Even after being informed of the hypnotic suggestion, 6 participants still insisted that they had been awakened by the noise (Laurence & Perry, 1983). These findings indicate the potential danger of hypnotically enhanced eyewitness testimony, particularly because juries put more trust in confident eyewitnesses (Sheehan & Tilden, 1983) and hypnotized eyewitnesses (Wagstaff, Vella, & Perfect, 1992).

hypermnesia The hypnotic enhancement of recall.

Behavioral Effects of Hypnosis

Though hypnosis can help some people, a debate has raged for more than a century about whether hypnosis can be used to induce harmful behavior (e.g., Liegois, 1899). Martin Orne and Frederick Evans (1965) demonstrated that hypnotized people could be induced to commit dangerous acts. Their study included a group of hypnotized participants and a group of participants who simulated being hypnotized. When instructed to do so, participants in both groups plunged their hands into what they were told was a nitric acid solution, threw the liquid in another person's face, and tried to handle a poisonous snake. Of course, the experimenters protected the participants (by immediately washing off the liquid, by actually having them throw water instead of acid, and by stopping them from touching the snake). Because both groups engaged in apparently dangerous acts, the research setting, rather than hypnosis, might have accounted for the results. In any case, there is no evidence that hypnotized people become mindless zombies who blindly obey orders to commit harmful acts (Gibson, 1991).

Similarly, some of the effects of stage hypnosis might have less to do with hypnosis than with the setting in which they occur. For example, you might have seen a stage hypnotist direct a hypnotized volunteer from the audience to remain as rigid as a plank while lying extended between two chairs. But highly motivated, non-hypnotized persons also can perform this "human plank" trick. According to researcher Theodore Barber, even the willingness of hypnotized participants to obey suggestions to engage in bizarre behaviors, such as clucking like a chicken, might be more attributable to the theatrical "anything goes" atmosphere of stage hypnosis than to the effect of hypnosis itself (Meeker & Barber, 1971).

The Nature of Hypnosis

In the late 19th century, most notably in France, practitioners of hypnosis disagreed whether hypnosis induced an altered, or trance, state of consciousness. One group argued that hypnosis induces a trancelike state called **dissociation,** in which parts of the mind become separated from one another and form independent streams of consciousness. Many distance runners use dissociation to divorce their conscious minds from possibly distressful bodily sensations while still remaining consciously aware of the racecourse ahead of them (Masters, 1992). Another group of French hypnotists argued that hypnosis does not induce a trance state. Instead, they insisted that it just induces a state of heightened

dissociation A state in which the mind is split into two or more independent streams of consciousness.

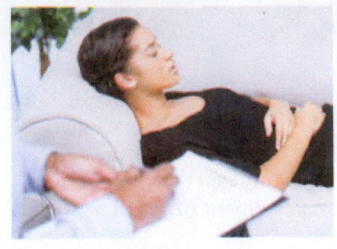

Hypnosis

Hypnotherapists make use of posthypnotic suggestions in the treatment of conditions such as chronic pain or anxiety.

Source: wavebreakmedia/Shutterstock.com.

neodissociation theory
The theory that hypnosis induces a dissociated state of consciousness.

hidden observer Ernest Hilgard's term for the part of the hypnotized person's consciousness that is not under the control of the hypnotist but is aware of what is taking place.

posthypnotic suggestions
Suggestions directing people to carry out particular behaviors or to have particular experiences after leaving hypnosis.

age regression A hypnotic state in which the individual apparently behaves as she or he did as a child.

suggestibility. This debate lingers on; some researchers view hypnosis as an altered state of consciousness, and others view it as a normal state of waking consciousness.

Hypnosis as a Dissociated State

Today, the main theory of hypnosis as an altered state is **neodissociation theory**. This theory originated in a classroom demonstration of hypnotically induced deafness by Ernest Hilgard (1904–2001), who directed a hypnotized blind student to raise an index finger if he heard a sound. When blocks were banged near his head, the student did not even flinch. But when asked if some part of his mind had actually heard the noise, his finger rose. Hilgard called this part of the mind the **hidden observer** (Hilgard, 1978). Hilgard helped make hypnosis scientifically legitimate when he founded his laboratory for hypnosis research at Stanford University in 1957 (Bowers, 1994).

Hilgard used the concept of the hidden observer to explain hypnotically induced pain relief. He relied on the cold pressor test, in which participants submerge an arm in ice water and are asked every few seconds to estimate their degree of pain. Though hypnotized participants who are told that they will feel less pain report that they feel little or no pain, the hidden observer, when asked, reports that it has experienced intense pain (Hilgard, 1973).

Additional evidence in favor of hypnosis as an altered state comes from experiments in which hypnotized participants experience physiological changes in response to hypnotic suggestions. In one study, highly hypnotizable participants learned lists of words and were given **posthypnotic suggestions** to forget them. Those who reported *posthypnotic amnesia* (their inability to recognize the words they had read) showed changes in components of their brain-wave patterns that are related to attention and recognition. This evidence indicates that posthypnotic amnesia is more than a state of heightened suggestibility (Allen, Iacono, Laravuso, & Dunn, 1995). Research studies using PET scans have shown that hypnosis is associated with activity in distinct regions of the brain that play critical roles in regulating consciousness (Rainville, Hofbauer, Bushnell, Duncan, & Price, 2002). More recent data using MRI have shown that hypnotic susceptible individuals do in fact show activation of distinct brain circuits. These circuits mimic the same circuits that are responsive during placebo analgesic effects (Huber, Lui, & Porro, 2013).

Hypnosis as Role Playing

The claim that hypnosis is an altered state of consciousness has not gone unchallenged. Critics insist that hypnotically induced effects are only responses to personal factors, such as the participant's motivation, and situational factors, such as the hypnotist's wording of suggestions. By arranging the right combination of factors, the hypnotist increases the likelihood that the participant will comply with hypnotic suggestions.

Evidence that hypnosis is a state of heightened suggestibility has also come from studies of hypnotic **age regression**, in which hypnotized participants are told to return to childhood. A hypnotized adult might use baby talk or play with an imaginary teddy bear. But a published review of research on hypnotic age regression found that adults do not adopt the true cognitive, behavioral, and physiological characteristics of children; they just act as though they were children (Nash, 1987). For example, in a classic study, Martin Orne (1927–2000) hypnotized college students and suggested that they regress back to their sixth birthday party. He then asked them to describe the people and activities at the party, which they did in great detail. When Orne asked the participants' parents to describe the same birthday party, he found that many of the participants' "memories" had been fabrications. They reported people and events they presumed would have been at their own sixth birthday party. There was no evidence that they actually reexperienced their sixth birthday party (Orne, 1951).

Neither side in the debate about the nature of hypnosis has provided sufficient evidence to discount the other side completely. As noted by William James more than a century ago, both sides might be correct: Hypnosis might be a dissociated state of consciousness that can be shaped by the social context and hypnotic suggestions (Kihlstrom & McConkey, 1990). After decades as a leading hypnosis researcher, Theodore Barber (2000) concluded that the all-or-none debate is fruitless. Instead, he believes researchers should study the three kinds of people he has identified as susceptible to hypnosis. The first are

Is Hypnosis an Altered State of Consciousness?

Rationale

In an experiment conducted by Nicholas Spanos (1942–1994) and Erin Hewitt of Carleton University in Ottawa, the hidden observer was made to give contradictory reports, depending on the hypnotist's suggestions (Spanos & Hewitt, 1980).

Method

The experiment recruited undergraduate participants who scored high on a hypnotizability scale and were then given suggestions for hypnotic analgesia. Two groups of participants were given contradictory suggestions. One group was told that the hypnotized part of their minds would have little awareness of the pain, while a hidden part would be more aware of the actual intensity of the pain. Another group was told that the hypnotized part of their minds would have little awareness of the pain, while a hidden part would be even less aware of the pain. Participants were asked to place a forearm in ice water, which induces pain. They were told to have the hypnotized parts of their minds state their level of pain on a scale from 0 to 20 every 5 seconds for 60 seconds. They also were told to hold a forearm in ice water while having their hidden observer report their level of pain (from 0 to 20) by tapping out a simple code on a response key every 5 seconds for 60 seconds.

Results and Discussion

When asked to report the intensity of the pain, the hidden observer reported what the participants had been led to expect. It experienced more pain than the hypnotized part when told it would be more aware and less pain when told it would be less aware. The results are presented in Figure 6-9. Thus, the hidden observer might simply be a result of the participant's willingness to act as though he or she has experienced suggested hypnotic effects. Spanos found that this willingness is not a case of faking but probably reflects the well-established ability of people to distract themselves from their pain. Moreover, the hidden observer never appears spontaneously—it appears only when explicitly asked to. This study, as well as others by Spanos, indicates that the hidden observer is a product not of the dissociation of consciousness, but instead of the participant's willingness to follow the hypnotist's suggestions.

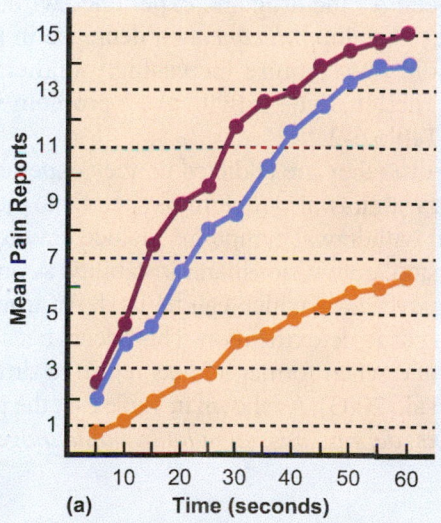 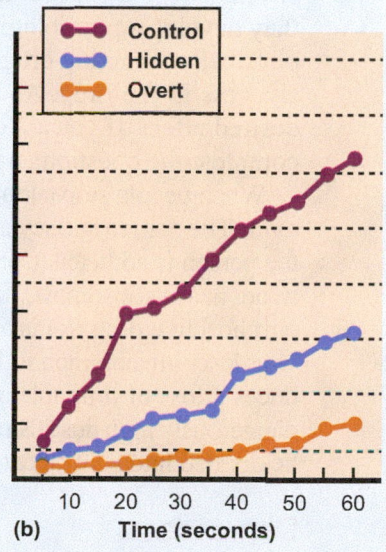

FIGURE 6-9 Pain Reports by the Hidden Observer

These two graphs show that the hidden observer might be merely the product of hypnotic suggestion rather than an objective perceiver of reality. *(a)* When told that it will be more aware, the hidden observer reports more pain. *(b)* When told that it will be less aware, the hidden observer reports less pain.

Source: From Spanos & Hewitt, *Journal of Personality and Social Psychology* 39: 1209. Copyright © 1980 by the American Psychological Association. Reprinted by permission

people who have had active fantasy lives since childhood. The second are people who are prone to dissociation and tend to repress undesirable thoughts, emotions, and memories. The third are people who are motivated to play the role of hypnotized participants.

Section Review: Hypnosis

1. How would you induce a state of hypnosis?

2. What are the benefits and risks of using hypnosis in enhancing the recall of memories?

3. Why do some researchers believe that hypnosis is not an altered state of consciousness?

Psychoactive Drugs

psychoactive drugs Chemicals that induce changes in mood, thinking, perception, and behavior by affecting neuronal activity in the brain.

Normal waking consciousness also can be altered by **psychoactive drugs,** which are chemicals that induce changes in mood, thinking, perception, and behavior by affecting neuronal activity. People seem drawn to psychoactive drugs. Many people consume alcohol to reduce social anxiety, take barbiturates to fall asleep, use narcotics to feel euphoric, drink coffee to get going in the morning, or smoke marijuana to enrich their perception of music.

Psychoactive drugs exert their effects by altering synaptic transmission, by either promoting or inhibiting it. But the effects of psychoactive drugs depend on a host of factors. These include the drugs' dosage, the user's experience with them, the user's expectations about their effects, and the setting in which they are taken.

Many psychoactive drugs can cause *psychological dependence*—an intense desire to achieve the intoxicated state induced by the drug. Most psychoactive drugs also can cause *physical dependence* (or *addiction*). That is, after people use the drug for a period of time, they develop a physiological need for the drug and experience withdrawal. As people use physically addicting drugs, they develop *tolerance*—a decrease in physiological responsiveness to the drug. As a result, they require increasingly higher doses to achieve the desired effect. If you are concerned that you might have a problem with substance abuse, complete the questionnaire in Table 6-2.

When people stop taking the drug they are addicted to, they experience *withdrawal symptoms.* The pattern and severity of withdrawal symptoms is specific to the kind of drug to which the person is addicted. Common withdrawal symptoms include craving, chills, headache, fatigue, nausea, insomnia, depression, convulsions, and irritability. A possible consequence of psychoactive drug use is a *drug overdose,* which can be fatal. An ironic finding is that drug overdoses are common following drug detoxification. This occurs because detoxification produces a loss of drug tolerance, and when former addicts return to drug use, they may use a dangerously high dose (Strang et al., 2003). As shown in Table 6-3, the psychoactive drugs can be divided into general categories: *depressants, stimulants, hallucinogens,* and *entactogens.*

Depressants

depressants Psychoactive drugs that inhibit activity in the central nervous system.

Depressants reduce arousal by inhibiting activity in the central nervous system. This section discusses several kinds of depressants: *alcohol, barbiturates,* and *opiates.*

Alcohol

ethyl alcohol (ethanol) A depressant found in beverages and commonly used to reduce social inhibitions.

Ethyl alcohol (or **ethanol**), an addictive drug, has been used—and abused—for thousands of years. Even the ancient Romans had to pass laws against drunk driving—of chariots (Whitlock, 1987). Drunk drivers are dangerous because they suffer from impaired judgment, perceptual distortions, and motor incoordination. Alcohol is involved in 50 percent of traffic accidents in the United States (Matthews, Best, White, Vandergriff, & Simon, 1996). Chronic alcoholics often lose their jobs, homes, and families and create a large toll on society. Many alcoholics die

TABLE 6-2 Are You Abusing a Drug?

Instructions: Listed below are eight criteria that the American Psychiatric Association uses to diagnose drug abuse (also known as *substance dependence*) in the DSM-5. If three or more of the following criteria describe your own behavior, you may have a problem with drug abuse.

Yes	No	
____	____	1. You take the drug in larger amounts or over a longer period than intended.
____	____	2. You have a persistent desire, or have made one or more unsuccessful efforts, to cut down or control drug use.
____	____	3. You spend a great deal of your time in activities necessary to get the drug (for example, theft), taking the drug (for example, chain smoking), or recovering from its effects (for example, alcohol hangovers) and do this while you are expected to fulfill obligations at work, school, or home, or when drug use is physically dangerous (for example, driving when intoxicated).
____	____	4. You experience strong urges for the drug that can occur anywhere but can be more intense in the context in which the drug is obtained or used, (for example, intense craving where the individual cannot think of anything else but the drug).
____	____	5. You give up or reduce in frequency important social, occupational, or recreational activities because of drug use.
____	____	6. You continue to use the drug despite recognizing its harmfulness to your social or interpersonal life.
____	____	7. You need increased amounts of the drug (at least 50 percent more) to achieve the desired effect and/or you experience a decreased effect with continued use of the same amount (tolerance).
____	____	8. You often take the drug to relieve or avoid withdrawal symptoms.

Source: Adapted from the American Psychiatric Association (2013).

from cirrhosis of the liver or chronic diseases associated with poor living conditions. Women who abuse alcohol while pregnant run the risk of giving birth to babies with fetal alcohol syndrome. This condition is characterized by malformations of the head and brain abnormalities and is accompanied by intellectual disabilities (see Chapter 4). Alcohol facilitates the actions of the neurotransmitter GABA, which inhibits neuronal transmission in the brain (Korpi, 1994), and blocks glutamate, which excites neuronal transmission in the brain. Given that the typical person metabolizes about one ounce of alcohol an hour, a person who drinks faster than that will become intoxicated. Men, due to their greater muscle mass and lower proportion of body fat, metabolize alcohol more efficiently than women do, so a woman might become intoxicated on less alcohol than it would take to intoxicate a man (Mumenthaler, Taylor, O'Hara, & Yesavage, 1999).

You probably have seen shy people become the life of the party, proper people become sexually indiscreet, or mild people become verbally or physically aggressive after a few drinks. Intoxicated men are less able to determine when sexual advances are unwelcome, perhaps contributing to the incidence of "acquaintance rape" (Marx, Gross, & Adams, 1999). One 15-month longitudinal study of men entering alcoholism and domestic violence treatment programs found that their wives and partners were significantly more likely to be physically assaulted on the days that the men drank (Fals-Stewart, 2003). And alcohol has been implicated in verbal and physical aggression among female and male heterosexual college students involved in abusive dating relationships (Shook et al., 2000). But the demonstration of an association between drinking alcohol and engaging in violence does not necessarily indicate a causal relationship between the two. Perhaps people who drink alcohol are more likely to be around other people, making aggressive encounters more likely. Or perhaps people who tend to be aggressive may prefer to drink more alcohol than do people who are not aggressive.

TABLE 6-3 Psychoactive Drugs and Their Effects on the Brain

Category	Drugs	Effects on the Brain	Sites of Action in Brain
Depressants	Alcohol (low doses inhibit anxiety; high doses produce sedation)	Removes social inhibitions Relieves anxiety Induces sleep Impairs judgment Causes disorientation and lack of coordination	Blocks glutamate receptors and facilitates GABA receptors
	Barbiturates	Remove social inhibitions Relieve anxiety Induce sleep Impair judgment Cause disorientation	Facilitates GABA
	Inhalants	Create detachment from immediate environment Cause disorientation	Blocks glutamate
	Opiates	Induce feelings of euphoria Relieve pain Induce sleep	Stimulates opiate receptors
Stimulants	Caffeine	Stimulates alertness Promotes wakefulness	Blocks adenosine receptors
	Nicotine	Stimulates alertness Relieves anxiety	Stimulates acetylcholine receptors
	Amphetamine and methamphetamine	Stimulate alertness Promote wakefulness and insomnia Create an overblown sense of confidence Induce feelings of elation Can cause symptoms of paranoia	Stimulates release of dopamine and norepinephrine
	Cocaine	Induces feelings of euphoria Creates an overblown sense of confidence	Blocks reuptake of dopamine and thus increases dopamine in the brain
Other Psychoactive Drugs	LSD	Causes visual hallucinations Creates a sense of oneness and timelessness Induces seemingly mystical insights	Stimulates serotonin receptors
	Marijuana	Induces relaxation Removes social inhibitions Intensifies sensory experience Interferes with memory formation	Stimulates cannabinoid receptors
	Entactogens or empathogens (MDE, MDMA)	Induces relaxation Induces positive mood Creates a sense of interpersonal closeness Enhances emotional sensitivity and feelings Alters perceptions of the time and physical environment	Stimulates release of serotonin

Evidence of a causal relationship between alcohol and aggression comes from experimental rather than correlational research. For example, experiments indicate that participants are, in fact, more likely to be aggressive after drinking alcohol than after drinking a placebo that merely tastes like alcohol (Dougherty, Cherek, & Bennett, 1996). Aside from alcohol's power to make people less inhibited by its direct effects on the brain, psychologists have identified other factors that account for alcohol's ability to weaken our inhibitions and increase risk-taking behavior. Alcohol researcher Claude Steele points to "alcohol myopia"—the inability of intoxicated people to foresee the negative consequences of their actions—as one reason why they will fail to inhibit undesirable behaviors (Steele & Josephs, 1990). For example, when college men are intoxicated, they report a greater willingness to engage in sexual intercourse without wearing condoms (MacDonald, MacDonald, Zanna, & Fong, 2000). Other researchers have found that because we are aware of alcohol's reputation for removing social inhibitions, we also might use it as an excuse for engaging in questionable behavior (Hull & Bond, 1986). This use is known as *self-handicapping* (see Chapter 14). If we can attribute our silliness, sexuality, or aggression to alcohol, we might feel less guilt and embarrassment for our actions when we sober up.

Barbiturates

Barbiturates are derived from barbituric acid. They produce effects similar to those of alcohol and likewise work by facilitating the actions of GABA (Yu & Ho, 1990). The barbiturate Seconal, which acts quickly to induce drowsiness, is used as a sleeping pill. The barbiturate Pentothal is used as a general anesthetic in surgery. Because mild doses of Pentothal induce a drunken, uninhibited state in which the intoxicated person is more willing to reveal private thoughts and feelings, it is popularly known as "truth serum," though it does not guarantee that the information revealed will be true.

barbiturates Depressants used to induce sleep or anesthesia.

opiates Depressants, derived from opium, used to relieve pain or to induce a euphoric state of consciousness.

Opiates

The opium poppy is the source of **opiates,** which include opium, morphine, heroin, and codeine. The opiates have been prized since ancient times for their ability to relieve pain and to induce euphoria. Sumerian clay tablets from about 4000 B.C. refer to the opium poppy as "the plant of joy" (Whitlock, 1987). Some 19th-century artists and writers used opiates to induce altered states of consciousness. Samuel Taylor Coleridge wrote his famous poem "Kubla Khan" under the influence of opium.

In the early 1860s, physicians used *morphine,* the main active ingredient in opium, to ease the pain of wounded soldiers in the American Civil War. Morphine was named after Morpheus, the Greek god of dreams, because it induces a state of blissful oblivion. In 1898 scientists used opium to derive a more potent drug—*heroin.* Heroin was named after the Greek god Hero because it was welcomed as a powerful painkiller and cure for morphine addiction. But physicians soon found that heroin simply replaced morphine addiction with heroin addiction. By the early 20th century, so many Americans had become addicted to opiates that in 1914 Congress passed the Harrison Narcotic Act banning their nonmedical use. Today, morphine, codeine, and the synthetic opiate Demerol are routinely prescribed to relieve severe pain. The euphoric and pain-relieving effects of the opiates are caused by their binding to endorphin receptors, which act to block pain impulses and stimulate the brain's pleasure centers (Levinthal, 1988).

Opium Poppy

Opium is extracted from the seed pods of the the plant opium poppy.
Source: ljansempoi/Shutterstock.com.

Stimulants

Whereas depressants reduce arousal, stimulants increase it. **Stimulants** include *caffeine, nicotine, amphetamines, methylphenidate,* and *cocaine.*

stimulants Psychoactive drugs that increase central nervous system activity.

Caffeine

Few of us go a day without ingesting the addictive drug **caffeine,** which is found in a variety of products, including coffee, tea, soft drinks, chocolate, cold pills, diet pills, energy drinks, and stimulant tablets. The mind-altering effects of caffeine have made it a popular drug for centuries. Chocolate, for example, was considered a gift from the gods by the Aztecs of Mexico, who drank cocoa during their religious rituals. In the late 19th century,

caffeine A stimulant used to increase mental alertness.

Coffea, the Source of Caffeine

Coffee is made from the seeds of the flowering plant, coffea.

Source: S_Photo/Shutterstock. com.

nicotine A stimulant used to regulate physical and cognitive arousal.

Tobacco

Many products containing nicotine are made from dried tobacco leaves.

Source: PunyaFamily/ Shutterstock.com

amphetamines Stimulants used to maintain alertness and wakefulness.

Americans' use of coffee accelerated after the introduction of the first commercial mix of coffee beans at a Nashville hotel called Maxwell House (Ray, 1983).

Today, caffeine is a popular means of maintaining cognitive alertness, apparently by stimulating the release of the excitatory neurotransmitter glutamate (Silinsky, 1989) and blocking the neurotransmitter adenosine. Caffeine reduces fatigue, improves attention, and facilitates information processing (Lorist & Tops, 2003). Unfortunately, caffeine's ability to enhance physiological arousal can interfere with nightly sleep, even if the coffee is ingested only early in the day (Landolt, Werth, Borbely, & Dijk, 1995). Because of its ability to increase alertness, caffeine is beneficial to night-shift workers. In one study, workers received either caffeinated or decaffeinated coffee for several nights during a simulated 8.5-hour night shift. The results showed that the caffeine group had decreased sleepiness and enhanced performance on an assembly-line task (Muehlbach & Walsh, 1995). If you are a habitual caffeine user and suddenly stop using it, you will find that caffeine withdrawal is marked by headaches and drowsiness (Hughes et al., 1991).

Nicotine

"If you can't send money, send tobacco" read a 1776 appeal from General George Washington (Ray, 1983). Washington's troops actually craved **nicotine,** a powerful addictive drug contained in tobacco. Nicotine works by stimulating certain acetylcholine receptors, which might increase the efficiency of information processing in the brain (Pritchard et al., 1995), a point not lost on students who smoke. And many smokers rely on nicotine to reduce anxiety (Kassel & Unrod, 2000). The World Health Organization estimates that 50% of smokers begin using this drug during adolescence. Adults who continue to smoke are at risk of experiencing smoking-related death or illness. Nicotine in combination with the other substances found in cigarettes can cause cancers of the lung, mouth, throat, and esophagus. Recently, there has been a rise in the use of "electronic" or e-cigarettes. These smokeless cigarettes vaporize the nicotine with a battery-powered device. There currently is a legislative debate about the regulation of their use; moreover, there is no scientific evidence of their safety or efficacy. They are being marketed as a smoking cessation tool; however, health professionals are advising instead the use of traditional nicotine replacement such as transdermal patches.

In regard to its addictiveness, nicotine is comparable to the addictiveness of cocaine, heroin, and alcohol (Stolerman & Jarvis, 1995) and has been attributed to more deaths than the so called "hard drugs." But why is it that some people get quickly addicted to nicotine, others smoke only occasionally, and still others avoid it totally? There seems to be a genetic basis for this variability. The more responsive users are to nicotine, the more quickly they develop tolerance and become dependent on it (Pomerleau, 1995). And nicotine is associated with intense withdrawal symptoms, which also may impair cognitive performance (Giannakoulas, Katramados, Melas, Diamantopoulos, & Chimonas, 2003). You can read more about the effects, treatment, and prevention of smoking in Chapter 16.

Amphetamines

Amphetamines—including Benzedrine, Dexedrine, and Methedrine—are addictive synthetic stimulants that are popularly known as "speed" and are more powerful than caffeine and nicotine. They exert their effects by stimulating the release of dopamine and norepinephrine and inhibiting their reuptake by the neurons that secrete them. In the 1930s, truck drivers discovered that amphetamines would keep them alert during long hauls, letting them drive for many hours without sleeping. For several decades, college students have used amphetamines to stay awake while cramming for final exams. Amphetamines even were used during Operation Desert Storm by the U.S. Air Force Tactical Air Command to stay alert during the Persian Gulf War against Iraq (Emonson & Vanderbeek, 1995). Because amphetamines also suppress appetite and increase the basal metabolic rate, they are commonly used as diet pills. But people who ingest high doses of amphetamines may develop symptoms of schizophrenia, including delusions, hallucinations, and thought disorders (Adeyemo, 2002). Methamphetamines are more potent forms of amphetamine and therefore have one of the highest potentials for abuse. These drugs damage dopamine neurons (Ares-Santos, Granado, & Moratalla, 2013) and serotonin neurons and cause the death of brain cells (Cadet, Jayanthi, & Deng, 2005).

Cocaine

During the 1980s, **cocaine,** an extract from the coca leaf, became the stimulant of choice for people who desired the brief but intense feeling of exhilaration and self-confidence that it induces. Cocaine prevents the reuptake of dopamine and norepinephrine by the neurons that secrete them (Gawin, 1991) and by facilitating activity at serotonin synapses (Aronson, Black, McDougle, & Scanley, 1995). Users snort or sniff cocaine in powdered form, smoke it in crystal form ("crack"), or inject it in solution form. The most common form of abuse is through sniffing, which allows the cocaine to come into contact with the nasal mucosa. This delivers the drug to the brain very rapidly.

People of the Andes have chewed coca leaves for more than a thousand years to induce euphoric feelings and to combat fatigue. In the 19th century, Sir Arthur Conan Doyle made his fictional character Sherlock Holmes a cocaine user. And Robert Louis Stevenson relied on cocaine to stay alert while taking just 6 days to write two drafts of *The Strange Case of Dr. Jekyll and Mr. Hyde.* In 1886 an Atlanta druggist named John Pemberton contributed to cocaine's popularity by introducing a stimulant soft drink that contained both caffeine and cocaine, which he named Coca-Cola.

Unfortunately, cocaine causes harmful side effects, as discovered by Sigmund Freud, who used it himself in part to help him function more efficiently (Karmel, 2003). In the 1880s, Freud praised cocaine as a wonder drug for combating depression, inducing local anesthesia, relieving asthmatic symptoms, and curing opiate addiction. But Freud stopped using and prescribing cocaine after discovering its ability to cause addiction, paranoia, and hallucinations (Freud, 1974). In the early 20th century, the dangers of cocaine use also led to its removal as an ingredient in Coca-Cola. Cocaine can stimulate the heart (Foltin, Fischman, & Levin, 1995), which may account for instances of sudden death in persons with cardiac dysfunctions.

cocaine A stimulant used to induce cognitive alertness and euphoria.

The Source of Cocaine

Extraction of cocaine from the coca plant requires many chemicals.
Source: Dr. Morley Read/ Shutterstock.com.

Other Psychoactive Drugs

Hallucinogens

The **hallucinogens** induce extreme alterations in consciousness. Users might experience visual hallucinations, a sense of timelessness, and feelings of depersonalization. It has been difficult to determine whether adverse personality changes associated with hallucinogens are caused mainly by the powerful effects of the drugs or by the tendency of people with psychological instability to use them (Strassman, 1984). The hallucinogens can induce psychological dependence, but there is little evidence that they can induce physical dependence. They exert their effects primarily by affecting serotonin neurons, stimulating some and inhibiting others (Glennon, 1990). The most commonly used hallucinogens include *psilocybin,* a chemical present in certain mushrooms, *mescaline,* a chemical in the peyote cactus, and *phencyclidine,* a synthetic drug better known as "PCP" or "angel dust." But perhaps the best-known hallucinogen is lysergic acid diethylamide (LSD).

hallucinogens Psychoactive drugs that induce extreme alterations in consciousness, including visual hallucinations, a sense of timelessness, and feelings of depersonalization.

LSD

On April 19, 1943, Albert Hofmann, director of research for the Sandoz drug company in Switzerland, accidentally experienced the effects of a microscopic amount of the chemical lysergic acid diethylamide (**LSD**). He evidently absorbed it through his skin. Hofmann reported that he felt as though he was losing his mind: "in a twilight state with my eyes closed . . . I found a continuous stream of fantastic images of extraordinary vividness and intensive kaleidoscopic colours" (Julien, 1981, p. 151). Hofmann found it a horrifying experience. Because many people in the 1960s and 1970s used LSD recklessly, Hofmann (1983) titled his autobiography *LSD: My Problem Child.*

LSD seems to exert its effects by affecting brain receptors for serotonin, most likely by inhibiting their activity (Aghajanian, 1994). A dose of LSD induces a "trip" that lasts up to 12 hours. The trip includes visual hallucinations, such as shifting patterns of colors, changes in the shapes of objects, and distortions in the sizes of body parts. Many people

LSD A hallucinogen derived from a fungus that grows on rye grain.

synesthesia The process in which an individual experiences sensations in one sensory modality that are characteristic of another.

who use LSD believe that it provides them with personal and philosophical insights and extreme perceptual changes (Prepeliczay, 2002). Even **synesthesia** is possible. This phenomenon occurs when stimulation of sensory receptors triggers sensory experiences that characterize another sense (Cytowic, 1989). Thus, someone listening to music while on an LSD trip might report seeing the notes as different colors. Users of LSD might also report a sense of timelessness, a feeling of oneness with the universe, and at times, mystical insights into the meaning of life. Nonetheless, mystical experiences induced by LSD are different from those induced by nondrug means (Smith & Tart, 1998).

The effects of LSD are so powerful that users can have "bad trips," in which the alteration in their consciousness is so disturbing that it induces feelings of panic (Miller & Gold, 1994). People who are more likely to have a bad trip are those who have unstable personalities, who are not told what to expect, or who are in stressful circumstances (McWilliams & Tuttle, 1973). LSD users also may report flashbacks (or *hallucinogen persisting perception disorder*), in which aspects of the trip are experienced long after the immediate effects of the drug have worn off (Lerner et al., 2002). Hofmann (1983), appalled by the indiscriminate use of LSD and the psychological harm it might do, questioned whether the human mind should be subjected to such extreme alteration. After all, the brain evolved to help us function by letting us perceive reality in a particular way, unaffected by hallucinogens like LSD.

Marijuana

tetrahydrocannabinol (THC) The psychoactive ingredient found in the cannabis sativa plant.

The most widely abused psychoactive drug is marijuana. Its active ingredient is **tetrahydrocannabinol (THC)**, present in the hemp plant *Cannabis sativa*. People smoke marijuana and potent hashish (another product from the plant) to induce an altered state of consciousness. Marijuana is a combination of the crushed stems, leaves, and flowers of the plant, and hashish is its dried resin. Marijuana and hashish exert their effects by stimulating THC receptors in the brain (Herkenhahn, Lynn, deCosta, & Richfield, 1991).

Marijuana has been used for thousands of years as a painkiller; the earliest reference to that use is in a Chinese herbal medicine book from 2737 B.C. (Julien, 1981). Marijuana relieves pain, inhibits vomiting, stimulates appetite (especially highly palatable foods), and reduces fluid pressure in the eye related to glaucoma (Nahas et al., 2002). Today most marijuana smokers use it for its mind-altering effects, which are related to its concentration of THC. Cancer patients use marijuana to reduce nausea produced by chemotherapy drugs. Moderately potent marijuana makes time seem to pass more slowly and induces rich sensory experiences in which music seems fuller and colors seem more vivid. Highly potent marijuana can induce visual hallucinations in which objects may appear to change their size and shape.

In 1937, after centuries of unregulated use, marijuana was outlawed in the United States because of claims that it induced bouts of wild sexual and aggressive behavior. Contrary to its popularity as an alleged aphrodisiac, marijuana at best causes disinhibition of the sex drive, which itself might be a placebo effect caused by its reputation as an aphrodisiac (Powell & Fuller, 1983). Moreover, marijuana does not promote aggression and might even inhibit it (Myerscough & Taylor, 1985). Today, while still illegal and considered a Schedule 1 drug at the federal level, some states have supported the regulated use of marijuana. This is highly controversial, and regulations for its use vary state by state.

Nevertheless, it would be unwise to drive or to operate machinery while under the influence of marijuana—or any other psychoactive drug. This is because marijuana impairs coordination (Navarro, Fernandex-Ruiz, de Miguel, & Hernandez, 1993) and the ability to concentrate on tasks without being distracted (Solowij, Michie, & Fox, 1995). And marijuana can disrupt memory formation by reducing acetylcholine levels in the hippocampus (Nava, Carta, Colombo, & Gessa, 2001). In fact, a review of high-quality research studies on the negative effects of marijuana found that the only consistently supported negative finding is that marijuana inhibits the formation of new long-term memories (Grant, Gonzalez, Carey, Natarajan, & Wolfson, 2003). Marijuana smokers also may exhibit amotivational syndrome (Cherek, Lane, & Dougherty, 2002), in which they prefer doing nothing rather than working or studying. But this finding raises the issue

Cannabis Sativa

The dried flowers and surrounding leaves of the *cannabis sativa* plant is the most widely consumed form of marijuana.

Source: RomboStudio/ Shutterstock.com.

of causation versus correlation. That is, though marijuana smoking might produce the syndrome, it is just as logical to assume that unmotivated people are drawn to marijuana.

Entactogens

The **entactogens,** also known as empathogens, are a new category of psychoactive drugs that have unique effects intermediate to those associated with hallucinogens and stimulants and produce distinct social and emotional effects. Drugs in this category include *methylenedioxyethylamphetamine* (*MDE* or "Eve") and *methylenedioxymethamphetamine* (*MDMA* or "Ecstasy").

entactogens A new category of psychoactive drugs that have unique effects intermediate to those associated with hallucinogens and stimulants.

The unique effects of the entactogen substance group were investigated in a study comparing doses of MDE, psilocybin, and methamphetamine in three groups of volunteer participants (Gouzoulis-Mayfrank et al., 1999). Participants who ingested MDE reported a sense of contentment, relaxation, peacefulness, and interpersonal closeness. In addition, some stimulant and hallucinogenic effects were observed as well—though the hallucinations were weaker than those reported by the participants in the psilocybin group. Similar effects have been reported by participants who receive a single dose of MDMA. These effects include a feeling of closeness with others, altered perceptions, enhanced mood and well-being, and increased emotional sensitivity (Vollenweider, Gamma, Liechti, & Huber, 1998). Though the two drugs are metabolized differently and have slightly different effects (Kovar, 1998), they appear to promote the release of the neurotransmitters dopamine, serotonin, norepinephrine, and acetylcholine. The euphoric effects of MDMA are associated with its stimulation of dopamine neurons, and its hallucinatory effects are associated with its stimulation of serotonin neurons (Liechti & Vollenweider, 2001).

The side effects of MDE and MDMA are difficult to assess. The results of animal studies indicate that serotonin levels are disrupted, and damage to the hippocampus and areas of the cortex are observed (Boot, McGregor, & Hall, 2000). Researchers who assess the effects on people conduct two types of studies: the effects of a single dose on nonusers and the cumulative effects of the drugs on long-term users. Not surprisingly, human studies of long-term use indicate more serious side effects, typically memory impairment (Verbaten, 2003). But because MDMA use is commonly associated with the use of marijuana—which impairs memory—it is impossible to determine the relative influence of MDMA and marijuana on the memory deficits displayed by MDMA users (Gouzoulois-Mayfrank, Becker, Pelz, Tuchtenhagen, & Daumann, 2002).

Entactogens have become known as "club drugs" because their use is common among young adults who attend raves and other social activities associated with polydrug use. Three surveys of users in Europe and Australia conclude that the side effects reported by users may be due to these confounding variables (Hammersley, Ditton, Smith, & Short, 1999; Pedersen & Skrondal, 1999; Topp, Hando, Dillon, Roche, & Solowij, 1999). What is certain, though, is that tolerance to these drugs develops rapidly (Boot, McGregor, & Hall, 2000).

Section Review: Psychoactive Drugs

1. What are the symptoms of physical dependency on drugs?

2. What are the effects and side effects of cocaine?

3. What are the effects and side effects of marijuana?

4. What are the effects and side effects of entactogens?

A Personal Study of Sleep and Dreams

Much of this chapter was devoted to a discussion of sleep and dreams. As noted earlier, formal scientific interest in the nature of sleep and dreams goes back to the 1890s, when Mary Whiton Calkins (1893) conducted her classic study. In this exercise you will record data about your sleep and dreams, analyze it statistically, and discuss it in the context of what you learned from reading this chapter. The student participants should agree on hypotheses about what they will find.

Method
Participants
The participants will be students from your introductory psychology course. The more who participate, the more secure you will be in drawing conclusions from your findings. But, as stressed in the discussion of research ethics in Chapter 2, participation must be voluntary, and any personal data must be kept strictly confidential.

Materials
All participants will maintain an anonymous daily sleep and dream diary on a one-page form created by the student participants. The form should include spaces for identifying the participant's sex, time of sleep onset, time of awakening in the morning, total amount of nightly sleep, number of awakenings during the night, any nap periods, and number of dreams recalled in part or whole. The form also should include spaces for recording responses to the following:

1. Was the dream about the previous day? How many of the dreams were?

2. Was the dream about a personal problem or conflict? How many of the dreams were?

3. How many men and how many women were in the dream?

4. Did the dream seem to incorporate any external stimuli?

If other aspects of sleep and dreams interest the participants, feel free to add them to the daily recording form.

Procedure
The participants will record their data for 7 days. On awakening in the morning, they should record their data on a separate form. To avoid influencing each other, participants should avoid discussing their sleep and dreams during the 7 days of the study.

Results
Each participant should calculate her or his mean for aspects of the data that are of interest to the participants, including the average length of nightly sleep, number of nightly awakenings, and number of dreams. The data from all the participants should be pooled, and group means for their data should be calculated. Group means should be used to create a graph showing both the average hours of sleep and the average number of dreams each night. (See Chapter 2 and Appendix C—available in the Online Edition.) Also use the data to calculate means for all the men and all the women.

Discussion
Discuss whether your results agree with your hypotheses. Do the results support what you read in the chapter, such as Calkins's (1893) findings from her classic research study? Do the results support any of the theories discussed in the chapter? Were there any differences between men and women? Are there any other conclusions that can be reached from the data?

As a researcher, you should also note any shortcomings of the study and things you would change to improve it. Finally, you should suggest a research study that would be a logical offshoot of this study.

Chapter Summary

The Nature of Consciousness

- Consciousness is the awareness of one's own cognitive activity.
- William James noted that consciousness is personal, selective, continuous, and changing.
- The selectivity of consciousness is the basis of research on attention.

- Perception without awareness is the unconscious perception of stimuli that exceed the absolute threshold but fall outside our focus of attention.
- We might experience perception without awareness whenever we use automatic rather than controlled processing of information.

- The Freudian unconscious is a portion of the mind containing thoughts and feelings that influence us without our awareness.
- Subliminal psychodynamic activation provides a means of scientifically studying the Freudian unconscious.

Sleep

- The sleep-wake cycle follows a circadian rhythm.
- The pineal gland and the suprachiasmatic nucleus help regulate circadian rhythms.
- The depth of sleep is defined by characteristic brain-wave patterns.
- REM sleep is associated with dreaming.
- Our nightly sleep duration and the percentage of time we spend in REM sleep decrease across the life span.
- The functions of sleep are still unclear. One theory views sleep as restorative.
- A second theory views it as adaptive inactivity, either because it protects us from danger when we are most vulnerable or because it conserves energy.
- The major sleep disorders include insomnia, sleep apnea, and narcolepsy.

Dreams

- Though we might fail to recall our dreams, everyone dreams.
- Most dreams deal with familiar people and situations.
- REM sleep can be disturbed by nightmares; NREM sleep can be disturbed by night terrors.
- In some cases we might incorporate into our dreams stimuli from the immediate environment.
- The major theories of dreaming view it as wish fulfillment, as problem solving, as an aid to memory, or as a by-product of spontaneous brain activity.

Hypnosis

- Hypnosis is a state in which one person responds to suggestions by another person for alterations in perception, thinking, feeling, and behavior.

- Hypnosis had its origin in mesmerism, a technique promoted by Franz Anton Mesmer to restore the balance of what he called animal magnetism.
- Hypnotic induction aims at the creation of a relaxed, passive, highly focused state of mind.
- Hypnosis may be useful in treating pain.
- Under certain conditions, hypnotized people—like nonhypnotized people—might obey suggestions to perform dangerous acts.
- The effects of stage hypnosis might result as much from the theatrical atmosphere as from being hypnotized.
- Researchers debate whether hypnosis is an altered state of consciousness or merely role playing.
- Ernest Hilgard put forth the concept of the hidden observer to support his neodissociation theory of hypnosis as an altered state.
- Neodissociation theory was challenged by Nicholas Spanos and his colleagues, who believe that hypnosis is a kind of role playing.

Psychoactive Drugs

- Psychoactive drugs induce changes in mood, thinking, perception, and behavior by affecting neuronal activity.
- Depressants reduce arousal by inhibiting activity in the central nervous system.
- The main depressants are alcohol, barbiturates, and opiates.
- Stimulants, which increase arousal, include caffeine, nicotine, amphetamines, methamphetamine, and cocaine.
- Hallucinogens induce extreme alterations in consciousness, including hallucinations, a sense of timelessness, and feelings of depersonalization.
- The main hallucinogens are psilocybin, mescaline, phencyclidine, LSD, and marijuana.
- Entactogens induce altered perceptions, a sense of well-being, and closeness with others.
- Common entactogens include MDE and MDMA.

Key Terms

Psychoactive Drugs

amphetamines (p. 228)
barbiturates (p. 227)
caffeine (p. 227)
Tetrahydrocannabinol (THC) (p. 230)
cocaine (p. 229)

depressants (p. 224)
entactogens (p. 231)
ethyl alcohol (ethanol) (p. 224)
hallucinogens (p. 229)
LSD (p. 229)

nicotine (p. 228)
opiates (p. 227)
psychoactive drugs (p. 224)
stimulants (p. 227)
synesthesia (p. 230)

Chapter Quiz

Note: Answers for the Chapter Quiz questions are provided at the end of the book.

1. Heroin's original purpose was to
   a. cure morphine addiction.
   b. help people overcome insomnia.
   c. induce mystical states of consciousness.
   d. enable truck drivers to make long hauls without sleeping.

2. The "cocktail party phenomenon" inspired research on
   a. attention.
   b. stage hypnosis.
   c. alcohol effects.
   d. biological rhythms.

3. Research has found that shift workers perform best when they move from the night shift to the day shift to the swing shift. In regard to biological rhythms, this is an example of phase
   a. delay.
   b. advance.
   c. inversion.
   d. acceleration.

4. Delta brain waves are most characteristic of
   a. stage 1 sleep.
   b. stage 2 sleep.
   c. stage 3 sleep.
   d. REM sleep.

5. Between infancy and adulthood, the percentage of a night's sleep spent in REM sleep
   a. decreases.
   b. increases.
   c. stays the same.
   d. increases and decreases unpredictably.

6. William James noted that the main qualities of consciousness are that it is changing, personal, selective, and
   a. cosmic.
   b. vestigial.
   c. continuous.
   d. superficial.

7. You would be most likely to be interrupted in the middle of a dream if you were awakened by a phone call
   a. shortly after falling asleep.
   b. in the middle of a night's sleep.
   c. just before you would wake up.
   d. about a half hour after falling asleep.

8. If you are experiencing a night terror, you are most likely to be in
   a. REM sleep.
   b. stage 1 sleep.
   c. stage 2 sleep.
   d. stage 4 sleep.

9. The term "animal magnetism" had its origin in
   a. mesmerism.
   b. neodissociation theory.
   c. transcendental meditation.
   d. research on biological rhythms.

10. The "hidden observer" is related to
    a. astral projection.
    b. hypnosis-induced dissociation.
    c. peyote-evoked hallucinations.
    d. subliminal psychodynamic activation.

11. A person has surgery to remove a brain tumor and experiences disruption of his circadian rhythm. The surgery most likely affected his
    a. thymus gland.
    b. thyroid gland.
    c. adrenal gland.
    d. pineal gland.

12. Research (Hull & Bond, 1986) indicates that people may ingest alcohol because
    a. they are fixated at the oral stage.
    b. we have evolved an inborn liking for the taste of alcohol.
    c. it provides them with an excuse to engage in socially disapproved behaviors.
    d. it acts as a central nervous system stimulant to make them more alert and energetic.

13. A man shows all the symptoms of drunkenness, but has not ingested alcohol. He has mostly likely ingested
    a. LSD.
    b. cocaine.
    c. an amphetamine.
    d. a barbiturate.

14. If you dreamed of flying like a bird, a psychoanalyst might interpret it to mean that you would like to be less socially inhibited. According to Sigmund Freud, the dream of your flying like a bird, itself, would be the
    a. latent content.
    b. abstract content.
    c. concrete content.
    d. manifest content.

15. A person is rushed to an emergency room experiencing hallucinations Given that she is not schizophrenic, she probably is a heavy user of
    a. opiates.
    b. amphetamines.
    c. barbiturates.
    d. marijuana.

16. A person suffering from a "bad trip" probably ingested the drug
    a. cocaine.
    b. amphetamine.
    c. nitrous oxide.
    d. LSD

17. Somnambulism does not occur during REM sleep because
    a. somnambulism is a myth.
    b. dreaming is distracting.
    c. we are blind during REM sleep.
    d. our limbs are paralyzed during REM sleep.

18. A habitual drug user is suffering from an inability to recall classroom and textbook material. He probably has been ingesting
    a. LSD.
    b. cocaine.
    c. marijuana.
    d. phencyclidine.

19. Research on dichotic listening and the Stroop effect most strongly supports
    a. subliminal advertising.
    b. perception without awareness.
    c. subliminal psychodynamic activation.
    d. Freud's notion of the motivated unconscious.

20. The deepest level of sleep tends to occur
    a. just before one normally arises.
    b. during the first half of a night's sleep.
    c. during the second half of a night's sleep.
    d. as much during the first half as during the second half of a night's sleep.

21. The sleep-deprivation experiences of Peter Tripp and Randy Gardner indicated that extended sleep loss
    a. has no apparent effects.
    b. proves that sleep in human beings is merely vestigial.
    c. produces symptoms that disappear after a night's sleep.
    d. induces personality changes that last for weeks afterwards.

22. Paradoxical intention has been used to
    a. help people overcome insomnia.
    b. induce obedience to subliminal messages.
    c. support the "trance" theory of hypnosis.
    d. explain the apparent mystical experiences induced by LSD.

23. The use of unconscious messages to stimulate unconscious fantasies is called
    a hypnagogia.
    b. hypermnesia.
    c. preconscious processing.
    d. subliminal psychodynamic activation.

24. According to activation-synthesis theory, dreams are
    a. wish fulfillments.
    b. prophecies from God.
    c. aids to problem solving.
    d. byproducts of brain activity.

25. An example of hypermnesia would be the use of
    a. hypnosis to have a person recall a phone number.
    b. subliminal perception to affect consumer behavior.
    c. depressant drugs to induce a profound, coma-like state.
    d. hypnosis to help a person forget a traumatic experience.

Thought Questions

1. How does research on people with brain damage support the existence of perception without awareness?

2. Given the nature of our circadian rhythms, why is it easier for people to travel across time zones going from east to west than going from west to east?

3. What evidence is there for the beneficial physical effects of sleep?

4. What would be the difference between Freudian theory and activation-synthesis theory in explaining a sexual dream?

5. How did the experiment by Spanos and Hewitt (1980) demonstrate that hypnosis might be role playing and not an altered state of consciousness?

6. What are the neurotransmitter mechanisms by which cocaine and amphetamines exert their effects?

7

Learning

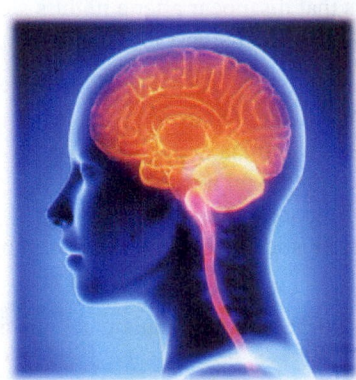

Source: CLIPAREA/Custom media/ Shutterstock.com.

Chapter Outline

Classical Conditioning
Operant Conditioning
Cognitive Learning

Growing up in Utah, Carl Gustavson (1946–1996) learned to love the wolves, coyotes, and other predators that abounded in his home state. Later, after becoming a wildlife psychologist (the application of psychological science to the protection of wildlife), he sought ways to ensure their survival. Coyotes in particular had long drawn the fury—and bullets—of sheep ranchers for their habit of preying on sheep. In 1974 Gustavson began research on psychological methods of fostering the survival of both coyotes and sheep (Gustavson, Garcia, Hawkins, & Rusiniak, 1974). Gustavson took advantage of the coyote's natural aversion to eating things that make it feel nauseous (Garcia & Gustavson, 1997). He inserted lithium chloride, a chemical that causes nausea, into sheep carcasses. When coyotes ate the tainted meat, they became nauseous. Gustavson predicted that the coyotes would associate the nausea with eating sheep and would stop killing them. He hoped this method would provide a happy compromise between ranchers who want to kill coyotes and conservationists who want to save them.

Gustavson began his research program in zoos, using captured coyotes, wolves, and a cougar. To his delight, the animals refused to eat meat from the kind of prey that had been associated with nausea; what psychologists refer to as a conditioned taste aversion was developed. More important, the predators also tended to shy away from the live animals themselves. Wolves and coyotes that had eaten tainted lamb and sheep meat avoided live lambs and sheep. Coyotes that had eaten tainted rabbit meat no longer attacked rabbits.

Other researchers successfully replicated this research using other predators, including hawks and ferrets. In one program, researchers scattered sheep meat laced with lithium chloride on a sheep range in Washington. This action was followed by a significant reduction in the killing of lambs by predators. Following the introduction of a similar program in southern California's Antelope Valley, the number of sheep kills was reduced to zero. The success of the method led to its adoption as the means of choice for controlling predators in Saskatchewan, Canada.

Despite its success in several field settings, Gustavson's method met with opposition from those with vested interests in killing coyotes. These included trappers who kill coyotes for fees and pelts and pilots who take hunters on flights to shoot coyotes from airplanes. Moreover, many sheep ranchers—more concerned with protecting their sheep than with the survival of coyotes—are reluctant to use the technique, preferring instead to simply eradicate the coyotes (Reese, 1986). Thus, a procedure that is scientifically feasible is not always one that will be practical.

Moreover, as is at times the case in scientific research, some researchers failed to replicate Gustavson's findings. For example, insertion of lithium chloride into meat inhibited some predators from eating, but not killing, their prey (Timberlake & Melcer, 1988). In a more recent study, two Alaskan Husky dogs that were given sheep meat laced with lithium chloride shunned sheep meat but still attacked sheep (Hansen, Bakken, & Braastad, 1997).

Regardless of the extent of its practicality and reliability, Gustavson's method illustrates the importance of **learning,** which is a relatively permanent change in knowledge or behavior that results from experience. What you learn is relatively permanent; it can be changed by future experience. This chapter will answer questions about the role of learning in a variety of areas, including these: How can children learn to stop bed-wetting? How can children receiving cancer chemotherapy learn to maintain their appetites? How do animal trainers apply learning principles in their work? How might psychological depression depend on learning?

Do not confuse learning with reflexes, instincts, or maturation. A *reflex* is an inborn, involuntary response to a specific kind of stimulus, such as automatically withdrawing your hand after touching a hot pot. An *instinct* is an inborn complex behavior found in members of a species (such as nest building in birds). And *maturation* is the sequential unfolding of inherited predispositions (such as walking in human infants, see Chapter 4). Moreover, because learning is more flexible, it enables us to adapt to ever-changing circumstances.

Psychologists began the scientific study of learning in the late 19th century. In keeping with Charles Darwin's theory of evolution, they viewed learning as a means of adapting to the environment. Because Darwin stressed the continuity between animals and human beings, psychologists became interested in studying learning in animals, hoping to identify principles that also might apply to human learning (Purdy, Harriman, & Molitorisz, 1993). As you will read, many of the principles of learning do indeed apply to both animals and people.

Psychologists have identified three kinds of learning. *Classical conditioning* considers the learning of associations between stimuli and responses. *Operant conditioning* considers the learning of associations between behaviors and their consequences. *Cognitive learning* considers learning as the acquisition of information.

learning A relatively permanent change in knowledge or behavior resulting from experience.

Classical Conditioning

Classical conditioning grew out of a tradition that can be traced back to Aristotle, who believed that learning depended on contiguity—the occurrence of events close together in time and space (such as lightning and thunder). British philosophers of the 17th and 18th centuries, most notably John Locke and David Hume, became known as associationists because they agreed with Aristotle's view that learning depends on associating contiguous events with one another.

In the early 20th century, the research of Ivan Pavlov (1849–1936) stimulated world-wide scientific interest in the study of *associative learning* (Delamater, 2011), which involves associating contiguous events with each other. Pavlov, a Russian physiologist, won a Nobel Prize in 1904 for his research on digestion in dogs, which attracted the interest of scientists around the world (Windholz & Kuppers, 1990). In his research, Pavlov would place meat powder on a dog's tongue, which stimulated reflexive salivation. He collected the saliva from a tube attached to one of the dog's salivary glands. He found that after repeated presentations of the meat powder, the dog would salivate in response to stimuli (that is, environmental events) associated with the meat powder. A dog would salivate at the sight of its food dish, the sight of the laboratory assistant who brought the food, or the sound of the assistant's footsteps. At first Pavlov was distressed by this phenomenon, which he called "psychic reflexes" or "conditional responses," because he could no longer control the onset of salivation by his dogs. But he eventually became so intrigued by the phenomenon that he devoted the rest of his career to studying it.

Pavlov was not alone in discovering this phenomenon, which was well known to scientists during the 19th century (Logan, 2002). Moreover, at the annual meeting of the American Psychological Association in 1904, the same year that Pavlov received his Nobel Prize, Edwin Twitmyer (1873–1943), an American graduate student at the University of Pennsylvania, reported the results of a study on the "knee jerk" reflex. As you may know from a past physical examination, when a physician strikes you with a rubber hammer on your patellar tendon just below your bent knee, your lower leg reflexively extends. In his study, Twitmyer rang a bell as a warning that the hammer was about to strike. After repeated trials in which the sound of the bell preceded the hammer strike, the sound of the bell alone caused extension of the lower leg (Twitmyer, 1974). But, to his disappointment, Twitmyer's presentation was met with indifference. In fact, William James, who chaired Twitmyer's session, was so bored (or hungry) that he adjourned the session for lunch—without providing the customary opportunity for discussion (Coon, 1982). North American psychologists did not begin to take serious note of this kind of learning until John B. Watson described Pavlov's research in his presidential address at the annual meeting of the American Psychological Association in 1914. Because of Pavlov's extensive early research on "conditional responses," the phenomenon earned the name of classical conditioning.

Principles of Classical Conditioning

As Pavlov first noted, in **classical conditioning** a stimulus comes to elicit (that is, bring about) a response (either an overt behavior or a physiological change) that it does not normally elicit. But how does this occur? It must be acquired.

Acquisition of the Classically Conditioned Response

To demonstrate classical conditioning (see Figure 7-1), you must first identify a stimulus that already elicits a reflexive response. The stimulus is called an **unconditioned stimulus (UCS),** and the response is called an **unconditioned response (UCR).** You then present several trials in which the UCS is preceded by a neutral stimulus—a stimulus that does not normally elicit the UCR. After one or more pairings of the neutral stimulus and the UCS, the neutral stimulus itself elicits the UCR. At that point the neutral stimulus has become a **conditioned stimulus (CS),** and the response to it is called a **conditioned response (CR).** Pavlov used the UCS of meat powder to elicit the UCR of salivation. He then used a tone as the neutral stimulus. After several trials in which the tone preceded the meat powder, the tone itself became a CS that elicited the CR of salivation. But does the CS directly elicit the CR? On the contrary, research indicates that the CS activates a memory trace representing the UCS, which then elicits the CR (Jacobs & Blackburn, 1995).

Higher-Order Conditioning In **higher-order conditioning,** a neutral stimulus can become a CS after being paired with an existing CS. In this case, the existing CS functions like a UCS. If the neutral stimulus precedes the existing CS, it elicits a CR similar to that elicited by the existing CS. Higher-order conditioning explains how neutral stimuli that have not been paired with a biological UCS such as food or other cues in our environment can gain control over our behavior. Higher-order conditioning might explain why music in commercials (such as those advertising fast-food restaurants) can affect our attitudes toward the products presented in the commercials (Blair & Shimp, 1992). The classical conditioning of an emotional response to a product is important in enhancing its appeal to consumers (Kim, Lim, & Bhargava, 1998).

Among the most important conditioned stimuli are words. This phenomenon is known as **semantic conditioning**. In a clever classroom demonstration of this, a college

---

classical conditioning
A form of learning in which a neutral stimulus comes to elicit a response after being associated with a stimulus that already elicits that response.

unconditioned stimulus (UCS)
In classical conditioning, a stimulus that automatically elicits a particular unconditioned response.

unconditioned response (UCR)
In classical conditioning, an unlearned, automatic response to a particular unconditioned stimulus.

conditioned stimulus (CS)
In classical conditioning, a neutral stimulus that comes to elicit a particular conditioned response after being paired with a particular unconditioned stimulus that already elicits that response.

conditioned response (CR)
In classical conditioning, the learned response given to a particular conditioned stimulus.

higher-order conditioning
In classical conditioning, the establishment of a conditioned response to a neutral stimulus that has been paired with an existing conditioned stimulus.

semantic conditioning
In classical conditioning, the use of words as conditioned stimuli.

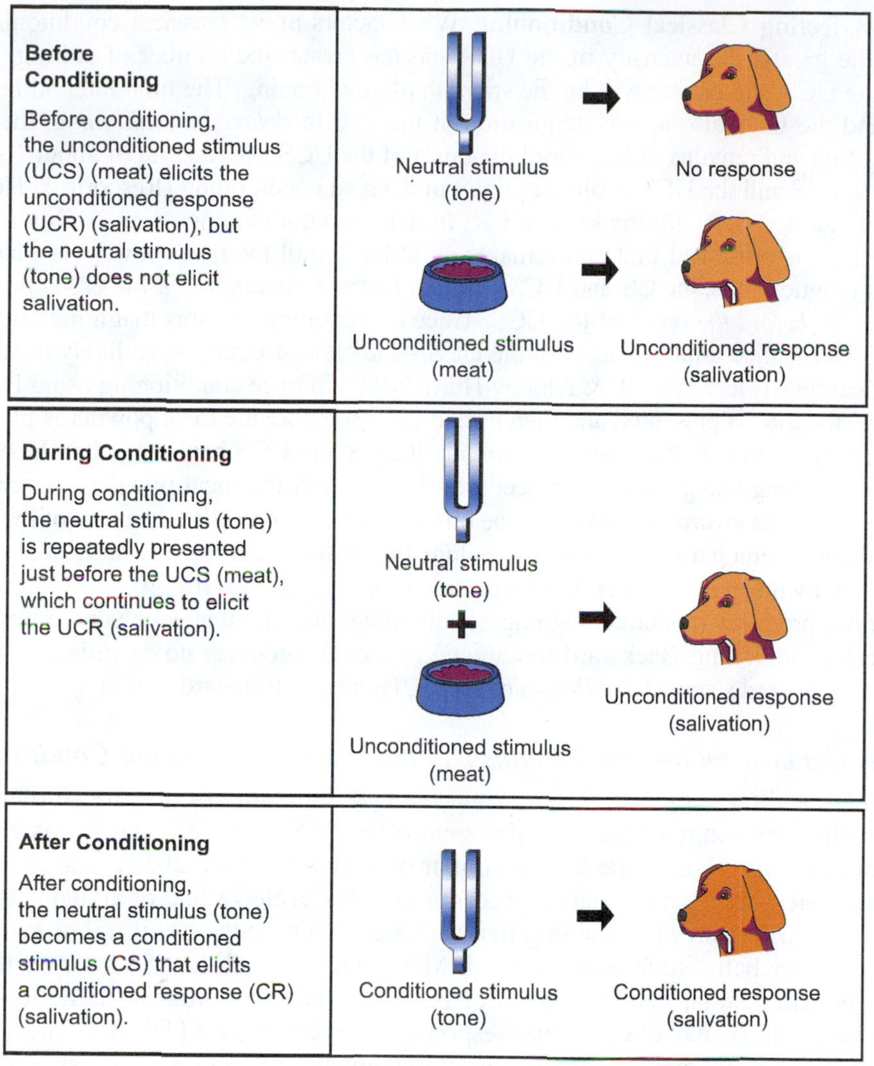

FIGURE 7-1
Classical Conditioning

Before Conditioning Before conditioning, the unconditioned stimulus (UCS) (meat) elicits the unconditioned response (UCR) (salivation), but the neutral stimulus (tone) does not elicit salivation.	Neutral stimulus (tone) → No response Unconditioned stimulus (meat) → Unconditioned response (salivation)
During Conditioning During conditioning, the neutral stimulus (tone) is repeatedly presented just before the UCS (meat), which continues to elicit the UCR (salivation).	Neutral stimulus (tone) + Unconditioned stimulus (meat) → Unconditioned response (salivation)
After Conditioning After conditioning, the neutral stimulus (tone) becomes a conditioned stimulus (CS) that elicits a conditioned response (CR) (salivation).	Conditioned stimulus (tone) → Conditioned response (salivation)

professor used the word *Pavlov* as a neutral stimulus (Cogan & Cogan, 1984). Student participants said "Pavlov" just before lemonade powder was placed on their tongues. The UCS of lemonade powder naturally elicited the UCR of salivation. After repeated pairings of "Pavlov" and the lemonade powder, *Pavlov* became a CS that elicited the CR of salivation. Classical conditioning might account, in part, for the power of words to elicit emotional responses. Perhaps the mere mention of the name of someone with whom you have a romantic relationship makes your heart flutter. Similarly, if someone repeatedly says something, such as "tickle, tickle," before tickling the sole of your foot, you might eventually learn to jerk away your foot as soon as you hear the words "tickle, tickle" (Newman, O'Grady, Ryan, & Hemmes, 1993).

Even bed-wetting, or *nocturnal enuresis,* in childhood can be controlled by classical conditioning. An effective technique, devised more than half a century ago (Mowrer & Mowrer, 1938), uses an electrified mattress pad that consists of a cloth sheet sandwiched between two thin metal sheets. The upper metal sheet contains tiny holes. When a drop of urine penetrates that sheet and soaks through the cloth sheet, the moisture completes an electrical circuit between the two metal sheets. This electrical circuit sets off a battery-powered alarm, which wakes the child, who then goes to the toilet. The alarm serves as a UCS, which elicits awakening as a UCR. After repeated trials, bladder tension, which precedes the alarm, becomes a CS, which then elicits awakening as a CR. The child eventually responds to bladder tension by awakening and going to the toilet instead of urinating in bed. This technique has become one of the most effective methods of treating nocturnal enuresis (Mellon & McGrath, 2000).

Factors Affecting Classical Conditioning What factors affect classical conditioning? In general, the greater the intensity of the UCS and the greater the number of pairings of the CS and the UCS, the greater will be the strength of conditioning. The time interval between the CS and the UCS also affects acquisition of the CR. In *delayed conditioning,* the CS is presented first and remains *at least* until the onset of the UCS. An interval of about 1 second between the CS and the UCS is often optimal in delayed conditioning (Rescorla & Holland, 1982), though it varies with the kind of CR. In delayed conditioning using Pavlov's procedure, the tone is presented first and remains on at least until the meat powder is placed on the dog's tongue. Thus, the CS and UCS overlap. In *trace conditioning,* the CS is presented first and ends *before the onset* of the UCS. Trace conditioning requires that a memory trace of the CS be retained until the onset of the UCS—the brain structure most likely involved is the hippocampus (Flesher, Butt, & Kinney-Hurd, 2011). In trace conditioning using Pavlov's procedure, the tone is presented and then turned off just before the meat powder is placed on the dog's tongue. In *simultaneous conditioning,* the CS and UCS begin together. In simultaneous conditioning using Pavlov's procedure, the tone and the meat powder are presented together. And in *backward conditioning,* the onset of the UCS precedes the onset of the CS. In backward conditioning using Pavlov's procedure, the meat powder is presented first, followed immediately by the tone. In general, delayed conditioning produces strong conditioning, trace conditioning produces moderately strong conditioning, and simultaneous conditioning produces weak conditioning. Backward conditioning generally produces no conditioning, though it sometimes is used successfully (Washio, Hayes, Hunter, & Pritchard, 2011).

Stimulus Generalization and Stimulus Discrimination in Classical Conditioning

In classical conditioning, the CR can occur in response to stimuli that are similar to the CS. This phenomenon is called **stimulus generalization.** A person who learns to fear a particular stimulus might come to fear similar ones (Glenn et al., 2012). For example, a child who undergoes a painful dental procedure might develop a fear of all dentists or the sound of any drill. Likewise, the dog that salivates to a particular bell might eventually salivate to other bells, such as a doorbell. Marketing research has found that, through stimulus generalization, generic brands of products that are similar in name to nationally known products may elicit similar responses from consumers (Till & Priluck, 2000). Thus, a cola soft drink manufactured by a small company may elicit a favorable response from people simply because they are familiar with the more famous national brand colas.

If a child undergoes painless dentistry with other dentists, she will eventually become afraid only of the dentist with whom she associated pain. This example is an instance of **stimulus discrimination,** in which the person or animal responds to the CS but not to stimuli that are similar to the CS. Similarly, the dog might eventually salivate only in response to the dinner bell if it learns that the other bells are not followed by food.

Extinction

In Pavlov's procedure, will a dog conditioned to salivate in response to a dinner bell do so forever? Not necessarily. If a CS is repeatedly presented without the UCS being presented, the CR will diminish and eventually stop occurring. This process is called **extinction.** A dog that has learned to salivate to a dinner bell (the CS) will eventually stop doing so unless presentations of the dinner bell are periodically followed by presentations of food (the UCS). Likewise, an animal that comes to fear a tone after it has been repeatedly followed by an electric shock will eventually stop acting fearful if the tone is repeatedly presented without being followed by the electric shock.

Though extinction inhibits the CR, it does not eliminate it (Bouton & Swartzentruber, 1991). In fact, after a CR has been subjected to extinction, it can reappear if the CS is reintroduced. For example, suppose you produce extinction of the CR of salivation by no longer presenting the dog with food after ringing the dinner bell. If you rang the dinner bell a few days later, the dog might respond again by salivating. This process, by which a CR that has been subjected to extinction will again be elicited by a CS, is called **spontaneous recovery.** In spontaneous recovery, however, the CR is weaker and extinguishes faster than it did originally. Thus, after spontaneous

---

stimulus generalization In classical conditioning, giving a conditioned response to stimuli similar to the conditioned stimulus.

stimulus discrimination In classical conditioning, giving a conditioned response to the conditioned stimulus but not to stimuli similar to it.

extinction
1. In classical conditioning, the gradual disappearance of the conditioned response when the conditioned stimulus is repeatedly presented without being paired with the unconditioned stimulus.

2. In operant conditioning, the gradual disappearance of a response that is no longer followed by a reinforcer.

spontaneous recovery
1. In classical conditioning, the reappearance after a period of time of a conditioned response that has been subjected to extinction.

2. In operant conditioning, the reappearance after a period of time of a behavior that has been subjected to extinction.

recovery the dog's salivation to the dinner bell will be weaker and subject to faster extinction than it was originally. Likewise, consider rats that have been conditioned to fear a tone that has repeatedly preceded an electric shock. If the tone is repeatedly presented without the electric shock, their fear of the tone will extinguish. But if the tone is again presented after a few days, they might exhibit complete spontaneous recovery; that is, they will display the same degree of fear of the tone as they had before extinction (Quirk, 2002). Figure 7-2 illustrates the acquisition, extinction, and spontaneous recovery of a classically conditioned response.

Applications of Classical Conditioning

In his 1932 novel *Brave New World,* Aldous Huxley warned of a future in which classical conditioning would mold people into narrow social roles. In the novel, classical conditioning is used to make children who have been assigned to become workers repulsed by any interests other than work. This repulsion is achieved by giving the children electric shocks (the UCS) in the presence of forbidden objects, such as books or flowers (the CS). Despite such fears of diabolical use, classical conditioning has, in reality, been applied in less ominous and often beneficial ways. Classical conditioning prepares the body for likely events and has been used to explain phobias, drug dependence, and learned taste aversions.

Classical Conditioning and Phobias

More than three centuries ago, John Locke (1690/1956) observed that children who had been punished in school for misbehaving became fearful of their books and other stimuli associated with school. Today we would say these children had been classically conditioned to develop school phobias. A phobia is an unrealistic or exaggerated fear, and a phobia was the subject of a classic research investigation of classical conditioning.

The study was conducted by John B. Watson and his graduate student Rosalie Rayner (Watson & Rayner, 1920). The participant was an 11-month-old boy, Albert B., later known as "Little Albert," who enjoyed playing with animals, including tame white rats. Watson and Rayner hoped to provide scientific evidence for the classical conditioning of emotional responses. This evidence would provide an alternative to the Freudian idea that phobias are symbolic manifestations of unconscious conflicts that arise from early childhood sexual conflicts (see Chapter 14). On several trials, just as Albert touched a white rat, Watson made a loud noise behind Albert's head by banging a steel bar with a hammer. Albert responded to the noise (the UCS) with fear (the UCR). He jumped violently, fell forward, and buried his face. After seven pairings of the rat and the noise (twice on the

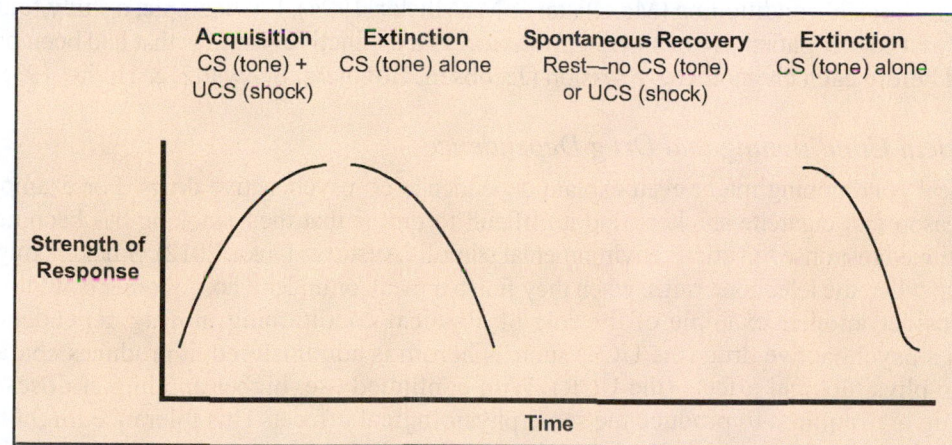

FIGURE 7-2

Processes in Classical Conditioning

During acquisition of the CR, repeatedly presenting the CS just before the UCS strengthens the CR. After acquisition of the CR, if the CS is repeatedly presented without being followed by the UCS, extinction of the CR occurs. Then, following a rest period during which neither the CS nor the UCS is presented, spontaneous recovery of the CR occurs. But extinction immediately takes place again, even more rapidly than the first time.

first day and five times a week later), Albert responded to the rat (the CS) with fear (the CR) by crying and showing distress.

When tested later, Albert showed stimulus generalization. He responded fearfully to other fur-like objects, including a dog, a rabbit, cotton wool, and a sealskin fur coat. Two months later he even showed fear of a Santa Claus mask. He had not shown fear of any of these objects at the age of 9 months. Watson and Rayner hypothesized that pleasurable stimulation paired with a feared object would reduce Albert's phobia. But Albert left the experiment before they had the opportunity to try that technique. As discussed in Chapter 15, Watson's student Mary Cover Jones (1924), who became a prominent psychologist, used it a few years later to relieve a child's animal phobia.

Current ethical standards of psychological research (see Chapter 2) would prevent the experimental induction of phobias in children. Though this study lacked the experimental control necessary for a convincing demonstration of a classically conditioned phobia, it led to sounder research studies demonstrating that fears and phobias can indeed be learned through classical conditioning (McAllister & McAllister, 1994). For example, a study found that breast cancer patients responded with anxiety to a distinctive stimulus that had been presented before each chemotherapy session (Jacobsen, Bovbjerg, Schwartz, & Hudis, 1995).

Classical Conditioning and Drug Dependence

Classical conditioning might even explain dependence on psychoactive drugs. For example, one reason that cigarette smokers find it difficult to quit is that their smoking has become a conditioned response to various environmental stimuli (Austin & Duka, 2012). Smokers might light up when the telephone rings, when they finish a meal, or under a host of other conditions.

Consider another example of the role of classical conditioning in drug dependence. When a psychoactive drug (the UCS) such as heroin is administered, it produces characteristic physiological effects (the UCR). With continued use, higher and higher doses of the drug are required to produce the same physiological effects. This tolerance might be, in part, the product of classical conditioning (Deffner-Rappold, Azorlosa, & Baker, 1996). Stimuli associated with the administration of certain drugs act as conditioned stimuli that elicit conditioned physiological responses opposite to those of the drug. For example, though heroin induces respiratory depression, stimuli associated with its administration induce respiratory excitation. Why would stimuli associated with drug taking elicit effects opposite to those of the drug itself? Perhaps it is an adaptive, compensatory mechanism that prevents the physiological response to the drug from becoming too extreme.

Consider heroin addiction and the phenomenon of tolerance. Tolerance to heroin might occur because stimuli associated with its administration, such as hypodermic needles and particular settings, can act as conditioned stimuli to counter the physiological effects produced by the drug. Tolerance might explain why heroin addicts sometimes die of respiratory failure from an "overdose" after injecting themselves with their normal dose of heroin in a setting different from that in which they normally administer the drug. By doing so, they remove the conditioned stimuli that elicit conditioned physiological responses that normally counter the unconditioned physiological responses elicited by the drug. As a consequence, their conditioned tolerance is reduced. The unconditioned physiological responses, particularly respiratory depression, to a normal dose might be stronger than usual—in some cases strong enough to be fatal (Siegel, Baptista, & Kim, 2000). This notion is supported by work with laboratory animals and often observed in people.

Classical Conditioning and Taste Aversions

Have you ever eaten something, by coincidence contracted a virus several hours later, become nauseated, and later found yourself repulsed by what you had eaten? If so, you have experienced a **conditioned taste aversion**—the classical conditioning of an aversion to a taste that has been associated with a noxious stimulus. The research program of Carl Gustavson that was described at the beginning of the chapter, in which he used classical conditioning to make coyotes nauseated by the taste of sheep meat, was an application of conditioned taste aversion. Research on conditioned taste aversion was prompted by the need to determine the effects of atomic radiation subsequent to the extensive atomic bomb testing of the 1950s. One of the leading researchers in that effort was John Garcia. Garcia and his colleagues exposed rats to radiation in special cages. He found that the rats failed to drink water in the radiation cages, yet drank normally in their own cages. They continued to refrain from drinking in the radiation cages even when they were no longer exposed to radiation in them. Garcia concluded that the plastic water bottles lent a distinctive taste to the water in the radiation cages, which created a conditioned taste aversion after being paired with radiation-induced nausea. Because the water bottles in the rats' own cages were made of glass, the rats did not associate the taste of water from them with nausea (Garcia, Kimeldorf, Hunt, & Davies, 1956).

Garcia also found that conditioned taste aversions could occur even when the animal did not become nauseous until hours after being exposed to the taste. In responding to Garcia's finding that a taste aversion could be learned even when the taste preceded feelings of nausea by hours, psychologists at first were shocked by this apparent violation of contiguity in classical conditioning, and many of them simply dismissed his findings as impossible (Garcia, 1981). How could the taste of food be associated with nausea that occurs hours later? (Tastes do not linger long enough for the contiguity of taste and nausea to be an explanation.) Through the persistence of Garcia and his colleagues, who replicated his findings, the conditioning of a taste aversion using a long interval between the CS and the UCS is now an accepted psychological phenomenon. Moreover, there even is evidence that learned taste aversions are more likely to occur when there is a longer interval between the CS and UCS than when there is a shorter interval. For example, a 30-minute interval is superior to a 10-second interval between presentation of a distinctive taste and presentation of a nausea-inducing chemical in the classical conditioning of an aversion to the taste (Schafe, Sollars, & Bernstein, 1995). One other special attribute of conditioned taste aversion is that it can occur, reliably and powerfully, with single trials or single experiences. If you have no previous experience with a food and then become ill after eating it, you will likely avoid that food in the future.

Had Garcia been less persistent, we might have been denied a potentially useful tool for combating the nausea-induced loss of appetite experienced by cancer patients undergoing chemotherapy. Their loss of appetite makes them eat less and lose weight, weakening them and impairing their ability to fight the disease.

conditioned taste aversion
A taste aversion induced by pairing a taste with gastrointestinal distress.

Can Classical Conditioning Help Maintain the Appetites of Children Undergoing Chemotherapy?

Rationale

Ilene Bernstein (1991), of the University of Washington, has conducted a program of research on taste aversion in chemotherapy patients. In one study, Bernstein (1978) determined whether children receiving chemotherapy would associate a novel taste with the nausea induced by chemotherapy.

Method

Bernstein assigned children receiving chemotherapy to one of three groups. The first group ate "Mapletoff" ice cream, which has a novel maple-walnut flavor, before each chemotherapy session. The second group ate Mapletoff on days when they did not receive chemotherapy. And the third group never ate Mapletoff. From 2 to 4 weeks later, the children were given the choice of eating Mapletoff or playing with a game. Later, at an average of 10 weeks after the first session, the children were asked to select Mapletoff or another novel-tasting ice cream.

Results and Discussion

As illustrated in Figure 7-3, when given the option of playing with a game or eating Mapletoff, 67 percent of the children who never ate Mapletoff and 73 percent of the children who ate it only on days when they did not receive chemotherapy chose Mapletoff. In contrast, only 21 percent of the children who ate Mapletoff on days they received chemotherapy chose Mapletoff. When given the option of choosing Mapletoff or another novel ice cream flavor, only 25 percent of those in the Mapletoff-plus-chemotherapy group chose Mapletoff, while 50 percent of the Mapletoff-only group and 66 percent of the no-Mapletoff group chose it. Thus, children exposed to Mapletoff plus chemotherapy developed a taste aversion to Mapletoff.

Based on these findings, and on findings that taste aversion is stronger in response to novel-tasting foods than to familiar-tasting foods (Kimble, 1981), perhaps cancer patients should be given a novel-tasting food before receiving chemotherapy. This practice might lead them to experience taste aversion in response only to the novel "scapegoat" food instead of to familiar foods, thereby helping them maintain their appetite for familiar, nutritious foods. Bernstein has, in fact, accomplished this conditioning with children receiving chemotherapy by using candies with unusual flavors (such as coconut) as scapegoats (Broberg & Bernstein, 1987).

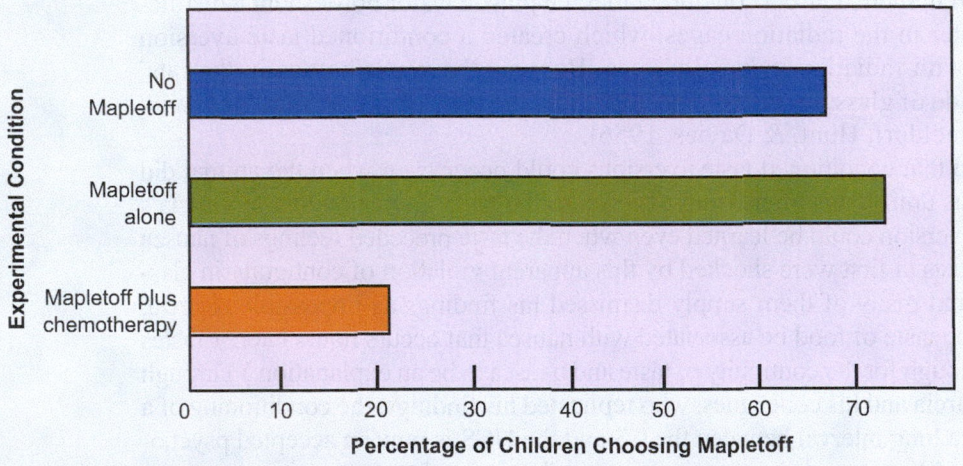

FIGURE 7-3

Chemotherapy and Conditioned Taste Aversion

Ilene Bernstein (1978) found that children undergoing cancer chemotherapy developed conditioned taste aversions to a novel flavor of ice cream (Mapletoff) eaten on the same days that they underwent treatment. The children might have developed the aversion to the flavor because it became associated with the nausea induced by the treatment. As the graph shows, when later given the choice of eating Mapletoff or playing a game, children who had eaten Mapletoff on the days they received treatment were less likely to choose Mapletoff than were children who had never eaten it or who had eaten it on days when they did not receive treatment.

Source: Data from Ilene L. Bernstein, "Learned Taste Aversions in Children Receiving Chemotherapy" in *Science,* 200: 1302–1303, American Association for the Advancement of Science, 1978.

Biological Constraints on Classical Conditioning

According to Ivan Pavlov (1928, p. 88), "Every imaginable phenomenon of the outer world affecting a specific receptive surface of the body may be converted into a conditioned stimulus." Until the past few decades, learning theorists agreed with Pavlov's proclamation. They assumed that any stimulus paired with an unconditioned stimulus could become a conditioned stimulus. But we now know that there are inherited biological constraints, perhaps the product of evolution, on the ease with which particular stimuli can be associated with particular responses. These constraints were demonstrated in an early study that tried to replicate Watson and Rayner's study on conditioned fear by using an opera glass instead of a white rat. The opera glass did not become a fear-inducing conditioned stimulus after being paired with an unconditioned stimulus that induced fear (Valentine, 1930). Nonetheless, as discussed in Chapter 14, some research studies have failed to support the role of biological preparedness in the development of phobias (de Jong & Merckelbach, 1997).

Biological constraints on classical conditioning were demonstrated in a study of classically conditioned taste aversion in which two groups of rats were presented with a CS consisting of three components: saccharin-flavored water, a flash of light, and a clicking sound (Garcia & Koelling, 1966). For one group the CS was followed by a strong electric shock (the UCS) that induced pain (the UCR). For another group the CS was followed by X-rays (the UCS) that induced nausea and dizziness (the UCR). The results indicated that the rats that had been hurt by the electric shock developed an aversion to the light and the click but not to the saccharin-flavored water. In contrast, the rats that had been made to feel ill developed an aversion to the saccharin-flavored water but not to the light and the click. This finding indicates that rats have a tendency, apparently inborn, to associate nausea and dizziness with tastes but not with sights and sounds, and to associate pain with sights and sounds but not with tastes. Thus, not all stimuli and responses are equally associable (Weiss, Panlilio, & Schindler, 1993).

Section Review: Classical Conditioning

1. How would you use classical conditioning to make a pet cat come running at the sound of a can opener?

2. How does Ilene Bernstein suggest using classical conditioning to help chemotherapy patients retain their appetite for nutritious foods by using scapegoat foods?

3. In what way did John Garcia demonstrate biological constraints on classical conditioning?

Operant Conditioning

In the late 1890s, while Russian physiologists were studying the relationship between stimuli and responses, an American psychologist named Edward Thorndike (1874–1949) was studying the relationship between actions and their consequences. While pursuing a doctoral degree at Harvard University, Thorndike studied learning in chicks by rewarding them with food for successfully negotiating a maze constructed of books. After his landlady objected to Thorndike's raising the chicks in his bedroom, William James, one of his professors, agreed to raise the chicks in his basement—much to the delight of the James children (Thorndike, 1961).

Thorndike left Harvard and completed his studies at Columbia University. At Columbia he conducted research using cats in so-called puzzle boxes (Hearst, 1999), which were constructed from wooden Heinz shipping crates (see Figure 7-4). In a typical puzzle box study, Thorndike (1898) put a hungry cat in the box and a piece of fish outside it. A sliding latch kept the door to the box closed. The cat could escape by stepping on a pedal or pulling a string that released the latch. At first the cat performed ineffective actions, such as biting the wooden slats or trying to squeeze between them. Eventually the cat accidentally performed the correct

FIGURE 7-4
Puzzle Boxes

Edward Thorndike, working under a limited budget, used Heinz shipping crates to create puzzle boxes for the conditioning of cats. In this example, the cat is prevented from escaping by panes of glass between the slats.

law of effect Edward Thorndike's principle that a behavior followed by a satisfying state of affairs is strengthened and a behavior followed by an annoying state of affairs is weakened.

instrumental conditioning A form of learning in which a behavior becomes more or less probable, depending on its consequences.

operant conditioning B. F. Skinner's term for instrumental conditioning, a form of learning in which a behavior becomes more or less probable, depending on its consequences.

Skinner box An enclosure that contains a bar or key that can be pressed to obtain food or water and that is used to study operant conditioning in rats, pigeons, or other small animals.

behavioral contingencies Relationships between behaviors and their consequences, such as positive reinforcement, negative reinforcement, extinction, and punishment.

positive reinforcement In operant conditioning, an increase in the probability of a behavior that is followed by a desirable consequence.

action, thereby releasing the latch, opening the door, and gaining access to the fish. Thorndike repeated this experiment for several trials and found that as the trials progressed, the cat took less and less time to escape, eventually escaping as soon as it was placed in the box.

The results of his puzzle box studies led Thorndike to develop the **law of effect**, which states that a behavior followed by a "satisfying" state of affairs is strengthened and a behavior followed by an "annoying" state of affairs is weakened. In the puzzle box experiments, behaviors that let the cat reach the fish were strengthened, and behaviors that kept it in the box were weakened. Because Thorndike studied the process by which behaviors are instrumental in producing certain consequences, the process became known as **instrumental conditioning**.

Principles of Operant Conditioning

Thorndike's work inspired B. F. Skinner (1904–1990), perhaps the best-known psychologist during the decades following World War II. In the 1930s Skinner called instrumental conditioning **operant conditioning**, because animals and people learn to "operate" on the environment to produce desired consequences instead of just responding reflexively (for example, salivation) to stimuli, as in classical conditioning. Following in Thorndike's footsteps, Skinner used chambers, now known as **Skinner boxes** or operant boxes, to study learning in animals—in particular, rats learning to press levers to obtain food pellets and pigeons learning to peck at lighted disks to obtain grain (see Figure 7-5). Skinner devoted his career to studying the relationships between behaviors and their consequences, which he called **behavioral contingencies:** positive reinforcement, negative reinforcement, extinction, and punishment (Lattal, 1995).

Positive Reinforcement

Over two centuries ago, while leading a fort-building expedition, Benjamin Franklin increased the likelihood of attendance at daily prayer meetings by withholding his men's rations of rum until they had prayed (Knapp & Shodahl, 1974). This action showed Franklin's appreciation of the power of reinforcement. A reinforcer is a consequence of a behavior that increases the likelihood that the behavior will occur again. In **positive reinforcement** a behavior (for example, praying) that is followed by the presentation of a desirable stimulus (for example, rum) becomes more likely to occur in the future. Skinner called the desirable stimulus a positive reinforcer. You certainly are aware of the effect of positive reinforcement in your own life. For example, if you find helping your parents or caregivers with household chores earns you their praise, you are more likely to help them in the future. Positive reinforcement has been used to condition bees to make specific antenna movements (Kisch & Erber, 1999) and to make police officers and staff more courteous (Wilson, Boni, & Hogg, 1997). However, what serves as a reinforcer for one person might not for another.

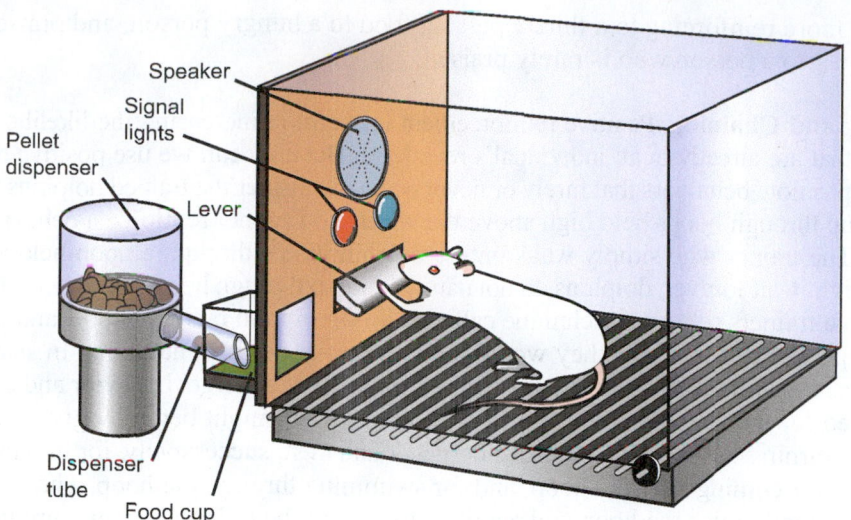

FIGURE 7-5
The Skinner Box

Rats placed in Skinner boxes, now more often referred to as operant boxes, learn to obtain food by pressing a bar, and pigeons placed in Skinner boxes learn to obtain food by pecking a lighted disk.

A handy approach to determining what will be an effective positive reinforcer is provided by the **Premack principle,** named for its discoverer, David Premack. Premack (1965) pointed out that a behavior that has a higher probability of occurrence can be used as a positive reinforcer for a behavior that has a lower probability. Parents use the Premack principle with their children when they make viewing television or using other electronic devices a positive reinforcer for the completion of homework. Even animals are trained using the Premack principle. For example, a study using rats as subjects successfully used wheel running, a higher-probability behavior, as a positive reinforcement for lever pressing, a lower-probability behavior (Iversen, 1993). Keep in mind that according to the Premack principle, something that is reinforcing to one individual might be less so to another (Timberlake & Farmer-Dougan, 1991). Parental praise might be a positive reinforcer to you, yet have little effect on your friend's behavior.

In general, positive reinforcement is strengthened by increasing the magnitude of the reinforcer, decreasing the interval between the behavior and the reinforcer, and increasing the number of pairings of the behavior and the reinforcer. There are two classes of positive reinforcers. A **primary reinforcer** is biological and unlearned, such as oxygen, food, water, and warmth. In contrast, a **secondary reinforcer** (also known as a conditioned reinforcer) is learned and becomes reinforcing by being associated with a primary reinforcer. Secondary reinforcers were demonstrated in a classic study in which chimpanzees could obtain grapes by inserting tokens into a vending machine (Wolfe, 1936). After using tokens to obtain grapes from the "chimp-o-mat," the chimps would steal tokens and hoard them. The tokens had become secondary reinforcers. Among the most powerful secondary reinforcers to people are praise, money, and prestige. How much time do you spend working for secondary reinforcers?

Why do behaviors that have been positively reinforced not occur continually? One reason is that behavior is controlled by discriminative stimuli, a process that Skinner calls stimulus control. A **discriminative stimulus** cues an individual when a behavior is likely to be reinforced. You would be silly to dial a telephone number on your landline if you did not first hear a dial tone, which acts as a discriminative stimulus to signal to you that dialing might result in positive reinforcement—reaching the person whom you are calling. Stimulus control even plays a role in drug abuse. Specific stimuli associated with drug use make drug use more likely in their presence (Falk, 1994), which explains, in part, why drug users who have undergone successful treatment often relapse when they return to the people and surroundings associated with their former drug use. Therapists emphasize the importance of addicts minimizing their exposure to situations, locations, and people that may elicit cravings for a particular drug.

A second reason that reinforced behaviors do not occur continually is the individual's relative degree of satiation in regard to the reinforcer. Reinforcement is more effective when the individual has been deprived of the reinforcer. In contrast, reinforcement is ineffective when the individual has been satiated by having free access to the reinforcer. So,

Premack principle
The principle that a more probable behavior can be used as a reinforcer for a less probable one.

primary reinforcer
In operant conditioning, an unlearned reinforcer that satisfies a biological need such as food, water, or oxygen.

secondary reinforcer
In operant conditioning, a neutral stimulus that becomes reinforcing after being associated with a primary reinforcer.

discriminative stimulus
In operant conditioning, a stimulus that indicates the likelihood that a particular response will be reinforced.

water is more reinforcing to a thirsty person, food to a hungry person, and praise is more reinforcing to a person who is rarely praised.

Shaping and Chaining Positive reinforcement is useful in increasing the likelihood of behaviors that are already in an individual's repertoire. But how can we use positive reinforcement to promote behaviors that rarely or never occur? Consider the trained dolphins you have seen jump through hoops held high above the water. You cannot reinforce a behavior until it occurs. The trainer who simply waits until a dolphin jumps through a hoop held above the water might wait forever; dolphins do not naturally jump through hoops held above the water.

shaping An operant conditioning procedure that involves the positive reinforcement of successive approximations of an initially improbable behavior to eventually bring about that behavior.

Animal trainers rely on a technique called **shaping** to train rats, dolphins, and other animals to perform actions that they would rarely or never perform naturally. In shaping, the individual is reinforced for successive approximations of the target behavior and eventually reinforced for the target behavior itself. A dolphin trainer might begin by giving a dolphin a fish for turning toward a hoop held underwater and then, successively, for moving toward the hoop, for coming near the hoop, and for swimming through the hoop. The trainer then would gradually raise the hoop and continue to reward the dolphin for swimming through it. Eventually the trainer would reward the dolphin for swimming through the hoop when it was held partly out of the water, then for jumping through the hoop when it was held slightly above the water, and finally, for jumping through the hoop when it was held several feet above the water. Shaping is also the process by which rats are taught to press levers and pigeons to peck at disks in Skinner boxes.

Shaping occurs naturally in the wild and may explain why wild rats living next to the Po River in Italy will dive to the river bottom to get shellfish to eat despite their inherent disinterest in swimming, whereas similar wild rats living next to other rivers will not (Galef, 1980). See Figure 7-6 for an illustration of the rats' behavior.

Shaping is not limited to animals. It also is useful in training people to perform novel behaviors. The successful application of what we now call shaping was reported as long ago as the 7th century, when it was used in England to help a mute person learn to speak (Cliffe, 1991). In a much more recent application, shaping was used to train a child with Down syndrome to jump over a hurdle in preparation for the Special Olympics (Cameron & Cappello, 1993).

chaining An operant conditioning procedure used to establish a desired sequence of behaviors by positively reinforcing each behavior in the sequence.

What if you wish to teach an individual or animal to perform a series of behaviors rather than single behaviors? You might use **chaining**, which involves the reinforcement of each behavior in a series. For example, in one study, chaining was used successfully to train adults with intellectual disabilities to perform the 18 separate steps required to make a corsage (Hur & Osborne, 1993). In *forward chaining,* a sequence of actions is taught by reinforcing the first action in the chain and then working forward, each time adding a behavioral segment to the chain, until the individual performs all the segments in sequence. Forward chaining has been successful in areas as diverse as teaching the use of a musical keyboard (Ash & Holding, 1990) and training children with autism spectrum disorders to speak more frequently (Taylor, Levin, & Jasper, 1999).

In *backward chaining,* a sequence of actions is taught by reinforcing the final action in the chain and then working backward until the individual performs all the segments in sequence (Hagopian, Farrell, & Amari, 1996). For example, a father could use chaining to teach his child to put on a shirt. The father would begin by putting the shirt on the child, leaving only the top button open. He then would work backward, first reinforcing the child for buttoning the top button, then for buttoning the top two buttons, and so on, until the child could perform the sequence of actions necessary for putting on a shirt. Even flight-training programs for pilots are more successful when they have trainees practice individual segments of a chain of actions they are to learn and combine them together through backward chaining (Wightman & Lintern, 1984).

continuous schedule of reinforcement A schedule of reinforcement that provides reinforcement for each instance of a desired response.

Schedules of Reinforcement Once an individual has been conditioned to perform a behavior, the performance of the behavior is influenced by its schedule of reinforcement—the pattern of reinforcements given for a desired behavior. In a **continuous schedule of reinforcement**, every instance of a desired behavior is reinforced. A rat in a Skinner box that receives a pellet of food each time it presses a bar is on a continuous schedule of reinforcement. Similarly, candy vending machines put you on a continuous schedule of reinforcement. Each time you insert the correct change, you receive a package of candy. If you do not receive the candy, you might pound on the machine, but you would, at best, insert coins only one more time. This example illustrates another characteristic of continuous schedules of reinforcement—they are subject to rapid extinction when reinforcement stops. Extinction is the decline in the probability of a behavior and its eventual disappearance as a result of its no longer being followed by a reinforcer.

In **partial schedules of reinforcement** (also known as intermittent schedules), reinforcement is given for only some instances of a desired behavior. Because partial schedules produce less predictable reinforcement, they are more resistant to extinction than are continuous schedules. Skinner (1956) discovered partial schedules by accident when he ran short of food pellets and decided not to reinforce each response but instead to reinforce responses only every so often. The rats kept responding and showed resistance to extinction. Partial schedules are further divided into ratio schedules and interval schedules. In a ratio schedule of reinforcement, reinforcement is provided after the individual makes a certain number of desired responses.

There are two kinds of ratio schedules: fixed and variable. A **fixed-ratio schedule of reinforcement** provides reinforcement after a specific number of desired responses. A rat in a Skinner box might be reinforced with a pellet of food after every 5 bar presses. Suppose

partial schedule of reinforcement A schedule of reinforcement that reinforces some, but not all, instances of a desired response.

fixed-ratio schedule of reinforcement A partial schedule of reinforcement that provides reinforcement after a set number of desired responses.

(a)

(b)

(c)

FIGURE 7-6
Shaping in the Wild on the Po River

Shaping might explain why wild rats living near the Po River in northern Italy will dive to the river bottom to get shellfish to eat, whereas similar wild rats living next to other rivers will not. The Po River experiences radical changes in depth. *(a)* At times, the rats living next to the Po can scamper across exposed areas of its bed to get shellfish. *(b)* As the water rises, the rats wade into the river and submerge their heads to get shellfish. *(c)* Eventually, when the water becomes deeper, they swim about in the river and dive to get shellfish. Thus, the natural changes in the depth of the river shape the rats' behavior by positively reinforcing them with shellfish for successive approximations of diving—until they are able to do full-fledged diving (Galef, 1980).

Gambling and Schedules of Reinforcement

Gamblers are on variable-ratio schedules of reinforcement, which makes their gambling highly resistant to extinction. This is one of the reasons why compulsive gambling is so difficult to treat.

Source: William Perugini/Shutterstock.com.

variable-ratio schedule of reinforcement A partial schedule of reinforcement that provides reinforcement after varying, unpredictable numbers of desired responses.

fixed-interval schedule of reinforcement A partial schedule of reinforcement that provides reinforcement for the first desired response made after a set length of time.

variable-interval schedule of reinforcement A partial schedule of reinforcement that provides reinforcement for the first desired response made after varying, unpredictable lengths of time.

negative reinforcement In operant conditioning, an increase in the probability of a behavior that is followed by the removal of an aversive stimulus.

a garment worker is paid with a voucher after every three shirts sewn. That person, too, would be on a fixed-ratio schedule. In one experiment, a fixed-ratio schedule of reinforcement increased the length of time exercisers rode stationary bicycles. In this case, 25-second video clips were presented after the riders completed a fixed number of pedal rotations (Cohen, Chelland, Ball, & LeMura, 2002). Fixed-ratio schedules produce high, steady response rates, with a brief pause in responding immediately after each reinforcement.

Unlike a fixed-ratio schedule, a **variable-ratio schedule of reinforcement** provides reinforcement after an unpredictable number of desired responses. The number of responses required will vary around an average. For example, a rat in a Skinner box might be reinforced with a food pellet after an average of 7 bar presses—perhaps 5 presses one time, 10 presses a second time, and 6 presses a third time. People playing slot machines are on a variable-ratio schedule because they cannot predict how many times they will have to play before they win. Even the archerfish, which hunts insects by spitting water at them as they fly by, continues to hunt that way (despite missing many times) because it is on a variable-ratio schedule of reinforcement (Goldstein & Hall, 1990).

Variable-ratio schedules produce high, steady rates of responding that are more resistant to extinction than are those produced by any other schedule of reinforcement. In fact, by using a variable-ratio schedule of reinforcement, Skinner conditioned pigeons to peck a lighted disk up to 10,000 times to obtain a single pellet of food. Variable-ratio schedules also offer one reason compulsive gamblers find it so difficult to quit—eventually they will receive positive reinforcement, though their reinforcement history is unpredictable (Horsley, Osborne, Norman, & Wells, 2012) and resistant to extinction.

Whereas ratio schedules of reinforcement provide reinforcement after a certain number of desired responses, interval schedules of reinforcement provide reinforcement for the first desired response after a period of time. As in the case of ratio schedules, there are two kinds of interval schedules: fixed and variable. A **fixed-interval schedule of reinforcement** reinforces the first desired response after a set period of time. For example, a rat in a Skinner box might be reinforced with a food pellet for its first bar press after intervals of 30 seconds. Bar presses that occur during the intervals would not be reinforced.

A fixed-interval schedule produces a drop in responses immediately after reinforcement and a gradual increase in responses as the time for the next reinforcement approaches. Suppose that you have a biology exam every 3 weeks. You would study before each exam to obtain a good grade—a positive reinforcer. But you would probably stop studying biology immediately after each exam and not begin studying it again until a few days before the next exam.

A **variable-interval schedule of reinforcement** provides reinforcement for the first desired response made after periods of time, which vary around an average. For example, a rat might be reinforced for its first bar press after 19 seconds, then after 37 seconds, then after 4 seconds, and so on, with the interval averaging 20 seconds. When you are fishing, you are on a variable-interval schedule of reinforcement because you cannot predict how long you will have to wait until a fish bites. Variable-interval schedules produce relatively slow, steady rates of responding that are highly resistant to extinction. An individual might continue to fish even if the fish are few and far between. And teachers who give periodic surprise quizzes make use of variable-interval schedules to promote more consistent studying by their students.

Ratio schedules produce faster response rates than do interval schedules because the number of responses, not the length of time, determines the onset of reinforcement. Variable schedules produce steadier response rates than do fixed schedules because the pattern of reinforcement is unpredictable. Figure 7-7 illustrates differences in response patterns under different schedules of reinforcement.

Negative Reinforcement

In **negative reinforcement,** a behavior that brings about the removal of an aversive stimulus becomes more likely to occur in the future. Note that both positive and negative reinforcement increase the likelihood of a behavior. Consider the boring lecture. Because daydreaming lets you escape from boring lectures, you are likely to daydream whenever

you find yourself listening to one. This form of negative reinforcement is called **escape learning**—learning to end something aversive. For example, you can terminate an irritating warning buzzer by putting on your automobile seat belt.

Of course your class might be so boring that you stop attending it. This form of negative reinforcement is called **avoidance learning**—learning to prevent something aversive. Thus, you can avoid the sound of a warning buzzer by buckling up before you start your automobile engine. And dormitory students at some schools quickly learn to scamper out of the shower when they hear a toilet being flushed to avoid being scalded when cold water is diverted to the toilet (Reese, 1986).

But if negative reinforcement involves engaging in a behavior that removes an aversive stimulus, how could avoidance learning (which only prevents an aversive stimulus) be a form of negative reinforcement? That is, what is the aversive stimulus that is being removed? Evidently, what is being removed is an internal aversive stimulus—the emotional distress caused by your anticipation of the aversive event, such as a boring class

escape learning Learning to perform a behavior that terminates an aversive stimulus, as in negative reinforcement.

avoidance learning Learning to prevent the occurrence of an aversive stimulus by giving an appropriate response to a warning stimulus.

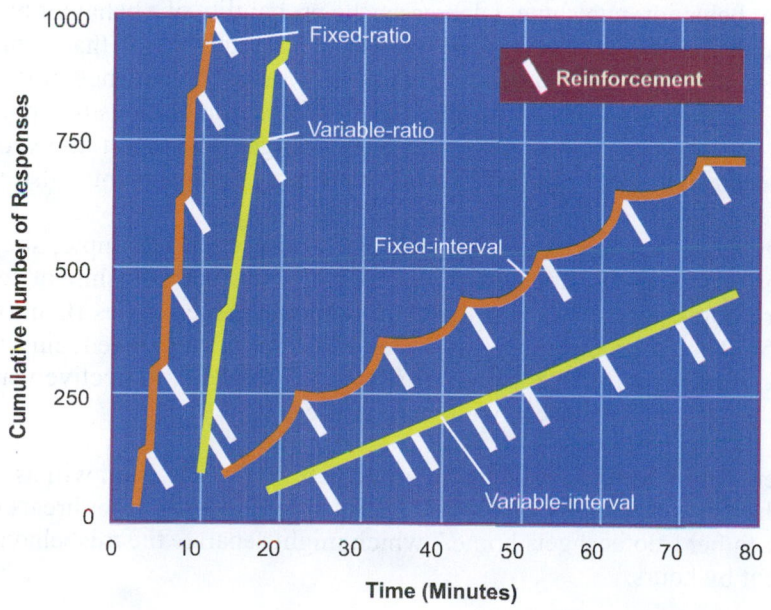

FIGURE 7-7
Schedules of Reinforcement

The hash marks show the delivery of reinforcement. Steeper slopes indicate higher rates of responding.

or a scalding shower. Thus, in escape learning, the aversive stimulus itself is removed, whereas in avoidance learning, the emotional distress caused by anticipation of that stimulus is removed (Mowrer, 1947). Even relatively simple animals engage in avoidance learning. For example, bees that get caught in spider webs—and are fortunate enough to escape—may learn to avoid them in the future (Craig, 1994).

Extinction

extinction
1. In classical conditioning, the gradual disappearance of the conditioned response when the conditioned stimulus is repeatedly presented without being paired with the unconditioned stimulus.
2. In operant conditioning, the gradual disappearance of a response that is no longer followed by a reinforcer.

As in classical conditioning, behaviors learned through operant conditioning are subject to **extinction.** Skinner discovered extinction by accident. In one of his early studies, he conditioned a rat in a Skinner box to press a bar to obtain pellets of food from a dispenser. On one occasion he found that the pellet dispenser had become jammed, preventing the release of pellets. Skinner noted that the rat continued to press the bar, though at a diminishing rate, until it finally stopped pressing at all. Extinction might occur when a student who raises her hand is no longer called on to answer questions. Because she is no longer being positively reinforced for raising her hand, she would eventually stop doing so.

When extinction begins, there is typically a burst in the response. This phenomenon is important in behavior therapy techniques that use extinction because the techniques might, at first, seem to be ineffective. Experienced therapists are aware of this burst and might promote appropriate behavior by reinforcing it while an undesired behavior is undergoing extinction (Lerman & Iwata, 1995). Extinction therapy is useful for individuals with phobias.

spontaneous recovery
1. In classical conditioning, the reappearance after a period of time of a conditioned response that has been subjected to extinction. 2. In operant conditioning, the reappearance after a period of time of a behavior that has been subjected to extinction.

Also, as with classical conditioning, a behavior that has been subjected to extinction can show **spontaneous recovery**—it might reappear after a period of time. Spontaneous recovery provides a functional advantage. For example, suppose that wild animals that visit a certain water hole normally obtain positive reinforcement by finding water. If they visit the water hole on several successive occasions and find that it has dried up, their behavior will undergo extinction; they will stop visiting the water hole. But after a period of time, the animals might exhibit spontaneous recovery, again visiting the water hole—in case it had become refilled with water.

Punishment

punishment In operant conditioning, the process by which an aversive stimulus decreases the probability of a response that precedes it.

Still another way of reducing the probability of behaviors is through **punishment,** in which the consequence of a behavior decreases its likelihood. Do not confuse punishment with negative reinforcement. Negative reinforcement is "negative" because it involves the removal of an aversive stimulus; it does not involve punishment. Negative reinforcement increases the probability of a behavior by removing something undesirable as a consequence of that behavior; punishment decreases the probability of a behavior by presenting something undesirable *(positive punishment)* as a consequence of that behavior or by removing something desirable *(negative punishment)* as a consequence of that behavior. For example, a driver who gets a speeding ticket—an example of positive punishment— is less likely to speed in the future. Likewise, a teenager who is not allowed to use the family car because of speeding—an example of negative punishment—also will be less likely to speed again.

Punishment is useful in animals, as well as in people. For example, social animals punish underlings who threaten group well-being. They use punishment to discipline offspring, promote cooperation, and maintain dominance hierarchies (Clutton-Brock & Parker, 1995). Though punishment can be an effective means of reducing undesirable behaviors, it often is ineffective. Consider some effective and ineffective ways of using punishment to discipline children (Walters & Grusec, 1977).

- Punishment for misbehavior should be immediate so that the child will associate the punishment with the misbehavior. A parent should not resort to threats of "wait until your father [mother] gets home," which might separate the misbehavior and punishment by hours.

- Punishment should be strong enough to stop the undesirable behavior but not excessive. You might punish a child for throwing clothes about his room by making him clean the room, but you would be using excessive punishment if you made him clean every room in the house. Punishment that is excessive induces resentment aimed at the person who administers the punishment.

- Punishment should be consistent. If parents truly want to reduce a child's misbehavior, they must punish the child each time it occurs. Otherwise the child learns only that her parents are unpredictable—that is, the child is on a variable-ratio schedule of reinforcement (which is highly resistant to extinction).

- Punishment should be aimed at the misbehavior, not at the child. For example, a child who is repeatedly called "stupid" for making mistakes while playing softball might feel incompetent and lose interest in softball and other sports.

- Punishing undesirable behavior merely suppresses the behavior in response to a specific discriminative stimulus, such as the parent who administers punishment and only teaches the child what not to do. To make sure that the child learns what to do, positive reinforcement of desirable behavior should also be used.

One of the main controversies concerning punishment is the use of physical punishment (Gershoff, 2002). Children imitate parental models. If they observe that their parents rely on physical punishment, they might rely on it in dealing with their friends, siblings, and eventually, their own children. Though physical punishment of children can suppress misbehavior in the short run, in the long run it is associated with problems such as juvenile delinquency and adult criminality (Straus, 1991). Being physically punished as a child also is associated with subsequent adult depression, suicidal tendencies, alcohol and spousal abuse (Straus & Kantor, 1994), and children resorting to physical violence during interpersonal disputes with their peers (Simons & Wurtele, 2010). Table 7-1 summarizes the differences among the behavioral contingencies of positive reinforcement, negative reinforcement, extinction, and punishment.

Applications of Operant Conditioning

B. F. Skinner (1986) claimed that many of our everyday problems could be solved by more widespread use of operant conditioning. As one example, consider the problem of injuries and deaths caused by automobile accidents. Operant conditioning has been effective in teaching children to use seat belts, thereby reducing their risk of injury (Roberts & Fanurik, 1986). Now consider several other ways in which operant conditioning has been applied to everyday life.

TABLE 7-1 Behavioral Contingencies

Contingency	Behavioral Consequence	Probability of Behavior	Example
Positive reinforcement	Brings about something desirable	Increases	You study for an exam and receive an A, which makes you more likely to study in the future.
Negative reinforcement	Removes something undesirable	Increases	You go to the dentist to have a cavity filled. This eliminates your toothache, which makes you more likely to visit the dentist in the future when you have a toothache.
Extinction	Fails to bring about something desirable	Decreases	You say hello to a person who repeatedly fails to greet you in return. This leads you to stop saying hello.
Punishment	Brings about something undesirable	Decreases	You overeat at a party and suffer from a severe upset stomach. In the future you become less likely to overeat.

Operant Conditioning and Animal Training

Skinner and some of his colleagues have been pioneers in the use of shaping and chaining to train animals to perform novel behaviors (Lukas, Marr, & Maple, 1998). Zoos rely on positive reinforcement, as in a popular otter-training program that was open to the public at Zoo Atlanta (Anderson, Kelling, Pressley-Keough, Bloomsmith, & Maple, 2003). Perhaps Skinner's most noteworthy feat in animal training occurred during World War II in "Project Pigeon." In this secret project, Skinner (1960) trained pigeons to guide missiles toward enemy ships by training them to peck at an image of the target ship shown on a display to obtain food pellets. Though this guidance system proved feasible, it was never used in combat.

More recently, pigeons have been trained to serve as air-sea rescue spotters in the Coast Guard's "Project Sea Hunt" (Stark, 1981). The pigeons are reinforced with food pellets for responding to red, orange, or yellow objects—the common colors of flotation devices. Three pigeons are placed in a compartment under a search plane so that they look out of windows oriented in different directions. When a pigeon spots an object floating in the sea, it pecks a key, which sounds a buzzer and flashes a light in the cockpit. Pigeons are superior to human spotters because they have the ability to focus over a wider area and to scan the sea for longer periods of time without becoming fatigued.

In another beneficial application of operant conditioning, psychologists have trained capuchin monkeys to serve as aides to physically disabled people (Mack, 1981). These monkeys act as extensions of the disabled person—bringing drinks, turning pages in books, changing television channels, and performing a host of other services. The person directs the monkey by using an optical pointer that focuses a beam of light on a desired object.

Operant Conditioning and Child Rearing

In 1945, Skinner shocked the public when he published the article "Baby in a Box," which described how he and his wife had reared an infant daughter in an enclosure called an *air crib*. The air crib filtered and controlled the temperature of the infant's air supply. Instead of diapers, it used a roll of paper that permitted sections to be placed under the baby and discarded when dirty. The parents could even pull down a shade over the front window of the air crib when the baby was ready to go to sleep. Skinner claimed that the air crib was a more convenient way to rear infants and allowed more time for social interaction with them. Critics disagreed with Skinner, claiming that his treatment of his daughter was dehumanizing. Over the past few decades, rumors have claimed that Skinner's daughter's experience with the air crib eventually led her to sue her father, to become mentally ill, or to commit suicide. In reality, she had a happy childhood and has pursued a successful career as an artist (Langone, 1983).

The air crib provoked fears of impersonal child rearing, and it was never widely used. Skinner had tried, unsuccessfully, to market the air crib under the clever brand name *Heir Conditioner* (Benjamin & Neilsen-Gammon, 1999). Nonetheless, operant conditioning has proved useful in child rearing. For example, parents have used extinction to eliminate their child's tantrums. When parents ignore the tantrums rather than give in to the child's demand for toys, candy, or attention, the tantrums might at first intensify but eventually will stop (Williams, 1959).

Operant Conditioning and Educational Improvement

Teachers likewise have used positive reinforcement to improve their students' classroom performance. For example, verbal praise has been used to increase participation in classroom discussions (Smith, Schumaker, Schaeffer, & Sherman, 1982), and positive reinforcement in the form of token economies has been used to promote desirable classroom behaviors (Swiezy, Matson, & Box, 1992). In a **token economy,** teachers use tokens to reward students for proper conduct and academic excellence. The students then use the tokens to purchase items such as toys or privileges such as extra recess time. Token economies have been used to increase classroom participation by college students (Boniecki & Moore, 2003) and appropriate behavior by adolescents in a drug and alcohol rehabilitation (Taylor & Mudford, 2012).

token economy An operant conditioning procedure that uses tokens as positive reinforcers in programs designed to promote desirable behaviors, with the tokens later used to purchase desired items or privileges.

Perhaps the most distinctive contribution that operant conditioning has made to education has been **programmed instruction,** which had its origin in the invention of the teaching machine by Sidney Pressey of Ohio State University in the 1920s. His machines provided immediate knowledge of results and a piece of candy to reward correct answers (Benjamin, 1988). But credit for developing programmed instruction is generally given to B. F. Skinner for his invention of a teaching machine that takes the student through a series of questions related to a particular subject, gradually moving the student from simple to more complex questions. After the student answers a question, the correct answer is revealed.

The teaching machine failed to catch on in the 1950s and 1960s because of fears that it would be dehumanizing, that it could teach only certain narrow subjects, and that teachers would lose their jobs. Nonetheless, supporters note that programmed instruction has several advantages over traditional approaches to education (Vargas & Vargas, 1991). Programmed instruction provides immediate feedback of results (positive reinforcement for correct answers and only mild punishment for incorrect answers), eliminates the need for anxiety-inducing exams, and permits the student to go at her or his own pace. Skinner (1984) claimed that if schools adopted programmed instruction, students would learn twice as much in the same amount of time.

Today's use of **computer-assisted instruction** (Skinner, 1989) is a descendant of Skinner's programmed instruction. Computer programs take the student through a graded series of items at the student's own pace. The programs even branch off to provide extra help on items that the student finds difficult. Though teaching machines and computers have not replaced teachers, they have added another teaching tool to the classroom. Computer-assisted instruction has proved useful, whether teaching academic skills to elementary school students (Christmann & Badgett, 2003), nursing skills to caregivers of elderly adults (Ponpaipan et al., 2010), or introductory psychology to college students (Pear & Crone-Todd, 1999). Computer-assisted instruction also is useful with special populations, such as children with autism spectrum disorder (Ploog, Scharf, Nelson, & Brooks, 2013), learning disabilities (Hall, Hughes, & Filbert, 2000), or intellectual disabilities (Patra & Rath, 2000).

Operant Conditioning and Psychological Disorders

Operant conditioning has enhanced our understanding of psychological disorders, particularly depression. The concept of **learned helplessness** has gained influence as an explanation for depression through the work of Martin Seligman (see Chapter 14). In his original research, Seligman exposed dogs restrained in harnesses to electric shocks. One group of dogs could turn off the shock by pressing a switch with their noses. A second group could not. The dogs then were tested in a shuttle box, which consisted of two compartments separated by an easily hurdled divider. A warning tone was sounded,

programmed instruction
A step-by-step approach, based on operant conditioning, in which the learner proceeds at his or her own pace through more and more advanced material and receives immediate knowledge of the results of each response.

computer-assisted instruction
The use of computer programs to provide programmed instruction.

learned helplessness
A feeling of futility caused by the belief that one has little or no control over events in one's life, which can make one stop trying and experience depressed mood.

Computer-Assisted Instruction

Students may benefit from computer-assisted instruction because it permits them to go at their own pace, receive immediate feedback on their progress, and, in some cases, obtain remedial help in areas of weakness.
Source: Robert Kneschke/ Shutterstock.com.

followed a few seconds later by an electric shock. Dogs in the first group escaped by jumping over the divider into the other compartment. In contrast, dogs in the second group whimpered but did not try to escape (Seligman & Maier, 1967).

Though replications of various versions of this study have produced inconsistent support for learned helplessness in animals (Klosterhalfen & Klosterhalfen, 1983), it is a model that is commonly used to elicit behaviors that resemble symptoms of depression and post-traumatic stress disorder (PTSD) in humans. Moreover, these behavioral changes respond to treatment with antidepressant medications (Hammack, Cooper, & Lezak, 2012). This study, as well as others, has demonstrated the effectiveness of this intervention in animals. However, it is not possible to use this method with people (Winefield, 1982). Nevertheless, the possibility that learned helplessness is a factor in depression has inspired hundreds of studies (Deuser & Anderson, 1995) and contributed to our understanding of the neurobiology that underlies the relationship between stress and depression. Depressed people experience less control over obtaining positive reinforcers and avoiding punishments. As a consequence, they are less likely to try to change their life situations—which further contributes to their feelings of depression. Consider adults whose everyday functioning can be reduced by uncontrollable pain. They might become depressed, reduce their activities even more, and perhaps become housebound (Kropp et al., 2012).

Operant conditioning also has been used to change maladaptive behaviors. This use is known as *behavior modification*. For example, token economies have been useful in training mental hospital patients to care for themselves (Morisse, Batra, Hess, & Silverman, 1996). Patients are trained to dress themselves, to use toilets, to brush their teeth, and to eat with utensils. They use the tokens to purchase merchandise or special privileges.

Operant Conditioning and Biofeedback

One day, more than three decades ago, the eminent learning researcher Neal Miller stood in front of a mirror trying to teach himself to wiggle one ear. By watching his ear in the mirror, he eventually was able to make it wiggle (Jonas, 1972). The mirror provided Miller with visual *feedback* of his ear's movement. This experience convinced him that people might learn to control physiological responses that are not normally subject to voluntary control if they were provided with feedback of those responses. Since the 1960s Miller and other psychologists have developed a technique called biofeedback to help people learn to control normally involuntary responses such as brain waves, blood pressure, and intestinal contractions.

biofeedback A form of operant conditioning that enables an individual to learn to control a normally involuntary physiological process or to gain better control of a normally voluntary one when provided with visual or auditory information indicating the state of that response.

Biofeedback is a form of operant conditioning that enables an individual to learn to control a normally involuntary physiological response or to gain better control of a normally voluntary one when provided with visual or auditory information indicating the state of that response. The feedback acts as a positive reinforcer for changes in the desired direction. The feedback might be provided by a light that changes in brightness as heart rate changes, a tone that changes in pitch as muscle tension changes, or any of a host of other visual or auditory stimuli that vary with changes in the target physiological response.

Biofeedback was popularized in the late 1960s by reports of participants who learned to control their alpha brain-wave patterns, which, as described in Chapter 6, are associated with a relaxed state of mind. But biofeedback did not become scientifically credible to many psychologists until Neal Miller reported success in training rats to gain voluntary control over physiological responses normally controlled solely by the autonomic nervous system. In his studies, Miller used electrical stimulation of the brain's reward centers (positive reinforcement) or, in some cases, escape or avoidance of shock (negative reinforcement) to train rats to increase or decrease their heart rate, intestinal contractions, urine production, or blood pressure. Because Miller was an eminent, hard-nosed researcher (Coons, 2002), serious scientists became more willing to accept the legitimacy of biofeedback. Ironically, for unknown reasons, attempts at replicating his rat studies generally have failed (Dworkin & Miller, 1986).

Disappointment at the failure to replicate Miller's rat studies and of biofeedback to fulfill early promises to induce mystical states of consciousness led to skepticism about its merits. But even though biofeedback has not proven to be an unqualified success, it has not proven to be a failure. Hundreds of studies have demonstrated the effectiveness of biofeedback in helping people learn to control a variety of physiological responses, such as chronic headaches (Blume, Brockman, & Breuner, 2012). Clinical applications have included reducing arrhythmia by training patients to regulate their own heart rates (Wheat & Larkin, 2010) and helping people with painfully cold hands to warm them by increasing blood flow (Sedlacek & Taub, 1996).

One of biofeedback's main uses has been in training people to gain better control of their skeletal muscles. For example, biofeedback has been used to train people with physical disabilities to maintain their balance (Milosevic & McConville, 2011), children with cerebral palsy to control their body movements (Bloom, Przekop, & Sanger, 2010), and people with panic disorder to reduce their symptoms by regulating their breathing (Meurat, Wilhelm, & Roth, 2001). Figure 7-8 shows how biofeedback can be used to control muscle tension.

Though biofeedback is widely used by psychologists and health professionals, it is not a panacea. In fact, there is controversy about its effectiveness and practicality. To demonstrate the effectiveness of biofeedback, one must show that self-regulation of physiological responses is caused by the feedback and not by extraneous factors (Heywood & Beale, 2003). For example, early biofeedback studies showed that feedback of alpha brain waves could increase them and induce a state of relaxation. But replications of those early studies showed that the effects were caused by the participants' sitting quietly with their eyes closed. The brain-wave feedback added nothing (Plotkin, 1979). Even when the results of a biofeedback study can be attributed to the feedback, the technique still might not be of practical use. Why?

- The typical biofeedback device costs hundreds or even thousands of dollars. Thus, clinicians must decide whether the benefits of biofeedback justify its cost, especially when other equally effective, less expensive treatments are available. Yet overall, treatment programs that include biofeedback have proved cost-effective in enhancing the quality of life and in reducing physician visits, medication use, medical care costs, hospital stays, and mortality (Schneider, 1987).

- Laboratory experiments on biofeedback can produce results that are statistically significant (a concept discussed in Chapter 2) and merit being reported but that are too small to be of practical use in clinical settings (Steiner & Dince, 1981). For example, biofeedback might produce a *statistically significant* reduction in blood pressure in hypertensive persons that is too small to be *clinically meaningful.*

- Biofeedback training in a clinician's office might produce results that do not last much beyond the training sessions. That is, there is a need for research on how to promote long-term maintenance of biofeedback-induced changes (McGrady, 2002). One way to promote the generalization of benefits from clinical training sessions to everyday life is to use portable biofeedback devices (Harrison, Gavin, & Isaac, 1988).

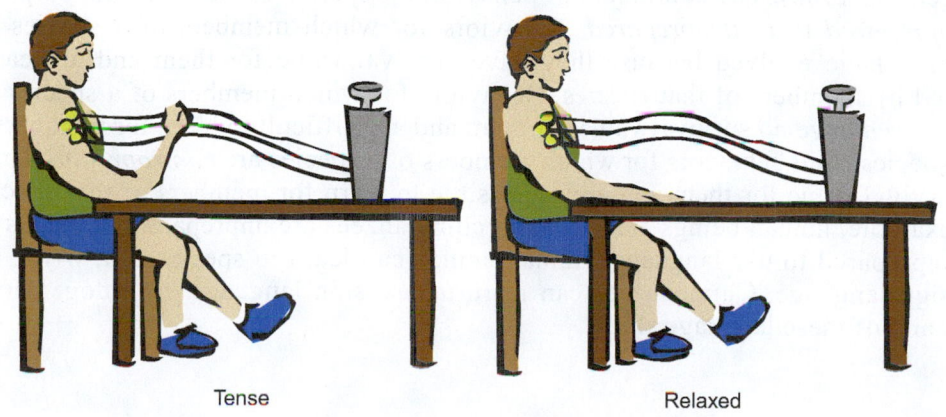

Tense   Relaxed

FIGURE 7-8
Biofeedback

People who are provided with feedback of physiological processes may gain some control over normally involuntary ones, such as blood pressure, or gain improved control over normally voluntary ones, such as muscle tension during physical rehabilitation. The individual shown here is undergoing physical rehabilitation using muscle biofeedback.

- The results of laboratory studies might not be applicable to the clinical setting. The therapist who uses biofeedback typically achieves success by combining biofeedback with other therapeutic approaches. Thus, biofeedback does not achieve its clinical effects by itself, as an antibiotic might do in curing a bacterial infection. That is, though it would be scientifically sound to compare a psychotherapy-plus-biofeedback group to a psychotherapy-alone group, it would be scientifically unsound to compare a psychotherapy-alone group to a biofeedback-alone group. As in other forms of therapy, emotional and cognitive factors play a role in the effectiveness of biofeedback therapy (Shahab, West, & McNeill, 2011).

Biological Constraints on Operant Conditioning

Around the turn of the 20th century, Edward Thorndike put forth the concept of *belongingness* to explain why he found it easier to train cats to escape from his puzzle boxes by stepping on a pedal than by scratching themselves. Thorndike observed that evolution seemed to have endowed animals with inherited tendencies to associate the performance of certain behaviors with certain consequences. Cats are more predisposed to escape by performing actions that affect the environment, such as stepping on a pedal, than by performing actions that affect their bodies, such as scratching themselves.

Thorndike's observation had little influence on his contemporaries, and it was not until the 1950s that psychologists rediscovered what he had observed. Among the first psychologists to make this rediscovery were Keller and Marian Breland, former students of B. F. Skinner who became renowned animal trainers (Timberlake, 2003). Since its founding in 1947, their Animal Behavior Enterprises in Hot Springs, Arkansas, trained animals to perform in zoos, fairs, movies, circuses, museums, amusement parks, department stores, and television commercials.

instinctive drift The reversion of animals to behaviors characteristic of their species even when being reinforced for performing other behaviors.

Despite their success in training animals, the Brelands were distressed by the tendency of some animals to "misbehave" (Breland & Breland, 1961). Their misbehavior was actually a reversion to behaviors characteristic of their species, which the Brelands called **instinctive drift**. For example, they used operant conditioning to train a chicken to hit a baseball by pulling a string to swing a miniature bat and then run to first base for food. Sometimes, instead, the chicken chased after the ball and pecked at it. This "misbehavior" of animals has distressed animal trainers, but it demonstrates that animals sometimes may revert back to species-specific behaviors even when being reinforced for other behaviors.

behavioral preparedness The degree to which members of a species are innately prepared to learn particular behaviors.

After considering instinctive drift and related problems in operant conditioning, psychologist Martin Seligman (1970) concluded that there is a continuum of **behavioral preparedness** for certain behaviors. For example, a hamster more easily learns to dig than to wash its face to obtain positive reinforcement (Shettleworth & Juergensen, 1980). The continuum of behavioral preparedness ranges from *prepared* to *unprepared* to *contraprepared*. Behaviors for which members of a species are prepared have evolved because they have survival value for them and are easily learned by members of that species. Behaviors for which members of a species are *unprepared* have no survival value for them and are difficult to learn for members of that species. And behaviors for which members of a species are *contraprepared* have no survival value for them and are impossible to learn for members of that species. For example, human beings are prepared, chimpanzees are unprepared, and dogs are contraprepared to use language. Human beings can learn to speak, read, write, and use sign language. Chimpanzees can learn to use sign language. And dogs cannot learn any of these language skills.

1. In what way was Edward Thorndike's instrumental conditioning the forerunner of B. F. Skinner's operant conditioning?

2. How would you use shaping to train children to straighten up their rooms?

3. In what ways are positive reinforcement and negative reinforcement similar, and in what ways are they different?

Cognitive Learning

Both classical conditioning and operant conditioning traditionally have been explained by the principle of contiguity—the mere association of events in time and space. Contiguity has been used to explain the association of a conditioned stimulus and an unconditioned stimulus in classical conditioning and the association of a behavior and its consequence in operant conditioning. Over the past few decades, the associationistic explanation of learning has been criticized for viewing human and animal learners as passive reactors to "external carrots, whips, and the stimuli associated with them" (Boneau, 1974, p. 308). These critics, influenced by the "cognitive revolution" in psychology, favor the study of cognitive factors in classical conditioning and operant conditioning, as well as the study of learning by observation, which had routinely been ignored by learning researchers (Wasserman, 1997).

Cognitive Factors in Associative Learning

The traditional view of classical conditioning and operant conditioning is that they are explained by contiguity alone. But evidence has accumulated that mere contiguity of a neutral stimulus and an unconditioned stimulus is insufficient to produce classical conditioning, and mere contiguity of a behavior and a consequence is insufficient to produce operant conditioning. This evidence has led to cognitive interpretations of associative learning, as in the case of operant conditioning. For example, secondary reinforcers traditionally have been thought to gain their reinforcing ability through mere contiguity with primary reinforcers. Cognitive theorists believe, instead, that secondary reinforcers gain their reinforcing ability because they have reliably *predicted* the occurrence of primary reinforcers (Rose & Fantino, 1978).

Suppose that you are using treats as positive reinforcers to train your dog to "shake hands." Just before giving your dog a treat, you might offer praise by saying "Good dog!" If you did so every time that your dog shook hands, the words "Good dog!" might become a secondary reinforcer. The traditional view of operant conditioning would claim that the praise became a secondary reinforcer by its mere *contiguity* with food. In contrast, the cognitive view would claim that the praise became a secondary reinforcer because it had become a good *predictor* of the food reward.

Psychologists also have provided cognitive explanations of classical conditioning that rule out mere contiguity as a sufficient explanation. The most influential of these explanations states that classical conditioning will occur only when the conditioned stimulus permits the individual to reliably predict the occurrence of the unconditioned stimulus (Siegel & Allan, 1996). The better the conditioned stimulus is as a predictor, the stronger the conditioning will be. Conditioning involves learning relations, or contingencies, among events in the environment (Rescorla, 1988).

Prediction was demonstrated by Robert Rescorla (1968), who favors a cognitive explanation of conditioning. In one experiment, he paired a buzzer (the neutral stimulus) with an electric shock (a UCS), which he administered to rats. All the rats received the same number of pairings of the buzzer and the electric shock. But some of the rats were given additional shocks not preceded by a buzzer. According to the traditional contiguity-based explanation of classical conditioning, because the buzzer and the electric shock had been paired an equal number of times for all the rats, the buzzer should have become an equally strong CS, eliciting a CR, for all of them. Yet, those for whom the buzzer always preceded the electric shock showed stronger conditioning.

Rescorla would explain this result cognitively—that is, in terms of the rats' knowledge of the relationship between the buzzer and the electric shock (Rescorla, 2003). The rats that always received an electric shock after the buzzer developed a stronger expectancy that an electric shock would follow the buzzer than did the rats that sometimes did and sometimes did not receive an electric shock after the buzzer. Consider this explanation in regard to Pavlov's studies of salivation in dogs. The dog learns that a tone is followed by meat powder. The more consistently the tone precedes the meat powder, the more predictable the relationship will be and, as a consequence, the stronger the conditioning will be.

Another source of evidence that supports the cognitive explanation of classical conditioning is the phenomenon of **blocking,** in which a neutral stimulus paired with a CS that already elicits a CR will fail to become a CS itself (Blaisdell, Gunther, & Miller, 1999). Blocking is illustrated in Table 7-2. Suppose that you have conditioned a dog to salivate to the sound of a bell by repeatedly presenting the bell before presenting meat powder. If you then repeatedly paired a light with the bell before presenting the meat powder, the principle of contiguity would make you expect that the light, too, would gain the ability to elicit salivation. But it will not. Instead, the CS (the bell) "blocks" the neutral stimulus (the light) from becoming a conditioned stimulus. According to the cognitive explanation, blocking occurs because the neutral stimulus (the light) adds nothing to the predictability of the UCS (the meat powder). The CS (the bell) already predicts the occurrence of the UCS. Blocking has been demonstrated in animals (Urushihara & Miller, 2010) and people (Hinchy, Lovibond, & Ter-Horst, 1995).

Still another source of evidence against a strictly contiguity-based view of classical conditioning comes from research on conditioned taste aversion. As you learned earlier, individuals who suffer gastrointestinal illness hours after eating novel food might avoid that food in the future. This finding contradicts the notion that events must be contiguous for us to learn to associate those events with each other.

Latent Learning

The "cognitive revolution" in psychology also has produced a trend to view learning less in terms of changes in overt behavior, as in classical or operant conditioning, and more in terms of the acquisition of knowledge (Greeno, 1980). Learning can occur without revealing itself

blocking The process by which a neutral stimulus paired with a conditioned stimulus that already elicits a conditioned response fails to become a conditioned stimulus.

TABLE 7-2 Blocking

In this example, in phase 1, rats in the experimental group are presented with a tone (the CS) immediately followed by an electric shock (the UCS), while rats in the control group receive neither stimulus. In phase 2, both groups are exposed to a tone and light, followed by a shock. In phase 3, both groups show fear (the CR) in response to the tone, but only the control group shows fear in response to the light. Because the tone already served as a reliable predictor of the shock for the experimental group, the tone blocked the light from becoming a CS for the rats in that group. That is, the light remained a neutral stimulus for the experimental group.

	Phase 1	Phase 2	Phase 3
Experimental Group	CS (tone) + UCS (shock)	CS (tone + light) + UCS (shock)	CS (tone)→CR (fear) Neutral stimulus (light)→No CR
Control Group	No training	CS (tone + light) + UCS (shock)	CS (tone)→CR (fear) CS (light)→CR (fear)

in observable behavior. For example, suppose that after studying many hours and mastering the material for a psychology exam, you fail the exam. Should your professor conclude that you had not learned the material? Not necessarily. Perhaps you failed the exam because the questions were ambiguous or because you were so anxious that your mind went blank. Your performance on the exam did not reflect how well you had learned the material.

But some researchers were interested in cognitive factors in learning decades before the onset of the cognitive revolution, even in regard to animal learning (Dewsbury, 2000). The first psychologist to stress the distinction between learning and performance was Edward Tolman (1932), who pointed out that learning can occur without rewards being given for overt actions, a process that he called **latent learning**. In latent learning, learning is not immediately revealed in performance but is revealed later when a reward is provided for performance. In a classic study, Tolman had three groups of rats run individually through a maze once a day for 10 days. One group received food as a positive reward for reaching the end of the maze, and the other two groups did not. The rewarded rats quickly learned to run through the maze with few wrong turns, while the nonrewarded rats did not. Beginning on the eleventh day, one of the groups of nonrewarded rats also was positively rewarded with food for reaching the end of the maze. The next day that group ran the maze as efficiently as the previously rewarded group did, while the remaining, still nonrewarded group continued to perform poorly. Tolman's study demonstrated latent learning. The rats that were not rewarded until the eleventh day had learned the route to the end of the maze, but they revealed this learning only when rewarded for doing so (Tolman & Honzik, 1930).

More recent research has provided additional support for latent learning. In one study, rats given an opportunity to observe a water maze before swimming through it for a food reward performed better than did rats that were not given such an opportunity (Keith & McVety, 1988). This experiment provided evidence that rats can form what Tolman called "cognitive maps"—mental representations of physical reality. But they use their cognitive maps only when rewarded for doing so. Nonetheless, some researchers have found that in similar experiments rats might be guided in their swimming not by cognitive maps but instead by visual cues in their environment (Prados, Chamizo, & MacKintosh, 1999).

latent learning Learning that occurs without the reinforcement of overt behavior.

Observational Learning

In the 1960s, research on latent learning stimulated interest in **observational learning**, in which an individual learns a behavior by watching others (models) perform it. That is, learning occurs without any overt behavior by the learner. Research on observational learning in animals dates back to at least 1881 (Robert, 1990). Observational learning has been demonstrated in a variety of animals, including cattle (Veissier, 1993), pigeons (Zentall, Sutton, & Sherburne, 1996), sea gulls (Obozova, Smirnova, & Zorina, 2011), horses (Ahrendt, Christensen, & Ladewig, 2012), dogs (Kupán, Miklósi, Gergely, & Topál, 2011), and even octopuses (Fiorito & Scotto, 1992). Consider rats. A rat that observes other rats eating foods will be more likely to eat those foods (Galef, 1993), infant rats that observe older rats opening pine cones will learn to do so themselves (Aisner & Terkel, 1992), and rats that observe other rats pushing a joystick in a particular direction to get food will learn to push it in that direction themselves (Heyes, Dawson, & Nokes, 1992).

There are numerous examples of observational learning in people (Ferrari, 1996). A few examples include basketball, baseball, ice hockey, and soccer players and their coaches learning athletic skills (Hancock, Rymal, & Ste-Marie, 2011), and students learning to behave properly by observing other students doing so (Hallenbeck & Kauffman, 1995). And in one study, 2-month-old infants watched a video of a woman responding positively or negatively to an object. Afterward, those who had seen the model respond negatively to the object tended to avoid it and to respond to it with negative emotionality (Mumme & Fernald, 2003).

Observational learning is central to Albert Bandura's **social learning theory**, which assumes that behavior is learned chiefly through observation and the mental processing of information. What accounts for observational learning? Bandura (1986) has identified four factors: First, you must pay attention to the model's actions; second, you must

observational learning Learning produced by observing the consequences that others receive for performing particular behaviors.

social learning theory A theory of learning that assumes that people learn behaviors mainly through observation and mental processing of information.

Critical Thinking About Psychology

Does Television Influence Children's Behavior?

Research on observational learning has contributed to concerns about the effects of the media on viewers, particularly children. For example, one study of children's television shows broadcast in the Los Angeles area found that 70 percent contained physical aggression, compared to 60 percent of nonchildren's shows. Moreover, children's shows contained three times more incidents of physical aggression than did nonchildren's shows (Wilson, Smith, Potter, Kunkel, Linz, Colvin, & Donnerstein, 2002). Concern about the effects of television on behavior is not new. It has existed ever since television became a popular medium in the 1950s (Carpenter, 1955). The first congressional report on the effects of television was a 1954 report on its impact on juvenile delinquency. Since then, reports on the social effects of television appeared in 1972 and 1982. Both reports found that violence on television led to aggressive behavior in children and adolescents and recommended a decrease in televised violence (Walsh, 1983). But critics of these reports claimed that, on the one hand, the results of laboratory experiments on the effects of televised violence might not generalize to real life and, on the other hand, field studies on the effects of televised violence failed to control all the other variables that might encourage violence (Fisher, 1983).

In a classic experiment by Bandura (1965) on the effect of television viewing on children, three groups of preschool children watched a film of an adult punching and verbally abusing a blow-up Bobo doll. Each group saw a different version of the film. In the first version the model was rewarded with candy, soda, and praise by another adult. In the second version the other adult scolded and spanked the model. And in the third version there were no consequences to the model. The children then played individually in a room with a Bobo doll and other toys. Those who had seen the model being rewarded for being aggressive were more aggressive in their play than were those who had seen the other two versions of the film. This experiment demonstrated that operant conditioning can occur vicariously, simply through observing others receiving positive reinforcement for engaging in the target behavior.

Over the past four decades, research and field studies have presented a complex picture of the effects of televised violence. A recent meta-analysis of relevant research studies found that there is a positive, significant correlation between televised violence and aggressive behavior (Paik & Comstock, 1994). Another meta-analysis found a causal relationship in which viewing televised aggression led to small increases in viewer aggression. This effect was stronger in cultures outside the United States (Hogben, 1998).

Children who watch television are exposed not only to antisocial models but also to prosocial models. Whereas children who watch violent programs tend to be more aggressive, children who watch altruistic programs such as *Mister Rogers' Neighborhood* tend to engage in more prosocial behaviors (Huston, Watkins, & Kunkel, 1989). In a recent study, Lawrence Rosenkoetter (1999) assessed whether elementary school-aged children understood the moral lessons in two situation comedies from the late 1980's and early 1990's, *The Cosby Show* and *Full House.* One-third of the first graders and one-half of the third graders in his sample were able to describe the prosocial theme of each show. Moreover, children's prosocial behavior was positively correlated with the frequency with which they viewed prosocial programs. This relationship was even stronger for the children who understood the underlying moral of the programming. Thus, children who watched such programs *and* understood their underlying messages engaged in more prosocial behavior.

As discussed in Chapter 4, television is only one of many influences on children's social development. The time children spend watching television is influenced by school and homework schedules, playing with other children, and other activities. One recent study of an ethnically diverse sample of children from low- and middle-income families found that participants who lived in more stimulating home environments and who had better educated mothers spent more of their television viewing time watching educational programming (Huston, Wright, Marquis, & Green, 1999). Thus, many psychologists believe that caregivers can exert considerable influence on children's viewing habits by using TV rating information to regulate television viewing and discussing program content with children (Abelman, 1999).

remember the model's actions; third, you must have the ability to produce the actions; and fourth, you must be motivated to perform the actions. Consider a gymnast learning to perform a flying dismount from the uneven bars. She might learn to perform this feat by first paying attention to a gymnast who can already perform it. To be able to attempt the feat, the learner would have to remember what the model did. But to perform the feat, the learner must have the strength to swing from the bars. Assuming that she paid attention to the model, remembered what the model did, and had the strength to perform the movement, she still might be motivated only to perform the feat in important competitions.

We are beginning to understand the neural circuits that might be responsible for observational learning and the imitation of others' actions. The neurons involved are called **mirror neurons.** The exact location of mirror neurons and their networks in the frontal and parietal cortex remains controversial, and studies in both monkeys and humans are helping us understand more. In monkeys or humans, these neurons fire during the observation of the same actions or behaviors done by other individuals. For example, this system might be useful for infants learning to express emotion and mimic their mothers, or these neurons might provide feedback for us to help us understand how people feel. Consider if you have ever mimicked someone's facial expression if they are telling you a sad story or you have felt empathy toward that person. Neurological disorders such as stroke, autism spectrum disorders, and schizophrenia are also providing evidence for mirror neurons. In stroke patients the action of observation followed by imitation is a useful approach for rehabilitation of disabilities (Small, Buccino, & Solodkin, 2012). Some researchers hypothesize that the social deficits seen in autism spectrum disorders and schizophrenia may arise from dysfunctional mirror neuron networks.

Observational learning can promote undesirable as well as desirable behavior. For example, we can develop phobias vicariously through observing people who exhibit them (Rachman, 1991). In fact, a study of people with spider phobia found that 71 percent traced it to observational learning, 57 percent to classical conditioning, and 45 percent to their knowledge of spiders (Merckelbach, Arntz, & de Jong, 1991). Even monkeys can develop fears through observing other monkeys (Mineka & Cook, 1993). For example, in a study that also found support for the concept of preparedness in the development of phobias through observation, rhesus monkeys watched videotapes of model monkeys showing fear of presumably fear-relevant stimuli (toy snakes or a toy crocodile) or presumably fear-irrelevant stimuli (flowers or a toy rabbit). The monkeys developed fears of the fear-relevant but not the fear-irrelevant stimuli (Cook & Mineka, 1989). Perhaps they are prepared by evolution to do so because such fears have survival value.

mirror neurons Neurons that appear to be involved in the neural circuits responsible for observational learning.

Section Review: Cognitive Learning

1. How do experiments on blocking support a cognitive interpretation of classical conditioning?

2. In what ways do latent learning and observational learning support a cognitive view of learning?

3. How might mirror neurons help individuals empathize with emotions of other people?

Shaping the Professor's Behavior—A Case Study

Shaping has proved to be a powerful tool in conditioning behaviors that have little or no chance of occurring spontaneously. Shaping has contributed to areas as diverse as industry, parenting, education, animal training, athletic training, and treating mental hospital patients. This activity will provide you with experience in shaping to condition the behavior of your introductory psychology professor.

Method
Participant
The participant will be your introductory psychology professor. Because you will be using shaping to condition your professor's behavior, the students should inform the professor that they intend to shape an unidentified but nonembarrassing behavior.

Materials
You will need a pen and a sheet of paper to record each of your professor's behaviors and each time he or she receives a positive reinforcer.

Procedure
The students should agree on a behavior to shape. Some possibilities include having the professor touch his or her face, lecture toward one side of the room, or lecture from a particular spot in the room. Feel free to choose another (nonembarrassing) behavior. Do not inform your professor of the specific behavior you will be shaping. Of course, you must first obtain your professor's permission to do this demonstration.

After you have obtained permission and have identified a behavior to shape, you must decide on the positive reinforcer to use. Possible positive reinforcers include smiling at the professor, making eye contact with the professor, raising one's hand to make a comment, and appearing to be studiously taking notes. Once you have decided on the positive reinforcer to use, the students should agree on the sequence of behaviors to positively reinforce as successive approximations of the target behavior. Then proceed to shape your professor's behavior during a class lecture. The students must reinforce each successive behavior immediately after it occurs.

The students should try to be subtle in providing positive reinforcement. If all the students suddenly smile or make eye contact or perform some other simultaneous action, it might become too obvious to the professor. Thus, it would be advisable to have only certain students assigned to provide the positive reinforcer. Continue this procedure for as many class sessions as it takes to achieve the target behavior.

Record how many reinforcements are required to establish the target behavior. Also record how long the professor engages in the target behavior during the class session after the one in which it first occurs. On the class session following the one in which the target behavior is established, stop the positive reinforcement. Measure how long the professor engages in the target behavior during the next three sessions.

Results
Using data recorded by each of the students and finding the mean, note how many sessions and reinforcements were needed to condition the target behavior. Also using the data recorded from each of the students and finding the mean, note how long the professor engaged in the target behavior on the day after it first appeared. Again using the data recorded from each of the students and finding the mean, note the average length of time the professor engaged in the behavior on the three nonreinforced sessions.

Discussion
Discuss how successful the students were in shaping the target behavior as well as any difficulties you encountered. Would you do anything different if you repeated this exercise? Did the professor become aware of the target behavior? If so, do you think that it helped or hindered the shaping of the target behavior? Suggest a related follow-up demonstration you would be interested in doing.

Chapter Summary

Classical Conditioning

- Learning is a relatively permanent change in knowledge or behavior resulting from experience.
- In the kind of learning called classical conditioning, a stimulus (the conditioned stimulus) comes to elicit a response (the conditioned response) that it would not normally elicit. It does so by being paired with a stimulus (the unconditioned stimulus) that already elicits that response (the unconditioned response).
- In stimulus generalization, the conditioned response occurs in response to stimuli that are similar to the conditioned stimulus.
- In stimulus discrimination, the conditioned response occurs only in response to the conditioned stimulus.
- In extinction, the conditioned stimulus is repeatedly presented without the unconditioned stimulus, causing the conditioned response to diminish and eventually stop.
- In spontaneous recovery, a conditioned response that has been extinguished will reappear after the passage of time.
- Classical conditioning has been applied in many ways, as in explaining phobias, drug dependence, and learned taste aversions.
- Research has shown that in classical conditioning there are biological constraints on the ease with which particular stimuli can be associated with particular responses.

Operant Conditioning

- Operant conditioning involves learning the relationship between behaviors and consequences.
- There are four behavioral contingencies between behaviors and consequences: positive reinforcement, negative reinforcement, extinction, and punishment.
- In shaping, positive reinforcement involving successive approximations of the desired behavior is used to increase the likelihood of a behavior that is not in an individual's repertoire.
- In chaining, positive reinforcement is used to teach an individual to perform a series of behaviors.
- In operant conditioning, behavior is affected by schedules of reinforcement.
- In a continuous schedule, every instance of a desired behavior is reinforced.
- In partial schedules, reinforcement is not given for every instance.
- Partial schedules include ratio schedules, which provide reinforcement after a certain number of responses, and interval schedules, which provide reinforcement for the first desired response after a certain interval of time.
- In negative reinforcement, a behavior followed by the removal of an aversive stimulus becomes more likely to occur in the future.

- Negative reinforcement is implicated in avoidance learning and escape learning.
- When a behavior is no longer followed by reinforcement, it is subject to extinction.
- But after a period of time the behavior might reappear, in so-called spontaneous recovery.
- In punishment, an aversive consequence of a behavior decreases the likelihood of the behavior.
- To be effective, punishment should be immediate, firm, consistent, aimed at the misbehavior rather than the individual, and coupled with reinforcement of desirable behavior.
- Operant conditioning has even more diverse applications than does classical conditioning; these include animal training, child rearing, educational improvement, and understanding and treating psychological disorders.
- Biofeedback is a form of operant conditioning that enables an individual to learn to control a normally involuntary physiological response or to gain better control of a normally voluntary physiological response when provided with visual or auditory feedback of the state of that response.
- Like classical conditioning, operant conditioning is subject to biological constraints because members of particular species are more evolutionarily prepared to perform certain behaviors than to perform others.

Cognitive Learning

- Cognitive psychologists have shown that contiguity might not be sufficient to explain learning.
- Mere contiguity of a neutral stimulus and an unconditioned stimulus is insufficient to produce classical conditioning, and mere contiguity of a behavior and a consequence is insufficient to produce operant conditioning.
- Instead, for learning to occur, active cognitive assessment of the relationship between stimuli or the relationship between behaviors and consequences appears to be essential.
- In latent learning, learning is revealed in overt behavior only when reinforcement is provided for that behavior.
- Albert Bandura's social learning theory considers how individuals learn through observing the behavior of others.
- Mirror neurons may play a role in observational learning.
- There is a relationship between watching television and aggression and prosocial behavior.
- But the extent to which this relationship is causal is unclear.

Classical Conditioning

classical conditioning (p. 238)
conditioned response (CR) (p. 238)
conditioned stimulus (CS) (p. 238)
conditioned taste aversion (p. 243)
extinction (p. 240)
higher-order conditioning (p. 238)
learning (p. 237)
semantic conditioning (p. 238)
spontaneous recovery (p. 240)
stimulus discrimination (p. 240)
stimulus generalization (p. 240)
unconditioned response (UCR) (p. 238)
unconditioned stimulus (UCS) (p. 238)

Operant Conditioning

avoidance learning (p. 251)
behavioral contingencies (p. 246)
behavioral preparedness (p. 258)
biofeedback (p. 256)

chaining (p. 248)
computer-assisted instruction (p. 255)
continuous schedule of reinforcement
   (p. 248)
discriminative stimulus (p. 247)
escape learning (p. 251)
extinction (p. 252)
fixed-interval schedule of reinforcement
   (p. 250)
fixed-ratio schedule of reinforcement
   (p. 249)
instinctive drift (p. 258)
instrumental conditioning (p. 246)
law of effect (p. 246)
learned helplessness (p. 255)
negative reinforcement (p. 251)
operant conditioning (p. 246)
partial schedule of reinforcement
   (p. 249)
positive reinforcement (p. 246)

Premack principle (p. 247)
primary reinforcer (p. 247)
programmed instruction (p. 255)
punishment (p. 252)
secondary reinforcer (p. 247)
shaping (p. 248)
Skinner box (p. 246)
spontaneous recovery (p. 252)
token economy (p. 254)
variable-interval schedule of
   reinforcement (p. 251)
variable-ratio schedule of reinforcement
   (p. 250)

Cognitive Learning

blocking (p. 260)
latent learning (p. 261)
mirror neurons (p. 263)
observational learning (p. 261)
social learning theory (p. 261)

Chapter Quiz

Note: Answers for the Chapter Quiz questions are provided at the end of the book.

1. You wear a new jacket and receive many compliments, which makes you more likely to wear the jacket. This is an example of
   a. extinction.
   b. spontaneous recovery.
   c. positive reinforcement.
   d. negative reinforcement.

2. You have a toothache, which motivates you to go to the dentist. The dentist fills a cavity, eliminating your pain. When you have a toothache in the future, you will be more likely to go to the dentist. This is an example of
   a. extinction.
   b. punishment.
   c. positive reinforcement.
   d. negative reinforcement.

3. A psychologist decides to teach a child with an autism spectrum disorder how to cook a meal. She uses pieces of a chocolate chip cookie to reinforce the child for each of the steps in cooking a meal, until the child is able to perform each of the steps in sequence. This technique is called
   a. latent learning.
   b. behavioral chaining.
   c. programmed instruction.
   d. intermittent reinforcement.

4. You meet someone who reminds you of a former romantic partner and your heart "flutters." This is an example of
   a. response discrimination.
   b. stimulus discrimination.
   c. response generalization.
   d. stimulus generalization.

5. According to the classical conditioning explanation of drug overdoses, they occur when the
   a. drug dose is preceded by a bell.
   b. unconditioned stimulus is no longer presented to the person.
   c. person self-administers a drug dose in unfamiliar circumstances.
   d. environment contains stimuli that are typically present when the individual self-administers a drug dose.

6. A particular child is more likely to draw pictures than to practice the piano. The child's parent does not permit him to draw until he has practiced the piano. This is an application of (the)
   a. chaining.
   b. latent learning.
   c. Premack principle.
   d. negative reinforcement.

7. A pigeon is reinforced for its first peck at a lighted disc after varying lengths of time. The pigeon is on a
   a. fixed ratio schedule.
   b. fixed interval schedule.
   c. variable ratio schedule.
   d. variable interval schedule.

8. A psychologist conditions a person to salivate to the word "Pavlov" by saying the word and then immediately placing lemon powder on the person's tongue. The lemon powder induces salivation. After several pairings of "Pavlov" and the lemon powder, the person salivates to the word "Pavlov" itself. The psychologist then presents the word "Skinner" before "Pavlov" and the lemon powder for several trials. Despite this, "Skinner" fails to elicit salivation. This is an example of
    a. blocking.
    b. extinction.
    c. latent learning.
    d. stimulus discrimination.

9. A child who plays with electrical outlets receives an electric shock, making her less likely to play with them in the future. In operant conditioning, this is an example of
    a. punishment.
    b. latent learning.
    c. spontaneous recovery.
    d. negative reinforcement.

10. A health psychologist conducts an experiment on the classical conditioning of the immune response to an allergen in guinea pigs. After she injects the guinea pigs with an allergen, they display an allergic (immune) response. She then presents a distinctive odor to the guinea pigs on several trials just before giving them the injection. The guinea pigs eventually display an allergic response to the odor. The odor is the
    a. conditioned response.
    b. conditioned stimulus.
    c. unconditioned response.
    d. unconditioned stimulus.

11. A child is reinforced with praise by his parents on some occasions that he brings home an "A" on a spelling test. Sometimes they praise the child, sometimes they do not—in a completely unpredictable manner. The child is on a
    a. fixed ratio schedule.
    b. fixed interval schedule.
    c. variable ratio schedule.
    d. variable interval schedule.

12. Each time you turn the ignition key in your car, the car starts. This means that you are on a
    a. continuous schedule of reinforcement.
    b. fixed-interval schedule of reinforcement.
    c. variable-ratio schedule of reinforcement.
    d. variable-interval schedule of reinforcement.

13. A form of operant conditioning that enables a person to learn to control a normally involuntary physiological process is called
    a. chaining.
    b. biofeedback.
    c. latent learning.
    d. spontaneous recovery.

14. When you see a green traffic light, you know that it is safe to drive across an intersection. According to B. F. Skinner, the light serves as a(n)
    a. primary reinforcer.
    b. unconditioned stimulus.
    c. discriminative stimulus.
    d. intermittent reinforcer.

15. A biopsychologist tries to condition constriction of the blood vessels of the skin in response to a tone. She sounds a tone, which is turned off before she directs a blast of cold air at the subject's right hand (which makes its peripheral vessels constrict). This would be an example of
    a. trace conditioning.
    b. delayed conditioning.
    c. backward conditioning.
    d. simultaneous conditioning.

16. Computer-assisted instruction, a descendant of teaching machines and programmed instruction, is most closely associated with
    a. latent learning.
    b. operant conditioning.
    c. classical conditioning.
    d. social-learning theory.

17. A child who normally throws temper tantrums in toy stores, and is reinforced by having his parents give in and buy him a toy, stops the tantrums when the parents no longer give in to them. But on visiting a toy store, after going three months without visiting one, the child again throws a tantrum. In operant conditioning, this is an example of
    a. punishment.
    b. latent learning.
    c. spontaneous recovery.
    d. negative reinforcement.

18. A relatively permanent change in knowledge or behavior resulting from experience is called
    a. instinct.
    b. learning.
    c. maturation.
    d. habituation.

19. A person decides to teach her dog to roll over. She uses dog treats to reinforce any slight rolling movement, then only larger rolling movements, and, eventually, only a complete roll. This technique makes use of
    a. shaping.
    b. latent learning.
    c. programmed instruction.
    d. secondary reinforcement.

20. Your friend, who drives a standard-shift car, suffers a leg injury and cannot drive home. Though you have only driven automatic-shift cars, you have observed other people drive cars with standard shifts. As a result, you succeed, despite shifting roughly, in driving your friend to the emergency room. This would be an example of
a. blocking.
b. latent learning.
c. instinctive drift.
d. learning without awareness.

21. A student calls her boyfriend every night just after 10 p.m., when he has returned home from his evening job. If she calls before 10, he is never home. If she calls after 10, she always reaches him. She is on a
a. fixed-ratio schedule.
b. fixed-interval schedule.
c. variable-ratio schedule.
d. variable-interval schedule.

22. You train a raccoon to take a tiny basketball and "dunk" it in a hoop. But, at times, the raccoon stops to wash the ball in a nearby puddle, much as it would wash food in the wild. This would be an example of
a. extinction.
b. latent learning.
c. instinctive drift.
d. spontaneous recovery.

23. The procedure in which a conditioned response is given to a neutral stimulus that has been paired with an existing conditioned stimulus is called
a. shaping.
b. chaining.
c. instinctive drift.
d. higher-order conditioning.

24. A dog learns that immediately after its owner opens the front door on returning home from work, food is placed in its food dish. The dog eventually salivates in response to the opening of the door. But the owner changes the dog's feeding schedule, placing food in the food dish an hour after returning home. The dog gradually stops salivating to the opening of the door. This is called
a. shaping.
b. extinction.
c. spontaneous recovery.
d. spontaneous remission.

25. On a quiz show, contestants are reinforced with $1000 after every three correct answers in a row. The contestants are on a
a. fixed-ratio schedule.
b. fixed-interval schedule.
c. variable-ratio schedule.
d. variable-interval schedule.

Thought Questions

1. How would you use shaping to teach a child to ride a tricycle?

2. What are the shortcomings of research on the use of conditioned taste aversion to prevent predators from killing sheep?

3. How does the phenomenon of blocking support a cognitive interpretation of classical conditioning?

4. How would you use the Premack principle to get a child to clean his room?

5. Why do researchers still disagree about the existence of a causal relationship between televised violence and real-life aggression?

Memory

In 1898 a survey of 179 middle-aged and elderly Americans asked, "Do you recall where you were when you heard that Lincoln was shot?" Of those surveyed, 127 claimed they could recall exactly where they were and what they were doing at that moment on April 14, 1865 (Colegrove, 1899). Such a vivid, long-lasting memory of an important, surprising, emotionally arousing event is called a **flashbulb memory** (Brown & Kulik, 1977). People with flashbulb memories of an event might recall who told them about it, where they were, and trivial things that occurred at the time.

Perhaps you have a flashbulb memory of your first kiss or an award you received. Depending on your age, you might have a flashbulb memory of the suicide airline attacks of September 11, 2001, the death of John F. Kennedy Jr., the massacre at Columbine High School in Colorado, or the death of Princess Diana (Hornstein, Brown, & Mulligan, 2003). Older adults might have a flashbulb memory from November 22, 1963, when they heard that President John F. Kennedy had been assassinated. A survey of over 600 Turkish residents found that flashbulb memories were more prevalent among participants who had personally experienced the 1999 Marmara earthquake than participants who had learned about the earthquake on the news. This finding supports research indicating that the formation of a flashbulb memory requires that an event be important and charged with emotion (Er, 2003).

What accounts for flashbulb memories? The answer is unclear and psychologists disagree on the mechanism responsible for this type of memory. You can imagine how hard it would be to simulate a surprising event in a laboratory setting that would result in such a memory. Some psychologists believe that flashbulb memories are the product of normal memory processes, such as thinking more often and more elaborately about such experiences (McCloskey, Wible, & Cohen, 1988). Likewise, other psychologists insist that the emotional nature of flashbulb memories can explain the phenomenon (Lanciano, Curci, & Semin, 2010).

One study tested the common belief that flashbulb memories are more accurate than everyday memories. On September 12, 2001, undergraduates completed questionnaires about their memories of the suicide airliner attacks on the United States and an unrelated event that occurred a few days before the attacks. One group of participants was retested 1 week later, a second group was retested 6 weeks later, and a third group was retested 32 weeks later. The accuracy of students' memories of the attacks and the everyday memories did not differ significantly; both memories declined with time. However, participants were significantly more confident about their memories

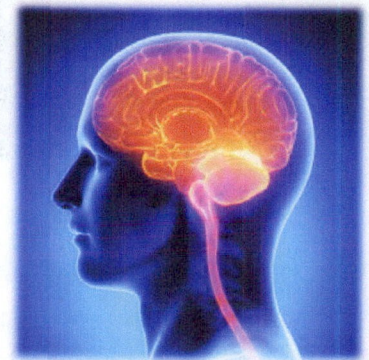

Source: CLIPAREA/Custom media/ Shutterstock.com.

Chapter Outline

Information Processing and Memory

Sensory Memory

Short-Term Memory

Long-Term Memory

Improving Your Memory

The Biopsychology of Memory

flashbulb memory A vivid, long-lasting memory of a surprising, important, emotionally arousing event.

of the attacks. These results indicate that flashbulb memories might seem special not because of a special mechanism but because of the undue confidence we place in them (Talarico & Rubin, 2003). Moreover, a survey of more than 3,000 residents of Great Britain regarding two major, unexpected events found that flashbulb memories might not be as vivid as commonly believed (Wright, Gaskell, & O'Muircheartaigh, 1998).

The exact nature of flashbulb memories will be discovered by research on **memory**, the process by which information is acquired, stored in the brain, later retrieved, and eventually possibly forgotten. As William James noted more than a century ago, memory provides our consciousness with its continuity over time. In the section "The Neuroanatomy of Memory," you will read about Henry Molaison, referred to before his death as H. M. for the purpose of participant anonymity, who suffered from brain damage that impaired his ability to maintain this continuity of consciousness. Memory also enables us to adapt to situations by letting us call on skills and information gained from our relevant past experiences. Your abilities to drive a car, to perform well on an exam, and to serve as a witness at a trial all depend on memory. Moreover, memory enriches our emotional lives. Your memory lets you re-experience events from your past, such as an uplifting family gathering.

In studying memory, psychologists consider several major "how" questions: How are memories formed? How are memories stored? How are memories retrieved? How are brain anatomy and brain chemistry related to memories? How dependable are eyewitness memories? This chapter addresses these questions.

memory The process by which information is acquired, stored in the brain, later retrieved, and eventually possibly forgotten.

Information Processing and Memory

During the past three decades, memory research has been driven by the "cognitive revolution" in psychology, which views the mind as an information processor. This predominance is reflected in the most influential model of memory, developed by Richard Shiffrin and Richard Atkinson (1969). Their model assumes that memory involves the processing of information in three successive stages: *sensory memory, short-term memory,* and *long-term memory.* **Sensory memory** stores, in *sensory registers,* exact replicas of stimuli impinging on the senses. Sensory memories last for a brief period—from less than 1 second

sensory memory The stage of memory that briefly (for at most a few seconds) stores exact replicas of sensations.

to several seconds. When you attend to information in sensory memory, it is transferred to **short-term memory**, which stores it for about 20 seconds unless you maintain it through mental rehearsal—as when you repeat a phone number to yourself long enough to dial it. Information transferred from short-term memory into **long-term memory** can be stored for up to a lifetime. Your ability to recall old memories indicates that information also passes from long-term memory into short-term memory.

The handling of information at each memory stage has been compared to information processing by a computer, which involves encoding, storage, and retrieval. **Encoding** is the conversion of information into a form that can be stored in memory. When you strike the keys on a computer keyboard, your actions are translated into a code that the computer understands. Similarly, information in your memory is stored in codes that your brain can process. **Storage** is the retention of information in memory. Computers typically store information on hard drives or CDs. In human and animal memory, information is stored in the brain. **Retrieval** is the recovery of information from memory. When you strike certain keys, you provide the computer with cues that make it retrieve the information you desire. Similarly, we often rely on cues to retrieve memories that have been stored in the brain. We are also subject to **forgetting**—the failure to retrieve information from memory. Forgetting is analogous to the erasing of information on a hard drive. Figure 8-1 summarizes this **information-processing model** of memory. Though some psychologists question the existence of separate information-processing stages for sensory memory, short-term memory, and long-term memory, there is strong evidence in support of them (Cowan, 1988).

short-term memory The stage of memory that can store a few items of unrehearsed information for up to about 20 seconds.

long-term memory The stage of memory that can store a virtually unlimited amount of information relatively permanently.

encoding The conversion of information into a form that can be stored in memory.

storage The retention of information in memory.

retrieval The recovery of information from memory.

forgetting The failure to retrieve information from memory.

information-processing model The view that the processing of memories involves encoding, storage, and retrieval.

Section Review: Information Processing and Memory

1. What evidence is there that flashbulb memories are not the product of a special brain mechanism?

2. How do sensory memory, short-term memory, and long-term memory differ from one another?

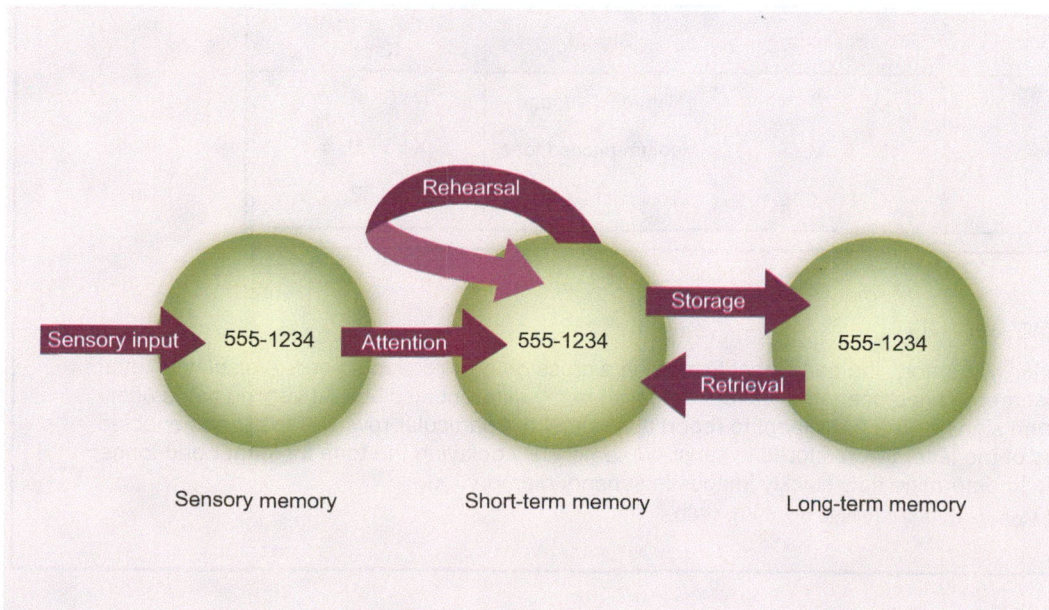

FIGURE 8-1
Memory Processes

The information-processing model of memory assumes that information (such as a phone number) passes from sensory memory to short-term memory to long-term memory. Information might also pass from long-term memory to short-term memory. Each of the stages involves information encoding, storage, and retrieval.

Do We Form Sensory Memories of All the Information That Stimulates Our Sensory Receptors?

Rationale

Though we have a sensory register for each of our senses, most research on sensory memory has been concerned with iconic memory. The classic experiment on iconic memory was carried out by a Harvard University doctoral student named George Sperling (1960). Sperling used an ingenious procedure to test the traditional wisdom that sensory memory stores only a small amount of the information that stimulates our sensory receptors.

Method

Sperling's procedure is illustrated in Figure 8-2. Participants, tested individually, stared at a screen on which Sperling projected sets of 12 letters, arranged in three rows of 4. Each presentation lasted for only 0.05 second—a mere flash. Sperling then asked the participants to report as many of the letters as possible. He found that the participants could accurately report an average of only 4 or 5 letters. Participants claimed, however, that they had briefly retained an image of the 12 letters, but by the time they had reported a few of them the remaining ones had faded away.

Rather than dismiss these claims, Sperling decided to test them experimentally by using a variation of this task. Instead of using whole report (asking participants to report as many of the 12 letters as possible), he used partial report (asking participants to report as many of the 4 letters as possible from a designated row). The task again included displays of 12 letters arranged in three rows of 4. But this time, at the instant the visual display was terminated, one of three different tones was sounded that indicated which row of letters was to be recalled.

Results and Discussion

When participants gave partial reports, they accurately reported an average of 3.3 of the 4 letters in a designated row. Because the participants did not know which row would be designated until after the display was terminated, the results indicated that, on the average, 9.9 of the 12 letters were stored in iconic memory. Sperling concluded that virtually all the information from visual receptors is stored as an image in iconic memory, but as his participants had claimed, the image fades rapidly.

These results inspired Sperling to seek the answer to another question: How fast does the information in iconic memory fade? He found the answer by repeating his partial-report procedure, but this time delaying the tone that signaled the participant to give a partial report. He varied the period of delay from 0.1 second to 1.0 second. As the delay lengthened, the participants' ability to recall letters in a designated row declined more and more. Sperling found that when the delay reached 1.0 second, the number of letters that could be recalled was about the same as when a whole report was used. Subsequent research has found that the typical duration of iconic memory is closer to 0.3 seconds than to 1.0 second (Loftus, Duncan, & Gehrig, 1992).

Fixation	Stimulus	Signal	Participant Report
＋	D G P R	High-pitched tone	D G P R
	X S M T	Medium-pitched tone	X S M T
	C H Z L	Low-pitched tone	C H Z L

Time →

FIGURE 8-2 Testing Sensory Memory

In Sperling's (1960) study of sensory memory, the participant fixated on a cross on a projection screen. A display of letters was then flashed briefly on the screen. This procedure was repeated with many different displays. At varying times after a display had been flashed, a tone signaled the participant to report the letters in a particular row. These reports enabled Sperling to determine how many of the letters were stored in sensory memory. By delaying the tone for longer and longer intervals, Sperling also was able to determine how quickly images in sensory memory fade.

Source: G. Sperling, *Psychological Monographs,* 74 (whole no. 498), 1960.

Sensory Memory

Think back to the last movie you saw. It was actually a series of frames, each containing a picture slightly different from the one before it. So why did you see smooth motion instead of a rapidly presented series of individual pictures? You did so because of your *visual sensory memory*, which stores images for up to a second. Visual sensory memory is called **iconic memory**; an image stored in it is called an *icon* (from the Greek word for "image"). The movie projector presented the frames at a rate (commonly 24 frames a second) that made each successive frame appear just before the previous one left your iconic memory, blending together the successive images and creating the impression of smooth motion. You can demonstrate iconic memory by rapidly swinging a pen back and forth. Notice how iconic memory lets you see a blurred image of the path taken by the pen. But how much of the information that stimulates our visual receptors is stored in iconic memory? That question inspired the classic experiment discussed in "The Research Process" box.

Auditory sensory memory serves a purpose analogous to that of visual sensory memory, blending together successive pieces of auditory information. Auditory sensory memory is called **echoic memory** because sounds linger in it. Echoic memory stores information longer than iconic memory does, normally holding sounds for 3 or 4 seconds but perhaps as long as 10 seconds (Samms, Hari, Rif, & Knuutila, 1993). The greater persistence of information in echoic memory lets you perceive speech by blending together successive spoken sounds that you hear (Ardila, Montanes, & Gempeler, 1986). A good demonstration of your echoic memory is when someone says something to you that you do not become aware of until a few seconds after it was said. Suppose that while you are enthralled by a television show a friend asks, "Where did you put the can opener?" After a brief delay, you might say, "What? . . . Oh, it's in the drawer to the left of the sink." Researchers have identified a precise region in the primary auditory cortex that processes echoic memories (Lu, Williamson, & Kaufman, 1992).

Based on Sperling's study and subsequent research, we know that sensory memory can store virtually all the information provided by our sensory receptors and that this information fades rapidly (though the fade rate varies among the senses). Nonetheless, we can retain information that is in sensory memory by attending to it and transferring it into short-term memory.

> **iconic memory** Visual sensory memory, which lasts up to about a second.

> **echoic memory** Auditory sensory memory, which lasts up to 4 or more seconds.

Section Review: Sensory Memory

1. How did George Sperling demonstrate that iconic memory stores more information than commonly believed?

2. How does the relatively long duration of echoic memory help us perceive speech?

Short-Term Memory

When you pay attention to information in your sensory memory or information retrieved from your long-term memory, the information enters your short-term memory, which has a limited capacity and holds information for about 0.2 to 60 seconds. Because you are paying attention to this sentence, it has entered your short-term memory. In contrast, other information in your sensory memory, such as the feeling of your tongue touching your teeth, will not enter your short-term memory until your attention is directed to it. And note that you are able to comprehend the words in this sentence because you have retrieved their meanings from your long-term memory. Because we use short-term memory to think about information provided by either sensory memory or long-term memory, it also is called *working memory*. Though some cognitive psychologists prefer to distinguish between short-term memory and working memory (Kail & Hall, 2001), they have yet to agree on the characteristics that would differentiate the two.

Information stored in short-term memory is encoded as sounds or visual images and then manipulated in working memory (Logie, 1999). We typically encode information as sounds—even when the information is visual. This phenomenon was demonstrated in a study in which participants were shown a series of 6 letters and immediately were asked to try to recall them. The participants' errors showed that they more often confused letters that sounded alike (for example, T and C) than letters that looked alike (for example, Q and O). The letters, though presented visually, had been encoded according to their sounds (Conrad, 1962).

In comparison to sensory memory or long-term memory, short-term memory has a relatively small storage capacity. You can demonstrate this for yourself by performing this exercise: Read the following numerals one at a time, and then (without looking at them) write them down in order on a sheet of paper: 6, 3, 9, 1, 4, 6, 5. Next, read the following numerals one at a time and write them down from memory: 5, 8, 1, 3, 9, 2, 8, 6, 3, 1, 7. If you have average short-term memory storage capacity, you were probably able to recall the 7 numbers in the first set but not the 11 numbers in the second set.

The normal limit of seven items in short-term memory was the theme of a famous article by psychologist George Miller (1956) entitled "The Magical Number Seven, Plus or Minus Two." Miller noted that short-term memory can hold, on the average, seven "chunks" of information, with a range of five to nine chunks. His observation has received support from other research studies (Logie, 2012), though some researchers have found that the normal range of capacity is greater than five to nine chunks (H. V. Smith, 1992). A *chunk* is a meaningful unit of information, such as a date, a word, or an abbreviation. For example, to a college student familiar with American culture, a list that includes the meaningful chunks CBS, NFL, and FBI would be easier to recall than a list that includes the meaningless combinations of letters JOL, OBS, and CWE.

Miller noted that the ability to chunk individual items of information can increase the amount of information stored in short-term memory (Baddeley, 1994). For example, after a 5-second look at the positions of pieces on a chessboard, expert chess players are significantly better than novice chess players at reproducing the positions of the pieces. Chess experts have a greater ability to chunk chess pieces into thousands of familiar configurations (Chase & Simon, 1973). Thus, though chess experts do not store more memory chunks in their short-term memory than novices do, their memory chunks contain more information (Gobet & Simon, 1998).

Given that about 7 chunks is the typical amount of information in short-term memory, how long will it remain stored? Without **maintenance rehearsal** (that is, without repeating the information to ourselves), we can store information in short-term memory for no more than about 20 seconds. But if we use maintenance rehearsal, we can store it in short-term memory indefinitely. You could use maintenance rehearsal to remember the items on a short grocery list long enough to select each of them at the store.

Early evidence that unrehearsed information in short-term memory lasts perhaps 20 seconds came from a study conducted by Lloyd and Margaret Peterson (1959) in which they orally presented trigrams that consisted of three consonants (for example, VRG) to their participants. Their procedure is presented in Figure 8-3. To distract the participants and prevent them from engaging in maintenance rehearsal of the trigrams, immediately after a trigram was presented a light signaled the participant to count backward from a 3-digit number by threes (for example, "657, 654, 651, . . ."). Following an interval that varied from 3 seconds to 18 seconds, a light signaled that the participants were to recall the trigram. The longer the interval, the less likely the participants were to recall the trigram. And when the interval was 18 seconds, the participants rarely could recall the trigram. Thus, the results indicated that unrehearsed information normally remains in short-term memory for no longer than about 20 seconds.

Information stored in short-term memory is commonly lost when other information interferes with it. For example, students who study while having the television playing in the background (Armstrong & Chung, 2000) often experience this loss. Background sounds interfere with the material that they have stored in short-term memory and prevent it from reaching long-term memory. Even low-volume irrelevant background sounds can markedly interfere with cognitive performance. Thus, simply turning down the volume will not be as beneficial as turning off the television.

maintenance rehearsal
Repeating information to oneself to keep it in short-term memory.

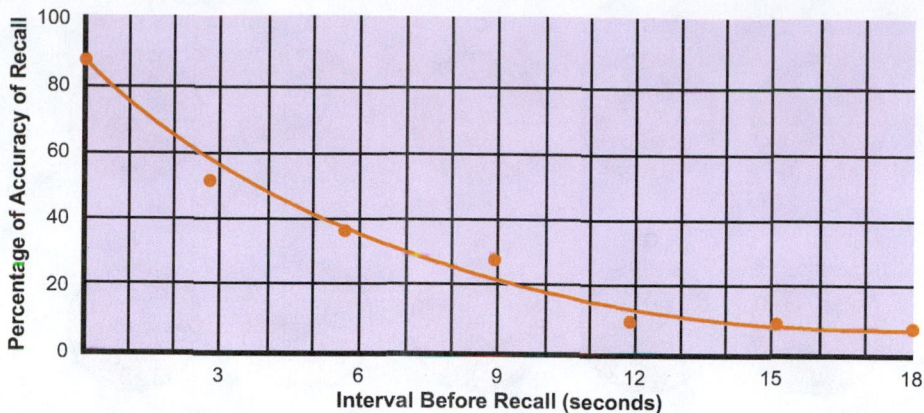

Interval Before Recall (seconds)

Y-axis: Percentage of Accuracy of Recall

FIGURE 8-3
The Duration of
Short-Term Memory

Peterson and Peterson
(1959) demonstrated that
the information in short-term
memory lasts no more than
20 seconds. A warning light
signaled that a trial was to
begin. The participant then
heard a 3-letter trigram and
a 3-digit number. To prevent
rehearsal of the trigram, the
participant counted backward
by threes from the number.
After a period of 3 to 18
seconds, a light signaled
the participant to recall the
trigram. The longer the delay
between presentation and
recall of the trigram, the less
likely the participant was to
recall it accurately.

Source: L. R. Peterson and M. J.
Peterson, "Short-Term Retention
of Individual Items" in *Journal of
Experimental Psychology*, 58:
193–198, 1959.

Section Review: Short-Term Memory

1. Why do psychologists believe that visual information tends to be stored acoustically in short-term memory?

2. How did Lloyd and Margaret Peterson demonstrate that short-term memories last about 20 seconds?

Long-Term Memory

As mentioned earlier, information moves back and forth between short-term memory and long-term memory. Information processing in long-term memory has been compared to the workings of a library. Information in a library is encoded in materials such as books or magazines, stored on shelves in a systematic way, retrieved via cues given by online catalogs, and forgotten when it is misplaced or its computer record is erased. Similarly, information in long-term memory is encoded in several ways, stored in an organized manner, retrieved via cues, and forgotten because of a failure to store it adequately or to use appropriate retrieval cues.

Encoding

William James (1890/1981, Vol. 1, p. 646) noted, "A curious peculiarity of our memory is that things are impressed better by active than by passive repetition." To appreciate James's claim, try to draw the face side of a United States penny from memory. Next, look at the drawings of pennies in Figure 8-4. Which one is accurate? Even if you have handled thousands of pennies over the years and realize that the front of a penny has a date and a profile of Abraham Lincoln, you probably were unable to draw every detail. And even when presented with several drawings to choose from, you still might have chosen the wrong one. If you had difficulty, you are not alone. A study of adult Americans found that few could draw a penny from memory, and less than half could recognize the correct drawing of one (Nickerson & Adams, 1979).

   What accounts for our failure to remember an image that is a common part of everyday life? The answer depends in part on the distinction between *maintenance rehearsal* and *elaborative rehearsal.* As noted earlier, in using maintenance rehearsal, we simply hold information in short-term memory without trying to transfer it into long-term memory, as when we remember a phone number just long enough to dial it. In **elaborative rehearsal**, we actively organize information and integrate it with information already stored in long-term memory, as when studying material from this chapter for an exam. Though maintenance rehearsal can encode some information (such as the main features of a penny) into long-term memory (Wixted, 1991), elaborative rehearsal encodes more information (such as the exact arrangement of the features of a penny) into long-term memory (Greene, 1987).

elaborative rehearsal
Actively organizing new information to make it more meaningful and integrating it with information already stored in long-term memory.

FIGURE 8-4
Can You Identify the Real Penny?

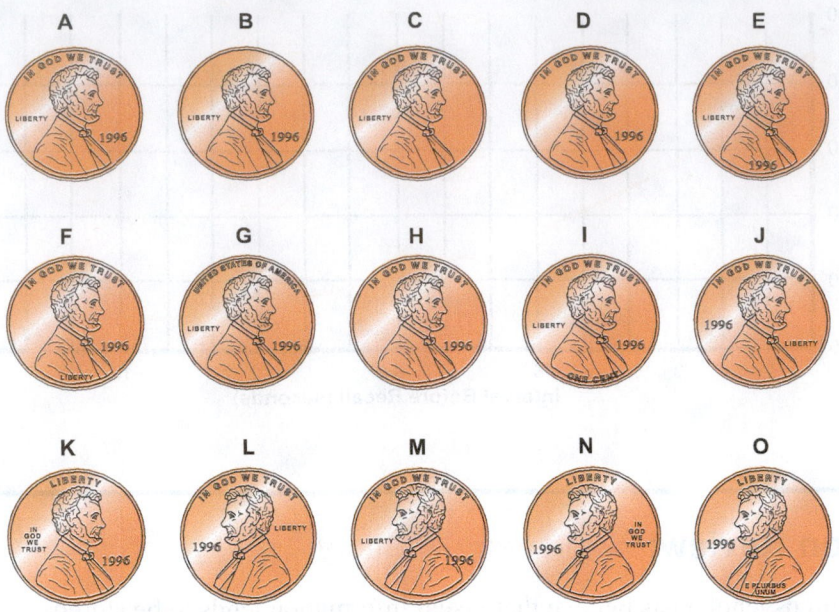

You can experience the benefits of elaborative rehearsal when you are confronted by new concepts in a textbook. If you try to understand a concept by integrating it with information already in your long-term memory, you will be more likely to encode the concept firmly into your long-term memory. For example, when the concept "flashbulb memory" was introduced at the beginning of this chapter, you would have been more likely to encode the concept into long-term memory if it provoked you to think about your own flashbulb memories. Elaborative rehearsal also has important practical benefits. In one study, sixth graders who were taught cardiopulmonary resuscitation showed better retention of what they learned if they used elaborative rehearsal (Rivera-Tovar & Jones, 1990).

levels of processing theory
The theory that the "depth" at which we process information determines how well it is encoded, stored, and retrieved.

The superior encoding of information through elaborative rehearsal supports the **levels of processing theory** of Fergus Craik and Robert Lockhart (1972), which originally was presented as an alternative to the information-processing model of memory. Craik and Lockhart believe that the level, or "depth," at which we process information determines how well it is encoded and, as a result, how well it is encoded in memory (Lockhart & Craik, 1990). When you process information at a shallow level, you attend to its superficial, sensory qualities—as when you use maintenance rehearsal of a telephone number. In contrast, when you process information at a deep level, you attend to its meaning—as when you use elaborative rehearsal of textbook material. Similarly, if you merely listen to the sound of a popular song over and over on the radio—a relatively shallow level of processing—you might recall the melody but not the lyrics. But if you listen to the lyrics and think about their meaning (perhaps even connecting them to personally significant events)—a deeper level of processing—you might recall both the words and the melody. Functional MRI and PET scans have provided support for the levels of processing theory by revealing that different brain regions are more active during shallow information processing than during deeper, more semantic information processing (Nyberg, 2002).

In a study that supported the levels of processing theory, researchers induced participants to process words at different levels by asking them different kinds of questions about each word just before it was flashed on a screen for a fifth of a second (Craik & Tulving, 1975). Imagine that you are replicating the study, and one of the words is *bread*. You could induce a shallow, *visual* level of encoding by asking how the word *looks*—for instance, "Is the word written in capital letters?" You could induce a somewhat deeper, *acoustic* level of encoding by asking how the word *sounds*—"Does the word rhyme with head?" And you could induce a much deeper, *semantic* level of encoding by asking a question related to what the word *means*—"Does the word fit in the sentence 'The boy used the ___ to make a sandwich'?" After repeating this procedure with several words,

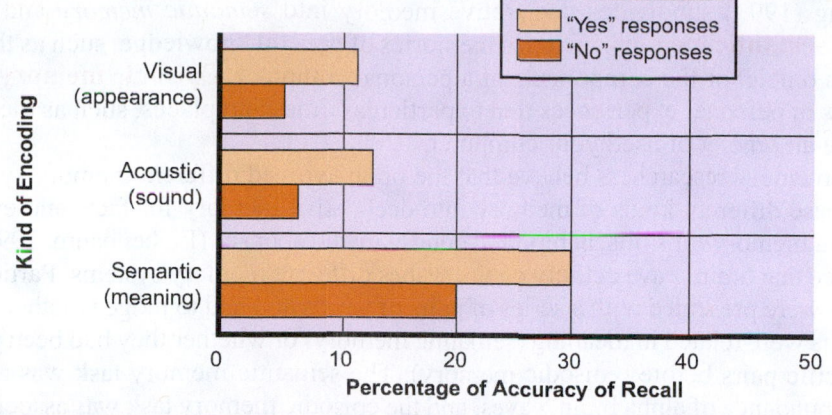

FIGURE 8-5
Levels of Processing
Craik and Tulving (1975) found that words that were processed at a deeper level were better remembered. Encoding words according to their meaning produced better recognition of them than did encoding them according to their sound or appearance.

Source: Data from F. I. M. Craik and E. Tulving, *Journal of Experimental Psychology: General,* 104: 268–294, American Psychological Association, 1975.

Level of Processing	Question	Answer	
		Yes	*No*
Visual (appearance)	Is the word presented in lowercase letters?	sofa	SOFA
Acoustic (sound)	Does the word rhyme with "look"?	book	DESK
Semantic (meaning)	Would the word fit in the sentence: "She left a _____ unlocked"?	DOOR	open

you would present participants with a list of words and ask them to identify which of the words had been presented before.

Craik and Tulving (1975) found that the deeper the level at which a word had been encoded, the more likely it was to be correctly identified (see Figure 8-5). Thus, the deeper the level at which information is encoded, the better it will be remembered. This conclusion has been supported by research showing that participants exhibited better recognition of previously presented words when they had attended to the words' meanings than when they had attended to the words' sounds (Ferlazzo, Conte, & Gentilomo, 1993). But some research findings indicate that the strength of the levels of processing effect depends on the nature of the material that is being processed in memory (Challis, Velichovsky, & Craik, 1996).

Storage

There are several major viewpoints on the nature of memory storage. Memory researchers look to *memory systems, semantic networks,* and *cognitive schemas* to explain the storage of memories.

Memory Systems

According to influential memory researcher Endel Tulving (1985), we store information in two kinds of long-term memory: **Procedural memory** includes memories of how to perform behaviors, such as making an omelet or using a word processor; **declarative memory** includes memories of facts. Declarative memory and procedural memory also are referred to, respectively, as **explicit memory** and **implicit memory** (Schacter, 1992). Implicit memory for odors can influence human behavior, as in a study of adults who performed creative, counting, and mathematical tests in unscented rooms or rooms weakly scented with jasmine or lavender. Though none of the participants reported smelling either odor, the results showed that jasmine hurt performance and lavender helped performance (Degel & Koester, 1999). Research on advertising has found that it can produce effects on both implicit and explicit memory. That is, we may be affected by memories of information that we may not be aware of (Northrup & Mulligan, 2013).

procedural memory
The long-term memory system that contains memories of how to perform particular actions.

declarative memory The long-term memory system that contains memories of facts.

explicit memory Conscious recollection of general information or personal experiences.

implicit memory Recollection of previous experiences demonstrated through behavior rather than through conscious, intentional remembering.

semantic memory
The subsystem of declarative memory that contains general information about the world.

episodic memory
The subsystem of declarative memory that contains memories of personal experiences tied to particular times and places.

Tulving (1993) subdivides declarative memory into *semantic memory* and *episodic memory*. **Semantic memory** includes memories of general knowledge, such as the definition of an omelet or the components of a personal computer. **Episodic memory** includes memories of personal experiences tied to particular times and places, such as the last time you made an omelet or used your computer.

Some memory researchers believe that the brain evolved different memory systems for storing these different kinds of memory into declarative memory for facts and events and procedural memory for skills, habits, and conditioned responses (Eichenbaum, 1997). There is evidence that brain-wave activity distinguishes different memory systems. Participants in one study were presented with a series of pairs of words and had to judge whether members of the pairs were related in meaning (semantic memory) or whether they had been presented with specific pairs before (episodic memory). The semantic memory task was associated with an abundance of alpha brain waves, and the episodic memory task was associated with an abundance of slower theta brain waves (Klimesch, 2012).

The main line of evidence in support of multiple memory systems in human beings comes from studies of people with brain damage. For example, either implicit or explicit memory can be intact while the other is impaired (Gabrieli Fleischman, Keane, & Reminger, 1995). In one case study (Schacter, 1983), a victim of Alzheimer's disease, which is a degenerative brain disorder marked by severe memory impairment, was able to play golf (procedural memory) and had good knowledge of the game (semantic memory) but could not find his tee shots (episodic memory). Though semantic memory and episodic memory are both forms of declarative memory, they may involve different brain systems. This conclusion is supported by PET scan studies that have found that different brain regions are involved in the performance of semantic and episodic memory tasks (Viard, Chételat, Lebreton, Desgranges, Landeau, de la Sayette, Eustache, & Piolino, 2011). Figure 8-6 illustrates the relationship of the different memory systems.

Nonetheless, some theorists believe that the selective loss of procedural, semantic, or episodic memories does not necessarily mean that we have separate memory systems (Horner, 1990). The question that many memory researchers seek to answer is this: Do different brain systems serve the different kinds of memory, or does a single brain system serve all of them? Regardless of how many memory systems we have, long-term memories must be stored in a systematic way. Unlike short-term memory, in which a few

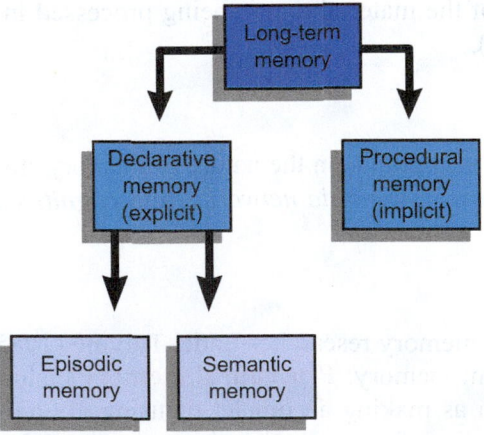

FIGURE 8-6
Memory Systems

Some memory researchers believe that there is sufficient behavioral and physiological evidence for the existence of memory systems that store different kinds of information. The declarative memory system stores explicit memories, which involve factual information that can be consciously recalled. Whereas the semantic memory system stores general information, the episodic memory system stores information about personal experiences. The procedural memory system stores implicit memories, which involve behavioral tendencies that can occur without conscious recollection of their origins. These memories include skills, habits, and conditioned responses.

unorganized items of information can be stored and retrieved efficiently, long-term memory requires that millions of pieces of information be stored in an organized rather than arbitrary manner. Otherwise, you might spend years searching your memory until you retrieved the memory you wanted, just as you might spend years searching the Library of Congress for William James's *The Principles of Psychology* if the library's books were shelved randomly. The better we are at organizing our memories, the better our recall of them is (Bjorklund & Buchanan, 1989). For example, a study of a server who could take 20 complete full-course dinner orders without writing them down found that he did so by quickly categorizing the items into meaningful groupings. When he was prevented from doing so, he was unable to recall all the orders (Ericsson & Polson, 1988).

Semantic Networks

A theory that explains how semantic information is meaningfully organized in long-term memory is the **semantic network theory**, which assumes that semantic memories are stored as nodes interconnected by links (see Figure 8-7). A *node* is a concept such as "pencil," "green," "uncle," or "cold," and a *link* is a connection between two concepts. More related nodes have shorter (that is, stronger) links between them. Even young children organize memories into semantic networks. For example, preschool children who enjoy playing with toy dinosaurs and listening to their parents read to them about dinosaurs may organize their knowledge of dinosaurs into semantic networks (Chi & Koeske, 1983). The dinosaurs would be represented as nodes (for example, "Brontosaurus" or *"Tyrannosaurus rex"*), and their relationships would be represented by links. The retrieval of a dinosaur's name from memory would activate nodes with which it is linked. So, retrieval of *Brontosaurus* would be more likely to activate nodes that contain the names of other plant-eating dinosaurs than nodes that contain the names of meat-eating dinosaurs, such as *Tyrannosaurus rex*. Deterioration of semantic networks may help account for the memory and language disruption seen in many people with schizophrenia (Brébion, et al., 2013) or Alzheimer's disease (Chan, Salmon, & De La Pena, 2001).

semantic network theory The theory that memories are stored as nodes interconnected by links that represent their relationships.

Cognitive Schemas

An alternative to the semantic network theory of memory organization is **schema theory**, which is used to explain both episodic memory and semantic memory. Schema theory was put forth decades ago by the English psychologist Frederic Bartlett (1932), who found that long-term memories are stored as parts of schemas. A *schema* is a cognitive structure that organizes knowledge about an event or an object and that affects the encoding, storage, and retrieval of information related to it (Alba & Hasher, 1983). Examples of schemas include "birthday party," "class clown," and "Caribbean vacation."

schema theory The theory that long-term memories are stored as parts of schemas, which are cognitive structures that organize knowledge about events or objects.

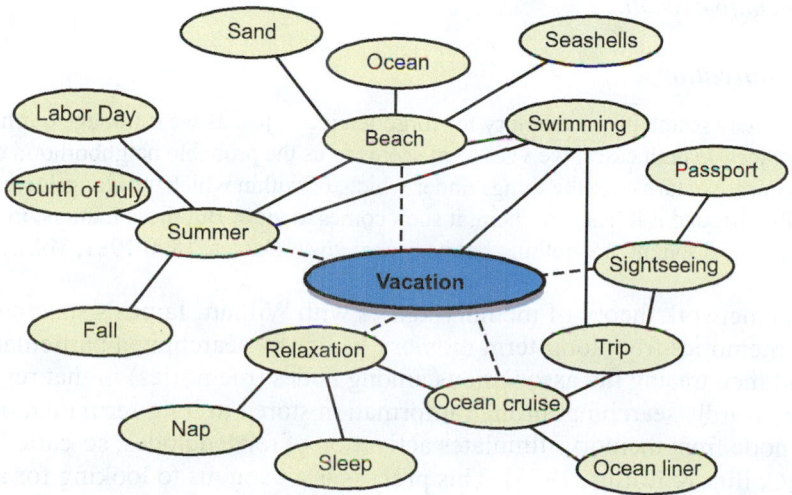

FIGURE 8-7
A Semantic Network Model

According to Collins and Loftus (1975), our long-term memories are organized into semantic networks in which concepts are interconnected by links. The shorter the link between two concepts, the stronger the association between them. After a retrieval cue has activated a concept, related concepts will also be activated and retrieved from long-term memory.

In a classic study, Bartlett instructed British college students to read a Native American folktale that told about a warrior fighting ghosts and later to write the story from memory. He found that the participants recalled the theme of the story but added, eliminated, or changed details to fit their own story schemas. For example, the participants added a moral, left out an event, or altered an aspect (such as changing a canoe to a boat). The reconfiguration of details in memory has received some support from more recent experiments (Ahlberg & Sharps, 2002).

Cultural schemas, which include the experiences, conventions, and expectations particular to one's culture, also can influence memory for stories. In a similar study, children from Papua, New Guinea, and the United States were read two fables ("The Boy Who Cried Wolf" and "Stone Soup"). Like the participants in Bartlett's study, the children changed many of the details in their retelling of the stories. Moreover, there were significant cross-cultural differences in the retelling of these stories, which were attributed to cultural differences in story schemas (Invernizzi & Abouzeid, 1995). Schema theory also has been used to explain gender differences in memory. In one study, children were taken to a playroom where they played with toys for 2 minutes. Half the toys were male-stereotyped (e.g., a space shuttle and train), and half were female-stereotyped (e.g., a Barbie doll and a tea set). Later, each child was asked to identify the toys from the playroom from a set of picture cards provided by the experimenter. Though there were no gender differences in the number of items identified, both girls and boys recognized more toys that were traditionally associated with their sex (Cherney & Ryalls, 1999). These results are consistent with studies that have reported similar biases in memory of masculine and feminine behaviors and female and male characters in children's literature (Signorella, Bigler, & Liben, 1997).

Other researchers have begun to investigate the influence of gender schemas on autobiographical memory in adults and children. In a series of studies, Penelope Davis (1999) found that women and girls reported more childhood memories—and accessed these memories more rapidly—than did men and boys. This gender difference was observed for events that were associated with both positive and negative emotions. In other words, female participants were more likely to recall incidents in which they, or others, were happy, sad, or fearful. Moreover, this gender difference also has been observed for everyday life events that are not associated with strong emotions (Seidlitz & Diener, 1998). The results of these studies have been attributed to gender differences in the socialization of emotional expression in men and women that influence the encoding of life events (Bauer, Stennes, & Haight, 2003).

Retrieval

Memory researchers are not only interested in how we encode and store memories but also in how we retrieve them. Psychologists who favor the semantic network theory study the role of *spreading activation,* and psychologists who favor schema theory study the role of *constructive recall.*

Spreading Activation

> In short, we may search in our memory for forgotten ideas, just as we rummage our house for a lost object. In both cases, we visit what seems to us the probable neighborhood of that which we miss. We turn over the things under which, or within which, or alongside which, it may possibly be; and if it lies near them, it soon comes to view. But these matters, in the case of a mental object sought, are nothing but its *associatives.* (James, 1890/1981, Vol. 1, p. 615)

The semantic network theory of memory agrees with William James's statement that the retrieval of memories from long-term memory begins by searching a particular region of memory and then tracing the associations among nodes (memories) in that region, rather than by haphazardly searching through information stored in long-term memory. The retrieval of a node from memory stimulates activation of related nodes, so-called *spreading activation* (Collins & Loftus, 1975). This process is analogous to looking for a book in a library. You would use the online catalog to give you a retrieval cue (a book number) to help you locate the book you want. Similarly, when you are given a memory retrieval cue, the relevant stored memories are activated, which in turn activate memories with which they are linked (Anderson, 1983). In keeping with this phenomenon, advertisers incorporate distinctive retrieval cues in their advertisements for specific products so that the repetition of those cues will evoke recall of those products. For example, a study found that the use of a visual cue helped children recall advertised cereal better and made them more likely to ask their parents to buy the cereal (Macklin, 1994).

To illustrate retrieval from a semantic network, suppose that you were given the cue "sensory memory." If your semantic network were well organized, the cue might activate nodes for "Sperling," "iconic," and "partial report." But if your semantic network were less well organized, the cue might also activate nodes for "amnesia," "chunks," or "Alzheimer's." And if your semantic network were poorly organized, the cue might activate nodes completely unrelated to sensory memory, such as "hallucination," "sensory deprivation," or "extrasensory perception."

Research findings indicate that spreading activation is important in a variety of contexts. The retrieval of mathematical facts depends on spreading activation within an arithmetic memory network (Niedeggen & Roesler, 1999). Word retrieval, as in the case of translation, among bilingual speakers also depends on spreading inactivation with the two language networks (Zhou & Li, 2013). And a study of radiologists found that their ability to make correct diagnoses from X-ray films depended in part on how well their relevant semantic networks facilitated spreading activation (Raufaste, Eyrolle, & Marine, 1998).

Constructive Recall

In contrast to semantic network theory, schema theory assumes that when we retrieve memories we might alter them to make them consistent with our schemas. An example of the schematic nature of memory retrieval, taken from testimony about the 1972 Watergate burglary that led to the resignation of President Richard Nixon, was provided by the eminent memory researcher Ulric Neisser (1981). Neisser described how a schema influenced the testimony of John Dean, former legal counsel to President Nixon, before the Senate Watergate Investigating Committee in 1973. Dean began his opening testimony with a 245-page statement in which he recalled the details of dozens of meetings that he had attended over a period of several years. Dean's apparently phenomenal recall of minute details prompted Senator Daniel Inouye of Hawaii to ask skeptically, "Have you always had a facility for recalling the details of conversations which took place many months ago?" (Neisser, 1981, p. 1).

Neisser found that Inouye's skepticism was well founded. In comparing Dean's testimony with tape recordings (secretly made by Nixon) of those conversations, Neisser found that Dean's recall of their themes was accurate, but his recall of many of the details was inaccurate. Neisser took this finding as evidence for Dean's reliance on a schema to retrieve memories. The schema reflected Dean's knowledge that there had been a cover-up of the Watergate break-in. Neisser (1984) used this analysis to support his conclusion that, in recalling real-life events, we rely on constructive recall more often than literal recall.

What Neisser called **constructive recall** is the distortion of memories by adding or changing details to fit a schema (Schacter, Norman, & Koutstaal, 1998). Schemas in the form of scripts for particular events even can affect eyewitness testimony. For example, the scripts we have for different crimes can affect our recall of events related to them. We might recall things that did not actually occur during a robbery if they fit our script for that kind of robbery (Garcia-Bajos & Migueles, 2003). Constructive recall might even explain why honest people have reported being abducted by aliens in UFOs. These people's memories might be constructed from nightmares, media attention, hypnotic suggestions during therapy, and support for their claims by alien-abduction groups (Clancy, 2007). But neither schema theory nor semantic network theory has yet emerged as the best explanation of the storage and retrieval of long-term memories. Perhaps a complete explanation requires both.

constructive recall
The distortion of memories by adding, dropping, or changing details to fit a schema.

Forgetting

According to William James (1890/1981, Vol. 1, p. 640), "If we remembered everything, we should on most occasions be as ill off as if we remembered nothing." James believed that forgetting is adaptive because it rids us of useless information that might impair our recall of useful information. But as you are sometimes painfully aware of when taking exams, even useful information that has been stored in memory is not always retrievable. The inability to retrieve previously stored information is called *forgetting*.

Measuring Forgetting

The first formal research on forgetting was conducted by the German psychologist Hermann Ebbinghaus (1885/1913). Ebbinghaus (1850–1909) made a purposeful decision to do for the study of memory what Gustav Fechner had done for the study of sensation—subject it to the scientific method (Postman, 1985). Ebbinghaus studied memory by repeating lists of items over and over until he could recall them in order perfectly. The items he used were called *nonsense syllables* (consisting of a vowel between two consonants, such as VEM) because they were not real words. He used nonsense syllables instead of words because he wanted a "pure" measure of memory, unaffected by prior associations with real words. Despite this effort, he discovered that even nonsense syllables varied in their meaningfulness, depending on how similar they were to words or parts of words.

Ebbinghaus found that immediate recall is worse for items in the middle of a list than for those at the beginning and end of a list (see Figure 8-8). His finding was replicated in the 1890s by Mary Whiton Calkins (Madigan & O'Hara, 1992). This differential forgetting is called the **serial-position effect** (Korsnes, Magnussen, & Reinvang, 1996). The better memory for items at the beginning of a list is called the *primacy effect,* and the better memory for items at the end of a list is called the *recency effect.* Thus, in memorizing a list of terms from this chapter, you would find it harder to memorize terms from the middle of the list than terms from the beginning or end of the list. The serial-position effect can even influence our memory for television commercials. A consumer psychology study demonstrated that when participants watched blocks of television commercials, their recall was worse for commercials in the middle of the blocks than at the beginning (especially) and end of the blocks. Television advertisers need to consider the relative placement of their advertisements for maximum impact on viewers' memories (Pieters & Bijmolt, 1997).

What accounts for the serial-position effect? The primacy effect seems to occur because the items at the beginning of a list are subjected to more rehearsal as a learner memorizes the list, firmly placing those items in long-term memory. And the recency effect seems to occur because items at the end of the list remain readily accessible in short-term memory. In contrast, items in the middle of the list are neither firmly placed in long-term memory nor readily accessible in short-term memory. Note that this explanation supports Shiffrin and

serial-position effect The superiority of immediate recall for items at the beginning and end of a list.

FIGURE 8-8
The Serial-Position Effect

This typical serial-position curve shows that items in the middle of a list are the most difficult to recall.

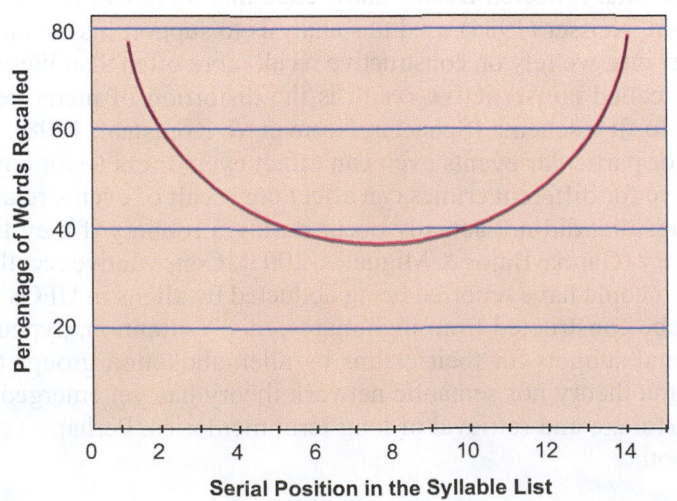

Atkinson's distinction between short-term memory and long-term memory. Before Ebbinghaus's work, knowledge of memory was based on common sense, anecdotal reports, and reasoning, with little supporting empirical evidence. Ebbinghaus moved memory from the philosophical realm into the psychological realm, making it subject to scientific research.

Ebbinghaus also introduced the **method of savings**, which is commonly called *relearning*, as a way to assess memory. In using the method of savings, Ebbinghaus memorized items in a list until he could recall them perfectly, noting how many trials he needed to achieve perfect recall. After varying intervals, during which he naturally forgot some of the items, Ebbinghaus again memorized the list until he could recall it perfectly. The delay varied from 20 minutes to 31 days. He found that it took him fewer trials to relearn a list than to learn it originally. He called the difference between the number of original trials and the number of relearning trials *savings* because he relearned the material more quickly the second time. The phenomenon of savings demonstrates that even when we cannot recall information, much of it still remains stored in memory, even though it is inaccessible to recall. If it were not still stored, we would take just as long to relearn material as we took to learn it originally.

When you study for a cumulative final exam, you experience savings. Suppose that your psychology course lasts 15 weeks, and you study your notes and readings for 6 hours a week to perform at an A level on exams given during the semester. You will have studied for a total of 90 hours. If you then studied for a cumulative final exam, you would not have to study for 90 hours to memorize the material to your original level of mastery. In fact, you would have to study for only a few hours to master the material again. Savings occurs because relearning improves the retrieval of information stored in memory (MacLeod, 1988).

Relearning is a method of testing implicit memory because it assesses information that has been retained without necessarily being accessible to conscious awareness prior to relearning. As another example of an implicit memory test, consider the word-stem completion test. Suppose you are exposed in passing to a list of words that includes *telephone*. Later, despite having no recollection of having seen the word, you would be more likely to take the word stem *tele-* and form the word *telephone* than if you had not been exposed to that word earlier.

You are more familiar with tests of explicit memory. A *recognition test* measures your ability to identify information that you have been exposed to previously when it is presented again. Recognition tests that you might encounter in college include matching, true/false, and multiple-choice exams. A *recall test* measures your ability to remember information without the information being presented to you. Recall tests that you might encounter in college include essay and fill-in-the-blanks exams. Ebbinghaus also found that once we have mastered a list of items, forgetting is initially rapid and then slows (see Figure 8-9). This phenomenon has been replicated many times (Wixted & Ebbesen,

method of savings
The assessment of memory by comparing the time or number of trials needed to memorize a given amount of information and the time or number of trials needed to memorize it again at a later time.

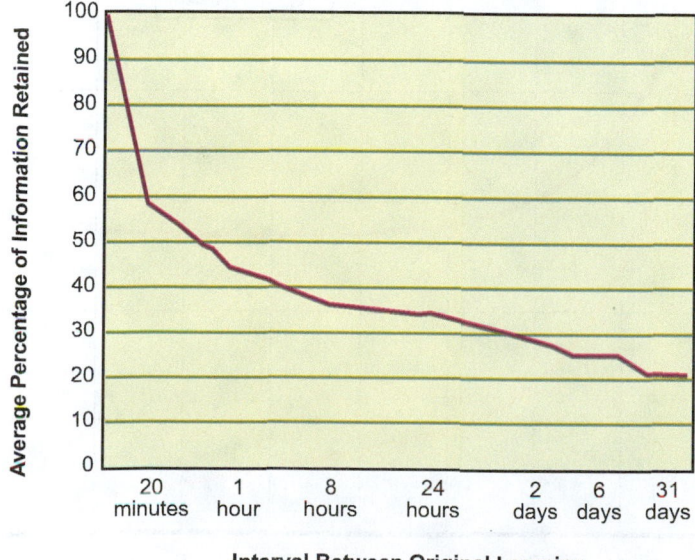

FIGURE 8-9
The Forgetting Curve

The graph presents the results of a study by Ebbinghaus on memory for nonsense syllables. It shows that forgetting is initially rapid and then levels off.

1991). So, if you memorized a list of terms from this chapter for an exam, you would do most of your forgetting in the first few days after the exam. But in keeping with the concept of levels of processing, meaningless nonsense syllables are initially forgotten more rapidly than is meaningful material, such as psychology terms.

Ebbinghaus's **forgetting curve**, which shows rapid initial forgetting followed by less and less forgetting over time, even holds for material learned decades before, as demonstrated in a recent study. Participants, aged 11 to 70 years, were former pupils of an elementary school in the Molenberg neighborhood of Heerlen in the Netherlands. Though some of the participants had not lived in the neighborhood for 50 years, they showed surprisingly good retention of the street names. Their forgetting was rapid in the first five years after leaving the neighborhood, but then it stabilized for more than 40 years after leaving. After a certain amount of time, memories that have not been forgotten can become permanently held, in a kind of "permastore" (Schmidt et al., 2000).

Explanations of Forgetting

During the past century, psychologists have provided several explanations of forgetting. These include *trace decay, interference, motivation,* and *encoding specificity.*

Trace Decay Plato, anticipating **decay theory**, likened memory to an imprint made on a block of soft wax: Just as soft-wax imprints disappear over time, memories fade over time. But decay theory has received little research support, and a classic study provided evidence against it. John Jenkins and Karl Dallenbach (1924) had participants memorize a list of 10 nonsense syllables and then either stay awake or immediately go to sleep for 1, 2, 4, or 8 hours. At the end of each period, the participants tried to recall the nonsense syllables. The researchers wondered whether sleep would prevent waking activities from interfering with the memories.

The graph in Figure 8-10 shows that participants had better recall if they slept than if they remained awake. There was some memory loss during sleep, providing modest support for decay theory, but if decay theory were an adequate explanation of forgetting, participants should have shown the same level of recall whether they remained awake or slept. Jenkins and Dallenbach concluded that participants forgot more of the nonsense syllables if they remained awake because experiences they had while awake interfered with their memories. In contrast, participants had forgotten fewer nonsense syllables after sleeping because they had few experiences while asleep that could interfere with their memories for the nonsense syllables. The durability of many childhood memories

forgetting curve A graph showing that forgetting is initially rapid and then slows.

decay theory The theory that forgetting occurs because memories naturally fade over time.

FIGURE 8-10
Interference and Recall

Jenkins and Dallenbach (1924) found that when participants learned a list of nonsense syllables and then slept, they forgot fewer of the nonsense syllables than when they stayed awake.

Source: J. G. Jenkins and K. M. Dallenbach, "Obliviscence During Sleeping and Waking" in *American Journal of Psychology,* 35: 605–612, 1924.

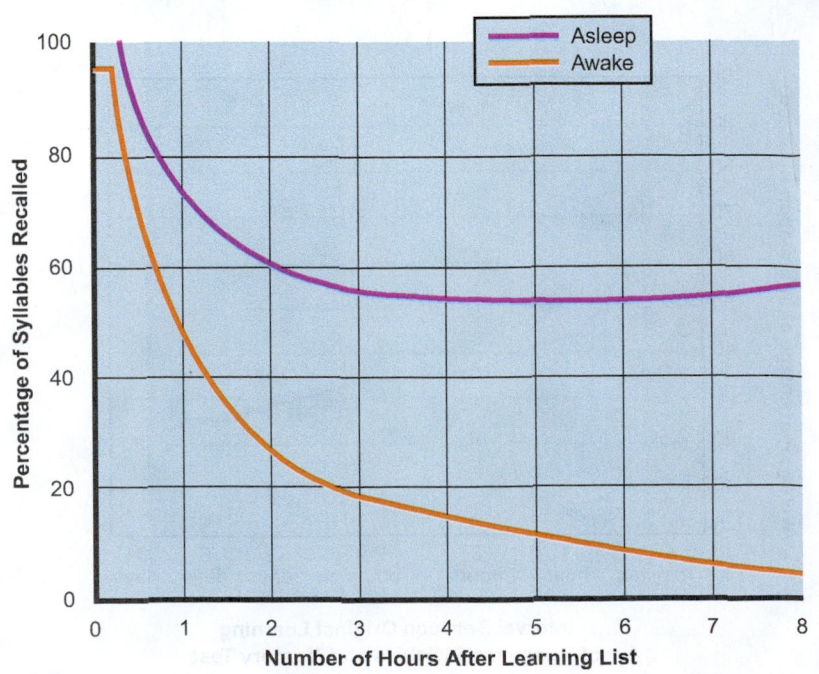

throughout adulthood, such as memories of your childhood neighborhood held in "permastore," also provides evidence against the decay theory.

Interference Since Jenkins and Dallenbach's classic study contradicting decay theory, psychologists have come to favor interference as a better explanation of forgetting. **Interference theory** assumes that forgetting results from particular memories' interfering with the retrieval of other memories. Interference occurs, for example, when we try to recall advertisements for the myriad of products we are exposed to in everyday life (Kumar, 2000). In **proactive interference**, old memories interfere with new memories (if you move to a new home, for instance, your memory of your old phone number might interfere with your ability to recall your new one). Proactive interference has been used to demonstrate that sign language and spoken language may be stored separately in human memory. A study found that there is less proactive interference in memory when old and new materials are each presented in a different language (that is, sign language and spoken language) than if both are presented in the same language (Hoemann & Keske, 1995). In **retroactive interference**, new memories interfere with old ones (your memory of your new phone number might interfere with your memory of your old one). Retroactive interference explains why learning a second language may interfere with our ability to retrieve words from our first language (Isurin & McDonald, 2001). Figure 8-11 illustrates the difference between proactive interference and retroactive interference.

You certainly have experienced both kinds of interference when taking an exam. Material you have studied for other courses sometimes interferes with your memories of the material on the exam. And interference is stronger when the materials are similar. Thus, biology material will interfere more than computer science material with your recall of psychology material. Because of the great amount of material you learn during a semester, proactive interference might be a particularly strong influence on your later exam performance (Dempster, 1985). So it would be best to study different subjects as far apart as possible rather than studying a bit of each every day. Moreover, be sure to study before going to sleep and right before your exam to reduce the effect of retroactive interference on your retrieval of relevant memories during the exam.

Motivation Sigmund Freud (1901/1965) claimed that we can forget experiences through **repression**, the process by which emotionally threatening experiences, such as witnessing a murder, are banished to the unconscious mind. Though research findings tend to contradict Freudian repression as an explanation of forgetting (Abrams, 1995), some studies suggest that we are more motivated to forget emotionally upsetting experiences than other kinds of experiences. Yet other studies find that there is no difference in recall of pleasant or unpleasant experiences (Bradley & Baddeley, 1990).

In an experiment that possibly demonstrated motivated forgetting, participants were shown one of two versions of a training film for bank tellers that depicted a simulated bank robbery. In one version, a shot fired by the robbers at pursuers hit a boy in the face. The boy fell to the ground, bleeding profusely. In the other version, instead of showing the boy being shot, the bank manager was shown talking about the robbery. When asked to recall details of the robbery, participants who had seen the violent version had poorer recall of the details of the crime than did participants who had seen the nonviolent version. One possible explanation is that

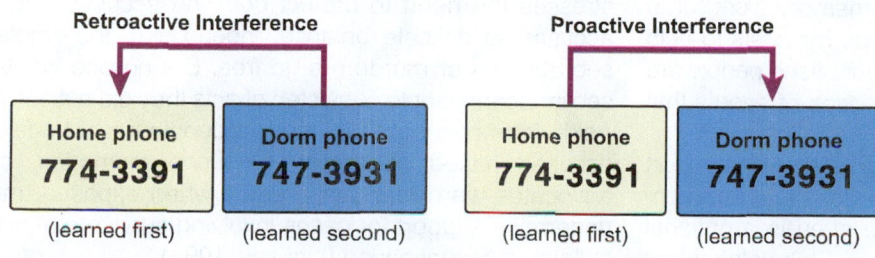

FIGURE 8-11
Proactive and Retroactive Interference

Forgetting takes place, in part, because memories interfere with each other. In proactive interference, old memories interfere with new memories. In retroactive interference, new memories interfere with old memories.

Should We Trust "Recovered Memories" of Childhood Abuse?

One day in 1989, Eileen Franklin-Lipsker looked into her 7-year-old daughter's eyes and was overcome by a horrible memory. Twenty years earlier, as an 8-year-old child, she had witnessed her father sexually assault and bludgeon to death her best friend, Susan Nason. Eileen recalled that her father, George Franklin, had warned her that he would kill her if she told anyone about the murder. Her attorney claimed that she had been so emotionally overwhelmed that she repressed the event for two decades—until the look in her daughter's eyes evoked the same feelings she had when looking into the eyes of Susan as she was being attacked. In 1990 George Franklin was convicted of murder (MacLean, 1993). The case was widely publicized by the media and was the basis of a made-for-television movie. In 1996 George Franklin's conviction was overturned on appeal because of a legal technicality.

During the 1990s, the media reported—and often sensationalized—several cases in which adults (usually women undergoing psychotherapy) suddenly recalled terrible childhood memories, most often of being sexually abused by an adult. Some of the people who have recalled these memories have made emotionally touching appearances on television talk shows to recount their stories of abuse. Many juries have convicted people based on such testimony, sending some defendants to prison and ordering others to make multimillion-dollar payments to their accusers.

Psychologists agree that most people with a history of childhood sexual assault remember all or part of their traumatic experiences. However, in a minority of cases, childhood memories of sexual abuse have resurfaced in adulthood. The media have become more skeptical in their treatment of such cases after finding that memory researchers are divided about whether to accept the validity of recovered memories. Researchers who support their validity believe that childhood trauma may result in total or partial amnesia and that memories may be recovered many years later (Alpert, Brown, & Courtois, 1998). Other researchers warn either that recovered memories are scientific fictions or that even if one accepts that phenomena such as dissociation or repression exists, therapists might purposely or unwittingly manipulate their clients into recalling vivid memories of events that never took place (Orenstein, Ceci, & Loftus, 1998). This manipulation becomes even more of an issue when therapists engage in "memory work" or in inappropriate use of techniques such as hypnosis to help their clients recover past memories. Hypnotized people are especially susceptible to forming memories of events that never took place (Wagstaff & Frost, 1996).

Researchers who believe there is little or no support for the validity of recovered memories call this phenomenon *false memory syndrome*. There even is a national False Memory Syndrome Foundation in Philadelphia that acts as a resource for people who claim they have been falsely accused of crimes based on recovered memories. People who claim they have been accused of crimes based on false recovered memories are suing therapists for implanting memories and convincing their clients of the reality of those memories. The notion that false memories may be created by therapists has a long history. In fact, the first documented creation of such a memory was reported in 1889 by the renowned French hypnotist Hippolyte Bernheim. Bernheim convinced a person that an extremely traumatic event had occurred, which led to the person's believing that this false memory was true (Rosen, Sageman, & Loftus, 2004). Nonetheless, supporters of the validity of recovered memories note that opposition to their existence comes primarily from memory researchers rather than from clinicians. Some clinicians insist that even though laboratory research has provided little support for this phenomenon, clinical experience with clients has convinced them that some cases of recovered memory are true (Critchlow, 1998). For example, clinicians have reported cases in which World War II veterans have recovered memories of traumatic, independently verified wartime experiences many years later—and obtained emotional relief by doing so (Karon & Widener, 1998).

But some memory researchers counter that these clinical reports are not reliable enough to support the validity of recovered memories (Lilienfeld & Loftus, 1998). Supporters of the validity of recovered memories point to scientific research indicating that recovered memories of childhood abuse can occur and that they are just as accurate as memories of abuse that have been recalled continuously from the time the events took place (Brown, Scheflin, & Whitfield, 1999). Other researchers claim that the memory processes of maltreated and healthy children are more similar than different (Howe, Toth, & Cicchetti, 2011). Memory researchers and clinicians do agree, though, that more research is necessary to identify the psychological processes that affect memory of childhood sexual abuse.

Expert memory researcher Elizabeth Loftus studies the fallibility of human memory. She insists that we might hold dearly to memories of events that never took place if we are led to believe they truly occurred through situations such as interviews conducted with leading questions. She stresses the need to protect both the accused and the accuser—a delicate balance, indeed. No one wants to see abusers or murderers go free. But no one wants to see innocent people convicted of acts they did not commit. Aside from concern that innocent people might be falsely accused based on therapist-induced memories, child advocates warn that such cases, when exposed, might undermine support for cases involving survivors of actual childhood sexual abuse (Lindsay, 1994).

Motivated Forgetting

According to Sigmund Freud, a person (such as children who experience trauma such as physical assault, warfare, or natural disasters) might forget a traumatic event by repressing its memory to the unconscious mind.
Source: kitty/Shutterstock.com.

the content of the violent version motivated participants to forget what they had seen (Loftus & Burns, 1982). However, in some cases, memory of traumatic events will be superior to memory of ordinary events (Christianson & Loftus, 1987).

Encoding Specificity Because the retrieval of long-term memories depends on adequate retrieval cues, forgetting sometimes can be explained by the failure to have or to use those cues. For example, odors that we associate with an event can aid our recall of it (Smith, Standing, & de Man, 1992). This explanation is known as *cue-dependence theory*. At times we might fail to find an adequate cue to activate the relevant portion of a semantic memory network. Consider the **tip-of-the-tongue phenomenon**, in which you cannot quite recall a familiar word—though you feel that you know it (Schwartz & Smith, 1997). As a demonstration, you might induce a tip-of-the-tongue experience by trying to recall the names of the seven dwarfs in the Snow White fairy tale. You might fail to recall one or two of them, yet still feel that you know them (Miserandino, 1991). The tip-of-the-tongue phenomenon indicates that when we speak, we might retrieve the meaning of a word before we retrieve its sound pattern (Vigliocco, Vinson, Martin, & Garrett, 1999). The frequency of tip-of-the-tongue experiences and the time that it takes to resolve them by retrieving the correct word increase with age (Heine, Ober, & Shenaut, 1999).

A study of the tip-of-the-tongue phenomenon presented college students with the faces of 50 celebrities and asked them to recall their names. The results indicated that the students searched for the names by using cues associated with the celebrities. The students tried to recall their professions, where they usually performed, and the last time they had seen them. Characteristics of the names also served as cues for recalling them. These cues included the first letters of the names, the first letters of similar-sounding names, and the number of syllables in the names (Yarmey, 1973). This study supports the concept of **encoding specificity**, which states that recall will be best when cues that were associated with the encoding of a memory are also present during attempts at retrieving the memory (Tulving & Thomson, 1973). Researchers interested in the role of encoding specificity in forgetting study *context-dependent memory* and *state-dependent memory*.

Context-Dependent Memory In an unusual experiment on encoding specificity, scuba divers memorized lists of words while either underwater or on a beach, and then tried to recall the words while either in the same location or in the other location (Godden & Baddeley, 1975). The participants communicated with the experimenter through a special intercom system. The results (see Figure 8-12) indicated that when participants memorized and recalled the words in different locations, they recalled about 30 percent fewer than when they memorized and recalled the words in the same location. This tendency for recall to be best when the environmental context present during the encoding of a memory also is present during attempts at retrieving it is known as **context-dependent memory**. The findings of the study even have practical implications. Instructions given to

tip-of-the-tongue phenomenon
The inability to recall information that one knows has been stored in long-term memory.

encoding specificity
The principle that recall will be best when cues that were associated with the encoding of a memory are also present during attempts at retrieving it.

context-dependent memory
The tendency for recall to be best when the environmental context present during the encoding of a memory is also present during attempts at retrieving it.

FIGURE 8-12
Context-Dependent
Memory

Godden and Baddeley
(1975) found that words
learned underwater were best
recalled underwater and that
words learned on land were
best recalled on land. This
is an example of improved
recall due to the fact that the
context of the environment
was the same at the time of
encoding and retrieval.

Source: Adapted from D. R.
Godden and A. D. Baddeley,
"Context-Dependent Memory
in Two Natural Environments:
On Land and Under Water" in
British Journal of Psychology, 66:
325–331. Copyright © 1975 British
Psychological Society, Leicester,
England. Reprinted by permission.

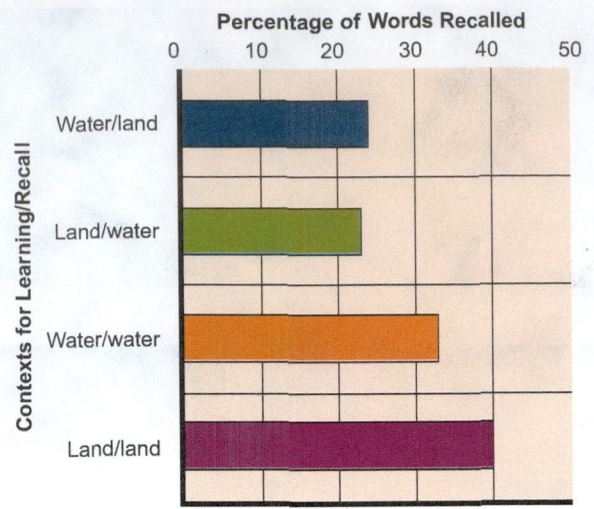

scuba divers should be given underwater as well as on dry land, and if divers are making observations about what they see underwater, they should record them there and not wait until they get on dry land (Baddeley, 1982).

When you return to your old school or neighborhood, long-lost memories might come flooding back, evoked by environmental cues that you had not been exposed to for years. This effect of environmental context on recall is not lost on theater directors, who hold dress rehearsals in full costume amid the scenery that will be used during actual performances. Similarly, even your academic performance can be affected by environmental cues (Parker & Gellatly, 1997), as in a study in which college students read an article in either noisy or silent conditions and then were tested on their comprehension of it in either noisy or silent conditions (Grant, et al., 1998). They performed better when they read the article and were tested under the same conditions (noisy-noisy or silent-silent) than when they did so under different conditions (noisy-silent or silent-noisy). Likewise, college students may perform worse when their exams are given in classrooms other than their normal ones (Abernethy, 1940). Perhaps you have noticed this phenomenon when you have taken a final exam in a strange room. If you find yourself in that situation, you might improve your performance by mentally reinstating the environmental context in which you learned the material (Smith, 1984).

There is controversy among memory researchers about whether the environmental context is important when *recall* is required but not when *recognition* is required. In other words, your performance on an essay exam might be impaired if you took the exam in a strange room, but your performance on a multiple-choice test would not. Perhaps tasks that require recognition include enough retrieval cues of their own, making environmental retrieval cues relatively less important (Eich, 1980). But some research indicates that even recognition memory is affected by environmental context. In one study, participants observed a person and then were asked to identify the individual in a photo lineup. Some participants had to identify the individual under the same environmental context, and some under different contexts. Recognition was better under the same context. In fact, participants who simply imagined the original context improved their recognition performance (Smith & Vela, 1992).

state-dependent memory
The tendency for recall to be best when one's emotional or physiological state is the same during the recall of a memory as it was during the encoding of that memory.

State-Dependent Memory Our recall of memories depends not only on cues from the external environment but also on cues from our internal states. The effect on recall of the similarity between a person's internal state during encoding and during retrieval is called **state-dependent memory**. For example, memories encoded while the person is in a psychoactive drug-induced state will be recalled better when the person is in that state. A variety of drugs induce state-dependent memory, a fact first noted in 1835 (Overton,

1991). These drugs include alcohol (Nakagawa & Iwasaki, 1996), nicotine (Peters & McGee, 1982), benzodiazepines (Sanday, Zanin, Patti, Tufkik, & Frussa-Filho, 2012), and barbiturates (Kumar, Ramalingam, & Karanth, 1994). Likewise, people who learn material while exercising on a bicycle ergometer will recall the material better if they do so while exercising on a bicycle ergometer (Miles & Hardman, 1998). Given this phenomenon, perhaps people who discuss business deals during aerobic exercise might have some difficulty recalling what they discussed when they return to their offices.

In a government-sponsored study on the possible state-dependent effects of marijuana (Eich, Weingartner, Stillman, & Gillin, 1975), one group of participants memorized a list of words after smoking marijuana, and a second group memorized the same list after smoking a placebo that tasted like marijuana. Participants were "blind"; that is, they did not know whether they were smoking marijuana or a placebo. Four hours later, half of each group smoked either marijuana or a placebo and then tried to recall the words they had memorized. Recall was better either when participants smoked the placebo on both occasions or when they smoked marijuana on both occasions than when they smoked marijuana on one occasion and the placebo on the other. You should *not* conclude that marijuana smoking improves memory. As noted in Chapter 6, marijuana actually impairs memory. And indeed, in this study the group who smoked the placebo on both occasions performed *better* than the groups who smoked marijuana on either occasion or both occasions.

Our internal states also involve our moods, which can play a role in a form of state-dependent memory called *mood-dependent memory,* in which our recall of information that has been encoded in a particular mood will be best when we are in that mood again. If you study material while listening to music that evokes a particular mood and then are tested on the material later, you might perform better if you are tested while listening to music that evokes a similar mood (Balch, Myers, & Papotto, 1999). Mood appears to act as a cue for the retrieval of memories. In one study, one group of undergraduates memorized a word list while in a state of fear, and a second group memorized a word list while in a state of relaxation. Recall was better for participants who learned and recalled the word lists in the same emotional state (Robinson & Rollings, 2011). Thus, if you have an emotional experience, you might be more likely to recall details of that experience when you are again experiencing the same emotion. Mood-dependent memory also might account for claims by some criminals who have committed violent crimes but have since calmed down, that they were so angry while committing the crimes that they cannot recall what they did (Swihart, Yuille, & Porter, 1999).

Section Review: Long-Term Memory

1. How does the superiority of elaborative rehearsal, compared to maintenance rehearsal, support the levels of processing theory of long-term memory encoding?

2. What is the difference between procedural memory and declarative memory?

3. What is the difference between proactive and retroactive interference?

4. What evidence is there to support the notion of state-dependent memory?

Memory, Forgetting, and Eyewitness Testimony

In August 1979, Father Bernard Pagano went on trial for a series of armed robberies. Eyewitnesses had identified him as the so-called gentleman bandit, a polite man who had robbed several convenience stores in Wilmington, Delaware. Father Pagano was arrested after several people who knew him told the police that he resembled published drawings of the bandit. Seven eyewitnesses, who were shown photographs in which Father Pagano wore his clerical collar, identified him as the robber. They might have been influenced by previous police reports that indicated that the perpetrator looked like a clergyman. Fortunately for Father Pagano, while he was on trial, another man, Ronald Clouser, confessed to the crimes (Rodgers, 1982).

There was little resemblance between Father Pagano and Ronald Clouser. The possibility of convicting innocent people or of exonerating guilty people based on inaccurate eyewitness testimony has led psychologists to study the factors that affect eyewitness memories. This concern is not new. Hugo Münsterberg (1908), a pioneer in the study of psychology and the law, warned us to consider the imperfections of human memory when evaluating the accuracy of **eyewitness testimony**. At about the same time, Alfred Binet, who gained fame for developing the first IQ test, championed the scientific study of eyewitness testimony. He introduced the *picture-description test,* which required participants to examine a picture of a scene and, after varying lengths of time, to recall as much as possible about the picture or to answer questions about it posed by an interrogator. Binet found that eyewitness testimony usually included inaccuracies and that testimony under questioning was less accurate than spontaneous testimony (Postman, 1985).

During the past few decades, psychologists have conducted many research studies of the factors that affect the accuracy of eyewitness testimony (Frenda, Nichols, & Loftus, 2011). Research on eyewitness memories shows that they are not like mental tape recordings that record and play back exact representations of events. Instead, eyewitness recollections are reconstructive, somewhat altering the events that they represent. For example, cognitive schemas can influence eyewitness testimony. When eyewitnesses are presented with an ambiguous crime schema, they are more likely to insert schema-consistent information that had not been present than schema-inconsistent information (Tuckey & Brewer, 2003).

The misidentification of Father Pagano would not surprise psychologists who study eyewitness testimony. They know that misidentifications from lineups of suspects are the single leading cause of wrongful criminal convictions (Lindsay & Pozzulo, 1999). Moreover, law enforcement and court procedures can contribute to misidentification of suspects. These procedures include the wording of questions, instructions for viewing lineups and mug shots, and exposing witnesses to information after the event (Kassin, Tubb, Hosch, & Memon, 2001).

The fragility of eyewitness testimony has been supported cross-culturally. In a study conducted in Japan based on a real-life event, customers (confederates of the researcher) visited stores and bought items from professional sales clerks. Three months later each clerk was asked to identify from a photograph the customer who had bought the items. Half the sales clerks recalled details of the event and the customer, but only two-thirds of those details were accurate. Of the two-thirds who claimed they could identify the customer from a photograph, only 14 percent were accurate (Naka, Itsukushima, & Itoh, 1996). And cross-cultural differences can influence eyewitness testimony. This finding was demonstrated in a study using 48 Spanish and 48 English undergraduates. Participants were shown two films, one of an event common in Spanish culture and one of an event common in English culture. Later they were asked to recall what they had seen. Perhaps contrary to common sense, recall accuracy was greater for the event that was not from the participants' own culture (Davies & Alonso-Quecuty, 1997).

A number of studies have found that recall is even less accurate when eyewitnesses are asked to recognize persons from other ethnic groups (Bothwell, Brigham, & Malpass, 1989). In one study, European American and African American participants were more accurate when they identified suspects from their own ethnic group (Devine & Malpass, 1985). These findings have been replicated with Latino (Platz & Hosch, 1988) and Asian samples (Ng & Lindsay, 1994). Two of the main topics of interest regarding eyewitness testimony are the accuracy of children's eyewitness testimony and the effects of questioning on eyewitness testimony.

Children as Eyewitnesses An issue that has concerned psychologists since the beginning of the 20th century is whether the testimony of children is trustworthy (Ceci & Bruck, 1993). As first demonstrated by the German psychologist William Stern, children

eyewitness testimony
Witnesses' recollections about events, most notably about criminal activity.

tend to be less accurate than adults in their eyewitness accounts of crimes, in part because they are more suggestible—that is, they are more susceptible to leading questions (Templeton & Wilcox, 2000). Concerns about children as eyewitnesses have been supported by research indicating that misleading information about events can distort children's memories of them. In an experiment that tested this finding, children aged 3 to 12 years listened to a story about a girl who had a *stomachache* after eating *eggs* too fast. When asked questions about the story, the children answered correctly almost all the time. But when asked if they remembered the story of a little girl who got a *headache* because she ate her *cereal* too fast, the children typically responded that they had. The effect of misleading questions was greater on the younger children than on the older ones (Ceci, Ross, & Toglia, 1987).

Other studies likewise have found that the younger the children, the less accurate their testimony tends to be. In one such study, children 3 to 4 years old or 6 years old were interviewed about real and fictitious events and were asked whether the events had happened to them. The younger children were more likely than the older ones to claim they had experienced an event that they had only thought about. Such studies might help explain some cases in which young children have falsely claimed they were sexually abused only after being interviewed in some detail about the alleged abuse (Ceci, Huffman, & Smith, 1994).

Children also are more likely to guess when testifying, as in a study in which kindergartners viewed a slide show of a staged theft and then were asked to identify the perpetrator from a lineup. Many identified a person in the lineup even when the perpetrator was not in the lineup. Moreover, some children who had made correct identifications when the perpetrator was present in the lineup later identified a person in a lineup in which the perpetrator was absent. Children may have a tendency to guess or make up answers when they testify repeatedly about the same event (Ackil & Zaragoza, 1998; Beal, Schmitt, & Dekle, 1995). In fact, children are more reliable eyewitnesses when they are given an option to say that they are not sure when they are providing their testimony (Brewer, Keast, & Sauer, 2010).

Not only are young children more fallible in their testimony than older children are, but also children tend to be less accurate in their testimony than adults are. One study compared adults and children in the accuracy of their memories for an event they experienced 2 years earlier. The children were less accurate in responding to yes/no questions and open-ended questions and were more likely to fabricate responses to a question about a man's occupation. This fallibility might have an effect on court cases that take a long time to reach trial (Poole & White, 1993).

Of course, especially because of the prevalence of child sexual and physical abuse, courts must achieve a delicate balance between believing children's testimony and being skeptical of it (Goodman & Schaaf, 1997). Fortunately, children can give accurate testimony provided that they are not given leading questions and provided that the questions are worded so that the children can understand them (Brooks & Siegel, 1991). To promote accuracy in children's testimony, the questioning of children should be done by neutral parties rather than by individuals who are biased either toward or against believing the children's stories of abuse. Failure to do so might induce children to testify in a manner consistent with the questioner's personal agenda.

Questioning the Eyewitness Though issues regarding the accuracy of children's eyewitness testimony have important social consequences, there has been even more research on the effects of questioning on adult eyewitness testimony. Because jurors attribute greater accuracy to the testimony of eyewitnesses who display confidence, an important factor in eyewitness testimony is how confident eyewitnesses are about their memories. In the 1972 case of *Neil v. Biggers*, the U.S. Supreme Court even ruled that one of the criteria that juries should use in judging the accuracy of an eyewitness's testimony is the degree of confidence expressed by the eyewitness. But this ruling might be misguided because eyewitnesses' level of confidence generally is unrelated to the accuracy of their testimony (Wells & Lindsay, 1985), and hypnotized witnesses may be subject to the formation of inaccurate "pseudo-memories" (Green, Lynn, & Malinoski, 1998). As a consequence, it can be unwise for jurors to assume that a confident eyewitness is necessarily an accurate eyewitness.

Can Leading Questions Alter Our Memories of Vivid Events?

One of the main factors potentially affecting eyewitness testimony is the wording of questions. If you saw an automobile accident and you were questioned about the automobile's speed, color, and direction, you probably would assume that your responses would be independent of these questions. Common sense tells you that being asked questions about your memory does not change your memories. In fact, a survey of university students found that they believed their own common sense was their single best source of information about eyewitness testimony (Shaw, Garcia, & McClure, 1999).

But Elizabeth Loftus, an expert on human memory and a contemporary pioneer in experimental research on eyewitness testimony, would disagree. Many of her research studies on eyewitness testimony have demonstrated that eyewitnesses might not only be subject to normal memory lapses but also to alterations in their memories produced by questioning by lawyers, prosecutors, and police officers. Judges and lawyers are taught to beware of leading questions, which can affect the testimony of eyewitnesses. Nonetheless, clever lawyers use subtle wording to influence testimony. In a dramatic study, Elizabeth Loftus and John Palmer (1974) examined the effect of leading questions regarding eyewitness accounts of an automobile accident.

Forty-five undergraduate participants viewed one of 7 driver education films of two-car automobile accidents lasting 5 to 30 seconds. Some participants were asked, "About how fast were the cars going when they smashed into each other?" Other participants were asked a similar question, with the word *smashed* replaced by *contacted, hit, bumped,* or *collided.* In a similar version of the experiment, another sample of 150 undergraduates likewise viewed films of two-car automobile accidents. Participants in one group were asked, "About how fast were the cars going when they smashed into each other?" and participants in a second group were asked, "About how fast were the cars going

when they hit each other?" A week later, participants were asked, "Did you see any broken glass?" To avoid sensitizing participants to its purpose, the question was embedded in a list of 10 questions. In reality, there was no broken glass at the accident scene.

Participants' estimates of the speed of the cars in the first part of the study were influenced by the severity of the word used in the question. The average estimates for *contacted, hit, bumped, collided,* and *smashed* were, respectively, 31.8, 34.0, 38.1, 39.3, and 40.8 miles per hour. In the second part of the study, though there had been no broken glass, participants in both groups recalled seeing some. But participants who had been given the question containing the word *smashed* were significantly more likely to report having seen broken glass than were participants who had been given the question containing the word *hit.*

Elizabeth Loftus

"One reason most of us, as jurors, place so much faith in eyewitness testimony is that we are unaware of how many factors influence its accuracy."

Source: Courtesy Elizabeth Loftus.

Section Review: Memory, Forgetting, and Eyewitness Testimony

1. What has research discovered about the accuracy of children's eyewitness testimony?

2. What concerns Elizabeth Loftus about the accuracy of eyewitness testimony?

Can Leading Questions Alter Our Memories of Vivid Events? *continued*

Loftus's findings have been replicated in other studies. In one study, college students were shown a videotaped mock crime. One week later they read a passage that described the crime. The passage contained leading, misleading, or control (no supplemental) information. When asked to recall the crime they had witnessed, the participants placed more confidence in the biased information presented by the experimenter than in their own memories (Ryan & Geiselman, 1991).

Studies like these demonstrate that the memories of eyewitnesses can be reconstructions, instead of exact replicas, of the events witnessed. This phenomenon was noted in 1846 in a trial that marked the first admission of hypnotically obtained testimony in an American court. Though the defendant was acquitted because of inadequate evidence, testimony by one expert noted that memory is often a reconstruction of events incorporating fact and fantasy (Gravitz, 1995).

Eyewitness memories can be altered by inaccurate information introduced during questioning. That is, "under some conditions misleading postevent information can impair the ability to remember what was witnessed and can lead people to believe that they witnessed things that they did not" (Lindsay, 1993, p. 86). To avoid such situations, leading questions are barred in courtroom proceedings. Though leading questions can affect the recall of eyewitnesses, research indicates that eyewitnesses might be less susceptible to them than had been suggested by earlier research (Kohnken & Maass, 1988).

Eyewitness memory can be improved by relatively simple procedures. One procedure, based on the principle of encoding specificity, improves recall by mentally reinstating the physical setting of the event. In one study, store clerks were asked to identify a previously encountered customer from an array of photographs. The original context was reinstated by providing physical cues from the encounter and by instructing the clerk to mentally recall events that led up to the customer's purchase. As discussed earlier, mentally reinstating the context in which you learned something can improve your recall of it. In this study, the reinstatement of the original context led to a significant increase in the accuracy of identifications (Krafka & Penrod, 1985).

We also can prevent misleading information from influencing the memories of eyewitnesses by warning them about that possibility. This was the finding of a study in which participants were warned just prior to the presentation of misleading information about a simulated crime. Participants viewed slides of a wallet being snatched from a woman's purse and then read descriptions of the crime. Participants who had been given warnings showed greater resistance to misleading information in the descriptions (Greene, Flynn, & Loftus, 1982). But some psychologists argue that informing jurors of the unreliability of eyewitness testimony might make already skeptical jurors too skeptical, perhaps leading to the exoneration of guilty persons (McCloskey & Egeth, 1983).

Regardless of the exact extent to which eyewitness testimony can be influenced by misleading information and the reasons for that influence, Elizabeth Loftus believes that eyewitness testimony is, in fact, too easily affected by such information. She expressed this belief in a statement that was a takeoff on John B. Watson's claim (quoted in Chapter 1) regarding his ability to condition infants to become any kind of person one desired. Loftus remarked:

> Give us a dozen healthy memories, well-informed, and our own specified world to handle them in. And we'll guarantee to take any at random and train it to become any type of memory that we might select—hammer, screwdriver, wrench, stop sign, yield sign, Indian chief—regardless of its origin or the brain that holds it. (Loftus & Hoffman, 1989, p. 103)

Improving Your Memory

More than a century ago William James (1890/1981) criticized those who claimed that memory ability could be improved by practice. To James, memory was a fixed, inherited ability and not subject to improvement. He concluded this after finding that practice in memorizing did not decrease the time it took him and other participants to memorize poetry or other kinds of literature. Regardless of the extent to which memory ability is inherited, we certainly can make better use of the ability we have by improving our study habits and by using *mnemonic devices*. For example, expert taxi drivers make good use of memory techniques to help them recall street names (Kalakoski & Saariluoma, 2001).

Using Effective Study Habits

Given two students with equal memory ability, the one with better study habits probably will perform better in school (Sanghvi, 1995). To practice good study habits, you would begin by setting up a schedule in which you would do the bulk of your studying when you are most alert and most motivated—whether in the early morning, in the late afternoon, or at some other time. You also should study in a quiet, comfortable place, free of distractions. If you study in a dormitory lounge with students milling around and holding conversations, you might find yourself distracted from the information being processed in your short-term memory, making it more difficult for you to transfer the information efficiently into your long-term memory. As for particular study techniques, you might consider using the *SQ3R method, overlearning,* and *distributed practice.*

The SQ3R Method

SQ3R method A study technique in which the student surveys, questions, reads, recites, and reviews course material.

In the **SQ3R method** (Robinson, 1970), SQ3R stands for Survey, Question, Read, Recite, and Review. This method has proved helpful to students in college (Carlston, 2011) and elementary school (Darch, Carnine, & Kameenui, 1986). It requires elaborative rehearsal, in which you process information at a relatively deep level. This process is distinct from rote memorization, in which you process information at a relatively shallow level. If you have ever found yourself studying for hours yet doing poorly on exams, it might be the consequence of failing to use elaborative rehearsal. For example, in one study students used either rote memory, writing down unfamiliar terms and their definitions, or elaborative rehearsal, writing down how the words might or might not describe them. One week later, students who had used elaborative rehearsal recalled significantly more definitions than did students who had used rote memory (Flannagan & Blick, 1989).

Suppose that you decide to use the SQ3R method to study the final section of this chapter. You would follow several steps.

- *Survey* the main headings and subheadings to create an organized framework in which to fit the information you are studying.

- As you survey the sections, ask yourself *questions* to be answered when you read them. For example, you might ask yourself, What is the physiological basis of memory?

- *Read* the material carefully, trying to answer your questions as you move through each section. In memorizing new terms, you might find it especially helpful to say them out loud. A study found that participants who read terms out loud remembered more of them than did participants who read them silently, wrote them down, or heard them spoken by someone else (Gathercole & Conway, 1988).

- After reading a section, *recite* information from it to see whether you understand it. Do not proceed to the next section until you understand the one you are studying.

Effective Study Habits

Good study habits include setting up a schedule and studying in a quiet place free of distractions.

Source: wavebreakmedia/ Shutterstock.com.

- Periodically (perhaps every few days) *review* the information in the entire section by quizzing yourself on it and then rereading anything you fail to recall. Asking questions of yourself as you read can increase elaborative rehearsal and the depth of processing, thereby improving your memory for the material (Andre, 1979). You also will find yourself experiencing savings; each time you review the material, it will take you less time to reach the same level of mastery.

Overlearning Material

You also might wish to apply other principles to improve your studying. Take advantage of **overlearning**. That is, study the material until you feel you know all of it—and then go over it several more times. A meta-analysis of research studies found that overlearning significantly improves the retention of material (Driskell, Willis, & Copper, 1992). Overlearning appears to work by making you less likely to forget material you have studied and more confident that you know it (Nelson, Leonesio, Shimamura, Landwehr, & Narens, 1982). This method might improve your exam performance by making you less anxious. The power of overlearning is revealed by the amazing ability people show for recognizing the names and faces of their high school classmates decades after graduation. This ability is attributable to their having overlearned the names and faces during their years together in school (Bahrick, Bahrick, & Wittlinger, 1975).

overlearning Studying material beyond the point of initial mastery

Distributed Practice

Use **distributed practice** instead of **massed practice**. The advantage of distributed practice over massed practice is especially important in studying academic material (Benjamin & Tullis, 2010). If you can devote a total of 5 hours to studying this chapter, you would be better off studying for 1 hour on five different occasions than studying for 5 hours on one occasion. Moreover, longer breaks between practice sessions have been found to facilitate memory in more complex tasks (Donovan & Radosevich, 1999). You might recognize this method as a suggestion to avoid cramming for exams. Note how the following explanation by William James for the negative effects of cramming anticipated recent research into the effects of elaborative rehearsal, overlearning, environmental cues, and semantic networks on memory:

distributed practice Spreading out the memorization of information or the learning of a motor skill over several sessions.

massed practice Cramming the memorization of information or the learning of a motor skill into one session.

> The reason why *cramming* is such a bad mode of study is now made clear. . . . Things learned thus in a few hours, on one occasion, for one purpose, cannot possibly have formed many associations with other things in the mind. . . . Speedy oblivion is the almost inevitable fate of all that is committed to memory in this simple way. . . . Whereas on the contrary, the same information taken in gradually, day after day, recurring in different contexts, considered in various relations, associated with other external incidents, and repeatedly reflected on, grow into a fabric, lie open to so many paths of approach, that they remain permanent possessions. (James, 1890/1981, Vol. 1, pp. 623–624)

Even students who are learning English as a second language can benefit from distributed practice, as in a study of economics and business students whose native language was Malay. The students were assigned to groups that received a total of 5 study sessions that consisted of 3 daily sessions over the period of a week or a session every 14 days. The students were tested on their understanding of English syntax 7 days after the training and 2 months later. The group that had received distributed practice performed significantly better on both occasions. The results indicate that those who teach languages to non-native speakers might be wise to divide long sessions into shorter ones (Bird, 2011).

Using Mnemonic Devices

Mnemonic devices are techniques for organizing information and providing memory cues to make it easier to recall, such as learning the names of U.S. presidents (Mastropieri, Scruggs, & Whedon, 1997) or learning the names of unfamiliar animals

mnemonic device Techniques for organizing information to be memorized to make it easier to remember.

(Carney & Levin, 2001). These devices are named after Mnemosyne, the Greek goddess of memory. You are familiar with certain mnemonic devices, such as *acronyms*. An **acronym** is a term formed from the first letters of a series of words. Examples of acronyms include *USA, NFL,* and even *SQ3R.* Many students have used the acronym *Roy G Biv* to help them recall the colors of the rainbow. Acronyms also have proved useful to psychiatrists, helping them recall the diagnostic criteria for psychological disorders (Pinkofsky, 1997).

You probably are familiar with the use of rhymes as mnemonic devices, as in *"I before e except after c"* and "Thirty days has September . . ." Though rhymes are useful mnemonic devices, they sometimes can impair memory. In one study, children who listened to stories presented in prose had better recall of them than did children who listened to the stories presented in verse. Evidently, the children who listened to verse processed the stories at a shallow level, as sounds, whereas the children who listened to prose processed the stories at a deeper level, in terms of their meaning (Hayes, Chemelski, & Palmer, 1982). The possible negative effect of using rhyming to help children learn academic material has been replicated in other research studies (Hayes, 1999). Moreover, a study in which adults listened to radio advertisements and then were randomly assigned to use either a rhyming mnemonic or no rhyming mnemonic found no difference in their ability to remember the advertisements a week later (Smith & Phillips, 2001). The major mnemonic devices include the *method of loci,* the *pegword method,* and the *link method.*

The Method of Loci

About 2,500 years ago the Greek poet Simonides stepped outside the banquet hall where he was to recite a poem in honor of a nobleman. While Simonides was outside, the hall collapsed, killing all the guests and maiming them beyond recognition. Yet, by recalling where each guest had been sitting, Simonides was able to identify each of them. He called this the **method of loci** (*loci* means "place" in Latin), which he recommended to orators because papers and pens were too expensive to waste on writing routine speeches (Bower, 1970). The method of loci is useful for memorizing lists of items. You might memorize concrete terms from this chapter by associating them with places and landmarks on your campus and then retrieving them while taking a mental walk across it. The method of loci has proved helpful in training patients who have undergone cardiac surgery to improve their memory and attention skills (Tourney-Jetté, Dupuis, Denault, Carter, & Bherer, 2012). Even the places on a Monopoly board have been used successfully to help students employ the method of loci (Schoen, 1996).

The Pegword Method

A mnemonic device that relies on both imagery and rhyming is the **pegword method**, which begins with memorizing a list of concrete nouns that rhyme with the numbers 1, 2, 3, 4, 5, and so on. For this method to work well, the image of the pegword object and the image of the object to be recalled should interact rather than just be paired with each other (Wollen, Weber, & Lowry, 1972). Suppose that you wanted to remember the grocery list presented in Figure 8-13. You might imagine, among other things, sugar being poured from a shoe, bees in a hive brushing their teeth, and a hen drinking from a soda bottle. To recall an item, you would simply imagine the pegword that is paired with a particular number, which would act as a cue for retrieving the image of the object that interacted with that pegword. Thus, if you imagined a shoe, you would automatically retrieve an image of sugar being poured from it. The pegword method has proved successful even when used by young children to learn nouns (Krinsky & Krinsky, 1996). The effectiveness of the pegword method also was demonstrated in a study in which one group of undergraduates memorized lists of facts such as the world's 10 highest mountains using the pegword method and a second group of undergraduates memorized the list without using it. When asked to

acronym A mnemonic device that involves forming a term from the first letters of a series of words that are to be recalled.

method of loci A mnemonic device in which items to be recalled are associated with landmarks in a familiar place and then recalled during a mental walk from one landmark to another.

pegword method A mnemonic device that involves associating items to be recalled with objects that rhyme with the numbers 1, 2, 3, and so on to make the items easier to recall.

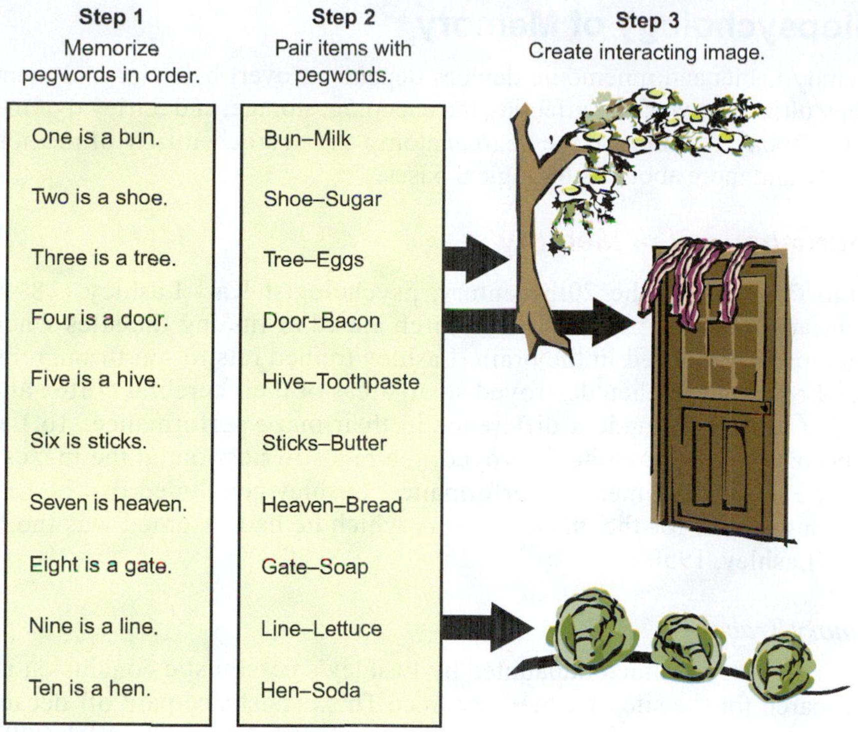

Step 1 Memorize pegwords in order.	Step 2 Pair items with pegwords.	Step 3 Create interacting image.
One is a bun.	Bun–Milk	
Two is a shoe.	Shoe–Sugar	
Three is a tree.	Tree–Eggs	
Four is a door.	Door–Bacon	
Five is a hive.	Hive–Toothpaste	
Six is sticks.	Sticks–Butter	
Seven is heaven.	Heaven–Bread	
Eight is a gate.	Gate–Soap	
Nine is a line.	Line–Lettuce	
Ten is a hen.	Hen–Soda	

FIGURE 8-13

The Pegword Method

The pegword method can be used to recall a grocery list. Each grocery item is paired with a pegword. Thus, the retrieval of a pegword will cue the retrieval of the associated grocery item.

recall the list immediately and 2 days later, the group that used the pegword method performed significantly better than the other group (Carney & Levin, 2011).

The Link Method

Still another mnemonic device that makes use of imagery is the **link method**, which takes images of the items to be memorized and connects them in sequence. One version of the link method is the *narrative method,* in which unrelated items are connected to one another in a story. In a study that showed the effectiveness of the narrative method, two groups of participants memorized 12 lists of 10 nouns. One group used the narrative method to memorize the nouns; the other group used ordinary mental rehearsal. Both groups showed nearly perfect immediate recall. But when later asked to recall all the lists, the narrative group recalled an average of 93 percent of the words, whereas the mental rehearsal group recalled an average of only 13 percent (Bower & Clark, 1969). More recent research has replicated the effectiveness of this technique (Hill, Allen, & McWhorter, 1991).

Ironically, despite the usefulness of mnemonic devices, a survey of college professors found that memory researchers were no more likely than other professors to use formal mnemonic devices. Instead, memory researchers and other professors alike recommended that memory be improved by writing things down, by organizing material to be learned, or by rehearsing material to be remembered (Park, Smith, & Cavanaugh, 1990). Like physicians who smoke, memory researchers might not practice what they preach.

link method A mnemonic device that involves connecting, in sequence, images of items to be memorized, to make them easier to recall.

Section Review: Improving Your Memory

1. What are some suggestions for improving your study habits?

2. How would you use the pegword method to recall lists of objects?

The Biopsychology of Memory

Though study habits and mnemonic devices depend on overt behavior and mental processes, they ultimately work by affecting the encoding, storage, and retrieval of memories in the brain. Today, research on the neuroanatomy and neurochemistry of memory is revealing more and more about its biological bases.

The Neuroanatomy of Memory

During the first half of the 20th century, psychologist Karl Lashley (1890–1958) carried out an ambitious program of research aimed at finding the sites where individual memories are stored in the brain. Lashley trained rats to run through mazes to obtain food rewards. He then destroyed small areas of their cerebral cortex and noted whether this procedure made a difference in their maze performance. To Lashley's dismay, no matter what area he destroyed, the rats still negotiated the mazes, showing at most a slight decrement in performance. Lashley concluded that he had failed in his lifelong search for the *memory trace,* which he had assumed was the basis of memories (Lashley, 1950).

Aplysia

The sea slug, aplysia, is a model organism to study learning and memory because it has approximately 20,000 neurons.

Source: LauraD/Shutterstock.com.

The Memory Trace

But many scientists remained undaunted by Lashley's pessimistic conclusion and continued to search for the site of a memory trace This persistence paid off decades later when a team of researchers began studying the sea snail *Aplysia* (Kandel, 2001). This creature has relatively few but large neurons, making it a simpler subject of study than animals with complex brains. Researchers have identified a neuronal event formed when *Aplysia* is classically conditioned to withdraw its gills in response to the movement of water (Kandel & Schwartz, 1982). This withdrawal (the conditioned response) occurs after several trials in which the movement of the water (the conditioned stimulus) has preceded an electric shock (the unconditioned stimulus) that automatically elicits gill withdrawal (the unconditioned response). Eric Kandel, along with several colleagues, won the Nobel Prize in 2000 for studying memory in this approach. His work set the stage for understanding the biochemical changes in neurons associated with learning and memory.

Evidence for the localization of memory traces in more complex animals comes from research that has identified neural substrates in the cerebellum (see Chapter 3), a brain structure that plays a role in both memory and the maintenance of equilibrium. The researchers classically conditioned rabbits to blink in response to a tone. Presentations of the tone (the conditioned stimulus) were followed by puffs of air (the unconditioned stimulus) directed at the rabbit's eyes, which elicited blinking (the unconditioned response). After several pairings of the tone and puffs of air, the tone itself elicited blinking (the conditioned response). After conditioning, the researchers found that electrical stimulation of a tiny site in the cerebellum of the rabbit elicited the conditioned eyeblink, whereas destruction of the site eliminated it—but not the unconditioned response. Thus, they had succeeded in locating a neural substrate for a classically conditioned memory (Krupa, Thompson, & Thompson, 1993)—undoubtedly, not the only site.

The Synapse

As for human memory, in 1894 Sigmund Freud and Santiago Ramón y Cajal independently speculated that learning produces changes in the efficiency of synaptic connections between neurons and that these changes might be the basis of memory formation. Their speculation has been supported by research findings that the formation of memories is associated with synaptic changes, including increases in the number of dendritic branches and the number of dendritic spines (protuberances on the dendrites) at certain sites (Martin & Morris, 2002). Recent research indicates that memory also might depend on the facilitation of neural impulses across synapses in the brain. The most widely studied phenomenon related to the facilitation of neural impulses is **long-term potentiation**, in which synaptic transmission of impulses between two neurons is made more efficient by brief electrical stimulation of specific neural pathways (Thompson, 2000). This phenomenon, discovered in the hippocampus and only demonstrated in animals, is viewed as a possible basis for long-term memory because long-term potentiation induced by specific experiences might strengthen synaptic connections in specific pathways (Martinez & Derrick, 1996). Long-term memories also depend on the actions of proteins that strengthen particular synaptic connections (Steward & Worley, 2002).

The Hippocampus

Researchers who study long-term potentiation are particularly interested in the *hippocampus,* which lies deep within the temporal lobes and helps consolidate memories (Norman & O'Reilly, 2003). Figure 8-14 illustrates the location of the hippocampus and other brain structures important in memory, including the thalamus (Van Der Werf et al., 2003), the amygdala (Seidenbecher et al., 2003), and as mentioned earlier, the cerebellum (Linden, 2003). The amygdala is particularly important in the formation of emotional memories (Pare, Collins, & Guillaume Pelletier, 2002).

Long-term potentiation in the hippocampus apparently promotes the storage of new memories but is required for only a limited period of time after a learning experience. Evidence for this finding comes from animal studies in which the hippocampus is purposely damaged at varying times after learning. The longer the delay before hippocampal damage, the less effect it has on the storage of the new memories (Zola-Morgan & Squire, 1990). More evidence for the importance of the hippocampus in the formation of long-term memories comes from research on Alzheimer's disease, which is marked by degeneration of neural pathways from the hippocampus (Teipel et al., 2003). Victims of Alzheimer's disease have a progressively more difficult time forming new long-term memories, particularly declarative memories (Davis et al., 2002). Alzheimer's disease also is characterized by the buildup of wanted proteins called *beta-amyloid* plaques. In animal models of Alzheimer's disease using transgenic mice with extra beta-amyloid, long-term potentiation is difficult to induce (Kimura,

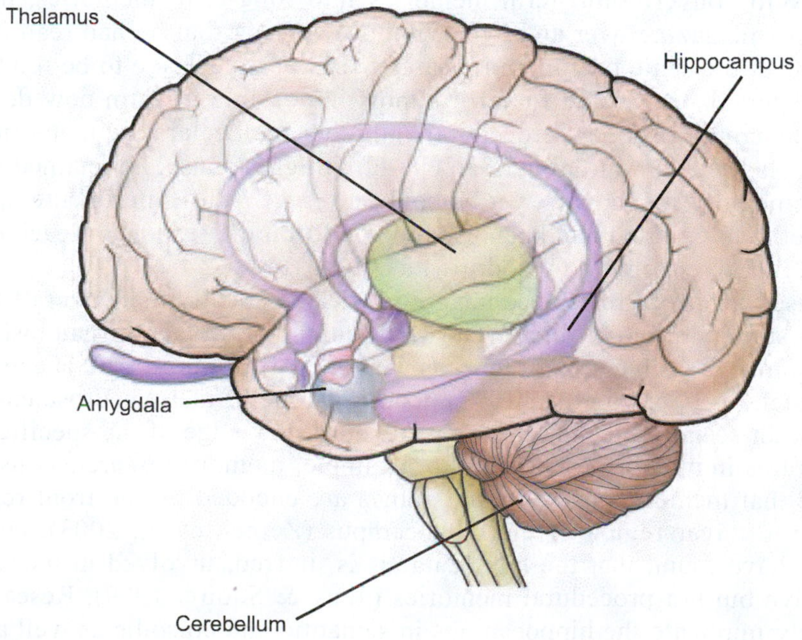

long-term potentiation
A phenomenon related to the facilitation of neural impulses in which synaptic transmission of impulses is made more efficient by brief electrical stimulation of specific neural pathways.

FIGURE 8-14
Anatomy of Memory

The brain contains no distinct memory center. Instead, memory depends on the integration of activity in several areas of the brain, including the thalamus, the amygdala, the cerebellum, and especially the hippocampus.

MacTavish, Yang, Westaway, & Jhamandas, 2012). Recently, advances were made in studying long-term potentiation-like events in humans using transcranial magnetic stimulation, a technique that places a magnetic field over the head. Researchers found that patients with Alzheimer's disease had impaired long-term potentiation signal events in their brains (Koch, et al., 2012). This indicates that this deficit accounts for the lack of plasticity and potential for learning and forming new memories. Nevertheless, we know that the hippocampus plays a role in the consolidation of short-term memory into long-term memory, but the exact sites of memory storage are unknown.

The hippocampus might provide an explanation for *infantile amnesia,* the inability to recall declarative memories from early childhood. A study of college students found that their earliest childhood memories were from age 2 for a hospitalization or the birth of a sibling and from age 3 for the death of a family member or a family move to a new home. If these events occurred earlier, the students were unable to recall them (Usher & Neisser, 1993). Perhaps infantile amnesia occurs because the hippocampus is too physically immature during infancy to consolidate short-term declarative memories into long-term ones. Note that we show perfectly good retention of procedural memories from infancy. Such memories, which involve skills, habits, and conditioned responses, do not seem to depend on the hippocampus.

The most celebrated single source of evidence for the role of the hippocampus and adjacent medial temporal lobe structures in memory comes from the case study of Henry Molaison (1926–2008), better known as H. M.. H. M. was studied most notably since the mid-1950s by Brenda Milner of the Montreal Neurological Institute (Scoville & Milner, 1957) and since the early 1960s by her former graduate student Suzanne Corkin of the Massachusetts Institute of Technology. H. M. had formed few new declarative memories since undergoing brain surgery in 1953, when he was 27 years old. The surgery, performed to relieve uncontrollable epileptic seizures, removed almost all of his hippocampus. As a result, H. M. developed anterograde amnesia, marked by the partial or complete inability to form new long-term declarative memories. After his surgery, H. M. was able to form several new semantic memories, but no episodic memories (Corkin, 2004). Because he could not recall events since his surgery, he felt that each moment of his life was like waking from a dream—short-term memories continually entered his consciousness and then faded away. H. M. and his condition inspired the film *Memento*.

H. M. could recall declarative memories from before his surgery, but because of his inability to convert short-term memories into long-term memories, he would read the same magazine over and over without realizing that he had read it before. He would meet the same person on repeated occasions, yet have to be reintroduced each time. Though H. M. had found it almost impossible to form new declarative memories, he could form new procedural and other nondeclarative memories. After undergoing classical conditioning of an eye-blinking response, he retained this nondeclarative memory for 2 years, yet he could not recall the experimenters, instructions, or methodology that had been used to condition the response—each of which involves declarative memory (Woodruff-Pak, 1993).

Corkin used magnetic resonance imaging (MRI) to specify the extent of the damage H. M.'s surgery did to his brain. The MRI found that, in fact, he had lost much of his hippocampus in each temporal lobe, as well as most of his amygdala and portions of other structures (Corkin et al., 1997). Corkin is one of many neuroscientists who are using brain-scanning techniques to refine our knowledge of the specific roles of brain structures in memory processes. For example, memory researchers using MRI have found that memories of faces and names are encoded by the front region and retrieved by the rear region of the hippocampus (Zeineh et al., 2003). Other neuroscientists have found that the hippocampus is, indeed, involved in the formation of declarative but not procedural memories (Teng & Squire, 1999). Research findings strongly implicate the hippocampus in semantic and episodic as well as spatial memory (Adeyemo, 2002).

The Neurochemistry of Memory

In 1959 James McConnell and his colleagues stunned the scientific world by reporting the results of an unusual experiment (McConnell, Jacobson, & Kimble, 1959). They had classically conditioned flatworms to contract their bodies in response to a light by repeatedly pairing presentations of the light with mild electric shocks. They then cut the flatworms in half. Because flatworms can regenerate themselves, both halves grew into whole flatworms. They then were retrained to contract in response to a light. As expected, the flatworms that had regenerated from the head (brain) ends showed memory savings— they took fewer trials to learn to respond to the light than had the original flatworms, which provided evidence that prior learning had been retained by the brain end. But to the researchers' surprise, the flatworms that had regenerated from the tail ends learned to respond to the light as fast as those that had regenerated from the brain ends. The memory of the classically conditioned response may have been encoded chemically and transported to the tail ends.

These findings led to a series of even more unusual experiments by a variety of researchers that seemed to demonstrate that memories could be transferred from one animal to another (Setlow, 1997). In one study, rats were trained to run to a lighted compartment instead of to a dark compartment (which they would normally favor) by shocking them whenever they entered the dark compartment. When extracts from the brains of these rats were injected into mice, the mice spent less time in the dark compartment than they normally would have. The researchers later isolated the proteinlike substance apparently responsible for this effect, which they called *scotophobin,* meaning "fear of the dark" (Unger, Desiderio, & Parr, 1972).

As you might assume, the results of successful memory transfer studies created controversy, leading 23 researchers to write a letter to the influential journal *Science* in which they reported their failure to produce memory transfer in 18 studies in seven laboratories (Byrne et al., 1966). Failure to replicate memory transfer studies became the main reason to reject those studies that found positive results (Rilling, 1996). But a few years later a published review of the research literature concluded that hundreds of studies of flatworms, goldfish, chickens, mice, rats, and hamsters had demonstrated the transfer of memories (Smith, 1974). Yet, because of the failure of other researchers to replicate those studies and to identify a physiological basis for the chemical transfer of memories, interest in the study of memory transfer has waned.

Perhaps interest has declined in part because the very notion of memory transfer seems better suited to science fiction than to science. Scientists in all disciplines, including biology, chemistry, and physics, tend to avoid topics that appear to violate accepted scientific paradigms (see Chapter 2). In contrast with the conflict generated by research on the chemical transfer of memories, there is no controversy about whether certain other neurochemical processes play a role in memory. Neuroscientists have concentrated their efforts on studying roles of the neurotransmitter *acetylcholine,* NMDA receptors from the amino acid neurotransmitter glutamate, *hormones,* and levels of blood *glucose* in memory.

Acetylcholine and Memory

The neurotransmitter that is most strongly implicated in memory processes is *acetylcholine* (Gold, 2003). Acetylcholine, the first neurotransmitter discovered, might be more important in the formation of declarative memories than in the formation of procedural memories. This relationship was implied by the results of a study in which one group of adult participants received a drug that blocked the effects of acetylcholine, and another group received a placebo (Nissen, Knopman, & Schacter, 1987). Those who received the active drug showed a reduced ability to recall and recognize stimuli presented previously (declarative memory) but no reduction in their ability to perform a reaction-time task they had learned previously (procedural memory).

But the most striking evidence of the role of acetylcholine in memory comes from studies of victims of Alzheimer's disease. Autopsies of victims of Alzheimer's

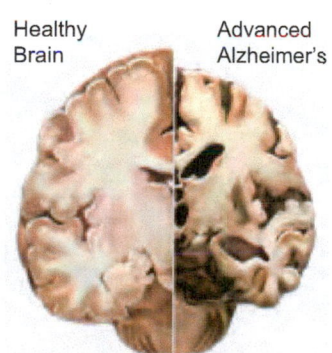

Healthy Brain   Advanced Alzheimer's

Brain Changes Caused by Alzheimer's Disease

Advanced Alzheimer's disease causes massive cell loss changes in the whole brain. This image shows a crosswise "slice" through the middle of the brain between the ears.

Source: © 2013 Alzheimer's Association. www.alz.org. All rights reserved. Illustrations by Stacy Jannis.

disease show degeneration of acetylcholine neurons that connect the hippocampus to other brain areas (Crews, 1994). In fact, when healthy participants are given drugs that inhibit the activity of acetylcholine neurons, they show memory losses similar to those seen in victims of Alzheimer's disease (McKinney & Richelson, 1984). Given this finding, it would seem logical that treatments aimed at elevating brain levels of acetylcholine would improve the ability of Alzheimer's victims to form new memories. One approach has been to administer *choline*—the dietary substance from which acetylcholine is synthesized and that is found in milk and eggs. Unfortunately, administration of high doses of choline has been only marginally effective in improving the cognitive functioning of Alzheimer's victims (Davidson et al., 1991). Evidently the degeneration of acetylcholine neurons prevents the additional choline from having a beneficial effect, just as adding gasoline to the empty tank of a car with no spark plugs would not make it more likely to start.

NMDA and Memory

Perhaps the most exciting area of current research on the chemical basis of memory concerns N-methyl-D-aspartate (NMDA) receptors (Steele, Stewart, & Rose, 1995). NMDA itself is an amino acid derivative that acts on the receptor for which it was named, the NMDA receptor. When NMDA is injected into animals, it acts like glutamate and binds to NMDA receptors in the hippocampus and enhances the efficiency of synaptic transmission along particular neural pathways. Blocking NMDA receptors in the amygdala prevents the formation of fear memories (Lee & Kim, 1998).

Consider a study of food preferences in rats. Rats, which are wary of unfamiliar foods, learn to prefer the foods eaten by neighboring rats—by smelling the scent of the food on another rat's breath. "Observer" rats were housed with a "demonstrator" rat that had eaten food laced with one of four spices (celery seed, anise, cloves, or marjoram). The experimental group received a dose of a drug that blocked NMDA receptors; the control group received a placebo injection. Then, each rat was provided with two sources of food. The familiar food was laced with the spice eaten by the demonstrator rat. The novel food was laced with one of the other spices. Both groups of rats preferred the familiar food shortly after the experimental procedure. When tested 72 hours later, the experimental group showed no food preference; the control group still preferred the familiar food. This study supports the role of NMDA receptors in the maintenance of long-term memory (Roberts & Shapiro, 2002). Additional support for the role of NMDA receptors in long-term memory consolidation comes from research on Alzheimer's disease. In the brains of victims of the disease, neural degeneration occurs in pathways rich in NMDA receptors (Maragos et al., 1987).

Hormones and Memory

Even hormones play a role in memory formation. The hormone *epinephrine* might have a special function in ensuring that we recall emotionally arousing events (McGaugh & Roozendaal, 2002). For example, in one study, participants were given injections of either an epinephrine blocker or a placebo. An hour later, they watched a series of slides accompanied by a neutral or an emotional story. When tested 1 week later, participants who received the epinephrine blocker had poorer recall of the emotional story than of the neutral story (Cahill et al., 1994). Given such findings, perhaps, if flashbulb memories are a real phenomenon, epinephrine plays a role in their formation. The effectiveness of epinephrine in promoting memory formation is independent of its role in stimulating the release of glucose from the liver (Gamaro et al., 1997).

Sex hormones, too, play a role in the formation of memory. Some studies have shown that estrogen replacement therapy promotes long-term memory and may reduce the risk of developing Alzheimer's disease in postmenopausal women (Zec & Trivedi, 2002). Other studies have found that testosterone replacement therapy has a similar effect on older men's long-term memory (Cherrier et al., 2001). The Women's

Health Initiative Memory Study, a double-blind clinical trial with a sample of more than 4,500 postmenopausal women, is the most comprehensive study of the effect of hormone replacement therapy on women's memory to date. The results indicated that hormone replacement therapy had no effect on participants' long-term memory and *doubled* the risk of Alzheimer's disease and stroke (Shumaker et al., 2003; Yaffe, 2003). The increased health risks were due to the therapy regimen: estrogen prescribed with progestins, which are combined to reduce women's risk of uterine cancer (Brinton & Nilsen, 2003). And the long-term effects of testosterone replacement therapy on men's health are unknown (Morley & Perry, 2003). Thus, memory researchers are faced with the challenge of devising an effective treatment for age-related memory loss that does not increase older adults' health risks.

Glucose and Memory

Still another topic of research interest regarding the chemical basis of memory is the effect of blood sugar, or glucose. There is a positive correlation between blood glucose levels and memory performance. For example, studies indicate that college students' performance on memory tasks is improved more by having a glucose drink than by having a placebo drink (Benton, Owens, & Parker, 1994). Dietary supplements of glucose also might improve memory in the elderly. In one study, adults at least 60 years old received doses of either glucose or saccharin (a placebo) before or after memorizing a brief prose passage. Their recall of the passage was tested 24 hours later. Those who had ingested glucose before or after memorizing the passage showed significantly better recall than those who had ingested saccharin. Evidently, the glucose promoted the storage of the prose passages in memory (Manning, Parsons, & Gold, 1992). Nonetheless, students should not conclude that it would be wise to ingest massive amounts of glucose. On the contrary, the greatest enhancement of memory is produced by moderate doses of glucose (Parsons & Gold, 1992).

As you can see, research on the biopsychology of memory cannot be divorced from the psychology of memory. And biopsychological research promises to discover ways of improving memory. Memory improvement would be a boon both to people with intact brains and to people with damaged brains.

Section Review: The Biopsychology of Memory

1. How did researchers demonstrate the presence of a classically conditioned memory trace in the cerebellum?

2. How does the case of H. M. support the role of the hippocampus in the consolidation of long-term memories?

3. Why do researchers believe that acetylcholine plays an important role in long-term memory?

Does the Pegword Method Improve Memory Performance?

Rationale

Research has found that we can improve our memory for lists of terms by connecting those terms to information we already have stored in memory. The pegword method, described in the section "Using Mnemonic Devices," involves memorizing a list of nouns that rhyme with numbers and then connecting terms to be learned to the nouns. In this exercise you will use the pegword method to memorize a grocery list.

Method
Participants

There should be at least 10 adult male and female participants (more would be even better) selected from among your friends, classmates, and relatives.

Materials

You will provide all the participants with two sheets, each with its own list of 10 grocery items to be memorized. One sheet will contain only a list of 10 items; the other sheet will contain a different list of 10 items and a list of pegwords paired with the numbers 1 through 10. Feel free to create your own number-pegword pairs or use the following: 1-bun, 2-shoe, 3-tree, 4-door, 5-hive, 6-sticks, 7-heaven, 8-gate, 9-line, and 10-hen.

Procedure

Have half the participants memorize the first list of grocery items for 2 minutes—without using any mnemonic devices. Have the other half memorize the same list of grocery items paired with pegwords, also for 2 minutes. Those using the pegword method should create vivid images of the pegwords and the items interacting together. At the end of 2 minutes, have the participants turn over their lists and immediately write down as many of the items as they can recall. They will have 2 minutes to do so. Then, using the second list of grocery items, have the two groups switch their methods in memorizing and then recalling the new list. Have the participants record the number of items they recalled correctly under each method.

Results and Discussion

Calculate the mean number of correct items under each of the two conditions of memorization. Draw a bar graph (see Appendix C in the Online Edition) representing these two means.

Did the two memorization conditions produce markedly different results in the average number of items that were correctly recalled? Why would it be better to use an inferential statistic (see Chapter 2 and Appendix C in the Online Edition) to make that judgment? Could any extraneous variables have accounted for your results? Could the results have had anything to do with the nature of the participants or the grocery lists themselves?

Chapter Summary

Information Processing and Memory

- Memory research has been influenced by the cognitive revolution in psychology.
- The most widely accepted model of memory assumes that memory processing involves the stages of sensory memory, short-term memory, and long-term memory.
- At each stage the processing of memories involves encoding, storage, retrieval, and forgetting.

Sensory Memory

- Stimulation of sensory receptors produces sensory memories.
- Visual sensory memory is called iconic memory, and auditory sensory memory is called echoic memory.
- George Sperling found that iconic memory contains more information than had been commonly believed and that almost all of it fades within a second.

Short-Term Memory

- Short-term memory is called working memory because we use it to manipulate information provided by either sensory memory or long-term memory.
- We tend to encode information in short-term memory as sounds.
- We can store an average of seven chunks of information in short-term memory without rehearsal.
- Memories in short-term memory last about 20 seconds without rehearsal.
- Forgetting in short-term memory is caused by decay and displacement of information.

Long-Term Memory

- Memories stored in long-term memory are relatively permanent.

- Elaborative rehearsal of information in short-term memory is more likely to produce long-term memories than is maintenance rehearsal.
- The levels of processing theory assumes that information processed at deeper levels will be more firmly stored in long-term memory.
- Researchers distinguish between procedural, semantic, and episodic memories.
- Semantic network theory assumes that memories are stored as nodes interconnected by links.
- Schema theory assumes that memories are stored as cognitive structures that affect the encoding, storage, and retrieval of information related to them.
- Hermann Ebbinghaus began the formal study of memory by employing the method of savings.
- Ebbinghaus identified the serial-position effect and the forgetting curve.
- The theories of forgetting include decay theory, interference theory, motivation theory, and encoding specificity theory.
- The main versions of encoding specificity theory are context-dependent memory and state-dependent memory.
- Research by Elizabeth Loftus and her colleagues has shown that eyewitness testimony often can be inaccurate.
- An important research finding is that eyewitnesses' confidence in their memories is not a good indicator of their accuracy.

- Another important finding is that leading questions can alter the recall of memories by eyewitnesses.
- Of special concern is the need for care in determining the accuracy of children's eyewitness testimony.

Improving Your Memory

- You can improve your memory by practicing good study habits and by using mnemonic devices.
- A useful study technique is the SQ3R method, in which you survey, question, read, recite, and review.
- Overlearning and distributed practice are also useful techniques.
- Mnemonic devices are memory aids that organize material to make it easier to recall.
- The main mnemonic devices include acronyms, the method of loci, the pegword method, and the link method.

The Biopsychology of Memory

- Though Karl Lashley failed in his search for the exact location of a memory trace, researchers have discovered some of the anatomical and chemical bases of memory.
- The hippocampus plays an important role in converting short-term memories into long-term memories.
- Research on NMDA receptors promises to contribute to our understanding of the physiological bases of memory.
- Neurotransmitters, particularly acetylcholine, and hormones play crucial roles in memory formation.
- Even blood glucose can facilitate memory formation.

Key Terms

flashbulb memory (p. 269)
memory (p. 270)

Information Processing and Memory

encoding (p. 271)
forgetting (p. 271)
information-processing model (p. 271)
long-term memory (p. 271)
retrieval (p. 271)
sensory memory (p. 270)
short-term memory (p. 271)
storage (p. 271)

Sensory Memory

echoic memory (p. 272)
iconic memory (p. 272)

Short-Term Memory

maintenance rehearsal (p. 274)

Long-Term Memory

constructive recall (p. 281)
context-dependent memory (p. 287)
decay theory (p. 284)
declarative memory (p. 277)
elaborative rehearsal (p. 275)
encoding specificity (p. 287)
episodic memory (p. 278)
explicit memory (p. 277)
eyewitness testimony (p. 290)
forgetting curve (p. 284)
implicit memory (p. 277)
interference theory (p. 285)
levels of processing theory (p. 276)
method of savings (p. 283)
proactive interference (p. 285)
procedural memory (p. 277)
repression (p. 285)
retroactive interference (p. 285)
semantic memory (p. 278)

semantic network theory (p. 279)
serial-position effect (p. 282)
state-dependent memory (p. 288)
tip-of-the-tongue phenomenon (p. 287)

Improving Your Memory

acronym (p. 296)
distributed practice (p. 295)
link method (p. 297)
massed practice (p. 295)
method of loci (p. 296)
mnemonic device (p. 296)
overlearning (p. 295)
pegword method (p. 296)
SQ3R method (p. 264)

The Biopsychology of Memory

long-term potentiation (p. 299)

Note: Answers for the Chapter Quiz questions are provided at the end of the book.

1. Certain drugs or hormones may enhance memory indirectly by stimulating the liver to release
   a. glucose.
   b. vitamin C.
   c. bile salts.
   d. hemoglobin.

2. "Working memory" is another name for
   a. encoding.
   b. sensory memory.
   c. long-term memory.
   d. short-term memory.

3. Your knowledge that the primary color pigments are red, blue, and yellow is an example of
   a. semantic memory.
   b. episodic memory.
   c. schematic memory.
   d. procedural memory.

4. The benefits of elaborative rehearsal provide support for the
   a. engram.
   b. decay theory.
   c. use of rote memorization.
   d. levels of processing theory.

5. In regard to eyewitness testimony, the confidence of eyewitnesses
   a. tends to be unrelated to their accuracy.
   b. is higher for female than male eyewitnesses.
   c. has no impact on jurors' perceptions of their accuracy.
   d. has been outlawed by the U.S. Supreme Court as a criterion of accuracy in jury decision-making about guilt or innocence.

6. A partygoer drinks alcohol and becomes inebriated. After sobering up she forgets where she put her car keys. After drinking enough to become inebriated again, she recalls where she put them. This is an example of
   a. mnemonic memory.
   b. schematic memory.
   c. state-dependent memory.
   d. context-dependent memory.

7. After suffering a stroke, a person recovers and learns how to cook gourmet meals, but forgets ever having learned how to cook them. This shows the difference between
   a. semantic memory and procedural memory.
   b. procedural memory and episodic memory.
   c. semantic memory and declarative memory.
   d. episodic memory and declarative memory.

8. Research by Elizabeth Loftus indicates that the accuracy of eyewitness recall may be affected by
   a. hypnosis.
   b. repression.
   c. leading questions.
   d. alcohol intoxication.

9. The blurring of a motion picture when the projector presents frames too fast is a phenomenon of
   a. mnemonics.
   b. sensory memory.
   c. long-term memory.
   d. short-term memory.

10. If you studied a list of concepts from this chapter until you went through the list perfectly once and then went through the list five more times perfectly, you would be taking advantage of
    a. overlearning.
    b. massed practice.
    c. distributed practice.
    d. maintenance rehearsal.

11. Many Americans have unusually vivid memories of the circumstances in which they heard that the World Trade Center had been attacked on September 11, 2001. These memories are called
    a. memory traces.
    b. mnemonics.
    c. echoic memories.
    d. flashbulb memories.

12. A person suffers damage to the hippocampus. She would be LEAST likely to have difficulty
    a. recalling where she had breakfast earlier today.
    b. remembering the names of people she met yesterday.
    c. studying this textbook chapter and taking an exam on it.
    d. learning how to use a CD player and retaining that ability later.

13. Your ability to use a word processor would be an example of
    a. semantic memory.
    b. episodic memory.
    c. procedural memory.
    d. declarative memory.

14. A football quarterback memorizes his team's playbook by studying 2 hours a day for 10 days, rather than trying to master it in one 20-hour session. He would be making use of
    a. overlearning.
    b. massed practice.
    c. distributed practice.
    d. maintenance rehearsal.

15. Under the condition of immediate partial report, George Sperling found that
    a. we can recall less information than under the condition of whole report.
    b. our preconscious mind can store much more information than our unconscious mind.
    c. we store virtually all available sensory information in sensory memory.
    d. we store only a tiny fraction of available sensory information in sensory memory.

16. If you were asked to recall your last visit to a beach, you might incorrectly recall certain events that are commonly associated with that activity (such as building a sand castle), but that you did not actually perform. This would support
    a. schema theory.
    b. state-dependent memory.
    c. semantic network theory.
    d. levels of processing theory.

17. Your memory of your first day in this class is an example of
    a. semantic memory.
    b. episodic memory.
    c. procedural memory.
    d. short-term memory.

18. If you tried to memorize a list of grocery items by associating it with a sequential list of places in your home, you would be making use of the
    a. method of loci.
    b. pegword method.
    c. in situ method.
    d. method of localization.

19. On Monday you study for a biology test. On Tuesday you study for a psychology test. On Wednesday you take a psychology test. If material you studied on Monday interferes with your ability to recall information you studied on Tuesday, you would experience
    a. retrograde amnesia.
    b. anterograde amnesia.
    c. proactive interference.
    d. retroactive interference.

20. The normal number of items that can be stored in short-term memory ranges from
    a. 3 to 5.
    b. 5 to 9.
    c. 9 to 12.
    d. 10 to 15.

21. The facilitation of certain neural pathways is called
    a. overlearning.
    b. neurotransmission.
    c. elaborative rehearsal.
    d. long-term potentiation.

22. Because of the serial-position effect, in studying a list of terms from this chapter, you should place
    a. the easiest words at the end of the list.
    b. the easiest words in the middle of the list.
    c. the easiest words at the beginning of the list.
    d. half of the easiest words at the beginning of the list and half at the end of the list.

23. You are introducing a new acquaintance to one of your friends, only to be embarrassed by your failure to recall the new person's name—despite your feeling that you know the name and your ability to conjure up the first letter. This is an example of the
    a. mnemonic effect.
    b. overlearning effect.
    c. schematic phenomenon.
    d. tip-of-the-tongue phenomenon.

24. A person witnesses a horrible accident in which people are maimed and killed. Weeks later he cannot recall the accident. According to Freud, he forgot the accident because of
    a. decay.
    b. decoding.
    c. expunging.
    d. repression.

25. A person suffers a stroke and can no longer form new memories. The stroke most likely affected the person's
    a. frontal lobes.
    b. parietal lobes.
    c. temporal lobes.
    d. occipital lobes.

Thought Questions

1. How might the notion of mood-congruent memory explain the difficulty that depressed people often have in getting rid of their depressed mood?

2. How would you use the concept of levels of processing to improve your memory for material you learn in your introductory psychology course?

3. Why should we be wary about the accuracy of eyewitness testimony?

4. What does the case of H. M. indicate about the role of the hippocampus in memory?

9

Thought and Language

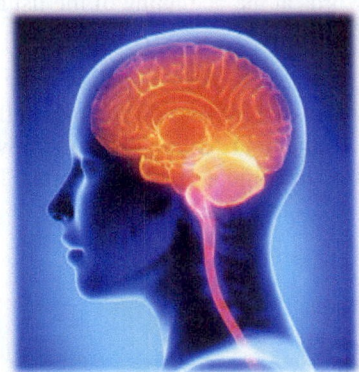

Source: CLIPAREA/Custom media/ Shutterstock.com.

Chapter Outline

Thought

Language

critical period A period in childhood when experience with language produces optimal language acquisition.

In 1800 a boy who appeared to be about 12 years old emerged from a forest near Aveyron, France, apparently having survived for many years without human contact (Hunter, 1993). The boy, named Victor by physician Jared Itard, became known as the "Wild Boy of Aveyron." Victor learned to use gestures, comprehend speech, and read and write on a basic level. Though Itard made an intensive effort to teach him to speak French, the only word Victor learned to say was "lait" (milk). Similar reports have provided evidence of a **critical period** for language acquisition that extends from infancy to adolescence, during which language learning is optimal. If people are not exposed to a language until after childhood, they might never become proficient in speaking it (Grimshaw, Adelstein, Bryden, & MacKinnon, 1998). There also seems to be a critical period for the acquisition of fluent sign language (Newman, Bavelier, Corina, Jezzard, & Neville, 2002).

A more recent and well-documented case described an American girl, Genie, who had been raised in isolation. In 1970, 13-year-old Genie was discovered by welfare workers in a room in which her father had kept her restrained in a harness and away from social contact—and language—since infancy. He communicated with her by barking and growling and beat her whenever she made a sound. By 1981, more than a decade after returning to society and undergoing intensive language training, Genie had acquired a large vocabulary but only a limited ability to speak. Like Victor, Genie might have been past her critical period for language acquisition when she returned to society (Pines, 1981).

Though the cases of Victor and Genie, as well as those of other children who have been reared in social isolation (Kenneally, Bruck, Frank, & Nalty, 1998), support the view that there is a critical period for language acquisition, you may recall from Chapter 2 that it is unwise to generalize too freely from case studies. For example, some children who have lived for years in social isolation, such as Kaspar Hauser, who was discovered in Nuremberg, Germany, in 1828 at age 17, have been able to learn language well even after reaching adolescence (Simon, 1979). Perhaps other factors could account for the findings in the cases of Victor and Genie. For example, suppose that Victor and Genie were born with brain disorders that interfered with their ability to acquire language. Even if they had been reared from birth in normal family settings, they still might have failed to acquire mature language.

Research on the acquisition of language and other topics related to how the brain processes information fall within the domain of *cognitive psychology*—perhaps the most influential field of psychology in recent years. In fact, the 1950s and 1960s saw a "cognitive revolution" in which the behaviorist perspective was countered by increased concern with the study of the mind (Miller, 2003). This revolution was inspired by an explosion of interest in the study of computer and cognitive sciences, cognitive processes, and language acquisition.

Cognitive psychology combines William James's concern with mental processes and John B. Watson's concern with observable behavior. Cognitive psychologists accomplish this combination by using techniques that permit them to infer cognitive processes from overt behavior (Greenwood, 1999). Cognitive psychologists who are interested in the neurological bases of cognitive processes pursue their research interests in **cognitive neuroscience**. A cognitive neuroscientist might, for example, use PET scans or functional MRI to assess brain activity that accompanies the performance of cognitive tasks such as language, memory, creativity, or decision making.

Thought and language are different, yet interrelated, cognitive activities. Chapter 8 describes the cognitive activity of memory, which permits you to store and retrieve information. Like memory, thought and language help you profit from experience and adapt to your environment. Your ability to think and to use language will enable you to comprehend the information conveyed in this chapter and to apply some of it, perhaps in your everyday life.

cognitive psychology
The field of psychology that studies cognitive processes such as thought and language.

cognitive neuroscience
The study of the neurological bases of cognitive processes.

Thought

Forming concepts. Solving problems. Being creative. Making decisions. Each of these processes depends on **thought**, which is the purposeful cognitive manipulation of words and images. Yet in 1925, John B. Watson, the founder of behaviorism and the psychologist who conducted the controversial "Little Albert" experiment described in Chapter 7, claimed that thought is not a mental activity. Instead, he insisted that it was no more than subvocal speech—activity of the speech muscles that is too subtle to produce audible sounds. Margaret Floy Washburn (1916), Watson's contemporary, made a similar claim in her *motor theory of thought*. There is an intuitive appeal to this claim because you might sometimes find yourself engaging in subvocal speech—perhaps even while reading this chapter. Moreover, physiological recordings of activity in the speech muscles have shown that some people do subvocalize while thinking (McGuigan, 1970).

But these findings do not necessarily support Watson's claim that subvocal speech *is* thought. Convincing evidence against Watson's claim came from a study in which a physician, Scott Smith, had himself paralyzed for half an hour by the drug that blocks acetylcholine—curare (Smith, Brown, Toman, & Goodman, 1947). He did so to assess its possible use in the induction of general anesthesia. Because curare paralyzes the skeletal muscles (see Chapter 3), including the breathing muscles, Smith was put on a respirator. After the curare wore off, he was able to report conversations that had taken place while he had been paralyzed. Because Smith was able to think and form memories while his speech muscles were paralyzed, thought does not depend on subvocal speech.

Most behaviorists did not equate thought with subvocal speech, but they agreed with Watson's position that cognitive processes were not the proper objects of study for psychologists. By the 1960s, though, dissatisfaction with the inability of strict behaviorism to explain memory, thought, and certain other psychological processes contributed to the cognitive revolution. This dissatisfaction reintroduced the study of mental processes, or "cognition," to psychology (Mandler, 2002). One of the basic cognitive processes is concept formation, the next topic in this chapter.

thought The cognitive manipulation of words and images, as in concept formation, problem solving, and decision making.

Concept Formation

concept A category of objects, events, qualities, or relations that share certain features.

If you encountered a snake while hiking, you would be more willing to pick up and hold a nonpoisonous snake than a poisonous snake. Similarly, you might be willing to pluck and eat a nonpoisonous mushroom but not a poisonous mushroom. Your actions would show that you understood the concepts "poisonous" and "nonpoisonous." A **concept** represents a category of objects, events, qualities, or relations whose members share certain features. For instance, poisonous objects share the ability to make you ill or kill you. During your life you have formed thousands of concepts, which provide the raw materials for thinking. Concepts enable us to respond to events appropriately and to store memories in an organized way. Cognitive psychologists distinguish between *logical concepts* (sometimes called *artificial concepts*) and *natural concepts* (Kalish, 2002).

Logical Concepts

logical concept A concept formed by identifying the specific features possessed by all things that the concept applies to.

How do we form concepts? Consider the case of a **logical concept,** which is formed by identifying the specific features possessed by all things that the concept applies to. "Great Lakes state" is a logical concept. Each of its members has the features of being a state and of bordering one or more of the Great Lakes. The book of Leviticus in the Old Testament of the Bible provides two of the oldest examples of logical concepts. Leviticus distinguishes between "clean" animals, which may be eaten, and "unclean" animals, which may not. As one example, "clean" sea animals have fins and scales, whereas "unclean" sea animals do not. Bass and trout are "clean" animals, and clams and lobsters are "unclean" animals (Murphy & Medin, 1985).

Logical concepts like those found in Leviticus refer to real-life concepts and have typically not been the kinds studied in the laboratory. Instead, laboratory studies generally have used logical concepts created by the researcher. The use of logical concepts lets the researcher exert more precise control over the definitions of particular concepts. An experiment on the formation of a logical concept might present participants with a series of symbols varying in size, shape, and color. The participant's task is to discover the features that define the concept. For example, a symbol might have to be large, square, and blue to be considered an example of the particular concept. Participants determine the features of the concept by testing hypotheses about its possible defining features on successive examples that are labeled as either positive or negative instances of it. A positive instance would include the defining features of the concept (in this case, large, square, and blue), whereas a negative instance would lack at least one of the defining features (for example, large, square, and red). Try to identify the concept presented in Figure 9-1.

Natural Concepts

natural concept A concept, typically formed through everyday experience, whose members possess some, but not all, of a common set of features.

Is baseball a sport? How about table tennis? fishing? foosball? golf? chess? mountain biking? professional wrestling? You have an intuitive sense of how "sportlike" each of these activities is. "Sport" is an example of a **natural concept,** a concept formed through everyday experience rather than by testing hypotheses about particular features that are common to all members of the concept. We might be unable to identify the defining features of natural concepts such as "sport." That is, natural concepts have "fuzzy borders." Such concepts include "love" (Regan, Kocan, & Whitlock, 1998), "emotion" (Russell, 1991), "moral" (Hart, 1998), "pleasure" (Dube & Le Bel, 2003), and "prejudice" (Inman

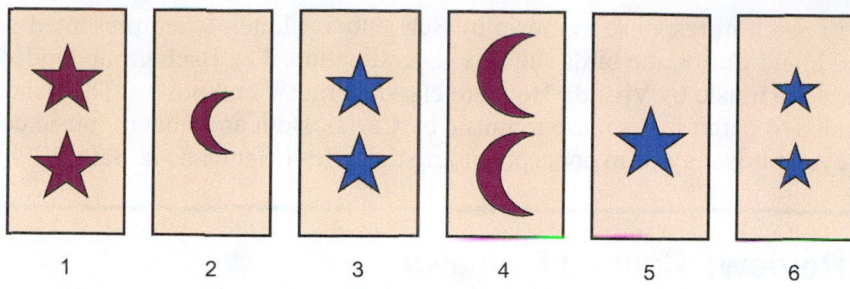

FIGURE 9-1
Concept Formation

Laboratory studies of the formation of logical concepts present participants with a series of examples varying on specific features. The participant's task is to identify the features that compose the concept. The figures in this example can vary in size (small or large), symbol (crescent or star), color (red or blue), or number (one or two). Given that the odd-numbered cards are members of the concept and the even-numbered cards are not, see how quickly you can identify the concept. (Answer is below.)

& Baron, 1996). Even Saint Augustine, in the fifth century, noted that a natural concept can have fuzzy borders when he remarked, "I know what 'time' is until someone asks me to define it" (Chadwick, 1986, p. 70).

The difficulty in defining natural concepts led psychologist Eleanor Rosch (1975) to propose that they are related to prototypes. A **prototype** is considered to be the best representative of a concept. According to Rosch, the more similarity between an example and a prototype, the more likely we are to consider the example to be a member of the concept represented by the prototype. A robin is a more prototypical bird than a penguin. Both have wings and feathers and hatch from eggs, but only the robin can fly. In regard to the concept "sport," baseball is more prototypical than golf, which in turn is more prototypical than foosball. The fuzziness of natural concepts can lead to arguments about whether a particular example is a member of a given concept (Medin, 1989). This problem was evident in 1988 in a series of letters to the editor of *The Sporting News* either supporting or opposing its coverage of Wrestlemania, the Indianapolis 500, and the World Chess Championship. Supporters considered these events to be examples of the concept "sport"; opponents did not.

Subsequent research has indicated that we do form concepts by creating prototypes of the relevant objects, events, qualities, or relations (Nosofsky, 1991). In regard to the concept "commitment," one experiment found that commitment is better understood from the prototype perspective than from the logical concept perspective. Commitment to friends, family, and spouse was considered most prototypical of "commitment"; commitment to one's work, education, or more distant relationships was considered less so (Fehr, 1999). Reliance on prototypes also can have practical benefits. Clinicians and trained laypeople can diagnose certain personality disorders when given a prototype of the disorder as well, if not better, than when they use the DSM-5 (see Chapter 14), a standardized reference of psychological disorders (Westen, DeFife, Bradley, & Hilsenroth, 2010).

Influenced by the work of Rosch, psychologists have become more interested in conducting laboratory studies of natural concept formation—the formation of concepts without logically testing hypotheses about their defining features. Consider the following study of the identification of artistic styles (Hartley & Homa, 1981). Participants who were naïve about artistic styles were shown works by the painters Manet, Renoir, and Matisse. Later, the participants were shown more paintings by these artists and by other artists, without being told the artists' identities. After viewing the second set of paintings, participants accurately matched particular paintings with the styles of the artists whose works they had seen in the first set of paintings. Participants used the first set to form concepts representing the styles of the three artists: a "Manet," a "Renoir," and a "Matisse." These results could not be explained as an example of logical concept formation because participants were unable to identify a set of features that distinguished a Manet from a Renoir from a Matisse. Similar approaches have been successful in teaching artistically naïve persons how to comprehend works of art (Seifert, 1996).

Other research studies have demonstrated that birds can form concepts of musical styles, as in a study in which one group of sparrows was reinforced for perch sitting only when music by Bach was played and a second group was reinforced for perch sitting only when music by Schoenberg was played. When presented with other music by those composers, the Bach group tended to perch in response to music by Bach and the Schoenberg

Answer: large stars.

prototype The best representative of a concept.

group tended to perch in response to music by Schoenberg. Later, when presented with music by Vivaldi and Carter, the birds showed generalization. The Bach group tended to perch in response to music by Vivaldi. Both are classical music composers. The Schoenberg group tended to perch in response to music by Carter. Both are modern music composers. Thus, even birds may form concepts of artistic styles (Watanabe & Sato, 1999).

Section Review: Concept Formation

1. What is the difference between a logical concept and a natural concept?

2. In what way do concepts such as "love" and "sport" have fuzzy borders?

Problem Solving

problem solving The thought process by which an individual overcomes obstacles to reach a goal.

One of the most important uses of concepts is in **problem solving,** the thought process that enables us to overcome obstacles to reach goals. Suppose that your car will not start. In looking for a solution to your problem, you might follow a series of steps commonly used in solving problems (Kramer & Bayern, 1984). First, you *identify the problem:* My car won't start. Second, you *gather information* relevant to the problem: Am I out of gas? Is my battery dead? Are my ignition wires wet? Third, you *try a solution:* I'm not out of gas, so I'll dry off the wires. Finally, you *evaluate the result:* The car started, so the wires were indeed wet. If the solution fails to work, you might try a different one: Drying off the wires didn't work, so I'll try a jump start.

Approaches to Problem Solving

Problem solving commonly involves one of several strategies, including *trial and error, insight, algorithms,* and *heuristics.*

trial and error An approach to problem solving in which the individual tries one possible solution after another until one works.

Trial and Error A common strategy for solving problems is **trial and error,** which involves trying one possible solution after another until one works. Ivan Pavlov, though best known for his research on classical conditioning, was one of the first scientists to stress the importance of trial and error (Windholz, 1992). Even the humble *E. coli* bacterium navigates by trial and error (Marken & Powers, 1989), and spiders pursue prey by using trial and error (Jackson, Carter, & Tarsitano, 2001). For an example of trial and error in human problem solving, imagine that your psychology professor asks you to get a timer from a laboratory and gives you a ring with 10 keys on it. Suppose that on reaching the laboratory you realize that you don't know which key opens the door to the laboratory. You would immediately identify the problem: finding the correct key. After assessing your situation, you probably would decide to use trial and error to solve the problem. You would try one key after another until you found one that opened the door.

Though trial and error often is effective, it is not always efficient. For example, a study of novice computer programmers found that the slower learners relied too much on trial and error (Green & Gilhooly, 1990). If your professor gave you a ring with 50 keys on it, you might find it more efficient to return and ask your professor to identify the correct key rather than waste time trying one key after another. Even worse, imagine learning how to use computer software by trying various combinations of keystrokes until you hit on the correct ones to perform desired functions (such as centering a line of text). It might take you years to complete even a brief term paper.

Trial and Error

You would likely use trial and error to figure out which key opens a specific door.

Source: DmitriMaruta/Shutterstock.com.

Insight In the third century B.C., the Greek physicist Archimedes was asked to solve a problem: Was King Hiero's new crown made of pure gold, or had the goldsmith cheated him by mixing cheap metals with the gold? Archimedes discovered a way to solve this problem when he noticed that if he sat in his bathtub, the water level rose. After shouting "Eureka!" he decided to submerge the crown in water and measure the volume of water it displaced. Reasoning that the volume of water displaced is proportionate to the weight of the object displacing it, he would compare the volume displaced by the crown to the volume displaced by an equal amount of metal that he knew to be pure gold. Archimedes found that the crown was indeed pure gold. To make this discovery, he relied on **insight,** an approach to problem solving that depends on cognitive manipulation of information rather than on overt trial and error.

Insight also is characterized by an "Aha!" moment or experience—the sudden realization of the solution to a problem (Topolonski & Reber, 2010)—as found in research by Janet Metcalfe. In a typical experiment, every 10 seconds Metcalfe asks participants working on either insight problems or non-insight problems (such as algebra) how "warm" they feel—that is, how close they feel they are to the correct solution. She has found that those working on insight problems are less accurate, indicating that solutions to non-insight problems are incremental and predictable, whereas solutions to insight problems are sudden and unpredictable (Metcalfe & Wiebe, 1987). Nonetheless, her interpretations of her research findings have been countered by recent research that suggests that what we call insight might seem to be sudden and unpredictable, but it is the product of the gradual accumulation of knowledge as one works on a problem (Hamel & Elshout, 2000; Novick & Sherman, 2003).

Assuming that insight does exist, can animals use it to solve problems? The classic study of insight in animals was conducted by Gestalt psychologist Wolfgang Köhler (1887–1967) on the island of Tenerife in the Canary Islands during World War I. Köhler (1925) presented a chimpanzee named Sultan with bananas, hanging them from the top of Sultan's cage, well out of his reach. But his cage also contained several crates. After trying fruitlessly to reach the bananas by jumping, Sultan suddenly hit on the solution. He piled the crates on top of one another, quickly climbed to the top, and grabbed a banana—just as the shaky structure came tumbling down.

The assumption that Sultan displayed insight was challenged more than a half century later by several behaviorists (Epstein, Kirshnit, Lanza, & Rubin, 1984). In a tongue-in-cheek study analogous to the one involving Sultan, they used food rewards to train a pigeon to first perform the separate acts of moving a tiny box, standing on the box, and pecking a plastic, miniature banana. When later confronted with the banana hanging out of reach from the top of its cage, the pigeon at first seemed confused but then suddenly moved the box under the banana, climbed on the box, and pecked at the banana to get a food reward. According to the researchers, if a pigeon can perform supposedly insightful behavior, then perhaps insight in animals—and even in people—is no more than the chaining together of previously rewarded behaviors (see Chapter 7). However, more recent research has found that birds, rats, and chimpanzees can demonstrate insight in laboratory tasks (Shettleworth, 2012; Panksepp & Panksepp, 2013).

It has long been known that nonhuman primates can display other complex emotions, such as empathy and insight, but can other species, such as rats? Electrophysiological studies performed by Durstewitz and colleagues (2010) with laboratory rats have demonstrated that groups of cells in the prefrontal cortex are activated during complex decision making that could be related to insight. The rats were trained in an instrumental conditioning set-shifting task and rewarded for pressing one of two levers that was illuminated by a light. After the rats learned this rule, the researchers then shifted the required response to press a lever in a specific location. This shift, from a visual to spatial cue, was the new rule the rat had to learn in order to receive a reward and was accompanied by changes in neuronal activation in the prefrontal cortex. The rat had to develop a new strategy and abandon an old strategy. This is related to insight because, as humans, we are faced with changes that require shifts in strategy, such as how to solve a difficult problem, that are distinct from trial-and-error processes.

Algorithms If you use the formula "length multiplied by width," you will obtain the area of a rectangle. A mathematical formula is an example of a problem-solving strategy called an algorithm. An **algorithm** is a rule that, when followed step by step, ensures that a solution to a problem will be found. Many physicians use algorithms to diagnose disorders, such as sexual dysfunctions, by noting specific combinations of symptoms and personal characteristics of patients (Hatzichristou, Bertero, & Goldstein, 1994). Researchers also have developed algorithms for the diagnosis of autism spectrum disorder (Kamp-Becker et al., 2013) and the most effective treatment strategies for anxiety

insight An approach to problem solving that depends on cognitive manipulation of information rather than overt trial and error and produces sudden solutions to problems.

algorithm A problem-solving rule or procedure that, when followed step by step, ensures that a correct solution will be found.

disorders (Culpepper, 2003). But some critics fear that the recent trend toward medical insurance providers requiring the use of algorithm-based treatments for psychological disorders—which at this time do not lend themselves to standardized treatments to the same extent that many medical illnesses do—is motivated more by the providers' desire to reduce costs than by their desire to ensure the provision of high-quality therapy (Slayton, 1998).

The notion of an algorithm is an offshoot of research in computer science by cognitive psychologists Allen Newell and Herbert Simon (1972). Many computer programs rely on algorithms to process information accurately. But, like trial and error, an algorithm can be an inefficient means of finding the solution to a problem. To appreciate this inefficiency, imagine that you are in the middle of a chess game. An algorithm for finding your best move would require tracing all possible sequences of moves from the current position. Because there is an average of 35 different moves that can be made in any single position in the middle of a chess game, you would need literally millions of years to find the best move by tracing all possible sequences of moves. Even using an algorithm to follow all possible sequences of just the next 3 moves in the middle of a chess game would require the analysis of an average of 1.8 billion moves (Waltz, 1982). Because a formal chess match has a typical time limit of 5 hours, even world chess champions do not rely on algorithms. Instead, they rely on problem-solving strategies called heuristics.

heuristic A general principle that guides problem solving, though it does not guarantee a correct solution.

Heuristics A **heuristic** is a general principle, or rule of thumb, that guides problem solving in everyday life and in scientific fields, such as biology (Baker & Dunbar, 2000). Unlike an algorithm, a heuristic does not guarantee a solution. But a heuristic can be more efficient because it rules out many useless alternatives before they are even attempted. A chess player might rely on heuristics, such as trying to control the center of the board or trading weaker pieces for stronger ones. A heuristic for studying and getting good grades might be to set aside at least 2–3 hours per class per week for reviewing class material.

Impediments to Problem Solving

Researchers who study problem solving are interested in obstacles that interfere with it. Two of the major obstacles are *mental sets* and *functional fixedness*.

Mental Sets Before reading on, try to solve the six problems presented in Figure 9-2, in which you must use three jars to measure out exact amounts of water. If you are like most research participants, you could easily solve the first five problems but ran into difficulty with the sixth.

FIGURE 9-2
Mental Sets

Luchins (1946) asked participants to use jars with the capacities shown in columns A, B, and C to obtain the amounts required in the right column. The first five problems led participants to overlook a simpler solution in the sixth problem.

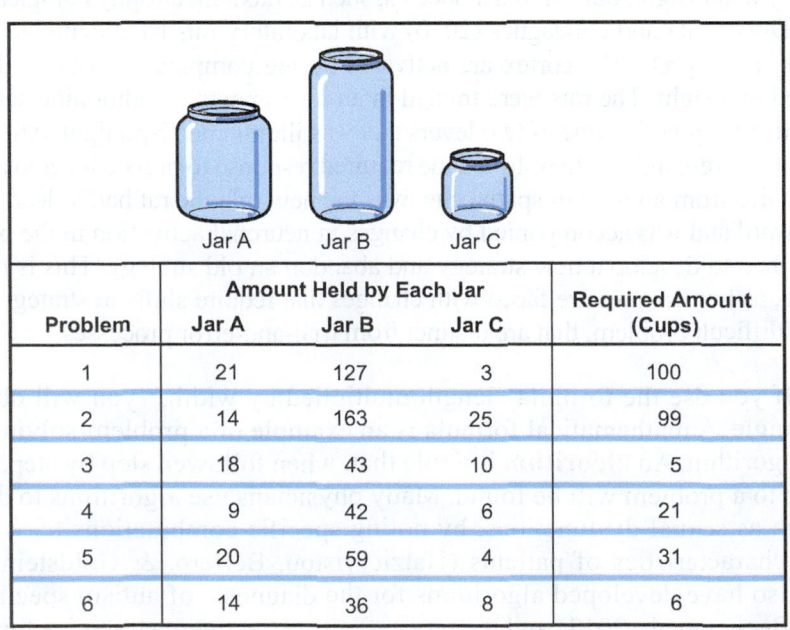

Problem	Amount Held by Each Jar			Required Amount (Cups)
	Jar A	Jar B	Jar C	
1	21	127	3	100
2	14	163	25	99
3	18	43	10	5
4	9	42	6	21
5	20	59	4	31
6	14	36	8	6

In an early study using the water-jar problem, participants quickly realized that the solution to the first problem was to fill jar B, pour enough water from it to fill jar A, and then pour enough water from jar B to fill jar C twice. These steps left the desired amount in jar B. The participants then found that the same strategy worked for each of the next four problems. But when they reached the sixth problem, two-thirds of them were unable to solve it. Those who failed to solve it had developed a strategy that was effective in solving previous examples but made the simple solution to problem 6 difficult to discover. In contrast, of participants who were asked to solve only the sixth problem, few had difficulty discovering the simple solution: fill jar A and pour enough water from it to fill jar C, leaving the desired amount in jar A (Luchins, 1946).

This study demonstrated that we sometimes are hindered by a **mental set**, a problem-solving strategy that has succeeded in the past but that can interfere with solving a problem that requires a new strategy. In one study, expert computer programmers and novice computer programmers were given a programming problem that could be solved by using a simple programming strategy that is more often used by novices. The results showed that the novices were more likely than the experts to solve the problem because the experts tried to use a more sophisticated but ineffective strategy that they had adopted during their careers as computer programmers. In other words, the experts had developed a mental set that blinded them to the simpler solution (Adelson, 1984). The possibility that expertise may create mental sets that blind problem solvers to simple solutions has been replicated in other research studies (Wiley, 1998). Even the bestseller book, *The Da Vinci Code,* contains an example of how a mental set can hamper an expert's ability to solve a problem that a novice might solve easily. In the novel, Sophie, an expert cryptographer, scolds herself for her failure to decipher a coded message that might help uncover an astounding biblical secret:

> Her shock over the anagram was matched only by her embarrassment at not having deciphered the message herself. Sophie's expertise in complex cryptanalysis had caused her to overlook simplistic word games, and yet she knew she should have seen it. After all, she was no stranger to anagrams—especially in English. (Brown, 2003, p. 99)

How can you overcome a mental set? One way is to make assumptions opposite to those you normally make. This approach might have helped the expert computer programmers who were unable to solve the problem that the novices were able to solve.

Functional Fixedness Another way in which past experience can impede our ability to solve problems is through **functional fixedness,** the inability to realize that a problem can be solved by using a familiar object in an unusual way. The term *functional fixedness* was coined by Gestalt psychologist Karl Duncker (1903–1940), who was a leader in the study of insight learning (Behrens, 2003). The role of functional fixedness in problem solving was demonstrated in a classic study (Maier, 1931) in which each participant was asked to perform the simple task of tying together two long strings hanging from a ceiling. The problem was that the two strings were too far apart for the participant to grasp them both at the same time. The room contained a variety of objects, including a table, a chair, an extension cord, and a pair of pliers.

Participants were given 10 minutes to solve the problem. Each time the participant identified a solution, the experimenter said, "Now do it a different way." One solution was to tie the extension cord to one string, grasp the other string, pull the strings toward one another, and then tie them together. Participants who discovered the solution that the experimenter was interested in tied the pliers to one of the strings and started it swinging like a pendulum. They then grabbed the other string, walked toward the swinging pliers, and tied the two strings together (Maier, 1931). To discover that solution, the participants had to realize that the pliers could be used as a weight and not solely as a tool. Only 39.3 percent of the participants discovered this solution on their own. More participants discovered it when the experimenter provided a hint by subtly setting one of the strings in motion.

As with mental sets, functional fixedness can be overcome. One of the best ways is to change or ignore the names of familiar objects. In a study that used this technique, participants were given a bulb, some wire, a switch, a wrench, and batteries. The participants were told to create a circuit that would light the bulb, even though they had too little wire

mental set A tendency to use a particular problem-solving strategy that has succeeded in the past but that may interfere with solving a problem requiring a new strategy.

functional fixedness The inability to realize that a problem can be solved by using a familiar object in an unusual way.

to complete the circuit. The solution was to use the wrench to complete it. Participants who were told to use nonsense names such as "jod" to refer to the wrench were more likely to solve the problem than were participants who called the wrench a "wrench" (Glucksberg & Danks, 1968). By using nonsense words to refer to the wrench, participants were less likely to think of it as just a mechanical tool.

More recently, researchers have facilitated this process by designing the *generic parts technique*. Using the above example, participants would be asked two questions. The first question, "Can this be decomposed further?" asks participants to break objects into subparts that might be useful in solving the problem. Thus, participants might think of pliers or wrenches as weights rather than tools to remove bolts or pins. The second question, "Does this imply a use?" asks participants to create descriptions of uses based on attributes of the object, such as shape or form. Thus, participants might think of pliers as creating a swing when tied to string or wrenches as providing additional metal to complete a circuit. One study found that participants trained in this method solved 67% more problems that generated functional fixedness than a control group (McCaffrey, 2012).

Section Review: Problem Solving

1. Why might heuristics be both superior and inferior to algorithms?

2. How do mental sets hamper problem solving in everyday life?

Creativity

In 1950, in his final address as president of the American Psychological Association, creativity researcher J. P. Guilford (1897–1987) expressed disappointment that of the more than 100,000 psychological studies published up until then, fewer than 200 dealt with creativity. Following Guilford's address, and influenced by the cognitive revolution, there was a striking increase in the number of scientific studies of creativity (Simonton, 2000). And this increase has not been limited to the United States. Scientific studies of creativity have spread around the world (Kaufman, 2010).

But what is creativity? Like other natural concepts, creativity cannot be defined by a specific set of features—that is, it has fuzzy borders. We might be able to distinguish between creative and noncreative behavior without being able to identify exactly what makes one example creative and another noncreative. Psychologists generally define **creativity** as a form of problem solving characterized by finding solutions that are novel as well as useful or socially valued (Mumford & Gustafson, 1988), whether practical, artistic, or scientific.

Of course, the works of many creative geniuses were not socially valued in their time. The exhibition of works by the French artist Paul Cézanne (1839–1906) that toured the world in 1996 drew millions of visitors to museums, attracted by the allure of an artist who many authorities believe inspired the development of modern art. Yet, in his own time, Cézanne was considered a technically inadequate artist whose paintings had little appeal to critics and laypeople alike. What is considered creative in one era or one culture might be considered inept in another.

Thus, in his time, Cézanne's works were considered novel but were not valued—novelty is not sufficient to demonstrate creativity (Epstein, 1991). Said the French mathematician Henri Poincaré (1948, p. 16), "To create consists precisely in not making useless combinations and in making those which are useful and which are only a small minority. Invention is discernment, choice." Thus, if you gave a monkey a canvas, a paintbrush, and a pallet of paint, it might produce novel paintings, but they would not be considered examples of creativity. Among the leading tools for measuring creativity are the Torrance Tests of Creative Thinking. These tests, developed by E. Paul Torrance, assess creativity using words or pictures (Palaniappan & Torrance, 2001).

creativity A form of problem solving that generates novel, socially valued solutions to problems.

Characteristics of Creative People

What characteristics are associated with creativity? Though creative people tend to have above-average intelligence, you do not have to be a genius to be highly creative (Nicholls, 1972). For example, a study of undergraduates found that their scores on a test of intelligence and a test of creative thinking correlated .24, indicating a positive but weak relationship between the two (Rushton, 1990). And a study of children found a positive correlation between their intelligence and their creativity up to an IQ of 120 (above average but not in the gifted range), but no relationship beyond that level of intelligence (Fuchs-Beauchamp, Karnes, & Johnson, 1993).

Creative people also tend to exhibit certain personality characteristics (Simonton, 1999). They tend to prefer novelty, favor complexity, and make independent judgments (Barron & Harrington, 1981). Creative people attend to stimuli that other people might screen from consciousness as being irrelevant to the task at hand (Carson, Peterson, & Higgins, 2003). They also tend to have a wide range of interests, be open to new experiences, and be nonconformists and unconventional (Simonton, 1999). For example, a recent study of university undergraduates investigated the relationship of multicultural experiences to creativity. The sample included three groups of participants. One group had studied abroad, another group had planned to study abroad, and the last group did not plan to study abroad. The participants who had studied abroad outperformed the other two groups on a standardized test of creativity as well as a culture-specific test (Lee, Therriault, & Linderholm, 2012). And creative people tend to be more creative when they are engaged in creative behavior for its own sake rather than to obtain some kind of reward (de Jesus, Rus, Lens, & Imaginário, 2013).

Creativity and the Sociocultural Environment

Psychologists also have studied the extent to which socialization and culture influence the development and expression of creativity in individuals. For example, historical eras characterized by political unrest or warfare tend to dampen creative expression and productivity (Simonton, 1984). Cultures, too, differ in the extent to which they encourage the expression of individuality and originality. One study compared musical innovation among dancers in four cultures. In two cultures, Samoan and Balinese, dancers are expected to emphasize their individuality as a form of artistic expression. In two other cultures, Japanese and Omaha Indian, individual expression is discouraged in favor of perfecting traditional form and style. Musical innovation was found to be more common in the Samoan and Balinese cultures (Colligan, 1983). Thus, cultural norms encouraging the expression of individualized style may support the expression of individual creativity. However, it also is important to remember that there are cultural differences in how creativity is conceptualized, the extent to which creativity is encouraged, and as in this instance, the nature of artistic and creative processes (Lubart, 1999).

Psychology versus Common Sense

Can Rewarding Creative Behavior Inhibit Creativity?

Common sense might lead us to presume that we can encourage people to become more creative by rewarding them when they engage in creative activities. But this commonsense bit of wisdom has been called into question by scientific research on creativity. According to creativity researcher Teresa Amabile (1989), creative people are more motivated by their intrinsic interest in creative tasks than by extrinsic factors such as fame, money, or approval. In fact, when people are presented with extrinsic reasons for performing intrinsically interesting creative tasks, they can lose their motivation to perform them. Amabile's 1985 study, presented here, provided further evidence of this loss of motivation.

Participants were recruited through advertisements asking for writers to participate in a study of people's reasons for writing. Most of the respondents were undergraduate or graduate students in English or creative writing. All the participants were asked to write two brief poems on designated themes (the first on snow, and the second on laughter). Each participant was assigned to one of three groups. After the participants wrote the first poem, one group completed a questionnaire that focused on intrinsic reasons for writing, such as the opportunity for self-expression, whereas a second group completed a questionnaire that focused on extrinsic reasons for writing, such as gaining public recognition. The third group served as a control group and was not given a questionnaire. Twelve experienced poets judged the creativity of the poems on a 40-point scale.

When the first poems were judged for their creativity, the three groups did not differ. However, when the second poems were judged for their creativity, the poems written by the group exposed to the questionnaire that focused on extrinsic reasons for writing were judged less creative than those written by the other two groups; the intrinsic-reasons group and the control group showed no change in creativity from the first poem to the second, but the extrinsic-reasons group showed a significant decrease. Thus, though concentrating on intrinsic reasons for creative writing did not improve creativity, concentrating on extrinsic reasons for creativity impaired it. Even the mere expectation of having one's performance evaluated will hamper creativity (Amabile, Goldfarb, & Brackfield, 1990). These findings agree with the experience of the noted American poet Sylvia Plath, who believed that her persistent writer's block was caused by her excessive concern about an extrinsic reason for writing—the recognition of her work by publishers, critics, and the public. Perhaps, given students who enjoy writing, teachers should avoid pointing out the extrinsic rewards for it, such as obtaining a better job or being accepted into graduate school. Chapter 11 discusses theories that explain the negative effects of extrinsic motivation on people's performance.

The example above supports the notion that psychology as a science is important and can rule out commonsense explanations. All sciences use an empirical approach. The empirical approach allows psychologists to use careful observation and experiments to gather facts and evidence.

Cross-cultural psychologists recently have investigated theories of creativity and the level of creative expression in Western and Asian cultures to assess both culture-specific and universal aspects of creativity. A recent review of cross-cultural studies revealed that Western and Asian participants have similar—but not identical—conceptions of creativity. And Western and Asian samples differ on some measures of creativity (Niu & Sternberg, 2002). The extent of these differences, however, is not as large as one would expect. In a recent study, 50 European American and 48 Chinese participants created original drawings of geometric shapes, a creative task that should be unaffected by cultural differences in artistic style. Six European American and eight Chinese judges were trained to evaluate the creativity expressed in the drawings. The judges demonstrated remarkable consensus in judging the creativity of the drawings created by European American and Chinese undergraduates. And there were no cross-cultural differences in the level of participants' creativity (Chen et al., 2002).

Creativity and Divergent Thinking

How many ways can you use a brick? If you could think of only such uses as "to build a house" or "to build a fireplace," you would exhibit convergent thinking. According to

Guilford, **convergent thinking** focuses on finding conventional "correct" solutions to problems. If you also thought of less conventional "correct" uses for a brick, such as "to prop open a door" or "to save water by putting it in a toilet tank," you would be engaging in divergent thinking. **Divergent thinking**, a hallmark of creativity (Guilford, 1984), involves freely considering a variety of potential solutions to artistic, literary, scientific, or practical problems. The importance of divergent thinking in creativity was noted as long ago as the mid-18th century (Puccio, 1991).

Overemphasis on convergent thinking can impair divergent thinking and, as a result, inhibit creativity (Reddy & Reddy, 1983). One way of inducing divergent thinking is brainstorming, in which thinkers are encouraged to conjure up as many solutions as possible to a problem. Brainstorming in small groups may result in more creative ideas than individual brainstorming, especially if the group is composed of diverse members and the exchange of ideas is encouraged (Brown & Paulus, 2002). Moreover, brainstorming is most effective in cases where the group is strongly committed to solving the problem (Litchfield, Fan, & Brown, 2011).

Performance on tests of divergent thinking correlates moderately highly with creative behavior (Runco, 1993). But creative ability in one area, such as writing poetry, might not correlate highly with creativity in another, such as writing stories. That is, divergent thinking might not be a general trait but instead might be limited to specific creative domains. This finding was illustrated in a study of seventh graders in which half were given divergent-thinking training in writing poetry and half were not. The students later were asked to write poems and short stories. Experts judged that the students who had received divergent-thinking training wrote more creative poetry than the ones who had not received special training. Moreover, the trained students showed greater creativity in their poems than in their short stories. Training in divergent thinking might affect performance on targeted tasks without affecting performance on presumably related tasks (Baer, 1996).

Divergent thinking can be cultivated. It is promoted by parents who raise their children to be open to a wide variety of experiences (Harrington, Block, & Block, 1987). Even adults can learn to use divergent thinking. This idea is not lost on industrial leaders, many of whom have their employees attend seminars so they can learn to think more creatively by engaging in divergent thinking (Basadur, Wakabayashi, & Takai, 1992). Divergent thinking also is promoted by positive emotional states (Vosburg, 1998). When you are anxious, for example, you are more likely to engage in convergent thinking (Byron & Khazanchi, 2011). Thus, teachers who evoke positive emotions in their students, and managers who evoke positive emotions in their employees, can encourage creative academic or vocational problem solving. For example, a study of physicians found that when positive emotions were induced in participants, they became more creative than control participants (Estrada, Isen, & Young, 1994).

convergent thinking
The cognitive process that focuses on finding conventional solutions to problems.

divergent thinking
The cognitive process by which an individual freely considers a variety of potential solutions to artistic, literary, scientific, or practical problems.

Decision Making

decision making A form of problem solving in which one tries to make the best choice from among alternative judgments or courses of action.

Each of our days is filled with decisions. They can be minor, such as deciding whether to take along an umbrella when leaving home, or major, such as deciding which college to attend. **Decision making** is a form of problem solving in which we try to make the best choice from among alternative courses of action to produce a desired outcome. Studies in the 1970s found that decision making also is subject to biases that can keep us from making objective decisions. Biases in decision making have been studied most extensively by two cognitive psychologists: Amos Tversky and Nobel Prize winner Daniel Kahneman. These researchers have found that our decision making often is biased by our reliance on heuristics (Kahneman, 2003). Judges, for example, sometimes use heuristics in making judicial decisions, such as setting the amount of bail in a criminal case (Dhami, 2003). Psychologists also understand that the biological basis of decision making and cognitive control is governed by the prefrontal cortex. This part of your brain helps govern self-control, self-restraint, and planning complex behavior. Human imaging studies using fMRI have shown that patients with lesions in the ventral portion of the prefrontal cortex perform worse on tasks associated with value-based decision making than healthy participants (Gläscher, et al., 2012). These studies suggest that it is likely that your prefrontal cortex helps guide your use of heuristics.

Heuristics in Decision Making

Kahneman and Tversky have identified several kinds of heuristics involved in decision making. Two that have been widely studied are the *representativeness heuristic* and the *availability heuristic*.

representativeness heuristic In decision making, the assumption that a small sample is representative of its population.

The Representativeness Heuristic In using the **representativeness heuristic**, we assume that a small sample is representative of its population (Kahneman & Tversky, 1973). For example, we use the representativeness heuristic when we eat at a fast-food restaurant and assume that other restaurants in the chain will be that good (or bad). Even young children use the representativeness heuristic (Davidson, 1995). Because a sample might not accurately represent its population, the use of the representativeness heuristic does not guarantee that our decisions will be correct ones. We may make unwise decisions under emotional stress because we are more likely to rely on the representativeness heuristic when we are in stressful situations (Shaham, Singer, & Schaeffer, 1992).

Consider a study of the effect of the representativeness heuristic in relation to undergraduates' perception of the timing of historic events (Moshinsky & Bar-Hillel, 2002). Hebrew University students were given lists of important events in American and European history from 1750 to 1961. The lists contained pairs of events, one American and one European. Half the pairs included an American event that occurred earlier than the European event, and half included a European event that occurred earlier than the American event. Participants were asked to mark the event that occurred earlier. Responses were correct 58 percent of the time, but the researchers analyzed the incorrect responses. Results indicated that when the earlier event occurred in America, the error rate was 36 percent. However, when the earlier event occurred in Europe, the error rate was 47 percent. The researchers concluded that participants were biased by thinking about America as the "New World" and Europe as the "Old World." Apparently, we assume that European historical events are representative of a longer history than American historical events. The representativeness heuristic guides decisions as varied as choosing a lottery ticket number (Holtgraves & Skeel, 1992), buying or selling stocks on the stock market (Andreassen, 1988), and judging the musical tastes of strangers based on a brief description (Lonsdale & North, 2012).

The Availability Heuristic To appreciate another kind of heuristic, answer the following question: In English, is the letter *k* more likely to be the first letter or the third letter of a word? Though the letter *k* is more likely to be the third letter, most people decide that it is more likely to be the first. This result is explained by what Tversky and Kahneman (1973) call the **availability heuristic,** which is the tendency to estimate the probability of an event by how easily instances of it come to mind. The more easily an instance comes to mind, the more probable we assume the event will be. But the ease with which instances come to mind might not reflect their actual probability. Instead, instances might come to mind because they are vivid, recent, or important. Thus, because it is easier to recall words that begin with *k,* such as *kick* or *kiss,* than words that have *k* as their third letter, such as *make* or *hike,* we conclude that more words have *k* as their first letter than as their third letter.

In a study of the impact of the availability heuristic, undergraduates were given lists containing equal numbers of male and female names of famous people and nonfamous people and were then asked to estimate whether the lists contained more male or female names. The students' estimates depended on whether the male names or the female names were more famous. Apparently, the availability heuristic affected the students' judgment of the relative number of names—even though the number of male and female names was always equal (McKelvie & Drumheller, 2001). A similar study found that children judged the names of famous people and cartoon characters to be more common than they actually are, presumably because they come to mind more easily than other names (Davies & White, 1994).

The practical effect of the availability heuristic was shown in a study in which participants estimated the prevalence of cheating by welfare recipients. Participants who first read a vivid case of welfare cheating overestimated its prevalence (Hamill, Wilson, & Nisbett, 1980). This finding reflects our tendency to respond to rare but vivid news reports of instances of welfare recipients living in luxurious comfort by overestimating the likelihood of welfare cheating. In fact, when we lack the information required for making an objective judgment, the availability of even a single instance of an event can make us overestimate the probability of other occurrences of that event (Lewicki, 1985). This tendency holds true when judging the prevalence of drug use (Eisenman, 1993), the probability of product failures (Folkes, 1988), and the likelihood of a person contracting HIV (Triplet, 1992). It also might explain why, until recently, New York City, though usually not one of the top 10 American cities in violent crime statistics, has the reputation of being the most dangerous American city. Perhaps the national media coverage given to horrible rapes and murders in New York creates, through the availability heuristic, the belief that individuals are more likely to become victims of violent crimes there than they actually are.

Framing Effects in Decision Making

Consider the following statements: "Dr. Jones fails 10 percent of his students" and "Dr. Jones passes 90 percent of his students." Though both statements report the same reality, you might be more inclined to enroll in Dr. Jones's course after hearing the second comment than you would be after hearing the first. Your inclination is an example of what Kahneman and Tversky call **framing effects**, biases introduced in the decision-making process by presenting a situation in a particular manner. Judges, lawyers, and prosecutors are aware of framing effects in the form of leading questions, which can bias jury decisions. Research also indicates that the manner in which television news coverage portrays social protests can create powerful framing effects that influence viewer decisions about the merits of the protesters' causes (McLeod & Detenber, 1999).

Framing effects also influence our everyday decisions. In one study (Levin, Schnittjer, & Thee, 1988), undergraduates rated the incidence of cheating at their school higher when told that "65 percent of students had cheated at some time in their college career" than when told that "35 percent of the students had never cheated." The undergraduates also were more likely

availability heuristic
In decision making, the tendency to estimate the probability of an event by how easily relevant instances of it come to mind.

framing effects Biases introduced into the decision-making process by presenting an issue or situation in a certain manner.

to rate a medical treatment as more effective, and were more apt to recommend it to others, when they were told it had a "50 percent success rate" than when told it had a "50 percent failure rate." A similar study found that undergraduates rated meat more highly when it was labeled "75 percent lean" than when it was labeled "25 percent fat" (Donovan & Jalleh, 1999). Note that in each study both statements present the same fact and differ only in how they frame the information. A recent meta-analysis of 136 studies found the overall effect size of framing on decision making to be small to moderate (Kuehberger, 1998).

To further appreciate framing effects, consider the following study by Kahneman and Tversky (1982), in which people were asked one of the following two questions: "If you lost a pair of tickets to a Broadway play for which you paid $40, would you purchase two more?" or "If you lost $40 on your way to purchase tickets at the box office, would you still purchase tickets?" Though in each case the participant would be $40 poorer, more participants answered yes to the second question. Thus, the way in which the questions were framed, not the amount of money the participants would lose, influenced their decision. Their subjective evaluation was more important than the objective situation. Framing effects influence a variety of decisions, including investment decisions (van de Heijden, Klein, Müller, & Potters, 2012), the choice of appropriate medical procedures for treating illnesses (Wang & Johnston, 1995), and decisions to engage in healthier behaviors, such as practicing regular breast self-examinations (Williams, Clarke, & Borland, 2001) and smoking cessation (Schneider et al., 2001). Framing effects even influence evaluations of a potential romantic partner as well as the anticipated success of the relationship (Knee & Boon, 2001).

Section Review: Decision Making

1. What is the availability heuristic?

2. How does the framing of leading questions influence decision making?

Artificial Intelligence

Researchers in the field of artificial intelligence use computers to simulate or improve human thought.

Source: maxuser/Shutterstock. com.

artificial intelligence (AI)
The field that integrates computer science and cognitive psychology in studying information processing through the design of computer programs that appear to exhibit intelligence.

Artificial Intelligence

Two centuries ago a Hungarian inventor named Wolfgang von Kempelen toured Europe with the Maezel Chess Automaton, a chess-playing machine. The Automaton defeated almost all the people who dared play against it. One of its admirers was the noted American author Edgar Allen Poe, who wrote an essay speculating—incorrectly—on how it worked. After years of defeating one challenger after another, the Automaton's mechanism was finally revealed. Inside it was a legless Polish army officer named Worouski, who was a master chess player ("Program Power," 1981).

During the past few decades, computer scientists have developed computer programs that actually can play chess. Computer chess programs are the offshoot of studies in **artificial intelligence (AI)**, a field founded by Nobel Prize winner Herbert Simon that integrates computer science and cognitive psychology. Researchers who study AI try to simulate or improve on human thought by using computer programs. For example, computer scientists have developed a program that answers political questions as though it were either a politically liberal or a politically conservative person (Abelson, 1981). Perhaps more important, some researchers in the field of peace psychology are now using AI to predict conflicts between countries and to promote successful conflict resolution (Hergovich & Olbrich, 2002).

Computer science and artificial intelligence researchers also are using artificial *neural networks,* which mimic human brain functioning, to help solve practical problems. For example, neural networks have been used in Milan, Italy, to help assess and prevent vehicular accidents at particular sites in that city (Mussone, Ferrari, & Oneta, 1999). Other applications of neural networks include diagnosing pancreatic cancer (Gorunescu, Gorunescu, Saftoiu, Vilmann, & Belciug, 2011), modeling insect navigation (Dale & Collett, 2001), assessing the IQ of people with intellectual disabilities (Di Nuovo, Nuovo, & Buono, 2012), and explaining posttraumatic stress disorder (Tryon, 1998). One of the central goals of this type of research is to improve the way we live our lives by pursuing innovative technologies.

Expert Systems

Many AI researchers are interested in developing computer programs, so-called **expert systems**, that display expertise in specific domains of knowledge. Computer chess programs have led the way in these efforts—and have contributed to the development of cognitive psychology itself (Charness, 1992). The first computer chess programs were developed in the 1950s at Los Alamos Laboratory in New Mexico and improved steadily during the next two decades until they finally began defeating expert chess players. In 1978 David Levy, the chess champion of Scotland, got a scare when a computer chess program defeated him in the fourth game of a six-game chess match. Levy had made a $2,500 bet that no chess program could defeat him in a match. But Levy won or drew the other five games and renewed his bet (Ehara, 1980). Despite his victory, Levy and world chess champions were doomed to eventual defeat by computer chess programs. An ominous sign occurred in 1979 at a backgammon match in Monte Carlo, when a computer program defeated the world backgammon champion, Luigi Villa of Italy. This was the first time a computer program had defeated a human world champion in an intellectual game ("Teaching a Machine the Shades of Gray," 1981).

In 1981, at the Virginia Open Chess Tournament, a computer chess program named Belle took fourth place in competition against master chess players ("Program Power," 1981). The only rating above master is grand master, the level achieved by the best chess players in the world. Whereas other computer chess programs relied on algorithms—searching for all possible sequences of moves, several moves deep—to find the best move in a given position, Belle took a more sophisticated, human approach by using heuristics. Though Belle could follow potential sequences of moves four moves deep, it did not follow each sequence to its conclusion. Instead, Belle stopped following a sequence as soon as it proved inferior to another that had already been identified. This heuristic approach made Belle perform faster and examine more potentially effective moves in a given time span than did other computer chess programs (Peterson, 1983). Expert computer programs have made great strides since the era of Belle. One chess program, KnightCap, achieved human master's level after only 3 days of online play on the Internet (Baxter, Tridgell, & Weaver, 2000). And in 1997, IBM's computer chess program Deep Blue defeated world chess champion Gary Kasparov. This was the first time that a computer chess program defeated a human world champion.

Though computer chess programs are the best known of expert systems, computer scientists have developed a variety of other systems. Among these expert systems, Mycin has helped physicians diagnose infectious diseases, Prospector has helped mining companies decide where to dig for minerals, and Dipmeter has helped analyze geological data from oil-well drillings (Davis, 1986). Expert systems also can help in the diagnosis and treatment of eating disorders (Todd, 1996). The program ES-MR helps select the best rehabilitation treatment for patients with stroke, brain injuries, and dementia (Man, Tam, & Hui-Chan, 2003), and the program Sexpert helps in the assessment and treatment of sexual dysfunctions (Ochs & Binik, 1998). Expert systems are helpful because in narrow domains of knowledge, they can analyze data more quickly and more objectively than human experts can.

Robotics

Though expert systems can analyze data more efficiently than can humans, AI researchers believe that an important difference between expert systems and human problem solving is that the latter occurs in the "real world." Experimental studies are being conducted with a new approach that uses robotics—machines operating within a physical environment rather than software programs that manipulate data. AI researchers interested in this approach believe that problem solving must be modeled with an embodied entity that is embedded in a physical context and, most important, exhibits actions that are modifiable by feedback based on the consequences of these actions (Ekbia, 2008).

expert systems Computer programs that display expertise in specific domains of knowledge.

Artificial Intelligence and Competitive Chess

Computer scientists can program a computer to play chess.
Source: maxuser/Shutterstock.com.

The study of robotics is based on the design of robots that interact with the physical environment through sensors as well as behavioral feedback. A network of systems guides the robot's actions by sensing obstacles and avoiding collisions and enables the robot to wander the environment. Another system may, for example, allow the robot to match features of objects in the environment to perceptual categories that have been programmed into the system. The machine receives feedback from yet another system. For example, if the machine grasps the incorrect object for the task, it may receive the feedback "failure; retry." Darwin VII is one robotic machine that has a complex neural network organization. It visually explores the environment, avoids obstacles during locomotion, and tracks and grips objects. Moreover, Darwin VII displays a simulated tasting process that is sensitive to learning. Pleasant tastes are sought out more frequently, and unpleasant tastes are avoided (Krichmar & Edelman, 2002). Thus, this new approach combines cognitive psychology with behaviorist principles to more effectively model everyday human problem solving. A more recent example of intuitive robotics is that of the daVinci Surgical System. This technology is being utilized by doctors to perform delicate and complex surgeries with tiny incisions and a precise robotic arm (Renaud et al., 2013).

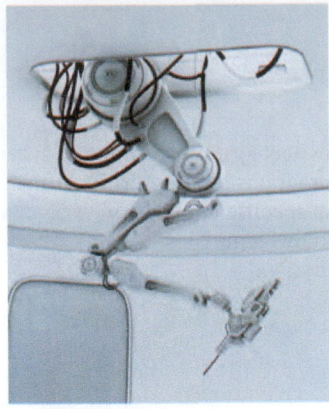

Robotics and Surgery

Today, many surgeries are performed with the assistance of programmable robots.

Source: Ociacia/Shutterstock.
com.

Section Review: Artificial Intelligence

1. Why are expert systems now capable of defeating the best chess players in the world?

2. How does the robotics approach differ from that of expert systems?

Language

language A formal system of communication involving symbols—whether spoken, written, or gestured—and rules for combining them.

Arguing about politics. Reading a newspaper. Using sign language. Each of these is made possible by **language**, a formal system of communication involving symbols—whether spoken, written, or gestured—and rules for combining them. In using language, we rely on spoken symbols to communicate through speech, written symbols to communicate through writing, and gestured symbols to communicate through sign language. We use language to communicate with other people, to store and retrieve memories, and to plan for the future.

But what makes a form of communication "language"? The world's several thousand languages share three characteristics: semanticity, generativity, and displacement. **Semanticity** is the conveying of the communicator's thoughts in a meaningful way to those who understand the language. For example, you know that *anti-* at the beginning of a word means being against something and *-ed* at the end of a word means past action. As discussed in Chapter 14, the language spoken by people with schizophrenia often lacks semanticity; it can be meaningless to other people.

semanticity The characteristic of language marked by the use of symbols to convey thoughts in a meaningful way.

Generativity is the combining of language symbols in novel ways, without being limited to a fixed number of combinations. In fact, each day you probably say or write things that have never been said or written by anyone before. This generativity of language accounts for baby talk, rap music, Brooklynese, and the works of Shakespeare.

generativity The characteristic of language marked by the ability to combine words in novel, meaningful ways.

Displacement is the use of language to refer to objects and events that are not present. The objects and events can be in another place or in the past or future. Thus, you can talk about someone in China, your fifth birthday party, or who will win the World Series next year.

displacement The characteristic of language marked by the ability to refer to objects and events that are not present.

Language is only one form of communication. Many animals, ourselves included, can communicate without using language. For example, researchers allowed dogs to witness a toy or treat being placed where the dogs could not access it. When their owners were present, the dogs would alternate their gaze between their owner and the unavailable object (Miklosi, Polgardi, Topal, & Csanyi, 2000). But are dogs using language? No, the only characteristic of language that dogs display is semanticity. Dogs do not exhibit generativity or displacement in their communications.

Other animals also communicate without using true language. A bee can communicate the location of nectar-containing flowers to residents of its hive. When a bee returns to its hive after finding nectar less than 50 yards away, it performs a "circle dance" on the wall of the hive. If the nectar is farther away, the bee does a "waggle dance," moving in a figure-eight pattern. The angle of the straight line in the figure-eight pattern relative to the sun indicates the direction to the nectar, and the duration of the dance indicates the distance to the nectar—the longer the duration, the farther away it is (Dyer, 2002). But these dances are merely a form of communication, not language. They have semanticity and displacement, but they lack generativity—they are not used to indicate anything other than the location of nectar.

Consider also how monkeys use different alarm calls to signal the presence of particular kinds of predators. In one study, researchers presented Vervet monkeys with tape recordings of alarm calls that signified the presence of an eagle, a boa constrictor, or a leopard. The monkeys responded to eagle alarms by looking up, to boa constrictor alarms by looking down, and to leopard alarms by climbing up into trees (Seyfarth, Cheney, & Marler, 1980). Though monkeys use alarm calls to communicate, they do not use true language. Their calls have semanticity because they communicate the presence of a particular kind of predator, but they lack generativity and displacement. Monkeys neither combine their calls in novel ways nor use them to refer to animals that are not present.

In contrast to dogs, bees, and monkeys, people use true language. Without language, we would be severely limited in our ability to communicate with one another. You would not even be reading this book; books would not exist. Even the book of Genesis from the Old Testament recognizes the importance of language. In the story of the Tower of Babel, God punishes people for their pride by having them speak different languages—restricting their ability to communicate and to engage in cooperative projects, such as building a tower to heaven.

The Structure of Language

English and all other languages have structures governed by rules known as **grammar**. The components of grammar include *phonology, syntax,* and *semantics.*

Phonology

All spoken languages are composed of **phonemes**—the basic sounds of a language. The study of phonemes is called **phonology**. Languages use as few as 20 and as many as 80 phonemes. English contains about 40—the number varies with the dialect. Each phoneme is represented by either a letter (such as the *o* sound in *go*) or a combination of letters (such as the *sh* sound in *should*). Words are combinations of phonemes, and each language permits only certain combinations. A native speaker of English would realize that the combination of phonemes in *cogerite* forms an acceptable word in English even though there is no such

grammar The set of rules that governs the proper use and combination of language symbols.

phoneme The smallest unit of sound in a language.

phonology The study of the sounds that compose languages.

word. That person also would realize that the combination of phonemes in *klputng* does not form an acceptable word in English. There is some evidence that women recognize and process phonemes faster than do men (Majeres, 1999).

One language might not include all the phonemes found in another language, and people learning to speak a foreign language might have more difficulty pronouncing the phonemes in the foreign language that are not in their native language. For example, native speakers of Japanese who learn English as adults have difficulty in distinguishing between *r* sounds, as in *rock,* and *l* sounds, as in *lock.* This difficulty may be due to differences in how phonemes are processed by the brain and early childhood experience with language—though providing training and feedback to native speakers of Japanese improves their ability to distinguish between the two sounds (McClelland, Fiez, & McCandliss, 2002). Catherine Best and Robert Avery investigated American and African adults' perception of *click consonants*—sounds produced by creating suction in the mouth and then releasing with the tongue, producing a sound that is similar to a "tsk" with an abrupt stop. English speakers process clicks acoustically—that is, as nonspeech sounds. In some African languages, clicks have linguistic significance and are perceived as consonants. Participants in the study were native speakers of English and Zulu and Xhosa, two African tone languages with click consonants. The experimental task involved identifying and matching click consonants and nonsense syllables. Results indicated that native Zulu and Xhosa speakers demonstrated more accurate performance on the experimental tasks, and the researchers attributed this finding to the fact that African tone language speakers processed the clicks linguistically rather than acoustically (Best & Avery, 2000).

morpheme The smallest meaningful units of language.

Individual phonemes and combinations of phonemes form **morphemes**, the smallest meaningful units of language. Words are composed of one or more morphemes. For example, the word *book* is composed of a single morpheme. In contrast, the word *books* is composed of two morphemes: *book,* which refers to an object, and *-s,* which indicates the plural of a word. One of the common morphemes that affect the meaning of words is the *-ing* suffix, which indicates ongoing action. Note that the 40 or so phonemes in English build more than 100,000 morphemes, which in turn build almost 500,000 words. Using these words, we can create a virtually infinite number of sentences. One of the outstanding characteristics of language is, indeed, its generativity.

Syntax

syntax The rules that govern the acceptable arrangement of words in phrases and sentences.

In addition to rules that govern the acceptable combinations of sounds in words, languages have **syntax**—rules that govern the acceptable arrangement of words in phrases and sentences. Because you know English syntax, you would say "She ate the ice cream" but not "She the ice cream ate" (though poets do have a "license" to violate normal syntax). And syntax varies from one language to another. The English sentence *John hit Bill* would be translated into its Japanese equivalent as *John Bill hit.* The normal order of the verb and the object in Japanese is the opposite of their normal order in English (Gliedman, 1983). As for adjectives, in English they usually precede the nouns they modify, whereas in Spanish adjectives usually follow the nouns they modify. The English phrase *the red book* would be *el libro rojo* in Spanish. Therefore, a Spanish-speaker learning English might say "the book red," whereas an English-speaker learning Spanish might say "el rojo libro."

Semantics

semantics The study of how language conveys meaning.

Not only must words be arranged appropriately in phrases and sentences, they must be meaningful. The study of how language conveys meaning is called **semantics**. Psycholinguist Noam Chomsky has been intrigued by our ability to convey the same meaning through different phrases and sentences. Consider the sentences *The boy fed the horse* and *The horse was fed by the boy.* Both express the same meaning, but they use different syntax. Moreover, the meaning expressed by these sentences can be expressed in French, Chinese, Swahili, and so on, though the sentences used to express it in those languages would be different from the English sentences.

To explain this ability to express the same meaning using different phrases or different languages, Chomsky distinguishes between a language's deep structure and its surface structure. The **deep structure** is the underlying meaning of a statement; the **surface structure** is the word arrangements that express the underlying meaning. Our ability to discern the deep structure of literary works, for example, lets us appreciate the motives of the main characters. **Transformational grammar** is the term that Chomsky gives to the rules by which languages generate surface structures out of deep structures, and deep structures out of surface structures. Language comprehension involves transforming the surface structure, which is the verbal message, into its deep structure, which is its meaning. Thus, the sentences *The boy fed the horse* and *The horse was fed by the boy* are transformed into the same deep structure, or meaning.

The meaning of a statement depends not only on its words and their arrangement but also on the social context in which the statement is made (Paradis, 1998). The branch of semantics that is concerned with the relationship between language and its social context is called **pragmatics**. To appreciate the relationship between language and its social context, consider the following statement made by a student about an upcoming meal in the cafeteria: "I can't wait to have dinner tonight." If spoken in an enthusiastic voice during Thanksgiving week, the statement might mean that the student expects to enjoy a delicious turkey dinner. Yet, if spoken in a sarcastic voice during a normal school week, the same statement might mean that the student expects to be confronted by the cafeteria's notorious "mystery meat."

Also consider the following embarrassing incident recounted by Elisabeth Kübler-Ross, the prominent death-and-dying researcher (see Chapter 4). She was reared in Switzerland but lived most of her adult life in the United States. "Last evening I spent 10 minutes trying to understand what a nurse was talking about when she invited me to attend a baby shower! Why should I want to look at a bathroom constructed for infants?" (Gill, 1980, p. 201). The incident is an example of the importance of a fund of cultural knowledge as a basis for language pragmatics (Reeder & Shapiro, 1993). Cross-cultural differences in the pragmatics that characterize Western and Asian languages include turn-taking (Lerner & Takagi, 1999) and directness of speech (Holtgraves, 1997).

The importance of pragmatics also is exemplified by the difficulty scientists have had in developing computer programs that can truly converse with people (Saygin & Cicekli, 2002). A program capable of comprehending speech would have to consider characteristics of the message, the speaker, and the situation. The difficulty in employing pragmatics in developing computer programs that can comprehend speech is illustrated in the following conversation (Gorman, 1985, p. 65) between a news reporter (R) and a computer "therapist" called Eliza (E):

R: Row, row, row your boat

E: What about your own boat?

R: Gently down the stream

E: Why do you say that?

R: Merrily, merrily, merrily, merrily

E: I am not sure I understand you fully.

R: Life is but a dream.

E: What does the dream suggest to you?

---

deep structure The underlying meaning of a statement.

surface structure The word arrangements used to express meaning.

transformational grammar The rules by which languages generate surface structures out of deep structures and deep structures out of surface structures.

pragmatics The relationship between language and its social context.

Section Review: The Structure of Language

1. What roles do semanticity, generativity, and displacement play in language?

2. What is the relationship between transformational grammar and the deep structure and surface structure of language?

The Acquisition of Language

What accounts for a child's ability to progress from a crying, gurgling infant to a talkative 3-year-old? The process of language acquisition seems to be universal, with infants in all cultures acquiring language in similar ways as they pass through distinct stages (Rice, 1989). Though the timing of the stages can vary among infants, the order does not.

Language Milestones

For the first few months after birth, infants are limited to communicating vocally through cooing, gurgling, and crying, which they use to indicate that they are content, happy, distressed, hungry, or in pain. Between 4 and 6 months of age, infants enter the babbling stage. When infants babble, they repeat sequences of phonemes, such as ba-ba-ba. Infants in all cultures begin babbling at about the same age and produce the same range of phonemes, including some that are not part of their parents' language (Roug, Landberg, & Lundberg, 1989). This similarity in phonemes might account for the prevalence of the words *mama, papa,* and *dada* to refer to parents in a variety of cultures. Even deaf infants begin babbling at the same age as infants who can hear, though their babbling is different from that of infants who can hear (Oller & Eilers, 1988). The universality of the onset and initial content of babbling indicates that it is a product of the maturation of an inborn predisposition, rather than a product of experience. Nonetheless, by the age of 9 months, infants begin to show the influence of experience, as they limit their babbling to the phonemes of the language, or languages, that they hear in their social environment.

When infants are about 1 year old, they begin to say their first words. Their earliest words typically refer to objects that interest them. Thus, common early words include *milk* and *doggie.* In using words, older infants exhibit **overextension**, applying words too broadly (Behrend, 1988). Consider an infant who refers to her cat as "kitty." If she also refers to dogs, cows, horses, and other four-legged animals as "kitty," she would be exhibiting overextension. In contrast, if she refers to her cat, but to no other cats, as "kitty," she would be exhibiting **underextension**—applying words too narrowly (Caplan & Barr, 1989). As infants gain experience with objects and language, they rapidly learn to apply their words to the correct objects.

After learning to say single words, infants begin using them in **holophrastic speech**, which is the use of single words to represent whole phrases or sentences. For example, an infant might say "car" on one occasion to indicate that the family car has pulled into the driveway and on another occasion to indicate that he would like to go for a ride. Between the ages of 18 and 24 months, infants go beyond holophrastic speech by speaking two-word phrases, typically including a noun and a verb in a consistent order. The infant is now showing a rudimentary appreciation of proper syntax, as in "Baby drink" or

overextension The tendency to apply a word to more objects or actions than it actually represents.

underextension The tendency to apply a word to fewer objects or actions than it actually represents.

holophrastic speech The use of single words to represent whole phrases or sentences.

Language Milestones

If this child refers to her cat as "kitty" and all other animals as "kitty," she would exhibit overextension. When she only refers to her cat—but no other cats—as "kitty," she would be exhibiting underextension.
Source: Oksana Kuzmina/ Shutterstock.com.

"Mommy go." Because, in the two-word stage, infants rely on nouns and verbs and leave out other parts of speech (such as articles and prepositions), their utterances are called **telegraphic speech**. To save time and money, people who used to write telegrams left out connecting parts of speech yet still communicated meaningful messages.

Until they are about 2 years old, infants use words to refer only to objects that are located in their immediate environment. At about age 2, children begin speaking sentences that include other parts of speech in addition to nouns and verbs. They also begin to exhibit displacement, as when a 2-year-old asks, "Grandma come tomorrow?" After age 2, children show a rapid increase in their vocabulary and in the length and complexity of their sentences. Psychologist Roger Brown (1973) invented a unit of measurement, the **mean length of utterance (MLU)**, to assess children's level of language maturation. The MLU is calculated by taking samples of a child's statements and finding their average length in morphemes. The MLU increases rapidly in early childhood, though there is some variability from one child to another. The MLU is a better predictor of overall language ability at younger ages than in later childhood (Scarborough, Rescorla, Tager-Flusberg, Fowler, & Sudhalter, 1991). The use of the MLU has proved useful in assessing language development with a variety of native languages, including Icelandic (Thordar-dottir & Weismer, 1998). The MLU also has been used to assess the language development of children with language disabilities (Barako, Arndt & Schuele, 2012).

The increased sophistication that young children show in their use of language is partly attributable to their application of language rules, which they learn from listening to the speech of those around them. From the day of their birth, infants are exposed to sophisticated language. In fact, studies have found that, contrary to popular impressions, staff members in hospital nurseries do not rely solely on baby talk and soothing sounds when speaking to newborn infants. Instead, staff members spend much of the time speaking to the infants with normal, though perhaps simple, phrases and sentences (Rheingold & Adams, 1980). The language rules that children in European American cultures learn are strongly influenced by their parents' speech—especially mothers' (Leaper, Anderson, & Sanders, 1998). In most non-Western cultures, however, children acquire language through interacting with a number of adults and other children (Mohanty & Perregaux, 1997).

Many languages, like English, have exceptions to grammatical rules. This inconsistency might explain the phenomenon of **overregularization**—the application of grammatical rules without making necessary exceptions (Maratsos, 2000). For example, at first children using the past tense will, correctly, say words such as *did, went*, and *brought*, which violate the -*ed* rule for forming the past tense. They learn these words by hearing the speech of older children and adults. But as children learn the -*ed* rule, they say words such as *doed, goed*, or *bringed*. Later, when they realize that grammatical rules have exceptions, they learn not to apply the -*ed* rule to irregular verbs, and again say *did, went*, and *brought* (Kolata, 1987). Thus, children tend at first to use correct wording, then begin to overregularize, and finally realize when to follow grammatical rules and when to break them (Marcus, 1995).

How do we know that infants learn rules rather than a series of specific instances of correct grammar? One source of evidence is a study by Jean Berko (1958), who reasoned that if children use correct grammar when confronted with words they have never heard, then they must be relying on rules, not rote memory. To test her assumption, Berko developed the "Wug test," which included drawings of imaginary creatures called "wugs." Berko found that children would, indeed, apply grammatical rules to novel words. For example, when shown a picture identified as a "wug" and then a picture with two of them, children completed the statement "There are two _____ " with the word *wugs*. This finding shows that they have learned to use the -*s* ending to indicate the plural.

Is There a Critical Period for Language Acquisition?

As described at the beginning of the chapter, many language researchers believe that there is a critical period for the acquisition of language during childhood. Children who are kept isolated from contact with language and not intensively exposed to language until adolescence—typically because they live in an abusive household—usually have great difficulty becoming proficient in their use of language. But such case studies do not permit

telegraphic speech Speech marked by reliance on nouns and verbs while other parts of speech, including articles and prepositions, are omitted.

mean length of utterance (MLU) A unit of measurement that assesses children's level of language maturation.

overregularization The application of a grammatical rule without making necessary exceptions to it.

us to know for certain whether these children would have shown normal language development had they been exposed to language beginning in infancy in a nurturing household.

Another, perhaps stronger, line of research on critical periods is concerned with adults who learn second languages. Second languages become progressively more difficult to learn as we get older (Birdsong & Molis, 2001). Support for this finding came from a study in which older Korean and Chinese immigrants to the United States found it more difficult to learn English than did younger immigrants—even though the groups were intellectually equal (Johnson & Newport, 1989). Nonetheless, this finding must be viewed with caution in light of the many other factors that could account for differences in the ease with which younger and older immigrants learn a new language.

Theories of Language Acquisition

Language researchers debate this question: Is language acquired solely through learning, or is it strongly influenced by the maturation of an inherited predisposition to develop language? Those who favor the learning position assume that if it were possible to raise two infants together with no exposure to language, they would not develop true language. In contrast, those who favor the view that language emerges from an inherited predisposition assume that the two infants might develop a rudimentary form of language marked by semanticity, generativity, and displacement. According to this position, learning normally determines only which language an infant will speak, whether English, French, or Navajo.

Language as the Product of Learning B. F. Skinner (1957) claimed that language is acquired solely through learning, chiefly through the positive reinforcement of appropriate speech. For example, a 1-year-old child might learn to say "milk" because her parents give her milk and praise her when she says "milk." Similarly, a 2-year-old child named Jane might be given a cookie and praise for saying "Give Jane cookie" but not for saying "Jane cookie give." As you can see, Skinner assumed that vocabulary and grammar are learned through positive reinforcement. In a study supportive of Skinner's position, two groups of infants between 2 and 7 months old were positively reinforced for producing different phonemes. The infants were reinforced by smiles, *tsk* sounds, and light stroking of the abdomen. One group was reinforced for making vowel sounds, whereas the other group was reinforced for making consonant sounds. The infants responded by increasing their production of the phonemes that were reinforced. This study showed that positive reinforcement can affect language acquisition (Routh, 1969). Of course, it does not indicate that language is acquired *solely* through learning.

Albert Bandura (1977), the influential cognitive-behavioral psychologist, stresses the role of observational learning in language acquisition. He assumes that children develop language primarily by imitating the vocabulary and grammatical constructions used by their parents and others in their everyday lives. In a study that supported his position, adults replied to statements

Modeling Language

The modeling of language by parents is an important factor in the acquisition of a particular language by children.

Source: rSnapshotPhotos/ Shutterstock.com.

made by 2-year-old children by purposely using slightly more complex syntax than the children normally would. After 2 months, the children had developed more complex syntax than did children who had not been exposed to the adult models (Nelson, 1977). Additional support for the effect of modeling comes from findings that 2-year-olds whose parents read to them acquire language more rapidly than do 2-year-olds whose parents do not (Whitehurst, Falco, Lonigan, Fischel, DeBaryshe, Valdez-Menchaca, & Caulfield, 1988). Yet, we cannot discount the possibility that other differences between the two groups of parents produced this effect.

Language as an Inherited Predisposition The assumption that language is acquired solely through learning has been challenged by the American linguist and scientist Noam Chomsky and his followers (Rondall, 1994). Chomsky insists that infants are born with the predisposition to develop language. He believes they inherit a *language acquisition device*—a hypothetical place in the brain that makes them sensitive to phonemes, syntax, and semantics. Chomsky has since refined this idea to the theory of *universal grammar,* which suggests that the ability to learn language is hard-wired, does not need to be taught, and is common to all humans. In analyzing the interactions of parents and children, Chomsky has found that children in different cultures progress through similar stages and learn their native languages without formal parental instruction. Children say things that adults never say, and their parents do not positively reinforce proper grammar (or correct improper grammar) in any consistent manner. Modeling, too, cannot explain all language learning because observations of children show that they vary greatly in the extent to which they imitate what their parents say (Snow, 1981).

What evidence is there to support Chomsky's position? One source of evidence comes from the Human Genome Project. In 2001 scientists discovered that the gene FOXP2 plays an important role in our ability to acquire spoken language (Marcus & Fisher, 2003). Another source of evidence is the universality in the basic features of language and the stages of language acquisition (Miller, 1990), which indicates that the tendency to develop language is inborn. Studies of deaf children and children of deaf parents support Chomsky's position. One study observed deaf children who were neither rewarded for using sign language nor exposed to a model who used it. Nonetheless, the children spontaneously developed their own gestural system in which they communicated by using signs with the characteristics of true language (Goldin-Meadow & Mylander, 1998). And infants born to deaf parents develop unique rhythmic hand movements that reflect the rhythmic patterns of language (Petitto, Holowka, Sergio, & Ostry, 2001).

Despite the evidence favoring language as innate and contradicting learning as an explanation for language acquisition, research has provided some support for the learning position (Stemmer, 1990). One study tested the claim made by those who favor Chomsky's position that adults typically ignore children's speech errors and fail to correct their ungrammatical statements. The study found that language acquisition does depend in part on feedback provided by adults who correct specific instances of improper grammar. Adults do so by repeating a child's grammatically incorrect statements in grammatically correct form or by asking the child to clarify his or her statements (Bohannon & Stanowicz, 1988).

It seems that the positions of Chomsky, Skinner, and Bandura must be integrated to explain how language is acquired. We appear to be born with a predisposition to develop language, which provides us with an innate sensitivity to grammar. But we might learn our specific language, including its grammar, mainly through operant conditioning and observational learning.

Section Review: The Acquisition of Language

1. What are the main characteristics of the stages of language development during infancy?

2. How do the theories of Skinner and Chomsky differ in regard to language development?

The Relationship Between Language and Thought

In his novel *1984,* George Orwell (1949) envisioned a totalitarian government that controlled citizen's thoughts by regulating their language. By adding, removing, or redefining words, the government used *Newspeak* to ensure that citizens would not think rebellious thoughts against their leader, "Big Brother." For example, in Newspeak the word *joycamp* referred to a forced labor camp. And the word *free* was redefined to refer only to physical reality, as in *The dog is free from lice,* rather than to political freedom. Even democratic government officials will, at times, resort to euphemisms reminiscent of Newspeak. For example, to reduce public outrage about deceptive government practices, American officials coined the word *misinformation* to replace the word *lying.* Businesspeople also understand the power of language to shape thought, as when used-car dealers refer to their vehicles as *previously owned* instead of *used.*

The Linguistic Relativity Hypothesis

linguistic relativity hypothesis
Benjamin Whorf's hypothesis that one's perception of the world is molded by one's language.

Orwell's view of the influence of language on thought was shared by the linguist-anthropologist Benjamin Lee Whorf (1897–1941), who expressed it in his **linguistic relativity hypothesis**, which assumes that our perception of the world is determined by the particular language we speak (Smith, 1996). Whorf (1956) pointed out that Inuit (once called "Eskimo") languages have several words for snow (such as words that distinguish between falling snow and fallen snow), whereas the English language has only one. According to the linguistic relativity hypothesis, the variety of words for snow in an Inuit language causes people who speak it to perceive differences in snow that people who speak English do not.

Critics argue that, on the contrary, thought determines language. Perhaps the greater importance of snow in their culture led the Inuits to coin several words for snow, each referring to a different kind. Moreover, English speakers to whom snow is important, such as avid skiers, use different adjectives to describe different kinds of snow. Their ability to distinguish between crusty, powdery, and granular snow indicates that even English speakers can perceive wide variations in the quality of snow. And the number of words for snow in Inuit languages might have been exaggerated in the early reports that influenced Whorf and other linguistic relativity theorists (Pullum, 1991).

What does formal research have to say about the linguistic relativity hypothesis? In an early study bearing on Whorf's hypothesis (Carmichael, Hogan, & Walter, 1932), participants were presented with ambiguous drawings of objects that were given either of two labels (see Figure 9-3). When later asked to draw the objects, participants drew pictures that looked more like the object that had been named than like the object they had seen. These results supported Whorf's hypothesis, at least in that language appeared to influence the participants' recall of objects.

Eleanor Rosch (1975) conducted a classic study to test whether language influences the perception of colors. She hypothesized that if the linguistic relativity hypothesis were correct, people who speak a language that has many color words would perceive colors differently than would people who speak a language with few color words.

When Rosch visited the Dani people of New Guinea, she found that the Dani language has two basic color words: *mili* for dark, cool colors, and *mola* for light, warm colors. In contrast, English has eleven basic color words: *black, white, red, green, yellow, blue, brown, purple, pink, orange,* and *gray.* To describe these colors, the Dani use relatively long phrases. Rosch wondered whether these differences in language would be associated with differences in the perception of colors. She decided to test this hypothesis by using "focal" colors, which are considered the best representatives of each of the colors (for example, "fire-engine red" for red), and nonfocal colors.

Dani and American participants were given a series of trials on which they were first shown a colored plastic chip for 5 seconds. After another 30 seconds, they were asked to select the chip from among 160 colored chips. Both the American participants and the Dani participants performed better when the chip to be recalled was a focal color than

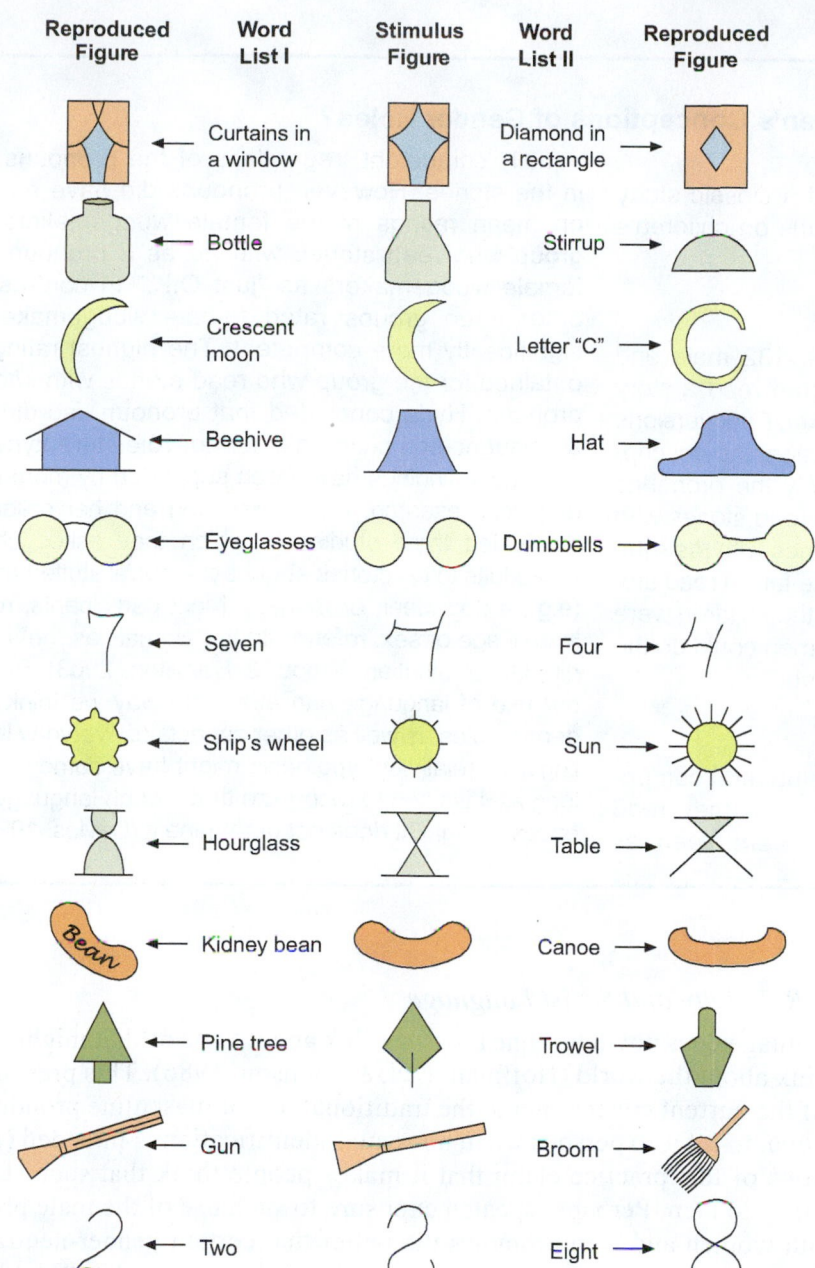

Reproduced Figure	Word List I	Stimulus Figure	Word List II	Reproduced Figure
	← Curtains in a window		Diamond in a rectangle →	
	← Bottle		Stirrup →	
	← Crescent moon		Letter "C" →	
	← Beehive		Hat →	
	← Eyeglasses		Dumbbells →	
	← Seven		Four →	
	← Ship's wheel		Sun →	
	← Hourglass		Table →	
	← Kidney bean		Canoe →	
	← Pine tree		Trowel →	
	← Gun		Broom →	
	← Two		Eight →	

FIGURE 9-3

The Effect of Labels on Recall

Participants were shown the pictures in the middle column with one of two different labels. When later asked to draw what they had seen, the participants drew pictures that were consistent with the labels, not with the pictures. This finding indicates that language can affect how we think about the world even though it might not affect how we perceive the world.

Source: Carmichael, L., Hogan, H. P., & Walter, A. (1932). An experimental study of the effect of language on the reproduction of visually perceived forms. *Journal of Experimental Psychology, 15,* 73–86.

when it was a nonfocal color. These results contradicted Whorf's hypothesis because, though the Dani use only two color names, they are as capable as English-speaking people of perceiving all the focal colors in the English language. Perhaps we are genetically prepared to perceive these focal colors regardless of whether our language takes special note of them.

During the past decades, though, interest in the relationship between language and thought has been spurred by recent research in cognitive linguistics. Cognitive linguistics researchers have found that language may influence cross-cultural variation in a number of ways, including noun-verb relations, conversational and story-telling patterns, cultural scripts that encourage or discourage particular ways of thinking, encoding of the meaning of words, and theories of the self (Goddard, 2003). For example, one study investigated 39 languages spoken in 71 cultures. Cultures with "pronoun drop languages"—languages that omit personal pronouns (*I* and *you*) in conversation—are less individualistic than are cultures with languages that include personal pronouns (Kashima & Kashima, 1998).

Does Language Influence Children's Conceptions of Gender Roles?

Rationale

Janet Shibley Hyde (1984) conducted a classic study to test the effects of gendered pronouns on children's stereotypes about women and men.

Method

The participants in Hyde's study were 132 male and female third and fifth graders. All children read a story about a fictitious occupation: *wudgemaker.* Four versions of the story were prepared. In each version, the description of wudgemakers was identical; only the pronouns used in each story differed. One group read stories with *he* for the pronoun, the second read stories with *they,* the third read stories with *he or she,* and the fourth read stories with *she.* After reading the stories, the children were asked to provide two ratings: how well men could do the job and how well women could do the job.

Results and Discussion

Children's ratings of the male wudgemakers' competence were not affected by the pronouns they read in their stories. Male wudgemakers were seen as equally competent, regardless of the pronouns used in the stories. However, pronouns did have an effect on mean ratings of the female wudgemakers. The group who read stories with *he* as a pronoun rated female wudgemakers as "just O.K." In contrast, the other three groups rated female wudgemakers as significantly more competent. The highest rating was obtained for the group who read stories with *she* as a pronoun. Hyde concluded that pronoun use did have an influence on children's gender-role stereotypes.

These findings have been supported by more recent empirical research. Mykol Hamilton and her colleagues conducted three studies in which they asked children and adults to tell stories about sex-neutral stuffed animals (e.g., a dog, deer, or mouse). Most participants, regardless of age or sex, referred to the animals as "he" (Lambdin, Greer, Jibotian, Wood, & Hamilton, 2003). Because our use of language can affect the way we think about gender roles as well as other aspects of everyday life, the linguistic relativity hypothesis might have some merit, as long as it is used to recognize that though language influences thought, it does not determine it (Davies, 1998).

Linguistic Relativity and Sexist Language

Though language does not determine how we think about the world, it might influence how we think about the world (Hoffman, Lau, & Johnson, 1986). This presumption is the basis of the current concern about the traditional use of masculine pronouns, such as *his* and *him,* to refer to persons when no sexual identification is intended (Prentice, 1994). Critics of this practice claim that it makes people think that such statements refer primarily to men. Perhaps repeated exposure to such use of the male pronoun to refer to both women and men promotes the belief that certain gender-neutral activities are more suitable for men than for women, the topic discussed in "The Research Process" box above.

Section Review: The Relationship Between Language and Thought

1. How does Orwell's concept of Newspeak embody the belief that language affects thought?

2. How are concerns about sexist language related to the linguistic relativity hypothesis?

Language in Apes

In the early 17th century, the philosopher René Descartes argued that language was the critical feature that distinguished people from other animals. Interest in teaching animals cognitive skills, such as language, that normally are associated with people was stimulated by the case of "Clever Hans," a horse who impressed onlookers by solving arithmetic problems in Germany in the early 20th century. Hans was trained to count out the answers to arithmetic problems by tapping one of his hooves until he reached the correct answer. He counted anything present, including persons, hats, or umbrellas. But a psychologist named Oskar Pfungst showed that Hans stopped counting when he noticed tiny movements of his questioner's head, which cued the initiation and termination of counting. When the questioner knew the answer, Hans was correct almost all the time. But when the questioner did not know the answer, Hans was wrong all the time. So, Hans might have been clever, but he had no idea how to perform arithmetic (Davis & Memmott, 1982).

As interest waned in teaching animals to perform arithmetic, interest in teaching them language grew. As you read earlier in the chapter, animals as diverse as bees, dogs, and monkeys can communicate in limited, stereotyped ways. But they do not use true language, which is characterized by semanticity, generativity, and displacement. Research on language learning in dolphins (Herman & Uyeyama, 1999) and sea lions (Gisiner & Schusterman, 1992) is promising but has yet to provide conclusive findings. A much larger body of research supports the belief that there is at least one kind of nonhuman animal capable of acquiring true language—the ape (Williams, Brakke, & Savage-Rumbaugh, 1997).

Teaching Chimpanzees to Use Language

More than 50 years ago, Winthrop and Luella Kellogg (1933) published a book about their experiences raising a chimpanzee named Gua with their infant son, Donald. Even after being exposed to speech as a member of the family, Gua could not speak a single word. Another couple, Cathy and Keith Hayes (Hayes, 1951), had only slightly better results with Viki, a chimpanzee they too raised as a member of their family. Despite their intensive efforts over a period of several years, Viki learned to say only four words: *mama, papa, cup,* and *up.* The Hayeses concluded that the vocal anatomy of apes is not designed for producing speech.

In 1925 the primatologist Robert Yerkes, wondering whether apes have lots to say but no way of saying it, suggested teaching them to use sign language instead of speech. His suggestion was not carried out until 1966, when Allen and Beatrix Gardner (1969) of the University of Nevada began teaching American Sign Language (ASL) to a 1-year-old chimpanzee named Washoe. They raised Washoe in a trailer next to their house. To encourage her to use ASL, they never spoke in her presence; instead, they signed to each other and Washoe, using simple words about various objects and everyday events (Dewsbury, 1996). They also asked Washoe simple questions, praised her correct signs, and tried to comply with her requests, just as parents do with young children. After 4 years of training, Washoe, had a repertoire of 132 signs, which she used to name objects and to describe qualities of objects. The Gardners later replicated their work with four other apes, teaching each to use sign language (Gardner, Gardner, & Van Cantfort, 1989).

Washoe also displayed the ability to generalize her signs to refer to similar things. For example, she used the sign for *open* to refer to doors on a car, a house, and a refrigerator. Washoe even seemed to show an important characteristic of true language—generativity. On seeing a swan for the first time, Washoe made the signs for *water bird.* And in a chimpanzee colony in Washington State, Washoe taught ASL to a young chimpanzee named Loulis, whom she had "adopted" (Cunningham, 1981). After 5 years, Loulis had acquired a vocabulary of more than 50 signs, which he could have learned only from Washoe and other chimpanzees, since all human signing was forbidden when Loulis was present (Gardner, Gardner, & Van Cantfort, 1989).

During the past few decades, several other apes have been taught to use sign language or other forms of language. Ann and David Premack taught a laboratory chimpanzee named Sarah to use plastic chips of different shapes and colors to represent

Can Chimpanzees Acquire Language?

Studying chimpanzees have helped us learn about the nature of language.

Source: MarcilSchauer/Shutterstock.com.

words (Premack, 1971). Sarah learned to answer questions by arranging the chips in different sequences on a board to form sentences. Duane Rumbaugh taught a chimpanzee named Lana to use a computer to create sentences by pressing large keys marked by lexigrams—geometric shapes representing particular words (Rumbaugh, Gill, & von Glasersfeld, 1973). Lana formed sentences by pressing keys in a particular order. Lana's language was called "Yerkish," in honor of Robert Yerkes. When Lana made grammatically correct requests, she was rewarded with food, toys, music, or other things she enjoyed.

Controversy About Ape-Language Research

Have Washoe, Sarah, and Lana learned to use true language? Do they exhibit semanticity, generativity, and displacement? That is, can they communicate meaningfully, create novel combinations of signs, and refer to objects that are not present? Columbia University psychologist Herbert Terrace, who once believed that apes can use language, says no (Terrace, Petitto, Sanders, & Bever, 1979). Terrace taught a chimpanzee named Nim Chimpsky to use sign language. (Nim was named after Noam Chomsky, who believes that apes cannot learn true language.) After 5 years of training, Nim had mastered 125 signs. At first, Terrace assumed that Nim had learned true language. But after analyzing videotapes of conversations with Nim and videotapes of other apes that had been taught sign language, he concluded that Nim and the other apes did not display true language.

On what did Terrace base his conclusion? He found that apes merely learned to make signs, arrange forms, or press computer keys in a certain order to obtain rewards. In other words, their use of language was no different from that of a pigeon that learns to peck a sequence of keys to get food rewards. No researcher would claim that the pigeon is using language. So, the ability of an ape to produce a string of words does not indicate that the ape has learned to produce a sentence. Terrace also claims that the apparent generativity of ape language might be a misinterpretation of their actions. For example, Washoe's apparent reference to a swan as a "water bird" might have been a reference to two separate things—a body of water and a bird.

As additional evidence against ape language, Terrace claims that many instances of allegedly spontaneous signing by chimpanzees are actually responses to subtle cues from trainers. Terrace found that Nim communicated primarily in response to prompting by his trainer or by imitating signs recently made by his trainer. Thus, he did not use language in an original or spontaneous way, and his signs were simply gestures prompted by cues from his trainer that produced consequences he desired—a kind of operant conditioning (Terrace, 1985).

Terrace's attack has not gone unchallenged. Francine Patterson taught a gorilla named Koko to use more than 300 signs ("Ape Language," 1981). Koko even displays generativity, as in spontaneously referring to a zebra as a "white tiger." Patterson criticized Terrace for basing his conclusions on his work with Nim and on isolated frames he has examined from films of other apes using ASL. She claimed that Nim's inadequate use of language might stem from his being confused by having 60 different trainers, which could account for Nim's failure to use sign language in a spontaneous way. In contrast, Patterson reported that Koko had only one primary trainer and used signs more spontaneously than Nim did. For example, Koko responded to a velvet hat by signing "that soft" (Patterson, Patterson, & Brentari, 1987).

In recent years, the strongest evidence in support of ape language comes from studies by Duane Rumbaugh and Sue Savage-Rumbaugh of the Language Research Center at Georgia State University. They trained two chimpanzees, Austin and Sherman, to communicate through Yerkish, the language used earlier by Lana. Austin and Sherman use language in a more sophisticated way than previous chimpanzees. In one study, Austin, Sherman, and Lana were taught to categorize three objects (an orange, a beancake, and a slice of bread) as "edible" and three objects (a key, a stick, and a pile of coins) as "inedible." When given other objects, Austin and Sherman, but not Lana, were able to categorize them as edible or inedible. Perhaps Lana could not learn this task because she had been trained to use language to associate labels with specific objects rather than to understand the concepts to which the labels referred (Savage-Rumbaugh, Rumbaugh, Smith & Lawson, 1980).

Even when housed in different rooms, Austin and Sherman can request objects from each other. This ability was demonstrated when one of the chimpanzees was given a box from which he could obtain food or drink only by using a tool located in the other chimpanzee's room. The chimpanzee in the room with the food indicated the tool he needed by striking a specific series of keys on a computer keyboard. The chimpanzee in the room with the tools then passed that tool to the other chimpanzee (Marx, 1980).

More recently, Sue Savage-Rumbaugh and her colleagues (1986) described their work with two pygmy chimpanzees, Kanzi and Mulika, who have achieved language ability superior to that of previous apes. Savage-Rumbaugh and her researchers exposed the chimpanzees to human language during everyday activities rather than as part of an artificial training program (Menzel, Savage-Rumbaugh, & Menzel, 2002). Kanzi learned Yerkish spontaneously by observing people and other chimpanzees (including his mother) pressing appropriate lexigrams on a keyboard (Savage-Rumbaugh, 1990). He also can identify symbols referred to in human speech. Previous apes depended on their own particular language system to comprehend human communications. Kanzi can even form requests in which other individuals are either the agent or the recipient of action—which reflects his appreciation of syntax (Savage-Rumbaugh, Murphy, Sevic, & Brakke, 1993). Before, apes such as Nim made spontaneous requests only in which they were the targets of a suggested action. Moreover, Kanzi shows displacement, using lexigrams to refer to things that are not present (Savage-Rumbaugh, 1987).

Nonetheless, some critics insist that even Kanzi does not display all the characteristics of true language (Kako, 1999). Savage-Rumbaugh has responded to this criticism by asking critics to stress the important language skills that Kanzi has exhibited rather than continually seeking to identify the relatively minor aspects of language that he has failed to exhibit (Shanker, Savage-Rumbaugh, & Taylor, 1999). Moreover, Allen Gardner has reported that Washoe and other language-trained chimpanzees who are living together in retirement converse with one another and with people in a manner similar to that of human children (Jensvold & Gardner, 2000).

Perhaps future studies using pygmy chimpanzees will succeed where others have failed in demonstrating convincingly that apes are capable of using true language. But even if apes can use true language, no ape has gone beyond the language level of a 3-year-old child. Is that the upper limit of ape language ability, or is it just the upper limit using current training methods? Research soon might provide the answer. In any case, we do know that apes are capable of more complex communication than simply grunting to convey crude emotional states.

Section Review: Language in Apes

1. What evidence is there that apes such as Washoe demonstrate the characteristics of true language?

2. Why do critics doubt that these apes have acquired true language?

Will the Replication of a Classic Research Study on Mental Sets Produce Similar Findings Today?

In the section titled "Problem Solving," you read about the cognitive impediment to problem solving called a mental set. A mental set is a predisposition to rely on an approach to solving a problem that has worked so well in the past that it blinds you to an effective solution to a current problem. The classic water-jar study supporting the negative effect of mental sets on problem solving was conducted more than 50 years ago (Luchins, 1946). In this exercise, you will conduct an approximate replication of the water-jar study to determine whether the original findings will hold up today.

Method
Participants
The participants will be 30 "naïve" fellow male and female students—that is, students who have not taken introductory psychology. Using students who have taken introductory psychology might threaten the validity of your study by including some who have learned about mental sets, perhaps even reading about the classic water-jar study.

Materials
You will use three versions of the water-jar problem discussed earlier in the chapter. You will need to present these problems to the participants in a written format or on a computer screen.

Procedure
Create three versions of the water-jar problem. One version should be identical to that described earlier in the chapter: The first five problems will be solvable by the same approach, and the sixth problem will not be solvable by that approach—though it will be solvable by a simpler approach. The second version should just present the sixth problem. The third version, added here to control for the possible effect of working on five problems before attempting the sixth, should present the same five problems as in the original study but the sixth problem should be solvable by the approach used in solving the first five.

Tell the participants that they will be participating in a study on problem solving, without revealing its exact purpose. Give 10 students the first version of the task, 10 students the second version, and 10 students the third version. To avoid biasing students who will be participating in the study later, ask your participants not to discuss the study with anyone else until it has been completed.

Results and Discussion
Count the number of correct responses to the problem in the second version and the sixth problem in the other two versions. Draw a bar graph (see Appendix C in the Online Edition) comparing the number of correct answers to those three problems.

Note how your results compare with those of Luchins (1946). Do the results appear to support the influence of a mental set? If not, try to explain why. Were there any confounding variables that might have adversely affected your study? Why would the use of an inferential statistic (see Chapter 2 and Appendix C in the Online Edition) have been preferable to subjectively judging the size of the differences between the three groups? Think of another study you could conduct to assess the effects of mental sets on problem solving.

Chapter Summary

Thought
- The past few decades have seen a cognitive revolution in psychology, with increased interest in the study of thought.
- Thought is the purposeful mental manipulation of words and images.

Concept Formation
- Thought depends on concepts, which are categories of objects, events, qualities, or relations whose members share certain features.
- A logical concept is formed by identifying specific features possessed by all members of the concept.
- A natural concept is formed through everyday experiences and has fuzzy borders.
- The best representative of a concept is called a prototype.

Problem Solving
- One of the most important uses of concepts is in problem solving, the thought process that enables us to overcome obstacles to reach goals.
- A basic method of solving problems is trial and error, which involves trying one possible solution after another until finding one that works.
- The problem-solving strategy called insight depends on the mental manipulation of information.
- An algorithm is a rule that, when followed step by step, ensures that a solution to a problem will be found.
- A heuristic is a general principle that guides problem solving but does not guarantee the discovery of a solution.
- A mental set is a problem-solving strategy that has succeeded in the past but that can interfere with solving a problem that requires a new strategy.

- Our past experience also can impede problem solving through functional fixedness, the inability to realize that a problem can be solved by using a familiar object in an unusual way.

Creativity

- Creativity is a form of problem solving characterized by novel solutions that also are useful or socially valued.
- Creative people tend to have above-average intelligence and are able to integrate different kinds of thinking.
- Creative people are more motivated by their intrinsic interest in creative tasks than by extrinsic factors.
- Sociocultural factors also may influence the development and expression of creativity.
- Creativity also depends on divergent thinking, in which a person freely considers a variety of potential solutions to a problem.

Decision Making

- In decision making we try to make the best choice from among alternative courses of action.
- In using the representativeness heuristic, we assume that a small sample is representative of its population.
- In using the availability heuristic, we estimate the probability of an event by how easily instances of it come to mind.
- We are also subject to framing effects, which are biases introduced in the decision-making process by presenting a situation in a certain manner.

Artificial Intelligence

- Artificial intelligence is a field that integrates computer science and cognitive psychology to try to simulate or improve on human thought by using computer programs.
- Computer programs called expert systems display expertise in specific domains of knowledge.
- Computer scientists are studying human performance by creating robots that engage in problem solving and intuitive movement while exploring and mapping the environment.

Language

- In using language, we rely on spoken symbols to communicate through speech, written symbols to communicate through writing, and gestured symbols to communicate through sign language.
- We use language to communicate with other people, to store and retrieve memories, and to plan for the future.

The Structure of Language

- True language is characterized by semanticity, generativity, and displacement.
- The rules of a language are its grammar.
- Phonemes are the basic sounds of a language, and morphemes are its smallest meaningful units.

- A language's syntax includes rules governing the acceptable arrangement of words and phrases.
- Semantics is the study of how language conveys meaning.
- Noam Chomsky calls the underlying meaning of a statement its deep structure and the words themselves its surface structure.
- We translate between the two structures by using transformational grammar.
- The branch of semantics concerned with the relationship between language and its social context is called pragmatics.

The Acquisition of Language

- Infants in all cultures progress through similar stages of language development.
- They begin babbling between 4 and 6 months of age and say their first words when they are about 1 year old.
- At first they use holophrastic speech, in which single words represent whole phrases or sentences.
- Between the ages of 18 and 24 months, infants begin speaking two-word sentences and use telegraphic speech.
- As infants learn their language's grammar, they may engage in overregularization, in which they apply grammatical rules without making necessary exceptions.
- There might be a critical period for language acquisition that extends from infancy to adolescence.
- B. F. Skinner and Albert Bandura believe that language is acquired solely through learning, whereas Noam Chomsky believes we have an innate predisposition to develop language.

The Relationship Between Language and Thought

- Benjamin Lee Whorf's linguistic relativity hypothesis assumes that our view of the world is determined by the particular language we speak.
- But research has shown that though language can influence thought, it does not determine it.

Language in Apes

- Researchers have taught apes to communicate by using sign language, form boards, and computers.
- The most well-known of these apes include the gorilla Koko and the chimpanzees Washoe, Sarah, and Lana.
- Herbert Terrace, the trainer of Nim Chimpsky, claims that apes have not learned true language; instead, they have learned to give responses that lead to rewards, just as pigeons learn to peck at keys to obtain food.
- Francine Patterson, Duane Rumbaugh, and Sue Savage-Rumbaugh have countered by providing evidence that the apes have indeed learned true language characterized by semanticity, generativity, and displacement.

Key Terms

cognitive neuroscience (p. 309)
cognitive psychology (p. 309)
critical period (p. 308)

Thought

thought (p. 309)

Concept Formation

concept (p. 310)
logical concept (p. 310)
natural concept (p. 310)
prototype (p. 311)

Problem Solving

algorithm (p. 313)
functional fixedness (p. 315)
heuristic (p. 314)
insight (p. 313)
mental set (p. 315)
problem solving (p. 312)
trial and error (p. 312)

Creativity

convergent thinking (p. 319)
creativity (p. 316)
divergent thinking (p. 319)

Decision Making

availability heuristic (p. 321)
decision making (p. 320)
framing effects (p. 321)
representativeness heuristic (p. 320)

Artificial Intelligence

artificial intelligence (AI) (p. 322)
expert systems (p. 323)

Language

displacement (p. 324)
generativity (p. 324)
language (p. 324)
semanticity (p. 324)

The Structure of Language

deep structure (p. 327)

grammar (p. 325)
morpheme (p. 326)
phoneme (p. 325)
phonology (p. 325)
pragmatics (p. 327)
semantics (p. 326)
surface structure (p. 327)
syntax (p. 326)
transformational grammar (p. 327)

The Acquisition of Language

holophrastic speech (p. 328)
mean length of utterance (MLU) (p. 329)
overextension (p. 328)
overregularization (p. 329)
telegraphic speech (p. 329)
underextension (p. 328)

The Relationship Between Language and Thought

linguistic relativity hypothesis (p. 332)

Chapter Quiz

Note: Answers for the Chapter Quiz questions are provided at the end of the book.

1. A computer program that could conduct psychotherapy would be an example of
   a. a heuristic.
   b. a prototype.
   c. an algorithm.
   d. an expert system.

2. A child who says "cup" whenever he is hungry would be exhibiting
   a. overextension.
   b. telegraphic speech.
   c. overregularization.
   d. holophrastic speech.

3. A computerized statistical program that always gives correct answers if numbers are entered into it properly is an example of
   a. a prototype.
   b. an algorithm.
   c. a heuristic.
   d. a mental set.

4. The speech of people with schizophrenia often is marked by incomprehensibility, arbitrary word orders, and bizarrely novel combinations of words. Given this, the characteristic of true language most often found in the speech of people with schizophrenia is
   a. syntax.
   b. semanticity.
   c. generativity.
   d. overregularization.

5. An experienced chess player who could checkmate her opponent in two moves fails to notice that opportunity and instead continues to follow a less effective approach that has worked in similar situations in the past. This failure to show flexibility in problem solving is an example of the influence of a
   a. prototype.
   b. mental set.
   c. expert system.
   d. framing effect.

6. A prime number can be evenly divided only by itself or one. "Prime number" is an example of
   a. an algorithm.
   b. a heuristic.
   c. a natural concept.
   d. a logical concept.

7. A child who says "I eated the lunch" or "I throwed the ball" would be exhibiting
   a. overextension.
   b. underextension.
   c. overregularization.
   d. holophrastic speech.

8. Though music by Alice in Chains or the Rolling Stones would be universally classified as rock, it might be difficult to agree on the classification of other music as rock. This difficulty indicates that "rock" is
   a. an algorithm.
   b. a heuristic.
   c. a logical concept.
   d. a natural concept.

9. The difficulty that computer programs such as Eliza have in comprehending speech is mainly related to
   a. syntax.
   b. pragmatics.
   c. holophrastic speech.
   d. linguistic relativity.

10. People high in creativity also are likely to
    a. combine different ways of thinking.
    b. filter out irrelevant stimuli to attend to the task at hand.
    c. display extrinsic motivation.
    d. be geniuses.

11. The linguistic relativity hypothesis is most relevant to
    a. George Orwell's *1984*.
    b. Joan Rivers's *Still Talking*.
    c. Mary Shelley's *Frankenstein*.
    d. J. D. Salinger's *The Catcher in the Rye*.

12. If you more easily recall media reports of street crime in city A than in city B, you may decide that city A is more crime-ridden than city B—even though city B may actually be the more crime-ridden city. This thinking would be an example of the
    a. availability heuristic.
    b. error of overextension.
    c. representative heuristic.
    d. fundamental attribution error.

13. The sentence "John the book gave to Jane" violates proper English
    a. syntax.
    b. semantics.
    c. pragmatics.
    d. displacement.

14. A man, trying to reach a wristwatch that has been swept out of his reach under a couch, searches in vain for a long, thin object that would enable him to reach it. He fails to realize that he could obtain such an object by untwisting a wire coat hanger and straightening it into a single long wire. His oversight would show the influence of
    a. underextension.
    b. overregularization.
    c. divergent thinking.
    d. functional fixedness.

15. Baseball strategies such as intentionally walking a good hitter in order to pitch instead to a weaker hitter and using a sacrifice bunt to move a runner from first base to second base are examples of
    a. prototypes.
    b. algorithms.
    c. heuristics.
    d. logical concepts.

16. An automobile company finds that customers are more likely to purchase one of its cars when it is advertised as being "safer than 18 of the top 20 sellers" than when it is advertised as being "safer than all but 2 of the top 20 sellers." This wording is an example of
    a. framing effects.
    b. the availability heuristic.
    c. the representative heuristic.
    d. the fundamental attribution error.

17. A child who enjoys playing the piano begins to play less often after his parents begin giving him five dollars every time he practices. His loss of interest was most likely the product of
    a. pragmatics.
    b. overextension.
    c. overregularization.
    d. extrinsic motivation.

18. The sentence "Yesterday, he zorked the brem in Antarctica" is most lacking in
    a. syntax.
    b. morphemes.
    c. semanticity.
    d. displacement.

19. If you meet three members of an ethnic group who act shy and soft-spoken and you decide that most members of that group share those traits, you would be exhibiting the
    a. availability heuristic.
    b. error of overextension.
    c. representative heuristic.
    d. fundamental attribution error.

20. A baby cries when it is in pain. The cry mainly exhibits
    a. syntax.
    b. semanticity.
    c. displacement.
    d. generativity.

21. The statement "They look great for their age" could be interpreted as either sarcasm or flattery, depending on its social context and the speaker's tone of voice. This interpretation is an example of
    a. syntax.
    b. pragmatics.
    c. generativity.
    d. linguistic relativity.

22. An infant's father has a beard. Because of this, she calls all men with beards "daddy." Her behavior is an example of
    a. generativity.
    b. overextension.
    c. overregularization.
    d. holophrastic speech.

23. Psychologists have been most successful in training apes to communicate by using
    a. speech.
    b. sign language.
    c. simple writing.
    d. facial expressions.

24. According to Noam Chomsky, language is acquired primarily through
    a. watching people model the use of language.
    b. an inborn biological language acquisition device.
    c. positive reinforcement of correct use of language.
    d. higher-order conditioning using words as conditioned stimuli.

25. The difficulty that people have in learning to pronounce certain words in a foreign language is related to
    a. syntax.
    b. phonemes.
    c. morphemes.
    d. pragmatics.

Thought Questions

1. Why might people be more likely to argue whether bowling is a true sport than whether tennis is a true sport?

2. How might heuristics contribute to ethnic prejudice?

3. How might calling people "senior citizens" rather than "elderly" and calling people "intellectually disabled" as opposed to "mentally retarded" be related to the linguistic relativity hypothesis?

4. What issues must be confronted by researchers who wish to demonstrate the acquisition of true language in apes?

Intelligence

In the 1988 movie *Rain Man,* which won an Academy Award for best picture, Dustin Hoffman portrays Raymond Babbitt, a man with **autism spectrum disorder (ASD)** who could perform amazing mental feats, such as memorizing restaurant menus, recalling the telephone number of anyone in the telephone book, and rapidly calculating complicated mathematical problems in his head. Raymond refuses to fly, basing his decision on the many airplane crashes he can recall, including the dates and fatalities of each one. Hoffman's performance won him the Academy Award for best actor. The film depicts a cross-country journey of self-discovery for his younger brother, Charlie, a self-centered young man whose father dies and leaves his $3 million estate to Raymond—a brother that Charlie never knew he had and whom he "kidnaps" from an institution, hoping to ransom him for half the money. Along the way, Raymond uses his unusual memory ability to help Charlie win almost $100,000 playing blackjack in Las Vegas. Charlie learns to be less self-centered and to accept—and even love—someone who is different from him.

The film is likewise a journey of discovery for viewers, who come to understand some aspects of ASD (see Chapter 14). For example, as is typical in ASD Raymond follows a strict routine—even insisting that pancake syrup always be put on the table before the pancakes arrive. He also shows the compulsive repetition of phrases and the difficulty in connecting emotionally to other people that is common. ASD is a term for a group of psychological disorders that are characterized by difficulties with social relationships, impaired language and communication, and repetitive behaviors.

Raymond not only suffers from ASD but also exhibits abilities that once would have had him labeled an *idiot savant* (French for "learned fool"). To avoid the negative connotation of the word *idiot,* idiot savants are now called *autistic savants,* or people with savant syndrome (Miller, 1999). An autistic savant is a person with ASD and below-average general intelligence but who has hyperdeveloped cognitive skills—typically in art (Hou et al., 2000), music (Heaton, Hermelin, & Pring, 1998), mechanics, or calculating (Kelly, Macaruso, & Sokol, 1997). These talents are developed beyond the person's level of functioning in other areas, and all involve exceptional memory ability. Studies suggest that 10 percent of individuals with ASD have savant skills (Bolte & Poustka, 2004; Corrigan, Richards, Treffert, & Dager, 2012).

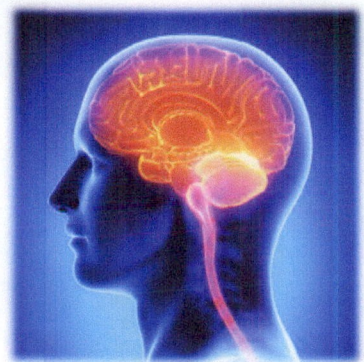

Source: CLIPAREA/Custom media/ Shutterstock.com.

Chapter Outline

Intelligence Testing

Extremes of Intelligence

Theories of Intelligence

Nature, Nurture, and Intelligence

autism spectrum disorder (ASD) A group of psychological conditions characterized by poor social relationships, impaired communication, and repetitive behaviors.

Dustin Hoffman *(left)* and Tom Cruise *(right)* are shown in a scene from *Rain Man,* in which Hoffman portrays an autistic savant.

Source: Photofest.

What we now call the savant syndrome was first noted in 1751 in a German magazine article that described the case of an uneducated farmhand with an extraordinary memory (Foerstl, 1989). In 1887 the phenomenon was named the idiot savant condition by John Langdon Down, the physician who also identified what we now call Down syndrome. In a much more recent case, a 12-year-old autistic savant could play unfamiliar piano pieces after listening to them once (Young & Nettelbeck, 1995). In another case, an autistic savant could give the day of the week for any date in the 20th century (Hurst & Mulhall, 1988). He had spent many hours memorizing the day of the week of each date, just as Dustin Hoffman's character spent many hours memorizing the telephone book. Because autistic savants tend to be socially isolated and persistent at tasks, they can spend the many hours needed to memorize large amounts of material (Heavey, Pring, & Hermelin, 1999) but also have the ability to retrieve the information at "lightning speed." Their feats are beyond the ability of children who memorize statistics from the backs of hundreds of baseball cards and then recall any statistic for any player.

The savant syndrome occurs in about 10 percent of people with ASD and six times more often in males than in females. Autistic savants vary in their ability to function in everyday life. Not all savants function at the level that Dustin Hoffman did in *Rain Man.* Though there are many autistic savants, fewer than 100 *prodigious savants*—the kind celebrated by the media—have been identified. A prodigious savant is a person with ASD who has a talent so highly developed that it would be remarkable even in a person of normal intellectual ability (Treffert, 1989).

There is no single accepted cause of the savant syndrome, but research findings implicate overdevelopment of certain structures of the right cerebral hemisphere that govern particular talents (Corrigan, Richards, Treffert, & Dager, 2012). Some speculation remains as to the exact underlying mechanisms of savant syndrome due to the inability to perform large-scale neuroimaging studies on these individuals. Nevertheless, researchers consistently find anatomical and neurochemical abnormalities within regions of the brain associated with learning and memory. The talents exhibited by autistic savants seem to be processed by implicit rather than explicit memory. As discussed in Chapter 8, the implicit memory system deals with memories that are processed without the conscious intention to do so. The outstanding talents of prodigious savants are probably strongly affected by heredity because their remarkable knowledge of the rules of art, music, or mathematics does not appear to be the product of practice alone (Treffert, 1989).

An autistic savant who memorizes enormous amounts of material is displaying *intelligence*. You certainly recognize intelligent behavior when you see it: someone getting an A on a calculus exam, or composing a great symphony, or discovering a cure for a disease. Recognizing intelligent behavior, though, is easier than defining intelligence itself. The word *intelligence* comes from the Latin word meaning "to understand," but the concept of intelligence is broader than that. Finding a universally acceptable definition of intelligence is difficult because intelligence is a natural concept. Natural concepts have "fuzzy borders"— they are not easily defined by a distinct set of features (see Chapter 9).

Decades ago, David Wechsler (1958), a leading intelligence researcher, put forth an influential definition of intelligence. He called **intelligence** the global capacity to act purposefully, to think rationally, and to deal effectively with the environment. In other words, intelligence reflects how well we *function*. This definition is in the spirit of the early school of psychology called functionalism (see Chapter 1), which stressed the importance of adaptive behavior in everyday life.

intelligence The global capacity to act purposefully, to think rationally, and to deal effectively with the environment.

Intelligence Testing

Modern interest in the study of intelligence began with the development of tests of cognitive abilities, which include achievement tests, aptitude tests, and intelligence tests. An **achievement test** assesses knowledge of a particular subject. For decades, New York State has required students to pass the Regents Exams, which are achievement tests designed to measure students' knowledge of major academic areas such as English, history, and mathematics. An **aptitude test** predicts your potential to benefit from instruction in a particular academic or vocational setting. Of course, an aptitude test is partly an achievement test—your performance on it depends on your previous experience with the material covered by the test. Aptitude tests are commonly used to screen job applicants and college applicants. In applying to colleges, you may have submitted the results of your performance on either the Scholastic Assessment Test (SAT) or the American College Test (ACT). These scores help admissions committees determine whether applicants have the potential to succeed in college. An **intelligence test**, the main topic of this section, is a kind of aptitude test that assesses overall mental ability, which influences our functioning in a variety of areas of life, including school and work (Brody, 1999).

achievement test A test that measures knowledge of a particular subject.

aptitude test A test designed to predict a person's potential to benefit from instruction in a particular academic or vocational setting.

intelligence test A test that assesses overall mental ability.

The History of Intelligence Testing

The use of tests of mental abilities has been traced back to 2200 B.C., when the Chinese appear to have used them to select talented individuals to serve as civil servants (Fox, 1981). But ability testing did not become the subject of scientific study until more than a century ago, when the English scientist Francis Galton (1822–1911) set up his Anthropometric Laboratory at the 1884 International Health Exhibition in London.

Francis Galton and Anthropometry

The word *anthropometric* means "human measurement." More than 9,000 visitors to Galton's laboratory paid to be measured on a variety of physical characteristics, including head size, grip strength, visual acuity, and reaction time to sounds (Morse, 1999). Galton was inspired by his cousin, Charles Darwin, and his theory of evolution. According to Darwin, individuals who are the most physically well adapted to their environment are the most likely to survive long enough to produce offspring, who would be likely to also have those physical characteristics. Galton similarly assumed that people with superior physical abilities, especially sensory and motor abilities, are better adapted for survival. He viewed such people as more intelligent than those with average or inferior physical abilities.

Galton's interest in studying physical differences reflected his interest in studying all sorts of individual differences, including the relative beauty of women from different countries. In a possible instance of experimenter bias, Galton found that the women of England, his home country, were the most beautiful. His research on individual differences established the field of **differential psychology**, which is concerned with the study of cognitive and behavioral differences among individuals. Differential psychology differs from traditional psychology in that modern psychologists study groups rather than individuals. Galton's anthropometric method was introduced to the United States by James McKeen Cattell (1860–1944), who administered Galton's tests—which Cattell called mental tests—to American students (Cattell, 1890). But anthropometry proved fruitless as a way of measuring general intelligence because many anthropometric measurements, such as grip strength, proved to have little or no relationship to mental measures of intelligence, such as reasoning ability. As discussed in the "Psychology Versus Common Sense" box, on page 358, however, more recent research has demonstrated a relationship between mental measurements and physical measures such as reaction time.

Alfred Binet, Theodore Simon, and the IQ Test

The first formal test of general intelligence—the *Binet-Simon scale* (and later modified and renamed the *Stanford-Binet IQ Test)*—appeared in 1905. It grew out of an 1881 French law that required all children to attend school even if they could not profit from a standard curriculum (Levine, 1976). This ruling led the French minister of public education to ask psychologist Alfred Binet (1857–1911) to develop a test to identify children who required special classes for slow learners. Binet collaborated with psychiatrist Theodore Simon (1873–1961) to develop a test that could assess children's ability to perform in school. Binet and Simon began by administering many questions related to language, reasoning, and arithmetic to elementary schoolchildren of all ages. Binet and Simon eliminated questions that tended to be answered the same by children of all ages. Questions that were answered correctly by more and more children at each successive age were retained and became the Binet-Simon scale.

The test was administered to children who needed to be placed in school. Each student was assigned a *mental age,* based on the number of test items she or he passed—the greater the number of items passed, the higher the mental age. A student with a mental age significantly below his or her chronological age was considered a candidate for placement in a class for slow learners. Binet urged that his test be used solely for class placement. He disagreed with those who claimed that the test measured a child's inherited level of intelligence or that a child's level of intelligence could not be improved by education.

The Binet-Simon scale proved useful, but the measure of mental age occasionally proved misleading. Suppose that a 10-year-old child had a mental age of 8 and a 6-year-old child had a mental age of 4. Both would be 2 years below their chronological ages, but the 6-year-old would be proportionately farther behind her or his age peers than the 10-year-old would be. This problem was solved by German psychologist William Stern (1871–1938), who recommended using the ratio of mental age to chronological age to determine a child's level of intelligence (Kreppner, 1992). A 10-year-old with a mental age of 8 has a ratio of 8/10 = 0.80, and a 6-year-old with a mental age of 4 has a ratio of 4/6 = 0.67. The 6-year-old is relatively further behind his or her age peers. Stanford University psychologist Lewis Terman eliminated the decimal point by multiplying the ratio by 100. Thus, 0.80 becomes 80, and 0.67 becomes 67. The formula (mental age/

---

differential psychology
The field of psychology that studies individual differences in physical, personality, and intellectual characteristics.

chronological age × 100) became known as the **intelligence quotient (IQ)**. As you can see, a child whose mental and chronological ages are the same has an IQ of 100, and a child who has a higher mental than chronological age has an IQ above 100.

intelligence quotient (IQ)
Originally, the ratio of mental age to chronological age; that is, mental age/chronological age × 100.

Lewis Terman and American Intelligence Testing

The Binet-Simon scale was translated into English and first used in the United States by the American psychologist Henry Goddard (1866–1957) in New Jersey at the Vineland Training School, which served children with intellectual disabilities (formerly referred to as mental retardation). In 1916 Lewis Terman (1877–1956) published a revised version of the Binet-Simon scale that was more suitable for children reared in American culture. The American version became known as the *Stanford-Binet Intelligence Scale* and still is used today. Terman also redesigned the Stanford-Binet to make it suitable for testing both children and adults. The test has been revised several times since 1916.

Because the Stanford-Binet is given individually and can take an hour or more to administer, it is not suitable for testing large groups of people in a brief period of time. The time factor became a problem during World War I, when the U.S. Army sought a way to assess the intelligence of large groups of recruits. The army wanted to reject recruits who did not have the intelligence to perform well and to identify recruits who would be good officer candidates. Terman and several other prominent psychologists provided the solution to this problem. They developed two group tests of intelligence—the Army Alpha Test and the Army Beta Test. The Army Alpha Test was given in writing to those who could read English, and the Army Beta Test was given orally to those who could not read English. The tests, reflecting their functionalist heritage, viewed intelligence as the ability to adapt to the environment (Mayrhauser, 1989). Descendants of these group intelligence tests include the Otis-Lennon Mental Abilities Tests and the Armed Forces Qualification Test.

David Wechsler and the Deviation IQ

After World War I, the Stanford-Binet became the most widely used intelligence test. But the ratio IQ devised by Stern, which was adequate for representing the intelligence of children, proved inadequate for representing the intelligence of adults. Because growth in mental age slows markedly after childhood, the use of the ratio IQ led to the absurdity of people with average or above-average intelligence becoming below average simply because their chronological age increased. For example, consider a 15-year-old girl with a mental age of 20. She would have an IQ of $(20/15) \times 100 = 133$. This score would put her in the mentally gifted range (that is, above 130). Suppose that at age 40 she had retained the mental age of 20. She would then have an IQ of $(20/40) \times 100 = 50$. This score would put her well within the range of intellectual disabilities (that is, below 70). Yet she might be a successful lawyer, physician, or professor.

This inadequacy of the ratio IQ was overcome by David Wechsler (1896–1981). He replaced Stern's ratio IQ with a deviation IQ, which compares a person's intelligence test score with the mean score of his or her age peers. Those persons who perform at exactly the mean of their age peers receive an IQ of 100, those who perform above the mean of their age peers receive an IQ above 100, and those who perform below the mean of their age peers receive an IQ below 100.

In 1939 Wechsler developed his own intelligence test. While working as chief psychologist at Bellevue Hospital in New York City, he sought a way to assess the intelligence of adult psychiatric patients with low verbal ability (Boake, 2002). Because the Stanford-Binet stressed verbal ability and was geared toward testing children, it was not suitable for that purpose. Wechsler was led to develop an adult intelligence test that tested nonverbal as well as verbal ability, which he called the *Wechsler-Bellevue Intelligence Scale*.

Wechsler later developed versions of his test for use with different age groups, beginning with the *Wechsler Intelligence Scale for Children (WISC)*, for ages 6 to 16; followed by the *Wechsler Adult Intelligence Scale (WAIS)*, for ages from late adolescence through adulthood; and concluding with the *Wechsler Preschool and Primary Scale of Intelligence (WPPSI)*, for ages 4 to 6-1/2. The Wechsler scales have been revised periodically. Each of the Wechsler intelligence scales contains 11 subtests that measure different aspects of verbal and nonverbal intelligence. The test taker receives a verbal IQ, a performance (nonverbal)

IQ, and an overall IQ. Research has supported the usefulness of distinguishing, as measured by the Wechsler scales, these three kinds of intelligence (LoBello & Gulgoz, 1991).

Standardization in Intelligence Testing

Formal tests must be standardized, reliable, and valid (see Chapter 2). *Standardization* refers to both the establishment of performance norms on a test and uniformity in how the test is administered and scored. When an intelligence test is standardized, the mean performance of the standardization group for each age range is given a score of 100, with a standard deviation of 15. The standard deviation is a measure of how variable a group of scores are around their mean. Figure 10-1 shows that IQ scores fall along a *normal curve*. For the Wechsler scales, about 68 percent of test takers will score between 85 and 115, and about 95 percent will score between 70 and 130. Average intelligence falls between 85 and 115. IQs below 70 fall in the range of intellectual disabilities, and IQs above 130 fall in the mentally gifted range. Though the word "standardized" can conjure up emotions of anxiety, imagine if a test of intelligence was not standardized. The opposite of a standardized test is unstandardized—a test with no clear questions or administered and scored under different conditions. The consistency provided by standardization can permit a reliable comparison of all test takers.

The Reliability of Intelligence Tests

You would have confidence in an intelligence test only if it were reliable. The *reliability* of a test is the degree to which it gives consistent results—or in other words, the repeatability of its scores. Suppose you took an IQ test and scored 102 (average) one month, 53 (within the range of intellectual disabilities) the next month, and 146 (mentally gifted) the third month. Your level of intelligence normally would not fluctuate that much in 3 months, and you would argue that the test is unreliable. Because the test-retest reliability correlation coefficients for the Stanford-Binet and Wechsler scales are at least .90 (out of a maximum of 1.00), the tests are reliable.

Though standardized IQ tests are reliable in the short run, an individual's IQ score can change over a period of years. The Berkeley Growth Study, conducted at the University of California at Berkeley, contradicted the once-popular belief that intelligence does not change during childhood. The study found that mental ability increases through adolescence and then levels off at about the age of 20 (Bayley, 1955). The nature of intellectual change later in life is discussed in Chapter 4.

The Validity of Intelligence Tests

A reliable test is not necessarily a valid one. A test's *validity* depends on whether the test measures what it is supposed to measure. The validity of IQ tests can be assessed by comparing their results to each other. A study of 40 children aged 6 to 16 years found a high correlation

FIGURE 10-1

The Normal Distribution of IQ Test Scores

Scores on standardized tests, such as the Wechsler intelligence scales, form what is known as a normal distribution (also called a "bell-shaped curve"). Given that the mean of the Wechsler scales is set at 100 and the standard deviation is 15, we can determine the percentage of individuals who fall above or below particular IQ scores and the percentage who fall between any two IQ scores.

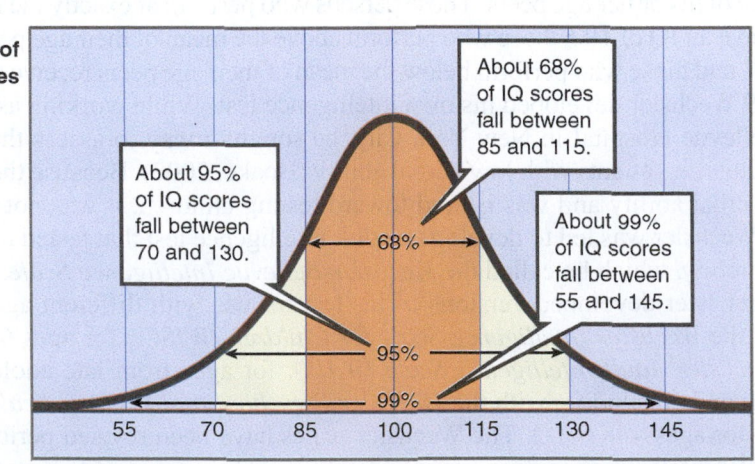

About 95% of IQ scores fall between 70 and 130.

About 68% of IQ scores fall between 85 and 115.

About 99% of IQ scores fall between 55 and 145.

between their scores on the Stanford-Binet Intelligence Scale and on the Wechsler Intelligence Scale for Children, as well as no statistically significant difference in the mean scores on the two tests (Lavin, 1996). The two tests are indeed measuring the same thing: "intelligence."

College Admissions Tests *Predictive validity* is especially important. Consider the SAT's ability to predict school performance. A published review of research on the SAT reported that the SAT correlated .41 with first-year college grade-point average. This correlation means that the SAT is a moderately good predictor. But high school grade-point average, which correlated .52 with first-year college grade-point average, is an even better predictor. Moreover, the combination of the SAT and high school grade-point average was a still better predictor, correlating .58 with first-year college grade-point average (Linn, 1982).

Claims that students with access to SAT preparation courses have an unfair advantage over students who do not might be unfounded. Such courses produce modest gains that are far less than promised by many of the organizations that offer SAT preparation courses (Powers & Rock, 1999). An increase of just 20 to 30 points on the verbal and mathematics subtests would require hours of study almost equivalent to full-time schooling (Messick & Jungeblut, 1981). The modest effects of preparatory courses appear to hold true across cultures, as in a study of the predictive validity of the Israeli Psychometric Entrance Exam. Students were randomly assigned to receive either preparatory coaching or no preparatory coaching. The results showed no difference in the predictive validity of the exam for the two groups of students regarding their subsequent performance in college (Allalouf & Ben-Shakhar, 1998).

Bias in Testing The Stanford-Binet and Wechsler scales correlate between .40 and .75 with school performance, depending on the aspect of school performance being measured (Aiken, 1982). These correlations indicate that the tests are good—but far from perfect—predictors of school performance. Because the correlations are less than a perfect 1.00, factors other than those measured by the SAT or IQ tests also contribute to school performance. The existence of other factors has made the fairness of intelligence tests one of the most controversial issues in contemporary psychology.

Critics argue that IQ tests and other tests of mental ability might be unfair to minority groups in the United States, most notably African Americans (Bender, Ponton, Crittenden, & Word, 1995), who score an average of 10 to 15 points lower than European Americans. A review of research on ethnic differences in intelligence found that environmental factors, such as socioeconomic status, had a stronger influence on IQ scores and might contribute to the disparity. There also has been a similar longstanding difference in scores on achievement tests between African Americans and European Americans. But this gap has been declining slowly in recent decades (Nisbett et. al., 2012). Critics of IQ testing allege that because African Americans are less likely to have the same cultural and educational experiences as European Americans, they tend, on the average, to perform more poorly on IQ tests that assume that both groups share common cultural and educational experiences (Brooks-Gunn, Klebanov, & Duncan, 1996). For example, one study found that European American participants outperformed African Americans in general vocabulary knowledge. However, this ethnic difference disappeared when participants were tested on newly learned words (Fagan & Holland, 2002). But does this finding mean that IQ tests are *biased* against African Americans?

The issue of the validity of IQ tests for African Americans reached the courts in the 1970s. In 1979 Judge Robert Peckham of the Federal District Court in San Francisco ruled that, without court approval, California schools could no longer base class placement of African American schoolchildren on IQ tests. His ruling came in the case of *Larry P. v. Wilson Riles* (Riles was the California superintendent of education), which was brought on behalf of six African American children in San Francisco who had been placed in classes for what was then called the educable mentally retarded (that is, those with mild intellectual disabilities). After hearing 10,000 pages of testimony from experts and advocates on both sides of the issue, Peckham ruled that the use of IQ tests violated the civil rights of African American children

Reliable, not valid

Low validity, low reliability

Not reliable, not valid

Both reliable and valid

Bull's Eye Example of Reliability and Validity

The principles of validity and reliability are displayed in this archery bull's-eye as an example of their roles in experimental design. Experimental findings should be both reliable and valid to be accepted.

because a proportionately greater number of these children than European American children were being placed in classes for children with intellectual disabilities. His decision convinced school districts in several other states to abandon the use of IQ tests for determining the school placement of African American children (Taylor, 1990).

But Peckham's decision also was met by arguments that IQ tests are not biased against African Americans because the tests have good predictive validity—they accurately predict the performance of both African American children and European American children in elementary school classes (Hunter & Schmidt, 2000). The differences in IQ scores between the two groups of children may reflect the fact that African American children might be more likely to be reared in socially disadvantaged circumstances that do not provide them with the opportunity to gain experiences that are important in doing well on IQ tests and in school (Lambert, 1981). A committee of scholars from several academic fields reported to the National Academy of Science that standardized tests are accurate predictors of school and job performance for all groups and therefore are not biased against any particular group ("NAS Calls Tests," 1982). This conclusion was supported by a study of Native American high school students that showed that their performance on the ACT accurately predicted their college performance (House, 1998). Thus, the consensus appears to be that tests of intellectual ability are not biased (Brown, Reynolds, & Whitaker, 1999).

Nonetheless, the issue has become as political as it is scientific. On the one side are the people, such as Judge Peckham, who believe that biased tests of cognitive abilities are being used to perpetuate discrimination against African American children by placing more of these children in slower classes and by preventing African American adults from obtaining desirable jobs. Peckham and his supporters favor outlawing the use of such tests. On the other side are those people who believe that blaming IQ tests for revealing the negative consequences of deprived upbringings is like killing the messenger who brings bad news. They favor changing the conditions that contribute to the lower average IQ test performance of African Americans and certain other minority groups (Elliott, 1988).

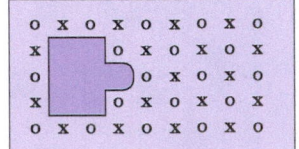

Raven Progressive Matrix

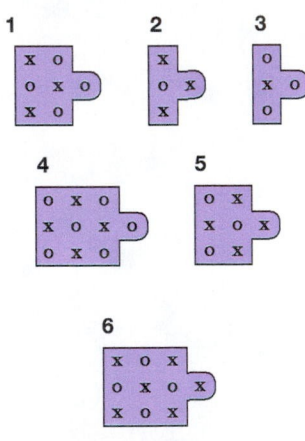

FIGURE 10-2

Raven Progressive Matrices

This figure is an example of the kind of matrix used in the Raven Progressive Matrices. In this "culture-fair" test, the person is presented with a series of incomplete matrices and must complete each by selecting the appropriate pattern from an accompanying group of patterns.

Culturally Unbiased Tests One possible solution to this controversy presents a compromise: Use tests that are not affected by the test taker's cultural background. The desirability of culturally unbiased tests has inspired research in a variety of cultures, including India (Misra, Sahoo, & Puhan, 1997) and South Africa (Claassen, 1997). But efforts to develop "culture-free" tests, beginning in the 1940s (Cattell, 1940), and "culture-fair" tests, beginning in the 1950s (Davis & Eels, 1953), produced disappointing results. These tests presented test takers with items that emphasized perceptual and spatial abilities rather than verbal abilities and avoided the use of items that would presume an extensive background in a particular culture. Figure 10-2 presents an example of the Raven Progressive Matrices, a nonverbal intelligence test that some educators have favored over the Stanford-Binet or Wechsler scales (Colom & Garcia-Lopez, 2003). But just like on traditional intelligence tests, people of higher socioeconomic status perform better on these nonverbal tests than do people of lower socioeconomic status (Jensen, 1980). And European Americans typically perform better than African Americans on tests of cognitive ability even when the tests are reworded to make them more comfortable to African American test takers (DeShon, Smith, Chan, & Schmitt, 1998).

Moreover, members of one culture may even perform the same on intelligence tests developed in another culture as they do on ones developed in their own culture. This finding was demonstrated in a study in which more than 600 grade school children from India and more than 1,000 grade school children from Holland were given two IQ tests, one developed in each country. The tests were slightly modified when given to students from the other country. The results showed that the students' performances were comparable on the two tests, indicating that cultural biases did not affect their IQ test performances (Bleichrodt, Hoksbergen, & Khire, 1999).

Stereotype Threat and IQ Test Performance According to psychologist Claude Steele, self-fulfilling prophecy may account for the poorer performance of African Americans on intelligence tests because of what he calls *stereotype threat* (Steele & Aronson, 2004). As discussed in Chapter 2, research has found that teachers' expectancies can help or hinder students' academic performance. Steele's twist is that in certain situations you become aware of others' expectations about your own stereotyped group; in turn, this awareness affects your performance. Because African Americans are aware of the negative stereotypes related to their academic abilities and achievement as early as middle childhood (McKown & Weinstein, 2003), they may become anxious and not perform as well on intelligence tests. In one study, Steele administered a verbal ability test to African American and European American college students approximately equal in their intellectual ability. Half of each group was told that the test simply served to assess how people solve problems. The other half was told that the test measured verbal reasoning ability.

The performance of African American and European American participants did not differ under the first condition, but African American participants performed worse than European American participants under the second condition. Steele concluded that under the second condition, African American participants succumbed to stereotype threat, became anxious, and thus performed more poorly (Steele & Aronson, 1995). Other research studies have found that stereotype threat has been shown to impair performance on cognitive tasks by increasing physiological arousal (O'Brien & Crandall, 2003) and reducing working memory capacity (Schmader & Johns, 2003) among participants from stigmatized groups.

Imagine how Alfred Binet would have reacted to the controversy that has arisen over the use of standardized tests, considering that he saw testing as an unbiased means of assessing students' abilities. In fact, despite the shortcomings of standardized tests, no alternative is as unbiased in assessing individuals without regard to irrelevant characteristics such as sex or ethnic background (Reilly & Chao, 1982). As Richard Weinberg, a leading intelligence researcher, has noted:

> In light of the effectiveness of current IQ tests to predict school performance, it is ironic that tests have been outlawed for the very purpose for which they were designed—to prevent subjective judgment and prejudice from being the basis for assigning students to special classes or denying them certain privileges. (Weinberg, 1989, p. 100)

Section Review: Intelligence Testing

1. What is an autistic savant?

2. How was Galton's view of intelligence influenced by his cousin Charles Darwin's theory of evolution?

Extremes of Intelligence

Another controversial issue regarding intelligence is the classification and education of people who fall at either extreme of the range of intelligence. As you learned in the section "Standardization in Intelligence Testing," 95 percent of the population score between 70 and 130 on IQ tests. Of the remaining 5 percent, half score below 70 and half score above 130. Those who score 70 or below fall in the range of intellectual disabilities, and those who score 130 or above fall in the mentally gifted range—though the classification of a person as having an intellectual disability or being mentally gifted is not based on IQ scores alone.

Intellectual Disabilities

Depending on the criteria used to define **intellectual disabilities**, from slightly more than 3 million to almost 7 million Americans have an intellectual disability. The estimate varies because a person's level of adaptive behavior, and not just level of intelligence, needs to be assessed before the person is classified as having an intellectual disability. In fact,

intellectual disabilities
Intellectual deficiency marked by an IQ of 70 or below and difficulties performing in everyday life.

the trend in classification has been to rely more on the person's everyday functioning and less on his or her IQ score (Haywood, Meyers, & Switzky, 1982).

Classification of Intellectual Disabilities

We have come a long way in our use of terms to classify persons with the condition once referred to as mental retardation. In the early 20th century, such persons were sorted into three categories, in terms of increasing degrees of mental retardation: moron (from a Greek word meaning "foolish"), imbecile (from a Latin word meaning "weak-minded"), and idiot (from a Greek word meaning "ignorant"). Fortunately, professionals no longer use these terms, but as you are well aware, they have become terms of disparagement in everyday language. In fact, because the term mental retardation itself has spawned disparaging terms and negative connotations, the American Association on Mental Retardation recently changed its name to the American Association on Intellectual and Developmental Disabilities, and the term has been changed to *intellectual disabilities*.

To be classified as having an intellectual disability, a person must have an IQ of 70 or below and, beginning in childhood, difficulties performing in everyday life (Landesman & Ramey, 1989)—including difficulties in self-care (such as eating and dressing), schoolwork (such as reading and arithmetic), and social relationships (such as conversing and developing friendships). Moreover, before a person can be classified as having an intellectual disability, alternative causes of the person's low IQ score and performance difficulties must be ruled out. These alternative causes include physical illness, impairment of vision or hearing, and coming from a family of people who are not native speakers of the language in which the IQ test was administered.

People with an intellectual disability suffer from varying degrees of cognitive deficits (Detterman, 1999). One of the most common deficits that they exhibit is inadequate use of language, in part related to difficulty with pragmatics. As described in Chapter 9, pragmatics is the aspect of language that involves using the sociocultural context of speech to help us give meaning to speech (Hatton, 1998). That is, people with an intellectual disability often interpret speech too literally, making them miss some of the subtleties of what is being said. Today, there are four categories of intellectual disabilities (American Psychiatric Association, 2013). Persons with IQs of 50 to 70 have *a mild intellectual disability* and constitute 85 percent of persons with intellectual disabilities. They are able to care for themselves, reach a sixth-grade level of education, hold responsible jobs, be married, and serve as adequate parents. Those with IQs of 35 to 49 have *a moderate intellectual disability* and constitute 10 percent of persons with intellectual disabilities. They might be trained to care for themselves, reach a second-grade level of education, and hold menial jobs, often in sheltered workshops, but they have difficulty maintaining social relationships, and they rarely marry.

Those with IQs between 20 and 34 have a *severe intellectual disability* and constitute 3 to 4 percent of persons with intellectual disabilities. They can learn rudimentary language and work skills but might be unable to care for themselves, benefit from schooling, hold jobs, or maintain normal social relationships. And those with IQs below 20 have a *profound intellectual disability* and constitute 1 to 2 percent of persons with intellectual disabilities. They have so few skills that they might spend their lives in institutions that provide them with no more than custodial care.

Causes of Intellectual Disabilities

In 1912 Henry Goddard traced the descendants of a Revolutionary War soldier he called Martin Kallikak. The soldier produced two lines of descendants. One line arose from his affair with a tavern maid who had what was described then as mental retardation. The other line arose from his marriage to a respectable woman of normal intelligence. Goddard found that the descendants of the tavern maid included many derelicts, prostitutes, and persons with mental retardation. In contrast, the descendants of his wife included few such people.

The differences between the two lines of descendants account for Goddard's use of the name *Kallikak*. The name is a combination of the Greek words *kalos* (meaning "good") and *kakos* (meaning "bad"). Goddard concluded that the descendants of the soldier's wife inherited the tendency to be moral and intelligent, whereas the descendants of the tavern maid inherited the tendency to be immoral and of lower intelligence. He discounted the effects of the markedly different sociocultural environments into which the children in each branch of the family were born as the probable causes of the differences.

Though some cases of intellectual disabilities may be linked to genetic factors (Winnepenninckx, Rooms, & Kooy, 2003), about 75 percent of cases of intellectual disabilities are caused by sociocultural deprivation. In fact, almost all persons with a mild intellectual disability come from such backgrounds. Their families might fail to provide them with adequate intellectual stimulation, such as discussing current events with them, encouraging them to read, helping them with homework, and taking them on trips to zoos, museums, and other educational settings. They also are more likely to attend inferior schools, to suffer from malnutrition, and to lack adequate medical care—each of which can impair intellectual growth.

Though some cases of intellectual disabilities are caused by sociocultural deprivation, many cases are caused by brain damage, which we can now identify by using modern brain-scanning techniques (Schaefer & Bodensteiner, 1999) such as MRI and PET. Brain damage in people with intellectual disabilities is often seen in the hippocampus, a structure associated with memory processes (see Chapter 8), and the cerebellum, a structure associated with motor coordination (Pulsifer, 1996). The brain damage that produces an intellectual disability is commonly caused by harmful environmental factors, sometimes related to parental health habits (Bryant & Maxwell, 1999) or prenatal environments. For example, pregnant women who ingest drugs or alcohol can cause brain damage in their offspring. And pregnant women who have certain diseases, such as the virus *rubella* (German measles) during the first three months of pregnancy (often referred to as the first trimester), also have a greater risk of giving birth to offspring with an intellectual disability. Pregnant women whose immune systems are activated due to bacterial or viral infections are at risk of their infants being diagnosed with ASD (Zerbo, et al., 2013).

Women who suffer from severe malnutrition during their pregnancies can give birth to infants with an intellectual disability and other neurodevelopmental disorders because of irreversible effects occurring at critical developmental periods. Animal studies have shown that the hippocampus and parts of the cortex are particularly vulnerable to malnutrition in early pregnancy (Penido et al., 2012). Additionally, studies have shown that *in utero* malnutrition can have long-lasting effects and affect individuals later in life. Prenatal exposure to X-rays can impair the normal migration of brain cells, increasing the possibility of intellectual disabilities (Schull, Norton, & Jensh, 1990). And a newborn infant who fails to breathe for several minutes after birth will experience *hypoxia*, a lack of oxygen to the brain. Hypoxia can cause the brain damage that characterizes **cerebral palsy**, a motor disorder often—but not always—accompanied by intellectual disabilities (Johnson, 2002).

Intellectual disabilities also are caused by genetic factors (Simonoff, Bolton, & Rutter, 1996), as in the case of **phenylketonuria (PKU)**. PKU is caused by an inherited lack of the enzyme required to metabolize the amino acid *phenylalanine*, which is found in milk and other common foods. This deficiency produces chemical changes that block the ability of brain cells to produce myelin (see Chapter 3), which leads to brain dysfunction and, as a result, an intellectual disability (Dyer, 1999). Fortunately, routine screening of newborns in the United States and other countries can detect PKU early enough to protect infants from brain damage by putting them on a diet that eliminates almost all their intake of phenylalanine (Sullivan & Chang, 1999).

Some cases of intellectual disabilities are produced by genetic defects that cause abnormal development during gestation, as in the case of **Down syndrome**. John Langdon Down identified the disorder in 1866 (Merrick, 2000). People normally have 23 pairs of chromosomes, with one member of each pair coming from each parent. A person with Down syndrome has an extra, third chromosome on the 21st pair. The extra chromosome can come from either the mother or the father. The chances of having a child with Down syndrome increase with age, being more common in middle-aged parents than in younger ones.

cerebral palsy A movement disorder that is caused by brain damage and is sometimes accompanied by intellectual disabilities.

phenylketonuria (PKU) A hereditary enzyme deficiency that, if left untreated in the infant, causes intellectual disabilities.

Down syndrome A form of intellectual disability, associated with certain physical deformities, that is caused by an extra, third chromosome on the 21st pair.

Down syndrome usually is characterized by moderate intellectual disability and distinctive physical characteristics. The risk of having a child with Down syndrome increases with age and is more common among middle-aged parents than among younger parents.

Source: Photo of Gertie Munholland, courtesy of Global Down Syndrome Foundation.

Down syndrome usually is characterized by moderate intellectual disability and distinctive physical characteristics. These characteristics include small ears and hands; short necks, feet, and fingers; protruding tongues; and a fold over the eyes, giving them an almond-shaped, Asian appearance. Because of this appearance, Down syndrome was originally called "mongolism." This term reflected the 20th-century Western belief that people with the disorder failed to develop beyond what was then presumed by Westerners to be the more primitive physical and intellectual level of Asians, such as Mongolians (Gould, 1981). Cognitive disorders often are associated with a loss or gain of functioning during development. For example, individuals with PKU are missing an enzyme and individuals with Down syndrome have an extra chromosome.

Education of People with Intellectual Disabilities

Over the centuries, people with an intellectual disability have been treated as everything from children of God who were believed to bring good luck, to subhumans who, it was believed, should be locked up as dangerous (Wolfensberger, 1972). Today psychologists interested in persons with an intellectual disability stress their potential to benefit from education and training. One reason why people with an intellectual disability do not perform as well as other people is that they fail to use effective methods of information processing. For example, when people with an intellectual disability are given a series of words or pictures to remember, they tend not to rehearse the items or group them into chunks—techniques that are commonly used by people who do not have an intellectual disability (Campione & Brown, 1979). As explained in Chapter 8, memory is enhanced by the rehearsal and chunking of information.

Today people with a mild intellectual disability are called "educable," and persons with a moderate intellectual disability are called "trainable." From the 1950s to the 1970s, persons who were categorized at the time as being educable mentally retarded were placed in special classes in which they received teaching tailored to their level of ability. But in the 1970s, dissatisfaction with the results of this approach led to mainstreaming, which places children with intellectual disabilities in as many normal classes as possible and encourages them to participate in activities with children who do not have intellectual disabilities. To promote mainstreaming in America, the Education for All Handicapped Children Act of 1975 mandated that children with intellectual disabilities be given instruction in the most normal academic setting that is feasible for them (Sussan, 1990).

The educational needs of individuals with intellectual disabilities are not limited to academic subjects. They also might need training in self-care skills (including eating, toileting, hygiene, dressing, and grooming), home management skills (including home maintenance,

The Mentally Gifted

Children and adolescents who are mentally gifted, like those who have an intellectual disability, benefit from special education programs to help them develop their skills.
Source: CREATISTA/ Shutterstock.com.

clothing care, food preparation, and home safety), consumer skills (including telephone use, money management, and shopping), and community mobility skills (including pedestrian safety and use of public transportation). Behavior modification has been especially useful in teaching self-care to people with intellectual disabilities (Huang & Cuvo, 1997). For example, behavior modification has been used successfully in training such persons to shower themselves (Matson, DiLorenzo, & Esveldt-Dawson, 1981).

A movement that has paralleled mainstreaming is *normalization,* the transfer of individuals with intellectual disabilities from large institutional settings into community settings so that they can live more normal lives. Given adequate support services, even people with severe and profound intellectual disabilities can progress in settings other than large, custodial institutions, with the greatest benefit shown in their ability to care for themselves (Lynch, Kellow, & Willson, 1997). But in too many instances, normalization has simply created smaller custodial settings rather than ones that truly encourage independent living (Sinson, 1994).

Mental Giftedness

The study of intellectual disabilities has been accompanied by interest in the study of **mental giftedness**. Francis Galton (1869) began the study of the mentally gifted in the late 19th century. Lewis Terman considered Galton himself to be mentally gifted. Terman based his assessment on Galton's early accomplishments, including his ability to recite the alphabet when he was 18 months old and read classical literature when he was 5 years old (Terman, 1917). Today the mentally gifted are people with IQs of 130 or above and with exceptionally high scores on achievement tests in specific subjects, such as mathematics (Fox, 1981). Ever since Leta Stetter Hollingworth founded the practice of special education for gifted students (Klein, 2000), the special needs of the mentally gifted generally have received less attention than those of persons with intellectual disabilities. Many gifted children feel isolated and unchallenged in their classes (Swiatek & Lupkowski-Shoplik, 2003). In the United States, there has been a decline in funding for research on the gifted and a lack of funding for the education of gifted children (Sternberg, 1996). One positive trend has been a greater attempt to identify gifted ethnic-minority children (Scott, Deuel, Jean-Francois, & Urbano, 1996). Perhaps the best-known organization dedicated to meeting the needs of the mentally gifted is MENSA (Serebriakoff, 1985), which limits its membership to those who are above age 14 and score in the top 2 percent on a standardized intelligence test.

One of the reasons for the traditional lack of interest in the mentally gifted was the belief in "early ripe, early rot." This belief assumed that children who are intellectually precocious are doomed to become academic, vocational, and social failures. The classic case study in support

mental giftedness Intellectual superiority marked by an IQ of 130 or above and exceptionally high scores on achievement tests in specific subjects, such as mathematics.

of this viewpoint was that of William James Sidis (1898–1944). He was named in honor of William James, a colleague of his father, Boris, at Harvard University. Sidis was a mathematically gifted boy who enrolled at Harvard in 1909 at the age of 11 and received national publicity a year later when he gave a talk on higher mathematics to the Harvard Mathematical Club. But constant pressure from his father to excel and the glare of publicity eventually led Sidis to retreat from the world. In his early twenties, Sidis left the faculty position he had taken at Rice Institute in Houston and spent the rest of his life working at menial jobs.

Years later, in 1937, James Thurber, writing under a pen name in the *New Yorker,* published a sarcastic article about Sidis entitled "April Fool" (Sidis was born on April 1). Thurber wrote that Sidis was a failure, living in a single room in a rundown section of Boston, which Thurber used as evidence of the dire consequences of being too intelligent at too young an age. Sidis sued the *New Yorker* for libel and won a modest settlement shortly before dying—in obscurity—in 1944 (Wallace, 1986).

Terman's Genetic Studies of Genius

Contrary to the case of William James Sidis, mentally gifted children do not tend to become failures. This finding was demonstrated in perhaps the most famous longitudinal study ever conducted, Lewis Terman's Genetic Studies of Genius (see "The Research Process" box), which still inspires interest today—more than 80 years after it began.

The Study of Mathematically Precocious Youth

Perhaps the best-known recent study of mentally gifted children is the longitudinal Study of Mathematically Precocious Youth by Camilla Benbow and Julian Stanley (1983) at Johns Hopkins University. Benbow and Stanley provided special programs for young adolescents who scored above 700 (out of a maximum of 800) on the mathematics subtest of the SAT. The programs offered intensive summer courses in science and mathematics, accelerated courses at universities, and counseling for parents to help them meet the academic and emotional needs of their gifted children (Barnett & Corazza, 1998). A 25-year follow-up found that participants in the study had many outstanding educational achievements and successful careers, particularly in the sciences, technology, engineering, and mathematics (Wai, Lubinski, Benbow, & Steiger, 2010). And contrary to popular belief, the participants also did not suffer academic burnout from their demanding course work (Swiatek, 1993). A 20-year follow-up of the adolescents involved in this program found that they tended to be high achievers and highly satisfied with their careers (Benbow, Lubinski, Shea, & Eftekhari-Sanji, 2000). Moreover, there is no evidence that gifted children are prone to the personal and social problems that plagued William James Sidis. In fact, a program such as the ones provided by Benbow and Stanley might have helped Sidis pursue a rewarding career as a mathematician instead of fading into obscurity.

Section Review: Extremes of Intelligence

1. What are some possible causes of intellectual disabilities?

2. In what way did Terman's Genetic Studies of Genius counter the notion of "early ripe, early rot"?

Theories of Intelligence

Is intelligence a general characteristic that affects all facets of behavior, or are there different kinds of intelligence, each affecting a specific facet of behavior? Today intelligence researchers tend to assume that there are several kinds of intelligence (Sternberg & Wagner, 1993). Consider, for example, a study of men who spent much of their recreational

What Is the Fate of Childhood Geniuses?

Rationale

Terman began his study in 1921, and it continued long after his death. He had hoped to counter the common-sense belief that being too intelligent too early led to later failure.

Method

Terman used the Stanford-Binet Intelligence Scale to identify California children with IQs above 135. He found 1,528 such children between the ages of 8 and 12. Their average IQ was 150. Reports on Terman's gifted children appeared periodically during the 20th century. After Terman's death in 1956, Robert Sears (who was a member of the original sample) and Pauline Sears of Stanford University continued the study.

Results and Discussion

The Terman Genetic Studies of Genius longitudinal study has shown that mentally gifted children tend to become socially, physically, vocationally, and academically superior adults. They are healthier and more likely to attend college, to have professional careers, and to have happy marriages. The 1972 report on Terman's participants, then at an average age of 62, found that they generally were satisfied with life, combining successful careers with rewarding family lives (Sears, 1977). Moreover, more recent follow-up studies found that participants who reported having lived up to their intellectual potential at age 49 were more satisfied with their work and family lives than were those who felt they had not realized their potential (Holahan, Holahan, & Wonacott, 1999).

Of course, Terman's study is not without certain weaknesses. Perhaps participants' awareness of being in such an important study affected how they performed in life—a kind of self-fulfilling prophecy. Also, could socioeconomic status, and not solely intelligence, have been a contributing factor? A follow-up study of samples of men from the original study found that those who maintained better health, had more stable marriages, and pursued more lucrative careers were less likely to come from families in which there was divorce, alcoholism, or other major family problems (Oden, 1968). Evidently, even for geniuses, the family environment is related to their success in life. A less ambitious replication of the Terman study involved 156 adults (aged 35 to 50 years) who had graduated from an elementary school for gifted children. As did their counterparts in the Terman study, these gifted individuals showed superior social, physical, and vocational well-being (Subotnik, Karp, & Morgan, 1989).

Opportunities for educational and occupational achievement differed for the men and women who participated in the Terman study. Two-thirds of the Terman women graduated from college—an astounding proportion considering they reached college age during the Great Depression of the 1930s—but only approximately half of the women were employed outside the home at some point in their adult lives (Tomlinson-Keasey, 1990). It is important to remember, though, that women of their generation were expected to devote themselves to their spouses and family, and the social context provided fewer professional opportunities for women than for men. Most (63 percent) of the Terman women expected to be wives and mothers, and many of them contributed to their spouse's career, worked in traditionally female occupations (typically teaching) after their children were grown, or dedicated themselves to volunteer organizations or the arts. Educational and employment opportunities for gifted women have improved over the last 50 years, however, and later studies find that the majority of gifted women—single or married—are employed in professional occupations. Nonetheless, a comparison of the Terman women, born in 1910, and a younger sample, born in 1940, revealed no differences in life satisfaction (Schuster, 1990).

Other studies have added to our understanding of mentally gifted people. A study of mathematically gifted adolescents supported the conclusions of Terman's study by finding that mentally gifted people are more socially competent (McCallister, Nash, & Meckstroth, 1996) and more psychologically well adjusted (Parker, 1996) than other people. Another study found that gifted high school students were more perfectionistic than other students, as shown by a greater need for order and more demands placed on themselves (Orange, 1997). Despite their high level of intelligence, mentally gifted people—as in Terman's study—rarely become recognized for extraordinarily creative achievements. Outstanding creativity involves skills and personality traits different from those of the typical mentally gifted person (Winner, 2000).

Are Faster Brains More Intelligent Brains?

We sometimes refer to people as being "quick-witted" or "fast thinkers," or being mentally swift in some other way. Common sense presumes that the faster our brains are at processing information, the more intelligent we are. Though we could argue about this commonsense belief—pro or con—by simply presenting arguments why we do or do not accept it, psychologists prefer to base their beliefs on empirical research findings. Many research studies have indeed found that people who score high on intelligence tests tend to be relatively faster in cognitive processing (Baumeister, 1998; Holm, Ullén, & Madison, 2011). For example, studies consistently have found a negative correlation between intelligence and reaction time (Neubauer, Riemann, Mayer, & Angleitner, 1997). That is, faster reaction times are associated with higher intelligence, and slower reaction times are associated with lower intelligence. One explanation for this relationship is that intelligence might partially depend on the speed of neural impulse conduction (Barrett, Daum, & Eysenck, 1990). Perhaps one can indeed be "quick-witted."

Researchers who support information-processing speed as a measure of intelligence have provoked criticism. This criticism has been particularly intense because one of the leading researchers whose research has supported a relationship between intelligence and information processing speed has been Arthur Jensen, who has attributed this relationship to heredity (Vernon, 1998). Jensen's belief that inherited ethnic differences in intelligence favor people of European descent over people of African descent has led some scientists to brand him a racist. This controversy is discussed in the section "The Influence of Heredity and Environment on Intelligence."

A major criticism of the research on the relationship between intelligence and information-processing speed is that researchers who claim a strong relationship between intelligence and the speed of information processing have exaggerated the implications of generally modest correlations between the two. A second criticism is that researchers have failed to explain the meaning of significant correlations between intelligence and the speed of information processing (Stankov & Roberts, 1997). In addition, the relationship between intelligence and reaction time varies in its strength across cultures. One study found, for example, that the size of the relationship between intelligence test scores and reaction time is smaller and in fact relatively weaker in rural Guatemalans than in residents from more urbanized environments (Choudhury & Gorman, 1999). It might be unwise to make sweeping statements about the importance of information-processing speed in intelligent behavior.

Still another, somewhat humorous, source of criticism comes from research comparing the information processing-speed of animals and humans. In one study, rhesus monkeys demonstrated faster reaction times on an information-processing task than human participants did (Washburn & Rumbaugh, 1997). But few people would use this finding to jump to the conclusion that monkeys are more intelligent than they are. At this time, the commonsense belief that people who are faster at information processing tend to be more intelligent than other people has some research backing, but the extent to which intelligence depends on information-processing speed remains to be determined.

---

time at racetracks betting on horse races. The results indicated that the men's ability to handicap races accurately was unrelated to their scores on a test of general intelligence. Handicapping horse races taps a specific kind of mental ability (Ceci & Liker, 1986).

Factor-Analytic Theories of Intelligence

At about the same time that Alfred Binet was developing his intelligence test, the British psychologist Charles Spearman (1863–1945) was developing a theory of intelligence. He considered intelligence a general ability that underlies most behaviors.

Spearman's Theory of General Intelligence

factor analysis A statistical technique that determines the degree of correlation between performances on various tasks to determine the extent to which they reflect particular underlying characteristics, which are known as factors.

In 1927, after more than two decades of research, Spearman published his conclusions about the nature of intelligence. He developed a statistical technique called **factor analysis**, which determines the degree of correlation between performances on various tasks (Bartholomew, 1995). If performances on certain tasks have a high positive correlation, then they are presumed to reflect the influence of a particular underlying factor. For example, if performances on a vocabulary test, a reading test, and a writing test correlate highly, they might reveal the influence of a "verbal ability" factor.

In using factor analysis, Spearman first gave a large group of people a variety of mental tasks. He found that scores on the tasks had high positive correlations with one another. In other words, participants tended to score high *or* moderate *or* low on all the tests. Spearman concluded that performance on all the tasks depended on the operation of a single underlying factor. He called this factor *g*—a general intelligence factor.

But because the correlations between the tasks were less than a perfect 1.00, Spearman concluded that performance on each task also depended, to a lesser extent, on its own specific factor, which he called *s*. For example, Spearman explained that scores on vocabulary tests and arithmetic tests tended to have a high positive correlation with each other because vocabulary ability and arithmetic ability are both influenced by a general intelligence factor. But because scores on vocabulary tests and arithmetic tests are not perfectly correlated, each ability must also depend on its own intelligence factor. Nonetheless, Spearman believed that the general intelligence factor was more important than any specific intelligence factor in governing a given ability. The existence of the factor *g* has received some research support. It appears to be associated mainly with activity in the frontal lobes of the brain (Duncan et al., 2000). Given that most intellectual tasks require attention and working memory, we know that neural networks in the frontal lobe are activated during cognitive processing. Researchers can attempt to study the neuroanatomical correlates of intelligence. In recent studies, 104 young adults were given 21 psychological tests of intelligence and then were placed in MRI scanners. Results indicated that tests of intelligence, working memory, attention, and processing speed all showed activation of portions of the frontal cortex as opposed to other cortical areas. This suggests that intelligence and cognitive factors are correlated, in part, due to shared specific regions in the brain (Colom et al., 2013).

Thurstone's Theory of Primary Mental Abilities

Like Spearman, Louis Thurstone (1887–1955) used factor analysis to determine the nature of intelligence. But unlike Spearman, Thurstone (1938) concluded that there was no general intelligence factor. Instead, based on a battery of tests that he gave to college students, he identified seven factors, which he called *primary mental abilities*: reasoning, word fluency, perceptual speed, verbal comprehension, spatial visualization, numerical calculation, and associative memory.

Though scores on tests measuring these abilities had moderately high positive correlations with one another, they did not correlate highly enough for Thurstone to assume the existence of a general underlying intelligence factor. Suppose that you took tests to assess your abilities in reasoning, verbal comprehension, and numerical calculation. Thurstone would insist that your performance on any single test would reflect, not the influence of a general intelligence factor, but instead the influence of a specific intelligence factor related to the particular ability assessed by that test. Like Thurstone, J. P. Guilford (1897–1987) rejected the notion of a general intelligence factor (Guilford, 1959). Instead of the mere seven factors in Thurstone's theory, though, Guilford identified 120 factors through the use of factor analysis. By the end of his life, Guilford (1985) had increased the number of factors to 180.

Horn and Cattell's Two-Factor Theory of Intelligence

A more recent theory of intelligence based on factor analysis was developed by John Horn and Raymond Cattell (1966), who identified two intelligence factors. **Crystallized intelligence** reflects the acquisition of skills and knowledge through schooling and everyday experience. Horn and Cattell found that crystallized intelligence increases or remains the same in late adulthood. **Fluid intelligence** reflects thinking ability, memory capacity, and speed of information processing. Whereas the ability to apply learned solutions to new problems depends on crystallized intelligence, the ability to find novel solutions to problems depends on fluid intelligence (Hunt, 1997). Short-term memory (discussed in Chapter 8) is strongly associated with fluid intelligence (Martínez et al., 2011).

crystallized intelligence
The form of intelligence that reflects knowledge acquired through schooling and in everyday life.

fluid intelligence The form of intelligence that reflects reasoning ability, memory capacity, and speed of information processing.

Horn and Cattell found that fluid intelligence is largely inherited, is affected little by training, and declines in late adulthood. Recent research studies confirm that fluid intelligence declines across late adulthood (Schretlen et al., 2000). Fluid intelligence has much in common with Spearman's notion of a general intelligence factor (Duncan, Burgess, & Emslie, 1995). Changes in fluid intelligence and crystallized intelligence across the life span are illustrated in Figure 10-3.

It remains for psychologists to determine which, if any, of the factor-analytic theories of intelligence is the best. Perhaps a more telling criticism of factor-analytic theories of intelligence is that they assume that intelligence primarily reflects those cognitive abilities related to academic performance. A more encompassing theory of intelligence would consider a broader range of abilities (Frederiksen, 1986). Theories proposed by Robert Sternberg and Howard Gardner have done so.

Sternberg's Triarchic Theory of Intelligence

As a child, Robert Sternberg performed poorly on IQ tests and suffered from severe test anxiety, yet he later earned a Ph.D. and became a leading researcher in cognitive psychology. His experience contributed to his belief that intelligence comprises more than the abilities measured by traditional intelligence tests (Trotter, 1986). To determine the views of laypersons on the nature of intelligence, Sternberg and his colleagues (1981) surveyed people reading in a college library, entering a supermarket, or waiting for a train. The participants were asked to list what they believed were the main characteristics of intelligent people. The results showed that respondents assumed that intelligent people had good verbal skills, social judgment, and problem-solving abilities.

Beginning in the early 1980s, Sternberg developed a **triarchic theory of intelligence,** which claims that intelligence comprises three kinds of abilities similar to those reported by the people in his earlier survey (Sternberg, 2000). He based his theory on his observations of how people process information. *Componential intelligence* is similar to the kind of intelligence considered by traditional theories of intelligence. It primarily reflects our information-processing ability, which helps in academic performance. *Experiential intelligence* is the ability to combine different experiences in insightful ways to solve novel problems based on past experience. In part, it reflects creativity, as exhibited by an artist, composer, or scientist. Creative geniuses, such as Leonardo da Vinci and Albert Einstein, had especially high levels of experiential intelligence. *Contextual intelligence* is the ability to function in practical, everyday social situations. It reflects "street smarts," as in negotiating the price of a new car. Though many situations require the use of all three kinds of intelligence, some people are better at using one kind than at using the other two (Sternberg & Clinkenbeard, 1995).

The triarchic theory recognizes that we must be able to function in settings other than school. According to Sternberg (1999), the triarchic theory of intelligence is a better basis for developing intelligence tests that account for cultural factors more than conventional intelligence tests do. Sternberg has developed the Sternberg Triarchic Abilities Test to assess

triarchic theory of intelligence
Robert Sternberg's theory of intelligence, which assumes that there are three main kinds of intelligence: componential, experiential, and contextual.

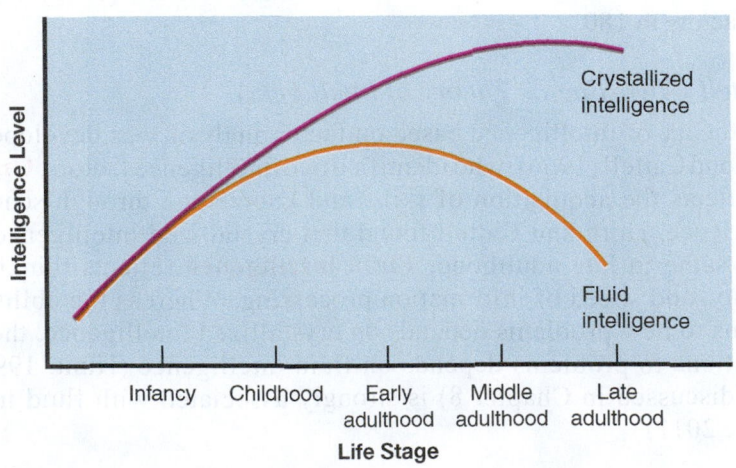

FIGURE 10-3

Life-Span Change in Intelligence

Whereas fluid intelligence tends to decline in old age, crystallized intelligence tends to increase.

Source: From J. L. Horn and G. Donaldson, "On the Myth of Intellectual Decline in Adulthood" in *American Psychologist,* 31: 701–719. Copyright © 1976 by the American Psychological Association.

the three kinds of intelligence, and he believes that each kind can be improved by special training (Sternberg, Castejon, Prieto, Hautamaeki, & Grigorenko, 2001). The triarchic theory received some support from a study of intellectually gifted adolescent students. They were superior to nongifted adolescent students in the cognitive abilities that are encompassed by componential intelligence. For example, they were more sophisticated and efficient in solving decision-making problems (Ball, Mann, & Stamm, 1994). Though Sternberg's theory goes beyond traditional theories by considering creative intelligence and practical intelligence as well as academic intelligence, more research is needed to determine its merits. In one of the few experimental studies of the triarchic theory, classroom instructional methods based on that theory (which involved analytical, creative, and practical instruction) produced better student performance among third graders and eighth graders on a variety of tests than was produced by traditional instructional methods (Sternberg, Torff, & Grigorenko, 1998). Sternberg more recently renamed his triarchic theory the *theory of successful intelligence*. He changed the name to stress his belief that intelligence is the ability to achieve success, given one's personal standards and sociocultural context (Sternberg, 2003).

Gardner's Theory of Multiple Intelligences

Whereas Sternberg based his theory on his study of information processing, Howard Gardner (1983) based his **theory of multiple intelligences** on his belief that the brain has evolved separate systems for different adaptive abilities that he calls "intelligences." According to Gardner, there are seven types of intelligence, each of which is developed to a different extent in each of us: linguistic, logical-mathematical, spatial, musical, bodily-kinesthetic, intrapersonal, and interpersonal. Gardner assumes that certain brain structures and pathways underlie the intelligences and that brain damage interferes with one or more of them. For example, damage to speech centers interferes with linguistic intelligence, and damage to the cerebellum interferes with bodily-kinesthetic intelligence.

Several of Gardner's kinds of intelligence are assessed by traditional intelligence tests. *Linguistic intelligence* is the ability to communicate through language. If you are good at reading textbooks, writing term papers, and presenting oral reports, you are high in linguistic intelligence. A person with high *logical-mathematical intelligence* is good at analyzing arguments and solving mathematical problems. And a person with high *spatial intelligence,* such as a skilled architect or carpenter, is good at perceiving and arranging objects in the environment.

The remaining kinds of intelligence are assessed little, if at all, by traditional intelligence tests. *Musical intelligence* is the ability to analyze, compose, or perform music. A person with good *bodily-kinesthetic intelligence* is able to move effectively, as in dancing or playing sports, or to manipulate objects effectively, as in using tools or driving a car. If you have high *intrapersonal intelligence,* you know yourself well and understand what motivates your behavior. For example, emotionally depressed people high in intrapersonal intelligence might be more likely to find ways to relieve their depression. And if you have high *interpersonal intelligence,* you function well in social situations because you are able to understand the needs of other people and to predict their behavior. People high in interpersonal intelligence are better at judging, for example, whether other people are trustworthy (Yamagishi, Kikuchi, & Kosugi, 1999).

Gardner's list of multiple intelligences has much in common with the kinds of intelligence targeted by the ancient Chinese educational program called the Six Arts (Chongde & Tsingan, 2003). According to Gardner, our ability to succeed in life depends on the degree to which we develop the kinds of intelligence that are needed to function well in our culture. For example, for most people in the United States, success depends more on linguistic intelligence than on musical intelligence. Success in a culture that relies on hunting skills would put a greater premium on spatial intelligence and bodily-kinesthetic intelligence. Gardner's theory has failed to generate sufficient scientific research to determine its merits, particularly research demonstrating valid means of assessing multiple intelligences (Plucker, Callahan, & Tomchin, 1996). But it is potentially superior to traditional theories of intelligence in its attention to the kinds of abilities needed to function in

theory of multiple intelligences Howard Gardner's theory of intelligence, which assumes that the brain has evolved separate systems for seven kinds of intelligence.

Musical Intelligence

According to Gardner's theory of multiple intelligences, an accomplished pianist would be high in musical intelligence.

Source: Kiselev Andrey Valerevich/Shutterstock.com.

both academic and nonacademic settings. The theory has been used to determine the relationship between multiple intelligences and academic performance among high school students (Snyder, 2000). Unfortunately, the theory sometimes has been used to develop academic programs in schools simply based on the assumption that programs that seem logically related to the theory will be effective—with little research evidence to support that belief (Mettetal, Jordan, & Harper, 1997).

A recent area of interest to intelligence researchers has been the concept of *emotional intelligence,* which overlaps intrapersonal intelligence and interpersonal intelligence. People who are high in emotional intelligence are more empathic (Davies, Stankov, & Roberts, 1998), more socially skilled (Schutte et al., 2001), better able to manage their emotional states (Ciarocchi, Chan, & Caputi, 2000), and more satisfied with their lives and less prone to depression (Martinez-Pons, 1997). But some researchers have criticized Gardner's theory for leaving out important intelligences. Psychologist Robert Emmons (2000) believes that, for example, the theory of multiple intelligences also should include spiritual intelligence. Gardner (2000) considers this proposal interesting but believes more research is needed before he would be willing to accept spirituality as an intelligence.

Section Review: Theories of Intelligence

1. What is the difference between Spearman's and Thurstone's factor-analytic theories of intelligence?

2. According to Gardner's theory of multiple intelligences, what kinds of intelligence are there?

Nature, Nurture, and Intelligence

In the 1983 movie *Trading Places,* two upper-class men argued about whether our social positions are determined more by heredity or by environment. They agreed to settle their argument by manipulating a rich European American (portrayed by Dan Ackroyd) and a poor African American (portrayed by Eddie Murphy) into trading homes (a mansion versus the street), vocations (big business versus panhandling), and financial status (wealth versus poverty). This movie illustrates the popular concern with the issue of nature versus nurture.

In the 1870s Francis Galton popularized the phrase *nature versus nurture* (Fancher, 1984). As a follower of his cousin Charles Darwin, Galton (1869) concluded that intelligence is inherited, after finding that eminent men had a higher proportion of eminent relatives than other men did. This conclusion led Galton to champion **eugenics** (Rabinowitz, 1984), the practice of encouraging supposedly superior people to reproduce while preventing supposedly inferior people from reproducing. Scientists today still argue about whether research on the relative contributions of nature and nurture will benefit humanity or instead have dehumanizing consequences (Turkheimer, 1998). Even at the turn of the 21st century, many people still believed in the practice of eugenics (Ouimet & de Man, 1998).

eugenics The practice of encouraging supposedly superior people to reproduce while preventing supposedly inferior people from reproducing.

Early Studies of Women

Gender differences in mental abilities were studied as early as 1900 when Helen Bradford Thompson (1874–1947)—later known by her married name, Helen Thompson Woolley—compared 25 men and 25 women on measures of motor and sensory abilities, intellect, and emotion. She concluded that the gender differences that she observed were due to socialization rather than to biological differences between women and men (Milar, 2000). In a later review of the psychological research on gender differences, she concluded, "There is perhaps no field aspiring to be scientific where flagrant personal bias, logic martyred in the cause of supporting a prejudice, unfounded assertions, and even sentimental rot and drivel, have run riot to such an extent as here" (Woolley, 1910, p. 340).

Despite this empirical evidence—and the fact that women were entering higher education in record numbers—belief in the superiority of the male intellect was unshaken. Differential psychologists turned to the *variability hypothesis* (Shields, 1982). The **variability hypothesis** was derived from evolutionary theory. It stated that men, as a group, are more variable than women. Variability within a group was seen as adaptive because it was thought to enable the species to evolve and adapt to changing circumstances. Thus, whereas groups of women and men might be equivalent on average—as Wooley's review reported—only men will be found at the extremes of human attributes. The variability hypothesis was used to explain why there were more men with extraordinary intellects—and more men with intellectual deficits—than women.

variability hypothesis
The prediction that men, as a group, are more variable than women.

The variability hypothesis was tested in a series of studies by Leta Stetter Hollingworth (1886–1939). In 1912 and 1913, she studied 1,000 female and male residents of the Clearing-House for Mental Defectives, where she administered Binet-Simon intelligence tests. She found that men and boys were admitted more frequently, but these data were biased. Male residents were admitted at an earlier age than female residents, which she attributed to the fact that women were identified as "mentally deficient" less often. In contrast, boys' deficits in intellectual abilities and functioning were more readily apparent. She concluded that many women escaped institutionalization because they could perform menial domestic tasks (Hollingworth, 1914). In another study, Helen Montague and Hollingworth (1914) examined the birth records of 2,000 infants in the New York Infirmary for Women and Children. They found that though male infants were larger than females, there were no gender differences in the variability of physical characteristics. Hollingworth's empirical research and her conclusion that social factors played an important role in the observed differences between women's and men's lives strongly influenced her contemporaries. By the 1920s the variability hypothesis was discredited, and prominent psychologists such as Lewis Terman began to consider the role of social discrimination in women's intellectual achievement (Benjamin & Shields, 1990).

Early Studies of Immigrants

In 1912 Henry Goddard became director of testing the intelligence of immigrants arriving at Ellis Island in New York Harbor. Goddard (1917) made the astonishing claim that 79 percent of Italians, 80 percent of Hungarians, 83 percent of Jews, and 87 percent of Russians scored in the "feebleminded" range on the Binet-Simon scale, which today we would call the range of mild intellectual disabilities. Even after later reevaluating his data, he claimed that an average of "only" 40 percent of these groups were "feebleminded" (Gelb, 1986). Goddard, following in the footsteps of Galton, concluded that these ethnic groups were by nature intellectually inferior.

You probably realize that Goddard discounted possible environmental causes for the poor test performance of immigrants. He failed to consider a lack of education, a long ocean voyage below deck, and anxiety created by the testing situation as causes of their poor performance. Moreover, even though the tests were translated into the immigrants' native languages, the translations were often inadequate. Despite the shortcomings of the tests, low test scores were used as the basis for deportation of many supposedly "feebleminded" immigrants. Ironically, at the 1915 meeting of the American Psychological Association in Chicago, a critic of Goddard's program of intelligence testing reported that the native-born mayor of Chicago had taken an IQ test and had scored in the feebleminded range (Gould, 1981).

Further support for Goddard's position was provided by the army's intelligence-testing program during World War I, headed by Robert Yerkes (1876–1956). One of Yerkes's colleagues, Carl Brigham (1923), published the results of the testing program. He found that immigrants scored lower on the IQ tests than their American-born counterparts did. Brigham attributed these differences in IQ scores to differences in heredity. The U.S. Congress passed the Immigration Act of 1924, which restricted immigration from eastern and southern Europe. There is disagreement among researchers who believe that Brigham's

Critical Thinking About Psychology

How Should We Respond to *The Bell Curve*?

Few books have provoked controversy in both professional journals and the popular media the way *The Bell Curve: Intelligence and Class Structure in American Life* did after it was published in 1994. For a while it was impossible to go a day without being confronted by media coverage of the controversy surrounding the book, which spent 15 weeks on *The New York Times* best-seller list and sold more than 500,000 copies within a few months of its publication. Reaction to *The Bell Curve* was in keeping with an earlier controversy over a book with a similar message, Arthur Jensen's (1980) *Bias in Mental Testing*. *The Bell Curve* provoked an even more intense and widespread controversy, inspiring hundreds of articles by critics and supporters of its content, implications, and scientific adequacy.

Books were published just to counter *The Bell Curve*'s claims, such as Steven Fraser's (1995) *The Bell Curve Wars,* a collection of commentaries on *The Bell Curve*. The controversy made the cover of *Newsweek* and *The New York Times Magazine.* And radio and television programs, including *Nightline, Charlie Rose,* and the *McNeil-Lehrer News Hour,* pitted the book's supporters and detractors against each other. But what was it about *The Bell Curve*—a book about intelligence—that created this furor?

The furor was created primarily by a conclusion implied by psychologist Richard Herrnstein and political scientist Charles Murray, the authors of *The Bell Curve.* They implied, without formally stating it, that research studies had convincingly demonstrated significant ethnic differences in intelligence, with people of European descent being intellectually superior to those of African descent. They also concluded that because intelligence is largely inherited, efforts to improve the intellectual abilities of children with lower socioeconomic status, such as Project Head Start, will have little effect. The authors urged that instead of fruitless efforts to improve the status of people who cannot improve, we should simply place people in the social positions they are genetically well suited for.

Many academics who opposed the book's premise accused its authors of basing their conclusions on flawed statistical analyses (Darlington, 1996) and weak scientific evidence (Poston & Winebarger, 1996). Some critics accused Herrnstein and Murray of using poor science to support their own unadmitted racist social and political agendas (Alderfer, 2003). Even the American Psychological Association established a task force on intelligence to assess the claims made in *The Bell Curve* (Neisser et al., 1996).

Other scholars noted that the authors, in tracing the history of attempts to examine the hereditary basis of intelligence, left out any instances in which claims of ethnic differences in intelligence were based on scientific fraud or biased interpretations of data (Samelson, 1997). In the early 20th century, these claims were often used to support prejudice and discrimination against ethnic minorities that were considered intellectually inferior. Yet some of these groups, such as Jews and Asians, have since surpassed the American average on IQ scores. The increases in intelligence from one generation to the next in many ethnic groups around the world was noted by Thomas Sowell, who offered perhaps the most intellectually balanced review of *The Bell Curve* in his article

---

findings influenced passage of the act (McPherson, 1985) and those who believe that they did not (Snyderman & Herrnstein, 1983).

Regardless, in 1930 Brigham stated that he had been wrong in assuming that the poorer performance of immigrants was overwhelmingly attributable to heredity. He noted that in their everyday lives, immigrants—living in their original cultures—might not have had the opportunity to encounter much of the material in the army IQ tests. To appreciate Brigham's point, consider the following multiple-choice items from the Army Alpha Test: "Crisco is a: patent medicine, disinfectant, toothpaste, food product [the correct answer];" and "Christy Mathewson is famous as a(n): writer, artist, baseball player [the correct answer], comedian" (Gould, 1981). Similarly, the poorer performance of African Americans on IQ tests was attributed to sociocultural deprivation caused by segregation (Rury, 1988).

The Influence of Heredity and Environment on Intelligence

After three decades of relative indifference to it, the issue of nature versus nurture reemerged in the 1960s when President Lyndon Johnson began Project Head Start, which provides preschool children from deprived socioeconomic backgrounds with enrichment programs to promote their intellectual development. Head Start was stimulated in part by

How Should We Respond to *The Bell Curve*? *continued*

"Ethnicity and IQ" in *The American Spectator* (February 1, 1995). Moreover, there is evidence that the consistent 15-point difference, on average, between European Americans and African Americans is the product of environment, not heredity. A study by psychologist Jeanne Brooks-Gunn and colleagues found that factors related to socioeconomic status explained the difference in intelligence test scores between European American and African American children. They found no evidence that the difference was attributable to heredity (Brooks-Gunn, Klebanov, & Duncan, 1996).

Though *The Bell Curve* received more criticism than support, some scholars have praised its scientific merits (Weidman, 1997) and conclusions (Carroll, 1997). Supporters accused the book's critics of ignoring strong evidence favoring its claims in order to support their own sociopolitical agendas (Rushton, 1997). In response to the widespread criticism of *The Bell Curve*, 52 international scholars in the field of intelligence signed a statement entitled "Mainstream Science on Intelligence" that was published in *The Wall Street Journal* (December 13, 1994) and that supported a number of the book's scientific conclusions. Few of the signees had ever been accused of letting racism guide their scientific practices. They refrained from endorsing some of the more inflammatory claims made in the book. Though supporting the reality of a genetic basis for IQ differences, they made no claims about the contribution of heredity to IQ differences among ethnic groups.

Perhaps the most astounding argument put forth by a psychologist in favor of the book's premise—to those who oppose it—is that many of the book's critics, especially college professors, are genetically predisposed to express moral outrage at it! According to this view, people who are genetically programmed to be more altruistic are drawn to helping occupations, such as education. This tendency, according to the argument, inclines them toward more liberal sociopolitical positions—such as opposing any evidence of a genetic basis for social status in favor of insisting that environmental manipulations can have profound effects on people's upward mobility (Ellis, 1998).

What is one to conclude? Though scientists, ideally, would use meticulous methodology, objective gathering of data, appropriate statistical analysis, and rational conclusions drawn from their research studies, they are limited because they are people with biases, emotions, and unique life histories. Thus, in regard to controversies about complicated topics—such as the possibility of inherited ethnic differences in intelligence—intelligent people easily can find reasons to support the position that agrees with their own biases and assumptions about human nature. Relatively few people would be able to approach such issues with an open mind (Rogers, 1996). In his highly critical article, noted naturalist Stephen Jay Gould (1994) concluded that, given what he believed to be the scientific impossibility of determining whether there are hereditary ethnic differences in intelligence, the best position to take is one of intellectual agnosticism toward the issue—though he believed that intellectuals should be free to study that and virtually any other topic.

the finding that African Americans scored lower than European Americans on IQ tests (Kagan, 2002). Supporters of Head Start attributed this difference to the poorer socioeconomic conditions in which African American children were more likely to be reared.

But in 1969 an article by psychologist Arthur Jensen questioned whether programs such as Head Start could significantly boost the intellectual level of deprived children. Jensen's doubts were based on the notion of **heritability**, the extent to which the variability in a characteristic within a population can be attributed to heredity. Jensen claimed that intelligence has a heritability of .80, which would mean that 80 percent of the variability in intelligence among the members of a group can be explained by heredity. He concluded that the IQ gap between European American and African American children was mainly attributable to heredity (Rushton & Jensen, 2003). But he was accused of making an unwarranted inference. Just because intelligence might have high heritability within a group does not mean that IQ differences between groups, such as African Americans and European Americans, are caused by heredity. Moreover, research has found that the heritability of intelligence is closer to .50 than to .80 (Casto, DeFries, & Fulker, 1995). Jensen's article led to accusations that he was a racist and to demonstrations against him when he spoke on college campuses, illustrating the tension between academic freedom and social sensitivity.

heritability The proportion of variability in a trait across a population attributable to genetic differences among members of the population.

In the tradition of eugenics, one of Jensen's chief supporters, William Shockley (1972), urged that the federal government pay Americans with below-average IQ scores (who would be disproportionately African American) to undergo sterilization. He recommended paying them $1,000 for each point by which their IQ scores were less than 100. Though Shockley was not a psychologist or even a social scientist, he gained media attention because he had won a 1956 Nobel Prize for inventing the transistor. Shockley and several other Nobel Prize winners even deposited their sperm in a sperm bank in California for use by women of superior intelligence who wished to produce highly intelligent offspring ("Superkids?" 1980).

A vigorous response to those who claimed that intelligence is chiefly the product of heredity came from Leon Kamin (1974). Kamin reported that important data supporting the hereditary basis of intelligence had been falsified. Cyril Burt (1883–1971), a British psychologist, had published findings from three studies showing that the positive correlation in IQ scores between identical twins reared apart was higher than the correlation in IQ of fraternal twins reared together. Because identical twins reared apart have the same genes but different environments, the data supported the greater influence of heredity on intelligence.

In each of his studies, supposedly using different sets of twins, Burt reported that the correlation in intelligence between identical twins reared apart was .771. But, as Kamin observed, the odds against finding the same correlation to three decimal places in three different studies are so high as to defy belief. Burt's findings were literally too good to be true. Even Burt's official biographer, who began as an admirer and who believed that Burt had not falsified his data, grudgingly concluded that the data were indeed fraudulent (Hearnshaw, 1979). These findings have not prevented others from coming to Burt's defense, trying to explain away his apparent falsification of data as the product of carelessness rather than the wholesale fabrication of data (Joynson, 2003). Whatever the explanation, Burt's data are not trustworthy (Butler & Petrulis, 1999). Ironically, less than a decade after Kamin's critique of Burt's research, the Minnesota Study of Twins Reared Apart found that identical twins reared apart had a correlation of .710 in their intelligence—not very different from what Burt had reported (Lykken, 1982).

Family Studies of Intelligence

Though the publicity generated by the discovery of Cyril Burt's deception struck a blow against the hereditary view of intelligence, other researchers have conducted legitimate family studies of intelligence. As shown in Figure 10-4, the closer the genetic relationship between relatives, the more similar they are in intelligence (Bouchard & McGue, 1981). But the closer the genetic relationship between relatives, the more likely they also are to share similar environments. Consequently, the size of the correlation in intelligence

FIGURE 10-4

Heredity versus Environment

The correlation in IQ between relatives increases as their hereditary or environmental similarity increases.

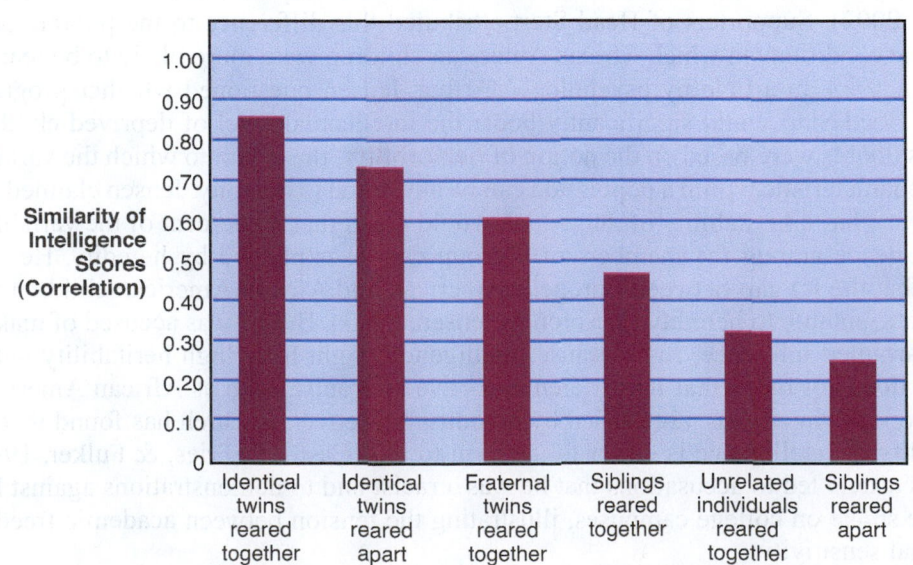

between relatives of varying degrees of genetic similarity is, by itself, inadequate to determine whether this similarity is caused primarily by hereditary factors or by environmental factors. But support for the relatively weak effect of environment on intelligence comes from "virtual twin" studies, in which unrelated children are reared in the same family from early infancy. A study of 90 pairs of virtual twins found that though there was a statistically significant correlation in their intelligence ($r = .26$), which indicates that the environment affects intelligence, their correlation in intelligence is lower than the correlation between nontwin siblings reared in the same family ($r = .50$). This finding indicates that heredity also affects intelligence (Segal, 2000).

Twin Studies Perhaps the higher correlation in intelligence between identical twins reared together than between fraternal twins reared together might be attributable to the more similar treatment received by identical twins. But research findings have provided strong evidence against this interpretation. When identical twins are mistakenly reared as fraternal twins, they become as similar in intelligence as identical twins who are reared as identical twins. Moreover, fraternal twins who are mistakenly reared as identical twins become no more similar in intelligence than do fraternal twins reared as fraternal twins (Scarr & Carter-Saltzman, 1979). These findings indicate that the similarity in intelligence between twins is determined more by their genetic similarity than by their environmental similarity.

Adoption Studies To separate the effects of heredity and environment, researchers have turned to adoption studies. Some of these studies compare the correlation in intelligence between adopted children and their adoptive parents to the correlation in intelligence between adopted children and their biological parents. A published review of adoption studies found the positive correlation in intelligence between adoptees and their biological parents is larger than the positive correlation between adoptees and their adoptive parents (Loehlin, Horn, & Willerman, 1994). This finding supports a genetic basis of intelligence; the genes inherited from the natural parents appear to exert a stronger influence on adoptees than does the environment provided by their adoptive parents (Bouchard & McGue, 1981).

Both the Colorado Adoption Project (Coon, Fulker, DeFries, & Plomin, 1990) and the Texas Adoption Project (Loehlin, Horn, & Willerman, 1994) have provided strong support for a hereditary component in intelligence. The influence of heredity on the variability in intelligence among children *increases* from infancy through childhood. For example, the Colorado Adoption Study has found that the heritability of intelligence is only .09 at age 1 but .36 at age 7 (Fulker, DeFries, & Plomin, 1988). As children spend more years in their home environment, the environment—counter to what common sense would predict—decreases in its influence on the variability in intelligence.

In addition to their support for the influence of heredity on intelligence, adoption studies have provided support for the effect of the environment on intelligence. If nature dominates nurture, then children from lower socioeconomic classes who are adopted by parents from higher socioeconomic classes should show little or no gain in IQ when compared to equivalent children who remain with their biological parents. This possibility was tested by Sandra Scarr and Richard Weinberg (1976) in the Minnesota Adoption Study. The study included African American children who had been adopted by European American couples of higher socioeconomic status than the children's biological parents. The study found that the children who had been adopted had an average IQ of 110. The environment had a strong effect on their intelligence because the adoptees scored about 20 points higher than the average IQ of African American children of the same socioeconomic status reared by their biological parents. These findings indicate that nurture as well as nature is important in intellectual development because children adopted into families of higher socioeconomic status have IQs that are higher than those of their biological parents, though lower than those of their adoptive parents (Weinberg, Scarr, & Waldman, 1992).

A study of adopted children in France found that these findings also held for European children. Participants in the study were 32 children who had been abandoned at birth by their lower-socioeconomic-class parents and adopted at an average age of 4 months by higher-socioeconomic-class professionals. When compared with their siblings who were reared by

The Nurturing of Intelligence

(a) Children from high socioeconomic backgrounds will be more likely than (b) children from lower socioeconomic backgrounds to receive the intellectual enrichment they need to reach their intellectual potential.

Sources: (a) Monkey Business Images/Shutterstock.com; *(b)* Nolte Lourens/Shutterstock.com.

(a)

(b)

their biological parents, the adoptees scored an average of 14 points higher in intelligence and were less likely to be left back in school (Schiff, Duyme, Dumaret, & Tomkiewicz, 1982). A more recent study in France included 87 adolescents given up at birth and adopted before 3 years of age into different socioeconomic classes. The results showed a significant negative correlation of –.37 between the social class of the adoptive families and the likelihood of repeating a grade in school. That is, as the socioeconomic class of the adoptive families increased, the likelihood of the adoptee having to repeat a grade decreased. This finding supported the importance of the environment in determining intellectual performance (Duyme, 1988). But other researchers have found that adopted children reared in families of higher socioeconomic status than that of their biological families show a smaller enhancement in intelligence than had been reported in previous studies (Locurto, 1990). Based on their review of adoption studies, Scarr and Weinberg (1983) concluded that intelligence is influenced by both heredity and environment, with neither dominating the other.

Family Configuration Studies An alternative source of support for the influence of the environment on intelligence comes from family configuration studies. A survey of 400,000 19-year-old men in the Netherlands found that the larger their families and the later they were in the birth order, the less intelligent they tended to be (Belmont & Marolla, 1973). This finding has been explained by Robert Zajonc's (1986) **confluence model**, which assumes that each child is born into an intellectual environment that depends on the intelligence level of his or her parents and siblings. The greater the number of children and the smaller the average interval between births, the lower will be what Zajonc calls the average intellectual environment into which a child is born (Zajonc & Mullally, 1997). One of the reasons for this drop may be the inevitable reduction in the attention parents give to each of their children after the birth of another child (Gibbs, Teti, & Bond, 1987).

In a bold gesture, Zajonc (1976) used the confluence model to predict that the decline in SAT scores that had begun in 1963 would stop in 1980 and then begin to rise. Zajonc based his prediction on the fact that high school students who took the SAT between 1963 and 1980 had been born into increasingly larger families during the post–World War II baby boom. But after 1980, high school students who would take the SAT would come from smaller and smaller families. Zajonc's prediction was supported: SAT scores continued to decline until 1980 and then began to rise. Of course, the decline could have a host of other explanations, including greater numbers of academically poor students taking the test (Astin & Garber, 1982).

Though Zajonc (1993) continues to present evidence supporting the confluence model, other researchers present evidence contradicting it (Barbut, 1993). For example, data from a study by the National Institutes of Health, which included 47,000 women and their 53,000 children, failed to find a relationship between the intelligence of the children and the average interval between the births in their families (Brackbill & Nichols, 1982).

confluence model Robert Zajonc's model of environmental influences on intelligence, which assumes that each child is born into an intellectual environment related to birth order and to the number and differences in age of her or his siblings.

Moreover, the confluence model has demonstrated, at best, a *correlational* rather than a causal relationship between family configuration and intelligence (Rodgers, Cleveland, van den Oord, & Rowe, 2000). That is, even if the relationship is real, perhaps other unidentified factors account for it.

Intellectual Enrichment Programs

Further support for the influence of the environment on intelligence comes from the finding that the difference between European American and African American performance on the SAT narrowed between 1976 and 1983 (Jones, 1984). Moreover, the difference between African American and European American children in IQ test scores is declining, possibly because more African American children have gained access to better educational and economic resources (Vincent, 1991). Access to enrichment programs such as Project Head Start also might play a role. Head Start ensures that poor children get medical care, helps their families gain access to social services, finds employment for parents, serves nutritious meals, provides intellectual stimulation, and helps children develop the social competence necessary to succeed in school (Zigler, 1999). Socioeconomically deprived children who attend Head Start show an average gain of 10 points in their IQ scores (Zigler, Abelson, Trickett, & Seitz, 1982) and greater improvement in their cognitive abilities compared to those not in such programs. This finding contradicts Jensen's (1969) prediction that Head Start would have no significant effect on intellectual growth. Unfortunately, the gains achieved by children in preschool enrichment programs often decline during grade school (Locurto, 1991), perhaps in part because these children typically attend inferior schools (Lee & Loeb, 1995). This finding indicates the need to continue enrichment programs beyond the preschool years.

Preschool enrichment programs other than Head Start also can have beneficial effects, as shown in a study of disadvantaged African American children who attended Head Start, other preschool, or no preschool programs. Children in the Head Start and other preschool programs showed greater improvement in several intellectual abilities than did those who did not attend either kind of program. This result could not be attributed to initial differences in intellectual abilities because the children were statistically matched on various relevant characteristics (Lee, Brooks-Gunn, Schnur, & Liaw, 1990).

Other countries also have found that intellectual enrichment programs can be beneficial. One of the most ambitious of all enrichment programs took place from 1979 to 1983 in Venezuela, under its minister of state for the development of intelligence (Gonzalez, 1989). The

Project Head Start

Intellectual enrichment programs, such as Project Head Start, provide a stimulating preschool environment that better prepares children for success in elementary school.
Source: Olesya Feketa/ Shutterstock.com.

program provided good prenatal care and infant nutrition, as well as sensory stimulation of preschoolers and special training in cognitive skills. New mothers watched videocassettes on proper child rearing while in their hospital rooms, schoolchildren attended "learning to think" classes, and television commercials promoted the need to develop the minds of Venezuelan children (Walsh, 1981). The more than 400 Venezuelan seventh graders who participated in a program to teach thinking skills (such as reasoning, problem solving, and decision making) achieved better academic performance than comparable control students who had not participated (Herrnstein, Nickerson, de Sanchez, & Swets, 1986).

Even more evidence of the influence of the environment on intelligence comes from the finding that IQ scores have increased from 5 to 25 points in 14 nations during the past few decades, apparently because of better nutrition, education, and health care (Flynn, 1987). And both Galton and Goddard would be surprised to find that today the Japanese, whom they considered intellectually inferior, score significantly higher than Americans on IQ tests that have been standardized on Americans. Japanese children score about 10 points higher than American children (Lynn, 1982). The Japanese increase in IQ scores parallels that country's increased emphasis on education, with children going to school more hours, attending school more days, and studying more hours than American children do. It is difficult to attribute this increase in IQ scores to accelerated evolution of Japanese brains.

Even the academic achievements of Asian Americans surpass those of European Americans and African Americans. What might account for this finding? Stanley Sue, a cross-cultural psychologist, insists that it is wrong to attribute these achievements to either an inborn intellectual superiority or a culture that places a high value on education. Instead, Sue looks to simple adaptive behavior. According to Sue, because Asian Americans have had cultural and discriminatory barriers to their upward mobility in careers that place less emphasis on education (such as sports, politics, entertainment, and corporate leadership), they have sought to pursue careers that provide fewer barriers. These more accessible alternatives (such as science, mathematics, and engineering) typically place a premium on academic excellence (Sue & Okazaki, 1990). Sue's hypothesis has not yet been adequately tested.

Some psychologists have suggested that it might not be in our best interest to study the relative importance of nature and nurture in intellectual development (Sarason, 1984). To do so might discover little of scientific import while providing apparent scientific support for discrimination against racial or ethnic minorities. Instead of examining the relative importance of nature versus nurture, it might be better to do what Anne Anastasi (1958), an authority on psychological testing, suggested more than three decades ago: determine *how* both achieve their effects (Turkheimer, 1991).

Section Review: Nature, Nurture, and Intelligence

1. What have adoption studies (especially studies of identical twins reared apart) discovered about the role of nature and nurture in intelligence?

2. What effects do programs such as Head Start have on deprived children's intellectual abilities?

What Would You Include in an IQ Test?

Rationale

Traditional IQ tests are descendants of the Binet-Simon Scale, which was designed to help place students in appropriate classes in French schools in the early 20th century. Because of their original use, as discussed in the sections "Sternberg's Triarchic Theory of Intelligence" and "Gardner's Theory of Multiple Intelligences," traditional IQ tests have been criticized for assessing narrow aspects of intelligence, primarily those related to verbal ability. Such criticisms have motivated some intelligence researchers to develop intelligence tests based on broader conceptions of intelligence, most notably Robert Sternberg's triarchic theory of intelligence and Howard Gardner's theory of multiple intelligences.

Assignment

Based on what you have learned about Sternberg's triarchic theory and Gardner's theory of multiple intelligences, write a proposal describing your own intelligence test. The test should assess more than the abilities necessary for performing well academically. Describe the rationale and the components of your test (that is, the kinds of talents and abilities that it would assess). Also, discuss how you would standardize the test, determine its reliability, and establish its validity.

Describe any similarities or differences between your test and traditional intelligence tests, such as the Wechsler and Stanford-Binet intelligence scales. Include a discussion of a relevant journal article that you found in Psychological Abstracts, perhaps by using *PsycInfo*.

Chapter Summary

Intelligence Testing

- Intelligence is the global capacity to act purposefully, to think rationally, and to deal effectively with the environment.
- An achievement test assesses knowledge of a particular subject, an aptitude test predicts the potential to benefit from instruction in a particular academic or vocational setting, and an intelligence test is a kind of aptitude test that assesses overall mental ability.
- Francis Galton began the study of mental abilities in the late 19th century and founded the field of differential psychology.
- The first formal test of general intelligence was the Binet-Simon scale, which was developed to help place children in school classes.
- The American version of the test became known as the Stanford-Binet Intelligence Scale.
- Today the Stanford-Binet Intelligence Scale and the Wechsler Intelligence Scales are the most popular intelligence tests.
- Tests must be standardized so that they are administered in a uniform manner and so that test scores can be compared with norms.
- A test must also be reliable, giving consistent results over time.
- And a test must be valid, meaning that it measures what it is supposed to measure.
- Controversy has arisen over whether intelligence testing is fair to minority groups, particularly African Americans.

- Opponents of intelligence testing claim that because African Americans, on the average, score lower than European Americans do, the tests are biased against African Americans.
- Proponents of intelligence testing claim that the tests accurately predict the academic performance of both African Americans and European Americans and typically attribute the differences in performance to the deprived sociocultural backgrounds that are more common among African American children.
- Attempts to develop tests that are not affected by the test taker's sociocultural background have failed.

Extremes of Intelligence

- To be classified as having an intellectual disability, a person must have an IQ of 70 or below and, beginning in childhood, difficulties performing in everyday life.
- The four categories of intellectual disabilities are mild intellectual disability, moderate intellectual disability, severe intellectual disability, and profound intellectual disability.
- Though most cases of intellectual disabilities are caused by sociocultural factors, some are caused by brain damage.
- Most people with an intellectual disability can benefit from education and training programs.
- To be classified as mentally gifted, a person must have an IQ of 130 or above and demonstrate unusual ability in at least one area, such as art, music, or mathematics.

- Lewis Terman's Genetic Studies of Genius have demonstrated that mentally gifted children tend to become successful in their academic, social, physical, and vocational lives.
- Social change and increased occupational opportunity for women are reflected in generational differences in gifted women's achievement.
- Benbow and Stanley's Study of Mathematically Precocious Youth identifies children with outstanding mathematical ability, provides them with special programs, and counsels their parents about how to help them reach their potential.

Theories of Intelligence

- Theories of intelligence traditionally have depended on factor analysis, a statistical technique for determining the abilities that underlie intelligence.
- The theories differ in the extent to which they view intelligence as a general factor or a combination of different factors.
- The most recent factor-analytic theory distinguishes between fluid intelligence and crystallized intelligence.
- Robert Sternberg's triarchic theory of intelligence (recently renamed the theory of successful intelligence) is based on his research on information processing.
- Sternberg's theory distinguishes between componential (academic) intelligence, experiential (creative) intelligence, and contextual (practical) intelligence.
- Sternberg also believes that people can be taught to process information more effectively, thereby increasing their level of intelligence.
- Howard Gardner's theory of multiple intelligences is a biopsychological theory, which assumes that the brain has evolved separate systems for different adaptive abilities that he calls "intelligences": linguistic, logical-mathematical, spatial, musical, bodily-kinesthetic, intrapersonal, and interpersonal intelligences.
- Each of us varies in the degree to which we have developed each of these kinds of intelligence.

Nature, Nurture, and Intelligence

- One of the most controversial issues in psychology has been the extent to which intelligence is a product of heredity or of environment.
- Early studies of women addressed gender differences and variability in physical and mental attributes.
- Few gender differences were observed, and the variability hypothesis was not supported.
- Early studies of immigrants concluded that many were "feebleminded."
- The examiners attributed this "feeblemindedness" to hereditary factors rather than to a host of cultural and environmental factors that actually accounted for that finding.
- Arthur Jensen created a stir by claiming that heredity is a much more powerful determinant of intelligence than is environment.
- Studies of twins, adopted children, family configuration effects, and enrichment programs indicate that neither heredity nor environment is a significantly more important determinant of intelligence.
- Though intelligence might be highly heritable, there is no widely accepted evidence that differences in intelligence among particular racial or ethnic groups are caused by heredity.

Key Terms

autism spectrum disorder (ASD) (p. 343)
intelligence (p. 345)

Intelligence Testing

achievement test (p. 345)
aptitude test (p. 345)
differential psychology (p. 346)
intelligence quotient (IQ) (p. 347)
intelligence test (p. 345)

Extremes of Intelligence

cerebral palsy (p. 353)

Down syndrome (p. 353)
intellectual disabilities (p. 351)
mental giftedness (p. 354)
phenylketonuria (PKU) (p. 353)

Theories of Intelligence

crystallized intelligence (p. 359)
factor analysis (p. 358)
fluid intelligence (p. 359)
theory of multiple intelligences (p. 361)
triarchic theory of intelligence (p. 360)

Nature, Nurture, and Intelligence

confluence model (p. 368)
eugenics (p. 362)
heritability (p. 365)
variability hypothesis (p. 363)

Chapter Quiz

Note: Answers for the Chapter Quiz questions are provided at the end of the book.

1. So-called culture-fair tests and culture-free tests have proved
   a. more biased than traditional IQ tests.
   b. less biased than traditional IQ tests.
   c. easier for people of lower socioeconomic status than of higher socioeconomic status.
   d. easier for people of higher socioeconomic status than of lower socioeconomic status.

2. Cerebral palsy, which sometimes involves intellectual disabilities, is associated with
   a. schizophrenia.
   b. movement disorders.
   c. interhemispheric interference.
   d. inability to form new memories.

3. According to the theory of multiple intelligences, if you realized why you had a short temper when confronted with minor frustrations, you would exhibit
   a. experiential intelligence.
   b. componential intelligence.
   c. interpersonal intelligence.
   d. intrapersonal intelligence.

4. According to the triarchic theory of intelligence, if you were a renowned abstract painter, you would be high in
   a. innate intelligence.
   b. contextual intelligence.
   c. componential intelligence.
   d. experiential intelligence.

5. Intellectual disabilities caused by phenylketonuria (PKU) can be prevented by
   a. dietary control.
   b. avoiding hypoxia at birth.
   c. Caesarean delivery.
   d. not exposing the fetus to rubella.

6. William Stern's formula for calculating IQ was inadequate when applied to
   a. adults.
   b. adolescents.
   c. people whose chronological age was greater than their mental age.
   d. people whose mental age was greater than their chronological age.

7. David Wechsler devised his first intelligence test to assess
   a. immigrants.
   b. army recruits.
   c. schoolchildren.
   d. psychiatric patients.

8. A test designed to predict your ability to benefit from training as a chef would be an
   a. aptitude test.
   b. expertise test.
   c. achievement test.
   d. intelligence test.

9. David Wechsler's definition of intelligence is in the spirit of
   a. structuralism.
   b. cognitivism.
   c. functionalism.
   d. psychoanalysis.

10. According to the triarchic theory of intelligence, if you can change a flat tire, feel at ease when meeting new people, and perform well when interviewing for a job, you are high in
    a. innate intelligence.
    b. contextual intelligence.
    c. componential intelligence.
    d. experiential intelligence.

11. Francis Galton was inspired by
    a. Cyril Burt's theory of eugenics.
    b. Charles Darwin's theory of evolution.
    c. Henry Goddard's theory of innate intelligence.
    d. Robert Sternberg's triarchic theory of intelligence.

12. Given a mental age of 8 and a chronological age of 16, a child would have an IQ of
    a. 2.
    b. 8.
    c. 50.
    d. 128.

13. A formal test of fans' knowledge of the rules, players, history, and all-time records in professional sports would be
    a. an aptitude test.
    b. an achievement test.
    c. a commonsense test.
    d. an intelligence test.

14. The case of *Larry P. v. Wilson Riles*
    a. outlawed federal funding for eugenics.
    b. ordered mainstreaming for elementary students with intellectual disabilities.
    c. provided special advanced classes for the mentally gifted.
    d. found that IQ tests violated the civil rights of African American children.

15. The original purpose of the intelligence test was to
    a. identify geniuses.
    b. find potential officer candidates for the military.
    c. place students in classes according to their ability.
    d. demonstrate the innate superiority of certain racial and ethnic groups.

16. You develop a new test of social intelligence and establish norms by administering it to groups varying in their sex, age, income, educational level, and geographic location. This procedure is an aspect of
    a. normalization.
    b. homogenization.
    c. standardization.
    d. factor analysis.

17. The extent to which variability in a characteristic within a group can be attributed to heredity is called
    a. eugenics.
    b. heritability.
    c. polygenicity.
    d. differential psychology.

18. To be classified as having an intellectual disability, a person must have a low IQ and
    a. lack the ability to communicate.
    b. medically verified brain damage.
    c. difficulty functioning in everyday life.
    d. complete dependence on others for self-care.

19. If you were an excellent problem solver and could rapidly perform mental arithmetic calculations, you would demonstrate excellent
    a. fluid intelligence.
    b. structural intelligence.
    c. experiential intelligence.
    d. crystallized intelligence.

20. A championship contestant on the television quiz show *Jeopardy* has acquired a great deal of knowledge from schooling and everyday life. This fund of information characterizes the kind of intelligence that increases across the life span, which is better known as
    a. fluid intelligence.
    b. structural intelligence.
    c. experiential intelligence.
    d. crystallized intelligence.

21. On a standardized intelligence test with a standard deviation of 15, the proportion of people who score between 70 and 130 is about
    a. 60 percent.
    b. 68 percent.
    c. 95 percent.
    d. 99 percent.

22. The belief that intelligence reflects both a general ability and several specific abilities was held by
    a. J. P. Guilford.
    b. Louis Thurstone.
    c. Raymond Cattell.
    d. Charles Spearman.

23. According to Robert Zajonc, the most intelligent child would probably be a 10-year-old girl with
    a. a 9-year-old sister and an 11-year-old sister.
    b. an 8-year-old brother and a 14-year-old sister.
    c. a 1-year-old brother and an 18-year-old sister.
    d. a 12-year-old brother and a 16-year-old brother.

24. If you claimed that only elite athletes and people who score above 1400 on the SAT should be permitted to reproduce, you would favor
    a. eugenics.
    b. polygenetics.
    c. evolutionary confluence.
    d. environmental determinism.

25. Research studies indicate that there is a larger positive correlation in intelligence between
    a. unrelated children reared together than between identical twins reared apart.
    b. fraternal twins reared together than between identical twins reared apart.
    c. adoptees and their biological parents than between adoptees and their adoptive parents.
    d. adoptees and their adoptive parents than between adoptees and their biological parents.

Thought Questions

1. In what ways have science, politics, and sociocultural factors become part of the debate on the relative roles of nature and nurture in intelligence?

2. Why do some psychologists believe that Gardner's theory of multiple intelligences might lead to intelligence tests that are superior to traditional ones?

3. How did Terman's longitudinal study of geniuses revise people's thinking about extremely intelligent people?

Motivation

On a beautiful spring day in 2000, hundreds of residents of the popular arts community comprising New Hope, Pennsylvania, and Lambertville, New Jersey, attended the funeral of a beloved man who had been known as "Mother" since he arrived in 1949, looking for work as a female impersonator. Mother, born Joseph Cavellucci in New York City in 1925, "came out of the closet" regarding his homosexuality as a teenager growing up in Philadelphia.

Mother's death left a void in the lives of those who were used to seeing him—dressed in female attire—on his daily walk, wearing pink slippers or high heels, across the bridge from his home in New Hope to do his grocery shopping in Lambertville. His death left a larger void in the lives of those who sought his wisdom and practical assistance (which accounted for his being called "Mother"). Cavellucci, who accepted being called either "he" or "she," never turned down a request to perform at an event to raise money for someone in need.

Mother was so beloved and well known that *The Philadelphia Inquirer* published a major obituary for him, calling him an icon of the gay community. His local daily newspaper, the Doylestown *Intelligencer Record,* called him "larger than life" and said, "Cavellucci achieved something many of us aspire to—he lived life on his own terms" (Duffy, 2000, p. A-1). Mother often behaved like a curmudgeon with a sense of humor. On one occasion, while working as a server (his long-time profession) at a canal-side restaurant, Mother responded to a woman who complained that her companion had one more shrimp than she had by simply tossing one of her partner's shrimp into the canal. He added, "Now you both have the same number."

As one of Mother's "family" remarked after his death, "She was truly the town's mother. She embraced everyone no matter what. But she could care for you and put you in your place at the same time" (Duffy, 2000, p. A-4). Mother's "children"—gay, lesbian, and straight—repaid his kindness by holding several fundraisers to pay for his long battle against cancer. They even kept paying the rent on his apartment, never giving up hope that he would one day return home. In his last days, Mother lived at Buckingham Valley Nursing Home, which he naturally renamed "Buckingham Palace," with himself as both king and queen. "I am the reigning man and woman," he announced. The nurses took turns putting on Mother's makeup and nail polish and styling his hair.

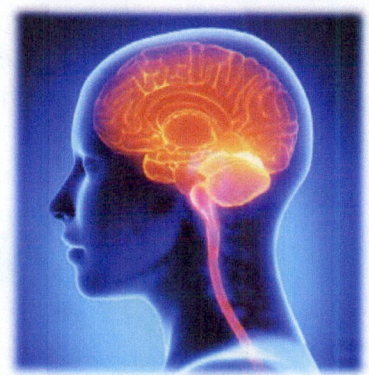

Source: CLIPAREA/Custom media/ Shutterstock.com.

Chapter Outline

The Nature of Motivation

The Hunger Motive

The Sex Motive

The Arousal Motive

The Achievement Motive

The Role of Motivation in Sports

Mother frequently worked as a female impersonator, appearing in extravaganzas throughout the United States, including the Gay Miss U.S.A. pageant. He loved dressing in shimmering gowns and wearing makeup, nail polish, and a bouffant hairdo when performing. He would bring down the house with his vocal stylings of "Hello, Dolly" and "God Bless America." A soulful rendition of the latter accompanied the long procession following his coffin out of St. John's Church in Lambertville. In eulogizing Mother, New Hope's mayor, Laurence Keller, recognized him as a pioneer for gay rights. (Mother was fond of saying, "Honey, I put the 'G' in gay.") Keller tearfully concluded his eulogy by saying, "I'll always remember the grand dame of New Hope" (Duffy, 2000, p. A-4).

After reading this brief passage on the life of Joseph "Mother" Cavellucci, you might ask: Why would a person born male be sexually attracted to other men? Why would a man prefer dressing in women's clothing? And why would a man claim to be both male and female? Possible answers to these questions are presented in the section on human sexuality. The chapter also discusses other kinds of human *motivation,* including hunger, arousal, and achievement.

The Nature of Motivation

motivation The psychological process that arouses, directs, and maintains behavior toward a goal.

Motivation is the psychological process that arouses, directs, and maintains behavior toward a goal. The hunger motive, for example, normally arouses us to take action, directs us to find food, and makes us eat until our hunger subsides. Because we cannot directly observe people's motivation, we must infer it from their behavior. We might infer that a person who drinks a quart of water is motivated by a strong thirst and that a person who becomes dictator of a country is motivated by a strong need for power. The concept of motivation also is useful in explaining fluctuations in behavior over time (Atkinson, 1981). If yesterday morning you ate three stacks of pancakes but this morning you ate only a piece of toast, your friends would not attribute your change in behavior to a change in your personality . Instead, they would attribute it to a change in your degree of hunger—your motivation.

Sources of Motivation

What are the main sources of motivation? In seeking answers to this question, psychologists have implicated *genes, drives,* and *incentives.*

Genes and Motivation

In the early 20th century, many psychologists, influenced by Charles Darwin's theory of evolution and led by William McDougall (1871–1938), attributed human and animal motivation to inherited *instincts.* An **instinct** is a complex, inherited (that is, unlearned) species-specific behavior pattern. Instincts are at work when birds build nests, spiders weave webs, and salmon swim upstream to their spawning grounds. But what of human instincts? McDougall (1908) claimed that people are guided by a variety of instincts, including instincts for "pugnacity," "curiosity," and "gregariousness." As discussed in Chapter 13, McDougall's contemporary, Sigmund Freud, based his theory of personality on instincts that supposedly motivate sex and aggression. And William James (1890/1981) claimed that humans are motivated by more instincts than any other animal.

instinct A complex, inherited behavior pattern characteristic of a species.

In the 1920s, psychologists, influenced by behaviorist John B. Watson, rejected instincts as factors in human motivation. Watson believed that human behavior depended on learning, not heredity. One reason why instinct theorists lost scientific credibility was that they had attempted to explain almost all human behavior as instinctive, in some cases compiling lists of thousands of alleged human instincts (Cofer, 1985). You might say, for example, that people paint because of an "aesthetic instinct" or play sports because of a "competitive instinct." A second reason why instinct theorists fell out of favor was their failure to explain the behaviors they labeled as instinctive. Consider the following hypothetical dialogue about an alleged "parenting instinct":

- Why do parents take care of their children?
- Because they have a parenting instinct.
- But how do you know parents have a parenting instinct?
- Because they take care of their children.

Such circular reasoning neither explains why parents take care of their children nor provides evidence of a parenting instinct. Each assertion is simply used to support the other. For these reasons, psychologists prefer not to refer to human instincts.

Though instinct theory, as applied to humans, has fallen into disfavor, some scientists believe that human social behavior does in fact have a genetic basis (Hoffman, 1995). The chief proponents of this belief work in the field of **sociobiology**, founded by Edward O. Wilson in the 1970s, which studies the hereditary basis of human and animal social behavior within the framework of evolution (Wilson, 1975). Sociobiological principles have been recognized for centuries in different cultures, as in the Japanese novel *The Tale of Genji,* written a millennium ago. This story is filled with sociobiological themes regarding human motivation (Thiessen & Umezawa, 1998).

But sociobiology has been criticized for overestimating the role of heredity in human social behavior (Hood, 1995). Critics fear that acceptance of sociobiology would lend support to the status quo, making us less inclined to change what many people believe has been "ordained by God or nature," such as the since-discredited theory of racial differences in criminality, social status, sexual behavior, and child neglect and abuse (Peregrine, Ember, & Ember, 2003). Nonetheless, research on personality and other topics lends support to some sociobiological notions. In fact, some personality researchers still see a role for evolutionary principles in the study of personality (Millon, 2003).

Drives and Motivation

Following the decline of the instinct theory of human motivation, the **drive-reduction theory** of Clark Hull (1884–1952) dominated psychology in the 1940s and 1950s (Webster & Coleman, 1992). According to Hull (1943), a **need** caused by physiological deprivation, such as a lack of food or water, induces a state of tension called a **drive**, which motivates the individual to reduce it. The thirst drive motivates drinking, the hunger drive motivates eating, and the sex drive motivates sexual behavior. Even the alleviation of a drug craving by the ingestion of a drug can be interpreted as an example of drive reduction (McMillan & Katz, 2002).

Drive reduction aims at the restoration of **homeostasis**, a steady state of physiological equilibrium. Consider your thirst drive. When your body loses water, as when you perspire, receptor cells in your hypothalamus (see Chapter 3) respond and make you feel thirsty. Thirst arouses you, signaling you that your body lacks water, and directs you to drink. By drinking, you reduce your thirst and restore homeostasis by restoring your body's normal water level. Undoubtedly, we are motivated to reduce drives such as thirst, hunger, and sex, but drive reduction cannot explain all human motivation. In some cases, we perform behaviors that do not reduce physiological drives, as in the case of Jim Abbott, who had only one hand yet pursued a successful career as a major league baseball pitcher.

Incentives and Motivation

Whereas a drive is an internal state of tension that "pushes" you toward a goal, an **incentive** is an external stimulus that "pulls" you toward a goal. Through experience, we learn that certain stimuli (such as a puppy) are desirable and should be approached, making them *positive* incentives. We also learn that other stimuli (such as elevator music) are undesirable and should

sociobiology The study of the hereditary basis of human and animal social behavior.

drive-reduction theory The theory that behavior is motivated by the need to reduce drives such as sex or hunger.

need A motivated state caused by physiological deprivation, such as a lack of food or water.

drive A state of psychological tension induced by a need.

homeostasis A steady state of physiological equilibrium.

incentive An external stimulus that pulls an individual toward a goal.

be avoided, making them *negative* incentives. Thus, we are pulled toward positive incentives and away from negative ones. Incentives often are used by teachers and employers to motivate students (Rassuli, 2012) and employees (Jeffrey & Adomdza, 2011).

Incentives often are associated with drives. For example, your thirst drive motivates you to replenish your body's water, but incentives determine what you choose to drink. Your thirst would push you to drink, but your favorite flavor would pull you toward a particular beverage. As with all incentives, your favorite flavor would partly depend on learning, which in this case would depend on your past experience with a variety of flavors. In the case of airline passengers who survived a crash in the Andes years ago and cannibalized the bodies of passengers who had died, a strong hunger drive made them respond to a weak incentive, human flesh (Read, 1974). The opposite can occur in your everyday life. Despite not feeling hungry, you might be motivated to eat in response to a strong incentive, such as an ice cream sundae.

Maslow's Hierarchy of Needs

If forced to make a choice, would you prefer enough food to eat or straight As in school? Would you prefer to have a warm home or close friends? In each case, though both options are appealing, you probably would choose the first; this quiz shows that some motives have priority over others. The fact that we have such preferences led the humanistic psychologist Abraham Maslow (1970) to develop a **hierarchy of needs** (see Figure 11-1), which ranks important needs by their priority. Maslow used the term *need* to refer to both physiological and psychological motives. According to Maslow, you must first satisfy your basic *physiological* needs, such as your needs for food and water, before you will be motivated to meet your higher needs for *safety* and *security,* and so on up the hierarchy from the need for *belongingness and love,* through the need for *esteem,* and ultimately to the needs for *self-actualization* (achievement of all your potentials) and *transcendence* (spiritual fulfillment). Though his theory has been criticized for its basis on Western and individualistic views on personal growth (Hanley & Abell, 2002), Maslow's concept of a hierarchy of needs has much in common with views of human motivation that are widely accepted in India (Satapathy, 2001).

Maslow believed that because most people are unable to satisfy all their lower needs, few people reach the two highest levels. Nonetheless, success in meeting lower-level needs in the hierarchy is positively correlated with psychological well-being (Lester, 1990). Though Maslow died before conducting much research on people who had reached transcendence, he did study the lives of people he considered self-actualized, including Abraham Lincoln and Eleanor Roosevelt (see Chapter 13).

Though some research on Maslow's hierarchy of needs—such as a study of the satisfaction of those needs in 88 countries from 1960 to 1994 (Hagerty, 1999)—has

hierarchy of needs Maslow's arrangement of needs in the order of their motivational priority, ranging from physiological needs to the needs for self-actualization and transcendence.

FIGURE 11-1
Maslow's Hierarchy of Needs

Abraham Maslow assumed that our needs are arranged in a hierarchy, with our most powerful needs at the bottom. We will be weakly motivated by higher needs until our lower needs are met.

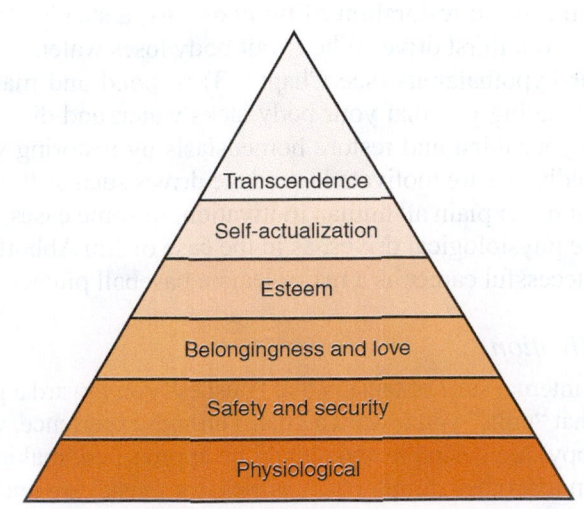

supported his sequence of need achievement, we do not always place a higher priority on lower-level needs (Goebel & Brown, 1981). This finding was supported by a study in which a survey given to 150 college students asked them to identify which of the needs in Maslow's hierarchy was most important to them. Both male and female undergraduates chose being in love as more important than any other need (Pettijohn, 1996). Moreover, martyrs such as Mahatma Gandhi will starve themselves for the sake of social justice. Now consider the biological motives of *hunger, sex,* and *arousal,* the social motive of *achievement,* and the role of motivation in sport.

Section Review: The Nature of Motivation

1. Why do some scientists criticize sociobiological explanations of human behavioral differences?

2. What are the different levels in Maslow's hierarchy of needs?

The Hunger Motive

The *hunger* motive impels you to eat to satisfy your body's need for nutrients. If you have just eaten, food might be the last thing on your mind. But if you have not eaten for a few days—or even for a few hours—food might be the only thing on your mind.

The Physiology of Hunger

Research on hunger and eating has grown in recent decades, largely because of concerns about the health risks associated with the increase in obesity and eating disorders in industrialized countries. One factor involved in body weight is heredity, which plays a role in the regulation of eating (De Castro, 1999). Much of this evidence has come from twin studies. The Minnesota Study of Twins Reared Apart compared monozygotic (identical) twins reared apart, dizygotic (fraternal) twins reared apart, and nontwins in regard to their dietary preferences. The results showed that the participants' dietary preferences were more strongly related to their degree of hereditary similarity than to their degree of environmental similarity (Hur, Bouchard, & Eckert, 1998). Though some researchers study the hereditary basis of eating regulation, most study bodily, brain, or environmental factors.

Bodily Factors and Hunger

The main bodily mechanisms that regulate hunger involve the mouth, the stomach, the small intestine, the liver, and the pancreas. Taste receptors on the tongue play a role in hunger by sending taste sensations to the brain, allowing you to perceive the taste of food. Though sensations from your mouth affect hunger, they are not its sole source. Your stomach also plays a role in hunger. In 1912, physiologist Walter Cannon (1871–1945) had his assistant Arthur Washburn swallow a balloon, which inflated in his stomach. The balloon was connected by a tube to a device that recorded stomach contractions by measuring changes they caused in the air pressure inside the balloon. Whenever Washburn felt a hunger pang, he pressed a key, producing a mark next to the recording of his stomach contractions. The recordings revealed that Washburn's hunger pangs were associated with stomach contractions, prompting Cannon and Washburn (1912) to conclude that stomach contractions cause hunger. Walter Cannon also coined the term "fight-or-flight" (see Chapter 12), an animal's response to threat, which can include changes in hunger.

Might they have interpreted their findings about hunger and stomach contractions in another way? Perhaps the opposite was true: Washburn's hunger might have caused the stomach contractions. Or, given that we now know that stomach contractions occur when the stomach contains food, perhaps the balloon itself caused Washburn's stomach contractions. Moreover, later research revealed that hunger sensations are not entirely dependent on the stomach; even people whose stomachs have been removed because of cancer or severe ulcers can experience hunger (Ingelfinger, 1944). Therefore, hunger also is regulated by other mechanisms.

Though the stomach is not necessary for the regulation of hunger, it does play an important role. Receptor cells in the stomach detect the amount of food it contains. After gorging yourself on a Thanksgiving dinner, you might become all too aware of the stretch receptors in your stomach that respond to the presence of food (Stricker & McCann, 1985). These receptors inform the brain of the amount of food in the stomach by sending neural impulses along the vagus nerve to the brain, reducing your level of hunger.

Food stored in the stomach eventually reaches the small intestine, the main site of digestion, where it stimulates the secretion of the hormone *cholecystokinin*, which in turn stimulates the vagus nerve to send neural impulses to the brain, reducing your level of hunger (Gosnell & Hsiao, 1984). In a study demonstrating the inhibitory effect of cholecystokinin on hunger, men received doses of either cholecystokinin or a saline placebo. Those who received doses of cholecystokinin reported less hunger than those who received the placebo (Greenough, Cole, Lewis, Lockton, & Blundell, 1998). Though the mouth, stomach, and small intestine each play a role in regulating hunger and eating, optimal regulation depends on the combination of signals from the three of them (Cecil, 2001).

Of special importance in the regulation of hunger are the hormones *insulin* and *ghrelin* (see Table 11-1). Insulin is secreted by the pancreas. It helps blood sugar enter body cells for use in metabolism, promotes the storage of fat, and induces feelings of hunger. Ghrelin is produced by cells in your stomach and released when your stomach is empty—in other words, when you are hungry. Ghrelin is considered an appetite-regulating hormone and hunger signal. In fact, hunger depends on interplay of several physiological feedback systems. For example, *glucose* is another important factor in the regulation of hunger. Glucose is a simple sugar that is absorbed directly into your bloodstream during digestion. It is the most important source of energy for your body and brain. Researchers have conducted studies in which the level of blood sugar was held constant by a continuous infusion of glucose while insulin levels were permitted to rise. Participants in those studies reported increased levels of hunger (Rodin, 1985).

Insulin and Hunger

The mere sight of rich, delicious food can stimulate your pancreas to secrete insulin, making you more hungry and, as a consequence, more likely to eat the food.

Source: cowardion/Shutterstock.com.

TABLE 11-1 Hormones Related to Hunger and Body Weight

Hormone	Function
Leptin	Regulates energy intake and expenditure
Insulin	Promotes the storage of fat and induces feelings of hunger
Ghrelin	Regulates appetite and serves as a hunger signal
Melanocortin	Regulates feelings of satiety
Cholecystokinin	Inhibits feelings of hunger

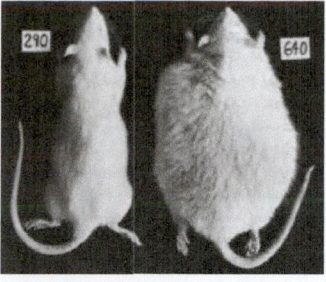

The VMH Rat

Destruction of the ventromedial hypothalamus induces overeating and gross obesity. A rat whose ventromedial hypothalamus has been destroyed might eat until it becomes three times its normal weight.

Source: From P. Teitelbaum, Appetite, *Proceedings of the American Philosophical Society,* *108,* 1964, 464–473.

Brain Factors and Eating

How does your brain decide when and what to eat? Signals from the body regulate hunger by their effects on the brain. In 1902 Viennese physician Alfred Fröhlich reported that patients with tumors of the pituitary gland (see Chapter 3) often became obese. Fröhlich concluded that the pituitary gland regulates hunger. But later research found that, in reality, the tumors influenced hunger by affecting the *hypothalamus*, which lies just above the pituitary gland. The neurotransmitter norepinephrine promotes eating by stimulating receptors in the hypothalamus (Towell, Muscat, & Willner, 1989).

Two areas of the hypothalamus are especially important in the regulation of hunger (see Figure 11-2). Electrical stimulation of the *ventromedial hypothalamus (VMH),* an area at the lower middle of the hypothalamus, inhibits eating, and its destruction induces eating. Rats whose VMH has been destroyed will eat until they became grossly obese and then eat enough to maintain their new, higher level of weight (Hetherington & Ranson, 1942). They have continuously high levels of insulin in their blood and store their meals as fat. They may weigh up to three times as much as a normal rat. Whereas the VMH has been implicated in reducing hunger, the *lateral hypothalamus (LH),* comprising areas on both sides of the hypothalamus, has been implicated in increasing it. Research findings indicate that one way in which cholecystokinin suppresses hunger is by inhibiting neuronal activity in the LH and stimulating it in the VMH (Shiraishi, 1990). Electrical stimulation of the LH promotes eating, whereas its destruction inhibits eating. Rats whose LH has been destroyed will stop eating and starve to death even in the presence of food (Anand & Brobeck, 1951). Though early experiments led to the conclusion that the LH acts as our "hunger center" and the VMH acts as our "satiety center," later experiments have shown that these sites are merely important components in the brain's complex system for regulating hunger and eating (Stricker & Verbalis, 1987).

But how does damage to the hypothalamus affect hunger? It does so in part by altering the body's **set point**—that is, its normal weight (Michel & Cabanac, 1999). People and animals maintain a fairly constant weight across their lifetime. Your set point depends on the level of *leptin,* a hormone that regulates energy intake and expenditure. Leptin receptors are located in the hypothalamus. Damage to the LH lowers the set point, reducing hunger

set point A specific body weight that the brain tries to maintain through the regulation of diet, activity, and metabolism.

FIGURE 11-2
The Hypothalamus and Hunger

The hypothalamus, located below the thalamus, is a portion of the brain that contains a number of small nuclei with a variety of functions, including regulating hunger. Each side of the brain has this grouping of nuclei. This image shows one side of the brain with the lateral hypothalamus on the outside edge and ventromedial hypothalamus in the bottom middle. These two areas are especially important in the regulation of hunger.

Source: Adapted from Alila Medical Media/Shutterstock.com.

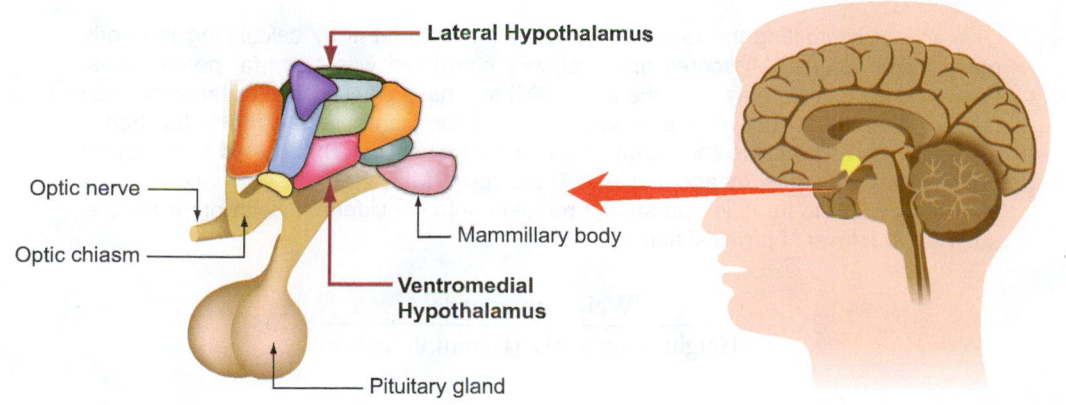

Lateral Hypothalamus

Optic nerve

Optic chiasm

Mammillary body

Ventromedial Hypothalamus

Pituitary gland

and making the animal eat less to maintain a lower body weight. In contrast, damage to the VMH raises the set point, increasing hunger and making the animal eat more to maintain a higher body weight (Keesey & Powley, 1986). Whereas signals from the body regulate changes in hunger from meal to meal, the set point regulates changes in hunger over months or years. Nonetheless, some researchers insist that there is relatively weak evidence of a role for a bodily set point in hunger and eating (Pinel, Assanand, & Lehman, 2000).

Sociocultural Influences That Regulate Hunger

Hunger, especially in humans, is regulated by external as well as internal factors. Food can act as an incentive to make you feel hungry. The taste, smell, sight, sound, and texture of food can pull you toward it. But how can the mere sight of food induce feelings of hunger? One way is by increasing the level of insulin in your blood. In fact, even daydreaming about food can stimulate your pancreas to release insulin, making you hungry and possibly sending you on a hunt for cake, candy, or ice cream (Rodin, 1985).

Obesity

obesity An unhealthy condition in men who have more than 25 percent body fat and women who have more than 30 percent body fat.

Obesity is a medical condition characterized by an excessive accumulation of body fat. It is defined by the ratio of lean body mass to fat (the body mass index [BMI]; see Figure 11-3). Men with more than 25 percent body fat and women with more than 30 percent body fat are considered to be obese. More than 60 percent of American adults are overweight, and more than one-third are clinically obese. Obesity is associated with health risks—notably, stroke, diabetes, heart disease, and some cancers (Ogden, Carroll, Kit, & Flegal, 2012)—and costs Americans approximately $147 billion a year in medical expenses (Finkelstein, Trogdon, Cohen, & Dietz, 2009).

In recent decades, obesity has been increasing among American adults, regardless of socioeconomic status (Ljungvall & Zimmerman, 2012). Obesity also has been increasing in other countries, particularly industrialized countries, though less than in the United States. Common sense and scientific opinion attribute the worldwide increase in obesity to higher calorie diets, larger portion sizes, and a decline in physical activity, but research evidence indicates that these are not the sole factors (Taubes, 1998). Obesity appears to depend on the interaction of several biopsychological and behavioral factors.

Biopsychological Factors in Obesity

Research studies are providing more and more evidence that obesity is prompted by several biopsychological factors. They include heredity and genetics, the body's set point, and basal metabolic rate.

Heredity and Obesity Thinness runs in families; research findings support a genetic basis for food and physical activity preferences (Wardle, Guthrie, Sanderson, Birch, & Plomin, 2001). Heredity influences our caloric intake (Faith, Rha, Neale, & Allison, 1999) and our degree of preference for fatty foods and sweet-tasting carbohydrates, all of which promote

FIGURE 11-3

Calculating Your Body Mass Index

One way of estimating the ratio of lean body mass to fat is by calculating the body mass index (BMI). BMI scores are positively correlated with body fat percentages. However, two people may have the same BMI and have different percentages of body fat. For example, a bodybuilder would have a lower percentage of body fat than a sedentary person with the same BMI. The correlation between BMI scores and body fat percentage also varies by age and sex. Thus, your BMI score is an estimation of your lean body mass to fat ratio and should be taken into consideration with other factors, such as your level of physical activity.

$$\text{BMI} = \frac{\text{Weight in pounds}}{(\text{Height in inches}) \times (\text{Height in inches})} \times 703$$

obesity (Reed, Bachmanov, Beauchamp, & Tordof, 1997). Twin, adoption, and family studies show that a person's obesity risk increases when he or she has obese relatives. The heritability of obesity is about 86 percent (Bulik, Sullivan, & Kendler, 2003). The role of heredity in obesity has been supported by studies of identical twins. Identical twins who have been reared together show a correlation of .75 in their amount of body fat. Even when identical twins have been reared apart, they show only a slightly lower correlation in their amount of body fat (Price & Gottesman, 1991). Evidence that heredity helps determine body weight also was provided by archival research on Danish adoption records. The results (see Figure 11-4) revealed a strong positive correlation between the weights of adoptees and the weights of their biological parents, but little relationship between the weights of adoptees and those of their adoptive parents. Heredity plays a more important role in obesity than do habits learned from the family in which one is reared (Stunkard, Stinnett, & Smoller, 1986).

Recent genetic studies in both humans and animals have linked the hormone *melanocortin* to body weight (see Table 11-1). People with melanocortin mutations are unable to feel full (a lack of satiety) and have severe early-onset obesity (Fani, Bak, Delhanty, van Rossum, & van den Akker, 2013). Mice that have mutated such that they lack melanocortin receptors become obese despite being born at normal weights. As they advance in age, they become extremely obese on a diet of regular rodent chow, though there are negligible differences in food intake between mutant and control mice. These mutant mice have increased fat tissue and leptin levels (Asai et al., 2013). It can be concluded that the gene for melanocortin contributes to body weight regulation in humans and animals; however, most cases of obesity are related to the combination of genes and the environment.

Set Point and Obesity An important factor in obesity is the body's set point, which reflects the amount of fat stored in the body. Though fat cells can increase in number and can increase or decrease in size, they cannot decrease in number. Once you have fat cells, they are yours forever. Obese people can lose weight only by shrinking the size of their fat cells. Because this effort induces constant hunger, it is difficult to maintain weight loss for an extended period of time (Kolata, 1985).

The set point seems to be affected by early nutrition, as shown by the results of an archival study of 300,000 men who years earlier had been exposed to a famine in Holland during World War II. Men who had been exposed to the famine during a critical period of development, which encompassed the third trimester of pregnancy and the first month after birth, were

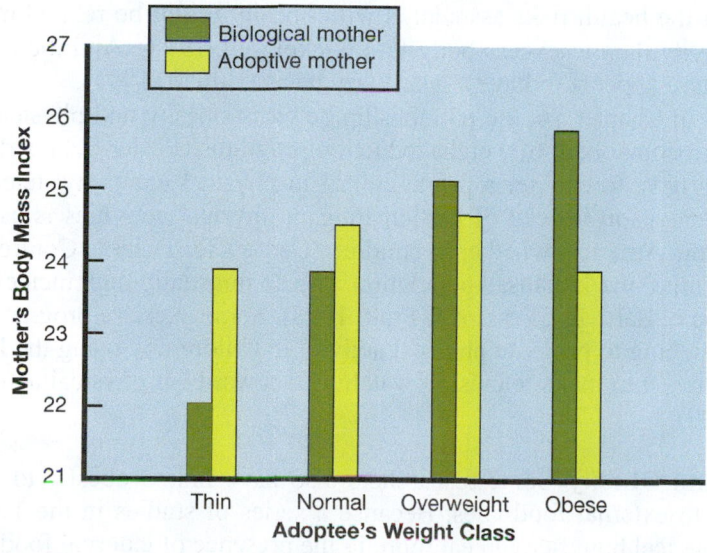

FIGURE 11-4
Heredity and Obesity

Data from Danish adoption records indicate a positive relationship between the weight of adopted children and that of their biological parents, but no relationship between the weight of adopted children and that of their adoptive parents. The graph illustrates the relationship between adoptees and their biological and adoptive mothers. The relationship also holds true for adoptees and their biological and adoptive fathers.

Source: Data from A. J. Stunkard et al., *New England Journal of Medicine,* 314: 193–198, Massachusetts Medical Society, 1986.

less likely to become obese than were men who had been exposed to the famine at other times during their early development (Ravelli, Stein, & Susser, 1976). The men exposed to the famine during the critical period might have developed lower set points than the other men. Even the results of the study of weight in Danish adoptees (Stunkard, Stinnett, & Smoller, 1986) might be explained by prenatal nutrition rather than by heredity. Perhaps adopted offspring are more similar in body weight to their biological mothers not because they share genes but because they spent their prenatal period in their mothers' wombs, where they were subjected to environmental influences such as nutrients provided by their mothers. These prenatal influences might affect their later body weight (Bonds & Crosby, 1986).

basal metabolic rate The rate at which the body burns calories just to keep itself alive.

Basal Metabolic Rate and Obesity Another important factor in obesity is the **basal metabolic rate,** the rate at which the body burns calories just to keep itself alive. The basal metabolic rate typically accounts for 65 to 75 percent of the calories that your body ingests (Shah & Jeffery, 1991). Ever wonder why one of your friends can habitually ingest a milkshake, two hamburgers, and a large order of french fries yet remain thin, whereas another gains weight by habitually ingesting a diet cola, a hamburger without a bun, and a few french fries? Your first friend might have a basal metabolic rate high enough to burn a large number of calories; your second friend might have a basal metabolic rate too low to burn even a modest number of calories, which forces the body to store much of the ingested food as fat. One way that aerobic exercise promotes weight loss is by elevating the basal metabolic rate (Davis, Sargent, Brayboy, & Bartoli, 1992).

Behavioral Factors in Obesity

The chief behavioral factors in promoting obesity are having easy access to food, eating large portions, eating foods high in fat, and failing to engage in regular physical activity (Hill & Peters, 1998). Scientists interested in the role of behavioral factors in obesity are particularly interested in studying the effects of physical inactivity, responsiveness to external food cues, and stress-related eating patterns.

Inactivity and Obesity Though Americans are modifying their eating habits, obesity continues to rise. One possible cause is physical inactivity (Sallis, Carlson, Mignano, Lemes, & Wagner, 2013). Sedentary children are more likely to become obese. Moreover, girls are less physically active than boys throughout childhood, thus increasing their risk of obesity (Prentice-Dunn & Prentice-Dunn, 2012). But the commonsense assumption that lack of exercise causes obesity is not necessarily correct. People who are obese might, as a result of being obese, engage in less physical activity. Moreover, some studies have found that the health risks associated with obesity might be related more to a lack of physical activity than to excess body fat (Wickelgren, 1998). And the tendency to be physically inactive appears to have a hereditary basis (Hewitt, 1997).

As discussed in Chapter 16, the relationship between obesity and physical inactivity is why exercise is a component of weight-reduction programs (Foster-Schubert et al., 2012). These programs have to counter a prime culprit in physical inactivity: television watching. Watching television instead of participating in physical activities is associated with obesity throughout America, whether in children (Centers for Disease Control and Prevention, 2011) or adult Pima Indians, a population with an unusually high incidence of obesity (Andersen, Crespo, Bartlett, Cheskin, & Pratt, 1998). Some exercise programs use the lure of television watching to promote physical activity in children by using the Premack principle (see Chapter 7) to make television watching a reward for physical activity (Jason & Brackshaw, 1999).

Eating Cues and Obesity Some researchers also have linked obesity to differences in responsiveness to external food cues. Because a series of studies in the 1960s indicated that obese people feel hungrier and eat more in the presence of external food cues, Stanley Schachter (1971) concluded that obese people are more responsive to those cues. Subsequent studies have provided some support for this belief. One study found that overweight children were more likely to overeat after being exposed to the enticing smell of tasty food or eating one bite of an appetizing snack. In fact, compared to lean children, overweight children salivated more in response to the smell and taste of food (Aspen, Stein, & Wilfley, 2012). Though studies like these support the belief that obese people are more responsive to food cues, the "externality" of obese people does not seem to cause their obesity. Instead, their obesity might cause their externality. How? Many obese people are constantly dieting, so they might be in a chronic state of hunger (Lowe, Foster, Kerzhnerman, Swain, & Wadden, 2001). Moreover, obesity researcher Judith Rodin (1981) has found that obese people may have chronically high levels of insulin, making them hungrier and, as a result, more responsive to food cues. This responsiveness gives the false impression that obese people become obese because they are more external than nonobese people.

In addition, an important environmental factor in eating involves the kinds of foods we eat when we are hungry. We tend to like foods more when we are hungry than when we are not, but this effect is stronger for fatty foods (Lozano, Crites, & Aikman, 1999). Perhaps people who are prone to obesity, being chronically hungry, are more motivated to eat fatty foods.

Stress and Obesity Another external factor—stress—can induce hunger and overeating (Sinha & Jastreboff, 2013). Stressful situations can induce negative emotions, such as anger, boredom, depression, and loneliness, and obese people are more likely than nonobese people to overeat when under stress (Laitinen, Ek, & Sovio, 2002). But how does stress induce overeating? One possibility is that stress stimulates the brain to secrete endorphins. As discussed in Chapters 3 and 5, endorphins are neurotransmitters that relieve pain. They also stimulate eating. One study found that endorphin levels were higher in obese women than in lean women (Perfetto, Piluso, Cagnacci, & Tarquini, 2002). Because endorphin levels increase when we are under stress, endorphins might contribute to stress-related overeating (Morley & Levine, 1980). Perhaps obese people eat more under stress than nonobese people do because stress induces greater increases in their endorphin levels. Stress also activates the *hypothalamic-pituitary-adrenal (HPA) axis*. The hormones of the HPA axis play an important role in regulating food intake, and dysregulation of the HPA axis may lead to the development of overeating.

Yet, stress does not always provoke overeating. A study of 95 adults who recorded their stress level and eating behavior for 12 weeks found a negative correlation between the two: As stress increased, eating decreased. This tendency was more pronounced in women than in men (Stone & Brownell, 1994). Thus, more research is needed to identify the conditions under which stress provokes overeating and the conditions under which it inhibits it.

Eating Disorders

Are you pleased with your physical appearance? As revealed by the study in the "Research Process" box, your answer might depend in part on whether you are a woman or man. Your satisfaction with your body also might influence the likelihood that you will develop an eating disorder. The ideal that women should be thin has permeated the Western media (Thompson & Heinberg, 1999). A recent study of the body measurements of female *Playboy* centerfolds found that the size of centerfold models has continued to decrease since the 1980s (Owen & Laurel-Seller, 2000). And another study compared the muscularity of male *Playgirl* centerfolds from 1973 to 1997. Whereas female centerfolds are becoming thinner, male centerfolds are becoming more muscular (Leit, Pope, & Gray, 2001).

Recent research indicates that the internalization of an ideal body type is a risk factor for distorted body image and eating disorders (Thompson & Stice, 2001). In one study, for example, children aged 6 through 12 were shown pictures of thin women in sexualized poses and muscular men with bare torsos. Girls and boys responded positively to the images of their own gender, but the effect was more pronounced for the girls (Murnen, Smolak, Mills, & Good, 2003). And among women and men, reading beauty or body-building magazines, respectively, is related to concerns about physical appearance, internalization of body ideals, and eating (Morry & Staska, 2001). Thus, internalization of unrealistic media images may be a powerful sociocultural influence on body satisfaction and the development of eating disorders.

How Satisfied Are Men and Women with Their Bodies?

Rationale

Some researchers believe that eating disorders, which are more common in women, can be promoted by distorted body images. This hypothesis inspired researchers April Fallon and Paul Rozin (1985) to examine the issue empirically.

Method

College students were presented with a set of nine drawings of body figures that ranged from very thin to very heavy. The participants were asked to indicate which figures were closest to their current physique, their ideal physique, and the physique they felt was most attractive to the other sex.

Results and Discussion

As shown in Figure 11-5, for men the current, the ideal, and the most attractive physiques were almost identical. For women, the current physique was heavier than

the most attractive, and the most attractive was heavier than the ideal. The women also thought men liked women thinner than the men actually reported. Moreover, women tended to be less satisfied with their own physiques than men were with their own physiques.

A study that replicated the essence of these findings found that adolescent girls preferred to be thinner than the average for their age and were more dissatisfied with their own bodies than adolescent boys were. Moreover, underweight adolescent boys were more dissatisfied with their own bodies than boys of average weight (Mäkinen, Puukko-Viertomies, Lindberg, Siimes, & Aalberg, 2012).

Perhaps this dissatisfaction contributes to women's greater tendency to develop eating disorders marked by excessive concern with weight control. In fact, people who disparage their own bodies for being fat, whether or not it is objectively true that they are fat, are more likely to develop eating disorders (Hsu & Sobkiewicz, 1991).

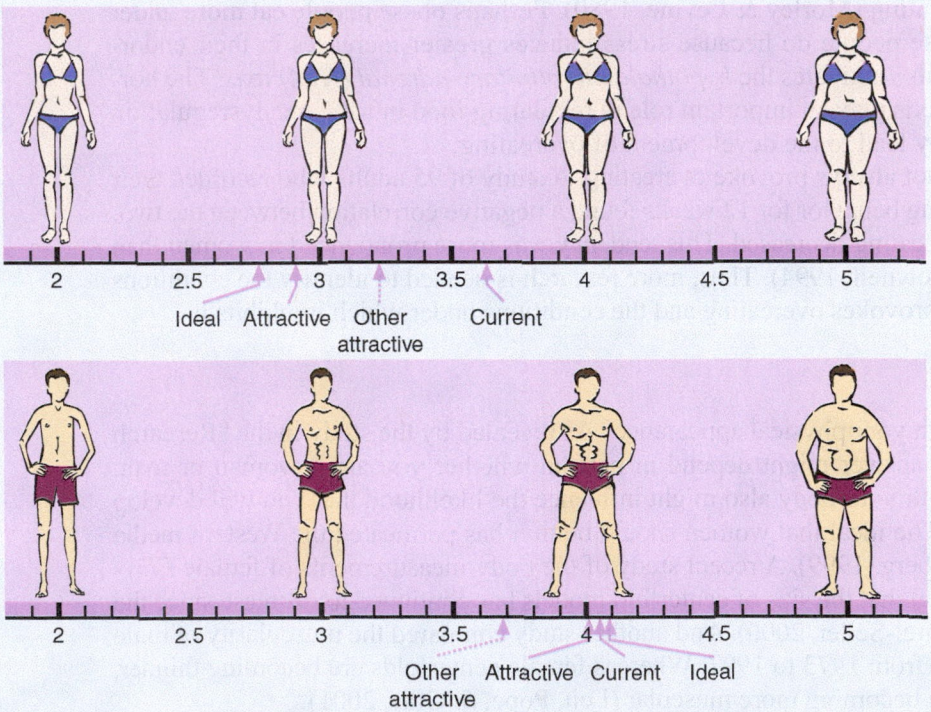

FIGURE 11-5 Gender Differences in Body Images

Fallon and Rozin (1985) found that for men (lower illustration), their self-perceived physique ("Current"), the physique that they believed was ideal ("Ideal"), and the physique that they believed was most attractive to women ("Attractive") were almost identical. The physique that they believed women preferred ("Attractive") was heavier than the one that women actually preferred ("Other attractive"). In contrast, for women (upper illustration), their self-perceived physique ("Current") was heavier than the physique that they believed was ideal ("Ideal") and the physique that they believed was most attractive to men ("Attractive"). Moreover, the physique that they believed men preferred ("Attractive") was thinner than the one that men actually preferred ("Other attractive").

Source: Fallon, A. E., & Rozin, P. (1985). Sex differences in perceptions of desirable body shape. *Journal of Abnormal Psychology, 94,* 102–105.

As Western culture exerts greater influence over other cultures, eating disorders among women have increased in those cultures—perhaps because they too have adopted Western ideals. For example, researchers studied eating attitudes and behaviors in Fijian adolescents. Participants' eating behaviors and attitudes were assessed before the introduction of television to the region, one month later, and three years later. Rates of binge eating and self-induced vomiting were significantly higher at the three-year follow-up. Moreover, participants reported a greater interest in losing weight in an attempt to look more like the television actors (Becker, Burwell, Herzog, Hamburg, & Gilman 2002). Acculturation also has been found to be related to body dissatisfaction among Guatemalan American female college students and Chinese women and girls living in the United States (Davis & Katzman, 1999; Franko & Herrera, 1997).

A review of research conducted during the second half of the 20th century found that gender differences in body image had increased, with women showing progressively more negative body images over that time period (Feingold & Mazzella, 1998). Though eating disorders are more prevalent among girls and women (Hoek & van Hoeken, 2003), the rate of male admissions to inpatient facilities for treatment of eating disorders between 1984 and 1997 increased (Braun, Sunday, Huang, & Halmi, 1999). Gender interacts with other sociocultural variables such that some groups are more at risk than others. For example, African American women are slightly less likely to develop eating disorders than European American women are (O'Neill, 2003). Research studies have found that African American women are more satisfied with their bodies than European American women (Walsh & Devlin, 1998) and are less likely to disparage large women, especially large African American women (Hebl & Heatherton, 1998).

Sexual orientation also influences the incidence of dissatisfaction with one's body and of eating disorders. Lesbians report greater satisfaction with their bodies, less frequent dieting, and fewer eating disorders than do heterosexual women (Lakkis, Ricciardelli, & Williams, 1999). The results of recent research suggest that lesbians are less likely than heterosexual women to have internalized cultural norms for thinness (Bergeron & Senn, 1998). In contrast, gay men express more dissatisfaction with their bodies and are more likely to engage in disordered eating than are heterosexual men (Lakkis, Ricciardelli, & Williams, 1999). The comparatively high rate of eating disorders among both gay men and heterosexual women may be due to a shared desire to attract men. One study found that heterosexual and gay men place a higher priority on physical appearance when judging a potential romantic partner than do heterosexual or lesbian women (Siever, 1994).

Though eating disorders are associated with sociocultural differences, they are influenced by many other factors. One factor is heredity. Though the heritability of many eating disorders has yet to be firmly established (Fairburn, Cowen, & Harrison, 1999), twin studies provide evidence that some people have a genetic predisposition to develop an eating disorder (Klump, McGue, & Iacono, 2002). Stressful life experiences also are important. Women who are under high psychological stress are more prone to eating disorders than are women who are under low psychological stress (Ball & Lee, 2000). Even personality factors are important. One study found that male and female university students who scored high on a measure of perfectionism were especially prone to eating disorders (Boone, Soenens, Vansteenkiste, & Braet, 2012).

Anorexia Nervosa

In 1983 the popular singer Karen Carpenter died of heart failure caused by starvation—despite having access to all the food she could want. She suffered from **anorexia nervosa**, a sometimes fatal disorder in which the victim is so desperate to lose weight that he or she goes on a starvation diet and becomes emaciated. People with anorexia nervosa view themselves as fat, even when they are objectively thin (as was Carpenter), and they are preoccupied with food—talking about it, cooking it, and urging others to eat it. Anorexia nervosa has a prevalence rate of 0.3 percent and is more common in young women (Hoek & Van Hoeken, 2003). Anorexia typically develops during late childhood and adolescence. Some women and men who participate in sports or activities that stress weight control (such as dancing, modeling, or wrestling) are more prone to develop eating disorders (Pierce &

anorexia nervosa An eating disorder marked by self-starvation.

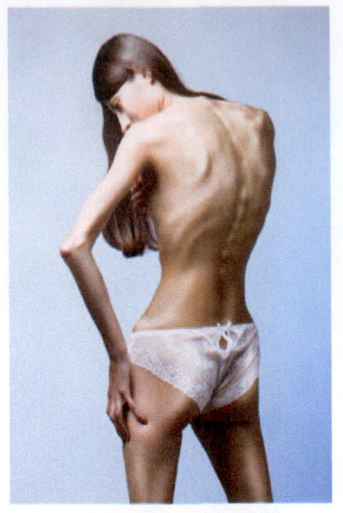

Anorexia Nervosa

People with anorexia nervosa see themselves as fat, though they are actually thin.
Source: PutilichD/Shutterstock.com.

Daleng, 1998). Moreover, a recent meta-analysis of the relationship of athletic participation to eating disorders among women concluded that elite athletes were most at risk. Among nonelite and high school athletes, however, sport served as a protective factor that reduced the risk of eating disorders among women (Smolak, Murnen, & Ruble, 2000).

Possible Causes of Anorexia Nervosa Possible causes of anorexia nervosa include heredity (Klump, Miller, Keel, McGue, & Iacono, 2001), excessive secretion of cholecystokinin (Cuntz et al, 2013), an emotionally enmeshed and critical family (Polivy & Herman, 2002), an excessive desire for self-control of eating (Fairburn, Shafran, & Cooper, 1999), obsessiveness and dependency (Rogers & Petrie, 2001), and a reaction to the tendency to accumulate unwanted body fat during puberty (Attie & Brooks-Gunn, 1989). Certain genes such as those that encode for leptin and melanocortin have been implicated in the development of anorexia nervosa. However, a recent meta-analysis indicated that genes did not play a significant role in its development (Hinney and Volckmar, 2013). Thus, researchers still have to discover a clear mechanism for this disorder.

Treatment of Anorexia Nervosa Because many people with anorexia nervosa are unwilling to seek treatment, their families often have to force them to receive it (Russell, 2001). Treatment of severe anorexia nervosa commonly begins with the provision of high-calorie nourishment (Agostino, Erdstein, & Di Meglio, 2013), often through intravenous feeding or feeding through a nasogastric tube. Therapists then typically use cognitive-behavioral therapy to promote more adaptive ways of eating, thinking about food, and perceiving one's body (Hay, Touyz, & Sud, 2012). Given that anorexia nervosa is associated with maladaptive family relationships, family therapy sometimes is included as a component of its treatment (Levitt, 2001).

Bulimia Nervosa

bulimia nervosa An eating disorder marked by binging and purging.

Persons with the related, more common, disorder called **bulimia nervosa** go on repeated eating binges in which they ingest thousands of calories at a time—they might eat a half gallon of ice cream, a two-pound box of chocolates, and other high-carbohydrate foods—but they maintain normal weight by then ridding themselves of the food by self-induced vomiting. People with bulimia nervosa tend to evaluate themselves in terms of their body weight and shape and to think obsessively about food. They also tend to have poor impulse control, binging in response to the presence of tempting food, and then purging to compensate for the binge (Polivy & Herman, 2002). The prevalence rates for bulimia nervosa are 1 percent of young women and 0.7 percent of young men (Hoek & Van Hoeken, 2003). Whereas the prevalence of anorexia is consistent across cultures, there are considerable cross-cultural differences in the prevalence of bulimia nervosa. Compared to anorexia nervosa, bulimia nervosa may be more influenced by sociocultural factors (Keel & Klump, 2003).

Possible Causes of Bulimia Nervosa There is some evidence that people with bulimia nervosa have a genetic predisposition to develop the disorder (Rowe, Pickles, Simonoff, Bulik, & Silberg, 2002). Another possible cause of bulimia nervosa is a low level of the neurotransmitter serotonin, which is associated with depression (Pichika et al., 2012). People with bulimia nervosa often try to elevate their moods or cope with stress by eating. Eating then leads to shame and guilt, which then is relieved by purging. The person becomes trapped in a vicious binge-and-purge cycle (Alpers & Tuschen-Caffier, 2001). This hypothesis is supported by research showing that antidepressant drugs that increase serotonin levels are useful in treating bulimia nervosa (Zhu & Walsh, 2002). In one study, women with bulimia nervosa were given fluoxetine (Prozac), an antidepressant that inhibits the reuptake of serotonin by the neurons that secrete it. While on the drug, participants snacked less frequently and ate less at each meal. Moreover, the drug inhibited binge eating (Wilcox, 1990).

Factors other than brain chemistry also play a role in bulimia nervosa. People who pursue activities that emphasize weight control are more likely to develop the disorder. For example, men with bulimia nervosa are often dancers, jockeys, or collegiate wrestlers (Striegel-Moore, Silberstein, & Rodin, 1986). People with bulimia nervosa tend to be perfectionistic (Boone et al., 2012), to have suffered a recent family disruption (Welch, Doll, & Fairburn, 1997), and to come from families who are critical, intrusive, and coercive (Polivy & Herman, 2002). And people with bulimia tend to respond to unhappy or stressful interpersonal experiences with self-criticism and negative moods (Steiger, Gauvin, Jabalpurwala, Séguin, & Stotland, 1999).

Treatment of Bulimia Nervosa The most common psychological treatment for bulimia nervosa is cognitive-behavioral therapy. This approach aims at changing irrational thinking about eating and body weight and altering maladaptive behaviors, particularly bingeing and purging. Research reviews consistently have found that cognitive-behavioral therapy is effective in treating bulimia nervosa (Wilson, Fairburn, Agras, Walsh, & Kraemer, 2002).

A medical approach to the treatment of bulimia nervosa is the use of antidepressants, an approach based on the finding that bulimia nervosa is commonly associated with lower levels of serotonin (Freeman, 1998). Drugs such as Prozac that increase levels of serotonin have achieved some success in treating bulimia (Narash-Eisikovits, Dierberger, & Westen, 2002). But cognitive-behavioral therapy is superior to drug therapy in treating the disorder (Whittal, Agras, & Gould, 1999). What about treatments that combine drug therapy and cognitive-behavioral therapy? Research findings are inconsistent about whether the combination is (Agras, 1997) or is not (Goldbloom et al., 1997) more effective than cognitive-behavioral therapy alone.

Section Review: The Hunger Motive

1. What is the role of the hypothalamus in eating?

2. What evidence is there for a hereditary basis of obesity?

3. What are some possible explanations for the greater incidence of eating disorders among heterosexual women and gay men?

The Sex Motive

Though some individuals, such as religious celibates, can live long lives without engaging in sexual intercourse, the survival of the species requires that many individuals engage in it. Had sexual intercourse not evolved into an extremely pleasurable behavior, we would have no inclination to seek it. But what factors account for the power of the sex motive?

Biopsychological Factors in Sexual Behavior

Sexual behavior is influenced by biopsychological factors. Many sex researchers study the physiological factors that affect human and animal sexual behavior. Some of these researchers focus on the physiology of the human sexual response cycle.

Physiological Factors and Sex

Important physiological factors in sexual motivation are sex hormones secreted by the **gonads**, the sex glands. The secretion of sex hormones is controlled by hormones secreted by the pituitary gland, which in turn is controlled by the hypothalamus. Sex hormones direct sexual development as well as sexual behavior (see Chapter 4). Though hormones exert a direct effect on human sexual development, they are less influential motivators of sexual behavior in humans than they are in animals. Research indicates

gonads The male and female sex glands.

that testosterone motivates both male and female sexual behavior (Apperloo et al., 2003), though women secrete less of it than men do.

The Sexual Response Cycle

Many Americans were shocked in the 1960s by reports of research conducted by William Masters and Virginia Johnson. Masters and Johnson were not content with just asking people about their sexual motivation and behavior. Instead, they studied ongoing sexual behavior and recorded physiological changes that accompanied it in hundreds of men and women. To study the human sexual response, they even invented devices that measured physiological changes in the penis and vagina during sexual arousal.

Based on their study of more than 10,000 orgasms experienced by more than 300 men and 300 women, Masters and Johnson (1966) identified four phases in the **sexual response cycle**: excitement, plateau, orgasm, and resolution (see Figure 11-6). During the *excitement phase,* mental or physical stimulation causes sexual arousal. In men the penis becomes erect as it becomes engorged with blood. In women the nipples become erect, the vagina becomes lubricated, and the clitoris protrudes as it too becomes engorged with blood in response to both direct stimulation and vaginal stimulation (Lavoisier, Aloui, Schmidt, & Watrelot, 1995).

During the *plateau phase*, heart rate, blood pressure, muscle tension, and breathing rate increase. In men the erection becomes firmer, and the testes are drawn closer to the body to prepare for ejaculation. Drops of semen, possibly containing sperm (and capable of causing pregnancy), may appear at the tip of the penis. In women the body flushes, lubrication increases, the clitoris retracts, and the breasts swell around the nipples (making the nipples seem to shrink).

The excitement and plateau phases compose the period of sexual foreplay. Men and women differ in the importance they assign to foreplay. A survey of young adults found that women chose foreplay as more important than either intercourse or afterplay, whereas men chose intercourse as most important. Women also preferred to spend more time on foreplay and afterplay than did men. Women reported more than men did that they enjoyed the verbal and physical affection of sexual behavior (Denney, Field, & Quadagno, 1984).

During the *orgasm phase,* heart rate and breathing rate reach their peak, men ejaculate semen (a fluid containing sperm), and both men and women experience intensely pleasurable sensations induced by rhythmic muscle contractions. There is evidence that the pleasure of orgasm might be caused by the release of *prolactin*, a hormone that targets the mammary glands, in men and women (Krueger, Haake, Hartmann, Schedlowski, & Exton, 2002). The subjective experience of orgasm also is similar for women and men. One study asked undergraduate

sexual response cycle During sexual activity, the phases of excitement, plateau, orgasm, and resolution.

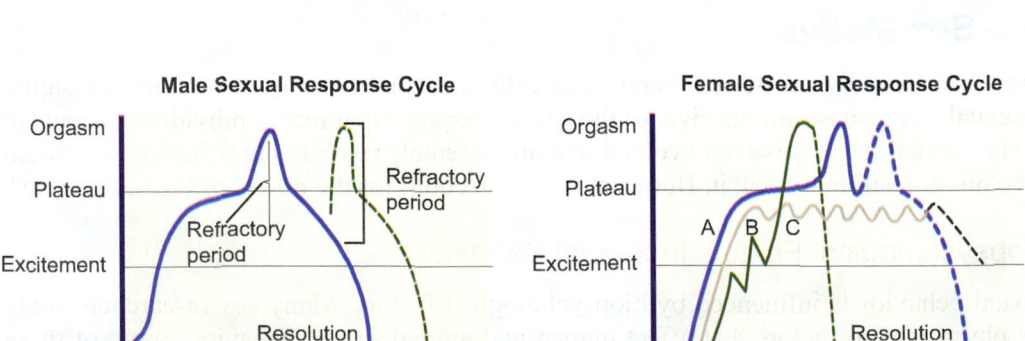

FIGURE 11-6
The Human Sexual Response Cycle

Masters and Johnson found that men and women have sexual response cycles comprising four phases: excitement, plateau, orgasm, and resolution. After reaching orgasm, men cannot achieve another orgasm until they have passed through a refractory period. In contrast, pattern A shows that women might experience more than one orgasm during a single cycle. Pattern B shows a cycle during which a woman has reached the plateau stage without proceeding to orgasm. Pattern C shows a cycle during which a woman has reached orgasm quickly. Men, too, may experience pattern B and pattern C.

participants to describe their most recent orgasmic experience on two occasions: during masturbation and during sex with a partner. Male and female participants' ratings of the physical sensations of their orgasmic experiences in both settings did not differ. But women and men rated their orgasms experienced with a partner as more pleasurable, ecstatic, and emotionally intimate than their orgasms experienced when alone. Whereas the physical experience of orgasm is unaffected by the circumstances in which it occurs, women and men find orgasms experienced with a partner as more emotionally and sexually satisfying (Mah & Binik, 2002).

Following the orgasm phase, the person enters the *resolution phase,* as blood leaves the genitals and sexual arousal lessens. This phase is associated with a *refractory period,* lasting from minutes to hours, during which the man cannot achieve orgasm. For many women, however, continued sexual stimulation can induce multiple orgasms. A survey of 720 women found that 43 percent had experienced multiple orgasms (Darling, Davidson, & Jennings, 1991).

Masters and Johnson's research has made a remarkable contribution to our understanding of human sexuality. However, it is not without controversy. Critics have pointed to the selective nature of their sample—primarily sexually experienced married men and women who were willing to engage in sexual activity in the laboratory. Perhaps more important, they failed to study individuals who had difficulty in experiencing orgasm and failed to consider individual differences in sexual responses and sexual desire (Tiefer, 1995). But their research has provided an important basis for the scientific study of the physiology of human sexuality.

Psychosocial Factors in Sexual Behavior

Though human sexuality is affected by biopsychological factors, it is strongly influenced by psychosocial factors as well. Researchers who study psychosocial factors in sexuality are particularly interested in the role of culture in sexual behavior. We know much about sexual behavior in American culture from surveys that have been carried out since the mid-20th century.

Culture and Sexual Behavior

Sex hormones are the main motivators of animal sexual behavior, but human sexual behavior depends more on sociocultural factors. Because in most animals sexual motivation is rigidly controlled by hormones, members of a given species vary little in their sexual behaviors. In contrast, because human sexual motivation is influenced more by sociocultural factors, we vary greatly in our sexual behavior. For example, breast caressing is a prelude to sexual intercourse among the Marquesan islanders of the Pacific but not among the Sirionian Indians of Bolivia (Klein, 1982).

In Western cultures, acceptable sexual behavior has varied over time. The ancient Greeks viewed bisexuality as normal and masturbation as a desirable way for youth to relieve their sexual tensions. In contrast, most Americans and Europeans of the Victorian era in the 19th century believed that all sexual activity should be avoided except when aimed at procreation. The Victorian emphasis on sexual denial led John Harvey Kellogg to invent what he claimed was a nutritional "cure" for masturbation—cornflakes (Money, 1986).

The liberalization of attitudes toward sexual behavior in Western industrialized countries during the 20th century was shown in 1983 when the *Journal of the American Medical Association* published an article on human sexuality. This event would not be noteworthy except that the article had been submitted for publication in 1899, near the end of the Victorian era. The article, based on a paper presented by gynecologist Denslow Lewis (1899/1983) at the annual meeting of the American Medical Association, concerned female sexuality. Lewis described the female sexual response, the need for sex education, the importance of sex for marital compatibility, and techniques for overcoming sexual problems. Lewis even made the radical (for his time) suggestion that wives be encouraged to enjoy sex as much as their husbands did. At the time, the editor of the journal refused to publish the paper, which a prominent physician called "filth" and another editor feared would bring charges of sending obscene material through the mail (Hollender, 1983).

Human Sexual Behavior

Human sexual behavior is guided by sex hormones, but even more important are sociocultural factors.
Source: Nina Vaclavova/ Shutterstock.com.

Surveys of Human Sexual Behavior

Denslow Lewis's critics would have been even more upset by research in human sexuality that has taken place in the past few decades, particularly the research studies of Masters and Johnson and Alfred Kinsey. Shortly after World War II, Kinsey (1894–1956), a biologist at Indiana University, found that he was unable to answer his students' questions about human sexual behavior because of a lack of relevant information. This dearth inspired him to conduct surveys to gather information on the sexual behavior of men (Kinsey, Pomeroy, & Martin, 1948) and women (Kinsey, Pomeroy, Martin, & Gebhard, 1953).

Kinsey's Findings Kinsey obtained his data from interviews with thousands of men and women and published his findings in two best-selling books. Kinsey's books (which contained statistics but no pictures) shocked the public because Kinsey reported that masturbation, oral sex, premarital sex, extramarital sex, homosexuality, and other sexual behaviors were more prevalent than commonly believed. Many Americans considered Kinsey's reports to be attacks on the moral order. J. Edgar Hoover, the FBI director, ordered that a dossier be compiled on Kinsey to determine whether he was a threat to the United States (Jones, 1997).

Among Kinsey's many findings were that most of the men and almost half of the women engaged in premarital sexual intercourse, and most of the women and almost all of the men masturbated. The public was particularly startled to learn that about one-third of men had engaged in at least one sexual act with another man to orgasm and that about 10 percent had more than casual homosexual relations. Kinsey concluded that most people were neither homosexual nor heterosexual but instead fit along a continuum that he developed (the *Kinsey Scale*) from exclusively heterosexual (0) to exclusively homosexual (6). Kinsey's survey of women was noteworthy because it challenged the widely held belief that women were uninterested in sex (Bullough, 1998).

Sex Surveys Since Kinsey Scientists warned that care should be taken in generalizing Kinsey's findings to all Americans because his sample was not representative of the American population; the sample included primarily European American, well-educated easterners and midwesterners who were willing to be interviewed about their sexual behavior. Moreover, what is true of people in one generation might not be true of those in another. For example, from the 1950s to the 1980s, premarital sexual activity in the United States increased. In the 1980s, however, premarital sexual activity with multiple partners tapered off because of increased fears about incurable sexually transmitted diseases, including AIDS, which is fatal, and genital herpes, which is painful and can harm romantic relationships (Gerrard, 1987). The transmission and prevention of AIDS are discussed in Chapter 16.

Changes in sexual behavior since Kinsey's day indicate that sexual norms do indeed depend on the time period during which they are studied. However, some gender differences in human sexual behavior appear to be unchanged despite considerable sociocultural change. Peterson and Janet Shibley Hyde (2010) conducted a meta-analysis of 730 research studies of 1,419,807 male and female participants from 87 countries on six continents published between 1993 and 2007. Of the 30 effect sizes computed, no large gender differences emerged. Four gender differences that were moderate in size were found: Men were somewhat more likely to use pornography, masturbate, have more positive attitudes toward casual sex, and engage in more casual sex than were women. To consider the size of these differences, you might want to contrast the effect sizes with those for the gender differences in cognitive abilities and social behavior reported in Chapter 4. Moreover, these effect sizes held steady regardless of the year of publication. The remaining gender differences were small to negligible. For example, men report more permissive attitudes toward extramarital sex and tend to have more permissive attitudes about sex overall. Moreover, men report having had more sex partners than do women, but these effect sizes are small. Gender similarities were the rule for a number of variables, such as sexual satisfaction, attitudes about masturbation, and incidence of some sexual behaviors other than sexual intercourse.

Sexual Dysfunctions

After Masters and Johnson had identified the phases of the human sexual response cycle, they became interested in studying **sexual dysfunctions**, which are chronic problems at phases in the sexual response cycle. Sexual dysfunctions are common among both sexes, with estimates ranging from 10 percent to 52 percent of men and 25 percent to 63 percent of women in the United States (Laumann, Paik, & Rosen, 1999). Sexual dysfunctions are associated with discord and conflict among partners (Metz & Epstein, 2002).

sexual dysfunction A chronic problem at a particular phase of the sexual response cycle.

Kinds of Sexual Dysfunctions

The most common male sexual dysfunctions include *erectile dysfunction* and *premature ejaculation*. About 5 percent to 10 percent of men suffer from an erectile dysfunction—failing either to attain an erection or to maintain it through the arousal phase (Spector & Carey, 1990). Causes of erectile dysfunction include physical factors, such as diabetes, and psychological factors, such as depression (Seidman, 2003). About one-third of all men experience premature ejaculation (Spector & Carey, 1990). Premature ejaculation is caused by psychological factors, such as performance anxiety or relationship problems, or physical factors, such as nerve damage, prostate inflammation, or withdrawal from certain drugs, particularly narcotics (Carver, 1998).

Among women, the most common sexual dysfunctions include *orgasmic disorder, dyspareunia,* and *vaginismus*. A woman with orgasmic disorder, present in 5 percent to 10 percent of women, is unable to reach the orgasm phase. Women who experience orgasmic disorder tend to have greater sexual guilt, difficulty discussing sexual activities, and more negative attitudes toward masturbation (Kelly, Strassberg, & Kircher, 1990). Women who suffer from dyspareunia experience pain during or after sexual intercourse, and those with vaginismus experience involuntary muscle spasms around the opening of the vagina. Dyspareunia and vaginismus appear to be caused by a complex interplay of genital pain, fear of pain, and history of abusive or distressing sexual experiences (Pukall, Payne, Binik, & Khalif, 2003; Reissing, Binik, Khalife, Cohen, & Amsel, 2004).

Treating Sexual Dysfunctions

Based on their research findings, Masters and Johnson (1970) concluded that the psychological causes of sexual dysfunctions are usually sexual guilt, sexual ignorance, or anxiety about sexual performance. Masters and Johnson's sex therapy is based on counseling clients to help them overcome their sexual guilt; educating them about sexual anatomy, sexual motivation, and sexual behavior; and teaching them specific ways of reducing performance anxiety.

The main technique in Masters and Johnson's sex therapy is **sensate focusing**, in which the partners first participate in nongenital caressing and only later proceed to genital stimulation, and finally engage in sexual intercourse. The partners at first are urged to concentrate on their pleasurable feelings instead of striving for erections and orgasms. They also are instructed to tell each other what kinds of stimulation they enjoy and what kinds they do not enjoy.

sensate focusing A technique, pioneered by Masters and Johnson, in which partners are urged to concentrate on their pleasurable feelings instead of striving for erections and orgasms.

Therapists trained in Masters and Johnson's sex therapy also teach their clients other techniques. In treating premature ejaculation, they might have the man's partner repeatedly stimulate his penis just to the point before orgasm to teach him to gain control over its timing. They might have a woman with an orgasmic disorder practice masturbating to orgasm as a step toward reaching orgasm during sexual intercourse, a more difficult feat. Another technique to promote female orgasm during heterosexual intercourse is to teach the couple ways of aligning their bodies to maximize penile stimulation of the clitoris.

Masters and Johnson (1970) reported that more than two-thirds of their sex therapy clients showed improvement. But they were criticized for not operationally defining what they meant by "improvement" and for failing to conduct follow-up studies of their clients to determine whether the positive effects of therapy were long lasting. Masters and Johnson also have been criticized for stressing sexual intercourse as a physical act and for ignoring factors such as sexual desire, love, and cultural differences in sexuality (Tiefer, 1994).

Some sexual dysfunctions respond well to medical as well as psychological treatments. Perhaps the best known of these medical treatments is the drug *sildenafil*, better known by its trade name, Viagra. Viagra is being studied as a potential treatment for sexual dysfunctions associated with the use of antidepressants in both men and women (Salerian et al., 2000). However, critics argue that such treatment neglects the social, psychological, and emotional factors in relationships, especially among older adults (Barnett, Robleda-Gomez, & Pachana, 2012). Thus, because sexual dysfunctions can affect self-esteem and romantic relationships, orgasmic dysfunctions might require both psychological and drug treatments (Zajecka et al., 2002).

During the past few decades, Masters and Johnson joined with other sex researchers in studying two other major topics in sexuality. These topics are **gender identity** (one's self-perceived sex) and **sexual orientation** (one's pattern of erotic attraction—whether to persons of one's own sex or of the other sex or both).

gender identity One's self-perceived sex.

sexual orientation A person's pattern of erotic attraction to persons of the same sex, other sex, or both sexes.

Gender Identity

In 1966 a 7-month-old boy lost most of his penis in a surgical accident. After consultation with sex researcher John Money, the 17-month-old child underwent sex reassignment surgery that involved castration, the removal of the remaining penile tissue, and the construction of a vagina. His parents were instructed to change his name, hairstyle, and clothing, and to raise him as a girl. Because the child had an identical twin brother who had not undergone surgery, Money was able to compare the development of the two children. Initial reports suggested that the child adopted feminine interests and behaviors and thought of herself as a girl, whereas the twin brother continued to think of himself as a boy. Based on these observations, Money concluded that gender identity was more strongly influenced by socialization than by genetic or hormonal factors (Money & Ehrhardt, 1972).

As the child entered puberty, however, it became clear that the sex reassignment was a failure. The teenager rejected hormonal therapy and began living as a young man, eventually marrying a woman and becoming a father to her young children (Colapinto, 2001; Diamond & Sigmundson, 1997). More recent research suggests that the development of gender identity involves a complex interaction of sociocultural and biopsychological influences. A sample of 16 genetic males aged 5 to 16 were treated at Johns Hopkins University for a rare congenital disorder that results in an absent penis and other medical problems. Fourteen children underwent sex reassignment surgery and were raised as girls; parents of two of the boys refused the surgery.

To date, the children and their families have been followed for 34 to 98 months. At the last reassessment, 6 of the 14 children who had been reassigned and raised as girls were living as boys—as were the two boys who had not undergone surgery. Five children were successfully living as girls. The remaining child angrily refused to be interviewed (Reiner & Gearhart, 2004). The results of this study are provocative and provide important information about the development of gender identity. These results suggest that sex reassignment may be successful in some cases but not in others. Moreover, as seen in the cases of the two children whose parents rejected sex reassignment, surgical correction of genitalia might not be necessary for the healthy establishment of gender identity.

Sexual Orientation

Gender identity should not be confused with sexual orientation, one's pattern of erotic attraction. For example, though Mother lived life as a man/woman, his sexual orientation would best be described as homosexual. *Homosexuals*—gay men or lesbians—are attracted to persons of the same sex; *heterosexuals* are attracted to persons of the other sex. And *bisexuals* have erotic feelings toward persons of both sexes. Today, attitudes toward homosexuality and bisexuality vary both among and within cultures. Moreover, there is considerable cross-cultural variation in same-sex behaviors and the expression of sexual orientations (Lippa & Tan, 2001).

Biopsychological Factors in Sexual Orientation

Given that our evolutionary history, reproductive anatomy, and contemporary cultural norms favor heterosexuality, why are an estimated 1 percent of women and 3 percent of men self-identified as homosexual (Laumann, Gagnon, Michael, & Michaels, 1994)?

Sexual Orientation

Whereas attitudes toward homosexuality and bisexuality vary both among and within cultures, there is considerable cross-cultural variation in same-sex behaviors and the expression of sexual orientations.
Source: Grigoriev Rusian/ Shutterstock.com.

Theories of sexual orientation abound, and none has gained universal acceptance. Biopsychological theories of homosexuality implicate hereditary and physiological factors.

Heredity, the Brain, and Sexual Orientation Homosexuality runs in families, providing circumstantial evidence for the role of genetic factors (Bailey, Dunne, & Martin, 2000). For example, lesbians are more likely than nonlesbians to have lesbians among their sisters, daughters, and nieces (Pattatucci & Hamer, 1995). Of course, it is impossible to determine, based on this evidence alone, whether this pattern is caused more by hereditary similarities or environmental similarities. Likewise, identical twins are more likely to both be homosexual than are fraternal twins, but again, the extent to which this difference is due to shared genetic or shared environmental influences is unclear. Moreover, the strength of sexual attraction and concordance rates differ for men and women (Bailey, Dunne, & Martin, 2000).

Stronger support for the hereditary basis of homosexuality comes from research showing the following regarding identical twins (who have the same genes) who have been adopted as infants by different families: If one of the twins is homosexual, the other twin has a higher likelihood of also being homosexual than does a nontwin sibling reared together in the same family with a homosexual sibling (Eckert, Bouchard, Bohlen, & Heston, 1986). And a study of 40 families containing two nontwin homosexual brothers indicated that 26 of the sibling pairs (64 percent) shared genetic markers on the X chromosome (Hamer, Hu, Magnuson, & Hu, 1993). These findings have been countered by researchers who believe that the evidence is not strong enough to connect homosexuality to a specific genetic factor (Risch, Squires-Wheeler, & Keats, 1993). For example, if homosexuality were completely genetically determined, then when one identical twin is homosexual, the other would always be homosexual.

It is well established that there are hormonal, functional, and structural differences between male and female brains. Researchers are just beginning to examine the neural correlates of gender identity and sexual orientation. The most well-studied region is a portion of the anterior hypothalamus called the INAH-3 that plays a role in the regulation of male sexual behavior. This region was examined in deceased adult men who died of AIDS. LeVay (1991) and colleagues found this region to be twice as large in heterosexual men than homosexual men (see the box "Critical Thinking about Psychology"). Given the inherent difficulty with studies of deceased persons, researchers have begun utilizing neuroimaging studies to examine sexual orientation. In one study, 26 healthy homosexual men and 26 age-matched healthy heterosexual men were assessed using MRI technology to assess functional connectivity, brain morphology, and neural activity. The participants' sexual orientation was evaluated using the Kinsey Scale (see page 392). The researchers found that homosexual men had reduced gyri

Is There a Gay Brain?

In 1991, Simon LeVay, then a neuroanatomist at the Salk Institute in La Jolla, California, published research findings indicating specific structural differences between the brains of homosexual and heterosexual men. As part of his study, LeVay examined hypothalamic tissue from 19 gay men (all of whom had died of AIDS), 16 heterosexual men (6 of whom had died of AIDS), and 6 heterosexual women (1 of whom had died of AIDS). LeVay (1991) found that a region of the anterior hypothalamus was significantly larger in heterosexual men than in gay men.

Because LeVay's report provided evidence that men's sexual orientation might be determined by localized brain differences—perhaps genetically based—it created a media sensation. For several years after the publication of LeVay's report, there was a flood of television stories and magazine and newspaper articles about the possible genetic basis of sexual orientation. The excitement generated by his research is reflected in the titles of some of these articles, which included "Hypothalamus Study Stirs Social Questions" in the *APA Monitor* (Adler, 1991), "Does DNA Make Some Men Gay?" in *Newsweek* (Begley & Hager, 1993), "Search for the Gay Gene" in *Time* (Thompson, 1995), and "The X Factor: The Battle Over the Ramifications of a Gay Gene" in *The New Yorker* (Kevles, 1995).

LeVay's report also attracted a mountain of commentary on its scientific weaknesses and social implications. Scientists criticized LeVay's study on several grounds. Isn't it possible, critics noted, that the presumed direction of causality might be opposite to what common sense would presume? That is, perhaps brain differences do not cause differences in sexual orientation, but instead, perhaps a lifetime of being homosexual, bisexual, or heterosexual produces the differences in hypothalamic structures that LeVay found. Moreover, LeVay's research failed to account for lesbians' sexual orientation.

Scientific critics also noted that the differences in the brains of the homosexual and heterosexual men in LeVay's study might have been the product of AIDS, which afflicted all of the gay men in his sample but only a few of the heterosexual men. Neuroanatomist William Byne reported that many men with AIDS suffer testicular atrophy before death, and animal research shows that certain gonadal hormones affect the size of hypothalamic structures. Because of these findings, Byne wondered whether LeVay's research would have produced the same results if he had compared the brains of homosexual and heterosexual men who had not died of AIDS (Byne, 1997). LeVay responded to this criticism by pointing out that the hypothalamic structure of interest was larger in the heterosexual men who had died of AIDS than in the gay men who had died of AIDS. If testicular atrophy related to AIDS in turn caused atrophy of that structure, it should have done so in both gay and heterosexual men. Ironically, Byne has conducted research indicating that differences in the structure of the hypothalamus are not the product of AIDS. Nonetheless, Byne cautions that we have little solid evidence of a causal relationship between specific brain structures and sexual orientation because most studies on the biological bases of sexual orientation are correlational, have not been replicated, or have been based on animal research that may not be generalizable to human beings.

Many gay men and lesbians were overjoyed by LeVay's research because it indicated that sexual orientation is not the product of a freely chosen lifestyle but instead is determined by brain differences—perhaps as the result of heredity. If so, this genetic basis would counter the contention of many conservative religious leaders and their followers that homosexuality is a matter of free choice and would weaken their claim that homosexual behavior is a sin.

But other homosexual activists warned that LeVay's contention that sexual orientation is produced by brain differences—possibly genetically based—might provide fuel to those who would use it to support their belief that homosexuality is the product of a genetic defect. They fear that this conclusion might lead to demands that scientists seek ways to "cure" gay men and lesbians of their brain disorder, perhaps by tinkering with a "gay gene" that might be identified. They also fear that many parents would choose to abort fetuses that they were told had a "gay gene." LeVay responded to these fears by noting that public opinion polls have found that people who believe sexual orientation is the product of free choice are more likely to be biased against lesbians and gay men than are people who believe sexual orientation is biologically determined.

and temporal lobe homogeneity. Regional homogeneity refers to the strength with which a particular brain region communicates with its immediate neighbors (Hu, 2013). Studies such as these will help us understand the neural basis of sexual orientation.

Prenatal Development and Sexual Orientation Male and female fetuses differ in hormonal concentrations as early as 8 weeks *in utero*. Additional support for the physiological basis of homosexuality comes from research on prenatal development—though some researchers warn against concluding that a correlation between prenatal hormonal exposure and later sexual orientation necessarily indicates a causal relationship between the two (Doell, 1995). Women exposed prenatally to excessively high levels of estrogens are more likely to be lesbians or bisexuals (Meyer-Bahlburg et al., 1995). Male homosexuality is associated with hormonal activity during a critical period between the second and the fifth month after conception that differs from that of heterosexual men. This hormonal activity might affect the development of the hypothalamus, which helps regulate sexual orientation, in a way that predisposes some men toward a homosexual orientation (Ellis & Ames, 1987).

An interesting hypothesis about the possible origin of brain differences in homosexual and heterosexual men implicates birth order. Researchers have hypothesized that pregnant women develop an immune response to H-Y antigens produced by the male fetus. With each male conception, the maternal immune response to the H-Y antigen, a substance foreign to her body, increases. One study found that homosexual men with older brothers had lower birth weights than heterosexual men with older brothers. The researchers concluded that a strong maternal immune response reduces the boy's birth weight and increases the likelihood of homosexuality (Blanchard & Ellis, 2001). Of course, this hypothesis fails to explain why many gay men are firstborns. Moreover, the theory does not explain the development of homosexuality in women.

An unusual piece of evidence of a possible prenatal influence on sexual orientation comes from a sample of almost 1,000 homosexual men and more than 4,000 heterosexual men interviewed by the Kinsey Institute between 1938 and 1963. The survey found that homosexual men, on average, had larger penises than heterosexual men. This finding supports the possibility that differences in prenatal hormone levels or other factors affecting the development of reproductive organs might affect sexual orientation (Bogaert & Hershberger, 1999). Also, a recent meta-analysis of 20 studies reported that gay men and lesbians had a 39 percent greater likelihood of being nonright-handed than heterosexual women and men, a difference also attributed to the influence of prenatal hormones (Lalumiere, Blanchard, & Zucker, 2000). However, it is important to be cautious in interpreting the results of studies that report physiological differences that vary by sexual orientation. Many researchers have studied a number of physical correlates of sexual orientation, most recently the structure and function of the cochlea (McFadden & Pasanen, 1999) and finger length patterns (Williams et al., 2000). Not only is it difficult to ascertain the direction of causality, but also critics assert that studies that report findings consistent with stereotypes about gender and sexual orientation may be more easily accepted by the scientific and lay communities than are studies that do not (Carroll, 1998).

Psychosocial Factors in Sexual Orientation

Traditional psychosocial explanations of sexual orientation have been influenced by psychoanalytic views of child development. They emphasize the family environment and early childhood experience.

Childhood Upbringing and Sexual Orientation The traditional view favored the Freudian notion that sexual orientation is determined by mothers' and fathers' relations with the preschool-aged children. However, there is no evidence that any particular pattern of childhood experiences alone determines one's sexual orientation (Bell, Weinberg, & Hammersmith, 1981). In addition, the importance of the family environment in determining sexual orientation is contradicted by research findings that the great majority of children who are raised in lesbian families develop a heterosexual orientation (Golombok & Tasker, 1996).

Gender and Sexual Orientation The patterns and development of sexual orientation among women do appear to differ from those of men. Lisa Diamond is conducting a longitudinal study investigating the determinants of sexual orientation, sexual attraction, and sexual behavior among lesbian, bisexual, and "unlabeled" adolescents and young women. Her research counters the notion that sexual orientation is stable and established in childhood—at least among women. A majority of her respondents reported that their sexual attractions varied over time and across situations, and they failed to consider themselves to be exclusively attracted to other women (Diamond, 1998). In a follow-up study two years later, she found that the vast majority of the 80 participants had changed their self-described sexual orientation at least once. Changes were more likely to be reported by bisexual and unlabeled women. Sexual behaviors also varied, with one quarter of the lesbians reporting having sex with men (Diamond, 2005).

The results of research investigating gender differences in women's and men's sexuality has prompted psychologist Roy Baumeister (2000) to suggest that women's sexuality is more flexible than men's. He suggests that women—lesbian, bisexual, or heterosexual—exhibit more variability in sexual behaviors and attractions and are more strongly influenced by situational and cultural influences than men. Perhaps most controversial is his assertion that women's sex drive may be weaker than men's (Baumeister, Catanese, & Vohs, 2001). Though his theory has been met with criticism—perhaps most notably that he neglects to consider the extent to which gender differences in sexual behavior and attitudes are far outweighed by gender similarities (Anderson, Cyranowski, & Aarestad, 2000) and that gender roles have a profound influence on women's sexual experiences (Hyde & Durik, 2000)—his theory provides intriguing hypotheses for future research in the sociocultural determinants of women's sexuality.

Current Status of Theories of Sexual Orientation

Despite numerous studies on the origins of sexual orientation, none has identified any physiological or social factor that by itself explains why one person develops a heterosexual orientation and another develops a homosexual orientation. As suggested by Alfred Kinsey more than 50 years ago, it might even be mistaken to view homosexuality and heterosexuality as mutually exclusive categories (Haslam, 1997). This was the finding of a study in which homosexual men and heterosexual men rated their degree of homosexuality-heterosexuality and the size of their penile erections was measured while they watched brief movie clips of nude men and nude women. The men's self-ratings and penile responses showed a positive correlation. As you might expect, the more homosexual their self-rating, the greater their penile response to nude men; and the more heterosexual their self-rating, the greater their penile response to nude women. Yet, both the gay men and the heterosexual men tended to respond at least somewhat both to nude men and nude women (McConaghy & Blaszcynski, 1991).

According to John Money (1987), sexual orientation is affected by the interaction of biological, psychological, and sociocultural factors, the relative influences of which vary. Money points, as an example, to the Sambia tribe of New Guinea, in which boys and young men between the ages of 9 and 19 are encouraged to engage in same-sex sexual behavior to become more manly. At age 19 the young men marry and switch to a heterosexual orientation. Thus, a complete explanation of human sexual orientation probably will have to include biological, psychological, and sociocultural factors (e.g., Bem, 2000; Diamond, 2003b).

Section Review: The Sex Motive

1. According to Masters and Johnson, what are the four phases of the human sexual response cycle?

2. Why were Kinsey's sex surveys controversial, and what are the best-established gender differences and similarities in sexual behavior and attitudes?

3. What biopsychological factors have been implicated in the development of sexual orientation?

The Arousal Motive

Though the hunger motive and the sex motive seem to dominate North American culture, people also are influenced by another biological motive, the **arousal motive**. *Arousal* is the general level of physiological activation of the brain and body. As noted in Chapter 3, the reticular formation regulates brain arousal, and the autonomic nervous system and endocrine system regulate bodily arousal. Three of the main areas of research interest regarding the arousal motive are *optimal arousal, sensory deprivation,* and *sensation seeking*.

arousal motive The motive to maintain an optimal level of physiological activation.

Optimal Arousal

In 1908 researchers reported that mice learned tasks best at moderate levels of external stimulation and that the more complex the task, the lower the level of optimal stimulation (Yerkes & Dodson, 1908). Later researchers, led by Donald Hebb (1955) of McGill University in Montreal, showed that people perform best at a moderate level of arousal, with performance deteriorating under excessively high or low arousal levels. This relationship between arousal and performance, represented by an inverted U-shaped curve (see Figure 11-7), became known as the **Yerkes-Dodson law**, after the researchers who had conducted the earlier animal study—even though that study dealt with the level of external stimulation rather than with the level of arousal (Teigen, 1994).

Yerkes-Dodson law The principle that the relationship between arousal and performance is best represented by an inverted U-shaped curve.

Hebb found that optimal arousal is higher for simple tasks than for complex tasks. For example, the optimal level of arousal for doing a simple addition problem would be higher than for doing a complex geometry problem. Hebb also found that optimal arousal is higher for well-learned tasks than for novel tasks. Your optimal level of arousal for reading is higher now than it was when you were first learning to read. Perhaps, when studying bores you, you find that playing music in the background helps you raise your level of brain arousal enough for you to maintain your concentration (Patton, Routh, & Stinard, 1986).

But how does arousal level affect performance? According to Hebb, it lets us concentrate and attend to tasks, such as exams. If you are underaroused, your mind might wander to irrelevant details, like when you make careless errors, such as darkening the letter C when you meant to darken the letter B on a multiple-choice exam. But if you are overaroused, your focus of attention might become too narrow, reducing your ability to shift to other details that might help you solve a problem, as when you find yourself so anxious that you stare at a particular exam question for several minutes. Overarousal impairs performance in part by interfering with the retrieval of information in short-term memory (Anderson, Revelle, & Lynch, 1989).

Though some research studies based on the Yerkes-Dodson law have tended to be methodologically flawed and inconsistent in their findings (Muse, Harris, & Feild, 2003), many studies have supported the notion of an optimal level of arousal for task performance (Robazza, Bortoli, & Nougier, 1998). In a study of arithmetic performance in third and fourth graders under time pressure, low-anxious children performed better than did moderately anxious or high-anxious children (Plass & Hill, 1986). How could the concept of optimal

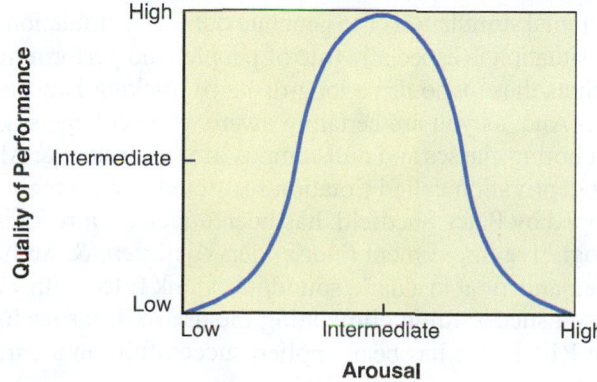

FIGURE 11-7
The Yerkes-Dodson Law

The graph depicts the relationship between arousal level and task performance. Note that the best performance occurs at a moderate level of arousal. Performance declines when arousal is below or above that level.

arousal explain these findings? Assume that before performing arithmetic, the low-anxious children began below their optimal level of arousal, the moderately anxious children began at their optimal level, and the high-anxious children began above their optimal level. The additional arousal induced by the arithmetic task might have boosted the arousal of the low-anxious children to their optimal level and the arousal of the moderately anxious children above their optimal level, while the arousal of the high-anxious children might have been boosted even further above their optimal level.

Though research has supported the notion of an optimal level of arousal for task performance, it has been inconsistent in supporting the belief that the optimal level of arousal will be lower for more difficult tasks than for easier tasks (Watters, Martin, & Schreter, 1997). Moreover, for any given task, there is no single optimal level of arousal; the optimal level varies from person to person (Ebbeck & Weiss, 1988). So an outstanding math student would have a higher optimal level of arousal for performing arithmetic than would a poor math student. As a consequence, the outstanding math student might have to "psych up" before an exam, and the poor math student might have to relax—each in an effort to reach an optimal arousal level.

Sensory Deprivation

Though people differ in the amount of arousal they prefer, they require at least a minimal amount for their brains to function properly. Anecdotal reports from Arctic explorers, shipwrecked sailors, and prisoners in solitary confinement made early psychologists aware that people require sensory stimulation for proper perceptual, cognitive, and emotional functioning.

sensory deprivation
The prolonged withdrawal of normal levels of external stimulation.

Sensory deprivation is the prolonged withdrawal of normal levels of external stimulation. When people are subjected to sensory deprivation, they may experience delusions, hallucinations, and emotional arousal caused by the brain's attempt to restore its optimal level of arousal. The experimental study of sensory deprivation began in the early 1950s when the Defense Research Board of Canada asked Donald Hebb to find ways of countering the "brainwashing" techniques that the Chinese communists used on prisoners during the Korean War. During brainwashing, prisoners were deprived of social and physical stimulation. This experience became so unpleasant that it motivated them to cooperate with their captors just to receive more stimulation (Hebb, 1958).

Hebb and his colleagues conducted studies of sensory deprivation in which each participant was confined to a bed in a soundproof room with only the monotonous hum of a fan and an air conditioner. The participants wore translucent goggles to reduce visual sensations, and cotton gloves and cardboard tubes over their arms to reduce touch sensations. They were permitted to leave the bed only to eat or to use the toilet. They stayed in the room for as many days as they could tolerate.

After many hours of sensory deprivation, some participants experienced hallucinations, emotional instability, and intellectual deterioration. Though the students who volunteered for the study were paid $20 a day (a tidy sum at the time) for participating, most quit within 48 hours. They found the lack of sensory stimulation so aversive that they preferred to forego the monetary incentive in favor of sensory stimulation (Bexton, Heron, & Scott, 1954).

Research on sensory deprivation demonstrates that inadequate external stimulation might motivate us to seek external stimulation or to generate our own stimulation through alterations in brain activity. This situation is especially true of people who perform monotonous tasks in relative isolation, such as those who drive long-distance trucking hauls or live for extended periods in outer space. And, as you are certainly aware, even college students seek external stimulation to combat boring classes and dull campus life (Weinstein & Almaguer, 1987).

A form of sensory deprivation called flotation restricted environmental stimulation (flotation REST), developed by Peter Suedfeld, has been effective in reducing arousal without causing distress or cognitive impairment (Norlander, Kjellgren, & Archer, 2000–2001). In flotation REST, participants float in a dark, soundproof tank filled with warm saltwater. Flotation REST has proved successful in eliminating the use of drugs such as nicotine (Suedfeld, 1990). Flotation REST also has been applied successfully in a variety of other ways, particularly in situations that call for a reduction in arousal. These applications include the treatment of high blood pressure (McGrady, Turner, Fine, & Higgins, 1987) and the relief of chronic back and neck pain (Kjellgren, Sundequist, Norlander, & Archer, 2001). Though flotation REST produces feelings of relaxation and even euphoria, the exact physiological basis of these effects remains to be determined (Schulz & Kaspar, 1994).

Sensation Seeking

Would you prefer to ride a roller coaster or lie on a beach? Would you prefer to attend a lively party or have a quiet conversation? Your preferences would depend in part on your degree of **sensation seeking**, which is your motivation to pursue sensory stimulation. People high in sensation seeking prefer activities that increase their arousal levels; those low in sensation seeking prefer activities that decrease their arousal. A study of personal relationships, Internet usage, and music preferences in college students found that those who scored higher in sensation seeking had more casual and close friends; used the Internet to download pornography, play games, and chat with friends; and preferred punk, heavy metal, and reggae music than did those who scored lower in sensation seeking (Weisskirch & Murphy, 2004). Another study of college students from 14 different countries who had studied in a foreign country as part of California State University's International Program found that they scored higher in sensation seeking than a control group with no study-abroad experience (Schroth & McCormack, 2000).

sensation seeking
The motivation to pursue sensory stimulation.

Sensation seeking varies by age, gender, and culture. Perhaps not surprisingly, younger people score higher in sensation seeking than do older people (Ball, Farnill, & Wangeman, 1984). Men, on average, have higher sensation-seeking scores than women, particularly on subscales that measure disinhibition and thrill and adventure seeking (Zuckerman, Eysenck, & Eysenck, 1978). Also, one cross-cultural study has found that Chinese respondents scored lower on sensation seeking than did Western samples (Wang et al., 2000).

Sensation seeking also is related to risky behavior. Those who score high in sensation seeking are more likely to gamble (Barrault & Varescon, 2013), engage in binge drinking and smoking marijuana (Moreno et al., 2012), and engage in risky behaviors such as Alpine skiing and snowboarding without a helmet (Ruedl, Abart, Ledochowski, Burtscher, & Kopp, 2012). The relationship between sensation seeking and risky behavior can be deadly. Sensation seeking is positively correlated with the frequency of risky sexual behavior such as cruising and casual sex among gay men (Bancroft et al., 2003) and men who have sex with prostitutes and other sex workers (Xantidis & McCabe, 2000). There is evidence that many people who are high in sensation seeking pursue such activities because of a desire to counteract a chronic inability to experience pleasure in their daily lives (Pierson, le Houezec, Fossaert, Dubal, & Jouvent, 1999). As discussed in Chapter 2, correlation does not necessarily imply causation. In this case, the association between sensation seeking and risky behaviors does not necessarily mean that sensation seeking in itself causes those behaviors.

Sensation Seeking

(a) People low in sensation seeking prefer activities that decrease their arousal levels. *(b)* People high in sensation seeking prefer activities that increase their arousal levels.
Sources: (a) Dudarev Mikhail/Shutterstock.com. *(b)* Vitalii Nesterchuk/Shutterstock.com.

1. How would the Yerkes-Dodson law explain poor exam performance by students who are either too relaxed or too anxious?

2. What evidence is there to support the effectiveness of flotation REST?

The Achievement Motive

achievement motive
The desire for mastery, excellence, and accomplishment.

People are motivated by social as well as physiological needs. Interest in studying social motivation was stimulated in the 1930s and 1940s by the work of Henry Murray (1938), who identified a variety of important social motives, including dominance, achievement, and affiliation. Since Murray's pioneering research, psychologists, led by John Atkinson and David McClelland, have been especially interested in studying the **achievement motive**, which is the desire for mastery, excellence, and accomplishment. In the context of Maslow's hierarchy of needs, the need for achievement would be associated with one of the higher levels, the need for esteem. This association means that the need for achievement would be stronger in cultures in which most people have satisfied their lower needs, such as in Canada and the United States. But even in the United States, the relative importance of the need for achievement has changed over time. Consider an archival study of children's readers published between 1800 and 1950 that found that the number of achievement themes in the readers increased until about 1890 and then decreased through 1950. This change was accompanied by a parallel change in the number of patents issued, indicating that changes in a country's achievement motivation can affect its practical achievements (DeCharms & Moeller, 1962). Nonetheless, it is not certain from the data that changes in achievement motivation caused changes in practical achievements. You will recall that a positive correlation between two variables does not necessarily mean that changes in one cause changes in the other. Of course, it does not preclude the possibility of a causal relationship, either.

Historical trends in the achievement motive also differ for men and women. From the late 1950s to the late 1970s, American men showed no change in their achievement motivation, whereas American women showed a marked increase. This increase has been attributed to the contemporary feminist movement of the past few decades, which encouraged women to pursue personal achievement outside traditional women's domains, such as homemaking (Veroff, Depner, Kulka, & Douvan, 1980).

Need for Achievement

The Achievement Motive

The social nature of the achievement motive is demonstrated not only by this boy's delight over his achievement, but also his mother's love and pride.
Source: Creativa/Shutterstock.com.

Henry Murray (1938) referred to the achievement motive as the *need for achievement,* which reveals itself in efforts to meet high standards of performance or to compete successfully against other people. How do psychologists measure the need for achievement? The most common means has been the *Thematic Apperception Test (TAT),* developed by Murray and his colleague Christiana Morgan (Morgan & Murray, 1935). The TAT is based on the assumption that our fantasies reveal our motives. The test consists of a series of drawings of people in ambiguous situations. Participants are asked to tell what is happening in the picture, what led up to it, how the people feel, and how the situation turns out. The responses are scored for any consistent themes. Individuals with a high need for achievement tend to tell stories in which people overcome obstacles, work hard to reach goals, and accomplish great things.

What do we know about people who score high on the need for achievement? Research shows that they persist at tasks in the face of difficulties, delay gratification in the pursuit of long-term goals, and are more successful than people with a low need for achievement. They also select moderately difficult challenges, neither so easy that they guarantee success nor so difficult that they guarantee failure (McClelland, 1985). One research team

investigated the relation of the achievement motive to migration in a sample of over 1,000 college students in Albania, the Czech Republic, and Slovenia. They found that students who wished to leave their country of birth scored higher on achievement motivation than did students who wished to stay. These results were replicated in a sample of American college students (Boneva, Frieze, Ferligoj, Pauknerova, & Orgocka 1998).

Though the importance of achievement motivation in situations such as academic courses has been demonstrated in different cultures (Jegede, Jegede, & Ugodulunwa, 1997), the achievement motive appears to be multidimensional and culture specific. In individualistic cultures, the achievement motive primarily is expressed in terms of individual achievement. In collectivist cultures, which value interdependence, achievement primarily is expressed through the family and other social groups (Niles, 1998). Moreover, bicultural individuals may express both motives. Angela Lew and her colleagues (1998) found that acculturation among Asian American college students was positively correlated with the achievement motive. However, students who endorsed both American and Asian values also had higher scores in individual-oriented and, to a lesser extent, social-oriented achievement.

The need for achievement varies with the achievement situation. People with a high need for achievement rarely seek success in more than a few areas of life. So your achievement behavior depends on more than just the strength of your general need for achievement. Your achievement behavior also depends on **incentive value,** the perceived rewards that accompany success in a particular area, and **expectancy**, the perceived probability of success in a particular area (Eccles & Wigfield, 1995). The combination of expectancy and incentive value even affects the choice of a college major by students (Sullins, Hernandez, Fuller, & Tashiro, 1995).

Consider your achievement motivation in regard to your achievement behavior in a psychology course. If you are high in achievement motivation, if you find that a good grade in the course has high incentive value for you, and if you expect that studying hard is likely to result in a good grade, you are more likely to work hard in the course. Yet, if you are high in achievement motivation but do not value a high grade in psychology (perhaps because it is only an elective course) or believe that you have little chance of success in the course (perhaps because the professor is a notoriously hard grader), you might not work as hard.

Research also has shown that the need for achievement can interact with arousal to determine a person's performance. As noted earlier, we perform best at our optimal level of arousal for a given task. In an arousing situation, such as giving a speech to a class, a student

incentive value The perceived rewards that accompany success in a particular area.

expectancy 1. The strength of the individual's beliefs about whether a particular outcome is attainable. 2. The perceived probability of success in a particular area.

with a low need for achievement might perform well because the situation raises the student to her optimal level of arousal. In the same situation, a student with a high need for achievement and already at an optimal level of arousal might perform poorly because the situation raises the student beyond his optimal level (Humphreys & Revelle, 1984).

Goal Setting

goal setting The use of goals to increase motivation and improve performance by providing incentives.

Suppose that you are high in the need for achievement in academics, sports, or some other area. How should you seek to fulfill that need? Hundreds of studies have demonstrated the importance of **goal setting**. Goals increase motivation and improve performance by providing incentives. Goal setting has been especially useful in business and industry in stimulating productivity (Nordstrom, Lorenzi, & Hall, 1990). Management by objectives, in which employees participate in setting goals, has been especially effective. Of 70 studies included in a review of research on the effectiveness of management by objectives, 68 found that it increased productivity (Rodgers & Hunter, 1991). Goal setting is useful in a variety of other circumstances as well. These include improving adult health behavior (Pierson, 2012), students' writing ability (Page-Voth & Graham, 1999), and college students' exam performance (Fleming, 2002).

But how should you set your goals? Research findings by Edwin Locke and his colleagues provide several suggestions (Locke & Latham, 2002). Specific, challenging goals (such as "I will increase my studying by one hour a night") produce better performance than do vague goals (such as "I will increase the time I spend studying"), easy goals (such as "I will increase my studying by 10 minutes a week"), or mere encouragement to do your best. Feedback on your progress (such as keeping a record of how much time you spend studying) will help you reach that goal. And a goal that you set yourself will motivate you more than a goal imposed on you (as when a parent forces a child to stay home and study every day after school). Though goal setting improves task performance, goal setting paired with performance feedback is superior to goal setting alone (McCalley & Midden, 2002). Thus, workers and students who set goals will tend to perform better if given feedback about their job or school performance.

Intrinsic Motivation

If you have ever written a term paper just to obtain a grade, you can appreciate William James's distress at having to complete his now-classic 1890 textbook for an extrinsic reason. According to Edward Thorndike (1961, p. 267), "James wrote the *Principles* with wailing and gnashing of teeth to fulfill a contract with a publishing firm." Though James enjoyed writing, he did not enjoy writing for money. He was not unusual because research has shown that receiving extrinsic rewards for performing intrinsically rewarding activities can reduce the motivation to perform them.

intrinsic motivation The desire to perform a behavior for its own sake.

extrinsic motivation The desire to perform a behavior in order to obtain an external reward, such as praise, grades, or money.

Intrinsic motivation is the desire to perform a behavior for its own sake. In contrast, **extrinsic motivation** is the desire to perform a task to gain external rewards, such as praise, grades, or money. For example, you might take a psychology course because you find it interesting (an intrinsic reason) or because it is a graduation requirement (an extrinsic reason).

Given the everyday observation that extrinsic rewards can increase achievement motivation, especially in people who initially have little or no motivation in a particular area (Cameron, Banko, & Pierce, 2001), why do extrinsic rewards sometimes decrease achievement motivation? Two theories provide possible answers.

Overjustification Theory

overjustification theory The theory that an extrinsic reward will decrease intrinsic motivation when a person attributes her or his performance to that reward.

Overjustification theory assumes that an extrinsic reward decreases intrinsic motivation when a person attributes his or her performance to the extrinsic reward. For example, in the "Psychology versus Common Sense" box, the students who were rewarded for drawing might have attributed their behavior to the reward rather than to their interest in drawing. Overjustification occurs when there is high intrinsic interest and the reward is perceived as more than adequate justification for performing the act. In a study of first and second graders, children played with an interesting or uninteresting toy and were rewarded or not rewarded. Rewards reduced the motivation to play with the interesting toy but not the uninteresting toy (Newman & Layton, 1984). A meta-analysis found strong support for overjustification theory (Tang & Hall, 1995), though some research studies indicate that it has limitations as an explanation for decreases in intrinsic motivation (Pittenger, 1996).

Cognitive-Evaluation Theory

An alternative theory, **cognitive-evaluation theory**, holds that a reward perceived as providing information about a person's competence in an activity will increase her or his intrinsic motivation to perform that activity (Deci, Nezlek, & Sheinman, 1981). But a reward perceived as an attempt to control a person's behavior will decrease his or her intrinsic motivation to perform that activity. The more controlling and less informative that students perceive a teacher to be, the lower will be the students' intrinsic motivation (Guay, Boggiano, & Vallerand, 2001).

Consider a student whose teacher rewards her for doing well in drawing. If the student believes that the reward is being used to provide information about her competence, her intrinsic motivation to perform that activity may increase. But if she believes that the reward is being used to control her behavior (perhaps to make her spend more time drawing), her intrinsic motivation to perform may decrease. Though there is strong research support for cognitive-evaluation theory (Rummel & Feinberg, 1988), some research findings have contradicted it (Carton, 1996).

cognitive-evaluation theory
The theory that a person's intrinsic motivation will increase when a reward is perceived as a source of information but will decrease when a reward is perceived as an attempt to exert control.

Section Review: The Achievement Motive

1. What are some basic rules for the effective use of goal setting?

2. What is the difference between overjustification theory and cognitive-evaluation theory in explaining the negative effects of extrinsic motivation?

The Role of Motivation in Sport

Near the end of the 19th century, Indiana University psychologist Norman Triplett (1898) observed that bicyclists rode faster when competing against other bicyclists than when competing against time. This study was perhaps the first in **sport psychology**, the field that studies the relationship between psychological factors and sport performance. Though Triplett began the scientific study of sport performance, magazines devoted to sport had advanced the desirability of a psychological approach to sport in the late 19th century (King, Raymond, & Simon-Thomas, 1995). One of the first celebrated participants in sport psychology research was baseball star Babe Ruth. In 1921 he performed tasks in a laboratory at Columbia University to help researchers discover what accounted for his extraordinary ability to hit home runs. The researchers hoped to use what they learned to help identify future baseball stars (Fuchs, 1998). Today, in studying motivation in sport, researchers are especially interested in the arousal motive and the achievement motive.

The Arousal Motive and Sport

Your arousal motive influences your sport performance. Of particular importance are your level of sensation seeking and your level of optimal arousal.

Sensation Seeking and Sport

Your level of sensation seeking might affect your choice of sports to pursue. People who score high on tests of sensation seeking are more likely to participate in risky activities such as skydiving, hang gliding, mountain climbing, and automobile racing (Jack & Ronan, 1998). And rugby and lacrosse players score higher in sensation seeking than do rowers and soccer players (Schroth, 1995).

Optimal Arousal and Sport

The arousal motive also is important to athletes in regard to their maintaining an optimal level of arousal for their sport performance. If you have ever played a competitive sport, you know what it is to choke—to be so anxious that you perform below your normal level of ability. Choking occurs when your anxiety makes you attend to the normally automatic movements involved in playing a sport. If you consciously attend to those movements, they will be disrupted (Baumeister, 1984). Consider the shooting of free throws in basketball. If you attend to each movement of your arm and hand as you shoot a free throw, you will disrupt the smooth sequence of movements that free-throw shooting requires. Athletes at an optimal level of arousal are less likely to be undermotivated or to choke, as shown in a study of female collegiate basketball players. Those with a moderate level of pregame anxiety performed better than did those with a low or high level (Sonstroem & Bernardo, 1982).

As mentioned earlier, the optimal level of arousal is lower for complex tasks than for simple tasks. This finding also is true in sports (Gardner, 1986). Your optimal level of arousal while hitting a golf ball (a relatively complex task) would be lower than your optimal level while playing shuffleboard (a relatively simple task). Moreover, the more skilled the athlete, the higher her optimal level of arousal will be. The golfer who makes a putt on the green to win the U.S. Open might be so skillful that he has a higher optimal level of arousal than does the golfer who chokes in the same situation. When teaching beginners to play golf, to ride a bicycle, or to serve a volleyball, you should try to keep their arousal levels from becoming too high. To avoid excess arousal, beginners should refrain from competition and not practice while being watched by people other than the coach or instructor.

One technique for achieving optimal arousal in athletes is flotation REST. Flotation REST has helped competitive archers maintain relaxed hand muscles (Norlander, Bergman, & Archer, 1999). And in a study of the effects of flotation REST on recreational basketball performance, college students who practiced flotation REST reported greater confidence and performed better than controls who did not practice it (Suedfeld & Bruno, 1990).

The Achievement Motive and Sport

On June 4, 1986, six weeks after setting the collegiate record for the 10,000-meter run, Kathy Ormsby, running among the leaders, veered off the track midway through the final race at the NCAA championships in Indianapolis. She left the stadium, ran to the nearby White River Bridge, and leaped 50 feet to the riverbank. The fall fractured her spine and paralyzed her from the waist down. Besides excelling at running, Ormsby had been her high school's valedictorian (with an average of 99 percent) and was a premedical student at North Carolina State University. Ormsby was certainly high in her motivation to succeed.

Ormsby had been overcome periodically by anxiety strong enough to force her to drop out of races. Though her high need for achievement certainly motivated her to compete, she apparently succumbed to her anxiety, finding it more and more difficult to motivate herself to compete against other elite athletes. Kathy Ormsby's tragic story shows that the achievement motive can be a powerful force in athletic competition as it is in other areas of life.

Motivation in Sport

Athletes' motivation can involve both the arousal motive and the achievement motive.

Source: Pete Saloutos/Shutterstock.com.

Need for Achievement and Sport

Athletes with a high need for achievement are motivated to seek competition that provides a fair test of their abilities. Early evidence for this finding came from a study in which college students played a game of ringtoss. Participants with a high need for achievement were more likely to stand at an intermediate distance from the peg, whereas participants with a low need for achievement were more likely to stand either close to the peg or far from it (Atkinson & Litwin, 1960). Similarly, if you were high in your need for achievement in tennis, you would probably choose to play someone of your own ability. In contrast, a person low in the need for achievement might prefer to play either someone who barely knows how to grip a racket, which would ensure success, or a professional tennis player, which would ensure that losing would be attributable to the professional opponent's excellence rather than to personal incompetence.

One way in which superior athletes make competition against lesser athletes more motivating is by giving themselves a handicap, making the competition a moderate challenge rather than a guaranteed success (Nicholls, 1984). If you are an excellent table tennis player, you might provide a moderate challenge for yourself by giving a lesser opponent 10 points in a 21-point game. Similarly, in the 1960s, Wilt Chamberlain, perhaps the most physically imposing athlete in history (who once averaged 50 points a game for a whole season in the National Basketball Association), developed a fadeaway jump shot to show that he could score even when giving up his greatest asset, his ability to score from near the basket because of his great strength and height (7 feet, 1 inch tall). By doing so, he made scoring a moderate rather than easy challenge for himself—often to the distress of his coaches. Chamberlain's use of intentional *self-handicapping* (see Chapter 13) is common among athletes in a variety of sports, including collegiate swimming and wrestling (Bailis, 2001).

Goal Setting and Sport

As in other areas of life, goal setting is important in sport motivation. A survey of 185 male and 143 female Olympic athletes found that all of them used goal setting to help enhance their performance and that they found it to be effective (Burton, Gillham, Weinberg, Yukelson, & Wiegand, 2013). A study of the effects of goal setting on college sharpshooters' performance found that sharpshooters who set specific goals improved more than those who set do-your-best goals (Boyce, 1992). Athletes whose performance can be improved by goal setting include football players (Ward

& Carnes, 2002), gymnasts (Lambert, Moore, & Dixon, 1999), and tennis players (Harwood & Swain, 2002).

Studies have demonstrated that goal setting is particularly useful in basketball. One study used what is known as an A-B-A design with multiple baselines to assess the effect of mental imagery and goal setting on the free-throw shooting of female collegiate basketball players. The participants were given several baseline sessions (A) during which they shot free throws. The length of the baseline sessions varied from one participant to another. The researchers varied the length of the baseline sessions to reduce the likelihood that another event (for example, the beginning of a new workout program on the very day that the participants began the test sessions that followed) could account for changes between the baseline sessions and the test sessions.

The participants then were given several test sessions (B) during which four participants used imagery, four used goal setting, and four used both imagery and goal setting to improve their free-throw shooting. The study concluded with another series of baseline sessions (A) during which the participants shot free throws without using imagery or goal setting. The results indicated that goal setting by itself produced the best results (Lerner et al., 1996).

Intrinsic Motivation and Sport

Athletes also are more motivated by intrinsic rewards than by extrinsic rewards (Vallerand & Losier, 1999). For example, a recent study found higher intrinsic motivation among Division I athletes who perceived that their coach's feedback focused on positive and informational feedback rather than control (Amorose & Horn, 2001). In terms of cognitive-evaluation theory, discussed earlier, rewards that are perceived as a means of control can decrease intrinsic motivation, and rewards that are perceived as a means of providing information about competence can increase intrinsic motivation (Ryan, 1980).

Intrinsic motivation also is important in adherence to exercise programs. A study of participants in aerobics, weight training, or tae kwon do found that those who were more motivated by intrinsic factors, such as enjoyment, social interaction, and improved competence, tended to adhere to their programs. In contrast, those who were more motivated by extrinsic factors, such as a desire to become more fit or attractive, tended not to adhere to their programs sooner (Ryan, Frederick, Lepes, Rubio, & Sheldon, 1997).

As you can see, motivational factors that are important in other areas of life also are important in sport. Athletes perform best at an optimal level of arousal, which varies with the individual, the sport, and the task. And athletes are influenced by their achievement motive; their level of motivation is enhanced by their need for achievement, proper use of goal setting, and reliance on intrinsic rewards.

Section Review: The Role of Motivation in Sport

1. How does the concept of optimal arousal explain why athletes perform differently in practice and in real competition?

2. Why would an athlete high in the need for achievement prefer an opponent of similar ability rather than one of much lower or much higher ability?

Can Mental Imagery Improve Sport Performance?

Rationale

Sport performance depends on several factors, including athletic ability, training techniques, physical conditioning, and personal motivation. A popular approach to improving performance is the use of mental imagery, which can improve technique and motivation. This activity will be an experiment comparing the effectiveness of two kinds of visual imagery in improving basketball free-throw shooting performance. The first kind of visual imagery, *internal imagery*, involves perceiving the task as though looking out through one's own eyes. The second kind of visual imagery, *external imagery*, involves perceiving the task as though looking through the eyes of an observer. Experiments have found that external imagery is superior to internal imagery for sport activities in which form is especially important, including karate, gymnastics, and rock climbing (Hardy & Callow, 1999).

Method
Participants

In this experiment you will need 30 female and male college students; 10 will be randomly assigned to each of three groups. The first group will use internal imagery, the second group will use external imagery, and the third group—the control group—will use no mental imagery. Be sure to include equal numbers of male and female participants in each group.

Materials

The participants will use the same basketball. You will need a data sheet to record the number of free throws made by each of the 30 participants.

Procedure

Each participant will take 20 free throws on an indoor basketball court, with those in the imagery groups using mental imagery before each free throw. Those in the internal imagery group will be told to close their eyes and imagine themselves shooting a successful free throw from their own visual perspective. Those in the external imagery group will be told to close their eyes and imagine themselves shooting a successful free throw from the perspective of someone observing them. Those in the no-imagery group will be told simply to try their best. Record the number of free throws made by each participant.

Results and Discussion

Calculate the mean number of free throws made for each of the three groups. Using these means, draw a bar graph (see Appendix C in the Online Edition). Are there any large differences between the means of the three groups? What do you conclude about the effectiveness of the imagery techniques? Why would scientists prefer to use inferential statistics (see Chapter 2 and Appendix C in the Online Edition) instead of subjective judgments of the differences between the means? What confounding variables might have affected the experiment? Among the possible factors to consider are the basketball, the setting, and the instructions given to participants.

If you were to perform the experiment again, how would you improve it? Given that research studies have provided some evidence that internal imagery is more effective for experts and external imagery is more effective for nonexperts, suggest an experiment that might test that hypothesis.

Chapter Summary

The Nature of Motivation

- Motivation is the psychological process that arouses, directs, and maintains behavior.
- The main sources of motivation include genes, drives, and incentives.
- Though William McDougall's instinct theory failed to achieve scientific credibility, interest in the hereditary basis of social behavior remains alive today in the field of sociobiology.
- Instinct theories gave way to the drive-reduction theory of Clark Hull, which assumes that physiological deprivation causes a need, which induces a state of tension called a drive.
- Drive reduction aims at restoring a steady state of physiological equilibrium called homeostasis.
- A drive "pushes" you toward a goal, whereas an incentive is an external stimulus that "pulls" you toward a goal.
- Abraham Maslow categorized human needs in a hierarchy, with the pursuit of higher needs contingent on the satisfaction of lower ones.

The Hunger Motive

- Hunger impels you to eat to satisfy your body's need for nutrients.
- Hunger is regulated by bodily, brain, and environmental factors.
- Areas of the hypothalamus regulate hunger by responding to signals from the blood and internal organs.

- External food-related cues also influence hunger and eating.
- The most common eating problem is obesity.
- Men with more than 25 percent body fat and women with more than 30 percent body fat are considered to be obese.
- Obesity depends on one's set point, basal metabolic rate, responsiveness to external cues, chronic level of blood insulin, and reactions to stress.
- Two of the most prevalent eating disorders are anorexia nervosa, which involves self-starvation, and bulimia nervosa, which typically involves binging and purging.

The Sex Motive

- Sex serves as both a drive and an incentive.
- Sex hormones direct sexual development and sexual behavior.
- Unlike in other animals, sexual behavior in human adults is controlled more by sociocultural factors than by sex hormones.
- Formal research on human sexuality began with surveys on men's and women's sexual behavior conducted by Alfred Kinsey and his colleagues.
- Later research by William Masters and Virginia Johnson showed that women and men have similar sexual response cycles.
- Masters and Johnson also developed sex therapy techniques that have been successful in helping men and women overcome sexual dysfunctions, which are chronic problems at phases in the sexual response cycle.
- Gender identity is one's self-perceived sex.
- Sexual orientation is one's pattern of erotic attraction.
- Gender identity and sexual orientation are influenced by biopsychological and sociocultural factors.

The Arousal Motive

- Arousal is the general level of physiological activation of the brain and body.
- The Yerkes-Dodson law holds that there is an optimal level of arousal for the performance of a given task, with the optimal level becoming lower as the task becomes more complex.
- Studies of sensory deprivation by Donald Hebb and his colleagues show that people are motivated to maintain at least a minimal level of sensory stimulation.

- Flotation REST has been successful in improving human physical and psychological functioning.
- People also differ in their degree of sensation seeking, which is the motivation to seek high or low levels of sensory stimulation.

The Achievement Motive

- The achievement motive is the desire for mastery, excellence, and accomplishment.
- Henry Murray and Christiana Morgan introduced the Thematic Apperception Test as a means of assessing the need for achievement.
- People with a high need for achievement persist at tasks in the face of difficulties, delay gratification in the pursuit of long-term goals, and achieve greater success than do people with a low need for achievement.
- People with a high need for achievement also prefer moderately difficult challenges.
- People's actual achievement behavior in a given situation depends on the strength of their need for achievement, the incentive value of success for them, and their expectancy of success.
- Goal setting increases motivation and improves performance by providing incentives.
- The best goals are specific and challenging, and feedback is useful for monitoring progress toward goals.
- The intrinsic motivation to engage in an activity can be reduced by extrinsic rewards.
- Overjustification theory and cognitive-evaluation theory provide different explanations for the detrimental effects of extrinsic rewards.

The Role of Motivation in Sport

- Sport psychology is the field that studies the relationship between psychological factors and sport performance, particularly the influence of motivation.
- To keep from choking during competition, athletes must learn to keep from rising above their optimal level of arousal.
- Athletic performance also is affected by other motivational factors, including the need for achievement, goal setting, and intrinsic motivation.

Key Terms

The Nature of Motivation

drive (p. 377)
drive-reduction theory (p. 377)
hierarchy of needs (p. 378)
homeostasis (p. 377)
incentive (p. 377)
instinct (p. 376)
motivation (p. 376)

need (p. 377)
sociobiology (p. 377)

The Hunger Motive

anorexia nervosa (p. 387)
basal metabolic rate (p. 384)
bulimia nervosa (p. 388)
obesity (p. 382)
set point (p. 381)

The Sex Motive

gender identity (p. 394)
gonads (p. 389)
sensate focusing (p. 393)
sexual dysfunction (p. 393)
sexual orientation (p. 394)
sexual response cycle (p. 390)

Chapter Quiz

Note: Answers for the Chapter Quiz questions are provided at the end of the book.

1. If you were high in your need for achievement, you would most likely seek to play basketball against
   a. an 8-year-old child.
   b. an Olympic basketball player.
   c. a person 6 inches shorter than you.
   d. a person similar in ability to you.

2. One of the criticisms of sociobiology is that it
   a. may simply support the status quo.
   b. favors "politically correct" science.
   c. has only been successful in explaining altruism.
   d. emphasizes social experiences over biological endowment.

3. Alfred Kinsey suggested viewing homosexuality and heterosexuality as
   a. genetically ordained.
   b. points on a continuum.
   c. products of free choice.
   d. mutually exclusive categories.

4. A person with anorexia nervosa
   a. engages in self-starvation.
   b. becomes morbidly overweight.
   c. binges on food and then vomits.
   d. exhibits conditioned taste aversions.

5. The Yerkes-Dodson law states that the relationship between arousal and performance is best represented by
   a. a U-shaped curve.
   b. an inverted U-shaped curve.
   c. a negatively accelerated curve.
   d. a positively accelerated curve.

6. Stress-related overeating is related to secretion of
   a. glucose.
   b. glucagon.
   c. endorphins.
   d. cholecystokinin.

7. Your self-perceived sex is your
   a. gender identity.
   b. sexual response.
   c. sexual orientation.
   d. gender role.

8. The notion that an extrinsic reward will decrease intrinsic motivation when a person attributes his or her performance to that reward is called
   a. overextension theory.
   b. overjustification theory.
   c. overregularization theory.
   d. cognitive-evaluation theory.

9. The thirst motive is regulated by the
   a. hypothalamus.
   b. aqueous humor.
   c. substantia nigra.
   d. medulla.

10. Reports of brainwashing during the Korean War inspired research on
    a. autism spectrum disorder.
    b. hypnosis.
    c. starvation.
    d. sensory deprivation.

11. Maslow's arrangement of motives in order of their motivational priority, ranging from physiological needs to the need for self-actualization and transcendence, is called the
    a. expectancy theory.
    b. intrinsic motives.
    c. hierarchy of needs.
    d. drive-reduction theory.

12. Hunger is reduced by the secretion of the hormone
    a. renin.
    b. thyroxin.
    c. cholecystokinin.
    d. prolactin.

13. Flotation REST is a kind of
    a. paraphilia.
    b. sex therapy.
    c. sensory deprivation.
    d. timeout used to enhance achievement motivation.

14. The set point is the
    a. body's normal weight.
    b. subject of research in sport psychology.
    c. degree of achievement that one finds satisfactory.
    d. amount of stimulation needed to trigger an orgasm.

15. Denslow Lewis's article, which he submitted to the *Journal of the American Medical Association,* was controversial because it
    a. promoted pedophilia.
    b. advocated premarital sex.
    c. encouraged women to enjoy sex.
    d. contained drawings of the sex organs.

16. The binge eating seen in bulimia nervosa may be an attempt to relieve feelings of
    a. mania.
    b. anxiety.
    c. depression.
    d. depersonalization.

17. According to Masters and Johnson, the order of phases in the human sexual response cycle is
    a. plateau, excitement, orgasm, resolution.
    b. excitement, plateau, orgasm, resolution.
    c. excitement, orgasm, resolution, plateau.
    d. excitement, orgasm, plateau, resolution.

18. The optimal level of arousal would probably be lowest for
    a. lifting weights.
    b. throwing a football.
    c. serving a tennis ball.
    d. making a shot on a pool table.

19. Controversial research by Simon LeVay has attributed one's sexual orientation to differences in
    a. early childhood rearing.
    b. part of the hypothalamus.
    c. genes on the X chromosome.
    d. prenatal hormone exposure.

20. The study of Danish adoption records by Stunkard et al. (1986) found that the body weight of adoptees is
    a. unrelated to the body weight of either the biological mother or the adoptive mother.
    b. more related to the body weight of the biological mother than the adoptive mother.
    c. more related to the body weight of the adoptive mother than the biological mother.
    d. more related to the body weight of the adoptive mother than the adoptive father.

21. You and several friends finish a meal and feel full. A server then gives a description of several delicious chocolate desserts, prompting an obese friend to order one. This reaction would most likely be a response to the secretion of
    a. glucose by the liver.
    b. insulin by the pancreas.
    c. glucagon by the pancreas.
    d. cholecystokinin by the small intestine.

22. One of the main criticisms of Kinsey's research is that
    a. it promoted the double standard.
    b. he used questionnaires instead of interviews.
    c. he observed people while they were engaged in sex.
    d. his sample of participants was not representative of the general population.

23. A man who would be most likely to develop bulimia nervosa would be a
    a. chef.
    b. psychologist.
    c. newspaper editor.
    d. collegiate wrestler.

24. The rate at which the body burns calories just to keep itself alive is called the
    a. set point.
    b. rate of homeostasis.
    c. basal metabolic rate.
    d. optimal caloric rate.

25. When you eat a meal, stretch receptors in your stomach reduce your hunger by sending impulses to the brain along the
    a. vagus nerve.
    b. gustatory nerve.
    c. trochlear nerve.
    d. trigeminal nerve.

Thought Questions

1. Given the factors that regulate hunger and eating, what are some ways to maintain a healthy body weight?

2. In what ways are sexual dysfunctions associated with different phases of the sexual response cycle?

3. How would the concept of optimal arousal explain your performance on an English exam?

4. How might research findings on the roles of intrinsic and extrinsic motivation explain why professional athletes who are paid millions of dollars to play games that children enjoy playing for free lose their desire to play?

Emotion

On September 16, 1999, CNN reported that U.S. Energy Secretary Bill Richardson had taken a polygraph test—popularly known as a lie detector test—during which he was asked if he had ever been a spy or met with foreign espionage agents. No results were made public, but it was presumed that he passed the test. Richardson took the test not because he was suspected of being a spy, but to demonstrate to nuclear weapons scientists that they had nothing to fear from mandatory polygraph testing. Following evidence of Chinese spying and lax security at weapons laboratories, Richardson urged that 5,000 scientists working for the Department of Energy submit to polygraph tests about security matters. Scientists with access to top-secret information about nuclear weapons were to be asked if they had ever illegally disclosed classified information; contacted foreign intelligence services without authorization; or committed espionage, sabotage, or terrorism. If they failed even one question, they would be subject to an FBI investigation.

Richardson's proposal was met by outrage from scientists, who claimed it threatened their sense of honor and violated their right to privacy. Scientists at the Lawrence Livermore National Laboratory in Livermore, California, argued that polygraph testing is neither valid nor reliable. Scientists at Los Alamos National Laboratory in New Mexico threatened to form a union to oppose the testing program.

In response, Richardson said, "I took the test. It was administered effectively, efficiently. It's easy and I believe scientifically sound. I respect the views of some of the lab scientists. But I think they have nothing to worry about." The U.S. Congress, backing Richardson and disregarding the scientists, passed a law permitting polygraph testing of employees with access to top-secret information. Directors of national laboratories insisted that the threat of this practice was hurting their efforts to recruit top scientists. Did scientists have good reason to fear the polygraph test? This question will be addressed later in the chapter. But to understand the nature and effectiveness of polygraph testing, it would be helpful to begin by learning about *emotion.*

How do you feel? Are you *anxious* about an upcoming exam, *depressed* by a recent loss, in *love* with a wonderful person, *angry* at a personal affront, or *happy* about your favorite team's performance? Such feelings are emotions. The word *emotion* comes from a Latin word meaning "to set in motion," and like motives (such as sex and hunger), emotions (such as love and anger) motivate behavior that helps us adapt to different situations (Ekman, 1992a). Though it is easy to recognize

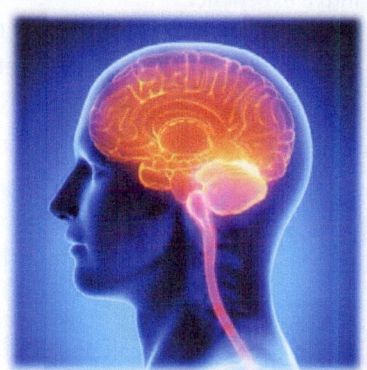

Source: CLIPAREA/Custom media/ Shutterstock.com.

Chapter Outline

The Biopsychology of Emotion

The Expression of Emotion

The Experience of Emotion

Theories of Emotion

an emotion, especially one that is a pure, prototypical example (such as extreme anger or intense romantic love), it is difficult to provide a formal definition of the concept itself (Russell, 1991). This difficulty led two prominent emotion researchers to observe, "Everyone knows what an emotion is, until asked to give a definition" (Fehr & Russell, 1984, p. 464).

Despite the difficulty of precisely defining the concept of emotion, most psychologists agree that an **emotion** is a motivated state that is marked by physiological arousal, expressive behavior, and cognitive experience. Emotions also vary in their intensity and pleasantness/unpleasantness (Buck, 1985). Consider an angry man. His heart might pound (a sign of physiological arousal), he might grit his teeth (an expressive behavior), and he might feel enraged (an intense, unpleasant mental experience). Emotions have evolved to motivate us to respond adaptively to changing environmental circumstances (Lang, Bradley, & Cuthbert, 1998). In trying to explain emotion, some psychologists prefer to study the biological level (the biopsychology of emotion), others the behavioral level (the expression of emotion), and still others the cognitive level (the experience of emotion).

emotion A motivated state marked by physiological arousal, expressive behavior, and cognitive experience.

The Biopsychology of Emotion

What are the physiological bases of emotion? To answer this question, psychologists study the autonomic nervous system, the brain, and neurochemicals.

The Autonomic Nervous System and Emotion

Both your emotional expression and your emotional experience depend on physiological arousal, which reflects activity in your *autonomic nervous system* (ANS). The system is called "autonomic" because it was thought to function independently, without the need for conscious, voluntary regulation by the brain. We now know that the brain and the spinal cord regulate the ANS; it does indeed operate below the level of consciousness. However, we still refer to the "autonomic" nervous system. Figure 12-1 illustrates the functions of the two branches of the autonomic nervous system: the *sympathetic nervous system* and the *parasympathetic nervous system*. The interplay of these two systems contributes to the ebb and flow of emotions and controls our internal organs such as the heart and intestines. The sympathetic nervous system relies on the neurotransmitter *norepinephrine* to regulate its target organs; the parasympathetic nervous system relies on the neurotransmitter *acetylcholine* to regulate its target organs.

Activation of the sympathetic nervous system can stimulate the **fight-or-flight response**, which evolved because it enabled our prehistoric ancestors to meet sudden physical threats (whether from nature, animals, or people) by either confronting them or running away from them. After a threat has been met or avoided, the sympathetic nervous system becomes less active and the parasympathetic nervous system becomes more active, calming the body. This system has been referred to as rest-and-digest. Yet, because the sympathetic nervous system stimulates the secretion of epinephrine and norepinephrine from the adrenal glands into the bloodstream, physiological arousal may last for a while after the threat has disappeared.

The fight-or-flight response is triggered not only by physical threats but also by psychological threats—such as academic demands that we feel are beyond our abilities. To appreciate the role of the autonomic nervous system in the emotional response to a psychological threat, imagine that you are about to give a classroom presentation for which you did not prepare adequately. As you walk to your class, you experience anxiety associated with physiological arousal induced by your sympathetic nervous system.

fight-or-flight response A state of physiological arousal that enables us to meet sudden threats by either confronting them or running away from them.

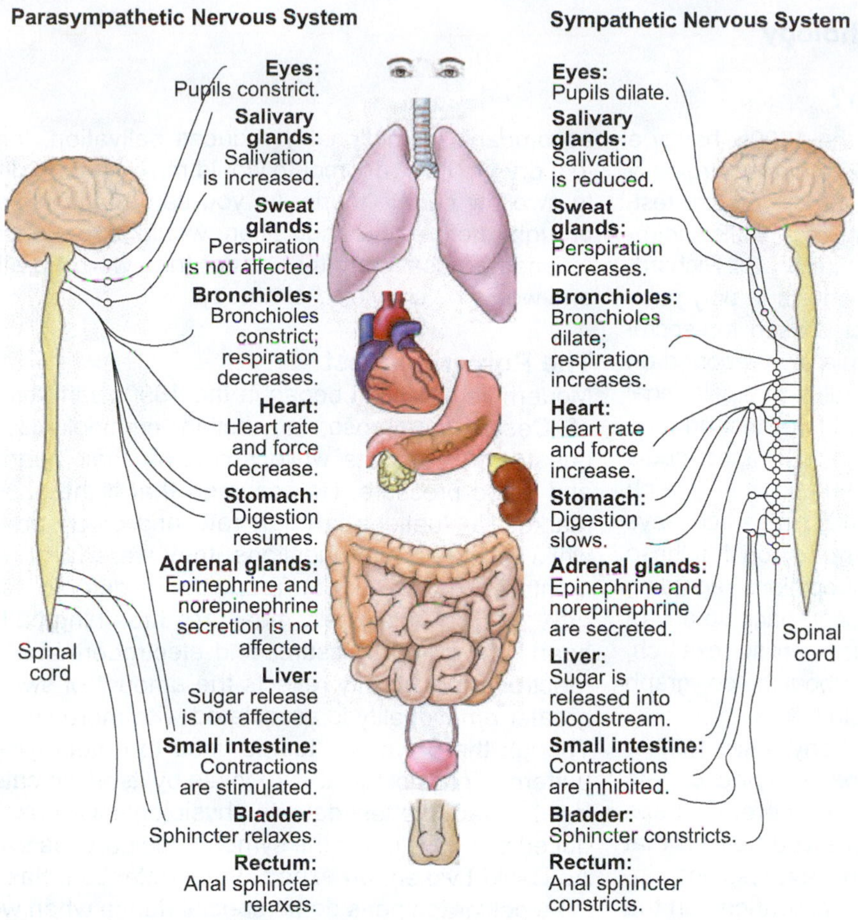

Parasympathetic Nervous System

Eyes: Pupils constrict.

Salivary glands: Salivation is increased.

Sweat glands: Perspiration is not affected.

Bronchioles: Bronchioles constrict; respiration decreases.

Heart: Heart rate and force decrease.

Stomach: Digestion resumes.

Adrenal glands: Epinephrine and norepinephrine secretion is not affected.

Liver: Sugar release is not affected.

Small intestine: Contractions are stimulated.

Bladder: Sphincter relaxes.

Rectum: Anal sphincter relaxes.

Spinal cord

Sympathetic Nervous System

Eyes: Pupils dilate.

Salivary glands: Salivation is reduced.

Sweat glands: Perspiration increases.

Bronchioles: Bronchioles dilate; respiration increases.

Heart: Heart rate and force increase.

Stomach: Digestion slows.

Adrenal glands: Epinephrine and norepinephrine are secreted.

Liver: Sugar is released into bloodstream.

Small intestine: Contractions are inhibited.

Bladder: Sphincter constricts.

Rectum: Anal sphincter constricts.

Spinal cord

FIGURE 12-1

The Autonomic Nervous System and Its Two Branches

Emotional responses involve the interplay of the two branches of the autonomic nervous system: the sympathetic nervous system, which tends to arouse us, and the parasympathetic nervous system, which tends to return us to a calmer state. The black lines represent clusters of neurons and their distribution to the organs. Both branches are constantly active, though one system can dominate depending on your arousal state.

As you enter the classroom, you become more alert and energetic as your circulatory system diverts blood rich in oxygen and other nutrients normally destined for your stomach and intestines to your brain and skeletal muscles. Your energy increases as your liver releases sugar into your bloodstream. Your heart pounds rapidly and strongly in response to epinephrine secreted by your adrenal glands. Your bronchioles dilate to permit more oxygen-rich air to enter your lungs, and you breathe more rapidly as your lungs work harder to expel carbon dioxide. A classmate might notice your pupils dilating, which improves your vision by letting more light into your eyes. And you might notice your mouth becoming dry, goose bumps appearing on your arms, and beads of perspiration forming on your forehead. Your dry mouth reflects a marked reduction in salivation. Your goose bumps are caused by hairs standing on end—a remnant of threat displays made by our furry prehistoric ancestors. And your perspiration provides a means of cooling off your aroused body.

Suppose that as you sit in class in this anxious, aroused state, your professor announces that a surprise guest speaker will lecture for the entire class period. You immediately feel relieved at not having to give your presentation; your arousal subsides partly because of activity in your autonomic nervous system. Your brain becomes less alert, your muscles less energetic, your heartbeat less noticeable, and your breathing more regular. Your pupils constrict to their normal size, your mouth becomes moist again, your goose bumps disappear, and you stop sweating. You might become so profoundly relaxed and relieved that you fall asleep during the guest speaker's lecture.

The Brain and Emotion

Though bodily arousal plays a role in emotionality, the brain is ultimately in control of emotional responses (LeDoux, 1995). Emotion researchers are especially interested in the roles of the limbic system and cerebral hemispheric lateralization in emotionality.

Do Lie Detectors Tell the Truth?

At times in the 1980s and again in the 1990s, hardly a week went by without the media reporting a controversy about the use of the polygraph test, or lie detector test. The chapter opened with a summary of a 1999 controversy about Department of Energy Secretary Bill Richardson's proposal to subject nuclear scientists to polygraph testing to ensure that they have not passed top-secret information to foreign spies. The media also reported on the role of polygraph testing in several high-profile legal cases, including the O. J. Simpson murder trial and the Bill Clinton–Monica Lewinsky sex scandal. But the media tend to report disagreements about the use of polygraph testing without reporting what scientific research says about its validity. One is left with the impression that these disagreements are simply clashes of opinions regarding its validity, with little scientific evidence to back up any of the competing claims. Consider what scientific research, as opposed to personal opinion, says about the polygraph as a means of identifying liars and truth tellers.

If you have ever detected a phony smile from a salesperson or politician, you probably noted certain cues indicating that the smile was insincere. Perhaps the smile lasted too long. Or perhaps you noticed that the smile was asymmetrical. Phony expressions, including smiles, will usually be more pronounced on the left side of the face than on the right side (Rinn, 1984). Nonetheless, in everyday life most people are poor at detecting deceit from facial expressions. One exception is U.S. Secret Service agents, who learn to attend to nonverbal cues in their efforts to protect the president from attack (Ekman & O'Sullivan, 1991). Other groups that are better than average at detecting deception from a person's demeanor include psychologists and law enforcement officers (Ekman, O'Sullivan, & Frank, 1999).

The detection of lies through interpretation of expressive behavior has a long history. The Old Testament describes a case in which King Solomon resolved a dispute between two women who claimed to be the mother of the same infant. Solomon wisely proposed cutting the infant in half, then giving one half to each woman. Whereas one of the women calmly agreed to this, the other pleaded with Solomon to give the infant to her adversary. Solomon reasoned that the pleading woman had to be the real mother because she was willing to lose the infant rather than see the child killed.

King Solomon inferred lying from expressive behavior, but lie detection has historically been based on the assumption that liars display increased physiological arousal. In the 15th century, interrogators for the Inquisition required suspected heretics to swallow pieces of bread and cheese. If the food stuck to the person's palate, he or she was considered guilty. As you will recall, the arousal of the sympathetic nervous system that accompanies emotionality reduces salivation, leading to a dry mouth. A dry mouth would make it more difficult to swallow certain foods. As you can imagine, people brought before the Inquisition would experience increased arousal—whether or not they were heretics—and would be convicted of heresy.

The Polygraph Test

Modern lie detection began in the 1890s with the work of Cesare Lombroso, an Italian criminologist who questioned suspects while recording their heart rate and blood pressure. He assumed that if they showed marked fluctuations in heart rate and blood pressure while responding to questions, they were lying (Kleinmuntz & Szucko, 1984b). Today the lie detector test, or **polygraph test**, typically measures breathing patterns, heart rate, blood pressure, and electrodermal activity. Electrodermal activity reflects the amount of sweating; greater emotionality is associated with more sweating. Though the polygraph test is used to detect lying, no pattern of physiological responses by itself indicates lying. Instead, the test detects physiological arousal produced by activation of the sympathetic nervous system. As David Lykken, an expert on lie detection, has said, "The polygraph pens do no special dance when we are lying" (Lykken, 1981, p. 10).

Given that no pattern of physiological responses indicates lying, how is the recording of physiological arousal used to detect lies? The typical polygraph test given to a criminal suspect begins with an explanation of the test and the kinds of questions to be asked. The suspect is then asked *control questions,* which are designed to provoke lying about minor transgressions common to almost everyone. For example, the suspect might be asked, "Have you ever stolen anything from an employer?" It is a rare person who has not stolen at least an inexpensive item, yet many people would answer no, creating an increase in physiological arousal; and even suspects who answer yes to a control question would probably experience some increase in physiological arousal in response to that question.

The suspect's physiological response to control questions is compared to her or his physiological response to *relevant questions,* which are concerned with facts about the crime, such as "Did you steal money from the bank safe?" Polygraphers assume that a guilty person will show greater physiological arousal in response to relevant questions and that an innocent person will show greater physiological arousal in response to control questions. Figure 12-2 shows a polygraph printout of differences in arousal in response to the different questions. The typical polygraph test asks about 12 relevant questions, which are repeated three or four times.

Do Lie Detectors Tell the Truth? *continued*

Issues in Lie Detection

Polygraph testing has provoked controversy because it is far from being a perfect measure of lying. One difficulty is that the accuracy of the polygraph test depends in part on the suspect's physiological reactivity. People with low reactivity exhibit a smaller difference between their responses to control questions and their responses to relevant questions than do people with high reactivity. This difference might cause an unemotional criminal to be declared innocent and an emotional innocent person to be declared guilty (Waid, Wilson, & Orne, 1981). Moreover, tranquilizers reduce the detectability of lying by reducing physiological arousal (Waid & Orne, 1982).

Criminals also are aware of countermeasures that can make them appear innocent on a polygraph test. Consider the case of Floyd Fay, an innocent man convicted in 1978 of murdering his best friend and sentenced to life in prison after failing a polygraph test that he had taken voluntarily. Two years later a public defender tracked down the real murderer. While in prison, Fay became an expert on lie detection and taught prisoners how to beat the polygraph test. Of 27 inmates who had admitted their guilt to him, 23 passed their polygraph tests (Kleinmuntz & Szucko, 1984a). One technique for fooling the polygraph test uses the properly timed induction of pain. For example, suppose that during control questions you bite your tongue or step on a tack hidden in your shoe. This would increase your level of physiological arousal in response to control questions, thereby reducing the difference between your physiological responses to control questions and relevant questions (Honts, Hodes, & Raskin, 1985).

Though aware that criminals can fool the polygraph machine, critics of the test are more concerned with the possibility that the polygraph will find innocent people guilty. In the 1980s millions of Americans were subjected to polygraph tests in criminal cases, employment screening, employee honesty checks, and security clearances (Kleinmuntz & Szucko, 1984b). In 1983 President Reagan gave an executive order to use the polygraph test to identify federal employees who reveal classified information. But a report commissioned by Congress found that the polygraph test was invalid in the situations favored by Reagan. The report concluded that the only justifiable use of the polygraph test is in criminal cases (Saxe, Dougherty, & Cross, 1985). Though the test might not be valid, it can elicit confessions from suspects who believe in its effectiveness (Simpson, 1986). Thus, the unreliability of the polygraph test makes its use to detect deception questionable (Fiedler, Schmid, & Stahl, 2002).

In June 1988 President Reagan, confronted with overwhelming opposition to the unrestricted use of polygraph tests, signed the Polygraph Protection Act banning their use for preemployment screening by private employers. But the law still permitted the use of polygraph tests in ongoing investigations of specific incidents. And drug companies, security services, government agencies, and private companies that have contracts with government intelligence agencies were exempted from the ban on using polygraph tests in employment screening (Bales, 1988).

What evidence led to the widespread opposition to the unrestricted use of the polygraph? Supporters of the polygraph test claim accuracy rates of 90 percent or better (Raskin & Podlesny, 1979). But research findings indicate

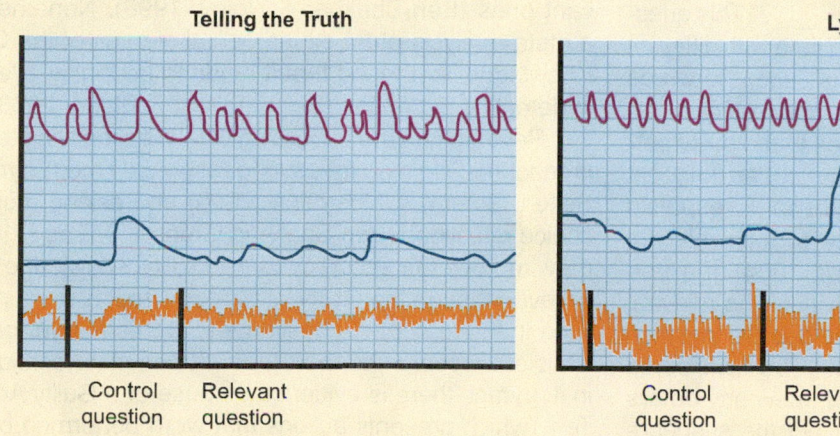

FIGURE 12-2 Relevant Questions versus Control Questions

The polygraph test compares physiological responses to relevant and control questions. The record on the left is of a person who responded less strongly to a question relevant to a crime than to an emotionally arousing control question not relevant to the crime. Such responses indicate to the examiner that the person is telling the truth. The record on the right is of a person who responded more strongly to a question relevant to a crime than to an emotionally arousing control question not relevant to the crime. Responses such as this one indicate to the examiner that the person is lying.

Do Lie Detectors Tell the Truth?   *continued*

that it is much less accurate than that, as revealed by the following study (Kleinmuntz & Szucko, 1984a). The polygraph printouts of 50 thieves and 50 innocent people were presented to six highly trained professional polygraphers. They were asked questions about real thefts. The results showed that the polygraphers correctly identified 76 percent of the guilty persons and 63 percent of the innocent persons. Though their performance was better than chance, these results also meant that they incorrectly identified 24 percent of the guilty persons as innocent and 37 percent of the innocent persons as guilty. The tendency of the polygraph test to produce unacceptably high rates of false positives (that is, identifying innocent persons as guilty) has been replicated in other studies (Horowitz, Kircher, Honts, & Raskin, 1997). The polygraph test's high rate of false positives can have tragic consequences for those who are unjustly denied jobs, fired from jobs, or prosecuted for crimes.

The Guilty Knowledge Test

A possible improvement over the control-question test is the **Guilty Knowledge Test,** developed by David Lykken (1974). If you have ever played the board game *Clue,* you have some understanding of the test. In contrast to the control-question test, Lykken's test assesses knowledge about a transgression rather than alleged anxiety about it. The Guilty Knowledge Test is useful only when details of the transgression are known to the transgressor but not to others who take the test. Consider its use in interrogating suspects in a bank robbery. A suspect would be asked questions about the victim, the site of the crime, and the commission of the crime. Instead of being asked, "Did you steal money from the bank safe?" the suspect would be asked, "Was the money stolen from the _____?" This question would be asked several times, each time with different words completing the statement. In this case, the words might be *bank safe, teller's drawer,* and *armored car.*

The Guilty Knowledge Test assumes that a guilty person (who knows details of the crime), but not an innocent person, will show more physiological arousal in response to the relevant words than in response to the irrelevant words (Verschuere, Crombez, & Koster, 2004). If a person shows greater physiological reactivity to the relevant words in a *series* of statements (a single positive instance would be insufficient), that person would be considered guilty. Of course, examiners should not know any details of the crime. Otherwise, they might affect the suspect's physiological response to relevant words (Elaad, 1997), perhaps by saying those words louder or softer. Researchers are developing a version of the Guilty Knowledge Test that would measure changes in brain-wave patterns to determine when a person has information that he or she is trying to conceal (Allen & Iacono, 1997).

A laboratory test in which undergraduates committed mock murders supported the assumption that guilt could be detected by differential physiological responses to relevant and irrelevant stimuli (Timm, 1982). In its first use in a study of real criminals, the Guilty Knowledge Test was given to 50 innocent and 48 guilty participants. The results supported the effectiveness of the test, particularly its ability to avoid false positives. Judges correctly classified 94 percent of the innocent and 65 percent of the guilty (Elaad, 1990). Research findings indicate that the Guilty Knowledge Test is biased toward false negatives, whereas control-question tests are biased toward false positives (McCauley & Forman, 1988). So, people more interested in protecting the innocent would favor the Guilty Knowledge Test, whereas those more interested in ferreting out transgressors would favor the control-question test.

Lykken, recognizing the merits of the Guilty Knowledge Test, urges its widespread adoption (Lykken, 1988). But research support for the superiority of the Guilty Knowledge Test has not been universal. Though one study found that it was effective in detecting individuals with knowledge relevant to a crime (Elaad, 1994), another study found that participants with guilty knowledge might not be detected reliably (Bradley & Warfield, 1984). Still another study found no difference in the success of the control-question test and Guilty Knowledge Test in detecting lying (Podlesny & Raskin, 1978). There also is evidence that guilty people can defeat the Guilty Knowledge Test by recalling emotional scenes from their past during the presentation of irrelevant items. This reduces differences in their physiological responses to relevant and irrelevant items, making them appear to have no more knowledge of relevant items than irrelevant ones (Ben-Shakhar & Dolev, 1996). Nonetheless, a meta-analysis of 80 experimental studies of the Guilty Knowledge Test found that it tends to be highly effective in detecting deception (Ben-Shakhar & Elaad, 2003).

Researchers are assessing whether modifying testing procedures, such as measuring response time (Seymour, Seifert, Shafto, & Mosmann, 2000) and asking multiple-choice questions (Ben-Shakhar, Gronau, & Elaad, 1999), may improve the accuracy of the Guilty Knowledge Test. So even though the Guilty Knowledge Test is more promising than the control-question test, it has not yet gained sufficient research support to merit complete confidence in it. In fact, there is evidence that use of a Guilty Actions Test (which presents actions that were performed by the perpetrator) might be superior to the Guilty Knowledge Test (Bradley, MacLaren, & Carle, 1996). Moreover, scientists have had some initial success in using brain-scanning techniques, such as functional MRI, to detect patterns of brain activity that are associated with deceptive responses (Lee et al., 2002).

The Limbic System and Emotion

As discussed in Chapter 3, autonomic nervous system arousal is regulated by the brain structure called the *hypothalamus,* a component of the *limbic system,* which also includes the *amygdala* and the *septum.* Among other things, the hypothalamus helps control changes in breathing and heart output during the fight-or-flight response (Spyer, 1989). The septum (a neural relay center in the brain) suppresses aversive emotional states. For example, electrical stimulation of the septum in rats reduces their tendency to avoid fear-inducing stimuli (Thomas, 1988).

The amygdala prompts us to react emotionally to environmental circumstances, enabling us to respond adaptively and to form memories of emotional situations (Pare, Collins, & Pelletier, 2002). The amygdala plays more of a role in recognizing unpleasant stimuli evoking emotionally negative feelings, such a fear or anger, than in recognizing pleasant stimuli evoking emotionally positive feelings (Hamann, Ely, Hoffman, & Kilts, 2002). Evidence supporting this finding comes from research on the effects of damage to the amygdala on the recognition of emotions. One study reported the case of a 54-year-old woman with amygdala damage who experienced difficulty in interpreting facial expressions of emotion. However, her ability to encode facial expressions of fear and other basic emotions was unaffected (Anderson & Phelps, 2000). In electrophysiological studies using animals, single neurons in the amygdala can become active when fearful stimuli are presented or retrieved from memory (Courtin, Karalis, Gonzalez-Campo, Wurtz, & Herry, 2013). These studies indicate the importance of the amygdala in processing information about environmental threats. The main limbic system structures are illustrated in Figure 12-3.

Hemispheric Lateralization and Emotion

Though the limbic system is important in the processing of emotions (Servan-Schreiber & Perlstein, 1998), the *cerebral cortex,* which covers the cerebral hemispheres, is important for our subjective experience of emotion. For example, though the limbic system tends to trigger rapid, automatic emotional reactions to stimuli, the frontal cortex modulates these reactions so that they are not excessive (Hariri, Bookheimer, & Mazziotta, 2000). Thus, a sudden noise might make you instantly experience fear generated by activity in your limbic system, but if you immediately realize that the noise was produced by your pet dog, your frontal cortex would prevent you from running away screaming or grabbing an object with which to defend yourself.

Research findings indicate that the cerebral hemispheres play different roles in emotion. For example, PET scans indicate that the right hemisphere is more active than the left when we try to assess emotional states from facial expressions (Nakamura et

polygraph test The lie detector test, which assesses lying by measuring changing patterns of physiological arousal in response to particular questions.

Guilty Knowledge Test A method that assesses lying by comparing physiological arousal in response to information that is relevant to a transgression and physiological arousal in response to information that is irrelevant to that transgression.

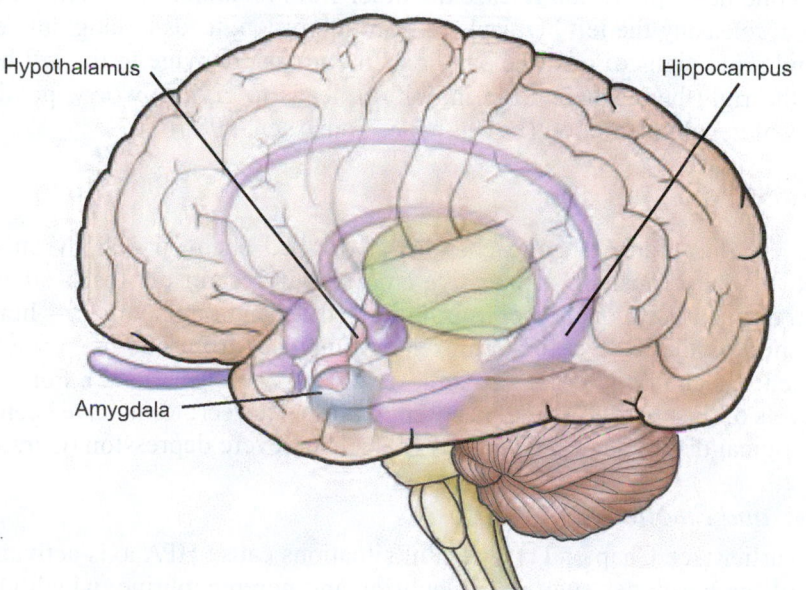

FIGURE 12-3
The Limbic System

A lateral view of the brain showing the limbic structures deep within the brain. Our emotional responses are regulated by activity in the limbic system, particularly in the amygdala, hippocampus, and hypothalamus.

Labels: Hypothalamus, Hippocampus, Amygdala

al., 1999). Research findings also suggest that each cerebral hemisphere is specialized to process different emotions, with the left hemisphere more involved in positive emotions and the right hemisphere more involved in negative emotions (Marosi et al., 2002). But keep in mind that particular emotions are not processed *solely* in one hemisphere or the other. Both cerebral hemispheres play a role in all emotional experience (Danko, Bechtereva, Shemyakina, & Antonova, 2003).

Much of our knowledge about the role of each hemisphere in emotional experience comes from studies, particularly those conducted by Richard Davidson, that have measured the relative degree of activity in each hemisphere during emotional arousal. For example, excessive activation of the left hemisphere is associated with euphoria, and excessive activation of the right hemisphere is associated with depression (Flor-Henry, 1983). One study measured electrical activity while participants watched emotionally positive or negative film clips to evoke positive or negative emotions in them. Those who experienced positive emotion had higher left-hemisphere activity; those who experienced negative emotion had higher right-hemisphere activity (Wheeler, Davidson, & Tomarken, 1993). A study that recorded electrical activity from the brains of 10-month-old infants found that hemispheric differences in the processing of emotions appear early in life. Greater activation of the left hemisphere was associated with a pleasant facial expression and a tendency to approach people. In contrast, greater activation of the right hemisphere was associated with an unpleasant facial expression and a tendency to withdraw from people (Fox & Davidson, 1988). Nonetheless, a published review of the relevant research literature found that the right hemisphere plays a greater role than the left hemisphere in regulating facial expressions of emotion (Borod, Haywood, & Koff, 1997).

The *Wada test,* which involves selective anesthesia of one cerebral hemisphere to determine hemispheric functions (particularly the site of the speech center), also has provided evidence of the lateralization of emotionality. In the Wada test, the anesthetic sodium amobarbital is injected into the left or right carotid artery of patients who are about to undergo brain surgery. Because the carotid arteries supply blood to the brain, injection of sodium amobarbital into one of them will anesthetize the associated hemisphere. Research using the Wada test shows that laughter and elation (positive emotionality) are more frequent after right-hemisphere anesthesia, whereas crying (negative emotionality) is more frequent after left-hemisphere anesthesia (Lee, Loring, Meader, & Brooks, 1990).

Further evidence that the left hemisphere is more related to positive emotions and the right hemisphere more related to negative emotions has been provided by studies of brain damage. Because each cerebral hemisphere inhibits the emotional activity of the other, we normally experience neither intensely positive nor intensely negative emotions. But damage to one hemisphere can release the other from its inhibition. Damage to the right hemisphere, releasing the left hemisphere from inhibition, leads to laughing, elation, optimism, and other signs of positive emotion. In contrast, damage to the left hemisphere, releasing the right hemisphere from inhibition, leads to crying, worry, pessimism, and other signs of negative emotion (Leventhal & Tomarken, 1986).

The Chemistry of Emotion

When we say that there is "good chemistry" or "bad chemistry" between people, we mean that they have positive or negative emotions in response to each other. Research has shown that our emotional responses do indeed depend on chemistry—hormones and neurotransmitters that convey emotion-related impulses from one neuron to another or between neurons and body organs (Baum, Grunberg, & Singer, 1992). For example, abnormal levels of the neurotransmitters norepinephrine and serotonin have been implicated in psychological disorders (see Chapter 14), such as severe depression (Curzon, 1982).

Hormones and Emotion

As noted earlier (see Chapter 11), stressful situations cause HPA axis activation and the secretion of the hormones such as epinephrine and norepinephrine, which also serve as neurotransmitters. In a study of psychologists and physicians, levels of these hormones were measured on a day when participants gave a public speech and on a day when they did not. Public speaking was associated with an increase in the level of both epinephrine and norepinephrine. Epinephrine increases glucose metabolism allowing for energy expenditure. Moreover, there was a rise in blood cholesterol on days when participants gave speeches relative to days when they did not. Perhaps stress hormones, by stimulating an increase in low-density lipoproteins (which are implicated in cardiovascular disease), provide one of the mechanisms by which emotional responses to stressful situations contribute to the development of cardiovascular disease (Bolm-Audorff, Schwammle, Ehlenz, & Kaffarnik, 1989). Another important hormone that regulates the stress response is *cortisol*. Cortisol is a glucocorticoid secreted from the adrenal glands in response to stress. The hypothalamus signals to the adrenal gland to increase or decrease production of cortisol and other hormones. There are glucocorticoid receptors in many parts of the brain, and activation of the receptors contributes to our neural response to stress. This interplay of hormonal and neural regulation is considered a feed-back loop.

Endorphins and Emotion

Endorphins, a class of neurotransmitters discussed in Chapters 3 and 5, contribute to emotional experiences by providing pain relief and evoking feelings of euphoria. For example, blood levels of endorphins rise markedly after bungee jumping and correlate positively with resulting feelings of euphoria (Hennig, Laschefski, & Opper, 1994). Even the emotional thrill we experience from a concert, a motion picture, or a dance performance may depend on endorphin activity. This finding was demonstrated in a study of college students who listened to a musical passage and then received an injection of either naloxone (a drug that blocks the effects of endorphins) or a placebo (in this case, a saline solution that does not block the effects of endorphins). Neither the participants nor the experimenter knew whether participants had received naloxone or a placebo (you might recognize this application of the *double-blind procedure* that was described in Chapter 2); the double-blind procedure prevented participant bias or experimenter bias from affecting the results. After receiving the injection, participants again listened to the musical passage. When asked to estimate the intensity of their emotional thrill in response to the music, participants who had received naloxone reported a significant decrease in intensity. Participants who had received a placebo reported no such decrease. Because naloxone blocks the effects of endorphins, but a placebo does not, the findings support the role of endorphins in positive emotional experiences (Goldstein, 1980).

Endorphins and Emotion

The emotional thrills experienced by fans at concert festivals might be caused by the release of endorphins in their brains.
Source: Franz Pfluegl/Shutterstock.com.

1. What evidence is there that positive and negative emotions are processed primarily in different brain hemispheres?

2. What evidence is there that endorphins are involved in feelings of euphoria?

The Expression of Emotion

How do you know how your fellow students feel? Because our emotional experiences are private, they cannot be directly observed by other people. Instead, emotions are inferred from descriptions of them or from expressive behaviors. Behaviors that express emotions include vocal qualities, body movements, and facial expressions. The expression of emotion varies across cultures. For example, people from collectivist cultures, such as Costa Rica, are less comfortable expressing negative emotions than are people from individualistic cultures, such as the United States (Stephan, Stephan, & de Vargas, 1996). Yet, there are basic facial expressions of emotion that are recognizable across cultures (Izard, 1994). Research studies also indicate that there might be gender differences in emotional expression. This research is discussed in Chapter 14.

Vocal Qualities and Emotion

prosody The vocal features of speech other than the words themselves.

When you speak, both your words and your voice convey emotion (Pell, Jaywant, Monetta, & Kotz, 2011). The vocal features of speech other than the words themselves are called **prosody**. Prosodic features include rate, pitch, and loudness. You can use the same spoken words to express different emotions by simply altering the prosodic features of your speech—the same statement can sound sincere or sarcastic depending on its vocal qualities. When you are happy, your voice goes up in pitch (just recall the last time you heard the voices of two people greeting each other after a long separation). Changes in vocal qualities indicative of changes in emotion tend to be consistent from one person to another and from one culture to another (Frick, 1985). Perhaps these common vocal patterns evolved in our prehistoric, prelanguage ancestors as a universal means of communicating emotional states in everyday social interaction.

Voice quality also affects social relations. Sometimes it can cause social rejection, as in a study in which undergraduates rated depressed or nondepressed fellow undergraduates who differed in how they spoke. Depressed participants were more likely to be rejected, in part because they spoke in soft, flat voices, with long pauses. This finding is important, because unappealing prosodic features can create a vicious cycle in which the depressed person alienates others, thereby reducing the likelihood of positive social interactions that might help the person overcome his or her depression (Paddock & Nowicki, 1986).

The prosodic features of speech are regulated primarily by the right cerebral hemisphere (Gandour, Larsen, Dechongkit, & Ponglorpisit, 1995), both when we speak (Graves & Landis, 1990) and when we listen to a speaker (Herrero & Hillix, 1990). Evidence for the role of the right hemisphere in prosody comes from studies of stroke victims and patients undergoing the Wada test. Patients with right-hemisphere strokes might retain their ability to speak but might speak with abnormal emotional tone (Gorelick & Ross, 1987). A study in which the Wada test was given to patients about to undergo brain surgery to relieve their epilepsy found that when the patients received injections of sodium amobarbital in the left carotid artery, they lost their ability to speak. When it was injected in their right carotid artery, they retained their ability to speak but lost the ability to impart emotion to their speech (Ross, Edmondson, Seibert, & Homan, 1988). In essence, it seems that "the left hemisphere provides the text [words], while the right hemisphere plays the accompaniment [emotional tone]" (Merewether & Alpert, 1990, p. 325). Though most research studies on the lateralization of prosody support a greater role for the right hemisphere, some also have found similar role for the left hemisphere (Pell,

1998). Pell (1999) suggests that damage to either the left or the right hemisphere can produce emotional prosody deficits. A recent functional MRI study also found evidence for bilateral processing of emotion in language (Kotz et al., 2003). Nevertheless, many newer fMRI studies point to a significant and distinct role for the right hemisphere in decoding emotional prosody (Wildgruber et al., 2005).

Body Movements and Emotion

Body Movements

Emotional cues from body movements are distinct from those provided by facial expressions and physical appearance.

Source: ostill/Shutterstock.com.

If you have observed the gestures of impatient drivers in heavy traffic on a hot summer day, you know that body movements can convey emotions. Even movements of the whole body can do so. The performance of basketball player Michael Jordan was especially appealing because his movements conveyed emotions.

But how do we know that we are responding to people's movements rather than simply to their facial expressions or physical appearances? The importance of body movements in expressing emotion has been demonstrated in studies that have eliminated other nonverbal emotional cues. In one study (Walk & Homan, 1984), college students watched a videotape of people performing dances that portrayed various emotions. To eliminate the influence of facial expressions and physical appearance, the dancers wore lights on their joints and danced in total darkness. Thus, participants saw only the movement of lights. Nonetheless, they accurately identified the emotions represented by the dances. This study indicates that the emotional cues provided by body movements are distinct from those provided by facial expressions or physical appearance.

The ability to decode nonverbal behavior is important in social interaction, as exemplified by the following research findings. Women are superior to men in decoding emotional states from body movements (Sogon & Izard, 1987). Elementary school children who are better at decoding nonverbal emotional cues are more popular (Nowicki & Duke, 1992). College roommates rate their relationship more positively when both are high in nonverbal decoding ability than when one or both are low in it (Hodgins & Zuckerman, 1990). And psychological counselors might be more effective when they are skillful in noting changes in their clients' nonverbal behavior (Hill & Stephany, 1990). The ability to recognize specific emotions from particular patterns of body movements develops across early childhood, with the ability to recognize basic emotions—including fear, anger, sadness, and happiness—present by age 8 (Boone & Cunningham, 1998).

We seem to prefer an optimal level of nonverbal interaction in everyday social interactions. We like people who are neither too nonverbally aloof nor too nonverbally intrusive. In a study that supported this finding, people who were walking on a college campus were asked to respond to a survey. During the brief interaction, they were randomly exposed to one of four conditions related to the interviewer's behavior: (1) eye contact and a momentary touch; (2) eye contact and no touch; (3) no eye contact and a momentary touch; or (4) no eye contact and no touch. At the end of the interaction, the interviewer dropped several folded questionnaires. Participants in the second or third conditions were more likely to help pick up the papers than were participants in the first or fourth. Thus, in agreement with the notion that there is an optimal level of nonverbal communication, participants responded more positively to a moderate level of nonverbal interaction (Goldman & Fordyce, 1983).

Facial Expressions and Emotion

Philip D. Chesterfield, an 18th-century British statesman, noted that our faces give away our emotions: "Look in the face of the person to whom you are speaking if you wish to know his real sentiments, for he can command his words more easily than his countenance." Chesterfield's observation may explain in part how teachers' expectations create the Pygmalion effect (see Chapter 2). Though teachers might believe that they are unbiased when speaking to their students, their facial expressions can communicate their true feelings, whether positive or negative, about particular students (Babad, Bernieri, & Rosenthal, 1989). But our recognition of facial expressions might depend on the social context. In one study, participants who displayed facial expressions of anger while in a frightening situation were judged to be afraid (Carroll & Russell, 1996).

Research has shown that facial expressions convey both the intensity and the pleasant-ness of our emotional states. Infants can express the emotions of joy and surprise as early as 4 months of age (Bennett, Bendersky, & Lewis, 2002). However, children's ability to recognize emotions from facial expressions develops more gradually. One study found that 5-month-old infants were able to discriminate between a smile and facial expressions of fear (Bornstein & Arterberry, 2003). And in another study, children aged 2 to 5 years were asked to identify and label facial expressions of basic emotions. The participants' ability to identify emotions improved with age. Whereas younger participants could reli-ably identify expressions of happiness, anger, and sadness, the older participants could more accurately identify expressions of fear, surprise, and disgust (Widen & Russell, 2003). As in the recognition of emotions from body movements, women are superior to men in recognizing emotions from facial expressions (Giovannini & Ricci Bitti, 1981)—a gender difference that emerges as early as infancy (McClure, 2000). Moreover, though men and women tend to respond empathetically by mimicking facial expressions, women do so more demonstratively (Lundqvist, 1995).

Does women's greater nonverbal expressivity reflect greater emotionality? One of the most consistent, long-standing gender stereotypes states just that—women are the emo-tional sex (e.g., Williams & Best, 1990). Two studies tested the relationship between gender role stereotypes and the interpretation of emotional expression in women (Plant, Hyde, Keltner, & Devine, 2000). A sample of 117 female and male undergraduates com-pleted a questionnaire assessing the frequency with which men and women experienced 19 emotions. Participants believed that most of these emotions (awe, embarrassment, fear, distress, happiness, guilt, sympathy, sadness, love, surprise, shame, and shyness) were experienced more frequently in women than in men. Men were thought to experi-ence only two emotions more frequently—pride and anger.

Another sample of over 150 male and female undergraduates then was asked to rate slides of two men and two women trained to pose facial expressions of four emotions. In two of the slides unambiguous emotions were posed; that is, pure expressions of anger and sadness. In two of the slides ambiguous emotions were posed; that is, facial expres-sions were a blend of anger and sadness.

Results indicated that gender-role stereotypes influenced ratings of emotional expres-sion by female stimuli. Participants rated women expressing ambiguous emotions as both sadder and less angry than men. This effect also was observed for the two slides depicting women posing unambiguous facial expressions of anger—participants rated these stimuli as a blend of anger and sadness. Thus, it appears that observers' interpretation of men's and women's emotional expression can be influenced by gender-role stereotypes. Women were perceived to be expressing greater sadness, a female-stereotyped emotion, whereas men were perceived to be expressing more anger, a male-stereotyped emotion.

Actors who feel the emotions they are portraying facially produce performances that are more emotionally convincing to audiences (Gosselin, Kirouac, & Dore, 1995). Knowledge of the relationship between facial expressions and emotions has enabled re-searchers to distinguish honest emotional expressions from fake ones. For example, the face reveals when smiles are sincere or false. Sincere smiles include muscular activity around the eyes, causing the skin to wrinkle, and around the mouth, causing the corners of the lips to rise (Quagflieg, Vermuelen, & Roisson, 2013). This natural smile is called the *Duchenne smile*. In contrast, when people display insincere smiles, perhaps to hide their negative emotional state, the corners of their lips are drawn downward and their upper lip curls up. In one experiment, participants were more likely to display the Duchenne smile when they watched a pleasant film than when they watched an unpleasant film. They also reported more positive emotions when they exhibited the Duchenne smile, verifying it as a sign of a pleasant emotional state (Ekman, Davidson, & Friesen, 1990).

Researchers studying smiling also have investigated the relationship between gender roles and emotional expression. In one creative study, school yearbooks—from kindergarten to col-lege—were collected, and photographs of students, staff, and faculty were coded for the pres-ence or absence of smiling. Gender differences were small to nonexistent until 4th grade—at which point girls smiled more frequently than did boys. This gender difference increased until

9th grade and remained steady through adulthood, a difference that the researchers attributed to gender-role socialization (Dodd, Russell, & Jenkins, 1999).

Heredity and Facial Expressions

Charles Darwin (1872/1965) believed that facial expressions evolved because they promoted survival by communicating emotions and helping individuals distinguish friend from foe. For example, the human facial expression of contempt might be a modification of the snarl found in dogs, apes, and our prehistoric ancestors (Izard & Haynes, 1988). Darwin's belief was supported in an experiment that measured how quickly participants could detect an angry face or a happy face in a crowd (Hansen & Hansen, 1988). Participants reported that a single angry face seemed to pop out of the crowd faster than a single happy face. The results supported the participants' impressions—they were able to detect an angry face faster than a happy face. Likewise, a more recent study has found that participants detect angry postures in a crowd faster than happy postures. Thus, angry faces and postures "pop out" from a crowd and are more quickly detected by people. Why might we have evolved the ability to detect angry faces and postures more quickly than other faces and postures? A possible reason is that it promotes our survival by motivating us to take more immediate action to confront or to escape from a person displaying an angry face (Gilbert, Martin, & Coulson, 2011).

Research by Carroll Izard (1990a) and his colleagues supports Darwin's view that facial expressions for basic emotions are inborn and universal. One line of research has found that even people who are blind from birth can use facial expressions to accurately communicate their emotional states to others (Galati, Miceli, & Sini, 2001). An early case study involved a 10-year-old girl who had been born deaf and blind. Despite her inability to see normal facial expressions or to receive spoken instructions on how to form them, she displayed appropriate facial expressions for the basic emotions, which include fear, anger, disgust, sadness, and surprise (Goodenough, 1932). Nonetheless, blind infants exhibit a more limited repertoire of facial expressions than do sighted infants (Troster & Brambring, 1992).

A second line of research support for the inborn, universal nature of facial expressions comes from studies showing that young infants produce facial expressions for the basic emotions (Izard, Huebner, Risser, McGinnes, & Dougherty, 1980). In one study, newborn infants were given solutions of sugar or quinine (which tastes bitter). Despite having no prior experience with those tastes, their facial expressions showed pleasure or displeasure, depending on which solution they had tasted. And the intensity of their facial expressions varied with the strength of the solutions (Ganchrow, Steiner, & Daher, 1983). Though infants can produce facial expressions for the basic emotions, their degree of expressiveness varies across cultures. Chinese infants are less facially expressive in smiling and crying than are Japanese or European American infants (Camras et al., 1998).

Culture and Facial Expressions

Further support for Darwin's evolutionary view of facial expressions comes from studies showing that facial expressions for the basic emotions are universal across cultures (Ekman, 1993; Izard, 1994). Examples of facial expressions of each of the basic emotions are presented in Figure 12-4. The research participants in one study were members of the Fore tribe of New Guinea, who had almost no contact with European Americans prior to the study (Ekman & Friesen, 1971). The tribe members listened to descriptions of a series of emotion-arousing situations representing joy, fear, anger, disgust, sadness, or surprise. The descriptions included situations such as "He is looking at something that smells bad" and "Her friends have come, and she is happy." After each description, the tribe members viewed a set of three photographs of European American faces expressing different emotions, from which they selected the face portraying the emotion of the person in the description they had just heard.

The tribe members correctly identified expressions portraying joy, anger, sadness, and disgust but failed to distinguish between expressions portraying fear and surprise. Perhaps

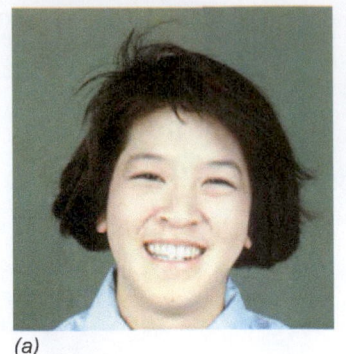

(a)

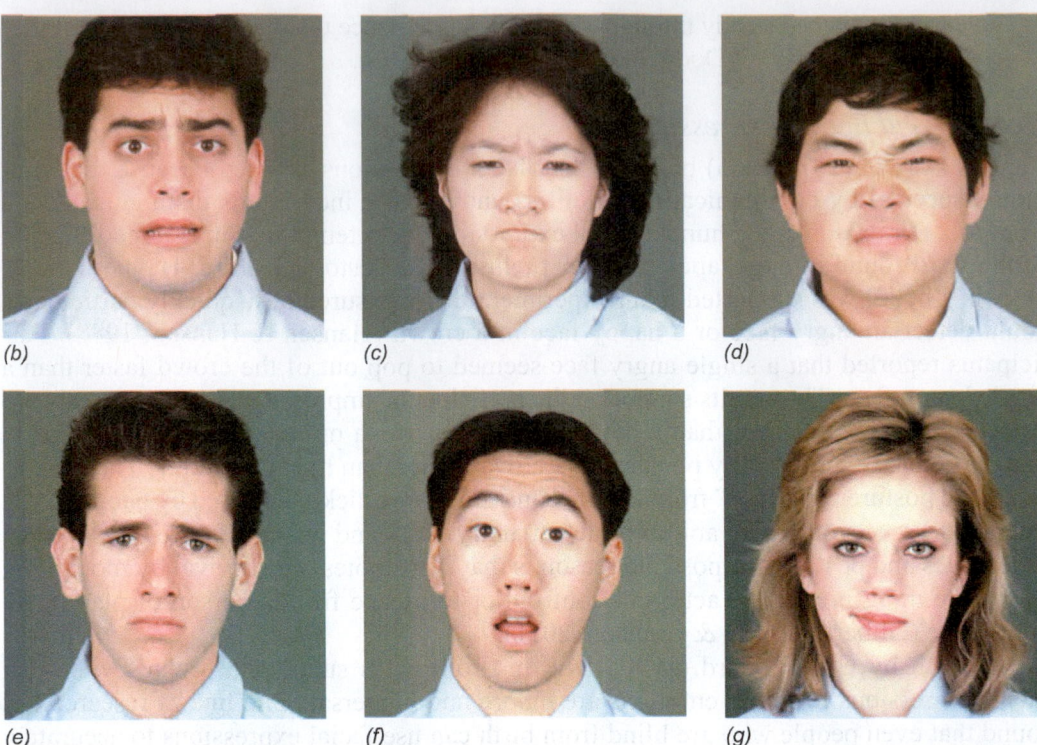

(b)　　　(c)　　　(d)

(e)　　　(f)　　　(g)

FIGURE 12-4
The Universality of Facial Expressions

Support for the inborn, universal nature of facial expressions representing the basic emotions comes from studies showing similar facial expressions in people from different cultures. Each of the photos here shows one of the following emotions: anger, sadness, happiness, contempt, surprise, disgust, and fear. Can you assign the correct emotion to each photo? (Answers are below.)

Source: © 1988–2004 David Matsumoto and Paul Ekman. Reprinted with permission.

Answers: (a) Happiness. (b) Fear. (c) Anger. (d) Disgust. (e) Sadness. (f) Surprise. (g) Contempt.

the tribe members' expressions for fear and surprise did not differ because similar situations (such as an enemy or a wild animal suddenly appearing from out of the jungle) evoke both fear and surprise in their culture. This study was replicated, with similar results, in a more recent study of people in 10 different cultures from around the world (Ekman et al., 1987). A meta-analysis of 97 studies supported the universality of certain emotional expressions. In more than 95 percent of the samples, emotions were universally recognized at levels greater than chance. The average cross-cultural accuracy rate was 58 percent. However, the cross-cultural accuracy rate was influenced by a number of factors. Recognition of facial expression of emotion was superior among members of the same national, ethnic, or regional group. This finding suggests that whereas there is remarkable universality in the facial expression of emotion, people are able to identify emotional expressions within their own cultural group with greater accuracy. However, this in-group advantage was found to be greater in culturally isolated groups. Thus, geographic proximity and cross-cultural interaction can reduce this ingroup advantage (Elfenbein & Ambady, 2002).

Nonetheless, some researchers have found that cross-cultural differences in the detection of universal facial expressions of emotion vary as a function of the methodology used in the studies (Frank & Stennett, 2001; Haidt & Keltner, 1999). And other researchers question whether research showing cross-cultural consistency in recognition of facial expressions has been sound enough to merit accepting the findings (Russell, 1994). That is, there are cross-cultural differences in the subjective feelings, physiological responses, and expressive behavior associated with emotions (Scherer & Wallbott, 1994). For example, one survey of more than 4,000 male and female participants in 30 countries investigated the influence of culture on people's moods after crying. The results indicated that the emotional response to a crying episode depended on cultural norms of emotional expression. In cultures where crying was common, participants reported feeling better after a cry. In cultures where crying was uncommon, participants reported feeling worse after a cry. As you might expect, cross-cultural differences in the frequency of crying were related to shameful feelings about shedding tears. Thus, crying in cultures that discourage such expressions of emotion is accompanied by a feeling of shame and a worsening of mood. And crying in cultures that encourage such expressions of emotion is accompanied by emotional relief (Becht & Vingerhoets, 2002).

Section Review: The Expression of Emotion

1. What gender differences have been found in nonverbal expressivity?
2. What evidence is there that certain emotional facial expressions are universal?

The Experience of Emotion

Though we have hundreds of words for emotions, there seem to be only a few basic emotions, from which all others are derived. One model of emotion, devised by Robert Plutchik (1980), considers joy, fear, anger, disgust, sadness, surprise, acceptance, and anticipation to be the basic emotions. More complex emotions arise from mixtures of these basic ones.

Charles Darwin assumed that the basic emotions evolved because they promoted our survival. For example, disgust (which means "bad taste") might have evolved because it prevented our ancient ancestors from ingesting poisonous substances. People in all cultures exhibit an early feeling of disgust at the sight and smell of feces—the "universal disgust object" (Rozin & Fallon, 1987). Note that disgust involves each of the major aspects of emotion: physiological change (stomach contractions causing nausea), expressive behavior (a contorted face), and cognitive experience (a feeling of revulsion). And the facial expression of disgust now has a social meaning as well, expressing revulsion at something that someone has said or done.

Folk wisdom holds that just as certain people are prone to experience unpleasant emotions, certain days—particularly so-called blue Mondays—are more likely to induce unpleasant emotions. In a study of the blue Monday effect researchers asked that people who insisted their moods were lowest on Mondays keep daily diaries of their emotional states (Stone, Hedges, Neale, & Satin., 1985). The results indicated that a given person's emotional states tended to be similar on Monday, Tuesday, Wednesday, and Thursday. But as you might expect, the person's emotional state on weekend days—Friday, Saturday, and Sunday—tended to be more positive than on weekdays. It might be that our blue Mondays owe their blueness to the contrast of returning to our normal weekday emotional state rather than to something unique about Mondays. In essence, we might have blue Mondays, but we also have equally blue Tuesdays, Wednesdays, and Thursdays. We simply notice more the contrast between bright Sunday and blue Monday. There also is evidence that the expectation that Mondays will be blue might account in part for individuals reporting less positive moods on Mondays (Croft & Walker, 2001). Older and retired participants also are less likely to report changes in mood over the course of the week (Stone, Schneider, & Harter, 2012).

The experience of emotion varies in both its intensity and its pleasantness. People who tend to experience intensely pleasant emotions (such as elation) also tend to experience intensely unpleasant emotions (such as despair). People who tend to experience mildly pleasant emotions (such as gladness) also tend to experience mildly unpleasant emotions (such as disappointment). This variation might be one reason why our happiness depends more on the frequency than on the intensity of our positive emotional experiences. A second reason is that intensely positive events can make less intense positive events seem even less positive. And a third reason is that the happier you are when you succeed at a task, the unhappier you will be when you fail at it (Diener, Colvin, Pavot, & Allman, 1991).

There is evidence, however, that culture influences the experience of positive and negative emotions. One study compared self-reported emotional experiences in a number of situations in samples of undergraduates recruited from the University of Michigan and the University of Beijing. Positive and negative emotions were negatively correlated in the American sample. Thus, in situations that American participants experienced as very joyful and loving, they reported experiencing *less* sadness and fear. In contrast, ratings of positive and negative emotions were positively correlated in the Chinese sample. In situations that Chinese participants experienced as very joyful and loving, they reported experiencing *more* sadness and fear. Though gender differences were observed across cultures—the correlation for women in both samples was stronger than that for men—the researchers attributed these findings to cultural differences in the interpretation of positive and negative events. Americans appear to adopt an optimistic *or* pessimistic perspective, depending on the circumstances. In Chinese culture, successes are not celebrated with elation, because things might not turn out so well in the future. And the blow of failure may be softened by the thought that things might turn out better next time (Bagozzi, Wong, & Yi, 1999).

People tend to view pleasant emotions, such as happiness, as normal, and unpleasant emotions, such as depression, as abnormal (Sommers, 1984). Yet, until the past few decades, psychologists had conducted many more studies of unpleasant emotions. In fact, *Psychological Abstracts,* traditionally the main research tool of psychologists, first published in the 1920s, did not include the term *happiness* in its index until 1973 (Diener, 1984). Another perusal of *Psychological Abstracts* found that it contained more emotion-related references under the category of "pathology" than under any other category (Whissell, 1984). To counter the traditional overemphasis placed on unpleasant emotions, and because unpleasant emotions such as anxiety and depression are discussed in later chapters, this chapter discusses the topics of happiness and humor.

Happiness

Many philosophers have considered happiness, what researchers in the field now call *subjective well-being,* the highest good (Diener, Suh, Lucas, & Smith, 1999). Thomas Jefferson even made happiness a central issue in the Declaration of Independence. Most people—regardless of age, nationality, or gender—report being at least moderately happy (Myers, 2000). Factors that correlate with happiness in cultures around the world include political systems that promote human rights and societal and economic equality (Diener, 2013). Financial satisfaction is positively correlated with life satisfaction—but only if it is associated with financial satisfaction and optimism (Diener, Tay, & Oishi, 2013). Happiness is positively correlated with intelligence, social skills, and family support (Diener & Fujita, 1995). Physical attractiveness has a positive correlation with happiness. But this relationship does not necessarily mean that physical attractiveness causes happiness. Perhaps happy people make themselves more physically attractive. For example, happy people are more likely to wear attractive clothing, jewelry, and hairstyles (Diener, Wolsic, & Fujita, 1995).

Happiness also is related to marital status. A cross-cultural study found that married people were, on average, happier than unmarried people. This finding held equally true for men and women. Happiness was more weakly associated with simply living together unmarried. The role of marriage in promoting happiness was linked to improved health and financial security (Stack & Eshleman, 1998), but the two most important factors in happiness are, first, one's state of health and, second, one's personality (DeNeve, 1999). Personality factors that correlate highly with happiness are trust, extraversion, agreeableness, self-esteem, emotional stability, and a sense of personal control (DeNeve & Cooper, 1998). Happiness is strongly related to what has been called *stable extraversion,* that is, being outgoing but not out of control (Steel & Ones, 2002). The association between extraversion and happiness has gained support from studies not only in Western cultures but also in non-Western cultures, such as China (Lu & Shih, 1997). And cross-cultural research has found that happy people place more emphasis on the best and most satisfying aspects of their lives when evaluating their levels of happiness (Diener, Lucas, Oishi, & Suh, 2002).

Cultural differences are found, though, in what makes people feel good. One research study investigated the correlates of positive emotions in a sample of 283 American and 630 Japanese male and female undergraduates. Results indicated that among Japanese participants—who live in a culture that values interdependence—positive emotions were correlated with social emotions (such as feeling friendly toward others). In contrast, among American participants—who live in a culture that values independence—positive emotions were correlated with personal emotions (such as feeling pride in a personal accomplishment) (Kitayama, Markus, & Kurokawa, 2000). As you will see in Chapter 13, these differences may be attributable to how the self is construed in individualistic and collectivistic cultures.

Social-Comparison Theory

Our happiness depends on comparisons we make between ourselves and others and between our current circumstances and our past circumstances (Diener, Oishi, & Lucas, 2003). Charles Montesquieu, an 18th-century French philosopher, noted: "If one only wished to be happy, this could be easily accomplished; but we wish to be happier than other people, and this is always difficult, for we believe others to be happier than they are." One of the most influential theories of happiness—**social-comparison theory**—shares Montesquieu's assumption about the nature of happiness. This theory considers happiness to be the result of estimating that one's life circumstances are more favorable than those of others (VanderZee, Buunk, & Sanderman, 1996), such as when you discover that your grade is one of the highest in the class. In one study, college students felt happier about themselves when in the presence of another person who was relatively worse off (Strack, Schwarz, Chassein, & Kern, 1990). Thus, you can make yourself happier with your own life by purposely comparing it with the lives of those who are less fortunate.

One factor in social comparison that is less important than commonly believed is wealth. Though there is an association between economic well-being and happiness (Schyns, 1998), wealth does not necessarily bring greater happiness. According to happiness researcher Edward Diener (1984), wealthy Americans are no happier than nonwealthy Americans, provided that the nonwealthy people have at least the basic necessities of life, such as a job, home, and family. Though this finding holds true in the United States, it does not hold true in all cultures. For example, a study of people in 39 other countries found a stronger relationship between high income and happiness than in the United States (Diener, Sandvik, Seidlitz, & Diener, 1993). Overall, based on surveys in countries throughout the world, Diener concludes that with the possible exception of people living in impoverished societies, most people are happy (Diener & Diener, 1996). In fact, most people believe they are happier than the average person, apparently because we attend to our own level of contentment more than other people's (Klar & Giladi, 1999).

Adaptation-Level Theory

Adaptation-level theory holds that happiness depends not on comparing yourself with other people but on comparing yourself with yourself. Thus, your current happiness depends in part on comparing your present circumstances and your past circumstances. Your present state of happiness is governed more by the most recent events in your life than by the more distant events (Suh, Diener, & Fujita, 1996). But as your circumstances improve, your standard of happiness becomes higher. This increase can have surprising emotional consequences for people who gain sudden financial success. Life's small pleasures might no longer make them happy—their standards of happiness might become too high, as revealed by a study of Illinois state lottery winners (Brickman, Coates, & Janoff-Bulman, 1978). Despite winning from $50,000 to $1 million, these winners were no happier than they had been in the past. In fact, they found less pleasure in formerly enjoyable everyday activities, such as watching television, shopping for clothes, or talking with a friend. So, though comparing our circumstances

social-comparison theory
The theory that happiness is the result of estimating that one's life circumstances are more favorable than those of others.

adaptation-level theory
The theory that happiness depends on comparing one's present circumstances with one's past circumstances.

Money Does Not Necessarily Buy Happiness

If you buy lottery tickets because you believe that winning the jackpot would make you happy, you might be in for a disappointment should you someday win. Lottery winners often are no happier after they win than when they were broke. In fact, they might no longer gain satisfaction from life's little pleasures.
Source: Ilya Shapovalov/ Shutterstock.com.

with those of less-fortunate people can make us happier, improvements in our own circumstances might make us adopt increasingly higher standards of happiness—making happiness more and more elusive. Recognizing this problem, the 19th-century clergyman Henry Van Dyke remarked, "It is better to desire the things we have than to have the things we desire."

Humor

Happiness is enhanced by humor, whether offered by friends, funny movies, situation comedies on television, or stand-up comedians in nightclubs. Psychologists have only recently begun to study humor scientifically. Research findings support the importance of humor in our everyday lives. Humor promotes romance (Lundy, Tan, & Cunningham, 1998), defuses interpersonal conflict (Brown & Keegan, 1999), contributes to effective teaching (Wanzer & Frymier, 1999), creates positive patient-physician rapport (Sala, Krupat, & Roter, 2002), and reduces the effects of stress (Abel, 2002), psychological distress, and anxiety (Szabo, 2003). Advertisers make good use of humor, realizing that viewers show better recall of humorous than nonhumorous advertisements (Krishnan & Chakravarti, 2003). And restaurant servers who display a sense of humor tend to get larger tips from customers (Guègen, 2002).

One surprising finding has been that humorous people might not feel as extraverted as they act. Consider the class clown, who sees humor in everything. Though that person might be popular, she might not be as sociable as you might expect; she might, instead, use humor as a way to avoid close personal relationships. For example, a study of humorous adolescents found that they often used humor to maintain their social distance from other people (Prasinos & Tittler, 1981). You may have been frustrated at one time or another by such people, who joke about everything, rarely converse in a serious manner, and never disclose their personal feelings. Evidence that some people use humor to maintain their social distance might explain anecdotal reports that many comedians, who might appear socially outgoing in public performances, are socially reclusive in their private lives. Johnny Carson, who retired in 1992 after 30 years as host of the *Tonight Show*, was humorous and engaging on stage but relatively somber and socially aloof off stage.

Granted that humorous people might not be as gregarious as they seem, we are still left with the question: What makes their humor amusing? The brain, particularly the right hemisphere, plays an important role. For example, damage to the right frontal lobe disrupts humor appreciation, including diminished smiling and laughing, more than damage to other parts of the brain (Shammi & Stuss, 1999). Though the brain is important in humor appreciation, we know more about psychological factors that affect our reactions to humor. For example, there are cross-cultural commonalities as well as differences in what people view as humorous, as demonstrated in a study of German and Italian adults' reactions to jokes and cartoons. The participants gave similar rankings for the quality of the jokes and cartoons, but Germans, compared to Italians, rated nonsense humor as funnier and sexual humor as less funny (Ruch & Forabosco, 1996). Another factor is the social context, such as night clubs, in which humor is expressed. To people who are inebriated, comedians who use blunt, simple humor will seem funnier than comedians who use subtle, complex humor (Weaver, Masland, Kharazmi, & Zillman, 1985). Thus, if you drank a few beers, you would probably find a Three Stooges movie more amusing and a Dennis Miller monologue less amusing. But what accounts for our responses to humor while in a sober state? The most popular theories are *disparagement theory, incongruity theory,* and *release theory* (Berger, 1987).

Disparagement Theory

According to C. L. Edson, a 20th-century American newspaper editor, "We love a joke that hands us a pat on the back while it kicks the other fellow down the stairs." Edson's comment indicates that he favored the **disparagement theory** of humor, first put forth by the 17th-century English philosopher Thomas Hobbes. Hobbes claimed that we feel amused when humor makes us feel superior to other people (Nevo, 1985). One study found that political conservatives found anti-left wing jokes as funnier and political liberals found anti-right wing jokes as funnier than jokes that disparaged members of their own political orientation (Braun & Preiser, 2013). Research supporting Hobbes's position

disparagement theory
The theory that humor is amusing when it makes one feel superior to other people.

has found that we are especially amused when we dislike those to whom we are made to feel superior (Wicker, Barron, & Willis, 1980). Satirists, newspaper columnists, and television commentators take this approach by disparaging certain commonly disliked groups, such as greedy lawyers, crooked politicians, and phony evangelists.

We also like disparaging humor better when we like the person doing the disparaging. Consider David Letterman, former host of the *Late Show*. Why is his disparaging humor perceived as funny? It is funny, in part, because many people find him likable. In a study in which students were presented with examples of Letterman's disparaging humor, those who found him likable rated his humor as funnier (Oppliger & Sherblom, 1992).

Incongruity Theory

In the 18th century, the German philosopher Immanuel Kant put forth an alternative theory of humor, **incongruity theory**. Incongruous humor brings together incompatible ideas in a surprising outcome that violates our expectations (Perlmutter, 2002), a technique commonly used in television commercials (Alden, Mukherjee, & Hoyer, 2000). Incongruous jokes tend to be perceived as more humorous than other jokes (Hillson & Martin, 1994). Incongruity theory explains why many jokes require timing and may lose something on the second hearing—bad timing or repetition can destroy the incongruity (Kuhlman, 1985). The appreciation of incongruous humor varies with age and conservatism. A study of more than 4,000 participants aged 14 to 66 found that older people and more conservative people preferred incongruous humor more, and nonsense humor less, than did younger people and more liberal people (Ruch, McGhee, & Hehl, 1990).

incongruity theory
The theory that humor is amusing when it brings together incompatible ideas in a surprising outcome that violates one's expectations.

Release Theory

Another theory of humor, **release theory**, is based on Sigmund Freud's claim that humor is a cathartic outlet for anxiety caused by repressed sexual or aggressive energy, as explained in his book *Jokes and Their Relationship to the Unconscious* (Freud, 1905). Humor can raise your level of anxiety—and then suddenly lower it, providing you relief so pleasurable that it can make you laugh (McCauley, Woods, Coolidge, & Kulick, 1983). Consider a study in which students were told they would be handling or taking blood samples from rats. As they approached the rats, they suddenly discovered that the rats were toys. The students then responded to questionnaires about their reactions to the situation. The more anxious and the more surprised they had been, the funnier they found the situation, thereby supporting release theory (Shurcliff, 1968). Release theory explains the popularity of humor that plays on our sexual anxieties by weaving a story that ends with a punch line that relieves our tension (Schill & O'Laughlin, 1984).

release theory The theory that humor relieves anxiety caused by sexual or aggressive energy.

In a study bearing on the release theory of humor in regard to aggression, high school students were given a frustrating exam. Afterward, they were more likely to respond aggressively to a subsequent frustrating situation. But students who were exposed after the exam to a humorous situation that provoked laughter became less likely to respond aggressively to the later frustration. According to release theory, the students' laughter provided a cathartic experience, which released energy that would have provoked later aggression (Ziv, 1987).

A recent study tested another prediction from Freud's theory—that hostility toward women may underlie sexist humor. A sample of college undergraduates completed a series of attitude and personality inventories and rated 10 sexist cartoons on perceived funniness. Enjoyment of the sexist cartoons was positively correlated with rape-related beliefs and psychological, physical, and sexual aggression among men but not women. That is, men who were more tolerant of rape and were more aggressive also found the sexist cartoons to be more enjoyable. Women found the cartoons to be less acceptable and less enjoyable than men did—though women were not less likely to retell them (Ryan & Kanjorski, 1998). The results of this study suggest that despite some research supportive of release theory, sexual or aggressive humor does not usually reduce sexual or aggressive tendencies (Nevo & Nevo, 1983).

The field of humor research is relatively young, and more research is needed to uncover the factors that make people find amusement in one kind of humor but not in another. Such research might explain, for example, why advertisers in some cultures employ humor in some cultures whereas advertisers in other cultures do not (Laroche, Nepomuceno, Huang, & Richard, 2011).

Section Review: The Experience of Emotion

1. What factors are associated with personal happiness?
2. What are the disparagement theory, the incongruity theory, and the release theory of humor?

Theories of Emotion

How do we explain emotional experience? Theories of emotion vary in their attention to physiology, behavior, and cognition.

Biopsychological Theories of Emotion

Though most theories of emotion recognize the importance of physiological factors, certain theories stress them.

The James-Lange Theory of Emotion

In the late 19th century, the American psychologist William James (1884) claimed that physiological changes precede emotional experiences. Because a Danish physiologist named Carl Lange (1834–1900) made the same claim at about the same time, it became known as the **James-Lange theory** (see Figure 12-5). Note that the theory violates the commonsense belief that physiological changes follow emotional experiences (see the "Psychology Versus Common Sense" box).

James-Lange theory
The theory that specific patterns of physiological changes evoke specific emotional experiences.

The Cannon-Bard Theory of Emotion

After rejecting the James-Lange theory of emotion, Walter Cannon (1927) and Philip Bard (1934) put forth their own theory, giving equal weight to physiological changes and cognitive processes. The **Cannon-Bard theory** (see Figure 12-5) claims that an emotion is produced when an event or object is perceived by the thalamus, a brain structure that conveys this information simultaneously to the cerebral cortex and to the skeletal muscles and sympathetic nervous system.

Cannon-Bard theory
The theory that an emotion is produced when an event or object is perceived by the thalamus, which conveys this information simultaneously to the cerebral cortex and the skeletal muscles and sympathetic nervous system.

The cerebral cortex then uses memories of past experiences to determine the nature of the perceived event or object, providing the subjective experience of emotion. Meanwhile, the muscles and sympathetic nervous system provide the physiological arousal that prepares the individual to take action to adapt to the situation that evoked the emotion. Unlike the James-Lange theory, the Cannon-Bard theory assumes that different emotions are associated with the same state of physiological arousal. The Cannon-Bard theory has failed to gain research support, because the thalamus does not appear to play the role the researchers envisioned. But if the theory is recast in terms of the limbic system instead of the thalamus, it is supported by research findings. For example, though the thalamus might not directly cause emotional responses, it does relay sensory information to the amygdala, which then processes the

FIGURE 12-5
Theories of Emotion

According to the James-Lange theory, specific patterns of physiological changes evoke specific emotional experiences. According to the Cannon-Bard theory, activity in the thalamus precedes both arousal and emotional experience.

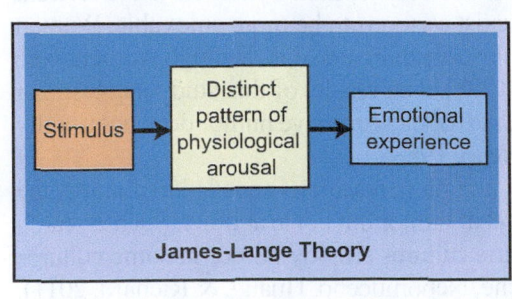

James-Lange Theory

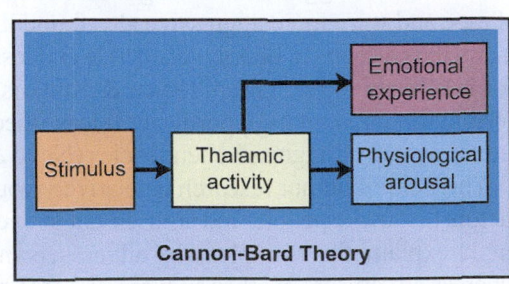

Cannon-Bard Theory

Do Emotional Experiences Depend on Physical Responses to Emotional Situations?

The main implication of the James-Lange theory is that particular emotional events stimulate specific patterns of physiological changes, each evoking a specific emotional experience (Lang, 1994). According to James (1890/1981, Vol. 2, p. 1065),

> Commonsense says, we lose our fortune, are sorry and weep; we meet a bear, are frightened and run; we are insulted by a rival, are angry and strike . . . the more rational statement is that we feel sorry because we cry, angry because we strike, afraid because we tremble.

Your own experience might provide evidence in support of this theory. If you have ever barely avoided an automobile accident, you may have noticed your pulse racing and your palms sweating, and then a moment later found yourself overcome by fear.

The James-Lange theory provoked criticism from the American physiologist Walter Cannon (1927). One of his criticisms was based on his assumption that individuals are unable to perceive many of the subtle physiological changes induced by the sympathetic nervous system. How could the perception of physiological changes be the basis of emotional experiences when we cannot perceive many of those changes? In part because of Cannon's criticisms, the James-Lange theory fell into disfavor for several decades.

But recent research has lent some support to the James-Lange theory (Barbalet, 1999). One line of support for the theory comes from research studies showing that fear can be evoked by threatening situations before we are consciously aware of them. We will react behaviorally to fear-inducing situations before we experience the emotion consciously. This process might have evolved because it is an adaptive, potentially life-saving process that permits us to react more quickly to confront or flee from a threat than we would if we had to first become consciously aware of it (Robinson, 1998). Other sources of evidence that we can react to emotional stimuli without being consciously aware of them (Mayer & Merckelbach, 1999) are discussed in Chapters 5 and 6.

Cannon also noted that different emotions are associated with the same pattern of physiological arousal. How could different emotions be evoked by the same pattern of arousal? In a study that supported the basic assumptions of the James-Lange theory, participants were directed to adopt facial expressions representing fear, anger, disgust, sadness, surprise, and happiness (Ekman, Levenson, & Friesen, 1983). Participants were told which muscles to contract or relax but were not told which emotions they were expressing. Recordings of heart rate and skin temperature were taken as they maintained the facial expressions. The results supported the assumption that the physiological changes underlying emotional responses to situations can occur before we consciously experience an emotion.

The results also supported the assumption that different behavioral reactions can induce different patterns of physiological activity. The facial expression of fear induced a large increase in heart rate and a slight decrease in finger temperature, whereas the facial expression of anger induced a large increase in both heart rate and finger temperature. Finger temperature varies with the amount of blood flow: A decrease in blood flow causes a decrease in temperature, and an increase in blood flow causes an increase in temperature. The presence of different patterns of autonomic activity for different emotions has been replicated in Western cultures (Christie & Friedman, 2004) and non-Western cultures, such as West Sumatra (Levenson, Ekman, Heider, & Friesen, 1992).

Note our everyday language: When we are afraid, we have "cold feet," and when we are angry, our "blood is boiling." The difference in the patterns of physiological arousal between fear and anger supports the assumption of the James-Lange theory that particular emotions are associated with particular patterns of physiological arousal. More recent studies have lent further support to the specificity of autonomic nervous system responses in different emotions. In one study, children watched the film *E.T., The Extraterrestrial* while being monitored physiologically. Scenes that evoked sadness were associated with greater variability in heart rate and blood oxygenation than were scenes that evoked happiness (Miller & Wood, 1997). In another study, participants had six of their autonomic nervous system responses, including heart rate and skin blood flow, monitored after inhaling five fragrances that produced different emotional responses. As predicted by the James-Lange theory, each of the fragrances was associated with its own pattern of autonomic activity (Alaoui-Ismaieli, Vernet-Maury, Dittmar, Delhomme, & Chanel, 1997).

---

information. This transfer can occur even when the cerebral cortex is removed; in one study, rats whose visual cortexes had been destroyed still learned to fear visual stimuli associated with pain (LeDoux, Romanski, & Xagoraris, 1989).

Research on victims of spinal cord damage has provided support for the Cannon-Bard theory while contradicting the James-Lange theory. Studies have found that even people with spinal cord injuries that prevent them from perceiving their bodily arousal experience distinct emotions just as intensely as people with intact spinal cords do (Cobos, Sanchez, Garcia, Vera, & Vila, 2002). This finding violates the James-Lange theory's assumption that emotional experience depends on the perception of bodily arousal, and supports the Cannon-Bard theory's assumption that emotional experience depends on the brain's perception of ongoing events. Of course, as you will learn later, research on victims of spinal cord damage does not rule out sensations from one's own facial expressions as a factor in emotional experience.

The Opponent-Process Theory of Emotion

In anticipating another theory of emotion, Plato, in the Phaedo, states:

> How strange would appear to be this thing that we call pleasure! And how curiously it is related to what is thought to be its opposite, pain! The two will never be found together in a man, and yet if you seek the one and obtain it, you are almost bound always to get the other as well, just as though they were both attached to one and the same head. . . . Wherever the one is found, the other follows up behind. So, in my case, since I had pain in my leg as a result of the fetters, pleasure seems to have come to follow it up.

If Plato were alive today, he might favor the **opponent-process theory** of emotion (see Figure 12-6), which holds that the mammalian brain has evolved mechanisms that counteract strong positive or negative emotions by evoking an opposite emotional response to maintain homeostasis. According to Richard Solomon (1980), who first put forth the theory, the opposing emotion begins sometime after the onset of the first emotion and lasts longer than the first emotion. If we experience the first emotion on repeated occasions, the opposing emotion grows stronger, and the emotion that is experienced becomes a compromise between the two opposing emotional states.

Suppose that you took up skydiving. The first time you parachuted from an airplane you would probably feel terror. After surviving the jump, your feeling of terror would be replaced by a feeling of relief. As you jumped again and again, you would feel anticipation instead of terror as you prepared to jump. And your initial post-jump feeling of relief might intensify into a feeling of exhilaration.

The opponent-process theory might help explain the "baby blues" that often follow the joy of childbirth or the euphoria that often follows the anxiety of final exams week. It might even explain why some blood donors become seemingly "addicted" to donating blood. When a person first donates blood, she might experience fear—but afterward might experience a pleasant feeling known as the "warm glow" effect. If the person repeatedly donates blood, the warm glow strengthens, leading the person to donate blood in order to induce that feeling (Piliavin, Callero, & Evans, 1982).

The opponent-process theory implies that our brains are programmed against hedonism, because people who experience intense pleasure are doomed to experience intense displeasure. This theory provides support for those who favor the "happy medium"—moderation in everything, including emotional experiences.

opponent-process theory
The theory that the brain counteracts a strong positive or negative emotion by evoking an opposite emotional response.

facial-feedback theory
The theory that particular facial expressions induce particular emotional experiences.

FIGURE 12-6
The Opponent-Process Theory

According to the opponent-process theory, when we experience an emotion (A), an opposing emotion (B) will counter the first emotion, dampening the experience of that emotion (as indicated by the steady level of A being lower than the peak of A). As we experience the first emotion (A') on repeated occasions, the opposing emotion (B') becomes stronger and the first emotion weaker, which leads to an even weaker experience of the first emotion (as indicated by the steady level of A' being lower than the peak of A'). For example, the first time you drove on a highway you might have experienced fear, followed by a feeling of relief. As you drove on highways on repeated occasions, your feeling of fear eventually gave way to a feeling of mild arousal.

Source: From R. L. Solomon, "The Opponent-Process Theory of Acquired Motivation: The Costs of Pleasure and Benefits of Pain" in *American Psychologist,* 35: 691–712. Copyright © 1980 by the American Psychological Association. Reprinted with permission.

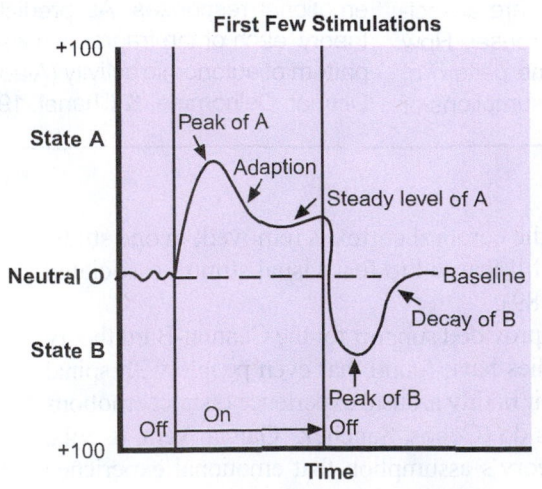
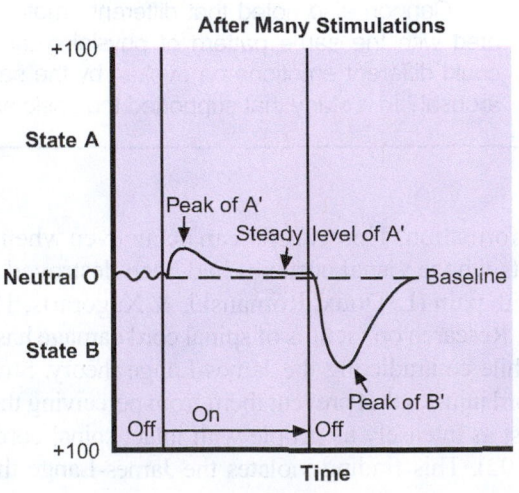

The Facial-Feedback Theory of Emotion

Benjamin Franklin claimed, "A cheerful face is nearly as good for an invalid as healthy weather." Have you ever received the advice "Put on a happy face" or "Keep a stiff upper lip" from people trying to help you overcome adversity? Both these bits of advice are commonsense versions of the **facial-feedback theory** of emotion (see Figure 12-7), which holds that our facial expressions affect our emotional experiences. Because it assumes that emotional experience is caused by the perception of physiological changes, the James-Lange theory inspired the facial-feedback theory (Izard, 1990b). As you learned in the discussion of the James-Lange theory, adopting a facial expression characteristic of a particular emotion can induce that emotion (Ekman, Levenson, & Friesen, 1983). But unlike the James-Lange theory, which primarily is concerned with the effects of autonomic nervous system activity on emotion, the facial-feedback theory is limited to the effects of facial expressions.

The facial-feedback theory was put forth in 1907 by the French physician Israel Waynbaum and recently has been restated in various versions. Waynbaum assumed that particular facial expressions alter the flow of blood to particular regions of the brain, thereby evoking particular emotional experiences. For example, smiling might increase the flow of blood to regions of the brain that elevate mood (Zajonc, 1985). A descendant of Waynbaum's theory, called the vascular theory, assumes that changes in facial expressions affect the volume of air flow through the nose, which alters brain temperature and, as a result, influences emotional states. The theory, assumes, that increased airflow cools the brain and induces positive moods, whereas decreased airflow warms the brain and induces negative moods. The theory, received support from a study in which participants who adopted negative facial expressions had reduced nasal airflow and experienced more negative moods (McIntosh, Zajonc, Vig, & Emerick, 1997). Because the vascular theory is relatively new, more research is needed to assess its validity.

Most contemporary facial-feedback theorists, led by Paul Ekman (1992b), assume that evolution has endowed us with facial expressions that provide different patterns of sensory feedback of muscle tension levels to the brain, thereby evoking different emotions. Support for the theory has come from studies that have found that emotional experiences follow facial expressions rather than precede them, and that sensory neurons convey information from facial muscles directly to the hypothalamus, which plays an important role in emotional arousal (Zajonc, 1985).

But the facial-feedback theory has not received unqualified support. Though there is a positive association between particular facial expressions and particular emotional experiences (Adelmann & Zajonc, 1989), the effect of facial feedback on emotional experience tends to be small (Matsumoto, 1987). Some studies also have found that emotional experience depends more on feedback from autonomic nervous system organs than on feedback from facial muscles (Buck, 1980). Another study found that facial feedback *and* body posture contributed to participants' emotional experience (Flack, Laird, & Cavallaro, 1999). And a case study of a woman with facial paralysis revealed that though she was unable to generate facial expressions of emotion, her self-reported responses to emotional stimuli did not differ from a healthy control sample (Keillor, Barrett, Crucian, Kortenkamp, & Heilman, 2002). Apparently, feedback from facial expressions is just one of several factors that govern our emotional experiences.

Though facial expressions might not be the sole cause of emotions, they can affect the intensity of ongoing emotions and induce emotions (McIntosh, 1996), with positive facial expressions inducing positive moods and negative facial expressions inducing negative moods (Kleinke, Peterson, & Rutledge, 1998). Try smiling and then frowning, and note the subtle differences they induce in your mood. For example, participants who respond with a genuine Duchenne smile to pleasant stimuli report more positive affect—and different patterns of autonomic arousal—than participants who view the same stimuli with pursed lips (Soussignan, 2002). In one study, heterosexual female participants were asked to imagine three pleasant scenes and three unpleasant scenes (McCanne & Anderson, 1987). The three pleasant scenes were "You get a 4.0 grade point average," "You inherit a million dollars," and "You meet the man of your dreams." The three unpleasant scenes were "Your mother dies," "You lose a really close friendship," and "You lose a limb in an accident."

Participants imagined each scene three times. The first time they simply imagined the scene. The second time they imagined the scene while maintaining increased muscle

Fear and Euphoria

According to the opponent-process theory of emotion, the fear that this skier experienced when he first learned to ski eventually gave way to a feeling of euphoria. *Source:* lm_photo/Shutterstock.com.

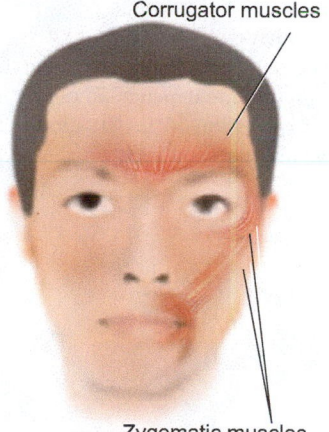

Corrugator muscles

Zygomatic muscles

FIGURE 12-7

The Facial-Feedback Theory

According to the facial-feedback theory of emotion, particular patterns of sensory feedback from facial expressions evoke particular emotions. Thus, sensory feedback from the corrugator muscles, which are active when we frown, might contribute to unpleasant emotional experiences. Similarly, sensory feedback from the zygomatic muscles, which are active when we smile, might contribute to pleasant emotional experiences.

tension in one of two muscle groups: either muscles that control smiling or muscles that control frowning. Through the use of biofeedback (see Chapter 7), participants learned to tense only the target muscles. The third time they imagined the scene, participants were instructed to suppress muscle tension in either their smiling muscles or their frowning muscles. On each occasion, participants were asked to report the degree of enjoyment or distress they experienced while imagining the scene. The results provided some support for the facial-feedback theory. Participants reported less enjoyment when imagining pleasant scenes while suppressing activity in their smiling muscles, and they reported less distress when imagining unpleasant scenes while suppressing activity in their frowning muscles.

Cognitive Theories of Emotion

More recent theories of emotion emphasize the importance of cognition. They assume that our emotional experiences depend on our subjective interpretation of situations in which we find ourselves.

The Two-Factor Theory of Emotion

two-factor theory The theory that emotional experience is the outcome of physiological arousal and the attribution of a cause for that arousal.

Stanley Schachter and Jerome Singer's **two-factor theory** (see Figure 12-8) views emotional experience as the outcome of two factors: physiological arousal and the attribution of a cause for it (see "The Research Process" box).

The Cognitive-Appraisal Theory of Emotion

cognitive-appraisal theory The theory that our emotion at a given time depends on our interpretation of the situation we are in at that time.

Though Schachter and Singer's two-factor theory has failed to gain strong support, it has stimulated interest in the cognitive basis of emotion. The purest cognitive theory of emotion is the **cognitive-appraisal theory** of Richard Lazarus (1993a). Unlike the two-factor theory, the cognitive-appraisal theory downplays the role of physiological arousal. Like the two-factor theory, the cognitive-appraisal theory assumes that our emotion at a given time depends on our interpretation of the situation we are in at that time. If we develop inflexible, maladaptive ways of appraising situations, we may develop emotional disorders (Lazarus, 1995). The cognitive appraisal of specific kinds of situations is consistent across different cultures, though cognitive appraisals vary somewhat from the norm in certain cultures. This conclusion was supported by a study of almost 3,000 people in 37 countries who had been asked to recall their cognitive appraisal of recent events associated with feelings of joy, fear, shame, guilt, anger, disgust, and sadness (Scherer, 1997).

This cognitive view of emotion is not new. In *Hamlet* Shakespeare wrote: "There is nothing either good or bad, but thinking makes it so." Cognitive appraisal can affect your emotions as you prepare for an exam. One study tracked college undergraduates' emotional states and appraisals of an upcoming exam. Compared to participants who appraised the exam as a threat, participants who appraised the exam as a challenge were more confident about their coping ability and experienced more positive emotions prior to the exam (Skinner & Brewer, 2002). People whose jobs require them to confront human pain, illness, and death find that cognitively reappraising situations, perhaps by finding meaning even in the worst disasters, helps them cope emotionally (McCammon, Durham, Allison, & Williamson, 1988).

An early study by Lazarus and his colleagues supported the cognitive-appraisal theory of emotion (Speisman, Lazarus, Mordkoff, & Davison, 1964). The participants watched a film about a tribal ritual in which incisions were made on adolescents' penises. Participants' level of emotional arousal was measured by recording their heart rate and skin conductance

FIGURE 12-8
The Two-Factor Theory

According to Schachter and Singer's two-factor theory, physiological arousal and a causal attribution combine to produce emotional experiences.

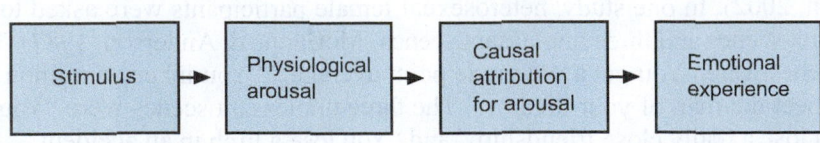

Do Emotions Depend on Our Attribution of a Cause for Our Physiological Arousal?

Rationale

According to Schachter and Singer, when you experience physiological arousal, you search for its source. Your attribution of a cause for your arousal determines the emotion that you experience. For example, if you experience intense physiological arousal in the presence of an appealing person, you might attribute your arousal to that person and, as a result, feel that you are attracted to him or her.

The two-factor theory resembles the James-Lange theory in assuming that emotional experience follows physiological arousal (Winton, 1990). But it is different from the James-Lange theory in holding, as does the Cannon-Bard theory, that all emotions involve similar patterns of physiological arousal. But the Cannon-Bard theory assumes that emotional experience and physiological arousal occur simultaneously; the two-factor theory assumes instead that emotion follows the attribution of a cause for one's physiological arousal.

Method

The original experiment on the two-factor theory provided evidence that when we experience physiological arousal, we seek to identify its source, and that what we identify as the source in turn determines our emotional experience (Schachter & Singer, 1962). Male college student volunteers participated one at a time and were told that they were getting an injection of a new vitamin called "Suproxin" to assess its effect on vision. In reality, they received an injection of the hormone epinephrine, which activates the sympathetic nervous system. The epinephrine caused hand tremors, a flushed face, a pounding heart, and rapid breathing. Some participants (the informed group) were told to expect these changes. Some participants (the misinformed group) were told to expect itching, numb feet, and headache, and some (the uninformed group) were told nothing about the effects. Other participants received a placebo injection of a saline solution instead of an injection of epinephrine and were told nothing about its physiological effects.

The participant then waited in a room with the experimenter's accomplice, a man who acted either happy or angry. When acting happy, the accomplice was cheerful and threw paper airplanes, played with a Hula Hoop, and shot wads of paper into a wastebasket. When acting angry, the accomplice acted upset, stomped around, and complained about a questionnaire given by the experimenter, which included questions about the bathing habits of the respondent's family and the sex life of his mother. The participant's emotional response to the accomplice was assessed by observing him through a one-way mirror and by having him complete a questionnaire about his feelings.

Results and Discussion

The results showed that the informed participants were unaffected by the accomplice's behavior, whereas the misinformed participants and uninformed participants expressed and experienced emotions similar to those of the accomplice. But the placebo group also expressed and experienced situation-appropriate emotions despite the lack of drug-induced physiological arousal. Schachter and Singer concluded that the informed participants attributed their arousal to the injection and did not experience situation-appropriate emotions. In contrast, the misinformed participants and the uninformed participants attributed their physiological arousal to the situation they were in, responding positively when the accomplice acted happy and responding negatively when the accomplice acted angry. Schachter and Singer assumed that the placebo participants became physiologically aroused in response to the emotional display of the accomplice and interpreted their own feelings as congruent with those of the accomplice.

Since the original studies of the two-factor theory in the early 1960s, research has produced inconsistent findings. Consider the theory's assumption that unexplained physiological arousal can just as well provoke feelings of joy as provoke feelings of sadness, depending on the person's interpretation of the source of the arousal. This assumption was contradicted by a study in which participants received injections of epinephrine without being informed of its true effects. The participants tended to experience negative emotions regardless of their immediate social environment. Even those in the presence of a happy person tended to experience unpleasant emotions (Marshall & Zimbardo, 1979). A review of research on Schachter and Singer's two-factor theory concluded that the only assumption of the theory that has been consistently supported is that physiological arousal misattributed to an outside source will intensify an emotional experience. There is little evidence that such a misattribution will cause an emotional experience (Reisenzein, 1983). More recent research has likewise provided mixed support for the two-factor theory (Mezzacappa, Katkin, & Palmer, 1999; Neumann, 2000).

(an increase in the electrical conductivity of the skin, caused by sweating). Each participant watched the same film but heard different sound tracks. Those in the *silent group* saw the film without a sound track. Those in the *trauma group* were told that the procedure was extremely painful and emotionally distressing. Those in the *intellectualization group* were told about the procedure in a detached, matter-of-fact way, with no mention of feelings. And those in the *denial group* were told that the procedure was not painful and that the boys were overjoyed because it signified their entrance into manhood.

Recordings of the participants' physiological arousal showed that the trauma group experienced greater arousal than the silent group, which in turn experienced greater arousal than the denial and intellectualization groups. These findings indicate that subjective appraisal of the situation, rather than the objective situation itself, accounted for participants' emotional arousal. Lazarus (1993b) has applied his theory of cognitive appraisal in helping individuals cope with stressful situations—a topic discussed in Chapter 16. More recent studies provide additional support for the assumption that your interpretation of a situation affects your emotional state (Wolgast, Lundh, & Viborg, 2011). Consider a situation that is all too familiar to people who fly frequently—lost luggage. A study of more than 100 airline passengers who had reported that their luggage was lost found that their emotional response to the loss depended on their cognitive appraisal of it (Scherer & Ceschi, 1997).

Moreover, there are cultural differences in the cognitive appraisal of personal experiences of success and failure. Participants were 67 European American students at the University of Michigan and 58 Japanese students at Kanazawa University. Participants rated their emotional responses to a situation involving personal success or failure (for example, getting a grade that was better or worse than usual) or social success or failure (for example, getting along well with someone versus not getting along well with someone). Results indicated that American participants felt proud of their successes and angry or unlucky when they failed. Japanese participants felt lucky when they succeeded and shameful when they failed. The researchers attributed these findings to cross-cultural differences in appraisals about the meaning of success and failure to the self. American participants attributed their successes to themselves and their failures to the situation or other external factors, whereas Japanese participants attributed their successes to the situation and their failures to themselves (Imada & Ellsworth, 2011). As you will read in Chapters 13 and 17, this is consistent with cross-cultural differences in construals of the self and causal attributions.

But the cognitive-appraisal theory has been challenged by Robert Zajonc (1984) and others, who insist that cognitive appraisal is not essential to the experience of emotion. For example, you probably have taken an instant liking or disliking to a person without knowing why. And, as noted in Chapter 6, research findings show that we can respond emotionally to stimuli we are unaware of (Dimberg, Thunberg, & Elmehed, 2000). This and other evidence indicates that emotional experience can take place without conscious cognitive appraisal (Izard, 1993).

There even is physiological evidence for this phenomenon, because of the direct pathways from the thalamus (which relays sensory input to other brain regions) to the limbic system (which plays an important role in emotional processing). These pathways bypass the cerebral cortex, the involvement of which seems required for conscious cognitive appraisal (see Figure 12-9). Thus, we can have emotional reactions to stimuli of which we are unaware (LeDoux, 1986).

What can we conclude from the variety of contradictory theories of emotion? The best we can do is to realize that none of them is sufficient to explain emotion, though each describes a process that contributes to it. Moreover, the theories illustrate the importance of the physiological, expressive, and experiential components of emotion.

FIGURE 12-9

Pathways for Emotion

This schematic drawing of a lateral view of the brain shows structures involved in the control and generation of emotion. The thalamus receives sensory input and relays information to the amygdala or cortex. Rapid responses of emotion, such as fear, are channeled through the amygdala. This pathway does not have cortical processing, which may explain why some emotions occur before any conscious appraisal. More careful assessment of emotions uses cortical circuits.

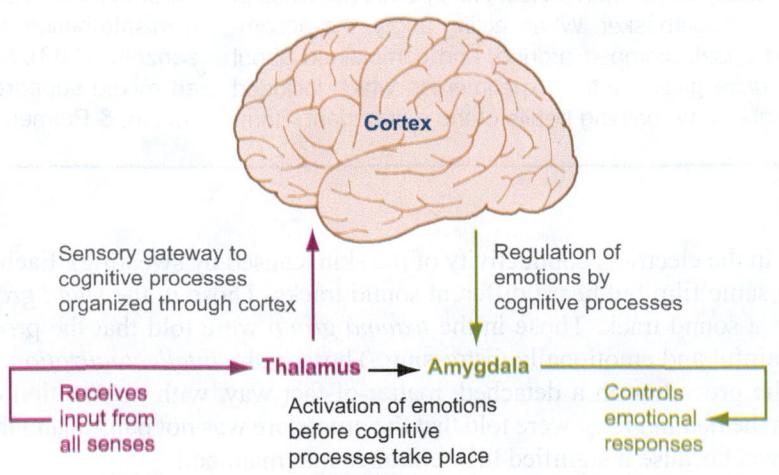

1. What evidence is there for and against the James-Lange theory of emotion?

2. How has research supported the facial-feedback theory of emotion?

3. What does research conducted since Schachter and Singer's classic study say about their two-factor theory of emotion?

Experiencing Psychology

Are Humorous Professors More Effective Teachers?

Rationale

As mentioned in the chapter section "Humor," research has found that humor is related to teaching effectiveness. To test this claim, you will be asked to conduct a study of the relationship between professors' use of humor and students' performance on exams. Feel free to alter the proposed study to suit your own circumstances.

Method
Participants

The participants will be college students and their professors. The more participants you use, the better. Be sure to ask your introductory psychology professor about ethical issues that will have to be addressed before conducting the study. These issues include deception, confidentiality, informed consent, and post-study debriefing.

Materials

The students will record instances of professorial humor during their lectures. You will have to agree on the kinds of behavior that will be considered examples of humor and create data sheets to record them.

Procedure

Have each student record instances of professorial humor (including bad humor) for three class lectures with each of the professors they have for lecture courses. No student should use data from the same professor. Add up the number of instances of humor for each class session. Also have the students write down their latest exam score (as a percentage) in each of their lecture classes. All data should be anonymous in regard to the names of the students and the names of the professors.

Results and Discussion

Find the mean number of instances of humor for each professor. Calculate a Pearson's correlation (see Appendix C in the Online Edition) pairing each professor's mean number of instances of humor and the associated student exam score. Draw a scattergram (see Appendix C in the Online Edition) of the relationship between instances of humor and student exam scores.

How strong is the correlation? What do you infer from that? What is the direction of the correlation? What do you infer from that? Would a large, positive correlation mean that professorial humor *causes* better student grades? Note any shortcomings of the study and suggest how to improve it.

Chapter Summary

The Biopsychology of Emotion

- Emotion is a motivated state marked by physiological arousal, expressive behavior, and cognitive experience.
- Emotional arousal depends on activity in the autonomic nervous system and the limbic system.
- The lie detector, or polygraph, test assumes that differences in physiological arousal in response to control questions and relevant questions can be used to determine whether a person is lying.

- Critics point out that the polygraph test can be fooled and that it has poor validity because it finds a large proportion of guilty people innocent and an even larger proportion of innocent people guilty.
- A promising alternative to the traditional polygraph test is the Guilty Knowledge Test, which depends on the guilty person's physiological arousal to important facts about his or her transgression.

- The left cerebral hemisphere plays a greater role in positive emotions; the right cerebral hemisphere plays a greater role in negative emotions.
- Neurotransmitters, including endorphins, alter our moods by affecting neuronal activity.

The Expression of Emotion

- We express our emotions behaviorally through changes in vocal qualities, body movements, and facial expressions.
- Charles Darwin believed that facial expressions evolved because they communicate emotions and help individuals distinguish friend from foe.
- The hereditary basis of facial expressions is supported by research showing cross-cultural similarity in the positive association between particular facial expressions and particular emotions.

The Experience of Emotion

- Robert Plutchik considers the basic emotions to be joy, fear, anger, disgust, sadness, surprise, acceptance, and anticipation.
- Emotions vary in their intensity and pleasantness; people who tend to experience intensely pleasant emotions are also likely to experience intensely unpleasant emotions.
- Psychologists have only recently begun to study pleasant emotions, such as happiness and humor-induced amusement, to the same extent as unpleasant emotions.
- According to social-comparison theory, happiness is the result of estimating that one's life circumstances are more favorable than those of others.
- According to adaptation-level theory, happiness depends on estimating that one's current life circumstances are more favorable than one's past life circumstances.

- Humor is explained by disparagement theory, incongruity theory, and release theory.

Theories of Emotion

- The James-Lange theory assumes that physiological changes precede emotional experiences and that different patterns of physiological arousal are associated with different emotions.
- The Cannon-Bard theory claims that the thalamus perceives an event and communicates this information to the cerebral cortex (which provides the subjective experience of emotion) and stimulates the physiological arousal characteristic of emotion.
- According to the opponent-process theory, the brain has evolved mechanisms that counteract strong positive or negative emotions by evoking an opposite emotional response.
- If the first emotion is repeated, the opposing emotion gradually strengthens and the first emotion gradually weakens, until a more moderate response becomes habitual.
- According to the facial-feedback theory, different emotions are caused by sensory feedback from different facial expressions.
- The two-factor theory views emotional experience as the consequence of attributing physiological arousal to a particular aspect of one's immediate environment.
- Cognitive-appraisal theory ignores the role of physiological arousal and considers emotional experience to be solely the result of a person's interpretation of her or his current circumstances.

Key Terms

emotion (p. 412)

The Biopsychology of Emotion

fight-or-flight response (p. 414)
Guilty Knowledge Test (p. 419)
polygraph test (p. 419)

The Expression of Emotion

prosody (p. 422)

The Experience of Emotion

adaptation-level theory (p. 429)
disparagement theory (p. 430)
incongruity theory (p. 431)
release theory (p. 431)

social-comparison theory (p. 429)

Theories of Emotion

Cannon-Bard theory (p. 432)
cognitive-appraisal theory (p. 436)
facial-feedback theory (p. 434)
James-Lange theory (p. 432)
opponent-process theory (p. 434)
two-factor theory (p. 436)

Note: Answers for the Chapter Quiz questions are provided at the end of the book.

1. A vicious dog runs after you. You run for your front door, pull it open, and escape into your home—just before the dog reaches you. You notice that you are sweating and breathing heavily and that your heart is beating rapidly. Only then do you notice that you feel terrified. This experience would provide circumstantial evidence for the
   a. James-Lange theory.
   b. Cannon-Bard theory.
   c. facial-feedback theory.
   d. opponent-process theory.

2. A study of the polygraph printouts of 50 thieves and 50 innocent people (Kleinmuntz & Szucko, 1984a) found that the polygraph test was
   a. equally good in detecting guilty and innocent people.
   b. better at detecting guilty people than innocent people.
   c. better at detecting innocent people than guilty people.
   d. no better than flipping a coin in detecting whether a person is guilty or innocent.

3. The bodily arousal that underlies emotional experience is associated mainly with activity in the
   a. central nervous system.
   b. somatic nervous system.
   c. autonomic nervous system.
   d. extrapyramidal motor system.

4. A person suffers a bullet wound of the brain and begins to respond inappropriately to threatening situations, often showing no concern for her own safety. The bullet probably damaged her
   a. amygdala.
   b. cerebellum.
   c. basal ganglia.
   d. medulla.

5. A construction worker is accidentally struck on the head by an iron beam. After recovering, he seems to always be happy and laughs at almost everything. The accident probably damaged his
   a. superior colliculus.
   b. inferior colliculus.
   c. left cerebral hemisphere.
   d. right cerebral hemisphere.

6. An emotion comprises mental experience, physiological arousal, and
   a. drive reduction.
   b. expressive behavior.
   c. affective vacillation.
   d. unconscious motivation.

7. An Olympic-class runner finds it difficult to be happy, because every time she improves her performance her standard of happiness becomes higher. This phenomenon is best explained by
   a. incongruity theory.
   b. disparagement theory.
   c. adaptation-level theory.
   d. social-comparison theory.

8. A study of the blue Monday effect (Stone et al., 1985) found that
   a. there is a general blue weekday effect.
   b. we tend to be bluer on Monday than on other weekdays.
   c. weekend days make us feel even bluer than does Monday.
   d. moods tend to be more positive on Monday than on any other day.

9. You return home and realize that your parents are angry with you—because of the rate, pitch, and loudness of their speech—even though the words they are using are not angry words. You are basing your judgment of their emotional state on
   a. prosody.
   b. kinesics.
   c. proxemics.
   d. physiognomy.

10. A victim of an automobile accident suffers a brain injury that disrupts her fight-or-flight response to stressful situations. The accident probably injured her
    a. hypothalamus.
    b. basal ganglia.
    c. occipital lobe.
    d. adrenal glands.

11. When you are physiologically aroused, epinephrine is secreted by your
    a. hypothalamus.
    b. adrenal glands.
    c. thyroid gland.
    d. pituitary gland.

12. Goldstein (1980) injected subjects with naloxone or a placebo and asked them to estimate the intensity of their emotional thrill in response to a musical passage. Because the placebo group experienced more intense feelings, his findings indicated that the positive feelings evoked by music may be related to the secretion of
    a. dopamine.
    b. endorphins.
    c. glutamic acid.
    d. acetylcholine.

13. Research indicates that negative emotions are primarily associated with activity in the
    a. thalamus.
    b. brainstem.
    c. left cerebral hemisphere.
    d. right cerebral hemisphere.

14. Target organs in the sympathetic nervous system are regulated by
    a. dopamine.
    b. epinephrine.
    c. acetylcholine.
    d. norepinephrine.

15. A scientist using sophisticated recording equipment finds that when you are happy you exhibit a consistent, specific pattern of physiological changes that slightly precede your emotional experience. This finding would support the
    a. two-factor theory.
    b. James-Lange theory.
    c. Cannon-Bard theory.
    d. opponent-process theory.

16. After a harrowing automobile ride to school over icy roads, you arrive physiologically aroused. You notice a fellow student whom you find to be more romantically attractive than you have in the past. The best explanation for your emotion would be provided by the
    a. two-factor theory.
    b. James-Lange theory.
    c. Cannon-Bard theory.
    d. opponent-process theory.

17. The Duchenne smile
    a. indicates lying.
    b. is a natural smile.
    c. indicates possible brain damage.
    d. is used in threat displays by animals.

18. The first time you canoe through white water on a river, you may be terrified. If you go white-water canoeing repeatedly, you will eventually instead feel exhilarated. This emotional experience would be explained best by the
    a. two-factor theory.
    b. James-Lange theory.
    c. Cannon-Bard theory.
    d. opponent-process theory.

19. "There is nothing either good or bad, but thinking makes it so." This line from Shakespeare's *Hamlet* bears a kinship to the
    a. James-Lange theory.
    b. Cannon-Bard theory.
    c. opponent-process theory.
    d. cognitive-appraisal theory.

20. The Polygraph Protection Act of 1988
    a. totally bans the use of the polygraph test.
    b. limits the use of the polygraph test to criminal cases.
    c. permits the use of the polygraph test by government intelligence agencies.
    d. protects polygraphers from being sued by suspects who are incorrectly accused of lying.

21. When you are physiologically aroused, sugar is released into your bloodstream by the
    a. liver.
    b. spleen.
    c. stomach.
    d. pancreas.

22. The interacting set of brain structures that regulate emotional arousal composes the
    a. basal ganglia.
    b. limbic system.
    c. superior colliculi.
    d. cerebral ventricles.

23. The Wada test is used for determining the
    a. validity of the lie detector.
    b. role of cerebrospinal fluid in emotionality.
    c. functions of the cerebral hemispheres in emotionality.
    d. relation between hormone levels and emotional intensity.

24. The importance of facial expressions in promoting survival was first noted by
    a. Sigmund Freud.
    b. Wilhelm Wundt.
    c. Charles Darwin.
    d. John B. Watson.

25. The study of Illinois state lottery winners (Brickman, Coates, & Janoff-Bulman, 1978) found that
    a. sudden wealth brings happiness.
    b. their reactions did not support adaptation-level theory.
    c. only winners who donated much of their winnings to charity felt happy.
    d. sudden wealth may make everyday sources of happiness less pleasurable.

Thought Questions

1. Why is it technically incorrect to refer to the polygraph test as a lie detector test?

2. What are the main sources of evidence supporting hemispheric lateralization of emotion?

3. How does research on implicit or unconscious processing support the James-Lange theory?

Personality

Years ago, a researcher placed a newspaper advertisement that offered a free, personalized astrological profile. Of the 150 persons who responded and received their personality profiles, 141 (94 percent) later said they had recognized their own personalities in the "personalized" profiles. The purpose of the study was to see how gullible people can be regarding astrological descriptions of personalities. Each of the respondents actually had received the same personality profile—the profile of a mass murderer who had terrorized France (Waldrop, 1984). Take a moment to see if you recognize yourself in the following personality profile:

> You have a strong need for other people to like and admire you. You have a tendency to be critical of yourself. You have a great deal of unused capacity, which you have not turned to your advantage. . . . Disciplined and controlled on the outside, you tend to be worrisome and insecure inside. . . . At times you are extraverted, affable, and sociable; at other times, you are introverted, wary, and reserved (Ulrich, Stachnik, & Stainton, 1963).

Study after study has shown that when people are given personality tests and then presented with a mock personality description like this one, they tend to accept their description as accurate. They do so because their description *is* accurate. But it—like the one used in the astrology study—is accurate because it contains traits that are shared by almost everyone; it says nothing that distinguishes one person from another. The acceptance of personality descriptions that are true of almost everyone is known as the "Barnum effect" (Meehl, 1956). This term reflects P. T. Barnum's saying that "There's a sucker born every minute." We are more likely to succumb to the Barnum effect when the personality description is flattering (MacDonald & Standing, 2002). The Barnum effect demonstrates that to be useful, personality descriptions must distinguish one person from another. You should no more accept a personality profile that fails to recognize your distinctive combination of personality traits than you would accept a physical description that merely states that you have a head, a torso, two eyes, ten toes, and other common physical characteristics.

Many times we refer to people as having a "good personality" or a "bad personality." But what exactly is personality? The word *personality* comes from the Latin word *persona,* meaning "mask." Just as masks distinguished one character from another in ancient Greek and Roman plays, your personality distinguishes you from other people. Your **personality** is your unique, relatively consistent pattern of thinking, feeling, and behaving.

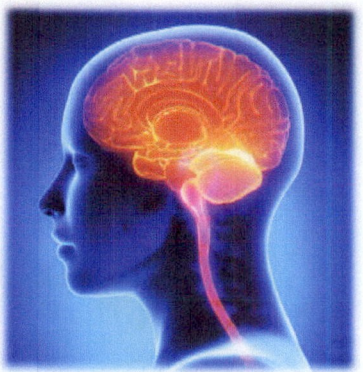

Source: CLIPAREA/Custom media/
Shutterstock.com.

Chapter Outline

The Psychoanalytic Approach to Personality

The Dispositional Approach to Personality

The Cognitive-Behavioral Approach to Personality

The Humanistic Approach to Personality

The Biopsychological Approach to Personality

personality An individual's unique, relatively consistent pattern of thinking, feeling, and behaving.

Given that each of us has a unique personality, how do we explain our distinctive patterns of thinking, feeling, and behaving? Personality theorists favor several approaches to this question. In reading about them, you will see that the theorists' own life experiences often color their personality theories (Atwood & Tomkins, 1976). The approaches to the study of personality differ on several dimensions, including the influence of unconscious motivation, the extent to which we are molded by learning, the role of cognitive factors, the importance of subjective experience, and the effects of biological factors.

The Psychoanalytic Approach to Personality

The *psychoanalytic approach* to personality is rooted in medicine and biology. Sigmund Freud, the founder of psychoanalysis, was a physician who hoped to find the biological basis of the psychological processes contained in his psychosexual theory.

Freud's Psychosexual Theory

Freud (1856–1939) was born in Moravia (a region in the Czech Republic) to Jewish parents; the family moved to Vienna when he was 4 years old. Though Freud desired a career as a physiology professor, anti-Semitism limited his choice of professions to law, business, or medicine. He chose medicine and practiced as a neurologist. Freud remained in Vienna until the Nazis threatened his safety. In 1938 he emigrated to England, where he died the following year after suffering for many years from mouth cancer.

Early in his career, Freud became interested in the effects of the mind on physical symptoms. He had studied with the French neurologist Jean Charcot, who demonstrated the power of hypnosis in treating *conversion hysteria,* a disorder characterized by physical symptoms such as deafness, blindness, or paralysis without a physical cause. Freud also was intrigued by a report that psychiatrist Josef Breuer had successfully used a "talking cure" to treat conversion hysteria. Breuer found that by encouraging his patients to talk freely about whatever came to mind, they became aware of the psychological causes of their physical symptoms and, as a result, experienced emotional release, or *catharsis.* Catharsis led to the disappearance of the symptoms.

Freud's personality theory reflected his time—the Victorian era of the late 19th century. The Victorians valued rationality and self-control of physical drives as characteristics that separated people from animals. Freud attributed the symptoms of conversion hysteria to unconscious sexual conflicts, which were symbolized in the symptoms. For example, paralyzed legs might represent a sexual conflict. Freud's claim that sexuality was an important determinant of human behavior shocked and disgusted many of his contemporaries (Rapp, 1988). After the carnage of World War I, Freud expanded his theory to include aggression as a central human motive. He claimed that we are motivated by both a life instinct, *Eros,* which promotes personal growth and development, and a death instinct, *Thanatos,* which promotes personal deterioration and destructiveness.

Levels of Consciousness

As described in Chapter 6, Freud divided the mind into three levels. The *conscious mind* is merely the "tip of the iceberg," representing a tiny region of the mind. The contents of the conscious mind are in a constant state of flux as feelings, memories, and perceptions enter and leave. Just below the conscious mind lies the *preconscious mind,* which includes accessible memories, that is, memories we can recall at will. The *unconscious mind,* the bulk of the mind, lies below both the conscious mind and the preconscious mind. It contains material we cannot recall at will.

Freud claimed that threatening thoughts or feelings are subject to *repression,* the banishment of conscious material into the unconscious. Because Freud assumed that unconscious thoughts and feelings are the most important influences on our behavior, he proclaimed: "The theory of repression is the cornerstone on which the whole structure of psychoanalysis rests" (Freud, 1914/1957, p. 16). The notion of repressed thoughts and feelings led to the concept of *psychic determinism*, which holds that all behavior is influenced by unconscious motives. Psychic determinism is exhibited in *Freudian slips*, unintentional statements that might reveal our repressed feelings (Reason, 2000). For instance, the slip "I loathe you . . . I mean, I love you" might reveal repressed hostility.

The Structure of Personality

As illustrated in Figure 13-1, Freud distinguished three structures of personality: the *id,* the *ego,* and the *superego.* The **id** is unconscious and consists of our inborn biological drives. In demanding immediate gratification of drives, most notably sex and aggression, the id obeys the **pleasure principle**.

The word *id* is Latin for "it," reflecting the id's impersonal nature. The classic 1950s science fiction movie *Forbidden Planet* portrays the amoral nature of the id: The id of a mad scientist is transformed into a being of pure energy that runs amok on an alien planet, blindly killing anyone in its path.

Through life experiences we learn that acting on every sexual or aggressive impulse is socially maladaptive. As a consequence, each of us develops an **ego,** Latin for "I." The ego obeys the **reality principle**, directing us to express sexual and aggressive impulses in socially acceptable ways. Suppose that a professor refuses to change your grade on an exam that was graded with an incorrect answer key. Your ego would encourage you to argue with the professor instead of punching him or her.

The **superego** (Latin for "over the I") counteracts the id, which is concerned only with immediate gratification, and the ego, which is concerned only with adapting to reality. The superego acts as our moral guide. It contains the *conscience,* which makes us feel guilty for doing or thinking wrong, and the *ego ideal,* which makes us feel good for doing or thinking right. To Freud, your personality is the outcome of the continual battle for dominance among the id, the ego, and the superego.

Defense Mechanisms

The ego might resort to **defense mechanisms**, which distort reality, to protect itself from the anxiety caused by id impulses, particularly those of sex and aggression. The ego also may use defense mechanisms to relieve the anxiety caused by unacceptable personal characteristics and unpleasant personal experiences, including traumatic experiences such as torture

id In Freud's theory, the part of the personality that contains inborn biological drives and that seeks immediate gratification.

pleasure principle The process by which the id seeks immediate gratification of its impulses.

ego In Freud's theory, the part of the personality that helps the individual adapt to external reality by making compromises between the id, the superego, and the environment.

reality principle The process by which the ego directs the individual to express sexual and aggressive impulses in socially acceptable ways.

superego In Freud's theory, the part of the personality that acts as a moral guide telling us what we should and should not do.

defense mechanism In Freud's theory, a process that distorts reality to prevent the individual from being overwhelmed by anxiety.

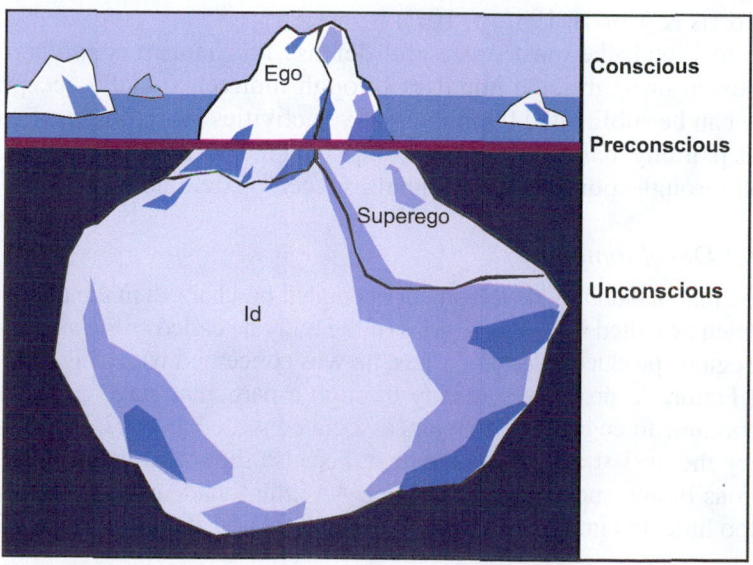

FIGURE 13-1
The Structure of Personality

Freud divided personality into the id, ego, and superego. The id is entirely unconscious and demands immediate gratification of its desires. The ego is partly conscious and partly unconscious. This permits it to balance the id's demands with the external demands of reality and the moralistic demands of the superego, which also is partly conscious and partly unconscious.

experienced by political prisoners (Punamaeki, Kanninen, Quota, & El-Sarr, 2002). Each of us uses defense mechanisms to varying extents, which contributes to the distinctiveness of our personalities. Researchers studying the role of unconscious processes in stress and coping have renewed scientific interest in defense mechanisms (P. Cramer, 2003). And as noted in Chapter 14, Freudians believe that excessive reliance on defense mechanisms contributes to the development of psychological disorders.

Because all defense mechanisms involve *repression,* we are not aware when we are using them. The memory of a traumatic event, such as an auto accident, might be repressed to relieve the anxiety that the memory produces. As discussed in Chapter 8, the defense mechanism of repression has become a controversial topic in the mass media because of the rise in reports of adults recalling apparently recovered memories of sexual abuse in early childhood (Loftus, Joslyn, & Polage, 1998).

We sometimes rely on immature kinds of defense mechanisms. In using *denial,* we simply refuse to admit a particular aspect of reality. For example, terminally ill patients might initially reduce their anxiety by denying they have a fatal disease. In resorting to the defense mechanism of *regression,* the individual displays immature behaviors that have relieved anxiety in the past. A child might respond to physical abuse by bed-wetting or refusing to be parted from a favorite stuffed toy (Finzi, Har-Even, & Weizman, 2003).

Other defense mechanisms rely on changing our perception of reality. When we resort to *rationalization,* we provide socially acceptable reasons for our inappropriate behavior. For example, a student whose semester grades include one D and four Fs might blame the four Fs on studying too much for the course in which he received a D. People who use *intellectualization* reduce anxiety by reacting to emotional situations in a detached, unemotional way. Instead of reacting to the death of a loved one by crying, they might react by saying, "Everyone must die sometime."

In some cases, defense mechanisms direct sexual or aggressive drives in safer directions. A person who fears the consequences of expressing her or his feelings toward a particular person might express them toward someone less threatening. This defense mechanism is known as *displacement.* For example, a worker who hates his boss but fears criticizing him might instead abuse his children with his hostility. If we cannot accept our own undesirable feelings, we might resort to *projection,* attributing our undesirable feelings to others. One experiment found, for example, that when people project onto other people their own feelings of anger or their belief that they are dishonest, they report that they feel less anger and believe that they are less dishonest (Schimel, Greenberg, & Martens, 2003). *Reaction formation* involves countering undesirable feelings by acting in a manner opposite to them. Samuel Johnson, the 18th-century writer and dictionary editor, reported a classic example of reaction formation. A pair of proper ladies who met him at a literary tea commented, "We see, Dr. Johnson, that you do not have those naughty words in your dictionary." Johnson replied, "And I see, dear ladies, that you have been looking for them" (Morris & Morris, 1985, p. 101).

According to Freud, the most successful defense mechanism is *sublimation,* the expression of sexual or aggressive impulses through indirect, socially acceptable outlets. The sex drive can be sublimated through creative activities (Kim, Zeppenfield, & Cohen, 2013), such as painting, ballet dancing, or composing music. And the aggressive drive can be sublimated through sports such as football, soccer, or field hockey.

Psychosexual Development

Freud assumed that personality development depended on changes in the distribution of sexual energy, which he called **libido**, in regions of the body he called *erogenous zones.* Stimulation of these regions produces pleasure. Thus, he was concerned with stages of *psychosexual development.* Failure to progress smoothly through a particular stage can cause *fixation,* a tendency to continue to engage in behaviors associated with that stage. Freud called the first year of infancy the **oral stage** of development, because the infant gains pleasure from oral activities such as biting, sucking, and chewing. An infant inadequately weaned, because of too much or too little oral gratification, might become fixated at the oral stage. Fixation might

Sublimation

According to Freud, the aggressive drive can be sublimated through participating in sports such as soccer.

Source: ostill/Shutterstock.com.

libido Freud's term for the sexual energy of the id.

oral stage In Freud's theory, the stage of personality development between birth and age 1 year, during which the infant gains pleasure from oral activities and faces a conflict over weaning.

lead to an *oral-dependent* personality, marked by passivity, dependency, and gullibility. The person will "swallow anything" and might become a "sucker." Or fixation might lead to an *oral-aggressive* personality, marked by cruelty and sarcastic, "biting" remarks.

At the age of one year, children enter the **anal stage**. They now obtain pleasure from defecation and experience an important conflict regarding toilet training. Freud claimed that inadequate toilet training, either premature or delayed, can lead to fixation at the anal stage. The main characters in the play, movie, and television series *The Odd Couple* represent two kinds of anal fixation. Felix represents the *anal-retentive* personality, marked by compulsive cleanliness, orderliness, and fussiness. Oscar represents the *anal-expulsive* personality, marked by sloppiness, carelessness, and informality.

Freud claimed that between the ages of 3 and 5, the child passes through the **phallic stage**, in which pleasure is gained from genital stimulation. This stage is associated with the **Oedipus complex**, in which the child sexually desires the parent of the other sex while fearing punishment from the parent of the same sex. Freud noted this conflict in Sophocles' play *Oedipus Rex,* in which Oedipus, abandoned as an infant, later kills his father and marries his mother—without knowing they are his parents.

Freud believed that the Oedipus story reflected a universal truth—the sexual attraction of each child to the other-sex parent. Resolution of the conflict leads to identification with the same-sex parent. The boy gives up his desire for his mother because of his *castration anxiety*—his fear that his father will punish him by removing his genitals. The girl, because of *penis envy,* becomes angry at her mother, whom she believes caused her to be born without a penis, and becomes attracted to her father. This stage is now known as the **Electra complex**, named by Carl Jung after a Greek character who had her mother killed (Kilmartin & Dervin, 1997). But, fearing the loss of maternal love, the girl identifies with her mother, hoping to still attract her father. Through the process of *identification,* boys and girls adopt parental values, develop a superego, and establish their gender identity and sexual orientation.

Freud called the period between age 5 and puberty the **latency stage**. He was relatively uninterested in this stage because he believed that the child experiences little psychosexual development during it. Instead, the child develops social skills and friendships. Finally, during adolescence, the child reaches the **genital stage** and becomes sexually attracted to other people. To Freud, the first three stages are the most important determinants of personality development. He assumed that personality is essentially fixed by the age of 5. Table 13-1 summarizes these psychosexual stages of development.

Because Freud's intellectual descendants modified his theory in developing their own, they became known as *neo-Freudians.* For example, a central concept of Erich Fromm's theory (1941) is the conflict between the need for freedom and the anxiety that freedom brings. And Harry Stack Sullivan (1953) emphasized the importance of healthy interpersonal relationships to personality development.

Adler's Theory of Individual Psychology

One of the most influential of Freud's followers was Alfred Adler (1870–1937). In 1902, Adler, a Viennese physician, joined the discussions of psychoanalysis at Freud's home and became a devoted disciple. But in 1911, Adler broke with Freud, downplaying the importance of sexual motivation and the unconscious mind. Adler (1927) developed his own theory, which he called *individual psychology.* The popularity of Adler's theory provoked Freud to complain, "I made a pygmy great" (Hergenhahn, 1984, p. 65).

Adler's childhood experiences inspired his theory of personality. He was a sickly child who saw himself as inferior to his stronger and healthier older brother. Adler assumed that because children feel small, weak, and dependent on others, they develop an *inferiority complex.* This complex motivates them to compensate by *striving for superiority*—that is, developing certain abilities to their maximum potential. Perhaps Adler compensated for his childhood frailty by becoming an eminent psychoanalyst.

Adler believed that striving for superiority is healthiest when it promotes active concern for the welfare of both oneself and others, which he called *social interest* (Adler, 1994). For example, both a physician and a criminal strive for superiority, but the physician expresses

Fixation

Is it too early or late for this child for toilet training? According to Freud, if this process is interrupted it could lead to a fixation.
Source: ARZTSAMUI/ Shutterstock.com.

anal stage In Freud's theory, the stage of personality development between ages 1 and 3, during which the child gains pleasure from defecation and faces a conflict over toilet training.

phallic stage In Freud's theory, the stage of personality development between ages 3 and 5, during which the child gains pleasure from the genitals and must resolve the Oedipus complex.

Oedipus complex In Freud's theory, a conflict, during the phallic stage, between the child's sexual desire for the parent of the other sex and fear of punishment from the same-sex parent.

Electra complex A term used by some psychoanalysts, but not by Freud, to refer to the Oedipus complex in girls.

latency stage In Freud's theory, the stage between age 5 and puberty, during which there is little psychosexual development.

genital stage In Freud's theory, the last stage of personality development, associated with puberty, during which the individual develops erotic attachments to others.

Zen

Zen is a school of Buddhism developed in China as early as the 6th century. This statue is located in Tian Tan.

Source: Blue Sky Studio/ Shutterstock.com.

this motive in a socially beneficial way. Cohesive, emotionally expressive families with low levels of conflict promote the development of social interest (Johnson, Smith, & Nelson, 2003). One study found that adolescent mentors with high social interest were more likely to continue as a mentor after the first year, to choose more challenging mentees, and to feel more connected with their school (Karcher & Lindwall, 2003). According to Adler, in striving for superiority we develop a *style of life* based on *fictional finalism,* which he referred to as the "guiding self ideal" (Watts & Holden, 1994). We are motivated by beliefs that might not be objectively true. A person guided by the belief that "nice guys finish last" might exhibit a ruthless, competitive style of life. In contrast, a person guided by the belief that "it is more blessed to give than to receive" might exhibit a helpful, altruistic style of life.

Horney's Theory of Feminine Psychology

Though Karen Horney (1885–1952) never studied with Freud she was a prominent neo-Freudian. She challenged many of his theoretical assumptions, beginning with a groundbreaking paper that she presented at the Seventh International Psychoanalytic Congress in 1922—at a session chaired by Freud. The paper was the first of a series of papers that ultimately formed the basis for her theory of feminine psychology (Horney, 1924). She criticized a number of Freud's concepts, such as penis envy and the Oedipal and Electra complexes. Most important, she believed that Freudian psychoanalytic theory neglected the role of sociocultural factors in personality development. She was an early advocate of a cross-cultural approach to psychology, and in her later years worked on integrating psychoanalysis and concepts from Zen Buddhism (Morvay, 1999).

Horney believed that psychoanalytic theory was *androcentric,* using male personality development as the norm by which to explain the development of women's personalities. In particular, she critiqued Freud's emphasis on penis envy, noting that men were just as likely to experience *womb envy.* In support of this notion, she pointed out that children often are in awe of women's ability to give birth (Horney, 1926/1967). She also believed that Freud overemphasized sexuality in the phallic stage. Horney asserted that girls were not envious of boys' genitalia but rather the fact that men held superior—and more powerful—positions in society (O'Connell, 1990). In her later work, she continued to emphasize the importance of gender roles, interpersonal power, and sociocultural factors influencing women's personality (Miletic, 2002).

Like Adler, Horney's childhood experiences are reflected in her theory. She was an anxious child who felt unwanted and struggled to gain her parents' love and approval. Later, in self-analysis, she realized that she felt hostile toward her parents, especially her authoritarian father. Horney theorized that children develop *basic anxiety* because of their emotional and physical dependency on adults—who have the power to give or withhold love. Basic anxiety leads to *basic hostility,* an emotional response that children must suppress to gain love and security from their parents. To combat these intense feelings of anxiety and hostility and to gain a sense of security, a child develops one of three coping styles: *moving toward others,* in which the child becomes compliant and affectionate; *moving against others,* in which the child becomes aggressive; or *moving away from others,* in which the child becomes detached and aloof (Coolidge, Moor, Yamazaki, Stewart, & Segal, 2001). These coping styles become part of one's personality. Neurotic people rigidly rely on one style; mentally healthy people are flexible and use each style when appropriate (Horney, 1950).

Jung's Theory of Analytical Psychology

Freud's favorite disciple was Carl Jung (1875–1961). Though Jung, a native of Switzerland, came from a family in which the men traditionally pursued careers as Protestant pastors, he was inspired to become a psychoanalyst after reading Freud's *The Interpretation of Dreams* (1900/1990). Beginning in 1906, Freud and Jung carried on a lively correspondence, and Freud hoped that Jung would become his successor as head of the psychoanalytic movement. But in 1914 they parted over revisions Jung made in Freud's theory, especially Jung's de-emphasis of the sex motive. Jung called his version of psychoanalysis *analytical psychology.*

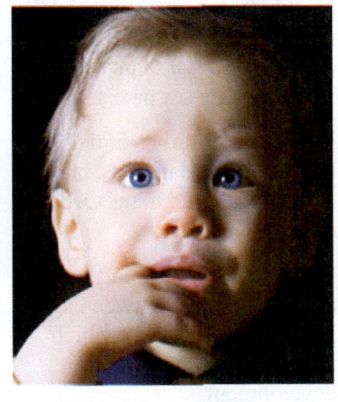

Basic Anxiety

According to Horney, children develop basic anxiety because of their emotional and physical dependency on adults.

Source: Stuart Monk/ Shutterstock.com.

TABLE 13-1 The Stages of Psychosexual Development

Stage	Age	Characteristics	
Oral	Birth to 1	Gratification from oral behaviors, such as sucking, biting, and chewing Conflict over weaning	
Anal	1 to 3	Gratification from defecation Conflict over toilet training	
Phallic	3 to 5	Gratification from genital stimulation Resolution of the Oedipus or Electra complex	
Latency	5 to puberty	Sexual impulses repressed Development of friendships	
Genital	Puberty on	Gratification from genital stimulation Development of intimate relationships	

Photo sources: Oral—Oksana Kuzmina/Shutterstock.com; Anal—Jamie Hooper/Shutterstock.com; Phallic—Rob Marmion/Shutterstock.com; Latency—Monkey Business Images/Shutterstock.com; Genital—swissmacky/Shutterstock.com.

The Mandala

Balanced, circular paintings such as these have been found in cultures throughout history and throughout the world. Jung claimed that they represent the complete congruence of the self and the persona.

Sources: (left) krishnasomya/ Shutterstock.com; *(right)* OkPic/ Shutterstock.com.

personal unconscious In Jung's theory, the individual's own unconscious mind, which contains repressed memories.

collective unconscious In Jung's theory, the unconscious mind that is shared by all people and that contains archetypal images passed down from our prehistoric ancestors.

archetypes In Jung's theory, inherited images that are passed down from our prehistoric ancestors and that reveal themselves as universal symbols in art, dreams, and religion.

extravert A person who is socially outgoing and prefers to pay attention to the external environment.

introvert A person who is socially reserved and prefers to pay attention to his or her private cognitive experiences.

projective test A psychoanalytic personality test based on the assumption that individuals project their unconscious feelings when responding to ambiguous stimuli.

Though Jung agreed with Freud that we each have our own unconscious mind (the **personal unconscious**), he claimed that we also share a common unconscious mind—the **collective unconscious.** Jung held that the collective unconscious contains inherited memories passed down from generation to generation. He called these memories **archetypes,** which are images that represent important aspects of the accumulated experience of humanity (McDowell, 2001). Jung claimed that archetypes influence our dreams, religious symbols, and artistic creations.

Jung (1959/1969) even connected the archetype of God to UFO sightings that began to be reported in the late 1940s, following the horrors of World War II and the advent of the atomic bomb. According to Jung, these sightings stemmed from the desire of people, inspired by the archetype of God, to have a more powerful force than themselves save humanity from self-destruction. Even the round shape of the flying saucer represented the archetypal image of godlike unity and perfection of the archetype of the *self.* Beginning in the 1950s with the movie *The Day the Earth Stood Still* and continuing with movies such as *Close Encounters of the Third Kind,* science fiction movies have reflected the Jungian theme of powerful aliens arriving in flying saucers to save us from ourselves.

The *persona* is another archetype related to the self. Whereas the self is the true, private personality, the persona is the somewhat false social "mask" that we wear in public. According to Jung, the persona and self of a psychologically healthy individual are fairly congruent. Jung also distinguished between the *anima,* the feminine archetype in men, and the *animus,* the masculine archetype in women. According to Jung, a psychologically healthy person, whether female or male, must maintain a balance between masculinity and femininity. A "macho" man who acts tough and rarely expresses tender emotions would be unhealthy, as would a "prissy" woman who acts passive and has little control over her emotions.

Jung even contributed to our everyday language by distinguishing between two personality types. **Extraverts** are socially outgoing and pay more attention to the surrounding environment; **introverts** are socially reserved and pay more attention to their private cognitive experiences. Jung applied this concept in his own life, viewing Freud as an extravert and Adler as an introvert (Monte, 1980).

Psychoanalytic Assessment of Personality

More than a century ago, Sir Arthur Conan Doyle popularized the use of handwriting analysis, or *graphology,* by having his fictional detective Sherlock Holmes use it to solve crimes. Graphology was an ancestor of psychoanalytic personality tests. Graphology is based on the assumption that because all children in a given culture learn to form written letters and words the same way, any deviations from the original prototypes reflect in part one's distinctive personality. Given the lack of experimental evidence in support of graphology, few psychologists today use it to assess personality.

Graphology has the same rationale as modern psychoanalytic assessment techniques, which are called **projective tests.** They are based on the assumption that we will "project" our repressed feelings and conflicts onto ambiguous stimuli. It is especially important that those who are interpreting responses to projective tests do not let their own preconceptions about the test takers affect their interpretations (Wiederman, 1999). Today the most popular projective tests are the *Rorschach test* and the *Thematic Apperception Test.*

The Rorschach Test

Have you ever seen animal shapes in cloud formations? Have you ever argued about images in abstract paintings? If so, you will have some appreciation for the *Rorschach test,* which asks participants to report what they see in inkblots. The Rorschach test was introduced in 1921 by the Swiss psychiatrist Hermann Rorschach (1884–1922), who died before he was able to conduct much research with it. The test consists of 10 bilaterally symmetrical inkblots. Some of the inkblots are in black and white, and the others include colors.

In responding to the inkblots, the person tells what he or she sees in each one and then reports the features of the inkblot that prompted the response. After scoring each response, based on formal criteria, the examiner uses clinical judgment and one of several available scoring systems to write a profile of the person's motives and conflicts. Such profiles have been used for purposes as diverse as diagnosing suicide risk among adolescents and young adults (Blasczyk-Schiep, Kazén, Kuhl, & Grygielski, 2011) and distinguishing between the personalities of murderers and nonviolent criminals (Coram, 1995).

The Thematic Apperception Test

The Thematic Apperception Test (TAT) (Morgan & Murray, 1935) was created by the American psychoanalyst Henry Murray and his associate Christiana Morgan (Morgan, 2002). The TAT consists of one blank card and 19 cards containing black-and-white pictures of people in ambiguous situations. The examiner asks several questions about each one: What is happening in the card? What events led up to that situation? Who are the people in the card? How do they feel? How does the situation turn out? Murray and Morgan assumed that people's responses would reveal their most important needs, such as the need for sex, power, achievement, or affiliation. The TAT is a moderately good predictor of real-life achievement, such as career success (Spangler, 1992). The TAT also has been used to measure changes in the use of defense mechanisms as a result of psychotherapy (Cramer, 1999).

The Rorschach Test

The basic assumption of the Rorschach test is that what we report seeing in a series of inkblots will reveal our unconscious motives and conflicts.

Source: michaeljung/Shutterstock.com.

Status of the Psychoanalytic Approach

Of all the psychoanalytic theories of personality, Freud's has been the most influential, but it has received limited support for its concepts (Fisher & Greenberg, 1985). As described in Chapter 6, there is substantial evidence demonstrating the effect of unconscious processes on human behavior (Dixon & Henley, 1991). And as described in Chapter 8, there is support for the Freudian view of repression from research showing that people are less likely to recall emotionally unpleasant personal experiences (Sparks, Pellechia, & Irvine, 1999), though the notion of total repression of traumatic emotional experiences has received only weak support (Bowers & Farvolden, 1996). Some research has supported the existence of several defense mechanisms, including projection and reaction formation. However, there is little support for certain other defense mechanisms, including displacement and sublimation (Baumeister, Dale, & Sommer, 1998).

There also has been little support for some of Freud's other concepts. For example, there is little evidence to support Freud's belief that resolution of the Oedipus and Electra complexes is essential for gender identity, sexual orientation, and superego development (Schrut, 1994). Perhaps the greatest weakness of Freudian theory is that many of its terms refer to processes that are neither observable nor measurable. Who has ever seen or measured an id? As noted in Chapter 2, we cannot conduct experiments on concepts that are not operationally defined.

Despite the limited support for certain psychoanalytic concepts, the psychoanalytic approach has contributed to our understanding of personality. It has revealed that much of our behavior is governed by motives of which we are unaware, as revealed in dreams, and it has stimulated interest in studying sexual behavior and sexual development. It has demonstrated the importance of early childhood experiences, such as infant attachment; it has contributed to the emergence of formal psychological therapies; and it has inspired research into the effects of psychological factors on illness. It also has influenced the works of artists, writers, and filmmakers (Highet, 1998).

Adler's theory of personality has influenced cognitive psychology and humanistic psychology (Watts & Critelli, 1997) through its emphasis on the importance of our subjective experiences of reality. Of the Adlerian concepts that impressed humanistic psychologists, the most influential were the concepts of social interest and style of life (Ansbacher, 1990). Moreover, his concept of a style of life that reflects our striving for superiority has an important descendant in the current interest in *Type A behavior,* which is discussed at length in Chapter 16 as a possible factor in coronary heart disease. Despite Adler's influence on humanistic and cognitive approaches to personality and psychotherapy, however, interest in individual psychology itself has declined in recent years (Freeman, 1999).

Horney's conceptualization of neurosis made a lasting contribution to American psychology and psychoanalysis (Ingram, 1985). Though there is little research directly testing Horney's theory, her work on human neurosis contributed to many of the principles and techniques of cognitive therapy and the treatment of anxiety and depression (see

Chapter 15). Like Adler, Horney influenced other psychological theorists. For example, her idea of basic anxiety is similar to Erikson's concept of basic trust-mistrust explained in Chapter 4. Moreover, her emphasis on sociocultural determinants of women's personality was carried forward in the work of contemporary feminist psychoanalytic theorists, such as Nancy Chodorow (1978), who explore the relation of gender roles, family relationships, and power to women's personality development.

And what of Jung's theory? Jung's concept of personality types has received research support. One study compared the styles of extraverted painters and introverted painters. Extraverted painters tended to use realistic styles, reflecting their greater attention to the external environment. In contrast, introverted painters tended to use abstract styles, reflecting their greater attention to private mental experience (Loomis & Saltz, 1984). Jung's concept of the archetype has been criticized because it violates known mechanisms of inheritance in its assumption that memories can be inherited. Nonetheless, research findings support the possibility that hereditary tendencies akin to archetypes affect human behavior (Neher, 1996). Evidence for this finding comes from research, explained in Chapter 14, showing that we have an inborn predisposition to develop phobias about snakes, heights, and other situations that were dangerous to our prehistoric ancestors. Thus, what Jung called archetypes might be inborn behavioral tendencies rather than inherited memories.

As for projective tests of personality, the Rorschach test and the TAT are frequently used by clinical and forensic psychologists. However, a recent review of the literature concluded that neither test has been shown to have greater validity than objective personality tests, such as the Minnesota Multiphasic Personality Inventory (MMPI), which is discussed in the section, "Dispositional Assessment of Personality." Moreover, it is unclear whether scoring procedures and norms for these tests are generalizable to different cultures and racial or ethnic groups (Lilienfeld, Wood, & Garb, 2000).

Section Review: The Psychoanalytic Approach to Personality

1. What does the Barnum effect indicate about the study of personality?

2. What is the relationship between the three structures of personality in Freud's theory?

3. What are the basic tenets of Adler's theory?

4. How did Horney broaden psychoanalytic theory to include social and cultural forces?

5. According to Jung, how do the collective unconscious and its archetypes affect our lives?

The Dispositional Approach to Personality

Personality theorists have traditionally assumed that personality is stable over time and consistent across situations. The *dispositional approach* to personality attributes this apparent stability and consistency to relatively enduring personal characteristics called *types* and *traits*.

Type Theories

In his book *Characters,* the Greek philosopher Theophrastus (ca. 372–ca. 287 B.C.) wondered why Greeks differed in personality despite sharing the same culture and geography. He concluded that personality differences arise from inborn predispositions to develop particular personality *types* dominated by a single characteristic. Like Theophrastus, we rely on personality typing when we call someone a "morning person" or an "evening person" (Mecacci & Rocchetti, 1998).

Today the most influential theory of personality types is Hans Eysenck's *three-factor theory* (Eysenck, 1990). Eysenck (1916–1997), a German psychologist, fled to England after refusing to become a member of Hitler's secret police. Eysenck used the statistical technique of factor analysis (see Chapter 10) in identifying three dimensions of personality. By measuring where a person falls on these dimensions, we can determine his or her personality type.

The dimension of *neuroticism* measures a person's level of stability/instability. Stable people are calm, even-tempered, and reliable; unstable people are moody, anxious, and unreliable. One study of moderate to heavy drinkers found that participants high in neuroticism engaged in more solitary drinking on days during which they had more negative interpersonal experiences than did participants low in neuroticism (Mohr et al., 2001). The dimension of *psychoticism* measures a person's level of tough-mindedness/tender-mindedness. Tough-minded people are hostile, ruthless, and insensitive, whereas tender-minded people are friendly, empathetic, and cooperative. Juvenile delinquents score high in psychoticism (Furnham & Thompson, 1991).

The dimension of *extraversion* measures a person's level of introversion/extraversion. Extraverts try to have fun, connect with other people, and tend to experience positive emotional states (McCabe & Fleeson, 2012). This dimension, first identified by Jung, has stimulated the most research interest. For example, studies have shown that there are proportionately more introverts among expert chess players than in the general population. Because introverted chess champions may be uncomfortable in social situations, they prefer to avoid victory parties, press conferences, and autograph hounds. They might even feel compelled to leave the chess scene itself. In 1972 the American Bobby Fischer generated unprecedented interest in chess with his brilliant play in winning the World Chess Championship, only to retire into seclusion soon after (Olmo & Stevens, 1984). Figure 13-2 illustrates the interaction of the dimensions of introversion/extraversion and stability/instability.

There is evidence that the dimensions in Eysenck's theory have a biological basis (Loehlin & Martin, 2001). For example, research on twins indicates that neuroticism, psychoticism, and extraversion have genetic bases. Heredity might explain why introverts are more physiologically reactive than extraverts are (Stelmack, 1990). This reactivity might in turn explain behavioral differences between introverts and extraverts. The greater physiological reactivity of introverts might explain why extraverts can work better than introverts under distracting conditions. Consider students who, perhaps like yourself, study while music is playing in the background. One study compared the effect of background music, office noise, and silence on reading comprehension, recall, and mental arithmetic tasks. Extraverts performed better while listening to background music or office noise, and introverts performed better in the silent condition. Thus, an introverted student would be wise to study in the library whereas an extraverted student may study effectively while listening to music (Furnham & Strbac, 2002).

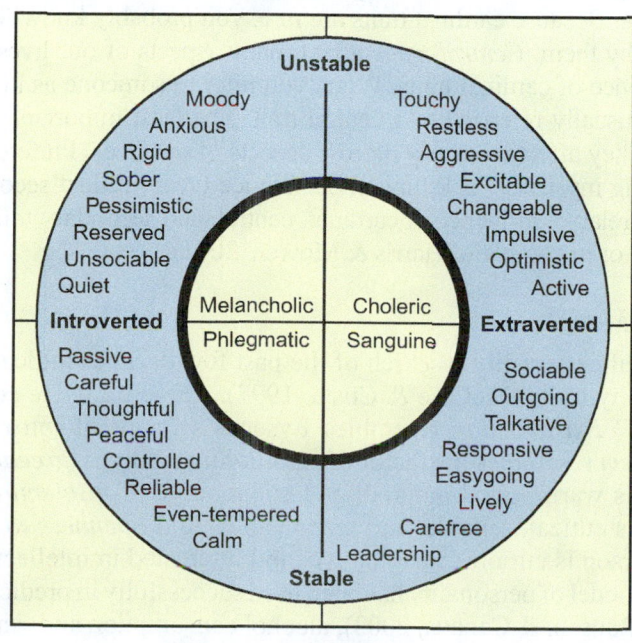

FIGURE 13-2
Eysenck's Personality Dimensions

The drawing shows the interaction of Eysenck's personality dimensions of introversion/extraversion and stability/instability.

Source: From Eysenck, S. B. G., & Eysenck, J. J. (1963). "The validity of questionnaire and rating assessments of extraversion and neuroticism, and their factorial stability" from *British Journal of Psychology, 54,* 51–62. Reprinted by permission of The British Psychological Society.

Another observable behavioral difference that can be measured is social withdrawal, which is related to introversion. Modern methods make it possible to search for genes associated with behavior characteristic of social withdrawal. Researchers collected genetic information from 551 six- to eighteen-year-olds in 187 families after administering two behavioral scales related to social withdrawal, the Child Behavior Checklist and the Withdrawn Behavior Subscale. The results indicated that genes regulating serotonin were associated with shyness and inhibition. And this relationship was particularly pronounced in young children (Rubin et al., 2013). This study and others indicate that some personality dimensions are biologically hereditable. But other researchers believe that people's personalities are as a result of environmental influences.

Trait Theories

trait A relatively enduring, cross-situationally consistent personality characteristic that is inferred from a person's behavior.

Instead of describing personality in terms of single types, trait theorists describe personality in terms of distinctive combinations of personal dispositions (McCrae & Costa, 1995). A **trait** is a relatively enduring, cross-situationally consistent personality characteristic that is inferred from a person's behavior. Eysenck's theory can be viewed as either a type theory or a trait theory, because the personality types in his theory are products of the interaction of certain trait dimensions. The most influential trait theory is that of Gordon Allport (1897–1967), who was a leader in making personality an important area of American psychological research in the 1920s and 1930s (Lombardo & Foschi, 2002).

Allport's Trait Theory

Early in his career, Allport had a brief meeting in Vienna with Sigmund Freud that convinced him that psychoanalysis was not the best approach to the study of personality. Confronted with a silent Freud, Allport broke the silence by describing a boy he had met on a train who had complained of dirty people and whose mother had acted annoyed at his behavior. Freud responded, "And was that little boy you?" Based on this meeting, Allport concluded that Freud was too concerned with finding hidden motives for even the most mundane behaviors (Allport, 1967).

Allport began his research by identifying all the English words that refer to personal characteristics. In 1936 Allport and his colleague Henry Odbert, using an unabridged dictionary, counted almost 18,000 such words. By eliminating synonyms and words referring to temporary states (such as *hungry*), they reduced the list to about 4,500 words. Allport then grouped the words into less than 200 clusters of related words, which became the original personality traits in his theory.

Allport distinguished three kinds of traits, the differences depending on how important they are in a given person's life. *Cardinal traits* are similar to personality types in that they affect every aspect of the person's life. For example, altruism was a cardinal trait in the personality of Mother Teresa. Because cardinal traits are rare, you probably know few people whose lives are governed by them. *Central traits* affect many aspects of our lives but do not have the pervasive influence of cardinal traits. When you refer to someone as kind, humorous, or conceited, you are usually referring to a central trait. The least important traits are *secondary traits,* because they affect relatively narrow aspects of our lives. Preferences for wearing cuffed pants, reading mysteries, or eating chocolate ice cream reflect secondary traits. One study looked at the relative influence of cardinal, central, and secondary traits on consumers' tendency to bargain or to complain (Harris & Mowen, 2001).

The Five-Factor Model

The most influential personality research of the past few decades indicates that there are five basic personality traits (McCrae & Costa, 1997). These traits are commonly known as "The Big Five." *Extraversion* resembles Eysenck's factor of introversion/extraversion, and *neuroticism* resembles his factor of stability/instability. *Agreeableness* indicates whether a person is warm, good-natured, and cooperative. *Conscientiousness* indicates whether a person is ethical, reliable, and responsible. And *openness to experience* indicates whether a person is curious, imaginative, and interested in intellectual pursuits.

The five-factor model of personality has been used successfully in predicting achievement orientation (Ross, Rausch, & Canada, 2003), alcohol consumption and grade-point average

(Paunonen, 2003), religiosity (McCullough, Tsang, & Brion, 2003), job strain (Tömroos et al, 2013), and personal values (Roccas, Sagi, Schwartz, & Knafo, 2002). The five-factor model has been applied to a wide range of behaviors, and it recently has been tested in many cultures. One study investigated the distribution of personality traits in more than 27,000 participants from 36 cultures. Personality traits were unrelated to most geographic variables, such as distance from the equator and average temperature. However, personality profiles of cultures in close proximity were more similar than those of distant cultures. And the researchers found differences between European American and Asian cultures similar to individualist and collectivist orientations. Whereas European American cultures scored higher in extraversion and openness to experience, Asian cultures scored higher on agreeableness (Allik & McCrae, 2004).

Dispositional Assessment of Personality

The dispositional assessment of personality relies on tests of personality types or traits. These tests are called *objective tests* because they present participants with straightforward statements rather than with ambiguous stimuli, as in projective tests.

Tests of Personality Types

One of the most popular objective tests is the *Myers-Briggs Type Indicator* (Briggs & Myers, 1943). The test assesses various personality characteristics, including personality types derived from Jung's analytical theory of personality. The participant is presented with pairs of statements and selects the statement in each pair that is closest to how she or he usually acts or feels. A typical item would be "At parties, do you (a) sometimes get bored or (b) always have fun?" An introvert would be more likely to select *a* and an extravert *b*. The test has satisfactory reliability (Capraro & Capraro, 2002) and validity (Murray, 1990) and has been used in a variety of research studies. One study found that psychological well-being, life satisfaction, and self-consciousness are related to specific personality profiles on the test (Harrington & Loffredo, 2001). A study that administered the Myers-Briggs Type Indicator to more than 1,000 participants found that the American population is equally divided into introverts and extraverts (Hammer & Mitchell, 1996).

Tests of Personality Traits

Researchers recently have developed personality tests based on the five-factor model of personality. These tests include the Five Factor Personality Inventory (Hendriks, Hofstee, & DeRaad, 1999) and the NEO Personality Inventory, which has been used to study relationships between personality traits and attitudes or behaviors, such as musical preferences (Rawlings & Ciancarelli, 1997). But the most widely used of all personality tests is the *Minnesota Multiphasic Personality Inventory (MMPI)*, which measures personality traits.

The MMPI was developed at the University of Minnesota by psychologist Starke R. Hathaway and psychiatrist John C. McKinley (1943) to diagnose psychological disorders. Hathaway and McKinley used the *empirical method* of test construction, which retains only those questions that discriminate between people who differ on the characteristics of interest. Hathaway and McKinley collected 1,000 statements, which they administered to 700 people, including nonpatients, medical patients, and psychiatric patients. Participants responded "True," "False," or "Cannot Say" to each statement, depending on whether it was true of them. Hathaway and McKinley kept those statements that tended to be answered the same way by people with particular psychiatric disorders. For example, they included the statement "Nothing in the newspaper interests me except the comics" solely because significantly more depressed people than nondepressed people responded "True" to that statement (Holden, 1986).

As shown in Table 13-2, the MMPI has 10 clinical scales that measure important personality traits. For example, *hypochondriasis* measures concern with bodily functions and symptoms, and *paranoia* measures suspiciousness and delusions of persecution. The MMPI also has four *validity scales* that test for evasiveness, defensiveness, lying to look good, and faking to look bad. For example, the Lie scale contains statements that describe common human failings to which almost all people respond "True." So, a person who

TABLE 13-2 Scales of the MMPI-2

Scales	Content
Clinical Scales	
Hypochondriasis	Items identifying people who are overly concerned with bodily functions and symptoms of physical illness
Depression	Items identifying people who feel hopeless and who experience slowing of thought and action
Hysteria	Items identifying people who avoid problems by developing mental or physical symptoms
Psychopathic deviate	Items identifying people who disregard accepted standards of behavior and have shallow emotional relationships
Masculinity-femininity	Items identifying people with stereotypically male or female interests
Paranoia	Items identifying people with delusions of grandeur or persecution who also exhibit pervasive suspiciousness
Psychasthenia	Items identifying people who feel guilt, worry, and anxiety and who have obsessions and compulsions
Schizophrenia	Items identifying people who exhibit social withdrawal, delusional thoughts, and hallucinations
Hypomania	Items identifying people who are overactive, easily excited, and recklessly impulsive
Social introversion	Items identifying people who are emotionally inhibited and socially shy
Validity Scales	
Cannot say	Items that are not answered, which may indicate evasiveness
Lie	Items indicating an attempt to make a positive impression
Frequency	Items involving responses that are rarely given by normal people, which may indicate an attempt to seem abnormal
Correction	Items revealing a tendency to respond defensively in admitting personal problems or shortcomings

Source: Clinical Scales and sample of Validity Scales taken from the MMPI®-2 (Minnesota Multiphasic Personality Inventory®-2) Manual for Administration, Scoring, and Interpretation, Revised Edition. Copyright © 2001 by the Regents of the University of Minnesota. Used by permission of the University of Minnesota Press. All rights reserved. "MMPI" and "Minnesota Multiphasic Personality Inventory" are trademarks owned by the Regents of the University of Minnesota.

responded "False" to statements such as "I sometimes have violent thoughts" might be lying to create a good impression (Rogers et al., 2003).

Psychologists commonly use the MMPI to screen applicants for positions in which people with serious psychological disorders might be dangerous, such as law enforcement. The MMPI has proved to be a valid means of diagnosing psychological disorders (Parker, Hanson, & Hunsley, 1988). But researchers found that by the 1980s the test was diagnosing a higher proportion of people as psychologically disordered than it did when it was first adopted. Did this finding mean that more people had psychological disorders than in the past? Or did it mean that the MMPI's norms were outdated? The latter seemed to be the case. As one critic noted more than three decades ago, "Whoever takes the MMPI today is being compared with the way a man or woman from Minnesota endorsed those items in the late 1930s and early 1940s" (Herbert, 1983, p. 228).

Because of this problem, the MMPI was restandardized in the 1980s. The revised 567-item MMPI (the MMPI-2) has added, deleted, or changed many statements. It also has new norms based on a more representative sample of the American population in regard to age, sex, ethnic background, educational level, and region of the country. These changes make the MMPI-2, though still imperfect, an improvement over the MMPI (Helmes & Reddon, 1993).

Uses of the MMPI-2 have included measuring social introversion (Ward & Perry, 1998), identifying sex offenders (Grover, 2011), evaluating parents in child custody and parental competency cases (Resendes & Lecci, 2012), and determining the relationship of personality to spirituality (MacDonald & Holland, 2003). Research findings indicate that the MMPI-2 is valid across many ethnic groups, including African Americans (Hall, Bansal, & Lopez, 1999) and Latinos (Fantoni-Salvador & Rogers, 1997), though there is some evidence that acculturation appears to influence Asian Americans' scores on nine subscales (Tsai & Pike, 2000). Translated versions of the MMPI have been found to be culturally equivalent and valid for use with diverse samples such as Vietnamese refugees (Dong & Church, 2003) and Latino adolescents (Scott, Butcher, Young, & Gomez, 2002).

Status of the Dispositional Approach

Though the dispositional approach to personality has been useful in *describing* personality differences, it is less successful in *explaining* those differences. Suppose that the results of testing with the Myers-Briggs Type Indicator reveal that one of your friends is an extravert. Someone might ask, "Why is she an extravert?" You might respond, "Because she likes to socialize." The person might then ask, "Why does she like to socialize?" To which you might reply, "Because she is an extravert." This circular reasoning would not explain why your friend is an extravert.

One of the few dispositional theories that tries to explain personality is Eysenck's three-factor theory. The existence of the three personality factors identified by Eysenck has been verified by other researchers (Zuckerman, Joireman, Kraft, & Kuhlma, 1999), and it has some support from cross-cultural research (Eysenck, Barrett, & Barnes, 1993). The introversion/extraversion dimension has received especially strong research support. One of Eysenck's assumptions is that a person's degree of introversion/extraversion depends on his or her customary level of physiological reactivity. As noted in the section, "Type Theories," introverts are more physiologically reactive to stimulation than extraverts are. As explained in Chapter 11, we have a tendency to try to adopt a moderate level of arousal. This tendency might explain why introverts avoid stimulation and extraverts seek it. For example, introverted students prefer to work in quieter conditions than extraverted students do (Geen, 1984), and extraverts are more likely than introverts to seek help from others in coping with stress (Swickert, Rosentreter, Hittner, & Mushrush, 2002).

There also is support for the possible universality of the five-factor model of personality (McCrae, Costa, Del Pila, Rolland, & Parker, 1998). One study found that the model, developed in the United States, holds up even when applied to personality profiles of people from China, Korea, Japan, Israel, Portugal, and Germany (McCrae & Costa, 1997). Nonetheless, psychologists who agree that there are five basic personality factors often fail to agree on their nature. Some researchers, for example, have failed to find support for the openness-to-experience factor (McKenzie, 1998). Other researchers have found the need to add a sixth factor: hedonism/spontaneity (Becker, 1999).

Introverts

According to Jung and Eysenck, introverts are socially reserved and pay more attention to their private mental experiences.
Source: Creativa/Shutterstock. com.

Section Review: The Dispositional Approach to Personality

1. What are the basic characteristics of Allport's trait theory of personality?

2. In what way is the MMPI based on an empirical approach to personality test construction?

3. What evidence is there that personality is more consistent across situations than Mischel believed?

Is Personality Consistent From One Situation to Another?

You might recall that the definition of personality includes the word *consistent*. But do people really behave consistently from one situation to another? Professors who write letters of recommendation for students assume so when they refer to their students as "mature," "friendly," and "conscientious." But will a student who has been mature, friendly, and conscientious in college necessarily exhibit those traits in a job or in graduate school? The degree of cross-situational consistency in personality has been one of the most controversial issues in personality research. Until the late 1960s commonsense belief among psychologists and nonpsychologists alike held that personality is consistent across different situations, with few researchers questioning that belief. But then some psychologists began reporting research findings indicating that personality might not be as cross-situationally consistent as was commonly believed.

Personality as Inconsistent

The debate over the consistency of personality began in 1968 with the publication of a book by the social-cognitive psychologist Walter Mischel. He reported that personality is much less consistent from one situation to another than was commonly believed. Mischel found that the correlation between any two behaviors presumed to represent the same underlying personality trait rarely exceeded a relatively modest .30. This finding means that we could not predict with confidence whether a person who scored high on the trait of generosity would behave in a generous manner in a given situation. For example, a person who scored high on a test measuring generosity might donate to a local charity but might not pick up the check in a restaurant—though both behaviors presumably would reflect the trait of generosity. Based on his review of research findings, Mischel concluded that our behavior is influenced more by the situations in which we find ourselves than by our personality characteristics. Though Mischel stimulated the recent debate over the issue of personality consistency, the issue is not new. Forty years before Mischel published his findings, psychologists reported research showing that children's honesty was inconsistent across situations. A child might cheat on a test but not in an athletic event, or lie at school but not at home (Hartshorne & May, 1928).

If personality is inconsistent across situations, why do we perceive it to be consistent in our everyday lives?

- We might confuse the consistency of behavior in a given situation over time with the consistency of that behavior across different situations (Mischel & Peake, 1982). If a student is consistently humorous in your psychology class, you might mistakenly infer that she is humorous at home, at parties, and in the dormitory.

- We tend to avoid situations that are inconsistent with our personalities (Snyder, 1983). If you view yourself as even-tempered, you might avoid situations that might make you lose your temper, such as a discussion about the abortion issue.

- Our first impression of a person can make us discount later behavior that is inconsistent with it (Hayden & Mischel, 1976). If someone is friendly to you the first time you meet but is rude to you the next time you meet, you might say that he was "not himself" at the second meeting.

- Our perception of cross-situational consistency in others might reflect a powerful situational factor—our presence in their environment (Lord, 1982). If others adapt their behavior to our presence, we might erroneously infer that they are consistent across situations.

Personality as Consistent

These attacks on cross-situational consistency have provoked responses from researchers who claim that there is more cross-situational consistency than Mischel and his allies believe (Kenrick & Funder, 1988).

- Individuals do show consistency on certain traits. But how do we know *which* traits? One way to find out is to ask. People who claim to be consistent on a given trait tend to exhibit behaviors reflecting that trait across situations (Zuckerman et al., 1988). In one study, students were asked to judge how consistent they were on the trait of friendliness. Those who claimed to be friendly across situations were, in fact, more consistently friendly than were students who did not claim to be—as verified by their peers, parents, and other observers (Bem & Allen, 1974).

- Cross-situational consistency in behavior depends on whether a person is a *high self-monitor* or a *low self-monitor*. High self-monitors are concerned about how people perceive them and adapt their behaviors to fit specific situations, whereas low self-monitors are less concerned about how people perceive them and do not adapt their behaviors as much to fit specific situations. This difference means that low self-monitors show greater cross-situational consistency in their behaviors than do high self-monitors (Gangestad & Snyder, 1985), though this effect is stronger among individualistic cultures than among collectivistic cultures (Church et al., 2006).

Is Personality Consistent From One Situation to Another? *continued*

- Many of the studies that Mischel reviewed were guaranteed to find low cross-situational consistency because they either correlated trait test scores with single instances of behaviors or correlated single instances of behaviors with each other. This situation would be like trying to predict your exact score on your next psychology test from your score on the Scholastic Assessment Test or from your score on a biology test. The prediction would most likely be wrong, because many factors influence your performance on any given academic test. Similarly, many factors other than a given personality trait influence your behavior in a given situation.

Psychologists have achieved greater success in demonstrating cross-situational consistency by using *behavioral aggregation.* In aggregating behaviors, you would observe a person's behavior across several situations. You then would determine how the person *typically,* but not necessarily *always,* behaves—much in the same way that you would find your average on several exams to determine your typical performance in a course. A "humorous" person would be humorous in many, but not all, situations. When we predict how a person will typically behave instead of how that person will behave in a specific situation, the corre-

lation between traits and behaviors becomes a relatively high .60 or more (Epstein & O'Brien, 1985). The importance of behavioral aggregation in determining personality consistency was demonstrated in the following classic study.

When behavioral aggregation was applied to the Hartshorne and May (1928) study, the correlation between the trait of honesty and honest behaviors rose considerably. Consider a similar study by George Dudycha (1936), which examined personality consistency in regard to punctuality. Dudycha noted that some people have reputations for always being punctual and others for always being late. He decided to study the phenomenon of punctuality in everyday life rather than set up artificial situations in which punctuality would be measured. Participants were 307 male and female undergraduates at Ripon College during the 1934–1935 academic year. Their punctuality was assessed on many occasions in six situations: 8 A.M. classes; dinnertime at a dining hall; conference appointments with professors; extracurricular activities (college band and college singers); church services; and entertainment programs (basketball, plays, and concerts). There were a total of 15,360 observations.

When correlations were computed between any two of these situations, students were inconsistent. This finding seemed to indicate that the situation, not personality traits, accounted for punctuality. But, as in the Hartshorne and May (1928) study, when behavioral aggregation was applied to the Dudycha study, college students showed much greater cross-situational consistency in their punctuality. Thus, though personality traits might not predict our behavior in particular situations, they might predict our typical behavior across a variety of related situations.

The cross-situational consistency debate has died down. Researchers now tend to agree that the best approach is to consider the interaction of the person and the situation in assessing cross-situational consistency (Mischel, Shoda, & Mendoza-Denton, 2002). Even Gordon Allport, the noted trait researcher, viewed human behavior as the product of those factors, with different traits aroused to different degrees by different situations (Zuroff, 1986). Of course, some situations (such as being in a worship service) are so powerful that almost all people—regardless of their personalities—will behave the same way in them (Monson, Hesley, & Chernick, 1982).

"Dad, I have commissioned my buddy to study your behaviour patterns."

Behavioral Aggregation

In aggregating behaviors, you would observe a person's behavior across several situations.

Source: Cartoonresource/Shutterstock.com.

The Cognitive-Behavioral Approach to Personality

Researchers who favor the *cognitive-behavioral approach* to personality discount biological factors, unconscious influences, and dispositional traits. Instead, they stress the importance of cognitive and situational factors (Staats, 1994). The cognitive-behavioral approach was influenced by B. F. Skinner (1953), whose operant conditioning theory is described in Chapter 7. He saw no use for concepts invoking biological predispositions, unconscious motives, personality traits, and the like. What we call *personality,* in Skinner's view, is simply a person's unique pattern of behavior, tied to specific situations (Skinner, 1974).

According to Skinner, we are what we do. And what we do in a particular situation depends on our experiences in that situation and similar situations. We tend to engage in behaviors that have been positively or negatively reinforced and to avoid engaging in behaviors that have been punished or extinguished. Thus, Skinner might assume that a gregarious person has a history of receiving attention or anxiety relief for being socially outgoing in a variety of situations. In contrast, a shy person might have a history of being criticized or ignored for being socially outgoing in a variety of situations.

Social-Cognitive Theory

Social-cognitive theory builds a bridge between Skinner's strict behavioral approach and a more cognitive approach to personality. Social-cognitive theory is similar to traditional behavioral theories in stressing the role of reinforcement and punishment in the development of personality. But it is different from traditional behavioral theories in arguing that behavior is affected by cognitive processes. That is, our interpretation of our own personal characteristics and environmental circumstances affects our behavior (Bandura, 1989).

Social-cognitive theory was developed by Albert Bandura (b. 1925), who was reared in Canada but became a professor in the United States and served as president of the American Psychological Association in 1974. Other social-cognitive theories have been developed by Julian Rotter and Walter Mischel. Bandura's theory of personality grew out of his research on observational learning, which also is described in Chapter 7. According to Bandura, we learn many of our behavioral tendencies by observing other people receiving rewards or punishments for particular behaviors. For example, children learn altruistic behavior from adults who behave in a helpful manner.

reciprocal determinism
Bandura's belief that cognitive factors, environmental factors, and overt behavior affect each other.

Bandura's (1986) theory of personality also stresses the concept of **reciprocal determinism,** which reflects his belief that neither personal dispositions nor environmental factors can by themselves explain behavior. You will note that reciprocal determinism differs from environmental determinism, which was favored by Skinner, and psychic determinism, which was favored by Freud. Environmental determinism assumes we are pawns controlled by external stimuli, and psychic determinism assumes we are pawns controlled by unconscious motives. Instead, as illustrated in Figure 13-3, Bandura assumes that cognitive factors, environmental factors, and overt behavior affect one another.

Research studies have found that reciprocal determinism can explain many kinds of behaviors, such as why depression is so difficult to overcome (Teichman & Teichman, 1990). A depressed person's negative thoughts and emotions might induce gloomy statements, sad facial expressions, and aloof social behavior. These outward indications might make other people avoid or respond negatively toward the depressed person. This social response would promote continued negative thoughts and emotions in the depressed person, thereby completing a vicious cycle that is difficult to break.

self-efficacy In Bandura's theory, a person's belief that she or he can perform behaviors that are necessary to bring about a desired outcome.

According to Bandura, one of the most important cognitive factors in reciprocal determinism is **self-efficacy**. Self-efficacy is the extent to which a person believes that she or he can perform behaviors that are necessary to bring about a desired outcome. Self-efficacy determines our choice of activities, our intensity of effort, and our persistence in the face of obstacles and unpleasant experiences, in part by reducing the anxiety that might interfere with engaging in the activity (Bandura, Reese, & Adams, 1982). Self-efficacy promotes motivation and the attainment of performance goals (Bandura & Locke, 2003), adherence to physical exercise programs (Short, Vendelanotte, Rebar, & Duncan, 2013), performance in academic courses (Robbins, Lauver, Davis, Langley, & Carlstrom, 2004), and adherence to addiction treatment regimens (Kelly & Greene, 2013) and chronic pain (da Menezes Costa, Maher, McAuley, Hancock, & Smeets, 2011).

But what determines whether you will have a feeling of self-efficacy in a given situation? The first determinant is *previous success*. You will have a greater feeling of self-efficacy in your psychology course if you have done well in previous courses. The second determinant is *vicarious experience*. You will have a greater feeling of self-efficacy if you know other students who have succeeded in the course. The third determinant is *verbal persuasion*. You will have a greater feeling of self-efficacy if you give yourself pep talks or your advisor convinces you that you have the ability to do well in the course. And the fourth determinant is *physiological arousal*. You will have a greater feeling of self-efficacy if you are at an optimal level of arousal (see Chapter 11).

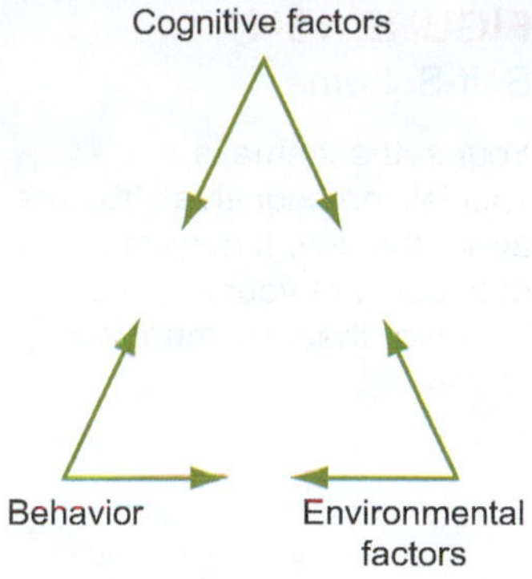

Bandura (2000) has continued to develop the concept of self-efficacy, noting that with increased interdependence between people, communities, and nations that individuals often have to work together to obtain a desired outcome. **Collective efficacy** refers to people's perception that with collaborative effort the group will obtain its desired outcome. Thus, whereas self-efficacy refers to the perception that "I think *I* can do it," collective efficacy refers to the perception that "I think *we* can do it." Collective efficacy has been found to predict family functioning and satisfaction with family life (Bandura, Caprara, Barbaranelli, Regalia, & Scabini, 2011), to predict engagement and performance in work groups (Salanova,Llorens, Cifre, Martinez, & Schaufeli, 2003), and to be higher among cohesive rugby teams (Kozub & McDonnell, 2000). Collective efficacy also has been used to explain the "home-court advantage" of basketball teams playing on their home court (Bray & Widmeyer, 2000).

Though collective efficacy is a relatively new concept and has not been subjected to rigorous empirical research as has the concept of self-efficacy, it provides a promising avenue by which researchers may investigate cultural variations in perceptions of control (Bandura, 2002) and the avenues by which people improve their lives through political activism and promotion of social change. For example, American bank tellers who scored high in personal control and high in self-efficacy experienced fewer stress-related health symptoms and lower job turnover than did tellers high in personal control and low in self-efficacy. A similar relationship was found for personal control and collective efficacy in a sample of bank tellers from Hong Kong. Tellers who scored high in personal control and high in collective efficacy experienced fewer stress-related health symptoms and lower job turnover than did tellers who scored high in personal control and low in collective efficacy (Schaubroeck, Lam, & Xie, 2000). Thus, perceptions of control and the belief that one can meet the demands of the job may reduce stress in individualistic cultures. And perceptions of control and the belief that with collaboration and cooperation the group can meet the demands of the job may reduce stress in collectivist cultures.

Schema Theory

During the past three decades cognitive theories of personality have moved toward an information-processing model, employing the concept of *schemas*. Schemas are cognitive structures that guide people's perception, organization, and processing of social information (see Chapters 4 and 9). Individual differences in personality are thought to be related to the different schemas people use to process information—in this case, about the self.

According to psychologist Hazel Markus (1977), **self-schemas** are specialized cognitive structures about the self. They develop through social experience and serve to organize and guide the processing of social information. Your self-schema consists of aspects of your life and behavior that are important to you (see Figure 13-4). Because each of us has different experiences and interests, not everything we do becomes part of our self-schema (Markus, 1983). For example, two college students may both be avid cyclists and fans of foreign cinema. But both activities may not be part of their self-schemas. If one student is training for a triathlon and describes herself as a serious recreational athlete, then cycling may be a part of her self-schema. If the other student has career aspirations to become an accomplished film director, then studying cinematography and attending

FIGURE 13-3
Reciprocal Determinism

Bandura's concept of reciprocal determinism considers the mutual influence of the person's cognitive factors, behavior, and environment. Each of the three factors can affect the other two.

collective efficacy People's perception that with collaborative effort the group will obtain its desired outcome.

self-schema In schema theory, specialized cognitive structures about the self.

FIGURE 13-4
Self-Schema

Your self-schema is a
specialized cognitive structure
about the self. It consists
of aspects of your life and
behavior that are important
to you.

foreign films may be part of his self-schema. Thus, activities, interests, and behaviors that are relevant to the self may become part of the self-schema.

Schema theory has been useful in research investigating the relationship between self-schemas and individual differences in a number of variables, including children's willingness to share and help others (Froming, Nasby, & McManus, 1998); women's attitudes toward mathematics (Oswald & Harvey, 2003); recovery from breast cancer surgery (Yurek, Farrar, & Andersen, 2000); adherence to exercise regimens (Whaley, 2003); the development of sexual identity among heterosexual men (Elder, Brooks, & Morrow, 2012); and gender differences in the impact of parenting on self-schemas (Morfei, Hooker, Fiese, & Cordeiro, 2001).

Schema theory has provided a glimpse into the cultural determinants of personality, especially the dimension of individualism versus collectivism (Triandis, 1989). Hazel Markus and Shinobu Kitayama (1991) have proposed that there are cross-cultural differences in the construal of self-schemas in individualistic and collectivistic cultures. These differences involve the concept of independence versus interdependence. Western cultures emphasize individual aspects of the self. People in Western cultures strive to be unique, engage in self-expression, and promote individual goals. In contrast, Asian cultures emphasize interdependent aspects of the self. People in Asian cultures value being part of a group, cooperating, and pursuing group goals. In this way, cultural values and social experiences become integrated into the self-schema. For example, cross-cultural differences in the nature of autobiographical memory (Wagar & Cohen, 2003) and consumers' responses to advertising (Forehand, Deshpande, & Reed, 2002; Wang, Briston, Mowen, & Chakraborty, 2000) have been attributed to cultural differences in self-schemas.

Cognitive-Behavioral Assessment of Personality

There are two main behavioral approaches to the assessment of personality. One approach examines overt behavior; the other examines cognitions that are closely tied to overt behavior.

Experience Sampling

Theorists who favor the examination of overt behavior believe that we should note what people actually do or say they would do in specific situations rather than simply record their responses to personality tests. One form of behavioral assessment uses the *experience-sampling method.* The person carries a beeper that is activated at random times, and on hearing the beep the person reports his or her experiences and behaviors at that time. This method reveals relationships between specific situations and the person's thoughts, feelings, and behaviors (Hormuth, 1986). Several studies have demonstrated the practical usefulness of experience sampling, such as studying depression (Telford, McCarthy-Jones, Corcoran, & Rowse, 2012), work-related stress and fatigue in medical residents (Zohar, Tzischinski, & Epstein, 2003), and cross-cultural differences in emotional experiences (Oishi, 2002). A study of elementary school children assessed their mental self-talk while they worked at their seats. Whenever the children heard a buzzer, they recorded their self-talk. The results showed that children who engaged in positive self-talk had higher academic achievement and more appropriate social behavior, whereas children who engaged in negative self-talk had poorer academic achievement and less appropriate social behavior (Manning, 1990). Of course, only experimental research could determine whether self-talk *causes* differences in academic achievement or social behavior.

The Locus of Control Scale

As an example of the cognitive assessment of personality, consider the *Internal-External Locus of Control Scale,* which was developed by Julian Rotter (1966) to measure what he calls the locus of control. Your *locus of control* is the degree to which you expect that you are in control of the outcomes of your behavior or that those outcomes are controlled by factors such as fate, luck, or chance (Rotter, 1990). In the former case you would have an internal locus of control, and in the latter case you would have an external locus of control. Rotter's concept of the locus of control has been so influential that his original study is one of the most frequently cited studies in the recent history of psychology (Sechrest, 1984).

The scale contains 29 pairs of statements, including 6 that serve to disguise the purpose of the test. A typical relevant pair would be similar to the following: "The more effort you expend, the more likely you are to succeed" and "Luck is more important than hard work in job advancement." Your responses would reveal whether you have an internal or an external locus of control. Just as your sense of self-efficacy might affect your behavior in everyday life, your locus of control might determine whether you try to exert control over real-life situations.

Locus of control has been the subject of numerous studies. People with an internal locus of control are less fatalistic, which makes them more likely to seek medical attention for their physical symptoms (Strickland, 1989). People with an internal locus of control are more likely to take protective action when warned of an impending natural disaster, such as an earthquake (McLure, Walkey, & Allen, 1999). An internal locus of control also is associated with higher job satisfaction and productivity, apparently because employees with an internal locus of control are more motivated and feel more competent (Erez & Judge, 2001; Judge & Bono, 2001). Drivers with an internal locus of control have fewer fatal accidents, perhaps because they are more cautious, attentive, and adept at avoiding dangerous situations (Montag & Comrey, 1987). And people reared in individualistic cultures, such as the United States, tend to be higher in their internal locus of control than are people from collectivist cultures (Rawdon, Willis, & Ficken, 1995), though some studies have found smaller differences when culture-specific measures are employed (e.g., Spector, Sanchez, Sui, Salgado, & Ma, 2004). Moreover, cross-cultural differences in locus of control may be attributed to the fact that in collectivist cultures an external locus of control may be more functional than in individualistic cultures (Cheng, Cheung, Chio, & Chang, 2013).

Status of the Cognitive-Behavioral Approach

B. F. Skinner's operant conditioning theory of personality has been praised for making psychologists more aware of the influence of environmental factors on personality. But the theory has been criticized by Hans Eysenck (1988) for ignoring the influence of heredity on individual differences in personality. The social-cognitive theorists have responded by recognizing the importance of cognitive and environmental factors. But traditional behavioral theorists argue that thoughts do not *cause* behavior. And psychoanalytic theorists criticize cognitive theories for ignoring the irrational, emotional bases of behavior.

How Effective Is Psychological Profiling in Identifying Criminals?

Over the years, you probably have read books or articles or seen television shows about FBI profilers, who provide descriptions of wanted criminals—typically serial killers or terrorists—with the hope of helping investigators narrow the range of potential suspects. Psychological profiling began in the mid-1970s at the FBI training center in Quantico, Virginia. There even was a television series in the 1990s, *Profiler,* that portrayed the exploits of an FBI profiler played by Robert Davi.

But how accurate are psychological profilers? Though the media might publicize individual cases in which psychological profiles have apparently helped solve crimes, there are other cases in which profilers have been inaccurate, sometimes even identifying the wrong person as a suspect. In December 1996, for example, security guard Richard Jewell won a settlement of more than $500,000 from NBC. Nightly news anchor Tom Brokaw had mentioned that Jewell was a suspect in the widely publicized bombing incident at the 1996 Summer Olympic Games in Atlanta that killed one person and injured more than 100 others. Brokaw noted that investigators believed that Jewell fit the psychological profile of other bombers. Nonetheless, investigators eventually cleared Jewell of any responsibility for the bombing.

More recently, with the rash of school shootings across the United States, psychological profiling is being used to help educators identify students at risk of violence (Drummond, 1999). But this application has led to claims that students who are not potential mass murderers are unfairly being brought under suspicion because they fit that psychological profile. In a widely publicized case in late 1999, nuclear scientist Wen Ho Lee accused the government of racism for imprisoning him after accusing him of spying for China and stealing military secrets while working at Los Alamos Laboratory in New Mexico. Lee claimed that he was the victim of overzealous psychological profiling.

If you are interested in learning how detectives develop formal psychological profiles of criminals, you might want to read the *Crime Classification Manual* by John Douglas, Ann Burgess, Allen Burgess, and Robert Ressler (1997). Richard Jewell hired Ressler, a renowned FBI profiler, to support his claim that he was the victim of an inappropriate use of FBI profiling. Ressler claimed that legal authorities were under so much pressure to find the Atlanta bomber that they arrested the first person they thought might be guilty.

Ressler, director of Forensic Behavioral Services, has his own website that describes his 30 years of investigative experience, including 20 with the FBI, and has written an autobiography, *Whoever Fights Monsters* (Ressler & Shachtman, 1992), which describes his work with violent serial and sexual criminals. His work influenced the creators of the book and movie *Silence of the Lambs* and the television series *The X Files.* Ressler

Bandura's concept of self-efficacy has been supported by research findings in a variety of areas in addition to those already mentioned. One study found that high school students' feelings of self-efficacy in mathematics were positively correlated with final exam scores (Pietsch, Walker, & Chapman, 2003). Another study found that people with feelings of self-efficacy for long-distance running are more likely to enter marathon races, train hard for those races, and continue running despite the pain and fatigue they experience (Okwumabua, 1985). A meta-analysis of more than 100 studies involving more than 21,000 participants found that self-efficacy is positively correlated with performance on work-related tasks (Stajkovic & Luthans, 1998). And the concept of collective self-efficacy has broadened our understanding of cross-cultural beliefs in the nature of control, motivation, and agency (Bandura, 2000).

Schema theory also has stimulated research investigating a range of topics such as the relationship of chronic pain, illness, and the self (Pincus & Morley, 2001), development of the self through adulthood (Cross & Markus, 1991), attributions about relapse from exercise regimens (Kendzierski, Sheffield, & Morganstein, 2002), and gender differences in perceptions of political leadership and power (Lips, 2000). Though some cross-cultural psychologists have disputed Markus and Kitayama's model (Matsumoto, 1999), self-schema theory has provided an important theoretical perspective for cross-cultural research investigating personality and motivation (Hernandez & Iyengar, 2001).

How Effective Is Psychological Profiling in Identifying Criminals? *continued*

and other profilers gained media attention regarding their views in the murder of JonBenet Ramsey, a child who was murdered December 26, 1996, in her Boulder, Colorado, home. Her parents, John and Patsy Ramsey, called on Gregg McCrary, a former FBI criminal profiler and colleague of Ressler's, to support their claim that they could not have committed the crime. After he refused to take their case, they hired John Douglas (Brennan, 1997a). McCrary claimed that Douglas's profile was vague and contained characteristics that could be true of many people. Ressler added, "It doesn't in any way resemble an FBI profile. In a nutshell, the profile is bogus. It has very little pertinence to what's going on here. It's so general, it could fit half of Boulder" (Brennan, 1997b). You might note this situation as a possible instance of the Barnum effect, discussed at the beginning of the chapter.

Given the popularity of psychological profiling, researchers are conducting research and publishing articles on it in professional journals. One reason for supporting psychological profiling is that some courts let prosecutors and defense attorneys consider the psychological state of the defendant (Cochran, 1999). Though personality profiling in criminal cases has gained media attention, its validity remains to be established (Kocsis, 2013). Nonetheless, there is evidence that specially trained FBI profilers do produce more accurate profiles than other people do. But even people who support the usefulness of psychological profiling insist that it should

be used to generate leads and direct investigations and that it should not be used by itself to identify particular suspects (Palermo, 2002). Moreover, the reasoning ability of profilers might be more important than the amount of experience that they have. In one study, for example, police detectives and undergraduate chemistry majors were presented with information about an actual homicide that an individual had been convicted of committing. Participants were asked to compose criminal profiles of the perpetrator. Contrary to what common sense would have predicted, the chemistry majors outperformed the police detectives—including detectives with many years of homicide investigative experience (Kocsis, Hayes, & Irwin, 2002).

Researchers are trying to provide a more scientific grounding for psychological profiling. In one study, profilers successfully developed psychological profiles that were useful in distinguishing between distinctly different kinds of arsonists (Kocsis, Irwin, & Hayes, 1998). Scientists now are attempting to develop psychological profiles that distinguish different kinds of burglars, (Fox & Farrington, 2012), child sex offenders (Marsa et al., 2004), stranger murderers (Salfati & Canter, 1999), and rapist-murderers (Keppel & Walter, 1999; Schlesinger & Revitch, 1999). The media certainly will continue to celebrate psychological profiling, but it will be up to science to determine whether psychological profiling is a valid technique.

Section Review: The Cognitive-Behavioral Approach to Personality

1. How does the social-cognitive theory of personality differ from the operant conditioning theory?

2. What is reciprocal determinism?

3. How does schema theory explain cross-cultural differences in individualism and collectivism?

4. How do psychologists use experience sampling in the assessment of personality?

The Humanistic Approach to Personality

The *humanistic approach* to personality, which emerged in the 1950s, holds that people are naturally good. This approach contrasts with psychoanalytic personality theorists, who believe that people are predisposed to be selfish and aggressive, and behavioral personality theorists, who believe that people are neither naturally good nor naturally evil.

The humanistic approach also contrasts with the psychoanalytic approaches in accepting subjective mental experience *(phenomenological experience)* as its subject matter. This acceptance makes the humanistic approach similar to the cognitive-behavioral approach, though more concerned with emotional experience. Moreover, the humanistic approach assumes that we have free will, meaning that our actions are not compelled by id impulses or environmental stimuli.

The Self-Actualization Theory of Personality

The first humanistic theory of personality was that of Abraham Maslow (1970), whose theory of motivation is discussed in Chapter 11. Maslow, reared in Brooklyn, was urged by his parents to attend law school. One day he found himself in a course in which he had no interest, and he bolted from the classroom.

Maslow never returned to law school. Instead, against his parents' wishes, he decided to pursue a career in psychology. This willingness to fulfill one's own needs rather than trying to please other people became a hallmark of humanistic theories of personality. As discussed in Chapter 11, Maslow believed we have a need for **self-actualization,** the predisposition to try to reach our potentials. The concept of self-actualization is a descendant of Adler's concept of striving for superiority (Crandall, 1980).

self-actualization In Maslow's theory, the individual's predisposition to try to fulfill her or his potentials.

But who is self-actualized? Maslow presented several candidates, including President Abraham Lincoln, psychologist William James, and humanitarian Eleanor Roosevelt. Table 13-3 presents a list of characteristics shared by self-actualized people. Maslow decided on these characteristics after testing, interviewing, or reading the works of individuals he considered self-actualized. Our psychological well-being is related in part to the extent to which we are self-actualized. For example, it seems that one of the reasons why extraverted people tend to be happier than other people is that they are more self-actualized than are more introverted people (Lester, 1990). Parents who score high on measures of self-actualization tend to practice authoritative parenting (Dominguez & Carton, 1997), a parenting style that is superior to permissive parenting and authoritarian parenting. These parenting styles are discussed in Chapter 4.

TABLE 13-3 Characteristics of Self-Actualized People

- Desire for privacy in certain personal areas of life
- Concern with solving problems more than serving selfish interests
- Nonconformist approach to life
- Means not confused with ends
- Nonhostile sense of humor
- Ability to be sociable while maintaining individual identity
- Objective, realistic outlook on life and others
- Accepting of self and others
- Egalitarian attitude toward others
- Interest in improving the lives of others
- Spontaneous, rather than constricted, in interpersonal relations
- Creative in relating to others and the world
- Preference for several intimate relationships rather than many superficial ones
- Spiritual, though not necessarily religious, experiences

Source: Data from A. H. Maslow (1971), *The Farther Reaches of Human Nature.* New York: Viking Press.

The Self Theory of Personality

Carl Rogers (1902–1987) was born near Chicago to a devoutly religious family. His religious upbringing led him to enter Union Theological Seminary in New York City. But Rogers left the seminary to pursue a career in psychology, eventually serving as president of the American Psychological Association in 1946.

The Self

Rogers pointed out that self-actualization requires acceptance of one's *self* or *(self-concept)*, which is your answer to the question "Who are you?" But each of us experiences some incongruence between the self and personal experience. We might learn to deny our feelings, perhaps claiming that we are not angry or embarrassed even when we are. This denial might make us feel phony or, as Rogers would say, not genuine. This incongruence between our self and our experience causes us anxiety, which in turn motivates us to reduce the incongruence by altering the self or reinterpreting the experience. Though complete congruence between the self and experience is impossible and would be maladaptive (we would have no motivation to improve the self if we did not experience some incongruence), people who have a great incongruence between the self and experience may develop psychological disorders (see Chapter 14).

How does incongruence between the self and experience develop? According to Rogers, children who do not receive *unconditional positive regard*—that is, complete acceptance—from their parents will develop incongruence by denying aspects of their experience. To gain acceptance from parents, a child might express thoughts, feelings, and behaviors that are acceptable to them. For example, a boy whose parents insist that "boys don't cry" might learn to deny his own painful physical and emotional experiences in order to gain parental approval. Such *conditions of worth* lead children to become rigid and anxious because of a failure to accept their experiences. Instead of becoming self-actualizing, such children may adopt a lifestyle of conformity and ingratiation (Baumeister, 1982). Rogers, like other personality theorists, reveals his own life experiences in his theory. He recalled that as a child he felt that his parents did not love him for himself apart from his accomplishments (Dolliver, 1995).

As shown in Figure 13-5, psychologically healthy people have greater congruence between the *actual self* (Rogers's *self*) and the *ideal self* (the person they would like to be). The more self-actualized the person, the less the incongruence between the person's actual self and ideal self and, as a result, the greater the person's self-esteem (Garcia & Hoskins, 2001). People with a great incongruence between their actual self and their ideal self have more self-doubts and fewer social skills. A study of undergraduates found that as the congruence between their actual and their ideal selves increased, their happiness increased (Drigotas, 2002).

Self-Handicapping

One way to protect the actual self is by *self-handicapping,* in which people claim that a task is too difficult or that factors beyond their control might contribute to their less-than-ideal behavior or performance (Jones & Berglas, 1978). People are more likely to engage in self-handicapping when their self-concept is threatened by potential failure. As you have certainly observed, self-handicapping is common among athletes (Gibson, Sachau, Doll, & Shumate, 2002) and students (Martin, Nejad, Colmar, & Liem, 2013). Thus, a student walking into class for a test might remind his classmates that the need to console a friend the night before prevented him from studying enough. Given these excuses, possible failure on the test would be less of a blow to the actual self. And if the student performs well on the test, the actual self would be elevated. One study found that undergraduates who were high self-handicappers reduced their study time and experienced more stress prior to an introduction to psychology exam. As you might expect, high self-handicappers received lower scores on the exam than did low self-handicappers. Nevertheless, despite their poor exam performance, high self-handicappers believed that they had the ability to do well in psychology, because they attributed their poor exam scores to lack of preparation rather than lack of ability (McCrea & Hirt, 2001).

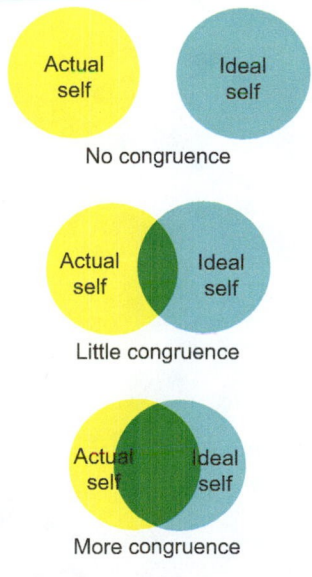

FIGURE 13-5

The Relationship of the Actual and Ideal Self

These diagrams show different degrees of congruence between the actual and ideal self. The more self-actualized the person, the less the incongruence between the actual and ideal self.

Self-Esteem

Childhood experiences have a marked influence on *self-esteem,* a person's sense of self-worth (Rosenberg, 1965). Children with warm, nurturant parents are higher in self-esteem (Pawlak & Klein, 1997). One study found that children and their mothers with low self-esteem felt less loved by one another than did children and mothers with high self-esteem (DeHart, Murray, Pelham, & Rose, 2003). And women who believe they have received unconditional positive regard from their fathers have higher self-esteem and less fear of intimate relationships (Scheffler & Naus, 1999). There also is hope for children who have low self-esteem. A meta-analysis found that formal programs aimed at enhancing children's self-esteem can be effective (Haney & Durlak, 1998).

Self-esteem also has important implications for adults. A longitudinal study found that children who had positive relationships with their parents during their transition into adulthood had higher self-esteem then and 20 years later (Roberts & Bengtson, 1996). The quality of romantic relationships is positively related to self-esteem (D. Cramer, 2003). And a study of adult romantic attachment styles found that those with secure or dismissive styles were higher in self-esteem than were those with fearful or preoccupied styles (Bylsma, Cozzarelli, & Sumer, 1997). Moreover, a recent meta-analysis of more than 100 longitudinal studies found that low self-esteem has been found to be correlated with both anxiety and depression across the lifespan (Sowislo & Orth, 2013).

According to *terror management theory,* self-esteem serves a protective function against death anxiety. People live their lives with an awareness of their own mortality and the inevitability of death. Numerous research studies have found that people high in self-esteem experience lower levels of anxiety. Likewise, people respond to reminders of their own mortality by bolstering their self-esteem (Pyszczynski, Greenberg, Solomon, & Arnst, 2004). Moreover, close relationships serve an additional protective function against death anxiety (Mikulincer, Florian, & Hirschberger, 2003). One study found that participants with secure attachment styles did not exhibit self-defensive responses when reminded of their own mortality. Instead, securely attached participants responded by desiring higher levels of intimacy than did anxious-ambivalent and avoidant participants (Mikulincer & Florian, 2000).

Self-esteem also is related to sociocultural factors. A meta-analysis of studies that included about 145,000 participants found that men tend to have a slightly higher level of self-esteem than women, though the overall effect size is small. The gender difference in self-esteem is greatest at late adolescence, which may be due in part to the increased influence of gender roles, dating, and cultural emphasis on physical appearance (Kling, Hyde, Showers, & Buswell, 1999). People from individualistic cultures tend to have higher self-esteem than do people from collectivist cultures. People from individualistic cultures also are more responsive to positive and negative social interactions than are people from collectivist cultures. Thus, the self-esteem of people from individualistic cultures will fluctuate more than the self-esteem of people from collectivist cultures in response to everyday social interactions (Tafarodi & Walters, 1999).

The Humanistic Assessment of Personality

How do humanistic psychologists assess personality? Two of the main techniques are the *Personal Orientation Inventory* and the *Q-sort.*

The Personal Orientation Inventory

Psychologists who wish to assess self-actualization commonly use the *Personal Orientation Inventory (POI)* (Shostrom, 1962). The POI determines the degree to which a person's values and attitudes agree with Maslow's description of self-actualized people, such as being governed by one's own motives and principles. The inventory contains items that force the person to choose between options, such as (a) "Impressing others is most important" and (b) "Expressing myself is most important." One study found POI scores were higher among older adults—who had mastered more developmental tasks—than among younger adults (Ivtzan, Gardner, Bernard, Sekhon, & Hart, 2013). A newer test of self-actualization, the Brief Index of Self-Actualization (Sumerlin & Bundrick, 1996), has yet to generate enough research to determine its usefulness.

The Q-Sort

The *Q-sort,* derived from Rogers's self theory, is used to measure the degree of congruence between a person's actual self and her or his ideal self. If you took a Q-sort test, you would be given a pile of cards with a self-descriptive statement on each. A typical statement might be "I feel comfortable with strangers." You would put the statements in several piles, ranging from a pile containing statements that are most characteristic of your actual self to a pile containing statements that are least characteristic of your actual self. You would then follow the same procedure for your ideal self, creating a second set of piles. The greater the degree of overlap between the two sets of piles, the greater the congruence between your actual self and your ideal self. Psychotherapists have used the Q-sort method to determine whether therapy has increased the congruence between a client's actual self and ideal self (Leaf, Krauss, Dantzig, & Alington, 1992). The Q-sort also has been used to assess developmental trends in psychological health from adolescence through old age (Jones & Meredith, 2000) and to predict international graduate students' acculturation and integration into university life (Bang & Montgomery, 2013).

Status of the Humanistic Approach

Research has produced mixed support for Maslow's concept of self-actualization. For example, a study of students who scored low in self-actualization on the POI at the beginning of a university preparatory course found they increased in self-actualization by the end of the course (Fogarty, 1994). But there have been inconsistent findings regarding the assumption that self-actualization increases with age. A cross-sectional study (see Chapter 4) of women aged 19 to 55 found an increase in their sense of autonomy. That is, older participants were more motivated by their own feelings than by the influence of other people—a characteristic of self-actualized people (Hyman, 1988). Yet a cross-sectional study of faculty members aged 30 to 68 found that their self-actualization did not increase with age (Hawkins, Hawkins, & Ryan, 1989). Researchers are working on cross-cultural approaches to identifying the universal characteristics of self-actualization and to develop a valid measure of it (Leclerc, Lefrancois, Dube, Hebert, & Gaulin, 1998).

There has been relatively more research on the self, per se, than on self-actualization. In fact, there has been a sprouting of a variety of "selves." A view of the self put forth by E. Tory Higgins (1987) considers the relationship between three selves: the *actual self,* the *ideal self,* and the *ought self.* Incongruence between the actual self and the ideal self will make a person feel depressed. Incongruence between the actual self and the ought self (which is similar to Freud's ego ideal in representing beliefs about one's moral duties) will make a person feel anxious (Strauman & Higgins, 1988). We are motivated to alleviate our personal distress by reducing the incongruence between these selves (Higgins, 1990).

The humanistic approach has been praised for countering psychologists' tendency to study the negative aspects of human experience by encouraging them to study love, creativity, and other positive aspects of human experience. The humanistic approach also has renewed interest in studying conscious mental experience, which was the original subject matter of psychology over a century ago (Singer & Kolligian, 1987). Moreover, the humanistic approach might best reflect popular views of personality. A survey of people in everyday life found that most people believe that others would know them best if others knew their private mental experiences rather than their overt behavior (Andersen & Ross, 1984). The humanistic approach also has contributed to the recent interest in self-development, including beginning a health and fitness regimen when faced with one's mortality (Arndt, Schimel, & Goldenberg, 2003).

But the humanistic approach has not escaped criticism. Critics accuse it of divorcing the person from both the environment and the unconscious mind and for failing to operationally define and experimentally test abstract concepts such as self-actualization (Daniels, 1982). And the assumption of the innate goodness of humanity has been called naïve even by the influential humanistic psychologist Rollo May (1982), who believes that innately good people would not have created the evil that the world has known. Moreover, cross-cultural psychologists question whether positive self-regard is a universal human need. For example, a self-critical focus is more characteristic of Japanese society than American culture (Heine, Lehman, Markus, & Kitayama, 1999), and self-enhancement is more characteristic of American culture (Taylor & Brown, 1988).

Maslow and Rogers have been accused of unintentionally promoting selfishness by stressing the importance of self-actualization without placing an equal emphasis on social responsibility (Geller, 1982). Critics assert that Maslow's model of self-actualization represents a Western model of individualistic growth at the expense of interpersonal relatedness (Hanley & Abell, 2002). But this accusation is countered by research showing that people who have developed a positive self-regard tend to have a greater regard for others than do people with a negative self-regard (Epstein & Feist, 1988). Thus, we must be careful not to confuse self-regard with self-centeredness.

Other researchers have questioned the importance and benefits of high self-esteem. Whereas self-esteem is positively correlated with many measures of mental health and negatively correlated with depression (Taylor & Brown, 1988), the direction of causality is unclear. Moreover there are instances when high self-esteem may be related to psychological and interpersonal problems—including aggression and antisocial behavior (Baumeister, Campbell, Krueger, & Vohs, 2003). Some researchers have investigated the correlates of inflated self-esteem, as assessed by comparing participants' self-descriptions with those of trained raters and their peers. People who self-aggrandize—that is, regard themselves more positively than others see them—tend to have poor social skills and exhibit some indices of psychological maladjustment (Colvin, Block, & Funder, 1995).

Though the humanistic approach to personality has received its share of criticism, Rogers has been widely praised for his contributions to the advancement of psychotherapy, which is discussed in Chapter 15. Today, no single approach to personality dominates the others. Each makes a valuable contribution to our understanding of personality.

Section Review: The Humanistic Approach to Personality

1. What are the principal characteristics of humanistic theories of personality?

2. What are some of the topics in research on the "self"?

3. How would you use the Q-sort to assess someone's personality?

The Biopsychological Approach to Personality

Personality researchers who favor the *biopsychological approach* warn that "any theory that ignores the evidence for the biological underpinnings of human behavior is bound to be an incomplete one" (Kenrick & Dantchik, 1983, p. 302). The biological basis of personality has been recognized by ancient and modern thinkers alike. The Greek physician-philosopher Hippocrates (460–377 B.C.) presented an early biological view of personality, which was elaborated on by the Greek physician Galen (A.D. 130–200). Hippocrates and Galen claimed that **temperament**, a person's predominant emotional state, reflects the relative levels of body fluids they called *humors*. They associated blood with a cheerful, or *sanguine,* temperament; phlegm with a calm, or *phlegmatic,* temperament; black bile with a depressed, or *melancholic*, temperament; and yellow bile with an irritable, or *choleric,* temperament. Research has failed to find a humoral basis for personality, though differences in temperaments show some relationship to specific patterns of brain activity (Robinson, 2001) and hormonal secretion (Gerra et al., 2000). But as discussed in section 13-2a, "Type Theories," Hans Eysenck's research supports the existence of these four basic temperaments (Stelmack & Stalikas, 1991).

Differences in fetal movement and heart rate are associated with differences in temperament in infancy. More active fetuses become more difficult and unadaptable infants than less active fetuses do. In other words, temperamental differences exist even prenatally (Dipietro et al., 2002). Thus, infants are born already differing in their temperaments. The personality you have today is the indirect product of your temperament as an infant (Rothbart, Ahadi, & Evans, 2000). Your behavior and the reactions of those around you when you were an infant were molded by your temperament. Infants who respond with distress to unfamiliar stimuli

temperament A person's characteristic emotional state, first apparent in early infancy and possibly inborn.

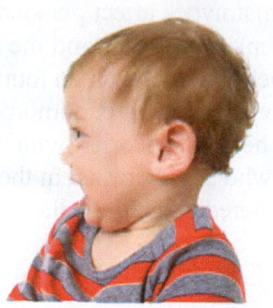

Temperament

Infants are born with different temperaments, which form the basis of personality.
Source: Hannamariah/ Shutterstock.com.

tend to become more fearful and subdued in childhood and adolescence (Kagan, 1997). Early life temperament also plays an important role in adult life. An fMRI study found that adults who had an inhibited temperament at 2 years of age had a greater amygdalar response (see Chapter 12, section 12-1b, "The Brain and Emotion") to unfamiliar faces than did adults who had been uninhibited children (Schwartz, Wright, Shin, Kagan, & Rauch, 2003). Likewise, some researchers think that this brain region, along with the hippocampus, might be responsible for influencing personality differences that contribute to temperament. Another fMRI study examined 39 participants that were separated into two groups: extremely inhibited or uninhibited temperaments. Participants were shown neutral faces on a screen while in a fMRI. In contrast to participants with uninhibited temperaments, the amygdala and hippocampus failed to habituate to novel faces in participants with inhibited temperaments (Blackford, Allen, Cowan, & Avery 2013). Thus, people with inhibited temperaments may be hypervigilant to strangers and social situations.

The humoral theory of personality was dominant until the late 18th century, when it was joined by phrenology and physiognomy. As described in Chapter 3 (see "Thinking Critically About Psychology"), *phrenology* is the study of the contours of the skull. Phrenologists assumed that specific areas of the brain controlled specific personality characteristics and that the bumps and depressions of the skull indicated the size of those brain areas. Those who believed in *physiognomy*, the study of physical appearance, held that personality was revealed by the features of the face.

Research failed to support phrenology and physiognomy. Like astrology, they were subject to the Barnum effect. Phrenologists did, however, spark interest in the study of the biological bases of personality, particularly the role of heredity (Hilts, 1982). The early 20th century saw biologically inclined personality researchers begin to study the relationship between physique and personality.

The Relationship Between Physique and Personality

The scientific study of the relationship between physique and personality began with the work of the German psychiatrist Ernst Kretschmer (1888–1964). Kretschmer (1925) measured the physique of hundreds of mental patients and found a relationship between thin physiques and schizophrenia and between rounded physiques and manic depression. But the researcher who did the most to advance the scientific study of the physique-personality relationship was the American physician and psychologist William Sheldon (1898–1977), whose inspiration to become a psychologist came from having William James as his godfather (Hilgard, 1987).

In formulating his *constitutional theory* of personality, Sheldon examined photographs of thousands of young men. He identified three kinds of physiques, each of which represents a different **somatotype**. The *ectomorph* has a thin, frail physique; the *mesomorph* has a muscular, strong physique; and the *endomorph* has a soft, rounded physique. Because Sheldon recognized that few people were pure somatotypes, he rated participants on a scale of 1 to 7 for each of the three kinds of physiques. Sheldon also administered personality tests to his research participants. He found that each somatotype was associated with a particular temperament. He called the shy, restrained, and introspective temperament of the ectomorph *cerebrotonia;* the bold, assertive, and energetic temperament of the mesomorph *somatotonia;* and the relaxed, sociable, and easy-going temperament of the endomorph *viscerotonia* (Sheldon & Stevens, 1942).

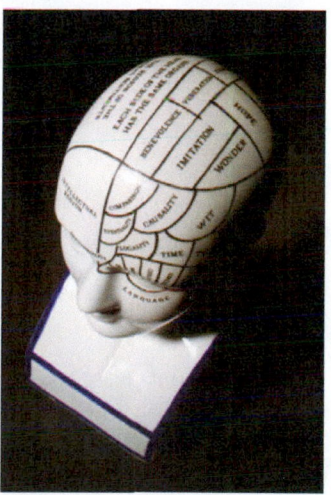

Phrenology

Phrenology was a pseudoscience that studied the contours of the skull.
Source: AMC Photography/ Shutterstock.com.

somatotype In Sheldon's theory, a physique associated with a particular temperament.

But how might somatotypes affect personality? Sheldon reasoned that their own somatotypes might affect people's behavior and the behavior of others toward them. For example, one study found that heterosexual women found mesomorphic men to be most sexually attractive, followed by ectomorphic and endomorphic men (Dixson, Halliwell, East, Wignarajah, & Anderson, 2003). Sheldon's theories, with some exceptions, are considered to be outdated. Today, psychologists who are interested in the biological bases of personality are more likely to study the effects of heredity and how heredity interacts with social experience.

The Relationship Between Heredity and Personality

More than a century ago Francis Galton insisted that "nature prevails enormously over nurture" (Holden, 1987, p. 598). Today, researchers like Galton who believe that heredity molds personality assume that evolution has provided us with inborn behavioral tendencies that differ from person to person (Bouchard & Loehlin, 2001). The field that studies the relationship between heredity and behavior is called *behavioral genetics* (see Chapters 3 and 4). For example, a behavioral genetics study found that the inherited tendency to be highly emotional is an important risk factor in regard to divorce (Jocklin, McGue, & Lykken, 1996).

Behavioral geneticists also study the manner in which heredity interacts with the environment. For example, mutations, in the gene that codes for the enzyme Monoamine Oxidase A (MAO-A), have been strongly associated with antisocial behavior. MAO-A is important for serotonin, norepinephrine, and dopamine signaling in brain regions associated with emotional processing. One recent study examined MAO-A as a marker for this behavioral trait. The researchers found that 7-year-old British boys with low MAO-A activity later developed mental health problems and that these individuals might be more susceptible to environmental stress (Kim-Cohen et al., 2006). Likewise, another recent study examined the same MAO-A mutation and the relationship between parenting and infant temperament. Participants, mothers and infants, were given assessments to examine maternal sensitivity and anger proneness, respectively. What researchers found was that low levels of MAO-A activity were dependent on both decreased maternal sensitivity and increased infant anger proneness (Pickles, 2013). MAO-A activity is an important mediator for predicting poor mental health outcomes for anger-prone individuals. This study and others contribute to our understanding of heredity and how heredity interacts with social experience.

How might these initial differences in temperament contribute to the development of differences in personality? They might affect how infants respond to other people and, in turn, how other people respond to them. For example, a placid infant would be less responsive to other people. As a consequence, others would be less responsive to the infant. This early lack of response might predispose the infant to become less sociable later in childhood, laying the groundwork for an introverted personality. Inherited differences in temperament contribute to the development of differences in specific personality characteristics, such as self-esteem (Kendler, Gardner, & Prescott, 1998). And as discussed above, genetics can affect behavior and can interact with social experience.

Biopsychological Assessment of Personality

In general, the closer the genetic relationship is between two persons, the more alike they will be in personality characteristics. But this relationship might reflect common life experiences rather than common genetic inheritance. For example, identical twins might respond similarly to personality tests because they are exposed to more similar environments than fraternal twins are (Schonemann & Schonemann, 1994). Because of the difficulty in separating genetic effects and environmental effects in studies of relatives who share similar environments, researchers have resorted to adoption studies. The Texas Adoption Project found that, in regard to personality, children tend to resemble their biological parents more than their adoptive parents (Loehlin, Horn, & Willerman, 1990). Such findings indicate that parent-child personality similarity is influenced more by common heredity than by common life experiences, as supported by the study described in "The Research Process: How Similar Are the Personalities of Identical Twins Reared Apart?"

The Research Process

How Similar Are the Personalities of Identical Twins Reared Apart?

Rationale

Since 1979, psychologist Thomas Bouchard of the University of Minnesota has conducted the most comprehensive study of identical twins reared apart and then reunited later in life. He has found amazing behavioral similarities between some of the twins. Consider the case of Oskar Stohr and Jack Yufe, who were born in Trinidad to a Jewish father and a Catholic mother. The twins were separated shortly after birth and reared in vastly different life circumstances. While Oskar was reared in Germany as a Nazi by his maternal grandmother, Jack was reared in Trinidad as a Jew by his father. Decades later, when they arrived at the airport in Minneapolis to take part in Bouchard's study, both Jack and Oskar sported mustaches, wire-rimmed glasses, and two-pocket shirts with epaulets. Bouchard found that they both preferred sweet liqueurs, stored rubber bands on their wrists, flushed the toilet before using it, read magazines from back to front, and dipped buttered toast in their coffee (Holden, 1980). Though there are probably no "flush toilet before using" genes, the men's identical genetic inheritance might have provided them with similar temperaments that predisposed them to develop certain behavioral similarities. In fact, Bouchard and his colleagues have found that the rearing environment has relatively little influence on the development of personality (Bouchard & McGue, 1990).

Studies of identical twins reared apart provide the strongest support for the hereditary basis of personality. Identical twins have 100 percent of their genes in common, whereas fraternal twins are no more alike genetically than nontwin siblings. Their shared genes might explain why identical twins who are adopted and reared by different families are more similar in personality than fraternal twins who are reared by their biological parents—even three decades after adoption (Tellegen et al., 1988).

Method

Participants were volunteers in the Minnesota Twin Study between 1970 and 1984. There were 217 identical twin pairs reared together, 114 fraternal twin pairs reared together, 44 identical twin pairs reared apart, and 27 fraternal twin pairs reared apart. The twins who had been reared apart had been separated, on the average, more than 30 years. Participants were given the Multidimensional Personality Questionnaire, which measures basic personality traits.

Results and Discussion

The results indicated that identical twins reared together and identical twins reared apart were highly similar in intelligence. Identical twins reared apart also were more similar than fraternal twins reared together. Overall, the heritability of personality was .48. (The heritability of personality is a population's proportion of the variability in personality that is caused by heredity.) Thus, the participants' personalities were strongly, though not solely, influenced by heredity.

One of the newer biopsychological approaches to personality assessment involves the measurement of brain activity. Much of the research has involved correlating brain activity with introversion and extraversion. One study found differences in the electrical activity of the brain, between extraverts and introverts in their response to emotional stimuli (Bartussek, Becker, Diedrich, & Naumann, 1996). Studies that have used the PET scan also have found differences in patterns of brain activity between introverts and extraverts (Fischer, Wik, & Fredrikson, 1997; Johnson et al., 1999). Studies using fMRI have examined the relationship between brain structure and personality as well. Researchers have found that amygdalar volume and cortical thickness and the way in which these structures communicate are positively correlated with externalizing behavior in children (Ameis et al., 2013). Further, extroverts with disorders such as oppositional defiant disorder or conduct disorder have problems making moral decisions. Imaging studies have shown that this might also be related to communication between structures such as the amygdala and cortex (Marsh et al., 2011). Therefore, brain structure and connectivity may contribute to personality traits.

Status of the Biopsychological Approach

Research has failed to find the strong relationship between somatotype and personality reported by Sheldon. One of the main problems with Sheldon's research was that *he* rated both the somatotypes and the temperaments of his participants. His close involvement provided room for experimenter bias, perhaps making his ratings support his theory more than they should have. Nonetheless, there is a modest relationship between physique and personality. For example, as predicted by Sheldon, mesomorphic men are more extra-verted, self-confident, and emotionally stable (Tucker, 1983). But a study in which staff members rated the personalities of children at a day-care center found no relationships between their physiques and their personalities (Lester, Kaminsky, & McGovern, 1993).

Even positive findings do not indicate that physique differences *cause* personality differences. Perhaps, instead, personality differences affect dietary and exercise habits, thereby causing differences in physique. Another possibility is that hereditary factors cause a relationship between physique and personality due to the interaction of heredity and social experience. For example, a study found that newborn ectomorphic infants were more emotionally responsive than infants with other physiques (Lester & Wosnack, 1990). This finding supported Sheldon's notion that the same genes might determine both physique and temperament (Sheldon & Stevens, 1942).

Putting aside the question of the relationship between physique and personality, how heritable is personality? Research has been mostly consistent, though results vary, in finding that the heritability of personality is about .30 to .60 (Benjamin, Ebstein, & Belmaker, 1997; Bouchard & Hur, 1998; Plomin, Corley, Caspi, Fulker, & DeFries, 1998). Moreover, there is some cross-cultural support for these estimates of the heritability of personality (Jang, McCrae, Angleitner, Riemann, & Livesley, 1998; Borkenau, Riemann, Angleitner, & Spinath, 2001). Studies in behavioral genetics have found, for example, genetic influences on the likelihood of marrying (Johnson et al., 2004), the degree of job satisfaction (Ilies & Judge, 2003), and the tendency to experience social anxiety (Stein, Jang, & Livesley, 2002). Research on the human genome has begun to identify specific genes associated with particular personality traits, including aggressiveness (Rujescu, Giegling, Gietl, Hartmann, & Moeller, 2003), and social detachment (Joensson et al., 2003).

As for environmental influences on personality, research findings have contradicted the commonsense belief that shared environmental experiences play a major role in personality similarity between close relatives. Research findings have consistently demonstrated that non-shared environmental experiences outweigh the effects of shared environmental experiences in affecting personality development (Hur, McGue, & Iacono, 1998; Saudino et al., 1999; Vernon, Jang, Harris, & McCarthy, 1997). Nonetheless, some personality traits, such as religious orthodoxy, do show substantial relationships to shared environmental experiences (Beer, Arnold, & Loehlin, 1998).

And what of Bouchard's research on identical twins reared apart? Care must be taken in drawing conclusions from the amazing behavioral similarities in some of the twins he has studied. Imagine that you and a fellow student were both asked thousands of questions (as Bouchard asks his participants). Undoubtedly you would find some surprising similarities between the two of you, even though you were not genetically related. This result was demonstrated in a study that found many similarities between pairs of strangers. For example, one pair of women were both Baptists, nursing students, active in tennis and volleyball, fond of English and mathematics, not fond of shorthand, and partial to vacations at historic places (Wyatt et al., 1984). Of course, by comparing twins' performances on formal personality tests, Bouchard does more than simply report selected instances of amazing similarities between certain ones. Given the evidence for both genetic and environmental influences, the best bet is to accept that they both strongly—apparently about equally—affect the development of personality.

Section Review: The Biopsychological Approach to Personality

1. What weaknesses are there in research on somatotypes and personality?

2. How do studies of identical twins who have been reunited provide evidence supporting the role of heredity in personality development?

Are Amazing Similarities in Personality Just the Result of Coincidence?

Rationale

As discussed in "The Research Process: How Similar Are the Personalities of Identical Twins Reared Apart?", amazing psychological and behavioral similarities between identical twins who were separated in infancy and reunited years later have provoked interest in the possible hereditary basis of personality. But researchers typically ask the reunited twins hundreds or even thousands of questions. Perhaps the amazing similarities we hear about have been research report examples selected by the media to support claims that personality development depends more on one's heredity than on one's environment. If, instead, we asked unrelated people many questions about themselves, we would find equally amazing similarities among them (Wyatt, Posey, Walker, & Seamonds, 1984).

Method
Participants

The participants will be the members of your introductory psychology class.

Materials

You and your classmates will complete the "Identical Twins Reunited Questionnaire" that accompanies this exercise. The questionnaire asks (not terribly personal) questions about behaviors, relationships, and personal characteristics.

Procedure

Have the students take the questionnaire anonymously. Go through the questionnaire responses to determine whether any pair of questionnaires has remarkable similarities in responses.

Results and Discussion

Describe your class findings. Were any similarities between students truly startling? If so, how might this finding affect your judgment of media reports of astounding similarities between identical twins reunited later in life? Why do research reports of similarities in personality between identical twins reared apart not suffer from the selection bias that might plague media reports of the same research?

Identical Twins Reunited Questionnaire

Give your responses to each of the following questions. If you prefer not to answer particular questions, feel free to leave them blank.

1. Academic major:
2. Favorite musical group/performer:
3. Mother's first name:
4. Favorite dessert:
5. Boyfriend's/girlfriend's first name:
6. Favorite television show:
7. Political affiliation (Dem/Rep/Indep/Other):
8. Favorite food:
9. Favorite actor:
10. Favorite actress:
11. Favorite movie:
12. Favorite hobby:
13. Favorite sport to watch:
14. Favorite sport to play:
15. Favorite professional sports team:
16. Favorite author:
17. Father's first name:
18. Most distinctive habit:
19. Favorite politician:
20. Favorite professional athlete:
21. Most disliked food:
22. Favorite automobile:
23. Favorite kind of pet animal:
24. Professional goal:
25. Most recent noncourse book read:

Chapter Summary

The Psychoanalytic Approach to Personality

- Your personality is your unique, relatively consistent pattern of thoughts, feelings, and behaviors.
- Freud's psychosexual theory emphasizes the conflict between biological drives and sociocultural prohibitions in the development of personality.
- Freud divided the mind into conscious, preconscious, and unconscious levels.

- Freud distinguished between the personality structures called the id, the ego, and the superego.
- According to Freud, we progress through oral, anal, phallic, latency, and genital stages of development.
- We may use defense mechanisms to protect us from being overwhelmed by anxiety.
- Freud's intellectual descendants altered his theory, generally downplaying the importance of sexuality and emphasizing the importance of social relationships.

- Alfred Adler's theory of individual psychology assumes that personality develops from our attempts to overcome early feelings of inferiority.
- Karen Horney's theory emphasized the role of social and cultural factors in personality development.
- Carl Jung's theory of analytical psychology assumes that we are influenced by both a personal unconscious and the archetypes in a collective unconscious.
- The Rorschach test and the Thematic Apperception Test are two of the main psychoanalytic assessment techniques.

The Dispositional Approach to Personality

- The dispositional approach to personality attributes the consistency we see in personality to relatively enduring personality attributes.
- Hans Eysenck's three-factor theory sees personality as dependent on the interaction of three dimensions: stability/instability, tough-minded/tender-minded, and introversion/extraversion.
- In his trait theory of personality, Gordon Allport distinguished three kinds of traits: cardinal traits, central traits, and secondary traits.
- Personality types are measured by tests such as the Myers-Briggs Type Indicator, and personality traits are measured by tests such as the MMPI.
- Walter Mischel provoked controversy by claiming that situations are more important determinants of behavior than are personality traits.
- Mischel based this conclusion on studies finding that individuals' behavior is not consistent across different situations.
- Research indicates that personality is neither as inconsistent as Mischel originally claimed nor as consistent as personality theorists had previously claimed.

The Cognitive-Behavioral Approach to Personality

- B. F. Skinner's operant conditioning theory assumes that what we call personality is simply a person's unique pattern of behavior.
- Albert Bandura's social-cognitive theory argues that cognitive factors influence behavior.
- Bandura's concept of reciprocal determinism points out the mutual influence of cognitive factors, overt behaviors, and environmental factors.

- One of the most important personality characteristics is self-efficacy, the extent to which a person believes that she or he can perform behaviors that are necessary to bring about a desired outcome.
- Self-schemas are cognitive structures about the self. Cross-cultural differences may be reflected in the construal of self-schemas.
- Behavioral assessment is accomplished through the experience-sampling method.
- Julian Rotter's Internal-External Locus of Control Scale is one of the main cognitive-behavioral assessment techniques.

The Humanistic Approach to Personality

- Abraham Maslow's self-actualization theory is based on his hierarchy of needs.
- Maslow assumes that we have a need to develop all our potentials, a process he called self-actualization.
- Maslow identified the characteristics of eminent people whom he believed were self-actualized.
- Carl Rogers's self theory holds that psychological well-being depends on the congruence between one's self and one's experience.
- Other researchers point to the importance of congruence between the actual self, the ideal self, and the ought self.
- Self-actualization is measured by the Personal Orientation Inventory.
- Congruence between the actual self and the ideal self is measured by the Q-sort.

The Biopsychological Approach to Personality

- Closely related to personality is temperament, a person's most characteristic emotional state.
- Sheldon's constitutional theory holds that different temperaments are associated with different physiques, or somatotypes.
- Research in behavioral genetics has found evidence of the hereditary basis of temperament and other aspects of personality.
- Heredity and its interaction with social experience play a role in personality development.

Key Terms

personality (p. 443)

The Psychoanalytic Approach to Personality

anal stage (p. 447)
archetypes (p. 450)
collective unconscious (p. 450)
defense mechanism (p. 445)

ego (p. 445)
Electra complex (p. 447)
extravert (p. 450)
genital stage (p. 447)
id (p. 445)
introvert (p. 450)
latency stage (p. 447)
libido (p. 446)

Oedipus complex (p. 447)
oral stage (p. 446)
personal unconscious (p. 450)
phallic stage (p. 447)
pleasure principle (p. 445)
projective test (p. 450)
reality principle (p. 445)
superego (p. 445)

The Dispositional Approach to Personality

trait (p. 454)

The Cognitive-Behavioral Approach to Personality

collective efficacy (p. 461)

reciprocal determinism (p. 460)
self-efficacy (p. 460)
self-schema (p. 460)

The Humanistic Approach to Personality

self-actualization (p. 466)

The Biopsychological Approach to Personality

somatotype (p. 471)
temperament (p. 470)

Chapter Quiz

Note: Answers for the Chapter Quiz questions are provided at the end of the book.

1. A student is tempted to cheat on an exam, but feels guilty and resists the impulse. A Freudian would attribute this to a strong
   a. id.
   b. ego.
   c. superego.
   d. archetype.

2. A person's characteristic emotional state, first apparent in early infancy, is called (the)
   a. ego.
   b. archetype.
   c. personality.
   d. temperament.

3. A researcher studies the hunger motive by providing participants with a buzzer randomly throughout the day. In response to the buzzer, the participants jot down the situation they are in and any of their immediate thoughts or feelings about food. This is an example of
   a. experience sampling.
   b. behavioral observation.
   c. reciprocal determinism.
   d. situational interviewing.

4. The role of self-esteem in protecting us from death anxiety is a central concept in
   a. self-schema theory.
   b. psychoanalytic theory.
   c. terror management theory.
   d. individual psychology.

5. A person who acts in a loud, boisterous manner in all situations would be low in
   a. somatotonia.
   b. extraversion.
   c. self-efficacy.
   d. self-monitoring.

6. The dimensions in Hans Eysenck's three-factor theory of personality are neuroticism, extraversion, and
   a. eroticism.
   b. psychoticism.
   c. obsessiveness.
   d. hypochondriasis.

7. According to William Sheldon, a person with an endomorphic physique has a temperament that he called
   a. adipotonia.
   b. somatotonia.
   c. cerebrotonia.
   d. viscerotonia.

8. The five-factor theory of personality includes the traits of extraversion, neuroticism, agreeableness, openness to experience, and
   a. melancholia.
   b. romanticism.
   c. aggressiveness.
   d. conscientiousness.

9. The view that personality is a person's unique pattern of behavior, tied to specific situations would most likely be held by
   a. B. F. Skinner.
   b. Abraham Maslow.
   c. Raymond Cattell.
   d. Harry Stack Sullivan.

10. A student who responds to the stress of final exams by sucking on lollipops, playing on a seesaw, and watching children's cartoon shows on television would most likely be resorting to the defense mechanism of
    a. denial.
    b. projection.
    c. regression.
    d. rationalization.

11. Carl Jung used the archetype of God to explain the
    a. Oedipus complex.
    b. striving for superiority.
    c. need for self-actualization.
    d. reports of flying saucers after World War II.

12. Walter Mischel (1968) argued that personality is not consistent because the correlation between behaviors that presumably represent the same trait rarely exceeded about
    a. .05.
    b. .10.
    c. .30.
    d. .60.

13. According to Hazel Markus and Shinobu Kitayama, people in Western cultures have a self-schema that is characterized by
    a. interdependence.
    b. independence.
    c. reciprocal determinism.
    d. constructive alternativism.

14. In Albert Bandura's theory, a person's belief that he or she can perform behaviors that are necessary to bring about a desired outcome is called
    a. self-efficacy.
    b. self-actualization.
    c. psychic determinism.
    d. reciprocal determinism.

15. According to Carl Rogers, personality development is affected by the degree of incongruence between the self and personal experience, which is affected by the degree of parental
    a. fixation.
    b. self-actualization.
    c. reciprocal determinism.
    d. unconditional positive regard.

16. According to researchers such as Gordon Allport, a relatively enduring, cross-situationally consistent personality characteristic is called a(n)
    a. trait.
    b. archetype.
    c. defense mechanism.
    d. personal construct.

17. One of the strongest criticisms of Freudian personality theory is that it
    a. does not operationally define its terms.
    b. has had little influence outside of psychotherapy.
    c. lacks any research support for unconscious motivation.
    d. gives more importance to adolescent experiences than to childhood experiences.

18. The Minnesota Multiphasic Personality Inventory (MMPI) was designed to
    a. reveal unconscious motives.
    b. diagnose psychological disorders.
    c. identify patterns of personal constructs.
    d. trace changes in personality across the life span.

19. The word *personality* comes from the Latin word for
    a. mask.
    b. character.
    c. individual.
    d. temperament.

20. According to Karen Horney, a person exhibiting a neurotic coping style might be submissive, aggressive, or
    a. manic.
    b. humorous.
    c. reclusive.
    d. extraverted.

21. According to Freud, the cornerstone of his theory is
    a. libido.
    b. free will.
    c. repression.
    d. early childhood experiences.

22. A psychologist shows you a series of pictures of people in ambiguous situations and asks you to tell her the story behind each. She is using the
    a. Q-sort.
    b. TAT.
    c. MMPI.
    d. Rorschach test.

23. In Alfred Adler's theory, the healthiest way of striving for superiority is expressed through
    a. sublimation.
    b. social interest.
    c. obeying one's archetypes.
    d. constructive alternativism.

24. The conflict between the need for freedom and the anxiety that freedom brings is a core concept in the personality theory of
    a. Erich Fromm.
    b. Karen Horney.
    c. Erik Erikson.
    d. Harry Stack Sullivan.

25. In his personality theory, Harry Stack Sullivan stressed the importance of
    a. somatotypes.
    b. behavioral consistency.
    c. healthy social relationships.
    d. sufficient numbers of personal constructs.

Thought Questions

1. How might Karen Horney's concept of basic anxiety explain the three major trends that she observed in how people relate to one another?

2. What are the arguments in favor of the cross-situational consistency of personality traits?

3. How might self-handicapping be used in everyday life in work, school, and sports?

Psychological Disorders

You might be surprised to learn that the United States once had a self-proclaimed emperor, the Emperor Norton I. He began his life as Joshua Norton, a man who left his family farm and built the first rice mill in California. Norton became a respected, seemingly normal San Francisco merchant. But after losing a hard-earned fortune of $40,000 and going bankrupt, in 1859 he deteriorated psychologically and placed an advertisement in *The San Francisco Bulletin* proclaiming himself Norton I, Emperor of the United States and Protector of Mexico. For the next two decades, he wore an officer's uniform and a beaver hat with a feather. He also carried a saber as he strolled the streets of the city, lifting the spirits of his "subjects." Though an emperor, he lived in an inexpensive rooming house, paying 50 cents a day for rent. Nonetheless, in his role as emperor, he abolished Congress and dissolved the United States.

The Emperor Norton (as he was affectionately known to his subjects) also declared streetcars to be free and issued bonds and collected taxes, which actually were donations to support him given by friendly bankers and shopkeepers. Norton became a renowned figure in the San Francisco Bay area. Though Jewish, he was welcomed into a different Christian church each Sunday—as part of his effort to prevent his subjects from believing that he favored one faith over another.

Norton received free meals at the finest restaurants, and he saw audiences rise in his honor when he arrived at the theater. And he did his best to protect his subjects. On one occasion, he prevented a frenzied crowd from attacking Chinese citizens by reciting the Lord's Prayer—shaming them into silence and freezing them in their place. He was so popular that when he was arrested for vagrancy, newspapers published editorials criticizing the police for their treatment of San Francisco's first citizen.

Though Norton was talkative, many of his speeches were virtually incomprehensible, consisting of his delusional thinking about the state of the country. Yet, some of his ideas were farsighted. In 1869 he placed an announcement in the *Oakland Daily News,* ordering the construction of a bridge across the bay. He was ridiculed for proposing such a "foolish" venture, an endeavor that was considered impossible at the time.

At the time of his death in 1880, the Emperor Norton had become the most famous and beloved person in San Francisco. But he died a pauper, his meager financial resources comprising $5.50 in coins and several Bonds of the Empire. The day after Norton's death, the *San Francisco Chronicle* carried the headline "Le Roi Est Mort" ("The King Is Dead"). Well-to-do friends paid for an elaborate funeral—fit for an emperor—attended by many thousands of Norton's subjects. Several

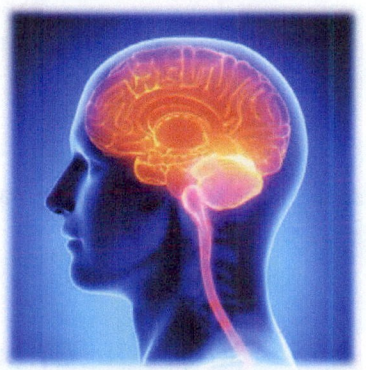

Source: CLIPAREA/Custom media/Shutterstock.com.

Chapter Outline

Characteristics of Psychological Disorders

Anxiety Disorders

Obsessive-Compulsive Disorder

Somatic Symptom and Related Disorders

Dissociative Disorders

Major Depressive Disorder and Related Disorders

Bipolar Disorder

Schizophrenia

Personality Disorders

Developmental Disorders

years later, Robert Louis Stevenson wrote that his favorite San Franciscan had been the Emperor Norton (McDonald, 1980). At Norton's final resting place, his friends erected a marble tombstone that read:

Norton I

Emperor of the United States and Protector of Mexico

Joshua A. Norton, 1819–1880

Aside from demonstrating that San Francisco has long been hospitable to people with unusual lifestyles, the story of Joshua Norton is an example of a person with the psychological disorder called *schizophrenia,* which often is marked by language problems, hallucinations, peculiar behavior, and delusions of grandeur, such as believing that one is a rich, famous, or powerful person. It also demonstrates that even a person with schizophrenia might be able to live a fulfilling life.

Characteristics of Psychological Disorders

How do psychologists determine whether a person has a psychological disorder? What are the causes of psychological disorders? And how are psychological disorders classified and diagnosed? Answers to these questions are provided by professionals with expertise in **psychopathology**—the study of psychological disorders. A diagnosis of a psychological disorder may interfere with a person's daily life, and many professionals are qualified to treat psychological disorders.

psychopathology The study of psychological disorders.

Criteria for Psychological Disorders

An ambitious study called the National Comorbidity Survey Replication (NCS-R) examined the prevalence of psychological disorders in the United States. This survey of more than 9,000 persons ages 15 to 54 years found that 32.4 percent had at least one psychological disorder within the past year (Kessler, Chiu, Demler, Merikangas, & Walters, 2005) and 48 percent had at least one during their lifetime (Kessler et al., 2004). You probably know people whose patterns of moods, thoughts, and actions make you suspect that they too suffer from a psychological disorder. But what are the criteria for determining that a person has a disorder? The main criteria are *abnormality, maladaptiveness,* and *personal distress.*

The Criterion of Abnormality

Abnormal behavior deviates from the behavior of the "typical" person—the *norm.* A norm can be qualitative or quantitative. *Qualitatively abnormal* behavior deviates from culturally accepted standards, perhaps even seeming bizarre. A railroad conductor who announces train stops would be normal. But a passenger who announces train stops would be abnormal. *Quantitatively abnormal* behavior deviates from the statistical average. A woman who washes her hands 3 times a day would be normal. But a woman who washes her hands 30 times a day would be abnormal.

By itself, abnormality is not a sufficient criterion for determining the presence of a psychological disorder. If qualitative abnormality were sufficient, then artistic innovators, political dissidents, and people who achieve rare accomplishments, such as a Nobel Prize winner or your student government president, would be considered psychologically disordered. And if quantitative abnormality were sufficient, then even a physician who washes her hands 30 times a day in the course of seeing patients would be considered psychologically disordered. Thus, the sociocultural context in which "abnormal" behavior occurs must be considered before deciding that it is symptomatic of a psychological disorder.

The Criterion of Maladaptiveness

According to the criterion of *maladaptiveness,* you would have a psychological disorder if your behavior seriously disrupted your social, academic, or vocational life. As an example, consider a person with the anxiety disorder called *agoraphobia,* which is the fear of being in public places. Such a person might be afraid to leave home and might consequently alienate friends, fail in school, and lose a job. Similarly, a person who uses drugs or alcohol excessively would be considered psychologically disordered because such behavior would interfere with everyday functioning. But maladaptive behavior is not always a sign of a psychological disorder. Though cramming for exams, failing to eat fruits and vegetables, and driving 90 miles an hour on a busy highway are maladaptive behaviors, they would not necessarily be symptomatic of a psychological disorder.

The Criterion of Personal Distress

The criterion of *personal distress* assumes that our subjective feeling of anxiety, depression, or other unpleasant emotions determines whether we have a psychological disorder. Nonetheless, personal distress might not be a sufficient criterion for determining the presence of a psychological disorder (Widiger & Trull, 1991). Some people, like the notorious John Wayne Gacy—a Chicago man who killed 33 boys and young men in the 1970s but expressed no guilt about it—might have a psychological disorder without feeling any distress.

Behavior that is abnormal, maladaptive, or personally distressing might indicate that a person has a psychological disorder. But there is no single point at which a person moves from being psychologically healthy to being psychologically disordered. Each of us varies on each of the criteria. Thus, there is a degree of subjectivity in even the best answers to the question of how abnormal, maladaptive, or personally distressing a person's behavior must be before we determine that he or she has a psychological disorder.

Viewpoints on Psychological Disorders

Even when psychologists agree on the presence of a particular psychological disorder, they may disagree on its causes. That is, they favor different viewpoints regarding the causes of psychological disorders. Since ancient times, people have tried to explain the unusual or distressing behavior patterns that we now call psychological disorders. Many ancient Greek authorities assumed that the gods inflicted psychological disorders on people to punish them for their misdeeds. But the Greek physician Hippocrates (ca. 460–ca. 377 B.C.) argued instead that psychological disorders had natural causes.

Despite the efforts of Hippocrates and his followers, supernatural explanations existed alongside naturalistic ones until the 19th century. The 16th-century Swiss physician Paracelsus (1493–1541) rejected the supernatural viewpoint. Instead of attributing unusual behavior to demons, he attributed it to the moon. Paracelsus called the condition *lunacy* and the people who exhibited it *lunatics.* These terms were derived from the Latin word for "moon." You probably have heard someone say, on an evening when people are acting oddly, "There must be a full moon tonight." Yet contrary to popular belief, the moon does not affect the incidence of crime, mental illness, or other abnormal behavior (Rotton & Kelly, 1985). This finding holds across countries. For example, a study of admissions to emergency psychiatric centers in Iran found no relationship between a full moon and the number of admissions (Kazemi-Bajestani, Amirsadri, Samari, & Akbar, 2011).

Current viewpoints on psychological disorders attribute them to natural factors. As shown in Table 14-1, the viewpoints differ in the extent to which they attribute psychological disorders to biological, mental, or environmental factors. But no single viewpoint provides an adequate explanation of psychological disorders. This lack of an explanation has led to the emergence of the **biopsychosocial model** (Figure 14-1), which holds that psychological disorders are the result of an interaction of biological, psychological, and social factors (Johnson, 2013). Often, professionals will have expertise in one aspect of this model, but very few would deny that all three aspects are important.

biopsychosocial model
The model that considers that psychological disorders are the result of an interaction of biological, psychological, and social factors.

TABLE 14-1 The Major Viewpoints on Psychological Disorders

Viewpoint	Causes of Psychological Disorders
Biopsychological	Inherited or acquired brain disorders involving imbalances in neurotransmitters or damage to brain structures
Psychoanalytic	Unconscious conflicts over impulses such as sex and aggression, originating in childhood
Behavioral	Reinforcement of inappropriate behaviors and punishment or extinction of appropriate behaviors
Cognitive	Irrational or maladaptive thinking about one's self, life events, and the world in general
Humanistic	Incongruence between one's actual self and public self as a consequence of trying to live up to the demands of others
Sociocultural	Sociocultural factors that influence psychological symptoms and the prevalence of psychological disorders

According to the biopsychosocial model, there can be many individual differences in the development of psychological disorders. For example, a person with a low sense of personal control might succumb to relatively low levels of stress due to factors such as a romantic breakup or academic failure. This person would be unlikely to cope well with most stressful situations. Likewise, a person with a high sense of personal control might not succumb to even moderate levels of stress, due to these same factors. This person would be likely to cope well with stressful situations by engaging in proactive strategies, such as recruiting the support of friends and family. Researchers often want to know what makes one person vulnerable to stress while another person is resilient to stress. Research findings indicate that the biopsychosocial model can explain the interaction of biological, psychological, and social factors to cause some psychological disorders, such as major depressive disorder (Schotte, Van Den Bossche, De Doncker, Claes, & Cosyns, 2006) and substance abuse that results from social anxiety (Buckner, Heimberg, Ecker, & Vinci, 2013). A core concept of this model is that all three features—biological, psychological, and social factors—interact with each other.

FIGURE 14-1

The Biopsychosocial Model

According to the biopsychosocial model, psychological disorders are the result of an interaction of biological, psychological, and social factors.

Source: (center image) art4all/ Shutterstock.com.

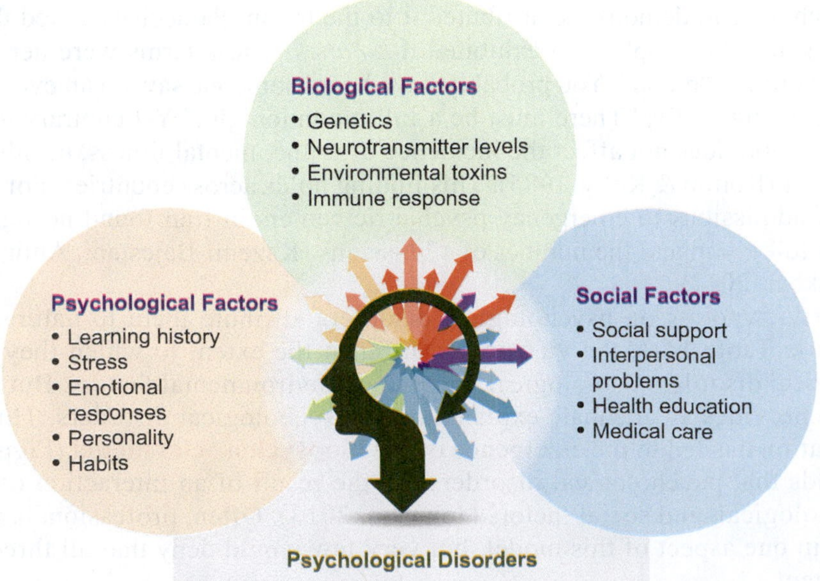

Biological Factors
- Genetics
- Neurotransmitter levels
- Environmental toxins
- Immune response

Psychological Factors
- Learning history
- Stress
- Emotional responses
- Personality
- Habits

Social Factors
- Social support
- Interpersonal problems
- Health education
- Medical care

Psychological Disorders

The Biopsychological Viewpoint

More than a century ago, Sigmund Freud remarked, "In view of the intimate connection between things physical and mental, we may look forward to a day when paths of knowledge will be opened up leading from organic biology and chemistry to the field of neurotic phenomena" (Taulbee, 1983, p. 45). As a physician and biologist, Freud might have approved of the *biopsychological viewpoint,* which favors the study of the biological causes of psychological disorders.

Modern interest in the biological causes of psychological disorders was stimulated in the late 19th century when early researchers discovered that a disorder called general paresis, marked by severe mental deterioration, was caused by brain damage due to untreated syphilis. Researchers in the 19th century also found that toxic chemicals could induce psychological disorders. In fact, the Mad Hatter in the book *Alice in Wonderland* exhibits psychological symptoms caused by exposure to the mercury that was used in making felt hats. This phenomenon was the origin of the phrase "mad as a hatter" (O'Carroll, Masterton, Dougall, Ebmeier, & Goodwin, 1995). We now know that mercury poisoning can cause neurocognitive disorders and other psychological symptoms due to the accumulation of heavy metals in the brain. Examples of the biological roots of psychological disorders include heredity, atypical brain development, excessive or deficient neurotransmitter activity, and variations in hormone levels. Some other contributing factors that might dependent on these biological roots are sleep disturbances, substance abuse, poor nutrition, and infectious diseases.

Today, biopsychological researchers are interested in how psychological factors interact with the biological roots of psychological disorders. Research supporting the possible role of heredity in the development of psychological disorders has found that monozygotic (identical) twins show higher correlations than dizygotic (fraternal) twins in traits that indicate psychopathology (Eaves et al., 1997). Moreover, monozygotic twins reared apart show higher correlations than ordinary siblings reared together in traits that indicate psychopathology (DiLalla, Carey, Gottesman, & Bouchard, 1996). One recent study examined the neural networks related to agoraphobia, a type of anxiety disorder in which people experience panic attacks in public or open spaces. Using fMRI, 72 participants with agoraphobia and their healthy matched controls were scanned while being shown images of open spaces. Researchers found that participants with agoraphobia had increased brain activity in regions associated with panic attacks, such as the basal ganglia, while viewing images or even anticipating viewing the images (Wittmann et al., 2014). Studies such as these contribute to our understanding of both the biology (brain activity) and psychology (perceptual processes) that contribute to the development of agoraphobia. Moreover, they will help researchers develop innovative treatments. Understanding psychological disorders is not a matter of biology versus psychology, but rather the interaction of both.

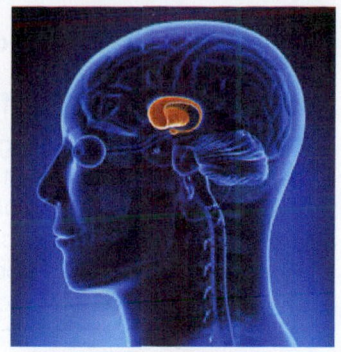

The Basal Ganglia

This image of the brain highlights the location of the basal ganglia.
Source: decade3d/Shutterstock.com.

The Psychoanalytic Viewpoint

The *psychoanalytic viewpoint,* which originated in medicine, grew out of the biopsychological viewpoint. But instead of looking for underlying biological causes of psychological disorders, the psychoanalytic viewpoint looks for unconscious causes. As discussed in Chapter 13, Sigmund Freud stressed the continual conflict between inborn biological drives, particularly sex and aggression, which demand expression, and the norms of society that inhibit their expression. According to Freud, conflicts about sex and aggression can be repressed into the unconscious mind. This repression can lead to feelings of anxiety caused by pent-up sexual or aggressive energy.

Freud claimed that we might gain partial relief of this anxiety by resorting to defense mechanisms. If your defense mechanisms are either too weak or too rigid, you might develop psychological disorders. Freud also stressed the importance of anxiety-provoking childhood experiences in promoting the development of psychological disorders. A major study, the NCS-R mentioned earlier in this chapter, found that some disorders were, in fact, associated with adverse experiences during childhood. For example, the more adverse events children experienced, the more likely they were to experience adult psychopathology. Additionally, there were gender differences in the development of adult psychological disorders. Among adult women, psychological disorders were related to childhood sexual abuse, whereas among adult men, psychological disorders were related to economic hardship in the family (Putnam, Harris, & Putnam, 2013).

Does the Insanity Defense Let Many Violent Criminals Escape Punishment?

More than 2,000 years ago, Plato noted that "someone may commit an act when mad or afflicted with disease . . . let him pay simply for the damage; and let him be exempt from other punishment" (quoted in Carson & Butcher, 1992, p. 32). Today, Plato would face opposition from those who argue against the insanity defense. Spurred by the media's coverage of the successful insanity plea of John Hinckley Jr. following his attempted assassination of President Ronald Reagan and the plea by Dan White after the murders of San Francisco mayor George Moscone and city supervisor Harvey Milk, critics believe that the insanity defense is a miscarriage of justice (Szasz, 1980). But do these and other cases portrayed in the media indicate that many people have gotten away with murder by using the insanity defense?

The Volitional Rule

A person who did not know what he or she was doing at the time of the crime could still use the insanity defense.
Source: Noel Powell/Shutterstock.com.

Characteristics of the Insanity Defense

Insanity is a legal, not a psychological or psychiatric, term attesting that a person is not responsible for his or her own actions. In criminal cases, insanity is usually determined by a jury. The insanity defense was formalized in 1843 in the case of Daniel M'Naghten, a man with schizophrenia who had tried to murder the English prime minister Robert Peel, who he believed was persecuting him. But M'Naghten killed Peel's secretary, Edward Drummond, by mistake. After a controversial trial that was sensationalized in magazines and newspapers, M'Naghten was ruled not guilty by reason of insanity and was committed to a mental hospital. The *M'Naghten rule* became a guiding principle in English law. The rule states that a person is not guilty if, at the time of a crime, the person did not know what she or he was doing or did not know that it was wrong.

Today the most widely used standard for determining insanity in the United States is that of the American Law Institute. The standard comprises two rules. First, the *cognitive rule,* similar to the M'Naghten rule, says that a person was insane at the time of a crime if the person did not know what he or she had done or did not know that it was wrong. Based on this rule, some defendants who have killed a person while sleepwalking have been acquitted of murder charges (Thomas, 1997).

Second, the *volitional rule* says that a person was insane at the time of a crime if the person was not in voluntary control of her or his behavior. In 1857, in an early use of the volitional rule, Abraham Lincoln—then an attorney in Illinois—prosecuted a case in which defense attorneys claimed that a defendant was insane at the time he committed a murder because he was under the influence of chloroform, a drug that can induce anesthesia (Spiegel & Suskind, 1998).

Controversy Concerning the Insanity Defense

In recent decades, several cases involving the insanity defense, including that of John Hinckley Jr., have provoked controversy. For example, in October 2002, John Allen Muhammad and Lee Boyd Malvo killed 10 people during a three-week period of random attacks in the Washington, D.C., area. The pair stalked people going about their daily lives in highways, shopping malls, and gas stations and then shot the victims with military precision using long-distance firearms. Muhammad, a 43-year-old Gulf War veteran, was sentenced to death by a Virginia court in March 2004. Malvo, who was 17 at the time of the shootings, pleaded not guilty by reason of insanity, claiming that Muhammad had brainwashed him while acting as his surrogate father. Nonetheless,

---

insanity A legal term attesting that a person is not responsible for his or her own actions, including criminal behavior.

The Behavioral Viewpoint

The *behavioral viewpoint* arose in opposition to psychological viewpoints that looked for mental causes of behavior. In the tradition of B. F. Skinner, psychologists who favor the behavioral viewpoint look to the environment and to the learning of maladaptive behaviors as the causes of psychological disorders. A psychological disorder might arise when a person is reinforced for inappropriate behavior or has appropriate behavior punished or extinguished. Social-cognitive behaviorists, such as Albert Bandura, would add that we might develop a psychological disorder by observing other people's behavior. For example, a person might develop a phobia (an unrealistic fear) of dogs after either being bitten by a dog or observing someone else being bitten by a dog.

Does the Insanity Defense Let Many Violent Criminals Escape Punishment? *continued*

Malvo was found guilty of his crimes and was sentenced to life in prison.

Despite media-driven concern about alleged abuses of the insanity defense, it rarely is used in felony crimes and is generally successful only with the most obviously disturbed persons. For example, an archival study of felony cases adjudicated in New York County from 1988 to 1997 found that less than 1 percent involved any type of insanity defense (Kirschner & Galperin, 2001). Even when the insanity defense is successful, the person is usually confined for an extended period (Lymburner & Roesch, 1999). This finding holds true in the United States as well as in other countries, such as Ireland (Gibbons, Mulryan, & O'Connor, 1997).

Guilty But Mentally Ill

The notoriety of cases such as those of John Hinckley, Dan White, and Lee Boyd Malvo prompted a reevaluation of the insanity defense by state legislatures and professional organizations. Some states have abandoned the insanity defense entirely, whereas others have adopted a rule of *guilty but mentally ill*. This rule requires that an insane person who committed a crime be placed in a mental hospital until she or he is no longer mentally ill, at which time the person would serve the remainder of the sentence in prison. This compromise verdict has provoked controversy regarding its wisdom (Melville & Naimark, 2002).

The American Psychiatric Association, the American Psychological Association, and the American Bar Association have their own positions regarding the insanity defense. The American Psychiatric Association position states that the insanity defense is a legal and moral question, not a psychiatric one, and that psychiatrists should testify only about a defendant's mental status—not about a defendant's responsibility for a crime (Herbert, 1983).

The American Psychological Association took a more cautious approach, calling for research on the effects of the insanity defense before deciding to eliminate it or replace it with a plea of guilty but mentally ill (Mervis, 1984). The past few decades have, in fact, seen a series of studies on the insanity defense. In an experiment on the effect of the guilty-but-mentally-ill verdict option, undergraduates participated as jurors in a mock trial. They then answered questions about the case. Participants who were given the guilty-but-mentally-ill verdict option showed a two-thirds reduction in the verdicts of either guilty or not guilty by reason of insanity when compared to participants not given that option (Poulson, 1990).

The American Bar Association would retain the cognitive rule but would eliminate the volitional rule in the insanity defense. A person who did not know what he or she was doing could still use the insanity defense. That is, someone who knowingly stole a smartphone, for example, would be legally responsible even if he believed that the smartphone was issuing instructions to him from Mars. Mental illness would be a defense only if a person were so psychotic that he thought he was squeezing an orange when he was strangling a child (Holden, 1983).

The volitional rule has come under especially strong attack because it might be impossible to determine whether a person has acted from free will or from an irresistible impulse. For example, in 1994 Lorena Bobbitt, in a celebrated case in which she cut off her husband Wayne's penis, was ruled not guilty by reason of insanity. Though she claimed that she had been driven to it after years of physical abuse, the prosecution claimed she should still be held criminally responsible for her act.

It remains to be seen whether legislatures will completely overturn our long tradition of not holding people with severe psychological disorders responsible for criminal actions. Both science and politics will determine the outcome of this issue, reflecting the battle between empiricism and emotionalism in regard to the insanity defense (Rogers, 1987).

Those who favor the behavioral viewpoint, with its emphasis on environmental factors, also would be more likely to consider the negative effects of socioeconomic conditions on psychological well-being. For example, poverty is a predisposing factor in a variety of psychological disorders. A survey found that poverty is associated with a higher risk of almost all psychological disorders. This finding holds true for young and old, men and women, and African Americans and European Americans (Bruce, Takeuchi, & Leaf, 1991). Moreover, a recent study found that psychiatric symptoms among children from families who moved out of poverty fell to the level of those who had never experienced poverty (Costello, Compton, Keeler, & Angold, 2003).

The Cognitive Viewpoint

The Greek Stoic philosopher Epictetus (A.D. ca. 60–ca. 120) taught that "men are disturbed not by things, but by the views which they take of things." This statement is the central assumption of the *cognitive viewpoint,* which holds that psychological disorders arise from maladaptive ways of thinking about oneself and the world. Many cognitive theorists assume that people with psychological disorders hold irrational beliefs that lead to emotional disturbances and maladaptive behaviors. For example, major depressive disorder is associated with a negative self-schema (see Chapter 13) and is exacerbated when people ruminate over their negative self-views (Dozois & Dobson, 2003; Sheppard & Teasdale, 2004). Yet, studies indicate that people with moderate levels of depression, termed *dysphoria,* may think more rationally and objectively than other people about themselves and the world (Taylor & Brown, 1988) and likely ruminate less. That is, if you are mentally healthy, you might be unrealistically optimistic and view the world through rose-colored glasses.

The Humanistic Viewpoint

As described in Chapter 13, psychologists who favor the *humanistic viewpoint,* most notably Carl Rogers and Abraham Maslow, stress the importance of self-actualization, which is the fulfillment of one's potential. According to Rogers and Maslow, psychological disorders occur when people fail to reach their potential, perhaps because others, especially their parents, discourage them from expressing their true desires, thoughts, and interests. This *conditional positive regard* may lead the person to develop a public self-image that is favorable to others but markedly different from his or her actual, private self. The distress caused by the failure to behave in accordance with one's own desires, thoughts, and interests can lead to the development of a psychological disorder.

The Sociocultural Viewpoint

One of the main influences on human diversity is culture, a factor that psychologists generally overlooked until the past 30 years. Psychologists who stress the importance of cultural influences on psychological disorders favor the *sociocultural viewpoint.* Instead of presuming that psychological disorders are identical in their prevalence and symptoms across cultures, these psychologists note that, though some disorders are universal, others are unique to particular cultures, and still others occur in most, but not all, cultures (Thakker, Ward, & Strongman, 1999). There is some cross-cultural universality in the symptoms of certain disorders, such as major depressive disorder and schizophrenia, but less universality in other disorders. Most psychological disorders show the influence of social, ethnic, and cultural factors (Draguns & Tanaka-Matsumi, 2003). For example, hunger, low-paid work under dangerous conditions, and chronic domestic violence are the social root of many mental health problems experienced by women worldwide. A recent study that examined over 5,500 Canadian Americans found an alarming relationship between

The Sociocultural Viewpoint

According to the sociocultural viewpoint, most psychological disorders show the influence of sociocultural factors, such as hunger.

Source: Stanislav Tiplyashin/ Shutterstock.com.

the lack of food and psychological disorders (Muldoon, Duff, Fielden, & Anema, 2013). Similarly, the social disruption, unemployment, and culture shock experienced by young male immigrants are risk factors for substance abuse (López & Guarnaccia, 2000).

In some cases, behavior that is considered disordered in one culture is considered normal in another. For example, Ethiopian immigrants who exhibit an altered state called *Zar,* which is considered normal in Ethiopia, have mistakenly been diagnosed as suffering from obsessive-compulsive disorder and treated with drug therapy by Western psychiatrists (Grisaru, Budowski, & Witztum, 1997). Given the importance of culture, it is desirable that the diagnosis of psychological disorders consider the individual's cultural background (Parron, 1997).

Classification of Psychological Disorders

Over the centuries, authorities have distinguished a variety of psychological disorders, each with its own set of symptoms. In 1883 German psychiatrist Emil Kraepelin (1856–1926) devised the first modern classification system (Weber & Engstrom, 1997). Today, the most widely used system of classification of psychological disorders is the fifth edition of the *Diagnostic and Statistical Manual of Mental Disorders (DSM-5),* published by the American Psychiatric Association. The *DSM-5* and all of its previous iterations have helped health care practitioners create a standardized system of diagnosing psychological disorders. This is useful because when a person is diagnosed with, for example, generalized anxiety disorder, it means approximately the same thing to different other practitioners. On a more practical level, a diagnosis from this manual helps guide important decisions about what insurers cover and what special services a child might receive in school.

The DSM

The *DSM-5,* published in 2013, is a revised version of the *DSM-IV,* which was published in 1994 (and revised in 2007 as the *DSM-IV-TR*). They were preceded by the *DSM-III,* which was published in 1980 (and revised in 1987 as the *DSM-III-R*), the *DSM-II,* which was published in 1968, and the *DSM-I* in 1952. The *DSM* provides a means of communication among mental health practitioners, offers a framework for research on the causes of disorders, and helps practitioners diagnose and choose the best treatment for particular disorders (Clark, Watson, & Reynolds, 1995).

The *DSM-I* and the *DSM-II,* which were based on psychoanalytic theory, divided disorders into neuroses and psychoses. A neurosis involved anxiety, moderate disruption of social relations, and relatively good contact with reality. A psychosis involved thought disturbances, bizarre behavior, severe disruption of social relations, and relatively poor contact with reality. The *DSM-III, DSM-IV,* and *DSM-5* dropped this psychoanalytic orientation and, consistent with the biopsychosocial model, consider the interaction of biological, psychological, and social factors in the diagnosis of psychological disorders.

The *DSM-IV* provided five axes for diagnosing psychological disorders. Axis I contained 16 major categories of psychological disorders. Axis II contained personality disorders and mental retardation, or as described in Chapter 10, intellectual disability disorder. Axis III contained medical conditions that might affect the person's psychological disorder. Axis IV contained social and environmental sources of stress that the person has been under recently. And Axis V contained an estimate of the person's level of functioning. The *DSM-5* introduced a major change in this system, noting that the multi-axial system was not necessary for the diagnosis of mental disorders. Instead, the *DSM-5* has adopted the World Health Organization's International Classification of Diseases (ICD). In addition to the ICD, clinicians must consider the psychological and environmental factors that an individual must face (Axis IV of the *DSM-TR*), and the World Health Organization's Disability Assessment Schedule (WHODAS) has been included—subject to future research—to replace Axis V.

Though the *DSM-5* has been recently published, there is a growing body of research examining its reliability and validity. The reliability of a diagnosis refers to the extent to which different evaluators make the same diagnosis. For example, will several clinical psychologists independently agree that a given person has schizophrenia? The validity of a diagnosis refers to the extent to which a diagnosis is accurate. For example, does a person who has been diagnosed as schizophrenic truly have schizophrenia? Though some critics accuse the *DSM-5* of having poor reliability and unknown validity (Jones, 2012), research indicates that the *DSM-5* has good to very good reliability (Narrow et al., 2013). Research trials assessing the validity of the *DSM-5* and various disorders are currently ongoing. Nevertheless, many psychologists agree that the *DSM-5* is an improvement over the *DSM-IV-TR* (Freedman et al., 2013). Moreover, though the *DSM-5* has been praised for being more culturally sensitive and gender-fair in diagnosing disorders (Kupfer, Kuhl, & Regier, 2013), it also has been criticized for not going far enough in doing so (e.g., Hinton & Lewis-Fernández, 2011; Swartz, 2013).

One advancement is the noticeable shift in considering gender-related issues. In the *DSM-5*, gender identity disorder has been replaced with the diagnosis *gender dysphoria*, which refers to transgender individuals whose gender identity is not consistent with their sex assigned at birth (see Chapter 11). Other notable changes include an intent to avoid inconsistencies and improve reliability in the diagnosis of autism spectrum disorder (ASD). For example, Asperger's syndrome, which is characterized by impaired social interactions, was once a subcategory of ASD. Now, it is diagnosed as ASD. As the *DSM* is a "living document," it is likely to change again in the future. This is evidenced by the purposeful change from Roman numerals to Arabic numbers. The next version will be *DMS-5.1* and so on.

Criticisms of the Diagnosis of Psychological Disorders

Despite the widespread reliance on the *DSM,* some professionals criticize the potential negative effects of the diagnosis of psychological disorders. This critical attitude was inspired in part by the classic study on the effects of diagnosis that is described in the "Psychology Versus Common Sense" feature.

Section Review: Characteristics of Psychological Disorders

1. How do the various viewpoints regarding the causes of psychological disorders differ from one another?

2. What is the difference between the cognitive rule and the volitional rule in regard to the insanity defense?

3. What is the main implication of Rosenhan's study of the diagnosis of psychological disorders?

Anxiety Disorders

anxiety disorder
A psychological disorder marked by persistent and unrealistic worry that disrupts everyday functioning.

You certainly have experienced anxiety when learning to drive, taking an important exam, or going on a first date. *Anxiety* is a feeling of apprehension accompanied by sympathetic nervous system arousal, which increases sweating, heart rate, and breathing rate and produces other physiological responses. Though anxiety is a normal and beneficial part of everyday life, warning us about potential threats, in **anxiety disorders,** it becomes intense, chronic, and disruptive of everyday functioning. About 33 percent of adult Americans suffer from anxiety disorders (Kessler, Petukhova, Sampson, Zaslavsky, & Wittchen, 2012), which briefly include *generalized anxiety disorder, panic disorder,* and *phobias,* such as *specific phobias, social anxiety disorder,* and *agoraphobia.*

Generalized Anxiety Disorder

generalized anxiety disorder
An anxiety disorder marked by a persistent state of worry that exists independently of any particular stressful situation and often interferes with daily functioning.

Though people normally experience anxiety in response to stressful situations, the person with a **generalized anxiety disorder** is in a continual state of worry that exists independent of any particular stressful situation. In essence, anxiety becomes one of the individual's cardinal personality traits (Rapee, 1991).

Can Mentally Healthy People Be Recognized in a Mental Hospital?

This classic study was conducted by psychologist David Rosenhan (1973). He wondered whether we should accept the commonsense belief that mentally healthy people, complaining of symptoms of schizophrenia, could gain admission to a mental hospital and, once admitted, be discovered by the staff. Rosenhan had eight apparently healthy persons, including himself, gain admission to mental hospitals by calling the hospitals for appointments and then complaining of hearing voices that said "empty, hollow, thud." Hearing imaginary voices is a symptom of schizophrenia.

The eight pseudopatients were admitted to 12 hospitals in five states; their stays ranged from 7 to 52 days. During their stays, they behaved normally, did not complain of hearing voices, and sometimes wrote hundreds of pages of notes about their experiences in the hospitals. Though no staff members discovered that the pseudopatients were faking, several real patients accused them of being journalists or professors investigating mental hospitals. Rosenhan concluded that the diagnosis of psychological disorders is influenced more by preconceptions and by the setting in which we find a person than by any objective characteristics of the person. According to his findings, the commonsense belief that professionals can easily determine whether someone has a psychological disorder is mistaken.

But Rosenhan's study provoked criticism from psychiatrist Robert Spitzer, who helped revise the *DSM* and who felt that Rosenhan had misinterpreted the results (Spitzer, 1975). First, the admission of the pseudopatients to the mental hospitals was justified because people who report hearing imaginary voices may have schizophrenia. Second, people with schizophrenia can go long periods of time without displaying obvious symptoms of the disorder. Thus, the staff members who observed the pseudopatients during their stays had no reason to conclude that they were faking.

Nonetheless, the suggestion that the label "mentally ill" has the power to color our judgment of a person was supported by another study. When participants observed people labeled as mental patients (who actually were not) or similar people not given that label, they were more likely to rate the alleged mental patients as being "unusual" (Piner & Kahle, 1984).

The diagnosis of psychological disorders also can be influenced by social class and gender role stereotypes. In two studies, clinicians (Landrine, 1987) and undergraduate psychology students (Landrine, 1989) read descriptions of women and men of different social classes and were asked to assign diagnoses to each case. Participants were cautioned that the descriptions might be of normal cases. Patterns of diagnosis varied by gender and social class. For example, descriptions of lower-class men were more likely to be labeled antisocial, and descriptions of married middle-class women were more likely to be labeled dependent. Thus, both clinicians and undergraduate psychology students perceived gender and social class patterns associated with psychopathology.

The leading critic of diagnostic labels is psychiatrist Thomas Szasz (1960), who has gone so far as to call mental illness, including schizophrenia, a "myth" (Dammann, 1997). He believes that the behaviors that earn the label of mental illness are "problems in living." According to Szasz, labeling people as mentally ill wrongly blames their maladaptive functioning on an illness. He believes that the notion of mental illness is a two-edged sword. On the one hand, it might excuse heinous behavior committed by those labeled mentally ill. On the other hand, it might enable governments to oppress nonconformists by labeling them mentally ill. Szasz's claim that mental illness is a myth has provoked critical responses from other mental health practitioners (Bentall & Pilgrim, 1993), as indicated in the following comment:

> This myth has a seductive appeal for many persons, especially if they do not have to deal clinically with individuals and their families experiencing the anguish, confusion, and terror of schizophrenia. Unfortunately, informing schizophrenics and their relatives that they are having a mythological experience does not seem to be appreciated by them and is not particularly helpful. (Kessler, 1984, p. 380)

The many mental health professionals who helped create the *DSM-5* do not view the psychological disorders it describes as myths. Among the most important categories of psychological disorders are *anxiety disorders, somatic symptom and related disorders, dissociative disorders, major depressive disorder and related disorders, schizophrenic disorders, personality disorders,* and *developmental disorders.* Figure 14-2 indicates the prevalence of several important psychological disorders in the United States.

Can Mentally Healthy People Be Recognized in a Mental Hospital?   *continued*

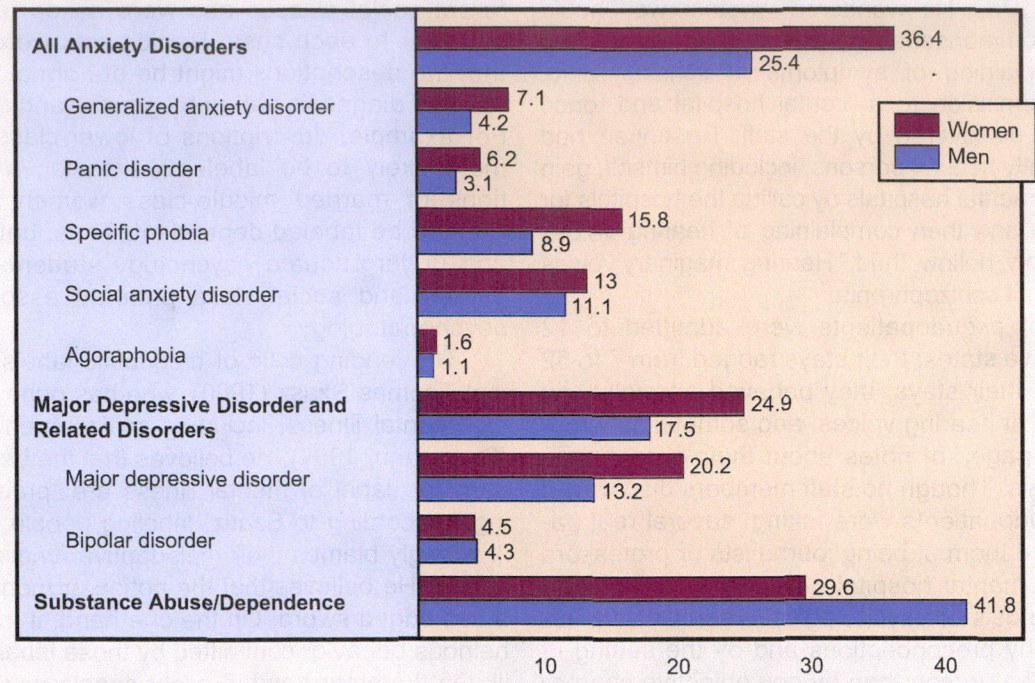

FIGURE 14-2 Prevalence of Some Major Psychological Disorders in the United States

Source: Data from Kessler, R. C., Berglund, P. A., Demler, O., Jin, R., Merikangas, K. R., and Walters, E. E. (2005). Lifetime prevalence and age-of-onset distributions of *DSM-IV* disorders in the National Comorbidity Survey Replication (NCS-R). *Archives of General Psychiatry, 62* (6), 593–602.

Characteristics of Generalized Anxiety Disorder

The central feature of generalized anxiety disorder is extreme and habitual worry. The person worries constantly about almost everything, including work, school, finances, and social relationships. About 6 percent of Americans suffer from generalized anxiety disorder sometime during their lifetime, with the disorder being more common in women than in men (Kessler, Petukhova, Sampson, Zaslavsky, & Wittchen, 2012). This gender difference emerges as early as age 6, with girls being twice as likely as boys to experience an anxiety disorder (Lewinsohn, Gotlib, Lewinsohn, Seeley, & Allen, 1998), though the size of the gender difference varies by culture (Gater et al., 1998). The experience of anxiety appears to be universal, though there are cross-cultural differences in symptoms and their meaning. For example, a common expression of anxiety among Latinos is *ataque de nervios,* characterized by fear, trembling, and bodily symptoms. These symptoms usually are related to disrupted family relationships and are socially acceptable manifestations of feeling "out of control" (López & Guarnaccia, 2000).

Causes of Generalized Anxiety Disorder

What accounts for the development of a generalized anxiety disorder? Biopsychological researchers look to heredity, neurochemistry, and brain activity for answers. The children of parents who suffer from anxiety disorders are seven times more likely to develop them than are children whose parents do not. Samuel Turner, a leading anxiety researcher, spent years examining the factors that make people prone to anxiety disorders. His early work suggested a possible genetic basis for anxiety disorders; however, it did not permit us to conclude that anxiety disorders are affected more by heredity than by life experiences (Turner, Beidel, & Costello, 1987). Turner's later work focused on parenting behavior as he studied the children of anxious and nonanxious parents. His results suggested that the "emotional climate" that anxious parents create in families may contribute to the increased risk for the development of anxiety disorders in children (Turner, Beidel, Roberson-Nay, & Tervo, 2003; Turner, Beidel, & Roberson-Nay, 2005). Stronger evidence for a hereditary basis of anxiety disorders comes from research that shows a higher concordance rate for identical twins, who share 100 percent of their genes, than for fraternal twins, who typically share 50 percent of their genes (Torgersen, 1983). The *concordance rate* is the likelihood that a person will develop a psychological disorder given that a particular relative has that disorder. Moreover, the heritability of generalized anxiety disorder appears to be the same in women and men (Hettema, Prescott, & Kendler, 2001).

Whether it is affected by heredity or not, generalized anxiety disorder is associated with an unusually strong stress response (Brawman-Mintzer & Lydiard, 1997) and unstable physiological responses, such as breathing rate (Wilhelm, Trabert, & Roth, 2001). Some genes also have been implicated in the development of anxiety disorder. For example, researchers have studied the role of the *MANEA* gene in the development of both panic disorder and social anxiety disorder (Jensen et al., 2014). These studies may lead to effective treatments tailored to the unique genetic makeup of people with anxiety disorders.

Psychoanalytic theorists view anxiety as the consequence of id impulses that threaten to overwhelm ego controls. Cognitive-behavioral theorists find that people with generalized anxiety disorder are more prone than other people to worry about finances, personal competence and achievement, and interpersonal relations. Moreover, they experience more distress over their worries because they perceive their worries to be more threatening and less controllable than other people do (Hazlett-Stevens & Craske, 2003). This continual worrying places the person in a constant fight-or-flight state of arousal. There is evidence that the higher prevalence of generalized anxiety disorder among women is due to the stress they experience related to gender role demands, interpersonal relationships, and adverse life events (Shear, Feske, & Greeno, 2000). Humanistic psychologists believe that anxiety arises from a discrepancy between the actual self and the ought self (Strauman & Higgins, 1988), as described in Chapter 13.

According to the humanistic perspective, people might develop generalized anxiety disorder when they feel that they have failed to live up to desirable standards of behavior. Despite the differing viewpoints of cause and effect, generalized anxiety disorders respond well to both antidepressant treatments such as Prozac (Baldwin, Woods, Lawson, & Taylor 2011) and cognitive-behavioral therapy (Mitte, 2005). In fact, Mitte (2005) found that overall dropout rates were lower for individuals receiving cognitive behavioral therapy, which suggests that this treatment is better tolerated by patients than drug therapy alone.

Panic Disorder

In describing the motivation for his painting *The Scream,* Norwegian artist Edvard Munch (1863–1944) remarked, "I was walking . . . and I felt a loud, unending scream piercing nature" (Blakemore, 1977, p. 155). The image in this painting conveys the intense anxiety and terror characteristic of a *panic attack,* which is a symptom of **panic disorder**.

Characteristics of Panic Disorder

Another refinement of the *DSM-5* is that panic disorder is no longer linked to agoraphobia and is considered to be its own anxiety disorder. Panic disorder is marked by sudden attacks of overwhelming anxiety, accompanied by dizziness, trembling, cold sweats, heart palpitations, shortness of breath, fear of dying, and fear of going crazy. People

panic disorder An anxiety disorder marked by sudden, unexpected attacks of overwhelming anxiety, often associated with the fear of dying or "losing one's mind."

experiencing panic attacks also might feel detached from their own bodies or feel that other people are not real. These panic attacks are now categorized as expected and unexpected. Though panic attacks usually last only a few minutes, they are so distressing that more people seek therapy for panic disorder than for any other psychological disorder (Boyd, 1986). About 2 percent of Americans experience panic disorder sometime in their lives, with women more likely to develop the disorder than men (Kessler et al., 2012), though there is evidence that men are less willing to report experiencing panic (Birchall, 1995). And symptoms of panic disorder differ by culture and gender. Women tend to report more respiratory symptoms, which have been attributed to gender differences in sensitivity to carbon dioxide levels (Sheikh, Leskin, & Klein, 2002). Japanese people with panic disorder, for example, show different patterns of symptoms than Americans with panic disorder (Shioiri, Murashita, Kato, & Fujii, 1996). Moreover, Taiwan has a much lower prevalence of panic disorder than does the United States (Weissman, Bland, Canino, & Faravelli, 1997).

Causes of Panic Disorder

Biopsychological researchers note that panic disorder runs in families, with a concordance rate among family members of about 20 percent (Crowe, 1990). The concordance rate is higher for identical twins than for fraternal twins (Stein, Jang, & Livesley, 1999). Again, these findings strongly suggest, but do not guarantee, a genetic predisposition for panic disorder. As mentioned earlier, a biopsychological factor that has gained substantial support is that people with panic disorder are hypersensitive to carbon dioxide levels in their blood. Instead of responding by breathing normally to reduce their carbon dioxide levels, they might at times respond as though they are being suffocated or hyperventilating—and experience a panic attack (van Beek et al., 2003). As discussed earlier, the *MANEA* gene has been found to have a relationship to the development of both panic disorder and social anxiety disorder (Jensen et al., 2014). Likewise, an imbalance of serotonin activity could be related to panic symptoms. A number of studies have linked variations in the enzyme *tryptophan hydroxylase 2*, which controls serotonin, to anxiety disorders, often in a gender-specific way. Researchers have recently studied men and women with panic disorder and found that women are particularly sensitive to the effect of tryptophan hydroxylase 2 (Maron et al., 2007).

Psychoanalytic theorists have had relatively little to say about panic disorder. Psychoanalytic theorists who consider panic disorder look to early childhood experiences as influences on its development (Vuksic-Mihaljevic, Mandic, Barkic, & Mrdenovic, 1998). For example, a meta-analysis of 25 studies found that adults with panic disorder tend to have experienced separation anxiety in childhood (Kossowsky et al., 2013). Separation anxiety evoked by recalling an important person in one's life whom one has lost is especially likely to instigate a panic attack (Horesh, Amir, Kedem, Goldberger, & Kotler, 1997). According to cognitive theorists, panic disorder results from faulty thinking. People prone to panic disorders engage in catastrophic thinking, misattributing physical symptoms of arousal caused by factors such as caffeine, exercise, mild stress, or emotional memories, to a serious mental or physical disorder (Schmidt, Lerew, & Jackson, 1999).

Phobias

phobia An anxiety disorder marked by excessive or inappropriate fear.

The word **phobia** comes from *Phobos,* the name of the Greek god of fear, and refers to the experience of excessive or inappropriate fear. People with a phobia realize that their fear is irrational but cannot prevent it.

Characteristics of Phobias

A subcategory of anxiety disorders includes phobias. Phobias can have maladaptive consequences. People with *claustrophobia* (the fear of enclosed places), for example, are sometimes too terrified to undergo diagnostic MRIs, which might require them to lie still in a cylinder for up to an hour or more (Kilborn & Labbe, 1990). The major classes of phobias are *specific phobias, social anxiety disorder,* and *agoraphobia.*

Specific Phobias A **specific phobia** is an intense, irrational fear of a specific object or situation, such as a spider or a height. Former television football announcer John Madden's flying phobia was so intense that to broadcast a game, he crossed the country in his own bus, even when forced to travel between the East Coast and the West Coast. In another case, a 14-year-old boy feared crickets so much that his fear hampered his academic performance (Jones & Friman, 1999). People with specific phobias might go to great lengths to avoid the object or situation they fear. Specific phobias are more common among women than men, and men and women differ in the likelihood of specific phobias and have a lifetime prevalence of over 15.8% (Kessler et al., 2012). Table 14-2 lists common specific phobias.

specific phobia A phobia of a specific object or situation.

Social Anxiety Disorder People with a **social anxiety disorder,** which affects about 12 percent of Americans (Kessler et al., 2012), fear social evaluation, which might lead them to avoid playing sports, making telephone calls, or performing music in public (Cox & Kenardy, 1993). The most common social anxiety disorder is the fear of public speaking (Kessler, Stein, & Berglund, 1998). Women are more likely than men to have social anxiety disorder, and women also experience more severe symptoms (Turk et al., 1998). This gender difference holds true across different cultures, as shown in a study that compared social anxiety disorder rates in Korea, Canada, Puerto Rico, and the United States (Weissman et al., 1996).

social anxiety disorder A phobia of situations that involve social evaluation.

A large proportion of the social anxiety disorders reported by East Asians comprises a culture-specific category: offensive social anxiety disorders. One type of offensive social anxiety disorder common among Koreans, for example, is characterized by a fear of being with others due to a pervasive sense that one's body odors are offensive to others (Lee & Oh, 1999). *Taijin kyofusho* is a Japanese form of social anxiety disorder that reflects an unreasonable fear of offending others with inappropriate behavior or an offensive physical appearance (Nagata et al., 2003). These cultural differences have been attributed to the collectivist orientation of Asian culture. Moreover, social anxiety disorder is more common among individuals with a collectivist orientation, regardless of culture (Dinnel, Kleinknecht, & Tanaka-Matsumi, 2002).

Social anxiety disorder seems to have its origins in childhood, with shy children more prone than outgoing children to develop social anxiety disorder in adulthood (Stein, Chavira,

TABLE 14-2 Specific Phobias

Phobia	Feared Object or Situation
Acrophobia	High places
Ailurophobia	Cats
Algophobia	Pain
Aquaphobia	Water
Arachnophobia	Spiders
Astraphobia	Lightning storms
Claustrophobia	Enclosed places
Cynophobia	Dogs
Hematophobia	Blood
Monophobia	Being alone
Mysophobia	Dirt
Nyctophobia	Darkness
Ocholophobia	Crowds
Thanatophobia	Death
Triskaidekaphobia	Number 13
Xenophobia	Strangers
Zoophobia	Animals

Acrophobia

A person with acrophobia might feel anxiety just looking at this photograph of a roller coaster.
Source: SIHASAKPRACHUM/ Shutterstock.com.

& Jang, 2001). Social anxiety disorder is maintained by increased self-focused attention in feared situations (Spurr & Stopa, 2003). Social anxiety disorder also is associated with perfectionism, making the person overly concerned with being evaluated (Rosser, Issakidis, & Peters, 2003). You have gotten a hint of this experience if you have noticed your mouth becoming dry, your palms sweating, and your heart beating strongly just before making an oral presentation in class.

Agoraphobia In 1992 former star football player Earl Campbell sat in his car listening to country music when suddenly he felt terrified, his heart racing out of control. After being hospitalized for a week for a suspected heart attack, he was diagnosed instead as suffering from panic disorder. His fear of having a panic disorder in public led him to stay home, afraid to venture outside even to check his mailbox. He had developed *agoraphobia.*

agoraphobia A fear of being in public, usually because the person fears the embarrassment of a panic attack.

Agoraphobia, which affects about 3 percent of Americans (Kessler et al., 2012), is the fear of being in public. The word *agoraphobia,* from the Greek term for "fear of the market-place," was coined in 1871 to describe the cases of four men who feared being in a city plaza (Boyd & Crump, 1991). People with agoraphobia typically have a history of panic attacks. They tend to avoid public places because they fear the embarrassment of having witnesses to their panic attacks (Amering et al., 1997). This fear makes them avoid parties, sporting events, shopping malls, and other public places. In extreme cases, the person can become a prisoner in her or his own home—terrified to leave for any reason. Because agoraphobia disrupts every aspect of the victim's life, including potentially destroying intimate relationships (McCarthy & Shean, 1996), it is a phobia commonly seen by psychotherapists.

Causes of Phobias

Phobias have been the target of much scientific research into their causes. Whereas many researchers search for biological factors, many others look to possible psychological factors.

Biopsychological Factors Some people have a biological, possibly hereditary, predisposition to develop phobias. One bit of evidence for this finding is that identical twins have a higher concordance rate than do fraternal twins (Lichtenstein & Annas, 2000). Moreover, research on the human genome has found that specific genetic markers are associated with the tendency to develop specific phobias (Gelernter et al., 2003); however, the genetic correlations are modest at best. According to psychologist Martin Seligman (1971), evolution has biologically prepared us to develop phobias of potentially dangerous natural objects or situations, such as fire, snakes, and heights. Whereas infants have an innate fear of loud startling noises, no one is born with a phobia; phobias develop over time. Early humans who were predisposed to avoid these dangers were more likely to survive long enough to reproduce and, as a result, pass on this predisposition to their offspring in their genes. This hypothesis might explain why phobias that involve potentially dangerous natural objects, such as snakes, are more persistent than phobias that involve usually safe, natural objects, such as flowers (McNally, 1987).

Agoraphobia

People with agoraphobia suffer from an excessive and debilitating fear of being in public places or open spaces.
Source: Mr.Tobin/Shutterstock. com.

Though some researchers question the existence of inherited preparedness to fear specific objects or situations (de Jong & Merckelbach, 1997), there is experimental research supporting it. For example, a recent twin study that compared the heritability of different phobias found that heredity had a moderate effect on fear of animals, whereas heredity had no effect on common situational fears (Skre, Onstad, Torgersen, Lygren, & Kringlen, 2000). The idea that we are genetically predisposed to fear certain things has some commonality with Jung's concept of archetypes (see Chapter 13).

Psychological Factors Psychoanalytic theorists trace the origin of phobias to early childhood experiences. For example, agoraphobia has been associated with separation anxiety in childhood (Hayward, Killen, & Taylor, 2003). The psychoanalytic viewpoint holds that phobias might be caused by anxiety displaced from a feared object or situation onto another object or situation. By displacing the anxiety, the person keeps the true source unconscious. The classic psychoanalytic case is that of little Hans, a 5-year-old boy who was afraid to go outside because of his fear of horses. Sigmund Freud attributed the phobia to inadequate resolution of the Oedipus complex. Freud claimed that Hans had an incestuous desire for his mother and a fear of being punished for it by being castrated by his father. Hans displaced his fear from his father to horses, permitting him to keep his incestuous feelings unconscious.

Behavioral psychologists view phobias as learned responses to life situations. Phobias develop because of learning, either through personal experience, observation of people with phobias, or exposure to information about fearful situations. Little Hans's phobia, for example, might have been attributable to a horrifying incident that he witnessed in which horses harnessed to a wagon fell and then struggled to get to their feet (Stafford-Clark, 1965). More recently, a study found that children's dog phobias arose, as predicted, from personal experience with dogs, observation of other people's experiences with dogs, or exposure to information about the dangerousness of dogs (King, Clowes-Hollins, & Ollendick, 1997).

Cognitive-behavioral explanations of phobias implicate self-efficacy (see Chapter 13). That is, people with phobias may believe that they lack the ability to cope with stressful situations. Research findings indicate that a person's feeling of self-efficacy in regard to the feared situation is a more important factor in phobias than is the person's anxiety level or perception of danger (Williams, Turner, & Peer, 1985). Cognitive explanations of phobias also stress the importance of exaggerated beliefs about the harmfulness of the fear-inducing object or situation (Thorpe & Salkovskis, 1995). For example, people with social anxiety disorder are more vigilant to potential social threats, such as angry faces (Mogg, Philippot, & Bradley, 2004); are more pessimistic about social events (Taylor & Wald, 2003); are more likely to be overly critical of their social behavior; and ruminate about their self-perceived social blunders (Abbott & Rapee, 2004). One form of cognitive-behavioral therapy that effectively treats patients with phobias is virtual reality therapy. Virtual reality therapy has been found to be as effective as group exposure therapy (Anderson et al., 2013). This technology is especially useful for phobias that are easy to simulate, such as fear of heights or elevators.

Virtual Reality Therapy

Virtual reality therapy can safely expose patients to the source of their phobias.
Source: Syda Productions/ Shutterstock.com.

Section Review: Anxiety Disorders

1. Why does agoraphobia prompt people to seek therapy more than any other phobia does?

2. How have psychologists connected the fear of suffocation and panic disorder?

Obsessive-Compulsive Disorder

Have you ever been unable to keep an advertising jingle from continually running through your mind? If so, you have experienced a mild *obsession,* which is a persistent, recurring thought. If you have ever repeatedly checked your alarm clock to make sure it was set the night before an early morning exam, you have experienced a mild *compulsion,* which is an action that you feel compelled to perform repeatedly. An obsession is a thought, and a compulsion is a behavior.

Characteristics of Obsessive-Compulsive Disorder

People whose obsessions and compulsions interfere with their daily functioning suffer from **obsessive-compulsive disorder (OCD).** Howie Mandel, a comedian and television host, became an unexpected mental health advocate in 2009 when he went public with his OCD diagnosis. His fist-bumps on the show *Deal or No Deal* may be his trademark, but they also are a hallmark of his symptoms of OCD. A very common feature of this disorder is irrational thoughts about contamination by germs. To avoid shaking hands, Mandel fist-bumps a person as an introduction. OCD is found in about 1 percent of the American population and is more common among women than men (Kessler et al., 2012). Cross-cultural research indicates that the prevalence of OCD is similar in Western and non-Western cultures (Al-Issa & Oudji, 1998), though symptoms may vary by culture (Lemelson, 2003). Obsessions can be self-perpetuating because the very act of trying to suppress a thought will make it more likely to enter consciousness (Wegner & Schneider,

obsessive-compulsive disorder (OCD) An anxiety disorder in which the person has recurrent, intrusive thoughts (obsessions) and recurrent urges to perform ritualistic actions (compulsions).

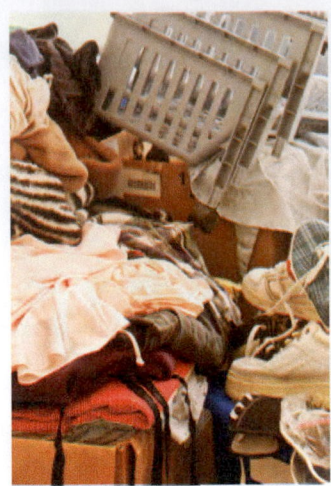

OCD and Hoarding

One potential symptom of OCD is hoarding. This is manifested by people who have difficulty discarding items that appear to others to have little or no value.

Source: MCarper/Shutterstock. com.

2003). The most common compulsive symptoms include hoarding, checking, washing, cleaning, ordering, and desiring excessive symmetry (Leckman, Grice, Boardman, & Zhang, 1997). In some cases, OCD can be so intrusive that it has potentially dangerous consequences, as in the case of a U.S. Air Force missile launch officer whose symptoms kept him from performing his job efficiently (Bourgeois & Bunn, 1996).

Causes of Obsessive-Compulsive Disorder

Some people appear to have a hereditary predisposition to develop OCD; this finding is based in part on research showing that OCD runs in families (Nestadt et al., 2000). Stronger support for the hereditary basis of OCD comes from a study of more than 400 pairs of twins, which found that heredity plays a role in the development of obsessions (Clifford, Murray, & Fulker, 1984). Heredity might predispose certain people to OCD because of its effects on the brain. OCD is associated with low levels of the neurotransmitter serotonin (Pogarell et al., 2003). Functional MRI and PET scans have found that people with OCD have abnormally high activity in the frontal lobes (Ursu, Stenger, Shear, Jones, & Carter 2003; Greenberg et al., 2000). This brain activity might mean that compulsive behavior serves to prevent anxiety from rising to uncomfortable levels. You might have encountered this experience in a milder form when you felt anxious about schoolwork, spent an hour rearranging your room, and as a result, felt less anxious after doing so. Even more convincing evidence suggests a dysfunction between the frontal cortex and basal ganglia. Neuroimaging studies have focused on the size and function of this neural network (Saxena and Rauch, 2000). Though OCD is typically treated with antidepressants, neurosurgical interventions (such as lesions or deep brain stimulation) are used for intractable cases of OCD (Greenberg, Rauch, & Haber, 2010).

According to psychoanalysts, OCD is caused by fixation at the anal stage, resulting from harsh toilet training. This fixation causes repressed anger directed at the parents. The child defends against the guilt generated by these feelings of anger and later transgressions by repeating certain thoughts and actions over and over. The obsessions and compulsions often have symbolic meaning, as portrayed in Shakespeare's *Macbeth* when Lady Macbeth engages in compulsive hand washing after murdering King Duncan. A study found that people with OCD do, in fact, feel more guilt than people without OCD (Shapiro & Stewart, 2011). Children with OCD also tend to suffer from separation anxiety, which might contribute to the development of OCD symptoms to relieve their distress (de Mathis et al., 2013). This psychoanalytic viewpoint is disputed by biopsychosocial theorists. For example, there is evidence that cases of OCD that develop in childhood differ in several ways from cases that develop in adulthood. And some researchers believe that childhood OCD is related to a *tic disorder,* such as Tourette's syndrome (Eichstedt & Arnold, 2001).

Behavioral theorists view obsessions and compulsions as ways of avoiding anxiety-inducing situations. So you might compulsively write and rewrite lists of things to do instead of studying for an upcoming final exam. Cognitive theorists note that OCD symptoms might be responses to imagined threats. In one study, for example, compulsive washing, checking, and hoarding were associated with exaggerated perceptions of threat, and compulsive ordering was associated with perfectionism (Tolin, Woods, & Abramowitz, 2003). Humanistic theorists, like psychoanalytic theorists, note the relationship between guilt and OCD, but they stress the importance of the conscious, rather than the unconscious, experience of guilt. Despite these explanations for OCD, it is likely that biological, psychological, and social factors interact to initiate and maintain this devastating disorder.

Section Review: Obsessive-Compulsive Disorder

1. What is the relationship between obsessive-compulsive disorder and anxiety?

2. What psychological factors are associated with obsessive-compulsive disorder?

Somatic Symptom and Related Disorders

Somatic means "bodylike." A **somatic symptom and related disorder** is characterized by heightened bodily sensations, such as back pain, joint pain, headache, and abdominal symptoms in the absence of disease or injury (Rief, Hessel, & Braehler, 2001). In previous versions of the *DSM*, these symptoms were thought to be caused, instead, by psychological factors or symptoms that were unable to be traced to a medical cause. Now, in the *DSM-5*, a person can be diagnosed with somatic symptom and related disorders with or without a diagnosis of a coexisting medical condition. This change now allows people suffering from both somatic symptom and related disorders and another medical diagnosis to get the help they need. Somatic symptom and related disorders run in families. The concordance rate for identical twins is three times greater than for fraternal twins (about 30 percent versus about 10 percent). But it is unclear whether the higher concordance rate for identical twins simply reflects greater genetic similarity or greater similarity in their life experiences (Torgersen, 1986). One particular challenge is diagnosing this disorder in pediatric patients.

Somatic symptom and related disorders affect less than 1 percent of the population, with women more likely to report somatic symptoms than men (Kroenke & Spitzer, 1998). Somatic symptom and related disorders also are more common among certain cultural groups. Chinese Americans, for example, report more somatic symptoms than do European Americans (Hsu & Folstein, 1997). Because of cultural differences in what is considered normal behavior and what is considered a symptom of a disorder, the diagnosis of somatic symptom and related disorders might be unreliable across cultures (Brown & Lewis-Fernández, 2011; Ono & Janca, 1999). Somatic symptom and related disorders include *illness anxiety disorder* and *conversion disorder.*

> **somatic symptom and related disorder** A psychological disorder characterized by physical symptoms in the absence of disease or injury.

Illness Anxiety Disorder

A person with **illness anxiety disorder**, once called hypochondriasis, interprets the slightest physical change in her or his body as evidence of a serious illness. To the person with illness anxiety disorder, a headache might indicate a brain tumor, and indigestion might signal an imminent heart attack. People with this disorder are also focused on the idea of being sick.

> **illness anxiety disorder** A somatic symptom and related disorder in which the person interprets the slightest physical changes as evidence of a serious illness.

Characteristics of Illness Anxiety Disorder

Many people with illness anxiety disorder go from physician to physician, searching for the one who will finally diagnose the disease that they are sure is causing their symptoms. Some medical students experience a mild form of illness anxiety disorder in the so-called "medical student disease," in which a mere cough might convince them they have lung cancer. As you read about the various psychological disorders, you should beware of developing a similar "psychology student syndrome," in which you interpret your normal variations in mood, thinking, and behavior as symptoms of a psychological disorder. Of course, if your symptoms become distressing, prolonged, or disruptive to your life, you should consider professional counseling.

Causes of Illness Anxiety Disorder

What accounts for illness anxiety disorder? Recent evidence demonstrates a remarkable similarity in the brain circuitry for people with illness anxiety disorder, OCD, and panic disorder. In one study, participants with all three anxiety disorders and a healthy control group were asked to perform a Tower of London Task, a widely used task of attentional and cognitive control, while undergoing fMRI scans. The researchers found reduced activity in the frontal cortex and basal ganglia in the anxiety disorder group versus the healthy control group (van den Heuvel et al., 2011). Psychoanalytic theorists see it as a defense against becoming aware of feelings of guilt or low self-esteem. Support for this view comes from the close association between fear of death, fear of separation, and illness anxiety disorder (Noyes, Stuarat, Longley, Langbehn, & Happel, 2002). Behavioral theorists point not only to positive reinforcement, such as being lavished with attention, and negative reinforcement, such as relief from work responsibilities, but also to parental modeling of bodily symptoms (Watt & Stewart, 2000).

Cognitive theorists note that people who develop illness anxiety disorder fear disease so much that they process normal physical symptoms through biased schema, thus noticing or exaggerating the slightest ones. In fact, this cognitive bias might generalize to other life experiences (Schwenzer & Mathiak, 2011).One study found that people with illness anxiety disorder were more likely to interpret ambiguous normal physical symptoms as indicative of disease (Schaefer, Egloff, & Witthöft, 2012). Explanations consistent with humanistic psychology see illness anxiety disorder as a form of self-handicapping. People with illness anxiety disorder, for example, are more likely to complain of symptoms when they know they are going to be evaluated (Smith, Snyder, & Perkins, 1983). There is evidence supporting each of these views, but none is clearly superior to the others.

Conversion Disorder

A girl whose legs were "paralyzed" for a year without any physical cause began walking again after simply being given biofeedback that provided her with evidence of activity in her leg muscles (Klonoff & Moore, 1986). She had been suffering from a **conversion disorder**.

Characteristics of Conversion Disorder

In typical cases, the person with conversion disorder experiences muscle paralysis, such as difficulty in speaking, or sensory loss, such as an inability to feel an object on the skin. But the apparently lost function is actually intact. Physicians suspect the presence of a conversion disorder when patients display *la belle indifference*—a lack of concern about their symptoms. As illustrated in Figure 14-3, a conversion disorder might also be diagnosed by a physician who notices that a patient's symptoms are anatomically impossible.

Causes of Conversion Disorder

Theories explaining conversion disorder have a long and sometimes bizarre history. An Egyptian papyrus dating from 1900 B.C. attributed the disorder, which was believed to be limited to women, to a wandering uterus (Jones, 1980). Hippocrates accepted this explanation and called the disorder *hysteria,* from the Greek word for "uterus." Because Hippocrates believed that the uterus wandered when a woman was sexually frustrated, he prescribed marriage as a cure. The wandering-womb view lost credibility in the face of 19th-century science.

In the late 19th century, Sigmund Freud claimed that hysteria resulted from anxiety generated by repressed sexual impulses and conflicts (Huopainen, 2002). The anxiety was converted into symbolic physical symptoms, such as paralyzed legs, that enabled a woman to avoid acting on her sexual impulses. Freud called such disorders *conversion hysteria.* Today, to avoid the implication that the disorder is strictly a female problem, it is called *conversion disorder.* There is evidence that severe childhood trauma, such as sexual or physical abuse, might contribute to the development of a conversion disorder (Roelofs, Keijsers, Hoogduin, Naering, & Moene, 2002).

Early biopsychological researchers conducted a case study of a 45-year-old woman with limb paralysis. They concluded that her paralysis might be associated with reduced activity in brain regions that stimulate movement in the affected limb and with increased activity in brain regions that inhibit movement of the affected limb (Marshall, Halligan, Fink, Wade, & Frackowiak, 1997). A more recent study using fMRI found a smaller left thalamus among participants with conversion disorder (Nicholson et al., 2014). As discussed in Chapter 3, the thalamus is a brain structure involved in relaying and integrating motor output (see Chapter 3). This study and only a handful of others indicate the brain structures that might be involved in conversion disorder.

Behavioral theorists assume that somatic symptom and related disorders occur because they are reinforced by increased attention or a reduction in responsibilities. Children may be prone to somatic symptom and related disorders after they observe other members of their family being reinforced for their physical symptoms (Mullins & Olson, 1990). And, as in the case of illness anxiety disorder, humanistic theorists may see conversion disorder as a form of self-handicapping. Whereas there is evidence supporting each of these views, none is clearly superior to the others.

conversion disorder
A somatic symptom and related disorder in which the person exhibits motor or sensory loss or the alteration of a physiological function without any apparent physical cause.

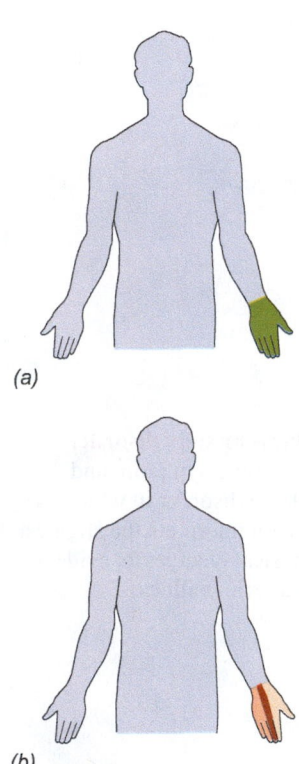

(a)

(b)

FIGURE 14-3
Conversion Disorder

(a) A person with "glove anesthesia" will complain of numbness in the hand from the wrist to the tips of the fingers. This condition is easily diagnosed as a conversion disorder because damage to the sensory nerves of the hand will not produce this pattern of sensory loss. *(b)* Different areas of the hand are served by the ulnar, radial, and median nerves. If a given nerve is injured, there will be numbness in only a portion of the hand. For example, damage to the ulnar nerve produces numbness only along the outer edge of the hand.

Section Review: Somatic Symptom and Related Disorders

1. How would you determine whether a person was displaying a somatic symptom related disorder?

2. What is "la belle indifference" in regard to conversion disorder?

Dissociative Disorders

In a **dissociative disorder**, the person's conscious mind loses access to certain of his or her thoughts, feelings, and memories. The dissociative disorders include *dissociative amnesia, dissociative fugue,* and *dissociative identity disorder.* About 3 percent of North Americans show symptoms of dissociative disorders (Waller & Ross, 1997). Though dissociative symptoms appear in all cultures, they are not always considered signs of a psychological disorder. The diagnosis of dissociative disorders should be made within the individual's cultural context (Lewis-Fernandez, 1998).

dissociative disorder
A psychological disorder in which thoughts, feelings, and memories become separated from conscious awareness.

Dissociative Amnesia and Fugue

While being interrogated about his assassination of Robert F. Kennedy in 1968, Sirhan Sirhan was unable to recall the incident (Bower, 1981). He apparently suffered from **dissociative amnesia**, the inability to recall personally significant memories (Coons & Milstein, 1992). In September 1980, a young woman was found wandering in Birch State Park in Florida. She could not recall who she was or where she was from. After an appearance on a nationally televised morning talk show, she was reunited with her family in Illinois. She suffered from **dissociative fugue**, which is marked by the memory loss characteristic of dissociative amnesia as well as the loss of one's identity and fleeing from one's prior life. The word *fugue* comes from the Latin word meaning "to flee."

dissociative amnesia
The inability to recall personally significant memories.

dissociative fugue Memory loss characteristic of dissociative amnesia as well as the loss of one's identity and fleeing from one's prior life.

Characteristics of Dissociative Amnesia and Fugue

In dissociative amnesia, the lost memories are usually related to a traumatic event, such as witnessing a catastrophe. But the lost memories typically return within hours or days. However, prolonged or repeated traumas may be more likely to lead to dissociative amnesia, especially if they occur in childhood (Joseph, 1997). In dissociative fugue, the person may adopt a new identity, only to emerge from the fugue state days, months, or years later, recalling nothing that happened during the intervening period (Kopelman, Christensen, Puffett, & Stanhope, 1994). In one case a 15-year-old girl assumed a new identity, spoke a foreign language she had learned in school, adopted new dress and grooming habits, and showed new skills, interests, and personality traits. Six days later she returned to her normal self (Venn, 1984).

Causes of Dissociative Amnesia and Fugue

The psychoanalytic viewpoint assumes that the repression of painful memories causes dissociative amnesia. This view was supported by a study in which people who viewed slides of normal and disfigured faces accompanied by verbal descriptions had poorer recall of the descriptions associated with the disfigured faces (Christianson & Nilsson, 1984). The most common factors implicated in dissociative amnesia are combat, adult rape, criminal acts, attempted suicide, disasters and accidents, and the violent death of a parent during childhood (Arrigo & Pezdek, 1997). People with dissociative amnesia experience *hypomnesia*—memory loss. There are often significant gaps in memories that involve the traumatic event.

There also is emerging evidence that biopsychological processes may contribute to dissociative amnesia. Researchers investigating the role of trauma in memory loss point to the impact of chronic elevations of stress hormones on impaired memory functioning.

In a recent study, 14 patients with dissociative amnesia that resulted from stressful or traumatic events submitted to PET scans. Researchers found decreased metabolism in the prefrontal cortex in this sample (Brand et al., 2009).The relationship of overwhelming stress and the resulting stress hormones to disrupted memory of traumatic events is complex, however, with some traumatized people displaying *hypermnesia*—stronger-than-normal recall of the traumatic event—and others displaying dissociative amnesia (Nadel & Jacobs, 1998). For example, a study of survivors of World War II concentration camps found that those who experienced traumatic events rarely reported dissociative amnesia (Merckelbach, Dekkers, Wessel, & Roefs, 2003), though this seems to be rare.

Dissociative Identity Disorder

In 1812 Benjamin Rush, the founder of American psychiatry, reported the following case involving a minister's wife:

> In her paroxysms of madness, she resumed her gay habits, spoke French, and ridiculed the tenets and practices of the sect to which she belonged. In the intervals of her fits, she renounced her gay habits, became zealously devoted to the religious principles and ceremonies of the Methodists, and forgot everything she did and said during the fits of her insanity. (Carlson, 1981, p. 668)

dissociative identity disorder
A dissociative disorder, formerly known as multiple personality disorder, in which the person has two or more distinct personalities that alternate with one another.

This case was one of the first well-documented cases of **dissociative identity disorder** (formerly called *multiple personality disorder*) in which a person has two or more distinct personalities that alternate with one another, as in the story of Dr. Jekyll and Mr. Hyde (Garcia, 1990).

Characteristics of Dissociative Identity Disorder

An individual's multiple personalities might include men and women, children and adults, and moral and immoral persons. A quiet, retiring, middle-aged woman might alternate with a flamboyant, promiscuous young man. Each personality might have its own way of walking, writing, and speaking (Hendrickson, McCarty, & Goodwin, 1990).

You might be familiar with two cases of dissociative identity disorder that were the subjects of popular movies: the story of Chris Cotner Sizemore, portrayed by Joanne Woodward in *The Three Faces of Eve,* and the story of Sybil Dorsett, portrayed by Sally Field in *Sybil.* According to her psychiatrists at the height of her disorder, Sizemore had 22 distinct personalities. Her personalities were finally integrated in 1975, and she went on speaking tours to discuss her experiences (Sizemore & Huber, 1988). Dissociative identity disorder has been popularized in more recent movies as well. In 2000, Jim Carrey starred in a slapstick comedy, *Me, Myself, and Irene,* in which he struggles with multiple personalities to control his shared body. More recently, in the 2014 movie, *The Lego Movie*, one Lego character played by Liam Neeson had two personalities—the good cop and bad cop.

Causes of Dissociative Identity Disorder

People who develop multiple personalities almost always have had traumatic experiences in early childhood, typically including sexual, physical, and emotional abuse, leading them to escape into their alternate personalities (Kluft, 1987). One longitudinal study followed 28 children with a history of sexual abuse and 71 nonabused children for one year. At the time of follow-up, the sexually abused children—especially boys—were far more likely to display dissociative symptoms, compared to the nonabused children (Bernier, Hébert, & Collin-Vézina, 2013). Psychoanalytic theorists believe that dissociative identity disorder arises from the child's impossible predicament—the need to escape intolerable abuse while maintaining emotional attachment to the abusive parent (Blizard, 1997).

Because of a marked increase in reported cases of dissociative identity disorder in the 1980s, some cognitive theorists believe that multiple personalities are being overdiagnosed and are simply the product of role playing. This possibility was demonstrated in a study in which students were hypnotized and asked to reveal the hidden personality of an accused multiple murderer called Harry Hodgins or Betty Hodgins. Eighty percent did so (Spanos, Weekes, & Bertrand, 1985). A more recent study found that hypnotized participants who were asked to role-play patients with dissociative identity disorder were more likely to report incidents of sexual or satanic ritual abuse than were hypnotized participants who were asked to role-play patients with depression or personal adjustment problems (Stafford & Lynn, 2002). This finding indicates that at least some reputed cases of dissociative identity disorder may be no more than role playing, whether intentional or not.

Despite these findings, a review of the research evidence found little support for the view that multiple personalities are induced by suggestions during psychotherapy (Gleaves, 1996). Clinical evidence supporting dissociative identity disorder comes from a survey of 425 psychotherapists, which found that most psychotherapists believe they had encountered a true case of dissociative personality disorder and that about one-third believed they had seen a feigned case (Cormier & Thelen, 1998). Even biopsychological evidence supports this view. One study found that when a middle-aged woman with dissociative identity disorder was switching from one personality to another, a functional MRI of her brain showed a distinctive pattern of changes in her hippocampus—the brain structure most important in memory for personal experiences and general information (Tsai, Condie, Wu, & Chang, 1999). In a well-designed fMRI study with multiple participants, results were similar. In this study, researchers were interested in adding to the biopsychological evidence that dissociative identity disorder is not an effect of fantasy or role playing. One group of female actors and another group of female patients with dissociative identity disorder were scanned while viewing neutral and angry faces. The actors had different neural and behavioral reactions, compared to the patients with dissociative identity disorder (Schlumpf et al., 2013). Researchers have also determined that there can be distinct physiological attributes for each personality, ranging from subjective reactions to trauma-related memories, cardiovascular responses, and cerebral activation patterns (Reinders et al., 2006). Taken together, it is possible that individuals with this disorder regulate emotions and memory differently than do healthy people.

Section Review: Dissociative Disorders

1. What kind of life experiences are common among people who develop dissociative identity disorder?

2. Why do some psychologists doubt the existence of dissociative identity disorder?

Major Depressive Disorder and Related Disorders

We all experience periodic fluctuations in our emotions, such as becoming briefly depressed after failing an exam or briefly elated after getting an A. But people with **major depressive disorder (MDD)** experience prolonged periods of extreme depression, often unrelated to their current circumstances, that disrupt their everyday functioning. Psychologists who study major depressive disorder also are interested in the causes and prevention of suicide.

major depressive disorder (MDD) A disorder marked by depression so intense and prolonged that the person may be unable to function in everyday life.

Major Depressive Disorder

People normally feel depressed after personal losses or failures; the frequency and intensity of depressive episodes vary from person to person. Since World War II, MDD has become 10 times more common among Americans (Seligman, 1989) and is considered the common cold of psychological disorders. Major depressive disorder is so prevalent and distressing that when Ann Landers (who wrote a syndicated advice newspaper column from 1943–2002) offered a pamphlet on MDD to her readers, 250,000 persons wrote away for it (Holden, 1986). People with major depressive disorder struggle to feel happiness from activities they once enjoyed. This disorder can be as debilitating as other chronic medical conditions.

Gender Differences in Depression

Women have higher rates of major depressive disorder, possibly due to rumination.

Source: Jochen Schoenfeld/Shutterstock.com.

Characteristics of Major Depressive Disorder

People with major depressive disorder experience extreme distress that disrupts their lives for weeks or months at a time. They commonly express despondency, helplessness, and loss of self-esteem. Their depressed mood is usually worse in the morning (Graw, Krauchi, Wirz-Justice, & Poldinger, 1991). They also may suffer from an inability to fall asleep or to stay asleep, lose their appetite or overeat, feel constantly fatigued, abandon good grooming habits, withdraw from social relations, lose interest in sex, find it difficult to concentrate, and fail to perform up to their normal academic and vocational standards. Symptoms also may vary by ethnicity (Avalon & Young, 2003) and culture (Yen, Robins, & Lin, 2000). About 13 percent of men and about 20 percent of women suffer from major depressive disorder (Kessler et al., 2005), and this gender difference is consistent across cultures (Weissman & Olfson, 1995). Why is MDD more common in women? The gender difference in the rates of major depressive disorder is complex and is not simply a difference in sex hormones. More likely, it is due to differences in how men and women process emotional events, especially the cognitive processes associated with rumination (see the "Research Process" feature).

Stress is a major trigger for the development of major depressive disorder as well as relapse. Usually, a series of events over time can lead to depressive states; however, large-scale disasters also can lead to increased rates of major depressive disorder. For example, in the 6-month period after the September 11, 2001, attacks on the World Trade Center in New York City, there was a 9 percent increase in major depressive disorder diagnoses in the New York City metropolitan area (Person, Tracy, & Galea, 2006). The prevalence of MDD is also higher among racial and ethnic minorities in the United States, who also are more likely than European Americans to report difficulties in meeting their basic needs (Plant & Sachs-Ericsson, 2004), and problems with acculturation or perceptions of racism (Liu & Lau, 2013). Higher rates of MDD have been reported among male college undergraduates who reported unwanted sexual contact (Larimer, Lydum, Anderson, & Turner, 1999) and a multiethnic sample of women who experienced child sexual abuse (Roosa, Reinholtz, & Angelini, 1999).

Causes of Major Depressive Disorder

What accounts for major depressive disorder? Each of the major viewpoints offers its own explanation.

The Biopsychological Viewpoint Major depressive disorder has a biological basis, apparently influenced by heredity. Identical twins have higher concordance rates for MDD (Lyons et al., 1998) than fraternal twins do. The fact that identical twins have the same genetic inheritance, whereas fraternal twins are no more genetically alike than ordinary siblings, provides evidence of a hereditary predisposition to develop mood disorders. But it is important to note that the effect of the environment, as well as behavioral predispositions, might be affected by hereditary tendencies. In fact, our sensitivity to stressful events, our ability to mobilize social support, and our choice of stressful environments to expose ourselves to are affected by genetic factors (Wade & Kendler, 2000). Nearly all people with major depressive disorder experience disturbances in their quality sleep time. Researchers have found that people with major depressive disorder enter REM sleep faster than healthy people (see Figure 14-4). However, reporting sleep disturbances does not replace a valid clinical judgment for diagnosis of major depressive disorder (Arfken et al., 2014). More recent studies have pointed to potential breathing abnormalities experienced during sleep. People with major depressive disorder exhibit higher rates of sleep-disordered breathing and sleep apnea, compared with healthy people (Cheng, Casement, Hoffmann, Armitage, & Deldin, 2013).

The hereditary predisposition to develop mood disorders might manifest itself by its effect on neurotransmitters. Major depressive disorder is related to abnormally low levels of *serotonin* and *norepinephrine* in the brain (Fava, 2003). One study measured levels of a chemical by-product of serotonin in the cerebrospinal fluid of people with MDD who had attempted suicide. Of those with above-average levels, none subsequently committed suicide. Of those with below-average levels, 20 percent subsequently did attempt suicide (Traskman, Asberg, Bertilsson, & Sjostrand, 1981). Many antidepressant drugs act by increasing levels of

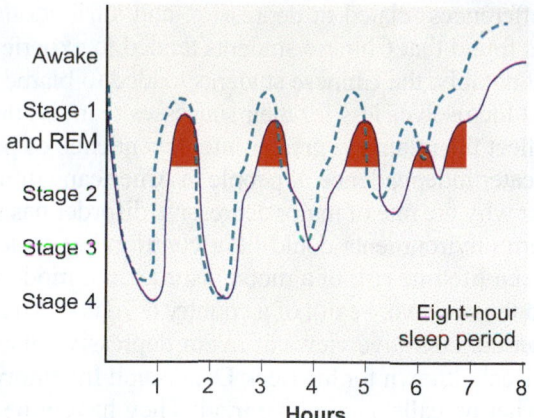

FIGURE 14-4

Sleep and Major Depressive Disorder

The solid line in the graph shows a normal sleep EEG pattern for healthy people. The dotted line shows an EEG pattern for people with major depressive disorder. People with depressed mood enter REM (rapid eye movement) sleep sooner and have more awakenings, compared to healthy people.

serotonin or norepinephrine (Nutt, 2002). Fluoxetine (Prozac), a well-known antidepressant, is a selective serotonin reuptake inhibitor (SSRI) and increases serotonin levels (see Chapter 15).

The Psychoanalytic Viewpoint The classic psychoanalytic view holds that the loss of a parent or rejection by a parent early in childhood predisposes the person to experience MDD whenever she or he suffers a personal loss, such as a job or a lover, later in life. Because these children feel that it is unacceptable to express anger at the lost or rejecting parent, they learn to turn their anger on themselves, creating feelings of guilt and self-loathing (Freud, 1917/1963). But research studies have found that this view cannot explain all cases of major depressive disorder. For example, both adults with and without MDD are equally likely to have suffered the loss of a parent in childhood (Crook & Eliot, 1980).

The Cognitive-Behavioral Viewpoint Behavioral explanations of major depressive disorder stress the role of learning and environmental factors. One of the most influential of these explanations is Peter Lewinsohn's reinforcement theory, which assumes that people with MDD lack the social skills needed to gain normal social reinforcement from others and might instead provoke negative reactions from them. For example, people with MDD stimulate less smiling, fewer statements of support, more unpleasant facial expressions, and more negative remarks from others than do healthy people (Gotlib & Robinson, 1982). Lewinsohn points out that the person with major depressive disorder is caught in a vicious cycle in which reduced social reinforcement leads to MDD, and depressed behavior further reduces social reinforcement (Youngren & Lewinsohn, 1980).

An influential cognitive-behavioral theory of major depressive disorder is based on Martin Seligman's attributional theory of depression. People with major depressive disorder attribute negative events in their lives to internal, stable, and global factors (Abramson, Seligman, & Teasdale, 1978). An internal factor is a characteristic of one's self rather than of the environment. A stable factor is unlikely to change. And a global factor affects almost all areas of one's life. This attributional style is associated with pessimistic expectations for the future (Peterson & Vaidya, 2001). Yet, many individuals rely on defensive pessimism—expecting the worst—to prepare themselves for negative outcomes (and, perhaps, to gain greater pleasure from positive outcomes). This approach is particularly prevalent in academic settings (Yamawaki, Tschanz, & Feick, 2004), as in the case of students who always claim that they have failed an exam—only to discover, more often than not, that they have done well.

Research on major depressive disorder has tended to find that, as predicted, people suffering from MDD make internal, stable, and global attributions for negative events in their lives (Sweeney, Anderson, & Bailey, 1986). For example, college freshmen who attribute their poor academic performance to internal, stable, and global factors, such as intelligence, become more depressed than do those who attribute their own poor academic performance to external, unstable, and specific factors, such as being assigned difficult teachers (Peterson & Barrett, 1987).

Seligman's attributional theory has also been supported in other cultures, such as Egypt, Turkey, and India (Aydin & Aydin, 1992; Duddu, Chaturvedi, & Isaac, 2003; Emam, 2013).

But there are cultural differences related to depression and attributions. A study of American and Chinese students found that Chinese students tended to experience MDD more than American students. Most notably, the Chinese students tended to blame themselves more for their failures and to credit themselves less for their successes than did the American students. This difference might reflect the relatively greater interdependence of people in Chinese culture and the relatively greater independence of people in American culture (Anderson, 1999). Researchers often wonder why the rate of major depressive disorder has increased. They often speculate that our modern environments could be a contributing factor. One review study found a correlation between lifetime risk of a mood disorder and modernization as measured by purchasing power and the national wealth of a country (Hidaka, 2012).

One of the most influential cognitive views of major depressive disorder is Aaron Beck's (1967) cognitive theory. Beck, known for his Beck Depression Inventory, has found that people with MDD exhibit what he calls a cognitive triad: They have a negative view of themselves, their current circumstances, and their future possibilities (Anderson & Skidmore, 1995). Moreover, this cognitive style appears to make people with major depressive disorder more reactive to day-to-day events than are healthy people (Nezlek & Gable, 2001). The cognitive triad is more common among people with MDD than among people with other psychological disorders (Jacobs & Joseph, 1997). This finding indicates that the triad is specific to major depressive disorder. The cognitive triad is maintained by the tendency of people with MDD to overgeneralize from negative events. For example, people with MDD tend to assume that a single failure means that they are incompetent (Carver & Ganellen, 1983).

As mentioned in the earlier section "Viewpoints on Psychological Disorders," people with psychological disorders may have more objective beliefs about themselves and the world than do people without such disorders. MDD researcher Lauren Alloy and her colleagues have found that this objectivity is especially true of people with major depressive disorder. Healthy people overestimate the likelihood of positive events and underestimate the likelihood of negative events (Crocker, Alloy, & Kayne, 1988). They also tend to have unrealistically positive self-evaluations (McKendree-Smith & Scogin, 2000). These findings lead to the surprising conclusion that if you have a healthy, positive mood, it might mean that you have an unrealistically positive view of reality and that people with MDD are more accurate in their view of their reality—so-called depressive realism (McKendree-Smith & Scogin, 2000). Nonetheless, some researchers have found that this difference between people with MDD and healthy people holds more in laboratory studies than in real-life emotional situations (Pacini, Muir, & Epstein, 1998). Moreover, depressive realism is more likely to be associated with only mild levels of depressed mood (Soderstrom, Davalos, & Vázquez, 2011).

Another cognitive view of major depressive disorder, put forth by Susan Nolen-Hoeksema, implicates continual rumination about one's plight. People who constantly think about and brood over the sad state of their lives—especially at night—experience more severe and more chronic depressed mood than do people who take action to improve their lives or who distract themselves by pursuing enjoyable activities (Takano & Tanno, 2011; Treynor, Gonzalez, & Nolen-Hoeksema, 2003). Nolen-Hoeksema believes that this rumination may explain why, after age 15, women are about twice as likely as men to experience MDD (Nolen-Hoeksema, 2001). Whereas women with MDD tend to ruminate about their plight, men with MDD tend to distract themselves from it (Nolen-Hoeksema, 2012). Thus, gender differences in MDD may reflect different cognitive coping strategies employed by men and women. In fact, Nolen-Hoeksema found that among college undergraduates, rumination was the single most important predictor of how long depressed mood would last. Because female undergraduates tended to ruminate more than male undergraduates, depressed women tended to have longer-lasting bouts of MDD (Butler & Nolen-Hoeksema, 1994). Moreover, rumination appears to contribute to a vicious cycle of uncertainty, chronic strain, and low sense of mastery—all contributing to depressive symptoms (Nolen-Hoeksema, Larson, & Grayson, 1999; Ward, Lyubomirsky, Sousa, & Nolen-Hoeksema, 2003).

The rumination hypothesis also has been found to be related to biological factors. Researchers have looked at the protein BDNF as a variable that contributes to a predisposition to rumination. One study identified a sample of adolescent girls at risk for developing major depressive disorder because they had a mother with a diagnosis of MDD. They assessed levels of BDNF, tendencies to ruminate, and depressive symptoms in mothers and daughters. The results indicated that mutations in BDNF levels predicted rumination and depressive symptoms in the young adolescent girls with mothers with major depressive disorder (Hilt, Sander, Nolen-Hoeksema, & Simen, 2007). Nolen-Hoeksema's response-style theory was tested in the study discussed in the "Research Process" feature.

The Humanistic Viewpoint Psychologists who favor the humanistic viewpoint attribute depression to the frustration of self-actualization. More specifically, people with major depressive disorder suffer from incongruence between their actual self and their ideal self (Weilage & Hope, 1999). The actual self is the person's subjective appraisal of his or her own qualities. The ideal self is the person's subjective judgment of the person he or she would like to become. If the actual self has qualities that are too distinct from those of the ideal self, the person becomes depressed.

The Sociocultural Viewpoint There are some cross-cultural commonalities in the manifestation of major depressive disorder but also great variability in the symptoms of MDD. The symptoms of MDD are the result of the interaction of universal tendencies and cultural factors (Draguns, 1995). Among the kinds of sociocultural factors in MDD are variables correlated with ethnicity, such as socioeconomic status. A survey of more than 2,000 Americans found that African Americans were more likely to experience MDD than European Americans. But when socioeconomic status was factored in, there were no differences. That is, African Americans and European Americans of the same socioeconomic class had equal rates of MDD. Thus, because African Americans on average have lower socioeconomic status, it is poverty, not ethnicity, that probably accounts for the ethnic difference (Biafora, 1995).

Seasonal Affective Disorder

Norman Rosenthal (1993) and his colleagues identified a form of depression called **seasonal affective disorder,** or **SAD** and pioneered the use of light therapy. People with SAD suffer from depressive symptoms during certain seasons, most commonly in the winter.

Characteristics of Seasonal Affective Disorder

SAD afflicts about 1 percent of Americans (Blazer, Kessler, & Swartz, 1998), though global population estimates vary by geographic latitude (Michalak & Lam, 2002). For

seasonal affective disorder (SAD) A mood disorder in which severe depressive symptoms occur during a particular season, usually the winter but sometimes the summer.

example, the rate of SAD can be as high as 2.9 percent in Canada (Westrin & Lam, 2007). Typically, people develop SAD at latitudes with shorter days in the winter season. It is three to four times more common in women than in men (Lee & Chan, 1999b).

Causes of Seasonal Affective Disorder

Seasonal affective disorder might be caused by an inability to adjust physiologically to seasonal changes in light levels. Seasonal affective disorder is treated by *phototherapy,* which involves extending the day by exposing the afflicted person to artificial bright light before sunrise or after sunset. Depressive symptoms have been alleviated with as little as two one-hour sessions of exposure to bright light (Reeves et al., 2012). Stronger light intensity tends to produce more relief of typical symptoms (Lee & Chan, 1999a). The exact mechanism of its effect is unknown; however, some research has indicated that exposure to bright light in specific wavelengths promotes the skin's production of vitamin D. Researchers have suggested that low levels of vitamin D are associated with depressed mood (Berk et al., 2007). One mystery is that SAD is found even in countries, such as India (Srivastava & Sharma, 1998), that have little variation in sunlight across the year.

Research into the causes of SAD has implicated genes that regulate serotonin activity in the brain (Thierry et al., 2004). SAD is related to depletion of serotonin. This finding was demonstrated in a double-blind experiment that compared light therapy and fluoxetine (Prozac) therapy. Participants (average age 41 years) had SAD and were randomly assigned to the conditions. Each participant received 1 week of placebo treatment and 5 weeks of active treatment. The active treatment consisted of fluoxetine plus a placebo light condition versus bright light plus a placebo drug. There were 20 participants in each of the two conditions. The results indicated that both treatments were effective, with 14 of the bright-light participants improving and 13 of the fluoxetine participants improving. Fluoxetine produced a faster effect on typical SAD symptoms (Ruhrmann et al., 1998).

Whereas there is not one species that perfectly replicates attributes of any psychological disorder, Randy Nelson has found that Siberian hamsters are a model organism with which to study SAD. Compared to rats and mice, these hamsters display specific depressive and anxiety-like behavior in response to short day length (Pyter and Nelson, 2006). Animal work also has helped us understand another mechanism that might contribute to the development of SAD. For example, some drugs that act on melatonin have been shown to produce antidepressant-like effects (Soumier et al., 2009). However many researchers speculate that there are many physiological processes that make an individual susceptible to SAD.

Suicide and Major Depressive Disorder

On January 22, 1987, at a televised news conference, Pennsylvania treasurer R. Budd Dwyer killed himself by putting the barrel of a pistol in his mouth and pulling the trigger. Dwyer had suffered from major depressive disorder after his conviction on charges of corruption. People who suffer from major depressive disorder are more susceptible to suicide.

Though some suicides are done for honor, as in the Japanese ritual of hara-kiri, or to escape intolerable pain, as in some cases of terminal illnesses, most are associated with major depressive disorder. There are more than 200,000 suicide attempts each year in the United States, with more than 25,000 fatalities. Though some suicide victims leave notes explaining why they killed themselves, the vast majority do not (O'Donnell, Farmer, & Catalan, 1993). The kinds of notes vary with age, with older victims citing factors associated with aging, such as illness and loneliness (Bauer et al., 1997). Overall, the most common issue addressed in suicide notes is the assignment of blame for the act (McClelland, Reicher, & Booth, 2000).

Factors in Suicide

Who commits suicide? Globally, more than one million people commit suicide every year, and it is the 13th leading cause of death (Bailey et al., 2011). Roy Baumeister (1990), a leading researcher on disorders of the self, believes that people commit suicide when their self-image becomes so negative that it is too painful to bear. Sex, ethnicity, and age are also factors. Women are much more likely than men to attempt suicide, yet many more men than women succeed

Seasonal Affective Disorder

Light therapy is useful for treating seasonal affective disorder.

Source: Image Point Fr/ Shutterstock.com.

(Spicer & Miller, 2000; Schmidtke et al., 1999). This difference is, in part, because men tend to use more lethal means, such as gunshots to the head, whereas women tend to use less lethal means, such as overdoses of depressants. This gender difference holds both in Western countries, such as the United States, and in Asian countries, such as China (He & Lester, 1998).

Widowed and divorced people are more likely to commit suicide than are single or married people (Canetto & Lester, 1995). There is some evidence that marriage has a stronger protective effect on men's risk of suicide relative to women's (Kposowa, 2000), possibly by reducing its acceptability (Stack, 1998). Traditionally, European Americans and Native Americans commit suicide more often than African Americans do, but in recent years, the suicide rate among young African Americans has increased (Willis, Coombs, Drentea, & Cockerham, 2003). There is increasing concern about the suicide rate among American military personnel, who are at risk of committing suicide only one month after being released from psychiatric care (Luxton, Trofimovich, & Clark, 2013). Elderly people have the highest suicide rate of any age group in the United States. The gender difference in suicide is dramatic among the elderly. Six out of seven suicides among those aged 65 or higher are men (Coren & Hewitt, 1999).

Though suicide rates are lower for high school and college students than for older people, suicide is one of the most common causes of death for the 15- to 24-year-old age group. Adolescent suicide often is associated with a dysfunctional family (Husain, 1990), blaming oneself for failure (Lester, 2003), and drug or alcohol abuse (Rowan, 2001). One study of 775 adolescents aged 12 to 19 living on the streets in San Francisco found that the mean number of suicide attempts was 6.2 for female and 5.1 for male participants. A history of sexual and physical abuse increased these adolescents' risk of suicide to 1.9 to 4.3 times the risk of nonabused adolescents (Molnar, Shade, Kral, Booth, & Watters, 1998). Because even young children commit suicide (Lester, 1995), parents and school personnel should be aware of the possibility in depressed, withdrawn children.

Suicide Prevention

During your lifetime, you will probably know people who you suspect are contemplating suicide. According to Edwin Shneidman (1994), a leading authority, at least 90 percent of people who attempt suicide give verbal or behavioral warnings before their attempts. People who have attempted suicide in the past are at especially high risk of trying again. A study of almost 400 youth suicides in Paris found that one-third of them had made earlier attempts (Lecomte & Fornes, 1998).

These statistics make it important to take threats seriously and to take appropriate actions to prevent suicide attempts. But a study of high school students found that few had knowledge of major warning signs and appropriate responses to suicidal threats by their peers (Norton, Durlak, & Richards, 1989). Major warning signs include changes in moods and habits associated with severe major depressive disorder, such as emotional apathy, social withdrawal, poor grooming habits, and loss of interest in recreational activities; giving away cherished belongings; tying up loose ends in their lives; and outright suicide threats (Shaughnessy & Nystul, 1985).

One of the obvious means of preventing suicide is to restrict access to means of suicide, especially guns (Brent & Bridge, 2003). But interpersonal action is also important. Shneidman suggests that because suicide attempts are usually cries for help, the simple act of providing an empathetic response might reduce the immediate likelihood of an actual attempt. Just talking about a problem may reduce its apparent dreadfulness and help the person realize possible solutions other than suicide. It may help to broaden the suicidal person's options to more than a choice between death and a hopeless, helpless life. An immediate goal should be to relieve the psychological pain of the person by intervening, if possible, with those who might be contributing to the pain, whether friends, lovers, teachers, or family members. You also should encourage the person to seek professional help, even if you have to make the appointment for the person and accompany him or her to it.

The U.S. Department of Health and Human Services sponsors a number of suicide prevention programs (DeMartino et al., 2003), as does the Canadian Association for Suicide Prevention (Leenaars, 2000), and 21 countries on 3 continents (Matsubayashi & Ueda, 2011). Many cities have 24-hour suicide hotlines or walk-in centers to provide emergency counseling.

School systems also have begun to implement suicide-prevention programs (Kalafat, 2003). With the advent of the Internet, professionals are even developing email approaches to suicide prevention (Wilson & Lester, 1998). In some college programs, resident assistants are trained to recognize warning signs of suicide. They also are taught how to respond to suicide threats, how to make referrals to professional counselors, and how to support those who seek therapy (Grosz, 1990). In the United States, the presence of suicide-prevention centers in a state is associated with a lowering of suicide rates (Lester, 1993). A study in Japan found that the more suicide-prevention centers there are in a region and the longer they are open, the relatively lower will be the suicide rate (Lester, Saito, & Abe, 1997).

Section Review: Major Depressive Disorder and Related Disorders

1. How does Seligman's attributional theory explain major depressive disorder?

2. How does rumination affect major depressive disorder?

3. What are Shneidman's suggestions for preventing someone from committing suicide?

Bipolar Disorder

A biblical story describes how King Saul stripped off his clothes in public, exhibited alternating bouts of elation and severe depression, and eventually committed suicide. Though the story attributes his behavior to evil spirits, psychologists might attribute it to bipolar disorder.

Characteristics of Bipolar Disorder

bipolar disorder A mood disorder marked by periods of mania alternating with longer periods of major depressive disorder.

mania A mood disorder marked by euphoria, hyperactivity, grandiose ideas, annoying talkativeness, unrealistic optimism, and inflated self-esteem.

Bipolar disorder, formerly called *manic depression*, is characterized by days or weeks of mania alternating with longer periods of major depressive disorder, typically separated by days or weeks of normal moods. **Mania** (from the Greek term for "madness") involves euphoria, hyperactivity, grandiose ideas, incoherent talkativeness, blind optimism, and inflated self-esteem. People with mania are sexually, physically, and financially reckless. They may also overestimate their own abilities, perhaps leading them to make rash business deals or to leave a sedentary job to train for the Olympics. At some time in their lives, about 4 percent of adults have bipolar disorder, which is equally common in men and women (Kessler et al., 2005), though there are gender differences in the nature of symptoms and the course of the disorder (Amsterdam, Brunswick, & O'Reardon, 2002).

Causes of Bipolar Disorder

There is compelling evidence that heredity plays a strong role in bipolar disorder. Identical twins have higher concordance rates for bipolar disorder (Mitchell, Mackinnon, & Waters, 1993) than do fraternal twins. A recent study in the United Kingdom of twins in which one twin was diagnosed with bipolar disorder found concordance rates of 67 percent among monozygotic twins and 19 percent among dizygotic twins (McGuffin et al., 2003). Additional evidence supportive of a hereditary basis for bipolar disorder was provided by a study by Janice Egeland of the Amish community in Lancaster County, Pennsylvania (Egeland et al., 1987). Because the Amish have an isolated community that includes descendants from 30 ancestors in the 18th century, only marrying among themselves, they provide an excellent opportunity to study the influence of heredity on psychological disorders. Egeland studied the families of Amish people with bipolar disorder, using blood tests to examine their chromosome structures.

Egeland found that Amish people who suffer from bipolar disorder share a defective gene on the 11th chromosome. But because only 63 percent of those with this defect develop the disorder, differences in life experience also play a role. Nonetheless, similar studies of families in which bipolar disorder follows a hereditary pattern have failed to find a genetic

The Amish Community

Members of the Amish community, because of their social and genetic isolation, may exhibit diseases likely to be seen in the general public, but at a higher rate.

Source: Arina P Habich/ Shutterstock.com.

marker for it on the 11th chromosome. These include a study of two Australian families (Mitchell, Waters, Morrison, & Shine, 1991) and a study of three Icelandic families (Kelsoe, Kristbjanarson, Bergesch, & Shilling 1993). These findings reinforce the importance of research replication, across different social groups, which was stressed in Chapter 2. Of course, it is possible that some cases of bipolar disorder are linked to the 11th chromosome, whereas others are linked to other chromosomes (Ewald, Mors, Flint, & Koed, 1995). More recent data from the National Institute of Mental Health study of more than 150 families with bipolar disorder implicate chromosomes 6, 10, 11, 16, and 20, which suggests that a single genetic cause for bipolar disorder is unlikely (McInnis et al., 2003). Molecular genetics has taken this field a bit further. A mutation on the cell membrane of neurons that regulate calcium flow has been found to be a risk factor for developing bipolar disorder. Carriers of this mutation are also at risk for developing major depressive disorder or schizophrenia (Green et al., 2010). The degree of overlap in the biological underpinnings of these psychological disorders indicates the complexity of this disorder.

Whereas major depressive disorder is associated with a combination of low levels of both serotonin and norepinephrine, mania is associated with a combination of low levels of serotonin and high levels of norepinephrine. Figure 14-5 shows that mania also is associated with unusually high levels of brain arousal, perhaps related to these neurotransmitter levels. Imaging studies have pointed to certain brain structures involved in bipolar disorder. Whereas some results are inconsistent, the most consistent findings focus on brain structures related to emotional processing. Compared to healthy control groups, people with bipolar disorder show altered activity in the amygdala, cingulate, and cortex when viewing emotional stimuli. Moreover, this group had difficulty in identifying fearful faces (Sagar, Dahlgren, Gönenç, & Gruber, 2013). Imaging studies also are helpful to reveal brain activity during manic episodes. Despite its biological roots, the course of bipolar disorder also is affected by stressful life events interacting with a biological vulnerability (Post, Leverich, Xing, & Weiss, 2001). This combination of factors is in keeping with the biopsychosocial model of psychological disorders.

Section Review: Bipolar Disorder

1. What are the interpersonal consequences experienced by people with mania?

2. Explain one reason why major depressive disorder and bipolar disorder are distinct psychological disorders?

FIGURE 14-5
Brain Activity in Bipolar Disorder

These PET scans show the brain activity of a rapid-cycling bipolar patient. The patient cycled between mania and depression every 24 to 48 hours. The top and bottom sets of scans were obtained during periods when the patient was depressed. The middle set of scans was obtained during a manic period. Note that the red areas indicate significantly higher brain activity during the manic period.

Source: Phelps, M. E., & Maziotta, J. C. (1985). Positron-emission tomography: Human brain function and biochemistry. *Science, 228,* 799–809. Courtesy of Drs. Lewis Baxter and Michael Phelps, UCLA School of Medicine.

schizophrenia A class of psychological disorders characterized by grossly impaired social, emotional, cognitive, and perceptual functioning.

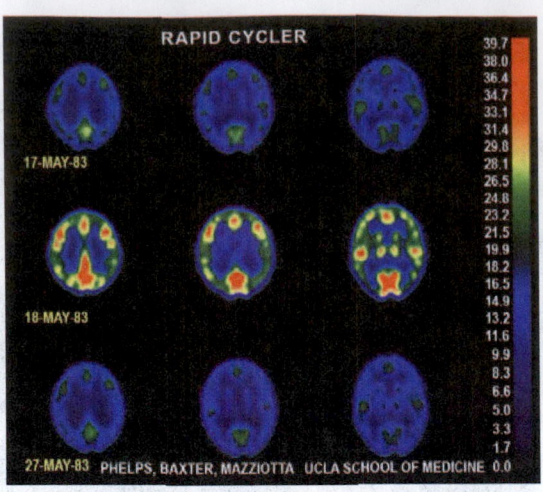

Schizophrenia

In middle age, Edvard Munch, the founder of modern expressionist painting referred to earlier in this chapter, began acting in odd ways. He became a social recluse, believed his paintings were his children, and claimed they were too jealous to be exhibited with other paintings (Wilson, 1967). Munch's actions were symptoms of **schizophrenia**, a severe psychological disorder characterized by impaired social, emotional, cognitive, and perceptual functioning.

The Nature of Schizophrenia

The modern classification of schizophrenia began in 1860 when the Belgian psychiatrist Benedict Morel used the Latin term *demence precoce* (meaning "premature mental deterioration") to describe the behavior of a brilliant, outgoing 13-year-old boy who gradually withdrew socially and deteriorated intellectually. The term was popularized by German psychiatrist Emil Kraepelin in his diagnostic system as *dementia praecox*. In 1911, the Swiss psychiatrist Eugen Bleuler (1857–1939) coined the term *schizophrenia* (from the Greek terms for "split mind") to refer to the disorder. This term reflected his belief that schizophrenia involved a splitting apart of the normally integrated functions of perceiving, feeling, and thinking. Whereas the *DSM-IV-TR* differentiated between discrete types of schizophrenia, the *DSM-5* considers schizophrenia to be a cluster of symptoms that can be demarcated by a series of stages of increasing psychosis (Häfner, Mauer, & vander Heiden, 2013). About 1 percent of the world's population are victims of schizophrenia, which is equally prevalent among men and women. Gender differences are apparent, though, in age of onset, psychosocial functioning, and the subtype of schizophrenia diagnosed (Tammings, 1997). Patients with schizophrenia occupy half the beds in American mental hospitals and cost the American economy billions of dollars each year. In contrast, there is some evidence that the course of schizophrenia is more favorable in developing countries, possibly due to a higher interdependence of the individual within the community and the role of the family in providing care and interpersonal support to mentally ill relatives (López & Guarnaccia, 2000).

Characteristics of Schizophrenia

Schizophrenia is associated with a diversity of potential symptoms. These include sensory-perceptual, cognitive, social-emotional, and motor symptoms. Particular kinds of brain dysfunctions might be associated with particular sets of schizophrenic symptoms. According to schizophrenia researcher Nancy Andreasen, there are two kinds of schizophrenic syndromes, characterized by either *positive symptoms* or *negative symptoms* (Andreasen & Flaum, 1991). Positive symptoms are psychotic behaviors that are not seen in healthy people and are active symptoms that include hallucinations, delusions, thought disorders, and bizarre behaviors. People with positive symptoms experience acute episodes and show progressively worsening symptoms. In contrast, negative symptoms are passive symptoms characterized by their absence in healthy people that include mutism, apathy, flat emotionality, social withdrawal, intellectual impairment, poverty of speech, and inability to experience pleasure.

Sensory-Perceptual Symptoms People with schizophrenia typically experience *hallucinations*, which are sensory experiences in the absence of sensory stimulation. Schizophrenic hallucinations are usually auditory, typically voices that may ridicule the person or order the person to commit harmful acts, perhaps violent ones (Zisook, Byrd, Kuck, & Jese, 1995). Researchers, however, have discovered that the type and prevalence of hallucinations can vary by culture (Bauer et al., 2011). Failure of the cognitive mechanism that normally helps people distinguish between experiences generated by the mind and experiences evoked by external stimuli can contribute to hallucinations (Beck & Rector, 2003). Researchers using fMRI and PET scans have demonstrated that schizophrenic hallucinations are associated with increased activity in the region of the cerebral cortex that normally processes the relevant sensory information. Auditory hallucinations, for example, are associated with increased activity in the temporal cortex, which processes sounds (Copolov et al., 2003).

Cognitive Symptoms Chief among the cognitive symptoms of schizophrenia is difficulty with attention. People with schizophrenia are easily distracted by irrelevant stimuli (Mirsky, Yardley, Jones, & Walsh, 1995) and have difficulty voluntarily switching their attention from one stimulus to another (Smith et al., 1998). This inability to control attention may account for the cognitive fragmentation that is a hallmark of schizophrenia. Because this fragmentation also is evident in schizophrenic speech, you might find it frustrating to converse with someone who suffers from schizophrenia. Schizophrenic speech might include invented words called *neologisms*, as in "The children have to have this 'accentuative' law so they don't go into the 'mortite' law of the church" (Vetter, 1969, p. 189). Schizophrenic speech might also include a meaningless jumble of words called a *word salad*, such as "The house burnt the cow horrendously always" (Vetter, 1969, p. 147).

Among the most distinctive cognitive disturbances in schizophrenia are delusions. A *delusion* is a belief that is held despite compelling evidence to the contrary, such as Edvard Munch's belief that his paintings were his children and were jealous of other paintings. The most common delusions are delusions of influence, such as the belief that one's thoughts are being beamed to all parts of the universe *(thought broadcasting)*.

Less common are *delusions of grandeur*, in which the person believes that she or he is a famous or powerful person. The fascinating book *The Three Christs of Ypsilanti* (Rokeach, 1964/1981) describes the cases of three men in a mental hospital who had the same delusion of grandeur: Each claimed to be Jesus Christ. The workings of the schizophrenic mind are vividly illustrated when they meet, and each man tries to explain why he is Jesus and the others merely impostors.

Delusions vary from culture to culture, as demonstrated in a large-scale study of German and Japanese people with schizophrenia. The study found that Germans were more likely to have delusions of direct persecution, such as poisoning. The Japanese were more likely to have delusions of reference, such as being slandered (Tateyama, Asai, Kamisada, & Hashimoto, 1993). These and other cognitive symptoms make it difficult to interact with people who have schizophrenia and can cause great distress to caregivers.

Social-Emotional Symptoms People with schizophrenia typically have flat or inappropriate emotionality. Emotional flatness is shown by an unchanging facial expression, a lack of expressive gestures, and an absence of vocal inflections. For example, people with schizophrenia are less facially responsive to emotional films than other people are (Blanchard, Kring, & Neale, 1994). Emotional inappropriateness is shown by bizarre outbursts, such as laughing when someone is seriously injured. And, as in the case of Edvard Munch, people with schizophrenia tend to be socially withdrawn, with few, if any, friends. This withdrawal usually first appears in childhood.

Motor Symptoms Schizophrenia also is associated with unusual motor behavior. The person might rock incessantly, make bizarre faces, pace back and forth, hold poses for hours, or trace patterns in the air.

The Western media have sensationalized periodic cases in which people with schizophrenia have committed violent crimes. This sensationalism might lead to the public's overestimating the incidence of violence by the mentally ill (Angermeyer & Schulze, 2001). But some researchers insist that people with schizophrenia are more likely to be violent and that this tendency might be inherited (Tehrani, Brennan, Hodgins, & Mednick, 1998). Other researchers have found a weak link between schizophrenia and violence (Walsh, Buchanan, & Fahy, 2002). Thus, violence by people with schizophrenia often is a product of factors, such as a history of victimization, personality disorders, substance abuse, or a violent environment (Serper, 2011).

Causes of Schizophrenia

The variety, complexity, and diversity of schizophrenic symptoms make the discovery of the causes of schizophrenia one of the most challenging of all tasks facing those who study the disorder (Andreasen, 1997). No single viewpoint can explain all cases of schizophrenia or why some people with certain risk factors develop schizophrenia and others do not.

The Biopsychological Viewpoint

Biopsychological theories of schizophrenia consider genetic, biochemical, and neurological factors.

Hereditary Factors Schizophrenia runs in families; the closer the genetic relationship is to a family member with schizophrenia, the more likely a person is to develop schizophrenia (Kety, Wender, Jacobsen, & Ingraham, 1994). Figure 14-6 shows that the concordance rates for schizophrenia appear to have a strong hereditary basis. A major study found a concordance rate of 48 percent for identical twins and only 4 percent for fraternal twins (Onstad, Skre, Torgerson, & Kringlen, 1991). Yet, the higher concordance rate might be caused by the more similar treatment that identical twins receive rather than by their identical genetic endowment. A recent meta-analysis of 12 twin studies concluded that schizophrenia is a result of a complex relationship of genetic and environmental factors (Sullivan, Kendler, & Neale, 2003). Schizophrenia also frequently coexists with other psychological disorders. For example, a common problem for people with schizophrenia is substance abuse, especially alcohol abuse. The European Schizophrenia Cohort Survey, a large-scale survey, reported that about 35 percent of people with schizophrenia also abused alcohol and/or drugs (Carrà et al., 2012).

To assess the relative contributions of heredity and experience, researchers have turned to adoption studies. Many of these studies have been conducted in Denmark, where the government maintains excellent birth and adoption records. The studies support the genetic

FIGURE 14-6

Heredity and the Risk of Schizophrenia

The concordance rates for schizophrenia between people become higher as their genetic similarity becomes greater. This finding provides evidence supportive of the hereditary basis of schizophrenia but cannot by itself rule out the influence of the degree of similarity in life experiences.

Source: Data from I. I. Gottesman and J. Shields (1982). *Schizophrenia: The epigenetic puzzle.* New York: Cambridge University Press.

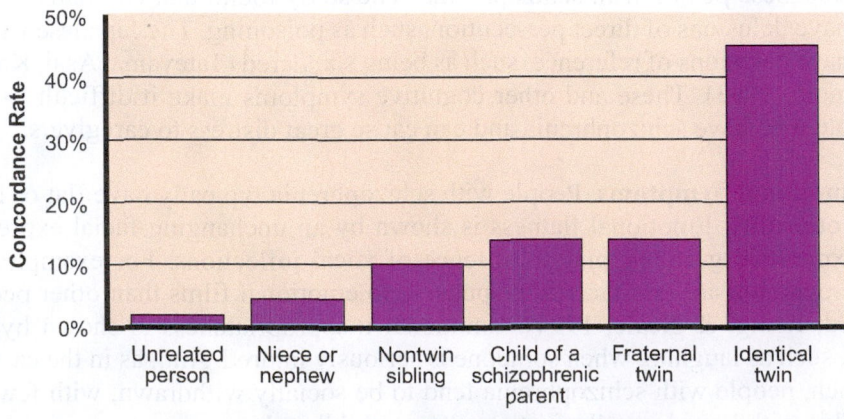

basis of schizophrenia. For example, schizophrenia is more common in the biological relatives of adoptees with schizophrenia than in their adoptive relatives, children adopted from parents with schizophrenia have a greater risk of schizophrenia than do children adopted from healthy parents, and children of healthy parents adopted by parents with schizophrenia do not show an increased risk of schizophrenia (Buchsbaum & Haier, 1983).

Consistent with the view that both heredity and experience contribute to the development of schizophrenia, it seems that schizophrenia is best explained by the biopsychological model, which sees it as the outcome of the interaction between a genetic predisposition and stressful life experiences (Conklin & Iacono, 2002). A review of research found that people with schizophrenia are predisposed to be more vulnerable to stressors, so stress that would hardly affect other people might cause them to develop symptoms of schizophrenia (Norman & Malla, 1993). For example, children who have both a genetic predisposition to develop schizophrenia and the stress of losing their father are more likely to develop schizophrenia than are children with only one of those factors (Walker, Hoppes, Emory, Mednick, & Schulsinger, 1981). The most convincing genetic information comes from a longitudinal family study. After studying a large Scottish family for decades, Millar et al. (2000) discovered a mutation in the gene called DISC1, abbreviated for *disrupted in schizophrenia-1*. This gene controls many cellular functions. However, as many advances were made as a result of this discovery, it is unlikely to be the sole explanation of the genetic effects on the risk of schizophrenia in every population (Bae et al., 2013).

Neurochemical Factors Given the apparent hereditary basis of schizophrenia, what biological differences might exist between people who develop schizophrenia and those who do not? One factor is the effect of genetic influences on activity of the neurotransmitter dopamine in the brain (Amin et al., 1999). Studies have found a relationship between schizophrenia and high levels of activity at synapses that use the neurotransmitters *dopamine* and *serotonin*.

What evidence is there of a dopamine basis for schizophrenia? First, drugs that are used to treat schizophrenia work by blocking dopamine (Silvestri et al., 2000) and serotonin receptors (Kapur and Remington, 1996). Second, drugs such as amphetamines, which increase dopamine levels in the brain, can induce schizophrenic symptoms in mentally healthy people (Adeyemo, 2002). Third, *L-dopa*, a drug used to treat Parkinson's disease because it increases dopamine levels in the brain, can induce schizophrenic symptoms in Parkinson's victims (Nicol & Gottesman, 1983). Fourth, brain-imaging studies have found overactivity of dopamine neurons in the brains of people with schizophrenia (Farde, 1997). And drugs that block both dopamine and serotonin receptors are effective in reducing symptoms of schizophrenia (O'Connor, 1998).

Season-of-Birth and Developmental Factors In seeking other factors in schizophrenia, biopsychological researchers are struck by one of the most well-replicated findings regarding schizophrenia: A disproportionate number of victims are born in the winter or early spring (Davies, Welham, Chant, Torrey, & McGrath, 2003). This finding has been confirmed in countries throughout the Northern Hemisphere, including Taiwan (Tam & Sewell, 1995), France (Amato, Rochet, Dalery, & Chauchat, 1994), Denmark (Mortensen et al., 1999), Holland (Pallast, Jongbloet, Straatman, & Zielhuis, 1994), and Switzerland (Modestin, Ammann, & Wurmle, 1995). But studies in the Southern Hemisphere, in countries such as Australia, have found that people with schizophrenia are born disproportionately in the Southern Hemisphere's spring and early summer (November, December, and January). Schizophrenia might be associated with certain months, not certain seasons (Berk, Terre-Blanche, Maude, & Lucas, 1996).

The observation that people are more likely to develop schizophrenia if they are born during certain months has inspired a search for a possible connection to influenza viruses prevalent during those months. These viruses might have infected the brains of people with schizophrenia prenatally, particularly during the second trimester, when brain development accelerates. The possible role of infections in the development of schizophrenia is supported by the tendency of the season-of-birth effect to hold more strongly in more crowded urban areas than in more sparsely populated rural areas ((Verdoux et al., 1997).

Many studies have investigated the relationship between a worldwide influenza epidemic in 1957 and the development of schizophrenia in people born shortly afterward. Unfortunately, findings have been inconsistent. Some studies have found that people exposed to influenza prenatally, especially during the second trimester, have higher rates of schizophrenia (Takei, Mortensen, Klaening, & Murray, 1996). But other studies have found that they do not (Mino, Oshima, Tsuda, & Okagami, 2000). Moreover, efforts to find viruses in the brains of people with schizophrenia have had little success (Taller, Asher, Pomeroy, & Eldadah, 1996), though this dearth of evidence does not mean they do not exist. Perhaps the viruses do their damage before ultimately being destroyed by the immune system (Sierra-Honigmann, Carbone, & Yolken, 1995).

A viral basis for schizophrenia might help explain why identical twins do not have 100 percent concordance rate for schizophrenia. For example, identical twins who share the same placenta have a higher concordance rate for schizophrenia than do identical twins with separate placentas. It is reasonable to assume that if one twin is infected by a virus, the other twin will be more likely to become infected if it shares the same placenta than if it does not (Davis & Phelps, 1995). Maternal health habits also has been found to play a role in the development of schizophrenia. Mothers who smoke can alter both oxygen levels and hormone levels of the fetus. One study compared the smoking rates of mothers of offspring with schizophrenia and a control group of mothers of healthy offspring. Approximately 44 percent of the mothers of offspring with schizophrenia smoked, whereas only 22 percent of the mothers of healthy offspring smoked. Thus, smoking while being pregnant is correlated with the development of schizophrenia among offspring (Stathopoulou, Beratis, & Beratis, 2013). This and other studies suggest that we cannot attribute the development of schizophrenia solely to genetics, but to a genetic/environment interaction.

Neurological Factors If viral infections play a role in schizophrenia, they would do so by affecting the brain. Brain-imaging studies have shown that schizophrenia is often associated with unusual brain activity. Schizophrenia is marked by greater abnormalities in activity in the left cerebral hemisphere than in the right cerebral hemisphere (Gur & Chin, 1999). In experiments that involve cognitive tasks, participants with schizophrenia also tend to have lower frontal-lobe activity than do healthy controls (Davidson & Heinrichs, 2003). As discussed in Chapter 3, the frontal lobes are important in thinking, planning, attention, and problem solving, each of which is likely to be deficient in schizophrenia.

As illustrated in Figure 14-7, some people with schizophrenia show atrophy of brain tissue, reducing the size of the amygdala and the hippocampus, as well as creating enlargement of the cerebral ventricles, the fluid-filled chambers inside the brain. A meta-analysis of MRI studies of biopsychological correlates of schizophrenia found that the largest difference between the brains of people with schizophrenia and healthy controls was found in the lateral ventricles (Wright et al., 2000). Because this enlargement can exist in people who have exhibited schizophrenic symptoms for only a brief time, it is not the consequence of prolonged drug treatments normally associated with chronic schizophrenia (Nopoulos, Torres, Flaum, & Andreasen, 1995). Andreasen and her associates have reported that some symptoms of schizophrenia are not consistently associated with ventricular enlargement (Andreasen, Flaum, Swayze, & Tyrrell, 1990). Moreover, it might be premature to divide schizophrenia into just two categories with either positive or negative symptoms. And the evidence is stronger for the existence of a syndrome of negative symptoms than for a syndrome of positive symptoms (Andreasen, Arndt, Alliger, & Miller, 1995).

The Psychoanalytic Viewpoint

According to the psychoanalytic viewpoint, people who develop schizophrenia fail to overcome their dependence on their mothers and, as a result, become fixated at the oral stage. This fixation gives them a weak ego that may fail to defend them against the anxiety caused

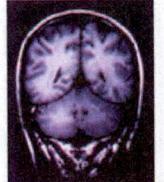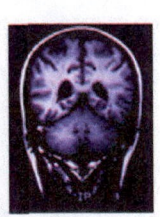

FIGURE 14-7
Schizophrenia and Neurological Abnormalities

CT scans of the brains of people with schizophrenia often show atrophy of brain tissue and enlarged ventricles. Notice that the ventricles (the dark areas) in the brain of the twin with schizophrenia *(right)* are much larger than those in the brain of the healthy twin *(left)*.
Source: Courtesy of Daniel R. Weinberger and E. Fuller Torrey.

by unconscious id impulses and external stressors. Instead, they cope with anxiety by resorting to behaviors characteristic of the oral stage, including fantasy, silly actions, incoherent speech, and irrational thinking.

Research in the spirit of the psychoanalytic viewpoint has found that parents high in what is known as *expressed emotion* might contribute to the maintenance or relapse of schizophrenia in their children. Parents who are high in expressed emotion criticize their children and become emotionally overprotective. Children's self-evaluations become more negative because of these critical attitudes, and the number of positive symptoms increases (Barrowclough, Tarrier, Humphreys, Ward, & Andrews, 2003). People with schizophrenia whose families are high in expressed emotion are more likely to suffer relapses (Hooley & Hiller, 2000). One study found that people with schizophrenia recalled more stressful memories about parents high in expressed emotion than parents low in expressed emotion (Cutting & Docherty, 2000). The notion of expressed emotion was developed in England and then in other Western countries, but the cross-cultural validity of the expressed emotion hypothesis is controversial (Cheng, 2002). Moreover, the relationship of expressed emotion to relapse varies by ethnicity (Subandi, 2011).

The Behavioral Viewpoint

Behavioral theories of schizophrenia, which stress the role of learning, assume that people with schizophrenia are rewarded for behaving in bizarre ways (Ullmann & Krasner, 1975). This situation was portrayed in the 1974 movie *A Woman Under the Influence,* in which a wife (played by Gena Rowlands) makes bizarre sounds to be rewarded with attention from her boorish husband (played by Peter Falk). Behavioral theorists also assume that a person who engages in bizarre behavior provokes social rejection from others, which in turn contributes to the suspiciousness and social withdrawal displayed by some people with schizophrenia.

The Cognitive Viewpoint

Proponents of the cognitive viewpoint point to disturbances of attention and thinking as the main factors in schizophrenia. As the leading schizophrenia researcher Eugen Bleuler observed early in the 20th century, people with schizophrenia seem "incapable of holding the train of thought in the proper channel" (Baribeau-Braun, Picton, & Gosselin, 1983). Children exposed to parents who communicate in confusing, irrational ways are predisposed to develop the disturbed cognitive activity of schizophrenia (Doane, West, Goldstein, Rodnick, & Jones, 1981).

The Humanistic Viewpoint

According to the humanistic viewpoint, schizophrenia is caused by extreme incongruence between the public self and the actual self. Psychologist R. D. Laing (1967) claimed that schizophrenia results when a person develops a false public self to confront an intolerable life situation. This retreat from reality permits the person to experience her or his actual self. The person's bizarre thinking, language, and behavior are indicative of this retreat from reality. In contrast to other humanistic psychologists, Laing recommended that family, friends, and professionals permit the person with schizophrenia to go on what he called a "voyage of self-discovery" into his or her actual self rather than interfering with that process through the administration of drugs or commitment to a mental hospital. According to Laing, traditional psychiatry and psychology unfairly try to force the person to conform to unfulfilling circumstances (Crossley, 1998).

Laing's critics claim that he romanticized schizophrenia, in the same way that 19th-century poets romanticized tuberculosis, by implying that it is somehow noble to have a serious psychological disorder. One of Laing's chief critics is Mark Vonnegut, son of the late novelist Kurt Vonnegut. Mark had been a follower of Laing's until he suffered several episodes of schizophrenia, as described in his autobiography *The Eden Express* (Vonnegut, 1975). When Mark recovered, he did not describe a voyage of self-discovery. Instead, he related a horrifying experience that he would have been better off without. Mark's disillusionment with Laing's view of schizophrenia led him to write a commentary for *Harper's* magazine entitled "Why I Want to Bite R. D. Laing" (Vonnegut, 1974).

The Sociocultural Viewpoint

Sociocultural factors can affect the precise pattern of symptoms in schizophrenia, but there is some cross-cultural universality in schizophrenic symptoms (Draguns & Tanaka-Matsumi, 2003). A study of French and North African participants with schizophrenia, for example, found little difference in their symptoms (Taleb, Rouillon, Petitjean, & Gorwood, 1996). Though the *DSM-5* considers sociocultural factors in schizophrenia more than prior editions did, critics insist that the *DSM* should pay even greater attention to them (Lake, 2012).

Section Review: Schizophrenia

1. What are the major symptoms of schizophrenia?

2. What evidence is there supporting the role of dopamine and serotonin in schizophrenia?

3. How do positive symptoms and negative symptoms of schizophrenia differ?

Personality Disorders

personality disorder
A psychological disorder characterized by enduring, inflexible, maladaptive patterns of behavior.

Personality disorders are long-standing, inflexible, maladaptive patterns of behavior. People with personality disorders exhibit certain personality traits to an inappropriate extreme. In essence, personality disorders are negative examples of what Alfred Adler called a style of life (see Chapter 13). Personality disorders are influenced by gender roles (Sprock, 2000), ethnicity (Chavira et al., 2003), and other sociocultural factors (Paris, 1998). Moreover, some critics assert that the *DSM-5* does not adequately represent the role of sociocultural factors in shaping personality disorders (Stone, 2012). Table 14-3 summarizes the personality disorders.

Borderline Personality Disorder

borderline personality disorder (BPD) A personality disorder marked by impulsivity, unstable moods, an inconsistent sense of identity, and difficulty maintaining intimate relationships.

A personality disorder of growing interest to psychologists is the **borderline personality disorder (BPD)**. This increase in interest is because BPD has become more prevalent, devastates the lives of its victims and their loved ones, and presents one of the greatest challenges to therapists. Though BPD occurs in all cultures, it is more prevalent in highly developed ones. This prevalence has been attributed in part to the breakdown of family ties (Paris, 1996).

Characteristics of Borderline Personality Disorder

The hallmark symptoms of BPD include impulsivity, unstable moods, an inconsistent sense of identity, and difficulty maintaining fulfilling intimate relationships. The impulsivity of people with BPD leads them into unwise behavior regarding sex, eating, driving, gambling, and spending (Hochhausen, Lorenz, & Newman, 2002). Such people can be in a friendly, lighthearted mood and suddenly become angry and vindictive for no apparent reason, reflecting their chronic emotional instability (Yen, Zlotnick, & Costello, 2002). Their sense of identity can be grandiose one moment and marked by suicidal self-loathing the next.

Perhaps of greatest pain to people with BPD and those close to them is their tendency to switch unpredictably between idealizing others and tearing them down, which professionals call splitting. People with BPD cannot retain a realistic view of people that combines positive and negative qualities. Instead, they rely on their latest interaction with the person to determine their feelings toward her or him.

TABLE 14-3 Personality Disorders

Disorders	Symptoms
Cluster A: Disorders Characterized by Odd or Eccentric Behavior	
Paranoid personality disorder	Unrealistic mistrust and suspiciousness of people
Schizoid personality disorder	Problems in forming emotional relationships with others
Schizotypal personality disorder	Oddities of thinking, perception, communication, and behavior not severe enough to be diagnosed as schizophrenia
Cluster B: Disorders Characterized by Dramatic, Emotional, or Erratic Behavior	
Antisocial personality disorder	Continually violating the rights of others, being prone to impulsive behavior, and feeling no guilt for the harm done to others
Borderline personality disorder	Instability in mood, behavior, self-image, and social relationships
Histrionic personality disorder	Overly dramatic behavior, self-centeredness, and a craving for attention
Narcissistic personality disorder	Grandiose sense of self-importance, an insistence on being the center of attention, and a lack of empathy for others
Cluster C: Disorders Characterized by Anxious or Fearful Behavior	
Avoidant personality disorder	Hypersensitivity to potential rejection by others, causing social withdrawal despite a desire for social relationships
Dependent personality disorder	Failure to take responsibility for own life, instead relying too much on others to make decisions
Obsessive-compulsive personality disorder	Preoccupation with rules, schedules, organization, and trivial details, and inability to express emotional warmth

People with BPD will desperately seek intimacy, only to run away when they find it. In romance, they can be charming and ingratiating at the first, superficial contact, only to become hostile and manipulative when true intimacy beckons. The author of the best-selling book on BPD, *I Hate You, Don't Leave Me,* stressed this problem by offering one intellectual's observation, "All is caprice. They love without measure those whom they will soon hate without reason" (Kreisman & Straus, 1989, p. 17). The chief reason for this behavior is that people with BPD desire love but are terrified at being engulfed by an intimate relationship. So they vacillate between clinging to their romantic partner and pushing their lover away (Chabrol, 1997). This inconsistency often leads to a romantic life marked by stormy, short-term relationships. Because of their inability to maintain healthy, intimate relationships, people with BPD tend to feel painfully alone. Given these feelings, experienced therapists know that that most of their clients with BPD will call them repeatedly for support between therapy sessions (Gunderson, 1996).

Causes of Borderline Personality Disorder

Borderline personality disorder (BPD) affects 2 percent of the population. Many studies find that BPD is more common among women; however, these findings are controversial (Sansone & Sansone, 2011). This prevalence among women might reflect the greater incidence of childhood sexual abuse of infants and girls because there is a relationship between BPD and sexual abuse (Johnson et al., 2003). The child who experiences sexual, physical, or emotional abuse develops a powerful conflict between his or her normal need for closeness and attachment, and fear of the pain that it might bring (Sable, 1997). However, a recent 10-year longitudinal twin study found no causal relationship between child emotional, physical, and sexual abuse and BPD. Whereas child sexual abuse was correlated with BPD, it also was correlated with genetic factors and behavioral problems. The researchers concluded that genetic factors interact with behavioral disorders and make the child more susceptible to developing BPD (Bornovalova et al., 2013). There also is evidence of a biological basis for BPD. For example, BPD is associated with a reduction in the size of the hippocampus, amygdala, and frontal lobes (Tebartz van Elst et al., 2003) and less active frontal lobes (De la Fuente et al., 1997). How these differences might contribute to BPD is unknown.

Antisocial Personality Disorder

antisocial personality disorder
A personality disorder marked by impulsive, manipulative, often criminal behavior, without any feelings of guilt in the perpetrator.

Until the recent surge of interest in BPD, the personality disorder of greatest interest to the general public was **antisocial personality disorder,** perhaps because it has been implicated in many notorious criminal cases. Between 1972 and 1978, a successful, civic-minded Chicago building contractor named John Wayne Gacy murdered 33 boys and young men and buried them under his house. After his capture, Gacy expressed no remorse and, instead, reported that his acts of cold-blooded murder had given him pleasure. Gacy's personal history indicated that he had an antisocial personality disorder.

Characteristics of Antisocial Personality Disorder

Antisocial personality disorder is found in about 3 percent of American men and less than 1 percent of American women. In the 19th century, it was called "moral insanity," and for most of the past century, it was called *psychopathy* or *sociopathy*. The disorder is characterized by maladaptive behavior beginning in childhood. This behavior includes lying, stealing, truancy, vandalism, fighting, drug abuse, physical cruelty, academic failure, and early sexual activity. Adults with antisocial personality disorder do not conform to social norms. They might fail to hold a job, to honor financial obligations, or to fulfill parental responsibilities. They also are more likely to become compulsive gamblers (Slutske et al., 2001).

Because people with antisocial personality disorder can be charming, lie with a straight face, and talk their way out of trouble, they may pursue careers as shyster lawyers, crooked politicians, or phony evangelists. Two hallmarks of the antisocial personality are impulsive behavior, such as reckless driving or promiscuous sexual relations, and a remarkable lack of guilt for the pain and suffering they inflict on others (Rogers, Duncan, Lynett, & Sewell, 1994). In extreme cases, people with an antisocial personality engage in criminal activities, yet fail to change their behavior even after being punished for it. Robert Hare, a noted researcher on antisocial personality disorder, has found that, fortunately for society, criminals with an antisocial personality tend to "burn out" after age 40 and commit fewer crimes than do other criminals (Hare, McPherson, & Forth, 1988).

Causes of Antisocial Personality Disorder

Antisocial personality disorder has been subjected to more research than any other personality disorder. Studies have provided evidence of a biological predisposition underlying it. Thomas Bouchard's University of Minnesota study of identical twins who were separated in infancy and then reunited years later (see Chapter 13) indicates that antisocial personality disorder has a genetic basis (Grove, Eckert, Heston, & Bouchard, 1990). Heredity seems to provide people who develop an antisocial personality disorder with an unusually low level of physiological reactivity to stress, most notably physical punishment (Arnett, Howland, Smith, & Newman, 1993). Given that people try to maintain an optimal level of physiological arousal (see Chapter 11), perhaps the unusually low level of arousal of people with an antisocial personality disorder motivates them to engage in behaviors that increase their level of arousal (Ellis, 1987). Whereas some people seek to increase their arousal by engaging in auto racing and similar socially acceptable activities, those with an antisocial personality disorder might learn to do so by committing bank robberies and similar antisocial activities. An MRI study found that men with antisocial personality disorder showed an 11 percent reduction in prefrontal gray matter, compared to healthy controls. The researchers believe that this deficit in the frontal lobe may underlie the low arousal, lack of conscience, and poor decision making that characterize antisocial personality disorder (Raine, Lencz, Bihrle, LaCasse, & Colletti, 2000).

But what makes one person with a low level of physiological arousal seek thrills through auto racing and another seek thrills through robbing banks? Behaviorists believe that antisocial personality disorder is caused by parents who reward, or fail to punish, their children for engaging in antisocial behaviors, such as lying, stealing, or aggression. However, a history of childhood conduct problems predicts antisocial personality disorder in adulthood independently of familial or social variables (Hill, 2003). There is some evidence that people with antisocial personality disorder, perhaps because of their low physiological reactivity, are less likely to learn from punishment for misdeeds. They do not show the normal increase in anxiety when exposed to punishment (Eysenck, 1982).

Section Review: Personality Disorders

1. Why do you think antisocial personality disorder at one time was called "moral insanity"?

2. What would be some signs that the person you are dating has a borderline personality disorder?

Developmental Disorders

Many theories address the origin of **developmental disorders,** which are psychological disorders originating in childhood that can be characterized by physical, learning, language, or behavioral impairments. None has been completely supported, but researchers ask question such as these: Do environmental factors disrupt normal development? Are the developmental abnormalities predetermined due to genetics? Could developmental disorders be a result of the combination of genetics and environment?

Autism Spectrum Disorder (ASD)

Autism spectrum disorder (ASD) is characterized by impaired social functioning that is present in early childhood. This disorder was first reported by Leo Kanner, when he published a case study in which he described three young children from his child psychiatry clinic at Johns Hopkins University "whose condition differs so markedly and uniquely from anything reported so far, that each case merits… a detailed consideration of its fascinating peculiarities" (Kanner, 1943, p. 217). He noted that these children had developmental delays in motor skills, extraordinary memory capabilities, poor verbal skills, and engaged in self-stimulating behavior, such as intense fascination with spinning blocks and other round objects.

Kanner used the word *autism,* previously associated with childhood schizophrenia, to describe these children. The term *autism* comes from the Greek word *autos*, or self. This term was coined to capture one of the core facets of autism: impaired social functioning. Kanner, in his original paper, called attention to what he observed as a lack of warmth among the fathers and mothers of autistic children. This promoted the misconception that this disorder was environmental in origin and caused by "refrigerator moms" who exhibited cold, distant, and insensitive parenting. Today, parents likely still feel a social stigma when their children diagnosed with ASD are perceived negatively by others in public settings. Social psychologists have found this to be the case when children with ASD are found to be high functioning intellectually yet still display noncompliant behaviors. Wales (2002) found that mothers feel the greatest impact from this social stigma.

developmental disorders Psychological disorders originating in childhood that can be characterized by physical, learning, language, or behavioral impairments. The disorder can improve or persist throughout a person's lifetime.

autism spectrum disorder (ASD) A psychological disorder characterized by poor social relationships, impaired communication, and repetitive behaviors.

Developmental Disorders

Developmental disorders are caused by impaired development of the brain. Diagnosing psychological disorders in young children can be challenging.

Source: Marcin Pawinski/Shutterstock.com.

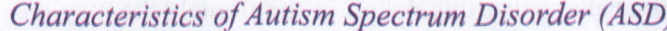

Characteristics of Autism Spectrum Disorder (ASD)

The defining characteristics of ASD according to the *DSM-5* (APA, 2013) are:

1. Deficits in social communication and social interaction (across multiple contexts).

2. Repetitive patterns of behavior (including self-stimulating behavior, extreme adherence to routines, difficulty in making transitions, rigidity and lack of flexibility in thought, and unusual sensory processes).

3. Symptoms are first present in early childhood.

In addition to these core symptoms, children with ASD show a variety of other symptoms. In previous versions of the *DSM,* children could be diagnosed into four separate but related disorders with a strict requirement that symptoms develop before the age of 3: *autistic disorder, Asperger's disorder, childhood disintegrative disorder,* or *pervasive developmental disorder not otherwise specified (PDD-NOS).* But now, to avoid inconsistencies and improve reliability in diagnosis and, ideally, treatment, people with the core symptoms noted are diagnosed with autism spectrum disorder (ASD). For example, Asperger's syndrome, which is characterized primarily by impaired social interactions, was once a subcategory of ASD. Now, it is diagnosed as ASD.

A recent study conducted by the Centers for Disease Control and Prevention estimated the prevalence of ASD in the United States as 11.3 in 1,000 (CDCP, 2012). ASD is approximately four times more common in boys than in girls, but girls appear to experience more disability from the disorder (Volkmar et al., 2014). Globally, there is more variation in prevalence rates. This is likely due to cultural differences and the fact that the *DSM* is still being revised. Fredrick Volkmar, a leading researcher who has spent decades improving diagnosis and treatment for individuals with ASD, suggests that the changes in the *DSM-5* will help practitioners differentiate between ASD and a variety of other disorders that develop in infancy and childhood. Many individuals with well-known genetic disorders, such as Down syndrome (see Chapter 10), display behaviors that mimic ASD. And these behaviors occasionally can coexist with a diagnosis of ASD (Moss, Richards, Nelson, & Oliver, 2013).

Developmental Characteristics of ASD

There is evidence that diagosis of ASD can occur as early as age 2 (Moore & Goodson, 2003). Family studies have indicated that there is a strong genetic basis for ASD. Siblings of people with ASD are nearly 100 times more likely to be at risk of developing the disorder, compared to that of the general population (Bolton et al., 1994). Researchers have begun to study abnormal brain structures that are common in people with ASD. In one recent study, the brains of infants at risk for developing ASD were scanned in modified MRI machines at 6 months, 12 months, and 24 months of age. The scans of infants that were ultimately diagnosed with ASD at 24 months of age indicated abnormal development of the axons of the neurons (Wolff et al., 2012). These results support a finding that has been replicated many times; that is, individuals with ASD have surprisingly large heads and brains (White, O'Reilly, & Frith, 2009).

Abnormal connections among neurons are not the only biopsychological relationship. Postmortem studies of the brains of individuals who had lived with ASD have found a number of abnormal brain structures, regardless of the age at which the person died. For example, the number of abnormal neurons in areas of the brain associated with emotion is increased, whereas the number of abnormal neurons in the cerebellum is decreased (Bauman and Kemper, 2005). Other researchers have investigated the relationship of neurotransmitters in the development of ASD. One neurotransmitter—serotonin—has received special attention. High blood levels of serotonin are found in people with ASD, and high levels of serotonin during childhood development can, in turn, alter brain function and behavior (Whitaker-Azmitia, 2001).

Autism Spectrum Disorder (ASD)

Children with ASD often engage in repetitive, self-stimulating behavior.

Source: viki2win/Shutterstock.com.

Maternal exposure to teratogens (see Chapter 4) and complications of pregnancy and childbirth can contribute to the development of ASD. Thalidomide, a drug previously used to treat the nausea often associated with the morning sickness experienced by pregnant women, has a long and sometimes notorious history. Whereas exposure to thalidomide *later* in pregnancy has been found to be associated with a loss of limbs in offspring, exposure to thalidomide very *early* in pregnancy has been found to be associated with ASD. The late Patricia Rodier was critical in helping ASD researchers link exposure to thalidomide during critical periods of the development of the fetal nervous system. She found that women who ingested thalidomide 20 to 24 days after conception were more likely to give birth to offspring with ASD than women who were not exposed to thalidomide (Rodier, Ingram, Tisdale, & Croog, 1997). And though there is no credible evidence that vaccines can cause ASD, the influence of maternal immune system reactions on the developing fetus have not been ruled out (Pardo, Vargas, & Zimmerman, 2005). It has taken many years, but researchers have ruled out a causal relationship between the administration of vaccines that contain mercury in childhood and ASD (Hviid, Stellfeld, Wohlfahrt, & Melbye, 2003). Thus, genetic and environmental factors also can contribute to the development of this disorder.

Attention Deficit Hyperactivity Disorder (ADHD)

Attention deficit hyperactivity disorder (ADHD) is a common childhood psychological disorder that can continue through adolescence and into adulthood. "Smart But Stuck" is how one leading clinical psychologist describes ADHD (Brown, 2014). This refers to bright children with ADHD who often must repeat grades in school (Kessler et al., 2013). It was not until 1968, when the *DSM-II* was published, that there was mention of a disorder that resembled ADHD, "hyperkinetic impulse disorder." Thus, this is a relatively new disorder listed in the DSM. Currently, there is no single test to diagnose ADHD and no cure. And many other psychological disorders can have symptoms that mimic those of ADHD. As described in "Smart But Stuck," people with ADHD can have high IQs (Antshel et al., 2010).

attention deficit hyperactivity disorder (ADHD)
A developmental disorder that begins in childhood and can persist into adulthood that is characterized by persistent lack of attention, distractibility when engaged in important tasks, impulsive behavior, hyperactivity, and failure to follow through with future plans.

Characteristics of Attention Deficit Hyperactivity Disorder (ADHD)

The defining characteristics for diagnosing a person with ADHD according to the *DSM-5* (APA, 2013) are:

1. *Inattention that is not age appropriate* (for example, failure to pay close attention to details, difficulty in maintaining attention to task, seemingly not listening when spoken to directly, failure to follow through on instructions, difficulty organizing tasks and activities, reluctance to perform tasks that require mental effort over a sustained period of time, frequent losses of personal belongings, and frequently being distracted and forgetful).

2. *Hyperactivity and impulsivity that is disruptive and age inappropriate* (for example, a tendency to physically fidget, inability to remain seated when expected to, tendency to run or climb in inappropriate settings, chronic restlessness, inability to participate in quiet activities, excessive talking, difficulty in waiting turns, and a tendency to interrupt others).

These symptoms must be present before the age of 12 and occur in multiple settings, such as at school, home, or work. Depending on the age of the person, a certain number of the characteristics listed must occur. And these symptoms must interfere with or reduce the quality of the person's social interactions or school and work performance. There are three subtypes of ADHD: *combined presentation, predominantly inattentive presentation,* and *predominantly hyperactive-impulsive presentation.*

Globally, prevalence rates of ADHD have been reported to be between 8 and 12 percent of the population (Faraone, Sergeant, Gillberg, & Biederman, 2003). One contemporary trend is the increasing rate of diagnosis of ADHD among children. The National Survey on Children's Health has recently reported that 2 million children and adolescents were diagnosed with ADHD in 2011. And adolescent boys are more likely than girls to have ever been diagnosed with ADHD (Visser et al., 2014). Studies also show that people with ADHD also are often diagnosed with mood disorders, disruptive behaviors, and substance abuse disorders (Kessler et al., 2013). Another study in which researchers reviewed insurance claims found a pronounced shift in care from pediatricians to psychiatrists for children with ADHD (Garfield et al., 2012). This study, as well as others, leads to the conclusion that close to two-thirds of children and adolescents diagnosed with ADHD are taking medication (Visser et al., 2014). This trend toward increased medication of children with ADHD—and children with ASD—demonstrates a need for pediatric psychiatrists for their treatment.

Despite the core symptoms noted earlier, clinicians are puzzled by the inconsistency of inattention symptoms. A person diagnosed with ADHD can abandon a boring task, yet then intensely focus on an interesting task. This *attentional bias* can influence the emotional processing in people with ADHD. Brown notes that attentional bias can cause emotional flare-ups and may contribute to poor motivation for achieving goals. He likens this phenomenon to viewing a spectator sport:

> For those with ADHD, life can be like trying to watch a basketball game through a telescope, which allows them to see only a small fragment of the action at any specific time. Sometimes, that telescope stays too long on one part of the court, missing out completely on important events occurring elsewhere at the same time. At other times, the telescope may randomly flit from one bit of action to another, losing track of where the ball is and what various players are in a position to do. To follow what is going on in a basketball game, a person needs to be able to watch the whole court, noting movements of the ball and rapidly shifting positions of players as they present multiple risks and opportunities in the game. (Brown, 2014, pp. 9–10.)

In fact, examining the brain structures involved in attentional, emotional, and motivational processing is one way researchers are attempting to understand the neurobiology of ADHD.

Developmental Causes of ADHD

Today, researchers are trying to identify the causes of ADHD. It is likely that there is more than one cause and more than one brain structure involved in the development of ADHD. Moreover, it is very likely that there are multiple causes that also might interact with each other. Nevertheless, research points to a very strong genetic link with high heritability rates (Larsson, Chang, D'Onofrio, & Lichtenstein, 2013). Children with parents or siblings with the disorder are two to eight times more likely to have ADHD (Faraone & Biederman). The average heritability estimates from 20 twin studies in the United States, Australia, Scandinavia, and the European Union are 76 percent (Faraone et al., 2005), indicating that ADHD is a highly heritable condition.

The brain areas researchers focus on are related to attention and cognitive control, particularly the *prefrontal cortex* (Carr, Henderson, & Nigg, 2010). The prefrontal cortex (see Chapter 3) is a sheet of cells covering our brain in the anterior portion of the frontal lobe. The prefrontal cortex is an important area that regulates attention, the planning of complex tasks, the shifting and dividing of attention in a task-appropriate manner, behavioral inhibition, and decision making. Typically, psychologists refer to this area as the "executive center." One famous neurobiologist—Patricia-Goldman Rakic—describes the prefrontal cortex as a "mental sketch pad" with special processing domains, allowing for the highest level of cognitive ability. She goes on to describe dysfunction in the domains as a "dysexecutive syndrome" characterized by disorganization, preservation, and distractibility (Goldman-Rakic, 1996).

Recently, fMRI studies have helped us understand the neural circuitry and structure of the prefrontal cortex. In one large study using fMRI, researchers scanned over 160 participants with ADHD. These scans were used to measure the thickness of the cortex across the brain. Children with ADHD had a general thinning of the cortex. This was most pronounced in regions associated with attention and cognition that were located in the prefrontal cortex (Shaw et al., 2006). This led researchers to question if development of the prefrontal cortex in people with ADHD is either delayed or dysfunctional. This same research group went on to scan over 200 more children and adolescents with ADHD and found that the cortical development in children with ADHD lagged behind that of a control group of healthy children. This lag in maturation was estimated to be equivalent to several years (Shaw et al., 2007a).

Genetic studies have identified genes in several neurotransmitter systems, including dopamine, norepinephrine, serotonin, and acetylcholine, that may be implicated in the development of ADHD (Gizer, Ficks, & Waldman, 2009). Particular attention has been paid to the dopamine system in the prefrontal cortex. Another study by Shaw and colleagues (2007) sought to examine the relationship between genetics and ADHD symptoms. In this longitudinal study, they looked at children with a particular version of a gene related to dopamine receptors and found, again, thinner cortical tissue in the prefrontal cortex. Interestingly, as the children grew up or took long-term medication, portions of their cortex developed to a normal thickness. This improvement in the cortical thickness was correlated with improved ADHD symptoms (Shaw et al., 2007b; Shaw, Gogtay, & Rapoport, 2010). Studies such as these highlight the plasticity of our brains and that ADHD might be a disorder related to this neuroplasticity.

Low doses of stimulants are effective in the treatment of ADHD. These medications enhance attention and cognitive skills. Stimulant medications that have been used in treating ADHD include *methyphenidate* (Ritalin), *mixed amphetamine salts* (Adderall), and the newer drug *lisdexamfetamine dimesylate* (Vyvanse). These medications work by increasing levels of dopamine in the neural synapses. Functional MRI studies demonstrate that stimulants reverse the underactivity found in the prefrontal cortex in people with ADHD (Bush, Valera, & Seidman, 2005). Animal studies also have confirmed the relationship between the effect of stimulants on the prefrontal cortex. Rats that have stimulants injected into their prefrontal cortex show improvements on cognitive tasks that are dependent on prefrontal cortex functioning (Spencer, Klein, & Berridge, 2012). Though it might seem counterintuitive to treat people with ADHD with stimulants, these medications work by improving focus and attention and reducing hyperactivity that is due to an understimulation of dopamine. The use of stimulants, especially those that have an extended release over the course of the day, help people with ADHD to improve their social functioning, school performance, behavior outside school, and ability to drive and to reduce disruptive behavior in general (Cox et al., 2006; Buitelaar & Medori, 2010; Swanson, Baler, & Volkow, 2011).

A noninvasive therapy that has received attention is neurofeedback. This technique uses biofeedback to help guide people with ADHD to regulate their brain activity, usually while playing video games. Some studies indicate that this treatment is effective (Butnik, 2005; Nazari, 2011), whereas others suggest that treatment efficacy was demonstrated to be less robust in randomized controlled and double-blinded studies (Moriyama et al., 2012). Researchers continue to study the relationship between brain structure and function and ADHD to identify the causes of this disorder and to optimize treatment interventions.

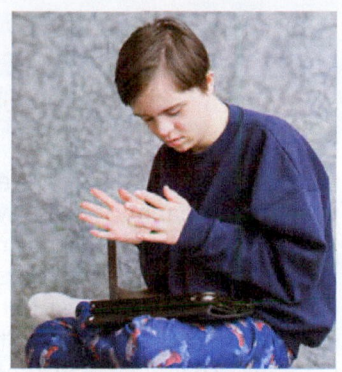

Interventions for Children with Developmental Disorders

In this photo, a boy diagnosed with both ASD and Down syndrome is clapping his hands as he plays with a tablet device. Tablet devices are powerful interventions that develop social interaction and communication skills. Touch-screen technology is just beginning to be studied for intervention in developmental disorders such as ASD.
Source: wallybird/Shutterstock. com.

Section Review: Developmental Disorders

1. Why was ASD once considered a disorder caused by environmental influences?

2. What is a consistent neurological correlate of people with ASD?

3. What are the major symptoms of ADHD, and how long can this disorder last?

How Do the Media Portray Psychological Disorders?

Rationale

Psychological disorders are a favorite topic of the media. You cannot go a day without reading about them on the Internet or in a magazine or newspaper, seeing people with disorders on daytime talk shows and soap operas, hearing about them on radio talk shows, or watching reports on them on the nightly television news. This activity asks you to keep a record of media portrayals of psychological disorders.

Procedure

Keep a 2-week diary of every instance in which you encounter a media portrayal of a person with a psychological disorder. Note such instances on the Internet, in movies, on television, and in books, magazines, or newspapers. Also note how often particular topics or disorders are presented and whether they are portrayed in a casual, scientific, or sensational manner.

Results and Discussion

Discuss your impression of how the media portray psychological disorders. How does the information presented in the media compare with the information presented in this chapter? What should the media present concerning psychological disorders that they do not do well enough?

Chapter Summary

Characteristics of Psychological Disorders

- Researchers in the field of psychopathology study psychological disorders.
- The criteria for determining the presence of a psychological disorder include abnormality, maladaptiveness, and personal distress.
- The major viewpoints on the causes of psychological disorders include the biopsychological, psychoanalytic, behavioral, cognitive, humanistic, and sociocultural viewpoints.
- The more recent biopsychosocial viewpoint sees psychological disorders as the result of an interaction of biological, psychological, and social factors.
- *The Diagnostic and Statistical Manual of Mental Disorders–Fifth Edition (DSM-5),* published by the American Psychiatric Association, is the accepted standard for classifying psychological disorders.
- Some psychologists and psychiatrists have questioned the reliability and validity of the *DSM-5.*
- Psychologist David Rosenhan and psychiatrist Thomas Szasz have noted certain dangers involved in diagnosing psychological disorders.
- Though the insanity defense is rarely used and is even more rarely successful in criminal cases, it has sparked controversy over concern that people guilty of violent crimes might escape punishment.

Anxiety Disorders

- Anxiety disorders are associated with anxiety that is intense and disruptive of everyday functioning.

- A generalized anxiety disorder is marked by a constant state of anxiety that exists independently of any particular stressful situation.
- A panic disorder is marked by sudden attacks of overwhelming anxiety accompanied by dizziness, trembling, cold sweats, heart palpitations, shortness of breath, fear of dying, and fear of going crazy.
- Phobias are excessive or inappropriate fears.
- A specific phobia involves a specific object or situation, a social anxiety disorder involves fear of social evaluation, and agoraphobia involves fear of being in public places.

Obsessive-Compulsive Disorder

- People with obsessions and compulsions that interfere with their daily functioning suffer from obsessive-compulsive disorder.
- An obsession is a persistent, recurring thought, and a compulsion is a repetitive action that one feels compelled to perform.

Somatic Symptom and Related Disorders

- The somatic symptom and related disorders are characterized by physical symptoms in the absence of disease or injury, with the symptoms caused instead by psychological factors.
- A person with illness anxiety disorder interprets the slightest physical changes in his or her body as evidence of a serious illness.
- A person with a conversion disorder exhibits loss or alteration of a physical function without any apparent physical cause.

Dissociative Disorders

- In a dissociative disorder, the person's conscious awareness becomes separated from certain aspects of her or his thoughts, feelings, and memories.
- A person with dissociative amnesia is unable to recall personally significant memories.
- A person with dissociative fugue suffers from dissociative amnesia and loss of identity and flees from home.
- A person with a dissociative identity disorder (formerly called multiple personality disorder) has two or more distinct personalities that may vie for dominance.

Major Depressive Disorder and Related Disorders

- People with major depressive disorder (MDD) experience depression that is so intense and prolonged that it causes severe distress and disrupts their lives.
- In cases of MDD, suicide is always a concern.
- People who attempt suicide usually give warnings, so suicidal threats should be taken seriously.

Bipolar Disorder

- In bipolar disorder, the person alternates between periods of mania and major depressive disorder.
- Mania is characterized by euphoria, hyperactivity, grandiose ideas, annoying talkativeness, inflated optimism, and inflated self-esteem.

Schizophrenia

- Schizophrenia is characterized by a severe disruption of perception, cognition, emotionality, behavior, and social relationships.

- The *DSM-5* considers schizophrenia to be a cluster of symptoms that can be demarcated by a series of stages of increasing psychosis.
- Biological theories of schizophrenia consider genetic, biochemical, developmental, and neurological factors.

Personality Disorders

- Personality disorders are long-standing, inflexible, maladaptive patterns of behavior.
- Of growing concern is the prevalence of the borderline personality disorder, marked by emotional instability and severely maladaptive social relationships.
- Of greatest concern is the antisocial personality disorder, associated with lying, stealing, fighting, drug abuse, physical cruelty, and lack of responsibility.

Developmental Disorders

- Developmental disorders are psychosocial disorders present in early childhood that can persist into adulthood
- Autism spectrum disorder (ASD) is characterized by poor social skills, poor communicative abilities, and repetitive behavior.
- People with attention deficit hyperactivity disorder (ADHD) have difficulty concentrating, remaining still, and staying on task at school or work.
- According to family studies, there is strong support for a genetic influence in both ASD and ADHD.

Key Terms

Characteristics of Psychological Disorders

biopsychosocial model (p. 481)
insanity (p. 484)
psychopathology (p. 480)

Anxiety Disorders

agoraphobia (p. 494)
anxiety disorder (p. 488)
generalized anxiety disorder (p. 488)
panic disorder (p. 491)
phobia (p. 492)
social anxiety disorder (p. 493)
specific phobia (p. 493)

Obsessive-Compulsive Disorder

obsessive-compulsive disorder (OCD) (p. 495)

Somatic Symptom and Related Disorder

conversion disorder (p. 498)
illness anxiety disorder (p. 497)
somatic symptom and related disorder (p. 497)

Dissociative Disorders

dissociative amnesia (p. 499)
dissociative disorder (p. 499)
dissociative fugue (p. 499)
dissociative identity disorder (p. 500)

Major Depressive Disorder and Related Disorders

major depressive disorder (p. 501)
seasonal affective disorder (SAD) (p. 505)

Bipolar Disorder

bipolar disorder (p. 508)
mania (p. 508)

Schizophrenia

schizophrenia (p. 510)

Personality Disorders

antisocial personality disorder (p. 518)
borderline personality disorder (BPD) (p. 516)
personality disorder (p. 516)

Developmental Disorders

autism spectrum disorder (ASD) (p. 519)
attention deficit hyperactivity disorder (ADHD) (p. 521)
developmental disorders (p. 519)

Note: Answers for the Chapter Quiz questions are provided at the end of the book.

1. The Swiss physician Paracelsus countered the supernatural view of psychological disorders by attributing them to
   a. neurotransmitters.
   b. phases of the moon.
   c. hallucinogenic substances.
   d. imbalances in body humors.

2. _____ involves the inability to develop normal social and communication skills and a tendency to be self-absorbed.
   a. Schizophrenia
   b. Parkinson's disease
   c. Autism spectrum disorder
   d. Attention deficit hyperactivity disorder

3. A woman subjected to horrible abuse from her husband suddenly loses her memory for herself, husband, and place of employment and begins a new life with a new identity in another state. This situation is most likely a case of
   a. hypermnesia.
   b. dissociative fugue.
   c. dissociative amnesia.
   d. conversion disorder.

4. A person likes to be by herself, laughs when she hears of tragedies, speaks gibberish, believes she is Catherine the Great, and hears voices that curse at her. This situation is most likely a case of
   a. schizophrenia.
   b. bipolar disorder.
   c. dissociative identity disorder.
   d. antisocial personality disorder.

5. Enlarged cerebral ventricles are associated with
   a. schizophrenia.
   b. bipolar disorder.
   c. conversion disorder.
   d. antisocial personality disorder.

6. Psychopathology is the study of
   a. psychopaths.
   b. schizophrenia.
   c. psychological disorders.
   d. physiological bases of mental illness.

7. Just before a major singing competition, one of the singers loses his voice. A physical examination reveals no medical cause for the condition. This situation is most likely a case of
   a. illness anxiety disorder.
   b. dissociative fugue.
   c. conversion disorder.
   d. obsessive-compulsive disorder.

8. According to R. D. Laing, whose belief was criticized by Mark Vonnegut, schizophrenia is a
   a. myth.
   b. mystical state.
   c. neurochemical disorder.
   d. voyage of self-discovery.

9. A friend of yours suddenly changes many of her habits. She stays in bed until late afternoon, rarely leaves her room, shows little appetite for food, no longer takes daily showers, and expresses no interest in spending time with friends. This situation is most likely a case of
   a. agoraphobia.
   b. schizophrenia.
   c. major depressive disorder.
   d. conversion disorder.

10. Parents high in expressed emotion may cause relapses in children with
    a. schizophrenia.
    b. major depressive disorder.
    c. dissociative amnesia.
    d. obsessive-compulsive disorder.

11. A young man enjoys getting into fights, has a history of stealing cars, and expresses no remorse for inflicting physical and emotional harm on others. This situation is most likely a case of
    a. mania.
    b. schizophrenia.
    c. dissociative identity disorder.
    d. antisocial personality disorder.

12. In 1843, Daniel M'Naghten became the first person to
    a. cure schizophrenia.
    b. use the insanity defense.
    c. demonstrate conversion hysteria in a man.
    d. be diagnosed with dissociative identity disorder.

13. According to research by Susan Nolen-Hoeksema, major depressive disorder is linked to
    a. chromosome 11.
    b. anger turned inward.
    c. ruminating about problems.
    d. faulty attributional processes.

14. According to the humanistic viewpoint, incongruence between the actual self and the ideal self causes
    a. major depressive disorder.
    b. schizophrenia.
    c. dissociative fugue.
    d. dissociative identity disorder.

15. According to Martin Seligman, depressed people tend to attribute negative events in their lives to
    a. stable, global, and internal factors.
    b. unstable, global, and internal factors.
    c. stable, specific, and external factors.
    d. unstable, specific, and external factors.

16. A psychological disorder in which depressive symptoms occur during particular times of the year is called
    a. neurosis.
    b. spring fever.
    c. bipolar disorder.
    d. seasonal affective disorder.

17. Janice Egeland and her colleagues (1987) found evidence, since disputed, that a defective gene on the 11th chromosome predisposed members of an extended Amish family to develop
    a. schizophrenia.
    b. bipolar disorder.
    c. seasonal affective disorder.
    d. antisocial personality disorder.

18. In regard to suicide,
    a. most attempters give warnings.
    b. most attempters leave notes explaining why.
    c. women tend to use more lethal means than men do.
    d. taking threats seriously will only instigate them.

19. The main criteria for diagnosing a psychological disorder are abnormality, personal distress, and
    a. insanity.
    b. delusions.
    c. maladaptiveness.
    d. auditory hallucinations.

20. A student who fails out of school becomes severely depressed and sees a psychologist for help. The psychologist attributes this depression to the frustration of the student's movement toward self-actualization. This situation indicates that the psychologist favors the
    a. cognitive viewpoint.
    b. behavioral viewpoint.
    c. humanistic viewpoint.
    d. psychoanalytic viewpoint.

21. A student who had been gloomy, unkempt looking, and socially aloof a week ago suddenly becomes wildly optimistic, impeccably groomed, and the "life of the party." This situation is most likely a case of
    a. agoraphobia.
    b. bipolar disorder.
    c. conversion disorder.
    d. disorganized schizophrenia.

22. David Rosenhan's (1973) study, in which pseudopatients had themselves admitted to mental hospitals, indicated that psychological diagnosis may be
    a. biased by preconceptions.
    b. more accurate than medical diagnosis.
    c. more accurate for psychoses than neuroses.
    d. affected by the socioeconomic status of the patient.

23. A college student faced with upcoming exams and term papers responds to his resulting feelings of anxiety by reorganizing his notes, rearranging his bookshelves, cleaning out his desk drawers, and straightening up his closet. He would be showing symptoms of
    a. claustrophobia.
    b. dissociative fugue.
    c. disorganized schizophrenia.
    d. obsessive-compulsive disorder.

24. While walking through a shopping mall, you suddenly have an intense feeling of dread, notice your heart beating strongly, feel as if you are suffocating, and find yourself running for the nearest exit. You would be exhibiting symptoms of
    a. mania.
    b. acrophobia.
    c. schizophrenia.
    d. panic disorder.

25. A student compulsively rearranges her room over and over. Her psychotherapist attributes this behavior to her desire to control an unconscious conflict over sex. The psychotherapist probably favors the
    a. cognitive viewpoint.
    b. behavioral viewpoint.
    c. humanistic viewpoint.
    d. psychoanalytic viewpoint.

Thought Questions

1. How would the three criteria for diagnosing psychological disorders be applied to agoraphobia?

2. Why might public concern about the use of the insanity defense in criminal cases be overblown?

3. A student becomes overwhelmed with anxiety when he is faced with major exams. How might the different viewpoints on psychological disorders explain this reaction?

15

Therapy

Source: CLIPAREA/Custom media/
Shutterstock.com.

Chapter Outline

catharsis In psychoanalysis, the release of repressed emotional energy as a consequence of insight into the unconscious causes of one's psychological problems.

From 1880 to 1882, Austrian physician Josef Breuer (1842–1925) treated a wealthy, intelligent, young woman he called Anna O. who suffered from *conversion hysteria*—that is, physical symptoms without any apparent physical cause (Van der Kolk, 2000). Her symptoms apparently were triggered by her difficulty dealing with her father's terminal illness, but also may have been complicated by morphine and chloral hydrate dependence (de Paula Ramos, 2003). She displayed a variety of symptoms that came and went, including eye squinting, loss of speaking ability, and paralyzed arms and legs.

Breuer found that when Anna O. spoke freely about her condition—at times under hypnosis—her symptoms disappeared. She called this experience her "talking cure" or "chimney sweeping." As she spoke freely, she often recalled distressing childhood experiences that had been repressed, sometimes violently reexperiencing the emotions she had felt in childhood. By talking about her feelings and experiences, she obtained emotional release, typically followed by the disappearance of her physical symptoms. Breuer called this process of emotional release **catharsis**. His treatment of Anna O. marked the beginning of modern psychotherapy. Breuer related the story of Anna O. to his young friend Sigmund Freud, who was so impressed by Breuer's approach that he began to use it himself. His use of it led to the founding of psychoanalysis, which Freud always attributed to his mentor, Breuer.

As for Anna O., she led a rich, productive life under her real name, Bertha Pappenheim (1859–1936). She became a founder of the social work profession (Swenson, 1994), championing the rights of the poor. She stressed the influence of poverty on crime and illness. Pappenheim also was an early feminist and wrote *A Woman's Right,* a play that denounced the exploitation of women (Kimball, 2000). Bertha Pappenheim's life is testimony to the power of psychotherapy to help individuals overcome psychological disorders and live full lives. At some time in your life you might develop a psychological disorder that leads you to seek professional help. If so, you will be in good company. Since the 1950s the percentage of Americans who seek psychotherapy during their lifetime has doubled (VandenBos, 1996).

The History of Therapy

The treatment of psychological disorders has come a long way since its ancient origins. Treatment practices have been influenced by their cultural, religious, and scientific contexts.

Ancient Practices

If you visit the Smithsonian Institution in Washington, D.C., you will encounter a display of Stone Age skulls with holes that were cut into them with stones—in the ancient practice of **trephining**. Some authorities assume that these ancient trephiners believed that they were releasing demons that caused abnormal behavior. Of course, without written records there is no way to know if demon release was the true reason. Perhaps, instead, trephining was performed for some unknown medical purpose.

The Greek philosopher Hippocrates (460–377 B.C.) turned away from supernatural explanations of psychological disorders, which attributed them to demons or punishment from the gods, in favor of naturalistic explanations. Hippocrates believed that many psychological disorders were caused by imbalances in fluids that he called humors, which included blood, phlegm, black bile, and yellow bile (see Chapter 14). For example, because Hippocrates believed that an excess of blood caused the agitated state of mania, he treated mania with bloodletting. As you would expect, people weakened by the loss of blood became less agitated.

Medieval and Renaissance Approaches

During the early Christian era, such naturalistic treatments existed side by side with supernatural ones. But by the late Middle Ages, treatments increasingly involved physical punishment. This inhumane treatment continued into the Renaissance, which also saw the advent of *insane asylums*. Though some of these institutions were pleasant communities in which residents received humane treatment, most were no better than prisons in which inmates lived under deplorable conditions. The most humane asylum was the town of Geel in Belgium, where people with mental disorders lived in the homes of townspeople, moved about freely, and worked to support themselves. In the 1990s, Geel continued to provide humane care for 800 individuals living with 600 families (Godemont, 1992).

Few Renaissance asylums were as pleasant as Geel. The most notorious one was St. Mary's of Bethlehem in London. In this nightmarish place, inmates were treated like animals in a zoo. On weekends, families would go on outings to the asylum, pay a small admission fee, and be entertained by the antics of the inmates. Visitors called the male inmates of St. Mary's "Tom Fools," contributing the word *tomfoolery* to our language. And the asylum became known as "Bedlam" (Harris, 2003b), reflecting the cockney pronunciation of Bethlehem.

18th- and 19th-Century Reforms

In 1792 inhumane conditions in French insane asylums and the positive model of Geel spurred physician Philippe Pinel (1745–1826) to institute what he called **moral therapy** at the Bicetre asylum in Paris (Harris, 2003a). Moral therapy was based on the premise that humane treatment, honest work, and pleasant recreation would promote mental well-being. Pinel had the inmates unchained, provided with good food, and treated with kindness. He even instituted the revolutionary technique of speaking with them about their problems. The first inmate released was a giant, powerful man who had been chained in a dark cell for 40 years after killing a guard with a blow from his manacles. Onlookers were surprised (and relieved) when he simply strolled outside, gazed up at the sky, and exclaimed, "Ah, how beautiful" (Bromberg, 1954, p. 83).

Pinel's moral therapy spread throughout Europe. It was introduced to the United States by Benjamin Rush (1745–1813), the founder of American psychiatry. As part of moral therapy, Rush prescribed work, music, and travel (Farr, 1944/1994). He also prescribed physical treatments that with hindsight we might view as barbaric, but which he believed

trephining An ancient technique in which sharp stones were used to chip holes in the skull, possibly to let out evil spirits that supposedly caused abnormal behavior.

Pinel Unchaining the Inmates of an Asylum

Philippe Pinel shocked and frightened many French citizens by freeing the inmates of an insane asylum and providing them with humane treatment. When opponents asked, "Citizen, are not you yourself crazy, that you would free these beasts?" Pinel replied, "I am convinced that these *people* are not incurable if they can have air and liberty" (Bromberg, 1954, p. 83).
Source: Anki Hoglund/ Shutterstock.com.

moral therapy An approach to therapy, developed by Philippe Pinel, that provided mental patients with humane treatment.

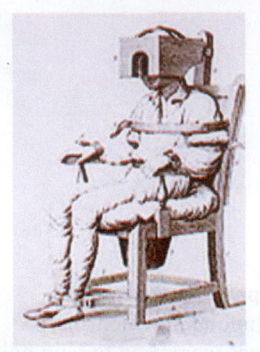

(a)

(b)

Nineteenth-Century Treatment Devices

Benjamin Rush invented *(a)* the "tranquilizing chair" to calm manic patients. Another device that was popular in the 19th century was *(b)* "the crib," which was used to restrain violent patients. The bed in which the patient would lie is on the left; the "cover" of the crib is on the right.

Source: (b) WIU Libraries Archives & Special Collections. All Rights Reserved. Reproduced with permission.

psychotherapy The treatment of psychological disorders through psychological means generally involving verbal interaction with a professional therapist.

cultural competence The consideration of sociocultural factors such as gender, ethnicity, sexual orientation, and religion in psychological training and practice.

had therapeutic value. For example, because Rush assumed that depressed people had too little blood in their brains, he whirled them around in special chairs to force blood from their bodies into their heads. One can imagine that, much as an amusement park ride can do today, this treatment induced a temporary feeling of elation.

In the 1840s Dorothea Dix (1802–1887), a Massachusetts schoolteacher, shocked the U.S. Congress with reports of the brutal treatment of the inmates confined to insane asylums. Because of her efforts, many state mental hospitals were built throughout the United States, usually in rural settings, that provided good food, social activities, and employment on farms. Though Canadian asylums were influenced more by Britain and France (Sussman, 1998), Dix also influenced Canadian reforms, including the establishment of the first mental hospital in Nova Scotia (Goldman, 1990). Unfortunately, over time many of these mental hospitals became human warehouses, providing little more than custodial care. This result contradicted the humane treatment that Dix had envisioned for asylum residents.

The Mental Health Movement

In the early 20th century, public concern about the deplorable conditions in state mental hospitals grew after the publication of *A Mind That Found Itself* by a Yale University graduate named Clifford Beers (Beers, 1908/1970). The book described the physical abuse Beers suffered during his 3 years in the Connecticut State Hospital. Beers (1876–1943) founded the mental health movement, which promotes the humane treatment of people with mental disorders. The mental health movement has seen mental hospitals joined by group homes, private practices, and counseling centers as alternative treatment sites for psychological disorders.

Today, specially trained professionals offer therapy for psychological disorders. Psychological therapy, or **psychotherapy**, involves the therapeutic interaction of a professional therapist with one or more persons suffering from a psychological disorder. Though there are many approaches to psychotherapy, most psychotherapists favor an *eclectic orientation,* in which they select techniques from different kinds of therapy that they believe will help particular clients. The first formal orientation toward the practice of psychotherapy was psychoanalysis, the topic of the next section.

A recent trend in psychotherapy is increased attention to sociocultural factors that might influence the course of therapy. For example, the 1999 National Multicultural Conference and Summit was a collaborative attempt by psychologists to broaden the concept of multiculturalism to include other variables relevant to the practice of psychology—culture, ethnicity, gender, and sexual orientation. The focus of the conference was the implementation of *cultural competence* in psychological training, research, and clinical practice (Sue, 2003). According to Stanley Sue, **cultural competence** is the "belief that people should not only appreciate and recognize other cultural groups but also be able to effectively work with them" (Sue, 1998, p. 440). Thus, cultural competence consists of cultural knowledge and the interpersonal skills to effectively use this knowledge.

The need for cultural competence is driven in part by changing demographics—about 50 percent of Americans will be members of ethnic minority groups by the year 2050. Therapists need to be aware of cross-cultural differences in beliefs and behaviors that they may encounter in therapy. For example, members of Western cultures disclose intimate details more readily than do members of Asian cultures (Toukmanian & Brouwers, 1998). And, as discussed in Chapter 13, there are cross-cultural differences in the construal of self-schema related to the dimensions of independence and interdependence (Hall, 2003). Failure to understand these cultural differences could affect assessment, the development of an empathetic relationship, and the effective provision of treatment. The University of South Dakota's clinical psychology training program for Native Americans, The Four Winds, is an example of the ways in which cultural competence can be incorporated into the psychological curriculum and practice. It presents traditional training in psychotherapy within a Native American cultural context. The program aims to increase the number of Native American psychotherapists and the availability of culturally sensitive psychotherapists to serve that ethnic group (Yutrzenka, Todd-Bazemore, & Caraway, 1999).

Section Review: The History of Therapy

1. Does the existence of trephined skulls necessarily mean that trephining was performed to release evil spirits?

2. What were some of the basic techniques used in moral therapy?

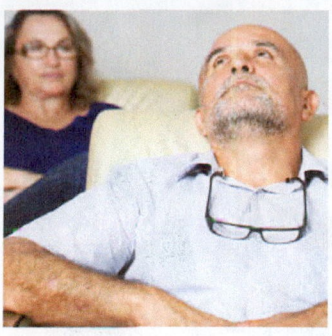

Psychoanalysis Today

The Psychoanalytic Orientation

As discussed at the beginning of the chapter, psychoanalysis grew out of Josef Breuer's case study of Anna O. Though Breuer was the first to describe this "talking cure," it was Sigmund Freud who elaborated it into a system of psychotherapy.

The Nature of Psychoanalysis

Freud believed that childhood emotional conflicts repressed into the unconscious mind cause the symptoms of psychological disorders, including conversion hysteria. Freud's aim was to make the person gain insight into his or her repressed conflicts, thereby inducing catharsis and relieving the underlying conflict. This approach led Freud to develop the form of therapy known as **psychoanalysis**. Traditional Freudian psychoanalysis takes place with the client reclining on a couch and the therapist sitting nearby, just out of sight. Freud claimed that this arrangement relaxes the client, thereby reducing inhibitions about discussing emotional topics. Traditional Freudian psychoanalysts might see clients three to five times a week for years.

Though most psychotherapists now favor seated, face-to-face interaction with their clients, some psychoanalytic psychotherapists still sit out of sight of the client, who reclines on a couch. *Source:* Adam Gregor/ Shutterstock.com.

psychoanalysis The early school of psychology that emphasized the importance of unconscious causes of behavior.

Techniques in Psychoanalysis

An important goal of psychoanalytic techniques is to make the client's unconscious conflicts conscious. To accomplish this goal, the therapist actively *interprets* the significance of what the client says. The therapist's interpretations are based on the analysis of *free associations, resistances, dreams,* and *transference.*

Analysis of Free Associations

The main technique of psychoanalysis is the **analysis of free associations**, which has much in common with Anna O.'s "talking cure." In free association, the client is urged to report any thoughts or feelings that come to mind—no matter how trivial or embarrassing they seem. Freud assumed, based on the principle of psychic determinism (see Chapter 1), that free association would unlock meaningful information related to the client's psychological disorder (Bronstein, 2002).

analysis of free associations In psychoanalysis, the process by which the therapist interprets the underlying meaning of the client's uncensored reports of anything that comes to mind.

Analysis of Resistances

In the **analysis of resistances**, the psychoanalyst notes behaviors that interfere with therapeutic progress. Signs of resistance include arriving late, missing sessions, abruptly changing topics, and talking about insignificant things. The client holds on dearly to resistances to block awareness of painful feelings, conflicts, or memories. By interpreting the meaning of the client's resistances, the therapist helps the client uncover these unconscious memories and conflicts. Suppose a client changes the topic whenever the therapist asks him about his father. The therapist might interpret this action as a sign that the client has unconscious emotional conflicts regarding his father. But resistances also might indicate that the client simply believes that the therapist is not empathetic enough (Messer, 2002).

analysis of resistances In psychoanalysis, the process by which the therapist interprets client behaviors that interfere with therapeutic progress toward uncovering unconscious conflicts.

Analysis of Dreams

Freud believed that the **analysis of dreams** was the "royal road to the unconscious" (see Chapter 6). He claimed that dreams symbolized unconscious sexual and aggressive conflicts.

analysis of dreams In psychoanalysis, the process by which the therapist interprets the symbolic, manifest content of dreams to reveal their true, latent content to the client.

Freud relied on his own dreams, as well as those of his clients, to illustrate his theory (Mautner, 1991). Having the client free-associate about the content of a series of dreams allows the psychoanalyst to interpret the symbolic, or *manifest,* content of the client's dreams to reveal the true, or *latent,* content—their true meaning.

Analysis of Transference

The key to a psychoanalytic cure is the **analysis of transference**. Transference is the tendency of the client to act toward the therapist in the way she or he acts toward important people in everyday life, such as a boss, spouse, parent, or teacher. Transference can be positive or negative. In *positive transference* the client expresses feelings of approval and affection toward the therapist. In *negative transference* the client expresses feelings of disapproval and rejection toward the therapist—such as criticizing the therapist's skill. By interpreting transference, the therapist helps the client gain insight into the earlier interpersonal origins of his or her current emotional problems.

Offshoots of Psychoanalysis

Traditional Freudian psychoanalysis inspired many offshoots. Nonetheless, psychoanalysis in its various forms went from being the choice of most therapists in the 1950s to being the choice of about 15 percent in the 1980s (Smith, 1982). One of the main reasons for this declining trend is that other less costly and less lengthy therapies are at least as effective as psychoanalysis (Fisher & Greenberg, 1985).

Today few therapists are strict Freudians. Instead, many practice what is called *psychodynamic therapy,* which employs aspects of psychoanalysis in face-to-face, once-a-week therapy lasting months instead of years. Psychodynamic therapists also rely more on discussions of past and present social relationships than on trying to uncover unconscious emotional conflicts. Psychodynamic therapy has proved effective in the treatment of a variety of psychological disorders (Shedler, 2010), though this conclusion has been criticized by others citing methodological problems in comparing different therapeutic approaches (Anestis, Anestis, & Lilienfeld, 2011).

Analysis of Resistances

In analysis of resistances, behaviors that interfere with therapeutic progress are noted.

Source: Ambrophoto/ Shutterstock.com.

analysis of transference
In psychoanalysis, the process by which the therapist interprets the feelings expressed by the client toward the therapist as being indicative of the feelings typically expressed by the client toward important people in his or her personal life.

Section Review: The Psychoanalytic Orientation

1. How do psychoanalysts employ the analysis of free associations?

2. How do psychoanalysts employ the analysis of resistances?

The Behavioral Orientation

behavior therapy
The therapeutic application of the principles of learning to change maladaptive behaviors.

In 1952 British psychologist Hans Eysenck coined the term **behavior therapy** to refer to treatments that favor changing maladaptive behaviors rather than providing insight into unconscious conflicts. Unlike traditional psychoanalysts, behavior therapists ignore unconscious conflicts, emphasize present behavior, and assume that therapy can be accomplished in weeks or months instead of years. To behavior therapists, abnormal behavior—like normal behavior—is learned and therefore can be unlearned (Tryon, 2000). Behavior therapists change maladaptive behaviors by applying the principles of classical conditioning, operant conditioning, and social learning theory. In their practices, behavior therapists often combine various behavioral techniques. Some behavior therapists stress the need to consider the cultural context of a person's behavior when working with clients. Misinterpretation of behaviors because of cultural ignorance might lead to the inappropriate application of behavioral change techniques (LaRoche & Lustig, 2013).

Classical Conditioning Therapies

Several kinds of behavior therapy have been derived from Ivan Pavlov's work on classical conditioning (Plaud, 2003). In classical conditioning, a stimulus associated with another stimulus that elicits a response may itself come to elicit that response (see Chapter 7). Therapies based on classical conditioning stress the importance of stimuli in controlling behavior. The goal of these therapies is the removal of the stimuli that control maladaptive behaviors or the promotion of more adaptive responses to those stimuli.

Counterconditioning

The classical conditioning technique of **counterconditioning** replaces unpleasant emotional responses to stimuli with pleasant ones, or vice versa. The procedure is based on the assumption that we cannot simultaneously experience an unpleasant feeling, such as anxiety, and a pleasant feeling, such as relaxation. Therapeutic counterconditioning was introduced by John B. Watson's student Mary Cover Jones (1896–1987). Watson had conditioned a toddler he called Little Albert to fear a white rat by pairing the rat with a loud sound (see Chapter 7). Watson proposed that the fear could be eliminated by pairing the rat with a pleasant stimulus, such as pleasurable stroking. Jones (1924) took Watson's suggestion and, under his advisement, tried to rid a 3-year-old boy named Peter of a rabbit phobia (see Chapter 14). Jones used what she called "direct conditioning," which is now known as counterconditioning. Jones presented Peter with candy and then brought a caged rabbit closer and closer to him. This therapy was done twice a day for 2 months.

At first, Peter cried when the rabbit was within 20 feet of him. Over the course of the study, he became less and less fearful of it. On the last day, he asked for the rabbit, petted it, tried to pick it up, and finally played with it on a windowsill. Evidently, the pleasant feelings Peter experienced in response to the candy gradually became associated with the rabbit. This association reduced his fear of the rabbit. Jones cautioned, however, that this procedure was delicate. If performed too rapidly, it could produce the opposite effect—fear of the candy. More recently, counterconditioning has been used effectively to treat posttraumatic stress disorder (PTSD) (Paunovic, 2003) and to reduce distress associated with a hypodermic injection (Slifer, Eischen, & Busby, 2002). In one application of counterconditioning, participants with spider phobias who were asked to imagine scenes of spiders paired with humorous scenes showed a significant reduction in the intensity of their phobias (Ventis, Higbee, & Murdock, 2001).

Systematic Desensitization

Today, the most widely used form of counterconditioning is **systematic desensitization**, developed by Joseph Wolpe (1915–1997) for treating phobias (Wolpe, 1958). Systematic desensitization involves three steps. The first step is for the client to practice *progressive relaxation,* a technique developed in the 1930s by Edmund Jacobson to relieve anxiety. To learn progressive relaxation, clients sit in a comfortable chair and practice successively tensing and relaxing each of the major muscle groups—including those of the head, arms, torso, and legs—until they gain the ability to relax their entire body.

The second step is the construction of an *anxiety hierarchy* (see Table 15-1), consisting of a series of anxiety-inducing scenes related to the person's phobia. The client lists 10 to 20 scenes, rating them on a 100-point scale from least to most anxiety inducing. A rating of zero would mean that the scene induces no anxiety; a rating of 100 would mean that the scene induces abject terror. Suppose that you have *arachnophobia*—a spider phobia. You might rate a photo of a spider a 5, a spider on your arm a 60, and a spider on your face an 85.

The third step involves imagining each of the anxiety-inducing responses in the anxiety hierarchy while relaxing. The therapist would start with the scene with the lowest rating, moving along the hierarchy from least to most threatening. For example, you first would learn to relax while imagining holding a photo of a spider. Once the relaxation response had been reliably conditioned to this stimulus, the therapist would move to the next scene on the anxiety hierarchy. In this way the new response, relaxation, would become conditioned to each of the anxiety-inducing stimuli.

Counterconditioning

One of the first uses of counterconditioning was eliminating a rabbit phobia in a young boy.
Source: Nagy-Bagoly Arpad/Shutterstock.com.

counterconditioning
A behavior therapy technique that applies the principles of classical conditioning to replace unpleasant emotional responses to stimuli with more pleasant ones.

systematic desensitization
A form of counterconditioning that trains the client to maintain a state of relaxation in the presence of imagined anxiety-inducing stimuli.

TABLE 15-1 A Test-Anxiety Hierarchy

Initial Rating of Distress	Fear-Inducing Scene
10	Registering for next semester's courses
15	Going over the course outline in class
20	Hearing the instructor announce that the midterm exam will take place in three weeks
30	Discussing the difficulty of the exam with fellow students
45	Reviewing your notes one week before the exam
50	Attending a review session three days before the exam
60	Listening to the professor explain what to expect on the exam the day before
65	Studying alone the day before the exam
70	Studying with a group of students the night before the exam
75	Overhearing superior students expressing their self-doubts about the exam
80	Realizing that you are running out of study time at 1:00 A.M. the day of the exam
90	Entering the class before the exam and having the professor remind you that one-third of your final grade depends on it
95	Reading the exam questions and discovering that you do not recognize several of them
100	Answering the exam questions while hearing other students hyperventilating and muttering about them

In Vivo Desensitization

A phobia sufferer might gain relief through in vivo desensitization, which involves gradual exposure to more and more anxiety-inducing situations related to the phobia. The woman on the left, suffering from a fear of heights (acrophobia), might have begun therapy by simply looking out of a first-floor window. She has progressed to the point that she is able to walk onto a balcony.

Source: bikeriderlondon/ Shutterstock.com.

in vivo desensitization
A form of counterconditioning that trains the client to maintain a state of relaxation in the presence of anxiety-inducing stimuli.

Systematic desensitization has been successful in treating a wide variety of phobias. These phobias include fear of dentists (Klepac, 1986), choking (Millikin & Braun-Janzen, 2013), and public speaking (Rossi & Seiler, 1989–1990). Given the success of systematic desensitization in treating phobias, what accounts for its effectiveness? This question is the topic of "The Research Process" box.

Of course, the ultimate test of systematic desensitization is the ability to face the actual source of your phobia. One way of ensuring such success is to use **in vivo desensitization**, which physically exposes the client to successive situations on the client's anxiety hierarchy. This technique is a variation of systematic sensitization and is in contrast to *in vitro desensitization* in which the patient simply imagines the source of the phobia. In vivo desensitization has been successful in treating claustrophobia (Edinger & Radtke, 1993), school phobia (Houlihan & Jones, 1989), and many other kinds of phobias. In one case, a woman who had chronic nightmares about snakes was relieved of them by an in vivo procedure that had her move closer and closer to a live, harmless snake (Eccles, Wilde, & Marshall, 1988). A newer refinement of these techniques is to use virtual reality technology to help patients with phobias. A recent study looked at active-duty members of the military who were diagnosed with post-traumatic stress disorder (see Chapter 16) related to service in Iraq or Afghanistan. The patients provided experimenters with information related to their most traumatic events during combat tours. The experimenters then took these scripts and converted them to virtual reality simulations that approximated the traumatic experiences the patients described. The results of the study concluded that virtual reality therapy was more effective than the control group that received combinations of cognitive processing therapy, eye movement desensitization, drug therapy,

The Research Process

Do Endorphins Mediate the Effect of Systematic Desensitization on Phobias?

Rationale

Might systematic desensitization exert its effects through the actions of endorphins? Perhaps pleasurable feelings induced by endorphins can counter phobic anxiety. This hypothesis was the rationale behind a study conducted by Kelly Egan, John Carr, Daniel Hunt, and Richard Adamson of the University of Washington (Egan, Hunt, Carr, & Adamson, 1988).

Method

Participants all suffered from specific phobias (see Chapter 14), such as fear of heights, fear of dogs, and fear of elevators. Participants were randomly assigned into two groups. Prior to sessions of systematic desensitization, 6 participants (the experimental group) received intravenous infusions of naloxone, a drug that blocks the effect of endorphins, and 5 participants (the control group) received intravenous infusions of a placebo, a saline solution with no specific effects. Because the study used the double-blind procedure, neither the participants nor the experimenter knew which participants received naloxone and which received the placebo. The double-blind procedure controlled for any participant or experimenter biases. Participants received 8 sessions over a period of 4 weeks.

Results and Discussion

The results indicated that participants who received the placebo experienced a significant decrease in the severity of their phobias, whereas those who received naloxone did not. Because naloxone blocks the effects of the endorphins, the results support the possible role of endorphins in the effects of systematic desensitization. The pleasant feelings produced by the endorphins may become conditioned to the formerly fear-inducing stimuli.

and other PTSD-related services (McLay et al., 2011). The results of this study suggest virtual reality therapy as a useful adjunct therapy to already exsisting PTSD therapies.

Aversion Therapy

The goal of **aversion therapy** is to make a formerly pleasurable, but maladaptive, behavior unpleasant. In aversion therapy, a stimulus that normally elicits a maladaptive response is paired with an unpleasant stimulus, leading to a reduction in the maladaptive response. Aversion therapy has been used to treat a variety of behavioral problems, including smoking, bed-wetting, and overeating.

But aversion therapy was originally introduced in the 1930s to treat alcoholism by administering painful electric shocks to alcoholic patients in the presence of the sight, smell, and taste of alcohol. Today aversion therapy for alcoholism uses drugs that make the individual feel deathly ill after drinking alcohol (see Figure 15-1). The drugs interfere with the metabolism of alcohol, leading to the buildup of a toxic chemical that induces nausea and dizziness. A study of more than 400 alcoholic patients who underwent a treatment program that included aversion therapy found that 60 percent were abstinent a year later (Smith & Frawley, 1993).

aversion therapy A form of behavior therapy that inhibits maladaptive behavior by pairing a stimulus that normally elicits a maladaptive response with an unpleasant stimulus.

Operant-Conditioning Therapies

Treatments based on operant conditioning change maladaptive behaviors by controlling their consequences. Popular forms of behavior modification rely on the behavioral contingencies of positive reinforcement, punishment, and extinction.

Positive Reinforcement

One of the most important uses of positive reinforcement has been in treating patients in mental hospitals. Residents of mental hospitals have traditionally relied on the staff to take care of all their needs. This reliance often leads to passivity, a decrease in self-care, and a general decline in dignified behavior. The development of the *token economy* provided a way to overcome this problem. The **token economy** provides tokens (often plastic poker chips) as positive reinforcement for desirable behaviors, such as making beds, taking showers, or wearing appropriate clothing. The patients use the tokens to purchase items such as books

token economy An operant conditioning procedure that uses tokens as positive reinforcers in programs designed to promote desirable behaviors, with the tokens later used to purchase desired items or privileges.

FIGURE 15-1
Aversion Therapy in the Treatment of Alcoholism

In aversion therapy, when alcoholics drink alcohol mixed with the drug Antabuse, they experience extreme nausea. The Antabuse serves as an unconditioned stimulus (UCS) that naturally elicits nausea as an unconditioned response (UCR). After repeated pairings of Antabuse and alcohol, classical conditioning takes place and alcohol becomes a conditioned stimulus (CS) that elicits nausea as a conditioned response (CR). Thus, alcohol, which previously had elicited a pleasant state of intoxication, now elicits an unpleasant state of nausea. This response increases the likelihood that the individual will stop drinking alcohol.

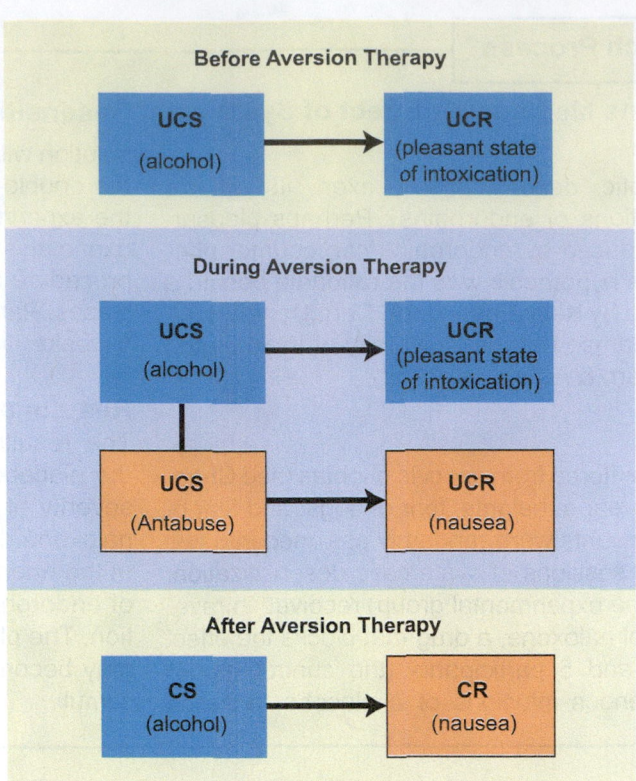

Before Aversion Therapy

UCS (alcohol) → UCR (pleasant state of intoxication)

During Aversion Therapy

UCS (alcohol) → UCR (pleasant state of intoxication)

UCS (Antabuse) → UCR (nausea)

After Aversion Therapy

CS (alcohol) → CR (nausea)

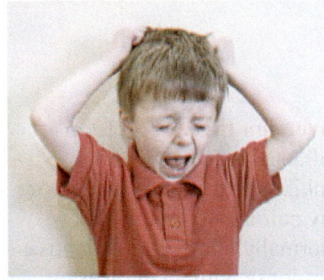

Operant-Conditioning Therapy for Autism Spectrum Disorder (ASD)

The combination of punishment and positive reinforcement has been effective in reducing self-injurious behaviors in children with ASD and promoting appropriate behaviors.

Source: Pixel Memoirs/Shutterstock.com.

flooding An extinction procedure in which a phobic client is exposed to a stimulus that evokes intense anxiety.

or candy and privileges such as television or passes to leave the hospital grounds. The use of token economies has proved successful, for example, in reducing self-injurious behavior and promoting positive social behavior by criminal inmates with psychological disorders (Seegert, 2003). Token economies also are employed in programs for people with intellectual disabilities. In one study, a token economy motivated a man with an intellectual disability to behave in a more socially appropriate manner (LeBlanc, Hagopian, & Maglieri, 2000).

Punishment

Though less desirable than positive reinforcement, punishment also can be effective in changing maladaptive behaviors. In fact, sometimes it may be the only way to prevent inappropriate, or even dangerous, behavior. In using punishment, the therapist provides aversive consequences for maladaptive behavior. A controversial application of punishment that was used in the past was mild electric shocks to reduce self-biting, head banging, and other self-destructive behaviors in children with autism spectrum disorder (ASD), who do not respond to talk therapy (see Chapter 14). Today, milder forms of punishment are used, such as sharply saying "no" when the child engages in the self-injurious behavior Once the behavior has stopped, the therapist uses positive reinforcement to promote more appropriate behaviors. The combination of punishment and positive reinforcement has been effective in improving the behavior of children with ASD (Ma, 2009).

Extinction

If a behavior—whether adaptive or maladaptive—is not reinforced, it will become extinguished. The technique of *flooding* takes advantage of this phenomenon in the elimination of intense fears and phobias. Unlike systematic desensitization, which trains the client to relax and experience a graded series of anxiety-inducing situations, **flooding** exposes the client to a situation that evokes intense anxiety. In *imaginal flooding,* the client is asked to hold in mind an image of the feared situation; in *in vivo flooding,* the client is placed in the actual feared situation. As clients experience the situation mentally or in reality, their anxiety diminishes because they are prevented from escaping and thereby negatively reinforcing their flight behavior through fear reduction. Of course, care must be taken to protect the client from being overwhelmed by fear. Flooding has helped clients overcome anxiety disorders such as panic disorder and agoraphobia (Siegmund et al., 2011), and PTSD (Foa et al., 1999).

Social-Learning Therapies

In treating Peter's rabbit phobia, Mary Cover Jones (1924) sometimes let Peter observe other children playing with a rabbit. By doing so, Jones made use of social learning (see Chapter 7). Therapists who use social learning have their clients watch other people model adaptive behaviors either in person or on videotape. Clients learn better social skills or to overcome phobias by performing the modeled behavior. Therapists also may use **participant modeling**, in which the therapist models the desired behavior while the client watches. The client then tries to perform the behavior. Participant modeling has been successful in helping individuals overcome their fears, including fears of dogs (May, Rudy, & Thomas, 2013) and post-traumatic stress disorder, even when the therapy is provided over the Internet (Mouthaan et al., 2011).

participant modeling A form of social-learning therapy in which the client learns to perform more adaptive behaviors by first observing the therapist model the desired behaviors.

Section Review: The Behavioral Orientation

1. How would you use systematic desensitization to treat a student who is terrified of making oral presentations in class?

2. How would you use a token economy to improve spelling and arithmetic performance by third graders?

The Cognitive Orientation

The Greek Stoic philosopher Epictetus (A.D. ca. 60–ca. 120) noted that irrational people tend to become emotionally upset. His observation explains the kinship between Stoic philosophy and the cognitive orientation in psychotherapy (Still & Dryden, 2003). Cognitive therapists believe that events in themselves do not cause maladaptive emotions and behaviors. Instead, it is our interpretation of events that does so. Given this assumption, cognitive therapists believe that changes in thinking can produce changes in maladaptive emotions or behaviors. Because cognitive therapies can include aspects of behavior therapy, they are commonly called *cognitive-behavior therapies*. They have been effective in treating many kinds of disorders, including compulsive gambling (Jiminez-Murcia et al., 2012), panic disorder (Stuart, Treat, & Wade, 2000), major depressive disorder, generalized anxiety disorder, social anxiety disorder, and posttraumatic stress disorder (Butler, Chapman, Forman, & Beck, 2006). Still, some cognitive therapists believe that the assumptions and practice of cognitive therapy may not translate well to other cultures. Beliefs and interpretations of events might be adaptive in one culture and maladaptive in others (Dowd, 2003).

Rational-Emotive Behavior Therapy

Albert Ellis (1962) developed the first form of cognitive therapy, which he called *rational-emotive therapy (R-E-T)*. He more recently renamed it **rational-emotive behavior therapy (R-E-B-T)** to emphasize the interaction of thinking, feeling, and behaving in maintaining psychological well-being (Ellis, 1999). A survey of therapists found that Ellis has been second only to Carl Rogers in his influence on the field of psychotherapy (Smith, 1982). Ellis's therapy is based on his *A-B-C theory* of emotion (Ziegler, 2001), in which *A* is an activating event, *B* is an irrational belief, and *C* is an emotional consequence (see Figure 15-2). Ellis points out that most of us believe that *A* causes *C*, when, in fact, *B* causes *C*.

rational-emotive behavior therapy (R-E-B-T) A type of cognitive therapy, developed by Albert Ellis, that treats psychological disorders by forcing the client to give up irrational beliefs.

FIGURE 15-2
The A-B-C Theory of Emotion

According to Albert Ellis's A-B-C theory of emotion, our emotions are caused by our beliefs about events, not the events themselves. That is, it is our cognitive interpretation of events that determines how they affect us emotionally.

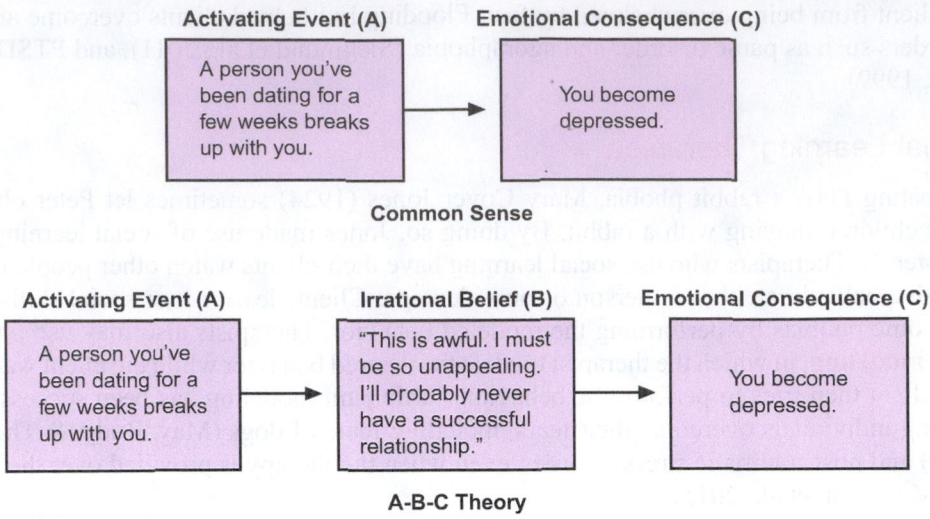

Activating Event (A)

A person you've been dating for a few weeks breaks up with you.

Emotional Consequence (C)

You become depressed.

Common Sense

Activating Event (A)

A person you've been dating for a few weeks breaks up with you.

Irrational Belief (B)

"This is awful. I must be so unappealing. I'll probably never have a successful relationship."

Emotional Consequence (C)

You become depressed.

A-B-C Theory

Cognitive Therapy

Cognitive therapy has been effective in treating the negative beliefs of depressed people.

Source: Burlingham/Shutterstock.com.

cognitive therapy A type of therapy, developed by Aaron Beck, that aims at eliminating exaggerated negative beliefs about oneself, the world, or the future.

Imagine that you fail an exam *(A)* and become depressed *(C)*. Ellis would attribute your depression not to your failure but to an irrational belief, such as the belief *(B)* that you must be perfect. Thus, your irrational belief, not your failure, causes your depression—and the behaviors it produces. Ellis has pointed out similarities between the Western practice of R-E-B-T and the Eastern practice of Zen Buddhism and urged that the two practices be integrated into an effective means of improving psychological well-being (Kwee & Ellis, 1998).

Though therapists who use R-E-B-T can develop warm, empathetic relationships with their clients, Ellis himself is more interested in demolishing, sometimes harshly, the irrational ideas of his clients (Johnson, DiGiuseppe, & Ulven, 1999). After identifying a client's irrational beliefs, Ellis challenges the client to provide evidence supporting them. Ellis then contradicts any irrational evidence, almost demanding that the client agree with him. Table 15-2 presents a verbatim transcript illustrating the use of R-E-B-T. Ellis (1997) has even described how R-E-B-T has helped him deal with a lifetime of physical disorders, including diabetes and deficient hearing.

A meta-analysis of research studies found that R-E-B-T is more effective than placebo treatment and as effective as other therapies (Engels, Garnefski, & Diekstra, 1993). It has helped people overcome depression (Macaskill & Macaskill, 1996), extreme jealousy (Ellis, 1996), and childhood sexual abuse (Rieckert & Moeller, 2000).

Cognitive Therapy

Psychiatrist Aaron Beck has found that depression is caused by negative beliefs about oneself, the world, and the future (Beck, 1997). Thus, depressed people tend to blame themselves rather than their circumstances for misfortunes, attend more to negative events than to positive events, and have a pessimistic view of the future (see Chapter 14). Depressed people also overgeneralize from rare or minor negative events in their lives. The goal of Beck's **cognitive therapy** is to change such exaggerated beliefs in treating psychological disorders, most notably depression.

Beck is less directive in his approach than Ellis is. Beck employs a Socratic technique, in which he asks clients questions that lead them to recognize their irrational beliefs. Beck has clients keep a daily record of their thoughts and urges them to note irrational beliefs and replace them with rational ones. A client who claims, "I am an awful student and will never amount to anything," might be encouraged to think, instead, "I am doing poorly in school because I do not study enough. If I change my study habits, I will graduate and pursue a desirable career." To promote positive experiences, Beck might begin by giving the client homework assignments that guarantee success, such as having a client who feels socially incompetent speak to a close friend on the telephone. Cognitive therapy has been especially successful in treating depression, which was its original purpose (Scott, Palmer, Paykel, Teasdale, & Hayhurst, 2003). Moreover, cognitive therapy is being used nationally in the Department of

TABLE 15-2 Rational-Emotive Behavioral Therapy

This transcript illustrates how the rational-emotive behavior therapist (T) challenges the client (C) to change irrational beliefs. The client is a 23-year-old young woman experiencing intense feelings of guilt for not living up to her parents' strict standards.

C: Well, this is the way it was in school, if I didn't do well in one particular thing, or even on a particular test—and little crises that came up—if I didn't do as well as I had wanted to do.

T: Right. You beat yourself over the head.

C: Yes.

T: But why? What's the point? Are you supposed to be perfect? Why the hell shouldn't human beings make mistakes, be imperfect?

C: Maybe you always expect yourself to be perfect.

T: Yes. But is that *sane*?

C: No.

T: Why do it? Why not give up that unrealistic expectation?

C: But then I can't accept myself.

T: But you're saying, "It's shameful to make mistakes." Why is it shameful? Why can't you go to somebody else when you make a mistake and say, "Yes, I made a mistake"? Why is that so awful? . . .

C: It might all go back to, as you said, the need for approval. If I don't make mistakes, then people will look up to me. If I do it all perfectly—

T: Yes, that's part of it. That is the erroneous belief; that if you never make mistakes everybody will love you and that it is necessary they do. That's right. That's a big part of it. But is it true, incidentally? Suppose you never did make mistakes—*would* people love you? They'd sometimes hate your guts, wouldn't they?

Source: Ellis, A. (1971). *Growth through reason.* Palo Alto, CA: Science & Behavior Books. Reprinted by permission.

Veteran Affairs to treat United States military and personnel who suffer from major depressive disorder (Karlin et al., 2012). Nonetheless, it also is effective in treating other disorders, such as panic disorder (Rathgeb-Feutsch, Kempter, Feil, Pollmächer, & Schuld, 2011) and obsessive-compulsive disorder (Sabine, 2000).

Section Review: The Cognitive Orientation

1. What are the basic assumptions and techniques of Ellis's rational-emotive behavior therapy?

2. What are the basic assumptions and techniques of Beck's cognitive therapy?

The Humanistic Orientation

Unlike the psychoanalytic orientation, the humanistic orientation stresses the present rather than the past, and conscious rather than unconscious experience. Unlike the behavioral orientation, the humanistic orientation stresses the importance of subjective cognitive experience rather than objective environmental circumstances. And unlike the cognitive orientation, the humanistic orientation encourages the expression of emotion rather than its control.

Person-Centered Therapy

person-centered therapy
A type of humanistic therapy, developed by Carl Rogers, that helps clients find their own answers to their problems.

The most popular kind of humanistic therapy is **person-centered therapy**, originally called *client-centered therapy*. It was developed in the 1950s by Carl Rogers (1902–1987) as one of the first alternatives to psychoanalysis. Rogers has been the most influential of all contemporary psychotherapists (Smith, 1982). Unlike the rational-emotive behavior therapist, who is *directive* in challenging the irrational beliefs of clients, the person-centered therapist is *nondirective* in encouraging clients to find their own answers to their problems (Bozarth, 2002). This approach is in keeping with the humanistic concept of self-actualization and is reminiscent of the Socratic method of self-discovery. Japanese psychologists have noted the similarity between person-centered therapy and the nondirective aspects of Taoist philosophy (Hayashi et al., 1998).

Given that person-centered therapists offer no advice, how do they help their clients? Their goal is to facilitate the pursuit of self-actualization, not by offering expertise but by providing a social climate in which clients feel comfortable being themselves. Person-centered therapists do so by promoting self-acceptance. Humanistic psychologists assume that psychological disorders arise from an incongruence between a person's public self and her or his actual self (see Chapter 14). This incongruence makes the person distort reality or deny feelings, trying to avoid the anxiety caused by failing to act in accordance with those feelings. The goal of person-centered therapy is to help individuals reduce this discrepancy by expressing and accepting their true feelings. The person-centered therapist promotes self-actualization through reflection of feelings, genuineness, accurate empathy, and unconditional positive regard (Rogers, 1957). Note that a close friend or relative whom you consider a "good listener" and valued counselor probably exhibits these characteristics, too.

Reflection of feelings is the main technique of person-centered therapy. The therapist is an active listener who serves as a therapeutic mirror, attending to the emotional content of what the client says and restating it to the client. This mirroring helps clients recognize their true feelings. By being *genuine* the therapist acts in a concerned, open, and sincere manner rather than in a detached, closed, and phony manner. This genuineness makes clients more willing to disclose their true feelings. During his career, Rogers increasingly stressed the importance of genuineness (Bozarth, 1990). The client also becomes more willing to share feelings when the therapist shows *accurate empathy,* which means that the therapist's words and actions indicate a true understanding of how the client feels (Meissner, 1996).

Perhaps the most difficult task for the person-centered therapist is the maintenance of *unconditional positive regard*—acting in a personally warm and accepting manner. The therapist must remain nonjudgmental, no matter how distasteful she or he finds the client's thoughts, feelings, and actions to be. This unconditional positive regard encourages clients to freely express and deal with even the most distressing aspects of themselves. Unconditional positive regard also promotes positive therapeutic outcomes by encouraging the client and the therapist to develop a mutually empathic and genuine relationship throughout the process of therapy (Murphy, Cramer, & Joseph, 2012). Table 15-3 presents a verbatim transcript that illustrates the use of person-centered therapy.

Gestalt Therapy

Gestalt therapy A type of humanistic therapy, developed by Fritz Perls, that encourages clients to become aware of their true feelings and to take responsibility for their own actions.

Fritz Perls (1893–1970), a former psychoanalytic psychotherapist and the founder of **Gestalt therapy**, claimed, "The idea of Gestalt therapy is to change paper people to real people" (Perls, 1973, p. 120). To Perls, paper people were people out of touch with their true feelings, which made them live "inauthentic lives." Like psychoanalysis, Gestalt therapy seeks to bring unconscious feelings into conscious awareness. Like person-centered therapy, Gestalt therapy tries to increase the client's emotional expressiveness. And like rational-emotive behavior therapy, Gestalt therapy may be confrontational in forcing clients to change maladaptive ways of thinking and behaving.

Despite its name, Gestalt therapy is not derived from Gestalt psychology, which is discussed in Chapter 1, except in stressing the need to achieve wholeness of the personality—meaning that one's emotions, language, and actions should be consistent with one another

TABLE 15-3 Person-Centered Therapy

This transcript illustrates how the person-centered therapist (T) acts as psychological mirror, reflecting back the feelings expressed in statements by the client (C). The client feels anxious about taking responsibility for her life. Notice how this therapist is less directive than the therapist in the transcript of rational-emotive behavior therapy in Table 15-2.

C: Um-hum. That's why I say . . . *(slowly and very thoughtfully)* well, with that sort of foundation, well, it's really up to me. I mean, it seems to be really apparent to me that I can't depend on someone else giving me an education. *(very softly)* I'll really have to get it myself.

T: It really begins to come home—there's only one person that can educate you—a realization that perhaps nobody else can give you an education.

C: Um-hum. *(long pause—while she sits thinking)* I have all the symptoms of fright. *(laughs softly)*

T: Fright: That this is a scary thing, is that what you mean?

C: Um-hum. *(very long pause—obviously struggling with feelings in herself)*

T: Do you want to say any more about what you mean by that? That it really does give you the symptoms of fright?

C: *(laughs)* I, uh . . . I don't know whether I quite know. I mean . . . Well, it really seems like I'm cut loose *(pause)*, and it seems that I'm very—I don't know—in a vulnerable position, but I, uh, I brought this up and it, uh, somehow it almost came out without saying it. It seems to be . . . it's something I let out.

T: Hardly a part of you.

C: Well, I felt surprised.

T: As though, "Well for goodness sake, did I say that?" *(both chuckle)*

Source: Excerpt from *On becoming a person* by Carl R. Rogers. Copyright © 1961 by Carl R. Rogers, renewed 1989 By David E. Rogers and Natalie Rogers. Reprinted by permission of Houghton Mifflin, Harcourt Company. All rights reserved.

(Polster & Polster, 1993). Gestalt therapists insist that clients take responsibility for their own behavior rather than blame other people or events for their problems and that clients live in the here and now rather than being concerned about events occurring at other places and times. Gestalt therapists also assume that people who are aware of their feelings can exert greater control over their reactions to events. The Gestalt therapist notes any signs that the client is not being brutally honest about his or her feelings, at times by observing the client's nonverbal communication posture, gestures, facial expressions, and tone of voice. For example, a client who denies feeling anxious while tightly clenching his fists would be accused of lying about his emotions.

Though research studies have found that Gestalt therapy can be effective with certain psychological disorders, such as phobias (Martinez, 2002), there has been a lack of scientific research on its effectiveness. Moreover, Perls has been criticized for promoting self-centeredness and emotional callousness, as in his "Gestalt prayer" (Perls, 1972, p. 70): "I do my thing and you do your thing. I am not in this world to live up to your expectations. And you are not in this world to live up to mine. You are you and I am I. And if by chance we find each other, it's beautiful. If not, then it can't be helped."

Section Review: The Humanistic Orientation

1. What are the basic characteristics of client-centered therapy?

2. How does Gestalt therapy differ from R-E-B-T?

The Social-Relations Orientation

The therapeutic orientations that have been discussed so far involve a therapist and a client. In contrast, the *social-relations orientation* assumes that because many psychological problems involve interpersonal relationships, additional people must be brought into the therapy process. Many psychotherapists insist that ethnic differences (Maiello, 1999), sexual orientation (Hartwell, Serovich, Gravsky, & Kerr, 2012), social class differences (Storck, 1997), and religious differences (Gopaul-McNicol, 1997) must be considered in any group approach to psychotherapy.

Group Therapy

In 1905 Joseph Pratt, a Boston physician, found that his tuberculosis patients gained relief from emotional distress by meeting in groups to discuss their feelings. Pratt's discovery marked the beginning of group therapy (Allen, 1990). Because group therapy allows a therapist to see more people (typically six to twelve in a group) in less time, more people can receive help at less cost per person. Group therapy provides participants with a range of role models, encouragement from others with similar problems, feedback about their own behavior, assurance that their problems are not unique, and the opportunity to try out new behaviors. Group therapy has been used to improve the emotional well-being of people as varied as cancer patients (Harman, 1991), bereaved relatives (Zimpfer, 1991), and people with major depressive disorder (Feng et al., 2012). Group therapy also has been used effectively in Botswana to provide treatment for the children who have been orphaned due to the HIV/AIDS epidemic in the region (Thamaku & Daniel, 2013). The procedures used in group therapy depend on the theoretical orientation of the therapist.

Transactional Analysis

transactional analysis (TA)
A form of psychoanalytic group therapy, developed by Eric Berne, that helps clients change their immature or inappropriate ways of relating to other people.

Group therapies derived from psychoanalysis emphasize insight and emotional catharsis. A form of group therapy inspired by psychoanalysis is **transactional analysis (TA)**, popularized in the 1960s by psychiatrist Eric Berne (1910–1970) in his best-selling book *Games People Play* (1964). Berne claimed that people act according to one of three roles: child, parent, or adult (Solomon, 2003). These roles resemble the Freudian personality structures of id, superego, and ego, respectively. The *child,* like the id, acts impulsively and demands immediate gratification. The *parent,* like the superego, is authoritarian and guides moral behavior. And the *adult,* like the ego, promotes rational and responsible behavior.

Each role is adaptive in certain situations and maladaptive in others. For example, acting childish might be appropriate at parties but not at job interviews. According to Berne, our relationships involve *transactions*—social interactions between these roles. *Complementary transactions,* in which both individuals act according to the same role, are usually best. *Crossed transactions,* as when one person acts as a child and the other acts as an adult, are maladaptive. The goal of TA is to analyze transactions between group members. For example, a person might engage in transactions that support her or his feelings of worthlessness and continually provoke responses from others that support those feelings. TA has been used to treat various problems, including personality disorders (Haimowitz, 2000).

Social-Skills Training

social-skills training A form of behavioral group therapy that improves the client's social relationships by improving her or his interpersonal skills.

assertiveness training A form of social-skills training that teaches clients to express their feelings constructively.

Psychologists who favor behavioral group therapies assume that changes in overt behavior will bring relief from emotional distress. A popular form of behavioral group therapy, also used in individual therapy, is **social-skills training**. Its goal is to improve social relationships by enhancing social skills, such as cultivating friendships or carrying on conversations. Participants are encouraged to rehearse new behaviors in the group setting. Members of the group may model more effective behaviors. Social-skills training has been used to help people with intellectual disabilities improve their social competence (Travis & Sturmey, 2013) and also has been used in the treatment of social anxiety disorder (van Dam-Baggen & Kraaimaat, 2000).

A form of social-skills training called **assertiveness training** helps people learn to express their feelings constructively in social situations. Many people experience poor social relations because they are unassertive. They are unable to ask for favors, to say no to requests, or to complain about poor service. By learning to express their feelings, formerly unassertive people relieve their anxiety and have more rewarding social relations. Members of assertiveness-training groups try out assertive behaviors in the group situation. Assertiveness training has improved the social skills of visually impaired adolescents (Kim, 2003) and has enabled female undergraduates to successfully resist sexual coercion (Rowe, Jouriles, McDonald, Platt, & Gomez, (2012). It also has been used to reduce drug use and risky sexual behavior in male methamphetamine users who are HIV-positive and have sex with other men (Semple, Strathdee, Zians, McQuaid, & Patterson, 2013).

Self-Help Groups

In the 1950s Carl Rogers introduced the encounter group, which comprised strangers who met to honestly assess their emotional and behavioral issues. The encounter group movement died out but led to the emergence of *self-help groups* for drug abusers, phobia sufferers, and others with specific shared problems. A survey of directors of substance abuse programs affiliated with the U.S. Department of Veterans Affairs found that 79 percent of their patients were referred to Alcoholics Anonymous (Humphreys, 1997). Self-help groups are conducted by people who have experienced those problems. For example, self-help groups for the elderly often are run by older adults (Gottlieb, 2000).

Family Therapy

Group therapy usually brings together unrelated people; **family therapy** brings together members of the same family. The basic assumption of family therapy is that a family member with problems related to her or his family life cannot be treated apart from the family. The main goals of family therapy are the constructive expression of feelings and the establishment of rules that family members agree to follow. The therapist helps family members establish an atmosphere in which no individual is blamed for all the family's problems. Like other kinds of group therapy, family therapy is paying greater attention to sociocultural factors, including ethnicity, sexual orientation, and religion (Carr, 2011).

Family therapists, such as the late Virginia Satir, who favor a *systems approach* may have family members draw diagrams of their relationships and discuss how certain of the relationships are maladaptive (Satir, Bitter, & Krestensen, 1988). Perhaps the family is too child-oriented, or perhaps a parent and child are allied against the other parent. The goal of the therapist is to have the family replace these maladaptive relationships with more effective ones. An offshoot of family therapy is *marital therapy,* which tries to improve relationships between married people. Because of the great number of committed couples who are not married, marital therapy has been joined by *couple therapy* (Gurman & Fraenkel, 2002). Research on couple therapy has found that it can have beneficial effects on both the couple's relationship and their individual emotional well-being. For example, when couple therapy reduces emotional depression, marital discord tends to decline. Likewise, when couple therapy improves marital discord, emotional depression tends to decline (Whisman & Beach, 2012).

Assertiveness Training

Members of assertiveness-training groups practice assertive behaviors in the group situation. Assertiveness training can lower anxiety and improve social skills.

Source: wavebreakmedia/Shutterstock.com.

family therapy A form of group therapy that encourages the constructive expression of feelings and the establishment of rules that family members agree to follow.

Section Review: The Social-Relations Orientation

1. What are the basic assumptions and techniques of transactional analysis?

2. What are the basic characteristics of assertiveness training?

The Biological Orientation

Though Sigmund Freud practiced psychoanalysis, he predicted that, as science progressed, therapies for psychological disorders would become more and more biological (Trotter, 1981). During the past few decades, the *biological orientation* has indeed become an

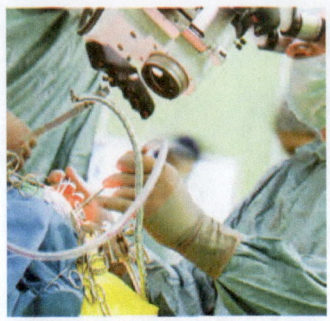

Psychosurgery

Today, psychosurgery is used less to destroy a region of the brain but more to modulate it. Psychosurgical techniques are much more refined as well. Instead of removing large sections of the frontal lobe, as in the early operations, neurosurgeons use computer-based magnetic resonance imaging to guide small electrodes to the brain region of interest.

Source: VILevi/Shutterstock.com.

psychosurgery The treatment of psychological disorders by destroying brain tissue.

electroconvulsive therapy (ECT) A biological therapy that uses brief electric currents to induce brain seizures in victims of major depressive disorder.

important approach to therapy. It is based on the assumption that psychological disorders are associated with brain dysfunctions and consequently will respond to treatments that alter brain activity. Biological treatments, because they involve medical procedures, can be offered only by psychiatrists and other physicians. The biological treatments include *psychosurgery, electroconvulsive therapy,* and *drug therapy.*

Psychosurgery

While attending a professional meeting in 1935, Portuguese neurologist Egas Moniz was impressed by a report that agitated chimpanzees became calmer after undergoing brain surgery that separated their frontal lobes from the rest of their brain. Moniz wondered whether such **psychosurgery** might benefit agitated mental patients. Moniz convinced neurosurgeon Almeida Lima to perform a *prefrontal leucotomy* (also known as a *prefrontal lobotomy*) on anesthetized patients. Lima drilled holes in the patient's temples, inserted a scalpel through the holes, and cut away portions of the frontal lobes. Moniz reported many successes in calming agitated patients (Moniz, 1937/1994). As a result, he won a Nobel Prize in 1949 for inventing psychosurgery, which was considered a humane alternative to the common practice of locking agitated patients in padded rooms or restraining them in straitjackets.

Psychosurgery was introduced to the United States in 1936 by neurosurgeon Walter Freeman and psychiatrist James Watts. They favored a technique called *transorbital leucotomy* (Freeman, 1948). The patient's eye socket (the *orbit*) was anesthetized (the brain itself is insensitive to pain), and a mallet was used to drive a surgical pick into the frontal lobe. The pick was then levered back and forth to separate portions of the lobe from the rest of the brain. By 1979, psychosurgery had been performed on about 35,000 mental patients in the United States. But the use of psychosurgery declined markedly and rightfully so. One reason was its unpredictable effects (Swayze, 1995)—some patients improved, others became apathetic, still others became violent, and a small percentage died. A second reason for its decline was the advent of drug therapies in the 1950s and 1960s, which provided safer, more effective, and more humane treatment (Tierney, 2000). And a third reason was public opposition to what seemed to be a barbaric means of behavior control.

Today, psychosurgery rarely is used in the United States; when it is used, it involves the use of electrodes inserted into the brain's limbic system to treat problems such as self-mutilation (Price et al., 2001). In this case a direct current is sent through the electrodes, destroying small amounts of tissue in precise areas of that brain region. This technique has achieved some success in treating cases of obsessive-compulsive disorder that have not responded to other treatments (Sachdev et al., 2001). A more common modification of psychosurgery is deep brain stimulation (DBS). This procedure increases surgical precision, minimizes risk of injury to the patient (Lapidus, Kopell, Ben-Haim, Rezai, & Goodman, 2013), and modulates the function of brain regions rather than destroying them. DBS is one of the treatments used for improving motor symptoms in patients with Parkinson's disease (Gervais-Bernard et al., 2009).

Electroconvulsive Therapy

In 1938, on a visit to a slaughterhouse, Italian psychiatrist Ugo Cerletti watched pigs being rendered unconscious by electric shocks. Cerletti reasoned that electric shock might be a safe alternative to drug-induced shock therapy in calming agitated patients with schizophrenia (Cerletti, 1954). This hypothesis inspired Cerletti and his fellow psychiatrist Lucio Bini to introduce **electroconvulsive therapy (ECT)**. ECT uses a brief electrical current to induce brain seizures. Though ECT originally was used for treating agitated patients, it proved more successful in elevating the mood of severely depressed patients who had failed to respond to drug therapy.

A psychiatrist administers ECT by attaching electrodes to one or both temples of a patient who is under general anesthesia and who has been given a muscle relaxant. The muscle relaxant prevents injuries that might otherwise be caused by violent contractions of the muscles. A burst of electricity of 70 to 150 volts is passed through the brain for about half a second. This electrical current induces a brain seizure, which is followed by a period of unconsciousness lasting up to 30 minutes. The patient typically receives three treatments a week for several weeks.

A major published review of the research literature found that it is unclear whether ECT or antidepressant drugs are best in the treatment of major depressive disorder (Piper, 1993). But because ECT produces more rapid improvement than antidepressant drugs, which can take several weeks, it is the treatment of choice for people with major depressive disorder in imminent danger of committing suicide (Persad, 1990). But ECT's mechanism of action in humans is unclear. For example, its antidepressant effect is unrelated to its induction of seizures (Sackeim, 1994). Because major depressive disorder is associated with reduced activity of serotonin and norepinephrine neurons in the brain, one explanation is that ECT stimulates an increase in the levels of those neurotransmitters. But a study found that the effectiveness of ECT in relieving major depressive disorder was unrelated to its effects on serotonin and norepinephrine neuronal activity (Markianos, Hatzimanolis, & Lykouras, 2002).

However, animal studies have offered a clue to the effectiveness of ECT. Researchers are studying *neurogenesis*, the birth of new neurons, which are identified by labeling them with a special compound. In one study, adult rats that were exposed to ECT experienced increased neurogenesis in the hippocampus (Scott, Wojtowicz, & Burnham, 2000). Adult-born neurons in the hippocampus have been linked to cognition and emotion (Snyder, Soumier, Brewer, Pickel, & Cameron, 2011). Because researchers are not able to measure neurogenesis in the human brain, studies of these also do not provide a definitive explanation for the effectiveness of ECT.

Despite evidence of its effectiveness in relieving major depressive disorder, there has been controversy about ECT's safety and effectiveness. In the past, the violence of the convulsions induced by ECT often broke bones and tore muscles. Today, muscle relaxants prevent such injury. But ECT still causes *retrograde amnesia*—the forgetting of events that occurred from minutes to days prior to the treatment. There also is conflicting evidence regarding the possibility that ECT can produce brain damage (Reisner, 2003). The debate about the desirability of using ECT remains as much emotional and political as scientific.

Drug Therapy

Since its introduction in the 1950s, drug therapy has become the most widely used form of biological therapy. Because many psychological disorders are associated with abnormal levels of neurotransmitters (see Chapter 14), drug therapies generally work by restoring neurotransmitter activity to more normal levels. But a common criticism of drug therapies is that they may relieve symptoms without changing the person's ability to adjust to everyday stress. Concurrent psychotherapy is desirable to help clients learn more adaptive ways of thinking and behaving. The following discussion uses well-known brand names for drugs, with their generic names in parentheses.

Antianxiety Drugs

Because of their calming effect, the **antianxiety drugs** were originally called *tranquilizers* or *anxiolytics*. Today the most widely prescribed are the *benzodiazepines,* such as Xanax (alprazolam) and Valium (diazepam). In fact, the prevalence of anxiety disorders has made the antianxiety drugs the most widely prescribed psychoactive drugs (Sand et al., 2000). In a double-blind study, participants received either Valium or a placebo. Those who received Valium showed a significantly greater reduction in their anxiety level than did those who received a placebo (Rickels, DeMartinis, & Aufdembrinke, 2000). The benzodiazepines act almost immediately and work by stimulating receptors in the brain that enhance the effects of the neurotransmitter GABA, which inhibits brain activity (Gorman, 2003). Benzodiazepines can also produce side effects, including drowsiness, depression, and dependence. A newer drug, Buspar (buspirone), is effective in relieving anxiety without the side effects of the older benzodiazepines, but it takes up to several weeks to have an effect. Buspar works by increasing serotonin levels in the brain (Haller, Halasz, & Makara, 2000).

antianxiety drugs
Psychoactive drugs that are used to treat anxiety disorders.

Antidepressant Drugs

The first **antidepressant drugs** were the *MAO inhibitors,* such as Nardil. Originally used to treat tuberculosis, they were prescribed as antidepressants after physicians noted that they induced euphoria in tuberculosis patients. The MAO inhibitors work by blocking enzymes that normally break down the neurotransmitters dopamine, serotonin, and nor-epinephrine. This blocking action increases the levels of those neurotransmitters in the brain, elevating the patient's mood. But the MAO inhibitors fell into disfavor because they can cause dangerously high blood pressure.

The MAO inhibitors gave way to the *tricyclic antidepressants,* such as Elavil (amitriptyline), Tofranil (imipramine), and Anafranil (clomipramine). The tricyclics increase serotonin and norepinephrine levels by preventing their reuptake by brain neurons that release them. Though the tricyclics are effective in treating major depressive disorder (Faravelli et al., 2003), they take 2 to 4 weeks to have an effect and also have undesirable side effects. This delay means that suicidal patients given antidepressants must be watched carefully during that period.

More recently, drugs known as *selective serotonin reuptake inhibitors (SSRIs)* have been added to the arsenal of antidepressants. These drugs relieve major depressive disorder by elevating serotonin levels by preventing its reuptake by neurons that release it. Among the most popular of these drugs are Zoloft (sertraline), Paxil (paroxetine), and most notably, Prozac (fluoxetine). A meta-analysis of studies with 10,706 participants found that SSRIs and tricyclic antidepressants are equally effective in the relief of major depressive disorder, with fewer patients discontinuing SSRIs due to side effects (Anderson, 2000).

But what is the relative effectiveness of drug therapy and psychotherapy for major depressive disorder? A meta-analysis compared the results of six studies evaluating the treatment outcomes of almost 600 depressed clients—some of whom received psychotherapy and some of whom received combined drug therapy and psychotherapy. In less severe cases of major depressive disorder, recovery rates for psychotherapy and combined therapy were not significantly different. However, in more severe cases, recovery rates for clients who received psychotherapy combined with drug therapy were higher (Thase et al., 1997). An alternative and noninvasive therapy that you have probably heard about is exercise. Exercise is inexpensive and does not require a doctor's prescription. Animal studies show that exercise increases neurogenesis in the hippocampus, and some researchers conclude that this might provide some relief to patients who suffer from psychological disorders, including major depressive disorder (DeCarolis & Eisch, 2010).

Mood Stabilizers

In the 1940s Australian physician John Cade (1949) observed that the chemical lithium calmed agitated guinea pigs. Cade then tried lithium on patients and found that it calmed those suffering from mania—apparently because of its ability to reduce abnormal firing patterns of brain neurons (Lenox & Hahn, 2000). Psychiatrists now prescribe antimanic drugs, also known as **mood stabilizers**, such as *lithium carbonate,* to prevent the extreme mood swings of bipolar disorder (Kleindienst & Greil, 2003). It is important for patients to stay on the drug because, of those who discontinue its use, 50 percent relapse within 3 months (Baker, 1994). Psychiatrists must vigilantly monitor patients taking lithium because it can produce dangerous side effects, including seizures, brain damage, and irregular heart rhythms. Another reason for careful monitoring of these patients is the risk that mood stabilizers will be consumed along with alcohol and other drugs. Substance abuse is significantly more common among individuals with bipolar disorder than among individuals with major depressive disorder (Moreno et al., 2012).

Antipsychotic Drugs

For centuries physicians in India prescribed the snakeroot plant for calming agitated patients. Beginning in the 1940s, a chemical derivative of the plant, *reserpine,* was used to reduce symptoms of mania and schizophrenia. But reserpine fell into disfavor because of its tendency to cause major depressive disorder and low blood pressure. The 1950s saw the development of safer **antipsychotic drugs** called *phenothiazines,*

antidepressant drugs
Psychoactive drugs that are used to treat major depressive disorder.

Antidepressant Medication

SSRIs such as Prozac (fluoxetine) are similar to tricyclic antidepressants but more specific in their effects.

Source: James Steidl/Shutterstock.com.

mood stabilizers Psychoactive drugs, most notably lithium carbonate, that are used to treat bipolar disorder.

antipsychotic drugs
Psychoactive drugs that are used to treat schizophrenia.

such as Thorazine (chlorpromazine), for treating people with schizophrenia. French physicians had noted that the drug, used to sedate patients before surgery, calmed psychotic patients.

The phenothiazines work by blocking brain receptor sites for the neurotransmitter dopamine (Schwartz et al., 2000). Unfortunately, long-term use of antipsychotic drugs can cause the motor side effects that characterize *tardive dyskinesia,* which include grimacing, lip smacking, and limb flailing. A newer antipsychotic drug, Clozaril (clozapine), produces fewer symptoms of tardive dyskinesia while effectively treating many cases of schizophrenia that have not responded well to the phenothiazines (Sachdev, 2000).

Section Review: The Biological Orientation

1. Why has the use of ECT been controversial?

2. How do the tricyclic antidepressants produce their results?

Community Mental Health

Since the 1960s psychologists have played a role in the community mental health movement. They have been involved in deinstitutionalization, community mental health centers, and the prevention of psychological disorders.

Deinstitutionalization

As discussed in the section, "The History of Therapy," for most of the 19th and 20th centuries, state mental hospitals served as the primary sites of treatment for people with serious psychological disorders. But since the 1950s there has been a movement toward **deinstitutionalization**, which promotes the treatment of people in community settings instead of in mental hospitals. Since the 1950s the number of occupied beds in state mental hospitals has decreased from 339 to just 29 per 100,000 members of the population (Lamb, 1998). What accounts for this trend?

deinstitutionalization
The movement toward treating people with psychological disorders in community settings instead of mental hospitals.

- The introduction of drug treatments made it more feasible for mental patients to function in the outside world.

- Mental hospitals had become underfunded, understaffed, and overcrowded. Community-based treatment seemed to be a cheaper, superior alternative.

- Increasing concern for the legal rights of mental patients made it more difficult to have people committed to mental hospitals and to keep them there.

- The Community Mental Health Centers Act of 1963, sponsored by President John F. Kennedy, mandated the establishment of federally funded centers in every community in the United States. These centers were to provide services to prevent and treat psychological disorders, further reducing the need for mental hospitals.

Despite its noble intentions and the fact that many people have benefited from it (Goldman, 1998), deinstitutionalization has worked better in theory than in practice. In many communities, funding has been inadequate to establish and run community mental health centers and to provide needed services. Even when funding is available for treatment facilities, such as halfway houses, homeowners often oppose the placement of such facilities in their neighborhoods (Piat, 2000). As a consequence,

Primary Prevention Programs

Primary prevention programs have been employed to provide treatment to people affected by natural disasters, such as those who survived this devastating tornado that hit Joplin, Missouri, with winds greater than 200 mph in 2011.
Source: Melissa Brandes/Shutterstock.com.

The Crisis Intervention Center

The community mental-health system is aided by crisis intervention centers. These centers handle emergencies such as rape cases, physical abuse, suicide threats, or other problems that require immediate help.
Source: Albert Lozano/Shutterstock.com.

former mental hospital patients who lack family support might have little choice but to live on the street. Others languish in prisons.

The potential benefits of adequately supported deinstitutionalization are evident in the results of a study that compared community care for former mental hospital patients in the comparable cities of Portland, Oregon, and Vancouver, British Columbia. At the time of the study, Portland provided few community mental health services, whereas Vancouver provided many private and public services. One year after their discharge, formerly hospitalized people with schizophrenia in Vancouver were less likely than those in Portland to have been readmitted and more likely to be employed and to report a greater sense of psychological well-being. Because the two groups were initially equivalent, the greater progress of the Vancouver group was attributed to community mental health services rather than to preexisting differences between the groups (Beiser et al., 1985). A more recent study assessed the effectiveness of a brief intervention focusing on psychosocial skills and continuity of care to people with schizophrenia living in a homeless shelter. Symptoms were assessed at the study's onset and six months after moving into the community. Men in the intervention group exhibited a significant decrease in some, but not all, symptoms of schizophrenia, compared to men in the control group (Herman et al., 2000). Thus, the provision of support services may have an impact on easing the transition of mental health patients into the community.

Prevention of Psychological Disorders

Community mental health centers have three main goals in the prevention of psychological disorders: primary prevention, secondary prevention, and tertiary prevention.

Primary prevention helps prevent psychological disorders by fostering social support systems, eliminating sources of stress, and strengthening individuals' ability to deal with stressors. These goals might be promoted, for example, by reducing unemployment and making low-cost housing available. Canada has instituted a community-based primary prevention program called *Better Beginnings, Better Futures* to prevent physical, cognitive, emotional, and behavioral problems in children from economically disadvantaged families (Peters, 1994). Primary prevention programs have, in fact, been effective in preventing social and behavioral problems in children (Leadbeater, Hoglund, & Woods, 2003), providing treatment to people affected by natural disasters (Bassilios, Reifels, & Pirkis, 2012), and immigrants and refugees (Kirmayer et al., 2011).

Secondary prevention provides early treatment for people at immediate risk of developing psychological disorders, sometimes through *crisis intervention*, as in the case of survivors of violence, natural disasters, or political terrorism (Everly, 2000). Secondary prevention has been used, for example, to prevent posttraumatic stress disorder in individuals who have experienced traumatic events (Pitman et al., 2002). A review of 130 secondary prevention programs for children and adolescents with early signs of maladjustment found that the programs were successful in preventing the development of full-blown psychological disorders (Durlak & Wells, 1998).

Tertiary prevention helps keep people who have full-blown psychological disorders from getting worse or having relapses after successful treatment for a disorder, such as drug dependence (Carroll, Tanneberger, & Monti, 1998). Tertiary prevention has been used in a Canadian program to prevent abusive parents from continuing to abuse their children. The program involves home visits by specially trained nurses who provide emotional support, education in proper child-rearing practices, and assistance to parents who are looking to obtain help from other human services (MacMillan & Thomas, 1993). Among the main community approaches to tertiary prevention are community residences that provide homelike, structured environments in which former mental hospital patients readjust to independent living. For example, tertiary prevention has been shown to reduce the rate of homelessness among people discharged from psychiatric care (Forchuk et al., 2013).

The Rights of the Therapy Client

Does a resident of a mental hospital have the right to refuse treatment? Does a resident of a mental hospital have the right to receive treatment? Is what a client reveals to a therapist privileged information? These questions have generated heated debate during the past few decades.

The Rights of Hospitalized Patients

In the United States, people who are committed to mental hospitals lose many of their rights, including their rights to vote, to marry, to divorce, and to sign contracts. Revelations about past psychiatric practices in the former Soviet Union show the extent to which the commitment process can be abused. Soviet psychiatrists used diagnoses such as "reformist delusions" and "schizophrenia with religious delirium" to commit political or religious dissidents to mental hospitals (Faraone, 1982).

Legally, only people who are judged to be dangerous to themselves or others can be involuntarily committed to mental hospitals. The need to demonstrate that people are dangerous before they can be committed was formalized by the U.S. Supreme Court in 1979 in *Addington v. Texas* (Hays, 1989). Commitment typically requires that two psychiatrists document that the person is dangerous. During the commitment process, the person has the right to a lawyer, to call witnesses, and to a hearing or a jury trial. The final decision on commitment is made by a judge or jury, not a psychiatrist.

The Right to Receive Treatment

Court decisions also have ruled that people committed to mental hospitals have a right to receive treatment. In 1975, in *Donaldson v. O'Connor,* the U.S. Supreme Court ruled that mental patients have a right to more than custodial care (Behnke, 1999). If they are not given treatment, are not dangerous, and can survive in the community, they must be released. The case was brought by Kenneth Donaldson, who had been confined for 15 years in a Florida mental hospital without treatment. But the court ruling in his case may be difficult to put into practice in particular cases. For example, it is difficult to predict whether a person will be dangerous if released from custodial care (Bernard, 1977). Legal decisions such as *Donaldson v. O'Connor* contributed to the deinstitutionalization movement by making it more difficult to keep mental patients hospitalized against their will.

The Right to Refuse Treatment

In 1983, in *Rogers v. Commissioner of Mental Health,* the Massachusetts Supreme Court ruled that mental patients also have a right to *refuse* treatment unless a court judges them to be incompetent to make their own decisions (Hermann, 1990). A person committed to a mental hospital is not automatically considered incompetent. When the Rogers case was in court, critics claimed that such a ruling would merely give mental patients the right to "rot with their rights on" (Appelbaum & Gutheil, 1980). Some patients are so psychologically disordered that they are unable to make a rational decision about whether they will accept treatment (Johnson, 1998). In reality, the decision appears to have had little influence. A Massachusetts study found that few cases of involuntary treatment were reviewed in court, and the ones that were reviewed were usually decided in favor of those who had prescribed treatment for a patient who had refused it (Veliz & James, 1987). Recent legal cases in Canada have expanded the right to refuse treatment there as well (Gratzer & Matas, 1994).

The Right to Confidentiality

But what of the rights of individuals receiving therapy? One of the most important is the right to confidentiality. In general, therapists are ethically, but not always legally, bound to keep confidential the information revealed by their clients. The extent to which this information is privileged varies from state to state. There are also fears, based on the movement to control costs, that third-party payers might demand more and more information that has traditionally been confidential (Kremer & Gesten, 1998).

The Tarasoff Decision

In recent decades, the most significant legal decision concerning confidentiality was the *Tarasoff* decision, a ruling by the California Supreme Court that a therapist who believes that a client might harm a particular person must protect or warn that person. The ruling came in the case of Prosenjit Poddar, who murdered his former lover, Tatiana Tarasoff. In 1969 Poddar had informed his therapist at the counseling center of the University of California at Berkeley that he intended to kill Tarasoff. The therapist reported the threat to the campus police, who ordered Poddar to stay away from Tarasoff. Two months later Poddar murdered her, leading her parents to sue the therapist, the police, and the university. In 1976 the court ruled in favor of the parents; the therapist should have directly warned Tarasoff about Poddar's threat (Mangalmurti, 1994). The *Tarasoff* decision upholding the duty to warn influenced similar decisions in other states and has become an issue in other countries, including Canada (Birch, 1992) and Australia (McMahon, 1992).

Controversy About the Duty to Warn

The duty to warn has provoked concern among therapists for several reasons. First, no therapist can reliably predict whether a threat made by a client is a serious one (Rubin & Mills, 1983). If a student in a moment of anger about an unfair exam says to a therapist, "I could just *kill* my psychology professor," should the therapist immediately warn the professor?

Second, it can be impractical to warn potential victims. In one case, a client threatened to kill "rich people." He then murdered a wealthy couple. Considering the duty to warn, this case prompted a therapist to ask whether a sign should have been posted reading, "All rich people watch out!" (Fisher, 1985). Moreover, the spread of HIV/AIDS has exacerbated the conflict between confidentiality and the duty to warn. Should a therapist warn the potential sex partners of clients who are HIV-positive (Alghazo, Upton, & Cioe, 2011)? How about breaking confidentiality to protect the life of a person with anorexia nervosa (Werth, Wright, Archambault, & Bardash, 2003)? Critics of the duty to warn also wonder why therapists should be required to reveal confidential information when the same legal jurisdiction might not require laypersons to do so (Wallace, 1988).

Third, the duty to warn might keep people from discussing hostile feelings or even seeking therapy at all (Appelbaum, 1998). This possibility was the basis of a 1988 ruling by the Court of Appeals in North Carolina in the case of *Currie v. United States*. The court ruled that psychiatrists did not have a duty to commit people to mental hospitals for threatening acts of violence. The case concerned a 1982 murder in which a man, who was under the care of Veterans Administration psychiatrists, shot a fellow IBM employee after making threats against IBM. The victim's relatives sued, claiming that the psychiatrists should have committed the man after he made threats against IBM. The court ruled that such a duty would prevent psychiatrists and clients from discussing hostile feelings, perhaps *increasing* the probability of violence (Bales, 1988).

Canadian legal decisions restricting client confidentiality have provoked similar alarm about the potential negative effects of the duty to disclose information on the client-therapist relationship (Glancy, Regehr, & Bryant, 1998). The implications of the *Tarasoff* decision continue to perplex therapists, who must balance the need to serve their clients while protecting themselves from potential lawsuits if their clients harm third parties (Monahan, 1993).

Section Review: The Rights of the Therapy Client

1. What are the possible ramifications of the right to refuse treatment and the right to receive treatment?

2. Why has the *Tarasoff* decision been controversial?

Finding the Proper Therapy

At times in your life, you or someone you know might face psychological problems that require more than friendly advice. When personal problems disrupt your social, academic, or vocational life or when you experience severe and prolonged emotional distress, you might be wise to seek the help of a therapist. You could receive therapy from a psychologist, a psychiatrist, or a variety of other kinds of therapists. You might even choose to read one of the many self-help books for specific psychological problems—an approach called *bibliotherapy.*

Selecting the Right Therapist

Just as there is no single way to find a physician, there is no single way to find a therapist. As explained in the section "Factors in the Effectiveness of Psychotherapy," in general the personal qualities of the therapist matter more than the kind of therapy she or he practices. How might you find a therapist? Your college counseling center would be a good place to start. You may have a friend, relative, or professor who can recommend a therapist or counseling center to you. Other potential sources of help or referral include community mental health centers, psychological associations, and mental health associations. In keeping with the growing use of the Internet, a relatively new source of psychotherapy is *e-therapy* provided by online therapists. A recent review indicates that e-therapy may be as effective as face-to-face therapy, but much more research is necessary to evaluate the effectiveness of e-therapy (Sucala et al., 2012).

After finding a therapist, try to assess her or his credentials, reputation, therapeutic approach, and interpersonal manner as best you can. Does the therapist have legitimate academic and clinical training? For example, is the therapist licensed or certified? Do you know anyone who will vouch for the therapist's competence? Does the therapist's approach make sense for your problem? The therapist should be warm, open, concerned, and empathetic. Clients prefer therapists whom they find helpful and likeable (Crosier, Scott, & Steinfeld, 2012).

Bibliotherapy as an Alternative

You can't visit a typical bookstore or shop online without noting the large section devoted to self-help books. Some traditional psychotherapists even have their clients read books relevant to their central problem. The use of books as a form of psychotherapy is called *bibliotherapy.* Many self-help books are written by people who make unrealistic claims about what they can offer you. Two task forces sponsored by the American Psychological Association found that perhaps the main weakness of bibliotherapy is that self-help books are rarely subjected to scientific research regarding their effectiveness and possible harmful consequences (Floyd, Scogin, McKendree-Smith, Floyd, & Rokke, 2004). Nonetheless, if you choose high-quality books written by credible

Bibliotherapy

Bibliotherapy can be effective if you choose high-quality books written by credible authors.

Source: kazoka/Shutterstock. com.

authors, bibliotherapy can be effective. Bibliotherapy has been used to treat disorders such as insomnia (Mimeault & Morin, 1999), alcoholism (Apodaca & Miller, 2003), panic disorder (Carlbring et al., 2011), and sexual dysfunctions (Mintz, Balzer, Zhao, & Bush, 2012).

Bibliotherapy has been widely used in treating major depressive disorder. In one study, participants received either 16 weeks of cognitive therapy or read a book on how to overcome depression. Participants in both groups had a greater reduction in depression than did those in a control group who had received no treatment. A three-month follow-up found that participants in both treatment groups maintained an equal reduction in depression (Floyd, McKendree-Smith, & Scogin, 2004). Psychotherapists commonly use bibliotherapy as one component of therapy, rather than as a form of therapy in itself. For example, cognitive-behavior therapists may recommend that their clients read books that are relevant to their particular problems (Broder, 2000).

Section Review: Finding the Proper Therapy

1. What are the major kinds of psychotherapists?

2. How would you advise a friend to go about seeking a psychotherapist?

The Effectiveness of Psychotherapy

In 1952 Hans Eysenck published an article that sparked a debate on the effectiveness of psychotherapy that has continued to this day. Based on his review of 24 studies of psychotherapy with people suffering from disorders involving moderate anxiety or depression, Eysenck concluded that about two-thirds of those who received psychotherapy improved. This analysis would have provided strong evidence in support of the effectiveness of psychoanalysis (then the dominant kind of psychotherapy), had Eysenck not also found that about two-thirds of control participants who had received *no* therapy also improved. He called improvement without therapy **spontaneous remission** and attributed it to beneficial factors that occurred in the person's everyday life. Because those who received no therapy were as likely to improve as those who received therapy, Eysenck concluded that psychotherapy is ineffective.

spontaneous remission
The improvement of some persons with psychological disorders without their undergoing formal therapy.

Eysenck's article provoked criticisms of its methodological shortcomings. One shortcoming was that many of the untreated people were under the care of physicians who prescribed drugs for them and provided informal counseling. Another shortcoming was that the treated groups and untreated groups were not equivalent, differing in educational level, socioeconomic status, and motivation to improve. These differences meant that the control group might have had a better initial prognosis than the treatment group had. Still another shortcoming was that Eysenck overestimated the rate of spontaneous remission, which later researchers found to be closer to 40 percent than to 65 percent (Bergin & Lambert, 1978). Many years later, Eysenck (1994) still insisted that psychotherapy does not produce improvement beyond that of spontaneous remission.

Evaluation of Psychotherapy

During the decades since Eysenck's article, hundreds of studies have assessed the effectiveness of psychotherapy. This scientific endeavor is difficult. One of the basic issues concerns what criteria to use in evaluating the success of psychotherapy.

Criteria of Success

The definition of *effective* varies with the orientation to therapy. Thus, the criteria of therapeutic success must consider the theoretical orientation of the therapy being evaluated.

Changing a specific target behavior, for example, might be a goal of behavioral therapy but not of humanistic therapy (Bohart, O'Hara, & Leitner, 1998).

Moreover, who is to judge whether desired changes have occurred? A survey of client satisfaction with psychotherapy found that most of those who responded said that they were pleased with their experience (Hollon, 1996). But clients as well as therapists can be biased in favor of reporting improvement. To avoid bias, friends, family members, teachers, or employers might also be asked for their assessment of the client's progress. Such examination provides cross-validation of client and therapist reports of improvement.

What has the admittedly imperfect research on the effectiveness of psychotherapy found? The general conclusion drawn from research conducted since Eysenck issued his challenge is that, overall, psychotherapy is more effective than placebo treatment, which in turn is more effective than no-treatment control conditions (Grissom, 1996). Placebo effects in psychotherapy are caused by factors such as the client's faith in the therapist's ability and the client's expectation of success.

Major Research Studies

Mary Lee Smith and her colleagues (1980) published a comprehensive meta-analysis that combined the results of 475 studies on the effectiveness of psychotherapy. They found that, on the average, the typical psychotherapy client is better off than 80 percent of untreated persons—and that there is little overall difference in the effectiveness of the various approaches to therapy (see Figure 15-3). So psychotherapy does work, but no single kind stands out as clearly more effective than the others. This finding has been supported by Lester Luborsky's more recent summary of meta-analyses of studies on the relative effectiveness of different kinds of psychotherapy (Luborsky et al., 2003).

Moreover, results of an ambitious $10 million U.S. government study—the National Institute of Mental Health (NIMH) Treatment of Depression Collaborative Research Program—in the 1980s have lent further support to the effectiveness of psychotherapy. The study randomly assigned 239 adult participants with major depressive disorder into four groups. One group received Beck's cognitive therapy. A second group received interpersonal psychotherapy (a form of psychoanalytic therapy). A third group received the antidepressant drug Tofranil (imipramine) plus a minimal amount of social support from a therapist. And a fourth group received a placebo

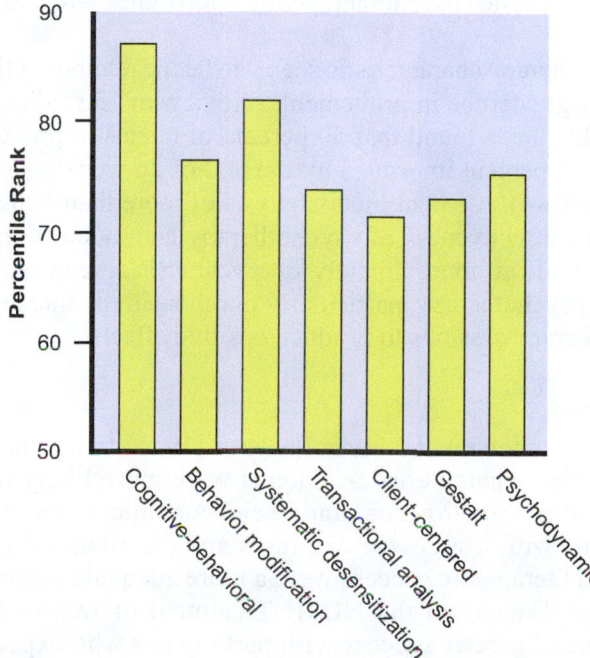

FIGURE 15-3

The Effectiveness of Psychotherapy

Research has found that psychotherapy is effective but that no kind of therapy is consistently better than any other kind. The figure shows the effectiveness of different kinds of therapy relative to no treatment. Overall, people given psychotherapy show, on the average, significantly greater improvement than about 80 percent of untreated people.

Source: Based on data from Smith, M. L., Glass, G. V., & Miller, T. I. (1980). *The benefits of psychotherapy.* Baltimore: Johns Hopkins University Press.

treatment consisting of an inactive pill plus a minimal amount of social support from a therapist (Stewart, Garfinkel, Nunes, Donovan, & Klein, 1998).

The participants were assessed after 16 weeks of therapy and again at a follow-up 18 months later. As expected, all the groups improved by the end of the 16 weeks; the three forms of active therapy eliminated depression in more than 50 percent of the participants, and the placebo therapy eliminated depression in 29 percent of the participants. There were no differences in effectiveness between the three active forms of therapy. Though drug therapy relieved symptoms more quickly, the two psychotherapies eventually caught up in their effectiveness (Mervis, 1986). But a follow-up study found that many of the participants relapsed, indicating that 16 weeks of therapy might be insufficient to produce lasting relief of depression (Shea, Elkin, Imber, & Sotsky, 1992).

Factors in the Effectiveness of Psychotherapy

Given the consensus that psychotherapy is usually effective and that no approach is significantly more effective than any other approach, researchers are faced with the question, What factors account for the effectiveness of psychotherapy? In trying to answer this question, researchers study the characteristics of therapies, clients, and therapists.

Therapy Characteristics

One of the first comprehensive reviews of therapy, client, and therapist factors, carried out by Lester Luborsky and his colleagues (1971), found that the poorest predictor of successful therapy was the nature of the therapy itself. More recent research studies have likewise found that the major kinds of psychotherapy are equally effective (Shapiro, 1995). Moreover, group therapy and individual psychotherapy are equally effective (McRoberts, Burlingame, & Hoag, 1998).

The inability to establish a reliable difference between psychotherapies in clinical outcomes has led some researchers to consider the *therapeutic alliance* to be a more important predictor of successful treatment. The therapeutic alliance refers to three aspects of the therapeutic context: the degree of collaboration, the quality of the emotional bond, and the ability of the client and the therapist to agree on the goals and means of treatment. A review of 79 studies found that the quality of the therapeutic alliance was positively correlated with therapeutic outcomes; the therapeutic alliance is a consistent predictor of therapeutic success regardless of the type of therapy (Martin, Garski, & Davis, 2000). These findings have led some researchers to argue that the therapeutic alliance is a common factor that underlies psychotherapeutic approaches—regardless of theoretical orientation.

The only important therapy characteristic seems to be the number of therapy sessions—the more sessions, the greater the improvement. A review of 15 studies of psychotherapy using more than 2,400 clients found that 50 percent of clients improved by the end of 8 weekly sessions and 75 percent improved by the end of 26 weekly sessions (Howard et al., 1986) (see Figure 15-4). A recent meta-analysis of more than 100 studies of clinical patients found that the effectiveness of psychotherapy continued to increase over time, with benefits leveling off at approximately one year (Shadish et al., 2000). Nonetheless, certain kinds of psychotherapy, particularly psychoanalytic therapy (Doidge, 1997), might require more therapy sessions to produce positive effects.

Client Characteristics

The classic review by Luborsky and his colleagues (1971) found that therapeutic success was related to client characteristics. Clients were more likely to improve if they were higher in education, intelligence, and socioeconomic status. Improvement also was greatest in clients with less severe disorders and disorders of recent onset. Other factors that promoted therapeutic success were a more adequate personality and greater motivation to change. Data from the NIMH Treatment of Depression Collaborative Research Program found greater success with participants who expected therapy to be

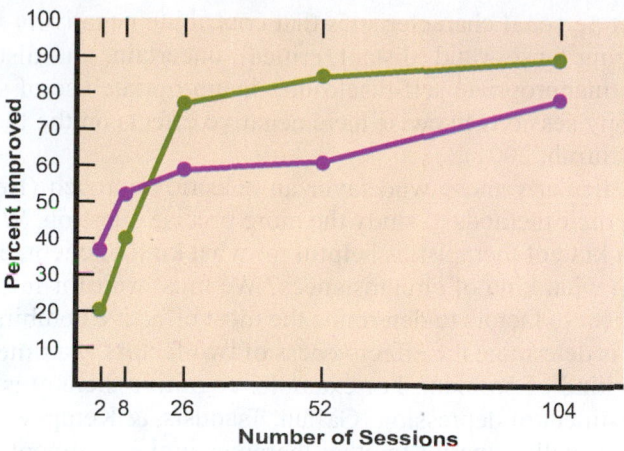

Note: Objective ratings at termination are shown by the top line; subjective ratings during therapy are shown by the bottom line.

FIGURE 15-4

The Relationship Between the Length of Therapy and Therapy Effectiveness

As the number of therapy sessions increases, the percentage of clients who improve increases. But after the 26th session, additional sessions help relatively few clients. Note the difference between objective ratings of improvement given by therapists (green line) and subjective ratings given by the clients themselves (purple line), though the general trend is similar for both.

Source: From Howard, K. I., Kopta, S. M., Krausse, M. S., & Orlinsky, D. E. (1986). "The dose-effect relationship in psychotherapy" from *American Psychologist, 41,* 159–164. Copyright © 1986 by the American Psychological Association. Reproduced with permission.

effective, apparently because they participated more constructively in therapy sessions (Meyer et al., 2002).

Unfortunately, no client characteristics have been documented that can serve as a basis for the selection of a particular treatment (Dance & Neufeld, 1988). And studies have tended to use European American clients to the exclusion of African Americans and members of other ethnic minority groups (Matt & Navarro, 1997). This exclusion makes it difficult to generalize research findings from the participants in psychotherapy studies to the population in general.

Therapist Characteristics

Research findings indicate that the nature of the therapist might be more important than the nature of the therapy (Charman, 2003). Therapy is an intense, intimate, vulnerable relationship between two people. Though it might be logical to assume that therapy would be best when the client and therapist are similar, there is little evidence that similarity in their sex (Bowman, Scogin, Floyd, & McKendree-Smith., 2001) or personality (Rinaldi, 1987) is a crucial factor in therapeutic outcomes. But research investigating ethnic similarity of clients and therapists has found that therapists' ratings of client functioning are higher when both are of the same ethnicity (Russell, Fujino, Sue, Cheung, & Snowden, 1996). And ethnic minority clients are less likely to drop out of therapy when they use mental health services designed to meet the needs of ethnic minority clients (Takeuchi, Sue, & Yee, 1995). A recent meta-analysis of relevant studies reported, however, that the effect size of ethnic similarity on the length of therapy and symptom improvement is small (Erdur, Rude, & Baron, 2003). Moreover, the effect of ethnic similarity on treatment outcomes varies by ethnic group (Cabral & Smith, 2011).

Just what therapist characteristics *are* important, then? The client's perception of therapist empathy has been consistently identified as an important factor in the effectiveness of psychotherapy (Keijsers, Schaap, & Hoogduin, 2000). In fact, one of the main factors in negative effects of psychotherapy is a lack of empathy by the therapist (Mohr, 1995). But empathy is not enough. Personal warmth has been found to be a factor that differentiates successful and unsuccessful therapists (Keijsers, Schaap, & Hoogduin, 2000). And professional training also is important. A meta-analysis found that highly trained therapists are more successful than less well-trained therapists, particularly in having fewer clients drop out of therapy (Stein & Lambert, 1995).

Researchers have become interested in investigating the therapist characteristics that promote or disrupt the therapeutic alliance. A review of relevant research findings found that therapist personal characteristics that contribute positively to the therapeutic alliance include being warm, open, honest, confident, respectful, trustworthy, and interested (Ackerman & Hilsenroth, 2003). In contrast, another review of relevant research findings found that therapist personal characteristics that contribute negatively to the therapeutic alliance include being tense, rigid, distant, critical, uncertain, and distracted. Therapist techniques such as inappropriate self-disclosure, inappropriate use of silence, and over-structuring of therapy sessions likewise have negative effects on the therapeutic alliance (Ackerman & Hilsenroth, 2001).

Researchers, particularly those who favor an eclectic approach (Beutler & Consoli, 1993), are refining their methods to study the more precise question, What kind of therapy, offered by what kind of therapist, is helpful for what kind of client, experiencing what kind of problem, in what kind of circumstances? We must wait for future studies testing interactions among these factors to determine the most effective combinations. Currently, the best we can do is determine the effectiveness of two factors at a time, such as the kind of therapy and the kind of problem. For example, cognitive therapy is superior to other therapies in the treatment of depression (Gaffan, Tsaousis, & Kemp-Wheeler, 1995), and behavior therapy is usually superior to other therapies in the treatment of phobias (Goisman, 1983) and for treating children and adolescents (Weisz et al., 1995).

Section Review: The Effectiveness of Psychotherapy

1. Why did Eysenck claim that psychotherapy produces no better results than spontaneous remission?
2. Are any therapist factors important in the effectiveness of psychotherapy?

Experiencing Psychology

How Do the Media Portray Drug Therapy?

Rationale

Drug therapy is a major approach to the treatment of psychological disorders. Drugs such as Prozac have inspired abundant media coverage. In this activity, you will examine the nature of drug therapy coverage in popular magazines and newspapers.

Method

Use your library and the Internet to find articles in popular magazines and newspapers about drug therapy from the past five years. Possible sources to peruse are

Time, Newsweek, The Washington Post, and *The New York Times.* Note which drugs are covered, the tone of the articles, and the positive and negative information presented.

Results and Discussion

Discuss the kinds of drugs that were covered, how sober or sensational the articles were, and any biases you came across. Based on what you read, what seem to be the disorders and drugs that are of greatest interest to the media? Why do you think this is so?

Chapter Summary

The History of Therapy

- In trephining, holes were cut in the skull, possibly to release evil spirits that were alleged to cause abnormal behavior.
- Hippocrates introduced a more naturalistic form of treatment, including procedures to restore the balance of body humors.

- The Renaissance saw the appearance of insane asylums; some, such as Bedlam, were awful places, but others, such as Geel, provided humane treatment.
- Near the end of the 18th century, Philippe Pinel released asylum inmates and championed moral therapy.
- Moral therapy was introduced to America by Benjamin Rush, who also used unusual devices for treating certain disorders.

- Through the efforts of Dorothea Dix, state mental hospitals were built throughout the United States.
- But the mental hospitals became crowded and deteriorated into mere human warehouses.
- In the early 20th century, a book by Clifford Beers, describing his horrible experiences in a mental hospital, led to the founding of the mental health movement, which promotes the prevention and humane treatment of psychological disorders.
- Increasing cultural diversity in the United States has prompted interest in developing cultural competence in psychological training and practice.

The Psychoanalytic Orientation

- After hearing Joseph Breuer's report of the benefits of catharsis in the case of Anna O., Sigmund Freud developed psychoanalysis.
- Psychoanalysis principally involves the analysis of free associations, dreams, resistances, and transference.
- The goal of these analyses is to have the client gain insight into unconscious conflicts and experience catharsis.

The Behavioral Orientation

- The behavioral orientation emphasizes the importance of learning and environmental influences.
- Two of the main kinds of behavioral therapy based on classical conditioning are systematic desensitization, which is useful in treating phobias, and aversion therapy, which makes formerly pleasurable but maladaptive behavior unpleasant.
- One of the main applications of the operant conditioning principle of positive reinforcement is the use of a token economy in institutional settings.
- The operant conditioning principle of punishment is useful in eliminating behaviors such as self-injurious behavior in autistic children.
- Social-learning theory has contributed participant modeling as a way to overcome phobias.

The Cognitive Orientation

- The cognitive orientation assumes that thoughts about events, rather than events themselves, cause psychological disorders.
- In Albert Ellis's rational-emotive behavior therapy, the client learns to change irrational thinking.
- Aaron Beck developed cognitive therapy to help depressed people think less negatively about themselves, the world, and the future.

The Humanistic Orientation

- The humanistic orientation emphasizes the importance of being aware of one's emotions and feeling free to express them.

- Carl Rogers's person-centered therapy, a form of nondirective therapy, helps clients find their own solutions to their problems.
- In contrast, Fritz Perls's Gestalt therapy is more directive in making clients face their true feelings and act on them.

The Social-Relations Orientation

- The social-relations orientation assumes that people cannot be treated as isolated individuals.
- In group therapy, people, usually strangers, are brought together for therapy.
- One form of group therapy derived from the psychoanalytic approach employs transactional analysis.
- Group therapy derived from the behavioral approach includes social-skills training and assertiveness training.
- In family therapy, family members gain insight into their unhealthy patterns of interaction and learn to change them.

The Biological Orientation

- The biological orientation uses medical procedures to treat psychological disorders.
- The main procedures include psychosurgery (rarely used today), modifications of psychosurgery such as deep brain stimulation, electroconvulsive therapy, and drug therapy.
- Psychiatrists may prescribe antianxiety drugs, antidepressant drugs, mood stabilizers, and antipsychotic drugs.

Community Mental Health

- The community mental health movement was stimulated by deinstitutionalization, the treatment of people in community settings instead of in mental hospitals.
- The failure to provide adequate housing and services for former mental hospital patients has contributed to the growing homelessness problem.
- Community mental health centers take a preventive approach to psychological disorders.

The Rights of the Therapy Client

- Laws require that formal procedures be followed before a person is committed to a mental hospital.
- Once in a mental hospital, patients have the right to refuse treatment and the right to receive treatment.
- What clients reveal in therapy sessions is normally confidential, but legal cases, most notably the *Tarasoff* decision, have led to the concept of the duty to warn.

Finding the Proper Therapy

- Most professional therapists are eclectic.
- You should be as careful in selecting a therapist as you are in selecting a physician.

The Effectiveness of Psychotherapy

- In 1952 Hans Eysenck challenged psychotherapists by claiming that people who received psychotherapy improved no more than did people who received no therapy.
- Subsequent research has shown that psychotherapy is better than no therapy and better than placebo therapy.

- No single kind of therapy stands out as clearly superior to the rest.
- More sophisticated research is required to determine the ideal combinations of therapy, therapist, and client factors for treating specific disorders.

Key Terms

catharsis (p. 528)

The History of Therapy

cultural competence (p. 530)
moral therapy (p. 529)
psychotherapy (p. 530)
trephining (p. 529)

The Psychoanalytic Orientation

analysis of dreams (p. 531)
analysis of free associations (p. 531)
analysis of resistances (p. 531)
analysis of transference (p. 532)
psychoanalysis (p. 531)

The Behavioral Orientation

aversion therapy (p. 535)
behavior therapy (p. 532)

counterconditioning (p. 533)
flooding (p. 536)
in vivo desensitization (p. 534)
participant modeling (p. 537)
systematic desensitization (p. 533)
token economy (p. 535)

The Cognitive Orientation

cognitive therapy (p. 538)
rational-emotive behavior therapy (R-E-B-T) (p. 537)

The Humanistic Orientation

Gestalt therapy (p. 540)
person-centered therapy (p. 540)

The Social-Relations Orientation

assertiveness training (p. 542)

family therapy (p. 543)
social-skills training (p. 542)
transactional analysis (TA) (p. 542)

The Biological Orientation

antianxiety drugs (p. 545)
antidepressant drugs (p. 546)
antipsychotic drugs (p. 546)
electroconvulsive therapy (ECT) (p. 544)
mood stabilizers (p. 546)
psychosurgery (p. 544)

Community Mental Health

deinstitutionalization (p. 547)

The Effectiveness of Psychotherapy

spontaneous remission (p. 552)

Chapter Quiz

Note: Answers for the Chapter Quiz questions are provided at the end of the book.

1. The duty to warn that a therapy client might be dangerous to another person was established in the
   a. *Tarasoff* decision.
   b. *Addington v. Texas* decision.
   c. *Donaldson v. O'Connor* decision.
   d. *Rogers v. Commissioner of Mental Health* decision.

2. An early hominid from the Stone Age claims he hears voices in his head, continually rants and raves, and makes bizarre movements with his hands. The tribe's medicine man treats him by using sharp rocks to cut holes in his head and release the evil spirits that are causing his behavior. This treatment is called
   a. trephining.
   b. aversion therapy.
   c. prefrontal lobotomy.
   d. transorbital leucotomy.

3. If a therapist noted that you tend to act childish when interacting with other adults and adult-like when playing with children, you are most likely undergoing
   a. counterconditioning.
   b. psychoanalysis.
   c. Gestalt therapy.
   d. transactional analysis.

4. In the 19th century, mental hospitals were built throughout the United States as a result of the work of
   a. Dorothea Dix.
   b. Benjamin Rush.
   c. Clifford Beers.
   d. Philippe Pinel.

5. The form of therapy that aims at contradicting exaggerated negative beliefs about oneself, the world, and the future is called
   a. moral therapy.
   b. cognitive therapy.
   c. counterconditioning.
   d. existential psychotherapy.

6. A therapist asks a client with a spider phobia to rate the degree of anxiety induced by imagined scenes involving spiders, such as a rubber spider, a spider on the wall, or a spider crawling on the client's arm. This procedure is most likely a component of
   a. flooding.
   b. aversion therapy.
   c. analysis of transference.
   d. systematic desensitization.

7. A community mental health center concerned with spousal abuse and child abuse institutes a stress management program for husbands and wives. This program is an example of
   a. primary prevention.
   b. tertiary prevention.
   c. secondary prevention.
   d. deinstitutionalization.

8. The token economy is based on principles derived from
   a. R-E-B-T.
   b. operant conditioning.
   c. transactional analysis.
   d. person-centered therapy.

9. During a therapy session, whenever the topic of the client's father arises, the client changes the topic and ridicules the therapist's ability. A psychoanalyst would consider this situation an example of
   a. catharsis.
   b. resistance.
   c. free association.
   d. counterconditioning.

10. Tardive dyskinesia is a side effect of long-term treatment with
   a. mood stabilizers,
   b. antianxiety drugs.
   c. antipsychotic drugs.
   d. antidepressant drugs.

11. A man who derives sexual pleasure from collecting used women's underwear is captured by police while stealing items from a laundromat. He enters therapy in which he is given a painful electric shock whenever he exhibits sexual arousal in the presence of women's underwear. This procedure is most likely a component of
   a. moral therapy.
   b. aversion therapy.
   c. in vivo desensitization.
   d. systematic desensitization.

12. A person who experiences intense anxiety in enclosed places is told by a therapist to imagine entering an elevator and remaining there even if terrified. This procedure is an example of
   a. flooding.
   b. catharsis.
   c. spontaneous remission.
   d. systematic desensitization.

13. Research (Egan et al., 1988) indicates that systematic desensitization might exert its effects through the actions of
   a. glycine.
   b. thyroxin.
   c. endorphins.
   d. epinephrine.

14. The American mental health movement was inspired by the publication of *A Mind That Found Itself* by
   a. Dorothea Dix.
   b. Benjamin Rush.
   c. Clifford Beers.
   d. Philippe Pinel.

15. The main technique of psychoanalysis is the analysis of
   a. dreams.
   b. resistances.
   c. transference.
   d. free association.

16. According to Albert Ellis's A-B-C theory of emotion, during therapy the client learns to change
   a. A.
   b. B.
   c. C.
   d. D.

17. A woman visits a therapist and complains that she is depressed because people criticize her. The therapist tries to convince the woman that her depression is caused by her unrealistic belief that she must be liked by everyone. The therapist's tactic is a component of
   a. moral therapy.
   b. counterconditioning.
   c. social-skills training.
   d. rational-emotive behavior therapy.

18. A client states, "I'm afraid to tell my parents that I didn't do too well this semester." The therapist replies, "It seems that you care very much what your parents think of you." The client adds, "I let them down." The therapist notes, "You seem to feel like a failure." This dialog would be most characteristic of
   a. R-E-B-T.
   b. participant modeling.
   c. assertiveness training.
   d. person-centered therapy.

19. A review of research studies on the effectiveness of psychotherapy (Luborsky et al., 1971) found that the most important therapy characteristic is the
   a. kind of therapy.
   b. location of therapy.
   c. number of therapy sessions.
   d. attention to unconscious conflicts.

20. The line from Shakespeare's *Hamlet,* "There is nothing either good or bad, but thinking makes it so," agrees with the basic premise of
   a. moral therapy.
   b. psychoanalysis.
   c. counterconditioning.
   d. rational-emotive behavior therapy.

21. The form of humanistic therapy that helps clients find their own answers to their problems by the reflection of feelings is called
   a. R-E-B-T.
   b. transactional analysis.
   c. person-centered therapy.
   d. existential psychotherapy.

22. A major review of 475 studies on the effectiveness of psychotherapy (Smith et al., 1980) found that the percentage of clients who improve more than untreated people is about
   a. 30 percent.
   b. 65 percent.
   c. 80 percent.
   d. 95 percent.

23. Research on therapy has found that an important therapist factor that promotes therapy's success is
   a. self-analysis.
   b. directiveness.
   c. accurate empathy.
   d. negative transference.

24. Tricyclic antidepressant drugs increase brain levels of
   a. GABA.
   b. glutamate.
   c. norepinephrine.
   d. monoamine oxidase.

25. A therapist accompanies a client with a fear of flying on several trips to the airport. They first simply go to the terminal, eventually sit in an airplane, and finally take off on a flight. This procedure is most likely a component of
   a. flooding.
   b. aversion therapy.
   c. in vivo desensitization.
   d. systematic desensitization.

Thought Questions

1. If a friend of yours had acrophobia (fear of heights), how would a therapist use systematic desensitization to treat it?
2. Why has deinstitutionalization not produced all the beneficial effects that were envisioned for it?
3. Why is the duty to warn a two-edged sword, with potentially both positive and negative consequences?
4. What criteria would you use to determine whether an approach to psychotherapy is effective?

Psychology and Health

In 1991 Earvin "Magic" Johnson, one of the greatest of all basketball players, announced that he had contracted the human immunodeficiency virus (HIV), which causes acquired immune deficiency syndrome (AIDS), by engaging in unprotected, nonmonogamous, heterosexual sex. Johnson's statement contradicted the common belief that AIDS was a disease restricted to gay men. The case of actor Rock Hudson, who had kept his homosexuality secret for decades, further dramatized the fact that no one—not even a wealthy, talented, popular movie star—is immune to HIV infection. These cases and the millions of other cases of HIV infection that have occurred worldwide since AIDS was first identified in the early 1980s show that we are not always passive victims of disease. In many cases we inflict illness or injury on ourselves—and others—through our own behavior, whether through ignorance or carelessness.

A meta-analysis of studies on the effects of Magic Johnson's announcement that he was HIV-positive found that the announcement was associated with positive effects on the public. It was associated with more accurate knowledge about HIV and AIDS, an increase in the number of persons who sought HIV testing, and a greater desire for information about HIV and AIDS. The announcement also was associated with an increased realization among adults that any sexually active person could be at risk of contracting HIV (Casey et al., 2003).

HIV infection is just one of many health issues related to our own behavior. Do you overeat, smoke cigarettes, drive recklessly, exercise rarely, drink excessive amounts of alcohol, respond ineffectively to stressful situations, or fail to follow your physician's medical recommendations? If you engage in any of these maladaptive behaviors, which are among the leading causes of death in the United States, you might be reducing your life span. A recent meta-analysis that analyzed 21 studies that included more than 530,000 participants over a period of more than 13 years assessed the influence of five lifestyle factors (i.e., obesity, alcohol consumption, smoking, diet, and physical activity) on all causes of mortality. Avoidance of at least four of these lifestyle factors was associated with a 66 percent reduction in mortality. Thus, adherence to a healthy lifestyle substantially reduces one's risk of mortality (Loef & Walach, 2012).

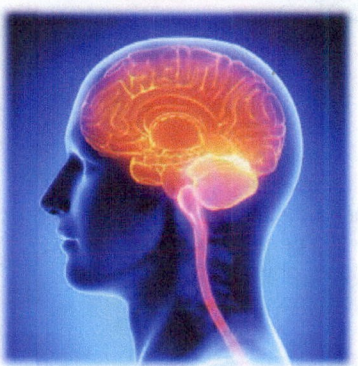

Source: CLIPAREA/Custom media/ Shutterstock.com.

Chapter Outline

Psychological Stress and Stressors

The Biopsychology of Stress and Illness

Factors That Moderate the Stress Response

Coping with Stress

Health-Promoting Habits

Reactions to Illness

Behavioral Causes of Illness and Death

More than half the mortality from the leading causes of death in the United States is influenced by unhealthy or dangerous behaviors, such as overeating, physical inactivity, and overexposure to the sun.
Source: Nomad_Soul/ Shutterstock.com.

health psychology The field that applies psychological principles to the prevention and treatment of physical illness.

This statement would not have been true at the beginning of the 20th century, when most North Americans died from infectious diseases such as influenza, pneumonia, or tuberculosis. But the development of vaccines and antibiotics, as well as improved hygiene and public sanitation practices, led to a decline in illness and mortality due to infectious diseases. This decline was accompanied by a surge in the prevalence of noninfectious diseases, especially those caused by dangerous or unhealthy behaviors. A century ago, cancer and cardiovascular disease, which are promoted by unhealthy lifestyles pursued over a span of decades, were relatively uncommon causes of death among Americans. Today, they are the two most common causes. We now are more likely to become ill or die because of our own actions than because of viruses or bacteria that invade our bodies. One of the main problems that psychologists who do research in *health psychology* study is the role of psychological factors in the onset and prevention of cancer, cardiovascular disease, and other illnesses that are affected by lifestyle and sociocultural variables associated with gender, ethnicity, and poverty.

Health psychology is the field that studies the role of biological, psychological, and sociocultural factors in the promotion of health and the prevention of illness. Health psychologists favor a *biopsychosocial model* of health and illness, which emphasizes the interaction of biological, psychological, and social factors (Suls, Krantz, & Williams, 2013). In contrast, the traditional *biomedical model* emphasizes biological factors and neglects psychological and social ones. The chief topics of interest to health psychologists are the relationship between stress and illness, the modification of health-impairing habits, and the promotion of adaptive reactions to illness.

Psychological Stress and Stressors

In the 1960s, undergraduates at Penn State University, recognizing their isolation in rural, peaceful State College, Pennsylvania, dubbed the town and its surroundings "Happy Valley." The students were vindicated in 1988, when California psychologist Robert Levine reported the results of his survey of living conditions in the United States. He concluded that State College had the distinction of being the least stressful place to live in America (Rossi, 1988).

But what is *stress*? According to Canadian endocrinologist Hans Selye (1907–1982), the founder of modern stress research, **stress** is the physiological response of the body to physical and psychological demands. Such demands are known as **stressors**. Though stress has been implicated as a factor in illness, some degree of stress is normal, necessary, and unavoidable. Stress motivates us to adjust our behavior to meet changing demands, as when we study for an upcoming exam or seek companionship when lonely. Stress can even be pleasurable, as when we attend a party or shoot river rapids on a raft. Selye called unpleasant stress *distress* and pleasant stress *eustress* (Spector, 1997). *Eustress* comes from the Greek for "good stress." The major sources of stress include *life changes* and *daily hassles*.

stress The physiological response of the body to physical and psychological demands.

stressor A physical or psychological demand that induces physiological adjustment.

Life Changes

Throughout life, each of us must adjust to life changes, both pleasant ones (such as moving into a new home) and unpleasant ones (such as the death of a loved one). Health psychologists who study the effects of life changes are mainly concerned with *life events* and *posttraumatic stress disorder.*

Life Events

Interest in the relationship between life changes and illness began when Thomas Holmes and Richard Rahe (1967) developed the Social Readjustment Rating Scale. Holmes and Rahe asked medical patients to report positive and negative life changes that they had experienced during the months before they became ill. This study generated a list of 43 kinds of life changes. (A recent revision of the Social Readjustment Rating Scale includes 51 life changes [Hobson & Delunas, 2001] but is only now beginning to be used by researchers.)

Participants in another sample were then asked to rate, on a 100-point scale, the degree of *adjustment* required by each of the 43 life changes. The scale includes both negative events, such as the foreclosure on a mortgage or loan, and positive events, such as Christmas. Your *life change score* is the sum of the scores for your life changes that occurred in a given period of time, generally the past year. Holmes and Rahe found that people who had a total life change score of more than 300 points in the preceding year were more than twice as likely to become ill as were people who had a total of less than 300 points. Similarly, a survey of adults found that the more life changes they had experienced, the more stress-related symptoms they had reported (Scully, Tosi, & Banning, 2000).

An important weakness of the Social Readjustment Rating Scale is that its very content might make researchers overestimate the relationship between life changes and illness. The scale contains some life changes that may be either causes or effects of illness (Zimmerman, 1983). The most obvious examples are "change in eating habits" and "personal injury or illness." Thus, a positive correlation between life changes and illness indicates only that there *might* be a causal relationship between the two.

But some experiments have provided evidence supporting the causal effect of life events on illness. One of these studies exposed 17 volunteers to a rhinovirus (which causes the common cold) and then isolated them individually for 5 days. The 12 participants who developed colds had experienced significantly more life changes in the previous year than had the 5 participants who did not (Stone, Bovberg, Neale, & Napoli, 1992). An explanation for this finding is provided by research studies that show that the greater the number of life changes that one experiences, the weaker one's immune response (Burns, Carroll, Drayson, Whitham, & Ring, 2003).

Though Holmes and Rahe assumed that adjustment to life changes induces stress, subsequent research has shown that it is the nature of the change, rather than change itself, that induces stress. Negative life changes induce more stress than neutral or positive life changes do (Monroe, 1982). One study of adolescent boys found that those with more positive changes in their lives had lower blood pressure than other adolescent boys had (Caputo, Rudolph, & Morgan, 1998). Moreover, there are gender and ethnic differences in the type of life events people experience. One study of children and adolescents found that girls reported more interpersonal stressors—such as parent-child conflicts—than did boys (Rudolph & Hammen, 1999). And a study of an ethnically diverse sample of undergraduates found that participants reported a number of ethnicity-related stressors. Whereas the type of stressors varied by ethnic group, participants reported stressors associated with perceived discrimination, stereotype confirmation concern, and conformity pressure from their own ethnic group (Contrada et al., 2001). These findings support Selye's distinction between distress and eustress.

Posttraumatic Stress Disorder

Traumatic events, such as wars or disasters, are particularly stressful and may lead to **posttraumatic stress disorder (PTSD)**, which can appear months or years after the event. As you might imagine, the suicide airline attacks on the World Trade Center and Pentagon on September 11, 2001, led to many studies on PTSD among the survivors as well as the rescuers and medical personnel who had worked to save lives after the attacks. For example, research studies have reported an unusually high incidence of PTSD among those who lived or worked near the World Trade Center or the Pentagon at the time of the attack. Moreover, survivors have reported symptoms up to 6 years after the attacks (Neria, DiGrande, & Adams, 2011).

posttraumatic stress disorder (PTSD) A syndrome of physical and psychological symptoms that appears as a delayed response after exposure to an extremely emotionally distressing event.

The syndrome of symptoms that characterize posttraumatic stress disorder first was formally identified among American and Canadian veterans of the Vietnam War. Lifetime prevalence rates for U.S. veterans who served in the Vietnam War have been found to be close to 20 percent, with approximately 10 percent still suffering from symptoms. And a strong positive correlation was found between the amount of combat exposure and PTSD diagnosis (Dohrenwend et al., 2006). In other words, greater combat stress was related to a greater likelihood of being diagnosed with PTSD. More recent research has investigated posttraumatic stress disorder among women and men who have served during the military conflicts in Iraq and Afghanistan. Tragically, this group of veterans—male and female—has reported the additional psychological burden associated with sexual abuse during their tours of duty (Worthen, 2011).

Emotional symptoms of PTSD include apathy, anxiety, and survivor guilt. Cognitive symptoms include hypervigilance, difficulty concentrating, recurring memories that are difficult to control, and flashbacks of the event. Behavioral symptoms include insomnia and social detachment. PTSD is especially common among rape survivors; those who were sexually abused as children are particularly vulnerable (Nishith, Mechanic, & Resick, 2000). Rape survivors initially experience intense anxiety and major depressive disorder, which tend to diminish gradually over the first year. Nonetheless, 20 percent of rape survivors have severe, long-lasting emotional scars (Hanson, 1990).

PTSD can affect children as well as adults. One factor that has been found to increase the risk of developing PTSD after trauma is growing up with parents who fail to cope effectively with trauma. For example, parents may express their distress and frustration by lashing out at others. One study was conducted of almost 400 families that were affected by Hurricane Katrina in New Orleans, Louisiana, in 2005. Researchers found that maladaptive coping by parents, such as resorting to physical punishment of their children, increased a child's risk for PTSD (Kelley et al., 2010). Perhaps providing positive support to parents experiencing stress from a traumatic event would protect their children from developing PTSD.

PTSD has been linked to the amygdala, a brain structure that maintains our vigilance against potential threats (see Chapter 3). A study that used functional magnetic resonance imaging found that combat veterans with PTSD had greater amygdala activity in response to threatening stimuli than did combat veterans without PTSD (Rauch et al., 2000). In another study, participants were scanned in an fMRI and shown a series of negative, neutral, or positive photographs. When participants with PTSD were presented with the negative emotional photographs, the scans demonstrated an exaggerated response from the amygdala. One week later, the participants returned and were give a recognition memory task, where they were presented with half of the original photographs. Scans in this session demonstrated that the hippocampus—a brain structure that plays a critical role in the formation of long-term memory—was overactive for the negative images that participants remembered. There was no change in the hippocampus for the negative images that participants had forgotten (Brohawn, Offringa, Pfaff, Hughes, & Shin, 2010). Together, these fMRI studies suggest that heightened brain processing in brain areas is associated with learning and memory and processing of trauma-related information.

PTSD also is associated with an increased risk of physical illness. For example, in 1980, the state of Washington was struck by a natural disaster—the eruption of the Mount Saint Helens volcano in the Cascade Mountains. Though more than 100 miles from the volcano, the town of Othello was covered by volcanic ash. Residents of that farming community suffered the distress of their fields being covered with ash, the fear of the effects of the ash on their health, and the dread that the volcano would erupt again. During the 6 months that followed the disaster, a local medical clinic reported an almost 200 percent increase in stress-related illnesses among the residents of Othello. There also was an almost 20 percent increase in the local death rate (Adams & Adams, 1984). Though the long-term health effects of volcanic ash exposure have not been studied, it is conceivable that exposure to the ash itself posed an additional health hazard (Baxter et al., 1999).

Daily Hassles

Though major life changes are important stress-inducing events, they are not the sole ones. Richard Lazarus (1922–2002) and his colleagues found other important, though less dramatic, stress-inducing events: the *hassles* of everyday life. A typical day can be filled with dozens of hassles, such as forgetting one's keys, being stuck in traffic, or dealing with a rude salesclerk. People who experience the cumulative effect of many daily hassles are more likely to suffer from health problems, including headaches, sore throats, and influenza (DeLongis, Folkman, & Lazarus, 1988).

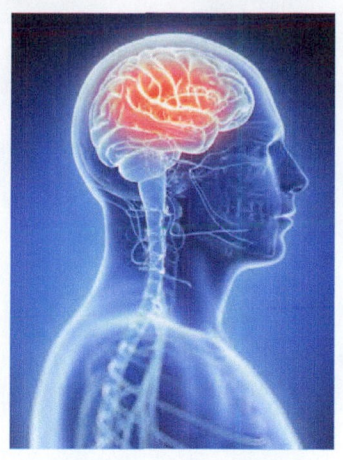

Cytokines and Inflammation

Chronic stress can lead to an increase in cytokine production by the nervous system. Cytokine plays a role in the development of psychological disorders. *Source:* Sebastian Kaulitzki/ Shutterstock.com.

Life Changes and Daily Hassles

Life changes can promote illness indirectly by increasing daily hassles. Some studies have even found that there is a stronger association between hassles and illness than between life changes and illness (Ruffin, 1993). For example, a study that examined 930 victims of a devastating hurricane found that the stress they experienced was due less to the hurricane itself and more to the chronic physical, family, and financial hassles it created for them (Norris & Uhl, 1993).

Our adrenal glands respond to stress by increasing their secretion of the hormones cortisol, epinephrine, and norepinephrine (see Figure 16-3). Though these hormones help us adapt to stressors, they also impair the immune system's ability to protect us from illness. And increases in daily hassles are indeed associated with adverse effects on the immune response (Peters, Godaert, Ballieux, & Heijnen, 2003). Daily hassles also can indirectly impair health by triggering unhealthy behaviors, including smoking more, exercising less, and eating fattier foods (Twisk, Snel, Kemper, & van Mechelen, 1999). Prolonged exposure to stress can decrease immune function, increase the release of *cytokines* (molecules that move cells toward areas of inflammation), alter the ability to cope with stressors, and affect brain regions associated with learning and memory (McEwen, 2004).

Prospective Studies of Daily Hassles

Most research on the relationship between daily hassles and illnesses makes it difficult to determine whether the two are just correlated with each other or whether hassles actually promote illness. This difficulty is because few *prospective* studies have been conducted on the relationship between hassles and health. A prospective study would investigate whether a person's current level of hassles is predictive of his or her future health. Prospective studies contrast with *retrospective* studies, which simply find that people who are ill report more hassles in their recent past.

One of the few prospective studies of the effects of daily hassles found that hassles do, in fact, promote illness. On two occasions, adolescent girls who served as participants in the study were asked to indicate, for each of 20 commonly experienced circumstances, whether it had occurred in their lives and whether they rated its occurrence as positive or negative. They also completed an illness symptoms checklist and a measure of depression. The results indicated that negative circumstances were associated with depressed mood and poor health. But this finding was true only when the girls also reported low levels of positive circumstances, or *uplifts*. Apparently, uplifts can buffer the effects of hassles, making them have fewer negative effects (Siegel & Brown, 1988).

These results, again, are in keeping with Selye's distinction between distress (such as hassles) and eustress (such as uplifts). In fact, the immune system response can be activated during periods of eustress, as well as during periods of distress. This finding was demonstrated in a study in which healthy university students were exposed to an *antigen* (that is, a substance that evokes an immune response). Three weeks later, those students who had experienced more "good stress" had higher lymphocyte proliferation, a measure of the immune response, than did those who had experienced more "bad stress" (Snyder, Roghmann, & Sigal, 1993). During times of maximum hassles, such as the last few weeks of a semester, students might do well to seek compensatory uplifts, such as visiting a friend, seeing a movie, or going to a party. However, it is well known that the immune system is activated during periods of distress, and the adverse effects of psychological stress can also be examined. The wear and tear of caring for aging relatives who suffer from the neuro-cognitive disorders associated with Alzheimer's disease can cause stress. Kiecolt-Glaser and colleagues made small wounds in the forearms of caregivers of family members with Alzheimer's disease and a control group who were not providing care to family members. When compared to the control group, the caregivers had slower rates of healing and lower levels of helpful immune cells (Kiecolt-Glaser, Marucha, Malarkey, Mercado, & Glaser, 1995). A more recent meta-analysis examining 11 studies of the wound-healing literature confirmed a link between psychological stress and impaired healing of wounds (Walburn, Vedhara, Hankins, Rixon, & Weinman, 2009). Together, these studies indicate that both high and chronic stress can impair the strength of your immune system.

Section Review: Psychological Stress and Stressors

1. Why are cancer and cardiovascular disease the most common causes of death today, though they were not a century ago?

2. Why do some researchers believe that life changes create stress through their effects on daily hassles?

3. What are the characteristics of posttraumatic stress disorder?

The Biopsychology of Stress and Illness

Whether it is caused by life changes or daily hassles, stress is marked by physiological arousal and, in some cases, diminished resistance to disease. In the 19th century, English physician Daniel Hack Tuke wrote one of the first books on the physiological effects of psychological stressors, *Illustrations of the Influence of the Mind on the Body* (Weiss, 1972). Today, Tuke's intellectual descendants study the effects of both physical and psychological stressors on physiological arousal. As explained in Chapter 12, physical and psychological stressors evoke the *fight-or-flight response,* first described by physiologist Walter Cannon (1915/1989). The fight-or-flight response involves activation of the sympathetic nervous system and secretion of stress hormones (including cortisol, epinephrine, and norepinephrine) by the adrenal glands.

The hormonal response to stress described in Chapter 12 does not vary significantly between the sexes. Recently, though, researchers have begun to investigate the role of one hormone produced in the hypothalamus and secreted by the pituitary gland—oxytocin—that might be related to gender differences in stress and coping. Both men and women under stress release oxytocin. However, oxytocin release is greater among women than men. Androgens appear to inhibit the release of oxytocin, and estrogens also modulate the effect of oxytocin, increasing its potential effect on women's stress response.

Fight-or-Flight? Or Tend-and-Befriend?

Men and women are affected differently by stressful relationships.

Source: PathDoc.Shutterstock.com.

The differential effects of oxytocin in female and male stress responses have led Shelley Taylor and her colleagues (Taylor et al., 2000) to wonder whether the fight-or-flight response is more descriptive of the male stress response. According to this model, men are likely to respond to stress with hostile and aggressive behaviors, but women are more likely to respond to stress with a *tend-and-befriend* response. The results of animal and human studies suggest that the release of oxytocin in the female stress response is associated with three biopsychosocial outcomes: reduced anxiety, increased affiliative behaviors, and increased nurturing behaviors. More recently, Taylor found that women in distressed relationships have higher levels of plasma oxytocin, whereas men in distressed relationships do not (Taylor, Saphire-Bernstein, & Seeman, 2010). As described in Chapter 4, gender-role socialization and family responsibilities have a profound influence on women's social lives—particularly in the domains of caregiving and interpersonal relationships. However, this research points to a biological factor that may contribute to gender differences in stress and coping.

General Adaptation Syndrome

Cannon's work influenced that of Hans Selye. Selye (1936) hoped to discover a new sex hormone. As part of his research, he injected rats with extracts of ovarian tissue. He found that the rats developed stomach ulcerations, enlarged adrenal glands, and atrophied spleens, lymph nodes, and thymus glands. Selye later observed that rats displayed this same response to a variety of stressors. This observation indicated that his initial findings were not necessarily caused by a sex hormone.

Selye also found that animals and people, in reacting to stressors, go through three stages, which he called the **general adaptation syndrome**. During the first stage, the *alarm reaction,* the body prepares to cope with the stressor by increasing activity in the sympathetic nervous system and adrenal glands (the fight-or-flight response). For example, medical students experiencing the stress of a series of academic exams respond with increased cortisol secretion (Malarkey, Pearl, Demers, & Kiecolt-Glaser, 1995). Selye noted that, during the alarm reaction, different stressors produce similar symptoms, including fatigue, fever, headache, and loss of appetite.

If the body continues to be exposed to the stressor, it enters the *stage of resistance,* during which it becomes more resistant to the stressor. Yet, during the stage of resistance, the body's resistance to disease may decline. During final exams week, you might be able to cope well enough to study for all your exams, but soon after finals are over, you might come down with the flu. If you succumb to disease, you might have entered the *stage of exhaustion.* At this point, the body's resistance to disease collapses; in extreme cases, the person might die. Figure 16-1 illustrates the stages of the general adaptation syndrome.

The fight-or-flight response evolved because it helped animals and human beings cope with periodic stressors, such as wildfires or animal attacks. Unfortunately, in modern industrialized countries, we are subjected to continual, rather than periodic, stressors. The infrequent saber-toothed-tiger attack has been replaced by three exams on one day and threats of muggers on city streets. The repeated activation of the fight-or-flight response takes its toll on the body, possibly causing or aggravating diseases. Stress-affected noninfectious diseases include asthma (Moran, 1991), diabetes (Fisher, Delamater, Bertelson, & Kirkley, 1982), gastric ulcers (Young, Richter, Bradley, & Anderson, 1987), and essential hypertension (Mellors, Boyle, & Roberts, 1994). Such diseases traditionally have been called *psychosomatic,* based on the assumption that they are caused or worsened by emotional factors (Fava & Sonino, 2000).

general adaptation syndrome
As first identified by Hans Selye, the body's stress response, which includes the stages of alarm, resistance, and exhaustion.

Stress and Cardiovascular Disease

Of all the diseases that might be affected by stress, coronary heart disease has received the most attention from health psychologists. Researchers study the effects of stress on the cardiovascular system and coronary-prone (so-called Type A) behavior.

Cardiovascular Effects of Stress

Coronary heart disease is caused by *atherosclerosis,* which is promoted by cholesterol deposits in the coronary arteries. Even the stress of everyday college life can affect the level of cholesterol in a person's blood. College students who merely anticipate an upcoming exam show significant increases in their levels of blood cholesterol (Van Doornen & van Blokland, 1987). Stress also can promote coronary heart disease by elevating heart rate and

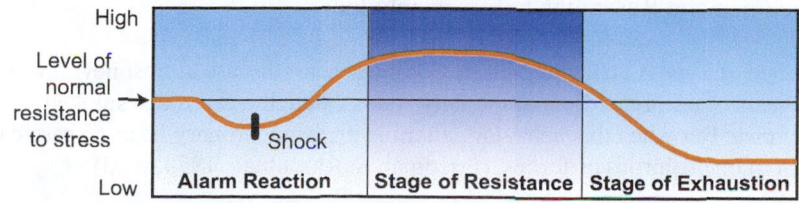

FIGURE 16-1 General Adaptation Syndrome

According to Hans Selye, when we react to stressors, we pass through one or more of the three stages of the general adaptation syndrome. These stages are the alarm reaction, the stage of resistance, and the stage of exhaustion.

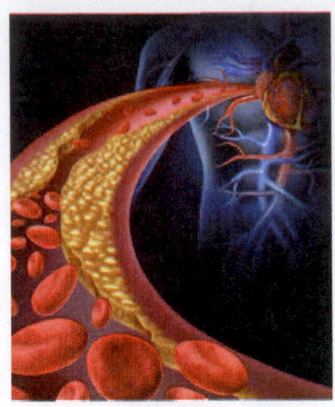

The Relationship of Stress to Atherosclerosis

Chronic stress can lead to overeating, which promotes glucose uptake. This promotes both an increase in body fat and atherosclerotic plaque buildup. Red blood cells are blocked as arteries narrow due to plaque buildup.
Source: Lightspring/Shutterstock.com.

Type A behavior

A syndrome—marked by impatience, hostility, and extreme competitiveness—that is associated with the development of coronary heart disease.

blood pressure, as well as by stimulating the release of stress hormones. These responses can damage the walls of the coronary arteries, making them more susceptible to the buildup of cholesterol plaques (Krantz & Manuck, 1984).

Type A Behavior and Cardiovascular Disease

On November 2, 1988, "Iron Mike" Ditka, the tough head coach of the Chicago Bears football team, was hospitalized with a mild heart attack. In a televised interview on ESPN, Ditka's physician reported that Ditka had none of the common physical risk factors for coronary heart disease. His only risk factor was a psychological one: *Type A behavior.* A published review of research on Type A behavior in middle-aged men (such as Mike Ditka) found that Type A behavior was present in 70 percent of those with coronary heart disease and in only 46 percent of those who were healthy (Miller, Turner, Tindale, Posavac, & Dugoni, 1991). And in men, Type A behavior is associated with an increased risk of cardiovascular disease, including strokes (Kim et al., 1998)—though its presence does not guarantee coronary heart disease, and its absence does not guarantee freedom from it.

Characteristics of Type A Behavior In the late 1950s, San Francisco cardiologist Meyer Friedman noticed that his patients were easily angered, highly competitive, and driven to do more and more in less and less time. Friedman, with his colleague Ray Rosenman, called this syndrome of behaviors **Type A behavior**. In contrast, *Type B behavior* is characterized by patience, an even temper, and willingness to do a limited number of things in a reasonable amount of time. The Type A person also might show time urgency by changing lanes to advance a single car length, chronic activation by staying busy most of every day, and *multiphasic activity* by texting, eating, and watching television at the same time. This lifestyle means that the Type A person is in a constant state of fight or flight. Would this lifestyle be associated with a greater risk of heart disease?

Friedman and Rosenman asked managers and supervisors of large companies to identify colleagues who fit the description of the Type A and Type B behavior patterns. They identified samples of men, including many executives, who fit each pattern. No women were included because, at the time, relatively few women were in executive positions. Participants were interviewed about their medical history and behavioral tendencies, such as being driven to succeed, feeling highly competitive, and feeling under chronic time pressure. They were observed for body movements, tone of voice, teeth clenching, and any observable signs of impatience. Based on the interview, 69 of the men were labeled pure Type A, and 58 of the men were labeled pure Type B.

Friedman and Rosenman found that the Type A participants had significantly higher levels of blood cholesterol than did the Type B participants. More important, 28 percent of the Type A participants had symptoms of coronary heart disease, but only 4 percent of the Type B participants had such symptoms. Before leaping to the conclusion that the study definitely demonstrated that Type A behavior promotes heart disease, note two other findings: First, the Type A participants smoked much more than the Type B participants did. Today, we know that smoking is a major risk factor in heart disease. Second, the Type A participants' parents had a higher incidence of coronary heart disease than did the Type B participants' parents. Perhaps the Type A participants inherited a genetic tendency to develop heart disease (Vogler, Mcclearn, Snieder, & Boomsma, 1997). Of course, there could just as well be a genetic tendency toward Type A behavior, which in turn might promote heart disease. In any case, Friedman and Rosenman contributed one of the first formal studies demonstrating a possible link between behavior and heart disease. Later, based on subsequent research findings, Friedman and Rosenman boldly concluded:

> In the absence of Type A behavior pattern, coronary heart disease almost never occurs before 70 years of age, regardless of the fatty foods eaten, the cigarettes smoked, or the lack of exercise. But when this behavior pattern is present, coronary heart disease can easily erupt in one's thirties or forties. (Friedman & Rosenman, 1974, p. xi)

In 1975, Friedman, Rosenman, and their colleagues reported the results of a study on coronary heart disease that began in 1960 and lasted 9 years—the Western Collaborative Group Study (Rosenman et al., 1975). They studied more than 3,000 middle-aged men who were free of heart disease at the beginning of the study. Each of the men was categorized as Type A or Type B, based on an interview. The results indicated that, during the period of the study, the men classified as Type A were more than twice as likely to develop coronary heart disease as were the men classified as Type B.

The pattern of behavior shown by Type A participants indicates that they are overconcerned with control of their environment. This concern leads to repeated physiological arousal when other people, time constraints, or personal responsibilities threaten their sense of control. Type A behavior is not just a style of responding to the environment; it can induce the very environmental circumstances that evoke it. This finding was illustrated in a study that compared Type A and Type B police radio dispatchers during work shifts. Type A dispatchers generated more job pressures by initiating extra work for themselves and attending to multiple tasks at the same time. Moreover, their coworkers and supervisors looked to them when there were additional tasks to be performed. So, Type A people can help create work conditions that maintain their driven, time-urgent, impatient behavioral style (Kirmeyer & Biggers, 1988).

But the role of Type A behavior in coronary heart disease was brought into question by the results of a 22-year follow-up of participants in a large-scale study of Type A behavior and coronary heart disease mortality (Ragland & Brand, 1988). In fact, Type A participants who had suffered a heart attack had a somewhat *lower* risk of a second heart attack. Of course, this result might have been due to other factors, such as greater medical attention given to Type A than to Type B heart attack victims. Though this study indicated that the *overall* pattern of Type A behavior is unrelated to coronary heart disease, research findings have been converging on a specific component of the Type A behavior pattern—*hostility*—as the factor most related to coronary heart disease (Miller, Smith, Turner, Guijarro, & Hallet, 1996). According to researcher Redford Williams, hostility has emerged as an independent risk factor for cardiovascular disease (Suarez, Kuhn, Schanberg, Williams, & Zimmermann, 1998).

Effects of Type A Behavior Regardless of whether hostility or some other aspect of Type A behavior promotes coronary heart disease, how might it do so? One way might be by inducing a chronic stress response. In fact, people who display hostility are more physiologically reactive to physical and emotional stressors (Smith, Cranford, & Mann, 2000). One study investigated the relationship between hostility and cardiovascular reactivity in social interactions among male and female undergraduates. The participants discussed a controversial topic with a confederate who was instructed to disagree with the participant. Female and male participants who scored high on a measure of hostility had greater increases in blood pressure during the discussion than did participants who scored low on hostility (Davis, Matthews, & McGrath, 2000).

High physiological reactivity also might unleash harmful effects through the actions of stress hormones. This hypothesis was confirmed in a study in which Redford Williams and his colleagues (1982) had Type A and Type B male college students compete in a stressful laboratory task. The results indicated that the Type A students displayed a significantly greater increase in levels of the adrenal gland stress hormones cortisol, epinephrine, and norepinephrine. These stress hormones promote the buildup of cholesterol plaques on the walls of arteries, increasing the risk of heart attacks.

The results of a study conducted in northern Ireland suggests that Type A behavior also might indirectly contribute to cardiovascular disease by promoting the eating of fast foods, which are convenient but also have higher levels of fat, salt, and sugar than more healthful food (Barker, Thompson, & McClean, 1996). Another possible factor mediating the effect of Type A behavior on coronary heart disease is the tendency of Type A people to ignore symptoms of illness. Before being hospitalized with his heart attack, Mike Ditka had ignored pain earlier in the week until his assistant coaches forced him to seek medical attention. This tendency of Type A people to discount their symptoms first appears in childhood. Type A children are less likely to complain of symptoms of illness, and Type A children who have surgery miss fewer days of school than do Type B children (Leikin, Firestone, & McGrath, 1988).

Development of Type A Behavior Though there is only weak evidence of a hereditary basis for Type A behavior, there is strong evidence that the pattern runs in families. Karen Matthews, a leading researcher on Type A behavior, points to child-rearing practices as

Multiphasic Activity

The Type A behavior pattern is associated with multiphasic activity, in which the person engages in several activities at once as part of a continual effort to do more and more in less and less time.
Source: Michael C. Gray/ Shutterstock.com.

the primary origin of Type A behavior. Parents of Type A children encourage them to try harder even when they do well and offer them few spontaneous positive comments. Type A children might be given no standards except "Do better," which makes it difficult for them to develop internal standards of achievement. They may then seek to compare their academic performance with the best in their class. This reaction might contribute to the development of the hard-driving component of the Type A behavior pattern (Matthews & Woodall, 1988).

There also are sociocultural differences in Type A behavior tendencies. One study found that low socioeconomic status was associated with increased cardiovascular reactivity in response to stress among African American and European American children (Gump, Matthews, & Raeikkoenen, 1999). And African American participants who experience stereotype threat (see Chapter 10) while performing a laboratory task have greater increases in blood pressure than do European American or African American participants who do not experience stereotype threat (Blascovich, Spencer, Quinn, & Steele, 2001). In fact, the term *John Henryism* has been coined to describe the psychological effects of trying to actively cope with chronic stress in the face of insurmountable odds—as many poor and ethnic minority individuals must do. John Henryism appears to be particularly lethal for African American men (Merritt, Bennett, Williams, Sollers, & Thayer, 2004).

Modification of Type A Behavior Because of the possible association between Type A behavior and coronary heart disease, its modification might be wise. But a paradox of Type A behavior is that Type A persons are not necessarily disturbed by their behavior. Why change a behavior pattern that is rewarded in competitive Western society? Programs to modify the Type A behavior of those who are willing to participate try to alter specific components of the Type A behavior pattern, particularly impatience, hostility, and competitiveness. One hostility-reduction program reduced diastolic blood pressure in participants compared to nonparticipants (Gidron, Davidson, & Bata, 1999). And a Swedish intervention study reduced both hostility and time pressure in Type A participants (Karlberg, Krakau, & Unden, 1998).

Stress and Immune Functioning

In 1884, a physician reported in a British medical journal that the depressed mood experienced by mourners at funerals predisposed them to develop illnesses (Baker, 1987). A century later, a research study provided a scientific basis for this observation that stress, depressed mood, and immune functioning are linked. As shown in Figure 16-2, the study found that men whose wives had died of breast cancer showed impaired functioning of their immune systems during the first 2 months of their bereavement (Schleifer, Keller, Camerino, Thornton, & Stein 1983). This finding agrees with research showing that major depressive disorder is associated with suppression of the immune system (McGuire, Kiecolt-Glaser, & Glaser, 2002). This research has led to the hypothesis that one cause of major depressive disorder is immunosuppression. More recent research has suggested

FIGURE 16-2

Immune Response to Bereavement

During the first 2 months after the death of their wives, widowers showed a decrease in the proliferation of lymphocytes in response to doses of antigens.

Source: Data from S. J. Schleifer et al., Suppression of lymphocytic stimulation following bereavement, *Journal of the American Medical Association*, 250, 374–377.

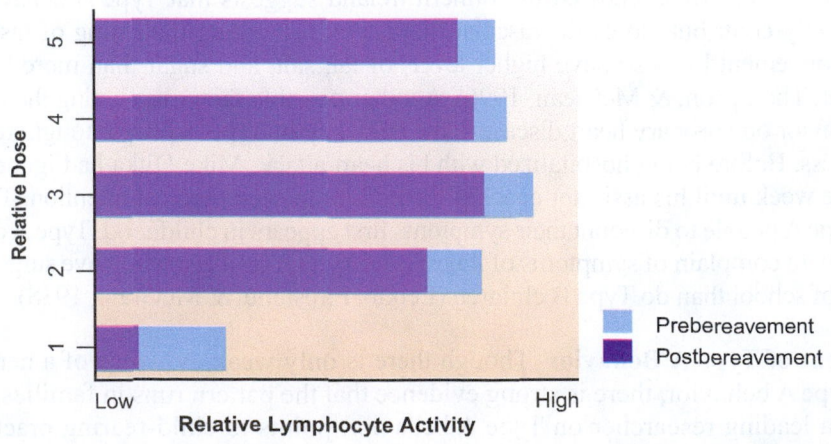

that this can be extended to inflammation (Savitz, Tan, Taylor, Drevets, & Teague, 2013) and has led to the new field of psychoneuroimmunology.

Psychoneuroimmunology

The realization that stressful events, such as the death of a loved one, can impair the immune system led to the emergence of **psychoneuroimmunology**, the interdisciplinary field that studies the relationship between psychological factors and illness, especially the effects of stress on the immune system (Ader, 2001). Though many of the mechanisms by which stress suppresses the immune system remain to be determined, one mechanism is well established (see Figure 16-3). Stress prompts the hypothalamus to secrete a hormone that stimulates the pituitary gland to secrete adrenocorticotropic hormone (ACTH), which then stimulates the adrenal cortex to secrete corticosteroids. The hypothalamus also increases activity in the sympathetic nervous system, which stimulates the adrenal medulla to secrete the hormones epinephrine and norepinephrine. As noted in the section "Daily Hassles," though adrenal hormones might make us more resistant to stressors, they also can impair our immune systems (Kiecolt-Glaser & Glaser, 1995).

A review of research studies found that major depressive disorder is consistently associated with large decreases in natural killer cell activity (Herbert & Cohen, 1993). *Natural killer cells* are lymphocytes responsible for triggering cytokine release. More recent evidence suggests that other immune cells also are involved in major depressive disorder. One study of men diagnosed with major depressive disorder who were not taking antidepressants found an increase in the number of white blood cells and a decrease in the number of specialized T-lymphocytes (Savitz, Tan, Taylor, Drevets, & Teague, 2013).

The cells chiefly responsible for the immunological response to infections are white blood cells called B-lymphocytes and T-lymphocytes. *B-lymphocytes* attack invading bacteria, and *T-lymphocytes* attack viruses, cancer cells, and foreign tissues (see Figure 16-4). The immunosuppressive effects of stress hormones might explain why Apollo astronauts, after returning to Earth from stressful trips to the moon, had impaired immune responses (Jemmott & Locke, 1984). But you do not have to go to the moon to experience stress-induced suppression of your immune response, as revealed in a study of college students. After the students had given speeches that were evaluated for their merit, they showed impairment of their immune response (Marsland, Manuck, Fazzari, & Stewart, 1995). And the chronic stress experienced by women who care for husbands suffering from Alzheimer's disease is associated with impaired immune functioning (Wu et al., 1999). In addition, there is a positive relationship between stressful life events and the progression of HIV disease (Leserman, 2003).

psychoneuroimmunology
The interdisciplinary field that studies the relationship between psychological factors and physical illness.

FIGURE 16-3
Stress Pathways

When the cerebral cortex processes stressful memories or stressful input from the immediate environment, it stimulates a physiological response by way of the endocrine system and the sympathetic nervous system. Both pathways involve the hypothalamus. The hypothalamus signals the pituitary gland, which secretes adrenocorticotropic hormone (ACTH). ACTH, in turn, stimulates the adrenal cortex to secrete corticosteroid hormones, which mobilize the body's energy stores, reduce tissue inflammation, and inhibit the immune response. The hypothalamus also sends signals through the sympathetic nervous system to the adrenal medulla, which in turn stimulates the release of epinephrine and norepinephrine. These hormones contribute to the physiological arousal characteristic of the fight-or-flight response.
Source: Alila Medical Media/ Shutterstock.com.

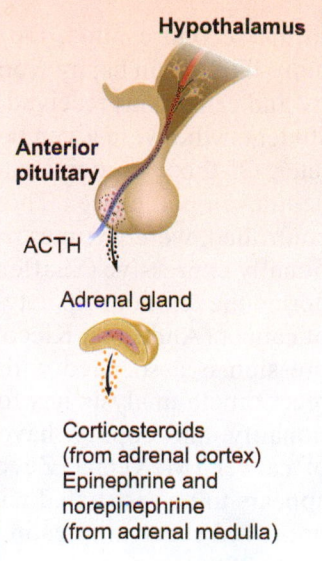

Source of stress
(memory or environment)
↓
Cerebral cortex, amygdala
(memory or environmental stimulus interpreted as stressful)
↓
Hypothalamus
(activates fight-or-flight response via pituitary gland and sympathetic nervous system)
↓   ↓
Pituitary gland   Sympathetic nervous system
(secretes ACTH)   (stimulates adrenal medulla)
↓   ↓
Adrenal cortex   Adrenal medulla
(secretes corticosteroids) (secretes epinephrine and norepinephrine)

Hypothalamus

Anterior pituitary

ACTH

Adrenal gland

Corticosteroids
(from adrenal cortex)
Epinephrine and norepinephrine
(from adrenal medulla)

FIGURE 16-4

CELL-MEDIATED IMMUNE RESPONSE

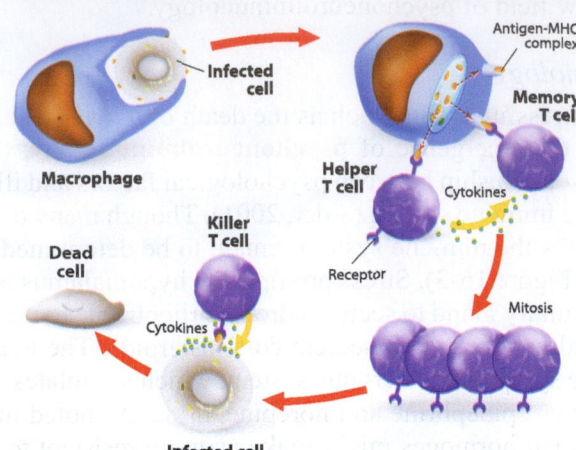

The Role of T-Lymphocytes in the Immune Response

This figure reflects one of many normal processes of immune activation, when the body detects an antigen (a substance that evokes an immune response). Macrophages recruit helper and memory T cells to multiply. The killer cells recognize and destroy cells infected with the antigen. After the process slows down, a small number of T cells live on as memory cells. Chronic stress can alter this process and can suppress the immune responses.

Source: Designua/Shutterstock.com.

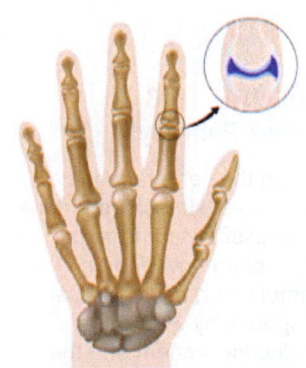

Normal

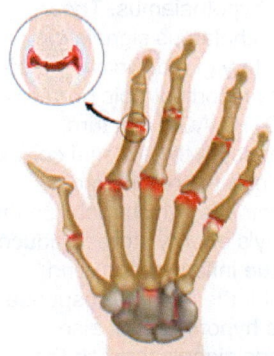

Rheumatoid arthritis

Stress and Rheumatoid Arthritis

Psychological stress aggravates rheumatoid arthritis. Though the exact mechanisms are unknown, cytokines likely play a role.

Source: Alila Medical Media/Shutterstock.com.

Conditioning the Immune Response

Given that the immune system is affected by stressful life experiences, is it conceivable that learning could alter the immune response? This question inspired the experiment described in "The Research Process" feature.

Perhaps classical conditioning one day will be applied clinically to enhance immune responses in people who have low resistance to infections, such as people who are HIV-positive or living with AIDS. People with AIDS experience stress induced by their illness, as well as hostile social reactions. Such stress might further impair the functioning of their immune systems, making them even more vulnerable to infections that often prove fatal (Ironson, Schneiderman, Kumar, & Antoni, 1994).

Classical conditioning also might be used to suppress undesirable immune responses, such as those that occur in *autoimmune diseases,* in which the immune system attacks a person's own body tissues as though they were foreign. One candidate for such treatment is rheumatoid arthritis, which is affected by stress (Evers, Kraaimaat, Geenen, Jacobs, & Bijlsma, 2003; McEwen, 2004). Preliminary research indicates that another beneficial application of conditioned immunosuppression might be in preventing the rejection of transplanted tissues and organs. In one study, heart transplants in rats were less likely to be rejected when the rats had been conditioned to suppress their immune response (Exton, Westermann, & Schedlowski, 2000).

Stress and Cancer

In the second century, the Greek physician Galen noted that depressed women were more likely than happy women to develop cancer. This relationship between emotionality and cancer has received support from modern research. Consider a study of medical students who were given personality tests in medical school and then assessed 30 years later. Of those participants who had been emotionally expressive, less than 1 percent had developed cancer. Those who had been loners, and presumably more emotionally controlled, were 16 times more likely to develop cancer than were those who were emotionally expressive (Shaffer, Graves, Swank, & Pearson, 1987). Other studies have supported the relationship between the tendency to suppress emotions and the development of cancer (Andersen, Kiecolt-Glaser, & Glaser, 1994), apparently because emotion suppression is associated with suppression of the immune response (Eysenck, 1994). A recent meta-analysis has found that psychosocial variables, such as personality, emotionality, and coping, have a modest but consistent relationship to the development of cancer (McKenna, Zevon, Corn, & Rounds, 1999). On the other hand, optimism appears to be associated with lower levels of stress, slower progression of disease, and improved survival rates in patients with certain cancers (Carver et al., 2005; de Moor et al., 2006).

Can the Immune Response Be Altered by Classical Conditioning?

Rationale

Certain chemicals can enhance or suppress the immune response. Researcher Robert Ader wondered whether such a chemical could be used as the basis for classically conditioning the immune response. He reasoned that a neutral stimulus paired with the chemical might come to have the same effect on the immune response. This possibility inspired him to test his hypothesis experimentally.

Method

Ader and his colleague Nicholas Cohen (1982) used the drug cyclophosphamide, which suppresses the immune system, as the unconditioned stimulus. When mice were injected with the drug, they experienced both nausea and immunosuppression—dual effects of the drug. Ader and Cohen used saccharin-flavored water as the neutral stimulus. They hoped that if the mice drank the water before being injected with the drug, the taste of sweet water would suppress their immune response to an antigen.

Results and Discussion

As Ader and Cohen expected, the mice developed an aversion to sweet-tasting water because they associated it with nausea caused by the drug. But when some of the mice were later forced to drink sweet-tasting water, several developed illnesses and died. Ader and Cohen attributed this result to conditioned suppression of the mice's immune response, with the sweet-tasting water having become a conditioned stimulus after being paired with the drug (see Figure 16-5). Many subsequent studies have provided additional evidence that the immune response is subject to classical conditioning (Ader, 2003). Animal research indicates that epinephrine and norepinephrine mediate conditioned immunosuppression (Lysle, Cunnick, & Maslonek, 1991).

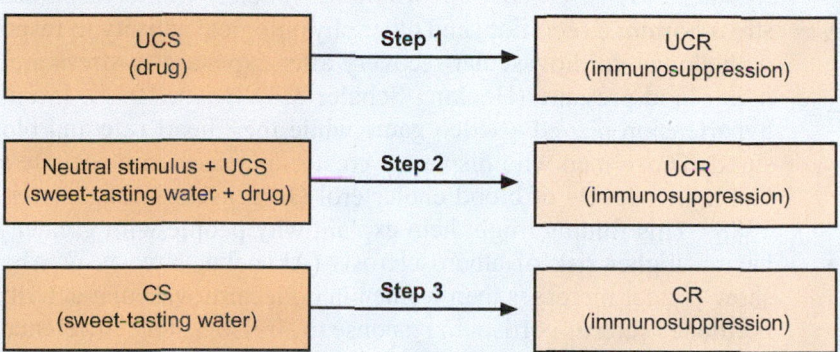

FIGURE 16-5 Conditioned Immunosuppression

When Ader and Cohen (1982) paired saccharin-sweetened water with cyclophosphamide, a drug that suppresses the immune response, they found that the sweet-tasting water itself came to elicit immunosuppression. (See Chapter 7 for a discussion of the relationship between the UCS, UCR, CS, and CR.)

Assuming that our emotions can affect the progress of cancer, what mechanisms might account for this relationship? Stress might indirectly promote cancer by affecting health behaviors, such as smoking tobacco, eating high-fat foods, and drinking too much alcohol. Stress also might directly interfere with the immune system's ability to defend against cancer. In fact, during periods when they are under intense academic pressure, medical students exhibit a reduction in the activity of natural killer cells, the lymphocytes responsible for detecting and destroying cancer cells (Glaser, Rice, Speicher, Stout, & Kiecolt-Glaser, 1986). And women who suffered repeated bouts of chronic depressed mood years earlier are more prone to developing breast cancer (Jacobs & Bovasso, 2000). Simply being diagnosed with cancer or being treated for cancer can induce stress-related suppression of the very immune responses that are needed to combat the cancer (Pompe, Antoni, & Heijnen, 1998). In reflecting on the link between psychological factors and cancer, note that though stress can *impair* the immune system's ability to destroy cancerous cells, there is little evidence that stress can directly *cause* normal cells to become cancerous (Levenson & Bemis, 1991).

Section Review: The Biopsychology of Stress and Illness

1. What is the relationship between stress and cancer?

2. How might stress impair immune system functioning?

3. What evidence is there that the immune response can be classically conditioned?

Factors That Moderate the Stress Response

More than 2,000 years ago, Hippocrates recognized the relationship between individual factors and physiological responses when he observed that it is more important to know what sort of person has a disease than to know what sort of disease a person has. Because of variability among individuals, a given stressor will not evoke the same response in every person. Our reactions to stress are moderated by a variety of factors. These factors include *physiological reactivity, cognitive appraisal, explanatory style, perceived control, psychological hardiness,* and *social support*

Physiological Reactivity

physiological reactivity
The extent to which a person displays increases in heart rate, blood pressure, stress hormone secretion, and other physiological activity in response to stressors.

People differ in their pattern of physiological responses to stressors (Walsh, Wilding, & Eysenck, 1994). **Physiological reactivity** refers to increased heart rate, blood pressure, stress hormone secretion, and other physiological activity in response to stressors. People with slower cardiovascular recovery after exposure to stress are more prone to develop high blood pressure (Hocking-Schuler & O'Brien, 1997). In one study, men with mild hypertension played a video game while their heart rate and blood pressure were measured. Those men who displayed greater increases in heart rate and blood pressure also had higher levels of blood cholesterol (Jorgensen, Nash, Lasser, Hymowitz, & Langer, 1988). This finding might help explain why people with greater physiological reactivity have a higher risk of atherosclerosis (Aheneku, Nwosu, & Aheneku, 2000). And men show greater increases than women in both cardiovascular activity and secretion of stress hormones such as cortisol in response to stressors. This difference might contribute to the greater vulnerability of men to coronary heart disease (Earle, Linden, & Weinberg, 1999).

More recent research supports the hypothesis that there is a genetic factor in physiological responses to stressors. Men who have a mutation in the receptor that responds to cortisol have enhanced cortisol secretion and heart rate responses to psychosocial stressors (DeRijk et al., 2006). Studying mutations in this receptor could help researchers understand physiological predispositions to psychological disorders related to stress and major depressive disorder.

Cognitive Appraisal

cognitive appraisal
The subjective interpretation of the severity of a stressor.

Though Hans Selye believed that all stressors produce similar patterns of physiological responses, more recent research indicates that different stressors may produce different patterns (Krantz & Manuck, 1984). Richard Lazarus, whose work on daily hassles was discussed earlier in the chapter, believed that one of the reasons that different stressors can produce different responses in the same person is that the person interprets the two stressors differently. This difference in interpretation is known as **cognitive appraisal** (Lazarus, 1993), which Lazarus also used as the basis of his theory of emotion (see Chapter 12).

Cognitive appraisal involves two stages: primary appraisal and secondary appraisal. In *primary appraisal,* you judge whether a situation requires a coping response. If you judge that a situation requires a coping response, you then engage in *secondary appraisal* by determining whether you have the ability to cope with the situation. The greater the perceived controllability of a stressful situation, the lower its perceived stressfulness (Peeters, Buunk, & Schaufeli, 1995). Consider final exams. Students who perceive their exams to be highly demanding and who lack confidence in their ability to perform well on them will experience greater stress than will students who perceive their upcoming exams as moderately demanding and are confident of their ability to perform well. This view has been supported by research finding more positive emotion and better coping among people who appraise stressors as challenging, rather than threatening (Folkman & Moskowitz, 2000).

Explanatory Style

People diagnosed with major depressive disorder (see Chapter 14) tend to have a pessimistic **explanatory style**. They attribute unpleasant events to *internal, stable,* and *global* characteristics of themselves. In other words, depressed people attribute unpleasant events to their own unchanging, pervasive, and personal characteristics. The possible role of a pessimistic explanatory style in the promotion of illness was supported by a retrospective study of 99 graduates of the Harvard University classes of 1942–1944. Graduates who had had a pessimistic explanatory style at the age of 25 (based on questionnaires they had completed at that time) became less healthy between the ages of 45 and 60 than did graduates who did not have a pessimistic explanatory style. All the graduates had been healthy at age 25 (Peterson, Seligman, & Vaillant, 1988).

The researchers hypothesized that pessimism might make people less likely to take actions to counter the effects of negative life events, leading to more severe stress in their lives. A pessimistic explanatory style might increase susceptibility to illness by leading to poor health habits, suppression of the immune system, and withdrawal from sources of social support. Each of these factors can promote illness. For example, one study found that older adults with a pessimistic explanatory style showed a weaker immune response to antigens than did older adults who did not exhibit a pessimistic explanatory style (Kamen-Siegel, Rodin, Seligman, & Dwyer, 1991).

One research study of male college students who were exposed to acute psychological stress found that higher levels of optimism were associated with smaller amounts of cytokines in their blood. Interestingly, there was no direct association between cytokine responses and negative mood. This finding suggests that the optimism-cytokine relationship is mediated by stress (Brydon, Walker, Wawrzyniak, Chart, & Steptoe, 2009). These findings were supported by a study in which college students with a pessimistic explanatory style were more likely to develop physical illnesses (Jackson, Sellers, & Peterson, 2002). Moreover, explanatory style is related to premature mortality. In particular, catastrophizing (operationally defined as making global attributions) has been found to predict mortality, especially among men (Peterson, Seligman, Yurko, Martin, & Friedman, 1998).

Fortunately, for many people, as demonstrated by health psychologist Shelley Taylor (Taylor, Lerner, Sherman, Sage, & McDowell, 2003), people with a more optimistic outlook on life—even a somewhat unrealistically positive one—are less susceptible to illness. For example, optimistic people are less likely than pessimistic people to develop cardiovascular disease (Kubzansky, Sparrow, Vokonas, & Kawachi, 2001).

Perceived Control

In a best-selling book describing his recovery from a massive heart attack, Norman Cousins, former editor of the *Saturday Review,* claimed that his insistence on taking personal responsibility for his recovery—including devising his own rehabilitation program—helped him regain his health. In contrast, as Cousins noted in his book, "good patients" (patients who remain passive) discover that "a weak body becomes weaker in a mood of total surrender" (Cousins, 1983, p. 223).

Research findings have supported Cousins's anecdotal report by converging on **perceived control** over stressors as one of the most important factors moderating the relationship between stress and illness. Perceived control over stressors reduces stress (Shirom, Melamed, & Nir-Dotan, 2000). People who work at demanding jobs and feel they have little control over job stressors are more likely to develop coronary heart disease (Krantz, Contrada, Hill, & Friedler, 1988). And consider impoverished residents of urban slums who are subjected to environmental factors out of their control, such as pollution, crowding, noise, and traffic. One study found that slum dwellers in Delhi, India, reported **learned helplessness**—the feeling that one has little control over events in one's life—in coping with these stressors (Siddiqui & Pandey, 2003) (see Chapter 7).

explanatory style The tendency to explain events optimistically or pessimistically.

perceived control The degree to which a person feels in control over life's stressors.

learned helplessness A feeling of futility caused by the belief that one has little or no control over events in one's life, which can make one stop trying and become depressed.

As mentioned in Chapter 13, there are cultural differences in perceived control (O'Connor & Shimizu, 2002). People with a sense of *primary control* believe that they can directly influence other people or the environment. People with a sense of *secondary control* accept and adjust to their environment. Whereas American culture emphasizes the importance of primary control, Japanese culture promotes secondary control (Weisz, Rothbaum, & Blackburn, 1984). For example, in one study American and Japanese participants in aerobics classes responded to a questionnaire assessing their reasons for choosing a class and their responses to being in a difficult class. American participants were more likely to choose a class based on convenience and to simplify moves they felt were too difficult. Japanese participants were more likely to choose classes based on their ability level and to work harder on moves that they felt were too difficult (Morling, 2000).

People in all walks of life benefit from a sense of control over the stressors that affect them. Residents of retirement homes who are given greater responsibility for self-care and everyday activities live longer and healthier lives than do residents whose lives are controlled by staff members (Langer & Rodin, 1976). People who feel a lack of control tend to secrete more adrenal hormones in response to stress (Peters et al., 1998), which in turn can impair their immune systems. In fact, people who lack a sense of control over their lives show reduced T helper cell (Brosschot et al., 1998) and natural killer cell (Reynaert, Janne, Bosly, & Staquet, 1995) activity in response to stressors. This reduction in cellular activity could impair their immunological defense against cancer.

Studying people's perceptions of stress is a complex task. Cognitive control does appear to decrease physiological responses to stress, and stressful events do appear to increase stress pathway responses (see Figure 16-3). Yet, successfully experiencing stressful events can help lead to a sense of cognitive control over future stressful events (Oldehinkel et al., 2011).

Nevertheless, a potential consequence of exposure to uncontrollable stress is the state of physical and psychological exhaustion called **burnout**. Burnout is especially common among human-service providers, including university professors and other teachers (Watts & Robertson, 2011), police officers (Gana & Boblique, 2000), athletic coaches (Price & Weiss, 2000), and medical personnel (Peltzer, Mashego, & Mabeba, 2003).

Children who experience stress early in life, such as separation from the primary caregiver, maltreatment, or neglect, have been found to have difficulty in regulating cognitive processes and elevated stress-related hormones. One fMRI study of adolescents who experienced such early life stress found that brain areas associated with cognitive control were impaired (Mueller et al., 2010).

burnout A state of physical and psychological exhaustion associated with chronic exposure to uncontrollable stress.

Psychological Hardiness

Psychologists Salvatore Maddi and Suzanne Kobasa were puzzled by the fact that while some people can work under chronic, intense pressure and remain healthy, others cannot. Maddi and Kobasa wondered whether this difference might be related to personality. To test this possibility scientifically, they gave a group of business executives a battery of personality tests and then conducted a 5-year, prospective study during which they periodically assessed the executives' health. Maddi and Kobasa found that those executives who were illness-resistant tended to share a set of personality characteristics that those who were illness-prone did not (Kobasa, Maddi, & Kahn, 1982).

Maddi and Kobasa called this set of personality characteristics **psychological hardiness**. They have found that people high in psychological hardiness are more resistant to stressors and, possibly as a result, are less susceptible to stress-related illness (Maddi, 2002). Other researchers have supported this finding as well. For example, a study of college undergraduates found that participants high in hardiness reported lower levels of stress and depression (Pengilly & Dowd, 2000). And a 10-week study of college students found a negative correlation between hardiness and visits to the college health center. That is, psychologically hardier students tended to be physically healthier than less hardy students were (Mathis & Lecci, 1999). And psychological hardiness has been found to reduce burnout (Lo Bue, Taverniers, Mylle, & Euwema, 2013) and posttraumatic disorder symptoms among military personnel (Escolas, Pitts, Safer, & Bartone, 2013).

psychological hardiness A set of personality characteristics marked by feelings of commitment, challenge, and control that promotes resistance to stress.

What characteristics do people high in psychological hardiness share? Kobasa found that hardy people face stressors with a sense of commitment, challenge, and control. People with a sense of *commitment* are wholeheartedly involved in everyday activities and social relationships, rather than being alienated from them. People with a sense of *challenge* view life's stressors as opportunities for personal growth rather than as burdens to be endured. And people with a sense of *control* believe they have the personal resources to cope with stressors, rather than being helpless in the face of them. Table 16-1 shows how individuals high or low in psychological hardiness might respond to stressors typically faced by college students.

But how does hardiness reduce susceptibility to illness? One way is by making hardy individuals less physiologically reactive to stressors, as demonstrated in a study of patients who were awaiting dental surgery (Solcova & Sykora, 1995). People who are higher in psychological hardiness also have a stronger immune response to antigens (Dolbier et al., 2001) and miss work less frequently (Hystad, Eid, & Brevik, 2011). Another way that hardiness reduces susceptibility to illness is by affecting health habits. People high in psychological hardiness, compared to people low in it, are more likely to maintain good health habits in the face of stress (Wiebe & McCallum, 1986). Thus, hardy students may be more resistant to illness because they are more likely to eat well, take vitamins, exercise more, and seek medical attention for minor ailments, even when under stress. Stress-management programs aimed at enhancing psychological hardiness have achieved initial success in increasing job satisfaction and reducing the severity of physical illness (Maddi, Kahn, & Maddi, 1998).

Social Support

People who have **social support** are less likely to become ill. For example, a lack of social support is a key factor in the "broken-heart phenomenon": the tendency of bereaved spouses to die sooner than people whose spouses are still alive. Those spouses who die sooner tend not to remarry, to live by themselves, to feel lonelier, and to have no one to talk to (Stroebe, 1994). Social support can be tangible, in the form of money or practical help, or intangible, in the form of advice or encouragement about how to eliminate or cope with stress. Social support promotes health by reducing the effects of stressful life events, promoting recovery from illness, and increasing adherence to medical regimens (Heitzmann & Kaplan, 1988).

social support The availability of support from other people, whether tangible or intangible.

People show lower cardiovascular reactivity in the face of a stressful situation when someone else accompanies them (Kamarck, Peterman, & Raynor, 1998). Social support can retard the progress of atherosclerosis by reducing stress-related increases in heart rate, blood pressure, and stress hormones (Knox & Uvnaes-Moberg, 1998). And social support is associated with a stronger immune response in HIV-positive patients (Cruess et al., 2000). This finding is important because HIV-positive individuals show reductions in the activity of natural killer cells and certain other important lymphocytes when facing stressful life events (Evans, Leserman, Perkins, & Stern, 1995).

TABLE 16-1 Psychological Hardiness

	Student High in Psychological Hardiness	Student Low in Psychological Hardiness
Commitment (vs. Alienation)	"Even though I'm a psychology major, I would like to learn all I can from my courses in English, history, and fine arts."	"I don't know why I have to waste my time taking courses that are not in my major."
Challenge (vs. Threat)	"My statistics course is difficult, but if I can master the material, I can do well in just about any course."	"My statistics course is too hard. Maybe I should drop the course so I don't get a low grade that hurts my GPA."
Control (vs. Helplessness)	"My Spanish professor wants us to make oral presentations of our term papers to the class. I suppose that if I practice enough, I should be able to do well."	"I can't believe that my Spanish professor wants us to make oral presentations of our term papers to the class. No matter how much I prepare, I'll just sound stupid."

But what experimental evidence is there that social support boosts the immune response? In one study, saliva samples were taken from healthy college students 5 days before their first final exam, during the final-exams period, and 14 days after their last final exam. The samples were analyzed for the level of immunoglobulin A, an antibody that provides immunity against infections of the upper respiratory tract, gastrointestinal tract, and urogenital system. Salivary concentrations of immunoglobulin A after the final-exams period were lower than before it. But students who reported more adequate social support during the pre-exam period had consistently higher immunoglobulin A concentrations than did their peers who reported less adequate social support (Jemmott & Magloire, 1988). These results indicate that social support may promote health by directly strengthening the immune response.

Can social support be studied at the level of brain and behavior? Social exclusion is one way to experimentally study the influence of social support. Researchers scanned participants in an fMRI while the participants were playing a virtual ball-tossing game in which they first participated and then were eventually excluded. One region of the brain—the anterior cingulate cortex—was active when the participant was excluded, which is a response similar to that of patients who experience pain (Eisenberger, Lieberman, & Williams, 2003). Another study showed that participants who interacted regularly with supportive individuals across a 10-day period had reduced activity in the anterior cingulate cortex and decreased cortisol reactivity in response to a social stressor (Eisenberger, Taylor, Gable, Hilmert, & Lieberman, 2007). Social support and its relation to health is an important area of research for health psychologists.

Another example of the importance of social support comes from the research on the consequences of bullying on children and adolescents. Bullies repeatedly make their victims feel sad, anxious, and unable to concentrate. Traditional or *direct bullying,* which might consist of hitting, name-calling, or social isolation among school-aged children, has been found to contribute to victims experiencing increased rates of depressed mood and poor academic grades (Hawker & Boulton, 2000), and this effect is more pronounced in boys (Rothon, Head, Klineberg, & Stansfeld, 2011). And Rothon and colleagues found that social support can have a protective effect against the negative consequences of bullying on school achievement and mental health. Cyberbullying is a form of *indirect bullying.* Cyberbullying involves the use of mobile phones and the Internet to bully a victim. In this modern form of bullying, women and girls are more likely to be both the bully and victim. Whereas social support has been found to be protective in direct forms of bullying, researchers are just beginning to examine the changing face of bullying (Law, Shapka, Olson, & Waterhouse, 2012) and the impact of cyberbullying on social interpersonal relationships and health.

There are sociocultural differences in the expressed need for social support in coping with illness. A study of European American, Chinese American, and Japanese American breast cancer patients found that European Americans desired more social support than the other two groups did (Wellisch et al., 1999). Another study found that European American participants tended to provide emotional social support, whereas Japanese participants not only provided emotional social support but also problem-focused support, such as helping a patient find a medical specialist. These findings were attributed to the cultural context, with Japanese support providers being motivated to maintain closeness with others, whereas European American support providers were motivated to maintain closeness but also to improve the self-esteem of others (Chen, Kim, Mojaverian, & Morling, 2012).

Social support groups are more likely to be sought out by people suffering from stigmatizing illnesses and health problems—such as AIDS, substance abuse, and cancer—than equally serious but less embarrassing disorders, such as heart disease (Davison, Pennebaker, & Dickerson, 2000). There also are gender differences in the effects of social support. In one study of 2,348 married or cohabiting heterosexual adults, social support from one's partner and family predicted psychological well-being among both women and men. However, women's psychological and physical health was more likely to suffer when their family was under stress. Moreover, whereas social support reduced stress among men and women in this sample, friends and family were more common sources of social support for women than for men (Walen & Lachman, 2000).

Cyberbullying

Cyberbullying is a new form of bullying that utilizes communication technologies and is becoming increasingly common. The bully's actions are repeated, hostile, and deliberate. Teenage girls engage in this behavior more often than do boys.

Source: oliveromg/Shutterstock.com.

Coping with Stress

Given that stress is unavoidable and often harmful, coping with stress is an important part of everyday life. One approach to coping divides it into task-oriented, emotion-oriented, and avoidance-oriented coping (Higgins & Endler, 1995). For example, suppose that you find it distressing to make oral presentations. You might engage in task-oriented coping by preparing carefully for oral presentations, emotion-oriented coping by cognitively reappraising the possible negative consequences of peer responses to your presentations, or avoidance-oriented coping by not enrolling in courses that require oral presentations. And the coping strategy you choose when under stress may be influenced by sociocultural factors, such as culture and gender. One study found that, when faced with difficult interpersonal situations, Nepalese children were more likely to engage in emotion-oriented coping, whereas American children were more likely to engage in task-oriented coping (Cole, Bruschi, & Tamang, 2002). Likewise, a recent meta-analysis found that women were more likely to use emotion-oriented coping strategies, such as ruminating about their problems, engaging in positive self-talk, and seeking emotional support (Tamres, Janicki, & Helgeson, 2002). These results are consistent with cross-cultural differences in emotional expression (see Chapter 12) and gender differences in rumination (see Chapter 14).

Cross-Cultural Differences in Coping

Compared to American children, these Nepalese girls are more likely to engage in emotion-oriented coping.

Source: nevenm/Shutterstock. com.

Of course, some people pursue more formal ways of coping with stress. Among the most common of these are stress-management programs, which have been effective in reducing angina pectoris (Gallacher, Hopkinson, Bennett, Burr, & Elwood, 1997) and high blood pressure (Garcia-Vera, Labrador, & Sanz, 1997). And an 8-week stress-management program for patients with multiple sclerosis resulted in decreased frequency and severity of physical symptoms, as well as reduced stress and depression (Artemiadis et al., 2012).

Emotional Release and Stress Management

Psychologist James Pennebaker and his colleagues have found that writing about our emotions is a stress-relieving practice that produces greater physical and psychological benefits than writing about superficial topics (Campbell & Pennebaker, 2003). Writing about stressful life experiences relieved symptoms in asthma and arthritis patients, when compared with patients who did not participate in writing (Stone, Smyth, Kaell, & Hurewitz, 2000). And undergraduates who wrote about traumatic experiences—the trauma itself, as well as how they grew or benefited from the experience—made fewer visits to the university health center compared to participants who did not write about their experiences (King & Miner, 2000). In contrast, suppressing our feelings while writing may adversely affect our immune system, as in a study in which participants wrote about their emotions or wrote while suppressing their emotions. Whereas those who wrote about their emotions showed increased lymphocyte activity, those who suppressed their emotions showed decreased lymphocyte activity (Petrie, Booth, & Pennebaker, 1998).

Humor and Stress Management

Humor relieves stress by inducing laughter, making stressors seem less negative, and evoking social support from other people (Nezu, Nezu, & Blissett, 1988). Moreover, people who use humor to cope with stress tend to be high in psychological hardiness. And the use of humor is even associated with a more effective immune response. For example, a study of women who had recently given birth found that those who used humor to cope with stress had fewer upper respiratory tract infections. Even their infants had fewer such infections, perhaps because they received more antibodies in their mother's milk (Dillon & Totten, 1989).

Research findings indicate that reliance on humor is associated with (1) a more positive self-concept when considered in terms of actual-ideal discrepancies, self-esteem, and standards for self-worth evaluation; (2) more positive and self-protective cognitive appraisals in the face of stress; and (3) more positive affect in response to both positive and negative life events. Research findings also support the proposal that humor, in addition to buffering the effects of stress, may play an important role in enhancing the enjoyment of positive life experiences (Martin, Kuiper, Olinger, & Dance, 1993).

Stress-Inoculation Training

stress-inoculation training
A type of cognitive therapy that helps clients change their pessimistic thinking into more positive thinking when in stressful situations.

A version of cognitive-behavior therapy called **stress-inoculation training**, introduced by Donald Meichenbaum (1985), helps clients change their pessimistic thinking into optimistic thinking when in stressful situations. A major review of 37 studies involving more than 1,800 participants found that stress-inoculation training is effective in reducing performance anxiety and improving work performance under stress (Saunders, Driskell, Johnston, & Salas, 1996). Stress-inoculation training also is effective in reducing anxiety in college students (Fontana, Diegman, Villeneuve, & Lepore, 1999) and law school students (Sheehy & Horan, 2004).

In a study of the effect of stress-inoculation training on anxiety and writing quality, participants were assigned to one of three conditions. The first condition combined stress-inoculation training with writing instruction, the second condition combined writing instruction with interpersonal attention, and the third condition (the control group) involved no treatment. Participants in the first two groups reported reductions in their anxiety levels that were greater than those reported by participants in the control group, but only the combination of stress-inoculation training and writing instruction improved writing quality—and significantly more of those in that group were able to pass a first-year college English equivalency examination (Salovey & Haar, 1990).

Stress-inoculation training also has proved effective in helping athletes during physical rehabilitation after arthroscopic surgery for torn cartilage, usually in a knee. A study of 60 athletes who underwent cartilage surgery found that those who received rehabilitation plus stress-inoculation training experienced less postsurgical pain and anxiety than did those who received rehabilitation alone. Those who received stress-inoculation training also regained use of their affected limbs more quickly (Ross & Berger, 1996).

Exercise and Stress Management

In the early 1960s, President John F. Kennedy, a physical fitness proponent, observed that "The Greeks knew that intelligence and skill can only function at the peak of their capacity when the body is healthy and strong—that hearty spirits and tough minds usually inhabit sound bodies" (Silva & Weinberg, 1984, p. 416). Kennedy would approve of the recent trend toward greater concern with personal fitness. The only way to achieve cardiovascular fitness is to maintain a program that includes regular aerobic exercise (exercise that markedly raises heart rate for at least 20 minutes). The possible beneficial effect of aerobic exercise was demonstrated in a longitudinal study (Brown & Siegel, 1988) that found that adolescents under high levels of stress who exercised regularly had a significantly lower incidence of illness than did adolescents who exercised little (see Figure 16-6).

Experimental research likewise shows that aerobic exercise programs improve both cardiovascular fitness and psychological well-being, regardless of age, occupation, or gender (Garcia, Archer, Moradi, & Andersson-Arntén, 2012). People who exercise become less physiologically reactive to stressors (Throne, Bartholomew, Craig, & Farrar, 2000) and more confident in their ability to cope (Steptoe, Moses, Edwards, & Mathews, 1993). There also is evidence that exercise can enhance the functioning of the immune system (Hong, 2000). The results of animal studies have indicated that exercise increases the generation of new neurons in the hippocampus, a brain structure involved in learning and memory (DeCarolis & Eisch, 2010)

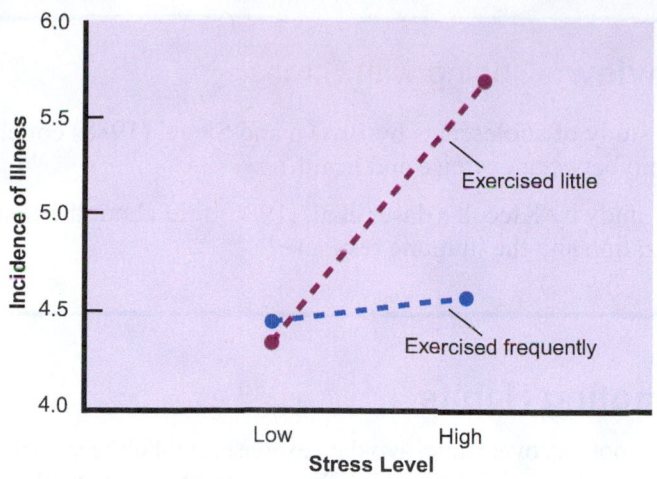

FIGURE 16-6
Exercise and Illness

A study of the relationship between exercise and illness found that adolescents who exercised little and adolescents who exercised regularly did not differ in their incidence of illness when under low levels of stress. In contrast, when under high levels of stress, those who exercised regularly had a significantly lower incidence of illness than did those who exercised little (Brown & Siegel, 1988).

Relaxation and Stress Management

Because stress is associated with physiological arousal, health psychologists emphasize the importance of relaxation training. Several techniques have proved effective in reducing psychological or physiological arousal. These include massage (Zeitlin, Keller, Shiflett, Schleifer, & Bartlett, 2000), hypnosis (Kiecolt-Glaser, Marucha, Atkinson, & Glaser, 2001), meditation (Speca, Carlson, Goodey, & Angen, 2000), biofeedback (Critchley, Melmed, Featherstone, Mathias, & Dolan, 2001), deep, rhythmic breathing (Gilbert, 2003), and restricted environmental stimulation training, or REST (Schulz & Kaspar, 1994). Hypnosis is discussed in Chapter 6, biofeedback in Chapter 7, and REST in Chapter 11.

The most basic relaxation technique is **progressive relaxation** (see Chapter 15). This technique was developed by Edmund Jacobson, who was inspired to evaluate the effect of relaxation on anxiety after noticing years earlier how distressed his father had become after losing some of his real estate in a fire (Jacobson, 1977). Progressive relaxation has been effective in reducing high blood pressure (Anthony et al., 2003). And heart-attack patients who receive training in breathing and relaxation develop a slower breathing rate and more normal heart rate (van Dixhoorn, 1998).

Progressive relaxation can even enhance the immunological response (Lekander, Fuerst, Rostein, Hursti, & Fredrikson, 1997). A study that compared children who practiced relaxation to children who did not found that the relaxation group had an increase in immunoglobulins, a measure of immune system functioning (Hewson-Bower & Drummond, 1996). Consider the following experiment that involved medical students, conducted by Janice Kiecolt-Glaser, a leading researcher on psychoneuroimmunology. Blood samples were taken from students 1 month before midterm exams and then again on the day of the exams. Half the students were randomly assigned to participate in relaxation practice during the month between the two measurement days. The students who were not assigned to practice relaxation, compared to the students who were, displayed a significantly greater decrease in natural killer cell activity between the first and second measurements (Kiecolt-Glaser et al., 1986). You will recall that natural killer cells are one of the body's main defenses against cancer cells.

As discussed earlier in this chapter, caregivers for patients with Alzheimer's disease experience chronic stress. A sample of caregivers participated in a study of the effects of meditation. Meditation, a form of relaxation, has been used for stress reduction for centuries. One group meditated for 12 minutes daily for 8 weeks. The other group listened to relaxing music for the same period of time. The researchers found that after 8 weeks of meditation, participants displayed increased immune functioning (Black et al., 2013). Whereas it is difficult for the researchers to conclude what exact features of meditation (e.g., chanting or breathing) might be responsible for these changes, practicing meditation daily might reverse the detrimental effects of chronic stress.

progressive relaxation
A stress-management procedure that involves the successive tensing and relaxing of each of the major muscle groups of the body.

Meditation and Stress

Recent evidence shows that daily structured meditation can help reverse the harmful effects of stress.
Source: luminaimages/Shutterstock.com.

Section Review: Coping with Stress

1. What did the study of adolescents by Brown and Siegel (1988) conclude about the relationship between exercise and health?

2. What did the study by Kiecolt-Glaser et al. (1986) find about the relationship between relaxation and the immune response?

Health-Promoting Habits

Habits as varied as smoking, overeating, avoiding exercise, and failing to wear seat belts sharply increase the chances of illness, injury, or death. Yet, a study found that college students tended to have an "it can't happen to me" attitude. Their estimate of the probability that their own risky behaviors would lead to illness or injury underestimated the actual probability. This feeling of invulnerability accounts for the greater tendency of young drivers to not use seat belts (Matsuura, Ishida, & Ishimatsu, 2002). Because of our inability to estimate the true riskiness of our behaviors, programs aimed at changing health-impairing habits must not only point out risky behaviors but also make participants realize that those habits make them more susceptible to unhealthy consequences than they might believe (Weinstein, 1984). An ambitious community program in New Zealand called Superhealth Basic used brief group sessions to help participants improve their behaviors related to sleep, stress, weight, smoking, drinking, exercise, and nutrition. Participants showed significant improvements in their mental health, physical health, management of stress, and sense of well-being (Raeburn, Atkinson, Dubignon, & Fitzpatrick, 1994).

One of the most important factors influencing whether people are motivated to engage in health-promoting behavior is their feeling of self-efficacy (Kelly, Zyzanski, & Alemagno, 1991). People high in self-efficacy feel that their actions will be effective. People with a high sense of self-efficacy in regard to health-promoting behaviors are more likely to see their benefits and to downplay barriers to performing them (Alexy, 1991). Feelings of self-efficacy are positively related to important health-promoting behaviors, including maintenance of smoking cessation, control of diet and body weight, and adherence to preventive health behaviors and medical regimens (O'Leary, 1985). For example, young adults with diabetes who are high in self-efficacy are more likely to practice procedures for keeping their disease under control (Griva, Myers, & Newman, 2000). Among the most important health-promoting habits are practicing safe sex, keeping physically fit, maintaining a healthy diet and body weight, and avoiding tobacco products.

Practicing Safe Sex

Today many health psychologists have turned their attention to risky sexual practices that contribute to the spread of sexually transmitted diseases, including AIDS, syphilis, gonorrhea, chlamydia, genital warts (the human papillomavirus), and genital herpes (the herpes simplex virus). But because it is usually fatal, AIDS has become of greatest interest to them.

HIV and AIDS

Acquired immune deficiency syndrome (AIDS) kills its victims by impairing their immune systems, making them eventually succumb to cancer or opportunistic infections—that is, infections that rarely occur in people with healthy immune systems. Since 1981, when it was first identified, AIDS has spread through much of the world with alarming rapidity. AIDS afflicts people of all ages, sexes, ethnicities, and sexual orientations. AIDS is caused by the human immunodeficiency virus (HIV). A person with HIV does not necessarily have AIDS but could develop AIDS in the future. Today, the use of antiviral therapy has helped delay or eliminate the progression of HIV-positive status to AIDS and can prevent noninfected sex partners from developing the disease (Cohen et al., 2011).

HIV is spread by infected protein-rich body fluids, such as blood or semen (Catania, Gibson, Chitwood, & Coates, 1990). Some HIV-positive people, most notably hemophiliacs, have acquired the virus in transfusions of contaminated blood. Drug addicts can acquire HIV by sharing hypodermic needles with infected addicts. The virus also can be transmitted through unprotected sexual activity, including anal sex and vaginal sex. Even infants born to HIV-positive mothers are at high risk of infection, especially if they are breast-fed. Transmission of the virus from infected dental or medical personnel to their patients, or from infected patients to dental or medical personnel, is much less likely. There is no evidence that kissing, simple touching, food handling, or other casual kinds of contact spread the virus.

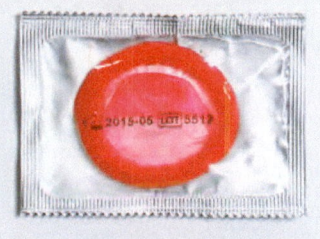

Prevention of HIV Infection

Blood, vaginal fluid, breast milk, and semen are the fluids that transmit HIV. Safe sex through the use of latex condoms is the primary prevention approach.
Source: kaarsten/Shutterstock. com.

Promoting Safe Sex

Because there is no cure for AIDS, prevention of HIV infection is crucial. One of the primary means of prevention is educating people to avoid risky behaviors. Foremost among the suggestions has been to practice "safe" sex (or at least "safer" sex). In regard to HIV infection, the safest sex is abstinence or limiting oneself to an uninfected partner. Many people do not abstain, however, and may have a series of sexual partners, so the next best suggestions are to use latex condoms and limit the number of sex partners.

Efforts to reduce risky behaviors have achieved some success. Though elsewhere in the world AIDS is more prevalent among heterosexuals, especially women, in North America, it has been more prevalent among gay men, Latinos, and African-Americans (Grossman, Purcell, Rotheram-Borus, & Veniegas, 2013). This prevalence has been attributed to the common practice of unprotected anal sex. The 10 percent of heterosexuals who practice anal sex also are at increased risk of infection (Voeller, 1991). Because AIDS has so ravaged the North American gay community, the earliest anti-AIDS programs were aimed at gay men. Cities with large gay and lesbian populations have instituted workshops on AIDS prevention for gay and bisexual men. For example, a survey of gay men in San Francisco, where there is a high level of AIDS education, found a significant increase in condom use (Catania, Coates, Stall, & Bye, 1991).

A review of research on the use of HIV-AIDS prevention videotapes found that they increase knowledge of HIV and AIDS and improve attitudes regarding risky sexual behavior. But it is unclear whether these changes translate into actual reductions in risky behavior (Kalichman, 1996). The National Institute of Mental Health conducted a program in 37 clinics across the United States that each had a high-risk population. The participants, compared to controls, showed a reduction in risky sexual behavior. They showed fewer acts of unprotected sex and increased use of condoms over a 12-month follow-up period (National Institute of Mental Health, 1998).

Keeping Physically Fit

People who exercise regularly are healthier and live longer than those who do not. Exercise promotes health and longevity, in part by boosting the immune system. A study found that HIV-positive people showed enhanced immunological responses after participating in an aerobic exercise program (Antoni, LaPerriere, Schneiderman, & Fletcher, 1991).

Beneficial Effects of Exercise

There is especially strong evidence for the effectiveness of exercise in preventing obesity and cardiovascular disease. Aerobic exercise (such as running, swimming, bicycling, brisk walking, or cross-country skiing) combats obesity by burning calories, raising the basal metabolic rate, and inhibiting the appetite. Aerobic exercise also reduces the cardiovascular risk factors of elevated cholesterol and high blood pressure.

The health risks of physical inactivity and the health benefits of exercise have led many sedentary people to start exercising. Unfortunately, of those who begin formal exercise programs, about 50 percent will drop out within 6 months. This attrition rate is unfortunate because participants in weight-control programs who continue to exercise after the programs end regain less weight than do those who stop exercising (Wadden, Vogt, Foster, & Anderson, 1998). According to Rod Dishman, an authority on exercise adherence, people who are obese or who have symptoms of cardiovascular disease—the very people who might benefit most from exercise—are the least likely to exercise (Dishman & Gettman, 1980). Physical inactivity is a greater health problem among African Americans and Latinos, who engage in less physical activity during leisure time than do European Americans. Moreover, this difference appears to be unrelated to social class (Crespo, Smit, Andersen, Carter-Pokras, & Ainsworth, 2000).

Adhering to an Exercise Program

Common reasons for failing to adhere to exercise programs are a lack of time and a lack of motivation (McAuley, Poag, Gleason, & Wraith, 1990). Moreover, a 2-year prospective study found that exercise adherence was lower among people who had experienced more than one major life event (Oman & King, 2000). One study conducted by the Centers for Disease Control and Prevention assessed barriers to physical activity in a multiethnic sample of young and middle-aged women. Regardless of ethnicity, family priorities were the main barrier to physical activity. Participants with multiple roles, such as wife, daughter, mother, and community member, reported having little time or energy for exercise (Eyler et al., 2002). Because of these responsibilities, home training may promote adherence relative to group training at an exercise facility (Perri, Martin, Leermakers, & Sears, 1997).

Other factors influence exercise adherence. People who practice dissociation (that is, blocking their conscious feelings of pain and fatigue) while running can exercise longer (Masters & Ogles, 1998). Intrinsic motivation (see Chapter 11) promotes exercise adherence. That is, people who exercise for enjoyment, competence, and social interaction show greater adherence than those who exercise just to improve their fitness or appearance (Ryan, Frederick, Lepes, Rubio, & Sheldon, 1997). In addition, one study found that people tend to adhere more to exercise programs that involve more frequent, lower-intensity workouts than to less frequent, higher-intensity workouts (Perri et al., 2002). And people who fail to adhere to exercise programs may have low self-efficacy—that is, a lack of confidence in their ability to meet the demands of the program. One study measured the self-efficacy of participants in a step-aerobics exercise class who participated in an 8-week program. There was a positive relationship between their self-efficacy levels and their attendance (Fontaine & Shaw, 1995).

The failure of people to maintain exercise programs has prompted health psychologists to study ways of increasing exercise adherence. One of the best ways to improve the motivation to exercise is to make exercising enjoyable (Wankel, 1993). Perhaps enjoyment explains the popularity of kickboxing classes and similar approaches to exercise. But some programs aimed at increasing adherence are more formal. In one study, groups of people engaged in jogging, aerobic dancing, or conditioning for skiing for 10 weeks. Some of the participants in each of the three groups also took part in a special program to increase their motivation to exercise. The program made participants more aware of obstacles to exercise and taught them how to cope with periodic exercise lapses instead of having an all-or-none attitude. Rather than giving up after exercise lapses, exercisers were urged to return immediately to their exercise programs. The results showed that those who participated in the adherence program, compared to those who did not, were indeed more likely to adhere to their exercise programs (Belisle, Roskies, & Levesque, 1987). Similar results have been found in a recent study that found that exercise adherence among older women was increased when they were provided with regularly scheduled telephone calls that offered assistance in coping with the demands of physical exercise and strategies to maintain their exercise regimen (Evers, Klusmann, Ziegelman, Schwarzer, & Heuser, 2012).

Maintaining a Healthy Diet and Body Weight

Health psychologists recognize the importance of maintaining a healthy diet and body weight. They are especially concerned with the relationship between diet and both diabetes and cardiovascular disease (Vidal, 2002). As mentioned earlier in this chapter, a high-fat diet is one of the main risk factors in cardiovascular disease. High-fat diets contribute to high blood pressure and high levels of cholesterol in the blood, which promote atherosclerosis by the buildup of plaque deposits that narrow the arteries. The narrowing of cerebral arteries and coronary arteries reduces blood flow, promoting strokes and heart attacks. Health psychologists have developed programs that combine nutritional education and cognitive-behavior modification to help people reduce their risks of cardiovascular disease by adopting healthier eating habits. For example, programs that reduce caloric intake produce significant reductions in blood pressure in participants with elevated blood pressure (Steffen et al., 2001).

Sociocultural Influences on Desirable Physiques

A high-fat diet also contributes to obesity—an important risk factor in illness for both men and women. Yet, in Western cultures, a leaner figure has been stylish for women only since the early 20th century, and a toned, muscular figure only in the past few decades. For the preceding 600 years, cultural standards favored a more rounded figure (Bennett & Gurin, 1982). You probably have seen this standard in Renaissance paintings that depict the ideal woman as being plump. Thus, what we consider an ideal body weight is regulated by cultural as well as biological and behavioral factors (Brownell & Wadden, 1991). Today, cultures differ in what they view as ideal physiques. A study found that Singaporeans rated muscular physiques as more attractive than British participants did. All participants rated muscular physiques as more attractive in men than in women. There was no difference in ratings given by male and female raters (Furnham & Lim, 1997).

But current Western standards of beauty, and concern with the health-impairing effects of obesity, make weight loss a major North American preoccupation (Dorian & Garfinkel, 2002). Weight reduction seems deceptively easy: You simply make sure that you burn more calories than you ingest. Yet, as noted by obesity researcher Kelly Brownell (1982), fewer than 5 percent of obese people maintain their weight loss long enough to be considered "cured." Some obesity researchers argue that this pessimistic figure represents only people who have been in formal weight-loss programs. In contrast, most people who try to lose weight on their own succeed. Perhaps those who seek treatment for obesity are a select group of people who are the least likely to succeed (Schachter, 1982). In fact, negative results typically come from university-based treatment programs. A small percentage of participants in these programs lose weight—but they differ from the general population of obese people. They tend to be more overweight, more likely to engage in binge eating, and more prone to psychological disorders (Brownell, 1993).

Because of the great cultural variability in perceptions of ideal body types and the difficulty that obese people have in maintaining weight loss, some critics believe it might be better to help obese people learn to accept their body types. There are group counseling programs that try to accomplish this acceptance. Participants discuss ways of maintaining their self-respect and social relationships despite being fat in a culture that frowns on fat people (Tenzer, 1989). In keeping with this approach, some authorities believe it would be better to promote weight control as a way to improve health, rather than as a way to achieve a particular body weight (Foreyt & Goodrick, 1994).

Approaches to Weight Control

Though many people do, in fact, desire to lose weight for health reasons, others desire to do so for social or aesthetic reasons. But how can people control their weight? A common but ineffective approach is dieting. People who diet may drastically reduce their caloric intake for weeks or months. Unfortunately, as dieters lose weight, their basal metabolic rate slows (Foreyt, 1987), forcing them to diet indefinitely to maintain their lower level of weight—an impossible feat. Because dieting cannot last for a lifetime, dieters eventually return to the same eating habits that contributed to their obesity. Moreover, dieting is unhealthy; 25 percent of diet-induced weight loss consists of lean body tissue, including skeletal muscle (Brownell, 1982).

Formal psychological approaches to weight loss rely on cognitive-behavior therapy in conjunction with aerobic exercise. In cognitive-behavior therapy programs, participants monitor their eating behaviors, change maladaptive eating habits, and correct misconceptions about eating. Aerobic exercise promotes weight loss not only by burning calories during exercise but also by raising the metabolic rate for hours afterward. This increase

The Ideal Female Figure

In Western cultures the ideal female figure has changed over time. The ideal has at times been represented by the plump Rubenesque nude of the early 17th century, the voluptuous actress Marilyn Monroe of the 1950s, and the muscular athlete Venus Williams of the early 21st century.

Source: Ammentorp Photography/Shutterstock.com.

counters dieting-induced decreases in the basal metabolic rate. Weight loss through aerobic exercise also is healthier than weight loss through dieting alone because only 5 percent of weight loss will be lean tissue (Brownell, 1982). Despite the effectiveness of aerobic exercise in weight control, most people who are trying to lose weight fail to increase their physical activity or engage in regular exercise (Gordon, Heath, Holmes, & Christy, 2000). Moreover, it is difficult for many obese people to maintain the intensity of exercise necessary to produce significant weight loss (Blix & Blix, 1995).

People who wish to lose weight often are impatient. But rapid weight loss does not guarantee long-term weight loss. This was the finding of a study of 49 obese women randomly assigned to a 52-week behavior-modification program combined with either moderate or severe restrictions on their daily caloric intake. Participants in the moderate-diet condition were limited to 1,200 calories a day throughout the study. Those in the severe-diet condition were limited to a 420-calorie liquid diet for 16 weeks and a 1,200-calorie diet for the remaining 36 weeks.

During the first 26 weeks, those in the severe-diet condition lost almost twice as much weight as those in the moderate-diet condition. But by the end of a 26-week follow-up after the study, those who had been in the severe-diet condition had gained so much weight that their net weight loss was slightly less than those who had been in the moderate-diet condition (Wadden, Foster, & Letizia, 1994). And though the past few decades have demonstrated the short-term effectiveness of behavioral modification in helping mildly or moderately obese people lose weight, no program has been able to halt the inevitable return to obesity by the great majority of participants. The typical 15-week weight-loss program of dieting or dieting plus exercise, for example, produces a loss of about 22 pounds, with 60 to 80 percent of participants maintaining weight loss for one year. But few participants maintain their weight after 3 to 5 years (Miller, 1999). Longer treatment programs that emphasize the importance of physical activity are more successful in promoting long-term weight loss (Jeffery et al., 2000).

Avoiding Tobacco Products

During the 1996 presidential campaign, Senator Robert Dole provoked controversy when he declared that smoking was not addictive. Dole's proclamation went against an enormous amount of evidence that smoking tobacco is addictive and is perhaps the single worst health-impairing habit. Despite the harmful effects of smoking, governments permit it—and even profit from it. In 1565, King James I of England, though viewing smoking as a despicable habit, chose to tax cigarettes rather than ban them, a practice governments still follow today.

The Effects of Smoking

Contrary to Dole's claim, smokers can become addicted to the nicotine in tobacco—though a small minority of smokers remain "chippers" who are able to smoke intermittently without becoming addicted (Davies, Willner, & Morgan, 2000). Though many addicted smokers insist that they smoke to relieve anxiety or to increase alertness, they actually smoke to avoid the unpleasant symptoms of nicotine withdrawal, which include irritability, hand tremors, heart palpitations, and difficulty concentrating. Thus, addicted smokers smoke to regulate the level of nicotine in their bodies (Parrott, 1995) and reduce craving (Gilbert & Warburton, 2000). Smoking is especially difficult to stop because it can become a conditioned response to many everyday situations, as in the case of smokers who light a cigarette when answering the telephone, after eating a meal, or on leaving a class.

Smoking produces harmful side effects through the actions of tars and other substances in cigarette smoke. Smoking causes fatigue by reducing the blood's ability to carry oxygen, making smoking an especially bad habit for athletes. But more important, smoking contributes to the deaths of more than 300,000 Americans each year from stroke, cancer, emphysema, and heart disease. Thus, its prevention is paramount.

The Prevention of Smoking

The ill effects of smoking make it imperative to devise programs to prevent the onset of smoking. Children are more likely to start smoking if their parents and peers smoke (Simons-Morton, 2002), especially boys (Nuño, Zhang, Harris, Wilkinson-Lee, & Wilhelm, 2011). Many smoking-prevention programs are based in schools and provide information about the immediate and long-term social and physical consequences of smoking (Ahmed, Ahmed, Bennett, & Hinds, 2002). But simply providing children with information about the ill effects of smoking is not enough to prevent them from starting. Smoking-prevention programs must also teach children how to resist peer pressure and advertisements that encourage them to begin smoking. Moreover, smoking prevention programs must address sociocultural factors that influence smoking in different ethnic groups. For example, culturally sensitive programs have been developed for Latinos (Gonzalez-Blanks, Lopez, & Garza, 2012), Native Americans (McKennitt & Currie, 2012), and Israeli Orthodox Jews (Knishkowi, Verbov, Amitai, Stein-Zamir, & Rosen, 2012). Overall, smoking-prevention programs have been effective, reducing the number of new smokers among participants by 50 percent (Flay, 1985).

The Treatment of Smoking

Though programs to prevent the onset of smoking are important, techniques to help people stop smoking are also essential. But quitting is difficult. A major University of Minnesota study followed 802 smokers for 2 years. Of those, 62 percent tried to quit, but only 16 percent succeeded, and 9 percent became chippers (Hennrikus, Jeffery, & Lando, 1995). People who do quit find it difficult to resist relapsing. The problem of relapse is such that the U.S. Public Health Service considers dependence on tobacco to be a chronic condition (Fiore, 2000). Moreover, relapse rates are higher among women. As yet, researchers are unable to account for this gender difference because women's relapse rates are not influenced by gender-related factors such as weight gain or weight concerns (Wetter et al., 1999).

Health psychologists use a variety of techniques to help people who cannot quit on their own. Participants are taught to expect the symptoms of nicotine withdrawal, which begin 6 to 12 hours after smoking cessation, peak in 1 to 3 days, and last 3 to 4 weeks (Hughes, Higgins, & Bickel, 1994). Even smoking non-nicotine (placebo) cigarettes reduces withdrawal symptoms (possibly because of classical conditioning) and might be useful in the transition period to total abstinence (Butschky, Bailey, Henningfield, & Pickworth, 1995). But certain consequences of quitting, including hunger, weight gain, and nicotine craving, may persist for 6 months or more (Hughes, Gust, Skoog, & Keenan, 1991). Nicotine prevents weight gain by reducing hunger and increasing metabolism (Winders & Grunberg, 1989). Thus, many smokers rightly fear that quitting will lead to weight gain.

Because tars and other chemicals in tobacco cause the harmful effects of smoking, some treatments aim at preventing smoking by providing participants with safer ways of obtaining nicotine. These nicotine-replacement techniques prevent some of the relapse caused by the desire to avoid weight gain (Nides, Rand, Dolce, & Murray, 1994) or withdrawal symptoms (Levin, Westman, Stein, & Carnahan, 1994).

Nicotine replacement therapy has proved successful. Though some smokers use nicotine nasal spray (Schneider et al., 2003), the two most common nicotine replacement techniques use *nicotine chewing gum* or a *nicotine patch,* which provides nicotine through the skin. A meta-analysis of well-controlled experiments found that, of participants who used a nicotine patch, 22 percent abstained from smoking after 6 months. Moreover, those who used a nicotine patch smoked less than those who used a placebo patch—that is, a patch without nicotine (Fiore, Smith, Jorenby, & Baker 1994). Higher-dose nicotine patches produce greater long-term abstinence than do lower-dose nicotine patches (Daughton et al., 1999). However, men appear to benefit from the nicotine patch more than women do. In a double-blind study using the nicotine patch and a placebo patch, the rate of sleep disturbances—which are related to withdrawal symptoms—was higher among women than men (Wetter et al., 1999). Smokers who

A Safe Cigarette?

A traditional cigarette is on the left, and an electronic cigarette is on the right. Electronic cigarettes vaporize nicotine. The safety of electronic cigarettes is currently under study, and their regulation is the subject of an ongoing debate.
Source: Gianluca Rasile/Shutterstock.com.

use the nicotine patch and chew nicotine gum are more successful in quitting than are those who use either technique alone (Fagerstrom, Schneider, & Lunell, 1993). A more recent trend in smoking cessation has been the use of electronic cigarettes as a form of nicotine replacement. However, the Food and Drug Administration has documented short- and long-term adverse health effects of electronic cigarettes (Chen, 2013), and studies of their use in formal smoking cessation programs need to be conducted to assess their efficacy (Odum, O'Dell, & Schepers, 2012).

Of course, though *replacement* therapy reduces the health risks of smoking, it does not help smokers overcome their *addiction* to nicotine. Those who wish to overcome their addiction do better if they are high in two of the factors that appear repeatedly as health promoters: a feeling of self-efficacy (Ockene et al., 2000) and the presence of social support (Nides, Rakos, Gonzales, & Murray, 1995). But a study of 210 smokers found that social support was more important in quitting for men than for women (Westmaas, Wild, & Ferrence, 2002).

For those who are motivated to overcome their addiction, *nicotine fading* is useful. This technique gradually weans smokers off nicotine by having them use cigarettes with lower and lower nicotine content until it has been reduced to virtually zero (Becona & Garcia, 1993). A more extreme technique is *rapid smoking,* a form of aversion therapy in which the smoker is forced to take a puff every 6 to 8 seconds for several minutes. This action induces feelings of nausea and dizziness, and after several sessions, the person may develop an aversion to smoking. Like nicotine fading, rapid smoking has proved effective (Tiffany, Martin, & Baker, 1986). Prescription medications also are effective for helping smokers quit. Varenicline (Chantix) is a drug that weakly stimulates nicotine receptors, and bupropion is an antidepressant. Both medications have been shown to be effective in clinical trials of smoking cessation programs. One recent meta-analysis examining 146 randomized controlled studies revealed that replacement therapy in any combination or alone (nicotine patch, varenicline, bupropion) was more effective than a placebo. Further, varenicline offered the best long-term treatment outcome (Mills et al., 2012).

Another approach to smoking cessation involves *self-management programs,* which employ behavior modification. The programs encourage smokers to avoid stimuli that act as cues for smoking, such as coffee breaks, alcoholic beverages, and other smokers. A potentially powerful way of teaching smokers self-management skills is to have their physicians educate them about how to quit. An ambitious study in England involved 1,200 heavy smokers and their primary-care physicians. The smokers received brief advice from their physician, a booklet on how to quit smoking, and nicotine patches or placebo patches that they wore for 16 hours a day for 18 weeks. A 1-year follow-up found that the nicotine patch was twice as effective as a placebo patch in promoting abstinence: 9.6 percent versus 4.8 percent, respectively (Stapleton, Russell, Feyerabend, & Wiseman, 1995). Effective smoking cessation involves behavioral change.

Section Review: Health-Promoting Habits

1. What behaviors can transmit HIV from one person to another?
2. What are the beneficial effects of regular aerobic exercise?
3. Why is it unwise to try to lose weight solely by dieting?

Reactions to Illness

Despite your best efforts to adapt to stress and to live a healthy lifestyle, you will periodically suffer from illness. Health psychologists study ways to encourage people to seek treatment for symptoms of illness, to reduce patient distress, and to increase patient adherence to medical regimens.

Seeking Treatment for Health Problems

What do you do when you experience a headache, nausea, diarrhea, dizziness, constipation, or nasal congestion? Your reaction would depend on your interpretation of the symptoms. This interpretation would depend, in turn, on your past experience with these symptoms, information you have received about them, their intensity, and their duration. Some people inappropriately seek medical attention for the most minor symptoms. However, many others deny, ignore, or misinterpret their symptoms, which might make them fail to seek help; as a consequence, many people let minor ailments become serious or delay treatment of serious ailments that might be cured by early treatment. Victims of heart attacks have a much better prognosis for recovery if they seek help within an hour of experiencing symptoms. But victims typically wait several hours from the time they first notice symptoms until they seek help (Walsh, Lynch, Murphy, & Daly, 2004).

Sociocultural factors influence the rates at which people make use of health-care services. A national survey of health attitudes and behaviors found that 33 percent of American men have no regular doctor, compared to 19 percent of American women. Moreover, women's greater tendency to seek regular medical care cannot be explained by medical visits due to pregnancy, reproductive health, and childbearing. Uninsured, younger, and less-educated men were especially likely to delay seeking treatment for a medical condition (Sandman, Simantov, & An, 2000). Many health psychologists believe that this gender difference in access to and use of medical care contributes to men's higher death rates and reduced longevity relative to women (Courtenay, 2000). Many ethnic groups, too, make use of home remedies, rituals, or folk practitioners, either alone or in conjunction with traditional medical treatment (Landrine & Klonoff, 1994).

The importance of seeking appropriate medical care has inspired health psychologists to study factors that motivate people to seek treatment. An important factor is social support. People with social support may be encouraged to seek treatment, may be referred to appropriate medical personnel, and may feel less anxious about seeking treatment (Roberts, 1988). Even one's explanatory style can affect the decision to seek medical treatment. A study of undergraduates found that those with a pessimistic explanatory style were less likely than optimistic students to seek medical treatment. Thus, the finding that pessimistic people are usually less healthy than optimistic ones might be caused by their greater passivity in the face of illness (Lin & Peterson, 1990).

One of the main factors in seeking treatment for symptoms is how one interprets them. A study of 366 older adults (average age 62 years) found that when they had ambiguous symptoms of illness, those who had experienced a stressful life event in the preceding 3 weeks were less likely to seek treatment than were those who had not experienced one. Evidently, those who did not seek treatment attributed their symptoms to the stress instead of an illness. When the symptoms were not ambiguous, there was no difference in the likelihood of seeking treatment (Cameron, Leventhal, & Leventhal, 1995).

Relieving Patient Distress

Illness, especially chronic illness or illness that requires surgery or painful procedures, is distressing. Patients differ in their ability to cope with illness or stressful medical procedures. One important factor is self-efficacy. For example, patients high in self-efficacy cope better with painful dental procedures (Litt, Nye, & Shafer, 1995).

Some patients also can benefit from psychological techniques that encourage effective coping with pain or stressful procedures. These patients include cancer patients (Cohen, 2002), children who undergo prolonged hospitalizations (Yap, 1988), and burn victims who must undergo excruciatingly painful skin debridement (Fauerbach, Lawrence, Haythornthwaite, & Richter, 2002). A meta-analysis found that psychological preparation for surgery is effective in reducing pain, distress, and length of stay. Informing surgery patients about the procedures they will undergo is especially effective (Johnston & Vogele, 1993).

A sensitive, comprehensive orientation program is especially important for patients about to undergo cancer treatment. In one study, a group of 150 breast cancer patients seen at an outpatient oncology clinic were assigned to an orientation program or a usual-care control condition. Those in the orientation program were given a guided tour, information about clinic operations, and a question-and-answer session with an oncology counselor. The results showed that the orientation group had less distress, anxiety, and depression (McQuellon et al., 1998).

Modeling has been a useful technique for reducing patient distress during unpleasant medical procedures (O'Halloran & Altmaier, 1995). In keeping with this technique, observing a patient who has undergone successful surgery can be beneficial to a patient about to undergo surgery. Patients waiting to undergo coronary bypass surgery who have a hospital roommate who has just undergone successful surgery of any kind are less anxious before surgery, walk more after surgery, and go home sooner than are similar patients who have a roommate who is about to undergo surgery. Apparently, simply observing a person who has survived surgery has a calming effect on patients anticipating surgery. Moreover, people who have undergone surgery can reduce the distress of patients about to undergo surgery by letting them know what to expect and suggesting ways to cope with the situation (Kulik & Mahler, 1987).

In some cases, relatively simple procedures can reduce illness-related distress. In a study of children undergoing chemotherapy for cancer, the experimental group played video games during their chemotherapy, and a control group did not. As shown in Figure 16-7, children in the experimental group reported less nausea. The children who played video games were apparently distracted from the unpleasant sensations caused by the chemotherapy (Redd et al., 1987).

There has been increasing interest in another factor related to patient distress: the quality of the relationship between patients and medical practitioners. A study found a negative correlation between the perceived empathy of nurses and patient anger, anxiety, and depression (Olson, 1995). Patients who perceive a lack of empathy in their physicians are more likely to sue them for malpractice (Frankel, 1995). There is a strong, positive correlation between the use of humor—both by physicians and their patients—and patient satisfaction (Sala, Krupat, & Roter, 2002). Research indicates that there are gender differences in the ways that physicians treat their patients. Female physicians tend to be more collaborative, rather than authoritarian, in relating to their patients. They are more likely to deal with feelings and emotions and to consider the patient's social and psychological context (Roter & Hall, 1998). Findings like these have prompted some health psychologists to suggest that health-care professionals receive education on improving patient interaction, including learning how to prepare patients for stressful medical and surgical procedures, as well as how to communicate with worried family members (Wilson-Barnett, 1994).

FIGURE 16-7
Controlling Patient Distress with Video Games

Children who played video games while undergoing cancer chemotherapy (the experimental group) showed a marked reduction in nausea. In contrast, children who did not play video games while undergoing cancer chemotherapy (the control group) showed little change in nausea.

Source: Data from W. H. Redd et al., "Cognitive/attentional distraction in the control of conditioned nausea in pediatric cancer patients receiving chemotherapy," in *Journal of Consulting and Clinical Psychology, 55,* 391–395.

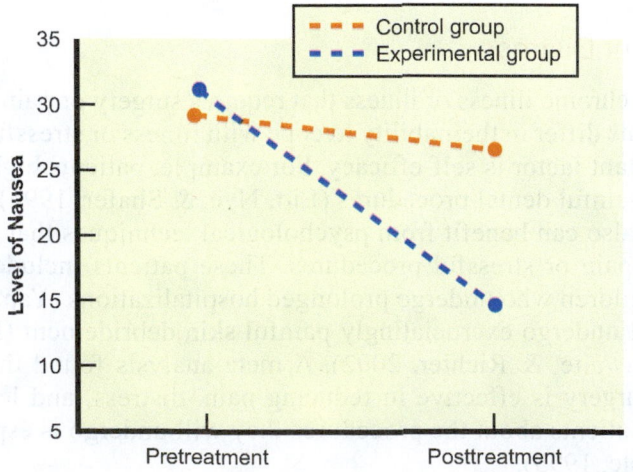

Encouraging Adherence to Medical Regimens

Recovery from illness often depends on following a medical regimen recommended by a physician. This regimen might include a prescription drug, a restricted diet, or an exercise program. Adherence is important in medical regimens aimed at controlling diabetes (DiMatteo, Sherbourne, Hays, & Ordway, 1993), treating obesity (Brownell & Cohen, 1995), controlling arthritis pain (Taal, Rasker, Seydel, & Wiegman, 1993), and lowering high blood pressure (Ibrahim, 2003). One of the main reasons that patients fail to follow treatment regimens is that they do not understand the physician's instructions (Glen & Anderson, 1989). The patient's personality also is a factor. A study based on the five-factor theory of personality (see Chapter 13) found that patients who scored high on the factor of conscientiousness were more likely to adhere to medication regimens (Christensen & Smith, 1995). A meta-analysis found that social support is an important factor in encouraging adherence to medical regimens (DiMatteo, 2004).

As is the case in the relief of patient distress, the relationship between the patient and the physician plays a key role in adherence to medical regimens. Patients are more likely to adhere to regimens prescribed by physicians they like. One of the most important factors determining whether a patient will be satisfied with a physician is the physician's emotional warmth during consultations. A physician who acts more like an automobile mechanic fixing a car than a health-care provider helping a suffering person will evoke negative reactions from patients. A longitudinal study of HIV-positive gay and bisexual men found that strong positive beliefs about their doctors and other health-care providers predicted adherence to protease inhibitor treatment regimens (Evans, Ferrando, Rabkin, & Fishman, 2000).

Sometimes, patients abandon their medical regimens prematurely because they no longer notice any symptoms. Consider a patient with essential hypertension (marked by chronic high blood pressure) who must take medication, watch her diet, and follow an exercise program. Because we have, at best, a slight ability to sense the level of our blood pressure (Pennebaker & Watson, 1988), the patient might assume, incorrectly, that because she does not feel like she has high blood pressure, she actually does not have high blood pressure—and abandon her prescribed medical regimen. This problem again points to the importance of adequate communication between the physician and the patient. Physicians need to communicate the risks and benefits of treatment and the specific details of the medical regimen (DiMatteo, Reiter, & Gambone, 1994). Even the simple act of asking patients to adhere to medical regimens can be effective. In one study, patients were put on 10-day antibiotic regimens to treat bacterial infections. The patients were divided into an experimental group and a control group. Those in the experimental group made oral and written commitments to adhere to the regimen. Those in the control group did not. The results showed that those in the experimental group were more likely than those in the control group to adhere to the regimen (Putnam, Finney, Barkley, & Bonner, 1994).

Health psychologists have demonstrated that we play an active role in maintaining our health, succumbing to disease, and recovering from illness. Though some diseases and injuries are unavoidable, we can no longer view ourselves as simply the passive victims of viruses, bacteria, or carcinogens. By learning to adapt effectively to stressors, to eliminate risky behaviors, to adopt health-promoting behaviors, and to respond appropriately to symptoms of disease, we can greatly reduce our chances of illness, injury, and death.

Section Review: Reactions to Illness

1. What are some factors that affect seeking treatment for symptoms of illness?

2. What role does the relationship between patient and health practitioner play in medical treatment?

Increasing Exercise Adherence

Rationale

Regular exercise is essential to physical health and stress management. But, as discussed in the section "Keeping Physically Fit," many people find it difficult to incorporate physical activity into their daily schedules. This activity asks you to keep a record of your physical activity and modify one variable that may be affecting your physical activity level.

Procedure

Keep a 1-week diary of your exercise habits. Note the date, time, and type of physical activity—for example, participation in an aerobics class, a brisk 20-minute walk, or a short spin on a bicycle, skateboard, or scooter. Note how long you exercised, whether you exercised alone or with others, and how you felt before, during, and after your exercise session. After 1 week, review the chapter section on exercise adherence and choose *one* variable that you feel might have influenced your physical activity during the preceding week. Identify the variable in your diary, and indicate how you will modify this variable. For example, if you feel that taking a walk by yourself is boring, indicate that you will recruit a friend to exercise with you. Then, continue to use your diary to monitor your physical activity for another week.

Results and Discussion

Compare your physical activity during the 2-week period recorded in your diary. Did manipulating the variable you identified increase the frequency and/or duration of your physical activity? What else could you do to increase your exercise adherence? If you are ambitious, review Chapters 7 and 15, and consider how you might employ cognitive-behavioral techniques to increase your physical activity.

Chapter Summary

Psychological Stress and Stressors

- Health psychology is the field that studies the role of psychological factors in the promotion of health and the prevention of illness and injury.
- One of the main topics of interest to health psychologists is stress, the physiological response of the body to physical and psychological demands.
- The chief psychological stressors are often categorized as either life changes or daily hassles.

The Biopsychology of Stress and Illness

- Hans Selye identified a pattern of physiological response to stress that he called the general adaptation syndrome, which includes the alarm reaction, the stage of resistance, and the stage of exhaustion.
- Stress has been linked to infectious and noninfectious diseases.
- The field that studies the relationship between psychological factors and illness is called psychoneuroimmunology.
- There is evidence that the immune response can be altered by classical conditioning.
- The main noninfectious diseases linked to stress are cardiovascular disease and cancer.

Factors That Moderate the Stress Response

- The relationship between stress and illness is mediated by the interaction of a variety of factors.

- The major factors include physiological reactivity, cognitive appraisal, explanatory style, perceived control, psychological hardiness, and social support.

Coping with Stress

- Health psychologists use stress-management programs to help people learn to cope with stress.
- Some of the main methods of reducing stress use stress-inoculation training, humor, formal exercise, and relaxation techniques.

Health-Promoting Habits

- Most deaths in the United States are associated with unhealthy habits, including unsafe sexual practices, lack of exercise, poor nutrition, and smoking.
- Programs aimed at changing these habits hold promise for reducing the incidence of illness and death.

Reactions to Illness

- Health psychologists study aspects of how people cope with illness, including the seeking of treatment, patient distress, and adherence to medical regimens.
- The patient-practitioner relationship is an important factor in adherence.

Key Terms

health psychology (p. 562)

Psychological Stress and Stressors

posttraumatic stress disorder (PTSD) (p. 563)
stress (p. 562)
stressor (p. 562)

The Biopsychology of Stress and Illness

general adaptation syndrome (p. 567)

psychoneuroimmunology (p. 571)
Type A behavior (p. 568)

Factors That Moderate the Stress Response

burnout (p. 576)
cognitive appraisal (p. 574)
explanatory style (p. 575)
learned helplessness (p.575)

perceived control (p. 575)
physiological reactivity (p. 574)
psychological hardiness (p. 576)
social support (p. 577)

Coping with Stress

progressive relaxation (p. 581)
stress-inoculation training (p. 580)

Chapter Quiz

Note: Answers for the Chapter Quiz questions are provided at the end of the book.

1. A century ago, North Americans were most likely to die from
   a. influenza.
   b. lung cancer.
   c. heart attacks.
   d. cerebral vascular accidents.

2. Hans Selye called pleasant stress
   a. eustress.
   b. pressure.
   c. endorphogenic stress.
   d. psychological hardiness.

3. Hormones that are most likely to impair the immune system are secreted by the
   a. pancreas.
   b. pineal gland.
   c. adrenal gland.
   d. thyroid gland.

4. Research on stress and cancer (Glaser, Rice, Speicher, Stout, & Kiecolt-Glaser, 1986) indicates that stress may promote cancer by reducing the activity of
   a. epinephrine.
   b. B-lymphocytes.
   c. corticosteroids.
   d. natural killer cells.

5. Research on the reasons for smoking indicates that habitual smokers smoke mainly to
   a. enhance self-esteem.
   b. make them more alert.
   c. conform to the behavior of their peers.
   d. regulate the level of nicotine in their bodies.

6. Research findings indicate that the component of Type A behavior that is most highly correlated with coronary heart disease is
   a. hostility.
   b. time pressure.
   c. chronic activation.
   d. multiphasic activity.

7. The Canadian scientist who founded modern stress research was
   a. Hans Selye.
   b. Meyer Friedman.

   c. Karen Matthews.
   d. Suzanne Kobasa.

8. One of the main weaknesses of the Social Readjustment Rating Scale is that it
   a. includes only negative life changes.
   b. ignores family-related life changes.
   c. includes life changes that can be either causes or effects of illness.
   d. has stimulated no research on its relationship to actual health status.

9. A student majoring in psychology registers for a course in behavioral statistics, a course that he anticipates will be stressful. The student's level of stress is reduced when he realizes that he has good logical and mathematical abilities. This realization is an example of what Richard Lazarus called
   a. primary appraisal.
   b. tertiary appraisal.
   c. secondary appraisal.
   d. preconscious appraisal.

10. Stress prompts the hypothalamus to secrete a hormone that stimulates the pituitary gland to secrete
    a. ACTH.
    b. adrenaline.
    c. lymphocytes.
    d. corticosteroids.

11. A professor feels in complete control of her courses, challenged by the need to prepare lively lectures, and committed to the teaching profession. She would most likely be high in
    a. burnout.
    b. Type A behavior.
    c. psychological hardiness.
    d. physiological reactivity.

12. A man tests HIV-positive. He most likely
    a. kissed someone who is HIV-positive.
    b. ate food prepared by a cook who is HIV-positive.
    c. used a toilet after a person who is HIV-positive.
    d. used a hypodermic needle used previously by a person who is HIV-positive.

13. Posttraumatic stress disorder became widely publicized as a result of interest in
    a. rape survivors.
    b. Vietnam War veterans.
    c. survivors of child abuse.
    d. survivors of the Mount Saint Helens volcano eruption.

14. Walter Cannon called the body's stress response the
    a. fight-or-flight syndrome.
    b. general adaptation syndrome.
    c. posttraumatic stress disorder.
    d. tend-or-befriend syndrome.

15. In Ader and Cohen's (1982) study of the classical conditioning of the immune response, in which sweetened water was paired with the immunosuppressive drug cyclophosphamide, the conditioned stimulus was
    a. nausea.
    b. sweetened water.
    c. cyclophosphamide.
    d. immunosuppression.

16. Edmund Jacobson was an early contributor to stress management through his research on
    a. burnout.
    b. Type A behavior.
    c. progressive relaxation.
    d. transcendental meditation.

17. Research indicates that of those people who begin formal exercise programs, the proportion who will drop out within 6 months is about
    a. 25 percent.
    b. 50 percent.
    c. 65 percent.
    d. 90 percent.

18. A major weakness in assessing the effect of daily hassles on health is that there has been little research using
    a. case studies.
    b. prospective studies.
    c. retrospective studies.
    d. naturalistic observation.

19. The field that studies the relationship between psychological factors and physical illness is called
    a. biofeedback.
    b. biopsychology.
    c. psychophysiology.
    d. psychoneuroimmunology.

20. B-lymphocytes are the body's main defense against
    a. viruses.
    b. bacteria.
    c. cancer cells.
    d. foreign tissues.

21. Worldwide, most victims of AIDS are
    a. gay men.
    b. hemophiliacs.
    c. heterosexuals.
    d. heroin addicts.

22. Smoking contributes to a yearly death rate of more than
    a. 50,000 Americans.
    b. 100,000 Americans.
    c. 300,000 Americans.
    d. 900,000 Americans.

23. Karen Matthews has found that children who engage in Type A behavior tend to have parents who
    a. pass on "Type A genes" to them.
    b. frown on the expression of anger.
    c. urge them to do better and better.
    d. stress the importance of punctuality.

24. For most of the past 1,000 years in Western cultures, the standard for the most attractive female physique has been
    a. thin.
    b. rounded.
    c. muscular.
    d. grossly obese.

25. Nicotine chewing gum
    a. leads to cigarette smoking.
    b. has no more than a placebo effect.
    c. eliminates the addiction to nicotine.
    d. may motivate weight-conscious smokers to stop smoking.

Thought Questions

1. Students commonly experience intense stress during the final weeks of the academic semester due to such factors as research papers, final exams, and lack of money. What physiological pathway might explain how these stressors could impair your immune system and make you more susceptible to illness immediately after the end of the semester?

2. Some researchers believe that major life events exert their harmful health effects through the daily hassles and related problems they create. How might getting divorced induce stress by this route?

3. Imagine that a friend of yours exhibits a pattern of Type A behavior. Which aspects of this pattern might it be best for her to alter?

4. What five risky or unhealthy behaviors would you be wisest to avoid?

Social Psychology

On March 26, 1997, millions around the world were shocked to learn of the mass suicide of 39 members of a cult known as Heaven's Gate in the wealthy California suburb of Rancho Santa Fe. In prearranged shifts over several days, cult members ingested lethal doses of phenobarbital, put plastic bags over their heads, and suffocated themselves. Their bodies were covered with identical purple shrouds. The chilling scene was made more so by its being meticulously neat and tidy, with identically clad people (down to their black Nike athletic shoes) lying peacefully on their backs, with their belongings (including lip balm and spiral notebooks) packed neatly in overnight bags stowed under their beds.

Cult members even left videotaped messages explaining why they took their lives. They committed suicide because their leader, Marshall Applewhite, had promised that they would be resurrected into a better life aboard a spaceship allegedly hidden behind the comet Hale-Bopp, which had appeared in the night sky. Applewhite, seeking more members to accompany the cult on its journey to Hale-Bopp, had taken out an advertisement in *USA Today* reading, "UFO Cult Resurfaces with Final Offer." The advertisement warned that it would be "the last chance to advance beyond human." Applewhite, an early advocate of the Internet as an advertising tool, also had created an elaborate Web page to entice others to join Heaven's Gate.

How could Applewhite, an outgoing former music teacher at the University of Alabama, transform himself into a charismatic cult leader? How could normal, intelligent adults be persuaded to forsake their families, abandon successful careers, and flee their "bodily containers" with a mere promise of a better life at the "Next Level"? The answers to these questions are sought by social psychologists, who study factors involved in human social interactions.

The scientific study of social psychology began more than a century ago. In the 1890s, bicycle racing was a major spectator sport in North America. As noted in Chapter 11, Norman Triplett (1898) observed that cyclists who raced against other riders rode faster than those who raced against the clock. He decided to study this phenomenon experimentally by having boys spin fishing reels as fast as they could while competing either against time or against another boy. He found that participants who competed against another boy performed faster. This study, the first experimental study of the relationship between psychological factors and sport performance, was possibly the first experiment in social psychology.

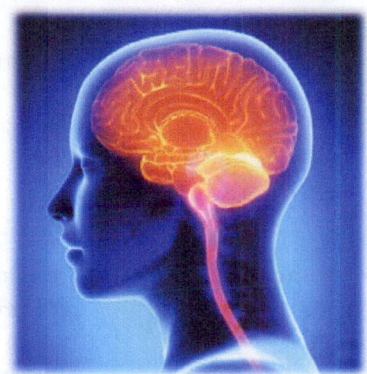

Source: CLIPAREA/Custom media/ Shutterstock.com.

Chapter Outline

Social Cognition

Interpersonal Attraction

Attitudes

Group Dynamics

Aggression

Prosocial Behavior

social psychology The field that studies how the actual, imagined, or implied presence of other people affects one's thoughts, feelings, and behaviors.

Social psychology is the field that studies behavior in its interpersonal context—that is, how the actual, imagined, or implied presence of other people affects one's thoughts, feelings, and behaviors. Though social-psychological research was conducted before the turn of the 20th century and the first social psychology textbooks were published in 1908 (Pepitone, 1981), social psychology did not become an important field of study until after World War II, when many psychologists became interested in the formal study of social behavior. This interest occurred largely through the earlier efforts of Floyd Allport, perhaps the leading pioneer in the development of social psychology (Parkovnick, 2000). The major topics of interest to social psychologists include social cognition, interpersonal attraction, attitudes, group dynamics, aggression, and prosocial behavior.

Social Cognition

social cognition The process of perceiving, interpreting, and predicting social behavior.

Psychologists who study **social cognition** are concerned with how we perceive, interpret, and predict social behavior. Though social cognition is usually accurate (Jussim, 1991), biases and subjectivity can distort it. Two of the main topics in social cognition are causal attribution and person perception.

Causal Attribution

causal attribution
The cognitive process by which we infer the causes of both our own and other people's social behavior.

As first noted in the 1940s by social psychologist Fritz Heider (1944), when we engage in **causal attribution,** we determine the extent to which a person's behavior is caused by the person or by the person's circumstances. There was so much research on causal attribution in the 1970s that the decade became known as "the decade of attribution theory in social psychology" (Weiner, 1985b, p. 74). The most influential attribution theorist of that decade was Harold Kelley (1921–2003); he identified factors that determine how we explain people's behavior.

When you decide that someone is primarily responsible for his or her behavior, you are making a dispositional attribution. That is, you would be attributing the behavior to personal qualities such as emotions, abilities, or personality traits. When you decide that circumstances are primarily responsible for a person's behavior, you are making a situational attribution. Consider explanations given for poverty. Two research studies, one using university students and one using nonstudents, found that political liberals and political conservatives tended to make different attributions (Zucker & Weiner, 1993). Whereas liberals tended to make situational attributions for poverty (blaming it on factors such as discrimination and lack of opportunities), conservatives tended to make dispositional attributions (blaming it on factors such as a lack of effort or ability). Moreover, there is increasing evidence that there are cultural differences in people's tendencies to make dispositional or situational attribution. One study compared Korean and American undergraduates' explanations for criminal behavior. Korean undergraduates held more lenient attitudes toward criminals and made more situational attributions for crime than did American undergraduates (Na & Loftus, 1998). Whereas people in Asian cultures favor situational factors when making attributions, people in Western cultures favor dispositional factors when making attributions (Kitayama, Duffy, Kawamura, & Larsen, 2003; Norenzayan, Choi, & Nisbett, 2002).

Dimensions of Causal Attribution

Kelley's theory of attribution was soon joined by one devised by Bernard Weiner (1985a). Whereas Kelley's theory has been used primarily to explain the behavior of others, Weiner's has been used primarily to explain how we make causal attributions for our own behavior (Martinko & Thomson, 1998). Weiner and his colleagues found that estimating the relative impact of dispositional and situational factors is important but cannot by itself account for the nature of causal attribution. Weiner identified three dimensions that govern the attribution process. The internal-external dimension is akin to Kelley's distinction between dispositional and situational attribution. The stable-unstable dimension refers to the degree to which we attribute a behavior to a factor that is stable or unstable. And the controllable-uncontrollable dimension indicates the extent to which we attribute a behavior to a factor that is controllable or uncontrollable. Weiner has found that people in a variety of cultures around the world use these dimensions in making attributions for their successes and failures (Schuster, Forsterling, & Weiner, 1989). Figure 17-1 illustrates the interaction of two of Weiner's attributional dimensions.

Weiner's three attributional dimensions are commonly used by students in explaining their academic performance (Anazonwu, 1995). In fact, students may use the dimensions in making excuses that both maintain their self-esteem and prevent professors from becoming angry at them (Weiner, Figueroa-Munoz, & Kakihara, 1991). Suppose you wanted to make an excuse for submitting a term paper late. Your excuse would be more effective if you attributed your behavior to external, unstable, and uncontrollable factors, such as a family emergency, than if you attributed it to internal, stable, and controllable factors, such as a difficulty in budgeting your time.

Attributions and Excuses

An effective strategy for making an excuse, such as being late, would include external, unstable, and uncontrollable factors, such as a family emergency.
Source: Dreaming Poet/Shutterstock.com.

Biases in Causal Attribution

If human beings were as rational and objective as Mr. Spock in *Star Trek,* the causal attribution process would be straightforward. But being somewhat irrational and subjective, we exhibit biases in the causal attributions we make. These biases include the fundamental attribution error and the self-serving bias.

The Fundamental Attribution Error One bias is the tendency to attribute other people's behavior to dispositional factors. This bias is known as the **fundamental attribution error** (Nisbett & Ross, 1980). In one study, college undergraduates read descriptions of an expectant mother or father who was anticipating staying at home with the baby or being employed after its birth. Participants rated the parents who expected to remain at home to care for their child as being more nurturing and family oriented and less independent and competitive than parents who expected to return to work. Moreover, these ratings were unaffected by information about whether parents' employment was a matter of choice or necessity (Riggs, 1998). Thus, in explaining why parents work outside the home, we might commit the fundamental attribution error by overemphasizing the role of personality (dispositional attributions) rather than situational factors.

Cross-cultural research finds that the fundamental attribution error, like other cognitive biases reported in this chapter, is more common in Western cultures. Cross-cultural studies indicate that Asian participants are *less* likely to attribute people's behavior to dispositional factors. A study relevant to this distinction compared how American and Japanese newspapers treated "rogue trader" financial scandals. Whereas American newspapers tended to focus on the individual traders as being responsible, Japanese newspapers tended to focus on the traders' organizations as being responsible (Menon, Morris, Chiu, & Hong, 1999). These cultural differences are attributable to East Asians' tendency to see people—and their behavior—as being constrained by social situations or circumstances (Nisbett, Peng, Choi, & Norenzayan., 2001).

The Self-Serving Bias We also are subject to a **self-serving bias,** which is the tendency to make dispositional attributions for our own successes and situational attributions for our own failures, especially when our self-esteem is threatened (Campbell & Sedikides, 1999). For example, a study of college students found that those who received high grades (As or Bs) tended to make dispositional attributions for their own performance, attributing their success to their own efforts and abilities. In contrast, students who received lower grades (Cs, Ds, or Fs) tended to make situational attributions, attributing their lack of success to bad luck and difficult tests (Bernstein, Stephan, & Davis, 1979). People who tend to attribute negative events to dispositional qualities in themselves might even induce physiological stress responses that impair their immune response. A study of HIV-positive gay men found that those who attributed negative events in their lives to aspects of themselves showed a more rapid decline in their immune response during the next 18 months than those who did not (Segerstrom, Taylor, Kemeny, Reed, & Visscher, 1996). The self-serving bias

	Internal	External
Stable	Ability	Task difficulty
Unstable	Effort	Luck

FIGURE 17-1
Two Dimensions of Causal Attribution

According to Bernard Weiner, we may explain our successes and failures by attributing them to internal or external causes that are either stable or unstable.

fundamental attribution error
The bias to attribute other people's behavior to dispositional factors.

self-serving bias
The tendency to make dispositional attributions for one's successes and situational attributions for one's failures.

Impression Management

Job applicants use impression management during job interviews.
Source: Africa Studio/ Shutterstock.com.

person perception The process of making judgments about the personal characteristics of others.

impression management The deliberate attempt to control the impression that others form of us.

is in keeping with evidence (see Chapter 13) that psychological well-being is associated with the maintenance of an unrealistically positive view of oneself (Taylor & Brown, 1988).

But is psychological well-being achieved only by focusing on oneself? People also may derive a sense of well-being from their group identity or collective achievements. There is evidence that in collectivist cultures attributions may follow a self-effacing rather than self-enhancing pattern. In one study, Japanese participants were more likely to make dispositional attributions following failure and less likely to make dispositional attributions following success on some achievement tasks (Kashima & Triandis, 1986). Moreover, Japanese students have been found to attribute the successes of others to dispositional factors and the failures of others to situational factors (Yamaguchi, 1988). This cross-cultural difference is even stronger for successes that are meaningful in individualist versus collectivist cultures (Leung, Kim, Zhang, Tam, & Chiu, 2012). Markus and Kitayama (1991) have coined the term *modesty bias* for this apparent reversal of the self-serving bias, noting its prevalence in collectivist cultures.

Person Perception

In addition to making causal attributions about the causes of behavior, we spend a great deal of our time making judgments about the personal characteristics of people, or engaging in **person perception**. Researchers interested in person perception study topics such as impression management, stereotypes, first impressions, and self-fulfilling prophecy.

Impression Management

Do you know a student who is considered "phony" by other students? The students might be reacting to that student's obvious attempt to convey an impression that is at odds with his or her true self. The deliberate attempt to control the impressions that others form of us is called **impression management** (Leary & Kowalski, 1990). Impression management is a normal part of everyday social relations. Job applicants use impression management when they write their résumés (Knouse, 1994) and during job interviews (Ellis, West, Ryan, & DeShon, 2002). And British banking executives found themselves in a double-bind when engaged in impression management during the UK banking inquiry that followed the 2008 global economic crisis. In order to avoid being held accountable by the press, they were faced with appearing to be either unethical or having poor professional credibility (Stapleton & Hargie, 2011). People who are good at impression management even may adapt better than those who are not when they find themselves in other cultures (Montagliani & Giacalone, 1998).

A common technique that we use in impression management is self-handicapping (see Chapter 13). When we self-handicap, we let others know that we are performing under a handicap. If we then do well, we look good to others. If we do poorly, others will attribute our poor performance to our "handicap." Consider a student who announces that he was too anxious to study for an exam. Success on the exam would reflect well on his ability; others would attribute failure on the exam to his anxiety rather than to lack of ability—thereby protecting his self-esteem. We would not be so lenient in judging his performance if he claimed he had not tried hard (Rhodewalt, Sanbonmatsu, Tschanz, & Feick, 1995).

Self-handicapping may protect self-esteem, but it also may have serious consequences for academic performance. One longitudinal study (see Chapter 4) found that undergraduates who scored high on a measure of self-handicapping had poorer academic records than low self-handicappers—in part due to poor study habits. Moreover, self-handicapping was correlated with poor adjustment and coping—which then led to even more self-handicapping (Zuckerman, Kiefer, & Knee, 1998). Thus, self-handicapping may lead to a vicious cycle of poor adjustment, ineffective coping, and increased self-handicapping. Moreover, self-handicapping may not always be an effective impression management strategy—especially in relationships with women. In one study male participants evaluated self-handicappers more positively and were more willing to accept excuses for their poor performance than were female participants. Female participants, however, were very critical of self-handicappers, viewing them with suspicion and believing that they were unmotivated. The researchers attributed these differences to women's tendency to value effort over ability when evaluating themselves and others (Hirt, McCrea, & Boris, 2003).

Stereotypes

College professor. Rock concert. Johnny Depp. Latina. Each of these concepts involves a **social schema,** which comprises the presumed characteristics of a role, event, person, or group. Social schemas bring order to what might otherwise be a chaotic social world by permitting us to interpret and predict the behavior of others. A **stereotype** is a social schema that includes characteristics that are ascribed to almost all members of a group. Note that stereotypes, though usually negative, can be positive. For example, American television commercials portray Asian Americans as a "model minority" consisting of people with a universally high work ethic. A study that analyzed more than 1,300 television commercials found that Asian Americans were overrepresented, appearing in 8.4 percent of the commercials though comprising only 3.6 percent of the population. But they were more likely than members of other minorities to appear in the background of commercials, with Asian American women rarely appearing in major roles. Moreover, the commercials support the stereotype of the hard-working Asian American by generally showing them in business situations and rarely at social functions or in family settings (Taylor & Stern, 1997).

Stereotypes are reinforced in part by our tendency to view members of our own group (our in-group) as more variable than members of another group (an out-group). For example, a study of college sororities found that they judged their own members as more variable than those of another sorority (Ryan & Bogart, 2001). This effect is stronger for groups with which we have little experience (Linville, Fischer, & Yoon, 1996). One study compared views of South Africans and European Americans about their own group and the other group. The results showed that both groups held relatively complex views of their own group but a relatively simplistic view of the other group (Bartsch, Judd, Louw, Park, & Ryan, 1997).

Stereotypes are more likely to be activated in certain situations. For example, stereotypes have a strong influence when we have little information about people other than their group membership. And we can inhibit the activation of stereotypes when we want to avoid prejudice (Kunda & Spencer, 2003). Of course, few people assume that all members of an out-group share the same characteristics. Thus, when confronted with someone who violates a stereotype, they simply assimilate that person into their out-group schema as an exception to the rule (Wilder, Simon, & Faith, 1996).

First Impressions

When we first meet a person, we might have little information about the individual other than her or his sex, ethnicity, apparent age, and physical appearance. Each of these characteristics might activate a particular social schema, which in turn will create a first impression of that person. A first impression functions as a social schema to guide our predictions of a person's behavior and our desire to interact with that person. First impressions are important in many situations, such as in determining whether college roommates will become friends (Berg, 1984). One clever study had trained coders evaluate the firmness of undergraduates' handshakes. A firm handshake was defined by duration and completeness of grip, vigor, strength, and amount of eye contact. Participants—especially females—with firm handshakes received more positive first impression ratings than did participants with weaker handshakes (Chaplin, Phillips, Brown, Clanton, & Stein, 2000). And even our exercise habits may contribute to the impressions we make on others. An experiment found that college students rated students described as exercisers more positively than students described as nonexercisers (Kanarek, Mathes, & D'Anci, 2012).

A classic experiment by Harold Kelley (1950) demonstrated the importance of a first impression on our evaluation of a stranger. Undergraduates were given a written description of a guest lecturer as "a rather warm person, industrious, critical, practical, and determined" or the same description with the word *warm* replaced by the word *cold.* After the lecture, which provided the opportunity for questions and discussion, the students were asked for their impressions of the lecturer. Students who had been told that the lecturer was warm rated him as more informal, sociable, and humorous than did those who were told he was cold. Those who had been told the lecturer was warm also asked more questions and participated in more discussions with him. These findings indicated that the students assimilated the lecturer's behavior into the schema they had created on the basis of the written description. This study has been replicated successfully using similar methodology (Widmeyer & Loy, 1988).

social schema A cognitive structure comprising the presumed characteristics of a role, an event, a person, or a group.

stereotype A social schema that incorporates characteristics, which can be positive or negative, supposedly shared by almost all members of a group.

First Impressions

Do these women bring different thoughts and feelings to mind? Your first impression of them might determine how you initially act toward them.
Source: (top) Zoom Team/ Shutterstock.com; (bottom) Angela Hawkey/Shutterstock. com.

Self-Fulfilling Prophecy

Self-Fulfilling Prophecy

Chronically insecure people may suffer from self-fulfilling prophecies of social rejection.
Source: CREATISTA/ Shutterstock.com.

self-fulfilling prophecy
The tendency for one person's expectations to influence another person to behave in accordance with them.

One of the important effects of first impressions is the **self-fulfilling prophecy,** which is the tendency for one person's expectations to make a second person behave in accordance with them. This phenomenon occurs because the social schema we have of the other person will make us act a certain way toward that person, which in turn will make the person respond in accordance with our expectations (Rosenthal, 2002). Thus, if you expect a person to be unfriendly and, as a result, act cold and aloof, you might elicit unfriendly behavior from that person—even if he or she would normally be inclined to be friendly. In fact, research shows that dating partners who expect to be rejected tend to behave in ways that provoke their partner to eventually reject them (Downey, Freitas, Michaelis, & Khouri, 1998). But in contrast, a 1-year longitudinal study found that dating partners who idealized each other at the beginning tended to create a self-fulfilling prophecy that produced the very relationship they sought (Murray, Holmes, & Griffin, 1996).

However, one recent longitudinal study found that chronically insecure college students' relationships can be enhanced by an intervention designed to influence their self-fulfilling prophecies of social rejection. At the beginning of the experiment, participants completed measures of relational security and also were rated by a trained nurse who rated their social demeanor (for example, calm/agitated, relaxed/anxious, and appreciative/unappreciative). Participants in the experimental condition engaged in a self-affirmation procedure in which they spent 15 minutes writing short paragraphs about why their values were important to them, their lives, and their self-image. Participants in the control condition spent 15 minutes writing about other people's values. This procedure was repeated approximately weekly over a period of 4 weeks. Results indicated that participants who wrote self-affirmations reported increased relational security and more positive social behavior ratings than participants in the control condition. Moreover, these effects persisted up to two months after the beginning of the experiment. Thus, a negative self-fulfilling prophecy can be mitigated by engaging in a process of positive self-affirmation (Stinson, Logal, Shepherd, & Zanna, 2011).

Stereotypes also may contribute to self-fulfilling prophecies. People perform better when they are unaware of negative stereotypes that others might hold. But what of positive stereotypes? Suppose you belong to two stereotyped groups, such as the case of Asian American women. As Asian Americans they are stereotypically viewed as good in mathematics. As women they are stereotypically viewed as poor in mathematics. In one study, Asian American women who completed a questionnaire that included items about their ethnicity then performed better on a mathematics test than did Asian American women who did not. But Asian American women who completed a questionnaire that included items about their gender then performed worse on a mathematics test than Asian American women who did not. Evidently, participants' performances depended on whether their ethnic or gender stereotype had been made salient to them (Shih, Pittinsky, & Ambady, 1999). And a replication study addressed the social costs of being a "model minority." In this study, Asians' *extremely* high performance in mathematics was made salient to Asian American women. Under these conditions, participants found it difficult to concentrate and performed more poorly. Hence, people's awareness of positive stereotypes that others might hold may lead to choking under pressure (Cheryan & Bodenhausen, 2000).

Section Review: Social Cognition

1. What are the three dimensions in Weiner's attribution model?

2. What is the self-serving bias?

3. How can a first impression create a self-fulfilling prophecy?

Interpersonal Attraction

While forming impressions of other people, we also develop interpersonal attraction toward some of them. By this point in the semester, you have probably become friendly with certain students; you might even have developed a romantic relationship with someone in particular. Social psychologists interested in interpersonal attraction seek answers to questions like these: Why do we like certain people more than others? What is the nature of romantic love?

Liking

Think of the students you have met this semester. Which ones do you like? Which ones do you not like? Among the factors that determine which ones you like are proximity, familiarity, physical attractiveness, similarity, and self-disclosure.

Proximity

You are more likely to develop a liking for someone who lives near you, works with you, or attends the same classes as you. Research has consistently supported the importance of proximity in the development of friendships, as in a classic study of the residents of apartments in a housing project for married students at the Massachusetts Institute of Technology. The closer that students lived to one another, the more likely they were to become friends. In fact, 41 percent of the students reported that their best friends lived next door. Because the students had been randomly assigned to apartments, their initial degree of liking for one another could not explain the findings (Festinger, Schachter, & Back, 1950). Proximity is important in dating relationships, too. But what effect does electronic communication and telecommuting have on people's friendships with coworkers? The Internet is quickly changing patterns of human interaction, especially inside the workplace. One study found that under these circumstances, physical proximity was the *least* important factor in friendship initiation. On the other hand, face-to-face communication in the workplace was the most important factor in maintaining satisfying friendships (Sias, Pedersen, Gallagher, & Kopaneva, 2012).

Familiarity

Proximity makes us more familiar with certain people. But contrary to the popular saying, familiarity tends to breed liking, not contempt. The more familiar we become with a stimulus, whether a car, a painting, or a professor, the more we will like it. So in general, the more we interact with particular people, the more we tend to like them (Moreland & Zajonc, 1982). In one study, participants who spoke with a person for a few minutes or simply waited quietly with a person were more likely to comply with a request from that person than were participants who were simply approached with a request (Burger, Soroka, Gonzago, Murphy, & Somervell, 2001). Of course, this tendency, called the *mere exposure effect*, holds only when people do not behave in negative ways. The effect of familiarity on liking is not lost on politicians, who enhance their popularity by making repeated television appearances. The more familiar we are with public figures (assuming they do nothing scandalous), the more we tend to like them (Harrison, 1969).

The mere exposure effect was supported by a clever experiment that used female college students as participants. For each participant, two photographs of the participant were presented to the participant and to a friend. One photograph was a direct image of the participant; the second was a mirror image—what the participant would see when looking at herself in a mirror. Mirror images and normal photographic images differ because our faces are not perfectly symmetrical—the left and right sides look different. Participants and friends were asked to choose which of the two photographs was preferable. Friends were more likely to choose the direct image, whereas participants were more likely to choose the mirror image. These results were evidence for the mere exposure effect because the friends were more familiar with the direct image, whereas the participants were more familiar with their own mirror image (Mita, Dermer, & Knight, 1977).

Physical Attractiveness

Cross-culturally, the results of research studies agree that "what is beautiful is good."
Source: TO COME FROM AUTHOR

Physical Attractiveness

Proximity not only lets us become familiar with people, it also lets us note their appearance. We tend to like physically attractive people more than physically unattractive ones. For example, one study found that both adults and children preferred physically attractive avatars from the Nintendo Wii console (Principe & Langlois, 2013). Contemporary films promote this tendency by associating positive personal characteristics with more physically attractive actors and actresses. A study that examined a random sample of five decades of top-grossing films found that physically attractive characters were portrayed more positively than physically unattractive ones. Moreover, after people view films that portray physically attractive characters as more appealing, they become more likely to evaluate physically attractive people in their own lives more positively, as when considering someone for admission to graduate school. These studies provide consistent findings that we believe that "what is beautiful is good" (Smith, McIntosh, & Bazzini, 1999).

Sensitivity to physical attractiveness begins early in life, with infants as young as 4 months old preferring to look at attractive faces instead of unattractive ones (Samuels, Butterworth, Roberts, & Graupner, 1994). This bias can have practical benefits for attractive people—especially physically attractive girls and women (Maner et al., 2003). Attractive adults and children are judged more positively and treated more positively by others. In turn—consistent with the self-fulfilling prophecy—attractive adults and children also exhibit more positive behaviors and personality traits (Langlois et al., 2000). For example, physically attractive people are perceived to be more intelligent (Jackson, Hunter, & Hodge, 1995) and more socially competent (Hope & Mindell, 1994). They also are more likely to be hired than are less attractive applicants with equivalent qualifications (Hosoda, Stone-Romero, & Coats, 2003). Physically attractive defendants are less likely to be convicted of crimes and, if convicted, less likely to be subjected to severe punishment (Mazzella & Feingold, 1994). And physically attractive college students are less likely to be asked for proof of age by bartenders (McCall, 1997).

Judgments of facial attractiveness have strong cross-cultural consistency (Langlois et al., 2000). In one study, native-born European Americans and newly arrived Asian and Hispanic students rated the attractiveness of photographs of African American, European American, Asian, and Latina women. The correlation in ratings, .93, was almost perfect. In a companion study, African and European American men rated the attractiveness of photos of African American women. Ratings of facial attractiveness correlated .94, but African Americans and European Americans differed in their judgments of body attractiveness (Cunningham, Roberts, Barbee, & Druen, 1995). In regard to facial attractiveness, there is cross-cultural evidence that we find symmetrical faces more attractive than faces that are not symmetrical (Rhodes et al., 2001). Moreover, this effect has been found among American children as young as 9 years of age (Vingilis-Jaremko & Larissa, 2013). Some researchers interpret this attraction as having a hereditary basis, perhaps one that is the product of evolution (Fink & Penton-Voak, 2002).

Physical attractiveness is an important factor in dating relationships. In an early experiment on the effect of physical attractiveness, first-year students at the University of Minnesota took part in a computer dating study. They completed personality and aptitude tests and were told that they would be paired based on their responses. In reality, they were paired randomly. Independent judges rated the physical attractiveness of each student. The couples then attended a dance that lasted several hours and rated their partners on a questionnaire. The results showed that physical attractiveness was the most important factor in determining whether participants liked their partners and whether they desired to date them again (Walster et al., 1966). More recent research has replicated this finding; both men and women value physically attractiveness in dating relationships (Eastwick, Eagly, Finkel, & Johnson, 2011).

Though we may prefer to have relationships with very attractive people, social sorting usually leads us to have friends (Cash & Derlega, 1978) and romantic partners (Folkes, 1982) who are similar to us in physical attractiveness. That is, though we may prefer more attractive people, they may reject us—just as we may reject people who are less attractive than we are. These rejections leave us in relationships with people whose level of attractiveness is similar to our own.

Similarity

Though we tend to develop relationships with people who are similar to us in physical attractiveness, do we seek people who are similar to us in other ways? Do opposites attract? Or do birds of a feather flock together? You may recall the experiment discussed in Chapter 2 that showed that we are more attracted to people whose attitudes are similar to our own (Byrne, Ervin, & Lamberth, 1970). The findings of that classic study have been replicated in many research studies, including recent experiments (Klohnen & Luo, 2003), and a recent meta-analysis has reported a large effect size for both actual and perceived similarity on attraction (Montoya, Horton, & Kirchner, 2008). But this interpretation has been challenged by research showing that we are likely to associate with people who hold similar attitudes simply by default because we are repulsed by those who have dissimilar ones. Life's circumstances simply put us in religious, political, recreational, and educational settings where we are likely to associate with people who share our attitudes (Rosenbaum, 1986).

But the results of recent research studies indicate that attitude similarity plays a more important role in interpersonal attraction in some contexts and that attitude dissimilarity plays a role in preventing interpersonal attraction in others (Singh & Ho, 2000). For example, we are attracted to people with similar attitudes if we expect to enjoy each other's company (Michinov & Monteil, 2002). And other research indicates that we like people who share our activity preferences even more than we like people who share our attitudes (Lydon, Jamieson, & Zanna, 1988). Thus, you might enjoy playing sports or going to music concerts with someone whose sexual, religious, and political values differ from yours. And in certain cases we are, indeed, more attracted to people who are not similar to us, particularly if we find that their personal characteristics are fulfilling to us. Such attraction may occur, for example, when one person is dominant and the other is submissive. These partners are more satisfied with their relationship than are partners who are similar in those personality characteristics (Dryer & Horowitz, 1997).

Self-Disclosure

To determine whether we share similar attitudes and interests with someone else, we must engage in self-disclosure, in which we reveal our beliefs, feelings, and experiences. Reciprocation of self-disclosure is important because we tend to like people more if they have disclosed personal information to us and if we have disclosed personal information to them (Collins & Miller, 1994). In social relationships, self-disclosure is best if it is gradual. When people disclose highly personal information to us too early in a relationship, we may become uneasy, suspicious, and less attracted to them. If someone you have just met has ever regaled you with his or her whole life story, including intimate details, you might have felt uncomfortable and uninterested in pursuing the relationship. Moreover, we must consider the cultural background of the person with whom we are interacting. For example, a study found that American college students preferred to engage in more self-disclosure than did Taiwanese college students (Chen, 1995).

Romantic Love

Love might make the world go round, but there were few scientific studies of romantic love until the 1970s. Since then, the findings of such research have been used to help prevent and relieve the emotional and physical suffering that is produced by unhappy romantic relationships, including spouse abuse, child abuse, and relationship dissolution. What have researchers discovered about the nature of romantic love? For one thing, the concept of love has "fuzzy borders" (see Chapter 9). That is, we know love when we see it or experience it, but we cannot define it by a single set of features without finding exceptions to any definition we put forth (Fehr & Russell, 1991).

Theories of Love

passionate love Love characterized by intense emotional arousal and sexual feelings.

companionate love Love characterized by feelings of affection and commitment to a relationship with another person.

Elaine Hatfield—undaunted by earning the first Golden Fleece Award (regularly bestowed by former U.S. senator William Proxmire for the project that he believed was the greatest waste of government funding) for the research she conducted with her colleague, Ellen Berscheid—distinguishes between passionate love and companionate love (Hatfield, 1988). **Passionate love,** commonly known as sexual love, involves intense emotional arousal, including sexual feelings. **Companionate love** involves feelings of affection and commitment to the relationship. Over time, romantic relationships tend to decline in passionate love and increase in companionate love.

More research has been conducted on passionate love than on companionate love. According to Berscheid and Hatfield, passionate love depends on three factors. First, the culture must promote the notion of passionate love. Passionate love has been important in Western cultures for only a few centuries, and even today some cultures have no concept of it. Second, the person must experience a state of intense emotional arousal. Third, the emotional arousal must be associated with a romantic partner (Berscheid & Walster, 1974).

Berscheid and Hatfield's theory of romantic love incorporates aspects of Stanley Schachter and Jerome Singer's two-factor theory of emotion. As explained in Chapter 12, Schachter and Singer's theory assumes that you will experience a particular emotion when you perceive that you are physiologically aroused, and you will attribute that arousal to an emotionally relevant aspect of the situation in which you find yourself. The two-factor theory assumes that romantic love is the result of being physiologically aroused in a situation that promotes the labeling of that arousal as romantic love.

The two-factor theory of romantic love was supported by a clever experiment that took place on two bridges in Vancouver, British Columbia (Dutton & Aron, 1974). One, the Capilano River Bridge, was 5 feet wide, 450 feet long, and 230 feet above rocky rapids. It had low handrails and was constructed of wooden boards attached to wire cables, making it prone to wobble back and forth, inducing fear-related physiological arousal in those who walked across it. The other bridge, over a tiny tributary of the Capilano River, was wide, solid, immobile, and only 10 feet above the water. These characteristics made that bridge less likely to induce arousal in those who walked across it.

Whenever a man walked across one of the bridges, he was met by an attractive woman who was the experimenter's confederate. The woman asked each man to participate in a psychology course project about the effects of scenic attractions on creativity. Each man was shown a picture of a man and a woman in an ambiguous situation and was asked to write a brief dramatic story about the picture. The woman then gave the man her telephone number in case he wanted to ask her any questions about the study. The results showed that, compared with the men on the solid bridge, the men who were on the bridge that induced physiological arousal wrote stories with more sexual content and were more likely to call the woman later.

According to the two-factor theory of romantic love, the men on the bridge that induced arousal had attributed their arousal to the presence of the attractive woman, leading them to experience romantic feelings toward her. But this interpretation of the results has been rejected by some researchers, who offer an alternative interpretation that assumes that the presence of the woman reduced the men's fear of the bridge, which, as a consequence, conditioned them to find her more attractive (Riordan & Tedeschi, 1983).

Nonetheless, results of studies similar to the Capilano River study have supported the two-factor theory of romantic love. In one such study, female and male participants who had just ridden a roller coaster rated photographs of persons of the other sex as more attractive and desirable than did participants who were waiting to ride the roller coaster (Meston & Frolich, 2003). A recent meta-analysis also found consistent effects of arousal on attraction, with effect sizes ranging from small to moderate across a number of conditions. For example, sexual arousal increased physical attraction, but not liking or interpersonal attraction (Foster et al., 1998).

Another prominent theory of love has been put forth by Robert Sternberg (1986). His triangular theory of love presumes that the experience of love depends on the interaction of three components. Passion encompasses drives that lead to romance, physical attraction,

Companionate Love

For romantic love to last after passionate love has waned somewhat, romantic partners must maintain the deep affection that characterizes companionate love.

Source: Monkey Business Images/Shutterstock.com.

and sexual relations. Intimacy encompasses feelings of closeness, bondedness, and connectedness. And decision/commitment encompasses, in the short term, the decision that one loves another and, in the long term, the commitment to maintain that love. The intensity of love depends on the individual strengths of these three components, whereas the kind of love that is experienced depends on the strengths of the three components relative to one another. For example, strong passion combined with little intimacy and weak decision/commitment is associated with infatuation, whereas strong passion and great intimacy combined with weak decision/commitment is associated with romantic love.

Though the triangular theory of love has been with us for more than two decades, it has inspired surprisingly little empirical research until more recently. There is some research evidence supporting the three components of the theory (Lemieux & Hale, 2002), its relationship to commitment in romantic relationships (Campbell, Foster, & Finkel, 2002), and gender differences in beliefs about love (Sprecher & Toro-Morn, 2002). A recent survey found that passionate love was higher among younger couples and companionate love higher among older couples. That does not mean that passionate love is doomed to die as the relationship endures. Whereas passionate love indeed waned over the first 20 years of a relationship, there was a "rebound" effect in which it grew stronger among couples in relationships that lasted longer than 20 years. This finding was attributed to family and life cycle transitions that enable older couples to enjoy each other more (Sheets, 2013). There also is research evidence that passion and intimacy are intertwined, with increases in intimacy associated with strong passion. When intimacy is stable, whether high or low, passion will be low (Baumeister & Bratslavsky, 1999).

There also are culture-related differences in the definition of romantic love (Landis & O'Shea, 2000) and the importance and expression of emotional intimacy (Seki, Matsumoto, & Imahori, 2002). One study compared love songs in the United States and Hong Kong and mainland China. In Chinese songs love was expected to come to an unhappy end that involved intense suffering. Though songs from both cultures depicted similar levels of desire, Chinese songs depicted love as being less individualistic and more influenced by family relationships and even the environment—a reflection of the Taoist principle of harmony with nature and society (Rothbaum & Tsang, 1998). In traditional Chinese culture many women and men consider the wishes of their family when choosing a mate. Thus, the prevalence of arranged marriages in traditional Chinese culture, which benefit the extended family, may be at odds with the Western concept of romantic love (Hsu, 1981). Recent surveys, however, point to individualistic trends, with more Chinese men and women preferring a love-based marriage (Xiaohe & Whyte, 1990).

Promoting Romantic Love

What factors promote romantic love? As in the case of personal liking, similarity is an important factor. We tend to choose romantic partners who are similar to us in attractiveness (Yela & Sangrador, 2001) as well as in religion, ethnic background, and educational level (Buss, 1985). One factor is an exception to the similarity rule—chronological age. Gay and heterosexual men prefer younger partners than do lesbian and heterosexual women (Silverthorne & Quinsey, 2000). A survey found that when men and women were asked to rate the personal factors that would make someone attractive as a romantic partner, a sense of humor was the most important one (Buss, 1988). A more recent survey of heterosexual college students found that both men and women viewed humorous people as more appealing for serious relationships, including marriage, but only when they perceived them as physically attractive (Lundy, Tan, & Cunningham, 1998). We also prefer romantic partners who view us as we see ourselves but who also bolster our self-esteem (Katz & Beach, 2000). And a study of 18-year-old dating couples found that those who engaged in mutual self-disclosure early in the relationship were more likely to be together 4 months later (Berg & McQuinn, 1986).

Another important factor in romantic relationships is equity, the belief that each partner is contributing equally to the relationship, which promotes long-term contentment and commitment, especially among men and women with nontraditional gender roles (Donaghue & Fallon, 2003). Even the mere promise of equity might be important in promoting romantic relationships. This finding has been shown in archival research on personal advertisements. A survey of 800 advertisements placed by individuals seeking romantic partners found that the advertisers tended to seek equitable relationships. But heterosexual women and men differed in complementary ways in the rewards they sought and offered. Men tended to seek attractive women while offering financial security in return. In contrast, women tended to seek financially secure men while offering physical attractiveness in return (Harrison, 1977). These findings have been replicated in a laboratory experiment (Buunk, Dijkstra, Fetchenhauer, & Kenrick, 2002) and in more recent archival research studies (Cicerello & Sheehan, 1995). These findings also hold across cultures, as in a study of the marital preferences of more than 1,500 heterosexual college students in Japan, Russia, and the United States (Hatfield & Sprecher, 1995). But the content of personal advertisements may vary with the individual's gender identity or sexual orientation. Two studies found, for example, that heterosexuals mentioned financial security more frequently than did gay men or lesbians. Physical characteristics were mentioned the most by gay men and the least by lesbians (Gonzales & Meyers, 1993).

Evolutionary psychologists would claim that these findings are not surprising because they reflect millions of years of evolution. According to evolutionary psychologists' interpretation of these findings, men prefer younger, physically attractive women because they would be more likely to have the ability to bear children and, as a result, pass on the men's genes. Similarly, women prefer men of higher financial status—especially those with personalities that are kind, caring, and loyal—because they would probably be more able and willing to care for the women and their offspring (Buss, 2003). Of course, this evolutionary psychology viewpoint, as it usually is, is an after-the-fact explanation for behaviors that might be explained just as well by learned cultural differences in male and female gender roles. This interpretation is supported by the results of a recent study that compared heterosexual women's and men's mate preferences in 37 cultures. Women (but not men) preferred mates with greater financial resources in cultures that limited reproductive freedom and educational equality for women (Kasser & Sharma, 1999).

Section Review: Interpersonal Attraction

1. What evidence is there that the mere exposure effect contributes to liking?

2. How does the two-factor theory explain romantic love?

3. How do personal advertisements for romantic partners support equity as a factor in romantic relationships?

Attitudes

attitude An evaluation—containing cognitive, emotional, and behavioral components—of an idea, event, object, or person.

What are your opinions about the insanity defense? Surprise parties? Abstract art? Sorority members? Your answers to these questions would reveal your attitudes. **Attitudes** are evaluations of ideas (such as the insanity defense), events (such as surprise parties), objects (such as cellular phones), or people (such as sorority members). In the 1930s, the noted psychologist Gordon Allport claimed that the concept of attitude was the single most important concept in social psychology. It no longer maintains such a lofty position, but it is still one of the most widely studied concepts in social psychology.

As shown in Figure 17-2, attitudes have emotional, cognitive, and behavioral components (Breckler, 1984). To appreciate these components, imagine that you have been asked to participate in a market research survey of attitudes toward a new low-cholesterol, fast-food hamburger called "Burger-Lo." The market researcher would determine your attitude toward Burger-Lo by measuring one or more of the three components of your attitude. Your emotional response might be measured by a questionnaire asking you to rate your feelings about Burger-Lo's taste, aroma, texture, and appearance. Your cognitive response might be measured by asking you to describe the thoughts that Burger-Lo brings to mind, such as "It's better than a Big Mac." And your behavioral response might

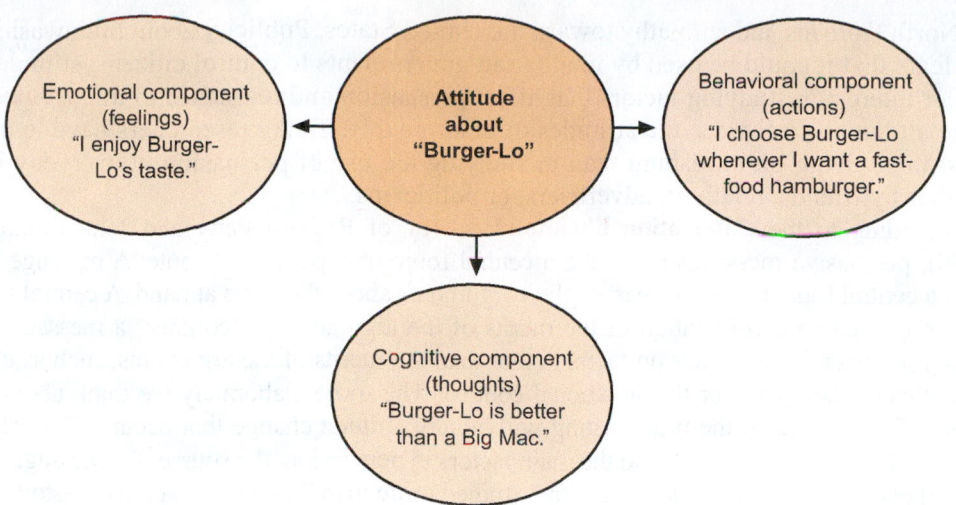

FIGURE 17-2
The Components of
Attitudes

Attitudes have emotional,
cognitive, and behavioral
components.

be measured by observing whether you choose Burger-Lo over several other fast-food hamburgers in a blind taste test.

The Formation of Attitudes

How are our attitudes formed? Some are learned through classical conditioning (see Chapter 7) by the pairing of a desirable or undesirable feeling with the object of the attitude (Olson & Fazio, 2002). If Burger-Lo tastes good, you will associate that experience with Burger-Lo and develop a positive attitude toward it. Research indicates that our food preferences are, in fact, influenced by classical conditioning (Rozin & Zellner, 1985). Advertisers of foods and other products take advantage of classical conditioning by pairing them with stimuli that are already desirable (Grossman & Till, 1998). Thus, advertisers often try to sell automobiles to consumers by associating them with attractive men and women in media advertisements.

Attitudes also can be formed through operant conditioning (see Chapter 7), as in an experiment conducted at the University of Hawaii (Insko, 1965). Undergraduates, contacted by telephone, were asked whether they agreed or disagreed with statements that favored or opposed a proposed "Springtime Aloha Week." The caller positively reinforced certain statements by saying "good." For half the telephone calls, the caller said "good" whenever the student agreed with a statement favoring the proposal. For the other half, the caller said "good" whenever the student agreed with a statement opposing the proposal. One week later the students were given a "local issues questionnaire." Among the items in the questionnaire was a question asking whether they favored or opposed the proposed Springtime Aloha Week. The responses to that question showed that students who earlier had been reinforced for making statements that favored the Springtime Aloha Week were more likely to favor it, whereas students who earlier had been reinforced for making statements that opposed it were more likely to oppose it.

According to social-learning theory, many of our attitudes are learned through observing others—particularly our parents, our peers, and characters on television shows—being punished or positively reinforced for engaging in particular behaviors (Kanekar, 1976). For example, cross-cultural differences and similarities in attitudes toward favorite foods are acquired through acculturation (Cervellon & Dube, 2002). Even our attitudes toward the use of drugs are affected by social learning. For example, adolescents have a more positive attitude toward alcohol use if they have consistently seen their peers, parents, and siblings drinking it (Ary, Tildesley, Hops, & Andrews, 1993).

The Art of Persuasion

In 1956, Edward Schein published an article that described the results of his interviews with United Nations soldiers who, as prisoners during the Korean War, had been subjected to so-called brainwashing, which in some cases made them express sympathy for

persuasion The attempt to influence the attitudes of other people.

elaboration likelihood theory A theory of persuasion that considers the extent to which messages take a central route or a peripheral route.

the North Koreans and antipathy toward the United States. Publicity about brainwashing, and fears that it could be used by totalitarian governments to control citizens, stimulated further interest in studying factors that affect persuasion and resistance to it. **Persuasion** is the attempt to influence the attitudes of other people. Today researchers have less interest in studying brainwashing than in studying the use of persuasion in everyday life, whether by friends, relatives, advertisers, or politicians.

According to the **elaboration likelihood theory** of Richard Petty and John Cacioppo (1990), persuasive messages may take a central route or a peripheral route. A message that takes a central route relies on clear, explicit arguments about the issue at hand. A central route encourages active consideration of the merits of the arguments. In contrast, a message that takes a peripheral route relies on factors other than the merits of the arguments, such as characteristics of the source or the situational context. The more elaborately we think about the merits of an argument, the more lasting will be any attitude change that occurs. The central and peripheral routes are related to the main factors in persuasion: the source, the message, and the audience. These three factors were first studied more than 2,000 years ago by Aristotle. He found that persuasion was most effective when the source had good character, the message was supported by strong evidence, and the audience was in a receptive frame of mind (Jones, 1985).

The Source and Persuasion

One of the important peripheral factors in persuasion is the source of the message. The greater the credibility of the source, the greater the persuasiveness of the message (Smith, De Houwer, & Nosek, 2013). Politicians realize this importance and gain votes by having credible supporters praise their merits and criticize their opponents' faults (Calantone & Warshaw, 1985). But what determines a source's credibility? Perhaps the most important factor is the source's expertise. A meta-analysis of 114 studies on the effects of source characteristics on persuasion found that expertise was the single most credibility-enhancing source characteristic (Wilson & Sherrell, 1993). For example, people who read stories about UFOs that include supportive statements from a scientific authority become more likely to express their belief in UFOs than people who read stories that do not include such statements (Sparks & Pellechia, 1997).

Another important factor in promoting source credibility is trustworthiness. When we perceive a source as trustworthy, we are less likely to critically scrutinize her or his message. Trust makes us more likely to be persuaded by the message (Priester & Petty, 2003). We perceive sources as especially trustworthy when their message is not an obvious attempt at persuasion, particularly when the message is contrary to the source's expected position (Wood & Eagly, 1981). For example, as noted in Chapter 10, Sir Cyril Burt's biographer concluded that Burt had fabricated data supporting a strong genetic basis for intelligence. The author of an article that discussed Burt's biography claimed, "The conclusion carries more weight because the author of the biography, Professor Leslie Hearnshaw, began his task as an admirer" (Hawkes, 1979, p. 673). If Hearnshaw had been a critic of Burt's work, his conclusion would have been less credible.

Sources who are attractive, because they are likable or physically appealing, also are more persuasive. Advertisers take advantage of this factor by having attractive actors appear in their commercials (Shavitt, Swan, Lowrey, & Wanke, 1994). Even the persuasiveness of politicians is affected by their attractiveness. Richard Nixon's unattractive appearance during a debate with John F. Kennedy may have cost him the 1960 presidential election. Nixon's five-o'clock shadow and tendency to perspire made him less attractive to voters who watched the debate on television. Surveys found that people who watched the debate on television rated Kennedy the winner of the debate, whereas those who listened to it on the radio rated Nixon the debate's winner (Weisman, 1988). Having learned from Nixon's mistake, today's politicians make sure that they appear as attractive as possible on television.

The Message and Persuasion

It might surprise you to learn that it is not always desirable to present arguments that support only your position. Simply acknowledging the other side of an issue while strongly supporting your own is at times more effective. A meta-analysis of research studies found

The Power of Persuasion

Attempts at persuasion pervade our everyday lives, as in this protest against genetically modified organisms, or GMOs.

Source: Glynnis Jones/Shutterstock.com.

Credibility and Persuasion

The effectiveness of a doctor's medical advice is based on perceived expertise and trustworthiness.

Source: XiXinXing/Shutterstock.com.

that two-sided messages are generally more effective than one-sided messages in changing attitudes (Allen, 1993). This finding was discovered by social psychologist Carl Hovland and his colleagues in the waning days of World War II, following the surrender of Germany (Hovland, Lumsdaine, & Sheffield, 1949). The military asked Hovland for advice on how to convince soldiers that the war against Japan would take a long time to win. The researchers presented soldiers with a 15-minute talk that presented either one-sided or two-sided arguments. In the one-sided argument, they presented only arguments about why the war would not be over soon, such as the fighting spirit of the Japanese. In the two-sided argument, they presented both that argument and arguments explaining why the war might end earlier, such as Allied air superiority. Before and after the message, participants were given surveys that included questions about how long they believed the war would last.

The results showed that those soldiers who originally believed that the war would take a long time to win were more influenced by the one-sided argument and became more extreme in their attitudes. But those who originally believed there would be an early end to the war were more influenced by the two-sided argument. As you can see, if the listener already favors your position or has no counterarguments handy, arguments that favor your position alone will be more persuasive. But if the listener opposes your position, arguments that acknowledge both sides of the issue will be more persuasive. Two-sided arguments are effective in part because they enhance the credibility of the source and decrease counterarguing by the listener (Bohner, Einwiller, Erb, & Siebler, 2003).

An intriguing aspect of persuasion is the **sleeper effect**. This effect occurs when a person initially fails to be convinced by a persuasive message, perhaps because the source lacks credibility, yet responds more favorably to it with the mere passage of time. A meta-analysis of research on the sleeper effect found that it is more likely to occur when the persuasive message had a strong initial impact but there was a strong reason for not responding positively to it (Kumkale & Albarracin, 2004). Thus, if you provide a well-presented argument that is initially rejected because, for example, you are perceived as lacking in expertise, it still might have a positive—though delayed—impact on its intended audience.

sleeper effect Responding favorably to a persuasive message following the mere passage of time after having initially rejected it because of a strong peripheral factor, such as not trusting the source of the message.

The Audience and Persuasion

Persuasion depends on the audience as well as the message and its source. An important audience factor is intelligence because it determines whether a message will be more effective using the central or the peripheral route. People of relatively high intelligence are more likely to be influenced by messages supported by rational arguments—the central route. People of relatively low intelligence are more likely to be influenced by messages supported by factors other than rational arguments—the peripheral route (Eagly & Warren, 1976). Overall, people of lower intelligence are more easily influenced than are people of higher intelligence (Rhodes & Wood, 1992).

Another important audience factor is whether the audience finds the message personally important (Zuwerink & Devine, 1996). A message's importance for a particular audience determines whether the central route or the peripheral route will be more effective (Petty & Cacioppo, 1990). When a message has high importance to an audience, the central route will be more effective. When a message has low importance, the peripheral route will be more effective. This finding came from a study that measured student attitudes toward recommended policy changes at a university. The changes would be instituted either the following year (high importance) or in 10 years (low importance). Students who were asked to respond to arguments about policy changes of high importance were influenced more by the quality of the arguments (central route) than by the expertise of the source (peripheral route). In contrast, students who were asked to respond to arguments about policy changes of low importance were influenced more by the expertise of the source than by the quality of the arguments (Petty, Cacioppo, & Goldman, 1981).

Attitudes and Behavior

Common sense tells us that if we know a person's attitudes, we can accurately predict her or his behavior. But the relationship is not that simple. For one thing, our behavior

Attitudes and Behavior

Market researchers are interested in measuring consumer attitudes to predict behavior. For example, if customers rate customer service highly, it is assumed that they will return.

Source: Brian A Jackson/ Shuttertock.com.

might not always agree with our attitudes. Perhaps more surprisingly, our behavior can sometimes affect our attitudes.

The Influence of Attitudes on Behavior

Until the late 1960s, most social psychologists accepted the commonsense notion that our behavior is consistent with our attitudes. But since then researchers have found that attitudes are not as consistent with behavior as previously believed (Scott & Willits, 1994). You have seen this inconsistency exhibited dramatically, for example, by television evangelists who preach sexual denial to their audience while they themselves engage in extramarital sexual relations.

Though widespread interest in the inconsistency between attitudes and behaviors is only a few decades old, evidence supporting the inconsistency between attitudes and behaviors appeared as early as the 1930s, when sociologist Richard LaPiere (1934) traveled with a young Chinese couple for 10,000 miles throughout the United States. They ate at 184 restaurants and stayed at 66 hotels, motels, and other places. Though anti-Chinese feelings were strong at that time, only 1 of the 250 establishments refused them service. Six months after the journey, LaPiere wrote to each of the establishments, asking whether they would serve Chinese people. Of the 128 that replied, 118 (92 percent) said they would not. LaPiere's conclusion was that our behaviors do not always agree with our attitudes. But the study had a major flaw. The people who served the couple (servers and desk clerks) may not have been the same people who responded to LaPiere's letter (owners and managers). Nonetheless, LaPiere's study stimulated interest in research on the ability of attitude questionnaires to predict real-life behavior (Dockery & Bedeian, 1989).

But what determines whether our attitudes and behaviors will be consistent? Attitudes that are strongly held (Kraus, 1995) or personally important (Crano & Prislin, 1995) are better predictors of behavior. For example, in one study researchers measured the strength of participants' attitudes toward Greenpeace, an international environmental advocacy group. A week later the participants were given the opportunity to donate money to Greenpeace. The results showed that the strength of the participants' attitudes toward Greenpeace was positively correlated with the likelihood of their donating money. That is, participants who had strongly positive attitudes were more likely to donate money than were those with less positive attitudes. Likewise, participants who had strongly negative attitudes were less likely to donate money than were those with less negative attitudes (Holland, Verplanken, & van Knippenberg, 2002).

Attitude-behavior consistency also is affected by the specificity of the attitude and the behavior. Your attitudes and behaviors are more consistent with one another when they are at similar levels of specificity (Weigel, Vernon, & Tognacci, 1974). For example, your attitude toward safe driving might not predict whether you will obey the speed limit tomorrow morning, but it will predict your general tendency, over time, to engage in safe driving behaviors, such as checking your tire pressure, using turn signals, and obeying the speed limit.

The Influence of Behavior on Attitudes

In the mid-1950s, Leon Festinger (1919–1989) and his colleagues were intrigued by a sect whose members believed they would be saved by aliens in flying saucers at midnight prior to the day of a prophesized worldwide flood (Festinger, Riecken, & Schachter, 1956). But neither the aliens nor the flood ever arrived. Did the members lose their faith? Some did, but many reported that their faith was strengthened. They simply concluded that the aliens had rewarded their faith by saving the world from the flood. These members simply changed their belief in order to justify their action.

The ability of the sect's members to relieve the emotional distress they experienced when the prophecy failed to come true stimulated Festinger's interest in attitude change and his development of the **cognitive dissonance theory**. Cognitive dissonance is an unpleasant state of tension associated with increased physiological (Harmon-Jones, Brehm, Greenberg, & Simon, 1996) and psychological (Elliot & Devine, 1994) arousal, caused by the realization that one holds beliefs that are inconsistent with each other or a belief that is inconsistent with one's behavior. Cognitive dissonance would occur in people who believe that smoking is dangerous, yet find themselves to be smokers. We are motivated to reduce the unpleasant

cognitive-dissonance theory
Leon Festinger's theory that attitude change is motivated by the desire to relieve the unpleasant state of arousal caused when one holds cognitions and/or behaviors that are inconsistent with each other.

arousal associated with cognitive dissonance by making our cognitions consistent. Thus, a smoker might stop smoking, simply discount reports of the health risks of smoking, or estimate that the risk is lower in his or her own case. Consider a person who drinks alcohol despite believing that drinking is wrong. A study of drinkers found that those who had negative attitudes toward drinking were more likely than those with positive attitudes to claim that other people drank more than they did, apparently to reduce their cognitive dissonance in response to performing a behavior they believed was inappropriate (Maekelae, 1997).

The theory of cognitive dissonance has practical applications in promoting positive behaviors. One study aroused cognitive dissonance in undergraduates by making them feel hypocritical about their willingness to help those in need. Researchers accomplished this arousal by getting some of the participants to recall times when they failed to help others while inducing high levels of empathy for a child with cancer. This inconsistency between their beliefs, emotions, and behavior was expected to arouse cognitive dissonance and, as a consequence, make the students change their behavior. The results supported this hypothesis because participants in the hypocrisy condition were more willing to help than were participants who were reminded of their past failures to help but who did not experience high levels of empathy toward the child (Harmon-Jones, Peterson, & Vaughn, 2003). According to cognitive dissonance theory, the participants in the hypocrisy condition reduced their distress by changing their behavior.

The more we feel responsible for the inconsistencies between our cognitions, the stronger will be our feelings of cognitive dissonance and the more motivated we will be to change them. This was the finding of a classic experimental study of cognitive dissonance (Festinger & Carlsmith, 1959). Students were asked to perform boring tasks, one of which was to arrange small spools on a tray, dump the tray, and arrange the spools again and again for half an hour. Each student was paid either $1 or $20 to tell the next student that the task was enjoyable. After the experiment was over, the students were asked to express their attitude toward the task. Their responses violated what common sense predicted. As shown in Figure 17-3, those who were paid less ($1) tended to rate the task as interesting, whereas those who were paid more ($20) tended to rate the task as boring.

What could account for this finding? According to the theory of cognitive dissonance, the students experienced unpleasant arousal because their claim that the task was interesting did not agree with their belief that the task was boring. But those who were paid $20 to lie about the task experienced weaker cognitive dissonance because they could justify their lies by attributing them to the large payment they received. In contrast, those who were paid only $1 to lie experienced stronger cognitive dissonance because they could not attribute their lies to such a paltry sum. Consequently, those who were paid only $1 reduced the dissonance between their cognitions by changing their attitudes toward the task, rating it as more interesting than it actually was.

The cognitive dissonance interpretation of attitude change has been challenged by a theory put forth by Daryl Bem (1967). According to his **self-perception theory,** attitude change is

self-perception theory
The theory that we infer our attitudes from our behavior in the same way that we infer other people's attitudes from their behavior.

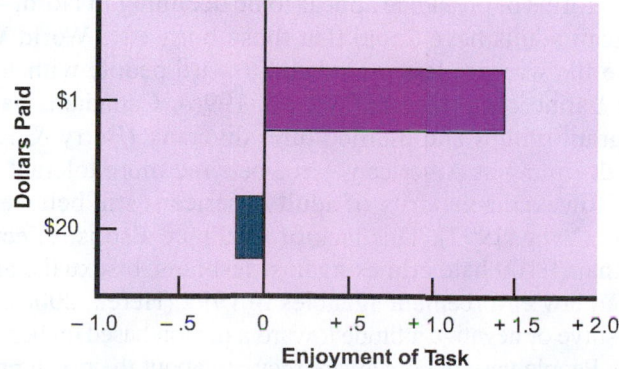

FIGURE 17-3
Cognitive Dissonance

In the classic study by Festinger and Carlsmith, participants who received $1 for telling other people that a boring task was interesting later rated the task as more enjoyable than did participants who received $20 for doing so.
Source: Data from L. Festinger and J. M. Carlsmith (1959), "Cognitive Consequences of Forced Compliance," *Journal of Abnormal and Social Psychology, 58,* 203–210.

Self-Perception Theory

Consider the predictions of self-perception theory and paying children to complete their homework or household chores. Is it wiser to pay large or small sums? Why?

Source: kitty/Shutterstock.com.

not motivated by our need to reduce cognitive dissonance. Instead, we infer our attitudes from our behavior in the same way that we infer other people's attitudes from their behavior. When we observe people behaving under no apparent external constraints, we use the behavior to make inferences about their attitudes. Likewise, when the situation we are in does not place strong constraints on our behavior, we might infer our attitudes from our behavior. Perhaps self-perception theory explains why we tend to favor our home sports teams. Because of our proximity to them, we are more likely to attend our home teams' games, watch our home teams on television, and read about them in the newspaper. When we observe ourselves engaging in these behaviors, we may infer that we like our home teams.

But how does self-perception theory explain why students who were paid $1 for lying showed greater attitude change than students who were paid $20? According to Bem, the students did not experience cognitive dissonance. Instead, they determined whether their behavior was attributable to themselves or to the situation. The students who were paid $20 attributed their behavior to being paid a relatively large sum of money. They had no reason to attribute their behavior to their attitude. In contrast, the students who were paid $1 could not attribute their behavior to such a small sum of money. Consequently, those students attributed their behavior to their attitude, perhaps saying to themselves, "If I told another student that the task was interesting and I was not induced to do so by a large amount of money, then the task must have been interesting to me."

Neither cognitive dissonance theory nor self-perception theory has emerged as the clearly superior explanation of the effect of behavior on attitudes. But each seems to be superior in certain circumstances. Whereas cognitive dissonance theory seems to be better at explaining the effect of behavior on well-defined attitudes, self-perception theory seems to be better at explaining the effect of behavior on poorly defined attitudes (Chaiken & Baldwin, 1981).

Prejudice

More than three decades ago, third-grade teacher Jane Elliott of Riceville, Iowa, gained national attention for a demonstration she gave of the devastating psychological effects of a particular kind of attitude: prejudice (Stewart, LaDuke, Bracht, Sweet, & Gamarel, 2003). She divided her students, who all were European American, into a blue-eyed group and a brown-eyed group. On the first day of the demonstration, Elliott declared that blue-eyed people were superior to brown-eyed people. The next day, she declared that brown-eyed people were superior to blue-eyed people.

Members of the superior group were given privileges, such as sitting where they wanted to in class, going to lunch early, and staying late at recess. Members of the inferior group were made to wear identification collars and were not permitted to play with members of the superior group. Elliott reported that during the two-day demonstration, students who were made to feel inferior became depressed and performed poorly on class work (Leonard, 1970). If prejudice could have this effect in an artificial, temporary situation, imagine the effect that prejudice has on children who are its targets in everyday life.

Fortunately, some forms of prejudice appear to be declining in North America. Surveys of European American adults have found that those born after World War II, compared to those born before the war, are less prejudiced toward people with Jewish, Asian, African American, or Latino backgrounds (Wilson, 1996). Canadians have become more accepting of immigrant groups and multicultural diversity (Berry & Kalin, 1995). And sexual prejudice is declining as Americans have become more tolerant of bisexuals, gay men, and lesbians. However, a majority of adult Americans still believe that homosexual behavior is "wrong" (Yang, 1997). This lack of tolerance also is reflected in a high rate of violence. More than 1,100 hate crimes against lesbians, bisexuals, and gay men were reported to American law enforcement agencies in 1997 (Herek, 2000).

prejudice A positive or negative attitude toward a person based on her or his membership in a particular group.

Prejudice is a positive or negative attitude toward a person based on her or his membership in a particular group. People vary in how aware they are about their own prejudiced attitudes. Some people are well aware of their prejudices; others may act in an explicitly prejudiced manner without even realizing they are implicitly prejudiced (Dovidio, Kawakami, & Gaertner, 2002). For example, a survey of four Western European countries found that respondents who scored high on a measure of blatant prejudice were more likely to endorse harsh exclusionary policies reducing immigration. In contrast, respondents who scored high on a measure of subtle prejudice shared exclusionary attitudes toward immigrants—however, they supported methods that were ostensibly nondiscriminatory (Meertens & Pettigrew, 1997). This *modern racism* is a subtle form of prejudice that could develop from social norms that discourage the expression of overt prejudice (McConahay, 1986). Modern racism is characterized by the beliefs that discrimination is no longer a problem, that ethnic minority groups' claims of inequality are unfounded, and that the gains ethnic minorities have made over the years may be unjustified.

The behavioral component of prejudice is discrimination, which involves treating persons differently, whether positively or negatively, based only on their group membership. For example, a study found that European American undergraduates who evaluated the employment applications of European American and African American candidates showed no racial discrimination in the case of strong or weak applications. However, European Americans did discriminate against African Americans in the case of ambiguous applications (Dovidio & Gaertner, 2000). Researchers who have applied the concept of modern racism to contemporary sexism believe that similar beliefs underlie negative attitudes toward affirmative action programs for women (Masser & Abrams, 1999). Moreover, this form of sexism is not unique to the United States. A cross-cultural study of 15,000 women and men found similar sexist beliefs in 19 countries (Glick et al., 2000).

Factors That Promote Prejudice

What factors account for the origin and maintenance of prejudice? As with all attitudes, learning plays an important role. Parents, peers, and the media all provide input, informing us of the supposed characteristics of particular groups. For example, an analysis of 1,699 television commercials found that they stereotyped European American men as powerful, European American women as sex objects, African American men as aggressive, and African American women as unimportant (Coltrane & Messineo, 2000). Even humor can promote prejudice. A Canadian study found that college students who were exposed to disparaging humor about an ethnic minority group became more prejudiced against that group than were students exposed to nondisparaging humor (Maio, Olson, & Bush, 1997).

Research has been especially concerned with factors that promote prejudice. The horrors of Nazism in the 1930s and 1940s led to a major research program at the University of California at Berkeley aimed at identifying the personality characteristics associated with fascist tendencies (Adorno, Frenkel-Brunswik, Levinson, & Sanford, 1950). Based on the results of tests and interviews with adult Californians, the researchers discovered what they called the **authoritarian personality**. People with an authoritarian personality tend to be obedient toward their superiors and domineering toward subordinates (authoritarianism), prejudiced in favor of their own groups and against other groups (ethnocentrism), and unwilling to admit their own faults but willing to place them on members of other groups (projection). In fact, the higher one's self-esteem, the less prejudiced one will tend to be against members of stereotyped groups (Fein & Spencer, 1997). Authoritarians tend to be prejudiced against other ethnic groups (Heaven & St. Quintin, 2003) as well as other out-groups, including people with AIDS

authoritarian personality
A personality type marked by the tendency to obey superiors while dominating subordinates, to favor one's own group while being prejudiced against other groups, and to be unwilling to admit one's own faults while projecting them onto members of other groups.

Prejudice and Social Learning

Adult models play a powerful role in determining whether children will become prejudiced against members of other groups.
Source: Monkey Business Images/Shutterstock.com.

(Cunningham et al., 1991), gay men and lesbians (Goodnight, Cook, Parrott, & Peterson, 2013), and mental hospital patients (Morrison, de Man, & Drumheller, 1993).

As mentioned in the section, "Liking," one of the most important factors in interpersonal attraction is attitude similarity. Prejudiced people perceive stereotyped groups as having attitudes that are different from those of their own groups. In fact, when there is little or no pressure to discriminate, ethnicity is less important than attitude similarity in determining racial or ethnic discrimination (Insko, Nacoste, & Moe, 1983). In a study of this phenomenon, participants were asked to choose a work partner. When they were given information about another's ethnicity and attitudes, their choices were influenced more by their similarity in attitudes than by their similarity in ethnicity (Rokeach & Mezei, 1966).

People also exhibit favoritism to their own kind. In a series of experiments, Henri Tajfel and Michael Billig (Tajfel, 1981; Tajfel & Billig, 1974) demonstrated that the social experience of becoming a member of a group can produce an in-group bias, or a tendency to exhibit favoritism toward members of one's group. Moreover, perceptions of threat to the in-group appear to increase this tendency. One study assessed the relationship between perceived threats to the in-group, intergroup anxiety, and negative stereotypes of Cuban, Mexican, and Asian immigrants in Florida, New Mexico, and Hawaii. Each of these factors was positively correlated with prejudice toward immigrants (Stephan, Ybarra, & Bachman, 1999). Similar results were found in a study of prejudice toward Moroccan, Russian, and Ethiopian immigrants in Spain and Israel (Stephan, Ybarra, Martinez, Schwarzwald, & Tur-Kaspa, 1998) and in a study of prejudice toward Turkish immigrants in Germany (Florack, Piontkowski, Bohman, Balzer, & Perzig, 2003). Likewise, a study of children and adults involved in the wars in the Republic of Georgia and Sierra Leone found that in-group biases were especially strong among individuals who were exposed to inter-ethnic conflict during middle childhood through early adulthood (Bauer, Cassar, Chytilová, & Heinrich, 2014).

Factors That Reduce Prejudice

Social psychologists also are concerned with finding ways to reduce prejudice. But this task is difficult because people are hesitant to revise personal judgments that are based on stereotypes. We modify the stereotypes we hold only gradually through individual experiences and by creating subtypes to accommodate instances that we cannot easily assimilate. As mentioned in the section, "Person Perception," we do not necessarily revise our stereotypes after experiencing a few dramatic exceptions to them (Weber & Crocker, 1983). Nonetheless, exceptions to stereotypes do make the out-group seem more variable, which tends to weaken the stereotypes somewhat (Hamburger, 1994).

In the 1950s, Gordon Allport (1954) insisted that prejudice could be reduced by increasing social contact between members of different social groups. At about the same time, in 1954, in the landmark case of *Brown v. Board of Education of Topeka*, the U.S. Supreme Court ruled that "separate but equal" schools did not provide African American children with the same benefits as European American children. The Court's decision was influenced by research, most notably by Kenneth B. Clark and Mamie Phipps Clark, showing that segregated schools hurt the self-esteem of African American children, increased racial prejudice, and encouraged European Americans to view African Americans as inferior (Benjamin & Crouse, 2002). For example, a study by the Clarks found that African American children believed European American dolls were better than African American ones and preferred to play with European American ones (Clark & Clark, 1947). A published review of studies of self-concept in African American children revealed that research findings differ according to whether the research was conducted before or after the civil rights movement of the 1960s. Earlier studies reported that African Americans had lower self-esteem than European Americans; more recent studies conducted after the civil rights movement have found that this conclusion is no longer true (Twenge & Crocker, 2002).

Events during the past few decades have shown that social contact alone might not produce the effects predicted by Allport and the Supreme Court. For contact between groups to reduce prejudice, the contact must be between group members of equal status (Spangenberg & Nel, 1983). If the contact is between group members of unequal status, then prejudice may actually increase. The effectiveness of equal-status contact in

Reducing Prejudice

For contact between groups to reduce prejudice, the contact must be between group members of equal status.

Source: Monkey Business Images/Shutterstock.com.

reducing racial prejudice was supported by a study of African American and European American high school athletes. European American athletes who played team sports with African American teammates had more positive attitudes toward African Americans as a group than did European American athletes who played individual sports (Brown, Brown, Jackson, Sellers, & Manuel, 2003). Contact with members of an out-group can weaken stereotypes by increasing the perceived heterogeneity of that group (Lee & Ottati, 1993).

Another way to reduce prejudice is to promote intergroup cooperation (Desforges et al., 1991). Unfortunately, cooperative efforts do not always increase liking. If cooperative efforts fail, members of one group may attribute responsibility for this failure to members of the other group. And if cooperative efforts succeed, members of one group will attribute responsibility for the success to a favorable situation rather than giving any credit to members of the other group (Brewer & Kramer, 1985). Thus, in certain situations, members of a cooperating group will be caught in a no-win situation.

Section Review: Attitudes

1. What factors influence the consistency between attitudes and behaviors?

2. What factors determine whether the central route or the peripheral route will be more effective in persuasion?

3. What does research say about the effect of contact between in-group members and out-group members on prejudice?

Group Dynamics

In everyday life we refer to any collection of people as a "group." But social psychologists favor a narrower definition of a **group** as a collection of two or more persons who interact and have mutual influence. Examples of groups include a sorority, a softball team, and the board of trustees of your school. In the late 1940s, hoping to understand the social factors that contributed to the Great Depression, the rise of European dictatorships, and World War II, social psychologists became more interested in studying the factors that affect relationships between members of groups (Zander, 1979). Group dynamics remains an important area of research in social psychology and includes the topics of group decision making, group effects on performance, and social influence.

group A collection of two or more persons who interact and have mutual influence on each other.

Group Decision Making

As members of groups, we often are called on to make group decisions. A family must decide which new house to buy, a jury must agree upon a verdict, college administrators must decide which proposed new academic majors to approve, and government officials must decide on air pollution standards. Decisions made by groups are not simply the outcome of rational give-and-take, with the wisest decision automatically emerging. They are affected by other factors as well.

Group Decision Making

Decisions made by groups, such as juries, are not simply the outcome of rational give-and-take, with the wisest decision automatically emerging. They are affected by other factors as well.

Source: bikeriderlondon/ Shutterstock.com.

Group Polarization

In the 1950s, social critic William H. Whyte (1956) claimed that groups, notably those within business and government organizations, tended to make safe, compromise decisions instead of risky, extreme decisions. Whyte assumed that this tendency explained why organizations failed to be as creative and innovative as individuals. In the 1960s, his view was challenged by studies that found a tendency for group decisions to be riskier than decisions made by individuals who composed those groups (Stoner, 1961). This tendency became known as the risky shift (Wallach, Kogan, & Bem, 1962). But later research found that groups tend to make decisions in either a risky or cautious direction, rather than in

group polarization
The tendency for groups to make more extreme decisions than their members would make as individuals.

only a risky direction. The tendency for groups to make more extreme decisions than their individual members would make is called **group polarization**. For example, when groups of high school students either high or low in racial prejudice discussed racial issues, groups that were low in prejudice became even less prejudiced and groups that were high in prejudice became even more prejudiced (Myers & Bishop, 1970).

What accounts for group polarization? Persuasive-argumentation theory assumes that group members who initially hold a moderate position about an issue will move in the direction of the most persuasive arguments, which will eventually move the group toward either a risky or a cautious decision (Mongeau & Garlick, 1988). Simply repeating an attitude over and over will tend to polarize a group in that direction (Brauer, Judd, & Gliner, 1995).

Minority Influence

Does the majority always determine the outcome of group decision making? In general, the answer is yes. This tendency becomes stronger as the size of the majority increases relative to the size of the minority (Bassili, 2003). The majority has the power to convince group members to go along with its decision, in part because of its ability to criticize and ostracize those who dissent. Yet, under certain circumstances, minorities may influence group decisions.

If you are part of a minority and wish to influence group decisions, you should follow several well-established principles.

- You must present rational rather than emotional reasons for your position. That is, you must take the central rather than the peripheral route of persuasion to make the majority consider your position. If minority arguments are of relatively higher quality than majority arguments, the minority will be more likely to influence the majority (Gordijn, De Vries, & De Dreu, 2002).

- You must appear absolutely confident in your position, with no wavering at all. If you are unsure or apologetic about your position, majority members will discount it.

- You must be consistent in your position over time to make the majority wonder whether there might actually be something to what you're saying. Again, if you are inconsistent, your opponents will discredit you. In fact, a meta-analysis of 97 relevant research studies found that the ability of the minority to be consistent in its position is an especially powerful factor in minority influence (Wood, Lundgren, Ouellette, & Busceme, 1994).

- Try to bring at least one other person over to your side (Clark, 2001). A minority of two is much more credible and influential than a minority of one. Each of the two will embolden and give credibility to the other.

- You must be patient. Though majorities may initially dismiss minority positions, the passage of time might make them privately ponder the evidence you have provided and gradually change their positions (Nemeth, 1986).

Groupthink

On January 28, 1986, the space shuttle *Challenger* exploded shortly after taking off from Cape Canaveral, Florida, killing the crew and shocking the millions of television viewers excited by the presence of the first teacher-astronaut, Christa McAuliffe. The committee that investigated this tragedy reported that the explosion was caused by a faulty joint seal in one of the rocket boosters. The decision to launch the shuttle had been made despite warnings from engineers that the joint might fail in cold weather. This ill-fated decision has been attributed to groupthink, which in this case put safety second to currying favor with the public and Congress (Moorhead, Ference, & Neck, 1991).

groupthink The tendency of small, cohesive groups to place unanimity ahead of critical thinking in making decisions.

The term **groupthink,** coined by psychologist Irving Janis (1918–1990), refers to a decision-making process in small, cohesive groups that places unanimity ahead of critical thinking and aims at premature consensus (Kerr & Tindale, 2004). Notice that groupthink is a form of group polarization. Groupthink is promoted by several factors: a charismatic leader, feelings of invulnerability, discrediting of contrary evidence, fear of criticism for disagreeing, the desire to maintain group harmony, isolation from outside influences, and disparaging outsiders as incompetent. A central factor in groupthink is a shared overestimate of the group's capabilities (Whyte, 1998). In criticizing the decision to launch the *Challenger,* Senator John Glenn of Ohio, the first American to orbit Earth, referred to feelings of invulnerability among the officials who made the decision: "The mindset of a few people in key positions at NASA had changed from an optimistic and supersafety conscious 'can do' attitude, when I was in the program, to an arrogant 'can't fail' attitude" (Zaldivar, 1986, p. 12-A). This change in attitudes was unfortunate because having dissenting views promotes consideration of alternatives (Nemeth, Connell, Rogers, & Brown,, 2001).

Janis's concept of groupthink has received support from experimental studies on group decision making. Groups with directive leaders consider fewer alternatives than do groups with leaders who encourage member participation, especially if the leader expresses her or his opinion early in deliberation (Leana, 1985). Group cohesiveness also has an effect. A meta-analysis of the effect of group cohesiveness on decision making found that if other conditions conducive to groupthink are present, group cohesiveness will promote groupthink; if those conditions are not present, cohesiveness actually will improve decision making (Mullen, Anthony, Salas, & Driskell, 1994). Of course, the groupthink phenomenon does not always occur during group decision making, and when it does occur, it does not always produce negative outcomes (Aldag & Fuller, 1993; Choi & Kim, 1999). Though the concept of groupthink seems convincing, evidence for it has come primarily from after-the-fact interpretations of well-known, misguided group decisions. In fact, there has been relatively little support for the groupthink phenomenon from experimental research (Park, 2000). More experimental research is needed to determine whether groupthink is a robust phenomenon and, if it does exist, to identify the factors that account for it.

Group Effects on Performance

One of the first topics to be studied by social psychologists was the influence of groups on the task performances of their members. Social psychologists have been especially interested in studying the effects of social facilitation and social loafing on performance.

Social Facilitation

As described at the beginning of the chapter, more than a century ago Norman Triplett (1898) observed that people performed faster when competing against other people than when competing against a clock. Two decades later Floyd Allport (1920) found that people performed a variety of tasks better when working in the same room than when working in separate rooms. Allport used the term **social facilitation** to describe the improvement in performance caused by the presence of other people.

But later studies found that the presence of others sometimes may impair performance. A review of 241 studies involving almost 24,000 participants found that the presence of other people improves performance on simple or well-learned tasks and impairs performance on complex or poorly learned tasks (Bond & Titus, 1983). For example, in one study, children tried to balance on a teeterboard for as long as possible. Children who were highly skilled performed better in the presence of others; children who were poorly skilled performed better when alone (MacCracken & Stadulis, 1985). Even college students learning to use personal computers may perform better when working alone than when working in the presence of an instructor (Schneider & Shugar, 1990).

What would account for these findings? The most influential explanation for both social facilitation and social inhibition is the drive theory of Robert Zajonc (1965), which was derived from a motivational theory put forth by Clark Hull (1943). According to Zajonc, the presence of other people increases physiological arousal, which energizes the performer's most likely responses to a task. For those who are good at a task, the most likely responses will be effective ones. Consequently, those people will perform better in the presence of others. In contrast, for those who are not good at a task, the most well-learned responses will be ineffective ones. Consequently, those people will perform worse in the presence of others.

social facilitation The effect of the presence of other people on a person's task performance, with performance on simple or well-learned tasks improved and performance on complex or poorly learned tasks impaired.

Social Facilitation

Cyclists ride faster when they are competing with others than when they are competing against the clock.
Source: Corepics VOF/ Shutterstock.com.

Social Loafing

Because of social loafing, these children will probably exert less individual effort than they would if they pulled by themselves.

Source: Diego Cervo/ Shutterstock.com.

social loafing A decrease in the individual effort exerted by group members when working together on a task.

conformity Behaving in accordance with group expectations with little or no overt pressure to do so.

Our drive level may increase in the presence of others because of evaluation apprehension. Consider a field study in which male and female runners were timed (without their being aware of it) as they ran along a 90-yard segment of a footpath. One-third of the participants ran alone, one-third encountered a woman facing them at the halfway point, and one-third encountered a woman seated with her back to them at the halfway point. Only the group who encountered a woman facing them (putting her in a position to evaluate them) showed a significant acceleration between the first and second halves of the segment (Worringham & Messick, 1983).

Social Loafing

Social facilitation is concerned with the effects of others on individual performance. But what of the effect of working in a group that has a common goal? In the 1880s, a French agricultural engineer named Max Ringelmann found that people exerted less effort when working in groups than when working alone. He had men pull on a rope attached to a meter that measured the strength of their pull. As the number of men pulling increased from one to eight, the average strength of each man's pull decreased. Ringelmann attributed this decrease to a loss of coordination when working with other people, a phenomenon that became known as the Ringelmann effect (Kravitz & Martin, 1986). His study has been replicated in other countries, including Japan (Kugihara, 1999) and Canada (Lichacz & Partington, 1996), but the effect diminishes markedly beyond a group size of three (Ingham, Levinger, Graves, & Peckham, 1974).

More recently, the Ringelmann effect has been attributed to a decrease in the effort exerted by individuals when working together, a phenomenon known as **social loafing**. This phenomenon supports the old saying "Many hands make light the work." In one experiment, high school cheerleaders cheered either alone or in pairs. Sound-level recordings found that individual cheerleaders cheered louder when alone than when cheering with a partner (Hardy & Latané, 1988). Social loafing has been demonstrated in sports such as elite rowing (Anshel, 1995) and high school swimming (Miles & Greenberg, 1993). A meta-analysis of 78 studies found that social loafing has been demonstrated across many different cultures, though it is more common in individualistic cultures such as Canada and the United States (Karau & Williams, 1993).

According to the concept of diffusion of responsibility, social loafing occurs when group members feel anonymous; believing that their individual performance will not be evaluated, they are less motivated to exert their maximum effort. Because of this lack of evaluation apprehension, group members often overestimate their contribution to the group's performance (Forsyth, Zyzniewski, & Giammanco, 2002). Ways to reduce social loafing include convincing group members that they will be held accountable (Weldon & Gargano, 1988), that their individual efforts will be evaluated (Hoeksema-van Orden, Gaillard, & Buunk, 1998), or that their individual effort will contribute to the group's performance (Shepperd & Taylor, 1999). Social loafing also can be overcome when a task is important to an individual and that person believes other group members lack the ability to perform better (Plaks & Higgins, 2000).

Social Influence

The groups we belong to influence our behavior in ways that range from subtle prodding to direct demands. We are influenced by police, bosses, clergy, parents, spouses, teachers, physicians, advertisers, politicians, salespersons, and a host of other people. Their influence is sometimes negative but often is positive, as, for example, in the case of exercise adherence. The influence of others tends to make us more likely to maintain a program of regular exercise (Carron, Hausenblas, & Mack, 1996). Among the most important kinds of social influence are conformity, compliance, and obedience.

Conformity

Do you dress the way you do because your friends dress that way? Do you hold certain religious beliefs because your parents hold them? If you answered yes to these questions, you would be exhibiting **conformity**, which means behaving in accordance with real or imagined group pressure. For example, a study of more than 100 men and 100 women found that people eating in a cafeteria were more likely to select a dessert if a dining companion did so (Guarino, Fridrich, & Sitton, 1994). And of greater importance, we are more likely to refuse to enter a vehicle with a drunk driver if a companion refuses than if the companion enters the vehicle (Powell & Drucker, 1997).

The power of conformity was demonstrated in a classic series of experiments conducted by psychologist Solomon Asch (1907–1996) in the 1950s. These experiments showed that even visual perception, something we take for granted, may be influenced by the social context (Gleitman, Rozin, & Sabini, 1997). In a typical experiment, a male college student who had volunteered to be a research participant was told that he would be taking part in a study of visual perception. He was seated at a table with six other "participants," who were actually the experimenter's confederates. As illustrated in Figure 17-4, the experimenter presented a series of trials in which he displayed two large white cards. One card contained three vertical lines of different lengths. The second card contained a single vertical line clearly equal in length to one of the three lines on the first card. On each of 18 trials, the participants were asked, one person at a time, to choose the line on the first card that was the same length as the line on the second card. The lengths of the lines varied from trial to trial. On the first 2 trials, each confederate chose the correct line. But on the 3rd trial, and on 11 of the succeeding trials, the confederates chose a line that was clearly not the same length as the single line.

On the first few bogus trials, the participant appeared uncomfortable but usually chose the correct line. Yet, over the course of the 12 bogus trials, the participant sometimes conformed to the erroneous choices made by the confederates. The results indicated that, overall, participants conformed on 37 percent of the bogus trials. Three-quarters of the participants conformed on at least one bogus trial. In other versions of the experiment, Asch varied the number of confederates from 1 to 15 persons. He found that the participants' tendency to conform increased dramatically until there were three confederates, with additional confederates inducing smaller increases in conformity (Asch, 1955).

Though some attempts to replicate Asch's study have failed (Lalancette & Standing, 1990), his research has been successfully replicated in different cultures, including studies using American (Larsen, 1990), Dutch (Vlaander & Van Rooijen, 1985), Kuwaiti (Amir, 1984), British (Nicholson, Cole, & Rocklin, 1985), and Australian (Walker & Andrade, 1996) participants. But a meta-analysis of 133 studies from 17 countries that used Asch's line-judgment task found that conformity has declined since the 1950s. And collectivist countries tended to show greater conformity than did individualistic countries (Bond & Smith, 1996). For example, Chinese college students tend to be more conforming than American college students (Zhang & Thomas, 1994).

These differences may be attributable to different cultural values related to uniqueness. In a series of experiments, East Asian and European American participants' preferences were assessed in a number of domains. In one version of the experiment, for example, participants were asked to select a ballpoint pen as a gift from a collection of five pens.

Standard line

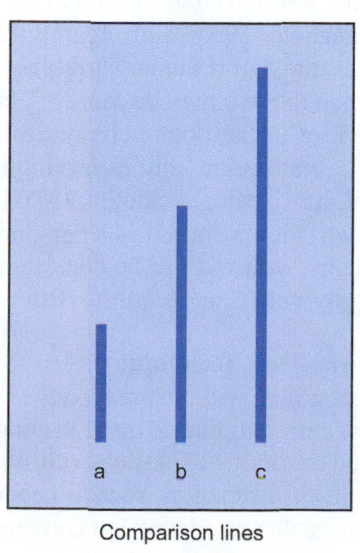
a   b   c
Comparison lines

FIGURE 17-4
The Asch Study

Participants in one of Solomon Asch's studies had to decide which of three lines was equal in length to another line.

At least one of the five pens was a different color from the rest of the group. Participants' choices were coded for uniqueness if they chose one of the pens that was different from the rest of the pens in the group. Participants' choices were coded for conformity if they chose one of the pens that did not differ from the rest of the group. European Americans were more likely to choose the unique pen, whereas East Asians were more likely to choose a pen that did not differ from the group (Kim & Markus, 1999).

In Asch's study, why did the participants conform to the obviously erroneous judgments of strangers? A few claimed that they really saw the lines as equal, and others assumed that the confederates knew something they did not. But their main reason for conforming was their need for social approval—they feared social rejection. Participants found, as do many people, that it is difficult to be the lone dissenter in a group. In variations of the experiment in which one of the confederates joined the participant in dissenting, participants conformed on less than one-tenth, rather than on one-third, of the bogus trials (Asch, 1955). Thus, like one of the principles mentioned for minority influence, dissent is more likely when we have fellow dissenters.

Compliance

We are continually bombarded with requests. A friend might want to borrow your car. A professor might ask you to help move laboratory equipment. An advertiser might urge you to purchase a particular deodorant. The process by which a person agrees to a request that is backed by little or no threat of punishment is called **compliance**. As discussed in Chapter 16, compliance often is lifesaving when it comes to medical regimens, dieting, and exercise. Two of the major means of inducing compliance are the foot-in-the-door technique and the door-in-the-face technique.

The Foot-in-the-Door Technique   Years ago, it was common for salespersons to go door-to-door trying to sell encyclopedias, vacuum cleaners, or other products. Every salesperson knew that a person who complied with the small request to be permitted inside to discuss or demonstrate a product would then be more likely to comply with the larger request to purchase the product. This phenomenon became known as the **foot-in-the-door technique** (Dillard, 1991).

This technique can produce extraordinary degrees of compliance. In one study, women were surveyed by telephone about the brand of soap they used. Three days later they were called again, as were a group of similar women who had not received the first call. This time the caller asked each woman for permission to send a team of men who would rummage through her cabinets to record the household items that she used. Of those who had complied with the first (small) request, 53 percent agreed to permit a team to visit their home. Of those who received only the second (large) request, just 22 percent agreed to permit a team to visit their home (Freedman & Fraser, 1966). The foot-in-the-door technique has proved so effective that it has even been used to encourage gynecological cancer check-ups (Dolin & Booth-Butterfield, 1995) and organ donations (Girandola, 2002). But the foot-in-the-door technique may fail if the larger request follows immediately after the smaller request. A delay between the two may be more effective (Chartrand, Pinckert, & Burger, 1999).

Why is the foot-in-the-door technique effective? Self-perception theory, which assumes that we infer our attitudes from observing our own behavior, provides an answer (Eisenberg, Cialdini, McCreath, & Shell, 1987). If you freely comply with a small, worthwhile request, you will view yourself as a person who has a positive attitude toward worthwhile requests. Because you wish to be consistent with your self-perception, you will be more likely to comply with other requests (Burger & Guadagno, 2003).

The Door-in-the-Face Technique   Salespeople also know that customers who refuse to purchase a particular item will be more likely to comply with a request to purchase a less expensive item. Fostering compliance by presenting a smaller request after a larger request has been denied is called the **door-in-the-face technique** (Dillard, 1991). We resort to this technique in our everyday lives in situations such as negotiating salaries (perhaps asking for several thousand dollars more than we expect) or convincing professors to give us extra time to complete

compliance Behaving in accordance with a request that is backed by little or no threat of punishment.

foot-in-the-door technique Increasing the likelihood that a person will comply with a request by first getting the person to comply with a smaller one.

Foot-in-the-Door Technique

Salespeople know that a person who complied with the small request to be permitted inside to discuss or demonstrate a product would then be more likely to comply with the larger request to purchase the product.

Source: Jaimie Duplass/Shutterstock.com.

door-in-the-face technique Increasing the likelihood that a person will comply with a request by first getting the person to reject a larger one.

term papers (boldly asking for an extra week when we would gladly settle for two extra days). Even charities use the technique. In one study, potential volunteers were asked to commit themselves to serve as a Big Brother or Big Sister at a juvenile detention center for 2 hours a week for 2 years. After they all rejected this large request, they were subjected to a much smaller request—to chaperone a group of low-income children on a single 2-hour visit to a zoo. Participants were significantly more likely to comply with this request than were those who had not been asked earlier to serve as a Big Brother or Big Sister (Cialdini et al., 1975).

The door-in-the-face technique depends on social norms that require that concessions offered by one negotiating party be met by concessions from the other party. The willingness of one person to reduce the size of an initial request would be a concession, imposing social pressure on the person who had refused the first request to comply with the second one (Cann, Sherman, & Elkes, 1975). Another explanation for the effectiveness of the foot-in-the-door technique assumes that the recipient complies with the second request to reduce guilt at refusing the first request (Millar, 2002). The foot-in-the door technique generally is more effective than the door-in-the-face technique (Fern, Monroe, & Avila, 1986).

Obedience

Would you assist in the cold-blooded murder of innocent people if your superior ordered you to? This question deals with the limits of **obedience**—the following of orders given by an authority. The limits of obedience were at the heart of the Nuremberg war crime trials held after World War II. The defendants were Nazis accused of crimes against humanity for their complicity in the executions of millions of innocent people during World War II, most notably the genocide of 6 million Jews. The defendants claimed that they were only following orders. In his journal Adolf Eichmann, who personally oversaw the deportation and murder of millions of Jews as a high-ranking Nazi official, described his role in the genocide as "the same as millions of others who had to obey" (Trounson, 2000, p. A1). The surprising extent to which people will obey orders to harm others was demonstrated in the classic study discussed in "The Research Process" box.

obedience Following orders given by an authority.

The Research Process

Would You Harm Someone Just Because an Authority Figure Ordered You To?

Rationale

Are people who obey orders to hurt innocent people unusually cruel, or are most human beings susceptible to obeying such orders? This question led psychologist Stanley Milgram (1933–1984) of Yale University to conduct perhaps the most famous—and controversial—of all psychology experiments (Milgram, 1963).

Method

Milgram's participants were adult men who had responded to an advertisement for volunteers to participate in a study of the effects of punishment on learning. On arriving at the laboratory, each participant was introduced to a pleasant, middle-aged man who also would participate in the experiment. In reality, the man was a confederate of the experimenter. The experimenter asked both men to draw a slip of paper out of a hat to determine who would be the "teacher" and who would be the "learner."

The drawing was rigged so that the participant was always the teacher. The teacher communicated with the learner over an intercom as the learner performed a memory task while strapped to an electrified chair in another room. The teacher sat at a control panel with a series of switches with labels ranging from "Slight Shock"(15 volts) to "Danger: Severe Shock" (450 volts) in 15-volt increments. The experimenter instructed the participant to administer an increasingly strong electric shock to the learner's hand whenever he made an error. At higher shock levels, the learner cried out in pain or begged the teacher to stop. Many participants responded to the learner's distress with sweating, trembling, and stuttering. If the participant hesitated to administer a shock, the experimenter might say, "You have no other choice, you must go on," and remind the teacher that he, the experimenter, was responsible for any ill effects. Note the similarity between this incremental approach and the foot-in-the-door technique (Gilbert, 1981).

continued

Would You Harm Someone Just Because an Authority Figure Ordered You To? *continued*

Results and Discussion

How far do you think you would have gone as the teacher in Milgram's study? Surveys of psychiatrists and Yale students had predicted that less than 2 percent of the participants would reach the maximum level. To Milgram's surprise, two-thirds of the participants reached the maximum level of shock, and none stopped before reaching 300 volts—the point at which the learner frantically banged on the wall and stopped answering questions. (By the way, the learner never received a shock. In fact, his "responses" were played on a tape recorder.)

Could the prestige of Yale University and the apparent legitimacy of a laboratory study have affected the participants? Milgram replicated the study in a run-down

office building in Bridgeport, Connecticut. The experimenter did not wear a laboratory coat, and he made no reference to Yale. He obtained impressive results nonetheless. Of those who participated, 48 percent reached the maximum level of shock. Would physically separating the teacher and the learner have an effect? Somewhat. When the participant sat near the learner, 40 percent reached the maximum. Even when the participant had to force the learner's hand onto a shock grid, 30 percent still reached the maximum (Milgram, 1974). No gender differences in obedience have been found in studies comparing male and female participants (Blass, 1999). Figure 17-5 shows how the results were affected by different experimental conditions. Milgram's original experiment also has been successfully replicated in other countries, which indicates that obedience to authority is common across cultures (Shanab & Yahya, 1977).

Milgram's research has disturbing implications. The line that separates us from war criminals may be thinner than we would like to believe. Many of us, given orders by someone we consider to be a legitimate authority and who we assume will be responsible for our actions, might be willing to harm an innocent person. Despite the insight that Milgram's research provided into the nature of obedience, it provoked criticism, most notably from Diana Baumrind (1964). She claimed that Milgram's use of deception increased distrust of psychological researchers and that his participants' self-esteem was damaged by the realization that they might harm an innocent person simply because an authority figure ordered them to.

In response to these criticisms, Milgram reported that 84 percent of the participants in his study were debriefed, that participants were glad they had participated, that there was no evidence that any of them developed long-term emotional distress, and that the importance of the findings made the use of deception worthwhile (Milgram, 1964). Given today's increased concern with the rights of research participants, partly in response to studies like Milgram's, it is unlikely that any researchers would replicate his studies. Milgram's research still sparks interest today, particularly in regard to people who disobey despite threats to their life and well-being—such as those who smuggled slaves out of Southern states via the underground railroad in the mid-19th century. One lesson is that those who resist early are more likely to maintain their defiance. For example, a reanalysis of audio recordings of participants in one of Milgram's replications of his original study found that the sooner participants resisted, the more likely they were to become defiant and refuse to give any more shocks (Modigliani & Rochat, 1995).

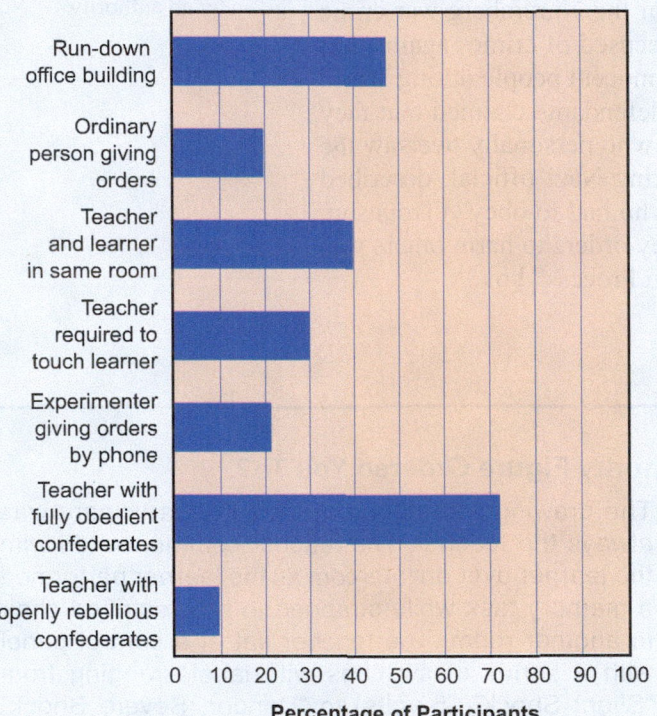

Percentage of Participants
Who Fully Obeyed Experimenter

FIGURE 17-5

Variables That Affect Obedience to Authority

In his series of classic experiments, Stanley Milgram varied the location of the experiment, the proximity of the teacher to the learner and the experimenter, and the presence of confederates.

Source: Data from S. Milgram, *Obedience to Authority: An Experimental View,* Harper and Row, Publishers, Inc., 1974; and S. Milgram, *The Individual in a Social World: Essays and Experiments,* Addison-Wesley Publishing Company, 1992.

Aggression

As much as people are capable of prosocial behavior, they are, unfortunately, just as capable of antisocial behavior. The most extreme form of antisocial behavior is **aggression**, which is verbal or physical behavior aimed at causing harm to another person. What accounts for the prevalence of aggression?

aggression Verbal or physical behavior aimed at harming another person.

Theories of Aggression

One class of theories views aggression as the product of physiology. A second class of theories views aggression as the product of experience. Obviously, both are important, including their interaction.

Aggression as the Product of Physiology

The earliest theories of aggression claimed that it was instinctive. An instinct is an inborn tendency, unaffected by learning, to engage in a relatively complex behavior that characterizes members of a species—such as nest building in birds. After observing the extraordinary violence of World War I, Sigmund Freud concluded that human aggression is caused by an instinct that he called Thanatos (Greek for "death"). According to Freud, Thanatos causes a buildup of aggressive energy, which must be released periodically through a process called catharsis. This release would prevent outbursts of extreme violence. You might experience catharsis by playing football, field hockey, or another aggressive sport.

Nobel-Prize–winning ethologist Konrad Lorenz (1966) agreed with Freud that we have an instinct for aggression. He claimed that all animals have a powerful aggressive drive that, like the sex drive, promotes the survival of their species. But because animals have evolved natural weapons such as fangs and claws that can kill, they also have evolved ritualistic behaviors to inhibit aggression and prevent unnecessary injuries and deaths. In contrast, because people have not evolved natural weapons that can kill, they have not evolved ritualistic behaviors to inhibit aggression against their own species. As a consequence, people are less inhibited in using artificial weapons such as clubs, spears, guns, and missiles against one another. Lorenz, like Freud, believed that outbursts of aggression could be avoided only by providing outlets for the cathartic release of aggressive energy through means such as sports (Leakey & Lewin, 1977). But research has failed to support the belief that aggression can be reduced through catharsis. In fact, participants who hit a punching bag while thinking about a person who angered them were more angry and more aggressive than participants who distracted themselves or did nothing at all (Bushman, 2002).

Evolutionary psychologists assume that there is a strong hereditary basis for aggression and other social behaviors (Buss, 1999). Twin studies have provided evidence supporting this hypothesis. Psychologists who study twins might compare the aggressiveness of identical twins reared together to the aggressiveness of fraternal twins reared together. These researchers assume that if heredity plays a role in aggression, identical twins (who are genetically identical) will be more similar in aggressiveness than will fraternal twins (who are no more

Catharsis and Violence

According to Freud, both the participants and the spectators of a violent sport, such as boxing or wrestling, should show a decrease in their tendencies toward violence as the result of catharsis. But research has found that, on the contrary, watching or taking part in violence will increase one's tendency to engage in it.
Source: Ersler Dmitry/Shutterstock.com.

frustration-aggression hypothesis The assumption that frustration causes aggression.

alike genetically than ordinary siblings). Twin studies have, indeed, found this correlation, providing evidence for the hereditary basis of aggressiveness (Beatty, Heisel, Hall, Levine, & LaFrance, 2002). Of course, this finding does not rule out the possibility that identical twins are more similar in aggressiveness because they are treated more alike than fraternal twins are.

What might be the physiological means by which heredity affects aggression? Several brain structures play important roles, particularly the left frontal cortex (Hortensius, Schutter, & Harmon-Jones, 2012) and structures in the limbic system, including the amygdala (Gopal et al., 2013) and the hypothalamus (Haller, 2013). A review of brain-imaging studies using CT, MRI, and PET scans found a relationship between frontal lobe abnormalities and aggressiveness (Mills & Raine, 1994). Another factor is the role of the hormones cortisol and especially testosterone (Montoya, Terburg, Bos, & van Honk, 2012). Violent criminals have higher levels of testosterone than do nonviolent criminals (Rubin, Reinisch, & Haskett, 1981). Athletes who use anabolic steroids, which are synthetic derivatives of testosterone, become more anxious and aggressive (Oberlander & Henderson, 2012). Testosterone levels are positively correlated with self-reported verbal and physical aggression in women (von der Pahlen, Lindman, Sarkola, Maekisalo, & Eriksson, 2002). The combination of psychotherapy and the administration of medications that lower testosterone levels may reduce sex-crime recidivism (Turner, Basdeskis-Jozsa, & Briken, 2013). And transgender individuals, who undergo testosterone treatment during female-to-male sex reassignment, report experiencing more aggression after starting hormone treatment (Slabbekoorn, Van Goozen, Gooren, & Cohen-Kettenis, 2001).

But some research has failed to find a relationship between testosterone levels and aggression. A recent meta-analysis found a weak positive relationship between increased testosterone levels and increased likelihood of aggression in humans (Book, Starzyk, & Quinsey, 2001). Other studies have found that men who receive testosterone injections may become more aggressive because of an expectancy effect—they act more aggressively simply because they believe they have received testosterone (Bjorkqvist, Nygren, Bjorklund, & Bjorkqvist, 1994). These negative findings have led some researchers to study the effect of experience on aggression (Albert, Walsh, & Jonik, 1993).

Aggression as the Product of Experience

Whereas some researchers look to hereditary factors, most look to life experiences as the main determinants of aggression. In the late 1930s, a team of behaviorists concluded that aggression is caused by frustration (Dollard, Doob, Miller, Mowrer, & Sears, 1939). This hypothesis became known as the **frustration-aggression hypothesis**. We experience frustration when we are blocked from reaching a goal. But the frustration-aggression hypothesis is an inadequate explanation of aggression because experiences other than frustration can cause aggression and because frustration does not always lead to aggression.

The inadequacies of the frustration-aggression hypothesis inspired psychologist Leonard Berkowitz to develop the revised frustration-aggression hypothesis. According to Berkowitz (1974), frustration does not directly provoke aggression. Instead, it directly provokes anger or another unpleasant emotion, such as anxiety or depression. The unpleasant emotion, in turn, will provoke aggression—particularly when stimuli (such as guns) that have been associated with aggression are present. Berkowitz demonstrated his hypothesis in a study in which male college students gave electric shocks to other students to induce feelings of anger in the shock recipients. When students who had received shocks were given the opportunity to give shocks to those who had shocked them, they gave more shocks when an aggressive stimulus such as a revolver, rather than a neutral stimulus such as a badminton racket, was left on the table (Berkowitz & LePage, 1967). Though some studies have failed to support the revised frustration-aggression hypothesis (Buss, Booker, & Buss, 1972), many have found that anger in the presence of aggressive stimuli does tend to provoke aggression (Rule & Nesdale, 1976). Moreover, unexpected frustrations, because they evoke stronger unpleasant emotions, are more likely to provoke aggression than are expected frustrations (Berkowitz, 1989). For example, one study found that participants who lost in a competitive video game demonstrated increased negative affect and aggression (Breuer, Scharkow, & Quandt, 2013).

As described in Chapter 7, much of our behavior is the product of social learning—learning by observing the behavior of others. Aggression is no exception to this rule.

We may learn to be aggressive by observing people who act aggressively. For example, women who observed their parents being aggressive are more likely to become aggressive themselves (White & Humphrey, 1994). And, as you read in Chapter 4, one explanation for the gender difference in aggression is gender-role socialization. However, many of the laboratory studies of aggression have relied on male samples and operational definitions of aggression based on physical aggression—like the application of electric shock to a stranger. When other measures of aggression are studied, levels of aggression observed among women and girls rise dramatically. In an extensive review of the literature, Jacquelyn White and Robin Kowalski (1994) found that gender differences in aggressive behavior reflect the social structure of women's and men's lives. For example, women are more likely to be verbally aggressive or sexually coercive within intimate relationships. In contrast, men are far more likely to be physically aggressive and to assault strangers in public places (Graham & Wells, 2001). Moreover, this gender difference is evident in childhood—across cultures. A cross-cultural study of American and Indonesian children aged 11 to 14 years found that boys were more likely to be engaged in physical aggression whereas girls were more likely to be engaged in relational aggression involving the spread of malicious rumors, the manipulation of relationships, or social ostracism (French, Jansen, & Pidada, 2002).

Group Violence

In the year A.D. 59, opposing fans rioted at the Pompeii amphitheater during a gladiatorial contest, prompting the Roman Senate to ban such contests in Pompeii for 10 years. Contemporary society also has seen its share of riots at athletic events. In June 2000, hundreds of basketball fans spilled into the streets the night that the Los Angeles Lakers won the NBA playoff, torching or destroying more than half a dozen vehicles—including police cars and an MTA bus. Within an hour, the crowd had grown to more than 6,000. Police eventually fired rubber bullets into the crowd in an attempt to regain control. The riot was finally quelled almost two hours later (Hall & Briggs, 2000). Group violence also can arise under more mundane circumstances. Less than 2 weeks before the riot in Los Angeles, sexual violence erupted in Central Park, New York, following a local parade. Roving groups of men sexually assaulted at least 24 women by spraying them with water, stripping off their clothes, and fondling and molesting them (Getlin, 2000).

Deindividuation

Deindividuation might lead to violence when people in large groups experience anonymity. *Source:* Pablo77/Shutterstock.com.

What makes normally peaceful individuals become violent when they are in groups? We are usually aware of our own thoughts, feelings, and perceptions and are concerned about being socially evaluated. But when in groups, we may become less aware of ourselves and less concerned about being socially evaluated. Leon Festinger named this process **deindividuation** (Festinger, Pepitone, & Newcomb, 1952). As the result of deindividuation, our behavior might no longer be governed by our social norms, which in turn can lead to the loss of normal restraints against undesirable behavior, making us more likely to conform to the behavior of the group (Postmes, Spears, Sakhel, & de Groot, 2001). Moreover, the anonymity provided by group membership can make us less concerned with how others are evaluating our behavior because we feel less accountable for our own actions (Prentice-Dunn & Rogers, 1982).

deindividuation The process by which group members become less aware of themselves as individuals and less concerned about being socially evaluated.

Even aggression by individuals who are not in groups is more likely when they feel anonymous. An experiment found that people driving convertibles with their tops up (high anonymity) will be more likely to honk their horns at cars that fail to proceed immediately at green lights than will people driving convertibles with their tops down (low anonymity). Those with tops up honk quicker, longer, and more frequently (Ellison, Govern, Petri, & Figler, 1995).

Deindividuation is most likely when the group is large and when the group members feel anonymous, have reduced self-awareness, and are emotionally aroused. These factors mean that large groups of people wearing masks, uniforms, or disguises and aroused by drugs, dancing, chanting, or oratory will be more likely to engage in violence. Disguised offenders engage in more acts of violence and vandalism than do nondisguised offenders (Silke, 2003). Despite theoretical support for deindividuation, research findings are far from convincing in supporting the existence of such a state of consciousness (Postmes & Spears, 1998).

Is This Altruism?

This woman is providing first aid by applying a thermal blanket over the victim. Her actions could be explained by two perspectives. Some researchers have found that prosocial behavior associated with feelings of empathy is truly altruistic, whereas prosocial behavior associated with the desire to relieve one's own distress is not.
Source: Halfpoint/Shutterstock.com.

prosocial behavior Behavior that helps others in need.

altruism The helping of others without the expectation of a reward.

negative state relief theory The theory that we engage in prosocial behavior to relieve our own state of emotional distress at another's plight.

1. What evidence is there for the role of testosterone in aggression?
2. What is the role of deindividuation in aggression?

Prosocial Behavior

On a spring day in 1986, 1-year-old Jennifer Kroll of West Chicago, Illinois, fell into her family's swimming pool. Jennifer's mother, after pulling Jennifer out of the pool and discovering that she was not breathing, ran outside and began screaming for help. Her screams were heard by James Patridge, who had been confined to a wheelchair since losing his legs in a land-mine explosion during the Vietnam War. Patridge responded by rolling his wheelchair toward the pool, until he encountered heavy brush, forcing him to crawl the final 20 yards. Patridge revived Jennifer by using cardiopulmonary resuscitation ("God's Hand," 1986). Patridge's heroic act led to offers of financial rewards, which he declined to accept, saying that saving Jennifer's life was reward enough.

Altruism

Patridge's act is an example of **prosocial behavior**—helping others in need. His behavior also is an example of **altruism**—helping others without the expectation of a reward in return. But are altruistic acts ever truly selfless? Perhaps people who engage in apparently altruistic behaviors do receive some kind of immaterial rewards. The most famous person to make this claim was Abraham Lincoln. During a train trip, Lincoln looked out his window and saw several piglets drowning. He ordered the train to stop so they could be saved. When praised for his action, Lincoln discounted altruism as his motive, claiming instead that his act was motivated by the selfish desire to avoid a guilty conscience (Batson et al., 1986).

Social psychologists interested in the study of altruism have been especially concerned with empathy, the ability to feel the emotions that someone else feels. Some researchers have found that prosocial behavior associated with feelings of empathy is truly altruistic (Batson, Bolen, Cross, & Neuringer-Benefiel, 1999), whereas prosocial behavior associated with the desire to relieve one's own distress is not (Maner et al., 2002). Research studies on the role of empathy in prosocial behavior have provided contradictory findings. In one study, participants completed a questionnaire that measured their level of sadness and their level of empathy for a person in need. Participants then were given the opportunity to help the person. The results indicated that the participants' willingness to help was related more to their sadness score than to their empathy score, indicating that they acted more out of a desire to reduce their own distress than out of a desire to reduce the distress of the other person. In fact, when the participants were given a "mood-fixing" placebo that allegedly (but not actually) made it impossible for them to alter their moods, fewer participants were willing to help, even when they had high empathy scores (Cialdini et al., 1987). This study provided support for the **negative state relief theory** of prosocial behavior of Robert Cialdini (Schaller & Cialdini, 1988).

But what about people whose prosocial behavior is associated with helpers' feelings of both distress and empathy? In an experiment, participants were empathetically aroused and led to anticipate an imminent mood-enhancing experience. The experimenters reasoned that if the motivation to help was directed toward the goal of negative state relief, then empathetically aroused individuals who anticipate mood enhancement should help less than those who do not. The rate of helping among high-empathy participants was no lower when they anticipated mood enhancement than when they did not. Regardless of anticipated mood enhancement, high-empathy participants helped more than low-empathy participants did. The results supported the empathy-altruism hypothesis (Batson et al., 1989). Reviews of relevant research have produced inconsistent findings in regard to the existence of altruistic helping (Carlson &

Miller, 1987; Cialdini & Fultz, 1990). So it still is unclear whether prosocial behavior is motivated more by empathy for others or by the desire to relieve one's own negative emotional states.

Bystander Intervention

Regardless of his motivation, James Patridge's rescue of Jennifer was an example of **bystander intervention,** the act of helping someone who is in immediate need of aid. Interest in the study of bystander intervention was stimulated by a widely publicized tragedy in which bystanders failed to help save a woman's life. At 3:20 A.M. on March 13, 1964, a 28-year-old woman named Kitty Genovese was returning home from her job as a bar manager. As she walked to her apartment building in the New York City borough of Queens, she was attacked by a mugger who repeatedly stabbed her. Thirty-eight of her neighbors reported that they had been awakened by her screams and had rushed to look out their windows but had not seen the attack. The assailant left twice, returning each time to continue his attack until, 30 minutes after her ordeal had begun, Kitty Genovese died.

How would you have responded had you been one of her neighbors? The neighbors' responses might surprise you. At no time during these three separate attacks did any of the 38 persons try to help Kitty Genovese or even call the police. When questioned by police and reporters, the witnesses gave a variety of explanations for why they had not called the police. Their reasons included feeling tired, assuming it was a lovers' quarrel, and believing that "it can't happen here" (Gansberg, 1964). The murder of Kitty Genovese gained national attention, and the apparent apathy of her neighbors was taken as a sign of the callous, impersonal nature of the residents of big cities.

But social psychologists John Darley and Bibb Latané rejected this commonsense explanation as too simplistic. Instead, they conducted research studies to determine the factors that affect the willingness of bystanders to intervene in emergencies. This intervention is as important today as it was when Kitty Genovese was murdered. In fact, a survey of more than 500 undergraduates and faculty members found that only 25 percent of those who had witnessed children being abused in public had ever intervened to help (Christy & Voight, 1994). Darley and Latané found that bystander intervention involves a series of steps, which are presented in Figure 17-6. The intervention process may continue through each of these steps or be halted at any one.

Noticing the Victim

To intervene in an emergency, you must first notice the event or the victim. James Patridge heard the screams of Jennifer Kroll's mother, and neighbors heard the screams of Kitty Genovese.

Interpreting the Situation as an Emergency

People's interpretations of an event as an emergency or nonemergency are influenced by their perceptions and attributions about the situation (Hoefnagels & Zwikker, 2001). James Patridge was confronted by an unambiguous situation. He interpreted the screams of Jennifer's mother as the sign of an emergency. In contrast, there was some ambiguity in Kitty Genovese's situation. In fact, bystanders tend to assume that an apparent confrontation between a man and a woman is a lovers' quarrel rather than a true emergency (Shotland & Straw, 1976). Because almost all of Kitty Genovese's neighbors interpreted the situation as a nonemergency, at that point there was little likelihood that any neighbors would help.

Taking Personal Responsibility

After interpreting the situation as an emergency, Patridge took responsibility for intervening. But not even those neighbors who may have interpreted Kitty Genovese's situation as an emergency took responsibility for helping her. Darley and Latané discovered a surprising reason for this lack of responsibility. Contrary to what you

bystander intervention
The act of helping someone who is in immediate need of aid.

FIGURE 17-6

Steps in Bystander Intervention

According to Latané and Darley (1968), bystanders go through certain steps before intervening in emergencies. The possibility of intervening can be inhibited at any of these steps.

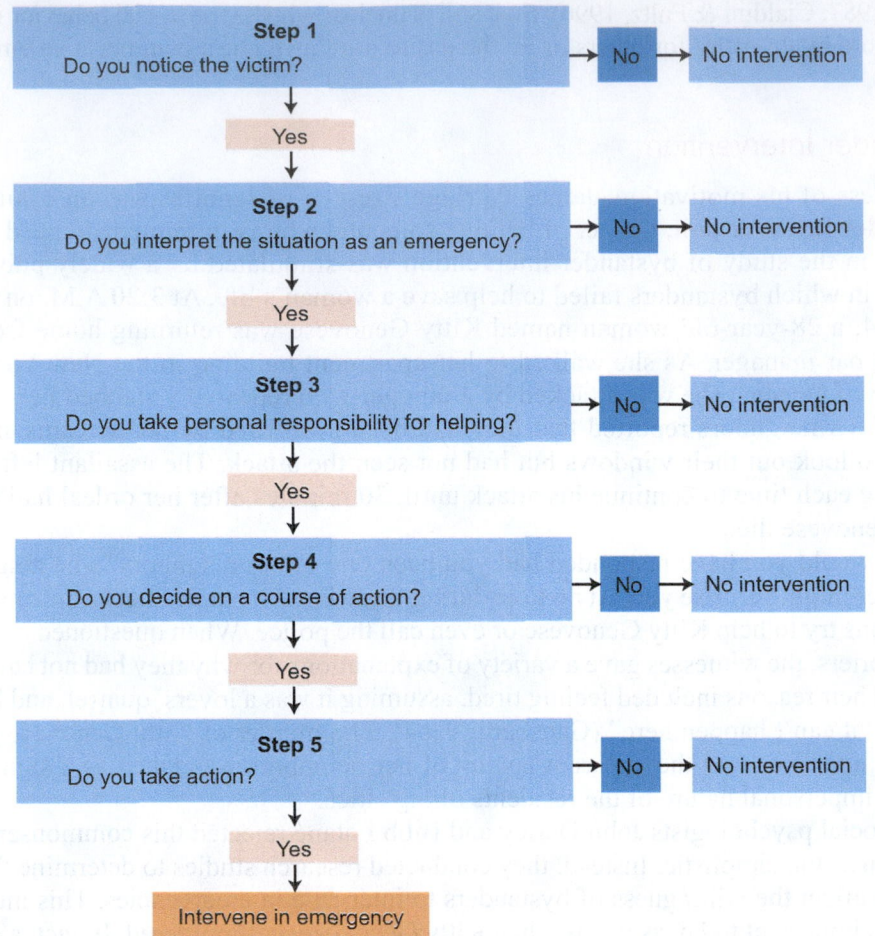

might expect, as the number of bystanders increases, the likelihood of a bystander's intervening decreases (Forsyth, Zyzniewski, & Giammanco, 2002). Note that this decrease in intervention is true only in situations involving strangers. In emergencies involving highly cohesive groups of people, such as friends or relatives, the probability of intervention will increase as the number of bystanders increases (Rutkowski, Gruder, & Romer, 1983).

The influence of the number of bystanders on bystander intervention was demonstrated in an early study by Darley and Latané (1968). They had college students meet to discuss the problems they faced in attending school in New York City. Each student was led to a room and told to communicate with other students over an intercom. The students were told that two, three, or six students were taking part in the discussion, but all the other students were the experimenter's confederates; in fact, the remarks of the other students were tape recordings. Early in the session the participant (the nonconfederate) heard another student apparently having an epileptic seizure and crying out for help.

Figure 17-7 shows that of those participants who believed they were a lone bystander, 85 percent sought help for the stricken person. Of those who believed they were one of two bystanders, 62 percent sought help. And of those who believed they were one of five bystanders, only 31 percent sought help. One reason for this decrease is the diffusion of responsibility: As the number of bystanders increases, the responsibility felt by each one decreases. So the students who were exposed to a mock epileptic seizure felt less responsibility for helping the victim when they believed other bystanders were present. In contrast to Kitty Genovese's neighbors, who assumed that other neighbors had been awakened, Patridge may have assumed that no one else could intervene, leaving him with the responsibility.

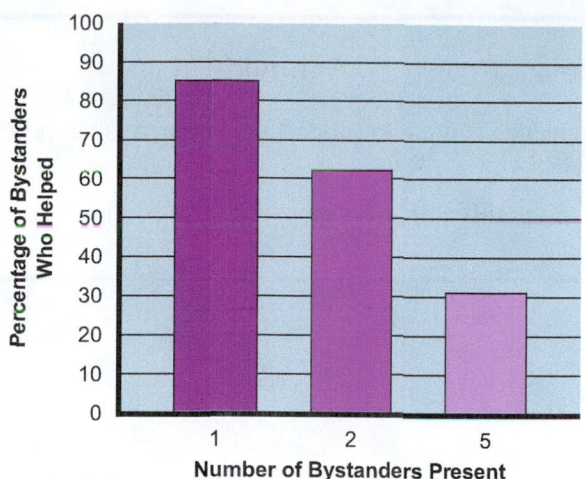

FIGURE 17-7
Diffusion of Responsibility

Darley and Latané found that as the number of bystanders increased, the likelihood of any of them going to the aid of a student apparently having an epileptic seizure decreased.
Source: Data from J. M. Darley and Bibb Latané, "Bystander Intervention in Emergencies: Diffusion of Responsibility," *Journal of Personality and Social Psychology, 8,* 377–383. Copyright © 1968 by the American Psychological Association.

Deciding on a Course of Action

The decision to intervene depends in part on whether the bystander feels competent to meet the demands of the situation (Clark & Word, 1974). Patridge decided to wheel himself toward the pool and then crawl to it. Because Patridge had training in cardiopulmonary resuscitation, whereas Jennifer Kroll's mother did not, he felt more competent to try to revive Jennifer. Though none did so until after Kitty Genovese was dead, her neighbors might have at least considered calling the police when they heard her screams. A study that interviewed people who had intervened in violent crimes, such as muggings and armed robberies, found that they were usually larger and stronger than those who did not. Moreover, they typically were better trained to cope with crimes and emergencies, having had more police training or emergency medical training. Thus, they felt more competent to help (Huston, Ruggiero, Conner, & Geis, 1981).

Taking Action

Patridge believed that the potential benefits of his intervention outweighed the potential costs. In one study, undergraduates reported the likelihood that they would help in a series of scenarios. The majority (76 percent) of their decisions reflected an assessment of the costs and benefits of each intervention (Fritzsche, Finkelstein, & Penner, 2000). This "bystander calculus" might explain why bystanders who believe that intervening in an emergency would place them in danger (as some might have believed in the case of Kitty Genovese) are less likely to intervene.

The characteristics of the victim also influence bystander intervention. One of the most important characteristics is the degree to which the victim appears responsible for his or her predicament. You might recognize this situation as an example of causal attribution. If we make dispositional attributions for a person's predicament, we will be less likely to help than if we make situational attributions for it (Weiner, 1980). We are more likely to help people in need when we perceive their situation to be the result of uncontrollable factors, such as a sudden illness, than when we perceive it to be the result of controllable factors, such as personal recklessness (Schmidt & Weiner, 1988).

As you can now appreciate, bystander intervention is not simply the product of a particular personality type. Instead, it is a complex process that depends on the interaction between characteristics of the victim, the bystander, and the situation. For example, a recent study found that women reported that they would be more likely to intervene when a child is being hit than when a dog or a woman is being hit. In contrast, men reported that they would be more likely to intervene when a woman is being hit than when a dog or a child is being hit (Laner, Benin, & Ventrone, 2001). These findings are consistent with the gender-role analysis of altruism discussed in Chapter 2.

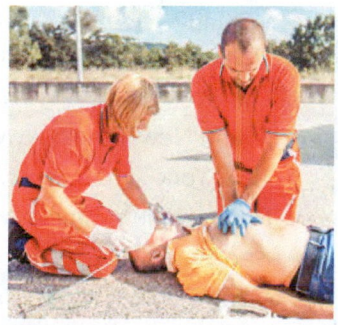

Expertise and Bystander Intervention

In dangerous situations, bystanders will be more likely to intervene when they feel competent to do so. A person specially trained to rescue people experiencing a heart attack or drowning, such as these two rescuers, will be more likely to intervene than will someone who is not.
Source: William Perugini/Shutterstock.com.

Section Review: Prosocial Behavior

1. What research evidence is there to support the negative state relief theory of seemingly altruistic behavior?

2. What is the role of the diffusion of responsibility in bystander intervention?

Experiencing Psychology

A Study of Personal Advertisements

As noted in the section, "Romantic Love," there are gender differences in the characteristics that women and men prefer when they are seeking a romantic partner. In this exercise, you will record data about age preferences in mate selection, analyze it statistically, and discuss it in the context of what you learned from reading this chapter. You should work in a group of three to four students and should agree on hypotheses about what you will find.

Method
Materials

Choose one of the websites that follow to serve as a source for your data. Each of these sites is the home page of a metropolitan newspaper that provides access to the personal advertisement area of their classified section.

- Atlanta Journal-Constitution: www.accessatlanta.com
- Chicago Tribune: www.chicagotribune.com/
- Denver Post: www.denverpost.com/
- Los Angeles Times: www.latimes.com/
- Miami New Times: www.miaminewtimes.com
- New York Times: www.nytimes.com/
- Phoenix New Times: www.phoenixnewtimes.com/
- San Francisco Chronicle: www.sfgate.com/
- Village Voice: http://villagevoice.com/
- Washington Post: www.washingtonpost.com/

Select 15 to 20 advertisements in each of the following categories: men seeking women, women seeking men, men seeking men, and women seeking women. Each of your advertisements must contain the following information: the advertiser's age, the advertiser's sex, the sex of the desired partner, and the exact age range desired. Do not include any advertisement that is ambiguous on any of these criteria.

Prepare four coding sheets, one for each of the advertiser categories (i.e., heterosexual men and women, gay men, and lesbians). Each coding sheet should have three columns: one for the advertiser's age, one for average age of desired partner, and one for a difference score that you will compute.

Procedure

Record your data for each of the advertisements you selected using the following procedure. Record the advertiser's age. Then compute an average age of desired partner by adding the minimum and maximum age in the range and divide by 2. For example, if an advertiser specified an age range of 20 to 30, the average age of desired partner would be 25. Then compute a difference score, the advertiser's age minus the average age of desired partner, and record this score on your data sheet. A negative score indicates that the advertiser is seeking an older partner; a positive score indicates that the advertiser is seeking a younger partner.

Results

Calculate group means for the difference scores for each of the four advertiser categories. Group means should be used for drawing a graph showing the difference scores for each of the four advertiser categories. (See Chapter 2 and Appendix C in the Online Edition.)

Discussion

Discuss whether your results agree with your hypotheses. Do the results support what you read in the chapter? Do the results support any of the theories discussed in the chapter? Were there any differences between men and women? Were there any differences between the heterosexual women and men, gay men, and lesbians? Are there any other conclusions that can be reached from the data?

As a researcher, you should also note any shortcomings of the study and aspects that you would change to improve it. Finally, you should suggest a research study that would be a logical offshoot of this study.

Chapter Summary

Social Cognition

- Social psychology is the field that studies behavior in its interpersonal context.
- The process by which we try to explain social behavior is called causal attribution.
- When you decide that a person is responsible for her or his own behavior, you are making a dispositional attribution.
- When you decide that circumstances are responsible for a person's behavior, you are making a situational attribution.
- Bernard Weiner's attribution theory looks at the interaction of the internal-external, stable-unstable, and controllable-uncontrollable dimensions.
- Biases in causal attribution include the fundamental attribution error and the self-serving bias.
- Person perception is the process by which we make judgments about the personal characteristics of people.
- Sometimes we try to affect other people's perceptions of us by engaging in impression management.
- Person perception also is affected by social schemas, which comprise the presumed characteristics of a role, an event, a person, or a group.
- Social schemas that we believe can be applied to almost all members of a group are called stereotypes.
- Our first impressions play an important role in person perception, in some cases creating a self-fulfilling prophecy.

Interpersonal Attraction

- Psychologists interested in studying social attraction are concerned with the factors that make us like or love other people.
- Liking depends on the factors of proximity, familiarity, physical attractiveness, similarity, and self-disclosure.
- Researchers who study love distinguish between passionate love and companionate love.
- According to Ellen Berscheid and Elaine Hatfield, romantic love depends on cultural support for the concept of romantic love, a state of physiological arousal, and the presence of an appropriate person to love.
- Robert Sternberg's triangular theory of love has received little empirical evaluation.
- Among the most important factors in promoting love are similarity, self-disclosure, and equity.

Attitudes

- Attitudes are evaluations of ideas, events, objects, or people.
- Attitudes have emotional, cognitive, and behavioral components.
- Classical conditioning, operant conditioning, and social-learning theory explain how attitudes are learned.
- We often are subjected to persuasive messages aimed at getting us to change our attitudes.

- Persuasive messages can take a central route or a peripheral route.
- Persuasiveness depends on the message, the source, and the audience.
- Sources that are more credible and attractive are more persuasive.
- Under certain circumstances, two-sided messages will be more effective than one-sided messages.
- The intelligence of the receiver and the relevance of the message also determine the effectiveness of persuasive messages.
- Our attitudes might not always accurately predict our behavior.
- Our behavior sometimes can affect our attitudes, a phenomenon that is explained by cognitive dissonance theory and self-perception theory.
- Prejudice is a positive or negative attitude toward others based on their membership in particular groups.
- The behavioral component of prejudice is discrimination.
- Among the important factors promoting prejudice are stereotypes and the authoritarian personality.
- Prejudice can be reduced when there is equal-status contact and intergroup cooperation.

Group Dynamics

- Psychologists interested in group dynamics study the effects of social relationships on thinking, feeling, and behaving.
- Decision making in groups can be affected by group polarization, which is the tendency for groups to make more extreme decisions than their members would make as individuals.
- Group decisions sometimes are characterized by groupthink, in which group members place greater emphasis on unanimity than on critical thinking.
- A minority can affect group decisions by being rational, confident, consistent, and patient.
- Groups can affect task performance through social facilitation, which is the improvement of performance caused by the presence of other people.
- Our performance can also be affected by social loafing, which is the tendency of individuals to exert less effort when performing in groups.
- Human relationships are characterized by conformity, compliance, and obedience.
- Conformity is behaving in accordance with group norms with little or no overt pressure to do so.
- Compliance is agreeing to a request that is backed by little or no threat of punishment.
- Two of the chief techniques for inducing compliance are the foot-in-the-door technique and the door-in-the-face technique.

- Obedience is following orders given by an authority.
- Stanley Milgram found that most people are all too willing to harm other people when ordered to do so by a legitimate authority figure.

Aggression

- Aggression is behavior aimed at causing harm to someone else.
- Physiological theories view aggression as biologically based, perhaps inborn.
- Sigmund Freud and Konrad Lorenz believed that aggression is instinctive, meaning that we have no choice but to engage in it periodically.
- Today most researchers reject the instinct theory of aggression but still study hormonal and hereditary influences on it.
- Most researchers look to life experiences as the main determinants of aggression.
- According to the frustration-aggression hypothesis, aggression becomes more likely after we have been blocked from reaching a goal.
- According to social-learning theory, we may learn to be aggressive by observing people who act aggressively.

- Group violence is promoted by deindividuation, which is the loss of self-awareness and the feeling of anonymity that comes from being part of a group.

Prosocial Behavior

- Prosocial behavior involves helping others in need.
- Altruism is helping others without the expectation of a reward in return.
- Some researchers have found that true altruism occurs only when prosocial behavior is done out of empathy rather than out of a desire to reduce one's own distress at the plight of another person.
- Other researchers have found, instead, that prosocial behavior is never truly altruistic—it always depends on the desire to reduce our own distress.
- Psychologists who study prosocial behavior are especially concerned with bystander intervention, the act of helping someone who is in immediate need of aid.
- Bystander intervention depends on noticing the victim, interpreting the situation as an emergency, taking personal responsibility, deciding on a course of action, and taking action to help.

Key Terms

social psychology (p. 596)

Social Cognition

causal attribution (p. 596)
fundamental attribution error (p. 597)
impression management (p. 598)
person perception (p. 598)
self-fulfilling prophecy (p. 600)
self-serving bias (p. 597)
social cognition (p. 596)
social schema (p. 599)
stereotype (p. 599)

Interpersonal Attraction

companionate love (p. 604)
passionate love (p. 604)

Attitudes

attitude (p. 606)
authoritarian personality (p. 613)
cognitive-dissonance theory (p. 610)
elaboration likelihood theory (p. 608)
persuasion (p. 608)
prejudice (p. 612)
self-perception theory (p. 611)
sleeper effect (p. 609)

Group Dynamics

compliance (p. 620)
conformity (p. 618)
door-in-the-face technique (p. 620)
foot-in-the-door technique (p. 620)
group (p. 615)

group polarization (p. 616)
groupthink (p. 616)
obedience (p. 621)
social facilitation (p. 617)
social loafing (p. 618)

Aggression

aggression (p. 623)
deindividuation (p. 625)
frustration-aggression hypothesis (p. 624)

Prosocial Behavior

altruism (p. 626)
bystander intervention (p. 627)
negative state relief theory (p. 626)
prosocial behavior (p. 626)

Chapter Quiz

Note: Answers for the Chapter Quiz questions are provided at the end of the book.

1. Richard LaPiere's (1934) study of prejudice against Chinese citizens by hotels and restaurants indicated that
   a. attitudes predict behavior.
   b. behavior predicts attitudes.
   c. attitudes may not predict behaviors.
   d. self-monitoring mediated attitude-behavior consistency.

2. In 1898, Norman Triplett conducted one of the first experiments in social psychology, which was influenced by his interest in
   a. persuasion.
   b. advertising.
   c. bicycle racing.
   d. pornography's effect on violence.

3. The student government decides to sponsor a spring picnic for the entire student body. But the student-government president insists that one person, rather than a committee, be responsible for it. The president most likely wishes to avoid
   a. social loafing.
   b. social facilitation.
   c. cognitive dissonance.
   d. self-fulfilling prophecy.

4. Two college students decide to see a horror movie together. They are terrified by the movie, become physiologically aroused, and immediately after the movie are surprised to find that they have romantic feelings toward each other. In regard to the emotional experience of romantic love, this situation would give the strongest support to the
   a. two-factor theory.
   b. James-Lange theory.
   c. Cannon-Bard theory.
   d. opponent-process theory.

5. According to Richard Petty and John Cacioppo (1990), persuasive messages that rely on characteristics of the source, instead of the merits of the arguments, take the
   a. direct route.
   b. central route.
   c. indirect route.
   d. peripheral route.

6. You receive a free sample of a new toothpaste, which, in reality, is no different from other kinds. After a period of using it, though your oral health is the same as it has always been, you develop a positive attitude toward the toothpaste—simply because you have been using it. Your attitude would be explained best by
   a. self-perception theory.
   b. self-serving bias theory.
   c. cognitive dissonance theory.
   d. self-fulfilling prophecy theory.

7. A basketball player is a notoriously poor "practice player" but performs well during actual games. This behavior would most likely be attributable to
   a. social loafing.
   b. social facilitation.
   c. cognitive dissonance.
   d. self-fulfilling prophecy.

8. If you decide that a fellow student has performed well on an exam because she is intelligent and conscientious, you have made a
   a. free will attribution.
   b. situational attribution.
   c. deterministic attribution.
   d. dispositional attribution.

9. Social psychologists interested in the study of altruism have been especially concerned with its relationship to
   a. empathy.
   b. egocentrism.
   c. social facilitation.
   d. cognitive dissonance.

10. You are asked to promote the building of a nuclear power plant in a community where most people oppose it. Based on the research of Carl Hovland and his associates near the end of World War II on factors involved in persuasion, you would be most persuasive if you
    a. denied the possibility of a nuclear meltdown.
    b. tried to convince the residents that they were being irrational.
    c. presented the financial and environmental benefits of nuclear energy, but none of its potential harmful effects.
    d. admitted the small probability of a nuclear meltdown, but stressed that nuclear energy produced less pollution than other sources of energy.

11. A political campaign asks you to volunteer to be a poll watcher on election day. After you say yes, you are then asked to call 50 potential voters in support of your favored candidate. The political campaign is making use of the
    a. jigsaw method.
    b. self-serving bias.
    c. door-in-the-face technique.
    d. foot-in-the-door technique.

12. Research by Kenneth and Mamie Phipps Clark (1947) on the effects of racial discrimination influenced the U.S. Supreme Court decision that
    a. African Americans should be guaranteed the right to vote.
    b. African Americans should be granted the same civil rights as European Americans.
    c. IQ tests should be banned from use with African American children.
    d. separate education for African Americans and European Americans was inherently unequal.

13. While enrolled in a course, you notice that one student is consistently late to class and conclude that she is irresponsible and lazy. This situation is an example of
    a. the fundamental attribution error.
    b. prejudice.
    c. self-serving bias.
    d. self-fulfilling prophecy.

14. In Stanley Milgram's (1963) classic study of the administration of electric shocks to a "learner," the proportion of participants who reached the maximum level of shock was about
    a. one-half.
    b. one-tenth.
    c. two-thirds.
    d. three-quarters.

15. Research indicates that interpersonal attraction between two persons is enhanced when
    a. both engage in gradual rather than rapid self-disclosure.
    b. both engage in immediate rather than long-term self-disclosure.
    c. neither person engages in self-disclosure, because "familiarity breeds contempt."
    d. one person engages in rapid self-disclosure and the other does not, because it flatters the recipient of the self-disclosure.

16. The individual members of the academic affairs committee of a college would like to make minor revisions in the college's curriculum. Yet, after discussing the topic for several meetings, arguing every side of the issue, and working independently of any powerful administrator, they produce a radical revision that changes every aspect of the old curriculum. This situation would most likely be an example of
    a. groupthink.
    b. group polarization.
    c. social facilitation.
    d. self-fulfilling prophecy.

17. In a debate during the presidential campaign of 1960, Richard Nixon's less attractive appearance made many people determine that John F. Kennedy was the winner of the debate. In regard to Richard Petty and John Cacioppo's (1990) theory of persuasion, this example shows the power of the
    a. direct route.
    b. central route.
    c. indirect route.
    d. peripheral route.

18. The study of friendship among residents of apartments in a housing project for married students at the Massachusetts Institute of Technology (Festinger et al., 1950) demonstrated the importance of
    a. proximity.
    b. similarity.
    c. familiarity.
    d. physical attractiveness.

19. The deliberate attempt to control the attitudes that others have toward us is called
    a. self-serving bias.
    b. fundamental attribution error.
    c. impression management.
    d. self-fulfilling prophecy.

20. If you continually insist that other people's misfortunes are caused by their own lack of ability or effort, you would be committing the
    a. self-serving bias.
    b. stereotype bias.
    c. fundamental attribution error.
    d. self-fulfilling prophecy effect.

21. The study in which participants' photographs representing true images or mirror images were shown to the participants and to their friends (Mita et al., 1977) demonstrated that social attraction is affected by
    a. proximity.
    b. similarity.
    c. familiarity.
    d. physical attractiveness.

22. If you tend to blame your academic failures on unfair exams and biased grading and to credit yourself for your academic successes, you would be committing the
    a. self-serving bias.
    b. modesty bias.
    c. fundamental attribution error.
    d. self-fulfilling prophecy effect.

23. According to research by John Darley and Bibb Latané, a person who collapsed on the street would be most likely to be helped if
    a. there are many witnesses to the event.
    b. there is a single witness to the event.
    c. witnesses are strangers rather than acquaintances.
    d. witnesses assumed that the person was drunk rather than a diabetic suffering from insulin shock.

24. According to Konrad Lorenz, people engage in widespread violence because they
    a. are easily frustrated.
    b. suffer from original sin.
    c. observe other people being aggressive.
    d. lack inborn ritualistic ways to inhibit aggression.

25. A social schema that includes characteristics that are ascribed to almost all members of a group is an example of
    a. a stereotype.
    b. a first impression.
    c. a causal attribution.
    d. an attitude.

Thought Questions

1. How might the attributions you make about a failed romantic relationship make you feel better about yourself?

2. In trying to persuade other students that your school's core curriculum should be made more rigorous, how might you use research findings on the role of the source, the message, and the audience?

3. How might you keep your family from succumbing to groupthink in making a decision on whether to buy a particular house?

4. If you were asked to coordinate a group of students in running a special lecture series, how might you prevent social loafing?

Answers to Section Review Questions

Chapter 1: The Nature of Psychology

The Historical Context of Psychology

1. The structuralists tried to analyze the mind into its component elements and discover how the elements interact.
2. Functionalism stressed the importance of how the mind helps us adapt to reality, and it expanded the kinds of methods, subjects, and settings used in psychological research.
3. Structuralism was criticized as being "brick-and-mortar psychology" for its attempt to analyze mental experience into discrete elements.
4. Behaviorism emerged when John B. Watson and other psychologists, seeking to make psychology an objective science, rejected the study of the unobservable mind in favor of studying observable behavior.

Contemporary Perspectives in Psychology

1. Like Gestalt psychologists, cognitive psychologists stress the active role of the mind in organizing perceptions, processing information, and interpreting experiences. Like behavioral psychologists, cognitive psychologists stress the need for objective, well-controlled, laboratory studies.
2. The three areas of interest to psychologists who favor the biopsychological perspective are the brain, the hormonal system, and the effects of heredity on psychological functions.
3. The sociocultural perspective is a reaction against the tendency to presume that psychological research findings in Western cultures are automatically generalizable to other cultures.

The Scope of Psychology

1. Basic research aims at contributing to knowledge, and applied research aims at solving practical problems.
2. A psychiatrist is a physician who has served a residency in psychiatry, which takes a medical approach to the treatment of psychological disorders.
3. Peace psychologists conduct research and seek to apply their findings to help prevent violence, reduce conflict, and avoid war.

Chapter 2: Psychology as a Science

Sources of Knowledge

1. The basic assumptions of science are that the universe is orderly, determinism is the best approach to explaining events, and skepticism is the proper scientific attitude.
2. Critical thinking is the systematic evaluation of claims by identifying the claim being made, examining evidence in support of the claim, and considering alternative explanations of the claim.
3. The steps in the scientific method include providing a rationale, conducting the study, analyzing the data, communicating the research findings, and replicating the study.

Goals of Scientific Research

1. Scientists use operational definitions to provide precise, concrete, and often quantitative definitions of events or characteristics in their research.
2. Science involves probabilistic prediction because so many variables are at work at any given time that it usually is impossible to be certain about the accuracy of one's predictions.
3. Scientific explanation in psychology involves the discovery of the causes of overt behaviors, mental experiences, cognitive processes, and physiological changes.

Methods of Psychological Research

1. A random sample permits generalization of survey findings from the sample to the population it represents.
2. The validity of a test is the extent to which it measures what it is supposed to measure.
3. The independent variable is manipulated by the experimenter, who determines its values before the experiment begins.
4. Internal validity is the extent to which changes in the dependent variable are attributable to the independent variable.

Statistical Analysis of Research Data

1. Measures of central tendency, which are used to represent a set of scores, include the mode, median, and mean.
2. Measures of variability, which are used to describe the degree of dispersion of a set of scores, include the range, the variance, and the standard deviation.
3. Statistical significance involves deciding whether the size of the difference between group performances is of sufficiently low probability to occur by chance that it can be attributed to the independent variable.
4. Meta-analysis combines the results of a large number of published and unpublished studies. After collecting the studies, the researcher computes the average size of the effect of the independent variable on the dependent variable.

Ethics of Psychological Research

1. Critics argue that the methodological benefits of deception do not outweigh the mistrust of psychological research it might create and the distress it might cause in deceived participants.
2. Debriefing involves informing participants of the purpose of the research study in which they participated and any unusual aspects, such as the use of deception.
3. Animal rights advocates oppose all laboratory research using animals, regardless of its scientific merit or practical benefits. Animal welfare advocates would permit laboratory research on animals as long as the animals are given humane care and the potential benefits of the research outweigh any pain and distress experienced by the animals.

Chapter 3: Biopsychological Bases of Behavior

Nature versus Nurture

1. Evolutionary psychology views human behavior through concepts from the theory of evolution. It assumes that human behaviors that exist today evolved because they had survival value for generation after generation of people.
2. The closer two persons are related biologically, the more genetically similar they will be, but also, in general, the more similar they will be in life experiences. Thus, we have no more right to attribute personal similarities between two closely related people solely to heredity than we do to attribute them solely to common life experiences.

Biological Communication Systems

1. The nervous system is divided into the central nervous system (including the brain and spinal cord) and the peripheral nervous system (including the somatic nervous system and the autonomic nervous system).
2. Whereas the endocrine glands secrete hormones into the bloodstream, exocrine glands secrete their chemicals into the body surface or into the body cavities. Moreover, endocrine secretions have many behavioral effects, but exocrine secretions have relatively few.

Neuronal Activity

1. The major structures of the neuron are the cell body (soma), the dendrites, axon, and synaptic terminals.
2. Neural impulses depend on the flow of positively charged ions into the neuron, which produces an action potential.

Brain Functions

1. The brain stem regulates breathing, heart rate, motor coordination, brain arousal, attention, and other important life functions. The limbic system regulates processes related to emotion, motivation, and memory. And the cerebral cortex contains motor areas that control body movements, sensory areas that process sensory input, association areas that permit the integration of information from different brain areas, and in people, language areas that permit the production and comprehension of speech.
2. Broca's area selects the muscle movements necessary for the expression of words and communicates them to the motor cortex. Wernicke's area selects words that convey meaning and communicates them to Broca's area.
3. Split-brain research shows that the left hemisphere predominates in speech because split-brain patients can respond orally only when information is presented to the left hemisphere. Likewise, we know the right hemisphere predominates in spatial relations because split-brain patients perform better on tests of spatial relations using the left hand than using the right hand.

Chapter 4: Human Development

Research Methods in Developmental Psychology

1. Maturation is the sequential unfolding of inherited abilities, such as an infant's progression from crawling to walking to standing.

2. Cross-sectional research designs assess age differences at one point in time. However, it may not be possible to generalize the results of cross-sectional research to other cohorts. Longitudinal research designs assess how individuals change over time. However, longitudinal designs require considerable financial support, and participants often drop out. If the participants who drop out differ from the remaining participants, the results of such studies might not be generalizable to the population of interest.

Prenatal Development

1. Cell-adhesion molecules direct the movement of cells and determine which cells will adhere to one another, thereby determining the size, shape, and location of organs in the embryo.

2. The hallmarks of fetal alcohol syndrome are facial deformities, hearing disorders, intellectual disability, attentional deficits, and poor impulse control.

Infant and Child Development

1. Depth perception is present in human infants by 6 months of age, and generally it develops in animals about the time when they can move about on their own.

2. Piaget assumed that the child proceeds through qualitatively different stages of cognitive development during which cognitive schemas are altered by the processes of assimilation and accommodation.

3. Securely attached infants have more successful peer relationships and more secure romantic attachments later in life.

4. Permissive parents set few rules and rarely punish misbehavior; authoritarian parents set strict rules and rely on punishment; and authoritative parents tend to be warm and loving, yet insist that their children behave appropriately. Authoritative parenting is the most successful, and the preferred, style of parenting.

Adolescent Development

1. Cultural and historical factors that are unique to particular cohorts can make those cohorts somewhat different from cohorts that precede or succeed them.

2. The person who has reached the formal operational stage can apply abstract principles and make predictions about hypothetical situations.

3. Adolescents develop a sense of identity by adopting their own set of values and social behaviors. This is a normal part of finding answers to questions such as these: What do I believe is important? What are my goals in life?

Adult Development

1. A reduction in caloric intake is associated with increased longevity.

2. Research indicates that fluid intelligence declines in old age but that crystallized intelligence does not.

3. Adults who achieve generativity become less self-absorbed and more concerned about being a productive worker, spouse, or parent.

Chapter 5: Sensation and Perception

Sensory Processes

1. Sensation is the process that detects stimuli from one's body or environment. Perception is the process that organizes sensations into meaningful patterns.

2. Psychophysics is the study of the relationship between the physical characteristics of stimuli and the corresponding psychological responses to them.

3. Sensory adaptation is the tendency of sensory receptors to respond less and less to an unchanging stimulus.

Visual Sensation

1. Light waves pass through the cornea, pupil, lens, and photoreceptors.

2. Trichromatic theory assumes that the retina has three kinds of receptors, each of which is maximally sensitive to red, green, or blue light. The relative degree of activity of these receptors determines the colors that we perceive.

Visual Perception

1. These are the principles of proximity, closure, similarity, and continuity.

2. Two binocular cues are binocular disparity and convergence.

Hearing

1. The major structures of the outer ear are the pinna, auditory canal, and tympanic membrane; the major structures of the middle ear are the eustachian tube and ossicles; and the major structures of the inner ear are the oval window, cochlea, basilar membrane, hair cells, and auditory nerve.

2. Place theory assumes that particular points on the basilar membrane vibrate maximally in response to sound waves of particular frequencies.

3. Sound localization depends on sounds reaching one ear slightly before reaching the other, on sounds being slightly more intense at the closer ear, and on the irregular shape of the pinna altering sounds differently depending on their location.

Chemical Senses

1. Pheromones are odorous chemicals that affect animals' behavior. Recent research suggests that pheromones may have some effect on humans' behavior and emotions.

2. The enjoyment of flavors depends on not only the sense of taste but also the sense of smell, which is diminished by a head cold.

Skin Senses

1. The blind person wears a camera on special eyeglasses and a computer-controlled electronic vest covered with a grid of tiny Teflon cones. Outlines of images provided by the camera are impressed onto the skin by vibrations of the cones.

2. The gate-control theory of pain assumes that pain impulses from the limbs or body pass through a part of the spinal cord that provides a "gate" for pain impulses, perhaps involving substance P neurons. Stimulation of neurons that convey touch sensations "closes" the gate, preventing input from neurons that convey pain sensations.

3. If human participants or animal subjects are given naloxone and the pain-relieving technique becomes less effective, it is assumed that the technique depends on the release of endorphins because naloxone blocks the effects of endorphins.

Body Senses

1. The kinesthetic sense informs you of the position of your joints, the tension in your muscles, and the movement of your arms and legs.

2. One of the major theories of motion sickness holds that it is produced by a conflict between sensory input to the eyes and sensory input to the vestibular organs.

Extrasensory Perception

1. The four paranormal abilities are mental telepathy, clairvoyance, precognition, and psychokinesis.

2. The major shortcomings of paranormal research are that it might involve poorly controlled demonstrations, chance events, fraud, or magic. Moreover, paranormal events cannot be explained by any known physical processes.

Chapter 6: Consciousness

The Nature of Consciousness

1. Automatic processing involves less conscious awareness and mental effort than controlled processing. As a result, it does not interfere with our performance of other activities.

2. The "cocktail party phenomenon" involves being engrossed in one conversation at a party yet noticing when your name is mentioned in another conversation.

3. Subliminal psychodynamic activation presents emotionally charged subliminal messages to alter the recipient's moods and behaviors by stimulating unconscious fantasies.

Sleep

1. The night typically involves four or five cycles in which the sleeper descends into the depths of NREM sleep, ascends to lighter stages of NREM sleep, and ends each cycle in REM sleep. During the second half of the night, the sleeper might not reach sleep deeper than stage 2 and will have longer REM periods.

2. The length of sleep varies negatively with how long it takes animals to find their daily food and positively with how secure they are from attack while asleep.

3. Persons with sleep-onset insomnia should avoid ingesting caffeine or doing exercise too close to bedtime. They also should avoid napping during the day; go to bed only when they feel sleepy; refrain from eating, reading, watching television, or listening to music while in bed; and get out of bed instead of tossing and turning.

Dreams

1. Among Calkins's findings were that we dream every night, that we have several dream periods each night, that we are more likely to dream during the second half of the night, that most dreams are mundane, that we can incorporate external stimuli into our dreams, that we can engage in "real thinking" while asleep, and that we can control our dreams.

2. Freud believed that dreams are often disguised forms of wish fulfillment in which the manifest content of the dream symbolically represents its true meaning; its latent content.

Hypnosis

1. During hypnotic induction you might have the person focus on a spot on the ceiling. You might then suggest that the person's eyelids are closing, feet are warming, muscles are relaxing, and breathing is slowing. You would gradually induce the person to relinquish more and more control of his or her perceptions, thoughts, and behaviors to you.

2. Hypnosis can help people recall memories but might make them overly confident in their recall of inaccurate "memories."

3. Some researchers believe that hypnosis is merely a state of heightened suggestibility in which people are willing to act out the suggestions given by the hypnotist. They also note that motivated nonhypnotized people can often perform the same feats as hypnotized people.

Psychoactive Drugs

1. The symptoms of physical drug dependency include tolerance and withdrawal symptoms.

2. Cocaine is a stimulant drug that induces a relatively brief state of euphoria. It can cause addiction, paranoia, hallucinations, and sudden death from cardiac arrest.

3. Marijuana alters sensory experiences and in higher doses can induce hallucinations. It impairs coordination, disrupts memory formation, and has been linked to a motivational syndrome.

4. Entactogens are a category of psychoactive drugs that induce altered perceptions, feelings of well-being, and interpersonal closeness and have been linked to memory impairment in chronic users.

Chapter 7: Learning

Classical Conditioning

1. You would repeatedly turn on the can opener just before presenting the cat with food. Eventually, the cat will come running at the sound of the can opener.

2. Bernstein suggests offering patients unusual, strange-tasting food before they have chemotherapy so that they will associate their resulting nausea with that food instead of with more common, nutritious foods.

3. Garcia found that rats have a tendency, apparently inborn, to associate nausea and dizziness with tastes, but not with sights and sounds, and to associate pain with sights and sounds, but not with tastes.

Operant Conditioning

1. Thorndike, like Skinner, found that behavior can be changed by altering its consequences.

2. You might train them by giving them a piece of cookie for looking at toys strewn on the floor, then for taking a step toward them, then for approaching them, then for touching one of them, then for picking it up, and finally for placing it in the toy box.

3. Both produce an increase in behavior, but whereas positive reinforcement involves the presentation of something appealing, negative reinforcement involves the removal of something unappealing.

Cognitive Learning

1. According to the cognitive explanation, blocking occurs because a new neutral stimulus adds nothing to the predictability of the UCS. The existing CS already predicts the occurrence of the UCS.

2. Latent learning and observational learning show that learning can take place without performing the relevant overt behavior.

3. Though the role of mirror neurons and their networks are still speculative, their functions have been observed in monkeys and humans. Mirror neurons fire when an animal learns to imitate the same action it just observed. This is thought to be an important physiological basis for observational learning and, thus, the phenomenon of empathy among humans.

Chapter 8: Memory

Information Processing and Memory

1. Some psychologists note that normal memory processes, such as thinking more often and more elaborately about certain experiences or being in a highly emotional state, can explain so-called flashbulb memories. Moreover, there is evidence that people are more confident in their flashbulb memories, even though those might be no more accurate than normal memories.

2. Sensory memory stores exact replicas of stimuli impinging on the senses for a brief period—from a fraction of second to several seconds. Short-term memory stores a limited amount of information in conscious awareness for about 20 seconds. And long-term memory stores a virtually unlimited amount of information for up to a lifetime.

Sensory Memory

1. By using partial report, Sperling demonstrated that iconic memory stores virtually all the information that strikes the photoreceptors, though the information fades so quickly that it seems that we store only a fraction of it.

2. Echoic memory helps us store speech sounds long enough to blend them with subsequent speech sounds, thereby letting us perceive a meaningful sequence of sounds.

Short-Term Memory

1. Research indicates that even when participants are tested on their short-term memory for letters presented visually, their errors indicate that they confuse letters based on their sounds more than on their appearance.

2. When they presented participants with trigrams to recall and prevented rehearsal of them, they found that after about 20 seconds participants could rarely recall the trigrams.

Long-Term Memory

1. Elaborative rehearsal involves processing the meaning of information instead of (as in maintenance rehearsal) its superficial qualities.

2. Procedural memory includes memories of how to perform behaviors, whereas declarative memory includes memories of facts.

3. In proactive interference, old memories interfere with new memories. In retroactive interference, new memories interfere with old ones.

4. Memories encoded while a person is in a specific state (such as a psychoactive drug-induced state) will be recalled better when the person is again in that state. There is also research showing that our recall of information that has been encoded in a particular mood will be best when we are in that mood again.

Memory, Forgetting, and Eyewitness Testimony

1. Children's eyewitness testimony is less accurate than that of adults, primarily because children are more suggestible and they are more likely to guess. The memories of preschool children are more fallible than the memories of older children.

2. Loftus believes that biased or leading questions can alter people's memory of past events. This becomes even more of an issue when hypnosis is used to recreate memories.

Improving Your Memory

1. You should set up a study schedule in a comfortable, nondistracting environment. You might also use the SQ3R method of studying. Other suggestions would be to use overlearning, distributed practice, and mnemonic devices.

2. You would memorize a list of concrete nouns that rhyme with numbers 1, 2, 3, 4, and so on. You would then imagine the objects to be recalled interacting with the objects represented by the concrete nouns. Then simply recall the concrete nouns associated with each number. This should automatically make you recall the interacting object.

The Biopsychology of Memory

1. After classically conditioning an eye-blink response in a rabbit, researchers found that electrical stimulation of a tiny site in the cerebellum of the rabbit elicited the conditioned eye blink and that destruction of the site eliminated it.

2. Since his hippocampus was removed decades ago, H. M. has been unable to form new long-term memories.

3. When participants are given a drug that blocks the effects of acetylcholine, they have trouble forming new long-term declarative memories. Other evidence comes from the loss of memory in victims of Alzheimer's disease, which is associated with the destruction of acetylcholine neurons in the brain.

Chapter 9: Thought and Language

Thought

1. Human development is characterized by critical periods during which the window for learning language is optimal.
2. Cognitive psychology combines William James's concern with mental processes and John B. Watson's concern with observable behavior.
3. Research indicates that we can think and form memories while our speech muscles are paralyzed; therefore, thought does not depend on subvocal speech.

Concept Formation

1. A logical concept is formed by identifying the specific features possessed by all things that the concept applies to. A natural concept is formed through everyday experience rather than by testing hypotheses about particular features that are common to all members of the concept.
2. They have fuzzy borders because it is difficult to identify their defining features.

Problem Solving

1. A heuristic can be more efficient because it rules out many useless alternatives before they are even attempted. But unlike an algorithm, a heuristic does not guarantee a correct solution.
2. Sometimes we are hindered by mental sets, which are commitments to problem-solving strategies that have succeeded in the past but that interfere with problem solving that requires a new strategy.

Creativity

1. Creative people tend to be above average in intelligence, imaginative, unconventional, and nonconforming; they also have a wide range of interests and are open to new experiences.
2. Amabile found that when students were given extrinsic reasons for writing poetry, they wrote less creative poems, whereas there was no decline in the creativity in poems by students who wrote for intrinsic reasons.

Decision Making

1. The availability heuristic is the tendency to estimate the probability of an event by how easily instances of it come to mind.
2. Leading questions affect people's decision making by the way in which they present the facts of a case, often as subtle as describing a 50 percent success rate versus a 50 percent failure rate.

Artificial Intelligence

1. Expert systems are using powerful computer programs that think more like world-class chess players rather than simply relying on brute calculation speed.
2. The study of neo-robotics is based on the belief that models of human problem solving must occur in a real-world context. AI researchers interested in this approach believe that problem solving must be modeled with a machine that operates within a physical environment and exhibits actions that are modifiable by feedback.

The Structure of Language

1. Semanticity is the conveying of the thoughts of the communicator in a meaningful way to those who understand the language. Generativity is the combining of language symbols in novel ways, without being limited to a fixed number of combinations. Displacement is the use of language to refer to objects and events that are not present.
2. In terms of transformational grammar, language comprehension involves transforming the surface structure, which is the verbal message, into its deep structure, which is its meaning.

The Acquisition of Language

1. Between 4 and 6 months of age, infants enter the babbling stage. When infants are about 1 year old, they begin to say their first words. Infants then begin using holophrastic speech, which is the use of single words to represent whole phrases or sentences. Next, in the two-word stage, infants use telegraphic speech.
2. Skinner believes that all aspects of language are learned. Chomsky believes that we have an inborn language mechanism that makes us sensitive to the rules of grammar.

The Relationship Between Language and Thought

1. In 1984 Orwell portrays a society in which the government changes the meaning of words or invents words to limit citizen's ability to think rebellious thoughts.
2. Research indicates that when male pronouns are used to represent people generically, those who read or hear them tend to take them to refer to males rather than to both males and females.

Language in Apes

1. Some apes have been able to use words meaningfully, use words in novel ways, and use words to refer to things that are not physically present.
2. Some researchers believe that apes do not use language spontaneously but instead use it to get things they want or simply as responses to prompting by their trainers.

Chapter 10: Intelligence

Intelligence Testing

1. An autistic savant is a person with autism spectrum disorder with below-average intelligence but with an outstanding ability, typically in art, music, memory, or calculating.
2. Galton similarly assumed that people with superior physical abilities, especially sensory and motor abilities, are better adapted for survival and, therefore, more intelligent.

Extremes of Intelligence

1. The possible causes of intellectual disability include hereditary defects, sociocultural deprivation, and brain damage.
2. Terman's Genetic Studies of Genius showed that mentally gifted children tend to become socially, physically, vocationally, and academically superior adults.

Theories of Intelligence

1. Spearman found that intelligence depends on a general intelligence factor more than on separate kinds of intelligence. In contrast, Thurstone found that intelligence depends more on separate kinds of intelligence than on a general intelligence factor.
2. The seven types of intelligence are linguistic, logical-mathematical, spatial, musical, bodily-kinesthetic, intrapersonal, and interpersonal.

Nature, Nurture, and Intelligence

1. In terms of intelligence, adopted children are more like their biological parents than like their adoptive parents. Moreover, identical twins reared apart are more alike in intelligence than ordinary siblings reared together are.
2. The beneficial effects of intellectual enrichment programs include gains in IQ scores and improved cognitive skills.

Chapter 11: Motivation

The Nature of Motivation

1. Critics fear that acceptance of sociobiology would lend support to the status quo, making us less inclined to change what many people believe has been "ordained by God or nature," such as racial differences, differences in sexual behavior, child neglect and abuse, criminality, and social status.

2. According to Maslow, you must first satisfy your basic physiological needs before you will be motivated to move on up the needs hierarchy to your higher needs of safety and security, belongingness and love, through the need for esteem, and ultimately, self-actualization and transcendence.

The Hunger Motive

1. Stimulation of the lateral hypothalamus provokes eating, and stimulation of the ventromedial hypothalamus inhibits eating. Nonetheless, the hypothalamus is only part of a complex physiological system that regulates hunger and eating.

2. The role of heredity in obesity has been supported by studies showing that the correlation in the amount of body fat between identical twins stays roughly the same whether they are reared together or apart. Moreover, adopted children are more similar in weight to their biological parents than to their adoptive parents.

3. Factors may include cultural emphasis on thinness, dissatisfaction with their bodies, and concerns about physical attractiveness.

The Sex Motive

1. The four phases of the human sexual response cycle are excitement, plateau, orgasm, and resolution.

2. Kinsey's surveys found that people engaged in more sex and a greater variety of sexual activities than was popularly believed. Women are less likely than men to have masturbated, and men are more likely to approve of casual sex.

3. Biopsychological factors influencing sexual orientation include genetics and prenatal exposure to sex hormones.

The Arousal Motive

1. According to the Yerkes-Dodson law, performance will be best at a moderate level of arousal.

2. Flotation REST has proved useful in reducing chronic pain and high blood pressure.

The Achievement Motive

1. Goals should be specific, challenging, and paired with performance feedback. Moreover, goals you set yourself will be more motivating than goals others impose on you.

2. Overjustification theory assumes that an extrinsic reward decreases intrinsic motivation when a person attributes his or her performance to the extrinsic reward. Cognitive-evaluation theory holds that a reward perceived as providing information about a person's competence in an activity will increase her or his intrinsic motivation to perform that activity, but a reward perceived as an attempt to control a person's behavior will decrease that person's intrinsic motivation to perform that activity.

The Role of Motivation in Sport

1. An athlete might be underaroused or overaroused in practice and optimally roused during a competition—or optimally aroused during practice and underaroused or overaroused during a competition.

2. Opponents of much lower or much higher ability would not be a fair test of the athlete's ability.

Chapter 12: Emotion

The Biopsychology of Emotion

1. Studies measuring brain activity or the effects of brain damage have found that increased activity in the left hemisphere is associated with positive emotions and increased activity in the right hemisphere is associated with negative emotions.

2. Endorphin levels rise markedly after activities that induce euphoria.

The Expression of Emotion

1. Women are superior to men in the expression and detection of emotion. And studies have found that people perceive women and men to experience emotions with different frequency. And people perceive women to be expressing more sadness, whereas men are perceived as expressing more anger.

2. One line of research has found that even people who are blind from birth exhibit facial expressions for the basic emotions. A second line of research shows that young infants produce facial expressions for the basic emotions. Some studies also show that facial expressions for the basic emotions are universal across cultures.

The Experience of Emotion

1. Happiness is positively correlated with physical health, an outgoing and agreeable personality, a sense of personal control, intelligence, social skills, and family support. Physical attractiveness has a low to moderate correlation with happiness. Our happiness also depends on comparisons we make between ourselves and others and between our current circumstances and our past circumstances.

2. According to disparagement theory, we feel amused when

humor makes us feel superior to other people. According to incongruity theory, incongruous humor brings together incompatible ideas in a surprising outcome that violates our expectations. And according to release theory, humor is a cathartic outlet for anxiety caused by repressed sexual or aggressive energy.

Theories of Emotion

1. Evidence for the theory comes from studies finding different patterns of physiological responses for different emotions. Evidence against the theory includes the findings that we are unable to perceive many of the subtle physiological changes induced by the sympathetic nervous system, that different emotions are associated with the same pattern of physiological arousal, and that physiological changes dependent on the secretion of hormones by the adrenal glands are too slow to be the basis of all emotions.

2. When participants alter their facial expressions, they report changes in their subjective emotional experience.

3. Participants who experience unexplained arousal will experience negative emotions, regardless of their social context, thereby contradicting the theory. The only consistent finding in favor of the theory is that misattribution of physiological arousal to an outside source will intensify an emotional experience.

Chapter 13: Personality

The Psychoanalytic Approach to Personality

1. The Barnum effect demonstrates that useful personality descriptions must distinguish one person from another.

2. The id is unconscious, consists of our inborn biological drives, and demands immediate gratification. The ego directs us to express sexual and aggressive impulses in socially acceptable ways. The superego, our moral guide, counteracts the id, which is concerned only with immediate gratification, and the ego, which is concerned only with adapting to reality.

3. Adler assumed that because children feel small, weak, and dependent on others, they develop an inferiority complex. This motivates them to compensate by striving for superiority.

4. Horney emphasized the role of gender roles, interpersonal power, and sociocultural factors in personality development, especially women's. She also was a proponent of cross-cultural research.

5. Jung claimed that archetypes influence our dreams, religious symbols, and artistic creations.

The Dispositional Approach to Personality

1. Allport believed we are guided by the interaction among our cardinal traits, central traits, and secondary traits.

2. The MMPI was constructed by retaining only those questions that discriminate between people who differ on the characteristics of interest.

3. First, individuals do show consistency on certain traits. Second, cross-situational consistency in behavior depends on whether a person is a high self-monitor or a low self-monitor. Third, many of the studies that Mischel reviewed were guaranteed to find low cross-situational consistency because they either correlated trait test scores with single instances of behaviors or correlated single instances of behaviors with each other. Psychologists have achieved greater success in demonstrating cross-situational consistency by using behavioral aggregation.

The Cognitive-Behavioral Approach to Personality

1. It is different from operant conditioning theory in arguing that behavior is affected by cognitive processes.

2. Reciprocal determinism reflects Bandura's belief that neither personal dispositions nor environmental factors can by themselves explain behavior. Instead, Bandura assumes that personality traits, environmental factors, and overt behavior affect one another.

3. Cultural values and social experiences become integrated into the self, producing differences in the construal of self-schema. People in Western cultures value independent aspects of the self; people in Asian cultures value interdependent aspects of the self.

4. In experience sampling, participants carry a portable device that beeps at random times, and on hearing the beep, the person reports her or his experiences and behaviors at that time.

The Humanistic Approach to Personality

1. The humanistic approach tends to have a positive view of human nature, studies subjective mental experience, and assumes we have free will.

2. Some of the research topics include self-actualization, self-schema, self-concept, self-development, and self-esteem.

3. You would have the person sort the cards twice, first into piles of statements that are or are not characteristic of the actual self and then into piles of statements that are or are not characteristic of the ideal self.

The Biopsychological Approach to Personality

1. Because Sheldon rated participants' somatotype and temperament, his findings possibly were influenced by experimenter bias. Also, whereas Sheldon found a modest relationship between somatotype and personality, other researchers have been unable to replicate his findings.

2. Researchers have found amazing similarities in the personalities of identical twins reared apart and reunited later in life.

Characteristics of Psychological Disorders

1. The biopsychological viewpoint emphasizes the role of genetic and biological factors. The psychoanalytic perspective emphasizes the role of the unconscious mind. The behavioral perspective emphasizes the role of the environment and learning in the development of maladaptive behaviors. The cognitive viewpoint emphasizes maladaptive thoughts. The humanistic perspective emphasizes failure in reaching one's human potential. And the sociocultural viewpoint emphasizes the role of cultural factors.

2. The cognitive rule says that a person was insane at the time of a crime if the person did not know what he or she had done or did not know that it was wrong. The volitional rule says that the person was insane at the time of the crime if the person was not in voluntary control of his or her actions.

3. Rosenhan's findings indicate that the diagnosis of psychological disorders is influenced more by the label provided by the diagnosis and the treatment setting than by behavioral or psychological attributes of the person.

Anxiety Disorders

1. Agoraphobia prompts so many people to seek therapy because it disrupts every aspect of the sufferer's life, including intimate relationships

2. Some people with panic disorder are hypersensitive to carbon dioxide levels in their blood. Instead of breathing normally to reduce carbon dioxide levels, they might respond as if they are being suffocated and experience a panic attack.

Obsessive-Compulsive Disorder

1. Obsessions and compulsions might be seen as ways of avoiding anxiety-inducing situations and responses to imagined threats.

2. People with obsessive-compulsive disorder report higher levels of guilt and a history of separation anxiety,

Somatic Symptom and Related Disorders

1. A malingerer would have no physical ailment. A person with illness anxiety disorder would exaggerate minor ailments. A person with conversion disorder would display sensory or motor loss or the alteration of a physiological function without any apparent physiological cause.

2. The person shows remarkable indifference to an apparently serious physical problem.

Dissociative Disorders

1. Most of them have suffered physical and sexual abuse as young children.

2. Some psychologists believe that people suffering from dissociative identity disorder are doing little more than role playing and do not, in fact, have more than one personality.

Major Depressive Disorder and Related Disorders

1. Seligman's theory explains major depressive disorder in terms of the attributions we make for events in our lives.

According to this theory, people with major depressive disorder attribute negative events in their lives to stable, global, internal factors.

2. People who constantly think about and brood over the sad state of their lives experience more severe and more chronic major depressive disorder than do people who take action to improve their lives or who distract themselves by pursuing enjoyable activities.

3. Shneidman suggests that because suicide attempts are usually cries for help, the simple act of providing an empathetic response can reduce the immediate likelihood of an actual attempt. Just talking about a problem might reduce its apparent dreadfulness and help the person realize that solutions other than suicide are possible and that his or her options include more than a choice between death and a hopeless, helpless life. An immediate goal should be to relieve the person's psychological pain by intervening, if possible, with those who might be contributing to the pain, whether friends, lovers, teachers, or family members. You should also encourage the person to seek professional help, even if you have to make the appointment for the person and accompany him or her to it.

Bipolar Disorder

1. People with mania are sexually, physically, and financially reckless. They may also overestimate their own abilities, perhaps leading them to make poor decisions.

2. People with major depressive disorder do not have alternating periods of mania.

Schizophrenia

1. The major symptoms of schizophrenia are hallucinations, problems maintaining attention, language disturbances, delusions, flat or inappropriate emotionality, unusual motor behavior, and social withdrawal.

2. First, drugs that are used to treat schizophrenia work by blocking dopamine and serotonin receptors. Second, drugs such as amphetamines, which increase dopamine levels in the brain, can induce schizophrenic symptoms in healthy people. Third, L-dopa, a drug used to treat Parkinson's disease because it increases dopamine levels in the brain, can induce schizophrenic symptoms in Parkinson's victims. Fourth, brain-imaging studies have found that people with schizophrenia have overactive dopamine neurons.

3. Positive symptoms are active symptoms and include hallucinations, delusions, thought disorders, and bizarre behaviors. Negative symptoms are passive symptoms and include mutism, apathy, flat affect, social withdrawal, intellectual impairment, poverty of speech, and inability to experience pleasure.

Personality Disorders

1. People with antisocial personality disorder show an appalling lack of conscience and have no qualms about harming other people.

2. People with borderline personality disorder are impulsive,

have unstable moods, and exhibit problems in establishing interpersonal relationships. At first, the person you are dating might seem to be pleasant and charming. As the relationship continues, though, she or he becomes hostile and manipulative—especially if the relationship is becoming more intimate.

Developmental Disorders

1. Early theories of autism spectrum disorder (ASD) that were driven by Leo Kanner's observations believed that ASD was acquired through interactions with parents who were cold and hostile toward their children. Hence, parents were blamed for their child's poor social skills and impaired communication. We now know that parents of children with ASD are just as warm and sociable as other parents.

2. People with ASD have larger brain volumes and an increased number of abnormal cells.

3. The major symptoms are inattention, hyperactivity, and impulsivity that can persist into adulthood.

Chapter 15: TherapyThe History of Therapy

The History of Therapy

1. No, it might have been done for other purposes, perhaps medical, religious, or punitive.

2. Moral therapy used humane treatment, honest work, and pleasant recreation to promote mental well-being.

The Psychoanalytic Orientation

1. In free association, the client is urged to report any thoughts or feelings that come to mind—no matter how trivial or embarrassing they seem. This is supposed to reveal important information that can help the client gain self-knowledge.

2. In the analysis of resistances, the psychoanalyst notes behaviors that interfere with therapeutic progress toward self-awareness. These resistances are interpreted to uncover the unconscious conflicts that underlie them.

The Behavioral Orientation

1. You would first use progressive relaxation to train the student to relax. You would then set up a hierarchy of scenes related to oral presentation. Finally, you would have the student relax while first imagining low-anxiety scenes and gradually progressing to higher-anxiety scenes.

2. You would give the students tokens for doing well in spelling and arithmetic and let them trade in the tokens for things or activities they enjoy.

The Cognitive Orientation

1. Ellis assumes that maladaptive emotions and behaviors are caused by irrational thinking. Therefore, his therapeutic techniques are aimed at making his clients think more rationally.

2. Beck assumes that major depressive disorder is caused by negative beliefs about oneself, the world, and the future. Beck's cognitive therapy teaches clients to recognize their negative beliefs and replace them with positive beliefs.

The Humanistic Orientation

1. Client-centered therapy strives to create greater congruence between the client's actual self and the client's ideal self by encouraging clients to express and accept their true feelings. The person-centered therapist promotes self-actualization through reflection of feelings, genuineness, accurate empathy, and unconditional positive regard.

2. Gestalt therapy attempts to help clients become aware of their unconscious feelings, increase their emotional expressiveness, and change their maladaptive thoughts and behaviors.

The Social-Relations Orientation

1. transactional analysis (TA) assumes that there are basic roles we all play and that these are sometimes adaptive, sometimes maladaptive. TA teaches group members to recognize the roles they play in their interactions (their transactions, or the "games" they play) and to use this understanding to improve their social relations.

2. Assertiveness training is a form of social-skills training that teaches people to express their feelings constructively in social situations.

The Biological Orientation

1. Critics believe that Electroconvulsive therapy (ECT) is dangerous because it can cause brain damage, memory loss, and other problems. Others say its dangers are outweighed by its ability to induce neurogenesis to relieve major depressive disorder and prevent suicide.

2. The tricyclics increase the levels of serotonin and norepinephrine in the brain by preventing their re-uptake by brain neurons that release them.

Community Mental Health

1. Four factors brought this movement about: (1) new drug treatments, (2) the underfunding and overcrowding of mental hospitals, (3) an increased concern for the legal rights of mental patients, and (4) the Community Mental Health Centers Act of 1963, which mandated the establishment of federally funded mental health centers in every community in the United States.

2. Primary prevention helps prevent psychological disorders by fostering social support systems, eliminating sources of stress, and strengthening individuals' ability to deal with stressors. Secondary prevention provides early treatment for people at immediate risk of developing psychological disorders. Tertiary prevention helps people with psychological disorders from getting worse or relapsing after successful treatment.

The Rights of the Therapy Client

1. The right to refuse treatment has led to some mental hospital patients not receiving necessary therapy. The right to receive treatment assures that patients who do not receive treatment must be released from custodial care.

2. The *Tarasoff* decision has been praised because it might help protect individuals whom a therapy client has threatened to harm. It has been criticized because it might inhibit people who feel hostile toward others from dealing with those feelings honestly in therapy and because it creates a legal obligation to inform that conflicts with the therapist's ethical obligation to maintain confidentiality.

Finding the Proper Therapy

1. Psychological therapy may be provided by a psychologist, a psychiatrist, or other mental health professionals.

2. The college counseling center might be a good place to start. A friend, relative, or professor might be able to recommend a therapist or counseling center to you. Other potential sources of help or referral include community mental health associations.

The Effectiveness of Psychotherapy

1. He found that about two-thirds of people with psychological disorders improve with or without psychotherapy.

2. The client's perception of therapist empathy has been consistently identified as an important factor in the effectiveness of psychotherapy. Personal warmth has also been found to be a factor that differentiates successful and unsuccessful therapists.

Chapter 16: Psychology and Health

Psychological Stress and Stressors

1. A century ago most people died young from infectious diseases. Today, with infectious diseases under control, people live longer and tend to succumb to behavior-related diseases, including cancer and cardiovascular disease.

2. Some studies have found that there is a stronger association between hassles and illness than between life changes and illness. Moreover, life changes might produce their negative effects by increasing daily hassles.

3. This is a disorder that appears months or years after a person experiences a traumatic event. It includes emotional, cognitive, and behavioral symptoms.

The Biopsychology of Stress and Illness

1. Stress can suppress the immune response, particularly natural killer cell activity, which might reduce the body's ability to destroy cancerous cells.

2. Stress stimulates the secretion of adrenal hormones, which have an immunosuppressive effect.

3. In animal studies, when a neutral stimulus is paired with a drug (an unconditioned stimulus) that alters the immune response (an unconditioned response), the neutral stimulus will become a conditioned stimulus that likewise alters the immune response (a conditioned response).

Factors That Moderate the Stress Response

1. Hardiness involves a sense of commitment, challenge, and control.

2. Social support promotes health by reducing the effects of stressful life events, promoting recovery from illness, and increasing adherence to medical regimens

Coping with Stress

1. The study found that adolescents under high levels of stress who exercised regularly had a significantly lower incidence of illness than did adolescents who exercised little.

2. The study found that the students who were not assigned to practice relaxation, compared to the students who were, displayed a significantly greater decrease in natural killer cell activity during final exams.

Health-Promoting Habits

1. HIV is most commonly transmitted by breastfeeding, the sharing of hypodermic needles by drug users, and unprotected anal and vaginal sex.

2. Aerobic exercise boosts the basal metabolic rate, promotes weight control, and reduces the risk of cardiovascular disease.

3. Dieting by itself slows the basal metabolic rate, cannot last a lifetime, promotes the loss of lean body tissue, and tends

to result in greater weight gain from rebound eating when the diet ends.

Reactions to Illness

1. Important factors include social support, explanatory style, and interpretation of symptoms.

2. A study found a negative correlation between the perceived empathy of nurses and patient anger, anxiety, and major depressive disorder. Patients who perceive a lack of empathy in their physicians are more likely to sue them for malpractice. And practitioners must communicate so that patients will adhere to medical regimens.

Chapter 17: Social Psychology

Social Cognition

1. The three dimensions in Weiner's attribution model are internal-external, stable-unstable, and controllable-uncontrollable.

2. The self-serving bias is the tendency to make dispositional attributions for our positive behaviors and situational attributions for our negative behaviors.

3. This occurs because the social schema we have of the other person will make us act a certain way toward that person, which in turn can make the person respond in accordance with our expectations.

Interpersonal Attraction

1. Evidence includes the fact that we like people more the more we are exposed to them. We even like images of our own faces that we see in mirrors more than images of our faces as they are seen by other people.

2. According to two-factor theory, the experience of physiological aroused in a situation that promotes the labeling of this arousal as love results in the development of romantic love.

3. Men offer financial status and seek physical attractiveness. Women seek financially well-off men and note their own physical attractiveness.

Attitudes

1. Attitudes that are strongly held or personally important are better predictors of behavior. Attitude-behavior consistency is also affected by the specificity of the attitude and the behavior.

2. A message that takes a central route relies on clear, explicit arguments about the issue at hand. A message that takes a peripheral route relies on factors other than the merits of the arguments, such as characteristics of the source or the situational context.

3. For such contact to reduce prejudice, it must be between people of equal status.

Group Dynamics

1. Groupthink can be prevented by not assigning a group leader and by encouraging group members to consider as many alternatives as possible.

2. Social facilitation enhances performance on easy or well-learned tasks. Social facilitation impairs performance on difficult tasks or tasks that are not well learned.

3. A good way to reduce social loafing is to convince group members that their individual efforts will be evaluated or that they will be held accountable. Social loafing can also be overcome when a task is important to an individual and that person believes other group members lack the ability to perform better.

4. Participants in Milgram's experiments were asked to increase shock gradually, in 15-volt increments. Their initial compliance in administering mild shock might have contributed to their obedience to the experimenter's instructions to administer higher levels of shock

Aggression

1. Violent criminals have higher levels of testosterone than nonviolent criminals do. Athletes who use anabolic steroids become more aggressive.

2. When people feel anonymous, are emotionally aroused, and experience reduced self-awareness, they are more likely to take part in group aggression.

Prosocial Behavior

1. Some research indicates that people will be more likely to help other people if they believe it will relieve their own negative feelings, such as guilt.

2. When strangers notice someone in trouble, as the number of strangers increases, their probability of helping decreases, apparently because each feels less responsible for helping.

Answers to Chapter Quiz Questions

Chapter 1

1. B	4. B	7. C	10. B	13. B	16. C	19. C	22. B	25. B
2. A	5. D	8. D	11. C	14. A	17. A	20. C	23. D	
3. A	6. B	9. D	12. D	15. D	18.. B	21. C	24. A	

Chapter 2

1. D	4. A	7. D	10. D	13. D	16. A	19. C	22. A	25. B
2. B	5. C	8. B	11. C	14. B	17. A	20. D	23. B	
3. B	6. B	9. B	12. D	15. C	18. B	21. B	24. A	

Chapter 3

1. A	4. C	7. B	10. A	13. A	16. C	19. D	22. B	25. C
2. B	5. A	8. A	11. C	14. C	17. D	20. D	23. C	
3. A	6. C	9. C	12. D	15. B	18. B	21. A	24. B	

Chapter 4

1. B	4. B	7. A	10. D	13. B	16. A	19. A	22. C	
2. C	5. C	8. C	11. C	14. A	17. B	20. A	23. A	
3. C	6. B	9. B	12. B	15. B	18. C	21. C	24. B	

Chapter 5

1. B	4. B	7. D	10. C	13. D	16. B	19. B	22. D	25. B
2. B	5. A	8. C	11. C	14. A	17. C	20. B	23. C	
3. C	6. B	9. D	12. D	15. A	18. B	21. D	24. C	

Chapter 6

1. A	4. C	7. C	10. B	13. D	16. D	19. C	22. A	25. A
2. A	5. A	8. D	11. D	14. D	17. D	20. B	23. D	
3. A	6. C	9. A	12. C	15. A	18. C	21. C	24. D	

Chapter 7

1. C	4. D	7. D	10. B	13. B	16. B	19. A	22. C	25. A
2. D	5. C	8. A	11. C	14. C	17. C	20. B	23. D	
3. B	6. C	9. A	12. A	15. A	18. B	21. B	24. B	

Chapter 8

1. A	4. D	7. B	10. A	13. C	16. A	19. C	22. B	25. A
2. D	5. A	8. C	11. D	14. C	17. B	20. B	23. D	
3. A	6. C	9. B	12. D	15. C	18. A	21. D	24. D	

Chapter 9

1. D	4. C	7. C	10. A	13. A	16. A	19. C	22. B	25. B
2. D	5. B	8. D	11. A	14. D	17. D	20. B	23. B	
3. B	6. D	9. B	12. A	15. C	18. C	21. B	24. B	

Chapter 10

1. D	4. D	7. D	10. B	13. B	16. C	19. A	22. D	25. C
2. B	5. A	8. A	11. B	14. D	17. B	20. D	23. C	
3. D	6. A	9. C	12. C	15. D	18. C	21. C	24. A	

Chapter 11

1. D	4. A	7. A	10. D	13. C	16. C	19. B	22. D	25. A
2. A	5. A	8. B	11. C	14. A	17. B	20. B	23. D	
3. B	6. D	9. A	12. C	15. C	18. D	21. B	24. C	

Chapter 12

1. A	4. A	7. C	10. A	13. C	16. A	19. D	22. B	25. D
2. B	5. D	8. A	11. B	14. D	17. B	20. C	23. C	
3. C	6. B	9. A	12. B	15. B	18. D	21. A	24. C	

Chapter 13

1. C	4. C	7. D	10. C	13. B	16. A	19. A	22. B	25. C
2. D	5. B	8. D	11. D	14. A	17. A	20. C	23. B	
3. A	6. B	9. A	12. C	15. D	18. B	21. C	24. A	

Chapter 14

1. B	4. A	7. C	10. A	13. C	16. D	19. C	22. A	25. D
2. D	5. A	8. D	11. D	14. A	17. A	20. C	23. D	
3. B	6. C	9. C	12. B	15. A	18. A	21. B	24. D	

Chapter 15

1. A	4. A	7. A	10. C	13. C	16. B	19. C	22. C	25. D
2. A	5. B	8. B	11. B	14. C	17. D	20. D	23. C	
3. D	6. D	9. B	12. A	15. D	18. D	21. C	24. C	

Chapter 16

1. A	4. D	7. A.	10. A	13. B	16. C	19. D	22. C	25. D
2. A	5. D	8. C	11. C	14. A	17. B	20. B	23. C	
3. C	6. A	9. C	12. D	15. B	18. B	21. C	24. B	

Chapter 17

1. C	4. A	7. B	10. D	13. A	16. B	19. C	22. A	25. A
2. C	5. D	8. D	11. D	14. C	17. D	20. C	23. B	
3. A	6. A	9. A	12. D	15. A	18. A	21. C	24. D	

Key Contributors

Chapter 1: The Nature of Psychology

The Historical Context of Psychology

Contemporary Perspectives in Psychology

Chapter 2: Psychology as a Science

Sources of Knowledge

Goals of Scientific Research

Methods of Psychological Research

Statistical Analysis of Research Data

Ethics of Psychological Research

Chapter 3: Biopsychological Bases of Behavior

Nature versus Nurture

Neuronal Activity

Brain Functions

Chapter 16: Psychology and Health

Chapter 17: Social Psychology

Glossary

A

absolute threshold The minimum amount of stimulation that an individual can detect through a given sense.

accommodation 1. The cognitive process that revises existing schemas to incorporate new information. 2. The process by which the lens of the eye increases its curvature to focus light from close objects or decreases its curvature to focus light from more distant objects.

achievement motive The desire for mastery, excellence, and accomplishment.

achievement test A test that measures knowledge of a particular subject.

acronym A mnemonic device that involves forming a term from the first letters of a series of words that are to be recalled.

action potential A series of changes in the electrical charge across the axonal membrane that occurs after the axon has reached its firing threshold.

activation-synthesis theory The theory that dreams are the by-products of the cortex's attempt to make sense of the spontaneous changes in physiological activity generated by the brain stem during REM sleep.

acupuncture A pain-relieving technique that relies on the insertion of fine needles into various sites on the body.

adaptation-level theory The theory that happiness depends on comparing one's present circumstances with one's past circumstances.

adolescence The transitional period lasting from the onset of puberty to the beginning of adulthood.

adrenal gland An endocrine gland that secretes hormones that regulate the excretion of minerals and the body's response to stress.

adulthood The period beginning when the individual assumes responsibility for her or his own life.

afterimage An image that persists after the removal of a visual stimulus.

age regression A hypnotic state in which the individual apparently behaves as she or he did as a child.

aggression Verbal or physical behavior aimed at harming another person.

agoraphobia A fear of being in public, usually because the person fears the embarrassment of a panic attack.

algorithm A problem-solving rule or procedure that, when followed step by step, ensures that a correct solution will be found.

all-or-none law The principle that once a neuron reaches its firing threshold, a neural impulse travels at full strength along the entire length of its axon.

altruism The helping of others without the expectation of a reward.

Alzheimer's disease A brain disorder characterized by difficulty in forming new memories and by general mental deterioration.

amphetamines Stimulants used to maintain alertness and wakefulness.

amygdala A limbic system structure that evaluates information from the immediate environment, contributing to feelings of fear, anger, or relief.

anal stage In Freud's theory, the stage of personality development between ages 1 and 3, during which the child gains pleasure from defecation and faces a conflict over toilet training.

analysis of dreams In psychoanalysis, the process by which the therapist interprets the symbolic, manifest content of dreams to reveal their true, latent content to the client.

analysis of free associations In psychoanalysis, the process by which the therapist interprets the underlying meaning of the client's uncensored reports of anything that comes to mind.

analysis of resistances In psychoanalysis, the process by which the therapist interprets client behaviors that interfere with therapeutic progress toward uncovering unconscious conflicts.

analysis of transference In psychoanalysis, the process by which the therapist interprets the feelings expressed by the client toward the therapist as being indicative of the feelings typically expressed by the client toward important people in his or her personal life.

analytic introspection A research method in which highly trained participants report the contents of their conscious mental experiences.

andropause The gradual decline of testosterone experienced by men after the age of 40.

anorexia nervosa An eating disorder marked by self-starvation.

antianxiety drugs Psychoactive drugs that are used to treat anxiety disorders.

antidepressant drugs Psychoactive drugs that are used to treat major depressive disorder.

antipsychotic drugs Psychoactive drugs that are used to treat schizophrenia.

antisocial personality disorder A personality disorder marked by impulsive, manipulative, often criminal behavior, without any feelings of guilt in the perpetrator.

anxiety disorder A psychological disorder marked by persistent and unrealistic worry that disrupts everyday functioning.

applied research Research aimed at improving the quality of life and solving practical problems.

aptitude test A test designed to predict a person's potential to benefit from instruction in a particular academic or vocational setting.

archetypes In Jung's theory, inherited images that are passed down from our prehistoric ancestors and that reveal themselves as universal symbols in art, dreams, and religion.

archival research The systematic examination of collections of letters, manuscripts, tape recordings, video recordings, or other records.

arousal motive The motive to maintain an optimal level of physiological activation.

artificial intelligence (AI) The field that integrates computer science and cognitive psychology in studying information processing through the design of computer programs that appear to exhibit intelligence.

assertiveness training A form of social-skills training that teaches clients to express their feelings constructively.

assimilation The cognitive process that interprets new information in light of existing schemas.

association area Regions of the cerebral cortex that integrate information from the primary cortical areas and other brain areas.

attention The process by which the individual focuses awareness on certain contents of consciousness while ignoring others.

attention deficit hyperactivity disorder (ADHD) A developmental disorder that begins in childhood and can persist into adulthood that is characterized by persistent lack of attention, distractibility when engaged in important tasks, impulsive behavior, hyperactivity, and failure to follow through with future plans.

attitude An evaluation—containing cognitive, emotional, and behavioral components—of an idea, event, object, or person.

audition The sense of hearing.

auditory cortex The area of the temporal lobes that processes sounds.

auditory nerve The nerve that conducts impulses from the cochlea to the brain.

authoritarian personality A personality type marked by the tendency to obey superiors while dominating subordinates, to favor one's own group while being prejudiced against other groups, and to be unwilling to admit one's own faults while projecting them onto members of other groups.

authoritative parenting An effective style of parenting in which the parent is warm and loving yet sets well-defined limits that he or she enforces in an appropriate manner.

autism spectrum disorder (ASD) A group of psychological conditions characterized by a range of poor social skills, impaired communication, and repetitive behaviors that are present in early childhood.

automatic processing Information processing that requires less conscious awareness and cognitive effort and that does not interfere with the performance of other ongoing activities.

autonomic nervous system The division of the peripheral nervous system that controls automatic, involuntary, physiological processes.

autonomy versus shame and doubt Erikson's developmental stage in which success is achieved by gaining a degree of independence from one's parents.

availability heuristic In decision making, the tendency to estimate the probability of an event by how easily relevant instances of it come to mind.

aversion therapy A form of behavior therapy that inhibits maladaptive behavior by pairing a stimulus that normally elicits a maladaptive response with an unpleasant stimulus.

avoidance learning Learning to prevent the occurrence of an aversive stimulus by giving an appropriate response to a warning stimulus.

axon The part of the neuron that conducts neural impulses to glands, muscles, or other neurons.

axonal conduction The transmission of a neural impulse along the length of an axon.

B

barbiturates Depressants used to induce sleep or anesthesia.

basal metabolic rate The rate at which the body burns calories just to keep itself alive.

basic research Research aimed at finding answers to questions out of theoretical interest or intellectual curiosity.

basilar membrane A membrane running the length of the cochlea that contains the auditory receptor (hair) cells.

behavior therapy The therapeutic application of the principles of learning to change maladaptive behaviors.

behavioral contingencies Relationships between behaviors and their consequences, such as positive reinforcement, negative reinforcement, extinction, and punishment.

behavioral genetics The study of the relative effects of heredity and life experiences on behavior.

behavioral neuroscience The field that studies the physiological bases of human and animal behavior and mental processes.

behavioral preparedness The degree to which members of a species are innately prepared to learn particular behaviors.

behaviorism The psychological viewpoint that rejects the study of mental processes in favor of the study of overt behavior.

binocular cues Depth perception cues that require input from the two eyes.

biofeedback A form of operant conditioning that enables an individual to learn to control a normally involuntary physiological process or to gain better control of a normally voluntary one when provided with visual or auditory information indicating the state of that response.

biological rhythms Repeating cycles of physiological changes.

biopsychosocial model The model that considers that psychological disorders are the result of an interaction of biological, psychological, and social factors.

biopsychological perspective The psychological viewpoint that stresses the relationship of physiological factors to behavior and mental processes.

bipolar disorder A mood disorder marked by periods of mania alternating with longer periods of major depressive disorder.

blocking The process by which a neutral stimulus paired with a conditioned stimulus that already elicits a conditioned response fails to become a conditioned stimulus.

borderline personality disorder (BPD) A personality disorder marked by impulsivity, unstable moods, an inconsistent sense of identity, and difficulty maintaining intimate relationships.

brain The structure of the central nervous system that is located in the skull and plays important roles in sensation, movement, and information processing.

brain stem A group of brain structures that provide life-support functions.

brightness constancy The perceptual process that makes an object maintain a particular level of brightness despite changes in the amount of light reflected from it.

Broca's area The region of the frontal lobe responsible for the production of speech.

bulimia nervosa An eating disorder marked by binging and purging.

burnout A state of physical and psychological exhaustion associated with chronic exposure to uncontrollable stress.

bystander intervention The act of helping someone who is in immediate need of aid.

C

caffeine A stimulant used to increase mental alertness.

Cannon-Bard theory The theory that an emotion is produced when an event or object is perceived by the thalamus, which conveys this information simultaneously to the cerebral cortex and the skeletal muscles and sympathetic nervous system.

case study An in-depth study of an individual.

cataplexy A sudden and temporary loss of muscle tone in the body while conscious that is triggered by laughing or crying.

catharsis In psychoanalysis, the release of repressed emotional energy as a consequence of insight into the unconscious causes of one's psychological problems.

causal attribution The cognitive process by which we infer the causes of both our own and other people's social behavior.

causation An effect of one or more variables on another variable.

central nervous system The division of the nervous system consisting of the brain and the spinal cord.

cerebellum A brain stem structure that controls the timing of well-learned movements.

cerebral cortex The outer covering of the brain.

cerebral hemisphere The left and right halves of the cerebrum.

cerebral palsy A movement disorder that is caused by brain damage and is sometimes accompanied by intellectual disability.

chaining An operant conditioning procedure used to establish a desired sequence of behaviors by positively reinforcing each behavior in the sequence.

childhood The period that extends from birth until the onset of puberty.

circadian rhythms Twenty-four-hour cycles of physiological changes, most notably the sleep-wake cycle.

clairvoyance The alleged ability to perceive objects or events without any sensory contact with them.

classical conditioning A form of learning in which a neutral stimulus comes to elicit a response after being associated with a stimulus that already elicits that response.

clinical psychology The field that applies psychological principles to the prevention, diagnosis, and treatment of psychological disorders.

cocaine A stimulant used to induce cognitive alertness and euphoria.

cochlea The spiral, fluid-filled structure of the inner ear that contains the receptor cells for hearing.

coefficient of correlation A statistic that assesses the degree of association between two or more variables.

cognitive appraisal The subjective interpretation of the severity of a stressor.

cognitive-appraisal theory The theory that our emotion at a given time depends on our interpretation of the situation we are in at that time.

cognitive-dissonance theory Leon Festinger's theory that attitude change is motivated by the desire to relieve the unpleasant state of arousal caused when one holds cognitions and/or behaviors that are inconsistent with each other.

cognitive-evaluation theory The theory that a person's intrinsic motivation will increase when a reward is perceived as a source of information but will decrease when a reward is perceived as an attempt to exert control.

cognitive neuroscience The study of the neurological bases of cognitive processes.

cognitive perspective The psychological viewpoint that favors the study of how the mind organizes perceptions, processes information, and interprets experiences.

cognitive psychology The field of psychology that studies cognitive processes such as thought and language.

cognitive therapy A type of therapy, developed by Aaron Beck, that aims at eliminating exaggerated negative beliefs about oneself, the world, or the future.

cohort A group of people of the same age group.

cohort-sequential research A research design that begins as a cross-sectional study by comparing different cohorts and then follows the cohorts longitudinally.

collateral sprouting The process in which branches from the axons of nearby healthy neurons grow into the pathways normally occupied by the axons of damaged neurons.

collective efficacy People's perception that with collaborative effort the group will obtain its desired outcome.

collective unconscious In Jung's theory, the unconscious mind that is shared by all people and that contains archetypal images passed down from our prehistoric ancestors.

color blindness The inability to distinguish between certain colors, most often red and green.

companionate love Love characterized by feelings of affection and commitment to a relationship with another person.

comparative psychology The field that studies similarities and differences in the physiology, behaviors, and abilities of different species of animals, including humans.

compliance Behaving in accordance with a request that is backed by little or no threat of punishment.

computed tomography (CT) A brain-scanning technique that relies on X-rays to construct computer-generated images of the brain or body.

computer-assisted instruction The use of computer programs to provide programmed instruction.

concept A category of objects, events, qualities, or relations that share certain features.

concrete operational stage The Piagetian stage, extending from 7 to 11 years of age, during which the child learns to reason logically about objects that are physically present.

conditioned response (CR) In classical conditioning, the learned response given to a particular conditioned stimulus.

conditioned stimulus (CS) In classical conditioning, a neutral stimulus that comes to elicit a particular conditioned response after being paired with a particular unconditioned stimulus that already elicits that response.

conditioned taste aversion A taste aversion induced by pairing a taste with gastrointestinal distress.

conduction deafness Hearing loss usually caused by blockage of the auditory canal, damage to the eardrum, or deterioration of the ossicles of the middle ear.

cones Receptor cells of the retina that play an important role in day vision and color vision.

confluence model Robert Zajonc's model of environmental influences on intelligence, which assumes that each child is born into an intellectual environment related to birth order and to the number and differences in age of her or his siblings.

conformity Behaving in accordance with group expectations with little or no overt pressure to do so.

confounding variable A variable whose unwanted effect on the dependent variable might be confused with that of the independent variable.

conscious mind The level of consciousness that includes the cognitive experiences that we are aware of at a given moment.

consciousness Awareness of one's own cognitive activity, including thoughts, feelings, and sensations.

conservation The realization that changing the form of a substance does not change its amount.

constructive recall The distortion of memories by adding, dropping, or changing details to fit a schema.

context-dependent memory The tendency for recall to be best when the environmental context present during the encoding of a memory is also present during attempts at retrieving it.

continuous schedule of reinforcement A schedule of reinforcement that provides reinforcement for each instance of a desired response.

control group The participants in an experiment who are not exposed to the experimental condition of interest.

controlled processing Information processing that involves conscious awareness and cognitive effort and that interferes with the performance of other ongoing activities.

conventional level In Kohlberg's theory, the level of moral reasoning characterized by concern with upholding laws and conventional values and by favoring obedience to authority.

convergent thinking The cognitive process that focuses on finding conventional solutions to problems.

conversion disorder A somatic symptom and related disorder in which the person exhibits motor or sensory loss or the alteration of a physiological function without any apparent physical cause.

cornea The round, transparent area in the front of the sclera that allows light to enter the eye.

corpus callosum A thick bundle of axons that provides a means of communication between the cerebral hemispheres and that is severed in so-called split-brain surgery.

correlation The degree of relationship between two or more variables.

correlational research Research that studies the degree of relationship between two or more variables.

correlational statistics Statistics that determine the relationship between two variables.

counseling psychology The field that applies psychological principles to help individuals deal with problems of daily living, generally less serious ones than those treated by clinical psychologists.

counterconditioning A behavior therapy technique that applies the principles of classical conditioning to replace unpleasant emotional responses to stimuli with more pleasant ones.

creativity A form of problem solving that generates novel, socially valued solutions to problems.

critical period A period in childhood when experience with language produces optimal language acquisition.

cross-cultural psychology An approach that tries to determine the extent to which research findings about human psychology hold true across cultures.

cross-sectional research A research design in which groups of participants of different ages are compared at the same point in time.

crystallized intelligence The form of intelligence that reflects knowledge acquired through schooling and in everyday life.

cultural competence The consideration of sociocultural factors such as gender, ethnicity, sexual orientation, and religion in psychological training and practice.

cultural psychology An approach that studies how cultural factors affect human behavior and mental experience.

D

dark adaptation The process by which the eyes become more sensitive to light when under low illumination.

debriefing A procedure, after the completion of a research study, that informs participants of the purpose of the study and aims to remove any physical or psychological distress caused by participation.

decay theory The theory that forgetting occurs because memories naturally fade over time.

decision making A form of problem solving in which one tries to make the best choice from among alternative judgments or courses of action.

declarative memory The long-term memory system that contains memories of facts.

deep structure The underlying meaning of a statement.

defense mechanism In Freud's theory, a process that distorts reality to prevent the individual from being overwhelmed by anxiety.

deindividuation The process by which group members become less aware of themselves as individuals and less concerned about being socially evaluated.

deinstitutionalization The movement toward treating people with psychological disorders in community settings instead of mental hospitals.

dèjá vu A feeling that you have experienced a present situation in the past and that you can anticipate what will happen next.

dendrites The branchlike structures of the neuron that receive neural impulses.

dependent variable A variable showing the effect of the independent variable.

depressants Psychoactive drugs that inhibit activity in the central nervous system.

depth perception The perception of the relative distance of objects.

descriptive research Research that involves the recording of behaviors that have been observed systematically.

descriptive statistics Statistics that summarize research data.

determinism The assumption that every event has physical, potentially measurable, causes.

developmental disorders Psychological disorders originating in childhood that can be characterized by physical, learning, language, or behavioral impairments. The disorder can improve or persist throughout a person's lifetime.

developmental psychology The field that studies physical, perceptual, cognitive, and psychosocial changes across the life span.

difference threshold The minimum amount of change in stimulation that can be detected.

differential psychology The field of psychology that studies individual differences in physical, personality, and intellectual characteristics.

discriminative stimulus In operant conditioning, a stimulus that indicates the likelihood that a particular response will be reinforced.

disparagement theory The theory that humor is amusing when it makes one feel superior to other people.

displacement The characteristic of language marked by the ability to refer to objects and events that are not present.

dissociation A state in which the mind is split into two or more independent streams of consciousness.

dissociative amnesia The inability to recall personally significant memories.

dissociative disorder A psychological disorder in which thoughts, feelings, and memories become separated from conscious awareness.

dissociative fugue Memory loss characteristic of dissociative amnesia as well as the loss of one's identity and fleeing from one's prior life.

dissociative identity disorder A dissociative disorder, more commonly known as multiple personality disorder, in which the person has two or more distinct personalities that alternate with one another.

distributed practice Spreading out the memorization of information or the learning of a motor skill over several sessions.

divergent thinking The cognitive process by which an individual freely considers a variety of potential solutions to artistic, literary, scientific, or practical problems.

door-in-the-face technique Increasing the likelihood that a person will comply with a request by first getting the person to reject a larger one.

double-blind technique A procedure that controls experimenter bias and participant bias by preventing experimenters and participants from knowing which participants have been assigned to particular conditions.

Down syndrome A form of intellectual disability, associated with certain physical deformities, that is caused by an extra, third chromosome on the 21st pair.

dream A storylike sequence of visual images, usually occurring during REM sleep.

drive A state of psychological tension induced by a need.

drive-reduction theory The theory that behavior is motivated by the need to reduce drives such as sex or hunger.

E

echoic memory Auditory sensory memory, which lasts up to 4 or more seconds.

educational psychology The field that applies psychological principles to help improve curriculum, teaching methods, and administrative procedures.

ego In Freud's theory, the part of the personality that helps the individual adapt to external reality by making compromises between the id, the superego, and the environment.

egocentrism The inability to perceive reality from the perspective of another person.

elaboration likelihood theory A theory of persuasion that considers the extent to which messages take a central route or a peripheral route.

elaborative rehearsal Actively organizing new information to make it more meaningful and integrating it with information already stored in long-term memory.

Electra complex A term used by some psychoanalysts, but not by Freud, to refer to the Oedipus complex in girls.

electroconvulsive therapy (ECT) A biological therapy that uses brief electric currents to induce brain seizures in victims of major depressive disorder.

electroencephalograph (EEG) A device used to record patterns of electrical activity produced by neuronal activity in the brain.

embryonic stage The prenatal period that lasts from the end of the second week through the eighth week.

emotion A motivated state marked by physiological arousal, expressive behavior, and cognitive experience.

empiricism The philosophical position that true knowledge comes through the senses.

encoding The conversion of information into a form that can be stored in memory.

encoding specificity The principle that recall will be best when cues that were associated with the encoding of a memory are also present during attempts at retrieving it.

endocrine system The physiological system whose glands secrete hormones into the bloodstream.

endorphins Neurotransmitters that play a role in pleasure, pain relief, and other functions.

engram A memory trace in the brain.

entactogens A new category of psychoactive drugs that have unique effects intermediate to those associated with hallucinogens and stimulants.

environmental psychology The field that applies psychological principles to help improve the physical environment, including the design of buildings and the reduction of noise.

episodic memory The subsystem of declarative memory that contains memories of personal experiences tied to particular times and places.

escape learning Learning to perform a behavior that terminates an aversive stimulus, as in negative reinforcement.

ethnic psychology The field that employs culturally appropriate methods to describe the experience of members of groups that historically have been underrepresented in psychology.

ethology The study of animal behavior in the natural environment.

ethyl alcohol (ethanol) A depressant found in beverages and commonly used to reduce social inhibitions.

eugenics The practice of encouraging supposedly superior people to reproduce while preventing supposedly inferior people from reproducing.

evolutionary psychology The study of the evolution of behavior through natural selection.

existential psychology A branch of humanistic psychology that studies how individuals respond to the basic philosophical issues of life, such as death, meaning, freedom, and isolation.

expectancy 1. The strength of the individual's beliefs about whether a particular outcome is attainable. 2. The perceived probability of success in a particular area.

experimental group Participants in an experiment who are exposed to the experimental condition of interest.

experimental method Research that manipulates one or more variables, while controlling other factors, to determine the effects on one or more other variables.

experimental psychology The field primarily concerned with laboratory research on basic psychological processes, including perception, learning, memory, thinking, language, motivation, and emotion.

experimenter bias effect The tendency of experimenters to let their expectancies alter the way they treat their participants.

expert systems Computer programs that display expertise in specific domains of knowledge.

explanatory style The tendency to explain events optimistically or pessimistically.

explicit memory Conscious recollection of general information or personal experiences.

external validity The extent to which the results of a research study can be generalized to other people, animals, or settings.

extinction 1. In classical conditioning, the gradual disappearance of the conditioned response when the conditioned stimulus is repeatedly presented without being paired with the unconditioned stimulus. 2. In operant conditioning, the gradual disappearance of a response that is no longer followed by a reinforcer.

extrasensory perception (ESP) The alleged ability to perceive events without the use of sensory receptors.

extravert A person who is socially outgoing and prefers to pay attention to the external environment.

extrinsic motivation The desire to perform a behavior in order to obtain an external reward, such as praise, grades, or money.

eyewitness testimony Witnesses' recollections about events, most notably about criminal activity.

F

facial-feedback theory The theory that particular facial expressions induce particular emotional experiences.

factor analysis A statistical technique that determines the degree of correlation between performances on various tasks to determine the extent to which they reflect particular underlying characteristics, which are known as factors.

family therapy A form of group therapy that encourages the constructive expression of feelings and the establishment of rules that family members agree to follow.

feature-detector theory The theory that we construct perceptions of stimuli from activity in neurons of the brain that are sensitive to specific features of those stimuli.

fetal alcohol syndrome A disorder, marked by physical defects and intellectual disability, that can afflict the offspring of women who drink alcohol during pregnancy.

fetal stage The prenatal period that lasts from the end of the eighth week through birth.

field experiment An experiment that is conducted in real-life as opposed to laboratory settings.

fight-or-flight response A state of physiological arousal that enables us to meet sudden threats by either confronting them or running away from them.

figure-ground perception The distinguishing of an object (the figure) from its surroundings (the ground).

fixed-interval schedule of reinforcement A partial schedule of reinforcement that provides reinforcement for the first desired response made after a set length of time.

fixed-ratio schedule of reinforcement A partial schedule of reinforcement that provides reinforcement after a set number of desired responses.

flashbulb memory A vivid, long-lasting memory of a surprising, important, emotionally arousing event.

flooding An extinction procedure in which a phobic client is exposed to a stimulus that evokes intense anxiety.

fluid intelligence The form of intelligence that reflects reasoning ability, memory capacity, and speed of information processing.

foot-in-the-door technique Increasing the likelihood that a person will comply with a request by first getting the person to comply with a smaller one.

forensic psychology The field that applies psychological principles to improve the legal system, including the work of police and juries.

forgetting The failure to retrieve information from memory.

forgetting curve A graph showing that forgetting is initially rapid and then slows.

formal operational stage The Piagetian stage, beginning at about age 11, marked by the ability to use abstract reasoning and to solve problems by testing hypotheses.

fovea A small area at the center of the retina that contains only cones and provides the most acute vision.

framing effects Biases introduced into the decision-making process by presenting an issue or situation in a certain manner.

frequency theory The theory of pitch perception that assumes that the basilar membrane vibrates as a whole in direct proportion to the frequency of the sound waves striking the eardrum.

frontal lobe A lobe of the cerebral cortex responsible for motor control and higher mental processes.

frustration-aggression hypothesis The assumption that frustration causes aggression.

functional fixedness The inability to realize that a problem can be solved by using a familiar object in an unusual way.

functional magnetic resonance imaging (fMRI) A brain-scanning technique that relies on strong magnetic fields to construct computer-generated images of physiological activity in the brain or body.

functionalism The early psychological viewpoint that studied how the conscious mind helps the individual adapt to the environment.

fundamental attribution error The bias to attribute other people's behavior to dispositional factors.

G

gate-control theory The theory that pain impulses can be blocked by the closing of a neuronal gate in the spinal cord.

gender identity One's self-perceived sex.

gender roles Behaviors that are considered appropriate for women or men in a given culture.

gender schema theory A theory of gender-role development that combines aspects of social learning theory and the cognitive perspective.

general adaptation syndrome As first identified by Hans Selye, the body's stress response, which includes the stages of alarm, resistance, and exhaustion.

generalized anxiety disorder An anxiety disorder marked by a persistent state of worry that exists independently of any particular stressful situation and often interferes with daily functioning.

generativity The characteristic of language marked by the ability to combine words in novel, meaningful ways.

generativity versus stagnation Erikson's developmental stage in which success is achieved by becoming less self-absorbed and more concerned with the well-being of others.

genital stage In Freud's theory, the last stage of personality development, associated with puberty, during which the individual develops erotic attachments to others.

genotype An individual's genetic inheritance.

germinal stage The prenatal period that lasts from conception through the second week.

Gestalt psychology The early psychological viewpoint that claimed that we perceive and think about wholes rather than simply combinations of separate elements.

Gestalt therapy A type of humanistic therapy, developed by Fritz Perls, that encourages clients to become aware of their true feelings and to take responsibility for their own actions.

glial cell A kind of cell that provides a physical support structure for the neurons, supplies them with nutrition, removes neuronal metabolic waste materials, facilitates the transmission of messages by neurons, and helps regenerate damaged neurons in the peripheral nervous system.

goal setting The use of goals to increase motivation and improve performance by providing incentives.

gonads The male and female sex glands.

grammar The set of rules that governs the proper use and combination of language symbols.

group A collection of two or more persons who interact and have mutual influence on each other.

group polarization The tendency for groups to make more extreme decisions than their members would make as individuals.

groupthink The tendency of small, cohesive groups to place unanimity ahead of critical thinking in making decisions.

Guilty Knowledge Test A method that assesses lying by comparing physiological arousal in response to information that is relevant to a transgression and physiological arousal in response to information that is irrelevant to that transgression.

gustation The sense of taste, which detects molecules of substances dissolved in the saliva.

H

hallucinogens Psychoactive drugs that induce extreme alterations in consciousness, including visual hallucinations, a sense of timelessness, and feelings of depersonalization.

health psychology The field that applies psychological principles to the prevention and treatment of physical illness.

heritability The proportion of variability in a trait across a population attributable to genetic differences among members of the population.

heuristic A general principle that guides problem solving, though it does not guarantee a correct solution.

hidden observer Ernest Hilgard's term for the part of the hypnotized person's consciousness that is not under the control of the hypnotist but is aware of what is taking place.

hierarchy of needs Maslow's arrangement of needs in the order of their motivational priority, ranging from physiological needs to the needs for self-actualization and transcendence.

higher-order conditioning In classical conditioning, the establishment of a conditioned response to a neutral stimulus that has been paired with an existing conditioned stimulus.

hippocampus A limbic system structure that contributes to the formation of memories.

holophrastic speech The use of single words to represent whole phrases or sentences.

homeostasis A steady state of physiological equilibrium.

hormones Chemicals, secreted by endocrine glands, that play a role in a variety of functions, including synaptic transmission.

hospice movement The providing of care for the dying patient with attention to alleviating the patient's physical, emotional, and spiritual suffering.

humanistic perspective The psychological viewpoint that holds that the proper subject matter of psychology is the individual's subjective mental experience of the world.

hypermnesia The hypnotic enhancement of recall.

hyperopia Visual farsightedness, which is caused by a shortened eyeball.

hypnosis An induced state of consciousness in which one person responds to suggestions by another person for alterations in perception, thinking, and behavior.

hypothalamus A limbic system structure that, through its effects on the pituitary gland and the autonomic nervous system, helps regulate aspects of motivation and emotion, including eating, drinking, sexual behavior, body temperature, and stress responses.

hypothesis A testable prediction about the relationship between two or more events or characteristics.

I

iconic memory Visual sensory memory, which lasts up to about a second.

id In Freud's theory, the part of the personality that contains inborn biological drives and that seeks immediate gratification.

identity versus role confusion Erikson's developmental stage in which success is achieved by establishing a sense of personal identity.

illness anxiety disorder A somatic symptom and related disorder in which the person interprets the slightest physical changes as evidence of a serious illness.

illusory contours The perception of nonexistent contours as if they were the edges of real objects.

implicit memory Recollection of previous experiences demonstrated through behavior rather than through conscious, intentional remembering.

impression management The deliberate attempt to control the impression that others form of us.

in vivo desensitization A form of counterconditioning that trains the client to maintain a state of relaxation in the presence of anxiety-inducing stimuli.

incentive An external stimulus that pulls an individual toward a goal.

incentive value The perceived rewards that accompany success in a particular area.

incongruity theory The theory that humor is amusing when it brings together incompatible ideas in a surprising outcome that violates one's expectations.

independent variable A variable manipulated by the experimenter to determine its effect on another, dependent, variable.

industrial/organizational psychology The field that applies psychological principles to improve productivity in businesses, industries, and government agencies.

industry versus inferiority Erikson's developmental stage in which success is achieved by developing a sense of competency.

infancy The period that extends from birth through 2 years of age.

inferential statistics Statistics used to determine whether changes in a dependent variable are caused by an independent variable.

information-processing model The view that the processing of memories involves encoding, storage, and retrieval.

initiative versus guilt Erikson's developmental stage in which success is achieved by behaving in a spontaneous but socially appropriate way.

insanity A legal term attesting that a person is not responsible for his or her own actions, including criminal behavior.

insight An approach to problem solving that depends on cognitive manipulation of information rather than overt trial and error and produces sudden solutions to problems.

insomnia Chronic difficulty in either falling asleep or staying asleep.

instinct A complex, inherited behavior pattern characteristic of a species.

instinctive drift The reversion of animals to behaviors characteristic of their species even when being reinforced for performing other behaviors.

instrumental conditioning A form of learning in which a behavior becomes more or less probable, depending on its consequences.

integrity versus despair Erikson's developmental stage in which success is achieved by reflecting back on one's life and finding that it has been meaningful.

intellectual disability Intellectual deficiency marked by an IQ of 70 or below and difficulties performing in everyday life.

intelligence The global capacity to act purposefully, to think rationally, and to deal effectively with the environment.

intelligence quotient (IQ) Originally, the ratio of mental age to chronological age; that is, mental age/chronological age × 100.

intelligence test A test that assesses overall mental ability.

interference theory The theory that forgetting results from some memories interfering with the ability to recall other memories.

internal validity The extent to which changes in a dependent variable can be attributed to one or more independent variables rather than to a confounding variable.

interneuron A neuron that conveys messages between neurons in the brain or spinal cord.

intimacy versus isolation Erikson's developmental stage in which success is achieved by establishing a relationship with a strong sense of emotional attachment and personal commitment.

intrinsic motivation The desire to perform a behavior for its own sake.

introvert A person who is socially reserved and prefers to pay attention to his or her private cognitive experiences.

iris The donut-shaped band of muscles behind the cornea that gives the eye its color and controls the size of the pupil.

J

James-Lange theory The theory that specific patterns of physiological changes evoke specific emotional experiences.

just noticeable difference (jnd) Weber and Fechner's term for the difference threshold.

K

kinesthetic sense The sense that provides information about the position of the joints, the degree of tension in the muscles, and the movement of the arms and legs.

L

language A formal system of communication involving symbols—whether spoken, written, or gestured—and rules for combining them.

latency stage In Freud's theory, the stage between age 5 and puberty, during which there is little psychosexual development.

latent content Sigmund Freud's term for the true, though disguised, meaning of a dream.

latent learning Learning that occurs without the reinforcement of overt behavior.

law of effect Edward Thorndike's principle that a behavior followed by a satisfying state of affairs is strengthened and a behavior followed by an annoying state of affairs is weakened.

learned helplessness A feeling of futility caused by the belief that one has little or no control over events in one's life, which can make one stop trying and experience depressed mood.

learning A relatively permanent change in knowledge or behavior resulting from experience.

lens The transparent structure behind the pupil that focuses light onto the retina.

levels of processing theory The theory that the "depth" at which we process information determines how well it is encoded, stored, and retrieved.

libido Freud's term for the sexual energy of the id.

limbic system A group of brain structures that, through their influence on emotion, motivation, and memory, promote the survival of the individual and, as a result, the continuation of the species.

linguistic relativity hypothesis Benjamin Whorf's hypothesis that one's perception of the world is molded by one's language.

link method A mnemonic device that involves connecting, in sequence, images of items to be memorized, to make them easier to recall.

logical concept A concept formed by identifying the specific features possessed by all things that the concept applies to.

longitudinal research A research design in which the same group of participants is tested or observed repeatedly over a period of time.

long-term memory The stage of memory that can store a virtually unlimited amount of information relatively permanently.

long-term potentiation A phenomenon related to the facilitation of neural impulses in which synaptic transmission of impulses is made more efficient by brief electrical stimulation of specific neural pathways.

loudness perception The subjective experience of the intensity of a sound, which corresponds most closely to the amplitude of the sound waves composing it.

LSD A hallucinogen derived from a fungus that grows on rye grain.

lucid dreaming The ability to be aware that one is dreaming and to direct one's dreams.

M

magnetic resonance imaging (MRI) A brain-scanning technique that relies on strong magnetic fields to construct computer-generated images of the brain or body based on blood flow.

magnetoencenphalography (MA) A functional neuroimaging technique to measure brain activity using magnetic fields. MEG is useful to map brain changes across time and is often used together with fMRI.

maintenance rehearsal Repeating information to oneself to keep it in short-term memory.

major depressive disorder (MDD) A disorder marked by depression so intense and prolonged that the person may be unable to function in everyday life.

mania A mood disorder marked by euphoria, hyperactivity, grandiose ideas, annoying talkativeness, unrealistic optimism, and inflated self-esteem.

manifest content Sigmund Freud's term for the verbally reported dream.

massed practice Cramming the memorization of information or the learning of a motor skill into one session.

maturation The sequential unfolding of inherited predispositions in physical and motor development.

mean The arithmetic average of a set of scores.

mean length of utterance (MLU) A unit of measurement that assesses children's level of language maturation.

measure of central tendency A statistic that represents the "typical" score in a set of scores.

measure of variability A statistic describing the degree of dispersion in a set of scores.

measurement The use of numbers to represent events or characteristics.

median The middle score in a set of scores that have been ordered from lowest to highest.

medulla A brain stem structure that regulates breathing, heart rate, blood pressure, and other life functions.

memory The process by which information is acquired, stored in the brain, later retrieved, and eventually possibly forgotten.

menarche The beginning of menstruation, usually occurring between the ages of 11 and 13.

menopause The cessation of menstruation, usually occurring between the ages of 40 and 55.

mental giftedness Intellectual superiority marked by an IQ of 130 or above and exceptionally high scores on achievement tests in specific subjects, such as mathematics.

mental set A tendency to use a particular problem-solving strategy that has succeeded in the past but that may interfere with solving a problem requiring a new strategy.

mental telepathy The alleged ability to perceive the thoughts of others.

meta-analysis A technique that combines the results of many similar studies to determine the effect size of a particular kind of independent variable.

method of loci A mnemonic device in which items to be recalled are associated with landmarks in a familiar place and then recalled during a mental walk from one landmark to another.

method of savings The assessment of memory by comparing the time or number of trials needed to memorize a given amount of information and the time or number of trials needed to memorize it again at a later time.

mirror neurons Neurons that appear to be involved in the neural circuits responsible for observational learning.

mnemonic devices Techniques for organizing information to be memorized to make it easier to remember.

mode The score that occurs most frequently in a set of scores.

monocular cues Depth perception cues that require input from only one eye.

mood stabilizers Psychoactive drugs, most notably lithium carbonate, that are used to treat bipolar disorder.

moon illusion The misperception that the moon is larger when it is at the horizon than when it is overhead.

moral therapy An approach to therapy, developed by Philippe Pinel, that provided mental patients with humane treatment.

morpheme The smallest meaningful units of language.

motivation The psychological process that arouses, directs, and maintains behavior toward a goal.

motor cortex The area of the frontal lobes that controls specific voluntary body movements.

motor neuron A neuron that sends messages from the central nervous system to smooth muscles, cardiac muscle, or skeletal muscles.

multicultural psychology The field that studies psychological similarities and differences across the subcultures that commonly exist within individual countries.

myelin A fatty white substance that forms sheaths around certain axons and increases the speed of neural impulses.

myopia Visual nearsightedness, which is caused by an elongated eyeball.

N

narcolepsy A condition in which an awake person suffers from repeated, sudden, and irresistible REM sleep attacks.

nativism The philosophical position that heredity provides individuals with inborn knowledge and abilities.

natural concept A concept, typically formed through everyday experience, whose members possess some, but not all, of a common set of features.

naturalistic observation The recording of the behavior of people or animals in their natural environments, with little or no intervention by the researcher.

near-death experience A phenomenon reported by dying people that in Western cultures often includes a peaceful state of mind and an out-of-body experience.

need A motivated state caused by physiological deprivation, such as a lack of food or water.

negative correlation A correlation in which variables tend to change values in opposite directions.

negative reinforcement In operant conditioning, an increase in the probability of a behavior that is followed by the removal of an aversive stimulus.

negative state relief theory The theory that we engage in prosocial behavior to relieve our own state of emotional distress at another's plight.

neodissociation theory The theory that hypnosis induces a dissociated state of consciousness.

nerve A bundle of axons that conveys information to or from the central nervous system.

nerve deafness Hearing loss caused by damage to the hair cells of the basilar membrane, the axons of the auditory nerve, or the neurons of the auditory cortex.

nervous system The chief means of communication in the body.

neural grafting The transplantation of healthy tissue into damaged nerves, brains, or spinal cords.

neural plasticity The brain's ability to learn from experience and to promote adaptive behavior.

neuron A cell specialized for the transmission of information in the nervous system.

neurotransmitter Chemicals secreted by neurons that provide the means of synaptic transmission.

nicotine A stimulant used to regulate physical and cognitive arousal.

night terror A frightening NREM experience, common in childhood, in which the individual may suddenly sit up, let out a bloodcurdling scream, speak incoherently, and quickly fall back to sleep, yet usually fails to recall it on awakening.

nightmare A frightening dream occurring during REM sleep.

norm A score, based on the test performances of large numbers of participants, that is used as a standard for assessing the performances of test takers.

NREM sleep The stages of sleep not associated with rapid eye movements and marked by relatively little dreaming.

O

obedience Following orders given by an authority.

obesity An unhealthy condition in men who have more than 25 percent body fat and women who have more than 30 percent body fat.

object permanence The realization that objects exist even when they are no longer visible.

observational learning Learning produced by observing the consequences that others receive for performing particular behaviors.

obsessive-compulsive disorder (OCD) An anxiety disorder in which the person has recurrent, intrusive thoughts (obsessions) and recurrent urges to perform ritualistic actions (compulsions).

occipital lobe A lobe of the cerebral cortex responsible for processing vision.

Oedipus complex In Freud's theory, a conflict, during the phallic stage, between the child's sexual desire for the parent of the other sex and fear of punishment from the same-sex parent.

olfaction The sense of smell, which detects molecules carried in the air.

operant conditioning B. F. Skinner's term for instrumental conditioning, a form of learning in which a behavior becomes more or less probable, depending on its consequences.

operational definition The definition of behaviors or qualities in terms of the procedures used to measure or produce them.

opiates Depressants, derived from opium, used to relieve pain or to induce a euphoric state of consciousness.

opponent-process theory 1. The theory that color vision depends on red-green, blue-yellow, and black-white opponent processes in the brain. 2. The theory that the brain counteracts a strong positive or negative emotion by evoking an opposite emotional response.

optic chiasm The point under the frontal lobes at which some axons from each of the optic nerves cross over to the opposite side of the brain.

optic nerve The nerve, formed from the axons of ganglion cells, that carries visual impulses from the retina to the brain.

oral stage In Freud's theory, the stage of personality development between birth and age 1 year, during which the infant gains pleasure from oral activities and faces a conflict over weaning.

otolith organs The vestibular organs that detect horizontal or vertical linear movement of the head.

ovaries The female gonads, which secrete hormones that regulate the development of the female reproductive system and secondary sex characteristics.

overextension The tendency to apply a word to more objects or actions than it actually represents.

overjustification theory The theory that an extrinsic reward will decrease intrinsic motivation when a person attributes her or his performance to that reward.

overlearning Studying material beyond the point of initial mastery.

overregularization The application of a grammatical rule without making necessary exceptions to it.

P

panic disorder An anxiety disorder marked by sudden, unexpected attacks of overwhelming anxiety, often associated with the fear of dying or "losing one's mind."

parapsychology The study of extrasensory perception, psychokinesis, and related phenomena.

parasympathetic nervous system The division of the autonomic nervous system that calms the body and performs maintenance functions.

parietal lobe A lobe of the cerebral cortex responsible for processing bodily sensations and perceiving spatial relations.

Parkinson's disease A degenerative disease of the dopamine pathway, which causes marked disturbances in motor behavior.

partial schedule of reinforcement A schedule of reinforcement that reinforces some, but not all, instances of a desired response.

participant bias The tendency of people who know they are participants in a study to behave differently than they normally would.

participant modeling A form of social-learning therapy in which the client learns to perform more adaptive behaviors by first observing the therapist model the desired behaviors.

passionate love Love characterized by intense emotional arousal and sexual feelings.

peace psychology The field that applies psychological principles to reducing conflict and maintaining peace.

pegword method A mnemonic device that involves associating items to be recalled with objects that rhyme with the numbers 1, 2, 3, and so on to make the items easier to recall.

perceived control The degree to which a person feels in control over life's stressors.

perception The process that organizes sensations into meaningful patterns.

perception without awareness The unconscious perception of stimuli that normally exceed the absolute threshold but fall outside our focus of attention.

peripheral nervous system The division of the nervous system that conveys sensory information to the central nervous system and motor commands from the central nervous system to the skeletal muscles and internal organs.

person-centered therapy A type of humanistic therapy, developed by Carl Rogers, that helps clients find their own answers to their problems.

person perception The process of making judgments about the personal characteristics of others.

personal unconscious In Jung's theory, the individual's own unconscious mind, which contains repressed memories.

personality An individual's unique, relatively consistent pattern of thinking, feeling, and behaving.

personality disorder A psychological disorder characterized by enduring, inflexible, maladaptive patterns of behavior.

personality psychology The field that focuses on factors accounting for the differences in behavior and enduring personal characteristics among individuals.

persuasion The attempt to influence the attitudes of other people.

phallic stage In Freud's theory, the stage of personality development between ages 3 and 5, during which the child gains pleasure from the genitals and must resolve the Oedipus complex.

phase advance Shortening the sleep-wake cycle, as occurs when traveling from west to east.

phase delay Lengthening the sleep-wake cycle, as occurs when traveling from east to west.

phenomenological psychology A branch of humanistic psychology primarily concerned with the study of subjective mental experience.

phenotype The overt expression of an individual's genotype (genetic inheritance) in his or her appearance or behavior.

phenylketonuria (PKU) A hereditary enzyme deficiency that, if left untreated in the infant, causes intellectual disability.

pheromone An odorous chemical secreted by an animal that affects the behavior of other animals.

phi phenomenon Apparent motion caused by the presentation of different visual stimuli in rapid succession.

phobia An anxiety disorder marked by excessive or inappropriate fear.

phoneme The smallest unit of sound in a language.

phonology The study of the sounds that compose languages.

photopigments Chemicals, including rhodopsin and iodopsin, that enable the rods and cones to generate neural impulses.

phrenology A discredited technique for determining intellectual abilities and personality traits by examining the bumps and depressions of the skull.

physiological reactivity The extent to which a person displays increases in heart rate, blood pressure, stress hormone secretion, and other physiological activity in response to stressors.

pineal gland An endocrine gland that secretes a hormone that has a general tranquilizing effect on the body and that helps regulate biological rhythms.

pitch perception The subjective experience of the highness or lowness of a sound, which corresponds most closely to the frequency of the sound waves that compose it.

pituitary gland An endocrine gland that regulates many of the other endocrine glands by secreting hormones that affect the secretion of their hormones.

place theory The theory of pitch perception that assumes that hair cells at particular points on the basilar membrane are maximally responsive to sound waves of particular frequencies.

placebo An inactive substance that might induce some of the effects of the drug for which it has been substituted.

pleasure principle The process by which the id seeks immediate gratification of its impulses.

polygraph test The lie detector test, which assesses lying by measuring changing patterns of physiological arousal in response to particular questions.

pons A brain stem structure that regulates the sleep-wake cycle.

population A group of individuals who share certain characteristics.

positive correlation A correlation in which variables tend to change values in the same direction.

positive reinforcement In operant conditioning, an increase in the probability of a behavior that is followed by a desirable consequence.

positron-emission tomography (PET) A brain-scanning technique that produces color-coded pictures showing the relative activity of different brain areas.

postconventional level In Kohlberg's theory, the level of moral reasoning characterized by concern with obeying mutually agreed-upon laws and by the need to uphold human dignity.

posthypnotic suggestions Suggestions directing people to carry out particular behaviors or to have particular experiences after leaving hypnosis.

posttraumatic stress disorder (PTSD) A syndrome of physical and psychological symptoms that appears as a delayed response after exposure to an extremely emotionally distressing event.

pragmatics The relationship between language and its social context.

precognition The alleged ability to perceive events in the future.

preconscious mind The level of consciousness that contains feelings and memories that we are unaware of at the moment but can become aware of at will.

preconventional level In Kohlberg's theory, the level of moral reasoning characterized by concern with the consequences that behavior has for oneself.

prejudice A positive or negative attitude toward a person based on her or his membership in a particular group.

Premack principle The principle that a more probable behavior can be used as a reinforcer for a less probable one.

preoperational stage The Piagetian stage, extending from two to seven years of age, during which the child's use of language becomes more sophisticated but the child has difficulty with the logical mental manipulation of information.

primary cortical area Regions of the cerebral cortex that serve motor or sensory functions.

primary reinforcer In operant conditioning, an unlearned reinforcer that satisfies a biological need such as food, water, or oxygen.

proactive interference The process by which old memories interfere with the ability to recall new memories.

problem solving The thought process by which an individual overcomes obstacles to reach a goal.

procedural memory The long-term memory system that contains memories of how to perform particular actions.

programmed instruction A step-by-step approach, based on operant conditioning, in which the learner proceeds at his or her own pace through more and more advanced material and receives immediate knowledge of the results of each response.

progressive relaxation A stress-management procedure that involves the successive tensing and relaxing of each of the major muscle groups of the body.

projective test A psychoanalytic personality test based on the assumption that individuals project their unconscious feelings when responding to ambiguous stimuli.

prosocial behavior Behavior that helps others in need.

prosody The vocal features of speech other than the words themselves.

prosopagnosia A condition in which an individual can recognize details in faces but cannot recognize faces as a whole.

prototype The best representative of a concept.

psychiatry The field of medicine that diagnoses and treats psychological disorders by using medical or psychological forms of therapy.

psychic determinism The Freudian assumption that all human behavior is influenced by unconscious motives.

psychoactive drugs Chemicals that induce changes in mood, thinking, perception, and behavior by affecting neuronal activity in the brain.

psychoanalysis The early school of psychology that emphasized the importance of unconscious causes of behavior.

psychokinesis (PK) The alleged ability to control objects with the mind alone.

psychological hardiness A set of personality characteristics marked by feelings of commitment, challenge, and control that promotes resistance to stress.

psychological test A formal sample of a person's behavior, whether written or performed.

psychology The science of behavior and cognitive processes.

psychoneuroimmunology The interdisciplinary field that studies the relationship between psychological factors and physical illness.

psychopathology The study of psychological disorders.

psychophysics The study of the relationship between the physical characteristics of stimuli and the conscious psychological experiences that are associated with them.

psychosurgery The treatment of psychological disorders by destroying brain tissue.

psychotherapy The treatment of psychological disorders through psychological means generally involving verbal interaction with a professional therapist.

puberty The period of rapid physical change that occurs during adolescence, including the development of the ability to reproduce sexually.

punishment In operant conditioning, the process by which an aversive stimulus decreases the probability of a response that precedes it.

pupil The opening at the center of the iris that controls how much light enters the eye.

R

random assignment The assignment of participants to experimental and control conditions so that each participant is as likely to be assigned to one condition as to another.

random sampling The selection of a sample from a population so that each member of the population has an equal chance of being included.

range A statistic representing the difference between the highest and lowest scores in a set of scores.

rational-emotive behavior therapy (REBT) A type of cognitive therapy, developed by Albert Ellis, that treats psychological disorders by forcing the client to give up irrational beliefs.

rationalism The philosophical position that true knowledge comes through correct reasoning.

reality principle The process by which the ego directs the individual to express sexual and aggressive impulses in socially acceptable ways.

reciprocal determinism Bandura's belief that cognitive factors, environmental factors, and overt behavior affect each other.

reflex An automatic, involuntary motor response to sensory stimulation.

release theory The theory that humor relieves anxiety caused by sexual or aggressive energy.

reliability The extent to which a test gives consistent results.

REM sleep The stage of sleep associated with rapid eye movements, an active brain-wave pattern, and vivid dreams.

replication The repetition of a research study, usually with some alterations in its methods or setting, to determine whether the principles derived from that study hold up under similar circumstances.

representativeness heuristic In decision making, the assumption that a small sample is representative of its population.

repression In psychoanalytic theory, the defense mechanism that involves banishing threatening thoughts, feelings, and memories into the unconscious mind.

resting potential The electrical charge of a neuron when it is not firing a neural impulse.

reticular formation A diffuse network of neurons, extending through the brain stem, that helps maintain vigilance and an optimal level of brain arousal.

retina The light-sensitive inner membrane of the eye that contains the receptor cells for vision.

retrieval The recovery of information from memory.

retroactive interference The process by which new memories interfere with the ability to recall old memories.

rods Receptor cells of the retina that play an important role in night vision and peripheral vision.

S

sample A group of participants selected from a population.

schema A cognitive structure that guides people's perception and information processing that incorporates the characteristics of particular persons, objects, events, procedures, or situations.

schema theory The theory that long-term memories are stored as parts of schemas, which are cognitive structures that organize knowledge about events or objects.

schizophrenia A class of psychological disorders characterized by grossly impaired social, emotional, cognitive, and perceptual functioning.

school psychology The field that applies psychological principles to improve the academic performance and social behavior of students in elementary, middle, and high schools.

scientific method A source of knowledge based on the assumption that knowledge comes from the objective, systematic observation and measurement of particular variables and the events they affect.

scientific paradigm A model that determines the appropriate goals, methods, and subject matter of a science.

sclera The tough, white, outer membrane of the eye.

seasonal affective disorder (SAD) A mood disorder in which depressive symptoms occur during a particular season, usually the winter but sometimes the summer.

secondary reinforcer In operant conditioning, a neutral stimulus that becomes reinforcing after being associated with a primary reinforcer.

self-actualization In Maslow's theory, the individual's predisposition to try to fulfill her or his potentials.

self-efficacy In Bandura's theory, a person's belief that she or he can perform behaviors that are necessary to bring about a desired outcome.

self-fulfilling prophecy The tendency for one person's expectations to influence another person to behave in accordance with them.

self-perception theory The theory that we infer our attitudes from our behavior in the same way that we infer other people's attitudes from their behavior.

self-schema In schema theory, specialized cognitive structures about the self.

self-serving bias The tendency to make dispositional attributions for one's successes and situational attributions for one's failures.

semantic conditioning In classical conditioning, the use of words as conditioned stimuli.

semantic memory The subsystem of declarative memory that contains general information about the world.

semantic network theory The theory that memories are stored as nodes interconnected by links that represent their relationships.

semanticity The characteristic of language marked by the use of symbols to convey thoughts in a meaningful way.

semantics The study of how language conveys meaning.

semicircular canals The curved vestibular organs of the inner ear that detect rotary movements of the head in any direction.

sensate focusing A technique, pioneered by Masters and Johnson, in which partners are urged to concentrate on their pleasurable feelings instead of striving for erections and orgasms.

sensation The process that detects stimuli from the body or surroundings.

sensation seeking The motivation to pursue sensory stimulation.

sensorimotor stage The Piagetian stage, from birth through the second year, during which the infant learns to coordinate sensory experiences and motor behaviors.

sensory adaptation The tendency of the sensory receptors to respond less and less to a constant stimulus.

sensory deprivation The prolonged withdrawal of normal levels of external stimulation.

sensory memory The stage of memory that briefly (for at most a few seconds) stores exact replicas of sensations.

sensory neuron A neuron that sends messages from sensory receptors to the central nervous system.

sensory receptors Specialized cells that detect stimuli and convert their energy into neural impulses.

sensory transduction The process by which sensory receptors convert stimuli into neural impulses.

serial-position effect The superiority of immediate recall for items at the beginning and end of a list.

set point A specific body weight that the brain tries to maintain through the regulation of diet, activity, and metabolism.

sexual dysfunction A chronic problem at a particular phase of the sexual response cycle.

sexual orientation A person's pattern of erotic attraction—whether to persons of one's own sex or of the other sex or both.

sexual response cycle During sexual activity, the phases of excitement, plateau, orgasm, and resolution.

shape constancy The perceptual process that makes an object appear to maintain its normal shape regardless of the angle from which it is viewed.

shaping An operant conditioning procedure that involves the positive reinforcement of successive approximations of an initially improbable behavior to eventually bring about that behavior.

short-term memory The stage of memory that can store a few items of unrehearsed information for up to about 20 seconds.

signal-detection theory The theory holding that the detection of a stimulus depends on both the intensity of the stimulus and the physical and psychological state of the individual.

simple phobia A phobia of a specific object or situation.

single photon emission computed tomography (SPECT) A brain-imaging technique that creates images of cerebral blood flow.

size constancy The perceptual process that makes an object appear to remain the same size despite changes in the size of the image it casts on the retina.

skepticism An attitude that doubts all claims not supported by solid research evidence.

skin senses The senses of touch, temperature, and pain.

Skinner box An enclosure that contains a bar or key that can be pressed to obtain food or water and that is used to study operant conditioning in rats, pigeons, or other small animals.

sleep apnea A condition in which a person awakens repeatedly in order to breathe.

sleeper effect Responding favorably to a persuasive message following the mere passage of time after having initially rejected it because of a strong peripheral factor, such as not trusting the source of the message.

smooth pursuit movements Eye movements controlled by the ocular muscles that keep objects focused on the fovea.

social anxiety disorder A phobia of situations that involve social evaluation.

social attachment A strong emotional relationship between an infant and a caregiver.

social clock The typical or expected timing of major life events in a given culture.

social cognition The process of perceiving, interpreting, and predicting social behavior.

social-comparison theory The theory that happiness is the result of estimating that one's life circumstances are more favorable than those of others.

social facilitation The effect of the presence of other people on a person's task performance, with performance on simple or well-learned tasks improved and performance on complex or poorly learned tasks impaired.

social learning theory A theory of learning that assumes that people learn behaviors mainly through observation and mental processing of information.

social loafing A decrease in the individual effort exerted by group members when working together on a task.

social psychology The field that studies how the actual, imagined, or implied presence of other people affects one another's thoughts, feelings, and behaviors.

social schema A cognitive structure comprising the presumed characteristics of a role, an event, a person, or a group.

social-skills training A form of behavioral group therapy that improves the client's social relationships by improving her or his interpersonal skills.

social support The availability of support from other people, whether tangible or intangible.

sociobiology The study of the hereditary basis of human and animal social behavior.

sociocultural perspective The psychological viewpoint that favors the scientific study of human behavior in its sociocultural context.

soma The cell body, which is the neuron's control center.

somatic nervous system The division of the peripheral nervous system that sends messages from the sensory organs to the central nervous system and messages from the central nervous system to the skeletal muscles.

somatic symptom and related disorder A psychological disorder characterized by physical symptoms in the absence of disease or injury.

somatosensory cortex The area of the parietal lobes that processes information from sensory receptors in the skin.

somatotype In Sheldon's theory, a physique associated with a particular temperament.

sound localization The process by which the individual determines the location of a sound.

spermarche The first ejaculation, usually occurring between the ages of 13 and 15.

spinal cord The structure of the central nervous system that is located in the spine and plays a role in bodily reflexes and in communicating information between the brain and the peripheral nervous system.

split-brain research A research technique for the study of cerebral hemispheric lateralization that involves people whose hemispheres have been surgically separated from each other.

spontaneous recovery 1. In classical conditioning, the reappearance after a period of time of a conditioned response that has been subjected to extinction. 2. In operant conditioning, the reappearance after a period of time of a behavior that has been subjected to extinction.

spontaneous remission The improvement of some persons with psychological disorders without their undergoing formal therapy.

sport psychology The field that applies psychological principles to help amateur and professional athletes improve their performance.

SQ3R method A study technique in which the student surveys, questions, reads, recites, and reviews course material.

standard deviation A statistic representing the degree of dispersion of a set of scores around their mean.

standardization 1. A procedure ensuring that a test is administered and scored in a consistent manner. 2. A procedure for establishing test norms by giving a test to large samples of people who are representative of those for whom the test is designed.

state-dependent memory The tendency for recall to be best when one's emotional or physiological state is the same during the recall of a memory as it was during the encoding of that memory.

statistical significance A low probability (usually less than 5 percent) that the results of a research study are due to chance factors rather than to the independent variable.

statistics Mathematical techniques used to summarize research data or to determine whether the data support the researcher's hypothesis.

stereotype A social schema that incorporates characteristics, which can be positive or negative, supposedly shared by almost all members of a group.

stimulants Psychoactive drugs that increase central nervous system activity.

stimulus discrimination In classical conditioning, giving a conditioned response to the conditioned stimulus but not to stimuli similar to it.

stimulus generalization In classical conditioning, giving a conditioned response to stimuli similar to the conditioned stimulus.

storage The retention of information in memory.

stress The physiological response of the body to physical and psychological demands.

stress-inoculation training A type of cognitive therapy that helps clients change their pessimistic thinking into more positive thinking when in stressful situations.

stressor A physical or psychological demand that induces physiological adjustment.

structuralism The early psychological viewpoint that sought to identify the components of the conscious mind.

subliminal perception The unconscious perception of stimuli that are too weak to exceed the absolute threshold for detection.

subliminal psychodynamic activation The use of subliminal messages to stimulate unconscious fantasies.

superego In Freud's theory, the part of the personality that acts as a moral guide telling us what we should and should not do.

surface structure The word arrangements used to express meanings.

survey A set of questions related to a particular topic of interest administered to a sample of people through an interview or questionnaire.

sympathetic nervous system The division of the autonomic nervous system that arouses the body to prepare it for action.

synapse The junction between a neuron and a gland, muscle, sensory organ, or another neuron.

synaptic transmission The conveying of a neural impulse between a neuron and a gland, muscle, sensory organ, or another neuron.

synesthesia The process in which an individual experiences sensations in one sensory modality that are characteristic of another.

syntax The rules that govern the acceptable arrangement of words in phrases and sentences.

systematic desensitization A form of counterconditioning that trains the client to maintain a state of relaxation in the presence of imagined anxiety-inducing stimuli.

T

taste buds Structures lining the grooves of the tongue that contain the taste receptor cells.

telegraphic speech Speech marked by reliance on nouns and verbs while other parts of speech, including articles and prepositions, are omitted.

temperament A person's characteristic emotional state, first apparent in early infancy and possibly inborn.

temporal lobe A lobe of the cerebral cortex responsible for processing hearing.

teratogen A noxious substance, such as a virus or drug, that can cause prenatal defects.

testes The male gonads, which secrete hormones that regulate the development of the male reproductive system and secondary sex characteristics.

tetrahydrocannabinol (THC) The psychoactive ingredient found in the *cannabis sativa* plant.

thalamus The brain stem structure that acts as a sensory relay station for taste, body, visual, and auditory sensations.

theory An integrated set of statements that summarizes and explains research findings and from which research hypotheses can be derived.

theory of multiple intelligences Howard Gardner's theory of intelligence, which assumes that the brain has evolved separate systems for seven kinds of intelligence.

thought The cognitive manipulation of words and images, as in concept formation, problem solving, and decision making.

timbre The subjective experience that identifies a particular sound and corresponds most closely to the mixture of sound waves composing it.

tip-of-the-tongue phenomenon The inability to recall information that one knows has been stored in long-term memory.

token economy An operant conditioning procedure that uses tokens as positive reinforcers in programs designed to promote desirable behaviors, with the tokens later used to purchase desired items or privileges.

trait A relatively enduring, cross-situationally consistent personality characteristic that is inferred from a person's behavior.

transactional analysis (TA) A form of psychoanalytic group therapy, developed by Eric Berne, that helps clients change their immature or inappropriate ways of relating to other people.

transcranial magnetic stimulation (TMS) An experimental manipulation of the brain that involves electrically stimulating the cerebral cortex of the brain by using pulsed magnetic fields administered near the scalp.

transcutaneous electrical nerve stimulation (TENS) The use of electrical stimulation of sites on the body to provide pain relief, apparently by stimulating the release of endorphins.

transformational grammar The rules by which languages generate surface structures out of deep structures and deep structures out of surface structures.

transitive inference The application of previously learned relationships to infer new relationships.

trephining An ancient technique in which sharp stones were used to chip holes in the skull, possibly to let out evil spirits that supposedly caused abnormal behavior.

trial and error An approach to problem solving in which the individual tries one possible solution after another until one works.

triarchic theory of intelligence Robert Sternberg's theory of intelligence, which assumes that there are three main kinds of intelligence: componential, experiential, and contextual.

trichromatic theory The theory that color vision depends on the relative degree of stimulation of red, green, and blue receptors.

trust versus mistrust Erikson's developmental stage in which success is achieved by having a secure social attachment with a caregiver.

two-factor theory The theory that emotional experience is the outcome of physiological arousal and the attribution of a cause for that arousal.

tympanic membrane The eardrum; a membrane separating the outer ear from the middle ear that vibrates in response to sound waves that strike it.

Type A behavior A syndrome—marked by impatience, hostility, and extreme competitiveness—that is associated with the development of coronary heart disease.

U

unconditioned response (UCR) In classical conditioning, an unlearned, automatic response to a particular unconditioned stimulus.

unconditioned stimulus (UCS) In classical conditioning, a stimulus that automatically elicits a particular unconditioned response.

unconscious mind The level of consciousness that contains thoughts, feelings, and memories that influence us without our awareness and that we cannot become aware of at will.

underextension The tendency to apply a word to fewer objects or actions than it actually represents.

unilateral neglect A disorder, caused by damage to a parietal lobe, in which the individual acts as though the side of her or his world opposite to the damaged lobe does not exist.

V

validity The extent to which a test measures what it is supposed to measure.

variability hypothesis The prediction that men, as a group, are more variable than women.

variable An event, behavior, condition, or characteristic that has two or more values.

variable-interval schedule of reinforcement A partial schedule of reinforcement that provides reinforcement for the first desired response made after varying, unpredictable lengths of time.

variable-ratio schedule of reinforcement A partial schedule of reinforcement that provides reinforcement after varying, unpredictable numbers of desired responses.

variance A measure based on the average deviation of a set of scores from their group mean.

vestibular sense The sense that provides information about the head's position in space and helps in the maintenance of balance.

visible spectrum The portion of the electromagnetic spectrum that we commonly call light.

vision The sense that detects objects by the light reflected from them into the eyes.

visual agnosia A condition in which an individual can see objects and identify their features but cannot recognize the objects.

visual cortex The area of the occipital lobes that processes visual input.

visual illusion A misperception of physical reality usually caused by the misapplication of visual cues.

volley theory The theory of pitch perception that assumes that sound waves of particular frequencies induce auditory neurons to fire in volleys, with one volley following another.

W

Wada test A technique in which a cerebral hemisphere is anesthetized to assess hemispheric lateralization.

Weber's law The principle that the amount of change in stimulation needed to produce a just noticeable difference is a constant proportion of the original stimulus.

Wernicke's area The region of the temporal lobe that controls the meaningfulness of speech.

Y

Yerkes-Dodson law The principle that the relationship between arousal and performance is best represented by an inverted U-shaped curve.

References

A

Abatzoglou, I., Anninos, P., Tsalafoutas, I., & Koukourakis, M. (2009). Multi-channel magnetoencephalogram on Alzheimer disease patients. *Journal of Integrative Neuroscience, 8,* 13–22.

Abbott, M. J., & Rapee, R. M. (2004). Post–event rumination and negative self–appraisal in social phobia before and after treatment. *Journal of Abnormal Psychology, 113,* 136–144.

Abel, M. H. (2002). Humor, stress, and coping strategies. *Humor: International Journal of Humor Research, 15,* 365–381.

Abelman, R. (1999). Preaching to the choir: Profiling TV advisory ratings users. *Journal of Broadcasting and Electronic Media, 43,* 529–550.

Abelson, R. P. (1981). Psychological status of the script concept. *American Psychologist, 36,* 715–729.

Abernethy, E. M. (1940). The effect of changed environmental conditions upon the results of college examinations. *Journal of Psychology, 10,* 293–301.

Abide, M. M., Richards, H. C., & Ramsay, S. G. (2001). Moral reasoning and consistency of belief and behavior: Decisions about substance abuse. *Journal of Drug Education, 31,* 367–384.

Abo, M., Chen, Z., Lai, L., Reese, T., & Bjelke, B. (2001). Functional recovery after brain lesion-contralateral neuromodulation: An fMRI study. *Neuroreport: For Rapid Communication of Neuroscience Research, 12,* 1543–1547.

Abokrysha, N. (2009). Ibn Sina (Avicenna) on pathogenesis of migraine compared with the recent theories. *Headache: Journal of Head and Neck Pain, 49,* 923–927.

Abou-Khalil, B. (2007). An update on determination of language dominance in screening for epilepsy surgery: The Wada test and newer noninvasive alternatives. *Epilepsia, 48,* 442–455.

Abrams, S. (1995). False memory syndrome versus total repression. *Journal of Psychiatry and the Law, 23,* 283–293.

Abramson, L. Y., Seligman, M. E. P., & Teasdale, J. D. (1978). Learned helplessness in humans: Critique and reformulation. *Journal of Abnormal Psychology, 87,* 49–74.

Ackerman, S. J., & Hilsenroth, M. J. (2001). A review of therapist characteristics and techniques negatively impacting the therapeutic alliance. *Psychotherapy: Theory, Research, Practice, Training, 38,* 171–185.

Ackerman, S. J., & Hilsenroth, M. J. (2003). A review of therapist characteristics and techniques positively impacting the therapeutic alliance. *Clinical Psychology Review, 23,* 1–33.

Ackil, J. K., & Zaragoza, M. S. (1998). Memorial consequences of forced confabulation; Age differences in susceptibility to false memories. *Developmental Psychology, 34,* 1358–1372.

Adams, P. R., & Adams, G. R. (1984). Mount Saint Helen's ashfall: Evidence for a disaster stress reaction. *American Psychologist, 39,* 252–260.

Adams, R. J., & Courage, M. L. (2002). A psychophysical test of the early maturation of infants' mid- and long-wavelength retinal cones. *Infant Behavior and Development, 25,* 247–254.

Adams, S. K., & Kisler, T. S. (2013). Sleep quality as a mediator between technology-related sleep quality, depression, and anxiety. *Cyberpsychology, Behavior, and Social Networking, 16,* 25–30.

Adams, W. L., Garry, P. J., Rhyne, R., & Hunt, W. C. (1990). Alcohol intake in the healthy elderly: Changes with age in a cross-sectional and longitudinal study. *Journal of the American Geriatrics Society, 38,* 211–216.

Adelmann, P. K., & Zajonc, R. B. (1989). Facial efference and the experience of emotion. *Annual Review of Psychology, 40,* 249–289.

Adelson, B. (1984). When novices surpass experts: The difficulty of a task may increase with expertise. *Journal of Experimental Psychology: Learning, Memory, and Cognition, 10,* 483–495.

Ader, R. (2001). Psychoneuroimmunology. *Current Directions in Psychological Science, 10,* 94–98.

Ader, R. (2003). Conditioned immunomodulation: Research needs and directions. *Brain, Behavior, and Immunity, 17,* S51–S57.

Ader, R., & Cohen, N. (1982). Behaviorally conditioned immunosuppression and murine systemic lupus erythematosus. *Science, 215,* 1534–1536.

Adeyemo, S. A. (2002). A review of the role of the hippocampus in memory. *Psychology and Education: An Interdisciplinary Journal, 39,* 46–63.

Adler, A. (1927). *Understanding human nature.* New York: Greenberg.

Adler, K. A. (1994). Socialist influences on Alderian psychology. *Individual Psychology: Journal of Adlerian Theory, Research, and Practice, 50,* 131–141.

Adler, T. (1991, November). Hypothalamus study stirs social questions. *APA Monitor,* pp. 8–9.

Adorno, T. W., Frenkel-Brunswik, E., Levinson, D. J., & Sanford, R. N. (1950). *The authoritarian personality.* New York: Harper & Row.

Afnan, S. M. (1958/1980). *Avicenna: His life and works.* Westport, CT: Greenwood.

Aghajanian, G. K. (1994). Serotonin and the action of LSD in the brain. *Psychiatric Annals, 24,* 137–141.

Agmo, A., & Berendfeld, R. (1990). Reinforcing properties of ejaculation in the male rat: Role of opioids and dopamine. *Behavioral Neuroscience, 104,* 177–182.

Agostino, H., Erdstein, J., & Di Meglio, G. (2013). Shifting paradigms: Continuous nasogastric feeding with high caloric intakes in anorexia nervosa. *Journal of Adolescent Health, 53,* 590–594.

Agras, W. S. (1997). Pharmacotherapy of bulimia nervosa and binge eating disorder: Long-term outcomes. *Psychopharmacology Bulletin, 33,* 433–436.

Agrawal, A., & Lynskey, M. T. (2008). Are there genetic influences on addiction? Evidence from family, adoption and twin studies. *Addiction, 103,* 1069–1081.

Aheneku, J. E., Nwosu, C. M., & Ahaneku, G. I. (2000). Academic stress and cardiovascular health. *Academic Medicine, 75,* 567–568.

Ahlberg, S. W., & Sharps, M. J. (2002). Bartlett revisited: Reconfiguration of long-term memory in young and older adults. *Journal of Genetic Psychology, 163,* 211–218.

Ahmed, N. U., Ahmed, N. S., Bennett, C. R., & Hinds, J. E. (2002). Impact of a Drug Abuse Resistance Education (D.A.R.E) program in preventing the initiation of cigarette smoking in fifth- and sixth-grade students. *Journal of the National Medical Association, 94,* 249–256.

Ahrendt, L. P., Christensen, J.-W., & Ladewig, J. (2012). The ability of horses to learn an instrumental task through social observation. *Applied Animal Behaviour Science, 139,* 105–113.

Aiken, L. R. (1982). *Psychological testing and assessment.* Boston: Allyn & Bacon.

Aisner, R., & Terkel, J. (1992). Ontogeny of pine cone opening behavior in the black rat, *Rattus rattus. Animal Behaviour, 44,* 327–336.

Akimova, I. M., Gurchin, F. A., Koroleva, N. Y., Melyucheva, L. A., Taits, E. A., & Khrakovskaya, M. G. (2000). Clinical use of the embryonic brain tissue grafts in epilepsy. *Human Physiology, 26,* 308–318.

Alaoui-Ismaieli, O., Vernet-Maury, E., Dittmar, A. Delhomme, G., & Chanel, J. (1997). Odor hedonics: Connection with emotional response estimated by autonomic parameters. *Chemical Senses, 22,* 237–248.

Alba, J. W., & Hasher, L. (1983). Is memory schematic? *Psychological Bulletin, 93,* 203–231.

Albert, D. J., Walsh, M. L., & Jonik, R. H. (1993). Aggression in humans: What is its biological foundation? *Neuroscience and Biobehavioral Reviews, 17,* 405–425.

Albright, T. D., Jessell, T. M., Kandel, E. R., & Posner, M. I. (2001). Progress in the neural sciences in the century after Cajal (and the mysteries that remain). *Annals of the New York Academy of Sciences, 929,* 11–40.

Aldag, R. J., & Fuller, S. R. (1993). Beyond fiasco: A reappraisal of the groupthink phenomenon and a new model of group decision processes. *Psychological Bulletin, 113,* 533–552.

Alden, D. L., Mukherjee, A., & Hoyer, W. D. (2000). The effects of incongruity, surprise, and positive moderators on perceived humor in television advertising. *Journal of Advertising, 29,* 1–15.

Alderfer, C. P. (2003). The science and nonscience of psychologists' responses to *The Bell Curve. Professional Psychology: Research and Practice, 34,* 287–293.

Aldrich, M. S. (1992). Narcolepsy. *Neurology, 42,* 34–43.

Alexy, B. B. (1991). Factors associated with participation or nonparticipation in a workplace wellness center. *Research in Nursing and Health, 14,* 33–40.

Alghazo, R., Upton, T. D., & Cioe, N. (2011). Duty to warn versus duty to protect confidentiality: Ethical and legal considerations relative to individuals with AIDS/HIV. *Journal of Applied Rehabilitation Counseling, 42,* 43–49.

Allen, M. G. (1990). Group psychotherapy: Past, present and future. *Psychiatricannals, 20,* 358–361.

Al–Issa, I., & Oudji, S. (1998). Culture and anxiety disorders. In S. S. Kazarian & D. R. Evans (Eds.), *Cultural clinical psychology: Theory, research, and practice (pp. 127–151).* New York: Oxford University Press.

Allalouf, A., & Ben-Shakhar, G. (1998). The effect of coaching on the predictive validity of scholastic aptitude tests. *Journal of Educational Measurement, 35,* 31–47.

Allen, J. J. B., & Iacono, W. G. (1997). A comparison of methods for the analysis of event-related potentials in deception detection. *Journal of Applied Psychology, 82,* 426–433.

Allen, J. J., Iacono, W. G., Laravuso, J. J., Dunn, L. A. (1995). An event–related potential investigation of posthypnotic recognition amnesia. *Journal of Abnormal Psychology, 104,* 421–430.

Allen, J., & Walsh, J. A. (2000). A construct-based approach to equivalence: Methodologies for cross-cultural/multicultural personality assessment research. In R. H. Dana (Ed.), *Handbook of cross-cultural and multicultural personality assessment* (pp. 63–85). Mahwah, NJ: Erlbaum.

Allen, M. (1993). Determining the persuasiveness of message sidedness: A prudent note about utilizing research summaries. *Western Journal of Communication, 57,* 98–103.

Allik, J., & McCrae, R. R. (2004). Toward a geography of personality traits: Patterns of profiles across 36 cultures. *Journal of Cross-CulturalPsychology, 35,* 13–28.

Allport, F. H. (1920). The influence of the group upon association and thought. *Journal of Experimental Psychology, 3,* 159–182.

Allport, G. W. (1954). *The nature of prejudice.* Reading, MA: Addison-Wesley.

Allport, G. W. (1967). Autobiography. In E. G. Boring & G. Lindzey (Eds.), *A history of psychology in autobiography, Vol. 5* (pp. 1–25). New York: Appleton-Century-Crofts.

Alpers, G. W., & Tuschen–Caffier, B. (2001). Negative feelings and the desire to eat in bulimia nervosa. *Eating Behaviors, 2,* 339–352.

Alpert, J. L., Brown, L. S., & Courtois, C. A. (1998). Symptomatic clients and memories of childhood abuse: What the abuse literature tells us. *Psychology, Public Policy, and Law, 4,* 941–995.

Althoff, R. R., Faraone, S. V., Rettew, D. C., Morley, C. P., & Hudziak, J. J. (2005). Family, twin, adoption, and molecular genetic studies of juvenile bipolar disorder. *Bipolar Disorders, 7,* 598–609.

Alto, L. T., Havton, L. A., Conner, J. M., Hollis II, E. R., Blesch, A., & Tuszynski, M. H. (2009). Chemotropic guidance facilitates axonal regeneration and synapse formation after spinal cord injury. *Nature Neuroscience, 12,* 1106–1115.

Alvarado, C. S. (1996). The place of spontaneous cases in parapsychology. *Journal of Broadcasting and Electronic Media, 41,* 345–359.

Alvarado, K. A., Templer, D. I., Bresler, C., & Thomas-Dobson, S. (1995). The relationship of religious variables to death depression and death anxiety. *Journal of Clinical Psychology, 51,* 202–204.

Amabile, T. M. (1989). *Growing up creative.* New York: Random House.

Amabile, T. M., Goldfarb, P., & Brackfield, S. C. (1990). Social influences on creativity: Evaluation, coaction, and surveillance. *Creativity Research Journal, 3,* 6–21.

Amato, P. R., & Keith, B. (1991). Parental divorce and the well-being of children: A meta-analysis. *Psychological Bulletin, 110,* 26–46.

d'Amato, T., Rochet, T., Dalery, J., & Chauchat, J. H. (1994). Seasonality of birth and ventricular enlargement in chronic schizophrenia. *Psychiatry Research: Neuroimaging, 55,* 65–73.

Ameis, S.H., Ducharme, S., Albaugh, M.D., Hudziak, J.J., Botteron, K.N., Lepage, C., . . . Karama, S., (2014). Cortical thickness, cortico-amygdalar networks, and externalizing behaviors in healthy children. *Biological Psychiatry, 75,* 65–72

Amen, D. G. (2010). High resolution brain SPECT imaging in a clinical substance abuse practice. *Journal of Psychoactive Drugs, 42,* 153–160.

American Psychiatric Association. (2013). *Diagnostic and statistical manual of mental disorders* (5th ed.). Washington, DC: Author.

Amering, M., Katschnig, H., Berger, P., Windhaber, J., Baischer, W., & Dantendorfer, K. (1997). Embarrassment about the first panic attack predicts agoraphobia in disorder patients. *Behaviour Research and Therapy, 35,* 517–521.

Amin, F., Silverman, J. M., Siever, L. J., Smith, C. J., Knott, P. J., & Davis, K. L. (1999). Genetic antecedents of dopamine dysfunction in schizophrenia. *Biological Psychiatry, 45,* 1143–1150.

Amir, T. (1984). The Asch conformity effect: A study in Kuwait. *Social Behavior and Personality, 12,* 187–190.

Amorose, A. J., & Horn, T. S. (2001). Pre- to post-season changes in the intrinsic motivation of first year college athletes: Relationship with coaching behavior and scholarship status. *Journal of Applied Sport Psychology, 13,* 355–373.

Amsterdam, J. D., Brunswick, D. J., & O'Reardon, J. (2002). Bipolar disorder in women. *Psychiatric Annals, 32,* 397–404.

Anand, B. K., & Brobeck, J. R. (1951). Hypothalamic control of food intake in rats and cats. *Yale Journal of Biology and Medicine, 24,* 123–140.

Anastasi, A. (1958). Heredity, environment, and the question "How?" *American Psychologist, 65,* 197–208.

Anastasi, A. (1972). The cultivation of diversity. *American Psychologist, 27,* 1091–1099.

Anastasi, A. (1985). Psychological testing: Basic concepts and common misconceptions. In A. M. Rogers & C. J. Scheirer (Eds.), *The G. Stanley Hall Lecture Series, Vol. 5* (pp. 87–120). Washington, DC: American Psychological Association.

Anazonwu, C. O. (1995). Locus of control, academic self-concept, and attribution of responsibility for performance in statistics. *Psychological Reports, 77,* 367–370.

Andersen, B. L., Kiecolt-Glaser, J. K., & Glaser, R. A (1994). A biobehavioral model of cancer stress and disease course. *American Psychologist, 49,* 389–404.

Andersen, R. E., Crespo, C. J., Bartlett, S. J., Cheskin, L. J., & Pratt, M. (1998). Associations among physical activity, television watching, and obesity in adult Pima Indians. *JAMA: Journal of the American Medical Association, 279,* 938–942.

Andersen, S. M., & Ross, L. (1984). Self-knowledge and social inference: I. The impact of cognitive/affective and behavioral data. *Journal of Personality and Social Psychology, 46,* 280–293.

Anderson, A. K., & Phelps, E. A. (2000). Expression without recognition: Contributions of the human amygdala to emotional communication. *Psychological Science, 11,* 106–111.

Anderson, B. L. (2003). The role of occlusion in the perception of depth, lightness, and opacity. *Psychological Review, 110,* 785–801.

Anderson, B. L., Cyranowski, J. M., & Aarestad, S. (2000). Beyond artificial, sex-linked distinctions to conceptualize female sexuality: Comment on Baumeister, 2000. *Psychological Bulletin, 126,* 380–384.

Anderson, C. A. (1999). Attributional style, depression, and loneliness: A cross–cultural comparison of American and Chinese students. *Personality and Social Psychology Bulletin, 25,* 482–499.

Anderson, D. C., Crowell, C. R., Doman, M., & Howard, G. S. (1988). Performance posting, goal setting, and activity-contingent praise as applied to a university hockey team. *Journal of Applied Psychology, 73,* 87–95.

Anderson, I. M. (2000). Selective serotonin reuptake inhibitors versus tricyclic antidepressants: A meta–analysis of efficacy and tolerability. *Journal of Affective Disorders, 58,* 19–36.

Anderson, J. R. (1983). Retrieval of information from long-term memory. *Science, 220,* 25–30.

Anderson, J. R. (2001). Obituary: Herbert A. Simon (1916–2001). *American Psychologist, 56,* 516–518.

Anderson, K. J., Revelle, W., & Lynch, M. J. (1989). Caffeine, impulsivity, and memory scanning: A comparison of two explanations for the Yerkes-Dodson effect. *Motivation and Emotion, 13,* 1–20.

Anderson, K. W., & Skidmore, J. R. (1995). Empirical analysis of factors in depressive cognition: The Cognitive Triad Inventory. *Journal of Clinical Psychology, 51,* 603–609.

Anderson, P. L., Price, M., Edwards, S.M., Obasaju, M. A., Schmertz, S.K., Zimand, E., Calamaras, M. R. (2013). Virtual reality exposure therapy for social anxiety disorder: A randomized controlled trial. *Journal of Consulting and Clinical Psychology, 81,* 751–760.

Anderson, R. A., Baron, R. S., & Logan, H. (1991). Distraction, control, and dental stress. *Journal of Applied Social Psychology, 21,* 156–171.

Anderson, S. W., & Rizzo, M. (1994). Hallucinations following occipital lobe damage: The pathological activation of visual representations. *Journal of Clinical and Experimental Neuropsychology, 16,* 651–663.

Anderson, U. S., Kelling, A. S., Pressley-Keough, R., Bloomsmith, M. A., & Maple, T. L. (2003). Enhancing the zoo visitor's experience by public animal training and oral interpretation at an otter exhibit. *Environment and Behavior, 35,* 826–841.

Anderson, W. S., Sheth, R. N., Bencherif, B., Frost, J. J., & Campbell, J. N. (2002). Naloxone increases pain induced by topical capsaicin in healthy human volunteers. *Pain, 99,* 207–216.

Andre, T. (1979). Does answering higher-level questions while reading facilitate productive learning? *Review of Educational Research, 49,* 280–318.

Andreasen, N. C. (1997). The evolving concept of schizophrenia: From Kraepelin to the present and future. *Schizophrenia Research, 28,* 105–109.

Andreasen, N. C., & Flaum, M. (1991). Schizophrenia: The characteristic symptoms. *Schizophrenia Bulletin, 17,* 27–49.

Andreasen, N. C., Arndt, S., Alliger, R., & Miller, D. (1995). Symptoms of schizophrenia: Methods, meanings, and mechanisms. *Archives of General Psychiatry, 52,* 341–351.

Andreasen, N. C., Flaum, M., Swayze, V. W., & Tyrrell, G. (1990). Positive and negative symptoms in schizophrenia: A critical reappraisal. *Archives of General Psychiatry, 47,* 615–621.

Andreassen, P. B. (1988). Explaining the price-volume relationship: The difference between price changes and changing prices. *Organizational Behavior and Human Decision Processes, 41,* 371–389.

Andrews, G., & Halford, G. S. (1998). Children's ability to make transitive inferences: The importance of premise integration and structural complexity. *Cognitive Development, 13,* 479–513.

Anestis, M. D., Anestis, J. C., & Lilienfeld, S. O. (2011). When it comes to evaluating psychodynamic therapy, the devil is in the details. *American Psychologist, 66,* 149–151.

Angermeyer, M. C., & Schulze, B. (2001). Reinforcing stereotypes: How the focus on forensic cases in news reporting may influence public attitudes towards the mentally ill. *International Journal of Law and Psychiatry, 24,* 469–486.

Anisfeld, M. (1996). Only tongue protrusion modeling is matched by neonates. *Developmental Review, 16,* 149–161.

Ansbacher, H. L. (1990). Alfred Adler's influence on the three leading cofounders of humanistic psychology. *Journal of Humanistic Psychology, 30,* 45–53.

Anshel, M. H. (1995). Examining social loafing among elite female rowers as a function of task duration and mood. *Journal of Sport Behavior, 18,* 39–49.

Anthony, B., Boudreaux, L., Dobbs, I., Jamal, S., Guerra, P., & Williamson, J. W. (2003). Can relaxation lower metaboreflex-mediated blood pressure elevations? *Medicine and Science in Sports and Exercise, 35,* 394–399.

Antoni, M. H., LaPerriere, A., Schneiderman, N., & Fletcher, M. A. (1991). Stress and immunity in individuals at risk for AIDS. *Stress Medicine, 7,* 35–44.

Antshel, K. M., Faraone, S. V, Maglione, K., Doyle, A. E., Fried, R., Seidman, L. J., & Biederman, J. (2010). Executive functioning in high-IQ adults with ADHD. *Psychological Medicine, 40,* 1909–18.

Antunano, M. J., & Hernandez, J. M. (1989). Incidence of airsickness among military parachutists. *Aviation, Space, and Environmental Medicine, 60,* 792–797.

Apodaca, T. R., & Miller, William R. (2003). Meta-analysis of the effectiveness of bibliotherapy for alcohol problems. *Journal of Clinical Psychology, 59*, 289–304.

Appel, J., Potter, E., Shen, Q., Pantol, G., Greig, M. T., Loewenstein, D., & Duara, R. (2009). A comparative analysis of structural brain MRI in the diagnosis of Alzheimer's disease. *Behavioural Neurology, 21.* 13–19.

Appelbaum, P. S. (1998). A "Health Information Infrastructure" and the threat to confidentiality of health records. *Psychiatric Services, 49,* 27–28, 33.

Appelbaum, P. S., & Gutheil, T. G. (1980). The Boston State Hospital case: "Involuntary mind control," the Constitution, and the "right to rot." *American Journal of Psychiatry, 137,* 720–723.

Apperloo, M. J. A., Van Der Stege, J. G., Hoek, A., Schultz, W., & Willibrord, C. M. (2003). In the mood for sex: The value of androgens. *Journal of Sex and Marital Therapy, 29,* 87–102.

Araújo, D. (2007). Ecological validity, representative design, and correspondence between experimental task constraints and behavioral setting: Comment on Rogers, Kadar, and Costall (2005). *Ecological Psychology, 19,* 69–78.

Ardila, A., Montanes, P., & Gempeler, J. (1986). Echoic memory and language perception. *Brain and Language, 29,* 134–140.

Ares–Santos, S., Granado, N., & Moratalla, R. (2013). The role of dopamine receptors in the neurotoxicity of methamphetamine. *Journal of Internal Medicine, 273,* 1365–2796.

Arfken, C.L., Joseph, A., Sandhu, G.R., Roehrs, T., Douglass, A. B., Boutros, .N. N. (2014). The status of sleep abnormalities as a diagnostic test for major depressive disorder. *Journal of Affective Disorders, 56,* 36–45.

Armario, A. (2006). The hypothalamic-pituitary-adrenal axis: What can it tell us about stressors? *CNS and Neurological Disorders: Drug Targets, 5,* 485–501.

Armstrong, G. B., & Chung, L. (2000). Background television and reading memory in context: Assessing TV interference and facilitative context effects on encoding versus retrieval processes. *Communication Research, 27,* 327–352.

Arndt, J., Schimel, J., & Goldenberg, J. L. (2003). Death can be good for your health: Fitness intentions as a proximal and distal defense against mortality salience. *Journal of Applied Social Psychology, 33,* 1726–1746.

Arnett, J. J. (1999). Adolescent storm and stress, reconsidered. *American Psychologist, 54,* 317–326.

Arnett, P. A., Howland, E. W., Smith, S. S., & Newman, J. P. (1993). Autonomic responsivity during passive avoidance in incarcerated psychopaths. *Personality and Individual Differences, 14,* 173–184.

Arnold, R. M., Miller, M., Mehta, R. S. (2012). Insomnia: Nonpharmacologic treatments #104. *Journal of Palliative Medicine, 15,* 242–243.

Arns, M., Heinrich, H., Strehl, U. (2014). Evaluation of neurofeedback in ADHD: The long and winding road. *Biological Psychology, 95,* 108–115.

Aronson, S. C., Black, J. E., McDougle, C. J., & Scanley, B. E. (1995). Serotonergic mechanisms of cocaine effects in humans. *Psychopharmacology, 119,* 179–185.

Arrigo, J. M., & Pezdek, K. (1997). Lessons from the study of psychogenic amnesia. *Current Directions in Psychological Science, 6,* 148–152.

Artemiadis, A. K., Vervainioti, A. A., Alexopoulos, E. C., Rombos, A., Anagnostouli, M. C., & Darviri, C. (2012). Stress management and multiple sclerosis: A randomized controlled trial. *Archives of Clinical Neuropsychology, 27,* 406–416

Ary, D. V., Tildesley, E., Hops, H., & Andrews, J. A. (1993). The influence of parent, sibling, and peer modeling and attitudes on adolescent use of alcohol. *International Journal of the Addictions, 28,* 853–880.

Asahina, M., Suzuki, A., Mori, M., Kanesaka, T., & Hattori, T. (2003). Emotional sweating response in a patient with bilateral amygdale damage. *International Journal of Psychophysiology, 17,* 87–93.

Asai, M., Ramachandrappa, S. Joachim, M., Shen, Y., Zhang, R. Nuthalapati, Ramanathan, Strolich, D. L., . . . Majzoub, J. A. (2013). Loss of function of the melanocortin 2 receptor accessory protein 2 is associated with mammalian obesity. *Science 341,* 275–278.

Asch, S. E. (1955, November). Opinions and social pressure. *Scientific American,* pp. 31–35.

Aseltine, R. H., Jr. (1996). Pathways linking parental divorce with adolescent depression. *Journal of Health and Social Behavior, 37,* 133–148.

Aserinsky, E., & Kleitman, N. (1953). Regularly occurring periods of eye motility and concomitant phenomena during sleep. *Science, 118,* 273–274.

Aserinsky, E., Lynch, J. A., Mack, M. E., Tzankoff, S. P., & Hurn, E. (1985). Comparison of eye motion in wakefulness and REM sleep. *Psychophysiology, 22,* 1–10.

Ash, D. W., & Holding, D. H. (1990). Backward versus forward chaining in the acquisition of a keyboard skill. *Human Factors, 32,* 139–146.

Aslin, R. N., & Smith, L. B. (1988). Perceptual development. *Annual Review of Psychology, 39,* 435–474.

Aspen, V. A., Stein, R. I., & Wilfley, D. E. (2012). An exploration of salivation patterns in normal weight and obese children. *Appetite, 58,* 539–542.

Astin, G. R., & Garber, H. (1982). *The rise and fall of national test scores.* New York: Academic Press.

Atkinson, D. R. (1983). Ethnic similarity in counseling psychology: A review of research. *Counseling Psychologist, 11,* 79–92.

Atkinson, J. W. (1981). Studying personality in the context of an advanced motivational psychology. *American Psychologist, 36,* 117–128.

Atkinson, J. W., & Litwin, G. H. (1960). Achievement motive and test anxiety concerned as motive to approach success and motive to avoid failure. *Journal of Abnormal and Social Psychology, 60,* 52–63.

Attie, I., & Brooks-Gunn, J. (1989). Development of eating problems in adolescent girls: A longitudinal study. *Developmental Psychology, 25,* 70–79.

Atwood, G. E., & Tomkins, S. S. (1976). On the subjectivity of personality theory. *Journal of the History of the Behavioral Sciences, 12,* 166–177.

Austin, A. J., & Duka, T. (2012). Mechanisms of attention to conditioned stimuli predictive of a cigarette outcome. *Behavioural Brain Research, 232,* 183–189.

Avalon, L, & Young, M. A. (2003) A comparison of depressive symptoms in African Americans and Caucasian Americans. *Journal of Cross-Cultural Psychology, 34,* 111–124.

Axmacher, N., Lenz, S., Haupt, S., Elger, C. E., & Fell, J. (2010). Electrophysiological signature of working and long-term memory interaction in the human hippocampus. *European Journal of Neuroscience, 31,* 177–188.

Ayabe-Kanamura, S., Schicker, I., Laska, M., Hudson, R., Distel, H., Kobayakawa, T., & Saito, S. (1998). Differences in perception of everyday odors: A Japanese-German cross-cultural study. *Chemical Senses, 23,* 31–38.

Aydin, G., & Aydin, O. (1992). Learned helplessness and explanatory style in Turkish samples. *Journal of Social Psychology, 132,* 117–119.

Aydt, H., & Corsaro, W. A. (2003). Differences in children's construction of gender across culture: An interpretative approach. *American Behavioral Scientist, 46,* 1306–1325.

B

Babad, E., Bernieri, F., & Rosenthal, R. (1989). When less information is more informative: Diagnosing teacher expectations from brief samples of behavior. *British Journal of Educational Psychology, 59,* 281–295.

Baban, A., & Craciun, C. (2007). Changing health risk behaviors: A review of theory and evidence-based interventions in health psychology. *Journal of Cognitive and Behavioral Psychotherapies, 7,* 45–67.

Baddeley, A. D. (1982). Domains of recollection. *Psychological Review, 89,* 708–729.

Baddeley, A. D. (1994). The magical number seven: Still magic after all these years? *Psychological Review, 101,* 353–356.

Bae, J. S., Kim, J. Y., Park, B.-L., Cheong, H. S., Kim, J.-H., Shin, J.-G, Woo, S.-I. (2013). Lack of association between DISC1 polymorphisms and risk of schizophrenia in a Korean population. *Psychiatry Research, 208,* 189–90.

Baer, J. (1996). The effects of task-specific divergent-thinking training. *Journal of Creative Behavior, 30,* 183–187.

Bagati, D., Nizamie, S. H., & Prakash, R. (2009). Effect of augmentatory repetitive transcranialmagnetic stimulation on auditory hallucinations in schizophrenia: Randomized controlled study. *Australian and New Zealand Journal of Psychiatry, 43,* 386–392.

Bagozzi, R. P., Wong, N., & Yi, Y. (1999). The role of culture and gender in the relationship between positive and negative affect. *Cognition & Emotion,13,* 641–672.

Bagwell, C. L., Newcomb, A. F., & Bukowski, W. M. (1998). Preadolescent friendship and peer rejection as predictors of adult adjustment. *Child Development, 69,* 140–153.

Bahill, A. T., & Karnavas, W. J. (1993). The perceptual illusion of baseball's rising fastball and breaking curveball. *Journal of Experimental Psychology: Human Perception and Performance, 19,* 3–14.

Bahill, A. T., & LaRitz, T. (1984). Why can't batters keep their eyes on the ball? *American Scientist, 72,* 249–253.

Bahrick, H. P., Bahrick, P. O., & Wittlinger, R. P. (1975). Fifty years of memory for names and faces: A cross–sectional approach. *Journal of Experimental Psychology: General, 104,* 54–75.

Bailey, C. J., Karhu, J., & Ilmoniemi, R. J. (2001). Transcranial magnetic stimulation as a tool for cognitive studies. *Scandinavian Journal of Psychology, 42,* 297–305.

Bailey, J. M., Dunne, M. P., & Martin, N. G. (2000). Genetic and environmental influences on sexual orientation and its correlates in an Australian twin sample. *Journal of Personality and Social Psychology, 78,* 524–536.

Bailey, J. M., Dunne, M. P., & Martin, N. G. (2000). Genetic and environmental influences on sexual orientation and its correlates in an Australian twin sample. *Journal of Personality and Social Psychology, 78,* 524–536.

Bailey, J. M., Pillard, R. C., Dawood, K., Miller, M. B., Farrer, L. A., Trivedi, S., & Murphy, R. L. (1999). A family history study of male sexual orientation using three independent samples. *Behavior Genetics, 29,* 79–86.

Bailey, R. K., Patel, T. C., Avenido, J., Patel, M., Jaleel, M., Barker, N., . . . Jabeen, S. (2011). Suicide: Current trends. *Journal of the National Medical Association, 103,* 614–617.

Bailey, S. P., Hall, E. E., Folger, S. E., & Miller, P. C. (2008). Changes in EEG during graded exercise on a recumbent cycle ergometer. *Journal of Sports Science and Medicine, 7,* 505–511.

Bailis, D. S. (2001). Benefits of self-handicapping in sport: A field study of university athletes. *Canadian Journal of Behavioural Science, 33,* 213–223.

Baird, J. C., & Wagner, M. (1982). The moon illusion: I. How high is the sky? *Journal of Experimental Psychology: General, 111,* 296–303.

Baisden, R. H. (1995). Therapeutic uses for neural grafts: Progress slowed but not abandoned. *Behavioral and Brain Sciences, 18,* 47–48.

Baker, G. H. B. (1987). Psychological factors and immunity. *Journal of Psychosomatic Research, 31,* 1–10.

Baker, J. P. (1994). Outcomes of lithium discontinuation: A meta-analysis. *Lithium, 5,* 187–192.

Baker, L. M., & Dunbar, K. (2000). Experimental design heuristics for scientific discovery: The use of "baseline" and "known standard" controls. *International Journal of Human-Computer Studies. Special Issue: Machine Discovery, 53,* 335–349.

Bala, N., Kang, L., Lindsay, R.C.L., & Talwar, V. (2010). The competency of children to testify: Psychological research informing Canadian law reform. *International Journal of Children's Rights, 18,* 53–77.

Balanovski, E., & Taylor, J. G. (1978). Can electromagnetism account for extra sensory phenomena? *Nature, 276,* 64–67.

Balch, W. R., Myers, D. M., & Papotto, C. (1999). Dimensions of mood in mood-dependent memory. *Journal of Experimental Psychology: Learning, Memory, and Cognition, 25,* 70–83.

Baldwin, D., Woods, R., Lawson, R., & Taylor, D. (2011). Efficacy of drug treatments for generalised anxiety disorder: Systematic review and meta-analysis. *British Medical Journal Open, 342,* 1–11.

Baldwin, E. (1993). The case for animal research in psychology. *Journal of Social Issues, 49,* 121–131.

Baldwin, M. W. (1954). Subjective measurements in television. *American Psychologist, 9,* 231–234.

Bales, J. (1988, August). Pre-work polygraph ban signed by Reagan. *APA Monitor,* p. 5.

Bales, J. (1988, March). Court rules no duty to commit in N.C. *APA Monitor,* p. 20.

Balkany, T. J, Hodges, A. V., Eshraghi, A. A., Butts, S., Bricker, K., Lingvai, J., . . . King, J. (2002). Cochlear implants in children: A review. *Acta Oto-Laryngologica, 122,* 356–362.

Ball, C., Mann, L., & Stamm, C. (1994). Decision-making abilities of intellectually gifted and non-gifted children. *Australian Journal of Psychology, 46,* 13–20.

Ball, I. L., Farnill, D., Wangeman, J. F. (1984). Sex and age differences in sensation seeking: Some national comparisons. *British Journal of Psychology, 75,* 257–265.

Ball, K., & Lee, C. (2000). Relationship between psychological stress, coping, and disordered eating. *Psychology and Health, 14,* 1007–1035.

Ballard, C. G., O'Brien, J. T., Reichelt, K. P., & Elaine K. (2002). Aromatherapy as a safe and effective treatment for the management of agitation in severe dementia: The results of a double-blind, placebo-controlled trial with Melissa. *Journal of Clinical Psychiatry, 63,* 553–558.

Bancroft, J., Janssen, E., Strong, D., Carnes, L., Vukadinovic, Z., & Long, J. S. (2003). Sexual risk-taking in gay men: The relevance of sexual arousability, mood, and sensation seeking. *Archives of Sexual Behavior, 32,* 555–572.

Bandura, A. (1965). Influence of model's reinforcement contingencies on the acquisition of imitative responses. *Journal of Personality and Social Psychology, 1,* 589–595.

Bandura, A. (1977). *Social learning theory.* Englewood Cliffs, NJ: Prentice-Hall.

Bandura, A. (1982). The psychology of chance encounters and life paths. *American Psychologist, 37,* 747–755.

Bandura, A. (1986). *Social foundations of thought and action: A social-cognitive theory.* Englewood Cliffs, NJ: Prentice Hall.

Bandura, A. (1989). Human agency in social cognitive theory. *American Psychologist, 44,* 1175–1184.

Bandura, A. (2000). Exercise of human agency through collective efficacy. *Current Directions in Psychological Science, 9,* 75–78.

Bandura, A. (2001). Social-cognitive theory: An agentic perspective. *Annual Review of Psychology, 52,* 1–26.

Bandura, A. (2002). Social cognitive theory in cultural context. *Applied Psychology, 51,* 269–290.

Bandura, A., Blanchard, E. B., & Ritter, B. (1969). The relative efficacy of desensitization and modeling approaches for inducing behavioral, affective, and attitudinal changes. *Journal of Personality and Social Psychology, 13,* 173–199.

Bandura, A., & Locke, E. A. (2003). Negative self-efficacy and goal effects revisited. *Journal of Applied Psychology, 88,* 87–99.

Bandura, A., Caprara, G. V., Barbaranelli, C., Regalia, C., & Scabini, E. (2011). Impact of family efficacy beliefs on quality of family functioning and satisfaction with family life. *Applied Psychology: An International Review, 60,* 421–448.

Bandura, A., Reese, L., & Adams, N. E. (1982). Microanalysis of action and fear arousal as a function of differential levels of perceived self-efficacy. *Journal of Personality and Social Psychology, 43,* 5–21.

Bang, H., & Montgomery, D. (2013). Understanding international graduate students' acculturation using Q methodology. *Journal of College Student Development, 54,* 343–360.

Bangerter, A., Grob, A., & Krings, F. (2001). Personal goals at age 25 in three generation of the twentieth century: Young adulthood in historical context. *Swiss Journal of Psychology –Schweizerische Zeitschrift fuer Psychologie – Revue Suisse de Psychologie, 60,* 59–64.

Banik, R. K., Kozaki, Y., Sato, J., Gera, L., & Mizumura, K. (2001). B2 receptor-mediated enhanced bradykinin sensitivity of rat cutaneous c-fiber nociceptors during persistent inflammation. *Journal of Neurophysiology, 86,* 2727–2735.

Banks, S. M., & Kerns, R. D. (1996). Explaining high rates of depression in chronic pain: A diathesis-stress framework. *Psychological Bulletin, 119,* 95–110.

Barako Arndt, K., & Schuele, C. M. (2012). Production of infinitival complements by children with specific language impairment. *Clinical Linguistics & Phonetics, 26,* 1–17.

Barbalet, J. M. (1999). William James' theory of emotions: Filling in the picture. *Journal for the Theory of Social Behaviour, 29,* 251–266.

Barbara, J. G. (2007). Louis Ranvier (1835–1922): The contribution of microscopy to physiology and the renewal of French general anatomy. *Journal of the History of the Neurosciences, 16,* 413–431.

Barber, T. X. (2000). A deeper understanding of hypnosis: Its secrets, its nature, its essence. *American Journal of Clinical Hypnosis, 42,* 208–272.

Barbut, M. (1993). Comments on a pseudo-mathematical model in social psychology. *European Journal of Social Psychology, 23,* 203–210.

Barclay, N. L. and Gregory, A. M. (2013). Quantitative genetic research on sleep: A review of normal sleep, sleep disturbances and associated emotional, behavioural, and health-related difficulties. *Sleep Medicine Reviews, 17,* 29–40.

Bard, P. (1934). On emotional experience after decortication with some remarks on theoretical views. *Psychological Review, 41,* 309–329.

Bargh, J. A. (1992). The ecology of automaticity: Toward establishing the conditions needed to produce automatic processing effects. *American Journal of Psychology, 105,* 181–199.

Baribeau-Braun, J., Picton, T. W., & Gosselin, J. Y. (1983). Schizophrenia: A neuropsychological evaluation of abnormal information processing. *Science, 219,* 874–876.

Barker, L. (2006). Teaching evolutionary psychology: An interview with David M. Buss. *Teaching of Psychology, 33,* 69–76.

Barker, M. E., Thompson, K. A., & McClean, S. I. (1996). Do type As eat differently? A comparison of men and women. *Appetite, 26,* 277–286.

Barker, R. A., Barrett, J. B., Mason, S. L., & Björklund, A. (2013). Fetal dopaminergic transplantation trials and the future of neural grafting in Parkinson's disease. *The Lancet Neurology, 12,* 84–91.

Barker-Collo, S., Read, J., & Cowie, S. (2012). Coping strategies in female survivors of childhood sexual abuse from two Canadian and two New Zealand cultural groups. *Journal of Trauma & Dissociation, 13,* 435–447.

Barnes, M. L., & Rosenthal, R. (1985). Interpersonal effects of experimenter attractiveness, attire, and gender. *Journal of Personality and Social Psychology, 48,* 435–446.

Barnes, R. C. (2000). Viktor Frankl's logotherapy: Spirituality and meaning in the new millennium. *TCA Journal, 28,* 24–31.

Barnett, L. B., & Corazza, L. (1998). Identification of mathematical talent and programmatic efforts to facilitate development of talent. *European Journal for Higher Ability, 9,* 48–61.

Barnett, Z. L., Robleda-Gomez, S., & Pachana, N. A. (2011). Viagra: The little blue pill with big repercussions. *Aging & Mental Health, 16,* 84–88.

Barrault, S., & Varescon, I. (2013). Impulsive sensation seeking and gambling practice among a sample of online poker players: Comparison between non pathological, problem, and pathological gamblers. *Personality and Individual Differences, 55,* 502–507.

Barrett, P. T., Daum, I., & Eysenck, H. J. (1990). Sensory nerve conduction and intelligence: A methodological study. *Journal of Psychophysiology, 4,* 1–13.

Barrowclough, C., Tarrier, N., Humphreys, L., Ward, G. L., & Andrews, B. (2003). Self-esteem in schizophrenia: Relationships between self–evaluation, family attitudes, and symptomatology. *Journal of Abnormal Psychology, 112,* 92–99.

Barry, T. D., Lochman, J. E., Fite, P. J., Wells, K. C., & Colder, C. R. (2012). The influence of neighborhood characteristics and parenting practices on academic problems and aggression outcomes among moderately to highly aggressive children. *Journal of Community Psychology, 40,* 372–379.

Bartholomew, D. J. (1995). Spearman and the origin and development of factor analysis. *British Journal of Mathematical and Statistical Psychology, 48,* 211–220.

Bartholomew, R. E., & Radford, B. (2003). *Hoaxes, myths, and manias: Why we need critical thinking.* Amherst, NY: Prometheus.

Bartlett, F. C. (1932). *Remembering: A study in experimental and social psychology.* Cambridge, England: Cambridge University Press.

Bartoshuk, L. M. (1991). Sensory factors in eating behavior. *Bulletin of the Psychonomic Society, 29,* 250–255.

Bartoshuk, L. M., & Beauchamp, G. K. (1994). Chemical senses. *Annual Review of Psychology, 45,* 419–449.

Bartoshuk, L. M., Cain, W. S., & Pfaffmann, C. (1985). Taste and olfaction. In G. A. Kimble & K. Schlesinger (Eds.), *Topics in the history of psychology, Vol. 1* (pp. 221–260). Hillsdale, NJ: Erlbaum.

Bartsch, R. A., Judd, C. M., Louw, D. A., Park, B., & Ryan, C. S. (1997). Cross-national outgroup homogeneity: United States and South African stereotypes. *South African Journal of Psychology, 27,* 166–170.

Bartussek, D., Becker, G., Diedrich, O., & Naumann, E. (1996). Extraversion, neuroticism, and event-related brain potentials in response to emotional stimuli. *Personality and Individual Differences, 20,* 301–312.

Basadur, M. S., Wakabayashi, M., & Takai, J. (1992). Training effects on the divergent thinking attitudes of Japanese managers. *International Journal of Intercultural Relations, 16,* 329–345.

Bassili, J. N. (2003). The minority slowness effect: Subtle inhibitions in the expression of views not shared by others. *Journal of Personality and Social Psychology, 84,* 261–276.

Bassilios, B., Reifels, L., & Pirkis, J. (2012). Enhanced primary mental health services in response to disaster. *Psychiatric Services, 63,* 868–874.

Bassuk, E. L. (1984, July). The homelessness problem. *Scientific American,* pp. 40–45.

Batson, C. D., Ahmad, N., Yin, J., Bedell, S. J., Johnson, J. W., Templin, C. M., & Whiteside, A. (1999). Two threats to the common good: Self-interested egoism and empathy and empathy-induced altruism. *Personality and Social Psychology Bulletin, 25,* 3–16.

Batson, C. D., Batson, J. G., Griffitt, C. A., Barrientos, S., Brandt, J. R., Sprengelmeyer, P., & Bayly, M. J. (1989). Negative-state relief and the empathy-altruism hypothesis. *Journal of Personality and Social Psychology, 56,* 922–933.

Batson, C. D., Bolen, M. H., Cross, J. A., & Neuringer-Benefiel, H. E. (1986). Where is the altruism in the altruistic personality? *Journal of Personality and Social Psychology, 50,* 212–220.

Bauer, D. G. (2005). Review of the endocrine system. *Medsurg Nursing, 14,* 335–337.

Bauer, M., Cassar, A., Chytilová, J., & Heinrich, J. (2014). War's enduring effects on the development of egalitarian motivations and in-group biases. *Psychological Science, 25,* 47–57.

Bauer, M. N., Leenaars, A. A., Berman, A. L., Jobes, D. A., Dixon, J. F., & Bibb, J. L. (1997). Late adulthood suicide: A life~span analysis of suicide notes. *Archives of Suicide Research, 3,* 91–108.

Bauer, P. J., Stennes, L., & Haight, J. C. (2003). Representation of the inner self in autobiography: Women's and men's use of internal states language in personal narratives. *Memory, 11,* 27–42.

Bauer, S. M., Schanda, H., Karakula, H., Olajossy-Hilkesberger, L., Rudaleviciene, P., Okribelashvili, N., . . . Stompe, T. (2011). Culture and the prevalence of hallucinations in schizophrenia. *Comprehensive Psychiatry, 52,* 319–325.

Baum, A., Grunberg, N. E., & Singer, J. E. (1992). Biochemical measurements in the study of emotion. *Psychological Science, 3,* 56–60.

Bauman, K. E., Carver, K., & Gleiter, K. (2001). Trends in parent and friend influence during adolescence. The case of adolescent cigarette smoking. *Addictive Behaviors, 26,* 349–361.

Bauman, M. L., & Kemper, T. L. (2005). Neuroanatomic observations of the brain in autism: A review and future directions. *International Journal of Developmental Neuroscience, 23,* 183–7.

Baumeister, A. A. (1998). Intelligence and the "personal equation." *Intelligence, 26,* 255–265.

Baumeister, R. F. (1982). A self-presentational view of social phenomena. *Psychological Bulletin, 91,* 3–26.

Baumeister, R. F. (1984). Choking under pressure: Self-consciousness and paradoxical effects of incentives on skillful performance. *Journal of Personality and Social Psychology, 46,* 610–620.

Baumeister, R. F. (1988). Should we stop studying sex differences altogether? *American Psychologist, 43,* 1092–1095.

Baumeister, R. F. (1990). Suicide as escape from self. *Psychological Review, 97,* 90–113.

Baumeister, R. F. (2000). Gender differences in erotic plasticity: The female sex drive as socially flexible and responsive. *Psychological Bulletin, 126,* 347–374.

Baumeister, R. F., & Bratslavsky, E. (1999). Passion, intimacy, and time: Passionate love as a function of change in intimacy. *Personality and Social Psychology Review, 3,* 49–67.

Baumeister, R. F., Campbell, J. D., Krueger, J. I., & Vohs, K. D. (2003). Does high self-esteem cause better performance, interpersonal success, happiness, or healthier lifestyles? *Psychological Science in the Public Interest, 4,* 1–44.

Baumeister, R. F., Catanese, K. R., Vohs, K. D. (2001). Is there a gender difference in strength of sex drive? Theoretical views, conceptual distinctions, and a review of relevant evidence. *Personality and Social Psychology Bulletin, 5,* 242–273.

Baumeister, R. F., Dale, K., & Sommer, K. L. (1998). Freudian defense mechanisms and empirical findings in modern social psychology: Reaction formation, projection, displacement, undoing, isolation, sublimation, and denial. *Journal of Personality, 66,* 1081–1124.

Baumrind, D. (1964). Some thoughts on ethics of research: After reading Milgram's "Behavioral Study of Obedience." *American Psychologist, 19,* 421–423.

Baumrind, D. (1966). Effects of authoritative control on child behavior. *Child Development, 37,* 887–907.

Baumrind, D. (1983). Rejoinder to Lewis's reinterpretation of parental firm control effects: Are authoritative families really harmonious? *Psychological Bulletin, 94,* 132–142.

Baumrind, D. (1985). Research using intentional deception: Ethical issues revisited. *American Psychologist, 40,* 165–174.

Baumrind, D. (2010). Differentiating being confrontive and coercive kinds of parental power–assertive disciplinary practices. *Human Development, 55,* 35–51.

Bavelier, D., Corina, D., Jezzard, P., Clark, V., Karni, A., Lalwani, A., . . . Neville, H. J. (1998). Hemispheric specialization for English and ASL: Left invariance–right variability. *Neuroreport, 9,* 1537–1542.

Baxter, J., Tridgell, A., & Weaver, L. (2000). Learning to play chess using temporal differences. *Machine Learning, 40,* 243–263.

Baxter, P. J., Bonadonna, C., Dupree, R., Hards, D. L., Kohn, S. C., Murphy, M. D., . . . Vickers, B. P. (1999). Cristobalite in volcanic ash of the Soufriere Hills volcano, Montserrat, British West Indies. *Science, 19,* 1142–1145.

Bayley, N. (1955). On the growth of intelligence. *American Psychologist, 10,* 805–818.

Bayton, J. A. (1975). Francis Sumner, Max Meenes, and the training of black psychologists. *American Psychologist, 30,* 185–186.

Beal, C. R., Schmitt, K. L., & Dekle, D. J. (1995). Eyewitness identification of children: Effects of absolute judgments, nonverbal response options, and event encoding. *Law and Human Behavior, 19,* 197–216.

Beatty, M. J., Heisel, A. D., Hall, A. E., Levine, T. R., & LaFrance, B. H. (2002). What can we learn from the study of twins about genetic and environmental influences on interpersonal affiliation, aggressiveness, and social anxiety? A meta-analytic study. *Communication Monographs, 69,* 1–18.

Beatty, W. W. (1984). Discriminating drunkenness: A replication. *Bulletin of the Psychonomic Society, 22,* 431–432.

Becht, M. C., & Vingerhoets, J. J. M. (2002). Crying and mood change: A cross-cultural study. *Cognition and Emotion, 16,* 87–101.

Beck, A. T. (1967). *Depression: Clinical, experimental and theoretical aspects.* New York: Harper & Row.

Beck, A. T. (1997). The past and future of cognitive therapy. *Journal of Psychotherapy Practice and Research, 6,* 276–284.

Beck, A. T. (2002). Cognitive patterns in dreams and daydreams. *Journal of Cognitive Psychotherapy, 16,* 23–28.

Beck, A. T., & Rector, N. A. (2003). A cognitive model of hallucinations. *Cognitive Therapy and Research, 27,* 19–52.

Becker, A. E., Burwell, R. A., Herzog, D. B., Hamburg, P., & Gilman, S. E. (2002). Eating behaviors and attitudes following prolonged exposure to television among ethnic Fijian adolescent girls. *British Journal of Psychiatry, 180,* 509–514.

Becker, J. B., Curran, E. J., & Freed, W. J. (1990). Adrenal medulla graft-induced recovery of function in an animal model of Parkinson's disease: Possible mechanisms of action. *Canadian Journal of Psychology, 44,* 293–310.

Becker, P. (1999). Beyond the Big Five. *Personality and Individual Differences, 26,* 511–530.

Becona, E., & Garcia, M. P. (1993). Nicotine fading and smoke-holding methods to smoking cessation. *Psychological Reports, 73,* 779–786.

Beebe, L. H., & Smith, K. (2010). Informed consent to research in persons with schizophrenia spectrum disorders. *Nursing Ethics, 17,* 425–434.

Beer, J. M., Arnold, R. D., & Loehlin, J. C. (1998). Genetic and environmental influences on MMPI factor scales: Joint model fitting to twin and adoption data. *Journal of Personality and Social Psychology, 74,* 818–827.

Beers, C. W. (1908/1970). *A mind that found itself.* New York: Doubleday.

Begley, S., & Hager, M. (1993, July 26). Does DNA make some men gay? *Newsweek,* p. 59.

Behnke, S. H. (1999). O'Connor v. Donaldson: Retelling a classic and finding some revisionist history. *Journal of the American Academy of Psychiatry and the Law, 27,* 115–126.

Behrend, D. A. (1988). Overextensions in early language comprehension: Evidence from a signal detection approach. *Journal of Child Language, 15,* 63–75.

Behrens, R. R. (2003). Thinking outside of the box: On Karl Duncker, functional fixedness, and the adaptive value of engaging in purposely deviant acts. *Gestalt Theory, 25,* 63–70.

Behrmann, M., & Kimchi, R. (2003). What does visual agnosia tell us about perceptual organization and its relationship to object perception? *Journal of Experimental Psychology: Human Perception and Performance, 29,* 19–42.

Beijersbergen, M. D., Juffer, F., Bakermans-Kranengurb, M. J., & van IJzendoorn, M. H. (2012). Remaining or becoming secure: Parental sensitive support predicts attachment continuity from infancy to adolescence in a longitudinal adoption study. *Developmental Psychology, 48,* 1277–1282.

Beiser, M., Shore, J. H., Peters, R., & Tatum, W. (1985). Does community care for the mentally ill make a difference? A tale of two cities. *American Journal of Psychiatry, 142,* 1047–1052.

Bekoff, M., Gruen, L., Townsend, S. E., & Rollin, B. E. (1992). Animals in science: Some areas revisited. *Animal Behaviour, 44,* 473–484.

Beleza-Meireles, A., & Al-Chalabi, A. (2009). Genetic studies of amyotrophic lateral sclerosis: Controversies and perspectives. *Amyotrophic Lateral Sclerosis. 10.* 1–14.

Belisle, M., Roskies, E., & Levesque, J. M. (1987). Improving adherence to physical activity. *Health Psychology, 6,* 159–172.

Bell, A. P., Weinberg, M. S., & Hammersmith, S. J. (1981). *Sexual preference: Its development in men and women.* Bloomington: Indiana University Press.

Bellisle, F. (1999). Glutamate and the Umami taste: Sensory, metabolic, nutritional and behavioural considerations. A review of the literature published in the last 10 years. *Neuroscience and Biobehavioral Reviews, 23,* 423–438.

Belmont, L., & Marolla, F. A. (1973). Birth order, family size, and intelligence. *Science, 182,* 1096–1101.

Belsky, J. (1988). The "effects" of infant day care reconsidered. *Early Childhood Research Quarterly, 3,* 235–272.

Belsky, J., & Hsieh, K. H. (1998). Patterns of marital change during the early childhood years: Parent personality, coparenting, and division–of–labor correlates. *Journal of Family Psychology, 12,* 511–528.

Belsky, J., & Pluess, M. (2009). The nature (and nurture?) of plasticity in early human development. *Perspectives on Psychological Science, 4,* 345–35l.

Bem, D. J. (1967). Self-perception: An alternative interpretation of cognitive dissonance phenomena. *Psychological Review, 74,* 183–200.

Bem, D. J. (2000). Exotic becomes erotic: Interpreting the biological correlates of sexual orientation. *Archives of Sexual Behavior, 29,* 531–548.

Bem, D. J., & Allen, A. (1974). On predicting some of the people some of the time: The search for cross-situational consistencies in behavior. *Psychological Review, 81,* 506–520.

Bem, D. J., & Honorton, C. (1994). Does psi exist? Replicable evidence for an anomalous process of information transfer. *Psychological Bulletin, 115,* 4–18.

Bem, S. L. (1981). Gender schema theory: A cognitive account of sex typing. *Psychological Review, 88,* 354—364.

Benbow, C. P. (1988). Sex differences in mathematical reasoning ability in intellectually talented preadolescents: Their nature, effect, and possible causes. *Behavioral and Brain Sciences, 11,* 169–232.

Benbow, C. P., & Stanley, J. C. (1983). Sex differences in mathematical reasoning ability: More facts. *Science, 222,* 1029–1031.

Benbow, C. P., Lubinski, D., Shea, D. L., & Eftekhari-Sanjani, H. (2000). Sex differences in mathematical reasoning ability at age 13: Their status 20 years later. *Psychological Science, 11,* 474–480.

Bender, S. L., Ponton, L. E., Crittenden, M. R., & Word, C. O. (1995). For underprivileged children, standardized intelligence testing can do more harm than good: Reply. *Journal of Developmental and Behavioral Pediatrics, 16,* 428–430.

Benham, B. (2008). The ubiquity of deception and the ethics of deceptive research. *Bioethics, 22,* 147–156.

Benjamin, A. S., & Tullis, J. (2010). What makes distributed practice effective? *Cognitive Psychology, 61,* 228–247.

Benjamin, J., Ebstein, R. P., & Belmaker, R. H. (1997). Personality genetics. *Israel Journal of Psychiatry and Related Sciences, 34,* 270–280.

Benjamin, L. T., Jr. (1988). A history of teaching machines. *American Psychologist, 43,* 703–712.

Benjamin, L. T., Jr. (2002). Marion White McPherson (1919–2000). *American Psychologist, 57,* 62.

Benjamin, L. T., Jr., & Crouse, E. M. (2002). The American Psychological Association's response to *Brown v. Board of Education*: The case of Kenneth B. Clark. *American Psychologist, 57,* 38–50.

Benjamin, L. T., Jr., & Nielsen-Gammon, E. (1999). B. F. Skinner and psychotechnology: The case of the heir conditioner. *Review of General Psychology, 3,* 155–167.

Benjamin, L. T., Jr., & Shields, S. A. (1990). Leta Stetter Hollingworth (1886-1939). In A. N. O'Connell & N. F. Russo (Eds.), *Women in psychology: A bio-bibliographic sourcebook* (pp. 173–183). NY: Greenwood Press.

Benjamin, L. T., Jr., Durkin, M., Link, M., Vestal, M., & Acord, J. (1992).Wundt's American doctoral students. *American Psychologist, 47,* 123–131.

Benjamin, L. T., Jr., Henry, K. D., & McMahon, L. R. (2005). Inez Beverly Prosser and the education of African Americans. *Journal of the History of the Behavioral Sciences, 41,* 43–62.

Bennett, D. S., Bendersky, M., & Lewis, M. (2002). Facial expressivity at 4 months: A context by expression analysis. *Infancy, 3,* 97–113.

Bennett, W., & Gurin, J. (1982). *The dieter's dilemma.* New York: Basic Books.

Ben-Shakhar, G., & Dolev, K. (1996). Psychophysiological detection through the guilty knowledge technique: Effect of mental countermeasures. *Journal of Applied Psychology, 81,* 273–281.

Ben-Shakhar, G., & Elaad, E. (2003). The validity of psychophysiological detection of information with the Guilty Knowledge Test: A meta-analytic review. *Journal of Applied Psychology, 88,* 131–151.

Ben-Shakhar, G., Gronau, N., & Elaad, E. (1999). Leakage of relevant information to innocent examinees in the GKT: An attempt to reduce false-positive outcomes by introducing target stimuli. *Journal of Applied Psychology, 84,* 651–660.

Ben-Shlomo, Y., Smith, G. D., Shipley, M., & Marmot, M. G. (1993). Magnitude and causes of mortality differences between married and unmarried men. *Journal of Epidemiology and Community Health, 47,* 200–205.

Bentall, R. P., & Pilgrim, D. (1993). Thomas Szasz, "crazy talk" and the myth of mental illness. *British Journal of Medical Psychology, 66,* 69–76.

Benton, D., Owens, D. S., & Parker, P. Y. (1994). Blood glucose influences memory and attention in young adults. *Neuropsychologia, 32,* 595–607.

Benton, T. R., Ross, D. F., Bradshaw, E., Thomas, W. N., & Bradshaw, G. S. (2006). Eyewitness memory is still not common sense: Comparing jurors, judges and law enforcement to Eyewitness experts. *Applied Cognitive Psychology, 20,* 115–129.

Berenbaum, S. A., & Hines, M. (1992). Early androgens are related to childhood sex–typed toy preferences. *Psychological Science, 3,* 203–206.

Berg, J. H. (1984). Development of friendship between roommates. *Journal of Personality and Social Psychology, 46,* 346–356.

Berg, J. H., & McQuinn, R. D. (1986). Attraction and exchange in continuing and noncontinuing dating relationships. *Journal of Personality and Social Psychology, 50,* 942–952.

Berger, A. A. (1987). Humor: An introduction. *American Behavioral Scientist, 30,* 6–15.

Berger, R. E., & Persinger, M. A. (1991). Geophysical variables and behavior: LXVII. Quieter annual geomagnetic activity and larger effect size for experimental psi (ESP) studies over six decades. *Perceptual and Motor Skills, 73,* 1219–1223.

Berger, R. J., & Phillips, N. H. (1995). Energy conservation and sleep. *Brain Research, 69,* 65–73.?

Bergeron, S. M., & Senn, C. Y. (1998). Body image and sociocultural norms: A comparison of heterosexual and lesbian women. *Psychology of Women Quarterly, 22,* 385–401.

Bergin, A. E., & Lambert, E. (1978). The evaluation of therapeutic outcome. In S. L. Garfield & A. E. Bergin (Eds.), *Handbook of psychotherapy and behavior change* (pp. 139–189). New York: Wiley.

Berk, M., Sanders, K. M., Pasco, J. A., Jacka, F. N., Williams, L. J., Hayles, A. L., & Dodd, S. (2007). Vitamin D deficiency may play a role in depression. *Medical Hypotheses, 69,* 1316–1319.

Berk, M., Terre-Blanche, M. J., Maude, C., & Lucas, M. D. (1996). Season of birth and schizophrenia: Southern hemisphere data. *Australian and New Zealand Journal of Psychiatry, 30,* 220–222.

Berko, J. (1958). The child's learning of English morphology. *Word, 14,* 150–177.

Berkowitz, L. (1974). Some determinants of impulsive aggression. *Psychological Review, 81,* 165–176.

Berkowitz, L. (1989). Frustration-aggression hypothesis: Examination and reformulation. *Psychological Bulletin, 106,* 59–73.

Berkowitz, L., & LePage, A. (1967). Weapons as aggression-eliciting stimuli. *Journal of Personality and Social Psychology, 7,* 202–207.

Berkowitz, M. W., Mueller, C. W., Schnell, S. V., & Padberg, U. (1986). Moral reasoning and judgments of aggression. *Journal of Personality and Social Psychology, 51,* 885–891.

Berlucchi, G. (2006). Revisiting the 1981 Nobel Prize to Roger Sperry, David Hubel, and Torsten Wiesel on the occasion of the centennial of the prize to Golgi and Cajal. *Journal of the History of the Behavioral Sciences, 15,* 369–375.

Bernard, J. L. (1977). The significance for psychology of *O'Connor v. Donaldson. American Psychologist, 32,* 1085–1088.

Berndt, T. J., & Hoyles, S. G. (1985) Stability and change in childhood and adolescent friendships. *Developmental Psychology, 21,* 1007–1015.

Berne, E. (1964). *Games people play.* New York: Grove Press.

Bernier, M.-J., Hébert, M., & Collin-Vézina, D. (2013). Dissociative symptoms over a year in a sample of sexually abused children. *Journal of Trauma & Dissociation, 14,* 455–472.

Berninger, V. W. (1988). Development of operational thought without a normal sensorimotor stage. *Intelligence, 12,* 219–230.

Bernstein, I. L. (1978). Learned taste aversions in children receiving chemotherapy. *Science, 200,* 1302–1303.

Bernstein, I. L. (1991). Aversion conditioning in response to cancer and cancer treatment. *Clinical Psychology Review, 11,* 185–191.

Bernstein, W. M., Stephan, W. G., & Davis, M. H. (1979). Explaining attributions for achievement: A path-analytic approach. *Journal of Personality and Social Psychology, 37,* 1810–1821.

Berry, J. W., & Kalin, R. (1995). Multicultural and ethnic attitudes in Canada: An overview of the 1991 national survey. *Canadian Journal of Behavioural Science, 27,* 301–320.

Bersagliere, A., & Achermann, P. (2010). Slow oscillations in human non-rapid eye movement sleep electroencephalogram: Effects of increased sleep pressure. *Journal of Sleep Research, 19,* 228–237.

Berscheid, E., & Walster, E. (1974). A little bit about love. In T. L. Houston (Ed.), *Foundations of interpersonal attraction.* (pp. 356-382) New York: Academic Press.

Bertelli, J. A., Orsal, D., & Mira, J. C. (1994). Median-nerve neurotization by peripheral nerve grafts directly implanted into the spinal cord: Anatomical, behavioral, and electrophysiological evidences of sensorimotor recovery. *Brain Research, 644,* 150–159.

Best, C. T., & Avery, R. A. (2000). Left-hemisphere advantage for click consonants is determined by linguistic significance and experience. *Psychological Science, 10,* 65–70.

Beutler, L. E., & Consoli, A. J. (1993). Matching the therapist's interpersonal stance to clients' characteristics: Contributions from systematic eclectic psychotherapy. *Psychotherapy, 30,* 417–422.

Bexton, W. H., Heron, W., & Scott, T. H. (1954). Effects of decreased variation in the sensory environment. *Canadian Journal of Psychology, 8,* 70–76.

Biafora, F. (1995). Cross–cultural perspective on illness and wellness: Implications for depression. *Journal of Social Distress and the Homeless, 4,* 105–129.

Bianchi, S. M. (1995). The changing demographic and socioeconomic characteristics of single parent families. *Marriage and Family Review, 20,* 71–97.

Bidzan, L., Mahableshwarkar, A. R., Jacobsen, P., Yan, M., & Sheehan, D. B. (2012). Vortioxetine (Lu AA21004) in generalized anxiety disorder: Results of an 8-week multinational, randomized, double-blind, placebo-controlled clinical trial. *European Neuropsychopharmacology, 22,* 847–857.

Binder, J. R., Rao, S. M., Hammeke, T. A., & Yetkin, F. Z. (1994). Functional magnetic resonance imaging of human auditory cortex. *Annals of Neurology, 35,* 662–672.

Binsted, G., & Elliott, D. (1999). The Mueller-Lyer illusion as a perturbation to the saccadic system. *Human Movement Science, 18,*103–117.

Birch, D. E. (1992). Duty to protect: Update and Canadian perspective. *Canadian Psychology, 33,* 94–104.

Birch, J. (1997). Efficiency of the Ishihara test for identifying red-green colour deficiency. *Ophthalmic and Physiological Optics, 17,* 403–408

Birchall, H. M. (1995). Reporting experiences of panic: Sex differences in a community sample. *Journal of Community and Applied Social Psychology, 5,* 167–172.

Bird, S. (2011). Effects of distributed practice on the acquisition of second language English syntax. *Applied Psycholinguistics, 32,* 437–452.

Birdsong, D., & Molis, M. (2001). On the evidence for maturational constraints in second-language acquisition. *Journal of Memory and Language, 44,* 235–249.

Bishop, D. V. M. (1990). *Handedness and developmental disorder.* Oxford, England: Mac Keith Press.

Bishop, D. V. M. (2001). Individual differences in handedness and specific speech and language impairment: Evidence against a genetic link. *Behavior Genetics, 31,* 339–351.

Bitgood, S. C. (2002). Environmental psychology in museums, zoos, and other exhibition centers. In R. B. Bechtel & A. Churchman (Eds.), *Handbook of environmental psychology* (pp. 461–480). New York: Wiley.

Bjork, D. W. (1988). *William James: The center of his vision.* New York: Columbia University Press.

Bjork, E. L., & Cummings, E. M. (1984). Infant search errors: Stage of concept development or stage of memory development. *Memory and Cognition, 12,* 1–19.

Bjorklund, D. F., & Buchanan, J. J. (1989). Developmental and knowledge-based differences in the acquisition and extension of a memory strategy. *Journal of Experimental Child Psychology, 48,* 451–471.

Bjorkqvist, K., Nygren, T., Bjorklund, A.-C., Bjorkqvist, S.-E. (1994). Testosterone intake and aggressiveness: Real effect or anticipation? *Aggressive Behavior, 20,* 17–26.

Bjorvatn, B., Grønli, J., & Pallesen, S. (2010). Prevalence of different parasomnias in the general population. *Sleep Medicine, 11,* 1031–1034.

Black, B., Herr, K., Fine, P., Sanders, S., Tang, X., Bergen–Jackson, K., Titler, M., & Forcucci, C. (2011). The relationships among pain, nonpain symptoms, and quality of life measures in older adults with cancer receiving hospice care. *Pain Medicine, 12,* 880–889.

Black, D. S., Cole, S. W., Irwin, M. R., Breen, E., St Cyr, N. M., Nazarian, N., Lavretsky, H. (2013). Yogic meditation reverses NF-Kb and IRF-related transcriptome dynamics in leukocytes of family dementia caregivers in a randomized controlled trial. *Psychoneuroendocrinology, 38,* 348–55.

Black, J. E., Isaacs, K. R., & Greenough, W. T. (1991). Usual vs. successful aging: Some notes on experiential factors. *Neurobiology of Aging, 12,* 325–328.

Blackford, J. U., Allen, A. H., Cowan, R. L., & Avery, S. N. (2013). Amygdala and hippocampus fail to habituate to faces in individuals with an inhibited temperament . *Social Cognitive and Affective Neuroscience, 8,* 143–150

Blair, M. E., & Shimp, T. A. (1992). Consequences of an unpleasant experience with music: A second-order negative conditioning perspective. *Journal of Advertising, 21,* 35–43.

Blaisdell, A. P., Gunther, L. M., & Miller, R. R. (1999). Recovery from blocking achieved by extinguishing the blocking CS. *Animal Learning and Behavior, 27,* 63–76.

Blakemore, C. (1977). *Mechanics of the mind.* New York: Cambridge University Press.

Blakemore, C., & Cooper, G. F. (1970). Development of the brain depends on the visual environment. *Nature, 228,* 477–478.

Blanchard, J. J., Kring, A. M., & Neale, J. M. (1994). Flat affect in schizophrenia: A test of neuropsychological models. *Schizophrenia Bulletin, 20,* 311–325.

Blanchard, R., & Ellis, L. (2001). Birth weight, sexual orientation and the sex of preceding siblings. *Journal of Biosocial Science, 33,* 451–467.

Blanchard, R., Zucker, K. J., Siegelman, M., Dickey, R., & Klassen, P. (1998). The relation of birth order to sexual orientation in men andd women. *Journal of Biosocial Science, 30,* 511–519.

Blanco-Centurion, C. A., & Salin-Pascual, R. J. (2001). Extracellular serotonin levels in the medullary reticular formation during normal sleep and after REM sleep deprivation. *Brain Research, 923,* 128–136.

Blaney, P. H. (1986). Affect and memory: A review. *Psychological Bulletin, 99,* 229–246.

Blankfield, R. P. (1991). Suggestion, relaxation, and hypnosis as adjuncts in the care of surgery patients: A review of the literature. *American Journal of Clinical Hypnosis, 33,* 172–186.

Blanton, H., & Jaccard, J. (2008). Representing versus generalizing: two approaches to external validity and their implications for the study of prejudice. *Psychological Inquiry, 19,* 99–105.

Blascovich, J., Spencer, S. J., Quinn, D., & Steele, C. (2001). African Americans and high blood pressure: The role of stereotype threat. *Psychological Science, 12,* 225–229.

Blasczyk-Schiep, S., Kazén, M., Kuhl, J., & Grygielski, M. (2011). Appraisal of suicidal risk among adolescents and young adults through the Rorschach Test. *Journal of Personality Assessment, 95,* 518–526.

Blass, T. (1999). The Milgram Paradigm after 35 years: Some things we now know about obedience to authority. *Journal of Applied Social Psychology, 29,* 955–978.

Blatt, I., Peled, R., Gadoth, N., & Lavie, P. (1991). The value of sleep recording in evaluating somnambulism in young adults. *Electroencephalography and Clinical Neurophysiology, 78,* 407–412.

Blazer, D. G., Kessler, R. C., & Swartz, M. S. (1998). Epidemiology of recurrent major and minor depression with a seasonal pattern: The National Comorbidity Survey. *British Journal of Psychiatry, 172,* 164–167.

Bleichrodt, N., Hoksbergen, R.A.C., & Khire, U. (1999). Cross-cultural testing of intelligence. *Cross-Cultural Research: The Journal of Comparative Social Science, 33,* 3–25.

Bliem, H. R., & Danek, A. (1999). Direct evidence for a consistent dissociation between structural facial discrimination and facial individuation in prosopagnosia. *Brain and Cognition, 40,* 48–52.

Blix, G. G., & Blix, A. G. (1995). The role of exercise in weight loss. *Behavioral Medicine, 21,* 31–39.

Blizard, R. A. (1997). The origins of dissociative identity disorder from an object relations and attachment theory perspective. *Dissociation: Progress in the Dissociative Disorders, 10,* 223–229.

Bloom, R., Przekop, A., & Sanger, T. D. (2010). Prolonged electromyogram biofeedback improves upper extremity function in children with cerebral palsy. *Journal of Child Neurology, 25,* 1480–1484.

Blume, H. K., Brockman, L. N, & Bruener, C. C. (2012). Biofeedback therapy for pediatric headache: Factors associated with response. *Headache: The Journal of Head and Face Pain, 52,* 1377–1386.

Blume-Marcovici, A. (2010). Gender differences in dreams: Applications to dream work with male clients. *Dreaming, 20,* 199–210.

Boake, C. (2002). From the Binet-Simon to the Wechsler-Bellevue: Tracing the history of intelligence testing. *Journal of Clinical and Experimental Neuropsychology, 24,* 383–405.

Boatwright, K., & Nolan, B. (2005). *Campaign for Mary Whiton Calkins: Update.* Paper presented at the Association of Women in Psychology National Conference, Tampa, FL.

Boddington, S. J. ., & Lavender, A. (1995). Treatment models for couples therapy: A review of the outcome literature and the Dodo's verdict. *Sexual and Marital Therapy, 10,* 69–81.

Bogaert, A. F., & Hershberger, S. (1999). The relation between sexual orientation and penile size. *Archives of Sexual Behavior, 28,* 213–221.

Bohannon, J. N., III, & Stanowicz, L. (1988). The issue of negative evidence: Adult responses to children's language errors. *Developmental Psychology, 24,* 684–689.

Bohart, A. C., O'Hara, M., & Leitner, L. M. (1998). Empirically violated treatments: Disenfranchisement of humanistic and other psychotherapies. *Psychotherapy Research, 8,* 141–157.

Bohner, G., Einwiller, S., Erb, H.-P., & Siebler, F. (2003). When small means comfortable: Relations between product attributes in two-sided advertising. *Journal of Consumer Psychology, 13,* 454–463.

Bolm-Audorff, U., Schwammle, J., Ehlenz, K., & Kaffarnik, H. (1989). Plasma level of catecholamines and lipids when speaking before an audience. *Work and Stress, 3,* 249–253.

Bolsover, S., Fabes, J., & Anderson, P. N. (2008). Axonal guidance molecules and the failure of axonal regeneration in the adult mammalian spinal cord. *Restorative Neurology and Neuroscience 26,* 117–130.

Bolte, S., & Poustka, F. (2004). Comparing the profiles of savant and non-savant individuals with autistic disorder. *Intelligence, 32,* 121–131.

Bolton, P., Macdonald, H., Pickles, A., Rios, P., Goode, S., Crowson, M., Bailey, A., & Rutter, M. (1994). A case–control family history study of autism. *Journal of Child Psychology and Psychiatry 35,* 877–900

Bond, C. F., Jr., & Titus, L. J. (1983). Social facilitation: A meta-analysis of 241 studies. *Psychological Bulletin, 94,* 265–292.

Bond, R., & Smith, P. B. (1996). Culture and conformity: A meta-analysis of studies using Asch's (1952b, 1956) line judgment task. *Psychological Bulletin, 119,* 111–137.

Bonds, D. R., & Crosby, L. O. (1986). "An adoption study of human obesity": Comment. *New England Journal of Medicine, 315,* 128.

Boneau, C. A. (1974). Paradigm regained? Cognitive behaviorism revisited. *American Psychologist, 29,* 297–309.

Boneva, B., Frieze, I. H., Ferligoj, A., Pauknerova, D., & Orgocka, A. (1998). Achievement, power, and affiliation motive as clues to (e) migration desires: A four-countries comparison. *European Psychologist, 3,* 247–254.

Boniecki, K. A., & Moore, S. (2003). Breaking the silence: Using a token economy to reinforce classroom participation. *Teaching of Psychology, 30,* 224–227.

Bonilla, C., Zurita, M., Otero, L., Aguayo, C., & Vaquero, J. (2009). Delayed intralesional transplantation of bone marrow stromal cells increases endogenous neurogenesis and promotes functional recovery after severe traumatic brain injury. *Brain Injury, 23,* 760–769.

Bonnefond, A., Muzet, A., Winter-Dill, A. S., Bailloeuil, C., Bitouze, F., & Bonneau, A. (2001). Innovative working schedule: Introducing one short nap during the night shift. *Ergonomics, 44,* 937–945.

Book, A. S., Starzyk, K. B., & Quinsey, V. L. (2001). The relationship between testosterone and aggression: A meta-analysis. *Aggression and Violent Behavior, 6,* 579–599.

Boone, L., Soenens, B., Vansteenkiste, M., & Braet, C. (2012). Is there a perfectionist in each of us? An experimental study on perfectionism and eating disorder symptoms. *Appetite, 59,* 531–540.

Boone, R. T., & Cunningham, J. G. (1998). Children's decoding of emotion in expressive body movement: The development of cue attunement. *Developmental Psychology, 34,* 1007–1016.

Boot, B. P., McGregor, I. S., & Hall, W. (2000). MDMA (Ecstasy) neurotoxicity: assessing and communicating the risks. *Lancet, 355,* 1818–1821.

Boring, E. G. (1950). *A history of experimental psychology.* New York: Appleton-Century-Crofts.

Borkenau, P., Riemann, R., Angleitner, A., & Spinath, F. M. (2001). Genetic and environmental influences on observed personality: Evidence from the German Observational Study of Adult Twins. *Journal of Personality and Social Psychology, 80,* 655–668.

Bornovalova, M. A., Huibregtse, B. M., Hicks, B. M., Keyes, M., McGue, M., & Iacona, W. (2013). Tests of a direct effect of childhood abuse on adult borderline personality disorder: A longitudinal discordant twin design. *Journal of Abnormal Psychology, 122,* 180–194.

Bornstein, M. H., & Arterberry, M. E. (2003). Recognition, discrimination, and categorization of smiling by 5-month-old infants. *Developmental Science, 6,* 585–599.

Borod, J. C., Haywood, C. S., & Koff, E. (1997). Neuropsychological aspects of facial asymmetry during emotional expression: A review of the normal adult literature. *Neuropsychology Review, 7,* 41–60.

Bors, D. A., & Forrin, B. (1995). Age, speed of information processing, recall, and fluid intelligence. *Intelligence, 20,* 229–248.

Bortz, W. M. II, Wallace, D. H., & Wiley, D. (1999). Sexual function in 1,202 aging males: Differentiating aspects. *Journals of Gerontology: Series A: Biological Sciences and Medical Sciences, 54A,* M237–M241.

Bosl, W., Tierney, A., Tager-Rusberg, H., & Nelson, C. (2011). EEG complexity as a biomarker for autism spectrum disorder risk. *BMC Medicine, 9,* 18–33.

Bothwell, R. K., Brigham, J. C., & Malpass, R. S. (1989). Cross-racial identification. *Personality and Social Psychology Bulletin, 15,* 19–25.

Bouchard, T. J., Jr., & Hur, Y.-M. (1998). Genetic and environmental influences on the continuous scales of the Myers-Briggs Type Indicator: An analysis based on twins reared apart. *Journal of Personality, 66,* 135–149.

Bouchard, T. J., Jr., & Loehlin, J. C. (2001). Genes, evolution, and personality. *Behavior Genetics, 31,* 243–273.

Bouchard, T. J., Jr., & McGue, M. (1981). Familial studies of intelligence: A review. *Science, 212,* 1055–1059.

Bouchard, T. J., Jr., & McGue, M. (1990). Genetic and rearing environmental influences on adult personality: An analysis of adopted twins reared apart. *Journal of Personality, 58,* 263–292.

Bouchard, T. J., Jr., Lykken, D. T., McGue, M., Segal, N. L., & Tellegen, A. (1990). Sources of human psychological differences: The Minnesota Study of Twins Reared Apart. *Science, 250,* 223–228.

Bouchard, T. J., Jr., McGue, M., Hur, Y.-M., & Horn, J. M. (1998). A genetic and environmental analysis of the California Psychological Inventory using adult twins reared apart and together. *European Journal of Personality, 12,* 307–320.

Boudreaux, R. (2000, March 28). Spaniards are missing their naps. *Los Angeles Times,* p. A1.

Bourgeois, J. A., & Bunn, A. (1996). Obsessive-compulsive disorder symptoms associated with military duty. *Military Medicine, 161,* 358–359.

Bouton, M. E., & Swartzentruber, D. (1991). Sources of relapse after extinction in Pavlovian and instrumental learning. *Clinical Psychology Review, 11,* 123–140.

Bower, G. H. (1970). Analysis of a mnemonic device. *American Scientist, 58,* 496–510.

Bower, G. H. (1981). Mood and memory. *American Psychologist, 36,* 129–148.

Bower, G. H., & Clark, M. C. (1969). Narrative stories as mediators for serial learning. *Psychonomic Science, 14,* 181–182.

Bower, G. H., & Mayer, J. D. (1989). In search of mood-dependent retrieval. *Bulletin of the Psychonomic Society, 4,* 121–156.

Bowers, K. S. (1994). A review of Ernest R. Hilgard's books on hypnosis, in commemoration of his 90th birthday. *Psychological Science, 5,* 186–189.

Bowers, K. S., & Farvolden, P. (1996). Revisiting a century-old Freudian slip—From suggestion disavowed to the truth repressed. *Psychological Bulletin, 119,* 355–380.

Bowlby, J. (1988). *A secure base: Parent-child attachment and healthy human development.* New York: Basic Books.

Bowmaker, J. K. (1998). Visual pigments and molecular genetics of color blindness. *Physiology, 13,* 63–69

Bowman, D., Scogin, F., Floyd, M., & McKendree-Smith, N. (2001). The effects of providing therapists with feedback on patient progress during psychotherapy: Are outcomes enhanced? *Psychotherapy Research, 11,* 49–68.

Boyce, B. A. (1992). The effects of goal proximity on skill acquisition and retention of a shooting task in a field–based setting. *Journal of Sport and Exercise Psychology, 14,* 298–308.

Boyce, W. T., Essex, M. J., Alkon, A., Smider, N. A., Pickrell, T., & Kagan, J. (2001). Temperament, tympanum and temperature: Four provisional studies of the biobehavioral correlates of tympanic membrane temperature asymmetries. *Child Development, 73,* 718–733.

Boyd, J. H. (1986). Use of mental health services for the treatment of panic disorder. *American Journal of Psychiatry, 143,* 1569–1574.

Boyd, J. H., & Crump, T. (1991). Westphal's agoraphobia. *Journal of Anxiety Disorders, 5,* 77–86.

Boynton, R. M. (1988). Color vision. *Annual Review of Psychology, 39,* 69–100.

Bozarth, J. D. (1990). The evolution of Carl Rogers as a therapist. *Person-Centered Review, 5,* 387–393.

Bozarth, J. D. (2002). Nondirectivity in the person-centered approach: Critique of Kahn's critique. *Journal of Humanistic Psychology, 42,* 78–83.

Brackbill, Y., & Nichols, P. L. (1982). A test of the confluence model of intellectual development. *Developmental Psychology, 18,* 192–198.

Bradbury, E. J., & McMahon, S. B. (2006). Spinal cord repair strategies: Why do they work? *Nature Reviews: Neuroscience, 7,* 644–653.

Bradley, B. P., & Baddeley, A. D. (1990). Emotional factors in forgetting. *Psychological Medicine, 20,* 351–355.

Bradley, M. T., & Warfield, J. F. (1984). Innocence, information, and the Guilty Knowledge Test in the detection of deception. *Psychophysiology, 21,* 683–689.

Bradley, M. T., MacLaren, V. V., & Carle, S. B. (1996). Deception and nondeception in guilty knowledge and guilty actions polygraph tests. *Journal of Applied Psychology, 81,* 153–160.

Bradshaw, M., & Ellison, C. G. (2009). The nature-nurture debate is over, and both sides lost! Implications for understanding gender differences in religiosity. *Journal for the Scientific Study of Religion, 48,* 241–251.

Brady, D. R., & Mufson, E. J. (1990). Amygdaloid pathology in Alzheimer's disease: Qualitative and quantitative analysis. *Dementia, 1,* 5–17.

Bramlett, R. K., Murphy, J. J., Johnson, J., Wallingsford, L., & Hall, J. D. (2002). Contemporary practices in school psychology: A national survey of roles and referral problems. *Psychology in the Schools, 39,* 327–335.

Branch, W. (1990). On interpreting correlation coefficients. *American Psychologist, 45,* 296.

Brand, G., & Millot, J. L. (2001). Sex differences in human olfaction: Between evidence and enigma. *Quarterly Journal of Experimental Psychology: Comparative and Physiology Psychology, 54B,* 259–270.

Brand, M., Eggers, C., Reinhold, N., Fujiwara, E., Kessler, J., Heiss, W., Markowitsch, H. J. (2009). Functional brain imaging in 14 patients with dissociative amnesia reveals right inferolateral prefrontal hypometabolism. *Psychiatry Research: Neuroimaging, 174,* 32–39.

Brattico, E., Pallesen, K. J., Varyagina, O., Bailey, C., Anourova, I., Järvenpää, M., Eerola, T., & Tervaniemi, M. (2009). Neural discrimination of nonprototypical chords in music experts and laymen: An MEG study. *Journal of Cognitive Neuroscience, 21,* 2230–2244.

Brauer, M., Judd, C. M., & Gliner, M. D. (1995). The effects of repeated expressions on attitude polarization during group discussions. *Journal of Personality and Social Psychology, 68,* 1014–1029.

Braun, A., & Preiser, S. (2013). The impact of disparaging humor content on the funniness of political jokes. *Humor: International Journal of Humor Research, 26,* 249–275.

Braun, D. L., Sunday, S. R., Huang, A., & Halmi, K. A. (1999). More males seek treatment for eating disorders. *International Journal of Eating Disorders, 25,* 415–424.

Brawman-Mintzer, O., & Lydiard, R. B. (1997). Biological basis of generalized anxiety disorder. *Journal of Clinical Psychiatry, 58,* 16–26.

Bray, S. R., & Widmeyer, W. N. (2000). Athletes' perceptions of the home advantage: An investigation of perceived causal factors. *Journal of Sport Behavior, 23,* 1–10.

Breathnach, C. S. (1989). Validation of language localization by computer-assisted tomographic and topographic techniques. *Irish Journal of Psychological Medicine, 6,* 11–18.

Brébion, G., Stephan-Otto, C., Huerta-Ramos, E., Usall, J., Ochoa, S., Roca, M., . . . Haro, J.-M. (2013). Abnormal functioning of the semantic network in schizophrenia patients with thought disorganization: An examplar production task. *Psychiatry Research, 205,* 1–6.

Breckler, S. J. (1984). Empirical validation of affect, behavior, and cognition as distinct components of attitude. *Journal of Personality and Social Psychology, 47,* 1191–1205.

Breier, J. I., Randle, S., Maher, L. M., & Papanicolaou, A. C. (2010). Changes in maps of language activation following melodic intonation therapy using magnetoencephalography: Two case studies. *Journal of Clinical and Experimental Neuropsychology, 32,* 309–314.

Breland, K., & Breland, M. (1961). The misbehavior of organisms. *American Psychologist, 16,* 681–684.

Brennan, C. (1997a, July 24). Killer's portrait "silly," profiler says. Former FBI agent says report issued by family "boilerplate 101." *Rocky Mountain News.*

Brennan, C. (1997b, July 25). Ramsey team distributes fliers of "profile." *Rocky Mountain News.*

Brent, D. A., & Bridge, J. (2003). Firearms availability and suicide: Evidence, interventions, and future directions. *American Behavioral Scientist, 46,* 1192–1210.

Bressan, P., Garlaschelli, L., & Barracano, M. (2003). Antigravity hills are visual illusions. *Psychological Science, 14.* 441–449.

Breuer, J., Scharkow, M., & Quandt, T. (2013). Sore losers? A reexamination of the frustration-aggression hypothesis for collocated video game play. *Psychology of Popular Media Culture,* December 23, 2013.

Brewer, M. B., & Kramer, R. M. (1985). The psychology of intergroup attitudes and behavior. *Annual Review of Psychology, 36,* 219–243.

Brewer, N., Keast, A., Sauer, J. D. (2010). Children's eyewitness identification and performance. Effects of a *Not Sure* response option and accuracy motivation. *Legal and Criminological Psychology, 15,* 261–277.

Bricklin, J. (1999). A variety of religious experience: William James and the non-reality of free will. *Journal of Consciousness Studies, 6,* 77–98.

Brickman, P., Coates, D., & Janoff-Bulman, R. (1978). Lottery winners and accident victims: Is happiness relative? *Journal of Personality and Social Psychology, 36,* 917–927.

Briggs, K. C., & Myers, I. B. (1943). *Myers-Briggs type indicator.* Palo Alto, CA: Consulting Psychologists Press.

Brigham, C. C. (1923). *A study of American intelligence.* Princeton, NJ: Princeton University Press.

Brigham, C. C. (1930). Intelligence tests of immigrant groups. *Psychological Review, 37,* 158–165.

Brigham, T. A. (1989). On the importance of recognizing the difference between experiments and correlational studies. *American Psychologist, 44,* 1077–1078.

Bringmann, M. W., Tyler, K. E., McAhren, P. E., Bringmann, W. G. (1989). A successful and unsuccessful replication of William Stern's eyewitness research. *Perceptual and Motor Skills, 69,* 619–625.

Brinton, R. D., & Nilsen, J. (2003). Effects of estrogen plus progestin on risk of dementia. *JAMA: Journal of the American Medical Association, 290,* 1706.

Brittain, A. E., & Lerner, R.M.(2013). Early influences and later outcomes associated with developmental trajectories of Eriksonian fidelity *Developmental Psychology, 49,* 722–735.

Broberg, D. J., & Bernstein, I. L. (1987). Candy as a scapegoat in the prevention of food aversions in children receiving chemotherapy. *Cancer, 60,* 2344–2347.

Broder, M. S. (2000). Making optimal use of homework to enhance your therapeutic effectiveness. *Journal of Rational and Cognitive Behavior Therapy, 18,* 3–18.

Brodnick, R. J., & Ree, M. J. (1995). A structural model of academic performance, socioeconomic status, and Spearman's g. *Educational and Psychological Measurement, 55,* 583–594.

Brody, N. (1999). What is intelligence? *International Review of Psychiatry, 11,* 19–25.

Brogaard, B. (2011). Are there unconscious perceptual processes? *Consciousness & Cognition: An International Journal, 20,* 449–463.

Brohawn, K. H., Offringa, R., Pfaff, D. L., Hughes, K. C., & Shin, L. M. (2010). The neural correlates of emotional memory in posttraumatic stress disorder. *Biological Psychiatry, 68,* 1023–30.

Bromberg, W. (1954). *Man above humanity: A history of psychotherapy.* Philadelphia: Lippincott.

Bronstein, C. (2002). On free association and psychic reality. *British Journal of Psychotherapy, 18,* 477–489.

Brooks, K., & Siegel, M. (1991). Children as eyewitnesses: Memory, suggestibility, and credibility. *Australian Psychologist, 26,* 84–88.

Brooks-Gunn, J., & Warren, M. P. (1989). Biological and social contributions to negative affect in young adolescent girls. *Child Development, 60,* 40–55.

Brooks-Gunn, J., Klebanov, P. K., & Duncan, G. J. (1996). Ethnic differences in children's intelligence test scores: Role of economic deprivation, home environment, and maternal characteristics. *Child Development, 67,* 396–408.

Brosschot, J. F, Godaert, G.L.R., Benschop, R. J., Olff, M., Ballieux, R. E., & Heijnen, C. J. (1998). Experimental stress and immunological reactivity: A closer look at perceived uncontrollability. *Psychosomatic Medicine, 60,* 359–361.

Broughton, R. S., & Perlstrom, J. R. (1992). PK in a competitive computer game: A replication. *Journal of Parapsychology, 56,* 291–305.

Brown, A. S. (1991). A review of the tip-of-the-tongue experience. *Psychological Bulletin, 109,* 204–223.

Brown, A. S. (2003). A review of the déjà vu experience. *Psychological Bulletin, 129,* 394–413.

Brown, D. A. (2006). Acetylcholine. *British Journal of Pharmacology, 147,* S120–S126.

Brown, D., Scheflin, A. W., & Whitfield, C. L. (1999). Recovered memories: The current weight of the evidence in science and the courts. *The Journal of Psychiatry and Law, 27,* 5–156.

Brown, J. D., & Siegel, J. M. (1988). Exercise as a buffer of life stress: A prospective study of adolescent health. *Health Psychology, 7,* 341–353.

Brown, K. T., Brown, T. N., Jackson, J. S., Sellers, R. M., & Manuel, W. J. (2003). Teammates on and off the field? White student athletes. *Journal of Applied Social Psychology, 33,* 1379–1403.

Brown, R. (1973). *A first language: The early stages.* Oxford, England: Harvard University Press.

Brown, R. B., & Keegan, D. (1999). Humor in the hotel kitchen. *Humor: International Journal of Humor Research, 12,* 47–70.

Brown, R. J., & Lewis-Fernández, R. (2011). Culture and conversion disorder: Implications for *DSM-5. Psychiatry, 74,* 187–206.

Brown, R. T., Reynolds, C. R., & Whitaker, J. S. (1999). Bias in mental testing since *Bias in Mental Testing. School Psychology Quarterly, 14,* 208–238.

Brown, R., & Kulik, J. (1977). Flashbulb memories. *Cognition, 5,* 73–99.

Brown, R., Price, R. J., King, M. G., & Husband, A. J. (1989). Interleukin–1B and muramyl depeptide can prevent decreased antibody response associated with sleep deprivation. *Brain, Behavior, and Immunity, 3,* 320–330.

Brown, T. E. (2014). *Smart but stuck: emotions in teens and adults with ADHD.* San Francisco, CA: Wiley.

Brown, V. R., & Paulus, P. B. (2002). Making group brainstorming more effective: Recommendations from an associative memory perspective. *Current Directions in Psychological Science, 11,* 208–212.

Brownell, K. D. (1982). Obesity: Understanding and treating a serious, prevalent, and refractory disorder. *Journal of Consulting and Clinical Psychology, 50,* 820–840.

Brownell, K. D. (1993). Whether obesity should be treated. *Health Psychology, 12,* 339–341.

Brownell, K. D., & Cohen, L. R. (1995). Adherence to dietary regimens: 1. An overview of research. *Behavioral Medicine, 20,* 149–154.

Brownell, K. D., & Wadden, T. A. (1991). The heterogeneity of obesity: Fitting treatments to individuals. *Behavior Therapy, 22,* 153–177.

Brozek, J. (1999). From "psichiologia" to "psychologia": A graphically documented archival study across three centuries. *Journal of the History of the Behavioral Sciences, 35,* 177–180.

Bruce, M. L., Takeuchi, D. T., & Leaf, P. J. (1991). Poverty and psychiatric status: Longitudinal evidence from the New Haven Epidemiologic Catchment Area study. *Archives of General Psychiatry, 48,* 470–474.

Brugger, P., & Taylor, K. I. (2003). ESP: Extrasensory perception or effect of subjective probability? *Journal of Consciousness Studies, 10,* 221–246.

Brummett, B. H., Boyle, S. H., Kuhn, C. M., Siegler, J. C., & Williams, R. B. (2009). Positive affect is associated with cardiovascular reactivity, norepinephrine level, and morning rise in salivary cortisol. *Psychophysiology, 46,* 862–869.

Bruner, J. S. (1956). Freud and the image of man. *American Psychologist, 11,* 463–466.

Bruno, G. (2009). Film, aesthetics, science: Hugo Münsterberg's laboratory of moving images. *Grey Room, 36,* 88–113.

Bryant, D. M., & Maxwell, K. L. (1999). The environment and mental retardation. *International Review of Psychiatry, 11,* 56–67.

Bryck, R. L., & Fisher, P. A. (2012). Training the brain: Practical applications of neural plasticity from the intersection of cognitive neuroscience, developmental psychology and prevention science. *American Psychologist, 67,* 87–100.

Brydon, L., Walker, C., Wawrzyniak, A. J., Chart, H., & Steptoe, A. (2009). Dispositional optimism and stress-induced changes in immunity and negative mood. *Brain, Behavior, and Immunity, 23,* 810–816.

Bryden, M. P. (1993). Perhaps not so sinister [Review of *The left-hander syndrome*]. *Contemporary Psychology, 38,* 71–72.

Bryden, M. P., Ardila, A., & Ardila, O. (1993). Handedness in native Amazonians. *Neuropsychologia, 31,* 301–308.

Buchsbaum, M. S., & Haier, R. J. (1983). Psychopathology: Biological approaches. *Annual Review of Psychology, 34,* 401–430.

Buck, R. (1980). Nonverbal behavior and the theory of emotion: The facial-feedback hypothesis. *Journal of Personality and Social Psychology, 38,* 811–824.

Buck, R. (1985). Prime theory: An integrated view of motivation and emotion. *Psychological Review, 92,* 389–413.

Buckley, K. W. (1989). *Mechanical man: John Broadus Watson and the beginnings of behaviorism.* New York: Guilford.

Buckner, J. D., Heimberg, R. G., Ecker, A. H., & Vinci, C. (2013). A biopsychosocial model of social anxiety and substance use. *Depression & Anxiety, 30,* 276–284.

Buechel, C., Price, C., Frackowiak, R.S.J., & Friston, K. (1998). Different activation patterns in the visual cortex of late and congenitally blind subjects. *Brain, 121,* 409–419.

Buitelaar, J., & Medori, R. (2010). Treating attention-deficit/hyperactivity disorder beyond symptom control alone in children and adolescents: A review of the potential benefits of long-acting stimulants. *European Child & Adolescent Psychiatry, 19,* 325–40.

Bulik, C. M., Sullivan, P. F., & Kendler, K. S. (1998). Heritability of binge-eating and broadly defined bulimia nervosa. *Biological Psychiatry, 44,* 1210–1218.

Bulik, C. M., Sullivan, P. F., & Kendler, K. S. (2003). Genetic and environmental contributions to obesity and binge eating. *International Journal of Eating Disorders, 33,* 293–298.

Bullough, V. L. (1998). Alfred Kinsey and the Kinsey Report: Historical overview and lasting contributions. *Journal of Sex Research, 35,* 127–131.

Bunge, M. (1992). The scientist's skepticism. *Skeptical Inquirer, 16,* 377–380.

Burchinal, M. R., Bryant, D. M., Lee, M. W., & Ramey, C. T. (1992). Early day care, infant-mother attachment, and maternal responsiveness in the infant's first year. *Early Childhood Research Quarterly, 3,* 383–396.

Burgard, S. A., & Ailshire, J. A. (2013). Gender and time for sleep among U.S. adults. *American Sociological Review, 78,* 51–69.

Burger, J. M., & Guadagno, R. E. (2003). Self-concept clarity and the foot-in-the-door procedure. *Basic and Applied Social Psychology, 25,* 79–86.

Burger, J. M., Soroka, S., Gonzago, K., Murphy, E., & Somervell, E. (2001). The effect of fleeting attraction on compliance to requests. *Personality and Social Psychology Bulletin, 27,* 1578–1586.

Burman, B., & Margolin, G. (1992). Analysis of the association between marital relationships and health problems: An interactional perspective. *Psychological Bulletin, 112,* 39–63.

Burnham, T. C., Chapman, J. F., Gray, P. B., McIntyre, M. H., Lipson, S. F., & Ellison, P. T. (2003). Men in committed, romantic relationships have lower testosterone. *Hormones and Behavior, 44,* 119–122.

Burns, V. E., Carroll, D., Drayson, M., Whitham, M., & Ring, C. (2003). Life events, perceived stress, and antibody response to influenza vaccination in young, healthy adults. *Journal of Psychosomatic Research, 55,* 569–572.

Bursik, K. (1998). Moving beyond gender differences: Gender-role comparisons of manifest dream content. *Sex Roles, 38,* 203–214.

Burton, D., Gillham, A., Weinberg, R., Yukelson, D., & Weigand, D., (2013). Goal setting styles: Examining the role of personality factors on the goal practices of prospective Olympic athletes. *Journal of Sport Behavior, 36,* 23–44.

Bush, G., Valera, E. M., & Seidman, L. J. (2005). Functional neuroimaging of attention-deficit/hyperactivity disorder: A review and suggested future directions. *Biological Psychiatry, 57,* 1273–1284.

Bushman, B. J. (2002). Does venting anger feed or extinguish the flame? Catharsis, rumination, distraction, anger, and aggressive responding. *Journal of Personality and Social Psychology, 28,* 724–731.

Bushman, B. J., & Anderson, C. A. (2001). Media violence and the American public: Scientific facts versus media misinformation. *American Psychologist, 56,* 477–489.

Buss, A., Booker, A., & Buss, E. (1972). Firing a weapon and aggression. *Journal of Personality and Social Psychology, 22,* 296–302.

Buss, A. R. (1976). Galton and the birth of differential psychology and eugenics: Social, political, and economic forces. *Journal of the History of the Behavioral Sciences, 12,* 47–58.

Buss, D. M. (1985). Human mate selection. *American Scientist, 73,* 47–51.

Buss, D. M. (1988). The evolution of human intrasexual competition. *Journal of Personality and Social Psychology, 54,* 616–628.

Buss, D. M. (1995). Psychological sex differences: Origins through sexual selection. *American Psychologist, 50,* 164–168.

Buss, D. M. (1999). *Evolutionary psychology: The new science of the mind.* Boston: Allyn & Bacon.

Buss, D. M. (2003). Sexual strategies: A journey into controversy. *Psychological Inquiry, 14,* 219–226.

Buss, D. M. Abbott, M., Angleitner, A., Asherian, A., Biaggio, A., Blanco-Villasenor, A. . . . Yang, K.-S. (1990). International preferences in selecting mates: A study of 37 cultures. *Journal of Cross-Cultural Psychology, 21,* 5–47.

Buss, D. M., Sarsen, R. J., Westen, D., & Semmelroth, J. (1992). Sex differences in jealousy: Evolution, physiology, and psychology. *Psychological Science, 3,* 251–255.

Bussey, K., & Bandura, A. (1999). Social cognitive theory of gender development and differentiation. *Psychological Review, 106,* 676–713.

Butler, A. C., Chapman, J. E., Forman, E. M., & Beck, A. T. (2006). The empirical status of cognitive-behavioral therapy: A review of meta-analyses. *Clinical Psychology Review, 26,* 17–31.

Butler, B. E., & Petrulis, J. (1999). Some further observations concerning Sir Cyril Burt. *British Journal of Psychology, 90,* 155–160.

Butler, L. D., & Nolen–Hoeksema, S. (1994). Gender differences in responses to depressed mood in a college sample. *Sex Roles, 30,* 331–346.

Butnik, S. M. (2005). Neurofeedback in adolescents and adults with attention deficit hyperactivity disorder. *Journal of Clinical Psychology, 61,* 621–625.

Butschky, M. F., Bailey, D., Henningfield, J. E., Pickworth, W. B. (1995). Smoking without nicotine delivery decreases withdrawal in 12-hour abstinent smokers. *Pharmacology, Biochemistry, and Behavior, 50,* 91–96.

Buunk, B. P., Angleitner, A., Oubaid, V., & Buss, D. M. (1996). Sex differences in jealousy in evolutionary and cultural perspective: Tests from the Netherlands, Germany, and the United States. *Psychological Science, 7,* 359–363.

Buunk, B. P., Dijkstra, P., Fetchenhauer, D., & Kenrick, D. T. (2002). Age and gender differences in mate selection criteria for various involvement levels. *Personal Relationships, 9,* 271–278.

Byars, K. C., Yolton, K., Rausch, J., Lanphear, B., Beebe, D. W. (2012). Prevalence, patterns, and persistence of sleep problems in the first 3 years of life. *Pediatraics, 129,* e276–e284.

Bylsma, W. H., Cozzarelli, C., & Sumer, N. (1997). Relation between adult attachment styles and global self-esteem. *Basic and Applied Social Psychology, 19,* 1–16.

Byne, W. (1997). Why we cannot conclude that sexual orientation is primarily a biological phenomenon. *Journal of Homosexuality, 34,* 73–80.

Byrne, D., Ervin, C. R., & Lamberth, J. (1970). Continuity between the experimental study of attraction and real-life computer dating. *Journal of Personality and Social Psychology, 16,* 157–165.

Byrne, W. L. and 22 cosigners. (1966). Memory transfer. *Science, 153,* 658–659.

Byrnes, J. P., Miller, D. C., & Schafer, W. D. (1999). Gender differences in risk taking: A meta-analysis. *Psychological Bulletin, 125,* 367–383.

Byron, K., & Khazanchi, S. (2011). A meta-analytic investigation of the relationship of state and trait anxiety to performance on figural and verbal creative tasks. *Personality & Social Psychological Bulletin, 37,* 269–283.

C

Cabral, R. R., & Smith, T. B. (2011). Racial/ethnic matching of clients and therapists in mental health services: A meta-analytic review of preferences, perceptions and outcomes. *Journal of Counseling Psychology, 58,* 537–554.

Cacioppo, J. T. Berntson, G. G., & Nusbaum, H. C. (2008). Neuroimaging as a new tool in the toolbox of psychological science. *Current Directions in Psychological Science, 17,* 62–67.

Cade, J. F. J. (1949). Lithium salts in the treatment of psychotic excitement. *Medical Journal of Australia, 2,* 349–352.

Cadet, J. L., Jayanthi, S., & Deng, X. (2005). Methamphetamine-induced neuronal apoptosis involves the activation of multiple death pathways. *Neurotoxicity Research, 8,* 199–206.

Cadoret, R. J., Yates, W. R., Troughton, E., & Woodworth, G. (1995). Adoption study demonstrating two genetic pathways to drug abuse. *Archives of General Psychiatry, 52,* 42–52.

Cadwallader, E. H. (1984). Values in Fritz Perls' Gestalt Therapy: On the dangers of half–truths. *Counseling and Values, 28,* 192–201.

Cahan, D. (2006). The "imperial chancellor of the sciences": Helmholtz between science and politics, *Social Research, 73,* 1093–1128.

Cahan, E. D., & White, S. H. (1992). Proposals for a second psychology. *American Psychologist, 47,* 224–235.

Cahill, L., Prins, B., Weber, M., & McGaugh, J. L. (1994). B-Adrenergic activation and memory for emotional events. *Nature, 371,* 702–704.

Calantone, R. J., & Warshaw, P. R. (1985). Negating the effects of fear appraisals in election campaigns. *Journal of Applied Psychology, 70,* 627–633.

Caldwell, J. L. (2000). The use of melatonin: An information paper. *Aviation, Space, and Environmental Medicine 71,* 238–244.

Calkins, M. W. (1893). Statistics of dreams. *American Journal of Psychology, 5,* 311–343.

Calkins, M. W. (1901). *An introduction to psychology.* New York: Macmillan.

Calkins, M. W. (1930). Mary Whiton Calkins. In C. Murchison (Ed.), *A history of psychology in autobiography, Vol. 1* (pp. 31–62). New York: Russell & Russell.

Camel, J. E., Withers, G. S., & Greenough, W. T. (1986). Persistence of visual cortex dendritic alterations induced by postweaning exposure to a "superenriched" environment in rats. *Behavioral Neuroscience, 100,* 810–813.

Cameron, J., Banko, K. M., & Pierce, W. D. (2001). Pervasive negative effects of rewards on intrinsic motivation: The myth continues. *Behavior Analyst, 24,* 1–44.

Cameron, L., Leventhal, E. A., & Leventhal, H. (1995). Seeking medical care in response to symptoms and life stress. *Psychosomatic Medicine, 57,* 37–47.

Cameron, M. J., & Cappello, M. J. (1993). "We'll cross that hurdle when we get to it": Teaching athletic performance within adaptive physical education. *Behavior Modification, 17,* 136–147.

Caminiti, R. (2009). Replacement of animals in research will never be possible. *Nature, 457,* 147.

Campbell, R. S., & Pennebaker, J. W. (2003). The secret life of pronouns: Flexibility in writing style and physical health. *Psychological Science, 14,* 60–65.

Campbell, W. K., Foster, C. A., & Finkel, E. J. (2002). Does self-love lead to love for others? A story of narcissistic game playing. *Journal of Personality and Social Psychology, 83,* 340–354.

Campbell, W. K., & Sedikides, C. (1999). Self-threat magnifies the self-serving bias: A meta-analytic integration. *Review of General Psychology, 3,* 23–43.

Campione, J. E., & Brown, A. L. (1979). Toward a theory of intelligence: Contributions from research with retarded children. *Intelligence, 2,* 279–304.

Camras, L. A., Oster, H., Campos, J., Campos, R., Ujiie, T., Miyake, K., . . . Meng, Z. (1998). Production of emotional facial expressions in European American, Japanese, and Chinese infants. *Developmental Psychology, 34,* 616–628.

Canel-Çınarbaş, D., Cui, Y., & Lauridsen, E. (2011). Cross-cultural validation of the Beck Depression Inventory-II across U.S. and Turkish samples. *Measurement and Evaluation in Counseling and Development, 44,* 77–91.

Canetto, S. S., & Lester, D. (1995). Gender and the primary prevention of suicide mortality. *Suicide and Life-Threatening Behavior, 25,* 58–69.

Cann, A., Sherman, S. J., & Elkes, R. (1975). Effects of initial request size and timing of a second request on compliance: The foot in the door and the door in the face. *Journal of Personality and Social Psychology, 32,* 774–782.

Cannon, D. S., & Baker, T. B. (1981). Emetic and electric shock alcohol aversion therapy: Assessment of conditioning. *Journal of Consulting and Clinical Psychology, 49,* 20–33.

Cannon, M., Jones, P., Huttunen, M. O., Tanskanen, A., Huttunen, T., Rabe-Hesketh, S., & Murray, R. M. (1999). School performance in Finnish children and later development of schizophrenia. *Archives of General Psychiatry, 56,* 457–463.

Cannon, W. B. (1915/1989). *Bodily changes in pain, hunger, fear, and rage.* Birmingham, AL: Gryphon.

Cannon, W. B. (1927). The James-Lange theory of emotions: A critical examination and an alternative. *American Journal of Psychology, 39,* 106–124.

Cannon, W. B., & Washburn, A. L. (1912). An explanation of hunger. *American Journal of Physiology, 29,* 444–454.

Caplan, L. J., & Barr, R. A. (1989). On the relationship between category intensions and extensions in children. *Journal of Experimental Child Psychology, 47,* 413–429.

Capraro, R. M., & Capraro, M. M. (2002). Myers-Briggs Type Indicator score reliability across studies: A meta-analytic reliability generalization study. *Educational and Psychological Measurement, 62,* 590–602.

Caputo, J. L., Rudolph, D. L., & Morgan, D. W. (1998). Influence of positive life events on blood pressure in adolescents. *Journal of Behavioral Medicine, 21,* 115–129.

Caqueret, A., Yang, C., Duplin, S., & Boucher, F. (2005). Looking for trouble: A search for developmental defects of the hypothalamus. *Hormone Research, 64,* 222–230.

Carlbring, P., Maurin, T., Sjömark, J., Maurin, L., Westling, B. E., Ekselius, L., . . . Anderssen, G. (2011). All at once or one at a time? A randomized controlled trial comparing two ways of delivering bibliotherapy for panic disorder. *Cognitive Behaviour Therapy, 40,* 228–235.

Carlson, D. (2011). Benefits of student-generated note packets: A preliminary investigation of SQ3R implementation. *Teaching of Psychology, 38,* 142–146.

Carlson, E. T. (1981). The history of multiple personality in the United States: I. The beginnings. *American Journal of Psychiatry, 138,* 666–668.

Carlson, M., & Miller, N. (1987). Explanation of the relation between negative mood and helping. *Psychological Bulletin, 102,* 91–108.

Carlsson, C. P. O., & Sjoelund, B. H. (2001). Acupuncture for chronic low back pain: A randomized placebo-controlled study with long-term follow-up. *Clinical Journal of Pain, 17,* 296–305.

Carmichael, L., Hogan, H. P., & Walter, A. (1932). An experimental study of the effect of language on the reproduction of visually perceived form. *Journal of Experimental Psychology, 15,* 73–86.

Carney, R. N., & Levin, J. R. (2001). Remembering the names of unfamiliar animals: Keywords as keys to their kingdom. *Applied Cognitive Psychology, 15,* 133–143.

Carney, R. N., & Levine, J. R. (2011). Delayed mnemonic benefits for a combined pegword strategy, time after time, rhyme after rhyme. *Applied Cognitive Psychology, 25,* 204–211.

Caron, S. L., Halteman, W. A., & Stacy, C. (1997). Athletes and rape: Is there a connection? *Perceptual and Motor Skills, 85,* 1379–1393.

Carpenter, C. R. (1955). Psychological research using television. *American Psychologist, 10,* 606–610.

Carr, A. (2011). Thematic review of family therapy journals 2010. *Journal of Family Therapy, 33,* 429–447.

Carr, A. S., Cardwe, C. R., McCarron, P. O., & McConville, J. (2010). A systematic review of population based epidemiological studies in myasthenia gravis. *BMC Neurology, 10,* 10–46.

Carr, L., Henderson, J., & Nigg, J. T. (2010). Cognitive control and attentional selection in adolescents with ADHD versus ADD. *Journal of Clinical Child and Adolescent Psychology, 39,* 726–740.

Carrà, G., Johnson, S., Bebbington, P., Angermeyer, M. C., Heider, D., Brugha, T., . . . Toumi, M. (2012). The lifetime and past-year prevalence of dual diagnosis in people with schizophrenia across Europe: Findings from the European Schizophrenia Cohort (EUROSC). *European Archives of Psychiatry and Clinical Neuroscience, 262*, 607–616.

Carretero, M., Escames, G., López, L. C., Venegas, C., Dayoub, J. C., Garcia, L., & Acuña-Castroviejo, D. (2009). Long-term melatonin administration protects brain mitochondria from aging. *Journal of Pineal Research, 47*, 192–200.

Carroll, J. (1999). The deep structure of literary representations. *Evolution and Human Behavior, 20*, 159–173.

Carroll, J. B. (1997). Psychometrics, intelligence, and public perception. *Intelligence, 24*, 25–52.

Carroll, J. F. X., Tanneberger, M., & Monti, T. C. (1998). Tertiary prevention strategy for drug–dependent clients completing residential treatment. *Alcoholism Treatment Quarterly, 16*, 51–61.

Carroll, J. M., & Russell, J. A. (1996). Do facial expressions signal specific emotions? Judging emotion from the face in context. *Journal of Personality and Social Psychology, 70*, 205–218.

Carroll, M. (1998). But fingerprints don't lie, eh? Prevailing gender ideologies and scientific knowledge. *Psychology of Women Quarterly, 22*, 739–749.

Carroll, M. E., & Overmier, J. B. (Eds.). (2001). *Animal research and human health: Advancing human welfare through behavioral science.* Washington, DC: American Psychological Association.

Carron, A. V., Hausenblas, H. A., & Mack, D. (1996). Social influence and exercise: A meta-analysis. *Journal of Sport and Exercise Psychology, 18*, 1–16.

Carson, R. C., & Butcher, J. N. (1992). *Abnormal psychology* (9th ed.). New York: HarperCollins.

Carson, S. H., Peterson, J. B., & Higgins, D. M. (2003). Decreased latent inhibition is associated with increased creative achievement in high-functioning individuals. *Journal of Personality and Social Psychology, 85*, 499–506.

Carton, J. S. (1996). The differential effects of tangible rewards and praise on intrinsic motivation: A comparison of cognitive evaluation theory and operant theory. *Behavior Analyst, 19*, 237–255.

Cartwright, R. D. (1978). *A primer on sleep and dreaming.* Reading, MA: Addison-Wesley.

Cartwright, R. D. (1991). Dreams that work: The relation of dream incorporation to adaptation to stressful events. *Dreaming: Journal of the Association for the Study of Dreams, 1*, 3–9.

Carver, C. (1998). Premature ejaculation: A common and treatable concern. *Journal of the American Psychiatric Nurses Association, 4*, 199–204.

Carver, C. S., & Ganellen, R. J. (1983). Depression and components of self-punitiveness: High standards, self–criticism, and overgeneralization. *Journal of Abnormal Psychology, 92*, 330–337.

Carver, C. S., Smith, R. G., Antoni, M.H., Petronis, V.M., Weiss, S., & Derhagopian, R. P. (2005). Optimistic personality and psychosocial well-being during treatment predict psychosocial well-being among long-term survivors of breast cancer. *Health Psychology, 24*, 508–516.

Case, L., & Smith, T. B. (2000). Ethnic representation in a sample of the literature of applied psychology. *Journal of Consulting and Clinical Psychology, 68*, 1107–1110.

Casey, M. K., Allen, M., Emmers-Sommer, T., Sahlstein, E., Degooyer, D., Winters, A. M., Wagner, . . . Dun, T. (2003). When a celebrity contracts a disease: The example of Earvin "Magic" Johnson's announcement that he was HIV positive. *Journal of Health Communication, 8*, 249–265.

Cash, T. F., & Derlega, V. J. (1978). The matching hypothesis: Physical attractiveness among same-sexed friends. *Personality and Social Psychology Bulletin, 4*, 240–243.

Casto, S. D., DeFries, J. C., & Fulker, D. W. (1995). Multivariate genetic analysis of Wechsler Intelligence Scale for Children-Revised (WISC-R) factors. *Behavior Genetics, 25*, 25–32.

Catania, J. A., Coates, T. J., Stall, R., & Bye, L. (1991). Changes in condom use among homosexual men in San Francisco. *Health Psychology, 10*, 190–199.

Catania, J. A., Gibson, D. R., Chitwood, D. D., & Coates, T. J. (1990). Methodological problems in AIDS behavioral research: Influences on measurement error and participation bias in studies of sexual behavior. *Psychological Bulletin, 108*, 339–362.

Catherwood, D. (1993). The haptic processing of texture and shape by 7- to 9-month-old infants. *British Journal of Developmental Psychology, 11*, 299–306.

Cattell, J. M. (1890). Mental tests and measurements. *Mind, 15*, 373–381.

Cattell, R. B. (1940). A culture free intelligence test: I. *Journal of Educational Psychology, 31*, 161–179.

Ceci, S. J., & Bruck, M. (1993). Suggestibility of the child witness: A historical review and synthesis. *Psychological Bulletin, 113*, 403–439.

Ceci, S. J., & Liker, J. J. (1986). A day at the races: A study of IQ, expertise, and cognitive complexity. *Journal of Experimental Psychology: General, 115*, 255–266.

Ceci, S. J., Huffman, M. L. C., & Smith, E. (1994). Repeatedly thinking about a non-event: Source misattributions among preschoolers. *Consciousness and Cognition: An International Journal, 3*, 388–407.

Ceci, S. J., Ross, D. F., & Toglia, M. P. (1987). Suggestibility of children's memory: Psychological implications. *Journal of Experimental Psychology: General, 116*, 38–49.

Cecil, J. E. (2001). Oral, gastric and intestinal influences on the control of appetite and feeding in humans. *Appetite, 36*, 235–236.

Centers for Disease Control and Prevention (2012). Prevalence of autism spectrum disorders—Autism and developmental disabilities monitoring network, 14 sites, United States, 2008. *Morbidity and Mortality Weekly Report, 61*, 1–19.

Centers for Disease Control and Prevention (2011). CDC grand rounds. Childhood obesity in the United States. *JAMA:Journal of the American Medical Association, 305*, 988–991.

Cerf-Ducastel, B., & Murphy, C. (2003). FMRI brain activation in response to odors is reduced in primary olfactory areas of elderly subjects. *Brain Research, 986*, 39–53.

Cerletti, U. (1954). Electroshock therapy. *Journal of Clinical and Experimental Psychopathology, 15*, 191–227.

Cervellon, M.-C., & Dube, L. (2002). Assessing the cross-cultural applicability of affective and cognitive components of attitude. *Journal of Cross-Cultural Psychology, 33*, 346–357.

Cha, K., Horch, K. W., & Normann, R. A. (1992). Mobility performance with a pixelized vision system. *Vision Research, 32*, 1367–1372.

Chabal, C., Fishbain, D. A., Weaver, M., & Heine, L. W. (1998). Long-term transcutaneous electrical nerve stimulation (TENS) use: Impact on medication utilization and physical therapy costs. *Clinical Journal of Pain, 14*, 66–73.

Chabrol, H. (1997). Abandonment and intrusion fears in borderline personality disorder. *American Journal of Psychiatry, 154*, 1329.

Chadwick, H. (1986). *Augustine.* New York: Oxford University Press.

Chaiken, S., & Baldwin, M. W. (1981). Affective-cognitive consistency and the effect of salient behavioral information on the self-perception of attitudes. *Journal of Personality and Social Psychology, 41*, 1–12.

Challis, B. H., Velichkovsky, B. M., & Craik, F. I. M. (1996). Levels-of-processing effects on a variety of memory tasks: New findings and theoretical implications. *Consciousness and Cognition: An International Journal, 5*, 142–164.

Chan, A. S., Salmon, D. P., & De La Pena, J. (2001). Abnormal semantic network for "animals" but not "tools" in patients with Alzheimer's disease. *Cortex, 37*, 197–217.

Chandler, M. J. (2009). Piaget on Piaget. *British Journal of Psychology, 100*, 225–228.

Chao, R. K. (1994). Beyond parental control and authoritarian parenting style: Understanding Chinese parenting through the cultural notion of training. *Child Development, 65*, 1111–1119.

Chao, R. K. (2001). Extending research on the consequences of parenting style for Chinese Americans and European Americans. *Child Development, 72*, 1832–1843.

Chaplin, W. F., Phillips, J. B., Brown, J. D., Clanton, N. R., & Stein, J. L. (2000). Handshaking, gender, personality, and first impressions. *Journal of Personality and Social Psychology, 79*, 110–117.

Charlton, H. (2008). Hypothalamic control of anterior pituitary function: A history. *Journal of Neuroendocrinology, 20*, 641–646.

Charman, D. (2003). Paradigms in current psychotherapy research: A critique and the case for evidence–based psychodynamic psychotherapy research. *Australian Psychologist, 38*, 39–45.

Charness, N. (1992). The impact of chess research on cognitive science. *Psychological Research, 54*, 4–9.

Chartrand, T., Pinckert, S., & Burger, J. M. (1999). When manipulation backfires: The effects of time delay and requester on the foot-in-the-door technique. *Journal of Applied Social Psychology, 29*, 211–221.

Chase, W. G., & Simon, H. A. (1973). Perception in chess. *Cognitive Psychology, 4*, 55–81.

Chaves, J. F. (1994). Recent advances in the application of hypnosis to pain management. *American Journal of Clinical Hypnosis, 37*, 117–129.

Chavira, D. A., Grillo, C. M., Shea, M. T., Yen, S., Gunderson, J. L. C., Skodol, . . . Mcglashan, T. (2003). Ethnicity and four personality disorders. *Comprehensive Psychiatry, 44*, 483–491.

Chen, C., Kasof, J., Himsel, A. J., Greenberger, E., Dong, Q., & Xue, G. (2002). Creativity in drawings of geometric shapes: A cross-cultural examination with the consensual assessment technique. *Journal of Cross-Cultural Psychology, 33*, 171–187.

Chen, C., Lee, S.-Y., & Stevenson, H. W. (1995). Response style and cross-cultural comparisons of rating scales among East Asian and North American students. *Psychological Science, 6*, 170–175.

Chen, G.-M. (1995). Differences in self-disclosure patterns among Americans versus Chinese: A comparative study. *Journal of Cross-Cultural Psychology, 26*, 84–91.

Chen, I.-L. (2013). FDA summary of adverse events on electronic cigarettes. *Nicotine & Tobacco Research, 15*, 615–616.

Chen, J. M., Kim, H. S., Mojaverian, T., & Morling, Beth (2012). Culture and social support provision: Who gives what and why? *Personality & Social Psychology Bulletin, 38*, 3–13.

Cheng, A. T. A. (2002). Expressed emotion: A cross–culturally valid concept? *British Journal of Psychiatry, 181*, 466–467.

Cheng, C., Cheung, S.-F., Chio, J. H. M., & Chan, M.-P. S. (2013). Cultural meaning of perceived control: A meta-analysis of locus of control and psychological symptoms across 18 cultural regions. *Psychological Bulletin, 139*, 152–188.

Cheng, P., Casement, M.D., Hoffmann, R. F., Armitage, R., & Deldin, P. J. (2013). Sleep-disordered breathing in major depressive disorder. *Journal of Sleep Research, 22*, 459–462

Cherek, D. R., Lane, S. D., & Dougherty, D. M. (2002). Possible amotivational effects following marijuana smoking under laboratory conditions. *Experimental and Clinical Psychopharmacology, 10*, 26–38.

Cherney, I. D., & Ryalls, B. O. (1999). Gender-linked differences in the incidental memory of children and adults. *Journal of Experimental Child Psychology, 72*, 305–328.

Cherrier, M. M., Asthana, S., Plymate, S., Baker, L., Matsumoto, A. M., Peskind, E., ...Craft, S. (2001). Testosterone supplementation improves spatial and verbal memory in healthy older men. *Neurology, 57*, 80–88.

Cherry, E. C. (1953). Some experiments on the recognition of speech with one and two ears. *Journal of the Acoustical Society of America, 25*, 975–979.

Cheryan, S., & Bodenhausen, G. V. (2000). When positive stereotypes threaten intellectual performance: The psychological hazards of "model minority" status. *Psychological Science, 11*, 399–402.

Chi, M. T. H., & Koeske, R. D. (1983). Network representation of a child's dinosaur knowledge. *Developmental Psychology, 19*, 29–39.

Chiao, J. Y., Iidaka T., Gordon H. L., Nogawa, J., Bar, M., Aminoff, E., Sadato, N., & Ambady N. (2008). Cultural specificity in amygdala response to fear faces. *Journal of Cognitive Neuroscience, 20*, 2167–2174.

Chichilnisky, E. J., & Wandell, B. A. (1999). Trichromatic opponent color classification. *Vision Research, 39*, 3444–3458.

Child, I. L. (1985). Psychology and anomalous observations: The question of ESP in dreams. *American Psychologist, 40*, 1219–1230.

Chipuer, H. M., Rovine, M. J., & Plomin, R. (1990). LISREL modeling: Genetic and environmental influences on IQ revisited. *Intelligence, 14*, 11–29.

Chodorow, N. (1978). *The reproduction of mothering.* Berkeley: University of California Press.

Choi, J. N., & Kim, M. U. (1999). The organizational application of groupthink and its limitations in organizations. *Journal of Applied Psychology, 84*, 297–306.

Chongde, L., & Tsingan, L. (2003). Multiple intelligence and the structure of thinking. *Theory and Psychology, 13*, 829–845.

Choudhury, N., & Gorman, K. S. (1999). The relationship between reaction time and psychometric intelligence in a rural Guatemalan adolescent population. *International Journal of Psychology, 34*, 209–217.

Christ, T. J. (2007). Experimental control and threats to internal validity of concurrent and nonconcurrent multiple baseline designs. *Psychology in the Schools, 44*, 451–459.

Christensen, A. J., & Smith, T. W. (1995). Personality and patient adherence: Correlates of the five-factor model in renal analysis. *Journal of Behavioral Medicine, 18*, 305–313.

Christensen, L. (1988). Deception in psychological research: When is its use justified? *Personality and Social Psychology Bulletin, 14*, 664–675.

Christensen, T. M., & Brooks, M. C. (2001). Adult children of divorce and intimate relationships: A review of the literature. *Family Journal-Counseling and Therapy for Couples and Families. 9*, 289–294.

Christianson, S. A., & Loftus, E. F. (1987). Memory for traumatic events. *Applied Cognitive Psychology, 1*, 225–239.

Christianson, S. A., & Nilsson, L. (1984). Functional amnesia as induced by a psychological trauma. *Memory and Cognition, 12*, 142–155.

Christie, D. J. (2006). What is peace psychology the psychology of? *Journal of Social Issues, 62*, 1–17.

Christie, I. C., & Friedman, B. H. (2004). Autonomic specificity of discrete emotion and dimensions of affective space: A multivariate approach. *International Journal of Psychophysiology, 51*, 143–153.

Christman, S. (2010). Eclectic lefty-hand: Conjectures on Jimi Hendrix, handedness, and Electric Ladyland. *Laterality, 15*, 253–269.

Christmann, E. P., & Badgett, J. L. (2003). A meta-analytic comparison of the effects of computer-assisted instruction on elementary students' academic achievement. *Information Technology in Childhood Education Annual, 15*, 91–104.

Christy, C. A., & Voigt, H. (1994). Bystander responses to public episodes of child abuse. *Journal of Applied Social Psychology, 24*, 824–847.

Church, A. T., Katigbak, M. S., Del Prado, A. M., Ortiz, F. A., Mastor, K. A., Harumi, Y., . . . Cabrera, H. F. (2006). Implicit theories and self-perceptions of traitedness across cultures: Toward integration of cultural and trait psychology perspectives. *Journal of Cross-Cultural Psychology, 37*, 694–716.

Cialdini, R. B., & Fultz, J. (1990). Interpreting the negative mood-helping literature via "mega"-analysis: A contrary view. *Psychological Bulletin, 107*, 210–214.

Cialdini, R. B., Schaller, M., Houlihan, D., Arps, K., Fultz, J., & Beaman, A. L. (1987). Empathy-based helping: Is it selflessly motivated? *Journal of Personality and Social Psychology, 52*, 749–758.

Cialdini, R. B., Vincent, J. E., Lewis, S. J., Catalan, J., Wheeler, D., & Darley, B. L. (1975). Reciprocal concessions procedure for inducing compliance: The door-in-the-face technique. *Journal of Personality and Social Psychology, 31*, 206–215.

Ciarrochi, J. V., Chan, A. Y.-C., Caputi, P. (2000). A critical evaluation of the emotional intelligence construct. *Personality and Individual Differences, 28*, 539–561.

Cicerello, A., & Sheehan, E. P. (1995). Personal advertisements: A content analysis. *Journal of Social Behavior and Personality, 10*, 751–756.

Cicerone, C. M., & Hayhoe, M. M. (1990). The size of the pool for bleaching in human rod vision. *Vision Research, 30*, 693–697.

Ciffone, J. (2007). Suicide prevention: An analysis and replication of a curriculum-based high school program. *Social Work, 52*, 41–49.

Ciftci Uruk, A., & Demir, A. (2003). The role of peers and families in predicting the loneliness level of adolescents. *Journal of Psychology, 137*, 179–193.

Cipolli, C., Bolzani, R., Tuozzi, G., & Fagioli, I. (2001). Active processing of declarative knowledge during REM-sleep dreaming. *Journal of Sleep Research, 10*, 277–284.

Claassen, D. O., & Rao, S. C. (2008). Locked-in or comatose? Clinical dilemma in acute pontine infarct. *Mayo Clinic Proceedings, 83*, 1197.

Claassen, N. C. W. (1997). Cultural differences, politics and test bias in South Africa. *European Review of Applied Psychology, 47*, 297–308.

Clancy, S. A. (2007). *Abducted: How People Come to Believe that They were Kidnapped by Aliens.* Cambridge, MA: Harvard University Press.

Clark, K. B., & Clark, M. P. (1947). Racial identification and preference in Negro children. In T. M. Newcomb & E. L. Hartley (Eds.), *Readings in social psychology* (pp. 169–178). New York: Holt.

Clark, L. A., Watson, D., & Reynolds, S. (1995). Diagnosis and classification of psychopathology: Challenges to the current system and future directions. *Annual Review of Psychology, 46*, 121–153.

Clark, R. D., III. (2001). Effects of majority defection and multiple minority sources on minority influence. *Group Dynamics, 5*, 57–62.

Clark, R. D., & Word, L. E. (1974). Where is the apathetic bystander? Situational characteristics of the emergency. *Journal of Personality and Social Psychology, 29*, 279–287.

Clark, S. A., McNally, R. J., Schachter, D. L., Lenzenweger, M. F., & Pitman, R. K. (2002). Memory distortion in people reporting abduction by aliens. *Journal of Abnormal Psychology, 111*, 455–461.

Clarke, P. G. H. (2010). Determinism, brain function, and free will. *Science and Christian Belief, 22*, 133–149.

Cliffe, M. J. (1991). Behaviour modification by successive approximation: Saxon age examples from Bede. *British Journal of Clinical Psychology, 30*, 367–369.

Clifford, C. A., Murray, R. M., & Fulker, D. W. (1984). Genetic and environmental influences on obsessional traits and symptoms. *Psychological Medicine, 14*, 791–800.

Clutton-Brock, T. H., & Parker, G. A. (1995). Punishment in animal societies. *Nature, 373*, 209–216.

Cobos, P., Sanchez, M., Garcia, C., Vera, M. N., & Vila, J. (2002). Revisiting the James versus Cannon debate on emotion: Startle and autonomic modulation in patients with spinal cord injuries. *Biological Psychology, 61*, 251–269.

Cochran, D. Q. (1999). Alabama v. Clarence Simmons: FBI "Profiler" testimony to establish an essential element of capital murder. *Law and Psychology Review, 23*, 69–89.

Cofer, C. N. (1985). Drives and motives. In G. A. Kimble & K. Schlesinger (Eds.), *Topics in the history of psychology, Vol. 2* (pp. 151–190). Hillsdale, NJ: Erlbaum.

Cofer, L. F., Grice, J. W., Sethre-Hofstad, L., Radi, C. J., Zimmerman, L. K., Palmer, Seal, D., & Santa Maria, G. (1999). Developmental perspectives on morningness-eveningness and social interactions. *Human Development, 42*, 169–198.

Cogan, D., & Cogan, R. (1984). Classical salivary conditioning: An easy demonstration. *Teaching of Psychology, 11*, 170–171.

Cohen, D. B. (1979). *Sleep and dreaming: Origins, nature and functions.* New York: Pergamon.

Cohen, J. (1969). *Statistical power analysis for the behavioral sciences.* New York: Academic Press.

Cohen, M. (2002). Coping and emotional distress in primary and recurrent breast cancer patients. *Journal of Clinical Psychology in Medical Settings, 9*, 245–251.

Cohen, M. S., Chen, Y. Q., McCauley, M., Gamble, T., Hosseinipour, M. C., Kumarasamy, N., & Fleming, T. R. (2011). Prevention of HIV-1 infection with early antiretroviral therapy. *New England Journal of Medicine, 365*, 493–505.

Cohen, N. J., & Squire, L. R. (1980). Preserved learning and retention of pattern-analyzing skill in amnesia: Dissociation of knowing how and knowing that. *Science, 210*, 207–210.

Cohen, S. L., Chelland, S., Ball, K. T., & LeMura, L. M. (2002). Effects of fixed ratio schedules on reinforcement on exercise by college students. *Perceptual and Motor Skills, 94*, 1177–1186.

Coke-Pepsi slugfest. (1976, July 26). *Time*, pp. 64–65.

Cokley, K., & Rosales, R. (2005). Book review: Handbook of multicultural competencies in counseling and psychology. *Measurement and Evaluation in Counseling and Development, 38*, 176–182.

Colace, C. (2003). Dream bizarreness reconsidered. *Sleep and Hypnosis, 5*, 105–128.

Colapinto, J. (2001). *As nature made him: The boy who was raised as a girl.* New York: HarperCollins.

Collaer, M. L., & Hines, M. (1995). Human behavioral sex differences: A role for gonadal hormones during early development? *Psychological Bulletin, 118*, 55–107.

Colcombe, S., & Kramer, A. F. (2003). Fitness effects on the cognitive function of older adults: A meta-analytic study. *Psychological Science, 14*, 125–130.

Cole, P. M., Bruschi, C. J., & Tamang, B. L. (2002). Cultural differences in children's emotional reactions to difficult situations. *Child Development, 73*, 983–996.

Colegrove, F. W. (1899). Individual memories. *American Journal of Psychology, 10*, 228–255.

Coleman-Mesches, K., & McGaugh, J. L. (1995). Differential involvement of the right and left amygdalae in expression of memory for aversively motivated training. *Brain Research, 670*, 75–81.

Collaer, M. L., Geffner, M. E., Kaufman, F. R., Buckingham, B., & Hines, M. (2002). Cognitive and behavioral characteristics of Turner syndrome: Exploring a role for ovarian hormones in female sexual differentiation. *Hormones and Behavior, 41*, 139–155.

Colligan, J. (1983). Musical creativity and social rules in four cultures. *Creative Child and Adult Quarterly, 8*, 39–44.

Collins, A. M., & Loftus, E. F. (1975). A spreading-activation theory of semantic processing. *Psychological Review, 82*, 407–428.

Collins, N. L., & Miller, L. C. (1994). Self-disclosure and liking: A meta-analytic review. *Psychological Bulletin, 116*, 457–475.

Colom, R., & Garcia-Lopez, O. (2003). Secular gains in fluid intelligence: Evidence from the Culture-Fair Intelligence Test. *Journal of Biosocial Science, 35*, 33–39.

Colom, R., Burgaleta, M., Román, F. J., Karama, S., Álvarez-Linera, J., Abad, F. J., . . . Haier, R. J. (2013). Neuroanatomic overlap between intelligence and cognitive factors: Morphometry methods provide support for the key role of the frontal lobes, *NeuroImage, 72*, 143–152.

Colon-Ramos, D. A., & Shen, K. (2008). Cellular conductors: Glial cells as guideposts during neural circuit development. *PLOS Biology, 6*, 672–674.

Coltrane, S., & Messineo, M. (2000). The perpetuation of subtle prejudice: Race and gender imagery in 1990s television advertising. *Sex Roles, 42*, 363–389.

Colvin, C. R., Block, J., & Funder, D. C. (1995). Overly positive evaluations and personality: Negative implications for mental health. *Journal of Personality and Social Psychology, 68*, 1152–1162.

Conklin, H. M., & Iacono, W. G. (2002). Schizophrenia: A neurodevelopmental perspective. *Current Directions in Psychological Science, 11*, 33–37.

Connie, F. O. Y., Kelvin, L. K. H., Chung, A, C., Diana, C. M. K., & Gilberto, L. K. K. (2008). Knowledge, acceptance and perception towards brainstem death among medical students in Hong Kong: A questionnaire survey on brainstem death. *Medical Teacher, 30*, 125–130.

Connors, A. (1988, February 5). At 91, she's stepping up in class. *Los Angeles Times*, p. 2.

Conrad, R. (1962). An association between memory errors and errors due to acoustic masking of speech. *Nature, 193*, 1314–1315.

Contrada, R. J., Ashmore, R. D., Gary, M. L., Coups, E., Egeth, J. D., Sewell, A., . . . Chasse, V. (2001). Measures of ethnicity-related stress: Psychometric properties, ethnic group differences, and associations with well-being. *Journal of Applied Social Psychology, 31*, 1775–1820.

Cook, M., & Mineka, S. (1989). Observational conditioning of fear to fear-relevant versus fear-irrelevant stimuli in rhesus monkeys. *Journal of Abnormal Psychology, 98*, 448–459.

Coolidge, F. L., Moor, C. J., Yamazaki, T. G., Stewart, S. E., & Segal, D. L. (2001). On the relationship between Karen Horney's tripartite neurotic type theory and personality disorder features. *Personality and Individual Differences, 30*, 1387–1400.

Coon, D. J. (1982). Eponymy, obscurity, Twitmyer, and Pavlov. *Journal of the History of the Behavioral Sciences, 18*, 255–262.

Coon, D. J. (2000). Salvaging the self in a world without soul: William James's The Principles of Psychology. *History of Psychology, 3*, 83–103.

Coon, H., Fulker, D. W., DeFries, J. C., & Plomin, R. (1990). Home environment and cognitive ability of seven-year-old children in the Colorado Adoption Project: Genetic and environmental etiologies. *Developmental Psychology, 26*, 459–468.

Coons, E. E. (2002). Neal Elgar Miller (1909-2002). *American Psychologist, 57*, 784–786.

Coons, P. M., & Milstein, V. (1992). Psychogenic amnesia: A clinical investigation of 25 cases. *Dissociation: Progress in the Dissociative Disorders, 5*, 73–79.

Cooper, J., & Cooper, G. (2002). Subliminal motivation: A story revisited. *Journal of Applied Social Psychology, 32*, 2213–2227.

Copolov, D. L., Seal, M. L., Maruff, P., Ulusoy, R., Wong, M. T. H., Tochon-Danguy, H. J., & Egan, G. F. (2003). Cortical activation associated with the human experience of auditory hallucinations and perception of human speech in schizophrenia: A PET correlation study. *Psychiatry Research: Neuroimaging, 122*, 139–152.

Coram, G. J. (1995). A Rorschach analysis of violent murderers and nonviolent offenders. *European Journal of Psychological Assessment, 11*, 81–88.

Corballis, M. C. (2001). Is the handedness gene on the X chromosome? Comment on Jones and Martin (2000). *Psychological Review, 108*, 805–810.

Corbetta, M., Kincades, M. J., Lewis, C., Snyder, A. Z., & Sapir, A. (2005). Neural basis and recovery of spatial attention deficits in spatial neglect. *Nature Neuroscience, 8*, 1603–1610.

Coren, S. (1996). *Sleep thieves: An eye–opening exploration into the science and mysteries of sleep.* New York: Free Press.

Coren, S., & Halpern, D. F. (1991). Left-handedness: A marker for decreased survival fitness. *Psychological Bulletin, 109*, 90–106.

Coren, S., & Hewitt, P. L. (1999). Sex differences in elderly suicide rates: Some predictive factors. *Aging and Mental Health, 3*, 112–118.

Coren, S., & Previc, F. H. (1996). Handedness as a predictor of increased risk of knee, elbow, or shoulder injury, fractures, and broken bones. *Laterality: Asymmetries of Body, Brain and Cognition, 1*, 139–152.

Coren, S., & Searleman, A. (1987). Left sidedness and sleep difficulty: The alinormal syndrome. *Brain and Cognition, 6*, 184–192.

Corkin, S. (2004, July 23). *Personal communication.*

Corkin, S., Amaral, D. G., Gonzalez, R. G., Johnson, K. A., & Hyman, B. T. (1997). H. M.'s medial temporal lobe lesion: Findings from magnetic resonance imaging. *Journal of Neuroscience, 17*, 3964–3979.

Cormier, J. F., & Thelen, M. H. (1998). Professional skepticism of multiple personality disorder. *Professional Psychology: Research and Practice, 29*, 163–167.

Corr, C. A. (1993). Coping with dying: Lessons that we should and should not learn from the work of Elisabeth Kübler-Ross. *Death Studies, 17*, 69–83.

Corrigan, N. M., Richards, T. L., Treffert, D. A., Dager, S. R. (2012). Toward a better understanding of the savant brain, *Comprehensive Psychiatry, 53*, 706–717.

Cosgrove, L. (2007). Humanistic psychology and the contemporary crisis of reason. *Humanistic Psychologist, 35*, 15–25.

Costello, E. J., Compton, S. N., Keeler, G., & Angold, A. (2003). Relationships between poverty and psychopathology. A natural experiment. *JAMA: Journal of the American Medical Association, 290*, 2023–2029.

Cotgrove, A. J., Zirinsky, L., Black, D., & Weston, D. (1995). Secondary prevention of attempted suicide in adolescence. *Journal of Adolescence, 18*, 569–577.

Courtenay, W. H. (2000). Engendering health: A social constructionist examination of men's health beliefs and behaviors. *Psychology of Men and Masculinity, 1*, 4–15.

Courtin, J., Karalis, N., Gonzalez-Campo, C., Wurtz, H., & Herry, C. (2013). Persistence of amygdala gamma oscillations during extinction learning predicts spontaneous fear recovery. *Neurobiology of Learning and Memory, 113*, 82-89.

Cousins, N. (1983). *The healing heart: Antidotes to panic and helplessness.* New York: W. W. Norton.

Cowan, N. (1988). Evolving conceptions of memory storage, selective attention, and their mutual constraints within the human information-processing systems. *Psychological Bulletin, 104*, 163–191.

Cowles, M. (1989). *Statistics in psychology: An historical perspective.* Hillsdale, NJ: Erlbaum.

Cowley, G. (1995, November 6). Melatonin mania. *Newsweek*, pp. 60–63.

Cox, D. J., Merkel, R. L., Moore, M., Thorndike, F., Muller, C., & Kovatchev, B. (2006). Relative benefits of stimulant therapy with OROS methylphenidate versus mixed amphetamine salts extended release in improving the driving performance of adolescent drivers with attention-deficit/hyperactivity disorder. *Pediatrics, 118*, 704–710.

Cox, K. S., Wilt, J, Olson, B., & McAdams, D. P.(2010). Generativity, the Big Five, and psychosocial adaptation in midlife adults. *Journal of Personality, 78*, 1185–1208.

Cox, W. E. (1984). Magicians and parapsychology. *Journal of the Society for Psychical Research, 52*, 383–386.

Cox, W. J., & Kenardy, J. (1993). Performance anxiety, social phobia, and setting effects in instrumental music students. *Journal of Anxiety Disorders, 7*, 49–60.

Coxon, P., & Valentine, T. (1997). The effects of the age of eyewitnesses on the accuracy and suggestibility of their testimony. *Applied Cognitive Psychology, 11*, 415–430.

Craft, S., Asthana, S., Cook, D. G., Baker, L. D., Cherrier, M., Purganan, K., . . . Kroohn, A. J. (2003). Insulin dose–response effects on memory and plasma amyloid precursor protein in Alzheimer's disease: Interactions with apolipoprotein E genotype. *Psychoneuroendocrinology, 28*, 809–822.

Craig, C. L. (1994). Limits to learning: Effects of predator pattern and colour on perception and avoidance-learning by prey. *Animal Behaviour, 47*, 1087–1099.

Craik, F. I. M., & Lockhart, R. S. (1972). Levels of processing: A framework for memory research. *Journal of Verbal Learning and Verbal Behavior, 11*, 671–684.

Craik, F. I. M., & Tulving, E. (1975). Depth of processing and the retention of words in episodic memory. *Journal of Experimental Psychology: General, 104*, 268–294.

Crain, W. (2009). Jane Goodall. *Encounter: Education for Meaning and Social Justice, 22*, 2–6.

Cramer, D. (2003). Acceptance and need for approval as moderators of self-esteem and satisfaction with a romantic relationship or closest friendship. *Journal of Psychology, 137*, 495–505.

Cramer, P. (1999). Future directions for the Thematic Apperception Test. *Journal of Personality Assessment, 72*, 74–92.

Cramer, P. (2000). Development of identity: Gender makes a difference. *Journal of Research in Personality, 34*, 42–72.

Cramer, P. (2003). Defense mechanisms and physiological reactivity to stress. *Journal of Personality, 71*, 221–244.

Crandall, J. E. (1980). Adler's concept of social interest: Theory, measurement, and implications for adjustment. *Journal of Personality and Social Psychology, 39*, 481–495.

Crano, W. D., & Prislin, R. (1995). Components of vested interest and attitude-behavior consistency. *Basic and Applied Social Psychology, 17*, 1–21.

Cranwell-Bruce, L. A. (2010). Drugs for Parkinson's disease. *Nursing Pharmacology, 19*, 347–355.

Cras, P. (2008). Glial neurobiology. *Spinal Cord, 46*, 463.

Crawford, H. J., Knebel, T., & Vendemia, J. M. C. (1998). The nature of hypnotic analgesia: Neurophysiological foundation and evidence. *Contemporary Hypnosis, 15*, 22–33.

Crepeau-Hobson, M. F., FiLaccio, M., & Gottfried, L. (2005). Violence prevention after Columbine: A survey of high school mental health professionals. *Children and Schools, 27*, 157–165.

Crespo, C. J., Smit, E., Andersen, R. E., Carter-Pokras, O., & Ainsworth, B. E. (2000). Race/ethnicity, social class, and their relation to physical inactivity during leisure time: Results from the Third National Health and Nutrition Examination Survey, 1988–1994. *American Journal of Preventive Medicine, 18*, 46–53.

Crews, F. T. (1994). Amyloid b protein disruption of cholinergic and growth factor phospholipase C signals could underlie cognitive and neurodegenerative aspects of Alzheimer's disease. *Neurobiology of Aging, 15*, S95–S96.

Critchley, H. D., Melmed, R. N., Featherstone, E., Mathias, C. J., & Dolan, R. J. (2001). Brain activity during biofeedback relaxation: A functional neuroimaging investigation. *Brain, 124*, 1003–1012.

References

Critchlow, S. (1998). False memory syndrome: Balancing the evidence for and against. *Irish Journal of Psychological Medicine, 15,* 64–67.

Crocker, J., Alloy, L. B., & Kayne, N. T. (1988). Attributional style, depression, and perceptions of consensus for events. *Journal of Personality and Social Psychology, 54,* 840–846.

Croft, G. P., & Walker, A. E. (2001). Are the Monday blues all in the mind? The role of expectancy in the subjective experience of mood. *Journal of Applied Social Psychology, 31,* 1133–1145.

Crohan, S. E. (1992). Marital happiness and spousal consensus on beliefs about marital conflict: A longitudinal investigation. *Journal of Social and Personal Relationships, 9,* 89–102.

Crook, T., & Eliot, J. (1980). Parental death during childhood and adult depression: A critical review of the literature. *Psychological Bulletin, 87,* 252–259.

Crosier, M., Scott, J., & Steinfeld, B. (2012). Improving satisfaction in patients receiving mental health care. A case study. *The Journal of Behavioral Health Services & Research, 39,* 42–54.

Cross, S., & Markus, H. (1991). Possible selves across the life span. *Human Development, 34,* 230–255.

Crossley, N. (1998). R. D. Laing and the British anti-psychiatry movement: A socio-historical analysis. *Social Science and Medicine, 47,* 877–889.

Crowe, R. R. (1990). Panic disorder: Genetic considerations. *Journal of Psychiatric Research, 24,* 129–134.

Crowley, J. J., & Lucki, I. (2006). Opportunities to discover genes regulating depression and antidepressant response from rodent behavioral genetics. *Current Pharmaceutical Design, 11,* 157–169.

Crowley, S. J., & Eastman, C. I. (2013). Melatonin in the afternoons of a gradually advancing sleep schedule enhances the circadian rhythm phase advance. *Psychopharmacology, 225,* 825–837.

Croy, I., Olgun, S., & Joraschky, P. (2011). Basic emotions elicited by odors and pictures. *Emotion, 11,* 1331–1335.

Crozier, J. B. (1997). Absolute pitch: Practice makes perfect, the earlier the better. *Psychology of Music, 25,* 110–119.

Cruess, S., Antoni, M., Cruess, D., Fletcher, M. A., Ironson, G., Kumar, M., . . . Schneiderman, N. (2000). Reductions in herpes simplex virus type 2 antibody titers after cognitive behavioral stress management and relationships with neuroendocrine function, relaxation skills, and social support in HIV-positive men. *Psychosomatic Medicine, 62,* 828–837.

Crum, B. (2009). It should be possible to replace animals in research. *Nature, 457,* 657.

Cruz, C., Boquet, A., Detwiler, C., & Nesthus, T. (2003). Clockwise and counterclockwise rotating shifts: Effects on vigilance and performance. *Aviation, Space, and Environmental Medicine, 74,* 606–614.

Cubit, K. (2010). Informed consent for research involving people with dementia: A grey area. *Contemporary Nurse, 34,* 230–236.

Cuellar, I., Roberts, R. E., Nyberg, B., & Maldonado, R. E. (1997). Ethnic identity and acculturation in a young adult Mexican-origin population. *Journal of Community Psychology, 25,* 535–549.

Culpepper, L. (2003). Use of algorithms to treat anxiety in primary care. *Journal of Clinical Psychiatry, 64,* 30–33.

Cunningham, J. A., Dollinger, S. J., Satz, M., & Rotter, N. S. (1991). Personality correlates of prejudice against AIDS victims. *Bulletin of the Psychonomic Society, 29,* 165–167.

Cunningham, M. R., Roberts, A. R., Barbee, A. P., & Druen, P. B. (1995). "Their ideas of beauty are, on the whole, the same as ours": Consistency and variability in the cross-cultural perception of female physical attractiveness. *Journal of Personality and Social Psychology, 68,* 261–279.

Cunningham, S. (1981, July). Chimps use sign language to talk to each other. *APA Monitor,* p. 11.

Cunningham, W. A., Preacher, K. J., & Banaji, M. R. (2001). Implicit attitude measures: Consistency, stability, and convergent validity. *Psychological Science, 12,* 163–170.

Cuntz, U., Enck, P., Frühauf, E., Lehnert, P., Riepl, R. L., Fichter, M. M., & Otto, B. (2013). Cholecystokinin revisited: CCK and the hunger trap in anorexia nervosa. *PLOS ONE, 8.* 454–457.

Curcio, C. A., Sloan, K. R., Jr., Packer, O., Hendrickson, A. E., & Kalina, R. E. (1987). Distribution of cones in human and monkey retina: Individual variability and radial asymmetry. *Science, 236,* 579–582.

Currie, C., Ahluwalia, N., Godeau, E., Gabhainn, S. N., Due, P., & Currie, D. B. (2012). Is obesity at individual and national level associated with lower age at menarche? Evidence from 34 countries in the Health Behaviour in School-aged Children Study. *Journal of Adolescent Health, 50,* 621–626.

Curzon, G. (1982). Transmitter amines in depression. *Psychological Medicine, 12,* 465–470.

Cutler, W. B., Friedmann, E., & McCoy, N. L. (1998). Pheromonal influences on sociosexual behavior in men. *Archives of Sexual Behavior, 27,* 1–13.

Cutting, L. P., & Docherty, N. M. (2000). Schizophrenia outpatients' perceptions of their parents: Is expressed emotion a factor? *Journal of Abnormal Psychology, 109,* 266–272.

Cytowic, R. E. (1989). Synesthesia and mapping of subjective sensory dimensions. *Neurology, 39,* 849–850.

Czeisler, C. A., Moore-Ede, M. C., & Coleman, R. M. (1982). Rotating shift work schedules that disrupt sleep are improved by applying circadian principles. *Science, 217,* 460–463.

Czyzewska, M. A. (2001). Implicit learning: Theoretical and methodological controversies. *Polish Psychological Bulletin, 32,* 45–52.

D

da C. Menezes Costa, L., Maher, C. G., McAuley, J. H., Hancoci, M. J., & Smeets, R. J. E. M. (2011). Self-efficacy is more important than fear of movement in mediating the relationship between pain and disability in chronic low back pain. *European Journal of Pain, 15,* 213–219.

Dabbs, J. M., Jr. (1997). Testosterone and puillary response to auditory sexual stimuli. *Physiology and Behavior, 62,* 909–912.

Dahlstrom, W. G. (1993). Tests: Small samples, large consequences. *American Psychologist, 48,* 393–399.

Daigen, V., & Holmes, J. G. (2000). Don't interrupt! A good rule for marriage? *Personal Relationships, 7,* 185–201.

Dale, K., & Collett, T. S. (2001). Using artificial evolution and selection to model insect navigation. *Current Biology, 11,* 1305–1316.

Dammann, E. J. (1997). "The myth of mental illness": Continuing controversies and their implications for mental health professionals. *Clinical Psychology Review, 17,* 733–756.

Dance, K. A., & Neufeld, R. W. J. (1988). Aptitude-treatment interaction research in the clinical setting: A review of attempts to dispel the "patient uniformity" myth. *Psychological Bulletin, 104,* 192–213.

Daniels, M. (1982). The development of the concept of self-actualization in the writings of Abraham Maslow. *Current Psychological Reviews, 2,* 61–75.

Danko, S. G., Bechtereva, N. P., Shemyakina, N. V., & Antonova, L. V. (2003). Electroencephalographic correlates of mental performance of emotional personal and scenic situations: I. Characteristics of local synchronization. *Human Physiology, 29,* 263–272.

Dantzer, J. M. (2006). Bursting on the scene: How thalamic neurons grab your attention. *PLOS Biology, 4,* 1100–1101.

Danziger, K. (1994). Does the history of psychology have a future? *Theory and Psychology, 4,* 467–484.

Darch, C. B., Carnine, D. W., & Kameenui, E. J. (1986). The role of graphic organizers and social structure in content area instruction. *Journal of Reading Behavior, 18,* 275–295.

Darley, J. M., & Latané, B. (1968). Bystander intervention in emergencies: Diffusion of responsibilities. *Journal of Personality and Social Psychology, 8,* 377–383.

Darling, C. A., Davidson, J. K., & Jennings, D. A. (1991). The female sexual response revisited: Understanding the multiorgasmic experience in women. *Archives of Sexual Behavior, 20,* 527–540.

Darling, N., & Steinberg, L. (1993). Parenting style as context: An integrative model. *Psychological Bulletin, 113,* 487–496.

Darlington, R. B. (1996). On race and intelligence: A commentary on affirmative action, the evolution of intelligence, the regression analyses in *The Bell Curve,* and Jensen's two-level theory. *Psychology, Public Policy, and Law, 2,* 635–645.

Darwin, C. (1859/1975). *The origin of species.* New York: W. W. Norton.

Darwin, C. (1872/1965). *The expression of the emotions in man and animals.* Chicago: University of Chicago Press.

Datta, S. (2002). Evidence that REM sleep is controlled by the activation of brain stem pedunculopontine tegmental kainate receptor. *Journal of Neurophysiology, 87,* 1790–1798.

Daughton, D. M., Fortmann, S. P., Glover, E. D., Hatsukami, D. K., Heatley, S. A., Lichtenstein, E., . . . Rennard, S. I. (1999). The smoking cessation efficacy of varying doses of nicotine patch delivery systems 4 to 5 years post-quit day. *Preventive Medicine: An International Journal Devoted to Practice and Theory, 28,* 113–118.

David, A. S., Woodruff, P. W. R., Howard, R., & Mellers, J. D. C. (1996). Auditory hallucinations inhibit exogenous activation of auditory association cortex. *Neuroreport: An International Journal for the Rapid Communication of Research in Neuroscience, 7,* 932–936.

David, S. S., Foot, H. C., & Chapman, A. J. (1990). Children's sensitivity to traffic hazard in peripheral vision. *Applied Cognitive Psychology, 4,* 471–484.

Davidson, D. (1995). The representativeness heuristic and the conjunction fallacy effect in children's decision making. *Merrill-Palmer Quarterly, 41,* 328–346.

Davidson, D. J., Zacks, R. T., & Williams, C. C. (2003). Stroop interference, practice, and aging. *Aging, Neuropsychology, and Cognition, 10,* 85–98.

Davidson, L. L., & Heinreichs, R. W. (2003). Quantification of frontal and temporal lobe brain-imaging findings in schizophrenia: A meta-analysis. *Psychiatry Research: Neuroimaging, 122,* 69–87.

Davies, G., & Alonso-Quecuty, M. (1997). Cultural factors in the recall of a witnessed event. *Memory, 5,* 601–614.

Davies, G., Welham, J., Chant, D., Torrey, E. F., & McGrath, J. (2003). A systematic review and meta-analysis of northern hemisphere season of birth studies in schizophrenia. *Schizophrenia Bulletin, 29,* 587–593.

Davies, G. M., Willner, P., & Morgan, M. J. (2000). Smoking-related cues elicit craving in tobacco "chippers": A replication and validation of the two-factor structure of the Questionnaire of Smoking Urges. *Psychopharmacology, 152,* 334–342.

Davies, I. R. L. (1998). A study of colour grouping in three languages: A test of linguistic relativity hypothesis. *British Journal of Psychology, 89,* 433–452.

Davies, M., Stankov, L., & Roberts, R. D. (1998). Emotional intelligence: In search of an elusive construct. *Journal of Personality and Social Psychology, 75,* 989–1015.

Davies, P. T., & Cummings, E. M. (1994). Marital conflict and child adjustment: An emotional security hypothesis. *Psychological Bulletin, 116,* 387–411.

Davis, A., & Eels, K. (1953). *Davis-Eels games*. Yonkers, NY: World Book.

Davis, C., & Katzman, M. A., (1999). Perfection as acculturation: Psychological correlates of eating problems in Chinese male and female students living in the United States. *International Journal of Eating Disorders, 25*, 65–70.

Davis, H., & Memmott, J. (1982). Counting behavior in animals: A critical evaluation. *Psychological Bulletin, 92*, 547–571.

Davis, J. M., Sargent, R. G., Brayboy, T. D., & Bartoli, W. P. (1992). Thermogenic effects of pre-prandial and post-prandial exercise in obese females. *Addictive Behaviors, 17*, 185–190.

Davis, J. O., & Phelps, J. A. (1995). Twins with schizophrenia: Genes or germs? *Schizophrenia Bulletin, 21*, 13–18.

Davis, J., Schiffman, H. R., & Greist-Bousquet, S. (1990). Semantic context and figure-ground organization. *Psychological Research, 52*, 306–309.

Davis, K. D., Lozano, A. M., Manduch, M., Tasker, R. R., Kiss, Z. H. T., & Dostrovsky, J. O. (1999). Thalamic relay site for cold perception in humans. *Journal of Neurophysiology, 81*, 1970–1973.

Davis, K. L., Price, C. C., Kaplan, E., & Libon, D. J. (2002). Error analysis of the nine-word California Verbal Learning Test (CVLT–9) among older adults with and without dementia. *Clinical Neuropsychologist, 16*, 81–89.

Davis, M. C., Matthews, K. A., & McGrath, C. E. (2000). Hostile attitudes predict elevated vascular resistance during interpersonal stress in men and women. *Psychosomatic Medicine, 62*, 17–25.

Davis, P. J. (1999). Gender differences in autobiographical memory for childhood emotional experiences. *Journal of Personality and Social Psychology, 76*, 498–510.

Davis, R. (1986). Knowledge-based systems. *Science, 231*, 957–963.

Davis, R. (1993). Biological tests of intelligence as culture fair. *American Psychologist, 48*, 695–696.

Davis, S. F., Thomas, R. L., & Weaver, M. S. (1982). Psychology's contemporary and all-time notables: Student, faculty, and chairperson viewpoints. *Bulletin of the Psychonomic Society, 20*, 3–6.

Davison, K. P., Pennebaker, J. W., & Dickerson, S. S. (2000). Who talks? The social psychology of illness support groups. *American Psychologist, 55*, 205–217.

De Castro, J. M. (1999). Heritability of hunger relationships with food intake in free-living humans. *Physiology and Behavior, 67*, 249–258.

de Gelder, B., & Rouw, R. (2000). Structural encoding precludes recognition of face parts in prosopagnosia. *Cognitive Neuropsychology, 17*, 89–102.

de Graaf, C., Polet, P., & van Staveren, W. A. (1994). Sensory perception and pleasantness of food flavors in elderly subjects. *Journals of Gerontology, 49*, P93–P99.

De Jesus, S. N., Rus, C. L., Lens, W., & Imaginário, S. (2013). Intrinsic motivation and creativity related to product: A meta-analysis of the studies published between 1990–2010. *Creativity Research Journal, 25*, 80–84.

de Jong, P. J., & Merckelbach, H. (1997). No convincing evidence for a biological preparedness explanation of phobias. *Behavioral and Brain Sciences, 20*, 362–363.

De la Fuente, J. M., Goldman, S., Stanus, E., Vizuete, C., Morlan, I., Bobes, J., & Mendlewicz, J. (1997). Brain glucose metabolism in borderline personality disorder. *Journal of Psychiatric Research, 31*, 531–541.

de Mathis, M. A., Diniz, J. B., Hounie, A. G., Shavitt, R. G., Fossaluza, V., Ferrão, Y., . . . Eurípedes, C. M. (2013). Trajectory in obsessive-compulsive disorder comorbidities. *European Neuropsychopharmacology, 23*, 594–601.

De Moor, J. S., de Moor, C. A, Basen-Engquist, K., Kudelka, A., Bevers, M. W., & Cohen, L.(2006). Optimism, distress, health-related quality of life, and change in cancer antigen 125 among patients with ovarian cancer undergoing chemotherapy. *Psychosomatic Medicine, 68*, 555–62.

de Paula Ramos, S. (2003). Revisiting Anna O.: A case of chemical dependence. *History of Psychology, 6*, 239–250.

de Valois, R. L., Abramov, I., & Jacobs, G. H. (1966). Analysis of response patterns of LGN cells. *Journal of the Optical Society of America, 56*, 966–977.

De Wolff, M., & van IJzendoorn, M. H. (1997). Sensitivity and attachment: A meta-analysis on parental antecedents of infant attachment. *Child Development, 68*, 571–591.

Deahl, M. (1991). Cannabis and memory loss. *British Journal of Addiction, 86*, 249–252.

Deaux, K. (1985). Sex and gender. *Annual Review of Psychology, 36*, 49–81.

Deaux, K., & Major, B. (1987). Putting gender into context: An interactive model of gender-related behavior. *Psychological Review, 94*, 369–389.

Debski, J., Spadafore, C. D., Jacob, S., Poole, D. A., & Hixson, M. D. (2007). Suicide intervention: training, roles, and knowledge of school psychologists. *Psychology in the Schools, 44*, 157–170.

DeCarolis, N. A, & Eisch, A. J. (2010). Hippocampal neurogenesis as a target for the treatment of mental illness: A critical evaluation. *Neuropharmacology, 58*, 884–893.

DeCharms, R., & Moeller, G. H. (1962). Values expressed in American children's readers: 1800–1950. *Journal of Abnormal and Social Psychology, 64*, 136–142.

Deci, E. L., Koestner, R., & Ryan, R. M. (1999). A meta-analytic review of experiments determining the effects of extrinsic rewards on intrinsic motivation. *Psychological Bulletin, 125*, 627–668.

Deci, E. L., Nezlek, J., & Sheinman, L. (1981). Characteristics of the rewarder and intrinsic motivation of the rewardee. *Journal of Personality and Social Psychology, 40*, 1–10.

Deffner-Rappold, C., Azorlosa, C., & Baker, J. D. (1996). Acquisition and extinction of context-specific morphine withdrawal. *Psychobiology, 24*, 219–226.

Degel, J., & Koester, E. P. (1999). Odors: Implicit memory and performance effects. *Chemical Senses, 24*, 317–325.

DeHart, T., Murray, S. L., Pelham, B. W., & Rose, P. (2003). The regulation of dependency in parent-child relationships. *Journal of Experimental Social Psychology, 39*, 59–67.

Del Giudice, M. (2011). Sex differences in romantic attachment: A meta-analysis. *Personality and Social Psychology Bulletin, 37*, 193–214.

Delamater, A. R. (2011). At the interface of learning and cognition: An associative learning perspective. *International Journal of Comparative Psychology, 24*, 389–411.

Delanoë, D., Hajri, S., Bachelot, A., Mahfoudg, D., Hassoun, D., Marsicano, E., & Ringa, V. (2012). Class, gender and culture in the experience of menopause: A comparative survey in Tunisia and France. *Social Science & Medicine, 75*, 401–409.

DeLongis, A., Folkman, S., & Lazarus, R. S. (1988). The impact of daily stress on health and mood: Psychological and social resources as mediators. *Journal of Personality and Social Psychology, 54*, 486–495.

DeMartino, R. E., Crosby, A. E., EchoHawk, M., Litts, D. A., Pearson, J., Reed, G A., & West, M. (2003). A call to collaboration: The federal commitment to suicide prevention. *Suicide and Life–Threatening Behavior, 33*, 101–110.

Dement, W. C. (1960). The effect of dream deprivation. *Science, 131*, 1705–1707.

Dement, W. C. (1976). *Some must watch while some must sleep*. New York: Norton.

Dement, W. C., & Wolpert, E. (1958). The relation of eye movements, body motility, and external stimuli to dream content. *Journal of Experimental Psychology, 53*, 543–553.

Dempster, F. N. (1985). Proactive interference in sentence recall: Topic similarity effects and individual differences. *Memory and Cognition, 13*, 81–89.

DeNeve, K. M. (1999). Happy as an extraverted clam? The role of personality for subjective well-being. *Current Directions in Psychological Science, 8*, 141–144.

DeNeve, K. M., & Cooper, H. (1998). The happy personality: A meta-analysis of 137 personality traits and subjective wellbeing. *Psychological Bulletin, 124*, 197–229.

Denmark, F. L. (1998).Women and psychology: An international perspective. *American Psychologist, 53*, 465–473.

Dennerstein, L., Dudley, E., & Guthrie, J. (2002). Empty nest or revolving door? A prospective study of women's quality of life in midlife during the phase of children leaving and re-entering the home. *Psychological Medicine, 32*, 545–550.

Denney, N. W., Field, J. K., & Quadagno, D. (1984). Sex differences in sexual needs and desires. *Archives of Sexual Behavior, 13*, 233–245.

Denny, K. (2009). Handedness and depression: Evidence from a large population survey. *Laterality, 14*, 246–255.

DeRijk, R. H., Wüst, S., Meijer, O. C., Zennaro, M.-C., Federenko, I. S., Hellhammer, D. H., . . . de Kloet, E. R. (2006). A common polymorphism in the mineralocorticoid receptor modulates stress responsiveness. *The Journal of Clinical Endocrinology and Metabolism, 91*, 5083–5090.

Desforges, D. M., Lord, C. G., Ramsey, S. L., Manson, J. A., van Leeuwen, M. D., West, S. C., & Lepper, M. R. (1991). Effects of structured cooperative contact on changing negative attitudes toward stigmatized social groups. *Journal of Personality and Social Psychology, 60*, 531–544.

DeShon, R. P., Smith, M. R., Chan, D., & Schmitt, N. (1998). Can racial differences in cognitive test performance be reduced by presenting problems in a social context? *Journal of Applied Psychology, 83*, 438–451.

DeSousa, E. A., Albert, R. H., & Kalman, B. (2002). Cognitive impairments in multiple sclerosis: A review. *American Journal of Alzheimer's Disease, 17*, 23–29.

Detterman, D. K. (1999). The psychology of mental retardation. *International Review of Psychiatry, 11*, 26–33.

Deuser, W. E., & Anderson, C. A. (1995). Controllability attributions and learned helplessness: Some methodological and conceptual problems. *Basic and Applied Social Psychology, 16*, 297–318.

Deutsch, D. (2002). The puzzle of absolute pitch. *Current Directions in Psychological Science. 11*, 200–204.

Devine, P. G., & Malpass, R. S. (1985). Orienting strategies in differential face recognition. *Personality and Social Psychology Bulletin, 11*, 33–40.

Deweer, B., Ergis, A. M., Fossati, P., & Pillon, B. (1994). Explicit memory, procedural learning and lexical priming in Alzheimer's disease. *Cortex, 30*, 113–126.

Dewsbury, D. A. (1990). Early interactions between animal psychologists and animal activists and the founding of the APA Committee on Precautions in Animal Experimentation. *American Psychologist, 45*, 315–327.

Dewsbury, D. A. (1996). Beatrix Tugendhat Gardner (1933–1995). *American Psychologist, 51*, 1332.

Dewsbury, D. A. (2000). Comparative cognition in the 1930s. *Psychonomic Bulletin and Review, 7*, 267–283.

Dhami, M. K. (2003). Psychological models of professional decision making. *Psychological Science, 14*, 175–180.

Di Nuovo, A. G., Nuovo, S. D., & Buono, S. (2012). Intelligent quotient estimation of mental retarded people from different psychometric instruments using artificial neural networks. *Artificial Intelligence in Medicine, 54*, 135–145.

Diaconis, P. (1978). Statistical problems in ESP research. *Science, 201*, 131–136.

Diamanduros, T., Downs, E., & Jenkins, S. J. (2008). The role of school psychologists in the assessment, prevention, and intervention of cyber bullying. *Psychology in the Schools, 45*, 693–704.

Diamond, L. M. (1998). Development of sexual orientation among adolescent and young adult women. *Developmental Psychology, 34*, 1085–1095.

Diamond, L. M. (2003a). Was it a phase? Young women's relinquishment of lesbian/bisexual identities over a 5-year period. *Journal of Personality & Social Psychology, 84,* 352–364.

Diamond, L. M. (2003b). What does sexual orientation orient? A biobehavioral model distinguishing romantic love and sexual desire. *Psychological Review, 110,* 173–192.

Diamond, M. C. (1988). *Enriching heredity: The impact of the environment on the anatomy of the brain.* New York: Free Press.

Diamond, M., & Sigmundson, H. K. (1997). Sex reassignment at birth: A long term review and clinical implications. *Archives of Pediatric & Adolescent Medicine, 151,* 298–304.

Dickson, D. (1984). Edinburgh sets up parapsychology chair. *Science, 223,* 1274.

Diego, M. A., Jones, N. A., Field, T., Hernandez-Reif, M., Schanberg, S., Kuhn, C., . . . Galamaga, M. (1998). Aromatherapy positively affects mood, EEG patterns of alertness and math computations. *International Journal of Neuroscience, 96,* 217–224.

Diener, E. (1984). Subjective well-being. *Psychological Bulletin, 95,* 542–575.

Diener, E. (2013). The remarkable changes in the science of subjective well-being. *Perspectives on Psychological Science, 8,* 663–666.

Diener, E., & Diener, C. (1996). Most people are happy. *Psychological Science, 7,* 181–185.

Diener, E., & Fujita, F. (1995). Resources, personal strivings, and subjective well-being: A nomothetic and idiographic approach. *Journal of Personality and Social Psychology, 68,* 926–935.

Diener, E., Colvin, C. R., Pavot, W. G., & Allman, A. (1991). The psychic costs of intense positive affect. *Journal of Personality and Social Psychology, 61,* 492–503.

Diener, E., Gohm, C. L., Suh, E., & Oishi, S. (2000). Similarity of the relations between marital status and subjective well-being across cultures. *Journal of Cross-Cultural Psychology, 31,* 419–436.

Diener, E., Lucas, R. E., Oishi, S., & Suh, E. M. (2002). Looking up and down: Weighting good and bad information in life satisfaction judgments. *Personality and Social Psychology Bulletin, 28,* 437–445.

Diener, E., Oishi, S., & Lucas, R. E. (2003). Personality, culture, and subjective well-being: Emotional and cognitive evaluations of life. *Annual Review of Psychology, 54,* 403–425.

Diener, E., Sandvik, E., Seidlitz, L., & Diener, M. (1993). The relationship between income and subjective well-being: Relative or absolute? *Social Indicators Research, 28,* 195–223.

Diener, E., Suh, E. M., Lucas, R. E., & Smith, H. L. (1999). Subjective well-being: Three decades of progress. *Psychological Bulletin, 125,* 276–302.

Diener, E., Tay, L., & Oishi, S. (2013). Rising income and the subjective well-being of nations. *Journal of Personality and Social Psychology, 104,* 267–276.

Diener, E., Wolsic, B., & Fujita, F. (1995). Physical attractiveness and subjective well-being. *Journal of Personality and Social Psychology, 69,* 120–129.

Digiuni, M., Jones, F. W., & Camic, P. M. (2013). Perceived social stigma and attitudes towards seeking therapy in training: A cross-national study. *Psychotherapy, 50,* 213–223.

DiLalla, D. L., Carey, G., Gottesman, I. I., & Bouchard, T. J., Jr. (1996). Heritability of MMPI personality indicators of psychopathology in twins reared apart. *Journal of Abnormal Psychology, 105,* 491–499.

Dillard, J. P. (1991). The current status of research on sequential-request compliance techniques. *Personality and Social Psychology Bulletin, 17,* 283–288.

Dillon, K. M., & Totten, M. C. (1989). Psychological factors, immunocompetence, and health of breast-feeding mothers and their infants. *Journal of Genetic Psychology, 150,* 155–162.

DiMatteo, M. R. (2004). Social support and patient adherence to medical treatment: A meta-analysis. *Health Psychology, 23,* 207–218.

DiMatteo, M. R., Reiter, R. C., & Gambone, J. C. (1994). Enhancing medication adherence through communication and informed collaborative choice. *Health Communication, 6,* 253–265.

DiMatteo, M. R., Sherbourne, C. D., Hays, R. D., & Ordway, L. (1993). Physicians' characteristics influence patients' adherence to medical treatment: Results from the Medical Outcomes Study. *Health Psychology, 12,* 93–102.

Dimberg, U., Thunberg, M., & Elmehed, K. (2000). Unconscious facial reactions to emotional facial expressions. *Psychological Science, 11,* 86–89.

Dimitrov, M., Phipps, M., Zahn, T. P., & Grafman, J. (1999). A thoroughly modern Gage. *Neurocase, 5,* 345–354.

Dindia, K., & Allen, M. (1992). Sex differences in self-disclosure: A meta-analysis. *Psychological Bulletin, 112,* 106–124.

Dinnel, D. L., Kleinknecht, R. A., & Tanaka–Matsumi, J. (2002). A cross–cultural comparison of social phobia symptoms. *Journal of Psychopathology and Behavioral Assessment, 24,* 75–84.

Dipietro, J. A., Bornstein, M. H., Costigan, K. A., Pressman, E. K., Hahn, C.-S., Painter, K., Smith, B. A., & Yi, L. J. (2002). What does fetal movement predict about behavior during the first two years of life? *Developmental Psychobiology, 40,* 358–371.

DiPietro, J. A., Hilton, S. C., Hawkins, M., Costigan, K. A., & Pressman, E. K. (2002). Maternal stress and affect influence fetal neurobehavioral development. *Developmental Psychology, 38,* 659–668.

Dishman, R. J., & Gettman, L. R. (1980). Psychobiologic influences on exercise adherence. *Journal of Sport Psychology, 2,* 295–310.

Distal, H., Ayabe-Kanamura, S., Martinez-Gomez, M., & Schicker, I., Kobayakawa, T., Saito, S., & Hudson, R. (1999). Perception of everyday odors: Correlations between intensity, familiarity and strength of hedonic judgement. *Chemical Senses, 24,* 191–199.

Ditunno, P. L., Patrick, M., Stineman, M., Morganti, B., Townson, A. F., & Ditunno, J. F. (2006). Cross-cultural differences in preference for recovery of mobility among spinal cord injury rehabilitation professionals. *Spinal Cord, 44,* 567–575.

Dixon, N. F., & Henley, S. H. (1991). Unconscious perception: Possible implications of data from academic research for clinical practice. *Journal of Nervous and Mental Disease, 179,* 243–252.

Dixson, A. F., Halliwell, G., East, R., Wignarajah, P., & Anderson, M. J. (2003). Masculine somatotype and hirsuteness as determinants of sexual attractiveness to women. *Archives of Sexual Behavior, 32,* 29–39.

Doane, J. A., West, K. L., Goldstein, M. J., Rodnick, E. H., & Jones, J. E. (1981). Parental communication deviance and affective style: Predictors of subsequent schizophrenia spectrum disorders in vulnerable adolescents. *Archives of General Psychiatry, 38,* 679–685.

Dobbins, A. C., Jeo, R. M., Fiser, J., Allman, J. M. (1998). Distance modulation of neural activity in the visual cortex. *Science, 281,* 552–555.

Dockery, T. M., & Bedeian, A. G. (1989). "Attitudes versus actions": LaPiere's (1934) classic study revisited. *Social Behavior and Personality, 17,* 9–16.

Dodd, D. K., Russell, B. L., & Jenkins, C. (1999). Smiling in school yearbook photos: Gender differences from kindergarten to adulthood. *Psychological Record, 49,* 543–554.

Doell, R. G. (1995). Sexuality in the brain. *Journal of Homosexuality, 28,* 345–354.

Dohrenwend, B. P., Turner, J. B., Turse, N. A, Adams, B. G., Koenen, K. C., & Marshall, R. (2006). The psychological risks of Vietnam for U.S. veterans: A revisit with new data and methods. *Science, 313,* 979–82.

Doi, Y., & Minowa, M. (2003). Gender differences in excessive daytime sleepiness among Japanese workers. *Social Science & Medicine, 56,* 883–894.

Doidge, N. (1997). Empirical evidence for the efficacy of psychoanalytical psychotherapies and psychoanalysis: An overview. *Psychoanalytic Inquiry [supplement],* 102–150.

Dolbier, C. L., Cocke, R. R., Leiferman, J. A., Steinhardt, M. A., Schapiro, S. J., Nehete, P. N., Perlman, J. E., & Sastry, J. (2001). Differences in functional immune responses of high vs. low hardy healthy individuals. *Journal of Behavioral Medicine, 24,* 219–229.

Dolin, D. J., & Booth-Butterfield, S. (1995). Foot-in-the-door and cancer prevention. *Health Communication, 7,* 55–66.

Dollard, J., Doob, I. W., Miller, N. E., Mowrer, O. H., & Sears, R. R. (1939). *Frustration and aggression.* New York: McGraw-Hill.

Dolliver, R. H. (1995). Carl Rogers's personality theory and psychotherapy as a reflection of his life and personality. *Journal of Humanistic Psychology, 35,* 111–128.

Dominguez, M. M., & Carton, J. S. (1997). The relationship between self-actualization and parenting style. *Journal of Social Behavior and Personality, 12,* 1093–1100.

Domino, E. F. (1999). Cannabinoids and the cholinergic system. In G. G. Nahas et al. (Eds.), *Marihuana and medicine* (pp. 223–226). Totowa, NJ: Humana Press.

Donaghue, N., & Fallon, B. J. (2003). Gender-role self-stereotyping and the relationship between equity and satisfaction in close relationships. *Sex Roles, 48,* 217–230.

Donaldson, K. D. (1976). *Insanity inside out: The personal story behind the landmark Supreme Court decision.* New York: Crown.

Donderi, D. C. (1994). Visual acuity, color vision, and visual search performance at sea. *Human Factors, 36,* 129–144.

Dong, Y. T., & Church, A. T. (2003). Cross-cultural equivalence and validity of the Vietnamese MMPI-2: Assessing psychological adjustment of Vietnamese refugees. *Psychological Assessment, 15,* 370–377.

Donovan, J. J., & Radosevich, D. J. (1999). A meta-analytic review of the distribution of practice effect: Now you see it, now you don't. *Journal of Applied Psychology, 84,* 795–805.

Donovan, R. J., & Jalleh, G. (1999). Positively versus negatively framed product attributes: The influence of involvement. *Psychology and Marketing, 16,* 613–630.

Donovan, W. L., Leavitt, L. A., & Walsh, R. O. (1997). Cognitive set and coping strategy affect mother's sensitivity to infant cries. *Child Development, 68,* 760–772.

Dorian, L., & Garfinkel, P. E. (2002). Culture and body image in Western culture. *Eating and Weight Disorders, 7,* 1–19.

Dorn, L. D., Susman, E. J., & Ponirakis, A. (2003). Pubertal timing and adolescent adjustment and behavior: Conclusions vary by rater. *Journal of Youth and Adolescence, 32,* 157–167.

Dougherty, D. M., Cherek, D. R., & Bennett, R. H. (1996). The effects of alcohol on the aggressive responding of women. *Journal of Studies on Alcohol, 57,* 178–186.

Dovidio, J. F., & Gaertner, S. L. (2000). Aversive racism and selection decisions: 1989 and 1999. *Psychological Science, 11,* 315–319.

Dovidio, J. F., Kawakami, K., & Gaertner, S. L. (2002). Implicit and explicit prejudice and interracial integration. *Journal of Social and Personality Psychology, 82,* 62–68.

Dowd, E. T. (2003). Cultural differences in cognitive therapy. *Behavior Therapist, 26,* 247–249.

Downey, G., Freitas, A. L., Michaelis, B., & Khouri, H. (1998). The self-fulfilling prophecy in close relationships: Rejection sensitivity and rejection by romantic partners. *Journal of Personality and Social Psychology, 75,* 545–560.

Doyle, A. C. (1930). *The complete Sherlock Holmes.* Garden City, NY: Doubleday.

Doyle, J. (1995). *The male experience* (3rd ed.). Madison, WI: Brown & Benchmark.

Dozois, D. J. A., & Dobson, K. S. (2003). The structure of the self-schema in clinical depression: Differences related to episode recurrence. *Cognition and Emotion, 17,* 933–941.

Draguns, J. G. (1995). Cultural influences upon psychopathology: Clinical and practical implications. *Journal of Social Distress and the Homeless, 4,* 79–103.

Draguns, J. G., & Tanaka-Matsumi, J. (2003). Assessment of psychopathology across and within cultures: Issues and findings. *Behaviour Research and Therapy, 41,* 755–776.

Dremencov, E., el Mansari, M., & Blier, P. (2009). Brain norepinephrine system as a target for antidepressant and mood stabilizing medications. *Current Drug Targets, 10,* 1061–1068.

Drews, F. A., Yazdani, H., Godfrey, C. N., Cooper, J. M., & Strayer, D. L. (2009). Text messaging during simulated driving. *Human Factors: The Journal of the Human Factors and Ergonomics Society, 51,* 762–770.

Drigotas, S. M. (2002). The Michelangelo phenomenon and personal well-being. *Journal of Personality, 70,* 59–77.

Driskell, J. E., Willis, R. P., & Copper, C. (1992). Effect of overlearning on retention. *Journal of Applied Psychology, 77,* 615–622.

Droesler, J. (2000). An n-dimensional Weber law and the corresponding Fechner law. *Journal of Mathematical Psychology, 44,* 330–335.

Drummond, T. (1999a, May 10). Battling the Columbine copycats. *Time.*

Dryer, D. C., & Horowitz, L. M. (1997). When do opposites attract? Interpersonal complementarity versus similarity. *Journal of Personality and Social Psychology, 72,* 592–603.

Dube, L., & Le Bel, J. L. (2003). The content and structure of laypeople's concept of pleasure. *Cognition & Emotion, 17,* 263–295.

Duddu, V., Chaturvedi, S. K., & Isaac, M. K. (2003). Amplification and attribution styles in somatoform and depressive disorders: A study from Bangalore, India. *Psychopathology, 36,* 98–103.

Dudycha, G. J. (1936). An objective study of punctuality in relation to personality and achievement. *Archives of Psychology, 29,* 1–53.

Duffy, J. F. (2000, May 9). New Hope bids farewell to "Mother." *Intelligencer Record,* pp. A1, A4.

Dufresne, T. (Ed.) (2007)). *Against Freud: Critics talk back.* Stanford, CA: Stanford University Press.

Duncan, J., Burgess, P., & Emslie, H. (1995). Fluid intelligence after frontal lobe lesions. *Neuropsychologia, 33,* 261–268.

Duncan, J., Seitz, R. J., Kolodny, J., Bor, D., Herzog, H., Ahmed, A., . . . Emslie, H. (2000). A neural basis for general intelligence. *Science, 289,* 457–460.

Dunn, R. L., & Schwebel, A. I. (1995). Meta-analytic review of marital therapy outcome research. *Journal of Family Psychology, 9,* 58–68.

Durand, K., & Lecuyer, R. (2002). Object permanence observed in 4-month-old infants with a 2D display. *Infant Behavior and Development, 35,* 269–278.

Durlak, J. ., & Wells, A. M. (1998). Evaluation of indicated preventive intervention (secondary prevention) mental health programs for children and adolescents. *American Journal of Community Psychology, 26,* 775–802.

Durstewitz, D., Vittoz, N.M., Floresco, S.B., & Seamans, J. K. (2010). Abrupt transitions between prefrontal neural ensemble states accompany behavioral transitions during rule learning. *Neuron, 66,* 438–448.

Dushanova, J., & Donoghue, J. (2010). Neurons in primary motor cortex engaged during action observation. *European Journal of Neuroscience, 31,* 386–398.

Dutton, D. G., & Aron, A. P. (1974). Some evidence for heightened sexual attraction under conditions of high anxiety. *Journal of Personality and Social Psychology, 30,* 510–517.

Duyme, M. (1988). School success and social class: An adoption study. *Developmental Psychology, 24,* 203–209.

Dworkin, B. R., & Miller, N. E. (1986). Failure to replicate visceral learning in the acute curarized rat preparation. *Behavioral Neuroscience, 100,* 299–314.

Dyer, C. A. (1999). Pathophysiology of phenylketonuria. *Mental Retardation and Developmental Disabilities Research Reviews, 5,* 104–112.

Dyer, F. C. (2002). When it pays to waggle. *Nature, 419,* 885–886.

Dym, R. J., Burns, J., Freeman, K., Lipton, M. L. (2011). Is functional MR imaging assessment of hemispheric language dominance as good as the Wada Test?:A meta-analysis. *Radiology 261,* 446–455

E

Eagle, M. (1997). Contributions of Erik Erikson. *Psychoanalytic Review, 84,* 337–347.

Eagly, A., & Steffen, V. J. (1983). Gender stereotypes stem from the distribution of women and men into social roles. *Journal of Personality and Social Psychology, 46,* 735–754.

Eagly, A. H. (1983). Gender and social influence: A social psychological analysis. *American Psychologist, 38,* 971–981.

Eagly, A. H. (1994). On comparing women and men. *Feminism and Psychology, 4,* 513–522.

Eagly, A. H. (1995). The science and politics of comparing women and men. *American Psychologist, 50,* 145–158.

Eagly, A. H., & Crowley, M. (1986). Gender and helping behavior: A meta-analytic review of the social psychology literature. *Psychological Bulletin, 100,* 283–308.

Eagly, A. H., & Steffen, V. J. (1986). Gender and aggressive behavior: A meta-analytic review of the social psychological literature. *Psychological Bulletin, 100,* 309–330.

Eagly, A. H., & Warren, R. (1976). Intelligence, comprehension, and opinion change. *Journal of Personality and Social Psychology, 44,* 226–242.

Earle, T. L., Linden, W., & Weinberg, J. (1999). Differential effects of harassment on cardiovascular and salivary cortisol stress reactivity and recovery in women and men. *Journal of Psychosomatic Research, 46,* 125–141.

Eastwick, P. W., Eagly, A. H., Finkel, E. J., & Johnson, S. E. (2011). Implicit and explicit prefeences for physical attractiveness in a romantic partner: A double dissociation in predictive validity. *Journal of Personality & Social Psychology, 101,* 993–1011.

Eaves, L. J., Silberg, J. L., Maes, H. H., Simonoff, E., Pickles, A., Rutter, M., . . . Hewitt, J. K. (1997). Genetics and developmental psychopathology: 2. The main effects of genes and environment on behavioral problems in the Virginia Twin Study of Adolescent Behavioral Development. *Journal of Child Psychology and Psychiatry and Allied Disciplines, 38,* 965–980.

Ebbeck, V., & Weiss, M. R. (1988). The arousal-performance relationship: Task characteristics and performance measures in track and field athletics. *Sport Psychologist, 2,* 13–27.

Ebbinghaus, H. (1885/1913). *Memory: A contribution to experimental psychology.* New York: Columbia University Press.

Eccles, A., Wilde, A., & Marshall, W. L. (1988). In vivo desensitization in the treatment of recurrent nightmares. *Journal of Behavior Therapy and Experimental Psychiatry, 19,* 285–288.

Eccles, J. S., & Wigfield, A. (1995). In the mind of the actor: The structure of adolescents' achievement task values and expectancy–related beliefs. *Personality & Social Psychology Bulletin, 21,* 215–225.

Ecenbarger, W. (1987, June 4). The forgotten sense. *Philadelphia Inquirer Magazine,* pp. 24–26, 34–35.

Eckert, E. D., Bouchard, T. J., Bohlen, J., & Heston, L. L. (1986). Homosexuality in monozygotic twins reared apart. *British Journal of Psychiatry, 148,* 421–425.

Edeline, J. M., & Weinberger, N. M. (1991). Subcortical adaptive filtering in the auditory system: Associative receptive field plasticity in the dorsal medial geniculate body. *Behavioral Neuroscience, 105,* 154–175.

Edinger, J. D., & Radtke, R. A. (1993). Use of in vivo desensitization to treat a patient's claustrophobic response to nasal CPAP. *Sleep, 16,* 678–680.

Egan, K. J., Carr, J. E., Hunt, D. D., & Adamson, R. (1988). Endogenous opiate system and systematic desensitization. *Journal of Consulting and Clinical Psychology, 56,* 287–291.

Egeland, J. A., Gerhard, D. S., Pauls, D. L., Sussex, J. N., Kidd, K. K., Allen, C. R., . . . Housman, D. E. (1987). Bipolar affective disorders linked to DNA markers on chromosome 11. *Nature, 325,* 783–787.

Egeth, H. (1992). Dichotic listening: Long–lived echoes of Broadbent's early studies. *Journal of Experimental Psychology: General, 121,* 124.

Ehara, T. H. (1980, December). On the electronic chess circuit. *Science 80, 78,* 80.

Ehrlichman, H., & Halpern, J. N. (1988). Affect and memory: Effects of pleasant and unpleasant odors on retrieval of happy and unhappy memories. *Journal of Personality and Social Psychology, 55,* 769–779.

Eich, E., Macaulay, D., & Ryan, L. (1994). Mood-dependent memory for events of the personal past. *Journal of Experimental Psychology General, 123,* 201–215.

Eich, J. E. (1980). The cue-dependent nature of state-dependent retrieval. *Memory and Cognition, 8,* 157–173.

Eich, J. E. (1995). Searching for mood-dependent memory. *Psychological Science, 6,* 67–75.

Eich, J. E., Weingartner, H., Stillman, R. C., & Gillin, J. C. (1975). State-dependent accessibility of retrieval cues in the retention of a categorized list. *Journal of Verbal Learning and Verbal Behavior, 14,* 408–417.

Eichenbaum, H. (1997). Declarative memory: Insights from cognitive neurobiology. *Annual Review of Psychology, 48,* 547–572.

Eichstedt, J. A., Arnold, S. L. (2001). Childhood-onset obsessive-compulsive disorder: A tic-related subtype of OCD? *Clinical Psychology Review, 21,* 137–157.

Eiden, R. D., Schuetze, P., & Coles, C. D. (2011). Maternal cocaine use and mother-infant interactions: Direct and moderated associations. *Neurotoxicology & Teratology, 33,* 120–128.

Eisdorfer, C. (1983). Conceptual models of aging: The challenge of a new frontier. *American Psychologist, 38,* 197–202.

Eisenberg, N., Cialdini, R. B., McCreath, H., & Shell, R. (1987). Consistency-based compliance: When and why do children become vulnerable? *Journal of Personality and Social Psychology, 52,* 1174–1181.

Eisenberg, N., & Lennon, R. (1983). Sex differences in empathy and related capacities. *Psychological Bulletin, 94,* 100–131.

Eisenberger, N. I., Lieberman, M. D., & Williams, K. D. (2003). Does rejection hurt? An fMRI study of social exclusion. *Science, 302,* 290–292.

Eisenberger, N. I., Taylor, S. E., Gable, S. L., Hilmert, C. J., & Lieberman, M. D. (2007). Neural pathways link social support to attenuated neuroendocrine stress responses. *NeuroImage, 35,* 1601–1612.

Eisenman, R. (1993). Belief that drug usage in the United States is increasing when it is really decreasing: An example of the availability heuristic. *Bulletin of the Psychonomic Society, 31,* 249–252.

Ekbia, H. R. (2008). *Artificial dreams: The quest for non-biological intelligence.* New York: Cambridge University Press.

Ekman, P. (1992a). An argument for basic emotions. *Cognition and Emotion, 6,* 169–200.

Ekman, P. (1992b). Facial expressions of emotion: New findings, new questions. *Psychological Science, 3,* 34–38.

Ekman, P. (1993). Facial expression and emotion. *American Psychologist, 48,* 384–392.

Ekman, P., & Friesen, W. V. (1971). Constants across cultures in the face and emotion. *Journal of Personality and Social Psychology, 17,* 124–129.

Ekman, P., & O'Sullivan, M. (1991). Who can catch a liar? *American Psychologist, 46,* 913–920.

Ekman, P., Davidson, R. J., & Friesen, W. V. (1990). The Duchenne smile: 2. Emotional expression and brain physiology. *Journal of Personality and Social Psychology, 58,* 342–353.

Ekman, P., Friesen, W. V., O'Sullivan, M., Chan, A., Diacoyanni-Tarlatzis, I., Heider, K., . . . Tzavaras, A. (1987). Universals and cultural differences in the judgments of facial expressions of emotion. *Journal of Personality and Social Psychology, 53,* 712–717.

Ekman, P., Levenson, R. W., & Friesen, W. V. (1983). Autonomic nervous system activity distinguishes among emotions. *Science, 221,* 1208–1210.

Ekman, P., O'Sullivan, M., & Frank, M. G. (1999). A few can catch a liar. *Psychological Science, 10,* 263–266.

Elaad, E. (1990). Detection of guilty knowledge in real-life criminal investigations. *Journal of Applied Psychology, 75,* 521–529.

Elaad, E. (1994). The accuracy of human decisions and objective measurements in psychophysiological detection of knowledge. *Journal of Psychology, 128,* 267–280.

Elaad, E. (1997). Polygraph examiner awareness of crime-relevant information and the Guilty Knowledge Test. *Law and Human Behavior, 21,* 107–120.

Elder, W. B., Brooks, G. R., & Morrow, S. L. (2012). Sexual self-schemas of heterosexual men. *Psychology of Men & Masculinity, 13,* 166–179.

Elfenbein, H. A., & Ambady, N. (2002). On the universality and cultural specificity of emotion recognition: A meta-analysis. *Psychological Bulletin, 128,* 203–235.

Elkind, D. (1996). Inhelder and Piaget on adolescence and adulthood: A postmodern appraisal. *Psychological Science, 7,* 216–220.

Elkins, R. L. (1987). An experimenter effect on place avoidance learning of selectively-bred taste-aversion prone and resistant rats. *Medical Science Research: Psychology and Psychiatry, 15,* 1181–1182.

Ellenberger, H. F. (1970). *The discovery of the unconscious: The history and evolution of dynamic psychiatry.* New York: Basic Books.

Elliot, A. J., & Devine, P. G. (1994). On the motivational nature of cognitive dissonance: Dissonance as psychological discomfort. *Journal of Personality and Social Psychology, 67,* 382–394.

Elliott, R. (1988). Tests, abilities, race, and conflict. *Intelligence, 12,* 333–350.

Ellis, A. (1962). *Reason and emotion in psychotherapy.* New York: Lyle Stuart.

Ellis, A. (1996). The treatment of morbid jealousy: A rational emotive behavior therapy approach. *Journal of Cognitive Psychotherapy, 10,* 23–33.

Ellis, A. (1997). Using Rational Emotive Behavior Therapy techniques to cope with disability. *Professional Psychology: Research and Practice, 28,* 17–22.

Ellis, A. (1999). Why rational-emotive therapy to rational emotive behavior therapy? *Psychotherapy, 36,* 154–159.

Ellis, A. P. J., West, B. J., Ryan, A. M., & DeShon, R. P. (2002). The use of impression management tactics in structured interviews: A function of question type? *Journal of Applied Psychology, 87,* 1200–1208.

Ellis, H. C. (1987). Recent developments in human memory. In V. P. Makosy (Ed.), *The G. Stanley Hall Lecture Series, Vol. 7,* (pp. 161–206). Washington, DC: American Psychological Association.

Ellis, L. (1987). Relationships of criminality and psychopathy with eight other apparent behavioral manifestations of sub-optimal arousal. *Personality and Individual Differences, 8,* 905–925.

Ellis, L. (1998). The evolution of attitudes about social stratification: Why many people (including social scientists) are morally outraged by *The Bell Curve. Personality and Individual Differences, 24,* 207–216.

Ellis, L., & Ames, M. A. (1987). Neurohormonal functioning and sexual orientation: A theory of homosexuality-heterosexuality. *Psychological Bulletin, 101,* 233–258.

Ellis, L., & Engh, T. (2000). Handedness and age of death: New evidence on a puzzling relationship. *Journal of Health Psychology, 5,* 561–565.

Ellis, R. R., & Lederman, S. J. (1998). The golf-ball illusion: Evidence for top-down processing in weight perception. *Perception, 27,* 193–201.

Ellison, P. A., Govern, J. M., Petri, H. L., & Figler, M. H. (1995). Anonymity and aggressive driving behavior: A field study. *Journal of Social Behavior and Personality, 10,* 265–272.

Ellison, W. J. (1987). State execution of juveniles: Defining "youth" as a mitigating factor for imposing a sentence of less than death. *Law and Psychology Review, 11,* 1–38.

Else-Quest, N. M., Hyde, J. S., & Linn, M. C. (2010). Cross-national patterns of gender differences in mathematics: A meta-analysis. *Psychological Bulletin, 136,* 103–127.

Else-Quest, N. M., Hyde, J. S., Goldsmith, H. H., Van Hulle, C. A. (2006). Gender differences in temperament: A meta-analysis. *Psychological Bulletin, 132,* 33–72.

Emam, M. M. (2013). Problem-solving orientation and attributional style as predictors of depressive symptoms in Egyptian adolescents with visual impairment. *British Journal of Visual Impairment, 31,* 150–163.

Emde Boas, W. van (1999). Juhn A. Wada and the sodium amytal test: The first (and last?) 50 years. *Journal of the History of the Neurosciences, 8,* 286–292.

Emmons, R. A. (2000). Is spirituality an intelligence? Motivation, cognition, and the psychology of ultimate concern. *International Journal for the Psychology of Religion, 10,* 3–26.

Emonson, D. L., & Vanderbeek, R. D. (1995). The use of amphetamines in U.S. Air Force tactical operations during Desert Shield and Storm. *Aviation, Space, and Environmental Medicine, 66,* 260–263.

Enders, C. K., Laurenceau, J. P., & Stuetzle, R. (2006). Teaching random assignment: A classroom demonstration using a deck of playing cards. *Teaching of Psychology, 33,* 239–242.

Enea, V., & Dafinoiu, I. (2013). Flexibility in processing visual information: Effects of mood and hypnosis. *International Journal of Clinical and Experimental Hypnosis, 61,* 55–70.

Engel, S. A. (1999). Using neuroimaging to measure mental representations: Finding color-opponent neurons in visual cortex. *Current Directions in Psychological Science, 8,* 23–27.

Engels, G. I., Garnefski, N., & Diekstra, R. F. W. (1993). Efficacy of rational-emotive therapy: A quantitative analysis. *Journal of Consulting and Clinical Psychology, 61,* 1083–1090.

Engstrom, M., & Söderfeldt, B. (2010). Brain activation during compassion meditation: A case study. *Journal of Alternative and Complementary Medicine, 16,* 597–599.

Epstein, M. H., & Synhhorst, L. (2008). Preschool Behavioral and Emotional Rating Scale (PreBERS): Test-retest reliability and inter-rater reliability. *Journal of Child and Family Studies, 17,* 853–862.

Epstein, R. (1991). Skinner, creativity, and the problem of spontaneous behavior. *Psychological Science, 2,* 362–370.

Epstein, R., Kirshnit, C. E., Lanza, R. P., & Rubin, I. C. (1984). "Insight" in the pigeon: Antecedents and determinants of an intelligent performance. *Nature, 308,* 61–62.

Epstein, S. (1994). Integration of the cognitive and the psychodynamic unconscious. *American Psychologist, 49,* 709–724.

Epstein, S., & Feist, G. J. (1988). Relation between self- and other-acceptance and its moderation by identification. *Journal of Personality and Social Psychology, 54,* 309–315.

Epstein, S., & O'Brien, E. J. (1985). The person-situation debate in historical and current perspective. *Psychological Bulletin, 98,* 513–537.

Er, N. (2003). A new flashbulb memory model applied to the Marmara earthquake. *Applied Cognitive Psychology, 17,* 503–517.

Erdur, O., Rude, S. S., & Baron, A. (2003). Symptom improvement and length of treatment in ethnically similar and dissimilar client–therapist pairings. *Journal of Counseling Psychology, 50,* 52–58.

Erel, O., & Burman, B. (1995). Interrelatedness of marital relations and parent-child relations: A meta-analytic review. *Psychological Bulletin, 118,* 108–132.

Erez, A., & Judge, T. A. (2001). Relationship of core self-evaluations to goal setting, motivation, and performance. *Journal of Applied Psychology, 86,* 1270–1279.

Ericsson, K. A., & Polson, P. G. (1988). An experimental analysis of the mechanisms of a memory skill. *Journal of Experimental Psychology: Learning, Memory, and Cognition, 14,* 305–316.

Erikson, E. (1963). *Childhood and society.* New York: W. W. Norton.

Erwin, P. G. (1994). Effectiveness of social skills training with children: A meta-analytic study. *Counselling Psychology Quarterly, 7,* 305–310.

Escolas, S. M., Pitts, B. L., Safer, M. A., & Bartone, P. T. (2013). The protective value of hardiness on military posttraumatic stress symptoms. *Military Psychology, 25,* 116–123.

Espejo, E. F., Gonzalez-Albo, M. C., Moraes, J. P., El Banoua, F., Flores, J. A., & Caraballo, I. (2001). Functional regeneration in a rat Parkinson's model after intrastriatal grafts of glial cell line-derived neurotrophic factor and transforming growth factor beta-sub-1-expressing extra-adrenal chromaffin cells of the Zuckerkandl's organ. *Journal of Neuroscience, 21,* 9888–9895.

Estrada, C. A., Isen, A. M., & Young, M. J. (1994). Positive affect improves creative problem solving and influences reported source of practice satisfaction in physicians. *Motivation and Emotion, 18,* 285–299.

Evans, D. L., Leserman, J., Perkins, D. O., & Stern, R. A. (1995). Stress-associated reductions of cytotoxic T lymphocytes and natural killer cells in asymptomatic HIV infection. *American Journal of Psychiatry, 152,* 543–550.

Evans, K. C., Wright, C. I., Wedig, M. M., Gold, A. L., Pollack, M. H., & Rauch, S. L. (2008). A functional MRI study of amygdala responses to angry schematic faces in social anxiety disorder. *Depression and Anxiety, 25,* 496–505.

Evans, S., Ferrando, S. J., Rabkin, J. G., & Fishman, B. (2000). Health locus of control, distress, and utilization of protease inhibitors among HIV-positive men. *Journal of Psychosomatic Research, 49,* 157–162.

Everly, G. S., Jr. (2000). Crisis management briefings (CMB): Large group crisis intervention in response to terrorism, disasters, and violence. *International Journal of Emergency Mental Health, 2,* 53–57.

Evers, A., Klusmann, V., Ziegelmann, J. P., Schwarzer, R., & Heuser, I. (2012). Long-term adherence to a physical activity intervention: The role of telephone-assisted vs. self-administered coping plans and strategy use. *Psychology & Health, 27,* 784–797.

Evers, A. W. M., Kraaimaat, F. W., Geenen, R., Jacobs, J. W. G., & Bijlsma, J. W. J. (2003). Stress-vulnerability factors as long-term predictors of disease activity in early rheumatoid arthritis. *Journal of Psychosomatic Research, 55,* 293–302.

Eviatar, Z. (2000). Culture and brain organization. *Brain and Cognition, 42,* 50–52.

Ewald, H. Mors, O., Flint, T., & Koed, K. (1995). A possible locus for manic depressive illness on chromosome 16p13. *Psychiatric Genetics, 5,* 71–81.

Ewin, D. M. (1994). Many memories retrieved with hypnosis are accurate. *American Journal of Clinical Hypnosis, 36,* 174–176.

Exton, M. S., Westermann, J., & Schedlowski, M. (2000). Behaviorally conditioned immunosuppression: Mechanisms and biological relevance. *Psychologische Beitrage, 42,* 118–129.

Eyler, A. A., Matson-Koffman, D., Vest, J. R., Evenson, K. R., Sanderson, B., Thompson, J. L., . . . Young, D. R. (2002). Environmental, policy, and cultural factors related to physical activity in a diverse sample of women: The Women's Cardiovascular Health Network Project—Summary and discussion. *Women and Health, 36,* 123–134.

Eysenck, H. J. (1982). *Personality, genetics, and behavior: Selected papers.* New York: Praeger.

Eysenck, H. J. (1988). Skinner, Skinnerism, and the Skinnerian in psychology. *Counseling Psychology Quarterly, 1,* 299–301.

Eysenck, H. J. (1990). Genetic and environmental contributions to individual differences: The three major dimensions of personality. *Journal of Personality, 58,* 245–261.

Eysenck, H. J. (1994). Cancer, personality, and stress: Prediction and prevention. *Advances in Behaviour Research and Therapy, 16,* 167–215.

Eysenck, H. J. (1994). The outcome problem in psychotherapy: What have we learned? *Behaviour Research and Therapy, 32,* 477–495.

Eysenck, S. B., Barrett, P. T., & Barnes, G. E. (1993). A cross-cultural study of personality: Canada and England. *Personality and Individual Differences, 14,* 1–9.

Ezzo, J., Berman, B., Hadhazy, V. A., Jadad, A. R., Lao, L., & Singh, B. B. (2000). Is acupuncture effective for the treatment of chronic pain? A systematic review. *Pain, 86,* 217–225.

F

Fabbro, F. (2000). Introduction to language and cerebellum. *Journal of Neurolinguistics, 13,* 83–94.

Fagan, J. F., & Holland, C. R. (2002). Equal opportunity and racial differences in IQ. *Intelligence, 30,* 361–387.

Fagan, M. M., & Ayers, K. (1983). Levinson's model as a predictor of the adult development of policemen. *International Journal of Aging and Human Development, 16,* 221–230.

Fagerstrom, K. O., Schneider, N. G., & Lunell, E. (1993). Effectiveness of nicotine patch and nicotine gum as individual versus combined treatments for tobacco withdrawal symptoms. *Psychopharmacology, 111,* 271–277.

Fairburn, C. G., Cowen, P. J., Harrison, P. J. (1999). Twin studies and the etiology of eating disorders. *International Journal of Eating Disorders, 26,* 349–358.

Fairburn, C. G., Shafran, R., & Cooper, Z. (1999). A cognitive behavioural theory of anorexia nervosa. *Behaviour Research and Therapy, 37,* 1–13.

Faith, M. S., Rha, S. S., Neale, M. C., & Allison, D. B. (1999). Evidence for genetic influences on human energy intake: Results from a twin study using measured observations. *Behavior Genetics, 29,* 145–154.

Falbo, T., & Polit, D. F. (1986). Quantitative review of the only-child literature: Research evidence and theory development. *Psychological Bulletin, 100,* 176–189.

Falk, J. L. (1994). The discriminative stimulus and its reputation: Role in the instigation of drug abuse. *Experimental and Clinical Psychopharmacology, 2,* 43–52.

Falk, R. (1998). Replication: A step in the right direction [Commentary on Sohn]. *Theory and Psychology, 8,* 313–321.

Fallace, T. D. (2010). The mind at every stage has its own logic: John Dewey as genetic psychologist. *Educational Theory, 60,* 129–146.

Fallon, A. E., & Rozin, P. (1985). Sex differences in perceptions of desirable body shape. *Journal of Abnormal Psychology, 94,* 102–105.

Fals-Stewart, W. (2003). The occurrence of partner physical aggression on days of alcohol consumption: A longitudinal diary study. *Journal of Consulting and Clinical Psychology, 71,* 41–52.

Fancher, R. E. (1984). Not Conley, but Burt and others: A reply. *Journal of the History of the Behavioral Sciences, 20,* 186.

Fancher, R. E. (1987). Henry Goddard and the Kallikak Family photographs: "Conscious skulduggery" or "Whig history"? *American Psychologist, 42,* 585–590.

Fani, L., Bak, S., Delhanty, P., van Rossum, E. F. C., & van den Akker, E. L. T. (2014). The melanocortin-4 receptor as target for obesity treatment: A systematic review of emerging pharmacological therapeutic options. *International Journal of Obesity, 38,* 163–169.

Fantoni-Salvador, P., & Rogers, R. (1997). Spanish versions of the MMPI-2 and PAI: An investigation of concurrent validity with Hispanic patients. *Assessment, 4,* 29–39.

Faraone, S. (1982). Psychiatry and political repression in the Soviet Union. *American Psychologist, 37,* 1105–1112.

Faraone, S. V, Perlis, R. H., Doyle, A. E., Smoller, J. W., Goralnick, J. J., Holmgren, M. A, & Sklar, P. (2005). Molecular genetics of attention-deficit/hyperactivity disorder. *Biological Psychiatry, 57,* 1313–1323.

Faraone, S. V, Sergeant, J., Gillberg, C., & Biederman, J. (2003). The worldwide prevalence of ADHD: Is it an American condition? *World Psychiatry, 2,* 104–113.

Faravelli, C., Cosci, F., Ciampelli, M., Scarpato, M. A., Spiti, R., & Ricca, V. (2003). A self-controlled, naturalistic study of selective serotonin reuptake inhibitors versus tricyclic antidepressants. *Psychotherapy and Psychosomatics. 72,* 95–101.

Farde, L. (1997). Brain imaging of schizophrenia: The dopamine hypothesis. *Schizophrenia Research, 28,* 157–162.

Farr, C. B. (1944/1994). Benjamin Rush and American psychiatry. *American Journal of Psychiatry, 151,* 65–73.

Farrimond, T. (1990). Effect of alcohol on visual constancy values and possible relation to driving performance. *Perceptual and Motor Skills, 70,* 291–295.

Farthing, G. W., Venturino, M., & Brown, S. W. (1984). Suggestion and distraction in the control of pain: Test of two hypotheses. *Journal of Abnormal Psychology, 93,* 266–276.

Fassbender, P. (1997). Parapsychology and the neurosciences: A computer-based content analysis of abstracts in the database "Medline" from 1975 to 1995. *Perceptual and Motor Skills, 84,* 452–454.

Fauerbach, J. A., Lawrence, J. W., Haythornthwaite, J. A., & Richter, L. (2002). Coping with the stress of a painful medical procedure. *Behaviour Research and Therapy, 40,* 1003–1015.

Faust, J., Olson, R., & Rodriguez, H. (1991). Same-day surgery preparation: Reduction of pediatric patient arousal and distress through participant modeling. *Journal of Consulting and Clinical Psychology, 59,* 475–478.

Fava, G. A., & Sonino, N. (2000). Psychosomatic medicine: Emerging trends and perspectives. *Psychotherapy and Psychosomatics, 69,* 184–197.

Fava, M. (2003). The role of the serotonergic and noradrenergic neurotransmitter systems in the treatment of psychological and physical symptoms of depression. *Journal of Clinical Psychiatry, 64,* 26–29.

Fava, M., & Rankin, M. (2002). Sexual functioning and SSRIs. *Journal of Clinical Psychiatry, 63,* 13–16.

Favreau, O. E. (1997). Sex and gender comparisons: Does null hypothesis testing create a false dichotomy? *Feminism and Psychology, 7,* 63–81.

Feather, S. R. (1983). Something different: A biographical sketch of Louisa Rhine. *Journal of Parapsychology, 47,* 293–302.

Fedoroff, I. C., Polivy, J., & Herman, C. P. (1997). The effect of pre-exposure to food cues on the eating behavior of restrained and unrestrained eaters. *Appetite, 28,* 33–47.

Feest, U. (2005). Operationism in psychology: What the debate is about, what the debate should be about. *Journal of the History of the Behavioral Sciences, 41,* 131–149.

Feest, U. (2007). Science and experience/science of experience: Gestalt psychology and the anti-metaphysical project of the aufbau. *Perspectives on Science, 15,* 1–25.

Fehr, B. (1999). Laypeople's conceptions of commitment. *Journal of Personality and Social Psychology, 76,* 90–103.

Fehr, B., & Russell, J. A. (1984). Concept of emotion viewed from a prototypic perspective. *Journal of Experimental Psychology: General, 113,* 464–486.

Fehr, B., & Russell, J. A. (1991). The concept of love viewed from a prototype perspective. *Journal of Personality and Social Psychology, 60,* 425–438.

Fein, D. (1990). Cerebral lateralization: A dominant question in developmental research [Review of *Brain lateralization in children: Developmental implications*]. *Contemporary Psychology, 35,* 676–677.

Fein, S., & Spencer, S. J. (1997). Prejudice as self-image maintenance: Affirming the self through derogating others. *Journal of Personality and Social Psychology, 73,* 31–44.

Feingold, A. (1994). Gender differences in personality: A meta-analysis. *Psychological Bulletin, 116,* 429–456.

Feingold, A., & Mazzella, R. (1998). Gender differences in body image are increasing. *Psychological Science, 9,* 190–195.

Feinstein, J. S., Rudrauf, D., Khalsa, S. S., Cassell, M. D., Bruss, J., Grabowski, T. J., & Tranel, D. (2010). Bilateral limbic system destruction in man. *Journal of Clinical and Experimental Neuropsychology, 32,* 88–106.

Feng, C.-Y., Chu, H., Chen, C.-H., Chang, Y.-S., Chen, T. H., Chou, Y.-H., . . . Chou, K. R. (2012). The effect of cognitive behavioral group therapy for depression: A meta-analysis. *World Views on Evidence-Based Nursing, 9,* 2–17.

Feng, D., Silverstein, M., Giarrusso, R., McArdle, J. J., & Bengtson, V. L. (2006). Attrition of older adults in longitudinal surveys: Detection and correction of sample selection bias using multigenerational data. *The Journals of Gerontology: Series B: Psychological Sciences and Social Sciences, 61,* S323–S328.

Feng, L. R., & Maguire-Zeiss, K. A. (2010). Gene therapy in Parkinson's disease: Rationale and current status. *CNS Drugs, 24,* 177–192.

Fenn, K. M., Nusbaum, H. C., & Margoliash, D. (2003). Consolidation during sleep of perceptual learning of spoken language. *Nature, 425,* 614–616.

Ferchiou, A., Schürhoff, F., Bulzacka, E., Leboyer, M., & Szöke, A. (2010). Selective attention impairment in schizophrenia: Can it explain source monitoring failure? *Journal of Nervous and Mental Disease, 198,* 779–781.

Ferlazzo, F., Conte, S., & Gentilomo, A. (1993). Event-related potentials and recognition memory within the "levels of processing" framework. *Neuroreport: An International Journal for the Rapid Communication of Research in Neuroscience, 4,* 667–670.

Fern, E. F., Monroe, K. B., & Avila, R. A. (1986). Effectiveness of multiple request strategies: A synthesis of research results. *Journal of Marketing Research, 23,* 144–152.

Ferrari, M. (1996). Observing the observer: Self-regulation in the observational learning of motor skills. *Developmental Review, 16,* 203–240.

Ferris, A. M., & Duffy, V. B. (1989). Effect of olfactory deficits on nutritional status: Does age predict persons at risk? *Annals of the New York Academy of Sciences, 561,* 113–123.

Fery, Y. A. (2003). Differentiating visual and kinesthetic imagery in mental practice. *Canadian Journal of Experimental Psychology, 57,* 1–10.

Festinger, L., & Carlsmith, J. M. (1959). Cognitive consequences of forced compliance. *Journal of Abnormal and Social Psychology, 58,* 203–210.

Festinger, L., Pepitone, A., & Newcomb, T. (1952). Some consequences of deindividuation in a group. *Journal of Abnormal and Social Psychology, 47,* 382–389.

Festinger, L., Riecken, H. W., & Schachter, S. (1956). *When prophecy fails.* New York: Harper & Row.

Festinger, L., Schachter, S., & Back, K. (1950). *Social pressures in informal groups: A study of a housing community.* Stanford, CA: Stanford University Press.

Fieckenstein, L. (1996, May 20). Trailblazing Hulda Crooks, 100: Loma Linda resident publishes memoirs. *The Press-Enterprise,* p. B03.

Fiedler, K., Schmid, J., & Stahl, T. (2002). What is the current truth about polygraph lie detection? *Basic and Applied Social Psychology, 24,* 313–324.

Field, T. M. (1991). Quality infant day-care and grade school behavior and performance. *Child Development, 62,* 863–870.

Field, T. M. (1996). Attachment and separation in young children. *Annual Review of Psychology, 47,* 541–561.

Field, T. M., Woodson, R., Greenberg, R., & Cohen, D. (1982). Discrimination and imitation of facial expressions by neonates. *Science, 218,* 179–181.

Field, T., Hernandez-Reif, M., Diego, M., Schanberg, S., & Kahn, C. (2005). Cortisol decreases and serotonin and dopamine increase following massage therapy. *International Journal of Neuroscience, 115,* 1397–1413.

Filsinger, E. E., Braun, J. J., Monte, W. C., & Linder, D. E. (1984). Human (Homo sapiens) responses to the pig (Sus scrofa) sex pheromone 5 alpha-androst-16-en-3-one. *Journal of Comparative Psychology, 98,* 219–222.

Fine, A., Meldrum, B. S., & Patel, S. (1990). Modulation of experimentally induced epilepsy by intracerebral grafts of fetal GABAergic neurons. *Neuropsychologia, 28,* 627–634.

Fink, B., & Penton-Voak, I. (2002). Evolutionary psychology of facial attractiveness. *Current Directions in Psychological Science,11,* 154–158.

Finkelstein, E. A., Trogdon, J. G., Cohen, J. W., & Dietz, W., (2009). Annual medical spending attributable to obesity: Payer-and-service-specific estimates. *Health Affairs, 28,* 822–831.

Finzi, R., Har-Even, D., & Weizman, A. (2003). Comparisons of ego defenses among physically abused children, neglected, and non-maltreated children. *Comprehensive Psychiatry, 44,* 388–395.

Fiore, M. C. (2000). A clinical practice guideline for treating tobacco use and dependence: A US Public Health Service Report. *JAMA: Journal of the American Medical Association, 283,* 3244–3254.

Fiore, M. C., Smith, S. S., Jorenby, D. E., & Baker, T. B. (1994). The effectiveness of the nicotine patch for smoking cessation: A meta-analysis. *JAMA: Journal of the American Medical Association, 271,* 1940–1947.

Fiorito, G., & Scotto, P. (1992). Observational learning in *Octopus vulgaris. Science, 256,* 545–547.

Fischer, A. R., Jome, L. M., & Atkinson, D. R. (1998). Back to the future of multicultural psychotherapy with a common factors approach. *Counseling Psychologist, 26,* 602–606.

Fischer, H., Wik, G., & Fredrikson, M. (1997). Extraversion, neuroticism, and brain function: A PET study of personality. *Personality and Individual Differences, 23,* 345–352.

Fischer, K. W., & Hencke, R. W. (1996). Infants' construction of actions in context: Piaget's contribution to research on early development. *Psychological Science, 7,* 204–210.

Fischer, K. W., & Silvern, L. (1985). Stages and individual differences in cognitive development. *Annual Review of Psychology, 36,* 613–648.

Fisher, C. B., & Fyrberg, D. (1994). Participant partners: College students weigh the costs and benefits of deceptive research. *American Psychologist, 49,* 417–427.

Fisher, C. B., Fried, A. L., & Feldman, L. G. (2009). Graduate socialization in the responsible conduct of research: A national survey on the research ethics training experiences of psychology doctoral students. *Ethics and Behavior, 19,* 496–518.

Fisher, E. B., Delamater, A. M., Bertelson, A. D., & Kirkley, B. G. (1982). Psychological factors in diabetes and its treatment. *Journal of Consulting and Clinical Psychology, 50,* 993–1003.

Fisher, K. (1983, February). TV violence. *APA Monitor,* pp. 7, 9.

Fisher, K. (1985, November). Duty to warn: Where does it end? *APA Monitor,* pp. 24–25.

Fisher, S., & Greenberg, R. P. (1985). *The scientific credibility of Freud's theories and therapy.* New York: Columbia University Press.

Fisher, S., & Greenberg, R. P. (1985). *The scientific credibility of Freud's theories and therapy.* New York: Columbia University Press.

Fiske, D. W., Conley, J. J., & Goldberg, R. P. (1987). E. Lowell Kelly (1905–1986). *American Psychologist, 42,* 511–512.

Fitzgerald, P. B., Hoy, K., Daskalakis, Z. J., & Kulkarni, J. (2009). A randomized trial of the anti-depressant effects of low- and high-frequency transcranial magnetic stimulation in treatment-resistant depression. *Depression and Anxiety, 26,* 229–234.

Flack, W. F., Jr., Laird, J. D., & Cavallaro, L. A. (1999). Separate and combined effects of facial expressions and bodily postures on emotional feelings. *European Journal of Social Psychology, 29,* 203–217.

Flannagan, D. A., & Blick, K. A. (1989). Levels of processing and the retention of word meanings. *Perceptual and Motor Skills, 68,* 1123–1128.

Flay, B. R. (1985). Psychosocial approaches to smoking prevention: A review of findings. *Health Psychology, 4,* 449–488.

Fleming, V. M. (2002). Improving students' exam performance by introducing study strategies and goal setting. *Teaching of Psychology, 29,* 115–119.

Flesher, M. M., Butt, A. E., & Kinney-Hurd, B. L. (2011). Differential acetylcholine release in the prefrontal cortex and hippocampus during Pavlovian trace and delay conditioning. *Neurobiology of Learning and Memory, 96,* 181–191.

Florack, A., Piontkowski, U., Bohman, A., Balzer, T., & Perzig, S. (2003). Perceived intergroup threat and attitudes of host community members toward immigrant acculturation. *Journal of Social Psychology, 143,* 633–648.

Flores, S. A., & Hartlaub, M. G. (1998). Reducing rape-myth acceptance in male college students: A meta-analysis of intervention studies. *Journal of College Student Development, 39,* 438–448.

Flor-Henry, P. (1983). Mood, the right hemisphere, and the implications of spatial information-perceiving systems. *Research Communications in Psychology, Psychiatry, and Behavior, 8,* 143–170.

Floyd, M., McKendree-Smith, N. L., & Scogin, F. R. (2004). Remembering the 1978 and 1990 task forces on self–help therapies: A response to Gerald Rosen. *Journal of Clinical Psychology, 60,* 115–117.

Floyd, M., Scogin, F., McKendree-Smith, N. L., Floyd, D. L., & Rokke, P. D. (2004). Cognitive therapy for depression: A comparison of individual psychotherapy and bibliotherapy for depressed older adults. *Behavior Modification, 28,* 297–318.

Flynn, J. R. (1987). Massive IQ gains in 14 nations: What IQ tests really measure. *Psychological Bulletin, 101,* 171–191.

Foa, E. B., Dancu, C. V., Hembree, E. A., Jaycox, L. H., Meadows, E. A., & Street, G. P. (1999). Comparison of exposure therapy, stress inoculation training, and their combination for reducing posttraumatic stress disorder in female assault victims. *Journal of Consulting and Clinical Psychology, 67,* 194–200.

Foerstl, J. (1989). Early interest in the idiot savant. *American Journal of Psychiatry, 146,* 566.

Fogarty, G. J. (1994). Using the Personal Orientation Inventory to measure change in student self-actualization. *Personality and Individual Differences, 17,* 435–439.

Fogel, R. B., Malhotra, A., Dalagiorgou, G., Robinson, M. K., Jakab, M., Kikinis, R., . . . White, D. P. (2003). Anatomic and physiologic predictors of apnea severity in morbidly obese subjects. *Sleep: Journal of Sleep and Sleep Disorders Research, 26,* 150–155.

Folkes, V. S. (1982). Forming relationships and the matching hypothesis. *Personality and Social Psychology Bulletin, 8,* 631–636.

Folkes, V. S. (1988). The availability heuristic and perceived risk. *Journal of Consumer Research, 15,* 13–23.

Fontaine, K. R., & Shaw, D. F. (1995). Effects of self-efficacy and dispositional optimism on adherence to step aerobic exercise classes. *Perceptual and Motor Skill, 81,* 251–255.

Fontana, A. M., Diegman, T., Villeneuve, A., & Lepore, A. J. (1999). Nonevaluative social support reduces cardiovascular reactivity in young women during acutely stressful performance situations. *Journal of Behavioral Medicine, 22,* 75–91.

Folkman, S., & Moskowitz, J. T. (2000). Stress, positive emotion, and coping. *Current Directions in Psychological Science, 9, 115–118.*

Foltin, R. W., Fischman, M. W., & Levin, F. R. (1995). Cardiovascular effects of cocaine in humans: Laboratory studies. *Drug and Alcohol Dependence, 37,* 193–210.

Forchuk, C., Godin, M., Hoch, J. S., Kingston-MacClure, S., Jeng, M. S., Puddy, L., . . . Jensen, E. (2013). Preventing homelessness after discharge from psychiatric wards: Perspectives of consumers and staff. *Journal of Psychosocial Nursing & Mental Health Services, 51,* 25–31.

Ford, B. D. (1993). Emergenesis: An alternative and a confound. *American Psychologist, 48,* 1294.

Forehand, M. R., Deshpanda, R., & Reed, A. (2002). Identity salience and the influence of the social self-schema on advertising response. *Journal of Applied Psychology, 87,* 1086–1099.

Foret, A., Quertainmont, R., Botman, O., Bouhy, D., Amabili, P., Brook, G., . . . Franzen, R. (2010). Stem cells in the adult rat spinal cord: Plasticity after injury and treadmill training exercise. *Journal of Neurochemistry, 112,* 762–772.

Foreyt, J. P. (1987). Issues in the assessment and treatment of obesity. *Journal of Consulting and Clinical Psychology, 55,* 677–684.

Foreyt, J. P., & Goodrick, G. K. (1994). Impact of behavior therapy on weight loss. *American Journal of Health Promotion, 8,* 466–468.

Forgas, J. P., Dunn, E., & Granland, S. (2008). Are you being served. . .? An unobtrusive experiment of affective influences on helping in a department store. *European Journal of Social Psychology, 38,* 333–343.

Forsyth, D. R., Zyzniewski, L. E., & Giammanco, C. A. (2002). Responsibility diffusion in cooperative collectives. *Personality and Social Psychology Bulletin, 28,* 54–65.

Foster, J. K., Lidder, P. G., & Suenram, S. I. (1998). Glucose and memory: Fractionation of enhancement effects? *Psychopharmacology, 137,* 259–270.

Foster-Schubert, K. E., Alfano, C. M., Duggan, C. R., Xiao, L., Campbell, K. L., Kong, A., . . . McTiernan, A. (2012). Effect of diet and exercise, alone or combined, on weight and body composition in overweight-to-obese postmenopausal women. *Obesity, 20,* 1628–1638.

Fox, B. H., & Farrington, D. P. (2012). Creating burglary profiles using latent class analysis: A new approach to offender profiling.. *Criminal Justice and Behavior, 39,* 1582–1611.

Fox, E., Lester, V., Russo, R., Bowles, R. J., Pichler, A., & Dutton, K. (2000). Facial expressions of emotion: Are angry faces detected more efficiently? *Cognition and Emotion, 14,* 61–92.

Fox, L. H. (1981). Identification of the academically gifted. *American Psychologist, 36,* 1103–1111.

Fox, N. A., & Davidson, R. J. (1988). Patterns of brain electrical activity during facial signs of emotion in 10-month-old infants. *Developmental Psychology, 24,* 230–236.

Fox, S. E., & Burns, D. J. (1993). The mere exposure effect for stimuli presented below recognition threshold: A failure to replicate. *Perceptual and Motor Skills, 76,* 391–396.

Fraley, C.R., Roisman, G. I., Booth-LaForce, C. Owen, M.T., & Holland, A. S. (2013). Interpersonal and genetic origins of adult attachment styles: A longitudinal study from infancy to early adulthood. *Journal of Personality and Social Psychology, 104,* 817–838.

France, C. R., France, J. L., al'Absi, M., Ring, C., & McIntyre, D. (2002). Catastrophizing is related to pain ratings, but not nociceptive flexion reflex threshold. *Pain, 99,* 459–463.

Frank, D. A., Brown, J., Johnson, S., & Cabral, H. (2002). Forgotten fathers: An exploratory study of mothers' report of drug and alcohol problems among fathers of urban newborns. *Neurotoxicology & Teratology, 24,* 339–347.

Frank, E., & Brandstaetter, V. (2002). Approach versus avoidance: Different types of commitment in intimate relationships. *Journal of Personality and Social Psychology, 82,* 208–221.

Frank, M. G., & Stennett, J. (2001). The forced-choice paradigm and the perception of facial expressions of emotion. *Journal of Personality and Social Psychology, 80,* 75–85.

Frankel, R. M. (1995). Emotion and the physician-patient relationship. *Motivation and Emotion, 19,* 163–173.

Franklin, B. et al. (1784/2002). Report by the commissioners charged by the King with the examination of animal magnetism [reprint]. *International Journal of Clinical and Experimental Hypnosis, 50,* 332–363.

Franko, D. L., & Herrera, I. (1997). Body image differences in Guatemalan-American and White college women. *Eating Disorders: The Journal of Treatment and Prevention, 5,* 119–127.

Fraser, S. (Ed.). (1995). *The bell curve wars: Race, intelligence, and the future of America.* New York: Basic Books.

Frederick, C. M., & Ryan, R. M. (1995). Self-determination in sport: A review using cognitive evaluation theory. *International Journal of Sport Psychology, 26,* 5–23.

Frederiksen, N. (1986). Toward a broader conception of human intelligence. *American Psychologist, 41,* 445–452.

Fredrikson, M., Annas, P., Fischer, H., & Wik, G. (1996). Gender and age differences in the prevalence of specific fears and phobias. *Behaviour Research and Therapy, 34,* 33–39.

Freedman, J. L. (1984). Effect of television violence on aggressiveness. *Psychological Bulletin, 96,* 227–246.

Freedman, J. L., & Fraser, S. C. (1966). Compliance without pressure. *Journal of Personality and Social Psychology, 4,* 195–202.

Freedman, M. A. (2002). Quality of life and menopause: The role of estrogen. *Journal of Women's Health, 11,* 703–718.

Freedman, R., Lewis, D. A., Michels, R., Pine, D. S., Schultz, Tamminga, C. A., . . . Yager, J. (2013). The initial field trials of DSM-5: New blooms and old thorns. *American Journal of Psychiatry, 170,* 1–5.

Freeman, A. (1999). Will increasing our social interest bring about a loss of our innocence? *Journal of Individual Psychology, 55,* 130–145.

Freeman, C. (1998). Drug treatment for bulimia nervosa. *Neuropsychobiology, 37,* 72–79.

Freeman, J., Palk, J., & Davey, J. (2010). Sex offenders in denial: A study into a group of forensic psychologists' attitudes regarding the corresponding impact upon risk assessment calculations and parole eligibility. *Journal of Forensic Psychiatry and Psychology, 21,* 39–51.

Freeman, R., Barabasz, A., Barabasz, M., & Warner, D. (2000). Hypnosis and distraction differ in their effects on cold pressor pain. *American Journal of Clinical Hypnosis, 43,* 137–148.

Freeman, W. (1948). Transorbital leucotomy. *Lancet, 255,* 371–373.

Freivalds, A., & Horii, K. (1994). An oculomotor test to measure alcohol impairment. *Perceptual and Motor Skills, 78,* 603–610.

French, D. C., Jansen, E. A., & Pidada, S. (2002). United States and Indonesian children's and adolescents' reports of relational aggression by disliked peers. *Child Development, 73,* 1143–1150.

French, S. E., & Holland, K. J. (2013). Condom negotiation strategies as a mediator of the relationship between self-efficacy and condom use. *Journal of Sex Research, 50,* 48–59.

Frenda, S. J., Nichols, R. M., & Loftus, E. F. (2011). Current issues and advances in misinformation research. *Current Directions in Psychological Science, 20,* 20–23.

Freud, S. (1900/1990). *The interpretation of dreams.* New York: Basic Books.

Freud, S. (1901/1965). *Psychopathology of everyday life.* New York: W. W. Norton.

Freud, S. (1901/2011). *The psychopathology of everyday life.* Eastford, CT: Martino.

Freud, S. (1905). *Jokes and their relationship to the unconscious.* London: Hogarth Press.

Freud, S. (1914/1957). On the history of the psychoanalytic movement. In J. Strachey (Ed.), *The standard edition of the complete psychological works of Sigmund Freud, Vol. 14* (pp. 7–66). London: Hogarth Press.

Freud, S. (1917/1963). Mourning and melancholia. In J. Strachey (Ed.), *The standard edition of the complete psychological works of Sigmund Freud, Vol. 14* (pp. 243–258). London: Hogarth Press.

Freud, S. (1974). *Cocaine papers* (R. Byck, Ed.). New York: Stonehill.

Freund, A. M., & Baltes, P. B. (1998). Selection, optimization, and compensation as strategies of life management: Correlations with subjective indicators of successful aging. *Psychology of Aging, 13,* 531–543.

Frick, R. W. (1985). Communicating emotion: The role of prosodic features. *Psychological Bulletin, 97,* 412–429.

Friedman, M., & Rosenman, R. H. (1974). *Type A behavior and your heart.* New York: Knopf.

Frisco, M. L., & Williams, K. (2003). Perceived housework equity, marital happiness, and divorce in dual-earner households. *Journal of Family Issues, 24,* 51–73.

Fritsch, G., & Hitzig, E. (1870/1960). *On the electrical excitability of the cerebrum.* Springfield, IL: Thomas

Fritzsche, B. A., Finkelstein, M. A., & Penner, L. A. (2000). To help or not to help: Capturing individuals' decision policies. *Social Behavior and Personality, 28,* 561–578.

Froming, W. J., Nasby, W., & McManus, J. (1998). Prosocial self-schemas, self-awareness, and children's prosocial behavior. *Journal of Personality and Social Psychology, 75,* 766–777.

Fromm, E. (1941). *Escape from freedom.* New York: Holt, Rinehart & Winston.

Froufe, M., & Schwartz, C. (2001). Subliminal messages for increasing self-esteem: Placebo effect. *Spanish Journal of Psychology, 4,* 19–25.

Fuchs, A. H. (1998). Psychology and "The Babe." *Journal of the History of the Behavioral Sciences, 34,* 153–165.

Fuchs, A. H., & Viney, W. (2002). The course in the history of psychology: Present status and future concerns. *Journal of the History of the Behavioral Sciences, 5,* 3–15.

Fuchs-Beauchamp, K. D., Karnes, M. B., & Johnson, L. J. (1993). Creativity and intelligence in preschoolers. *Gifted Child Quarterly, 37,* 113–117.

Fudin, R. (2001). Problems in Silverman's work indicate the need for a new approach to research on subliminal psychodynamic activation. *Perceptual and Motor Skills, 92,* 611–622.

Fujita, K. (1996). Linear perspective and the Ponzo illusion: A comparison between rhesus monkeys and humans. *Japanese Psychological Research, 38,* 136–145.

Fujita, K., Blough, D. S., & Blough, P. M. (1993). Effects of the inclination of context lines on perception of the Ponzo illusion by pigeons. *Animal Learning and Behavior, 21,* 29–34.

Fulker, D. W., DeFries, J. C., & Plomin, R. (1988). Genetic influence on general mental ability increases between infancy and middle childhood. *Nature, 336,* 767–769.

Fullerton, A. S., & Dixon, J. C. (2010). Generational conflict or methodological artifact? Reconsidering the relationship between age and policy attitudes in the U.S., 1984–2008. *Public Opinion Quarterly, 74,* 643–673.

Fundytus, M. E. (2001). Glutamate receptors and nociception: Implications for the drug treatment of pain. *CNS Drugs, 15,* 29–58.

Furman, W. (2002). The emerging field of adolescent romantic relationships. *Current Directions in Psychological Science, 11,* 177–180.

Furnham, A., & Lim, A.-N. (1997). Cross-cultural differences in the perception of male and female body shapes as a function of exercise. *Journal of Social Behavior and Personality, 12,* 1037–1053.

Furnham, A., & Strbac, L. (2002). Music is as distracting as noise: The differential distraction of background music and noise on the cognitive test performance of introverts and extraverts. *Ergonomics, 45,* 203–217.

Furnham, A., & Thompson, J. (1991). Personality and self-reported delinquency. *Personality and Individual Differences, 12,* 585–593.

Furumoto, L. (1980).Mary Whiton Calkins (1863–1930). *Psychology of Women Quarterly, 5,* 94–102.

G

Gabrieli, J. D. E., Fleischman, D. A., Keane, M. M., & Reminger, S. L. (1995). Double dissociation between memory systems underlying explicit and implicit memory in the human brain. *Psychological Science, 6,* 76–82.

Gaffan, E. A., Tsaousis, J., & Kemp-Wheeler, S. M. (1995). Researcher allegiance and meta-analysis: The case of cognitive therapy for depression. *Journal of Consulting and Clinical Psychology, 63,* 966–980.

Galak, J., LeBoeuf, R. A., Nelson, L. D., & Simmons, J. P. (2012). Correcting the past: Failures to replicate psi. *Journal of Personality & Social Psychology, 103,* 933–948.

Galanter, E. (1962). *New directions in psychology.* New York: Holt, Rinehart & Winston.

Galati, D., Miceli, R., & Sini, B. (2001). Judging and coding facial expression of emotions in congenitally blind children. *International Journal of Behavioral Development, 25,* 268–278.

Galef, B. G. (1993). Functions of social learning about food: A causal analysis of effects of diet novelty on preference transmission. *Animal Behaviour, 46,* 257–265.

Galef, B. G., Jr. (1980). Diving for food: Analysis of a possible case of social learning in wild rats (*Rattus norvegicus*). *Journal of Comparative and Physiological Psychology, 94,* 416–425.

Gallacher, J. E. J., Hopkinson, C. A., Bennett, P., Burr, M. L., & Elwood, P. C. (1997). Effect of stress management on angina. *Psychology and Health, 12,* 523–532.

Galton, F. (1869). *Hereditary genius.* London: Macmillan.

Gamaro, G. D., Denardin, J. D., Michalowski, M. B., Catelli, D., Correa, J. B., Xavier, M. H., & Dalmaz, C. (1997). Epinephrine effects on memory are not dependent on hepatic glucose release. *Neurobiology of Learning and Memory, 68,* 221–229.

Gana, K., & Boblique, C. (2000). Coping and burnout among police officers and teachers: Test of a model. *European Review of Applied Psychology, 50,* 423–430.

Ganchrow, J. R., Steiner, J. E., & Daher, M. (1983). Neonatal facial expressions in response to different qualities and intensities of gustatory stimuli. *Infant Behavior and Development, 6,* 189–200.

Gandour, J., Larsen, J., Dechongkit, S., & Ponglorpisit, S. (1995). Speech prosody in affective contexts in Thai patients with right hemisphere lesions. *Brain & Language, 51,* 422–443.

Gangestad, S., & Snyder, M. (1985). "To carve nature at its joints": On the existence of discrete classes in personality. *Psychological Review, 92,* 317–349.

Gannon, L., Luchetta, T., Rhodes, K., Pardie, L., & Segrist, D. (1992). Sex bias in psychological research: Progress or complacency? *American Psychologist, 47,* 389–396.

Ganong, L., Coleman, M., Fine, M., & Martin, P. (1999). Stepparents' affinity-seeking and affinity-maintaining strategies with stepchildren. *Journal of Family Issues, 20,* 299–327.

Gansberg, M. (1964, March 27). Thirty-seven who saw murder didn't call the police. *New York Times,* pp. 1, 38.

Garcia, D., Archer, T., Moradi, S., & Andersson-Arntén, A.-C. (2012). Exercise frequency, high activation positive affect, and psychological well-being: Beyond age, gender, and occupation. *Psychology, 3,* 328–336.

Garcia, E. E. (1990). A brief note on "Jekyll and Hyde" and MPD. *Dissociation: Progress in the Dissociative Disorders, 3,* 165–166.

Garcia, J. (1981). Tilting at the paper mills of academe. *American Psychologist, 36,* 149–158.

Garcia, J., & Gustavson, A. R. (1997, January). Carl R. Gustavson (1946-1996): Pioneering wildlife psychologist. *APS Observer,* pp. 34–35.

Garcia, J., & Koelling, R. A. (1966). The relation of cue to consequence in avoidance learning. *Psychonomic Science, 4,* 123–124.

Garcia, J., Kimeldorf, D. J., Hunt, E. L., & Davies, B. P. (1956). Food and water consumption of rats during exposure to gamma radiation. *Radiation Research, 4,* 33–41.

Garcia, L. T., & Hoskins, R. (2001). Actual-ideal self discrepancy and sexual esteem and depression. *Journal of Psychology and Human Sexuality, 13,* 49–61.

Garcia-Bajos, E., & Migueles, M. (2003). False memories for script actions in a mugging account. *European Journal of Cognitive Psychology, 15,* 195–208.

Garcia-Larrea, L., Perchet, C., Perrin, F., & Amenedo, E. (2001). Interference of celular phone conversations with visuomotor tasks: An ERP study. *Journal of Psychophysiology, 15,* 14–21.

Garcia-Vera, M. P., Labrador, F. J., & Sanz, J. (1997). Stress-management training for essential hypertension: A controlled study. *Applied Psychophysiology and Biofeedback, 22,* 261–283.

Gardener, H., Munrer, K., Chitnis, T., Spiegelman, D., & Ascherio, A.(2009). The relationship between handedness and risk of multiple sclerosis. *Multiple Sclerosis, 15,* 587–592.

Gardner, D. G. (1986). Activation theory and task design: An empirical test of several new predictions. *Journal of Applied Psychology, 71,* 411–418.

Gardner, H. (1983). *Frames of mind: The theory of multiple intelligences.* New York: Basic Books.

Gardner, H. (2000). A case against spiritual intelligence. *International Journal for the Psychology of Religion, 10,* 27–34.

Gardner, R. A., Gardner, B. T., & Van Cantfort, T. E. (Eds.). (1989). *Teaching sign language to chimpanzees.* Albany: State University of New York Press.

Garfield, C. F., Dorsey, E. R., Zhu, S., Huskamp, H. A, Conti, R., Dusetzina, S. B., . . . Alexander, G. C. (2012). Trends in attention deficit hyperactivity disorder ambulatory diagnosis and medical treatment in the United States, 2000–2010. *Academic Pediatrics, 12,* 110–6.

Garmon, L. C., Basinger, K. S., Gregg, V. R., & Gibbs, J. C. (1996). Gender differences in stage and expression of moral judgment. *Merrill-Palmer Quarterly, 42,* 418–437.

Garonzik, R. (1989). Hand dominance and implications for left-handed operation of controls. *Ergonomics, 32,* 1185–1192.

Garrison, D. W., & Foreman, R. D. (1994). Decreased activity of spontaneous and noxiously evoked dorsal horn cells during transcutaneous electrical nerve stimulation (TENS). *Pain, 58,* 309–315.

Gater, R., Tansella, M., Korten, A., Tiemens, G. B., Mavreas, V. G., & Olatawura, M. O. (1998). Sex differences in the prevalence and detection of depressive and anxiety disorders in general health care settings: Report from the World Health Organization collaborative study on psychological problems in general health care. *Archives of General Psychiatry, 55,* 405–413.

Gathercole, S. E., & Conway, M. A. (1988). Exploring long-term modality effects: Vocalization leads to best retention. *Memory and Cognition, 16,* 110–119.

Gaukroger, S. (2009). The role of natural philosophy in the development of Locke's empiricism. *British Journal for the History of Philosophy, 17,* 55–83.

Gauld, A. O. (1990). The early history of hypnotic skin marking and blistering. *British Journal of Experimental and Clinical Hypnosis, 7,* 139–152.

Gawin, F. H. (1991). Cocaine addiction: Psychology and neurophysiology. *Science, 251,* 1580–1586.

Gay, P. (1988). *Freud: A life for our time.* New York: W.W. Norton.

Gay, V. (1986). Augustine: The reader as self-object. *Journal for the Scientific Study of Religion, 25,* 64–76.

Gazzaniga, M. S. (1967, August). The split brain in man. *Scientific American,* pp. 24–29.

Gazzaniga, M. S. (1983). Right hemisphere language following brain bisection: A 20-year perspective. *American Psychologist, 38,* 525–537.

Gazzaniga, M. S. (2005). Forty-five years of split-brain research and still going strong. *Nature Reviews; Neuroscience, 6,* 653–659.

Gazzola, N., & Stalikas,a. (1997). An investigation of counselor interpretations in client–centered therapy. *Journal of Psychotherapy Integration, 7,* 313–327.

Geen, R. G. (1984). Preferred stimulation levels in introverts and extraverts: Effects on arousal and performance. *Journal of Personality and Social Psychology, 46,* 1303–1312.

Gelb, S. A. (1986). Henry H. Goddard and the immigrants, 1910–1917: The studies and their social context. *Journal of the History of the Behavioral Sciences, 22,* 324–332.

Gelernter, J., Page, G. P., Bonvicini, K., Woods, S. W., Pauls, D. L., & Kruger, S. (2003). A chromosome 14 risk locus for simple phobia: Results from a genomewide linkage scan. *Molecular Psychiatry, 8,* 71–82.

Geller, L. (1982, Spring). The failure of self-actualization theory: A critique of Carl Rogers and Abraham Maslow. *Journal of Humanistic Psychology, 22,* 56–73.

Gelman, D., Foote, D., Barrett, T., & Talbot, M. (1992, February 24). Born or bred? *Newsweek,* pp. 46–53.

Geracioti, T. D., & Liddle, R. A. (1988). Impaired cholecystokinin secretion in bulimia nervosa. *New England Journal of Medicine, 319,* 683–688.

Gerra, G., Zaimovic, A., Timpano, M., Zambelli, U., Delsignore, R., & Brambilla, F. (2000). Neuroendocrine correlations of temperamental traits in humans. *Psychoneuroendocrinology, 25,* 479–496.

Gerrard, M. (1987). Sex, sex guilt, and contraceptive use revisited: The 1980s. *Journal of Personality and Social Psychology, 52,* 975–980.

Gershoff, E. T. (2002). Corporal punishment by parents and associated child behaviors and experiences: A meta-analytic and theoretical review. *Psychological Bulletin, 128,* 539–579.

Gervais-Bernard, H., Xie–Brustolin, J., Mertens, P., Polo, G., Klinger, H., Adamec, D., . . . Thobois, S. (2009). Bilateral subthalamic nucleus stimulation in advanced Parkinson's Disease: Five year follow-up. *Journal of Neurology, 256,* 225–233.

Gescheider, G. A., Beiles, E. J., Checkosky, C. M., & Bolanowski, S. J. (1994). The effects of aging on information processing channels in the sense of touch: II. Temporal summation in the P channel. *Somatosensory and Motor Research, 11,* 359–365.

Geschwind, N. (1979, September). Specializations of the human brain. *Scientific American,* pp. 180–199.

Getlin, J. (2000, June 15). Outrage in N.Y. over assaults: Giuliani says videotapes will be used to identify attackers of women in Central Park, and allegedly uncaring police. *Los Angeles Times,* p. A5.

Gfellner, B. M., & Hundleby, J. D. (1994). Developmental and gender differences in drug use and problem behaviour during adolescence. *Journal of Child and Adolescent Substance Abuse, 3,* 59–74.

Giannakoulas, G., Katramados, A., Melas, N., Diamantopoulos, I., & Chimonas, E. (2003). Acute effects of nicotine withdrawal syndrome in pilots during flight. *Aviation, Space, and Environmental Medicine, 74,* 247–251.

Gibbons, B. (1986). The intimate sense of smell. *National Geographic, 170,* 324–361.

Gibbons, P., Mulryan, N., & O'Connor, A. (1997). Guilty but insane: The insanity defence in Ireland, 1850–1995. *British Journal of Psychiatry, 170,* 467–472.

Gibbs, E. D., Teti, D. M., & Bond, L. A. (1987). Infant-sibling communication: Relationships to birth-spacing and cognitive and linguistic development. *Infant Behavior and Development, 10,* 307–323.

Gibson, B., Sachau, D., Doll, B., & Shumate, R. (2002). Sandbagging in competition: Responding to the pressure of being the favorite. *Personality and Social Psychology Bulletin, 28,* 1119–1130.

Gibson, E. J., & Walk, R. D. (1960, April). The visual cliff. *Scientific American,* pp. 67–71.

Gibson, H. B. (1991). Can hypnosis compel people to commit harmful, immoral and criminal acts? A review of the literature. *Contemporary Hypnosis, 8,* 129–140.

Gibson, J. J. (1979). *The ecological approach to visual perception.* Boston: Houghton Mifflin.

Gidron, Y., Davidson, K., & Bata, I. (1999). The short-term effects of a hostility-reduction intervention on male coronary heart disease patients. *Health Psychology, 18,* 416–420.

Giesler, G. J., Katter, J. T., & Dado, R. J. (1994). Direct spinal pathways to the limbic system for nociceptive information. *Trends in Neurosciences, 17,* 244–250.

Gilbert, A. K. (2003). The contribution of descending fibers from the rostral ventromedial medulla to nociception, and to opioid and non-opioid analgesia. *Dissertation Abstracts International: Section B: The Sciences and Engineering, 63,* 3507.

Gilbert, C. (2003). Clinical applications of breathing regulation: Beyond anxiety management. *Behavior Modification, 27,* 692–709.

Gilbert, H. M., & Warburton, D. M. (2000). Craving: A problematic concept in smoking research. *Addiction Research, 8,* 381–397.

Gilbert, S. J. (1981). Another look at the Milgram obedience studies: The role of the graduated series of shocks. *Personality and Social Psychology Bulletin, 7,* 690–695.

Gilbert, T., Martin, R., & Coulson, M. (2010). Attentional biases using the body in the crowd task: Are angry body postures detected more rapidly? *Cognition and Emotion, 25,* 700–708.

Gilchrist, H., Povey, R., Dickinson, A., & Povey, R. (1995). The Sensation Seeking Scale: Its use in a study of the characteristics of people choosing "adventure holidays." *Personality and Individual Differences, 19,* 513–516.

Gill, D. (1980). *Quest: The life of Elisabeth Kübler-Ross.* New York: Harper & Row.

Gillam, B. (1980, January). Geometrical illusions. *Scientific American,* pp. 102–111.

Gillam, B. (1992). The status of perceptual grouping 70 years after Wertheimer. *Australian Journal of Psychology, 44,* 157–162.

Gilligan, C. (1982). *In a different voice: Psychological theory and women's development.* Cambridge, MA: Harvard University Press.

Gilman, S., Chervin, R. D., Koeppe, R. A., Consens, F. B., Little, R., An, H., . . . Heumann, M. (2003). Obstructive sleep apnea is related to a thalamic cholinergic deficit in MSA. *Neurology, 61,* 35–39.

Ginandes, C., Brooks, P., Sando, W., Jones, C., & Aker, J. (2003). Can medical hypnosis accelerate post-surgical wound healing? Results of a clinical trial. *American Journal of Clinical Hypnosis, 45,* 333–351.

Girandola, F. (2002). Sequential requests and organ donation. *Journal of Social Psychology, 142,* 171–178.

Ginis, K. A. M., Jetha, A., Dack, D. E., & Hetz, S. (2010). Physical activity and subjective well-being among people with spinal cord injury: A meta-analysis. *Spinal Cord, 48,* 65–72.

Giovanni, G. D. (2008). Will it ever become possible to prevent dopaminergic neuronal degeneration? *CNS and Neurological Disorders, 7,* 28–44.

Giovannini, D., & Ricci Bitti, P. E. (1981). Culture and sex effect in recognizing emotions by facial and gestural cues. *Italian Journal of Psychology, 8,* 95–102.

Gisiner, R., & Schusterman, R. J. (1992). Sequence, syntax, and semantics: Responses of a language-trained sea lion (*Zalophus californianus*) to novel sign combinations. *Journal of Comparative Psychology, 106,* 78–91.

Gitau, R., Modi, N., Gianakoulopoulos, X., Bond, C., Glover, V., & Stevenson, J. (2002). Acute effects of maternal skin-to-skin contact and massage on saliva cortisol in preterm babies. *Journal of Reproductive and Infant Psychology, 20,* 83–88.

Gizer, I. R., Ficks, C., & Waldman, I. D. (2009). Candidate gene studies of ADHD: A meta-analytic review. *Human Genetics, 126,* 51–90.

Glancy, G. D., Regehr, C., & Bryant, A. G. (1998). Confidentiality in crisis: Part II—Confidentiality of treatment records. *Canadian Journal of Psychiatry, 43,* 1006–1011.

Gläscher, J., Adolphs, R., Damasio, H., Bechara, A., Rudrauf, D., Calamia, M., . . . Trane, D. (2012). Lesion mapping of cognitive control and value-based decision making in the prefrontal cortex. *Proceedings of the National Academy of Sciences, 109,* 14681–14686.

Glaser, R., Rice, J., Speicher, C. E., Stout, J. C., & Kiecolt-Glaser, J. K. (1986). Stress depresses interferon production by leukocytes concomitant with a decrease in natural killer cell activity. *Behavioral Neuroscience, 100,* 675–678.

Gleaves, D. H. (1996). The sociocognitive model of dissociative identity disorder: A reexamination of the evidence. *Psychological Bulletin, 120,* 42–59.

Gleitman, H., Rozin, P., & Sabini, J. (1997). Solomon E. Asch (1907–1996): Obituary. *American Psychologist, 52,* 984–985.

Glen, L., & Anderson, J. A. (1989). Medication and the elderly: A review. *Journal of Geriatric Drug Therapy, 4,* 59–89.

Glenn, C. R., Klein, D. N., Lissek, S., Britton, J. C., Pine, D. S., & Hajcak, G. (2012). The development of fear learning and generalization in 8–13 year-olds. *Developmental Psychobiology, 54,* 675–684.

Glenn, S. S., & Ellis, J. (1988). Do the Kallikaks look "menacing" or "retarded"? *American Psychologist, 43,* 742–743.

Glennon, R. A. (1990). Do classical hallucinogens act as 5-HT-sub-2 agonists or antagonists? *Neuropsychopharmacology, 3,* 509–517.

Glick, P., Fiske, S. T., Mladinic, A., Saiz, J. L., Abrams, D., Masser, B., . . . Lopez, W. L. (2000). Beyond prejudice as simple antipathy: Hostile and benevolent sexism across cultures. *Journal of Personality and Social Psychology, 79,* 763–775.

Glickstein, M., Waller, J., Baizer, J. S., Brown, B., & Timmann, D. (2005). Cerebellum lesions and finger use. *Cerebellum, 4,* 189–197.

Gliedman, J. (1983, November). Interview with Noam Chomsky. *Omni,* pp. 112–118, 171–174.

Gloor, P. (1994). Is Berger's dream coming true? *Electroencephalography and Clinical Neurophysiology, 90,* 253–266.

Glover, E., & Ginsberg, M. (1934). A symposium on the psychology of peace and war. *British Journal of Medical Psychology, 14,* 274–293.

Gluck, M. A., & Myers, C. E. (1995). Representation and association in memory: A neurocomputational view of hippocampal function. *Current Directions in Psychological Science, 4,* 23–29.

Glucksberg, S., & Danks, J. H. (1968). Effects of discriminative labels and of nonsense labels upon availability of novel functions. *Journal of Verbal Learning and Verbal Behavior, 7,* 72–76.

Gobet, F., & Simon, H. A. (1998). Expert chess memory: Revisiting the chunking hypothesis. *Memory, 6,* 225–255.

Goddard, C. (2003). Thinking across language and cultures: Six dimensions of variation. *Cognitive Linguistics, 14,* 109–140.

Goddard, H. H. (1912). *The Kallikak family: A study in the heredity of feeblemindedness.* New York: Macmillan.

Goddard, H. H. (1917). Mental tests and the immigrant. *Journal of Delinquency, 2,* 243–277.

Godden, D. R., & Baddeley, A. D. (1975). Context-dependent memory in two natural environments: On land and under water. *British Journal of Psychology, 66,* 325–331.

Godemont, M. (1992). Six hundred years of family care in Geel, Belgium: 600 years of familiarity with madness in town life. *Community Alternatives: International Journal of Family Care, 4,* 155–168.

"God's hand": Legless veteran crawls to save life of a baby. (1986, June 6). *Philadelphia Inquirer,* pp. 1-A, 24-A.

Goebel, B. L., & Boeck, B. E. (1987). Ego integrity and fear of death: A comparison of institutionalized and independently living older adults. *Death Studies, 11,* 193–204.

Goebel, B. L., & Brown, D. R. (1981). Age differences in motivation related to Maslow's need hierarchy. *Developmental Psychology, 17,* 809–815.

Goisman, R. M. (1983). Therapeutic approaches to phobia: A comparison. *American Journal of Psychotherapy, 37,* 227–234.

Gold, M. S., Pottash, A. L. C., Sweeney, D. R., Martin, D. M., & Davies, R. K. (1980). Further evidence of hypothalamic-pituitary dysfunction in anorexia nervosa. *American Journal of Psychiatry, 137,* 101–102.

Gold, P. E. (2003). Acetylcholine modulation of neural systems involved in learning and memory. *Neurobiology of Learning & Memory, 80,* 194–210.

Goldberg, M. A., & Remy-St. Louis, G. (1998). Understanding and treating pain in ethnically diverse patients. *Journal of Clinical Psychology in Medical Settings, 5,* 343–356.

Goldbloom, D. S., Olmsted, M., Davis, R., Clewes, J., Heinmaa, M., Rockert, W., & Shaw, B. (1997). A randomized controlled trial of fluoxetine and cognitive behavioral therapy for bulimia nervosa: Short-term outcome. *Behaviour Research and Therapy, 35,* 803–811.

Golden-Meadow, S., & Mylander, C. (1998). Spontaneous sign systems created by deaf children in two cultures. *Nature, 391,* 279–281.

Golding, J. F., Bles, W., Bos, J. E., Haynes, T., & Gresty, M. A. (2003). Motion sickness and tilts of the inertial force environment: Active suspension systems vs. active passengers. *Aviation, Space, and Environmental Medicine, 74,* 220–227.

Goldman, D. L. (1990). Dorothea Dix and her two missions of mercy in Nova Scotia. *Canadian Journal of Psychiatry, 35,* 139–143.

Goldman, H. H. (1998). Deinstitutionalization and community care: Social welfare policy as mental health policy. *Harvard Review of Psychiatry, 6,* 219–222.

Goldman, M., & Fordyce, J. (1983). Prosocial behavior as affected by eye contact, touch, and voice expression. *Journal of Social Psychology, 121,* 125–129.

Goldman-Rakic, P. S. (1996). The prefrontal landscape: implications of functional architecture for understanding human mentation and the central executive. *Philosophical Transactions of the Royal Society of London. Series B, Biological Sciences, 35,* 1445–1453.

Goldstein, A. (1980). Thrills in response to music and other stimuli. *Physiological Psychology, 8,* 126–129.

Goldstein, S. R., & Hall, D. (1990). Variable ratio control of the spitting response in the archer fish (*Toxotes jaculator*). *Journal of Comparative Psychology, 104,* 373–376.

Golombok, S., & Tasker, F. (1996). Do parents influence the sexual orientation of their children? Findings from a longitudinal study of lesbian families. *Developmental Psychology, 32,* 3–11.

Gonzalez, A. B., Salas, D., & Umpierrez, G. E. (2011). Special considerations on the management of Latino patients with type 2 diabetes mellitus. *Current Medical Research and Opinion, 27,* 969–979.

Gonzales, M. H., & Meyers, S. A. (1993). "Your mother would like me": Self-presentation in the personals ads of heterosexual and homosexual men and women. *Personality and Social Psychology Bulletin, 19,* 131–142.

Gonzalez, R. (1989). Ministering intelligence: A Venezuelan experience in the promotion of cognitive abilities. *International Journal of Mental Health, 18,* 5–18.

Gonzalez-Blanks, A. G., Lopez, S. G., & Garza, R. T. (2012). Collectivism in smoking prevention programs for Hispanic preadolescents: Raising the ante on cultural sensitivity. *Journal of Child & Adolescent Substance Abuse, 21,* 427–439.

Goodall, J. (1990). *Through a window: My thirty years with the chimpanzees of Gombe.* Boston: Houghton Mifflin.

Goode, D. (2002). Mental retardation is dead: Long live mental retardation! *Mental Retardation, 40,* 57–59.

Goodenough, F. L. (1932). Expression of the emotions in a blind-deaf child. *Journal of Abnormal and Social Psychology, 27,* 328–333.

Goodman, G. S., & Schaaf, J. M. (1997). Over a decade of research on children's eyewitness testimony: What have we learned? Where do we go from here? *Applied Cognitive Psychology, 11,* S5–S20.

Goodnight, B. L., Cook, S. L., Parrott, D. J., & Peterson, J. L. (2013). Effects of masculinity, authoritarianism, and prejudice on anti-gay aggression: A path analysis of gender-role enforcement. *Psychology of Men & Masculinity, 16,* 3–17.

Goodwin, C. J. (1985). On the origins of Titchener's experimentalists. *Journal of the History of the Behavioral Sciences, 21,* 383–389.

Gopal, A., Clark, E., Allgair, A., Amato, C. D., Furman, M., Gansler, D. A., & Fulwiler, C. (2013). Dorsal/ventral parcellation of the amygdala: Relevance to impulsivity and aggression. *Psychiatry Research: Neuroimaging, 211,* 24–30.

Gopaul-McNicol, S. (1997). The role of religion in psychotherapy: A cross-cultural examination. *Journal of Contemporary Psychotherapy, 27,* 37–48.

Gordijn, E. H., De Vries, N. K., & De Dreu, C. K. W. (2002). Minority influence on focal and related attitudes: Change in size, attributions, and information processing. *Personality and Social Psychology Bulletin, 28,* 1315–1326.

Gordon, I. E., & Earle, D. C. (1992). Visual illusions: A short review. *Australian Journal of Psychology, 44,* 153–156.

Gordon, P. M., Heath, G. W., Holmes, A., & Christy, D. (2000). The quantity and quality of physical activity among those trying to lose weight. *American Journal of Preventive Medicine, 18,* 83–86.

Gorelick, P. B., & Ross, E. D. (1987). The aprosodias: Further functional-anatomical evidence for the organization of affective language in the right hemisphere. *Journal of Neurology, Neurosurgery, and Psychiatry, 50,* 553–560.

Gorman, J. (1985, February). My fair software. *Discover,* 64–65.

Gorman, J. M. (2003). New molecular targets for antianxiety interventions. *Journal of Clinical Psychiatry, 64,* 28–35.

Gorrese, A., & Ruggieri, R. (2012). Peer attachment: A meta-analytic review of gender and age differences and associations with parent attachment. *Journal of Youth & Adolescence, 41,* 650–672.

Gorunescu, F., Gorunescu, M., Saftoiu, A., Vilmann, P., & Belciug, S. (2011). Competitive/collaborative neural computing system for medical diagnosis in pancreatic cancer detection. *Expert Systems: International Journal of Knowledge Engineering & Neural Networks, 28,* 33–48.

Gosnell, B. A., & Hsiao, S. (1984). Effects of cholecystokinin on taste preference and sensitivity in rats. *Behavioral Neuroscience, 98,* 452–460.

Gosselin, P., Kirouac, G., & Dore, F. Y. (1995). Components and recognition of facial expression in the communication of emotion by actors. *Journal of Personality and Social Psychology, 68,* 83–96.

Goswami, M. (1998). The influence of clinical symptoms on quality of life in patients with narcolepsy. *Neurology, 50,* S31–S36.

Gotlib, I. H., & Robinson, L. A. (1982). Responses to depressed individuals: Discrepancies between self-report and observer-rated behavior. *Journal of Abnormal Psychology, 91,* 231–240.

Gottlieb, B. H. (2000). Self–help, mutual aid, and support groups among older adults. *Canadian Journal on Aging, 19,* 58–74.

Gould, S. J. (1981). *The mismeasure of man.* New York: W. W. Norton.

Gouzoulis-Mayfrank, E., Becker, S., Pelz, S., Tuchtenhagen, F., & Daumann, J. (2002). Neuroendocrine abnormalities in recreational ecstasy (MDMA) users: Is it ecstasy or cannabis? *Biological Psychiatry, 51,* 766–769.

Gouzoulis-Mayfrank. E., Thelen, B., Habermeyer, E., Kunert, H. J., Kovar, K. A., Lindenblatt, H., . . . Sass, H. (1999). Psychopathological, neuroendocrine and autonomic effects of 3,4-methylenedioxyethylamphetamine (MDE), psilocybin, and d-methamphetamine in healthy volunteers. *Psychopharmacology, 142,* 41–50.

Graham, K., & Wells, S. (2001). The two worlds of aggression for men and women. *Sex Roles, 45,* 595–622.

Grace, M. S., Woodward, O. M., Church, D. R., & Calisch, G. (2001). Prey targeting by the infrared-imaging snake Python: Effects of experimental and congenital visual deprivation. *Behavioural Brain Research, 119,* 23–31.

Graham, A. L., Papandonatos, G. D., DePue, J. D., Pinto, B. M., Borrelli, B., Neighbors, C. J. . . . Abrams, D. B. (2008). Lifetime characteristics of participants and non-participants in a smoking cessation trial: implications for external validity and public health impact. *Annals of Behavioral Medicine, 35,* 295–307.

Graham, M. J., Larsen, U., & Xu, X. (1999). Secular trend in age at menarche in China: A case study of two rural counties in Anhui province. *Journal of Biosocial Science, 31,* 257–267.

Grant, H. M., Bredahl, L. C., Clay, J., Ferrie, J., Groves, J. E., McDorman, T. A., & Dark, V. J. (1998). Context-dependent memory for meaningful material: Information for students. *Applied Cognitive Psychology, 12,* 617–623.

Grant, I., Gonzalez, R., Carey, C. L., Natarajan, L., & Wolfson, T. (2003). Non-acute (residual) neurocognitive effects of cannabis use: A meta-analytic study. *Journal of the International Neuropsychological Society, 9,* 679–689.

Grattan, D. R., Pi, X. J., Andrews, Z. B., Augustine, R. A., Kokay, I. C., Summerfield, M. R., . . . Bunn, S. J. (2001). Prolactin and receptors in the brain during pregnancy and lactation: Implications for behavior. *Hormones and Behavior, 40,* 115–124.

Gratzer, T. G., & Matas, M. (1994). The right to refuse treatment: Recent Canadian developments. *Bulletin of the American Academy of Psychiatry and the Law, 22,* 249–256.

Graves, R., & Landis, T. (1990). Asymmetry in mouth opening during different speech tasks. *International Journal of Psychology, 25,* 179–189.

Gravitz, M. A. (1995). First admission (1846) of hypnotic testimony in court. *American Journal of Clinical Hypnosis, 37,* 326–330.

Gravius, A., Pietraszek, M., Dekundy, A., & Danysz, W. (2010). Metabotropic glutamate receptors as therapeutic targets for cognitive disorders. *Current Topics in Medicinal Chemistry, 10,* 187–206.

Graw, P., Krauchi, K., Wirz-Justice, A., & Poldinger, W. (1991). Diurnal variation of symptoms in seasonal affective disorder. *Psychiatry Research, 37,* 105–111.

Gray, D.E., (2002). Everybody just freezes. Everybody is just embarrassed: Felt and enacted stigma among parents of children with high functioning autism. *Sociology of Health and Illness, 24,* 734–749.

Greeff, A. P., & de Bruyne, Tanya (2000). Conflict management style and marital satisfaction. *Journal of Sex and Marital Therapy, 26,* 321–334.

Green, A. J. K., & Gilhooly, K. J. (1990). Individual differences and effective learning procedures: The case of statistical computing. *International Journal of Man-Machine Studies, 33,* 97–119.

Green, C. D., & Powell, R. (1990). Comment on Kimble's generalism. *American Psychologist, 45,* 556–557.

Green, E. K., Grozeva, D., Jones, I., Jones, L., Kirov, G., Caesar, S., . . . Craddock, N. (2010). The bipolar disorder risk allele at CACNA1C also confers risk of recurrent major depression and of schizophrenia. *Molecular Psychiatry, 15,* 1016-1022.

Green, J. P., Lynn, S. J., & Malinoski, P. (1998). *Applied Cognitive Psychology, 12,* 431–444.

Greenberg, B. D., Ziemann, U., Cora-Locatelli, G., Harmon, A., Murphy, D. L., Keel, J. C., & Wassermann, E. M. (2000). Altered cortical excitability in obsessive-compulsive disorder. *Neurology, 54,* 142–147.

Greenberg, B.D., Rauch, S.L., & Haber, S. N. (2010). Invasive circuitry-based neurotherapeutics: Stereotactic ablation and deep brain stimulation for OCD. *Neuropsychopharmacology. 35,* 317–336

Greene, E., Flynn, M. S., & Loftus, E. F. (1982). Inducing resistance to misleading information. *Journal of Verbal Learning and Verbal Behavior, 21,* 207–219.

Greene, R. L. (1987). Effects of maintenance rehearsal on human memory. *Psychological Bulletin, 102,* 403–413.

Greeno, J. G. (1980). Psychology of learning, 1960–1980: One participant's observations. *American Psychologist, 35,* 713–728.

Greenough, A., Cole, G., Lewis, J., Lockton, A., & Blundell, J. (1998). Untangling the effects of hunger, anxiety, and nausea on energy intake during intravenous cholecystokinin octapeptide (CCK–8) infusion. *Physiology and Behavior, 65,* 303–310.

Greenwood, J. D. (1999). Understanding the "cognitive revolution" in psychology. *Journal of the History of the Behavioral Sciences, 35,* 1–22.

Gregory, A. M., Light-Häusermann, J. H., Rijsdijk, F., & Eley, T. C. (2009). Behavioral genetic analyses of prosocial behavior in adolescents. *Developmental Science, 12,* 165–174.

Gregory, C. M., Bowden, M. G., Jayaraman, A., Shah, P., Behrman, A., Kautz, S. A., & Vandenborne, K. (2007). Resistance training and locomotor recovery after incomplete spinal cord injury: A case series. *Spinal Cord, 45,* 522–530.

Greskoo, R. B., & Karlsen, A. (1994). The Norwegian program for the primary, secondary, and tertiary prevention of eating disorders. *Eating Disorders: The Journal of Treatment and Prevention, 2,* 57–63.

Grey, W. (1994). Philosophy and the paranormal, Part 1: The problem of "psi." *Skeptical Inquirer, 18,* 142–149.

Gribble, J. R. (2000). The psychosocial crisis of industry versus inferiority and self-estimates of vocational competence in high school students. *Dissertation Abstracts International: Section B. The Sciences and Engineering, 60,* 3618.

Griffies, W. S. (2010). Believing in the patient's capacity to know his mind: A psychoanalytic case study of fibromyalgia. *Psychoanalytic Inquiry, 30,* 390–404.

Grimshaw, G. M., Adelstein, A., Bryden, M. P., & MacKinnon, G. E. (1998). First-language acquisition in adolescence: Evidence for a critical period for verbal language development. *Brain and Language, 63,* 237–255.

Grisaru, N., Budowski, D., & Witztum, E. (1997). Possession by the "Zar" among Ethiopian immigrants to Israel: Psychopathology or culture-bound syndrome? *Psychopathology, 30,* 223–233.

Grissom, R. J. (1996). The magical number 7 + − 2: Meta-meta-analysis of the probability of superior outcome in comparisons involving therapy, placebo, and control. *Journal of Consulting and Clinical Psychology, 64,* 973–982.

Griva, K., Myers, L. B., & Newman, S. (2000). Illness perceptions and self-efficacy beliefs in adolescents and young adults with insulin dependent diabetes mellitus. *Psychology and Health, 15,* 733–750.

Gross, C. G. (2007). The discovery of motor cortex and its background. *Journal of the History of the Neurosciences, 16,* 320–331.

Gross, M., & Lavie, P. (1994). Dreams in sleep apnea patients. *Dreaming: Journal of the Association for the Study of Dreams, 4,* 195–204.

Grossman, C. I., Purcell, D. W., Rotheram-Borus, M. J., & Veniegas, R. (2013). Opportunities for HIV combination prevention to reduce racial and ethnic health disparities. *American Psychologist, 68,* 237–246.

Grossmann, K., Grossmann, K. E., Fremmer-Bombik, E., Kindler, H., Scheuerer-Englisch, H., & Zimmerman, P. (2002). The uniqueness of the child-father attachment relationship: Fathers' sensitive and challenging play as a pivotal variable in a 16-year longitudinal study. *Social Development, 11,* 307–331.

Grossman, R. P., & Till, B. D. (1998). The persistence of classically conditioned brand attitudes. *Journal of Advertising, 27,* 23–31.

Grosz, R. D. (1990). Suicide: Training the resident assistant as an interventionist. *Journal of College Student Psychotherapy, 4,* 179–194.

Grouios, G., Tsorbatzoudis, H., Alexandris, K., & Barkoukis, V. (2000). Do left-handed competitors have an innate superiority in sports? *Perceptual and Motor Skills, 90,* 1273–1282.

Grove, W. M., Eckert, E. D., Heston, L., & Bouchard, T. J. (1990). Heritability of substance abuse and antisocial behavior: A study of monozygotic twins reared apart. *Biological Psychiatry, 27,* 1293–1304.

Grover, B. L. (2011). The validity of MMPI-2 scores with a correctional population and convicted sex offenders. *Psychology, 2,* 638–642.

Grutzendler, J., Kasthuri, N., & Gan, W. B. (2002). Long-term dendritic spine stability in the adult cortex. *Nature, 420,* 812–816.

Guarino, M., Fridrich, P., & Sitton, S. (1994). Male and female conformity in eating behavior. *Psychological Reports, 75,* 603–609.

Guay, F., Boggiano, A. K., & Vallerand, R. J. (2001). Autonomy support, intrinsic motivation, and perceived competence. *Personality & Social Psychology Bulletin, 27,* 643–650.

Gubernskaya, Z. (2010). Changing attitudes toward marriage and children in six countries. *Sociological Perspectives, 53,* 179–200.

Guègen, N. (2002). The effects of a joke on tipping when it is delivered at the same time as the bill. *Journal of Applied Social Psychology, 32,* 1955–1963.

Guhu, N., Sönksen, P. H., & Holt, R. I. G. (2010). Growth hormone abuse: A threat to elite sport. *The Biologist, 57,* 185–190.

Guilford, J. P. (1959). Three faces of intellect. *American Psychologist, 14,* 469–479.

Guilford, J. P. (1984). Varieties of divergent production. *Journal of Creative Behavior, 18,* 1–10.

Guilford, J. P. (1985). The structure of intellect model. In B. B. Wolman (Ed.), *Handbook of Intelligence* (pp. 225–266). New York: Wiley.

Gulevich, G., Dement, W., & Johnson, L. (1966). Psychiatric and EEG observations on a case of prolonged (264 hours) wakefulness. *Archives of General Psychiatry, 15,* 29–35.

Gump, B. B., Matthews, K. A., & Raeikkoenen, K. (1999). Modeling relationships among socioeconomic status, hostility, cardiovascular reactivity, and left ventricular mass in African American and White children. *Health Psychology, 18,* 140–150.

Gunderson, J. G. (1996). Borderline patient's intolerance of aloneness: Insecure attachments and therapist availability. *American Journal of Psychiatry, 153,* 752–758.

Gunderson, V. M., Yonas, A., Sargent, P. L., & Grant-Webster, K. S. (1993). Infant macaque monkeys respond to pictorial depth. *Psychological Science, 4,* 93–98.

Gunter, T. D., Vaughn, M. G., & Philibert, R. A. (2010). Behavioral genetics in antisocial spectrum disorders and psychopathy: A review of the recent literature. *Behavioral Sciences and the Law, 28,* 148–173.

Gur, R. E., & Chin, S. (1999). Laterality in functional brain imaging studies of schizophrenia. *Schizophrenia Bulletin, 25,* 141–156.

Gurman, A. S., & Fraenkel, P. (2002). The history of couple therapy: A millennial review. *Family Process, 41,* 199–260.

Gustavson, C. R., Garcia, J., Hawkins, W. G., & Rusiniak, K. W. (1974). Coyote predation control by aversive conditioning. *Science, 184,* 581–583.

Guttler, F., Guldberg, P., & Henriksen, K. F. (1993). Mutation genotype of mentally retarded patients with phenylketonuria. *Developmental Brain Dysfunction, 6,* 92–96.

Guttman, S. R. (2006). Hysteria as a concept: A survey of its history in the psychoanalytic literature. *Modern Psychoanalysis, 31,* 182–228.

H

Haase, A. M., Prapavessis, H., & Owens, R. G. (2002). Perfectionism, social physique anxiety, and disordered eating: A comparison of male and female elite athletes. *Psychology of Sport and Exercise, 3,* 209–222.

Haber, R. N. (1980). How we perceive depth from flat pictures. *American Scientist, 68,* 370–380.

Habert, M. O., Cruz de Souza, L., Lamari, F., Daragon, N., Desarnaud, S., Jardel, C., . . . Sarazin, M. (2010). Brain perfusion SPECT correlates with CSF biomarkers in Alzheimer's disease. *European Journal of Nuclear Medicine and Molecular Imaging, 37,* 589–593.

Hadjikhani, N., & de Gelder, B. (2002). Neural basis of prosopagnosia: An fMRI study. *Human Brain Mapping, 16,* 176–182.

Hadjikhani, N., & Tootell, R. B. H. (2000). Projection of rods and cones within human visual cortex. *Human Brain Mapping, 9,* 55–63.

Hadley, J. (2009). Animal rights extremism and the terrorism question. *Journal of Social Philosophy, 40,* 363–378.

Häffner, H, Maurer, K., & an der Heiden, W. (2013). ABC schizophrenia study: An overview of results since 1996. *Social Psychiatry and Psychiatric Epidemiology, 48,* 1021–1031.

Hagan, L. D., & Hagan, A. C. (2008). Custody evaluations without psychological testing: Prudent practice or fatal flaw? *Journal of Psychiatry and Law, 36,* 67–106.

Hagerty, M. R. (1999). Testing Maslow's hierarchy of needs: National quality-of-life across time. *Social Indicators Research, 46,* 249–271.

Hagopian, L. P., Farrell, D. A., & Amari, A. (1996). Treating total liquid refusal with backward chaining and fading. *Journal of Applied Behavior Analysis, 29,* 573–575.

Haidt, J., & Keltner, D. (1999). Culture and facial expression: Open-ended methods find more expressions and a gradient of recognition. *Cognition and Emotion, 13,* 225–266.

Haight, B. K., Michel, Y., & Hendrix, S. (2000). The extended effects of the life review in nursing home residents. *International Journal of Aging and Human Development, 50,* 151–168.

Haimowitz, C. (2000). Maybe it's not "kick me"afterall: Transactional analysis and schizoid personality disorder. *Transactionalanalysis Journal, 30,* 84–90.

Haist, F., Song, A. W., Wild, K., Faber, T. L.,Popp, C. A., & Morris, R. D. (2001). Linking sight and sound: fMRI evidence of primary auditory cortex activation during visual word recognition. *Brain and Language, 76,* 340–350.

Hall, C., & Briggs, J. (2000, June 20). NBA Championship: Lakers 116–Pacers 111: Vandalism mars L.A.'s euphoria. *Los Angeles Times,* p. A1.

Hall, C. S. (1966). *The meaning of dreams.* New York: McGraw-Hill.

Hall, G. C. N. (2003). The self in context: Implications for psychopathology and psychotherapy. *Journal of Psychotherapy, 13,* 66–82.

Hall, G. C. N., Bansal, A., & Lopez, I. R. (1999). Ethnicity and psychopathology: A meta-analytic review of 31 years of comparative MMPI/MMPI-2 research. *Psychological Assessment, 11,* 186–197.

Hall, G. S. (1904). *Adolescence.* New York: Appleton.

Hall, H. K., & Byrne, A. T. J. (1988). Goal setting in sport: Clarifying recent anomalies. *Journal of Sport and Exercise Psychology, 10,* 184–198.

Hall, M. , Baum, A., Buysse, D. J., Prigerson, H. G., Kupfer, D., & Reynolds, C. F. III (1998). Sleep as a mediator of the stress-immune relationship. *Psychosomatic Medicine, 60,* 48–56.

Hall, T. E., Hughes, C. A., & Filbert, M. (2000). Computer-assisted instruction in reading for students with learning disabilities: A research synthesis. *Education and Treatment of Children, 23,* 173–193.

Hallenbeck, B. A., & Kauffman, J. M. (1995). How does observational learning affect the behavior of students with emotional or behavioral disorders? A review of research. *Journal of Special Education, 29,* 45–71.

Haller, J. (2013). The neurobiology of abnormal manifestations of aggression—A review of hypothalamic mechanisms in cats, rodents, and humans. *Brain Research Bulletin, 93,* 97–109.

Haller, J., Halasz, J., & Makara, G. B. (2000). Housing conditions and the anxiolytic efficacy of buspirone: The relationship between main and side effects. *Behavioural Pharmacology, 11,* 403–412.

Halpern, D. F. (1994). Stereotypes, science, censorship, and the study of sex differences. *Feminism & Psychology, 4,* 523–530.

Halpern, D. F. (1995). Cognitive gender differences: Why diversity is a critical research issue. In H. Landrine (Ed.), *Bringing cultural diversity to feminist psychology* (pp. 77–92). Washington, DC: American Psychological Association.

Halpern, D. F. (2000). *Sex differences in cognitive abilities* (3rd ed.). Mahwah, NJ: Erlbaum.

Halpern, D. F., & Coren, S. (1988). Do right-handers live longer? *Nature, 333,* 213.

Halpern, D. F., & Coren, S. (1993). Left-handedness and life span: A reply to Harris. *Psychological Bulletin, 114,* 235–241.

Halpern, D. F., & LeMay, M. L. (2000). The smarter sex: A critical review of sex differences in intelligence. *Educational Psychology Review, 12,* 229–246.

Halpern, D. F., Gilbert, R., & Coren, S. (1996). PC or not PC? Contemporary challenges to unpopular research findings. *Journal of Social Distress and the Homeless, 5,* 251–271.

Halpern, L., Blake, R., & Hillerbrand, J. (1986). Psychoacoustics of a chilling sound. *Perception and Psychophysics, 39,* 77–80.

Hamann, S. B., Ely, T. D., Hoffman, J. M., & Kilts, C. D. (2002). Ecstasy and agony: Activation of human amygdala in positive and negative emotion. *Psychological Science, 13,* 135–141.

Hamarman, S., Pope, K. H., & Czaja, S. J. (2002). Emotional abuse in children: Variations in legal definitions and rates across the United States. *Child Maltreatment: Journal of the American Professional Society on the Abuse of Children, 7,* 303–311.

Hamburger, Y. (1994). The contact hypothesis reconsidered: Effects of the atypical outgroup member on the outgroup stereotype. *Basic and Applied Social Psychology, 15,* 339–358.

Hamel, R., & Elshout, J. J. (2000). On the development of knowledge during problem solving. *European Journal of Cognitive Psychology, 12,* 289–322.

Hamer, D. H., Hu, S., Magnuson, V. L., & Hu, N. (1993). A linkage between DNA markers on the X chromosome and male sexual orientation. *Science, 261,* 321–327.

Hamill, R., Wilson, T. D., & Nisbett, R. E. (1980). Insensitivity to sample bias: Generalizing from atypical cases. *Journal of Personality and Social Psychology, 39,* 578–589.?

Hammack,S.E., Cooper, M. A., & Lezak, K. R. (2012). Overlapping neurobiology of learned helplessness and conditioned defeat: Implications for PTSD and mood disorders. *Neuropharmacology, 62,* 565–575.

Hammer, A. L., & Mitchell, W. D. (1996). The distribution of MBTI types in the U.S. by gender and ethnic group. *Journal of Psychological Type, 37,* 2–15.

Hammersley, R., Ditton, J., Smith, I., & Short, E. (1999). Patterns of ecstasy use by drug users. *British Journal of Criminology, 39,* 625–647.

Hammond, G. (2002). Correlates of human-handedness in primary motor cortex: A review and hypothesis. *Neuroscience and Biobehavioral Reviews, 26,* 285–292.

Hampstead, B. M., & Koffler, S. P. (2009). Thalamic contributions to anterograde, retrograde, and implicit memory: A case study. *Clinical Neuropsychologist, 23,* 1232–1249.

Hamson-Utley. J. J., Martin, S., & Walters, J. (2009). Athletic trainers' and physical therapists' perceptions of the effectiveness of psychological skills within sport injury rehabilitation programs. *Journal of Athletic Training, 43,* 258–264.

Han, D. H., Kim, Y. S., Lee, Y. S., Min, K. J., & Renshaw, P. F. (2010). Changes in cue-induced, prefrontal cortex activity with video-game play. *Cyberpsychology, Behavior, and Social Networking, 13,* 655–661.

Hancock, D. J., Rymal, A. M., & Ste-Marie, D. M. (2011). A triadic comparison of the use of observational learning amongst team sport athletes, coaches, and officials. *Psychology of Sport & Exercise, 12,* 236–241.

Haney, P., & Durlak, J. A. (1998). Changing self-esteem in children and adolescents: A meta-analytic review. *Journal of Clinical Child Psychology, 27,* 423–433.

Hanley, S. J., & Abell, S. C. (2002). Maslow and relatedness: Creating an interpersonal model of self-actualization. *Journal of Humanistic Psychology, 42,* 37–56.

Hanna, G., Kundiger, E., & Larouche, C. (1990). Mathematical achievement of grade 12 girls in fifteen countries. In L. Burton (Ed.), *Gender and mathematics: An international perspective* (pp. 87–98). New York: Cassell.

Hansen, L., Bakken, M., & Braastad, B. O. (1997). Failure of LiCl-conditioned taste aversion to prevent dogs from attacking sheep. *Applied Animal Behaviour Science, 54,* 251–256.

Hansen, C. H., & Hansen, R. D. (1988). Finding the face in the crowd: An anger superiority effect. *Journal of Personality and Social Psychology, 54,* 917–924.

Hanson, R. K. (1990). The psychological impact of sexual assault on women and children: A review. *Annals of Sex Research, 3,* 187–232.

Harbach, H., Hell, K., Gramsch, C., Katz, N., Hempelmann, G., & Teschemacher, H. (2000). Beta-endorphin (1-31) in the plasma of male volunteers undergoing physical exercise. *Psychoneuroendocrinology, 25,* 551–562.

Harbin, G., Durst, L., & Harbin, D. (1989). Evaluation of oculomotor response in relationship to sports performance. *Medicine and Science in Sports and Exercise, 21,* 258–262.

Hardy, C. J., & Latané, B. (1988). Social loafing in cheerleaders: Effects of team membership and competition. *Journal of Sport and Exercise Psychology, 10,* 109–114.

Hardy, L., & Callow, N. (1999). Efficacy of external and internal visual imagery perspectives for the enhancement of performance on tasks in which form is important. *Journal of Sport and Exercise Psychology, 21,* 95–112.

Hare, R. D., McPherson, L. M., & Forth, A. E. (1988). Male psychopaths and their criminal careers. *Journal of Consulting and Clinical Psychology, 56,* 710–714.

Hariri, A. R., Bookheimer, S. Y., & Mazziotta, J. C. (2000). Modulating emotional responses: Effects of a neocortical network on the limbic system. *Neuroreport: For Rapid Communication of Neuroscience Research, 11,* 43–48.

Harlow, H. F., & Zimmerman, R. R. (1959). Affectional responses in the infant monkey. *Science, 130,* 421–432.

Harlow, J. M. (1993). Recovery from the passage of an iron bar through the head. *History of Psychiatry, 4,* 271–281.

Harman, M. J. (1991). The use of group psychotherapy with cancer patients: A review of recent literature. *Journal for Specialists in Group Work, 16,* 56–61.

Harmer, C. J., Hill, S. A., Taylor, M. J., Cowen, P. J., & Goodwin, G. M. (2003). Toward a neuropsychological theory of antidepressant drug action: Increase in positive emotional bias after potentiation of norepinephrine activity. *American Journal of Psychiatry, 160,* 990–992.

Harmon-Jones, E., Brehm, J. W., Greenberg, J., & Simon, L. (1996). Evidence that the production of aversive consequences is not necessary to create cognitive dissonance. *Journal of Personality and Social Psychology, 70,* 5–16.

Harmon-Jones, E., Peterson, H., & Vaughn, K. (2003). The dissonance-inducing effects of an inconsistency between experienced empathy and knowledge of past failures to help: Support for the action-based model of dissonance. *Basic and Applied Social Psychology, 25,* 69–78.

Harrington, D. M., Block, J. H., & Block, J. (1987). Testing aspects of Carl Rogers' theory of creative environments: Childrearing antecedents of creative potential in young adolescents. *Journal of Personality and Social Psychology, 52,* 851–856.

Harrington, R., & Loffredo, D. A. (2001). The relationship between life satisfaction, self-consciousness, and the Myers-Briggs Type Inventory dimensions. *Journal of Psychology, 135,* 439–450.

Harris, C. R. (2003). A review of sex differences in sexual jealousy, including self-report data, psychophysiological resonses, interpersonal violence, and morbid jealousy. *Personality and Social Psychology Review, 7,* 102–128.

Harris, E. G., & Mowen, J. C. (2001). The influence of cardinal-, central-, and surface-level personality traits on consumers' bargaining and complaint intentions. *Psychology and Marketing, 18,* 1155–1185.

Harris, J. C. (2003a). Pinel orders the chains removed from the insane at Bicetre. *Archives of General Psychiatry, 60,* 442.

Harris, J. C. (2003b). A rake's progress: "Bedlam." *Archives of General Psychiatry, 60,* 338–339.

Harris, L. J. (1993). Do left-handers die sooner than right-handers? Commentary on Coren and Halpern's (1991) "Left-handedness: A marker for decreased survival fitness." *Psychological Bulletin, 114,* 203–234.

Harris, L. J. (1999). Early theory and research on hemispheric specialization. *Schizophrenia Bulletin, 25,* 11–39.

Harris, M. J. (1994). Self-fulfilling prophecies in the clinical context: Review and implications for clinical practice. *Applied and Preventive Psychology, 3,* 145–158.

Harris, R. L., Ellicott, A. M., & Holmes, D. S. (1986). The timing of psychosocial transitions and changes in women's lives: An examination of women aged 45 to 60. *Journal of Personality and Social Psychology, 51,* 409–416.

Harrison, A. A. (1969). Exposure and popularity. *Journal of Personality, 37,* 359–377.

Harrison, A. A. (1977). Let's make a deal: An analysis of revelations and stipulations in lonely hearts advertisements. *Journal of Personality and Social Psychology, 35,* 257–264.

Harrison, D. W., Gavin, M. R., & Isaac, W. (1988). A portable biofeedback device for autonomic responses. *Journal of Psychopathology and Behavioral Assessment, 10,* 217–224.

Hart, D. (1998). Can prototypes inform moral developmental theory? *Developmental Psychology, 34,* 420–423.

Hartley, J., & Homa, D. (1981). Abstraction of stylistic concepts. *Journal of Experimental Psychology: Human Learning and Memory, 7,* 33–46.

Hartmann, E., & Basile, R. (2003). Dream imagery becomes more intense after 9/11/01. *Dreaming: Journal of the Association for the Study of Dreams, 13,* 61–66.

Hartshorne, H., & May, M. A. (1928). *Studies in deceit.* New York: Macmillan.

Hartup, W. W. (1989). Social relationships and their developmental significance. *American Psychologist, 44,* 120–126.

Hartwell, E. E., Serovich, J. M., Gravsky, E. L., & Kerr, Z. Y. (2012). Coming out of the dark: Content analysis of articles pertaining to gay, lesbian, and bisexual issues in couple and family therapy journals. *Journal of Marital & Family Therapy, 38,* 227–243.

Harwood, C., & Swain, A. (2002). The development and activation of achievement goals within tennis: II. A player, parent, and coach intervention. *Sport Psychologist, 16,* 111–137.

Hasebe, S., Graf, E. W., & Schor, C. (2001). Fatigue reduces tonic accommodation. *Ophthalmic and Physiological Optics, 21,* 151–160.

Haslam, N. (1997). Evidence that male sexual orientation is a matter of degree. *Journal of Personality and Social Psychology, 73,* 862–870.

Hassett, J. (1978). *A primer of psychophysiology.* San Francisco: Freeman.

Hatfield, E. (1988). Passionate and companionate love. In R. J. Sternberg & M. L. Barnes (Eds.), *The psychology of love* (pp. 191-218). New Haven, CT: Yale University Press.

Hatfield, E., & Sprecher, S. (1995). Men's and women's preferences in marital partners in the United States, Russia, and Japan. *Journal of Cross-Cultural Psychology, 26,* 728–750.

Hatfield, G. (2002). Psychology, philosophy, and cognitive science: Reflections on the history and philosophy of experimental psychology. *Mind and Language, 17,* 207–232.

Hathaway, S. R., & McKinley, J. C. (1943). *Minnesota Multiphasic Personality Inventory.* New York: Psychological Corporation.

Hatton, C. (1998). Pragmatic language skills in people with intellectual disabilities: A review. *Journal of Intellectual and Developmental Disability, 23,* 79–100.

Hatzichristou, D. G., Bertero, E. B., & Goldstein, I. (1994). Decision making in the evaluation of impotence: The patient profile–oriented algorithm. *Sexuality and Disability, 12,* 29–37.

Hawker, D. S., & Boulton, M. J. (2000). Twenty years' research on peer victimization and psychosocial maladjustment: A meta-analytic review of cross-sectional studies. *Journal of Child Psychology and Psychiatry, and Allied Disciplines, 41,* 441–55.

Hawkes, N. (1979). Tracing Burt's descent to scientific fraud. *Science, 205,* 673–675.

Hawkins, D. L., Pepler, D. J., & Craig W. M. (2001). Naturalistic observations of peer interventions in bullying. *Social Development, 10,* 512–527.

Hawkins, M. J., Hawkins, W. E., & Ryan, E. R. (1989). Self-actualization as related to age of faculty members at a large midwestern university. *Psychological Reports, 65,* 1120–1122.

Hawkins, R. F. M. (2001). A systematic meta-review of hypnosis as an empirically supported treatment for pain. *Pain Reviews, 8,* 47–73.

Hay, P. J., Touyz, S., & Sud, R. (2012). Treatment for severe and enduring anorexia nervosa: A review. *Australian and New Zealand Journal of Psychiatry, 46,* 1136–1144.

Hayashi, S., Kuno, T., Morotomi, Y., Osawa, M., Shimizu, M., & Suetake, Y. (1998). Client-centered therapy in Japan: Fujio Tomoda and taoism. *Journal of Humanistic Psychology, 38,*103–124.

Hayden, T., & Mischel, W. (1976). Maintaining trait consistency in the resolution of behavioral inconsistency: The wolf in sheep's clothing? *Journal of Personality, 44,* 109–132.

Hayes, D. S. (1999). Young children's exposure to rhyming and nonrhyming stories: A structural analysis of recall. *Journal of Genetic Psychology, 160,* 280–293.

Hayes, D. S., Chemelski, B. E., & Palmer, M. (1982). Nursery rhymes and prose passages: Preschoolers' liking and short-term retention of story events. *Developmental Psychology, 18,* 49–56.

Hayes, R. L., Pechura, C. M., Katayama, Y., Povlishuck, J. T., Giebel, M. L., & Becker, D. P. (1984). Activation of pontine cholinergic sites implicated in unconsciousness following cerebral concussions in the cat. *Science, 223,* 301–303.

Hayflick, L. (1980, January). The cell biology of human aging. *Scientific American,* pp. 58–65.

Haykin, S., & Chen, Z. (2005). The cocktail party problem. *Neural Computation, 17,* 1875–1902.

Hays, J. R. (1989). The role of Addington v. Texas on involuntary civil commitment. *Psychological Reports, 65,* 1211–1215.

Hays, P. J., Touyz, S., & Sud, R. (2012). Treatment for severe and enduring anorexia nervosa: A review. *Australian & New Zealand Journal of Psychiatry, 46,* 1136–1144.

Hays, W.S. T. (2003). Human pheromones: have they been demonstrated? *Behavioral Ecology and Sociobiology, 54,* 89–97.

Hayward, C., Killen, J. D., & Taylor, C. B. (2003). The relationship between agoraphobia symptoms and panic disorder in a non-clinical sample of adolescents. *Psychological Medicine, 33,* 733–738.

Haywood, H. C., Meyers, C. E., & Switzky, H. N. (1982). Mental retardation. *Annual Review of Psychology, 33,* 309–342.

Hazelrigg, P. J., Cooper, H., & Strathman, A. J. (1991). Personality moderators of the experimenter expectancy effect: A reexamination of five hypotheses. *Personality and Social Psychology Bulletin, 17,* 569–579.

Hazlett–Stevens, H., & Craske, M. G. (2003). The catastrophizing worry process in generalized anxiety disorder: A preliminary investigation of an analog population. *Behavioral and Cognitive Psychotherapy, 31,* 387–401.

He, Z.-X., & Lester, D. (1998). Methods for suicide in mainland China. *Death Studies, 22,* 571–579.

Hearne, K. M. (1989). A nationwide mass dream–telepathy experiment. *Journal of the Society for Psychical Research, 55,* 271–274.

Hearnshaw, L. S. (1979). *Cyril Burt: Psychologist.* Ithaca: Cornell University Press.

Hearnshaw, L. S. (1985). Francis Bacon: Harbinger of scientific psychology. *Revista de Historia de la Psicologia, 6,* 5–14.

Hearst, E. (1999). After the puzzle boxes: Thorndike in the 20th century. *Journal of the Experimental Analysis of Behavior, 72*, 441–446.

Heath, D. T., & Orthner, D. K. (1999). Stress and adaptation among male and female single parents. *Journal of Family Issues, 20*, 557–587.

Heaton, P., Hermelin, B., & Pring, L. (1998). Autism and pitch processing: A precursor for savant musical ability. *Music Perception, 15*, 291–305.

Heavey, L., Pring, L., & Hermelin, B. (1999). A date to remember: The nature of memory in savant calendrical calculators. *Psychological Medicine, 29*, 145–160.

Heaven, P. C., L., & St. Quintin, D. (2003). Personality factors predict racial prejudice. *Personality and Individual Differences, 34*, 625–634.

Hebb, D. O. (1955). Drives and the C.N.S. (conceptual nervous system). *Psychological Review, 62*, 243–254.

Hebb, D. O. (1958). The motivating effects of exteroceptive stimulation. *American Psychologist, 13*, 109–113.

Hebl, M. R., & Heatherton, T. F. (1998). The stigma of obesity in women: The difference is black and white. *Personality and Social Psychology Bulletin, 24*, 417–426.

Hechinger, N. (1981, March). Seeing without eyes. *Science 81*, pp. 38–43.

Hedges, L. V. (1987). How hard is hard science, how soft is soft science? The empirical cumulativeness of research. *American Psychologist, 42*, 443–455.

Hedges, L. V., & Nowell, A. (1999). Changes in the Black-White gap in achievement test scores. *Sociology of Education, 72*, 111–135.

Heffner, H. E. (1983). Hearing in large and small dogs: Absolute thresholds and size of the tympanic membrane. *Behavioral Neuroscience, 97*, 310–318.

Heidelberger, M. (2004). *Nature from within: Gustav Theodor Fechner and his psychophysical worldview.* Pittsburgh: University of Pittsburgh Press.

Heider, F. (1944). Social perception and phenomenal causality. *Psychological Review, 51*, 358–374.

Heine, M. K., Ober, B. A., & Shenaut, G. K. (1999). Naturally occurring and experimentally induced tip-of-the-tongue experiences in three adult age groups. *Psychology and Aging, 14*, 445–457.

Heine, S. H., Lehman, D. R., Markus, H. R., & Kitayama, S. (1999). Is there a universal need for positive self-regard? *Psychological Review, 106*, 766–794.

Heitzmann, C. A., & Kaplan, M. (1988). Assessment of methods for measuring social support. *Health Psychology, 7*, 75–109.

Hellekant, G., Ninomiya, Y., & Danilova, V. (1998). Taste in chimpanzees. I: Labeled-line coding in sweet taste. *Physiology and Behavior, 65*, 191–200.

Helmes, E., & Reddon, J. R. (1993). A perspective on developments in assessing psychopathology: A critical review of the MMPI and MMPI-2. *Psychological Bulletin, 113*, 453–471.

Hendrick, C. (1990). Replications, strict replications, and conceptual replications: Are they important? *Journal of Social Behavior and Personality, 5*, 41–49.

Hendrickson, K. M., McCarty, T., & Goodwin, J. M. (1990). Animal alters: Case reports. *Dissociation: Progress in the Dissociative Disorders, 3*, 218–221.

Hendriks, A. A. J., Hofstee, W. K. B., & De Raad, B. (1999). The Five-Factor Personality Inventory (FFPI). *Personality and Individual Differences, 27*, 307–325.

Henle, M. (1978). One man against the Nazis: Wolfgang Köhler. *American Psychologist, 33*, 939–944.

Henle, M. (1993). Man's place in nature in the thinking of Wolfgang Köhler. *Journal of the History of the Behavioral Sciences, 29*, 3–7.

Hennig, J., Laschefski, U., & Opper, C. (1994). Biopsychological changes after bungee jumping: b-Endorphin immunoreactivity as a mediator of euphoria? *Neuropsychobiology, 29*, 28–32.

Hennrikus, D. J., Jeffery, R. W., & Lando, H. A. (1995). The smoking cessation process: Longitudinal observations in a working population. *Preventive Medicine: An International Journal Devoted to Practice and Theory, 24*, 235–244.

Henrich, J., Heine, S. J., & Norenzayan, A. (2010). The weirdest people in the world? *Behavioral and Brain Sciences, 33*, 61–135.

Hepper, P. G., Shahidulla, S., & White, R. (1991). Handedness in the human fetus. *Neuropsychologia, 29*, 1107–1111.

Herbert, T. B., & Cohen, S. (1993). Depression and immunity: A meta-analytic review. *Psychological Bulletin, 113*, 472–486.

Herbert, W. (1983). MMPI: Redefining normality for modern times. *Science News, 134*, 228.

Herbert, W. (1983). Remembrance of things partly. *Science News, 124*, 378–381.

Herek, G. M. (2000). The psychology of sexual prejudice. *Current Directions in Psychological Science, 9*, 19–22.

Hergenhahn, B. R. (1984). *An introduction to theories of personality.* Englewood Cliffs, NJ: Prentice-Hall.

Hergovich, A., & Olbrich, A. (2002). What can artificial intelligence do for peace psychology? *Review of Psychology, 9*, 3–11.

Herkenhahn, M., Lynn, A. B., deCosta, B. R., & Richfield, E. K. (1991). Neuronal localization of cannabinoid receptors in the basal ganglia of the rat. *Brain Research, 547*, 267–274.

Herman, D., Opler, L., Felix, A., Valencia, E., Wyatt, R. J., & Susser, E. (2000). A critical time intervention with mentally ill homeless men: Impact on psychiatric symptoms. *Journal of Nervous and Mental Disease, 188*, 135–140.

Herman, L. M., & Uyeyama, R. K. (1999). The dolphin's grammatical competency: Comments on Kako (1999). *Animal Learning and Behavior, 27*, 18–23.

Hermann, D. H. (1990). Autonomy, self determination, the right of involuntarily committed persons to refuse treatment, and the use of substituted judgment in medication decisions involving incompetent persons. *International Journal of Law and Psychiatry, 4*, 361–385.

Hernandez, M., & Iyengar, S. S. (2001). What drives whom? A cultural perspective on human agency. *Social Cognition, 19*, 269–294.

Herning, R. I. (1985). Cocaine increases EEG beta: A replication of Hans Berger's historic experiments. *Electroencephalography and Clinical Neurophysiology, 60*, 470–477.

Herrero, J. V., & Hillix, W. A. (1990). Hemispheric performance in detecting prosody: A competitive dichotic listening task. *Perceptual and Motor Skills, 71*, 479–486.

Herrnstein, R. J. (1994). *The bell curve: Intelligence and class structure in American life.* New York: Free Press.

Herrnstein, R. J., Nickerson, R. S., de Sanchez, M., & Swets, J. A. (1986). Teaching thinking skills. *American Psychologist, 41*, 1279–1289.

Hersen, M., Kazdin, A. E., & Bellack, A. S. (Eds.). (1983). *The clinical psychology handbook.* New York: Pergamon.

Hershberger, S. L. (1997). A twin registry study of male and female sexual orientation. *Journal of Sex Research, 34*, 212–222.

Hershenson, D. B. (2008). Ahead of its time: Career counseling's roots in phrenology. *Career Development Quarterly, 57*, 181–190.

Hertenstein, M. J. (2002). Touch: Its communicative functions in infancy. *Human Development, 45*, 70–94.

Herter, C. J., & Rhine, J. B. (1945). An exploratory investigation of the PK effect. *Journal of Parapsychology, 9*, 17–25.

Hertwig, R., & Ortmann, A. (2008). Deception in experiments: Revisiting the arguments in its defense. *Ethics and Behavior, 18*, 59–92.

Herz, R. S., & Cupchik, G. C. (1992). An experimental characterization of odor-evoked memories in humans. *Chemical Senses, 17*, 519–528.

Hetherington, A. W., & Ranson, S. W. (1942). The spontaneous activity and food intake of rats with hypothalamic lesions. *American Journal of Physiology, 136*, 609–617.

Hettema, J. M., Prescott, C. A., & Kendler, K. S. (2001). A population-based twin study of generalized anxiety disorder in men and women. *Journal of Nervous and Mental Disease, 189*, 413–420.

Hewitt, J. K. (1997). Behavior genetics and eating disorders. *Psychopharmacology Bulletin, 33*, 355–358.

Hewitt, J. K. (1997). The genetics of obesity: What have genetic studies told us about the environment? *Behavior Genetics, 27*, 353–358.

Hewlett, B. S., Lamb, M. E., Shannon, D., Leyendecker, B., & Schoelmerich, A. (1998). Culture and early infancy among central African foragers and farmers. *Developmental Psychology, 34*, 653–661.

Hewson-Bower, B., & Drummond, P. D. (1996). Secretory immunoglobulin A increases during relaxation in children with and without recurrent upper respiratory tract infections. *Journal of Developmental and Behavioral Pediatrics, 17*, 311–316.

Heyes, C. M., Dawson, G. R., & Nokes, T. (1992). Imitation in rats: Initial responding and transfer evidence. *Quarterly Journal of Experimental Psychology Comparative and Physiological Psychology, 45B*, 229–240.

Heywood, C., & Beale, I. L. (2003). EEG biofeedback vs. placebo treatment for attention-deficit/hyperactivity disorder: A pilot study. *Journal of Attention Disorders, 7*, 43–55.

Hiatt, S. W., Campos, J. J., & Emde, R. N. (1980). Facial patterning and infant emotional expression: Happiness, surprise, and fear. *Annual Progress in Child Psychiatry and Child Development*, 95–121.

Hicks, A. U., Lappalainen, R. S., Narkilahti, S., Suuronen, R., Corbett, D., Sivenius, J., . . . Jolkkonen, J. (2009). Transplantation of human embryonic stem cell-derived neural precursor cells and enriched environment after cortical stroke in rats: Cell survival and functional recovery. *European Journal of Neuroscience, 29*, 563–574.

Hicks, R. A., Johnson, C., & Pellegrini, R. J. (1992). Changes in the self–reported consistency of normal habitual sleep duration of college students (1978 and 1992). *Perceptual and Motor Skills, 75*, 1168–1170.

Hicks, R. A., Johnson, C., Cuevas, T., & Debaro, D. (1994). Do right-handers live longer? An updated assessment of baseball player data. *Perceptual and Motor Skills, 78*, 1243–1247.

Hidaka, B. (2012). Depression as a disease of modernity: Explanations for increasing prevalence. *Journal of Affective Disorders, 140*, 205–214.

Higashiyama, A., & Kitano, S. (1991). Perceived size and distance of persons in natural outdoor settings: The effects of familiar size. *Psychologia: An International Journal of Psychology in the Orient, 34*, 188–199.

Higgins, E. T. (1987). Self-discrepancy: A theory relating self and affect. *Psychological Review, 94*, 319–340.

Higgins, E. T. (1990). Self-state representations: Patterns of interconnected beliefs with specific holistic meanings and importance. *Bulletin of the Psychonomic Society, 28*, 248–253.

Higgins, J. E., & Endler, N. S. (1995). Coping, life stress, and psychological and somatic distress. *European Journal of Personality, 9*, 253–270.

Highet, A. (1998). Casablanca, Humphrey Bogart, the Oedipus complex, and the American male. *Psychoanalytic Review, 85*, 761–774.

Hilgard, E. (1987). *Psychology in America: A historical survey.* San Diego: Harcourt Brace Jovanovich.

Hilgard, E. R. (1973). A neodissociative interpretation of pain reduction in hypnosis. *Psychological Review, 80*, 403–419.

Hilgard, E. R. (1978, January). Hypnosis and consciousness. *Human Nature*, pp. 42–49.

Hill, C. E., & Stephany, A. (1990). Relation of nonverbal behavior to client reactions. *Journal of Counseling Psychology, 37*, 22–26.

Hill, J. (2003). Early identification of individuals at risk for antisocial personality disorder. *British Journal of Psychiatry, 182*, S11–S14.

Hill, J. L., Waldfogel, J., Brooks-Gunn, J., & Han, W. J. (2005). Maternal employment and child development: A fresh look using newer methods. *Developmental Psychology, 41*, 833–850

Hill, J. O., & Peters, J. C. (1998). Environmental contributions to the obesity epidemic. *Science, 280*, 1371–1374.

Hill, R. D., Allen, A. C., & McWhorter, P. (1991). Stories as a mnemonic aid for older learners. *Psychology and Aging, 6*, 484–486.

Hillson, T. R., & Martin, R. A. (1994). What's so funny about that? The domains-interaction approach as a model of incongruity and resolution in humor. *Motivation and Emotion, 18*, 1–29.

Hilt, L. M., Sander, L. C., Nolen–Hoeksema, S., & Simen, A. A. (2007). The BDNF Val66Met polymorphism predicts rumination and depression differently in young adolescent girls and their mothers. *Neuroscience Letters, 429*, 12–16.

Hilts, V. L. (1982). Obeying the laws of hereditary descent: Phrenological views on inheritance and eugenics. *Journal of the History of the Behavioral Sciences, 18*, 62–77.

Hinchy, J., Lovibond, P. F., & Ter-Horst, K. M. (1995). Blocking in human electrodermal conditioning. *Quarterly Journal of Experimental Psychology Comparative and Physiological Psychology, 48*, 2–12.

Hines, T. M. (1998). Comprehensive review of biorhythm theory. *Psychological Reports, 83*, 19–64.

Hinney, A., & Volckmar A. L. (2013). Genetics of eating disorders. *Current Psychiatry Reports, 15*, 17–33.

Hinton, D. E., & Lewis–Fernández, R. (2011). The cross–cultural validity of posttraumatic stress disorder: Implications for *DSM-5*. *Depression & Anxiety, 28*, 783–801.

Hirata, Y., Kuriki, S., & Pantev, C. (1999). Musicians with absolute pitch show distinct neural activities in the auditory cortex. *Neuroreport: For Rapid Communication of Neuroscience Research, 10*, 999–1002.

Hirsch, H. V. B., & Spinelli, D. N. (1970). Visual experience modifies distribution of horizontally and vertically oriented receptive fields in cats. *Science, 168*, 869–871.

Hirt, E. R., McCrea, S. M., & Boris, H. I. (2003). "I know you self-handicapped last exam": Gender differences in reactions to self-handicapping. *Journal of Personality and Social Psychology, 84*, 177–193.

Hobson, C. J., & Delunas, L. (2001). National norms and life-event frequencies for the revised Social Readjustment Rating Scale. *International Journal of Stress Management, 8*, 299–314.

Hobson, J. A. (1988). *The dreaming brain.* New York: Basic Books.

Hobson, J. A., & McCarley, R. W. (1977). The brain as a dream state generator: An activation-synthesis hypothesis of the dream process. *American Journal of Psychiatry, 134*, 1335–1348.

Hobson, J. A., Pace-Schott, E. F., & Stickgold, R. (2000). Dream science 2000: A response to commentaries on "Dreaming and the brain." *Behavioral and Brain Sciences, 23*, 1019–1035, 1083–1121.

Hochhausen, N. M., Lorenz, A. R., & Newman, J. R. (2002). Specifying the impulsivity of female inmates with borderline personality disorder. *Journal of Abnormal Psychology, 111*, 495–501.

Hocking-Schuler, J. L., & O'Brien, W. H. (1997). Cardiovascular recovery from stress and hypertension risk factors: A meta-analytic review. *Psychophysiology, 34*, 649–659.

Hodgins, H. S., & Zuckerman, M. (1990). The effect of nonverbal sensitivity on social interaction. *Journal of Nonverbal Behavior, 14*, 155–170.

Hoefnagels, C., & Zwikker, M. (2001). The bystander dilemma and child abuse: Extending the Latané and Darley model to domestic violence. *Journal of Applied Social Psychology, 31*, 1158–1183.

Hoek, H. W., & Van Hoeken, D. (2003). Review of the prevalence and incidence of eating disorders. *International Journal of Eating Disorders, 34*, 383–396.

Hoeksema-van Orden, C. Y. D., Gaillard, A. W. K., & Buunk, B. P. (1998). Social loafing under fatigue. *Journal of Personality and Social Psychology, 75*, 1179–1190.

Hoemann, H. W., & Keske, C. M. (1995). Proactive interference and language change in hearing adult students of American Sign Language. *Sign Language Studies, 86*, 45–61.

Hoffman, C., Lau, I., & Johnson, D. R. (1986). The linguistic relativity of person cognition: An English-Chinese comparison. *Journal of Personality and Social Psychology, 51*, 1097–1105.

Hoffman, N. (1995). The social "instinct." *Journal of the American Academy of Psychoanalysis and Dynamic Psychiatry, 23*, 197–206.

Hofmann, A. (1983). *LSD: My problem child.* Los Angeles: Tarcher.

Hogan, J. D. (2003). Anne Anastasi: Master of differential psychology and psychometrics. In G. Kimble & M. Wertheimer (Eds.), *Portraits of pioneers in psychology, Vol. 5* (pp. 263–296). Mahwah, NJ: Erlbaum.

Hogben, M. (1998). Factors moderating the effect of televised aggression on viewer behavior. *Communication Research, 25*, 220–247.

Holahan, C. K., Holahan, C. J., & Wonacott, N. L. (1999). Self-appraisal, life satisfaction, and retrospective life choices across one and three decades. *Psychology and Aging, 14*, 238–244.

Holden, C. (1980, November). Twins reunited: More than the faces are familiar. *Science, 80*, pp. 55–59.

Holden, C. (1983). Insanity defense reexamined. *Science, 222*, 994–995.

Holden, C. (1986). Depression research advances, treatment lags. *Science, 233*, 723–726.

Holden, C. (1986). Researchers grapple with problems of updating classic psychological test. *Science, 233*, 1249–1251.

Holden, C. (1987). Animal regulations: So far, so good. *Science, 237*, 598–601.

Holden, C. (1987). The genetics of personality. *Science, 237*, 598–601.

Holland, L. N., Goldstein, B. D., & Aronstam, R. S. (1993). Substance P receptor desensitization in the dorsal horn: Possible involvement of receptor-G protein complexes. *Brain Research, 600*, 89–96.

Holland, R. W., Verplanken, B., & van Knippenberg, A. (2002). On the nature of attitude-behavior relations: The strong guide, the weak follow. *European Journal of Social Psychology, 32*, 869–876.

Hollender, M. H. (1983). The 51st landmark article. *Journal of the American Medical Association, 250*, 228–229.

Hollingworth, L. S. (1914). Variability as related to sex differences in achievement. *American Journal of Sociology, 19*, 510–530.

Hollins, M., Delemos, K. A., & Goble, A. K. (1991). Vibrotactile adaptation on the face. *Perception and Psychophysics, 49*, 21–30.

Hollist, C. S., Miller, R. B., Falceto, O. G., & Fernandes, C. L. C. (2007). Marital satisfaction and depression: A replication of the marital discord model in a Latino sample. *Family Process, 46*, 485–498.

Hollon, S. D. (1996). The efficacy and effectiveness of psychotherapy relative to medications. *American Psychologist, 51*, 1025–1030.

Holm, L., Ullén, F., & Madison, G. (2011). Intelligence and temporal accuracy of behavior: Unique and shared associations with reaction time and motor timing. *Experimental Brain, Research, 214*, 175–183.

Holmes, D. S. (1974). Investigations of repression: Differential recall of material experimentally or naturally associated with ego threat. *Psychology Bulletin, 81*, 632–653.

Holmes, J. D., & Beins, B. C. (2009). Psychology is a science: At least some students think so. *Teaching of Psychology, 36*, 5–11.

Holmes, T. H., & Rahe, R. H. (1967). The Social Readjustment Rating Scale. *Journal of Psychosomatic Research, 11*, 213–218.

Holroyd, J. (1996). Hypnosis treatment of chronic pain: Understanding why hypnosis is useful. *International Journal of Clinical and Experimental Hypnosis, 44*, 33–51.

Holtgraves, T. (1997). Styles of language use: Individual and cultural variability in conversational indirectness. *Journal of Personality and Social Psychology, 73*, 624–637.

Holtgraves, T., & Skeel, J. (1992). Cognitive biases in playing the lottery: Estimating the odds and choosing the numbers. *Journal of Applied Social Psychology, 22*, 934–952.

Holton, R. (2009). Determinism, self-efficacy, and the phenomenology of free will. *Inquiry, 52*, 412–428.

Honchar, M. P., Olney, J. W., & Sherman, W. R. (1983). Systematic cholinergic agents induce seizures and brain damage in lithium-treated rats. *Science, 220*, 323–325.

Hong, S. (2000). Exercise and psychoneuroimmunology. *International Journal of Sport Psychology, 31*, 204–227.

Honts, C. R., Hodes, R. L., & Raskin, D. C. (1985). Effects of physical countermeasures on the physiological detection of deception. *Journal of Applied Psychology, 70*, 177–187.

Hood, K. E. (1995). Social psychology and sociobiology: Which is the metatheory? *Psychological Inquiry, 6*, 54–56.

Hooley, J. M., & Hiller, J. B. (2000). Personality and expressed emotion. *Journal of Abnormal Psychology, 109*, 40–44.

Hope, D. A., & Mindell, J. A. (1994). Global social skill ratings: Measures of social behavior or physical attractiveness? *Behaviour Research and Therapy, 32*, 463–469.

Hopkins, J. R. (1995). Erik Homburger Erikson (1902–1994). *American Psychologist, 50*, 796–797.

Horesh, N., Amir, M., Kedem, P., Goldberger, Y., & Kotler, M. (1997). Life events in childhood, adolescence, and adulthood and the relationship to panic disorder. *Acta Psychiatrica Scandinavica, 96*, 373–378.

Hormuth, S. E. (1986). The sampling of experiences in situ. *Journal of Personality, 54*, 262–293.

Horn, J. L., & Cattell, R. C. (1966). Refinement and test of the theory of fluid and crystallized general intelligences. *Journal of Educational Psychology, 57*, 253–270.

Horn, J. L., & Donaldson, G. (1976). On the myth of individual decline in adulthood. *American Psychologist, 31*, 701–719.

Horne, J. A., & Reyner, L. A. (1996). Counteracting driver sleepiness: Effects of napping, caffeine, and placebo. *Psychophysiology, 33*, 306–309.

Horner, M. D. (1990). Psychobiological evidence for the distinction between episodic and semantic memory. *Neuropsychology Review, 1*, 281–321.

Horney, K. (1924). On the genesis of the castration complex in women. *International Journal of Psychoanalysis, 5*, 50–65.

Horney, K. (1926/1967). The flight from womanhood. In K. Horney, *Feminine psychology* (H. Kelman, Ed., pp. 54–70). New York: W. W. Norton.

Horney, K. (1950). *Neurosis and human growth.* New York: Norton.

Hornstein, S. L., Brown, A. S., & Mulligan, N. W. (2003). Long-term flashbulb memory for learning of Princess Diana's death. *Memory, 11*, 293–306.

Horowitz, F. D. (1992). John B. Watson's legacy: Learning and environment. *Developmental Psychology, 28*, 360–367.

Horowitz, S. W., Kircher, J. C., Honts, C. R., & Raskin, D. C. (1997). The role of comparison questions in physiological detection of deception. *Psychophysiology, 34*, 108–115.

Horsley, R. R., Osborne, M., Norman, C., & Wells, T. (2012). High-frequency gamblers show increased resistance to extinction following partial reinforcement. *Behavioural Brain Research, 229*, 438–442.

Hortensius, R., Schutter, D. J. L. G., & Harmon-Jones, E. (2012). When anger leads to aggression: Induction of relative left frontal cortical activity with transcranial direct current stimulation increases the anger-aggression relationship. *Social Cognitive & Affective Neuroscience, 7,* 342–347.

Hosoda, M., Stone-Romero, E. F., & Coats, G. (2003). The effects of physical attractiveness on job-related outcomes: A meta-analysis of experimental studies. *Personnel Psychology, 56,* 431–462.

Hou, C., Miller, B. L., Cummings, J. L., Goldberg, M., Mychack, P., Bottino, V., & Benson, D. F. (2000). Artistic savants. *Neuropsychiatry, Neuropsychology, and Behavioral Neurology, 13,* 29–38.

Houlihan, D. D., & Jones, R. N. (1989). Treatment of a boy's school phobia with in vivo systematic desensitization. *Professional School Psychology, 4,* 285–293.

House, J. D. (1998). High school achievement and admissions test scores as predictors of course performance of American Indian and Alaska Native students. *Journal of Psychology, 132,* 680–682.

Hovland, C. I., Lumsdaine, A., & Sheffield, F. (1949). *Experiments on mass communication.* Princeton, NJ: Princeton University Press.

Howard, K. I., Kopta, S. M., Krausse, M. S., & Orlinsky, D. E. (1986). The dose-effect relationship in psychotherapy. *American Psychologist, 41,* 159–164.

Howarth, H.V.C., & Griffin, M. J. (2003). Effect of roll oscillation frequency on motion sickness. *Aviation, Space, and Environmental Medicine, 74,* 326–331.

Howe, M. J., & Smith, J. (1988). Calendar calculating in "idiot savants": How do they do it? *British Journal of Psychology, 79,* 371–386.

Howe, M., Toth, S. L., & Cicchetti, D. (2011). Can maltreated children inhibit true and false memories for emotional information? *Child Development, 82,* 967–981.

Hsu, F. L. K. (1981). *Americans and Chinese: Passage to differences* (3rd ed.). Honolulu: The University of Hawaii Press.

Hsu, L. G., & Sobkiewicz, T. A. (1991). Body image disturbance: Time to abandon the concept for eating disorders? *International Journal of Eating Disorders, 10,* 15–30.

Hsu, L. G., Chester B. E., & Santhouse, R. (1990). Bulimia nervosa in eleven sets of twins: A clinical report. *International Journal of Eating Disorders, 9,* 275–282.

Hsu, L. K. G., & Folstein, M. F. (1997). Somatoform disorders in Caucasian and Chinese Americans. *Journal of Nervous and Mental Disease, 185,* 382–387.

Hu, S., Xu, D., Peterson, B. S., Wang, Q., He, X., Hu, J., . . . Xu, Y. (2013) Association of cerebral networks in resting state with sexual preference of homosexual men: A study of regional homogeneity and functional connectivity. *PLOS ONE 8(3),* e59426.

Hu, L. W., Gorenstein, C., & Fuentes, D. (2007). Portuguese version of Corah's Dental Anxiety Scale: Transcultural adaptation and reliability analysis. *Depression and Anxiety, 24,* 467–471.

Hu, S., & Stern, R. M. (1999). The retention of adaptation to motion sickness eliciting stimulation. *Aviation, Space, and Environmental Medicine, 70,* 766–768.

Huang, W., & Cuvo, A. J. (1997). Social skills training for adults with mental retardation in job-related settings. *Behavior Modification, 21,* 3–44.

Hubel, D. H., & Wiesel, T. N. (1979, September). Brain mechanisms of vision. *Scientific American,* pp. 130–144.

Huber, A., Lui, F., Porro, C. A. (2013). Hypnotic susceptibility modulates brain activity related to experimental placebo analgesia, *Pain 154,* 1509–1518.

Huberfeld,G., Habert, M. O., Clemenceau, S., Maksud, P., Baulac, M., & Adam, C. (2006). Ictal brain hyperperfusion contralateral to seizure onset: The SPECT mirror image. *Epilepsia, 47,* 123–133.

Hublin, C., Partinen, M., Koskenvuo, M., & Kaprio, J. (2013). Genetic gactors in evolution of sleep length—A longitudinal twin study in Finnish adults. *Journal of Sleep Research, 22,* 513–518.

Hudesman, J., Page, W., & Rautiainen, J. (1992). Use of subliminal stimulation to enhance learning mathematics. *Perceptual and Motor Skills, 74,* 1219–1224.

Hugdahl, K., Satz, P., Mitrushina, M., & Miller, E. N. (1993). Left-handedness and old age: Do left-handers die earlier? *Neuropsychologia, 31,* 325–333.

Hughes, B. M. (2001). Just noticeable differences in 2D and 3D bar charts: A psychophysical analysis of chart readability. *Perceptual and Motor Skills, 92,* 495–503.

Hughes, J. R., & Callas, P. W. (2010). Data to assess the generalizability of samples from studies of adult smokers. *Nicotine and Tobacco Research, 12,* 73–76.

Hughes, J. R., Gust, S. W., Skoog, K., & Keenan, R. (1991). Symptoms of tobacco withdrawal: A replication and extension. *Archives of General Psychiatry, 48,* 52–59.

Hughes, J. R., Higgins, S. T., & Bickel, W. K. (1994). Nicotine withdrawal versus other drug withdrawal syndromes: Similarities and dissimilarities. *Addiction, 89,* 1461–1470.

Hughes, J. R., Higgins, S. T., Bickel, W. K., Hunt, W. K., Fenwick, J. W., Gulliver, S. B., & Mireault, G. C. (1991). Caffeine self-administration, withdrawal, and adverse effects among coffee drinkers. *Archives of General Psychiatry, 48,* 611–617.

Hughes, J., Gabbay, M., Funnell, E., & Dowrick, C. (2012). Exploratory review of placebo characteristics reported in randomized placebo controlled antidepressant drug trials. *Pharmacopsychiatry, 45,* 20–27.

Hughes, J., Smith, T. W., Kosterlitz, H. W., Fothergill, L. A., Morgan, B. A., & Morris, H. R. (1975). Identification of two related pentapeptides from the brain with potent opiate agonistic activity. *Nature, 258,* 577–579.

Hui, K. K. S., Liu, J., Makris, N., Gollub, R. L., Chen, A. J. W., Moore, C. I., . . . Kwong, K. K. (2000). Acupuncture modulates the limbic system and subcortical gray structures of the human brain: Evidence from fMRI studies in normal subjects. *Human Brain Mapping, 9,* 13–25.

Hull, C. L. (1943). *Principles of behavior.* New York: Appleton-Century-Crofts.

Hull, J. G., & Bond, C. F., Jr. (1986). Social and behavioral consequences of alcohol consumption and expectancy: A meta-analysis. *Psychological Bulletin, 99,* 347–360.

Hulme, C., & Roodenrys, S. (1995). Verbal working memory development and its disorders. *Journal of Child Psychology and Psychiatry and Allied Disciplines, 36,* 373–398.

Hultsch, D. F., Hertzog, C., Small, B. J., & Dixon, R. A. (1999). Use it or lose it: Engaged lifestyle as a buffer of cognitive decline in aging? *Psychology and Aging, 14,* 245–263.

Humphreys, K. (1997). Clinicians' referral and matching of substance abuse patients to self-help groups after treatment. *Psychiatric Services, 48,* 1445–1449.

Humphreys, M. S., & Revelle, W. (1984). Personality, motivation, and performance: A theory of the relationship between individual differences and information processing. *Psychological Review, 91,* 153–184.

Hunsberger, B., Pratt, M., & Pancer, S. M. (2001). Adolescent identity formation: Religious exploration and commitment. *Identity, 1,* 365–386.

Hunt, E. (1997). The status of the concept of intelligence. *Japanese Psychological Research, 39,* 1–11.

Hunter, J. E., & Schmidt, F. L. (2000). Racial and gender bias in ability and achievement tests: Resolving the apparent paradox. *Psychology, Public Policy, and Law, 6,* 151–158.

Huopainen, H. (2002). Freud's view of hysteria in light of modern trauma research. *Scandinavian Psychoanalytic Review, 25,* 92–107.

Hur, J., & Osborne, S. (1993). A comparison of forward and backward chaining methods used in teaching corsage making skills to mentally retarded adults. *British Journal of Developmental Disabilities, 39,* 108–117.

Hur, Y.-M., Bouchard, T. J., Jr., & Eckert, E. (1998). Genetic and environmental influences on self-reported diet: A reared-apart twin study. *Physiology and Behavior, 64,* 629–636.

Hur, Y.-M., McGue, M., & Iacono, W. G. (1998). The structure of self-concept in female preadolescent twins: A behavioral genetic approach. *Journal of Personality and Social Psychology, 74,* 1069–1077.

Hurst, L. C., & Mulhall, D. J. (1988). Another calendar savant. *British Journal of Psychiatry, 152,* 274–277.

Hurvich, Leo M. (1969). Hering and the scientific establishment. *American Psychologist, 24,* 497–514.

Husain, S. A. (1990). Current perspective on the role of psychosocial factors in adolescent suicide. *Psychiatric Annals, 20,* 122–127.

Huston, A. C., Watkins, B. A., & Kunkel, E. (1989). Public policy and children's television. *American Psychologist, 44,* 424–433.

Huston, A. C., Wright, J. C., Marquis, J., & Green, S. B. (1999). How young children spend their time: Television and other activities. *Developmental Psychology, 35,* 912–925.

Huston, T. L., Ruggiero, M., Conner, R., & Geis, G. (1981). Bystander intervention into crime: A study based on naturally-occurring episodes. *Social Psychology Quarterly, 44,* 14–23.

Huttenlocher, P. R. (1990). Morphometric study of human cerebral-cortex development. *Neuropsychologia, 28,* 517–527.

Huxley, A. F. (1959). Ion movements during nerve activity. *Annals of the New York Academy of Sciences, 81,* 221–246.

Hviid, A., Stellfeld, M., Wohlfahrt, J., & Melbye, M. (2003). Association between thimerosal-containing vaccine and autism. *Journal of the American Medical Association, 290,* 1763–1766.

Hyde, J. S. (1984). Children's understanding of sexist language. *Developmental Psychology, 20,* 697–706.

Hyde, J. S. (1994). Can meta-analysis make feminist transformations in psychology? *Psychology of Women Quarterly, 18,* 451–462.

Hyde, J. S. (2007). New directions in the study of gender similarities and differences. *Current Directions in Psychological Science, 16,* 259–263.

Hyde, J. S., & Durik, A. M. (2000). Gender differences in erotic plasticity—Evolutionary or sociocultural forces? Comment on Baumeister, 2000. *Psychological Bulletin, 126,* 375–379.

Hyde, J. S., & Linn, M. C. (1988). Gender differences in verbal ability: A meta-analysis. *Psychological Bulletin, 104,* 53–69.

Hyde, J. S., & Plant, E. A. (1995). Magnitude of psychological gender differences: Another side of the story. *American Psychologist, 50,* 159–161.

Hyde, J. S., Fennema, E., & Lamon, S. J. (1990). Gender differences in mathematics performance: A meta-analysis. *Psychological Bulletin, 107,* 139–155.

Hyland, B. (1998). Neural activity related to reaching and grasping in rostral and caudal regions of rat motor cortex. *Behavioural Brain Research, 94,* 255–269.

Hyman, R. B. (1988). Four stages of adulthood: An exploratory study of growth patterns of inner-direction and time-competence in women. *Journal of Research in Personality, 22,* 117–127.

Hynan, D. J. (1990). Client reasons and experiences in treatment that influence termination of psychotherapy. *Journal of Clinical Psychology, 46,* 891–895.

Hystad, S.W., Eid, J., & Brevik, J.I., (2011). Effects of psychological hardiness, job demands, and job control on sickness absence: A prospective study. *Journal of Occupational Health Psychology, 16,* 265–278.

I

Ibrahim, S. A. (2003). Hypertension and medication adherence among African Americans: A potential factor in cardiovascular disparities. *Journal of the National Medical Association, 95,* 28–29.

Ickes, W., Gesn, P. R., & Graham, T. (2000). Gender differences in empathic accuracy: Differential ability or differential motivation? *Personal Relationships, 7,* 95–109.

Iijima, M., Osawa, M., Nishitan, N., & Iwata, M. (2009). Effects of incense on brain function: Evaluation using electroencephalograms and event-related potentials. *Neuropsychobiology, 59,* 80–86.

Ilies, R., & Judge, T. A. (2003). On the heritability of job satisfaction: The mediating role of personality. *Journal of Applied Psychology, 88,* 750–759.

Imada, T., & Ellsworth, P. C. (2011). Proud Americans and lucky Japanese: Cultural differences in appraisal and corresponding emotion. *Emotion, 11,* 329–345.

Immergluck, L. (1964). Determinism-freedom in contemporary psychology: An ancient problem revisited. *American Psychologist, 19,* 270–281.

Ingelfinger, F. J. (1944). The late effects of total and subtotal gastrectomy. *New England Journal of Medicine, 231,* 321–327.

Ingham, A. G., Levinger, G., Graves, J., & Peckham, V. (1974). The Ringelmann effect: Studies of group size and group performance. *Journal of Experimental Social Psychology, 10,* 371–384.

Ingram, D. H. (1985). Karen Horney at 100: Beyond the frontier. *American Journal of Psychoanalysis, 45,* 305–309.

Inman, M. L., & Baron, R. S. (1996). Influence of prototypes on perceptions of prejudice. *Journal of Personality and Social Psychology, 70,* 727–739.

Inouye, S., Honda, K., & Komoda, Y. (1995). Sleep as neuronal detoxification and restitution. *Behavioural Brain Research, 69,* 91–96.

Insko, C. A. (1965). Verbal reinforcement of attitude. *Journal of Personality and Social Psychology, 2,* 621–623.

Insko, C. A., Nacoste, R. W., & Moe, J. L. (1983). Belief congruence and racial discrimination: Review of the evidence and critical evaluation. *European Journal of Social Psychology, 13,* 153–174.

Invernizzi, M. A., & Abouzeid, M. P. (1995). One story map does not fit all: A cross-cultural analysis of children's written story retellings. *Journal of Narrative & Life History, 5,* 1–19.

Iqbal, H. M., & Shayer, M. (2000). Accelerating the development of formal thinking in Pakistan secondary school students: Achievement effects and professional development issues. *Journal of Research in Science Teaching, 37,* 259–274.

Irnich, D., Behrens, N., Gleditsch, J. M., Stor, W., Schreiber, M. A., Schops, P., . . . Beyer, A. (2002). Immediate effects of dry needling and acupuncture at distant points in chronic neck pain: Results of a randomized, double-blind, sham-controlled crossover trial. *Pain, 99,* 83–89.

Ironson, G., Schneiderman, H., Kumar, M., & Antoni, M. H. (1994). Psychosocial stress, endocrine, and immune response in HIV-1 disease. *Homeostasis in Health and Disease, 35,* 137–148.

Irwin, M., Mascovich, A., Gillin, J. C., & Willoughby, R. (1994). Partial sleep deprivation reduced natural killer cell activity in humans. *Psychosomatic Medicine, 56,* 493–498.

Ishai, A., Ungerleider, L. G., Martin, A., & Haxby, J. V. (2000). The representation of objects in the human occipital and temporal cortex. *Journal of Cognitive Neuroscience, 12,* 35–51.

Ishizawa, Y., Ma, H.-C., Dohi, S., & Shimonaka, H. (2000). Effects of cholinomimetic injection into the brain stem reticular formation on halothane anesthesia and antinociception in rats. *Journal of Pharmacology and Experimental Therapeutics, 293,* 845–851.

Ispa, J. M., Thornburg, K. R., & Gray, M. M. (1990). Relations between early childhood care arrangements and college students' psychosocial development and academic performance. *Adolescence, 25,* 529–542.

Isurin, L., & McDonald, J. L. (2001). Retroactive interference from translation equivalents: Implications for first language forgetting. *Memory and Cognition, 29,* 312–319.

Iversen, I. H. (1993). Techniques for establishing schedules with wheel running as reinforcement in rats. *Journal of the Experimental Analysis of Behavior, 60,* 219–238.

Ivry, G. B., Ogle, C. A., & Shim, E. K. (2006). Role of sun exposure in melanoma. *Dermatological Surgery, 32,* 481–492.

Ivtzan, I., Gardner, H. E., Bernard, I., Sekhon, M., & Hart, R. (2013). Wellbeing through self-fulfilment: Examining developmental aspects of self-actualization. *The Humanistic Psychologist, 41,* 119–132.

Iyengar, S. S., & Lepper, M. R. (1999). Rethinking the value of choice: A cultural perspective on intrinsic motivation. *Journal of Personality and Social Psychology, 76,* 349–366.

Izard, C. E. (1990a). Facial expressions and the regulation of emotions. *Journal of Personality and Social Psychology, 58,* 487–498.

Izard, C. E. (1990b). The substrates and functions of emotion feelings: William James and current emotion theory. *Personality and Social Psychology Bulletin, 16,* 626–635.

Izard, C. E. (1993). Four systems for emotion activation: Cognitive and noncognitive processes. *Psychological Review, 100,* 68–90.

Izard, C. E. (1994). Innate and universal facial expressions: Evidence from developmental and cross-cultural research. *Developmental Psychology, 115,* 288–299.

Izard, C. E., & Haynes, O. M. (1988). On the form and universality of the contempt expression: A challenge to Ekman and Friesen's claim of discovery. *Motivation and Emotion, 12,* 1–16.

Izard, C. E., Huebner, R. R., Risser, D., McGinnes, G. C., & Dougherty, L. M. (1980). The young infant's ability to produce discrete emotion expressions. *Developmental Psychology, 16,* 132–140.

J

Jack, S. J., & Ronan, K. R. (1998). Sensation seeking among high- and low-risk sports participants. *Personality and Individual Differences, 25,* 1063–1083.

Jacklin, C. N. (1989). Female and male: Issues of gender. *American Psychologist, 44,* 127–133.

Jackson, B., Sellers, R. M., & Peterson, C. (2002). Pessimistic explanatory style moderates the effect of stress on physical illness. *Personality and Individual Differences, 32,* 567–573.

Jackson, G. R., Owsley, C., & McGwin, Gerald, Jr. (1999). Aging and dark adaptation. *Vision Research, 39,* 3975–3982.

Jackson, L. A., Hunter, J. E., & Hodge, C. N. (1995). Physical attractiveness and intellectual competence: A meta-analytic review. *Social Psychology Quarterly, 58,* 108–122.

Jackson, R. R., Carter, C. M., &Tarsitano, M. S. (2001). Trial-and-error solving of a confinement problem by a jumping spider, *Portia fimbriata. Behaviour, 138,* 1215–1234.

Jacobs, G. H., Neitz, M., Deegan, J. F., & Neitz, J. (1996). Trichromatic colour vision in New World monkeys. *Nature, 382,* 156–158.

Jacobs, J. R., & Bovasso, G. B. (2000). Early and chronic stress and their relation to breast cancer. *Psychological Medicine, 30,* 669–678.

Jacobs, L., & Joseph, S. (1997). Cognitive Triad Inventory and its association with symptoms of depression and anxiety in adolescents. *Personality and Individual Differences, 22,* 769–770.

Jacobs, W. J., & Blackburn, J. R. (1995). A model of Pavlovian conditioning: Variations in representations of the unconditional stimulus. *Integrative Physiological and Behavioral Science, 30,* 12–33.

Jacobsen, P. B., Bovbjerg, D. H., Schwartz, M. D., & Hudis, C. A. (1995). Conditioned emotional distress in women receiving chemotherapy for breast cancer. *Journal of Consulting and Clinical Psychology, 63,* 108–114.

Jacobson, E. (1977). The origins and development of progressive relaxation. *Journal of Behavior Therapy and Experimental Psychiatry, 8,* 119–123.

Jaencke, L., Shah, N. J., & Peters, M. (2000). Cortical activations in primary and secondary motor areas for complex bimanual movements in professional pianists. *Cognitive Brain Research, 10,* 177–183.

Jaffee, S., & Hyde, J. S. (2000). Gender differences in moral orientation: A meta-analysis. *Psychological Bulletin, 126,* 703–726.

James, W. (1884). What is an emotion? *Mind, 9,* 188–205.

James, W. (1892/1985). *Psychology: Briefer course.* Cambridge, MA: Harvard University Press.

James, W. (1902/1992). *The varieties of religious experience.* New York: Gryphon.

Jancke, L., & Steinmetz, H. (2003). Brain size: A possible source of interindividual variability in corpus callosum morphology. In E. Zaidel & M. Iacoboni (Eds.), *The parallel brain: The cognitive neuroscience of the corpus callosum* (pp. 51–63). Cambridge, MA: MIT Press.

Jang, K. L., McCrae, R. R., Angleitner, A., Riemann, R., & Livesley, W. J. (1998). Heritability of facet-level traits in a cross-cultural twin sample: Support for a hierarchical model of personality. *Journal of Personality and Social Psychology, 74,* 1556–1565.

Jason, L. A., & Brackshaw, E. (1999). Access to TV contingent on physical activity: Effects on reducing TV-viewing and body weight. *Journal of Behavior Therapy and Experimental Psychiatry, 30,* 145–151.

Jeffery, R. W., Epstein, L. H., Wilson, G. T., Drewnowski, A., Stunkard, A. J., & Wing, R. R. (2000). Long-term maintenance of weight loss: Current status. *Health Psychology, 19,* 5–16.

Jeffrey, S. A., & Adomdza, G. K. (2011). Incentive salience and improved performance. *Human Performance, 24,* 47–59.

Jeffries, S., & Konnert, C. (2002). Regret and psychological well-being among voluntarily and involuntarily childless women and mothers. *International Journal of Aging and Human Development, 54,* 89–106.

Jegede, J. O., Jegede, R. T., & Ugodulunwa, C. A. (1997). Effects of achievement motivation and study habits on Nigerian secondary school students' academic performance. *Journal of Psychology, 131,* 523–529.

Jemmott, J. B., & Locke, S. E. (1984). Psychosocial factors, immunologic mediation, and human susceptibility to infectious diseases: How much do we know? *Psychological Bulletin, 95,* 78–108.

Jemmott, J. B., & Magloire, K. (1988). Academic stress, social support, and secretory immunoglobulin A. *Journal of Personality and Social Psychology, 55,* 803–810.

Jenkins, J. G., & Dallenbach, K. M. (1924). Obliviscence during sleep and waking. *American Journal of Psychology, 35,* 605–612.

Jensen, A. R. (1969). How much can we boost IQ and scholastic achievement? *Harvard Educational Review, 39,* 1–123.

Jensen, A. R. (1980). *Bias in mental testing.* New York: Free Press.

Jensen, K. P, Stein, M.B., Kranzler, H.R., Yang, B.Z., Farrer, L.A., & Gelernter (2014). The α-endomannosidase gene (*manea*) is associated with panic disorder and social anxiety disorder. *Translational Psychiatry, 4,* 1–6.

Jensvold, M.L.A., & Gardner, R. A. (2000). Interactive use of sign language by cross-fostered chimpanzees (Pan troglodytes). *Journal of Comparative Psychology, 114,* 335–346.

Jeynes, W. H. (2002). The relationship between the consumption of various drugs by adolescents and their academic achievement. *American Journal of Drug and Alcohol Abuse, 28,* 15–35.

Jiminez-Murcia, S., Ayamí, N., Gómez-Peña, M., Santamaría, J. J. Álvarez-Moya, E., Fernández-Aranda, F., . . . Menchón, J. M. (2012). Does exposure and response prevention improve the results of group cognitive-behavioral therapy for male slot-machine gamblers? *British Journal of Clinical Psychology, 51,* 54–71.

Jocklin, V., McGue, M., & Lykken, D. T. (1996). Personality and divorce: A genetic analysis. *Journal of Personality and Social Psychology, 71,* 288–299.

Joensson, E. G., Cichon, S., Gustavsson, J. P., Gruenhage, F., Forslund, K., Mattila-Evenden, M., . . . Noethen, M. M. (2003). Association between a promoter dopamine D-sub-2 receptor gene variant and the personality trait detachment. *Biological Psychiatry, 53,* 577–584.

Johnson, A. (2002). Prevalence and characteristics of children with cerebral palsy in Europe. *Developmental Medicine and Child Neurology, 44,* 633–640

Johnson, C., & Flach, A. (1985). Family characteristics of 105 patients with bulimia. *American Journal of Psychiatry, 142,* 1321–1324.

Johnson, D. L. (1998). The right to refuse medication: Freedom and responsibility. *Psychiatric Rehabilitation Journal, 21,* 252–254.

Johnson, D. L., Swank, P. R., Owen, M. J., Baldwin, C. D., Howie, V. M., & McCormick, D. P.(2000). Effects of early middle ear effusion on child intelligence at three, five, and seven years of age. *Journal of Pediatric Psychology, 25,* 5–13.

Johnson, D. L., Wiebe, J. S., Gold, S. M., Andreasen, N. C., Hichwa, R. D., Watkins, G. L., & Ponto, L. L. B. (1999). Cerebral blood flow and personality: A positron emission tomography study. *American Journal of Psychiatry, 156,* 252–257.

Johnson, D. M., Shea, M. T., Yen, S., Battle, C. L., Zlotnick, C., Sanislow, C. A., . . . McGlashan, T. (2003). Gender differences in borderline personality disorder: Findings from the Collaborative Longitudinal Personalitiy Disorders Study. *Comprehensive Psychiatry, 44,* 284–292.

Johnson, M. E., & Hauck, C. (1999). Beliefs and opinions about hypnosis held by the general public. *American Journal of Clinical Hypnosis, 42,* 10–20.

Johnson, P., Smith, A. J., & Nelson, M. D. (2003). Predictors of social interest in young adults. *Journal of Individual Psychology, 59,* 281–292.

Johnson, S. B. (2013). Increasing psychology's role in health research and health care. *American Psychologist, 68,* 311–321.

Johnson, T. J., & Cropsey, K. L. (2000). Sensation seeking and drinking game participation in heavy-drinking college students. *Addictive Behaviors, 25,* 109–116.

Johnson, W., McGue, M., Krueger, R. F., & Bouchard, T. J., Jr. (2004). Marriage and personality: A genetic analysis. *Journal of Personality and Social Psychology, 86,* 285–294.

Johnson, W. B., Digiuseppe, R., & Ulven, J. (1999). Albert Ellis as mentor: National survey results. *Psychotherapy: Theory, Research, Practice, Training, 36,* 305–312.

Johnston, M., & Vogele, C. (1993). Benefits of psychological preparation for surgery: A meta-analysis. *Annals of Behavioral Medicine, 15,* 245–256.

Johnston, M. V. (2009). Plasticity in the developing brain: Implications for rehabilitation. *Developmental Disabilities Research Reviews, 15,* 94–101.

Jonah, B. A. (1997). Sensation seeking and risky driving: A review and synthesis of the literature. *Accident Analysis and Prevention, 29,* 651–665.

Jonas, G. (1972). *Visceral learning: Toward a science of self-control.* New York: Viking.

Jones, C. J., & Meredith, W. (2000). Developmental paths of psychological health from early adolescence to later adulthood. *Psychology and Aging, 15,* 351–360.

Jones, E. E. (1985). History of social psychology. In G. A. Kimble & K. Schlesinger (Eds.), *Topics in the history of psychology, Vol. 2* (pp. 371–407). Hillsdale, NJ: Erlbaum.

Jones, E. E., & Berglas, S. (1978). Control of attributions about the self through self-handicapping strategies: The appeal of alcohol and the role of underachievement. *Personality & Social Psychology Bulletin, 4,* 200–206.

Jones, J. H. (1997, August 25/September 1). Dr. Yes. *The New Yorker,* pp. 98–113.

Jones, K. D. (2012). A critique of the *DSM-5* field trials. *Journal of Nervous & Mental Disease, 200,* 517–519.

Jones, K. M., & Friman, P. C. (1999). A case study of behavioral assessment and treatment of insect phobia. *Journal of Applied Behavior Analysis, 32,* 95–98.

Jones, L. (1900). Education during sleep. *Suggestive Therapeutics, 8,* 283–285.

Jones, L. V. (1984). White-black achievement differences: The narrowing gap. *American Psychologist, 39,* 1207–1213.

Jones, M. C. (1924). The elimination of children's fears. *Journal of Experimental Psychology, 7,* 383–390.

Jones, M. M. (1980). Conversion disorders: Anachronism or evolutionary form? A review of the neurologic, behavioral, and psychoanalytic literature. *Psychological Bulletin, 87,* 427–441.

Jones, R. B. (2003). Have cholinergic therapies reached their clinical boundary in Alzheimer's disease? *International Journal of Geriatric Psychiatry, 18,* S7–S13.

Jones, S. (2008). Nature and nurture in the development of social smiling. *Philosophical Psychology, 21,* 349–357.

Jorgensen, R. S., Nash, J. K., Lasser, N. L., Hymowitz, N., & Langer, A. W. (1988). Heart rate acceleration and its relationship to total serum cholesterol, triglycerides, and blood pressure. *Psychophysiology, 25,* 39–44.

Joseph, R. (1997). Traumatic amnesia, repression, and hippocampus injury due to emotional stress, corticosteroids, and enkephalins. *Child Psychiatry and Human Development, 29,* 169–185.

Jousselin-Hosaja, M., Venault, P., Tobin, C., Joubert, C., Delacour, J., & Chapouthier, G. (2001). Involvement of adrenal medulla grafts in the open field behavior. *Behavioural Brain Research, 121,* 29–37.

Joyce, J. (1916/1967). *A portrait of the artist as a young man.* New York: Viking.

Joynson, R. B. (2003). Selective interest and psychological practice: A new interpretation of the Burt affair. *British Journal of Psychology, 94,* 409–426.

Judge, S. J., & Cumming, B. G. (1986). Neurons in the monkey midbrain with activity related to convergence eye movement and accommodation. *Journal of Neurophysiology, 55,* 915–930.

Judge, T. A., & Bono, J. E. (2001). Relationship of core self-evaluation traits—self-esteem, generalized self-efficacy, locus of control, and emotional stability—with job satisfaction and job performance: A meta-analysis. *Journal of Applied Psychology, 86,* 80–92.

Julien, R. M. (1981). *A primer of drug action.* San Francisco: Freeman.

Jung, C. G. (1959/1969). *Flying saucers: A modern myth of things seen in the sky.* New York: Signet.

Jussim, L. (1991). Social perception and social reality: A reflection-construction model. *Psychological Review, 98,* 54–73.

K

Kagan, J. (1997). Temperament and the reactions to unfamiliarity. *Child Development, 68,* 139–143.

Kagan, J. (2002). Empowerment and education: Civil rights, expert-advocates, and parent politics in Head Start, 1964–1980. *Teachers College Record, 104,* 516–562.

Kahan, T. L., & LaBerge, S. (1994). Lucid dreaming as metacognition: Implications for cognitive science. *Consciousness and Cognition: An International Journal, 3,* 246–264.

Kahneman, D. (2003). A perspective on judgment and choice: Mapping bounded rationality. *American Psychologist, 58,* 697–720.

Kahneman, D., & Tversky, A. (1973). On the psychology of prediction. *Psychological Review, 80,* 237–251.

Kahneman, D., & Tversky, A. (1982, January). The psychology of preferences. *Scientific American,* pp. 160–173.

Kail, R., & Hall, L. K. (2001). Distinguishing short-term memory from working memory. *Memory and Cognition, 29,* 1–9.

Kako, E. (1999). Elements of syntax in the systems of three language-trained animals. *Animal Learning and Behavior, 27,* 1–14.

Kalafat, J. (2003). School approaches to youth suicide prevention. *American Behavioral Scientist, 46,* 1211–1223.

Kalakoski, V., & Saariluoma, P. (2001). Taxi drivers' exceptional memory of street names. *Memory & Cognition, 29,* 634–638.

Kalbfleisch, M. L. (2008). Introduction to the special issues on the cognitive neuroscience of giftedness. *Roeper Review, 30,* 159–161.

Kalichman, S. C. (1996). HIV-AIDS prevention videotapes: A review of empirical findings. *Journal of Primary Prevention, 17,* 259–280.

Kalish, C. (2002). Gold, jade, and emeruby: The value of naturalness for theories of concepts and categories. *Journal of Theoretical and Philosophical Psychology, 22,* 45–66.

Kaltiala-Heino, R., Koivisto, A.-M., Marttunen, M., & Fröjd, S. (2011). Pubertal timing and substance use in middle adolescence: A 2-year follow-up study. *Journal of Youth and Adolescence, 40,* 1288–1301.

Kalueff, A. V., & Nutt, D. J. (2007). Role of GABA in anxiety and depression. *Depression and Anxiety, 24,* 495–517.

Kamarck, T. W., Peterman, A. H., & Raynor, D. A. (1998). The effects of the social environment on stress-related cardiovascular activation: Current findings, prospects, and implications. *Annals of Behavioral Medicine, 20,* 247–256.

Kamen-Siegel, L., Rodin, J., Seligman, M. E., & Dwyer, J. (1991). Explanatory style and cell-mediated immunity in elderly men and women. *Health Psychology, 10,* 229–235.

Kamin, L. J. (1974). *The science and politics of IQ.* New York: Wiley.

Kamp-Becker, I., Ghahreman., M., Heinzel-Gutenbrunner, M., Peters, M., Remschmidt, H., & Becker, K. (2013). Evaluation of the revised algorithm of Autism Diagnostic Observation Schedule (ADOS) in the diagnostic investigation of high-functioning children and adolescents with autism spectrum disorders. *Autism, 17,* 87–102.

Kanarek, R. B., Mathes, W. F., & D'Anci, K. E. (2012). Exercise promotes positive first impression formation towards both men and women. *Appetite, 58,* 786–789.

Kanda, M., Nagamine, T., Ikeda, A., Ohara, S., Kunieda, T., Fujiwara, N., . . . Shibasaki, H. (2000). Primary somatosensory cortex is actively involved in pain processing in human. *Brain Research, 853,* 282–289.

Kandel, E. R. (2001). The molecular biology of memory storage: A dialogue between genes and synapses. *Science, 294,* 1030–1038.

Kandel, E. R., & Schwartz, J. H. (1982). Molecular biology of learning: Modulation of transmitter release. *Science, 218,* 433–443.

Kanekar, S. (1976). Observational learning of attitudes: A behavioral analysis. *European Journal of Social Psychology, 6,* 5–24.

Kanner, L. (1943). Autistic disturbances of affective contact. *Nervous Child, 2,* 217–250.

Kansaku, K., & Kitazawa, S. (2001). Imaging studies on sex differences in lateralization of language. *Neuroscience Research, 41,* 333–337.

Kapur, S., & Remington, G. (1996). Serotonin-dopamine interaction and its relevance to schizophrenia. *American Journal of Psychiatry, 153,* 466–476.

Karama, S., LeCours, A. R., Leroux, J.-M., Bourgouin, P., Beaudoin, G., Joubert, S., & Beauregard, M. (2002). Areas of brain activation in males and females during viewing of erotic film excerpts. *Human Brain Mapping, 16,* 1–13.

Karau, S. J., & Williams, K. D. (1993). Social loafing: A meta-analytic review and theoretical integration. *Journal of Personality and Social Psychology, 65,* 681–706.

Karcher, M. J., & Lindwall, J. (2003). Social interest, connectedness, and challenging experiences: What makes high school mentors persist? *Journal of Individual Psychology, 59,* 293–315.

Karlberg, L., Krakau, I., & Unden, A.-L. (1998). Type A behavior intervention in primary health care reduces hostility and time pressure: A study in Sweden. *Social Science and Medicine, 46,* 397–402.

Karlin, B. E., Brown, G. K., Trockel, M., Cunning, D., Zeiss, A. M., & Taylor, C. B. (2012). National dissemination of cognitive behavioral therapy for depression in the Department of Veteran Affairs health care system: Therapist and patient-level outcomes. *Journal of Consulting & Clinical Psychology, 80,* 707–718.

Karmel, R. (2003). Freud's "Cocaine Papers" (1884–1887): A commentary. *Canadian Journal of Psychoanalysis, 11,*161–169.

Karney, B. R., & Bradbury, T. N. (2000). Attributions in marriage: State or trait? A growth curve analysis. *Journal of Personality and Social Psychology, 78,* 295–309.

Karnovsky, M. L. (1986). Progress in sleep. *New England Journal of Medicine, 315,* 1026–1028.

Karon, B. P., & Widener, A. (1998). Repressed memories: The real story. *Professional Psychology: Research and Practice, 29,* 482–487.

Kashima, E. S., & Kashima, Y. (1998). Culture and language: The case of cultural dimensions and personal pronoun use. *Journal of Cross-Cultural Psychology, 29,* 461–486.

Kashima, Y., & Triandis, H. C. (1986). The self-serving bias in attributions as a coping strategy: *Journal of Cross-Cultural Psychology, 17,* 83–97.

Kassel, J. D., & Unrod, M. (2000). Smoking, anxiety, and attention: Support for the role of nicotine in attentionally mediated anxiolysis. *Journal of Abnormal Psychology, 109,* 161–166.

Kasser, T., & Sharma, Y. S. (1999). Reproductive freedom, educational equality, and females' preference for resource-acquisition characteristics in mates. *Psychological Science, 10,* 374–377.

Kassin, S. M., Tubb, V. A., Hosch, H. M., & Memon, A. (2001). On the "general acceptance" of eyewitness testimony research. *American Psychologist, 56,* 405–416.

Katata, K., Sakai, N., Doi, K., Kawamitsu, H., Fujii, M., Sugimura K., & Nibu, K. I.(2009). Functional MRI of regional brain responses to "pleasant" and "unpleasant" odors. *Acta Oto-Lryngologica, 129,* 85–90.

Katz, J., & Beach, S. R. H. (2000). Looking for love? Self-verification and self-enhancement effects on initial romantic attraction. *Personality and Social Psychology Bulletin, 26,* 1526–1539.

Katz, J., & Schneider, M. E. (2013). Casual hook-up sex during the first year of college: Prospective associations with attitudes about sex and love relationships. *Archives of Sexual Behavior, 42,* 1451–1462.

Kaufman, I., & Rock, I. (1962, July). The moon illusion. *Scientific American,* 120–130.

Kaufman, J. C. (2010). Editor's introduction. *The International Journal of Creativity & Problem Solving, 20,* 5.

Kavšek, M., Yonas, A., & Granrud, C. E. (2012). Infants' sensitivity to pictorial depth cues: A review and meta-analysis of looking studies. *Infant Behavior & Development, 35,* 109–128.

Kazemi-Bajestani, S. M. R., Amirsadri, A., Samari, S. A. A., & Akbar, J. A. (2011). Lunar phase cycle and psychiatric hospital emergency visits, inpatient admissions and aggressive behavior. *Asian Journal of Psychiatry, 4,* 45–50.

Kebbell, M. R. (2000). The law concerning the conduct of lineups in England and Wales: How well does it satisfy the recommendations of the American Psychology-Law Society? *Law and Human Behavior, 24,* 309–315.

Kebbell, M. R., & Wagstaff, G. F. (1997). An investigation into the influence of hypnosis on the confidence and accuracy of eyewitness recall. *Contemporary Hypnosis, 14,* 157–166.

Kebbell, M. R., & Wagstaff, G. F. (1998). Hypnotic interviewing: The best way to interview eyewitnesses? *Behavioral Sciences and the Law, 16,* 115–129.

Keegan, J., Parva, M., Finnegan, M., Gerson, A., & Beldon, M. (2010). Addiction in pregnancy. *Journal of Addictive Diseases, 29,* 175–191.

Keen, R., Carrico, R. L., Sylvia, M. R., & Berthier, & N. E. (2003). How infants use perceptual information to guide action. *Developmental Science, 6,* 221–231.

Keesey, R. E., & Powley, T. L. (1986). The regulation of body weight. *Annual Review of Psychology, 37,* 109–133.

Keijsers, G. P. J., Schaap, C. P. D. R., & Hoogduin, C. A. L. (2000). The impact of interpersonal patient and therapist behavior on outcome in cognitive-behavioral therapy: A review of empirical studies. *Behavior Modification, 24,* 264–297.

Keillor, J. M., Barrett, A. M., Crucian, G. P., Kortenkamp, S., & Heilman, K. M. (2002). Emotional experience and perception in the absence of facial feedback. *Journal of the International Neuropsychological Society, 8,* 130–135.

Keith, J. R., & McVety, K. M. (1988). Latent place learning in a novel environment and the influences of prior training in rats. *Psychobiology, 16,* 146–151.

Keller, F. S. (1991). Burrhus Frederic Skinner (1904–1990). *Journal of the History of the Behavioral Sciences, 27,* 3–6.

Kelley, H. H. (1950). The warm-cold variable in first impressions of personality. *Journal of Personality, 18,* 431–439.

Kelley, H. H. (1992). Commonsense psychology and scientific discovery. *Annual Review of Psychology, 43,* 1–23.

Kelley, M. Lou, Self-Brown, S., Le, B., Bosson, J. V., Hernandez, B. C., & Gordon, A. T. (2010). Predicting posttraumatic stress symptoms in children following Hurricane Katrina: A prospective analysis of the effect of parental distress and parenting practices. *Journal of Traumatic Stress 23,* 582–590.

Kelly, E. W., Greyson, B., & Stevenson, I. (1999–2000). Can experiences near death furnish evidence of life after death? *Omega: Journal of Death and Dying, 40,* 513–519.

Kelly, J. F., & Greene, M. C. (2013). Where there's a will there's a way: A longitudinal investigation of the interplay between recovery motivation and self-efficacy in predicting treatment outcome. *Psychology of Addictive Behaviors,* Retrieved from http://psycnet.apa.org/psycinfo/2013-40800-001/, 4/20/14.

Kelly, M. P., Strassberg, D. S., & Kircher, J. R. (1990). Attitudinal and experiential correlates of anorgasmia. *Archives of Sexual Behavior, 19,* 165–177.

Kelly, R. B., Zyzanski, S. J., & Alemagno, S. A. (1991). Prediction of motivation and behavior change following health promotion: Role of health beliefs, social support, and self-efficacy. *Social Science and Medicine, 32,* 311–320.

Kelly, S. J., Macaruso, P., & Sokol, S. M. (1997). Mental calculation in an autistic savant: A case study. *Journal of Clinical and Experimental Neuropsychology, 19,* 172–184.

Kelly, W. E., Kelly, K. E., & Clanton, R. C. (2001). The relationship between sleep length and grade point average among college students. *College Student Journal, 35,* 84–86.

Kelsoe, J. R., Kristbjanarson, H., Bergesch, P., & Shilling, P. (1993). A genetic linkage study of bipolar disorder and 13 markers on chromosome 11 including the D-sub-2 dopamine receptor. *Neuropsychopharmacology, 9,* 293–301.

Kemp, B., Krause, J. S., & Adkins, R. (1999). Depression among African Americans, Latinos, and Caucasians with spinal cord injury: An exploratory study. *Rehabilitation Psychology, 44,* 235–247.

Kendler, K. S., Gardner, C. O., & Prescott, C. A. (1998). A population-based twin study of self-esteem and gender. *Psychological Medicine, 28,* 1403–1409.

Kendzierski, D., Sheffield, A., & Morganstein, M. S. (2002). The role of schema in attributions for own versus other's exercise lapse. *Basic and Applied Social Psychology, 24,* 251–260.

Kenneally, S. M., Bruck, G. E., Frank, E. M., & Nalty, L. (1999). Language intervention after thirty years of isolation: A case study of a feral child. *Education and Training in Mental Retardation and Developmental Disabilities, 33,* 13–23.

Kenrick, D. T., & Dantchik, A. (1983). Interactionism, idiographics, and the social psychological invasion of personality. *Journal of Personality, 51,* 286–307.

Kenrick, D. T., & Funder, D. C. (1988). Profiting from controversy: Lessons from the person-situation debate. *American Psychologist, 43,* 23–34.

Keppel, R. D., & Walter, R. (1999). Profiling killers: A revised classification model for understanding sexual murder. *International Journal of Offender Therapy and Comparative Criminology, 43,* 417–437.

Kerkhoff, G., & Rossetti, Y. (2006). Plasticity in spatial neglect—Recovery and rehabilitation. *Restorative Neurology and Neuroscience, 24,* 201–206.

Kerr, N. L., & Tindale, R. S. (2004). Group performance and decision making. *Annual Review of Psychology, 55,* 623–655.

Kessler, R. C., Adler, L. A., Berglund, P., Green, J. G., McLaughlin, K. A., Fayyad, J., . . . Zaslavsky, A. M. (2013). The effects of temporally secondary co-morbid mental disorders on the associations of *DSM-IV* ADHD with adverse outcomes in the U.S. National Comorbidity Survey Replication Adolescent Supplement (NCS-A). *Psychological Medicine/FirstView,* 1–14.

Kessler, R. C., Berglund, P., Demler, O., Jin, R., Merikangas, K. R., & Walters, E. E. (2005). Lifetime prevalence and age-of-onset distributions of *DSM–IV* disorders in the National Comorbidity Survey Replication. *Archives of General Psychiatry, 62,* 593–602.

Kessler, R. C., Chiu, W. T., Demler, O., Merikangas, K. R., & Walters, E. E. (2005). Prevalence, severity, and comorbidity of twelve-month *DSM-IV* disorders in the National Comorbidity Survey Replication (NCS–R). *Archives of General Psychiatry, 62,* 617–627.

Kessler, R. C., Petukhova, M., Sampson, N. A., Zaslavsky, A. M., & Wittchen, H.-U. (2012). Twelve-month and lifetime prevalence and lifetirme morbid risk of anxiety and mood disorders in the United States. *International Journal of Methods in Psychiatric Research, 21,* 169–184.

Kessler, R. C., Stang, P. E., Wittchen, H.-U., Ustun, T. B., Roy-Burne, P. P., & Walters, E. E. (1998). Lifetime panic-depression comorbidity in the National Comorbidity Survey. *Archives of General Psychiatry, 55,* 801–808.

Kessler, R. C., Stein, M. B., & Berglund, P. (1998). Social phobia subtypes in the National Comorbidity Survey. *American Journal of Psychiatry, 155,* 613–619.

Kessler, S. (1984). The myth of mythical disease [Review of *Schizophrenia: Medical diagnosis or moral verdict?*]. *Contemporary Psychology, 29,* 380–381.

Kety, S. S., Wender, P. H., Jacobsen, B., & Ingraham, L. J. (1994). Mental illness in the biological and adoptive relatives of schizophrenic adoptees: Replication of the Copenhagen study in the rest of Denmark. *Archives of General Psychiatry, 51,* 442–455.

Kevles, D. J. (1995, April 3). The X factor: The battle over the ramifications of the gay gene. *The New Yorker,* pp. 85–90.

Kidd, J. A. (2003). The need for improved operational definition of suicide attempts: Illustrations from the case of street youth. *Death Studies, 27,* 449–455.

Kiecolt-Glaser, J. K., & Glaser, R. (1995). Psychoneuroimmunology and health consequences: Data and shared mechanisms. *Psychosomatic Medicine, 57,* 269–274.

Kiecolt-Glaser, J. K., Glaser, R., Strain, E. C., Stout, J. C., Tarr, K. L., Holliday, J. E., & Speicher, C. E. (1986). Modulation of cellular immunity in medical students. *Journal of Behavioral Medicine, 9,* 5–21.

Kiecolt-Glaser, J. K., Marucha, P. T., Malarkey, W. B., Mercado, A M., & Glaser, R. (1995). Slowing of wound healing by psychological stress. *Lancet, 346,* 1194–1196.

Kiecolt-Glaser, J. K., Marucha, P. T., Atkinson, C., & Glaser, R. (2001). Hypnosis as a modulator of cellular immune dysregulation during acute stress. *Journal of Consulting and Clinical Psychology, 69,* 674–682.

Kiecolt-Glaser, J. K., Newton, T., Cacioppo, J. T., MacCallum, R. C., Glaser, R., & Malarkey, W. (1996). Marital conflict and endocrine function: Are men really more physiologically affected than women? *Journal of Consulting and Clinical Psychology, 64,* 324–332.

Kiernan, B. D., Dane, J. R., Phillips, L. H., & Price, D. D. (1995). Hypnotic analgesia reduces R-III nociceptive reflex: Further evidence concerning the multifactorial nature of hypnotic analgesia. *Pain, 60,* 39–47.

Kihlstrom, J. F., & McConkey, K. M. (1990). William James and hypnosis: A centennial reflection. *Psychological Science, 1,* 174–178.

Kilborn, L. C., & Labbe, E. E. (1990). Magnetic resonance imaging scanning procedures: Development of phobic response during scan and at one-month follow-up. *Journal of Behavioral Medicine, 13,* 391–401.

Kilmartin, C. T., & Dervin, D. (1997). Inaccurate representation of the Electra complex in psychology textbooks. *Teaching of Psychology, 24,* 269–271.

Kim, D., Adipudi, V., Shibayama, M., Giszter, S., Tessler, A., Murray, M., & Simansky, K. J. (1999). Direct agonists for serotonin receptors enhance locomotor function in rats that received neural transplants after neonatal spinal transection. *Journal of Neuroscience, 19,* 6213–6224.

Kim, E., Zeppenfeld, V., & Cohen, D. (2013). Sublimation, culture, and creativity. *Journal of Personality & Social Psychology, 105,* 639–666.

Kim, H., & Markus, H. R. (1999). Deviance or uniqueness, harmony or conformity? A cultural analysis. *Journal of Personality and Social Psychology, 77,* 785–800.

Kim, J., Lim, J.-S., & Bhargava, M. (1998). The role of affect in attitude formation: A classical conditioning application. *Journal of the Academy of Marketing Science, 26,* 143–152.

Kim, J. E., & Moen, P. (2001). Is retirement good or bad for subjective well-being? *Current Directions in Psychological Science, 10,* 83–86.

Kim, J. S., Yoon, S. S., Lee, S. I., Yoo, H. J., Kim, C. Y., Choi-Kwon, S., & Lee, B. C. (1998). Type A behavior and stroke: High tenseness dimension may be a risk factor for cerebral infarction. *European Neurology, 39,* 168–173.

Kim, Y. I. (2003). The effects of assertiveness training on enhancing the social skills of adolescents with visual impairments. *Journal of Visual Impairment and Blindness, 97,* 285–297.

Kim-Cohen, J., Caspi, A., Taylor, A., Williams, B., Newcombe, R., Craig, I. W., Moffitt, T. E. (2006). MAOA, maltreatment, and gene-environment interaction predicting children's mental health: New evidence and a meta-analysis. *Molecular Psychiatry 11,* 903–913

Kimball, M. M. (1989). A new perspective on women's math achievement. *Psychological Bulletin, 105,* 198–214.

Kimball, M. M. (1995). *Gender and math: What makes a difference? Feminist visions of gender similarities and differences.* New York: Harrington Park Press.

Kimball, M. M. (2000). From "Anna O." to Bertha Pappenheim: Transforming private pain into public action. *History of Psychology, 3,* 20–43.

Kimble, G. A. (1981). Biological and cognitive constraints on learning. In L. T. Benjamin, Jr. (Ed.), *The G. Stanley Hall Lecture Series, Vol. 1* (pp. 11–60). Washington, DC: American Psychological Association.

Kimura, D. (1987). Are men's and women's brains really different? *Canadian Psychology, 28,* 133–147.

Kimura, D., & Hampson, E. (1994). Cognitive pattern in men and women is influenced by fluctuations in sex hormones. *Current Directions in Psychological Science, 3,* 57–61.

Kimura, R., MacTavish, D., Yang, J., Westaway, D., & Jhamandas, J. H. (2012). Beta amyloid-induced depression of hippocampal long-term potentiation is mediated through the amylin receptor. *Journal of Neuroscience, 32,* 17401–17406.

King, D. B., Raymond, B. L., & Simon-Thomas, J. A. (1995). History of sport psychology in cultural magazines of the Victorian era. *Sport Psychologist, 9,* 376–390.

King, L. A., & Miner, K. N. (2000). Writing about the perceived benefits of traumatic events: Implications for physical health. *Personality and Social Psychology Bulletin, 26,* 220–230.

King, N. J., Clowes-Hollins, V., & Ollendick, T. H. (1997). The etiology of childhood dog phobia. *Behaviour Research and Therapy, 35,* 77.

King, R. (1998). Evidence-based practice: Where is the evidence? The case of cognitive behaviour therapy and depression. *Australian Psychologist, 33,* 83–88.

Kinsey, A. C., Pomeroy, W. D., & Martin, C. E. (1948). *Sexual behavior in the human male.* Philadelphia: Saunders.

Kinsey, A. C., Pomeroy, W. D., Martin, C. E., & Gebhard, T. H. (1953). *Sexual behavior in the human female.* Philadelphia: Saunders.

Kirmayer, L. J., Narasiah, L., Munoz, M., Rashid, M., Ryder, A. G., Guzder, J., . . . Pottie, K. (2011). Common mental health problems in immigrants and refugees: General approach in primary care. *Canadian Medical Association Journal, 183,* e959–e967.

Kirmeyer, S. L., & Biggers, K. (1988). Environmental demand and demand engineering behavior: An observational analysis of the Type A patterns. *Journal of Personality and Social Psychology, 54,* 997–1005.

Kirsch, I. (1996). Hypnotic enhancement of cognitive-behavioral weight loss treatments: Another meta-reanalysis. *Journal of Consulting and Clinical Psychology, 64,* 517–519.

Kirschner, S. M., & Galperin, G. J. (2001). Psychiatric defenses in New York County: Pleas and results. *Journal of the American Academy of Psychiatry and the Law, 29,* 194–201.

Kisch, J., & Erber, J. (1999). Operant conditioning of antennal movements in the honey bee. *Behavioural Brain Research, 99,* 93–102.

Kisilevsky, B. S., & Hains, S. M. J. (2011). Onset and maturation of fetal heart rate response to the mother's voice over late gestations. *Developmental Science, 14,* 214–223.

Kisner, M. J. (2005). Scepticism and the early Descartes. *British Journal for the History of Philosophy, 13,* 207–235.

Kitayama, S., Duffy, S., Kawamura, T., & Larsen, J. T. (2003). Perceiving object and its context in different cultures. *Psychological Science, 14,* 201–206.

Kitayama, S., Markus, H. R., & Kurokawa, M. (2000). Culture, emotion, and well-being: Good feelings in Japan and the United States. *Cognition and Emotion, 14,* 93–124.

Kittlerova, P., & Valouskova, V. (2000). Retinal ganglion cells regenerating through the peripheral nerve graft retain their electroretinographic responses and mediate light-induced behavior. *Behavioural Brain Research, 112,* 187–194.

Kittrell, D., (1998). A comparison of the evolution of men's and women's dreams in Daniel Levinson's theory of adult development. *Journal of Adult Development, 5,* 105–115.

Kjellgren, A., Sundequist, U., Norlander, T., & Archer, T. (2001). Effects of flotation-REST on muscle tension pain. *Pain Research & Management, 6,* 181–189.

Klahr, A. M., Rueter, M. A., McGue, M., Iacono, W. G., & Alexandra, B. S. (2011). The relationship between parent-child conflict and adolescent antisocial behavior: Confirming shared environmental mediation. *Journal of Abnormal Child Psychology, 39,* 683–694.

Klar, Y., & Giladi, E. E. (1999). Are most people happier than their peers, or are they just happy? *Personality and Social Psychology Bulletin, 25,* 585–594.

Kleiber, C., & Harper, D. C. (1999). Effects of distraction on children's pain and distress during medical procedures: A meta-analysis. *Nursing Research, 48,* 44–49.

Klein, A. G. (2000). Fitting the school to the child: The mission of Leta Stetter Hollingworth, founder of gifted education. *Roeper Review, 23,* 97–103.

Klein, P. D. (1997). Multiplying the problems of intelligence by eight: A critique of Gardner's theory. *Canadian Journal of Education, 22,* 377–394.

Klein, S. B. (1982). *Motivation: Biosocial approaches.* New York: McGraw-Hill.

Kleindienst, N., & Greil, W. (2003). Lithium in the long-term treatment of bipolar disorders. *European Archives of Psychiatry and Clinical Neuroscience, 253,* 120–125.

Kleinke, C. L., Peterson, T. R., & Rutledge, T. R. (1998). Effects of self-generated facial expressions on mood. *Journal of Personality and Social Psychology, 74,* 272–279.

Kleinmuntz, B., & Szucko, J. J. (1984a). A field study of the fallibility of polygraph lie detection. *Nature, 308,* 449–450.

Kleinmuntz, B., & Szucko, J. J. (1984b). Lie detection in ancient and modern times: A call for contemporary scientific study. *American Psychologist, 39,* 766–776.

Klepac, R. K. (1986). Fear and avoidance of dental treatment in adults. *Annals of Behavioral Medicine, 8,* 17–22.

Klimesch, W., (2012). Alpha-band oscillations, attention, and controlled access to stored information. *Trends in Cognitive Sciences, 16,* 606–617.

Kling, K. C., Hyde, J. S., Showers, C. J., & Buswell, B. N. (1999). Gender differences in self-esteem: A meta-analysis. *Psychological Bulletin, 125,* 470–500.

Kling, K. C., Hyde, J. S., Showers, C. J., & Buswell, B. N. (1999). Gender differences in self-esteem: A meta-analysis. *Psychological Bulletin, 125,* 470–500.

Klohnen, E. C., & Luo, S. (2003). Interpersonal attraction and personality: What is attractive— Self similarity, ideal similarity, complementarity, or attachment security? *Journal of Personality and Social Psychology 85,* 709–722.

Klonoff, E. A., Janata, J. W., & Kaufman, B. (1986). The use of systematic desensitization to overcome resistance to magnetic resonance imaging (MRI) scanning. *Journal of Behavior Therapy and Experimental Psychiatry, 17,* 189–192.

Klonoff, E. A., & Moore, D. J. (1986). "Conversion reactions" in adolescents: A biofeedback-based operant approach. *Journal of Behavior Therapy and Experimental Psychiatry, 17,* 179–184.

Klosterhalfen, W., & Klosterhalfen, S. (1983). A critical analysis of the animal experiments cited in support of learned helplessness. *Psychologische Beitrage, 25,* 436–458.

Kluft, R. P. (1987). An update on multiple personality disorder. *Hospital and Community Psychiatry, 38,* 363–373.

Klump, K. L., McGue, M., & Iacono, W. G. (2002). Genetic relationship between personality and eating attitudes and behaviors. *Journal of Abnormal Psychology, 111,* 380–389.

Klump, K. L., Miller, K. B., Keel P. K., McGue, M., & Iacono, W. G. (2001). Genetic and environmental influences on anorexia nervosa syndromes in a population–based twin sample. *Psychological Medicine, 31,* 737–740.

Klüver, H., & Bucy, P. C. (1937). "Psychic blindness" and other symptoms following bilateral temporal lobectomy in rhesus monkeys. *American Journal of Physiology, 119,* 352–353.

Kmiecik-Małecka, E., Małecki, A., Pawlas, N., Woźniakova, Y., & Pawlas, K. (2009). The effect of blood lead concentration on EEG, brain electrical activity mapping and psychological test results in children. *Polish Journal of Environmental Studies, 18,* 1021–1027.

Knapp, T. J., & Shodahl, S. A. (1974). Ben Franklin as a behavior modifier: A note. *Behavior Therapy, 5,* 656–660.

Knee, C. R., & Boon, S. D. (2001). When the glass is half-empty: Framing effects and evaluations of a romantic partner's attributes. *Personal Relationships, 8,* 249–263.

Knishkowy, B., Verbov, G., Amitai, Y., Stein-Zamir, C., & Reinvang, I. (2012). Reaching Jewish ultra-orthodox adolescents: Results from a targeted smoking prevention trial. *International Journal of Adolescent Medicine & Health, 24,* 173–179.

Knouse, S. B. (1994). Impressions of the resume: The effects of applicant education, experience, and impression management. *Journal of Business and Psychology, 9,* 33–45.

Knox, S. S., & Uvnaes-Moberg, K. (1998). Social isolation and cardiovascular disease: An atherosclerotic pathway? *Psychoneuroendocrinology, 23,* 877–890.

Knudsen, E. I. (1981, December). The hearing of the barn owl. *Scientific American,* pp. 112–113, 115–116, 118–125.

Kobasa, S. C., Maddi, S. R., & Kahn, S. (1982). Hardiness and health: A prospective study. *Journal of Personality and Social Psychology, 42,* 168–177.

Kobayakawa, T., Ogawa, H., Kaneda, H., Ayabe-Kanamura, S., Endo, H., & Saito, S. (1999). Spatio-temporal analysis of cortical activity evoked by gustatory stimulation in humans. *Chemical Senses, 24,* 201–209.

Koch, G., Di Lorenzo, F., Bonnì, S., Ponzo, V., Caltagagirone, C., & Martorana, A., (2012). Impaired LTP-but not LTD-like cortical plasticity in Alzheimer's Disease patients. *Journal of Alzheimer's Disease, 31,* 593–599.

Kocsis, R. N. (2013). The criminal profiling reality: What is actually behind the smoke and mirrors? *Journal of Forensic Psychology Practice, 13,* 79–91.

Kocsis, R. N., Hayes, A. F., & Irwin, H. J. (2002). Investigative experience and accuracy in psychological profiling of a violent crime. *Journal of Interpersonal Violence, 17,* 811–823.

Kocsis, R. N., Irwin, H. J., & Hayes, A. F. (1998). Organised and disorganised criminal behaviour syndromes in arsonists: A validation study of a psychological profiling concept. *Psychiatry, Psychology, and Law, 5,* 117–131.

Koehler, J. J., & Conley, C. A. (2003). The "hot hand" myth in professional basketball. *Journal of Sport and Exercise Psychology, 25,* 253–259.

Kohlberg, L. (1981). *Essays on moral development.* New York: Harper & Row.

Köhler, W. (1925). *The mentality of apes.* New York: Harcourt Brace Jovanovich.

Köhler, W. (1959). Gestalt psychology today. *American Psychologist, 14,* 727–734.

Kohnken, G., & Maass, A. (1988). Eyewitness testimony: False alarms on biased instructions. *Journal of Applied Psychology, 73,* 363–370.

Kolata, G. (1985). Why do people get fat? *Science, 227,* 1327–1328.

Kolata, G. (1987). Associations or rules in learning language? *Science, 237,* 133–134.

Komisaruk, B. R., & Whipple, B. (2005). Functional MRI of the brain during orgasm in women. *Annual Review of Sex Research, 16,* 62–86.

Koole, S. L., Greenberg, J., & Pyszczynski, T. (2006). Introducing psychology to the science of the soul: Experimental existential psychology. *Current Directions in Psychological Science, 15,* 212–216.

Koopmans, J. R., Boomsma, D. I., Heath, A. C., & van Doornen, L. J. P. (1995). A multivariate genetic analysis of sensation seeking. *Behavior Genetics, 25,* 349–356.

Kopelman, M. D., Christensen, H., Puffett, A., & Stanhope, N. (1994). The great escape: A neuropsychological study of psychogenic amnesia. *Neuropsychologia, 32,* 675–691.

Koppe, S. (1983). The psychology of the neuron: Freud, Cajal, and Golgi. *Scandinavian Journal of Psychology, 24,* 1–12.

Koretz, J., & Gutheil, T. G. (2009). "I can't let anything go": A case study with psychological testing of a patient with pathologic hoarding. *American Journal of Psychotherapy, 63,* 257–266.

Korpi, E. R. (1994). Role of GABA-sub(A) receptors in the actions of alcohol and in alcoholism: Recent advances. *Alcohol and Alcoholism, 29,* 115–129.

Korsnes, M. S., Magnussen, S., & Reinvang, I. (1996). Serial position effects in visual short-term memory for words and abstract spatial patterns. *Scandinavian Journal of Psychology, 37,* 62–73.

Kosmicki, F. X., & Glickauf–Hughes, C. (1997). Catharsis in psychotherapy. *Psychotherapy, 34,* 154–159.

Kossowsky, J., Pfaltz, M. C., Schneider, S., Taeymans, J., Locher, C., & Gaab, J. (2013). The separation anxiety hypothesis of panic disorder revisited: A meta-analysis. *American Journal of Psychiatry, 170,* 768–781.

Kotani, H. (1999). Aspects of intrapsychic, interpersonal and cross-cultural dynamics in Japanese group psychotherapy. *International Journal of Group Psychotherapy, 49,* 93–104.

Kotz, S. A., Meyer, M., Alter, K., Besson, M., von Cramon, D. Y., & Friederici, A. D. (2003). On the lateralization of emotional prosody: An event-related functional MR investigation. *Brain and Language, 86,* 366–376.

Kovac, S. H., & Range, L. M. (2000). Writing projects: Lessening undergraduates' unique suicidal bereavement. *Suicide and Life-Threatening Behavior, 30,* 50–60.

Kovar, K. A. (1998) Chemistry and pharmacology of hallucinogens, entactogens, and stimulants. *Pharmacopsychiatry, 31,* 69–72.

Kozub, S. A., & McDonnell, J. F. (2000). Exploring the relationship between cohesion and collective efficacy in rugby teams. *Journal of Sport Behavior, 23,* 120–129.

Kposowa, A. J. (2000). Marital status and suicide in the National Longitudinal Mortality Study. *Journal of Epidemiology and Community Health, 54,* 254–261.

Krafka, C., & Penrod, S. (1985). Reinstatement of context in a field experiment on eyewitness identification. *Journal of Personality and Social Psychology, 49,* 58–69.

Krakow, B., Schrader, R., Tandberg, D., Hollifield, M., Koss, M. P., Yau, C. L., & Cheng, D. T. (2002). Nightmare frequency in sexual assault survivors with PTSD. *Journal of Anxiety Disorders, 16,* 175–190.

Kralikova, E., Kozak, J. T., Rasmussen, T., Gustavsson, G., & Le Houezec, J. (2009). Smoking cessation or reduction with nicotine replacement therapy: A placebo-controlled double blind trial with nicotine gum and inhaler. *BMC Public Health, 9,* 433–440.

Kramer, D. E., & Bayern, C. D. (1984). The effects of behavioral strategies on creativity training. *Journal of Creative Behavior, 18,* 23–24.

Krantz, D. S., Contrada, R. J., Hill, D. R., & Friedler, E. (1988). Environmental stress and biobehavioral antecedents of coronary heart disease. *Journal of Consulting and Clinical Psychology, 56,* 333–341.

Krantz, D. S., & Manuck, S. B. (1984). Acute psychophysiologic reactivity and risk of cardiovascular disease: A review and methodologic critique. *Psychological Bulletin, 96,* 435–464.

Kraus, S. J. (1995). Attitudes and the prediction of behavior: A meta-analysis of the empirical literature. *Personality and Social Psychology Bulletin, 21,* 58–75.

Krause, J. S. (1998). Subjective well-being after spinal-cord injury: Relationship to gender, race-ethnicity, and chronologic age. *Rehabilitation Psychology, 43,* 282–296.

Kravitz, D. A., & Martin, B. (1986). Ringelmann rediscovered: The original article. *Journal of Personality and Social Psychology, 50,* 936–941.

Kreisman, J. J., & Straus, H. (1989). *I hate you-Don't leave me: Understanding the borderline disorder.* New York: Avon Books.

Kremer, J. F., & Dietzen, L. L. (1991). Two approaches to teaching accurate empathy to undergraduates: Teacher-intensive and self-directed. *Journal of College Student Development, 32,* 69–75.

Kremer, T. G., & Gesten, E. L. (1998). Confidentiality limits of managed care and clients' willingness to self-disclose. *Professional Psychology: Research and Practice, 29,* 553–558.

Kreppner, K. (1992). William L. Stern, 1871–1938: A neglected founder of developmental psychology. *Developmental Psychology, 28,* 539–547.

Kretch, K. S., & Adolph, K. E. (2013). Cliff or step? Posture-specific learning at the edge of a drop-off. *Child Development, 84,* 226–240.

Kretschmer, E. (1925). *Physique and character.* New York: Harcourt, Brace.

Krichmar, J. L., & Edelman, G. M. (2002). Machine psychology: Autonomous behavior, perceptual categorization and conditioning in a brain-based device. *Cerebral Cortex, 12,* 818–830.

Krinsky, R., & Krinsky, S. G. (1994). The peg-word mnemonic facilitates immediate but not long-term memory in fifth-grade children. *Contemporary Educational Psychology, 19,* 217–229.

Krippner, S. (1995). Psychical research in the postmodern world. *Journal of the American Society for Psychical Research, 89,* 1–18.

Krippner, S., & Thompson, A. (1996). A 10-factor model of dreaming applied to dream practices of 16 Native-American cultural groups. *Dreaming: Journal of the Association for the Study of Dreams, 6,* 71–96.

Krippner, S., Braud, W., Child, I. L., & Palmer, J. (1993). Demonstration research and meta-analysis in parapsychology. *Journal of Parapsychology, 57,* 275–286.

Krippner, S., Vaughan, A., & Spottiswoode, S. J. P. (2000). Geomagnetic factors in subjective precognitive dream experiences. *Journal of the Society for Psychical Research, 64,* 109–117.

Krishnan, H. S., & Chakravarti, D. (2003). A process analysis of the effects of humorous advertisng executions on brand claims memory. *Journal of Consumer Psychology, 18,* 230–245.

Krishnan, R. V., Sankar, V., & Muthusamy, R. (2001). Recovery of locomotor function in adult paraplegic frogs by inductive lability in the distal isolated spinal cord neural networks. *International Journal of Neuroscience, 108,* 43–54.

Kroenke, K., & Spitzer, R. L. (1998). Gender differences in the reporting of physical and somatoform symptoms. *Psychosomatic Medicine, 60,* 150–155.

Kropp, P., Brecht. I.-B., Niederberger, U., Kowalski, J., Schröder, D., Thome, J., . . . Gerber, W. D. (2012). Time-dependent post-imperative negative variation indicates adaptation and problem-solving in migraine patients. *Journal of Neural Transmission, 119,* 1213–1221.

Krueger, T. H. C., Haake, P., Hartmann, U., Schedlowski, M., & Exton, M. S. (2002). Orgasm-induced prolactin secretion: Feedback control of sexual drive? *Neuroscience and Biobehavioral Reviews, 26,* 31–44.

Krupa, D. J., Thompson, J. K., & Thompson, R. F. (1993). Localization of a memory trace in the mammalian brain. *Science, 260,* 989–991.

Krupnick, J. L., Sotsky, S. M., Simmens, S., & Moyer, J. (1996). The role of the therapeutic alliance in psychotherapy and pharmacotherapy outcome: Findings in the National Institute of Mental Health Treatment of Depression Collaborative Research Program. *Journal of Consulting and Clinical Psychology, 64,* 532–539.

Kübler-Ross, E. (1969). *On death and dying.* New York: Macmillan.

Kübler-Ross, E. (1974). *Questions and answers on death and dying.* New York: Macmillan.

Kubzansky, L. D., Sparrow, D., Vokonas, P., & Kawachi, I. (2001). Is the glass half empty or half full? A prospective study of optimism and coronary heart disease in the normative aging study. *Psychosomatic Medicine, 63,* 910–916.

Kudo, F. T., Longhofer, J. L., & Floersch, J. E. (2012). On the origins of early leadership: The role of authoritative parenting practices and mastery orientation. *Leadership, 8,* 345–375.

Kuehberger, A. (1998). The influence of framing on risky decisions: A meta-analysis. *Organizational Behavior and Human Decision Processes, 75,* 23–55.

Kuelbelbeck, A. (1991, August 23). A real high point. *Los Angeles Times,* p. E1.

Kugel, W. (1990-91). Amplifying precognition: Two experiments with roulette. *European Journal of Parapsychology, 8,* 85–97.

Kugihara, N. (1999). Gender and social loafing in Japan. *Journal of Social Psychology, 139,* 516–526.

Kuhlman, T. L. (1985). A study of salience and motivational theories of humor. *Journal of Personality and Social Psychology, 49,* 281–286.

Kuhlmann, H. (2005). *Living Walden Two: B. F. Skinner's behaviorist utopia and experimental communities.* Champaign, IL: University of Illinois Press.

Kuhn, T. S. (1970). *The structure of scientific revolutions.* Chicago: University of Chicago Press.

Kukla, A. (1989). Nonempirical issues in psychology. *American Psychologist, 44,* 785–794.

Kulik, J. A., & Mahler, H. I. M. (1987). Effects of preoperative roommate assignment and preoperative anxiety and recovery from coronarybypass surgery. *Health Psychology, 6,* 525–543.

Kumar, A. (2000). Interference effects of contextual cues in advertisements on memory for ad content. *Journal of Consumer Psychology, 9,* 155–166.

Kumar, K. B., Ramalingam, S.,& Karanth, K. S. (1994). Phenytoin and phenobarbital: A comparison of their state-dependent effects. *Pharmacology, Biochemistry, and Behavior, 47,* 951–956.

Kumari, V., Hemsley, D. R., Cotter, P. A., Checkley, S. A., & Gray, J. A. (1998). Haloperidol-induced mood and retrieval of happy and unhappy memories. *Cognition and Emotion, 12,* 437–508.

Kumkale, G. T., & Albarracin, D. (2004). The sleeper effect in persuasion: A meta-analytic review. *Psychological Bulletin, 130,* 143–172.

Kuncel, N. R., Hezlett, S. A., & Ones, D. S. (2001). A comprehensive meta-analysis of the predictive validity of the graduate record examinations: Implications for graduate student selection and performance. *Psychological Bulletin, 127,* 162–181.

Kunda, Z., & Schwartz, S. H. (1983). Undermining intrinsic moral motivation: External reward and self-presentation. *Journal of Personality and Social Psychology, 45,* 763–771.

Kunda, Z., & Spencer, S. J. (2003). When do stereotypes come to mind and when do they color judgment? A goal-based theoretical framework for stereotype activation and application. *Psychological Bulletin, 129,* 522–544.

Kuo, L. E., Kitlinska, J. B., Tilan, J. U., Li, L., Baker, S. B., Johnson, M. D., . . . Zukowska, Z. (2007). Neuropeptide Y acts directly in the periphery on fat tissue and mediates stress-induced obesity and metabolic syndrome. *Nature Medicine, 1,* 803–811.

Kupán, K., Miklósi, Á., Gergely, G., & Topál, J. Why do dogs (*Canis familiaris*) select the empty container in an observational learning task? *Animal Cognition, 14,* 259–268.

Kupfer, D. J., Kuhl, E. A., & Regier, D. A. *DSM-5*—The future arrived. *JAMA: Journal of the American Medical Association, 309,* 1691–1692.

Kurdek, L. A. (1998). Relationship outcomes and their predictors: Longitudinal evidence from heterosexual married, gay cohabiting, and lesbian cohabiting couples. *Journal of Marriage and the Family, 60,* 553–568.

Kurdek, L. A. (1999). The nature and predictors of the trajectory of change in marital quality for husbands and wives over the first 10 years of marriage. *Developmental Psychology, 35,* 1283–1296.

Kwee, M., & Ellis, A. (1998). The interface between rational emotive behavior therapy (REBT) and Zen. *Journal of Rational-Emotive and Cognitive Behavior Therapy. 16,* 5–43.

L

La Roche, M., & Lustig,K. Being mindful about the assessment of culture: A cultural analysis of culturally adapted acceptance-based behavior therapy approaches. *Cognitive and Behavioral Practice, 20,* 60–63.

La Vaque, T. J. (1999). History of EEG Hans Berger: Psychophysiologist. A historical vignette. *Journal of Neurotherapy, 3,* 1–9.

LaBar, K. S., & Cabeza, R. (2006). Cognitive neuroscience of emotional memory. *Nature Reviews, 7,* 54–64.

LaFrance, M., Hecht, M. A., & Paluck, E. L. (2003). The contingent smile: A meta-analysis of sex differences in smiling. *Psychological Bulletin, 129,* 305–334.

Laing, R. D. (1967). *The politics of experience.* New York: Ballantine Books.

Laitinen, J., Ek, E., & Sovio, U. (2001). Stress–related eating and drinking behavior and body mass index and predictors of this behavior. *Preventive Medicine, 34,* 29–39.

Lake, A. E., III, & Saper, J. R. (2002). Chronic headache: New advances in treatment strategies. *Neurology, 59,* S8–S13.

Lake, C. R. (2012). *Schizophrenia is a misdiagnosis: Implications for the DSM-5 and ICD-11.* New York: Springer.

Lakkis, J., & Ricciardelli, L. A., & Williams, R. J. (1999). Role of sexual orientation and gender-related traits in disordered eating. *Sex Roles, 41,* 1–16.

Lal, S. (2002). Giving children security: Mamie Phipps Clark and the racialization of child psychology. *American Psychologist, 57,* 20–28.

Lalancette, M. F., & Standing, L. G. (1990). Asch fails again. *Social Behavior and Personality, 18,* 7–12.

Lalumiere, M. L., Blanchard, R., & Zucker, K. J. (2000). Sexual orientation and handedness in men and women: A meta-analysis. *Psychological Bulletin, 126,* 575–592.

Lam, D.C.K., Salkovskis, P. M., & Warwick, H. M. C. (2005). An experimental investigation of the impact of biological versus psychological explanations of the cause of "mental illness." *Journal of Mental Health, 14,* 453–464.

Lamb, M. E. (1996). Effects of nonparental child care on child development: An update. *Canadian Journal of Psychiatry, 41,* 330–342.

Lamb, M. E. (2012). Mothers, fathers, families and circumstances: Factors affecting children's adjustment. *Applied Developmental Science, 16,* 98–111.

Lamb, R. H. (1998). Deinstitutionalization at the beginning of the new millennium. *Harvard Review of Psychiatry, 6,* 1–10.

Lamb, T. (1999). Obituary: Alan Hodgkin (1914–98). *Nature, 397,* 112.

Lambdin, J. R., Greer, K. M., Jibotian, K. S., Wood, K. R., & Hamilton, M. C. (2003). The animal = male hypothesis: Children's and adults' beliefs about the sex of non-sex-specific stuffed animals. *Sex Roles, 48,* 471–482.

Lambert, M. J. (1989). The individual therapist's contribution to psychotherapy process and outcome. *Clinical Psychology Review, 9,* 469–485.

Lambert, N. M. (1981). Psychological evidence in *Larry P. v. Wilson Riles. American Psychologist, 36,* 937–952.

Lambert, S. M., Moore, D. W., & Dixon, R. S. (1999). Gymnasts in training: The differential effects of self- and coach-set goals as a function of locus of control. *Journal of Applied Sport Psychology, 11,* 72–82.

Lamme, V. A. F. (1995). The neurophysiology of figure-ground segregation in primary visual cortex. *Journal of Neuroscience, 15,* 1605–1615.

Lanciano, T., Curci, A., & Semin, G. R. (2010). The emotional and reconstructive determinants of emotional memories: An experimental approach to flashbulb memory investigation. *Memory, 18,* 473–485.

Landers, S. (1987, December). Aversive device sparks controversy. *APA Monitor,* p. 15.

Landesman, S., & Ramey, C. (1989). Developmental psychology and mental retardation: Integrating scientific principles with treatment practices. *American Psychologist, 44,* 409–415.

Landis, D., & O'Shea, W. A. (2000). Cross-cultural aspects of passionate love: An individual differences analysis. *Journal of Cross-Cultural Psychology, 31,* 752–777.

Landolt, A. S., & Milling, L. S. (2011). The efficacy of hypnosis as an intervention for labor and delivery pain: A comprehensive methodological review. *Clinical Psychology Review, 31,* 1022–1031.

Landolt, H. P., Werth, E., Borbely, A. A., & Dijk, D. J. (1995). Caffeine intake (200 mg) in the morning affects human sleep and EEG power spectra at night. *Brain Research, 675,* 67–74.

Landrine, H. (1987). On the politics of madness: A preliminary analysis of the relationship between social roles and psychopathology. *Psychology Monographs, 113,* 341–406.

Landrine, H. (1989). The politics of personality disorder. *Psychology of Women Quarterly, 13,* 325–339.

Landrine, H., & Klonoff, E. A. (1994). Cultural diversity in causal attributions for illness: The role of the supernatural. *Journal of Behavioral Medicine, 17,* 181–194.

Landy, F. J. (1997). Early influences on the development of industrial and organizational psychology. *Journal of Applied Psychology, 86,* 467–477.

Laner, M. R., Benin, M. H., & Ventrone, N. A. (2001). Bystander attitudes toward victims of violence: Who's worth helping? *Deviant Behavior, 22,* 23–42.

Lang, A. J., Craske, M. G., Grown, M., & Ghaneian, A. (2001). Fear–related state dependent memory. *Cognition and Emotion, 15,* 695–703.

Lang, P. J. (1994). The varieties of emotional experience: A meditation on James-Lange theory. *Psychological Review, 101,* 211–221.

Lang, P. J., Bradley, M. M., & Cuthbert, B. N. (1998). Emotion, motivation, and anxiety: Brain mechanisms and psychophysiology. *Biological Psychiatry, 44,* 1248–1263.

Langenbucher, J. W., & Nathan, P. E. (1983). Psychology, public policy, and the evidence for alcohol intoxication. *American Psychologist, 38,* 1070–1077.

Langer, E. J., & Rodin, J. (1976). The effects of choice and enhanced personal responsibility for the aged: A field experiment in an institutional setting. *Journal of Personality and Social Psychology, 34,* 191–198.

Langlois, J. H., Kalakanis, L., Rubenstein, A. J., Larson, A., Hallam, M., & Smoot, M. (2000). Maxims or myths of beauty? A meta-analytic and theoretical review. *Psychological Bulletin, 126,* 390–423.

Langone, J. (1983, September). B. F. Skinner: Beyond reward and punishment. *Discover,* pp. 38–46.

Lantz, J., & Gregoire, T. (2000). Existential psychotherapy with couples facing breast cancer: A twenty year report. *Contemporary Family Therapy, 22,* 315–327.

Lapidus, K. A. B., Kopell, B. H., Ben-Haim, S., Rezai, A. R., & Goodman, W. K. (2013). History of psychosurgery: A psychiatrist's perspective. *World Neurosurgery, 80,* 1–16.

LaPiere, R. T. (1934). Attitudes versus action. *Social Forces, 13,* 230–237.

Larimer, M. E., Lydum, A. R., Anderson, B. K., & Turner, A. P. (1999). Male and female recipients of unwanted sexual contact in a college student sample: Prevalence rates, alcohol use, and depression symptoms. *Sex Roles, 40,* 295–308.

Lariviere, W. R., Wilson, S. G., Laughlin, T. M., Kokayeff, A., West, E. E., Adhikari, S. M., Wan, Y., & Mogil, J. S. (2002). Heritability of nociception. III. Genetic relationships among commonly used assays of nociception and hypersensitivity. *Pain, 97,* 75–86.

Laroche, M., Nepomuceno, M. V., Huang, L., & Richard, M. (2011). What's so funny? The use of humor in magazine advertising in the United States, China, and France. *Journal of Advertising Research, 51,* 404–416.

Larsen, K. S. (1990). The Asch conformity experiment: Replication and transhistorical comparisons. *Journal of Social Behavior and Personality, 5,* 163–168.

Larsson, H., Chang, Z., D'Onofrio, B. M., & Lichtenstein, P. (2013). The heritability of clinically diagnosed attention deficit hyperactivity disorder across the lifespan. *Psychological Medicine/FirstView,* 1–7.

Lashley, K. S (1950). In search of the engram. In *Symposium of the Society for Experimental Biology* (Vol. 4, pp. 454–482). New York: Cambridge University Press.

Laska, M., Scheuber, H.-P., Sanchez, E. C., & Luna, E. R. (1999). Taste difference thresholds for sucrose in two species of nonhuman primates. *American Journal of Primatology, 48,* 153–160.

Lassonde, M., & Sauerwein, H. C. (2003). Agenesis of the corpus callosum. In K. Hugdahl & R. J. Davidson (Eds.), *The asymmetrical brain* (pp. 619–649). Cambridge, MA: MIT Press.

Latané, B., & Darley, J. M. (1968). Group inhibition of bystander intervention in emergencies. *Journal of Personality and Social Psychology, 10,* 215–221.

Lattal, K. A. (1995). Contingency and behavior analysis. *Behavior Analyst, 18,* 209–224.

Laumann, E. O., Gagnon, J. H., Michael, R. T., & Michaels, S. (1994). *The social organization of sexuality.* Chicago: University of Chicago Press.

Laumann, E. O., Paik, A., & Rosen, R. C. (1999). Sexual dysfunction in the United States: Prevalence and predictors. *Journal of the American Medical Association, 281,* 537–544.

Laurence, J. R., & Perry, C. (1983). Hypnotically created memory among highly hypnotizable subjects. *Science, 222,* 523–524.

Laursen, B., Coy, K. C., & Collins, W. A. (1998). Reconsidering changes in parent-child conflict across adolescence: A meta-analysis. *Child Development, 69,* 817–832.

Laver, A. B. (1972). Precursors of psychology in ancient Egypt. *Journal of the History of the Behavioral Sciences, 8,* 181–195.

Lavie, P. (2000). Sleep-wake as a biological rhythm. *Annual Review of Psychology, 52,* 277–303.

Lavin, C. (1996). The Wechsler Intelligence Scale for Children-third edition and the Stanford-Binet Intelligence Scale–fourth edition: A preliminary study of validity. *Psychological Reports, 78,* 491–496.

Lavoisier, P., Aloui, R., Schmidt, M. H., & Watrelot, A. (1995). Clitoral blood flow increases following vaginal pressure stimulation. *Archives of Sexual Behavior, 24,* 37–45.

Law, D. M., Shapka, J. D., Hymel, S., Olson, B. F., & Waterhouse, T. (2012). The changing face of bullying: An empirical comparison between traditional and internet bullying and victimization. *Computers in Human Behavior, 28,* 226–232.

Lawson, T. J. (1999). Assessing psychological critical thinking as a learning outcome for psychology majors. *Teaching of Psychology, 26,* 207–209.

Lawton, C. A. (2001). Gender and regional differences in spatial referents used in direction giving. *Sex Roles, 44,* 321–337.

Lazarus, A. A. (1989). Brief psychotherapy: The multimodal model. *Professional Psychology, 26,* 6–10.

Lazarus, R. S. (1993a). Coping theory and research: Past, present, and future. *Psychosomatic Medicine, 55,* 234–247.

Lazarus, R. S. (1993b). From psychological stress to the emotions: A history of changing outlooks. *Annual Review of Psychology, 44,* 1–21.

Lazarus, R. S. (1995). Cognition and emotion from the RET viewpoint. *Journal of Rational-Emotive and Cognitive Behavior Therapy, 13,* 29–54.

Leadbeater, B., Hoglund, W., & Woods, T. (2003). Changing contents? The effects of a primary prevention program on classroom levels of peer relational and physical victimization. *Journal of Community Psychology, 31,* 397–418.

Leaf, R. C., Krauss, D. H., Dantzig, S. A., & Alington, D. E. (1992). Educational equivalents of psychotherapy: Positive and negative mental health benefits after group therapy exercises by college students. *Journal of Rational Emotive and Cognitive Behavior Therapy, 10,* 189–206.

Leakey, R. E., & Lewin, R. (1977, November). Is it our culture, not our genes, that makes us killers? *Smithsonian,* pp. 56–64.

Leana, C. R. (1985). A partial test of Janis' groupthink model: Effects of group cohesiveness and leader behavior on defective decision making. *Journal of Management, 11,* 5–17.

Leaper, C., Anderson, K. J., & Sanders, P. (1998). Moderators of gender effects on parents' talk to their children: A meta-analysis. *Developmental Psychology, 34,* 3–27.

Leary, M. R., & Kowalski, R. M. (1990). Impression management: A literature review and two-component model. *Psychological Bulletin, 107,* 34–47.

Leary, M. R., Kowalski, R. M., Smith, L., & Phillips, S. (2003). Teasing, rejection, and violence: Case studies of the school shootings. *Aggressive Behavior, 29,* 202–214.

LeBlanc, L. A, Hagopian, L. P., & Maglieri, K. A. (2000). Use of a token economy to eliminate excessive inappropriate social behavior in an adult with developmental disabilities. *Behavioral Interventions, 15,* 135–143.

Lebow, J. (2000). What does the research tell us about couple and family therapy? *Journal of Clinical Psychology, 56,* 1083–1094.

Leckman, J. F., Grice, D. E., Boardman, J., & Zhang, H. (1997). Symptoms of obsessive-compulsive disorder. *American Journal of Psychiatry, 154,* 911–917.

Leclerc, G., Lefrancois, R., Dube, M., Hebert, R., & Gaulin, P. (1998). The self-actualization concept: A content validation. *Journal of Social Behavior and Personality, 13,* 69–84.

Lecomte, D., & Fornes, P. (1998). Suicide among youth and young adults, 15 through 24 years -of age: A report of 392 cases from Paris, 1989–1996. *Journal of Forensic Sciences, 43,* 964–968.

Ledezma, E., & Monroig, R. (1997). Parapsychology in Mexico. *Journal of the American Society for Psychical Research, 91,* 122–132.

LeDoux, J. E. (1986). Sensory systems and emotion: A model of affective processing. *Integrative Psychiatry, 4,* 237–243.

LeDoux, J. E. (1995). Emotion: Clues from the brain. *Annual Review of Psychology, 46,* 209–235.

LeDoux, J. E., Romanski, L., & Xagoraris, A. (1989). Indelibility of subcortical emotional memories. *Journal of Cognitive Neuroscience, 1,* 238–243.

Lee, C. S., Therriault, D. J., & Linderholm, T. (2012). On the cognitive benefits of cultural experience: Exploring the relationship between studying abroad and creative thinking. *Applied Cognitive Psychology, 26,* 768–778.

Lee, E. H., Kim, J. H., & Yu, B. H. (2009). Reliability and validity of the self-report version of the panic disorder severity scale in Korea. *Depression and Anxiety, 26,* E120–E123.

Lee, G. P., Loring, D. W., Meador, K. J., & Brooks, B. B. (1990). Hemispheric specialization for emotional expression: A reexamination of results from intracarotid administration of sodium amobarbital. *Brain and Cognition, 12,* 267–280.

Lee, H., & Kim, J. J. (1998). Amygdalar NMDA receptors are critical for new fear learning in previously fear-conditioned rats. *Journal of Neuroscience, 18,* 8444–8454.

Lee, J.-H., & Beitz, A. J. (1992). Electroacupuncture modifies the expression of c-fos in the spinal cord induced by noxious stimulation. *Brain Research, 577,* 80–91.

Lee, M. S., Choi, J., Posadzki, P., & Ernst, E. (2012). Aromatherapy for health care: An overview of systematic reviews. *Maturitas, 71,* 257–260.

Lee, M. G., Hassani, O. K., & Jones, B. E. (2005). Discharge of identified orexin/hypocretin neurons across the sleep-wakingcycle. *The Journal of Neuroscience, 25,* 6716–6720.

Lee, S., & Lee, A. M. (2000). Disordered eating in three communities of China: A comparative study of female high school students in Hong Kong, Shenzhen, and rural Hunan. *International Journal of Eating Disorders, 27,* 317–327.

Lee, S. H., & Oh, K. S. (1999). Offensive type of social phobia: Cross-cultural perspectives. *International Medical Journal, 6,* 271–279.

Lee, T. M. C., & Chan, C. C. H. (1999a). Dose-response relationship of phototherapy for seasonal affective disorder: A meta-analysis. *Acta Psychiatrica Scandinavica, 99,* 315–323.

Lee, T. M. C., & Chan, C. C. H. (1999b). Vulnerability by sex to seasonal affective disorder. *Perceptual and Motor Skills, 87,* 1120–1122.

Lee, T. M. C., Liu, H. L., Tan, L. H., Chan, C. C. H., Mahankali, S., Feng, C. M., . . . Gao, J. H. (2002). Lie detection by functional magnetic resonance imaging. *Human Brain Mapping, 15,* 157–164.

Lee, V. E., & Loeb, S. (1995). Where do head start attendees end up? One reason why preschool effects fade out. *Educational Evaluation and Policy Analysis, 17,* 62–82.

Lee, V. E., Brooks-Gunn, J., Schnur, E., & Liaw, F.-R. (1990). Are Head Start effects sustained? A longitudinal follow-up comparison of disadvantaged children attending Head Start, no preschool, and other preschool programs. *Child Development, 61,* 495–507.

Lee, Y. T., & Ottati, V. (1993). Determinants of in-group and out-group perceptions of heterogeneity: An investigation of Sino-American stereotypes. *Journal of Cross-Cultural Psychology, 24,* 298–318.

Leenaars, A. A. (2000). Suicide prevention in Canada: A history of a community approach. *Canadian Journal of Community Mental Health, 19,* 57–73.

Leeson, F. J., & Nixon, R. D. V. (2011). The role of children's appraisals on adjustment following psychological maltreatment: A pilot study. *Journal of Abnormal Child Psychology, 39,* 759–771.

Lei, T. (1994). Being and becoming moral in a Chinese culture: Unique or universal? *Cross-Cultural Research: The Journal of Comparative Social Science, 28,* 58–91.

Leibowitz, H. W., & Pick, H. A., Jr. (1972). Cross-cultural and educational aspects of the Ponzo perspective illusion. *Perception and Psychophysics, 12,* 430–432.

Leigland, S. (2000). On cognitivism and behaviorism. *American Psychologist, 55,* 273–274.

Leikin, L., Firestone, P., & McGrath, P. (1988). Physical symptom reporting in Type A and Type B children. *Journal of Consulting and Clinical Psychology, 56,* 721–726.

Leit, R. A., Pope, H. G., & Gray, J. J. (2001). Cultural expectations of muscularity in men: The evolution of Playgirl centerfolds. *International Journal of Eating Disorders, 29,* 90–93.

Leitenberg, H. (1995). Cognitive-behavioural treatment of bulimia nervosa. *Behaviour Change, 12,* 81–97.

Lekander, M., Fuerst, C. J., Rostein, S., Hursti, T. J., & Fredrikson, M. (1997). Immune effects of relaxation during chemotherapy for ovarian cancer. *Psychotherapy and Psychosomatics, 66,* 185–191.

Lemelson, R. (2003). Obsessive-compulsive disorder in Bali: The cultural shaping of a neuropsychiatric disorder. *Transcultural Psychiatry, 40,* 377–408.

Lemere, F. (1993). "Homeless mentally ill or mentally ill homeless?": Comment. *American Journal of Psychiatry, 150,* 989.

Lemieux, R., & Hale, J. L. (2002). Cross-sectional analysis of intimacy, passion, and commitment: Testing the assumptions of the triangular theory of love. *Psychological Reports, 90,* 1009–1014.

Lenox, R. H., & Hahn, C. G. (2000). Overview of the mechanism of action of lithium in the brain: Fifty–year update. *Journal of Clinical Psychiatry, 61,* 5–15.

Leonard, J. (1970, May 8). Ghetto for blue eyes in the classroom. *Life,* p. 16.

Leong, T. T. L., Zachar, P., Conant, L., & Tolliver, D. (2007). Career specialty preferences among psychology majors: Cognitive processing styles associated with scientist and practitioner interests. *Career Development Quarterly, 55,* 328–338.

Leung, A. K.-Y., Kim, Y.-H., Zhang, Z.-X., Tam, K. P., & Chiu, C.-Y. (2012). Cultural construction of success and epistemic motives moderate American-Chinese differences in reward allocation biases. *Journal of Cross-Cultural Psychology, 43,* 46–52.

Lepper, M. R., Greene, D., & Nisbett, R. E. (1973). Undermining children's intrinsic interest with extrinsic reward: A test of the "overjustification" hypothesis. *Journal of Personality and Social Psychology, 28,* 129–137.

Lerman, D. C., & Iwata, B. A. (1995). Prevalence of the extinction burst and its attenuation during treatment. *Journal of Applied Behavior Analysis, 28,* 93–94.

Lerner, A. G., Gelkopf, M., Skladman, I., Oyffe, I., Finkel, B., Sigal, M., & Weizman, A. (2002). Flashback and hallucinogen persisting perception disorder: Clinical aspects and pharmacological treatment approach. *Israel Journal of Psychiatry and Related Sciences, 39,* 92–99.

Lerner, B. S., Ostrow, A. C., Yura, M. T., & Etzel, E. F. (1996). The effects of goal-setting and imagery training programs on the free-throw performance of female collegiate basketball players. *Sport Psychologist, 10,* 382–397.

Lerner, E. (1943). Preface to the psychology of peace and reconstruction. *Journal of Psychology, 15,* 3–25.

Lerner, G. H., & Takagi, T. (1999). On the place of linguistic resources in the organization of talk-in-interaction: A co-investigation of English and Japanese grammatical practices. *Journal of Pragmatics, 31,* 49–75.

Lescaudron, L., & Stein, D. G. (1990). Functional recovery following transplants of embryonic brain tissue in rats with lesions of visual, frontal, and motor cortex: Problems and prospects for future research. *Neuropsychologia, 28,* 588–599.

Leserman, J. (2003). HIV disease progression: Depression, stress, and possible mechanisms. *Biological Psychiatry, 54,* 295–306.

Leslie, K., & Ogilvie, R. (1996). Vestibular dreams: The effect of rocking on dream mentation. *Dreaming, 6,* 1–16.

Lester, D. (1990). Maslow's hierarchy of needs and personality. *Personality and Individual Differences, 11,* 1187–1188.

Lester, D. (1993). The effectiveness of suicide prevention centers. *Suicide and Life-Threatening Behavior, 23,* 263–267.

Lester, D. (1995). Myths about childhood suicide. *Psychological Reports, 77,* 330.

Lester, D. (2003). Adolescent suicide from an international perspective. *American Behavioral Scientist, 46,* 1157–1170.

Lester, D., & Wosnack, K. (1990). An exploratory test of Sheldon's theory of personality in neonates. *Perceptual and Motor Skills, 71,* 1282.

Lester, D., Kaminsky, S., & McGovern, M. (1993). Sheldon's theory of personality in young children. *Perceptual and Motor Skills, 77,* 1330.

Lester, D., Saito, Y., & Abe, K. (1997). The effect of suicide prevention centers on suicide in Japan. *Crisis, 18,* 48.

LeVay, S. (1991). A difference in hypothalamic structure between heterosexual and homosexual men. *Science, 253,* 1034–1037.

Levenson, J. L., & Bemis, C. (1991). The role of psychological factors in cancer onset and progression. *Psychosomatics, 32,* 124–132.

Levenson, R. W., Ekman, P., Heider, K., & Friesen, W. V. (1992). Emotion and autonomic nervous system activity in the Minangkabau of West Sumatra. *Journal of Personality and Social Psychology, 62,* 972–988.

Leventhal, H., & Tomarken, A. J. (1986). Emotion: Today's problems. *Annual Review of Psychology, 37,* 565–610.

Levin, B. E. (2009). Synergy of nature and nurture in the development of childhood obesity. *International Journal of Obesity, 33,* 553–556.

Levin, E. D., & Simon, B. B. (1998). Nicotinic acetylcholine involvement in cognitive function in animals. *Psychopharmacology, 138,* 217–230.

Levin, E. D., Westman, E. C., Stein, R. M., & Carnahan, E. (1994). Nicotine skin patch treatment increases abstinence, decreases withdrawal symptoms, and attenuates rewarding effects of smoking. *Journal of Clinical Psychopharmacology, 14,* 41–49.

Levin, I. P., Schnittjer, S. K., & Thee, S. L. (1988). Information framing effects in social and personal decisions. *Journal of Experimental Social Psychology, 24,* 520–529.

Levin, R. B., & Gross,a. M. (1985). The role of relaxation in systematic desensitization. *Behaviour Research and Therapy, 23,* 187–196.

Levine, J. S., & MacNichol, E. F., Jr. (1982, February). Color vision in fishes. *Scientific American,* pp. 140–149.

Levine, M. (1976). The academic achievement test: Its historical context and social functions. *American Psychologist, 31,* 228–238.

Levine, S. C., Huttenlocher, J., Taylor, A., & Langrock, A. (1999). Early sex differences in spatial skill. *Developmental Psychology, 35,* 940–949.

Levinson, D. J. (1978). *The seasons of a man's life.* New York: Knopf.

Levinson, D. J. (1986). A conception of adult development. *American Psychologist, 41,* 3–13.

Levinthal, C. F. (1988). *Messengers of paradise.* New York: Anchor/Doubleday.

Levis, D. J. (1999). The negative impact of the cognitive movement on the continued growth of the behavior therapy movement: A historical perspective. *Genetic, Social, and General Psychology Monographs, 125,* 157–171.

Levitt, D. H. (2001). Anorexia nervosa: Treatment in the family context. *Family Journal. 9,* 159–163.

Levy, G. D. (1999). Gender-typed and non-gender-typed category awareness in toddlers. *Sex Roles, 41,* 851–873.

Levy, J. (1983). Language, cognition, and the right hemisphere: A response to Gazzaniga. *American Psychologist, 38,* 538–541.

Levy, N. (2002). Reconsidering cochlear implants: The lessons of Martha's Vineyard. *Bioethics. 16,* 134–153.

Lew, A. S., Allen, R., Papouchis, N., & Ritzler, B. (1998). Achievement orientation and fear of success in Asian American college students. *Journal of Clinical Psychology, 54,* 97–108.

Lew, M. W., Kravits, K., Garberoglio, C., & Williams, A. C. (2011). Use of preoperative hypnosis to reduce postoperative pain and anesthesia-related side effects. *International Journal of Clinical & Experimental Hypnosis, 59,* 406–423.

Lewicki, P. (1985). Nonconscious biasing effects of single instances on subsequent judgments. *Journal of Personality and Social Psychology, 48,* 563–574.

Lewinsohn, P. M., Gotlib, I. H., Lewinsohn, M., Seeley, J. R., & Allen, N. B. (1998). Gender differences in anxiety disorders and anxiety symptoms in adolescents. *Journal of Abnormal Psychology, 107,* 109–117.

Lewis, D. (1899/1983). The gynecologic consideration of the sexual act. *Journal of the American Medical Association, 250,* 222–227.

Lewis, J. (1981). *Something hidden: A biography of Wilder Penfield.* New York: Doubleday.

Lewis-Fernandez, R. (1998). A cultural critique of the *DSM–IV* dissociative disorders section. *Transcultural Psychiatry, 35,* 387–400.

Leyendecker, B., Lamb, M. E., Fracasso, M. P., Schölmerich, A., & Larson, C. (1997). Playful interaction and the antecedents of attachment. A longitudinal study of Central American and Euro-American mothers and infants. *Merrill-Palmer Quarterly, 43,* 24–47.

Lichacz, F. M., & Partington, J. T. (1996). Collective efficacy and true group performance. *International Journal of Sport Psychology, 27,* 146–158.

Lichtenstein, P., & Annas, P. (2000). Heretability and prevalence of specific fears and phobias in childhood. *Journal of Child Psychology and Psychiatry and Allied Disciplines, 41,* 927–937.

Lieberman, D. A. (1979). Behaviorism and the mind: A (limited) call for a return to introspection. *American Psychologist, 34,* 319–333.

Liechti, M. E., & Vollenweider, F. X. (2001). Which neuroreceptors mediate the subjective effects of MDMA in humans? A summary of mechanistic studies. *Human Psychopharmacology: Clinical and Experimental, 16,* 589–598.

Liegois, M. J. (1899). The relation of hypnotism to crime. *Suggestive Therapeutics, 6,* 18–21.

Lightdale, J. R., & Prentice, D. A. (1994). Rethinking sex differences in aggression: Aggressive behavior in the absence of social roles. *Personality and Social Psychology Bulletin, 20,* 34–44.

Lilienfeld, S. O., & Loftus, E. F. (1998). Repressed memories and World War II: Some cautionary notes. *Professional Psychology: Research and Practice, 29,* 471–475.

Lilienfeld, S. O., Wood, J. M.,& Garb, H. N. (2000). The scientific status of projective techniques. *Psychological Science in the Public Interest, 1,* 27–66.

Lin, E. H., & Peterson, C. (1990). Pessimistic explanatory style and response to illness. *Behaviour Research and Therapy, 28,* 243–248.

Lindberg, A. C., Kelland, A., & Nicol, C. J. (1999). Effects of observational learning on acquisition of an operant response in horses. *Applied Animal Behaviour Science, 61,* 187–199.

Lindberg, S. M., Hyde, J. S., Petersen, J. L., & Linn, M. C. (2010). New trends in gender and mathematics performance: A meta-analysis. *Psychological Bulletin, 136,* 1123–1135.

Linden, D. J. (2003). From molecules to memory in the cerebellum. *Science, 301,* 1682–1683, 1685.

Lindholm, T., & Christianson, S.-A. (1998). Intergroup biases and eyewitness testimony. *Journal of Social Psychology, 138,* 710–723.

Lindsay, D. S. (1993). Eyewitness suggestibility. *Current Directions in Psychological Science, 2,* 86–89.

Lindsay, D. S. (1994). Contextualizing and clarifying criticisms of memory work. *Consciousness and Cognition: An International Journal, 3,* 426–437.

Lindsay, G. (2007). Educational psychology and the effectiveness of inclusive education/mainstreaming. *British Journal of Educational Psychology, 77,* 1–24.

Lindsay, R.C.L., & Pozzulo, J. D. (1999). Sources of eyewitness identification error. *International Journal of Law and Psychiatry, 22,* 347–360.

Lindvall, O., Brundin, P., Widner, H., Rehncrona, S., Gustavii, B., Frackowiak, R., . . . Bjorklund, A. (1990). Grafts of fetal dopamine neurons survive and improve motor function in Parkinson's disease. *Science, 247,* 574–577.

Link, S. W. (1994). Rediscovering the past: Gustav Fechner and signal detection theory. *Psychological Science, 5,* 335–340.

Linn, R. L. (1982). Admissions testing on trial. *American Psychologist, 37,* 279–291.

Linville, P. W., Fischer, G. W., & Yoon, C. (1996). Perceived covariation among the features of ingroup and outgroup members: The outgroup covariation effect. *Journal of Personality and Social Psychology, 70,* 421–436.

Liossi, C., & Hatira, P. (2003). Clinical hypnosis in the alleviation of procedure-related pain in pediatric oncology patients. *International Journal of Clinical and Experimental Hypnosis, 51,* 4–28.

Lipman, J. J., Miller, B. E., Mays, K. S., & Miller, M. N. (1990). Peak B endorphin concentration in cerebrospinal fluid: Reduced in chronic pain patients and increased during the placebo response. *Psychopharmacology, 102,* 112–116.

Lippa, R. A., & Tan, F. D. (2001). Does culture moderate the relationship between sexual orientation and gender-related personality traits? *Cross-Cultural Research: The Journal of Comparative Social Science, 35,* 65–87.

Lips, H. M. (2000). College students' visions of power and possibility as moderated by gender. *Psychology of Women Quarterly, 24,* 39–43.

Lipton, R. B., Stewart, W. F., Diamond, S., Diamond, M. L., & Reed, M. (2001). Prevalence and burden of migraine in the United States: Data from the American Migraine Study II. *Headache, 41,* 646–657.

Litchfield, R. C., Fan, J., & Brown, V. R. (2011). Directing idea generation using brainstorming with specific novelty goals. *Motivation & Emotion, 35,* 135–143.

Litt, M. D., Nye, C., & Shafer, D. (1995). Preparation for oral surgery: Evaluating elements of coping. *Journal of Behavioral Medicine, 18,* 435–459.

Littner, M., Johnson, S. F., McCall, W. V., Anderson, W. M., Davila, D., Hartse, K., ... Woodson, B. T. (2001). Practice parameters for the treatment of narcolepsy: An update for 2000. *Sleep: Journal of Sleep and Sleep Disorders Research, 24,* 451–466.

Liu, H., Bravata, D. M., Olkin, I., Friedlander, A., Liu, V., Roberts, B., . . . Hoffman, A. R. (2008). Systematic review: The effects of growth hormone on athletic performance. *Annals of Internal Medicine, 148,* 747–758.

Liu, L. L., & Lau, A. S. (2013). Teaching about race/ethnicity and racism matters: An examination of how perceived ethnic racial socialization processes are associated with depression symptoms. *Cultural Diversity & Ethnic Minority Psychology, 19,* 383–394.

Liu, X., Uchiyama, M., Kim, K., Okawa, M., Shibui, K., Kudo, Y., . . . Ogihara, R. (2000). Sleep loss and daytime sleepiness in the general adult population of Japan. *Psychiatry Research, 93,* 1–11.

Ljungvall, A., & Zimmerman, F. J. (2012). Bigger bodies: Long-term trends and disparities in obesity and body-mass index among U.S. adults, 1960–2008. *Social Science & Medicine, 75,* 109–119.

Llorente, M. D., Currier, M. B., Norman, S. E., & Mellman, T. A. (1992). Night terrors in adults: Phenomenology and relationship to psychopathology. *Journal of Clinical Psychiatry, 53,* 392–394.

Lo Bue, S., Taverniers, J., Mylle, J., & Euwema, M. (2013). Hardiness promotes work engagement, prevents burnout, and moderates their relationship. *Military Psychology, 25,* 105–115.

LoBello, S. G., & Gulgoz, S. (1991). Factor analysis of the Wechsler Preschool and Primary Scale of Intelligence-Revised. *Psychological Assessment, 3,* 130–132.

Lockart, R. S., & Craik, F. I. (1990). Levels of processing: A retrospective commentary on a framework for memory research. *Canadian Journal of Psychology, 44,* 87–112.

Locke, E. A., & Latham, G. P. (2002). Building a practically useful theory of goal setting and task motivation: A 35-year odyssey. *American Psychologist, 57,* 705–717.

Locke, J. (1690/1959). *An essay concerning human understanding.* New York: Dover.

Lockhart, R. S., & Craik, F. I. (1990). Levels of processing: A retrospective commentary on a framework for memory research. *Canadian Journal of Psychology, 44,* 87–112

Locurto, C. (1990). The malleability of IQ as judged from adoption studies. *Intelligence, 14,* 275–292.

Locurto, C. (1991). Beyond IQ in preschool programs? *Intelligence, 15,* 295–312.

Loef, M., & Walach, H. (2012). The combined effects of healthy lifestyle behaviors on all-cause mortality. *Preventive Medicine: An International Journal Devoted to Practice & Theory, 55,* 163–170.

Loehlin, J. C., & Martin, N. G. (2001). Age changes in personality traits and their heritabilities during the adult years: Evidence from Australian twin registry samples. *Personality and Individual Differences, 30,* 1147–1160.

Loehlin, J. C., Horn, J. M., & Willerman, L. (1990). Heredity, environment, and personality change: Evidence from the Texas Adoption Project. *Journal of Personality, 58,* 221–243.

Loehlin, J. C., Horn, J. M., & Willerman, L. (1994). Differential inheritance of mental abilities in the Texas Adoption Project. *Intelligence, 19,* 325–336.

Loewi, O. (1960). An autobiographical sketch. *Perspectives in Biology and Medicine, 3,* 3–25.

Loftus, E. F. (1993). The reality of repressed memories. *American Psychologist, 48,* 518–537.

Loftus, E. F., & Burns, T. E. (1982). Mental shock can produce retrograde amnesia. *Memory and Learning, 10,* 318–323.

Loftus, E. F., & Hoffman, H. G. (1989). Misinformation and memory: The creation of new memories. *Journal of Experimental Psychology: General, 118,* 100–104.

Loftus, E. F., & Palmer, J. C. (1974). Reconstruction of automobile destruction: An example of the interaction between language and memory. *Journal of Verbal Learning and Verbal Behavior, 13,* 585–589.

Loftus, E., Joslyn, S., & Polage, D. (1998). Repression: A mistaken impression? *Development and Psychopathology, 10,* 781–792.

Loftus, G. R., Duncan, J., & Gehrig, P. (1992). On the time course of perceptual information that results from a brief visual presentation. *Journal of Experimental Psychology: Human Perception and Performance, 18,* 530–549.

Logan, C. (2002). When scientific knowledge becomes scientific discovery: The disappearance of classical conditioning before Pavlov. *Journal of the History of the Behavioral Sciences, 38,* 393–403.

Logie, R. H. (1999). Working memory. *Psychologist, 12,* 174–178.

Logie, R. H. The functional organization and capacity limits of working memory. *Current Directions in Psychological Science, 20,* 240–245.

Lombardo, G. P., & Foschi, R. (2002). The European origins of "personality psychology." *European Psychologist, 7,* 134–145.

Long, M. E., Hammons, M. E., Davis, J. L., Frueh, B. C., Khan, M. M., Klhai, J. D., & Teng, E. J. (2011). Imagery rescripting and exposure group treatment of posttraumatic nightmares in veterans with PTSD. *Journal of Anxiety Disorders, 25,* 531–535.

Lonner, W. J., & Malpass, R. S. (Eds.). (1994). *Psychology and culture.* Boston: Allyn & Bacon.

Lonsdale, A. J., & North, A. C. (2012). Musical taste and the representativeness heuristic. *Psychology of Music, 40,* 131–142.

Lonsway, K. A., Klaw, E. L., Berg, D. R., Waldo, C. R., Kothari, C., Mazurek, C. J., & Hegeman, K. E. (1998). Beyond "no means no": Outcomes of an intensive program to train campus acquaintance rape educators. *Journal of Interpersonal Violence, 13,* 73–92.

Loomis, A. L., Harvey, E. N., & Hobart, G. A. (1937). Electrical potentials of the human brain. *Journal of Experimental Psychology, 21,* 127–144.

Loomis, M., & Saltz, E. (1984). Cognitive styles as predictors of artistic styles. *Journal of Personality, 52,* 22–35.

Loose, R., Kaufmann, C., Auer, D. P., & Lange, K. W. (2003). Human prefrontal and sensory cortical activity during divided attention tasks. *Human Brain Mapping, 18,* 249–259.

López, S. R., & Guarnaccia, P. J. J. (2000). Cultural psychopathology: Uncovering the social world of mental illness. *Annual Review of Psychology, 51,* 571–598.

Lord, C. G. (1982). Predicting behavioral consistency from an individual's perception of situational similarities. *Journal of Personality and Social Psychology, 42,* 1076–1088.

Lorenz, K. Z. (1966). *On aggression.* New York: Harcourt Brace Jovanovich.

Lorist, M. M., & Tops, M. (2003). Caffeine, fatigue, and cognition. *Brain and Cognition, 53,* 82–94.

Lottes, I. L. (1993). Nontraditional gender roles and the sexual experiences of heterosexual college students. *Sex Roles, 29,* 645–669.

Lou, L., & Chen, J. (2003). Attention and blind-spot phenomenology. *Psyche: An Interdisciplinary Journal of Research on Consciousness, 9,* 02.

Lovell, P. G., Bloj, M., & Harris, J. M. (2012). Optimal integration of shading and binocular disparity for depth perception. *Journal of Vision, 12,* 1–18.

Lovie, A. D., & Lovie, P. (1993). Charles Spearman, Cyril Burt, and the origins of factor analysis. *Journal of the History of the Behavioral Sciences, 29,* 308–321.

Loving, T. J., Gleason, M. J., & Pope, M. T. (2009). Transition novelty moderates daters' cortisol responses when talking about marriage. *Personal Relationships, 16,* 187–2003.

Lowe, G. (1982). Alcohol-induced state-dependent learning: Differentiating stimulus and storage hypotheses. *Current Psychological Research, 2,* 215–222.

Lowe, M. R., Foster, G. D., Kerzhnerman, I., Swain, R. M., & Wadden, T. A. (2001). Restrictive dieting vs. "undieting": Effects on eating regulation in obese clinic attenders. *Addictive Behaviors, 26,* 253–266.

Lozano, D. I., Crites, S. L., Jr., & Aikman, S. N. (1999). Changes in food attitudes as a function of hunger. *Appetite, 32,* 207–218.

Lu, L., & Shih, J. B. (1997). Personality and happiness: Is mental health a mediator? *Personality and Individual Differences, 22,* 249–256.

Lu, Z. L., Williamson, S. J., & Kaufman, L. (1992). Behavioral lifetime of human auditory sensory memory predicted by physiological measures. *Science, 258,* 1668–1670.

Lubar, J. F. (1991). Discourse on the development of EEG diagnostics and biofeedback for attention-deficit/hyperactivity disorders. *Biofeedback and Self-Regulation, 16,* 201–225.

Lubart, T. I. (1999). Creativity across cultures. In R. J. Sternberg (Ed.), *Handbook of creativity* (pp. 339–350). NY: Cambridge University Press.

Lubek, I., Innis, N. K., Kroger, R. O., McGuire, G. R., Stam, H. J., & Herrmann, T. (1995). Faculty genealogies in five Canadian universities: Historiographical and pedagogical concerns. *Journal of the History of the Behavioral Sciences, 31,* 52–72.

Lubinski, D., Benbow, C. P., Shea, D. L., Eftekhari-Sanjani, H., & Halvorson, B. J. (2001). Men and women at promise for scientific excellence: Similarity not dissimilarity. *Psychological Science, 12,* 309–317.

Luborsky, L., Chandler, M., Auerbach, A. H., Cohen, J., & Bachrach, H. M. (1971). Factors influencing the outcome of psychotherapy: A review of quantitative research. *Psychological Bulletin, 75,* 145–185.

Luborsky, L., Rosenthal, R., Diguer, L., Andrusyna, T. P., Levitt, J. T., Seligman, D. A., . . . Krause, E. D. (2003). Are some psychotherapies much more effective than others? *Journal of Applied Psychoanalytic Studies, 5,* 455–460.

Luce, G. G., & Segal, J. (1966). *Sleep.* New York: Coward McCann.

Luchins, A. (1946). Classroom experiments on mental sets. *American Journal of Psychology, 59,* 295–298.

Luders, E., Narr, K. I., Bilder, R. M., Szeszko, P. R., Gurbani, M. N., Hamilton, L., . . . Gaser, C. (2008). Mapping the relationship between cortical convolution and intelligence: Effects of gender. *Cerebral Cortex, 18,* 2019–2026.

Luhmann, M., Lucas, R. E., Eid M., & Diener, E. (2013). The prospective effect of life satisfaction on life events. *Social Psychological & Personality Science, 4,* 39–45.

Lukas, K. E., Marr, M. J., & Maple, T. L. (1998). Teaching operant conditioning at the zoo. *Teaching of Psychology, 25,* 112–116.

Lundqvist, L.-O. (1995). Facial EMG reactions to facial expressions: A case of facial emotional contagion? *Scandinavian Journal of Psychology, 36,* 130–141.

Lundstrom, J. N., Goncalves, M., Esteves, F., & Olsson, M. J. (2003). Psychological effects of subthreshhold exposure to the putative human pheromone 4, 16-androstadien-3-one. *Hormones and Behavior, 44,* 395–401.

Lundy, D. E., Tan, J., & Cunningham, M. R. (1998). Heterosexual romantic preferences: The importance of humor and physical attractiveness for different types of relationships. *Personal Relationships, 5,* 311–325.

Luo, J., Phan, T. X., Yang, Y., Garelick, M. G., & Storm, D. R. (2013). Increases in cAMP, MAPK activity, and CREB phosphorylation during REM sleep: Implications for REM sleep and memory consolidation. *The Journal of Neuroscience, 33,* 6460–6468.

Lutz, J., Means, L. W., & Long, T. E. (1994). Where did I park? A naturalistic study of spatial memory. *Applied Cognitive Psychology, 8,* 439–451.

Luxton, D. D., Trofimovich, L., & Clark, L. L. (2013). Suicide risk among U.S. service members after psychiatric hospitalization, 2002–2011. *Psychiatric Services, 64,* 626–629.

Lydon, J. E., Jamieson, D., & Zanna, M. P. (1988). Interpersonal similarity and the social and intellectual dimensions of first impressions. *Social Cognition, 6,* 269–286.

Lykken, D. T. (1974). Psychology and the lie detector industry. *American Psychologist, 29,* 725–739.

Lykken, D. T. (1981). *A tremor in the blood: Uses and abuses of the lie detector.* New York: McGraw-Hill.

Lykken, D. T. (1982). Research with twins: The concept of emergenesis. *Psychophysiology, 19,* 361–373.

Lykken, D. T. (1988). Detection of guilty knowledge: A comment on Forman and McCauley. *Journal of Applied Psychology, 73,* 303–304.

Lykken, D. T., Bouchard, T. J., Jr., McGue, M., & Tellegen, A. (1993). Heritability of interests: A twin study. *Journal of Applied Psychology, 73,* 303–304.

Lykken, D. T., McGue, M., Tellegen, A., & Bouchard, T. J., Jr. (1992). Emergenesis: Genetic traits that may not run in families. *American Psychologist, 47,* 1565–1577.

Lymburner, J. A., & Roesch, R. (1999). The insanity defense: Five years of research (1993–1997). *International Journal of Law and Psychiatry, 22,* 213–240.

Lynch, P. S., Kellow, J. T., & Willson, V. L. (1997). The impact of deinstitutionalization on the adaptive behavior of adults with mental retardation: A meta-analysis. *Education and Training in Mental Retardation and Developmental Disabilities, 32,* 255–261.

Lynn, R. (1982). IQ in Japan and the United States shows a growing disparity. *Nature, 297,* 222–223.

Lynn, S. J., Rhue, J. W., & Weekes, J. R. (1990). Hypnotic involuntariness: A social-cognitive analysis. *Psychological Review, 97,* 169–184.

Lyons, J. (2002). Factors contributing to low back pain among professional drivers: A review of current literature and possible ergonomic controls. *Work: Journal of Prevention, Assessment and Rehabilitation, 19,* 95–102.

Lyons, M. J., Eisen, S. A., Goldberg, J., True, W., Lin, N., Meyer, J. M., . . . Tsuang, M. T. (1998). A registry-based twin study of depression in men. *Archives of General Psychiatry, 55,* 468–472.

Lysle, D. T., Cunnick, J. E., & Maslonek, K. A. (1991). Pharmacological manipulation of immune alterations induced by an aversive conditioned stimulus: Evidence for a-adrenergic receptor-mediated Pavlovian conditioning process. *Behavioral Neuroscience, 105,* 443–449.

Lytton, H., & Romney, D. M. (1991). Parents' differential socialization of boys and girls: A meta-analysis. *Psychological Bulletin, 109,* 267–296.

M

Ma, H.-H. (2009). The effectiveness of intervention on the behavior of individuals with autism: A meta-analysis using percentage of data point exceeding the median of baseline phase (PEM). *Behavior Modification, 33,* 339–359.

Ma, H. K., Shek, D. T. L., Cheung, P. C., Oi Bun Lam, C. (2000). Parental, peer, and teacher influences on the social behavior of Hong Kong Chinese adolescents. *Journal of Genetic Psychology, 161,* 65–78.

Maag, U., Vanasse, C., Dionne, G., & Laberge-Nadeau, C. (1997). Taxi drivers' accidents: How binocular vision problems are related to their rate and severity in terms of the number of victims. *Accident Analysis and Prevention, 29,* 217–224.

Maass, A., & Russo, A. (2003). Directional bias in the mental representation of spatial events: Nature or culture? *Psychological Science, 14,* 296–301.

Macaskill, N. D., & Macaskill, A. (1996). Rational-emotive therapy plus pharmacotherapy versus pharmacotherapyalone in the treatment of high cognitive dysfunction depression. *Cognitive Therapy and Research, 20,* 575–592.

Macchi, M. M., Boulos, Z., Ranney, T., Simmons, L., & Campbell, S. S. (2002). Effects of an afternoon nap on nighttime alertness and performance in long–haul drivers. *Accident Analysis and Prevention, 34,* 825–834.

Maccoby, E. E., & Jacklin, C. N. (1974). *The psychology of sex differences* (2 vols.). Stanford, CA: Stanford University Press.

Maccoby, E. E., & Lewis, C. C. (2003). Less day care or different day care? *Child Development, 74,* 1069–1075.

MacCracken, M. J., & Stadulis, R. E. (1985). Social facilitation of young children's dynamic balance performance. *Journal of Sport Psychology, 7,* 150–165.

MacDonald, D. A., & Holland, D. (2003). Spirituality and the MMPI-2. *Journal of Clinical Psychology, 59,* 399–410.

MacDonald, D. J., & Standing, L. G. (2002). Does self-serving bias cancel the Barnum effect? *Social Behavior and Personality, 30,* 625–630.

MacDonald, T. K., MacDonald, G., Zanna, M. P., Fong, G. (2000). Alcohol, sexual arousal, and intentions to use condoms in young men: Applying alcohol myopia theory to risky sexual behavior. *Health Psychology, 19,* 290–298.

Macera, M. H., & Cohen, S. H. (2006). Psychology as a profession: An effective career exploration and orientation course for undergraduate psychology majors. *Career Development Quarterly, 54,* 367–371.

MacFarlane, J. G., Cleghorn, J. M., Brown, G. M., & Streiner, D. L. (1991). The effects of exogenous melatonin on the total sleep time and daytime alertness of chronic insomniacs: A preliminary study. *Biological Psychiatry, 30,* 371–376.

Mack, A., Heuer, F., Villardi, K., & Chambers, D. (1985). The dissociation of position and extent in Müller-Lyer figures. *Perception and Psychophysics, 37,* 335–344.

Mack, S. (1981). Novel help for the handicapped. *Science, 212,* 26–27.

Macklin, M. C. (1994). The effects of an advertising retrieval cue on young children's memory and brand evaluations. *Psychology and Marketing, 11,* 291–311.

MacLean, H. N. (1993). *Once upon a time: A true story of memory, murder, and the law.* New York: HarperCollins.

MacLeod, C. M. (1988). Forgotten but not gone: Savings for pictures and words in long-term memory. *Journal of Experimental Psychology: Learning, Memory, and Cognition, 14,* 195–212.

MacMillan, H. L., & Thomas, B. H. (1993). Public health nurse home visitation for the tertiary prevention of child maltreatment: Results of a pilot study. *Canadian Journal of Psychiatry, 38,* 436–442.

Macmillan, M. (2000). Nineteenth-century inhibitory theories of thinking: Bain, Ferrier, Freud (and Phineas Gage). *History of Psychology, 3,* 187–217.

Maddi, S. R. (2002). The story of hardiness: Twenty years of theorizing, research, and practice. *Consulting Psychology Journal: Practice and Research, 54,* 175–185.

Maddi, S. R., Kahn, S., & Maddi, K. L. (1998). The effectiveness of hardiness training. *Consulting Psychology Journal: Practice and Research, 50,* 78–86.

Madigan, M. W., & O'Hara, R. (1992). Short-term memory at the turn of the century: Mary Whiton Calkins's memory research. *American Psychologist, 47,* 170–174.

Maekelae, K. (1997). Drinking, the majority fallacy, cognitive dissonance, and social pressure. *Addiction, 92,* 729–736.

Maganaris, C. N., Collins, D., & Sharp, M. (2000). Expectancy effects and strength training: Do steroids make a difference? *Sport Psychologist, 14,* 272–278.

Magee, W. J., Eaton, W. W., Wittchen, H.-W., McGonagle, K. A., & Kessler, R. C. (1996). Agoraphobia, simple phobia, and social phobia in the national comorbidity survey. *Archives of General Psychiatry, 53,* 159–168.

Mah, K., & Binik, Y. M. (2002). Do all orgasms feel alike? Evaluating a two–dimensional model of the orgasm experience across gender and sexual context. *Journal of Sex Research, 39,* 104–113.

Maiello, S. (1999). Encounter with an African healer: Thinking about the possibilities and limits of cross-cultural psychotherapy. *Journal of Child Psychotherapy, 25,* 217–238.

Maier, N. R. (1931). Reasoning in humans. *Journal of Comparative Psychology, 12,* 181–194.

Maier, S. F. (1984). Learned helplessness and animal models of depression. *Progress in Neuro-Psychopharmacology and Biological Psychiatry, 8*(3), 435–446.

Maio, G. R., Olson, J. M., & Bush, J. E. (1997). Telling jokes that disparage social groups: Effects on the joke teller's stereotypes. *Journal of Applied Social Psychology, 27*, 1986–2000.

Majde, J.A., Krueger, J. M. (2005). Links between the innate immune system and sleep. *Journal of Allergy and Clinical Immunology, 116*, 188–1198.

Majeres, R. L. (1999). Sex differences in phonological processes: Speeded matching and word reading. *Memory and Cognition, 27*, 246–253.

Majhi, P., Bagga, R., Kalra, J., & Sharma, M. (2009). Intravaginal use of natural micronised progesterone to prevent pre-term birth: A randomised trial in India. *Journal of Obstetrics and Gynaecology, 29*, 493–498.

Mäkinen, M., Puukko-Viertomies, L.-R, Lindberg, N., Siimes, M. A., & Aalberg, V. (2012). Body dissatisfaction and body mass in girls and boys transitioning from early to mid-adolescence: Additional role of self-esteem and eating habits. *BMC Psychiatry, 12*, 1-8.

Malamuth, N. M., Hald, G. M., & Koss, M. (2012). Pornography, individual differences in risk and men's acceptance of violence against women in a representative sample. *Sex Roles, 66*, 427–439.

Malarkey, W. B., Pearl, D. K., Demers, L. M., & Kiecolt-Glaser, J. K. (1995). Influence of academic stress and season on 24-hour mean concentrations of ACTH, cortisol, and b-endorphin. *Psychoneuroendocrinology, 20*, 499–508.

Malik, R., Paraherakis, A., Joseph, S., & Ladd, H. (1996). The method of subliminal psychodynamic activation: Do individual thresholds make a difference? *Perceptual and Motor Skills, 83*, 1235–1242.

Malinowski, C. I., & Smith, C. P. (1985). Moral reasoning and moral conduct: An investigation prompted by Kohlberg's theory. *Journal of Personality and Social Psychology, 49*, 1016–1027.

Malmberg, A. B., & Basbaum, A. I. (1998). Partial sciatic nerve injury in the mouse as a model of neuropathic pain: Behavioral and neuroanatomical correlates. *Pain, 76*, 215–222.

Man, D. W. K., Tam, S. F., & Hui-Chan, C. W. Y. (2003). Learning to live independently with expert systems in memory rehabilitation. *NeuroRehabilitation, 18*, 21–29.

Mandai, O., Guerrien, A., Sockeel, P., & Dujardin, K. (1989). REM sleep modifications following a Morse code learning session in humans. *Physiology and Behavior, 46*, 639–642.

Mandel, D. R., Jusczyk, P. W., & Pisoni, D. B. (1995). Infants' recognition of the sound patterns of their own names. *Psychological Science, 6*, 314–317.

Mandler, G. (2002). Origins of the cognitive (r)evolution. *Journal of the History of the Behavioral Sciences, 38*, 339–353.

Maner, J. K., Kenrick, D. T., Becker, D. V., Delton, A .W., Hofer, B., Wilbur, C. J., & Neuberg, S. L. (2003). Sexually selective cognition: Beauty captures the mind of the beholder. *Journal of Personality and Social Psychology, 85*, 1107–1120.

Maner, J. K., Luce, C. L., Neuberg, S. L., Cialdini, R. B., Brown, S., & Sagarin, B. J. (2002). The effects of perspective taking on motivations for helping: Still no evidence for altruism. *Personality and Social Psychology Bulletin, 28*, 1601–1610.

Mangalmurti, V. S. (1994). Psychotherapists' fear of a Tarasoff: All in the mind? *Journal of Psychiatry and Law, 22*, 379–409.

Manley, R. S., Smye, V., & Srikameswaran, S. (2001). Addressing complex ethical issues in the treatment of children and adolescents with eating disorders: Application of a framework for ethical decision-making. *European Eating Disorders Review, 9*, 144–166.

Mann, K., Pankok, J., Connemann, B., & Roeschke, J. (2003). Temporal relationship between nocturnal erections and rapid eye movement episodes in healthy men. *Neuropsychobiology, 47*, 109–114.

Manning, B. H. (1990). A categorical analysis of children's self-talk during independent school assignments. *Journal of Instructional Psychology, 17*, 208–217.

Manning, C. A., Parsons, M. W., & Gold, P. E. (1992). Anterograde and retrograde enhancement of 24-hour memory by glucose in elderly humans. *Behavioral and Neural Biology, 58*, 125–130.

Mansell, W., & Carey, T. A. (2009). A century of psychology and psychotherapy: Is an understanding of "control" the missing link between theory, research, and practice? *Psychology and Psychotherapy: Theory, Research, and Practice, 82*, 337–353.

Mansfield, N. J., & Griffin, M. J. (2000). Difference thresholds for automobile seat vibration. *Applied Ergonomics, 31*, 255–261.

Maragos, W. F., Greenamyre, J. T., Penney, J. B., & Young, A. B. (1987). Glutamate dysfunction in Alzheimer's disease: A hypothesis. *Trends in Neuroscience, 10*, 65–68.

Maranto, G. (1984, December). Aging: Can we slow the inevitable? *Discover*, pp. 17–21.

Maratsos, M. (2000). More overregularizations after all: New data and discussion on Marcus, Pinker, Ullman, Hollander, Rosen and Xu. *Journal of Child Language, 27*, 183–212.

Marchand, S., Charest, J., Li, J., & Chenard, J. R. (1993). Is TENS purely a placebo effect? A controlled study on chronic low back pain. *Pain, 54*, 99–106.

Marcus, G. F. (1995). Children's overregularization of English plurals: A quantitative analysis. *Journal of Child Language, 22*, 447–459.

Marcus, G. F., & Fisher, S. E. (2003). FOXP2 in focus: What can genes tell us about speech and language? *Trends in Cognitive Sciences, 7*, 257–262.

Marder, S. R., Wirshing, W. C., Mintz, J., & McKenzie, J. (1996). Two-year outcome of social skills training and group psychotherapy for outpatients with schizophrenia. *American Journal of Psychiatry, 153*, 1585–1592.

Maren, S., & Baudry, M. (1995). Properties and mechanisms of long–term synaptic plasticity in the mammalian brain: Relationships to learning and memory. *Neurobiology of Learning and Memory, 63*, 1–18.

Margolis, R. B., & Mynatt, C. R. (1986). The effects of external and self-administered reward on high base rate behavior. *Cognitive Therapy and Research, 10*, 109–122.

Marken, R. S., & Powers, W. T. (1989). Random-walk chemotaxis: Trial and error as a control process. *Behavioral Neuroscience, 103*, 1348–1355.

Markianos, M., Hatzimanolis, J., & Lykouras, L. (2002). Serotonergic and dopaminergic neuroendocrine responses of male depressive patients before and after a therapeutic ECT course. *European Archives of Psychiatry and Clinical Neuroscience, 252*, 172–176.

Markowitsch, H. J. (1998). Cognitive neuroscience of memory. *Neurocase: Case Studies in Neuropsychology, Neuropsychiatry, and Behavioural Neurology, 4*, 429–435.

Marks, I. M. (1995). Advances in behavioral-cognitive therapy of social phobia. *Journal of Clinical Psychiatry, 56*, 25–31.

Markus, E., Lange, A., & Pettigrew, T. F. (1990). Effectiveness of family therapy: A meta-analysis. *Journal of Family Therapy, 12*, 205–221.

Markus, H. (1977). Self-schemata and processing information about the self. *Journal of Personality and Social Psychology, 35*, 63–78.

Markus, H. (1983). Self-knowledge: An expanded view. *Journal of Personality, 51*, 543–565.

Markus, H. R., & Kitayama, S. (1991). Culture and the self: Implications for cognition, emotion, and motivation. *Psychological Review, 98*, 224–253.

Maron, E., Tõru, I. Must, A., Tasa, G., Toover, E., Vasar, V., . . . Shlik, J. (2007). Association study of tryptophan hydroxylase 2 gene polymorphisms in panic disorder. *Neuroscience Letters, 411*, 180–184

Marosi, E., Bazan, O., Yanez, G., Bernal, J., Fernandez, T., Rodriguez, M., . . . Reyes, A. (2002). Narrow-band spectral measurements of EEG during emotional tasks. *International Journal of Neuroscience, 112*, 871–891.

Marsa, F., O'Reilly, G., Carr, A., Murphy, P., O'Sullivan, M., Cotter, A., & Hevey, D. (2004). Attachment styles and psychological profiles of child sex offenders in Ireland. *Journal of Interpersonal Violence, 19*, 228–251.

Marsden, J. (2011). Cerebellar ataxia: Pathophysiology and rehabilitation. *Clinical Rehabilitation, 25*, 195–216.

Marsh, A. A., Finger, E. C., Fowler, K. A., Jurkowitz, I., Schechter, J. C., Yu, H. H., . . . Blair, R. J. R., (2011). Reduced amygdala–orbitofrontal connectivity during moral judgments in youths with disruptive behavior disorders and psychopathic traits. *Psychiatry Research: Neuroimaging, 194*, 279–286

Marshall, G. D., & Zimbardo, P. G. (1979). Affective consequences of inadequately explained physiological arousal. *Journal of Personality and Social Psychology, 37*, 970–988.

Marshall, J. C., Halligan, P. W., Fink, G. R., Wade, D. T., & Frackowiak, R. S. J. (1997). The functional anatomy of a hysterical paralysis. *Cognition, 64*, B1–B8.

Marshall, M. (1990). The theme of quantification and the hidden Weber in the early work of Gustav Theodor Fechner. *Canadian Psychology, 31*, 45–63.

Marsland, A. L., Manuck, S. B., Fazzari, T. V., & Stewart, C. J. (1995). Stability of individual differences in cellular immune responses to acute psychological stress. *Psychosomatic Medicine, 57*, 295–298.

Martin, A. J., Nejad, H. G., Colmar, S., & Liem, G. A. D. (2013). Adaptability: How students' responses to uncertainty and novelty predict their academic and nonacademic outcomes. *Journal of Educational Psychology, 105*, 728–746.

Martin, D. J., Garske, J. P., & Davis, M. K. (2000). Relation of the therapeutic alliance with outcome and other variables: A meta-analytic review. *Journal of Consulting and Clinical Psychology, 68*, 438–450.

Martin, R. A., Kuiper, N. A., Olinger, L. J., & Dance, K. (1993). Humor, coping with stress, self-concept, and psychological well-being. *Humor: International Journal of Humor Research, 6*, 89–104.

Martin, S. J., & Morris, R. G. M. (2002). New life in an old idea: The synaptic plasticity and memory hypothesis revisited. *Hippocampus, 12*, 609–636.

Martinez, H. R., Gonzalez-Garza, M. T., Moreno-Cuevas, J. E., Caro, E., Gutierrez-Jimenez, E., & Segura, J. J. (2009). Stem-cell transplantation into the frontal motor cortex in amyotrophic lateral sclerosis patients. *Cytotherapy, 11*, 26–34.

Martinez, J. L., Jr., & Derrick, B. E. (1996). Long-term potentiation and learning. *Annual Review of Psychology, 47*, 173–203.?

Martínez, K., Burgaleta, M., Román, F. J., Escorial, S., Shih, P. C., Ángeles Quiroga, M., & Colom, 2011. Can fluid intelligence be reduced to "simple" short-term storage? *Intelligence, 39*, 473–480.

Martinez, M., Brezun, J. M., Zennou-Azogui, Y., Baril, N., & Xerri,C. (2009). Sensorimotor training promotes functional recovery and somatosensory cortical map reactivation following cervical spinal cord injury. *European Journal of Neuroscience, 30*, 2356–2367.

Martinez, M. E. (2002). Effectiveness of operationalized Gestalt therapy role playing in the treatment of phobic behaviors. *Gestalt Review, 6*, 148–167.

Martinez-Pons, M. (1997). The relation of emotional intelligence with selected areas of personal functioning. *Imagination, Cognition and Personality, 17*, 3–13.

Martinko, M. J., & Thomson, N. F. (1998). A synthesis and extension of the Weiner and Kelley attribution models. *Basic and Applied Social Psychology, 20*, 271–284.

Martins, I. P., & Parriera, E. (2001). Behavioral response to headache: A comparison between migraine and tension-type headache. *Headache, 41*, 546–553.

Marx, B., Gross, A. M., & Adams, H. E. (1999). The effect of alcohol on the responses of sexually coercive and noncoercive men to an experimental rape analog. *Sexual Abuse: Journal of Research and Treatment, 11*, 131–145.

Marx, J. L. (1980). Ape-language controversy flares up. *Science, 207*, 1330–1333.

Masling, J., Bornstein, F. R., Fishman, I., & Davila, J. (2002). Can Freud explain women as well as men? A meta-analytic review of gender differences in psychoanalytic research. *Psychoanalytic Psychology, 19*, 328–347.

Maslow, A. H. (1970). *Motivation and personality.* New York: Harper & Row.

Masoro, E. J., Shimokawa, I., Higami, Y., & McMahan, C. A. (1995). Temporal pattern of food intake not a factor in the retardation of aging processes by dietary restriction. *Journals of Gerontology: Series A: Biological Sciences and Medical Sciences, 50A*, B48–B53.

Masserano, J. M., Takimoto, G. S., & Weiner, N. (1981). Electroconvulsive shock increases tyrosine hydroxylaseactivity via the brain and adrenal gland of the rat. *Science, 214*, 662–665.

Masser, B., & Abrams, D. (1999). Contemporary sexism: The relationships among hostility, benevolence, and neosexism. *Psychology of Women Quarterly, 23*, 503–517.

Masters, K. S. (1992). Hypnotic susceptibility, cognitive dissociation, and runner's high in a sample of marathon runners. *American Journal of Clinical Hypnosis, 34*, 193–201.

Masters, K. S., & Knestel, A. (2011). Religious orientation among a random sample of community-dwelling adults: Relations with health status and health-relevant behaviors. *International Journal for the Psychology of Religion, 21*, 63–76.

Masters, K. S., & Ogles, B. M. (1998). Associative and dissociative cognitive strategies in exercise and running: 20 years later, what do we know? *Sport Psychologist, 12*, 253–270.

Masters, W. H., & Johnson, V. E. (1966). *Human sexual response.* Boston: Little, Brown.

Mastropieri, M. A., Scruggs, T. E., & Whedon, C. (1997). Using mnemonic strategies to teach information about U.S. presidents: A classroom-based investigation. *Learning Disability Quarterly, 20*, 13–21.

Mathew, R. J., Wilson, W. H., Turkington, T. G., Hawk, T. C., Coleman, R. E., DeGrado, T. R., & Provenzale, J. (2002). Time course of tetrahydrocannabinol-induced changes in regional cerebral blood flow measured with positron emission tomography. *Psychiatry Research: Neuroimaging, 116*, 173–185.

Mathis, M., & Lecci, L. (1999). Hardiness and college adjustment: Identifying students in need of services. *Journal of College Student Development, 40*, 305–309.

Matlock, J. G. (1991). Records of the Parapsychology Laboratory: An inventory of the collection in the Duke University library. *Journal of Parapsychology, 55*, 301–314.

Matson, J. L., DiLorenzo, T. M., & Esveldt-Dawson, K. (1981). Independence training as a method of enhancing self-help skills acquisition of the mentally retarded. *Behaviour Research and Therapy, 19*, 399–405.

Matsubayashi, T., & Ueda, M. (2011). The effect of national suicide prevention programs on suicide rates in 21 OECD nations. *Social Science & Medicine, 73*, 1395–1400.

Matsumoto, D. (1987). The role of facial response in the experience of emotion: More methodological problems and a meta-analysis. *Journal of Personality and Social Psychology, 52*, 769–774.

Matsumoto, D. (1999). Culture and self: An empirical assessment of Markus and Kitayama's theory of independent and interdependent self-construal. *Asian Journal of Social Psychology, 2*, 289–310.

Matsuura, T., Ishida, T., & Ishimatsu, K. (2002). Changes in seatbelt use after licensing: A developmental hypothesis for novice drivers. *Transportation Research Part F: Traffic Psychology and Behaviour, 5*, 1–13.

Matt, G. E., & Navarro, A. M. (1997). What meta-analyses have and have not taught us about psychotherapy effects: A review and future directions. *Clinical Psychology Review, 17*, 1–32.

Matt, G. E., Vazquez, C., & Campbell, W. K. (1992). Mood-congruent recall of affectively toned stimuli: A meta-analytic review. *Clinical Psychology Review, 12*, 227–255.

Mattai, P. R. (2002). The multifaceted needs, concerns and responses to educating all children: Editor's comments. *Child Study Journal, 32*, 1–3.

Mattanah, J. F., Pratt, M. W., Cowan, P. A., & Cowan, C. P. (2005). Authoritative parenting, parental scaffolding of long-division mathematics, and children's academic competence in fourth grade. *Journal of Applied Developmental Psychology, 26*, 85–106.

Matthews, D. B., Best, P. J., White, A. M., Vandergriff, J. L., & Simon, P. E. (1996). Ethanol impairs spatial cognitive processing: New behavioral and electrophysiological findings. *Current Directions in Psychological Science, 5*, 111–115.

Matthews, K. A., & Woodall, K. L. (1988). Childhood origins of overt Type A behaviors and cardiovascular reactivity to behavioral stressors. *Annals of Behavioral Medicine, 10*, 71–77.

Mautner, B. (1991). Freud's Irma dream: A psychoanalytic interpretation. *International Journal of Psycho-Analysis, 72*, 275–286.

May, R. (1982, Summer). The problem of evil: An open letter to Carl Rogers. *Journal of Humanistic Psychology*, pp. 10–21.

Mayer, B., & Merckelbach, H. (1999). Unconscious processes, subliminal stimulation, and anxiety. *Clinical Psychology Review, 19*, 571–590.

Mazzella, R., & Feingold, A. (1994). The effects of physical attractiveness, race, socioeconomic status, and gender of defendants and victims on judgments of mock jurors: A meta-analysis. *Journal of Applied Social Psychology, 24*, 1315–1344.

McAdams, D. P., de St. Aubin, E., & Logan, R. L. (1993). Generativity among youth, midlife, and older adults. *Psychology and Aging, 8*, 221–230.

McAllister, D. E., & McAllister, W. R. (1994). Extinction and reconditioning of classically conditioned fear before and after instrumental learning: Effects of depth of fear extinction. *Learning and Motivation, 25*, 339–367.

McAlpine, D., & Grothe, B. (2003). Sound localization and delay lines: Do mammals fit the model? *Trends in Neurosciences, 26*, 347–350.

McAuley, E., Poag, K., Gleason, A., & Wraith, S. (1990). Attrition from exercise programs: Attributional and affective perspectives. *Journal of Social Behavior and Personality, 5*, 591–602.

McCabe, K. O., & Fleeson, W. (2012). What is extraversion for? Integrating trait and motivational perspectives and identifying the purpose of extraversion. *Psychological Science, 23*,1498–1505.

McCaffrey, T. (2012). Innovation relies on the obscure: A key to overcoming the classic problem of functional fixedness. *Psychological Science, 23*, 215–218.

McCall, M. (1997). The effects of physical attractiveness on gaining access to alcohol: When social policy meets social decision making. *Addiction, 92*, 597–600.

McCalley, L. T., & Midden, C. J. H. (2002). Energy conservation through product–integrated feedback: The roles of goal-setting and social orientation. *Journal of Economic Psychology, 23*, 589–603.

McCallister, C., Nash, W. R., & Meckstroth, E. (1996). The social competence of gifted children: Experiments and experience. *Roeper Review, 18*, 273–276.

McCammon, S., Durham, T. W., Allison, E. J., & Williamson, J. E. (1988). Emergency workers' cognitive appraisal and coping with traumatic events. *Journal of Traumatic Stress, 1*, 353–372.

McCanne, T. R., & Anderson, J. A. (1987). Emotional responding following experimental manipulation of facial electromyographic activity. *Journal of Personality and Social Psychology, 52*, 759–768.

McCarthy, L., & Shean, G. (1996). Agoraphobia and interpersonal relationships. *Journal of Anxiety Disorders, 10*, 477–487.

McCauley, C., & Forman, R. F. (1988). A review of the Office of Technology Assessment report on polygraph validity. *Basic and Applied Social Psychology, 9*, 73–84.

McCauley, C., Woods, K., Coolidge, C., & Kulick, W. (1983). More-aggressive cartoons are funnier. *Journal of Personality and Social Psychology, 44*, 817–823.

McClelland, J. L., Fiez, J. A., & McCandliss, B. D. (2002). Training the /r/-/l/ discrimination to Japanese adults: Behavioral and neural aspects. *Physiology & Behavior, 77*, 657–662.

McClelland, J. L., McNaughton, B. L., & O'Reilly, R. C. (1995). Why there are complementary learning systems in the hippocampus and neocortex: Insights from the successes and failures of connectionist models of learning and memory. *Psychological Review, 102*, 419–437.

McClelland, L., Reicher, S., & Booth, N. (2000). A last defence: The negotiation of blame within suicide notes. *Journal of Community and Applied Social Psychology, 10*, 225–240.

McCloskey, M., & Egeth, H. E. (1983). Eyewitness identification: What can a psychologist tell a jury? *American Psychologist, 38*, 550–563.

McCloskey, M., Wible, C. G., & Cohen, N. J. (1988). Is there a special flashbulb-memory mechanism? *Journal of Experimental Psychology: General, 117*, 171–181.

McClure, E. B. (2000). A meta-analytic review of sex differences in facial expression processing and their development in infants, children, and adolescents. *Psychological Bulletin, 126*, 424–453.

McComas, A., & Upton, A. (2009). Therapeutic transcranial magnetic stimulation in migraine and its implications for a neuroinflammatory hypothesis. *Inflammopharmacology, 17*, 68–75.

McConahay, J. B. (1986). Modern racism, ambivalence, and the Modern Racism Scale. In J. F. Dovidio & S. L. Gaertner (Eds.), *Prejudice, discrimination, and racism* (pp. 91-125). London: Academic Press.

McConaghy, N., & Blaszczynski, A. (1991). Initial stages of validation by penile volume assessment that sexual orientation is distributed dimensionally. *Comprehensive Psychiatry, 32*, 52–58.

McConnell, J. V., Cutler, R. L., & McNeil, E. B. (1958). Subliminal stimulation: An overview. *American Psychologist, 13*, 229–242.

McConnell, J. V., Jacobson, A. L., & Kimble, D. P. (1959). The effects of regeneration upon retention of a conditioned response in the planarian. *Journal of Comparative and Physiological Psychology, 52*, 1–5.

McCrae, R. R., & Costa, P. T., Jr. (1995). Trait explanations in personality psychology. *European Journal of Personality, 9*, 231–252.

McCrae, R. R., & Costa, P. T., Jr. (1997). Personality trait structure as a human universal. *American Psychologist, 52*, 509–516.

McCrae, R. R., Costa, P. T., Jr., Del Pilar, G. H., Rolland, J.-P., & Parker, W. D. (1998). Cross-cultural assessment of the five-factor model: The Revised NEO Personality Assessment. *Journal of Cross-Cultural Psychology, 29*, 171–188.

McCrea, D. A. (1992). Can sense be made of spinal interneuron circuits? *Behavioral and Brain Sciences, 15*, 633–643.

McCrea, S. M., & Hirt, E. R. (2001). The role of ability judgments in self-handicapping. *Personality and Social Psychology Bulletin, 27*, 1378–1389.

McCullough, M. E., Tsang, J.-A., & Brion, S. (2003). Personality traits in adolescence as predictors of religiousness in early adulthood: Findings from the Terman longitudinal study. *Personality and Social Psychology Bulletin, 29*, 980–991.

McDonald, D. N. (2007). Differing conceptions of personhood within the psychology and philosophy of Mary Whiton Calkins. *Transactions of the Charles S. Peirce Society, 43*, 753–768.

McDonald, M. S. (1980, September 10). Emperor Norton. *American West*, pp. 30–32, 51, 61.

McDougal, Y. B., Crowe, G. W., & Holland, S. M. (2003). Motion parallax: Is it presented accurately in textbooks? *Teaching of Psychology, 30*, 256–258.

McDougall, W. (1908). *Social psychology*. New York: G. Putnam & Sons.

McDowell, M. J. (2001). Principle of organization: A dynamic-systems view of the archetype-as-such. *Journal of Analytical Psychology, 46*, 637–654.

McEwen, B. S. (2004). Protection and damage from acute and chronic stress: Allostasis and allostatic overload and relevance to the pathophysiology of psychiatric disorders. *Annals of the New York Academy of Sciences, 1032*, 1–7.

McFadden, D. (1998). Sex differences in the auditory system. *Developmental Neuropsychology, 14*, 261–298.

McFadden, D. (2002). Masculinization effects in the auditory system. *Archives of Sexual Behavior, 31*, 99–111

McFadden, D., & Pasanen, E. G. (1999). Spontaneous otoacoustic emissions in heterosexuals, homosexuals, and bisexuals. *Journal of the Acoustical Society of America, 105*, 2403–2413.

McGaha, A. C., & Korn, J. H. (1995). The emergence of interest in the ethics of psychological research with humans. *Ethics and Behavior, 5*, 147–159.

McGaugh, J. L., & Roozendaal, B. (2002). Role of adrenal stress hormones in forming lasting memories in the brain. *Current Opinion in Neurobiology, 12*, 205–210.

McGrady, A. (2002). A commentary on "Problems inherent in assessing biofeedback efficacy studies." *Applied Psychophysiology and Biofeedback, 27*, 111–112.

McGrady, A., Turner, J. W., Fine, T. H., & Higgins, J. T. (1987). Effects of biobehaviorally assisted relaxation training on blood pressure, plasma renin, cortisol, and aldosterone levels in borderline essential hypertension. *Clinical Biofeedback and Health, 10*, 16–25.

McGue, M., Bacon, S., & Lykken, D. T. (1993). Personality stability and change in early adulthood: A behavioral genetic analysis. *Developmental Psychology, 29*, 96–109.

McGuffin, P., Rijsdijk, F., Andrew, M., Sham, P., Katz, R., & Cardno, A. (2003). The heritability of bipolar affective disorder and the genetic relationship to unipolar depression. *Archives of General Psychiatry, 60*, 497–502.

McGuigan, F. J. (1970). Covert oral behavior during the silent performance of language tasks. *Psychological Bulletin, 74*, 309–326.

McGuire, L., Kiecolt-Glaser, J. K., & Glaser, R. (2002). Depressive symptoms and lymphocyte proliferation in older adults. *Journal of Abnormal Psychology, 111*, 192–197.

McInnis, M. G., Dick, D. M., Willour, V. L., Avramopoulos, D., MacKinnon, D. F., Simpson, S., . . . Foroud, T. M. (2003). Genome-wide scan and conditional analysis in bipolar disorder: Evidence for genomic interaction in the National Institute of Mental Health genetics initiative bipolar pedigrees. *Biological Psychiatry, 54*, 1265–1273.

McIntosh, D. N. (1996). Facial feedback hypotheses: Evidence, implications, and directions. *Motivation and Emotion, 20*, 121–147.

McIntosh, D. N., Zajonc, R. B., Vig, P. S., & Emerick, S. W. (1997). Facial movement, breathing, temperature, and affect: Implications of the vascular theory of emotional efference. *Cognition and Emotion, 11*, 171–195.

McKelvie, S. J., & Drumheller, A. (2001). The availability heuristic with famous names: A replication. *Perceptual & Motor Skills, 92*, 507–516.

McKendree-Smith, N., & Scogin, F. (2000). Depressive realism: Effects of depression severity and interpretation time. *Journal of Clinical Psychology, 56*, 1601–1608.

McKenna, M. C., Zevon, M. A., Corn, B., & Rounds, J. (1999). Psychosocial factors and the development of breast cancer: A meta-analysis. *Health Psychology, 18*, 520–531.

McKennitt, D. S., & Currie, C. L. (2012). Does a culturally sensitive smoking prevention program reduce smoking intentions among aboriginal children? A pilot study. *American Indian and Alaska Native Mental Health Research, 19*, 55–63.

McKenzie, J. (1998). Fundamental flaws in the Five Factor Model: A re-analysis of the seminal correlation matrix from which the "openness-to-experience" factor was extracted. *Personality and Individual Differences, 24*, 475–480.

McKinney, M., & Richelson, E. (1984). The coupling of the neuronal muscarinic receptor to responses. *Annual Review of Pharmacology and Toxicology, 24*, 121–146.

McKown, C., & Weinstein, R. S. (2003). The development and consequences of stereotype consciousness in middle childhood. *Child Development, 74*, 498–515.

McLay, R. N., Wood, D. P., Webb-Murphy, J., Spira, J. L., Wiederhold, M. D., Pyne, J. M., & Wiederhold, B. K. (2011). A randomized, controlled trial of virtual reality-graded exposure therapy for post-traumatic stress disorder in active duty service members with combat-related post-traumatic stress disorder. *Cyberpsychology, Behavior and Social Networking, 14*, 223–229.

McLeod, D. M., & Detenber, B. H. (1999). Framing effects of television news coverage of social protest. *Journal of Communication, 49*, 3–23.

McLure, J., Walkey, F., & Allen, M. (1999). When earthquake damage is seen as preventable: Attributions, locus of control, and attitudes to risk. *Applied Psychology: An International Review, 48*, 239–256.

McMahon, M. (1992). Dangerousness, confidentiality, and the duty to protect. *Australian Psychologist, 27*, 12–16.

McManus, C., Nicholls, M., & Vallortigara, G. (2009). Editorial commentary: Is LRRTM1 the gene for handedness? *Laterality, 14*, 1–2.

McMillan, D. E., & Katz, J. L. (2002). Continuing implications of the early evidence against the drive–reduction hypothesis of the behavioral effects of drugs. *Psychopharmacology, 163*, 251–264.

McMinn, M. R., Vogel, M. J., & Heyne, L. K. (2010). A place for the church within professional psychology. *Journal of Psychology and Theology, 38*, 267–274.

McNatt, D. B. (2000). Ancient Pygmalion joins contemporary management: A meta-analysis of the result. *Journal of Applied Psychology, 85*, 314–322.

McNelles, L. R., & Connolly, J. A. (1999). Intimacy between adolescent friends: Age and gender differences in intimate affect and intimate behaviors. *Journal of Research on Adolescence, 9*, 143–159.

McPherson, K. S. (1985). On intelligence testing and immigration legislation. *American Psychologist, 40*, 242–243.

McQuellon, R. P., Wells, M., Hoffman, S., Craven, B., Russell, G., Cruz, J., . . . Savage, P. (1998). Reducing distress in cancer patients with an orientation program. *Psycho-Oncology, 7*, 207–217.

McRoberts, C., Burlingame, G. M., & Hoag, M. J. (1998). Comparative efficacy of individual and group psychotherapy: A meta–analytic perspective. *Group Dynamics, 2*, 101–117.

McWilliams, S. A., & Tuttle, R. J. (1973). Long-term psychological effects of LSD. *Psychological Bulletin, 79*, 341–351.

Meana, M., & Binik, Y. M. (1994). Painful coitus: A review of female dyspareunia. *Journal of Nervous and Mental Disease, 182*, 264–272.

Mecacci, L., & Rocchetti, G. (1998). Morning and evening types: Stress-related personality aspects. *Personality and Individual Differences, 25*, 537–542.

Medin, D. L. (1989). Concepts and conceptual structure. *American Psychologist, 44*, 1469–1481.

Medland, S. E., Geffen, G., & McFarland, K. (2002). Lateralization of speech production using verbal/manual dual tasks: Meta-analysis of sex differences and practice effects. *Neuropsychologia, 40*, 1233–1239.

Meehan, J. W., & Day, R. H. (1995). Visual accommodation as a cue for size. *Ergonomics, 38*, 1239–1249.

Meehl, P. E. (1956). Wanted: A good cookbook. *American Psychologist, 11*, 263–272.

Meeker, W. B., & Barber, T. X. (1971). Toward an explanation of stage hypnosis. *Journal of Abnormal Psychology, 77*, 61–70.

Meert, T. F., Vissers, K., Geenen, F., & Kontinen, V. K. (2003). Functional role of exogenous administration of substance P in chronic constriction injury model of neuropathic pain in gerbils. *Pharmacology, Biochemistry and Behavior, 76*, 17–25.

Meertens, R. W., & Pettigrew, T. F. (1997). Is subtle prejudice really prejudice? *Public Opinion Quarterly, 61*, 54–71.

Mehu, M, & Dunbar, R. I. M. (2008). Naturalistic observations of smiling and laughter in human group interactions. *Behaviour, 145*, 1747–1780.

Meichenbaum, D. (1985). *Stress-inoculation training*. New York: Pergamon.

Meichenbaum, D. H., Bowers, K. S., & Ross, R. R. (1969). A behavioral analysis of teacher expectancy effect. *Journal of Personality and Social Psychology, 13*, 306–316.

Meisenzahl, E. M., Schmitt, G. J., Scheuerecker, J., & Möller, H. J. (2007). The role of dopamine for the pathophysiology of schizophrenia. *International Review of Psychiatry, 19*, 337–345.

Meissner, W. W. (1996). Empathy in the therapeutic alliance. *Psychoanalytic Inquiry, 16*, 39–53.

Melanoma risk and socio-economic class (1983). *Science News, 124*, 232.

Mellon, M. W., & McGrath, M. L. (2000). Empirically supported treatments in pediatric psychology: Nocturnal enuresis. *Journal of Pediatric Psychology, 25*, 193–214.

Mellors, V., Boyle, G. J., & Roberts, L. (1994). Effects of personality, stress, and lifestyle on hypertension: An Australian twin study. *Personality and Individual Differences, 16*, 967–974.

Melmed, S. (2009). Acromegaly pathogenesis and treatment. *Journal of Clinical Investigation, 119*, 3189–3202.

Melville, J. D., & Naimark, D. (2002). Punishing the insane: The verdict of guilty but mentally ill. *Journal of the American Academy of Psychiatry and the Law, 30*, 553–555.

Melzack, R. (1993). Pain: Past, present and future. *Canadian Journal of Experimental Psychology, 47*, 615–629.

Melzack, R., & Wall, P. D. (1965). Pain mechanisms: A new theory. *Science, 150*, 971–979.

Menachemi, N. (2011). Assessing response bias in a web survey at a university faculty. *Evaluation and Research in Education, 24*, 5–15.

Menchetti1, M., Bortolotti1, B., Rucci, P., Scocco, P., Bombi1, A., & Berardi, D. (2010). Depression in primary care: Interpersonal counseling vs selective serotonin reuptake inhibitors. The DEPICS Study: A multicenter randomized controlled trial—Rationale and design. *BMC Psychiatry, 10*, 97–105.

Mendelson, W. B., Maczaj, M., & Holt, J. (1991). Buspirone administration to sleep apnea patients. *Journal of Clinical Psychopharmacology, 11*, 71–72.

Menéndez-Colino, L. M., Falco, C., Traserra, J., Berenguer, J., Pujo, T., Doménech, J., & Bernal-Prekelsen, M. (2007). Activation patterns of the primary auditory cortex in normal-hearing subjects: a functional magnetic resonance imaging study. *Acta Oto-Laryngologica, 127*, 1283–1291.

Mengel, M. K. C., Stiefenhofer, A. E., Jyvasjarvi, E., & Kniffki, K. D. (1993). Pain sensation during cold stimulation of the teeth: Differential reflection of Ad and C fibre activity? *Pain, 55*, 159–169.

Menon, T., Morris, M. W., Chiu, C.-Y., & Hong, Y.-Y. (1999). Culture and the construal of agency: Attribution to individual versus group dispositions. *Journal of Personality and Social Psychology, 76,* 701–717.

Menzel, C. R., Savage-Rumbaugh, E. S., & Menzel, E, W. (2002). Bonobo *(Pan paniscus)* spatial memory and communication in a 20-hectare forest. *International Journal of Primatology, 23,* 601–619.

Mercier, M., Schwartz, S., Michel, C. M., & Blanke, O. (2009). Motion direction tuning in human visual cortex. *European Journal of Neuroscience, 29,* 424–434.

Merckelbach, H., Arntz, A., & de Jong, P. (1991). Conditioning experiences in spider phobics. *Behaviour Research and Therapy, 29,* 333–335.

Merckelbach, H., Dekkers, T., Wessel, I., & Roefs, A. (2003). Dissociative symptoms and amnesia in Dutch concentration camp survivors. *Comprehensive Psychiatry, 44,* 65–69.

Merckelbach, H., Muris, P., & Kop, W. J. (1994). Handedness, symptom reporting, and accident susceptibility. *Journal of Clinical Psychology, 50,* 389–392.

Merewether, F. C., & Alpert, M. (1990). The components and neuroanatomical bases of prosody. *Journal of Communication Disorders, 23,* 325–336.

Merikle, P. M., Smilek, D., & Eastwood, J. D. (2001). Perception without awareness: Perspectives from cognitive psychology. *Cognition, 79,* 115–134.

Merrick, J. (2000). Aspects of Down syndrome. *International Journal of Adolescent Medicine and Health, 12,* 5–17.

Merritt, M. M., Bennett, G. G., Williams, R. B., Sollers, J. J., III, & Thayer, J. F. (2004). Low educational attainment, John Henryism, and cardiovascular reactivity to and recovery from personally relevant stress. *Psychosomatic Medicine, 66,* 49–55.

Mervis, J. (1984, March). Council ends forums trial, opens way for new divisions. *APA Monitor,* pp. 10–11.

Mervis, J. (1986, July). NIMH data point way to effective treatment. *APA Monitor,* pp. 1, 13.

Messer, S. B. (2002). A psychodynamic perspective on résistance in psychotherapy: Vive la resistance. *Journal of Clinical Psychology, 58,* 157–163.

Messer, W. S., & Griggs, R. A. (1989). Student belief and involvement in the paranormal and performance in introductory psychology. *Teaching of Psychology, 16,* 187–191.

Messick, S., & Jungeblut, A. (1981). Time and method in coaching for the SAT. *Psychological Bulletin, 89,* 191–196.

Messier, C. (1997). Object recognition in mice: Improvement of memory by glucose. *Neurobiology of Learning and Memory, 67,* 172–175.

Messier, C., Pierre, J., Desrochers, A., & Gravel, M. (1998). Dose-dependent action of glucose on memory processes in women: Effect on serial position and recall priority. *Cognitive Brain Research, 7,* 221–233.

Meston, C. M., & Frolich, P. F. (2003). Love at first fright: Partner salience moderates roller-coaster–induced excitation transfer. *Archives of Sexual Behavior, 32,* 537–544.

Metcalfe, J., & Wiebe, D. (1987). Intuition in insight and noninsight problem solving. *Memory and Cognition, 15,* 238–246.

Mettetal, G., Jordan, C., & Harper, S. (1997). Attitudes toward a multiple intelligences curriculum. *Journal of Educational Research, 91,* 115–122.

Metz, M. E., & Epstein, N. (2002). Assessing the role of relationship conflict in sexual dysfunction. *Journal of Sex & Marital Therapy, 28,* 139–164.

Meuret, A. E., Wilhelm, F. H., & Roth, W. T. (2001). Respiratory biofeedback-assisted therapy in panic disorder. *Behavior Modification, 25,* 584–605.

Meyer, B., Pilkonis, P., Krupnick, J. L., Egan, M. K., Simmens, S. J., & Sotsky, S. M. (2002). Treatment expectancies, patient alliance and outcome: Further analyses from the National Institute of Mental Health Treatment of Depression Collaborative Research Program. *Journal of Consulting and Clinical Psychology, 70,* 1051–1055.

Meyer-Bahlburg, H. F. L., Ehrhardt, A. A., Rosen, L. R., Guren, R. S., Veridiano, N. P., Vann, F. H., & Neuwalder, H. F. (1995). Prenatal estrogens and the development of homosexual orientation. *Developmental Psychology, 31,* 12–21.

Meyer-Bisch, C. (1996). Epidemiological evaluation of hearing damage related to strongly amplified music (personal cassette players, discotheques, rock concerts): High-definition audiometric survey on 1364 subjects. *Audiology, 35,* 121–142.

Mezzacappa, E. S., Katkin, E. S., & Palmer, S. N. (1999). Epinephrine, arousal, and emotion: A new look at two-factor theory. *Cognition and Emotion, 13,* 181–199.

Miaskowski, C. (1999). The role of sex and gender in pain perception and response to treatment. In R. J. Gatchel et al. (Eds.), *Psychosocial factors in pain: Critical perspectives* (pp. 401–411). New York: Guilford Press.

Michalak, E. E., & Lam, R. W. (2002). Seasonal affective disorder: The latitude hypothesis revisited. *Canadian Journal of Psychiatry, 47,* 787–788.

Michel, C., & Cabanac, M. (1999). Lipectomy, body weight, and body weight set point in rats. *Physiology and Behavior, 66,* 473–479.

Michinov, E., & Monteil, J.-M. (2002). The similarity-attraction relationship revisited: Divergence between the affective and behavioral facets of attraction. *European Journal of Social Psychology, 32,* 485–500.

Miczek, K. A., Thompson, M. L., & Shuster, L. (1982). Opioid-like analgesia in defeated mice. *Science, 215,* 1520–1523.

Middlebrooks, J. C., & Green, D. M. (1991). Sound localization by human listeners. *Annual Review of Psychology, 42,* 135–159.

Midgley, N. (2006). The "inseparable bond between cure and research": Clinical case study as a method of psychoanalytic inquiry. *Journal of Child Psychotherapy, 32,* 122–147.

Miklosi, A., Polgardi, R., Topal, J., & Csanyi, V. (2000). Intentional behavior in dog-human communication: An experimental analysis of "showing" behavior in the dog. *Animal Cognition, 3,* 159–166.

Mikulincer, M., & Florian, V. (2000). Exploring individual differences in reactions to mortality salience: Does attachment style regulate terror management mechanisms? *Journal of Personality and Social Psychology, 79,* 260–273.

Mikulincer, M., Florian, V., & Hirschberger, G. (2003). The existential function of close relationships: Introducing death into the science of love. *Personality and Social Psychology Review, 7,* 20–40.

Milan, R. J., Kilmann, P. R., & Boland, J. P. (1988). Treatment outcome of secondary orgasmic dysfunction: A two- to six-year follow-up. *Archives of Sexual Behavior, 17,* 463–480.

Milar, K. S. (2000). The first generation of women psychologists and the psychology of women. *American Psychologist, 55,* 616–619.

Miles, C., & Hardman, E. (1998). State-dependent memory produced by aerobic exercise. *Ergonomics, 41,* 20–28.

Miles, J. A., & Greenberg, J. (1993). Using punishment threats to attenuate social loafing effects among swimmers. *Organizational Behavior and Human Decision Processes, 56,* 246–265.

Miletic, M. P. (2002). The introduction of a feminine psychology to psychoanalysis: Karen Horney's legacy. *Contemporary Psychoanalysis, 38,* 287–299.

Milgram, S. (1963). Behavioral study of obedience. *Journal of Abnormal and Social Psychology, 67,* 371–378.

Milgram, S. (1964). Issues in the study of obedience: A reply to Baumrind. *American Psychologist, 19,* 848–852.

Milgram, S. (1974). *Obedience to authority.* New York: Harper & Row.

Millar, J. K., Wilson-Annan, J. C., Anderson, S., Christie, S., Taylor, M. S., Semple, C. A., . . . Porteous, D. J. (2000). Disruption of two novel genes by a translocation co-segregating with schizophrenia. *Human Molecular Genetics, 9,* 1415–1423

Millar, M. (2002). Effects of a guilt induction and guilt reduction on door in the face. *Communication Research, 29,* 666–680.

Miller, B. D., & Wood, B. L. (1997). Influence of specific emotional states on autonomic reactivity and pulmonary function in asthmatic children. *Journal of the American Academy of Child and Adolescent Psychiatry, 36,* 669–677.

Miller, C. (2003). Ethical guidelines in research. In J. C. Thomas & M. Hersen (Eds.), *Understanding research in clinical and counseling psychology* (pp. 271–293). Mahwah, NJ: Erlbaum.

Miller, D. L., & Kelley, M. L. (1994). The use of goal setting and contingency contracting for improving children's homework performance. *Journal of Applied Behavior Analysis, 27,* 73–84.

Miller, E. (1996). Phrenology, neuropsychology, and rehabilitation. *Neuropsychological Rehabilitation, 6,* 245–255.

Miller, E. M. (1994). Intelligence and brain myelination: A hypothesis. *Personality and Individual Differences, 17,* 803–832.

Miller, G. A. (1956). The magical number seven, plus or minus two: Some limits on our capacity for processing information. *Psychological Review, 63,* 81–97.

Miller, G. A. (2003). The cognitive revolution: A historical perspective. *Trends in Cognitive Sciences, 7,* 141–144.

Miller, H. A., Watkins, R. J., & Webb, D. (2009). The use of psychological testing to evaluate law enforcement leadership competencies and development. *Police Practice and Research, 10,* 49–60.

Miller, J. (1983). Three constructions of transference in Freud, 1895–1915. *Journal of the History of the Behavioral Sciences, 19,* 153–172.

Miller, L. K. (1999). The Savant syndrome: Intellectual impairment and exceptional skill. *Psychological Bulletin, 125,* 31–46.

Miller, N. E. (1985). The value of behavioral research on animals. *American Psychologist, 40,* 423–440.

Miller, N. S., & Gold, M. S. (1994). LSD and Ecstasy: Pharmacology, phenomenology, and treatment. *Psychiatric Annals, 24,* 131–133.

Miller, S. C., Mor, V., Wu, N., Gozalo, P., & Lapane, K. (2002). Does receipt of hospice care in nursing homes improve the management of pain at the end of life? *Journal of the American Geriatrics Society, 50,* 507–515.

Miller, T. Q., Smith, T. W., Turner, C. W., Guijarro, M. L., & Hallet, A. J. (1996). Meta-analytic review of research on hostility and physical health. *Psychological Bulletin, 119,* 322–348.

Miller, T. Q., Turner, C. W., Tindale, R. S., Posavac, E. J., & Dugoni, B. L. (1991). Reasons for the trend toward null findings in research on Type A behavior. *Psychological Bulletin, 110,* 469–485.

Miller, W. C. (1999). How effective are traditional dietary and exercise interventions for weight loss? *Medicine and Science in Sports and Exercise, 31,* 1129–1134.

Miller-Jones, D. (1989). Culture and testing. *American Psychologist, 44,* 360–366.

Millikin, C., & Braun-Janzen, C. (2013). Collaborative treatment of choking phobia in an older adult. *Clinical Case Studies, 12,* 263–277.

Milling, L. S. (2012). The Spanos Attitudes Toward Hypnosis Questionnaire: Psychometric characteristics and normative data. *American Journal of Clinical Hypnosis, 54,* 202–212.

Millon, T. (2003). It's time to rework the blueprints: Building a science for clinical psychology. *American Psychologist, 58,* 948–961.

Mills, E., Wu, P., Seely, D., & Guatt, G. (2005). Melatonin in the treatment of cancer: A systematic review of randomized controlled trials and meta-analysis. *Journal of Pineal Research, 39,* 360–366.

Mills, E. J., Wu, P., Lockhart, I., Thorlund, K., Puhan, M., & Ebbert, J. O. (2012). Comparisons of high-dose and combination nicotine replacement therapy, varenicline, and bupropion for smoking cessation: A systematic review and multiple treatment meta-analysis. *Annals of Medicine, 44,* 588–597.

Mills, S., & Raine, A. (1994). Neuroimaging and aggression. *Journal of Offender Rehabilitation, 21,* 145–158.

Milosevic, M.,& McConville, K. M. V. (2011). Audiovisual biofeedback system for postural control. *International Journal on Disability and Human Development, 10,* 321–324.

Mimeault, V., & Morin, C. M. (1999). Self-help treatment for insomnia: Bibliotherapy with and without professional guidance. *Journal of Consulting & Clinical Psychology, 67,* 511–519.

Mindell, J. A., & Barrett, K. M. (2002). Nightmares and anxiety in elementary-aged children: Is there a relationship? *Child: Care, Health and Development, 28,* 317–322.

Mineka, S., & Cook, M. (1993). Mechanisms involved in the observational conditioning of fear. *Journal of Experimental Psychology General, 122,* 23–38.

Minini, L., Parker, A. J., & Bridge, H. (2010). Neural modulation by binocular disparity in human dorsal visual stream. *Journal of Neurophysiology, 104,* 169–178.

Mino, Y., Oshima, I., Tsuda, T., & Okagami, K. (2000). No relationship between schizophrenic birth and influenza epidemics in Japan. *Journal of Psychiatric Research, 34,* 133–138.

Mintz, L. B., Balzer, A. M., Zhao, X., & Bush, H. E. (2012). Bibliotherapy for low sexual desire: Evidence for effectiveness. *Journal of Counseling Psychology, 59,* 471–478.

Minuchin, S. (1974). *Families and family therapy.* Cambridge, MA: Harvard University Press.

Mirsky, A. F., Yardley, S. L., Jones, B. P., & Walsh, D. (1995). Analysis of the attention deficit in schizophrenia: A study of patients and their relatives in Ireland. *Journal of Psychiatric Research, 29,* 23–42.

Mischel, W., & Peake, P. J. (1982). Beyond déjà vu in the search for cross-situational consistency. *Psychological Review, 89,* 730–755.

Mischel, W., Shoda, Y., & Mendoza-Denton, R. (2002). Situation-behavior profiles as a locus of consistency in personality. *Current Directions in Psychological Science, 11,* 50–54.

Miserandino, M. (1991). Memory and the seven dwarfs. *Teaching of Psychology, 18,* 169–171.

Mishkin, M., & Appenzeller, T. (1987). The anatomy of memory. *Scientific American,* pp. 80–89.

Misra, G., Sahoo, F. M., & Puhan, B. N. Cultural bias in testing: India. *European Review of Applied Psychology, 47,* 309–317.

Mita, T. H., Dermer, M., & Knight, J. (1977). Reversed facial images and the mere-exposure hypothesis. *Journal of Personality and Social Psychology, 35,* 597–601.

Mitchell, P., & Taylor, L. M. (1999). Shape constancy and theory of mind: Is there a link? *Cognition, 70,* 167–190.

Mitchell, P., Mackinnon, A. J., & Waters, B. (1993). The genetics of bipolar disorder. *Australian and New Zealand Journal of Psychiatry, 27,* 560–580.

Mitchell, P., Waters, B., Morrison, N., & Shine, J. (1991). Close linkage of bipolar disorder to chromosome 11 markers is excluded in two large Australian pedigrees. *Journal of Affective Disorders, 21,* 23–32.

Mitte, K. (2005). Meta-analysis of cognitive-behavioral treatments for generalized anxiety disorder: A comparison with pharmacotherapy. *Psychological Bulletin, 5,* 785–795.

Mobbs, D., & Watt, C. (2011). There is nothing paranormal about near-death experiences: How neuroscience can explain seeing bright lights, meeting the dead, or being convinced that you are one of them. *Trends in Cognitive Sciences, 15,* 447–449.

Modestin, J., Ammann, R., & Würmle, O. (1995). Season of birth: Comparison of patients with schizophrenia, affective disorders, and alcoholism. *Acta Psychiatrica Scandinavica, 91,* 140–143.

Modigliani, A., & Rochat, F. (1995). The role of interaction sequences and the timing of resistance in shaping obedience and defiance to authority. *Journal of Social Issues, 51,* 107–123.

Moen, M. D. (2010). Bevacizumab in previously treated glioblastoma. *Drugs, 70,* 181–189.

Mogg, K., Philippot, P., & Bradley, B. P. (2004). Selective attention to angry faces in clinical social phobia. *Journal of Abnormal Psychology, 113,* 160–165.

Mohanty, A. K., & Perregaux, C. (1997). Language acquisition and bilingualism. In J. W. Berry, P. R. Dasen, & T. S. Saraswathi (Eds.), *Handbook of cross-cultural psychology: Vol. 2. Basic processes and human development* (2nd ed., pp. 217–253). Boston: Allyn & Bacon.

Mohr, C. D., Armeli, S., Tennen, H., Carney, M. A., Affleck, G., & Hromi, A. (2001). Daily interpersonal experiences, context, and alcohol consumption: Crying in your beer and toasting good times. *Journal of Personality and Social Psychology, 80,* 489–500.

Mohr, D. C. (1995). Negative outcome in psychotherapy: A critical review. *Clinical Psychology: Science and Practice, 2,* 1–27.

Molchan, G., & Keilis-Borok, V. (2008). Earthquake prediction: Probabilistic aspect. *Geophysical Journal International, 173,* 1012–1017.

Molina, M., & Jouen, F. (1998). Modulation of the palmar grasp behavior in neonates according to texture property. *Infant Behavior and Development, 21,* 659–666.

Molnar, B. E., Shade, S. B., Kral, A. H., Booth, R. E., & Watters, J. K. (1998). Suicidal behavior and sexual/physical abuse among street youth. *Child Abuse and Neglect, 22,* 213–222.

Monahan, J. (1993). Limiting therapist exposure to Tarasoff liability: Guidelines for risk containment. *American Psychologist, 48,* 242–250.

Money, J. (1986). *Venuses penuses: Sexology, sexosophy, and exigency theory.* Buffalo, NY: Prometheus.

Money, J. (1987). Sin, sickness, or status? Homosexual gender identity and psychoneuroendocrinology. *American Psychologist, 42,* 384–399.

Money, J., & Ehrhardt, A. A. (1972). *Man and woman, boy and girl: Differentiation and dimorphism of gender identity from conception to maturity.* Oxford, England: Johns Hopins University Press.

Mongeau, P. A., & Garlick, R. (1988). Social comparison and persuasive arguments as determinants of group polarization. *Communication Research Reports, 5,* 120–125.

Moniz, E. (1937/1994). Prefrontal leucotomy in the treatment of mental disorders. *American Journal of Psychiatry, 151,* 237–239.

Monroe, S. M. (1982). Life events and disorder: Event-symptom associations and the course of disorder. *Journal of Abnormal Psychology, 91,* 14–24.

Monson, T. C., Hesley, J. W., & Chernick, L. (1982). Specifying when personality traits can and cannot predict behavior: An alternative to abandoning the attempt to predict single-act criteria. *Journal of Personality and Social Psychology, 43,* 385–399.

Montag, I., & Comrey, A. L. (1987). Internality and externality as correlates of involvement in fatal driving accidents. *Journal of Applied Psychology, 72,* 339–343.

Montagliani, A., & Giacalone, R. A. (1998). Impression management and cross-cultural adaptation. *Journal of Social Psychology, 138,* 598–608.

Montague, H., & Hollingworth, L. S. (1914). The comparative variability of the sexes at birth. *American Journal of Sociology, 20,* 335–370.

Monte, C. F. (1980). *Beneath the mask: An introduction to theories of personality.* New York: Holt, Rinehart & Winston.

Montgomery, G., & Kirsch, I. (1996). Mechanisms of placebo pain reduction: An empirical investigation. *Psychonomic Science, 7,* 174–176.??

Montgomery, G. H., DuHamel, K. N., & Redd, W. H. (2000). A meta-analysis of hypnotically induced analgesia: How effective is hypnosis? *International Journal of Clinical & Experimental Hypnosis, 48,* 138–153.

Montour, K. (1977). William James Sidis: The broken twig. *American Psychologist, 32,* 265–279.

Montoya, E. R., Terburg, D., Bos, P. A., & van Honk, J. (2012). Testosterone, cortisol, and serotonin as key regulators of social aggression: A review and theoretical perspective. *Motivation & Emotion, 36,* 65–73.

Montoya, R. M., Horton, R. S., & Kirchner, J. (2008). Is actual similarity necessary for attraction? A meta-analysis of actual and perceived similarity. *Journal of Social & Personal Relationships, 25,* 889–922.

Mooney, G., Speed, J., & Sheppard, S. (2005). Factors related to recovery after mild traumatic brain injury. *Brain Injury, 19,* 975–987.

Moore, C., & Engel, S. A. (1999). Visual perception: Mind and brain see eye to eye. *Current Biology, 9,* R74–R76.

Moore, J. (1990). On mentalism, privacy, and behaviorism. *Journal of Mind and Behavior, 11,* 19–36.

Moore, M. S. (2002). Psychophysical measurement and prediction of digital video quality. *Dissertation Abstracts International: Section B. The Sciences and Engineering, 63,* 2955.

Moore, V., & Goodson, S. (2003). How well does early diagnosis of autism stand the test of time? Follow-up study of children assessed for autism at age 2 and development of an early diagnostic service. *Autism, 7,* 47–63.

Moorhead, G., Ference, R., & Neck, C. P. (1991). Group decision fiascoes continue: Space shuttle Challenger and a revised groupthink framework. *Human Relations, 44,* 539–550.

Moran, M. G. (1991). Psychological factors affecting pulmonary and rheumatologic diseases: A review. *Psychosomatics, 32,* 14–23.

Morawski, J. G. (1982). Assessing psychology's moral heritage through our neglected utopias. *American Psychologist, 37,* 1082–1095.

Moreland, R. L., & Zajonc, R. B. (1982). Exposure effects in person perception: Familiarity, similarity, and attraction. *Journal of Experimental Social Psychology, 18,* 395–415.

Moreno, M., Estevez, A. F., Zaldivar, F., Montes, J. M. G., Guttiérez–Ferre, V. E., Esteban, L., . . . Flores, P. (2012). Impulsivity differences in recreational cannabis users and binge drinkers in a university population. *Drug & Alcohol Dependence, 124,* 355–362.

Moreno, C., Hasin, D. S., Arango, C., Oquendo, M. A, Vieta, E., Liu, S., . . . Blanco, C. (2012). Depression in bipolar disorder versus major depressive disorder: Results from the National Epidemiologic Survey on Alcohol and Related Conditions. *Bipolar Disorders, 14,* 271–82.

Morfei, M. Z., Hooker, K., Fiese, B. H., & Cordeiro, A. M. (2001). Continuity and change in parenting possible selves: A longitudinal follow-up. *Basic and Applied Social Psychology, 23,* 217–223.

Morgan, C., & Murray, H. A. (1935). A method of investigating fantasies. *Archives of Neurology and Psychiatry, 4,* 310–329.

Morgan, W. G. (2002). Origin and history of the earliest thematic apperception test pictures. *Journal of Personality Assessment, 79,* 422–445.

Mori, T., Sugimura, T., & Minami, M. (1996). Effects of prior knowledge and response bias upon recognition memory for a story: Implications for children's eyewitness testimony. *Japanese Psychological Research, 38,* 39–46.

Morin, A. (2001). The split-brain debate revisited: On the importance of language and self-recognition for right hemispheric consciousness. *Journal of Mind and Behavior, 22,* 107–118.

Morisse, D., Batra, L., Hess, L., & Silverman, R. (1996). A demonstration of a token economy for the real world. *Applied and Preventive Psychology, 5,* 41–46.

Moriyama, T. S., Polanczyk, G., Caye, A., Banaschewski, T., Brandeis, D., & Rohde, L. A. (2012). Evidence-based information on the clinical use of neurofeedback for ADHD. *Neurotherapeutic, 9,* 588–598.

Morley, J. E. (2001). Androgens and aging. *Maturitas, 38,* 61–73.

Morley, J. E., & Levine, A. S. (1980). Stres-induced eating is mediated through endogenous opiates. *Science, 209,* 1259–1261.

Morley, J. E., & Perry, H. M. (2003). Andropause: An old concept in new clothing. *Clinics in Geriatric Medicine, 19,* 507–528.

Morling, B. (2000). "Taking" an aerobics class in the U.S. and "entering" an aerobics class in Japan: Primary and secondary control in a fitness context. *Asian Journal of Social Psychology, 3,* 73–85

Morris, S. (1980, April). Interview: James Randi. *Omni,* pp. 76–78, 104, 106, 108.

Morris, W., & Morris, M. (1985). *Harper dictionary of contemporary usage.* New York: Harper & Row.

Morrison, A. R. (1983, April). A window on the sleeping brain. *Scientific American,* pp. 94–102.

Morrison, M., de Man, A. F., & Drumheller, A. (1993). Correlates of socially restrictive and authoritarian attitudes toward mental patients in university students. *Social Behavior and Personality, 21,* 333–338.

Morrongiello, B. A., Fenwick, K. D., & Chance, G. (1990). Sound localization acuity in very young infants: An observer-based testing procedure: Correction. *Developmental Psychology, 26,* 1003.

Morry, M. M., & Staska, S. L. (2001). Magazine exposure: Internaliation, self-objectification, eating attitudes, and body satisfaction in male and female university students. *Canadian Journal of Behavioural Science, 33,* 269–279.

Morse, C. K. (1999). Age and variability in Francis Galton's data. *Journal of Genetic Psychology,160,* 99–104.

Mortensen, P. B., Pedersen, C. B., Westergaard, T., Wohlfahrt, J., Ewald, H., Mors, O., . . . Melbye, M. (1999). Effects of family history and place and season of birth on the risk of schizophrenia. *New England Journal of Medicine, 340,* 603–608.

Moruzzi, G., & Magoun, H. W. (1949). Brain-stem reticular formation and activation of the EEG. *Electroencephalography and Clinical Neurophysiology, 1,* 455–473.

Morvay, Z. (1999). Horney, Zen, and the real self: Theoretical and historical connections. *American Journal of Psychoanalysis, 59,* 25–35.

Moscovitch, M. (1995). Recovered consciousness: A hypothesis concerning modularity and episodic memory. *Journal of Clinical and Experimental Neuropsychology, 17,* 276–290.

Moshinsky, A., & Bar-Hillel, M. (2002). Where did 1850 happen first—in America or in Europe? A cognitive account for a historical bias. *Psychological Science, 13,* 20–26.

Moss, J., Richards, C., Nelson, L., & Oliver, C. (2013). Prevalence of autism spectrum disorder symptomatology and related behavioural characteristics in individuals with Down syndrome. *Autism.The International Journal of Research and Practice, 17,* 390–404.

Mouratidis, A., & Michou, A. (2011). Self-determined motivation and social achievement goals in children's emotions. *Educational Psychology, 31,* 67–86.

Mouthaan, J., Sijbrandij, M., Reitsma, J. B., Luitse, J. S. K., Goslings, J. C., & Olff, M. (2011). Trauma tips: An Internet-based intervention to prevent posttraumatic stress disorder in injured trauma patients. *Journal of CyberTherapy & Rehabilitation, 4,* 331–340.

Mowrer, O. H. (1947). On the dual nature of learning—A reinterpretation of "conditioning" and "problem solving." *Harvard Educational Review, 17,* 102–148.

Mowrer, O. H., & Mowrer, W. M. (1938). Enuresis: A method for its study and treatment. *American Journal of Orthopsychiatry, 8,* 436–559.

Moy, S. S., & Nadler, J. J. (2008). Advances in behavioral genetics: Mouse models of autism. *Molecular Psychiatry, 13,* 4–25.

Muccio, C. F., De Simone, M., Esposito, G., De Blasio, E., Vittori, C., & Cerase, A. (2009). Reversible post-traumatic bilateral extensive restricted diffusion of the brain. A case study and review of the literature. *Brain Injury, 23,* 466–472.

Muehlbach, M. J., & Walsh, J. K. (1995). The effects of caffeine on simulated night-shift work and subsequent daytime sleep. *Sleep, 18,* 22–29.

Mueller, C. G. (1979). Some origins of psychology as a science. *Annual Review of Psychology, 30,* 9–29.

Mueller, S. C., Maheu, F. S., Dozier, M., Peloso, E., Mandell, D., Leibenluft, E., & Ernst, M. (2010). Early-life stress is associated with impairment in cognitive control in adolescence: An fMRI study. *Neuropsychologia, 48,* 3037–3044.

Muir-Broaddus, J., King, T., Downey, D., & Petersen, M. (1998). Conservation as a predictor of individual differences in children's susceptibility to leading questions. *Psychonomic Bulletin and Review, 5,* 454–458.

Muldoon, K.A., Duff, P.K., Fielden, S., & Anema, A. (2013). Food insufficiency is associated with psychiatric morbidity in a nationally representative study of mental illness among food insecure Canadians. *Social Psychiatry and Psychiatric Epidemiology, 48,* 795–803.

Mullen, B., Anthony, T., Salas, E., & Driskell, J. E. (1994). Group cohesiveness and quality of decision making: An integration of tests of the groupthink hypothesis. *Small Group Research, 25,* 189–204.

Mulligan, T., & Moss, C. R. (1991). Sexuality and aging in male veterans: A cross-sectional study of interest, ability, and activity. *Archives of Sexual Behavior, 20,* 17–25.

Mullins, L. L., & Olson, R. A. (1990). Familial factors in the etiology, maintenance, and treatment of somatoform disorders in children. *Family Systems Medicine, 8,* 159–175.

Mumenthaler, M. S., Taylor, J. L., O'Hara, R., & Yesavage, J. A. (1999). Gender differences in moderate drinking effects. *Alcohol Research and Health, 23,* 55–61.

Mumford, M. D., & Gustafson, S. B. (1988). Creativity syndrome: Integration, application, and innovation. *Psychological Bulletin, 103,* 27–43.

Mumme, D. L., & Fernald, A. (2003). The infant as onlooker: Learning from emotional reactions observed in a television scenario. *Child Development, 74,* 221–237.

Munakata, Y., McClelland, J. L., Johnson, M. H., & Siegler, R. S. (1997). Rethinking infant knowledge: Toward an adaptive process account of successes and failures in object permanence tasks. *Psychological Review,104,* 686–713.

Münsterberg, H. (1908). *On the witness stand.* New York: Doubleday.

Murnen, S. K., Smolak, L., Mills, J. A., & Good, L. (2003). Thin, sexy women and strong, muscular men: Grade-school children's responses to objectified images of women and men. *Sex Roles, 49,* 427–437.

Murphy, D., Cramer, D., & Joseph, S. (2012). Mutuality in person-centered therapy: A new agenda for research and practice. *Person-Centered and Experiential Psychotherapies, 11,* 109–123.

Murphy, G. L., & Medin, D. L. (1985). The role of theories in conceptual coherence. *Psychological Review, 92,* 289–316.

Murphy, T. (2001). Near-death experiences in Thailand. *Journal of Near-Death Studies, 19,* 161–178.

Murray, H. A. (1938). *Explorations in personality.* New York: Oxford University Press.

Murray, J. B. (1990). Review of research on the Myers-Briggs Type Indicator. *Perceptual and Motor Skills, 70,* 1187–1202.

Murray, S. L., Holmes, J. G., & Griffin, D. W. (1996). The self-fulfilling nature of positive illusions in romantic relationships: Love is not blind, but prescient. *Journal of Personality and Social Psychology, 71,* 1155–1180.

Muse, L. A., Harris, S. G., & Feild, H. S. (2003). Has the inverted-U theory of stress and job performance had a fair test? *Human Performance,16,* 349–364.

Musikantow, R. (2011). Thinking in circles: Power and responsibility in hypnosis. *American Journal of Clinical Hypnosis, 54,* 83–85.

Mussone, L., Ferrari, A., & Oneta, M. (1999). An analysis of urban collisions using an artificial intelligence model. *Accident Analysis and Prevention, 31,* 705–718.

Myers, D. G. (2000). The funds, friends, and faith of happy people. *American Psychologist, 55,* 56–67.

Myerscough, R., & Taylor, S. (1985). The effects of marijuana on human physical aggression. *Journal of Personality and Social Psychology, 49,* 1541–1546.

Myers, D. G., & Bishop, G. D. (1970). Discussion effects on racial attitudes. *Science, 169,* 778–779.

N

Na, E. U., & Loftus, E. F. (1998). Attitudes toward law and prisoners, conservative authoritarianism, attribution, and internal-external locus of control: Korean and American law students and undergraduates. *Journal of Cross-Cultural Psychology, 29,* 595–615.

Nadel, L., & Jacobs, W. J. (1998). Traumatic memory is special. *Current Directions in Psychological Science, 7,* 154–156.

Nagata, T., Oshima, J., Wada, A., Yamada, H., Iketani, T., & Kiriike, N. (2003). Open trial of milnacipran for Taijin-Kyofusho in Japanese patients with social anxiety disorder. *International Journal of Psychiatry in Clinical Practice, 7,* 107–112.

Nagata, T., Yamada, H., Teo, A. R., Yoshimura, C., Nakajima, T., & van Vliet, I. (2013). Comorbid social withdrawal (hikikomori) in outpatients with social anxiety disorder: Clinical characteristics and treatment response in a case series. *International Journal of Social Psychiatry, 59 ,* 73–78.

Nahas, G., Harvey, D. J., Sutin, K., Turndorf, H., & Cancro, R. (2002). A molecular basis of the therapeutic and psychoactive properties of cannabis (Delta-sup-9 tetrahydrocannabinol). *Progress in Neuro-Psychopharmacology and Biological Psychiatry, 26,* 721–730.

Najavits, L. M., & Strupp, H. H. (1994). Differences in the effectiveness of psychodynamic therapists: A process-outcome study. *Psychotherapy, 31,* 114–123.

Naka, M., Itsukushima, Y., & Itoh, Y. (1996). Eyewitness testimony after three months: A field study on memory for an incident in everyday life. *Japanese Psychological Research, 38,* 14–24.

Nakagawa, Y., & Iwasaki, T. (1996). Ethanol-induced state-dependent learning is mediated by 5hydroxytryptamine-sub-3 receptors but not by Nmethyl-D-aspartate receptor complex. *Brain Research, 706,* 227–232.

Nakamura, K., Kawashima, R., Ito, K., Sugiura, M., Kato, T., Nakamura, A., . . . Kojima, S. (1999). Activation of the right inferior frontal cortex during assessment of facial emotion. *Journal of Neurophysiology, 82,* 1610–1614.

Nakano, T., Shimomura, T., Takahashi, K., & Ikawa, S. (1993). Platelet substance P and 5-hydroxytryptamine in migraine and tension-type headache. *Headache, 33,* 528–532.

Nakayama, K. (1994). James J. Gibson: An appreciation. *Psychological Review, 101,* 329–335.

Narash-Eisikovits, O., Dierberger, A., & Westen, D. (2002). A multidimensional meta-analysis of pharmacotherapy for bulimia nervosa: Summarizing the range of outcomes in controlled clinical trials. *Harvard Review of Psychiatry, 10,* 193–211.

Narita, E., Echizenya, M., Takeshima, M., Inomata, Y., &Shimizu, T. (2011). Core body temperature rhythms in circadian rhythm sleep disorder, irregular sleep-wake type. *Psychiatry & Clinical Neurosciences, 65,* 679–680.

Narita, M., Hashimoto, K., Amano, T., Narita, M., Niikura, K., Nakamura, A., & Suzuki, T. (2008). Post-synaptic action of morphine on glutamatergic neuronal transmission related to the descending antinociceptive pathway in the rat thalamus. *Journal of Neurochemistry, 104,* 469–478.

Narrow, W. E., Clarke, D. E., Kuramoto, S. J., Kraemer, H. C., Kupfer, D. J., Greiner, L., & Regier, D. A. (2013). *DSM-5* field trials in the United States and Canada. Part III: Development and reliability testing of a cross-cutting symptom assessment for *DSM-5. American Journal of Psychiatry, 170,* 71–82.

NAS calls tests fair but limited. (1982, April). *APA Monitor,* p. 2.

Nash, M. (1987). What, if anything, is regressed about hypnotic age regression? A review of the empirical literature. *Psychological Bulletin, 102,* 42–52.

National Institutes of Mental Health. (1998). The NIMH Multisite HIV Prevention Trial: Reducing HIV sexual risk behavior. *Science, 280,* 1889–1894.

National Sleep Foundation. (2011). *2011 Sleep in America Poll: Communications technology in the bedroom.* Retrieved from http://www.sleepfoundation.org/article/sleep-america-polls/2011-communications-technology-use-and-sleep. Retrieved 11/17/2013.

Natsoulas, T. (1997–1998). The stream of consciousness, XVII: James in recent context (1991–1996). *Imagination, Cognition, and Personality, 17,* 345–364.

Nava, F., Carta, G., Colombo, G., & Gessa, G. L. (2001). Effects of chronic Delta-sup-9-tetrahydrocannabinol treatment on hippocampal extracellular acetycholine concentration and alternation performance in the T-maze. *Neuropharmacology, 41,* 392–399.

Navarro, M., Fernandez-Ruiz, J. J., de Miguel, R., & Hernandez, M. L. (1993). Motor disturbances induced by an acute dose of d-sup-9-tetrahydrocannabinol: Possible involvement of nigrostriatal dopaminergic alterations. *Pharmacology, Biochemistry, and Behavior, 45,* 291–298.

Nayak, S., Shiflett, S. C., Eshun, S., & Levine, F. M. (2000). Culture and gender effects in pain beliefs and the prediction of pain tolerance. *Cross-Cultural Research, 34,* 135–151.

Nazari, M. A. (2011). Effectiveness of EEG biofeedback as compared with methylphenidate in the treatment of attention-deficit/hyperactivity disorder: A clinical outcome study. *Neuroscience & Medicine, 2,* 78–86.

Nazzi, T., Floccia, C., & Bertoncini, J. (1998). Discrimination of pitch contours by neonates. *Infant Behavior and Development, 21,* 779–784.

Neher, A. (1996). Jung's theory of archetypes: A critique. *Journal of Humanistic Psychology, 36,* 61–91.

Neisser, U. (1981). John Dean's memory: A case study. *Cognition, 9,* 1–22.

Neisser, U. (1984). Interpreting Harry Bahrick's discovery: What confers immunity against forgetting? *Journal of Experimental Psychology: General, 113,* 32–35.

Neisser, U., & Becklen, R. (1975). Selective looking: Attending to visually specified events. *Cognitive Psychology, 7,* 480–494.

Neisser, U., Boodoo, G., Bouchard, T. J., Jr., Boykin, A. W., Brody, N., Ceci, S. J., . . . Urbina, S. (1996). Intelligence: Knowns and unknowns. *American Psychologist, 51,* 77–101.

Nejime, Y., & Moore, B. C. J. (1998). Evaluation of the effect of speech rate slowing on speech intelligibility in noise using a simulation of cochlear hearing loss. *Journal of the Acoustical Society of America, 103,* 572–576.

Nelson, K. E. (1977). Facilitating children's syntax acquisition. *Developmental Psychology, 18,* 101–107.

Nelson, T. O. (1996). Consciousness and metacognition. *American Psychologist, 51,* 102–116.

Nelson, T. O., Leonesio, R. J., Shimamura, A. P., Landwehr, R. F., & Narens, L. (1982). Overlearning and the feeling of knowing. *Journal of Experimental Psychology: Learning, Memory, and Cognition, 8,* 279–288.

Nemeth, C. J. (1986). Differential contributions of majority and minority influence. *Psychological Review, 93,* 23–32.

Nemeth, C. J., Connell, J. B., Rogers, J. D., & Brown, K. S. (2001). Improving decision making by means of dissent. *Journal of Applied Social Psychology, 31,* 48–58.

Nenty, H. J. (1986). Cross-culture bias analysis of Cattell Culture-Fair Intelligence Test. *Perspectives in Psychological Researches, 9,* 1–16.

Neria, Y., DiGrande, L., & Adams, B. G. (2011). Posttraumatic stress disorder following the September 11, 2001 terrorist attacks: A review of the literature among highly exposed populations. *American Psychologist, 66,* 429–466.

Nesheim, B. I., Kinge, R., Berg, B., Alfredsson, B., Allgot, E., Hove, G., . . . Solberg, S. (2003). Acupuncture during labor can reduce the use of meperidine: A controlled clinical study. *Clinical Journal of Pain, 19,* 187–191.

Nestadt, G., Samuels, J., Riddle, M., Bienvenu, J., Liang, K.-Y., LaBuda, M., Walkup, J., . . . Hoehn-Saric, R. (2000). A family study of obsessive-compulsive behavior. *Archives of General Psychiatry, 57,* 358–363.

Neubauer, A. C., Riemann, R., Mayer, R., & Angleitner, A. (1997). Intelligence and reaction times in the Hick, Sternberg and Posner paradigms. *Personality and Individual Differences, 22,* 885–894.

Neugebauer, V., Schaible, H. G., Weiretter, F., Freudenberger, U. (1994). The involvement of substance P and neurokinin-1 receptors in the responses of rat dorsal horn neurons to noxious but not to innocuous mechanical stimuli applied to the knee joint. *Brain Research, 666,* 207–215.

Neumann, R. (2000). The causal influences of attributions on emotions: A procedural priming approach. *Psychological Science, 11,* 179–182.

Nevo, O. (1985). Does one ever really laugh at one's own expense? *Journal of Personality and Social Psychology, 49,* 799–807.

Nevo, O., & Nevo, B. (1983). What do you do when asked to answer humorously? *Journal of Personality and Social Psychology, 44,* 188–194.

Newcomb, A. F., & Bagwell, C. L. (1995). Children's friendship relations: A meta-analytic review. *Psychological Bulletin, 117,* 306–347.

Newcomb, A. F., Bukowski, W. M., & Pattee, L. (1993). Children's peer relations: A meta-analytic review of popular, rejected, neglected, controversial, and average sociometric status. *Psychological Bulletin, 113,* 99–128.

Newcombe, N. S. (2002). The nativist-empiricist controversy in the context of recent research on spatial and quantitative development. *Psychological Science, 13,* 395–401.

Newell, A., & Simon, H. A. (1972). *Human problem solving.* Oxford, England: Prentice-Hall.

Newman, A. J., Bavelier, D., Corina, D., Jezzard, P., & Neville, H. J. (2002). A critical period for right hemisphere recruitment in American Sign Language processing. *Nature Neuroscience, 5,* 76–80.

Newman, B., O'Grady, M. A., Ryan, C. S., & Hemmes, N. S. (1993). Pavlovian conditioning of the tickle response of human subjects: Temporal and delay conditioning. *Perceptual and Motor Skills, 77,* 779–785.

Newman, J., & Layton, B. D. (1984). Overjustification: A self–perception perspective. *Personality and Social Psychology Bulletin, 10,* 419–425.

Nezlek, J. B., & Gable, S. L. (2001). Depression as a moderator of relationships between positive daily events and day-to-day psychological adjustment. *Personality and Social Psychology Bulletin, 27,* 1692–1704.

Nezu, A. M., Nezu, C. M., & Blissett, S. E. (1988). Sense of humor as a moderator of the relation between stressful events and psychological distress: A prospective analysis. *Journal of Personality and Social Psychology, 54,* 520–525.

Ng, W.-J., & Lindsay, R. C. L. (1994). Cross-race facial recognition: Failure of the contact hypothesis. *Journal of Cross-Cultural Psychology, 25,* 217–232.

NICHD Early Child Care Research Network (1997). The effects of infant child care on infant-mother attachment security: Results of the NICHD study of early child care. *Child Development, 68,* 860–879.

Nicholls, J. G. (1972). Creativity in the person who will never produce anything original and useful: The concept of creativity as a normally distributed trait. *American Psychologist, 27,* 717–727.

Nicholls, J. G. (1984). Achievement motivation: Conceptions of ability, subjective experience, task choice, and performance. *Psychological Review, 91,* 328–346.

Nichols, A. L., & Maner, J. K. (2008). The good-subject effect: Investigating participant demand characteristics. *Journal of General Psychology, 135,* 151–165.

Nichols, M. P., & Efran, J. S. (1985). Catharsis in psychotherapy: A new perspective. *Psychotherapy, 22,* 46–58.

Nicholson, N., Cole, S. G., & Rocklin, T. (1985). Conformity in the Asch situation: A comparison between contemporary British and U.S. university students. *British Journal of Social Psychology, 24,* 59–63.

Nicholson, T.R., Aybek, S., Kempton, M.J., Daly, E.M., Murphy, D.G., David, D.G., & Kanaan, R. A. (2014). A structural MRI study of motor conversion disorder: evidence of reduction in thalamic volume. *Journal of Neurology and Neuropsychiatry, 85,* 227–229.

Nickerson, R. S., & Adams, M. J. (1979). Long-term memory for a common object. *Cognitive Psychology, 11,* 287–307.

Nicol, S. E., & Gottesman, I. I. (1983). Clues to the genetics and neurobiology of schizophrenia. *American Scientist, 71,* 398–404.

Nicoll, R. A., & Madison, D. V. (1982). General anesthetics hyperpolarize neurons in the vertebrate nervous system. *Science, 217,* 1055–1057.

Nicolson, P. (2002). Psychology, evolution, and gender: Editorial. *Psychology, Evolution, and Gender, 4,* 1–2.

Nides, M. A., Rakos, R. F., Gonzales, D., & Murray, R. P. (1995). Predictors of initial smoking cessation and relapse through the first 2 years of the Lung Health Study. *Journal of Consulting and Clinical Psychology, 63,* 60–69.

Nides, M., Rand, C., Dolce, J., & Murray, R. (1994). Weight gain as a function of smoking cessation and 2-mg nicotine gum use among middle-aged smokers with mild lung impairment in the first 2 years of the Lung Health Study. *Health Psychology, 13,* 354–361.

Niedeggen, M., & Roesler, F. (1999). N400 effects reflect activation spread during retrieval of arithmetic facts. *Psychological Science, 10,* 271–276.

Nielsen, T. A. (1993). Changes in the kinesthetic content of dreams following somatosensory stimulation of leg muscles during REM sleep. *Dreaming: Journal of the Association for the Study of Dreams, 3,* 99–113.

Niemann, Y. F., O'Connor, E., & McClorie, R. (1998). Intergroup stereotypes of working class Blacks and Whites: Implications for stereotype threat. *Western Journal of Black Studies, 22,* 103–108.

Niles, S. (1998). Achievement goals and means: A cultural comparison. *Journal of Cross-Cultural Psychology, 29,* 656–667.

Nisbett, R. E., Aronson, J., Blair, C., Dickens, W., Flynn, J., Halpern, D. F., & Turkheimer, E. (2012). Intelligence: New findings and theoretical developments. *American Psychologist, 67,* 130–159.

Nisbett, R. E., Peng, K., Choi, I., & Norenzayan, A. (2001). Culture and systems of thought: Holistic versus analytic cognition. *Psychological Review, 108*, 291–310.

Nisbett, R. E., & Ross, L. (1980). *Human inference: Strategies and shortcomings of social judgment.* Englewood Cliffs, NJ: Prentice-Hall.

Nishikawa, T., Okuda, J., Mizuta, I., Ohno, K., Jamshidi, J., Tokunaga, H., . . . Takeda, M. (2001). Conflict of intentions due to callosal disconnection. *Journal of Neurology, Neurosurgery, and Psychiatry, 71*, 462–471.

Nishimura, H., Hashikawa, K., Doi, K., Iwaki, T., Watanabe, Y., Kusuoka, H., Nishimura, T., & Kubo, T. (1999). Sign language "heard" in the auditory cortex. *Nature, 397*, 116.

Nishith, P., Mechanic, M. B., & Resick, P. A. (2000). Prior interpersonal trauma: The contribution to current PTSD symptoms in female rape victims. *Journal of Abnormal Psychology, 109*, 20–25.

Nissen, M. J., Knopman, D. S., & Schacter, D. L. (1987). Neurochemical dissociation of memory systems. *Neurology, 37*, 789–794.

Niu, W., & Sternberg, R. (2002). Contemporary studies on the concept of creativity. The East and the West. *Journal of Creative Behavior, 36*, 269–288.

Nolen-Hoeksema, S. (2001). Gender differences in depression. *Current Directions in Psychological Science, 10*, 173–176.

Nolen-Hoeksema, S. (2012). Emotion regulation and psychopathology: The role of gender. *Annual Review of Clinical Psychology, 8*, 61–87.

Nolen-Hoeksema, S., & Morrow, J. (1993). Effects of rumination and distraction on naturally occurring depressed mood. *Cognition and Emotion, 7*, 561–570.

Nolen-Hoeksema, S., Larson, J., & Grayson, C. (1999). Explaining the gender difference in depression. *Journal of Personality and Social Psychology, 77*, 1061–1072.

Nopoulos, P., Torres, I., Flaum, M., & Andreasen, N. C. (1995). Brain morphology in first-episode schizophrenia. *American Journal of Psychiatry, 152*, 1721–1723.

Norcross, J. C., Strausser, D. J., & Faltus, F. J. (1988). The therapist's therapist. *American Journal of Psychotherapy, 42*, 53–66.

Nordblom, J. Persson, J. K. E., Svensson, M.,.& Mattsson, P. (2009). Peripheral nerve grafts in a spinal cord prosthesis result in regeneration and motor evoked potentials following spinal cord resection. *Restorative Neurology and Neuroscience 27*, 285–295.

Nordstrom, R., Lorenzi, P., & Hall, R. V. (1990). A review of public posting of performance feedback in work settings. *Journal of Organizational Behavior Management, 11*, 101–123.

Norenzayan, A., Choi, I., & Nisbett, R. E. (2002). Cultural similarities and differences in social inferences: Evidence from behavioral predictions and lay theories of behavior. *Personality and Social Psychology Bulletin, 28*, 109–120.

Norlander, T., Bergman, H., & Archer, T. (1999). Primary process in competitive archery performance: Effects of flotation REST. *Journal of Applied Sport Psychology, 11*, 194–209.

Norlander, T., Kjellgren, A., & Archer, T. (2000–2001). The experience of flotation-rest as a function of setting and previous experience of altered state of consciousness. *Imagination, Cognition & Personality, 20*, 161–178.

Norman, K. A., & O'Reilly, R. C. (2003). Modeling hippocampal and neocortical contributions to recognition memory: A complementary-learning-systems approach. *Psychological Review, 110*, 611–646.

Norman, R. M., & Malla, A. K. (1993). Stressful life events and schizophrenia: I. A review of the research. *British Journal of Psychiatry, 162*, 161–166.

Norris, F. H., & Uhl, G. A. (1993). Chronic stress as a mediator of acute stress: The case of Hurricane Hugo. *Journal of Applied Social Psychology, 23*, 1263–1284.

Norris, N. P. (1978). Fragile subjects. *American Psychologist, 33*, 962–963.

Northrup, T., & Mulligan, N. (2013). Conceptual implicit memory in advertising research. *Applied Cognitive Psychology, 27*, 127–136.

Norton, E. M., Durlak, J. A., & Richards, M. H. (1989). Peer knowledge of and reactions to adolescent suicide. *Journal of Youth and Adolescence, 18*, 427–437.

Nosofsky, R. M. (1991). Relation between the rational model and the context model of categorization. *Psychological Science, 2*, 416–421.

Notz, W. W. (1975). Work motivation and the negative effects of extrinsic rewards: A review with implications for theory and practice. *American Psychologist, 30*, 884–891.

Novick, L. R., & Sherman, S. J. (2003). On the nature of insight solutions: Evidence from skill differences in anagram solution. *Quarterly Journal of Experimental Psychology: Human Experimental Psychology, 56A*, 351–382.

Nowicki, S., & Duke, M. P. (1992). The association of children's nonverbal decoding abilities with their popularity, locus of control, and academic achievement. *Journal of Genetic Psychology, 153*, 385–393.

Noyes, R., Jr., Stuart, S., Longley, S. L., Langbehn, D. R., & Happel, R. L. (2002). Hypochondriasis and fear of death. *Journal of Nervous and Mental Disease, 190*, 503–509.

Nunn, J., & Hodges, H. (1994). Cognitive deficits induced by global cerebral ischaemia: Relationship to brain damage and reversal by transplants. *Behavioral Brain Research, 65*, 1–31.

Nuño, V. L., Zhang, Q., Harris, R. B., Wilkinson-Lee, A. M., & Wilhem, M. S. (2011). Smoking susceptibility among students followed from grade six to eight. *Addictive Behaviors, 36*, 1261–1266.

Nutt, D. J. (2002). The neuropharmacology of serotonin and noradrenaline in depression. *International Clinical Psychopharmacology, 17*, S1–S12.

Nutt, D. J., Ballenger, J. C., Sheehan, D., & Wittchen, H.-U. (2002). Generalized anxiety disorder: Comorbidity, comparative biology, and treatment. *International Journal of Neuropsychopharmacology, 5*, 315–325.

Nyberg, L. (2002). Levels of processing: A view from functional brain imaging. *Memory, 10*, 345–348.

O

O'Brien, L. T., & Crandall, C. S. (2003). Stereotype threat and arousal: Effects on women's math performance. *Personality and Social Psychology Bulletin, 29*, 782–789.

O'Carroll, R. E., Masterton, G., Dougall, N., Ebmeier, K. P., & Goodwin, G. M. (1995). The neuropsychiatric sequelae of mercury poisoning: The Mad Hatter's disease revisited. *British Journal of Psychiatry, 167*, 95–98.

O'Connell, A. N. (1990). Karen Horney (1885–1952). In A. N. O'Connell & N. F. Russo (Eds.), *Women in psychology: A bio-bibliographic sourcebook* (pp. 184–185). New York: Greenwood Press.

O'Connell, A. N., & Russo, N. F. (Eds.). (1990). *Women in psychology: A bio-bibliographic sourcebook.* New York: Greenwood.

O'Connor, D. B., & Shimizu, M. (2002). Sense of personal control, stress, and coping style: A cross-cultural study. *Stress and Health, 18*, 173–183.

O'Connor, F. L. (1998). The role of serotonin and dopamine in schizophrenia. *Journal of the American Psychiatric Nurses Association, 4*, S30–S34.

O'Connor, P. J., Lewis, R. D., & Kirchner, E. M. (1995). Eating disorder symptoms in female college gymnasts. *Medicine and Science in Sports and Exercise, 27*, 550–555.

O'Donnell, I., Farmer, R., & Catalan, J. (1993). Suicide notes. *British Journal of Psychiatry, 163*, 45–48.

O'Halloran, C. M., & Altmaier, E. M. (1995). The efficacy of preparation for surgery and invasive medical procedures. *Patient Education and Counseling, 25*, 9–16.

O'Leary, A. (1985). Self-efficacy and health. *Behaviour Research and Therapy, 23*, 437–451.

O'Leary, K. D., & Smith, D. A. (1991). Marital interactions. *Annual Review of Psychology, 42*, 191–212.

O'Malley, R. C., Wallauer, W., Murray, C. M., & Goodall, J. (2012). The appearance and spread of ant fishing among the Kasekela chimpanzees of Gombe: A possible case of intercommunity cultural transmission. *Current Anthropology, 53*, 650–663.

O'Neil, W. M. (1995). American behaviorism: A historical and critical analysis. *Theory and Psychology, 5*, 285–305.

O'Neill, S. K. (2003). African American women and eating disturbances: A meta-analysis. *Journal of Black Psychology, 29*, 3–16.

O'Shea, R. P., Govan, D. G., & Sekuler, R. (1997). Blur and contrast as pictorial depth cues. *Perception, 26*, 599–612.

Oberlander, J. G., & Henderson, L. P. (2012). The *Sturm und Drang* of anabolic steroid use: Angst, anxiety, and aggression. *Trends in Neurosciences, 35*, 382–392.

Obozova, T. A., Smirnova, A. A., & Zorina, Z. A. (2011). Observational learnng in a glaucous-winged gull natural colony. *International Journal of Comparative Psychology, 24*, 226–234.

Ochs, E. P. P., & Binik, Y. M. (1998). A sex-expert computer system helps couples learn more about their sexual relationship. *Journal of Sex Education and Therapy, 23*, 145–155.

Ockene, J. K., Mermelstein, R. J., Bonollo, D. S., Emmons, K. M., Perkins, K. A., Voorhees, C. C., & Hollis, J. F. (2000). Relapse and maintenance issues for smoking cessation. *Health Psychology, 19*, 17–31.

Oden, G. C. (1984). Dependence, independence, and emergence of word features. *Journal of Experimental Psychology: Human Perception and Performance, 10*, 394–405.

Oden, M. H. (1968). The fulfillment of promise: 40-year followup of the Terman gifted group. *Genetic Psychology Monographs, 77*, 3–93.

Odum, L. E., O'Dell, K. A., & Schepers, J. S. (2012). Electronic cigarettes: Do they have a role in smoking cessation? *Journal of Pharmacy Practice, 25*, 611–614.

Ogden, C. L., Carroll, M. D., Kit, B. K., & Flegal, K. M. (2012). *Prevalence of obesity in the United States 2009–2010. NCHS Data Brief, no. 82.* Hyattsville, MD: National Center for Health Statistics.

Ogilvie, R. D., McDonagh, D. M., Stone, S. N., & Wilkinson, R. T. (1988). Eye movements and the detection of sleep onset. *Psychophysiology, 25*, 81–91.

Ohayon, M. M., Guilleminault, C., & Priest, R. G. (1999). Night terrors, sleepwalking, and confusional arousals in the general population. *Journal of Clinical Psychiatry, 60*, 268–276.

Öhman, A. (2009). Of snakes and faces: An evolutionary perspective on the psychology of fear. *Scandinavian Journal of Psychology, 50*, 543–552.

Oishi, S. (2002). The experiencing and remembering of well-being: A cross-cultural analysis. *Personality and Social Psychology Bulletin, 28*, 1398–1406.

Okano, H., Sakaguchi, M., Ohki, K., Suzuki, N., & Sawamoto, K. (2007). Regeneration of the central nervous system using endogenous repair mechanisms. *Journal of Neurochemistry, 102*, 1459–1465.

Okogbaa, O., Shell, R. L., & Filipusic, D. (1994). On the investigation of the neurophysiological correlates of knowledge worker mental fatigue using the EEG signal. *Applied Ergonomics, 25,* 355–365.

Oku, Y., & Okada, M. (2008). Periodic breathing and dysphagia associated with a localized lateral medullary infarction. *Respirology, 13,* 608–610.

Okwumabua, T. M. (1985). Psychological and physical contributions to marathon performance: An exploratory investigation. *Journal of Sport Behavior, 8,* 163–171.

Oldehinkel, A. J., Ormel, J., Bosch, N. M., Bouma, E. M. C., Van Roon, A. M., Rosmalen, J. G. M., & Riese, H. (2011). Stressed out? Associations between perceived and physiological stress responses in adolescents: The TRAILS study. *Psychophysiology, 48,* 441–452.

Olds, J. (1956, October). Pleasure centers in the brain. *Scientific American,* pp. 105–116.

Olds, J., & Milner, P. (1954). Positive reinforcement produced by electrical stimulations of septal area and other regions of rat brain. *Journal of Comparative and Physiological Psychology, 47,* 419–427.

Oliver, M. B., & Hyde, J. S. (1993). Gender differences in sexuality: A meta-analysis. *Psychological Bulletin, 114,* 29–51.

Oller, D. K., & Eilers, R. E. (1988). The role of audition in infant babbling. *Child Development, 59,* 441–449.

Olmo, R. J., & Stevens, G. L. (1984, August). Chess champs: Introverts at play. *Psychology Today,* pp. 72, 74.

Olsen, S., Smith, S. S., Oei, T.P.S., & Douglas, J. (2012). Motivational interviewing (MINT) improves continuous positive airway pressure (CPAP) acceptance and adherence: A randomized controlled trial. *Journal of Consulting and Clinical Psychology, 80,* 151–163.

Olson, J. K. (1995). Relationships between nurse-expressed empathy, patient-perceived empathy and patient distress. *IMAGE: Journal of Nursing Scholarship, 27,* 317–322.

Olson, M. A., & Fazio, R. H. (2002). Implicit acquisition and manifestation of classically conditioned attitudes. *Social Cognition, 20,* 89–104.

Oman, R. F., & King, A. C. (2000). The effect of life events and exercise program formation on the adoption and maintenance of exercise behavior. *Health Psychology, 19,* 605–612.

Ono, Y., & Janca, A. (1999). Rethinking somatoform disorders. *Journal of Psychosomatic Research, 46,* 537–539.

Onstad, S., Skre, I., Torgersen, S., & Kringlen, E. (1991). Twin concordance for *DSM-III-R* schizophrenia. *Acta Psychiatrica Scandinavica, 83,* 395–401.

Oosterveld, W. J. (1987). The combined effect of Cinnarizine and domperidone on vestibular susceptibility. *Aviation, Space, and Environmental Medicine, 58,* 218–223.

Oppliger, P. A., & Sherblom, J. C. (1992). Humor: Incongruity, disparagement, and David Letterman. *Communication Research Reports, 9,* 99–108.

Orange, C. (1997). Gifted students and perfectionism. *Roeper Review, 20,* 39–41.

Orenstein, P. A., Ceci, S. J., & Loftus, E. F. (1998). Adult recollections of childhood abuse: Cognitive and developmental perspectives. *Psychology, Public Policy, and Law, 4,* 1025–1051.

Orne, M. T. (1951). The mechanisms of hypnotic age regression: An experimental study. *Journal of Abnormal and Social Psychology, 46,* 213–225.

Orne, M. T., & Evans, F. J. (1965). Social control in the psychological experiment: Antisocial behavior and hypnosis. *Journal of Personality and Social Psychology, 1,* 189–200.

Osawa, A., & Maeshima, S. (2010). Family participation can improve unilateral spatial neglect in patients with acute right hemispheric stroke. *European Neurology, 63,* 170–175.

Osberg, T. M. (1993). Psychology is not just common sense: An introductory psychology demonstration. *Teaching of Psychology, 20,* 110–111.

Oswald, D. L., & Harvey, R. D. (2003). A Q-methodological study of women's subjective perspectives on mathematics. *Sex Roles, 49,* 133–142.

Oudiette, D., & Paller, K. A. (2013). Upgrading the sleeping brain with targeted memory reactivation. *Trends in Cognitive Sciences, 17,* 142–149.

Ouimet, J., & De Man, A. F. (!998). Correlates of attitudes toward the application of eugenics to the treatment of people with intellectual disabilities. *Social Behavior and Personality, 26,* 69–74.

Overton, D. A. (1991). Historical context of state dependent learning and discriminative drug effects. *Behavioural Pharmacology, 2,* 253–264.

Owen, P. R., & Laurel–Seller, E. (2000). Weight and shape ideals: Thin is dangerously in. *Journal of Applied Social Psychology, 30,* 979–990.

Ozbay, H., Goka, E., Ozturk, E., & Gungor, S. (1993). Therapeutic factors in an adolescent psychodrama group. *Journal of Group Psychotherapy, Psychodrama, and Sociometry, 46,* 3–11.

P

Pacini, R., Muir, F., & Epstein, S. (1998). Depressive realism from the perspective of cognitive-experiential self–theory. *Journal of Personality and Social Psychology, 74,* 1056–1068.

Paddock, J. R., & Nowicki, S. (1986). Paralanguage and the interpersonal impact of dysphoria: It's not what you say but how you say it. *Social Behavior and Personality, 14,* 29–44.

Padian, K. (2008). Darwin's enduring legacy. *Nature, 451,* 632–634.

Page, S. J., Martin, S. B., & Wayda, V. K. (2001). Attitudes toward seeking sport psychology consultation among wheelchair basketball athletes. *Adapted Physical Activity Quarterly, 18,* 183–192.

Page-Voth, V., & Graham, S. (1999). Effects of goal setting and strategy use on the writing performance and self–efficacy of students with writing and learning problems. *Journal of Educational Psychology, 91,* 230–240.

Paik, H., & Comstock, G. (1994). The effects of television violence on antisocial behavior: A meta-analysis. *Communication Research, 21,* 516–546.

Paikoff, R. L., & Brooks-Gunn, J. (1991). Do parent-child relationships change during puberty? *Psychological Bulletin, 110,* 47–66.

Palaniappan, A. K., & Torrance, E. P. (2001). Comparison between regular and streamlined versions of scoring of Torrance Tests of Creative Thinking. *Korean Journal of Thinking and Problem Solving, 11,* 5–7.

Palencik, J. T. (2007). William James and the psychology of emotion: From 1884 to the present. *Transactions of the Charles S. Peirce Society, 43,* 769–786.

Palermo, G. B. (2002). Criminal profiling: The uniqueness of the killer. *International Journal of Offender Therapy and Comparative Criminology, 46,* 383–385.

Pallast, E. G. M., Jongbloet, P. H., Straatman, H. M., & Zielhuis, G. A. (1994). Excess seasonality of births among patients with schizophrenia and seasonal ovopathy. *Schizophrenia Bulletin, 20,* 269–276.

Palmer, J. A., Honorton, C., & Utts, J. (1989). Reply to the National Research Council Study on parapsychology. *Journal of the American Society for Psychical Research, 83,* 31–49.

Pan, Y., Chen, M., Yin, J., An, X., Zhang, X., Lu, Y., . . . Wang, W. (2012). Equivalent representation of real and illusory contours in macque V4. *The Journal of Neuroscience, 32,* 6760–6770.

Panksepp, J., & Panksepp, J. B. (2013). Toward a cross-species understanding of empathy. *Trends in Neurosciences, 36,* 489–496.

Pantev, C., Roberts, L. E., Schulz, M., Engelien, A., & Ross, B. (2001). Timbre-specific enhancement of auditory cortical representations in musicians. *Neuroreport: For Rapid Communication of Neuroscience Research, 12,* 169–174.

Paradis, M. (1998). The other side of language: Pragmatic competence. *Journal of Neurolinguistics, 11,* 1–10.

Pardo, C.A., Vargas, D.L., & Zimmerman, A. W. (2005). Immunity, neuroglia and neuroinflammation in autism. *International Reviews of Psychiatry, 17,* 485–495.

Pare, D., Collins, D. R., & Guillaume Pelletier, J. (2002). Amygdala oscillations and the consolidation of emotional memories. *Trends in Cognitive Sciences, 6,* 306–314.

Paris, J. (1996). Cultural factors in the emergence of borderline pathology. *Psychiatry: Interpersonal and Biological Processes, 59,* 185–192.

Paris, J. (1998). Personality disorders in sociocultural perspective. *Journal of Personality Disorders, 12,* 289–301.

Park, D. C., Smith, A. D., & Cavanaugh, J. C. (1990). Metamemories of memory researchers. *Memory and Cognition, 18,* 321–327.

Park, R. L. (2008). Fraud in science. *Social Research, 75,* 1135–1150.

Park, W. W. (2000). A comprehensive empirical investigation of the relationship among variables of the groupthink model. *Journal of Organizational Behavior, 21,* 873–887.

Parker, A. (2001). What can cognitive psychology and parapsychology tell us about near-death experiences? *Journal of the Society for Psychical Research, 65,* 225–240.

Parker, A., & Gellatly, A. (1997). Moveable cues: A practical method for reducing context-dependent forgetting. *Applied Cognitive Psychology, 11,* 163–173.

Parker, K. C. H., Hanson, R. K., & Hunsley, J. (1988). MMPI, Rorschach, and WAIS: A meta-analytic comparison of reliability, stability, and validity. *Psychological Bulletin, 103,* 367–373.

Parker, S. (1990). A note on the growth of the use of statistical tests in perception and psychophysics. *Bulletin of the Psychonomic Society, 28,* 565–566.

Parker, W. D. (1996). Psychological adjustment in mathematically gifted students. *Gifted Child Quarterly, 40,* 154–157.

Parkovnick, S. (2000). Contextualizing Floyd Allport's social psychology. *Journal of the History of the Behavioral Sciences, 36,* 429–441.

Parra, A. (1997). Parapsychological developments in Argentina (1990-1995). *Journal of the American Society for Psychical Research, 91,* 103–109.

Parron, D. L. (1997). The fusion of cultural horizons: Cultural influences on the assessment of psychopathology on children. *Applied Developmental Science, 1,* 156–159.

Parrott, A. C. (1995). Smoking cessation leads to reduced stress, but why? *International Journal of the Addictions, 30,* 1509–1516.

Parsons, M. W., & Gold, P. E. (1992). Glucose enhancement of memory in elderly humans: An inverted-U dose-response curve. *Neurobiology of Aging, 13,* 401–404.

Partala, T., & Surakka, V. (2003). Pupil size variation as an indication of affective processing. *International Journal of Human-Computer Studies, 59,* 185–198.

Parten, M. B. (1932). Social participation among preschool children. *Journal of Abnormal and Social Psychology, 27,* 243–269.

Pates, J., Maynard, I., & Westbury, T. (2001). An investigation into the effects of hypnosis on basketball performance. *Journal of Applied Sport Psychology, 31,* 84–102.

Patra, J., & Rath, P. K. (2000). Computer and pedagogy: Replacing telling with computer assisted instruction for teaching arithmetic skills to mentally retarded children. *Journal of Adolescent Health, 26,* 244–251.

Pattatucci, A. M. L., & Hamer, D. H. (1995). Development and familiality of sexual orientation in females. *Behavior Genetics, 25,* 407–420.

Patterson, D. R., & Jensen, M. P. (2003). Hypnosis and clinical pain. *Psychological Bulletin, 129,* 495–521.

Patterson, D. R., Adcock, R. J., & Bombardier, C. H. (1997). Factors predicting hypnotic analgesia in clinical burn pain. *International Journal of Clinical and Experimental Hypnosis, 45,* 377–395.

Patterson, F. G., Patterson, L. H., & Brentari, D. K. (1987). Language in child, chimp, and gorilla. *American Psychologist, 42*, 270–272.

Patton, J. E., Routh, D. K., & Stinard, T. A. (1986). Where do children study? Behavioral observations. *Bulletin of the Psychonomic Society, 24*, 439–440.

Paul, M. A., Miller, J. C., Gray, G. W., Love, R. J., Lieberman, H. R., & Arendt, J. (2010). Melatonin treatment for eastward and westward travel preparation. *Psychopharmacology, 208*, 377–386.

Paulsen, F. (1899/1963). *Immanuel Kant: His life and doctrine*. New York: Ungar

Paunonen, S. V. (2003). Big Five factors of personality and replicated predictions of behavior. *Journal of Personality and Social Psychology, 84*, 411–422.

Paunovic, N. (2003). Prolonged exposure counterconditioning as a treatment for chronic posttraumatic stress disorder. *Journal of Anxiety Disorders, 17*, 479–499.

Pavlov, I. P. (1928). *Lectures on conditioned reflexes*. New York: Liveright.

Pawlak, J. L., & Klein, H. A. (1997). Parental conflict and self-esteem: The rest of the story. *Journal of Genetic Psychology, 158*, 303–313.

Pear, J. J., & Crone-Todd, D. E. (1999). Personalized system of instruction in cyberspace. *Journal of Applied Behavior Analysis, 32*, 205–209.

Pearce, J. M. S. (2007). Corpus callosum. *European Neurology, 57*, 249–250.

Pearce, J. M. S. (2009). Marie-Jean-Pierre Flourens (1794–1867) and cortical localization. *European Neurology, 61*, 311–314.

Pearson, E. S. (2012). Goal setting as a health behavior change strategy in overweight and obese adults: A systematic literature review examining intervention components. *Patient Education and Counseling, 87*, 32–42.

Pedersen, W., & Skrondal, A. (1999). Ecstasy and new patterns of drug use: A normal population study. *Addiction, 94*, 1695–1706.

Peeters, M. C. W., Buunk, B. P., & Schaufeli, W. B. (1995). A micro-analysis exploration of the cognitive appraisal of daily stressful events at work: The role of controllability. *Anxiety, Stress, and Coping: An International Journal, 8*, 127–139.

Pejovic, S., Basta, M., Vgontzas, A. N., Kritikou, I., Shaffer, M. L., Tsaoussoglou, M., . . . Chrousos, G. P. (2013). Effects of recovery sleep after one work week of mild sleep restriction on interleukin–6 and cortisolsecretion and daytime sleepiness and performance. *American Journal of Physiology—Endocrinology and Metabolism, 305*, 890–896.

Pell, M. D. (1998). Recognition of prosody following unilateral brain lesion: Influence of functional and structural attributes of prosodic contours. *Neuropsychologia, 36*, 701–715.

Pell, M. D., Jaywant, A., Monetta, L., & Kotz, S. A. (2011). Emotional speech processing: Disentangling the effects of prosody and semantic cues. *Cognition and Emotion, 25*, 834–853.

Peltzer, K., Mashego, T. A., & Mabeba, M. (2003). Occupational stress and burnout among South African medical practitioners. *Psychology and Health, 18*, 677–684.

Penfield, W. (1975). *The mystery of the mind*. Princeton, NJ: Princeton University Press.

Pengilly, J. W., & Dowd, E. T. (2000). Hardiness and social support as moderators of stress. *Journal of Clinical Psychology, 56*, 813–820.

Penido, A. B., Rezende, G. H., Abreu, R. V., Oliveira, A. C., Guidine, P. A., Schenatto-Pereira G., . . . Moraes, M. F. (2012). Malnutrition during central nervous system growth and development impairs permanently the subcortical auditory pathway. *Nutritional neuroscience, 15*, 31–36.

Pennebaker, J. W., & Watson, D. (1988). Blood pressure estimation and beliefs among normotensives and hypertensives. *Health Psychology, 7*, 309–328.

Pepitone, A. (1981). Lessons from the history of social psychology. *American Psychologist, 36*, 972–985.

Peregrine, P. N., Ember, C. R., & Ember, M. (2003). Cross-cultural evaluation of predicted associations between race and behavior. *Evolution and Human Behavior, 24*, 357–364.

Perelman, M. A. (1998). Commentary: Pharmacological agents for erectile dysfunction and the human sexual response cycle. *Journal of Sex and Marital Therapy, 24*, 309–312.

Peretz, I., Kolinsky, R., Tramo, M., & Labrecque, R. (1994). Functional dissociations following bilateral lesions of auditory cortex. *Brain, 117*, 1283–1301.

Perfetto, F., Piluso, A., Cagnacci, A., & Tarquini, R. (2002). Circadian pattern of serum leptin and beta-endorphin levels in obese and non obese women. *Biological Rhythm Research, 33*, 287–302.

Perl, D. P. (2010). Neuropathology of Alzheimer's disease. *Mount Sinai Journal of Medicine, 77*, 32–42.

Perlman, D. (1999, October 15). Odds on the big one. *The San Francisco Chronicle*, p. A1.

Perlmutter, D. D. (2002). On incongruities and logical inconsistencies in humor: The delicate balance. *Humor: International Journal of Humor Research, 15*, 155–168.

Perls, F. (1972). Interview with Frederick Perls. In A. Bry (Ed.), *Inside psychotherapy* (pp. 58–70). New York: Basic Books.

Perls, F. (1973). *The Gestalt Approach and Eyewitness to Therapy*. Palo Alto, CA: Science & Behavior Books.

Perosa, S. L., & Perosa, L. M. (1993). Relationships among a Minuchin's structural family model, identity achievement, and coping style. *Journal of Counseling Psychology, 40*, 479–489.

Perri, M. G., Anton, S. D., Durning, P. E., Ketterson, T. U., Sydeman, S. J., Berlant, N. E., . . . Martin, A. D. (2002). Adherence to exercise prescriptions: Effects of prescribing moderate versus higher levels of intensity and frequency. *Health Psychology, 21*, 452–458.

Perri, M. G., Martin, A. D., Leermakers, E. A., & Sears, S. F. (1997). Effects of group-versus home-based exercise in the treatment of obesity. *Journal of Consulting and Clinical Psychology, 65*, 278–285.

Perronia, B. F., Tessitorea, C. A., Cibellid, G., Lupoa, C., D'Artibalea. E., Cortisa, E. C., . . . Capranica, L. (2009). Effects of simulated firefighting on the responses of salivary cortisol, alpha-amylase and psychological variables. *Ergonomics, 52*, 484–491.

Persad, E. (1990). Electroconvulsive therapy in depression. *Canadian Journal of Psychiatry, 35*, 175–182.

Person, C., Tracy, M., & Galea, S. (2006). Risk factors for depression after a disaster. *The Journal of Nervous and Mental Disease, 194*, 659–666.

Pert, C. B., & Snyder, S. H. (1973). Opiate receptor: Demonstration in nervous tissue. *Science, 179*, 1031–1034.

Peters, M. L., Godaert, G. L., Ballieux, R. E., & Heijnen, C. J. (2003). Moderation of physiological stress responses by personality traits and daily hassles: Less flexibility of immune system responses. *Biological Psychology, 65*, 21–48.

Peters, M. L., Godaert, G. L., Ballieux, R. E., van Vliet, M., Willemsen, J. J., Sweep, F. C. G. J., & Heijnen, C. J. (1998). Cardiovascular and endocrine responses to experimental stress: Effects of mental effort and controllability. *Psychoneuroendocrinology, 23*, 1–17.

Peters, R., & McGee, R. (1982). Cigarette smoking and state-dependent memory. *Psychopharmacology, 76*, 232–235.

Peters, R. D. (1994). Better beginnings, Better futures: A community-based approach to primary prevention. *Canadian Journal of Community Mental Health, 13*, 183–188.

Petersen, J. L., & Hyde, J. S. (2010). A meta-analytic review of research on gender differences in sexuality: 1993–2007. *Psychological Bulletin, 136*, 21–38.

Peterson, B. E., & Gerstein, E. D. (2005). Fighting and flying: Archival analysis of threat, authoritarianism, and the North American comic book. *Political Psychology, 26*, 887–904.

Peterson, C., & Barrett, L. C. (1987). Explanatory style and academic performance among university freshmen. *Journal of Personality and Social Psychology, 53*, 603–607.

Peterson, C., Seligman, M. E. P., & Vaillant, G. E. (1988). Pessimistic explanatory style is a risk factor for physical illness: A 35-year longitudinal study. *Journal of Personality and Social Psychology, 55*, 23–27.

Peterson, C., Seligman, M. E. P., Yurko, K. H., Martin, L. R., & Friedman, H. S. (1998). Catastrophizing and untimely death. *Psychological Science, 9*, 127–130.

Peterson, C., & Vaidya, R. S. (2001). Explanatory style, expectations, and depressive symptoms. *Personality and Individual Differences, 31*, 1217–1223.

Peterson, C. C. (1996). The ticking of the social clock: Adults' beliefs about the timing of transition events. *International Journal of Aging and Human Development, 42*, 189–203.

Peterson, I. (1983). Playing chess bit by bit. *Science News, 124*, 236–237.

Peterson, J. L., & Hyde, J. S. (2010). A meta-analytic review of research on gender differences in sexuality: 1993–2007. *Psychological Bulletin, 136*, 21–38.

Peterson, L. R., & Peterson, M. (1959). Short-term retention of individual verbal items. *Journal of Experimental Psychology, 58*, 193–198.

Peterson, M. A., & Gibson, B. S. (1994). Must figure-ground organization precede object recognition? An assumption in peril. *Psychological Science, 5*, 253–259.

Petitto, L. A., Holowka, S., Sergio, L. E., & Ostry, D. (2001). Language rhythms in baby hand movements. *Nature, 413*, 35–36.

Petrie, K. J., Booth, R. J., & Pennebaker, J. W. (1998). The immunological effects of thought suppression. *Journal of Personality and Social Psychology, 75*, 1264–1272.

Pettersen, L., Yonas, A., & Fisch, R. O. (1980). The development of blinking in response to impending collision in preterm, full-term, and postterm infants. *Infant Behavior and Development, 3*, 155–165.

Pettijohn, T. F., II. (1996). Perceived happiness of college students measured by Maslow's hierarchy of needs. *Psychological Reports, 79*, 759–762.

Petty, R. E., & Cacioppo, J. T. (1990). Involvement and persuasion: Tradition versus integration. *Psychological Bulletin, 107*, 367–374.

Petty, R. E., Cacioppo, J. T., & Goldman, R. (1981). Personal involvement as a determinant of argument-based persuasion. *Journal of Personality and Social Psychology, 41*, 847–855.

Pfeffer, K., & Barnecutt, P. (1996). Children's auditory perception of movement of traffic sounds. *Child: Care, Health & Development, 27*, 129–137.

Phelps, E. A., & LeDoux J. E. (2005). Contributions of the amygdala to emotion processing: From animal models to human behavior. *Neuron, 48*, 175–187.

Phillips, R. D., Wagner, S. H., Fells, C. A., & Lynch, M. (1990). Do infants recognize emotion in facial expressions? Categorical and "metaphorical" evidence. *Infant Behavior and Development, 13*, 71–84.

Phinney, J. S. (1990). Ethnic identity in adolescents and adults: Review of research. *Psychological Bulletin, 108*, 499–514.

Phinney, J. S., & Ong, A. D. (2002). Adolescent-parent disagreements and life satisfaction in families from Vietnamese- and European-American backgrounds. *International Journal of Behavioral Development, 26*, 556–561.

Phinney, J. S., Cantu, C. L., & Kurtz, D. A. (1997). Ethnic and American identity as predictors of self-esteem among African American, Latino, and White adolescents. *Journal of Youth and Adolescence, 26*, 165–185.

Phinney, J. S., Ong, A., & Madden, T. (2000). Cultural values and intergenerational value discrepancies in immigrant and nonimmigrant families. *Child Development, 71*, 528–539.

Piaget, J. (1932). *The moral judgment of the child*. New York: Harcourt, Brace & World.

Piaget, J. (1952). *The origins of intelligence in children*. New York: International Universities Press.

Piat, M. (2000). The NIMBY phenomenon: Community residents' concerns about housing for deinstitutionalized people. *Health and Social Work, 25,* 127–138.

Pichika, R., Buchsbaum, M. S., Bailer, U., Hoh, C., DeCastro, A., Buchsbaum, B. R., & Kaye, W. (2012). Serotonin transporter binding after recovery from bulimia nervosa. *International Journal of Eating Disorders, 45,* 345–352.

Pichon, S., & Kell, C. A. (2013). Affective and sensorimotor components of emotional prosody generation. *The Journal of Neuroscience, 33,* 1640–1650

Pickles, A., Hill, J., Breen, G., Quinn, J., Abbott, K., Jones, H., Sharp, H. (2013). Evidence for interplay between genes and parenting on infant temperament in the first year of life: Monoamine oxidase a polymorphism moderates effects of maternal sensitivity on infant anger proneness. *The Journal of Child Psychology and Psychiatry 54,* 1308–1317

Pierce, E. F., & Daleng, M. L. (1998). Distortion of body image among elite female dancers. *Perceptual and Motor Skills, 87,* 769–770.

Pierce, E. F., Eastman, N. W., Tripathi, H. L., & Olson, K. G. (1993). B-endorphin response to endurance exercise: Relationship to exercise dependence. *Perceptual and Motor Skills, 77,* 767–770.

Pieri, L. F., & Campbell, D. A. (1999). Understanding the genetic predisposition to anorexia nervosa. *European Eating Disorders Review, 7,* 84–95.

Pierrehumbert, B., Santelices, M. P., Ibáñez, M., Alberdi, M., Ongari, B., Roskam, I., . . . Borghini, A., (2009). Gender and attachment representations in the preschool years: Comparisons between five countries. *Journal of Cross-Cultural Psychology, 40,* 543–566.

Pierson, A., le Houezec, J., Fossaert, A., Dubal, S., & Jouvent, R. (1999). Frontal reactivity and sensation seeking an ERP study in skydivers. *Progress in Neuro-Psychopharmacology & Biological Psychiatry, 23,* 447–463.

Pieters, R. G. M., & Bijmolt, T. H. A. (1997). Consumer memory for television advertising: A field study of duration, serial position, and competition effects. *Journal of Consumer Research, 23,* 362–372.

Pietsch, J., Walker, R., & Chapman, E. (2003). The relationship between self-concept, self-efficacy, and performance in mathematics during secondary school. *Journal of Educational Psychology, 95,* 589–603.

Piko, B. F., & Balázs, M. Á. (2012). Authoritative parenting style and adolescent smoking and drinking. *Addictive behaviors, 37,* 353–356.

Pilcher, J. J., Lambert, B. J., & Huffcutt, A. I. (2000). Differential effects of permanent and rotating shifts on self-report sleep length: A meta-analytic review. *Sleep: Journal of Sleep and Sleep Disorders Research, 23,* 155–163.

Piliavin, J. A., Callero, P. L., & Evans, E. E. (1982). Addiction to altruism: Opponent-process theory and habitual blood donation. *Journal of Personality and Social Psychology, 43,* 1200–1213.

Pincus, T., & Morley, S. (2001). Cognitive-processing bias in chronic pain: A review and integration. *Psychological Bulletin, 127,* 599–617.

Pinel, J. P. J., Assanand, S., & Lehman, D. R. (2000). Hunger, eating, and ill health. *American Psychologist, 55,* 1105–1116.

Piner, K. E., & Kahle, L. R. (1984). Adapting to the stigmatizing label of mental illness: Foregone but not forgotten. *Journal of Personality and Social Psychology, 47,* 805–811.

Pines, M. (1981, September). The civilizing of Genie. *Psychology Today,* pp. 28–34.

Pinkofsky, H. B. (1997). Mnemonics for *DSM–IV* personality disorders. *Psychiatric Services, 48,* 1197–1198.

Pinquart, M. (2003). Loneliness in married, widowed, divorced, and never-married older adults. *Journal of Social and Personal Relationships, 20,* 31–53.

Pinquart, M., & Soerensen, S. (2003). Differences between caregivers and noncaregivers in psychological health and physical health: A meta-analysis. *Psychology and Aging, 18,* 250–267.

Piper, A. (1993). Tricyclic antidepressants versus electroconvulsive therapy: A review of the evidence for efficacy in depression. *Annals of Clinical Psychiatry, 5,* 13–23.

Piper, B. J., Gray, H. M., & Birkett, M. A. (2012). Maternal smoking cessation and reduced academic and behavioral problems in offspring. *Drug and Alcohol Dependence, 121,* 62–67.

Pitman, R. K., Sanders, K. M., Zusman, R. M., Healy, A. R., Cheema, F., Lasko, N. B., . . . Orr, S. P. (2002). Pilot study of secondary prevention of posttraumatic stress disorder with propranolol. *Biological Psychiatry, 51,* 189–192.

Pittenger, D. J. (1996). Reconsidering the overjustification effect: A guide to critical resources. *Teaching of Psychology, 23,* 234–236.

Pittenger, D. J. (2002). Deception in research: Distinctions and solutions from the perspective of utilitarianism. *Ethics and Behavior, 12,* 117–142.

Plaks, J. E., & Higgins, E. T. (2000). Pragmatic use of stereotyping in teamwork: Social loafing and compensation as a function of inferred partner-situation fit. *Journal of Personality and Social Psychology, 79,* 962–974.

Plant, E. A., & Sachs-Ericsson, N. (2004). Racial and ethnic differences in depression: The roles of social support and meeting basic needs. *Journal of Consulting and Clinical Psychology, 72,* 41–52.

Plant, E. A., Hyde, J. S., Keltner, D., & Devine, P. G. (2000). The gender stereotyping of emotion. *Psychology of Women Quarterly, 24,* 81–92.

Plass, J. A., & Hill, K. T. (1986). Children's achievement strategies and test performance: The role of time pressure, evaluation, anxiety, and sex. *Developmental Psychology, 22,* 31–36.

Platz, S. J., & Hosch, H. M. (1988). Cross-racial/ethnic eyewitness identification: A field study. *Journal of Applied Social Psychology, 18,* 972–984.

Plaud, J. J. (2003). Pavlov and the foundation of behavior therapy. *Spanish Journal of Psychology, 6,* 147–154.

Ploeger, A., van der Maas, H. L. J., & Raijmakers, M. E. J. (2008). Is evolutionary psychology a metatheory for psychology? A discussion of four major issues in psychology from an evolutionary developmental perspective. *Psychological Inquiry, 19,* 1–18.

Plomin, R., & Asbury, K. (2001). Nature and nurture in the family. *Marriage and Family Review, 33,* 273–281.

Plomin, R., Asbury, K., & Dunn, J. (2001). Why are children in the same family so different? Nonshared environment a decade later. *Canadian Journal of Psychiatry, 46,* 225–233.

Plomin, R., Corley, R., Caspi, A., Fulker, D. W., & DeFries, J. (1998). Adoption results for self-reported personality: Evidence for nonadditive genetic effects? *Journal of Personality and Social Psychology, 75,* 211–218.

Ploog, B. O., Scharf, A., Nelson, D., & Brooks, P. J. (2013). Use of computer-assisted technologies (CAT) to enhance social communicative, and language development in children with autism spectrum disorders. *Journal of Autism and Developmental Disorders, 43,* 301–322.

Plotkin, W. B. (1979). The alpha experience revisited: Biofeedback in the transformation of psychological state. *Psychological Bulletin, 86,* 1132–1148.

Plous, S. (1991). An attitude survey of animal rights activists. *Psychological Science, 2,* 194–196.

Plucker, J. A., Callahan, C. M., & Tomchin, E. M. (1996). Wherefore art thou, multiple intelligences? Alternative assessments for identifying talent in ethnically diverse and low income students. *Gifted Child Quarterly, 40,* 81–92.

Plutchik, R. (1980, February). A language for the emotions. *Psychology Today,* pp. 68–78.

Podlesny, J. A., & Raskin, D. C. (1978). Effectiveness of techniques and physiological measures in the detection of deception. *Psychophysiology, 15,* 344–359.

Pogarell, O., Hamann, C., Popperi, G., Juckel, G., Chouker, M., Zaudig, M., . . . Tatsch, K. (2003). Elevated brain serotonin transporter availability in patients with obsessive-compulsive disorder. *Biological Psychiatry, 54,* 1406–1413.

Poincaré, H. (1948, August). Mathematical creation. *Scientific American,* pp. 14–17.

Poldrack, R. A., & Wagner, A. D. (2008). The interface between neuroscience and psychological science. *Current Directions in Psychological Science, 17,* 61.

Politis, M. (2010). Dyskinesias after neural transplantation in Parkinson's disease: What do we know and what is next? *BMC Medicine, 8,* 80–84.

Polivy, J., & Herman, C. P. (2002). Causes of eating disorders. *Annual Review of Psychology 53,* 187–213.

Pollack, M. H., Otto, M. W., Kaspi, S. P., & Hammerness, P. G. (1994). Cognitive behavior therapy for treatment-refractory panic disorder. *Journal of Clinical Psychiatry, 55,* 200–205.

Pollak, S. D., & Tolley-Schell, S. A. (2003). Selective attention to facial emotion in physically abused children. *Journal of Abnormal Psychology, 112,* 323–338.

Pollard, I. (2000). Substance abuse and parenthood: Biological mechanisms—Bioethical challenges. *Women and Health, 30,* 1–24.

Polster, E., & Polster, M. (1993). Frederick Perls: Legacy and invitation. *Gestalt Journal, 16,* 23–25.

Pomerantz, J. R., & Portillo, M. C. (2011). Grouping and emergent features in vision: Toward a theory of basic gestalts. *Journal of Experimental Psychology: Human Perception & Performance, 37,* 1331–1349.

Pomerleau, O. F. (1995). Individual differences in sensitivity to nicotine: Implications of genetic research on nicotine dependence. *Behavior Genetics, 25,* 161–177.

Pompe, G. van der, Antoni, M. H., & Heijnen, C. J. (1998). The effects of surgical stress and psychological stress on the immune function of operative cancer patients. *Psychology and Health, 13,* 1015–1026.

Ponpaipan, M., Srisuphan, W., Jitapunkul, S., Panuthai, S., Tonmukayakul, O., & White, A. (2011). Multimedia computer-assisted instruction for carers on exercise for older people: Development and testing. *Journal of Advanced Nursing, 67,* 308–316.

Poole, D. A., & White, L. T. (1993). Two years later: Effect of question repetition and retention interval on the eyewitness testimony of children and adults. *Developmental Psychology, 29,* 844–853.

Poppen, P. J. (1994). Adolescent contraceptive use and communication: Changes over a decade. *Adolescence, 29,* 503–514.

Popplestone, J. A., & McPherson, M. W. (1976). Ten years at the Archives of the History of American Psychology. *American Psychologist, 31,* 533–534.

Populin, L. C., & Yin, T. C. T. (1998). Pinna movements of the cat during sound localization. *Journal of Neuroscience, 18,* 4233–4243.

Porac, C., & Coren, S. (1981). *Lateral preferences and human behavior.* New York: Springer-Verlag.

Porreca, F., & Gebhart, G. F. (2002). Chronic pain and medullary descending facilitation. *Trends in Neurosciences, 25,* 319–325.

Porro, C. A., Baraldi, P., Pagnoni, G., Serafini, M., Facchin, P., Maieron, M., & Nichelli, P. (2002). Does anticipation of pain affect cortical nociceptive systems? *Journal of Neuroscience, 22,* 3206–3214.

Post, R. M., Leverich, G. S., Xing, G., & Weiss, S. R. B. (2001). Developmental vulnerabilities to the onset and course of bipolar disorder. *Development and Psychopathology, 13,* 581–598.

Postman, L. (1985). Human learning and memory. In G. A. Kimble & K. Schlesinger (Eds.), *Topics in the history of psychology, Vol. 1* (pp. 69–134). Hillsdale, NJ: Erlbaum.

Postmes, T., & Spears, R. (1998). Deindividuation and antinormative behavior: A meta-analysis. *Psychological Bulletin, 123,* 238–259.

Postmes, T., Spears, R., Sakhel, K., & de Groot, D. (2001). Social influence on computer-mediate communication: The effects of anonymity on group behavior. *Personality and Social Psychology Bulletin, 27,* 1243–1254.

Poston, W. S. II, & Winebarger, A. A. (1996). The misuse of behavioral genetics in prevention research, or for whom the "Bell Curve" tolls. *Journal of Primary Prevention, 17,* 133–147.

Potts, M. (2002). The evidential value of near-death experiences for belief in life after death. *Journal of Near-Death Studies, 20,* 233–258.

Poulson, R. L. (1990). Mock juror attribution of criminal responsibility: Effects of race and the guilty but mentally ill (GBMI) verdict option. *Journal of Applied Social Psychology, 20,* 1596–1611.

Pourtois, G., Schwartz, S., Seghier, M. L., Lazeyras, F., & Vuilleumier, P. (2005). Portraits or people? Distinct representations of face identity in the human visual cortex. *Journal of Cognitive Neuroscience 17,* 1043–1057.

Powell, D. J., & Fuller, R. W. (1983). Marijuana and sex: Strange bedpartners. *Journal of Psychoactive Drugs, 15,* 269–280.

Powell, J. L., & Drucker, A. D. (1997). The role of peer conformity in the decision to ride with an intoxicated driver. *Journal of Alcohol and Drug Education, 43,* 1–7.

Powers, D. E., & Rock, D. A. (1999). Effects of coaching on SAT I: Reasoning Test scores. *Journal of Educational Measurement, 36,* 93–118.

Prados, J., Chamizo, V. D., & MacKintosh, N. J. (1999). Latent inhibition and perceptual learning in a swimming-pool navigation task. *Journal of Experimental Psychology: Animal Behavior Processes, 25,* 37–44.

Prasinos, S., & Tittler, B. I. (1981). The family relationships of humor-oriented adolescents. *Journal of Personality, 47,* 295–305.

Pratkanis, A. R. (1992). The cargo-cult science of subliminal persuasion. *Skeptical Inquirer, 16,* 260–272.

Pratto, F., & Hegarty, P. (2000). The political psychology of reproductive strategies. *Psychological Science, 11,* 57–62.

Premack, D. (1965). Reinforcement theory. In D. Levine (Ed.), *Nebraska symposium on motivation* (pp. 123–188). Lincoln: University of Nebraska Press.

Prentice-Dunn, H., & Prentice-Dunn, S. (2012). Physical activity, sedentary behavior, and childhood obesity: A review of cross-sectional studies. *Psychology, Health & Medicine, 17,* 255–273.

Prentice-Dunn, S., & Rogers, R. W. (1982). Effects of public and private self-awareness on deindividuation and aggression. *Journal of Personality and Social Psychology, 3,* 503–513.

Prepeliczay, S. (2002). Socio-cultural and psychological aspects of contemporary LSD use in Germany. *Journal of Drug Issues, 32,* 431–458.

Price, B. H., Baral, I., Cosgrove, G. R., Rauch, S. L., Nierenberg, A. A., Jenike, M. A., & Cassem, E. H. (2001). Improvement in severe self-mutilation following limbic leucotomy: A series of 5 consecutive cases. *Journal of Clinical Psychiatry, 62,* 925–932.

Price, M. S., & Weiss, M. R. (2000). Relationships among coach burnout, coach behaviors, and athletes' psychological responses. *Sport Psychologist, 14,* 391–409.

Price, R., & Gottesman, I. I. (1991). Body fat in identical twins reared apart: Roles for genes and environment. *Behavior Genetics, 21,* 1–7.

Price-Williams, E., Gordon, W., & Ramirez, M. (1969). Skill and conservation: A study of pottery-making children. *Developmental Psychology, 1,* 769.

Priester, J. R., & Petty, R. E. (2003). The influence of spokesperson trustworthiness on message elaboration, attitude strength, and advertising effectiveness. *Journal of Consumer Psychology, 13,* 408–421.

Principe, C. P., & Langlois, J. H. (2013). Children and adults use attractiveness as a social cue in real people and avatars. *Journal of Experimental Child Psychology, 115,* 590–597.

Pritchard, W. S., Robinson, J. H., deBethizy, J. D., & Davis, R. A. (1995). Caffeine and smoking: Subjective, performance, and psychophysiological effects. *Psychophysiology, 32,* 19–27.

Prochaska, J. O. (1984). *Systems of psychotherapy: A transtheoretical approach.* Homewood, IL: Dorsey.

Proctor, R. W., & Kim-Phuong, L. V. (2006). The cognitive revolution at age 50: Has the promise of the human information-processing approach been fulfilled? *International Journal of Human-Computer Interaction, 21,* 253–284.

Prud'homme, M. J. L., Cohen, D. A. D., & Kalaska, J. F. (1994). Tactile activity in primate primary somatosensory cortex during active arm movements: Cytoarchitectonic distribution. *Journal of Neurophysiology, 71,* 173–181.

"A psychic Watergate." (1981, June). *Discover,* p. 8.

Puccio, G. J. (1991). William Duff's eighteenth century examination of original genius and its relationship to contemporary creativity research. *Journal of Creative Behavior, 25,* 1–10.

Pukall, C. F., Payne, K. A., Binik, Y. M., & Khalife, S. (2003). Pain measurement in vulvodynia. *Journal of Sex & Marital Therapy, 29,* 111–120.

Pullum, G. K. (1991). *The great Eskimo vocabulary hoax.* Chicago: University of Chicago Press.

Pulsifer, M. B. (1996). The neuropsychology of mental retardation. *Journal of the International Neuropsychological Society, 2,* 159–176.

Punamacki, R. L., & Joustie, M. (1998). The role of culture, violence, and personal factors affecting dream content. *Journal of Cross-Cultural Psychology, 29,* 320–342.

Punamaeki, R.-L., Kanninen, K., Quota, S., & El-Sarraj, E. (2002). The role of psychological defences in moderating between trauma and post-traumatic symptoms among Palestinian men. *International Journal of Psychology, 37,* 286–296.

Purdy, J. E., Harriman, A., & Molitorisz, J. (1993). Contributions to the history of psychology: XCV. Possible relations between theories of evolution and animal learning. *Psychological Reports, 73,* 211–223.

Purselle, D. C., & Nemeroff, C. B. (2003). Serotonin transporter: A potential substrate in the biology of suicide. *Neuropsychopharmacology, 28,* 613–619.

Putnam, D. E., Finney, J. W., Barkley, P. L., & Bonner, M. J. (1994). Enhancing commitment improves adherence to a medical regimen. *Journal of Consulting and Clinical Psychology, 62,* 191–194.

Putnam, F. W. (2003). Ten-year research update review: Child sexual abuse. *Journal of the American Academy of Child and Adolescent Psychiatry, 42,* 269–278.

Putnam, K. T., Harris, W. H., & Putnam, F. W. (2013). Synergistic childhood adversities and complex adult psychopathology. *Journal of Traumatic Stress, 26,* 435–442.

Pyszczynski, T., Greenberg, J., Solomon, S., Arndt, J., & Schimel, J. (2004). Why do people need self-esteem? A theoretical and empirical review. *Psychological Bulletin, 130,* 435–468.

Pyter, L.M., & Nelson, R. J. (2006). Enduring effects of photoperiod and affective behaviors in Siberian hamsters. *Behavioral Neuroscience, 120,* 125–134.

Q

Qian, Y., Zeng, B. F., Zhang, X. L., & Jiang, Y. (2008). High levels of substance P and CGRP in pseudosynovial fluid from patients with aseptic loosening of their hip prosthesis. *Acta Orthopaedica, 79,* 342–345.

Quadflieg, S., Vermeulen, N., & Rossion, B., (2013). Differential reliance on the Duchenne marker during smile evaluations and person judgments. *Journal of Nonverbal Behavior, 37,* 69–77.

Quigley, N., Green, J. F., Morgan, D., Idzikowski, C., & King, D. J. (2000). The effect of sleep deprivation on memory and psychomotor function in healthy volunteers. *Human Psychopharmacology: Clinical and Experimental, 15,* 171–177.

Quintana, S. M., Aboud, F. E., Chao, R. K., Contreras-Grau, J., Cross, W. E. Jr., Hudley, C., . . . Vietze, D. L. (2006). Race, ethnicity, and culture in child development: Contemporary research and future directions. *Child Development, 77,* 1129–1141.

Quirk, G. J. (2002). Memory for extinction of conditioned fear is long-lasting and persists following spontaneous recovery. *Learning and Memory, 9,* 402–407.

R

Rabin, J., & Wiley, R. (1994). Switching from forward-looking infrared to night vision goggles: Transitory effects on visual resolution. *Aviation, Space, and Environmental Medicine, 65,* 327–329.

Rabinowitz, F. M. (1984). The heredity-environment controversy: A Victorian legacy. *Canadian Psychology, 25,* 159–166.

Racagni, G., & Brunello, N. (1999). Physiology to functionality: The brain and neurotransmitter activity. *International Clinical Psychopharmacology, 14,* S3–S7.

Rachman, S. (1991). Neo-conditioning and the classical theory of fear acquisition. *Clinical Psychology Review, 11,* 155–173.

Rachman, S. J. (1993). Statistically significant difference or probable nonchance difference. *American Psychologist, 48,* 1093.

Racine, M., Tousignant-Laflamme, Y., Kloda, L. A., Dion, D., Dupuis, G., & Choiniere, M. (2012). A systematic literature review of 10 years of research on sex/gender and pain perception—Part 2: Do biopsychosocial factors alter pain sensitivity differently in women and men? *Pain, 153,* 619–635.

Radin, D. (2007). Review of C. Carter (2007), Parapsychology and the skeptics: A scientific argument for the existence of ESP. *Journal of Parapsychology, 71,* 184–185.

Raeburn, J. M., Atkinson, J. M., Dubignon, J. M., & Fitzpatrick, J. (1994). Superhealth basic: Development and evaluation of a low-cost community-based lifestyle change programme. *Psychology and Health, 9,* 383–395.

Ragland, D. R., & Brand, R. J. (1988). Type A behavior and mortality from coronary heart disease. *New England Journal of Medicine, 318,* 65–69.

Rahim-Williams, B., Riley, J. L., Williams, A. K. K., & Fillingham, R. (2012). A quantitative review of ethnic group differences in experimental pain response: Do biology, psychology, and culture matter? *Pain Medicine, 13,* 522–540.

Raine, A., Lencz, T., Bihrle, S., LaCasse, L., & Colletti, P. (2000). Reduced prefrontal gray matter volume and reduced autonomic activity in antisocial personality disorder. *Archives of General Psychiatry, 57,* 119–127.

Rainville, P., Hofbauer, R. K., Bushnell, M. C., Duncan, G. H., & Price, D. D. (2002). Hypnosis modulates activity in brain structures involved in the regulation of consciousness. *Journal of Cognitive Neuroscience, 14,* 887–901.

Rajan, R. (2000). Centrifugal pathways protect hearing sensitivity at the cochlea in noisy environments that exacerbate the damage induced by loud sound. *Journal of Neuroscience, 20,* 6684–6693.

Raloff, J. (1982). Noise can be hazardous to your health. *Science News, 121,* 377–381.

Ramón y Cajal, S. (1937/1966). *Recollections of my life.* Cambridge, MA: MIT Press.

Randall, J. L. (1998). Physics, philosophy and precognition: Some reflections. *Journal of the Society for Psychical Research, 63,* 1–11.

Range, L. M., Kovac, S. H., & Marion, M. S. (2000). Does writing about the bereavement lessen grief following sudden, unintentional death? *Death Studies, 24,* 115–134.

Rapee, R. M. (1991). Generalized anxiety disorder: A review of clinical features and theoretical concepts. *Clinical Psychology Review, 11,* 419–440.

Rapp, D. (1988). The reception of Freud by the British press: General interest and literary magazines, 1920–1925. *Journal of the History of the Behavioral Sciences, 24,* 191–201.

Raskin, D. C., & Podlesny, J. A. (1979). Truth and deception: A reply to Lykken. *Psychological Bulletin, 86,* 54–59.

Rasmussen, T., & Penfield, W. (1947). Further studies of the sensory and motor cerebral cortex of man. *Federation Proceedings, 6,* 452–460.

Rassuli, A. (2012). Engagement in classroom learning: Creating temporal participation incentives for extrinsically motivated students through bonus credits. *Journal of Education for Business, 87,* 86–93.

Rathgeb–Feutsch, M., Kempter, G., Feil, A., Pollmächer, T., & Schuld, A. (2011). Short- and long-term efficacy of cognitive behavioral therapy for *DSM–IV* panic disorder in patients with and without severe psychiatric morbidity. *Journal of Psychiatric Research, 45,* 1264–1268.

Rauch, S. L., Whalen, P. J., Shin, L. M., McInerney, S. C., Macklin, M. L., Lasko, N. B., . . . Pitman, R. K. (2000). Exaggerated amygdala response to masked facial stimuli in posttraumatic stress disorder: A functional MRI study. *Biological Psychiatry, 47,* 769–776.

Raufaste, E., Eyrolle, H., & Marine, C. (1998). Pertinence generation in radiological diagnosis: Spreading activation and the nature of expertise. *Cognitive Science, 22,* 517–546.

Ravelli, G. P., Stein, Z. A., & Susser, M. W. (1976). Obesity in young men after famine exposure in utero in early infancy. *New England Journal of Medicine, 295,* 349–353.

Raw, S. (2003). Professional and legislative issues. *The Behavior Therapist, 26,* 322–324.

Rawdon, V. A., Willis, F. N., & Ficken, E. J. (1995). Locus of control in young adults in Russia and the United States. *Perceptual and Motor Skills, 80,* 599–604.

Rawlings, D., & Ciancarelli, V. (1997). Music preference and the five-factor model of the NEO Personality Inventory. *Psychology of Music, 25,* 120–132.

Ray, C. G., & Finley, J. K. (1994). Did CMHCs fail or succeed? Analysis of the expectations and outcomes of the community mental health movement. *Administration and Policy in Mental Health, 21,* 283–293.

Ray, O. (1983). *Drugs, society, and human behavior.* St. Louis: Mosby.

Read, P. P. (1974). *Alive: The story of the Andes survivors.* Philadelphia: Lippincott.

Reason, J. (2000). The Freudian slip revisited. *Psychologist, 13,* 610–611.

Rebeta, J. L., Brooks, C. I., O'Brien, J. P., & Hunter, G. A. (1993). Variations in trait-anxiety and achievement motivation of college students as a function of classroom seating position. *Journal of Experimental Education, 61,* 257–267.

Redd, W. H., Jacobsen, P. B., Die-Trill, M., Dermatis, H., McEvoy, M., & Holland, J. C. (1987). Cognitive/attentional distraction in the control of conditioned nausea in pediatric cancer patients receiving chemotherapy. *Journal of Consulting and Clinical Psychology, 55,* 391–395.

Reddon, J. R., Whippler, S. M., & Reddon, J. E. (2007). Seemingly anomalous WISC-IV full scale IQ scores in the American and Canadian standardization samples. *Current Psychology, 26,* 60–69.

Reddy, A. V., & Reddy, P. B. (1983). Creativity and intelligence. *Psychological Studies, 28,* 20–24.

Redfern, S., Dancey, C. P., & Dryden, W. (1993) Empathy: Its effect on how counsellors are perceived. *British Journal of Guidance and Counselling, 21,* 300–309.

Reed, D. R., Bachmanov, A. A., Beauchamp, G. K., & Tordoff, M. G. (1997). Heritable variation in food preferences and their contribution to obesity. *Behavior Genetics, 27,* 373–387.

Reeder, K., & Shapiro, J. (1993). Relationship between early literate experience and knowledge and children's linguistic pragmatic strategies. *Journal of Pragmatics, 19,* 1–22.

Reese, E. P. (1986). Learning about teaching from teaching about learning: Presenting behavioral analysis in an introductory survey course. In V. P. Makosky (Ed.), *The G. Stanley Hall Lecture Series, Vol. 6,* (pp. 65–127). Washington, DC: American Psychological Association.

Reeve, J. M., Bolt, E., & Cai, Y. (1999). Autonomy-supportive teachers: How they teach and motivate students. *Journal of Educational Psychology, 91,* 537–548.

Reeves, G. M., Nijjar, G. V., Langenberg, P., Johnson, M. A., Khabazghazvini, B., Sleemi, A., . . . Snitker, S. (2012). Improvement in depression scores after 1 hour of light therapy treatment in patients with seasonal affective disorder. *Journal of Nervous and Mental Disease, 200,* 51–55.

Regan, P. C., Kocan, E. R., & Whitlock, T. (1998). Ain't love grand! A prototype analysis of the concept of romantic love. *Journal of Social and Personal Relationships, 15,* 411–420.

Regan, T., & Woods, K. (2000). Teachers' understandings of dyslexia: Implications for educational psychology practice. *Educational Psychology in Practice, 16,* 333–347.

Regehr, C., Edward, M., & Bradford, J. (2000). Research ethics and forensic patients. *Canadian Journal of Psychiatry, 45,* 892–898.

Reggiani, P., & Weerts, A. H. (2008). Probabilistic quantitative precipitation forecast for flood prediction: An application. *Journal of Hydrometeorology, 9,* 76–95.

Rehbein, F., Kleimann, M., & Mödle, T. (2010). Prevalence and risk factors of video gamedependency in adolescence: Results of a German nationwide survey, *Cyberpsychology, Behavior, and Social Networking, 13,* 269–277.

Reifman, A., Villa, L. C., Amans, J. A., Rethinam, V., & Telesca, T. Y. (2001). Children of divorce in the 1990s: A meta-analysis. *Journal of Divorce and Remarriage, 36,* 27–36.

Reilly, R. R., & Chao, G. R. (1982). Validity and fairness of some alternative employee selection procedures. *Personnel Psychology, 35,* 1–62.

Reinders, A. A. T., Nijenhuis, E. R. S., Quak, J., Korf, J., Haaksma, J., Paans, A. M. J., . . . den Boer, J. A. (2006). Psychobiological characteristics of dissociative identity disorder: a symptom provocation study. *Biological Psychiatry, 60,* 730–740.

Reiner, W. G., & Gearhart, J. P. (2004). Discordant sexual identity in some genetic males with cloacal exstrophy assigned to female sex at birth. *New England Journal of Medicine, 350,* 333–341.

Reis, S. (1989). Reflections on policy affecting the education of gifted and talented students: Past and future perspectives. *American Psychologist, 44,* 399–408.

Reisenzein, R. (1983). The Schachter theory of emotion: Two decades later. *Psychological Bulletin, 94,* 239–264.

Reisner, A. D. (2003). The electroconvulsive therapy controversy: Evidence and ethics. *Neuropsychology Review, 13,* 199–219.

Reissing, E. D., Binik, Y. M., Khalife, S., Cohen, D., & Amsel, R. (2004). Vaginal spasm, pain, and behavior: An empirical investigation of the diagnosis of vaginismus. *Archives of Sexual Behavior, 33,* 5–17.

Renart, A., Parga, N., & Rolls, E. T. (1999). Backward projections in the cerebral cortex: Implications for memory storage. *Neural Computation, 11,* 1349–1388.

Renn, J. A., & Calvert, S. L. (1993). The relation between gender schemas and adults' recall of stereotyped and counterstereotyped televised information. *Sex Roles, 28,* 449–459.

Renner, J. W., Abraham, M. R., Grzybowski, E. B., & Marek, E. A. (1990). Understandings and misunderstandings of eighth graders of four physics concepts found in textbooks. *Journal of Research in Science Teaching, 27,* 35–54.

Rescorla, R. A. (1968). Probability of shock in the presence and absence of CS in fear conditioning. *Journal of Comparative and Physiological Psychology, 66,* 1–5.

Rescorla, R. A. (1988). Pavlovian conditioning: It's not what you think it is. *American Psychologist, 43,* 151–160.

Rescorla, R. A. (2003). Contemporary study of Pavlovian conditioning. *Spanish Journal of Psychology, 6,* 185–195.

Rescorla, R. A., & Holland, P. C. (1982). Behavioral studies of associative learning in animals. *Annual Review of Psychology, 33,* 265–308.

Resendes, J., & Lecci, L. (2013). Comparing the MMPI-2 scale scores of parents involved in parental competency and child custody assessments. *Psychological Assessment, 24,* 1054–1059.

Ressler, R. K., & Shachtman, T. (1992). *Whoever fights monsters.* New York: St. Martin's Press.

Reynaert, C., Janne, P., Bosly, A., & Staquet, P. (1995). From health locus of control to immune control: Internal locus of control has a buffering effect on natural killer cell activity decrease in major depression. *Acta Psychiatrica Scandinavica, 92,* 294–300.

Rheingold, H. L., & Adams, J. L. (1980). The significance of speech to newborns. *Developmental Psychology, 16,* 397–403.

Rhine, J. B. (1974). Security versus deception in parapsychology. *Journal of Parapsychology, 38,* 99–121.

Rhodes, G., Yoshikawa, S., Clark, A., Lee, K., McKay, R., & Akamatsu, S. (2001). Attractiveness of facial averageness and symmetry in non-Western cultures: In search of biologically based standards of beauty. *Perception, 30,* 611–625.

Rhodes, N., & Wood, W. (1992). Self-esteem and intelligence affect influenceability: The mediating role of message reception. *Psychological Bulletin, 111,* 156–171.

Rhodewalt, F., Sanbonmatsu, D. M., Tschanz, B., & Feick, D. L. (1995). Self-handicapping and interpersonal trade-offs: The effects of claimed self-handicaps on observers' performance evaluations and feedback. *Personality and Social Psychology Bulletin, 21,* 1042–1050.

Rice, M. L. (1989). Children's language acquisition. *American Psychologist, 44,* 149–156.

Rickels, K., DeMartinis, N., & Aufdembrinke, B. (2000). A double-blind, placebo-controlled trial of abecarniland diazepam in the treatment of patients with generalized anxiety disorder. *Journal of Clinical Psychopharmacology, 20,* 12–18.

Rieber, R. W. (Ed.). (1980). *Wilhelm Wundt and the making of a scientific psychology.* New York: Plenum.

Rieckert, J., & Moeller, A. T. (2000). Rational-emotive behavior therapy in the treatment of adult victims of childhood sexual abuse. *Journal of Rational-Emotive and Cognitive Behavior Therapy, 18,* 87–102.

Ried, K., Sullivan, T., Fakler, P., Frank, O. R., & Stocks, N, P. (2010). Does chocolate reduce blood pressure? A meta-analysis. *BMC Medicine, 8,* 39–49.

Rief, W., Hessel, A., & Braehler, E. (2001). Somatization symptoms and hypochondriacal features in the general population. *Psychosomatic Medicine, 63,* 595–602.

Ries, M. L., Carlsson, C. M., Rowley, H. A., Sager, M. A., Gleason, C. E., Asthana, S., & Johnson, S. C. (2008). Magnetic resonance imaging characterization of brain structure and function in mild cognitive impairment: A review. *Journal of the American Geriatrics Association, 56,* 920–934.

Riggs, J. M. (1998). Social roles we choose and don't choose: Impressions of employed and unemployed parents. *Sex Roles, 39,* 431–443.

Riggs, L. A. (1985). Sensory processes: Vision. In G. A. Kimble & K. Schlesinger (Eds.), *Topics in the history of psychology, Vol. 1* (pp. 165–220). Hillsdale, NJ: Erlbaum.

Riley, J. L., Robinson, M. E., Wise, E. A., Myers, C. D., & Fillingim, R. B. (1998). Sex differences in the perception of noxious experimental stimuli: A meta-analysis. *Pain, 74,* 181–187.

Riley, K., Snowdon, D. A., & Markesbery, W. R. (2002). Alzheimer's neurofibrillary pathology and the spectrum of cognitive function: Findings from the Nun Study. *Annals of Neurology, 51,* 567–577.

Rilling, M. (1996). The mystery of the vanished citations: James McConnell's forgotten 1960s quest for planarian learning, a biochemical engram, and celebrity. *American Psychologist, 51,* 589–598.

Rinaldi, R. C. (1987). Patient-therapist personality similarity and the therapeutic relationship. *Psychotherapy in Private Practice, 5,* 11–29.

Rinn, W. E. (1984). The neuropsychology of facial expression: A review of the neurological and psychological mechanisms for producing facial expressions. *Psychological Bulletin, 95,* 52–77.

Riordan, C. A., & Tedeschi, J. T. (1983). Attraction in aversive environments: Some evidence for classical conditioning and negative reinforcement. *Journal of Personality and Social Psychology, 44,* 683–692.

Risch, N., Squires-Wheeler, E., & Keats, B. J. B. (1993). Male sexual orientation and genetic evidence. *Science, 262,* 2063–2065.

Rittenhouse, C. D., Stickgold, R., & Hobson, J. A. (1994). Constraint on the transformation of characters, objects, and settings in dream reports. *Consciousness and Cognition: An International Journal, 3,* 100–113.

Rivera-Tovar, L. A., & Jones, R. T. (1990). Effect of elaboration on the acquisition and maintenance of cardiopulmonary resuscitation. *Journal of Pediatric Psychology, 15,* 123–138.

Robazza, C., Bortoli, L., & Nougier, V. (1998). Physiological arousal and performance in elite archers: A field study. *European Psychologist, 3,* 263–270.

Robbins, S. B., Lauver, K., Le, H., Davis, D., Langley, R., & Carlstrom, A. (2004). Do psychological and study skill factors predict college outcomes? A meta-analysis. *Psychological Bulletin, 130,* 261–288.

Robert, M. (1990). Observational learning in fish, birds, and mammals: A classified bibliography spanning over 100 years of research. *Psychological Record, 40,* 289–311.

Roberts, M. C., & Fanurik, D. (1986). Rewarding elementary school children for their use of safety belts. *Health Psychology, 5,* 185–196.

Roberts, M., & Shapiro, M. (2002). NMDA receptor antagonists impair memory for nonspatial, socially transmitted food preferences. *Behavioral Neuroscience, 116,* 1059–1069.

Roberts, R. E. L., & Bengtson, V. L. (1996). Attachment styles, self-esteem, and patterns of seeking feedback from romantic partners. *Social Psychology Quarterly, 59,* 96–106.

Roberts, R. E., Phinney, J. S., Masse, L. C., Chen, Y. R., Roberts, C. R., & Romero, A. (1999). The structure of ethnic identity of young adolescents from diverse ethnocultural groups. *Journal of Early Adolescence, 19,* 301–322.

Roberts, S. J. (1988). Social support and help seeking: Review of the literature. *Advances in Nursing Science, 10,* 1–11.

Robins, R.W., Gosling, S. D., & Craik, K. H. (1999). An empirical analysis of trends in psychology. *American Psychologist, 54,* 117–128.

Robinson, D. L. (1993). The EEG and intelligence: An appraisal of methods and theories. *Personality and Individual Differences, 15,* 695–716.

Robinson, D. L. (2001). How brain arousal systems determine different temperament types and the major dimensions of personality. *Personality and Individual Differences, 31,* 1233–1259.

Robinson, F. P. (1970). *Effective study.* New York: Harper & Row.

Robinson, J., & Briggs, P. (1997). Age trends and eye-witness suggestibility and compliance. *Psychology, Crime and Law, 3,* 187–202.

Robinson, M. D. (1998). Running from William James' bear: A review of preattentive mechanisms and their contributions to emotional experience. *Cognition and Emotion, 12,* 667–696.

Robinson, S. J., & Rollings, L. J. L. (2011). The effect of mood-context on visual recognition and recall memory. *Journal of General Psychology, 138,* 66–79.

Roccas, S., Sagiv, L., Schwartz, S. H., & Knafo, A. (2002). The Big Five personality factors and personal values. *Personality and Social Psychology Bulletin, 28,* 789–801.

Rock, I., Gopnik, A., & Hall, S. (1994). Do young children reverse ambiguous figures? *Perception, 23,* 635–644.

Rockwell, T. (1979). Pseudoscience or pseudocriticism? *Journal of Parapsychology, 43,* 221–231.

Rodgers, J. E. (1982, June). The malleable memory of eyewitnesses. *Science, 82,* pp. 32–35.

Rodgers, J. L., Cleveland, H. H., van den Oord, E., & Rowe, D. C. (2000). Resolving the debate over birth order, family size, and intelligence. *American Psychologist, 55,* 599–612.

Rodgers, R., & Hunter, J. E. (1991). Impact of management by objectives on organizational productivity. *Journal of Applied Psychology, 76,* 322–336.

Rodier, P. M., Ingram, J. L., Tisdale, B., & Croog, V. J. (1997). Linking etiologies in humans and animal models : Studies of autism. *Reproductive Toxicology, 11,* 417–422.

Rodin, J. (1981). Current status of the internal-external hypothesis for obesity: What went wrong? *American Psychologist, 36,* 361–372.

Rodin, J. (1985). Insulin levels, hunger, and food intake: An example of feedback loops in body weight regulation. *Health Psychology, 4,* 1–23.

Roelofs, K., Keijsers, G. P. J., Hoogduin, K. A. L., Naering, G. W. B., & Moene, F. C. (2002). Childhood abuse in patients with conversion disorder. *American Journal of Psychiatry, 159,* 1908–1913.

Rogers, A. E., Aldrich, M. S., & Lin, X. (2001). A comparison of three different sleep schedules for reducing daytime sleepiness in narcolepsy. *Sleep: Journal of Sleep and Sleep Disorders Research, 24,* 385–391.

Rogers, C. R. (1957). The necessary and sufficient conditions of therapeutic personality change. *Journal of Consulting Psychology, 21,* 95–103.

Rogers, C. R. (1961). *On becoming a person: A therapist's view of psychotherapy.* Boston: Houghton Mifflin.

Rogers, C. R. (1968). Interpersonal relationships. *Journal of Applied Behavioral Science, 4,* 1–12.

Rogers, C. R. (1985). Toward a more human science of the person. *Journal of Humanistic Psychology, 25,* 7–24.

Rogers, K. B. (1996). What *The Bell Curve* says and doesn't say: Is a balanced view possible? *Roeper Review, 18,* 252–255.

Rogers, L. J. (2000). Evolution of hemispheric specialization: Advantages and disadvantages. *Brain and Language, 73,* 236–253.

Rogers, R. (1987). APA's position on the insanity defense: Empiricism versus emotionalism. *American Psychologist, 42,* 840–848.

Rogers, R. L., & Petrie, T. A. (2001). Psychological correlates of anorexia and bulimic symptomatology. *Journal of Counseling and Development, 79,* 178–187.

Rogers, R. L., Meyer, J. S., & Mortel, K. F. (1990). After reaching retirement age physical activity sustains cerebral perfusion and cognition. *Journal of the American Geriatrics Society, 38,* 123–128.

Rogers, R., Duncan, J. C., Lynett, E., & Sewell, K. W. (1994). Prototypical analysis of antisocial personality disorder: *DSM–IV* and beyond. *Law and Human Behavior, 18,* 471–484.

Rogers, R., Sewell, K. W., Martin, M. A., & Vitacco, M. J. (2003). Detection of feigned mental disorders: A meta-analysis of the MMPI-2 and malingering. *Assessment, 10,* 160–177.

Rogge, R. D., & Bradbury, T. N. (1999). Till violence does us part: The differing roles of communication and aggression in predicting adverse marital outcomes. *Journal of Consulting and Clinical Psychology, 67,* 340–351.

Rogoff, B., & Chavajay, P. (1995). What's become of research on the cultural basis of cognitive development? *American Psychologist, 50,* 459–477.

Röhl, M., Kollmeier, B., & Uppenkamp, S. (2011). Spectral loudness summation takes place in the primary auditory cortex. *Human Brain Mapping, 32,* 1483–1496.

Rohsenow, D. J. (2005). Understanding the interactions of nicotine and alcohol: How basic research can help guide treatment for alcoholic smokers. *Brown University Digest of Addiction Theory and Application, 24,* 8.

Roig, M. (1993). Summarizing parapsychology in psychology textbooks: A rejoinder to Kalat and Kohn. *Teaching of Psychology, 20,* 174–175.

Rokeach, M. (1964/1981). *The three Christs of Ypsilanti.* New York: Columbia University Press.

Rokeach, M., & Mezei, L. (1966). Race and shared belief as factors in social choice. *Science, 151,* 167–172.

Roll, R., Kavounoudias, A., & Roll, J. P. (2002). Cutaneous afferents from human plantar sole contribute to body posture awareness. *Neuroreport: For Rapid Communication of Neuroscience Research, 13,* 1957–1961.

Rollman, G. B. (1998). Culture and pain. In S. S. Kazarian, D. R. Evans (Eds.). *Cultural clinical psychology: Theory, research, and practice* (pp. 267–286). NY: Oxford University Press.

Rondall, J. A. (1994). Pieces of minds in psycholinguistics: Steven Pinker, Kenneth Wexler, and Noam Chomsky. *International Journal of Psychology, 29,* 85–104.

Rook, K. S., Catalano, R., & Dooley, D. (1989). The timing of major life events: Effects of departing from the social clock. *American Journal of Community Psychology, 17,* 233–258.

Roosa, M. W., Reinholtz, C., & Angelini, P. J. (1999). The relation of child sexual abuse and depression in young women: Comparisons across four ethnic groups. *Journal of Abnormal Child Psychology, 27,* 65–76.

Roozendaal, B., McEwen, B. S., & Chattarji, S. (2009). Stress, memory and the amygdala. *Nature Reviews: Neuroscience, 10,* 423–433.

Rosch, E. (1975). Cognitive representation of semantic categories. *Journal of Experimental Psychology: General, 104,* 192–233.

Rose, D. (2011) Growing our kids in "Healthy Soil": New research on environmental influences on children's food intake. *Journal of Adolescent Health, 48,* 3–4.

Rose, J. E., & Fantino, E. (1978). Conditioned reinforcement and discrimination in second-order schedules. *Journal of the Experimental Analysis of Behavior, 29,* 393–418.

Rosen, G. M., Sageman, M., & Loftus, E. (2004). A historical note on false traumatic memories. *Journal of Clinical Psychology, 60,*137–139.

Rosenbaum, M. E. (1986). The repulsion hypothesis: On the nondevelopment of relationships. *Journal of Personality and Social Psychology, 51,* 1156–1166.

Rosenberg, M. (1965). *Society and the adolescent self-image.* Princeton, NJ: Princeton University Press.

Rosenbloom, T., & Wolf, Y. (2002). Signal detection in conditions of everyday life traffic dilemmas. *Accident Analysis and Prevention, 34,* 763–772.

Rosenhan, D. L. (1973). On being sane in insane places. *Science, 179,* 250–258.

Rosenkoetter, L. I. (1999). The television situation comedy and children's prosocial behavior. *Journal of Applied Social Psychology, 29,* 979–993.

Rosenman, R. H., Brand, R. J., Jenkins, D., Friedman, M., Straus, R., & Wurm, M. (1975). Coronary heart disease in the Western Collaborative Group Study: Final follow-up experience of 8 1/2 years. *Journal of the American Psychological Association, 233*, 872–877.

Rosenthal, N. E. (1993). *Winter blues: Seasonal affective disorder—What it is and how to overcome it*. New York: Guilford.

Rosenthal, R. (1995). Ethical issues in psychological science: Risk, consent, and scientific quality. *Psychological Science, 6*, 322–323.

Rosenthal, R. (2002). Covert communication in classrooms, clinics, courtrooms, and cubicles. *American Psychologist, 57*, 839–849.

Rosenthal, R., & DiMatteo, M. R. (2002). Meta-analysis. In. H. Pashler & J. Wixted (Eds.), *Stevens' handbook of experimental psychology: Vol. 4. Methodology in experimental psychology* (3rd ed., pp. 391–428). New York: Wiley.

Rosenthal, R., & Fode, K. L. (1963). The effect of experimenter bias on the performance of the albino rat. *Behavioral Science, 8*, 183–189.

Rosenthal, R., & Jacobson, L. (1968). *Pygmalion in the classroom*. New York: Holt, Rinehart & Winston.

Rosenwald, R. R. (2009). The future of research into growth hormone responsiveness. *Hormone Research, 71*, 71–74.

Rosenzweig, M. R., & Bennett, E. L. (1996). Psychobiology of plasticity: Effects of training and experience on brain and behavior. *Behavioral Brain Research, 78*, 57–65.

Ross, E. (1999, June 18). Einstein's brain was exceptional. *The Philadelphia Inquirer*, p. A-1.

Ross, E. D., Edmondson, J. A., Seibert, G. B., & Homan, R. W. (1988). Acoustic analysis of affective prosody during right-sided Wada test: A within-subjects verification of the right hemisphere's role in language. *Brain and Language, 33*, 128–145.

Ross, E. D., Thompson, R. D., & Yenkosky, J. (1997). Lateralization of affective prosody in brain and the callosal integration of hemispheric language functions. *Brain and Language, 56*, 27–54.

Ross, M. J., & Berger, R. S. (1996). Effects of stress inoculation training on athletes' postsurgical pain and rehabilitation after orthopedic injury. *Journal of Consulting and Clinical Psychology, 64*, 406–410.

Ross, S. R., Rausch, M. K., & Canada, K. E. (2003). Competition and cooperation in the five-factor model: Individual differences in achievement orientation. *Journal of Psychology, 137*, 323–337.

Rosser, S., Issakidis, C., & Peters, L. (2003). Perfectionism and social phobia: Relationship between the constructs and impact on cognitive behavior therapy. *Cognitive Therapy and Research, 27*, 143–151.

Rossi, A. F., Rittenhouse, C. D., & Paradiso, M. A. (1996). The representation of brightness in primary visual cortex. *Science, 273*, 1104–1107.

Rossi, A. M., & Seiler, W. J. (1989–1990). The comparative effectiveness of systematic desensitization and an integrative approach in treating public speaking anxiety: A literature review and a preliminary investigation. *Imagination, Cognition, and Personality, 9*, 49–66.

Rossi, B., & Creatti, L. (1993). The sensation seeking in mountain athletes as assessed by Zuckerman's Sensation Seeking Scale. *International Journal of Sport Psychology, 24*, 417–431.

Rossi, F. (1988, November 8). Stress test. *Philadelphia Inquirer*, pp. 1-E, 10-E.

Roter, D. L., & Hall, J. A. (1998). Why physician gender matters in shaping the physician-patient relationship. *Journal of Women's Health, 7*, 1093–1097.

Roth, T. (1995). An overview of the report of the National Commission on Sleep Disorders Research. *European Psychiatry, 10*, 109s–113s.

Roth, L. W., & Polotsky, A. J. (2012). Can we live longer by eating less? A review of caloric restriction and longevity. *Maturitas, 71*, 315–319.

Rothbart, M. K., Ahadi, S. A., & Evans, D. E. (2000). Temperament and personality: Origins and outcomes. *Journal of Personality and Social Psychology, 78*, 122–135.

Rothbaum, F., & Tsang, B. Y. P. (1998). Love songs in the United States and China: On the nature of romantic love. *Journal of Cross-Cultural Psychology, 29*, 306–319.

Rothon, C., Head, J., Klineberg, E., & Stansfeld, S. (2011). Can social support protect bullied adolescents from adverse outcomes? A prospective study on the effects of bullying on the educational achievement and mental health of adolescents at secondary schools in East London. *Journal of Adolescence, 34*, 579–88.

Rothschild, A. J. (2000). New directions in the treatment of antidepressant–induced sexual dysfunction. *Clinical Therapeutics: The International Journal of Drug Therapy, 22*, A42–A57.

Rotter, J. B. (1966). Generalized expectancies for internal versus external control of reinforcement. *Psychological Monographs, 80*, 1–28.

Rotter, J. B. (1990). Internal versus external control of reinforcement: Case history of a variable. *American Psychologist, 45*, 489–493.

Rotton, J., & Kelly, I. W. (1985). Much ado about the full moon: A meta-analysis of lunar-lunacy research. *Psychological Bulletin, 97*, 286–306.

Roug, L., Landberg, I., & Lundberg, L. J. (1989). Phonetic development in early infancy: A study of four Swedish children during the first eighteen months of life. *Journal of Child Language, 16*, 19–40.

Rouillon, F. (1997). Epidemiology of panic disorder. *Human Psychopharmacology: Clinical and Experimental, 12*, S7–S12.

Routh, D. K. (1969). Conditioning of vocal response differentiation in infants. *Developmental Psychology, 1*, 219–226.

Rowan, A. B. (2001). Adolescent substance abuse and suicide. *Depression and Anxiety, 14*, 186–191.

Rowe, L. S., Jouriles, E. N., McDonald, R., Platt, C. G., & Gomez, G. S. (2012). Enhancing women's resistance to sexual coercion: A randomized controlled trial of the DATE program. *Journal of American College Health, 60*, 211–218.

Rowe, R., Pickles, A., Simonoff, E., Bulik, C. M., & Silberg, J. L. (2002). Bulimic symptoms in the Virginia twin study of adolescent behavioral development: Correlates, comorbidity, and genetics. *Biological Psychiatry, 51*, 172–182.

Rowsell, H. C. (1988). The status of animal experimentation in Canada. *International Journal of Psychology, 23*, 377–381.

Rozin, P. (2005). The meaning of food in our lives: A cross-cultural perspective on eating and well-being. *Journal of Nutrition Education and Behavior, 37*, S107–S112.

Rozin, P., & Fallon, A. E. (1987). A perspective on disgust. *Psychological Review, 94*, 23–41.

Rozin, P., & Zellner, D. (1985). The role of Pavlovian conditioning in the acquisition of food likes and dislikes. *Annals of the New York Academy of Sciences, 443*, 189–202.

Rubin, D. H., Althoff, R. R., Ehli, E. A., Davies, G. E., Rettew, D. C., Crehan, E. T., Walkup, J. T., & Hudziak, J. J. (2013). Candidate gene associations with withdrawn behavior. *Journal of Child Psychology and Psychiatry, 54*, 1337–1345

Rubin, J. R., Provenzano, F. J., & Luria, Z. (1974). The eye of the beholder: Parents' views on sex of newborns. *American Journal of Orthopsychiatry, 44*, 512–519.

Rubin, L. C., & Mills, M. J. (1983). Behavioral precipitants to civil commitment. *American Journal of Psychiatry, 140*, 603–606.

Rubin, R. T., Reinisch, J. M., & Haskett, R. F. (1981). Postnatal gonadal steroid effects on human behavior. *Science, 211*, 1318–1324.

Rubin, Z. (1985). Deceiving ourselves about deception: Comment on Smith and Richardson's "Amelioration of deception and harm in psychological research." *Journal of Personality and Social Psychology, 48*, 252–253.

Ruch, W., & Forabosco, G. (1996). A cross-cultural study of humor appreciation: Italy and Germany. *Humor: International Journal of Humor Research, 9*, 1–18.

Ruch, W., McGhee, P. E., & Hehl, F. J. (1990). Age differences in the enjoyment of incongruity-resolution and nonsense humor during adulthood. *Psychology and Aging, 5*, 348–355.

Ruda, M. A. (1982). Opiates and pain pathways: Demonstration of enkephalin synapses on dorsal horn projection neurons. *Science, 215*, 1523–1525.

Rudolph, K. D., & Hammen, C. (1999). Age and gender as determinants of stress exposure, generation, and reactions in youngsters: A transactional perspective. *Child Development, 70*, 660–677.

Rudy, D., & Grusec, J. E. (2001). Correlates of authoritarian in individualistic and collectivist cultures and implications for understanding the transmission of values. *Journal of Cross-Cultural Psychology, 32*, 202–212.

Ruedl, G., Abart, M., Ledochowski, L., Burtscher, M., & Kopp, M. (2012). Self reported risk taking and risk compensation in skiers and snowboarders are associated with sensation seeking. *Accident Analysis and Prevention, 48*, 292–296.

Ruffin, C. L. (1993). Stress and health: Little hasslers vs. major life events. *Australian Psychologist, 28*, 201–208.

Ruffman, T. K., & Olson, D. R. (1989). Children's ascriptions of knowledge to others. *Developmental Psychology, 25*, 601–606.

Ruhrmann, S., Kasper, S., Hawellek, B., Martinez, B., Hoeflich, G., Nickelsen, T., & Moeller, H.-J. (1998). Effects of fluoxetine versus bright light in the treatment of seasonal affective disorder. *Psychological Medicine, 28*, 923–933.

Ruiter, M. E., DeCoster, J., Jacobs, L., & Lichstein, K. L. (2011). Normal sleep in African-Americans and Caucasian-Americans: A meta-analysis. *Sleep Medicine, 12*, 209–214.

Ruiz, G., & Baños, J. E. (2009). Heat hyperalgesia induced by endoneurial nerve growth factor and the expression of substance p in primary sensory neurons. *International Journal of Neuroscience, 119*, 185–203.

Rujescu, D., Giegling, I., Gietl, A., Hartmann, A. M., & Moeller, H. J. (2003). A functional single nucleotide polymorphism (V158M) in the COMT gene is associated with aggressive personality traits. *Biological Psychiatry, 54*, 34–39.

Rule, B. G., & Nesdale, A. R. (1976). Emotional arousal and aggressive behavior. *Psychological Bulletin, 83*, 851–863.

Rummel, A., & Feinberg, R. (1988). Cognitive evaluation theory: A meta-analytic review of the literature. *Social Behavior and Personality, 16*, 147–164.

Runco, M. A. (1993). Divergent thinking, creativity, and giftedness. *Gifted Child Quarterly, 37*, 16–22.

Runco, M. A., & Johnson, D. J. (2002). Parents' and teachers implicit theories of children's creativity: A cross-cultural perspective. *Creativity Research Journal, 14*, 427–438.

Rungger-Brändle, E., Ripperger, J. A., Steiner, K., Conti, A., Stieger, A., Soltanieh, S., & Rungger, D. (2010). Retinal patterning by Pax6-dependent cell adhesion molecules. *Developmental Neurobiology, 70*, 764–780.

Rury, J. L. (1988). Race, region, and education: An analysis of Black and White scores on the 1917 Army Alpha Intelligence Test. *Journal of Negro Education, 57*, 51–65.

Ruscio, A. M., Stein, D. J., Chiu, W. T., & Kessler, R. C. (2010). The epidemiology of obsessive-compulsive disorder in the National Comorbidity Survey Replication. *Molecular Psychiatry, 15*, 53–63.

Rushton, J. P. (1997). Race, IQ, and the APA report on *The Bell Curve. American Psychologist, 52*, 69–70.

Rushton, J. P., & Ankney, C. D. (2009). Whole brain size and general mental ability: A review. *International Journal of Neuroscience, 119,* 692–732.

Rushton, J. P., & Jensen, A. R. (2003). African-White IQ differences from Zimbabwe on the Wechsler Intelligence Scale for Children-Revised are mainly on the g factor. *Personality and Individual Differences, 34,* 177–183.

Rushton, J. P. (1990). Creativity, intelligence, and psychoticism. *Personality and Individual Differences, 11,* 1291–1298.

Russell, G. F. M. (2001). Involuntary treatment in anorexia nervosa. *Psychiatric Clinics of North America, 24,* 337–349.

Russell, G. L., Fujino, D. C., Sue, S., Cheung, M.-K., & Snowden, L. R. (1996). The effects of therapist-client ethnic match in the assessment of mental health functioning. *Journal of Cross-Cultural Psychology, 27,* 598–615.

Russell, J. A. (1991). In defense of a prototype approach to emotion concepts. *Journal of Personality and Social Psychology, 60,* 37–47.

Russell, J. A. (1994). Is there universal recognition of emotion from facial expressions? A review of the cross-cultural studies. *Psychological Bulletin, 115,* 102–141.

Russell, M. J. (1976). Human olfactory communication. *Nature, 260,* 520–522.

Rust, J., Golombok, S., Hines, M., Johnston, K., & Golding, J. (2000). The role of brothers and sisters in the gender development of preschool children. *Journal of Experimental Child Psychology, 77,* 292–303.

Rutherford, A. (2000). Radical behaviorism and psychology's public: B. F. Skinner in the popular press, 1934–1990. *History of Psychology, 3,* 371–395.

Rutkowski, G. K., Gruder, C. L., & Romer, D. (1983). Group cohesiveness, social norms, and bystander intervention. *Journal of Personality and Social Psychology, 44,* 545–552.

Ruys, K. K., & Aarts, H. (2012). I didn't mean to hurt you! Unconscious origins of experienced self-agency over others' emotions. *Emotion, 12,* 132–141.

Ryan, C. S., & Bogart, L. M. (2001). Longitudinal changes in the accuracy of new group members' in-group and out-group stereotypes. *Journal of Experimental Social Psychology, 37,* 118–133.

Ryan, E. D. (1980). Attribution, intrinsic motivation, and athletics: A replication and extension. In C. H. Nadeau, W. R. Halliwell, K. M. Newell, & G. C. Roberts (Eds.), *Psychology of motor behavior and sport-1979* (pp. 19–26). Champaign, IL: Human Kinetics.

Ryan, J. J., Sattler, J. M., & Lopez, S. J. (2000). Age effects in Wechsler Adult Intelligence Scale-III subtests. *Archives of Clinical Neuropsychology, 15,* 311–317.

Ryan, K. M., & Kanjorski, J. (1998). The enjoyment of sexist humor, rape attitudes, and relationship aggression in college students. *Sex Roles, 38,* 743–756.

Ryan, R. H., & Geiselman, R. E. (1991). Effects of biased information on the relationship between eyewitness confidence and accuracy. *Bulletin of the Psychonomic Society, 29,* 7–9.

Ryan, R. M., Frederick, C. M., Lepes, D., Rubio, N., & Sheldon, K. M. (1997). Intrinsic motivation and exercise adherence. *International Journal of Sport Psychology, 28,* 335–354.

S

Sabatini, B. L., & Regehr, W. G. (1999). Timing of synaptic transmission. *Annual Review of Psychology, 61,* 521–542.

Sabbagh, M., & Cunnings, J. (2011). Progressive cholinergic decline in Alzheimer's disease: Consideration for treatment with donepezil 23 mg in patients with moderate to severe symptomatology. *BMC neurology. 11,* 21–26.

Sabine, W. (2000). Cognitive therapy for obsessive-compulsive disorder. *Journal of Cognitive Psychotherapy, 14,* 245–259.

Sable, P. (1997). Attachment, detachment, and borderline personality disorder. *Psychotherapy, 34,* 171–181.

Sachdev, P. (2000). The current status of tardive dyskinesia. *Australian and New Zealand Journal of Psychiatry, 34,* 355–369.

Sachdev, P., Trollor, J., Walker, A., Wen, W., Fulham, M., Smith, J. S., & Matheson, J. (2001). Bilateral orbitomedial leucotomy for obsessive-compulsive disorder: A single-case study using positron emission tomography. *Australian and New Zealand Journal of Psychiatry, 35,* 684–690.

Sachdeva, S., Singh, P., & Medin, D. (2011). Culture and the quest for universal principles in moral reasoning. *International Journal of Psychology, 46,* 161–176.

Sackeim, H. A. (1994). Central issues regarding the mechanisms of action of electroconvulsive therapy: Directions for future research. *Psychopharmacology Bulletin, 30,* 281–308.

Sacks, O. (1985). *The man who mistook his wife for a hat and other clinical tales.* New York: Summit.

Saczynski, J. S. (2002). Cognitive training gains in the Seattle longitudinal study: Individual predictors and mediators of training effects. *Dissertation Abstracts International: Section B. The Sciences and Engineering, 62,* 6001

Sadeh, A., Raviv, A., & Gruber, R. (2000). Sleep patterns and sleep disruptions in school-age children. *Developmental Psychology, 36,* 291–301.

Sadigh-Lindell, B., Sylven, C., Hagerman, I., Berglund, M., Terenius, L., Franzen, O., & Eriksson, B. E. (2001). Oscillation of pain intensity during adenosine infusion: Relationship to beta-endorphin and sympathetic tone. *Neuroreport: For Rapid Communication of Neuroscience Research, 12,* 1571–1575.

Sagar, K. A., Dahlgren, M. K., Gönenç, A., & Gruber, S. A. (2013). Altered affective processing in bipolar disorder: an fMRI study. *Journal of Affective Disorders, 150,* 1192–1196.

Sagie, A., Elizur, D., & Yamauchi, H. (1996). The structure and strength of achievement motivation: A cross–cultural comparison. *Journal of Organizational Behavior, 17,* 431–444.

Sala, F., Krupat, E., & Roter, D. (2002). Satisfaction and the use of humor by physicians and patients. *Psychology and Health, 17,* 269–280.

Salanova, M., Llorens, S., Cifre, E., Martinez, I. M., & Schaufeli, W. B. (2003). Perceived collective efficacy, subjective well-being, and task performance among electronic work groups: An experimental study. *Small Group Research, 34,* 43–73.

Salerian, A. J., Deibler, W. E., Vittone, B. J., Geyer, S. P., Drell, L., Mirmirani, N., . . . Fleisher, S. (2000). Sildenafil for psychotropic-induced sexual dysfunction in 31 women and 61 men. *Journal of Sex and Marital Therapy, 26,* 133–140.

Sales, B.D., & Folkman, S. (2000). *Ethics in research with human participants.* Washington, DC: American Psychological Association.

Salfati, C. G., & Canter, D. V. (1999). Differentiating stranger murders: Profiling offender characteristics from behavioral styles. *Behavioral Sciences and the Law, 17,* 391–406.

Sallis, J. F., Carlson, J. A., Mignano, A. M., Lemes, A., & Wagner, N. (2013). Trends in presentations of environmental and policy studies related to physical activity, nutrition, and obesity at society of behavioral medicine, 1995–2010: A commentary to accompany the Active Living Research supplement to *Annals of Behavioral Medicine. Annals of Behavioral Medicine, 45,* S14–S17.

Salovey, P., & Haar, M. D. (1990). The efficacy of cognitive-behavior therapy and writing process training for alleviating writing anxiety. *Cognitive Therapy and Research. 14,* 513–526.

Salthouse, T. A. (1991). Mediation of adult age differences in cognition by reductions in working memory and speed of processing. *Psychological Science, 2,* 179–183.

Salvatore, J., & Maracek, J. (2010). Gender in the gym: Evaluation concerns as barriers to women's weight lifting. *Sex Roles, 63,* 556–567.

Samelson, F. (1997). On the uses of history: The case of *The Bell Curve. Journal of the History of the Behavioral Sciences, 33,* 129–133.

Sameroff, A. (2010). A unified theory of development: A dialectic integration of nature and nurture. *Child Development, 81,* 6–22.

Samms, M., Hari, R., Rif, J., & Knuutila, J. (1993). The human auditory sensory memory trace persists about 10 sec: Neuromagnetic evidence. *Journal of Cognitive Neuroscience, 5,* 363–370.

Samuels, C. A., Butterworth, G., Roberts, T., & Graupner, L. (1994). Facial aesthetics: Babies prefer attractiveness to symmetry. *Perception, 23,* 823–831.

Sand, P., Kavvadias, D., Feineis, D., Riederer, P., Schreier, P., Kleinschnitz, M., . . . Beckmann, H. (2000). Naturally occurring benzodiazepines: Current status of research and clinical implications. *Journal of Clinical Psychopharmacology, 20,* 12–18.

Sanday, L., Zanin, K. A., Patti, C. L., Tufik, S., & Frussa-Filho, R. (2012). Role of state-dependency in memory impairment inducted by acute administration of midazolam in mice. *Progress in Neuro-Psychophamalogy & Biological Psychiatry, 37,* 1–7.

Sander, K., Brechmann, A., & Scheich, H. (2003). Audition of laughing and crying leads to right amygdala activation in a low-noise fMRI setting. *Brain Research Protocol, 11,* 81–91.

Sandman, D., Simantov, E., & An, C. (2000). Out of touch: American men and the health care system (Publication No. 374). New York: The Commonwealth Fund.

Sanghvi, C. (1995). Efficacy of study skills training in managing study habits and test anxiety of high test anxious students. *Journal of the Indian Academy of Applied Psychology, 21,* 71–75.

Sansone, R. A., & Sansone, L. A. (2011). Gender patterns in borderline personality disorder. *Innovations in Clinical Neuroscience, 8,* 16–20.

SantaCruz, K. S., Sonnen, J. A., Pezhough, M. K., Desrosiers, M. F., Nelson, P., & Tyas, S. L. (2011). Alzheimer disease pathology in subjects without dementia in 2 studies of aging: The Nun Study and the Adult Changes in Thought Study. *Journal of Neuropathology & Experimental Neurology, 70,* 832–840.

Santucci, A. C., Gluck, R., Kanof, P. D., & Haroutunian, V. (1993). Induction of memory and cortical cholinergic neurochemical recovery with combined fetal transplantation and GMI treatments in rats with lesions of the NBM. *Dementia, 4,* 272–281.

Sapp, M., Farrell, W. C., Jr., Johnson, J. H., Jr., & Hitchcock, K. (1999). Attitudes toward rape among African American male and female college students. *Journal of Counseling and Development, 77,* 204–208.

Sarason, S. (1984). If it can be studied or developed, should it be? *American Psychologist, 39,* 477–485.

Sargent-Cox, K. A., Anstey, K. J., & Luszcz, M. A. (2010). Patterns of longitudinal change in older adults' self-rated health, the effect of the point of reference. *Health Psychology, 29,* 143–152.

Satapathy, B. (2001). Getting the best out of your people: The Indian way. *Social Science International, 17,* 37–45.

Satir, V., Bitter, J. R., & Krestensen, K. K. (1988). Family reconstruction: The family within—A group experience. *Journal for Specialists in Group Work, 13,* 200–208.

Sato, T., & Beidler, L. M. (1997). Broad tuning of rat taste cells for four basic taste stimuli. *Chemical Senses, 22,* 287–293.

Satoh, M., Takeda, K., Nagata, K., Hatazawa, J., & Kuzuhara, S. (2001). Activated brain regions in musicians during an ensemble: A PET study. *Cognitive Brain Research, 12*, 101–108.

Saudino, K. J., Gagne, J. R., Grant, J., Ibatoulina, A., Marytuina, T., Ravich-Scherbo, I., & Whitfield, K. (1999). Genetic and environmental influences on personality in adult Russian twins. *International Journal of Behavioral Development, 23*, 375–389.

Saunders, C. (1996). Hospice. *Mortality, 1*, 317–322.

Saunders, T., Driskell, J. E., Johnston, J. H., & Salas, E. (1996). The effect of stress- inoculation training on anxiety and performance. *Journal of Occupational Health Psychology, 1*, 170–186.

Savage-Rumbaugh, E. S., Rumbaugh, D. M., Smith, S. T., & Lawson, J. (1980). Reference: The linguistic essential. *Science, 210*, 922–925.

Savitz, J., Tan, C., Taylor, A., Drevets, W., & Teague, K., (2013). Abnormalities in regulatory T cells and natural killer cells in major depressive disorder (P3127). *The Journal of Immunology, 190*, 25–43.

Sawatzky, J. V., & Naimark, B. J. (2002). Physical activity and cardiovascular health in aging women: A health-promotion perspective. *Journal of Aging and Physical Activity, 10*, 396–412.

Saxe, L., Dougherty, D., & Cross, T. (1985). The validity of polygraph testing: Scientific analysis and public controversy. *American Psychologist, 40*, 355–366.

Saxena, S., & Rauch, S. L. (2000). Functional neuroimaging and the neuroanatomy of obsessive-compulsive disorder. *Psychiatric Clinics of North America, 23*, 563–586.

Saygin, A. P., & Cicekli, I. (2002). Pragmatics in human-computer conversations. *Journal of Pragmatics, 34*, 227–258.

Scammell, T. E. (2001). Wakefulness: An eye-opening perspective on orexin neurons. *Current Biology, 11*, R769–R771.

Scammell, T. E. (2003). The neurobiology, diagnosis, and treatment of narcolepsy. *Annals of Neurology, 53*, 154–166.

Scarborough, H. S., Rescorla, L., Tager-Flusberg, H., Fowler, A. E., & Sudhalter, V. (1991). The relation of utterance length to grammatical complexity in normal and language-disordered groups. *Applied Psycholinguistics, 12*, 23–45.

Scarr, S. (1998). American child care today. *American Psychologist, 53*, 95–108.

Scarr, S., & Carter-Saltzman, L. (1979). Twin method: Defense of a critical assumption. *Behavior Genetics, 9*, 527–542.

Scarr, S., & Weinberg, R. A. (1976). IQ test performance of black children adopted by white families. *American Psychologist, 31*, 726–739.

Scarr, S., & Weinberg, R. A. (1983). The Minnesota Adoption Studies: Genetic differences and malleability. *Child Development, 54*, 260–267.

Schaal, B., Marlier, L., & Soussignan, R. (1998). Olfactory function in the human fetus: Evidence from selective neonatal responsiveness to the odor of amniotic fluid. *Behavioral Neuroscience, 112*, 1438–1449.

Schaap, J., & Meijer, J. H. (2001). Opposing effects of behavioural activity and light on neurons of the suprachiasmatic nucleus. *European Journal of Neuroscience, 13*, 1955–1962.

Schachter, S. (1971). Some extraordinary facts about obese humans and rats. *American Psychologist, 26*, 129–144.

Schachter, S. (1982). Recidivism and self-cure of smoking and obesity. *American Psychologist, 37*, 436–444.

Schachter, S., & Singer, J. E. (1962). Cognitive, social, and physiological determinants of emotional state. *Psychological Review, 69*, 379–399.

Schacter, D. L. (1983). Amnesia observed: Remembering and forgetting in a natural environment. *Journal of Abnormal Psychology, 92*, 236–242.

Schacter, D. L. (1992). Understanding implicit memory: A cognitive neuroscience approach. *American Psychologist, 47*, 559–569.

Schacter, D. L., Norman, K. A., & Koutstaal, W. (1998). The cognitive neuroscience of constructive memory. *Annual Review of Psychology, 49*. 289–318.

Schaefer, G. B., & Bodensteiner, J. B. (1999). Developmental anomalies of the brain in mental retardation. *International Review of Psychiatry, 11*, 47–55.

Schaefer, M., Egloff, B., & Witthöft, M. (2012). Is interoceptive awareness really altered in somatoform disorders? Testing competing theories with two paradignms of heartbeat perception. *Journal of Abnormal Psychology, 121*, 719–724.

Schafe, G. E., Sollars, S. I., & Bernstein, I. L. (1995). The CS-US interval and taste aversion learning: A brief look. *Behavioral Neuroscience, 109*, 799–802.

Schaie, K. W. (1989). Perceptual speed in adulthood: Cross-sectional and longitudinal studies. *Psychology and Aging, 4*, 443–453.

Schaie, K. W., & Hertzog, C. (1983). Fourteen-year cohort-sequential analyses of adult intellectual development. *Developmental Psychology, 19*, 531–543.

Schaie, K. W., Labouvie, G. V., & Barrett, T. J. (1973). Selective attrition effects in a 14-year study of adult intelligence. *Journal of Gerontology, 28*, 328–334.

Schaller, M., & Cialdini, R. B. (1988). The economics of empathic helping: Support for a mood management motive. *Journal of Experimental Social Psychology, 24*, 163–181.

Schaubroeck, J., Lam, S. S. K., & Xie, J. L. (2000). Collective efficacy versus self-efficacy in coping responses to stressors and control: A cross-cultural study. *Journal of Applied Psychology, 85*, 512–525.

Schechter, E. (2012). The switch model of split-brain consciousness. *Philosophical Psychology, 25*, 203–226.

Scheffler, T. S., & Naus, P. J. (1999). The relationship between fatherly affirmation and a woman's self-esteem, fear of intimacy, comfort with womanhood, and comfort with sexuality. *Canadian Journal of Human Sexuality, 8*, 39–45.

Scheflin, A. W., & Brown, D. (1996). Repressed memory or dissociative amnesia: What the science says. *Journal of Psychiatry and Law, 24*, 143–188.

Scherer, K. R. (1997). Profiles of emotion-antecedent appraisal: Testing theoretical predictions across cultures. *Cognition and Emotion, 11*, 113–150.

Scherer, K. R., & Ceschi, G. (1997). Lost luggage: A field study of emotion-antecedent appraisal. *Motivation and Emotion, 21*, 211–235.

Scherer, K. R., & Wallbott, H. G. (1994). Evidence for universality and cultural variation of differential emotion response patterning. *Journal of Personality and Social Psychology, 66*, 310–328.

Schiff, M., Duyme, M., Dumaret, A., & Tomkiewicz, S. (1982). How much could we boost scholastic achievement and IQ scores? A direct answer from a French adoption study. *Cognition, 12*, 165–196.

Schiffman, S. S., Sattely-Miller, E. A., Suggs, M. S., & Graham, B. G. (1995). The effect of pleasant odors and hormone status on mood of women at midlife. *Brain Research Bulletin, 36*, 19–29.

Schill, T., & O'Laughlin, M. S. (1984). Humor preference and coping with stress. *Psychological Reports, 55*, 309–310.

Schimel, J., Greenberg, J., & Martens, A. (2003). Evidence that projection of a feared trait can serve a defensive function. *Personality and Social Psychology Bulletin, 29*, 969–979.

Schlegel, P. A., & Roth, A. (1997). Tuning of electroreceptors in the blind cave salamander, *Proteus anguinus* L. *Brain, Behaviour, and Evolution, 49*, 132–136.

Schleifer, S. J., Keller, S. E., Camerino, M., Thornton, J. C., & Stein, M. (1983). Suppression of lymphocytic stimulation following bereavement. *Journal of the American Medical Association, 250*, 374–377.

Schlenker, B. R., Phillips, S. T., Boniecki, K. A., & Schlenker, D. R. (1995). Championship pressures: Choking or triumphing in one's own territory? *Journal of Personality and Social Psychology, 68*, 632–643.

Schlesinger, L. B., & Revitch, E. (1999). Sexual burglaries and sexual homicide: Clinical, forensic, and investigative considerations. *Journal of the American Academy of Psychiatry and the Law, 27*, 227–238.

Schlumpf, Y. R., Nijenhuis, E. R. S., Chalavi, S., Weder, E. V, Zimmermann, E., Luechinger, R., . . . Jäncke, L. (2013). Dissociative part-dependent biopsychosocial reactions to backward masked angry and neutral faces: An fMRI study of dissociative identity disorder. *NeuroImage. Clinical, 3*, 54–64.

Schmader, T., & Johns, M. (2003). Converging evidence that stereotype threat reduces working memory capacity. *Journal of Personality & Social Psychology, 85*, 440–452.

Schmeidler, G. R. (1985). Belief and disbelief in psi. *Parapsychology Review, 16*, 1–4.

Schmeidler, G. R. (1993). William James: Pioneering ancestor of modern parapsychology. In M. E. Donnelly (Ed), *Reinterpreting the legacy of William James* (pp. 339–352). Washington, DC: American Psychological Association.

Schmeidler, G. R. (1997). Psi-conducive experimenters and psi-permissive ones. *European Journal of Parapsychology, 13*, 83–94.

Schmid, H. (2003). The mystery of the moon illusion. Exploring size perception. *Swiss Journal of Psychology, 62*, 200–201.

Schmidt, G., & Weiner, B. (1988). A attribution-affect-action theory of behavior: Replications of judgments of help-giving. *Personality and Social Psychology Bulletin, 14*, 610–621.

Schmidt, H. G., Peeck, V. E., Paas, F., & Van Breukelen, G. J. P. (2000). Remembering the street names of one's childhood neighbourhood: A study of very long-term retention. *Memory, 8*, 37–49.

Schmidt, L. A., Trainor, L. J., & Santesso, D. L. (2003). Development of frontal electroencephalogram (EEG) and heart rate (ECG) responses to affective musical stimuli during the first 12 months of post-natal life. *Brain and Cognition, 52*, 27–32.

Schmidt, N. B., Lerew, D. R., & Jackson, R. J. (1999). Prospective evaluation of anxiety sensitivity in the pathogenesis of panic: Replication and extension. *Journal of Abnormal Psychology, 108*, 532–537.

Schmidt, S., & Walach, H. (2000). Electrodermal activity (EDA): State-of-the-art measurement and techniques for parapsychological purposes. *Journal of Parapsychology, 64*, 139–163.

Schmidtke, A., Weinacker, B., Apter, A., Batt, A., Berman, A., Bille–Brahe, U., . . . Wasserman, D. (1999). Suicide rates in the world: Update. *Archives of Suicide Research, 5*, 81–89.

Schmitt, I., Bitoun, E. I., & Manto, M. (2009). PTPRR, cerebellum, and motor coordination. *Cerebellum, 8*, 71–73.

Schmitt-Rodermund, E., & Vondracek, F. W. (1999). Breadth of interests, exploration, and identity development in adolescence. *Journal of Vocational Behavior, 55*, 298–317.

Schneider, B. H., Atkinson, L., & Tardif, C. (2001). Child-parent attachment and children's peer relatins: A quantitative review. *Developmental Psychology, 37*, 86–100.

Schneider, C. J. (1987). Cost effectiveness of biofeedback and behavioral medicine treatments: A review of the literature. *Biofeedback and Self-Regulation, 12*, 71–92.

Schneider, H. G., & Shugar, G. J. (1990). Audience and feedback effects in computer learning. *Computers in Human Behavior, 6*, 315–321.

Schneider, M. P., van Melle, G., Uldry, C., Huynh-Ba, M., Stubi, C. L. F., Iorillo, D., . . . Zellweger, J. P. (2003). Electronic monitoring of long-term use of the nicotine nasal spray and predictors of success in a smoking cessation program. *Nicotine and Tobacco Research, 5*, 719–727.

Schneider, P., Scherg, M., Dosch, H. G., Specht, H. J., Gutschalk, A., & Rupp, A. (2002). Morphology of Heschl's gyrus reflects enhanced activation in the auditory cortex of musicians. *Nature Neuroscience, 5,* 688–694.

Schneider, T. R., Salovey, P., Pallonen, U., Mundorf, N., Smith, N. F., & Steward, W. T. (2001). Visual and auditory message framing effects on tobacco smoking. *Journal of Applied Social Psychology, 31,* 667–682.

Schneider-Rosen, K., & Burke, P. B. (1999). Multiple attachment relationships within families: Mothers and fathers with two young children. *Developmental Psychology, 35,* 436–444.

Schoen, L. M. (1996). Mnemopoly: Board games and menomics. *Teaching of Psychology, 23,* 30–32.

Schonemann, P. H., & Schonemann, R. D. (1994). Environmental versus genetic models for Osborne's personality data on identical and fraternal twins. *Cahiers de Psychologie, 13,* 141–167.

Schooler, C., Mulatu, M. S., & Oates, G. (1999). The continuing effects of substantively complex work on the intellectual functioning of older workers. *Psychology and Aging, 14,* 483–506.

Schott, R. L. (1995). The childhood and family dynamics of transvestites. *Archives of Sexual Behavior, 24,* 309–327.

Schotte, C. K. W., Van Den Bossche, B., De Doncker, D., Claes, S., & Cosyns, P. (2006). A biopsychosocial model as a guide for psychoeducation and treatment of depression. *Depression & Anxiety, 23,* 312–324.

Schretlen, D., Pearlson, G. D., Anthony, J. C., Aylward, E. H., Augustine, A. M., Davis, A., & Barta, P. (2000). Elucidating the contributions of processing speed, executive ability, and frontal lobe volume to normal age-related differences in fluid intelligence. *Journal of the International Neuropsychological Society, 6,* 52–61.

Schroth, M. L. (1995). A comparison of sensation seeking among different groups of athletes and nonathletes. *Personality and Individual Differences, 18,* 219–222.

Schroth, M. L., & McCormack, W. A. (2000). Sensation seeking and need for achievement among study-abroad students. *Journal of Social Psychology, 140,* 533–535.

Schrut, A. H. (1994). The Oedipus complex: Some observations and questions regarding its validity and universal existence. *Journal of the American Academy of Psychoanalysis, 22,* 727–751.

Schull, W. J., Norton, S., & Jensh, R. P. (1990). Ionizing radiation and the developing brain. *Neurotoxicology and Teratology, 12,* 249–260.

Schulz, D., Mirrione, M. M., & Henn, F. a. (2010). Cognitive aspects of congenital learned helplessness and its reversal by the monoamine oxidase (MAO)-B inhibitor deprenyl. *Neurobiology of Learning and Memory, 93,* 291–301.

Schulz, P., & Kaspar, C. H. (1994). Neuroendocrine and psychological effects of restricted environmental stimulation technique in a flotation tank. *Biological Psychology, 37,* 161–175.

Schulz, R., & Curnow, C. (1988). Peak performance and age among superathletes: Track and field, swimming, baseball, tennis, and golf. *Journal of Gerontology, 43,* 113–120.

Schuster, B., Forsterling, F., & Weiner, B. (1989). Perceiving the causes of success and failure: A cross-cultural examination of attributional concepts. *Journal of Cross-Cultural Psychology, 20,* 191–213.

Schuster, D. T. (1990). Fulfillment of potential, life satisfaction, and competence: Comparing four cohorts of gifted women at midlife. *Journal of Educational Psychology, 82,* 471–478.

Schutte, N. S., Malouff, J. M., Bobik, C., Coston, T. D., Greeson, C., Jedlicka, C., . . . Wendorf, G. (2001). Emotional intelligence and interpersonal relations. *Journal of Social Psychology, 141,* 523–536.

Schwaninger, J., Eisenberg, P. R., Schechtman, K. B., & Weiss, A. N. (2002). A prospective analysis of near-death experiences in cardiac arrest patients. *Journal of Near-Death Studies, 20,* 215–232.

Schwartz, B. L., & Smith, S. M. (1997). The retrieval of related information influences tip-of-the-tongue states. *Journal of Memory and Language, 36,* 68–86.

Schwartz, C. E., Wright, C. I., Shin, L. M., Kagan, J., & Rauch, S. L. (2003). Inhibited and uninhibited infants "grown up": Adult amygdalar responses to novelty. *Science, 300,* 1952–1953.

Schwartz, J. C., Diaz, J., Pilon, C., & Sokoloff, P. (2000). Possible implications of the dopamine D–sub–3 receptor in schizophrenia and in antipsychotic drug actions. *Brain Research Reviews, 31,* 277–287.

Schwarz, T., Loewenstein, J., & Isenberg, K. E. (1995). Maintenance ECT: Indications and outcome. *Convulsive Therapy, 11,* 14–23.

Schweizer, T. A., Alexander, M. P., Gillingham, S., Cusimano, M., & Stuss, D. T. (2010). Lateralized cerebellar contributions to word generation: A phonemic and semantic fluency study. *Behavioral Neurology, 23,* 31–37.

Schwenzer, M., & Mathiak, K. (2011). Hypochondriacal attitudes may reflect a general cognitive bias that is not limited to illness-related thoughts. *Psychology & Health, 26,* 965–973.

Schyns, P. (1998). Cross-national differences in happiness: Economic and cultural factors explored. *Social Indicators, 43,* 3–26.

Scopesi, A., Zanobini, M., & Carossino, P. (1997). Childbirth in different cultures: Psychophysical reactions of women delivering in U.S., German, French, and Italian hospitals. *Journal of Reproductive and Infant Psychology, 15,* 9–30.

Scott, B. W., Wojtowicz, J. M., & Burnham, W. M. (2000). Neurogenesis in the dentate gyrus of the rat following electroconvulsive shock seizures. *Experimental Neurology, 165,* 231–236.

Scott, D., & Willits, F. K. (1994). Environmental attitudes and behavior: A Pennsylvania survey. *Environment and Behavior, 26,* 239–260.

Scott, J., Palmer, S., Paykel, E., Teasdale, J., & Hayhurst, H. (2003). Use of cognitive therapy for relapse prevention in chronic depression: Cost-effectiveness study. *British Journal of Psychiatry, 182,* 221–227.

Scott, K. G., & Carran, D. T. (1987). The epidemiology and prevention of mental retardation. *American Psychologist, 42,* 801–804.

Scott, M. S., Deuel, L.L.S., Jean-Francois, B., & Urbano, R. C. (1996). Identifying cognitively gifted ethnic minority children. *Gifted Child Quarterly, 40,* 147–153.

Scott, R. L., Butcher, J. N., Young, T. L., & Gomez, N. (2002). The Hispanic MMPI-A across five countries. *Journal of Clinical Psychology, 58,* 407–417.

Scoville, W. B., & Milner, B. (1957). Loss of recent memory after bilateral hippocampal lesions. *Journal of Neurology, Neurosurgery, and Psychiatry, 20,* 11–21.

Scully, J. A., Tosi, H., & Banning, K. (2000). Life events checklists: Revisiting the Social Readjustment Rating Scale after 30 years. *Educational and Psychological Measurement, 60,* 864–876.

Sears, R. R. (1977). Source of life satisfaction of the Terman gifted men. *American Psychologist, 32,* 119–128.

Sechrest, L. (1984). Review of the development and application of social language theory: Selected papers. *Journal of the History of the Behavioral Sciences, 20,* 228–230.

Sedlacek, K., & Taub, E. (1996). Biofeedback treatment of Raynaud's disease. *Professional Psychology: Research and Practice, 27,* 548–553.

Seegert, C. R. (2003). Token economies and incentive programs: Behavioral improvement in mental health inmates housed in state prisons. *Behavior Therapist, 208,* 210–211.

Segal, N. L. (2000). Virtual twins: New findings on within-family environmental influences on intelligence. *Journal of Educational Psychology, 92,* 442–448.

Segall, M. H., Dasen, P. R., Berry, J. W., & Poortinga, Y. H. (1990). *Human behavior in global perspective: An introduction to cross-cultural psychology.* New York: Pergamon.

Segerstrom, S. C., Taylor, S. E., Kemeny, M. E., Reed, G. M., & Visscher, B. R. (1996). Causal attributions predict rate of immune decline in HIV-seropositive gay men. *Health Psychology, 15,* 485–493.

Segovia, C., Hutchinson, I., Laing, D. G., & Jinks, A. L. (2002). A quantitative study of fungiform papillae and taste pore density in adults and children. *Developmental Brain Research, 138,* 135–146.

Seidenbecher, T., Laxmi, T. R., Stork, O., & Pape, H. C. (2003). Amygdalar and hippocampal theta rhythm synchronization during fear memory revisited. *Science, 301,* 846–850.

Seidlitz, L., & Diener, E. (1998). Sex differences in the recall of affective experiences. *Journal of Personality and Social Psychology, 74,* 262–271.

Seidman, S. M. (2003). The aging male: Androgens, erectile dysfunction, and depression. *Journal of Clinical Psychiatry, 64,* 31–37.

Seifert, L. S. (1996). On the use of concept formation tasks to educate naive observers about the visual arts. *Visual Arts Research, 22,* 11–19.

Seki, K., Matsumoto, D., & Imahori, T. T. (2002). The conceptualization and expression of intimacy in Japan and the United States. (2002). *Journal of Cross-Cultural Psychology, 33,* 303–319.

Selcuk, E., & Ong, A. D. (2013). Perceived partner responsiveness moderates the association between received emotional support and all-cause mortality. *Health Psychology, 32,* 231–235.

Self, D. J., & Baldwin, D. C., Jr. (1998). Does medical education inhibit the development of moral reasoning in medical students? A cross-sectional study. *Academic Medicine, 73,* S91–S93.

Seligman, M. E. P. (1970). On the generality of the laws of learning. *Psychological Review, 77,* 406–418.

Seligman, M. E. P. (1971). Phobias and preparedness. *Behavior Therapy, 2,* 307–320.

Seligman, M. E. P. (1989). Research in clinical psychology: Why is there so much depression today? In I. S. Cohen (Ed.), *The G. Stanley Hall Lecture Series, Vol. 9* (pp. 75–96). Washington, DC: American Psychological Association.

Seligman, M. E. P., & Maier, S. F. (1967). Failure to escape traumatic shock. *Journal of Experimental Psychology, 74,* 1–9.

Selye, H. (1936). A syndrome produced by diverse nocuous agents. *Nature, 138,* 32.

Seyfarth, R. M., Cheney, D. L., & Marler, P. (1980). Monkey responses to three different alarm calls: Evidence of predator classification and semantic communication. *Science, 210,* 801–803.

Semendeferi, K., Lu, A., Schenker, N., & Damasio, H. (2002). Humans and great apes share a large frontal cortex. *Nature Neuroscience, 5,* 272–276.

Semple, S. J., Strathdee, S. A., Zians, J., McQuaid, J. R., & Patterson, T. L. (2013). Drug assertiveness and sexual risk-taking behavior in a sample of HIV-positive, methamphetamine-using men who have sex with men. *Journal of Substance Abuse Treatment, 41,* 265–272.

Serebriakoff, V. (1985). *Mensa: The society for the highly intelligent.* New York: Stein & Day.

Serok, S., & Levi, N. (1993). Application of Gestalt therapy with long-term prison inmates in Israel. *Gestalt Journal, 16,* 105–127.

Serper, M. R. (2011). Aggression in schizophrenia. *Schizophrenia Bulletin, 37,* 897–898.

Servan-Schreiber, D., & Perlstein, W. M. (1998). Selective limbic activation and its relevance to emotional disorders. *Cognition and Emotion, 12,* 331–352.

Setlow, B. (1997). Georges Ungar and memory transfer. *Journal of the History of the Neurosciences, 6,* 181–192.

Seto, M. C., Lalumiere, M. L., & Quinsey, V. L. (1995). Sensation seeking and males' sexual strategy. *Personality and Individual Differences, 19,* 669–675.

Seymour, T. L., Seifert, C. M., Shafto, M. G., & Mosmann, A. L. (2000). Using response time measures to assess "guilty knowledge." *Journal of Applied Psychology, 85,* 30–37.

Shackelford, T. K., Buss, D. M., & Weekes-Shackelford, V. A. (2003). Wife killings committed in the context of a lover's triangle. *Basic and Applied Social Psychology, 25,* 137–143.

Shadish, W. R., Navarro, A. M., Matt, G. E., & Phillips, G. (2000). The effects of psychological therapies under clinically representative conditions: A meta-analysis. *Psychological Bulletin, 126,* 512–529.

Shaffer, J. W., Graves, P. L., Swank, R. T., & Pearson, T. A. (1987). Clustering of personality traits in youth and the subsequent development of cancer among physicians. *Journal of Behavioral Medicine, 10,* 441–447.

Shah, M., & Jeffery, R. W. (1991). Is obesity due to overeating and inactivity, or to a defective metabolic rate? A review. *Annals of Behavioral Medicine, 13,* 73–81.

Shahab, L., West, R., & McNeill, A. (2011). A randomized, controlled trial of adding expired carbon monoxide feedback to brief stop smoking advice: Evaluation of cognitive and behavioral effects. *Health Psychology, 30,* 49–57.

Shaham, Y., Singer, J. E., & Schaeffer, M. H. (1992). Stability/instability of cognitive strategies across tasks determine whether stress will affect judgmental processes. *Journal of Applied Social Psychology, 22,* 691–713.

Shammi, P., & Stuss, D. T. (1999). Humour appreciation: A role of the right frontal lobe. *Brain, 122,* 657–666.

Shanab, M. E., & Yahya, K. A. (1977). A behavioral study of obedience in children. *Journal of Personality and Social Psychology, 35,* 530–536.

Shanker, S. G., Savage-Rumbaugh, E. S., & Taylor, T. J. (1999). Kanzi: A new beginning. *Animal Learning and Behavior, 27,* 24–25.

Shapiro, C. M., Bortz, R., Mitchell, D., Bartel, P., & Jooste, P. (1981). Slow-wave sleep: A recovery period after exercise. *Science, 214,* 1253–1254.

Shapiro, D. (1995). Finding out how psychotherapies help people change. *Psychotherapy Research, 5,* 1–21.

Shapiro, J. K. (1995). Dr. Kohlberg goes to Washington: Using congressional debates to teach moral development. *Teaching of Psychology, 22,* 245–247.

Shapiro, L. A. (2005). Can psychology be a unified science? *Philosophy of Science, 72,* 953–963.

Shapiro, L. J., & Stewart, S. E. (2011). Pathological guilt: A persistent yet overlooked treatment factor in obsessive-compulsive disorder. *Annals of Clinical Psychiatry, 23,* 63–70.

Sharpe, D., & Faye, C. (2009). A second look at debriefing practices: Madness in our method? *Ethics and Behavior, 19,* 432–447.

Sharpley, A. L. (2002). Sleep: Slow wave and non–REM stages. In E. Perry et al. (Eds.), *Neurochemistry of consciousness: Neurotransmitters in mind* (pp. 105–122). Amsterdam, Netherlands: John Benjamins.

Shaughnessy, M. F., & Nystul, M. S. (1985). Preventing the greatest loss—Suicide. *Creative Child and Adult Quarterly, 10,* 164–169.

Shavitt, S., Swan, S., Lowrey, T. M., & Wanke, M. (1994). The interaction of endorser attractiveness and involvement in persuasion depends on the goal that guides message processing. *Journal of Consumer Psychology, 3,* 137–162.

Shaw, J. S. III, Garcia, L. A., & McClure, K. A. (1999). A lay perspective on the accuracy of eyewitness testimony. *Journal of Applied Social Psychology, 29,* 52–71.

Shaw, P., Eckstrand, K., Sharp, W., Blumenthal, J., Lerch, J. P., Greenstein, D., . . . Rapoport, J. L. (2007). Attention-deficit/hyperactivity disorder is characterized by a delay in cortical maturation. *Proceedings of the National Academy of Sciences of the United States of America, 104,* 19649–19654.

Shaw, P., Gogtay, N., & Rapoport, J. (2010). Childhood psychiatric disorders as anomalies in neurodevelopmental trajectories. *Human Brain Mapping, 31,* 917–925.

Shaw, P., Gornick, M., Lerch, J., Addington, A., Seal, J., Greenstein, D., . . . Rapoport, J. L. (2007). Polymorphisms of the dopamine D4 receptor, clinical outcome, and cortical structure in attention-deficit/hyperactivity disorder. *Archives of General Psychiatry, 64,* 921–931.

Shaw, P., Lerch, J., Greenstein, D., Sharp, W., Clasen, L., Evans, A., . . . Rapoport, J. (2006). Longitudinal mapping of cortical thickness and clinical outcome in children and adolescents with attention-deficit/hyperactivity disorder. *Archives of General Psychiatry, 63,* 540–549.

Shea, J. D. (2003). Hypnosis with cancer patients. *Australian Journal of Clinical Hypnotherapy and Hypnosis, 24,* 98–111.

Shea, M. T., Elkin, I., Imber, S. D., & Sotsky, S. M. (1992). Course of depressive symptoms over follow-up: Findings from the National Institute of Mental Health Treatment of Depression Collaborative Research Program. *Archives of General Psychiatry, 49,* 782–787.

Shear, M. K., Feske, U., & Greeno, C. (2000). Gender differences in anxiety disorders: Clinical implications. In E. Frank (Ed.), *Gender and its effects on psychopathology* (pp. 151–165). Washington, DC: American Psychiatric Publishing.

Shedler, J. (2010). The efficacy of psychodynamic psychotherapy. *American Psychologist, 65,* 98–109.

Sheehan, P. W., & Tilden, J. (1983). Effects of suggestibility and hypnosis on accurate and distorted retrieval from memory. *Journal of Experimental Psychology: Learning, Memory, and Cognition, 9,* 283–293.

Sheehy, R., & Horan, J. J. (2004). Effects of stress inoculation training for 1st-year law students. *International Journal of Stress Management, 11,* 41–55.

Sheets, V. L. (2013). Passion for life: Self-expansion and passionate love across the life span. *Journal of Social & Personal Relationships, 28,* 748–771.

Shefler, G., Dasberg, H., & Ben-Shakhar, G. A. (1995). A randomized controlled outcome and follow-up study of Mann's limited psychotherapy. *Journal of Consulting and Clinical Psychology, 63,* 585–593.

Sheikh, J. I., Leskin, G. A., & Klein, D. F. (2002). Gender differences in panic disorder: Findings from the National Comorbidity survey. *American Journal of Psychiatry, 159,* 55–58.

Sheiner, E. K., Sheiner, E., Shoham-Vardi, I., Mazor, M., & Katz, M. (1999). Ethnic differences influence care giver's estimates of pain during labour. *Pain, 81,* 299–305.

Sheldon, W. H., & Stevens, S. S. (1942). *The varieties of temperament: A psychology of constitutional differences.* New York: Harper.

Shepard, R. N. (1984). Ecological constraints on internal representation: Resonant kinematics of perceiving, imagining, and dreaming. *Psychological Review, 91,* 417–447.

Sheppard, L. C., & Teasdale, J. D. (2004). How does dysfunctional thinking decrease during recovery from major depression? *Journal of Abnormal Psychology, 113,* 64–71.

Shepperd, J. A., & Taylor, K. M. (1999). Social loafing and expectancy-value theory. *Personality and Social Psychology Bulletin, 25,* 1147–1158.

Sherwood, S. J., & Roe, C. A. (2003). A review of dream ESP studies conducted since the Maimonides dream ESP studies. *Journal of Consciousness Studies, 10,* 85–109.

Shettleworth, S. J. (2012). Do animals have insight, and what is insight anyway? *Canadian Journal of Experimental Psychology, 66,* 217–226.

Shettleworth, S. J., & Juergensen, M. R. (1980). Reinforcement of the organization of behavior in golden hamsters: Brain stimulation reinforcement for seven action patterns. *Journal of Experimental Psychology: Animal Behavior Processes, 6,* 352–375.

Shevell, S. K., & He, J. C. (1997). The visual photopigments of simple deuteranomalous trichromats inferred from color matching. *Vision Research, 37,* 1115–1127.

Shields, S. A. (1975). Functionalism, Darwinism, and the psychology of women: A study in social myth. *American Psychologist, 30,* 739–754.

Shields, S. A. (1982). The variability hypothesis. *Signs, 7,* 769–797.

Shiffrin, R. M., & Atkinson, R. C. (1969). Storage and retrieval processes in long-term memory. *Psychological Review, 76,* 179–193.

Shih, M., Pittinsky, T. L., & Ambady, N. (1999) Stereotype susceptibility: Identity salience and shifts in quantitative performance. *Psychological Science, 10,* 80–83.

Shinskey, J. L. (2012). Disappearing décalage: Object search in light and dark at 6 months. *Infancy, 17,* 272–294.

Shioiri, T., Murashita, J., Kato, T., & Fujii, K. (1996). Characteristic clinical features and clinical course in 270 Japanese outpatients with panic disorder. *Journal of Anxiety Disorders, 10,* 163–172.

Shiraishi, T. (1990). CCK as a central satiety factor: Behavioral and electrophysiological evidence. *Physiology and Behavior, 48,* 879–885.

Shirom, A., Melamed, S., & Nir-Dotan, M. (2000). The relationships among objective and subjective environmental stress levels and serum uric acid: The moderating effect of perceived control. *Journal of Occupational Health Psychology, 5,* 374–385.

Shneidman, E. (1987, March). At the point of no return. *Psychology Today,* pp. 54–58.

Shneidman, E. S. (1994). Clues to suicide reconsidered. *Suicide and Life-Threatening Behavior, 24,* 395–397.

Shockley, W. (1972). Dysgenics, geneticity, raceology: A challenge to the intellectual responsibility of educators. *Phi Delta Kappan, 53,* 297–307.

Shook, N. J., Gerrity, D. A., Jurich, J., & Segrist, A. E. (2000). Courtship violence among college students: A comparison of verbally and physically couples. *Journal of Family Violence, 15,* 1–22.

Short, A., Vandelanotte, C., Rebar, A., & Duncan, M. J. (2013). A comparison of correlates associated with adult physical activity behavior in major cities and regional settings. *Health Psychology.*

Shostrom, E. L. (1962). *Personal orientation inventory.* San Diego: EDITS.

Shotland, R. L., & Straw, M. J. (1976). Bystander response to an assault: When a man attacks a woman. *Journal of Personality and Social Psychology, 34,* 990–999.

Shumaker, S. A., Legault, C., Rapp, S. R., Thal, L., Wallace, R. B., Ockens, J. K., . . . Wactawski-Wende, J. (2003). Estrogen plus progestin and the incidence of dementia and mild cognitive impairment in postmenopausal women: The Women's Health Initiative Memory Study: A randomized controlled trial. *JAMA: Journal of the American Medical Association, 289,* 2651–2662.

Shurcliff, A. (1968). Judged humor, arousal, and the relief theory. *Journal of Personality and Social Psychology, 8,* 360–363.

Sias, P. M., Pedersen, H., Gallagher, E. B., & Kopaneva, I. (2012). Workplace friendship in the electronically connected organization. *Human Communication Research, 38,* 253–279.

Siddiqui, R. N., & Pandey, J. (2003). Coping with environmental stressors by urban slum dwellers. *Environment and Behavior, 35,* 589–604.

Siegel, J. M., & Brown, J. D. (1988). A prospective study of stressful circumstances, illness symptoms, and depressed mood among adolescents. *Developmental Psychology, 24,* 715–721.

Siegel, S., & Allan, L. G. (1996). The widespread influence of the Rescorla-Wagner model. *Psychonomic Bulletin and Review, 3,* 314–321.

Siegel, S., Baptista, M. A. S., & Kim, J. (2000). Pavlovian psychopharmacology: The associative basis of tolerance. *Experimental and Clinical Psychopharmacology, 8,* 276–293.

Siegmund, A., Köster, L., Meves, A. M., Plag, J., Stoy, M., & Ströhe, A. (2011). Stress hormones during flooding therapy and their relationship to therapy outcomes in patients with panic disorder and agoraphobia. *Journal of Psychiatric Research, 45*, 339–346.

Sierra-Honigmann, A. M., Carbone, K. M., & Yolken, R. H. (1995). Polymerase chain reaction (PCR) search for viral nucleic acid sequences in schizophrenia. *British Journal of Psychiatry, 166*, 55–60.

Siever, M. D. (1994). Sexual orientation and gender as factors in socioculturally acquired vulnerability to body dissatisfaction and eating disorders. *Journal of Consulting and Clinical Psychology, 62*, 252–260.

Signorella, M. L., Bigler, R. S., & Liben, L. S. (1997). A meta-analysis of children's memories for own-sex and other-sex information. *Journal of Applied Developmental Psychology, 18*, 429–445.

Silinsky, E. M. (1989). Adenosine derivatives and neuronal function. *Seminars in the Neurosciences, 1*, 155–165.

Silke, A. (2003). Deindividuation, anonymity, and violence: Findings from Northern Ireland. *Journal of Social Psychology, 143*, 493–499.

Silva, J. M. III, & Weinberg, R. S. (1984). *Psychological foundations of sport.* Champaign, IL: Human Kinetics.

Silverman, I. W. (2003). Gender differences in delay of gratification: A meta-analysis. *Sex Roles, 49*, 451–463.

Silverthorne, Z. A., & Quinsey, V. L. (2000). Sexual partner age preferences of homosexual and heterosexual men and women. *Archives of Sexual Behavior, 29*, 67–76.

Silverstein, L. B., & Auerbach, C. F. (1999). Deconstructing the essential father. *American Psychologist, 54*, 397–407.

Silvestri, S., Seeman, M. V., Negrete, J.-C., Houle, S., Shammi, C. M., Remington, G. J., . . . Seeman, P. (2000). Increased dopamine D-sub-2 receptor binding after long-term treatment with antipsychotics in humans: A clinical PET study. *Psychopharmacology, 152*, 174–180.

Simon, H. A. (1995). The information-processing theory of mind. *American Psychologist, 50*, 507–508.

Simon, N. (1979). Kaspar Hauser's recovery and autopsy: A perspective on neurological and sociological requirements for language development. *Annual Progress in Child Psychiatry & Child Development*, 215–228.

Simon, R. I. (1997). Video voyeurs and the covert videotaping of unsuspecting victims: Psychological and legal consequences. *Journal of Forensic Sciences, 42*, 884–889.

Simonoff, E., Bolton, P., & Rutter, M. (1996). Mental retardation: Genetic findings, clinical implications and research agenda. *Journal of Child Psychology and Psychiatry and Allied Disciplines, 37*, 259–280.

Simons, D. A., & Wurtele, S. K. (2010). Relationship between parents' use of corporal punishment and their children's endorsement of spanking and hitting other children. *Child Abuse & Neglect, 34*, 639–646.

Simons-Morton, B. G. (2002). Prospective analysis of peer and parent influences on smoking initiation among early adolescents. *Prevention Science, 3*, 275–283.

Simonton, D. K. (1984). *Genius, creativity, and leadership: Historimetric inquiries.* Cambridge, MA: Harvard University Press.

Simonton, D. K. (1999). Creativity and genius. In L. Pervin & O. John (Eds.), *Handbook of personality theory and research* (2nd ed., pp. 629–652). NY: Guilford.

Simonton, D. K. (2000). Creativity: Cognitive, personal, developmental, and social aspects. *American Psychologist, 55*, 151–158.

Simpson, B. A. (1986). The polygraph: Concept, usage, and validity. *Psychology: A Quarterly Journal of Human Behavior, 23*, 42–45.

Simpson, D. (2005). Phrenology and the neurosciences: contributions of F. J. Gall and J. G. Spurzheim. *Australian and New Zealand Journal of Surgery, 75*, 472–482.

Singer, A. G., & Macrides, F. (1990). Aphrodisin: Pheromone or transducer? *Chemical Senses, 15*, 199–203.

Singer, J. D., Fuller, B., Keiley, M. K., & Wolf, A. (1998). Early child-care selection: Variation by geographic location, maternal characteristics, and family structure. *Developmental Psychology, 34*, 1129–1144.

Singer, J. L., & Kolligian, J., Jr. (1987). Personality: Developments in the study of private experience. *Annual Review of Psychology, 38*, 533–574.

Singh, A.K., Mahlios, J., Mignot, E. (2013). Genetic association, seasonal infections and autoimmune basis of narcolepsy. *Journal of Autoimmunity, 43*, 26–31.

Singh, R., & Ho, S. Y. (2000). Attitudes and attraction: A new test of the attraction, repulsion and similarity-dissimilarity hypotheses. *British Journal of Social Psychology, 39*, 197–211.

Sinha, R., & Jastreboff, A. M. (2013). Stress as a common risk factor for obesity and addiction. *Biological Psychiatry, 73*, 827–835.

Sinson, J. C. (1994). Normalization and community integration of adults with severe mental handicap relocated to group homes. *Journal of Developmental and Physical Disabilities, 6*, 255–270.

Sirridge, M. (2005). Dream bodies and dream pains in Augustine's "De natura et origine animae." *Vivarium, 43*, 213–249.

Sizemore, C. C., & Huber, R. J. (1988). The 22 faces of Eve. *Individual Psychology: Journal of Adlerian Theory, Research, and Practice, 44*, 53–62.

Skinner, B. F. (1945, October). Baby in a box. *Ladies Home Journal*, pp. 30–31.

Skinner, B. F. (1948).*Walden two.* New York: Macmillan.

Skinner, B. F. (1953). *Science and human behavior.* New York: Macmillan.

Skinner, B. F. (1956). A case history in scientific method. *American Psychologist, 11*, 221–233.

Skinner, B. F. (1957). *Verbal behavior.* New York: Appleton-Century-Crofts.

Skinner, B. F. (1960). Pigeons in a pelican. *American Psychologist, 15*, 28–37.

Skinner, B. F. (1974). *About behaviorism.* New York: Knopf.

Skinner, B. F. (1984). The shame of American education. *American Psychologist, 39*, 947–954.

Skinner, B. F. (1986). What is wrong with daily life in the Western world? *American Psychologist, 41*, 220–222.

Skinner, B. F. (1989). Teaching machines. *Science, 243*, 1535.

Skinner, N. F. (1983). Switching answers on multiple-choice questions: Shrewdness or shibboleth? *Teaching of Psychology, 10*, 220–222.

Skinner, N., & Brewer, N. (2002). The dynamics of threat and challenge appraisals prior to stressful achievement events. *Journal of Personality and Social Psychology, 83*, 678–692.

Skoe, E. E. A., Cumberland, A., Eisenberg, N., Hansen, K., & Perry, J. (2002). The influence of sex and gender-role identity on moral cognition and prosocial personality traits. *Sex Roles, 46*, 295–309.

Skoe, E. E. A., Hansen, K. L., Morch, W.-T., Bakke, I., Hoffmann, T., Larsen, B., & Aasheim, M. (1999). Care-based moral reasoning in Norwegian and Canadian early adolescents: A cross-national comparison. *Journal of Early Adolescence, 19*, 280–291.

Skre, I., Onstad, S., Torgersen, S., Lygren, S., & Kringlen, E. (2000). The heritability of common phobic fear: A twin study of a clinical sample. *Journal of Anxiety Disorders, 14*, 549–562.

Slabbekoorn, D., Van Goozen, S. H. M., Gooren, L. J. G., & Cohen-Kettenis, P. T. (2001). Effects of cross-sex hormone treatment on emotionality in transsexuals. *International Journal of Transgenderism, 5*, 2.

Slater, A. (1992). The visual constancies in early infancy. *Irish Journal of Psychology, 13*, 412–425.

Slater, C. L. (2003). Generativity versus stagnation: An elaboration of Erikson's adult stage of human development. *Journal of Adult Development, 10*, 53–65.

Slavik, S., & Croake, J. (2006). Individual psychology perspectives on the phenomenology of depression. *Journal of Individual Psychology, 62*, 429–442.

Slayton, J. M. (1998). Treatment algorithms: Bane or boon to mental health? *Harvard Review of Psychiatry, 6*, 225–227.

Slife, B. D. (2005). The Kant of psychology: Joseph Rychlak and the bridge to postmodern psychology, *Journal of Constructivist Psychology, 18*, 297–306.

Slifer, K. J., Eischen, S. E., & Busby, S. (2002). Using counterconditioning to treat behavioural distress during subcutaneous injections in a paediatric rehabilitation patient. *Brain Injury, 16*, 901–916.

Sliškovic, A., Seršić, D. M., & Burić, I. (2011). Work locus of control as a mediator of the relationship between sources and consequences of occupational stress among university teachers. *Review of Psychology, 18*, 109–118.

Slob, A. K., Steyvers, C. L., Lottman, P. E. M., van der Werfften Bosh, J. J., & Hop, W. C. J. (1998). Routine psychophysiological screening of 384 men with erectile dysfunction. *Journal of Sex and Marital Therapy, 24*, 273–279.

Slutske, W. S., Eisen, S., Xian, H., True, W. R., Lyons, M. J., Goldberg, J., & Tsuang, M. (2001). A twin study of the association between pathological gambling and antisocial personality disorder. *Journal of Abnormal Psychology, 110*, 297–308.

Small, S. L., Buccino, G., & Solodkin, A. (2012). The mirror neuron system and treatment of stroke. *Developmental Psychobiology, 54*, 293–310.

Smith, A. L., & Tart, C. T. (1998). Cosmic consciousness experience and psychedelic experiences: A first-person comparison. *Journal of Consciousness Studies, 5*, 97–107.

Smith, B. D., Cranford, D., & Mann, M. (2000). Gender, cynical hostility, and cardiovascular function: Implications for differential cardiovascular disease risk? *Personality and Individual Differences, 29*, 659–670.

Smith, B. M., Schumaker, J. B., Schaeffer, J., & Sherman, J. A. (1982). Increasing participation and improving the quality of discussion in seventh-grade social studies classes. *Journal of Applied Behavior Analysis, 15*, 97–110.

Smith, C. T., De Houwer, J., & Nosek, B. A. (2013). Consider the source: Persuasion of implicit evaluations is moderated by source credibility. *Personality & Social Psychology Bulletin, 39*, 193–205.

Smith, D. (1982). Trends in counseling and psychotherapy. *American Psychologist, 37*, 802–809.

Smith, D. G., Standing, L., & de Man, A. (1992). Verbal memory elicited by ambient odor. *Perceptual and Motor Skills, 74*, 339–343.

Smith, D. V., & Margolis, F. L. (1999). Taste processing: Whetting our appetites. *Current Biology, 9*, R453–R455.

Smith, G. L., Large, M. M., Kavanagh, D. J., Karayanidis, F., Barrett, N. A., Michie, P. T., & O'Sullivan, B. T. (1998). Further evidence for a deficit in switching attention in schizophrenia. *Journal of Abnormal Psychology, 107*, 390–398.

Smith, H. V. (1992). Is there a magical number 7 ± 2? The role of exposure duration and information content in immediate recall. *Irish Journal of Psychology, 13*, 85–97.

Smith, H. F. (1995). Introduction: Gedo and Freud on working through. *Journal of the American Psychoanalytic Association, 43*, 331–392.

Smith, J. D. (1988). Fancher on Gould, Goddard, and historical interpretation: A reply. *American Psychologist, 43*, 744–745.

Smith, J. L., & White, P. H. (2002). An examination of implicitly activated, explicitly activated, and nullified stereotypes on mathematical performance: It's not just a woman's issue. *Sex Roles, 47,* 179–191.

Smith, J. W., & Frawley, P. J. (1993). Treatment outcome of 600 chemically dependent patients treated in a multimodal inpatient program including aversion therapy and pentothal interviews. *Journal of Substance Abuse Treatment, 10,* 359–369.

Smith, K. K. (2000). Symptom management in the adult headache population. *Dissertation Abstracts International: Section B: The Sciences and Engineering, 60,* 50–52.

Smith, L. D. (2002). On prediction and control: B. F. Skinner and the technological ideal of science. In W. E. Pickren & D. A. Dewsbury (Eds.), *Evolving perspectives on the history of psychology* (pp. 255–272). Washington, DC: American Psychological Association.

Smith, L. T. (1974). The interanimal transfer phenomenon: A review. *Psychological Bulletin, 81,* 1078–1095.

Smith, M. C. (1983). Hypnotic memory enhancement of witnesses: Does it work? *Psychological Bulletin, 94,* 387–407.

Smith, M. C., & Phillips, M. R., Jr. (2001). Age differences in memory for radio advertisements: The role of mnemonics. *Journal of Business Research, 53,* 103–109.

Smith, M. L., Glass, G. V., & Miller, T. I. (1980). *The benefits of psychotherapy.* Baltimore: Johns Hopkins University Press.

Smith, S. M. (1984). A comparison of two techniques for reducing context-dependent forgetting. *Memory and Cognition, 12,* 477–482.

Smith, S. M., Brown, H. O., Toman, J. E. P., & Goodman, J. S. (1947). The lack of cerebral effects of d-tubercurarine. *Anesthesiology, 8,* 1–14.

Smith, S. M., McIntosh, W. D., & Bazzini, D. G. (1999). Are the beautiful good in Hollywood? An investigation of the beauty-and-goodness stereotype on film. *Basic and Applied Social Psychology, 21,* 69–80.

Smith, S. M., & Vela, E. (1992). Environmental context-dependent eyewitness recognition. *Applied Cognitive Psychology, 6,* 125–139.

Smith, S. S., & Richardson, D. (1983). Amelioration of deception and harm in psychological research: The important role of debriefing. *Journal of Personality and Social Psychology, 44,* 1075–1082.

Smith, T., Snyder, C. R., & Perkins, S. C. (1983). The self-serving function of hypochondriacal complaints: Physical symptoms as self-handicapping strategies. *Journal of Personality and Social Psychology, 44,* 787–797.

Smits, M. G., Nagtegaal, E. E., van der Heijden, J., Coenen, A. M. L., & Kerkhof, G. A. (2001). Melatonin for chronic sleep onset insomnia in children: A randomized placebo-controlled trial. *Journal of Child Neurology, 16,* 86–92.

Smolak, L., Murnen, S. K., & Ruble, A. E. (2000). Female athletes and eating problems: A meta-analysis. *International Journal of Eating Disorders, 27,* 371–380.

Snarey, J. R., Reimer, J., & Kohlberg, L. (1985). Development of social-moral reasoning among kibbutz adolescents: A longitudinal cross-cultural study. *Developmental Psychology, 21,* 3–17.

Sneed, J. R., Whitbourne, S. K., Schwartz, S. J., & Huang, S. (2012). The relationship between identity, intimacy, and midlife well-being: Findings from the Rochester Adult Longitudinal Study. *Psychology and Aging, 27,* 318–323.

Snow, C. E. (1981). The uses of imitation. *Journal of Child Language, 8,* 205–212.

Snow, D. S. (2000). The emotional basis of linguistic and nonlinguistic intonation: Implications for hemispheric specialization. *Developmental Neuropsychology, 17,* 1–28.

Snow, W. G., & Sheese, S. (1985). Lateralized brain damage, intelligence, and memory: A failure to find sex differences. *Journal of Consulting and Clinical Psychology, 33,* 940–941.

Snyder, B. K., Roghmann, K. J., & Sigal, L. H. (1993). Stress and psychosocial factors: Effects on primary cellular immune response. *Journal of Behavioral Medicine, 16,* 143–161.

Snyder, J. S., Soumier, A., Brewer, M., Pickel, J., & Cameron, H. A. (2011). Adult hippocampal neurogenesis buffers stress responses and depressivebehaviour. *Nature, 476,* 458–461.

Snyder, M. (1983). The influence of individuals on situations: Implications for understanding the links between personality and social behavior. *Journal of Personality, 51,* 497–516.

Snyder, R. F. (2000). The relationship between learning styles/multiple intelligences and academic achievement of high school students. *High School Journal, 83,* 11–20.

Snyder, S. H. (2002). Forty years of neurotransmitters: A personal account. *Archives of General Psychiatry, 59,* 983–994.

Snyderman, M., & Herrnstein, R. J. (1983). Intelligence tests and the Immigration Act of 1924. *American Psychologist, 38,* 986–995.

Soderstrom, N. C., Davalos, D. B., & Vázquez, S. M. (2011). Metacognition and depressive realism: Evidence for the level-of-depression account. *Cognitive Neuropsychiatry, 16,* 461–472.

Soffer–Dudek, N., & Shahar, G. (2010). Effect of exposure to terrorism on sleep-related experiences in Israeli young adults. *Psychiatry:Interpersonal & Biological Processes, 73,* 264–276.

Sogon, S., & Izard, C. E. (1987). Sex differences in emotion recognition by observing body movements: A case of American students. *Japanese Psychological Research, 29,* 89–93.

Solcova, I., & Sykora, J. (1995). Relation between psychological hardiness and physiological response. *Homeostasis in Health and Disease, 36,* 30–34.

Solomon, C. (2003). Transactional analysis theory: The basics. *Transactional Analysis Journal, 33,* 15–22.

Solomon, P. R., & Morse, D. L. (1981). Teaching the principles of operant conditioning through laboratory experience: The rat Olympics. *Teaching Psychology, 8,* 111–112.

Solomon, R. L. (1980). The opponent-process theory of acquired motivation: The costs of pleasure and the benefits of pain. *American Psychologist, 35,* 691–712.

Solomon, S., & Guglielmo, K. M. (1985). Treatment of headache by transcutaneous electrical stimulation. *Headache, 25,* 12–15.

Solowij, N., Michie, P. T., & Fox, A. M. (1995). Differential impairments of selective attention due to frequency and duration of cannabis use. *Biological Psychiatry, 37,* 731–739.

Sommer, B., Avis, N., Meyer, P., Ory, M., Madden, T, Kagawa-Singer, M., . . . Adler, S. (1999). Attitudes toward menopause and aging across ethnic/racial groups. *Psychosomatic Medicine, 61,* 868–875.

Sommers, S. (1984). Reported emotions and conventions of emotionality among college students. *Journal of Personality and Social Psychology, 46,* 207–215.

Sonino, N., Navarrini, C., Ruini, C., Fallo, F., Boscaro, M., & Fava, G. A. (2004). Life events in the pathogenesis of hyperprolactinemia. *European Journal of Endocrinology, 151,* 61–65.

Sonstroem, R. J., & Bernardo, P. (1982). Intraindividual pregame state anxiety and basketball performance: A re-examination of the inverted-U curve. *Journal of Sport Psychology, 4,* 235–245.

Soumier, A., Banasr, M., Lortet, S., Masmejean, F., Bernard, N., Kerkerian-Le-Goff, L., . . . Daszuta, A. (2009). Mechanisms contributing to the phase-dependent regulation of neurogenesis by the novel antidepressant, agomelatine, in the adult rat hippocampus. *Neuropsychopharmacology, 34,* 2390–2403.

Sourkes, T. L. (2009). Acetylcholine: From vagusstoff to cerebral neurotransmitter. *Journal of the History of the Neurosciences, 18,* 47–58.

Soussignan, R. (2002). Duchenne smile, emotional experience, and autonomic reactivity: A test of the facial feedback hypothesis. *Emotion, 2,* 52–74.

Sowislo, J. F., & Orth, U. (2013). Does low self-esteem predict depression and anxiety? A meta-analysis of longitudinal studies. *Psychological Bulletin, 139,* 213–240.

Spangenberg, E. R., Crowley, A. E., & Henderson, P. W. (1996). Improving the store environment: Do olfactory cues affect evaluations and behaviors? *Journal of Marketing, 60,* 67–80.

Spangenberg, J., & Nel, E. M. (1983). The effect of equal-status contact on ethnic attitudes. *Journal of Social Psychology, 121,* 173–180.

Spangler, W. D. (1992). Validity of questionnaire and TAT measures of need for achievement: Two meta-analyses. *Psychological Bulletin, 112,* 140–154.

Spanos, N. P., & Hewitt, E. C. (1980). The hidden observer in hypnotic analgesia: Discovery or experimental creation? *Journal of Personality and Social Psychology, 49,* 1201–1214.

Spanos, N. P., Burgess, C. A., Burgess, M. F., Samuels, C., & Blois, W. G. (1999). Creating false memories of infancy with hypnotic and nonhypnotic procedures. *Applied Cognitive Psychology, 13,* 201–218.

Spanos, N. P., McNeil, C., & Stam, H. J. (1982). Hypnotically "reliving" a prior burn: Effects on blister formation and localized skin temperature. *Journal of Abnormal Psychology, 91,* 303–305.

Spanos, N., Weekes, J. R., & Bertrand, L. (1985). Multiple personality: A social psychological perspective. *Journal of Abnormal Psychology, 94,* 362–376.

Sparks, G. G., & Pellechia, M. (1997). The effect of news stories about UFOs on readers' UFO beliefs: The role of confirming or disconfirming testimony from a scientist. *Communication Reports, 10,* 165–172.

Sparks, G. G., Pellechia, M., & Irvine, C. (1999). The repressive coping style and fright reactions to mass media. *Communication Research, 26,* 176–192.

Speca, M., Carlson, L. E., Goodey, E., & Angen, M. (2000). A randomized, wait-list controlled clinical trial: The effect of a mindfulness meditation-based stress reduction program on mood and symptoms of stress in cancer outpatients. *Psychosomatic Medicine, 62,* 613–622.

Spector, I. P., & Carey, M. P. (1990). Incidence and prevalence of the sexual dysfunctions: A critical review of the empirical literature. *Archives of Sexual Behavior, 19,* 389–408.

Spector, N. H. (1997). The great Hans Selye and the great "stress" muddle. *Developmental Brain Dysfunction, 10,* 538–542.

Spector, P. E., Sanchez, J. I., Sui, O. L., Salgado, J., & Ma., J. (2004). Eastern versus Western control beliefs at work: An investigation of secondary control, socioinstrumental control, and work locus of control in China and the US. *Applied Psychology, 53,* 38–60.

Speisman, J. C., Lazarus, R. S., Mordkoff, A., & Davison, L. (1964). Experimental reduction of stress based on ego-defense theory. *Journal of Abnormal and Social Psychology, 68,* 367–380.

Spencer, R. C., Klein, R. M., & Berridge, C. W. (2012). Psychostimulants act within the prefrontal cortex to improve cognitive function. *Biological Psychiatry, 72,* 221–227

Spengler, F., Godde, B., & Dinse, H. R. (1995). Effects of ageing on topographic organization of somatosensory cortex. *Neuroreport: An International Journal for the Rapid Communication of Research in Neuroscience, 6,* 469–473.

Sperling, G. (1960). The information available in brief visual presentations. *Psychological Monographs, 74* (498).

Sperry, R. W. (1982). Some effects of disconnecting the cerebral hemispheres. *Science, 217,* 1223–1226.

Sperry, R. W. (1984). Consciousness, personal identity, and the divided brain. *Neuropsychologia, 22,* 661–673.

Spicer, R. S., & Miller, T. R. (2000). Suicide acts in 8 states: Incidence and case fatality rates by demographics and method. *American Journal of Public Health, 90,* 1885–1891.

Spiegel, A. D., & Suskind, P. B. (1998). Chloroform-induced insanity defense confounds lawyer Lincoln. *History of Psychiatry, 8,* 487–500.

Spierings, E. L. H. (2003). Pathogenesis of the migraine attack. *Clinical Journal of Pain, 19,* 255–262.

Spillmann, J., & Spillmann, L. (1993). The rise and fall of Hugo Münsterberg. *Journal of the History of the Behavioral Sciences, 29,* 322–338.

Spinella, M., Znamensky, V., Moroz, M., Ragnauth, A., & Bodnar, R. J. (1999). Actions of NMDA and cholinergic receptor antagonists in the rostral ventromedial medulla upon beta-endorphin analgesia elicited from the ventrolateral periaqueductal gray. *Brain Research, 829,* 151–159.

Spitzer, R. L. (1975). On pseudoscience in science, logic in remission, and psychiatric diagnosis: A critique of Rosenhan's "On being sane in insane places." *Journal of Abnormal Psychology, 84,* 442–452.

Spotts, E. L., Lichtenstein, P., Pedersen, N., Neiderhiser, J. M., Hansson, K., Cederblad, M., & Reiss, D. (2005). Personality and marital satisfaction: A behavioural genetic analysis. *European Journal of Personality, 19,* 205–227.

Sprecher, S., & Toro-Morn, M. (2002). A study of men and women from different sides of earth to determine if men are from Mars and women are from Venus in their beliefs about love and romantic relationships. *Sex Roles, 46,* 131–147.

Springer, S. P., & Deutsch, G. (1998). *Left brain, right brain* (5th ed.). New York: Freeman.

Sprock, J. (2000). Gender-typed behavioral examples of histrionic personality disorder. *Journal of Psychopathology and Behavioral Assessment, 22,* 107–122.

Spurr, J. M., & Stopa, L. (2003). The observer perspective: Effects on social anxiety and performance. *Behaviour Research and Therapy, 41,* 1009–1028.

Spyer, K. M. (1989). Neural mechanisms involved in cardiovascular control during affective behavior. *Trends in Neurosciences, 12,* 506–513.

Squire, L. R. (1992). Declarative and nondeclarative memory: Multiple brain systems supporting learning and memory. *Journal of Cognitive Neuroscience, 4,* 232–243.

Srivastava, S., & Sharma, M. (1998). Seasonal affective disorder: Report from India (latitude 26" 45' N). *Journal of Affective Disorders, 49,* 145–150.

Staats, A. W. (1994). Psychological behaviorism and behaviorizing psychology. *Behavior Analyst 17,* 93–114.

Stack, S. (1998). Gender, marriage, and suicide acceptability: A comparative analysis. *Sex Roles, 38,* 501–520.

Stack, S., & Eshleman, J. R. (1998). Marital status and happiness: A 17-nation study. *Journal of Marriage and the Family, 60,* 527–536.

Stafford, J., & Lynn, S. J. (2002). Cultural scripts, memories of childhood abuse, and multiple identities: A study of role-played enactments. *International Journal of Clinical and Experimental Hypnosis, 50,* 67–85.

Stafford-Clark, D. (1965). *What Freud really said.* New York: Schocken Books.

Stairs, A. (1992). Self-image, world-image: Speculations on identity from experiences with Inuit. *Ethos, 20,* 116–126.

Stajkovic, A. D., & Luthans, F. (1998). Self-efficacy and work-related performance: A meta-analysis. *Psychological Bulletin, 124,* 240–261.

Stamps, J. J., Bartoshuck, L. M., & Heilman, K. M. (2013). A brief olfactory test for Alzheimer's disease. *Journal of the Neurological Sciences, 333,* 19–24.

Stankov, L., & Roberts, R. D. (1997) Mental speed is not the "basic" process of intelligence. *Personality and Individual Differences, 22,* 69–84.

Stanley C. Krippner: Award for Distinguished Contributions to the International Advancement of Psychology. (2003). *American Psychologist, 57,* 960–962.

Stapleton, J. A., Russell, M.A.H., Feyerabend, C., & Wiseman, S. M.(1995). Dose effects and predictors of outcome in a randomized trial of transdermal nicotine patches in general practice. *Addiction, 90,* 31–42.

Stapleton, K., & Hargie, O. (2011). Double-bind accountability dilemmas: Impression management and accountability strategies used by senior banking executives. *Journal of Language & Social Psychology, 30,* 266–289.

Stark, E. (1981, September). Pigeon patrol. *Science, 81,* pp. 85–86.

Stark, E., Drori, R., Asher, I., Ben-Shaul, Y., & Abeles, M. (2007). Distinct movement parameters are represented by different neurons in the motor cortex. *European Journal of Neuroscience, 26,* 1055–1066.

Stark-Wroblewski, K., Wiggins. T. L., & Ryan, J. J. (2006). Assessing student interest and familiarity with professional psychology specialty areas. *Journal of Instructional Psychology, 33,* 273–277.

Stathopoulou, A., Beratis, I. N., & Beratis, S. (2013). Prenatal tobacco smoke exposure, risk of schizophrenia, and severity of positive/negative symptoms. *Schizophrenia Research, 148,* 105–106.

Steel, P., & Ones, D. S. (2002). Personality and happiness: A national-level analysis. *Journal of Personality and Social Psychology, 83,* 767–781.

Steele, C. M., & Aronson, J. (1995). Stereotype threat and the intellectual test performance of African Americans. *Journal of Personality and Social Psychology, 69,* 797–811.

Steele, C. M., & Aronson, J. A. (2004). Stereotype threat does not live by Steele and Aronson (1995) alone. *American Psychologist, 59,* 47–48.

Steele, C. M., & Josephs, R. A. (1990). Alcohol myopia: Its prized and dangerous effects. *American Psychologist, 45,* 921–933.

Steele, R. J., Stewart, M. G., & Rose, S. P. R. (1995). Increases in NMDA receptor binding are specifically related to memory formation for a passive avoidance task in the chick: A quantitative autoradiographic study. *Brain Research, 674,* 352–356.

Steeves, R., Kahn, D., Ropka, M. E., & Wise, C. (2001). Ethical considerations in research with bereaved families. *Family and Community Health, 23,* 75–83.

Steffen, P. R., Sherwood, A., Gullette, E. C. D., Georgiades, A., Hinderliter, A., & Blumenthal, J. A. (2001). Effects of exercise and weight loss on blood pressure during daily life. *Medicine and Science in Sports and Exercise, 33,* 1635–1640.

Steiger, H., Gauvin, L., Jabalpurwala, S., Séguin, J. R., & Stotland, S. (1999). Hypersensitivity to social interactions in bulimic syndromes. Relationship to binge eating. *Journal of Consulting and Clinical Psychology, 67,* 765–775

Stein, D. M., & Lambert, M. J. (1995). Graduate training in psychotherapy: Are therapy outcomes enhanced? *Journal of Consulting and Clinical Psychology, 63,* 182–196.

Stein, M. B., Chavira, D. A., & Jang, K. L. (2001). Bringing up bashful baby: Developmental pathways to social phobia. *Psychiatric Clinics of North America, 24,* 661–675.

Stein, M. B., Jang, K. L., & Livesley, W. J. (1999). Heritability of anxiety sensitivity: A twin study. *American Journal of Psychiatry, 156,* 246–251.

Stein, M. B., Jang, K. L., & Livesley, W. J. (2002). Heritability of social anxiety-related concerns and personality characteristics: A twin study. *Journal of Nervous and Mental Disease, 19,* 219–224.

Steiner, S. S., & Dince, W. M. (1981). Biofeedback efficacy studies: A critique of critiques. *Biofeedback and Self-Regulation, 6,* 275–288.

Steinkamp, F. (2000). Acting on the future: A survey of precognitive experiences. *Journal of the American Society for Psychical Research, 94,* 37–59.

Steinkamp, F., Milton, J., & Morris, R. L. (1998). A meta-analysis of forced-choice experiments comparing clairvoyance and precognition. *Journal of Parapsychology, 62,* 193–218.

Stelmack, R. M. (1990). Biological bases of extraversion: Psychophysiological evidence. *Journal of Personality, 58,* 293–311.

Stelmack, R. M., & Stalikas, A. (1991). Galen and the humour theory of temperament. *Personality and Individual Differences, 12,* 255–263.

Stemmer, N. (1990). Skinner's verbal behavior, Chomsky's review, and mentalism. *Journal of the Experimental Analysis of Behavior, 54,* 307–315.

Stephan, K. E., Marshall, J. C., Friston, K. J., Rowe, J. B., Ritzl, A., Zilles, K., & Fink, G. R. (2003). Lateralized cognitive processes and lateralized task control in the human brain. *Science, 301,* 384–386.

Stephan, W. G., Stephan, C. W., & de Vargas, M. C. (1996). Emotional expression in Costa Rica and the United States. *Journal of Cross-Cultural Psychology 27,* 147–160.

Stephan, W. G., Ybarra, O., & Bachman, G. (1999). Prejudice toward immigrants. *Journal of Applied Social Psychology, 29,* 2221–2237.

Stephan, W. G., Ybarra, O., Martinez, C. M., Schwarzwald, J., & Tur-Kaspa, M. (1998). Prejudice toward immigrants to Spain and Israel: An integrated threat theory analysis. *Journal of Cross-Cultural Psychology, 29,* 559–576.

Stephan, Y., & Maiano, C. (2007). On the social nature of global self-esteem: A replication study. *Journal of Social Psychology, 147,* 573–575.

Steptoe, A., Moses, J., Edwards, S., & Mathews, A. (1993). Exercise and responsivity to mental stress: Discrepancies between the subjective and physiological effects of aerobic training. *International Journal of Sport Psychology, 24,* 110–129.

Sterling, R. C. (2002). Researching the treatment of drinking problems: A call for external as well as internal validity. *Addiction, 97,* 294–295.

Sternberg, R. J. (1986). A triangular theory of love. *Psychological Review, 93,* 119–135.

Sternberg, R. J. (1996). The sound of silence: A nation responds to its gifted. *Roeper Review, 18,* 168–172.

Sternberg, R. J. (1999). A triarchic approach to the understanding and assessment of intelligence in multicultural populations. *Journal of School Psychology, 37,* 145–159.

Sternberg, R. J. (2000). Patterns of giftedness: A triarchic analysis. *Roeper Review, 22,* 231–235.

Sternberg, R. J. (2003). A broad view of intelligence: The theory of successful intelligence. *Consulting Psychology Journal: Practice and Research, 55,*139–154.

Sternberg, R. J., & Clinkenbeard, P. B. (1995). The triarchic model applied to identifying, teaching, and assessing gifted children. *Roeper Review, 17,* 231–235.

Sternberg, R. J., & Wagner, R. K. (1993). The geocentric view of intelligence and job performance is wrong. *Current Directions in Psychological Science, 2,* 1–5.

Sternberg, R. J., Castejon, J. L., Prieto, M. D., Hautamaeki, J., & Grigorenko, E. L. (2001). Confirmatory factor analysis of the Sternberg Triarchic Abilities Test in three international samples: An empirical test of the triarchic theory of intelligence. *European Journal of Psychological Assessment, 17,* 1–16.

Sternberg, R. J., Conway, B. E., Ketron, J. L., & Bernstein, M. (1981). People's conceptions of intelligence. *Journal of Personality and Social Psychology, 41,* 37–55.

Sternberg, R. J., Torff, B., & Grigorenko, E. L. (1998). Teaching triarchically improves school achievement. *Journal of Educational Psychology, 90,* 374–384.

Sterrenberg, P., & Thunnissen, M. M. (1995). Transactional analysis as a cognitive treatment for borderline personality disorder. *Transactional Analysis Journal, 25,* 221–227.

Stessman, J., Maaravi, Y., Hammerman-Rozenberg, R, & Cohen, A. (2000). The effects of physical activity on mortality in the Jerusalem 70-year-olds longitudinal study. *Journal of the American Geriatrics Society, 48,* 499–504.

Stevens, P. (1998-99). Remote psychokinesis. *European Journal of Parapsychology, 14,* 68–79.

Steward, O., & Worley, P. (2002). Local synthesis of proteins at synaptic sites on dendrites: Role in synaptic plasticity and memory consolidation? *Neurobiology of Learning & Memory, 78,* 508–527.

Stewart, J. W., Garfinkel, R., Nunes, E. V., Donovan, S., & Klein, D. F. (1998). Atypical features and treatment response in the National Institute of Mental Health Treatment of Depression Collaborative Research Program. *Journal of Clinical Psychopharmacology, 18,* 429–434.

Stewart, M. G., Lowndes, M. Hunter, A., & Doubell, T. (1992). Memory storage in chicks involves an increase in dendritic spine number and synaptic density. *Brain Dysfunction, 5,* 50–64.

Stewart, T. L., LaDuke, J. R., Bracht, C., Sweet, B. A. M., & Gamarel, K. E. (2003). Do the "eyes" have it? A program evaluation of Jane Elliott's "blue-eyes/brown-eyes" diversity training exercise. *Journal of Applied Social Psychology, 33,* 1898–1921.

Still, A., & Dryden, W. (2003). Elli sand Epictetus: Dialogue vs. method in psychotherapy. *Journal of Rational-Emotive and Cognitive Behavior Therapy, 21,* 37–55.

Stinson, D. A., Logel, C., Shepherd, S., & Zanna, M. P. (2011). Rewriting the self-fulfilling prophecy of social rejection: Self-affirmation improves relational security and social behavior up to 2 months later. *Psychological Science, 22,* 1145–1149.

Stoiber, K. C., & Waas, G. A. (2002). A contextual and methodological perspective on the evidence-based movement within school psychology in the United States. *Educational and Child Psychology, 19,* 7–21.

Stolerman, I. P., & Jarvis, M. J. (1995). The scientific case that nicotine is addictive. *Psychopharmacology, 117,* 2–10.

Stone, A. A., Bovberg, D. H., Neale, J. M., & Napoli, A. (2002). Development of common cold symptoms following experimental rhinovirus infection is related to prior stressful life events. *Behavioral Medicine, 18,* 115–120.

Stone, A. A., & Brownell, K. D. (1994). The stress-eating paradox: Multiple daily measurements in adult males and females. *Psychology and Health, 9,* 425–436.

Stone, A. A., Hedges, S. M., Neale, J. M., & Satin, M. S. (1985). Prospective and cross-sectional mood reports offer no evidence of a "blue Monday" phenomenon. *Journal of Personality and Social Psychology, 49,* 129–134.

Stone, A. A., Schneider, S., & Harter, J. K. (2012). Day-of-week mood patterns in the United States: On the existence of "Blue Monday," "Thank God It's Friday," and weekend effects. *Journal of Positive Psychology, 7,* 306–314.

Stone, A. A., Smyth, J. M., Kaell, A., & Hurewitz, A. (2000). Structured writing about stressful events: Exploring potential psychological mediators of positive health effects. *Health Psychology, 19,* 619–624.

Stone, M. H. (2012). Disorder in the domain of personality disorders. *Psychodynamic Psychiatry, 40,* 23–46.

Stoner, J. A. F. (1961). *A comparison of individual and group decisions involving risk.* Unpublished master's thesis, Massachusetts Institute of Technology, Cambridge.

Storck, L. E. (1997). Cultural psychotherapy: A consideration of psychosocial class and cultural differences in group treatment. *Group, 21,* 331–349.

Storey, A. E., Walsh, C. J., Quintin, R. L., & Wynne-Edwards, K. E. (2000). Hormonal correlates of paternal responsiveness in new and expectant fathers. *Evolution and Human Behavior, 21,* 79–95.

Storm, L., Tressoldi, P. E., & DiRisio, L. (2010). Meta-analysis of free-response studies, 1992–2008: Assessing the noise reduction model in parapsychology. *Psychological Bulletin, 136,* 471–485.

Storms, M. D. (1981). A theory of erotic orientation development. *Psychological Review, 88,* 340–353.

Strack, F., Schwarz, N., Chassein, B., & Kern, D. (1990). Salience of comparison standards and the activation of social norms: Consequences for judgements of happiness and their communication. *British Journal of Social Psychology, 29,* 303–314.

Straneva, P. A., Maixner, W., Light, K. C., Pedersen, C. A., Costello, N. L., & Girdler, S. S. (2002). Menstrual cycle, beta-endorphins, and pain sensitivity in premenstrual dysphoric disorder. *Health Psychology, 21,* 358–367.

Strang, J., McCambridge, J., Best, D., Beswick, T., Bearn, J., Rees, S., & Gossop, M. (2003). Loss of tolerance and overdose mortality after inpatient opiate detoxification: Follow up study. *BMJ: British Medical Journal, 326,* 959–960.

Strassman, R. J. (1984). Adverse reactions to psychedelic drugs: A review of the literature. *Journal of Nervous and Mental Disease, 172,* 577–595.

Strauman, T. J., & Higgins, E. T. (1988). Self-discrepancies as predictors of vulnerability to distinct syndromes of chronic emotional distress. *Journal of Personality, 56,* 685–707.

Strauman, T. J., & Higgins, E. T. (1988). Self-discrepancies as predictors of vulnerability to distinct syndromes of chronic emotional distress. *Journal of Personality, 56,* 246–253.

Straus, M. A. (1991). Discipline and deviance: Physical punishment of children and violence and other crime in adulthood. *Social Problems, 38,* 133–154.

Straus, M. A., & Kantor, G. K. (1994). Corporal punishment of adolescents by parents: A risk factor in the epidemiology of depression, suicide, alcohol abuse, child abuse, and wife beating. *Adolescence, 29,* 543–561.

Strayer, D. L., & Kramer, A. F. (1990). Attentional requirements of automatic and controlled processing. *Journal of Experimental Psychology: Learning, Memory, and Cognition, 16,* 67–82.

Strecher, V. J., Seijts, G. H., Kok, G. J., & Latham, G. P. (1995). Goal setting as a strategy for health behavior change. *Health Education Quarterly, 22,* 190–200.

Streitmatter, J. (1993). Gender differences in identity development: An examination of longitudinal data. *Adolescence, 28,* 55–66.

Stricker, E. M., & McCann, M. J. (1985). Visceral factors in the control of food intake. *Brain Research Bulletin, 14,* 687–692.

Stricker, E. M., & Verbalis, J. G. (1987). Biological bases of hunger and satiety. *Annals of Behavioral Medicine, 9,* 3–8.

Strickland, B. R. (1989). Internal-external control expectancies: From contingency to creativity. *American Psychologist, 44,* 1–12.

Striegel-Moore, R. H., Silberstein, L. R., & Rodin, J. (1986). Toward an understanding of risk factors in bulimia. *American Psychologist, 41,* 246–263.

Stroebe, M. S. (1994). The broken heart phenomenon: An examination of the mortality of bereavement. *Journal of Community and Applied Social Psychology, 4,* 47–61.

Stroebe, W., Stroebe, M. S., & Abakoumkin, G. (1999). Does differential social support cause sex differences in bereavement outcome? *Journal of Community and Applied Social Psychology, 9,* 1–12.

Struch, N., Schwartz, S. H., & van der Kloot, W. A. (2002). Meanings of basic values for women and men: A cross-cultural analysis. *Personality and Social Psychology Bulletin, 28,* 16–28.

Stuart, G. L., Treat, T. A., & Wade, W. A. (2000). Effectiveness of an empirically based treatment for panic disorder delivered in a service clinic setting: 1 year follow-up. *Journal of Consulting and Clinical Psychology, 68,* 506–512.

Stumbrys, T., & Daniels, M. (2010). An exploratory study of creative problem-solving in lucid dreams: Preliminary findings and methodological considerations. *International Journal of Dream Research, 3,* 121–129.

Stunkard, A. J., Stinnett, J. L., & Smoller, J. W. (1986). Psychological and social aspects of the surgical treatment of obesity. *American Journal of Psychiatry, 143,* 417–429.

Sturgeon, R. S., Cooper, L. M., & Howell, R. J. (1989). Pupil response: A psychophysiological measure of fear during analogue desensitization. *Perceptual and Motor Skills, 69,* 1351–1367.

Stuss, D. T., Gow, C. A., & Hetherington, C. R. (1992). "No longer Gage": Frontal lobe dysfunction and emotional changes. *Journal of Consulting and Clinical Psychology, 60,* 349–359.

Suarez, E., Kuhn, C. M., Schanberg, S. M., Williams, R B., Jr., & Zimmermann, E. A. (1998). Neuroendocrine, cardiovascular, and emotional responses of hostile men: The role of interpersonal challenge. *Psychosomatic Medicine, 60,* 78–88.

Subandi, M. A. (2011). Family expressed emotion in a Javanese cultural context. *Culture, Medicine, & Psychiatry, 35,* 331–346.

Subotnik, R F., Karp, D. E., & Morgan, E. R. (1989). High IQ children at midlife: An investigation into the generalizability of Terman's genetic studies of genius. *Roeper Review, 11,* 139–144.

Sucala, M., Schnur, J. B., Constantino, M. J., Miller, S. J., Brackman, E. H., & Montgomery, G. H., (2012). The therapeutic relationship in e-therapy for mental health: A systematic review. *Journal of Medical Internet Research, 14,* 175–187.

Sue, S. (1998). In search of cultural competence in psychotherapy and counseling. *American Psychologist, 53,* 440–448.

Sue, S. (1999). Science, ethnicity, and bias: Where have we gone wrong? *American Psychologist, 54,* 1070–1077.

Sue, S. (2003). In defense of cultural competency in psychotherapy and treatment. *American Psychologist, 58,* 964–970.

Sue, S., Fujino, D., Hu, L., Takeuchi, D., & Zane, N. (1991). Community mental health services for ethnic minority groups: A test of the cultural responsiveness hypothesis. *Journal of Clinical and Consulting Psychology, 59,* 533–540.

Sue, S., & Okazaki, S. (1990). Asian-American educational achievements: A phenomenon in search of an explanation. *American Psychologist, 45,* 913–920.

Suedfeld, P. (1990). Restricted environmental stimulation and smoking cessation: A 15-year progress report. *International Journal of the Addictions, 25,* 861–888.

Suedfeld, P., & Bruno, T. (1990). Flotation REST and imagery in the improvement of athletic performance. *Journal of Exercise and Exercise Psychology, 12,* 82–85.

Suedfeld, P., & Coren, S. (1989). Perceptual isolation, sensory deprivation, and REST: Moving introductory psychology texts out of the 1950s. *Canadian Psychology, 30,* 17–29.

Suedfeld, P., & Steel, G. D. (2000). The environmental psychology of capsule habitats. *Annual Review of Psychology, 51,* 227–253.

Sufka, K. J., & Price, D. D. (2002). Gate control theory reconsidered. *Brain and Mind, 3,* 277–290.

Suh, E., Diener, E., & Fujita, F. (1996). Events and subjective well-being: Only recent events matter. *Journal of Personality and Social Psychology, 70,* 1091–1102.

Sullins, E. S., Hernandez, D., Fuller, C., & Tashiro, J. S. (1995). Predicting who will major in a science discipline: Expectancy-value theory as part of an ecological model for studying academic communities. *Journal of Research in Science Teaching, 32,* 99–119.

Sullivan, H. S. (1953). *An interpersonal theory of psychiatry.* New York: W. W. Norton.

Sullivan, J. E., & Chang, P. (1999). Review: Emotional and behavioral functioning in phenylketonuria. *Journal of Pediatric Psychology, 24,* 281–299.

Sullivan, P. F., Kendler, K. S., & Neale, M. C. (2003). Schizophrenia as a complex trait: Evidence from a meta-analysis of twin studies. *Archives of General Psychiatry, 60,* 1187–1192.

Suls, J., Krantz, D. S., & Williams, G. C. (2013). Three strategies for bridging different levels of analysis and embracing the biopsychosocial model. *Health Psychology, 32,* 597–601.

Sumerlin, J. R., & Bundrick, C. M. (1996). Brief index of self-actualization: A measure of Maslow's model. *Journal of Social Behavior and Personality, 11,* 253–271.

Superkids? A sperm bank for Nobelists. (1980, March 10). *Time,* p. 49.

Sussan, T. A. (1990). How to handle the process litigation effectively under the Education for All Handicapped Children Act of 1975. *Journal of Reading, Writing, and Learning Disabilities International, 6,* 63–70.

Sussman, S. (1998). The first asylums in Canada: A response to neglectful community care and current trends. *Canadian Journal of Psychiatry, 43,* 260–264.

Swann, W. B., Jr., Hixon, J. G., & De La Ronde, C. (1992). Embracing the bitter "truth": Negative self-concepts and marital commitment. *Psychological Science, 3,* 118–121.

Swanson, J., Baler, R. D., & Volkow, N. D. (2011). Understanding the effects of stimulant medications on cognition in individuals with attention-deficit hyperactivity disorder: a decade of progress. *Neuropsychopharmacology, 36,* 207–26.

Swartz, S. (2013). Feminism and psychiatric diagnosis: Reflections of a feminist practitioner. *Feminism & Psychology, 23,* 41–48.

Swayze, V. W. (1995). Frontal leucotomy and related psychosurgical procedures in the era before antipsychotics (1935–1954): A historical overview. *American Journal of Psychiatry, 152,* 505–515.

Sweat, J. A., & Durm, M. W. (1993). Psychics: Do police departments really use them? *Skeptical Inquirer, 17,* 148–158.

Sweeney, P. D., Anderson, K., & Bailey, S. (1986). Attributional style in depression: A meta-analytic review. *Journal of Personality and Social Psychology, 50,* 974–991.

Swenson, C. R. (1994). Freud's "Anna O.": Social work's Bertha Pappenheim. *Clinical Social Work Journal, 22,* 149–163.

Swenson, R. S., Danielsen, E. H., Klausen, B. S., & Erlich, E. (1989). Deficits in beam walking after neonatal motor cortical lesions are not spared by fetal cortical transplants in rats. *Journal of Neural Transplantation, 1,* 129–133.

Swiatek, M. A. (1993). A decade of longitudinal research on academic acceleration through the study of mathematically precocious youth. *Roeper Review, 15,* 120–124.

Swiatek, M. A., & Lupkowski-Shoplik, A. (2003). Elementary and middle school student participation in gifted programs: Are gifted students underserved? *Gifted Child Quarterly, 47,* 118–130.

Swickert, R. J., Rosentreter, C. J., Hittner, J. B., & Mushrush, J. E. (2002). Extraversion, social support processes, and stress. *Personality and Individual Differences, 32,* 877–891.

Swiezy, N. B., Matson, J. L., & Box, P. (1992). The Good Behavior Game: A token reinforcement system for preschoolers. *Child and Family Behavior Therapy, 14,* 21–32.

Swihart, G., Yuille, J., & Porter, S. (1999). The role of state-dependent memory in "red-outs." *International Journal of Law and Psychiatry, 22,* 199–212.

Swindale, N. V. (1982). The development of columnar systems in the mammalian visual cortex: The role of innate and environmental factors. *Trends in Neurosciences, 5,* 235–241.

Swindale, N. V. (2000). How many maps are there in visual cortex? *Cerebral Cortex, 10,* 633–643.

Szabo, A. (2003). The acute effects of humor and exercise on mood and anxiety. *Journal of Leisure Research, 35,* 152–162.

Szasz, T. (1960). The myth of mental illness. *American Psychologist, 15,* 113–118.

Szasz, T. (1980). "J'Accuse": Psychiatry and the diminished American capacity for justice. *Journal of Mind and Behavior, 1,* 111–120.

T

Taal, E., Rasker, J. J., Seydel, E. R., & Wiegman, O. (1993). Health status, adherence with health recommendations, self-efficacy and social support in patients with rheumatoid arthritis. *Patient Education and Counseling, 20,* 63–76.

Tafarodi, R. W., & Walters, P. (1999). Individualism-collectivism, life events, and self-esteem: A test of two trade-offs. *European Journal of Social Psychology, 29,* 797–814.

Taits, I. (2011). Learning lucid dreaming and its effect on depression in undergraduates. *International Journal of Dream Research, 4,* 117–126.

Tajfel, H. (1981). *Human groups and social categories: Studies in social psychology.* London: Cambridge University Press.

Tajfel, H., & Billig, M. (1974). Familarity and categorization in intergroup behavior. *Journal of Experimental Social Psychology, 10,* 159–170.

Takagi, M., Toda, H., Yoshizawa, T., & Hara, N. (1992). Ocular convergence-related neuronal responses in the lateral suprasylvian area of alert cats. *Neuroscience Research, 15,* 229–234.

Takahata, Y., Hasegawa, T., & Nishida, T. (1984). Chimpanzee predation in the Mahale Mountains from August 1979 to May 1982. *International Journal of Primatology, 5,* 213–233.

Takano, K., & Tanno, Y. (2011). Diurnal variation in rumination. *Emotion, 11,* 1046–1058.

Takei, N., Mortensen, P. B., Klaening, U., & Murray, R. M. (1996). Relationship between in utero exposure to influenza epidemics and risk of schizophrenia in Denmark. *Biological Psychiatry, 40,* 817–824.

Takei, Y., Kumano, S., Hattori, S., Uehara, T., Kawakubo, Y., Kasai, K., Fukuda, M., & Mikuni, M. (2009). Preattentive dysfunction in major depression: A magnetoencephalography study using auditory mismatch negativity. *Psychophysiology, 46,* 52–61.

Takeuchi, D. T., Sue, S., & Yeh, M. (1995). Return rates and outcomes from ethnicity-specific mental health programs. *American Journal of Public Health, 85,* 638–643.

Takeuchi, M. S., Miyaoka, H., Tomoda, A., Suzuki, M., Liu, Q., & Kitamura, T. (2010). The effect of interpersonal touch during childhood on adult attachment and depression: A neglected area of family and developmental psychology? *Journal of Child and Family Studies, 19,* 109–117.

Talarczyk, M. (2011). The authorial model of the therapy used in night terrors and sleep disorders in children. *Archives of Psychiatry & Psychotherapy, 13,* 45–51.

Talarico, J. M., & Rubin, D. C. (2003). Confidence, not consistency, characterizes flashbulb memories. *Psychological Science, 14,* 455–461.

Taleb, M., Rouillon, F., Petitjean, F., & Gorwood, P. (1996). Cross-cultural study of schizophrenia. *Psychopathology, 29,* 85–94.

Taller, A. M., Asher, D. M., Pomeroy, K. L., & Eldadah, B. A. (1996). Search for viral nucleic acid sequences in brain tissues of patients with schizophrenia using nested polymerase chain reaction. *Archives of General Psychiatry, 53,* 32–40.

Tam, W.-C. C., & Sewell, K. W. (1995). Seasonality of birth in schizophrenia in Taiwan. *Schizophrenia Bulletin, 21,* 117–127.

Tammings, C. A. (1997). Gender and schizophrenia. *Journal of Clinical Psychiatry, 58,* 33–37.

Tamres, L. K., Janicki, D., & Helgeson, V. S. (2002). Sex differences in coping behavior: A meta-analytic review and examination of relative coping. *Personality and Social Psychology Review, 6,* 2–30.

Tan, G., Jensen, M. P., Robinson-Whelen, S., Thornby, J. I., Monga, T., Taylor, W. R., & Vaney, D. I. (2003). New directions in retinal research. *Trends in Neurosciences, 26,* 379–385.

Tang, S. H., & Hall, V. C. (1995). The overjustification effect: A meta-analysis. *Applied Cognitive Psychology, 9,* 365–404.

Tankard, J. W. (1984). *The statistical pioneers.* Cambridge, MA: Schenkman.

Tardieu, D., & McAdams, S. (2012). Perceptions of dyads of impulsive and sustained instrument sounds. *Music Perception, 30,* 117–128.

Tarricone, B. J., Simon, J. R., Li, Y. J., & Low, W. C. (1996). Neural grafting of cholinergic neurons in the hippocampal formation. *Behavioural Brain Research, 74,* 25–44.

Tateyama, M., Asai, M., Kamisada, M., & Hashimoto, M. (1993). Comparison of schizophrenic delusions between Japan and Germany. *Psychopathology, 26,* 151–158.

Taubes, G. (1998). As obesity rates rise, experts struggle to explain why. *Science, 280,* 1367–1370.

Tauer, C. A. (1994). The NIH trials of growth hormone for short stature. *IRB: A Review of Human Subjects Research, 16,* 1–9.

Taulbee, P. (1983). Solving the mystery of anxiety. *Science News, 124,* 45.

Taylor, B. A., Levin, L., & Jasper, S. (1999). Increasing play-related statement in children with autism toward their siblings: Effects of video modeling. *Journal of Development and Physical Disabilities, 11,* 253–264.

Taylor, C. R., & Stern, B. B. (1997). Asian-Americans: Television advertising and the "model minority" stereotype. *Journal of Advertising, 26,* 47–61.

Taylor, D. J., & Roane, B. M. (2010). Treatment of insomnia in adults and children: A practice-friendly review of research. *Journal of Clinical Psychology, 66,* 1137–1147.

Taylor, J., Iacono, W. G., & McGue, M. (2000). Evidence for a genetic etiology of early-onset delinquency. *Journal of Abnormal Psychology, 109,* 634–643.

Taylor, R. L. (1990). The *Larry P.* decision a decade later: Problems and future directions. *Mental Retardation, 28,* iii–vi.

Taylor, S., & Wald, J. (2003). Expectations and attributions in social anxiety disorder: Diagnostic distinctions and relationship to general anxiety and depression. *Cognitive Behaviour Therapy, 32,* 166–178.

Taylor, S., & Goritsas, E. (1994). Dimensions of identity diffusion. *Journal of Personality Disorders, 8,* 229–239.

Taylor, S. A., & Mudford, O. C. (2012). Improving behavior in a residential service for youth in drug and alcohol rehabilitation. *Behavioral Intervention, 27,* 109–128.

Taylor, S. E., & Brown, J. D. (1988). Illusion and well-being: A social psychological perspective on mental health. *Psychological Bulletin, 103,* 193–210.

Taylor, S. E., Klein, L. C., Lewis, B. P., Gruenewald, T. L., Gurung, R. A. R., & Upegraff, J. A. (2000). Biobehavioral responses to stress in females: Tend-and-befriend, not fight-or-flight. *Psychological Review, 107,* 411–429.

Taylor, S. E., Lerner, J. S., Sherman, D. K., Sage, R. M., & McDowell, N. K. (2003). Are self-enhancing cognitions associated with healthy or unhealthy biological profiles? *Journal of Personality and Social Psychology, 85,* 605–615.

Taylor, S. E., Saphire-Bernstein, S., & Seeman, T. E. (2010). Are plasma oxytocin in women and plasma vasopressin in men biomarkers of distressed pair-bond relationships? *Psychological Science, 21,* 3–7.

Teasdale, N., Forget, R., Bard, C., & Paillard, J. (1993). The role of proprioceptive information for the production of isometric forces and for handwriting tasks. *Acta Psychologica, 82,* 179–191.

Tebartz van Elst, L., Hesslinger, B., Thiel, T., Geiger, E., Haegele, K., Lemieux, L., . . . Ebert, D. (2003). Frontolimbic abnormalities in patients with borderline personality disorder: A volumetric magnetic resonance imaging study. *Biological Psychiatry, 54,* 163–171.

Tehrani, J. A., Brennan, P. A., Hodgins, S., & Mednick, S. A. (1998). Mental illness and criminal violence. *Social Psychiatry and Psychiatric Epidemiology, 33* (Suppl. 1), S81–S85.

Teichman, Y., & Teichman, M. (1990). Interpersonal view of depression: Review and integration. *Journal of Family Psychology, 3,* 349–367.

Teigen, K. H. (1984). A note on the origin of the term "nature and nurture": Not Shakespeare and Galton, but Mulcaster. *Journal of the History of the Behavioral Sciences, 20,* 363–364.

Teigen, K. H. (1994). Yerkes-Dodson: A law for all seasons. *Theory and Psychology, 4,* 525–547.

Teipel, S. J., Bayer, W., Alexander, G. E., Bokde, A. L. W., Zebuhr, Y., Teichberg, D., . . . Hampel, H. (2003). Regional pattern of hippocampus and corpus callosum atrophy in Alzheimer's disease in relation to dementia severity: Evidence for early neocortical degeneration. *Neurobiology of Aging, 24,* 85–94.

Telford, C., McCarthy-Jones, S., Corcoran, R., & Rowse, G. (2012). Experience sampling methodology studies of depression: The state of the art. *Psychological Medicine, 42,* 1119–1129.

Tellegen, A., Lykken, D. T., Bouchard, T. J., Jr., Wilcox, K. J., Segal, N. L., & Rich, S. (1988). Personality similarity in twins reared apart and together. *Journal of Personality and Social Psychology, 54,* 1031–1039.

Templeton, L. M., & Wilcox, S. A. (2000). A tale of two representations: The misinformation effect and children's developing theory of mind. *Child Development, 71,* 402–416.

Tenenbaum, H. R., & Leaper, C. (2002). Are parents' gender schemas related to their children's gender-related cognitions? A meta-analysis. *Developmental Psychology, 38,* 615–630.

Teng, E., & Squire, L. R. (1999). Memory for places learned long ago is intact after hippocampal damage. *Nature, 400,* 675–677.

Tenzer, S. (1989). Fat acceptance therapy (F.A.T.): A non-dieting group approach to physical wellness, insight, and self-acceptance. *Women and Therapy, 8,* 39–47.

Terman, L. (1925). *Genetic studies of genius, Vol. I: Mental and physical traits of a thousand gifted children.* Stanford, CA: Stanford University Press.

Terman, L. M. (1917). The intelligence quotient of Francis Galton in childhood. *American Journal of Psychology, 28,* 209–215.

Terman, L. M. (1918). Expert testimony in the case of Alberto Flores. *Journal of Delinquency, 3,* 145–164.

Terrace, H. S., Petitto, L. A., Sanders, R. J., & Bever, T. G. (1979). Can an ape create a sentence? *Science, 206,* 891–902.

Terry-McElrath, Y. M., & O'Malley, P. M. (2011). Substance use and exercise participation among young adults: Parallel trajectories in a national cohort-sequential study. *Addiction, 106,* 1855–1865.

Thakker, J., Ward, T., & Strongman, K. T. (1999). Mental disorder and cross-cultural psychology: A constructivist perspective. *Clinical Psychology Review, 19,* 843–874.

Thamaku, M., & Daniel, M. (2013). Exploring responses to transformative group therapy for orphaned children in the context of mass orphaning in Botswana. *Death Studies, 37,* 413–447.

Thase, M. E., Greenhouse, J. B., Frank, E., Reynolds, C. F., Pilkonis, P. A., Hurley, K., . . . Kupfer, D. J. (1997). Treatment of major depression with psychotherapy or psychotherapy-pharmacotherapy combinations. *Archives of General Psychiatry, 54,* 1009–1015.

Thierry, N., Willeit, M., Praschak-Rieder, N., Zill, P., Hornik, K., Neumeister, A., . . . Kasper, S. (2004). Serotonin transporter promoter gene polymorphic region (5-HTTLPR) and personality in female patients with seasonal affective disorder and in healthy controls. *European Neuropsychopharmacology, 14,* 53–58.

Thiessen, D., & Umezawa, Y. (1998). The sociobiology of everyday life: A new look at a very old novel. *Human Nature, 9,* 293–320.

Thomas, E. (1988). Forebrain mechanisms in the relief of fear: The role of the lateral septum. *Psychobiology, 16,* 36–44.

Thomas, H. (1993). A theory explaining sex differences in high mathematical ability has been around for some time. *Behavioral and Brain Sciences, 16,* 187–189.

Thomas, T. N. (1997). Sleepwalking disorder and *mens rea:* A review and case report. *Journal of Forensic Sciences, 42,* 17–24.

Thompson, A., Hollis, C., & Richards, D. (2003). Authoritarian parenting attitudes as a risk for conduct problems: Results from a British national cohort study. *European Child and Adolescent Psychiatry, 12,* 84–91.

Thompson, B. (2002). "Statistical," "practical," and "clinical": How many kinds of significance do counselors need to consider? *Journal of Counseling and Development, 80,* 64–71.

Thompson, B., Diamond, K. E., McWilliam, R., Snyder, P., & Snyder, S. W. (2005). Evaluating the quality of evidence from correlational research for evidence-based practice. *Exceptional Children, 71,* 181–194.

Thompson, J. K., & Heinberg, L. J. (1999). The media's influence on body image disturbance and eating disorders: We've reviled them, now can we rehabilitate them? *Journal of Social Issues, 55,* 339–353.

Thompson, J. K., & Stice, E. (2001). Thin-ideal internalization: Mounting evidence for a new risk factor for body-image disturbance and eating pathology. *Current Directions in Psychological Science, 10,* 181–183.

Thompson, K., Biddle, K. R., Robinson-Long, M., Poger, J., Wang, J., Yang, Q. X., & Eslinger, P. J. (2009). Cerebral plasticity and recovery of function after childhood prefrontal cortex damage. *Developmental Neurorehabilitation, 12,* 298–312.

Thompson, L. (1995, June 12). Search for a gay gene. *Time,* 60–61.

Thompson, N. J., Coker, J., Krause, J. S., & Henry, E. (2003). Purpose in life as a mediator of adjustment after spinal cord injury. *Rehabilitation Psychology, 48,* 100–108.

Thompson, R. F. (1991). Are memory traces localized or distributed? *Neuropsychologia, 29,* 571–582.

Thompson, S. M. (2000). Synaptic plasticity: Building memories to last. *Current Biology, 10,* R218–R221.

Thordardottir, E. T., & Weismer, S. E. (1998). Mean length of utterance and other language sample measures in early Icelandic. *First Language, 18,* 1–32.

Thorndike, E. L. (1898). Animal intelligence: An experimental study of the associative processes in animals. *Psychological Review Monograph Supplement, 2* (No. 8).

Thorndike, E. L. (1961). Edward Lee Thorndike. In C. Murchison (Ed.), *A history of psychology in autobiography, Vol. 1* (pp. 263–270). New York: Russell & Russell.

Thorpe, S. J., & Salkovskis, P. M. (1995). Phobia beliefs: Do cognitive factors play a role in specific phobias? *Behaviour Research and Therapy, 33,* 805–816.

Throne, L. C., Bartholomew, J. B., Craig, J., & Farrar, R. P. (2000). Stress reactivity in fire fighters: An exercise intervention. *International Journal of Stress Management, 7,* 235–246.

Thurstone, L. L. (1938). *Primary mental abilities.* Chicago: University of Chicago Press.

Tiedt, A. D. (2013). Cross-national comparisons of gender differences in late-life depressive symptoms in Japan and the United States. *The Journals of Gerontology: Series B: Psychological Sciences and Social Sciences, 68,* 443–454.

Tiefer, L. (1995). *Sex is not a natural act.* Boulder, Co: Westview Press.

Tierney, A. J. (2000). Egas Moniz and the origins of psychosurgery: A review commemorating the 50th anniversary of Moniz's Nobel Prize. *Journal of the History of the Neurosciences, 9,* 22–36.

Tiffany, S. T., Martin, E. M., & Baker, T. B. (1986). Treatments for cigarette smoking: An evaluation of the contributions of aversion and counseling procedures. *Behaviour Research and Therapy, 24,* 437–452.

Till, B. D., & Priluck, R. L. (2000). Stimulus generalization in classical conditioning: An initial investigation and extension. *Psychology and Marketing, 17,* 55–72.

Tilley, A. J., & Empson, J. A. (1978). REM sleep and memory consolidation. *Biological Psychology, 6,* 293–300.

Timberlake, W. (2003). Marian Breland Bailey: Many lives (SQAB, May 25, 2002, Toronto, Canada). *Behavioural Processes, 62,* 1–4.

Timberlake, W., & Farmer-Dougan, V. A. (1991). Reinforcement in applied settings: Figuring out ahead of time what will work. *Psychological Bulletin, 110,* 379–391.

Timberlake, W., & Melcer, T. (1988). Effects of poisoning on predatory and ingestive behavior toward artificial prey in rats (*Rattus norvegicus*). *Journal of Comparative Psychology, 102,* 182–187.

Timm, H. W. (1982). Effect of altered outcome expectancies stemming from placebo and feedback treatments on the validity of the guilty knowledge technique. *Journal of Applied Psychology, 67,* 391–400.

Timmann, D., Lee, P., Watts, S., & Hore, J. (2008). Kinematics of arm joint rotations in cerebellar and unskilled subjects associated with the inability to throw fast. *Cerebellum, 7,* 366–378.

Timney, B., & Keil, K. (1996). Horses are sensitive to pictorial depth cues. *Perception, 25,* 1121–1128.

Tobach, E. (2006). Identity of comparative psychology: Its status and advances in evolutionary theory and genetics. *International Journal of Comparative Psychology, 19,* 129–150.

Todd, L. K. (1996). A computer-assisted expert system for clinical diagnosis of eating disorders: A potential tool for practitioners. *Professional Psychology: Research and Practice, 27,* 184–187.

Todman, D. (2008). Henry Dale and the discovery of chemical synaptic transmission. *European Neurology, 60,* 162–164.

Tolin, D. F., Woods, C. M., & Abramowitz, J. S. (2003). Relationship between obsessive beliefs and obsessive-compulsive symptoms. *Cognitive Therapy and Research, 27,* 657–669.

Tolman, E. C. (1932). *Purposive behavior in animals and man.* New York: Appleton-Century-Crofts.

Tolman, E. C., & Honzik, C. H. (1930). Introduction and removal of reward, and maze performance in rats. *University of California Publications in Psychology, 4,* 257–275.

Tomfohr, L., Pung, M. A., Edwards, K. M., & Dimsdale, J. E. (2012). Racial differences in sleep architecture: The role of ethnic discrimination. *Biological Psychology, 89,* 34–38.

Tomlinson-Keasey, C. (1990). The working lives of Terman's gifted women. In H. Y. Grossman & N. L. Chester (Eds.), *The experience and meaning of work in women's lives* (pp. 213–240). Hillsdale, NJ: Erlbaum.

Tonello, G. (2008). Seasonal affective disorder: Lighting research and environmental psychology. *Lighting Research and Technology, 40,* 103–110.

Topolinski, S., & Reber, R. (2010). Gaining insight into the "aha" experience. *Current Directions in Psychological Science, 19,* 402–405.

Topp, L., Hando, J., Dillon, P., Roche, A., & Solowij, N. (1999). Ecstasy use in Australia: Patterns of use and associated harm. *Drug and Alcohol Dependence, 55,* 105–115.

Torgersen, S. (1983). Genetic factors in anxiety disorders. *Archives of General Psychiatry, 40,* 1085–1089.

Torgersen, S. (1986). Genetics of somatoform disorders. *Archives of General Psychiatry, 43,* 502–505.

Törnroos, M., Hintsanen, M., Hintsa, T., Jokela, M., Pulkki-Råback, L., & Hutri-Kähönen, N. (2013). Associations between five-factor model traits and perceived job strain: A population-based study. *Journal of Occupational Health Psychology, 18,* 492–500.

Torri, G., Cecchettin, M., Bellometti, S., & Galzigna, L. (1995). Analgesic effect and beta-endorphin and substance P levels in plasma after short-term administration of a ketoprofen-lysine salt or acetylsalicylic acid in patients with osteoarthrosis. *Current Therapeutic Research, 56,* 62–69.

Toth, C., McNeil, S., & Feasby, T. (2005). Peripheral nervous system injuries in sport and recreation. *Sports Medicine, 35,* 717–738.

Toth, L. A., & Krueger, J. M. (1990). Somnogenic, pyrogenic thermatologic effects of experimental pasteurellosis in rabbits. *American Journal of Physiology, 258,* R536–R542.

Toufexis, A. (1990, December 17). Drowsy America. *Time,* pp. 78–85.

Toukmanian, S. G., & Brouwers, M. C. (1998). Cultural aspects of self-disclosure and psychotherapy. In S. S. Kazarian & D. R. Evans (Eds.), *Cultural clinical psychology: Theory, research, and practice* (pp. 106–124). New York: Oxford University Press.

Tourney-Jetté, E., Dupuis, G., Denault, A., Carter, R., & Bherer, L. (2012). The benefits of cognitive training after a coronary artery bypass graft surgery. *Journal of Behavioral Medicine, 35,* 557–568.

Towell, A., Muscat, R., & Willner, P. (1989). Noradrenergic receptor interactions in feeding elicited by stimulation of the paraventricular hypothalamus. *Pharmacology, Biochemistry, and Behavior, 32,* 133–139.

Tracey, I., Ploghaus, A., Gati, J. S., Clare, S., Smith, S., Menon, R. S., & Matthews, P. M. (2002). Imaging attentional modulation of pain in the periaqueductal gray in humans. *Journal of Neuroscience, 22,* 2748–2752.

Tranel, D. (1995). Where did my arm go? [Review of *Unilateral neglect: Clinical and experimental studies*]. *Contemporary Psychology, 40,* 885–887.

Tranel, D., & Damasio, A. R. (1985). Knowledge without our awareness: An automatic index of facial recognition by prosopagnosics. *Science, 228,* 1453–1454.

Trappey, C. (1996). A meta-analysis of consumer choice and subliminal advertising. *Psychology and Marketing, 13,* 517–530.

Traskman, L., Asberg, M., Bertilsson, L., & Sjostrand, L. (1981). Monoamine metabolites in CSF and suicidal behavior. *Archives of General Psychiatry, 38,* 631–636.

Travis, R. W., & Sturmey, P. (2013). Using behavioural skills training to treat aggression in adults with mild intellectual disability in a forensic setting. *Journal of Applied Research in Intellectual Disabilities, 26,* 481–488.

Treede, R. D. (2002). Spinothalamic and thalamocortical nociceptive pathways. *Journal of Pain, 3,* 109–112.

Treffert, D. A. (1989). *Extraordinary people: Understanding savant syndrome.* New York: Harper & Row.

Trenton, A. J., & Currier, G. W. (2005). Behavioural manifestations of anabolic steroid use. *CNS Drugs, 19,* 571–595.

Trevethan, C. T., & Sahraie, A. (2003). Spatial and temporal processing in a subject with cortical blindness following occipital surgery. *Neuropsychologia, 41,* 1296–1306.

Treynor, W., Gonzalez, R., & Nolen–Hoeksema, S. (2003). Rumination reconsidered: A psychometric analysis. *Cognitive Therapy and Research, 27,* 247–259.

Triandis, H. C. (1989). The self and social behavior in differing cultural contexts. *Psychological Review, 96,* 506–520.

Triandis, H. C. (1990). Theoretical concepts that are applicable to the analysis of ethnocentrism. In R. W. Brislin (Ed.), *Applied cross-cultural psychology* (pp. 34–55). Newbury Park, CA: Sage.

Triarhou, L. C. (1995). The cerebellar model of neural grafting: Structural integration and functional recovery. *Brain Research Bulletin, 39,* 127–138.

Trice, A. D., & Ogden, E. P. (1987). Informed consent: Effects of the withdrawal clause in longitudinal research. *Perceptual and Motor Skills, 65,* 135–138.

Triplet, R. G. (1992). Discriminatory biases in the perception of illness: The application of availability and representativeness heuristics to the AIDS crisis. *Basic and Applied Social Psychology, 13,* 303–322.

Triplett, N. (1898). The dynamogenic factors in pacemaking and competition. *American Journal of Psychology, 9,* 507–553.

Troster, H., & Bambring, M. (1992). Early social-emotional development in blind infants. *Child Care, Health, and Development, 18,* 207–227.

Trotter, R. J. (1981). Psychiatry for the 80's. *Science News, 119,* 348–349.

Trotter, R. J. (1986, August). Three heads are better than one. *Psychology Today,* pp. 56–62.

Trounson, R. (2000, March 1). Eichmann rationalizes his Nazi role in jail notebooks. *Los Angeles Times,* p. A1.

Truax, C. B. (1966). Reinforcement and nonreinforcement in Rogerian psychotherapy. *Journal of Abnormal Psychology, 71,* 1–9.

Tryon, W. W. (1998). A neural network explanation of posttraumatic stress disorder. *Journal of Anxiety Disorders, 12,* 373–385.

Tryon, W. W. (2000). Behavior therapy as applied learning theory. *Behavior Therapist, 23,* 131–133.

Tsai, D. C., & Pike, P. L. (2000). Effects of acculturation on the MMPI-2 scores of Asian American students. *Journal of Personality Assessment, 74,* 216-230.

Tsai, G. E., Condie, D., Wu, M.-T., & Chang, I.-W. (1999). Functional magnetic resonance imaging of personality switches in a woman with dissociative identity disorder. *Harvard Review of Psychiatry, 7,* 119–122.

Tsao, J.C.I., Fanurik, D., & Zeltzer, L. K. (2003). Long-term effects of a brief distraction intervention on children's laboratory pain reactivity. *Behavior Modification, 27,* 217–232.

Tsutsui, K. I., Sakata, H., Naganuma, T., & Taira, M. (2002). Neural correlates for perception of 3D surface orientation from texture gradient. *Science, 298,* 409–412.

Tucker, L. A. (1983). Muscular strength: A predictor of personality in males. *Journal of Sports Medicine and Physical Fitness, 23,* 213–220.

Tucker, W. H. (1994). Fact and fiction in the discovery of Sir Cyril Burt's flaws. *Journal of the History of the Behavioral Sciences, 30,* 335–347.

Tucker, W. H. (1997). Re-reconsidering Burt: Beyond a reasonable doubt. *Journal of the History of the Behavioral Sciences, 33,* 145–162.

Tuckey, M. R., & Brewer, N. (2003). The influence of schemas, stimulus ambiguity, and interview schedule on eyewitness memory over time. *Journal of Experimental Psychology: Applied, 9,* 101–118.

Tulsky, F. N. (1986, March 28). $988,000 is awarded in suit over lost psychic power. *Philadelphia Inquirer,* p. 1-A.

Tulving, E. (1985). How many memory systems are there? *American Psychologist, 40,* 385–398.

Tulving, E. (1993). What is episodic memory? *Current Directions in Psychological Science, 2,* 67–70.

Tulving, E., & Markowitsch, H. J. (1998). Episodic and declarative memory: Role of the hippocampus. *Hippocampus, 8,* 198–204.

Tulving, E., & Thomson, D. M. (1973). Encoding specificity and retrieval processes in episodic memory. *Psychological Review, 80,* 352–373.

Turk, C. L., Heimberg, R. G., Orsillo, S. M., Holt, C. S., Gitow, A., Street, L. L., . . . Liebowitz, M. R. (1998). An investigation of gender differences in social phobia. *Journal of Anxiety Disorders, 12,* 209–223.

Turkheimer, E. (1991). Individual and group differences in adoption studies of IQ. *Psychological Bulletin, 110,* 392–405.

Turkheimer, E. (1998). Heritability and biological explanation. *Psychological Review, 105,* 782–791.

Turnbull, C. M. (1961). Some observations regarding the experiences of the Bambuti Pygmies. *American Journal of Psychology, 74,* 304–308.

Turner, D., Basdekis-Jozsa, R., & Briken, P. (2013). Prescription of testosterone-lowering medications for sex offender treatment in German forensic-psychiatric institutions. *Journal of Sexual Medicine, 10,* 570–578.

Turner, S. M., Beidel, D. C., & Costello, A. (1987). Psychopathology in the offspring of anxiety disorder patients. *Journal of Consulting and Clinical Psychology, 55,* 229–235.

Turner, S. M., Beidel, D.C., Roberson-Nay, R. (2005). Offspring of anxious parents: Reactivity, habituation, and anxiety-proneness. *Behavioral Research Therapy, 10,* 1263–1279.

Turner, S.M., Beidel, D.C., Roberson-Nay, R., & Tervo, K. (2003). Parenting behaviors in parents with anxiety disorders. *Behavioral Research Therapy, 5,* 541–554.

Twenge, J. M., & Crocker, J. (2002). Race and self-esteem: Meta-analyses comparing Whites, Blacks, Hispanics, Asians, and American Indians and comment on Gray-Little and Hafdahl, 2000. *Psychological Bulletin, 128,* 371–408.

Twisk, J. W. R., Snel, J., Kemper, H. C. G., & van Mechelen, W. (1999). Changes in daily hassles and life events and the relationship with coronary heart disease risk factors: A 2-year longitudinal study in 27–29-yr-old males and females. *Journal of Psychosomatic Research, 46,* 229–240.

Twitmyer, E. B. (1974). A study of the knee jerk. *Journal of Experimental Psychology, 103,* 1047–1066.

U

Ullman, M., Krippner, S., & Vaughan, A. (1973). *Dream telepathy.* New York: Macmillan.

Ullmann, L. P., & Krasner, L. (1975). *Psychological approaches to abnormal behavior.* Englewood Cliffs, NJ: Prentice-Hall.

Ulrich, R. E., Stachnik, T. J., & Stainton, N. R. (1963). Student acceptance of generalized personality interpretations. *Psychological Reports, 13,* 831–834.

Unal, E., Koksal, Y., Baysal, T., Energin, M., Aydin, K., & Caliskan, U. (2007). Klüver-Bucy syndrome in a boy with non-Hodgkin lymphoma. *Pediatric Hematology and Oncology, 24,* 149–152.

Underwood, G. (1994). Subliminal perception on TV. *Nature, 370,* 103.

Unger, G., Desiderio, D. M., & Parr, W. (1972). Isolation, identification and synthesis of a specific-behavior-inducing brain peptide. *Nature, 238,* 198–202.

Ursu, S., Stenger V. A., Shear, M. K., Jones, M. R., & Carter, C. S. (2003). Overactive action monitoring in obsessive-compulsive disorder: Evidence from functional magnetic resonance imaging. *Psychological Science, 14,* 347–353.

Urushihara, K., & Miller, R. R. (2010). Backward blocking in first-order conditioning. *Journal of Experimental Psychology: Animal Behavior Processes, 36,* 281–295.

Usher, J. A., & Neisser, U. (1993). Childhood amnesia and the beginnings of memory for four early life events. *Journal of Experimental Psychology General, 122,* 155–165.

V

Vaidya, C. J., & Stollstorff, M. (2008). Cognitive neuroscience of attention deficit hyperactivity disorder: Current status and working hypotheses. *Developmental Disabilities, 14,* 261–267.

Vaillant, G. E., & Milofsky, E. (1980). Natural history of male psychological health: IX. Empirical evidence for Erikson's model of the life cycle. *American Journal of Psychiatry, 137,* 1348–1359.

Vakil, E., Blachstein, H., Sheinman, M., & Greenstein, Y. (2009). Developmental changes in attention test norms: Implications for the structure of attention. *Child Neuropsychology, 15,* 21–39.

Valentine, C. W. (1930). The innate bases of fear. *Journal of Genetic Psychology, 37,* 485–497.

Vallerand, R. J., & Losier, G. F. (1999). An integrative analysis of intrinsic and extrinsic motivation in sport. *Journal of Applied Sport Psychology, 11,* 142–169.

van Beek, N., Perna, G., Schruers, K., Verburg, K., Cucchi, M., Bellodi, L., & Griez, E. (2003). Vulnerability to 35% CO2 of panic disorder patients with a history of respiratory disorders. *Psychiatry Research, 120,* 125–130.

Van Boven, R. W., Hamilton, R. H., Kauffman, T., Keenan, J. P., & Pascual-Leone, A. (2000). Tactile spatial resolution in blind Braille readers. *Neurology, 54,* 2230–2236.

Van Dam-Baggen, R., & Kraaimaat, F. W. (2000). Social skills training in two subtypes of psychiatric inpatients with generalized social phobia. *Scandinavian Journal of Behaviour Therapy, 29,* 14–21.

Van de Water, T. J. (1997). Psychology's entrepreneurs and the marketing of industrial psychology. *Journal of Applied Psychology, 82,* 486–499.

van den Heuvel, O.A., Mataix-Cols, D., Zwitser, G., Cath, D.C., van der Werf, Y.D., Groenewegen, H. J., . . . Veltman, D. J. (2011). Common limbic and frontal-striatal disturbances in patients with obsessive-compulsive disorder, panic disorder and hypochondriasis. *Psychological Medicine, 41,* 2399–2410.

Van der Heijden, E., Klein, T. J., Müller, W., & Potters, J. (2012). Framing effects and impatience: Evidence from a large-scale experiment. *Journal of Economic Behavior & Organization, 84,* 701–711.

Van der Kolk, B. A. (2000). Trauma, neuroscience, and the etiology of hysteria: An exploration of the relevance of Breuer and Freud's 1893 article in light of modern science. *Journal of the American Academy of Psychoanalysis, 28,* 237–262.

Van Der Werf, Y. D., Jolles, J., Witter, M. P., & Uylings, H. B. M. (2003). Contributions of thalamic nuclei to declarative memory functioning. *Cortex, 39,* 1047–1062.

Van Dixhoorn, J. (1998). Cardiorespiratory effects of breathing and relaxation instruction in myocardial infarction patients. *Biological Psychology, 49,* 123–135.

Van Doorn, M. D., Branje, S. J. T., & Meeus, W. H. J. (2011). Developmental changes in conflict resolution styles in parent-adolescent relationships: A four-wave longitudinal study. *Journal of Youth & Adolescence, 40,* 97–107.

Van Doornen, L. J. P., & van Blokland, R. (1987). Serum-cholesterol: Sex specific psychological correlates during rest and stress. *Journal of Psychosomatic Research, 31,* 239–249.

van Lankveld, J. J. D. M. (1998). Bibliotherapy in the treatment of sexual dysfunctions: A meta-analysis. *Journal of Consulting & Clinical Psychology, 66,* 702–708.

van Ommen, G. J. B. (2005). The human genome, revisited. *European Journal of Human Genetics, 13,* 265–270.

Van Wyk, P. H., & Geist, C. S. (1995). Biology of bisexuality: Critique and observations. *Journal of Homosexuality, 28,* 357–373.

VandenBos, G. R. (1996). Outcome assessment of psychotherapy. *American Psychologist, 51,* 1005–1006.

VanderZee, K., Buunk, B., & Sanderman, R. (1996). The relationship between social comparison processes and personality. *Personalityand Individual Differences, 201,* 551–565.

Vargas, E. A., & Vargas, J. S. (1991). Programmed instruction: What it is and how to do it. *Journal of Behavioral Education, 1,* 235–251.

Varner, L. J., & Ellis, H. C. (1999). Cognitive activity and physiological arousal: Processes that mediate mood-congruent memory. *Memory and Cognition, 26,* 939–950.

Vecera, S. P., & O'Reilly, R. C. (1998). Figure-ground organization and object recognition processes: An interactive account. *Journal of Experimental Psychology: Human Perception and Performance, 24,* 441–462.

Vein, A. M., Sidorov, A. A., Martazaev, M. S., & Karlov, A. V. (1991). Physical exercise and nocturnal sleep in healthy humans. *Human Physiology, 17,* 391–397.

Veissier, I. (1993). Observational learning in cattle. *Applied Animal Behaviour Science, 35,* 235–243.

Veliz, J., & James, W. S. (1987). Medicine court: Rogers in practice. *American Journal of Psychiatry, 144,* 62–67.

Vella-Zarb, R. A., & Elgar, F. J. (2009). The "freshman 5": A meta-analysis of weight gain in the freshman year of college. *Journal of American College Health, 58,* 161–166.

Veneroso, C., Tuñón, M. J., González-Gallego, J., & Collado, P. S. (2009). Melatonin reduces cardiac inflammatory injury induced by acute exercise. *Journal of Pineal Research, 47,* 184–191.

Venn, J. (1984). Family etiology and remission in a case of psychogenic fugue. *Family Process, 23,* 429–435.

Ventis, W. L., Higbee, G., & Murdock, S. . (2001). Using humor in systematic desensitization to reduce fear. *Journal of General Psychology,128,* 241–253.

Verbaten, M. N. (2003). Specific memory deficits in ecstasy users? The results of a meta-analysis. *Human Psychopharmacology: Clinical and Experimental, 18,* 281–290.

Verdoux, H., Takei, N., Cassou de Saint-Mathurin, R., Murray, R. M., & Bourgeois, M. L. (1997). Seasonality of birth in schizophrenia: The effect of regional population density. *Schizophrenia Research, 23,* 175–180.

Verissimo, M., Santos, A. J., Vaughn, B. E., Torres, N., Monteiro, L., & Santos, O. (2011). Quality of attachment to father and mother and number of reciprocal friends. *Early Child Development and Care, 181,* 27–38.

Vermetten, E., & Bremner, J. D. (2003). Olfaction as a traumatic reminder in posttraumatic stress disorder: Case reports and review. *Journal of Clinical Psychiatry, 64,* 202–207.

Vernon, P. A. (1998). From the cognitive to the biological: A sketch of Arthur Jensen's contributions to the study of g. *Intelligence, 26,* 267–271.

Vernon, P. A., Jang, K. L., Harris, J. A., & McCarthy, J. M. (1997). Environmental predictors of personality differences: A twin and sibling study. *Journal of Personality and Social Psychology, 72,* 177–183.

Veroff, J., Depner, C., Kulka, R., & Douvan, E. (1980). Comparison of American motives: 1957 versus 1976. *Journal of Personality and Social Psychology, 39,* 1249–1262.

Verschuere, B., Crombez, G., & Koster, E. H. W. (2004). Orienting to guilty knowledge. *Cognition and Emotion, 18,* 265–279.

Vertes, R. P., & Eastman, K. E. (2000). The case against memory consolidation in REM sleep. *Behavioral and Brain Sciences, 23,* 867–876, 904–1018, 1083–1121.

Vetter, H. J. (1969). *Language behavior and psychopathology.* Chicago: Rand McNally.

Viard, A., Chételat, G., Lebreton, K., Desgranges, B., Landeau, B., de la Sayette, V., . . . Piolino, P. (2011). Mental time travel into the past and future in healthy aged adults: An fMRI study. *Brain & Cognition, 75,* 1–9.

Vidal, J. (2002). Updated review on the benefits of weight loss. *International Journal of Obesity and Related Metabolic Disorders, 26,* S25–S28.

Vigliocco, G., Vinson, D. P., Martin, R. C., & Garrett, M. F. (1999). Is "count" and "mass" information available when the noun is not? An investigation of tip-of-the-tongue states and anomia. *Journal of Memory and Language, 40,* 534–558.

Vincent, K. R. (1991). Black/white IQ differences: Does age make the difference? *Journal of Clinical Psychology, 47,* 266–270.

Viney, W. (1993). *A history of psychology: Ideas and context.* Boston: Allyn & Bacon.

Vingilis-Jaremo, L., & Maurer, D. (2013). The influence of symmetry on children's judgments of facial attractiveness. *Perception, 42,* 302–320.

Visser, S. N., Danielson, M. L., Bitsko, R. H., Holbrook, J. R., Kogan, M. D., Ghandour, R. M., . . . Blumberg, S. J. (2014). Trends in the parent-report of health care provider-diagnosed and medicated attention-deficit/hyperactivity disorder: United States, 2003–2011 *Journal of the American Academy of Child and Adolescent Psychiatry, 53,* 34–46.

Vitiello, B. (2008). Effectively obtaining informed consent for child and adolescent participation in mental health research. *Ethics and Behavior, 18,* 182–198.

Vlaander, G. P., & Van Rooijen, L. (1985). Independence and conformity in Holland: Asch's experiment three decades later. *Gedrag: Tijdschrift voor Psychologie, 13,* 49–55.

Voeller, B. (1991). AIDS and heterosexual anal intercourse. *Archives of Sexual Behavior, 20,* 233–276.

Vogel, J. J., Bowers, C. A., & Vogel, D. S. (2003). Cerebral lateralization of spatial abilities: A meta-analysis. *Brain and Cognition, 52,* 197–204.

Vogler, G. P., Mcclearn, G. E., Snieder, H., & Boomsma, D. I. (1997). Genetics and behavioral medicine: Risk factors for cardiovascular disease. *Behavioral Medicine, 22,* 141–149.

Vokey, J. R., & Read, J. D. (1985). Subliminal messages: Between the devil and the media. *American Psychologist, 40,* 1231–1239.

Volkmar, F., Siegel, M., Woodbury-Smith, M., King, B., McCracken, J., & State, M. (2014). Practice parameter for the assessment and treatment of children and adolescents with autism spectrum disorder. *Journal of the American Academy of Child and Adolescent Psychiatry, 53,* 237–257.

Vollenweider, F. X., Gamma, A., Liechti, M., & Huber, T. (1998). Psychological and cardiovascular effects and short-term sequelae of MDMA ("Ecstasy") in MDMA-naive healthy volunteers. *Neuropsychopharmacology, 19,* 241–251.

von Békésy, G. (1957, August). The ear. *Scientific American,* pp. 66–78.

von der Pahlen, B., Lindman, R., Sarkola, T., Maekisalo, H., & Eriksson, C. J. P. (2002). An exploratory study on self-evaluated aggression and androgens in women. *Aggressive Behavior, 28,* 273–280.

von Hofsten, C., Kellman, P., & Putaansuu, J. (1992). Young infants' sensitivity to motion parallax. *Infant Behavior and Development, 15,* 245–264.

von Mayrhauser, R. T. (1989). Making intelligence functional: Walter Dill Scott and applied psychological testing in World War I. *Journal of the History of the Behavioral Sciences, 25,* 60–72.

von Senden, M. (1960). *Space and sight: The perception of space and shape in the congenitally blind before and after operation.* Oxford, England: Free Press of Glencoe.

Vonnegut, M. (1974, April). Why I want to bite R. D. Laing. *Harper's Magazine,* pp. 90–92.

Vonnegut, M. (1975). *The Eden express.* New York: Bantam Books.

Vosburg, S. K. (1998). The effects of positive and negative mood on divergent-thinking performance. *Creativity Research Journal, 11,* 165–172.

Votruba-Drzal, E., Coey, R. L., Maldonado-Carreño, Li-Grining, C. P., & Chase-Lansdale, P. L. (2010). Child care and the development of behavior problems among economically disadvantaged children in middle childhood. *Child Development, 81,* 1460–1474.

Voyer, D., & Flight, J. (2001). Gender differences in laterality on a dichotic task: The influence of report strategies. *Cortex, 37,* 345–362.

Voyer, D., & Rodgers, M. A. (2002). Reliability of laterality effects in a dichotic listening task with nonverbal material. *Brain and Cognition, 48,* 602–606.

Voyer, D., Voyer, S., & Bryden, M. P. (1995). Magnitude of sex differences in spatial abilities: A meta-analysis and consideration of critical variables. *Psychological Bulletin, 117,* 250–270.

Vrbova, G., Mehra, N., Shanmuganathan, H., Tyreman, N., Schachner, M., & Gordon, T. (2009). Chemical communication between regenerating motor axons and Schwann cells in the growth pathway. *European Journal of Neuroscience, 30,* 366–375.

Vuksic-Mihaljevic, Z., Mandic, N., Barkic, J., & Mrdenovic, S. (1998). A current psychodynamic understanding of panic disorder. *British Journal of Medical Psychology, 71,* 27–45.

Vulliemoz, S., Lemieux, L., Daunizeau, J., Michel, C. M., & Duncan, J. S. (2010). The combination of EEG source imaging and EEG-correlated functional MRI to map epileptic networks. *Epilepsia, 51,* 491–505.

W

Wadden, T. A., Foster, G. D., & Letizia, K. A. (1994). One-year behavioral treatment of obesity: Comparison of moderate and severe caloric restriction and the effects of weight maintenance therapy. *Journal of Consulting and Clinical Psychology, 62,* 165–171.

Wadden, T. A., Vogt, R. A., Foster, G. D., & Anderson, D. A. (1998). Exercise and the maintenance of weight loss: 1-year follow-up of a controlled clinical trial. *Journal of Consulting and Clinical Psychology, 66,* 429–433.

Wade, A. G., Ford, I., Crawford, G., McConnachie, A., Nir, T., Laudon, M., & Zisapel, M. (2010). Nightly treatment of primary insomnia with prolonged release melatonin for 6 months: A randomized placebo controlled trial on age and endogenous melatonin as predictors of efficacy and safety. *BMC Medicine, 8,* 51–69.

Wade, T. D., & Kendler, K. S. (2000) The relationship between social support and major depression: Cross-sectional, longitudinal, and genetic perspectives. *Journal of Nervous and Mental Disease, 188,* 251–258.

Wade, T. D., Bulik, C. M., Sullivan, P. F., Neale, M. C., & Kendler, K. S. (2000). The relation between risk factors for binge eating and bulimia nervosa: A population-based female twin study. *Health Psychology, 19,* 115–123.

Wagar, B. M., & Cohen, D. (2003). Culture, memory, and the self: An analysis of the personal and collective self in long-term memory. *Journal of Experimental Social Psychology, 39,* 468–475.

Wagemans, J. Elder, J. H., Kubovy, M., Palmer, S. E., Peterson, M. A., Singh, M., & von der Heyt, R. (2012). A century of Gestalt psychology in visual perception: I. Perceptual grouping and figure-ground organization. *Psychological Bulletin, 138,* 1172–1217.

Wagemans, J., Feldman, J., Gepshtein, S., Kimchi, R., Pomerantz, J. R., van der Helm, P. A., & van Leeuwen, C. (2012). A century of Gestalt psychology in visual perception: II. Conceptual and theoretical foundations. *Psychological Bulletin, 138,* 1218–1252.

Wagner, A. M., & Houlihan, D. D. (1994). Notes and shorter communications: Sensation seeking and trait anxiety in hang-glider pilots and golfers. *Personality and Individual Differences, 16,* 975–977.

Wagner, R. V. (2006). Terrorism: A peace psychological analysis. *Journal of Social Issues, 62,* 155–171.

Wagner, U., Gais, S., & Born, J. (2001). Emotional memory formation is enhanced across sleep intervals with high amounts of rapid eye movement sleep. *Learning and Memory, 8,* 112–119.

Wagstaff, G. F., & Frost, R. (1996). Reversing and breaching posthypnotic amnesia and hypnotically created pseudomemories. *Contemporary Hypnosis, 13,* 191–197.

Wagstaff, G. F., Vella, M., & Perfect, T. (1992). The effect of hypnotically elicited testimony on jurors' judgments of guilt and innocence. *Journal of Social Psychology, 132,* 591–595.

Wahlsten, D. (1999). Single-gene influences on behavior. *Annual Review of Psychology, 50,* 599–624.

Wai, J., Lubinski, D., Benbow, C. P., & Steiger, J. H. (2010). Accomplishment in science, technology, engineering, and mathematics (STEM) and its relation to STEM educational dose: A 25-year longitudinal study. *Journal of Educational Psychology, 102,* 860–871.

Waid, W. M., & Orne, M. T. (1982). The physiological detection of deception. *American Scientist, 70,* 402–409.

Waid, W. M., Wilson, S. K., & Orne, M. T. (1981). Cross-modal physiological effects of electrodermal ability in the detection of deception. *Journal of Personality and Social Psychology, 40,* 1118–1125.

Wainright, J. L., Russell, S. T., & Patterson, C. J. (2004). Psychosocial adjustment, school outcomes, and romantic relationships of adolexents with same-sex parents. *Child Development, 75,* 1886–1898.

Walker, L. J. (1986). Experiential and cognitive sources of moral development in adulthood. *Human Development, 29,* 113–124.

Wakeman, D. R., Dodiya, H. B., & Kordower, J. H. (2011). Cell transplantation and gene therapy in Parkinson's disease. *Mount Sinai Journal of Medicine, 78,* 126–158.

Walburn, J., Vedhara, K., Hankins, M., Rixon, L., & Weinman, J. (2009). Psychological stress and wound healing in humans: A systematic review and meta-analysis. *Journal of Psychosomatic Research, 67,* 253–271.

Walczyk, J. J. (2000). The interplay between automatic and control processes in reading. *Reading Research Quarterly, 35,* 554–566.

Wald, G. (1964). The receptors of human color vision. *Science, 145,* 1007–1017.

Waldhauser, F., Saletu, B., & Trinchard, L. I. (1990). Sleep laboratory investigations on hypnotic properties of melatonin. *Psychopharmacology, 100,* 222–226.

Waldrop, M. M. (1984). Artificial intelligence in parallel. *Science, 225,* 608–610.

Walen, H. R., & Lachman, M. E. (2000). Social support and strain from partner, family, and friends: Costs and benefits for men and women in adulthood. *Journal of Social and Personal Relationships, 17,* 5–30.

Walk, R. D., & Homan, C. P. (1984). Emotion and dance in dynamic light displays. *Bulletin of the Psychonomic Society, 22,* 437–440.

Walker, E., Hoppes, E., Emory, E., Mednick, S., & Schulsinger, F. (1981). Environmental factors related to schizophrenia in psychophysiologically labile high-risk males. *Journal of Abnormal Psychology, 90,* 313–320.

Walker, L. J. (1989). A longitudinal study of moral reasoning. *Child Development, 60,* 157–166.

Walker, M. B., & Andrade, M. G. (1996). Conformity in the Asch task as a function of age. *Journal of Social Psychology, 136,* 367–372.

Walker, M. M., Dennis, T. E., & Kirschvink, J. L. (2002). The magnetic sense and its use in long-distance navigation by animals. *Current Opinion in Neurobiology, 12,* 735–744.

Wallace, A. (1986). *The prodigy.* New York: Dutton.

Wallace, R. E. (1988). Abolish the duty to protect: It's time to release the scapegoats. *Psychotherapy in Private Practice, 6,* 55–63.

Wallace, W. (2003). The vibrating nerve impulse in Newton, Willis, and Gassendi: First steps in a mechanical theory of communication. *Brain and Cognition, 51,* 66–94.

Wallach, H., & Marshall, F. J. (1986). Shape constancy in pictorial representation. *Perception and Psychophysics, 39,* 233–235.

Wallach, M. A., Kogan, N., & Bem, D. J. (1962). Group influence on individual risk taking. *Journal of Abnormal and Social Psychology, 65,* 75–86.

Waller, N. G., & Ross, C. A. (1997). The prevalence and biometric structure of pathological dissociation in the general population: Taxometric and behavior genetic findings. *Journal of Abnormal Psychology, 106,* 499–510.

Waller, N. G., Kojetin, B. A., Bouchard, T. J., & Lykken, D. T. (1990). Genetic and environmental influences on religious interests, attitudes, and values: A study of twins reared apart and together. *Psychological Science, 1,* 138–142.

Wallis, C. (1984, June 11). Unlocking pain's secrets. *Time,* pp. 58–66.

Walsh, B. T., & Devlin, M. J. (1998). Eating disorders: Progress and problems. *Science, 280,* 1387–1390.

Walsh, E., Buchanan, A., & Fahy, T. (2002). Violence and schizophrenia: Examining the evidence. *British Journal of Psychiatry, 180,* 490–495.

Walsh, J. (1981). A plenipotentiary for human intelligence. *Science, 214,* 640–641.

Walsh, J. (1983). Wide world of reports. *Science, 220,* 804–805.

Walsh, J. C., Lynch, M., Murphy, A. W., & Daly, K. (2004). Factors influencing the decision to seek treatment for symptoms of acute myocardial infarction: An evaluation of the self-regulatory model of illness behaviour. *Journal of Psychosomatic Research, 56,* 67–73.

Walsh, J. J., Wilding, J. M., & Eysenck, M. W. (1994). Stress responsivity: The role of individual differences. *Personality and Individual Differences, 16,* 385–394.

Walsleben, J. A., Norman, R. G., Novak, R. D., O'Malley, E. B., Rapoport, D. M., & Strohl, K. P. (1999). Sleep habits of Long Island Railroad commuters. *Sleep, 22,* 728–734.

Walster, E., Aronson, V., Abrahams, D., & Rottman, L. (1966). Importance of physical attractiveness in dating behavior. *Journal of Personality and Social Psychology, 4,* 508–516.

Walters, G. C., & Grusec, J. E. (1977). *Punishment.* San Francisco: Freeman.

Waltz, D. L. (1982, October). Artificial intelligence. *Scientific American,* pp. 118–133.

Wang, C. L., Briston, T., Mowen, J. C., & Chakraborty, G. (2000). Alternative modes of self-construal: Dimensions of connectedness-separateness and advertising appeals to the cultural and gender-specific self. *Journal of Consumer Psychology, 9,* 107–115.

Wang, J. Q., Mao, L., & Han, J.-S. (1992). Comparison of the antinociceptive effects induced by electroacupuncture and transcutaneous electrical nerve stimulation in the rat. *International Journal of Neuroscience, 65,* 117–129.

Wang, M. Q., Nicholson, M. E., Mahoney, B. S., & Li, Y. (1993). *Perceptual and Motor Skills, 77,* 83–88.

Wang, W., & Viney, L. L. (1997). The psychosocial development of children and adolescents in the People's Republic of China: An Eriksonian approach. *International Journal of Psychology, 32,*139–153.

Wang, W., Wu, Y. X., Peng, Z. G., Lu, S. W., Yu, L., Wang, G. P., . . .Wang, Y. H. (2000). Test of sensation seeking in a Chinese sample. *Personality and Individual Differences, 28,* 169–179.

Wang, X. T., & Johnston, V. S. (1995). Perceived social context and risk preference: A re-examination of framing effects in a life-death decision problem. *Journal of Behavioral Decision Making, 8,* 279–293.

Wankel, L. M. (1993). The importance of enjoyment to adherence and psychological benefits from physical activity. Special Issue: Exercise and psychological well-being. *International Journal of Sport Psychology, 24,* 151–169.

Wanzer, M. B., & Frymier, A. B. (1999). The relationship between student perceptions of instructor humor and student's reports of learning. *Communication Education, 48,* 48–62.

Ward, A., Lyubomirsky, S., Sousa, L., & Nolen-Hoeksema, S. (2003). Can't quite commit: Rumination and uncertainty. *Personality and Social Psychology Bulletin, 29,* 96–107.

Ward, L. C., & Perry, M. S. (1998). Measurement of social introversion by the MMPI-2. *Journal of Personality Assessment, 70,* 171–182.

Ward, P., & Carnes, M. (2002). Effects of posting self-set goals on collegiate football players' skill execution during practice and games. *Journal of Applied Behavior Analysis, 35,* 1–12.

Wardle, J., Guthrie, C., Sanderson, S., Birch, L., & Plomin, R. (2001). Food and activity preferences in children of lean and obese parents. *International Journal of Obesity & Related Metabolic Disorders, 25,* 971–977.

Warwick-Evans, L. A., Symons, N., Fitch, T., & Burrows, L. (1998). Evaluating sensory conflict and postural instability: Theories of motion sickness. *Brain Research Bulletin, 47,* 465–469.

Washburn, D. A., & Rumbaugh, D. M. (1997). Faster is smarter, so why are we slower? A comparative perspective on intelligence and processing speed. *American Psychologist, 52,* 1147–1148.

Washburn, M. F. (1916). *Movement and mental imagery.* Oxford, England: Houghton Mifflin.

Washio, Y., Hayes, L. J., Hunter, K. W., & Pritchard, J. K. (2011). Backward conditioning of tumor necrosis factor-cc in a single trial. Changing intervals between exposures to lipopolysaccharide and saccharin taste. *Physiology & Behavior, 102,* 239–244.

Wasserman, E. A. (1997). What's elementary about associative learning? *Annual Review of Psychology, 48,* 573–607.

Watanabe, S., & Sato, K. (1999). Discriminative stimulus properties of music in Java sparrows. *Behavioural Processes, 47,* 53–57.

Waterhouse, J., Reilly, T., Atkinson, G., & Edwards, B. (2007). Jet lag: Trends and coping strategies. *The Lancet, 369,* 1117–1129.

Waters, E., Merrick, S., Treboux, D., Crowell, J., & Albersheim, L. (2000). Attachment security in infancy and early adulthood: A twenty-year longitudinal study. *Child Development, 71,* 684–689.

Waters, E., Weinfield, N. S., & Hamilton, C. E. (2000). The stability of attachment security from infancy to adolescence and early adulthood: General discussion. *Child Development, 71,* 703–706.

Waters, R. S., Samulack, D. D., Dykes, R. W., & McKinley, P. A. (1990). Topographic organization of baboon primary motor cortex: Face, hand, forelimb, and shoulder representation. *Somatosensory and Motor Research, 7,* 485–514.

Watson, J. B. (1913). Psychology as the behaviorist views it. *Psychological Review, 20,* 158–177.

Watson, J. B. (1930). *Behaviorism.* New York: W.W. Norton.

Watson, J. B., & Rayner, R. (1920). Conditioned emotional reactions. *Journal of Experimental Psychology, 3,* 1–14.

Watt, M. C., & Stewart, S. H. (2000). Anxiety sensitivity mediates the relationships between childhood learning experiences and elevated hypochondriacal concerns in young adulthood. *Journal of Psychosomatic Research, 49,* 107–118.

Watten, R. G., Lie, I., & Birketvedt, O. (1994). The influence of long-term visual near-work on accommodation and convergence: A field study. *Journal of Human Ergology, 23,* 27–39.

Watters, P. A., Martin, F., & Schreter, Z. (1997). Caffeine and cognitive performance: The nonlinear Yerkes-Dodson Law. *Human Psychopharmacology Clinical and Experimental, 12,* 249–257.

Watts, B. L. (1982). Individual differences in circadian activity rhythms and their effects on roommate relationships. *Journal of Personality, 50,* 374–384.

Watts, J., & Robertson, N. (2011), Burnout in university teaching staff: A systematic literature review. *Educational Research, 53,* 33–50.

Watts, R. E., & Critelli, J. W. (1997). Roots of contemporary cognitive theories in the individual psychology of Alfred Adler. *Journal of Cognitive Psychotherapy, 11,* 147–156.

Watts, R. E., & Holden, J. M. (1994). Why continue to use "fictional finalism"? *Individual Psychology: Journal of Adlerian Theory, Research, and Practice, 50,* 161–163.

Wax, M. L., (1999). The angel of dreams: Toward an ethnology of dream interpreting. *Journal of the American Academy of Psychoanalysis, 27,* 417–429.

Weaver, C. A. (1993). Do you need a "flash" to form a flashbulb memory? *Journal of Experimental Psychology: General, 122,* 39–46.

Weaver, J. B., Masland, J. L., Kharazmi, S., & Zillman, D. (1985). Effect of alcoholic intoxication on the appreciation of different types of humor. *Journal of Personality and Social Psychology, 49,* 781–787.

Webb, W. B. (1981). An essay on consciousness. *Teaching of Psychology, 8,* 15–19.

Webb, W. B. (1985). Sleep and dreaming. In G. A. Kimble & K. Schlesinger (Eds.), *Topics in the history of psychology, Vol. 2* (pp. 191–217). Hillsdale, NJ: Erlbaum.

Webb, W. B. (1992). *Sleep: The gentle tyrant* (2nd ed.). Boston: Anker.

Weber, M. M., & Engstrom, E. J. (1997). Kraepelin's "diagnostic cards": The confluence of clinical research and preconceived categories. *History of Psychiatry, 8,* 375–385.

Weber, R., & Crocker, J. (1983). Cognitive processes in the revision of stereotype beliefs. *Journal of Personality and Social Psychology, 45,* 961–977.

Webster, S., & Coleman, S. R. (1992). The reception of Clark L. Hull's behavior theory, 1943–1960. *Psychological Reports, 70,* 1063–1071.

Wechsler, D. (1958). *Measurement and appraisal of adult intelligence.* Baltimore: Williams & Wilkins.

Weekes, J. R., Lynn, S. J., Green, J. P., & Brentar, J. T. (1992). Pseudomemory in hypnotized and task-motivated subjects. *Journal of Abnormal Psychology, 101,* 356–360.

Wegner, D. M., & Schneider, D. J. (2003). The white bear story. *Psychological Inquiry, 14,* 326–329.

Weidman, N. (1997). Heredity, intelligence and neuropsychology; or, why *The Bell Curve* is good science. *Journal of the History of the Behavioral Sciences, 33,* 141–144.

Weigel, R. H., Vernon, D. T. A., & Tognacci, L. N. (1974). Specificity of the attitude as a determinant of attitude-behavior congruence. *Journal of Personality and Social Psychology, 30,* 724–728.

Weilage, M., & Hope, D. A. (1999). Self-discrepancy in social phobia and dysthymia. *Cognitive Therapy and Research, 23,* 637–650.

Weinberg, R. A. (1989). Intelligence and IQ: Landmark issues and great debates. *American Psychologist, 44,* 98–104.

Weinberg, R. A., Scarr, S., & Waldman, I. D. (1992). The Minnesota Transracial Adoption Study: A follow-up of IQ test performance at adolescence. *Intelligence, 16,* 117–135.

Weinberger, J., & Silverman, L. H. (1990). Testability and empirical verification of psychoanalytic dynamic propositions through subliminal psychodynamic activation. *Psychoanalytic Psychology, 7,* 299–339.

Weinberger, J., & Smith, B. (2011). Investigating merger: Subliminal psychodynamic activation and oneness motivation research. *Journal of the American Psychoanalytic Association, 59,* 553–570.

Weiner, B. (1980). A cognitive (attribution)-emotion-action model of motivated behavior: An analysis of judgments of help-giving. *Journal of Personality and Social Psychology, 39,* 186–200.

Weiner, B. (1985a). An attributional theory of achievement motivation and emotion. *Psychological Review, 92,* 548–573.

Weiner, B. (1985b). "Spontaneous" causal thinking. *Psychological Bulletin, 97,* 74–84.

Weiner, B., Figueroa-Munoz, A., & Kakihara, C. (1991). The goals of excuses and communication strategies related to causal perceptions. *Personality and Social Psychology Bulletin, 17,* 4–13.

Weinstein, L., & Almaguer, L. L. (1987). "I'm bored!" *Bulletin of the Psychonomic Society, 25,* 389–390.

Weinstein, N. D. (1984). Reducing unrealistic optimism about illness susceptibility. *Health Psychology, 3,* 431–457.

Weisfeld, G. E., Czilli, T., Phillips, K. A., Gall, J. A., & Lichtman, C. M. (2003). Possible olfaction-based mechanisms in human kin recognition and inbreeding avoidance. *Journal of Experimental Child Psychology, 85,* 279–295.

Weisman, J. (1988, November 19–25). Remembering JFK: Our first TV president. *TV Guide,* pp. 2–4, 6–8.

Weiss, J. M. (1972, June). Psychological factors in stress and disease. *Scientific American,* pp. 104–113.

Weiss, M. G. (1995). Eating disorders and disordered eating in different cultures. *Psychiatric Clinics of North America, 18,* 537–553.

Weiss, S. J., Panlilio, L. V., & Schindler, C. W. (1993). Single-incentive selective associations produced solely as a function of compound-stimulus conditioning context. *Journal of Experimental Psychology Animal Behavior Processes, 19,* 284–294.

Weisskirch, R. S., & Murphy, L. C. (2004). Friends, porn, and punk: Sensation seeking in personal relationships, Internet activities and music preference among college students. *Adolescence, 39,* 189–201.

Weissman, M. M., Bland, R. C., Canino, G. J., & Faravelli, C. (1997). The cross-national epidemiology of panic disorder. *Archives of General Psychiatry, 54,* 305–309.

Weissman, M. M., Bland, R. C., Canino, G. J., Greenwald, S., Lee, C.-K., Newman, S. C., . . . & Wickramaratne, P. J. (1996). The cross-national epidemiology of social phobia: A preliminary report. *International Clinical Psychopharmacology, 11,* 9–14.

Weissman, M.M., & Olfson, M. (1995). Depression in women: Implications for health care research. *Science, 269,* 799–801.

Weisz, J. R., Rothbaum, F. M., & Blackburn, T. C. (1984). Standing out and standing in: The psychology of control in America and Japan. *American Psychologist, 39,* 955–969.

Weisz, J. R., Weiss, B., Han, S. S., & Granger, D. (1995). Effects of psychotherapy with children and adolescents revisited: A meta-analysis of treatment outcome studies. *Psychological Bulletin, 117,* 450–468.

Weitzenhoffer, A. M., & Hilgard, E. R. (1962). *Stanford Scale of Hypnotic Susceptibility, Form C.* Palo Alto, CA: Consulting Psychologists Press.

Welch, S. L., Doll, H. A., & Fairburn, C. G. (1997). Life events and the onset of bulimia nervosa: A controlled study. *Psychological Medicine, 27,* 515–522.

Welch-Ross, M. K., & Schmidt, C. R. (1996). Gender-schema development and children's constructive story memory: Evidence for a developmental model. *Child Development, 67,* 820–835.

Weldon, E., & Gargano, G. M. (1988). Cognitive loafing: The effects of accountability and shared responsibility on cognitive effort. *Personality and Social Psychology Bulletin, 14,* 159–171.

Weller, S. (2012). Evolving creativity in qualitative longitudinal research with children and teenagers, *International Journal of Social Research Methodology: Theory & Practice, 15,* 119–133.

Wellisch, D., Kagawa-Singer, M., Reid, S. L., Lin, Y. J., Nishikawa-Lee, S., & Wellisch, M., (1999). An exploratory study of social support: A cross-cultural comparison of Chinese-, Japanese-, and Anglo-American breast cancer patients. *Psycho-Oncology, 8,* 207–219.

Wells, G. L., & Lindsay, R. C. L. (1985). Methodological notes on the accuracy-confidence relation in eyewitness identification. *Journal of Applied Psychology, 70,* 413–419.

Wenderoth, P. (1994). On the relationship between the psychology of visual perception and the neurophysiology of vision. *Australian Journal of Psychology, 46,* 1–6.

Wendorf, C. A. (2001). History of American morality research, 1894–1932. *History of Psychology, 4,* 272–288.

Wermter, A. K., Laucht, M., Schimmelmann, B. G., Banaschweski, T., Sonuga-Barke, E. J. S., Rietschel, M., & Becker, K. (2010). From nature versus nurture, via nature and nurture, to gene 3 environment interaction in mental disorders. *European Child and Adolescent Psychiatry, 19,* 199–210.

Werth, J. L. Jr., Wright, K. S., Archambault, R. J., & Bardash, R. (2003). When does the "duty to protect" apply with a client who has anorexia nervosa? *Counseling Psychologist, 31,* 427–450.

Wertheimer, M. (1978). Humanistic psychology and the humane but tough-minded psychologist. *American Psychologist, 33,* 739–745.

Wertheimer, M., & King, D. B. (1994). Max Wertheimer's American sojourn, 1933–1943. *History of Psychology Newsletter, 26,* 3–15.

Wesp, R., & Montgomery, K. (1998). Developing critical thinking through the study of paranormal phenomena. *Teaching of Psychology, 25,* 275–278.

Wesson, G. (1997, November 25). Mountain climber Hulda Crooks dies at 101. *The Press-Enterprise,* p. B06A.

Westen, D., DeFife, J. A., Bradley, B., & Hilsenroth, M. J. (2010). Prototype personality diagnosis in clinical practice: A viable alternative for *DSM-5* and *ICD-11. Professional Psychology: Research & Practice, 41,* 482–487.

Westermeyer, J. F. (2004). Predictors and characteristics of Erikson's life cycle model among men: A 32-year longitudinal study. *The International Journal of Aging & Human Development, 58,* 29–48.

Westmaas, J. L., Wild, T. C., & Ferrence, R. (2002). Effects of gender in social control of smoking cessation. *Health Psychology, 21,* 368–376.

Westrin, A., & Lam, R. W. (2007). Seasonal affective disorder: A clinical update. *Annals of Clinical Psychiatry: Official Journal of the American Academy of Clinical Psychiatrists, 19,* 239–46.

Wetter, D. W., Fiore, M. C., Young, T. B., McClure, J. B., deMoor, C. A., & Baker, T. B. (1999). Gender differences in response to nicotine replacement therapy: Objective and subjective indexes of tobacco withdrawal. *Experimental and Clinical Psychopharmacology, 7,* 135–144.

Wetter, D. W., Kenford, S. L., Smith, S. S., Fiore, M. C., Jorenby, D. E., & Baker, T. B. (1999). Gender differences in smoking cessation. *Journal of Consulting and Clinical Psychology, 67,* 555–562.

Wever, E. G., & Bray, C. W. (1937). The perception of low tones and the resonance volley theory. *Journal of Psychology, 3,* 101–114.

Whaley, D. E. (2003). Future-oriented self-perceptions and exercise behavior in middle-aged women. *Journal of Aging and Physical Activity, 11,* 1–17.

Wheat, A. L., & Larkin, K. T. (2010). Biofeedback of heat rate variability and related physiology: A critical review. *Applied Psycholphysiology & Biofeedback, 35,* 229–242.

Wheeler, R. E., Davison, R. J., & Tomarken, A. J. (1993). Frontal brain asymmetry and emotional reactivity: A biological substrate of affective style. *Psychophysiology, 30,* 82–89.

Whelan, B. M., Murdoch, B. E., Theodoros, D. G., Silburn, P., & Hall, B. (2002). A role for the dominant thalamus in language? A linguistic comparison of two cases subsequent to unilateral thalamotomy procedures in the dominant and nondominant hemispheres. *Aphasiology, 16,* 1213–1226.

Wheldall, K., & Benner, H. (1993). Conservation without conversation revisited: A replication and elaboration of the Wheldall-Poborca findings on the nonverbal assessment of conservation of liquid quantity. *Educational Psychology, 13,* 49–58.

Whisman, M. A., & Beach, S. R. H. (2012). Couple therapy for depression. *Journal of Clinical Psychology, 68,* 526–535.

Whissell, C. M. (1984). Emotion: A classification of current literature. *Perceptual and Motor Skills, 59,* 599–609.

Whitaker-Azmitia, P. M. (2001). Serotonin and brain development: Role in human developmental diseases.'

Whitbourne, S. K., & Hulicka, I. M. (1990). Ageism in undergraduate psychology texts. *American Psychologist, 45,* 1127–1136.

White, G. L., & Taytroe, L. (2003). Personal problem-solving using dream incubation: Dreaming, relaxation, or waking cognition? *Dreaming: Journal of the Association for the Study of Dreams, 13,* 193–209.

White, J. W., & Humphrey, J. A. (1994). Women's aggression in heterosexual conflicts. *Aggressive Behavior, 20,* 195–202.

White, J. W., & Kowalski, R. M. (1994). Deconstructing the myth of the nonaggressive woman: A feminist analysis. *Psychology of Women Quarterly, 18,* 487–508.

White, S. H. (1990). Child study at Clark University. *Journal of the History of the Behavioral Sciences, 26,* 131–150.

White, S. H. (1994). Hilgard's vision of psychology's history. *Psychological Science, 5,* 192–194.

White, S., O'Reilly, H., & Frith, U. (2009). Big heads, small details and autism. *Neuropsychologia, 47,* 1274–81.

Whitehurst, G. J., Falco, F. L., Lonigan, C. J., Fischel, J. E., DeBaryshe, B. D., Valdez-Menchaca, M. C., & Caulfield, M. (1988). Accelerating language development through picture book reading. *Developmental Psychology, 24,* 552–559.

Whitlock, F. A. (1987). Addiction. In R. L. Gregory (Ed.), *Oxford companion to the mind* (pp. 3–5). New York: Oxford University Press.

Whittal, M. L., Agras, W. S., & Gould, R. A. (1999). Bulimia nervosa: A meta-analysis of psychosocial and pharmacological treatments. *Behavior Therapy, 30,* 117–135.

Whorf, B. L. (1956). Science and linguistics. In J. B. Carroll (Ed.), *Language, thought, and reality: Selected writings of Benjamin Lee Whorf* (pp. 202–219). Cambridge, MA: MIT Press.

Whyte, G. (1998). Recasting Janis's groupthink model: The key role of collective efficacy in decision fiascoes. *Organizational Behavior and Human Decision Processes, 73,* 185–209.

Whyte, W. H. (1956). *The organization man.* New York: Simon & Schuster.

Wichstrom, L. (2001). The impact of pubertal timing on adolescents' alcohol use. *Journal of Research on Adolescence, 11,* 131–150.

Wickelgren, I. (1998). Obesity: How big a problem? *Science, 280,* 1364–1367.

Wicker, F. W., Barron, W. L., & Willis, A. C. (1980). Disparagement humor: Dispositions and resolutions. *Journal of Personality and Social Psychology, 39,* 701–709.

Wickramasekera, I. E., II, & Szlyk, J. P. (2003). Could empathy be a predictor of hypnotic ability? *International Journal of Clinical and Experimental Hypnosis, 51,* 390–399.

Widen, S. C., & Russell, J. A. (2003). A closer look at preschoolers' freely produced labels for facial expressions. *Developmental Psychology, 39,* 114–128.

Widiger, T. A., & Trull, T. J. (1991). Diagnosis and clinical assessment. *Annual Review of Psychology, 42,* 109–133.

Widmeyer, W. N., & Loy, J. W. (1988). When you're hot, you're hot: Warm-cold effects in first impressions of persons and teaching effectiveness. *Journal of Educational Psychology, 80,* 118–121.

Wiebe, D. J., & McCallum, D. M. (1986). Health practices and hardiness as mediators in the stress-illness relationship. *Health Psychology, 5,* 425–438.

Wiederman, M. W. (1999). A classroom demonstration of potential biases in the subjective interpretation of projective tests. *Teaching of Psychology, 26,* 37–39.

Wiederman, M. W. (1999). Volunteer bias in sexuality research using college student participants. *Journal of Sex Research, 36,* 59–66.

Wiederman, M. W., & Kendall, E. (1999). Evolution, sex, and jealousy: Investigation with a sample from Sweden. *Evolution and Human Behavior, 20,* 121–128.

Wiesmann, U., & Hannich, H.-J. (2011). A salutogenic analysis of developmental tasks and ego integrity vs. despair. *The International Journal of Aging & Human Development, 73,* 351–369.

Wightman, D. C., & Lintern, G. (1984, August). Part-task training of tracking in manual control. *NAVTRAEQUIPCEN* (Technical Report 81-C-0105-2).

Wijk, R. G., van (2009). From statistical significance to clinical relevance. *Clinical and Experimental Allergy, 40,* 197–199.

Wilcox, J. A. (1990). Fluoxetine and bulimia. *Journal of Psychoactive Drugs, 22,* 81–82.

Wilder, D. A., Simon, A. F., & Faith, M. (1996). Enhancing the impact of counterstereotypic information: Dispositional attributions for deviance. *Journal of Personality and Social Psychology, 71,* 276–287.

Wildgruber, D., Riecker, A., Hertrich, I. Erb, M., Grodd, W., Ethoger T., & Ackerman, H. (2005). Identification of emotional intonation evaluated by fMRI. *Neuroimage, 24,* 1233–1241.

Wilding, J., Rashid, W., Gilmore, D., & Valentine, E. (1986). A comparison of two mnemonic methods in learning medical information. *Human Learning: Journal of Practical Research and Applications, 5,* 211–217.

Wiles, R., Crow, G., Heath, S., & Charles, V. (2008). The management of confidentiality and anonymity in social research. *International Journal of Social Research Methodology, 11,* 417–428.

Wiley, J. (1998). Expertise as mental set: The effects of domain knowledge in creative problem solving. *Memory and Cognition, 26,* 716–730.

Wilhelm, F. H., Trabert, W., & Roth, W. T. (2001). Physiologic instability in panic disorder and generalized anxiety disorder. *Biological Psychiatry, 49,* 596–605.

Wilkins, P. (2000). Unconditional positive regard reconsidered. *British Journal of Guidance and Counselling, 28,* 23–36.

Wilson, C., Boni, D., & Hogg, A. (1997). The effectiveness of task clarification, positive reinforcement, and corrective feedback in changing courtesy among police staff. *Journal of Occupational Behavior Management, 17,* 65–99.

Williams, C. D. (1959). The elimination of tantrum behavior by extinction procedures. *Journal of Abnormal and Social Psychology, 59,* 269.

Williams, J. D., & Klug, M. G. (1996). Aging and cognition: Methodological differences in outcome. *Experimental Aging Research, 22,* 219–244.

Williams, J. E., & Best, D. L. (1990). *Measuring sex stereotypes: A multination study.* Newbury Park, CA: Sage.

Williams, J., Merritt, J., Rittenhouse, C., & Hobson, J. A. (1992). Bizarreness in dreams and fantasies: Implications for the activation-synthesis hypothesis. *Consciousness and Cognition: An International Journal, 1,* 172–185.

Williams, L., Forster, G., & Petrak, J. (1999). Rape attitudes amongst British medical students. *Medical Education, 33,* 24–27.

Williams, R. B. Jr., Kuhn, C. M., Melosh, W., White, A. D., & Schonberg, S. M. (1982). Type A behavior and elevated physiological and neuroendocrine responses to cognitive tasks. *Science, 218,* 483–485.

Williams, S. L., Brakke, K. E., & Savage-Rumbaugh, E. S. (1997). Comprehension skills of language-competent and nonlanguage-competent apes. *Language and Communication, 17,* 301–317.

Williams, S. L., Turner, S. M., & Peer, D. F. (1985). Guided mastery and performance desensitization treatments for severe acrophobia. *Journal of Consulting and Clinical Psychology, 53,* 237–247.

Williams, T. J., Pepitone, M. E., Christensen, S. E., Cooke, B. M., Huberman, A. D., Breedlove, N. J., . . . Breedlove, S. M. (2000). Finger length patterns and human sexual orientation. *Nature, 404,* 455–456.

Williams, T. L., Clarke, V., & Borland, R. (2001). Effects of message framing on breast-cancer-related beliefs and behaviors: The role of mediating factors. *Journal of Applied Social Psychology, 31,* 925–950.

Willis, L. A., Coombs, D. W., Drentea, P., & Cockerham, W. C. (2003). Uncovering the mystery: Factors of African American suicide. *Suicide and Life-Threatening Behavior, 33,* 412–429.

Wilson, B. J., Smith, S. L., Potter, W. J., Kunkel, D., Linz, D., Colvin, C. M., & Donnerstein, E. (2002). Violence in children's television programming: Assessing the risks. *Journal of Communication, 52,* 5–35.

Wilson, E. J., & Sherrell, D. L. (1993). Source effects in communication and persuasion research: A meta-analysis of effect size. *Journal of the Academy of Marketing Science, 21,* 101–112.

Wilson, E. O. (1975). *Sociobiology: The new synthesis.* Cambridge, MA: Harvard University Press.

Wilson, G. D. (1987). Male-female differences in sexual activity, enjoyment, and fantasies. *Personality and Individual Differences, 8,* 125–127.

Wilson, G. T., Fairburn, C. C., Agras, W. S., Walsh, B. T., & Kraemer, H. (2002). Cognitive-behavioral therapy for bulimia nervosa: Time course and mechanisms of change. *Journal of Consulting and Clinical Psychology, 70,* 267–274.

Wilson, G., & Lester, D. (1998). Suicide prevention by e-mail. *Crisis Intervention and Time–Limited Treatment, 4,* 81–87.

Wilson, J. R. (1967). *The mind.* New York: Time.

Wilson, T. C. (1996). Cohort and prejudice: Whites' attitudes toward Blacks, Hispanics, Jews, and Asians. *Public Opinion Quarterly, 60,* 253–274.

Wilson-Barnett, J. (1994). Preparing patients for invasive medical and surgical procedures: III. Policy implications for implementing specific psychological interventions. *Behavioral Medicine, 20,* 23–26.

Winders, S. E., & Grunberg, N. E. (1989). Nicotine, tobacco smoke, and body weight: A review of the animal literature. *Annals of Behavioral Medicine, 11,* 125–133.

Windholz, G. (1992). Pavlov's conceptualization of learning. *American Journal of Psychology, 105,* 459–469.

Windholz, G., & Kuppers, J. R. (1990). Pavlov and the Nobel Prize award. *Pavlovian Journal of Biological Science, 25,* 155–162.

Winefield, A. H. (1982). Methodological difficulties in demonstrating learned helplessness in humans. *Journal of General Psychology, 107,* 255–266.

Winer, R. S. (1999). Experimentation in the 21st century: The importance of external validity. *Journal of the Academy of Marketing Science, 27,* 349–358.

Winnepenninckx, B., Rooms, L., & Kooy, R. F. (2003). Mental retardation: A review of the genetic causes. *British Journal of Developmental Disabilities, 49,* 29–44.

Winner, E. (2000). The origins and ends of giftedness. *American Psychologist, 55,* 159–169.

Winsky-Sommerer, R. (2009). Role of GABAA receptors in the physiology and pharmacology of sleep. *European Journal of Neuroscience, 29,* 1779–1794.

Winter, Y., Lopez, J., & von Helversen, O. (2003). Ultraviolet vision in a bat. *Nature, 425,* 612–614.

Winton, W. M. (1990). Jamesian aspects of misattribution research. *Personality and Social Psychology Bulletin, 16,* 652–664.

Wittmann, A., Schlagenhauf, F., Guhn, A., Lueken, U., Gaehlsdorf, C., Stoy, M., . . . Ströhle, A. (2014). Anticipating agoraphobic situations: The neural correlates of panic disorder with agoraphobia. *Psychological Medicine/First View,* 1–12.

Wixted, J. T. (1991). Conditions and consequences of maintenance rehearsal. *Journal of Experimental Psychology: Learning, Memory, and Cognition, 17,* 963–973.

Wixted, J. T., & Ebbesen, E. B. (1991). On the form of forgetting. *Psychological Science, 2,* 409–415.

Wolfe, J. (1936). Effectiveness of token rewards for chimpanzees. *Comparative Psychology Monographs, 12* (No. 5).

Wolfensberger, W. (1972). *Normalization.* Toronto: National Institute on Mental Retardation.

Wolfensohn, S., & Maguire, M. (2010). What has the animal rights movement done for animal welfare? *Biologist, 57,* 22–27.

Wolff, J. J., Gu, H., Gerig, G., Elison, J. T., Styner, M., Gouttard, S., . . . Piven, J. (2012). Differences in white matter fiber tract development present from 6 to 24 months in infants with autism. *American Journal of Psychiatry, 169,* 589–600.

Wolgast, M., Lundh, L.-G., & Viborg, G. (2011). Cognitive reappraisal and acceptance: An experimental comparison of two emotion regulation strategies. *Behaviour Research & Therapy, 49,* 858–866.

Wolkowitz, O. M., Gertz, B., Weingartner, H., & Beccaria, L. (1990). Hunger in humans induced by MK-329, a specific peripheral-type cholecystokinin receptor antagonist. *Biological Psychiatry, 28,* 169–173.

Wollen, K. A., Weber, A., & Lowry, D. H. (1972). Bizarreness versus interaction of mental images as determinants of learning. *Cognitive Psychology, 3,* 518–523.

Wolpe, J. (1958). *Psychotherapy by reciprocal inhibition.* Stanford, CA: Stanford University Press.

Wolpe, J. (1988). Obituary: Mary Cover Jones 1896–1987. *Journal of Behavior Therapy and Experimental Psychiatry, 19,* 34.

Wolpin, M., Marston, A., Randolph, C., & Clothier, A. (1992). Individual difference correlates of reported lucid dreaming frequency and control. *Journal of Mental Imagery, 16,* 231–236.

Wood, J. M., Bootzin, R. R., Kihlstrom, J. F., & Schacter, D. L. (1992). Implicit and explicit memory for verbal information presented during sleep. *Psychological Science, 3,* 236–239.

Wood, J. M., Bootzin, R. R., Rosenhan, D., Nolen-Hoeksema, S., & Jourden, F. (1992). Effects of the 1989 San Francisco earthquake on frequency and content of nightmares. *Journal of Abnormal Psychology, 101,* 219–224.

Wood, W., & Eagly, A. H. (1981). Stages in the analysis of persuasive messages: The role of causal attributions and message comprehension. *Journal of Experimental and Social Psychology, 40,* 246–259.

Wood, W., & Eagly, A. H. (2000). A call to recognize the breadth of evolutionary perspectives: Sociocultural theories and evolutionary psychology. *Psychological Inquiry, 11,* 52–55.

Wood, W., Lundgren, S., Ouellette, J. A., & Busceme, S. (1994). Minority influence: A meta-analytic review of social influence processes. *Psychological Bulletin, 115,* 323–345.

Woodruff-Pak, D. S. (1993). Eyeblink classical conditioning in H. M.: Delay and trace paradigms. *Behavioral Neuroscience, 107,* 911–925.

Woods, C. J. P. (1996). Gender differences in moral development and acquisition: A review of Kohlberg's and Gilligan's models of justice and care. *Social Behavior and Personality, 24,* 375–384.

Woolley, H. T. (1910). A review of recent literature on the psychology of sex. *Psychological Bulletin, 7,* 335–342.

Worringham, C. J., & Messick, D. M. (1983). Social facilitation of running: An unobtrusive study. *Journal of Social Psychology, 121,* 23–29.

Worthen, M. (2011). The anger between traumatic exposures, posttraumatic stress disorder, and anger in male and female veterans. *23,* 188–201.

Wright, D. B., Gaskell, G. D., & O'Muircheartaigh, C. A. (1998). Flashbulb memory assumptions: Using national surveys to explore cognitive phenomena. *British Journal of Psychology, 89,* 103–121.

Wright, I. C., Rabe-Hesketh, S., Woodruff, P. W. R., David, A. S., Murray, R. M., & Bullmore, E. T. (2000). Meta-analysis of regional brain volumes in schizophrenia. *American Journal of Psychiatry, 157,* 16–25.

Wright, S., Grogan, S., & Hunter, G. (2000). Motivations for anabolic steroid use among bodybuilders. *Journal of Health Psychology, 5,* 566–571.

Wu, H., Wang, J., Cacioppo, J. T., Glaser, R., Kiecolt-Glaser, J. K., & Malarkey, W. B. (1999). Chronic stress associated with spousal caregiving of patients with Alzheimer's dementia is associated with downregulation of B-lymphocyte GH mRNA. *Journals of Gerontology, 54A,* M212–M215.

Wu, J., Witkiewitz, K., McMahon, R. J., & Dodge, K.A. (2010). A parallel process growth mixture model of conduct problems and substance use with risky sexual behavior. *Drug and Alcohol Dependence, 111,* 207–214.

Wyatt, J. W. (1993). Identical twins, emergenesis, and environments. *American Psychologist, 48,* 1294–1295.

Wyatt, J. W., Posey, A., Walker, W., & Seamonds, C. (1984). Natural levels of similarities between identical twins and between unrelated people. *Skeptical Inquirer, 9,* 62–66.

Wynn, K. (1995). Infants possess a system of numerical knowlege. *Current Directions in Psychological Science, 4,* 172–177.

Wysocki, C. J., & Preti, G. (1998). Pheromonal influences. *Archives of Sexual Behavior, 27,* 627–629.

X

Xantidis, L., & McCabe, M. P. (2000). Personality characteristics of male clients of female commercial sex workers. *Archives of Sexual Behavior, 29,* 165–176.

Xiao, Q., & Frost, B. J. (2013). Motion parallax processing in pigeon (*Columba livia*) pretectal neurons. *European Journal of Neuroscience, 37,* 1103–1111.

Xiaohe, X., & Whyte, M. K. (1990). Love matches and arranged marriages: A Chinese replication. *Journal of Marriage and the Family, 52,* 709–722.

Xie, L., Kang, H., Xu, Q., Chen, M. J., Liao, Y., Thiyagarajan, M., . . . Nedergaard, M. (2013). Sleep drives metabolite clearance from the adult brain. *Science 342,* 373–377.

Y

Yaccarino, M. E. (1993). Using Minuchin's structural family therapy techniques with Italian–American families. *Contemporary Family Therapy: An International Journal, 15,* 459–466.

Yaffe, K. (2003). Hormone therapy and the brain: Déjà vu all over again? *JAMA: Journal of the American Medical Association, 289,* 2717–2719.

Yamagishi, T., Kikuchi, M., & Kosugi, M. (1999). Trust, gullibility, and social intelligence. *Asian Journal of Social Psychology, 2,* 145–161.

Yamaguchi, H. (1988). Effects of actor's and observer's roles on causal attribution by Japanese subjects for success and failure in competitive situations. *Psychological Reports, 63,* 619–626.

Yamamiya, Y., Shroff, H., & Thompson, J. K. (2008). The tripartite influence model of body image and eating disturbance: A replication with a Japanese sample. *International Journal of Eating Disorders, 41,* 88–91.

Yamawaki, N., Tschanz, B. T., & Feick, D. L. (2004). Defensive pessimism, self-esteem instability, and goal strivings. *Cognition and Emotion, 18,* 233–249.

Yanchar, S. C. (1997).William James and the challenge of methodological pluralism. *Journal of Mind and Behavior, 18,* 425–442.

Yang, A. (1997). Trends: Attitudes toward homosexuality. *Public Opinion Quarterly, 61,* 477–507.

Yang, C. M., & Spielman, A. J. (2001). The effect of a delayed weekend sleep pattern on sleep and morning functioning. *Psychology and Health, 16,* 715–725.

Yap, J. N. (1988). The effects of hospitalization and surgery on children: A critical review. *Journal of Applied Developmental Psychology, 9,* 349–358.

Yarmey, A. D. (1973). I recognize your face but I can't remember your name: Further evidence on the tip-of-the-tongue phenomenon. *Memory and Cognition, 1,* 287–290.

Yela, C., & Sangrador, J. L. (2001). Perception of physical attractiveness throughout loving relationships. *Current Research in Social Psychology, 6,* 57–75.

Yen, S., Robins, C. J., & Lin, N. (2000). A cross-cultural comparison of depressive symptom manifestation: China and the United States. *Journal of Consulting and Clinical Psychology, 68,* 993–999.

Yen, S., Zlotnick, C., & Costello, E. (2002). Affect regulation in women with borderline personality disorder traits. *Journal of Nervous and Mental Disease, 190,* 693–696.

Yerkes, R. M., & Dodson, J. D. (1908). The relation of strength of stimulus to rapidity of habit formation. *Journal of Comparative Neurology and Psychology, 18,* 459–482.

Young, L. D., Richter, J. E., Bradley, L. A., & Anderson, K. O. (1987). Disorders of the upper gastrointestinal system: An overview. *Annals of Behavioral Medicine, 9,* 7–12.

Young, R. L., & Nettelbeck, T. (1995). The abilities of a musical savant and his family. *Journal of Autism and Developmental Disorders, 25,* 231–248.

Youngren, M. A., & Lewinsohn, P. M. (1980). The functional relation between depression and problematic interpersonal behavior. *Journal of Abnormal Psychology, 89,* 333–341.

Yu, S., & Ho, I. K. (1990). Effects of acute barbiturate administration, tolerance and dependence on brain GABA system: Comparison to alcohol and benzodiazepines. *Alcohol, 7,* 261–272.

Yuan, W., Ming, Z., Rana, N., Hail, L., Chen-Wang, J., & Shao-Hui, M. (2010). A functional magnetic resonance imaging study of human brain in pain-related areas induced by electrical stimulation with different intensities. *Neurology India, 58,* 922–927.

Yurek, D., Farrar, W., & Andersen, B. L. (2000). Breast cancer surgery: Comparing surgical groups and determining individual differences in postoperative sexuality and body change stress. *Journal of Consulting and Clinical Psychology, 68,* 697–709.

Yutrzenka, B. A., Todd-Bazemore, E., & Caraway, S. J. (1999). Four winds: The evolution of culturally inclusive clinical psychology training for Native Americans. *International Review of Psychiatry, 11,* 129–135.

Z

Zach, U., & Keller, H. (1999). Patterns of the attachment-exploration balance of 1-year-old infants from the United States and northern Germany. *Journal of Cross-Cultural Psychology, 30,* 381–388.

Zadra, A. L., & Pihl, R. O. (1997). Lucid dreaming as a treatment for recurrent nightmares. *Psychotherapy and Psychosomatics, 66,* 50–55.

Zadra, A. L., O'Brien, S. A., & Donderi, D. C. (1998). Dream content, dream recurrence, and well-being: A replication with a younger sample. *Imagination, Cognition, and Personality, 17,* 293–311.

Zajecka, J., Dunner, D. L., Gelenberg, A. J., Hirschfeld, R. M. A., Kornstein, S. G., Ninan, P. T., . . . Keller, M. B. (2002). Sexual function and satisfaction in the treatment of chronic major depression with nefazodone, psychotherapy and their combination. *Journal of Clnical Psychiatry, 63,* 709–716.

Zajonc, R. B. (1965). Social facilitation. *Science, 149,* 269–274.

Zajonc, R. B. (1976). Family configuration and intelligence. *Science, 192,* 227–236.

Zajonc, R. B. (1984). On the primacy of affect. *American Psychologist, 39,* 117–123.

Zajonc, R. B. (1985). Emotion and facial efference: A theory revisited. *Science, 228,* 15–21.

Zajonc, R. B. (1986). The decline and rise of scholastic aptitude scores: A prediction derived from the confluence model. *American Psychologist, 41,* 862–867.

Zajonc, R. B. (1993). The confluence model: Differential or difference equation. *European Journal of Social Psychology, 23,* 211–215.

Zajonc, R. B., & Mullally, P. R. (1997). Birth order: Reconciling conflicting effects. *American Psychologist, 52,* 685–699.

Zaldivar, R. A. (1986, June 10). Panel faults NASA on shuttle. *Philadelphia Inquirer,* pp. 1-A, 12-A.

Zander, A. (1979). The psychology of group processes. *Annual Review of Psychology, 30,* 417–451.

Zangariand, W., & Machado, F. R. (2001). Parapsychology in Brazil: A science entering young adulthood. *Journal of Parapsychology, 65,* 351–356.

Zanoto de Luca, M. C., Brandao, M. L., Motta, V. A., & Landeira-Fernandez, J. (2003). Antinociception induced by stimulation of ventrolateral periaqueductal gray at the freezing threshold is regulated by opioid and 5-HT-sub(2A) receptors as assessed by the tail-flick and formalin tests. *Pharmacology, Biochemistry and Behavior, 75,* 459–466.

Zatorre, R. J., Belin, P., & Penhune, V. B. (2002). Structure and function of auditory cortex: Music and speech. *Trends in Cognitive Sciences, 6,* 37–46.

Zatorre, R. J., Bouffard, M., Ahad, P., & Belin, P. (2002). Where is "where" in the human auditory cortex? *Nature Neuroscience, 5,* 905–909.

Zec, R. F., & Trivedi, M. A. (2002). The effects of estrogen replacement therapy on neuropsychologial functioning in postmenopausal women with and without dementia: A critical and theoretical review. *Neuropsychology Review, 12,* 65–109.

Zentall, T. R., Sutton, J. E., & Sherburne, L. M. (1996). True imitative learning in pigeons. *Psychological Science, 7,* 343–346.

Zeitlin, D., Keller, S. E., Shiflett, S. C., Schleifer, S. J., & Bartlett, J. A. (2000). Immunological effects of massage therapy during acute academic stress. *Psychosomatic Medicine, 62,* 83–84.

Zerbo, O., Qian, Y., Yoshida, C., Grether, J. K., Van de Water, J., & Croen, L. A. (2013). Maternal infection during pregnancy and autism spectrum disorders. *Journal of Autism and Developmental Disorders, 40,* 1423-1430.

Zhang, J., & Thomas, D. L. (1994). Modernization theory revisited: A cross-cultural study of adolescent conformity to significant others in mainland China, Taiwan, and the USA. *Adolescence, 29,* 885–903.

Zhang, X., & Nurmi, J.-E. (2012). Teacher-child relationships and social competence: A two-year longitudinal study of Chinese preschoolers. *Journal of Applied Developmental Psychology, 33,* 125–135.

Zhou, Q., Wang, Y., Deng, X., Eisenberg, N., Wolchik, S. A., & Tein, J.-Y. (2008). Relations of temperament and temperament to Chinese children's experience of negative life events, coping efficacy, and externalizing problems. *Child Development, 79,* 493–513.

Zhou, X., & Li, P. (2013), Simulating cross-language priming with a dynamic computational model of the lexicon. *Bilingualism: Language & Cognition, 16,* 288–303.

Zhu, A. J., & Walsh, B. T. (2002). In review: Pharmacologic treatment of eating disorders. *Canadian Journal of Psychiatry, 47,* 227–234.

Zhu, Z., Disbrow, E. A., Zumer, J. M., McGonigle, D. J., & Nagarajan, S. S. (2007). Spatiotemporal integration of tactile information in human somatosensory cortex. *BMC Neuroscience, 8,* 21–34.

Zickar, M. J. (2003). Remembering Arthur Kornhauser: Industrial psychology's advocate for worker well-being. *Journal of Applied Psychology, 88,* 363–369.

Ziegler, D. J. (2001). The possible place of cognitive appraisal in the ABC model underlying Rational-Emotive Behavior Therapy. *Journal of Rational-Emotive and Cognitive Behavior Therapy, 19,* 137–152.

Zigler, E. (1999). Head Start is not child care. *American Psychologist, 54,* 142.

Zigler, E., Abelson, W. D., Trickett, P. K., & Seitz, V. (1982). Is an intervention program necessary in order to improve economically disadvantaged children's IQ scores? *Child Development, 33,* 340–348.

Zimmerman, M. (1983). Methodological issues in the assessment of life events: A review of issues and research. *Clinical Psychology Review, 3,* 339–370.

Zimpfer, D. G. (1991). Groups for grief and survivorship after bereavement: A review. *Journal for Specialists in Group Work, 16,* 46–55.

Zimprich, D., & Martin, M. (2002). Can longitudinal changes in processing speed explain longitudinal age changes in fluid intelligence? *Psychology and Aging, 17,* 690–695.

Zisook, S., Byrd, D., Kuck, J., & Jeste, D. V. (1995). Command hallucinations in outpatients with schizophrenia. *Journal of Clinical Psychiatry, 56,* 462–465.

Ziv, A. (1987). The effect of humor on aggression catharsis in the classroom. *Journal of Psychology, 121,* 359–364.

Zohar, D., Tzischinski, O., & Epstein, R. (2003). Effects of energy availability on immediate and delayed emotional reactions to work events. *Journal of Applied Psychology, 88,* 1082–1093.

Zola-Morgan, S. M., & Squire, L. R. (1990). The primate hipppocampal formation: Evidence for a time-limited role in memory storage. *Science, 250,* 288–290.

Zomlaiski, N., Dyrborg, J., Rasmussen, H., Schumann, T., Koch, S. V., & Bilenberg, N. (2010). Validity and clinical feasibility of the ADHD rating scale (ADHD-RS):A Danish nationwide multicenter study. *Acta Pediatrica, 98,* 397–402.

Zucker, G. S., & Weiner, B. (1993). Conservatism and perceptions of poverty: An attributional analysis. *Journal of Applied Social Psychology, 23,* 925–943.

Zuckerman, M. (1990). The psychophysiology of sensation seeking. *Journal of Personality, 58,* 313–345.

Zuckerman, M., Eysenck, S. B., & Eysenck, H. J. (1978). Sensation seeking in England and America: Cross-cultural, age and sex comparisons. *Journal of Consulting and Clinical Psychology, 46,* 139–149.

Zuckerman, M., Joireman, J., Kraft, M., & Kuhlman, D. M. (1999). Where do motivational and emotional traits fit within three-factor models of personality? *Personality and Individual Differences, 26,* 487–504.

Zuckerman, M., Kieffer, S. C., & Knee, C. R. (1998). Consequences of self-handicapping: Effects on coping, academic performance, and adjustment. *Journal of Personality and Social Psychology, 74,* 1619–1628.

Zuckerman, M., Koestner, R., DeBoy, T., Garcia, T., Maresca, B. C., & Sartoris, J. M. (1988). To predict some of the people some of the time: A reexamination of the moderator variable approach in personality theory. *Journal of Personality and Social Psychology, 54,* 1006–1019.

Zuroff, D. C. (1986). Was Gordon Allport a trait theorist? *Journal of Personality and Social Psychology, 51,* 983–1000.

Zuwerink, J. R., & Devine, P. G. (1996). Attitude importance and resistance to persuasion: It's not just the thought that counts. *Journal of Personality and Social Psychology, 70,* 931–944.

Zwislocki, J. J. (1981). Sound analysis in the ear: A history of discoveries. *American Scientist, 69,* 184–192.

Name Index

Bennett, R. H., 96, 227
Bennett, W., 585
Ben-Shakhar, G., 349, 418
Ben-Shaul, Y., 88
Ben-Shlomo, Y., 141
Bentall, R. P., 489
Benton, D., 303
Benton, T. R., 26
Beratis, I. N., 514
Beratis, S., 514
Berenbaum, S. A., 138
Berg, J. H., 599, 605
Berger, A. A., 430
Berger, R. S., 580
Bergeron, S. M., 387
Bergesch, P., 509
Bergin, A. E., 552
Berglas, S., 467
Berglund, P., 490, 493
Bergman, H., 406
Berk, M., 506, 513
Berko, J., 329
Berkowitz, L., 624
Berkowitz, M. W., 125
Berlucchi, G., 15
Bernard, I., 468
Bernardo, P., 406
Berndt, T. J., 122
Bernier, M.-J., 500
Bernieri, F., 423
Berninger, V. W., 114
Bernstein, I. L., 243–244
Bernstein, W. M., 597
Berntson, G. G., 82
Berridge, C. W., 523
Berry, J. W., 114, 612
Bersagliere, A., 81
Berscheid, E., 604
Bertelli, J. A., 99
Bertelson, A. D., 567
Bertero, E. B., 313
Berthier, N. E., 114
Bertilsson, L., 502
Bertoncini, J., 111
Bertrand, L., 501
Best, C. T., 326
Best, D. L., 424
Best, P. J., 224
Beutler, L. E., 556
Bever, T. G., 336
Bexton, W. H., 400
Bhargava, M., 238
Bherer, L., 296
Biafora, F., 505
Bianchi, S. M., 143
Bickel, W. K., 587
Bidzan, L., 41
Biederman, J., 521
Biggers, K., 569
Bigler, R. S., 280
Bihrle, S., 519
Bijlsma, J. W. J., 572
Bijmolt, T. H. A., 282
Bilder, R. M., 95
Billig, M., 614

Binder, J. R., 88
Binik, Y. M., 323, 391, 393
Binsted, G., 172
Birch, D. E., 550
Birch, J., 163
Birch, L., 382
Birchall, H. M., 492
Bird, S., 295
Birdsong, D., 330
Birkett, M. A., 109
Birketvedt, O., 167
Bishop, D. V. M., 92, 93
Bishop, G. D., 616
Bitgood, S. C., 20
Bitoun, E. I., 84
Bitter, J. R., 543
Bjelke, B., 97
Bjork, D. W., 61
Bjork, E. L., 114
Björklund, A., 99
Bjorklund, A. C., 624
Bjorklund, D. F., 279
Bjorkqvist, K., 624
Bjorvatn, B., 207
Blachstein, H., 36
Black, B., 144
Black, D. S., 581
Black, J. E., 135, 229
Blackburn, J. R., 238
Blackburn, T. C., 576
Blackford, J. U., 471
Blair, M. E., 238
Blaisdell, A. P., 260
Blake, R., 178
Blakemore, C., 172, 491
Blanchard, J. J., 511
Blanchard, R., 397
Blanco-Centurion, C. A., 84
Bland, R. C., 492
Blanke, O., 89
Blanton, H., 44
Blascovich, J., 570
Blaszczyk-Schiep, S., 451
Blass, T., 622
Blaszcynski, A., 398
Blazer, D. G., 505
Bleichrodt, N., 350
Bles, W., 187
Blick, K. A., 294
Blier, P., 76
Blissett, S. E., 579
Blix, A. G., 586
Blix, G. G., 586
Blizard, R. A., 500
Block, J. H., 319
Block, J., 319, 470
Blois, W. G., 221
Bloj, M., 167
Bloom, R., 257
Bloomsmith, M. A., 254
Blough, D. S., 173
Blume, H. K., 257
Blume-Marcovici, A., 215
Blundell, J., 380
Boake, C., 347

Boardman, J., 496
Boatwright, K., 8
Boblique, C., 576
Bodenhausen, G. V., 600
Bodensteiner, J. B., 353
Bodnar, R. J., 77
Boeck, B. E., 144
Bogaert, A. F., 397
Bogart, L. M., 599
Boggiano, A. K., 405
Bohannon, J. N., III 331
Bohart, A. C., 553
Bohlen, J., 395
Bohman, A., 614
Bohner, G., 609
Bolanowski, S. J., 183
Bolen, M. H., 626
Bolm-Audorff, U., 421
Bolsover, S., 97
Bolt, E., 119
Bolte, S., 343
Bolton, P., 353, 520
Bolzani, R., 217
Bombardier, C. H., 186
Bond, C. F., Jr., 227
Bond, C. F., 617
Bond, L. A., 368
Bond, R., 619
Bonds, D. R., 384
Boneau, C. A., 259
Boneva, B., 403
Boni, D., 246
Boniecki, K. A., 254
Bonilla, C., 100
Bonnefond, A., 209
Bonner, M. J., 591
Bonni, S., 300
Bono, J. E., 463
Book, A. S., 624
Booker, A., 624
Bookheimer, S. Y., 419
Boomsma, D. I., 568
Boon, S. D., 322
Boone, L., 387, 389
Boone, R. T., 423
Boot, B. P., 231
Booth, N., 506
Booth, R. E., 507, 579
Booth-Butterfield, S., 620
Booth-LaForce, C., 119
Bootzin, R. R., 200
Boquet, A., 205
Borbely, A. A., 228
Boring, E. G., 5
Boris, H. I., 598
Borkenau, P., 474
Borland, R., 322
Born, J., 218
Bornovalova, M. A., 518
Bornstein, M. H., 10, 424
Borod, J. C., 420
Bortoli, L., 399
Bortz, R., 210
Bortz, W. M., II, 134
Bos, J. E., 187

Bos, P. A., 624
Bosl, W., 81
Bosly, A., 576
Bothwell, R. K., 290
Bouchard, T. J., Jr., 64–65, 366–367, 379, 472–474, 483, 518
Bouchard, T. J., 395
Boucher, F., 85
Boudreaux, R., 209
Bouffard, M., 179
Boulos, Z., 209
Boulton, M. J., 578
Bourgeois, J. A., 496
Bouton, M. E., 240
Bovasso, G. B., 573
Bovberg, D. H., 563
Bovbjerg, D. H., 242
Bower, G. H., 296, 297, 499
Bowers, C. A., 95
Bowers, K. S., 45, 222, 451
Bowlby, J., 117
Bowman, D., 555
Box, P., 254
Boyce, B. A., 407
Boyce, W. T., 174
Boyd, J. H., 492, 494
Boyle, G. J., 567
Boyle, S. H., 69
Boynton, R. M., 163
Bozarth, J. D., 540
Braastad, B. O., 237
Bracht, C., 612
Brackbill, Y., 368
Brackfield, S. C., 318
Brackshaw, E., 384
Bradbury, E. J., 97
Bradbury, T. N., 141–142
Bradford, J., 53
Bradley, B. P., 285, 495
Bradley, B., 311
Bradley, L. A., 567
Bradley, M. M., 414
Bradley, M. T., 418
Bradshaw, E., 26
Bradshaw, M., 65
Braehler, E., 497
Braet, C., 387
Brakke, K. E., 335
Bramlett, R. K., 20
Branch, W., 48
Brand, G., 180
Brand, M., 500
Brand, R. J., 569
Brandao, M. L., 184
Brandstaetter, V., 142
Branje, S. J. T., 132
Bratslavsky, E., 605
Brattico, E., 82
Brauer, M., 616
Braun, A., 430
Braun, D. L., 387
Braun-Janzen, C., 534
Brawman-Mintzer, O., 491
Bray, C. W., 177
Bray, S. R., 461

Brayboy, T. D., 384
Breathnach, C. S., 90
Brébion, G., 279
Brechmann, A., 85
Breckler, S. J., 606
Bredahl, L. C., 288
Brehm, J. W., 610
Breier, J. I., 82
Breland, K., 258
Bremner, J. D., 180
Brennan, C., 465
Brennan, P. A., 512
Brent, D. A., 507
Brentar, J. T., 221
Brentari, D. K., 336
Bresler, C., 144
Breuer, J., 624
Brevik, J. I., 577
Brewer, M. B., 615
Brewer, M., 545
Brewer, N., 290–291, 436
Brezun, J. M., 97
Bricklin, J., 28
Brickman, P., 429
Bridge, H., 166
Bridge, J., 507
Briggs, J., 625
Briggs, K. C., 455
Brigham, C. C., 363
Brigham, J. C., 38, 290
Briken, P., 624
Brinton, R. D., 303
Brion, S., 455
Briston, T., 462
Brittain, A. E., 131
Brobeck, J. R., 381
Broberg, D. J., 244
Brockman, L. N., 257
Broder, M. S., 552
Brogaard, B., 201
Brohawn, K. H., 564
Bromberg, W., 529
Bronstein, C., 531
Brooks, B. B., 420
Brooks, G. R., 462
Brooks, K., 291
Brooks, M. C., 122
Brooks, P., 220
Brooks, P. J., 255
Brooks-Gunn, J., 121,128–129, 349, 365, 369, 388
Brosschot, J. F., 576
Broughton, R. S., 190
Brouwers, M. C., 530
Brown, A. L., 354
Brown, A. S., 50, 189, 269, 315, 615
Brown, B., 84
Brown, D., 286, 350, 430
Brown, D. A., 74
Brown, D. R., 379
Brown, H. O., 309
Brown, J. D., 469, 470, 486, 565, 580–582, 598–599
Brown, K. S., 617
Brown, L. S., 286

Brown, R., 212, 269, 329
Brown, R. J., 319, 497
Brown, S. W., 220
Brown, T. E., 521–522
Brown, V. R., 109, 319
Brownell, K. D., 385, 585–586, 591
Brozek, J., 2
Bruce, M. L., 485
Bruck, G. E., 308
Bruck, M., 290
Bruener, C. C., 257
Brugger, P., 190
Brummett, B. H., 69
Brunello, N., 76
Bruner, J. S., 10
Bruno, G., 7
Bruno, T., 407
Brunswick, D. J., 508
Bruschi, C. J., 579
Bryant, A. G., 550
Bryant, D. M., 121, 353
Bryck, R. L., 111
Bryden, M. P., 92–93, 136, 308
Brydon, L., 575
Buccino, G., 263
Buchanan, A., 512
Buchanan, J. J., 279
Buchsbaum, M. S., 513
Buck, R., 414, 435
Buckingham, B., 109
Buckley, K. W., 11
Buckner, J. D., 482
Bucy, P. C., 86
Budowski, D., 487
Buechel, C., 159
Buitelaar, J., 523
Bukowski, W. M., 122
Bulik, C. M., 383, 388
Bullough, V. L., 392
Bulzacka, E., 199
Bundrick, C. M., 468
Bunge, M., 29
Bunn, A., 496
Buono, S., 322
Burchinal, M. R., 121
Burgard, S. A., 207
Burger, J. M., 601, 620
Burgess, C. A., 221
Burgess, P., 360
Buric, I., 35
Burke, P. B., 119
Burlingame, G. M., 554
Burman, B., 121
Burnham, W. M., 545
Burns, D. J., 152
Burns, J., 92
Burns, T. E., 287
Burns, V. E., 563
Burr, M. L., 579
Burrows, L., 188
Bursik, K., 215
Burton, D., 407
Burwell, R. A., 387
Busby, S., 533
Busceme, S., 616

Bush, G., 523
Bush, H. E., 552
Bush, J. E., 613
Bushman, B. J., 39, 623
Bushnell, M. C., 222
Buss, A., 624
Buss, A. R., 5, 136
Buss, D. M., 15, 62, 138, 141, 605–606, 623
Bussey, K., 123
Buswell, B. N., 137, 468
Butcher, J. N., 457, 484
Butler, A. C., 537
Butler, B. E., 366
Butler, L. D., 504
Butnik, S. M., 523
Butschky, M. F., 587
Butt, A. E., 240
Butterworth, G., 602
Buunk, B. P., 62, 429, 574, 606, 618
Byars, K. C., 216
Bye, L., 583
Bylsma, W. H., 468
Byne, W., 396
Byrd, D., 511
Byrne, D., 30, 53, 603
Byrne, W. L., 301
Byrnes, J. P., 138
Byron, K., 319

C

Cabanac, M., 381
Cabeza, R., 15
Cabral, H., 109
Cabral, R. R., 555
Cacioppo, J. T., 82, 608–609
Cade, J. F. J., 546
Cadet, J. L., 228
Cadoret, R. J., 64
Cagnacci, A., 385
Cahan, D., 4
Cahan, E. D., 15
Cahill, L., 302
Cai, Y., 119
Cain, W. S., 182
Calantone, R. J., 608
Caldwell, J. L., 204
Calisch, G., 155
Calkins, M. W., 8, 214–216, 232
Callahan, C. M., 361
Callas, P. W., 45
Callero, P. L., 434
Callow, N., 409
Caltagagirone, C., 300
Calvert, S. L., 123
Camel, J. E., 111
Camerino, M., 570
Cameron, H. A., 545
Cameron, J., 404
Cameron, L., 589
Cameron, M. J., 248
Camic, P. M., 16
Caminiti, R., 55
Campbell, D. A., 597

Campbell, J. D., 470, 579
Campbell, J. N., 184, 209, 605
Campione, J. E., 354
Camras, L. A., 425
Canada, K. E., 454
Canel-Çinarbas, D., 37
Canetto, S. S., 507
Canino, G. J., 492
Cann, A., 621
Cannon, M., 64
Cannon, W. B., 432–433, 566
Canter, D. V., 465
Cantu, C. L., 132
Caplan, L. J., 328
Cappello, M. J., 248
Caprara, G. V., 461
Capraro, M. M., 455
Capraro, R. M., 455
Caputi, P., 362
Caputo, J. L., 563
Caqueret, A., 85
Caraway, S. J., 530
Carbone, K. M., 514
Cardwe, C. R., 76
Carey, C. L., 230
Carey, G., 483
Carey, M. P., 393
Carey, T. A., 32
Carlbring, P., 552
Carle, S. B., 418
Carlsmith, J. M., 611
Carlson, D., 294
Carlson, E. T., 500
Carlson, J. A., 384
Carlson, L. E., 581
Carlson, M., 626
Carlsson, C. P. O., 186
Carlstrom, A., 460
Carmichael, L., 332
Carnahan, E., 587
Carnes, M., 408
Carney, R. N., 296–297
Carnine, D. W., 294
Carossino, P., 185
Carpenter, C. R., 262
Carr, A., 543
Carr, A. S., 76, 522
Carr, J. E., 535
Carrà, G., 512
Carretero, M., 26
Carrico, R. L., 114
Carroll, D., 563
Carroll, J. B., 365
Carroll, J. M., 423
Carroll, M., 397, 548
Carroll, M. E., 55
Carron, A. V., 618
Carson, R. C., 484
Carson, S. H., 317
Carta, G., 230
Carter, C. M., 312
Carter, C. S., 496
Carter, R., 296
Carter-Pokras, O., 584
Carter-Saltzman, L., 367

Karhu, J., 79
Karlberg, L., 570
Karlin, B. E., 539
Karlov, A. V., 210
Karmel, R., 229
Karnavas, W. J., 160
Karnes, M. B., 317
Karney, B. R., 142
Karnovsky, M. L., 212
Karon, B. P., 286
Karp, D. E., 356
Kashima, E. S., 333
Kashima, Y., 598
Kaspar, C. H., 401, 581
Kassel, J. D., 228
Kasser, T., 606
Kassin, S. M., 290
Kasthuri, N., 71
Katata, K., 82
Katkin, E. S., 437
Kato, T., 492
Katramados, A., 228
Katter, J. T., 184
Katz, J., 107
Katz, J. L., 377
Katz, M., 185
Katz, N., 605
Katzman, M. A., 387
Kauffman, J. M., 261
Kauffman, T., 183
Kaufman, F. R., 109
Kaufman, I., 171
Kaufman, J. C., 316
Kaufman, L., 272
Kaufmann, C., 199
Kavounoudias, A., 183
Kavšek, M., 167
Kawachi, I., 575
Kawakami, K., 612
Kawamura, T., 596
Kayne, N. T., 504
Kazemi-Bajestani, S. M. R., 481
Kazén, M., 451
Keane, M. M., 278
Keast, A., 291
Keats, B. J. B., 395
Kebbell, M. R., 20
Kedem, P., 492
Keegan, D., 430
Keegan, J., 109
Keel, P. K., 388
Keeler, G., 485
Keen, R., 114
Keenan, J. P., 183
Keenan, R., 587
Keesey, R. E., 382
Keijsers, G. P. J., 498, 555
Keil, K., 173
Keiley, M. K., 121
Keilis-Borok, V., 32
Keillor, J. M., 435
Keith, B., 122
Keith, J. R., 261
Keller, F. S., 12
Keller, H., 118

Keller, S. E., 570, 581
Kelley, H. H., 26, 599
Kelley, M., 564
Kelling, A. S., 254
Kellow, J. T., 355
Kelly, E. W., 145
Kelly, I. W., 481
Kelly, J. F., 461
Kelly, M. P., 393
Kelly, R. B., 582
Kelly, S. J., 343
Kelly, W. E., 209
Kelsoe, J. R., 509
Keltner, D., 424, 426
Kelvin, L. K. H., 83
Kemeny, M. E., 597
Kemp, B., 67
Kemper, H. C. G., 565
Kemper, T. L., 520
Kempter, G., 539
Kemp-Wheeler, S. M., 556
Kenardy, J., 493
Kendall, E., 62
Kendler, K. S., 383, 472, 491, 502,
    512
Kendzierski, D., 464
Kenneally, S. M., 308
Kenrick, D. T., 458, 470, 606
Keppel, R. D., 465
Kerkhoff, G., 60
Kern, D., 429
Kerns, R. D., 183
Kerr, N. L., 616
Kerr, Z. Y., 542
Kerzhnerman, I., 385
Keske, C. M., 285
Kessler, R. C., 45, 480, 488, 490,
    492–495, 502, 505, 508, 521, 522
Kessler, S., 489
Kety, S. S., 512
Kevles, D. J., 396
Khalife, S., 393
Kharazmi, S., 430
Khazanchi, S., 319
Khire, U., 350
Khouri, H., 600
Kidd, J. A., 31
Kiecolt-Glaser, J. K., 69, 220,
    566–567, 570–573, 581–582
Kiefer, S. C., 598
Kiernan, B. D., 186
Kihlstrom, J. F., 200, 222
Kikuchi, M., 361
Kilborn, L. C., 492
Killen, J. D., 494
Kilmartin, C. T., 447
Kilts, C. D., 419
Kim, D., 67, 617, 620
Kim, H. S., 578
Kim, J. E., 143
Kim, J. H., 37
Kim, J., 238, 302, 568
Kim, J. Y., 446
Kim, K., 243
Kim, Y. I., 543

Kim, Y. S., 89
Kim, Y. H., 598
Kimball, M. M., 137, 528
Kimble, D. P., 301
Kimble, G. A., 244
Kimchi, R., 150
Kim-Cohen, J., 472
Kimeldorf, D. J., 243
Kim-Phuong, L. V., 14
Kimura, D., 138–139
Kimura, R., 299
Kincades, M. J., 60
King, D. B., 8, 406
King, D. J., 209, 579, 584
King, M. G., 212
King, N. J., 495
King, T., 115
Kinney-Hurd, B. L., 240
Kinsey, A. C., 392
Kircher, J. C., 418
Kircher, J. R., 393
Kirchner, J., 603
Kirkley, B. G., 567
Kirmayer, L. J., 548
Kirmeyer, S. L., 569
Kirouac, G., 424
Kirsch, I., 185
Kirschner, S. M., 485
Kirschvink, J. L., 151
Kirshnit, C. E., 313
Kisch, J., 246
Kisilevsky, B. S., 109
Kisler, T. S., 211
Kisner, M. J., 3
Kit, B. K., 382
Kitano, S., 167
Kitayama, S., 428, 462, 469, 596, 598
Kitazawa, S., 95
Kittlerova, P., 99
Kittrell, D., 143
Kitano, S., 167
Klaening, U., 514
Klahr, A. M., 121
Klar, Y., 429
Klausen, B. S., 99
Klebanov, P. K., 349, 365
Kleiber, C., 186
Kleimann, M., 35
Klein, A. G., 355
Klein, D. F., 492, 554
Klein, D. N., 322, 523
Klein, P. D., 468
Klein, S. B., 391
Kleindienst, N., 546
Kleinke, C. L., 435
Kleinknecht, R. A., 493
Kleinmuntz, B., 416–418
Kleitman, N., 207
Klepac, R. K., 534
Klimesch, W., 278
Klineberg, E., 578
Kling, K. C., 137, 468
Klohnen, E. C., 603
Klonoff, E. A., 498, 589
Klosterhalfen, W., 256

Kluft, R. P., 500
Klug, M. G., 107
Klump, K. L., 387–388
Klusmann, V., 584
Klüver, H., 86
Kmiecik-Malecka, E., 36
Knafo, A., 455
Knapp, T. J., 246
Knebel, T., 186
Knee, C. R., 322, 598
Knestel, A., 36
Kniffki, K. D., 183
Knight, J., 601
Knishkowy, B., 587
Knopman, D. S., 301
Knouse, S. B., 598
Knox, S. S., 577
Knudsen, E. I., 179
Knuutila, J., 272
Kobasa, S. C., 576
Kobayakawa, T., 182
Kocan, E. R., 310
Koch, G., 300
Kocsis, R. N., 465
Koed, K., 509
Koehler, J. J., 26
Koelling, R. A., 245
Koeske, R. D., 279
Koester, E. P., 277
Koestner, R., 405
Koff, E., 420
Kogan, N., 615
Kohlberg, L., 124, 126
Köhler, W., 14, 313
Kohnken, G., 293
Koivisto, A.-M., 129
Kojetin, B. A., 64
Kolata, G., 329, 383
Kolinsky, R., 176
Kolligian, J., Jr., 469
Kollmeier, B., 177
Komisaruk, B. R., 82
Komoda, Y., 209
Konnert, C., 142
Kontinen, V. K., 183
Koole, S. L., 14
Kooy, R. F., 353
Kop, W. J., 93
Kopaneva, I., 601
Kopell, B. H., 544
Kopelman, M. D., 499
Koppe, S., 73
Kordower, J. H., 99
Koretz, J., 34
Korn, J. H., 52
Korpi, E. R., 225
Korsnes, M. S., 282
Kortenkamp, S., 435
Koskenvuo, M., 208
Koss, M., 36
Kossowsky, J., 492
Koster, E. H. W., 418
Kosugi, M., 361
Kotler, M., 492
Kotz, S. A., 422–423

Mack, M. E., 172
Mack, S., 254
Mackinnon, A. J., 508
MacKinnon, G. E., 308
MacKintosh, N. J., 261
Macklin, M. C., 281
MacLaren, V. V., 418
MacLean, H. N., 286
MacLeod, C. M., 283
MacMillan, H. L., 548
Macmillan, M., 89
MacNichol, E. F., Jr., 161
Macrides, F., 181
MacTavish, D., 300
Maczaj, M., 213
Madden, T., 132
Maddi, K. L., 577
Maddi, S. R., 576–577
Madigan, M. W., 282
Madison, D. V., 72
Madison, G., 358
Maekelae, K., 611
Maekisalo, H., 624
Maeshima, S., 60
Maganaris, C. N., 69
Maglieri, K. A., 536
Magloire, K., 578
Magnuson, V. L., 395
Magnussen, S., 282
Magoun, H. W., 84
Maguire, M., 55
Maguire-Zeiss, K. A., 76
Mah, K., 391
Mahableshwarkar, A. R., 41
Maher, C. G., 461
Maher, L. M., 82
Mahler, H. I. M., 590
Mahlios, J., 214
Mahoney, B. S., 187
Maiano, C., 45
Maiello, S., 542
Maier, N. R., 315
Maier, S. F., 256
Maio, G. R., 613
Majde, J. A., 212
Majeres, R. L., 326
Majhi, P., 69
Major, B., 123
Makara, G. B., 545
Mäkinen, O., 386
Malamuth, N. M., 36
Malarkey, W. B., 566–567
Maldonado, R. E., 132
Malecki, A., 36
Malik, R., 203
Malinoski, P., 291
Malinowski, C. I., 126
Malla, A. K., 513
Malpass, R. S., 15, 290
Man, D. W. K., 323
Mandai, O., 218
Mandel, D. R., 112
Mandic, N., 492
Mandler, G., 309
Maner J. K., et al., 626

Maner, J. K., 42, 602
Mangalmurti, V. S., 550
Manley, R. S., 53
Mann, K., 207
Mann, L., 361
Mann, M., 569
Manning, B. H., 463
Manning, C. A., 303
Mansell, W., 32
Mansfield, N. J., 153
Manto, M., 84
Manuck, S. B., 568, 571, 574
Manuel, W. J., 615
Mao, L., 186
Maple, T. L., 254
Maracek, J., 38
Maragos, W. F., 302
Maranto, G., 135
Maratsos, M., 329
Marchand, S., 186
Marcus, G. F., 329, 331
Marek, E. A., 130
Margoliash, D., 217
Margolis, F. L., 181
Marine, C., 281
Marion, M. S., 144
Marken, R. S., 312
Markianos, M., 545
Markus, H., 461–462, 464
Markus, H. R., 428, 469, 620
Marler, P., 325
Marlier, L., 111
Marmot, M. G., 141
Marolla, F. A., 368
Maron, E., 492
Marosi, E., 420
Marquis, J., 262
Marr, M. J., 254
Marsa, F., 465
Marsden, J., 84
Marsh, A. A., 473
Marshall, F. J., 169
Marshall, G. D., 437
Marshall, J. C., 498
Marshall, M., 4
Marshall, W. L., 534
Marsland, A. L., 571
Marston, A., 216
Martazaev, M. S., 210
Martens, A., 446
Martin, A. J., 467
Martin, B., 618
Martin, C. E., 392
Martin, E. M., 588
Martin, F., 400, 584
Martin, L. R., 575
Martin, N. G., 20, 64, 159, 395, 453, 554
Martin, P., 120, 287
Martin, R., 425
Martin, R. A., 431, 580
Martin, S., 20
Martin, S. J., 139, 298
Martinez, B., 614
Martinez, H. R., 97, 99

Martinez, I. M., 461
Martinez, J. L., Jr., 299
Martinez, M. E., 541
Martinez-Pons, M., 362
Martinko, M. J., 596
Martins, I. P., 183
Martorana, A., 300
Marttunen, M., 129
Marucha, P. T., 220, 566, 581
Marx, B., 225
Marx, J. L., 337
Mashego, T. A., 576
Masland, J. L., 430
Masling, J., 10
Maslonek, K. A., 573
Maslow, A. H., 378, 466
Mason, S. L., 99
Masoro, E. J., 135
Masser, B., 613
Masters, K. S., 36, 221, 584
Masterton, G., 483
Mastropieri, M. A., 295
Matas, M., 550
Mathes, W. F., 599
Mathew, R. J., 82
Mathews, A., 580
Mathiak, K., 498
Mathias, C. J., 581
Mathis, M., 576
Matlock, J. G., 190
Matson, J. L., 254, 355
Matsubayashi, T., 507
Matsumoto, D., 435, 464, 605
Matsuura, T., 582
Matt, G. E., 555
Mattai, P. R., 37
Mattanah, J. F., 120
Matthews, D. B., 224
Matthews, K. A., 569–570
Mattsson, P., 99
Maude, C., 513
Maurer, K., 510
Mautner, B., 532
Maxwell, K. L., 353
May, M. A., 458–459
May, R., 469
Mayer, B., 433
Mayer, R., 358
Mazor, M., 185
Mazzella, R., 387, 602
Mazziotta, J. C., 419
McAdams, D. P., 143
McAdams, S., 178
McAllister, D. E., 242
McAlpine, D., 179
McArdle, J. J., 106
McAuley, E., 584
McAuley, J. H., 461
McCabe, K. O., 453
McCabe, M. P., 401
McCaffrey, T., 316
McCall, M., 602
McCalley, L. T., 404
McCallister, C., 356
McCallum, D. M., 577

McCammon, S., 436
McCandliss, B. D., 326
McCann, M. J., 380
McCanne, T. R., 435
McCarley, R. W., 218
McCarron, P. O., 76
McCarthy, J. M., 474
McCarthy, L., 494
McCarty, T., 500
McCarthy-Jones, S., 463
McCauley, C., 418, 431
McClean, S. I., 569
Mcclearn, G. E., 568
McClelland, J. L., 114, 326, 402
McClelland, L., 506
McCloskey, M., 269, 293
McClure, E. B., 424
McClure, K. A., 292
McComas, A., 79
McConaghy, N., 398
McConahay, J. B., 613
McConkey, K. M., 222
McConnell, J. V., 152, 301
McConville, J., 76
McConville, K. M. V., 257
McCormack, W. A., 401
McCrae, R. R., 454–455, 457, 474
McCrea, D. A., 70
McCrea, S. M., 467, 598
McCreath, H., 620
McCullough, M. E., 455
McDonagh, D. M., 206
McDonald, D. N., 8
McDonald, J. L., 285
McDonald, M. S., 480
McDonald, R., 543
McDonnell, J. F., 461
McDorman, T. A., 288
McDougal, Y. B., 167
McDougall, W., 376
McDougle, C. J., 229
McDowell, M. J., 450
McDowell, N. K., 575
McEwen, B. S., 85, 565, 572
McFadden, D., 173, 397
McFarland, K., 95
McGaha, A. C., 52
McGaugh, J. L., 302
McGee, R., 289
McGhee, P. E., 431
McGinnes, G. C., 425
McGonigle, D. J., 88
McGovern, M., 474
McGrady, A., 257, 401
McGrath, J., 513
McGrath, M. L., 239, 569
McGrath, P., 569
McGregor, I. S., 231
McGue, M., 62, 64–65, 121, 366–367, 387–388, 472–474
McGuffin P., et al., 508
McGuigan, F. J., 309
McGuire, G. R., 7
McGuire, L., 570
McGwin, G., Jr., 161

Nyberg, L., 276
Nye, C., 589
Nygren, T., 624
Nystul, M. S., 507

O

O'Brien, E. J., 459
O'Brien, L. T., 351
O'Brien, W. H., 574
O'Carroll, R. E., 483
O'Connell, A. N., 7, 448
O'Connor, A., 485
O'Connor, D. B., 576
O'Connor, F. L., 513
O'Dell, K. A., 588
O'Donnell, I., 506
O'Halloran, C. M., 590
O'Hara, M., 553
O'Hara, R., 225
O'Laughlin, M. S., 431
O'Leary, A., 582
O'Malley, E. B., 208
O'Malley, P. M., 107
O'Malley, R. C., 34
O'Neil, W. M., 11
O'Neill, S. K., 387
O'Reardon, J., 508
O'Reilly, H., 520
O'Reilly, R. C., 299
O'Shea, W. A., 605
O'Sullivan, M., 416
Oates, G., 135
Ober, B. A., 287
Oberlander, J. G., 624
Obozova, T. A., 261
O'Brien, J. T., 180
O'Brien, S. A., 215
Ochoa, S., 279
Ochs, E. P. P., 323
Ockene, J. K., 588
Oden, G. C., 165
Oden, M. H., 356
Odum, L. E., 588
Oei, T. P. S., 213
Offringa, R., 564
Ogden, C. L., 382
Ogden, E. P., 53
Ogilvie, R., 216
Ogilvie, R. D., 206
Ogle, C. A., 39
Ogles, B. M., 584
O'Grady, M. A., 239
Oh, K. S., 493
O'Hara, R., 282
Ohayon, M. M., 216
Ohki, K., 97
Öhman, A., 61
Oi Bun Lam, C., 131
Oishi, S., 141, 428–429, 463
Okada, M., 84
Okagami, K., 514
Okano, H., 97
Okazaki, S., 370

Okogbaa, O., 81
Oku, Y., 83
Okwumabua, T. M., 464
Olbrich, A., 322
Oldehinkel, A. J., 576
Olds, J., 85
O'Leary, K. D., 141
Olfson, M., 502
Olgun, S., 180
Olinger, L. J., 580
Oliver, C., 520
Ollendick, T. H., 495
Oller, D. K., 328
Olmo, R. J., 453
Olsen, S., 213
Olson, B., 143
Olson, B. F., 578
Olson, D. R., 115
Olson, J. K., 590
Olson, J. M., 613
Olson, K. G., 77
Olson, M. A., 607
Olson, R. A., 498
Olsson, M. J., 181
Oman, R. F., 584
O'Muircheartaigh, C. A., 270
Ones, D. S., 37, 428
Oneta, M., 322
Ong, A. D., 132, 141
Ong, A., 132
Ono, Y., 497
Onstad, S., 494, 512
Opper, C., 77, 421
Oppliger, P. A., 431
Orange, C., 356
Ordway, L., 591
Orenstein, P. A., 286
Orgocka, A., 403
Orne, M. T., 221–222, 417
Orsal, D., 99
Orth, U., 468
Orthner, D. K., 143
Ortmann, A., 54
Osawa, A., 60
Osawa, M., 81
Osberg, T. M., 25
Osborne, M., 250
Osborne, S., 248
O'Shea, R. P., 167
Oshima, I., 514
Ostry, D., 331
Oswald, D. L., 462
Ottati, V., 615
Oubaid, V., 62
Oudji, S., 495
Ouellette, J. A., 616
Ouimet, J., 362
Overmier, J. B., 55
Overton, D. A., 288
Owen, M. J., 385
Owen, M. T., 119
Owens, D. S., 303
Owsley, C., 161

P

Pace-Schott, E. F., 214
Pachana, N. A., 394
Pacini, R., 504
Packer, O., 158
Padberg, U., 125
Paddock, J. R., 422
Padian, K., 5
Page, S. J., 20
Page, W., 203
Page-Voth, V., 404
Paik, A., 393
Paik, H., 262
Paikoff, R. L., 128
Paillard, J., 187
Palaniappan, A. K., 316
Palencik, J. T., 7
Palermo, G. B., 465
Palk, J., 20
Pallast, E. G. M., 513
Pallesen, S., 207
Palmer, J. A., 190
Palmer, J. C., 292
Palmer, M., 296
Palmer, S., 538
Palmer, S. N., 437
Paluck, E. L., 51
Pan, Y., 165
Pancer, S. M., 131
Pandey, J., 575
Pankok, J., 207
Panksepp, J., 313
Panlilio, L. V., 245
Pantev, C., 176, 178
Papanicolaou, A. C., 82
Papotto, C., 289
Paradis, M., 327
Paradiso, M. A., 159
Paraherakis, A., 203
Pardo, C. A., 521
Pare, D., 299, 419
Paris, J., 516
Park, B., 599
Park, D. C., 297
Park, R. L., 52
Park, W. W., 617
Parker, A., 145, 288
Parker, A. J., 166
Parker, G. A., 252
Parker, K. C. H., 456
Parker, P. Y., 303
Parker, S., 46
Parker, W. D., 356, 457
Parkovnick, S., 596
Parr, W., 301
Parra, A., 188
Parriera, E., 183
Parron, D. L., 487
Parrott, A. C., 586
Parrott, D. J., 614
Parsons, M. W., 303
Partala, T., 156
Parten, M. B., 122
Partinen, M., 208

Partington, J. T., 618
Parva, M., 109
Pasanen, E. G., 397
Pascual-Leone, A., 183
Patel, S., 99
Patra, J., 255
Pattatucci, A. M. L., 395
Pattee, L., 122
Patterson, C. J., 120
Patterson, D. R., 186
Patterson, F. G., 336
Patterson, L. H., 336
Patterson, T. L., 543
Patti, C. LO., 289
Patton, J. E., 399
Pauknerova, D., 403
Paul, M. A., 26
Paulsen, F., 4
Paulus, P. B., 319
Paunonen, S. V., 455
Paunovic, N., 533
Pavlov, I. P., 245
Pavot, W. G., 427
Pawlak, J. L., 468
Pawlas, N., 36
Paykel, E., 538
Payne, K. A., 393
Peake, P. J., 458
Pear, J. J., 255
Pearce, J. M. S., 4, 95
Pearl, D. K., 567
Pearson, T. A., 572
Peckham, V., 618
Pedersen, C. B., 231
Pedersen, H., 601
Peer, D. F., 495
Peeters, M. C. W., 574
Pejovic, S., 212
Pelham, B. W., 468
Pell, M. D., 422
Pellechia, M., 451, 608
Pellegrini, R. J., 209
Pelletier, J., 419
Peltzer, K., 576
Pelz, S., 231
Penfield, W., 78, 88
Peng, K., 597
Pengilly, J. W., 576
Penhune, V. B., 88
Penido, A. B., 353
Pennebaker, J. W., 578–579, 591
Penner, L. A., 629
Penrod, S., 293
Penton-Voak, I., 602
Pepitone, A., 596, 625
Pepler, D. J., 33
Perchet, C., 199
Peregrine, P. N., 377
Peretz, I., 176
Perfect, T., 221
Perfetto, F., 385
Perkins, D. O., 577
Perkins, S. C., 498
Perl, D. P., 86

Schimel, J., 446, 469
Schindler, C. W., 245
Schlegel, P. A., 151
Schleifer, S. J., 570, 581
Schlesinger, L. B., 465
Schlumpf, Y. R., 501
Schmader, T., 351
Schmeidler, G. R., 190–191
Schmid, H., 172
Schmid, J., 417
Schmidt, F. L., 190, 284, 350
Schmidt, G., 629
Schmidt, L. A., 81
Schmidt, M. H., 390
Schmidt, N. B., 492
Schmidtke, A., 507
Schmitt, G. J., 76
Schmitt, I., 84
Schmitt, K. L., 291
Schmitt, N., 350
Schmitt-Rodermund, E., 131
Schneider, B. H., 322
Schneider, C. J., 257
Schneider, D. J., 495, 587
Schneider, H. G., 617
Schneider, M. E., 107
Schneider, N. G., 588
Schneider, P., 89
Schneider, S., 427
Schneiderman, H., 572
Schneiderman, N., 583
Schneider-Rosen, K., 119
Schnell, S. V., 125
Schnittjer, S. K., 321
Schnur, E., 369
Schoelmerich, A., 116
Schoen, L. M., 296
Schölmerich, A., 118
Schonemann, P. H., 472
Schooler, C., 135
Schor, C., 156
Schotte, C. K. W., 482
Schreter, Z., 400
Schroth, M. L., 401, 406
Schrut, A. H., 451
Schuele, C. M., 329
Schuetze, P., 109
Schuld, A., 539
Schull, W. J., 353
Schulsinger, F., 513
Schultz, W., 69
Schulz, M., 178
Schulz, P., 401, 581
Schulz, R., 134
Schulze, B., 512
Schumaker, J. B., 254
Schürhoiff, F., 199
Schuster, B., 597
Schuster, D. T., 356
Schusterman, R. J., 335
Schutte, N. S., 362
Schutter, D. J. L. G., 624
Schwammle, J., 421
Schwaninger, J., 145

Schwartz, B. L., 287
Schwartz, C., 153
Schwartz, C. E., 471
Schwartz, J. C., 547
Schwartz, J. H., 298
Schwartz, M. D., 242
Schwartz, S. H., 138, 455
Schwartz, S., 89
Schwartz, S. J., 106, 140
Schwarz, N., 429
Schwarzer, R., 584
Schwarzwald, J., 614
Schweizer, T. A., 84
Schwenzer, M., 498
Schyns, P., 429
Scogin, F., 504, 555
Scogin, F. R., 551–552
Scopesi, A., 185
Scott, B. W., 545
Scott, D., 610
Scott, J., 538, 551
Scott, M. S., 355
Scott, R. L., 457
Scott, T. H., 400
Scotto, P., 261
Scoville, W. B., 86, 300
Scruggs, T. E., 295
Scully, J. A., 563
Seamonds, C., 475
Searleman, A., 93
Sears, R. R., 356, 624
Sears, S. F., 584
Sechrest, L., 463
Sedikides, C., 597
Sedlacek, K., 257
Seegert, C. R., 536
Seeley, J. R., 490
Seely, D., 26
Seeman, T. E., 566
Segal, D. L., 448
Segal, J., 197
Segal, N. L., 64, 367
Segall, M. H., 114
Segerstrom, S. C., 597
Seghier, M. L., 89
Segovia, C., 182
Séguin, J. R., 389
Seibert, G. B., 422
Seidenbecher, T., 299
Seidlitz, L., 280, 429
Seidman, L. J., 523
Seidman, S. M., 393
Seifert, C. M., 418
Seifert, L. S., 311
Seiler, W. J., 534
Seitz, V., 369
Sekhon, M., 468
Seki, K., 605
Sekuler, R., 167
Selcuk, E., 141
Self, D. J., 107
Seligman, M. E. P., 256, 258, 494,
    501, 503, 575
Seligman, M. E., 575
Sellers, R. M., 575, 615

Selye, H., 567
Semendeferi, K., 89
Semin, G. R., 269
Semmelroth, J., 61
Semple, S. J., 543
Senn, C. Y., 387
Serebriakoff, V., 355
Sergeant, J., 521
Sergio, L. E., 331
Serovich, J. M., 542
Serper, M. R., 512
Seršic, D. M., 35
Servan-Schreiber, D., 419
Setlow, B., 301
Sewell, K. W., 513, 518
Seydel, E. R., 591
Seyfarth, R. M., 325
Seymour, T. L., 418
Shachtman, T., 464
Shackelford, T. K., 62
Shade, S. B., 507
Shadish, W. R., 554
Shafer, D., 589
Shaffer, J. W., 572
Shafran, R., 388
Shafto, M. G., 418
Shah, M., 384
Shah, N. J., 88
Shahab, L., 258
Shaham, Y., 320
Shahar, G., 216
Shahidulla, S., 91
Shammi, P., 430
Shanab, M. E., 622
Shanker, S. G., 337
Shannon, D., 116
Shapiro, C. M., 210
Shapiro, J. K., 125, 554
Shapiro, J., 327
Shapiro, L. A., 13
Shapiro, L. J., 496
Shapiro, M., 302
Shapka, J. D., 578
Sharma, M., 69, 506
Sharma, Y. S., 606
Sharp, M., 69
Sharpe, D., 54
Sharpley, A. L., 207
Sharps, M. J., 280
Shaughnessy, M. F., 507
Shavitt, S., 608
Shaw, D. F., 584
Shaw, J. S., III, 292
Shaw, P., 523
Shayer, M., 130
Shea, D. L., 139, 357
Shea, M. T., 220, 554
Shean, G., 494
Shear, M. K., 491, 496
Shedler, J., 532
Sheehan, D. B., 41
Sheehan, E. P., 606
Sheehan, P. W., 221
Sheehy, R. A., 580
Sheese, S., 139

Sheets, V. L., 605
Sheffield, A., 464
Sheffield, F., 609
Sheikh, J. I., 492
Sheiner, E. K., 185
Sheinman, L., 405
Sheinman, M., 36
Shek, D. T. L., 131
Sheldon, K. M., 408, 584
Sheldon, W. H., 471, 474
Shell, R. L., 81
Shell, R., 620
Shemyakina, N. V., 420
Shen, K., 70
Shenaut, G. K., 287
Shepherd, S., 600
Sheppard, L. C., 486
Sheppard, S., 98
Shepperd, J. A., 618
Sherblom, J. C., 431
Sherbourne, C. D., 591
Sherburne, L. M., 261
Sherman, J. A., 254
Sherman, S. J., 313, 575, 621
Sherrell, D. L., 608
Sherwood, S. J., 189
Sheth, R. N., 184
Shettleworth, S. J., 258, 313
Shevell, S. K., 163
Shields, S. A., 136, 363
Shiffrin, R. M., 270
Shiflett, S. C., 184, 581
Shih, J. B., 428
Shih, M., 600
Shilling, P., 509
Shim, E. K., 39
Shimamura, A. P., 295
Shimizu, M., 576
Shimizu, T., 211
Shimokawa, I., 135
Shimomura, T., 76
Shimonaka, H., 84
Shimp, T. A., 238
Shin, L. M., 471
Shin, L. M., 564
Shine, J., 509
Shinskey, J. L., 114
Shioiri, T., 492
Shipley, M., 141
Shiraishi, T., 381
Shirom, A., 575
Shneidman, E. S., 507
Shneidman, E., 143
Shockley, W., 366
Shoda, Y., 459
Shodahl, S. A., 246
Shoham-Vardi, I., 185
Shook, N. J., 225
Short, A., 460
Short, E., 231
Shostrom, E. L., 468
Shotland, R. L., 627
Showers, C. J., 137, 468
Shroff, H., 45
Shugar, G. J., 617

Z

Subject Index

Note: Page numbers in italics identify illustrations. An italic *t* next to a page number (e.g., 517*t*) indicates information that appears in a table.

National Institute of Mental Health (NIMH)
  Treatment of Depression Collaborative Research
  Program, 553
Nativism, 3
Natural concepts, 310–312, 345
Naturalistic observation, 33–34
Natural killer cells, 212, 571
Natural selection, 5, 61
Nature-versus-nurture debate
  early theorists, 4
  evolutionary psychology and, 61
  on intelligence, 362–370
Nazi war crimes, 621
Near-death experiences, 145
Nearsightedness, 157
Need for achievement, 402–404
  sport and, 407
Need-motive-value perspective, B-9
Needs, 377, 378–379
Negative correlations, 38, 48
Negative incentives, 377–378
Negative reinforcement, 250–252, 253t
Negative state relief theory, 626
Negative symptoms, of schizophrenia, 510, 514
Negative transference, 532
Neil v. Biggers, 291
Neodissociation theory, 222
Neo-Freudians, 10, 447
Neologisms, 511
Nerve deafness, 177
Nerve growth factor, 97
Nerve impulses, 4
Nerves, 67
Nervous system overview, 66–67, *66*
Neural grafting, 99
Neural networks, 322
Neural plasticity, 96–100
Neural transplantation, 98–100
Neuroanatomy of memory, 298–300
Neurological factors, in schizophrenia, 514
Neurological view, 189
Neuromodulators, 77
Neuronal membrane, 72
Neuron doctrine, 74
Neurons, 66, 70–77, *71*
Neuropeptides, 76
Neuropeptide Y, 76
Neuroses, 451, 487
Neuroticism, 453, 454
Neurotransmitters
  basic functions, 74
  bipolar disorder and, 509
  developmental disorders and, 520
  drug effects on, 75–76, 225, 228, 231
  major depressive disorder and, 502
  memory functions, 301
  pain, 184
  role in emotion, 420–421
  schizophrenia and, 513
  sleep regulation, 207
Newborns. *See* Infant and child development
Newspeak, 332
Newsweek magazine, 26
Newton, Isaac, 71
Ngandu culture, 116

Nicotine, 226t, 228, 586–588
Nicotine chewing gum, 587
Nicotine replacement therapy, 587–588
Nightingale, Florence, 46
Nightmares, 216
Night terrors, 216
Nim Chimpsky (chimpanzee), 336
Nixon, Richard, 608
NMDA receptors, 302
N-methyl-D-aspartate (NMDA) receptors, 302
Nociceptors, 183
Nocturnal emissions, 128
Nocturnal enuresis, 239
Nodes, in semantic network theory, 279
Nodes of Ranvier, 73
Nolen-Hoeksema, Susan, 504
Nonjudgmental performance measures, B-6
Nonsense syllables, 282, *283*, 284
Nonverbal behavior, 423
Norepinephrine, 414
  bipolar disorder and, 509
  major depressive disorder and, 76, 502, 546
  role in emotion, 420–421
  source, 69
Normal curve, 348
Normalization, 355
Normative commitment, B-12
Norms, in testing, 36
Norton, Joshua, 479–480
NREM sleep, 206–207
Nun Study, 139
Nuremberg war crimes trials, 621
Nutrition, prenatal, 384

O

Obedience, 621
Obesity
  behavioral factors in, 384–385
  biopsychological factors in, 382–384
  causes, 382–385
  cultural influences, 585
  health risks, 583–584
  heredity and, *383*
  weight control approaches, 585–586
Objective tests, 455
Object permanence, 114
Observational learning, 261–263, 330
Observation, naturalistic, 33–34
Obsessive-compulsive disorder (OCD), 495–496,
  544
Obsessive-compulsive personality disorder, 517t
Occipital lobes, 89, 159
Occlusion, 167, *168*
Odors, sensing, 179–181
Oedipus complex, 123, 447
Offensive social anxiety disorders, 493
Ohrwall, Hjalmar, 182
Olds, James, 85
Olfaction, 179–181
Olfactory nerves, 180, *181*
Oligodendrocytes, 70
One-sided messages, 609
Online therapy, 551
On-the-job training, B-8

Open-minded skepticism, 28
Openness to experience, 454
Operant conditioning
  applications, 253–258
  attitude formation by, 607
  for autism spectrum disorder (ASD), 536
  biological constraints, 258
  cognitive factors, 259
  origins, 245–246
  principles, 246–253, 253t
  therapies, 535–537
Operational definitions, 31
Operations, in Piaget's theory, 115
Opiate receptors in brain, 77
Opiates, 226t, 227
Opium poppy, 227
Opponent-process theory, 434
  of color vision, 162
Optic chiasm, 158, *159*
Optic nerves, 157, 158, *159*
Optimal arousal, 399–400, 403–404, 406–407
Oral stage, 446–447, 449, 514–515
Orexin, 207
Orgasmic disorder, 393
Orgasm phase, 390
Orientation programs, for cancer patients, 590
Origin of Species, 5
Ormsby, Kathy, 407
Orne, Martin, 222
Ossicles, 175, *175*, 177
Othello, Washington, 564
Otolith organs, 187, *188*
Ought self, 469
Outer ear, 174, *175*
Out-groups, 599
Out-of-body experiences, 145
Oval window, 175, 176
Ovaries, 69, 108, *128*
Overextension, 328
Overjustification theory, 404–405
Overlearning, 295
Overregularization, 328
Oxytocin, 566

P

Pagano, Bernard, 289–290
Pain perception, 183–186, 220
Pain relief, 77
Panic disorder, 491–492
Papillae, 181–182
Pappenheim, Bertha, 528
Paracelsus, 481
Paradoxical intention, 211
Paradoxical sleep, 206–207
Parallel play, 122
Paranoia scale, 455, 456t
Paranoid personality disorder, 517t
Parapsychology, 188–192
Parasympathetic nervous system, 67, 414, 415
Parental conflict, 121–122
Parent-child relationships, 120–122
Parenting influences, 142–143
Parenting styles, 120–121, 466
Parents, adolescent relationships with, 132–133